QuickPass™ More Than a Textbook

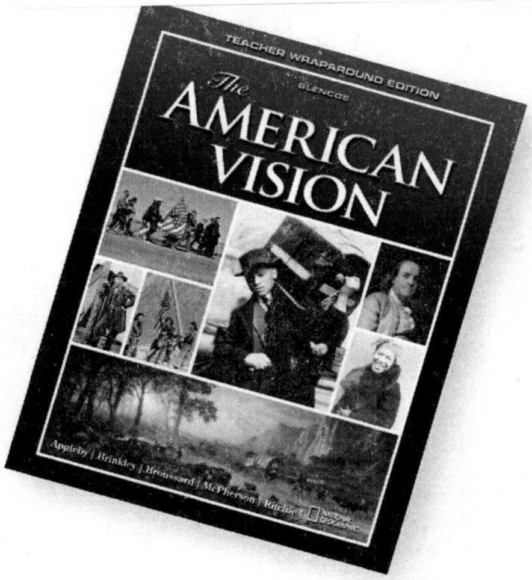

- **More online resources**

  Go to **History ONLINE** at glencoe.com.

- **More convenient**

  Enter a QuickPass™ chapter code to go directly to the chapter resources you need.

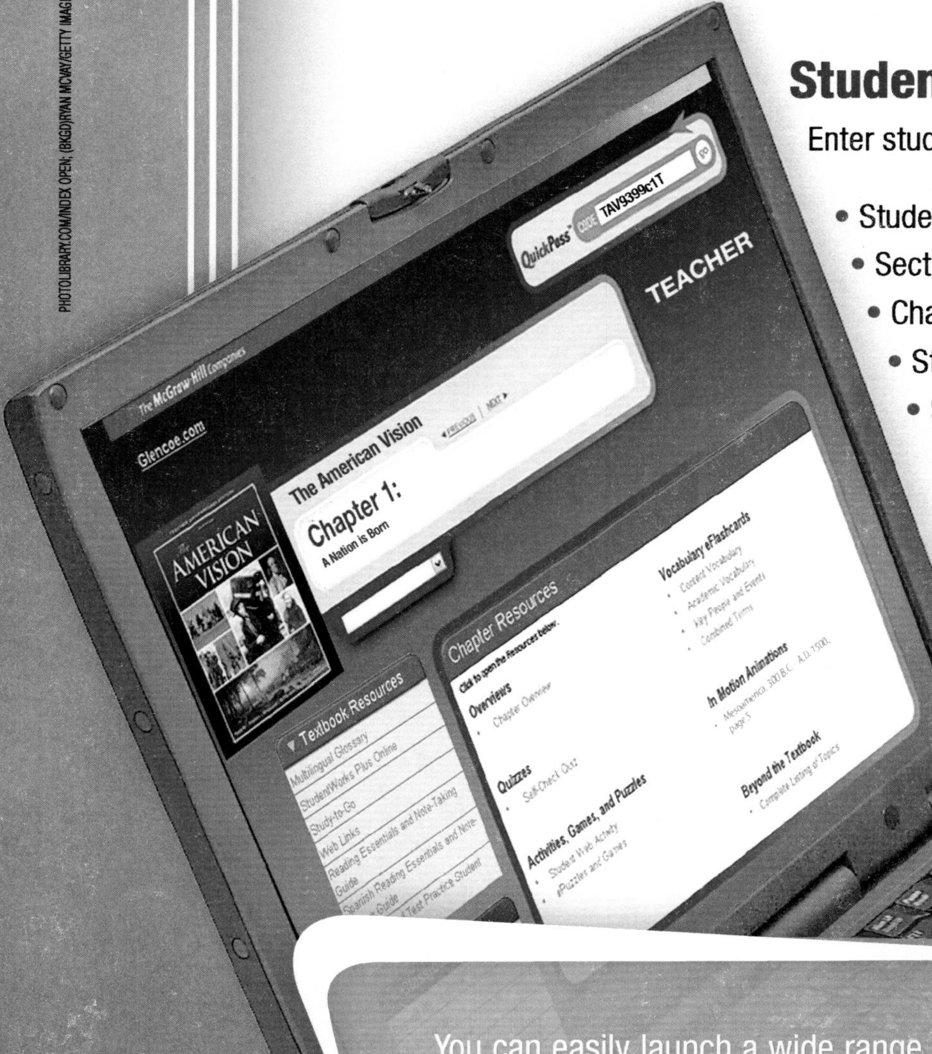

Student QuickPass™

Key in chapter number.

Enter student code TAV9846c1 to access these resources:

- StudentWorks™ Plus Online
- Section Spotlight Video
- Chapter Overview
- Study Central™
- Study-to-Go
- Chapter Audio
- In Motion Animations
- Student Web Activity
- Self-Check Quiz

...and more

Teacher QuickPass™

Key in chapter number.

Enter teacher code TAV9399c1T to access these resources:

- All student materials
- Web resources
- Teacher resources

...and more

You can easily launch a wide range of digital products from your computer's desktop with the McGraw-Hill Social Studies widget.

TeacherWorks

★★ Make history ★★

COME ALIVE

with GLENCOE'S

TECHNOLOGY TOOLS

Students can review lesson content, take notes, and build vocabulary at Study Central!

Help students learn key vocabulary with eFlashcards!

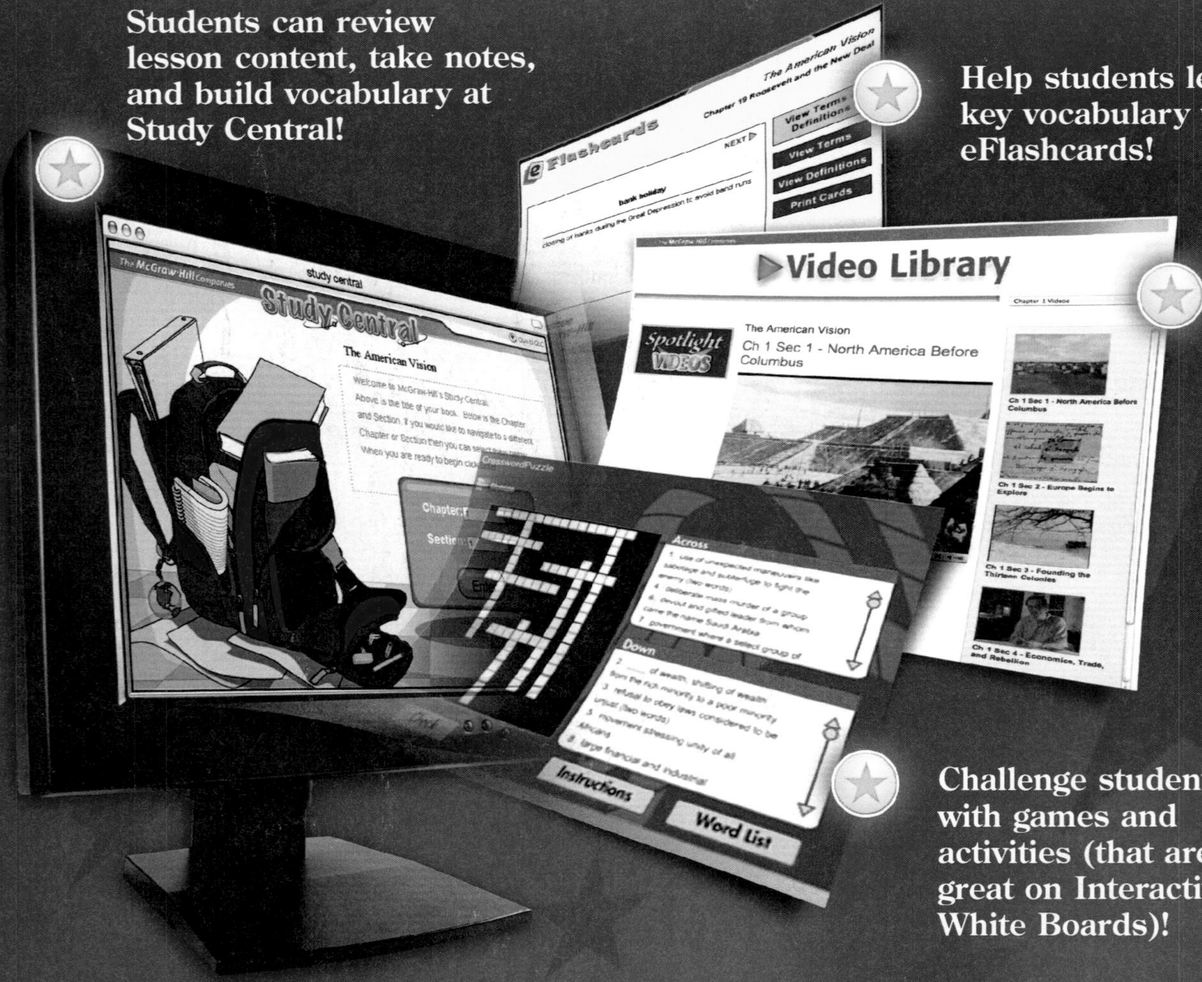

Bring the sights and sounds of history to your classroom with Spotlight Videos, rich with primary source images!

Challenge students with games and activities (that are great on Interactive White Boards)!

Students can find maps in motion, interactive graphic organizers, and more technology tools on StudentWorks™ Plus or online at glencoe.com.

TEACHER WRAPAROUND EDITION

The AMERICAN VISION

Joyce Appleby, Ph.D. Alan Brinkley, Ph.D. Albert S. Broussard, Ph.D.
James M. McPherson, Ph.D. Donald A. Ritchie, Ph.D.

NATIONAL GEOGRAPHIC

McGraw Hill Glencoe

About the Cover The images on the cover are (from left to right): the March on Selma, a Polish immigrant arriving at Ellis Island, Benjamin Franklin, Ulysses S. Grant, firefighters raising the U.S. flag on 9/11, Zora Neale Hurston, and *Oregon Trail* by Alfred Bierstadt.

Teacher Wraparound Edition Text Acknowledgment: page 627 "Brother, Can You Spare a Dime?" Words by E.Y. Harburg. Music by Jay Gorney Copyright © 1932 by Gorney Music and Glocca Morra Music. Copyright renewed. All rights administered by Next Decade Entertainment, Inc. International Copyright Secured. All rights reserved.

The McGraw-Hill Companies

Glencoe

Send all inquiries to:
Glencoe/McGraw-Hill
8787 Orion Place
Columbus, OH 43240-4027

ISBN 978-0-07-890939-9 *(Teacher Wraparound Edition)*
MHID 0-07-890939-2 *(Teacher Wraparound Edition)*
ISBN 978-0-07-879984-6 *(Student Edition)*
MHID 0-07-879984-8 *(Student Edition)*

Printed in the United States of America

3 4 5 6 7 8 9 MER 13 12 11

Joyce Appleby, Ph.D., is Professor Emerita of History at UCLA. Dr. Appleby's published works include *Inheriting the Revolution: The First Generation of Americans; Capitalism and a New Social Order: The Jeffersonian Vision of the 1790s;* and *Ideology and Economic Thought in Seventeenth-Century England,* which won the Berkshire Prize. She served as president of both the Organization of American Historians and the American Historical Association, and chaired the Council of the Institute of Early American History and Culture at Williamsburg. Dr. Appleby has been elected to the American Philosophical Society and the American Academy of Arts and Sciences, and is a Corresponding Fellow of the British Academy.

Alan Brinkley, Ph.D., is Allan Nevins Professor of American History at Columbia University. His published works include *Voices of Protest: Huey Long, Father Coughlin, and the Great Depression,* which won the 1983 National Book Award; *The End of Reform: New Deal Liberalism in Recession and War; The Unfinished Nation: A Concise History of the American People;* and *Liberalism and Its Discontents.* He received the Levenson Memorial Teaching Prize at Harvard University and the Great Teacher Award at Columbia.

Albert S. Broussard, Ph.D., is Professor of History at Texas A&M University from which he received a Distinguished Teaching Award and has served as a distinguished lecturer. Before joining the Texas A&M faculty, Dr. Broussard was Assistant Professor of History and Director of the African American Studies Program at Southern Methodist University. Among his publications are the books *Black San Francisco: The Struggle for Racial Equality in the West, 1900–1954* and *African American Odyssey: The Stewarts, 1853–1963.* Dr. Broussard has also served as president of the Oral History Association and was chair of the Nominating Committee for the Organization of American Historians.

James M. McPherson, Ph.D., is George Henry Davis Professor of American History, Emeritus at Princeton University. Dr. McPherson is the author of 14 books about the Civil War era. These include *Battle Cry of Freedom: The Civil War Era,* for which he won the Pulitzer Prize in 1989, and *For Cause and Comrades: Why Men Fought in the Civil War,* for which he won the 1998 Lincoln Prize. He is a member of many professional historical associations, including the Civil War Preservation Trust.

Donald A. Ritchie, Ph.D., is Associate Historian of the United States Senate Historical Office. Dr. Ritchie received his doctorate in American history from the University of Maryland after service in the U.S. Marine Corps. He has taught American history at various levels, from high school to university. He edits the Historical Series of the Senate Foreign Relations Committee and is the author of several books, including *Doing Oral History; Electing FDR: The New Deal Campaign of 1932; Reporting from Washington: The History of the Washington Press Corps;* and *Press Gallery: Congress and the Washington Correspondents,* which received the Organization of American Historians Richard W. Leopold Prize. Dr. Ritchie has served as president of the Oral History Association and as a council member of the American Historical Association.

The National Geographic Society, founded in 1888 for the increase and diffusion of geographic knowledge, is the world's largest nonprofit scientific and educational organization. Since its earliest days, the Society has used sophisticated communication technologies, from color photography to holography, to convey knowledge to its worldwide membership. The School Publishing Division supports the Society's mission by developing innovative educational programs—ranging from traditional print materials to multimedia programs including CD-ROMs, DVDs, and software.

Contributing Author

Dinah Zike, M.Ed., is an award-winning author, educator, and inventor known for designing three-dimensional hands-on manipulatives and graphic organizers known as Foldables®. Foldables are used nationally and internationally by teachers, parents, and educational publishing companies. Dinah has developed over 150 supplemental educational books and materials. She is the author of *The Big Book of United States History, The Big Book of World History,* and *The Big Book of Books and Activities,* which was awarded Learning Magazine's Teachers' Choice Award. In 2004 Dinah was honored with the CESI Science Advocacy Award. Dinah received her M.Ed. from Texas A&M, College Station, Texas.

Consultants & Reviewers

Academic Consultants

David Berger
Broeklundian Professor of History
Brooklyn College and the Graduate Center
City University of New York
Brooklyn, New York

Paul Cimbala
Professor of History
Fordham University, Rose Hill Campus
Bronx, New York

Linda Clemmons
Assistant Professor of History
Illinois State University
Normal, Illinois

Charles Eagles
Professor of History
University of Mississippi
University, Mississippi

Neil Foley
Associate Professor of History
University of Texas at Austin
Austin, Texas

Allison Gough
Assistant Professor of History
Hawaii Pacific University
Honolulu, Hawaii

K. Austin Kerr
Emeritus Professor of History
The Ohio State University
Columbus, Ohio

Jeffrey Ogbar
Associate Professor of History and Director of the Institute for African American Studies
University of Connecticut, Storrs
Storrs, Connecticut

Elizabeth Pleck
Professor of History
University of Illinois at Urbana-Champaign
Urbana, Illinois

William Bruce Wheeler
Emeritus Professor of History
University of Tennessee
Knoxville, Tennessee

Shawn Johansen
Professor of History
Brigham Young University Idaho
Rexburg, Idaho

Teacher Reviewers

Joanna Ackley
John F. Kennedy High School
Taylor, Michigan

Pat Ambrose
Adlai E. Stevenson High School
Lincolnshire, Illinois

Sharon K. Anderson
Cookeville High School
Cookeville, Tennessee

Fred Barnett
Cibola High School
Albuquerque, New Mexico

Shawn Barnum
Tonawanda High School
Tonawanda, New York

Vincent Beasley
Eastern Wayne High School
Goldsboro, North Carolina

Jeremiah Bergan
Baker High School
Baldwinsville, New York

Randy Bishop
Middleton High School
Middleton, Tennessee

Patrick Boyd
Ravenwood High School
Brentwood, Tennessee

Suzanne Brock
Vestavia Hills High School
Vestavia Hills, Alabama

Joyce Brown
LaFayette High School
LaFayette, Georgia

David Chapman
Bentonville High School
Bentonville, Arkansas

Teresa Cooper
Battle Creek Central High School
Battle Creek, Michigan

Timothy Davish
Lakota East High School
Liberty Township, Ohio

Peter DeWolf
First Colonial High School
Virginia Beach, Virginia

Glenn DiTomaso
Norwell High School
Norwell, Massachusetts

Kimberly Dunn
Chase High School
Forest City, North Carolina

Bre England
Warren Central High School
Indianapolis, Indiana

Robert Fenster
Hillsborough High School
Hillsborough, New Jersey

James A. Field
Morgantown High School
Morgantown, West Virginia

Shane Gardner
Freedom High School
Morganton, North Carolina

Diane Gebel
Attica High School
Attica, New York

James Gill
Binghamton High School
Binghamton, New York

Mary Ellen Goergen
Amherst High School
Amherst, New York

Teacher Reviewers

Robert Haley
Cleveland Hill High School
Cheektowaga, New York

Ken Hall
Larkin High School
Elgin, Illinois

Anne Harper
Del Sol High School
Las Vegas, Nevada

Roberta Heath
Capital High School
Charleston, West Virginia

Cliff Hong
Liverpool High School
Liverpool, New York

George Irby
Miami Killian Senior High School
Miami, Florida

JeTaun Jamerson
Lake View High School
Chicago, Illinois

Carol Johnson
Cary High School
Cary, North Carolina

Harry F. Jones
Panther Creek High School
Cary, North Carolina

Shirley Jones
Hillcrest High School
Memphis, Tennessee

Joe Leonard
Southport High School
Indianapolis, Indiana

Tom Long
Buffalo Gap High School
Swoope, Virginia

Rebecca Mabrey
Central Cabarrus High School
Concord, North Carolina

Amy MacIntosh
Fairfield Warde High School
Fairfield, Connecticut

Shannon W. McDonald
Harding University High School
Charlotte, North Carolina

Chad McGee
Warren County High School
McMinnville, Tennessee

Marty McNeil
Akron East High School
Akron, Ohio

Kathryn Merritt
Hillcrest High School
Tuscaloosa, Alabama

Rita Morgan
Beaverton High School
Beaverton, Oregon

Jimmy Neal
Beech High School
Hendersonville, Tennessee

Teresa Pardee
East Mecklenburg High School
Charlotte, North Carolina

Patricia Radigan
Thomas Dale High School
Chester, Virginia

Steven Reeder
Cordova High School
Cordova, Tennessee

Debi Reeves
Liberty High School
Bedford, Virginia

Connie Schlieker
Atherton High School
Louisville, Kentucky

Mark Schuler
North Springs High School
Atlanta, Georgia

Russ Smith
Ashley High School
Wilmington, North Carolina

Mitzi Terry
Franklin High School
Franklin, Tennessee

Dal Tomlinson
Dixon High School
Holly Ridge, North Carolina

Penny Toneatti
Half Hollow Hills High School East
Dix Hills, New York

Lisa Valentine
Harding University High School
Charlotte, North Carolina

Stan Vickers
Westview High School
Martin, Tennessee

Danielle Walsh
Emmaus High School
Emmaus, Pennsylvania

Joshua White
Charlotte High School
Rochester, New York

Gerald Wild II
Alden High School
Alden, New York

Amy Working
Central High School
Memphis, Tennessee

Table of Contents

Unit 2

Table of Contents

Unit 3

Unit 4

NO MOLLY-CODDLING HERE

Unit 5

Imperialism and Progressivism 486
1890–1920

Unit 6

Table of Contents

Unit 7

Unit 8

Table of Contents

Unit 9

Appendix

Features

TECHNOLOGY & HISTORY

NATIONAL GEOGRAPHIC GEOGRAPHY & HISTORY

TIME NOTEBOOK

People IN HISTORY

Analyzing Primary Sources

Debates in History

Turning Point

Analyzing Supreme Court Cases

Features

POLITICAL CARTOONS PRIMARY SOURCE

PAST & PRESENT

Time Lines

Primary Source Quotes

A variety of quotations and excerpts throughout the text express the thoughts, feelings, and life experiences of people, past and present.

Primary Source Quotes

CHAPTER 14 • Becoming a World Power, 1872–1917

CHAPTER 15 • The Progressive Movement, 1890–1920

CHAPTER 16 • World War I and Its Aftermath, 1914–1920

CHAPTER 17 • The Jazz Age, 1921–1929

CHAPTER 18 • The Great Depression Begins, 1929–1932

CHAPTER 19 • Roosevelt and the New Deal, 1933–1941

CHAPTER 20 • A World in Flames, 1931–1941

CHAPTER 21 • America and World War II, 1941–1945

CHAPTER 22 • The Cold War Begins, 1945–1960

CHAPTER 23 • Postwar America, 1945–1960

CHAPTER 24 • The New Frontier and the Great Society, 1961–1968

Primary Source Quotes

Maps

Maps In MOtion See *StudentWorks™ Plus* or glencoe.com.

Maps labeled with the In Motion icon have been specially enhanced on the StudentWorks™ Plus DVD and on glencoe.com. These In Motion maps allow you to interact with layers of displayed data and to listen to audio components.

Entries in **blue** are In Motion maps.

Maps

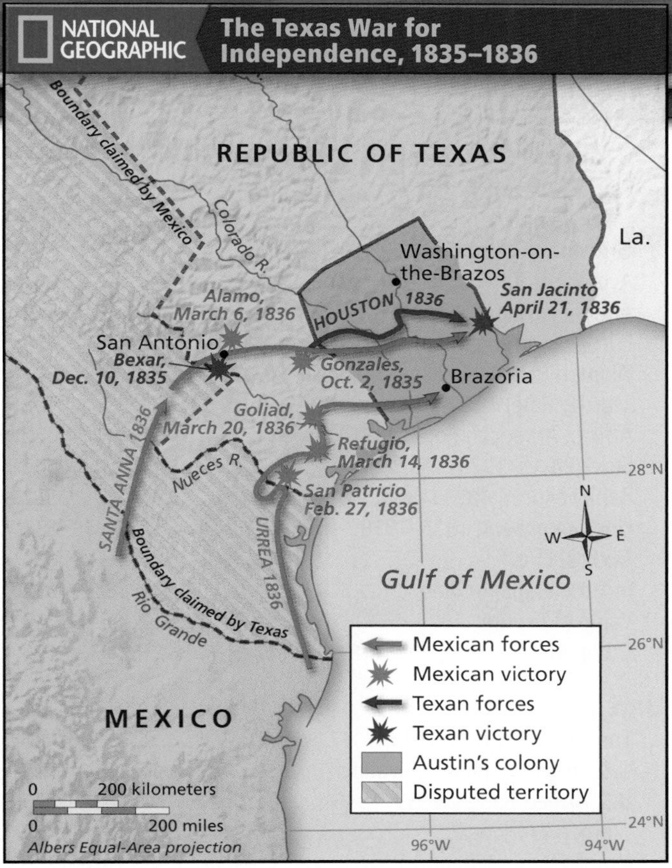

Unit 6

Unit 7

Unit 8

Unit 9

Charts & Graphs

The American Vision contains a wealth of information. The trick is to know where to look to access all the information in the book. If you go through this scavenger hunt, either alone or with your teacher or parents, you will quickly learn how the textbook is organized and how to get the most out of your reading and study time. Let's get started!

1. How many units and chapters are in the book? 9 units, 31 chapters
2. What is the difference between the glossary and the index? glossary: defines terms; index: lists page numbers for various topics
3. Most sections of a chapter open with a primary source—a document or other testimony dating from the period. Where else can you find primary sources in the textbook? in Analyzing Primary Sources features, and in Documents in American History and American Literature Library in the Appendix
4. In what special feature can you find the definition of a physical map, a political map, and a special-purpose map? the Geography Handbook
5. If you want to quickly find all the maps, charts, and graphs about World War II, where in the front do you look? look in the Table of Contents
6. How can you find information about William Penn's colonization of Pennsylvania? look in the Index
7. Where can you find a graphic organizer that summarizes the major events of the Civil War discussed in Chapter 9? in the Visual Summary at the end of the chapter
8. What are the key terms and names for Chapter 8, Section 3, and how are they highlighted in the text? listed in the Guide to Reading and Section Review; boldfaced and highlighted in yellow in the text
9. The Web site for the book is listed ten times in Chapter 16. After finding all ten, list how the Web site can help you. provides previews, additional activities and resources, and practice tests
10. Which of the book's main features will provide you with strategies for improving your studying and writing skills? The Skillbuilder Handbook in the Appendix

Big Ideas in History

Themes in the American Vision

As you read THE AMERICAN VISION, *you will be given help in sorting out all the information you encounter. This textbook organizes the events of your nation's past and present around 10 themes. A theme is a concept, or main idea, that happens again and again throughout history. By recognizing these themes, you will better understand events of the past and how they affect you today.*

Culture and Beliefs

Being aware of cultural differences helps us understand ourselves and others. People from around the world for generations have sung of the "land of the Pilgrims' pride, land where our fathers died," even though their ancestors arrived on these shores long after these events occurred.

Past and Present

Recognizing our historic roots helps us understand why things are the way they are today. This theme includes political, social, religious, and economic changes that have influenced the way Americans think and act.

Geography and History
Understanding geography helps us understand how humans interact with their environment. The United States succeeded in part because of its rich natural resources and its vast open spaces. In many regions, the people changed the natural landscape to fulfill their wants and needs.

Individual Action
Responsible individuals have often stepped forward to help lead the nation. Americans' strong values helped create such individuals. These values spring in part from earlier times when the home was the center of many activities, including work, education, and spending time with one's family.

Group Action
Identifying how political and social groups and institutions operate helps us work together. From the beginning, Americans formed groups and institutions to act in support of their economic, political, social, and religious beliefs.

Government and Society
Understanding the workings of government helps us become better citizens. Abraham Lincoln explained the meaning of democracy as "government of the people, by the people, for the people." Democracy, at its best, is "among" the people.

Science and Technology
Americans have always been quick to adopt innovations. The nation was settled and built by people who gave up old ways in favor of new. Americans' lives are deeply influenced by technology, the use of science, and machines. Perhaps no machine has so shaped modern life as the automobile. Understanding the role of science and technology helps us see their impact on our society and the roles they will play in the future.

Economics and Society
The free enterprise economy of the United States is consistent with the nation's history of rights and freedoms. Freedom of choice in economic decisions supports other freedoms. Understanding the concept of free enterprise is basic to studying American history.

Trade, War, and Migration
Events much bigger than any individual also shape the course of history. Being aware of global interdependence helps us make decisions and deal with the difficult issues we will encounter. Trade, war, and the movement of people between nations have altered the nation's history.

Struggles for Rights
For a democratic system to survive, its citizens must take an active role in government. The foundation of democracy is the right of every person to take part in government and to voice one's views on issues. An appreciation for the struggle to preserve these freedoms is vital to the understanding of democracy.

Using the Big Ideas

You will find Big Ideas at the beginning of every section of every chapter. You are asked questions that help you put it all together to better understand how ideas and themes are connected across time—and to see why history is important to you today.

Correlation of
The American Vision to the NCSS Thematic Strands

Theme and Performance Expectations	Student Pages
I. *Culture* The study of culture helps students understand similarities and differences within groups of people. By studying a culture's beliefs, values, and traditions, students begin to gain a perspective that helps them relate to different groups. In high school, students can understand and use complex cultural concepts such as adaptation, assimilation, and acculturation to explain how culture and cultural systems function.	
***The American Vision* Related Theme: Culture and Traditions**	
A. Analyze and explain the ways groups, societies, and cultures address human needs and concerns.	4–13, 24–41, 54–73, 104–109, 136–248, 284–308, 458–469, 470–475, 520–542, 604–609, 774–781, 838–844, 850–876, 910–926, 968–973
B. Predict how data and experiences may be interpreted by people from diverse cultural perspectives and frames of reference.	9, 104–109
C. Apply an understanding of culture as an integrated whole that explains the functions and interactions of language, literature, the arts, traditions, beliefs and values, and behavior patterns.	4–11, 28–31, 86–91, 230–235, 260–263, 442–447, 450–457, 458–461, 464–467, 468–469, 604–607, 610–615, 616–621, 634–637, 800–802, 804–807, 910–925, 1002–1005
D. Compare and analyze societal patterns for preserving and transmitting culture while adapting to environmental or social change.	28–33, 42–45, 254–257, 260–263, 392–393, 394–397, 442–447, 452–457
E. Demonstrate the value of cultural diversity, as well as cohesion, within and across groups.	4–11, 742, 982–987, 1016–1019
F. Interpret patterns of behavior reflecting values and attitudes that contribute or pose obstacles to cross-cultural understanding.	4–23, 34–51, 212–215, 242–247, 260–263, 442–449, 604–609, 694–701, 810–815, 848–876, 1016–1026, 1036–1038
G. Construct reasoned judgments about specific cultural responses to persistent human issues.	R7–R14
H. Explain and apply ideas, theories, and modes of inquiry drawn from anthropology and sociology in the examination of persistent issues and social problems.	4, 459–460, 464–466, 810
II. *Time, Continuity, and Change* Understanding time, continuity, and change involves being knowledgeable about what things were like in the past and how things change and develop over time. Knowing how to read and reconstruct the past helps students gain a historical perspective. In high school, students examine the past's relationship with the present while extrapolating into the future. They also integrate individual stories about people, events, and situations to form a more complete conception, in which continuity and change persist in time and across cultures. Students will use their knowledge of history to make informed choices and decisions in the present.	
***The American Vision* Related Theme: Continuity and Change**	
A. Demonstrate that historical knowledge and the concept of time are socially influenced constructions that lead historians to be selective in the questions they seek to answer and the evidence they use.	62–63, 66, 210–211, 266, 304, 334–335, 412, 448–449, 524, 562–563, 654, 660–661, 700–701, 738, 748, 860, 868–869, 1020–1021, 1044, R19, R20
B. Apply key concepts such as time, chronology, causality, change, conflict, and complexity to explain, analyze, and show connections among patterns of historical change and continuity.	19, 66, 72, 166, 223, 224, 243, 266, 304, 306, 326, 360, 368, 388, 412, 474, 506, 524, 554, 578, 620, 654, 656, 706, 738, 748, 784, 812, 840, 854, 860, 984, 1037, 1044, R3, R17
C. Identify and describe significant historical periods and patterns of change within and across cultures, such as the development of ancient cultures and civilizations, the rise of nation-states, and social, economic, and political revolutions.	4–23, 52–95, 312–353, 354–381, 408–439, 848–879, 914–929, 1002–1007
D. Systematically employ the processes of critical historical inquiry to reconstruct and reinterpret the past, such as using a variety of sources and checking their credibility, validating and weighing evidence for claims, and searching for causality.	62–63, 210–211, 334–335, 448–449, 562–563, 660–661, 700–701, 868–869, 1020–1021, R3, R19, R20

Theme and Performance Expectations	Student Pages
E. Investigate, interpret, and analyze multiple historical and contemporary viewpoints within and across cultures related to important events, recurring dilemmas, and persistent issues, while employing empathy, skepticism, and critical judgment.	62–63, 70–71, 112–113, 210–211, 272–273, 298–299, 334–335, 448–449, 464–465, 500–501, 532–533, 552–553, 562–563, 660-661, 664–665, 700–701, 750–751, 762–763, 868–869, 886–887, 916–917, 976–977, 1010–1011, 1020–1021, R5, R8, R11, R13, R18, R19, R20
F. Apply ideas, theories, and modes of historical inquiry to analyze historical and contemporary developments, and to inform and evaluate actions concerning public policy issues.	19, 72, 166, 171, 191, 223, 243, 297, 306, 326, 360, 474, 429, 531, 554, 559, 620, 671, 706, 733, 779, 784, 822, 853, 854, 901, 943, 1037
III. *People, Places, and Environments* The study of people, places, and environments will help students as they create their spatial views and geographic perspectives of the world. Students begin to make informed and critical decisions about the relationship between humans and their environment. In high school, geographic concepts become central to students' comprehension of global connections as they expand their knowledge of diverse cultures, both historical and contemporary.	
***The American Vision* Related Theme: Geography and History**	
A. Refine mental maps of locales, regions, and the world that demonstrate understanding of relative locations, direction, size and shape.	GH9, 5, 9, 17, 21, 32, 39, 43, 84, 99, 163, 169, 213, 218, 227, 231, 256, 265, 289, 292, 387, 390, 395, 411, 443, 505, 509, 516, 549, 571, 585, 683, 684, 685, 689, 698, 705, 761, 764, 769, 883, 884, 970, 991, 992, 1023, 1038
B. Create, interpret, use, and synthesize information from various representations of the earth, such as maps, globes, and photographs.	GH3–GH13, 5, 9, 17, 21, 28, 32, 35, 37, 39, 43, 44, 45, 50, 55, 57, 69, 81, 83, 84, 89, 94, 99, 100, 102, 111, 118, 163, 169, 179, 180, 184, 189, 192, 195, 203, 206, 207, 213, 218, 223, 227, 231, 250, 256, 265, 268, 271, 274, 278, 289, 292, 303, 306, 322, 323, 325, 337, 345, 347, 352, 362, 374, 376, 380, 387, 390, 395, 399, 411, 417, 419, 431, 443, 445, 477, 498, 499, 505, 509, 516, 525, 537, 538, 544, 549, 565, 568, 569, 571, 578, 580, 585, 620, 624, 629, 646, 656, 676, 683, 684, 685, 689, 698, 705, 723, 724, 731, 737, 741, 744, 747, 756, 761, 764, 769, 770, 771, 790, 797, 798, 825, 834, 878, 883, 884, 888, 896, 906, 928, 949, 964, 970, 991, 992, 994, 1023, 1033, 1038, 1049, 1058
C. Use appropriate resources, data sources, and geographic tools such as aerial photographs, satellite images, geographic information systems (GIS), map projections, and cartography to generate, manipulate, and interpret information such as atlases, databases, grid systems, charts, graphs, and maps.	GH3–GH13, 5, 9, 17, 21, 28, 32, 35, 37, 39, 43, 44, 45, 50, 55, 57, 69, 81, 83, 84, 89, 94, 99, 100, 102, 111, 118, 163, 169, 179, 180, 184, 189, 192, 195, 203, 206, 207, 213, 218, 223, 227, 231, 250, 256, 265, 268, 271, 274, 278, 289, 292, 303, 306, 322, 323, 325, 337, 345, 347, 352, 362, 374, 376, 380, 387, 390, 395, 399, 411, 417, 419, 431, 443, 445, 477, 498, 499, 505, 509, 516, 525, 537, 538, 544, 549, 565, 568, 569, 571, 578, 580, 585, 620, 624, 629, 646, 656, 676, 683, 684, 685, 689, 698, 705, 723, 724, 731, 737, 741, 744, 747, 756, 761, 764, 769, 770, 771, 790, 797, 798, 825, 834, 878, 883, 884, 888, 896, 906, 928, 949, 964, 970, 991, 992, 994, 1023, 1033, 1038, 1049, 1058
D. Calculate distance, scale, area, and density, and distinguish spatial distribution patterns.	99, 395, 419, 443, 445, 624, 988
E. Describe, differentiate, and explain the relationships among various regional and global patterns of geographic phenomena such as landforms, soils, climate, vegetation, natural resources, and population.	4–13, 24–33, 194–211, 254–263, 386–397, 410–411, 958–962
F. Use knowledge of physical system changes such as seasons, climate and weather, and the water cycle to explain geographic phenomena.	396–397, 635, 638–639
G. Describe and compare how people create places that reflect culture, human needs, government policy, and current values and ideals as they design and build specialized buildings, neighborhoods, shopping centers, urban centers, industrial parks, and the like.	450–457, 982–983, 988
H. Examine, interpret, and analyze physical and cultural patterns and their interactions, such as land use, settlement patterns, cultural transmission of customs and ideas, and ecosystem changes.	4–13, 24–41, 194–211, 254–263, 264–269, 386–397, 442–449, 635, 638–639, 958–959, 1026

Theme and Performance Expectations	Student Pages
I. Describe and assess ways that historical events have been influenced by, and have influenced, physical and human geographic factors in local, regional, national, and global settings.	4–13, 34–41, 194–211, 254–263, 386–397, 442–449, 470–475, 490–514, 548–555, 635, 638–639, 682–693, 760–765, 830–837, 882–891, 958–959, 1022–1026, 1036–1053
J. Analyze and evaluate social and economic effects of environmental changes and crises resulting from phenomena such as floods, storms, and drought.	396–397, 522–523, 635, 638–639, 958–959, 1052–1053
K. Propose, compare, and evaluate alternative policies for the use of land and other resources in communities, regions, nations, and the world.	386–397, 410–421, 532-533, 635, 638–639, 958–962, 988
IV. *Individual Development and Identity* People and culture influence a person's identity. Examining the different forms of human behavior improves one's understanding of social relationships and the development of personal identity. The study of human behavior helps students become aware of how social processes influence a person's identity. In high school, students use methods from the behavioral sciences to examine individuals, societies, and cultures.	
The American Vision **Related Theme: Individual Action**	
A. Articulate personal connections to time, place, and social/cultural system.	242–247, 388, 412–413, 428–435, 476–481, 498, 564–573
B. Identify, describe, and express appreciation for the influence of various historical and contemporary cultures on an individual's daily life.	458–467, 520–527, 616–621, 718–729, 724, R62–R81
C. Describe the ways family, religion, gender, ethnicity, nationality, socioeconomic status, and other group and cultural influences contribute to the development of a sense of self.	393, 402, 424–425, 435, 483–484, 524–525
D. Apply concepts, methods, and theories about the study of human growth and development, such as physical endowment, learning, motivation, behavior, perception, and personality.	402, 424–425, 426
E. Examine the interaction of ethnic, national, or cultural influences in specific situations or events.	392–393, 482–487, 497–498, 540–543
F. Analyze the role of perceptions, attitudes, values, and beliefs in the development of personal identity.	434, 528–533, 560–561
G. Compare and evaluate the impact of stereotyping, conformity, acts of altruism, and other behaviors on individuals and groups.	398–403, 483–484, 541, 570–573
H. Work independently and cooperatively within groups and institutions to accomplish goals.	176–181, 650–659
I. Examine factors that contribute to and damage one's mental health and analyze issues related to mental health and behavioral disorders in contemporary society.	458–467, 527, 957
V. *Individuals, Groups, and Institutions* Institutions, such as schools, governments, and churches, influence people and often reflect a society's values. Because of the vital role that institutions play in people's lives, it is important that students know how institutions develop, what controls and influences them, and how humans react to them. High school students must understand the traditions and theories that support social and political traditions.	
The American Vision **Related Theme: Groups and Institutions**	
A. Apply concepts such as role, status, and social class in describing the connections and interactions of individuals, groups, and institutions in society.	222–229, 366–371, 428–435, 529, 668–673
B. Analyze group and institutional influences on people, events, and elements of culture in both historical and contemporary settings.	212–215, 222–229, 230–235, 264–267, 294–301, 314–317, 328–333, 356–363, 366–371, 428–435, 520–527, 616–621, 640–643, 650–659, 668–673, 714–721, 958–961
C. Describe the various forms institutions take, and explain how they develop and change over time.	212–215, 222–229, 236–241, 264–269, 294–301, 314–319, 356–363, 366–371, 429–435, 616–621, 640–643, 650–659
D. Identify and analyze examples of tensions between expressions of individuality and efforts used to promote social conformity by groups and institutions.	230–235, 328–333, 356–363, 714–721, 910–913
E. Describe and examine belief systems basic to specific traditions and laws in contemporary and historical movements.	212–215, 264–267, 294–301, 328–333, 482–484, 542, 616–621, 668–673, 714–721, 958–961, 968–973

Theme and Performance Expectations	Student Pages
F. Evaluate the role of institutions in furthering both continuity and change.	212–215, 222–229, 264–267, 314–317, 328–333, 356–363, 428–435, 520–527, 616–621, 640–643, 650–659, 958–961
G. Analyze the extent to which groups and institutions meet individual needs and promote the common good in contemporary and historical settings.	230–235, 366–371, 428–435, 520–527, 640–643, 650–659, 958–961
H. Explain and apply ideas and modes of inquiry drawn from behavioral science and social theory in the examination of persistent issues and social problems.	4, 459–460, 464–466, 810

VI. *Power, Authority, and Governance*

Studying structures of power, authority, and governance and their functions in the United States and around the world is important for developing a notion of civic responsibility. Students will identify the purpose and characteristics of various types of government and how people try to resolve conflicts. Students will also examine the relationship between individual rights and responsibilities. High school students study the various systems that have been developed over time to allocate and employ power and authority in the governing process.

The American Vision **Related Theme: Government and Democracy**

Theme and Performance Expectations	Student Pages
A. Examine persistent issues involving the rights, roles, and status of the individual in relation to the general welfare.	54–73, 104–119, 202–211, 222–229, 236–248, 284–308, 326, 356–365, 470–475, 476–481, 520–527, 729–732, 733, 850–875, 910–925, 968–973
B. Explain the purpose of government and analyze how its powers are acquired, used, and justified.	74–77, 98–119, 120–149, 171, 191, 297, 326, 360, 479, 531, 559, 671, 733, 779, 827, 853, 901, 943
C. Analyze and explain ideas and mechanisms to meet needs and wants of citizens, regulate territory, manage conflict, establish order and security, and balance competing conceptions of a just society.	120–129, 171, 191, 222–229, 236–248, 284–308, 314–350, 356–378, 398–404, 428–436, 470–475, 479, 520–542, 559, 650–667, 671, 733, 779, 827, 850–876, 901, 910–926, 943
D. Compare and analyze the ways nations and organizations respond to conflicts between forces of unity and forces of diversity.	442–449, 604–609, 952–957, 1016–1021
E. Compare different political systems (their ideologies, structure, institutions, processes, and political cultures) with that of the United States, and identify representative political leaders from selected historical and contemporary settings.	14–33, 264–269, 682–687, 694–701, 760–765, 990–998, 1036–1047
F. Analyze and evaluate conditions, actions, and motivations that contribute to conflict and cooperation within and among nations.	162–167, 188–193, 212–216, 264–276, 284–308, 356–365, 398–404, 490–514, 548–555, 576–582, 682–707, 760–773, 830–837, 882–903, 990–995, 1036–1047
G. Evaluate the role of technology in communications, transportation, information-processing, weapons development, or other areas as it contributes to or helps resolve conflicts.	15, 196, 203, 318, 388–389, 396, 41–413, 418, 451, 566, 598, 691, 783, 832–833, 982–983, 1002–1007
H. Explain and apply ideas, theories, and modes of inquiry drawn from political science to the examination of persistent ideas and social problems.	40–41, 45–47, 810, 936
I. Evaluate the extent to which governments achieve their stated ideals and policies at home and abroad.	86–91, 180–181, 372–377, 403, 570–572, 640–643, 668–673, 682–693, 746–753, 842–843, 898–903, 950–951, 980–981, 990–995
J. Prepare a public policy paper and present and defend it before an appropriate forum in school or community.	545

VII. *Production, Distribution, and Consumption*

Societies try to meet people's needs and wants by trying to answer the basic economic questions: What is to be produced? How should goods be produced? How should goods and services be distributed? How should land, labor, capital, and management be allocated? By studying how needs and wants are met, students learn how trade and government economic policies develop. In high school, students develop economic perspectives and a deeper understanding of key economic concepts and processes.

The American Vision **Related Theme: Economic Factors**

Theme and Performance Expectations	Student Pages
A. Explain how the scarcity of productive resources (human, capital, technological, and natural) requires the development of economic systems to make decisions about how goods and services are to be produced and distributed.	14–41, 194–211, 410–427, 442–449, 490–495, 628–633, 1022–1025
B. Analyze the role that supply and demand, prices, incentives, and profits play in determining what is produced and distributed in a competitive market system.	34–41, 194–201, 202–204, 390–391, 422–427, 628–633, 982–983
C. Consider the costs and benefits to society of allocating goods and services through private and public sectors.	34–41, 194–211, 386–397, 410–435, 520–541, 556–563, 628–633, 650–667, 728–735, 838–843, 982–983, 1022–1025

Theme and Performance Expectations	Student Pages
D. Describe the relationships among the various economic institutions that comprise economic systems such as households, business firms, banks, government agencies, labor unions, and corporations.	372–377, 422–427, 428–435, 548–550, 628–633, 794–799, 974–981, 1002–1005
E. Analyze the role of specialization and exchange in economic processes.	372–377, 422–427
F. Compare how values and beliefs influence economic decisions in different societies.	4–11, 372–377, 386–393, 414–415, 430, 590–595, 794–799, 968–973, 990–995, 1002–1005, 1008–1015
G. Compare basic economic systems according to how rules and procedures deal with demand, supply, prices, the role of government, banks, labor and labor unions, savings and investments, and capital.	429–435, 470–475, 526–530, 534–535, 538–540, 974–981
H. Apply economic concepts and reasoning when evaluating historical and contemporary social developments and issues.	570
I. Distinguish between the domestic and global economic systems, and explain how the two interact.	386–393, 470–475, 490–495
J. Apply knowledge of production, distribution, and consumption in the analysis of a public issue such as the allocation of health care or the consumption of energy, and devise an economic plan for accomplishing a socially desirable outcome related to that issue.	838–843, 958–961, 1008–1015, 1022–1025
K. Distinguish between economics as a field of inquiry and the economy.	590–595, 668–673, 974–981

VIII. *Science, Technology, and Society*

The study of science, technology, and society is ever changing. It raises questions about who will benefit from it and how fundamental values and beliefs can be preserved in a technology-driven society. In high school, students will confront issues that balance the benefits of science and technology against the accompanying social consequences.

The American Vision **Related Theme: Science and Technology**

Theme and Performance Expectations	Student Pages
A. Identify and describe both current and historical examples of the interaction and interdependence of science, technology, and society in a variety of cultural settings.	14–23, 194–201, 203, 254–257, 389, 396–397, 450–455, 504–511, 596–603, 650–659, 830–835, 858–867, 882–889, 982–987, 1002–1005
B. Make judgments about how science and technology have transformed the physical world and human society and our understanding of time, space, place, and human-environment interactions.	12–13, 14–23, 194–201, 254–257, 196–197, 203, 318, 396, 418, 450–455, 512–513, 566, 596–603, 650–659, 691, 782–787, 830–835, 982–987, 1002–1005
C. Analyze how science and technology influence the core values, beliefs, and attitudes of society, and how core values, beliefs, and attitudes of society shape scientific and technological change.	14–23, 194–201, 596–603, 774–781, 830–835, 982–987, 1002–1005
D. Evaluate various policies that have been proposed as ways of dealing with social changes resulting from new technologies, such as genetically engineered plants and animals.	512–513, 958–961, 1002–1005
E. Recognize and interpret varied perspectives about human societies and the physical world using scientific knowledge, ethical standards, and technologies from diverse world cultures.	12–13, 14–23, 1022–1025
F. Formulate strategies and develop policies for influencing public discussions associated with technology-society issues, such as the greenhouse effect.	958–961, 1024–1025

IX. *Global Connections*

As countries grow more interdependent, understanding global connections among world societies becomes important. Students will analyze emerging global issues in many different fields. They will also investigate relationships among the different cultures of the world. High school students will address critical issues such as peace, human rights, trade, and global ecology.

The American Vision **Related Theme: Global Connections**

Theme and Performance Expectations	Student Pages
A. Explain how language, art, music, belief systems, and other cultural elements can facilitate global understanding or cause misunderstanding.	14–23, 24–33, 42–47, 604–621, 782–787, 1032–1055

Theme and Performance Expectations	Student Pages
B. Explain conditions and motivations that contribute to conflict, cooperation, and interdependence among groups, societies, and nations.	59–115, 176–181, 188–193, 212–215, 264–275, 280–377, 496–511, 546–581, 678–787, 880–925, 990–995, 1036–1047
C. Analyze and evaluate the effects of changing technologies on the global community.	202–211, 230–235, 410–421, 610–615, 800–809, 958–964, 1002–1006
D. Analyze the causes, consequences, and possible solutions to persistent, contemporary, and emerging global issues, such as health, security, resource allocation, economic development, and environmental quality.	648–673, 838–843, 848–875, 908–925, 952–961, 968–973, 1030–1055
E. Analyze the relationships and tensions between national sovereignty and global interests, in such matters as territory, economic development, nuclear and other weapons, use of natural resources, and human rights concerns.	52–91, 176–181, 490–511, 548–555, 682–687, 746–753, 758–787, 830–837, 880–891, 934–939, 958–961, 990–996, 1036–1047
F. Analyze or formulate policy statements demonstrating an understanding of concerns, standards, issues, and conflicts related to universal human rights.	14–23, 42–47, 682–687, 694–699, 850–875, 910–925
G. Describe and evaluate the role of international and multinational organizations in the global arena.	760–765, 766–773, 1008–1015, 1022–1025
H. Illustrate how individual behaviors and decisions connect with global systems.	1008–1015, 1022–1025, 1032–1055
X. *Civic Ideals and Practices* **Understanding civic ideals and practices is crucial to complete participation in society and is the main purpose of social studies. Students will learn about civic participation and the role of the citizen within his or her community, country, and world. High school students learn, through experience, to identify social needs, setting directions for public policy, and working to support both individual dignity and the common good.**	
***The American Vision* Related Theme: Civic Rights and Responsibilities**	
A. Explain the origins and interpret the continuing influence of key ideals of the democratic republican form of government, such as individual human dignity, liberty, justice, equality, and the rule of law.	54–61, 74–77, 120–148, 284–293, 824–829, 870–875, 910–925, 952–955, 1016–1019
B. Identify, analyze, interpret, and evaluate sources and examples of citizens' rights and responsibilities.	54–61, 284–293, 694–699, 774–781
C. Locate, access, analyze, organize, synthesize, evaluate, and apply information about selected public issues—identifying, describing, and evaluating multiple points of view.	162–167, 284–293, 302–307, 356–363, 774–781, 824–829, 870–875, 892–897
D. Practice forms of civic discussion and participation consistent with the ideals of citizens in a democratic republic.	247, 829, 857, 889, 897, 919, 939, 951, 973, 981, 1019, 1025, 1035, 1041
E. Analyze and evaluate the influence of various forms of citizen action and public policy.	242–251, 428–435, 470–475
F. Analyze a variety of public policies and issues from the perspective of formal and informal political actors.	242–251, 428–435, 470–475
G. Evaluate the effectiveness of public opinion in influencing and shaping public policy developments and decision-making.	242–251, 428–435, 470–475
H. Evaluate the degree to which public policies and citizen behaviors reflect or foster the stated ideals of a democratic republican form of government.	162–167, 212–215, 230–247, 254–279, 284–307, 354–377, 428–435, 440–481, 490–495, 504–11, 518–541, 588–621, 626–645, 648–673, 792–815, 822–843, 848–875, 908–925, 932–961, 966–995, 1008–1015, 1030–1055
I. Construct a policy statement and an action plan to achieve one or more goals related to an issue of public concern.	247, 887, 889, 897, 919, 973, 981, 1019, 1025
J. Participate in activities to strengthen the "common good," based upon careful evaluation of possible options for citizen action.	857, 987, 1041

Using the Teacher Wraparound Edition

To Teachers:

Welcome to the Teacher Wraparound Edition of *The American Vision*. We have created this teacher edition based on input from experienced teachers and educational consultants. Our goal is to provide you with teaching strategies and activities that are labeled for you at point-of-use. The following pages will show the structure of the Teacher Wraparound Edition.

Student-Based Instruction

Point-of-Use

- Strategies and activities apply directly to student content.

Differentiated Instruction

- Leveled activities and options for differentiated instruction help meet the needs of all your students, including English language learners.

Review and Reinforcement

- Reading and critical thinking skills are reinforced throughout the lesson.

Assessment and Intervention

- Chapter Assessments provide standardized test practice.
- Assessments gauge student mastery of content.
- Additional resources provide intervention options.

Planning and Teaching the Unit

Planning pages appear at the beginning of each unit.

Pacing Chart

Provides time management suggestions for teaching the unit

Author Note

Highlights author's ideas for teaching the unit

Teacher to Teacher

Includes activities from the classrooms of successful teachers

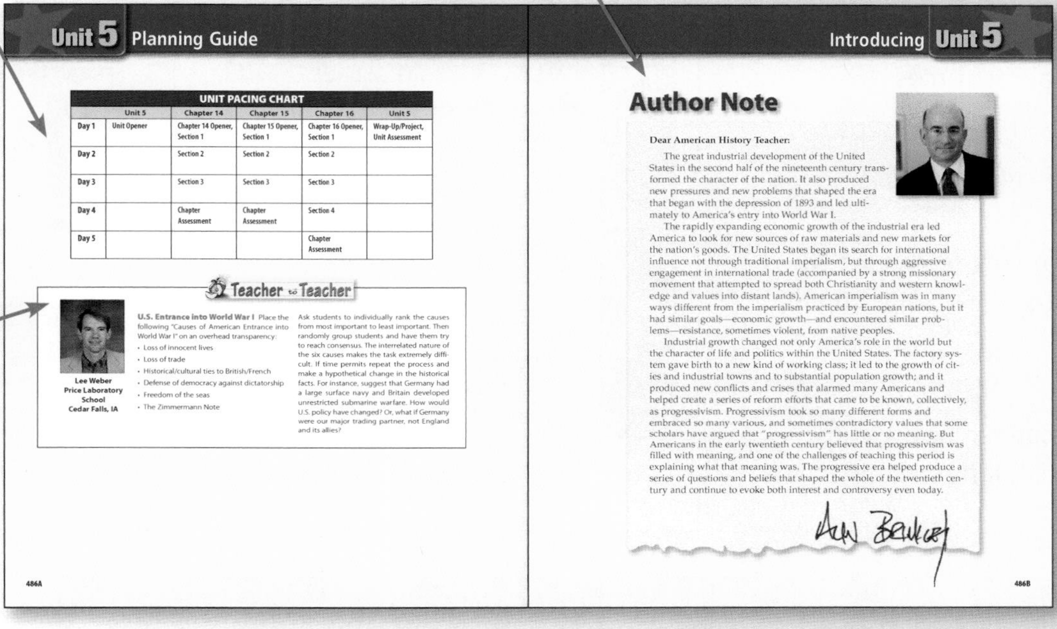

Unit 5 Planning Guide

UNIT PACING CHART					
	Unit 5	Chapter 14	Chapter 15	Chapter 16	Unit 5
Day 1	Unit Opener	Chapter 14 Opener, Section 1	Chapter 15 Opener, Section 1	Chapter 16 Opener, Section 1	Wrap-Up/Project, Unit Assessment
Day 2		Section 2	Section 2	Section 2	
Day 3		Section 3	Section 3	Section 3	
Day 4		Chapter Assessment	Chapter Assessment	Section 4	
Day 5				Chapter Assessment	

Teacher to Teacher

Lee Weber
Price Laboratory School
Cedar Falls, IA

U.S. Entrance into World War I Place the following "Causes of American Entrance into World War I" on an overhead transparency:

- Loss of innocent lives
- Loss of trade
- Historical/cultural ties to British/French
- Defense of democracy against dictatorship
- Freedom of the seas
- The Zimmermann Note

Ask students to individually rank the causes from most important to least important. Then randomly group students and have them try to reach consensus. The interrelated nature of the six causes makes the task extremely difficult. If time permits repeat the process and make a hypothetical change in the historical facts. For instance, suggest that Germany had a large surface navy and Britain developed unrestricted submarine warfare. How would U.S. policy have changed? Or, what if Germany were our major trading partner, not England and its allies?

486A

Introducing Unit 5

Author Note

Dear American History Teacher:

The great industrial development of the United States in the second half of the nineteenth century transformed the character of the nation. It also produced new pressures and new problems that shaped the era that began with the depression of 1893 and led ultimately to America's entry into World War I.

The rapidly expanding economic growth of the industrial era led America to look for new sources of raw materials and new markets for the nation's goods. The United States began its search for international influence not through traditional imperialism, but through aggressive engagement in international trade (accompanied by a strong missionary movement that attempted to spread both Christianity and western knowledge and values into distant lands). American imperialism was in many ways different from the imperialism practiced by European nations, but it had similar goals—economic growth—and encountered similar problems—resistance, sometimes violent, from native peoples.

Industrial growth changed not only America's role in the world but the character of life and politics within the United States. The factory system gave birth to a new kind of working class; it led to the growth of cities and industrial towns and to substantial population growth; and it produced new conflicts and crises that alarmed many Americans and helped create a series of reform efforts that came to be known, collectively, as progressivism. Progressivism took so many different forms and embraced so many various, and sometimes contradictory values that some scholars have argued that "progressivism" has little or no meaning. But Americans in the early twentieth century believed that progressivism was filled with meaning, and one of the challenges of teaching this period is explaining what that meaning was. The progressive era helped produce a series of questions and beliefs that shaped the whole of the twentieth century and continue to evoke both interest and controversy even today.

486B

Why It Matters

Provides an activity to help students discover why the events they will study are important

Skill Practice

Point-of-use skill-based activities help students practice historical analysis and geography skills

Team Teaching Activity

Introduce the unit by relating history to other social studies disciplines

Introducing Unit 5

Focus

Why It Matters
Tell students that today many people consider the United States the world's only superpower. Ask students if they agree with that assessment and why or why not. OL

Connecting to Past Learning
Have students identify nations that they think are powerful. **Ask:** What makes a nation powerful? *(Answers might include a strong military, a robust economy, industry, and political influence.)* Tell students that in this unit they will learn about how the United States became a world power and became increasingly involved in world events. OL

Unit Launch Activity
Making Connections Have students brainstorm a list of weapons used in warfare today. List students' answers on the board. **Ask:** Which of these weapons existed at the beginning of the twentieth century? *(Answers will vary.)* Discuss with the class how new weaponry has changed warfare since the early 1900s. OL

Unit 5

Imperialism and Progressivism
1890–1920

CHAPTER 14
Becoming a World Power
1872–1917

CHAPTER 15
The Progressive Movement
1890–1920

CHAPTER 16
World War I and Its Aftermath
1914–1920

Why It Matters
Between 1890 and 1920 two very important developments took place in American history. First, the United States began its rise to the global superpower it is today. Second, reformers began changing the government to solve problems caused by industrialism. Government became more involved in society than ever before.

Team Teaching Activity

Sociology Read to the students the following lines written by poet Sarah Cleghorn in the early 1900s: "The golf links lie so near the mill/That almost every day/The laboring children can look out/And see the men at play." **Ask:** What do you think this quote tells you about the economic and social conditions in the United States in 1900? *(There were no child labor laws; children worked in factories; wealthy men played golf.)* Have the economics teacher come and explain the evolution of child labor laws and their impact on the business world. OL

486

U.S. warships battle the Spanish off the coast of Cuba, 1898.

487

More About the Photo

The U.S. fleet set out for Havana Harbor during the Spanish-American War. The quick American victory in that war made the nation an imperialist power.

Introducing Unit 5

Teach

S1 Skill Practice
Visual Literacy Have students study the unit painting.
Ask: What impression or feeling is the artist trying to convey in this painting? *(The United States is militarily strong; the Spanish fleet is weak.)* BL

S2 Skill Practice
Concluding Have students again review the unit painting.
Ask: What is the topic of the painting? *(America's military power)* Discuss with the class why reformers might be opposed to the nation's growing military power at the beginning of the twentieth century. OL

NCLB No Child Left Behind

Teaching Tip The NCLB Act emphasizes reading. Have students make a time line that begins with 1872 and ends with 1919. Have them keep the time line with them and add key events as they read the unit. Students can use the time line while studying to help understand the sequence of events.

487

Planning the Chapter

Chapter Planning Guides provide a snapshot of the scope of resources available to enhance and extend learning in each chapter.

Incorporating Resources

Utilizes a structured lesson plan to incorporate additional resources

Leveled Activities

Organizes resources by appropriate ability levels

*Spanish Resources

Indicates resources for English language learners

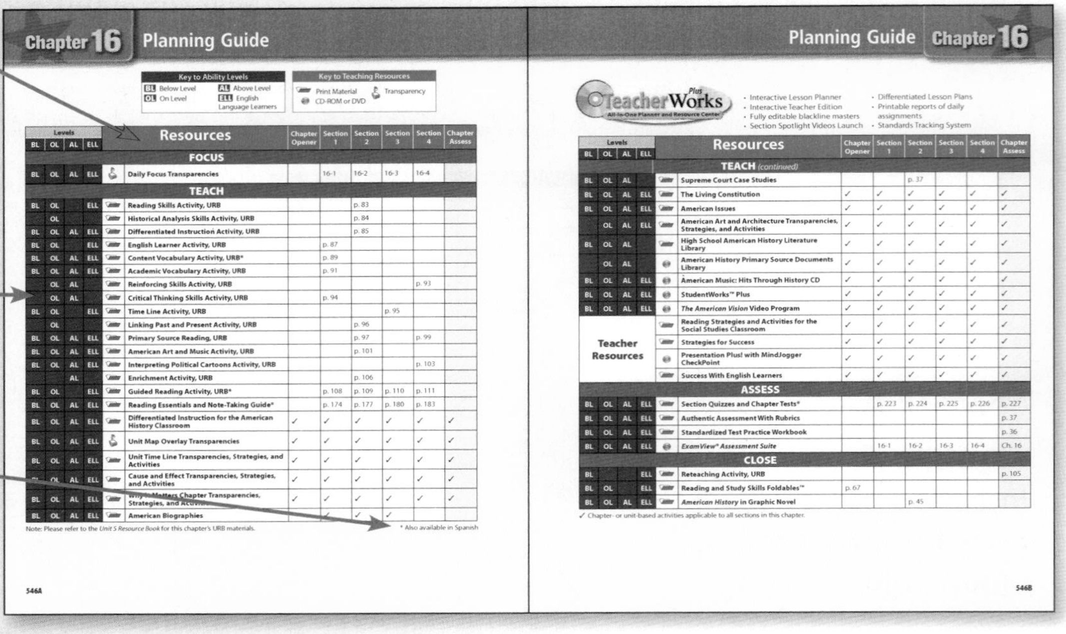

Additional Resources

Identifies resources for supplementing the chapter

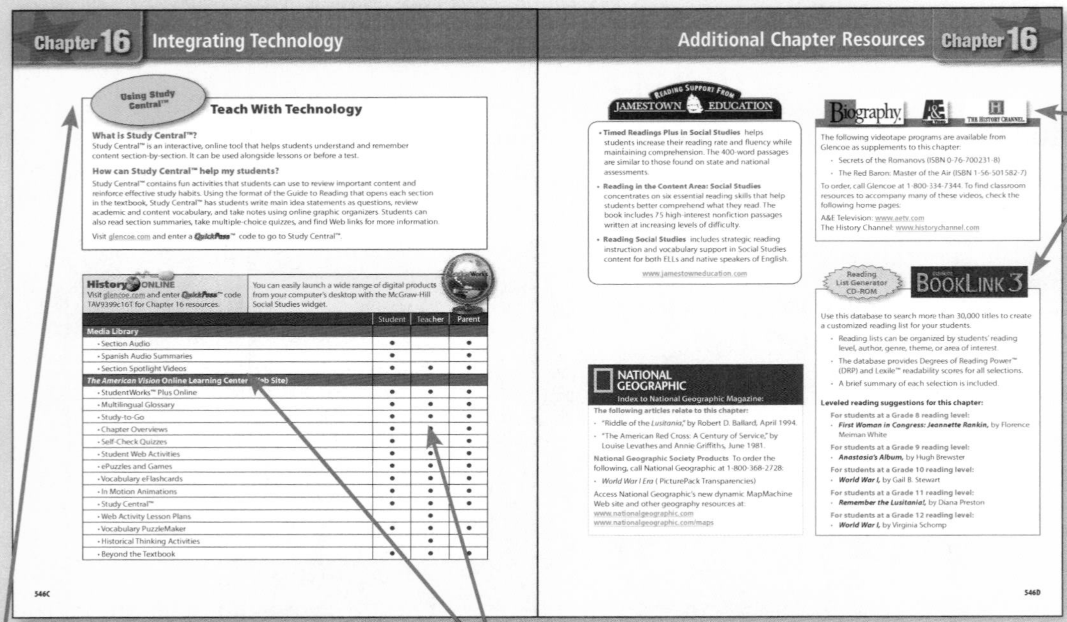

Teaching with Technology

Explains how to incorporate different Glencoe technology resources in the classroom

Online Learning and *QuickPass*™

Easily access engaging online content using a *QuickPass*™ code that takes you directly to resources for the chapter you are teaching

Teaching the Chapter

The Big Ideas and Essential Question at the beginning of the chapter help you teach the most important chapter contents.

Making Connections

Introductory questions lead to an exploration of big ideas. These questions activate students' prior knowledge and lead students to see not only the "big picture," but also the relevancy of what they are learning. These lesson launcher activities compel students to consider the big idea of the chapter.

The Big Ideas

Big Ideas are themes, issues, concepts, questions, or ideas tied to the main concepts of the chapter and of each section. The Essential Question leads to an understanding of Big Ideas. These questions are broad and have no right or wrong answers. Essential Questions are thought-provoking, challenge old assumptions, and stimulate discussion. Student activities throughout the chapter will refer back to the Essential Question, leading to a greater comprehension of chapter themes.

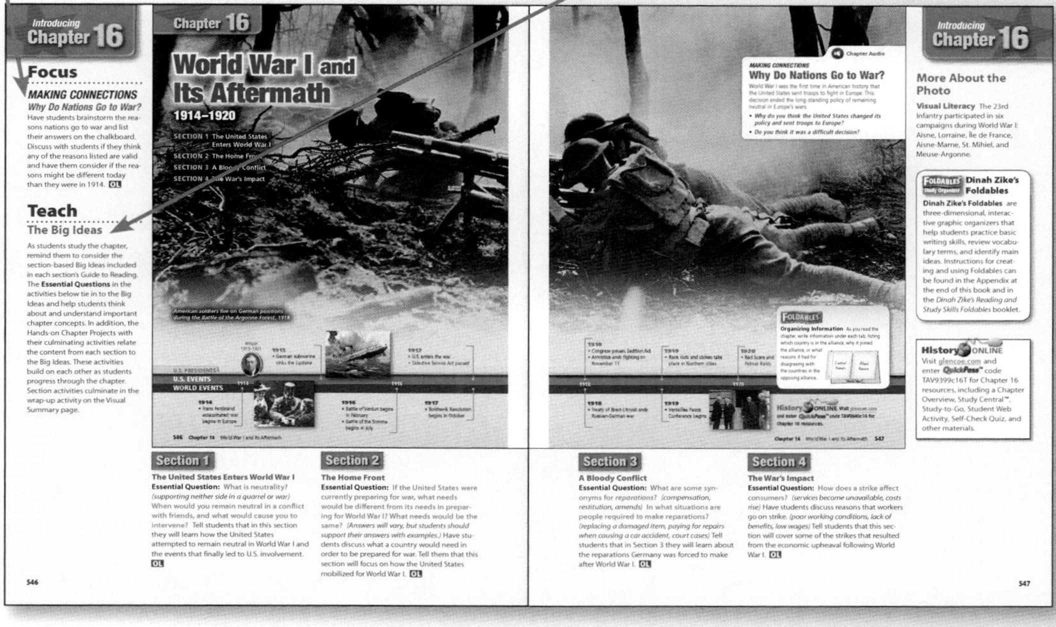

Introducing Chapter 16

Focus

MAKING CONNECTIONS
Why Do Nations Go to War?
Have students brainstorm the reasons nations go to war and list their answers on the chalkboard. Discuss with students if they think any of the reasons listed are valid and have them consider if the reasons might be different today than they were in 1914. OL

Teach

The Big Ideas

As students study the chapter, remind them to consider the section-based Big Ideas included in each section's Guide to Reading. The **Essential Questions** in the activities below tie in to the Big Ideas and help students think about and understand important chapter concepts. In addition, the Hands-on Chapter Projects with their culminating activities relate the content from each section to the Big Ideas. These activities build on each other as students progress through the chapter. Section activities culminate in the wrap-up activity on the Visual Summary page.

Chapter 16

World War I and Its Aftermath
1914–1920

SECTION 1 The United States Enters World War I
SECTION 2 The Home Front
SECTION 3 A Bloody Conflict
SECTION 4 The War's Impact

American soldiers fire on German positions during the Battle of the Argonne Forest, 1918

U.S. PRESIDENTS
Wilson 1913–1921
U.S. EVENTS
WORLD EVENTS
1914 • Franz Ferdinand assassinated; war begins in Europe
1915 • German submarine sinks the *Lusitania*
1916 • Battle of Verdun begins in February • Battle of the Somme begins in July
1917 • U.S. enters the war • Selective Service Act passed
1917 • Bolshevik Revolution begins in October

546 Chapter 16 World War I and Its Aftermath

Chapter Audio

MAKING CONNECTIONS
Why Do Nations Go to War?
World War I was the first time in American history that the United States sent troops to fight in Europe. This decision ended the long-standing policy of remaining neutral in Europe's wars.
- *Why do you think the United States changed its policy and sent troops to Europe?*
- *Do you think it was a difficult decision?*

FOLDABLES
Organizing Information As you read the chapter, write information under each tab, listing which country is in the alliance, why it joined the alliance, or what reasons it had for disagreeing with the countries in the opposing alliance.

1918 • Congress passes Sedition Act • Armistice ends fighting on November 11
1919 • Race riots and strikes take place in Northern cities
1920 • Red Scare and Palmer Raids
1918 • Treaty of Brest-Litovsk ends Russian-German war
1919 • Versailles Peace Conference begins

History ONLINE Visit glencoe.com and enter QuickPass™ code TAV9399c16 for Chapter 16 resources.

Chapter 16 World War I and Its Aftermath 547

Introducing Chapter 16

More About the Photo

Visual Literacy The 23rd Infantry participated in six campaigns during World War I: Aisne, Lorraine, Île de France, Aisne-Marne, St. Mihiel, and Meuse-Argonne.

Dinah Zike's Foldables

Dinah Zike's Foldables are three-dimensional, interactive graphic organizers that help students practice basic writing skills, review vocabulary terms, and identify main ideas. Instructions for creating and using Foldables can be found in the Appendix at the end of this book and in the *Dinah Zike's Reading and Study Skills Foldables* booklet.

History ONLINE
Visit glencoe.com and enter QuickPass™ code TAV9399c16T for Chapter 16 resources, including a Chapter Overview, Study Central™, Study-to-Go, Student Web Activity, Self-Check Quiz, and other materials.

Section 1

The United States Enters World War I
Essential Question: What is neutrality? *(supporting neither side in a quarrel or war)* When would you remain neutral in a conflict with friends, and what would cause you to intervene? Tell students that in this section they will learn how the United States attempted to remain neutral in World War I and the events that finally led to U.S. involvement. OL

Section 2

The Home Front
Essential Question: If the United States were currently preparing for war, what needs would be different from its needs in preparing for World War I? What needs would be the same? *(Answers will vary, but students should support their answers with examples.)* Have students discuss what a country would need in order to be prepared for war. Tell them that this section will focus on how the United States mobilized for World War I. OL

Section 3

A Bloody Conflict
Essential Question: What are some synonyms for *reparations*? *(compensation, restitution, amends)* In what situations are people required to make reparations? *(replacing a damaged item, paying for repairs when causing a car accident, court cases)* Tell students that in Section 3 they will learn about the reparations Germany was forced to make after World War I. OL

Section 4

The War's Impact
Essential Question: How does a strike affect consumers? *(services become unavailable, costs rise)* Have students discuss reasons that workers go on strike. *(poor working conditions, lack of benefits, low wages)* Tell students that this section will cover some of the strikes that resulted from the economic upheaval following World War I. OL

546

547

Lesson Structure

Each lesson in *The American Vision* is presented in a structured lesson plan: Focus, Teach, Assess, and Close.

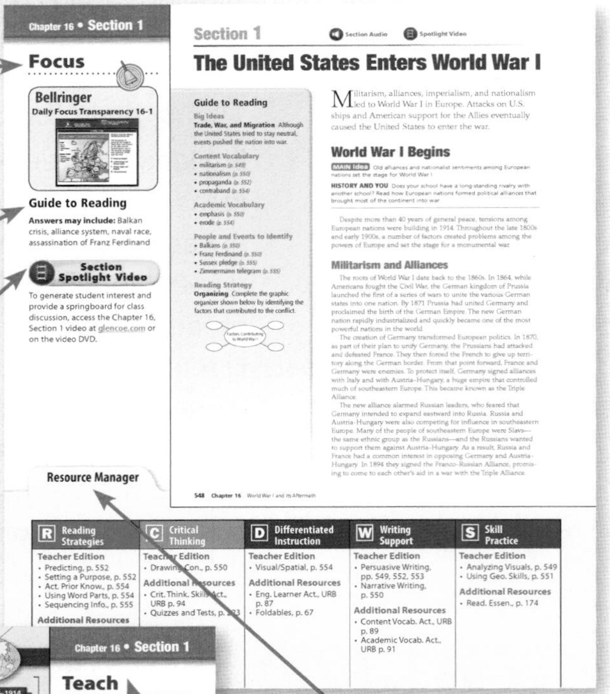

FOCUS

Includes a Bellringer activity to help your students think about the lesson topic

Guide to Reading

Provides pre-reading strategies to improve comprehension

Spotlight Video

Engages students with the content using a short BBC video

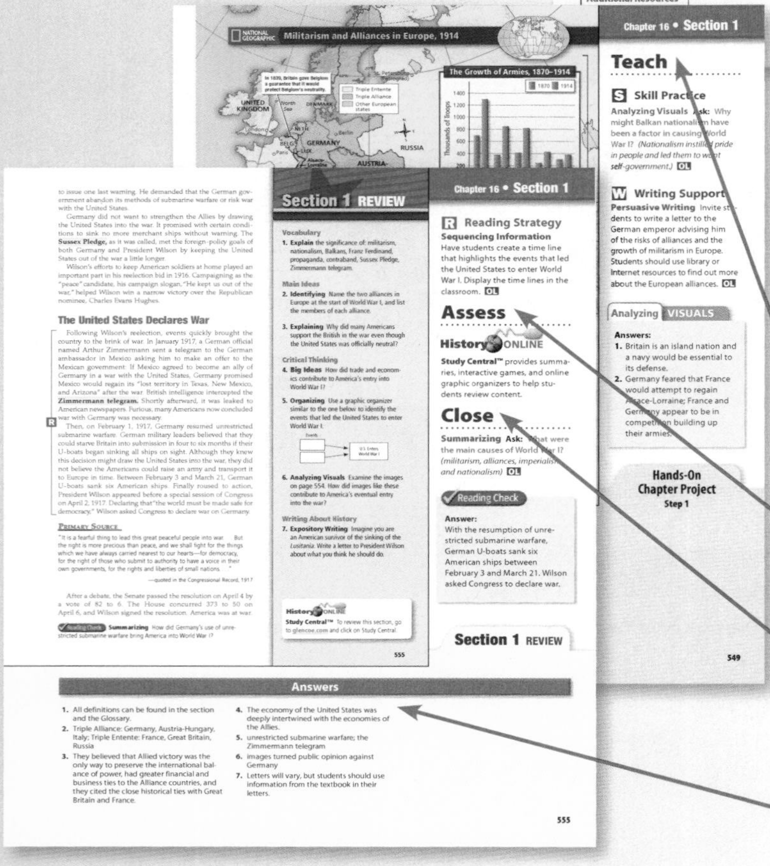

Resource Manager

Provides a list of teacher edition and supplemental resources that support lesson content and reinforce skills

TEACH

Stimulate learning and interest using leveled activities

ASSESS

Identifies assessment resources

CLOSE

Gauges comprehension of section content

Answers

Lists the answers to Student Edition questions

Understanding the Brackets and Letters

Brackets

Brackets on the reduced Student Edition page correspond to teaching strategies and activities in the Teacher Wraparound Edition. As you teach the section, the brackets show you exactly where to teach these strategies and activities.

Letters*

The letters on the reduced Student Edition page identify the type of strategy or activity. See the key below to learn about the different types of strategies and activities.

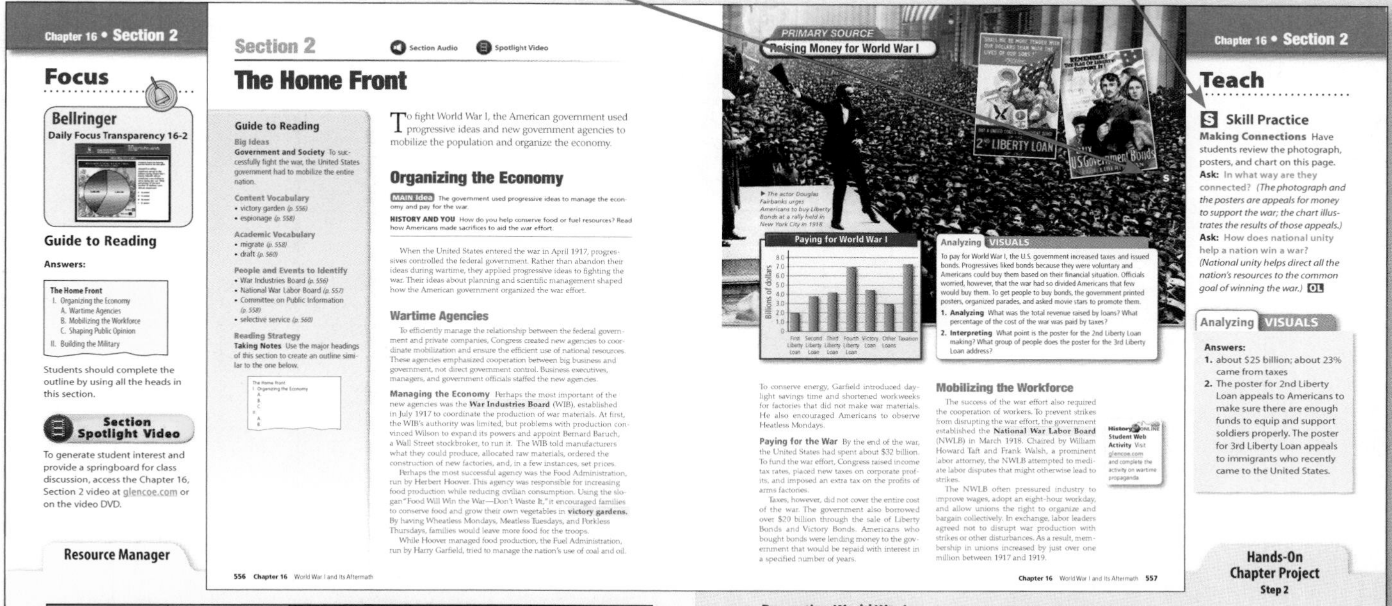

R Reading Strategies	C Critical Thinking	D Differentiated Instruction	W Writing Support	S Skill Practice
Teacher Edition • Understanding Vocab., p. 560 **Additional Resources** • Prim. Source Read., URB p. 97 • Guid. Read. Act., URB p. 109 • Am. History in Graphic Novel, p. 45 • Reading Skills Act., URB p. 83	**Additional Resources** • Enrichment Act., URB p. 106 • Linking Past and Present, URB p. 96 • Supreme Court Case Studies, p. 37 • Quizzes and Tests, p. 224	**Teacher Edition** • Special Ed., p. 558 • Verbal/Ling., p. 560 **Additional Resources** • Diff. Instr. Act., URB p. 85 • Am. Art and Music Act., URB p. 101	**Teacher Edition** • Narrative Writing, p. 561 **Additional Resources** • Enrichment Act., URB p. 106	**Teacher Edition** • Making Conn., p. 557 • Using Geo. Skills, p. 558 **Additional Resources** • Hist. Analysis Skills Act., URB p. 84 • Read. Essen., p. 177

KEY for Using the Teacher Wraparound Edition

R **Reading Strategies** activities help you teach reading skills and vocabulary.

C **Critical Thinking** strategies help students apply and extend what they have learned.

D **Differentiated Instruction** activities provide differentiated instruction for students learning to speak English, along with suggestions for teaching various types of learners.

S **Skill Practice** strategies help students practice historical analysis and geography skills.

W **Writing Support** activities provide writing opportunities to help students comprehend the text.

* Letters are followed by a number when there is more than one of the same type of strategy or activity on the page.

Hands-On Chapter Projects

Extend student learning with unique and interactive Hands-On Chapter Projects. These activities allow students to take principles and put them to practical use. Projects progress through each section and culminate in a wrap-up discussion. Students conceptualize, plan, and execute their vision in a hands-on approach that makes people and places in history come alive.

Steps

Each lesson includes a self-contained activity, with one lesson building on knowledge gained from previous lessons.

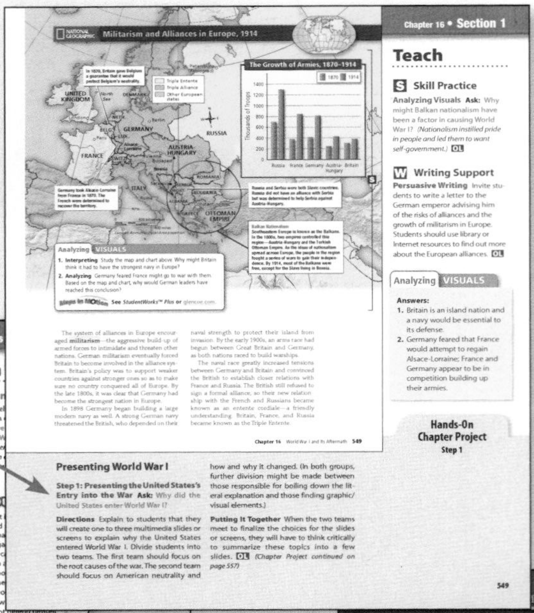

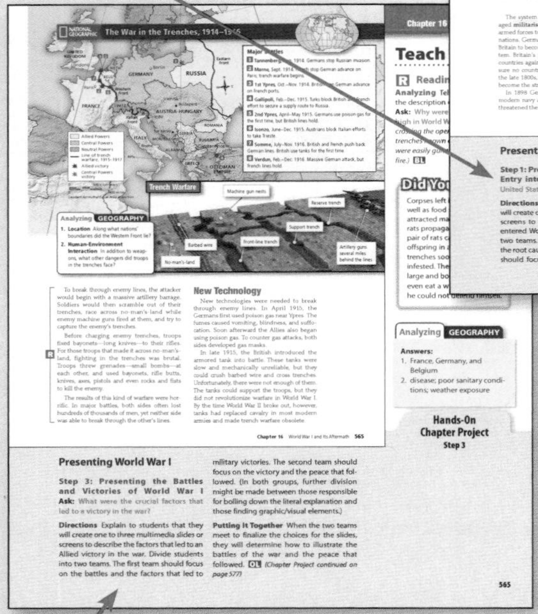

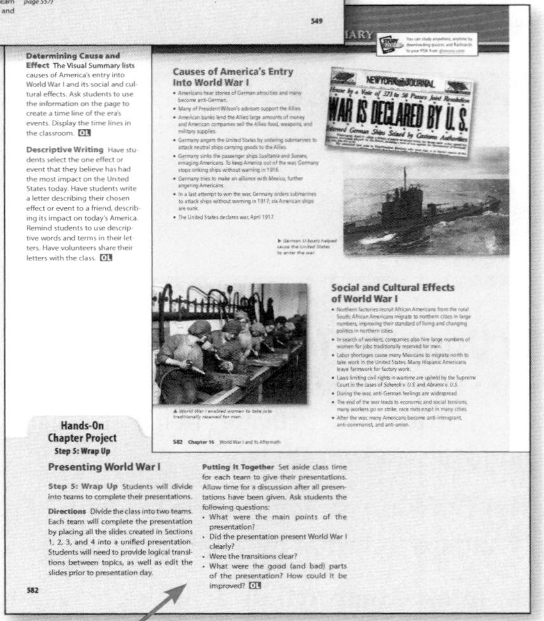

Hands-On

Students utilize diverse learning styles and creativity and work cooperatively to create their projects.

Results

The Hands-On project culminates in an interactive discussion where students synthesize what they have learned and draw conclusions.

Differentiated Instruction

Each section of the Teacher Wraparound Edition of *The American Vision* provides differentiated instruction activities to meet the diverse needs of every student.

Differentiated Activities

Innovative ideas meet each student's interests and learning styles through point-of-use activities

Additional Resources

Provides suggestions for incorporating additional resources based on students' different learning abilities

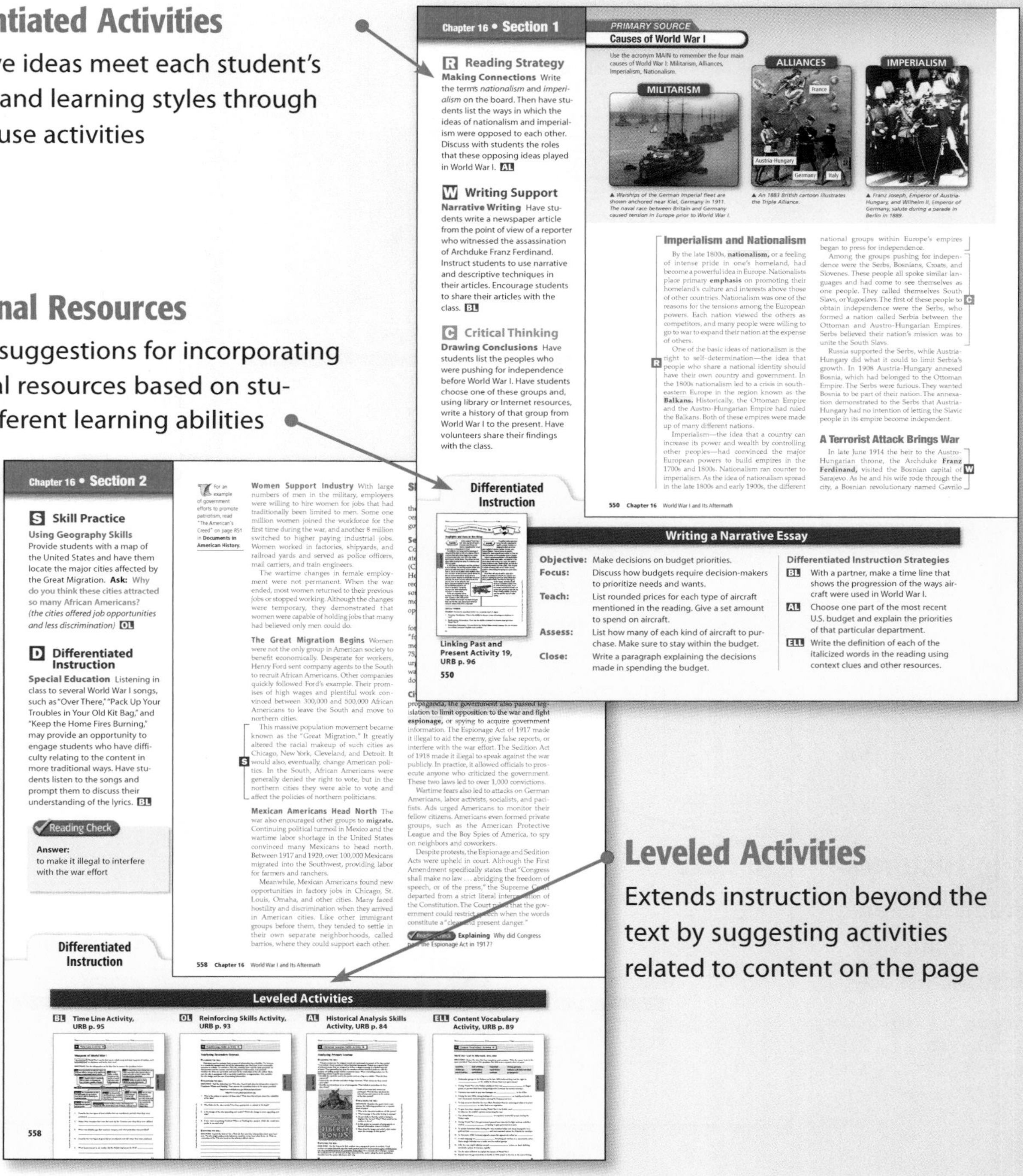

Chapter 16 • Section 1

R Reading Strategy
Making Connections Write the terms *nationalism* and *imperialism* on the board. Then have students list the ways in which the ideas of nationalism and imperialism were opposed to each other. Discuss with students the roles that these opposing ideas played in World War I. AL

W Writing Support
Narrative Writing Have students write a newspaper article from the point of view of a reporter who witnessed the assassination of Archduke Franz Ferdinand. Instruct students to use narrative and descriptive techniques in their articles. Encourage students to share their articles with the class. BL

C Critical Thinking
Drawing Conclusions Have students list the peoples who were pushing for independence before World War I. Have students choose one of these groups and, using library or Internet resources, write a history of that group from World War I to the present. Have volunteers share their findings with the class.

PRIMARY SOURCE
Causes of World War I

Use the acronym MAIN to remember the four main causes of World War I: Militarism, Alliances, Imperialism, Nationalism.

MILITARISM / ALLIANCES / IMPERIALISM

Imperialism and Nationalism

A Terrorist Attack Brings War

550 Chapter 16 World War I and Its Aftermath

Differentiated Instruction

Linking Past and Present Activity 19, URB p. 96

Writing a Narrative Essay

Objective: Make decisions on budget priorities.
Focus: Discuss how budgets require decision-makers to prioritize needs and wants.
Teach: List rounded prices for each type of aircraft mentioned in the reading. Give a set amount to spend on aircraft.
Assess: List how many of each kind of aircraft to purchase. Make sure to stay within the budget.
Close: Write a paragraph explaining the decisions made in spending the budget.

Differentiated Instruction Strategies
BL With a partner, make a time line that shows the progression of the ways aircraft were used in World War I.
AL Choose one part of the most recent U.S. budget and explain the priorities of that particular department.
ELL Write the definition of each of the italicized words in the reading using context clues and other resources.

Chapter 16 • Section 2

S Skill Practice
Using Geography Skills Provide students with a map of the United States and have them locate the major cities affected by the Great Migration. **Ask:** Why do you think these cities attracted so many African Americans? *(the cities offered job opportunities and less discrimination)* OL

D Differentiated Instruction
Special Education Listening in class to several World War I songs, such as "Over There," "Pack Up Your Troubles in Your Old Kit Bag," and "Keep the Home Fires Burning," may provide an opportunity to engage students who have difficulty relating to the content in more traditional ways. Have students listen to the songs and prompt them to discuss their understanding of the lyrics. BL

Reading Check
Answer: to make it illegal to interfere with the war effort

Women Support Industry / The Great Migration Begins / Mexican Americans Head North

558 Chapter 16 World War I and Its Aftermath

Differentiated Instruction

Leveled Activities

BL Time Line Activity, URB p. 95
OL Reinforcing Skills Activity, URB p. 93
AL Historical Analysis Skills Activity, URB p. 84
ELL Content Vocabulary Activity, URB p. 89

Leveled Activities

Extends instruction beyond the text by suggesting activities related to content on the page

Dynamic Features

Use these creative features to dig deep into the fascinating people, places, and cultures covered in the text.

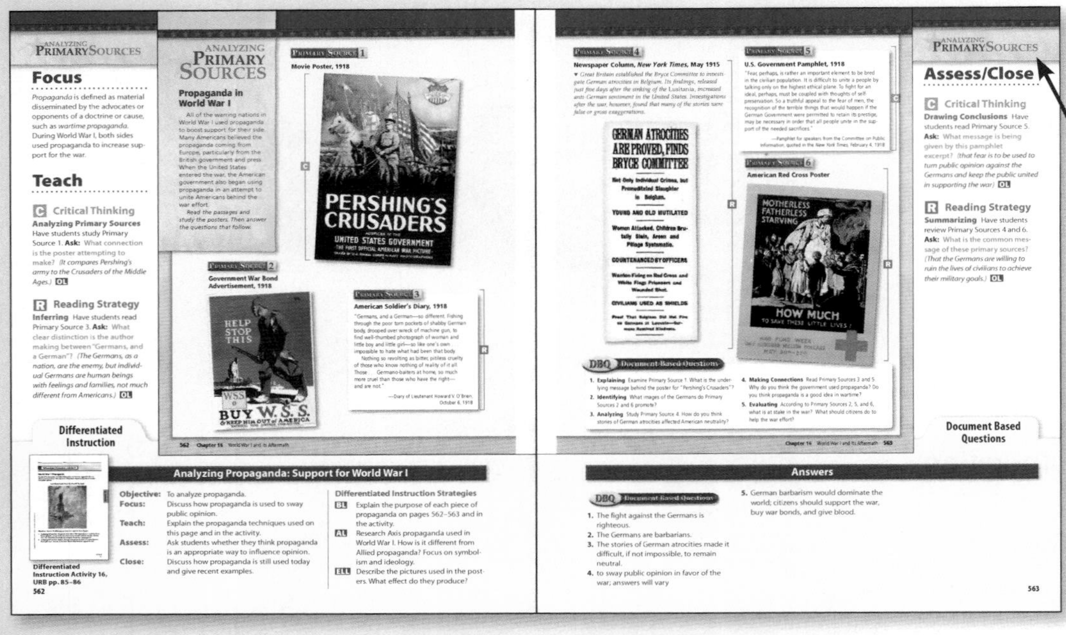

Analyzing Primary Sources

Primary Source readings provide opportunities for historical analysis and discussion

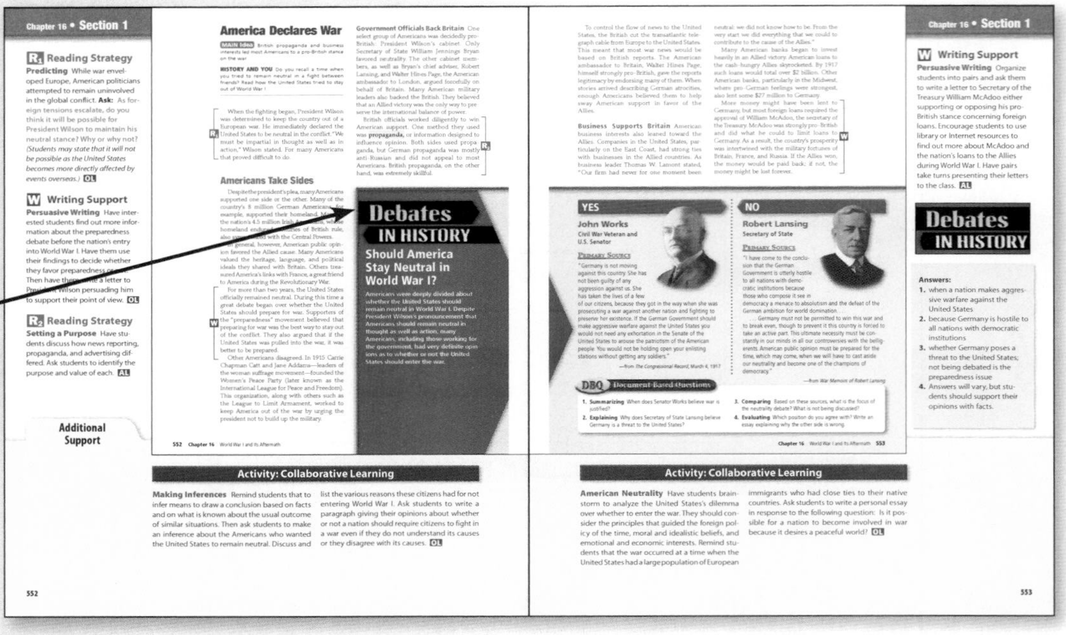

Debates in History

Teaches students to analyze different points-of-view on historical issues

Chapter Summary and Assessment

Visual Summary

Summary activities help students to synthesize major chapter themes.

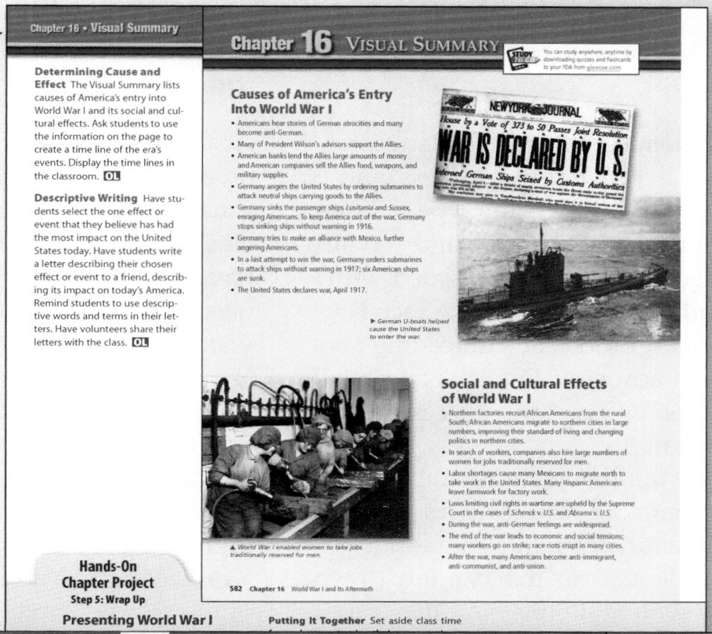
Chapter 16 • Visual Summary

Determining Cause and Effect The Visual Summary lists causes of America's entry into World War I and its social and cultural effects. Ask students to use the information on the page to create a time line of the era's events. Display the time lines in the classroom. OL

Descriptive Writing Have students select the one effect or event that they believe has had the most impact on the United States today. Have students write a letter describing their chosen effect or event to a friend, describing its impact on today's America. Remind students to use descriptive words and terms in their letters. Have volunteers share their letters with the class. OL

Chapter 16 VISUAL SUMMARY

Causes of America's Entry Into World War I

- Americans hear stories of German atrocities and many become anti-German.
- Many of President Wilson's advisors support the Allies.
- American banks lend the Allies large amounts of money and American companies sell the Allies food, weapons, and military supplies.
- Germany angers the United States by ordering submarines to attack neutral ships carrying goods to the Allies.
- Germany sinks the passenger ships *Lusitania* and *Sussex*, enraging Americans. To keep America out of the war, Germany stops sinking ships without warning in 1916.
- Germany tries to make an alliance with Mexico, further angering Americans.
- In a last attempt to win the war, Germany orders submarines to attack ships without warning in 1917; six American ships are sunk.
- The United States declares war, April 1917.

NEW YORK JOURNAL — WAR IS DECLARED BY U.S.

▶ German U-boats helped cause the United States to enter the war.

▲ World War I enabled women to take jobs traditionally reserved for men.

Social and Cultural Effects of World War I

- Northern factories recruit African Americans from the rural South; African Americans migrate to northern cities in large numbers, improving their standard of living and changing politics in northern cities.
- In search of workers, companies also hire large numbers of women for jobs traditionally reserved for men.
- Labor shortages cause many Mexicans to migrate north to take work in the United States. Many Hispanic Americans leave farmwork for factory work.
- Laws limiting civil rights in wartime are upheld by the Supreme Court in the cases of *Schenck v. U.S.* and *Abrams v. U.S.*
- During the war, anti-German feelings are widespread.
- The end of the war leads to economic and social tensions; many workers go on strike; race riots erupt in many cities.
- After the war, many Americans become anti-immigrant, anti-communist, and anti-union.

582 Chapter 16 World War I and Its Aftermath

Hands-On Chapter Project Step 5: Wrap Up — Presenting World War I

Putting It Together Set aside class time

Standardized Test Practice

Answers incorporate analysis and identify potential student pitfalls, challenges, distracters, and test-taking strategies.

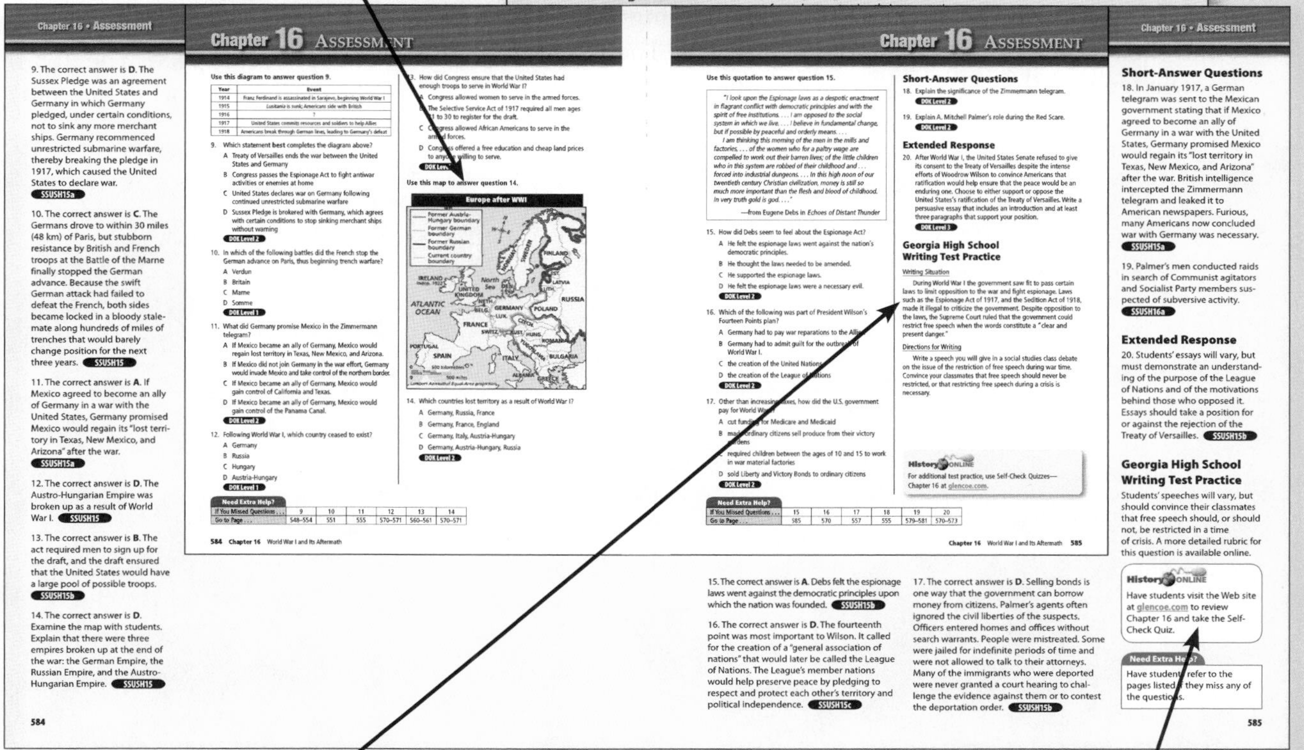
Chapter 16 • Assessment

9. The correct answer is **D**. The Sussex Pledge was an agreement between the United States and Germany in which Germany pledged, under certain conditions, not to sink any more merchant ships. Germany recommenced unrestricted submarine warfare, thereby breaking the pledge in 1917, which caused the United States to declare war. SSUSH15a

10. The correct answer is **C**. The Germans drove to within 30 miles (48 km) of Paris, but stubborn resistance by British and French troops at the Battle of the Marne finally stopped the German advance. Because the swift German attack had failed to defeat the French, both sides became locked in a bloody stalemate along hundreds of miles of trenches that would barely change position for the next three years. SSUSH15

11. The correct answer is **A**. If Mexico agreed to become an ally of Germany in a war with the United States, Germany promised Mexico would regain its "lost territory in Texas, New Mexico, and Arizona" after the war. SSUSH15a

12. The correct answer is **D**. The Austro-Hungarian Empire was broken up as a result of World War I. SSUSH15

13. The correct answer is **B**. The act required men to sign up for the draft, and the draft ensured that the United States would have a large pool of possible troops. SSUSH15b

14. The correct answer is **D**. Examine the map with students. Explain that there were three empires broken up at the end of the war: the German Empire, the Russian Empire, and the Austro-Hungarian Empire. SSUSH15

584

Chapter 16 ASSESSMENT

Chapter 16 ASSESSMENT

Short-Answer Questions

Extended Response

Georgia High School Writing Test Practice

584 Chapter 16 World War I and Its Aftermath

Chapter 16 World War I and Its Aftermath 585

15. The correct answer is **A**. Debs felt the espionage laws went against the democratic principles upon which the nation was founded. SSUSH15b

16. The correct answer is **D**. The fourteenth point was most important to Wilson. It called for the creation of a "general association of nations" that would later be called the League of Nations. The League's member nations would help preserve peace by pledging to respect and protect each other's territory and political independence. SSUSH15c

17. The correct answer is **D**. Selling bonds is one way that the government can borrow money from citizens. Palmer's agents often ignored the civil liberties of the suspects. Officers entered homes and offices without search warrants. People were mistreated. Some were jailed for indefinite periods of time and were not allowed to talk to their attorneys. Many of the immigrants who were deported were never granted a court hearing to challenge the evidence against them or to contest the deportation order. SSUSH15b

Chapter 16 • Assessment

Short-Answer Questions

18. In January 1917, a German telegram was sent to the Mexican government stating that if Mexico agreed to become an ally of Germany in a war with the United States, Germany promised Mexico would regain its "lost territory in Texas, New Mexico, and Arizona" after the war. British intelligence intercepted the Zimmermann telegram and leaked it to American newspapers. Furious, many Americans now concluded war with Germany was necessary. SSUSH15a

19. Palmer's men conducted raids in search of Communist agitators and Socialist Party members suspected of subversive activity. SSUSH16a

Extended Response

20. Students' essays will vary, but must demonstrate an understanding of the purpose of the League of Nations and of the motivations behind those who opposed it. Essays should take a position for or against the rejection of the Treaty of Versailles. SSUSH15b

Georgia High School Writing Test Practice

Students' speeches will vary, but should convince their classmates that free speech should, or should not, be restricted in a time of crisis. A more detailed rubric for this question is available online.

History ONLINE — Have students visit the Web site at glencoe.com to review Chapter 16 and take the Self-Check Quiz.

Need Extra Help? — Have students refer to the pages listed if they miss any of the questions.

585

Georgia High School Writing Test Practice

Provides persuasive writing practice on chapter-specific content

History Online

Provides additional assessment opportunities

Classroom Solutions

Academic Vocabulary

How Can I Help My Students Learn Academic Vocabulary?

What Is Academic English?

Academic English is the language used in academics, business, and courts of law. It is the type of English used in textbooks, and contains linguistic features associated with academic disciplines like social studies. Proficiency in reading and using academic English is especially related to long-term success in all parts of life.

By reinforcing academic English, teachers can help learners to access authentic, academic texts—not simplified texts that dummy down the content. In this way, they can provide information that will help build their students' background knowledge rapidly.

What Is Academic Vocabulary?

Academic vocabulary is based on academic English. By the time children have completed elementary school, they must have acquired the knowledge needed to understand academic vocabulary. How many words should they acquire to be able to access their textbooks? A basic 2,000-word vocabulary of high-frequency words makes up 87% of the vocabulary of academic texts. Eight hundred other academic words comprise an additional 8% of the words. Three percent of the remaining words are technical words. The remaining 2% are low-frequency words. There may be as many as 123,000 low-frequency words in academic texts.

Why Should Students Learn Academic Vocabulary?

English learners who have a basic 2,000-word vocabulary are ready to acquire most general words found in their texts.

Knowledge of academic words and general words can significantly boost a student's comprehension level of academic texts. Students who learn and practice these words before they graduate from high school are likely to master academic material with more confidence and speed. They waste less time and effort in guessing words or

Superstudio/Getty Images

consulting dictionaries than those who only know the basic 2,000 words that characterize general conversation.

How Do I Include Academic Vocabulary and Academic English in My Teaching?

Teachers can provide students with academic vocabulary and help students understand the academic English of their text.

To develop academic English, learners must have already acquired basic proficiency in the grammar of everyday English.

Academic English should be taught within contexts that make sense. In terms of instruction, teaching academic English includes providing students with access to core curriculum—in this case Social Studies.

Academic English arises in part from social practices in which academic English is used. The acquisition of academic vocabulary and grammar is necessary to advance the development of academic English.

Tips for Teaching Academic Vocabulary:

- ✔ **Expose Students to Academic Vocabulary** You do not need to call attention to words students are learning because they will acquire them subconsciously.
- ✔ **Do Not Correct Students' Mistakes When Using the Vocabulary Words** All vocabulary understanding and spelling errors will disappear once the student reads more.
- ✔ **Help Students Decode the Words Themselves** Once they learn the alphabet, they should be able to decode words. Decoding each word they don't recognize will help them more than trying to focus on sentence structure. Once they can recognize the words, they can read "authentic" texts.
- ✔ **Do Not Ignore the English Learner in This Process** They can learn academic vocabulary before they are completely fluent in oral English.
- ✔ **Helping Students Build Academic Vocabulary Leads to Broader Learning** Students who have mastered the basic academic vocabulary are ready to continue acquiring words from the rest of the groups. To help determine which words are in the 2,000-word basic group, refer to *West's General Service List of English Words,* 1953. The list is designed to serve as a guide for teachers and as a checklist and goal list for students. For additional information about the list, visit: http://www.vuw.ac.nz/lals/research/awl

Guidelines for Teaching Academic Vocabulary	
1. Direct and planned instruction **2.** Models—that have increasingly difficult language **3.** Attention to form—pointing out linguistic features of words	**4.** Practice **5.** Motivation **6.** Instructional feedback **7.** Assessment—on a regular basis

Classroom Activity

Writing About Modern America

Give students a brief writing assignment. Ask them to write a short essay about one of the topics listed below in the left column. Have students use as many of the academic vocabulary words in the right column as they can in their essay. When completed, ask student volunteers to share their writing. Note what academic vocabulary words they use.

Topic	Academic Vocabulary
The challenges of reducing poverty in America	sufficient
	minimum
	medical
	income
Recent technological advances	innovate
	technology
	media
	potential
	data
	transmit

Meeting the Diverse Needs of Our Students

by Douglas Fisher, Ph.D.

Today's classroom contains students from a variety of backgrounds with a variety of learning styles, strengths, and challenges. As teachers we are facing the challenge of helping students reach their educational potential. With careful planning, you can address the needs of all students in the social studies classroom. The basis for this planning is universal access. When classrooms are planned with universal access in mind, fewer students require specific accommodations.

What Is a Universal Access Design for Learning?

Universal design was first conceived in architectural studies when business people, engineers, and architects began making considerations for physical access to buildings. The idea was to plan the environment in advance to ensure that everyone had access. As a result, the environment would not have to be changed later for people with physical disabilities, people pushing strollers, workers who had injuries, or others for whom the environment would be difficult to negotiate. The Center for Universal Design at www.design.ncsu.edu/cud defines Universal Design as:

The design of products and environments to be usable by all people, to the greatest extent possible, without the need for adaptation or specialized design.

Universal Design and Access in Education

Researchers, teachers, and parents in education have expanded the development of built-in adaptations and inclusive accommodations from architectural space to the educational experience, especially in the area of curriculum.

In 1998, the National Center to Improve the Tools of Educators (NCITE), with the partnership of the Center for Applied Special Technology (CAST), proposed an expanded definition of universal design focused on education:

In terms of learning, universal design means the design of instructional materials and activities that allows the learning goals to be achievable by individuals with wide differences in their abilities to see, hear, speak, move, read, write, understand English, attend, organize, engage, and remember.

How Does Universal Design Work in Education?

Universal design and access, as they apply to education and schooling, suggest the following:

✔ **Inclusive Classroom Participation** Curriculum should be designed with all students and their needs in mind. The Glencoe/McGraw-Hill social studies texts and materials were designed with a wide range of students in mind. For example, understanding that English learners and students who struggle with reading would be using this textbook, vocabulary is specifically taught and reinforced. Similarly, the teacher-support materials provide multiple instructional points to be used depending on the needs of the students in the class. Further, the text is written such that main ideas are identified for all learners. Activating prior knowledge is also taken into consideration by the text. Connections between what students know and think about are made within the text.

- ✔ **Maximum Text Readability** In universally designed classrooms that provide access for all students, texts use direct language, clear noun-verb agreements, and clear construct-based wording. In addition to these factors, the Glencoe Social Studies text uses embedded definitions for difficult terms, provides for specific instruction in reading skills, uses a number of visual representations, and includes note-taking guides.
- ✔ **Adaptable and Accommodating** The content in this textbook can be easily translated, read aloud, or otherwise changed to meet the needs of students in the classroom. The section and end-of-chapter assessments provide students with multiple ways of demonstrating their content knowledge while also ensuring that they have practice with thinking in terms of multiple-choice questions. Critical thinking and analysis skills are also practiced.

How Is Differentiated Instruction the Key to Universal Access?

To differentiate instruction, teachers must acknowledge student differences in background knowledge and current reading, writing, and English language skills. They must also consider student learning styles and preferences, interests, and needs, and react accordingly. There are a number of general guidelines for differentiating instruction in the classroom to reach all students, including:

- ✔ **Link Assessment With Instruction** Assessments should occur before, during, and after instruction to ensure that the curriculum is aligned with what students do and do not know. Using assessments in this way allows you to plan instruction for whole groups, small groups, and individual students. Backward planning, where you establish the assessment before you begin instruction, is also important.
- ✔ **Clarify Key Concepts and Generalizations** Students need to know what is essential and how this information can be used in their future learning. In addition, students need to develop a sense of the **Big Ideas**—ideas that transcend time and place.
- ✔ **Emphasize Critical and Creative Thinking** The content, process, and products used or assigned in the classroom should require that students think about what they are learning. While some students may require support, additional motivation, varied tasks, materials, or equipment, the overall focus on critical and creative thinking allows for all students to participate in the lesson.
- ✔ **Include Teacher- and Student-Selected Tasks** A differentiated classroom includes both teacher- and student-selected activities and tasks. At some points in the lesson or day, the teacher must provide instruction and assign learning activities. In other parts of the lesson, students should be provided choices in how they engage with the content. This balance increases motivation, engagement, and learning.

How Do I Support Individual Students?

The vast majority of students will thrive in a classroom based on universal access and differentiated instruction. However, wise teachers recognize that no single option will work for all students and that there may be students who require unique systems of support to be successful.

Classroom Activity

Display a map of westward United States expansion between 1840 and 1860. Discuss with students the general causes of westward expansion during this time period and have them list the different areas of the country settled during this time period.

To differentiate this activity:

- Have students imagine they are living during this period of westward expansion from 1840 to 1860. Have them write a letter to a family member back home about their journey west.
- Have students record the different areas settled during this time period. Have students create a chart of the various destinations of the expansionists.
- Have students compose a song or poem about the hardships of the trail.
- Have students write a three-page paper discussing the risks and rewards these emigrants faced on their journey west.

Tips For Instruction

The following tips for instruction can support your efforts to help all students reach their maximum potential.

- ✔ Survey students to discover their individual differences. Use interest inventories of their unique talents so you can encourage contributions in the classroom.
- ✔ Be a model for respecting others. Adolescents crave social acceptance. The student with learning differences is especially sensitive to correction and criticism, particularly when it comes from a teacher. Your behavior will set the tone for how students treat one another.
- ✔ Expand opportunities for success. Provide a variety of instructional activities that reinforce skills and concepts.
- ✔ Establish measurable objectives and decide how you can best help students meet them.
- ✔ Celebrate successes and make note of and praise "work in progress."
- ✔ Keep it simple. Point out problem areas if doing so can help a student effect change. Avoid overwhelming students with too many goals at one time.
- ✔ Assign cooperative group projects that challenge all students to contribute to solving a problem or creating a product.

How Do I Reach Students With Learning Disabilities?

- ✔ Provide support and structure. Clearly specify rules, assignments, and responsibilities.
- ✔ Practice skills frequently. Use games and drills to help maintain student interest.
- ✔ Incorporate many modalities into the learning process. Provide opportunities to say, hear, write, read, and act out important concepts and information.
- ✔ Link new skills and concepts to those already mastered.
- ✔ If possible, allow students to record answers on audiotape.
- ✔ Allow extra time to complete assessments and assignments.
- ✔ Let students demonstrate proficiency with alternative presentations, including oral reports, role plays, art projects, and musical presentations.
- ✔ Provide outlines, notes, or tape recordings of lecture material.
- ✔ Pair students with peer helpers, and provide class time for pair interaction.

How Do I Reach Students With Behavioral Challenges?

- ✔ Provide a structured environment with clear-cut schedules, rules, seat assignments, and safety procedures.
- ✔ Reinforce appropriate behavior and model it for students.
- ✔ Cue distracted students back to the task through verbal signals and teacher proximity.
- ✔ Set goals that can be achieved in the short term. Work for long-term improvement in the big areas.

How Do I Reach Students With Physical Challenges?

- ✔ Openly discuss with the student any uncertainties you have about when to offer aid.
- ✔ Ask parents or therapists and students what special devices or procedures are needed and whether any special safety precautions need to be taken.
- ✔ Welcome students with physical challenges into all activities, including field trips, special events, and projects.
- ✔ Provide information to assist class members and adults in their understanding of support needed.

How Do I Reach Students with Visual Impairments?

- ✔ Facilitate independence. Modify assignments as needed.
- ✔ Teach classmates how and when to serve as visual guides.
- ✔ Limit unnecessary noise in the classroom if it distracts the student with visual impairments.
- ✔ Provide tactile models whenever possible.
- ✔ Foster a spirit of inclusion. Describe people and events as they occur in the classroom. Remind classmates that the student with visual impairments cannot interpret gestures and other forms of nonverbal communication.
- ✔ Provide taped lectures and reading assignments for use outside the classroom.
- ✔ Team the student with a sighted peer for written work.

How Do I Reach Students With Hearing Impairments?

- ✔ Seat students where they can see your lip movements easily and where they can avoid any visual distractions.
- ✔ Avoid standing with your back to the window or light source.
- ✔ Use an overhead projector so you can maintain eye contact while writing information for students.
- ✔ Seat students where they can see speakers.
- ✔ Write all assignments on the board, or hand out written instructions.
- ✔ If the student has a manual interpreter, allow both student and interpreter to select the most favorable seating arrangements.
- ✔ Teach students to look directly at each other when they speak.

How Do I Reach English Learners?

- ✔ Remember, students' ability to speak English does not reflect their academic abilities.
- ✔ Try to incorporate the students' cultural experience into your instruction. The help of a bilingual aide may be effective.
- ✔ Avoid any references in your instruction that could be construed as cultural stereotypes.
- ✔ Preteach important vocabulary and concepts.
- ✔ Encourage students to preview text before they begin reading, noting headings.
- ✔ Remind students not to ignore graphic organizers, photographs, and maps since there is much information in these visuals.
- ✔ Use memorabilia and photographs whenever possible to build background knowledge and understanding. An example of this would be coins in a foreign currency or a raw cotton ball to reinforce its importance in history.

How Do I Reach Gifted Students?

- ✔ Make arrangements for students to take selected subjects early and to work on independent projects.
- ✔ Ask "what if" questions to develop high-level thinking skills. Establish an environment safe for risk taking in your classroom.
- ✔ Emphasize concepts, theories, ideas, relationships, and generalizations about the content.
- ✔ Promote interest in the past by inviting students to make connections to the present.
- ✔ Let students express themselves in alternate ways such as creative writing, acting, debates, simulations, drawing, or music.
- ✔ Provide students with a catalog of helpful resources, listing such things as agencies that provide free and inexpensive materials, appropriate community services and programs, and community experts who might be called upon to speak to your students.
- ✔ Assign extension projects that allow students to solve real-life problems related to their communities.

Douglas Fisher is a professor at San Diego State University, San Diego, CA.

Classroom Activity

Students respond eagerly to a subject when they can relate it to their own experiences. With the growing number of students who come from other world regions, explaining history through a global theme can give them a worldwide as well as a regional perspective. Have students use the library or the Internet to research the effect revolution has had around the world and the influence of the American Revolution on revolutions in other countries, such as France and Latin America. Ask students the following questions:

- What influence has the American Revolution had upon revolutions throughout the world?
- Where have some of these other revolutions occurred?
- How successful have these revolutions and their resulting new governments been as compared to the United States?

Encourage students to do additional research and share what they find with the class.

Classroom Solutions

Backward Mapping

How Can My Instruction Help Students Succeed in a Standards-Based System?

by Emily M. Schell, Ed.D.

Content standards articulate what students should know and be able to do in every social studies classroom. Effective instructional planning based in the standards and maximizing available resources is essential for meaningful teaching and learning of social studies. Planning instruction with educational goals in mind makes for the most effective teaching.

How Do I Map My Curriculum?

Mapping the curriculum from beginning to end, and from the end to the beginning—backward mapping—makes for solid instruction. Mapping out the curriculum allows teachers to achieve several goals. These goals include a better understanding of the standards and content-specific objectives, organization and pacing of the curriculum, and focused assessment related to specific goals and objectives.

- ✔ **Begin the Process of Curriculum Mapping** To begin, teachers analyze the body of content standards for one grade level. They then compare and contrast these standards to additional sources of information that support effective teaching and learning at that grade level and in that subject area. This process works best with same-grade colleagues who bring varying perspectives and expertise to teaching this subject. As a result of this collaboration, strengths and weaknesses of the standards become apparent. Teachers will have a better understanding of the standards and identify concerns and questions for follow-up while mapping.
- ✔ **Analyze the Organization of the Standards-Based Content** Most social studies teachers agree with researchers that history is best taught in chronological order. However, some grade-level standards either do not or cannot present the content in chronological order. Rich discussions about themes and concepts tend to emerge, and teachers identify meaningful methods for presenting complex and overlapping information. In this way students will see the connections that transcend chronology.
- ✔ **Identify the Content and Order of Teaching** A plan is developed to present certain content first, then second, then third and so on. Folding in content that is either missing from the standards or essential in building background knowledge with students enters the curriculum map as well. Outside resources brought into the classroom are good supplements.
- ✔ **Separate Overlapping Units** Identify areas of instruction for the topics, themes, big ideas, or concepts. It is at this stage that backward planning is introduced for the development of instructional units, which will support the grade-level curriculum map. The instruction must support the planned assessment.
- ✔ **Map Curriculum at Each Grade Level** Curriculum planning should be shared among grade levels. Teachers will have a better understanding of what knowledge and skills students bring to their coursework if they take into consideration what has been learned previously.

How Do I Use Backward Mapping?

After a year-long course of study is mapped out, each unit must be further developed through backward mapping. You will start with the end in mind—knowing your curricular goals and objectives at the

Ariel Skelley/CORBIS

outset, which are often found in the content standards and articulated in the curriculum maps. Once goals have been determined, teachers develop assessments that will show progress toward those goals and objectives. In the final step of this backward mapping process, teachers determine meaningful teaching and learning strategies and identify useful resources that support the assessment.

To use backward mapping in developing your units of instruction, consider the following steps:

Step One: Know Your Targets

First, identify exactly what students must know and do in this unit. Analyze content standards and any other resources that support curricular goals and objectives for this unit. As you plan, ask yourself:

- ✔ What do I want my students to know as a result of this unit?
- ✔ What skills will students develop during the course of this unit?
- ✔ How do I describe these goals clearly and concisely to my students so they understand where we should be at the end of this unit?
- ✔ What essential knowledge will students need to access to make sense of this information?
- ✔ Do my instructional goals align with strategies identified in the curriculum map?
- ✔ Have I introduced any Big Ideas that are pertinent to this content?

Step Two: Identify and Develop Assessments

- ✔ Second, consider the multiple forms of formal and informal assessments that will help you determine to what degree each student has achieved the stated goals and objectives seen in Step One. Some assessments are embedded throughout the instructional unit, while others come at the end of the unit. Some assessments are performance-based, while others are not. Some are authentic applications of information and skills, while others require the formal recall of information. Ask yourself:
- ✔ What do I want to know and see from each student?
- ✔ What are the best methods for students to demonstrate what they know and can do based on the goals and objectives?
- ✔ How many assessments do I need to determine what students know and can do?
- ✔ How will I balance informal and formal assessments?
- ✔ How will I assess students with diverse learning styles, skills, and abilities?
- ✔ How can I prepare and support students?
- ✔ How will these assessments promote student progress in social studies?
- ✔ At what time(s) during the unit will I administer these assessments?

Step Three: Develop Meaningful Instruction

After the assessments for the unit have been determined, consider the meaningful and effective teaching strategies that will support learning and student achievement on assessments. While developing lesson plans for instruction, ask yourself:

- ✔ How will students learn what they are expected to know?
- ✔ How will I engage students in the studies of this unit?
- ✔ In what ways might students relate or connect to this information?
- ✔ What research-based strategies will be most effective with my students and in these studies?
- ✔ How will I differentiate my instruction to meet the diverse needs of my students?
- ✔ How will I scaffold or provide access to the curriculum for my English learners?
- ✔ What vocabulary requires attention in this unit?
- ✔ How much time will I have to effectively teach this unit?
- ✔ How will I use the textbook and other resources to support the goals and objectives for this unit?
- ✔ What lessons will I develop?
- ✔ In what sequence will I teach these lessons during this unit?
- ✔ How will these lessons support the assessments from Step Two?

Step Four: Locate and Manage Resources

Effective teaching and learning of social studies requires the use of multiple forms of text and varied resources. Consider what you have available in your classroom, including your textbook, and identify resources you will add in order to teach this unit successfully. Ask yourself:

- ✔ What parts of the textbook are required for the lessons determined in Step Three?
- ✔ What ancillary materials are needed for the lessons in this unit?
- ✔ What Web sites will I recommend to students to support these lessons?
- ✔ Do I need to contact guest speakers or obtain outside resources?
- ✔ What literature resources are available to support this unit?

Emily Schell is Visiting Professor, San Diego State University; and Social Studies Education Director, SDSU City Heights Educational Collaborative, San Diego, CA

Teaching Maps, Graphs, and Charts

How Can I Use Visuals to Improve Students' Reading Comprehension?

Maps, graphs, and charts are visual tools. By using images rather than words, these tools present complex information in an easy-to-understand format. Teach students the following generalized viewing strategies, and encourage them to apply these strategies as they study each chapter.

- ✔ **Asking Questions** Students should start by looking over the graphic and asking themselves questions, such as "What is my purpose for looking at this image?" Then students can identify questions they hope to answer, such as "What is being compared?" or "What are the most important features?"
- ✔ **Finding Answers** Next, students should use the graphic's features, such as the title, labels, colors, and symbols, to help them find answers to their questions. If the source of the graphic is available, students should also determine its reliability.
- ✔ **Drawing Conclusions** After studying the visual, students should summarize its main points and draw conclusions.
- ✔ **Connecting** Students also should relate what they learned from the visual with what they gained from reading the text selection. Students can examine how the visual supports or extends the meaning of the text.

Maps

Maps show the relative size and location of specific geographic areas. Two of the most common general purpose maps are political maps and physical maps.

Parts of Maps

All maps contain parts that assist in interpreting the information. Help students learn to identify the following map parts.

- ✔ **Title** The map title identifies the area shown on the visual. The title can also identify a map's special focus.
- ✔ **Map Key** The map key, or legend, explains the symbols presented on the map, thus unlocking the map's information.
- ✔ **Compass Rose** A compass rose is a direction marker. It is a symbol that points out where the cardinal directions—north, south, east, and west—are positioned.
- ✔ **Scale** A measuring line, often called a scale bar, indicates the relationship between the distances on the map and the actual distances on Earth.
- ✔ **Latitude and Longitude** Mapmakers use lines of latitude and longitude to pinpoint exact locations on maps and globes. The imaginary horizontal lines that circle the globe from east to west are lines of latitude, also called parallels. The imaginary vertical lines are lines of longitude, also called meridians. Both parallels and meridians are measured in degrees.

Europe: Vegetation

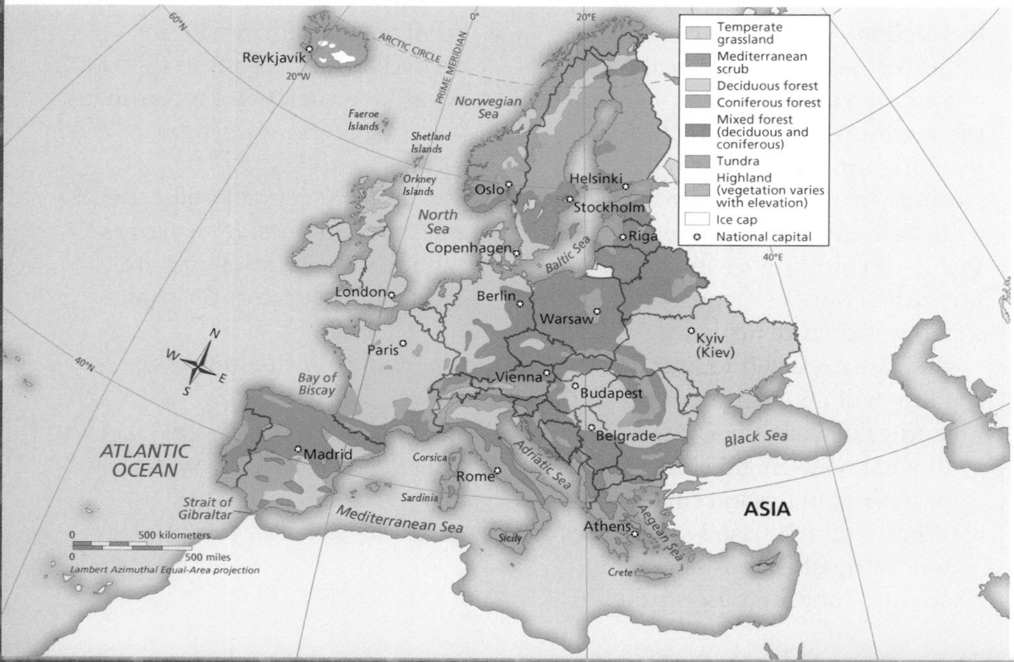

Graphs

Graphs are a way of showing numbers or statistics in a clear, easy-to-read way. Because graphs summarize and present information visually, readers have an easier time understanding the data and drawing conclusions. The most common types of graphs are bar graphs, line graphs, circle graphs, and pictographs.

- ✔ **Bar Graphs** A bar graph shows how two or more subjects or statistics compare. It provides information along two sides or axes. The horizontal axis is the line across the bottom of the graph. The vertical axis is the line along the side. The bars may be either vertical or horizontal. In most cases the labels on one axis show quantity, while the labels on the opposite axis show the categories of data being compared.
- ✔ **Line Graphs** A line graph shows change over time. Like a bar graph, it organizes information along the horizontal and vertical axes. The horizontal axis usually shows passing time, such as months, years, or decades. The vertical axis usually shows quantity or amount. Sometimes more than one set of data is shown in a line graph. A double-line graph, for instance, plots data for two related quantities, which may be represented in different colors or patterns.
- ✔ **Circle Graphs** A circle graph, also called a pie graph, shows how each part or percentage relates to the whole. A circle graph enables a viewer to make comparisons between parts and to analyze the relationship of each part to the whole.
- ✔ **Pictograph** A pictograph uses rows of small symbols or pictures, each representing a particular amount. Like a bar graph, a pictograph is useful for making comparisons.

World Population, 2005

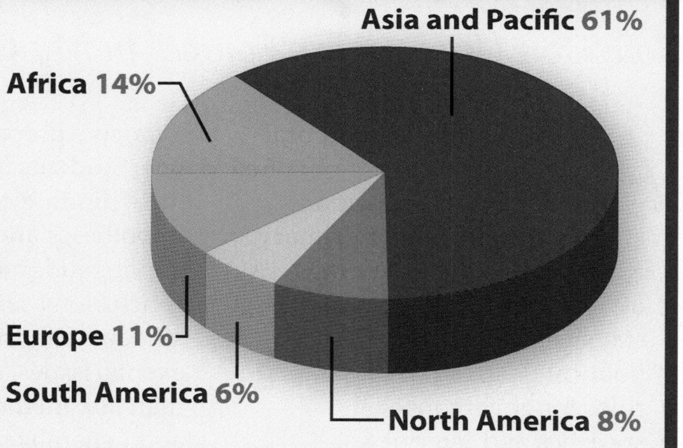

Source: *World Population Data Sheet*, 2005.

Charts

While all charts present information or data in a visual way, the type of chart is often dictated by the nature of the information and by the chart-maker's purposes.

- ✔ **Tables** Tables show information, including numerical data, in columns and rows. This organized arrangement facilitates comparisons between categories of information. Labels are usually located at the top of each column and on the left-hand side of the table.
- ✔ **Diagrams** Diagrams are specialized drawings. They can show steps in a process; point out parts of an object, organization, or idea; or explain how something works. Arrows or lines may join parts of a figure and can show relationships between parts or the flow of steps.

Classroom Activity

Create a Graph

Graphs can be difficult to interpret and understand. Help students by having them create their own graphs. First, separate students into small groups. Then have each group take a survey of classmates and make a graph to show their results. Suggest that students select a bar graph, line graph, circle graph, or pictograph to show their data. To prompt students' thinking, ask the following questions.

- *Do you play on a sports team? Which sport(s)?*
- *What do you plan to do after high school?*
- *About how much time do you spend watching TV each day? About how much time did you spend on TV when you were 10 years old? When you were five years old?*

After students have these graphs completed, invite each group to share its work. Discuss the types of graphs students made and their reasons for choosing them. Each group should then take the graph done by another group and transfer the information to another type of graph.

Primary Source Strategies

How Do I Use Primary Sources in My Classroom?

A primary source is an oral or written account obtained from actual participants in an event. Examples of primary sources include the following:

- ✔ official documents (records, statistics)
- ✔ political declarations, laws, and rules for governance
- ✔ speeches and interviews
- ✔ diaries, memoirs, and oral histories
- ✔ autobiographies
- ✔ recipes and cookbooks
- ✔ advertisements and posters
- ✔ letters
- ✔ physical objects, such as tools, dishes, fine art, photographs, maps, films, and videotapes
- ✔ songs and audio recordings

Why Use Primary Sources in Your Classroom?

Using primary sources transforms the study of social studies from a passive process to an active one. Students become investigators—finding clues, formulating hypotheses and drawing inferences, making judgments, and reaching conclusions. Using primary sources, students can think critically about events, issues, and concepts rather than just memorizing dates, names, and generalizations. Thinking critically then becomes a habit that can help students become good citizens.

How Do I Introduce Students to Primary Sources?

Carefully explain the nature of primary sources to students. Alert students to the fact that primary sources contain biases and prejudices and must be approached with caution. Every primary source reflects the creator's point of view. Students must consider the authorship and why the primary source was written.

Choosing Primary Sources

Expose students to a variety of sources, including historic photographs, folk or popular music, financial records as well as letters, journals, and historic documents.

When choosing print sources, consider the interests and reading levels of your students. Many texts contain challenging vocabulary and unfamiliar sentence structure. You may need to create a reader's guide that defines key vocabulary and paraphrases the main points of the reading.

Some documents may be too long. Decide whether using an excerpt will provide enough information for students to draw conclusions. You also may need to provide different primary sources to expose students to a variety of perspectives.

Decide how students will access the primary sources: through the Internet, the library, a museum, or other print resources. Consider the possibility of an Internet virtual field trip for students. Students can visit museum sites and other Web pages to view artifacts, interpret data, and read journals, letters, and official documents.

Interpreting a Primary Source

Before students interpret a primary source, they need to know the source's context. Then they can use guidelines, such as those on the next page, to help them analyze and interpret the primary source.

Interpreting a Primary Source

Print Sources

- Who created the source, and what was the purpose for doing so?
- Did the writer personally experience or witness the event(s)?
- Who was the intended audience?
- Was the writer trying to record facts, express an opinion, or persuade others to take action?
- What bias does it reflect?
- What information about the topic can you gather from this document?
- Compare this document with what you know about the topic. Does it confirm those ideas or introduce a new perspective?
- How might other accounts about this topic support or modify the message this source delivers?

Visual Sources

- Who created the source, and what was the purpose for doing so?
- What does the image show?
- Who or what dominates the image or catches your eye?
- How does the view impact the message?
- What is excluded from view?
- What bias does the visual reflect?
- What information about the topic can you gather from this visual?
- How might other visuals about this topic support or modify the message this one delivers?

Audio Sources

- Who created the source? What was the purpose for creating this source?
- What is the main idea of the audio?
- What bias does the audio text reflect?
- What information about the topic can you gather from this audio source?
- Compare the information in this source with what you already know about the topic. Does it confirm those ideas or introduce a new perspective?
- How might other sources about this topic support or modify the message that this one delivers?

Exploring Information

Provide a variety of primary sources related to a topic or time period. Have students compare and contrast the items, analyzing the information, making inferences, and drawing conclusions about the period.

Evaluation Activities

Have students evaluate a primary source and tell how it supports or refutes what they learned in the textbook, or have students read a primary source document that provides one perspective on a topic and have students write their own account, presenting another perspective or opinion.

Prereading Activities

Present a primary source for students to study at the beginning of a new chapter or topic. Have students analyze the source, using the questions and guidelines presented above. Then have students make predictions about what they might learn in the upcoming lessons.

Classroom Activity

Use this activity to explore the use of primary sources. This activity is especially beneficial when a less-proficient reader is paired with a more-proficient reader.

1. Before class make a list of student reading partners. Make sure one of the two is a good reader.
2. Have students read a primary source document, taking turns as they go. They should "mark" any words that they do not understand.
3. After each paragraph, the student pair should stop and restate what it says in their own words.
4. Students should look up unfamiliar words they've marked and create an illustrated dictionary entry for each term.
5. Ask student pairs to present their paraphrased primary source to the rest of the class.

Classroom Solutions

Test-Taking Strategies

How Can I Help My Students Succeed on Tests?

It's not enough for students to learn social studies facts and concepts—they must be able to show what they know in a variety of test-taking situations.

How Can I Help My Students Do Well on Objective Tests?

Objective tests may include multiple choice, true/false, and matching questions. Applying the strategies below can help students do their best on objective tests.

How Can I Help My Students Do Well on Essay Tests?

Essay tests require students to provide well-organized written responses, in addition to telling what they know. Help students use the following strategies on essay tests.

- ✔ **Analyze** To analyze means to systematically and critically examine all parts of an issue or event.
- ✔ **Classify or Categorize** To classify or categorize means to put people, things, or ideas into groups, based on a common set of characteristics.
- ✔ **Compare and Contrast** To compare is to show how things are similar, or alike. To contrast is to show how things are different.
- ✔ **Describe** To describe means to present a sketch or impression. Rich details, especially details that appeal to the senses, flesh out a description.
- ✔ **Discuss** To discuss means to systematically write about all sides of an issue or event.
- ✔ **Evaluate** To evaluate means to make a judgment and support it with evidence.
- ✔ **Explain** To explain means to clarify or make plain.
- ✔ **Illustrate** To illustrate means to provide examples or to show with a picture or other graphic.
- ✔ **Infer** To infer means to read between the lines or to use knowledge and experience to draw conclusions.
- ✔ **Justify** To justify means to prove or to support a position with specific facts and reasons.
- ✔ **Predict** To predict means to tell what will happen in the future, based on an understanding of prior events and behaviors.
- ✔ **State** To state means to briefly and concisely present information.
- ✔ **Summarize** To summarize means to give a brief overview of the main points of an issue or event.
- ✔ **Trace** To trace means to present the steps in sequential order.

Objective Tests

Multiple-Choice Questions

- Students should read the directions carefully to learn what answer the test requires—the best answer or the right answer. This is especially important when answer choices include "all of the above" or "none of the above."
- Advise students to watch for negative words in the questions, such as *not, except, unless, never,* and *so forth*. If the question contains a negative, the correct answer choice is the one that does not fit.
- Students should try to mentally answer the question before reading the answer choices.
- Students should read all the answer choices and cross out those that are obviously wrong. Then they should choose an answer from those that remain.

True/False Questions

- It is important that students read the entire question before answering. For an answer to be true, the entire statement must be true. If one part of a statement is false, the answer should be marked False.
- Remind students to watch for words like *all, never, every,* and *always*. Statements containing these words are often false.

Matching Questions

- Students should read through both lists before they mark any answers.
- Unless an answer can be used more than once, students should cross out each choice as they use it.
- Using what they know about grammar can help students find the right answer. For instance, when matching a word with its definition, the definition is often the same part of speech (noun, verb, adjective, and so forth) as the word.

Read the Question

The key to writing successful essay responses lies in reading and interpreting questions correctly. Teach students to identify and underline key words in the questions, and to use these words to guide them in understanding what the question asks. Help students understand the meaning of some of the most common key words, listed on the previous page.

Plan and Write the Essay

After students understand the question, they should follow the writing process to develop their answer. Encourage students to follow the steps below to plan and write their essays.

1. **Map out an answer.** Make lists, webs, or an outline to plan the response.
2. **Decide on an order** in which to present the main points.
3. **Write an opening statement** that directly responds to the essay question.
4. **Write the essay.** Expand on the opening statement. Support key points with specific facts, details, and reasons.
5. **Write a closing statement** that brings the main points together.
6. **Proofread** to check for spelling, grammar, and punctuation.

How Can I Help My Students Prepare for Standardized Tests?

Students can follow the steps below to prepare for standardized assessments they are required to take.

- ✔ **Read About the Test** Students can familiarize themselves with the format of the test, the types of questions that will be asked, and the amount of time they will have to complete the test. Emphasize that it is very important for students to budget their time during test-taking.
- ✔ **Review the Content** Consistent study throughout the school year will help students build social studies knowledge and understanding. If there are specific objectives or standards that are tested on the exam, help students review these facts or skills to be sure they are proficient.
- ✔ **Practice** Provide practice, ideally with real released tests, to build students' familiarity with the content, format, and timing of the real exam. Students should practice all the types of questions they will encounter on the test.
- ✔ **Pace** Students should pace themselves differently depending on how the test is administered. If the test is timed, students should not allow themselves to become stuck on any one question. If the test is untimed, students should work slowly and carefully. If students have trouble with an item, they should mark it and come back to it later.
- ✔ **Analyze Practice Results** Help students improve test-taking performance by analyzing their test-taking strengths and weaknesses.

Spend time discussing students' completed practice tests. Help students identify what kinds of questions they had the most difficulty with. Look for patterns in errors and then tailor instruction to review appropriate skills or content.

Classroom Activity

Below is an example of an assessment review activity. Reviewing graded tests is a great way for students to assess their test-taking skills. It also helps teachers teach test-taking strategies and review content. As the class rereads each test question, guide students to think logically about their answer choices. Show students how to:

1. Read each question carefully to determine its meaning.
2. Look for key words in the question to support their answers.
3. Recognize synonyms in the answer choices that may match phrases in the question.
4. Narrow down answer choices by eliminating ones that don't make sense.
5. Anticipate the answer before looking at the answer choices.
6. Circle questions of which they are unsure and go back to them later. Sometimes a clue will be found in another question on the test.

Classroom Solutions

Project CRISS

How Can I Teach My Students How to Learn Social Studies?

by Carol M. Santa, Ph.D.

We all know that teaching social studies involves far more than teaching just course content. We understand that students need to become engaged, confident learners. Achieving that goal means helping them to understand, organize, and retain information.

Teaching Both Content and Skills

In other words, we want our students to have the skills and confidence to be lifelong learners. With its rich content, social studies offer an ideal arena for teaching both content and skills.

- ✔ **A Dual Responsibility** Let's take a moment to consider why the dual responsibility of teaching both content and skills is so important. Think back to your own middle and high school years. What do you remember about the content you learned? If I recall my experiences, I find I remember remarkably little content. What did I learn in biology or history? What did my textbooks look like? As the years go by, I don't even remember the names of most of my teachers.
- ✔ **An Inspiring Teacher** Yet I have vivid memories of my eighth-grade social studies teacher, who came out of retirement to fill in for a history teacher who left on maternity leave. I remember how fascinated I became with ancient history; I recall giving oral reports and how she helped me become comfortable speaking before a group. In fact, I remember more from her class than any other I took during high school.
- ✔ **Teach How to Learn** More important, I now understand that she taught me how to learn to learn. She showed me how to underline, how to organize information using different note-taking formats, and how to write coherent answers on essay tests. She taught me the need to test myself on what I knew. And during that vulnerable, adolescent year, I went from being a mediocre student to being an excellent one.

This inspirational teacher did something else for me. At some point during that eighth-grade year, I decided to become a teacher. Later I realized that she had launched me on my professional mission—to spread her wisdom to others. Eventually this led to Project CRISS.

What Is CRISS?

CRISS stands for CReating Independence through Student-owned Strategies. It is a staff development program that I created in collaboration with middle and high school teachers in Kalispell, Montana.

- ✔ **Origin of CRISS** CRISS had its start 20 years ago in a lunchtime conversation in a teachers' lounge. One of the social studies teachers said, "My students aren't doing a good job of answering chapter questions. In fact, I don't think they even read my assignments. My reading assignments are becoming a waste of time!" His words struck a chord. "My students don't have a clue about how to study, and they don't write very well either," another teacher lamented.
- ✔ **Evolving Strategies** Supported by a state grant, we started working together to find practical ways to help students read, write, and learn content. We met in teams, read professional literature, and designed studies to test classroom strategies. From these efforts, we evolved a project to help students become better readers, writers, and learners. Once the project took shape, we shared our discoveries with other teachers by offering a two- or three-day CRISS workshop to schools and districts in the state.
- ✔ **Constant Growth** Over the last two decades, Project CRISS has spread from teacher to teacher across this country, into Canada, and to several European countries. The project seems to sell itself. Teachers who use CRISS principles and strategies find that their students attain a deeper understanding of course content and become better readers, writers, and learners at the same time. In fact, data from numerous quantitative studies shows that using CRISS strategies improves student learning. (For the most recent data and for information on CRISS workshops, see www.projectcriss.com)

CRISS Strategies in the Teacher Edition

When the editors of Glencoe/McGraw-Hill asked me and my colleagues to help them integrate CRISS strategies into their social studies texts, we welcomed the opportunity. In this teacher wraparound edition, we offer many references to CRISS strategies. We have packed the pages with strategies that help students gain a deeper understanding of specific content.

CRISS Training

We have one word of caution, however: the integration of CRISS strategies within this teacher wraparound edition does not take the place of a Project CRISS workshop, which provides an in-depth knowledge of CRISS. So, if you haven't yet participated in a CRISS workshop, we encourage you to do so. During a workshop, CRISS trainers take you step-by-step through the philosophy and instructional strategies. Participants are actively involved in all aspects of the program—practicing, adapting, and applying strategies to meet teaching needs.

Long-lasting change occurs when teachers and administrators work together to share, extend ideas, and problem solve. The most effective implementations occur when the initial workshop is supported by follow-up sessions, including a specific follow-up day. At this session, teachers bring examples of strategies they have used since the initial training. Part of this time may be spent in review and in learning new strategies. The rest of the time is for sharing applications. Additional ongoing support can occur in teacher planning periods.

In any case, for those of you unfamiliar with Project CRISS, let's begin with a little background knowledge. In this way you will have some context for the various activities suggested throughout the teacher wraparound edition.

The CRISS Philosophy

The first thing to know is that Project CRISS is more than a collection of learning strategies. Its underlying power rests not on the individual strategies but on the teaching philosophy behind them. This philosophy integrates work from cognitive psychology, social learning theory, and neurological research about how the brain learns. It includes these overlapping principles:

- ✔ background knowledge and purposeful reading
- ✔ author's craft
- ✔ active involvement
- ✔ discussion
- ✔ organization
- ✔ writing
- ✔ teacher modeling

Let's look at each of these principles in more detail, along with examples of instructional strategies that illustrate them.

Background knowledge and purposeful reading are powerful determinants of reading comprehension.

Teachers involved in Project CRISS often talk about the importance of background knowledge. Readers are far more likely to learn new information when they have some previous knowledge and have a purpose in mind before they read or listen.

- ✔ **More Than Simply Reading** We warn students not to simply begin reading. We ask them, "What might you already know about the topic? What questions do you have about the topic?" We also remind them to preview the assignment and think about their goals for reading. We often have to be very explicit about the goals. For example, we might tell students, "After reading this selection, you should be able to . . . ," or, "After viewing the video, you should be able to identify . . ."
- ✔ **KWLH** In the teaching strategies included for each chapter in this book, we offer ideas for helping students tap into their background knowledge. For example, we suggest that students preview their reading assignment and consider what they already know about a topic. Or, we might develop a whole-class KWLH chart (Know, Want to learn, Learned, How to learn more), where students work on this task together. They can generate questions about what they want to learn, and then, after completing the assignment, they can list the new information they have learned and how they can learn more.

K	W	L	H
What I **Know**	What I **Want** to Find Out	What I **Learned**	**How** I Can Learn More

- ✔ **Reading Goals** We also suggest ways to make sure your students have clear goals for their reading. Each section opener lists reading strategies and main ideas that outline reading goals. Most students will skip over this material and simply start reading. Teachers need to help students understand that the reading goals are important tools for understanding. We tell students, *"Don't ignore your purposes for reading. Take time to think about them before delving into your reading."* Project CRISS also provides hints about how to get students to use these purpose statements to evaluate whether they have understood their reading.

Reading social studies materials has its own special considerations. CRISS specialist Malla S. Kolhoff shares this advice:

"As educators, it is our responsibility to set a purpose for historical reading. Students often must struggle to connect history with their own lives. To compare and contrast, establish cause and effect, and sequence events in chronological order presents a challenge for even the best reader. CRISS strategies allow students to move beyond words to the real significance for their society. With CRISS, my students are able to become engaged in the learning process through:

a. background knowledge
b. active reading, listening, and learning
c. discussion
d. metacognition
e. writing
f. organization
g. understanding

I have found that these strategies help my students attain a higher level of historical thinking and understanding."

Good readers have an intuitive understanding of the author's craft.

When students know how authors craft their writing, they can more readily understand and remember what they read.

✔ **Pay Attention** Good readers and writers know that paying attention to how text is organized—its headings and paragraphs, for example—makes it easier to comprehend its content. Good readers will analyze the author's style of presentation as they read. They might ask themselves, "What is this author doing to help me learn key concepts? How does the writer lead me from one idea to the next?" When students become aware of what the author is doing to impart content, they have a clearer idea of what the author is saying.

✔ **The Walk Through** Walk students through the first lesson of the text. Point out the parts of the lesson to help students discover the author's style of presentation. Point out the surface structure (headings, bold print, color coding of topical headings, italicized words), but also point out main ideas in sample paragraphs to analyze how the author elaborates on key topics.

Effective learners are actively involved when they listen and read.

We learn best when we act on the information presented. We can do this by using a variety of organizing activities that require us to write, talk, and transform the information we are absorbing. None of us learns much from reading alone—it's far too passive.

CRISS strategies encourage active engagement in learning. We might ask students to read a section and describe what they are learning to a partner, or we might be more elaborate and have students develop concept maps or write summaries.

Students need many opportunities to talk with one another about what they are learning.

Discussion is critical to learning. The discussions we advocate are different from those in which the teacher remains the authority figure, with students simply reciting answers to questions. If discussion becomes mere recitation and there is little interaction among students, little learning occurs. Thus we focus on how to get students to lead their own discussions about a topic. We want them to understand that it is their discussing, their oral grappling with meaning—not ours—that leads to deeper understanding.

Competent readers know several ways to organize information for learning.

Learning depends on organization. We show students different ways to organize information. They can take notes, underline selectively, develop concept maps, and summarize ideas in charts. Once we have taught students these techniques, we tell them, "You have to do more than just read this assignment. How are you going to organize the information from this assignment? You have to change it, to transform it so that it becomes your own."

For each chapter of this text, we offer ideas for assisting students in organizing information. Once students have learned a variety of organizing systems, we suggest ways to help them apply these structures independently.

Students deserve opportunities to write about what they are learning.

Writing is an integral part of the CRISS project. Writing lets us figure out what we know and what we still need to know. We cannot write about something we do not understand. While we teach students how to write expository papers and essay exams, we also encourage students to write more informally by questioning, speculating, and writing explanations in learning logs. We make sure that students are writing continually about what they are learning.

For each chapter of this text, we offer ideas for assisting students in organizing information. Once students have learned a variety of organizing systems, we suggest ways to help them apply these structures independently.

Teaching involves explanation and modeling.

Our final principle has to do with our own teaching. Students learn to think strategically when we use these processes as part of our instruction. Our demonstrations are especially critical for struggling readers. Most have never been taught how to learn. We have to show them how.

- ✔ **Take Center Stage** When you introduce a new strategy, you should take the center stage: showing, telling, modeling, demonstrating, and explaining not only the content but the process of active reading. As students learn, gradually release responsibility to them. Strategy instruction involves two overlapping steps. First, we explain what the strategy is and why students should use it. If students do not know why they are performing an activity, they will rarely use the activity on their own. Next, we demonstrate and talk about procedures for carrying out the strategy. We discuss, demonstrate, and think aloud while modeling. Then, students practice under our guidance and feedback.

- ✔ **A Systematic Approach** Project CRISS is a valuable basis for instruction. It provides a systematic approach for using what we now know about teaching and learning. The following chart lists questions we need to continually ask ourselves while we are teaching. Use this chart to monitor your efforts to incorporate CRISS principles into your teaching.

CRISS Principles	The CRISS Philosophy	Yes	No	Somewhat
Background Knowledge:	Did I assist students in thinking about what they already knew about the topic before beginning the unit? Did I develop necessary concepts before students read?			
Purpose/ Setting:	Did my students have a clear purpose about what they were going to learn before beginning the lesson?			
Author's Craft:	Can my students use the author's style of presentation to facilitate their understanding?			
Active Involvement:	Were my students engaged in the topic? Did I help students become actively involved in their learning?			
Discussion:	Did my students have opportunities to talk about what they were learning?			
Organization:	Did my students organize information in a variety of ways?			
Writing:	Did my students write about what they were learning?			
Teacher Modeling:	Did I do enough teacher modeling of learning strategies so that students could begin doing them on their own?			

REFERENCE ATLAS

NATIONAL GEOGRAPHIC

ATLAS KEY

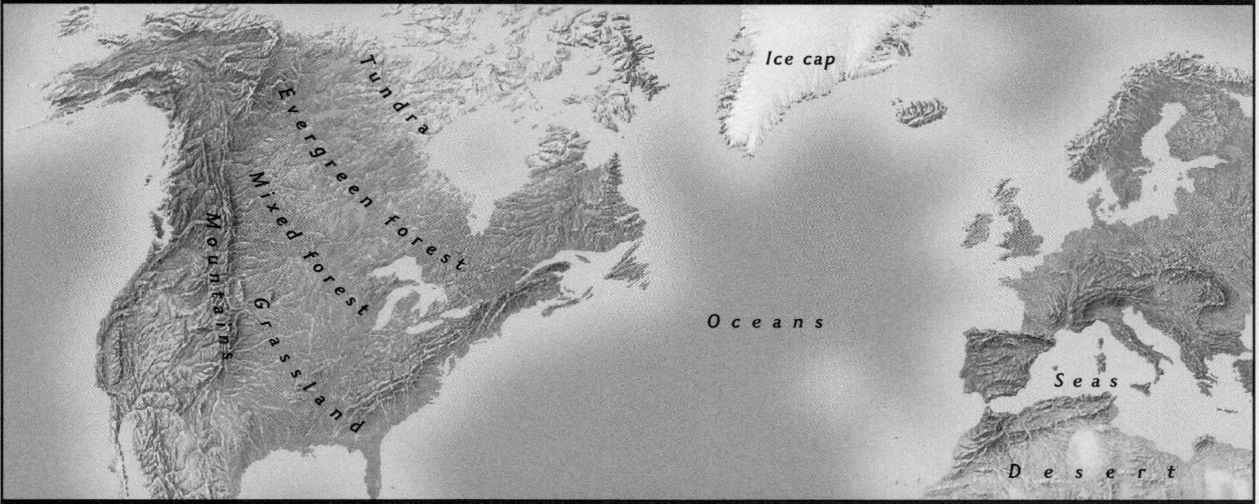

SYMBOL KEY

- Canal
- Claimed boundary
- International boundary
- Depression
- Elevation
- National capital
- Towns
- Below sea level
- Dry salt lake
- Lake
- Rivers
- Lava
- Sand
- Swamp

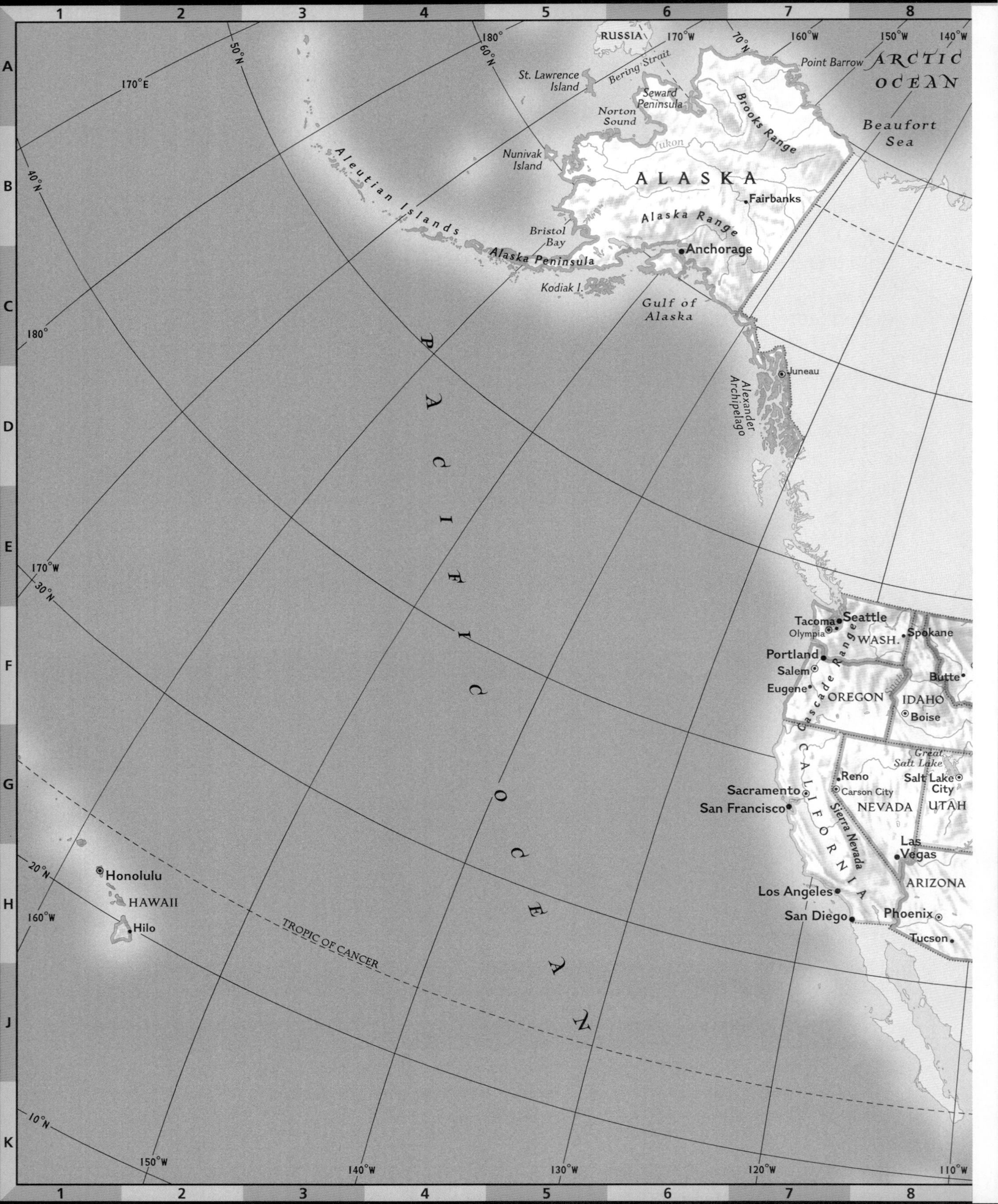
RUSSIA
St. Lawrence Island
Bering Strait
Seward Peninsula
Norton Sound
Point Barrow
ARCTIC OCEAN
Beaufort Sea
Brooks Range
Yukon
Nunivak Island
ALASKA
Fairbanks
Alaska Range
Aleutian Islands
Bristol Bay
Alaska Peninsula
Anchorage
Kodiak I.
Gulf of Alaska
Juneau
Alexander Archipelago
PACIFIC OCEAN
Tacoma
Seattle
Olympia
WASH.
Spokane
Portland
Salem
Eugene
Cascade Range
OREGON
Snake
IDAHO
Boise
Butte
Great Salt Lake
Salt Lake City
UTAH
Reno
Carson City
NEVADA
Sacramento
San Francisco
CALIFORNIA
Sierra Nevada
Las Vegas
ARIZONA
Los Angeles
San Diego
Phoenix
Tucson
Honolulu
HAWAII
Hilo
TROPIC OF CANCER
170°E
180°
50°N
60°N
70°N
40°N
30°N
20°N
10°N
170°W
160°W
150°W
140°W
130°W
120°W
110°W
1
2
3
4
5
6
7
8
A
B
C
D
E
F
G
H
J
K

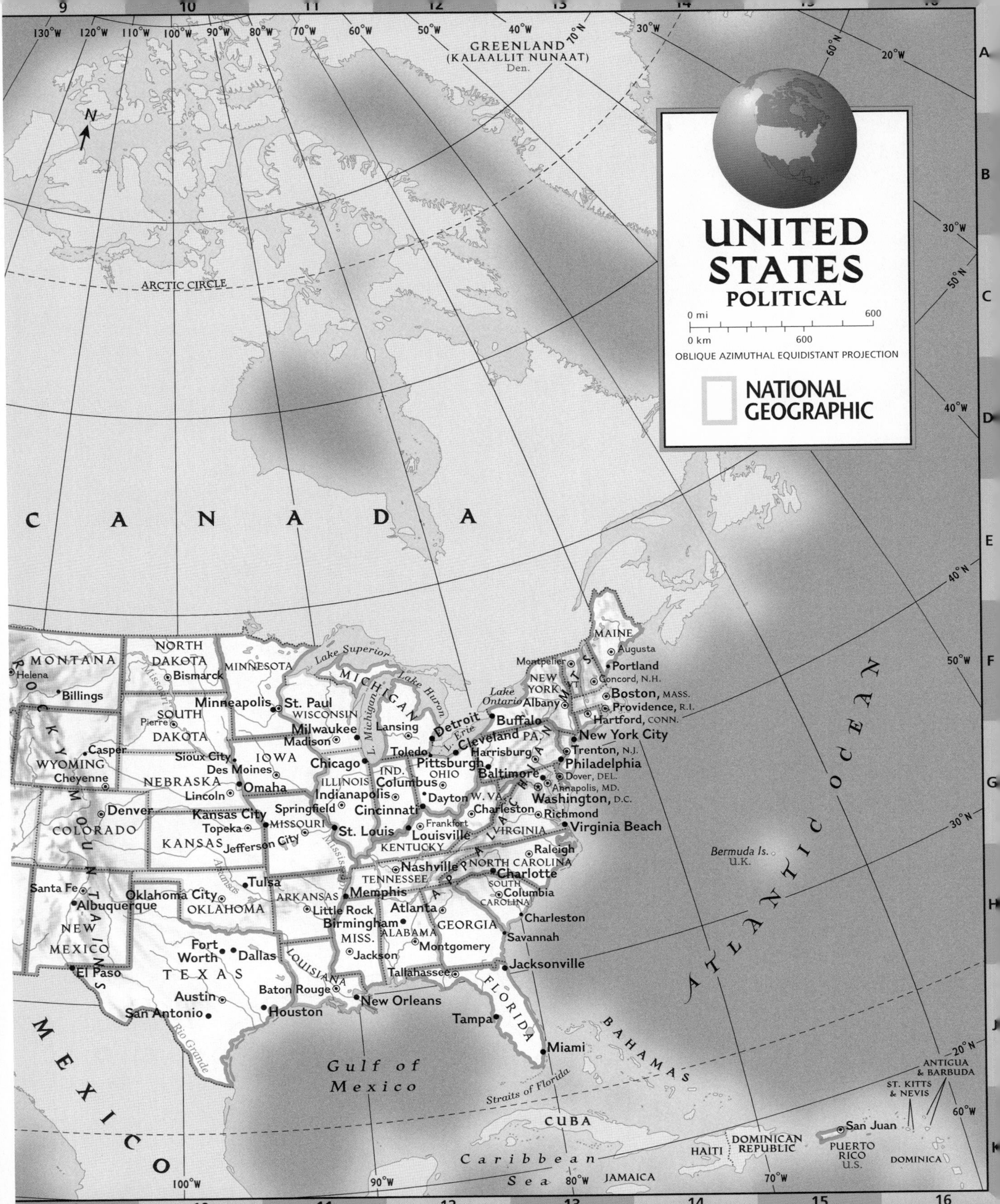

UNITED STATES
POLITICAL
0 mi 600
0 km 600
OBLIQUE AZIMUTHAL EQUIDISTANT PROJECTION
NATIONAL GEOGRAPHIC
GREENLAND (KALAALLIT NUNAAT) Den.
ARCTIC CIRCLE
CANADA
MONTANA
Helena
Billings
NORTH DAKOTA
Bismarck
MINNESOTA
Minneapolis
St. Paul
SOUTH DAKOTA
Pierre
WYOMING
Casper
Cheyenne
NEBRASKA
Lincoln
Omaha
IOWA
Sioux City
Des Moines
WISCONSIN
Milwaukee
Madison
MICHIGAN
Lansing
Detroit
Lake Superior
Lake Huron
L. Michigan
L. Erie
Lake Ontario
Chicago
ILLINOIS
Springfield
IND.
Indianapolis
OHIO
Columbus
Dayton
Cincinnati
Toledo
Cleveland
Pittsburgh
PA.
Harrisburg
Buffalo
NEW YORK
Albany
Montpelier
VT.
N.H.
MAINE
Augusta
Portland
Concord, N.H.
Boston, MASS.
Providence, R.I.
Hartford, CONN.
New York City
Trenton, N.J.
Philadelphia
Baltimore
Dover, DEL.
Annapolis, MD.
Washington, D.C.
W. VA.
Charleston
Richmond
VIRGINIA
Virginia Beach
Denver
COLORADO
Kansas City
Topeka
KANSAS
Jefferson City
MISSOURI
St. Louis
Frankfort
Louisville
KENTUCKY
Nashville
TENNESSEE
NORTH CAROLINA
Raleigh
Charlotte
SOUTH CAROLINA
Columbia
Charleston
ROCKY MOUNTAINS
APPALACHIAN MTS.
Santa Fe
Albuquerque
NEW MEXICO
Tulsa
Oklahoma City
OKLAHOMA
ARKANSAS
Little Rock
Memphis
Atlanta
GEORGIA
Savannah
Birmingham
ALABAMA
MISS.
Jackson
Montgomery
Fort Worth
Dallas
TEXAS
El Paso
Austin
San Antonio
Houston
LOUISIANA
Baton Rouge
New Orleans
Tallahassee
Jacksonville
FLORIDA
Tampa
Miami
Rio Grande
Missouri
Mississippi
Arkansas
MEXICO
Gulf of Mexico
ATLANTIC OCEAN
Bermuda Is. U.K.
BAHAMAS
Straits of Florida
CUBA
HAITI
DOMINICAN REPUBLIC
PUERTO RICO U.S.
San Juan
JAMAICA
Caribbean Sea
ANTIGUA & BARBUDA
ST. KITTS & NEVIS
DOMINICA
130°W
120°W
110°W
100°W
90°W
80°W
70°W
60°W
50°W
40°W
30°W
20°W
70°N
60°N
50°N
40°N
30°N
20°N
100°W
90°W
80°W
70°W
60°W
50°W
40°W
30°W
9
10
11
12
13
14
15
16
A
B
C
D
E
F
G
H
J
K

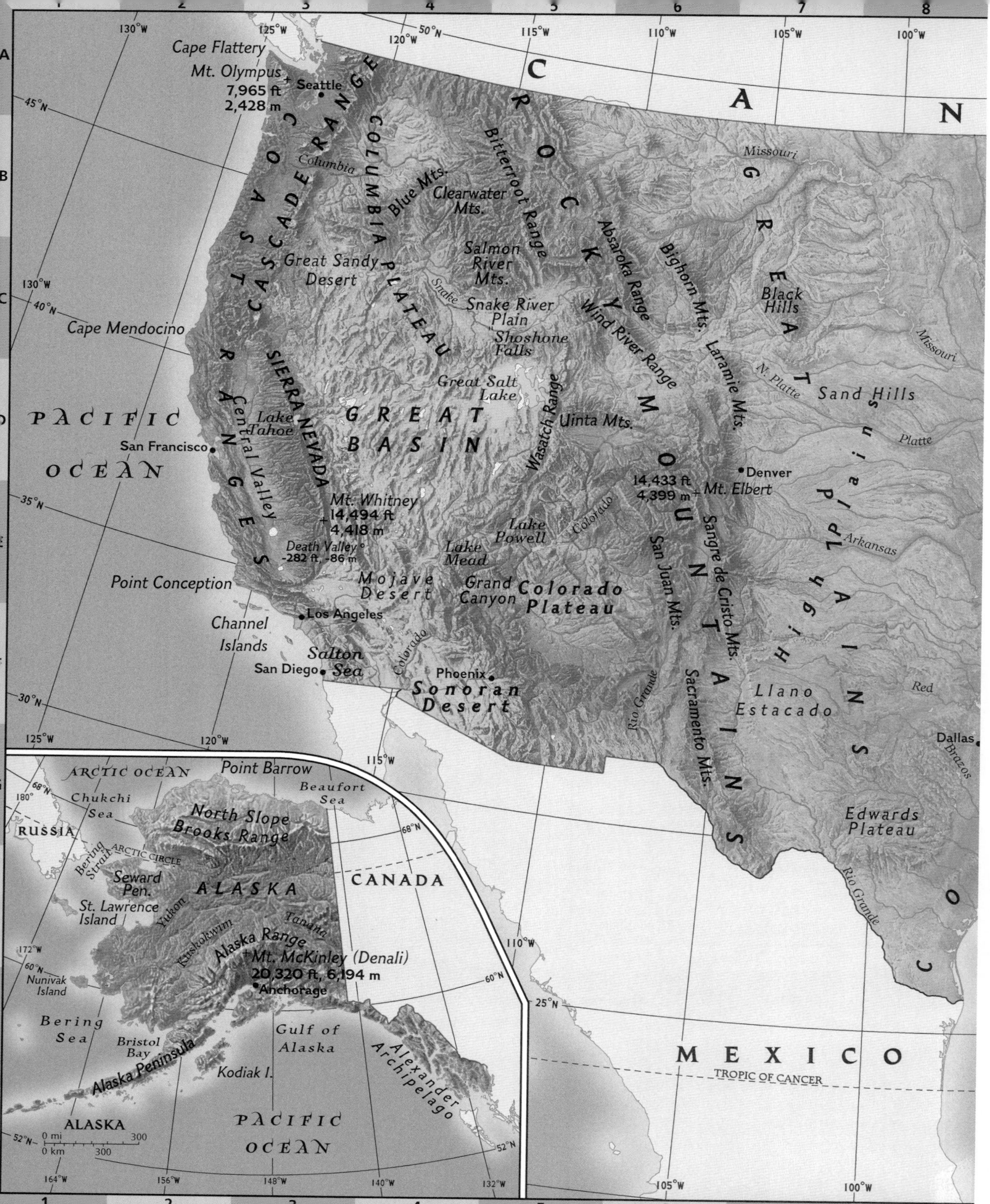

Cape Flattery
Mt. Olympus
7,965 ft
2,428 m
Seattle
COAST RANGES
CASCADE RANGE
COLUMBIA PLATEAU
Columbia
Blue Mts.
Clearwater Mts.
Bitterroot Range
ROCKY MOUNTAINS
CANADA
Missouri
GREAT PLAINS
Salmon River Mts.
Absaroka Range
Bighorn Mts.
Black Hills
Great Sandy Desert
Snake
Snake River Plain
Shoshone Falls
Wind River Range
Laramie Mts.
Cape Mendocino
SIERRA NEVADA
Great Salt Lake
Wasatch Range
N. Platte
Sand Hills
PACIFIC OCEAN
Lake Tahoe
GREAT BASIN
Uinta Mts.
Platte
San Francisco
Central Valley
Denver
14,433 ft
4,399 m
Mt. Elbert
Mt. Whitney
14,494 ft
4,418 m
Colorado
Lake Powell
Sangre de Cristo Mts.
Arkansas
Death Valley
-282 ft, -86 m
Lake Mead
San Juan Mts.
High Plains
Point Conception
Mojave Desert
Grand Canyon
Colorado Plateau
Los Angeles
Channel Islands
Salton Sea
San Diego
Phoenix
Sonoran Desert
Rio Grande
Sacramento Mts.
Llano Estacado
Red
Dallas
Brazos
Edwards Plateau
MEXICO
TROPIC OF CANCER
ARCTIC OCEAN
Point Barrow
Chukchi Sea
Beaufort Sea
RUSSIA
North Slope
Brooks Range
Bering Strait
ARCTIC CIRCLE
Seward Pen.
ALASKA
CANADA
St. Lawrence Island
Yukon
Tanana
Kuskokwim
Alaska Range
Mt. McKinley (Denali)
20,320 ft, 6,194 m
Nunivak Island
Anchorage
Bering Sea
Bristol Bay
Gulf of Alaska
Alexander Archipelago
Alaska Peninsula
Kodiak I.
ALASKA
PACIFIC OCEAN
0 mi 300
0 km 300

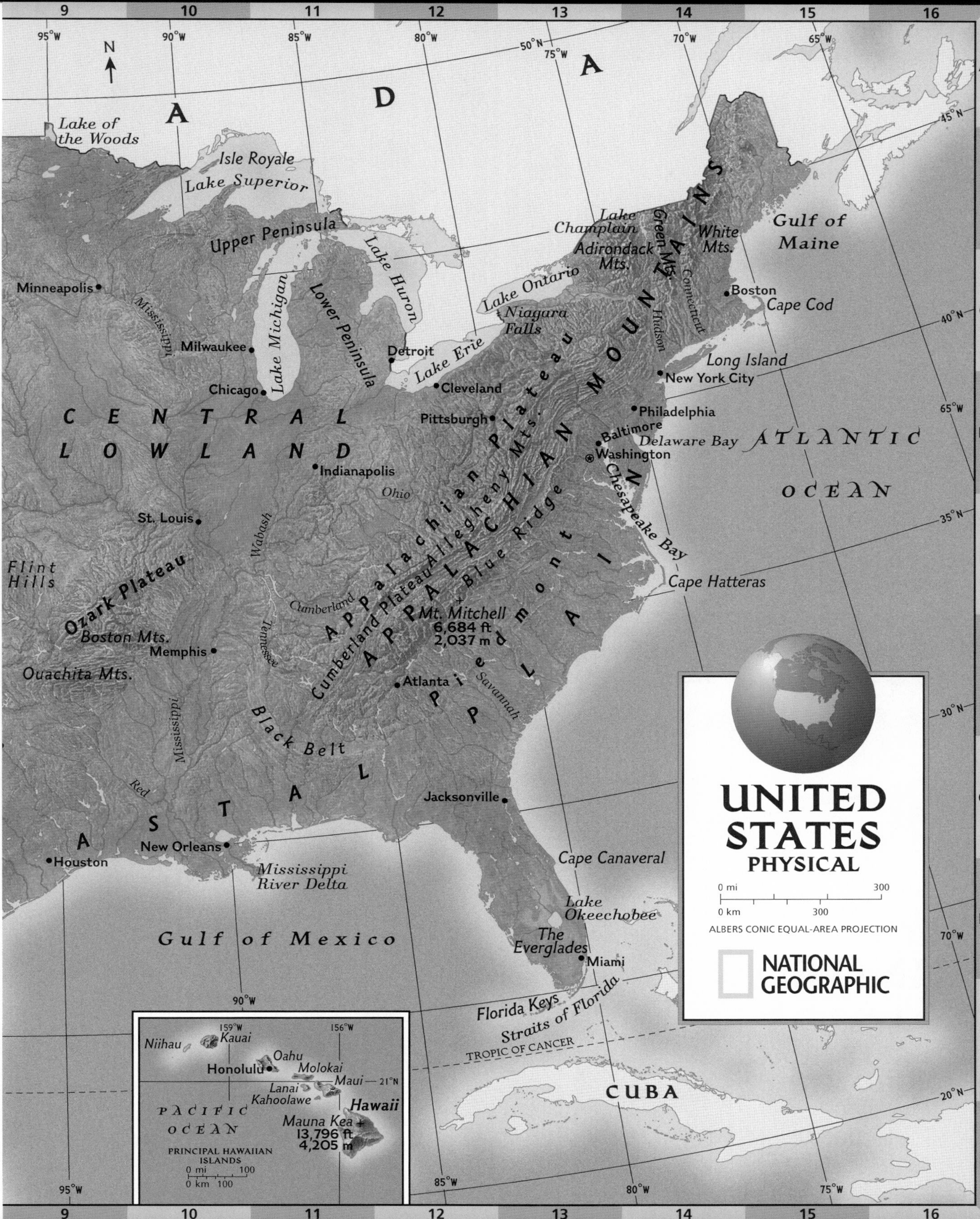
UNITED STATES
PHYSICAL
0 mi 300
0 km 300
ALBERS CONIC EQUAL-AREA PROJECTION
NATIONAL GEOGRAPHIC
C A N A D A
Lake of the Woods
Isle Royale
Lake Superior
Upper Peninsula
Lake Michigan
Lower Peninsula
Lake Huron
Lake Erie
Lake Ontario
Niagara Falls
Lake Champlain
Adirondack Mts.
Green Mts.
White Mts.
Gulf of Maine
Boston
Cape Cod
Long Island
New York City
Philadelphia
Baltimore
Washington
Delaware Bay
Chesapeake Bay
Cape Hatteras
ATLANTIC OCEAN
Minneapolis
Milwaukee
Chicago
Detroit
Cleveland
Pittsburgh
Indianapolis
St. Louis
Memphis
Atlanta
Jacksonville
New Orleans
Houston
Miami
CENTRAL LOWLAND
Flint Hills
Ozark Plateau
Boston Mts.
Ouachita Mts.
Appalachian Plateau
Allegheny Mts.
Cumberland Plateau
Blue Ridge
APPALACHIAN MOUNTAINS
Piedmont
Mt. Mitchell 6,684 ft 2,037 m
COASTAL PLAIN
Black Belt
Mississippi
Wabash
Ohio
Cumberland
Tennessee
Savannah
Red
Hudson
Connecticut
Mississippi River Delta
Gulf of Mexico
Cape Canaveral
Lake Okeechobee
The Everglades
Florida Keys
Straits of Florida
TROPIC OF CANCER
CUBA
Niihau
Kauai
Oahu
Honolulu
Molokai
Maui
Lanai
Kahoolawe
Hawaii
Mauna Kea 13,796 ft 4,205 m
PACIFIC OCEAN
PRINCIPAL HAWAIIAN ISLANDS
0 mi 100
0 km 100
159°W
156°W
21°N
95°W
90°W
85°W
80°W
75°W
70°W
65°W
50°N
45°N
40°N
35°N
30°N
20°N
9
10
11
12
13
14
15
16
A
B
C
D
E
F
G
H
J
K

UNITED STATES TERRITORIAL GROWTH

NATIONAL GEOGRAPHIC

A New Nation, 1787

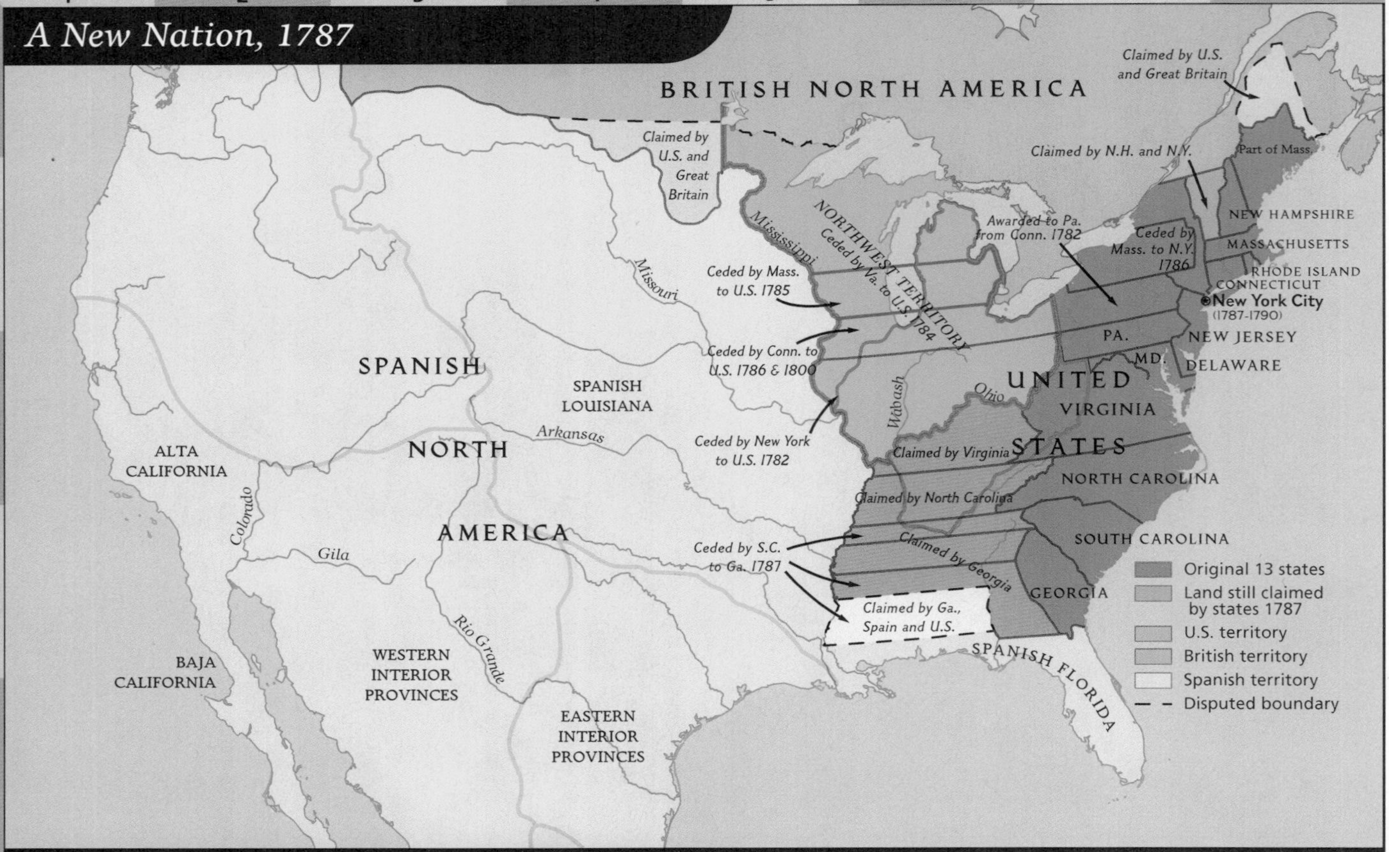

Coming of Age, 1821

Expanding West of the Mississippi, 1803

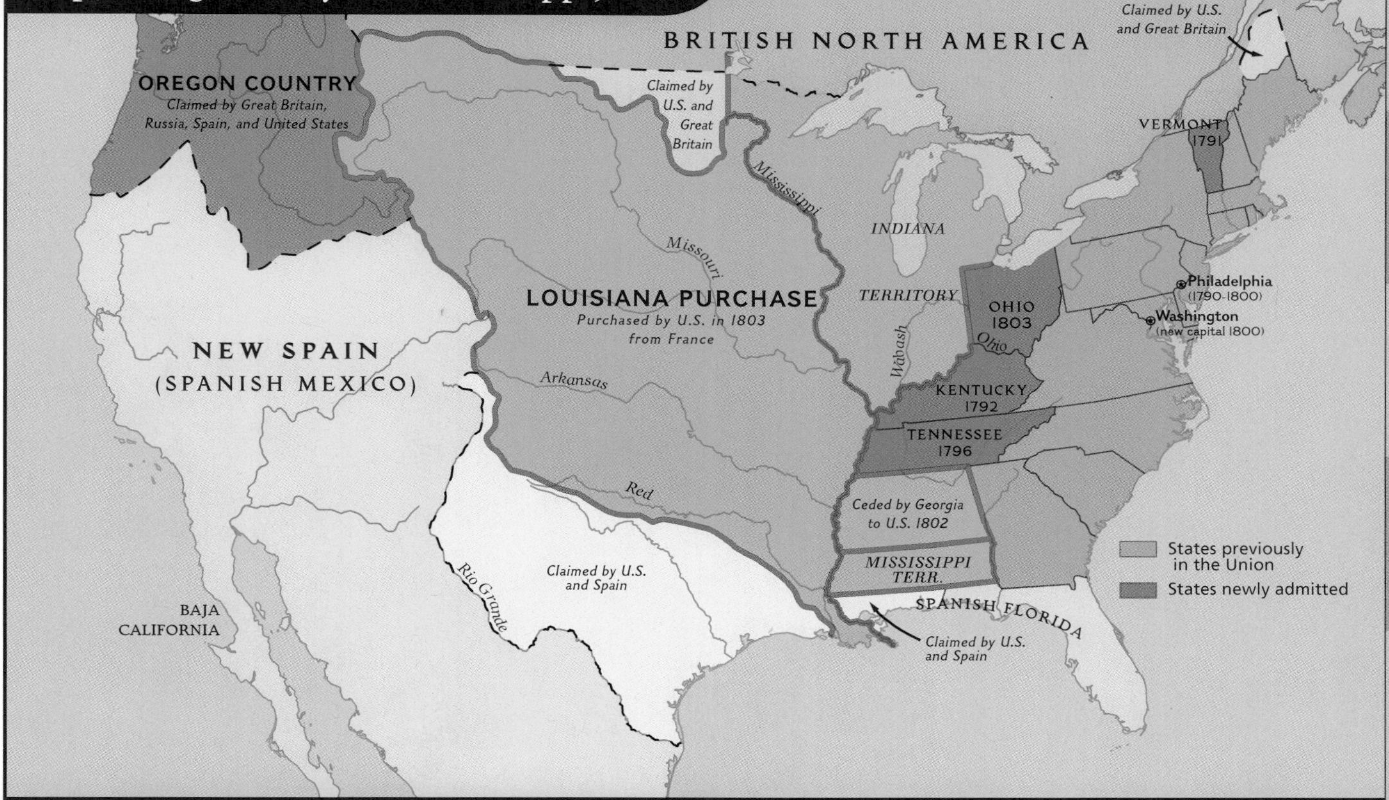

Coast to Coast, 1850 and beyond

MIDDLE AMERICA
PHYSICAL/POLITICAL
0 mi
400
0 km
400
AZIMUTHAL EQUIDISTANT PROJECTION
NATIONAL GEOGRAPHIC
UNITED STATES
MEXICO
Gulf of Mexico
PACIFIC OCEAN
CENTRAL AMERICA
Tijuana
Mexicali
Sonoran Desert
Baja California
Gulf of California
BAJA CALIFORNIA
BAJA CALIFORNIA SUR
SONORA
CHIHUAHUA
Ciudad Juarez
Chihuahua
Rio Grande
COAHUILA
Sierra Madre Occidental
Sierra Madre Oriental
SINALOA
DURANGO
Nuevo Laredo
Monterrey
NUEVO LEON
Matamoros
TAMAULIPAS
La Paz
False Cape
Mazatlan
ZACATECAS
SAN LUIS POTOSI
San Luis Potosi
Ciudad Madero
Tampico
NAYARIT
AGUASCALIENTES
Guadalajara
Leon
JALISCO
QUERETARO
VERACRUZ
TLAXCALA
HIDALGO
Revillagigedo Islands
Mex.
GUANAJUATO
COLIMA
MICHOACAN
Mexico City
Bay of Campeche
Orizaba
18,855 ft
5,747 m
Popocatepetl
17,802 ft
5,426 m
PUEBLA
Veracruz
DISTRITO FEDERAL
MEXICO
MORELOS
Sierra Madre del Sur
GUERRERO
Acapulco
OAXACA
Isthmus of Tehuantepec
TABASCO
CHIAPAS
Sierra Madre
Gulf of Tehuantepec
CAMPECHE
YUCATAN
Merida
Yucatan Peninsula
QUINTANA ROO
Cozumel Island
Belize City
Belmopan
BELIZE
Gulf of Honduras
HON
GUATEMALA
Guatemala
Tegucigalpa
EL SALVADOR
San Salvador
Leon
Cocos Island
C.R.
N
30°N
20°N
10°N
0°
110°W
100°W
90°W

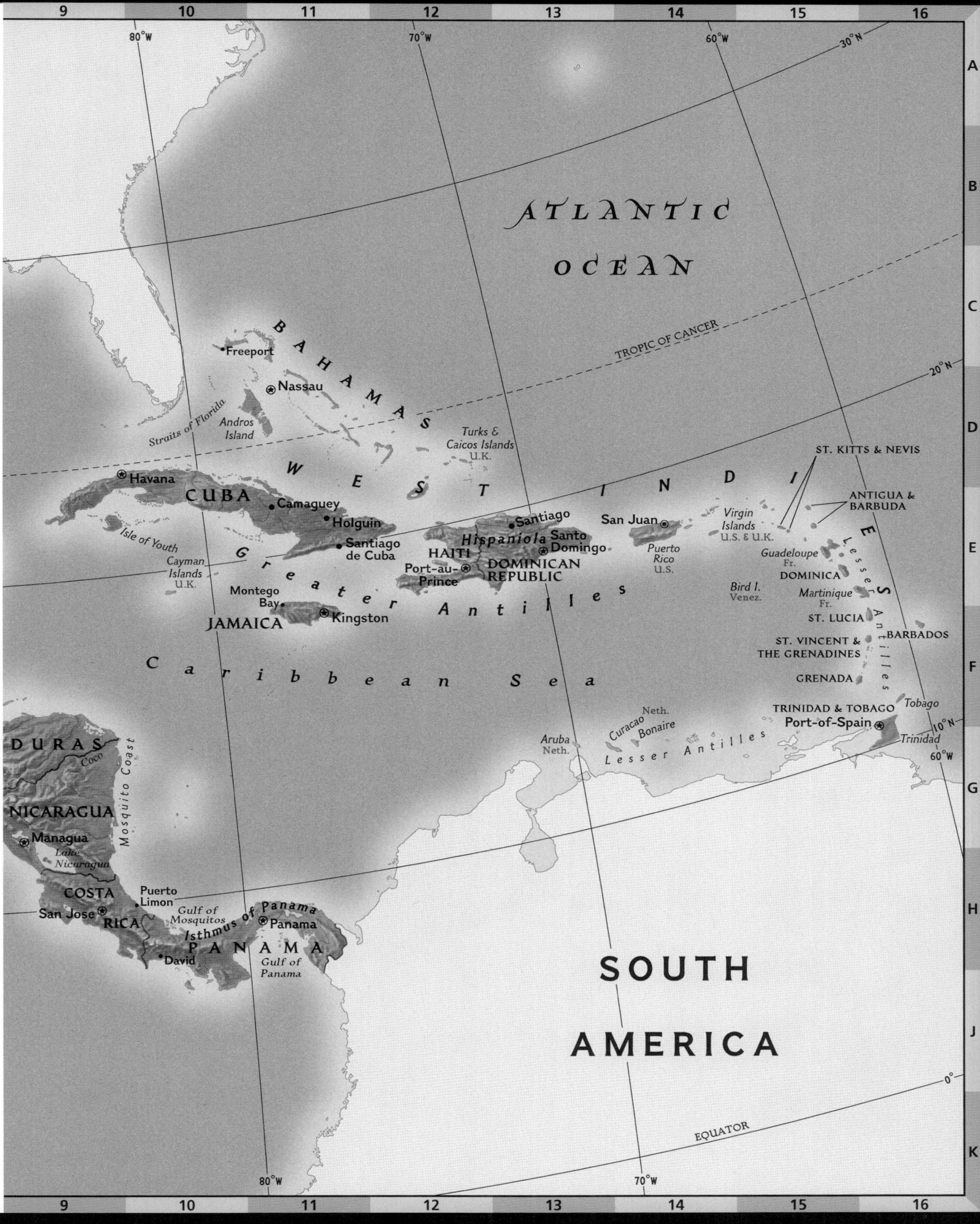

ATLANTIC OCEAN
TROPIC OF CANCER
30°N
20°N
10°N
0°
80°W
70°W
60°W
BAHAMAS
Freeport
Nassau
Andros Island
Straits of Florida
Turks & Caicos Islands U.K.
WEST INDIES
Havana
CUBA
Camaguey
Holguin
Santiago de Cuba
Isle of Youth
Cayman Islands U.K.
Greater Antilles
Montego Bay
Kingston
JAMAICA
HAITI
Port-au-Prince
Hispaniola
Santiago
Santo Domingo
DOMINICAN REPUBLIC
San Juan
Puerto Rico U.S.
Virgin Islands U.S. & U.K.
ST. KITTS & NEVIS
ANTIGUA & BARBUDA
Guadeloupe Fr.
DOMINICA
Martinique Fr.
ST. LUCIA
BARBADOS
ST. VINCENT & THE GRENADINES
GRENADA
Lesser Antilles
Bird I. Venez.
TRINIDAD & TOBAGO
Port-of-Spain
Tobago
Trinidad
Caribbean Sea
Aruba Neth.
Curacao
Neth. Bonaire
Lesser Antilles
DURAS
Coco
Mosquito Coast
NICARAGUA
Managua
Lake Nicaragua
COSTA RICA
San Jose
Puerto Limon
Gulf of Mosquitos
Isthmus of Panama
Panama
PANAMA
David
Gulf of Panama
SOUTH AMERICA
EQUATOR

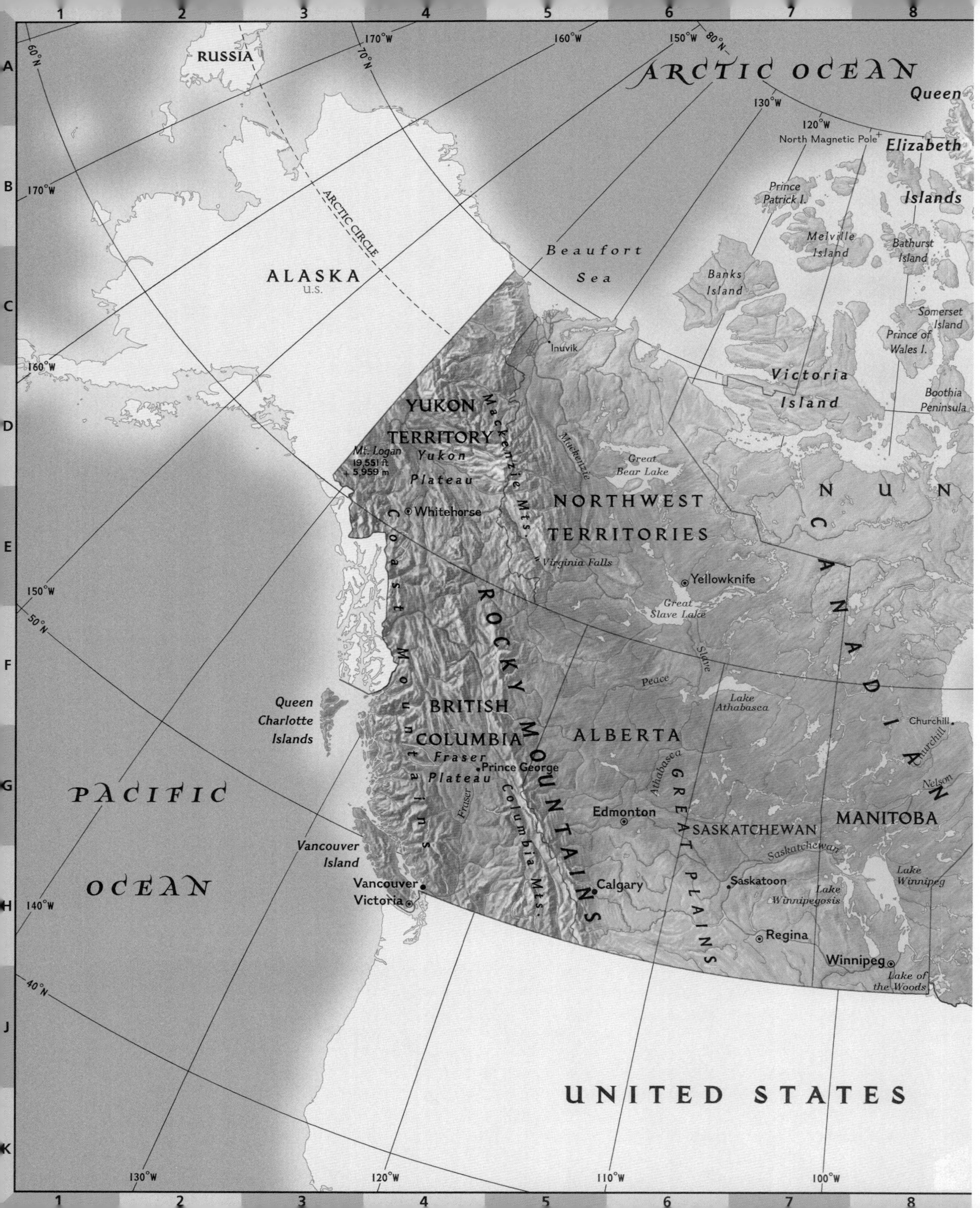
RUSSIA
ARCTIC OCEAN
Queen
Elizabeth
Islands
North Magnetic Pole
Prince
Patrick I.
Melville
Island
Bathurst
Island
Banks
Island
Somerset
Island
Prince of
Wales I.
Victoria
Island
Boothia
Peninsula
Beaufort
Sea
ALASKA
U.S.
ARCTIC CIRCLE
Inuvik
YUKON
TERRITORY
Mt. Logan
19,551 ft
5,959 m
Yukon
Plateau
Mackenzie Mts.
Mackenzie
Great
Bear Lake
NORTHWEST
TERRITORIES
NUNAVUT
CANADIAN
Whitehorse
Virginia Falls
Yellowknife
Great
Slave Lake
Coast Mountains
ROCKY MOUNTAINS
Slave
Peace
Lake
Athabasca
Queen
Charlotte
Islands
BRITISH
COLUMBIA
ALBERTA
Churchill
Churchill
Nelson
Fraser
Plateau
Prince George
Athabasca
GREAT PLAINS
PACIFIC
OCEAN
Fraser
Columbia Mts.
Edmonton
SASKATCHEWAN
MANITOBA
Saskatchewan
Vancouver
Island
Vancouver
Victoria
Calgary
Saskatoon
Lake
Winnipegosis
Lake
Winnipeg
Regina
Winnipeg
Lake of
the Woods
UNITED STATES
170°W
160°W
150°W
140°W
130°W
120°W
110°W
100°W
80°N
70°N
60°N
50°N
40°N
1
2
3
4
5
6
7
8
A
B
C
D
E
F
G
H
J
K

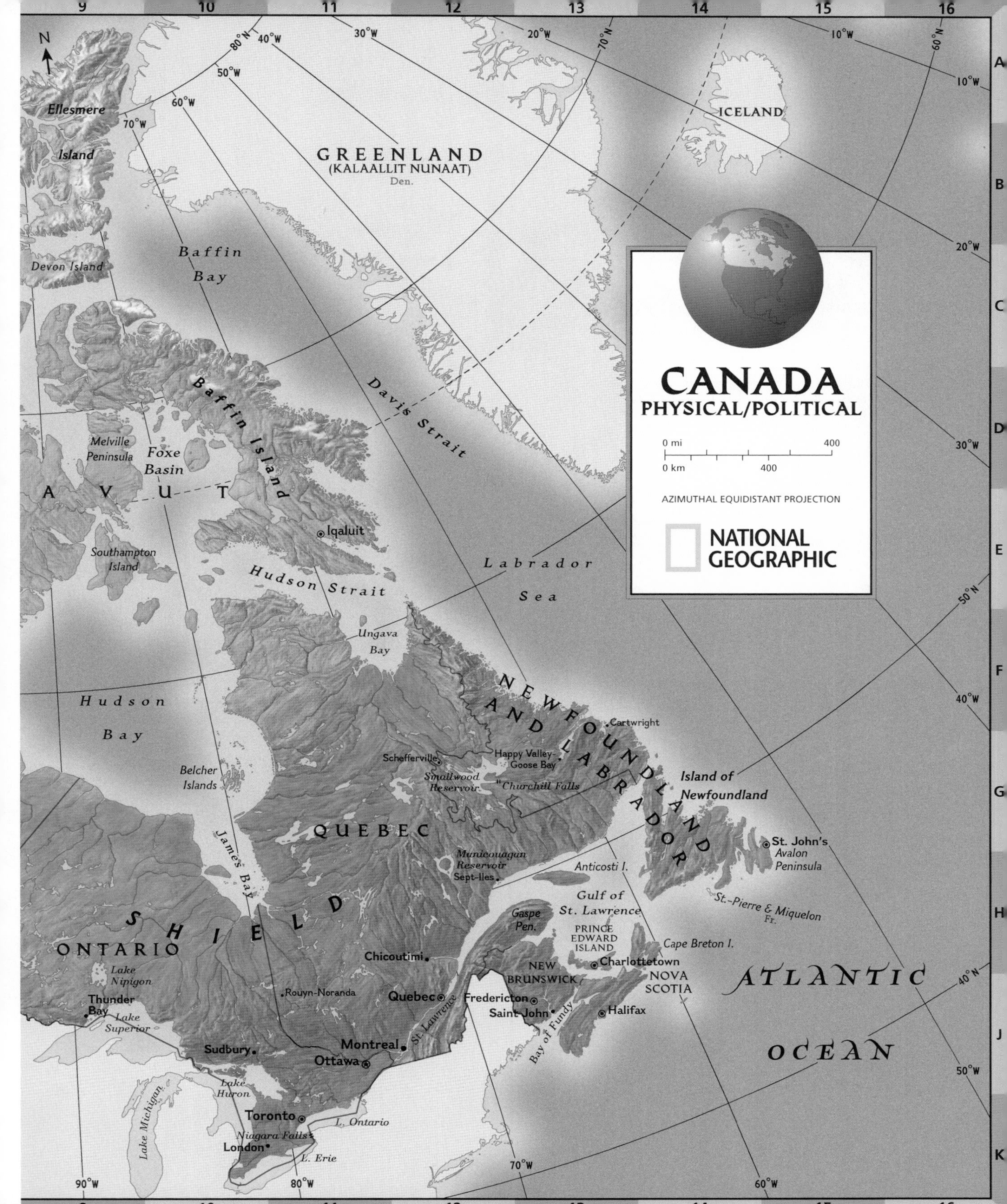
CANADA
PHYSICAL/POLITICAL
0 mi 400
0 km 400
AZIMUTHAL EQUIDISTANT PROJECTION
NATIONAL GEOGRAPHIC
GREENLAND
(KALAALLIT NUNAAT)
Den.
ICELAND
Ellesmere Island
Devon Island
Baffin Bay
Baffin Island
Davis Strait
Melville Peninsula
Foxe Basin
Iqaluit
Southampton Island
Hudson Strait
Labrador Sea
Ungava Bay
Hudson Bay
Belcher Islands
James Bay
QUEBEC
NEWFOUNDLAND AND LABRADOR
Cartwright
Schefferville
Happy Valley-Goose Bay
Smallwood Reservoir
Churchill Falls
Island of Newfoundland
St. John's
Avalon Peninsula
Manicouagan Reservoir
Sept-Iles
Anticosti I.
Gulf of St. Lawrence
St.-Pierre & Miquelon Fr.
Gaspe Pen.
PRINCE EDWARD ISLAND
Cape Breton I.
Charlottetown
NEW BRUNSWICK
NOVA SCOTIA
ATLANTIC OCEAN
Fredericton
Saint John
Halifax
Bay of Fundy
Chicoutimi
Quebec
St. Lawrence
Montreal
Ottawa
SHIELD
ONTARIO
Lake Nipigon
Rouyn-Noranda
Thunder Bay
Lake Superior
Sudbury
Lake Huron
Lake Michigan
Toronto
L. Ontario
Niagara Falls
London
L. Erie
A V U T

1
2
3
4
5
6
7
8
A
B
C
D
E
F
G
H
J
K
10°E
20°E
30°E
40°E
40°N
30°N
EUROPE
Black Sea
Sea of Marmara
Istanbul
ANATOLIA
Ankara
TURKEY
Tunis
TUNISIA
Taurus Mountains
Aleppo
Mediterranean Sea
CYPRUS
SYRIA
Tripoli
LEBANON
Damascus
Beirut
ISRAEL
Syrian Desert
Jerusalem
Amman
Alexandria
JORDAN
Cairo
El Giza
LIBYA
Sinai Pen.
See inset below
EGYPT
Nile R.
Hejaz
Aswan High Dam
Red Sea
SAHARA
Boundary claimed by Sudan
SUDAN
AFRICA
Khartoum
Eastern Mediterranean Area
30°E
TURKEY
N
Aleppo
CYPRUS
SYRIA
LEBANON
Mediterranean Sea
Beirut
Damascus
Sea of Galilee
Golan Heights
Jordan River
Tel Aviv–Jaffa
West Bank
Jerusalem
Amman
Suez Canal
Gaza Strip
Dead Sea
ISRAEL
JORDAN
El Giza
Cairo
30°N
EGYPT
SAUDI ARABIA
Nile River
Gulf of Suez
Gulf of Aqaba
0 mi 100
0 km 100
Red Sea

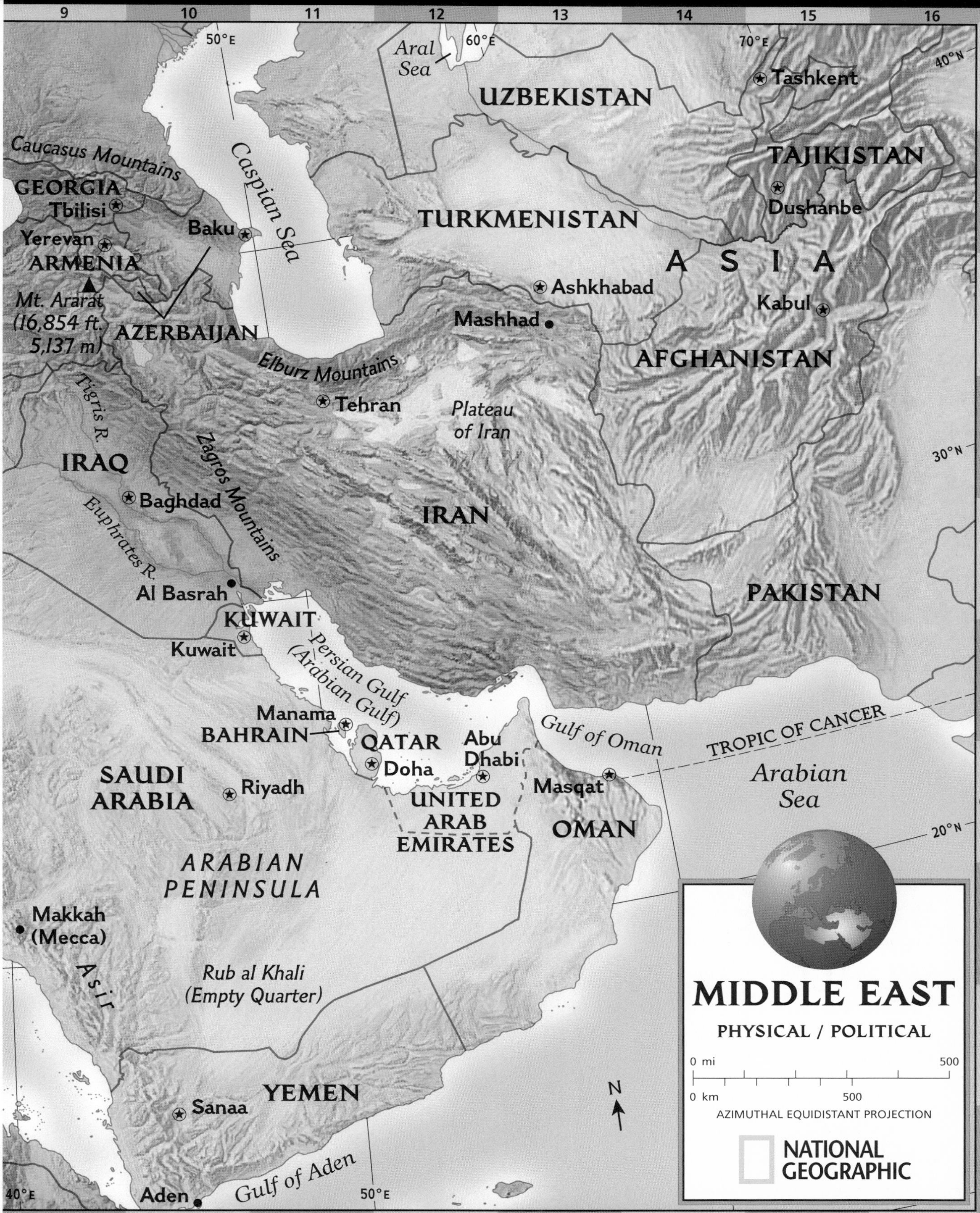

MIDDLE EAST
PHYSICAL / POLITICAL
0 mi 500
0 km 500
AZIMUTHAL EQUIDISTANT PROJECTION
NATIONAL GEOGRAPHIC
Aral Sea
Caspian Sea
Caucasus Mountains
GEORGIA
Tbilisi
Baku
Yerevan
ARMENIA
Mt. Ararat (16,854 ft. 5,137 m)
AZERBAIJAN
UZBEKISTAN
Tashkent
TAJIKISTAN
Dushanbe
TURKMENISTAN
ASIA
Ashkhabad
Mashhad
Kabul
AFGHANISTAN
Elburz Mountains
Tehran
Plateau of Iran
Tigris R.
IRAQ
Zagros Mountains
Baghdad
Euphrates R.
IRAN
Al Basrah
KUWAIT
Kuwait
PAKISTAN
Persian Gulf (Arabian Gulf)
Manama
BAHRAIN
QATAR
Doha
Abu Dhabi
Gulf of Oman
TROPIC OF CANCER
Arabian Sea
Masqat
SAUDI ARABIA
Riyadh
UNITED ARAB EMIRATES
OMAN
ARABIAN PENINSULA
Makkah (Mecca)
Asir
Rub al Khali (Empty Quarter)
YEMEN
Sanaa
Aden
Gulf of Aden
N
40°N
30°N
20°N
40°E
50°E
60°E
70°E

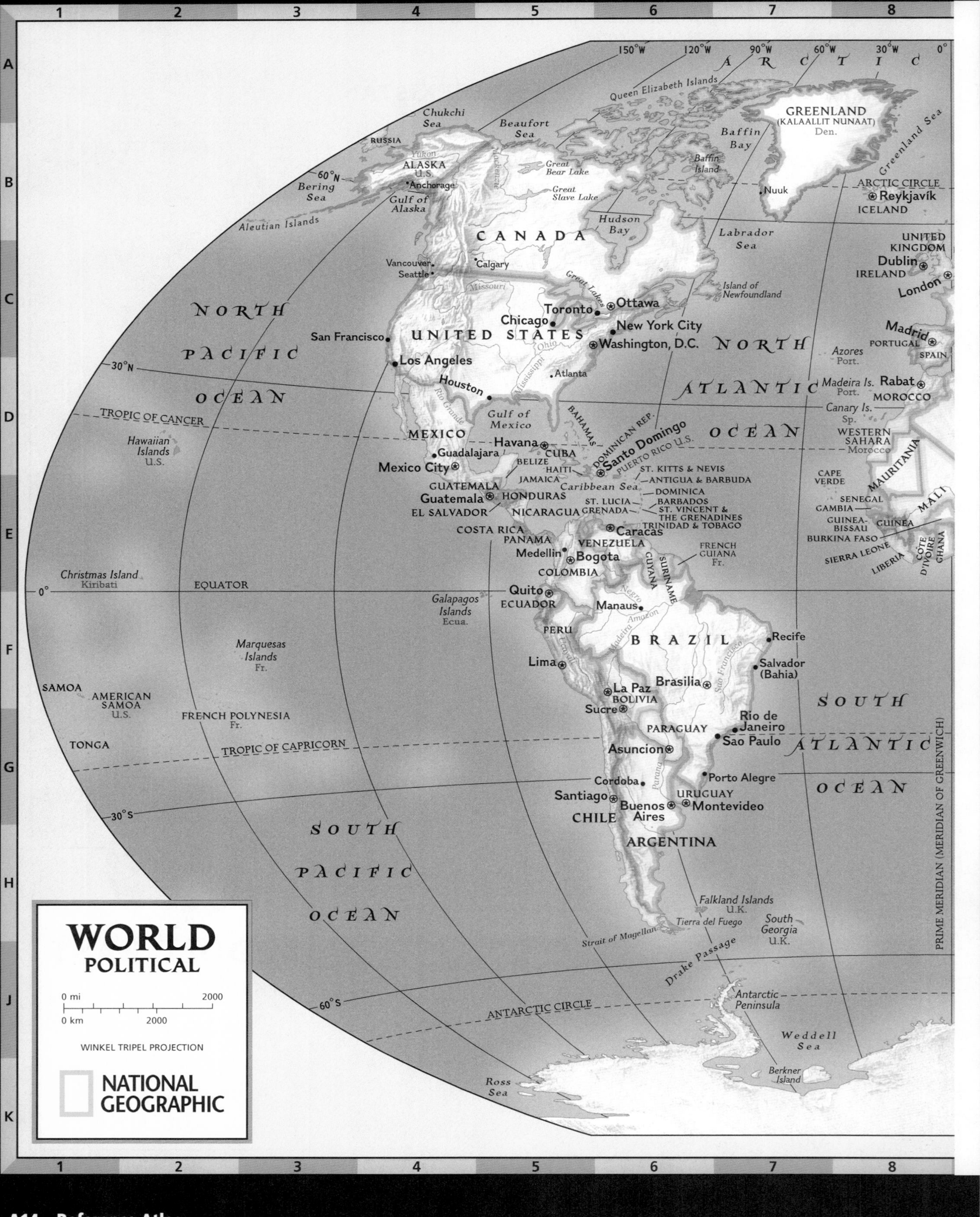
WORLD
POLITICAL
0 mi 2000
0 km 2000
WINKEL TRIPEL PROJECTION
NATIONAL GEOGRAPHIC
1 2 3 4 5 6 7 8
A B C D E F G H J K
150°W 120°W 90°W 60°W 30°W 0°
60°N
30°N
0°
30°S
60°S
ARCTIC
Queen Elizabeth Islands
GREENLAND (KALAALLIT NUNAAT) Den.
Greenland Sea
Chukchi Sea
Beaufort Sea
Baffin Bay
Baffin Island
RUSSIA
Yukon
ALASKA U.S.
Mackenzie
Great Bear Lake
Great Slave Lake
Bering Sea
Anchorage
Gulf of Alaska
Nuuk
ARCTIC CIRCLE
Reykjavík
ICELAND
Aleutian Islands
Hudson Bay
CANADA
Labrador Sea
UNITED KINGDOM
Dublin
IRELAND
London
Vancouver
Seattle
Calgary
Missouri
Great Lakes
Island of Newfoundland
NORTH PACIFIC OCEAN
Toronto
Ottawa
Chicago
New York City
San Francisco
UNITED STATES
Ohio
Washington, D.C.
NORTH ATLANTIC OCEAN
Madrid
PORTUGAL
SPAIN
Azores Port.
Los Angeles
Mississippi
Atlanta
Houston
Rio Grande
Madeira Is. Port.
Rabat
MOROCCO
Canary Is. Sp.
TROPIC OF CANCER
Gulf of Mexico
BAHAMAS
DOMINICAN REP.
Santo Domingo
Hawaiian Islands U.S.
MEXICO
Havana
CUBA
PUERTO RICO U.S.
WESTERN SAHARA Morocco
MAURITANIA
Guadalajara
BELIZE
Mexico City
HAITI
ST. KITTS & NEVIS
CAPE VERDE
JAMAICA
Caribbean Sea
ANTIGUA & BARBUDA
GUATEMALA
DOMINICA
SENEGAL
MALI
Guatemala
HONDURAS
ST. LUCIA
BARBADOS
GAMBIA
EL SALVADOR
NICARAGUA
GRENADA
ST. VINCENT & THE GRENADINES
GUINEA-BISSAU
GUINEA
TRINIDAD & TOBAGO
COSTA RICA
Caracas
BURKINA FASO
PANAMA
VENEZUELA
FRENCH GUIANA Fr.
SIERRA LEONE
LIBERIA
CÔTE D'IVOIRE
GHANA
Medellín
Bogota
GUYANA
SURINAME
COLOMBIA
Christmas Island Kiribati
EQUATOR
Quito
ECUADOR
Negro
Galapagos Islands Ecua.
Manaus
Amazon
PERU
Madeira
BRAZIL
São Francisco
Recife
Marquesas Islands Fr.
Lima
Salvador (Bahia)
La Paz
Brasilia
BOLIVIA
SAMOA
AMERICAN SAMOA U.S.
FRENCH POLYNESIA Fr.
Sucre
SOUTH ATLANTIC OCEAN
Rio de Janeiro
PARAGUAY
Sao Paulo
TONGA
TROPIC OF CAPRICORN
Asuncion
Parana
Porto Alegre
Cordoba
URUGUAY
Santiago
Buenos Aires
Montevideo
CHILE
ARGENTINA
SOUTH PACIFIC OCEAN
Falkland Islands U.K.
Tierra del Fuego
South Georgia U.K.
Strait of Magellan
Drake Passage
PRIME MERIDIAN (MERIDIAN OF GREENWICH)
Antarctic Peninsula
ANTARCTIC CIRCLE
Weddell Sea
Berkner Island
Ross Sea

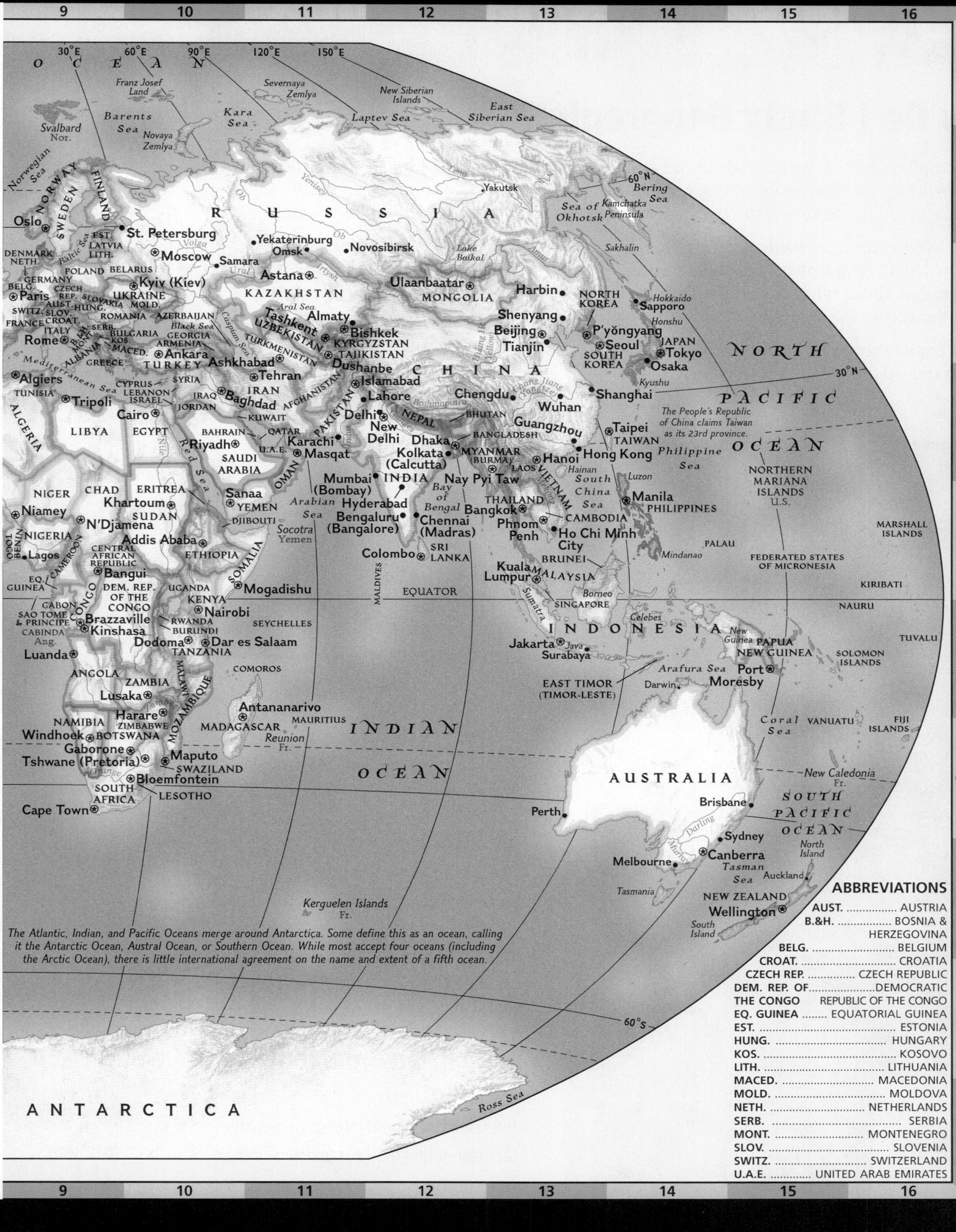

ABBREVIATIONS

AUST.	AUSTRIA
B.&H.	BOSNIA & HERZEGOVINA
BELG.	BELGIUM
CROAT.	CROATIA
CZECH REP.	CZECH REPUBLIC
DEM. REP. OF THE CONGO	DEMOCRATIC REPUBLIC OF THE CONGO
EQ. GUINEA	EQUATORIAL GUINEA
EST.	ESTONIA
HUNG.	HUNGARY
KOS.	KOSOVO
LITH.	LITHUANIA
MACED.	MACEDONIA
MOLD.	MOLDOVA
NETH.	NETHERLANDS
SERB.	SERBIA
MONT.	MONTENEGRO
SLOV.	SLOVENIA
SWITZ.	SWITZERLAND
U.A.E.	UNITED ARAB EMIRATES

Geography Skills Handbook

How Do I Study Geography?

Geographers have tried to understand the best way to teach and learn about geography. In order to do this, geographers created the *Five Themes of Geography*. The themes acted as a guide for teaching the basic ideas about geography to students like yourself.

People who teach and study geography, though, thought that the Five Themes were too broad. In 1994, geographers created 18 national geography standards. These standards were more detailed about what should be taught and learned. The Six Essential Elements act as a bridge connecting the Five Themes with the standards.

These pages show you how the Five Themes are related to the Six Essential Elements and the 18 standards.

5 Themes of Geography

1 Location

Location describes where something is. Absolute location describes a place's exact position on the Earth's surface. Relative location expresses where a place is in relation to another place.

2 Place

Place describes the physical and human characteristics that make a location unique.

3 Regions

Regions are areas that share common characteristics.

4 Movement

Movement explains how and why people and things move and are connected.

5 Human-Environment Interaction

Human-Environment Interaction describes the relationship between people and their environment.

6 Essential Elements

18 Geography Standards

I. The World in Spatial Terms
Geographers look to see where a place is located. Location acts as a starting point to answer "Where Is It?" The location of a place helps you orient yourself as to where you are.

1 How to use maps and other tools
2 How to use mental maps to organize information
3 How to analyze the spatial organization of people, places, and environments

II. Places and Regions
Place describes physical characteristics such as landforms, climate, and plant or animal life. It might also describe human characteristics, including language and way of life. Places can also be organized into regions. **Regions** are places united by one or more characteristics.

4 The physical and human characteristics of places
5 How people create regions to interpret Earth's complexity
6 How culture and experience influence people's perceptions of places and regions

III. Physical Systems
Geographers study how physical systems, such as hurricanes, volcanoes, and glaciers, shape the surface of the Earth. They also look at how plants and animals depend upon one another and their surroundings for their survival.

IV. Human Systems
People shape the world in which they live. They settle in certain places but not in others. An ongoing theme in geography is the movement of people, ideas, and goods.

V. Environment and Society
How does the relationship between people and their natural surroundings influence the way people live? Geographers study how people use the environment and how their actions affect the environment.

7 The physical processes that shape Earth's surface
8 The distribution of ecosystems on Earth's surface
9 The characteristics, distribution, and migration of human populations
10 The complexity of Earth's cultural mosaics
11 The patterns and networks of economic interdependence
12 The patterns of human settlement
13 The forces of cooperation and conflict
14 How human actions modify the physical environment
15 How physical systems affect human systems
16 The meaning, use, and distribution of resources

VI. The Uses of Geography
Knowledge of geography helps us understand the relationships among people, places, and environments over time. Applying geographic skills helps you understand the past and prepare for the future.

17 How to apply geography to interpret the past
18 How to apply geography to interpret the present and plan for the future

NATIONAL GEOGRAPHIC

Contents

Geography Skills Handbook

Throughout this text, you will discover how geography has shaped the course of events in United States history. Landforms, waterways, climate, and natural resources all have helped or hindered human activities. Usually people have learned either to adapt to their environments or to transform it to meet their needs. The resources in this handbook will help you get the most out of your textbook—and provide you with skills you will use for the rest of your life.

The study of geography is more than knowing a lot of facts about places. Rather, it has more to do with asking questions about the Earth, pursuing their answers, and solving problems. Thus, one of the most important geographic tools is inside your head: the ability to think geographically.

Globes and Maps

A **globe** is a scale model of the Earth. Because Earth is round, a globe presents the most accurate depiction of geographic information such as area, distance, and direction. However, globes show little close-up detail. A printed **map** is a symbolic representation of all or part of the planet. Unlike globes, maps can show small areas in great detail.

From 3-D to 2-D

Think about the surface of the Earth as the peel of an orange. To flatten the peel, you have to cut it like the globe shown here. To create maps that are not interrupted, mapmakers, or **cartographers**, use mathematical formulas to transfer information from the three-dimensional globe to the two-dimensional map. However, when the curves of a globe become straight lines on a map, distortion of size, shape, distance, or area occurs.

globe accurately shows a great circle route, as indicated on the map below. However, as shown on the flat map, the great circle distance (dotted line) between Tokyo and Los Angeles appears to be far longer than the true direction distance (solid line). In fact, D the great circle distance is 345 miles (555 km) shorter.

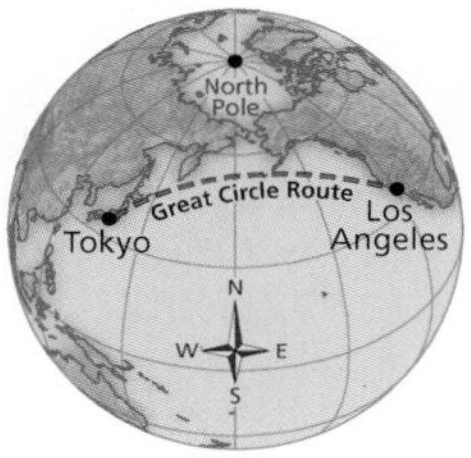

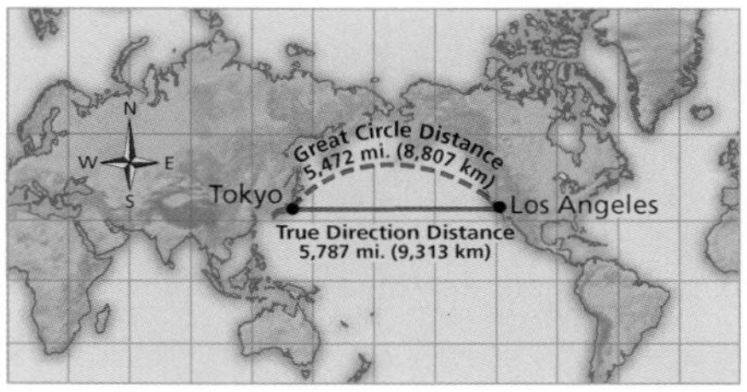

Great Circle Routes

A straight line of true direction—one that runs directly from west to east, for example—is not always the shortest distance between two points. This is due to the curvature of the Earth. To find the shortest distance, stretch a piece of string around a globe from one point to the other. The C string will form part of a *great circle*, an imaginary line the follows the curve of the Earth. Ship captains and airline pilots use these **great circle routes** to reduce travel time and conserve fuel.

The idea of a great circle route is an important difference between globes and maps. A round

Practicing SKILLS

1. **Explain** the significance of: globe, map, cartographer, great circle route.
2. **Describe** the problems that arise when the curves of a globe become straight lines on a map.
3. **Use** a Venn diagram like the one below to identify the similarities and differences between globes and maps.

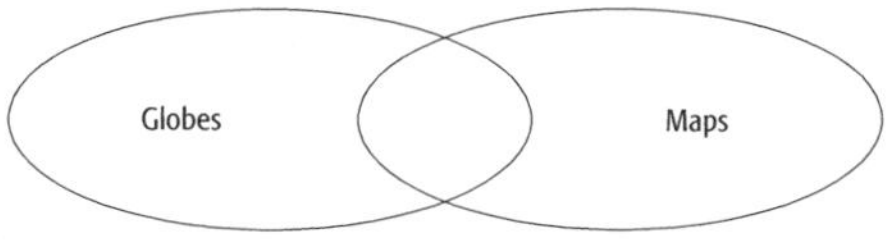

Teach

D Differentiated Instruction

Visual/Spatial Use an orange to illustrate the challenges of transferring measurements from a three-dimensional to a two-dimensional form. Sketch an outline of the continents and two or three lines of longitude and latitude onto an orange. Then carefully remove the peel (in one piece, if possible) and gently flatten it. Allow students to examine the peel, and point out how lines and shapes are distorted when the curved peel is flattened. **OL**

C Critical Thinking

Making Inferences Have students use a piece of string and a globe to find the shortest route from New York to Hong Kong. (over the top of the globe) **OL**

PRACTICING SKILLS

Answers

1. globe: scale model of the Earth; map: symbolic representation of all or part of the planet; cartographer: mapmakers; great circle route: routes that follow the great circle along the curve of the Earth
2. Size, shape, distance, or area becomes distorted.
3. Globes present the most accurate depiction of geographic information such as area, distance, and direction, but do not show close-up detail. Maps are symbolic representations of all or part of the planet and can show areas in great detail. Both show information about places on the Earth.

C Critical Thinking

Identifying Central Issues

Ask: Why do map makers use projections? *(Projections help in transferring information from a three-dimensional surface to a two-dimensional surface.)* **OL**

D Differentiated Instruction

Kinesthetic If students are struggling with the concept of projection, give them a large sheet of paper or poster board and a globe. Have students place the paper and the globe in the same physical relationships shown in the illustrations. Check to make sure students can visualize how each projection offers a different approximation of the sphere. **BL**

Projections

To create maps, cartographers project the round Earth onto a flat surface—making a **map projection.** Distance, shape, direction, or size **C** may be distorted by a projection. As a result, the purpose of the map usually dictates which projection is used. There are many kinds of map projections, some with general names and some named for the cartographers who developed them. Three basic categories of map projections are shown here: **planar, cylindrical,** and **conic.**

Planar Projection

A planar projection shows the Earth centered in such a way that a straight line coming from the center to any other point represents the shortest distance. Also known as an azimuthal projection, it is most accurate at its center. As a result, it is often used for maps of the Poles.

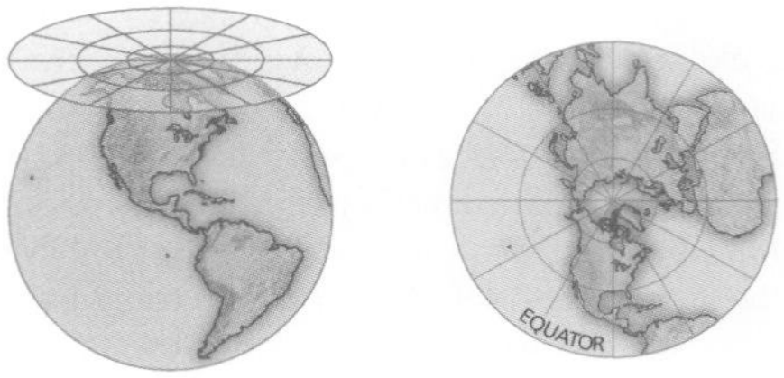

Cylindrical Projection

A cylindrical projection is based on the projec- **D** tion of the globe onto a cylinder. This projection is most accurate near the Equator, but shapes and distances are distorted near the Poles.

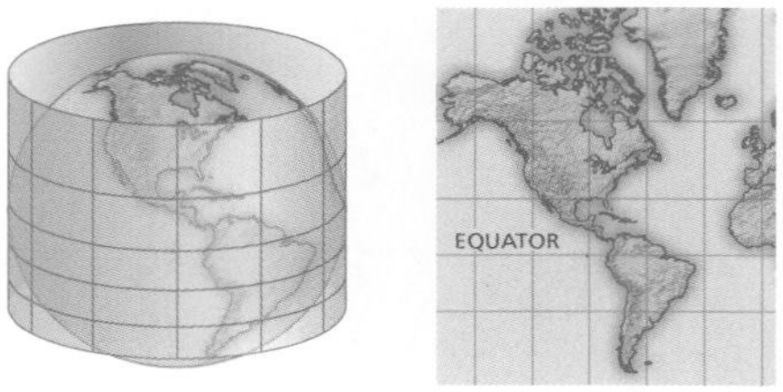

Conic Projection

A conic projection comes from placing a cone over part of a globe. Conic projections are best suited for showing limited east-west areas that are not too far from the Equator. For these uses, a conic projection can indicate distances and directions fairly accurately.

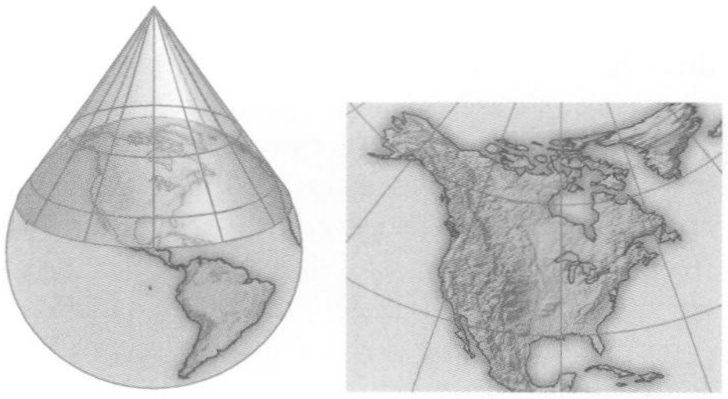

Differentiated Instruction

Activity: Creating a Graphic Organizer

Visual/Spatial To help students remember the several different categories and examples of maps discussed in this section, guide them in creating a graphic organizer entitled "Types of Maps." Branching this main head should be three boxes labeled "Political," "Physical," and "Special-Purpose." Have students complete the organizer by taking notes on each of the different types of maps. **OL**

Common Map Projections

Each type of map projection has advantages and some degree of inaccuracy. Four of the most common projections are shown here.

Winkel Tripel Projection

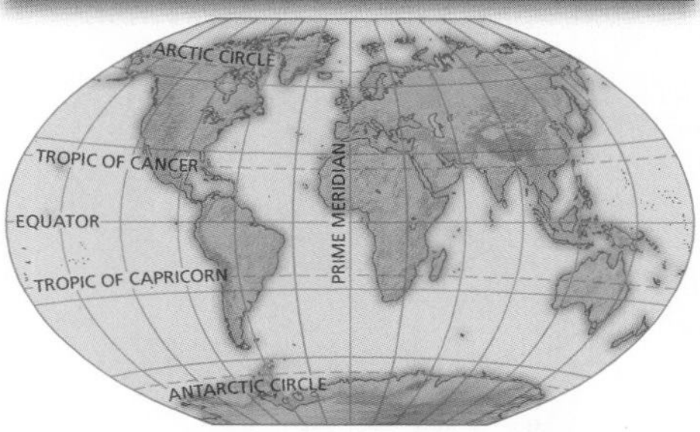

Most general reference world maps are the Winkel Tripel projection. It provides a good balance between the size and shape of land areas as they are shown on the map. Even the polar areas are depicted with little distortion of size and shape.

Goode's Interrupted Equal-Area Projection

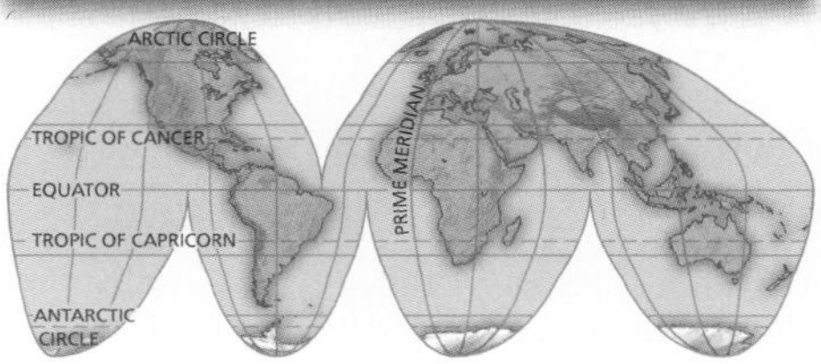

An **interrupted projection** resembles a globe that has been cut apart and laid flat. Goode's Interrupted Equal-Area projection shows the true size and shape of Earth's landmasses, but distances are generally distorted.

Robinson Projection

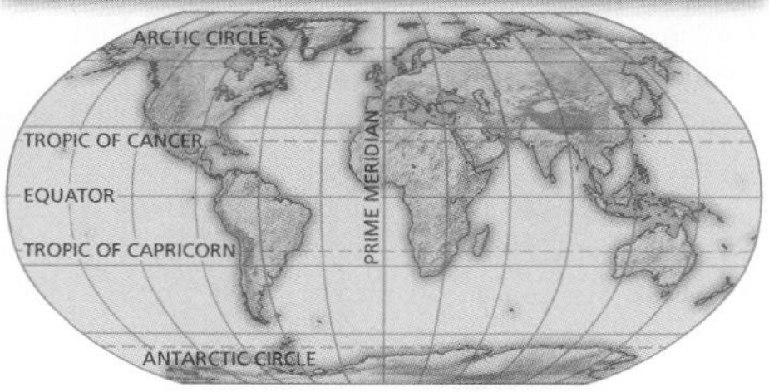

The Robinson projection has minor distortions. The sizes and shapes near the eastern and western edges of the map are accurate, and outlines of the continents appear much as they do on the globe. However, the polar areas are flattened.

Mercator Projection

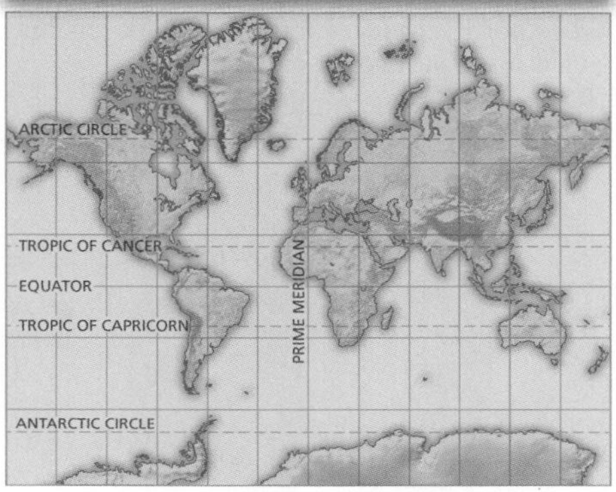

The Mercator projection increasingly distorts size and distance as it moves away from the Equator. However, Mercator projections do accurately show true directions and the shapes of landmasses, making these maps useful for sea travel.

C Critical Thinking

Comparing and Contrasting

Ask students to cover the text and look at the selected projections. **Ask:** What is one similarity and one difference between the Winkle Tripel Projection and the Goode's Interrupted Equal-Area Projection? *(similarity: both show all of the continents; difference: Goode's projection splits Antarctica into four pieces, while the Winkel Tripel projection does not.)* **BL**

R Reading Strategy

Analyzing Text Structure

Have students read the selected captions. **Ask:** How is the information structured in these captions? *(Both captions propose a benefit of the projection, followed by a drawback.)* **OL**

Practicing SKILLS

1. **Explain** the significance of: map projection, planar, cylindrical, conic, interrupted projection.
2. **How** does a cartographer determine which map projection to use?
3. **How** is Goode's Interrupted Equal-Area projection different from the Mercator projection?
4. **Which** of the four common projections described above is the best one to use when showing the entire world? Why?
5. **Use** a Venn diagram like the one below to identify the similarities and differences between the Winkel Tripel and Mercator projections.

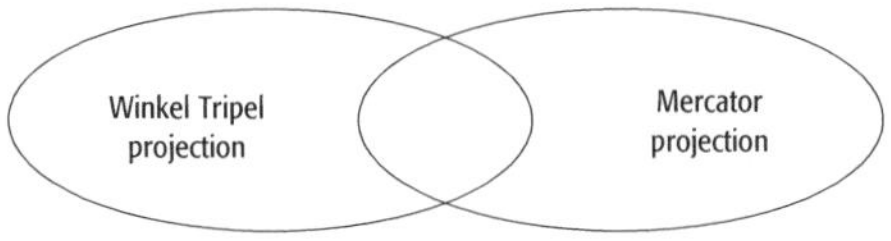

PRACTICING SKILLS

Answers

1. map projection: projecting image of earth onto a flat surface to make a map, different projections have their advantages/disadvantages. planar: shows shortest distance between points, most often used for maps of the Poles; cylindrical: most accurate near the Equator; conic: best for limited east-west areas not too far from the Equator; interrupted projection: shows true size and shape of Earth but distorts distances
2. by deciding what it will be used for to determine the least distortion
3. Goode distorts distances while showing the true size and shape. Mercator distorts size and distances but shows true directions.
4. Winkel Tripel, because it distorts the size and shape of landmasses the least.
5. Both show all continents with little to no distortion of shape. Mercator shows true direction, but distorts land size and distance. Winkel Tripel shows little size distortion.

S Skill Practice

Visual Literacy Have students study the selected figures. **Ask:** What are two differences between longitude and latitude? *(Lines of latitude run horizontally and are parallel. Lines of longitude run vertically and intersect at the poles.)* **OL**

D Differentiated Instruction

Logical/Mathematical Have students use the Internet or library resources to determine their exact absolute location. If you have access to GPS equipment, you may wish to let students use it to check their work. **OL**

Determining Location

Geography is often said to begin with the question: *Where?* The basic tool for answering the question is **location.** Lines on globes and maps provide information that can help you locate places. These lines cross one another forming a pattern called a **grid system,** which helps you find exact places on the Earth's surface.

A **hemisphere** is one of the halves into which the Earth is divided. Geographers divide the Earth into hemispheres to help them classify and describe places on Earth. Most places are located in two of the four hemispheres.

Latitude

Lines of **latitude,** or parallels, circle the Earth parallel to the Equator and measure the distance north or south of the Equator in degrees. The Equator is measured at 0° latitude, while the Poles lie at latitudes 90°N (north) and 90°S (south). Parallels north of the Equator are called north latitude. Parallels south of the Equator are called south latitude.

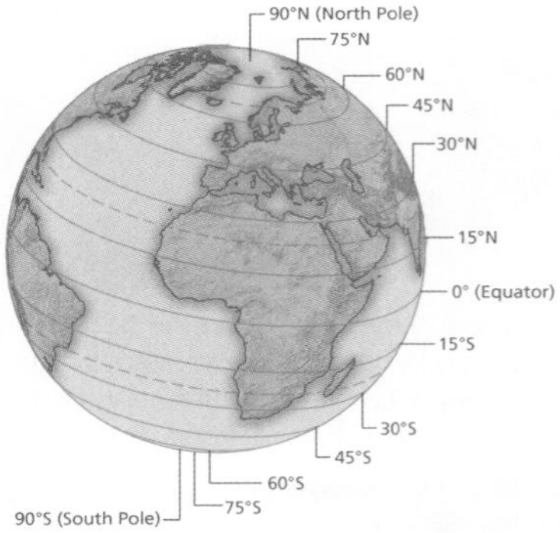

S

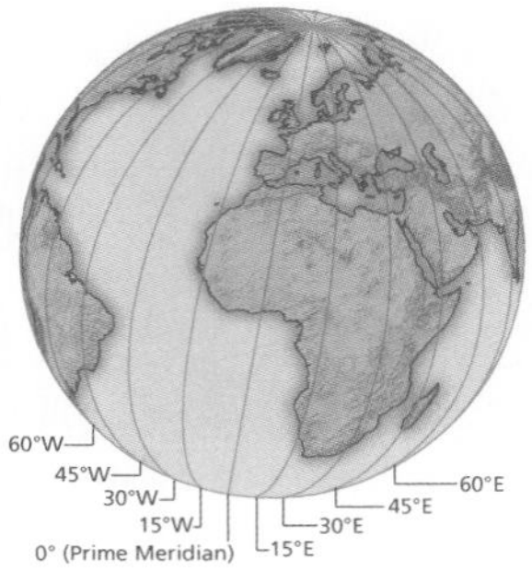

Longitude

Lines of **longitude,** or meridians, circle the Earth from Pole to Pole. These lines measure distance east or west of the **Prime Meridian** at 0° longitude. Meridians east of the Prime Meridian are known as east latitude. Meridians west of the Prime Meridian are known as west longitude. The 180° meridian on the opposite side of the Earth is called the International Date Line.

The Global Grid

Every place has a global address, or **absolute location.** You can identify the absolute location of a place by D naming the latitude and longitude lines that cross exactly at that place. For example, Tokyo, Japan, is located at 36°N latitude and 140°E longitude. For more precise readings, each degree is further divided into 60 units called minutes.

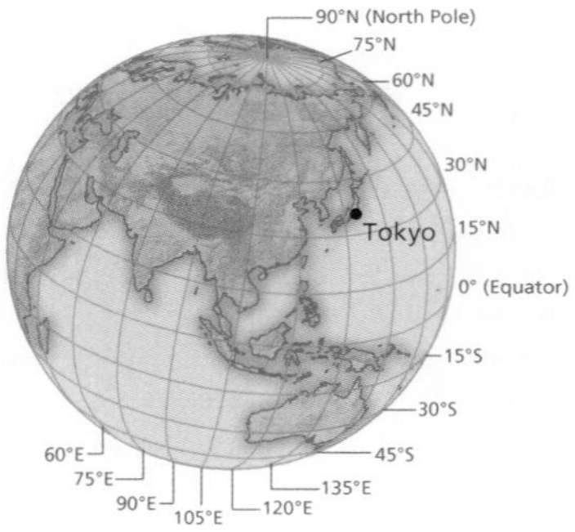

Hands-On Chapter Project

Creating a Global Treasure Hunt

Directions Organize students into teams and have each team choose 10 places on Earth to research and study. Students may choose places that are well known or unfamiliar. However, all places should be on land and located at least 50 miles (80 km) from each other. Tell students to make a list of 8–10 interesting facts about each place.

Putting It Together Tell students to "bury" their treasure in each of the locations. Then have students use the facts they learned about the place to create clues for a Treasure Atlas. Clues will be locations, that, when followed, will lead to the buried treasure. The correct response to each clue will be a place name and coordinates that can be easily looked up. Clues should be written on index cards. Students should list all the clues with their answers on a separate sheet of paper. Each correct answer earns another clue to a new location, eventually leading to the buried treasure, so remind students to make sure their clues follow a logical route. **OL**

Northern and Southern Hemispheres

The diagram below shows that the Equator divides the Earth into the Northern and Southern Hemispheres. Everything north of the Equator is in the **Northern Hemisphere.** Everything south of the Equator is in the **Southern Hemisphere.**

Northern Hemisphere

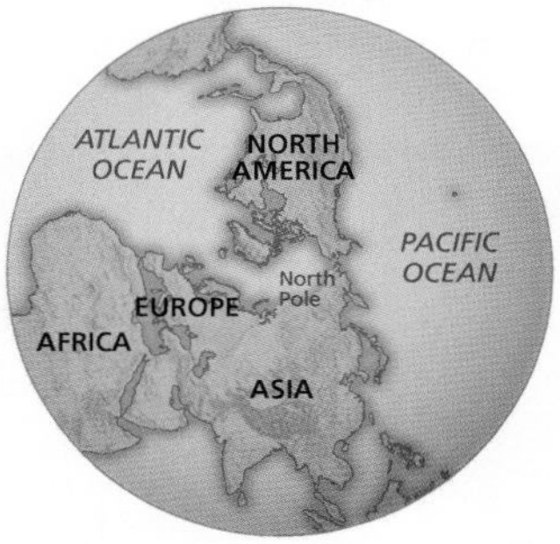

Southern Hemisphere

Eastern and Western Hemispheres

The Prime Meridian and the International Date Line divide the Earth into the Eastern and Western Hemispheres. Everything east of the Prime Meridian for 180° is in the **Eastern Hemisphere.** Everything west of the Prime Meridian for 180° is in the **Western Hemisphere.**

Eastern Hemisphere

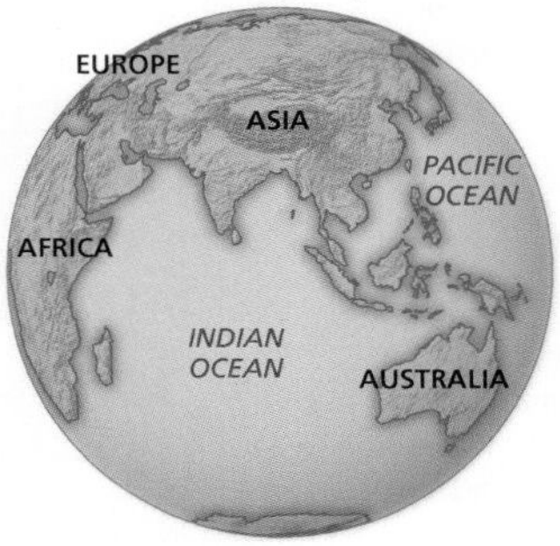

Western Hemisphere

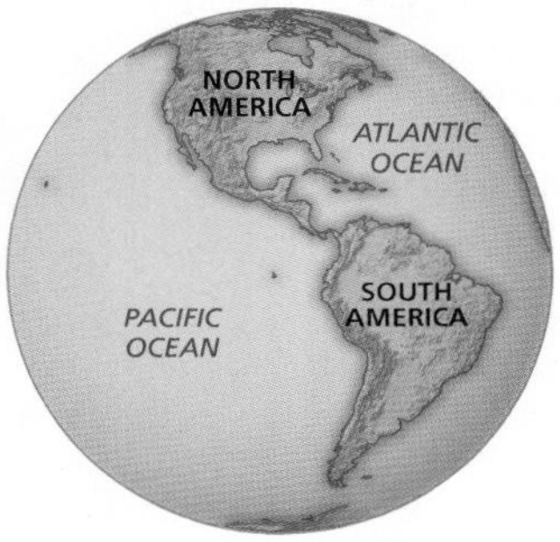

Practicing SKILLS

1. **Explain** the significance of: location, grid system, hemisphere, Northern Hemisphere, Southern Hemisphere, Eastern Hemisphere, Western Hemisphere, latitude, longitude, Prime Meridian, absolute location.
2. **Why** do all maps label the Equator 0° latitude and the Prime Meridian 0° longitude?
3. **Which** lines of latitude and longitude divide the Earth into hemispheres?
4. **Using** the Reference Atlas maps, fill in a chart like the one below by writing the latitude and longitude of three world cities. Have a partner try to identify the cities.
5. **Use** a chart like the one below to identify the continents in each hemisphere. Some may be in more than one hemisphere.

Hemisphere	Continents
Northern	
Southern	
Eastern	
Western	

S Skill Practice

Visual Literacy Point out that most people probably are not used to seeing the globe from these angles. **Ask:** What view do these illustrations show? *(the globe viewed from the top and the bottom)* **Ask:** How do you generally view the globe? *(from the side, along the Equator)* If students still struggle to understand the difference between these views, use an actual globe to show them the view reflected in the illustration. **BL**

C Critical Thinking

Detecting Bias Ask: Since planet Earth has no true top or bottom, why do globes show Europe on the top half of Earth? *(early map makers and explorers were from Europe)* **AL**

PRACTICING SKILLS

Answers

1. location: a specific place on Earth; grid system: pattern formed as the lines of latitude and longitude cross one another; hemisphere: half of a sphere or globe; Northern Hemisphere: everything north of the Equator; Southern Hemisphere: everything south of the Equator; Eastern Hemisphere: everything east of the Prime Meridian for 180°; Western Hemisphere: everything west of the Prime Meridian for 180°
2. They are where the division between north/south (N/S) and east/west (E/W) occur, respectively.
3. Equator and Prime Meridian
4. Answers will vary according to cities chosen.
5. Northern: North America, Asia, Europe, Africa; Eastern: Asia, Europe, Africa, Australia; Southern: Antarctica, Australia, South America, Africa; Western: North America, South America

S Skill Practice

Using Geography Skills Have students use the scale bar on the map to calculate the distance in kilometers between Paris and Stockholm. First, have students use a ruler to measure the distance between the cities on the map in centimeters (4.5 cm). Then, have students measure the map's scale in centimeters. (600 km = 1.7 cm) **Ask:** How can you use this to find the distance between Paris and Stockholm? *(set up a proportion:*

$$\frac{600\ km}{1.7\ cm} = \frac{x}{4\ cm}$$

$$x = \frac{600\ km \times 4\ cm}{1.7\ cm}$$

x = 1,412 km) **OL**

R Reading Strategy

Reading Maps **Ask:** According to the map, what is the capital of Russia? *(St. Petersburg)* **Ask:** What major city is located southeast of Vienna? *(Budapest)* **OL**

Additional Support

Reading a Map

In addition to latitude and longitude, maps feature other important tools to help you interpret the information they contain. Learning to use these map tools will help you read the symbolic language of maps more easily.

Title

The title tells you what kind of information the map is showing.

Key

The **key** lists and explains the symbols, colors, and lines used on the map. The key is sometimes called a legend.

Scale Bar

S The **scale bar** shows the relationship between map measurements and actual distances on the Earth. By laying a ruler along the scale bar, you can calculate how many miles or kilometers are represented per inch or centimeter. The map projection used to create the map is often listed near the scale bar.

Compass Rose

The **compass rose** indicates directions. The four **cardinal directions**—north, south, east, and west—are usually indicated with arrows or the points of a star. The **intermediate directions**—northeast, northwest, southeast, and southwest—may also be shown.

Cities

Cities are represented by a dot. Sometimes the relative sizes of cities are shown using dots of different sizes.

R

Capitals

National capitals are often represented by a star within a circle.

Boundary Lines

On political maps of large areas, boundary lines highlight the borders between different countries or states.

Activity: Technology Connection

Contrasting Have students use an Internet mapping Web site to help them understand scale. Tell students to find a particular location, such as their school or home address. Then have them use the map's zoom function to help visualize the benefits of increasing and decreasing scale when viewing a location. **Ask:** To find the nearest lake, would you use a distant or a close view? *(distant view)* **Ask:** What view would show the names of neighboring streets? *(closer view)* Point out that a distant view corresponds to an increase in scale: it allows you to view a wider area but you cannot see much detail. Conversely, a close view corresponds to a decrease in scale: detail is increased, but the size of the area is diminished. **OL**

Using Scale

All maps are drawn to a certain scale. **Scale** is a consistent, proportional relationship between the measurements shown on the map and the measurement of the Earth's surface.

W **Small-Scale Maps** A small-scale map, like this political map of France, can show a large area but little detail. Note that the scale bar on this map indicates that about 1 inch is equal to 200 miles.

Large-Scale Maps A large-scale map, like this map of Paris, can show a small area with a great amount of detail. Study the scale bar. Note that the map measurements correspond to much smaller distances than on the map of France.

France: Political

The City of Paris

Absolute and Relative Location

D As you learned on page GH6, absolute location is the exact point where a line of latitude crosses a line of longitude. Another way to indicate location is by **relative location**, or the location of one place in relation to another. To find relative location, find a reference point—a location you already know—on a map. Then look in the appropriate direction for the new location. For example, locate Paris (your reference point) on the map of France above. The relative location of Lyon can be described as southeast of Paris.

Practicing SKILLS

1. **Explain** the significance of: key, compass rose, cardinal directions, intermediate directions, scale bar, scale, relative location.
2. **Describe** the elements of a map that help you interpret the information displayed on the map.
3. **How** does the scale bar help you determine distances on the Earth's surface?
4. **Describe** the relative location of your school in two different ways.
5. **Use** a Venn diagram to identify the similarities and differences of small-scale maps and large-scale maps.

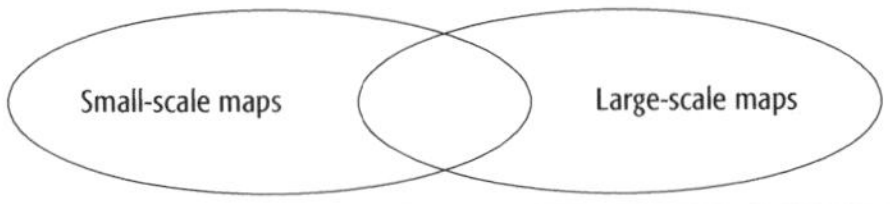

W Writing Support

Expository Writing To give students practice thinking about scale, have them write about two imaginary experiences. First, have students imagine they are an ant beginning to climb a tree. Next, have them imagine they are giants bending down to look at a nest in the top of the same tree. **OL**

D Differentiated Instruction

Kinesthetic Have two students stand side-by-side, but 10 feet (3 m) apart. **Ask:** What is the relative position of each student to the other? *(One is 10 feet (3 m) to the left. The other is 10 feet (3 m) to the right.)* **BL**

PRACTICING SKILLS

Answers

1. key: lists and explains symbols, colors, and lines on map; compass rose: indicates direction; cardinal directions: north, south, east, and west; intermediate directions: northeast, northwest, southeast, and southwest; scale bar: shows relationship between map measurements and actual distances on Earth; scale: consistent, proportional relationship between measurements shown on map and measurement of Earth's surface; relative location: location of one place in relation to another
2. title tells kind of information shown on map; key lists and explains symbols, colors, and lines used on map; scale bar shows relationship between map measurements and actual distances on Earth; compass rose indicates direction
3. shows the relationship between map measurements and actual distances
4. Answers will vary according to school.
5. Small scale shows large areas but little detail. Large scale shows small area with great detail. Both show location.

W Writing Support

Narrative Writing Have interested students research and write a story about a physical feature that affected history. Students can explore how mountain ranges and cliffs have served as protection, how frozen lakes and straits allowed for travel, or even how the construction of a canal changed transportation. **AL**

C Critical Thinking

Making Generalizations

Ask: What can relief and elevation tell you about rivers? *(Both elements give a sense of direction: water flows downhill so rivers flow from high elevation to lower elevation.)* **OL**

Physical Maps

W A **physical map** shows the location and the **topography,** or shape of the Earth's physical features. A study of a country's physical features often helps to explain the historical development of the country. For example, mountains may be barriers to transportation, and rivers and streams can provide access into the interior of a country.

Water Features

Physical maps show rivers, streams, lakes, and other water features.

Landforms

C Physical maps may show landforms such as mountains, plains, plateaus, and valleys.

Relief

Physical maps use shading and texture to show general **relief**—the differences in **elevation,** or height, of landforms.

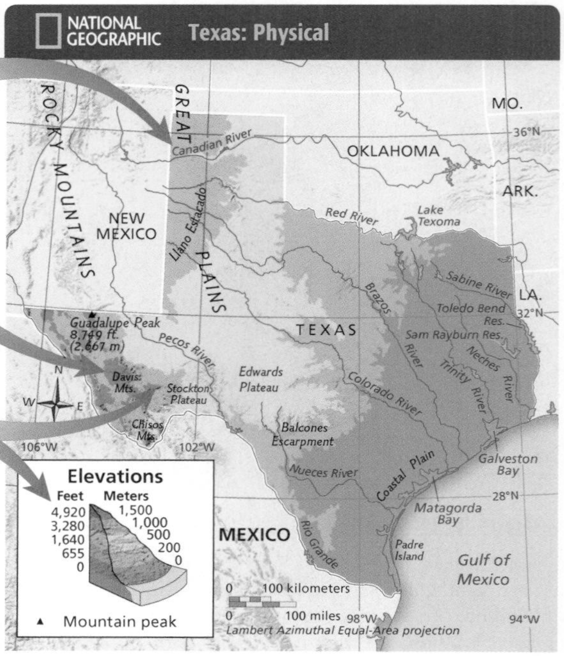

Practicing SKILLS

1. **Explain** the significance of: physical map, topography, relief, elevation.
2. **Complete** a table like the one to the right to explain what you can learn from the map about each of the physical features listed.

Physical Feature	What You Can Learn from the Map
Davis Mountains	
Red River	
Gulf Coastal Plains	

PRACTICING SKILLS

Answers

1. physical map: shows location and topography of Earth's physical features; topography: shape of Earth's physical features; relief: difference in elevation of landforms; elevation: height
2. Davis Mountains: location, elevation, length; Red River: location, length, route; Gulf Coastal Plains: location, elevation, length

Political Maps

A **political map** shows the boundaries and locations of political units such as countries, states, counties, cities, and towns. Many features depicted on a political map are **human-made,** or determined by humans rather than by nature. Political maps can show the networks and links that exist within and between political units. **D**

NATIONAL GEOGRAPHIC Texas: Political

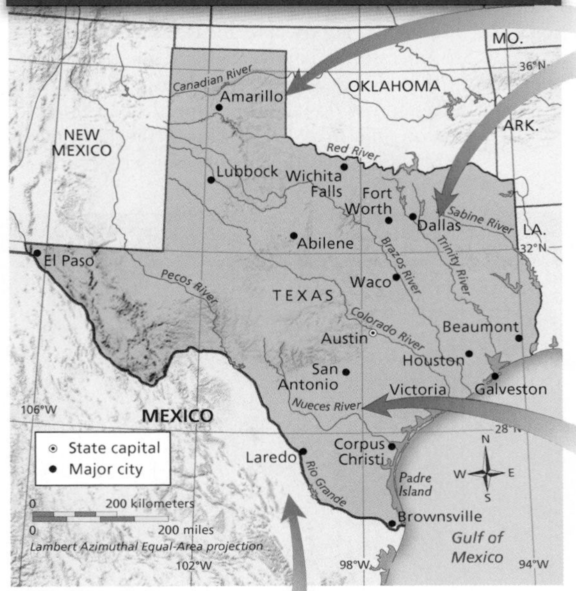

Human-Made Features

Political maps show human-made features such as boundaries, capitals, cities, roads, highways, and railroads. **C**

Physical Features

Political maps may show some physical features such as relief, rivers, and mountains.

Nonsubject Area

Areas surrounding the subject area of the map are usually a different color to set them apart. They are labeled to give you a context for the area you are studying.

Practicing SKILLS

1. **Explain** the significance of: political map, human-made.
2. **What** types of information would you find on a political map that would not appear on a physical map?
3. **Complete** a table like the one to the right to explain what you can learn from the map about each of the human-made features listed.

Human-Made Feature	What You Can Learn from the Map
Austin	
El Paso	
Texas state boundary	

D Differentiated Instruction

Gifted and Talented Political maps change more rapidly than physical maps. Have interested students select an area and research how political maps of this area have changed over time. Students may be interested to learn how their own state or region has changed politically, or they may wish to study another area. Have students create a presentation of their findings. **AL**

C Critical Thinking

Comparing and Contrasting

Ask: When you fly in an airplane and look down at the ground, what human-made features can you see? *(roads, buildings, farms, dams, some lakes, railroads)* **Ask:** What human-made features can you not see? *(boundaries, capital designation)* **BL**

PRACTICING SKILLS

Answers

1. political map: shows boundaries and locations of political units such as countries, states, counties, cities, and towns; human-made: determined by humans rather than nature
2. capitals, cities, roads, highways, railroads
3. Austin: location, that it is the capital city of Texas; El Paso: location; Texas state boundary: what states border Texas, what river forms its southern border

S Skill Practice

Visual Literacy Have students study the "Europe: Slavic Migrations" map. **Ask:** What do the arrows on this map represent? *(The main routes of migration taken by Slavic peoples in c. 700.)* **Ask:** How is color used to present information on this map? *(It distinguishes the three major groups of Slavs by their place of origin.)* **Ask:** How would you explain the forks that appear in several arrows? *(These indicate places where immigrants from the same area of origin diverged into two groups.)* **OL**

Thematic Maps

Maps that emphasize a single idea or a particular kind of information about an area are called **thematic maps**. There are many kinds of thematic maps, each designed to serve a different need. This textbook includes thematic maps that show exploration and trade, migration of peoples, economic activities, and war and political conflicts.

Qualitative Maps

Maps that use colors, symbols, lines, or dots to show information related to a specific idea are called **qualitative maps**. Such maps are often used to depict historical information. For example, the qualitative map below shows the spread of farming in Latin America over time.

Flow-Line Maps

Maps that illustrate the movement of people, animals, goods, and ideas, as well as physical processes like hurricanes and glaciers, are called **flow-line maps**. Arrows are usually used to represent the flow and direction of movement. The flow-line map below shows the movement of Slavic peoples throughout Europe.

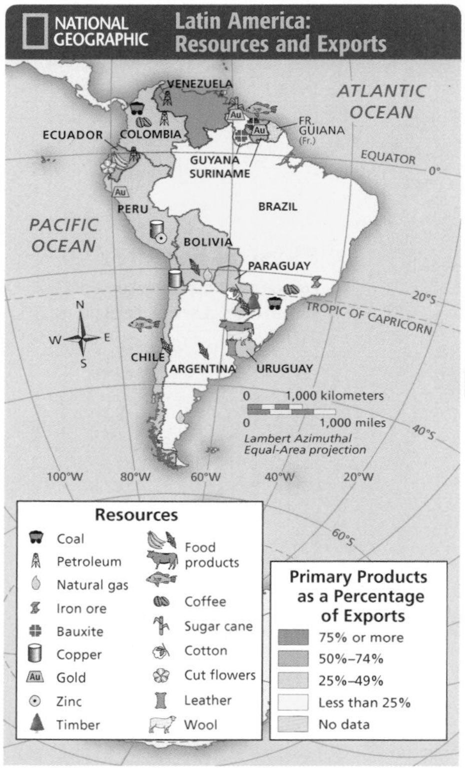

Additional Support

Teacher Tip

Collaborative Learning Ask students if they have difficulty distinguishing one color from another on the map above. If so, these students may benefit from other resources, such as maps that make distinctions using shading or symbols rather than color.

Activity: Collaborative Learning

Making Thematic Maps Divide the class into several groups. Each group will research a theme that interests them and create a thematic map to present to the class. Themes may be national (for example, a U.S. map showing the location of roller coasters or professional football stadiums) or local (for example, a city map displaying the location of public libraries or city parks). After groups choose their themes, each group should designate tasks (research, drawing maps, creating the presentation) among themselves so that each group member participates. Schedule a period for all the groups to present their maps to the class. **OL**

Geographic Information Systems

Modern technology has changed the way maps are made. Most cartographers use computers with software programs called **geographic information systems (GIS)**. A GIS is designed to accept data from different sources—maps, satellite images, printed text, and statistics. The GIS converts the data into a digital code, which arranges it in a database. Cartographers then program the GIS to process the data and produce maps. With GIS, each kind of information on a map is saved as a separate electronic layer.

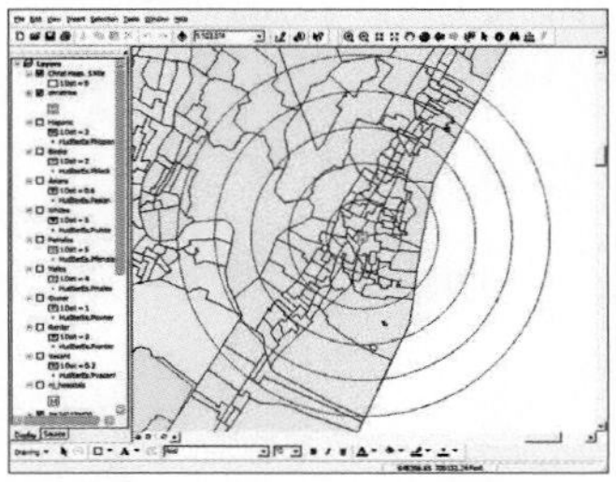

1 The first layer of information in a GIS pinpoints the area of interest. This allows the user to see, in detail, the area he or she needs to study. In this case, the area of study is a 5 mile (8 km) radius around Christ Hospital in Jersey City, New Jersey.

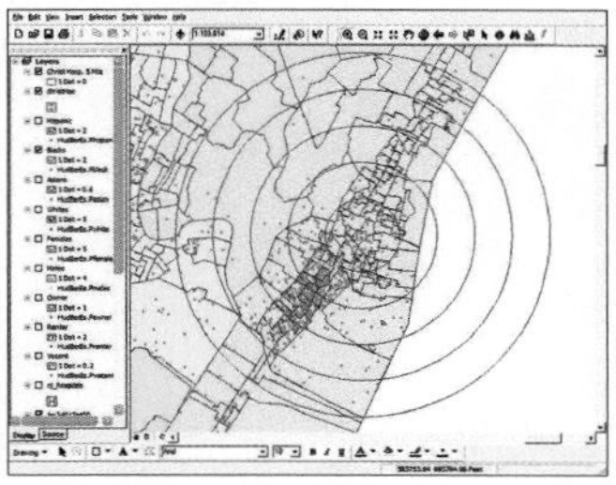

2 Additional layers of information are added based on the problem or issue being studied. In this case, hospital administrators want to find out about the population living in neighborhoods near the hospital so they can offer the community what it needs. A second layer showing African Americans who live within the 5 mile (8 km) radius has been added to the GIS.

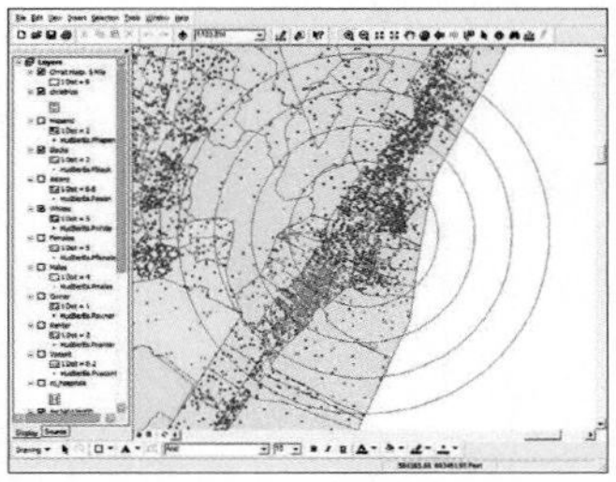

3 Complex information can be presented using more than one layer. For example, the hospital's surrounding neighborhoods include other groups in addition to African Americans. A third layer showing whites who live within the 5 mile (8 km) radius has been added to the GIS. Administrators can now use this information to help them make decisions about staffing and services associated with the hospital.

S

Practicing SKILLS

1. **Explain** the significance of: thematic map, qualitative maps, flow-line maps.
2. **Which** type of thematic map would best show the spread of Islam during Muhammad's time?
3. **Which** type of thematic map would best show average income per capita in the United States?
4. **How** does GIS allow cartographers to create maps and make changes to maps quickly and easily?
5. **Complete** a chart like the one below by identifying three examples of each type of thematic map found in this textbook. Note the page numbers of each.

Qualitative Maps	Flow-Line Maps

S Skill Practice

Visual Literacy Ask: How could you make GIS maps without a computer? *(You could draw the data on transparencies, and layer the transparencies.)* **OL**

Assess

Summarizing Have students work in pairs to make study cards for the Geography Handbook. Students can use main headings and subheadings to organize the section material. When the cards are finished, have students take turns testing each other on what they have learned. **OL**

Close

Identifying Ask: What are the four main types of maps? *(physical, political, qualitative, and flow-line)*

PRACTICING SKILLS

Answers

1. thematic map: emphasizes a single idea or particular kind of information about an area; qualitative map: uses colors, symbols, lines, or dots to show information related to a specific idea; flow-line map: illustrates movement of people, animals, goods, and ideas, as well as physical processes like hurricanes and glaciers
2. qualitative
3. flow-line
4. by allowing information to be stored and displayed on separate electronic layers
5. Answers will vary. Note that most maps in the text are qualitative maps; most climate maps are qualitative and flow-line.

Geographic Dictionary

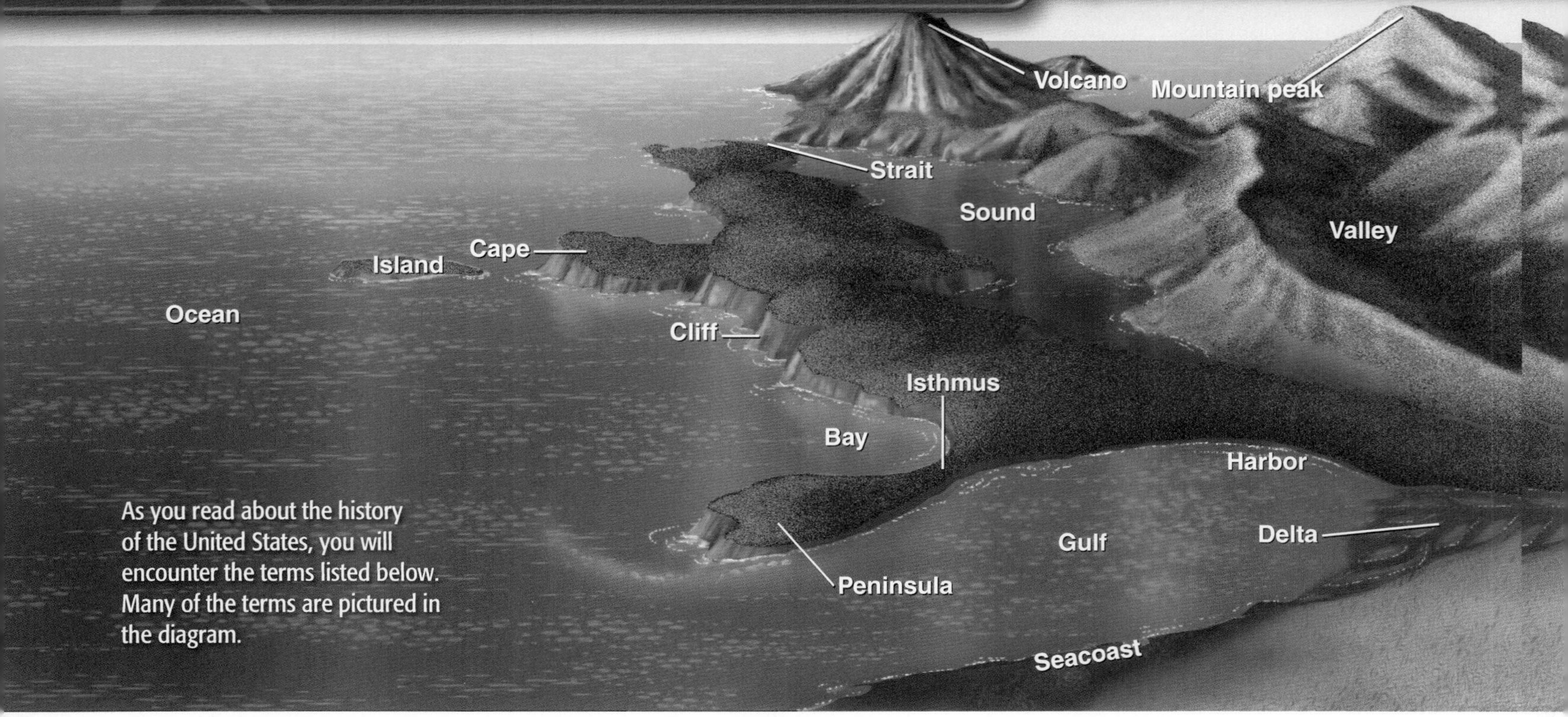

As you read about the history of the United States, you will encounter the terms listed below. Many of the terms are pictured in the diagram.

absolute location exact location of a place on the earth described by global coordinates

basin area of land drained by a given river and its branches; area of land surrounded by lands of higher elevations

bay part of a large body of water that extends into a shoreline, generally smaller than a gulf

canyon deep and narrow valley with steep walls

cape point of land that extends into a river, lake, or ocean

channel wide strait or waterway between two landmasses that lie close to each other; deep part of a river or other waterway

cliff steep, high wall of rock, earth, or ice

continent one of the seven large landmasses on the earth

cultural feature characteristic that humans have created in a place, such as language, religion, housing, and settlement pattern

delta flat, low-lying land built up from soil carried downstream by a river and deposited at its mouth

divide stretch of high land that separates river systems

downstream direction in which a river or stream flows from its source to its mouth

elevation height of land above sea level

Equator imaginary line that runs around the earth halfway between the North and South Poles; used as the starting point to measure degrees of north and south latitude

glacier large, thick body of slowly moving ice

gulf part of a large body of water that extends into a shoreline, generally larger and more deeply indented than a bay

harbor a sheltered place along a shoreline where ships can anchor safely

highland elevated land area such as a hill, mountain, or plateau

hill elevated land with sloping sides and rounded summit; generally smaller than a mountain

island land area, smaller than a continent, completely surrounded by water

isthmus narrow stretch of land connecting two larger land areas

lake a large inland body of water

latitude distance north or south of the Equator, measured in degrees

longitude distance east or west of the Prime Meridian, measured in degrees

lowland land, usually level, at a low elevation

map drawing of the earth shown on a flat surface

meridian one of many lines on the global grid running from the North Pole to the South Pole; used to measure degrees of longitude

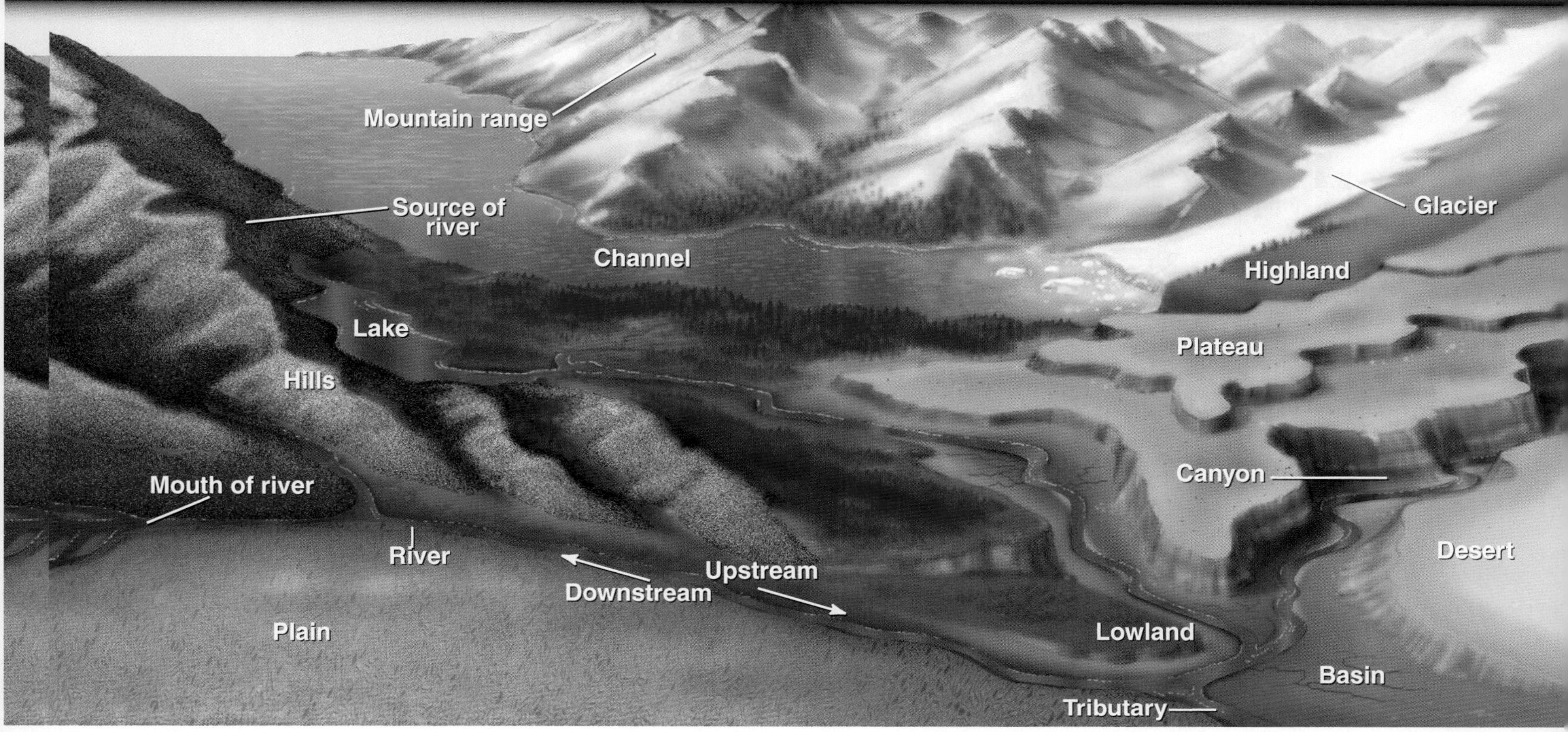

mesa broad, flat-topped landform with steep sides; smaller than a plateau

mountain land with steep sides that rises sharply (1,000 feet or more) from surrounding land; generally larger and more rugged than a hill

mountain peak pointed top of a mountain

mountain range a series of connected mountains

mouth (of a river) place where a stream or river flows into a larger body of water

ocean one of the four major bodies of salt water that surround the continents

ocean current stream of either cold or warm water that moves in a definite direction through an ocean

parallel one of many lines on the global grid that circle the earth north or south of the Equator; used to measure degrees of latitude

peninsula body of land jutting into a lake or ocean, surrounded on three sides by water

physical feature characteristic of a place occurring naturally, such as a landform, body of water, climate pattern, or resource

plain area of level land, usually at a low elevation and often covered with grasses

plateau large area of flat or rolling land at a high elevation, about 300–3,000 feet high

Prime Meridian line of the global grid running from the North Pole to the South Pole at Greenwich, England; starting point for measuring degrees of east and west longitude

relief changes in elevation over a given area of land

river large natural stream of water that runs through the land

sea large body of water completely or partly surrounded by land

seacoast land lying next to a sea or ocean

sea level position on land level with surface of nearby ocean or sea

sound body of water between a coastline and one or more islands off the coast

source (of a river) place where a river or stream begins, often in highlands

strait narrow stretch of water joining two larger bodies of water

tributary small river or stream that flows into a larger river or stream; a branch of the river

upstream direction opposite the flow of a river; toward the source of a river or stream

valley area of low land between hills or mountains

volcano mountain created as ash or liquid rock erupts from inside the earth

Unit 1 Planning Guide

UNIT PACING CHART					
	Unit 1	**Chapter 1**	**Chapter 2**	**Chapter 3**	**Unit 1**
Day 1	Unit Opener	Chapter 1 Opener, Section 1	Chapter 2 Opener, Section 1	Chapter 3 Opener, Section 1	Wrap-Up/Project, Unit Assessment
Day 2		Section 2	Section 2	Sections 2 & 3	
Day 3		Section 3	Section 3	Chapter Assessment	
Day 4		Section 4	Section 4		
Day 5		Section 5	Chapter Assessment		
Day 6		Chapter Assessment			

Teacher to Teacher

Kelly Baker
Cleveland Hill High School
Cheektowaga, New York

Role Play and Debate Divide your class into two groups. One group will be representatives of Great Britain. The other group will act as national leaders in the colony. In this activity, the members of each group will work together to draft a letter to the other side. Britain's representatives will explain to the colonists why colonization is necessary. They should outline the benefits of imperialism and highlight any sacrifices they made for the benefit of the colony. The nationalists' group should focus on the negative impacts of imperialism on the colonists. They should try to convince Britain to free them. Once the letters have been drafted, each group will present their letters and then debate the issues.

Author Note

Dear American History Teacher,

As you begin to teach this unit, there are themes that recur that you will want to point out to students.

Developments in politics, social life, religion, and the economy laid the foundation for the United States. The significant nation-building acts like declaring independence, winning a war with Great Britain, securing a fair peace treaty, and writing a new constitution are the most salient events in this period. Yet students need to know how ordinary Americans reacted to their new status as Americans rather than subjects of the King of England. For many, this new freedom prompted them to move west. Others, particularly young people, seized opportunities to leave their family farm and take up occupations like teaching school or tending a store. The huge debt incurred in fighting the war and the closure of many trades based in Great Britain affected everyone.

Most observers did not expect that the thirteen original states that formed the Confederation would be able to strengthen the ties that bound them together. Students should realize just how difficult it was to forge the compromises necessary to form a new nation. The Constitution created citizens of the United States and the Bill of Rights made explicit the liberties the Americans had fought for.

Not everyone benefited from these decades of change and innovation. Native Americans were forced to move farther West as white settlers sought land in the unsettled parts of the country. Although the Revolution was fought in the name of natural rights, enslaved men and women, who composed a fifth of the nation's population, did not receive their freedom. Soon, the cultivation of cotton would make slavery's shackles stronger. Women, by and large, had a slightly wider ambit for their ambitions. This is one of the most exciting periods in American history. Students can feel this if they are taught about the daunting challenges the country faced.

Senior Author

Focus

Why It Matters

Point out to students that the United States has a blended culture made up of many others, although its historic political roots are from Europe, and mainly Britain. Have students explain how they think the blending of cultures continues to have an impact on the lives of Americans. **OL**

Connecting to Past Learning

Ask students to recall what they may have learned about cultures in Europe and Africa and about Native American cultures. In Unit 1 they will study how these cultures came together in North America, the results of those encounters, and the subsequent blending of new political and social ideas.

Unit Launch Activity

Discuss with students what they know about early colonial life in North America. For example, they may know that the first permanent English settlement was at Jamestown, or they may know that the oldest European settlement still in existence is St. Augustine, Florida. Have students suggest some of the challenges explorers and settlers faced when they arrived. **OL**

Unit 1

Creating A Nation

Beginnings to 1789

CHAPTER 1
Colonizing America
Prehistory to 1754

CHAPTER 2
The American Revolution
1754–1783

CHAPTER 3
Creating a Constitution
1781–1789

Why It Matters

The settlement of North America brought together three cultures—European, African, and Native American—and created several new colonial societies. In 1776 anger at British policies caused thirteen British colonies to declare independence and create the United States of America. The American Revolution led to a new form of government. Americans created a democratic republic with a federal constitution and began expanding across the continent.

Team Teaching Activity

Geography Ask: Do you think that the land in 1500 looked different than it looks today? Explain that in the late 1400s when Europeans began their explorations, the eastern part of North America was covered by thick forests. Marshland stretched along much of Europe's Mediterranean coast and covered vast areas of northern Germany and Russia. Have interested students research the environment of each continent in 1500. Have them create a world vegetation map for that year based on their research. Ask them to discuss their findings with the class. **OL**

Signing the Declaration of Independence

1

Teach

Skill Practice

Visual Literacy Have students study the painting. **Ask:** How does the position of the five men who helped to draft the Declaration show their importance? Why do you think that Thomas Jefferson is shown handing the document to president of Congress John Hancock? *(Possible answer: The five men are the focus of the painting, which underscores their involvement in drafting it. Jefferson is shown delivering the document because he was the primary author.)* **BL**

Skill Practice

Visual Literacy Have students study the painting. **Ask:** What is the tone of this painting? What does this painting indicate about the event? *(Answers will vary, but students should recognize that the painting expresses the formality and solemnity of the occasion, and that it was painted to record what is essentially the founding of the United States.)* **OL**

More About the Painting

Visual Literacy Explain to students that this famous painting, titled *Declaration of Independence*, is by John Trumbull and was commissioned in 1817 for display in the U.S. Capitol's rotunda. The image captures the moment before the signing of the Declaration and features the men who helped to draft it: John Adams, Robert Livingston, Roger Sherman, Thomas Jefferson, and Benjamin Franklin. John Hancock, president of the Continental Congress and famous signer, is shown seated on the right, receiving the document from Thomas Jefferson, its primary author.

NCLB No Child Left Behind

Teaching Tip Help students become proficient users of technology in an academic context by:
- Asking students to find relevant materials on the Internet.
- Encouraging students to use computer-presentation software.

Chapter 1 Planning Guide

Key to Ability Levels	
BL Below Level	**AL** Above Level
OL On Level	**ELL** English Language Learners

Key to Teaching Resources	
Print Material	Transparency
CD-ROM or DVD	

Levels				Resources	Chapter Opener	Section 1	Section 2	Section 3	Section 4	Section 5	Chapter Assess
BL	**OL**	**AL**	**ELL**								
FOCUS											
BL	OL	AL	ELL	**Daily Focus Skills Transparencies**		1-1	1-2	1-3	1-4	1-5	
TEACH											
	OL	AL		**Geography and History, URB**		p. 3					
	OL	AL		**History Simulations and Problem Solving, URB**				p. 9			
		AL		**American Literature Reading, URB**				p. 13			
BL	OL		ELL	**Reading Essentials and Note-Taking Guide***		p. 1	p. 4	p. 8	p. 11	p. 14	
	OL			**Historical Analysis Skills Activity, URB**						p. 22	
BL	OL		ELL	**Guided Reading Activities, URB***		p. 48	p. 49	p. 50	p. 51	p. 52	
BL	OL	AL	ELL	**Content Vocabulary Activity, URB***		p. 27					
BL	OL	AL	ELL	**Academic Vocabulary Activity, URB**		p. 29					
	OL	AL		**Critical Thinking Skills Activity, URB**		p. 32					
BL	OL		ELL	**Reading Skills Activity, URB**		p. 21					
BL			ELL	**English Learner Activity, URB**						p. 25	
	OL	AL		**Reinforcing Skills Activity, URB**			p. 31				
BL	OL	AL	ELL	**Differentiated Instruction Activity, URB**				p. 23			
BL	OL		ELL	**Time Line Activity, URB**				p. 33			
	OL			**Linking Past and Present Activity, URB**		p. 34					
BL	OL	AL	ELL	**American Art and Music Activity, URB**				p. 39			
BL	OL	AL	ELL	**Interpreting Political Cartoons Activity, URB**			p. 41				
		AL		**Enrichment Activity, URB**					p. 45		
BL	OL	AL	ELL	**American Biographies**		✓	✓	✓	✓		
BL	OL	AL	ELL	**Primary Source Reading, URB**		p. 35				p. 37	
BL	OL	AL	ELL	**The Living Constitution***	✓	✓	✓	✓	✓		✓
	OL	AL		**American History Primary Source Documents Library**	✓	✓	✓	✓	✓		✓
BL	OL	AL	ELL	**Unit Map Overlay Transparencies**	✓	✓	✓	✓	✓		✓
BL	OL	AL	ELL	**Differentiated Instruction for the American History Classroom**	✓	✓	✓	✓	✓		✓

Note: Please refer to the *Unit 1 Resource Book* for this chapter's URB materials.

* Also available in Spanish

TeacherWorks Plus
All-In-One Planner and Resource Center

- Interactive Lesson Planner
- Interactive Teacher Edition
- Fully editable blackline masters
- Section Spotlight Videos Launch
- Differentiated Lesson Plans
- Printable reports of daily assignments
- Standards Tracking System

Levels: BL	OL	AL	ELL	Resources	Chapter Opener	Section 1	Section 2	Section 3	Section 4	Section 5	Chapter Assess
				TEACH *(continued)*							
BL	OL	AL	ELL	StudentWorks™ Plus	✓	✓	✓	✓	✓	✓	✓
BL	OL	AL	ELL	American Music Hits Through History CD	✓	✓	✓	✓	✓	✓	✓
BL	OL	AL	ELL	Unit Time Line Transparencies and Activities	✓	✓	✓	✓	✓	✓	✓
BL	OL	AL	ELL	Cause and Effect Transparencies, Strategies, and Activities	✓	✓	✓	✓	✓	✓	✓
BL	OL	AL	ELL	Why It Matters Transparencies, Strategies, and Activities	✓	✓	✓	✓	✓	✓	✓
BL	OL	AL	ELL	American Issues	✓	✓	✓	✓	✓	✓	✓
	OL	AL	ELL	American Art and Architecture Transparencies, Strategies, and Activities	✓	✓	✓	✓	✓	✓	✓
BL	OL	AL		High School American History Literature Library	✓	✓	✓	✓	✓	✓	✓
BL	OL	AL	ELL	*The American Vision* Video Program	✓	✓	✓	✓	✓	✓	✓
Teacher Resources				Strategies for Success	✓	✓	✓	✓	✓	✓	✓
Teacher Resources				Success with English Learner	✓	✓	✓	✓	✓	✓	✓
Teacher Resources				Reading Strategies and Activities for the Social Studies Classroom	✓	✓	✓	✓	✓	✓	✓
Teacher Resources				Presentation Plus! with MindJogger CheckPoint	✓	✓	✓	✓	✓	✓	✓
				ASSESS							
BL	OL	AL	ELL	Section Quizzes and Chapter Tests*		p. 5	p. 6	p. 7	p. 8	p. 9	p. 11
BL	OL	AL	ELL	Authentic Assessment With Rubrics							p. 7
BL	OL	AL	ELL	Standardized Test Practice Workbook							p. 1
BL	OL	AL	ELL	*ExamView® Assessment Suite*		1-1	1-2	1-3	1-4	1-5	CH. 1
				CLOSE							
BL			ELL	Reteaching Activity, URB							p. 43
BL	OL		ELL	Reading and Study Skills Foldables™							p. 46
BL	OL	AL	ELL	*American History* in Graphic Novel							p. 1

✓ Chapter- or unit-based activities applicable to all sections in this chapter.

Chapter 1 Integrating Technology

Using QuickPass™

Teach With Technology

What is a QuickPass™ code?

A *QuickPass*™ code is a shortcut that takes students and teachers from glencoe.com directly to resources for each chapter in this book. You can enter a *QuickPass*™ code at glencoe.com or with the McGraw-Hill Social Studies widget.

How can a QuickPass™ code help my students and me?

A *QuickPass*™ code takes you directly to each chapter's resources. *QuickPass*™ codes in the Student Edition go directly to student resources, while codes in the Teacher Wraparound Edition go to teacher resources. The *T* at the end of the code indicates a teacher version.

Find a *QuickPass*™ code on the Chapter Opener pages of the textbook. Visit glencoe.com and enter a *QuickPass*™ code to go directly to resources for each chapter.

History ONLINE
Visit glencoe.com and enter *QuickPass*™ code TAV9399c1T for Chapter 1 resources.

You can easily launch a wide range of digital products from your computer's desktop with the McGraw-Hill Social Studies widget.

	Student	Teacher	Parent
Media Library			
• Section Audio	●		●
• Spanish Audio Summaries	●		●
• Section Spotlight Videos	●	●	●
***The American Vision* Online Learning Center (Web Site)**			
• StudentWorks™ Plus Online	●	●	●
• Multilingual Glossary	●	●	●
• Study-to-Go	●	●	●
• Chapter Overviews	●	●	●
• Self-Check Quizzes	●	●	●
• Student Web Activities	●	●	●
• ePuzzles and Games	●	●	●
• Vocabulary eFlashcards	●	●	●
• In Motion Animations	●	●	●
• Study Central™	●	●	●
• Web Activity Lesson Plans		●	
• Vocabulary PuzzleMaker	●	●	●
• Historical Thinking Activities		●	
• Beyond the Textbook	●	●	●

Reading Support From Jamestown Education

- **Timed Readings Plus in Social Studies** helps students increase their reading rate and fluency while maintaining comprehension. The 400-word passages are similar to those found on state and national assessments.
- **Reading in the Content Area: Social Studies** concentrates on six essential reading skills that help students better comprehend what they read. The book includes 75 high-interest nonfiction passages written at increasing levels of difficulty.
- **Reading Social Studies** includes strategic reading instruction and vocabulary support in Social Studies content for both ELLs and native speakers of English.

www.jamestowneducation.com

National Geographic

Index to National Geographic Magazine:

The following articles relate to this chapter:

- "Mystery Mountain of the Inca" by Peter Frost, February 2004.
- "Dawn of Humans: The First Americans," by Kenneth Garrett, December 2000.

National Geographic Society Products To order the following, call National Geographic at 1-800-368-2728:

- *The Age of Exploration* (CD-ROM)

Access National Geographic's new, dynamic MapMachine Web site and other geography resources at:

www.nationalgeographic.com
www.nationalgeographic.com/maps

Biography — A&E Home Video — The History Channel

The following videotape programs are available from Glencoe as supplements to this chapter:

- Christopher Columbus: Explorer of the New World (ISBN 1-56-501667-X)
- The Aztec Empire (ISBN 0-76-700542-2)

To order, call Glencoe at 1-800-334-7344. To find classroom resources to accompany many of these videos, check the following home pages:

A&E Television: www.aetv.com
The History Channel: www.historychannel.com

Reading List Generator CD-ROM — Glencoe BookLink 3

Use this database to search more than 30,000 titles to create a customized reading list for your students.

- Reading lists can be organized by students' reading level, author, genre, theme, or area of interest.
- The database provides Degrees of Reading Power™ (DRP) and Lexile™ readability scores for all selections.
- A brief summary of each selection is included.

Leveled reading suggestions for this chapter:

For students at a Grade 8 reading level:
- ***Christopher Columbus***, by Peggy Pancella

For students at a Grade 9 reading level:
- ***The Landing of the Pilgrims***, by James Daugherty

For students at a Grade 10 reading level:
- ***Forgotten Voyager: The Story of Amerigo Vespucci***, by Ann Fitzpatrick Alper

For students at a Grade 11 reading level:
- ***Colonial American Home Life***, by John F. Warner

For students at a Grade 12 reading level:
- ***Mayflower 1620: A New Look at a Pilgrim Voyage***, by Peter Arenstam

Introducing
Chapter 1

Focus

MAKING CONNECTIONS
Why Do People Migrate to New Lands?

Ask students to suggest reasons why people migrate to new lands. Have students categorize their reasons as either "push" or "pull" factors. Activate students' prior knowledge about migration by asking them why they think the Pilgrims came to America. Students may recall that the Pilgrims came to be free to practice their religion. Point out to students that while many came to what is now the United States for religious freedom, individuals and groups came for many other reasons, including to gain wealth and to acquire land. The colonies Europeans developed in the Americas took on different social, cultural, and economic characters depending on who founded them and where they were located.

Teach

Big Ideas

As students study the chapter, remind them to consider the section-based Big Ideas included in each section's Guide to Reading. The **Essential Question** in the activities below tie in to the Big Ideas and help students think about and understand important chapter concepts. In addition, the Hands-on Chapter Projects with their culminating activities relate the content from each section to the Big Ideas. These activities build on each other as students progress through the chapter. Section activities culminate in the wrap-up activity on the Visual Summary page.

Chapter 1

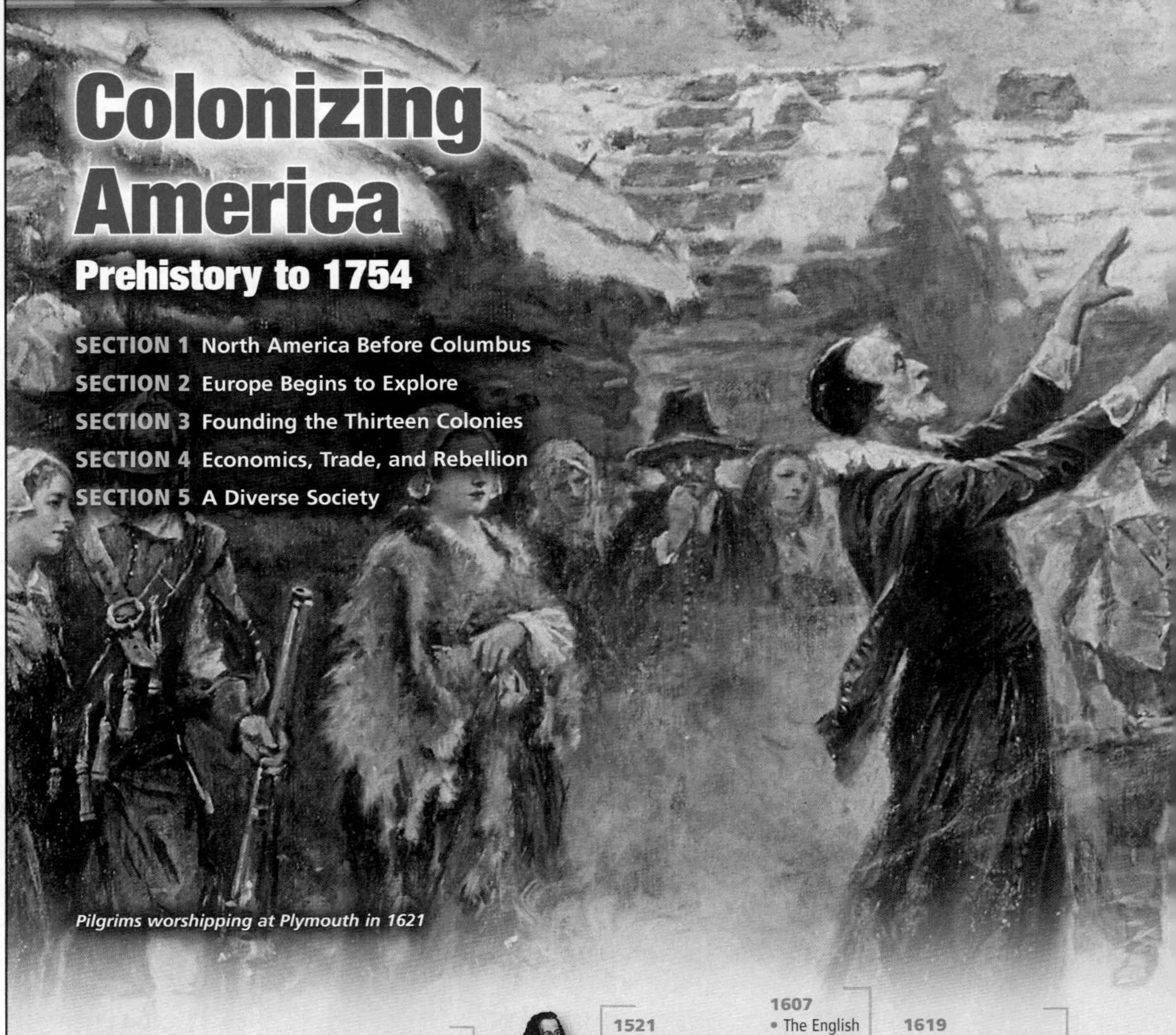

Colonizing America

Prehistory to 1754

Pilgrims worshipping at Plymouth in 1621

U.S. EVENTS

- **1492** • Christopher Columbus lands in the Caribbean

- **1521** • Hernán Cortés conquers the Aztec
- **1607** • The English found Jamestown in Virginia
- **1619** • First Africans arrive in Virginia via Dutch traders

1450 — 1500 — 1550 — 1600

WORLD EVENTS

- **c. 1450** • Songhai Empire expands in West Africa
- **1498** • Vasco da Gama sails around Africa to India, locating a water route to Asia from Europe
- **1520** • Ferdinand Magellan sails into Pacific Ocean
- **1534** • Henry VIII breaks with Catholic Church

- **1588** • English defeat Spanish Armada
- **1603** • Tokugawa period of feudal rule begins in Japan

Section 1

North America Before Columbus

Essential Question: How did regional geography affect the development of Native American cultures? *(Customs and traditions of the various Native American culture groups were affected by the environment in which they lived. Differences in landforms and climate created differences in the types of food people ate, what they wore, and the style of home in which they lived.)* **OL**

Section 2

Europe Begins to Explore

Essential Question: How did advancements during the Renaissance lead to European exploration? *(Revenue from increased trade and the creation of strong states, along with new technologies in navigation and shipping facilitated exploration.)* **OL**

Chapter Audio

MAKING CONNECTIONS
Why Do People Migrate to New Lands?

Europeans began leaving their continent in the 1500s to settle in the Americas. Their colonies reflected the values and traditions of their homelands, but they were also shaped by the geography of the new land they settled.

- ***Why do you think Europeans came to America?***
- ***How might the location of a colony affect its development?***

1630
- Massachusetts Bay Colony is established

1660
- British Navigation Acts regulate American colonial trade

1681
- William Penn receives charter for Pennsylvania

1735
- Libel trial of publisher John Peter Zenger helps establish free press

1650 — 1700 — 1750

1642
- English Civil War begins

1688
- Glorious Revolution establishes limited monarchy in England

1707
- Act of Union creates Great Britain

FOLDABLES

Analyzing Colonial Experiments Create a Two-Tab Book Foldable to help analyze the colonial experiences of the French and Spanish. As you read, identify the successes and failures for each country under its tab.

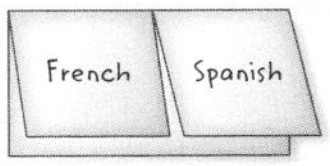

History ONLINE Visit glencoe.com and enter *QuickPass*™ code TAV9846c1 for Chapter 1 resources.

Introducing Chapter 1

More About the Photo

Visual Literacy Explain to students that Plymouth was the second English settlement in North America. This painting depicts the first sermon given at the colony upon landing.

FOLDABLES Study Organizer **Dinah Zike's Foldables**

Dinah Zike's Foldables are three-dimensional, interactive graphic organizers that help students practice basic writing skills, review vocabulary terms, and identify main ideas. Instructions for creating and using Foldables can be found in the Appendix at the end of this book and in the *Dinah Zike's Reading and Study Skills Foldables* booklet.

History ONLINE

Visit glencoe.com and enter *QuickPass*™ code TAV9399c1T for Chapter 1 resources, including a Chapter Overview, Study Central™, Study-to-Go, Student Web Activity, Self-Check Quiz, and other materials.

Section 3

Founding the Thirteen Colonies

Essential Question: What were the main causes of English settlement in North America? *(The English began to colonize North America to compete with their Spanish rivals to gain wealth and territory, to escape religious persecution, and because of the enclosure of lands in England.)* **OL**

Section 4

Economics, Trade, and Rebellion

Essential Question: How did development of the English colonies form distinct regions? *(The colonies developed based on their geography and economies. The South had a structured society based on cash-crop agriculture. The Middle Colonies had cities, industry, and good soil for farming. People in New England farmed their own land or worked in shipping or related trades.)* **OL**

Section 5

A Diverse Society

Essential Question: What contributed to the diversity of the 13 English colonies? *(Enormous rates of immigration and the forced emigration of enslaved Africans, different occupations and religions as well as new ideas and movements contributed to the cultural diversity of the 13 English colonies.)* **OL**

Focus

Bellringer

Daily Focus Transparency 1-1

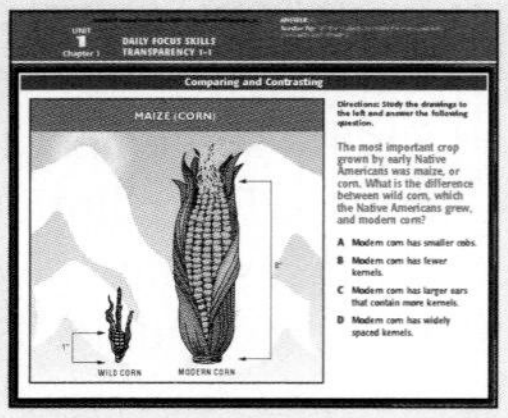

Guide to Reading

Region	Groups
Mesoamerica	Olmec, Maya, Toltec, Aztec
West	Hohokam, Anasazi, Zuni, Hopi and Pueblo peoples, Apache, Navajo, Tlingit, Haida, Kwakiutl, Nootka, Chinook, and Salish peoples
Midwest	Mississippians, Cherokee, Choctaw, Chickasaw, Natchez, Creek, Pawnee, Kansas, Iowa, Sioux
Northeast	Algonquian peoples and Iroquois Confederacy

Section Spotlight Video

To generate student interest and provide a springboard for class discussion, access the Chapter 1, Section 1 video at glencoe.com or on the video DVD.

Section 1 — Section Audio — Spotlight Video

North America Before Columbus

Guide to Reading

Big Ideas

Geography and History Native American groups developed cultures based on the geography of the region in which they lived.

Content Vocabulary
- agricultural revolution *(p. 4)*
- tribute *(p. 6)*
- kiva *(p. 7)*
- pueblo *(p. 7)*

Academic Vocabulary
- decline *(p. 5)*
- technology *(p. 6)*
- eventually *(p. 8)*

People and Events to Identify
- Beringia *(p. 4)*
- Mesoamerica *(p. 4)*
- Maya *(p. 5)*
- Aztec *(p. 6)*
- Cahokia *(p. 8)*
- Iroquois Confederacy *(p. 11)*

Reading Strategy

Categorizing Complete a chart similar to the one below by filling in the names of the groups who lived in each region.

Region	Groups
Mesoamerica	
West	
Midwest	
Northeast	

Before 1492 the peoples of the Americas had almost no contact with the rest of the world. The societies and languages that developed varied widely. In North America, some Native Americans lived as nomadic hunters, while others lived in large, complex cities.

Mesoamerican Cultures

MAIN Idea An agricultural revolution led to the first civilizations in Mesoamerica, whose people built large, elaborate cities.

HISTORY AND YOU What is the largest city you have visited? Read to learn about the origins of Mexico City, the largest city in North America.

No one knows for certain when the first people arrived in the Americas. Current scientific evidence suggests that the first humans arrived between 15,000 and 30,000 years ago. Based on DNA tests and other evidence, some scientists think the earliest Americans came from northeast Asia. Some may have arrived during the last Ice Age, when much of the earth's water became frozen and created a land bridge between Alaska and Asia along the Bering Strait. Along this stretch of land, known as **Beringia,** nomadic hunters may have crossed to the Americas as they followed large prey, such as the wooly mammoth, antelope, and caribou. These people did not come all at once, and some may have come by boat.

Over time, the descendants of these early settlers spread southward and eastward across the Americas. Between 9,000 and 10,000 years ago, some early Americans learned to plant and raise crops. This **agricultural revolution** began in **Mesoamerica,** the region that today includes central and southern Mexico and Central America. The agricultural revolution made possible the rise of Mesoamerica's first civilizations.

Anthropologists think the first people to develop a civilization in Mesoamerica were the Olmec. Olmec culture emerged between 1500 and 1200 B.C., near where Veracruz, Mexico, is located today. The Olmec developed a sophisticated society with large villages, temple complexes, and pyramids. They also sculpted huge monuments, including 8-foot-high heads weighing up to 20 tons, from a hard rock known as basalt. Olmec culture lasted until about 300 B.C.

Olmec ideas spread throughout Mesoamerica, influencing other peoples. One of these peoples constructed the first large city in the Americas, called Teotihuacán (TAY•oh•TEE•wah•KAHN), about 30 miles northeast of where Mexico City is today. The city was built near a volcano, where there were large deposits of obsidian, or volcanic glass. Obsidian was very valuable. Its sharp, strong edges were perfect for tools and weapons.

Resource Manager

R Reading Strategies	C Critical Thinking	D Differentiated Instruction	W Writing Support	S Skill Practice
Teacher Edition • Previewing, p. 5 • Monitoring, p. 7 • Comparing, p. 10 • Und. Q/A Relationships, p. 11 **Additional Resources** • Guid. Read. Act., URB p. 48 • RENTG, p. 1	**Teacher Edition** • Compare/Contrast, p. 6 • Ident. Cent. Issues, p. 7 • Det. Cause/Effect, p. 8 **Additional Resources** • Quizzes/Tests, p. 5 • Crit. Think. Act., URB p. 32	**Teacher Edition** • English Learners, p. 9 **Additional Resources** • English Learner Activity, URB p. 25	**Additional Resources** • Cont. Vocab. Act., URB p. 27 • Academic Vocab. Act, URB p. 29 • Pri. Source Read., URB p. 35	**Teacher Edition** • Using Geo. Skills, pp. 5, 9 • Analyzing Sources, p. 10 **Additional Resources** • Geography and History, URB p. 3 • Read. Skills Act., URB p. 21 • Linking Past and Present, URB p. 34

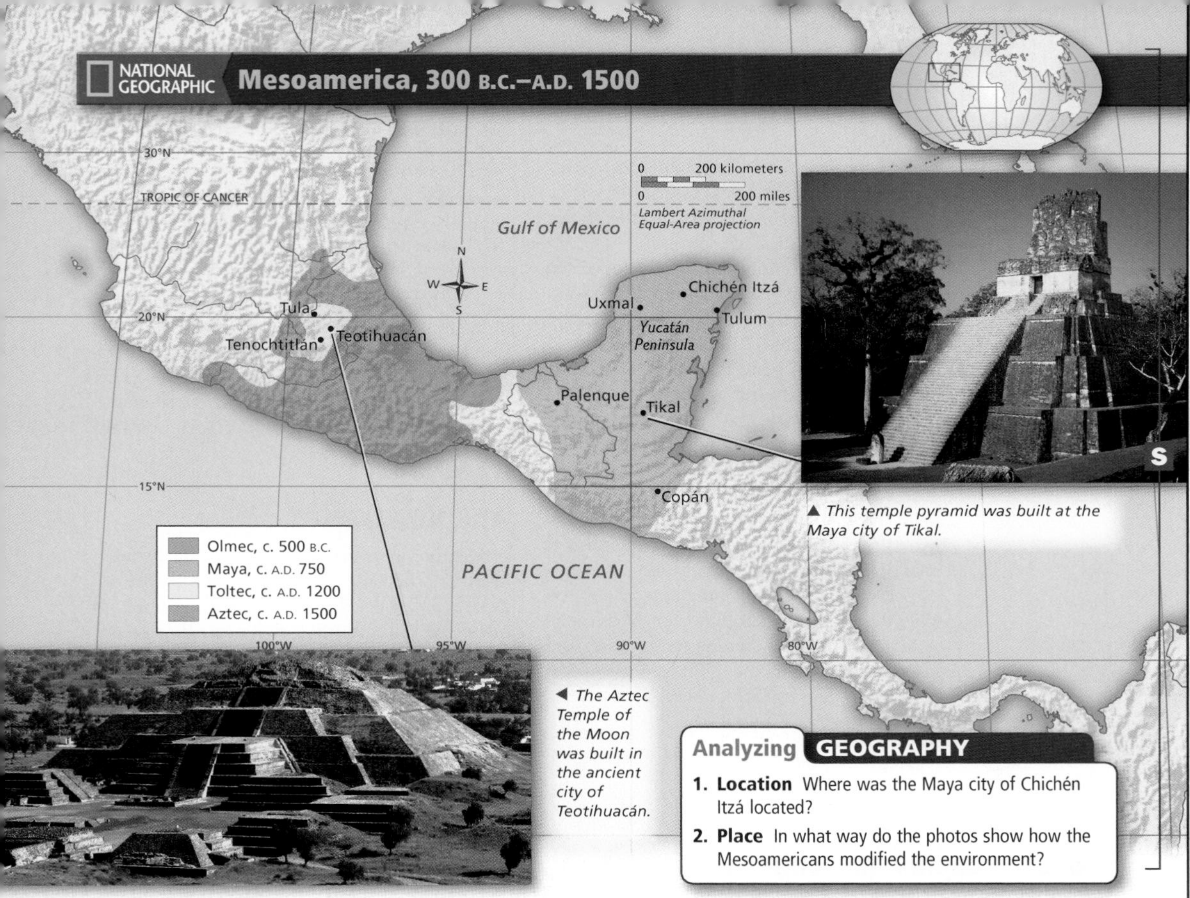

▲ *This temple pyramid was built at the Maya city of Tikal.*

◀ *The Aztec Temple of the Moon was built in the ancient city of Teotihuacán.*

Analyzing GEOGRAPHY

1. **Location** Where was the Maya city of Chichén Itzá located?
2. **Place** In what way do the photos show how the Mesoamericans modified the environment?

The people of Teotihuacán built up a trade network based on obsidian, which influenced the development of Mesoamerica. The city lasted from about 300 B.C. to about A.D. 650.

R The Maya

Around A.D. 200, as Teotihuacán's influence spread, the Maya civilization emerged in the Yucatán Peninsula and expanded into what is now Central America and southern Mexico. The **Maya** had a talent for engineering and mathematics. They developed complex and accurate calendars linked to the positions of the stars. They also built great temple pyramids. These pyramids formed the centerpieces of Maya cities, such as Tikal and Chichén Itzá. Marvels of engineering, some pyramids were 200 feet (61 m) high. At the top of each pyramid was a temple where priests performed ceremonies dedicated to the many Maya gods.

Although trade and a common culture linked the Maya, they were not unified. Each city-state controlled its own territory. Because of the fragmented nature of their society, the different cities frequently went to war.

The Maya continued to thrive until the A.D. 900s, when they abandoned their cities in the Yucatán for unknown reasons. Some anthropologists believe Maya farmers may have exhausted the region's soil. This in turn would have led to famine, riots, and the collapse of the cities. Others believe that invaders from the north devastated the region. Maya cities in what is today Guatemala flourished for several more centuries, although by the 1500s they too were in **decline.**

History ONLINE
Student Web Activity Visit glencoe.com and complete the activity on American prehistory.

Teach

R Reading Strategy

Previewing Tell students: Preview the text's structure before you begin reading. Text structures include time order, compare-contrast, description, cause-and-effect, and problem-solution. Noticing how ideas are organized will help you to better understand what you read. BL

S Skill Practice

Using Geography Skills

Ask: About how far did the Aztec Empire extend from north to south? *(about 500 miles or 800 kilometers)* OL

Analyzing GEOGRAPHY

Answers:
1. on the northern Yucatán Peninsula
2. Possible answer: They had to clear the land to build large cities and temple complexes.

Hands-On Chapter Project
Step 1

Establishing a Colony in North America

Step 1: Researching Conditions in North America Essential Question: What do colonists need to know about the land and people in North America to create a successful colony?

Directions Organize students into small groups. Have them assume the role of English people living around 1600. Each group of students will explore what area of North America is most likely to sustain a colony.

Students should first make a list of criteria for a successful colony. For example, a colony will need a source of freshwater, timber for building, food sources, be in a defensible location, have a good harbor, and so on. Students should also research the locations and cultures of Native Americans living on the Atlantic coast.

Next, students should create a map indicating the locations or availability of the resources on their list of criteria as well as any major landforms, such as mountains, rivers, or natural harbors. The map should also include the locations of Native American groups. Students should then determine the exact location for their colony.

Summarizing Have representatives for each group share the chosen location with the class and summarize the benefits and challenges of settling in that location. OL

(Chapter Project continued in Section 2, p. 15)

C Critical Thinking

Comparing and Contrasting Have students write a paragraph to compare and contrast aspects of the Aztec capital Tenochtitlán with their own community. Have them consider what types of activities people did then that they do today, buildings that your community and Tenochtitlán may have in common, such as a sports field or arena, and so on. OL

Analyzing VISUALS

Answers:
1. the Great Temple
2. A hearth provides warmth and enables people to cook food, which is needed to survive. Fire might have symbolized the sun or life to the Aztec.

Reading Check

Answers: Some anthropologists believe that Maya farmers may have exhausted the region's soil, and this would have led to famine, riots, and the collapse of the cities. Others believe that invaders from the north devastated the region.

Additional Support

The Toltec and the Aztec

North of the Maya civilization, the Toltec people built a large city called Tula. The Toltec were master architects. They built large pyramids and huge palaces with pillared halls. They were among the first American peoples to use gold and copper in art and jewelry.

About A.D. 1200, Tula fell to invaders from the north, known as the Chichimec. One group of Chichimec, called the Mexica, built the city of Tenochtitlán (tay•NAWCH•teet•LAHN) in 1325 on the site of what is today Mexico City. The Mexica took the name **Aztec** for themselves, from the name of their original homeland, Aztlán. Aztlán is thought to have been located in the American Southwest.

The Aztec created a mighty empire by conquering neighboring cities. Using their military power, they controlled trade in the region and demanded **tribute,** or payment, from the cities they conquered. They also brought some of the people they conquered to Tenochtitlán to sacrifice in their religious ceremonies. When the Europeans arrived in the 1500s, an estimated 5 million people were living under Aztec rule.

Reading Check **Examining** What are some of the theories that explain the decline of Maya cities?

Western Cultures

MAIN Idea Depending on their local environment, the Native Americans of western North America pursued agriculture, fishing, and hunting.

HISTORY AND YOU Do you have a particular household chore assigned to you? Read how some Native American families divided household work.

North of Mesoamerica, other peoples developed their own cultures. Many anthropologists think that agricultural **technology** spread from Mesoamerica into the American Southwest and up the Mississippi River. There, it transformed many hunter-gatherer societies into farming societies.

The Hohokam

Beginning in A.D. 300, in what is now south-central Arizona, a group called the Hohokam built a system of irrigation canals. The Hohokam used the Gila and Salt Rivers as their water supply. Their canals carried water hundreds of miles to their farms.

The Hohokam grew corn, cotton, beans, and squash. They also made decorative red-on-buff-colored pottery and turquoise pen-

PRIMARY SOURCE

The Aztec Capital, Tenochtitlán

The Aztec were master builders who filled their cities with wide plazas and spectacular temples.

▲ At the top, Aztecs sit in their home in front of the hearth, which was sacred to them, while an Aztec is shown cooking below.

Analyzing VISUALS

1. **Identifying** What was the main feature of the city of Tenochtitlán?
2. **Making Inferences** Why would the hearth be sacred to the Aztecs?

Activity: Interdisciplinary Connection

Visual Arts Ask: What do you know about the styles and subjects of pre-Columbian art? Have students conduct research about pre-Columbian artwork using library, museum, and Internet resources. Ask students to focus their research on one of the cultures addressed in this section. Based on their findings, have students prepare an oral presentation. Tell students to bring printouts or books containing examples of the artwork they will discuss to share with classmates during their presentation. If possible, encourage students to create their presentation using presentation software. OL dants, and used cactus juice to etch shells. Hohokam culture flourished for more than 1,000 years, but in the 1300s they began to abandon their irrigation systems, likely due to floods and increased competition for farmland. By 1500, the Hohokam had left the area.

The Anasazi

Between A.D. 700 and 900, the people living in villages in what is called the Four Corners area—where Utah, Colorado, Arizona, and New Mexico now meet—developed another culture. We know these people by the name the Navajo gave them—Anasazi, or "ancient ones." Today they are often called "ancestral Puebloan" people. In the harsh desert, the Anasazi accumulated water by building networks of basins and ditches to channel rain into stone-lined depressions.

Between A.D. 850 and 1100, the Anasazi living in Chaco Canyon in what is now northwest New Mexico began constructing large, multistory buildings of adobe and cut stone, with connecting passageways and circular ceremonial rooms called **kivas.** Early Spanish explorers called these structures **pueblos,** the Spanish word for "villages." Those who built them are sometimes referred to as Pueblo people. R

The Anasazi built these pueblos at junctions where streams of rainwater ran together. A pueblo in Chaco Canyon, called Pueblo Bonito, had 600 rooms and probably housed at least 1,000 people. Later, at Mesa Verde in what is today southwestern Colorado, the Anasazi built impressive cliff dwellings.

Beginning around A.D. 1130, Chaco Canyon experienced a devastating drought that lasted at least 50 years. This probably caused the Anasazi to abandon their pueblos. The Mesa Verde pueblos lasted for another 200 years, but when another drought struck in the 1270s, they too were abandoned.

The Southwest

The descendants of the Anasazi and Hohokam live in the arid Southwest. At the time of European contact, there were over 50 groups. These groups included the Zuni, Hopi, and other Pueblo peoples. Corn was essential to their survival in the arid climate because its long taproot could reach moisture deep beneath the surface. The farmers also grew squash and beans.

The Pueblo people assigned different tasks to men and women. Men farmed, performed most ceremonies, made moccasins, and wove clothing and blankets. Women made the meals, crafted pottery and baskets, and hauled water. The men and women worked together when harvesting crops and building houses.

Sometime between A.D. 1200 and 1500, two other peoples—the Apache and the Navajo—came to the region from the far northwest of North America. Some anthropologists think that their arrival might have been what drove the Chichimec people into Mexico, where they formed the Aztec Empire. Although many of the Apache remained primarily nomadic hunters, the Navajo learned farming from the Pueblo people and lived in widely dispersed settlements.

The Pacific Coast

Many different groups, including the Tlingit, Haida, Kwakiutl, Nootka, Chinook, and Salish peoples, lived in the lands bordering the Pacific Ocean from what is now southeastern Alaska to Washington State. Although they did not practice agriculture, these groups dwelt in permanent settlements. They looked to the dense coastal forests for lumber, which they used not only to build homes and to fashion oceangoing canoes, but also to create elaborate works of art, ceremonial masks, and totem poles. They were able to stay in one place because the region's coastal waters and many rivers teemed with fish. C

In what is today central California, several groups hunted the abundant wildlife and flourished in the mild climate. The Pomo, for example, gathered acorns, caught fish in nets and traps, and snared small game and birds. Pomo hunters, working together, would drive deer toward a spot where the village's best archer waited, hidden and disguised in a deerhead mask. Sometimes, the hunters stampeded game into a corral, where the animals could be easily killed. When game was scarce, however, the Pomo relied on the acorn, which they had learned to convert from a hard, bitter nut into edible flour.

Reading Check **Analyzing** How did societies of the Southwest cope with the dry climate?

R Reading Strategy

Monitoring Tell students that they will find that some text selections are more difficult to read than others. Because of this, they must learn to check their understanding and to make adjustments to their reading rate accordingly. Remind students to slow down when they encounter difficult concepts or words, connections to previous ideas, new vocabulary, or text that contains a great deal of information. OL

C Critical Thinking

Identifying Central Issues
Ask: What about the local geography made it unnecessary for the peoples of the Pacific Northwest to become nomads? *(The ocean and rivers provided a constant and plentiful supply of food.)* OL

Reading Check

Answer:
They built basins to collect water and grew plants, such as corn, that were adapted to a dry climate.

Extending the Content

Totem poles are carved and painted cedar logs created by Native American peoples who lived along the northwest Pacific coast. These poles were positioned upright and often placed in front of dwellings, graves, and bodies of water. Totem poles have specific traditional significance, such as to memorialize a dead family member or someone special in the community. Some of the stylized animal figures on the poles are family or clan symbols, or totems, while others are figures from mythology. Some of the most familiar are ravens, bears, beavers, and fish. Totemic figures were also carved into supporting structures in the architecture of this culture group.

C Critical Thinking

Determining Cause and Effect Clarify that horses are not native to the Americas, but were brought initially by the Spanish. **Ask:** How did the arrival of the horse change the culture of some Native Americans on the Great Plains? *(Tribal groups, such as the Sioux, used horses to hunt and in war. The Sioux and others like them became some of the world's greatest mounted hunters and warriors.)* **OL**

Reading Check

Answer:
Many aspects of Mississippian culture survived in the Southeast until the Europeans arrived. Almost all the people in the Southeast lived in towns arranged around a central plaza, with stockades. The houses were built out of poles and covered with grass, mud, or thatch. Women did most of the farming, while the men hunted.

Additional Support

Mississippian Culture and Its Descendants

MAIN Idea Along the Mississippi River, Native Americans built Cahokia and other large cities, while those on the Great Plains hunted buffalo herds.

HISTORY AND YOU Have you seen photos of pyramids in Egypt or Mexico? Read to learn about the large pyramids built in the Mississippi River valley.

Between A.D. 700 and 900, as agricultural technology and improved strains of maize and beans spread north from Mexico and up the Mississippi River, another new culture—the Mississippian—emerged. It began in the Mississippi River valley, where the rich soil of the floodplains was perfectly suited to the intensive cultivation of maize and beans.

The Mississippians were great builders. Eight miles from what is now St. Louis, Missouri, are the remains of one of their largest cities, which anthropologists named **Cahokia.** At its peak between about A.D. 1050 and 1250, Cahokia covered five square miles (13 sq km), contained more than 100 flat-topped pyramids and mounds, and was home to an estimated 16,000 people. Most of the people lived in pole-and-thatch houses that spread out over 2,000 acres (810 ha). The largest pyramid, named Monks Mound, was 100 feet (30.5 m) high, had four levels, and covered 16 acres (6.5 ha)—more than any pyramid in Egypt or Mexico. A log wall with watchtowers and gates surrounded the central plaza and the larger pyramids.

As it expanded across the American South, Mississippian culture led to the rise of at least three other large cities with flat-topped mounds—at present-day Spiro, Oklahoma; Moundville, Alabama; and Etowah, Georgia. Mississippian culture also spread north and west along the great rivers of the region: the Missouri, Ohio, Red, and Arkansas.

Peoples of the Southeast

The population of Cahokia mysteriously declined around A.D. 1300. The city may have been attacked by other Native Americans or its population may have become too large to support, resulting in famine and emigration. Another possibility is that the city was struck by an epidemic.

Although Cahokia came to an end, many aspects of Mississippian culture survived in the Southeast until the Europeans arrived. Almost all the people in the Southeast lived in towns. The buildings were arranged around a central plaza. Stockades usually surrounded the towns, although moats and earthen walls were also used. The houses were built out of poles and covered with grass, mud, or thatch. Women did most of the farming, while men hunted deer, bear, wildfowl, and even alligator.

The Cherokee were the largest group in the Southeast. They were located in what is today western North Carolina and eastern Tennessee. About 20,000 Cherokee lived in some 60 towns when the Europeans arrived. Other peoples in the Southeast included the Choctaw, Chickasaw, Natchez, and Creek. The Creek were a large group living in some 50 villages spread across Georgia and Alabama.

The Great Plains

When Europeans arrived, the people of the Great Plains were nomads, who had only recently abandoned farming. Until about 1500 the societies of the Great Plains had been shaped by Mississippian culture. The people of the region lived near rivers, where they could plant corn and find wood to build their homes.

Around the year 1500, the peoples of the western Plains abandoned their villages and became nomads, possibly because of war or drought. Those in the east, including the Pawnee, Kansas, and Iowa peoples, continued to farm, as well as hunt. Peoples of the western Plains, including the Sioux, became nomadic. They hunted migrating buffalo herds on foot and lived in cone-shaped tents called tepees.

Life for the Sioux and others on the Great Plains changed dramatically after they began taming horses. The Spanish brought horses to North America in the 1500s. Over the next few centuries, as horses either escaped or were stolen, the animals spread northward, **eventually** reaching the Great Plains. There, the Sioux encountered and mastered them. The Sioux soon became some of the world's greatest mounted hunters and warriors. C

Reading Check **Contrasting** How did the Mississippian culture affect the peoples of the Southeast?

Activity: Collaborative Learning

Dramatizing a Myth **Ask:** What is your favorite myth or legend? Have students work in small groups to research a myth or traditional tale from one of the North American culture groups covered in this section. Students should collaborate on writing a script to dramatize this tale, create necessary costumes, and design any special lighting or sound effects. Provide time for students to act out the tale for the class. **OL**

NATIONAL GEOGRAPHIC Native American Cultures, c. 1500

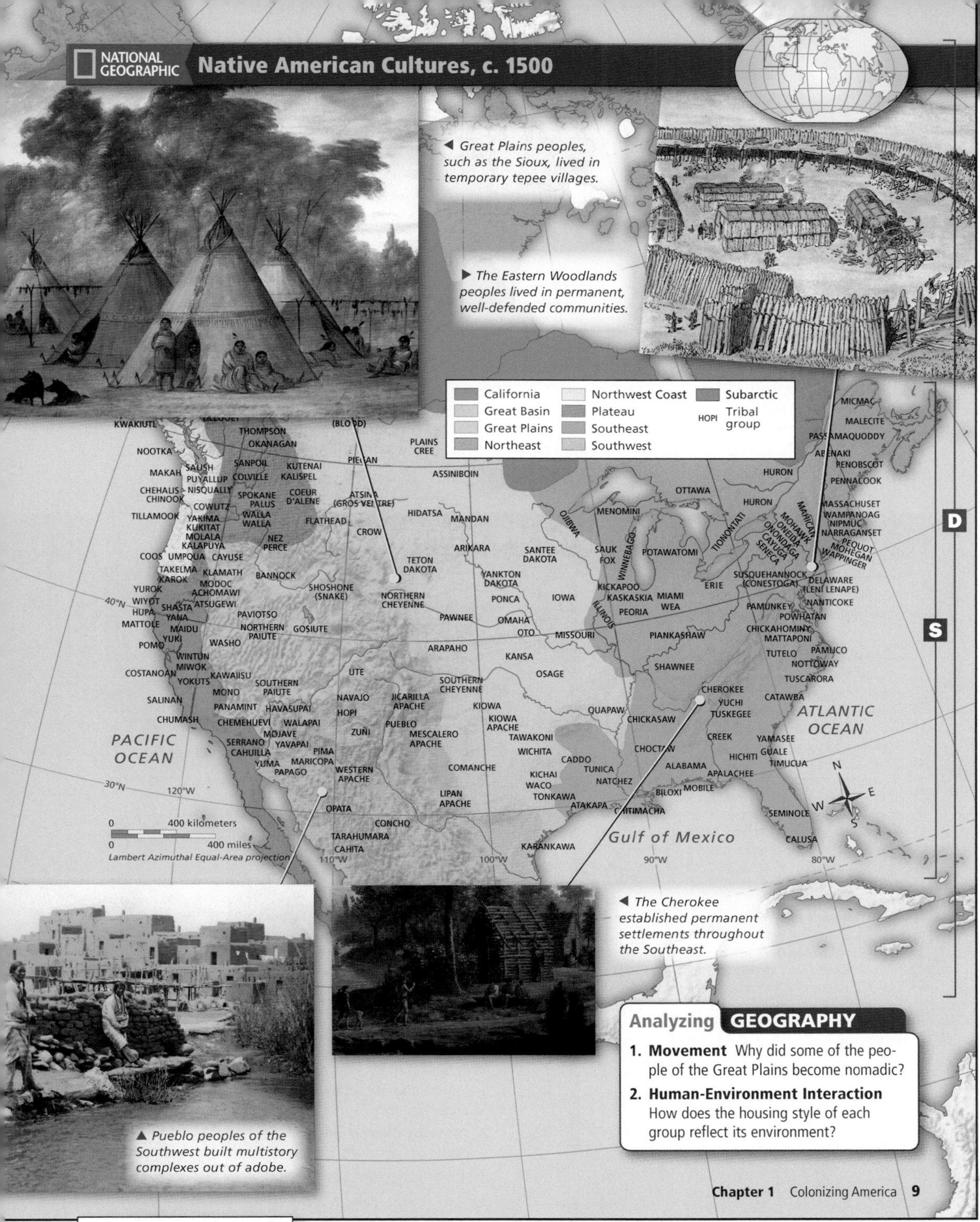

◀ *Great Plains peoples, such as the Sioux, lived in temporary tepee villages.*

▶ *The Eastern Woodlands peoples lived in permanent, well-defended communities.*

▲ *Pueblo peoples of the Southwest built multistory complexes out of adobe.*

◀ *The Cherokee established permanent settlements throughout the Southeast.*

Analyzing GEOGRAPHY

1. **Movement** Why did some of the people of the Great Plains become nomadic?
2. **Human-Environment Interaction** How does the housing style of each group reflect its environment?

D Differentiated Instruction

English Learners Have students work in pairs using dictionary or Internet resources to look up the correct pronunciation of the names of each Native American culture discussed in the section. Have students practice saying the names aloud as they write them down. **ELL**

S Skill Practice

Using Geography Skills Have students study the map and identify several tribal groups who lived in or nearest to your community. **OL**

Analyzing GEOGRAPHY

Answers:

1. They became nomadic possibly because of war or drought.
2. Each group used local materials, such as hides from buffalo on the plains or wooden houses and stockades in the eastern woodlands.

Differentiated Instruction

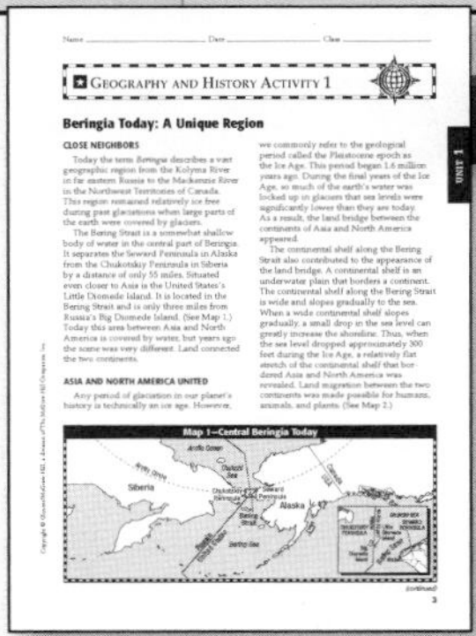

Geography and History Activity, URB p. 3–6

Drawing Conclusions: Traveling to Beringia

Objective: Draw a conclusion about how visitors reach the Bering Land Bridge National Preserve.

Focus: Have students locate the Bering Land Bridge National Preserve on Map 3. Identify the nearest cities.

Teach: List the physical features of the Preserve.

Assess: Write a paragraph describing how visitors could reach the Preserve.

Close: Create a brochure describing the Preserve.

Differentiated Instruction Strategies

BL List three physical features of the Preserve that would attract visitors.

AL Research the native peoples of the Beringia region. Include how they use the natural resources of the area in their lives.

ELL Make a list of vocabulary words. Write a definition for each.

S Skill Practice

Analyzing Sources Have students study the excerpt from the *Great Binding Law of the Five Nations.* **Ask:** How many war chiefs did each nation in the Confederacy have and what were their duties? *(There was one war chief for each member nation. They had to carry messages for their leaders and to fight in case of emergency.)* **BL**

DBQ Document Based Questions

Answers:

1. The Lords of the Confederacy must ask the people what they want to do and the people's wishes will "affect the decision of the Confederate Council."
2. Possible answer: They did not want warriors, who have the most to gain from war, to make decisions about whether or not the Confederacy would fight.

History ONLINE
Student Skill Activity To learn how to create and modify a database, visit glencoe.com and complete the skill activity.

For an example of Native American storytelling, read the selections on pages R64–R65 in the **American Literature Library.**

Northeastern Peoples

MAIN Idea Most Eastern Woodlands peoples spoke Algonquian or Iroquoian languages; combined hunting, fishing, and farming; and lived in small villages.

HISTORY AND YOU Can you think of an organization intended to stop conflict between nations today? Read on to learn about the origins and purpose of the Iroquois Confederacy.

When Europeans arrived, almost a million square miles of woodlands lay east of the Mississippi River and south of the Great Lakes. This landscape supported an amazing range of plant and animal life. Almost all the Eastern Woodlands peoples provided for themselves by combining hunting and fishing with farming. Deer were plentiful in the region, and deer meat regularly supplemented the corn, beans, and squash the people planted. Deer hide was also used for clothing.

The Algonquian Peoples

Most peoples in the Northeast belonged to one of two language groups: those who spoke Algonquian languages and those who spoke Iroquoian languages. The Algonquian-speaking peoples included most of the groups living in the area known today as New England. Among these peoples were the Wampanoag in Massachusetts, the Narragansett in Rhode Island, and the Pequot in Connecticut. Farther south, in what is today Virginia, lived the Algonquian-speaking peoples of the Powhatan Confederacy. Native Americans in New England and Virginia were among the first to encounter English settlers.

NATIONAL GEOGRAPHIC The Native Americans of the Northeast, c. 1600

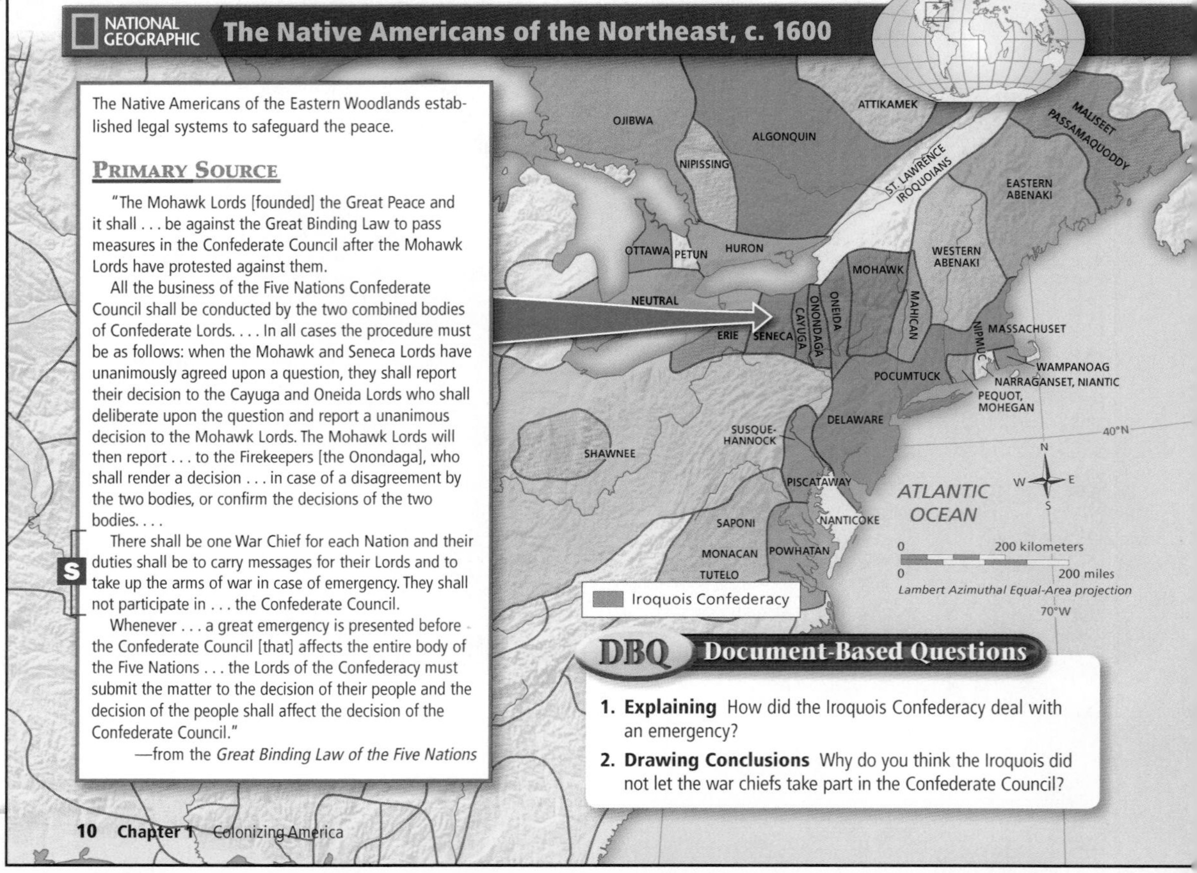

The Native Americans of the Eastern Woodlands established legal systems to safeguard the peace.

PRIMARY SOURCE

"The Mohawk Lords [founded] the Great Peace and it shall . . . be against the Great Binding Law to pass measures in the Confederate Council after the Mohawk Lords have protested against them.

All the business of the Five Nations Confederate Council shall be conducted by the two combined bodies of Confederate Lords. . . . In all cases the procedure must be as follows: when the Mohawk and Seneca Lords have unanimously agreed upon a question, they shall report their decision to the Cayuga and Oneida Lords who shall deliberate upon the question and report a unanimous decision to the Mohawk Lords. The Mohawk Lords will then report . . . to the Firekeepers [the Onondaga], who shall render a decision . . . in case of a disagreement by the two bodies, or confirm the decisions of the two bodies. . . .

S There shall be one War Chief for each Nation and their duties shall be to carry messages for their Lords and to take up the arms of war in case of emergency. They shall not participate in . . . the Confederate Council.

Whenever . . . a great emergency is presented before the Confederate Council [that] affects the entire body of the Five Nations . . . the Lords of the Confederacy must submit the matter to the decision of their people and the decision of the people shall affect the decision of the Confederate Council."

—from the *Great Binding Law of the Five Nations*

DBQ Document-Based Questions

1. **Explaining** How did the Iroquois Confederacy deal with an emergency?
2. **Drawing Conclusions** Why do you think the Iroquois did not let the war chiefs take part in the Confederate Council?

Leveled Activities

BL Reteaching Activity, URB p. 43

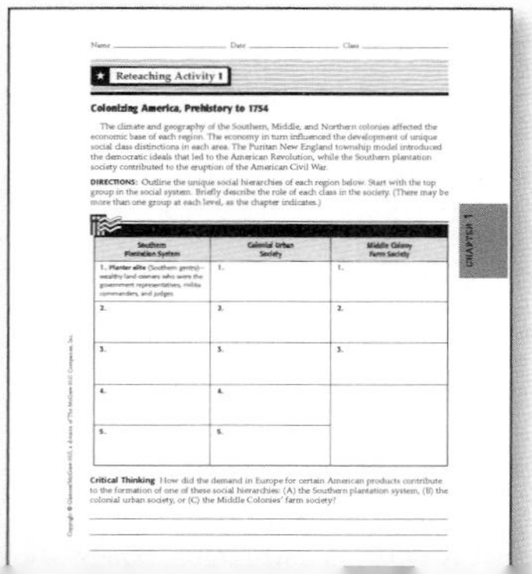

OL Academic Vocabulary Activity, URB p. 29

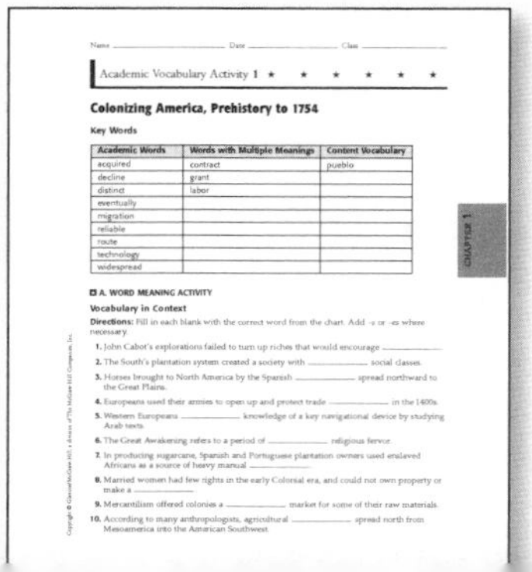

AL Primary Source Reading, URB p. 35

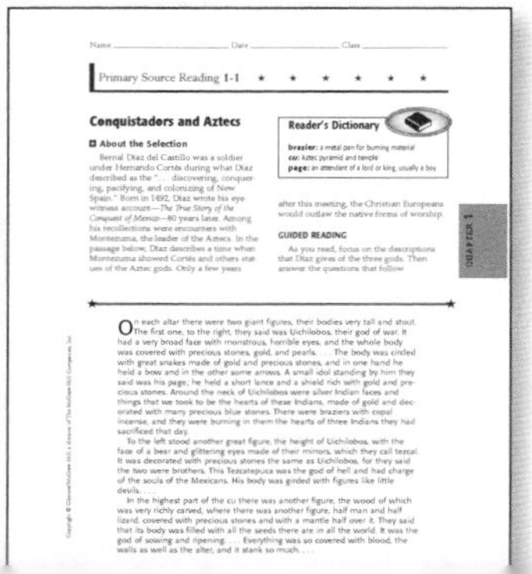

ELL English Learner Activity, URB p. 25

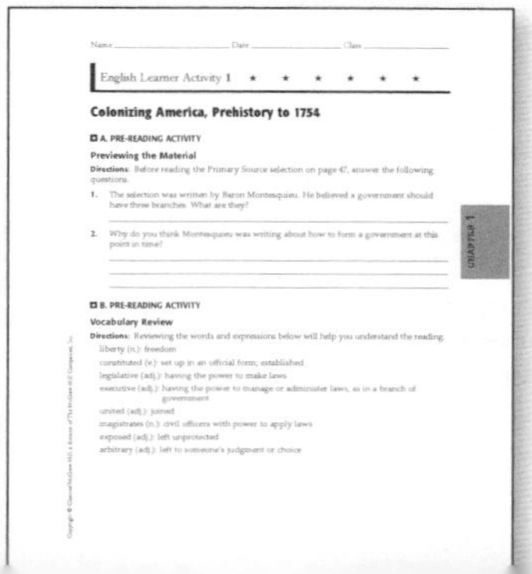

Other Algonquian peoples included the Delaware, who lived near the Delaware River in what is today eastern Pennsylvania and New Jersey; and the Shawnee, who lived in the Ohio River valley. Words from the Algonquian language used in English today include *succotash, hominy, moccasin,* and *papoose.*

Many peoples in the Northeast, including the Algonquians and the Iroquoians, practiced slash-and-burn agriculture. By cutting down parts of forests and burning the wood, they were left with nitrogen-rich ashes. They then worked the ashes into the soil, making it more fertile for a few years. After exhausting the soil, the people of the village would move to a new location and burn down another section of forest for farming.

Native Americans of the Northeast built several types of houses. Many villages had large rectangular longhouses with barrel-shaped roofs covered in bark. Other groups built wigwams. These dwellings were either conical or dome-shaped and were formed using bent poles covered with hides or bark.

The Iroquois Confederacy

Stretching west from the Hudson River across what is today New York and southern Ontario and north to Georgian Bay lived the Iroquoian-speaking peoples. They included the Huron, Neutral, Erie, Wenro, Seneca, Cayuga, Onondaga, Oneida, and Mohawk.

All the Iroquoian peoples had similar cultures. They lived in longhouses in large towns, which they protected by building stockades. **R** Women were responsible for the planting and harvesting of crops while men hunted. The people lived in large kinship groups, or extended families, headed by the elder women of each kinship group. Up to 10 related families lived together in each longhouse.

Iroquois women occupied positions of power and importance in their communities. Although all 50 chiefs of the Iroquois ruling council were men, the women who headed the kinship groups selected them. Council members were appointed for life, but the women could remove an appointee if they disagreed with his actions. In this way, Iroquois women enjoyed considerable political influence.

War often erupted among the Iroquoians. In the late 1500s, five of the nations in western New York—the Seneca, Cayuga, Onondaga, Oneida, and Mohawk—formed an alliance to maintain peace and oppose their common enemy—the more powerful Huron people, who lived across the Niagara River in what is now southwestern Ontario. This alliance was later called the **Iroquois Confederacy.** Europeans called these five nations the Iroquois, even though other nations spoke Iroquoian as well.

According to Iroquoian tradition, Dekanawidah, a shaman or tribal elder, and Hiawatha, a chief of the Mohawk, founded the confederacy. They were worried that war was tearing the five nations apart when the more powerful Huron people threatened them all. The five nations agreed to the Great Binding Law, an oral constitution that defined how the confederacy worked.

✓ Reading Check **Analyzing** How did some Eastern Woodlands groups increase their crop yield?

Section 1 REVIEW

Vocabulary

1. **Explain** the significance of: Beringia, agricultural revolution, Mesoamerica, Maya, Aztec, tribute, kiva, pueblo, Cahokia, Iroquois Confederacy.

Main Ideas

2. **Describing** What route did humans take when they first came to North America?
3. **Identifying** What happened to change life for the peoples of the Great Plains?
4. **Explaining** Why did the Iroquoians form a confederacy?

Critical Thinking

5. **Big Ideas** How did geography and climate affect the cultures and traditions of Native American groups?
6. **Categorizing** Use a graphic organizer to list North American regions and the ways in which groups living in these regions obtained food.

Region	Methods of Getting Food

7. **Analyzing Visuals** Examine the map on page 10. Which groups are members of the Iroquis Confederacy?

Writing About History

8. **Expository Writing** Using library or Internet resources, find more information about the groups discussed in this section. Use the information to create a database about these civilizations. Write a one-page report with your findings.

History ONLINE
Study Central™ To review this section, go to glencoe.com and click on Study Central.

11

R Reading Strategy

Comparing Have students make a two-column chart to compare and contrast the Algonquian and Iroquoian peoples. Have students include information about location, languages, food production, and so on. **BL**

✓ Reading Check

Answer:
They practiced slash-and-burn agriculture.

Assess

History ONLINE

Study Central™ provides summaries, interactive games, and online graphic organizers to help students review content.

Close

Summarizing **Ask:** **What were the main culture groups in the Americas before the arrival of Europeans?** *(Mesoamerican, Southwest, Pacific Coast, Great Plains, Mississippian, Eastern Woodlands)* **OL**

Section 1 REVIEW

Answers

1. All definitions can be found in the section and the Glossary.
2. They came over the land bridge known as Beringia from Asia 15,000 to 30,000 years ago.
3. They began to tame and use horses for hunting and in war.
4. The five nations often fought. They formed the alliance to maintain peace among themselves and to oppose their common enemy, the more powerful Huron people.
5. Answers will vary. Students should note how customs and traditions were affected by geography and climate, using examples from the text.
6. Southwest: farmed; Pacific Coast: fished, hunted, gathered acorns; Southeast: farmed and hunted; Great Plains: hunted and farmed; Northeast: hunted, fished, farmed
7. the Seneca, Cayuga, Onondaga, Oneida, and Mohawk
8. Students' reports will vary. Reports should focus on one culture group and provide information beyond what is found in the student text.

GEOGRAPHY & HISTORY

Focus

Tell students that the Columbian Exchange had unintended consequences. For example, weeds and germs new to the Americas arrived along with the intended crops and livestock.

Teach

R Reading Skill

Sequencing Have students make charts ordering the events of the Columbian Exchange. *(Possible answer: Europe: brought crops, animals, diseases; took home food, animals. Native Americans: died from diseases. Africa: people enslaved in Americas; food taken to Africa.)* OL

C Critical Thinking

Contrasting Have students propose an alternative to enslaved labor. Ask them to consider models that worked at least for a time in other places. *(Possible answers: prisoners in penal colonies, such as Georgia, Australia; indentured servants.)* OL

Additional Support

NATIONAL GEOGRAPHIC

GEOGRAPHY & HISTORY

R The Columbian Exchange

The arrival of Europeans in the Americas set in motion a series of complex interactions between peoples and environments. These interactions, called the Columbian Exchange, permanently altered the world's ecosystems and changed nearly every culture around the world.

Native Americans introduced Europeans to new crops. Corn, squash, pumpkins, beans, sweet potatoes, tomatoes, chili peppers, peanuts, chocolate, and potatoes all made their way to Europe, as did tobacco and chewing gum. Perhaps the most significant import for Europeans was the potato. European farmers learned that four times as many people could live off the same amount of land when potatoes were planted instead of grain.

The Europeans introduced Native Americans to wheat, oats, barley, rye, rice, onions, bananas, coffee, and citrus fruits such as lemons and oranges. They also brought over livestock such as cattle, pigs, sheep, and chickens. Perhaps the most important form of livestock was the horse—which dramatically changed life for many Native Americans on the Great Plains.

How Did Geography Shape the Exchange?

C The isolation of the Americas from the rest of the world meant that Native Americans had no resistance to diseases that were common in other parts of the world, such as influenza, measles, chicken pox, mumps, typhus, and smallpox. The consequences were devastating. Epidemics killed millions of Native Americans. This catastrophe also reduced the labor supply available to Europeans, who then turned to the slave trade, eventually bringing millions of Africans to the Americas.

Analyzing GEOGRAPHY

1. Movement What new crops were introduced in Europe from the Americas? How did these crops improve the diet of Europeans?
2. Human-Environment Interaction How did geography play a role in the spread of diseases?

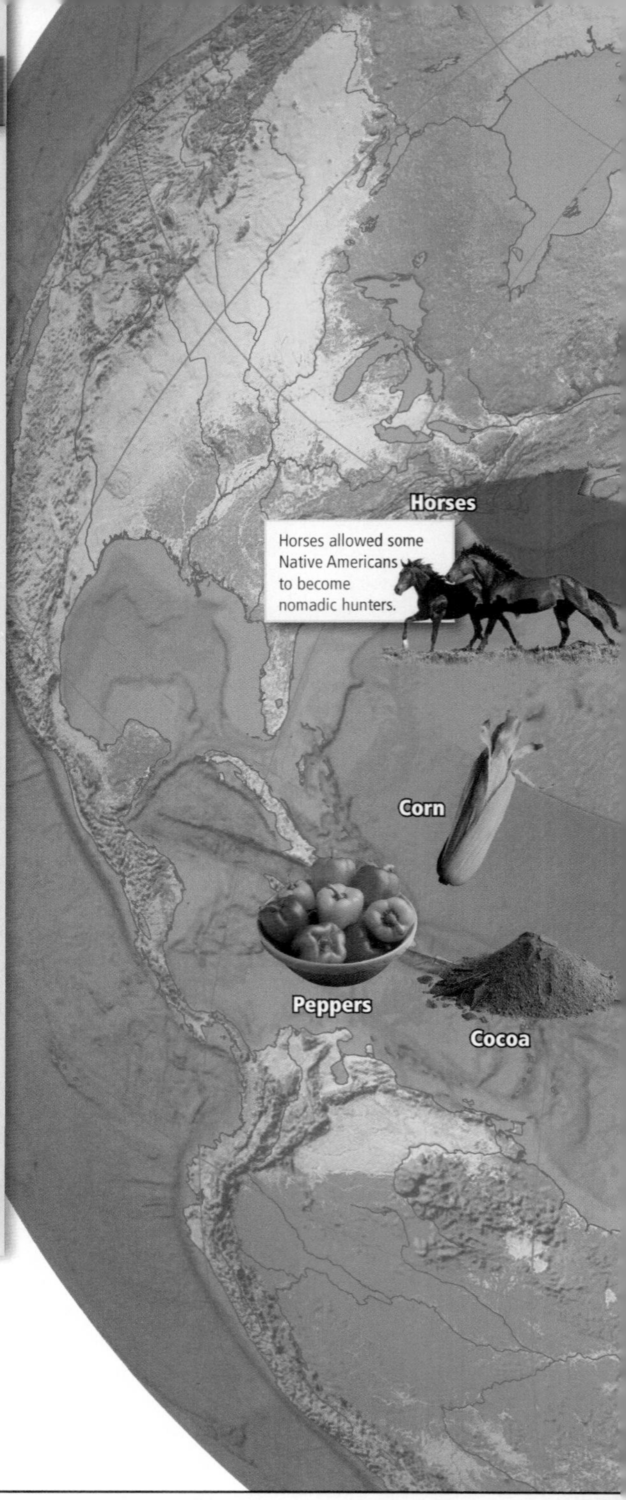

Extending the Content

World Population Growth As a result of the increased number of calories in the European diet produced by the Columbian Exchange, the world population boomed in the years following 1700 at a rate faster than at any time in human history. From 1700 to 1750 the world population jumped from 610 million to 720 million. From 1750 to 1800 total population expanded from 720 million to 900 million. Despite the loss of life due to the spread of diseases, the increased nutrition in diets offset the losses.

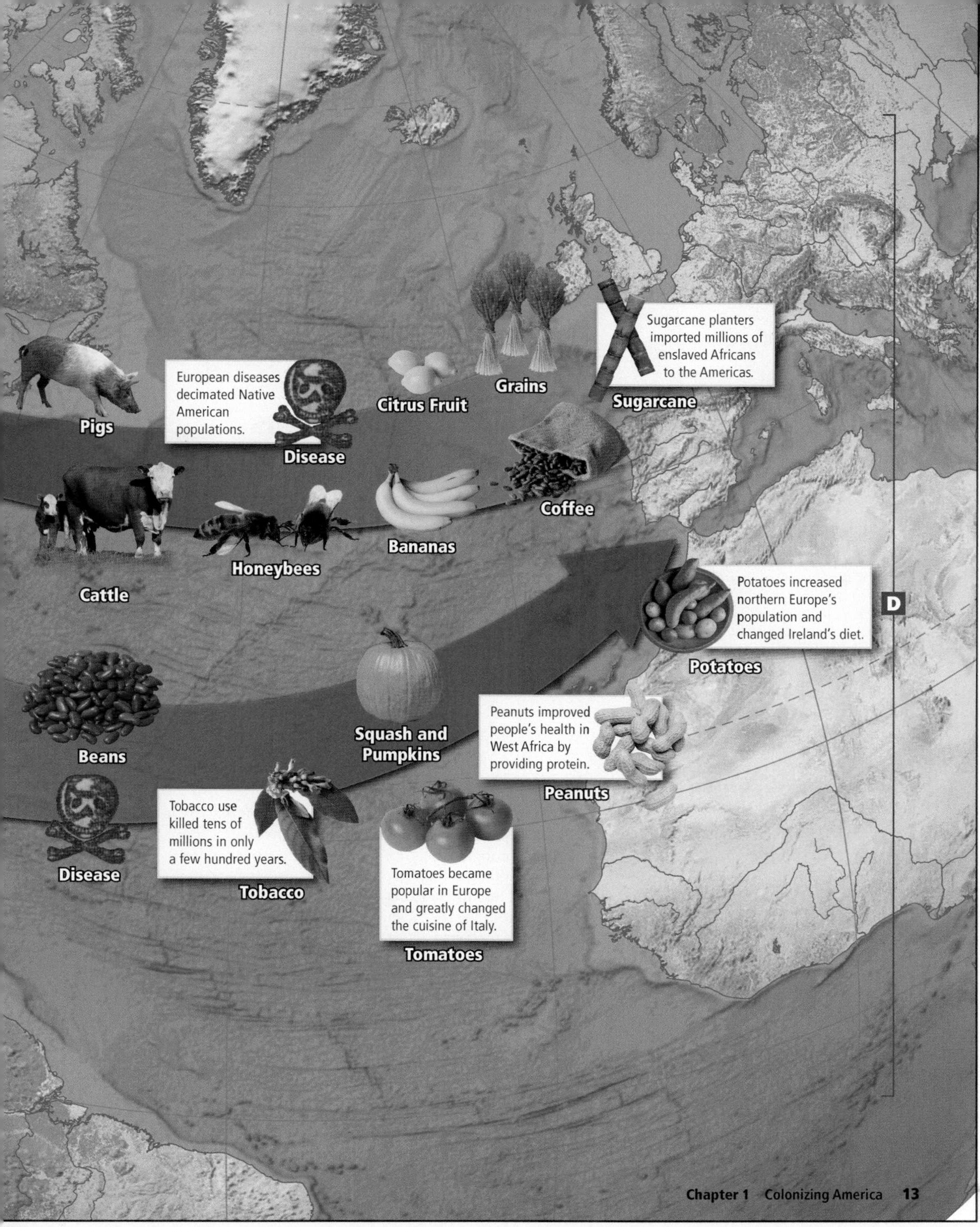

D

GEOGRAPHY & HISTORY

Assess/Close

D Differentiated Instruction

Naturalist Invite students to choose one of the elements of the Columbian Exchange and use the library or Internet resources to become a specialist on that one aspect. Have them report their findings to the class. **AL**

Analyzing GEOGRAPHY

Answers:

1. American crops included corn, squash, pumpkins, beans, sweet potatoes, tomatoes, chili peppers, peanuts, chocolate, and potatoes. Europeans could feed more people off the same amount of land by planting potatoes, and tomatoes changed Italy's cuisine.
2. Because the Americas were isolated, the inhabitants had no resistance to common European diseases. Epidemics killed millions of Native Americans.

Interdisciplinary Connection: Science

Contemporary Exchanges Invite students to find out more about the current situation with invasive species in the United States and to report on efforts to control them. You may wish to divide the class into groups, assigning each group one of the following categories: animals, aquatic species, plants, or microbes. Groups can report on the effects of invasive species on habitats and the economy and on the federal government's response. The USDA Natural Agricultural Library Web site is a good starting point for research.

Focus

Bellringer

Daily Focus Transparency 1-2

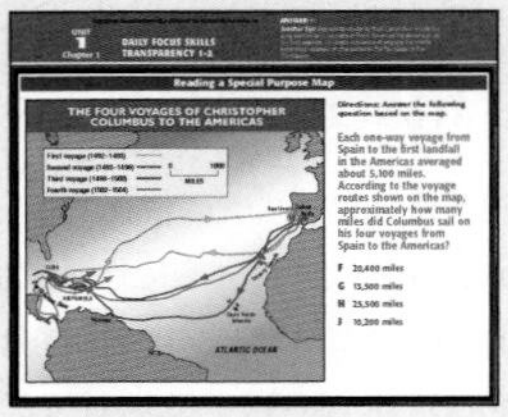

Guide to Reading

Answers:

Exploration	Outcome
Columbus	began exploration of the Americas
Vespucci	continued exploration and mapping, and Americas are named for him
Balboa	first European to reach the Pacific coast of the Americas
Magellan	named the Pacific Ocean and led the crew that was the first to circumnavigate the globe

Section Spotlight Video

To generate student interest and provide a springboard for class discussion, access the Chapter 1, Section 2 video at glencoe.com or on the video DVD.

Section 2 Section Audio Spotlight Video

Europe Begins to Explore

Guide to Reading

Big Ideas

Science and Technology The Renaissance brought about a scientific revolution that enabled Europeans to explore the world.

Content Vocabulary
- astrolabe *(p. 16)*
- caravel *(p. 16)*
- circumnavigate *(p. 19)*
- conquistador *(p. 20)*
- *encomienda (p. 22)*

Academic Vocabulary
- route *(p. 15)*
- acquire *(p. 16)*
- labor *(p. 17)*

People and Events to Identify
- Henry the Navigator *(p. 16)*
- Amerigo Vespucci *(p. 18)*
- Hernán Cortés *(p. 20)*
- Francisco Pizarro *(p. 20)*
- Samuel de Champlain *(p. 23)*

Reading Strategy

Organizing Complete a chart similar to the one below by filling in the outcome of each exploration listed in the chart.

Exploration	Outcome
Columbus	
Vespucci	
Balboa	
Magellan	

During the Renaissance, increased trade and new technology led Europeans to embark on overseas exploration. First, Europeans sailed around Africa to reach Asia. Later, Christopher Columbus sailed west and reached the Americas. Spain became the first European colonial power in the Americas.

European Explorations

MAIN Idea Beginning in the 1400s, Europe entered a new era of intellectual and technological advancement known as the Renaissance.

HISTORY AND YOU Have you tried food from a different culture? Read to learn how Europeans developed a taste for spices and produce from Asia.

For centuries, the Roman Empire dominated Europe, imposing a unified and stable social and political order. By A.D. 500, however, the Roman political and economic system collapsed, disconnecting western Europe from the rest of the world. Without a central authority, the region experienced a decline in trade, and the political system became more fragmented. Most people lived on manors or in villages ruled by local lords, who kept the peace only in the lands they controlled. This period, lasting from roughly A.D. 500 to 1500, is known as the Middle Ages.

Expanding Horizons

In 1095 Pope Urban II called for Christians to free their religion's holy places in the Middle East from Muslim control. The resulting Crusades brought western Europeans into contact with the Arab civilization of the Middle East. The Europeans began trading with the Arabs, and in particular, began buying luxury goods that Arab traders obtained from East Asia: spices, sugar, melons, tapestries, silk, and other items. As demand for East Asian goods increased, Italian city-states such as Venice, Pisa, and Genoa grew wealthy moving goods between the Middle East and western Europe. By 1200, Italian and Arab merchants controlled most of the trade in the eastern Mediterranean and charged high prices for the goods that western Europeans wanted.

By the 1300s, Europeans had a strong economic motive to begin exploring the world for a route to Asia that bypassed the Italian city-states and the Arab kingdoms. Yet western Europe did not have the technology or wealth to begin exploring. All that started to change in the 1400s. The rise of towns and the merchant class provided kings

Resource Manager

R Reading Strategies	C Critical Thinking	D Differentiated Instruction	W Writing Support	S Skill Practice
Teacher Edition • Questioning, p. 15 • Academic Vocab, p. 17 • Act. Prior Know., p. 18 • Summarizing, pp. 20, 22 • Using Word Parts, p. 21 • Reading Charts, p. 22 **Additional Resources** • Guid. Read. Act, URB p. 49	**Teacher Edition** • Ident. Cent. Issues, p. 16 • Ident. Points of View, p. 18 **Additional Resources** • Interpreting Political Cartoons, URB p. 41 • Quizzes/Tests, p. 6	**Teacher Edition** • Kinesthetic, p. 15 • Visual/Spatial, p. 19	**Teacher Edition** • Expository, p. 20	**Teacher Edition** • Using Geo. Skills, p. 21 **Additional Resources** • Reinforcing Skills Act., URB p. 31 • RENTG, p. 4

Age of Exploration New or newly discovered technologies helped launch the European age of exploration in the 1400s.

The triangular lateen sail caught wind that blew perpendicular to the ship, providing more maneuverability and the ability to sail against the wind.

Relocating the rudder to the back of the ship made it much easier to steer.

▲ The caravel was perfect for exploration. These small ships ranged from 70 to 90 feet (23 to 27 m). They were highly maneuverable and very fast. Their smaller size enabled them to sail along shallow coastlines and explore up rivers much farther than other ships.

▲ The astrolabe helped sailors stay on course by using the position of the sun and stars to determine time, direction, and latitude.

◀ The compass was invented by the Chinese. Made using a lodestone, it would always point to magnetic north.

Analyzing VISUALS

1. **Explaining** How did lateen sails improve navigation?
2. **Making Inferences** How would knowing the time help sailors navigate?

and queens with a new source of wealth they could tax. They used their armies to open up and protect trade **routes** and to enforce uniform trade laws and a common currency within their kingdoms.

The revenue from trade meant rulers in western Europe did not have to rely as much upon the nobility for support. Increasingly, they unified their kingdoms and created strong central governments. By the mid-1400s, four strong states—Portugal, Spain, England, and France—had emerged. Starting with Portugal in the early 1400s, all four began financing exploration in the hope of expanding their trade by finding a new route to Asia.

Scientific Advances

The political and economic changes that encouraged western Europeans to explore the world would not have mattered had they not had the technology necessary to launch their expeditions. In order to find a water route to Asia, western Europeans needed navigational instruments and ships capable of long-distance travel. Fortunately, at about the same time that the new, unified kingdoms were emerging in western Europe, an intellectual revolution known as the Renaissance began as well. It quickly led to new scientific and technological advances.

Lasting from about 1350 to 1600, the Renaissance marked an artistic flowering and a rebirth of interest in ancient Greece and Rome. European scholars rediscovered the works of ancient poets, philosophers, geographers, and mathematicians. In their quest for learning, they also read the teachings of Arab scholars.

The Renaissance started with a renewed interest in the past, but it quickly led to a renewed commitment to reason, which later helped trigger a scientific revolution.

Teach

R Reading Strategy

Questioning Explain to students that they can check their own comprehension by formulating questions about what they have read. If they do not understand an important idea, they will need to reread, review, or read on to clarify what is unclear. **BL** **ELL**

D Differentiated Instruction

Kinesthetic Have students choose a technological advancement mentioned in the section and create a display showing how the technology worked and how it was used. **OL**

Analyzing VISUALS

Answers:

1. They caught winds blowing perpendicular to the ship allowing more maneuverability and sailing against the wind.
2. It could help determine how far the ship had traveled and its location.

Hands-On Chapter Project Step 2

Establishing a Colony in North America

Step 2: Planning the Initial Voyage

Directions Returning to their groups, students should use library or Internet resources and their textbook to find out what types of sailing ships were available by 1610 and then select a model. Then, based on the passenger and cargo capacity of their chosen ship model, each group should make a table that includes the following information: starting date of the voyage—remind students that they probably do not want to arrive too much before or after planting season unless they can devise other sources of food; the duration of the voyage; when they plan to arrive; the total number of colonists making the voyage; and the type and quantity of resources they will need during the voyage and for a time after they have arrived. Remind students that they need to deduct the number of crew from the total number of passengers a ship can carry and that the total weight of the goods they want to bring cannot exceed the cargo capacity of the ship but must provide for all the colonists.

Putting It Together Have volunteers from each group explain why they included some of the specific materials, foods, weapons, tools, or resources they listed in their table. Have groups adjust their lists of resources based on the discussion with the other groups. **OL**

(Chapter Project continued in Section 3, page 25)

C Critical Thinking

Identifying Central Issues
Point out to students the importance of the caravel at this time. **Ask:** Why was the development of the caravel so important in the development of European exploration? *(It was large enough to carry 130 tons of cargo, enabling Europeans to make lengthy journeys. The ship needed little water to sail which allowed it to sail close to shore, and was small enough so that it could be beached for repairs with relative ease.)* **BL**

Reading Check

Answer:
Kingdoms centralized and developed enough wealth to finance expeditions, and new technologies, such as the astrolabe, compass, and caravel, were found or developed that enabled ships to make long voyages.

By studying Arab texts, western Europeans **acquired** the knowledge of a key navigational instrument, the **astrolabe**—a device invented by the ancient Greeks and refined by Arab navigators. An astrolabe uses the position of the sun to determine direction, latitude, and local time. Europeans also acquired the compass from Arab traders. Invented in China, the compass reliably shows the direction of magnetic north.

Navigational tools were vital to exploration, but the most important requirement was a ship capable of long-distance travel. Late in the 1400s, European shipwrights began to outfit ships with triangular-shaped lateen sails perfected by Arab traders. These sails made it possible for ships to sail against the wind. Shipwrights also began using multiple masts with several smaller sails hoisted one above the other, which made the ships travel much faster. They also moved the rudder from the side to the stern, making ships easier to steer.

C In the 1400s a Portuguese ship called the caravel incorporated all of these improvements. A **caravel** was a small vessel capable of carrying about 130 tons (118 t) of cargo. A caravel needed little water to sail, so it allowed explorers to venture up shallow inlets and to beach their ships to make repairs.

Portuguese Exploration

Sailing their caravels, Portuguese explorers became the first Europeans to search for a sea route to Asia. In 1419 Prince Henry of Portugal, known as **Henry the Navigator,** set up a center for astronomical and geographical studies at Sagres on Portugal's southwestern tip. He invited mapmakers, astronomers, and shipbuilders from throughout the Mediterranean world to come there to study and plan voyages of exploration.

In 1420 Portuguese explorers began mapping Africa's west coast. In 1488 a Portuguese ship commanded by Bartholomeu Dias reached the southern tip of Africa. A decade later, four ships commanded by Vasco da Gama sailed from Portugal, rounded Africa, and reached the southwest coast of India. The long-sought water route to eastern Asia had been found.

Reading Check **Examining** What developments made it possible for Europeans to begin exploring the world?

African Cultures

MAIN Idea Three great empires arose in West Africa and prospered from the gold trade.

HISTORY AND YOU What are some of the valuable things countries trade today? Read how trade influenced the rise and fall of African states.

Three great empires arose in West Africa between the 400s and 1400s. All three gained wealth and power by controlling the trade in gold and salt. Between the A.D. third and fifth centuries, Arab merchants began using camels to transport salt, gold, ivory, ostrich feathers, and furs from regions south of the Sahara to North Africa. Around the northern and southern boundaries of the Sahara, large trading settlements developed. Ideas, as well as goods, traveled the African trade routes. The Muslim nomads who controlled the caravans spread Islam into West Africa as well.

The Empires of West Africa

In the A.D. 400s the empire of Ghana emerged. Located between the salt mines of the Sahara and the gold mines to the south, Ghana prospered by taxing trade. Ghana became a Muslim kingdom in the 1100s, but frequent wars with the Muslims of the Sahara took their toll. Equally damaging was a decline in food production. Intensive cultivation had left Ghana's land exhausted and its farmers unable to feed its people. At the same time, new gold mines opened to the east. Trade routes to these mines bypassed Ghana and, by the early 1200s, the empire collapsed.

East of Ghana the empire of Mali arose. Mali also built its wealth and power by controlling the salt and gold trade. By the mid-1300s, Mali had extended eastward along the Niger River past the trading center of Timbuktu and westward to the Atlantic Ocean. Although the rulers and merchants of Mali adopted Islam, many of the people clung to their traditional belief in "spirits of the land," who they thought ensured the growth of their crops.

Mali reached its peak in the 1300s under the leadership of Mansa Musa. By that time, the opening of new gold mines had shifted the trade routes farther east and helped make Timbuktu a great center of trade and Muslim scholarship.

Additional Support

Activity: Interdisciplinary Connection

Performing Arts Have students research the influence of African music and dance on American music and dance. **Ask:** What influence has African music and dance had on American music and dance? Encourage students to learn about traditional African musical instruments and styles. Also suggest that students explore African music and dance through live and recorded performances. **OL**

NATIONAL GEOGRAPHIC Portuguese Exploration and African Empires, c. 1450

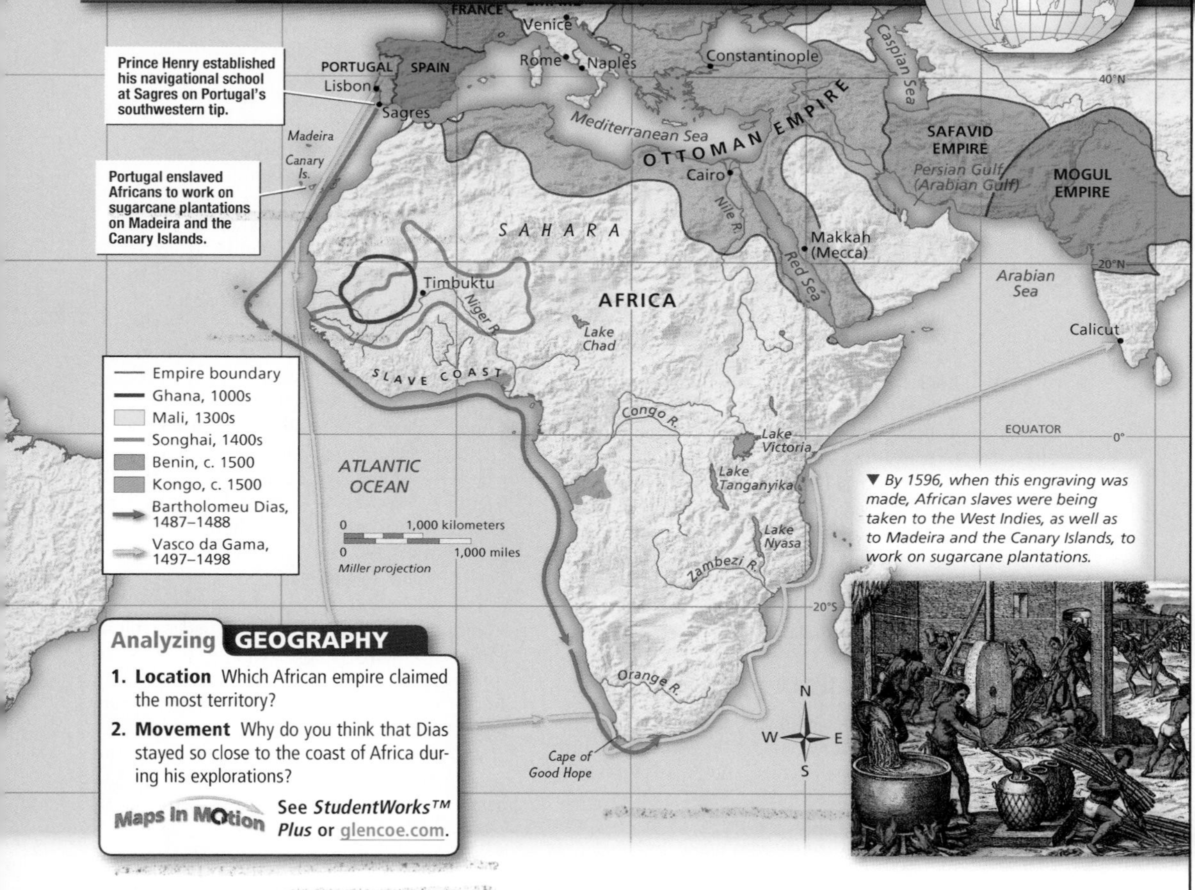

▼ *By 1596, when this engraving was made, African slaves were being taken to the West Indies, as well as to Madeira and the Canary Islands, to work on sugarcane plantations.*

Analyzing GEOGRAPHY

1. **Location** Which African empire claimed the most territory?
2. **Movement** Why do you think that Dias stayed so close to the coast of Africa during his explorations?

Maps in MOtion See *StudentWorks™ Plus* or glencoe.com.

Along the Niger River, the empire of Songhai emerged. When Mali began to decline, the ruler of Songhai, Sonni Ali, seized Timbuktu in 1468. He then pushed north into the Sahara and south along the Niger River. According to legend, Sonni Ali's army never lost a battle. Songhai remained a powerful empire until 1591, when Moroccan troops shattered its army.

Slavery and Sugar

As in other parts of the world, slavery existed in African society. Most of the people enslaved in African societies had been captured in war. Most African societies would either ransom captives back to their people or absorb them into their own society. West African slavery began to change with the arrival of Arab traders, who exchanged horses, cotton, and other goods for enslaved people.

Sugar growers from Spain and Portugal also sought enslaved Africans. In the 1400s Spain and Portugal established sugarcane plantations on the Canary and Madeira Islands. The climate and soil there were favorable for growing sugarcane, a crop that requires much manual **labor.** Sugarcane must be chopped with heavy knives. Sugar growers brought in enslaved Africans to do the work. **R**

Reading Check **Analyzing** Why did Europeans begin to acquire enslaved Africans?

R Reading Strategy

Academic Vocabulary Have students locate and then read the sentence that includes the academic vocabulary term *labor*. **Ask:** What is a synonym for the word *labor*? Invite volunteers to use the word *labor* in a sentence of their own. **BL** **ELL**

Analyzing GEOGRAPHY

Answers:

1. Songhai
2. Since no European had been that far down the African coast before and there were no maps, Dias probably did not want to venture too far from land.

Reading Check

Answer:
They began to grow sugarcane, a crop that required massive numbers of workers to produce.

Additional Support

Activity: Technology Connection

Using Geography Skills Have students locate Sagres on the map on this page. This is the site where Prince Henry the Navigator established the headquarters for his school of navigation. Scholars came to the school to teach and study. Captains of successful voyages brought back nautical knowledge and taught of the Atlantic currents, wind systems, and cartography. **Ask:** Why do you think Henry established his school at this point? Then ask: Why do you think that the Portuguese began their explorations down the coast of Africa and not across the Atlantic Ocean? *(The coast of Africa was close to Portugal, and it was safer to explore along a coast, close to shore, rather than to set off across an ocean when no one knew how wide it was.)*

Have students work in groups to research the voyages of discovery sponsored by Henry. Students should prepare a brief narrative of a voyage of discovery, and how technology made the voyage possible. **OL**

R Reading Strategy

Activating Prior Knowledge

Before students begin to acquire new information, prepare them by bringing to mind what they already know about Christopher Columbus. **Ask:** How did Columbus pay for his explorations? What was the goal of his first exploration? How many voyages did he make? What were some effects of his "discoveries"? Use these questions to encourage students to think about the topic and share ideas. As they read the section, have them locate the answers to these and other questions. BL

C Critical Thinking

Identifying Points of View

Ask students to express their opinion about who "discovered" America. Have them discuss the appropriateness of the word *discovered* in this context. **Ask:** Is it always wrong to use that word, or does it depend on a particular point of view? *(Answers will vary; accept all reasoned responses.)* OL

Exploring America

R **MAIN Idea** Spain led in the early European exploration and colonization of the Americas.

HISTORY AND YOU Do you know how your community got its name? Read to find out how the names for Florida and the Pacific Ocean came about.

NB:

By the 1400s, most educated Europeans knew that the world was round. On European maps of the time, only the Mediterranean, Europe, the Middle East, and Africa's northern coast were shown in any detail. At that time, Europeans rediscovered the works of Claudius Ptolemy, written in the A.D. 100s. His *Geography* became very influential. His basic system of lines of latitude and longitude is still used today.

European mariners also consulted the work of a twelfth-century Arab geographer named al-Idrisi. In 1154 al-Idrisi published a geographical survey of as much of the world as was then known to Europeans and Arabs. By studying the maps of Ptolemy and al-Idrisi, Western mariners finally obtained a reliable idea of the geography of the eastern African coast and the Indian Ocean.

Spain Claims America

Despite its usefulness, Ptolemy's *Geography* seriously underestimated the size of the earth. Basing his own calculations on Ptolemy's, Italian mariner Christopher Columbus predicted with wild optimism that "the end of Spain and the beginning of India are not far apart."

Columbus needed financial backing to make a voyage across the Atlantic to Asia. For six years he tried to persuade various European rulers to fund his expedition. Finally, in 1492, Spain's King Ferdinand and Queen Isabella agreed to finance his venture.

C Columbus and his three ships—the *Niña*, the *Pinta*, and the *Santa Maria*—left Spain in August 1492. He sailed westward across the uncharted Atlantic until he reached the Bahamas in October. He probably landed on present-day San Salvador Island. There, Columbus encountered the Taino people. He called them "Indians" because he thought he had reached the fabled Indies. He then headed farther into the Caribbean, searching for gold. He found the islands of Cuba and Hispaniola.

In March 1493 Columbus made a triumphant return to Spain with gold, parrots, spices, and Native Americans. Ferdinand and Isabella were pleased with Columbus's findings and prepared to finance further expeditions. However, they were now involved in a competition with Portugal, which had claimed control over the Atlantic route to Asia. To resolve the rivalry, the two nations appealed to the pope. In 1493 Pope Alexander VI established a line of demarcation, an imaginary line running down the middle of the Atlantic. Spain would control everything west of the line; Portugal would control everything to the east.

In 1494, in the Treaty of Tordesillas, the demarcation line was approved by both countries. The treaty confirmed Portugal's right to control the route around Africa to India. It also confirmed Spain's claim to most of the Americas.

In the meantime, Columbus headed back across the Atlantic with 17 ships and over 1,200 Spanish colonists. Later, they accused Columbus of misleading them with false promises of gold, and many of them headed back to Spain to complain.

Hoping to find more gold and save his reputation, Columbus began exploring Hispaniola. He discovered enough loose gold to make mining worthwhile. He then decided to enslave the local Taino people and force them to mine gold and plant crops.

In 1496 Columbus returned to Spain. In the meantime, his brother Bartholomew founded a town named Santo Domingo on the south coast of Hispaniola, closer to the gold mines. Santo Domingo became the first capital of Spain's empire in America. Columbus made two more trips to America, mapping part of the coastline of South America and Central America. He died without obtaining the riches he had hoped to find.

Naming America In 1499 an Italian named **Amerigo Vespucci,** sailing under the Spanish flag, repeated Columbus's attempt to sail west to Asia. Exploring the coast of South America, Vespucci, like Columbus, assumed he had reached outermost Asia. In 1501 he made another voyage, this time for Portugal. After sailing along the coast of South America, he realized that this landmass could not be part of Asia. In 1507 a German mapmaker proposed that the new continent be named *America* for "Amerigo, the discoverer."

Additional Support

Activity: Technology Connection

Longitude Explain to students that although people figured out how to determine latitude almost 1,000 years ago, longitude was a tougher problem to solve and no one really did so until the eighteenth century. **Ask:** Why was knowing longitude necessary, and how was the problem of determining longitude solved? Have students research the history of longitude and write a short report on the technology that was developed to help sailors determine their east-west position. OL

Turning Point

▶ *Although no images of Christopher Columbus exist from his lifetime, this painting from about 1525 is considered to be the closest likeness.*

▲ *The Landing of Columbus* was painted by American artist Albert Bierstadt in 1892, the year of the 400th anniversary of Columbus's arrival in North America. Note that the artist portrayed the indigenous people as shrouded in darkness and shadow, emerging to kneel worshipfully before the Europeans, who bring with them the "light" of civilization. Unfortunately, the arrival of Europeans did more to destroy the indigenous cultures than to enlighten them.

Columbus Arrives in America

Columbus's first voyage to the Americas was a major turning point in world history. For Europeans, it opened up new areas of exploration and discovery, and provided vast wealth through trade. The event was devastating, however, for native peoples of the Americas whose cultures were changed or destroyed by war, disease, and enslavement.

ANALYZING HISTORY Describe one positive and one negative effect of Columbus's voyage to the Americas.

Later Spanish Expeditions In 1513 the Spanish governor of Puerto Rico, Juan Ponce de León, sailed north. Legend has it that he was searching for a fountain that could magically restore youth. He never found the fabled fountain, but he did discover a land full of blooming wildflowers and fragrant plants. He claimed the area for Spain and named it *Florida*, which means "land of flowers."

Spanish explorers continued to search for a passage to China and India. In 1510 Vasco de Balboa, a planter from Hispaniola, founded a colony on the Isthmus of Panama. After hearing tales of a "south sea" that led to an empire of gold, he hacked his way across steamy, disease-ridden jungles and swamps until he reached the opposite coast. There, in 1513, Balboa became the first European to reach the Pacific coast of America.

D

In 1520 Ferdinand Magellan, a Portuguese mariner working for Spain, discovered the strait later named for him at the southern tip of South America. After navigating its stormy narrows, he sailed into the ocean Balboa had seen. Its waters seemed so calm that Magellan named it *Mare Pacificum*, Latin for "peaceful sea"—the Pacific Ocean. Although Magellan was killed in the Philippine Islands, his crew continued west, arriving in Spain in 1522. They became the first known people to **circumnavigate**, or sail around, the globe.

(C. 1480–1521)

Reading Check **Describing** What were the results of Columbus's voyages across the Atlantic?

D Differentiated Instruction

Visual/Spatial Have visual learners trace and label the voyages of Juan Ponce de León, Vasco de Balboa, and Ferdinand Magellan on a world map or on a globe using colored push pins. BL

Turning Point

Answer:
Student answers should provide examples based on the feature or the section content.

Reading Check

Answer:
Spain claimed most of Central and South America; Native Americans were conquered and enslaved or died of disease; other explorers came, such as Magellan who circumnavigated the globe. The pope established a line of demarcation, splitting the newly discovered territories between Spain and Portugal.

Extending the Content

Adventures and Consequences The consequences of the diseases Europeans unwittingly brought to the Americas were devastating to Native Americans. Some groups suffered a 90 percent population loss in the first century after European contact. This catastrophe reduced the labor supply available to Europeans in the Americas, who then turned to enslaving Africans. Thus, modern slavery in the Western Hemisphere is traceable in part to the Columbian Exchange.

Another adventurer seeking a route to India, Pedro Álvares Cabral, ended up landing along the coast of South America in present-day Brazil. One of the plants he transported back to Portugal was a hardwood tree known as brazilwood. The core of the tree produced bright red dye used by clothmakers. The color became favored among the wealthiest Europeans. The French especially valued the dye and French traders were soon competing with the Portuguese to supply the demand. Largely due to the brazilwood trade, the Portuguese government established permanent settlements in present-day Brazil to deter the French from making claims there.

W Writing Support

Expository Writing Have students select a person mentioned in this section and do research to write a biography of him or her. You may want to encourage students to work in groups to plan and write their biographies so that there is no duplication and then have students create a class booklet or a Web site titled *Biographies of Spanish America.* OL

New Spain

MAIN Idea After defeating the Aztec Empire, the Spanish established the colony of New Spain.

W

HISTORY AND YOU Have you seen unusual animals at the zoo? Read how one Spanish explorer went looking for gold but found only "shaggy cows."

In 1519 a Spaniard named **Hernán Cortés** sailed from Cuba to explore the Yucatán Peninsula with 11 ships, 550 men, and 16 horses. Soon after arriving, thousands of warriors attacked Cortés's party. Although outnumbered, the Spanish had superior weapons. Their swords, crossbows, guns, and cannons quickly killed more than 200 warriors. As a peace offering, the Native Americans gave Cortés 20 women, including Malinche, who helped translate for Cortés. He had her baptized and called her Doña Marina.

From local rulers, Cortés learned that the Aztec had conquered many people and were at war with others, including the powerful Tlaxcalan. Cortés wanted the Tlaxcalan to join him against the Aztec. His army helped him gain their support. The local people had never seen horses before. Their foaming muzzles and glistening armor astonished them. Equally amazing were the "shooting sparks" of the Spanish cannons. Impressed, the Tlaxcalan agreed to ally with Cortés against the Aztec.

Meanwhile, the Aztec emperor Montezuma was worried. He believed in a prophecy that Quetzalcóatl—a fair-skinned, bearded deity—would someday return to conquer the Aztec. Montezuma did not know if Cortés was Quetzalcóatl, but he sent envoys promising a yearly payment to the Spanish king if Cortés halted his advance. Cortés refused to stop.

With the Spanish and Tlaxcalan heading toward him, Montezuma tried to ambush them at the city of Cholula. Warned in advance, the Spanish struck first, killing over 6,000 Cholulans. Believing Cortés was unstoppable, Montezuma allowed the Spanish troops to enter Tenochtitlán peacefully.

Defeat of the Aztec

Sitting on an island in the center of a lake, the city of Tenochtitlán impressed the Spanish. Larger than most European cities, Tenochtitlán had more than 200,000 residents and an elaborate system of canals. In the central plaza, a large double pyramid and a huge rack displayed thousands of human skulls.

Surrounded by thousands of Aztec, Cortés decided to take Montezuma hostage. Montezuma did not resist. Following orders from Cortés, he stopped all human sacrifices and had statues of the Aztec gods replaced with Christian crosses and images of the Virgin Mary. Aztec priests were furious and organized a rebellion in early 1520. The battle raged for days before the Spanish retreated to Tlaxcala. Over 450 Spaniards and more than 4,000 Aztec had died, including Montezuma.

Meanwhile, smallpox erupted in the region, devastating the defenders of Tenochtitlán. As one Aztec recounted:

PRIMARY SOURCE

"While the Spaniards were in Tlaxcala, a great plague broke out here in Tenochtitlán. . . . Sores erupted on our faces, our breasts, our bellies; we were covered with agonizing sores from head to foot. The illness was so dreadful that no one could walk or move."

—from *The Broken Spears: The Aztec Account of the Conquest of Mexico*

In 1521 Cortés returned with reinforcements and destroyed Tenochtitlán. On its ruins, the Spanish built Mexico City, which became the capital of the colony of New Spain. Cortés then sent several expeditions to conquer the rest of Central America. The men who led these expeditions became known as **conquistadors,** or "conquerors."

New Explorations In 1526 Spanish explorer **Francisco Pizarro** reached Peru. Six years later he returned with a small band of infantry. With superior weapons, Pizarro's force plundered the wealthy Inca Empire.

The Spanish had heard tales of the Seven Golden Cities of Cíbola, rumored to exist north of New Spain. In 1540, hoping to find Cíbola, Francisco Vásquez de Coronado led an expedition northward and explored the region between the Colorado River and the Great Plains. Instead of cities of gold, however, Coronado found only windswept plains and "shaggy cows," as he described the buffalo.

Additional Support

Teacher Tip

Collaborative Learning This activity requires students to work individually and then with a partner and to complete several distinct steps. To provide extra support to English language learners, pair them with students who are proficient with reading in the English language.

Activity: Collaborative Learning

Using Think-Write-Pair-Share This strategy engages students in their subject matter through discussions. Have students think silently about what they know concerning the influence of the Spanish and French colonies in the Americas. Ask them to write down three to five influences these colonies had. Then have students pair up and share their ideas with a partner. Then conclude with a class share discussion.

Ask: What impact did the Spanish and French have in the Americas? *(Answers will vary, but should be supported by information from the text.)* OL

Spain's New World Empire, c. 1600

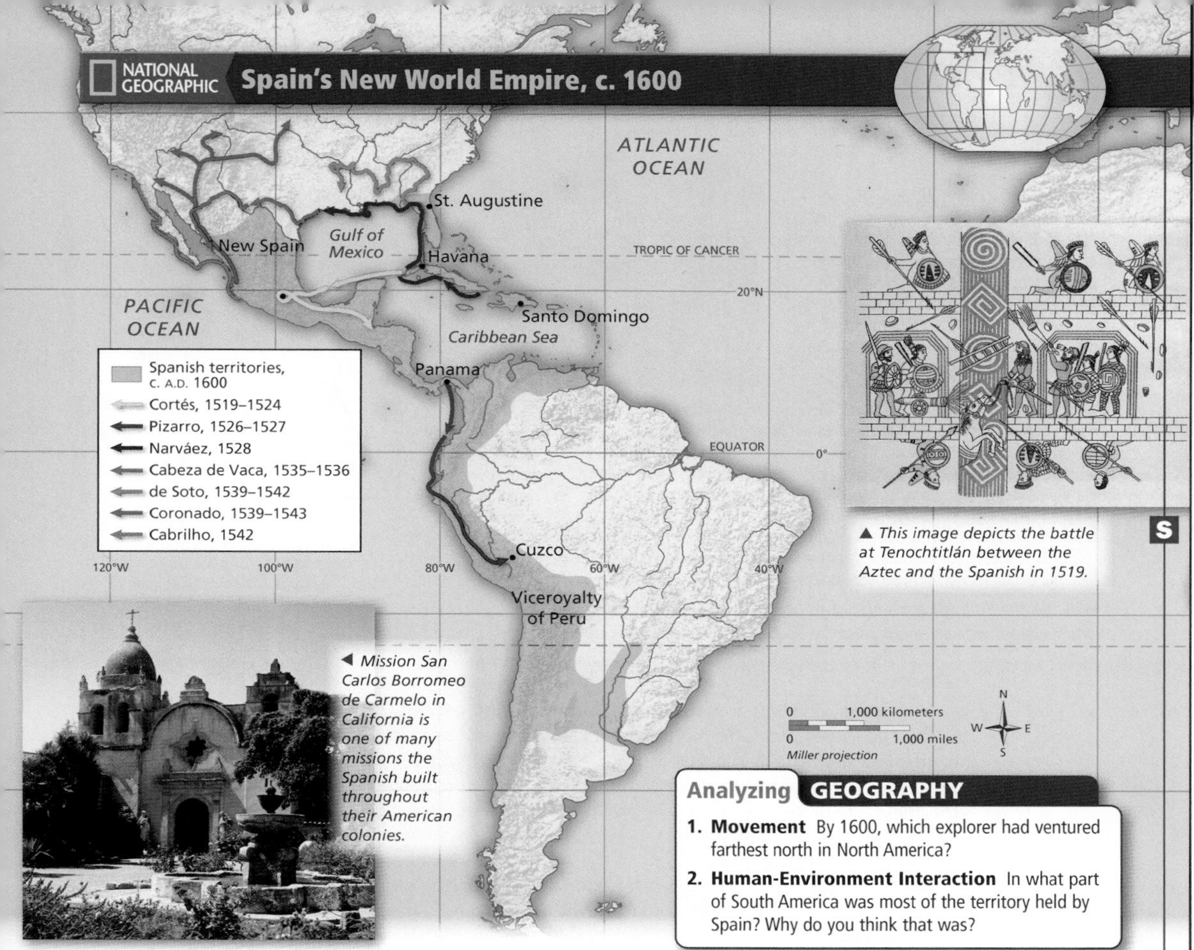

▲ *This image depicts the battle at Tenochtitlán between the Aztec and the Spanish in 1519.*

◀ *Mission San Carlos Borromeo de Carmelo in California is one of many missions the Spanish built throughout their American colonies.*

Analyzing GEOGRAPHY

1. **Movement** By 1600, which explorer had ventured farthest north in North America?
2. **Human-Environment Interaction** In what part of South America was most of the territory held by Spain? Why do you think that was?

Meanwhile, Hernando de Soto led an expedition into the region north of Florida, exploring parts of what are today North Carolina, Tennessee, Alabama, Arkansas, and Texas. As they crisscrossed the region, the Spanish killed many local people and raided their villages for supplies. De Soto became ill and died; soon after, his men abandoned the mission and headed home.

Settling the Southwest Because no gold or other wealth was found north of New Spain, Spanish settlement of the region was slow. It was not until 1598 that settlers, led by Juan de Oñate, pushed north of the Rio Grande. When they finally reached the Rio Grande, the survivors organized a feast to give thanks to God. This "Spanish Thanksgiving" is still celebrated each April in El Paso, Texas.

The Spanish gave the name New Mexico to the territory north of New Spain. Throughout the region, they built forts called presidios to protect settlers and serve as trading posts. Despite these efforts, few Spaniards settled in the harsh region. Instead, the Catholic Church began colonizing the Southwest.

In the 1600s and 1700s, Spanish priests built missions and spread the Christian faith among the Navajo and Pueblo peoples of the Southwest. Beginning in 1769, missionaries, led by Franciscan priest Junípero Serra, took control of California by establishing a chain of missions from San Diego to just north of San Francisco.

S Skill Practice

Using Geography Skills Have students trace the route of each explorer on the map and then use their own words to describe the places that person visited. **BL**

R Reading Strategy

Using Word Parts Write on the board the words *mission* and *missionaries*. Underline the common word part, *mission*, in both words. **Ask:** What do missionaries have to do with a mission? *(Missionaries are religious people who set up a* mission *to convert others to their beliefs.)* **BL** **ELL**

Analyzing GEOGRAPHY

Answers:
1. Coronado
2. the west coast; Answers may vary. Some students may suggest the location was related to the Spanish territorial rights under the line of demarcation.

Additional Support

Activity: Interdisciplinary Connection

Statistics Have interested students work together to create a fact or fiction survey based on the material in this section or in the chapter. Prepare copies of the survey and have each student obtain at least five completed surveys from friends and family members. Score the surveys and create a graph showing the results. Use the graph as the basis for a classroom discussion about the level of knowledge most Americans have about the exploration and settlement of the Americas. **AL**

R1 Reading Strategy

Summarizing Have students summarize the intended purpose of the *encomienda* system and how it led to the abuse of Native Americans. **OL**

R2 Reading Strategy

Reading Charts Have students study the pyramid chart of society in New Spain. **Ask:** What was the important criterion that determined into which level of colonial society you would be born? *(It depended on how recently one or both parents had lived in Spain.)* **OL**

People IN HISTORY

Answer:
The *encomienda* system gave the *encomenderos* official power and authority over Native Americans that they might not have had otherwise. Ending that control would help to end the abuses.

Reading Check

Answer:
They found silver in Mexico and then set up cattle ranches to feed the many mine workers.

People IN HISTORY

Bartolomé de Las Casas
1474–1566

In the years following the Spanish conquest, many people began to protest against the abuses of the *encomienda* system. Among them was Bartolomé de Las Casas, Bishop of Chiapas. In 1502 Las Casas traveled to Hispaniola and was horrified by what he saw. The Spanish tortured, burned, and cut off the hands and noses of Native Americans to force them to obey.

Las Casas maintained that the Church and the king had a duty to protect Native Americans. In this view, he had the support of the pope who declared the Native Americans should not be enslaved. Las Casas wrote several books that were widely read in Europe, describing the treatment of the Native Americans. In response, the Spanish government stopped granting *encomiendas* and banned Native American slavery. Slowly, as *encomiendos* died without heirs, the *encomienda* system came to an end. However, Las Casas died outraged. "Surely," he wrote in his will, "God will wreak his fury and anger against Spain some day for the unjust wars waged against American Indians."

Why did the Spanish government think that ending the encomienda system was a way to stop the abuses of Native Americans?

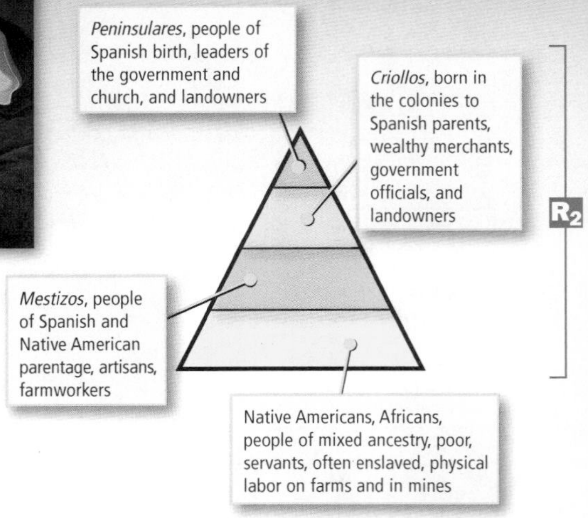

The priests and missionaries in California forced the mostly nomadic Native Americans to live in villages near the missions. In New Mexico, the priests and missionaries adapted their efforts to fit into the lifestyle of the Pueblo peoples. They built churches near where the Pueblo people lived and farmed.

The Spanish priests tried to end traditional Pueblo religious practices that conflicted with Catholic beliefs. Some priests beat and whipped Native Americans who defied them. In response, a Pueblo religious leader named Popé organized an uprising in 1680. Some 17,000 warriors destroyed most of the missions in New Mexico. It took the Spanish more than a decade to regain control of the region.

Spanish American Society

R1 Cortés rewarded his men by giving them control of some towns in the Aztec Empire. This became the ***encomienda*** system. Each Spaniard deserving a reward was made an *encomendero,* or commissioner, and was given control over a group of villages. Villagers paid their *encomendero* a share of the harvest and also worked part-time for him for free. The *encomendero* was supposed to protect them and convert them to Christianity. Sadly, many *encomenderos* abused their power and worked the Native Americans to death.

New Spain had a highly structured society based on birth, income, and education. At the top were *peninsulares,* those who were born in Spain. They held the top government and church positions. Next were the *criollos*—those born in the colonies to Spanish parents. Many *criollos* were wealthy, but they held slightly lesser positions. Next came the *mestizos,* people of Spanish and Native American parentage. Their social status could vary, but most were poor and relegated to the lowest class, along with people of other mixed ancestry, Native Americans, and Africans. These people provided most of the labor for New Spain's farms, mines, and ranches.

In the 1540s the Spanish discovered silver ore in northern Mexico and set up mining camps using Native American labor. Work in the dark, damp mineshafts was very difficult. Explosions and cave-ins killed many miners. Others died from exhaustion. To feed the miners, the Spanish established large cattle ranches called haciendas.

Reading Check **Describing** Why did the Spanish set up mines and cattle ranches in Mexico?

Extending the Content

Background Las Casas was following his own conscience in his protests against the *encomienda* system but he also was carrying out the dictates of his superior, the pope. Pope Paul III had declared, "The said Indians are by no means to be deprived of their liberty or the possessions of their property…nor should they in any way be enslaved." Since the pope had made this declaration, it was the official policy of the Roman Catholic Church. **Ask:** How did the Catholic Church take moral leadership over the treatment of Native Americans? *(Answers will vary, but students will probably recognize that the Church did not approve of how the Spanish treated Native Americans, at least under the* encomienda *system and was powerful enough to be taken seriously.)*

New France

MAIN Idea France claimed a vast territory in North America, but its colony had a small French population.

HISTORY AND YOU Did you know that one-third of Canadians speak French? Read to learn about French settlements in North America.

In 1524 King Francis I of France sent Giovanni da Verrazano to find the Northwest Passage—the hoped-for northern route through North America to the Pacific. Verrazano explored the Atlantic coast from North Carolina to Newfoundland, but found no sign of a passage. Ten years later, Jacques Cartier made three trips to North America, exploring and mapping the St. Lawrence River.

In 1602 King Henry IV of France authorized a group of French merchants to establish a colony. The merchants hired **Samuel de Champlain** to help them. In 1608 Champlain founded Quebec, which became the capital of the colony of New France.

The company that founded New France wanted to make money from the fur trade, so they did not need settlers to clear the land and build farms. As a result, the colony grew slowly. Most of the fur traders preferred to make their homes among the Native Americans with whom they traded. Jesuit missionaries, known as "black robes," likewise lived among the local people. In 1663 King Louis XIV made New France a royal colony and sent 4,000 new settlers. By the 1670s, New France had nearly 7,000 people, and by 1760, more than 60,000.

As their colony grew, the French continued to explore North America. In 1673 a fur trader named Louis Joliet and a Jesuit priest named Jacques Marquette began searching for a waterway the Algonquian people called the "big river." The two men finally found it—the Mississippi. In 1682 René-Robert Cavelier de La Salle followed the Mississippi all the way to the Gulf of Mexico, becoming the first European to do so. He claimed the region for France and named the territory Louisiana in honor of Louis XIV.

The geography of the lower Mississippi hindered settlement. The oppressive heat caused food to spoil quickly and mosquito-filled swamps made the climate unhealthy. The first permanent French settlement in the region was Biloxi, founded in 1699. Mobile, New Orleans, and several forts followed. The French in Louisiana realized that the crops that could be grown there, such as sugar, rice, and indigo, required abundant labor. As a result, they began importing enslaved Africans to work on their plantations.

The Spanish had always been concerned about the French in North America. Indeed, they founded St. Augustine, Florida, in 1565 to counter French settlement attempts in what became the Carolinas. St. Augustine prospered and became the first permanent town established by Europeans in what is today the United States. The arrival of the French at the mouth of the Mississippi River convinced the Spanish in 1690 to build their first mission in East Texas, San Francisco de los Tejas. Spanish settlers arrived in 1716 to secure Spain's claim and block French expansion in the area.

Reading Check **Explaining** Why do you think the French established forts and settlements in Louisiana?

Section 2 REVIEW

Vocabulary

1. **Explain** the significance of: astrolabe, caravel, Henry the Navigator, Amerigo Vespucci, circumnavigate, Hernán Cortés, conquistador, Francisco Pizarro, *encomienda*, Samuel de Champlain.

Main Ideas

2. **Examining** What led Europeans to begin exploring in the 1400s?

3. **Identifying** On what did African kingdoms base their wealth and power?

4. **Explaining** How did the Americas receive that name?

5. **Organizing** Use a graphic organizer similar to the one below to list characteristics of Spanish colonies in the Americas.

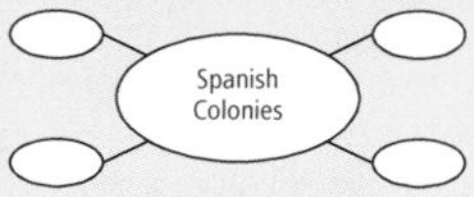

6. **Explaining** Why was New France so sparsely populated?

Critical Thinking

7. **Big Ideas** How did scientific advancements affect geographic knowledge?

8. **Analyzing Visuals** Study the photograph of the mission on page 21. How did the Catholic Church contribute to the Spanish settlement in North America?

Writing About History

9. **Descriptive Writing** Take on the role of a sailor on Columbus's first voyage to the Americas. Write a journal entry about the Caribbean islands you explore.

History ONLINE
Study Central™ To review this section, go to glencoe.com and click on Study Central.

Reading Check

Answer:
Answers may include to claim and establish control of the Mississippi river; to protect claims from the Spanish

Assess

History ONLINE

Study Central™ provides summaries, interactive games, and online graphic organizers to help students review content.

Close

Summarizing Ask: What were the effects of European exploration on Native Americans, Africans, and Europeans? *(Native Americans died in the millions from disease, war, and enslavement. Africans prospered through trade, but also suffered mass enslavement by Europeans. Europeans suffered from diseases native to the Americas, but also benefited from the conquest of Native American cultures and their wealth.)* **OL**

Section 2 REVIEW

Answers

1. All definitions can be found in the section and the Glossary.
2. European rulers desired their own trade with Asia to bypass the high costs charged by Muslim and Italian traders. Technological advances and the rise of strong and wealthy rulers made exploration possible.
3. the gold and salt trades
4. Vespucci suggested that the newly discovered land was not part of Asia. In 1507, a German mapmaker proposed that the new continent be named *America*, for "Amerigo, the discoverer."
5. built forts called *presidios*; Catholic Church a primary force that built missions and spread the Christian faith; highly structured society; encomienda system used to organize and govern territory
6. The backers of the colony wanted to focus on the fur trade. So most people were there for the furs and spent their time in the forests trapping with Native Americans, not building and living in settlements.
7. made it possible for explorers to map the coastline of Africa, travel to Asia and the Americas, and circumnavigate the globe
8. They established missions to convert Native Americans to Catholicism and teach European culture, and they also enslaved and controlled the local native people.
9. Students' journal entries will vary but should include a thoughtful discussion of what Columbus and his men might have seen in the Caribbean on the first voyage.

Focus

Bellringer

Daily Focus Transparency 1-3

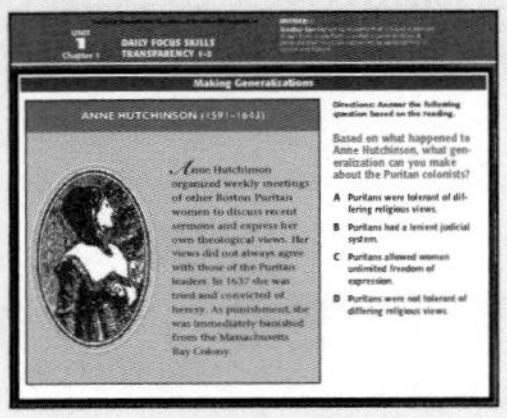

Guide to Reading

Answers:
food shortages, lawlessness, sickness, the location was low, swampy, colonists did not know how to hunt, fish, or farm, some would not do menial labor, there was a lack of consensus and leadership

Section Spotlight Video

To generate student interest and provide a springboard for class discussion, access the Chapter 1, Section 3 video at glencoe.com or on the video DVD.

Resource Manager

Section 3

Section Audio Spotlight Video

Founding the Thirteen Colonies

Guide to Reading

Big Ideas
Geography and History The headright system provided English settlers with a new way to acquire more land.

Content Vocabulary
- joint-stock company *(p. 25)*
- privateer *(p. 26)*
- headright *(p. 27)*
- proprietary colony *(p. 27)*
- heretic *(p. 29)*

Academic Vocabulary
- migration *(p. 24)*
- grant *(p. 26)*

People and Events to Identify
- Jamestown *(p. 26)*
- Powhatan Confederacy *(p. 26)*
- John Winthrop *(p. 29)*
- Roger Williams *(p. 30)*
- Anne Hutchinson *(p. 30)*
- Henry Hudson *(p. 31)*

Reading Strategy
Organizing Complete a graphic organizer similar to the one below by listing the problems faced by the Jamestown colonists.

England was late to establish colonies in the Americas. Joint-stock companies established the first English colonies with the intention of making profits. Many settlers, however, went to the Americas to escape religious persecution.

England's First Colonies

MAIN Idea While Spain was establishing an overseas empire in the 1500s, England was distracted by problems at home.

HISTORY AND YOU Religion and politics were inseparable in the 1500s and led to many conflicts. Can you think of some religious-based conflicts in the world today? Read on to learn how the Reformation divided Europe.

The first English expedition to arrive in North America was led by Italian navigator John Cabot. In 1497 Cabot sailed to present-day Nova Scotia, hoping to discover a sea route through North America to China. For the next 80 years, the English made no effort to settle in America. Cabot had found no riches that would spur **migration.** In the late 1500s, religious, economic, and political changes encouraged the founding of the first English colonies in North America.

The Protestant Reformation

At the time Cabot sailed to America, most of western Europe was Roman Catholic. This unity began to break apart in 1517, when a German monk named Martin Luther published an attack on the Church, accusing it of corruption. Luther's call for reform launched the Protestant Reformation. The Catholic Church excommunicated, or expelled, Luther, but his ideas continued to spread.

In England the rebellion against Catholicism began in 1527, when Henry VIII asked the pope to annul his marriage to Catherine of Aragon. The pope refused. Infuriated, Henry broke with the Church and declared himself the head of England's church. He then arranged his own divorce. The new church, the Anglican Church, was Protestant, but its organization and rituals retained many Catholic elements.

Some English people supported the new church, but others wanted to go further. Puritans wanted to "purify" the Anglican Church of any remaining Catholic elements. They also disapproved of the monarch having the power to appoint bishops to run the church. In their view, each congregation should elect its own leaders.

The Puritan cause suffered a serious setback in 1603, when James I became king. Although King James was Protestant, he refused to tolerate any changes in the structure of the Anglican Church. James's

R Reading Strategies	C Critical Thinking	D Differentiated Instruction	W Writing Support	S Skill Practice
Teacher Edition • Sequencing, p. 26 • Using Word Parts, p. 27 • Analyzing Text Structure, p. 29 • Predicting, p. 31 **Additional Resources** • American Lit. Read., URB p. 13 • Guid. Read Act, URB p. 50	**Teacher Edition** • Making Inferences, p. 30 **Additional Resources** • History Simulations and Prob. Solv. Act., URB p. 9 • Quizzes/Tests, p. 7	**Teacher Edition** • EL/Special Ed., p. 27 • EL, p. 32 **Additional Resources** • American Art and Music Act., URB p. 39 • Diff. Inst. Act., URB p. 23	**Teacher Edition** • Expository, pp. 25, 29 • Descriptive Writing, p. 31	**Teacher Edition** • Using Geo. Skills, pp. 28, 32 **Additional Resources** • Time Line Act., URB p. 33 • RENTG, p. 8

PRIMARY SOURCE

The Causes of English Settlement in America

Three major factors led the English to found colonies in the Americas.

RELIGIOUS PERSECUTION

◀ English Puritans and non-Anglicans faced prejudice and legal harassment. Many fled to North America where they could worship as they wished.

ECONOMIC CHANGES

▲ The enclosure movement displaced thousands of tenant farmers. Many English leaders thought that having colonies would help absorb England's unemployed people.

RIVALRY WITH SPAIN

◀ The Protestant English wanted to share the riches of the Americas that Catholic Spain was monopolizing.

Analyzing VISUALS

1. **Determining Cause and Effect** How did England's rivalry with Spain drive the nation to establish new colonies in North America?
2. **Explaining** Why did religious groups found colonies?

refusal to reform the Anglican Church eventually caused many Puritans to leave England—some for America.

Economic Changes in England

Economic changes in England also created a motive to found colonies in America. Traditionally, English nobles who owned large estates rented their land to tenant farmers. In the 1500s, however, a large market for wool cloth developed. Landowners discovered they could make more money by evicting their tenants, enclosing the land, and raising sheep. This left thousands of tenant farmers homeless and destitute. At the same time, England's population was rising rapidly in the 1500s. Many English leaders concluded that colonies were necessary to provide land and work to the kingdom's rising number of unemployed.

The wool market had another impact on American settlement. To market their woolen goods, some merchants began organizing **joint-stock companies**. By joining together and issuing stock, merchants were able to raise large amounts of money to fund major projects. Joint-stock companies could also afford the cost of setting up colonies in other parts of the world.

England Returns to America

Hoping to share in the lucrative trade with Asia, English merchants also began searching for a water route through North America to Asia. England's new interest in the Americas contributed to its growing rivalry with Spain. England was the leading Protestant power, while Spain remained strongly Catholic.

Teach

W Writing Support

Expository Writing Ask students to take on the role of an ordinary English person in the early period of North American colonization and, based on the information about economic and religious issues in England, write a letter to a family member explaining their reasons for emigrating to the colonies. OL

Analyzing VISUALS

Answers:

1. Because England wanted greater riches to compete with Spain and also naval bases from which to attack Spanish shipping, England was driven to establish new colonies in North America.
2. They wanted to emigrate so that they could worship as they wished.

Hands-On Chapter Project Step 3

Establishing a Colony in North America

Step 3: Governing the Colony in North America

Directions Returning to their groups, students should review their plans, lists, and map. Using their textbook as a reference, have groups agree on the purpose of their colonies—for example, do they want to achieve religious freedom or to make money? They should also determine the type of colony—will it be a joint-stock venture, a proprietary colony, or a royal colony?

Then using the textbook and reference resources, have students create a governing document for their colony, similar to the *Mayflower Compact*. As they work to draft their document, students should consider the purpose and type of colony, some basic aspects of English law, ideas about land distribution, as well as the circumstances and the needs of an isolated community.

Putting It Together Have volunteers from each group present the group's governing document to the class. Discuss the strengths and weaknesses of each document as a class. Have groups revise their governing documents, as necessary, based on ideas that came up during the class discussion. OL

(Chapter Project continued in Section 4, p. 35)

R Reading Strategy

Sequencing Information

Have students create a diagram or time line of English monarchs, from Henry VIII through George II. Final products should include the start and end dates of each reign and the North American colonies established during each monarch's rule. BL

People IN HISTORY

In 1614, John Smith continued his adventures, exploring and mapping for the Plymouth Company the region he named New England.

Answer:

He led the Jamestown settlement successfully and established a foothold for England in North America. He promoted colonization of Virginia when he returned to England.

People IN HISTORY

Captain John Smith
1580–1631

John Smith had a lifetime of adventures before he set foot in Virginia. Smith began his career as a soldier, fighting for the Dutch in their war against Spain. He later fought with the Austrians against the Turks in eastern Europe. Smith was a prolific writer, and many details about his life come from his own accounts.

After returning to England, Smith joined the expedition that settled Jamestown. He quickly began exploring the region and trading with the local Native Americans. It was on one such expedition that Smith later claimed he was taken prisoner by Chief Powhatan and that Pocahontas saved him from being killed. After Smith became president of Jamestown in 1608, he instituted rigid discipline. He required all members of the colony to work, declaring "he that does not worke shall not eate." Smith's rules led to fewer deaths. In 1609 he returned to England, where he continued to promote colonization of Virginia.

How did Smith contribute to English efforts to colonize America?

▲ *Captain John Smith helped save early Jamestown by trading with the local Native Americans.*

When the Spanish tried to suppress Protestantism in the Netherlands, the Dutch rebelled. To help the Dutch, Queen Elizabeth I allowed English **privateers** to attack Spanish ships. Privateers are privately owned ships licensed by the government to attack ships of other countries.

To attack Spanish ships in the Caribbean, Elizabeth's advisers recommended that England establish outposts in the Americas. Elizabeth agreed, but the early attempts at colonization were not promising.

R In 1578 and 1583 Sir Humphrey Gilbert tried to create a colony but failed. After Gilbert was lost at sea, his half-brother, Walter Raleigh, sent two ships to scout the American coastline. Along the outer banks of what is now North Carolina, the ships found an island the Native Americans called Roanoke. Impressed, Queen Elizabeth knighted Raleigh, who had named the colony Virginia—in honor of Elizabeth, "the Virgin Queen."

Raleigh sent settlers to Roanoke Island twice, once in 1585 and again in 1587. The first group returned to England after a difficult winter. The fate of the second group is unknown. When English ships arrived in 1590, the colonists had vanished.

"lost Colony of Roanoke"

The Chesapeake Colonies

In 1606 King James I **granted** a charter to a new company—the Virginia Company—giving its stockholders permission to start colonies in Virginia. The company sent three small ships and 144 men to Virginia in late 1606. After a difficult trip, the ships sailed into Chesapeake Bay in the spring of 1607. The 104 men who survived the trip founded a settlement on the James River, which they named **Jamestown** in honor of their king.

Early Troubles Most of Jamestown's colonists were townspeople who knew little about living in the woods. They did not know how to fish or hunt for food, nor could they raise livestock or cultivate crops. Furthermore, the "gentlemen" among them refused to do manual labor. Lawlessness, sickness, and food shortages were the result. In late 1607, with winter approaching and the colony short of food, Captain John Smith began bartering goods for food with the **Powhatan Confederacy.** This trade helped the colony survive the next two winters.

To entice settlers, the company offered free land to anyone who worked for the colony for

Additional Support

Extending the Content

Until 1996 the exact location of Jamestown's fort was not known. From written descriptions, archaeologists knew that the fort lay along the James River, but they did not know its precise location. The only drawing of the fort that existed was a rough sketch made in 1608 by Pedro Zuniga, a Spanish spy. Researchers believed that remains of the fort had been destroyed by erosion along the banks of the James as it altered its course over time. However, in 1996, archaeologists finally discovered evidence of a fortification that matched historical descriptions of the structure.

Tell students that the colony at Roanoke Island is often referred to as "the Lost Colony." What happened to the colonists there remains one of the great mysteries of history. Ask students to speculate about what might have happened to colony members. Encourage interested students to do additional research to find out about the various theories suggested by historians about the colonists' fate. OL seven years. The offer produced results, and 400 new settlers arrived in Jamestown in 1609. The arrival of so many settlers created a crisis. There was not enough food, nor could enough be grown before winter. As winter neared, settlers began raiding the food stores of local Native Americans. In response, Powhatan cut off trade with the colonists, and his warriors began attacking settlers.

The winter of 1609–1610 became known as the "starving time." In their hunger, colonists resorted to extreme measures. George Percy, an early settler, described their desperation:

PRIMARY SOURCE

"Having fed upon horses and other beasts as long as they lasted, we were glad to make shift with vermin, as dogs, cats, rats, and mice. . . . Nothing was spared to maintain life and to do those things which seem incredible, as to dig up corpses out of graves and to eat them."

—from *The Jamestown Adventure*

D

By spring, only 60 settlers were still alive. The survivors abandoned Jamestown and headed downriver. On the way, they met three English ships bringing supplies, 150 more settlers, and the new governor, Lord De La Warr, who convinced the settlers to stay. His deputy, Thomas Dale, then drafted a harsh law code. Settlers were organized into work gangs and had to work at least six hours per day. The death penalty was imposed for many crimes, including rape, swearing, desertion, theft, lying, and expressing disrespect for the Bible.

Tobacco Saves the Colony The colony still had to find a way to make a profit. The solution was a cash crop: tobacco. Smoking tobacco had become popular in Europe, although King James had condemned tobacco as a "vile weed [of] black stinking fumes [that are] baleful to the nose, harmful to the brain, and dangerous to the lungs."

The Jamestown settlers had tried growing tobacco, but the local variety was too bitter. A colonist named John Rolfe then began to experiment with seeds from Trinidad. He also developed a new method for curing tobacco, and in 1614 sent his first shipment to England. Rolfe's tobacco sold for a good price, and the settlers began planting large quantities of it.

In 1618 the Virginia Company granted the colonists the right to elect a lawmaking body. Virginia's first general assembly met in the Jamestown church on July 30, 1619. The new government included a governor, six councilors, and 20 representatives—two from each of the colony's 10 towns. The representatives were called burgesses, and the assembly was called the House of Burgesses.

The Virginia Company also introduced the system of **headrights.** Settlers who paid their own passage to Virginia received 50 acres of land. Settlers also received 50 acres of land for each family member over 15 years of age and each servant they transported to Virginia.

In 1619 the first Africans were brought to Virginia. A Dutch slave ship stopped to trade for supplies, and the Jamestown settlers purchased 20 African men as "Christian servants," not slaves. Within a few years, however, enslaved Africans were being brought to the colony.

By 1622, more than 4,500 settlers had arrived in Virginia. This alarmed the Native Americans, and they attacked Jamestown in March 1622. They burned homes, destroyed food supplies, and killed nearly 350 settlers. The settlers eventually put an end to the uprising, but the colony was devastated. After blaming the Virginia Company, an English court revoked its charter. Virginia became a royal colony run by a governor who was appointed by the king.

Maryland Is Founded In England, Catholics were persecuted because they did not accept the monarch as head of the Church. They were viewed as potential traitors who might help Catholic countries overthrow the English monarchy. Catholics were forbidden to practice law or teach school. They were also fined for not attending Anglican services.

The persecution of his fellow Catholics convinced George Calvert, who held the title Lord Baltimore, to found a colony where Catholics could practice their religion freely. In 1632 King Charles granted him a large area of land northeast of Virginia. Baltimore named the new colony Maryland.

Lord Baltimore owned Maryland, making it a **proprietary colony.** The proprietor, or owner, had almost unlimited authority over the colony. He could appoint a government, establish courts, coin money, impose taxes, grant lands, create towns, and raise an army. The only restriction on a proprietor was that he could do nothing that was contrary to established English law.

R

D Differentiated Instruction

English Learners and Special Education Review with Special education or English language learners the primary source quotation on this page to check their understanding and to clarify any challenging terms or figurative language. For example, you might need to define the word *vermin* and explain the meaning of the idiom "to make shift with." ELL BL

R Reading Strategy

Using Word Parts Remind students that they can use knowledge of word parts to figure out or remember the meanings of new words. Have students locate the vocabulary term *proprietary colony* and the word *proprietor* in the next sentence. Point out the common word part *prop-* in both words. Explain to students that these words share the same root as the more familiar word *property*, or "something that is owned." BL ELL

Additional Support

Activity: Collaborative Learning

Designing a Flag Have students work in small groups to design a flag for one of the colonies mentioned in this section. **Ask:** What are the main characteristics of a particular English colony? Have students work together on sketches for a design based on what they have learned about their chosen colony and then reach a consensus on its appearance and prepare a final drawing of their flag. Then have groups write a brief explanation of the colors and symbols used in their flag. Display flags and explanations around the classroom. BL

S Skill Practice

Using Geography Skills Have students study the map on this page. **Ask:** Why do you think that more people immigrated to New England than to the Chesapeake colonies? *(Possible answer: There were more and larger English settlements already established in New England than in the Chesapeake colonies. If most of the immigrants were Protestants that would also draw them to settle in Protestant communities in New England.)* **OL**

Analyzing VISUALS

Answers:

1. Chesapeake colonies: 5,000; New England colonies: 20,000
2. It was established for the "better ordering and preservation" of the colony.

Reading Check

Answer:
as a refuge for English Catholics

For the complete text of The Mayflower Compact, see page R39 in **Documents in American History.**

Lord Baltimore died shortly before settlers arrived in his colony. In 1634, 20 gentlemen, mostly Catholic, and 200 servants and artisans, mostly Protestant, arrived from England. Despite Baltimore's hope that Maryland would become a Catholic refuge, most of its settlers were Protestant, although the government officials and most owners of large estates were Catholic. As in England, religious differences led to social conflict. To reduce friction between the two groups, the colonial assembly passed the Toleration Act in 1649. This act mandated religious toleration for all Christians but made denying the divinity of Jesus a crime punishable by death.

1649 !

Reading Check **Analyzing** Why was Maryland founded?

Mandated religious tolerance For trinitarian Christians.

Pilgrims and Puritans

MAIN Idea Both the Pilgrims and the Puritans founded colonies to escape religious persecution.

HISTORY AND YOU Have you ever thought that an authority figure was too strict? Read on to learn what happened to those who challenged Puritan authorities.

In England, a group of Puritans, called Separatists, concluded that the Anglican Church was too corrupt to be reformed. They formed their own congregations, and in 1608, one group fled to the Netherlands to escape persecution. These Separatists, later known as Pilgrims, later sailed to America in 1620.

In 1654, only 5 yrs after its passage, the act was repealed.

NATIONAL GEOGRAPHIC The Puritan Migration to America, 1620–1640

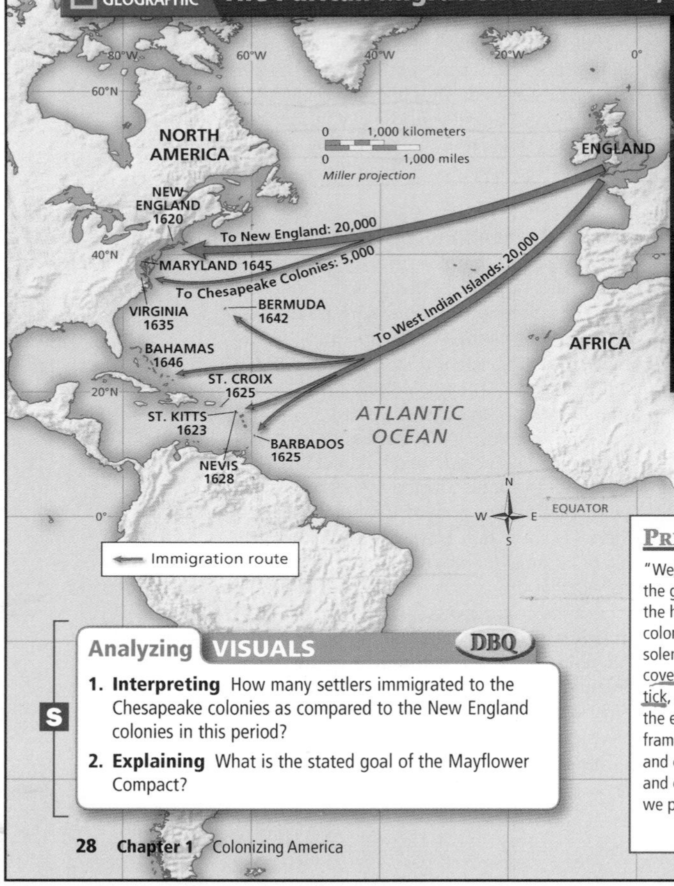

▲ *On November 21, 1620, while still aboard the Mayflower, 41 colonists signed the Mayflower Compact. It was the first self-government plan ever put into effect in the English colonies.*

PRIMARY SOURCE

"We, whose names are underwritten . . . having undertaken for the glory of God, and advancement of the Christian faith, and the honour of our king and country, a voyage to plant the first colony in the northern parts of *Virginia;* do by these presents, solemnly and mutually, in the presence of God and one another, covenant and combine ourselves together into a civil body politick, for our better ordering and preservation, and furtherance of the ends aforesaid: and by virtue hereof do enact, constitute, and frame, such just and equal laws, ordinances, acts, constitutions, and officers, from time to time, as shall be thought most meet and convenient for the general good of the colony; unto which we promise all due submission and obedience."

Source: *The Mayflower Compact*

S **Analyzing VISUALS** **DBQ**

1. **Interpreting** How many settlers immigrated to the Chesapeake colonies as compared to the New England colonies in this period?
2. **Explaining** What is the stated goal of the Mayflower Compact?

Additional Support

Activity: Collaborative Learning

Identifying Central Issues Discuss with students the relatively radical nature of the Toleration Act passed in Maryland in 1649. **Ask:** What was the significance of the Toleration Act? *(Rarely had religious tolerance been legislated before in the colonies or in England.)* Explain that at the time of the act, in England there was no such law guaranteeing religious tolerance, and Puritan forces were warring with their Anglican king, whom they suspected of harboring Catholic sympathies. When Protestants began to outnumber Catholics in Maryland, the colony's leaders decided to ensure the religious toleration of Catholics by passing the act. Along with the charter of Rhode Island that guaranteed religious liberty, the Toleration Act helped to set a precedent for religious freedom later in the United States. **OL**

Plymouth Colony R

Before crossing the Atlantic, the Pilgrims returned to England, where they joined other emigrants aboard a ship called the *Mayflower.* On September 16, 1620, 102 passengers set sail for Virginia. The Pilgrims, however, decided to settle farther north. In December they settled in the Cape Cod area known as "Plymouth."

After constructing a "common house," the settlers built modest homes of frame construction and thatched roofs. Soon, however, a plague swept through the colony, sparing only about 50 settlers.

The surviving Pilgrims might have perished were it not for the help of Squanto, a Wampanoag man who helped them grow corn and catch fish. The following autumn, the Pilgrims joined with the Wampanoag in a three-day festival to celebrate the harvest and give thanks to God for their good fortune. This celebration later became the basis for the Thanksgiving holiday.

Massachusetts Bay Colony

In 1625 Charles I took the throne, and persecution of the Puritans increased. At the same time, a depression struck England's wool industry. The depression caused high unemployment, particularly in the southern and eastern counties where large numbers of Puritans lived.

As he watched his fellow Puritans suffering both religious and economic hardships, **John Winthrop** grew concerned. Winthrop and several other wealthy Puritans were stockholders in the Massachusetts Bay Company. The company had already received a charter from King Charles to create a colony in New England. Winthrop decided to turn his business investment into a refuge for Puritans in America.

Other Puritans embraced the idea, and in 1630, 11 ships carrying about 900 settlers set sail. En route, in a sermon titled "A Model of Christian Charity," John Winthrop preached that the new colony should be an example to the world: "We shall be like a City upon a Hill; the eyes of all people are on us."

As conditions in England worsened, large numbers of people began to leave in what was later called the Great Migration. By 1643, an estimated 20,000 settlers had arrived in New England.

The charter of the Massachusetts Bay Company defined the colony's government. People who owned stock in the company were called "freemen." All the freemen of the colony together constituted the General Court. The General Court was to make the laws and elect the governor. John Winthrop was chosen as the first governor. He ignored the charter, however, and told the settlers that only he and his assistants could make laws for the colony. No one knew that this violated the charter, W because Winthrop kept it locked in a chest.

The freemen elected Winthrop in four consecutive, annual elections. In 1634 the freemen demanded to see the charter. Winthrop had no grounds to refuse. As they read the charter, they realized that the General Court was supposed to make the laws. When the General Court assembled, they reorganized the government. The General Court became a representative assembly, with the freemen from each town electing deputies to send to the Court each year.

The Puritans believed that each congregation should control its own church. Although only church members could vote and hold office, Puritans kept the governance of church and state separate. The General Court passed laws regulating moral behavior and collected taxes for the support of their churches.

As the Puritan population grew, religion's power to order society weakened. This social shift was expressed in various ways. The Halfway Covenant simplified new church membership by allowing the children of members to join without a public statement of conversion. These halfway members were not, however, allowed to vote in church assemblies. The Salem witchcraft trials of 1692, while unusually intense, reflected the tensions behind social change. Historians believe that the string of accusations reflected either farmers' fear of new merchant lifestyles in the developing commercial industries or were aimed at women who did not conform to the subordinate place demanded of Puritan females.

Puritans did not tolerate the expression of different religious ideas. **Heretics**—people who disagree with established religious beliefs—were considered a threat to the community. Those who voiced ideas that contradicted Puritan beliefs could be charged with heresy and banished.

R Reading Strategy

Analyzing Text Structure Remind students that textbooks have a head structure that can help them better understand and recall what they read. Tell students that they can preview a section by reading the headings before they actually read the text. Also, they can use the headings as an outline to help them organize their notes. BL

W Writing Support

Expository Writing Have students assume the role of one of the Pilgrims. Ask students to write four brief journal entries describing their activities or feelings. The dates for the journal entries are: autumn 1620, winter 1620, summer 1621, winter 1621. OL

Did You Know?

The term *pilgrim* refers to someone who travels to a shrine or sacred place. It can also mean "a traveler." It seems appropriate that William Bradford would describe the group who arrived in Plymouth on the *Mayflower* as "Pilgrims."

Additional Support

Activity: Technology Connection

Preserving Historical Documents Invite an archivist or historian from a local historical society, museum, or college to visit your class to talk about the importance of and methods for preserving historical documents, such as the copy of the *Mayflower Compact* made by William Bradford in his manuscript for his book *History of Plymouth Plantation*. Ask the speaker to give a short history on how documents have been preserved in the past and to explain the technological innovations that are currently used in preservation. Encourage students to ask questions at the end of the presentation. Have students write a paragraph summarizing what they learned. **Ask:** What role does technology play in preserving important historical documents? (*Answer should include new and old techniques introduced during the presentation.*) OL

C Critical Thinking

Making Inferences Discuss with students the significance of Thomas Hooker's beliefs about the church and the government. **Ask:** How did Thomas Hooker's beliefs promote the idea of the separation of church and state? *(Hooker thought that all adult men should be allowed to vote and take part in governing a community—not just male church members.)* OL

People IN HISTORY

Answer:

Roger Williams
In his colony of Rhode Island, Williams established the idea of religious freedom, which later became an important American principle.

Anne Hutchinson
Hutchinson challenged Puritan doctrine on how to achieve salvation and questioned the authority of several ministers. Since Massachusetts was ruled by Puritans, these ideas undermined their authority.

People IN HISTORY

Roger Williams
1603?–1683

Shortly after his arrival in Boston in 1631, Roger Williams declared he was a Separatist and began criticizing Puritan leaders. He served as a minister in Salem, moved briefly to Plymouth Colony in 1632, and then returned to preach at Salem.

When Williams returned to Salem, he continued to criticize Puritan leaders for not making a complete break from the corrupt Anglican Church. He also insisted on greater separation of church and state. Finally, he denounced Massachusetts Bay's charter because it assumed the king had the right to give away land belonging to Native Americans. As Puritan leaders prepared to banish him, Williams fled.

In 1636 he founded Providence—later to be part of Rhode Island—on land he purchased from the Narragansetts. In his new colony, Williams created a haven for Quakers, Separatists, Jews, and others whose religious practices or views were not tolerated elsewhere. Most important, Williams championed religious freedom, which later became an important American principle.

What significant contribution to civil rights did Roger Williams make?

Anne Hutchinson
1591–1643

Anne Hutchinson, an experienced midwife and the wife of a prosperous merchant, arrived in Boston in 1634. There, she began to hold meetings with other women to discuss sermons, express her own beliefs, and evaluate the ministers.

Hutchinson stirred up controversy with her discussions of how salvation could be obtained. To most Puritans, this was heresy. In 1637 Hutchinson was tried for sedition by the Massachusetts General Court. Hutchinson did not repent. She said that God "hath let me see which was the clear [correct] ministry and which the wrong. . . ." When asked how God let her know, she replied that God spoke to her "by an immediate revelation." The Court ordered her banished.

Hutchinson, her family, and some of her followers founded a settlement in what is today Rhode Island. After the death of her husband, she moved to Long Island. In 1643 she and all but one of her children were killed in an attack by Native Americans. Some Puritans viewed her tragic death as God's judgment against a heretic.

How did Hutchinson challenge Puritan authority in the Massachusetts Bay Colony?

Puritan efforts to suppress other religious beliefs inevitably sparked conflict. Eventually, Puritan intolerance led to the founding of other colonies in New England.

Rhode Island and Dissent

In 1631 a young minister named **Roger Williams** arrived in Massachusetts. Williams was a Separatist who believed Puritans corrupted themselves by staying within the Anglican Church. Williams angered many people by condemning the Puritan churches, as well as declaring that the king had no right to give away land belonging to Native Americans.

In 1635 the Massachusetts General Court ordered him to be deported back to England, but Williams instead escaped south with a few followers. He then purchased land from the Narragansett people and founded the town of Providence in 1636. In Providence, the government had no authority over religious matters. Different religious beliefs were tolerated rather than suppressed.

In the midst of the uproar over Roger Williams, a devout Puritan named **Anne Hutchinson** began causing a stir in Boston. Hutchinson held religious discussion meetings in her home and questioned the authority of several ministers. In late 1637 the General Court charged her with heresy and banished her. Hutchinson and a few followers headed south and settled in Rhode Island.

Over the next few years, Massachusetts banished other dissenting Puritans. They too headed south and founded Newport in 1639 and Warwick in 1643. In 1644 these two towns joined Portsmouth and Providence to become the single colony of Rhode Island and Providence Plantations. Religious freedom became a key part of the new colony's charter.

New England Expands

C In 1636 Reverend Thomas Hooker asked the General Court of Massachusetts for permission to move his congregation to the Connecticut River valley. Hooker was frustrated by the Massachusetts political system. He thought that voting should not be limited to male church members. The General Court granted Hooker's request, and he and some 100 settlers headed to the Connecticut River

Extending the Content

Background Although the Puritans came to North America to escape religious persecution, ironically they did not extend any tolerance to those who did not follow their beliefs. Roger Williams and Anne Hutchinson both challenged the beliefs and leadership in the Massachusetts Bay Colony and both were banished. **Ask:** What did Roger Williams and Anne Hutchinson have in common? *(They both challenged Puritan beliefs and authority of the Puritan leaders in Massachusetts and both were banished.)*

To help better understand the establishment of the thirteen English colonies, have students create a time line that includes the founder and founding date for each colony. Encourage them to include any other important events in the period, such as the English Civil War, King Philip's War, or the passage of the Toleration Act. OL and founded the town of Hartford. Two years later, Hooker helped write the Fundamental Orders of Connecticut, a constitution that allowed all adult men, not just church members, to vote and serve in government. This marked the beginning of the colony of Connecticut.

Much of the territory north of Massachusetts had been granted to two men, Sir Fernando Gorges and Captain John Mason. Mason took the southern part and named it New Hampshire, while Gorges's territory in the north came to be called Maine. The government of Massachusetts claimed both New Hampshire and Maine and challenged the claims of Mason and Gorges in court. In 1677 an English court ruled against Massachusetts. Two years later, New Hampshire became a royal colony. Massachusetts, however, bought Maine from Gorges's heirs, and Maine remained part of Massachusetts until 1820.

R King Philip's War (1675-78)

In 1637 war broke out between the English settlers and the Pequot people of New England. This conflict ended with the near extermination of the Pequot people. In the following decades, however, English settlers and Native Americans lived in relative peace.

The fur trade, in particular, facilitated peace. It enabled Native Americans to acquire tools, guns, and other European goods in exchange for furs. By the 1670s, however, the fur trade was in decline. At the same time, colonial governments began to demand that Native Americans follow English laws and customs. Native Americans reacted angrily, considering such demands arrogant and insulting.

W Tensions peaked in 1675 when Plymouth Colony arrested, tried, and executed three Wampanoag men for murder. This touched off what came to be called King Philip's War, named after the Wampanoag leader Metacomet, whom the settlers called King Philip. Colonists killed Metacomet in 1676 and then mounted his head on a pike and paraded it through their settlements. By the time the war ended in 1678, few Native Americans were left in New England.

Reading Check **Explaining** Why were Roger Williams and Anne Hutchinson banished from Massachusetts?

England's Civil War and New Colonies

MAIN Idea The English Civil War interrupted colonization. After it ended, new colonies were founded.

HISTORY AND YOU Have you ever watched television programs about New York City? Read to learn how it became an English colony.

For an excerpt from the Fundamental Orders of Connecticut, see page R40 in **Documents in American History.**

The English Civil War arose from a power struggle between King Charles I and Parliament. In 1642 this struggle erupted into armed conflict after the king sent troops into the Puritan-dominated Parliament to arrest Puritan leaders. In response, Parliament organized an army. After years of battles, Parliament's forces defeated the king's troops and beheaded him in 1649. Oliver Cromwell, the commander of Parliament's army, then seized power, took the title "Lord Protector," and in a few years ruled as a dictator of the new English Commonwealth.

After Cromwell died in 1658 and his son unsuccessfully tried to rule in his place, Parliament invited King Charles's son, Charles II, to take the throne. With the monarchy restored in 1660, the English government began backing a new round of colonization in America.

New York and New Jersey

Located between England's Chesapeake and New England colonies was a Dutch colony. In 1609 the Dutch East India Company hired English navigator **Henry Hudson** to search for a river that flowed through North America. Instead, he found the wide river that came to bear his name. The Dutch claimed the region, named it New Netherland, and established a settlement at New Amsterdam on Manhattan Island.

The colony grew slowly, partly because the fur trade was the focus of activity. To increase the population, the Dutch allowed anyone from any country to buy land. The strategy worked. By 1664 the population of the colony exceeded 10,000 people, with immigrants from the Netherlands, Britain, Scandinavia, Germany, and France. The first enslaved Africans arrived in the 1620s.

R Reading Strategy

Predicting Refer students to the heading "King Philip's War," and explain that it was a conflict between English colonists in New England and Native Americans. Ask students to write one prediction about the cause of this conflict and one predicted effect. Tell students to then read the information under the heading to check the accuracy of their predictions. **BL**

W Writing Support

Descriptive Writing Have students write a one-page description of what they think life in the English colonies would have been like if the settlers and Native Americans had collaborated more effectively. **OL**

Reading Check

Answer: They were both considered heretics because they proposed ideas that were not approved by the Puritan leaders.

Additional Support

Activity: Collaborative Learning

Making an Oral Presentation Divide the class into seven groups and assign each group one of the seven colonies founded after the English Civil War. Instruct students to use the textbook and library and Internet resources to gather information about their assigned colony in preparation for an oral presentation. Presentations should include various media, such as charts, graphs, and images, and give the history of the founding of the colony, important events in its colonial history, and include any characteristics from its early existence that are still present in the state today. **AL**

D Differentiated Instruction

English Learners Have students work with a proficient student to check their pronunciation for each of the names of the thirteen colonies. If necessary, have partners create phonetic respellings so that English Learners can practice on their own. ELL

S Skill Practice

Using Geography Skills
Have students study the map and list each colony and the cities labeled in those colonies. Then have students use a modern map of the United States to determine if any of these colonial cities went on to become state capitals. OL

Analyzing GEOGRAPHY

Answers:

1. because it gave quicker access to ships for re-supply and the ocean for food
2. Georgia

Additional Support

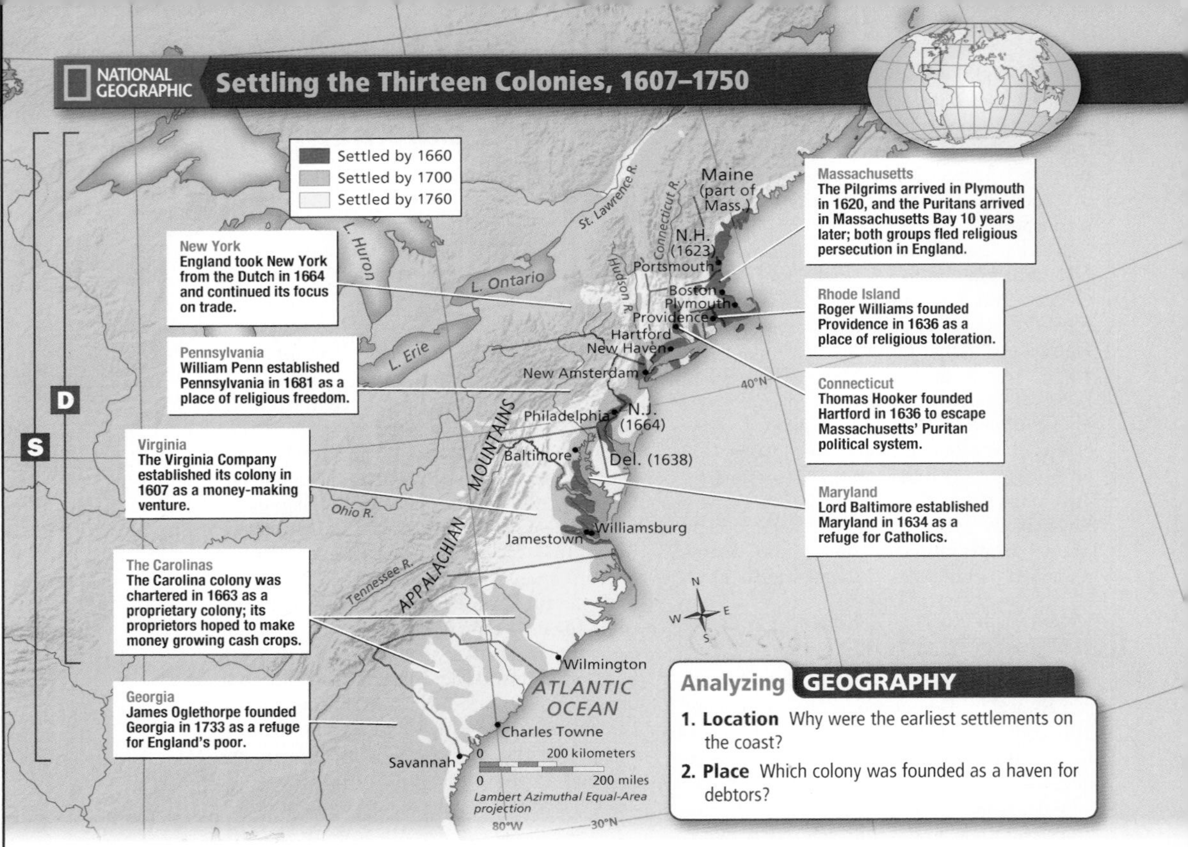

Analyzing GEOGRAPHY

1. **Location** Why were the earliest settlements on the coast?
2. **Place** Which colony was founded as a haven for debtors?

England and the Netherlands were commercial rivals. In 1664 Charles II successfully took New Netherland from the Dutch. The king granted the land to his brother, James, Duke of York, who renamed the colony New York. James also received land between Delaware Bay and the Connecticut River. James later granted some of this land to two of the king's advisers and named it New Jersey. To attract settlers, New Jersey offered generous land grants, religious freedom, and the right to have a legislative assembly.

Pennsylvania and Delaware

The origins of the colony of Pennsylvania lay in a persecuted religious group and a large unpaid debt. The religious group was the Society of Friends, also known as the Quakers (because of founder George Fox's instruction to "tremble at the word of the Lord"). The debt was owed by King Charles II to the deceased father of William Penn.

William Penn was a member of the Quakers. The Quakers were considered a radical group because they saw no need for ministers and viewed the Bible as less important than each person's "inner light" from God. Quakers believed in religious toleration and pacifism, or opposition to war.

In 1681, to settle the debt owed to Penn's father, Charles II granted William Penn a large tract of land between New York and Maryland. Penn wanted his new colony of Pennsylvania to be a place where complete political and religious freedom would be practiced. He also tried to treat Native Americans fairly, and many years of peaceful relations resulted.

Penn named the capital of the colony Philadelphia, Greek for "city of brotherly love." The colony's government provided for an elected assembly and guaranteed religious

Activity: Interdisciplinary Connection

Mathematics Using a ruler and the map scale for the map "Settling the Thirteen Colonies," have students work in pairs to calculate the distances between one city and the other 13 and list the results in a chart. Then have students do research to find out the average distance a person can travel by horse. Then they determine how long it would take a person on horseback to travel between their chosen city and the others and add that information to their chart. Have students conclude by comparing and discussing results with other partners. **Ask:** What might be the effects on the development of society, culture, or government when it took so long to travel among the colonies? *(Students should note that the colonies developed distinct and independent governing bodies, economies, and societies.)* OL freedom. The right to vote was limited, however, to Christian men who owned 50 acres of land.

Greater religious freedom and available land attracted immigrants of a variety of faiths from England, Scotland, Ireland, Scandinavia, and Germany. By 1684, Pennsylvania had more than 7,000 residents, and by 1760, Philadelphia was the largest city in the colonies. In 1682 Penn bought three counties south of Pennsylvania from the Duke of York. These "lower counties" became the colony of Delaware.

The Carolinas

Charles II also took a keen interest in the unsettled land between Virginia and Spanish Florida. Charles awarded much of this territory to eight friends in 1663. The land was named Carolina—Latin for "Charles."

Although Carolina was not divided into two distinct colonies until 1729, it developed as two separate regions. North Carolina was home to a small and scattered population of farmers. The lack of good harbors hindered its growth. Eventually, the farmers began growing tobacco as a cash crop. They also used native pine to make and export shipbuilding supplies.

The proprietors of Carolina were far more interested in the southern half of their holdings, where they hoped to cultivate sugarcane. In 1670 the first settlers arrived in South Carolina. They named their first settlement Charles Town. Sugarcane, however, did not grow well there. Instead, early colonists sold deerskins obtained from nearby Native Americans and started a slave trade in Native American prisoners of war.

The Georgia Experiment

Georgia began as a refuge for England's "worthy poor." In the 1720s James Oglethorpe, a member of Parliament, investigated English prisons. He was appalled to find that so many of the imprisoned were debtors, not strictly criminals. Oglethorpe asked the king for a colony where the poor could start over. In 1732 King George II made Oglethorpe and 19 other philanthropists the trustees for the territory between the Savannah and Altamaha rivers. Oglethorpe named the new colony Georgia, in honor of the king. Settlers arrived in 1733.

Oglethorpe and his fellow trustees banned slavery, rum, and brandy in Georgia, and they limited the size of land grants. Still, the colony attracted settlers from all over Europe. Increasingly, the settlers objected to the colony's strict rules. In the 1740s the trustees lifted the restrictions on brandy, rum, and slavery; in 1751 they granted the settlers their own elected assembly. The next year, Georgia became a royal colony.

By 1775, roughly 2.5 million people lived in England's thirteen American colonies. Despite the stumbling starts in Roanoke and Jamestown, the English had succeeded in building a large and prosperous society on the east coast of North America.

Reading Check **Summarizing** How did William Penn acquire Pennsylvania?

Section 3 REVIEW

Vocabulary

1. **Explain** the significance of: joint-stock company, privateer, grant, Jamestown, Powhatan Confederacy, headright, proprietary colony, John Winthrop, heretic, Roger Williams, Anne Hutchinson, Henry Hudson.

Main Ideas

2. **Summarizing** How did the Protestant Reformation affect England's colonization efforts?
3. **Explaining** Why did people leave the Massachusetts Bay Colony to begin new colonies?
4. **Describing** On what principles did William Penn develop his colony?

Critical Thinking

5. **Big Ideas** How did the headright system encourage settlement in the English colonies?
6. **Organizing** Use a graphic organizer similar to the one below to list the colonies and the reasons for their founding.

Colony	Reason for Founding

7. **Analyzing Visuals** Study the painting of the signing of the Mayflower Compact on page 28. Why did the Pilgrims feel that it was necessary to create their own government?

Writing About History

8. **Persuasive Writing** Take the role of Captain John Smith. Write a speech explaining to your fellow Jamestown colonists why trading with the Powhatan Confederacy is a good survival strategy.

History ONLINE
Study Central™ To review this section, go to glencoe.com and click on Study Central.

Reading Check

Answer:
Charles II gave Penn the colony to pay off a debt he owed to Penn's father.

Assess

History ONLINE

Study Central™ provides summaries, interactive games, and online graphic organizers to help students review content.

Close

Summarizing Ask: What motivated the English government and English people to establish colonies in North America? *(The English government was motivated to establish colonies in North America because it wanted to compete for riches with its rival Spain and to set up naval bases to attack Spanish shipping. The English people came to North America to escape religious persecution, to find new economic opportunities, and to own land.)* **OL**

Section 3 REVIEW

Answers

1. All definitions can be found in the section and the Glossary.
2. It caused people who did not follow the Anglican Church—radical Protestants as well as Catholics—to think about establishing places in the Americas where they might worship freely.
3. They did not agree with the way in which the Massachusetts Bay Colony was ruled, with church leaders controlling the government.
4. He based his colony on political and religious freedom, as well as good treatment of Native Americans.
5. People were given 50 acres of land if they paid their own transport to the colony, and 50 acres for each family member over 15 as well as for each servant they brought. This not only encouraged settlement, but encouraged large families to emigrate.
6. Jamestown: as an investment; Maryland: as a refuge for English Catholics; Plymouth: for religious freedom; Massachusetts Bay: for religious freedom; Rhode Island: for religious freedom; New York: to force the Dutch from the English colonies and remove them as a commercial rival; Pennsylvania: as a refuge for persecuted people; Georgia: as a place for debtors to start new lives
7. to organize the colony and help it to succeed
8. Students' speeches will vary, but should include valid reasons for trading with the Powhatan Confederacy.

Focus

Bellringer

Daily Focus Transparency 1-4

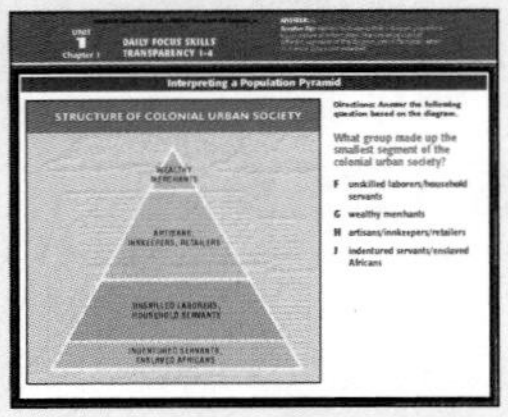

Guide to Reading

Answers:
From the top to the bottom, the social order in the Southern Colonies included: the planter elite, backcountry farmers, landless tenant farmers, indentured servants, enslaved Africans

Section Spotlight Video

To generate student interest and provide a springboard for class discussion, access the Chapter 1, Section 4 video at glencoe.com or on the video DVD.

Section 4

Section Audio | Spotlight Video

Economics, Trade, and Rebellion

Guide to Reading

Big Ideas

Geography and History Geography shaped the development of distinct regions within the English colonies.

Content Vocabulary
- indentured servant *(p. 34)*
- town meeting *(p. 38)*
- triangular trade *(p. 38)*
- mercantilism *(p. 40)*

Academic Vocabulary
- distinct *(p. 35)*
- reliable *(p. 40)*

People and Events to Identify
- Nathaniel Bacon *(p. 36)*
- English Bill of Rights *(p. 41)*

Reading Strategy

Organizing Complete a graphic organizer similar to the one below showing the ranking of classes in the colonial South.

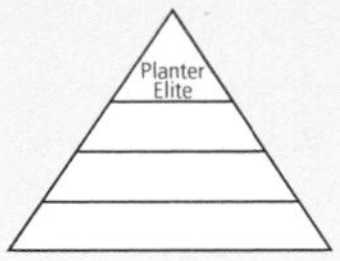

Differences in geography and patterns of settlement caused colonies to develop differently. Political changes in England affected the economy and governance of the thirteen colonies because they were part of the English imperial system.

Southern Society

MAIN Idea Society in the Southern Colonies was sharply divided between the wealthy elite and the backcountry farmers.

HISTORY AND YOU What kinds of produce are grown in your state? Read on to learn how the cultivation of cash crops helped the economies of the Southern colonies to grow.

In the South, wealthy planters stood on society's top rung and led very different lives from small farmers in the middle and enslaved Africans at the bottom. What linked all groups, however, was an economy based on growing crops for export. Tobacco was the South's first successful cash crop, or crop grown primarily to be sold at market. It was grown in Virginia and Maryland and, to a lesser extent, in North Carolina. In early colonial days, there was plenty of land, but not enough workers to produce the crop.

England had the opposite problem. The English enclosure movement had forced many farmers off their land. Many of them, hoping to acquire their own land in America, left England, agreeing to become **indentured servants** to cover the cost of their transportation to the colonies. Indentured servants were not enslaved, but neither were they free. The person who bought a servant's contract, or indenture, promised to provide food, clothing, and shelter to the servant until the indenture expired. In return, the servant agreed to work for the owner of the contract for a specific number of years, which varied from four to seven.

For most of the 1600s, indentured servitude benefited tobacco planters. Indentured servants could produce five times the price of their contracts in tobacco in the first year alone. Under the headright system, every indentured servant transported to America also earned the landowner another 50 acres of land. As indentured servants arrived in Virginia and Maryland, tobacco production rose steadily.

Unfortunately, almost half the indentured servants who came to Virginia and Maryland in the 1600s died before earning their freedom. Of those who survived their term of servitude, less than half ever acquired their own land.

In South Carolina, meanwhile, after trying unsuccessfully to grow sugarcane, settlers turned to rice. This failed at first, but in the 1690s a

Resource Manager

R Reading Strategies	C Critical Thinking	D Differentiated Instruction	W Writing Support	S Skill Practice
Teacher Edition • Categorizing, p. 37 • Making Connections, p. 40 **Additional Resources** • Guid. Read Act, URB p. 51 • RENTG, p. 11	**Teacher Edition** • Comparing, p. 36 • Det. Cause/Effect, p. 38 **Additional Resources** • Enrichment Act., URB p. 45 • Quizzes/Tests, p. 8	**Teacher Edition** • Special Ed., p. 35	**Teacher Edition** • Persuasive Writing, p. 36	**Teacher Edition** • Reading Graphs, p. 37 • Using Geo. Skills, p. 39 • Making Tables, p. 40

NATIONAL GEOGRAPHIC The Economy of the Colonial South, c. 1750

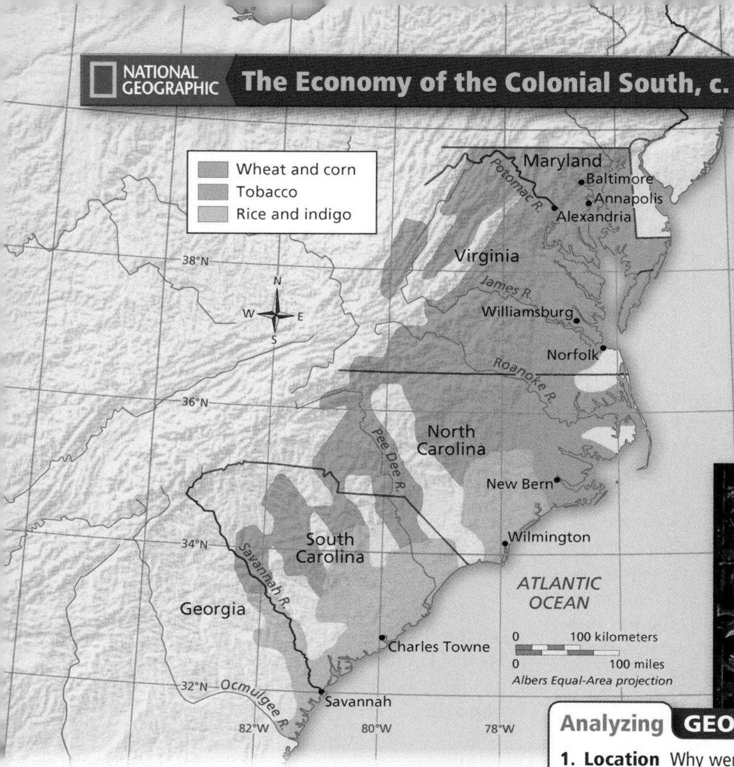

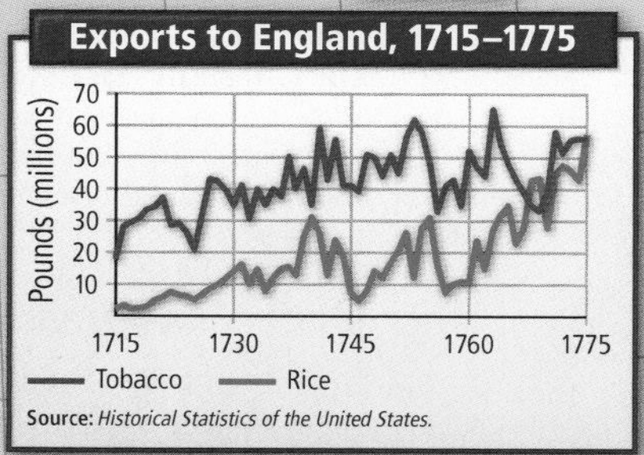

Source: *Historical Statistics of the United States.*

▲ Harvesting tobacco in colonial Virginia

Analyzing GEOGRAPHY

1. **Location** Why were tobacco and rice plantations located on or near rivers?
2. **Movement** About how much tobacco was exported to England from the Southern Colonies in 1745?

new variety was introduced, and planters imported enslaved Africans to cultivate it. West Africans had grown rice for centuries and knew how to raise and harvest it. Rice rapidly became a major cash crop in South Carolina and Georgia.

Planters had also tried another crop, indigo, without much success. Indigo was used to make blue dye for cloth. It was rare and in high demand, and anyone who could grow it could make a large profit. In the early 1740s a 17-year-old named Eliza Lucas discovered that indigo needed high ground and sandy soil, not the wetlands that suited rice. Indigo quickly became another important cash crop.

Disparities in Wealth

Although many immigrants to the Southern Colonies hoped to become wealthy, very few succeeded. The plantation system tended to create a society with **distinct** social classes.

The wealthy plantation owners, sometimes referred to as the Southern gentry or the planter elite, were few in number, and they enjoyed enormous economic and political influence. They served in the governing councils and assemblies, commanded the local militias, and became county judges. With few towns or roads in the region, their plantations functioned as self-contained communities. The residents lived near each other in a group of buildings, including the planter's great house, stables, barns, and the workers' cabins. **D** Plantations often had a school, a chapel, and workshops for blacksmiths, carpenters, weavers, coopers, and leatherworkers.

The majority of landowners in the colonial South, however, were small farmers living inland. These "backcountry" farmers worked small plots of land and lived in tiny houses. Although they grew some tobacco, they largely practiced subsistence farming, producing only enough to feed their families.

Teach

D Differentiated Instruction

Special Education Divide this section of the chapter into three parts using the main headings as a guide. Assign text under each section head to at least one student. Have students read their assigned text and become familiar with it. Invite students to write or give an oral summary of their assigned text. **OL**

Did You Know?

Making Contracts The contract of an indentured servant was "indented," or folded and torn along the indenture. Each party to the contract kept half.

Analyzing GEOGRAPHY

Answers:

1. Students should speculate that rivers provided water for irrigation and transportation of the crop to market
2. about 40 million pounds

Hands-On Chapter Project Step 4

Establishing a Colony in North America

Step 4: Determining the Economic Nature of the Colony

Directions Have students return to their groups. Each group should assume that they successfully established a colony in their chosen location and determine in which real colony it would be located in the year 1750. Using the maps in this section of the textbook that show the economic activities of the various English colonies, as well as library or Internet resources, each group makes a map of a major community in their colony, showing various structures, such as churches, businesses, government buildings, or colonists' homes, roads, areas of farmland, docks and a harbor, and so on. Maps may be based on an existing map of a real community, such as Boston or Charles Town, or may be of a fictional community based solely on historical facts and research. Each map should include a key and an extended caption summarizing the colony's economic activities.

Putting It Together Have a volunteer from each group present their map to the class and explain the major features and economic activities of the colonial community. As a class, discuss the differences among the colonies and the geographic and cultural reasons for these differences. **OL**

(Chapter Project continued in Section 5, p. 43)

W Writing Support

Persuasive Writing Have students write an advertisement to recruit indentured servants. The advertisement should include information about where the servant will work, what the master or mistress is willing to provide, what the servant must agree to do, and the length and any other terms of service. OL

C Critical Thinking

Comparing To help students understand the significance of geography and economics in history, have them focus on agriculture in the Southern colonies. Have students create a table to compare and contrast commercial agriculture and subsistence farming. The table should include information about crops, land use, transportation, and labor. OL

Reading Check

Answer:
The government opposed expanding into Native American lands and refused to sanction military action against Native Americans.

Additional Support

W Landless tenant farmers made up another large group in the South. Although land itself was easy to acquire, many settlers and former indentured servants could not afford the costs of the deed, land survey, tools, seed, and livestock. Instead, they worked land that they rented from the planter elite. Tenant farmers led difficult lives but had higher social status than indentured servants.

Bacon's Rebellion

By the 1660s, Virginia's government was dominated by wealthy planters led by the governor, Sir William Berkeley. Berkeley assembled a majority of supporters in the House of Burgesses and arranged to restrict the vote to people who owned property. This cut the number of voters in half. Berkeley also exempted himself and his councilors from taxation. These actions angered backcountry and tenant farmers. Ultimately, however, it was the governor's policies toward Native American lands that led to a rebellion.

C Acquiring land was the goal of most colonists. Many indentured servants and tenant farmers wanted to own farms eventually. Backcountry farmers wanted to increase their holdings. By the 1670s, however, most uncultivated land was in areas belonging to Native Americans in the Piedmont, the region of rolling hills between the coastal plains and the Appalachians.

Most wealthy planters lived near the coast in the region known as the Tidewater. They had no interest in the backcountry and did not want to endanger their plantations by risking war with the Native Americans. Therefore, they opposed expanding Virginia's territory into Native American lands.

In 1675 war broke out between backcountry settlers and the Susquehannock people. When Berkeley refused to support further military action, backcountry farmers were outraged. In April 1676, **Nathaniel Bacon,** a well-to-do but sympathetic planter on the governor's council, took up their cause. Bacon organized his own militia and attacked the Susquehannock. He then won a seat in the House of Burgesses. The assembly then authorized another attack on the Native Americans. It also restored the right to vote to all free white men and took away the tax exemptions Berkeley had given his supporters.

These reforms did not satisfy Bacon, however. He marched to Jamestown in July 1676 with several hundred armed men and charged Berkeley with corruption. Berkeley fled to raise his own army, and a civil war erupted. The two sides battled for control of the colony. In September 1676 Bacon's army burned Jamestown to the ground. The following month, the rebellion ended abruptly when Bacon became sick and died. Without his leadership, his army rapidly fell apart, and Berkeley returned to power.

Bacon's Rebellion convinced many wealthy planters that land should be made available to backcountry farmers. From the 1680s onward, Virginia's government generally supported expanding the colony westward, regardless of the impact on Native Americans.

The Rise of Slavery

Bacon's Rebellion also accelerated an existing trend in Virginia. By the 1670s, many planters had begun using enslaved Africans instead of indentured servants to work their plantations. In the 1680s, after the rebellion, the number of Africans brought to the colony rose rapidly.

Planters began to switch to enslaved African labor for several reasons. Enslaved workers did not have to be freed and would never have to be given their own land. In addition, when cheap land became available in the 1680s in other colonies, fewer English settlers were willing to become indentured servants.

At the same time, the English government adopted policies that encouraged slavery. English law limited trade between the English colonies and other countries. Before the 1670s, if settlers wanted to acquire enslaved Africans, they had to buy them from the Dutch or Portuguese, which was difficult to arrange. In 1672, however, King Charles II granted a charter to the Royal African Company to engage in the slave trade. This made it easier to acquire enslaved people. Planters also discovered another advantage to slavery; because enslaved Africans, unlike indentured servants, were considered property, planters could use them as collateral to borrow money and expand their plantations.

Reading Check **Identifying** What government policies caused backcountry farmers in Virginia to rebel?

Extending the Content

Indentured Servants In 1750 Gottlieb Mittelberger traveled to Pennsylvania on the ship the "Osgood" with indentured servants. Mittelberger was not an indentured servant, but came to Pennsylvania to serve as a schoolmaster and organist. He later wrote about his experiences and the experiences of the indentured servants on the ship in an essay titled, "On the Misfortune of Indentured Servants." He noted that if a child's parents died during the voyage to the colonies, the child had to serve long enough to pay for the parents' passage as well as his or her own. When they finally paid off their expenses and finished their service, indentured servants were to be given a new set of clothes. Depending on the terms of service, some male servants also received a horse, while female servants received a cow.

New England Society

MAIN Idea New England's economy was based on fishing, family farms, and lumber mills.

HISTORY AND YOU Have you attended a meeting of your local government? Read on to learn about early New England town meetings.

New England's thin and rocky soil was ill-suited to cash crops and the development of large plantations. Instead, on small farms from Connecticut to Maine, New England colonists practiced subsistence farming. The main crop was wheat, but farmers also grew other grains and vegetables, tended apple orchards, and raised dairy cattle, sheep, and pigs.

More than any other industry, fishing and whaling brought prosperity to New England. Nearby lay the Grand Banks, a shallow area in the Atlantic Ocean that teemed with cod, mackerel, halibut, and herring. In addition, New England had good harbors and plenty of timber for building fishing boats. Colonists found markets for their fish in the colonies, southern Europe, and the Caribbean. Whale blubber was used to make candles and lamp oil, and whale bones were used to fashion buttons, combs, and other items.

New England also developed a thriving lumber industry. Maine and New Hampshire had many waterfalls near the coast that could power sawmills. Demand for lumber never waned. It was used for furniture, buildings, and products such as barrels, which were used to ship almost everything in the colonial era.

Shipbuilding also became an important business. With forests and sawmills close to the coast, ships could be built quickly and cheaply—for 30 to 50 percent less than in England. By the 1770s, one out of every three English ships was built in America.

While self-sufficient plantations defined the social unit in the South, New England's social life centered on the towns. Puritans believed that Christians should form groups united by a church covenant—a voluntary agreement to worship together. The commitment to a church covenant encouraged the development of small towns surrounded by farms.

NATIONAL GEOGRAPHIC **New England and the Middle Colonies, c. 1750**

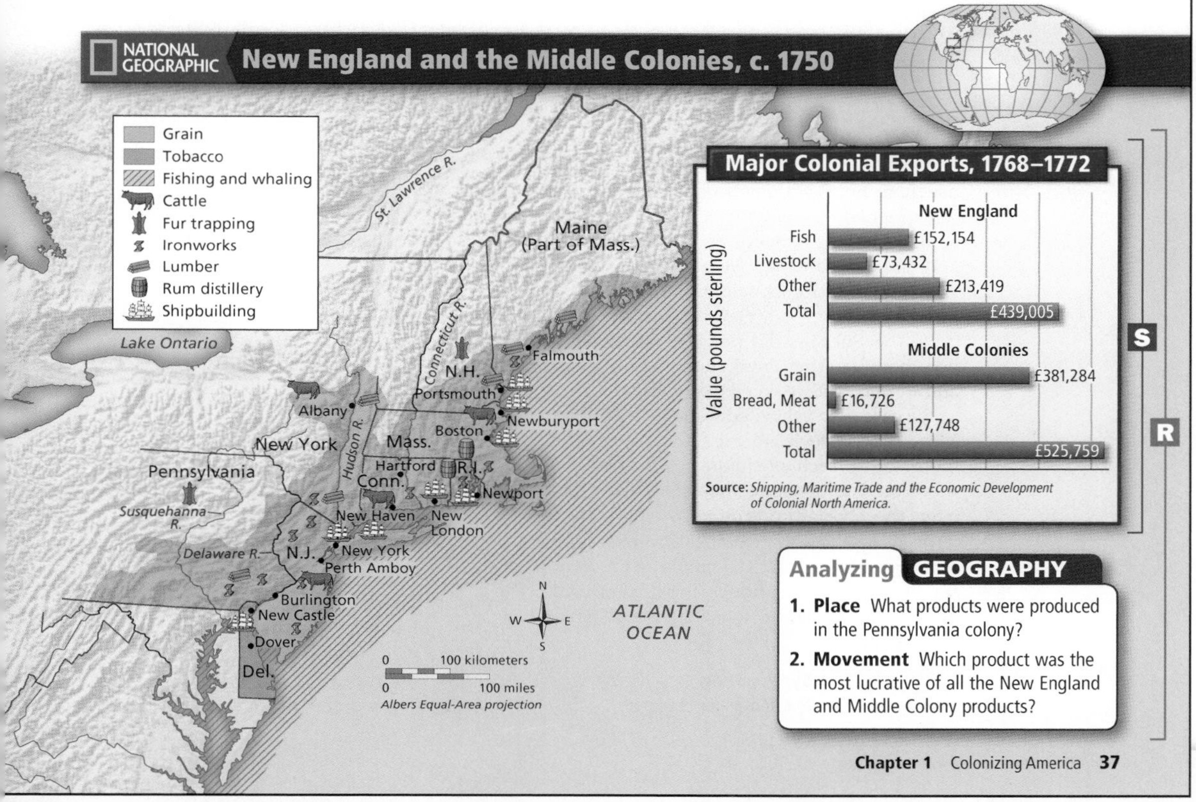

Analyzing GEOGRAPHY

1. **Place** What products were produced in the Pennsylvania colony?
2. **Movement** Which product was the most lucrative of all the New England and Middle Colony products?

R Reading Strategy

Categorizing As students read about New England and the Middle Colonies, have them complete a two-column chart. The first column should be labeled "Resources" and the second column, "Industries." Have students fill in their charts to illustrate how the availability of resources affected economic development. **BL**

S Skill Practice

Reading Graphs Have students synthesize the information in the map and bar graph in the feature on this page and write a summary describing how the geography of New England and of the Middle Colonies worked to form their basic economies. **OL**

Analyzing GEOGRAPHY

Answers:

1. lumber, wheat and corn, fur, iron
2. grain

Additional Support

Activity: Technology/Economics Connection

Have students build a working model of a water-powered mill. Ask students to share their models with the class to demonstrate how water was used by such mills to provide power for industry. **Ask:** **In what ways has the use of waterpower changed or remained the same since colonial times?** *(Student answers will vary, but should be based on facts and knowledge gained during their research of water-powered mills.)* **AL**

C Critical Thinking

Determining Cause and Effect To help them organize the information under the heading "Local Government," have students illustrate, in flowchart form, the cause-and-effect chain from what caused the town meeting to develop to the effects of town meetings on later events, such as the American Revolution. **Ask:** What caused the development of the town meeting form of government? *(Townspeople began to meet in town meetings to discuss local affairs. They developed into local governments.)* BL

Reading Check

Answer: Throughout New England, town meetings established a tradition of self-government, which people began to see as a right. Town meetings helped set the stage for the American Revolution and the emergence of democratic government in the United States.

Additional Support

Life in these small communities revolved around a "town common," or open public area. The marketplace, school, and "meetinghouse" (or church) bordered the common. Each family had a home lot where they could build a house and storage buildings and plant a garden.

Local Government

In the early days of colonial New England, the General Court appointed town officials and managed the town's affairs. Over time, however, townspeople began discussing local problems and issues at **town meetings.** These developed into local governments, with landowners holding the right to vote and pass laws. They elected selectmen to oversee town matters and appoint clerks, constables, C and other officials. Any resident, however, could attend a town meeting and express an opinion.

Because the settlers in New England, unlike English tenants, were allowed to participate in local government, they developed a strong belief in their right to govern themselves. Town meetings thus helped set the stage for the American Revolution and the emergence of democratic government.

Puritan Society

New England Puritans valued religious devotion, hard work, and obedience to strict rules regulating daily life. Card playing and gambling were banned, and "stage-players" and "mixed dancing" were frowned upon. Watching over one's neighbors' behavior, or "holy watching," was elevated to a religious duty. The Puritans did not lead pleasureless lives, however. They drank rum, enjoyed music, and wore brightly colored clothing.

Puritans also valued education. In 1642 the Massachusetts legislature required parents and ministers to teach all children to read so that they could understand the Bible. Five years later, the legislature ordered towns with at least 50 families to establish an elementary school and those with 100 families or more to set up secondary schools. Soon afterward, other New England colonies adopted similar legislation.

Reading Check **Synthesizing** How did town meetings prepare the colonists for the future?

Trade and the Rise of Cities

MAIN Idea Cities prospered and grew through trade with England, Africa, and other colonies.

HISTORY AND YOU Does today's society have distinct social classes? Read on to learn how social classes developed in the colonies.

In the early colonial era, settlers lacked money to invest in local industry. As a result, they had to import most manufactured goods from England. Unfortunately, they produced few goods that England wanted in return.

Triangular Trade

Instead of trading directly with England, colonial merchants developed systems of **triangular trade** involving a three-way exchange of goods. New England merchants, for example, traded fish, lumber, and meat to sugar planters in the Caribbean. In return, they received raw sugar or bills of exchange—credit slips from English merchants. New England merchants would then trade the bills and sugar to English merchants for hardware, linens, and other English goods.

Trade with the Caribbean sugar plantations made many New England merchants rich. With their new wealth, they built factories to refine raw sugar and distilleries to turn molasses into rum. They also traded with the Southern Colonies, exchanging fish, rum, and grain for rice, tobacco, and indigo.

A New Urban Society

The rise of trade caused several Northern ports—including Boston, New York City, and Philadelphia—to grow into cities. In the South, trade made Charles Town, South Carolina, the region's largest urban center. In all of these cities and others, a new society with distinct social classes developed.

At the top of the social structure were wealthy merchants who controlled the city's trade. These rich merchants composed a tiny minority. Skilled artisans and their families made up nearly half of the urban population. Artisans were skilled workers such as carpenters, smiths, glassmakers, coopers, bakers, masons, and shoemakers. Alongside the

Activity: Collaborative Learning

Holding a Town Meeting Organize the class into small groups. Ask them to identify school rules or practices that they would like to see changed. Have each group member think of at least two examples. Then have group members meet to discuss their responses. With one group member acting as a recorder, have the groups put together a descriptive listing of their ideas to present to the class for discussion. After all groups have made their presentations, have students compile a master list representing all the accepted ideas. Finally, initiate a class "town meeting," to determine what steps should be taken to make the recommended changes. OL

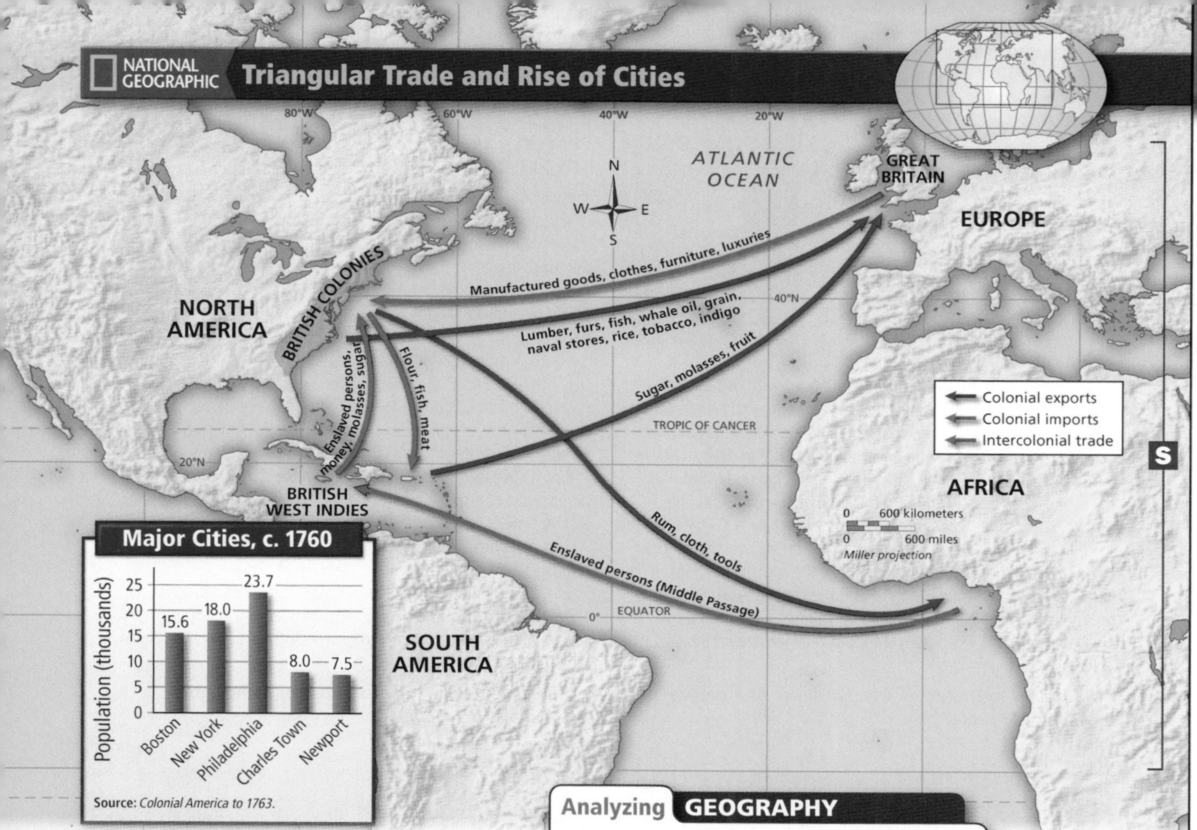

Analyzing GEOGRAPHY

1. **Movement** What commodities were shipped from the colonies to West Africa?
2. **Human-Environment Interaction** What types of goods did the American colonies export?

artisans in social status were innkeepers and retailers who owned their own businesses.

Beneath the artisans in urban society were people without skills or property. Many of these people loaded and serviced ships at the harbor. Others worked as servants. These people made up about 30 percent of urban society. Below them in status were indentured servants and enslaved Africans. Relatively few enslaved people lived in the North. Those who did usually lived in cities, making up between 10 and 20 percent of the population.

Life in the Middle Colonies

The Middle Colonies—Pennsylvania, New York, New Jersey, and Delaware—combined aspects of New England's economy with that of the South. As in New England, trade led to the rise of cities along the coast. As in the South, colonists benefited from fertile soil and a long growing season. Farmers produced abundant crops of rye, oats, barley, potatoes, and especially wheat. And just as the Southern economy was based on exporting cash crops, so too did the Middle Colonies develop an economy with an important cash crop: wheat.

As merchants in the Middle Colonies began selling wheat and flour to colonies in the Caribbean, they benefited from the region's geography. Three wide rivers—the Hudson, the Delaware, and the Susquehanna—ran deep into the interior, making it easy for farmers to ship their crops to the coast.

In the early and mid-1700s, the demand for wheat soared, thanks to population growth in Europe resulting from a decline of disease. Between 1720 and 1770, wheat prices more than doubled, bringing great prosperity.

S Skill Practice

Using Geography Skills

Discuss with students aspects of the triangular trade. Ask questions that lead to student understanding of the goods and materials that flowed to and from each point in the system. **Ask:** **What goods were traded from the North American colonies to West Africa and what was traded back to the British West Indies and then to North American colonies in exchange?** *(From North America to West Africa: rum, tools, cloth; from West Africa to the West Indies: enslaved people; to the North American colonies: enslaved people, money, molasses, sugar)* **OL**

Analyzing GEOGRAPHY

Answers:

1. rum, cloth, tools
2. rum, cloth, tools, lumber, furs, fish, whale oil, naval stores, rice, tobacco, indigo, flour, meat, grain

Additional Support

Activity: Interdisciplinary Connection

Literature Invite a literature teacher or librarian to speak to your class about themes in American literature written between 1640 and 1740. Ask the speaker to also share examples of poetry, tales, and books that might help students gain a better understanding of the colonial period. After the presentation, ask students the following questions: **What topics did colonial writers address on which writers today still focus? What are some differences between colonial literature and contemporary literature?** *(Student answers will vary.)* **OL**

R Reading Strategy

Making Connections Point out the vocabulary term *mercantilism* in the text and discuss with students how mercantilism is related to the triangular trade. **Ask:** How did the triangular trade support England's mercantilist goals? *(In the triangular trade system, England's colonies supplied it with raw materials, while the colonies provided markets for English finished goods.)* OL

S Skill Practice

Making Tables Have students use information in the text as well as additional research to make a table listing each of the Navigation Acts, including the year of each law's passage and its main provisions. OL

People IN HISTORY

Answer:

John Locke
Locke believed the government's right to rule comes from the people it governs.

Benjamin Franklin
Franklin began with a humble life. His education and hard work placed him in colonial society's elite.

People IN HISTORY

John Locke
1632–1704

The Glorious Revolution of 1688 importantly suggested that there were times when revolution was justified. In 1690, John Locke, a philosopher allied with those who had overthrown King James II, wrote *Two Treatises of Government* on this topic.

He argued that a government's right to rule came from the people, who were born with certain natural rights, including the right to life, liberty, and property. People created government to protect their rights, making a contract to obey the government's laws while the government protected their rights. If a ruler violated those rights, the people were justified in rebelling.

Locke's ideas greatly influenced the American colonists. The Mayflower Compact and the Fundamental Orders of Connecticut were agreements between the people and their government. The colonists saw Locke's "natural rights" as the specific rights of Englishmen set out in the Magna Carta and the English Bill of Rights. By the 1770s, the American colonies would put these ideas into practice when they launched their own revolution against Britain.

According to Locke, what is the source of a government's right to rule?

Benjamin Franklin
1706–1790

This famous patriot is an example of the social mobility ideal that has driven many Americans, while also demonstrating the Enlightenment ideal that one could unlock the laws of nature through rational exploration.

Franklin grew up humbly, the son of a Boston candle and soap maker. At sixteen, Franklin's passion for books and writing led him to Philadelphia: "I was dirty from my journey . . . and I knew no soul nor where to look for lodging . . . my whole stock of cash consisted of a Dutch dollar and about a shilling in copper." He eventually achieved success as a printer, writer, scientist, and philosopher. By the time he was 42, the man who popularized the proverb "Time is money" could afford to retire and devote himself to public life.

In this retirement, he began his scientific investigations. Most famously, his kite experiments proved that lightning was electrical in nature and gained him an international reputation as an Enlightenment thinker.

How did Franklin's life experiences demonstrate American social mobility?

For an excerpt from the *Second Treatise of Government,* see page R42 in **Documents in American History.**

The wheat boom created a new group of wealthy capitalists who had money to invest in businesses. Industry did not develop on a large scale in the colonial era, but these capitalists did build many large mills near New York and Philadelphia that produced vast quantities of flour for export. Other capitalists in the Middle Colonies established glass and pottery works.

The Imperial System

Mercantilism is an economic theory about the world economy. Mercantilists believed that to become wealthy, a country must acquire gold and silver. A country could do this by selling more goods to other countries than it buys from them. This would cause more gold and silver to flow into the country than flowed out to pay for products from other countries. Mercantilists also argued that a country should be self-sufficient in raw materials. If it had to buy raw materials from another country, gold and silver would flow out to pay for them. Thus to be self-sufficient, a country needed colonies where raw materials were available. The home country would then buy raw materials from its colonies and sell them manufactured goods in return.

Mercantilism provided some benefits to colonies. It gave them a **reliable** market for some of their raw materials and an eager supplier of manufactured goods. Mercantilism also had drawbacks, however. It prevented colonies from selling goods to other nations, even if they could get a better price. Furthermore, if a colony produced nothing the home country needed, it could not acquire gold or silver to buy manufactured goods. This was a serious problem in New England, and it partly explains why merchants there turned to the triangular trade and smuggling.

The Navigation Acts When Charles II assumed the throne in 1660, he and his advisers were determined to generate wealth for England in America and they established policies based on mercantilist ideas. Beginning in 1660, the king asked Parliament to pass a series

Extending the Content

Background Although John Locke is best known for his political writings, he had other talents. Although he never completed a medical degree, he was known as "Dr. Locke" in some circles. In 1666 he successfully performed an operation on the Earl of Shaftesbury to clean out an abscess in his chest. In return, the earl allowed Locke to live at his home, which enabled Locke to devote his time to writing. **Ask:** How do you think the ideas of John Locke would later contribute to the revolutionary ideas in the American colonies? *(Locke's ideas about a contract between the government and the people, justifiable rebellion, and natural rights would later inspire the American colonists to rebel against Britain.)*

of Navigation Acts that imposed restrictions on colonial trade. These acts required that all goods shipped to and from the colonies be carried on English ships, and listed specific products that could be sold only to England or other English colonies. Many of these goods—including sugar, tobacco, lumber, cotton, wool, and indigo—were the major products that earned money for the American colonies.

Anger at the Navigation Acts encouraged colonists to break the new laws. New England merchants began smuggling goods to Europe, the Caribbean, and Africa in large quantities. In 1686, soon after King James II succeeded his brother Charles, England took decisive action to end the smuggling. Massachusetts, Plymouth, and Rhode Island were merged into a new royal province called the Dominion of New England to be governed by an English governor-general appointed by the king. The following year, Connecticut and New Jersey were added to the Dominion, and by early 1688, New York was added as well.

King James II appointed Sir Edmund Andros to be the Dominion's first governor-general. Andros became very unpopular because he levied new taxes and rigorously enforced the Navigation Acts. Equally disturbing to Puritans were Andros's efforts to undermine their congregations. For example, he declared that only marriages performed in Anglican churches were legal.

The Glorious Revolution While Andros was angering New England colonists, James II was losing support in England. He offended many by disregarding Parliament, revoking town charters, prosecuting Anglican bishops, and practicing Catholicism.

The birth of James's son in 1688 triggered a crisis. Opponents of James had been content to wait until he died, because they expected his Protestant daughter Mary to succeed him. The son, however, was now first in line for the throne, and would be raised Catholic. To prevent a Catholic dynasty, Parliament invited Mary and her Dutch husband, William of Orange, to claim the throne. James fled in what became known as the Glorious Revolution.

Soon afterward, the colonists ousted Governor-General Andros. William and Mary permitted Rhode Island and Connecticut to resume their previous forms of government, but in 1691 they merged Massachusetts Bay, Plymouth, and Maine into the new royal colony of Massachusetts. The colony was headed by a governor appointed by the king, but the colonists were allowed to elect an assembly.

Before assuming the throne, William and Mary had to swear their acceptance of the **English Bill of Rights.** This document, written in 1689, said monarchs could not suspend Parliament's laws or create their own courts, nor could they impose taxes or raise an army without Parliament's consent. The Bill of Rights also guaranteed freedom of speech within Parliament, banned excessive bail and cruel and unusual punishments, and guaranteed every English subject the right to an impartial jury in legal cases. The ideas in this document would later help shape the American Bill of Rights.

Reading Check **Examining** In what ways did the Navigation Acts affect trade in the colonies?

Section 4 REVIEW

Vocabulary

1. **Explain** the significance of: indentured servant, Nathaniel Bacon, town meeting, triangular trade, mercantilism, English Bill of Rights.

Main Ideas

2. **Explaining** How did the development of cash crops in the Southern colonies encourage the trade in enslaved people?
3. **Identifying** How did Puritan ideals lead to the development of town meetings?
4. **Analyzing** How did life in the Middle Colonies differ from life in the Southern Colonies?
5. **Categorizing** Complete a graphic organizer similar to the one below by filling in the benefits of mercantilism.

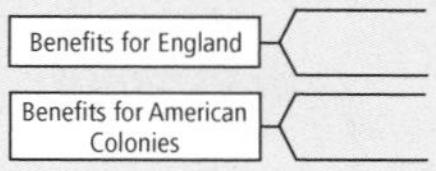

Critical Thinking

6. **Big Ideas** What role did geography play in developing different economies in the colonies?
7. **Analyzing Visuals** Study the bar graph showing the populations of major colonial cities on page 39 and the product map and graph on page 37. Why do you think Philadelphia was the largest city at this time?

Writing About History

8. **Expository Writing** Take on the role of a colonial merchant. Write a letter to a relative in England explaining how the Navigation Acts have affected your business.

History ONLINE
Study Central™ To review this section, go to glencoe.com and click on Study Central.

Reading Check

Answer:
They encouraged colonists to break the new laws by smuggling goods to places where they were forbidden to sell them.

Assess

History ONLINE

Study Central™ provides summaries, interactive games, and online graphic organizers to help students review content.

Close

Summarizing Ask: What were the main characteristics of the three regions of English colonies? *(Southern Colonies: well-defined class structure; economy based on agriculture, mainly cash crops. Middle Colonies: most cities and industry; good land for agriculture; exported large amounts of wheat; class structure less rigid. New England: shipping and industry were important to the economy; subsistence farming; people lived in small communities; few class differences.)* **OL**

Section 4 REVIEW

Answers

1. All definitions can be found in the section and the Glossary.
2. Cash crops required more labor, so plantation owners turned to enslaved people as a labor force.
3. Puritans worshipped together in small groups. This led to a settlement pattern of a small town centered on the church, and church meetings probably evolved into political discussions of town issues, which became town meetings.
4. South: planter elite was the top of the social class and had power in local government, militias and courts; Middle Colonies: capitalists invested in mills, glass, and pottery works.
5. For England: increased flow of gold and silver, provided markets for finished goods, provided sources of raw materials; For Colonies: provided markets for some raw materials, provided supplies of finished goods.
6. South: huge tracts of fertile land led to cash crops; New England: rugged landscape and infertile soil led to subsistence farming; Middle: fertile soil led to wheat cash crop and large cities led to industry and trade.
7. Philadelphia was the main port in the Middle Colonies. They were very prosperous, due to trade with Britain.
8. Letters should include references to shipping costs, raw materials, and the high cost of imports.

Focus

Bellringer

Daily Focus Transparency 1-5

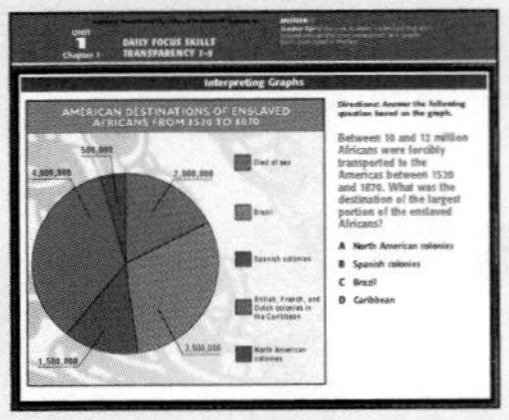

Guide to Reading

Answers:

Germans: settled in Pennsylvania; came to escape religious wars

Scots-Irish: settled on the frontier, backcountry of Pennsylvania, or the Southern Colonies; came to escape rising taxes, bad harvests, and religious persecution

Jews: settled in the large cities; came to escape religious persecution

Section Spotlight Video

To generate student interest and provide a springboard for class discussion, access the Chapter 1, Section 5 video at glencoe.com or on the video DVD.

Resource Manager

R Reading Strategies	C Critical Thinking	D Differentiated Instruction	W Writing Support	S Skill Practice
Teacher Edition • Analyzing, p. 43 • Det. Importance, p. 46 **Additional Resources** • Guid. Read. Act., URB p. 52 • RENTG, p. 14	**Teacher Edition** • Det. Cause/Effect, p. 44 **Additional Resources** • Pri. Source Read., URB p. 37 • Quizzes/Tests, p. 9	**Additional Resources** • Eng. Learner Act., URB p. 25 • Reteaching Act., URB p. 43 • Graphic Novel, p. 1	**Teacher Edition** • Expository Writing, p. 45 **Additional Resources** • Foldables, p. 46	**Teacher Edition** • Using Geo. Skills, p. 43 • Making Graphs, p. 44 **Additional Resources** • Hist. Analysis Act., URB p. 22 • Reteaching Act., URB p. 43 • Authentic Assess., p. 7

Section 5 — Section Audio — Spotlight Video

A Diverse Society

Guide to Reading

Big Ideas

Trade, War, and Migration Immigrants from Europe and those brought by force from Africa greatly increased the population of the American colonies in the 1700s.

Content Vocabulary
- slave code *(p. 44)*
- rationalism *(p. 45)*
- pietism *(p. 47)*
- revival *(p. 47)*

Academic Vocabulary
- contract *(p. 43)*
- widespread *(p. 47)*

People and Events to Identify
- Cotton Mather *(p. 42)*
- Stono Rebellion *(p. 45)*
- John Locke *(p. 46)*
- Baron Montesquieu *(p. 47)*
- Jonathan Edwards *(p. 47)*
- George Whitefield *(p. 47)*

Reading Strategy

Categorizing Complete a graphic organizer similar to the one below by identifying why immigrants settled in the colonies.

Group	Where They Settled	Reasons for Immigrating
Germans		
Scots-Irish		
Jews		

The American colonies experienced rapid growth through natural increase and immigration. The importation of enslaved Africans continued even as colonists engaged in philosophical and religious discussions about the rights of individuals.

Colonial America Grows

MAIN Idea The American colonies experienced tremendous growth due to high birthrates, long life spans, and immigration.

HISTORY AND YOU Do you remember getting vaccinated against certain diseases? Read to find out how inoculation was introduced in the colonies.

The population of the American colonies grew rapidly in the eighteenth century. A major factor was the era's high birthrate. Most women married in their early twenties, typically to men about the same age. On average, colonial women gave birth to seven children, although giving birth to twice that number of children was not uncommon. Between 1640 and 1700, the colonial population increased from 25,000 to more than 250,000. In the 1700s the population doubled every 25 years. By the time of the American Revolution, the colonial population had reached roughly 2.5 million.

An important factor in population growth was improved housing and sanitation. Although women often died in childbirth, many adults lived into their early sixties. Contagious diseases, however, such as typhoid fever, tuberculosis, cholera, diphtheria, and scarlet fever, continued to ravage residents in colonial cities.

When an epidemic of deadly smallpox swept through Boston in 1721, Reverend **Cotton Mather,** a Puritan leader, promoted "the new Method used by the Africans and Asiaticks, to prevent and abate the Dangers of the Small-Pox." This method, inoculation, proved highly successful. Of 6,000 people who were not inoculated and caught smallpox, about 900, or 15 percent, died. In contrast, only 6 of the 241 people who received inoculation died of the disease.

Immigration

Immigration also contributed to population growth. Some 300,000 European immigrants arrived between 1700 and 1775. Most settled in the Middle Colonies, especially eastern Pennsylvania. Many others headed to the frontier, where land was free, and settled in the backcountry of Pennsylvania and the colonial South. At the same time, traders brought large numbers of enslaved Africans to America, mostly to the Southern Colonies.

NATIONAL GEOGRAPHIC Ethnic Diversity in Colonial America, 1760

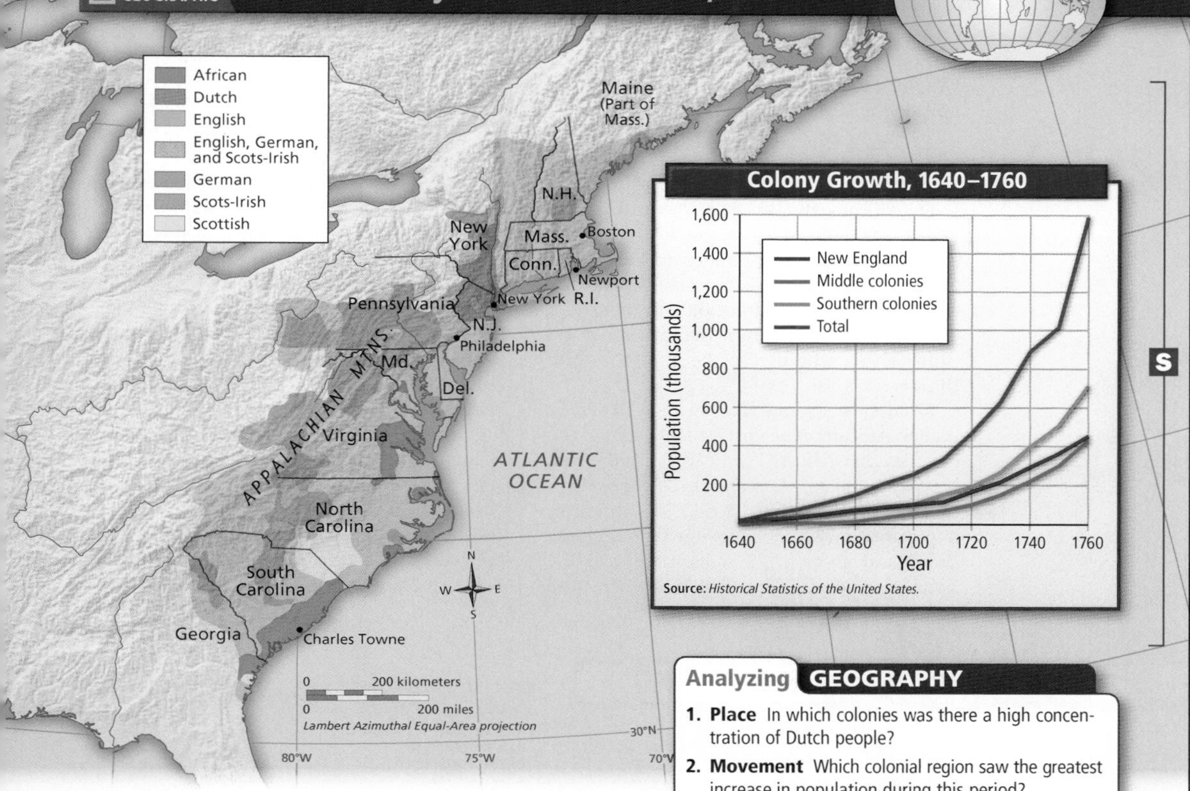

Source: *Historical Statistics of the United States.*

Analyzing GEOGRAPHY

1. **Place** In which colonies was there a high concentration of Dutch people?
2. **Movement** Which colonial region saw the greatest increase in population during this period?

In 1683 German Mennonites had come to Pennsylvania to escape religious wars at home, and by the early 1700s, a large wave of German immigration had begun. By 1775, more than 100,000 Germans lived in the colony, making up about one-third of the population. Most were farmers.

The Scots-Irish were descendants of the Scots who had helped England claim control of Northern Ireland. Beginning in 1717, rising taxes, poor harvests, and religious persecution convinced many to flee Ireland. An estimated 150,000 Scots-Irish came to the American colonies between 1717 and 1776. Most headed for the western frontier, settling in the backcountry of Pennsylvania and the South. R

Jews seeking religious tolerance also began moving to America in colonial times. In 1654 a small group of Dutch Jews from Brazil arrived in New York, which was then called New Amsterdam. There they founded one of the first synagogues in North America. By 1776, approximately 1,500 Jews lived in the colonies. R

Women

Women did not have equal rights in colonial America. In the early colonial era, married women could not own property or make **contracts** or wills. Husbands were the sole guardians of the children and were allowed to physically discipline both them and their wives. Single women and widows, however, had more rights. They could own property, file lawsuits, and run businesses.

Teach

R Reading Strategy

Analyzing Organize students into groups of four or five. Assign each group one of the immigrant groups listed in this section. After students have read the section, have the groups review the information on their assigned immigrant group to determine why these people immigrated to the colonies, and where they settled. Have groups present their findings in an oral presentation to the class. BL ELL

S Skill Practice

Using Geography Skills Have students study the map and write a summary of the information, describing the ethnic makeup of the population of each of the three colonial regions in 1760. OL

Analyzing GEOGRAPHY

Answers:
1. New York and New Jersey
2. the Southern Colonies

Hands-On Chapter Project
Step 5

Establishing a Colony in North America

Step 5: Encouraging Immigration

Directions Have students return to their groups. Each group should assume that their colony is relatively prosperous, but that it requires additional immigrants.

Using the textbook as well as library or Internet resources, each group researches the "pull" factors for immigrants in the region in which their colony is located around the year 1750, as well as the "push" factors at the time in Europe that might have encouraged immigration. Then have students create an informational pamphlet on the benefits of immigrating to their colony. Students should include a description of the geography, the economic activities and opportunities, examples of individuals who prospered in the colony, and any possible indenture contracts or other deals that they might want to offer to entice immigrants to move there. Encourage students to use page layout or word-processing software to plan and create their pamphlets.

Putting It Together Have a volunteer from each group present the pamphlet to the class. Discuss the various attractions, benefits, and challenges for immigrants in each colony. Then, as a class, vote on the colony which students feel would be likely to attract the most new immigrants. OL

(Chapter Project continued on the Visual Summary, p. 48)

C Critical Thinking

Determining Cause and Effect Discuss with students what slavery was like before and after the institution of the slave codes. **Ask:** How did the fact that English law did not recognize chattel slavery affect the development of slavery in the colonies? *(Slavery was slow to develop initially, and Africans were treated more like indentured servants than slaves.)* Why were the slave codes passed, and what was their effect? *(The number of Africans increased in the colonies and there was a desire to make hereditary, chattel slavery legal. After the slave codes were instituted, enslaved people no longer had any rights at all, but were property.)* OL

S Skill Practice

Making Graphs Have students make a circle graph using the data in the text about the numbers and fates of enslaved Africans between 1450 and 1870. Discuss with students the effects of the Atlantic slave trade on the enslaved people as well as the societies and economies of the slave holding people. OL

Additional Support

By the 1700s, the status of married women had improved. In most colonies, for example, a husband could not sell or mortgage his land without his wife's signature on the contract. Despite legal limitations, many women worked outside the home.

Africans in the Colonies

For Africans, the voyage to America usually began with a forced march to the West African coast, where they were traded to Europeans, branded, and crammed onto ships. Chained together in the ships' filthy holds for more than a month, they were given minimal food and drink. Those who died or became sick were thrown overboard.

S Historians estimate that between 10 and 12 million Africans were enslaved and sent to the Americas between 1450 and 1870. On the way, roughly 2 million died at sea. Of the 8 to 10 million Africans who reached the Americas, approximately 3.6 million went to Portuguese Brazil and another 1.5 million went to the Spanish colonies. The British, French, and Dutch colonies in the Caribbean imported nearly 3.7 million others to work on their plantations. Approximately 500,000 Africans were transported to British North America.

When the first Africans arrived in Virginia in 1619, English law did not recognize chattel slavery—the actual ownership of one human being by another. As a result, slavery developed slowly in the Chesapeake colonies. The first Africans brought to Virginia and Maryland were treated in a manner similar to indentured servants, and children born to Africans were not always considered enslaved.

At first, enslaved Africans could obtain their freedom by converting to Christianity. To many C English settlers, enslaving Africans was acceptable, not because they were not white, but because they were not Christian. Over time, as the number of Africans increased, their status changed. By the 1660s, new laws changed slavery into a hereditary system based on race.

Finally, in 1705 Virginia created a **slave code**—a set of laws defining the relationship between enslaved people and free people. Other colonies followed suit. Enslaved persons

PRIMARY SOURCE
The Atlantic Slave Trade c. 1500–1800

In 1619 the first Africans arrived in the English colonies, beginning the brutal African slave trade. After a nearly fatal voyage across the Atlantic, known as the Middle Passage, under stifling, dirty, and crowded conditions, those starved and exhausted Africans who managed to survive were sold in markets or at auction.

Captured Africans on a slave ship

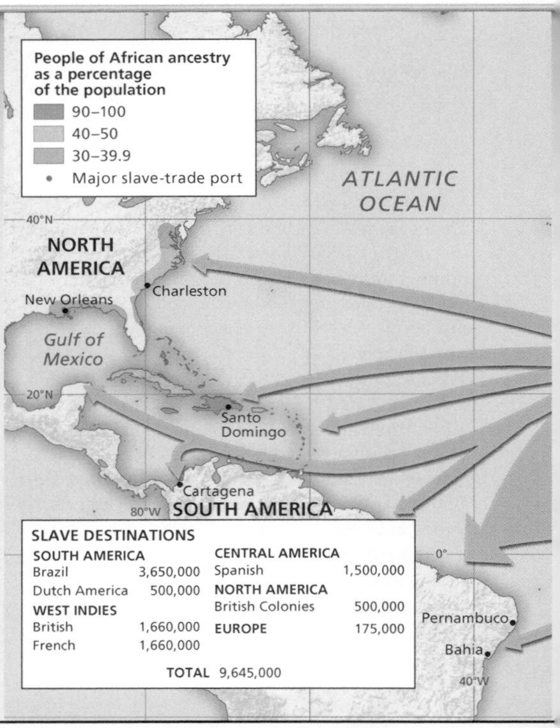

Activity: Interdisciplinary Connection

Literature and Folklore Have students use library and Internet resources to learn about traditional storytelling in Africa. **Ask:** How are traditional African folktales the same as or different from American folktales? What are some American folktales with African roots? Encourage students to find English-language translations of African folktales and legends and to compare stories and themes with familiar American folktales and legends. Have students write a short report about their findings. OL could not own property, testify against whites in court, move about freely, or assemble in large numbers. By the early 1700s, slavery had become generally accepted in colonial society. By 1775, roughly 20 percent of the colonial population was of African heritage.

No group in the American colonies endured lower status or more hardship than enslaved Africans. Most lived on Southern plantations, where they worked long days and were beaten and branded by planters. Planters also controlled enslaved Africans by threatening to sell them away from their families.

Family and religion helped the enslaved Africans maintain their dignity. Some resisted by escaping to the North; others refused to work hard or broke or lost their tools. In 1739 a group of Africans living near the Stono River in South Carolina rebelled against their white overseers and tried to escape to Spanish Florida. The militia quickly ended the **Stono Rebellion,** which took the lives of 21 whites and 44 Africans. **W**

Reading Check **Summarizing** In what ways did enslaved people resist their enslavement?

New Ideas

MAIN Idea The ideas of the Enlightenment and the Great Awakening made the colonists question their role as subjects of the English monarchy.

HISTORY AND YOU Have you ever read a book that changed the way you thought about a subject? Read how two cultural developments influenced American colonists.

During the 1700s the English colonies came under the influence of the Enlightenment and the Great Awakening. The first championed human reason, while the second stressed a new personal relationship with God.

The Enlightenment

Enlightenment thinkers came to believe that natural laws applied to social, political, and economic relationships, and that people could figure out these natural laws if they employed reason. This emphasis on logic and reasoning was known as **rationalism.**

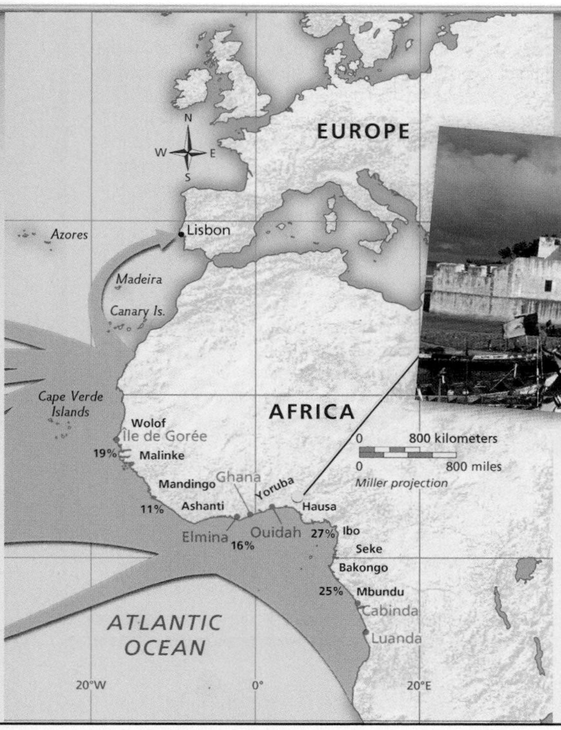

▼ In West Africa, the Castle of St. George held captured Africans until they were shipped to America.

▲ Most enslaved Africans spent their lives at hard agricultural labor or as domestic house slaves.

Analyzing VISUALS

1. **Specifying** About how many captured Africans were taken to the British colonies in North America?
2. **Explaining** Why do you think so many people died during the Middle Passage?

W Writing Support

Expository Writing Have students write a newspaper report about the Stono Rebellion. Reports should focus on facts, not opinions, and should be written in a formal style. Suggest to students that they use the questions: *Who? What? When? Where? Why?* and *How?* as a guide to what to include in their reports. **OL**

Analyzing VISUALS

Answers:
1. 500,000
2. Conditions were crowded and dark in the hold of the ship; people did not get enough fresh air, exercise, food and water. Also, they were probably very anxious and frightened about what was going to happen.

Reading Check

Answer:
They refused to work hard, broke or lost tools on purpose, or escaped. One group rebelled.

Additional Support

Activity: Technology Connection

The Middle Passage Refer students to the chart in the feature on this page. Ask them a series of questions to help them analyze the data. **Ask:** To which destination were most enslaved people taken? *(Brazil)* Where were the fewest enslaved people taken? *(Europe)* Why do you think so many enslaved people were taken to Brazil and so few were taken to Europe? *(Brazil probably had a plantation economy and needed large amounts of labor, while Europe did not need to import labor.)*

Then have students find out more about the Middle Passage, the route between Africa and America aboard the slave trader ships. Tell students of one of the most famous slave revolts that occurred along the Middle Passage on the *Amistad.* In this incident, a group of captives revolted during the voyage across the Atlantic, killing the captain and members of the crew. The *Amistad* captives landed in the United States, were charged with murder, but were acquitted and eventually returned to Africa.

Have students work individually or in groups to present their research on the Middle Passage in multimedia or slide show presentations. **OL**

R Reading Strategy

Determining Importance
Discuss with students the fact that the Zenger case is considered by most political scientists and historians to be a landmark event in the development of democracy, especially in the United States.
Ask: Why do you think that the Zenger case is considered so important? *(Answers will vary, but students should indicate an understanding that the case established a precedent for a free press, which is crucial in a democracy.)* OL

DBQ Document Based Questions

Answers:

1. He is pointing out that people are free to express their opinions about religion—which they were not free to do 200 years earlier—but are seemingly not free to express their opinions about the government.
2. They will become enslaved.

John Locke One of the earliest and most influential Enlightenment writers was **John Locke.** His contract theory of government and natural rights profoundly influenced the thinking of American political leaders. In his work *Two Treatises of Government,* Locke attempted to use reason to discover natural laws that applied to politics and society:

PRIMARY SOURCE

"123. If man in the state of nature be so free . . . why will he part with his freedom? . . . [T]he enjoyment of the property he has in this state is very unsafe, very unsecure. This makes him willing . . . to join in society with others . . . for the mutual *preservation* of their lives, liberties and estates. . . .

192. For no government can have a right to obedience from a people who have not freely consented to it; which they can never be supposed to do till . . . they are put in a full state of liberty to choose their government. . . ."

—from *Two Treatises of Government*

Equally important was Locke's *Essay on Human Understanding.* In this work he argued that, contrary to what most Christians believed, people were not born sinful. Instead, their minds were blank slates that could be shaped by society and education, making people better. These ideas, that all people have rights and that society can be improved, became core beliefs in American society.

Rousseau and Montesquieu French thinker Jean Jacques Rousseau carried Locke's ideas further. In *The Social Contract,* he argued that a government should be formed by the consent of the people, who would then make

PRIMARY SOURCE

The Trial of John Peter Zenger, 1735

R In 1733 John Peter Zenger began printing the *New York Weekly Journal,* a newspaper highly critical of New York Governor William Cosby. Unable to identify the anonymous writers and publisher, Cosby ordered Zenger's arrest for printing libel. The jury found Zenger not guilty. In doing so, the jury engaged in "jury nullification." Zenger was clearly guilty—but the jury, in effect, decided the law itself was wrong and refused to convict Zenger.

▲ *The Zenger case established a precedent for a free press in the colonies, and later in the United States.*

In his summation to the jury, Zenger's attorney Andrew Hamilton compared free speech and free press to freedom of religion and noted that liberty depends upon the ability to publish criticisms of the government:

PRIMARY SOURCE

". . . we well know that it is not two centuries ago that a man would have been burnt as an heretic for owning such opinions in matters of religion as are publicly wrote and printed at this day. . . . I think it is pretty clear that in New York a man may make very free with his God, but he must take special care what he says of his governor. It is agreed upon by all men that this is a reign of liberty, and while men keep within the bounds of truth I hope they may with safety both speak and write their sentiments of the conduct of men in power. I mean of that part of their conduct only which affects the liberty or property of the people under their administration; were this to be denied, then the next step may make them slaves; For what notions can be entertained of slavery beyond that of suffering the greatest injuries and oppressions without the liberty of complaining, or if they do, to be destroyed, body and estate, for so doing?"

—from *A Brief Narrative of the Case and Trial of John Peter Zenger*

DBQ Document-Based Questions

1. **Interpreting** What point is Hamilton making when he says that "a man may make very free with his God," but must be careful about what he says about the governor?
2. **Identifying Central Issues** What does Hamilton say will happen if people are not allowed to express their opinions about those in the government?

Additional Support

Activity: Collaborative Learning

Comparing and Contrasting Tell students that although most colonists had probably never heard of John Locke, his philosophy would prove to be of great importance to colonial Americans. The idea of natural rights and responsible government became the basis of protest and revolt in the colonies.

Have students work in small groups to do research to find out more about the ideas of Locke, Rousseau, and Montesquieu. Students should prepare a report that compares and contrasts the ideas of these three important Enlightenment figures. Students' reports should also discuss their influence on the men who wrote the U.S. Constitution and discuss which of their ideas appear in that document. AL their own laws. Another influential writer was **Baron Montesquieu.** In his work, *The Spirit of Laws,* Montesquieu suggested that there were three types of political power—executive, legislative, and judicial. These powers should be separated into different branches to protect people's liberty:

PRIMARY SOURCE

"In order to have this liberty, it is necessary the government be so constituted as one man need not be afraid of another.

When the legislative and executive powers are united in the same body of magistrates, there can be no liberty. . . .

Again, there is no liberty, if the judiciary power be not separated from the legislative and executive. Were it joined with the legislative, the life and liberty of the subject would be exposed to arbitrary [control], for the judge would be then the legislator. Were it joined to the executive power, the judge might behave with violence and oppression."

—from *The Spirit of Laws*

Montesquieu's ideas were widely debated. They had a great influence on the leaders who wrote the United States Constitution.

The Great Awakening

While some Americans turned away from a religious world view, others renewed their Christian faith. Many Americans embraced a European religious movement called **pietism,** which stressed an individual's piety (devoutness) and an emotional union with God. Throughout the colonies, ministers held **revivals**—large public meetings for preaching and prayer. This **widespread** resurgence of religious fervor became known as the Great Awakening.

In 1734 a Massachusetts preacher named **Jonathan Edwards** helped launch the Great Awakening. In powerful, terrifying sermons, he invoked the "forbearance of an incensed [angry] God" and argued that a person had to repent and convert. His emotional, as opposed to rational, style of preaching was typical of the fervor of the Great Awakening. **George Whitefield,** an Anglican minister from England, also attracted and inspired many listeners.

The Great Awakening peaked around 1740. Many churches split into factions called the New Lights and the Old Lights. Those who embraced the new ideas—including Baptists, some Presbyterians and Congregationalists, and a new group called Methodists—won many converts, while traditional churches lost members.

In the South, the Baptists gained a strong following among poor farmers. Baptists also welcomed Africans at their revivals and condemned slavery. Despite violent attempts by planters to break up Baptist meetings, about 20 percent of Virginia's whites and thousands of enslaved Africans had become Baptists by 1775.

The Enlightenment and the Great Awakening had different origins, but both profoundly affected colonial society. The Enlightenment provided arguments against British rule. The Great Awakening undermined allegiance to traditional authority.

Reading Check **Determining Cause and Effect** Why did the Great Awakening cause division in established churches?

Section 5 REVIEW

Vocabulary

1. **Explain** the significance of: Cotton Mather, slave code, Stono Rebellion, rationalism, John Locke, Baron Montesquieu, pietism, revival, Jonathan Edwards, George Whitefield.

Main Ideas

2. **Describing** What was slavery like in the early colonies?
3. **Identifying** What are two beliefs of John Locke that later became core American values?

Critical Thinking

4. **Big Ideas** What factors and motivations brought people to the American colonies in the 1700s?
5. **Organizing** Use a graphic organizer similar to the one below to explain the reasons for the population increase in the colonies in the 1700s.

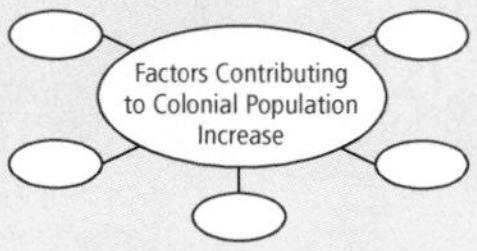

6. **Analyzing Visuals** Examine the map on pages 44–45. In which area of the Americas did African Americans become the greatest percentage of the population?

Writing About History

7. **Persuasive Writing** Suppose that you are a German immigrant to the colonies in 1725. Write a letter to relatives in Germany explaining what your life in the colonies has been like and encouraging them to join you.

History ONLINE
Study Central™ To review this section, go to glencoe.com and click on Study Central.

47

Reading Check

Answer:
Some people wanted to follow the traditional, existing ways of worship, while others were inspired by the new spirit of piety of the Great Awakening to establish a new church with new ways of worshipping.

Assess

History ONLINE

Study Central™ provides summaries, interactive games, and online graphic organizers to help students review content.

Close

Summarizing Ask: What contributed to the diversity in colonial society? *(Large numbers of immigrants came to the colonies in this period, as well as enslaved Africans. Also new movements, such as the Enlightenment and the Great Awakening, created an atmosphere in which people explored new ideas about government, society, and religion.)* OL

Section 5 REVIEW

Answers

1. All definitions can be found in the section and the Glossary.
2. At first, there was no concept of chattel slavery and not all enslaved people were treated as such, but more like indentured servants. Also, enslaved people who became Christians were sometimes freed, because their enslavement was based not on their skin color, but on the fact that they were not Christians. Lastly, slavery was not assumed to be hereditary. Later, the colonies established slave codes that defined enslavement as hereditary, chattel slavery.
3. that all people have natural rights and the rights of government come from the people
4. pursuit of religious freedom; escape from religious wars, rising taxes, poor harvests, enslavement
5. enslavement of Africans, immigration, improved housing and sanitation, smallpox inoculation, higher birthrate
6. Caribbean
7. Letters should include descriptive language of daily life and reasons why the relative should emigrate to the colonies.

Determining Cause and Effect Discuss with students the information provided in the Visual Summary for this chapter. **Ask:** What information does the Visual Summary provide? *(the causes and effects of European exploration and colonization in the Americas)* Have students identify at least one effect for each cause or one cause for each effect in one category in the Visual Summary. Tell students that they may use information already in the Visual Summary as well as from within the chapter. **OL**

Narrative Writing Have students select one cause, effect, or image in the Visual Summary as a story starter and then write a short story based on that item. Stories should be realistic fiction. Encourage students to do additional research to find historical details that will enrich their work. Once you have read the stories and students have made final revisions, collect them into a single volume for your classroom or the school library. **OL**

Chapter 1 Visual Summary

STUDY TO GO — You can study anywhere, any time by downloading quizzes and flashcards to your PDA from glencoe.com.

Causes of European Exploration

- The Crusades broaden European horizons and stimulate interest in luxury goods from Asia.
- The rise of towns and the growth of the merchant class enrich monarchs and make them less dependent on the nobility.
- Monarchs want to find trade routes to Asia, by passing Italy and the Muslim states.
- The Renaissance promotes a scientific view of the world.
- New technologies such as the compass and astrolabe make sea exploration possible.

▲ *Trading ships like these vessels of the Dutch East India Company carried goods around the world.*

▲ *The English founded their first permanent colony in North America at Jamestown in 1607.*

Causes of English Colonization

- The wealth Spain acquired from conquering the Aztec and mining gold encourages others to consider creating colonies.
- The Protestant Reformation in England leads to the rise of Puritans who are persecuted by the English government, as are Catholics and others who disagree with the Anglican Church.
- Puritans, Catholics, and other religious dissenters, such as the Quakers, seek religious freedom by migrating to America.
- The growth of trade and the rising demand for English wool lead to landowners evicting peasants so as to raise sheep. Some of the peasants migrate to America to escape poverty and obtain land.

Effects of European Colonization

- Europeans explore West Africa; they begin enslaving Africans and forcing them to work on sugarcane plantations.
- European explorers land in the Americas, map the eastern coastline, and begin exploring the interior.
- Beginning with Cortés, Spanish conquistadors conquer Mexico, Peru, and the Maya people of Central America.
- An exchange of plants, animals, goods, and ideas begins between Europe and the Americas; European diseases devastate Native American populations; American diseases spread to Europe.
- Spain establishes colonies in the Caribbean; France establishes colonies along the St. Lawrence River; England establishes colonies along the east coast, from Massachusetts to Georgia.
- Cash crops, such as rice, tobacco, and sugarcane, allow Southern Colonies to flourish; they also lead to the rise of the slave trade.
- Triangular trade allows northern American colonies to prosper and leads to the rise of cities along the American East Coast.

▲ *In the South, a plantation economy developed in which many planters grew rich by exporting their cash crops to Britain.*

Hands-On Chapter Project
Step 6: Wrap Up

Establishing a Colony in North America

Step 6: Evaluating the Colonial Experience Students will synthesize what they have learned in Steps 1, 2, 3, 4, and 5.

Directions Have the groups of students review their colonial experience—their plans, the location they selected, their goals, the government they established, the colony's economy and growth, and then summarize the challenges they learned about as they worked on the project.

Putting It Together Then have students discuss and evaluate as a class the challenges and dangers real colonists must have faced in establishing a colony. **OL**

Chapter 1 ASSESSMENT

Reviewing Vocabulary

Directions: Choose the word or words that best complete the sentence.

1. The Aztec demanded ______ from the areas they conquered.
   - **A** praise
   - **B** maize
   - **C** silver
   - **D** tribute

2. The Portuguese used a ship known as a ______ to better explore the shallow inlets of the Americas.
   - **A** astrolabe
   - **B** *encomienda*
   - **C** caravel
   - **D** lateen

3. Because Pennsylvania was owned by William Penn, it was considered
   - **A** a charter colony.
   - **B** a joint-stock company.
   - **C** a proprietary colony.
   - **D** part of the headright system.

4. Individuals who signed contracts to cover the cost of transportation to the colonies were called
   - **A** serfs.
   - **B** indentured servants.
   - **C** mercantilists.
   - **D** subsistence farmers.

5. The Enlightenment encouraged a renewed emphasis on logic called
   - **A** pietism.
   - **B** mercantilism.
   - **C** activism.
   - **D** rationalism.

Reviewing Main Ideas

Directions: Choose the best answer for each of the following questions.

Section 1 *(pp. 4–11)*

6. Which of the following was a feature of the Mississippian culture?
   - **A** ocean-going canoes
   - **B** pyramids
   - **C** pueblos
   - **D** giant basalt sculptures

7. The Iroquois Confederacy was formed to
   - **A** stop the constant warfare.
   - **B** unite against the English.
   - **C** better compete with the Algonquian peoples.
   - **D** invade the Great Lakes region.

Section 2 *(pp. 14–23)*

8. The Treaty of Tordesillas established which of the following?
   - **A** European Christians would fight the Crusades to retake holy places from Muslims in the Middle East.
   - **B** Spain, Portugal, England, and France would all have equal rights to colonies in the Americas.
   - **C** The Aztec would surrender their lands and possessions to Hernán Cortés and the rulers of Spain.
   - **D** Spain would control everything west of a line of demarcation; Portugal would control everything to the east.

TEST-TAKING TIP

When possible, depending on the form of the test, underline or circle key words in the question stem so that you know what to focus on as you read the answer choices. For example, some questions ask for a specific number of items in an answer.

Need Extra Help?

If You Missed Questions . . .	1	2	3	4	5	6	7	8
Go to Page . . .	6	16	32–33	32–33	45–46	8	11	18

GO ON

Reviewing Vocabulary

1. D Some students may be confused by choice *A*, which can be a synonym for tribute. Remind students that tribute in this sense means "payment."

2. C The caravel was highly maneuverable, fast, and small enough to sail beside shallow coastlines and farther up the mouths of rivers.

3. C Proprietary colonies were owned by a single person, or proprietor. Since Pennsylvania was owned by a single person, students should be able to immediately eliminate *B*, because a joint-stock company is composed of more than one person. Charter colonies were started with the granting of a charter usually to a group of people. The headright system is not related to ownership of colonies.

4. B Students may have trouble choosing between *A* and *B*. Students should understand the difference between serfs, who had no freedom, and indentured servants, who worked to pay off a debt, and would be free once the debt had been paid off.

5. D This is a good question to help students understand the importance of carefully reading the question. In this case, students are looking for the answer choice that encouraged a renewed "emphasis on logic." Rationalism is the most closely related: "rational" and "logical" are synonymous.

Reviewing Main Ideas

6. B Considering the geography of the United States may help students who are confused eliminate *A* and *C*, which are characteristics of southwestern and northwestern cultures, respectively.

7. A The Iroquois Confederacy, with its binding oral constitution, is a good example of a democratic government. Explain to students that, although the two types of governments are not similar, both the Confederacy and the United States had constitutions that spelled out the rules of governing. The Confederacy was formed to stop constant warfare and set out rules that allowed different tribes to work together.

8. D Although students should be able to immediately eliminate *A*, they may be confused by the remaining choices. *C* is incorrect, because Cortés and his men defeated the Aztec; they did not sign a treaty. *B* and *D* are similar, but the Treaty of Tordesillas was between Spain and Portugal and no other nations. Spain, Portugal, England, and France never signed any agreements to divide up colonies in the Americas.

9. B Students can approach this question as if it were a true/false question. They must look for the answer that is a correct motivation for the creation of English colonies. *A, C,* and *D* are all false or untrue. Therefore, they cannot be correct. It is true that new religious groups sought religious freedom outside of Britain.

10. C One of the most interesting facets of Rhode Island is the religious tolerance that was practiced there. In fact, Newport is home to the oldest synagogue in the United States, the Touro Synagogue. In addition, government had no control over religious practices.

11. A The farmers in the backcountry wanted to take more land from Native Americans, but they were not supported in this by the wealthy planters, who did not want to be involved in a fight with Native Americans. Therefore, the rebellion began over land. Remind students that most fights with Native Americans took place over land issues or disputes.

12. D Students should always look for answer choices they can immediately eliminate to increase their chances of choosing the correct answer. In this case, *B* should be eliminated immediately, because it contradicts the question. Students should also realize that slavery was never illegal in the colonies because enslavement began very soon after the founding of the colonies and this suggests that both answers *(A)* and *(C)* can be eliminated.

Chapter 1 ASSESSMENT

Section 3 *(pp. 24–33)*

9. The Reformation encouraged the creation of English colonies because
   - **A** the English monarchs wanted to banish all non-Anglicans.
   - **B** new religious groups sought religious freedom outside of England.
   - **C** Protestants wanted land for new churches.
   - **D** Martin Luther told his followers to leave their homes and start new lives.

10. In Roger Williams's colony of Rhode Island,
   - **A** only Puritans could worship publicly.
   - **B** the government controlled all aspects of daily life.
   - **C** different religious practices were tolerated.
   - **D** Native Americans were assimilated into English culture.

Section 4 *(pp. 34–41)*

11. Bacon's Rebellion began because
   - **A** farmers wanted to take more land from Native Americans.
   - **B** farmers were tired of paying high taxes.
   - **C** farmers were not allowed in the House of Burgesses.
   - **D** farmers wanted to acquire enslaved Africans.

Section 5 *(pp. 42–47)*

12. Why did slavery slowly develop in the colonies?
   - **A** English law made it illegal to enslave colonists.
   - **B** King Charles II granted a charter that encouraged the slave trade in the colonies.
   - **C** Africans were allowed to sue for their freedom.
   - **D** England did not allow trade with other nations, some of whom controlled the slave trade.

13. In the 1700s the English colonies were affected by a resurgence of religious zeal known as
   - **A** the Enlightenment.
   - **B** the Glorious Revolution.
   - **C** the Renaissance.
   - **D** the Great Awakening.

Critical Thinking

Directions: Choose the best answers to the following questions.

14. The geography of the region in which they lived affected how Native American groups
   - **A** developed language.
   - **B** gathered their food.
   - **C** governed themselves.
   - **D** conducted trade.

Base your answers to question 15 on the map below and on your knowledge of Chapter 1.

Settlement of the Colonies, 1587–1700

15. Which of the following colonies had the largest settled areas by 1660?
   - **A** Massachusetts
   - **B** North Carolina
   - **C** New Hampshire
   - **D** Virginia

Need Extra Help?

If You Missed Questions . . .	9	10	11	12	13	14	15
Go to Page . . .	24–25	30	36	44–45	47	4–11	32

GO ON

13. D Of the movements mentioned in the answer choices, only the Great Awakening was a religious movement. If students are unsure of the correct answer, review briefly the other movements. Point out that the Enlightenment and Renaissance were social movements, and that the Glorious Revolution was political.

Critical Thinking

14. B This type of question requires a bit of common sense reasoning. Students should ask themselves which of the answer choices would most likely be affected by geography. Remind students that for multiple-choice questions, they must always look for the *best* answer to the question among the choices given. Physical geography would most likely affect food gathering or trade. In this case, based on the information in the chapter, *B* is the best answer.

15. A Careful reading of the map makes map questions easy to answer. The question specifically asks for areas settled by 1660, so students should use the map key to identify those areas settled by 1660.

16. Which of the following is true about the early colonies of Jamestown and Plymouth?

A They were started by people interested in establishing a new nation.

B Disease caused a huge loss of life.

C Tobacco was the primary source of income.

D They were started by religious separatists.

Analyze the painting and answer the questions that follow. Base your answers on the painting and on your knowledge of Chapter 1.

17. In this painting, William Penn is most likely

A asking Native Americans for permission to take over Pennsylvania.

B telling Native Americans in Pennsylvania about the benefits of being Quakers.

C explaining to Native Americans in Pennsylvania that he was their new king.

D signing a treaty with Native Americans who lived in Pennsylvania.

18. The overall mood of the subjects in the painting is

A tense and suspicious.

B friendly and open.

C jolly and laughing.

D angry and ranting.

Document-Based Questions

Directions: Analyze the document and answer the short-answer questions that follow the document.

In 1519 conquistador Hernán Cortés and his soldiers conquered the Aztec and entered their capital, Tenochtitlán. The following excerpt is from an Aztec account of the event:

> "When the Spaniards were installed in the palace, they asked Motecuhzoma [Montezuma] about the city's resources and reserves. . . . They questioned him closely and then demanded gold. Motecuhzoma guided them to it. . . . When they arrived at the treasure house called Teucalco, the riches of gold and feathers were brought out to them. . . . Next they went to Motecuhzoma's storehouse, in the place called Totocalco, where his personal treasures were kept. The Spaniards grinned like little beasts and patted each other with delight. When they entered the hall of treasures, it was as if they had arrived in Paradise. They searched everywhere and coveted everything; they were slaves to their own greed. . . . They seized these treasures as if they were their own, as if this plunder were merely a stroke of good luck."
>
> —quoted in *The Broken Spears: The Aztec Account of the Conquest of Mexico*

19. How does the author of this account characterize the Spanish?

20. What is the overall tone of this account?

Extended Response

21. The Spanish, English, and French who settled in the Americas each related to or treated the native peoples they encountered differently. Write an expository essay comparing and contrasting how each of the three groups generally interacted with Native Americans. In your essay, include an introduction and at least three paragraphs to describe the various relationships with supporting details from Chapter 1.

STOP

History ONLINE

For additional test practice, use Self-Check Quizzes—Chapter 1 at glencoe.com.

Need Extra Help?

If You Missed Questions . . .	16	17	18	19	20	21
Go to Page . . .	24–33	R18	R18	51	R19	14–23

16. B This question asks students to find a similarity between the two colonies. Students may have a difficult time with this question, because some of the answer choices are true of one of the two colonies. It is important that students understand that the correct answer will be true of both colonies.

17. D Explain to students that when they analyze historical art, they should always keep the historical circumstances in mind. Students should recognize that Penn has a treaty in the painting. The statements in the other answer choices are all untrue, and therefore, cannot be correct.

18. B Students should pay attention to the expressions on the faces of the participants and their body language. There is nothing to suggest that the meeting is tense, suspicious, angry, or ranting; the overall feeling of the painting is positive. However, jolly and laughing do not fit the situation. Friendly and open best captures the mood. You may want to walk through the picture and discuss answer choices with the class if students have trouble interpreting the painting.

Document-Based Questions

19. The author describes them as greedy beasts. This question asks for specific information, so students should refer back to the passage specifically looking for the description. The author specifically uses the words *greedy* and *beasts*, so students' answers should contain some form of this description.

20. The tone is one of anger and disgust. This question should be easy to answer after students answer question 18. If students have trouble with this one, it may be helpful to read the passage aloud and ask the class what feelings the passage evokes in them as they hear it. Relate these feelings to tone.

Extended Response

21. Students' essays will vary, but should clearly and logically compare and contrast the relations between each of the three European groups and Native Americans, with supporting details and examples from the chapter. Be sure that students followed directions properly and include an introduction and at least three paragraphs.

History ONLINE

Have students visit the Web site at glencoe.com to review Chapter 1 and take the Self-Check Quiz.

Need Extra Help?

Have students refer to the pages listed if they miss any of the questions.

Chapter 2 Planning Guide

Key to Ability Levels	
BL Below Level	**AL** Above Level
OL On Level	**ELL** English Language Learners

Key to Teaching Resources	
Print Material	Transparency
CD-ROM or DVD	

Levels					Resources	Chapter Opener	Section 1	Section 2	Section 3	Section 4	Chapter Assess
BL	OL	AL	ELL								
					FOCUS						
BL	OL	AL	ELL		**Daily Focus Skills Transparencies**		2-1	2-2	2-3	2-4	
					TEACH						
BL	OL		ELL		**Reading Essentials and Note-Taking Guide***		p. 17	p. 20	p. 23	p. 26	
	OL				**Historical Analysis Skills Activity, URB**					p. 56	
BL	OL		ELL		**Guided Reading Activities, URB***		p. 80	p. 81	p. 82	p. 83	
BL	OL	AL	ELL		**Content Vocabulary Activity, URB***	p. 61					
BL	OL	AL	ELL		**Academic Vocabulary Activity, URB**	p. 63					
	OL	AL			**Critical Thinking Skills Activity, URB**			p. 66			
BL	OL		ELL		**Reading Skills Activity, URB**					p. 55	
BL			ELL		**English Learner Activity, URB**			p. 59			
	OL	AL			**Reinforcing Skills Activity, URB**		p. 65				
BL	OL	AL	ELL		**Differentiated Instruction Activity, URB**			p. 57			
BL	OL		ELL		**Time Line Activity, URB**					p. 67	
	OL				**Linking Past and Present Activity, URB**		p. 68				
BL	OL	AL	ELL		**American Art and Music Activity, URB**			p. 73			
BL	OL	AL	ELL		**Interpreting Political Cartoons Activity, URB**		p. 75				
		AL			**Enrichment Activity, URB**	p. 78					
BL	OL	AL	ELL		**American Biographies**		✓	✓	✓		
BL	OL	AL	ELL		**Primary Source Reading, URB**			p. 69		p. 71	
BL	OL	AL	ELL		**The Living Constitution***	✓	✓	✓	✓	✓	✓
	OL	AL			**American History Primary Source Documents Library**	✓	✓	✓	✓	✓	✓
BL	OL	AL	ELL		**Unit Map Overlay Transparencies**	✓	✓	✓	✓	✓	✓
BL	OL	AL	ELL		**Differentiated Instruction for the American History Classroom**	✓	✓	✓	✓	✓	✓
BL	OL	AL	ELL		**StudentWorks™ Plus**	✓	✓	✓	✓	✓	✓

Note: Please refer to the *Unit 1 Resource Book* for this chapter's URB materials.

* Also available in Spanish

TeacherWorks Plus
All-In-One Planner and Resource Center

- Interactive Lesson Planner
- Interactive Teacher Edition
- Fully editable blackline masters
- Section Spotlight Videos Launch
- Differentiated Lesson Plans
- Printable reports of daily assignments
- Standards Tracking System

Levels: BL	OL	AL	ELL	Resources	Chapter Opener	Section 1	Section 2	Section 3	Section 4	Chapter Assess
				TEACH *(continued)*						
BL	OL	AL	ELL	American Music Hits Through History CD	✓	✓	✓	✓	✓	✓
BL	OL	AL	ELL	Unit Time Line Transparencies and Activities	✓	✓	✓	✓	✓	✓
BL	OL	AL	ELL	Cause and Effect Transparencies, Strategies, and Activities	✓	✓	✓	✓	✓	✓
BL	OL	AL	ELL	Why It Matters Transparencies, Strategies, and Activities	✓	✓	✓	✓	✓	✓
BL	OL	AL	ELL	American Issues	✓	✓	✓	✓	✓	✓
	OL	AL	ELL	American Art and Architecture Transparencies, Strategies, and Activities	✓	✓	✓	✓	✓	✓
BL	OL	AL		High School American History Literature Library	✓	✓	✓	✓	✓	✓
BL	OL	AL	ELL	*The American Vision* Video Program	✓	✓	✓	✓	✓	✓
Teacher Resources				Strategies for Success	✓	✓	✓	✓	✓	✓
Teacher Resources				Success with English Learner	✓	✓	✓	✓	✓	✓
Teacher Resources				Reading Strategies and Activities for the Social Studies Classroom	✓	✓	✓	✓	✓	✓
Teacher Resources				Presentation Plus! with MindJogger CheckPoint	✓	✓	✓	✓	✓	✓
				ASSESS						
BL	OL	AL	ELL	Section Quizzes and Chapter Tests*		p. 19	p. 20	p. 21	p. 22	p. 23
BL	OL	AL	ELL	Authentic Assessment With Rubrics						p. 9
BL	OL	AL	ELL	Standardized Test Practice Workbook						p. 3
BL	OL	AL	ELL	*ExamView® Assessment Suite*		2-1	2-2	2-3	2-4	Ch. 2
				CLOSE						
BL			ELL	Reteaching Activity, URB						p. 77
BL	OL		ELL	Reading and Study Skills Foldables™	p. 49					
BL	OL	AL	ELL	*American History* in Graphic Novel			p. 7			

✓ Chapter- or unit-based activities applicable to all sections in this chapter

Chapter 2 Integrating Technology

Using a Widget

Teach With Technology

What is a widget?

The McGraw-Hill Social Studies widget is a program for any computer with Internet access that acts as a one-stop launching pad for both software- and online-based programs.

How can the widget help my students and me?

The widget is a convenient way for you and your students to access McGraw-Hill's technology tools, both software-based and online. Some of the features of the widget include:

- customizable links to frequently used Glencoe Web pages
- recognition of, and compatibility with, Glencoe DVD and CD-ROM programs
- QuickPass entry for fast access to chapter content and activities

Visit glencoe.com to download the free student and teacher versions of the McGraw-Hill Social Studies widget.

History ONLINE
Visit glencoe.com and enter ***QuickPass***™ code TAV9399c2T for Chapter 2 resources.

You can easily launch a wide range of digital products from your computer's desktop with the McGraw-Hill Social Studies widget.

	Student	Teacher	Parent
Media Library			
• Section Audio	●		●
• Spanish Audio Summaries	●		●
• Section Spotlight Videos	●	●	●
***The American Vision* Online Learning Center (Web Site)**			
• StudentWorks™ Plus Online	●	●	●
• Multilingual Glossary	●	●	●
• Study-to-Go	●	●	●
• Chapter Overviews	●	●	●
• Self-Check Quizzes	●	●	●
• Student Web Activities	●	●	●
• ePuzzles and Games	●	●	●
• Vocabulary eFlashcards	●	●	●
• In Motion Animations	●	●	●
• Study Central™	●	●	●
• Web Activity Lesson Plans		●	
• Vocabulary PuzzleMaker	●	●	●
• Historical Thinking Activities		●	
• Beyond the Textbook	●	●	●

Reading Support From Jamestown Education

- **Timed Readings Plus in Social Studies** helps students increase their reading rate and fluency while maintaining comprehension. The 400-word passages are similar to those found on state and national assessments.
- **Reading in the Content Area: Social Studies** concentrates on six essential reading skills that help students better comprehend what they read. The book includes 75 high-interest nonfiction passages written at increasing levels of difficulty.
- **Reading Social Studies** includes strategic reading instruction and vocabulary support in Social Studies content for both ELLs and native speakers of English.

www.jamestowneducation.com

National Geographic

Index to National Geographic Magazine:

The following articles relate to this chapter:

- "WILLIAM BARTRAM A Naturalist's Vision of Frontier America" by Glenn Oeland, March 2001.

National Geographic Society Products To order the following, call National Geographic at 1-800-368-2728:

- *The American Revolution* (PicturePack Transparencies)

Access National Geographic's new, dynamic MapMachine Web site and other geography resources at:

www.nationalgeographic.com
www.nationalgeographic.com/maps

Biography · A&E Home Video · The History Channel

The following videotape programs are available from Glencoe as supplements to this chapter:

- Founding Fathers, DVD (ISBN 1-76-703093-1)
- Paul Revere: The Midnight Rider (ISBN 1-56-501596-7)

To order, call Glencoe at 1-800-334-7344. To find classroom resources to accompany many of these videos, check the following home pages:

A&E Television: www.aetv.com
The History Channel: www.historychannel.com

Reading List Generator CD-ROM — Glencoe BookLink 3

Use this database to search more than 30,000 titles to create a customized reading list for your students.

- Reading lists can be organized by students' reading level, author, genre, theme, or area of interest.
- The database provides Degrees of Reading Power™ (DRP) and Lexile™ readability scores for all selections.
- A brief summary of each selection is included.

Leveled reading suggestions for this chapter:

For students at a Grade 8 reading level:
- ***America's Ethan Allen***, by Stewart Holbrook

For students at a Grade 9 reading level:
- ***Guns for General Washington***, by Seymour Reit

For students at a Grade 10 reading level:
- ***Abigail Adams: Witness to a Revolution***, by Natalie S. Bober

For students at a Grade 11 reading level:
- ***George Washington***, by Marian Leighton

For students at a Grade 12 reading level:
- ***Black Heroes of the American Revolution***, by Burke Davis

Introducing

Chapter 2

Focus

MAKING CONNECTIONS

Why Do People Rebel?

Ask students to suggest reasons why people have rebelled against their governments. Activate students' prior knowledge about revolution and rebellion by asking if they recall any reasons why American colonists rebelled against Great Britain. Students may recall that one reason was that the colonists were angered over what they claimed was "taxation without representation." Ask students to recall John Locke's ideas about the contract between the people and their government from Chapter 1. Ask students what would constitute a government breaking that contract, which would justify a rebellion by the people. **OL**

Teach

Big Ideas

As students study the chapter, remind them to consider the section-based Big Ideas included in each section's Guide to Reading. The **Essential Question** in the activities below tie in to the Big Ideas and help students think about and understand important chapter concepts. In addition, the Hands-on Chapter Projects with their culminating activities relate the content from each section to the Big Ideas. These activities build on each other as students progress through the chapter. Section activities culminate in the wrap-up activity on the Visual Summary page.

Chapter 2

The American Revolution

1754–1783

George Washington at Valley Forge

1754
- French and Indian War begins

1765
- Parliament passes the Stamp Act, triggering protests throughout the colonies

1770
- British troops fire on colonists in Boston Massacre

U.S. PRESIDENTS
U.S. EVENTS
WORLD EVENTS

1745 — 1755 — 1765

1748
- Montesquieu's *Spirit of Laws* is published

1751
- Chinese invade Tibet and control succession to the throne

1755
- Samuel Johnson's *Dictionary of the English Language* is published

1769
- Steam engine is patented by James Watt

Section 1

The Colonies Fight for Their Rights

Essential Question: How did the relationship between Britain and its colonies begin to disintegrate after the mid-1700s? *(The French and Indian War led Britain to establish several rounds of economic policies and new taxes that angered many colonists, leading to unrest.)* Point out that in Section 1 students will learn how Britain's renewed controls over the colonies led to resistance and protests. **OL**

Section 2

The Revolution Begins

Essential Question: What led to the American Revolution and the establishment of the United States? *(A series of restrictions and reprisals established by the British on their American colonies led to increased tensions and rebellion in 1775.)* Explain that in Section 2, students will learn how relations between Britain and its colonies deteriorated, leading to rebellion and the colonists' formation of their own government. **OL**

Chapter Audio

MAKING CONNECTIONS

Why Do People Rebel?

Even today, Americans grow frustrated when the government raises taxes. In the early colonial era, Americans grew accustomed to running their own affairs. So when Britain tried to reestablish control, tensions mounted over taxes and basic rights.

- *Why do you think colonists became angry at Britain?*
- *When do you think it is acceptable to rebel against a government?*

1775
- First shots of the War are fired at Lexington and Concord

1776
- Declaration of Independence is signed

1781
- Cornwallis surrenders at Yorktown, marking the end of the Revolutionary War

1783
- Treaty of Paris is signed, officially recognizing the independence of the United States

1775 — 1785

1776
- Adam Smith's treatise on mercantilism, *Wealth of Nations*, is published

1780
- Empress Maria Theresa of Austria-Hungary dies

FOLDABLES

Generalizing on the American Revolution Create a Concept-Map Book Foldable that details the causes and the course of the American Revolutionary War. Select the most important causes of the war and list them inside one-half of the Concept-Map. Use the other half to list the outcomes of battles during the war.

American Revolution | Causes of the War | Course of the War

History ONLINE Visit glencoe.com and enter *QuickPass*™ code TAV9846c2 for Chapter 2 resources.

More About the Photo

Visual Literacy Tell students that this painting, titled *The March to Valley Forge*, by William B. T. Trego depicts colonial troops on their way to Valley Forge, Pennsylvania, the Continental Army's headquarters during the winter of 1777–1778. The winter at Valley Forge became celebrated for the troops' dedication in the face of terrible cold, hunger, and lack of essential supplies. Valley Forge was a serious test of the colonists' will to continue their fight against Britain—a test they passed due to their loyalty to Washington and to his leadership abilities.

FOLDABLES Study Organizer **Dinah Zike's Foldables**

Dinah Zike's Foldables are three-dimensional, interactive graphic organizers that help students practice basic writing skills, review vocabulary terms, and identify main ideas. Instructions for creating and using Foldables can be found in the Appendix at the end of this book and in the *Dinah Zike's Reading and Study Skills Foldables* booklet.

Section 3

The War for Independence

Essential Question: How did the American colonists win the war for independence against Britain? *(They persevered over a struggle of several years, and through timely victories, good leadership, and the support of powerful allies.)* Point out that in Section 3 students will learn how the smaller and less-professional colonial forces were able to win the American Revolution against the more-powerful British. **OL**

Section 4

The War Changes American Society

Essential Question: How did the Revolution change society in America? *(The experience of the war and the Republican ideals on which it was based led to an expansion of voting rights and to greater freedoms for many Americans.)* Tell students that they will learn in Section 4 how American society was affected by the experiences of and ideas that evolved during the American Revolution. **OL**

History ONLINE

Visit glencoe.com and enter *QuickPass*™ code TAV9399c2T for Chapter 2 resources, including a Chapter Overview, Study Central™, Study-to-Go, Student Web Activity, Self-Check Quiz, and other materials.

Focus

Bellringer

Daily Focus Transparency 2-1

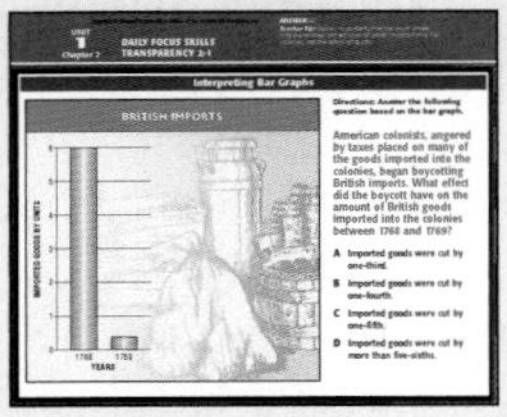

Guide to Reading

Answers: dispute over control of the Ohio River valley, building of French forts from Lake Ontario to the Ohio River

Section Spotlight Video

To generate student interest and provide a springboard for class discussion, access the Chapter 2, Section 1 video at glencoe.com or on the video DVD.

Resource Manager

Section 1

Section Audio Spotlight Video

The Colonies Fight for Their Rights

Guide to Reading

Big Ideas

Struggles for Rights The colonists used economic protest to fight the power of the British Parliament.

Content Vocabulary

- customs duty *(p. 57)*
- inflation *(p. 58)*
- nonimportation agreement *(p. 59)*
- writ of assistance *(p. 60)*

Academic Vocabulary

- dominance *(p. 54)*
- substitute *(p. 59)*

People and Events to Identify

- Albany Plan of Union *(p. 55)*
- French and Indian War *(p. 56)*
- Stamp Act *(p. 58)*
- Sons of Liberty *(p. 59)*
- Townshend Acts *(p. 60)*
- Boston Massacre *(p. 61)*

Reading Strategy

Organizing Complete a graphic organizer similar to the one below by listing the causes of the French and Indian War.

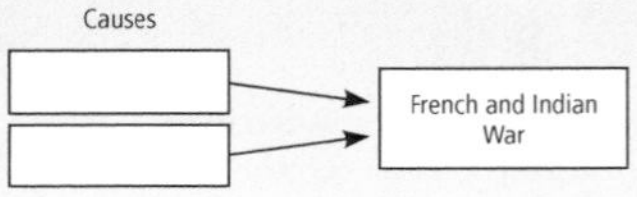

In the mid-1700s, England and France fought a war for control of North America. Britain emerged from the conflict victorious. After the war Parliament's attempts to raise revenue from the colonies met with resistance and protests.

The French and Indian War

MAIN Idea Rivalry between France and England turned into a war for control of North America.

HISTORY AND YOU During the colonial era, France and England were frequently at war. Can you think of similar national conflicts today? Read on to learn about George Washington's role in the French and Indian War.

The French and English had been vying for **dominance** in Europe since the late 1600s, fighting three major wars between 1689 and 1748. Most of the fighting took place in Europe, but whenever France and England were at war, their colonies went to war as well. In 1754 a fourth struggle began.

The First Skirmish

In the 1740s, the British and French both became interested in the Ohio River valley. By crossing from Lake Ontario to the Ohio River and following the river south to the Mississippi River, the French could travel from New France to Louisiana very easily. Meanwhile, British fur traders had begun entering the Ohio River valley, and British land speculators—people who bought empty land hoping to sell it to settlers for a profit—had become interested in the region.

To block British claims in the region, the French built a chain of forts from Lake Ontario to the Ohio River. The British governor of Virginia tried to counter the French by building a British fort in western Pennsylvania. Before the British fort was completed, the French seized it and built Fort Duquesne at the site. Virginia's governor then asked George Washington, a young officer in the Virginia militia, to raise a force and expel the French.

As Washington's troops marched toward the Ohio River in the spring of 1754, they encountered a small French force near Great Meadows. After a brief battle, Washington retreated a short distance and built a stockade named Fort Necessity. A little over a month later, a large French force arrived and forced Washington to surrender. As the fighting between France and Britain expanded into a world war, the 22-year-old Washington became a hero in the colonies for his courageous attempt to resist the French.

R Reading Strategies	C Critical Thinking	D Differentiated Instruction	W Writing Support	S Skill Practice
Teacher Edition • Sequencing, p. 56 • Paraphrasing, p. 58 • Academic Vocab., p. 59 **Additional Resources** • Guid. Read. Act., URB p. 80	**Teacher Edition** • Analyzing Info., p. 55 • Compare/Contrast, p. 56 • Ident. Cent. Issues, p. 58 **Additional Resources** • Linking Past and Present, URB p. 68 • Interp. Polit. Cartoons, URB p. 75 • Quizzes and Tests, p. 19	**Teacher Edition** • English Learners, p. 57 **Additional Resources** • Content Vocab. Act., URB p. 61 • Academic Vocab. Act., URB p. 63		**Teacher Edition** • Using Geo. Skills, pp. 55, 57 **Additional Resources** • Reinforcing Skills Act., URB p. 65 • Read. Essen., p. 17

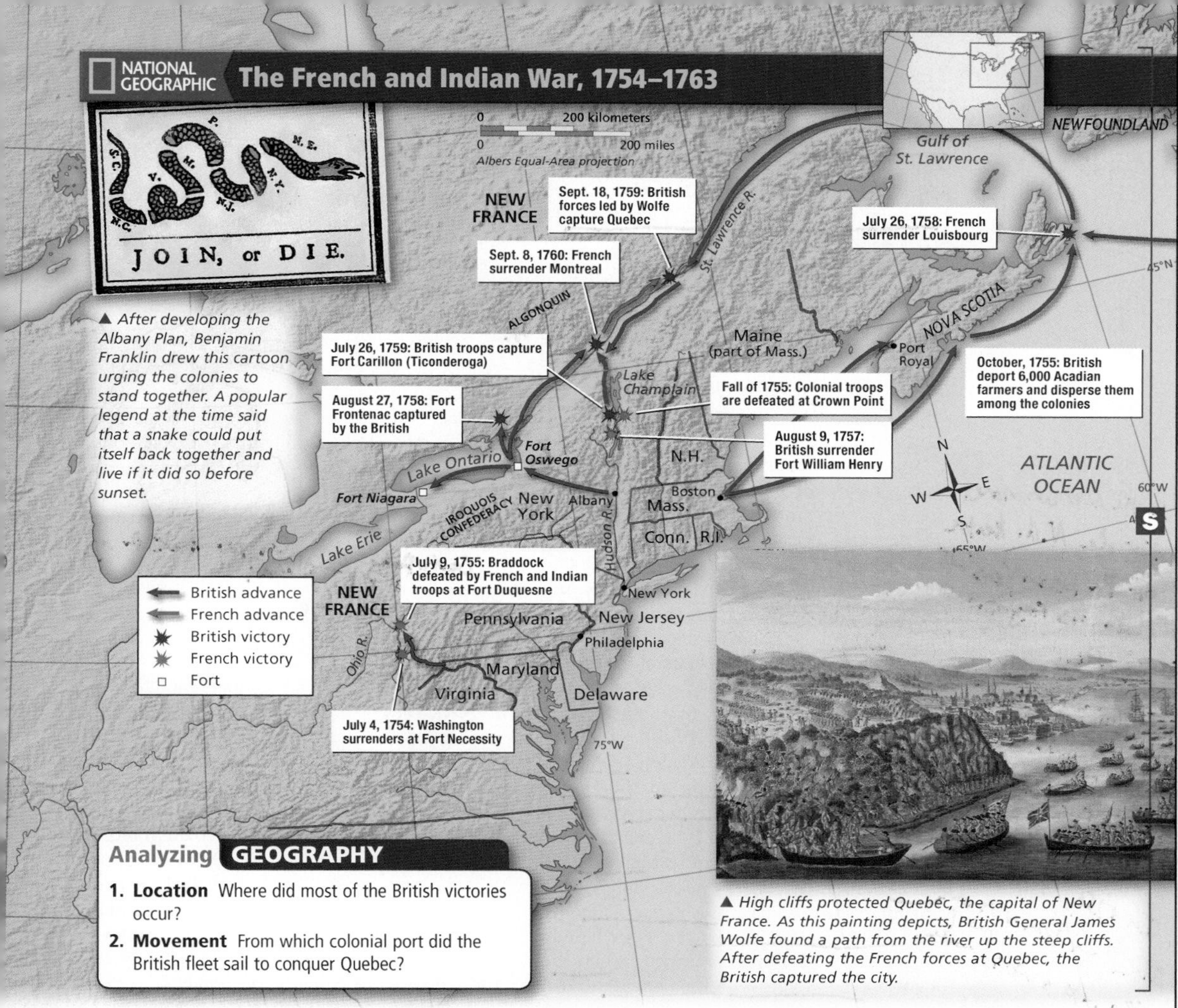

▲ After developing the Albany Plan, Benjamin Franklin drew this cartoon urging the colonies to stand together. A popular legend at the time said that a snake could put itself back together and live if it did so before sunset.

▲ High cliffs protected Quebec, the capital of New France. As this painting depicts, British General James Wolfe found a path from the river up the steep cliffs. After defeating the French forces at Quebec, the British captured the city.

Analyzing GEOGRAPHY

1. **Location** Where did most of the British victories occur?
2. **Movement** From which colonial port did the British fleet sail to conquer Quebec?

The Albany Conference

Even before fighting started, the British government had urged its colonies to work together to prepare for the coming war. The government also suggested that the colonies negotiate an alliance with the Iroquois. The Iroquois controlled western New York—territory the French had to pass through to reach the Ohio River. In response, delegates from seven colonies met with Iroquois leaders at Albany, New York, in June 1754.

This meeting, known as the Albany Conference, achieved several things. Although the Iroquois refused an alliance with the British, they did promise to remain neutral. The colonies agreed that Britain should appoint one supreme commander of all British troops in the colonies. The conference also issued the **Albany Plan of Union,** a proposal developed by a committee led by Benjamin Franklin. The Plan of Union proposed that the colonies unite to form a federal government. **C** Although the colonies rejected the plan, it showed that many colonial leaders had begun to think about joining together for their common defense.

Teach

C Critical Thinking

Analyzing Information

Discuss the advantages and disadvantages of the Albany Plan of Union. Encourage students to consider how U.S. history might have been different if the colonies had adopted the plan. **OL**

S Skill Practice

Using Geography Skills

Discuss the causes and the events of the French and Indian War.

Ask: Why do you think the battles occurred where they did? *(Students should note that the British were fighting the French, so naturally many of the battles would be along the border between New France and the British colonies. Also, the war included Native Americans who were trying to hold off expansion along the Appalachian Mountains and in the Ohio River valley.)* **OL**

Analyzing GEOGRAPHY

Answers:

1. New France
2. Boston

Hands-On Chapter Project
Step 1

War Correspondence

Step 1: Understanding the Colonists' Point of View Working in small groups, students will compile a list of complaints the American colonists had about British rule.

Directions Ask: What actions did the king and Parliament take that most angered the colonists? Students will summarize the actions. Students' list of complaints as American colonists should reflect the actions of the king and Parliament.

Composing Organize students into small groups. Have them assume the role of colonists in 1775 and write a letter to King George III explaining their grievances. **OL**

(Chapter Project continued on page 65)

C Critical Thinking

Comparing and Contrasting
Explain to students that General Braddock underestimated the fighting abilities of his enemy, the Native Americans. **Ask:** What are some other examples of times in history when underestimating the enemy has had dire consequences? *(Answers will vary; students may recall the fate of Custer at Little Bighorn, Hitler's mistaken ideas about the resolve of the British during World War II, the United States's experience in Vietnam, Saddam Hussein's underestimation of the effects of UN troops in the first Gulf War, or the United States's underestimation of the effort needed in the second Gulf War.)* **AL**

Reading Check

Answer:
The French used the Ohio River valley to travel from Lake Ontario to the Mississippi River. The Ohio River thus connected the rest of New France to the port of New Orleans. The British were interested in the region for fur trade and land speculation.

Additional Support

The British Triumph

In 1755 the new British commander in chief, General Edward Braddock, arrived in Virginia with 1,400 British troops. After linking up with 450 local militia troops, Braddock appointed Lieutenant Colonel George Washington to serve as his aide. He then marched west intending to attack Fort Duquesne.

Seven miles from the fort, French and Native American forces ambushed the British. Braddock was killed. His troops panicked and only Washington saved them from disaster. As shots whizzed past him—leaving four holes in his hat and clothes—Washington rallied the men and organized a retreat.

C The successful ambush emboldened the Delaware people, and they began attacking British settlers in western Pennsylvania. For the next two years, the **French and Indian War,** as it was called, raged along the frontier. In 1756 the fighting between Britain and France spread to Europe, where it later became known as the Seven Years' War.

Gradually, the British fleet cut off the flow of supplies and reinforcements to the colonies from France. The Iroquois, realizing the tide was turning in favor of the British, pressured the Delaware to end their attacks. With their Native American allies giving up, the French found themselves badly outnumbered. In 1759 a British fleet commanded by General James Wolfe sailed to Quebec, the capital of New France. After defeating the French troops defending the city, the British seized Quebec and took control of New France. Elsewhere in the world, the fighting continued. When the Spanish joined forces with the French in 1761, Britain seized Spain's colonies in Cuba and the Philippines.

The Treaty of Paris finally ended the war in 1763. Except for a few offshore islands, the treaty eliminated French power in North America. All French territory east of the Mississippi River, except New Orleans, became part of the British Empire. To get Cuba and the Philippines back, Spain gave Florida to Britain. To compensate Spain, the French then signed a separate treaty giving the Spanish control of New Orleans and all French territory west of the Mississippi.

Reading Check **Examining** Why were the French and the British interested in the Ohio River valley?

Growing Discontent

MAIN Idea The British decision to stop colonists from settling new western lands and to impose new taxes led to widespread protests.

HISTORY AND YOU The English Bill of Rights guarantees certain individual rights. Can you recall some of these rights? Read on to learn how Parliament denied these rights to colonists.

Great Britain's victory in 1763 left the country deeply in debt. It had to pay not only the cost of the war but also the cost of governing and defending its new territories. Many British officials thought that the colonies should pay part of the costs, especially the cost of stationing British troops there. As the British government adopted new policies to solve its financial problems, resentment began to grow in the American colonies.

The Proclamation of 1763

In the spring of 1763, Pontiac, the chief of the Ottawa people, decided to go to war against the British. After uniting several Native American groups, including the Ottawa, Delaware, Shawnee, and Seneca peoples, Pontiac's forces attacked forts along the frontier and burned down several towns before British troops were able to stop them. Pontiac's War did not surprise British officials. They had been expecting trouble since 1758, when reports first indicated that settlers were moving into western Pennsylvania in defiance of the colony's treaty with the region's Native Americans.

British leaders did not want to bear the cost of another war. Many officials also owned shares in fur-trading companies operating in the region, and they knew a war would disrupt trade. They decided that the best solution was to limit western settlement until new treaties could be negotiated.

In early October, King George III issued the Proclamation of 1763. The Proclamation drew a line from north to south along the Appalachian Mountains and declared that colonists could not settle west of that line without the British government's permission. This enraged many farmers and land speculators, who wanted access to the land.

Activity: Economics Connection

Making Maps **Ask:** What has been the economic significance of the Ohio River in American history? Have students use library and Internet resources to learn more about the economic significance of the Ohio River and the economic activities in the region during the period of the Proclamation of 1763. In addition, have students research how the Ohio River currently contributes to the economy of the country. Have students create a thematic map to illustrate the economic activities in the region in 1763 and today. Students' maps should be clearly labeled, and should include a map key, a title, and a compass rose. **AL**

The Proclamation of 1763 and Grenville's Reforms

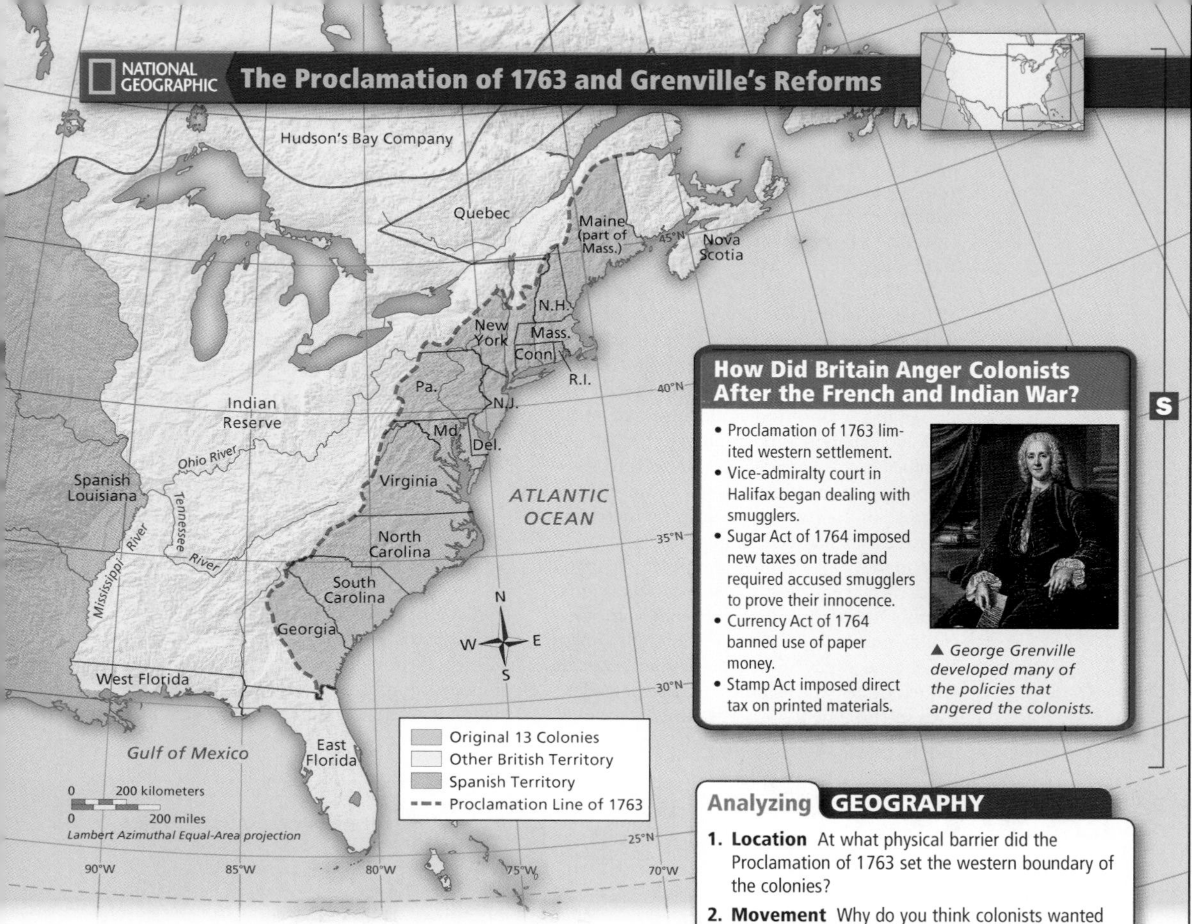

How Did Britain Anger Colonists After the French and Indian War?

- Proclamation of 1763 limited western settlement.
- Vice-admiralty court in Halifax began dealing with smugglers.
- Sugar Act of 1764 imposed new taxes on trade and required accused smugglers to prove their innocence.
- Currency Act of 1764 banned use of paper money.
- Stamp Act imposed direct tax on printed materials.

▲ *George Grenville developed many of the policies that angered the colonists.*

S

Analyzing GEOGRAPHY

1. **Location** At what physical barrier did the Proclamation of 1763 set the western boundary of the colonies?
2. **Movement** Why do you think colonists wanted to move west of that boundary?

Customs Reform

At the same time the Royal Proclamation Act was angering western farmers, eastern merchants were objecting to new tax policies. In 1763 George Grenville became prime minister and first lord of the Treasury. Grenville had to find a way to reduce Britain's debt and pay for the 10,000 British troops now stationed in North America.

Grenville knew that merchants were smuggling many goods into and out of the colonies without paying **customs duties,** taxes on imports and exports. He convinced Parliament to pass a law allowing smugglers to be tried at a new vice-admiralty court in Halifax, Nova Scotia. Unlike colonial courts, where the juries were often sympathetic to smugglers, vice-admiralty courts were run by naval officers. These courts had no juries and did not follow British common law because Admiralty cases involved property not people. Still colonists objected, particularly to having to go to Nova Scotia to prove the legality of their property. D

Among those tried by the vice-admiralty court was John Hancock. Hancock had made a fortune in the sugar trade, smuggling molasses from French colonies in the Caribbean. Defending Hancock was a young lawyer named John Adams. Adams argued that the use of vice-admiralty courts denied colonists their rights as British citizens.

D Differentiated Instruction

English Learners Point out to students the term *customs duties*. Explain that both words in this term have other meanings. For example, the word *custom* usually refers to a longstanding way of doing something. It also refers to doing business or exchanging goods, which explains why a *customs duty* is a fee on trade goods. Explain that students may know that the word *duty* means "a fee or tax" but that it can also mean "a task." **ELL**

S Skill Practice

Using Geography Skills Have students study the map of North America at the time of the Proclamation of 1763. Ask them to write three questions that can be answered using information on the map and exchange them with a partner to answer. **OL**

Analyzing GEOGRAPHY

Answers:

1. the Appalachian Mountains
2. Farmers and land speculators wanted access to more land.

Additional Support

Activity: Interdisciplinary Connection

Art Ask: **What were the main issues that developed between the colonists and the British in the 1760s?** *(Answers may include taxes and civil rights.)* Have students select a person or event from the struggles between the British and the colonists over economic issues after the French and Indian War. Events may include the Proclamation of 1763, the Stamp Act, the Sons of Liberty, and so on. Have students create a cartoon depicting their chosen person or event. The cartoon should express a strongly held opinion of the time period about the subject. Have students share their completed cartoons with the class. **OL**

C Critical Thinking

Identifying Central Issues Discuss with students the reactions in the colonies to the Sugar Act. **Ask:** What provisions of the Sugar Act most angered the colonists? *(Merchants were angered because they felt that the act hurt trade. Many were also furious because the act violated many traditional English rights, such as the presumption of innocence and due process and the ability to sue when goods had been improperly seized.)* **OL**

R Reading Strategy

Paraphrasing Write the phrase "no taxation without representation" on the board. Ask students to use the information on this page and their own words to explain what the phrase means. **BL**

The Sugar Act

In addition to stepping up enforcement of customs duties, Grenville introduced the American Revenue Act of 1764, better known as the Sugar Act. The act raised the tax rates on imports of raw sugar and molasses. It also placed new taxes on silk, wine, coffee, pimento, and indigo.

C Merchants throughout the colonies complained to Parliament that the Sugar Act hurt trade. Many were also furious that the act violated several traditional English rights. Under the act, the property of merchants accused of smuggling was seized and presumed illegal until its legality had been proved. The act also let officials seize goods without due process—proper court procedures—in some circumstances, and prevented lawsuits by merchants whose goods had been improperly seized.

R In many colonial cities, pamphlets circulated condemning the Sugar Act. In one pamphlet James Otis argued that although Parliament could impose taxes to regulate trade, taxing Americans to pay for British programs was different because the colonies had no representatives in Parliament. Otis's arguments gave rise to the popular expression, "No taxation without representation."

Despite the protests, the Sugar Act remained in force, and Grenville pressed ahead with other new policies. To slow **inflation,** Parliament passed the Currency Act of 1764. This act banned the use of paper money in the colonies, because it tended to lose its value quickly. The act angered colonial farmers and artisans who liked paper money precisely because it lost value quickly. They could use paper money to repay their loans, and since the money was not worth as much as when they borrowed it, the loans were easier to pay back.

The Stamp Act Crisis

Although the Sugar Act began to bring in revenue for Britain, Grenville did not believe it would cover all of the government's expenses in America. To raise more money, he asked Parliament to pass the **Stamp Act.**

Enacted in March 1765, the Stamp Act taxed almost all printed materials, including newspapers, pamphlets, posters, wills, mortgages, deeds, licenses, diplomas, and even playing

PAST & PRESENT

Protesting Government Actions

Americans have a long tradition of exercising freedom of speech and assembly to protest unpopular government actions. In 1765, for example, the British Stamp Act enraged the colonists. Many, like Patrick Henry of Virginia, spoke publicly against the act. At the same time, groups such as the Sons of Liberty organized demonstrations and other forms of protest. The tradition continues today. In Seattle, Washington, in 2002, thousands of angry protesters demonstrated for days against United States involvement in the World Trade Organization (WTO). These demonstrators believed the WTO's support for globalization damages local economies at home and abroad.

▲ *Patrick Henry speaks out in protest against the Stamp Act in the Virginia House of Burgesses.*

Differentiated Instruction

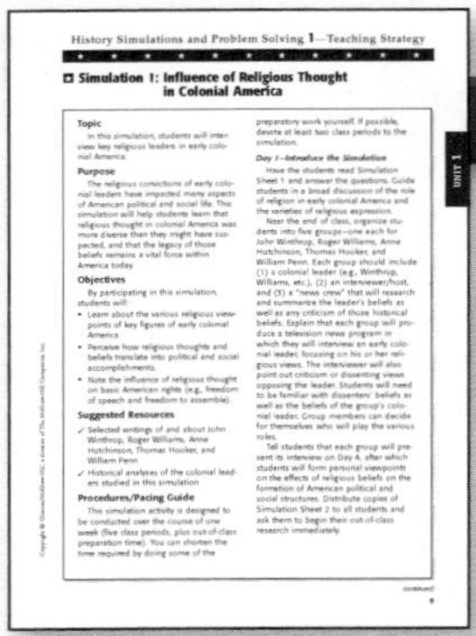

History Simulation and Problem Solving Activity, URB p. 9–12

Applying Information: Craft an Interview

Objective: Develop a script to role-play an interview with a key religious figure in colonial America.

Focus: Have students compare information from Simulation Sheet 2 and compile a group sheet.

Teach: Using the group sheet, script as many questions as possible to ask in the interview.

Assess: Organize the questions to form a logical, coherent script for the interview.

Close: Write a paragraph describing what makes a good interview question.

Differentiated Instruction Strategies

BL Using a sample script as a model, write 2 to 3 interview questions based on the information in Simulation Sheet 2.

AL Select two of the religious figures and write a short essay comparing and contrasting their beliefs, using the topics in Simulation Sheet 2 as a guide.

ELL Write a phrase or short sentence to describe or define each of the topics.

cards. Unlike previous taxes, which had always been imposed on trade, the stamp tax was a direct tax—the first Britain had ever levied on the colonists.

As word of the Stamp Act spread through the colonies in the spring of 1765, a huge debate began. Roused by Patrick Henry's speeches, the Virginia House of Burgesses passed resolutions declaring that Virginians were entitled to the rights of British people and could be taxed only by their own representatives. Other colonial assemblies passed similar resolutions.

By the summer of 1765, a group called the **Sons of Liberty** was organizing huge demonstrations and intimidating stamp distributors. In August, a crowd in Boston hung effigies—crude stuffed figures meant to represent persons—of several British officials, including Boston's stamp agent.

In October, representatives from nine colonies met for what became known as the Stamp Act Congress. Together, they issued the Declaration of Rights and Grievances, drafted by a wealthy lawyer from Pennsylvania named John Dickinson. The resolutions declared that because taxation depended upon representation, only the colonists' political representatives, and not Parliament, had the right to tax them. The congress further petitioned King George III for relief and asked Parliament to repeal the Stamp Act.

When the Stamp Act went into effect on November 1, 1765, the colonists ignored it. Instead, they began to boycott all British goods. People **substituted** sage and sassafras for imported tea. They stopped buying British cloth. In New York, 200 merchants signed a **nonimportation agreement,** pledging not to buy any British goods until Parliament repealed the Stamp Act. R

The boycott had a powerful effect in Britain. Thousands of workers lost their jobs as orders from the colonies were cancelled, and British merchants could not collect money the colonies owed them. With protests mounting in both Britain and the American colonies, British lawmakers repealed the act in 1766. To assert its authority, Parliament passed the Declaratory Act. This act affirmed that Parliament had the power to make laws for the colonies.

Reading Check **Evaluating** How was the Stamp Act different from other taxes Britain had imposed on the colonies?

2002

▼ *Thousands gathered in Seattle, Washington, to protest policies of the World Trade Organization.*

MAKING CONNECTIONS

1. **Identifying Central Issues** What were the reasons for the protests in 1765 and 2002?
2. **Comparing** How were the protests in 1765 against the Stamp Act similar to the protests in 2002 against the WTO policies?

R Reading Strategy

Academic Vocabulary Have students locate the term *substitute(d)* on this page. Point out the prefix *sub-* in this word. Explain that in this case, *sub-*, which often means "below," means "in place of." The entire word comes from Latin and means "to stand in place of." Have students write a sentence of their own using the word *substitute.* **BL** **ELL**

MAKING CONNECTIONS

Answers:

1. In 1765 Americans protested against the Stamp Act, a tax imposed by the British government that they felt was unfair. In 2002 Americans protested the World Trade Organization, whose globalization policies were seen by many as damaging to local economies.
2. In both cases, individuals protested policies they believed violated their rights.

Reading Check

Answer:
The Stamp Act was the first direct tax paid by the colonists.

Additional Support

Activity: Interdisciplinary Connection

Political Science In 1774 the widely respected literary figure Samuel Johnson wrote the following: "He that accepts protection, stipulates obedience. We have always protected the Americans. We may, therefore, subject them to government." Johnson believed that one of the government's roles was to protect its subjects. Imposing taxes to pay for that protection was, in his view, entirely justified. **Ask:** **If subjects enjoy the protection of the government, does that mean that the government has certain rights, including taxation to pay for that protection?** Ask students to list reasons why they support or disagree with Johnson's position. **OL**

People IN HISTORY

Background Samuel Adams wrote a pamphlet entitled "The Rights of the Colonists." In the pamphlet, he explores three themes: the rights of the colonists as men, the rights of the colonists as Christians, and the rights of the colonists as subjects. He also argues for rights that will later be incorporated into the founding documents of the United States. Among these are the rights of life, liberty, private property, and the free exercise of religion.

Question for Discussion: Why do you think Samuel Adams is considered to be one of the important figures in the American Revolution? *(Answers will vary, but students should recognize his contributions to the cause of independence, starting with his organization of the protests in Boston over the British tax laws.)*

Answer:
He organized the Boston chapter of the Sons of Liberty, wrote pamphlets, and united different social classes and got them to work together to protest the British tax laws.

Additional Support

The Townshend Acts

MAIN Idea Colonists continued to deny that Parliament had the right to tax them and began organizing resistance to new taxes.

HISTORY AND YOU Have you ever disagreed with a policy at your school? Did you speak up about it? Read on to learn how the colonists reacted to the Townshend Acts.

During the Stamp Act crisis, Britain's financial problems worsened. Protests in Britain forced Parliament to lower property taxes there, yet somehow the government had to pay for its troops in America. In 1767 Charles Townshend, the new chancellor of the Exchequer, introduced new regulations and taxes. These came to be called the **Townshend Acts.**

One of the Townshend Acts was the Revenue Act of 1767. This act put new customs duties on glass, lead, paper, paint, and tea imported by the colonies. Violators of the Revenue Act had to face trial in vice-admiralty courts, which did not have juries or follow the common law. The Townshend Acts, like the Sugar Act, also allowed officials to seize private property under certain circumstances without following due process.

To help customs officers arrest smugglers, the Revenue Act legalized the use of **writs of assistance.** The writs were general search warrants that enabled customs officers to enter any location during the day to look for evidence of smuggling.

Action and Reaction

The Townshend Acts infuriated many colonists. During the winter of 1767–1768, John Dickinson published a series of essays entitled *Letters From a Farmer in Pennsylvania.* Dickinson reasserted that only assemblies elected by the colonists had the right to tax them. In addition, he called on the colonies to become "firmly bound together" to "form one body politic" to resist the Townshend Acts.

Less than a month after Dickinson's first essay appeared, the Massachusetts assembly

People IN HISTORY

Samuel Adams
1722–1803

A passionate defender of colonial rights, Boston's Sam Adams was either a saint or a scoundrel—depending on who was describing him. Adams enjoyed his reputation as a fiery agitator. "Where there is a spark of patriotic fire," he once declared, "we will enkindle it."

Born in Boston, Adams graduated from Harvard College in 1740. He briefly studied law, worked as a clerk and merchant, and managed a brewery before being elected tax collector for Boston. As tensions with Britain increased, Adams discovered his true talents: speaking out against British tax laws and organizing resistance against them. He helped organize the Boston chapter of the Sons of Liberty. Adams forged an anti-British alliance of merchants, lawyers, and other members of the social elite with artisans, shopkeepers, and common laborers, all of whom worked together to protest British tax policies.

How did Sam Adams become a leader in the protests against British tax laws?

Sam Adams played an important role in organizing resistance to the Stamp Act and the Townshend Acts in Boston. To the right, an engraving shows protestors in Boston burning British stamps. The British cartoon above shows George Grenville carrying a tiny coffin labeled "Miss Ame-Stamp born 1765 died 1766."

Activity: Economics Connection

Analyzing Discuss with students why the British government continued to insist on taxing the American colonies. **Ask:** Do you think that the Townshend Acts were justified? Explain. *(Answers will vary. Some students may feel that Great Britain was justified in taxing the colonies to pay for their own protection.)* **Ask:** Do you think that there might have been a way for Britain to tax the colonies yet not cause anger among the colonists? Explain. *(Answers will vary, but students might suggest that if Britain had simply taxed the colonies without also violating their rights, resistance may have been less. Britain might also have agreed to allow representatives from the colonies to sit in Parliament.)* **AL**

began organizing resistance against Britain. Among the leaders of this resistance was Sam Adams, cousin of John Adams. In February 1768, Sam Adams, with the help of James Otis, drafted a "circular letter" for the Massachusetts assembly to pass and circulate to other colonies criticizing the Townshend Acts. British officials ordered the Massachusetts assembly to withdraw the letter. The assembly refused. Furious, the British government ordered the Massachusetts assembly dissolved. In August 1768, the merchants of Boston and New York responded by signing nonimportation agreements, promising not to import any goods from Britain. Philadelphia's merchants joined the boycott in March 1769.

In May 1769 Virginia's House of Burgesses passed the Virginia Resolves, stating that only the House could tax Virginians. When Britain dissolved the House of Burgesses, its leaders—including George Washington, Patrick Henry, and Thomas Jefferson—immediately called the members to a convention. This convention then passed a nonimportation law, blocking the sale of British goods in Virginia.

As the boycott spread, Americans again stopped drinking British tea and buying British cloth. Women's groups, known as the Daughters of Liberty, began spinning their own rough cloth, called "homespun." Wearing homespun became a sign of patriotism. Throughout the colonies, the Sons of Liberty encouraged people to support the boycotts. In 1769 colonial imports from Britain declined sharply from what they had been in 1768.

The Boston Massacre

In the fall of 1768, as violence against customs officers in Boston increased, Britain dispatched roughly 1,000 troops to the city to maintain order. Bostonians referred to the British troops stationed there as "lobster backs" because of the red coats they wore. Crowds constantly heckled and harassed the troops. On March 5, 1770, a crowd of colonists began taunting and throwing snowballs at a British soldier guarding a customs house. His call for help brought Captain Thomas Preston and a squad of soldiers.

In the midst of the tumult, the troops began firing into the crowd. According to accounts, the first colonist to die was a man of African and Native American descent known as both Michael Johnson and Crispus Attucks. When the smoke cleared, three people lay dead, two more would die later, and six others were wounded. The shootings became known as the **Boston Massacre.** Colonial newspapers portrayed the British as tyrants who were willing to kill people who stood up for their rights.

News of the Boston Massacre raced like lightning across the colonies. It might have set off a revolution, but only a few weeks later, news arrived that the British had repealed almost all of the Townshend Acts. Parliament kept one tax—a tax on tea—to uphold its right to tax the colonies. At the same time, it allowed the colonial assemblies to resume meeting. Peace and stability returned to the colonies, but only temporarily.

Reading Check **Examining** What was stated in the Virginia Resolves passed by Virginia's House of Burgesses?

Section 1 REVIEW

Vocabulary

1. **Explain** the significance of: Albany Plan of Union, French and Indian War, customs duty, inflation, Stamp Act, Sons of Liberty, nonimportation agreement, Townshend Acts, writ of assistance, Boston Massacre.

Main Ideas

2. **Explaining** What did the Albany Plan of Union demonstrate?
3. **Describing** How did the colonists fight the Stamp Act, and what was the result?
4. **Stating** What did John Dickinson suggest that the colonies should do in his *Letters From a Farmer in Pennsylvania?*

Critical Thinking

5. **Big Ideas** What argument did the Stamp Act Congress make in protest against the British taxes?
6. **Categorizing** Use a graphic organizer similar to the one below to list the acts passed by the British Parliament and the colonists' reactions to each.

Act		Colonists' Reactions
________	→	________
________	→	________
________	→	________
________	→	________
________	→	________

7. **Analyzing Visuals** Study the political cartoon on page 55, and then summarize its main idea.

Writing About History

8. **Persuasive Writing** Suppose that you are a member of the Sons of Liberty. Write a pamphlet explaining what your group does and urging other colonists to join.

History ONLINE
Study Central™ To review this section, go to glencoe.com and click on Study Central.

Reading Check

Answer:
Only the Virginia House of Burgesses had the right to tax Virginians.

Assess

History ONLINE

Study Central™ provides summaries, interactive games, and online graphic organizers to help students review content.

Close

Summarizing Ask: How did the relationship between the British government and the American colonies change after the French and Indian War? *(Before the French and Indian War, the colonists had been largely left to govern themselves; after the war, the British government began to impose taxes and other economic policies that led to resistance and protest among the colonists.)* OL

Section 1 REVIEW

Answers

1. All definitions can be found in the section and the Glossary.
2. that some colonial leaders recognized the need for the colonies to unite in common defense
3. The Sons of Liberty organized demonstrations and intimidated customs officers; representatives from nine colonies met for what became known as the Stamp Act Congress. Together they issued the Declaration of Rights and Grievances and petitioned the king and Parliament to repeal the Stamp Act; many colonists boycotted British goods through nonimportation agreements. As a result, thousands of British workers lost their jobs and the British Parliament repealed the Stamp Act.
4. He called on the colonies to form one political unit to oppose the Townshend Acts.
5. Only the colonists' political representatives, not Parliament, had the right to tax them.
6. Students' answers should include the most important acts mentioned in the section and accurately match the section content.
7. If the colonies did not unite politically, they would be destroyed.
8. Students' pamphlets will vary but should include information about the activities of the group and a call for colonists to join it.

ANALYZING PRIMARY SOURCES

Focus

As a busy port city, colonial Boston became a focus for protests against British economic policies that hurt trade and cut profits. Soon, groups such as the Sons of Liberty formed to fight the British reprisals against the city, and tensions escalated. The friction between British troops and angry citizens exploded in the Boston Massacre. The event pushed relations between Britain and her colonies near the breaking point.

Teach

Remind students that for about 70 years Britain had allowed the colonies a great deal of self-rule. Historians often take into account this salutary, or beneficial, neglect when analyzing the reaction to attempts by Britain to exert control. Many British leaders were puzzled by the reaction.

Using the sources in this feature, discuss the goals of British policies in the 1760s. **Ask:** Was the British government wrong to tax the colonies? *(Answers will vary).* **OL**

Additional Support

ANALYZING PRIMARY SOURCES

Boston: Hotbed of Revolution

The growing dispute between colonists and British authorities centered on the extent of Parliament's power over the colonies, particularly the power to levy taxes. Boston was a center of protest against British policies. When, on the night of March 5, 1770, British soldiers fired into a crowd, killing or injuring 11 people, colonists were quick to declare the event a "massacre," even though exactly what occurred is debatable.

Study these primary sources and answer the questions that follow.

PRIMARY SOURCE 1

Engraving, 1774

▼ *"The Bostonians Paying the Excise-man, or Tarring and Feathering" depicts the Sons of Liberty tarring and feathering a British customs officer.*

PRIMARY SOURCE 2

Political Essay, 1767

"From what has been said, I think this uncontrovertible conclusion may be deduced, that when a ruling state obliges a dependent state to take certain commodities from her alone, it is implied in the nature of that obligation; is essentially requisite to give it the least degree of justice; and is inseparably united with it, in order to preserve any share of freedom to the dependent state; that those commodities should never be loaded with duties, FOR THE SOLE PURPOSE OF LEVYING MONEY ON THE DEPENDENT STATE.

Upon the whole, the single question is, whether the parliament can legally impose duties to be paid by the people of these colonies only, FOR THE SOLE PURPOSE OF RAISING A REVENUE, on commodities which she obliges us to take from her alone, or, in other words, whether the parliament can legally take money out of our pockets, without our consent."

—John Dickinson, "Letter From a Farmer in Pennsylvania, to the Inhabitants of the British Colonies," *Pennsylvania Gazette,* December 10, 1767

PRIMARY SOURCE 3

Political Essay, 1774

"To suppose, that by sending out a colony, the nation established an independent power; that when, by indulgence and favour, emigrants are become rich, they shall not contribute to their own defence, but at their own pleasure; and that they shall not be included, like millions of their fellow subjects, in the general system of representation; involves such an accumulation of absurdity, as nothing but the show of patriotism could palliate.

He that accepts protection, stipulates obedience. We have always protected the Americans; we may therefore subject them to government.

The less is included in the greater. That power which can take away life, may seize upon property. The parliament may enact, for America, a law of capital punishment; it may therefore establish a mode and proportion of taxation."

—Samuel Johnson, *The Patriot*

Activity: Technology Connection

Comparing and Contrasting Have students compare the effectiveness of Source 1 and Source 5 as propaganda. Explain that Source 1 was created by a British artist and remind students that Paul Revere, the engraver of Source 5, was a colonist and member of the Sons of Liberty.

Tell students to copy or print from the library or on the Internet a larger version of each image. They will then mount the copies side-by-side on a large piece of paper under the title "Two Examples of Pre-Revolution Propaganda." Students should then research and write informational callouts that explain the details and elements in each image, and a summarizing paragraph that compares and contrasts the purpose and effectiveness of each as propaganda. **AL**

PRIMARY SOURCE 4

Letter, 1770

"[T]he Mob proceeded to a [S]entinel posted upon the Custom House, at a small Distance from the Guard, and Attacked him. . . . Captain Preston . . . hearing the [S]entinel was in Danger of being Murdered, he detached a sergeant and twelve Men to relieve him. . . . This Party as well as the [S]entinel was immediately attacked, Some [colonists] throwing Bricks, Stones, Pieces of Ice and Snow-Balls at them, whilst others advanced up to their Bayonets, and endeavored to close with them, to use their Bludgeons and Clubs; calling out to [the soldiers] to fire if they dared, and provoking them to it by the most Opprobrious Language.

Captain Preston stood between the Soldiers and the Mob . . . using every conciliating Method to perswade [sic] them to retire peaceably. . . . All he could say had no Effect, and one of the Soldiers, receiving a violent Blow, instantly fired . . . and the Mob . . . attacked with greater Violence, continually Striking at the Soldiers and pelting them, and calling out to them to fire. The Soldiers at length perceiving their Lives in Danger, and hearing the Word Fire all round them, three or four of them fired one after another, and again three more in the same hurry and Confusion. . . .

Some have swore Captain Preston gave Orders to fire; others who were near, that the Soldiers fired without Orders from the Provocation they received. None can deny the Attack made upon the Troops, but differ in the Degree of violence in the Attack."

—Thomas Gage, commander in chief of all British North American soldiers, explaining the events of March 5, 1770

PRIMARY SOURCE 5

Engraving, 1770

▼ *The Bloody Massacre,* by Paul Revere

PRIMARY SOURCE 6

Newspaper Account, 1770

"Thirty or forty persons, mostly lads, being . . . gathered in King-street, Capt. Preston, with a party of men with charged bayonets, came from the main guard to the Commissioners house, the soldiers pushing their bayonets, crying, Make way! They took place by the custom-house, and continuing to push to drive the people off, pricked some in several places; on which [the colonists] were clamorous, and, it is said, threw snow-balls. On this, the Captain commanded them to fire, and more snow-balls coming, he again said, Damn you, Fire, be the consequence what it will! One soldier then fired . . . [and] the soldiers continued the fire, successively, till 7 or 8, or as some say 11 guns were discharged."

—"A Particular Account of the Most Barbarous and Horrid Massacre," *Essex [Mass.] Gazette,* March 6, 1770

DBQ Document-Based Questions

1. **Identifying** Consider the image presented in Source 1 from a British point of view. What is going on in the picture? What image of American colonists is presented?
2. **Contrasting** Compare the arguments made in Source 2 and Source 3. How do they differ on the right of Parliament to tax the colonists?
3. **Contrasting** How do the accounts of the events of March 5, 1770, differ in Source 4 and Source 6? Which do you find more convincing?
4. **Analyzing** How does the engraving in Source 5 portray the Boston Massacre? Does this depiction more accurately reflect the account given in Source 4 or Source 6? Why?

ANALYZING PRIMARY SOURCES

Assess/Close

Have students write a brief summary of the arguments on each side in the conflict between the British and the Bostonians, based on Sources 1–6.

DBQ Document Based Questions

Answers:

1. tarring and feathering: The Bostonians are depicted as lawless thugs.
2. Dickinson argues that Parliament is putting taxes on items without representation in Parliament. Johnson argues that the colonists are British subjects and as such must be ruled by the British government.
3. Gage says the soldiers were assaulted and provoked into firing, while the newspaper says the group threw snowballs after they had been pricked with bayonets. Students' opinions will vary.
4. as a massacre: It reflects Source 6.

Additional Support

Activity: Economics Connection

Debating the Issues Ask: What arguments did people make on both sides of the political and economic issues in the colonies? Have students work with a partner to research and then write essays arguing for or against British economic policies in the colonies. Students should use information from their textbook, library resources, and the Internet to find out more about what individuals in the colonies and in Britain thought about a particular issue of the time. Partners should select together an issue to debate, determine who will assume which point of view, and then each write an essay of at least 500 words that supports, with evidence, the point of view. Partners should then peer review each other's essays and compare points to make sure they are clearly expressing different points of view over the same issue. They should also make any additional edits to create a final draft. OL

Focus

Bellringer

Daily Focus Transparency 2-2

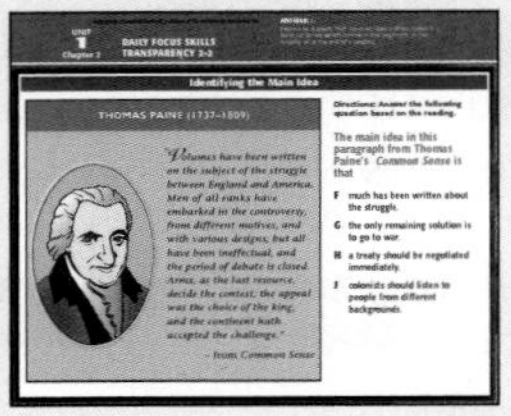

Guide to Reading

Answers:

Students' outlines should include the following main heads.

I. Massachusetts Defies Britain
II. The Revolution Begins
III. The Decision to Declare Independence

Section Spotlight Video

To generate student interest and provide a springboard for class discussion, access the Chapter 2, Section 2 video at glencoe.com or on the video DVD.

Section 2 — Section Audio — Spotlight Video

The Revolution Begins

Guide to Reading

Big Ideas

Government and Society The colonists formed the Continental Congress to act as a government during the American Revolution.

Content Vocabulary
- committee of correspondence *(p. 64)*
- minuteman *(p. 68)*

Academic Vocabulary
- enforce *(p. 67)*
- submit *(p. 73)*

People and Events to Identify
- Boston Tea Party *(p. 66)*
- Intolerable Acts *(p. 67)*
- Loyalist *(p. 68)*
- Patriot *(p. 68)*
- Battle of Bunker Hill *(p. 70)*
- Thomas Paine *(p. 73)*
- Declaration of Independence *(p. 73)*

Reading Strategy

Organizing Use the major headings of the section to create an outline similar to the one below, with information about the rising tensions between the colonies and Britain.

The Revolution Begins
I. Massachusetts Defies Britain
A.
B.
C.
D.
II.

After years of escalating tensions, a true revolt against British rule began in the colonies in the 1770s. The colonists established a new government for themselves and organized militias to combat what they saw as British tyranny.

Massachusetts Defies Britain

MAIN Idea When Parliament punished Massachusetts for the Boston Tea Party, the colonists organized the First Continental Congress.

HISTORY AND YOU Is it ever acceptable to break the law to make a political point? Read how some colonists responded to unpopular laws.

Despite the tragedy of the Boston Massacre, the British decision to repeal the Townshend Acts had ended another crisis in colonial relations. For more than two years, the situation remained calm. Then, in the spring of 1772, a new crisis began. Britain introduced several new policies that again ignited the flames of rebellion in the American colonies. This time the fire could not be put out.

The *Gaspee* Affair

After Britain repealed the Townshend Acts, trade with the American colonies resumed, and so did smuggling. To intercept smugglers, the British sent customs ships to patrol North American waters. One such ship was the *Gaspee,* stationed off the coast of Rhode Island. Many Rhode Islanders hated the commander of the *Gaspee* because he often searched ships without a warrant and sent his crew ashore to seize food without paying for it. In June 1772, when the *Gaspee* ran aground, some 150 colonists seized and burned the ship.

The attack outraged the British. They sent a commission to investigate and gave it authority to take suspects to Britain for trial. This angered the colonists, who believed it violated their right to a trial by a jury of their peers. Rhode Island's assembly then sent a letter to the other colonies asking for help.

After the Virginia House of Burgesses received the letter in March 1773, one of its members, Thomas Jefferson, suggested that each colony create a **committee of correspondence** to communicate with the other colonies about British activities. These committees of correspondence helped unify the colonies and shape public opinion. They also helped colonial leaders coordinate their plans for resisting the British.

Resource Manager

R Reading Strategies	C Critical Thinking	D Differentiated Instruction	W Writing Support	S Skill Practice
Teacher Edition • Making Connections, p. 66 • Identifying, p. 68 • Setting a Purpose, p. 70 • Summarizing, p. 73 **Additional Resources** • Prim. Source Read., URB p. 69 • Guid. Read Act., URB p. 81	**Teacher Edition** • Det. Cause/Effect, p. 65 • Making Inferences, p. 67 **Additional Resources** • Crit. Think. Skills Activity, URB p. 66 • Quizzes and Tests, p. 20	**Teacher Edition** • Visual/Spatial, p. 70 • Kinesthetic, p. 72 **Additional Resources** • Differentiated Instr., URB p. 57 • English Learner Act., URB p. 59 • Am. History in Graphic Novel, p. 7	**Teacher Edition** • Persuasive Writing, p. 68 • Expository Writing, p. 71	**Teacher Edition** • Reading Time Lines, p. 66 • Using Geo. Skills, p. 69 **Additional Resources** • Time Line Activity, URB p. 67 • Read. Essen., p. 20 • Am. Art & Music Act., URB p. 73

PRIMARY SOURCE

The Boston Tea Party, December 1773

Some 150 raiders disguised themselves as Native Americans, boarded the British ships, and threw the tea overboard.

A large crowd gathered on the pier to cheer the raiders and to make it difficult for any British troops that might arrive to get to the ships.

▲ *This lithograph, titled* The Destruction of Tea at Boston Harbor, *was created by engravers Currier & Ives in 1846. The engravers depict the scene in daylight—most likely to make the image clearer—although it happened at night.*

What Were the Coercive Acts?

Britain responded to the Boston Tea Party with four acts intended to punish Massachusetts and reassert British authority:

1. Boston Port Act
   - Closed the port of Boston until Massachusetts paid for the tea
2. Massachusetts Government Act
   - Banned town meetings
   - Required all sheriffs, council members, and judges to be appointed by the British governor
3. Administration of Justice Act
   - Allowed trials of British soldiers and officials to be transferred to Britain to protect them from American juries
4. Quartering Act
   - Required local officials to lodge British troops at the scene of a disturbance; in private homes, if necessary

Analyzing VISUALS

1. **Explaining** What was the purpose of the Boston Port Act?
2. **Drawing Conclusions** Why would the British want to ban town meetings?

The Boston Tea Party

C

In May 1773, Britain's new prime minister, Lord North, made a serious mistake. He decided to help the struggling British East India Company. Corrupt management and costly wars in India had put the company deeply in debt. At the same time, British taxes on tea had encouraged colonial merchants to smuggle in cheaper Dutch tea. As a result, the company had in its warehouses over 17 million pounds of tea that it needed to sell quickly.

To help the company, Parliament passed the Tea Act of 1773. The Tea Act refunded four-fifths of the taxes the company had to pay to ship tea to the colonies, leaving only the Townshend Tax. East India Company tea could now be sold at lower prices than smuggled Dutch tea. The act also allowed the East India Company to sell directly to shopkeepers, bypassing American merchants who usually distributed the tea. The Tea Act enraged the colonial merchants, who feared it was the first step by the British to squeeze them out of business.

In October 1773, the East India Company shipped 1,253 chests of tea to Boston, New York, Philadelphia, and Charles Town. The committees of correspondence decided that they must not allow the tea to be unloaded. When the first shipments arrived in New York and Philadelphia, the colonists forced the agents for the East India Company to return home with the tea. In Charles Town, customs officers seized the tea and stored it in a local warehouse where it remained unsold.

C Critical Thinking

Determining Cause and Effect Discuss with students why the Boston Tea Party occurred and why it had such serious results. **Ask:** Why did Boston merchants hate the Tea Act so much? *(Because it took away their business and they were concerned that it was the first step by the British to squeeze them out of business.)* **Ask:** How did the British react to the Tea Party? *(It was the last straw for the British government, which now felt that they had been too lenient with the colonists and must now punish them. This led Parliament to pass laws known as the Coercive Acts.)* **OL**

Analyzing VISUALS

Answers:

1. to force the Bostonians to pay for the ruined tea
2. because group meetings could provide leaders with further opportunities to plan protests and also lead to unrest

Hands-On Chapter Project
Step 2

War Correspondence

Step 2: Understanding the British Point of View Have students use Internet or library materials to learn more about Parliament and how the English regarded taxation.

Directions Returning to their groups, students place themselves in the role of the British Prime Minister and respond to the petition they wrote in Section 1.

Summarizing Students will summarize their actions and reasoning into a governmental action plan. **OL**

(Chapter Project continued on page 79)

R Reading Strategy

Making Connections Discuss with students what the reaction might be today if a group of citizens dressed up in costume and dumped the contents of a ship into the harbor. **Ask:** What would the public reaction be to the Boston Tea Party if it occurred today? *(Answers will vary; students may feel that it would not be approved of today and would be considered an act of vandalism, if not terrorism.)* **OL**

S Skill Practice

Reading Time Lines Work with students who may need extra help by asking a series of questions to provide them with opportunities to practice analyzing time lines. **Ask:** What happened in 1768? *(Colonial merchants began the nonimportation campaign.)* **Ask:** Which happened first—the Sugar Act or the Stamp Act? *(the Sugar Act)* In what year did the Boston Massacre happen? *(1770)* You may suggest that students also work in pairs to quiz each other on the time line information. **BL** **ELL**

Additional Support

The most dramatic event occurred in Boston Harbor, shortly after the tea ships arrived. On December 17, 1773, the night before customs officials planned to bring the tea ashore, a group of approximately 150 men secretly gathered at the Boston dock. One of the men was George Hewes, a struggling Boston shoemaker who had grown to despise the British. Hewes had taken offense when British soldiers stopped and questioned him on the street and when they refused to pay him for shoes. After witnessing the Boston Massacre, his hatred grew deeper and more political.

So, after he "daubed his face and hands with coal dust, in the shop of a blacksmith," Hewes gladly joined the other volunteers as they prepared to sneak aboard several British ships anchored in Boston Harbor and destroy the tea stored on board:

PRIMARY SOURCE

"When we arrived at the wharf . . . they divided us into three parties for the purpose of boarding the three ships which contained the tea. . . . We then were ordered by our commander to open the hatches and take out all the chests of tea and throw them overboard, and we immediately proceeded to execute his orders, first cutting and splitting the chests with our tomahawks, so as thoroughly to expose them to the effects of the water. . . . In about three hours . . . we had thus broken and thrown over board every tea chest . . . in the ship."

—quoted in *The Spirit of 'Seventy-Six*

Several thousand people on the shore cheered as Hewes and the other men dumped 342 chests of tea into Boston Harbor. Although the men were disguised as Native Americans, many knew who they were. A witness later testified that Sam Adams and John Hancock were among those who boarded the ships. The raid came to be called the **Boston Tea Party.** R

The Coercive Acts

The Boston Tea Party was the last straw for the British. King George III informed Lord North that "concessions have made matters worse. The time has come for compulsion." In the spring of 1774, Parliament passed four new

Countdown to Revolution, 1763–1776

S

1763 Proclamation of 1763 bans colonists from settling west of the Proclamation Line

1764 Sugar Act imposes new taxes on trade; James Otis argues that taxation without representation violates colonists' liberties

1765 Stamp Act Congress issues Declaration of Rights and Grievances

1765 The Stamp Act imposes taxes on printed materials; Sons of Liberty organize protests and boycotts

1767 Townshend Acts impose new taxes on trade goods; violators to be tried in vice admiralty courts

1768 Colonial merchants begin nonimportation campaign, refuse to import British goods; Daughters of Liberty help by spinning cloth

1770 British troops shoot colonists at Boston Massacre; most Townshend Acts are repealed

1764 1766 1768 1770

Activity: Interdisciplinary Connection

Art and Design **Ask:** How is effective propaganda created? *(Student responses may include characterizing the opposing side in an unfavorable light.)* Have students choose one entry from the time line that begins on this page and create a piece of propaganda, similar to Paul Revere's engraving of the Boston Massacre on page 63. Encourage students to include one or more images depicting or related to the event, an evocative headline, and text that expresses a clear point of view of either the colonial or the British side of the conflict. **AL**

laws that came to be known as the Coercive Acts. These laws were intended to punish Massachusetts and end colonial challenges to British authority.

The first act was the Boston Port Act. It shut down Boston's port until the city paid for the tea that had been destroyed. The second act was the Massachusetts Government Act. It required all council members, judges, and sheriffs in Massachusetts to be appointed by the governor instead of being elected. This act also banned most town meetings.

The third act, the Administration of Justice Act, allowed the governor to transfer trials of British soldiers and officials to Britain to protect them from American juries. The final act was a new Quartering Act. It required local officials to provide lodging for British soldiers, in private homes if necessary. To **enforce** the acts, the British moved 2,000 troops to New England and appointed General Thomas Gage as the new governor of Massachusetts.

The Coercive Acts violated several traditional English rights, including the right to trial by a jury of one's peers and the right not to have troops quartered in one's home. The king was also not supposed to maintain a standing army in peacetime without Parliament's consent. Although the British Parliament had authorized the troops, colonists believed that their own local assemblies had to give their consent as well.

In July 1774, a month after the last Coercive Act had become law, the British introduced the Quebec Act. This law had nothing to do with events in the American colonies, but it, too, angered colonists. The Quebec Act stated that a governor and council appointed by the king would run Quebec. It also extended Quebec's boundaries to include much of what is today Ohio, Illinois, Michigan, Indiana, and Wisconsin. If colonists moved west, they would have to live in territory where they had no elected assembly. The Quebec Act, coming so soon after the Coercive Acts, seemed to imply that the British were trying to seize control of the colonial governments. **C**

As other colonies learned of the harsh measures imposed on Massachusetts, they reacted with sympathy and outrage. The Coercive Acts and the Quebec Act together became known as the **Intolerable Acts.**

1773
At Boston Tea Party, colonists toss British tea into Boston Harbor

1774
Britain imposes Coercive Acts; First Continental Congress meets, passes the Suffolk Resolves, and issues Declaration of Rights and Grievances

January 1776
Tom Paine publishes *Common Sense*, arguing for independence

July 4, 1776
Congress issues Declaration of Independence

1772 1774 1776

1775
British battle colonial militia at Lexington and Concord; Second Continental Congress meets, selects George Washington to head Continental Army

Analyzing TIME LINES

1. **Stating** When and under what circumstances did the concept of "taxation without representation" first appear?
2. **Specifying** Which occurred first—the Boston Tea Party or the battles at Lexington and Concord?

C Critical Thinking

Making Inferences Discuss the Quebec Act with students. **Ask:** Why did the Quebec Act enrage the American colonists even though it did not directly affect them? *(It extended Quebec's borders to the region west of the colonies and put Quebec under the control of a royal governor and council. The colonists knew if they moved west, they would be in an area without an elected assembly. They felt this implied that the British were trying to do away with the colonial governments.)* **Ask:** What do you think will happen next between the colonists and the British government? *(Answers will vary, but may include fighting or war.)* **OL**

Analyzing TIME LINES

Answers:
1. In 1764, in reaction to the Sugar Act, James Otis argues that taxation without representation violates colonists' rights.
2. Boston Tea Party

Additional Support

Activity: Collaborative Learning

Creating a Poster Have students work in small groups to research boycotts that have been conducted. Each group should select a boycott and create a poster that educates the class about it. Each poster should include a title, at least one relevant photo, and text that answers these questions: Who? What? Where? When? Why? How? The "How" section should explain how the group organized the boycott and how successful it was. Examples of boycotts might be the national grape boycott led by United Farm Workers Union (1967–1970); the boycott of Jewish businesses in Poland (1935–1945); or any recent boycott of goods for political or ethical reasons. **OL** **AL**

R Reading Strategy

Identifying Discuss with students the reasons why the colonists formed the First Continental Congress. **Ask:** What did the First Continental Congress accomplish or decide? *(It endorsed the Suffolk Resolves; it issued the Declaration of Rights and Grievances; it approved the Continental Association; and it agreed to hold a second congress in May 1775 if the crisis was not yet resolved.)* Explore with students how these actions and decisions represented the wide range of opinions of the delegates. **OL**

W Writing Support

Persuasive Writing Tell students to compose a pamphlet urging other students to join either the Loyalists or the Patriots. Encourage them to research the position they choose to support as well as the position of the opposing group. Have students share their pamphlets with the class. **OL**

Reading Check

Answer:
They enacted the Coercive Acts and the Quebec Act.

Additional Support

The First Continental Congress

In May 1774, the Virginia House of Burgesses declared the arrival of British troops in Boston a "military invasion" and called for a day of fasting and prayer. When Virginia's governor dissolved the House of Burgesses, its members went to a nearby tavern and issued a resolution urging the colonies to suspend trade with Britain and to send delegates to a colonial congress to discuss what to do next. At least one burgess, Patrick Henry, was ready for war: "I know not what course others may take, but as for me, give me liberty or give me death!"

In New York and Rhode Island, similar calls for a congress had already been made. The committees of correspondence coordinated the different proposals, and on September 5, 1774, the First Continental Congress met in Philadelphia. The 55 delegates to the Congress represented 12 of Britain's North American colonies. Florida, Georgia, Nova Scotia, and Quebec did not attend. The delegates from the 12 colonies represented a wide range of opinion. Moderate delegates opposed the Intolerable Acts but believed a compromise was possible. Other, more radical, delegates believed the time had come to fight.

R The Congress's first order of business was to endorse the Suffolk Resolves. These resolutions, prepared by Bostonians and other residents of Suffolk County, Massachusetts, urged colonists not to obey the Coercive Acts. They also called on the people of Suffolk County to arm themselves and stop buying British goods.

While discussing what other steps to take, the Congress learned that the British had suspended the Massachusetts assembly. In response, the Congress voted to issue the Declaration of Rights and Grievances. The declaration expressed loyalty to the king, but it also condemned the Coercive Acts and stated that the colonies would form a nonimportation association. Several days later, the delegates approved the Continental Association, a plan for every county and town to form committees to enforce a boycott of British goods. The delegates then agreed to hold a second Continental Congress in May 1775 if the crisis had not been resolved.

Reading Check **Examining** How did the British react to the Boston Tea Party?

The Revolution Begins

MAIN Idea Colonists organized alternative governments and formed militias to oppose British "tyranny."

HISTORY AND YOU Your political views are partly shaped by your personal background. Read on to learn why some colonists supported the British while others fought for independence.

In October 1774, members of the suspended Massachusetts assembly defied the British and organized the Massachusetts Provincial Congress. They then formed the Committee of Safety and chose John Hancock to lead it, giving him the power to call up the militia. In effect, the Provincial Congress had made Hancock a rival governor to General Gage.

A full-scale rebellion was now underway. Militias began to drill and practice shooting. The town of Concord created a special unit of men trained and ready to "stand at a minute's warning in case of alarm." These were the famous **minutemen.** All through the summer and fall of 1774, British control of the colonies weakened as colonists created provincial congresses and militias raided military depots for ammunition and gunpowder. These rebellious acts infuriated British officials.

Loyalists and Patriots

Although many colonists did not agree with Parliament's policies, they were still loyal to the king and to Britain and believed that British law should be upheld. Americans who supported the British side in the conflict became known as **Loyalists** or Tories.

W Loyalists came from all parts of American society. Many were government officials or Anglican ministers. Others were prominent merchants and landowners. Many backcountry farmers on the frontier remained loyal as well, because they regarded the king as their protector against the planters and merchants who controlled the local governments.

On the other side were those who believed that the British had become tyrants. These people were known as **Patriots** or Whigs. Patriots also represented a wide cross-section of society. They were artisans, farmers, merchants, planters, lawyers, and urban workers. The Patriots were strong in New England and Virginia, while

Activity: Technology Connection

Analyzing Organize students into two groups, and ask the first group to assume the role of the aides to the leaders of the Continental Congress. For the First Continental Congress held in September 1774, they will create a multimedia presentation to outline the intended outcomes of the Congress. Ask students to use their textbook and other resources to investigate the Suffolk Resolves and the Continental Association, and to include specific information about each in the multimedia presentation.

For the second Continental Congress held in May 1775, the second group of students will create a presentation that is representative of the defensive and governmental actions of the Congress. Students should include information about the formation of the Continental Army, the election of George Washington, the offering of the Olive Branch Petition, and the formation of the postal system. Have groups make their presentations to the class. **AL**

NATIONAL GEOGRAPHIC The Battles of Lexington and Concord, April 1775

◀ *This engraving, one of a famous series by Amos Doolittle, shows the initial exchange of fire on Lexington Green between the colonists and the British soldiers.*

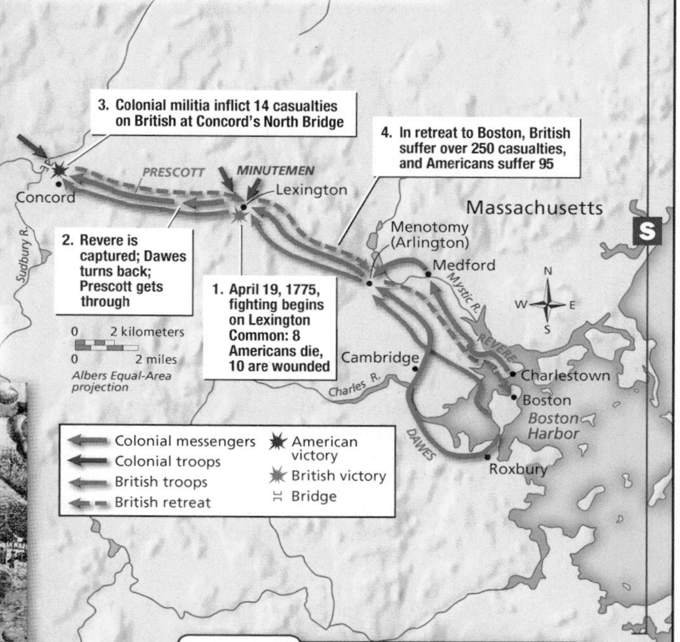

▼ *Later in the battle at Lexington, the colonial militia took cover behind stone walls, and harassed the British as they moved out of town toward Concord.*

Analyzing GEOGRAPHY

1. **Movement** Which side suffered the highest number of casualties at Lexington and Concord?
2. **Location** About how far was Lexington from Boston?

most of the Loyalists lived in Georgia, the Carolinas, and New York. Political differences divided communities and even split families. The American Revolution was not simply a war between the Americans and the British. It was also a civil war between Patriots and Loyalists.

Even before the Revolution, Patriot groups brutally enforced the boycott of British goods. They tarred and feathered Loyalists, and broke up Loyalist gatherings. Loyalists fought back, but there were not as many of them and they were not as well organized. Caught between the two groups were many people, possibly a majority, who did not favor either side and would support whichever side won.

Lexington and Concord

In April 1775, the British government ordered General Gage to arrest the Massachusetts Provincial Congress, even if it meant risking armed conflict. Gage did not know where the Congress was sitting, so he decided to seize the militia's supply depot at Concord instead. On April 18, about 700 British troops set out for Concord on a road that took them through the town of Lexington.

S Skill Practice

Using Geography Skills Have students study the map of the battles of Lexington and Concord. Explain that Samuel Prescott was a citizen of Concord, so he knew the area better than the other two and was able to escape from the British. **Ask:** How were the routes to Lexington by Revere and Dawes different? Why do you think this is the case? *(Revere left Boston and rode north from Charlestown and Dawes rode south from Boston. They were both trying to avoid the British troops who were taking the main route out of the city. Being on horseback and taking two routes would increase the chances of one of them accomplishing their mission.)* OL

Analyzing GEOGRAPHY

Answers:
1. the British
2. about 15 miles

Additional Support

Activity: Interdisciplinary Connection

Art Ask students to read the description of events at Lexington and Concord and then study the Doolittle engravings on this page. **Ask:** Based on what you have read and can see in the pictures, visualize what it must have been like on Lexington Green when the colonists confronted the British. What are some sights, sounds, and smells you might have experienced if you had been there? *(Answers will vary. Possible answers include: musket fire, screaming and yelling, gunpowder, smoke, wet ground, sweat, blood, people crying, fire, British accents. Accept all reasonable responses).* OL ELL

R Reading Strategy

Setting a Purpose Tell students that setting a goal before they begin can help focus their reading. To set a purpose for reading "The Second Continental Congress," **ask:** **What was the main concern of the Second Continental Congress when it first met?** *(It was concerned with defense and it adopted the militia army around Boston and named it the Continental Army.)* BL

D Differentiated Instruction

Visual/Spatial Have students create a map of colonial Boston, labeling major geographic features and indicating the positions of the colonial militia and British troops just after the Battle of Bunker Hill. Then have students write a paragraph explaining how the British troops became trapped in the city by the colonial militia. OL

Reading Check

Answer:
It helped build confidence by showing that the largely untrained colonial militia could stand up to the British army.

Additional Support

Patriot leaders heard about the plan and sent Paul Revere and William Dawes to spread the alarm. The two men made it to Lexington and warned people that the British were coming. Along with a third man, Dr. Samuel Prescott, they then headed for Concord. A British patrol stopped Revere and Dawes, but Prescott got through in time to warn Concord.

On April 19, British troops arrived in Lexington and spotted some 70 minutemen lined up on the village green. The British marched onto the field and ordered them to disperse. The minutemen had begun to back away when a shot was fired; no one is sure by whom. The British soldiers then fired at the minutemen, killing 8 and wounding 10.

The British then headed to Concord, where they found that most of the military supplies had been removed. When they tried to cross the North Bridge on the far side of town, they ran into some 400 colonial militia. A fight broke out, forcing the British to retreat.

As the British headed back to Boston, militia and farmers fired at them from behind trees, stone walls, barns, and houses. By the time the British reached Boston, they had lost 99 men, and another 174 were wounded. The colonial forces had lost 49 militia, and another 46 were wounded. News of the fighting spread across the colonies. Militia from all over New England raced to the area to help fight the British. By May 1775, the militia had surrounded Boston, trapping the British.

R The Second Continental Congress

Three weeks after the battles at Lexington and Concord, the Second Continental Congress met in Philadelphia. The first issue was defense. The Congress voted to "adopt" the militia army surrounding Boston, and they named it the Continental Army. On June 15, 1775, the Congress selected George Washington to command the new army.

Before Washington could get to his new command, however, the British landed reinforcements in Boston. Determined to gain control of the area, the British decided to seize the hills north of the city. Warned in advance, the militia acted first. On June 16, 1775, they dug in on Breed's Hill near Bunker Hill and began building a fort at the top.

The following day, General Gage sent 2,200 troops to take the hill. According to legend, an American commander named William Prescott told his troops, "Don't fire until you see the whites of their eyes." When the British closed to within 50 yards, the Americans fired. They stopped two British attacks and were forced to retreat only after running out of ammunition.

D The **Battle of Bunker Hill,** as it came to be called, helped to build American confidence. It showed that the colonial militia could stand up to one of the world's most feared armies. The British suffered more than 1,000 casualties in the fighting. Shortly afterward, General Gage resigned and was replaced by General William Howe. The situation became a stalemate, with the British troops encircled by colonial militia.

Reading Check **Interpreting** Why was the Battle of Bunker Hill important to the Americans?

Debates IN HISTORY

Should the American Colonies Declare Independence?

Although it may seem like the only natural course today, in 1776 independence was not the obvious choice for the 13 British colonies. While many were fed up with British actions and thought that it was time to institute true self-rule, others felt loyalty to what they considered their mother country and wanted to pursue a resolution of their grievances through political and diplomatic, not military, means. British-born Thomas Paine was one who strongly supported independence, as he discussed in his famous pamphlet, *Common Sense.* American-born John Dickinson, while angered at the behavior of the British, expressed in a speech to the Congress his arguments against splitting from Great Britain.

Activity: Interdisciplinary Connection

Political Science Explain to students that the debate over independence even took place among the clergy and in churches. Independence drew powerful support from the Congregational, Presbyterian, and other Christian churches with no official ties to England. In contrast, the Anglican clergy in America opposed independence. As representatives of the state religion, they saw opposition to British rule as a danger to all authority. Their support of Britain drew widespread acceptance among colonial aristocracy, particularly in the Southern colonies. **Ask:** **In what ways did the debate over independence sometimes depend on the feelings of individuals?** *(Some people felt a loyalty to the British king and saw themselves as British people. Others felt a loyalty or affinity to their colony over Britain.)* OL

The Decision to Declare Independence

MAIN Idea After more than a year of war, the Continental Congress issued the Declaration of Independence.

HISTORY AND YOU Have you ever tried to mediate a disagreement between siblings or friends? Read on to learn about the Olive Branch Petition and how it failed to achieve peace.

Despite the onset of fighting, many colonists in the summer of 1775 were not prepared to break away from Great Britain. Most members of the Second Continental Congress wanted the right to govern themselves, but they did not want to break with the British Empire. By 1776, however, opinions had changed. Frustrated by Britain's refusal to compromise, many Patriot leaders began to call for independence.

Efforts at Peace

In July 1775, as the siege of Boston continued, the Continental Congress sent a document known as the Olive Branch Petition to King George III. Written by John Dickinson, the petition stated that the colonies were still loyal to the king and asked him to call off hostilities and resolve the situation peacefully.

In the meantime, the radical delegates of the Congress convinced the body to order an attack on the British troops based in Quebec. They hoped the attack would convince the French in Quebec to rebel and join in fighting the British. The American forces captured the city of Montreal, but the French did not rebel.

HistoryONLINE Student Web Activity Visit glencoe.com and complete the activity on the American Revolution.

YES

Thomas Paine
Writer

PRIMARY SOURCE

"It is the good fortune of many to live distant from the scene of present sorrow; . . . But let our imaginations transport us for a few moments to Boston. . . . The inhabitants of that unfortunate city who but a few months ago were in ease and affluence, have now no other alternative than to stay and starve, or turn out to beg. . . .

Men of passive tempers look somewhat lightly over the offenses of Britain and, still hoping for the best, are apt to call out, *Come, come we shall be friends again for all this.* But examine the passions and feelings of mankind; Bring the doctrine of reconciliation to the touchstone of nature, and then tell me whether you can hereafter love, honour, and faithfully serve the power that hath carried fire and sword into your land?"

—from *Common Sense*

NO

John Dickinson
Delegate, Continental Congress

PRIMARY SOURCE

"Even those Delegates who are not restrained by Instructions [from their legislatures] have no Right to establish an independent separate Government for a Time of Peace. . . . without a full & free Consent of the People plainly exprest [sic]. . . . We are now acting on a principle of the English Constitution in resisting the assumption or Usurpation of an unjust power. We are now acting under that Constitution. Does that Circumstance [support] its Dissolution? But granting the present oppression to be a Dissolution, the Choice of . . . Restoring it, or forming a new one is vested in our Constituents, not in Us. They have not given it to Us. We may pursue measures that will force them into it. But that implies not a Right so to force them."

—from *Letters of Delegates to Congress, 1774–1789*

W

DBQ Document-Based Questions

1. **Finding the Main Idea** What are the main ideas in Paine's argument?
2. **Paraphrasing** Why does Dickinson believe that the Congress has no right to form a new government?
3. **Assessing** Which argument do you think is the most logical? Explain.

W Writing Support

Expository Writing Have students write a Q-and-A style interview about independence with either Thomas Paine or John Dickinson. Students should include five to ten questions about events in 1775 and 1776 and answers that their subjects might have supplied. Have pairs of volunteers act out their interviews for the class. OL

Debates IN HISTORY

Answers:

1. Paine argues that after the British have "carried fire and sword" into the colonies, it is impossible to trust or honor them again and so they have lost their right to rule.
2. Dickinson argues that the Congress does not have the right to create a new government because most of the people they represent do not want it, and under the English constitution they then do not have the authority to declare independence.
3. Answers will vary, but students' choices should be supported with logical reasoning and arguments based on the excerpts.

Additional Support

Teacher Tip

This activity requires students to work in groups to discuss a specific topic. Before groups begin, encourage them to appoint the member who will be reporting to the class, as well as another member who will act as recorder during the discussion.

Activity: Collaborative Learning

Discussing a Topic Organize the class into groups of four or five. **Ask:** **When, if ever, was there a point during the events discussed in this section when reconciliation between the British government and the colonists was possible, and, if so, what would have been required of both parties?** *(Answers will vary.)* After sufficient discussion time, instruct groups to take a yes/no vote on the question and the group's conclusions. Have one person in each group report the group's vote and the reasons for it. OL

D Differentiated Instruction

Advanced Learners Ask students to draw a political cartoon about the colonies declaring independence. The cartoon can be either from the Loyalist or Patriot perspective. Then have students share their cartoons and solicit constructive feedback. **AL**

Turning Point

Answer:
The publication of the Declaration was a turning point because it was the first time a colony had declared itself independent of its ruling nation in a written document specifying why, and the precedent set by this event was repeated over the next two hundred years around the world; also, the language of the Declaration was used by women and minority groups seeking their civil rights.

Additional Support

Turning Point

▼ *Colonists in Manhattan pull down a statue of King George III upon hearing the news of the Declaration.*

▲ *Benjamin Franklin, John Adams, and Thomas Jefferson are shown here working to draft the Declaration of Independence.*

D The Colonies Declare Independence

The Declaration of Independence was an important turning point in the political history of the world. Not until this event had a colony declared itself truly independent of its ruling nation in a written document that specified the legal and moral reasons for that separation. The precedent set by the Declaration and the American Revolution was repeatedly followed over the next two hundred years by other colonies and nations. Additionally, in the United States, minority groups and women would use the language of the Declaration in their arguments for increased equality and civil rights.

ANALYZING HISTORY Why was the Declaration of Independence a turning point in political history?

D

▲ *In this 1779 English cartoon, a horse named "America" throws its rider, King George.*

History ONLINE Student Web Activity Visit glencoe.com and complete the activity on the Declaration of Independence.

The attack on Quebec convinced British officials that there was no hope of reconciliation. When the Olive Branch Petition arrived in Britain, King George III refused to look at it. Instead he proclaimed that the colonies were now "open and avowed enemies" and ordered the military to suppress the rebellion in America.

With no compromise likely, the Continental Congress increasingly began to act like an independent government. It sent people to negotiate with the Native Americans and established a postal system, a Continental Navy, and a Marine Corps. By March 1776, the Continental Navy had raided the Bahamas and had begun seizing British merchant ships.

The Fighting Spreads

As the Revolution began, Governor Dunmore of Virginia organized two Loyalist armies to assist the British troops in Virginia, one composed of white Loyalists, the other of enslaved Africans. Dunmore proclaimed that Africans enslaved by rebels would be freed if they fought for the Loyalists. The announcement convinced many Southern planters that the colonies had to declare independence. Otherwise, they might lose their lands and labor force. They also increased their efforts to raise a large Patriot army.

In December 1775, the Patriot troops attacked and defeated Dunmore's forces near Norfolk,

Activity: Interdisciplinary Connection

Government Tell students that Jefferson later recalled his experience in drafting the Declaration. He wrote: "[The committee members] unanimously pressed on myself alone to undertake the draught. I consented; I drew it; but before I reported it to the committee I communicated it separately to Dr. Franklin and Mr. Adams requesting their correction. . ." One of most controversial changes requested by the Continental Congress was the deletion of Jefferson's condemnation of King George's support of slavery. Jefferson disagreed with the decision to delete this passage, but agreed to modify the document to keep from alienating the Southern colonies. **How was the Declaration a model for other freedom movements?** *(It was written to explain why the first colony in history was going to declare itself independent of its ruling nation, and the language is simple, but elegant, as well. Later groups turned to this document as a source or a model when they wanted to make similar statements.)*

Virginia. The British then pulled their soldiers out of Virginia, leaving the Patriots in control. In North Carolina, Patriot troops dispersed Loyalists at the Battle of Moore's Creek in February 1776. The British then decided to seize Charles Town, South Carolina, but the city militia thwarted their attack.

While fighting raged in the South, Washington ordered his troops to capture the hills south of Boston. After the Americans seized the hills by surprise and surrounded Boston, the British navy evacuated the British troops, leaving the Patriots in control.

Despite their defeats, it was clear that the British were not backing down. In December 1775 the king issued the Prohibitory Act, shutting down trade with the colonies and ordering a naval blockade. The British also began expanding their army by recruiting mercenaries, or soldiers for hire, from Germany.

Common Sense and Independence

As the war dragged on, more and more Patriots began to think that the time had come to declare independence, although they feared that most colonists were still loyal to the king. In January 1776, however, public opinion began to change when **Thomas Paine** published a lively and persuasive pamphlet called *Common Sense.* Until *Common Sense* appeared, nearly everyone viewed Parliament, not the king, as the enemy. In *Common Sense,* Paine attacked King George III. Parliament, he wrote, did nothing without the king's support. Paine argued that monarchies had been set up by seizing power from the people. King George III was a tyrant, and it was time to declare independence: **R**

PRIMARY SOURCE

"Everything that is right or reasonable pleads for separation. The blood of the slain, the weeping voice of nature cries, 'TIS TIME TO PART. . . . Every spot of the old world is over-run with oppression. Freedom hath been hunted round the globe . . . and England hath given her warning to depart. Oh receive the fugitive, and prepare in time an asylum for mankind."

—from *Common Sense*

Within three months, *Common Sense* had sold 100,000 copies. George Washington noted that "*Common Sense* is working a powerful change in the minds of men." One by one the provincial congresses and legislatures told their representatives at the Continental Congress to vote for independence.

In early July a committee comprised of John Adams, Benjamin Franklin, Roger Sherman, Robert Livingston, and Thomas Jefferson **submitted** a document that Jefferson drafted, explaining why it was time for independence. On July 4, 1776, the Continental Congress issued this **Declaration of Independence.** The colonies had now become the United States of America. The American Revolution had begun.

Reading Check **Analyzing** How did Thomas Paine help persuade colonists to declare independence?

Section 2 REVIEW

Vocabulary

1. **Explain** the significance of: committee of correspondence, Boston Tea Party, Intolerable Acts, minuteman, Loyalist, Patriot, Battle of Bunker Hill, Thomas Paine, Declaration of Independence.

Main Ideas

2. **Summarizing** What were the first two actions of the First Continental Congress?
3. **Explaining** What was significant about the battles at Lexington and Concord?
4. **Making Connections** What motivated the Southern colonists to join the Revolution?

Critical Thinking

5. **Big Ideas** After King George III rejected the Olive Branch Petition, in what ways did the Continental Congress begin to act like an independent government?
6. **Organizing** Use a graphic organizer similar to the one below to indicate ways in which colonists defied Britain after the repeal of the Townshend Acts.

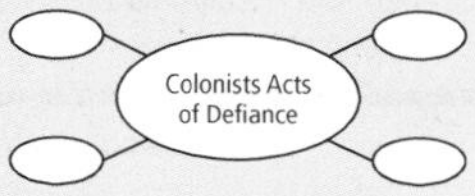

7. **Analyzing Visuals** Study the painting of the colonists toppling King George's statue on page 72. What did the colonists hope to accomplish by this act?

Writing About History

8. **Descriptive Writing** Suppose that you were a participant in the Boston Tea Party. Write a diary entry describing the event.

History ONLINE
Study Central™ To review this section, go to glencoe.com and click on Study Central.

R Reading Strategy

Summarizing Invite interested students to read Thomas Paine's *Common Sense* and write a summary of the main ideas in the work. **AL**

Reading Check

Answer:
He wrote the pamphlet *Common Sense.*

Assess

History ONLINE

Study Central™ provides summaries, interactive games, and online graphic organizers to help students review content.

Close

Summarizing Ask: Why did the last efforts at peace fail and the American Revolution begin? *(George III rejected the Olive Branch Petition when it was learned that American colonists had attacked British troops stationed in Quebec.)* **OL**

Section 2 REVIEW

Answers

1. All definitions can be found in the section and the Glossary.
2. It endorsed the Suffolk Resolves and approved the Continental Association.
3. They were the first armed engagements of the Revolution, and the British were forced to retreat.
4. Governor Dunmore of Virginia offered enslaved people their freedom if they would fight with the Loyalists against the rebels.
5. It began negotiations with Native Americans and established a postal system, a navy, and a marine corps.
6. Boston Tea Party, boycotts, burning of the *Gaspee*, formed committees of correspondence
7. By toppling the statue, the colonists were symbolically overthrowing the king.
8. Students' entries will vary but should be written from the perspective of participants.

Focus

MAKING CONNECTIONS

Have students speculate why the Founders thought it was important to formally declare independence and write their suggestions on the board. Then have them skim the Declaration of Independence to determine if Thomas Jefferson, the document's author, gave his readers any reasons. *(Answers will vary, but students may point out that the Declaration justifies independence as an inalienable right that is derived from the consent of the people [the governed]. Jefferson also lists numerous grievances against King George III.)*

Teach

D Differentiated Instruction

English Learners Choose a student to read aloud the first paragraph under "Declaration of Natural Rights" on this page. Discuss with students any unfamiliar terms such as *self-evident* and *unalienable*. Then have students close their textbook and write a paraphrase of the first paragraph. ELL

Additional Support

THE DECLARATION OF INDEPENDENCE

In Congress, July 4, 1776. The unanimous Declaration of the thirteen united States of America,

[Preamble]

When in the Course of human events, it becomes necessary for one people to dissolve the political bands which have connected them with another, and to assume among the Powers of the earth, the separate and equal station to which the Laws of Nature and of Nature's God entitle them, a decent respect to the opinions of mankind requires that they should declare the causes which **impel** them to the separation.

What It Means
The Preamble The Declaration of Independence has four parts. The Preamble explains why the Continental Congress drew up the Declaration.

impel *force*

[Declaration of Natural Rights]

D We hold these truths to be self-evident, that all men are created equal, that they are **endowed** by their Creator with certain unalienable Rights, that among these are Life, Liberty, and the pursuit of Happiness.

That to secure these rights, Governments are instituted among Men, deriving their just powers from the consent of the governed,

That whenever any Form of Government becomes destructive of these ends, it is the Right of the People to alter or to abolish it, and to institute new Government, laying its foundation on such principles and organizing its powers in such form, as to them shall seem most likely to effect their Safety and Happiness. Prudence, indeed, will dictate that Governments long established should not be changed for light and transient causes; and accordingly all experience hath shown, that mankind are more disposed to suffer, while evils are sufferable, than to right themselves by abolishing the forms to which they are accustomed. But when a long train of abuses and usurpations, pursuing invariably the same Object evinces a design to reduce them under absolute **Despotism,** it is their right, it is their duty, to throw off such Government, and to provide new Guards for their future security.

What It Means
Natural Rights The second part, the Declaration of Natural Rights, states that people have certain basic rights and that government should protect those rights. John Locke's ideas strongly influenced this part. In 1690 Locke wrote that government was based on the consent of the people and that people had the right to rebel if the government did not uphold their right to life, liberty, and property.

endowed *provided*

despotism *unlimited power*

[List of Grievances]

Such has been the patient sufferance of these Colonies; and such is now the necessity which constrains them to alter their former Systems of Government. The history of the

What It Means
List of Grievances The third part of the Declaration lists the colonists' complaints against the British government. Notice that King George III is singled out for blame.

Extending the Content

The Real Title Strictly speaking, the title of this famous document is not the "Declaration of Independence," but rather "The Unanimous Declaration of the Thirteen United States of America." The document was not the act by which independence was declared. That had been done on July 2, when the Continental Congress adopted Richard Henry Lee's resolution.

Also, point out to students that their textbook uses the spelling and punctuation from the original document. Thus, in the introduction to the document, for example, the term *united* is not capitalized—just as Jefferson wrote.

present King of Great Britain is a history of repeated injuries and **usurpations,** all having in direct object the establishment of an absolute Tyranny over these States. To prove this, let Facts be submitted to a candid world.

He has refused his Assent to Laws, the most wholesome and necessary for the public good.

He has forbidden his Governors to pass Laws of immediate and pressing importance, unless suspended in their operation till his Assent should be obtained; and when so suspended, he has utterly neglected to attend to them.

He has refused to pass other Laws for the accommodation of large districts of people, unless those people would **relinquish** the right of Representation in the Legislature, a right **inestimable** to them and formidable to tyrants only.

He has called together legislative bodies at places unusual, uncomfortable, and distant from the depository of their Public Records, for the sole purpose of fatiguing them into compliance with his measures.

He has dissolved Representative Houses repeatedly, for opposing with manly firmness his invasions on the rights of the people.

He has refused for a long time, after such dissolutions, to cause others to be elected; whereby the Legislative Powers, incapable of **Annihilation,** have returned to the People at large for their exercise; the State remaining in the mean time exposed to all the dangers of invasion from without, and **convulsions** within.

He has endeavoured to prevent the population of these States; for that purpose obstructing the Laws for **Naturalization of Foreigners;** refusing to pass others to encourage their migrations hither, and raising the conditions of new Appropriations of Lands.

He has obstructed the Administration of Justice, by refusing his Assent to Laws for establishing Judiciary Powers.

He has made Judges dependent on his Will alone, for the **tenure** of their offices, and the amount and payment of their salaries.

He has erected a multitude of New Offices, and sent hither swarms of Officers to harass our people, and eat out their substance.

He has kept among us, in times of peace, Standing Armies without the Consent of our legislature.

He has affected to render the Military independent of and superior to the Civil Power.

He has combined with others to subject us to a jurisdiction foreign to our constitution, and unacknowledged by our laws; giving his Assent to their acts of pretended legislation:

For **quartering** large bodies of troops among us:

For protecting them, by a mock Trial, from Punishment for any Murders which they should commit on the Inhabitants of these States:

R C

usurpations *unjust uses of power*

relinquish *give up*
inestimable *priceless*

annihilation *destruction*

convulsions *violent disturbances*

Naturalization of Foreigners *process by which foreign-born persons become citizens*

tenure *term*

quartering *lodging*

C Critical Thinking

Comparing and Contrasting The Declaration lists many accusations against King George III. **Ask:** **Why would Great Britain have been opposed to allowing more immigrants to come to the colonies?** *(An influx of immigrants would increase the power of the colonies; by restricting immigration, Britain could restrict the size of the colonial militias.)* Ask students to research the current U.S. policy on immigration. Have them write a one-page report explaining how today's immigration regulations compare with the restrictions placed on immigration to the colonies by the British before the Revolutionary War. **AL**

R Reading Strategy

Summarizing Have students read the list of grievances against King George III. Then have them select five of the complaints and summarize them in their own words. **OL**

Additional Support

Extending the Content

The Original Document The original copy of the Declaration of Independence is housed in the Rotunda for the Charters of Freedom in the National Archives Building in Washington, D.C. Its condition is poor, in part due to early improper preservation techniques.

S Skill Practice

Organizing Organize the class into small groups. Assign each group one or two of the grievances listed in the Declaration of Independence. Have the groups use their textbooks, the Internet, or library resources to find specific events, acts, or statements made by the king or Parliament that relate to the grievance. Have students read aloud the grievances that they were assigned and state the information that relates to the grievance. **OL**

W Writing Support

Persuasive Writing Tell students to write an editorial about the Declaration of Independence to an influential Loyalist newspaper in Boston. Point out that their editorials should support the position of the newspaper and therefore should explain why the colonists should remain loyal to Great Britain. **AL**

Additional Support

render *make*

abdicated *given up*

perfidy *violation of trust*

insurrections *rebellions*

petitioned for redress *asked formally for a correction of wrongs*

unwarrantable jurisdiction *unjustified authority*

consanguinity *originating from the same ancestor*

For cutting off our Trade with all parts of the world:

For imposing taxes on us without our Consent:

For depriving us in many cases, of the benefits of Trial by Jury:

For transporting us beyond Seas to be tried for pretended offences:

For abolishing the free System of English Laws in a neighbouring Province, establishing therein an Arbitrary government, and enlarging its Boundaries so as to **render** it at once an example and fit instrument for introducing the same absolute rule into these Colonies:

For taking away our Charters, abolishing our most valuable Laws, and altering fundamentally the Forms of our Governments:

For suspending our own Legislature, and declaring themselves invested with Power to legislate for us in all cases whatsoever.

S He has **abdicated** Government here, by declaring us out of his Protection and waging War against us.

He has plundered our seas, ravaged our Coasts, burnt our towns, and destroyed the lives of our people.

He is at this time transporting large armies of foreign mercenaries to compleat the works of death, desolation and tyranny, already begun with circumstances of Cruelty & **perfidy** scarcely paralleled in the most barbarous ages, and totally unworthy the Head of a civilized nation.

He has constrained our fellow Citizens taken Captive on the high Seas to bear Arms against their Country, to become the executioners of their friends and Brethren, or to fall themselves by their Hands.

He has excited domestic **insurrections** amongst us, and has endeavoured to bring on the inhabitants of our frontiers, the merciless Indian Savages, whose known rule of warfare, is an undistinguished destruction of all ages, sexes and conditions.

In every stage of these Oppressions We have **Petitioned for Redress** in the most humble terms: Our repeated Petitions have been answered only by repeated injury. A Prince, whose character is thus marked by every act which may define a Tyrant, is unfit to be the ruler of a free People.

Nor have We been wanting in attention to our British brethren. We have warned them from time to time of attempts by their legislature to extend an **unwarrantable jurisdiction** over us. W We have reminded them of the circumstances of our emigration and settlement here. We have appealed to their native justice and magnanimity, and we have conjured them by the ties of our common kindred to disavow these usurpations, which, would inevitably interrupt our connections and correspondence. They too have been deaf to the voice of justice and of **consanguinity.** We must, therefore, acquiesce in the necessity, which denounces our Separation, and hold them, as we hold the rest of mankind, Enemies in War, in Peace Friends.

Extending the Content

Jefferson and the Declaration In June 1776, Thomas Jefferson was assigned to a committee to draft the Declaration of Independence. Jefferson found it difficult to work in his current lodgings in the heart of Philadelphia, so he rented rooms in the home of Jacob Graff. The Graff home, located on the outskirts of the city, provided the peace and quiet Jefferson needed to write. He was able to complete the Declaration in less than three weeks.

The Graff home was torn down in 1883, but photographs of the site enabled the National Park Service to build a faithful recreation of the original building in 1975. Today, the rebuilt house includes a recreation of the rooms Jefferson rented on the second floor furnished with period furnishings.

[Resolution of Independence by the United States] C

We, therefore, the Representatives of the united States of America, in General Congress, Assembled, appealing to the Supreme Judge of the world for the **rectitude** of our intentions, do, in the Name, and by Authority of the good People of these Colonies, solemnly publish and declare, That these United Colonies are, and of Right ought to be Free and Independent States; that they are Absolved from all Allegiance to the British Crown, and that all political connection between them and the State of Great Britain, is and ought to be totally dissolved; and that as Free and Independent States, they have full Power to levy War, conclude Peace, contract Alliances, establish Commerce, and to do all other Acts and Things which Independent States may of right do.

And for the support of this Declaration, with a firm reliance on the Protection of Divine Providence, we mutually pledge to each other our Lives, our Fortunes and our sacred Honor.

John Hancock
President from Massachusetts

Georgia
Button Gwinnett
Lyman Hall
George Walton

North Carolina
William Hooper
Joseph Hewes
John Penn

South Carolina
Edward Rutledge
Thomas Heyward, Jr.
Thomas Lynch, Jr.
Arthur Middleton

Maryland
Samuel Chase
William Paca
Thomas Stone
Charles Carroll of Carrollton

Virginia
George Wythe
Richard Henry Lee
Thomas Jefferson
Benjamin Harrison
Thomas Nelson, Jr.
Francis Lightfoot Lee
Carter Braxton

Pennsylvania
Robert Morris
Benjamin Rush
Benjamin Franklin
John Morton
George Clymer
James Smith
George Taylor
James Wilson
George Ross

Delaware
Caesar Rodney
George Read
Thomas McKean

New York
William Floyd
Philip Livingston
Francis Lewis
Lewis Morris

New Jersey
Richard Stockton
John Witherspoon
Francis Hopkinson
John Hart
Abraham Clark

New Hampshire
Josiah Bartlett
William Whipple
Matthew Thornton

Massachusetts
Samuel Adams
John Adams
Robert Treat Paine
Elbridge Gerry

Rhode Island
Stephen Hopkins
William Ellery

Connecticut
Samuel Huntington
William Williams
Oliver Wolcott
Roger Sherman

What It Means
Resolution of Independence The final section declares that the colonies are "Free and Independent States" with the full power to make war, to form alliances, and to trade with other countries.

rectitude *rightness*

What It Means
Signers of the Declaration The signers, as representatives of the American people, declared the colonies independent from Great Britain. Most members signed the document on August 2, 1776.

Assess

C Critical Thinking

Analyzing Primary Sources
Have students create a chart listing the four sections of the Declaration of Independence and providing a brief summary and explanation of the purpose of each section. OL

S Skill Practice

Making Oral Presentations
Organize the class into groups. Assign each group one of the following: the French Revolution, Latin American independence movements, or the breakup of the Soviet Union. Have groups use library or Internet resources to learn about their assigned movement and the effects that the Declaration of Independence had on the movement. Have groups prepare an oral report on their findings. OL

Close

Organizing Information
Have students list the powers that the newly independent states planned to claim. OL

Additional Support

Extending the Content

John Hancock Most people have heard of John Hancock and the large signature he placed on the Declaration of Independence, but it is also important to understand his other contributions to history. Hancock was an important Patriot and political leader. He served in the Continental Congress from 1775 to 1780 and as its president from May 1775 to October 1777. He was also the first member to sign the Declaration of Independence. After the revolution, he continued to serve in a variety of political capacities, including nine terms as the governor of Massachusetts.

Focus

Bellringer

Daily Focus Transparency 2-3

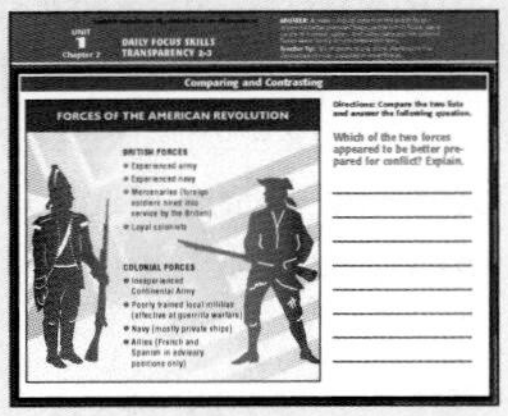

Guide to Reading

Answer: Students should include a battle, its importance, and outcomes for each year from 1776 to 1781.

Section Spotlight Video

To generate student interest and provide a springboard for class discussion, access the Chapter 2, Section 3 video at glencoe.com or on the video DVD.

Section 3

Section Audio | Spotlight Video

The War for Independence

Guide to Reading

Big Ideas

Trade, War, and Migration Hostility between France and Britain caused France to enter the Revolution on the side of the colonies.

Content Vocabulary

- guerrilla warfare *(p. 78)*
- letter of marque *(p. 82)*

Academic Vocabulary

- equip *(p. 78)*
- objective *(p. 83)*

People and Events to Identify

- William Howe *(p. 78)*
- Nathan Hale *(p. 80)*
- Valley Forge *(p. 81)*
- Marquis de Lafayette *(p. 81)*
- Saratoga *(p. 82)*
- John Paul Jones *(p. 82)*
- Charles Cornwallis *(p. 84)*
- Battle of Kings Mountain *(p. 84)*
- Treaty of Paris *(p. 85)*

Reading Strategy

Sequencing Complete a time line similar to the one below to record the major battles of the American Revolution and their outcomes.

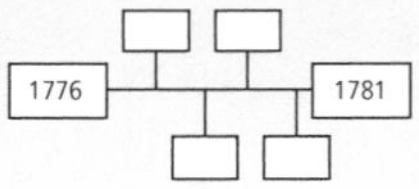

The Continental Army experienced several setbacks while fighting against the British military in a war that lasted many years. Eventually, the Americans, with the help of the French and other nations, were able to foil the British war strategy to win independence.

The Opposing Sides

MAIN Idea The Continental Army and local militias had to fight more experienced and better equipped British troops.

HISTORY AND YOU Have you ever tried something new without having time to prepare? Read on to learn how the Americans fought a war without proper training or equipment.

On the same day that the Continental Congress voted for independence, the British began landing troops in New York Harbor. By mid-August, they had assembled an estimated 32,000 men under the command of General **William Howe.** British officials did not expect the rebellion to last long. Their troops were disciplined, well trained, and well **equipped.**

Compared to the British troops, the Continental Army was inexperienced and poorly equipped. Although more than 230,000 men served in the Continental Army at various times, it rarely numbered more than 20,000 at any one time. Many soldiers deserted or refused to reenlist when their term was up. Others left their posts and returned to their farms at planting or harvest time.

Paying for the war was equally difficult. Lacking the power to tax, the Continental Congress issued paper money. These "Continentals" were not backed by gold or silver and became almost worthless very quickly. Fortunately, Robert Morris, a wealthy Pennsylvania merchant and banker, personally pledged large amounts of money for the war effort. Morris also set up an efficient method of buying rations and uniforms, arranged for foreign loans, and convinced the Congress to create the Bank of North America to finance the military.

Not only did the British have to worry about fighting the Continental Army, they also had to contend with the local militias. The militias were poorly trained, but they fought differently. They did not always line up for battle. They hid behind trees and walls and ambushed British troops and supply wagons. This kind of fighting is called **guerrilla warfare,** and it is very difficult to defeat.

Another problem for the British was that they were not united at home. Many merchants and members of Parliament opposed the war. The British had to win quickly and cheaply; otherwise, opinions in Parliament would shift against the war. The United States did not have

Resource Manager

R Reading Strategies	C Critical Thinking	D Differentiated Instruction	W Writing Support	S Skill Practice
Teacher Edition • Inferring, p. 80 • Summarizing, p. 81 • Predicting, p. 83 **Additional Resources** • Guid. Read. Act., URB p. 82	**Teacher Edition** • Ident. Cent. Issues, p. 79 • Det. Cause/Effect, p. 81 • Drawing Con., p. 82 • Det. Importance, p. 84 **Additional Resources** • Quizzes and Tests, p. 21	**Teacher Edition** • Adv. Learners, p. 80	**Teacher Edition** • Descriptive Writing, p. 84	**Teacher Edition** • Using Geo. Skills, p. 83 **Additional Resources** • Read. Essen., p. 23

PRIMARY SOURCE

Why Did Britain Lose the Revolutionary War?

At the time of the Revolution, the British military was among the most powerful forces in the world. Pitted against this formidable fighting machine, the ragtag colonial forces did not seem to have a chance. Yet perseverance and the desire to secure individual freedoms eventually tipped the scales in the colonists' favor.

▶ *The British army, though extremely disciplined and well-trained, fought in the traditional way, by marching forward across an open space in tight formation. This approach made the soldiers easy targets when colonial troops fought in a guerrilla style.*

The Opposing Sides

Colonial Advantages	British Advantages
• Fighting on home ground • Good decisions by generals • Fighting for their rights and freedoms • French alliance providing loans, naval support, and troops • Time: the longer the war dragged on, the more likely the British were to give up	• Well-trained, well-supplied army and navy • Wealthy nation with substantial resources • Strong central government
Colonial Disadvantages	**British Disadvantages**
• Untrained soldiers • Food and ammunition shortages • Weak and divided central government	• Fighting in unfamiliar, hostile territory • Fighting far from Britain • Many troops were mercenaries, many indifferent to the cause • Half-hearted support at home

C

Analyzing VISUALS

1. **Comparing** How did different approaches to warfare sometimes give the Americans the advantage over the better-trained and better-supplied British army?
2. **Summarizing** What other advantages did the Americans have in the war?

to defeat Britain—it simply had to survive until the British became tired of paying for the war.

The European balance of power also hampered the British. The French, Dutch, and Spanish were all eager to exploit Britain's problems. As a result, Britain had to station much of its military elsewhere in the world to defend its empire. The European balance of power also meant that the Patriots might be able to find allies against the British.

All these factors meant that the British had to win quickly. To do so, they had to convince Americans that their cause was hopeless and that they could safely surrender without being hanged for treason. General Howe's strategy, therefore, had two parts. First, he sent a large number of troops to capture New York City. This would separate New England from the South and demonstrate to Americans that they could not win. The second part of Howe's strategy was diplomatic. He invited delegates from the Continental Congress to a peace conference. Howe promised that rebels who laid down their arms and swore loyalty to the king would be pardoned. When the Americans realized that Howe had no authority to negotiate a compromise, they refused to talk further.

✓Reading Check **Identifying** What three major disadvantages did the British face in the American Revolution?

Teach

C Critical Thinking

Identifying Central Issues Discuss the advantages and disadvantages of each side during the Revolution. **Ask:** Why did the Continental army not need to defeat the British militarily to win? *(Many in Britain would not support a long, costly war.)* **BL**

Analyzing VISUALS

Answers:

1. Sometimes the Americans' guerrilla approach gave them an advantage against a more formal British advance because they could shoot from protected positions.
2. They were fighting on home ground, they had the support of the French, and their generals made many good decisions.

✓Reading Check

Answer:
guerrilla warfare, opposition at home, the struggle to maintain the balance of power in Europe

Hands-On Chapter Project Step 3

War Correspondence

Step 3: Justifying the War Have students choose a role to take—either a member of the British army or a member of the Continental Army. Students will research the advantages and disadvantages of each opposing side at the beginning of the war.

Directions As a member of the chosen army, students will write a letter home describing why they are fighting and why they believe that they will win this war.

Justifying Students will use facts to justify their arguments in a written letter. **OL**
(Chapter Project continued on page 87)

D Differentiated Instruction

Advanced Learners Have students consider what it would have been like to be one of the following: a Continental soldier, a French volunteer, a wife waiting for news of her husband, a merchant smuggling supplies to the troops, or a woman spying for the Continental army. Ask students to write a letter about the dangers they faced and the reasons for their commitment to the cause. AL

R Reading Strategy

Inferring Have students read the last paragraph under "Crossing the Delaware." **Ask:** What about the timing of the American attack on Trenton may have contributed to its success? *(Not only was the attack in the winter, when both sides in a conflict usually ceased fighting, but it was also Christmas. It is possible that British troops were even less alert and more relaxed than usual on this holiday, so the element of surprise was increased.)* OL

Additional Support

Battles in the North

MAIN Idea Early setbacks plagued the Continental Army, but the victory at Saratoga convinced France to enter the war.

HISTORY AND YOU Can you think of other wars in which the weaker side managed to defeat a stronger power? Read on to learn how the Battle of Saratoga was a turning point in the war.

Although the British had sent a huge force to seize New York City, the Congress asked Washington to try to defend it. Congressional leaders feared that if New York fell without a fight it would hurt American morale. Washington moved much of his army to Long Island.

The inexperience of Washington's troops became obvious when British troops attacked them in the summer of 1776. Many American soldiers fled, and some 1,500 were wounded or killed. Fortunately, the British were slow to advance, and the surviving American troops rejoined the remainder of Washington's army defending New York City. Even so, the British captured New York and used it as their headquarters for the rest of the war.

D About this time, Washington sent volunteer Captain **Nathan Hale** to spy on the British. Although Hale was disguised as a Dutch schoolteacher, he was caught by the British and hanged. Brave until the end, Hale's last words were: "I only regret that I have but one life to lose for my country." Shortly afterward, Washington moved most of his troops from Manhattan Island to White Plains, New York.

Crossing the Delaware

At the Battle of White Plains in October 1776, the British forced Washington to retreat again. Then they surprised him. Instead of coming after the Continental Army, the British troops headed toward Philadelphia, where the Continental Congress was meeting. Caught by surprise, Washington's troops had to move quickly to get there ahead of the British.

While this march was taking place, Thomas Paine wrote another pamphlet to help boost American morale. In *The American Crisis,* he reminded Americans that "the harder the conflict, the more glorious the triumph":

PRIMARY SOURCE

"These are the times that try men's souls. The summer soldier and the sunshine patriot will in this crisis shrink from the service of their country; but he that stands it now deserves the love and thanks of man and woman."

—from *The American Crisis*

As the armies headed toward Philadelphia, the British stopped their advance and dispersed into winter camps in New Jersey. In the 1700s, armies did not usually fight in the winter because of the weather and scarce food supplies.

At this point Washington tried something daring—a winter attack. On December 25, 1776, he led some 2,400 men across the icy Delaware River and attacked a British camp at Trenton in the middle of a sleet storm. They killed or captured almost 1,000 British. Several days later, Washington's forces scattered three British regiments near Princeton. After these R small victories, Washington headed into the hills of northern New Jersey for the winter. Washington did not have a significant victory in the early years of the war, but he managed to keep his fluctuating number of troops together while avoiding a resounding defeat that might have ended the revolutionary effort.

Philadelphia Falls

In March 1777 General John Burgoyne, based in Quebec, developed a plan to isolate New England from the other American states. Burgoyne proposed a three-pronged attack on New York. He would take a large force south from Montreal. Another force would move from Montreal up the St. Lawrence River to Lake Ontario, and then head east into New York. A third force, led by General Howe, would march north from New York City. The three forces would meet near Albany and then march east into New England.

Unfortunately for the British, they did not coordinate the plan. By the time Burgoyne began marching south, General Howe had already moved 13,000 men by ship to Maryland and attacked Philadelphia from the south. Howe believed capturing Philadelphia and the Continental Congress would cripple the Revolution and convince Loyalists to rise up and take control of Pennsylvania.

Howe's action was a military success but a political failure. He defeated Washington at the Battle of Brandywine Creek and captured

Activity: Interdisciplinary Connection

Art Invite an art teacher or artist to speak to the class about various types of artwork related to the American Revolution. Ask the speaker to give examples of works that inspired patriotism during the war and works that illustrate historical events but were created after the war. Encourage the speaker to talk about how artists learned about the historical events they depicted. Allow time for students to ask the speaker questions about art and the American Revolution. OL

NATIONAL GEOGRAPHIC The War for Independence, 1776–1777

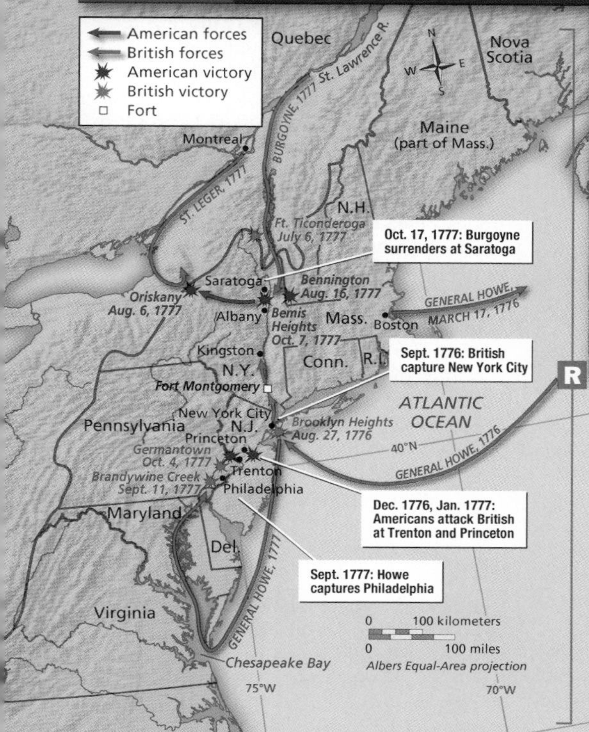

▲ *The famous* Washington Crossing the Delaware *was painted by Emanuel Gottlieb Leutze in 1851.*

▲ *This painting depicts the surrender of British General John Burgoyne to American General Horatio Gates at Saratoga on October 17, 1777. The American victory there encouraged the French to support the Americans.*

Analyzing GEOGRAPHY

1. **Location** What are two colonial victories that occurred in New Jersey?
2. **Movement** What was the role of the British navy in the Revolution?

Philadelphia, but the Continental Congress escaped and no Loyalist uprising occurred.

Howe also failed to destroy the Continental Army, which set up its winter camp at **Valley Forge.** There, bitter cold and food shortages killed nearly 2,500 men.

Joining Washington at Valley Forge were two European military officers, the **Marquis de Lafayette** from France and Baron Friedrich von Steuben from Prussia. These officers helped Washington improve discipline and boost morale among the weary troops despite the camp's harsh conditions.

The Battle of Saratoga

General Burgoyne did not know Howe had gone south to attack Philadelphia. In June 1777, he and an estimated 8,000 troops marched south from Quebec into New York. Another 900 troops under the command of Colonel Barry St. Leger headed down the St. Lawrence to the eastern end of Lake Ontario. There they joined more than 1,000 Iroquois warriors and headed east toward Albany. The Iroquois had allied with the British hoping to keep American settlers off Iroquois lands. C

R Reading Strategy

Summarizing Have visual learners and students who are acquiring English use the map on this page to summarize British General Burgoyne's three-pronged plan and why it failed. BL ELL

C Critical Thinking

Determining Cause and Effect Discuss Burgoyne's plan and the reasons for its failure. **Ask:** Why did General Howe not follow Burgoyne's plan and what were the consequences? *(He felt that capturing Philadelphia and the Continental Congress was more important than dividing the colonies, so he made that his goal. However, his success in doing so had little effect on the colonial effort, as the Congress escaped and so did Washington's troops. His failure to follow the plan may have caused Burgoyne to lose at Saratoga, which was a turning point in the war.)* OL

Analyzing GEOGRAPHY

Answers:
1. Trenton and Princeton
2. transporting troops, supplies, and equipment

Additional Support

Extending the Content

Valley Forge During the winter of 1777–1778, approximately 12,000 men from the Continental Army were quartered at Valley Forge, Pennsylvania, located about 25 miles (40 km) west of Philadelphia. Although the weather is blamed for many of the 2,500 deaths in the camp that winter, the temperatures and precipitation, including rain and snow, were typical for winter in this area of the state. What made the winter particularly dangerous for the troops was the lack of proper shelter and clothing. Long marches had destroyed the men's boots, and ragged clothes were seldom replaced.

C Critical Thinking

Drawing Conclusions Discuss the effects of the American Revolution on Native American groups in the region. **Ask:** Why might Native American groups, such as the Iroquois and the Cherokee, have fought on the British side during the Revolution? *(The British had tried to control westward expansion of the colonies to protect Native American lands. If the British won, they would most likely help their allies by continuing to limit expansion west of the Appalachians.)* OL

Reading Check

Answer:
In this treaty, France became the first country to recognize the United States as an independent nation.

Additional Support

At first, Burgoyne's march south went smoothly. His troops easily seized Fort Ticonderoga with its large store of gunpowder and supplies. In response, the Congress fired the commander defending the region and replaced him with General Horatio Gates.

After this early victory, Burgoyne's march slowed to a crawl. American troops felled trees in front of the British army and removed all the crops and cattle from the region in an effort to cut off the British food supply. Meanwhile, the British and Iroquois forces marching east from Lake Ontario were ambushed by militia and then driven back by American troops under General Benedict Arnold.

In desperation, Burgoyne retreated to **Saratoga,** where he was quickly surrounded by an American army nearly three times the size of his own. On October 17, 1777, he surrendered to General Gates. More than 5,000 British soldiers were taken prisoner. The American victory at Saratoga was astonishing and marked a turning point in the war. It not only dramatically improved American morale, it also convinced the French that the time had come to commit troops to the American cause.

Both Spain and France had been secretly sending arms and supplies to the United States well before Saratoga. The Congress appreciated the supplies but wanted the French to send troops, too. In September 1776, the Congress sent Benjamin Franklin, Arthur Lee, and Silas Deane to France to ask for troops. The French, however, were not willing to risk war until they believed the Americans could win. The victory at Saratoga convinced them, and shortly afterward they began negotiations to enter the war against Britain.

On February 6, 1778, the United States signed its first two treaties. In the first treaty, France became the first country to recognize the United States as an independent nation. The second treaty was an alliance between the United States and France. By June 1778, Britain and France were at war. In 1779 Spain entered the war as well, as an ally of France but not of the United States.

The War in the West

Not all the fighting in the Revolutionary War took place in the East. In 1778 Patriot George Rogers Clark took 175 troops down the Ohio River and captured several towns. By February 1779, the British had surrendered, giving the Americans control of the region.

While Clark fought the British in the West, Chief Joseph Brant, also known as Thayendanegea, convinced four Iroquois nations to join the British. In July 1778, British troops and Iroquois warriors attacked western Pennsylvania, burning towns and killing over 200 militia. The following summer, American troops defeated the British and Iroquois in western New York. These battles destroyed the power of the Iroquois people. C

Farther south, the Cherokee people suffered a similar fate. After the Revolution began, a delegation of Shawnee, Delaware, and Mohawk convinced the Cherokee that the time had come to drive American settlers off Cherokee lands. The Cherokee attacked settlers in Virginia and North Carolina, but the American militia units were too strong. By 1780, militia units had burned down hundreds of Cherokee towns.

The War at Sea

Americans fought the British at sea, as well as on land. Instead of attacking the British fleet directly, American warships attacked British merchant ships. To further disrupt British trade, the Congress began issuing **letters of marque** (mark), or licenses, to private ship owners authorizing them to attack British merchant ships. By the war's end, millions of dollars of cargo had been seized, seriously harming Britain's trade and economy.

Perhaps the most famous naval battle of the war involved the American naval officer **John Paul Jones.** Jones commanded a ship named the *Bonhomme Richard.* While sailing near Britain in September 1779, Jones encountered a group of British merchant ships protected by the warships *Serapis* and *Countess of Scarborough.* Jones attacked the *Serapis,* but the heavier guns of the British ship nearly sank the *Bonhomme Richard.* With the American ship in distress, the British commander called on Jones to surrender. Jones replied, "I have not yet begun to fight." He lashed his ship to *Serapis* so it could not sink, and then boarded the British ship. The battle lasted more than three hours before the British surrendered.

Reading Check **Summarizing** What was significant about the first U.S. treaty with France?

Extending the Content

Bernardo de Gálvez Bernardo de Gálvez (1746–1786) was born in Malága, Spain. Gálvez came to New Spain as a member of the Spanish military. In 1769, Gálvez was placed in command of Spanish forces on New Spain's northern frontier. In 1777 he was appointed governor of Louisiana.

Even before Spain entered the Revolution, Gálvez took steps to aid the Americans. He used his authority as governor to secure the Mississippi River against the British, while allowing Spanish, French, and American ships access to smuggle arms to American forces. When Spain declared war on Britain, Gálvez raised an army, fought British troops near Baton Rouge and Natchez, and captured British forts at Mobile and Pensacola. His campaigns were important to the American victory because they tied down British troops that might otherwise have fought farther north. The city of Galveston, Texas, is named in his honor.

Battles in the South

MAIN Idea The British strategy to control the Southern states failed with their surrender at Yorktown.

HISTORY AND YOU Have you ever changed your opinion about an event because of the actions of the people or groups involved? Read on to learn how the Battle of Kings Mountain encouraged Southern farmers to organize forces.

After the British defeat at Saratoga, General Howe resigned. He was replaced by Sir Henry Clinton, who ordered the British troops in Philadelphia to abandon the city and return to New York City. Clinton wanted to gather all his forces in one place before beginning a new campaign. Washington ordered his forces at Valley Forge to intercept the British. The two sides met at the Battle of Monmouth—the largest battle of the war. Neither side won, but for the first time American troops were able to stand against the British in a regular battle.

After Clinton reached New York, he was ordered to begin a campaign in the South, where the British had the strongest Loyalist support. The Southern states were also valuable because they produced tobacco and rice. The British hoped they could keep the South, even if they lost the North. **S**

The Struggle in the Carolinas

In December 1778, some 3,500 British troops captured Savannah, Georgia. They seized control of Georgia's backcountry and returned the British royal governor to power. The next **objective** was to capture Charles Town, South Carolina—the largest city in the South.

NATIONAL GEOGRAPHIC The War for Independence, 1778–1781

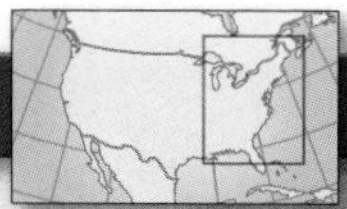

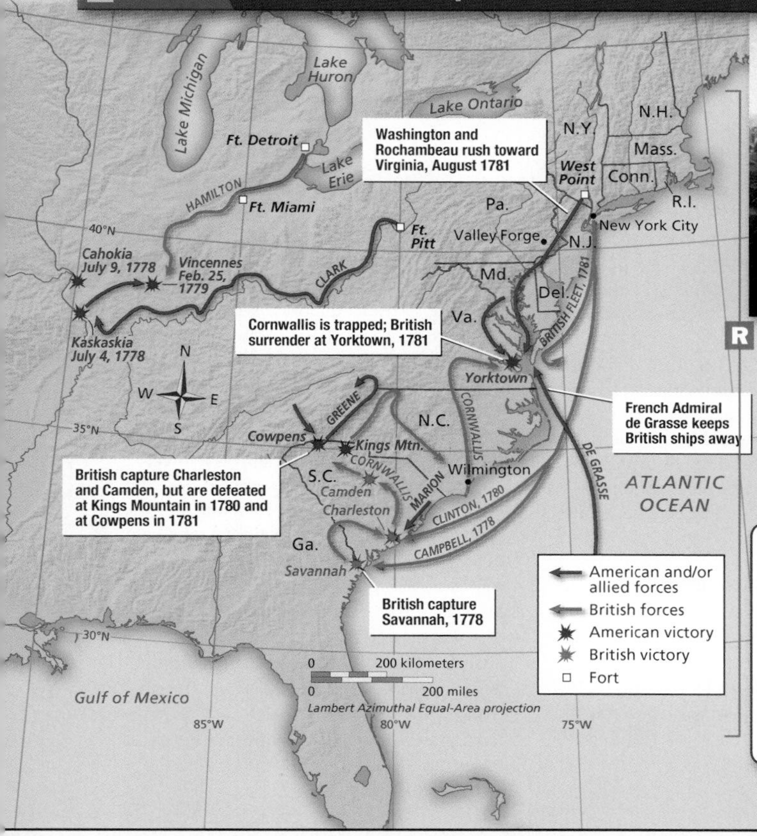

▲ *This painting celebrates the courage of Mary Ludwig Hays, known as "Molly Pitcher," who according to tradition carried water to the troops during the Battle of Monmouth and helped fire a cannon after the crew was killed.*

Analyzing GEOGRAPHY

1. **Movement** How did the French help the American forces?
2. **Location** Where did the final battle of the war occur?

Maps In MOtion See *StudentWorks™ Plus* or glencoe.com.

Chapter 2 The American Revolution 83

S Skill Practice

Using Geography Skills Discuss how British war goals began to shift by 1778. **Ask:** To where did the focus of the war move after 1778? Why was this the case? *(It moved to the South. The British felt that they would get assistance there from the many Loyalists in the region; also, they wanted to keep the South even if they lost the North because of the valuable cash crops produced in the region.)* **OL**

R Reading Strategy

Predicting Have students select one of the major battles of the American Revolution and ask them to consider what would have happened if the other side had won. Have them also consider what advantage the winning side would then have gained and what its next likely move would have been. Have students share their predictions as part of a class discussion. **OL**

Analyzing GEOGRAPHY

Answers:

1. They blocked British ships so that Cornwallis could not escape or be re-supplied.
2. Yorktown

Additional Support

Activity: Collaborative Learning

Building a Model **Ask:** How do historians and artists learn details of past events? *(Answers may include primary sources such as diaries, images, and documents.)* Have students work in small groups to build a model depicting one of the events mentioned in this section. Encourage students to use library and Internet resources to locate descriptions and images to help them recreate the scene. Suggest that students create a handout to accompany their model. Make arrangements to display the models at your school, the local library, or other appropriate venues. **AL**

C Critical Thinking

Determining Importance Discuss with students why the British, who had initial success in the South, then began to experience setbacks. **Ask:** Why was the Battle of Kings Mountain a turning point in the war in the South? *(Southern farmers began to organize against the British because of British mistreatment.)* Explore with students what the British did wrong and what the Americans did right during this phase of the war. **OL**

W Writing Support

Descriptive Writing Have students do additional research to find out more about Francis Marion and his role in the war effort. Ask students to use this information to write a short essay describing Marion's contributions and their importance in the American victory. **OL**

Analyzing GEOGRAPHY

Answers:

1. north: British Canada and the Great Lakes; south: Gulf of Mexico and Spanish Florida; west: Mississippi River
2. Britain and Spain

Additional Support

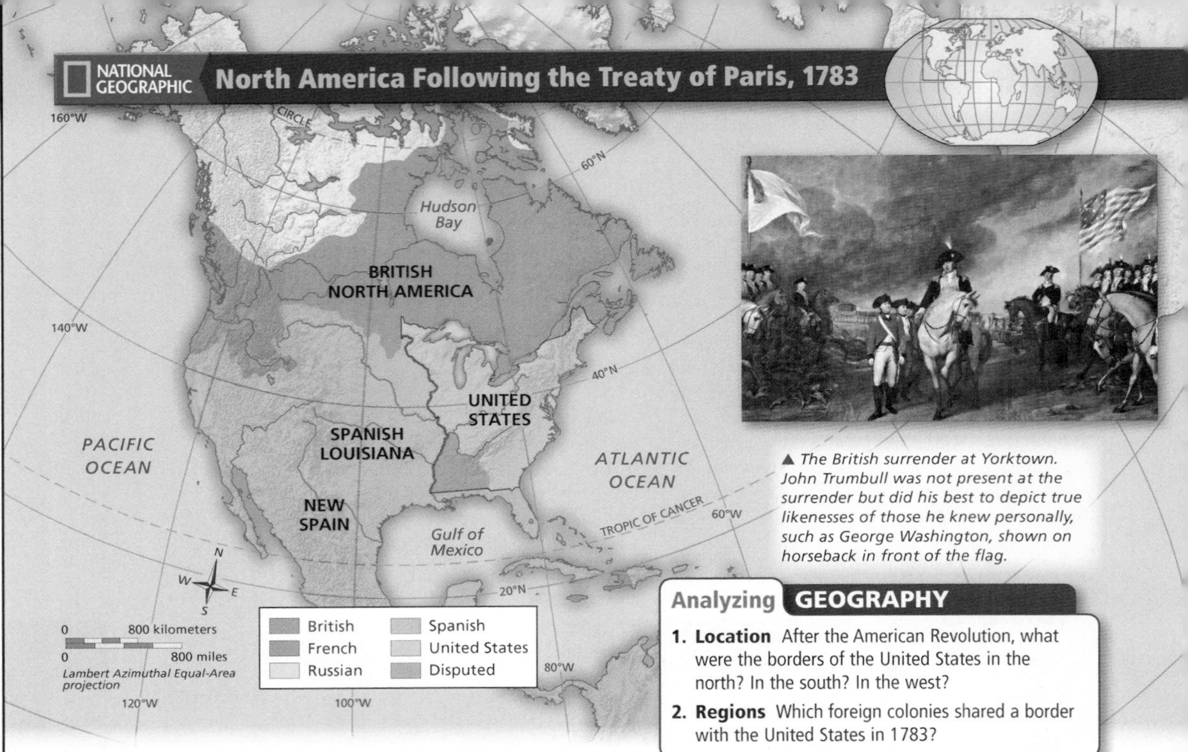

▲ The British surrender at Yorktown. John Trumbull was not present at the surrender but did his best to depict true likenesses of those he knew personally, such as George Washington, shown on horseback in front of the flag.

Analyzing GEOGRAPHY

1. **Location** After the American Revolution, what were the borders of the United States in the north? In the south? In the west?
2. **Regions** Which foreign colonies shared a border with the United States in 1783?

Charles Town Falls Clinton attacked Charles Town with nearly 14,000 British soldiers. His forces quickly surrounded the city, trapping the American forces inside. On May 12, 1780, the Americans surrendered. Nearly 5,500 Americans were taken prisoner, the greatest American defeat in the war.

After capturing Charles Town, Clinton returned to New York, leaving General **Charles Cornwallis** in command. The Continental Congress then sent General Horatio Gates, the hero of Saratoga, to defend the South Carolina backcountry. Gates attempted to destroy a British supply base at Camden, South Carolina, but failed.

The Battle of Kings Mountain After the Battle of Camden, the British began subduing the Carolina backcountry. At first, everything went well for them. Many of the settlers were Loyalists and agreed to fight for Britain. Two British cavalry officers, Banastre Tarleton and Patrick Ferguson, led many of the Loyalist forces in the region. These troops became known for their brutality.

Ferguson finally went too far when he tried to subdue the people living in the Appalachian Mountains. Enraged at his tactics, the "overmountain" men, as they were known, put together a militia. They intercepted Ferguson at Kings Mountain on October 7, 1780, and destroyed his army. The **Battle of Kings Mountain** was a turning point in the South. Southern farmers, furious with British treatment, began organizing their own forces.

The new American commander in the region, General Nathanael Greene, decided to wear down the British in battle while militia destroyed their supplies. He organized the militia into small units to carry out hit-and-run raids against British camps and supply wagons. Francis Marion, known as the "Swamp Fox," led the most famous of these units. The strategy worked. By late 1781, the British controlled very little of the South except for Savannah, Charles Town, and Wilmington.

Extending the Content

Surrender Washington is pictured in Trumbull's painting, but he did not receive the British surrender. This is because Cornwallis refused to surrender to Washington, whom he felt was of inferior rank, and so sent his second-in-command, General O'Hara, shown in the red uniform, standing in the center. O'Hara first tried to surrender to the French army commander Rochambeau as more suitable than a lowly colonial general. Rochambeau refused to accept it, and sent O'Hara, rightly, to Washington. However, Washington would not accept the surrender from anyone less than Cornwallis, so sent his own subordinate, Major-General Lincoln, who is pictured here on horseback in the center, to accept it from O'Hara. In that way the surrender finally was accomplished.

The Battle of Yorktown

In late April 1781, Cornwallis marched into Virginia. As long as the Americans controlled Virginia, he believed, new troops and supplies could keep coming south. With more French troops on the way to America, the British knew they had very little time left to win the war. They had to secure Virginia.

When he reached Virginia, Cornwallis linked up with forces under the command of Benedict Arnold. Arnold had been an American general early in the war but had later sold military information to the British. When his treason was discovered, Arnold fled to British-controlled New York City. There, he was given command of British troops and ordered to Virginia.

After Arnold's forces joined those of Cornwallis, the British began to conquer Virginia. Their combined forces encountered very little resistance until June 1781, when a large American force led by General Anthony Wayne arrived in Virginia. Outnumbered and too far inland, Cornwallis retreated to the coastal town of Yorktown to protect his supplies and to maintain communications by sea.

Cornwallis's retreat created an opportunity for the Americans and their French allies. The previous year, 6,000 French troops had arrived in New England. With this support, Washington decided to march on New York City. As the troops headed to New York, the French general Rochambeau learned that a French fleet commanded by Admiral de Grasse was on its way north from the Caribbean.

When he learned of the French fleet, Washington canceled the attack on New York City. Instead, he and Rochambeau headed to Yorktown. As their troops raced south, Admiral de Grasse moved into Chesapeake Bay near Yorktown. His fleet cut off the flow of supplies to Cornwallis and prevented him from escaping by sea.

On September 28, 1781, American and French forces surrounded Yorktown and began to bombard it. On October 14, Washington's aide, Alexander Hamilton, led an attack that captured key British defenses. Three days later, Cornwallis began negotiations to surrender, and on October 19, 1781, approximately 8,000 British soldiers marched out of Yorktown and laid down their weapons.

The Treaty of Paris

When Lord North, the British prime minister, learned of the surrender at Yorktown, he knew the war was over. In March 1782, Parliament voted to begin peace negotiations. John Adams, Benjamin Franklin, and John Jay conducted most of the negotiations for the United States.

The final settlement, known as the **Treaty of Paris,** was signed on September 3, 1783. In this treaty, Britain recognized the United States of America as a new nation, with the Mississippi River as its western border. Britain also gave Florida back to Spain. France received colonies in Africa and the Caribbean that the British had seized from them in 1763. On November 24, 1783, the last British troops left New York City. The American Revolution was over. The creation of a new nation was about to begin.

Reading Check **Describing** How was the war won at Yorktown?

Section 3 REVIEW

Vocabulary

1. **Explain** the significance of: William Howe, guerrilla warfare, Nathan Hale, Valley Forge, Marquis de Lafayette, Saratoga, letter of marque, John Paul Jones, Charles Cornwallis, Treaty of Paris.

Main Ideas

2. **Explaining** Why did the Continental Congress have trouble paying for the war?
3. **Describing** Before they officially joined the war effort, how were European countries helping the Americans fight the British?
4. **Summarizing** What was General Nathaniel Greene's strategy for fighting the British in the South?

Critical Thinking

5. **Big Ideas** Why were the French at first reluctant to make an alliance with the colonies?
6. **Categorizing** Use a graphic organizer similar to the one below to list the provisions of the Treaty of Paris.

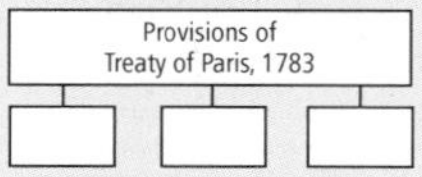

7. **Analyzing Visuals** Study the map on page 84. Which nation controlled most of North America at the end of the American Revolution?

Writing About History

8. **Persuasive Writing** Suppose that you are a colonial leader during the American Revolution. Write a letter to convince the ruler of a European nation to support the Americans in the war.

History ONLINE
Study Central™ To review this section, go to glencoe.com and click on Study Central.

85

Reading Check

Answer:
American and French forces surrounded the British at Yorktown, cutting off their access to supplies and to escape by sea.

Assess

History ONLINE

Study Central™ provides summaries, interactive games, and online graphic organizers to help students review content.

Close

Summarizing Ask: How were the colonists able to win the American Revolution? *(The colonial forces achieved timely victories, had several excellent leaders, and, later, the support of powerful allies. They also employed non-traditional tactics, such as guerrilla warfare, that worked well against the British forces, who used more formal military approaches.)* **OL**

Section 3 REVIEW

Answers

1. All definitions can be found in the section and the Glossary.
2. The Congress did not have the power to tax, so to pay for the war it issued Continentals, paper money that soon became worthless.
3. France and Spain sent money and supplies. Also, the Marquis de Lafayette came from France to help in the military effort, as did Prussian General Von Steuben.
4. He decided to wear down the British in battle while militia destroyed their supplies, and he organized the militia into small units to carry out hit-and-run guerrilla raids against British camps and supply wagons.
5. The French were not willing to send troops until they believed that the Americans could win.
6. Britain recognized the United States as a new nation with the Mississippi River as its western border; Spain reclaimed Florida; France regained colonies in Africa and the Caribbean.
7. Spain
8. Students' letters will vary but should make an argument and include the benefits for a European country if it supports the Americans.

Focus

Bellringer

Daily Focus Transparency 2-4

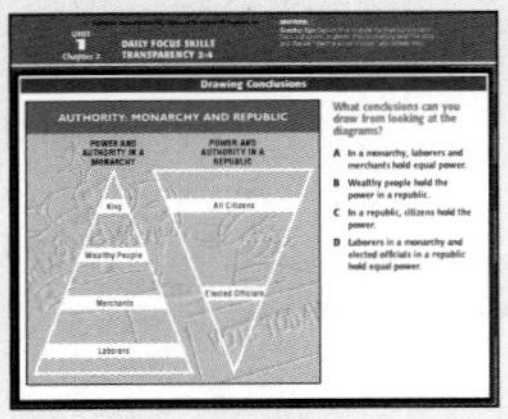

Guide to Reading

Answers: established a republic, elected representatives to govern according to laws or constitution, expanded voting rights, protected freedom of religion

Section Spotlight Video

To generate student interest and provide a springboard for class discussion, access the Chapter 2, Section 4 video at glencoe.com or on the video DVD.

Resource Manager

R Reading Strategies	C Critical Thinking	D Differentiated Instruction	W Writing Support	S Skill Practice
Teacher Edition • Reading Graphs, p. 87 **Additional Resources** • Pri. Source Reading, URB p. 71 • Guid. Read. Act., URB p. 83	**Teacher Edition** • Ident. Cent. Issues, pp. 88, 90 **Additional Resources** • Quizzes and Tests, p. 22	**Teacher Edition** • Verbal/Linguistic, p. 88 **Additional Resources** • Time Line Act., URB p. 67 • Reteaching Act., URB p. 77	**Additional Resources** • Authentic Assessment p. 9	**Teacher Edition** • Using Geo. Skills, p. 89 **Additional Resources** • Hist. Analysis Skills Act., URB p. 56 • Read. Skills Act., URB p. 55 • Read. Essen., p. 26

Section 4 — Section Audio — Spotlight Video

The War Changes American Society

Guide to Reading

Big Ideas

Culture and Beliefs As the American Revolution ended, a unique culture arose in the new United States.

Content Vocabulary
- republic *(p. 86)*
- emancipation *(p. 89)*
- manumission *(p. 90)*

Academic Vocabulary
- contradiction *(p. 86)*
- revolutionary *(p. 88)*

People and Events to Identify
- Virginia Statute for Religious Freedom *(p. 88)*
- John Trumbull *(p. 91)*
- Charles Willson Peale *(p. 91)*

Reading Strategy

Organizing Complete a graphic organizer similar to the one below by listing the features of the U.S. political system set up after the Revolution.

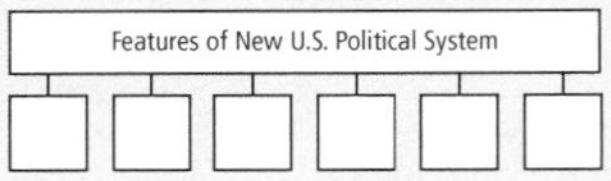

The American Revolution changed society in a variety of ways. New forms of government encouraged new political ideas. Additionally, many of those who had been loyal to Britain left; this strengthened the development of a new, American cultural identity.

New Political Ideas

MAIN Idea Republican ideals changed American government by allowing some citizens voting rights and granting greater religious freedom.

HISTORY AND YOU Have you ever made up your own rules for a game? Read on to learn how the Founders experimented with new forms of government.

When American leaders declared independence and founded the United States of America, they were very much aware that they were creating something new. By breaking away from the king, they had established a **republic.** A republic is a form of government in which power resides with a body of citizens entitled to vote. The power is exercised by elected officials who are responsible to the citizens and who must govern according to laws or a constitution.

While many Europeans viewed a republic as radical and dangerous, Americans believed it could be better than other forms of government. In an ideal republic, all citizens are equal under the law, regardless of their wealth or social class. These ideas conflicted with many traditional beliefs, including ideas about slavery, about women not being allowed to vote or own property, and about certain families being "better" than others. Despite these **contradictions,** republican ideas began to change American society after the war.

New State Constitutions

Events before the Revolution led many Americans to believe that each state's constitution should be written down and that it should limit the government's power over the people. At the same time, many, including John Adams, worried that democracy could endanger a republican government and lead to tyranny. When Adams used the word *democracy,* he meant a society where the majority rules. He and other founders feared that in a pure democracy, minority groups would not have their rights protected. For example, the poor might vote to take everything away from the rich. Adams argued that government needed "checks and balances" to prevent any group in society from becoming strong enough to take away the rights of the minority.

PRIMARY SOURCE

The Revolution Changes Government

▲ *After the Revolution, voting rights expanded. The New Jersey constitution adopted in 1776 granted the right to vote to "all inhabitants" who owned a certain amount of wealth. This wording (probably unintentionally) allowed unmarried women who owned property to vote. Married women did not have property rights.*

Wealth of Elected Officials

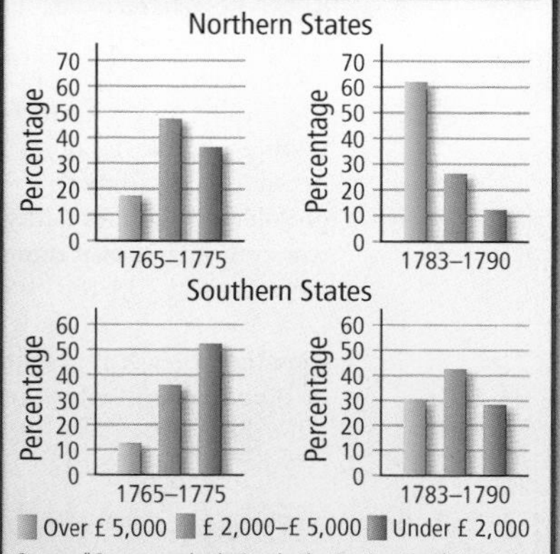

Source: "Government by the People: The American Revolution and the Democratization of the Legislatures."

Analyzing VISUALS

1. **Analyzing** In the North after the Revolution, how much did the percentage of wealthy officeholders increase?
2. **Specifying** In which region did the greater number of middle-class people enter public office after the Revolution?

Adams favored a "mixed government" with a separation of powers; he believed the executive, legislative, and judicial branches should be independent of one another. He also argued that the legislature should be bicameral; that is, it should have two houses: a senate to represent people of property and an assembly to protect the rights of the common people. Adams's ideas influenced several states as they drafted new constitutions during the Revolution. Virginia's constitution of 1776, New York's constitution of 1777, and Massachusetts's constitution of 1780 all established an elected governor, senate, and assembly. By the 1790s, most of the other states had created similar institutions.

Many states also attached a list of rights to their constitutions. This began in 1776, when George Mason drafted Virginia's Declaration of Rights, which guaranteed Virginians freedom of speech, freedom of religion, the right to bear arms, and the right to trial by jury. It barred the state from searching anyone's home without a warrant or taking their property without proper court proceedings.

Voting Rights Expand

The Revolution led to an expansion of voting rights. The experience of fighting side by side with people from every social class and region increased Americans' belief in equality. If all men were fighting for the same cause and risking death for the same ideas, then all deserved the right to vote for their leaders.

The war also weakened feelings of deference toward the upper class. The war had shown many farmers and artisans that they were equal to the rich planters and merchants they fought beside. While sitting in a tavern with farmers who were spitting and pulling off their muddy boots, one wealthy Virginian noted: "Every one who bore arms esteems himself upon an equal footing with his neighbors. . . . Each of these men considers himself, in every respect, my equal."

As a result of these ideas, in almost every state, the new constitutions made it easier for men to gain the right to vote. Many states allowed any white male who paid taxes to vote, whether or not he owned property.

Teach

R Reading Strategy

Reading Graphs Have students study the graph about the wealth of elected officials. Ask them to summarize the changes in each region by comparing the percentages of the wealth of elected officials before and after the American Revolution. OL

Analyzing VISUALS

Answers:
1. about 45 percent
2. the South

Hands-On Chapter Project Step 4

War Correspondence

Step 4: Understanding the New Republic Have students read the text, but also use other library and Internet sources to research state constitutions and the provisions included in them.

Directions Students will list the provisions that they believe must be included in their state's new constitution.

Making Generalizations Students will support their opinions with evidence and generalize why the provisions that they have included in their state's constitution will result in a strong state and nation. OL

(Chapter Project continued on the Visual Summary page)

C Critical Thinking

Identifying Central Issues

Have students review the information on the Virginia Statute for Religious Freedom presented in this section. **Ask:** What important influence did this statute have upon the central government? *(Answers should include that it led to changes in the relationships between church and state.)* **OL**

D Differentiated Instruction

Verbal/Linguistic Write the word *revolutionary* on the board. Have students look up the definition in the dictionary. As a class list the different revolutionary ideas the citizens and political leaders had during the early years of the country. **BL**

Reading Check

Answer:
It guaranteed Virginians freedom of speech, freedom of religion, the right to bear arms, and the right to trial by jury. It banned the state from searching anyone's home without a warrant or taking their property without proper court proceedings.

Differentiated Instruction

Although voting rights expanded, people still had to own a certain amount of property to hold elective office, although usually much less than before the Revolution. The practice of giving veterans land grants as payment for their military service increased the number of people eligible to hold office. In the North, before the Revolution, over 80 percent of people elected were wealthy. Ten years after the war, only a little over one-third of officeholders were wealthy. In the South, higher property qualifications kept the wealthy in power, but their numbers dropped from almost 90 percent of officeholders before the war to 70 percent after the war.

For the text of the Virginia Statute for Religious Freedom, see page R43 in **Documents in American History.**

Freedom of Religion

The Revolution also led to changes in the relationship between church and state. Many of the Revolution's leaders feared "ecclesiastical tyranny"—the power of a church, backed by the government, to make people worship in a certain way. In Virginia, Baptists led **C** a movement to abolish taxes collected to support the Anglican Church. Governor Thomas Jefferson wrote the **Virginia Statute for Religious Freedom,** and James Madison convinced the legislature to pass it in 1786. The statute declared:

PRIMARY SOURCE

"[N]o man shall be compelled to . . . support any religious worship, place, or Ministry . . . nor shall otherwise suffer on account of his religious opinions or belief; but that all men shall be free to profess . . . their opinion in matters of religion."

—from the Virginia Statute for Religious Freedom

The statute also declared that Virginia no longer had an official church and that the state could not collect taxes for churches.

The idea of denying tax support to churches spread slowly. In Massachusetts, the state constitution originally provided for the collection of funds to support churches. Quakers and Baptists were permitted to assign their taxes to their own churches instead of to the Congregational churches (the successors to the Puritan churches), but the state did not abolish religious taxes entirely until 1833.

Reading Check **Examining** Which freedoms did Virginia's constitution guarantee in its bill of rights?

The War and American Society

MAIN Idea After the war, women gained more rights, Northern states outlawed slavery, and many Loyalists fled the new nation.

HISTORY AND YOU Can you think of modern examples of how war changes the way people live? Read on to learn how the Revolution changed American society.

The American ideals of equality and liberty did not generally apply to women and African Americans. Both groups did, however, find their lives changed by the Revolution, as did the Loyalists who had supported Britain.

Women at War

Women played a vital role in the Revolutionary War, contributing on both the home front and the battlefront. With their husbands, brothers, and sons at war, some women took over running family farms. Others traveled with the army—cooking, washing, and nursing the wounded. Women also served as spies and couriers, and a few even joined the fighting. Deborah Samson of Massachusetts fought in the Continental Army disguised as a man under the name Robert Shurtleff. Margaret Corbin accompanied her husband to battle, and after his death she took his place at his cannon until the battle ended.

D After the war, as Americans began to think about what their **revolutionary** ideals implied, women made some advances. They could more easily obtain a divorce and gained greater access to education. In 1779 Judith Sargent Murray wrote an essay entitled "On the Equality of the Sexes." The essay argued that women were as intelligent as men but lacked the education needed to achieve more in life. After the Revolution, many schools for girls were founded, and the number of women who were able to read increased.

African Americans

Thousands of enslaved African Americans obtained their freedom during the Revolution. Although British officials seized numerous enslaved people and shipped them to British plantations in the Caribbean, they also freed

Leveled Activities

BL Reteaching Activity, URB p. 77

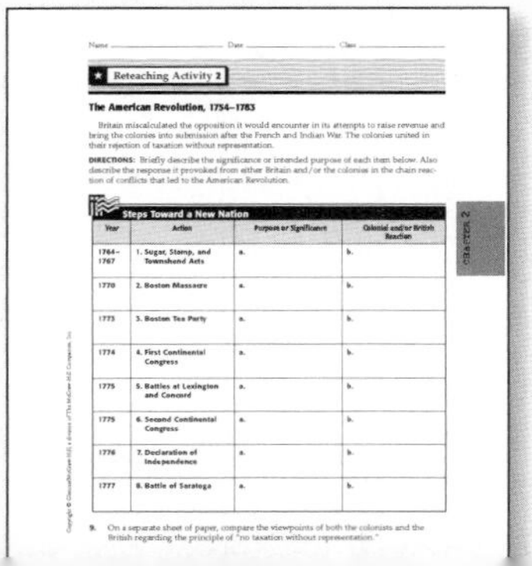

OL American Art and Music Activity, URB p. 73

AL Enrichment Activity, URB p. 78

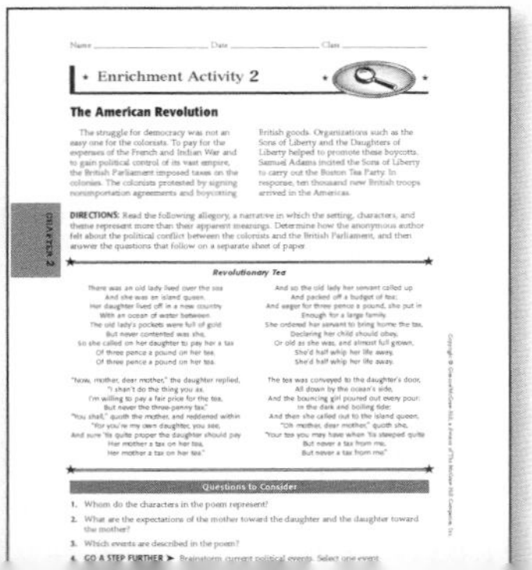

ELL English Learner Activity, URB p. 59

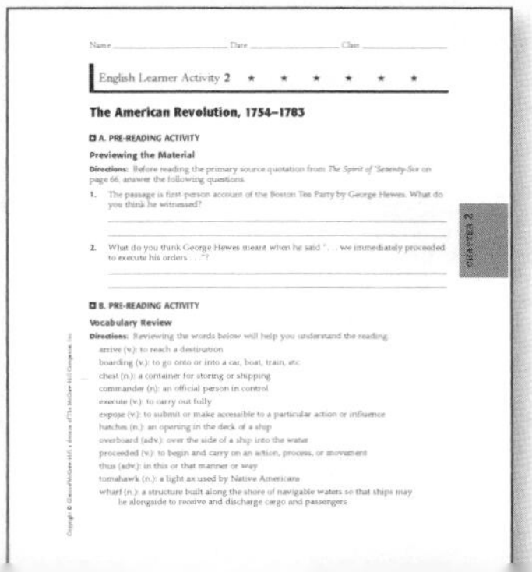

Emancipation After Independence, 1780–1784

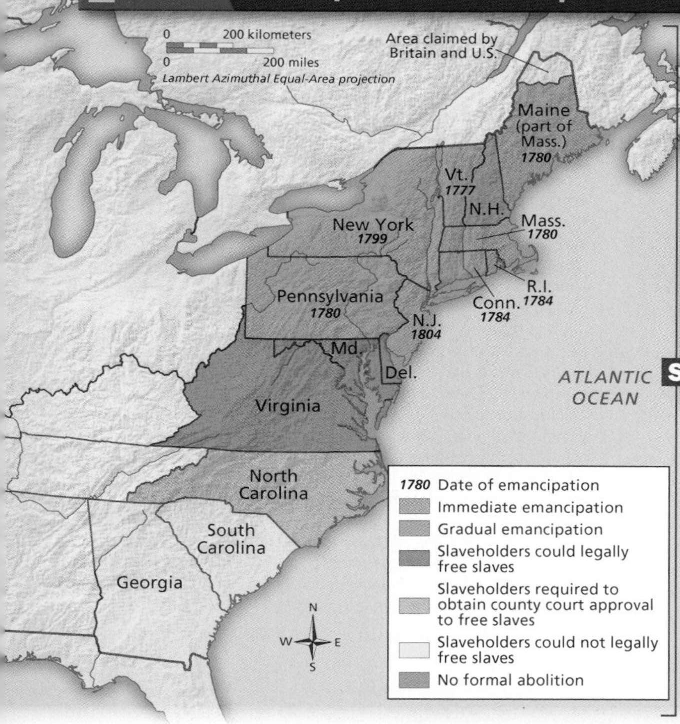

S

▲ *Dinah Morris of Vermont was granted her freedom in 1777. She was the first enslaved person to be freed in the North.*

Analyzing GEOGRAPHY

1. **Region** Which region made it difficult to emancipate enslaved people?
2. **Human-Environment Interaction** Why do you think slavery remained firmly entrenched in certain areas?

many others in exchange for military service. Many planters freed slaves who agreed to fight the British, and General Washington permitted African Americans to join the Continental Army. He also urged state militias to admit African Americans and to offer freedom to all who served. About 5,000 African Americans served in the militias and the Continental Army during the American Revolution.

After the Revolution, many Americans realized that enslaving people did not fit in with the new ideals of liberty and equality. Opposition to slavery had been growing steadily even before the Revolution, especially in the Northern and middle states. After the war began, **emancipation,** or freedom from enslavement, became a major issue. Many Northern states took steps to end slavery. Vermont banned slavery in 1777. In 1780 Pennsylvania freed all children born enslaved when they reached age 28. Rhode Island decreed in 1784 that enslaved men born thereafter would be freed when they turned 21 and enslaved women when they turned 18. In 1799 New York freed enslaved men born in that year or later when they reached age 28 and women when they reached age 25. The eradication of slavery in the North was thus a gradual process that took several decades, but it demonstrated that slavery could be abolished.

Discrimination against African Americans did not disappear with emancipation, however. African Americans were often unable to get more than menial jobs—digging, carrying, or sweeping. Free African Americans also faced voting restrictions, segregation, and possible kidnapping and transportation to the South, where they would again be enslaved. Despite the hardships, freedom offered choices. Once free, many African Americans moved to the cities to find employment. Some found opportunities in previously barred occupations, such as artists or ministers.

S Skill Practice

Using Geography Skills

Have students study the map about emancipation after the Revolution. **Ask:** **Which states passed immediate emancipation? In what year was it granted?** *(Massachusetts and Vermont; 1780 and 1777 respectively.)* **Which Northern state was the last to pass emancipation?** *(New Jersey in 1804)* **OL**

Analyzing GEOGRAPHY

Answers:

1. South
2. Slavery was needed to support the economy

Additional Support

Activity: Interdisciplinary Connection

Language Arts Point out to students the vocabulary term *emancipation* on this page and *manumission* on the next page. **Ask:** **What root do these two words have in common?** *(man-)*. Explain that *man-* is the root of both these terms and comes from the Latin word *manus*, which means "hand." In these words the root refers to slavery, or being "held by" or "under the hand of" another person. *Emancipation* means "to gain one's freedom from enslavement," while *manumission* refers to the act of a slaveholder freeing enslaved people. Make sure that students understand the difference. Ask students to think of other terms that have the root *man-* and to speculate out how the root relates to the word's meaning. (Examples include *manipulate*, *manual*, and *manner*.) **OL**

C Critical Thinking

Identifying Central Issues Discuss with students the precarious situation in which Loyalists found themselves after the war. **Ask:** Why did most Loyalists flee the United States after the Revolution? *(because they feared for their lives or did not want to live under the new government)* **Ask:** What do you think should have been done with Loyalist property—do you agree with New York or Massachusetts on this issue? *(Answers will vary; accept all reasonable responses.)* OL

People IN HISTORY

Elizabeth Freeman
Answer:
Her case helped to end slavery in Massachusetts.

Quock Walker
Answer:
The constitution states that all men are born free and equal, and so it cannot support slavery.

Additional Support

People IN HISTORY

Elizabeth Freeman (Mumbet)
c. 1742–1829

Elizabeth Freeman, later called Mumbet, began life as an enslaved African American. At the age of six months she was acquired, along with her sister, by John Ashley, a wealthy western Massachusetts lawyer and businessman. The family called her Betty or Bett. For nearly 40 years, Bett worked for the Ashley family. One day, Ashley's wife tried to strike Bett's sister with a shovel. Bett intervened and took the blow instead. Furious, she stormed out of the house and refused to come back. When the Ashleys tried to force her to return, Bett consulted a local lawyer named Thomas Sedgewick. With his help, Bett sued for her freedom.

While serving the Ashleys, Bett had listened to many discussions about the new Massachusetts constitution. If the constitution said that all people were free and equal, then she thought that should apply to her. In 1781 a jury agreed, and Bett won her freedom—and took Freeman as her last name. Elizabeth Freeman was the first enslaved person in Massachusetts to gain freedom under the new constitution. Her case helped to end slavery in Massachusetts.

What is the significance of Elizabeth Freeman's court case?

Quock Walker
1753–?

▲ *Chief Justice William Cushing*

Between 1781 and 1783, an enslaved Massachusetts man named Quock Walker also took the extraordinary step, in a series of cases, of suing a white man who had assaulted him. That man, Nathaniel Jennison, also claimed to own Walker, who had escaped from Jennison's farm after a severe beating.

Given the times, this was a bold step, but Walker believed, as Freeman did, that the law was on his side. Massachusetts's new constitution referred to the "inherent liberty" of all men. The judge, Chief Justice William Cushing, agreed and found in his favor. "Our [state] Constitution," Cushing said, "sets out with declaring that all men are born free and equal . . . and in short is totally repugnant to the idea of [people] being born slaves. This being the case, I think the idea of slavery is inconsistent with our own conduct and Constitution."

While the Walker and Freeman cases did not abolish slavery, they demonstrated that the Massachusetts courts would not support the institution. As a result of the rulings and various antislavery efforts, slavery ceased to exist in Massachusetts by 1790.

How was slavery "inconsistent" with the Massachusetts constitution?

A small group of African Americans achieved some wealth and social status. The discrimination they faced encouraged them to build their own distinct culture. Religion played an important role in that emerging culture, and African Americans created their own style of worship. In 1816 African American church leaders formed the first independent African American denomination, the African Methodist Episcopal (AME) Church.

The story was quite different in the South. The South relied heavily on enslaved labor to sustain its agricultural economy. As a result, Southern leaders showed little interest in abolishing slavery. Only Virginia took steps toward ending the institution. In 1782 the state passed a law encouraging **manumission,** or the voluntary freeing of enslaved people, especially for those who had fought in the Revolution. Through this law, about 10,000 slaves obtained their freedom, but the vast majority remained in bondage.

The Loyalists Flee

Many women and African Americans found their lives little changed as a result of the Revolution, but for many Loyalists, the end of the war changed everything. Because of their support for the British, Loyalists often found themselves shunned by former friends, and state governments sometimes seized their property.

Unwilling to live under the new government and often afraid for their lives, approximately 100,000 Loyalists fled the United States after the war. Some went to Great Britain or the British West Indies, but most moved to British North America, particularly to Nova Scotia, New Brunswick, and the region near Niagara Falls. This region was part of Quebec at the time, but in 1791 Britain made it a separate colony called Upper Canada. Today it is the province of Ontario. C

Americans grappled with what to do with the property and assets of Loyalists. In North

Activity: Interdisciplinary Connection

Mathematics Present the data at right to students. Ask them to use it to create a bar graph that illustrates the relationship between the number of enslaved people and the total population of Virginia between 1790 and 1830. Ask students to write a paragraph in which they offer an explanation of the population trends. OL

Virginia Population Data

No. of Enslaved Persons

1790	1800	1810	1820	1830
292,627	346,671	392,518	425,153	469,757

Total Population

1790	1800	1810	1820	1830
747,550	885,171	974,622	1,065,379	1,211,405

Carolina, Patriots confiscated Loyalist lands outright. Officials in New York also seized Loyalists' lands and goods, claiming the "sovereignty of the people of this state in respect to all property." Other public officials opposed such actions. The Massachusetts Constitution of 1780, for example, extended the rights of "life, liberty, and property" to Loyalists, and gave much of the land seized from departing Loyalists to their agents or relatives who had remained.

An American Culture Emerges

In the United States, victory over the British united Americans and created powerful nationalist feelings. The Revolution helped this process in two ways. First, Americans in all the states had battled a common enemy. Soldiers from all over the country had fought side by side in each other's states. Second, stories of the Revolution and its heroes encouraged Americans to think of themselves as all belonging to the same group.

American Painters The Revolution also sparked the creativity of American painters, including **John Trumbull** and **Charles Willson Peale.** Their work and that of other artists contributed to an American identity. Trumbull served in the Continental Army as an aide to Washington. He is best known for his depiction of battles and important events in the Revolution. Peale fought at Trenton and Princeton and survived the winter at Valley Forge. He is best known for his portraits of Washington and other Patriot leaders.

Changes in Education As they started a new nation, American leaders considered an educated public to be critical to the republic's success. Jefferson called it the "keystone of our arch of government." Several state constitutions provided for government-funded universities. In 1795 the University of North Carolina became the first state university in the nation. At the same time, elementary schools instituted an American-centered style of teaching. Tossing out British textbooks, they taught republican ideas and the history of the struggle for independence.

Noah Webster, a teacher from Connecticut, was one of the educators who believed that Americans needed to develop their own educational system based on their own culture. In 1783 he wrote a textbook titled *A Grammatical Institute of the English Language,* which included *The American Spelling Book.* American teachers used this textbook for over 100 years, and it is still in print. Although he also published magazines and newspapers, as well as his best-selling textbook, Webster is probably most famous for his *American Dictionary of the English Language,* published in 1828. In that two-volume work, he purposefully set out to regularize American English, but especially to underscore its differences from British English.

As Americans began to build a national identity separate from Britain's, leaders of the United States turned their attention to the creation of a government that could promote the ideals and beliefs that the colonists had fought so hard to secure.

Reading Check **Summarizing** How did life change for women, African Americans, and Loyalists after the Revolutionary War?

Section 4 REVIEW

Vocabulary

1. **Explain** the significance of: republic, Virginia Statute for Religious Freedom, emancipation, manumission, John Trumbull, Charles Willson Peale.

Main Ideas

2. **Describing** What ideas of John Adams did Massachusetts and other states include in their constitutions?

3. **Explaining** How did the Revolution help to create powerful nationalist feelings in the United States?

Critical Thinking

4. **Big Ideas** What new aspects of culture emerged after the American Revolution?

5. **Categorizing** Use a graphic organizer similar to the one below to list the position of women, African Americans, and Loyalists in American society after the Revolution.

	Position in American Society
Women	
African Americans	
Loyalists	

6. **Analyzing Visuals** Review the graph on the wealth of elected officials on page 87. Which group lost the greatest percentage of representation among elected officials in both regions?

Writing About History

7. **Expository Writing** Suppose that you are on a committee to write a new state constitution. List the freedoms you want protected in that constitution, and explain why you feel it is important to guarantee each one.

History ONLINE
Study Central™ To review this section, go to glencoe.com and click on Study Central.

Reading Check

Answer:
Women could more easily obtain a divorce, and they had greater access to education. Many African Americans in Northern states gained their freedom, but they still faced discrimination. Loyalists were shunned and in some cases their property was seized. Many left the United States.

Assess

History ONLINE

Study Central™ provides summaries, interactive games, and online graphic organizers to help students review content.

Close

Summarizing **Ask:** How did culture and society change in America after the Revolution? *(There was an expansion of voting rights and greater freedoms for many Americans; many African Americans were emancipated. There was a rise in patriotic symbols and common folklore; and a new emphasis on American, non-British education.)* **OL**

Section 4 REVIEW

Answers

1. All definitions can be found in the section and the Glossary.
2. Adams argued that government needed "checks and balances" to prevent any group in society from becoming strong enough to take away the rights of the minority. He favored a "mixed government" with a separation of powers: the executive, legislative, and judicial branches should be independent of one another. Adams also argued that the legislature should be bicameral; that is, it should have two houses: a senate to represent people of property and an assembly to protect the rights of the common people.
3. Fighting a common enemy united the states and gave rise to patriotic symbols, national heroes, and a common folklore.
4. Possible answers include the following: new emphasis on a new style of American, non-British education, widespread rejection of ideas of social class, equality of all men
5. Women: could obtain divorce, more access to education; African Americans: many gained freedom in North, but faced discrimination; Loyalists: lost property, shunned.
6. people with wealth under £2,000
7. Students' lists will vary but should include an explanation of the importance of each freedom.

Determining Importance Discuss with students the information provided in the Visual Summary for this chapter. **Ask:** What information does the Visual Summary provide? *(It provides a summary of the causes and effects of the chapter content focus, the American Revolution.)* Have students identify what they feel are the three most significant causes and three most significant effects of the American Revolution, and invite them to explain their choices in a whole-class discussion. **OL**

Creating a Time Line Have students use their textbook and library and Internet resources to research the expansion of voting rights in the United States from 1780 to 1980. Have students use that information to create a voting-rights time line. Encourage students to add images to the basic information in their time lines. **OL**

Chapter 2 Visual Summary

STUDY TO GO — You can study anywhere, anytime by downloading quizzes and flashcards to your PDA from glencoe.com.

Causes of the American Revolution

- Defending the colonies in the French and Indian War costs Britain a great deal of money; Britain seeks ways to cover the costs incurred.
- Britain issues the Proclamation Act of 1763, banning colonists from moving west of the Proclamation line.
- The British crack down on smuggling by enforcing customs duties and creating a vice-admiralty court to try smugglers; merchants are angered, and colonists believe their rights are being violated.
- The Sugar Act is attacked by colonists as taxation without representation.
- The Currency Act banning paper money angers farmers and artisans.
- The 1765 Stamp Act leads to widespread colonial protests, the holding of the Stamp Act Congress, and a boycott of British goods.
- The 1767 Townshend Acts lead to further protests and another boycott.
- The Boston Massacre convinces many that the British are tyrants.
- In 1773, British efforts to help the East India Company lead to the Boston Tea Party and other protests against the tea shipments.
- Britain issues the Coercive Acts, banning Massachusetts town meetings, closing Boston's port, and quartering troops in private homes.
- Neither King George nor British officials agree to compromise with the Continental Congress, and Congress orders a boycott of British goods.
- British troops fire on militia at Lexington and Concord; the Revolution begins; and the Declaration of Independence is issued, July 4, 1776.

▲ *From the first shots fired at Lexington (above), the will to fight to preserve their liberties and independence helped the Americans to win the Revolution against the much more powerful British.*

▲ *The British surrender at Saratoga. The victory at Saratoga boosted morale and helped Americans gain the support of France and Spain.*

Effects of the American Revolution

- The American colonies form a new nation: the United States of America.
- A Revolutionary War between American forces led by George Washington, and British forces, rages from 1775–1780.
- The American victory at Saratoga brings France into the war as an American ally.
- The American victory at Yorktown leads to Britain agreeing to negotiate; the Treaty of Paris of 1783 formally ends the Revolutionary War.
- American states begin writing constitutions based on republican ideas.
- Voting rights expand.
- Northern American states adopt laws that gradually end slavery.
- Americans loyal to Britain flee north, leading to the creation of the new colonies of Upper and Lower Canada.
- A new American culture emerges based on the republican values.

Hands-On Chapter Project

Step 5: Wrap Up

War Correspondence

Step 5: Resolving Disputes Have students review the letters that they have written for the class project. They will take on an opposing role and respond to the letter.

Directions Students should write a brief response to each of their letters from the opposing point of view. For example, have students return to their role as colonists and discuss whether they are satisfied with the Prime Minister's response to their list of grievances.

Drawing Conclusions Have volunteers present a letter and the opposing side's response. Encourage students to discuss what actions should be taken next by either side. **OL**

Chapter 2 Assessment

Reviewing Vocabulary

Directions: Choose the word or words that best complete the sentence.

1. To protest the Stamp Act, the colonists signed a ________, pledging not to buy British goods.
   - **A** writ of assistance
   - **B** proclamation
   - **C** committee of correspondence
   - **D** nonimportation agreement

2. Massachusetts towns formed militia groups known as ________ in case of British aggression.
   - **A** committees
   - **B** minutemen
   - **C** privateers
   - **D** the Sons of Liberty

3. The American militias were poorly trained, but the use of ________ made it difficult for the British troops to defeat them.
   - **A** guerilla warfare
   - **B** letters of marque
   - **C** habeas corpus
   - **D** the astrolabe

4. To disturb British trade, the Congress would issue ________, allowing a private American ship to attack British merchant ships.
   - **A** an act
   - **B** writs of assistance
   - **C** letters of marque
   - **D** a bill of rights

5. After the Revolution, many people hoped to end slavery gradually through voluntary ________, rather than all at once by force.
   - **A** proclamation
   - **B** manumission
   - **C** declaration
   - **D** adoption

Reviewing Main Ideas

Directions: Choose the best answer for each of the following questions.

Section 1 *(pp. 54–61)*

6. The significance of the Albany Plan of Union was that it
   - **A** marked the first time that the colonists had met with Native Americans.
   - **B** explained clearly to the British why independence was necessary.
   - **C** created a new nation out of the 13 separate colonies.
   - **D** demonstrated an interest in unifying the colonies.

7. King George III issued the Proclamation of 1763 to
   - **A** make peace with the French and Spanish.
   - **B** give more lands to the colonists.
   - **C** make peace with Native Americans.
   - **D** punish the port of Boston.

8. In which of the following documents did John Dickinson urge colonial unity to resist the Townshend Acts?
   - **A** *Letters From a Farmer in Pennsylvania*
   - **B** *Common Sense*
   - **C** *The American Crisis*
   - **D** the Declaration of Rights

Section 2 *(pp. 64–73)*

9. The First Continental Congress was formed in reaction to the
   - **A** Coercive Acts.
   - **B** Tea Act.
   - **C** Townshend Acts.
   - **D** Stamp Act.

TEST-TAKING TIP

As you read each question, be sure to look for main ideas. A main idea or a key word repeated in an answer choice may be a clue that it is the right answer.

Need Extra Help?

If You Missed Questions . . .	16	17	18	19	20	21
Go to Page . . .	24–33	R18	R18	51	R19	14–23

GO ON

Answers and Analyses
Reviewing Vocabulary

1. D Looking closely at the vocabulary used in the answer choices will lead students to the correct answer. Goods from Britain sold in the colonies were *imported*. The word *import* appears in the correct answer. A pledge is an agreement.

2. B Minutemen were supposed to "stand at a minute's warning in case of alarm." In other words, they would be ready at a minute's notice. A good way to remember that Massachusetts militiamen were called minutemen is to focus on the shared first letter, M.

3. A Colonial guerilla warfare involved hiding behind trees and stone walls. The colonial soldiers attacked supply wagons and ambushed British troops rather than lining up in orderly ranks on the battlefield.

4. C Choice *A* is too general. A writ of assistance was a search warrant, not a permission to attack, so *B* is not correct. A bill of rights would list rights of certain people.

5. B Remind students that they must consider the definitions of each answer choice in a vocabulary question. A proclamation and a declaration are kinds of statements, either written or spoken. Neither is appropriate in this case. Adoption does not make sense. To manumit is to free someone from slavery.

Reviewing Main Ideas

6. D The Albany Plan of Union was issued during the Albany Conference as a plan to unite the colonies to form a federal government. The plan was rejected, but it did show that there was interest in unifying the colonies. Although colonists met with the Iroquois at the Conference, it was not the first time colonists met with Native Americans.

7. C The Proclamation of 1763 came about in response to Pontiac's War and had long-lasting effects on the relationship between the colonies and Great Britain. Because it put a limit on western settlement, it angered colonists who wanted the land, especially western farmers who wanted to expand.

8. A Thomas Paine wrote both *Common Sense* and *The American Crisis.* Dickinson did draft the Declaration of Rights, but he wrote it before the Townshend Acts.

9. A A good mnemonic to help students remember that the First Continental Congress was formed in reaction to the Coercive Acts is to remember the letter c: the "**c**ause" of the **C**ontinental **C**ongress was the **C**oercive Acts.

10. C The Battle of Bunker Hill provided patriots with a necessary shot of confidence. The British suffered large casualties, and the colonial forces proved they could handle fighting with the British Army.

11. C This question presents a good example to illustrate process of elimination in selecting the correct answer. Choice *A* does not make sense; Great Britain was a wealthy nation that could pay its soldiers. In addition, they had a great navy, not an inexperienced one. Again, because Great Britain was a world power, it would not need France's help. In addition, France and Great Britain were not allies. This leaves choice *C*.

12. B Hopefully, students will be able to eliminate *C* and *D*. Settlers had not yet explored or reached the Rockies or the Pacific. Students may be tempted to choose the Appalachian Mountains, but remind them that settlers had already expanded west of the Appalachians by the time of the Revolution.

13. C Civil rights are the basic rights that all citizens are entitled to, such as the right to life, liberty, and fair treatment by government. Students must remember to read questions keeping the context and time period in mind—in this case, the Revolution.

14. A Nationalism is an intense feeling of national pride or patriotism. Be sure that students fully grasp this concept. Nationalism was not based on cheerfulness; it was based on winning the war. The colonists had banded together and defeated Britain and its professional army. The American flag was a symbol that represented the feelings of nationalism, not a cause. Choice *D* does not make sense.

Chapter 2 Assessment

Section 3 *(pp. 78–85)*

10. The Battle of Bunker Hill demonstrated that

- **A** British leaders did not know the geography around Boston.
- **B** colonial cannons were better handled than British cannons.
- **C** the colonial militia could stand up to a professional army.
- **D** more people were loyal to the British than Patriot leaders had thought.

11. Which of the following was one disadvantage the British faced during the Revolution?

- **A** They did not have enough money to pay their soldiers.
- **B** Their navy was weak and inexperienced.
- **C** The war did not have total support at home.
- **D** They could not get France to fight against the colonists.

12. Under the Treaty of Paris ending the Revolution, the western boundary of the United States would become the

- **A** Appalachian Mountains.
- **B** Mississippi River.
- **C** Rocky Mountains.
- **D** Pacific Ocean.

Section 4 *(pp. 86–91)*

13. Virginia's Declaration of Rights was written to protect

- **A** land rights.
- **B** fishing rights.
- **C** civil rights.
- **D** mining rights.

14. The American Revolution created a new spirit of nationalism based on which of the following?

- **A** The colonists had struggled against a common enemy.
- **B** Everyone loved the new American flag, which provided a unified symbol.
- **C** Winning the war made everyone feel more cheerful.
- **D** No one wanted to speak the English language anymore.

Critical Thinking

Directions: Choose the best answers to the following questions. Base your answer to question 15 on the map below and on your knowledge of Chapter 2.

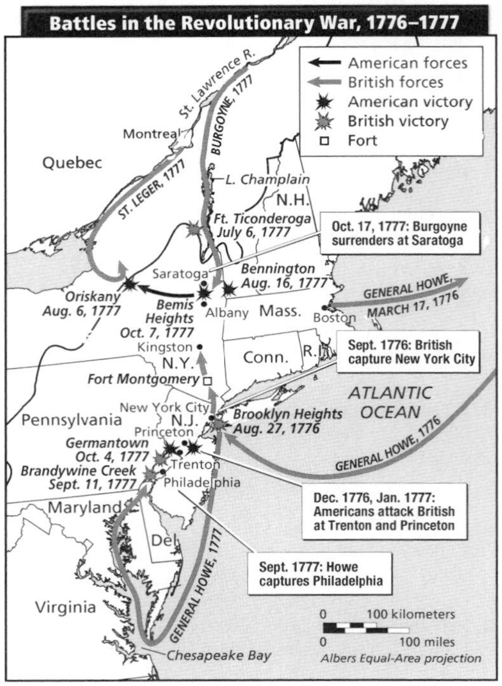

15. How did American troops slow Burgoyne's march to seal off New England from the rest of the United States?

- **A** American troops defeated the British at Philadelphia.
- **B** American troops retreated from Ft. Ticonderoga, where the British gained supplies.
- **C** American troops cut off the British food supply by removing cattle and crops from the region.
- **D** American warships attacked British merchant ships to disrupt trade.

Need Extra Help?						
If You Missed Questions . . .	10	11	12	13	14	15
Go to Page . . .	78	85	87	91	55	81–82

GO ON

Critical Thinking

15. C The question asks how American troops *slowed down* Burgoyne's march, so the answer is not likely that American troops defeated the British. Choice *B* does not make sense in the context of the question. *D* is incorrect, because troops sealed off a march, which means that whatever happened took place on land, not in the water.

16. The colonists complained about having to pay British taxes while not being allowed to vote for members of Parliament. Which of the following quotations best expresses their complaint?
   - **A** "Give me liberty or give me death!"
   - **B** "Taxation without representation is tyranny."
   - **C** "These are the times that try men's souls."
   - **D** "Don't fire until you see the whites of their eyes."

Analyze the cartoon and answer the question that follows. Base your answer on the cartoon and on your knowledge of Chapter 2.

17. What was John Dickinson's belief about English taxation in the colonies?
   - **A** He favored the English Magna Carta and opposed colonial resistance to British taxation.
   - **B** He favored the Stamp Act and was loyal to the guidelines it established.
   - **C** He was against English taxation in the colonies and believed only elected colonial assemblies had the right to tax the colonists.
   - **D** He favored the Stamp Act as a way to raise revenue to protect the colonies from attacks by Native Americans.

Document-Based Questions

Directions: Analyze the document and answer the short-answer question that follows the document.

In 1766 Benjamin Franklin testified before Parliament about the colonists' reaction to the Stamp Act. The excerpt below is from his testimony:

> **Q.** "Don't you know that the money [tax] arising from the stamps was all to be laid out in America?
> **A.** I know it is appropriated by the act to the American service; but it will be spent in the conquered colonies where the soldiers are, not in the colonies that pay it. . . .
>
> **Q.** Do you think it right that America should be protected by this country and pay no part of the expense?
> **A.** That is not the case. The colonies raised, clothed, and paid, during the last war, near 25,000 men and spent many millions.
>
> **Q.** Were you not reimbursed by Parliament?
> **A.** We were only reimbursed what, in your opinion, we had advanced beyond our proportion, or beyond what might reasonably be expected from us; and it was a very small part of what we spent. Pennsylvania, in particular, disbursed about 500,000 pounds, and the reimbursements, in the whole, did not exceed 60,000 pounds. . . ."
>
> —from Benjamin Franklin's testimony before Parliament, 1766

18. Why does Franklin say that the tax is unfair?

Extended Response

19. After the American Revolution, a new culture emerged in the United States. Write an expository essay that compares and contrasts American culture before and after the Revolution in these areas: government, society, the arts, and education. In your essay, include an introduction and at least three paragraphs.

STOP

History ONLINE
For additional test practice, use Self-Check Quizzes—Chapter 2 at glencoe.com.

Need Extra Help?

If You Missed Questions . . .	16	17	18	19
Go to Page . . .	58	60	95	86–91

Extended Response

19. Students' essays will vary, but must cover each of the areas listed using information from the chapter. In addition, essays must be written in a compare/contrast format as stated in the prompt. Essays must include an introduction, three body paragraphs, and a conclusion.

16. B The answer can be found in the wording of the question, "complained about taxes…not being allowed to vote…" Although all of the other quotes relate to the American Revolution, they do not fit the question.

17. C Dickinson, a member of the Sons of Liberty, wrote about his views against English taxation in favor of colonial assemblies when he drafted the Declaration of Rights and Grievances.

Document-Based Questions

18. Franklin says the tax is unfair because the colonies were already paying more than their share. If students have trouble analyzing this source, consider reading each question and answer aloud, discussing each one with the class.

History ONLINE
Have students visit the Web site at glencoe.com to review Chapter 2 and take the Self-Check Quiz.

Need Extra Help?
Have students refer to the pages listed if they miss any of the questions.

Chapter 3 Planning Guide

Key to Ability Levels	
BL Below Level	**AL** Above Level
OL On Level	**ELL** English Language Learners

Key to Teaching Resources	
Print Material	Transparency
CD-ROM or DVD	

Levels				Resources	Chapter Opener	Section 1	Section 2	Section 3	Chapter Assess
BL	OL	AL	ELL						
FOCUS									
BL	OL	AL	ELL	Daily Focus Skills Transparencies		3-1	3-2	3-3	
TEACH									
BL	OL		ELL	Reading Skills Activity, URB			p. 87		
	OL			Historical Analysis Skills Activity, URB				p. 88	
BL	OL	AL	ELL	Differentiated Instruction Activity, URB			p. 89		
BL			ELL	English Learner Activity, URB		p. 91			
BL	OL	AL	ELL	Content Vocabulary Activity, URB	p. 93				
BL	OL	AL	ELL	Academic Vocabulary Activity, URB	p. 95				
	OL	AL		Reinforcing Skills Activity, URB		p. 97			
	OL	AL		Critical Thinking Skills Activity, URB				p. 98	
BL	OL		ELL	Time Line Activity, URB			p. 99		
	OL			Linking Past and Present Activity, URB			p. 100		
BL	OL	AL	ELL	Primary Source Reading, URB		p. 101	p. 103		
BL	OL	AL	ELL	American Art and Music Activity, URB			p. 105		
BL	OL	AL	ELL	Interpreting Political Cartoons Activity, URB				p. 107	
		AL		Enrichment Activity, URB			p. 110		
BL	OL		ELL	Guided Reading Activity, URB		p. 112	p. 113	p. 114	
BL	OL		ELL	Reading Essentials and Note-Taking Guide		p. 29	p. 32	p. 35	
BL	OL	AL	ELL	Differentiated Instruction for the American History Classroom	✓	✓	✓	✓	✓
BL	OL	AL	ELL	Unit Map Overlay Transparencies	✓	✓	✓	✓	✓
BL	OL	AL	ELL	Unit Time Line Transparencies and Activities	✓	✓	✓	✓	✓
BL	OL	AL	ELL	Cause and Effect Transparencies, Strategies, and Activities	✓	✓	✓	✓	✓
BL	OL	AL	ELL	Writer's Guidebook	✓	✓	✓	✓	✓

Note: Please refer to the *Unit 1 Resource Book* for this chapter's URB materials.

* Also available in Spanish

TeacherWorks Plus
All-In-One Planner and Resource Center

- Interactive Lesson Planner
- Interactive Teacher Edition
- Fully editable blackline masters
- Section Spotlight Videos Launch
- Differentiated Lesson Plans
- Printable reports of daily assignments
- Standards Tracking System

Levels BL	Levels OL	Levels AL	Levels ELL		Resources	Chapter Opener	Section 1	Section 2	Section 3	Chapter Assess
					TEACH *(continued)*					
BL	OL	AL	ELL		**American Biographies**	✓		✓		✓
BL	OL	AL	ELL		**The Living Constitution**	✓		✓		✓
BL	OL	AL	ELL		**American Issues**	✓	✓	✓	✓	✓
	OL	AL	ELL		**American Art and Architecture Transparencies**	✓	✓			✓
BL	OL	AL			**High School American History Literature Library**	✓	✓			✓
	OL	AL			**American History Primary Source Documents Library**	✓	✓			✓
BL	OL	AL	ELL		**American Music: Hits Through History CD**	✓	✓			✓
BL	OL	AL	ELL		**StudentWorks™ Plus**	✓	✓			✓
BL	OL	AL	ELL		***The American Vision* Video Program**	✓	✓	✓	✓	✓
Teacher Resources					**Reading Strategies and Activities for the Social Studies Classroom**	✓	✓	✓	✓	✓
					Strategies for Success	✓	✓	✓	✓	✓
					Presentation Plus! with MindJogger CheckPoint	✓	✓	✓	✓	✓
					Success with English Learners	✓	✓	✓	✓	✓
					ASSESS					
BL	OL	AL	ELL		**Section Quizzes and Chapter Tests**		p. 31	p. 32	p. 33	p. 35
BL	OL	AL	ELL		**Authentic Assessment With Rubrics**					p. 11
BL	OL	AL	ELL		**Standardized Test Practice Workbook**					p. 5
BL	OL	AL	ELL		***ExamView® Assessment Suite***		3-1	3-2	3-3	Ch. 3
					CLOSE					
BL			ELL		**Reteaching Activity, URB**					p. 109
BL	OL		ELL		**Reading and Study Skills Foldables™**	p. 50				

✓ Chapter- or unit-based activities applicable to all sections in this chapter

Using Reproducible Lesson Plans

Teach With Technology

What are Reproducible Lesson Plans?

Reproducible Lesson Plans (RLPs) are detailed lesson plans that teachers may use to prepare their lessons throughout the year.

How can RLPs help me teach?

RLPs are organized by chapter and also by section, suggesting where the wide variety of technology and ancillary products can be used within the book. RLPs are organized two ways:

- Teaching activities and ancillaries are presented using the FOCUS, TEACH, ASSESS, CLOSE organization of the Teacher Wraparound Edition.
- Teaching activities and ancillaries are also grouped by skill level, which helps you identify the activities that are appropriate for the students in your classroom.

RLPs are available on TeacherWorks™ Plus.

History ONLINE
Visit glencoe.com and enter ***QuickPass***™ code TAV9399c3T for Chapter 3 resources.

You can easily launch a wide range of digital products from your computer's desktop with the McGraw-Hill Social Studies widget.

	Student	Teacher	Parent
Media Library			
• Section Audio	●		●
• Spanish Audio Summaries	●		●
• Section Spotlight Videos	●	●	●
The American Vision **Online Learning Center (Web Site)**			
• StudentWorks™ Plus Online	●	●	●
• Multilingual Glossary	●	●	●
• Study-to-Go	●	●	●
• Chapter Overviews	●	●	●
• Self-Check Quizzes	●	●	●
• Student Web Activities	●	●	●
• ePuzzles and Games	●	●	●
• Vocabulary eFlashcards	●	●	●
• In Motion Animations	●	●	●
• Study Central™	●	●	●
• Web Activity Lesson Plans		●	
• Vocabulary PuzzleMaker	●	●	●
• Historical Thinking Activities		●	
• Beyond the Textbook	●	●	●

Reading Support From Jamestown Education

- **Timed Readings Plus in Social Studies** helps students increase their reading rate and fluency while maintaining comprehension. The 400-word passages are similar to those found on state and national assessments.
- **Reading in the Content Area: Social Studies** concentrates on six essential reading skills that help students better comprehend what they read. The book includes 75 high-interest nonfiction passages written at increasing levels of difficulty.
- **Reading Social Studies** includes strategic reading instruction and vocabulary support in Social Studies content for both ELLs and native speakers of English.

www.jamestowneducation.com

National Geographic
Index to National Geographic Magazine:

The following articles relate to this chapter:

- "James Madison: Architect of the Constitution" by Alice J. Hall, September 1987.
- "Two Revolutions" by Charles McCarry, August 2000.

National Geographic Society Products To order the following, call National Geographic at 1-800-368-2728:

- *ZipZapMap! USA* (ZipZapMap!)

Access National Geographic's new dynamic MapMachine Web site and other geography resources at:
www.nationalgeographic.com
www.nationalgeographic.com/maps

Biography / A&E Home Video / The History Channel

The following videotape programs are available from Glencoe as supplements to this chapter:

- George Washington: Founding Father (ISBN 1-56-501377-8)
- Independence Day: History of July 4th (ISBN 0-76-700359-4)

To order, call Glencoe at 1-800-334-7344. To find classroom resources to accompany many of these videos, check the following home pages:

A&E Television: www.aetv.com
The History Channel: www.historychannel.com

Reading List Generator CD-ROM — Glencoe BookLink 3

Use this database to search more than 30,000 titles to create a customized reading list for your students.

- Reading lists can be organized by students' reading level, author, genre, theme, or area of interest.
- The database provides Degrees of Reading Power™ (DRP) and Lexile™ readability scores for all selections.
- A brief summary of each selection is included.

Leveled reading suggestions for this chapter:

For students at a Grade 8 reading level:
- ***George Washington,*** by Genevieve Foster

For students at a Grade 9 reading level:
- ***The U.S. Constitution,*** by Joan Banks

For students at a Grade 10 reading level:
- ***Our Constitution,*** by Linda Carlson Johnson

For students at a Grade 11 reading level:
- ***The United States Constitution,*** by Kristal Leebrick

For students at a Grade 12 reading level:
- ***The Constitution,*** by Hal Marcovitz

Introducing Chapter 3

Focus

MAKING CONNECTIONS
How Are Governments Created?

Discuss with students the two questions posed on page 97. Activate students' prior knowledge by reminding them that the founders were suspicious of the tyranny of monarchs and that they wanted to find a way to have strong leadership balanced with fair representation. Help students think of a current example of checks and balances in practice, such as attempts by Congress to limit a president's war powers or confirmation hearings for Supreme Court justices. As part of the discussion, ask students to speculate about what American government and society would be like without this system of checks and balances. **OL**

Teach

The Big Ideas

As students study the chapter, remind them to consider the section-based Big Ideas included in each section's Guide to Reading. The **Essential Questions** in the activities below tie in to the Big Ideas and help students think about and understand important chapter concepts. In addition, the Hands-on Chapter Projects with their culminating activities relate the content from each section to the Big Ideas. These activities build on each other as students progress through the chapter. Section activities culminate in the wrap-up activity on the Visual Summary page.

Chapter 3

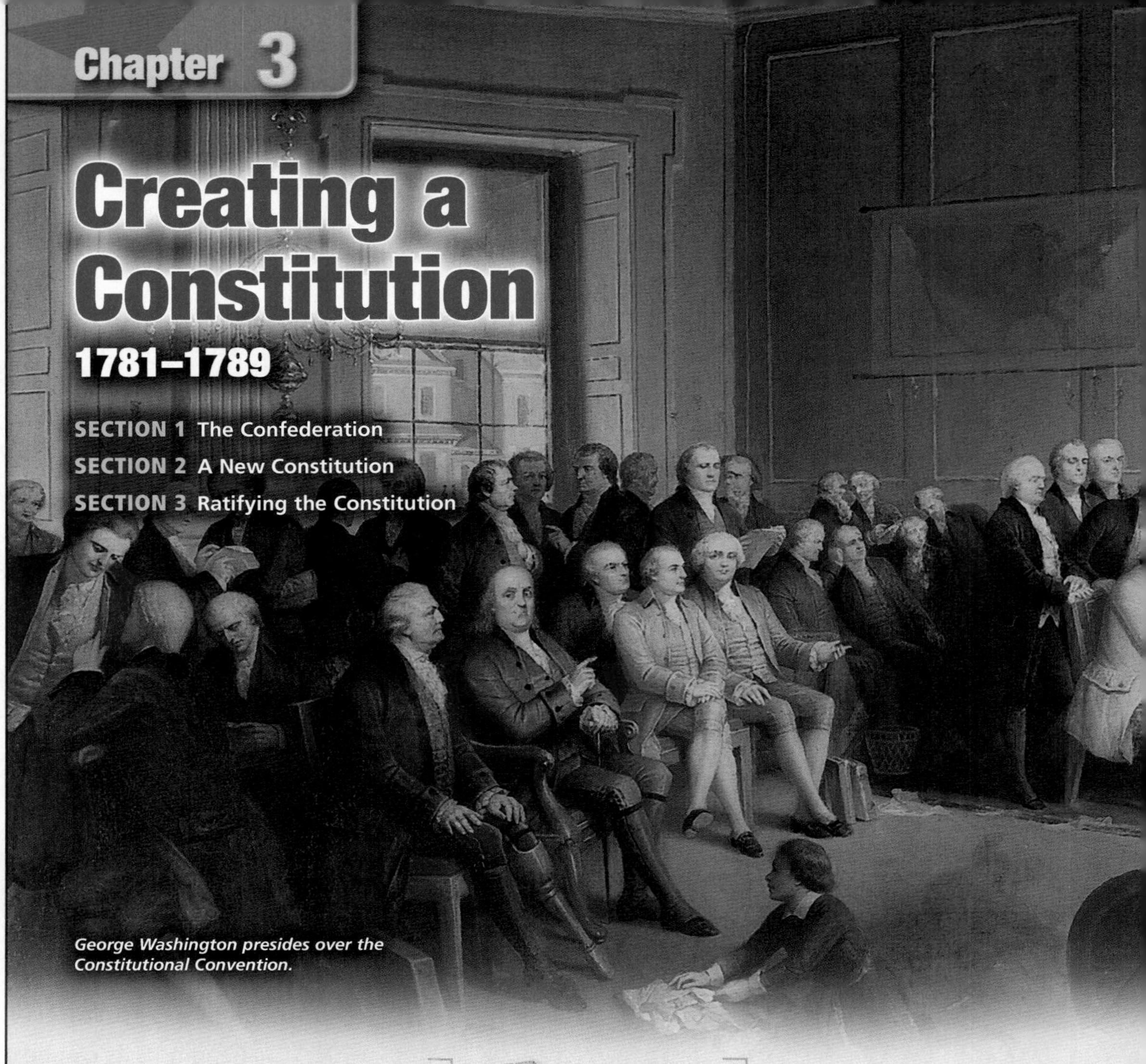

Creating a Constitution

1781–1789

SECTION 1 The Confederation
SECTION 2 A New Constitution
SECTION 3 Ratifying the Constitution

George Washington presides over the Constitutional Convention.

U.S. PRESIDENTS
U.S. EVENTS
WORLD EVENTS

1781
- The Articles of Confederation are ratified by the states

1783
- Treaty of Paris ends Revolutionary War

1784
- American ships begin trading with China at the port of Canton

1781 — 1783 — 1785

1781
- William Herschel discovers the planet Uranus using a telescope

1783
- Latin American soldier and statesman Simón Bolívar is born

Section 1

The Confederation

Essential Question: **What problems were caused by the Articles of Confederation?** *(The Articles created a Congress made up of representatives from the states. The central government was weak, and Congress had only limited powers. For example, it could not impose taxes or regulate trade. Each state was independent and did not always follow the lead of other states.)* Point out that in Section 1 students will learn about the first national constitution of the United States. **OL**

Section 2

A New Constitution

Essential Question: **What new form of government did the delegates to the Constitutional Convention create?** *(They created a system of checks and balances and a balance of power between the states and national government.)* Point out that in Section 2 students will learn how the Framers of the Constitution achieved their goal by making compromises. **OL**

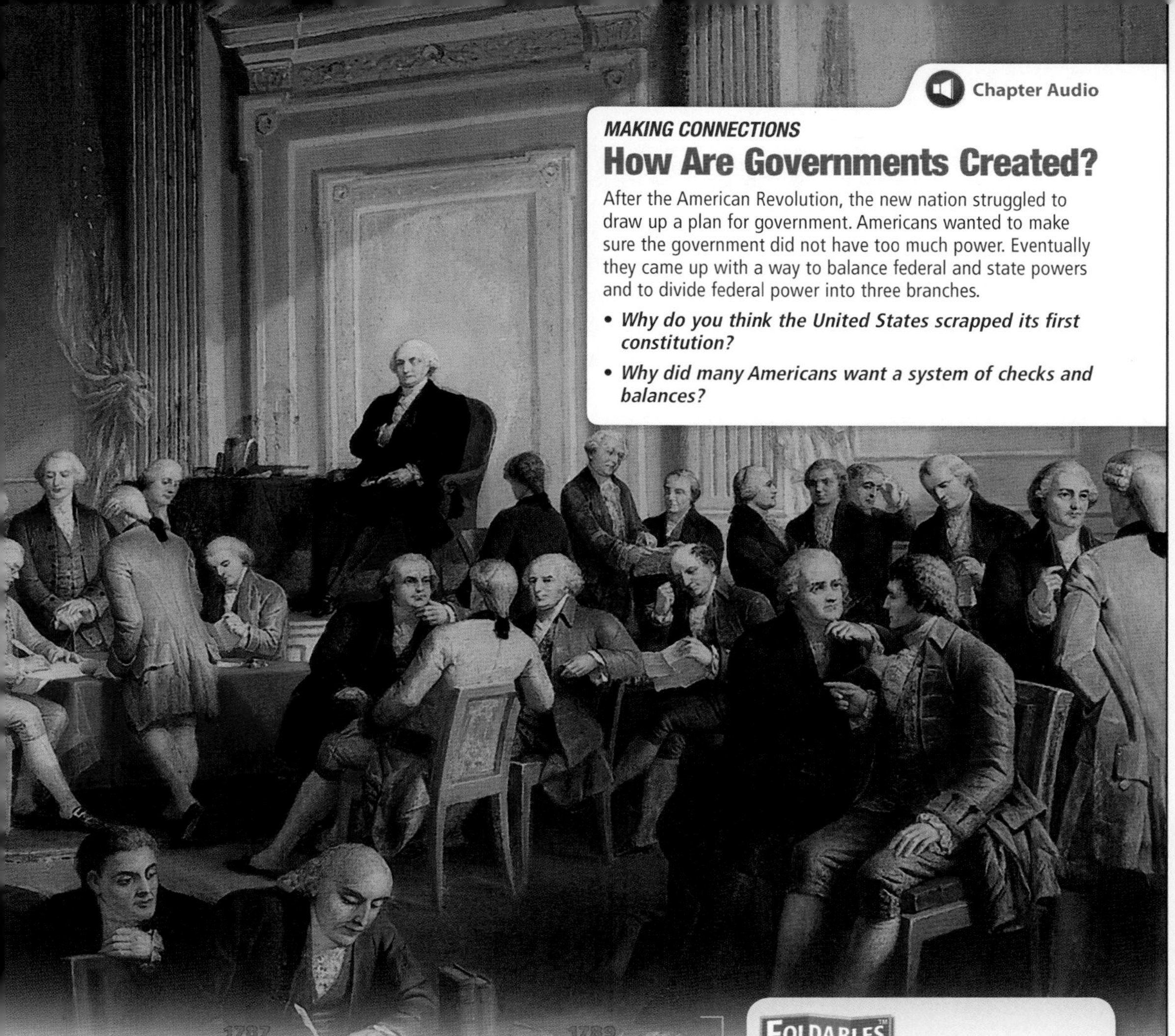

Chapter Audio

MAKING CONNECTIONS

How Are Governments Created?

After the American Revolution, the new nation struggled to draw up a plan for government. Americans wanted to make sure the government did not have too much power. Eventually they came up with a way to balance federal and state powers and to divide federal power into three branches.

- ***Why do you think the United States scrapped its first constitution?***
- ***Why did many Americans want a system of checks and balances?***

1786
- Shays's Rebellion begins in western Massachusetts

1787
- Constitutional Convention in Philadelphia drafts the Constitution of the United States

1788
- Constitution is ratified by 11 of 13 states and goes into effect

1789
- George Washington is elected president of the United States

Washington 1789–1797

1787

1789

1786
- British appoint Cornwallis to be Governor-General of British India

1787
- Sierra Leone is founded by freed Africans

1789
- French Revolution begins

FOLDABLES

Analyzing Constitutional Powers Create a Trifold Book to analyze the Constitution by listing the various functions of government using a Venn diagram. As you read the chapter, list the powers exclusive to the state, those exclusive to the nation, and the shared powers.

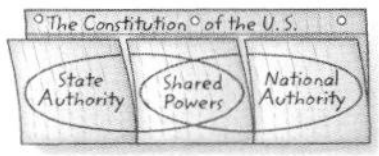

History ONLINE Visit glencoe.com and enter ***QuickPass***™ code TAV9846c3 for Chapter 3 resources.

Section 3

Ratifying the Constitution

Essential Question: Why did some people oppose ratification of the Constitution? *(They thought it gave the national government too much power and worried that the states would lose their independence. They also worried because it did not contain a bill of rights to protect individual liberties.)* Point out that in Section 3 students will learn about the issues debated by the states as they considered ratifying the Constitution. **OL**

More About the Painting

Visual Literacy As can be seen from the painting, the delegates to the Constitutional Convention in Philadelphia dressed formally, in woolen pants and coats and powdered wigs, in spite of the fact that the climate was humid and the temperature often exceeded 90 degrees. The room in which the delegates met that summer was cramped. It was also extremely hot and stuffy, as the doors and windows were locked tightly to keep the proceedings private.

FOLDABLES™ Study Organizer **Dinah Zike's Foldables**

Dinah Zike's Foldables are three-dimensional, interactive graphic organizers that help students practice basic writing skills, review vocabulary terms, and identify main ideas. Instructions for creating and using Foldables can be found in the Appendix at the end of this book and in the *Dinah Zike's Reading and Study Skills Foldables* booklet.

History ONLINE

Visit glencoe.com and enter ***QuickPass***™ code TAV9399c3T for Chapter 3 resources, including a Chapter Overview, Study Central™, Study-to-Go, Student Web Activity, Self-Check Quiz, and other materials.

Focus

Bellringer

Daily Focus Transparency 3-1

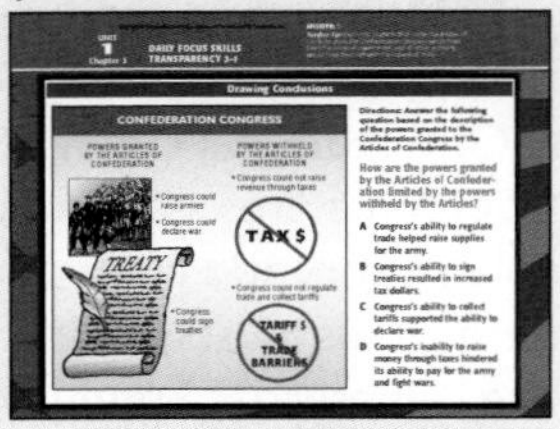

Guide to Reading

Answers may include the following: [top right] establishment of a system for surveying the Northwest Territory under the Land Ordinance of 1785, [top left] passage of the Northwest Ordinance, [bottom right] promotion of trade through trade treaties, [bottom left] led the warring United States during the years of the Revolution

Section Spotlight Video

To generate student interest and provide a springboard for class discussion, access the Chapter 3, Section 1 video at glencoe.com or on the video DVD.

Section 1 — Section Audio — Spotlight Video

The Confederation

Guide to Reading

Big Ideas

Government and Society The Articles of Confederation provided a workable but faulty national government.

Content Vocabulary

- duty *(p. 101)*
- recession *(p. 102)*

Academic Vocabulary

- explicitly *(p. 98)*
- occupy *(p. 101)*

People and Events to Identify

- Articles of Confederation *(p. 98)*
- Northwest Ordinance *(p. 99)*
- Shays's Rebellion *(p. 103)*

Reading Strategy

Organizing Complete a graphic organizer similar to the one below by listing the achievements of the Congress.

The Articles of Confederation became the first national constitution of the United States. Written during the Revolutionary War, the Articles of Confederation created a weak national government, which proved to be ineffective.

Congress Under the Articles of Confederation

MAIN Idea The Articles of Confederation gave the national government few powers.

HISTORY AND YOU Have you ever tried an experiment that failed? Read on to learn about the first national government of the United States.

Even before independence was declared, Patriot leaders at the Continental Congress realized that the colonies needed to be united under some type of central government. In November 1777 the Continental Congress adopted the Articles of Confederation and Perpetual Union—a plan for a loose union of the states under the authority of the Congress.

The Articles of Confederation

The **Articles of Confederation** established a very weak central government. The states had spent several years fighting for independence from Britain. They did not want to give up that independence to a new central government that might become tyrannical.

Under the Articles, once a year, each state would select a delegation to send to the capital city. This group, generally referred to as the Congress, was the entire government. There were no separate executive and judicial branches.

The Congress had the right to declare war, raise armies, and sign treaties. Although these powers were significant, the Congress was not given the power to impose taxes, and it was **explicitly** denied the power to regulate trade.

Western Policies

Lacking the power to tax or regulate trade, the Confederation depended on state contributions to fund the government. Congress also raised money by selling the land it controlled west of the

Resource Manager

R Reading Strategies	C Critical Thinking	D Differentiated Instruction	W Writing Support	S Skill Practice
Teacher Edition • Academic Vocab., p. 101 **Additional Resources** • Prim. Source Read, URB p. 101 • Guid Read Act., URB p. 112	**Teacher Edition** • Analyzing Info., p. 99 **Additional Resources** • Quizzes and Tests, p. 31	**Teacher Edition** • Verbal/Linguistic, p. 100 • Special Ed., p. 101 • Intrapersonal, p. 102 **Additional Resources** • Eng. Learner Act., URB p. 91	**Teacher Edition** • Expository Writing, p. 101	**Teacher Edition** • Using Geo. Skills, p. 99 **Additional Resources** • Reinforcing Skills Act., URB p. 97 • Read. Essen., p. 29

The Northwest Ordinance, 1787

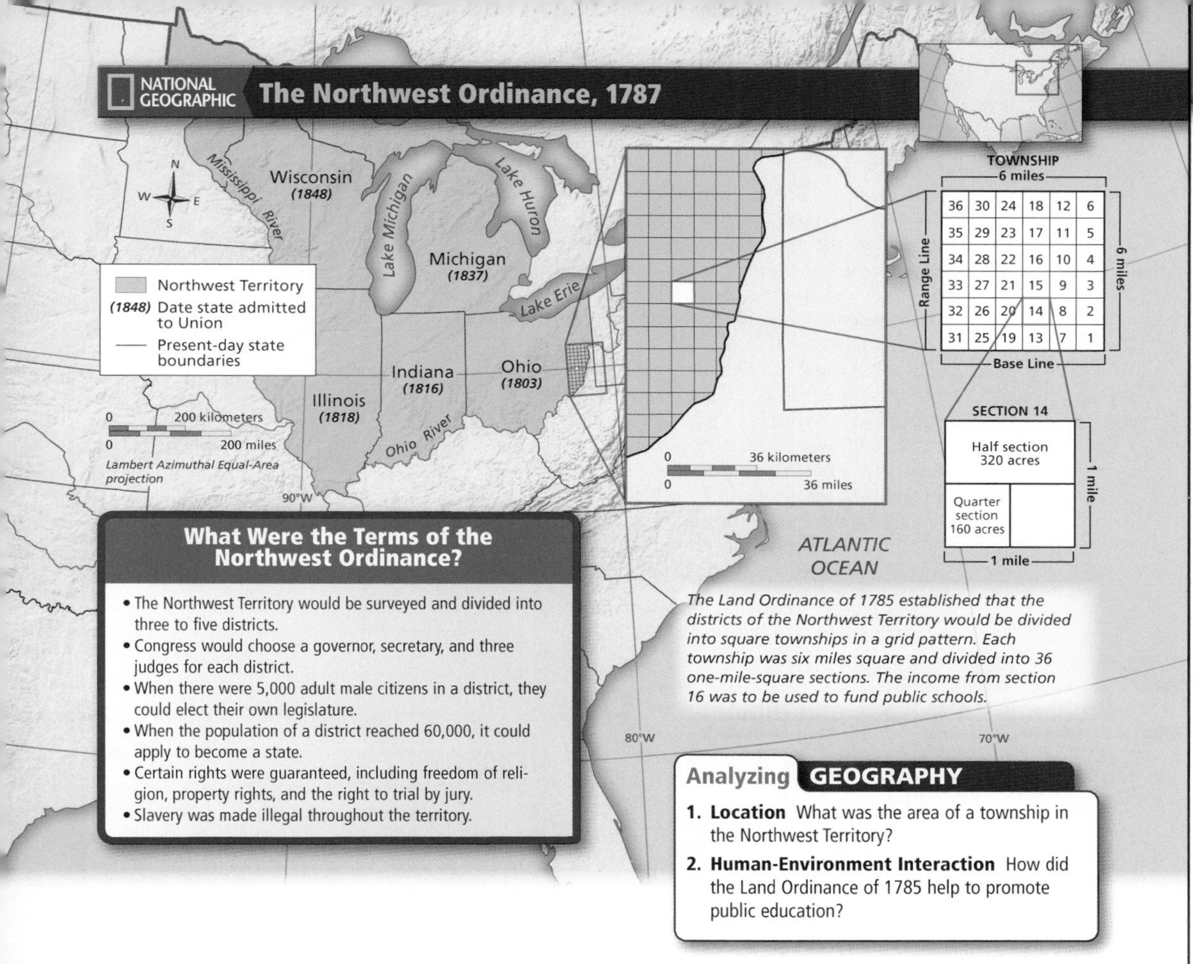

The Land Ordinance of 1785 established that the districts of the Northwest Territory would be divided into square townships in a grid pattern. Each township was six miles square and divided into 36 one-mile-square sections. The income from section 16 was to be used to fund public schools.

What Were the Terms of the Northwest Ordinance?

- The Northwest Territory would be surveyed and divided into three to five districts.
- Congress would choose a governor, secretary, and three judges for each district.
- When there were 5,000 adult male citizens in a district, they could elect their own legislature.
- When the population of a district reached 60,000, it could apply to become a state.
- Certain rights were guaranteed, including freedom of religion, property rights, and the right to trial by jury.
- Slavery was made illegal throughout the territory.

Analyzing GEOGRAPHY

1. **Location** What was the area of a township in the Northwest Territory?
2. **Human-Environment Interaction** How did the Land Ordinance of 1785 help to promote public education?

Appalachian Mountains. To get people to buy the land and settle in the region, the Congress established an orderly system for dividing and selling the land and governing the new settlements. The Land Ordinance of 1785 set up a **S** method for surveying the western lands. It arranged the land into townships, six miles square. Each township was divided into 36 sections, one mile square.

Two years later, the Congress passed the **Northwest Ordinance,** which provided the basis for governing much of the western territory. The law created a new territory north of the Ohio River and east of the Mississippi, which could eventually be divided into three to five states. Initially the Congress would choose a governor, a secretary, and three judges for the territory. When 5,000 adult male citizens had settled in a territory, they could elect a territorial legislature. When the population of a territory reached 60,000, the territory could apply to become a state "on an equal footing with the original states."

The Northwest Ordinance also guaranteed certain rights to people living in the territory. These included freedom of religion, property rights, and the right to trial by jury. The ordinance also stated that "there [would] be neither slavery nor involuntary servitude in the **C** said territory." The exclusion of slavery from the Northwest Territory meant that as the United States expanded in future years, it would be divided between Southern slaveholding states and Northern free states.

Teach

S Skill Practice

Using Geography Skills Have students use a local road map to understand the size of the townships created by the Land Ordinance of 1785. Have students outline an area six miles square that includes their current location. **BL** **ELL**

C Critical Thinking

Analyzing Information Ask: Why might settlers have wanted to move to the Northwest Territory? *(They might have wanted the independence and adventure of moving to a new region. They might also have been attracted by the exclusion of slavery and by freedom of religion, property rights, and right to trial by jury.)* **OL**

Analyzing GEOGRAPHY

Answers:

1. six miles square
2. The income from section 16 in a township would be used to fund public schools.

Differentiated Instruction

Leveled Activites

BL Reteaching Activity, URB p. 109

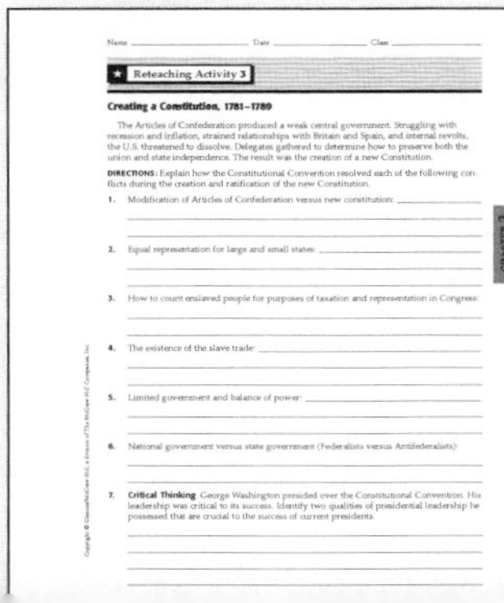

OL Reinforcing Skills Activity, URB p. 97

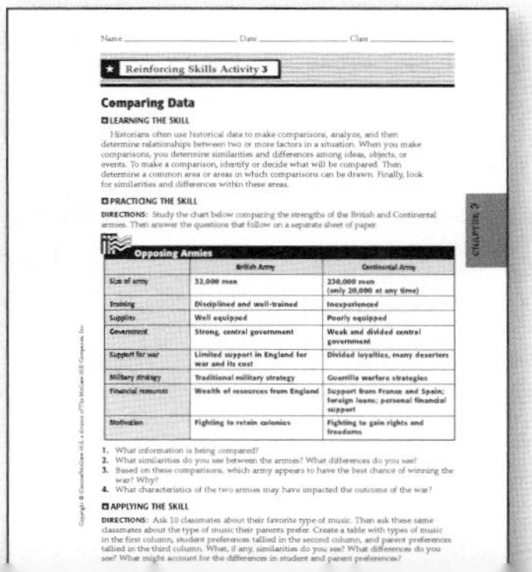

AL Enrichment Activity, URB p. 110

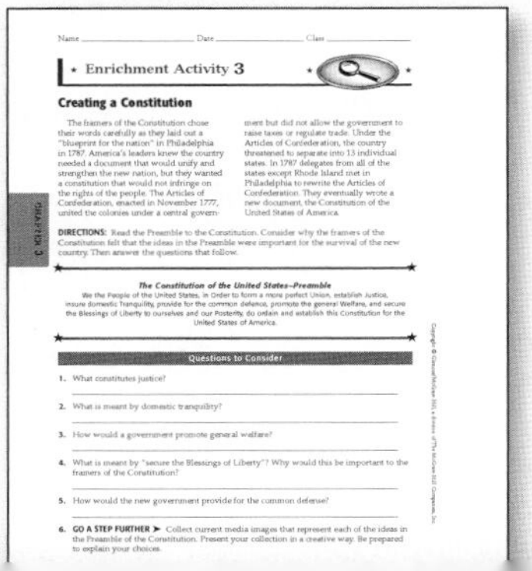

ELL English Learner Activity, URB p. 91

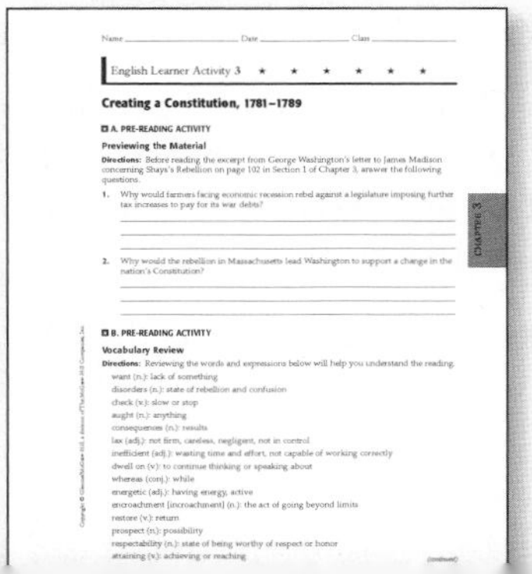

D Differentiated Instruction

Verbal/Linguistic Assign different students the map, the graph, or the chart on page 100. Ask them to write a paragraph summarizing the information in the visual. Then lead a discussion to clarify the relationship among the visuals. **BL**

Analyzing VISUALS

Answers:

1. The Revolution ended in 1783 and the U.S. government had no way of regulating imports.
2. States imposed trade restrictions and tariffs.

Reading Check

Answer: When 5,000 adult male citizens had settled in a territory, they could elect a legislature. When the population reached 60,000, the territory could apply for statehood. Freedom of religion, property rights, and the right to trial by jury were guaranteed. Slavery was excluded.

Success in Trade

In addition to organizing western settlement, the Congress tried to promote trade with other nations. After the Revolutionary War ended, the British government imposed sharp restrictions on American access to British colonies in the Caribbean. American ships could still carry goods to Britain, but only goods from their respective states. A ship from Massachusetts, for example, could not carry New York goods.

To solve these problems, representatives from the Congress negotiated trade treaties with other countries, including Holland, Prussia, and Sweden. A previous commercial treaty with France also permitted American merchants to sell goods to French colonies in the Caribbean. By 1790, the trade of the United States was greater than the trade of the American colonies before the Revolution.

Reading Check **Describing** What were the provisions of the Northwest Ordinance of 1787?

The Congress Falters

MAIN Idea The first national government could not regulate trade, collect taxes, or enforce treaties, which led to calls for a stronger national government.

HISTORY AND YOU Is it better for government to be too strong or too weak? Read on to learn about problems facing the Congress.

The Congress's commercial treaties and its system of settling the West were two of its major achievements. Other problems were not so easily solved.

Problems With Trade

During the boycotts of the 1760s and the Revolutionary War, American artisans and manufacturers had prospered by making goods that people had previously bought from the British. After the war ended, British merchants flooded the United States with inexpensive

HISTORY AND GEOGRAPHY

Problems With Trade and Diplomacy

The weak confederation government was powerless to solve economic and diplomatic problems.

Imports from England

Source: *Historical Statistics of the United States.*

D

British Forts in the United States, 1787

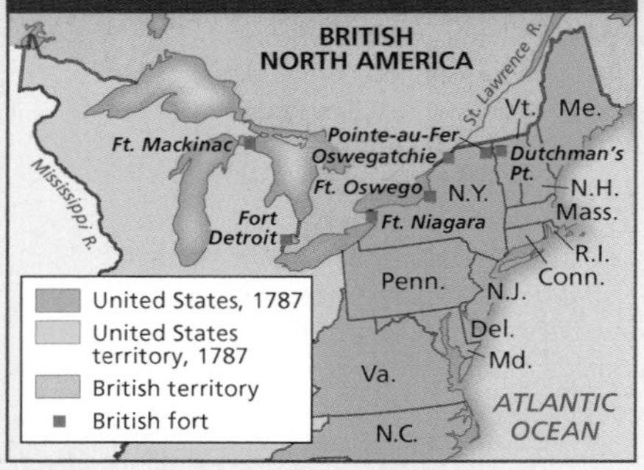

◀ *Americans resented the continued British military presence in the United States.*

How Did the Articles of Confederation Affect Foreign Policy?

Weakness	Problem Caused
• No power to regulate commerce • No power to compel states to obey international treaties signed by the Congress • Cannot declare war without unanimous support of all states	• States impose trade restrictions and tariffs • States restrict Britain's ability to collect American debts; Congress cannot reach a financial settlement with Britain; Britain refuses to evacuate forts on American soil • Spain denies Americans permission to deposit goods at mouth of Mississippi; Congress has no leverage with Spain

Analyzing VISUALS

1. **Explaining** Why did imports from England increase so sharply after 1782?
2. **Determining Cause and Effect** What was the effect of the national government's inability to regulate interstate trade under the Articles of Confederation?

Hands-On Chapter Project Step 1

Designing a Film Treatment

Step 1: Seeing the "Big Picture" Have students work in groups to develop a film treatment of the chapter content.

Ask What concerns did people have about the form of government in the United States, and what steps did they take to develop a Constitution?

Directions Tell students they are going to plan a film treatment of the events leading up to the Constitutional Convention and the subsequent fight for ratification.

First, have groups discuss the structure of the film. Will it be a sweeping narrative, or will the story be told from the point of view of specific individuals, leaders, and so on? Remind students as they read the chapter to look for events and ideas that have the most conflict and dramatic "punch." Each section of the film should correspond to a section of the chapter and include at least one dramatic event.

Next, have group members divide the responsibilities for planning the film. Each group will need people to create a storyboard and outline a script. Groups should choose scene designers, costume designers, and sound designers. Location scouts will identify settings for the film.

Putting It Together Ask each group to report on the preliminary choices they have made. **OL**

(Chapter Project continued on page 105)

British goods, driving many American artisans out of business.

British trade practices convinced many states to fight back by restricting British imports. Unfortunately, the states did not all impose the same **duties,** or taxes, on imported goods. The British would then take their goods to the states that had the lowest taxes or fewest restrictions. Once British goods were in the United States, they moved overland into the states that had tried to keep them out.

Because the Articles of Confederation did not allow the Congress to regulate commerce, the states began setting up customs posts on their borders to prevent the British from exploiting the different trade laws. They also levied taxes on each other's goods to raise revenue. New York, for example, taxed firewood from Connecticut and cabbage from New Jersey. New Jersey retaliated by charging New York for a harbor lighthouse on the New Jersey side of the Hudson River. Each state was beginning to act as an independent country, and this behavior threatened the unity of the new United States. W

Problems With Diplomacy D

The Articles of Confederation also created problems for Congress in other areas of foreign policy. The first problems surfaced immediately after the Treaty of Paris, which ended the Revolutionary War, was signed. Neither Britain nor the United States carried out the terms of the treaty, primarily because the Congress lacked the power to uphold its side of the treaty. Problems also arose with America's ally Spain soon after the war ended.

Problems With Britain Before the war, many American merchants and planters had borrowed money from British lenders. In the peace treaty, the United States had agreed that the states should allow British creditors to recover their prewar debts by suing in American courts. The Congress had no power to compel the states to do this, however, and many states placed restrictions on Britain's ability to collect its debts.

Even when the British were able to get the matter into court, they often found that American judges and juries sided with the American debtors. The United States had also agreed that the states should return the property that had been confiscated from Loyalists during the war. Again, the Congress could not compel the states to do this, further angering the British.

In retaliation, the British refused to evacuate American soil, as specified in the treaty. British forces continued to **occupy** a string of frontier posts south of the Great Lakes, inside American territory. The Congress had no way to resolve these problems. It did not have the power to impose taxes, so it could not raise the money to pay a financial settlement to Britain for the debts and Loyalist property. It also could not afford to raise an army to expel the British from American territory. R

Problems With Spain American dealings with Spain also showed the weaknesses of the Articles of Confederation. After the revolutionary war, Spain's support for the United States came to an end. Instead, Spain began to regard the United States as a rival wanting to claim land in North America that Spain also claimed.

The first major dispute between Spain and the United States involved the border between Spanish territory and the state of Georgia. To pressure the United States into accepting the border where Spain wanted it to be, the Spanish withdrew permission for Americans to deposit their goods on Spanish territory at the mouth of the Mississippi River. This effectively closed the Mississippi River to frontier farmers, who used the river to ship their goods to market.

Unfortunately, the negotiators for the Congress had no leverage to pressure the Spanish to change their policy. The best American negotiators could do was to get Spain to agree to a trade treaty, in exchange for the United States withdrawing its demand for navigation rights on the Mississippi.

The proposed treaty enraged people in the Southern states. They believed the Northern states had given in on the issue simply to help Northern merchants increase their trade with Spain. Without Southern support, the treaty could not pass Congress and was withdrawn from consideration. The dispute over Georgia's border and navigation on the Mississippi remained unresolved. Again, the limited powers of the Congress under the Articles of Confederation had prevented any diplomatic solution from being worked out.

W Writing Support

Expository Writing Have interested students research a current court case that involves states' rights versus the rights of the federal government. Ask students to prepare a one-page summary of the state's position and a one-page summary of the federal government's position. AL

D Differentiated Instruction

Special Education Have students with reading difficulties work in pairs to outline the section "Problems with Diplomacy." Suggest that they use the headings and paragraph breaks to structure their outlines. BL

R Reading Strategy

Academic Vocabulary Ask: What is a synonym for *occupy*? *(inhabit, live in)* Read aloud the first sentence of the paragraph, emphasizing the phrase "refused to evacuate." Make sure that students understand that *evacuate* means "leave." Then help them see that the phrase, "continued to occupy," means the opposite.) BL

Additional Support

Teacher Tip

Paired Activity This activity requires students to take on the roles of teacher and student. Mixed-ability learners have the opportunity to work together, and the activity is also an excellent opportunity for English learners to develop better fluency and pronunciation. This activity can be used to reteach content throughout the textbook.

Activity: Collaborative Learning

Explaining Have students select one portion of Section 1 to teach to another student. Ask students to read the passage and then to teach it to a partner. Have the student that is teaching ask questions about the section. Direct the "teacher" to review any concepts that the "learner" did not understand. Then have students switch roles to study another portion of the section. BL ELL

D Differentiated Instruction

Intrapersonal To help illustrate the economic concepts, have students role-play some of the relationships described in "The Economic Crisis." Assign students to play the parts of farmers, other debtors, merchants and planters, and representatives of the states. Review the content of the section to clarify each group's concerns and then ask them to role-play a conversation and/or argument between the participants in which they try to find a solution to their various problems. **AL**

DBQ Document Based Questions

Answers:

1. second after South Carolina
2. He felt that it showed the weaknesses of the central government under the Articles of Confederation, which caused the states to work against each other and the national government.

Additional Support

PRIMARY SOURCE

Shays's Rebellion

▲ *Rebels occupy a courthouse in western Massachusetts.*

Revolutionary Debt

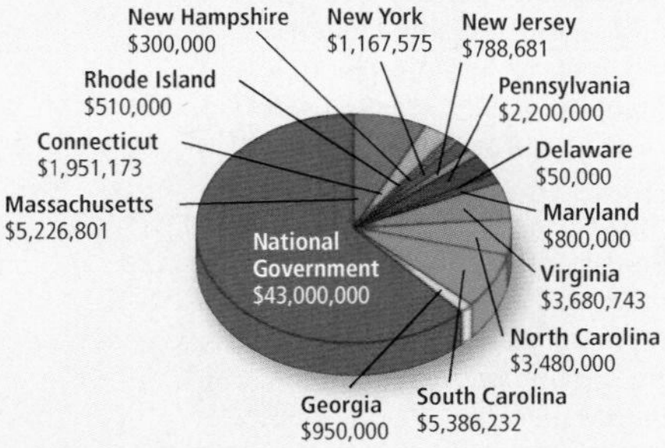

Sources: *The American States During and After the Revolution; The Price of Liberty: The Public Debt of the American Revolution.*

In the midst of Shays's Rebellion, George Washington wrote to James Madison agreeing that the rebellion showed the need to revise the Articles of Confederation:

"What stronger evidence can be given of the want of energy in our governments than these disorders? If there exists not a power to check them, what security has a man for life, liberty, or property? To you, I am sure I need not add aught on this subject, the consequences of a lax, or inefficient government, are too obvious to be dwelt on. Thirteen Sovereignties pulling against each other, and all tugging at the federal head will soon bring ruin on the whole; whereas a liberal, and energetic Constitution, well guarded and closely watched, to prevent incroachments, might restore us to that degree of respectability and consequence, to which we had a fair claim, and the brightest prospect of attaining."

—from George Washington's letter to James Madison, November 5, 1786

DBQ Document-Based Questions

1. **Specifying** Where did Massachusetts rank among the states in terms of the amount of its Revolutionary debt?
2. **Explaining** What did Washington feel was the significance of Shays's Rebellion?

D The Economic Crisis

While the Congress struggled with diplomatic issues, many other Americans were struggling financially. The end of the Revolutionary War and the decline of trade with Britain had plunged the United States into a severe economic **recession.**

Farmers were among those most affected by the recession. They were not earning as much money as they once did, and they had to keep borrowing to get their next crop in the ground. Many also had mortgages to pay. At the same time, the Revolutionary War had left both the Congress and many states in debt. To pay for the war, many states had issued bonds as a way to borrow money from wealthy merchants and planters. With the war over, the people holding those bonds wanted them to be redeemed for gold or silver.

To pay off their debts, the states could raise taxes, but farmers and other people in debt urged the state governments to issue paper money instead. They also wanted the states to make the paper money available to farmers through government loans on farm mortgages.

Since paper money would not be backed up by gold and silver, and people would not trust it, inflation—a decline in the value of money—began. Debtors would be able to pay their debts using paper money that steadily lost its value. This would let them pay off their debts more easily. Lenders, on the other hand, including many merchants and importers, strongly opposed paper money because they would not be receiving the true amount they were owed. Beginning in 1785, seven states began issuing paper money.

In Rhode Island, paper money eventually became so worthless that merchants refused to

Activity: Economics Connection

Economic Relationships Invite an economics teacher or economist to speak to the class about the relationship among taxes, inflation, and the issuance of currency. If possible, ask the speaker to provide an activity or pretest that the students can complete before he or she comes to speak. After the presentation, have students reread "The Economic Crisis" in the paragraphs above and use a graphic organizer to summarize the concepts. Then have students discuss how these economic concepts affect their daily lives. **AL**

accept it. After an angry mob rioted against the merchants, Rhode Island's assembly passed a law forcing people to accept the paper money. Those who refused could be arrested and fined.

The violence in Rhode Island demonstrated two things to many American leaders. The Rhode Island assembly, influenced by the mob, had forced wealthy creditors to accept worthless money. This showed that unless a government was properly designed, the people could use the power of government to steal from the wealthy. The events also suggested that a strong central government was needed to take on the country's debts and stabilize the currency.

Shays's Rebellion

Property owners' fears seemed justified when a rebellion, known as **Shays's Rebellion,** erupted in Massachusetts in 1786. The conflict started when the government of Massachusetts decided to raise taxes instead of issuing paper money to pay off its debts. The taxes fell most heavily on farmers, particularly poor farmers in the western part of the state. As the recession grew worse, many found it impossible to pay their debts. Those who could not pay often faced the loss of their farms.

Angry at the legislature's indifference to their plight, farmers in western Massachusetts rebelled in late August 1786. They closed down several county courthouses to prevent farm foreclosures and then marched to the state supreme court. At this point, Daniel Shays, a former captain in the Continental Army who was now a bankrupt farmer, emerged as one of the rebellion's leaders.

In January 1787 Shays and about 1,200 farmers headed to a state arsenal intending to seize weapons before marching on Boston. In response, the governor sent a force under the command of General Benjamin Lincoln to defend the arsenal. Before Lincoln arrived, Shays attacked, and the militia defending the arsenal opened fire. Four farmers died in the fighting. The rest scattered. The next day Lincoln's troops arrived and ended the rebellion. The fears the rebellion had raised, however, were harder to disperse.

People with greater income and social status tended to see the rebellion, as well as inflation and an unstable currency, as signs that the republic itself was at risk. They feared that as state legislatures became more democratic and responsive to poor people, they would weaken property rights and vote to take property from the wealthy. As General Henry Knox, a close aide to George Washington, concluded: "What is to afford our security against the violence of lawless men? Our government must be braced, changed, or altered to secure our lives and property."

These concerns were an important reason that many people, including merchants, artisans, and creditors, began to argue for a stronger central government, and several members of the Congress called on the states to correct "such defects as may be discovered to exist" in the present government. The Confederation's failure to deal with conditions that might lead to rebellion, as well as the problems with trade and diplomacy, only added fuel to their argument.

Reading Check **Explaining** What caused Shays's Rebellion?

Section 1 REVIEW

Vocabulary

1. **Explain** the significance of: Articles of Confederation, Northwest Ordinance, duty, recession, Shays's Rebellion.

Main Ideas

2. **Describing** What were some accomplishments of the U.S. government under the Articles of Confederation?
3. **Explaining** Why did Shays's Rebellion lead to a call for a stronger national government?

Critical Thinking

4. **Big Ideas** What do you think was the most serious flaw of the Articles of Confederation? Explain.
5. **Organizing** Use a graphic organizer similar to the one below to list the weaknesses of the Congress.

6. **Analyzing Visuals** Study the map of the Northwest Ordinance on page 99. What significant provision of this law would contribute to dividing the nation into competing regions?

Writing About History

7. **Persuasive Writing** Take on the role of a newspaper publisher during the time of the Congress. Write an editorial expressing your opinion of Shays's Rebellion, and suggest how the government might handle such situations better in the future.

History ONLINE
Study Central™ To review this section, go to glencoe.com and click on Study Central.

Reading Check

Answer:
Poor farmers in western Massachusetts found it impossible to pay their taxes, mortgages, and other debts. They rebelled to close down the courts where they were being declared bankrupt.

Assess

History ONLINE

Study Central™ provides summaries, interactive games, and online graphic organizers to help students review content.

Close

Summarizing Ask: What were the strengths and weaknesses of the Articles of Confederation? *(Strengths: It gave Congress under the Articles of Confederation the right to declare war, raise armies, and sign treaties. Weaknesses: The central government could not raise taxes, states made independent decisions, and the central government could not respond effectively to internal conflict.)* **OL**

Section 1 REVIEW

Answers

1. All definitions can be found in the section and the Glossary.
2. The Congress passed the Land Ordinance of 1785, which established a method for surveying western lands. Congress passed the Northwest Ordinance, which provided the basis for governing much of the western territory and outlined an orderly method for achieving statehood. The Congress was also successful in promoting trade through treaties.
3. Americans with greater assets were concerned about the national government's inability to maintain stability and to protect property rights.
4. Answers will vary but should include a specific flaw of the government under the Articles of Confederation.
5. no power to impose taxes, regulate trade, force states to abide by the Treaty of Paris, or regulate currency
6. The exclusion of slavery in the Northwest Territory would lead to increased competition and friction between the Northern free states and the Southern slave-holding states as new free states joined the Union.
7. Students' editorials will vary. Editorials should express an opinion on the issue and offer at least one suggestion for improvement.

Focus

Bellringer

Daily Focus Transparency 3-2

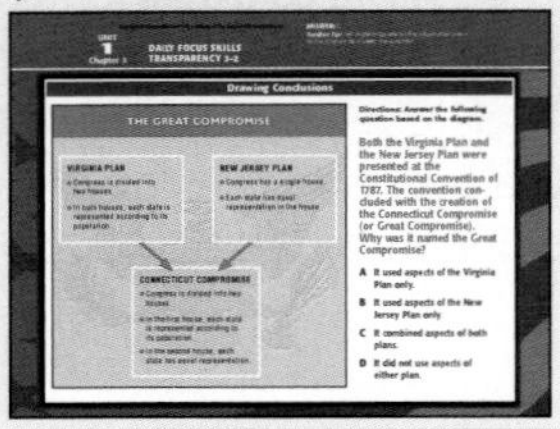

Guide to Reading

Answer:

A New Constitution
I. The Constitutional Convention
  A. The Framers
  B. The Virginia Plan
II. A Union Built on Compromise
  A. The Connecticut Compromise
  B. Compromise Over Slavery
III. A Framework for Limited Government
  A. Checks and Balances
  B. Amending the Constitution

Section Spotlight Video

To generate student interest and provide a springboard for class discussion, access the Chapter 3, Section 2 video at glencoe.com or on the video DVD.

Resource Manager

Section 2

Section Audio Spotlight Video

A New Constitution

Guide to Reading

Big Ideas

Government and Society In the new Constitution, the Framers tried to uphold the rights of the states while providing needed national authority.

Content Vocabulary

- popular sovereignty *(p. 108)*
- federalism *(p. 108)*
- separation of powers *(p. 108)*
- checks and balances *(p. 109)*
- veto *(p. 109)*
- amendment *(p. 109)*

Academic Vocabulary

- financier *(p. 104)*

People and Events to Identify

- James Madison *(p. 104))*
- Great Compromise *(p. 106)*
- Three-Fifths Compromise *(p. 107)*

Reading Strategy

Categorizing As you read, use the major headings of the section to fill in an outline similar to the one below.

A New Constitution
I. The Constitutional Convention
  A.
  B.
II.
  A.
  B.

In 1787 the delegates to the Constitutional Convention intended to revise the Articles of Confederation. Instead, they began drafting a constitution for a new national government. The delegates negotiated many difficult compromises before agreeing on the framework for the new federal system.

The Constitutional Convention

MAIN Idea The delegates to the convention tried to create a stronger national government that gave fair representation to big and small states.

HISTORY AND YOU Who do you think should be chosen to create a government? Should it be the smartest people or the richest, or should other criteria be used? Read to learn about the men who designed the Constitution.

The political and economic problems facing the United States in 1787 worried many American leaders. They believed that the new nation would not survive without a strong central government and that the Articles of Confederation had to be revised or replaced. People who supported a stronger central government became known as "nationalists." Prominent nationalists included Benjamin Franklin, George Washington, John Adams, and the **financier** Robert Morris.

One of the most influential nationalists was **James Madison,** a member of the Virginia Assembly and head of its commerce committee. As head of the commerce committee, Madison was well aware of Virginia's trade problems with the other American states and with Britain. He firmly believed that a stronger national government was needed.

In 1786 Madison convinced Virginia's assembly to call a convention of all the states to discuss trade and taxation problems. Representatives from the states were to meet in Annapolis, Maryland, but when the convention began, delegates from only five states were present, too few to reach a final decision on the problems facing the states. The delegates did discuss the weakness of the Articles of Confederation and expressed interest in modifying them.

Another important nationalist, New York delegate Alexander Hamilton, recommended that the Congress itself call for a convention. Members of the Congress were initially reluctant to call a convention, but news of Shays's Rebellion changed many minds. In February 1787, Congress called for a convention of the states "for the sole purpose of revising the Articles of Confederation."

Every state except Rhode Island sent delegates to what became known as the Constitutional Convention. In May 1787 the delegates

R Reading Strategies	C Critical Thinking	D Differentiated Instruction	W Writing Support	S Skill Practice
Teacher Edition • Making Connections, p. 106 • Summarizing, p. 109 **Additional Resources** • Read. Skills Act., URB p. 87 • Prim. Source Read, URB p. 103 • Guid. Read Act., URB p. 113	**Teacher Edition** • Making Inferences, p. 105 **Additional Resources** • Linking Past and Present Act., URB p. 100 • Quizzes and Tests, p. 32	**Teacher Edition** • Visual/Spatial, p. 108 • English Learners, p. 108 **Additional Resources** • Diff. Inst. Act., URB p. 89 • American Art and Music, URB p. 105 • Enrichment Act., URB p. 110	**Teacher Edition** • Persuasive Writing, p. 106	**Additional Resources** • Time Line Act., URB p. 99 • Read. Essen., p. 32

PRIMARY SOURCE
Creating a Constitution

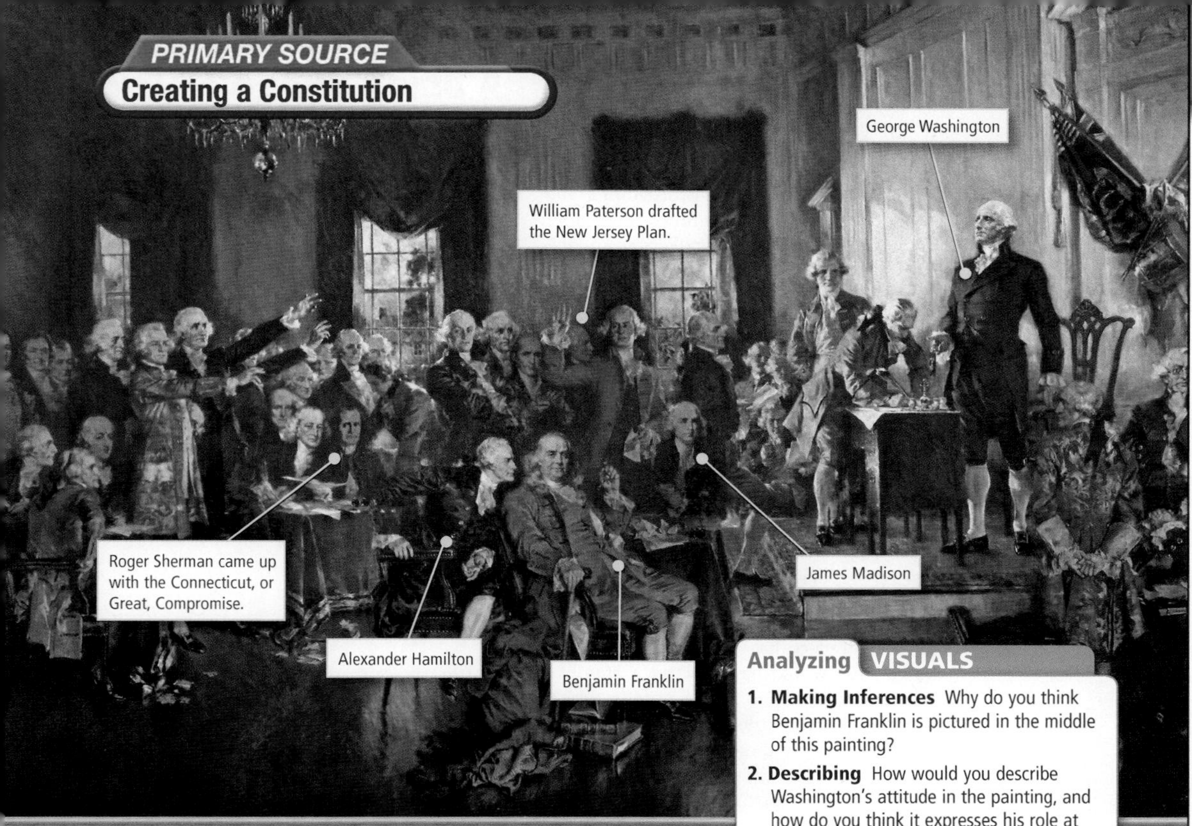

Analyzing VISUALS

1. **Making Inferences** Why do you think Benjamin Franklin is pictured in the middle of this painting?
2. **Describing** How would you describe Washington's attitude in the painting, and how do you think it expresses his role at the Convention?

took their places in the Pennsylvania statehouse in Philadelphia. They knew they faced a daunting task: to balance the rights of the states with the need for a stronger national government.

The Framers

The 55 delegates who attended the convention in Philadelphia included some of the shrewdest and most distinguished leaders in the United States. The majority were attorneys, and most of the others were planters and merchants. Most had experience in colonial, state, or national government. Seven had served as state governors. Thirty-nine had been members of the Congress. Eight had signed the Declaration of Independence. In the words of Thomas Jefferson, who was unable to attend the convention because he was serving as American minister to France, the convention in Philadelphia was no less than "an assembly of demigods."

The delegates chose George Washington of Virginia, hero of the American Revolution, as presiding officer. Benjamin Franklin was a delegate from Pennsylvania. Now 81 years old, he tired easily and had other state delegates read his speeches for him. He provided assistance to many of his younger colleagues, and his experience and good humor helped smooth the debates.

Other notable delegates included New York's Alexander Hamilton and Connecticut's Roger Sherman. Virginia sent a well-prepared delegation, including the scholarly James Madison, who kept a record of the debates. Madison's records provide the best source of information about what went on in the sessions. The meetings were closed to the public to help ensure honest and open discussion free from outside political pressures. **C**

Teach

C Critical Thinking

Making Inferences Ask: The convention was held behind closed doors. Who do you think the delegates worried might try to interfere with the proceedings? *(They might have been concerned that strong states or other special interests would press their case for more power under the new Constitution).* **OL**

Analyzing VISUALS

Answers:

1. Answers will vary. Students might suggest it is to show respect for Franklin and the influence he had on the formation of the government from the Revolution through the Convention.
2. Possible answer: He is prominently placed in the picture and is standing in a proud and commanding way. It reinforces the importance of his role as presiding officer of the Convention and that he was a figure worthy of great respect.

Hands-On Chapter Project
Step 2

Designing a Film Treatment

Step 2: Making Key Decisions Students will begin nailing down some crucial decisions based on what they have learned in Section 1.

Directions At this stage, groups will need to identify the film's main characters. Suggest that students find ways to incorporate the speakers of primary source quotations as characters in the film. Then have them discuss possible actors to play those roles. At this point, groups will have to make final, firm decisions about the structure and point of view of the film—the storyboard and outline should begin to take shape and key scenes identified. Costume and scene designers will make some preliminary sketches, and background music and sound effects will be chosen. (Students may enjoy researching these period details.) Location scouts will explain where various scenes might be filmed. Remind students that, although they have specific responsibilities, they should keep the overall project in mind and contribute their ideas about areas that are not their primary responsibility.

Putting It Together Have students share preliminary storyboards, outlines, and sketches. As a group, have students evaluate the progress they have made toward completion of the film treatment. Discuss any key events in Sections 1 and 2 that they find difficult to convey. **OL**

(Chapter Project continued on page 113)

W Writing Support

Persuasive Writing Have students reread "The Connecticut Compromise" and write a speech by Roger Sherman, in which he sets forth his arguments for the Great Compromise. Encourage students to review the information about the Virginia Plan and the New Jersey Plan so they can include specific details in their speech. Their speeches should directly address the fears and concerns of the delegates. **AL**

R Reading Strategy

Making Connections Ask: Do you think it was fair that the most committed delegates were left off the committee? How would you feel if you were not allowed to express strong opinions when a compromise needed to be made? *(Students' responses will vary but should refer to the material.)* **BL**

Reading Check

Answer:
Smaller states feared that larger states would outvote them if representation was based only on population.

Additional Support

A Union Built on Compromise

MAIN Idea American leaders created a new constitution based on compromise.

HISTORY AND YOU Have you ever had to compromise on something you felt strongly about? Read on to learn how slavery divided the delegates at the Constitutional Convention.

As the convention worked out the details of the new constitution, the delegates found themselves divided geographically. The small states demanded changes that would protect them from the voting power of the big states. At the same time, Northern and Southern states were divided over how to treat slavery in the new constitution. The only way to resolve the differences was through compromise.

The Virginia Plan

History ONLINE Student Web Activity Visit glencoe.com and complete the activity on the Constitution.

The Virginia delegation arrived at the convention with a detailed plan—mostly the work of James Madison—for a new national government. A few days into the proceedings, the governor of Virginia, Edmund Randolph, introduced the plan. "A national government," he declared, "ought to be established, consisting of a supreme Legislative, Executive, and Judiciary." The Virginia Plan, as it came to be called, proposed scrapping the Articles of Confederation and creating a new national government with the power to make laws binding upon the states and to raise its own money through taxes.

The Virginia Plan proposed that the legislature be divided into two houses. The voters in each state would elect members of the first house. Members of the second house would be nominated by the state governments but actually elected by the first house. In both houses, the number of representatives for each state would reflect that state's population. The Virginia Plan would benefit large states like Virginia, New York, and Massachusetts, which had more votes than the smaller states.

The Virginia Plan drew sharp reactions. The delegates accepted the idea of dividing the government into executive, legislative, and judicial branches, but the smaller states strongly opposed having representation based on population. They feared that larger states would outvote them. William Paterson, a New Jersey delegate, offered a counterproposal that came to be called the New Jersey Plan.

The New Jersey Plan did not abandon the Articles of Confederation. Instead it modified them to make the central government stronger. Under the plan, Congress would have a single house in which each state was equally represented, but it would also have the power to raise taxes and regulate trade.

The delegates had to choose one plan for further negotiation. After debating on June 19, the convention voted to proceed with the Virginia Plan. With this vote, the convention delegates decided to go beyond their original purpose of revising the Articles of Confederation. Instead, they began work on a new constitution for the United States.

Reading Check **Explaining** Why did small states oppose the Virginia Plan?

The Connecticut Compromise

After the convention voted to proceed with the Virginia Plan, tempers flared as delegates from the small states insisted that each state had to have an equal vote in Congress. Angry delegates from the larger states threatened to walk out. By July 1787, the convention had reached a turning point. As a delegate from North Carolina warned, "If we do not concede on both sides, our business must soon end." **W**

R The convention appointed a special committee to negotiate a compromise. Delegates who were strongly committed to one side or the other were left off the committee, leaving only those who were undecided or willing to change their minds. Benjamin Franklin chaired the proceedings.

The compromise the committee worked out was based on an idea proposed by Roger Sherman of Connecticut. Although sometimes called the Connecticut Compromise, it is also known as the **Great Compromise.** The committee proposed that in one house of Congress—the House of Representatives—the states would be represented according to the size of their populations. In the other house—the Senate—each state would have equal representation. Voters in each state would elect the House of Representatives, but the state legislatures would choose the senators.

Interdisciplinary Connection

Mathematics Write the approximate population of the states in 1790 on the board: Connecticut: 238,000; Delaware: 59,000; Maryland: 320,000; Massachusetts: 379,000; New Hampshire: 142,000; New Jersey: 184,000; New York: 340,000; North Carolina: 395,000; Pennsylvania: 434,000; Rhode Island: 69,000; South Carolina: 249,000; and Virginia: 750,000.

Have students compare the populations of the states listed on the board. **Ask:** Which states do you think were most likely to support the Virginia Plan? Why? *(Virginia, North Carolina, Pennsylvania, Maryland, Massachusetts, New York; they had the largest populations, and under the Virginia Plan, representation would be determined by population.)*

People IN HISTORY

James Madison
1751–1836

Although many individuals contributed to the framing of the U.S. Constitution, the master builder was James Madison. In the year preceding the Constitutional Convention, the 36-year-old Virginia planter read volume after volume on political history. "From a spirit of industry and application," said one colleague, Madison was "the best-informed man on any point in debate."

Based on his experience in helping to draft Virginia's constitution, Madison created the Virginia Plan. Perhaps his greatest achievement was in defining the true source of political power. He argued that all power, at all levels of government, flowed ultimately from the people.

At the Convention, Madison served his nation well. The ordeal, he later said, almost killed him. In the years to come, though, the nation would call on him again. In 1801 he became President Thomas Jefferson's secretary of state. In 1808 he was elected the fourth president of the United States.

How did Madison contribute to the drafting of the U.S. Constitution?

Roger Sherman
1721–1793

Roger Sherman was born in Massachusetts but in 1743 moved to Connecticut, where he studied law and eventually became a superior court judge. Sherman was enormously respected for his knowledge, judgment, and integrity. He was a delegate to the Continental Congress and was a member of the group who drafted the Declaration of Independence. He also helped to write the Articles of Confederation.

A skilled legislator and master of political compromise, Sherman was a logical choice to serve as one of Connecticut's delegates to the Constitutional Convention. There, he ably defended the interests of the smaller states and developed the famous Connecticut Compromise that saved the convention from breaking up. Sherman was elected to the House of Representatives, where he helped to prepare the Bill of Rights. He is the only person to have signed the Declaration of Independence, the Articles of Confederation, and the Constitution—and he played an important role in drafting all three.

Why do you think that Sherman is not as well-known as some other Founders?

Compromise Over Slavery

Franklin's committee also proposed that each state could elect one member to the House of Representatives for every 40,000 people in the state. This caused a split between Northern and Southern delegates. Southern delegates wanted to count enslaved people when determining how many representatives they could elect. Northern delegates objected, pointing out that the enslaved could not vote.

Northern delegates also suggested that if slaves were counted for representation, they should be counted for purposes of taxation as well. In the end, a solution, referred to as the **Three-Fifths Compromise,** was worked out. Every five enslaved people would count as three free people for determining both representation and taxes.

The dispute over how to count enslaved people was not the only issue dividing North and South. Southerners feared that a strong national government might impose taxes on the export of farm products or ban the import of enslaved Africans. The Southern delegates insisted that the new constitution forbid interference with the slave trade and limit Congress's power to regulate trade. Northern delegates, on the other hand, knew that Northern merchants and artisans needed a government capable of controlling foreign imports into the United States.

Eventually, another compromise was worked out. The delegates agreed that the new Congress could not tax exports. They also agreed that it could not ban the slave trade until 1808 or impose high taxes on the importation of slaves. The Great Compromise and the compromises between Northern and Southern delegates ended most of the major disputes between the state delegations. This enabled the convention to focus on the details of how the new government would operate.

By mid-September, the delegates had completed their task. Although everyone made compromises, the 39 delegates who signed the new Constitution believed it was a vast improvement over the Articles of Confederation. On September 20, they sent it to the Congress for approval. Eight days later, the Congress voted to submit the Constitution to the states for approval. The Constitution specified that nine of the thirteen states had to ratify the Constitution for it to take effect.

Reading Check **Describing** What was the Three-Fifths Compromise, and why was it necessary?

People IN HISTORY

James Madison

Answer:
He did a great deal of research on political history beforehand, so he was able to provide information on various points during the discussions. He drafted the Virginia Plan.

Roger Sherman

Answer:
Students may suggest that Sherman is less well known because he did not become president.

Reading Check

Answer:
It was a compromise between free states and slave-holding states in which each five enslaved people would be equal, for purpose of representation and taxation, to three free people. At the time, it was necessary to continue the work of the Convention and prevent the nation from splitting apart.

Additional Support

Extending the Content

James Madison and Roger Sherman each contributed powerful ideas to the Constitutional Convention. The two men, however, had very different backgrounds. Madison was highly educated but unsure what profession to follow. He considered the law, but had no taste for it. Sherman, on the other hand, did not receive a formal education, as his family did not have the means to send him to college. He worked on his father's farm and also learned the shoe making trade from him. Eventually he turned his attention to law, and after he was admitted to the bar he rose rapidly in a professional career.

D1 Differentiated Instruction

Visual/Spatial Have students create a diagram that shows the powers granted to each branch of government and how each branch can limit the power of the other two branches. **BL** **ELL**

D2 Differentiated Instruction

English Learners Some English learners may have trouble with the difficult vocabulary and dense summary of information in this chart. Suggest that students work together to write sentences linking each pair of facts portrayed on the chart. **BL**

Analyzing VISUALS

Answers:

1. Members of the Congress were appointed by state legislatures annually; members of the House of Representatives are elected by voters every two years.
2. It gave the federal government the power over the states to regulate interstate and foreign trade.

A Framework for Limited Government

MAIN Idea The Framers created a federal system that provided for a separation of powers along with checks and balances to keep any one branch of government from becoming too powerful.

HISTORY AND YOU Can you think of situations when dividing responsibilities makes it harder to get things done? Read to learn why the Framers created checks and balances.

The new constitution that the states were considering was based on the idea of **popular sovereignty,** or rule by the people. Rather than a direct democracy, it created a representative system of government in which elected officials represented the voice of the people. The new constitution also established a **federal** system. It divided government power between the federal, or national, government and the state governments.

D1 The United States Constitution provides for a **separation of powers** among the three branches of the federal government. The two houses of Congress compose the legislative branch of the government. They make the laws. The executive branch, headed by a president, implements and enforces the laws passed by Congress. The judicial branch—a system of

INFOGRAPHIC
Comparing Constitutions

D2

The Articles of Confederation		The Federal Constitution
One—the Congress	**How Many Houses in the Legislature?**	Two—the House of Representatives and the Senate
Members of Congress appointed annually by state legislatures	**How Are Delegates Chosen?**	Representatives elected every two years by voters; senators originally chosen by state legislatures for a six-year term (today voters elect senators as well)
No separate executive; members of the Congress elect a president annually; government departments are run by committees created by the Congress	**How Is Executive Power Exercised?**	Separate executive branch; president elected every four years by Electoral College; president conducts policy, selects officers to run government departments, appoints ambassadors and judges
Judicial matters left to the states and local courts; the Congress acts as a court for disputes between states	**How Is Judicial Power Exercised?**	Separate judicial branch with a Supreme Court and lower courts created by Congress; judges appointed by the president but confirmed by the Senate
Only states can levy taxes	**What Taxes Can Be Levied?**	Federal government can levy taxes
The Congress regulated foreign trade but had no power to regulate interstate trade	**Can Trade Be Regulated?**	Federal government regulates both interstate commerce and foreign commerce

Analyzing VISUALS

1. **Contrasting** How was the election of members of the House of Representatives different from the election of members of the Congress?
2. **Evaluating** How did the Constitution solve the problems experienced under the Articles with interstate and foreign trade?

Differentiated Instruction

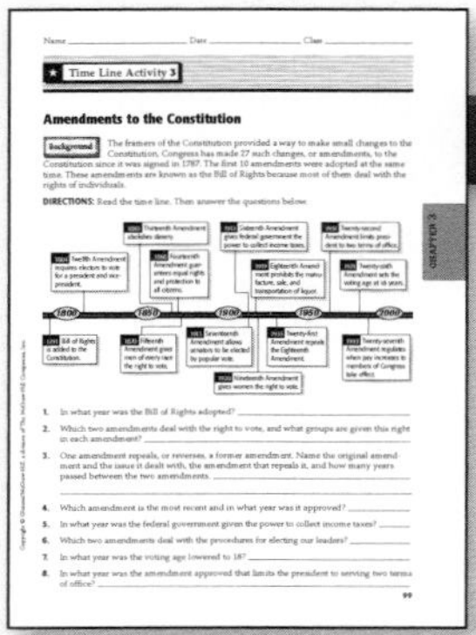

Time Line Activity 3, URB p. 99

Evaluating Information: Changing the Constitution

Objective: Evaluate the process followed to amend the U.S. Constitution.

Focus: Identify amendments to the Constitution.

Teach: Discuss the process of amending the Constitution. Draw a diagram or flow chart to visualize the process.

Assess: Make a list of the pros and cons of the amendment process.

Close: Write a paragraph stating whether you agree or disagree with the amendment.

Differentiated Instruction Strategies

BL With a partner, write a few sentences that describe the amendment process.

AL Research a more recent amendment or one that failed to be ratified. Give a brief presentation that includes the reasons the amendment passed or failed.

ELL Make a chart or poster illustrating the amendment process. Be sure to label each step clearly.

federal courts—interprets federal laws and renders judgment in cases involving those laws. No one serving in one branch can serve in any other branch at the same time.

Checks and Balances

In addition to separating the powers of the government into three branches, the delegates to the convention created a system of **checks and balances** to prevent any one of the three branches from becoming too powerful. Within this system, each branch has some ability to limit the power of the other branches.

Under the Constitution, the president—as head of the executive branch—is given far-reaching powers. The president can propose legislation, appoint judges, put down rebellions, and **veto,** or reject, acts of Congress. The president is also the commander in chief of the armed forces. According to one delegate in Philadelphia, these powers might not have been so great "had not many of the members cast their eyes towards George Washington as president."

Although the president can veto acts of Congress, the legislature can override a veto with a two-thirds vote in both houses. The Senate also has to approve or reject presidential appointments to the executive branch as well as any treaties. Furthermore, Congress can, if necessary, impeach, or formally accuse of misconduct, and then remove the president or other high officials.

Members of the judicial branch of government can hear all cases arising under federal law and the Constitution. The powers of the judiciary are balanced by the other two branches. The president can nominate members of the judiciary, but the Senate has to confirm or reject such nominations. Once appointed, however, federal judges serve for life, thus ensuring their independence from both the executive and the legislative branches.

Amending the Constitution

The delegates in Philadelphia recognized that the new constitution might need to be amended, or changed over time. To ensure this, they created a clear system for making **amendments,** or changes. To prevent the constitution from being changed constantly, they made the process difficult.

The amendment process had two steps—proposal and ratification. An amendment could be proposed by a vote of two-thirds of the members of both houses of Congress. Alternatively, two-thirds of the states could call a constitutional convention to propose new amendments. The proposed amendment then had to be ratified by three-fourths of the state legislatures or by conventions in three-fourths of the states. R

The success of the Philadelphia Convention in creating a government that reflected the country's many different viewpoints was, in Washington's words, "little short of a miracle." The convention, John Adams declared, was "the single greatest effort of national deliberation that the world has ever seen."

Reading Check **Explaining** How is power divided under the system of federalism?

Section 2 REVIEW

Vocabulary

1. **Explain** the significance of: James Madison, Great Compromise, Three-Fifths Compromise, popular sovereignty, federalism, separation of powers, checks and balances, veto, amendment.

Main Ideas

2. **Contrasting** How did the New Jersey Plan differ from the Virginia Plan?
3. **Explaining** How did the Great Compromise meet the needs of both large and small states?
4. **Identifying** What provision did the Framers make in the Constitution to limit the powers of each branch of the government?

Critical Thinking

5. **Big Ideas** How did the Constitution uphold the rights of the states while strengthening the national government?
6. **Organizing** Use a graphic organizer to list the compromises that the Framers reached in creating the new Constitution.

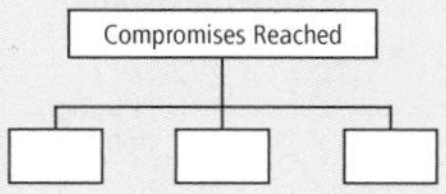

7. **Analyzing Visuals** Study the chart on page 108. What was significant about the fact that the federal government under the new Constitution could now levy taxes?

Writing About History

8. **Descriptive Writing** Imagine you are at the Constitutional Convention. Write a journal entry describing the arguments from each side as well as your own opinion on them.

History ONLINE
Study Central™ To review this section, go to glencoe.com and click on Study Central.

109

R Reading Strategy

Summarizing Ask: How can the Constitution be amended? *(Two-thirds of both houses of Congress can propose an amendment, or two-thirds of the states can call a convention; the amendment must be ratified by three-fourths of the state legislatures or state conventions.)* **OL**

Reading Check

Answer:
Power is divided between the national government and the state governments.

Assess

History ONLINE

Study Central™ provides summaries, interactive games, and online graphic organizers to help students review content.

Close

Summarizing Ask: What issues did delegates to the convention consider? *(representation, balance of power, checks and balances)* **OL**

Section 2 REVIEW

Answers

1. All definitions can be found in the section and the Glossary.
2. New Jersey Plan: Congress consists of single house with each state equally represented; Virginia Plan: Congress divided into two houses, state representation in both houses based on population.
3. It created two houses—the House of Representatives, based on population, which satisfied the large states, and the Senate, based on equal representation, which satisfied the small states.
4. They included a system of checks and balances to limit the power of each branch of government.
5. It gave more power to the national government than had existed under the Articles of Confederation. At the same time, it established a representative government. The system is also a federal system, so power is shared between the states and the national government.
6. Connecticut or Great Compromise, Three-Fifths Compromise, compromises on Congress's powers to tax trade
7. Under the Articles, the national government could not levy taxes, so it had no way to raise the substantial revenue needed to run the government and pay for things such as an army and navy to execute its laws. Under the Constitution, it now could raise taxes and fund itself.
8. Students' journal entries should include events and issues discussed in the section.

Focus

Bellringer

Daily Focus Transparency 3-3

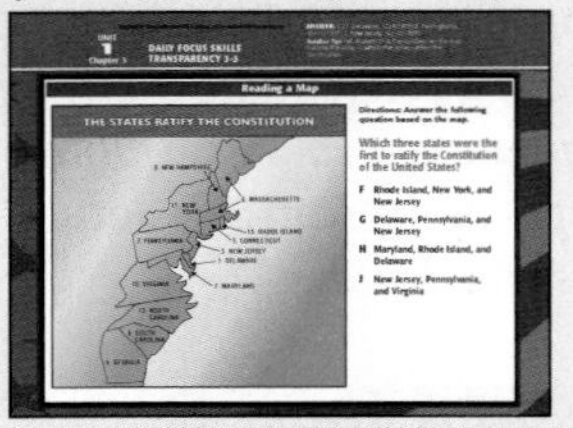

Guide to Reading

Federalists' supporters: large landowners, merchants, artisans, coastal farmers;	**Anti-Federalists' supporters: western farmers, those who wanted a bill of rights;**
goal: federal system that divided power between an effective national government and the states; a strong central government that could regulate trade consistently	**goal: national government with limited powers and a bill of rights**

Section Spotlight Video

To generate student interest and provide a springboard for class discussion, access the Chapter 3, Section 3 video at glencoe.com or on the video DVD.

 Section Audio Spotlight Video

Ratifying the Constitution

Guide to Reading

Big Ideas

Government and Society
Ratification of the Constitution moved to the states, where Federalists and Anti-Federalists argued their opposing views.

Content Vocabulary
- bill of rights *(p. 113)*

Academic Vocabulary
- framework *(p. 112)*
- specific *(p. 113)*

People and Events to Identify
- Federalist *(p. 110)*
- Anti-Federalist *(p. 111)*
- John Hancock *(p. 111)*
- Patrick Henry *(p. 111)*

Reading Strategy
Complete a graphic organizer similar to the one below by listing the supporters and goals of the Federalists and Anti-Federalists.

	Federalists	Anti-Federalists
Source of Support		
Goals		

Once the work of the Constitutional Convention was complete, the campaign for ratification began. Each state elected delegates to a convention to vote on the new framework of government. Nine of the thirteen states had to ratify it to put it into effect.

A Great Debate

MAIN Idea Federalists supported the Constitution, but Anti-Federalists thought it endangered states' independence and gave the national government too much power.

HISTORY AND YOU Has a political advertisement ever changed your mind on an issue? Read on to learn about the tactics used by Federalists to promote their cause.

As soon as the Philadelphia Convention ended, delegates rushed home to begin the campaign for ratification. Each state would elect a convention to vote on the new constitution. Nine states had to vote for the Constitution to put it into effect. As Americans learned about the new Constitution, they began to argue over whether it should be ratified. The debate took place in state legislatures, in mass meetings, in the columns of newspapers, and in everyday conversations.

Federalists and Anti-Federalists

Supporters of the Constitution called themselves **Federalists.** The name was chosen with care. It emphasized that the Constitution would create a federal system. They believed that power should be divided between a central government and regional governments. They hoped the name would remind Americans who feared a central government that the states would retain many of their powers.

Supporters of the Federalists and the new Constitution included large landowners who wanted the property protection a strong central government could provide. Supporters also included merchants and artisans living in large coastal cities. The inability of the Congress to regulate trade had hit these citizens hard. They believed that an effective federal government that could impose taxes on foreign goods would help their businesses.

Many farmers who lived near the coast or along rivers that led to the coast also supported the Constitution, as did farmers who shipped goods across state borders. These farmers depended on trade for their livelihood and had been frustrated by the different tariffs and duties the states imposed. They wanted a strong central government that could regulate trade consistently.

Resource Manager

R Reading Strategies	C Critical Thinking	D Differentiated Instruction	W Writing Support	S Skill Practice
Teacher Edition • Reading Graphs, p. 111 • Sequencing, p. 115 **Additional Resources** • Guide Read Act., URB p. 114	**Teacher Edition** • Making Inferences, p. 112 • Making Connections, p. 114 **Additional Resources** • Critical Thinking Skills Act., URB p. 98 • Interp. Political Cartoons, URB p. 107 • Quizzes and Tests, p. 33	**Teacher Edition** • English Learners, p. 113 • Advanced Learners, p. 114	**Teacher Edition** • Persuasive Writing, p. 112	**Additional Resources** • Historical Skills Analysis, URB p. 88 • Read. Essen., p. 35

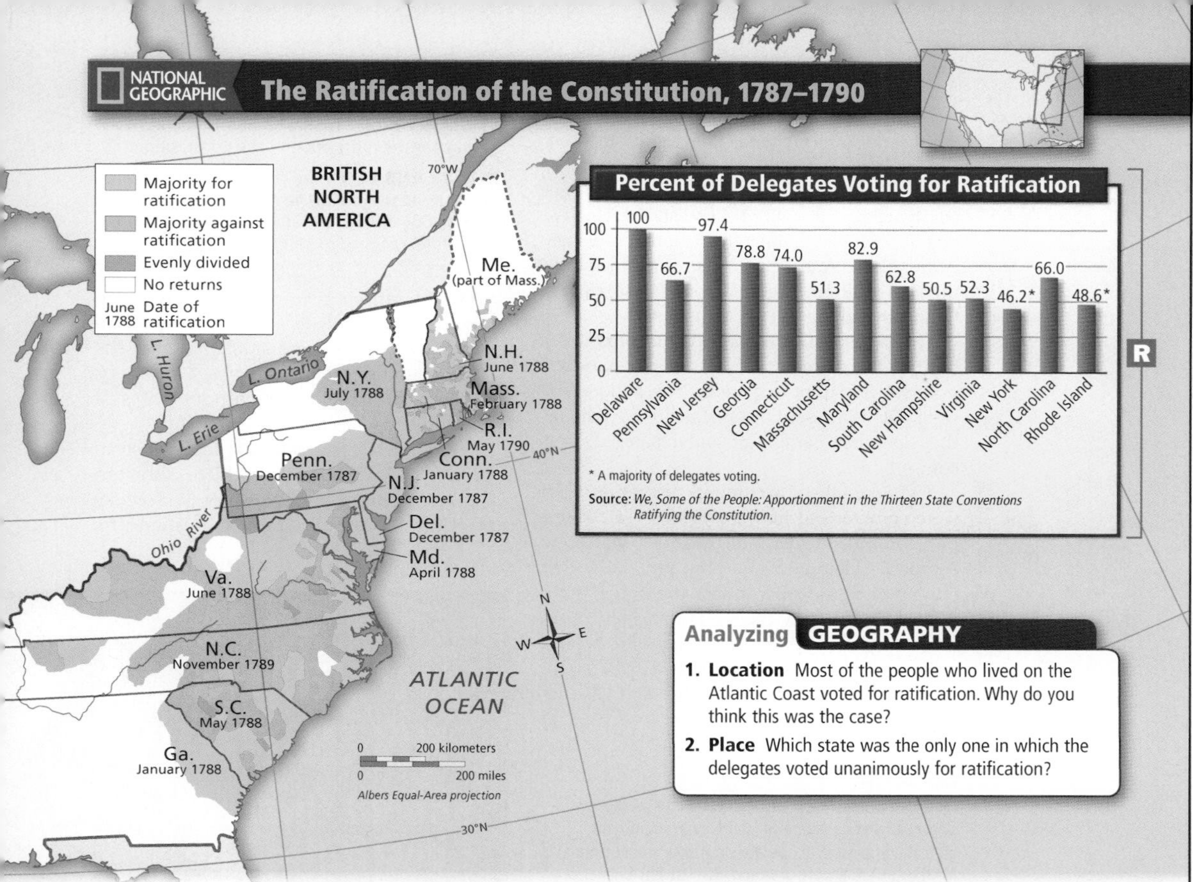

Analyzing GEOGRAPHY

1. **Location** Most of the people who lived on the Atlantic Coast voted for ratification. Why do you think this was the case?
2. **Place** Which state was the only one in which the delegates voted unanimously for ratification?

Opponents of the Constitution were called **Anti-Federalists,** a misleading name, as they were not against federalism. They accepted the need for a national government. The real issue for them was whether the national government or the state governments would be supreme. Prominent Anti-Federalists included **John Hancock, Patrick Henry,** Richard Henry Lee of Virginia, and George Clinton, governor of New York. Two members of the Constitutional Convention, Edmund Randolph and George Mason, became Anti-Federalists because they believed the new Constitution should have included a bill of rights. Sam Adams agreed. He opposed the Constitution because he believed it endangered the independence of the states.

Many Anti-Federalists were western farmers living far from the coast. These people considered themselves self-sufficient and were suspicious of the wealthy and powerful. Many of them were also deeply in debt and suspected that the new Constitution was simply a way for wealthy creditors to get rid of paper money and foreclose on their farms. A farmer named Amos Singletary expressed views shared by many western farmers:

PRIMARY SOURCE

"These lawyers and men of learning, and moneyed men, that talk so finely, and gloss over matters so smoothly, to make us poor, illiterate people swallow down the pill, expect to get into Congress themselves; they expect to be managers of this Constitution, and get all the power and all the money into their own hands, and then they will swallow up all us little folks. . . ."

—*The Massachusetts Gazette,* February 15, 1788

Teach

R Reading Strategy

Reading Graphs Ask: How many states had more than 50 percent of delegates vote for ratification? Which states had the most support for ratification? *(11; Delaware, New Jersey, and Maryland)* BL

Analyzing GEOGRAPHY

Answers:

1. Most people there were probably merchants or other business people who wanted a strong national government to control trade.
2. Delaware

Additional Support

Activity: Technology Connection

Creating a Demographic Database Have students use library or Internet resources to find more demographic information about Americans in various states during this period, such as statistics about population, occupation, education, newspaper circulation, and so on. Then have them use graphic design software to create bar graphs and other visual representations of the data they acquire. Students with access to page-making software may create a booklet with both text and graphics. OL

W Writing Support

Persuasive Writing Have students read James Madison's essay No. 10 from *The Federalist Papers.* One of his most famous and important essays, it discusses the danger posed by factions to a stable government. Next, have students write a letter to James Madison, explaining why they do or do not agree with his philosophy. Suggest that they incorporate examples from present-day political circumstances and conflicts to support their point of view. AL

C Critical Thinking

Making Inferences Ask: About what kinds of issues might the present-day judiciary consult the Constitution, even though the Framers of the Constitution did not address those issues directly? *(Possible answers: gun control, separation of church and state in education, capital punishment)* AL

Reading Check

Answer:
large landowners, merchants, artisans, and farmers who exported crops

Additional Support

The Federalist

For excerpts from *Federalist 10, Federalist 51,* and *Federalist 59,* see pages R44–R45 in **Documents in American History.**

Although many influential leaders in the young nation opposed the newly drafted Constitution, several factors worked against the Anti-Federalists. First of all, their campaign was a negative one. The Federalists presented a definite program to meet the nation's problems. Although the Anti-Federalists complained that the Constitution failed to protect basic rights, they had nothing to offer in its place.

The Federalists were also better organized than their opponents. Most of the nation's newspapers supported them. The Federalists were able to present a very convincing case in their speeches, pamphlets, and debates in state conventions.

W The Federalists' arguments for ratification were summarized in *The Federalist*—a collection of 85 essays written by James Madison, Alexander Hamilton, and John Jay. Under the joint pen name of Publius, the three men published most of the essays in New York newspapers in late 1787 and early 1788 before collecting them in *The Federalist.* Federalist No. 1, the first essay in the series, tried to set the **framework** for the debate:

PRIMARY SOURCE

"After an unequivocal experience of the inefficacy of the subsisting Foederal [sic] Government, you are called upon to deliberate on a new Constitution for the United States of America. . . . It has been frequently remarked that it seems to have been reserved to the people of this country, by their conduct and example, to decide the important question, whether societies of men are really capable or not of establishing good government from reflection and choice, or whether they are forever destined to depend for their political constitutions on accident and force."

—from *The Independent Journal,* October 27, 1787

C The essays explained how the new Constitution worked and why it was needed. The essays were very influential. Even today, judges, lawyers, legislators, and historians rely upon *The Federalist* to help them interpret the Constitution and understand what the original Framers intended.

Reading Check **Summarizing** Which groups of people in the United States tended to support the new Constitution?

Battle for Ratification

MAIN Idea The promise of a Bill of Rights paved the way for the ratification of the Constitution.

HISTORY AND YOU Have you ever had to convince a friend to do something? Read on to learn why some states quickly decided to ratify the Constitution, but others states required more convincing.

As the ratifying conventions began to gather, the Federalists knew that they had clear majorities in some states but that the vote was going to be much closer in others, including the large and important states of Massachusetts, Virginia, and New York.

The first state conventions took place in December 1787 and January 1788. Although Delaware, Pennsylvania, New Jersey, Georgia, and Connecticut all quickly ratified the

Debates IN HISTORY

Should the Federal Constitution Be Ratified?

The debate over ratification of the Constitution was often heated. Many important figures of the time, such as Patrick Henry, were concerned about the loss of state power and the fact that the Constitution did not mention protections of civil liberties. Others, such as James Madison, were convinced that only a strong federal government would protect people's liberties and ensure the success of the new United States of America.

Extending the Content

The Federalist Papers One of the most famous of the Federalist Papers, No. 78, written by Alexander Hamilton, addresses the issue of judicial power:

> "The interpretation of the laws is the proper and peculiar province of the courts. A constitution is in fact, and must be, regarded by the judges, as a fundamental law. It therefore belongs to them to ascertain its meaning as well as the meaning of any particular act proceeding from the legislative body."

Hamilton and others supported this position, but the Constitution does not specifically give the Supreme Court judicial review—the power to review federal and state laws to determine whether or not they are constitutional. Judicial review was established definitively in the 1803 Supreme Court decision in *Marbury* v. *Madison,* when the Supreme Court declared an act of Congress to be unconstitutional, thus placing an additional check on the legislative branch. (Another check, from the executive branch, is the presidential veto.)

Constitution, the most important battles still lay ahead.

The Debate in Massachusetts

In Massachusetts, opponents of the Constitution held a clear majority when the convention met in January 1788. Among the opponents were Massachusetts Governor John Hancock and Samuel Adams, both of whom had signed the Declaration of Independence. Adams refused to support the new Constitution unless Federalists could give him a guarantee "that the said Constitution be never construed to authorize Congress to infringe the just liberty of the press, or the rights of conscience; or to prevent the people of the United States . . . from keeping their own arms; . . . or to subject the people to unreasonable searches and seizures of their persons, papers or possessions."

Federalists moved quickly to meet Adams's objections to the Constitution. **Specifically,** Federalists promised to attach a **bill of rights** to the Constitution once it was ratified. Federalists also agreed to support an amendment that would reserve for the states all powers not specifically granted to the federal government.

These concessions, combined with most artisans siding with the Federalists, persuaded Adams to vote for ratification. John Hancock and his supporters were won over by hints from local Federalists that they would support him for president of the United States. In the final vote, 187 members of the convention voted in favor of the Constitution, while 168 voted against it.

YES

James Madison
Delegate to the Constitutional Convention

PRIMARY SOURCE

"In a single republic . . . usurpations are guarded against by a division of the government into distinct and separate departments. In the compound republic of America, the power surrendered by the people, is first divided between two distinct governments, and then the portion allotted to each, subdivided among the rights of the people. The different governments will controul [sic] each other; at the same time that each will be controuled [sic] by itself. . . .

In the extended republic of the United States, and among the great variety of interests, parties and sects which it embraces, a coalition of a majority of the whole society could seldom take place on any other principles than those of justice and the general good."

—from *Federalist No. 51*

NO

Patrick Henry
Member of the Virginia Ratifying Convention

PRIMARY SOURCE

"This proposal of altering our federal government is of a most alarming nature: make the best of this new government—say it is composed by anything but inspiration—you ought to be extremely cautious, watchful, jealous of your liberty; for instead of securing your rights, you may lose them forever. . . . My political curiosity . . . leads me to ask, who authorized [the Framers] to speak the language of *We, the People*, instead of *We, the States*? States are the characteristics, and the soul of a confederation. If the states be not the agents of this compact, it must be one great consolidated national government, of the people of all the states."

—from *The Debates in the Several State Conventions on the Adoption of the Federal Constitution*

D

DBQ Document-Based Questions

1. **Summarizing** According to Madison, how is power to be divided under the Constitution?
2. **Explaining** According to Henry, why should people be cautious about the new national government?
3. **Identifying Points of View** How do Madison and Henry disagree over the role of the states in the federal republic?

D Differentiated Instruction

English Learners Tell students that the English used in the late 1700s is difficult for many modern readers to understand. Have students work in pairs to define unknown vocabulary by using a dictionary and locating context clues. Then have them identify the beginning and ending of each complete thought, as well as the subject and verb of each clause. Ask them to restate each clause in contemporary speech. **BL** **ELL**

Debates IN HISTORY

Answers:

1. It is divided between the national government, the state governments, and the people.
2. Because the new Constitution takes power away from the states, Henry feels that it jeopardizes people's freedoms.
3. Henry feels that more power should be retained by the states than Madison does.

Hands-On Chapter Project
Step 3

Designing a Film Treatment

Step 3: Complete the Film Treatment Students will put the finishing touches on their film treatment.

Directions Have each group member display and describe his or her contribution. At this point, all members of the group should see sketches, the storyboard, and outline, and provide their summaries of details such as music, sound effects, and location. Have them agree upon a title for their film.

Putting It Together Ask students to describe which parts of the film treatment they think are strongest and which need to be expanded, revised, or cut. More research might be necessary to flesh out certain scenes. **OL**

(Chapter Project continued on Visual Summary page)

D Differentiated Instruction

Advanced Learners Ask students to select an event or issue in this section and draw a political cartoon to illustrate it. Then have students share their cartoons and solicit constructive feedback **AL**

C Critical Thinking

Making Connections Ask: As a delegate at your state's ratification convention who was disappointed by the convention's vote, what recourse might you have to change the Constitution to be more to your liking? *(You could propose an amendment to the Constitution and work toward its ratification.)* **OL**

Analyzing VISUALS

Answers:

1. Hamilton was a New Yorker and a major promoter of the Constitution.
2. New York is being added, North Carolina and Rhode Island are about to be added.

Additional Support

The Debate in Virginia

By the end of June 1788, Maryland, South Carolina, and New Hampshire had ratified the Constitution. The Federalists had reached the minimum number of states required to put the new Constitution into effect, but Virginia and New York still had not ratified. Without the support of these two large states, many feared the new government would not succeed.

Patrick Henry, Richard Henry Lee, George Mason, and other Anti-Federalists argued strongly against ratification. George Mason raised an argument similar to the one Sam Adams had made in Massachusetts:

PRIMARY SOURCE

"... the State Legislatures have no Security for the Powers now presumed to remain to them; or the People for their Rights. There is no Declaration of any kind, for preserving the Liberty of the Press, or the [trial] by Jury in civil [causes]; nor against the Danger of standing [armies] in time of Peace."

—George Mason, from "Objections to This Constitution of Government," 1787

C George Washington and James Madison presented the arguments for ratification to the Virginia convention. In the end, Madison's promise to add a bill of rights won the day for the Federalists. Upon hearing the proposal for a bill of rights, Virginia Governor Edmund Randolph agreed to support the new Constitution. Randolph had attended the Constitutional Convention but had refused to sign the final document, worried that it lacked sufficient protections of the people's rights. His decision to change sides convinced others to change their votes as well. The Virginia convention voted narrowly for the new Constitution, 89 in favor and 79 against.

PRIMARY SOURCE
Ratifying the Constitution

▲ *On July 26, 1788, New Yorkers celebrated the ratification of the Constitution.*

D

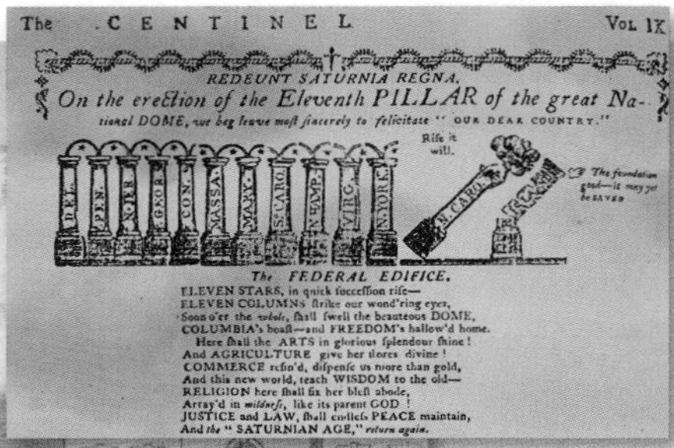

▲ *This famous cartoon published in 1788 in the Massachusetts* Centinel *depicts the states as pillars creating the federal "edifice," or government.*

Analyzing VISUALS

1. **Explaining** Why do you think a float in this parade was named for Hamilton?
2. **Specifying** Which is the last "pillar" shown being added to the federal "edifice"?

Activity: Collaborative Learning

Creating a Newspaper Editorial Divide the class into groups. Have each group review the arguments of the Federalists and Anti-Federalists about the Constitution. Have each group write a newspaper editorial that might have been published during that time, either supporting or opposing the Constitution. Groups can write their editorials from the viewpoint of one of the colonists, such as a western farmer, a merchant in a coastal city, or a large landowner.

New York Votes to Ratify

In New York, two-thirds of the members elected to the state convention, including New York Governor George Clinton, were Anti-Federalists. During the debate over ratification, the Federalists, led by Alexander Hamilton and John Jay, repeatedly tried to assure the Anti-Federalists that the new federal government would pose no threat to liberty. Hamilton stressed that the new constitution had been specifically designed to limit the growth of tyranny:

PRIMARY SOURCE

"On whatever side we view this subject, we discover various and powerful checks to the encroachments of Congress. The true and permanent interests of the members are opposed to corruption. Their number is vastly too large for easy combination. The rivalship between the houses will forever prove an insuperable obstacle. The people have an obvious and powerful protection in their state governments. Should any thing dangerous be attempted, these bodies of perpetual observation will be capable of forming and conducting plans of regular opposition."

—from "Speech Urging Ratification of the Constitution by New York State, 1788"

The Federalists managed to delay the final vote until news arrived that New Hampshire and Virginia had both ratified the Constitution and that the new federal government was now in effect. If New York refused to ratify, it would be in a very awkward position. It would have to operate independently of all of the surrounding states. Soon after, delegates from New York City warned that the city would secede from the state of New York and join the United States independently if the new Constitution was not ratified. These arguments convinced enough Anti-Federalists to change sides. The vote was very close, 30 to 27, but the Federalists won.

By July 1788, all the states except Rhode Island and North Carolina had ratified the Constitution. Because ratification by nine states was all that the Constitution required, the new government could be launched without them. In mid-September 1788, the Congress established a timetable for the election of the new government. It chose March 4, 1789, as the date for the first meeting of the new Congress.

The two states that had held out finally ratified the Constitution after the new government was in place. North Carolina waited until a bill of rights had actually been proposed, then voted to ratify the Constitution in November 1789. Rhode Island, still nervous about losing its independence, did not ratify the Constitution until May 1790, and even then the vote was very close—34 to 32.

R The United States now had a new government, but no one knew if the new Constitution would work any better than the Articles had. With both anticipation and nervousness, the American people waited for their new government to begin. Many expressed great confidence, because George Washington was the first president under the new Constitution.

Reading Check **Examining** Why was it important for Virginia and New York to ratify the Constitution, even after the required nine states had done so?

Section 3 REVIEW

Vocabulary

1. **Explain** the significance of: Federalist, Anti-Federalist, John Hancock, Patrick Henry, bill of rights.

Main Ideas

2. **Explaining** What did supporters of the Constitution hope to achieve with the selection of the name *Federalists*?
3. **Identifying** What two promises did Federalists make to win the support of those who initially opposed the Constitution?

Critical Thinking

4. **Big Ideas** Do you think it was important for all the states to ratify the Constitution? Why or why not?
5. **Organizing** Use a graphic organizer similar to the one below to list the factors that worked against the Anti-Federalists.

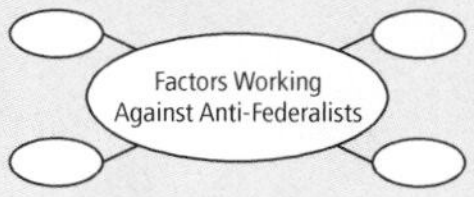

6. **Analyzing Visuals** Study the cartoon on page 114. The Latin phrase at the top means "a return to the Age of Saturn," or a golden age. Why do you think that phrase was included in this cartoon?

Writing About History

7. **Persuasive Writing** Take on the role of a Federalist or an Anti-Federalist at a state ratifying convention. Write a speech in which you try to convince your audience to either accept or reject the new Constitution.

History ONLINE
Study Central™ To review this section, go to glencoe.com and click on Study Central.

R Reading Strategy

Sequencing Information

Have students create an annotated time line of the battle for ratification, beginning in December 1787 and ending in May 1790. OL

Reading Check

Answer:
They were large, populous states.

Assess

History ONLINE

Study Central™ provides summaries, interactive games, and online graphic organizers to help students review content.

Close

Summarizing Ask: What concerns did opponents of ratification have? *(They worried that the national government might become too powerful and dominate the states, and that the Constitution did not contain a bill of rights.)* OL

Section 3 REVIEW

Answers

1. All definitions can be found in the section and the Glossary.
2. They wanted to remind Americans who worried about the consequences of a strong national government that power would be shared with the states, and that the states would retain many of their powers.
3. They promised to add a bill of rights and an amendment that would reserve for the states all powers not specifically granted to the federal government.
4. Students should offer a logical opinion, supported by evidence in the text.
5. negative campaign, not well organized, did not have support of newspapers, probably were not as wealthy as the Federalists
6. Answers will vary, but students should recognize that the phrase is propaganda used by Federalists to promote ratification of the Constitution. Students may make the connection between the classical pillars and the "golden age" of the republics of the ancient world.
7. Students' speeches will vary but should address the concerns of their audience.

Determining Cause and Effect To review the material, have students complete a cause-and-effect chain about key events described in this chapter. For example, the first cause might be the Congress's need to raise money, the effect of which was the passage of the Land Ordinance of 1785. **OL**

Predicting Consequences
Ask: How would life in the United States today be different if it were governed under the Articles of Confederation or a similar document instead of the Constitution? *(Possible answer: Without a strong national government, it would be difficult to create and regulate services such as transportation, health care, and so on. None of these services could be paid for without taxation. Without a strong executive branch, it might be difficult to enforce international treaties. Without a judicial branch, justice would vary from state to state, and there would be little or no protection for individuals.)* **OL**

Chapter 3 Visual Summary

STUDY TO GO — You can study anywhere, anytime by downloading quizzes and flashcards to your PDA from glencoe.com.

The Articles of Confederation

Weaknesses

- No power to regulate commerce
- No power to compel states to obey international treaties signed by the Congress
- No power to tax
- No power to print or coin money

Effects

- States impose trade restrictions and tariffs on each other's goods
- States restrict Britain's ability to collect debts from Americans; Congress cannot reach a financial settlement with Britain; Britain refuses to evacuate forts on American soil
- Spain denies Americans permission to deposit goods at mouth of Mississippi; Congress has no leverage to force Spain to negotiate
- States issue money, inflation makes the currency worthless; debt problems lead to rebellion in Massachusetts and riots in Rhode Island

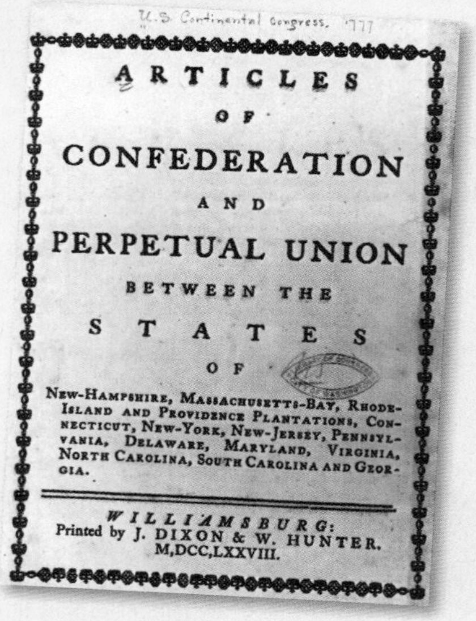
ARTICLES OF CONFEDERATION AND PERPETUAL UNION BETWEEN THE STATES OF NEW-HAMPSHIRE, MASSACHUSETTS-BAY, RHODE-ISLAND AND PROVIDENCE PLANTATIONS, CONNECTICUT, NEW-YORK, NEW-JERSEY, PENNSYLVANIA, DELAWARE, MARYLAND, VIRGINIA, NORTH CAROLINA, SOUTH CAROLINA AND GEORGIA.

WILLIAMSBURG:
Printed by J. DIXON & W. HUNTER.
M,DCC,LXXVIII.

▲ *The Articles of Confederation*

◀ *George Washington headed the Constitutional Convention that drafted a new plan of government.*

▼ *Many Americans celebrated the ratification of the new Constitution and hoped for greater stability and less chaos.*

The Federal Constitution

Decisions at the Constitutional Convention

- New Jersey Plan to amend the Articles of Confederation is rejected
- Virginia Plan to create a federal Constitution is approved
- Connecticut Compromise (Great Compromise) gets both small and large states to support the constitution: Congress will have House of Representatives elected by the people and a Senate, whose members are chosen by the states, and each state has equal representation
- Three-Fifths Compromise gets Southern and Northern states to support the constitution: enslaved people will count as three-fifths of a free person for determining representation in Congress and taxes owed

Checks and Balances of the Federal Constitution

- Federal government has three branches: executive (headed by a president), legislative (Congress), and judicial
- President can veto laws but Congress can override a veto
- President commands the military; Congress votes all funds and taxes
- President selects his cabinet and nominates judges, but the Senate must approve the nominations
- Congress can impeach the president and judges and remove them from office
- To get the Constitution ratified, supporters also promised to add a bill of rights (Amendments 1–10) to further limit federal power

Hands-On Chapter Project
Step 4: Wrap-Up

Designing a Film Treatment

Step 4: Make a Pitch to a Producer Students will synthesize what they have learned in Steps 1, 2, and 3 by pitching their film treatment to a producer.

Directions Write the Essential Question on the board and have students evaluate how well they have answered this question in their film treatment. Ask volunteers from each group to discuss the most interesting and most challenging elements of the project and describe the choices the group made to address these elements.

Putting It Together Have one group member assume the role of a film producer. He or she should ask questions, make suggestions, interview each contributor, and evaluate the pitch. **OL**

Reviewing Vocabulary

Directions: Choose the word or words that best complete the sentence.

1. Under the Articles of Confederation, each state could set a ________ on goods it imported.
- **A** recession
- **B** duty
- **C** stamp
- **D** bounty

2. The U.S. Constitution was based on the concept of dividing governmental powers between the national and state governments, which was called
- **A** nationalism.
- **B** mutualism.
- **C** popular sovereignty.
- **D** federalism.

3. The presidential power of the ________ checks and balances the power of Congress.
- **A** vote
- **B** deletion
- **C** veto
- **D** correction

4. The ________ process may begin when either a two-thirds majority of both houses of Congress agrees or if two-thirds of the states call for a convention to propose Constitutional changes.
- **A** veto
- **B** federalist
- **C** recession
- **D** amendment

5. Many Anti-Federalist fears were laid to rest when the Federalists agreed to add a ________ to the Constitution.
- **A** preamble
- **B** supreme court
- **C** bill of rights
- **D** compromise

Reviewing Main Ideas

Directions: Choose the best answer for each of the following questions.

Section 1 *(pp. 98–103)*

6. The Northwest Ordinance outlined the process for
- **A** ratifying the Constitution.
- **B** achieving statehood.
- **C** negotiating international treaties.
- **D** extending slavery north of the Ohio River.

7. Shays's Rebellion was viewed by many powerful people as
- **A** evidence that the Articles were working.
- **B** a righteous fight of the oppressed.
- **C** a sign that the national government was too weak.
- **D** a major blow to democracy.

8. Under the Articles of Confederation, governmental power
- **A** was shared equally by the central government and the states.
- **B** was balanced among the three branches of government.
- **C** belonged to a strong chief executive leading a unified central government.
- **D** rested much more with the states than with the central government.

Section 2 *(pp. 104–109)*

9. At the Constitutional Convention of 1787, the Great Compromise resolved the issue of
- **A** representation.
- **B** taxation.
- **C** slavery.
- **D** control of trade.

TEST-TAKING TIP

Pace yourself when taking a test so that you will have time to go back and check your answers or try to answer any questions you may have skipped.

Need Extra Help?

If You Missed Questions . . .	1	2	3	4	5	6	7	8	9
Go to Page . . .	100–101	108–109	108–109	109	112–113	98–99	103	98	106–107

GO ON

Answers and Analyses

1. B Although Congress could not regulate trade, each state could impose a duty on imported goods. The British took their products into the states with the lowest duties and then moved them into other states. To counter this and to raise revenue, each state could set up customs posts and impose a duty on products coming across its borders.

2. D Popular sovereignty and nationalism are concepts that relate to the work of the Framers of the Constitution, but federalism is the concept behind the division of power between the national and state governments.

3. C If the president disagrees with a bill that Congress passes, he or she may veto the bill, which then requires that, in order for the bill to become law, both houses of the Congress must vote in favor of it by a two-thirds majority. This is one of the ways that the balance of power between Congress and the president is maintained.

4. D Veto refers to a presidential power to block legislation. Federalists were supporters of the Constitution. While both terms relate to the Constitution, amendment is the only term that correctly completes the sentence.

5. C The first, second, and fourth answer choices relate to the creation of the Constitution, but only the addition of a bill of rights answered some of the objections of the Anti-Federalists.

6. B Students should recall that the Northwest Ordinance had nothing to do with ratifying the Constitution, negotiating international treaties, or extending slavery. Its purposes were to provide an effective temporary government for the area, an orderly process to establish statehood, and protection of basic rights for residents.

7. C Many powerful people saw the rebellion as a sign that the national government was too weak. They wanted a stronger national government that would protect property rights.

8. D Students should recall that those creating the Articles of Confederation wanted a weak central government with most of the power resting with the states. Governmental power was not shared equally. The separation of powers did not exist until the Constitution was ratified.

9. A The convention did consider issues of taxation, slavery, and trade, but only the Great (Connecticut) Compromise addressed the issue of representation.

10. A The Virginia Plan proposed that the legislature be made up of two houses, with voters electing members of the first house, and members of the second house nominated by the state governments but elected by the first house. There was no Missouri Plan. The New Jersey Plan proposed a Congress with a single house. The Three-Fifths Compromise was about slavery.

11. D The delegates knew that the Constitution might have to be changed in later years, so they devised a way of amending it. So that changes did not occur too quickly or easily, they made this process complicated and difficult.

12. A Students may find this question a bit confusing because, although the last three answers do in fact refer to elements in the Constitution, only the first answer, by mentioning the three separate branches of the federal government, relates to the idea of a balance of power between these three branches.

13. C The Anti-Federalists objected to the Constitution because they thought it gave too much power to the national government and did not protect civil liberties.

14. B These 85 essays by James Madison, Alexander Hamilton, and John Jay, published mostly in New York newspapers, were written to gain support for ratification of the Constitution.

15. C The strongest supporters of a strong federal government were landowners and merchants. They were motivated by fears that a weak government would not be able to protect their interests.

16. D By studying the map, students will see that Virginia had claimed all of the area that became the Northwest Territory.

Chapter 3 Assessment

10. Which of the following proposed a legislature that was divided into two houses?

A the Virginia Plan
B the New Jersey Plan
C the Three-Fifths Compromise
D the Missouri Plan

11. The Framers ensured that the Constitution could evolve over time by

A establishing a process for replacing it.
B establishing a bill of rights.
C establishing that the states could veto federal laws.
D establishing a process for amending it.

12. The Framers provided for a separation of powers in the federal government by

A establishing executive, legislative, and judicial branches.
B giving the president the power to command the army.
C making the Supreme Court the most important court in the nation.
D establishing a process of changing the Constitution.

Section 3 *(pp. 110–115)*

13. Most Anti-Federalists were against ratifying the Constitution because it

A had been written by Federalists.
B gave too much power to the states.
C did not protect civil liberties or states' rights.
D gave more power to the Northern states than the Southern states.

14. *The Federalist* essays were published in 1787 and 1788 to help gain support for

A a bill of rights.
B the ratification of the Constitution.
C a weaker central government.
D the abolition of slavery.

Critical Thinking

Directions: Choose the best answers to the following questions.

15. Large landowners and merchants supported the Constitution because it

A allowed states to trade with foreign powers with fewer regulations.
B enabled the original states to settle lands in the West.
C gave the national government power to protect property and regulate trade.
D eased trade laws and lowered taxes on land and businesses.

Base your answer to question 16 on the map below and on your knowledge of Chapter 3.

16. Which state had the largest land claims in the West?

A Massachusetts
B North Carolina
C Georgia
D Virginia

Need Extra Help?

If You Missed Questions . . .	10	11	12	13	14	15	16
Go to Page . . .	106	108–109	108–109	110–111	112	110	118

GO ON

17. Which of the following is an *opinion* about the Constitution?

A By 1790, all states had ratified the Constitution.

B A major concern in writing the Constitution was how many representatives each state would have.

C Under the Constitution, the federal government could raise money to operate.

D Because of the Constitution, the United States has the best government in the world.

Analyze the cartoon and answer the questions that follow. Base your answers on the cartoon and on your knowledge of Chapter 3.

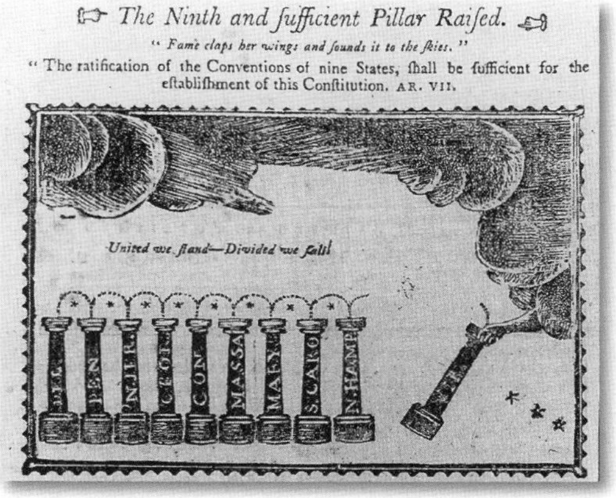

18. To what does the cartoonist compare the states that have ratified the Constitution?

A pillars supporting the nation

B storm clouds of controversy

C stepping stones to ratification

D a woven basket of unity

19. Which two states were the last to ratify the Constitution?

A Massachusetts and Virginia

B New York and Delaware

C Rhode Island and North Carolina

D Virginia and Rhode Island

Document-Based Questions

Directions: Analyze the document and answer the short-answer questions that follow the document.

In this excerpt from his 1789 textbook, *The American Geography*, the Reverend Jedediah Morse discusses the defects of the Articles of Confederation:

> *"[The Articles of Confederation] were framed during the rage of war, when a principle of common safety supplied the place of a coercive power in government. . . .*
>
> *When resolutions were passed in Congress, there was no power to compel obedience. . . . Had one state been invaded by its neighbour, the union was not constitutionally bound to assist in repelling the invasion. . . ."*
>
> —from *The American Geography*

20. What defects in the Articles does Morse mention?

21. Why does Morse think that the Articles were effective during the American Revolution but not afterwards?

Extended Response

22. The Constitutional Convention met in 1787 to address weaknesses in the government under the Articles of Confederation. Soon the delegates agreed that the Articles had failed and that the Confederation should be replaced with a new form of government. In an essay, explain the three most important changes that the delegates made from the Articles to the Constitution. Explain the change in detail and why it was an improvement. Your essay should include an introduction, at least three paragraphs, and a conclusion.

STOP

History ONLINE

For additional test practice, use Self-Check Quizzes—Chapter 3 at glencoe.com.

Need Extra Help?

If You Missed Questions . . .	17	18	19	20	21	22
Go to Page . . .	110–115	119	113–115	119	119	104–109

17. D The first three answer choices are not opinions because they can be verified by an examination of historical facts. The last option is not verifiable and is an opinion. For example, citizens of other countries may believe that their own government is best.

18. A They are pillars "standing" together to support the nation.

19. C Although approval of the new Constitution was achieved when nine states had voted for ratification, it was considered highly desirable that the other states join in. Rhode Island and North Carolina were the final two to do so.

20. Congress did not have the power to enforce laws.

21. During the war, the need for unity against a common enemy compelled states to cooperate; during peace there was nothing that compelled cooperation.

22. Students' essays will vary but should include a discussion, based on supporting details and examples from the chapter, of three selected weaknesses of the Articles and how the Constitution dealt with those weaknesses.

History ONLINE

Have students visit the Web site at glencoe.com to review Chapter 3 and take the Self-Check Quiz.

Need Extra Help?

Have students refer to the pages listed if they miss any of the questions.

Focus

Making Connections Have students speculate why they think it might be important for a nation to have a written constitution and write their ideas on the board. **Ask:** **What might happen if a nation did not have a written constitution?** *(Answers will vary, but students might note that laws would not be clear; the government might assume too much power; people would not know their civil rights.)* **OL**

Guide to Reading

Answers to Graphic:

I. Major Principles
   A. Popular Sovereignty and Republicanism
   B. Limited Government
   C. Federalism
   D. Separation of Powers
   E. Checks and Balances
   F. Individual Rights

Students should complete the outline by including all heads in the section.

Additional Support

THE CONSTITUTION HANDBOOK

Guide to Reading

Big Ideas

Government and Society A written contract between the people and their government can preserve natural rights and allow for change over time.

Content Vocabulary

- popular sovereignty *(p. 120)*
- federalism *(p. 120)*
- enumerated powers *(p. 121)*
- reserved powers *(p. 121)*
- concurrent powers *(p. 122)*
- impeach *(p. 123)*
- bill *(p. 124)*
- cabinet *(p. 125)*
- judicial review *(p. 127)*
- due process *(p. 127)*

Academic Vocabulary

- grant *(p. 121)*
- responsive *(p. 129)*

Reading Strategy

Taking Notes As you read about the Constitution, use the major headings of the handbook to fill in an outline.

I. Major Principles
A.
B.
C.
D.
E.
F.
II.

Serving as the framework of national government and the source of American citizens' basic rights, the Constitution is the most important document of the United States. To preserve self-government, all citizens need to understand their rights and responsibilities.

Major Principles

MAIN Idea The Constitution's basic principles assure people's rights and provide for a balance among the different branches of government.

HISTORY AND YOU If you had to create the rules for a new organization, would you give all members an equal voice? Read on to learn how the Constitution reflects representative government.

The principles outlined in the Constitution were the Framers' solution to the complex problems of a representative government. The Constitution rests on seven major principles of government: (1) **popular sovereignty,** (2) republicanism, (3) limited government, (4) **federalism,** (5) separation of powers, (6) checks and balances, and (7) individual rights.

Popular Sovereignty and Republicanism

The opening words of the Constitution, "We the people," reinforce the idea of popular sovereignty, or "authority of the people." In the Constitution, the people consent to be governed and specify the powers and rules by which they shall be governed.

The Articles of Confederation's government had few powers, and it was unable to cope with the many challenges facing the nation. The new federal government had greater powers, but it also had specific limitations. A system of interlocking responsibilities kept any one branch of government from becoming too powerful.

Voters are sovereign, that is, they have ultimate authority in a republican system. They elect representatives and give them the responsibility to make laws and run the government. For most Americans today, the terms republic and representative democracy mean the same thing: a system of limited government where the people are the final source of authority.

Extending the Content

Constitutions The United States has the oldest written national constitution still in effect. Compared to other written constitutions, it might be characterized as succinct. The average federal constitution contains about 26,500 words, while the U.S. Constitution with its 27 amendments has fewer than 7,500 words.

Limited Government

Although the Framers agreed that the nation needed a stronger central authority, they feared misuse of power. They wanted to prevent the government from using its power to give one group special advantages or to deprive another group of its rights. By creating a limited government, they restricted the government's authority to specific powers **granted** by the people.

The delegates to the Constitutional Convention were very specific about the powers granted to the new government. C1 Their decision to provide a written outline of the government's structure also served to show what they intended. Articles I, II and III of the Constitution describe the powers of the federal government and the limits on those powers. Other limits are set forth in the Bill of Rights, which guarantees certain rights to the people.

Federalism

In establishing a strong central government, the Framers did not deprive states of all authority. The states gave up some powers to the national government but retained others. This principle of shared power is called federalism. The federal system allows the people of each state to deal with their needs in their own way, but at the same time, it lets the states act together to deal with matters that affect all Americans.

The Constitution defines three types of government powers. Certain powers belong only to the federal government. These **enumerated powers** include the power to C2 C1 coin money, regulate interstate and foreign trade, maintain the armed forces, and create federal courts (Article I, Section 8).

The second kind of powers are those retained by the states, known as **reserved powers,** including the power to establish schools, set marriage and divorce laws, and regulate trade within the state. Although reserved powers are not specifically listed in the Constitution, the Tenth Amendment says that all powers not granted to the federal government "are reserved to the States."

Teach

C1 Critical Thinking

Identifying Central Issues Have students read through and define in their own words each of the Constitution's major underlying principles. Students should then locate at least one part of the Constitution that addresses each principle. **Ask:** Which constitutional principle affects your life the most today? *(Answers will vary.)* **OL**

C2 Critical Thinking

Making Inferences Write the enumerated powers of the federal government on the board. **Ask:** Why do you think the Framers thought it was important to list the powers of the federal government? *(Students may suggest that the Framers wanted to avoid confusion over what the federal government could and could not do.)* **OL**

Additional Support

Extending the Content

Independence Hall The red brick building in which the Framers met to draw up the Constitution is now known as Independence Hall. Several important events took place there, including the meeting of the First and Second Continental Congresses and Jefferson's reading of the Declaration of Independence. On July 4, 2003, the National Constitution Center opened a few blocks from Independence Hall. This museum explains the importance of the Constitution and its role in the history of the United States.

D Differentiated Instruction

English Learners Pair students and ask each pair to write for five minutes about what they believe the phrase "the supreme Law of the Land" means. Then ask students to read one another's writing and discuss their opinions with each other. **ELL**

R Reading Strategy

Organizing Information Ask students to create a table listing the following presidents: Ulysses S. Grant, Franklin D. Roosevelt, Harry S. Truman, Richard M. Nixon, and Ronald Reagan. Have students research the following information for each president and add it in separate columns of their table: the total number of vetoes, the number of overturned vetoes, and the numbers of "pocket" vetoes. Then have students compare each president's acts and offer possible explanations for any differences they see. **OL**

Reading Check

Answer:
Legislative, Executive, Judicial

Additional Support

The third set of powers defined by the Constitution is **concurrent powers**—powers the state and federal governments share. They include the right to raise taxes, borrow money, provide for public welfare, and administer criminal justice. Conflicts between state law and federal law must be settled in a federal court. The Constitution declares that it is "the supreme Law of the Land."

Separation of Powers

To prevent any single group or institution in government from gaining too much authority, the Framers divided the federal government into three branches: legislative, executive, and judicial. Each branch has its own functions and powers. The legislative branch, Congress, makes the laws. The executive branch, headed by the president, carries out the laws. The judicial branch, consisting of the Supreme Court and other federal courts, interprets and applies the laws.

In addition to giving separate responsibility to separate branches, the membership of each branch is chosen in different ways. The president nominates federal judges and the Senate confirms the appointments. People vote for members of Congress. Voters cast ballots for president, but the method of election is indirect. On Election Day the votes in each state are counted. Whatever candidate receives a majority receives that state's electoral votes, which total the number of senators and representatives the state has in Congress. Electors from all states meet to formally elect a president. A candidate must receive at least 270 of 538 electoral votes to win.

Checks and Balances

The Framers who wrote the Constitution deliberately created a system of checks and balances in which each branch of government can check, or limit, the power of the other branches. This system helps balance the power of the three branches and prevents any one branch from becoming too powerful. For example, imagine that Congress passes a law. The president can reject the law by vetoing it. However, Congress can override, or reverse, the president's veto if two-thirds of the members of both the Senate and the House of Representatives vote again to approve the law.

Individual Rights

Ten amendments to the Constitution were approved in 1791 to protect certain basic rights, including freedom of speech, religion, and the right to a trial by jury. These ten amendments are referred to as the Bill of Rights. Over the years, 17 more amendments were added to the Constitution. Some give additional rights to Americans and some modify how the government works. Included among them are amendments that abolish slavery, guarantee voting rights, authorize an income tax, and set a two-term limit on the presidency.

Reading Check **Explaining** What are the three branches of government?

INFOGRAPHIC
The Federal Government

The Constitution divides power in three ways:

1. Between the federal and state governments
2. Between three branches of government
3. By providing checks and balances

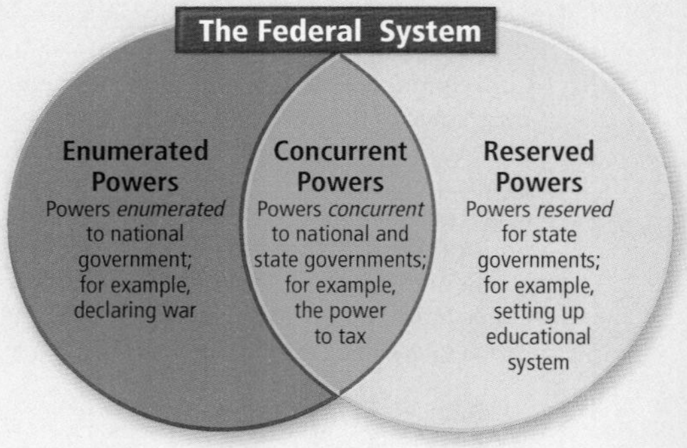

Extending the Content

Mr. President When George Washington became the nation's first President, no one knew what to call him. John Adams, the first Vice President, suggested, "His Highness, The President of the United States and Protector of Their Liberties." Washington felt that a less formal title was more appropriate. He chose the title "Mr. President," which is still used to this day.

The Legislative Branch

MAIN Idea The Legislative branch makes the nation's laws and appropriates funds.

HISTORY AND YOU Have you ever written to your representative to support or oppose a bill? Read to find out how Congress makes laws.

The legislative branch includes the two houses of Congress: the Senate and the House of Representatives. Congress's two primary roles are to make the nation's laws and to decide how federal funds are spent.

The government cannot spend any money unless Congress appropriates, or sets aside, funds. All tax and spending bills must originate in the House of Representatives and be approved in both the House and the Senate before moving to the president for signature.

Congress also monitors the executive branch and investigates possible abuses of power. The House of Representatives can **impeach,** or bring formal charges against, any federal official it suspects of wrongdoing or misconduct. If an official is impeached, the Senate acts as a court and tries the accused official. Officials who are found guilty may be removed from office. **W**

The Senate has certain additional powers. Two-thirds of the Senate must ratify treaties made by the president. The Senate must also confirm presidential appointments of federal officials such as department heads, ambassadors, and federal judges.

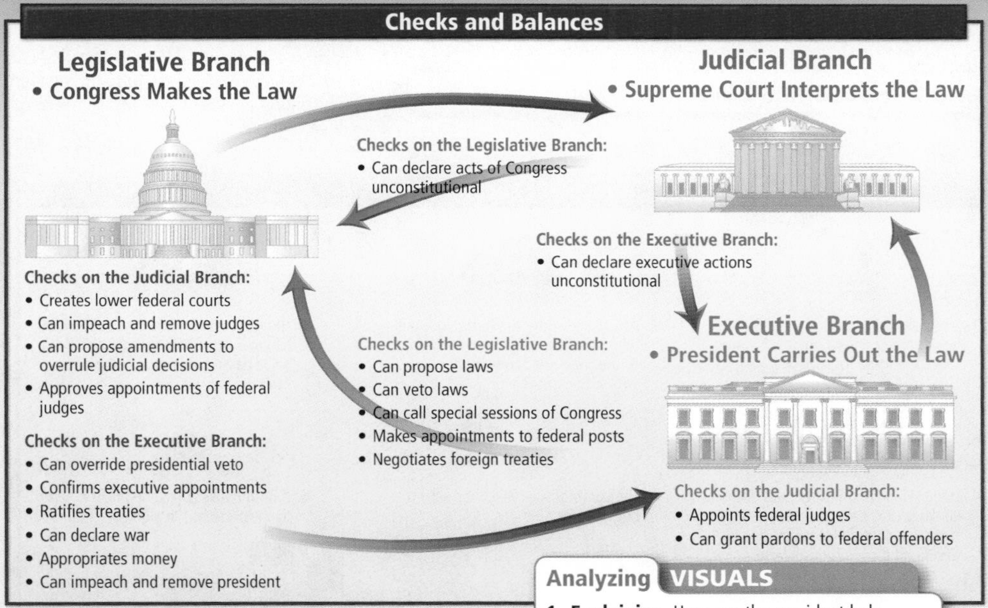

Analyzing VISUALS

1. **Explaining** How can the president help control the judiciary?
2. **Summarizing** What checks does the legislative branch have on the president?

123

W Writing Support

Expository Writing Have students use library and Internet resources to research the impeachment trial of President William Clinton. Tell them to summarize the key events of the trial in a one-page report. Encourage students to share their reports with the class. **OL**

Analyzing VISUALS

Answers:

1. The president appoints federal judges and can grant pardons to federal offenders.
2. can override presidential veto; confirms executive appointments; ratifies treaties; can declare war; appropriates money; can impeach and remove the president

Additional Support

Extending the Content

Representative Government Since January 1789, Americans have voted every other year on persons to represent them in their national government. This has not stopped despite a civil war, two world wars, and an economic depression. The American people reaffirm in every election James Madison's belief in the people's right to choose the government they will live by.

R Reading Strategy

Connecting Have students use Internet resources to research and identify your state senators and representatives. Ask students to compose and send e-mails to one of those representatives describing an important issue in your community. Keep track of the responses students receive, and post those responses in the classroom. OL

Reading Check

Answer: making law

All members of Congress have the responsibility to represent their constituents, the people of their home states and districts. As a constituent, you can expect your senators and representative to promote national and state R interests. Thousands of **bills**—proposed laws—are introduced in Congress every year. Because individual members of Congress cannot possibly study all these bills carefully, both houses use committees of selected members to evaluate proposed legislation.

Standing committees are permanent committees in both the House and the Senate that specialize in a particular topic, such as agriculture, commerce, or veterans' affairs. These committees are usually divided into subcommittees that focus on a particular aspect of an issue. The House and the Senate also form temporary select committees to deal with issues requiring special attention. These committees meet only until they complete their task.

Occasionally the House and the Senate form joint committees with members from both houses. These committees meet to consider specific issues. One type of joint committee, a conference committee, has a special function. If the House and the Senate pass different versions of the same bill, a conference committee meets to work out a compromise bill acceptable to both houses.

Once a committee in either house of Congress approves a bill, it is sent to the full Senate or House for debate. After debate the bill may be passed, rejected, or returned to the committee for further changes. When both houses pass a bill, it goes to the president. If the president approves the bill and signs it, the bill becomes law. If the president vetoes the bill, it does not become law unless Congress takes it up again and votes to override the veto.

Reading Check **Analyzing** What is the most important power of the legislative branch?

INFOGRAPHIC

How a Bill Becomes Law

The legislative process is complex. It begins with a representative in Congress introducing a bill and eventually works its way to the president who either signs the bill into law or vetoes it.

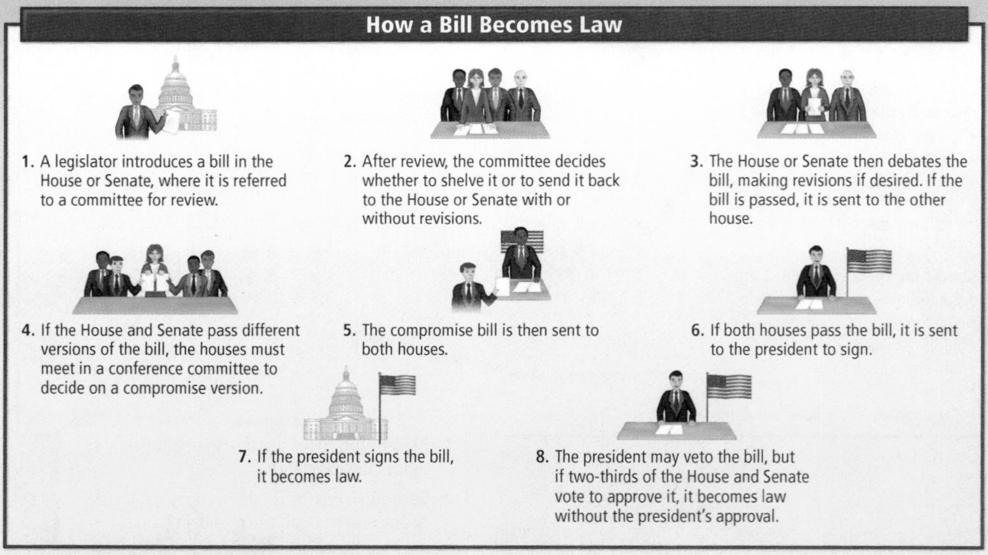

Additional Support

Extending the Content

Congressional Debate A *filibuster* is an attempt to delay for as long as possible or stop altogether the passage of a bill through the Senate. A filibuster exploits the long-held tradition in the Senate of not limiting debate. A senator can hold the floor as long as he or she wants to, as long as he or she continues talking. The Senate can halt a filibuster by passing a vote of cloture to force a vote.

The Executive Branch

MAIN Idea As the nation's leader, the president carries out laws with the help of executive offices, departments, and agencies.

HISTORY AND YOU What would you do if you were the student council president? Read on to learn about the roles of the U.S. president.

The executive branch of government includes the president, the vice president, and various executive offices, departments, and agencies. The executive branch executes, or carries out, the laws that Congress passes.

The President's Roles

The president plays a number of different roles in government. These roles include serving as the nation's chief executive, chief diplomat, commander in chief of the military, chief of state, and legislative leader.

▲ *President Bush signs the Voting Rights Act of 2006.*

Analyzing VISUALS

1. **Describing** What is the role of a conference committee?
2. **Analyzing** How can a bill become law without the approval of the president?

Chief Executive As chief executive, the president is responsible for carrying out the nation's laws. As chief diplomat, the president directs foreign policy, appoints ambassadors, and negotiates treaties with other nations.

Commander in Chief As commander in chief of the armed forces, the president can give orders to the military and direct its operations. The president cannot declare war; only Congress holds this power. The president can send troops to other parts of the world for up to 60 days but must notify Congress when doing so. The troops may remain longer only R if Congress gives its approval or declares war.

Chief of State As chief of state, the president is symbolically the representative of all Americans. The president fulfills this role when receiving foreign ambassadors or heads of state, visiting foreign nations, or honoring Americans.

Legislative Leader The president serves as a legislative leader by proposing laws to Congress and working to see that they are passed. In the annual State of the Union address, the president presents his goals for legislation in the upcoming year.

The Executive at Work

Many executive offices, departments, and independent agencies help the president carry out and enforce the nation's laws. The Executive Office of the President (EOP) is made up of individuals and agencies that directly assist the president. Presidents rely on the EOP for advice and for gathering information needed for decision making.

The executive branch has 15 executive departments, each responsible for a different area of government. For example, the Department of State carries out foreign policy, and the Department of the Treasury manages the nation's finances. The department heads have the title of secretary, and are members of the president's **cabinet.** The cabinet helps the president set policies and make decisions.

Reading Check **Explaining** What are the major roles of the president?

R Reading Strategy

Evaluating Have students review the key roles of the president: chief executive and chief diplomat, commander in chief, chief of state, and legislative leader. **Ask:** Which of these roles is most important? Why? *(Students should cite evidence or examples to logically support their opinions.)* OL

Analyzing VISUALS

Answers:

1. resolves differences between versions of bills passed by the Senate and the House
2. If the president vetoes a bill and two-thirds of the House and Senate override the veto, the bill becomes law without the president's approval.

Reading Check

Answer:
Chief Executive, Commander in Chief, Chief of State, Legislative leader

Additional Support

Extending the Content

Washington and His Cabinet George Washington's first cabinet included some of the nation's most influential founding fathers. Thomas Jefferson, the primary writer of the Declaration of Independence, served as Secretary of State; Alexander Hamilton, one of the writers of *The Federalist* and tireless champion of Constitutional ratification, served as Secretary of the Treasury. Henry Knox, Secretary of War, was a general from the American Revolution and had served as Secretary of War under the Articles of Confederation. Edmund Randolph, the former governor of Virginia, became the Attorney General. Like Hamilton and Washington, he was a delegate to the Constitutional Convention, and presented the Virginia Plan.

W Writing Support

Descriptive Writing Organize students into nine groups. Tell each group to use library or Internet resources to research one of the current Supreme Court justices. Have groups present their findings in one-page reports that include each justice's background information, political stance, and role in important or controversial court decisions. Encourage each group to share its reports with the class. OL

Did You Know?

Careful Selection Of the approximately 7,000 cases that get sent to the U.S. Supreme Court every year, the Court agrees to hear only 160 or so. Many cases are rejected simply because they were improperly filed.

Additional Support

The Judicial Branch

MAIN Idea The judicial branch consists of different federal courts that review and evaluate laws and interpret the Constitution.

HISTORY AND YOU The Constitution did not specifically give the judicial branch the power to review laws. Do you think it is a reasonable task? Read to learn about the role of federal judges and the Supreme Court.

Article III of the Constitution calls for the creation of a Supreme Court and "such inferior [lower] courts as Congress may from time to time ordain and establish." Today the judicial branch consists of three main categories of courts, including:

District and Appellate Courts

United States district courts are the lowest level of the federal court system. These courts consider criminal and civil cases that come under federal authority, such as kidnapping, federal tax evasion, claims against the federal government, and cases involving constitutional rights, such as free speech. There are 94 district courts, with at least one in every state.

The appellate courts, or appeals courts, consider district court decisions in which the losing side has asked for a review of the verdict. If an appeals court disagrees with the lower court's decision, it can overturn the verdict or order a retrial. There are 14 appeals courts, one for each of 12 federal districts, one military appeals court, and an appellate court for the federal circuit.

The Supreme Court

The Supreme Court is the final authority in the federal court system. It consists of a chief justice and eight associate justices. Most of the Supreme Court's cases come from appeals of lower court decisions. Only cases involving foreign ambassadors or disputes between states can begin in the Supreme Court. W

INFOGRAPHIC

The Federal Court System

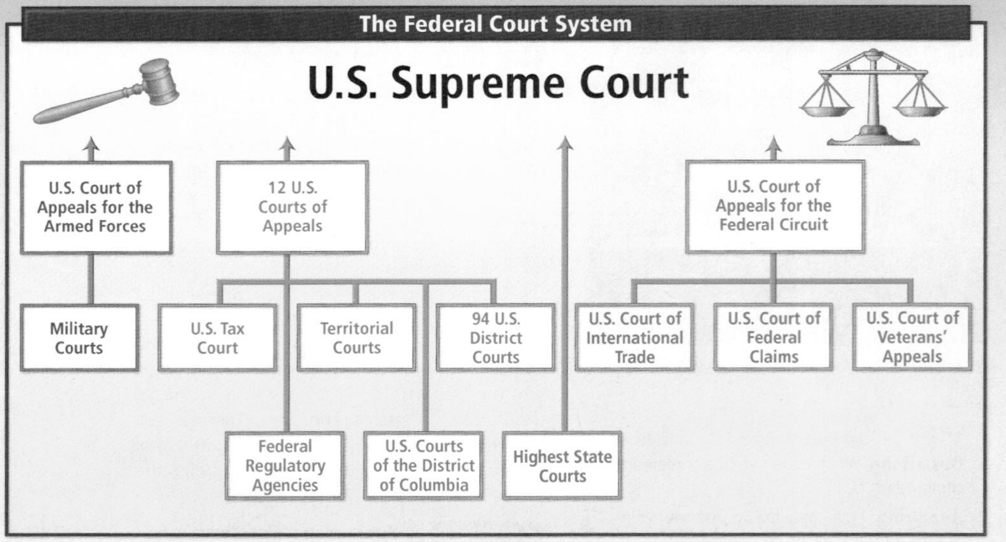

Extending the Content

Washington and the First Justices As the first president, George Washington had the responsibility of appointing the first six justices, as specified in the Judiciary Act of 1789. In naming the first justices, Washington paid close attention to their politics, which essentially meant loyalty to the new Constitution. Of his six original appointees, three attended the Constitutional Convention in Philadelphia and the other three supported the document's ratification. John Jay, the first chief justice, was coauthor with James Madison and Alexander Hamilton of *The Federalist*, a series of articles that supported the Constitution. During his two terms of office, Washington appointed five other Supreme Court justices—for a record total of eleven appointments to the Court.

Washington also considered geographical balance in his appointments. Among his first six appointees were three northerners and three southerners.

Supreme Court Independence The president appoints the Court's justices for life, and the Senate confirms the appointments. The public has no input. The Framers hoped that by appointing judges, they would be free to evaluate the law with no concern for pleasing voters.

Judicial Review The role of the judicial branch is not described in detail in the Constitution, but the role of the courts has grown as powers implied in the Constitution have been put into practice. In 1803 Chief Justice John Marshall expanded the power of the Supreme Court by striking down an act of Congress in the case of *Marbury* v. *Madison*. Although not mentioned in the Constitution, judicial review has become a major power of the judicial branch. **Judicial review** gives the Supreme Court the ultimate authority to interpret the meaning of the Constitution.

Reading Check **Analyzing** How does the Supreme Court protect the Constitution?

▲ *The U.S. Supreme Court, front row, left to right, Justices Anthony Kennedy and John Paul Stevens, Chief Justice John Roberts, Justices Antonin Scalia and David Souter; back row, left to right, Justices Stephen Breyer, Clarence Thomas, Ruth Bader Ginsburg, Samuel Alito*

Analyzing VISUALS

1. **Interpreting** How many routes to the U.S. Supreme Court are depicted in the chart?
2. **Analyzing** How would a case originating in Puerto Rico be appealed to the U.S. Supreme Court?

Rights and Responsibilities

MAIN Idea The Constitution and the Bill of Rights provide Americans with protection and freedoms.

HISTORY AND YOU How do you think the Constitution protects your rights as a student? Read on to find out about the major rights of Americans.

All American citizens have certain basic rights, but they also have specific responsibilities. Living in a system of self-government means ultimately that every citizen is partly responsible for how their society is governed and for the actions the government takes on their behalf.

The Rights of Americans

The rights of Americans fall into three broad categories: the right to be protected from unfair actions of the government, to receive equal treatment under the law, and to retain certain basic freedoms.

Protection from Unfair Actions Parts of the Constitution and the Bill of Rights protect all Americans from unfair treatment by the government or the law. Among these rights are the right to a lawyer when accused of a crime and the right to trial by jury when charged with a crime. In addition, the Fourth Amendment protects us from unreasonable searches and seizures. This provision requires police to have a court order before searching a person's home for criminal evidence. To obtain this, the police must have a very strong reason to suspect the person of committing a crime. **S**

Equal Treatment All Americans, regardless of race, religion, or political beliefs, have the right to be treated the same under the law. The Fifth Amendment states that no person shall "be deprived of life, liberty, or property, without due process of law." **Due process** means that the government must follow procedures established by law and guaranteed by the Constitution, treating all people equally. The Fourteenth Amendment requires every state to grant its citizens "equal protection of the laws."

S Skill Practice

Identifying Point of View Have students use library or Internet resources to learn about the exclusionary rule. *(keeps illegally obtained evidence from being admissible in a court of law)* Use students' findings to discuss the exclusionary rule as a class. Then ask students to write a paragraph either in favor of the exclusionary rule or opposed to it. *(Pro: protects Fourth and Fourteenth Amendment rights; Con: criminals may go free based on "technicalities")* **AL**

Analyzing VISUALS

Answers:
1. four
2. from the Territorial courts through one of the U.S. Courts of Appeals

Reading Check

Answer:
It ensures that all laws are constitutional.

Additional Support

Activity: Interdisciplinary Connection

Art Have interested students use library or Internet resources to find paintings, sketches, or photographs that illustrate the rights and freedoms guaranteed by the First Amendment. Have students use these images as models to create their own posters depicting the freedoms guaranteed by the First Amendment. Display the posters around the classroom. **OL**

W Writing Support

Expository Writing Remind students that while the First Amendment guarantees an individual's right to free speech, it does not give individuals the right to yell "fire" in a crowded theater. Have students write a two-page paper that discusses the government's need to balance an individual's constitutional rights with society's need for order and safety. **OL**

C Critical Thinking

Making Generalizations Have students write a short paragraph answering the following questions: Should communities permit rallies by unpopular groups, such as the KKK, even though such rallies may upset some members of the community or could possibly incite violence? Why or why not? *(Answers will vary.)* **OL**

Analyzing VISUALS

Answers:

1. States must ratify amendments; two-thirds of the states may request a national convention to request amendments.
2. three-fourths of the state legislatures

Additional Support

Basic Freedoms The basic freedoms are described in the First Amendment—freedom of speech, freedom of religion, freedom of the press, freedom of assembly, and the right to petition. In a democracy, power rests in the hands of the people. Therefore, citizens in a democratic society must be able to exchange ideas freely. The First Amendment allows citizens to criticize the government, in speech or in the press, without fear of punishment.

In addition, the Ninth Amendment states that the rights of Americans are not limited to those in the Constitution. This has allowed Americans to assert other basic rights over the years that have been upheld in court, or assured by amending the Constitution.

Limits on Rights The rights of Americans are not absolute. They are limited based on the principle of respecting everyone's rights equally. For example, many cities and towns require groups to obtain a permit to march on city streets. Such laws do limit free speech, but they also protect the community by ensuring that the march will not endanger other people.

In this and other cases, the government balances an individual's rights, the rights of others, and the community's health and safety. Most Americans are willing to accept some limitations on their rights to gain these protections as long as the restrictions are reasonable and apply equally to all. A law banning all marches would violate the First Amendment rights of free speech and assembly and be unacceptable. Similarly, a law preventing only certain groups from marching would be unfair because it would not apply equally to everyone.

Citizens' Responsibilities

Citizens in a democratic society have both duties and responsibilities. Duties are actions required by law. Responsibilities are voluntary actions. Fulfilling both your duties and your responsibilities helps ensure good government and protects your rights.

Duties One basic duty of all Americans is to obey the law. Laws serve three important functions. They help maintain order; they protect

INFOGRAPHIC
Amending the Constitution

Article V of the Constitution enables Congress and the states to amend, or change, the Constitution.

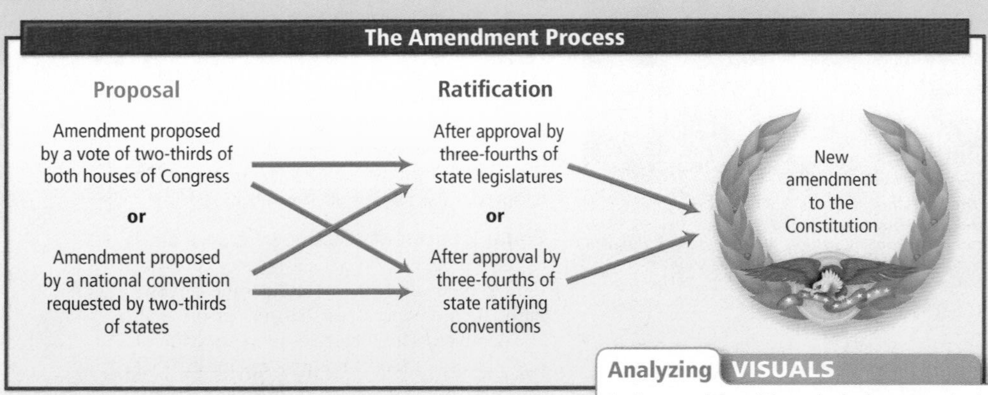

Analyzing VISUALS

1. **Summarizing** What role do the states play in the amendment process?
2. **Explaining** How many approvals by state legislatures are required for an amendment to the Constitution?

Activity: Cooperative Learning

Debating Rights Organize the class into five groups, one for each of the five rights incorporated into the First Amendment. Tell students they will have 10 minutes to prepare an outline about the right assigned to their group. Also tell them they will have five minutes to persuade the class that the right they represent is more important than the other four. Tell them to include as many factual details and real-life scenarios as possible. After each group has presented, have the class vote on which right they think is most important.

the health, safety, and property of all citizens; and they make it possible for people to live together peacefully. If you believe a law is wrong, you can work through your representatives to change it.

Americans also have a duty to pay taxes. The government uses tax money to defend the nation, to build roads and bridges, and to assist people in need. Americans benefit from services provided by the government. Another duty of citizens is to defend the nation. All males aged 18 and older must register with the government in case the nation needs to call on them for military service. Military service is not automatic, but a war could make it necessary.

The Constitution guarantees all Americans the right to a trial by a jury of their equals. For this reason, you may be called to jury duty when you reach the age of 18. Having a large group of jurors on hand is necessary to guarantee the right to a fair and speedy trial. You also have a duty to serve as a trial witness if called to do so.

Most states require you to attend school until a certain age. School is where you gain the knowledge and skills needed to be a good citizen. In school you learn to think more clearly, to express your opinions more accurately, and to analyze the ideas of others. These skills will help you make informed choices when you vote.

Responsibilities The responsibilities of citizens are not as clear-cut as their duties, but they are as important because they help maintain the quality of government and society. One important responsibility is to be well informed. You need to know what is happening in your community, your state, your country, and the world. Knowing what your government is doing and expressing your thoughts about its actions helps to keep it **responsive** to the wishes of the people. You also need to be informed about your rights and to assert them when necessary. Knowing your rights helps preserve them. Other responsibilities include accepting responsibility for your actions, and supporting your family.

To enjoy your rights to the fullest, you must be prepared to respect the rights of others. Respecting the rights of others also means respecting the rights of people with whom you disagree. Respecting and accepting others regardless of race, religion, beliefs, or other differences is essential in a democracy.

Vote, Vote, Vote! Perhaps the most important responsibility of American citizens is to vote when they reach the age of 18. Voting allows you to participate in government and to guide its direction. When you vote for people to represent you in government, you will be exercising your right of self-government. If you disapprove of the job your representatives are doing, it will be your responsibility to help elect other people in the next election. You can also let your representatives know what you think about issues through letters, telephone calls, and petitions and by taking part in public meetings or political rallies.

Reading Check **Describing** What are the major rights and responsibilities of an American citizen?

Constitution Handbook REVIEW

Vocabulary

1. **Explain** the significance of: popular sovereignty, federalism, enumerated powers, reserved powers, concurrent powers, impeach, bill, cabinet, judicial review, due process.

Main Ideas

2. **Explaining** What are the provisions of the First Amendment?
3. **Summarizing** How are popular sovereignty and voting connected?

Critical Thinking

4. **Big Ideas** What is the difference between a duty and a responsibility?
5. **Organizing** Use a graphic organizer similar to the one below to list reasons why the framers of the Constitution provided for separation of powers.

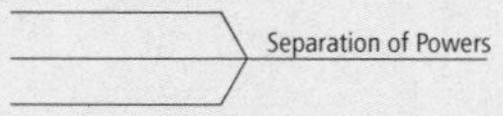

6. **Analyzing Visuals** Study the photograph on page 127. How has the composition of the Supreme Court changed over time?

Writing About History

7. **Expository Writing** Working with a partner, choose one of the constitutional rights listed below. Write a report that traces the right's historical development, from the time the Constitution was ratified to the present.

suffrage
freedom of speech
freedom of religion
equal protection of law

History ONLINE
Study Central™ To review this section, go to glencoe.com and click on Study Central.

Reading Check

Answer:
Rights: protection from unfair actions; equal treatment; freedom of speech; freedom of religion; freedom of the press; freedom of assembly; right to petition; right to a fair and speedy trial. Responsibilities: obey the law; pay taxes; serve on jury duty; be responsible for your actions; support your family; vote.

Assess

History ONLINE

Study Central™ provides summaries, interactive games, and online graphic organizers to help students review content.

Close

Summarizing Ask: In what ways does the Constitution protect our rights? *(Answers will vary, but students should note that the Constitution is designed to prevent any one branch from becoming too powerful; also, the Bill of Rights and the other amendments protect our rights.)* **OL**

Constitution Handbook REVIEW

Answers

1. All definitions can be found in the section and the Glossary.
2. freedom of speech, religion, and the press; right of assembly; and right to petition
3. The people express their wishes through voting.
4. Duties are actions required by law; responsibilities are voluntary.
5. to prevent one branch of government from becoming too powerful; to provide a system for each branch of government to check and balance the others; to protect individual rights
6. Women and African Americans are now represented on the Court.
7. Reports will vary, but students should use historically accurate information.

Focus

Making Connections Have students suggest ways in which they think the U.S. Constitution affects their daily life and write their ideas on the board. **Ask:** Why is it important to know about the Constitution's main provisions? *(Answers will vary, but students might note that good citizens know about how their nation is governed; citizens would better understand if any laws passed by state or local governments might be unconstitutional.)* **OL**

Teach

D Differentiated Instruction

English Learners Ask students to read the Preamble and help students understand any difficult words or terms. Then have them identify which purpose is most important to them personally. **ELL**

Additional Support

THE CONSTITUTION OF THE UNITED STATES

The Constitution of the United States is a truly remarkable document. It was one of the first written constitutions in modern history. The entire text of the Constitution and its amendments follow. For easier study, those passages that have been set aside or changed by the adoption of amendments are printed in blue. Also included are explanatory notes that will help clarify the meaning of important ideas presented in the Constitution.

A burst of fireworks over the Lincoln Memorial in Washington, D.C.

Extending the Content

Sergeants-at-Arms House and Senate sergeants-at-arms are the police officers of Congress. They enforce the rules and maintain order. When they walk down the aisle of the legislature, carrying the ceremonial staff called a mace, Congress must be orderly. Any member of Congress who persists in disorderly conduct is guilty of contempt. The sergeants-at-arms also maintain security within the Capitol and associated buildings and supervise the Capitol police force. Sometimes the sergeants-at-arms round up members for floor votes, personally escorting any member who refuses to attend.

Preamble

We the People of the United States, in Order to form a more perfect Union, establish Justice, insure domestic Tranquility, provide for the common defence, promote the general Welfare, and secure the Blessings of Liberty to ourselves and our Posterity, do ordain and establish this **Constitution** for the United States of America. D

Article I

Section 1

All legislative Powers herein granted shall be vested in a Congress of the United States, which shall consist of a Senate and House of Representatives.

Section 2

[1.] The House of Representatives shall be composed of Members chosen every second Year by the People of the several States, and the Electors in each State shall have the Qualifications requisite for Electors of the most numerous Branch of the State Legislature.

[2.] No person shall be a Representative who shall not have attained to the Age of twenty five Years, and been seven Years a Citizen of the United States, and who shall not, when elected, be an Inhabitant of that State in which he shall be chosen.

[3.] Representatives and direct Taxes shall be apportioned among the several States which may be included within this Union, according to their respective Numbers, which shall be determined by adding to the whole Number of free Persons, including those bound to Service for a Term of Years, and excluding Indians not taxed, three fifths of all other Persons. The actual **Enumeration** shall be made within three Years after the first Meeting of the Congress of the United States, and within every subsequent Term of ten Years, in such Manner as they shall by Law direct. The Number of Representatives shall not exceed one for every thirty Thousand, but each State shall have at Least one Representative; and until such enumeration shall be made, the State of New Hampshire shall be entitled to chuse three; Massachusetts eight, Rhode-Island and Providence Plantations one, Connecticut five, New-York six, New Jersey four, Pennsylvania eight, Delaware one, Maryland six, Virginia ten, North Carolina five, South Carolina five, and Georgia three. C

[4.] When vacancies happen in the Representation from any State, the Executive Authority thereof shall issue Writs of Election to fill such Vacancies.

[5.] The House of Representatives shall chuse their Speaker and other Officers; and shall have the sole Power of **Impeachment.**

The Preamble introduces the Constitution and sets forth the general purposes for which the government was established. The Preamble also declares that the power of the government comes from the people.

The printed text of the document shows the spelling and punctuation of the parchment original.

Article I. The Legislative Branch

The Constitution contains seven divisions called articles. Each article covers a general topic. For example, Articles I, II, and III create the three branches of the national government—the legislative, executive, and judicial branches. Most of the articles are divided into sections.

Section 1. Congress

Lawmaking The power to make laws is given to a Congress made up of two chambers to represent different interests: the Senate to represent the states and the House to be more responsive to the people's will.

Section 2.
House of Representatives

Division of Representatives Among the States The number of representatives from each state is based on the size of the state's population. Each state is entitled to at least one representative. The Constitution states that each state may specify who can vote, but the Fifteenth, Nineteenth, Twenty-fourth, and Twenty-sixth Amendments have established guidelines that all states must follow regarding the right to vote. What are the qualifications for members of the House of Representatives?

Vocabulary

preamble: *introduction*
constitution: *principles and laws of a nation*
enumeration: *census or population count*
impeachment: *bringing charges against an official*

C Critical Thinking

Analyzing Information Have students research data from the 1990 and 2000 censuses. Students should create a chart of the populations of each state and the number of representatives each state had in 1990. Then students should list the populations each state had in 2000 and whether that state lost or gained representation in the House of Representatives. Have students identify which states gained the most seats and speculate as to why those states gained population. OL

Answer: A member of the House of Representatives must be at least 25 years old, be a citizen for at least seven years, and be an inhabitant of the state from which he or she was elected.

Additional Support

Extending the Content

Committee of Style The delegates to the Constitutional Convention appointed five of their members—William Samuel Johnson, Alexander Hamilton, Gouverneur Morris, James Madison, and Rufus King—to write the final draft of the Constitution. The members completed the task in four days and presented their version to the delegates on September 12, 1787. Some additional changes were made before the Constitution was adopted on September 17, 1787.

C1 Critical Thinking

Analyzing Primary Sources Write on the board the following, which George Washington supposedly said to Thomas Jefferson in defense of the Senate: "We pour legislation into the senatorial saucer to cool it." **Ask:** What do you think Washington meant by this? *(The Senate was the more deliberative of the two houses of Congress.)* **OL**

C2 Critical Thinking

Making Generalizations Call on students to list the qualifications for serving in Congress as set forth in the Constitution. Then ask students what other qualifications, if any, they think should be applied to members of Congress. Discuss with students whether they would like to serve in Congress. (Note: For information on serving in the House, see Article I, Section 2, on page 131.) **OL**

Answer: The Senate has the power to remove impeached officials from office and disqualify them from holding office in the future.

Additional Support

Section 3. The Senate
Voting Procedure Originally, senators were chosen by the legislators of their own states. The Seventeenth Amendment changed this, so that senators are now elected by their state's people. There are 100 senators, 2 from each state.

What Might Have Been
Electing Senators South Carolina delegate Charles Pinckney suggested during the Convention that the members of the Senate come from four equally proportioned districts within the United States and that the legislature elect the executive every seven years.

Section 3. The Senate
Trial of Impeachments One of Congress's powers is the power to impeach—to accuse government officials of wrongdoing, put them on trial, and, if necessary, remove them from office. The House decides if the offense is impeachable. The Senate acts as a jury, and when the president is impeached, the Chief Justice of the United States serves as the judge. A two-thirds vote of the members present is needed to convict impeached officials. What punishment can the Senate give if an impeached official is convicted?

Section 3

[1.] The Senate of the United States shall be composed of two Senators from each State, chosen by the Legislature thereof, for six Years; and each Senator shall have one Vote.

[2.] Immediately after they shall be assembled in Consequence of the first Election, they shall be divided as equally as may be into three Classes. The Seats of the Senators of the first Class shall be vacated at the Expiration of the second Year, of the second Class at the Expiration of the fourth Year, and of the third Class at the Expiration of the sixth Year, so that one third may be chosen every second Year; and if Vacancies happen by Resignation, or otherwise, during the Recess of the Legislature of any State, the Executive thereof may make temporary Appointments until the next Meeting of the Legislature, which shall then fill such Vacancies.

[3.] No Person shall be a Senator who shall not have attained to the Age of thirty Years, and been nine Years a Citizen of the United States, and who shall not, when elected, be an Inhabitant of that State for which he shall be chosen. C1 C2

[4.] The Vice President of the United States shall be President of the Senate, but shall have no Vote, unless they be equally divided.

[5.] The Senate shall chuse their other Officers, and also a **President pro tempore,** in the Absence of the Vice-President, or when he shall exercise the Office of the President of the United States.

[6.] The Senate shall have the sole Power to try all Impeachments. When sitting for that Purpose, they shall be on Oath or Affirmation. When the President of the United States is tried, the Chief Justice shall preside: And no Person shall be convicted without the Concurrence of two thirds of the Members present.

[7.] Judgment in Cases of Impeachment shall not extend further than to removal from Office, and disqualification to hold and enjoy any Office of honor, Trust or Profit under the United States: but the Party convicted shall nevertheless be liable and subject to Indictment, Trial, Judgment and Punishment, according to Law.

Section 4

[1.] The Times, Places and Manner of holding Elections for Senators and Representatives, shall be prescribed in each State by the Legislature thereof; but the Congress may at any time by Law make or alter such Regulations, except as to the Places of chusing Senators.

[2.] The Congress shall assemble at least once in every Year, and such Meeting shall be on the first Monday in December, unless they shall by Law appoint a different Day.

Section 5

[1.] Each House shall be the Judge of the Elections, Returns and Qualifications of its own Members, and a Majority of each shall constitute a **Quorum** to do Business; but a smaller Number may **adjourn** from day to day, and may be

Vocabulary

president pro tempore: *presiding officer of Senate who serves when the vice president is absent*
quorum: *minimum number of members that must be present to conduct sessions*
adjourn: *to suspend a session*

Extending the Content

Female Representatives Republican and pacifist Jeanette Rankin of Montana was the first woman elected to the House of Representatives in 1916. In 1917 she and 49 House colleagues voted against entering World War I. In 1941 she was the only member of Congress to vote against declaring war on Japan.

In 2007 Nancy Pelosi of California became the first female Speaker of the House of Representatives.

authorized to compel the Attendance of absent Members, in such Manner, and under such Penalties as each House may provide.
[2.] Each House may determine the Rules of its Proceedings, punish its Members for disorderly Behaviour, and, with the **Concurrence** of two thirds, expel a Member.
[3.] Each House shall keep a Journal of its Proceedings, and from time to time publish the same, excepting such Parts as may in their Judgment require Secrecy; and the Yeas and Nays of the Members of either House on any question shall, at the Desire of one fifth of those Present, be entered on the Journal.
[4.] Neither House, during the Session of Congress, shall, without the Consent of the other, adjourn for more than three days, nor to any other Place than that in which the two Houses shall be sitting.

Section 6

[1.] The Senators and Representatives shall receive a Compensation for their Services, to be ascertained by Law, and paid out of the Treasury of the United States. They shall in all Cases, except Treason, Felony and Breach of the Peace, be privileged from Arrest during their Attendance at the Session of their respective Houses, and in going to and returning from the same; and for any Speech or Debate in either House, they shall not be questioned in any other Place.
[2.] No Senator or Representative shall, during the Time for which he was elected, be appointed to any civil Office under the Authority of the United States, which shall have been created, or the **Emoluments** whereof shall have been encreased during such time; and no Person holding any Office under the United States, shall be a Member of either House during his Continuance in Office.

Section 7

[1.] All Bills for raising **Revenue** shall originate in the House of Representatives; but the Senate may propose or concur with Amendments as on other **Bills.**
[2.] Every Bill which shall have passed the House of Representatives and the Senate, shall, before it become a Law, be presented to the President of the United States; If he approve he shall sign it, but if not he shall return it, with his Objections to that House in which it shall have originated, who shall enter the Objections at large on their Journal, and proceed to reconsider it. If after such Reconsideration two thirds of that House shall agree to pass the Bill, it shall be sent, **W** together with the Objections, to the other House, by which it shall likewise be reconsidered, and if approved by two thirds of that House, it shall become a Law. But in all such Cases the Votes of both Houses shall be determined by yeas and Nays, and the Names of the Persons voting for and against the Bill shall be entered on the Journal of each House respectively. If any Bill shall not be returned by the President within ten Days (Sundays excepted) after it shall have been presented to him, the Same shall be a Law, in like Manner as if he had signed it, unless the Congress by their Adjournment prevent its Return, in which Case it shall not be a Law.

Vocabulary

R

concurrence: *agreement*
emoluments: *salaries*
revenue: *income raised by government*
bill: *draft of a proposed law*

Section 6. Privileges and Restrictions
Pay and Privileges To strengthen the federal government, the Founders set congressional salaries to be paid by the United States Treasury rather than by members' respective states. Originally, members were paid $6 per day. In 2002, all members of Congress received a base salary of $150,000.

Section 7. Passing Laws
Revenue Bill All tax laws must originate in the House of Representatives. This ensures that the branch of Congress that is elected by the people every two years has the major role in determining taxes.

Section 7. Passing Laws
How Bills Become Laws A bill may become a law only by passing both houses of Congress and by being signed by the president. The president can check Congress by rejecting–vetoing–its legislation. How can Congress override the president's veto?

R Reading Strategy

Using Context Clues Have students work in pairs to create a study card for each vocabulary word listed on this page. Instruct students to write the term on one side of a blank note card. Have students use the other side to write an explanation of how the term relates to the Constitution. Have students take turns quizzing each other using their study cards. **OL**

W Writing Support

Expository Writing Point out that because of the heavy volume of legislation, both houses of Congress have committees that do much of the work in preparing bills. Each committee deals with a particular issue, such as banking, foreign affairs, or natural resources. Encourage students to write letters asking representatives and senators from your state about the committees on which they serve. Invite volunteers to share the replies they receive. **OL**

Answer: A bill can become law, despite not being signed by the president, if two-thirds of the House of Representatives and two-thirds of the Senate approve the bill.

Additional Support

Extending the Content

Congressional Salaries Wanting to reduce the influence of the states, the Framers decided the members of Congress would be paid from the United States treasury, rather than by the individual states. In 1789 members of Congress received $6.00 per day. The chart shows the increase of congressional pay.

Selected Years	Congressional Salary*
1789	$1,500
1817	$2,000
1855	$3,000
1865	$5,000
1874	$5,000
1907	$7,500
1925	$10,000

Selected Years	Congressional Salary*
1932	$9,000
1935	$10,000
1947	$12,500
1955	$22,500
1965	$30,000
1975	$44,600
1977	$57,500

Selected Years	Congressional Salary*
1983	$69,800
1990	$96,600
1991	$125,100
1998	$136,700
2001	$145,100
2003	$154,700
2007	$168,000

*Daily rates have been converted to an annual salary, based on a hypothetically possible 250-day session.

C Critical Thinking

Drawing Conclusions Organize students into groups of five to consider one of the expressed powers of Congress: taxing and spending; regulating commerce, foreign policy, and national defense; or providing for the nation's growth. Have each group discuss why the power it selected was delegated to Congress, rather than to the executive branch. Then ask each group to share their answers with the class. AL

S Skill Practice

Conducting Research Have students work in pairs to research the naturalization process. Each pair should present the information in a flowchart or other graphic organizer. **Ask:** Why is the process of becoming a U.S. citizen so difficult? Do you think it should be easier? Why or why not? *(Each pair should respond in a short paragraph. Have the pairs copy their paragraphs onto a poster board along with their flowchart or graphic organizer and display the posters around the classroom.)* AL

Answer: Article I, Section 8, Clause 11

Additional Support

Section 8. Powers Granted to Congress
Expressed Powers Expressed powers are those powers directly stated in the Constitution. Most of the expressed powers of Congress are itemized in Article I, Section 8. These powers are also called enumerated powers because they are numbered 1 to 18. Which clause gives Congress the power to declare war?

[3.] Every Order, **Resolution,** or Vote to which the Concurrence of the Senate and House of Representatives may be necessary (except on a question of Adjournment) shall be presented to the President of the United States; and before the Same shall take Effect, shall be approved by him, or being disapproved by him, shall be repassed by two thirds of the Senate and House of Representatives, according to the Rules and Limitations prescribed in the Case of a Bill.

Section 8

[1.] The Congress shall have the Power to lay and collect Taxes, Duties, Imposts and Excises, to pay the Debts and provide for the common Defence and general Welfare of the United States; but all Duties, Imposts and Excises shall be uniform throughout the United States;
[2.] To borrow Money on the credit of the United States;
[3.] To regulate Commerce with foreign Nations, and among the several States, and with the Indian Tribes;
[4.] To establish an uniform Rule of **Naturalization,** and uniform Laws on the subject of Bankruptcies throughout the United States;
[5.] To coin Money, regulate the Value thereof, and of foreign Coin, and fix the Standard of Weights and Measures;
[6.] To provide for the Punishment of counterfeiting the Securities and current Coin of the United States;
[7.] To establish Post Offices and post Roads;
[8.] To promote the Progress of Science and useful Arts, by securing for limited Times to Authors and Inventors the exclusive Right to their respective Writings and Discoveries;
[9.] To constitute Tribunals inferior to the supreme Court;
[10.] To define and punish Piracies and Felonies committed on the high Seas, and Offences against the Law of Nations;
[11.] To declare War, grant Letters of Marque and Reprisal, and make Rules concerning Captures on Land and Water;
[12.] To raise and support Armies, but no Appropriation of Money to that Use shall be for a longer Term than two Years;
[13.] To provide and maintain a Navy;
[14.] To make Rules for the Government and Regulation of the land and naval Forces;
[15.] To provide for calling forth the Militia to execute the Laws of the Union, suppress Insurrections and repel Invasions;
[16.] To provide for organizing, arming, and disciplining, the Militia, and for governing such Part of them as may be employed in the Service of the United States, reserving to the States respectively, the Appointment of the Officers, and the Authority of training the Militia according to the discipline prescribed by Congress;
[17.] To exercise exclusive Legislation in all Cases whatsoever, over such District (not exceeding ten Miles square) as may, by Cession of particular States, and the Acceptance of Congress, become the Seat of Government of the United States, and to exercise like Authority over all Places purchased by the Consent of the Legislature of the State in which the Same shall be, for the Erection of Forts, Magazines, Arsenals, dock-Yards, and other needful Buildings; And

Vocabulary

resolution: *legislature's formal expression of opinion*
naturalization: *procedure by which a citizen of a foreign nation becomes a citizen of the United States*

Extending the Content

Experience, Not Age The title Senior Senator refers to the senator from each state who has more experience as a senator. A senior senator may actually be younger than the other senator from his or her state.

[18.] To make all Laws which shall be necessary and proper for carrying into Execution the foregoing Powers, and all other Powers vested by this Constitution in the Government of the United States, or in any Department or Officer thereof.

Section 9

[1.] The Migration or Importation of such Persons as any of the States now existing shall think proper to admit, shall not be prohibited by the Congress prior to the Year one thousand eight hundred and eight, but a Tax or duty may be imposed on such Importation, not exceeding ten dollars for each Person.
[2.] The Privilege of the Writ of Habeas Corpus shall not be suspended, unless when in Cases of Rebellion or Invasion the public Safety may require it. **R**
[3.] No Bill of Attainder or ex post facto Law shall be passed.
[4.] No Capitation, or other direct, Tax shall be laid, unless in Proportion to the Census or Enumeration herein before directed to be taken.
[5.] No Tax or Duty shall be laid on Articles exported from any State.
[6.] No Preference shall be given by any Regulation of Commerce or Revenue to the Ports of one State over those of another: nor shall Vessels bound to, or from, one State, be obliged to enter, clear, or pay Duties in another.
[7.] No Money shall be drawn from the Treasury, but in Consequence of Appropriations made by Law; and a regular Statement and Account of the Receipts and Expenditures of all public Money shall be published from time to time.
[8.] No Title of Nobility shall be granted by the United States:And no Person holding any Office of Profit or Trust under them, shall, without the Consent of the Congress, accept of any present, Emolument, Office, or Title, of any kind whatever, from any King, Prince, or foreign State.

Section 10

[1.] No State shall enter into any Treaty, Alliance, or Confederation; grant Letters of Marque and Reprisal; coin Money; emit Bills of Credit; make any Thing but gold and silver Coin a Tender in Payment of Debts; pass any Bill of Attainder, ex post facto Law, or Law impairing the Obligation of Contracts, or grant any Title of Nobility.
[2.] No State shall, without the Consent of the Congress, lay any Imposts or Duties on Imports or Exports, except what may be absolutely necessary for executing it's inspection Laws: and the net Produce of all Duties and Imposts, laid by any State on Imports and Exports, shall be for the Use of the Treasury of the United States; and all such Laws shall be subject to the Revision and Controul of the Congress.
[3.] No State shall, without the Consent of Congress, lay any Duty of Tonnage, keep Troops, or Ships of War in time of Peace, enter into any Agreement or Compact with another State, or with a foreign Power, or engage in War, unless actually invaded, or in such imminent Danger as will not admit of delay.

Section 8. Powers Granted to Congress

Elastic Clause The final enumerated power is often called the "elastic clause." This clause gives Congress the right to make all laws "necessary and proper" to carry out the powers expressed in the other clauses of Article I. It is called the elastic clause because it lets Congress "stretch" its powers to meet situations the Founders could not have anticipated.

What does the phrase "necessary and proper" in the elastic clause mean? It was a subject of dispute from the beginning. The issue was whether a strict or a broad interpretation of the Constitution should be applied. The dispute was first addressed in 1819, in the case of *McCulloch* v. *Maryland*, when the Supreme Court ruled in favor of a broad interpretation. The Court stated that the elastic clause allowed Congress to use its powers in any way that was not specifically prohibited by the Constitution. **D**

Section 9. Powers Denied to the Federal Government

Original Rights A writ of habeas corpus issued by a judge requires a law official to bring a prisoner to court and show cause for holding the prisoner. A bill of attainder is a bill that punishes a person without a jury trial. An "ex post facto" law is one that makes an act a crime after the act has been committed. What does the Constitution say about bills of attainder?

Section 10. Powers Denied to the States

Limitations on Powers Section 10 lists limits on the states. These restrictions were designed, in part, to prevent an overlapping in functions and authority with the federal government.

D Differentiated Instruction

Interpersonal Organize the class into groups of five. **Ask:** What does the phrase "necessary and proper" in the elastic clause mean? How much should members of Congress be able to "stretch" the powers of the Constitution? Have each group write a statement answering the questions. *(Group's responses will vary.)* Have a volunteer from each group present their group's statement, inviting the rest of the class to respond. **OL**

R Reading Strategy

Evaluating Article 1, Section 9, prohibits the suspension of the writ of habeas corpus. Discuss with students the protection this offers. **Ask:** Is this an outdated principle or still necessary to the Constitution? *(Most students will likely see this as a major principle of our legal system.)* **OL**

Answer: No bills of attainder shall be passed.

Additional Support

Extending the Content

The Electoral College The electors in the Electoral College almost always vote as expected. Exceptions are rare. There have been only a small number of "faithless electors" among the more than 17,000 electors chosen since 1789. For example, in 1988 Democratic nominee Michael Dukakis was denied one of his 112 electoral votes when a West Virginia elector cast her ballot for Dukakis's running mate, Senator Lloyd Bentsen. She gave her vice-presidential vote to Dukakis. In 2004 Democratic nominee John Kerry received one electoral vote less than the expected 252 when a Minnesota elector cast a ballot for his running mate, John Edwards.

C Critical Thinking

Analyzing Information Point out that one of the difficult questions for the Framers of the Constitution concerned the chief executive—exactly how much power should the president have? **Ask:** Why did the Framers set up an office of president with limited powers? *(Discussion should focus on the Framers' fear of a single leader with uncontrolled powers.)* OL

R Reading Strategy

Evaluating Tell students that the Constitution originally did not limit the number of terms the president could serve. George Washington set a precedent by serving only two terms. Until Franklin D. Roosevelt, no president had served more than two terms. Many people opposed Roosevelt's four terms in office. This opposition eventually led to the 1951 ratification of the Twenty-second Amendment, which limited presidents to two terms. **Ask:** Do you think that presidents should be limited to two terms in office? Why or why not? *(Answers will vary.)* As a class, make a list of pros and cons for a two-term limit for presidential office. BL

Additional Support

Article II. The Executive Branch

C Article II creates an executive branch to carry out laws passed by Congress. Article II lists the powers and duties of the president, describes qualifications for office and procedures for electing the president, and provides for a vice president.

What Might Have Been
Term of Office Alexander Hamilton also provided his own governmental outline at the Constitutional Convention. Some of its most distinctive elements were that both the executive and the members of the Senate were "elected to serve during good behaviour," meaning there was no specified limit on their time in office.

Section 1.
President and Vice President
Former Method of Election In the election of 1800, the top two candidates received the same number of electoral votes, making it necessary for the House of Representatives to decide the election. To eliminate this problem, the Twelfth Amendment, added in 1804, changed the method of electing the president stated in Article II, Section 3. The Twelfth Amendment requires that the electors cast separate ballots for president and vice president.

Section 1.
President and Vice President
Qualifications The president must be a citizen of the United States by birth, at least 35 years of age, and a resident of the United States for 14 years.

What Might Have Been
Qualifications At the Constitutional Convention, the New Jersey Amendments, sponsored by the smaller states, raised the possibility of making the executive a committee of people rather than a single individual. Also, executives were not allowed to run for a second term of office under this plan.

Article II
Section 1

[1.] The executive Power shall be vested in a President of the United States of America. He shall hold his Office during the Term of four Years, and, together with the Vice-President, chosen for the same Term, be elected, as follows
[2.] Each State shall appoint, in such Manner as the Legislature thereof may direct, a Number of Electors, equal to the whole Number of Senators and Representatives to which the State may be entitled in the Congress: but no Senator or Representative, or Person holding an Office of Trust or Profit under the United States, shall be appointed an Elector.
[3.] The Electors shall meet in their respective States, and vote by Ballot for two Persons, of whom one at least shall not be an Inhabitant of the same State with themselves. And they shall make a List of all the Persons voted for, and of the Number of Votes for each; which List they shall sign and certify, and transmit sealed to the Seat of the Government of the United States, directed to the President of the Senate. The President of the Senate shall, in the Presence of the Senate and House of Representatives, open all the Certificates, and the Votes shall then be counted. The Person having the greatest Number of Votes shall be the President, if such Number be a Majority of the whole Number of Electors appointed; and if there be more than one who have such Majority, and have an equal Number of Votes, then the House of Representatives shall immediately chuse by Ballot one of them for President; and if no person have a Majority, then from the five highest on the List the said House shall in like Manner chuse the president. But in chusing the President, the Votes shall be taken by States, the Representation from each State having one Vote; A quorum for this Purpose shall consist of a Member or Members from two thirds of the States, and a Majority of all the States shall be necessary to a Choice. In every Case, after the Choice of the President, the Person having the greatest Number of Votes of the Electors shall be the Vice-President. But if there should remain two or more who have equal Votes, the Senate shall chuse from them by Ballot the Vice President.
[4.] The Congress may determine the Time of chusing the Electors, and the Day on which they shall give their Votes; which Day shall be the same throughout the United States.
R **[5.]** No Person except a natural born Citizen, or a Citizen of the United States, at the time of the Adoption of this Constitution, shall be eligible to the Office of President; neither shall any Person be eligible to that Office who shall not have attained to the Age of thirty five Years, and been fourteen Years a Resident within the United States.
[6.] In Case of the Removal of the President from Office, or of his Death, Resignation, or Inability to discharge the Powers and Duties of the said Office, the Same shall devolve on the Vice-President, and the Congress may by Law provide for the Case of Removal, Death, Resignation

Extending the Content

Incapacitated Presidents The United States has had a disabled president several times in its history. In the 1880s James Garfield remained bedridden for 80 days before dying from injuries sustained by an assassin's bullet. In 1901 William McKinley was struck by an assassin and lingered until he died eight days later. Woodrow Wilson suffered a severe stroke and was incapacitated from October 1919 until April 1920. During that time First Lady Edith Wilson controlled all access to the president; she maintained that although the president was bedridden, his mental abilities were unimpaired. President Wilson did not see any document that she did not wish him to see and she was his only spokesperson.

or Inability, both of the President and Vice-President, declaring what Officer shall then act as President, and such Officer shall act accordingly, until the Disability be removed, or a President shall be elected.

[7.] The President shall, at stated Times, receive for his Services, a Compensation, which shall neither be encreased nor diminished during the Period for which he shall have been elected, and he shall not receive within that Period any other Emolument from the United States, or any of them.

[8.] Before he enter on the Execution of his Office, he shall take the following Oath or Affirmation—"I do solemnly swear (or affirm) that I will faithfully execute the Office of President of the United States, and will to the best of my Ability, preserve, protect and defend the Constitution of the United States."

Section 2

[1.] The President shall be Commander in Chief of the Army and Navy of the United States, and of the Militia of the several States, when called into the actual Service of the United States; he may require the Opinion, in writing, of the principal Officer in each of the executive Departments, C1 upon any Subject relating to the Duties of their respective Offices, and he shall have Power to grant Reprieves and Pardons for Offences against the United States, except in Cases of Impeachment.

[2.] He shall have Power, by and with the Advice and Consent of the Senate, to make Treaties, provided two thirds of the Senators present concur; and he shall nominate, and by and with the Advice and Consent of the Senate, shall appoint Ambassadors, other public Ministers and Consuls, Judges of the supreme Court, and all other Officers of the United States, whose Appointments are not herein otherwise provided for, and which shall be established by Law: but the Congress may by Law vest the Appointment of such inferior Officers, as they think proper, in the President alone, in the Courts of Law, or in the Heads of Departments. C2

[3.] The President shall have Power to fill up all Vacancies that may happen during the Recess of the Senate, by granting Commissions which shall expire at the End of their next Session.

Section 3

He shall from time to time give to the Congress Information of the State of the Union, and recommend to their Consideration such Measures as he shall judge necessary and expedient; he may, on extraordinary Occasions, convene both Houses, or either of them, and in Case of Disagreement between them, with Respect to the Time of Adjournment, he may adjourn them to such Time as he shall think proper; he shall receive Ambassadors and other public Ministers; he shall take Care that the Laws be faithfully executed, and shall Commission all the Officers of the United States.

Section 1. President and Vice President

Vacancies If the president dies, resigns, is removed from office by impeachment, or is unable to carry out the duties of the office, the vice president becomes president.

Section 1. President and Vice President

Salary Originally, the president's salary was $25,000 per year. The president's current salary is $400,000 plus a $50,000 expense account per year. The president also receives living accommodations in the White House and Camp David.

Section 2. Powers of the President

Cabinet Mention of "the principal officer in each of the executive departments" is the only suggestion of the president's cabinet to be found in the Constitution. The cabinet is an advisory body, and its power depends on the president. Section 2, Clause 1 also makes the president the head of the armed forces. This established the principle of civilian control of the military.

Section 2. Powers of the President

Treaties The president is responsible for the conduct of relations with foreign countries. What role does the Senate have in approving treaties?

Section 3. Duties of the President

Executive Orders An important presidential power is the ability to issue executive orders. An executive order is a rule or command the president issues that has the force of law. Only Congress can make laws under the Constitution, but executive orders are considered part of the president's duty to "take care that the laws be faithfully executed." This power is often used during emergencies. Over time the scope of executive orders has expanded. Decisions by federal agencies and departments are also considered to be executive orders.

C1 Critical Thinking

Analyzing Information Ask students to discuss why the Framers of the Constitution make the president commander in chief of the armed forces and any state militias called to serve the United States. *(The Framers wanted to ensure civilian control of the military.)* **OL**

C2 Critical Thinking

Determining Cause and Effect Discuss the increase in presidential power during the twentieth and twenty-first centuries. For example, increasing globalization has expanded the president's foreign relations responsibilities. Write the following on the board: "The increase in presidential power has been related to crises, whether domestic or foreign." **Ask:** Do you think this is the true cause of the increase in presidential power? Why or why not? If not, what do you think caused the increase? *(Some students may agree that globalization is the cause of increased presidential importance. Others may point to the role of the media in focusing attention on one individual.)*

Answer: Two-thirds of the Senators must concur in order for a treaty to be approved.

Additional Support

Extending the Content

Presidential Elections In the first election, the American people had no problem selecting a president. George Washington was the unanimous choice, winning 69 electoral votes—the maximum possible in 1789. No other president has matched that feat, although Franklin D. Roosevelt came close in 1936 with 98.5 percent of the electoral vote. Most other presidential elections have been more competitive, sometimes creating issues the Founders did not foresee.

C Critical Thinking

Identifying Central Issues Ask students to consider the meaning of the phrase "respect for the law." Guide their discussion by asking the following questions: What is the law? How can the law affect individuals and society? Why is respect for the law necessary for good government? *(Answers will vary.)* OL

R Reading Strategy

Evaluating Have students underline the definition of treason in the Constitution (Article III, Section 3, Clause 1). Tell students that this specific definition cannot be modified by Congress and can only be changed by a constitutional amendment. Have students use library or Internet resources to research U.S. citizens who have been guilty of treason. **Ask:** Do you think the person was guilty of treason? Did the person's crime fit the definition presented in the Constitution? *(Answers will vary.)* Invite students to share their findings and responses with the class. OL

Additional Support

Section 4. Impeachment
Reasons for Removal From Office This section states the reasons for which the president and vice president may be impeached and removed from office. Only Andrew Johnson and Bill Clinton have been impeached by the House. Richard Nixon resigned before the House could vote on possible impeachment.

Section 4

The President, Vice-President and all civil Officers of the United States, shall be removed from Office on Impeachment for, and Conviction of, Treason, Bribery, or other high Crimes and Misdemeanors.

Article III. The Judicial Branch
The term *judicial* refers to courts. The Constitution set up only the Supreme Court but provided for the establishment of other federal courts. The judiciary of the C United States has two different systems of courts. One system consists of the federal courts, whose powers derive from the Constitution and federal laws. The other includes the courts of each of the 50 states, whose powers derive from state constitutions and laws.

Article III

Section 1

The judicial Power of the United States, shall be vested in one supreme Court, and in such inferior Courts as the Congress may from time to time ordain and establish. The Judges, both of the supreme and inferior Courts, shall hold their Offices during good Behaviour, and shall, at stated Times, receive for their Services, a Compensation, which shall not be diminished during their Continuance in Office.

Section 2. Jurisdiction
General Jurisdiction Federal courts deal mostly with "statute law," or laws passed by Congress, treaties, and cases involving the Constitution itself.

Section 2. Jurisdiction
The Supreme Court A court with "original jurisdiction" has the authority to be the first court to hear a case. The Supreme Court generally has "appellate jurisdiction" in that it mostly hears cases appealed from lower courts.

Section 2. Jurisdiction
Jury Trial Except in cases of impeachment, anyone accused of a crime has the right to a trial by jury. The trial must be held in the state where the crime was committed. Jury trial guarantees were strengthened in the Sixth, Seventh, Eighth, and Ninth Amendments.

Section 2

[1.] The judicial Power shall extend to all Cases, in Law and Equity, arising under this Constitution, the Laws of the United States, and Treaties made, or which shall be made, under their Authority;—to all Cases affecting Ambassadors, other public Ministers and Consuls;—to all Cases of admiralty and maritime Jurisdiction;—to Controversies to which the United States shall be a Party;—to Controversies between two or more States;—between a State and Citizens of another State;—between Citizens of different States,—between Citizens of the same State claiming Lands under Grants of different States, and between a State, or the Citizens thereof, and foreign States, Citizens or Subjects.

[2.] In all Cases affecting Ambassadors, other public Ministers and Consuls, and those in which a State shall be Party, the supreme Court shall have **original Jurisdiction.** In all the other Cases before mentioned, the supreme Court shall have **appellate Jurisdiction,** both as to Law and Fact, with such Exceptions, and under such Regulations as the Congress shall make.

[3.] The Trial of all Crimes, except in Cases of Impeachment, shall be by Jury; and such Trial shall be held in the State where the said Crimes shall have been committed; but when not committed within any State, the Trial shall be at such Place or Places as the Congress may by Law have directed.

Section 3

[1.] Treason against the United States, shall consist only in levying War against them, or in adhering to their Enemies, giving them Aid and Comfort. No Person shall be convicted R of Treason unless on the Testimony of two Witnesses to the same overt Act, or on Confession in open Court.

[2.] The Congress shall have Power to declare the Punishment of Treason, but no Attainder of Treason shall work Corruption of Blood, or Forfeiture except during the Life of the Person attainted.

Vocabulary

original jurisdiction: *authority to be the first court to hear a case*
appellate jurisdiction: *authority to hear cases that have been appealed from lower courts*

Extending the Content

Supreme Court Justices To date, all except four members of the U.S. Supreme Court have been white men. Thurgood Marshall, the first African American, was nominated to the Court by President Lyndon Johnson in 1967; after Marshall's retirement, he was replaced in 1991 by another African American, Clarence Thomas, who was nominated by President George H.W. Bush. President Ronald Reagan appointed the first woman to the Court—Sandra Day O'Connor—in 1981. President William Clinton appointed the second woman to the Court—Ruth Bader Ginsburg—in 1993.

Article IV

Section 1

Full Faith and Credit shall be given in each State to the public Acts, Records, and judicial Proceedings of every other State. And the Congress may by general Laws prescribe the Manner in which such Acts, Records and Proceedings shall be proved, and the Effect thereof.

Section 2

[1.] The Citizens of each State shall be entitled to all Privileges and Immunities of Citizens in the several States.
[2.] A Person charged in any State with **Treason,** Felony, or other Crime, who shall flee from Justice, and be found in another State, shall on Demand of the executive Authority of the State from which he fled, be delivered up, to be removed to the State having Jurisdiction of the Crime.
[3.] No Person held to Service of Labour in one State, under the Laws thereof, escaping into another, shall, in Consequence of any Law or Regulation therein, be discharged from such Service or Labour, but shall be delivered up on Claim of the Party to whom such Service or Labour may be due.

Section 3

[1.] New States may be admitted by the Congress into this Union; but no new State shall be formed or erected within the Jurisdiction of any other State; nor any State be formed by the Junction of two or more States, or Parts of States, without the Consent of the Legislatures of the States concerned as well as of the Congress. **S**
[2.] The Congress shall have Power to dispose of and make all needful Rules and Regulations respecting the Territory or other Property belonging to the United States; and nothing in this Constitution shall be so construed as to Prejudice any Claims of the United States, or of any particular State.

Section 4

The United States shall guarantee to every State in this Union a Republican Form of Government, and shall protect each of them against Invasion; and on Application of the Legislature, or of the Executive (when the Legislature cannot be convened) against domestic Violence.

Article V

The Congress, whenever two thirds of both Houses shall deem it necessary, shall propose **Amendments** to this Constitution, or, on the Application of the Legislatures of two thirds of the several States, shall call a Convention for proposing Amendments, which, in either Case, **C** shall be valid to all Intents and Purposes, as Part of this Constitution, when ratified by the Legislatures of three fourths of the several States, or by Conventions in three fourths thereof, as the one or the other Mode of **Ratification** may be proposed by the Congress; Provided

Article IV. Relations Among the States

Article IV explains the relationship of the states to one another and to the national government. This article requires each state to give citizens of other states the same rights as its own citizens, addresses the admission of new states, and guarantees that the national government will protect the states.

Section 1. Official Acts

Recognition by States This provision ensures that each state recognizes the laws, court decisions, and records of all other states. For example, a marriage license issued by one state must be accepted by all states.

Vocabulary

treason: *violation of the allegiance owed by a person to his or her own country, for example, by aiding an enemy*

amendment: *a change to the Constitution*

ratification: *process by which an amendment is approved*

Section 3. New States and Territories

New States Congress has the power to admit new states. It also determines the basic guidelines for applying for statehood. Two states, Maine and West Virginia, were created within the boundaries of another state. In the case of West Virginia, President Lincoln recognized the West Virginia government as the legal government of Virginia during the Civil War. This allowed West Virginia to secede from Virginia without obtaining approval from the Virginia legislature.

Article V. The Amendment Process

Article V explains how the Constitution can be amended, or changed. All of the 27 amendments were proposed by a two-thirds vote of both houses of Congress. Only the Twenty-first Amendment was ratified by constitutional conventions of the states. All other amendments have been ratified by state legislatures. What is an amendment?

S Skill Practice

Conducting Research Have students use library or Internet resources to research a current U.S. territory, including the history of the territory's relationship with the United States. Tell them to present their findings in a three-page report. Encourage students to supplement their reports with photographs, maps, and drawings that provide information about the territory. **AL**

C Critical Thinking

Identifying Central Issues

Ask students to recall weaknesses of the Articles of Confederation government. *(inability to tax states, unanimous approval needed to change the government)* **Ask:** How did the Framers make the new Constitution easier to amend? *(It does not require all states to agree before a change goes into effect. Amendments can be proposed by the state legislatures or by the congressional chambers. Ratification of the amendments can be either by state legislatures or by state conventions.)* **OL**

Answer: An amendment is a change to the Constitution.

Additional Support

Activity: Collaborative Learning

Predicting Outcomes Organize students into groups to present either the pros or cons of federal judges being elected rather than appointed. Give groups time to prepare their arguments and encourage group members to be responsible for different parts of the research. As each group presents its arguments, note major points on the board.

C Critical Thinking

Analyzing Information

Inform students that one political scientist has called the supremacy clause (Article VI, Section 2) "the most important single provision of the Constitution." **Ask:** Why do you think this might be so? *(This clause made it clear that the national Constitution and laws are supreme over state constitutions.)* OL

Did You Know?

Ratification The first five states to ratify the Constitution—Delaware, Pennsylvania, New Jersey, Georgia, and Connecticut—did so quickly and by large majorities. The last two of the original thirteen states ratified the Constitution after George Washington had been inaugurated as the first president on April 30, 1789—North Carolina on November 21, 1789, and Rhode Island on May 29, 1790.

that no Amendment which may be made prior to the Year One thousand eight hundred and eight shall in any Manner affect the first and fourth Clauses in the Ninth Section of the first Article; and that no State, without its Consent, shall be deprived of its equal Suffrage in the Senate.

Article VI. Constitutional Supremacy
Article VI contains the "supremacy clause." This clause establishes that the Constitution, laws passed by Congress, and treaties of the United States "shall be the supreme Law of the Land." The "supremacy clause" recognizes the Constitution and federal laws as supreme when in conflict with those of the states. C

Article VI

[1.] All Debts contracted and Engagements entered into, before the Adoption of this Constitution, shall be as valid against the United States under this Constitution, as under the Confederation.

[2.] This Constitution, and the Laws of the United States which shall be made in Pursuance thereof; and all Treaties made, or which shall be made, under the Authority of the United States, shall be the supreme Law of the Land; and the Judges in every State shall be bound thereby, any Thing in the Constitution or Laws of any State to the Contrary notwithstanding.

[3.] The Senators and Representatives before mentioned, and the Members of the several State Legislatures, and all executive and judicial Officers, both of the United States and of the several States, shall be bound by Oath or Affirmation, to support this Constitution; but no religious Test shall ever be required as a Qualification to any Office or public Trust under the United States.

Article VII. Ratification
Article VII addresses ratification and states that, unlike the Articles of Confederation, which required approval of all thirteen states for adoption, the Constitution would take effect after it was ratified by nine states.

Article VII

The Ratification of the Conventions of nine States, shall be sufficient for the Establishment of this Constitution between the States so ratifying the same.

Done in Convention by the Unanimous Consent of the States present the Seventeenth Day of September in the Year of our Lord one thousand seven hundred and Eighty seven and of the Independence of the United States of America the Twelfth. In witness whereof We have hereunto subscribed our Names,

Signers

George Washington,
President and Deputy from Virginia

New Hampshire
John Langdon
Nicholas Gilman

Massachusetts
Nathaniel Gorham
Rufus King

Connecticut
William Samuel Johnson
Roger Sherman

New York
Alexander Hamilton

New Jersey
William Livingston
David Brearley
William Paterson
Jonathan Dayton

Pennsylvania
Benjamin Franklin
Thomas Mifflin
Robert Morris
George Clymer
Thomas FitzSimons
Jared Ingersoll
James Wilson
Gouverneur Morris

Delaware
George Read
Gunning Bedford, Jr.
John Dickinson
Richard Bassett
Jacob Broom

Maryland
James McHenry
Daniel of St. Thomas Jenifer
Daniel Carroll

Virginia
John Blair
James Madison, Jr.

North Carolina
William Blount
Richard Dobbs Spaight
Hugh Williamson

South Carolina
John Rutledge
Charles Cotesworth Pinckney
Charles Pinckney
Pierce Butler

Georgia
William Few
Abraham Baldwin

Attest:
William Jackson,
Secretary

Additional Support

Extending the Content

Signers of the Constitution Of the 55 delegates who attended the Constitutional Convention, only 39 signed the document. The thirty-ninth signature—that of John Dickinson—was written by George Read at Dickinson's request. Elbridge Gerry of Massachusetts and Edmund Randolph and George Mason of Virginia refused to sign while 13 other delegates left the convention early.

Amendment I

Congress shall make no law respecting an establishment of religion, or prohibiting the free exercise thereof; or abridging the freedom of speech, or of the press; or the right of the people peaceably to assemble, and to petition the Government for a redress of grievances.

Amendment II

A well regulated Militia, being necessary to the security of a free State, the right of the people to keep and bear Arms, shall not be infringed.

Amendment III

No Soldier shall, in time of peace be **quartered** in any house, without the consent of the Owner, nor in time of war, but in a manner to be prescribed by law.

Amendment IV

The right of the people to be secure in their persons, houses, papers, and effects, against unreasonable searches and seizures, shall not be violated, and no **Warrants** shall issue, but upon **probable cause,** supported by Oath or affirmation, and particularly describing the place to be searched, and the persons or things to be seized.

Amendment V

No person shall be held to answer for a capital, or otherwise infamous crime, unless on a presentment or indictment of a Grand Jury, except in cases arising in the land or naval forces, or in the Militia, when in actual service in time of War or public danger; nor shall any person be subject for the same offence to be twice put in jeopardy of life or limb; nor shall be compelled in any criminal case to be a witness against himself, nor be deprived of life, liberty, or property, without due process of law; nor shall private property be taken for public use without just compensation.

Amendment VI

In all criminal prosecutions, the accused shall enjoy the right to a speedy and public trial, by an impartial jury of the State and district wherein the crime shall have been committed, which district shall have been previously ascertained by law, and to be informed of the nature and cause of the accusation; to be confronted with the witnesses against him; to have compulsory process for obtaining Witnesses in his favor, and to have the assistance of counsel for his defence.

Amendment VII

In Suits at common law, where the value in controversy shall exceed twenty dollars, the right of trial by jury shall be preserved, and no fact tried by a jury, shall be otherwise reexamined in any Court of the United States, than according to the rules of **common law.**

The Amendments

This part of the Constitution consists of changes and additions. The Constitution has been amended 27 times throughout the nation's history. **R**

The Bill of Rights

The first 10 amendments are known as the Bill of Rights (1791). These amendments limit the powers of the federal government. The First Amendment protects the civil liberties of individuals in the United States. The amendment freedoms are not absolute, however. They are limited by the rights of other individuals. What freedoms does the First Amendment protect?

Vocabulary

quarter: *to provide living accommodations*

warrant: *document that gives police particular rights or powers*

probable cause: *police must have a reasonable basis to believe a person is linked to a crime*

Amendment 5

Rights of the Accused This amendment contains important protections for people accused of crimes. One of the protections is that government may not deprive any person of life, liberty, or property without due process of law. This means that the government must follow proper constitutional procedures in trials and in other actions it takes against individuals. According to Amendment V, what is the function of a grand jury?

Amendment 6

Right to Speedy and Fair Trial A basic protection is the right to a speedy, public trial. The jury must hear witnesses and evidence on both sides before deciding the guilt or innocence of a person charged with a crime. This amendment also provides that legal counsel must be provided to a defendant. In 1963, in *Gideon* v. *Wainwright*, the Supreme Court ruled that if a defendant cannot afford a lawyer, the government must provide one to defend him or her. Why is the right to a "speedy" trial important?

Vocabulary

common law: *law established by previous court decisions*

R Reading Strategy

Categorizing Information

As they read the amendments, have students list in a table each amendment according to the following headings: *Personal Freedoms, Relations Among States, Process of Government*, and *Citizenship*. Students should keep in mind the substance of the amendment and its effect on American life. Remind them that some amendments might fit into more than one category. **OL**

Answer: freedom of religion, freedom of speech, freedom of the press, freedom to peaceably assemble, and freedom to petition the government for a redress of grievances

Answer: A grand jury evaluates whether there is enough evidence to bring an accused person to trial.

Answer: The requirement of a "speedy" trial ensures that an accused person will not be held in jail for a lengthy period as a means of punishing the accused without a trial.

Additional Support

Activity: Collaborative Learning

Writing Reports Organize students into four groups and assign to each group one of the four sections of Article I (Sections 2, 3, 4, and 9) that has been modified by amendment. Have each group research how, why, and when the amendment to its assigned section was made. Encourage groups to present their findings to the rest of the class in brief written reports.

S Skill Practice

Conducting Research Point out that the Electoral College has been criticized as obsolete, and various reforms have been suggested for changing it or abolishing it altogether. Ask students to research some of these suggestions or reforms. Lead a discussion about the 2000 and 2004 presidential elections, which continued the debate over the role of the Electoral College, and discuss how potential reforms might or might not have affected the elections' outcomes. AL

Answer: the House of Representatives

Vocabulary

bail: *money that an accused person provides to the court as a guarantee that he or she will be present for a trial*

Amendment 9
Powers Reserved to the People This amendment prevents government from claiming that the only rights people have are those listed in the Bill of Rights.

Amendment 10
Powers Reserved to the States This amendment protects the states and the people from the federal government. It establishes that powers not given to the national government and not denied to the states by the Constitution belong to the states or to the people. These are checks on the "necessary and proper" power of the federal government, which is provided for in Article I, Section 8, Clause 18.

Amendment 11
Suits Against States The Eleventh Amendment (1795) provides that a lawsuit brought by a citizen of the United States or a foreign nation against a state must be tried in a state court, not in a federal court. The Supreme Court had ruled in *Chisholm* v. *Georgia* (1793) that a federal court could try a lawsuit brought by citizens of South Carolina against a citizen of Georgia.

Vocabulary

majority: *more than half*

Amendment 12
Election of President and Vice President The Twelfth Amendment (1804) corrects a problem that had arisen in the method of electing the president and vice president, which is described in Article II, Section 1, Clause 3. This amendment provides for the Electoral College to use separate ballots in voting for president and vice president. If no candidate receives a majority of the electoral votes, who elects the president?

Amendment VIII

Excessive **bail** shall not be required, nor excessive fines imposed, nor cruel and unusual punishments inflicted.

Amendment IX

The enumeration in the Constitution, of certain rights, shall not be construed to deny or disparage others retained by the people.

Amendment X

The powers not delegated to the United States by the Constitution, nor prohibited by it to the States, are reserved to the States respectively, or to the people.

Amendment XI

The Judicial power of the United States shall not be construed to extend to any suit in law or equity, commenced or prosecuted against one of the United States by Citizens of another State, or by Citizens or Subjects of any Foreign State.

Amendment XII

The electors shall meet in their respective states and vote by ballot for President and Vice-President, one of whom, at least, shall not be an inhabitant of the same state with themselves; they shall name in their ballots the person voted for as President, and in distinct ballots the person voted for as Vice-President, and they shall make distinct lists of all persons voted for as President, and of all persons voted for as Vice-President, and of the number of votes for each, which lists they shall sign and certify, and transmit sealed to the seat of the government of the United States, directed to the President of the Senate;—The President of the Senate shall, in the presence of the Senate and House of Representatives, open all the certificates and the votes shall then be counted;—The person having the greatest number of votes for President, shall be the President, if such number be a **majority** of the whole number of Electors appointed; and if no person have such majority, then from the persons having the highest numbers not exceeding three on the list of those voted for as President, the House of Representatives shall choose immediately, by ballot, the President. But in choosing the President, the votes shall be taken by states, the representation from each state having one vote; a quorum for this purpose shall consist of a member or members from two-thirds of the states, and a majority of all the states shall be necessary to a choice. And if the House of Representatives shall not choose a President whenever the right of choice shall devolve upon them, before the fourth day of March next following, then the Vice-President shall act as President, as in the case of the death or other constitutional disability of the President. The person having the greatest number of votes as Vice-President, shall be the Vice-President, if such number be a S

Additional Support

Extending the Content

The Twelfth Amendment Only once since ratification of the Constitution has an amendment been adopted that changed the method of electing the president. The election of 1800 was the first in which the Constitution's election procedures were put to the test and the House elected the president. The Federalists nominated John Adams for a second term and chose Charles Cotesworth Pinckney as his running mate. The Democratic-Republicans chose Vice President Thomas Jefferson for president and Aaron Burr for vice president.

The electors met in each state on December 4, with the following results: Jefferson and Burr, 73 electoral votes each; Adams, 65; Pinckney, 64; and John Jay, 1. The Federalists had lost, but because the Democratic-Republicans had neglected to withhold one electoral vote from Burr, their presidential and vice-presidential candidates were tied, and the election was thrown into the House.

The Jefferson-Burr contest clearly illustrated the dangers of the double-balloting system established by the Constitution, and pressure began to build for an amendment requiring separate votes for president and vice president. Congress approved the Twelfth Amendment in December 1803.

majority of the whole number of Electors appointed, and if no person have a majority, then from the two highest numbers on the list, the Senate shall choose the Vice-President; a quorum for the purpose shall consist of two-thirds of the whole number of Senators, and a majority of the whole number shall be necessary to a choice. But no person constitutionally ineligible to the office of President shall be eligible to that of Vice-President of the United States.

Amendment XIII

Section 1

Neither slavery nor involuntary servitude, except as a punishment for crime whereof the party shall have been duly convicted, shall exist within the United States, or any place subject to their jurisdiction.

Section 2

Congress shall have power to enforce this article by appropriate legislation.

Amendment XIV

Section 1

All persons born or naturalized in the United States, and subject to the jurisdiction thereof, are citizens of the United States and of the State wherein they reside. No State shall make or enforce any law which shall **abridge** the privileges or immunities of citizens of the United States; nor shall any State deprive any person of life, liberty, or property, without due process of law; nor deny to any person within its jurisdiction the equal protection of the laws. C D

Section 2

Representatives shall be apportioned among the several States according to their respective numbers, counting the whole number of persons in each State, excluding Indians not taxed. But when the right to vote at any election for the choice of electors for President and Vice-President of the United States, Representatives in Congress, the Executive and Judicial officers of a State, or the members of the Legislature thereof, is denied to any of the male inhabitants of such State, being twenty-one years of age, and citizens of the United States, or in any way abridged, except for participation in rebellion, or other crime, the basis of representation therein shall be reduced in the proportion which the number of such male citizens shall bear to the whole number of male citizens twenty-one years of age in such State.

Section 3

No person shall be a Senator or Representative in Congress, or elector of President and Vice-President, or hold any office, civil or military, under the United States, or under any State, who, having previously taken an oath, as a member of Congress, or as an officer of the United States, or as a member of any State legislature, or as an executive or judicial officer of any State, to support the Constitution

Amendment 13
Abolition of Slavery Amendments Thirteen (1865), Fourteen, and Fifteen often are called the Civil War amendments because they grew out of that conflict. The Thirteenth Amendment outlaws slavery.

Amendment 14
Rights of Citizens The Fourteenth Amendment (1868) originally was intended to protect the legal rights of the freed slaves. Its interpretation has been extended to protect the rights of citizenship in general by prohibiting a state from depriving any person of life, liberty, or property without "due process of law." In addition, it states that all citizens have the right to equal protection of the laws in all states.

Amendment 14. Section 2
Representation in Congress This section reduced the number of members a state had in the House of Representatives if it denied its citizens the right to vote. Later civil rights laws and the Twenty-fourth Amendment guaranteed the vote to African Americans.

Vocabulary

abridge: *to reduce*

Amendment 14. Section 3
Penalty for Engaging in Insurrection The leaders of the Confederacy were barred from state or federal offices unless Congress agreed to remove this ban. By the end of Reconstruction, all but a few Confederate leaders were allowed to return to public service.

D Differentiated Instruction

Visual/Spatial Have students make a time line that includes each of the amendments and the year of ratification. Display the time lines in the classroom. BL

C Critical Thinking

Drawing Conclusions Inform students that the constitutional provisions protecting personal liberties have been tested. One such test occurred during World War II, when more than 100,000 Japanese Americans were put into relocation camps. **Ask:** In times of crisis, can the government suspend personal liberties? *(Answers will vary.)* Ask students to cite specific evidence when answering. OL

Additional Support

Extending the Content

Civil War Amendments The Thirteenth, Fourteenth, and Fifteenth Amendments represent attempts to use the Constitution to end slavery, to extend citizenship to formerly enslaved men and women, and to guarantee male African Americans the right to vote. Literacy tests, poll taxes, and grandfather clauses, however, continued to keep large numbers of African Americans from voting until the passage of the Civil Rights Act of 1965.

R Reading Strategy

Categorizing Information Have students work together in three groups to research one of the following: poll taxes, literacy tests, or grandfather clause. Remind students to pay particular attention to how the provision was used to keep African Americans from voting. Then ask the groups to combine their information and present it in a chart or graphic organizer that lists the provision, a definition or explanation of the provision, and the impact of the provision on African American voting rights. OL

Answer: Former slaveholders could not collect compensation for the loss of their slaves.

Answer: six years

Additional Support

Amendment 14. Section 4
Public Debt The public debt acquired by the federal government during the Civil War was valid and could not be questioned by the South. However, the debts of the Confederacy were declared to be illegal. Could former slaveholders collect payment for the loss of their slaves?

R

Amendment 15
Voting Rights The Fifteenth Amendment (1870) prohibits the government from denying a person's right to vote on the basis of race. Despite the law, many states denied African Americans the right to vote by such means as poll taxes, literacy tests, and white primaries.

Amendment 16
Income Tax The origins of the Sixteenth Amendment (1913) date back to 1895, when the Supreme Court declared a federal income tax unconstitutional. To overturn this decision, this amendment authorizes an income tax that is levied on a direct basis.

Amendment 17
Direct Election of Senators The Seventeenth Amendment (1913) states that the people, instead of state legislatures, elect United States senators. How many years are in a Senate term?

of the United States, shall have engaged in insurrection or rebellion against the same, or given aid or comfort to the enemies thereof. But Congress may by a vote of two-thirds of each House, remove such disability.

Section 4
The validity of the public debt of the United States, authorized by law, including debts incurred for payment of pensions and bounties for service, in suppressing insurrection or rebellion, shall not be questioned. But neither the United States nor any State shall assume or pay any debt or obligation incurred in aid of **insurrection** or rebellion against the United States, or any claim for the loss or emancipation of any slave; but all such debts, obligations and claims shall be held illegal and void.

Section 5
The Congress shall have power to enforce, by appropriate legislation, the provisions of this article.

Amendment XV
Section 1
The right of citizens of the United States to vote shall not be denied or abridged by the United States or by any State on account of race, color, or previous condition of servitude.

Section 2
The Congress shall have power to enforce this article by appropriate legislation.

Amendment XVI
The Congress shall have power to lay and collect taxes on incomes, from whatever source derived, without **apportionment** among the several States and without regard to any census or enumeration.

Amendment XVII
Section 1
The Senate of the United States shall be composed of two Senators from each State, elected by the people thereof, for six years; and each Senator shall have one vote. The electors in each State shall have the qualifications requisite for electors of the most numerous branch of the State legislatures.

Section 2
When **vacancies** happen in the representation of any State in the Senate, the executive authority of such State shall issue writs of election to fill such vacancies: *Provided*, That the legislature of any State may empower the executive thereof to make temporary appointments until the people fill the vacancies by election as the legislature may direct.

Vocabulary
insurrection: *rebellion against the government*
apportionment: *distribution of seats in House based on population*
vacancy: *an office or position that is unfilled or unoccupied*

Extending the Content

Racial Discrimination and the Constitution The Thirteenth, Fourteenth, and Fifteenth Amendments represent attempts to use the Constitution to end slavery, to extend citizenship to formerly enslaved persons, and to guarantee male African Americans the right to vote. Literacy tests, poll taxes, and grandfather clauses, however, continued to keep large numbers of African Americans from voting in many Southern states after Reconstruction.

Section 3

This amendment shall not be so construed as to affect the election or term of any Senator chosen before it becomes valid as part of the Constitution.

Amendment XVIII

Section 1

C After one year from ratification of this article, the manufacture, sale, or transportation of intoxicating liquors within, the importation thereof into, or the exportation thereof from the United States and all territory subject to the jurisdiction thereof for beverage purposes is hereby prohibited.

Section 2

The Congress and the several States shall have concurrent power to enforce this article by appropriate legislation.

Section 3

This article shall be inoperative unless it shall have been ratified as an amendment to the Constitution by the legislatures of the several States, as provided in the Constitution, within seven years from the date of the submission hereof to the States by the Congress.

Amendment XIX

Section 1

S The right of citizens of the United States to vote shall not be denied or abridged by the United States or by any state on account of sex.

Section 2

Congress shall have power by appropriate legislation to enforce the provisions of this article.

Amendment XX

Section 1

The terms of the President and Vice President shall end at noon on the 20th day of January, and the terms of the Senators and Representatives at noon on the 3rd day of January, of the years in which such terms would have ended if this article had not been ratified; and the terms of their successors shall then begin.

Section 2

The Congress shall assemble at least once in every year, and such meeting shall begin at noon on the 3rd day of January, unless they shall by law appoint a different day.

Amendment 18
Prohibition The Eighteenth Amendment (1919) prohibited the production, sale, or transportation of alcoholic beverages in the United States. Prohibition proved to be difficult to enforce. This amendment was later repealed by the Twenty-first Amendment.

Amendment 19
Woman Suffrage The Nineteenth Amendment (1920) guaranteed women the right to vote. By then women had already won the right to vote in many state elections, but the amendment made their right to vote in all state and national elections constitutional.

Amendment 20
"Lame Duck" The Twentieth Amendment (1933) sets new dates for Congress to begin its term and for the inauguration of the president and vice president. Under the original Constitution, elected officials who retired or who had been defeated remained in office for several months. For the outgoing president, this period ran from November until March. Such outgoing officials, referred to as "lame ducks," could accomplish little. What date was fixed as Inauguration Day?

C Critical Thinking

Predicting Consequences Inform students that Prohibition successfully reduced the consumption of alcohol in the United States, thus decreasing the number of alcohol-related deaths and accidents. **Ask:** What do you think happened to this number after Prohibition was repealed in 1933? *(Answers will vary.)* Have students check their predictions by using library or Internet resources to locate statistics on alcohol-related deaths and accidents during the early twentieth century. **AL**

S Skill Practice

Conducting Research Have students use library or Internet resources to research one of the women involved in the movement to achieve national woman suffrage. Tell students to use this data to create posters profiling the individual and her achievements. Encourage students to use captioned photographs and drawings, as well as written information, and to include titles for their posters. Display the posters in the classroom. **OL**

Answer: January 20

Additional Support

Extending the Content

Early Women's Suffrage Early in our history, women in one state—New Jersey—had the vote. The state's first constitution granted suffrage to "any person" who met certain property qualifications. Many women took advantage of this provision to vote. However, the state legislature took this right away from women in 1807.

C Critical Thinking

Analyzing Information Make sure students understand the "lame-duck" issue by reminding them that lame ducks are presidents and members of Congress waiting to leave office after retiring or failing to gain reelection. Since lame ducks were often members of the defeated party, they were in a position to affect legislation even though they no longer spoke for the majority of voters. **Ask:** How did the Twentieth Amendment address the problem of lame ducks? *(It shortened the waiting period between Election Day and the beginning of a new term.)* **OL**

D Differentiated Instruction

Visual/Spatial Have students create political cartoons illustrating the Twenty-first Amendment. Remind them to include titles and captions, if necessary. Then ask students to write paragraphs explaining their cartoons. Display the cartoons in the classroom as you discuss the Twenty-first Amendment. **ELL**

Additional Support

Amendment 20. Section 3
Succession of President and Vice President This section provides that if the president-elect dies before taking office, the vice president-elect becomes president.

Vocabulary

president-elect: *individual who is elected president but has not yet begun serving his or her term*

Amendment 21
Repeal of Prohibition The Twenty-first Amendment (1933) repeals the Eighteenth Amendment. It is the only amendment ever passed to overturn an earlier amendment. It is also the only amendment ratified by special state conventions instead of state legislatures.

Section 3

If, at the time fixed for the beginning of the term of the President, the President elect shall have died, the Vice President elect shall become President. If a President shall not have been chosen before the time fixed for the beginning of his term, or if the **President elect** shall have failed to qualify, then the Vice President elect shall act as President until a President shall have qualified; and the Congress may by law provide for the case wherein neither a President elect nor a Vice President elect shall have qualified, declaring who shall then act as President, or the manner in which one who is to act shall be selected, and such person shall act accordingly until a President or Vice President shall have qualified.

Section 4

The Congress may by law provide for the case of the death of any of the persons from whom the House of Representatives may choose a President whenever the right of choice shall have devolved upon them, and for the case of the death of any of the persons from whom the Senate may choose a Vice President whenever the right of choice shall have devolved upon them.

Section 5

Sections 1 and 2 shall take effect on the 15th day of October following the ratification of this article.

Section 6

This article shall be inoperative unless it shall have been ratified as an amendment to the Constitution by the legislatures of three-fourths of the several States within seven years from the date of its submission.

Amendment XXI

Section 1

The eighteenth article of amendment to the Constitution of the United States is hereby repealed.

Section 2

The transportation or importation into any State, Territory, or possession of the United States for delivery or use therein of intoxicating liquors, in violation of the laws thereof, is hereby prohibited.

Section 3

This article shall be inoperative unless it shall have been ratified as an amendment to the Constitution by conventions in the several States, as provided in the Constitution, within seven years from the date of the submission hereof to the States by the Congress.

Activity: Cooperative Learning

Discussing a Concept Organize students into groups to present either the pros or cons of Prohibition. Give groups time to prepare their arguments and encourage group members to be responsible for different parts of the research. As each group presents its arguments, note major points on the board.

Amendment XXII

Section 1

No person shall be elected to the office of the President more than twice, and no person who had held the office of President, or acted as President, for more than two years of a term to which some other person was elected President shall be elected to the office of the President more than once. But this Article shall not apply to any person holding the office of President when this Article was proposed by the Congress, and shall not prevent any person who may be holding the office of President, or acting as President, during the term within which this Article becomes operative from holding the office of President or acting as President during the remainder of such term.

Section 2

This article shall be inoperative unless it shall have been ratified as an amendment to the Constitution by the legislatures of three-fourths of the several States within seven years from the date of its submission to the States by the Congress.

Amendment 22
Presidential Term Limit The Twenty-second Amendment (1951) limits presidents to a maximum of two elected terms. The amendment wrote into the Constitution a custom started by George Washington. It was passed largely as a reaction to Franklin D. Roosevelt's election to four terms between 1933 and 1945. It also provides that anyone who succeeds to the presidency and serves for more than two years of the term may not be elected more than one more time.

Amendment XXIII

Section 1

The District constituting the seat of Government of the United States shall appoint in such manner as the Congress may direct:

A number of electors of President and Vice President equal to the whole number of Senators and Representatives in Congress to which the District would be entitled if it were a State, but in no event more than the least populous State; they shall be in addition to those appointed by the States, but they shall be considered, for the purposes of the election of President and Vice President, to be electors appointed by a State; and they shall meet in the District and perform such duties as provided by the twelfth article of amendment. **S** **W**

Section 2

The Congress shall have power to enforce this article by appropriate legislation.

Amendment 23
D.C. Electors The Twenty-third Amendment (1961) allows citizens living in Washington, D.C., to vote for president and vice president, a right previously denied residents of the nation's capital. The District of Columbia now has three presidential electors, the number to which it would be entitled if it were a state.

Amendment XXIV

Section 1

The right of citizens of the United States to vote in any primary or other election for President or Vice President, for electors for President or Vice President, or for Senator or Representative in Congress, shall not be denied or abridged by the United States or any State by reason of failure to pay any poll tax or other tax.

Amendment 24
Abolition of the Poll Tax The Twenty-fourth Amendment (1964) prohibits poll taxes in federal elections. Prior to the passage of this amendment, some states had used such taxes to keep low-income African Americans from voting. In 1966 the Supreme Court banned poll taxes in state elections as well.

W Writing Support

Expository Writing Write the following statement on the board: "That the people of Washington, D.C., have no representation in Congress is a violation of their democratic rights." Ask students to write a one-page paper expressing their feelings and point of view on this statement. **OL**

S Skill Practice

Identifying Point of View Have students write two newspaper editorials. The first editorial should be written from the perspective of someone in favor of the Twenty-third Amendment, and the second from the perspective of someone who is against the amendment. **OL**

Additional Support

Extending the Content

Presidential Term Limits The Framers were concerned about giving the executive branch of the new government too much power. They originally considered having the president serve one seven-year term with no opportunity for reelection. However, many delegates thought that a seven-year term was too long. The final decision set the presidential term of office at four years and allowed presidents to run for reelection.

C Critical Thinking

Drawing Conclusions Congress has the authority to determine presidential and vice presidential succession, as it did by proposing the Twenty-fifth Amendment. **Ask:** Why is it important to have plans for an orderly transition of power? *(Answers will vary, but students might note that, especially since the events of September 11, 2001, it is more important than ever to be certain that governmental power and authority is clear in case of any national emergency.)* OL

W Writing Support

Descriptive Writing Have students write a letter to the president identifying the necessary qualifications for someone to be appointed as vice president if the post became vacant. Remind students that they need to include the constitutional requirements, as well as other qualities they deem essential. Have volunteers read their letters to the class. OL

Answer: the president pro tempore of the Senate (the vice president) and the Speaker of the House of Representatives

Amendment 25
Presidential Disability and Succession The Twenty-fifth Amendment (1967) established a process for the vice president to take over leadership of the nation when a president is disabled. It also set procedures for filling a vacancy in the office of vice president.

This amendment was used in 1973, when Vice President Spiro Agnew resigned from office after being charged with accepting bribes. President Richard Nixon then appointed Gerald R. Ford as vice president in accordance with the provisions of the Twenty-fifth Amendment. A year later, President Nixon resigned during the Watergate scandal, and Ford became president. President Ford then had to fill the vice presidency, which he had left vacant upon assuming the presidency. He named Nelson A. Rockefeller as vice president. Thus individuals who had not been elected held both the presidency and the vice presidency. Whom does the president inform if he or she cannot carry out the duties of the office?

Section 2
The Congress shall have power to enforce this article by appropriate legislation.

Amendment XXV
Section 1
In case of the removal of the President from office or his death or resignation, the Vice President shall become President.

Section 2
W Whenever there is a vacancy in the office of the Vice President, the President shall nominate a Vice President who shall take the office upon confirmation by a majority vote of both Houses of Congress.

Section 3
Whenever the President transmits to the President pro tempore of the Senate and the Speaker of the House of Representatives his written declaration that he is unable to discharge the powers and duties of his office, and until he transmits to them a written declaration to the contrary, such powers and duties shall be discharged by the Vice President as Acting President.

Section 4
C Whenever the Vice President and a majority of either the principal officers of the executive departments or of such other body as Congress may by law provide, transmit to the President pro tempore of the Senate and the Speaker of the House of Representatives their written declaration that the President is unable to discharge the powers and duties of his office, the Vice President shall immediately assume the power and duties of the office of Acting President.

Thereafter, when the President transmits to the President pro tempore of the Senate and the Speaker of the House of Representatives his written declaration that no inability exists, he shall resume the powers and duties of his office unless the Vice President and a majority of either the principal officers of the executive department or of such other body as Congress may by law provide, transmit within four days to the President pro tempore of the Senate and the Speaker of the House of Representatives their written declaration that the President is unable to discharge the powers and duties of his office. Thereupon Congress shall decide the issue, assembling within forty-eight hours for that purpose if not in session. If the Congress, within twenty-one days after receipt of the latter written declaration, or, if Congress is not in session, within twenty-one days after Congress is required to assemble, determines by two-thirds vote of both Houses that the President is unable to discharge the powers and duties of his office, the Vice President shall continue to discharge the same as Acting President; otherwise, the President shall resume the power and duties of his office.

Additional Support

Extending the Content

Gerald R. Ford Gerald R. Ford became the thirty-eighth president of the United States in 1974. He was the only president who was not elected either president or vice president. He replaced Spiro T. Agnew when Agnew resigned as vice president, then replaced President Richard Nixon, who resigned on August 9, 1974.

Amendment XXVI

Section 1

D C The right of citizens of the United States, who are eighteen years of age or older, to vote shall not be denied or abridged by the United States or by any State on account of age.

Section 2

The Congress shall have power to enforce this article by appropriate legislation.

Amendment XXVII

No law, varying the compensation for the services of Senators and Representatives, shall take effect, until an election of representatives shall have intervened.

Amendment 26
Voting Age of 18 The Twenty-sixth Amendment (1971) lowered the voting age in both federal and state elections to 18.

Amendment 27
Congressional Salary Restraints The Twenty-seventh Amendment (1992) makes congressional pay raises effective during the term following their passage. James Madison offered the amendment in 1789, but it was never adopted. In 1982 Gregory Watson, then a student at the University of Texas, discovered the forgotten amendment while doing research for a school paper. Watson made the amendment's passage his crusade.

C Critical Thinking

Analyzing Information Inform students that people aged 18 to 25 have historically low voter turnout (the lowest of any group). **Ask:** Why don't many young people vote? *(Answers will vary. Students may note that young people are not interested or do not feel connected to political issues.)* Organize students into small groups to answer the following question: What can be done to increase voter turnout among 18- to 25-year-olds? Have groups come up with plans to increase voter turnout in this age group and present their recommendations to the class. **OL**

D Differentiated Instruction

Visual/Spatial Have students work in pairs to create a poster informing 18-year-olds of their right and responsibility to vote. Remind them to include illustrations on their posters, as well as information about how, when, and where to register to vote. Display the posters in a high-traffic area of the school, such as the lunchroom or the hallway outside your classroom. **BL**

Additional Support

Extending the Content

The Twenty-sixth Amendment Many people used the Vietnam War to justify the adoption of the Twenty-sixth Amendment. These people argued that those old enough to fight and die for their country were also old enough to vote. The Twenty-sixth Amendment was ratified more quickly than any other. It was proposed by Congress on March 23, 1971, and President Richard Nixon formally certified the Twenty-sixth Amendment on July 1, 1971, after it was ratified by three-fourths of the states.

Unit 2 Planning Guide

UNIT PACING CHART						
	Unit 2	**Chapter 4**	**Chapter 5**	**Chapter 6**	**Chapter 7**	**Unit 2**
Day 1	Unit Opener	Chapter 4 Opener, Section 1	Chapter 5 Opener, Section 1	Chapter 6 Opener, Section 1	Chapter 7 Opener, Section 1	Wrap-Up/Project, Unit Assessment
Day 2		Section 2	Section 2	Section 2	Section 2	
Day 3		Section 3	Sections 3 & 4	Sections 3 & 4	Section 3	
Day 4		Section 4	Chapter Assessment	Chapter Assessment	Section 4	
Day 5		Chapter Assessment			Chapter Assessment	

Teacher to Teacher

Heather W. Riehl
Ewing Township Public Schools
Ewing, NJ

Manifest Destiny Debate Organize the class into groups of three or four students. Assign members of each group the roles of Speaker, Recorder, Traveler, and Checker. Provide half of the groups this statement: "It is neither the right nor the duty of the United States to expand to the Pacific Ocean." Provide the other half of the groups this statement: "It is the right and the duty of the United States to expand to the Pacific Ocean."

Have the students brainstorm information to support their statement. The Checker should make sure each student contributes an idea; the Recorder should write down each idea.

After three minutes, send each Traveler to another group that is defending the same statement. Have him or her listen to the group's ideas and let him or her share any other ideas from his/her group. Continue moving the Travelers from group to group until they have visited all groups. Move the desks into two groups now facing each other and ask the Speakers to take turns sharing their arguments to the other side.

Author Note

Dear American History Teacher:

In the early years of the Republic, men and women who had played no part in the revolutionary movement came to maturity. The most stunning political development after 1789 was the emergence of an opposition to George Washington's administration. Although we see the two-party system as a norm, no one then had anticipated this development. Thomas Jefferson criticized the government for being too aristocratic in its values and too pro-British in its policies.

From 1793 to 1815, Europe was engaged in warfare with few years of peace. This brought both prosperity and problems to the United States. Prosperity resulted as warring France and England used the American merchant marine as safe shippers from the Caribbean to Europe. Problems occurred because neither side recognized the idea of "neutral carriers" and attacked Americans on the high seas. Washington issued a Neutrality Proclamation, but it did not stop the conflict. Domestic politics added complications because the Jeffersonians ardently championed the French who had rebelled against their king, and the Federalists favored all things English.

With Jefferson's election as president, the direction of America toward a more open society and popular, political participation was set. Religious revivals also swept across the country during the early decades of the nineteenth century, bringing to Americans a more intimate and emotional form of worship. Political and religious freedoms converged and ignited dozens of reforms like prohibition and abolition.

By 1803, each one of the Northern states had put slavery on a course toward extinction, turning the Mason-Dixon line into a vibrant divide between free and slave labor. Defending slavery pushed the Southern states further and further away from the American mainstream.

Joyce Appleby
Senior Author

Introducing **Unit 2**

Focus

Why It Matters

Tell students that the world they see today would not exist without the development of industry in the 1800s. **Ask:** How did industrial development change the United States? What people probably benefited the most? *(Possible response: It led to manufacturing, new technology, and the growth of cities. The people most likely to benefit would be owners of industry.)* Point out that the most populous cities in the United States at this time were in the North and that the South would have a distinct technological disadvantage during the Civil War. **AL**

Connecting to Past Learning

In Unit 1, students learned about how the early leaders of the United States came together to create a strong government. In Unit 2, they will study the challenges facing the new republic as it strode onto the world stage.

Unit Launch Activity

Remind students of the system of checks and balances designed by the Framers of the Constitution. Tell them that after the Constitution was ratified, this system was tested in many situations that the Framers could not have imagined. Discuss the kinds of issues that might arise today regarding political party and regional divisions. Tell students that the system of checks and balances was tested, and held, during the growing pains of the early republic, just as it continues to be held today. **OL**

Unit 2

The Young Republic

1789–1850

Why It Matters

Internal improvements and industrial development began to transform the United States in the early 1800s, but these changes also highlighted the growing differences between the North and South and set the stage for civil war. At the same time, Americans fought a war with Mexico and continued to expand west, building a nation that stretched from the Atlantic to the Pacific.

Team Teaching Activity

Civics Review with students what they know about how presidential elections are conducted. Then form groups of students, and ask each group to research a presidential election of the early republic (1789–1844). Have groups create a 10-question quiz based on what they know about modern presidential elections and what they have learned about the election they researched. Encourage the groups to give the quiz to a variety of people they know and chart the accuracy of the responses. Have the class as a whole discuss how and why the procedures for holding elections changes over time. **OL**

The bustle and excitement of an Election Day in Philadelphia in the early 1800s

151

More About the Art

John Krimmel (1789–1821) is considered one of America's first genre painters. His work expresses democratic and moralizing themes within the political and social changes affecting Philadelphia and the nation. Krimmel, born in Germany, immigrated to the United States in 1810. Much of his work, including *Election Day in Philadelphia*, contains hints of sarcasm.

Teach

Skill Practice

Visual Literacy Have students look closely at the painting, and remind them of the title, *Election Day in Philadelphia.* **Ask:** What aspects of campaigning do you see in the painting? How does this scene compare with modern elections? *(Possible responses: putting up posters, people arguing and giving speeches; today, there is much less public activity. People wait to hear the election results at home, and campaigning near polling places is not allowed.)* BL

Skill Practice

Reading Time Lines Have students skim ahead and study the time lines that open each chapter. **Ask:** When were the U.S. presidents elected, and how long did they serve? What was one significant event during each president's tenure? *(dates elected, years of service, and major events will vary)* OL

NCLB No Child Left Behind

Teaching Tip Wherever possible, give students the opportunity to use Internet search engines and electronic databases to extend their learning on topics about which they are especially interested and to make interdisciplinary connections between American history and other subject areas.

Chapter 4 Planning Guide

Key to Ability Levels	
BL Below Level	**AL** Above Level
OL On Level	**ELL** English Language Learners

Key to Teaching Resources	
Print Material	Transparency
CD-ROM or DVD	

Levels: BL	OL	AL	ELL		Resources	Chapter Opener	Section 1	Section 2	Section 3	Section 4	Chapter Assess
					FOCUS						
BL	OL	AL	ELL	Transparency	**Daily Focus Skills Transparencies**		4-1	4-2	4-3	4-4	
					TEACH						
		AL		Print Material	**American Literature Reading, URB**					p. 13	
BL	OL		ELL	Print Material	**Reading Essentials and Note-Taking Guide***		p. 38	p. 41	p. 44	p. 47	
	OL			Print Material	**Historical Analysis Skills Activity, URB**				p. 22		
BL	OL		ELL	Print Material	**Guided Reading Activities, URB***		p. 46	p. 47	p. 48	p. 49	
BL	OL	AL	ELL	Print Material	**Content Vocabulary Activity, URB***	p. 27					
BL	OL	AL	ELL	Print Material	**Academic Vocabulary Activity, URB**	p. 29					
	OL	AL		Print Material	**Critical Thinking Skills Activity, URB**			p. 32			
BL	OL		ELL	Print Material	**Reading Skills Activity, URB**		p. 21				
BL			ELL	Print Material	**English Learner Activity, URB**	p. 25					
	OL	AL		Print Material	**Reinforcing Skills Activity, URB**			p. 31			
BL	OL	AL	ELL	Print Material	**Differentiated Instruction Activity, URB**				p. 23		
BL	OL		ELL	Print Material	**Time Line Activity, URB**				p. 33		
	OL			Print Material	**Linking Past and Present Activity, URB**						p. 34
BL	OL	AL	ELL	Print Material	**American Art and Music Activity, URB**					p. 39	
BL	OL	AL	ELL	Print Material	**Interpreting Political Cartoons Activity, URB**				p. 41		
		AL		Print Material	**Enrichment Activity, URB**			p. 44			
BL	OL	AL	ELL	Print Material	**American Biographies**				✓		
BL	OL	AL	ELL	Print Material	**Primary Source Reading, URB**		p. 35		p. 37		
BL	OL	AL	ELL	Print Material	**The Living Constitution***	✓	✓	✓	✓	✓	✓
	OL	AL		CD-ROM or DVD	**American History Primary Source Documents Library**	✓	✓	✓	✓	✓	✓
BL	OL	AL	ELL	Transparency	**Unit Map Overlay Transparencies**	✓	✓	✓	✓	✓	✓
BL	OL	AL	ELL	Print Material	**Differentiated Instruction for the American History Classroom**	✓	✓	✓	✓	✓	✓
BL	OL	AL	ELL	CD-ROM or DVD	**StudentWorks™ Plus**	✓	✓	✓	✓	✓	✓

Note: Please refer to the *Unit 2 Resource Book* for this chapter's URB materials.

* Also available in Spanish

TeacherWorks Plus
All-In-One Planner and Resource Center

- Interactive Lesson Planner
- Interactive Teacher Edition
- Fully editable blackline masters
- Section Spotlight Videos Launch
- Differentiated Lesson Plans
- Printable reports of daily assignments
- Standards Tracking System

Levels					Resources	Chapter Opener	Section 1	Section 2	Section 3	Section 4	Chapter Assess
BL	OL	AL	ELL								
TEACH *(continued)*											
BL	OL	AL	ELL	CD	American Music Hits Through History CD	✓	✓	✓	✓	✓	✓
BL	OL	AL	ELL	Folder	Unit Time Line Transparencies and Activities	✓	✓	✓	✓	✓	✓
BL	OL	AL	ELL	Folder	Cause and Effect Transparencies, Strategies, and Activities	✓	✓	✓	✓	✓	✓
BL	OL	AL	ELL	Folder	Why It Matters Transparencies, Strategies, and Activities	✓	✓	✓	✓	✓	✓
BL	OL	AL	ELL	Folder	American Issues	✓	✓	✓	✓	✓	✓
	OL	AL	ELL	Folder	American Art and Architecture Transparencies, Strategies, and Activities	✓	✓	✓	✓	✓	✓
BL	OL	AL		Folder	High School American History Literature Library	✓	✓	✓	✓	✓	✓
BL	OL	AL	ELL	CD	*The American Vision* Video Program	✓	✓	✓	✓	✓	✓
Teacher Resources				Folder	Strategies for Success	✓	✓	✓	✓	✓	✓
Teacher Resources				Folder	Success with English Learner	✓	✓	✓	✓	✓	✓
Teacher Resources				Folder	Reading Strategies and Activities for the Social Studies Classroom	✓	✓	✓	✓	✓	✓
Teacher Resources				CD	Presentation Plus! with MindJogger CheckPoint	✓	✓	✓	✓	✓	✓
ASSESS											
BL	OL	AL	ELL	Folder	Section Quizzes and Chapter Tests*		p. 51	p. 52	p. 53	p. 54	p. 55
BL	OL	AL	ELL	Folder	Authentic Assessment With Rubrics						p. 13
BL	OL	AL	ELL	Folder	Standardized Test Practice Workbook						p. 7
BL	OL	AL	ELL	CD	*ExamView® Assessment Suite*		4-1	4-2	4-3	4-4	Ch. 4
CLOSE											
BL			ELL	Folder	Reteaching Activity, URB						p. 43
BL	OL		ELL	Folder	Reading and Study Skills Foldables™	p. 51					

✓ Chapter- or unit-based activities applicable to all sections in this chapter

Using the Lesson Planner

Teach With Technology

What is the Lesson Planner?

The TeacherWorks™ Plus Lesson Planner is a practical tool for creating and organizing daily lesson plans using an interactive calendar.

How can the Lesson Planner help me?

The Lesson Planner makes it easy to see, at a glance, the resources you have chosen to use for each class on any given day. Using a simple drag-and-drop format, you can generate lesson plans using any number of ancillary titles included in the TeacherWorks™ Plus software, as well as Internet links, documents, files, and programs of your choosing. Once a lesson plan is created, the Lesson Planner serves as a launching point for these resources.

The Lesson Planner is a feature of TeacherWorks™ Plus.

History ONLINE
Visit glencoe.com and enter ***QuickPass***™ code TAV9399c4T for Chapter 4 resources.

You can easily launch a wide range of digital products from your computer's desktop with the McGraw-Hill Social Studies widget.

	Student	Teacher	Parent
Media Library			
• Section Audio	●		●
• Spanish Audio Summaries	●		●
• Section Spotlight Videos	●	●	●
***The American Vision* Online Learning Center (Web Site)**			
• StudentWorks™ Plus Online	●	●	●
• Multilingual Glossary	●	●	●
• Study-to-Go	●	●	●
• Chapter Overviews	●	●	●
• Self-Check Quizzes	●	●	●
• Student Web Activities	●	●	●
• ePuzzles and Games	●	●	●
• Vocabulary eFlashcards	●	●	●
• In Motion Animations	●	●	●
• Study Central™	●	●	●
• Web Activity Lesson Plans		●	
• Vocabulary PuzzleMaker	●	●	●
• Historical Thinking Activities		●	
• Beyond the Textbook	●	●	●

Reading Support From Jamestown Education

- **Timed Readings Plus in Social Studies** helps students increase their reading rate and fluency while maintaining comprehension. The 400-word passages are similar to those found on state and national assessments.
- **Reading in the Content Area: Social Studies** concentrates on six essential reading skills that help students better comprehend what they read. The book includes 75 high-interest nonfiction passages written at increasing levels of difficulty.
- **Reading Social Studies** includes strategic reading instruction and vocabulary support in Social Studies content for both ELLs and native speakers of English.

www.jamestowneducation.com

Biography | A&E Home Video | The History Channel

The following videotape programs are available from Glencoe as supplements to this chapter:

- Thomas Jefferson: Philosopher of Freedom (ISBN 1-56-501502-9)
- Lewis and Clark (ISBN 1-56-501592-4)

To order, call Glencoe at 1-800-334-7344. To find classroom resources to accompany many of these videos, check the following home pages:

A&E Television: www.aetv.com
The History Channel: www.historychannel.com

National Geographic

Index to National Geographic Magazine:

The following articles relate to this chapter:

- "Lewis and Clark's lost Missouri: a mapmaker re-creates the river of 1804 and changes the course of history" by Cathy Riggs Salter, April 2002.
- "Pioneer Explorers, Botanical Collectors," May 2000.

National Geographic Society Products To order the following, call National Geographic at 1-800-368-2728:

- *Lewis and Clark* (CD-ROM)

Access National Geographic's new, dynamic MapMachine Web site and other geography resources at:

www.nationalgeographic.com
www.nationalgeographic.com/maps

Reading List Generator CD-ROM — Glencoe BookLink 3

Use this database to search more than 30,000 titles to create a customized reading list for your students.

- Reading lists can be organized by students' reading level, author, genre, theme, or area of interest.
- The database provides Degrees of Reading Power™ (DRP) and Lexile™ readability scores for all selections.
- A brief summary of each selection is included.

Leveled reading suggestions for this chapter:

For students at a Grade 8 reading level:
- ***Thomas Jefferson***, by Lucia Raatma

For students at a Grade 9 reading level:
- ***Thomas Jefferson: Father of Our Democracy***, by David A. Adler

For students at a Grade 10 reading level:
- ***Thomas Jefferson: Letters from a Philadelphia Bookworm***, by Jennifer Armstrong

For students at a Grade 11 reading level:
- ***Sacagawea: Westward with Lewis and Clark***, by Alana J. White

For students at a Grade 12 reading level:
- ***The Incredible Journey of Lewis and Clark***, by Rhoda Blumberg

Introducing Chapter 4

Focus

MAKING CONNECTIONS
Why Do People Form Political Parties?

Discuss with students the two questions posed on page 153. Ask students what they know about how the major parties in the United States function at the local, state, and national level. Discuss whether the Framers were right about parties being a bad idea in a democracy, or whether parties best represent the interest of American citizens and cause the government to work more effectively and efficiently. Encourage students to explore how the two major parties function in today's government. **OL**

Teach

The Big Ideas

As students study the chapter, remind them to consider the section-based Big Ideas included in each section's Guide to Reading. The **Essential Questions** in the activities below tie in to the Big Ideas and help students think about and understand important chapter concepts. In addition, the Hands-on Chapter Projects with their culminating activities relate the content from each section to the Big Ideas. These activities build on each other as students progress through the chapter. Section activities culminate in the wrap-up activity on the Visual Summary page.

Chapter 4

Federalists and Republicans

1789–1816

SECTION 1 Washington and Congress
SECTION 2 Partisan Politics
SECTION 3 Jefferson in Office
SECTION 4 The War of 1812

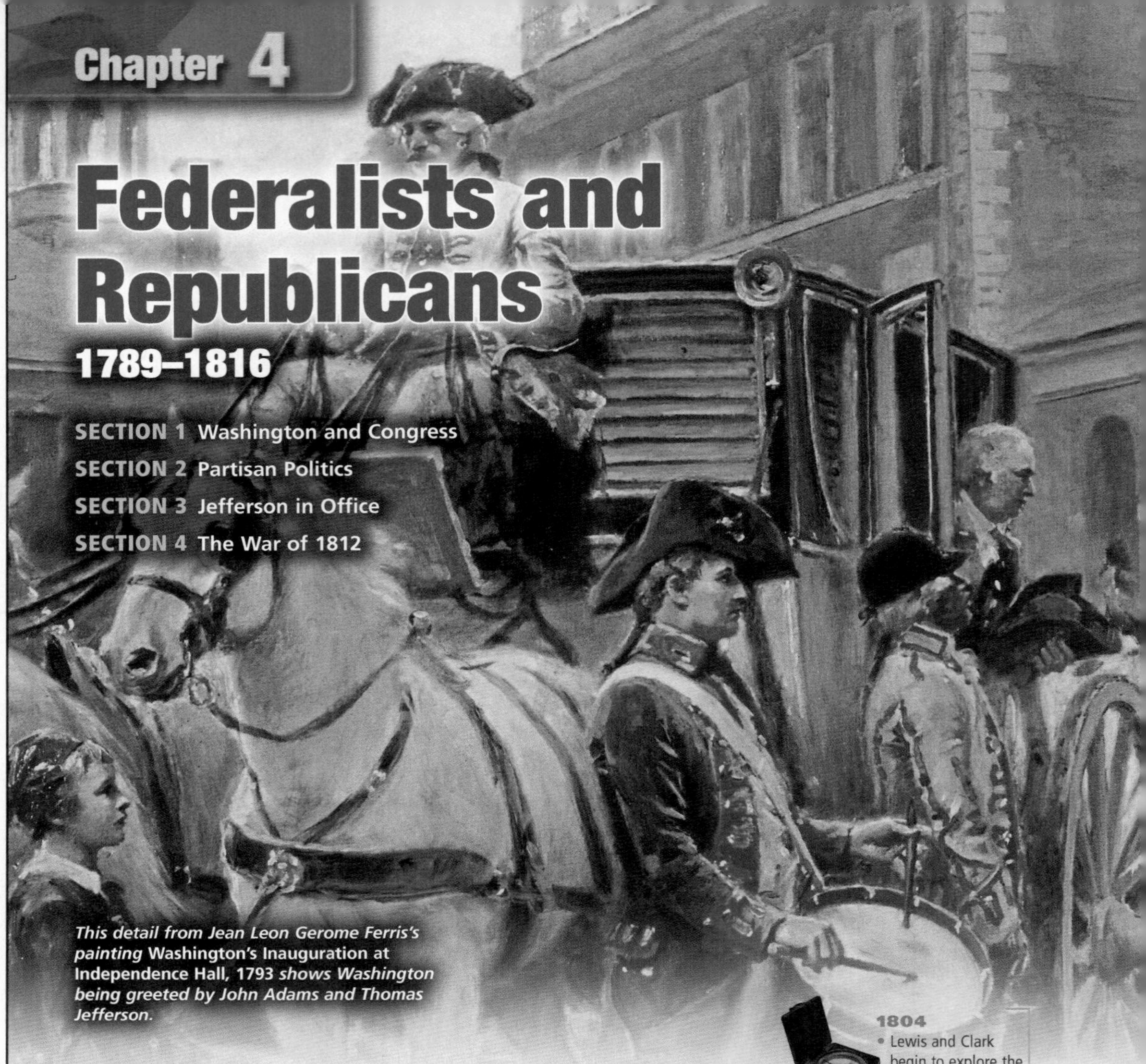

This detail from Jean Leon Gerome Ferris's painting Washington's Inauguration at Independence Hall, 1793 *shows Washington being greeted by John Adams and Thomas Jefferson.*

U.S. PRESIDENTS
Washington 1789–1797
J. Adams 1797–1801
Jefferson 1801–1809

U.S. EVENTS
1789 • Washington becomes president
1794 • Jay's Treaty is signed
1803 • Louisiana Purchase doubles size of the nation
1804 • Lewis and Clark begin to explore the Louisiana Purchase

1790 — 1795 — 1800

WORLD EVENTS
1789 • French Revolution begins
1793 • Louis XVI is guillotined during French Revolution
1798 • Quasi-War between France and the U.S. begins

Section 1

Washington and Congress

Essential Question: **What key events occurred during George Washington's presidency?** *(The Bill of Rights was passed, controversial tariffs were enacted, the Bank of the United States was established, and political parties began to develop.)* Point out that in Section 1 students will learn about how George Washington helped define the new presidency. **OL**

Section 2

Partisan Politics

Essential Question: **How did trade with other nations, westward expansion, and the rise of political parties affect the new nation?** *(The United States avoided war with France and Britain; acquired land from Spain, and began settling the Northwest Territory. Conflicts erupted between the Federalist and Democratic-Republican parties.)* Point out that in Section 2 students will learn about the growing pains of the new republic. **OL**

Chapter Audio

MAKING CONNECTIONS

Why Do People Form Political Parties?

The Constitution does not mention political parties, and the Founders thought they were a bad idea in a democracy, yet almost immediately after the federal government was created, political parties began to take shape.

- ***What role do you think political parties played in the early Congress?***
- ***Are parties necessary for government to work?***

Madison 1809–1817

1811
- Battle of Tippecanoe breaks up Tecumseh's confederacy

1814
- Hartford Convention meets
- Treaty of Ghent is signed

1812
- United States declares war on Britain

1805 | 1810 | 1815

1805
- British navy wins Battle of Trafalgar
- Russia begins building forts in Alaska

1812
- Napoleon invades, then retreats from Russia

1816
- Argentina declares independence

FOLDABLES

Analyzing Political Parties Create a Concept Map Foldable that compares the different points of each political party. List the groups that supported them and their attitudes toward territorial expansion and a national bank.

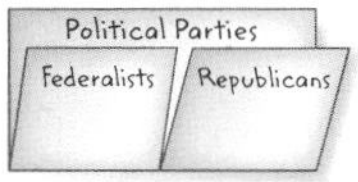

History ONLINE Visit glencoe.com and enter **QuickPass™** code TAV9846c4 for Chapter 4 resources.

Section 3

Jefferson in Office

Essential Question: What are the main legacies of Jefferson's administration? *(the Louisiana Purchase and subsequent exploration, keeping the United States out of war with Britain and France)* Point out that in Section 3 students will learn about how Thomas Jefferson acquired land for westward expansion and tried to contain international tensions. **OL**

Section 4

The War of 1812

Essential Question: What issues sparked the War of 1812? *(British impressments of American soldiers, trade issues with France and Britain, a British-Native American alliance against the United States in the Northwest Territory)* Point out that in Section 4 students will learn about the causes of the War of 1812, strategies for fighting, and the war's outcome. **OL**

Introducing
Chapter 4

More About the Art

Visual Literacy Washington's first inauguration took place in New York City on the balcony of Federal Hall. The second inauguration occurred at Congress Hall in Philadelphia, Pennsylvania. The cupola of Congress Hall can be seen on the far left side of the painting. Philadelphia served as the nation's capital from 1790 to 1800.

FOLDABLES Study Organizer **Dinah Zike's Foldables**

Dinah Zike's Foldables are three-dimensional, interactive graphic organizers that help students practice basic writing skills, review vocabulary terms, and identify main ideas. Instructions for creating and using Foldables can be found in the Appendix at the end of this book and in the *Dinah Zike's Reading and Study Skills Foldables* booklet.

History ONLINE

Visit glencoe.com and enter **QuickPass™** code TAV9399c4T for Chapter 4 resources, including a Chapter Overview, Study Central™, Study-to-Go, Student Web Activity, Self-Check Quiz, and other materials.

Focus

Bellringer

Daily Focus Transparency 4-1

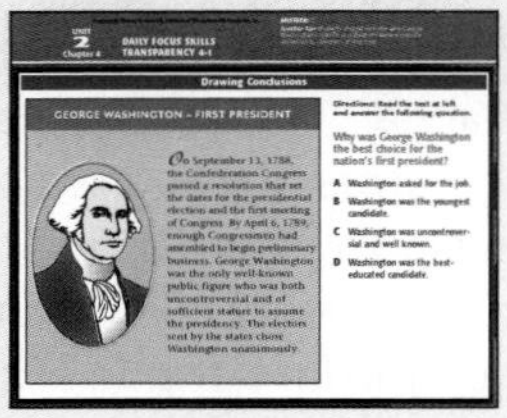

Guide to Reading

Answers: organized executive branch by creating departments, organized judicial branch, introduced the Bill of Rights, financed government by imposing tariffs and tonnage rates, created a national bank, accepted debt of Continental Congress at full value to establish credit

Section Spotlight Video

To generate student interest and provide a springboard for class discussion, access the Chapter 4, Section 1 video at glencoe.com or on the video DVD.

Section 1

Section Audio   Spotlight Video

Washington and Congress

Guide to Reading

Big Ideas

Individual Action George Washington helped define the new American presidency.

Content Vocabulary

- cabinet *(p. 154)*
- bond *(p. 156)*
- speculator *(p. 157)*
- enumerated powers *(p. 157)*
- implied powers *(p. 157)*
- agrarianism *(p. 159)*

Academic Vocabulary

- revenue *(p. 155)*
- creditor *(p. 156)*

People and Events to Identify

- Tariff of 1789 *(p. 156)*
- Bank of the United States *(p. 158)*
- Whiskey Rebellion *(p. 158)*

Reading Strategy

Organizing Complete a graphic organizer similar to the one below by indicating the tasks completed by the first Congress under the Constitution.

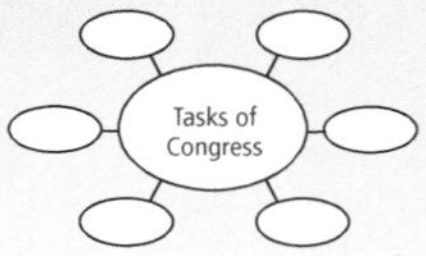

President Washington and the First Congress had to decide how to make the new government function effectively. The conflicting philosophies of Thomas Jefferson and Alexander Hamilton became the basis for two new political parties.

Creating a New Government

MAIN Idea With the adoption of the Constitution, American leaders had to establish a new national government to deal effectively with the challenges facing the nation.

HISTORY AND YOU Have you ever had to accomplish something based on a complicated plan? Read on to find out how American leaders carried out the specifications of the new Constitution.

The Philadelphia Convention had given the nation a new Constitution. George Washington's task, and the task facing the newly elected Congress, was to take the words of the Constitution and turn them into an effective government for the United States. To get the government up and running, the president needed a bureaucracy to handle different responsibilities. In 1789 Congress created the Department of State, the Department of the Treasury, the Department of War, and the Office of the Attorney General.

To manage these departments, Washington wanted individuals who were "disposed to measure matters on a Continental Scale," instead of thinking only of their own states. He chose Thomas Jefferson as secretary of state, Alexander Hamilton as secretary of the treasury, and General Henry Knox as secretary of war. For attorney general, Washington selected Edmund Randolph, the former governor of Virginia. Washington regularly met with these men to ask for their advice. The department heads came to be known as the **cabinet,** a group of advisers to the president.

Congress also established the federal judiciary. In the Judiciary Act of 1789, Congress established 13 district courts, three courts of appeal, and the Supreme Court. With the Senate's consent, Washington chose the federal judges and selected John Jay to become the first chief justice of the United States.

The Bill of Rights

One of the most important acts of Congress was the introduction of the Bill of Rights. During the campaign to ratify the Constitution, the Federalists had promised to add such amendments. James Madison, one of the leaders in Congress, made the passage of a bill of rights top

Resource Manager

R Reading Strategies	C Critical Thinking	D Differentiated Instruction	W Writing Support	S Skill Practice
Teacher Edition • Academic Vocab., p. 155 • Summarizing, p. 157 **Additional Resources** • Pri. Source Read. Act., URB p. 35 • Guide Read, URB p. 46	**Teacher Edition** • Comparing and Contrasting, p. 158 **Additional Resources** • Quizzes and Tests, p. 51	**Teacher Edition** • Visual/Spatial, p. 156 • Special Ed., p. 156	**Additional Resources** • Content Vocab. Act., URB p. 27 • Academic Vocab. Act., URB p. 29	**Additional Resources** • Reading Skills Act., URB p. 21 • Read. Essen., p. 38

INFOGRAPHIC

Origins of the Bill of Rights

Basic Rights	Magna Carta (1215)	English Bill of Rights (1689)	Virginia Declaration of Rights (1776)	Virginia Statute for Religious Freedom (1786)	American Bill of Rights (1791)
No state religion				●	●
Freedom of worship		● limited	●	●	●
Freedom of speech		●	●		●
Right to petition		● limited			●
Right to bear arms					●
No quartering troops in private homes without permission					●
No searches and seizures without a specific search warrant	●		●		●
Government cannot take away life, liberty, or property unless it follows proper court procedures (due process)	●	●	●		●
Right to a speedy public trial by jury and to a lawyer	●	●	●	●	●
No excessive bail, fines, or cruel and unusual punishment	●	●	●		●

Steps to the Bill of Rights

In creating the Bill of Rights, the first ten amendments to the Constitution, James Madison drew on the great founding documents of English legal history and tradition: the Magna Carta, the English Bill of Rights, the Virginia Declaration of Rights, and the Virginia Statute for Religious Freedom. Beginning in 1215, these and other documents had established protections of individual rights and freedoms designed to safeguard citizens from oppression and tyrannical government.

Analyzing VISUALS

1. **Specifying** Which right was established in the Magna Carta and appears in all subsequent documents?
2. **Explaining** Which two rights are the only ones unique to the American Bill of Rights, and why do you think that is?

priority. He hoped it would demonstrate the good faith of federal leaders and build support for the new government.

In drafting the Bill of Rights, Madison relied heavily on the Virginia Declaration of Rights that George Mason prepared in 1776 and the Virginia Statute for Religious Freedom that Thomas Jefferson wrote in 1786. In late September 1789, Congress agreed on 12 constitutional amendments. They were then sent to the states for ratification, but only 10 were approved. These 10 went into effect and are generally referred to as the Bill of Rights. The first eight protect the rights of individuals against actions of the federal government. The last two set limits on the powers of the new national government. The Ninth Amendment states that the people have other rights not listed. The Tenth Amendment states that any powers not specifically given to the federal government are reserved for the states.

Financing the Government

Having organized the new federal government, the next most pressing need was a source of **revenue.** Without money, the government could not operate. Madison and Hamilton responded to this need with different plans for financing the government. R

Teach

R Reading Strategy

Academic Vocabulary Ask: What is a synonym for *revenue*? *(income)* Remind students that they can use context clues to understand unknown words. Point out that the sentence following the word *revenue* begins with "Without money." Show students how they might rephrase this sentence: "They needed revenue, because they were without money." **BL**

Analyzing VISUALS

Answers:

1. the right to a speedy trial by jury and to a lawyer
2. The unique rights are the right to bear arms and no quartering of troops in private homes. Most will assume that these rights grew out of the dependence on citizen militias at the beginning of the Revolution and the opposition to forced quartering by the British.

Hands-On Chapter Project Step 1

Presidential Customs

Step 1: Precedents Set by Washington Students will work individually to research the presidential customs initiated by President George Washington.

Directions Point out that as the first United States President, George Washington set the precedent for many customs of the office. Have students research the presidency of Washington. Have each student list three examples of such precedents.

Interpreting Information Students will need to research online or print sources to find descriptions of the Washington presidency. They will then determine which of Washington's actions influenced the presidency. **OL**

(Chapter Project continued on page 163)

D1 Differentiated Instruction

Visual/Spatial Have students create a political cartoon supporting or opposing the Tariff of 1789. Encourage students to look at styles of political cartoons from the era and to use the types of tools that a satirist of the era may have used. Have students display their cartoons around the classroom. **AL**

D2 Differentiated Instruction

Special Education Ask students to think about the way debts and income work in their daily lives. Point out that on the chart of the United States's finances in 1792, the total debt was 75 times the amount of income. Discuss what their own personal finances would be like if they owed 75 times the amount of money they had. Use this analogy to help students understand why Hamilton believed the bonds should be redeemed at full value. **Ask:** How can paying off a debt generate more income? *(Possible answer: It might encourage other creditors to loan money.)* **BL**

Differentiated Instruction

The Tariff of 1789 James Madison suggested that the federal government raise most of its money by taxing imports. After much discussion, Congress passed the **Tariff of 1789.** This law required importers to pay a percentage of the value of their cargo when they landed it in the United States. Shippers also had to pay tonnage—a tax based on how much their ships carried. **D1**

The tariffs and tonnage rates angered many Southern planters. High tonnage rates meant they would be charged higher rates to ship their rice and tobacco to Europe. The new tariff also meant that the imported goods the South needed would cost more. Many Southerners began to suspect that the federal government was opposed to their region's interests.

Hamilton's Financial Program Hamilton supported the Tariff of 1789, but he believed the government also needed the ability to borrow money. To fund the Revolutionary War, the Congress under the Articles of Confederation had issued **bonds**—paper notes promising to repay money after a certain length of time with interest. By 1789, the United States owed roughly $40 million to American citizens and another $11.7 million to lenders in France, Spain, and the Netherlands. Few believed the bonds would be repaid in full, and they had fallen in value to as little as 10 cents on the dollar. In 1790 Hamilton asked Congress to redeem the bonds at full value.

Hamilton believed that if the United States accepted these debts at full value, then wealthy **creditors,** bankers, and merchants who owned the bonds would have enough confidence in its financial stability to lend it money in the future. Hamilton had described the importance of debt several years earlier:

Primary Source

"A national debt if it is not excessive will be to us a national blessing; it will be a powerfull cement of our union. It will also create a necessity for keeping up taxation . . . which without being oppressive, will be a spur to industry. . ."

—from Alexander Hamilton, letter to Robert Morris, April 30, 1781

Opposition to Hamilton's Plan Led by Madison, critics argued that Hamilton's plan was unfair to the original purchasers of the bonds. These people—who included farmers, war veterans, and widows—fearing they would

PRIMARY SOURCE

Funding a New Government

For the new federal government to succeed, it needed money. Secretary Alexander Hamilton wanted the government to do four things to secure its ability to raise money: 1. tax imports, 2. take on the debts of the Continental Congress, 3. establish a national bank, and 4. impose an excise tax on whiskey. All were controversial.

1. THE TARIFF OF 1789

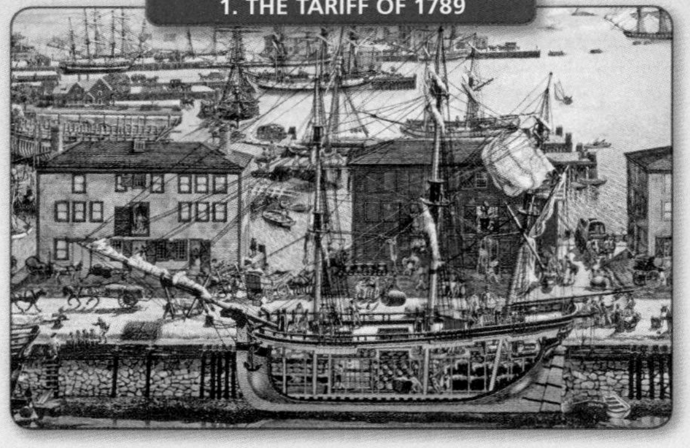

◀ *The Tariff of 1789 levied a tax on the value of goods imported and on the weight of the shipment (tonnage).*

2. THE NATION'S FINANCES, 1792 **D2**

Debts	
• Foreign debt:	$11.7 million
• State debt the federal government agreed to pay:	$21.5 million
• Domestic debts (bonds):	$42.4 million
• Total:	$75.6 million
Annual interest on the debts (must be paid every year):	$4.6 million
Income	
• Customs revenue (tariffs and tonnage):	$4.4 million
• Excise taxes (whiskey tax):	$1.2 million
• Funds remaining (after paying interest):	$1.0 million

▲ *Hamilton believed that establishing a national bank that would take on prior debts would give lenders a stake in the new government's success.*

Leveled Activities

BL Reteaching Activity, URB p. 43

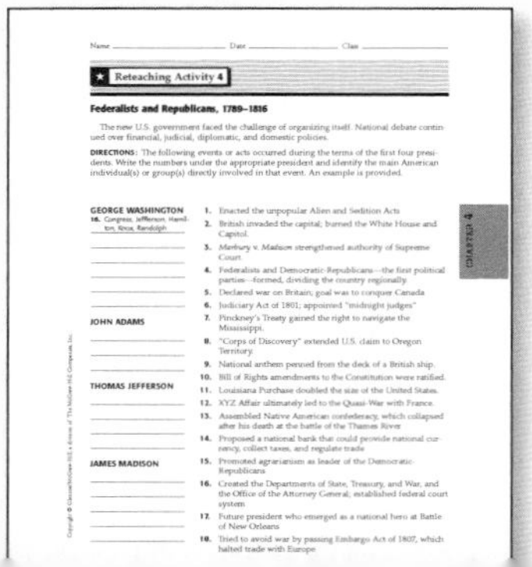

OL Reinforcing Skills Activity, URB p. 31

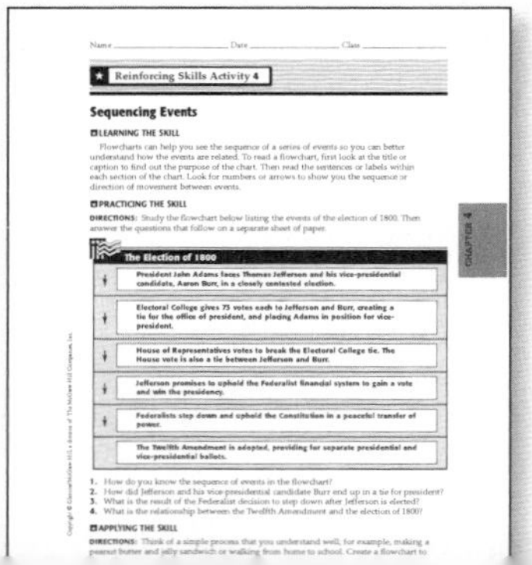

AL Historical Analysis Skills Activity, URB p. 22

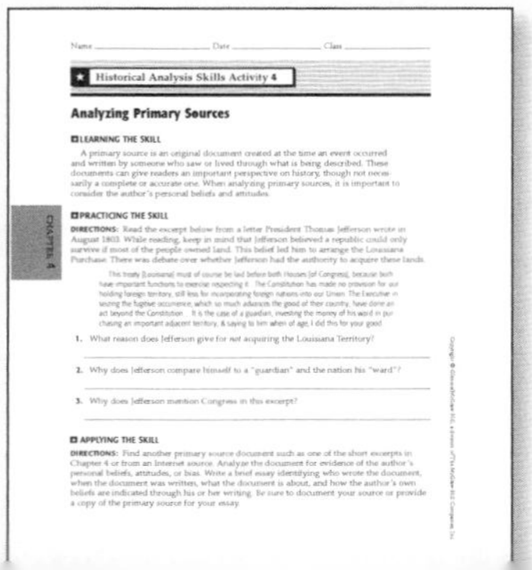

ELL English Learner Activity, URB p. 25

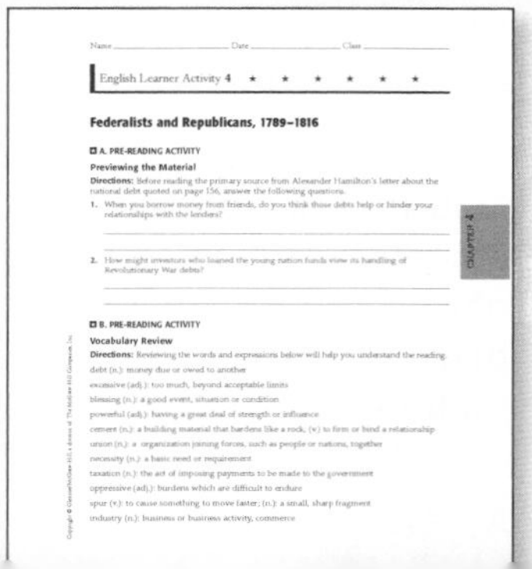

never be paid, had sold their bonds to **speculators.** Madison was outraged that speculators who had paid as little as $10 for a $100 bond would now receive full value.

Madison and other Southerners were also upset because Northerners owned most of the bonds, while much of the tax money that would be used to pay off the bonds would come from the South. Madison also worried that creditors would eventually dominate American society and endanger liberty.

The debate over Hamilton's proposals raged for months. Finally, in July 1790, Hamilton, Madison, and Jefferson struck a deal. Madison and Jefferson would use their influence to convince Southerners in Congress to vote for Hamilton's plan. In return, the United States capital would move from New York City to an area along the Potomac River to be called the District of Columbia. Southerners believed that having the capital in the South would help offset the strength of the Northern states.

The Bank of the United States

With his system of public credit finally in place, Hamilton asked Congress to create a national bank. He argued that the government needed the bank to manage its debts and interest payments. The bank would also issue bank notes—paper money. The notes would provide a national currency that would promote trade, encourage investment, and stimulate economic growth.

Southerners opposed the plan. They pointed out that Northern merchants would own most of the bank's stock. Madison argued that Congress could not establish a bank because **R** it was not among the federal government's **enumerated powers,** or powers specifically mentioned in the Constitution.

Despite Madison's objections, Congress passed the bank bill. Washington realized that his decision to sign the bill or to veto it would set an important precedent. Attorney General Randolph and Secretary of State Jefferson argued that the Constitution did not give the federal government the power to create a bank. Hamilton disagreed, noting that Article I, Section 8, of the Constitution gave the federal government the power "to make all laws which shall be necessary and proper" to execute its responsibilities. The "necessary and proper" clause created **implied powers**—powers not listed in the Constitution but necessary for the government to do its job.

3. THE NATIONAL BANK

Hamilton explains why a national bank is constitutional:

"[I]f the measure have an obvious relation to that end, and is not forbidden by any particular provision of the Constitution—it may safely be deemed to come within the compass of the national authority. There is also this further criterion, which may materially assist the decision. Does the proposed measure abridge a preexisting right of any State or of any individual? If it does not, there is a strong presumption in favour of its constitutionality. . . ."

—from Alexander Hamilton, *Opinion on the Constitutionality of Establishing a National Bank,* February 23, 1791

Jefferson argues that a national bank is unconstitutional:

"I consider the foundation of the Constitution as laid on this ground that 'all powers not delegated to the U.S. by the Constitution, nor prohibited by it to the States, are reserved to the States or to the people.' . . . To take a single step beyond the boundaries thus specially drawn around the powers of Congress, is to take possession of a boundless feild [sic] of power, no longer susceptible of any definition."

—from Thomas Jefferson, *Opinion on the Constitutionality of Establishing a National Bank,* February 15, 1791

4. EXCISE TAXES

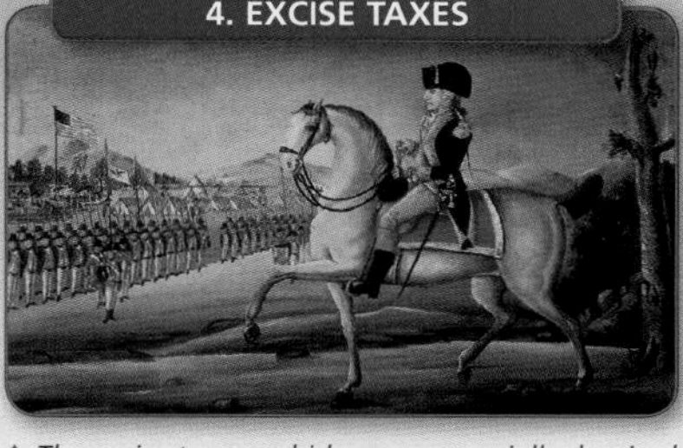

▲ *The excise tax on whiskey was especially despised and led to a rebellion in 1794 quelled by federal troops sent by George Washington.*

DBQ Document-Based Questions

1. **Synthesizing** Why did Hamilton want to establish credit for the new nation?
2. **Explaining** Why did Jefferson argue against a national bank?

R Reading Strategy

Summarizing Ask: What is the difference between enumerated and implied powers? *(Enumerated powers are spelled out in the Constitution. Implied powers are not specifically listed in the Constitution; however, the federal government is given authority to make "necessary and proper" laws.)* **BL**

Did You Know?

The founding of the Bank of the United States did not end the controversy surrounding it. In 1811 the bank's 20-year charter was not renewed.

DBQ Document Based Questions

Answers:

1. to give lenders a stake in the government's success and to gain credit for the new government
2. He felt that it was unconstitutional because the power to establish it was not explicitly included in the Constitution.

Additional Support

Activity: Economics Connection

The National Debt Have students use the Treasury Department's Web site to research the national debt for the years 1800, 1900, and 2000. Have students explain why it is not appropriate to compare these numbers directly. Encourage students to use an inflation calculator to calculate the debt figures in comparable dollars. Provide students with the Internet addresses shown below to do this research. Finally, have students prepare a line graph displaying the relative total national debt over time. Then have partners discuss their findings. **AL**

The Public Debt Online—
http://www.treasurydirect.gov/govt/govt.htm

CJR Dollar Conversion Calculator—
http://cjr.org/tools/inflation

C Critical Thinking

Comparing and Contrasting

Ask: What parallels can you draw between the Whiskey Rebellion and Shays's Rebellion (see page 103)? How did the ratification of the Constitution affect President Washington's ability to intervene in the Whiskey Rebellion? *(Both rebellions were sparked by the imposition of new taxes. In the case of the Whiskey Rebellion, the president could put down the rebellion by military means.)* **AL**

People IN HISTORY

Answers:

Hamilton: wrote about the weaknesses of the Articles of Confederation, called for the Constitutional Convention, wrote many of the Federalist Papers, and promoted a strong central government

Jefferson: a national government with limited powers

Reading Check

Answer:
He argued that Congress could not establish a bank because it was not among the federal government's enumerated powers.

Additional Support

A national bank, Hamilton argued, was necessary to collect taxes, regulate trade, and provide for defense. Jefferson agreed that implied powers existed, but believed "necessary and proper" meant absolutely necessary, not simply convenient. After studying the issue, Washington agreed to sign the bill. In 1791 the **Bank of the United States** was created with a 20-year charter.

The Whiskey Rebellion

History ONLINE **Student Web Activity** Visit glencoe.com and complete the activity on the rise of political parties.

Hamilton also believed the government had to establish its right to impose direct taxes. In 1791 Congress imposed a tax on the manufacture of whiskey. The new tax enraged western farmers who distilled their grain into whiskey before shipping it to market. The **Whiskey Rebellion** erupted in western Pennsylvania in 1794. Farmers terrorized tax collectors, stopped court proceedings, and robbed the mail. In August 1794, Washington sent about 15,000 troops to crush the rebellion. The rebels dispersed without a fight. This willingness to use armed troops against civilians, however, worried many people.

Reading Check **Explaining** Why did Madison object to Hamilton's plan for a national bank?

The Rise of Political Parties

MAIN Idea Federalists backed a stronger government and manufacturers; Republicans supported a weaker government and farmers.

HISTORY AND YOU The Federalists were more popular in some parts of the nation, the Democratic-Republicans in others. Is one political party more popular than others in your state?

During Washington's first term in office, the debate over Hamilton's financial program divided Congress into factions based on their views of the federal government's role. These factions became the nation's first political parties. Hamilton's supporters called themselves Federalists. His opponents, led by Madison and Jefferson, took the name Democratic-Republicans, although most people at the time referred to them as Republicans.

Decades later, the Democratic-Republicans became known as the Democrats, the name they are known by today. The party known today as the Republican Party is a different party that was founded in 1854. The Federalist Party does not exist today.

People IN HISTORY

Alexander Hamilton
1755/57–1804

Alexander Hamilton was born in the British West Indies and immigrated to America in 1772. An attorney by profession, Hamilton represented New York at the Constitutional Convention of 1787 and, as author of many of the *Federalist* papers, was instrumental in getting the Constitution ratified.

As secretary of the treasury in the new government, Hamilton advocated his vision for a powerful national government, a national bank, and the assumption of Revolutionary-era debts. His ideas became the foundation of the Federalist Party.

Hamilton resigned as treasury secretary in 1795, but remained influential. In 1804 he was killed in a duel with Aaron Burr, a political enemy. An ambitious, brilliant, pragmatic, and innovative statesman, Alexander Hamilton's legacy is the strong national government we have today.

How did Alexander Hamilton contribute to the formation of the U.S. government?

Thomas Jefferson
1743–1826

Thomas Jefferson was a man of contradictions. He wrote elegantly about American ideals of rights and liberties, yet he was a slaveholder. Jefferson was the chief drafter of the Declaration of Independence and the author of the Virginia Statute for Religious Freedom.

During the Revolution, Jefferson served as United States minister to France. He remained in that post until 1789, when he returned to the United States to become secretary of state in Washington's administration.

With James Madison, Jefferson formed the Democratic-Republican Party in opposition to the Federalists, whom he felt were betraying the ideals of the American Revolution by attempting to set up a government as authoritarian as the British monarchy. Jefferson believed that the power of the national government should be minimized. In 1800 he was elected to be the third president of the United States.

What was Jefferson's vision for the nation?

Extending the Content

Hamilton and Jefferson Alexander Hamilton and Thomas Jefferson were similar in many respects. They devoted most of their lives to public service. President George Washington appointed both men to serve in his first cabinet. They were eloquent speakers and gifted writers. However, they frequently clashed. As a Federalist, Hamilton believed that the security of the nation depended on a strong central government. Jefferson, a leader of the Democratic-Republican Party, worried that such a government might imperil personal freedom. Jefferson advocated close relations with France, while Hamilton believed the United States should have closer ties with Britain.

Hamilton and the Federalists

Hamilton favored a strong national government. He believed that democracy was dangerous to liberty and stated that "the people are turbulent and changing; they seldom judge or determine right." This distrust led him to favor putting government into the hands of the "rich, well born, and able."

Hamilton also believed that manufacturing and trade were the basis of national wealth and power. He favored policies that would support these areas of the economy. Supporters of the Federalist Party often included artisans, merchants, manufacturers, and bankers. The party also attracted urban workers and Eastern farmers who benefited from trade.

Jefferson and the Republicans

Although James Madison led the opposition to Hamilton's program in Congress, Thomas Jefferson emerged as the leader of the Democratic-Republicans. Jefferson believed that the strength of the United States was its independent farmers. His ideas are sometimes referred to as **agrarianism.** Jefferson argued that owning land enabled people to be independent. As long as most people owned their own land, they would fight to preserve the Republic.

Jefferson feared that too much emphasis on commerce would lead to a society sharply divided between the rich, who owned everything, and the poor, who worked for wages. He also believed that the wealthy would corrupt the government and threaten the rights and liberties of ordinary people.

PRIMARY SOURCE

"Dependence begets subservience and venality, suffocates the germ of virtue. . . . While we have land to labour . . . let us never wish to see our citizens occupied at a work-bench, or twirling a distaff. . . .[L]et our work-shops remain in Europe. It is better to carry provisions and materials to workmen there, than bring them to the provisions and materials, and with them their manners and principles. . . . The mobs of great cities add just so much to the support of pure government, as sores do to the strength of the human body."

—from *Notes on the State of Virginia*

In general, Democratic-Republicans supported agriculture over commerce and trade. They also expressed concern that Hamilton's policies tended to favor the North. Over time, they became the party that stood for the rights of states against the federal government.

The development of America's first two political parties divided the country regionally. The rural South and West tended to support the Republicans, while the more urban Northeast tended to support the Federalists. Although these parties emerged during the dispute over Hamilton's programs, events in Europe would deepen the divisions between them and create new crises for the young nation.

✓Reading Check **Classifying** What were the nation's first two political parties, and what issues did they favor?

Section 1 REVIEW

Vocabulary

1. **Explain** the significance of: cabinet, Tariff of 1789, bond, speculator, enumerated powers, implied powers, Bank of the United States, Whiskey Rebellion, agrarianism.

Main Ideas

2. **Listing** What actions of the new federal government started and ended the Whiskey Rebellion?
3. **Identifying** Who was the main leader of each of the new American political parties?

Critical Thinking

4. **Big Ideas** What precedents did George Washington set as president of the United States?
5. **Categorizing** Use a graphic organizer similar to the one below to list the first political parties in the United States, their supporters, and the issues they promoted.

Political Party	Supporters	Issues Supported

6. **Analyzing Visuals** Study the chart on the Bill of Rights on page 155. What new protection originated in the Virginia Statute for Religious Freedom?

Writing About History

7. **Persuasive Writing** Suppose you are James Madison. Write a speech to persuade others not to support Alexander Hamilton's financial program.

History ONLINE
Study Central™ To review this section, go to glencoe.com and click on Study Central.

✓Reading Check

Answer:
The Federalists and the Democratic-Republicans; the Federalists favored policies that would help create national wealth and power; the Democratic-Republicans supported agriculture and states' rights.

Assess

History ONLINE

Study Central™ provides summaries, interactive games, and online graphic organizers to help students review content.

Close

Summarizing Ask: What were the major differences in opinion between Alexander Hamilton and James Madison? *(Possible response: Hamilton believed in a strong national government, which would exercise firm control over the economy; he suggested taxation to overcome debt. Madison disagreed about how to pay off debt, he opposed a national bank.)* **OL**

Section 1 REVIEW

Answers

1. All definitions can be found in the section and the Glossary.
2. Started: The federal government laid a tax on whiskey. Ended: The federal government called in troops to put down the rebellion.
3. Alexander Hamilton led the Federalists, while Thomas Jefferson led the Democratic-Republicans.
4. He met regularly with his cabinet, which was made up of the heads of the major governmental departments. He served only two terms.
5. Federalist supporters included merchants, artisans, manufacturers, and bankers; issues: strong national government, manufacturing, and trade; Democratic-Republican supporters included independent farmers, rural South and West; issues: agriculture and states' rights
6. the prohibition against a state religion
7. Speeches should use persuasive language, appeal to the intended audience, and reflect Madison's beliefs.

Focus

Have students read George Washington's list of rules of civil behavior. Ask them to state these rules in modern language, and then ask volunteers to share their versions. **Ask:** Why do you think some rules of civil behavior change little over time, while others change significantly? *(Possible response: Today's more casual society lives by different rules, but some behaviors will always apply.)*

Teach

W Writing Support

Descriptive Writing Have students read aloud Lucy Knox's quotation in the Verbatim section and the statistics in the Numbers section. Point out that, while many of the events described in the textbook involved men, women and children were equally affected by these events. Encourage groups to research the lives of women and children during the late 1700s, and write a description of daily life away from the battlefield and halls of government. OL

Additional Support

TIME NOTEBOOK

HULTON GETTY

GEORGE WASHINGTON *At the age of 16, George Washington carefully transcribed in his own hand the* Rules of Civility and Decent Behaviour in Company and Conversation. *Among the rules our first president lived by:*

- Every action done in company ought to be with some sign of respect to those that are present.
- When in company, put not your hands to any part of the body, not usually [un]covered.
- Put not off your clothes in the presence of others, nor go out your chamber half dressed.
- Sleep not when others speak.
- Spit not in the fire, nor stoop low before it. Neither put your hands into the flames to warm them, nor set your feet upon the fire, especially if there is meat before it.
- Shake not the head, feet or legs. Roll not the eyes. Lift not one eyebrow higher than the other. Wry not the mouth, and bedew no man's face with your spittle, by approaching too near him when you speak.
- Show not yourself glad at the misfortune of another though he were your enemy.
- Be not hasty to believe flying reports to the disparagement of any.
- Think before you speak.
- Cleanse not your teeth with the Table Cloth.

VERBATIM

WAR'S END

"I hope you will not consider yourself as commander-in-chief of your own house, but be convinced, that there is such a thing as equal command." W

LUCY FLUCKER KNOX, *to her husband Henry Knox, upon his return as a hero from the Revolutionary War*

"The American war is over, but this is far from being the case with the American Revolution. Nothing but the first act of the drama is closed."

BENJAMIN RUSH, *signer of the Declaration of Independence and member of the Constitutional Convention*

"You could not have found a person to whom your schemes were more disagreeable."

GEORGE WASHINGTON, *to Colonel Lewis Nicola, in response to his letter urging Washington to seize power and proclaim himself king*

"It appears to me, then, little short of a miracle that the delegates from so many states . . . should unite in forming a system of national government."

GEORGE WASHINGTON, *in a letter to the Marquis de Lafayette at the close of the Constitutional Convention*

"It astonishes me to find this system approaching to near perfection as it does; and I think it will astonish our enemies."

LEONARD DESEL VA/CORBIS

BENJAMIN FRANKLIN, *remarking on the structure of the new United States government*

Extending the Content

American Spelling Book Noah Webster's Elementary Spelling Book was used by schoolchildren for nearly a century. It had a blue-green cover and was nicknamed "the blue-backed speller." The book contains a large collection of maxims, proverbs, fables, and some very stern views of how children should behave, including the following quote: "As for those boys and girls that mind not their books, and love not the church and school, but play with such as tell tales, tell lies, curse, swear, and steal, they will come to some bad end, and must be whipt till they mend their ways."

Annual Salaries

Annual federal employee salaries, 1789

President (he refused it)	$25,000
Vice President	$5,000
Secretary of State	$3,500
Chief Justice	$4,000
Senator	$6 per day
Representative	$6 per day
Army Captain	$420
Army Private	$48

CORBIS

1780s WORD PLAY

Dressing the "Little Pudding Heads"

Can you match these common items of Early American clothing with their descriptions?

1. clout	**a.** a band of strong fabric wrapped around a baby to suppress the navel
2. stays	**b.** a diaper
3. surcingle	**c.** the wool cover worn over a diaper
4. pilch	**d.** a head covering for a child learning to walk to protect its brain from falls
5. pudding cap	**e.** a garment worn by children to foster good posture, made from linen and wood or baleen splints

answers: 1. b; 2. e; 3. a; 4. c; 5. d

Milestones

SETTLED, 1781. LOS ANGELES, by a group of 46 men and women, most of whom are of Native American and African descent.

CALLED, 1785. LEMUEL HAYNES, as minister to a church in Torrington, Connecticut. Haynes, who fought at Lexington during the Revolutionary War, is the first African American to minister to a white congregation. A parishioner insulted Haynes by refusing to remove his hat in church, but minutes into the sermon, the parishioner was so moved that the hat came off. He is now a prayerful and loyal member of the congregation.

PUBLISHED, 1788. *THE ELEMENTARY SPELLING BOOK,* by Noah Webster, a 25-year-old teacher from Goshen, N.Y. The book standardizes American spelling and usage that differs from the British.

NUMBERS

5 **Number of years younger average American bride compared to her European counterpart**

6 **Average number of children per family to survive to adulthood**

7 **Average number of children born per family**

8 **Number of Daniel Boone's surviving children**

68 **Number of Daniel Boone's grandchildren**

$5 **Average monthly wage for male agricultural laborer, 1784** W

$3 **Average monthly wage for female agricultural laborer, 1784**

PIX/FPG

CRITICAL THINKING

1. *Contrasting* Benjamin Rush made a distinction between the American war and the American Revolution. What do you think he meant by his statement?

2. *Making Inferences* Based on the rules George Washington lived by, how would you describe his character?

W Writing Support

Expository Writing Have students research one of the people mentioned in the feature. Ask students to write a one-page essay about the person's contribution to history. OL

Assess/Close

Summarizing Ask students to discuss which part of the spread they found most interesting, entertaining, or surprising. **Ask:** **How do these details give you a better picture of life during the period?** *(Answers will vary.)* OL

Visit the TIME Web site at www.time.com for up-to-date news, weekly magazine articles, editorials, online polls, and an archive of past magazine and Web articles.

Critical Thinking Answers:

1. Possible response: The revolution to come would be a change in thinking about the proper role of the government.
2. Possible response: He was modest, considerate, polite, and open-minded.

Additional Support

Activity: Interdisciplinary Connection

Language Arts Tell students that many of the concerns of the people of the time—both in government and in private life—were similar to the ones they have today. Invite students to choose one of the quotations in the Verbatim section. Have them identify contemporary issues in government and international relations similar to the ones addressed by the speakers. For example, the quotation by George Washington could be related to contemporary issues of presidential authority. Ask students to write brief synopses of these contemporary issues and then share these with the class. OL

Focus

Bellringer

Daily Focus Transparency 4-2

Guide to Reading

Answers: Jay's Treaty: Britain had the right to seize cargo bound for French ports, and agreed to international arbitration. British gave up forts in American territory and gave the U.S. most-favored nation status. Pinckney's Treaty: U.S. given the right to navigate the Mississippi and to deposit goods in New Orleans. Convention of 1800: U.S. gave up claims against France for damage to American shipping, and France released the U.S. from the Treaty of 1778.

Section Spotlight Video

To generate student interest and provide a springboard for class discussion, access the Chapter 4, Section 2 video at glencoe.com or on the video DVD.

Section 2

Section Audio   Spotlight Video

Partisan Politics

Guide to Reading

Big Ideas

Government and Society
Disagreements between the political parties early in the nation's history threatened citizens' rights.

Content Vocabulary

- most-favored nation *(p. 163)*
- alien *(p. 166)*
- sedition *(p. 166)*
- interposition *(p. 167)*
- nullification *(p. 167)*

Academic Vocabulary

- radical *(p. 162)*
- neutral *(p. 162)*

People and Events to Identify

- Jay's Treaty *(p. 163)*
- Pinckney's Treaty *(p. 164)*
- Quasi-War *(p. 165)*
- Alien and Sedition Acts *(p. 166)*

Reading Strategy

Categorizing Complete a graphic organizer by listing the provisions of treaties made by the United States.

Treaty	Provisions
Jay's Treaty	
Pinckney's Treaty	
Convention of 1800	

Although Washington wanted to remain neutral in the ongoing war between France and Britain, staying out of the conflict was not easy. In 1800 the United States underwent its first transfer of political power—from the Federalist Party to the Democratic-Republican Party.

Trade and Western Expansion

MAIN Idea During Washington's presidency, the United States faced several challenges in foreign policy and territorial expansion; the French Revolution and conflict between Britain and France divided Americans.

HISTORY AND YOU Have you ever been involved in a dispute between two friends? Read on to find out how events in France forced Americans to take sides in political struggles at home.

Shortly after George Washington was inaugurated in 1789, the French Revolution began in Europe. At first, most Americans sympathized with the revolutionaries, who seemed to be fighting for the same rights Americans had won a few years earlier. By the spring of 1793, however, a new group of French **radicals** had seized control. They stripped aristocrats of their property and executed thousands of people, including the king and queen. These events divided Americans. Many Federalists, horrified by the violence and chaos, opposed the revolutionaries, but many Republicans supported them, despite the bloodshed, because they seemed to be fighting for liberty.

When France declared war on Britain, President Washington found himself in a difficult position. Both Britain and France traded with the United States. Furthermore, the Treaty of 1778 with France required the United States to help defend France's colonies in the Caribbean. Fulfilling this agreement might mean war with Great Britain. In April 1793, Washington declared the United States to be "friendly and impartial" toward both warring powers.

Jay's Treaty

Despite Washington's declaration, the British began intercepting all **neutral** ships carrying goods to French ports, including hundreds of American ships. At the same time, reports appeared that the British, operating out of forts they still occupied on American territory, were inciting Native Americans to attack western settlers. Together, these events pushed Congress to the brink of war in 1794.

Determined to avoid war, Washington sent John Jay to Britain to seek a solution. The British were busy fighting France. They did not want to fight the Americans, but they knew that the United States

Resource Manager

R Reading Strategies	C Critical Thinking	D Differentiated Instruction	W Writing Support	S Skill Practice
Teacher Edition • Reading Maps, p. 163 • Summarizing, p. 166 **Additional Resources** • Guide Read. Act., URB p. 47	**Teacher Edition** • Making Inferences, p. 164 **Additional Resources** • Critical Thinking Skills Act., URB p. 32 • Quizzes and Tests, p. 52	**Teacher Edition** • Visual/Spatial, p. 164 **Additional Resources** • Enrichment Act., URB p. 44	**Teacher Edition** • Persuasive Writing, pp. 165, 166	**Additional Resources** • Reinf. Skills Act., URB p. 31 • Read. Essen., p. 41

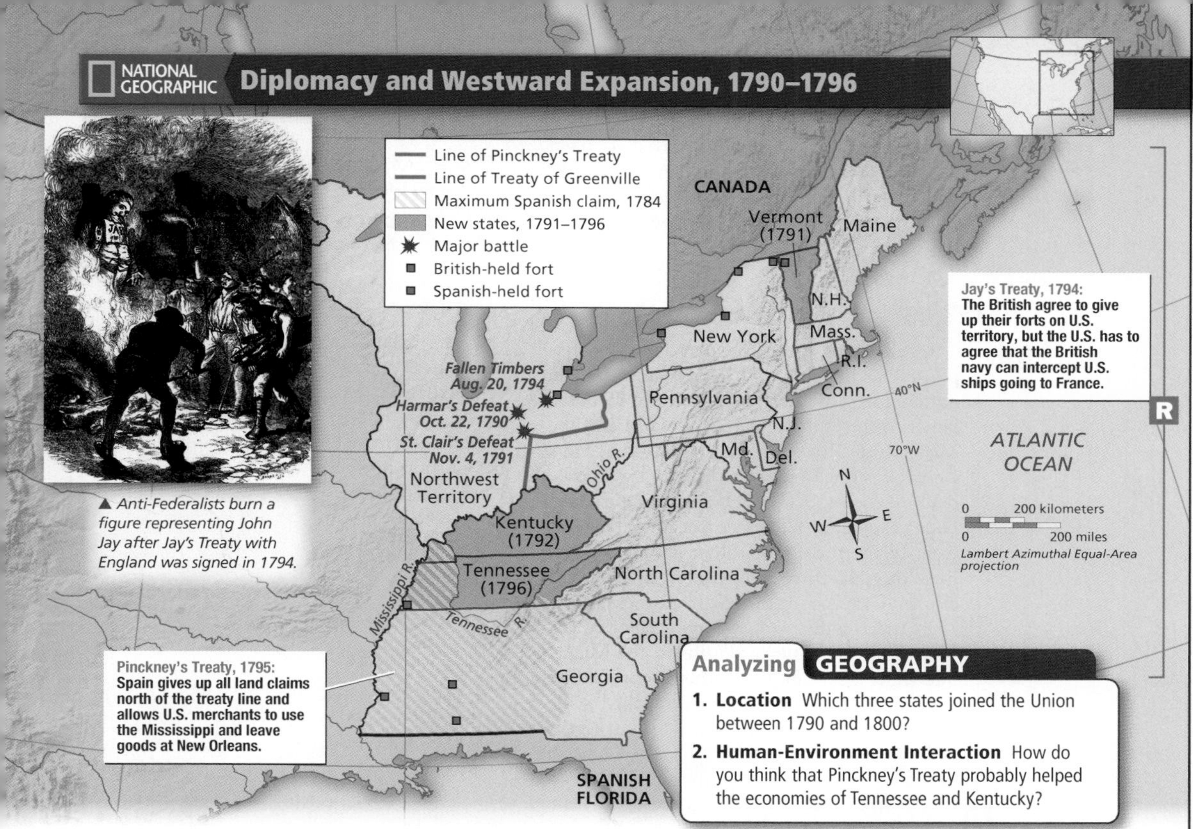

▲ *Anti-Federalists burn a figure representing John Jay after Jay's Treaty with England was signed in 1794.*

Analyzing GEOGRAPHY

1. **Location** Which three states joined the Union between 1790 and 1800?
2. **Human-Environment Interaction** How do you think that Pinckney's Treaty probably helped the economies of Tennessee and Kentucky?

depended on trade with Britain. They agreed to sign a treaty but drove a hard bargain.

Jay was forced to agree that Britain had the right to seize cargoes bound for French ports. He also failed to get compensation for merchants whose goods had been seized. The British did agree, however, to submit the issue to international arbitration—a hearing by neutral third countries. The British also agreed to give up their forts on American territory and granted the United States **most-favored nation** status. American merchants would no longer be discriminated against when trading with Britain. They were also allowed limited trade with Britain's colonies in the Caribbean.

When **Jay's Treaty** was sent to the Senate for ratification, the senators were shocked by its terms and tried to keep them secret. Although they eventually ratified the treaty, news of its terms leaked to the public. The Republicans immediately attacked the treaty, accusing the Federalists of being pro-British. Across much of the country, public protests were held condemning the treaty. After prolonged deliberation, Washington agreed to implement the treaty. The decision prevented war with Great Britain and protected the fragile American economy.

Pinckney's Treaty

Jay's Treaty also helped the United States win concessions from Spain, which still controlled Florida and territory west of the Mississippi River. In 1795 Spain joined France in its war against Britain. The signing of the treaty had raised fears in Spain that the British and Americans might now join forces to seize Spain's North American holdings. Spain quickly offered to negotiate all outstanding issues with the United States. Washington sent Thomas Pinckney to Spain to negotiate.

Teach

R Reading Strategy

Reading Maps Ask: What established a boundary between the United States and Spain's western territory? Why do you think control of that boundary was important? *(Possible response: the Mississippi River; rivers are essential to trade—gave the United States an important trade advantage.)* BL

Analyzing GEOGRAPHY

Answers:

1. Vermont, Kentucky, Tennessee
2. Possible answer: Pinckney's Treaty probably helped the economies of the two states because farmers and others could use the Mississippi River to get their goods to market and ship them around the world from New Orleans.

Hands-On Chapter Project
Step 2

Presidential Customs

Step 2: The Legacy of George Washington Students will share their research (from Step 1) in groups.

Directions Divide the class into small groups. Each student will share his or her three examples of presidential precedents set by George Washington. Groups will work together to describe the origins of these precedents and why they have impacted the presidency.

Causes and Effects Students will determine why certain presidential customs and procedures are in place. OL

(Chapter Project continued on page 169)

D Differentiated Instruction

Visual/Spatial Have students reread the passage "Westward Expansion" on page 164. Then ask them to create a flowchart documenting events leading up to the end of Native American resistance in the Northwest Territory. The flowchart should begin with the arrival of white settlers and end with the signing of the Treaty of Greenville. BL

C Critical Thinking

Making Inferences Have students research the origins and practices of the Electoral College. Point out that there were 139 electoral votes cast in the presidential election of 1796. Today the Electoral College casts 538 votes. **Ask:** Why were fewer electoral votes needed to win the election in 1796 than in 2004? *(There were fewer electoral votes because there were fewer states.)* BL

Reading Check

Answer:
to defend Native American lands against white settlement

Additional Support

In 1795 the Spanish signed the Treaty of San Lorenzo—better known as **Pinckney's Treaty.** The treaty granted the United States the right to navigate the Mississippi and to deposit goods at the port of New Orleans. The treaty won broad acceptance, especially among western farmers who wanted to use the Mississippi to get crops to market.

Westward Expansion

In the 1780s, drawn by abundant land, fertile soil, wide rivers, and a wide variety of fish and game, Americans flocked to the area between the Appalachian Mountains and the Mississippi River. In less than a decade, Kentucky grew from a few hundred settlers to over 70,000, and in 1792, it became a state. Four years later, Tennessee became a state as well. In the meantime, other settlers moved into the Northwest Territory, where they clashed with the region's Native Americans.

In the Northwest Territory, a chief of the Miami named Little Turtle united the Miami, Shawnee, Delaware, and other groups into a confederacy to defend their lands against white settlers. In late 1790, Little Turtle's forces defeated American troops led by General Josiah Harmar. A year later, they ambushed an American force led by General Arthur St. Clair, killing nearly half his men. D

After these disasters, Washington sent General Anthony Wayne to stop the Native American attacks. In August 1794, a large force made up of Shawnee, Ottawa, Chippewa, and Potawatomi warriors, led by the Shawnee chief Blue Jacket, attacked Wayne's troops at the Battle of Fallen Timbers. Wayne's forces won the battle, inflicting heavy losses.

Wayne's victory dealt a decisive blow to Native American resistance in the Northwest Territory. In August 1795, 12 Native American nations signed the Treaty of Greenville. They agreed to give up part of southern Ohio and Indiana in exchange for a yearly payment of $10,000 from the federal government. They also gave up land near where Chicago, Detroit, and Vincennes, Indiana, are located today. After the treaty was signed, the flow of settlers into the region rapidly increased. By 1803, Ohio had enough settlers to become a state.

Reading Check **Examining** Why did Little Turtle form a confederacy?

The War Between the Parties

MAIN Idea Conflict between Federalists and Republicans began to threaten social stability.

HISTORY AND YOU Do you think that the federal government should be able to suspend civil rights? Read on to learn how the Federalists suppressed criticism of their leadership.

With Washington stepping down, the United States held its first openly contested election. The Federalists rallied around John Adams for president, while the Republicans nominated Thomas Jefferson. Anger over Jay's Treaty made the election close, but when the electoral votes were tallied, John Adams edged out Jefferson 71 to 68 and became the second president of the United States. C

The Quasi-War With France

President Adams faced troubled times at home and abroad. Enraged by Jay's Treaty, the French began stopping American ships en route to Britain and seizing their goods. France's actions led many Federalists to call for war. Although critical of the French, Adams, like Washington, was reluctant to go to war. Instead, he sent Charles Pinckney, Elbridge Gerry, and John Marshall to Paris to negotiate with the French government.

After weeks of waiting, three agents representing Charles Maurice de Talleyrand, the French minister of foreign affairs, approached the Americans. They asked for a bribe of $250,000 just to initiate talks, and also sought an American loan of $12 million. In a letter, John Marshall recounted an exchange with "Mr. X," one of the agents:

PRIMARY SOURCE

"Mr. X. again returned to the subject of money; said he, Gentlemen, you do not speak to the point—it is money: it is expected that you will offer money. We said we had spoken to that point very explicitly: we had given an answer. No, said he, you have not; what is your answer? We replied, it is no; no; not a sixpence."

—from *Official Correspondence . . . Between C. C. Pinckney, John Marshall, and Elbridge Gerry*

Extending the Content

Chief Blue Jacket Some historians believe that the Shawnee chief Blue Jacket was Marmaduke Van Swearingen, a white teenager who was captured by the Shawnee. There is little hard evidence to substantiate this claim, and DNA samples from the descendants of Blue Jacket and the Van Swearingen family indicate that the families are not related. The controversy continues because there is some dispute over whether the DNA samples were from bona fide descendants.

PRIMARY SOURCE

Washington's Farewell Address, 1796

Before leaving office, George Washington wrote a letter to the American people. Widely reprinted, Washington's Farewell Address warned Americans against sectionalism, political parties, and the dangers of becoming too attached to any foreign nation:

"... The name of American, which belongs to you in your national capacity, must always exalt the just pride of patriotism.... With slight shades of difference, you have the same religion, manners, habits, and political principles. You have in a common cause fought and triumphed together; the independence and liberty you possess are the work of joint counsels, and joint efforts of common dangers, sufferings, and successes.

... In contemplating the causes which may disturb our Union, it occurs as matter of serious concern that any ground should have been furnished for characterizing parties by geographical discriminations, Northern and Southern, Atlantic and Western.... You cannot shield yourselves too much against the jealousies and heartburnings which spring from these misrepresentations.

... Let me now take a more comprehensive view, and warn you in the most solemn manner against the baneful effects of the spirit of party generally.... The disorders and miseries, which result, gradually incline the minds of men to seek security and repose in the absolute power of an individual.

... Of all the dispositions and habits which lead to political prosperity, religion and morality are indispensable supports. In vain would that man claim the tribute of patriotism, who should labor to subvert these great pillars of human happiness, these firmest props of the duties of men and citizens....

... The great rule of conduct for us in regard to foreign nations is in extending our commercial relations, to have with them as little political connection as possible.... It is our true policy to steer clear of permanent alliances with any portion of the foreign world.... we may safely trust to temporary alliances for extraordinary emergencies."

—From "A Letter to the American People," Sept. 17, 1796

▲ *George Washington at Versailles, France, 1796*

DBQ Document-Based Questions

1. **Identifying** About what three main issues does Washington warn Americans?
2. **Discussing** How do you think Washington would feel about the activities of the national government today?

When President John Adams informed Congress of the incident, he referred to the French agents as X, Y, and Z. Newspapers began referring to the incident as the XYZ Affair. Federalist newspapers later turned Pinckney's response into a stirring campaign slogan, "Millions for defense, but not one cent for tribute." **W**

Irate Americans, who had been angry with Britain a few years earlier, now called for war against France. Resolutions and mass meetings further aroused the public. In June 1798 Congress suspended trade with France and directed the navy to capture French ships.

The two nations were soon fighting an undeclared war at sea that came to be known as the **Quasi-War.** In the fall of 1798, France proposed new negotiations. In September 1800 the two countries signed the Convention of 1800. The United State gave up all claims against France for damages to American shipping. In return, France released the United States from the Treaty of 1778. The signing of the Convention of 1800 brought the Quasi-War to an end.

The Alien and Sedition Acts

The Quasi-War also affected domestic politics in the United States. Many Federalists resented the harsh criticisms printed in Republican newspapers. They remembered the angry Republican crowds that had protested Jay's Treaty. Now, the Quasi-War had reversed the situation, and Federalists decided to strike back at the Republicans.

W Writing Support

Persuasive Writing Have students conduct additional research about the XYZ affair. Using the information they find, in addition to the information on this page, have them write a newspaper article calling for war against France or calling for peace. They should cite reasons and examples to support their opinions. Have students "publish" their articles and discuss which articles best support the writers' opinions. **AL**

DBQ Document Based Questions

Answers:

1. sectionalism, political parties, foreign alliances
2. Students' answers will vary, but most will feel that Washington would be unhappy with the national government today. Political parties are strong and often antagonistic, and the United States has many foreign alliances.

Additional Support

Extending the Content

The Real Washington Have students study the painting of George Washington reproduced on page 165. Explain that early sculptures and paintings, such as this one, tended to make Washington a regal, unapproachable figure. As time progressed, his image was used commercially and, by the mid-1800s, artists had made Washington a more human figure. Artists in the late 1800s and early 1900s returned Washington to a lofty pedestal during the Colonial Revival Movement. Artists included in the Colonial Revival Movement include J.L.G. Ferris, Norman Rockwell, and N.C. Wyeth.

R Reading Support

Summarizing **Ask:** How would the Alien and Sedition Acts harm the Republicans? *(They targeted recent immigrants, who tended to vote Republican.)* OL

W Writing Support

Persuasive Writing Have students write a position paper in which they explain whether or not they feel the Alien and Sedition Acts were unconstitutional. Responses should be supported by a logical explanation for the position taken. Encourage students to review Chapter 3 and the Constitution Handbook before taking their position. AL

Turning Point

Answer:
It was a peaceful transfer of power between deeply hostile political parties, so it demonstrated a commitment to the Constitution and to a democratic republic.

Additional Support

Turning Points

The Election of 1800

The election of 1800 was a major turning point in American political history. This is because it was the first transfer of power between parties under the federal Constitution, and, despite the enormous political and personal hatred between the party members, it was accomplished peacefully. It demonstrated the commitment on all sides to the Constitution and to a democratic republic despite partisan passions.

ANALYZING HISTORY **What made the election of 1800 so significant in American political history?**

▲ *This cartoon reveals the emotions in American politics and the divisive nature of the relationship between the parties in the early years of the nation. The scene depicts a fight in the House of Representatives in 1798, begun when Federalist Roger Griswold of Connecticut assaulted Republican Matthew Lyon of Vermont.*

Presidential Election of 1800

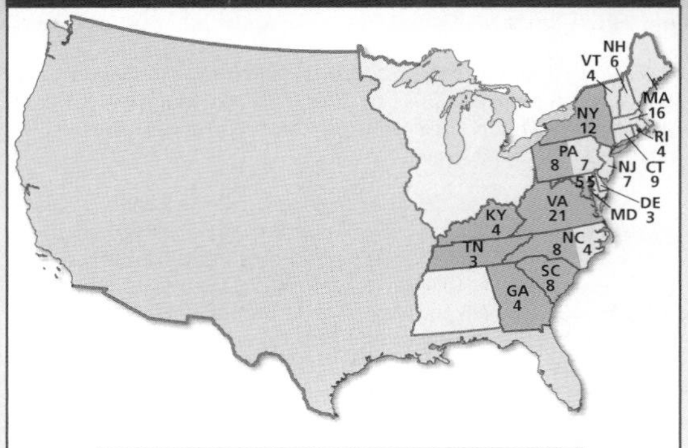

Presidential Candidate	Popular Votes	% of Popular Vote	Electoral Votes
Jefferson	*	*	73
Adams	*	*	65

*Electors were not chosen by popular vote, but by state legislatures.

According to the original terms of the Constitution, each elector in the Electoral College voted for two people in a presidential election. The person receiving the most votes became president, and the person receiving the second-highest number of votes became vice president. Under this system a tie was possible, as happened in the case of the tie between Thomas Jefferson and Aaron Burr in 1800. The House of Representatives then elected Jefferson after 35 rounds of voting in which there was no clear winner. To prevent such confusion in the future, the Twelfth Amendment was added to the Constitution in 1804. The amendment stipulates that electoral votes for president and vice president are counted and listed separately.

For the text of the Kentucky Resolution, see page R47 in **Documents in American History.**

At the height of public anger at France in 1798, the Federalists pushed four laws through Congress. These laws became known as the **Alien and Sedition Acts.**

The first three laws were aimed at **aliens**—people living in the country who were not citizens. The Federalists knew that many recent immigrants had come from France and Ireland. W These immigrants were often anti-British and R tended to vote for the Republicans when they became citizens.

The first law changed the period for people waiting to become citizens from 5 to 14 years. The next two laws gave the president the power to deport without trial any alien deemed dangerous to the nation.

The fourth law tried to prevent **sedition,** or incitement to rebellion. This law made it illegal to say or print anything "false, scandalous, and malicious" about the federal government or any government officer. In short, the act deprived citizens of their right to criticize public officials. The government indicted 21 people W and convicted 11 under this act, most of them Republican newspaper editors and politicians.

In 1798 and 1799, the Republican-controlled legislatures of Kentucky and Virginia passed resolutions, secretly written by Jefferson and Madison, criticizing the Alien and Sedition Acts. Both resolutions argued that since the states had created the Constitution, they could declare federal laws unconstitutional.

Extending the Content

The Federalists By the election of 1800, sometimes referred to as "the Revolution of 1800," a number of crises had led to deep divisions in the country. Both the Republican and Federalist parties were concerned that the other party, if it obtained power, would betray the ideals of the Revolution and overthrow the Constitution. During the balloting, many feared that civil war might erupt if the vote remained deadlocked. According to one eyewitness, over a hundred thousand people filled the streets of Washington, anxiously waiting for a winner to be declared.

In his inaugural address of March 4, 1801, Jefferson said: "Let us, then, fellow citizens, unite with one heart and one mind. Let us restore to social intercourse that harmony and affection without which liberty and even life itself are but dreary things. . . . We have called by different names brethren of the same principle. We are all Republicans, we are all Federalists." OL

The Virginia Resolutions introduced the theory of **interposition.** They argued that if the federal government did something unconstitutional, the state could interpose between the federal government and the people and stop the illegal action. The Kentucky Resolutions advanced the theory of **nullification.** According to this theory, if the federal government passed an unconstitutional law, the states had the right to nullify the law, or declare it invalid. Although these resolutions had little effect in 1800, states used these ideas in later decades to defend their regional interests.

The Election of 1800

John Adams hoped to win reelection in 1800 but he faced an uphill battle. The Alien and Sedition Acts had angered many people, as had new taxes on houses, land, and enslaved Africans. The Republican nominees, Thomas Jefferson for president and Aaron Burr for vice president, campaigned against the taxes and the national bank. They accused the Federalists of favoring monarchy and discouraging political participation.

The election was closely contested and had an unexpected outcome, one that revealed a flaw in the system for selecting the president. The Constitution does not let citizens vote directly for the chief executive. Instead, each state chooses electors—the same number as it has senators and representatives. This group, known as the Electoral College, then votes for the president.

According to the original terms of the Constitution, each elector in the Electoral College voted for two people. The normal practice was for an elector to cast one vote for his party's presidential candidate and another for the vice presidential candidate. To avoid a tie between Jefferson and Burr, the Republicans had intended for one elector to refrain from voting for Burr, but when the votes were counted, Jefferson and Burr each had 73. Since no candidate had a majority, the Federalist-controlled House of Representatives had to choose a president.

Many Federalists despised Jefferson and wanted to choose Burr, but Alexander Hamilton preferred Jefferson. He urged his followers to support Jefferson, leading to a tie in the House of Representatives. Finally, in February 1801, Federalist James Bayard cast a blank ballot so that Jefferson received more votes than Burr and became president. Historians are not sure why this happened. They have inferred that Bayard did it because Jefferson had let him know that if elected, he would keep Hamilton's financial system and not fire all Federalists in the government.

The election of 1800 was an important turning point in American history. At the time, the Federalists controlled the army, the presidency, and the Congress. They could have refused to step down and overthrown the Constitution. Instead, they respected the people's right to choose the president. The election of 1800 demonstrated that power in the United States could be peacefully transferred despite strong disagreements between the parties.

Reading Check **Analyzing** What was the purpose of the Alien and Sedition Acts?

Section 2 REVIEW

Vocabulary

1. **Explain** the significance of: most-favored nation, Jay's Treaty, Pinckney's Treaty, Quasi-War, Alien and Sedition Acts, alien, sedition, interposition, nullification.

Main Ideas

2. **Identifying** What were the positive outcomes of Jay's Treaty?
3. **Determining Cause and Effect** What were the causes of the Quasi-War?

Critical Thinking

4. **Big Ideas** How did the Alien and Sedition Acts interfere with the lives of Americans?
5. **Organizing** Use a graphic organizer similar to the one below to list the foreign policy challenges that Washington and Adams faced during their presidencies.

6. **Analyzing Visuals** Study the map of the presidential election of 1800 on page 166. Which three states split their electoral votes between Adams and Jefferson?

Writing About History

7. **Persuasive Writing** Assume the role of an American citizen in 1798. Write a letter to the editor explaining why you do or do not support the Alien and Sedition Acts.

History ONLINE
Study Central™ To review this section, go to glencoe.com and click on Study Central.

167

Reading Check

Answer:
to limit rights of immigrants and suppress criticism of the government, also reduced Republican power as many immigrants tended to vote Republican

Assess

History ONLINE

Study Central™ provides summaries, interactive games, and online graphic organizers to help students review content.

Close

Summarizing Ask: What were the major domestic and international issues of Adams's presidency? *(the passage of the Alien and Sedition Acts threatened immigrants' security and made criticizing the government a crime; the XYZ affair; the Quasi-War with France)* **OL**

Section 2 REVIEW

Answers

1. All definitions can be found in the section and the Glossary.
2. The treaty prevented war with Great Britain, thus protecting the fragile U.S. economy.
3. In response to Jay's Treaty, the French began to seize American ships. When Adams sent diplomats to negotiate with the French, they requested bribes. This incident, called the XYZ Affair, enraged Americans, and in June 1798 Congress suspended trade with France and directed the navy to capture French ships. This began an undeclared war with France.
4. The Acts required immigrants to wait 14 years before they could become citizens, allowed the president to deport aliens without trial, and deprived citizens of the right to criticize the government.
5. Washington: British interference with U.S. shipping, French Revolution, struggle with Native Americans over Northwest Territory, Spain's control of the Mississippi; Adams: XYZ Affair, Quasi-War, French interference with U.S. shipping
6. Pennsylvania, Maryland, North Carolina
7. Letters to the editor should express an opinion about the Alien and Sedition Acts based on students' ideas and information from the section.

Focus

Bellringer

Daily Focus Transparency 4-3

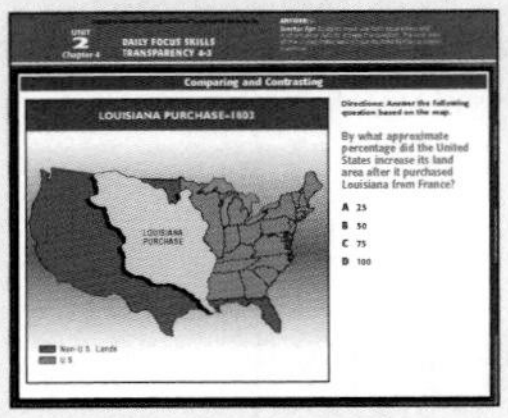

Guide to Reading

Answers may include: 1801: Jefferson took office, Judiciary Act of 1801 repealed; 1803: *Marbury* v. *Madison* decision, Louisiana Purchase expands nation; 1804: Supreme Court Justice Samuel Chase impeached, Lewis and Clark begin expedition, Burr murders Hamilton; 1805: Pike maps upper Mississippi; 1806: Pike travels to Colorado, Britain issues Orders in Council; 1807: Embargo Act passed; 1809: Embargo Act repealed

Section Spotlight Video

To generate student interest and provide a springboard for class discussion, access the Chapter 4, Section 3 video at glencoe.com or on the video DVD.

Resource Manager

Section 3 — Section Audio — Spotlight Video

Jefferson in Office

Guide to Reading

Big Ideas

Government and Society Jefferson worked to limit the scope of the government, obtain the Louisiana Territory, and keep the nation out of European wars.

Content Vocabulary
- judicial review *(p. 170)*
- embargo *(p. 173)*

Academic Vocabulary
- license *(p. 173)*

People and Events to Identify
- Louisiana Purchase *(p. 169)*
- Meriwether Lewis *(p. 169)*
- William Clark *(p. 169)*
- Sacagawea *(p. 170)*
- John Marshall *(p. 170)*

Reading Strategy

Sequencing Complete a time line similar to the one below to record the major events of Thomas Jefferson's presidency.

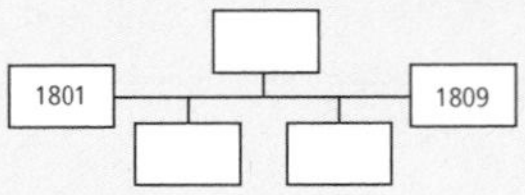

President Thomas Jefferson worked to limit the scope of the federal government, purchased the Louisiana Territory, and tried to keep the United States out of European conflicts. The Supreme Court, under John Marshall, established the power of judicial review.

Jefferson's Administration

MAIN Idea During Jefferson's presidency the nation more than doubled in size, while the federal judiciary established its authority.

HISTORY AND YOU Today, we await a Supreme Court decision to determine whether a law is constitutional. However, the Court did not start out with this power. Read on to find out how the Supreme Court established this authority.

Thomas Jefferson privately referred to his election as the "Revolution of 1800." He believed that Washington and Adams had acted too much like royalty, and he tried to create a less formal style for the presidency. He rode horseback rather than traveling in carriages. In place of formal receptions, he entertained at more intimate dinners around a circular table so that, as he said, "When brought together in society, all are perfectly equal."

Although Jefferson set a new style for the presidency, he did not overturn all of the Federalists' policies. Instead he sought to integrate Republican ideas into the policies that the Federalists had already put in place. A strong believer in small government, Jefferson hoped to limit federal power. He began paying off the federal debt, cut government spending, and did away with the hated whiskey tax. Instead of a standing army, he planned to rely on local militia.

Jefferson's economic ideas had worried many Federalists, who expected the new president to close the national bank. Jefferson's choice of Albert Gallatin as secretary of the treasury reassured them. Gallatin was a skilled financier who supported Hamilton's system.

The Louisiana Purchase

One of Jefferson's strongest beliefs was that a republic could survive only if most of the people owned land. This belief led him to support the idea of expanding the country farther west.

In 1800 French leader Napoleon Bonaparte convinced Spain to give Louisiana back to France in exchange for helping Spain take control of part of Italy. Napoleon's deal worried Jefferson because it gave France control of the lower Mississippi. Jefferson believed that having France back in North America would force the United States

R Reading Strategies	C Critical Thinking	D Differentiated Instruction	W Writing Support	S Skill Practice
Additional Resources • Prim. Source Read., URB p. 37 • Guide Read. Act., URB p. 48	**Additional Resources** • Inter. Pol. Cartoons, URB p. 41 • Quizzes and Tests, p. 53	**Teacher Edition** • Kinesthetic, p. 170 **Additional Resources** • Diff. Instruction Activity, URB p. 23	**Teacher Edition** • Narrative Writing, p. 170	**Teacher Edition** • Using Geo. Skills, pp. 169, 172 **Additional Resources** • Historical Analysis Skills Act., URB p. 22 • Time Line Activity, URB p. 33 • Read. Essen., p. 44

The Louisiana Purchase, 1803

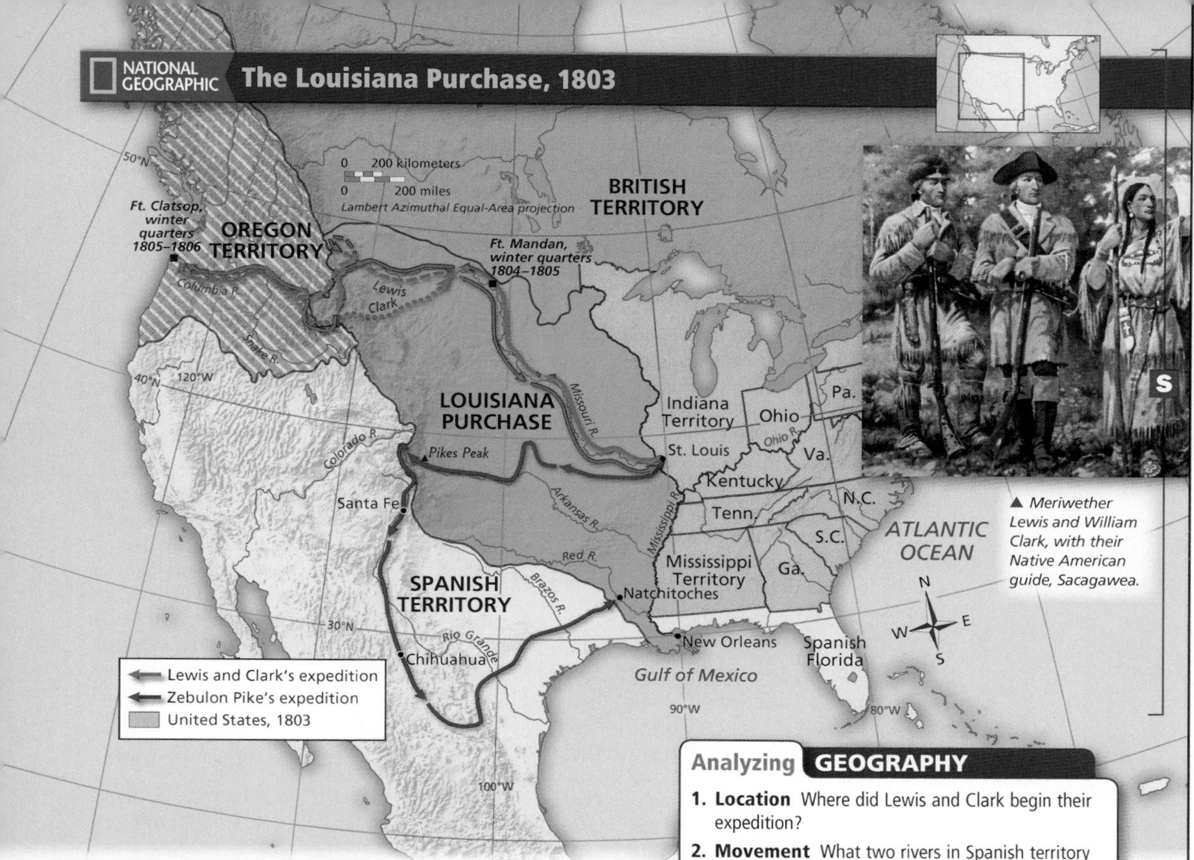

▲ *Meriwether Lewis and William Clark, with their Native American guide, Sacagawea.*

Analyzing GEOGRAPHY

1. **Location** Where did Lewis and Clark begin their expedition?
2. **Movement** What two rivers in Spanish territory did Pike cross during his explorations?

into an alliance with the British, whom Jefferson despised. Jefferson ordered Robert Livingston, his ambassador to France, to try to block the deal or gain concessions for the United States. Livingston arrived in Paris in the spring of 1801, but he accomplished little until 1803.

By 1803, Napoleon had begun making plans to conquer Europe. If France resumed its war against Britain, the last thing the French wanted was an alliance between the United States and Great Britain. Furthermore, France's government was short on funds. In 1803, therefore, Napoleon offered to sell all of the Louisiana Territory, as well as New Orleans, to the United States. Livingston immediately accepted.

On April 30, 1803, the United States bought Louisiana from France for $11.25 million. It also agreed to take on French debts owed to American citizens. These debts were worth about $3.75 million, making the total cost about $15 million. The Senate overwhelmingly approved the **Louisiana Purchase.** The deal more than doubled the size of the United States and gave the nation control of the entire Mississippi River.

Lewis and Clark Even before Louisiana became a part of the United States, Jefferson asked Congress to fund a secret expedition into the Louisiana Territory to trace the Missouri River and find a route to the Pacific Ocean. After Congress approved the expedition, Jefferson chose **Meriwether Lewis,** his private secretary, and **William Clark,** the brother of Revolutionary War hero George Rogers Clark, to lead the expedition.

S Skill Practice

Using Geography Skills Have students study the arrows showing the origin, path, and ending point of each expedition and identify the territories and regions through which each expedition passed. **Ask:** In what ways did the routes of the expeditions differ from each other? *(Much of Lewis and Clark's expedition was in a northwestern direction, following, for long distances, the courses of rivers—the Missouri and the Columbia. Pike's expedition followed a more circuitous route—west, south, and then northeast again.)* **BL**

Analyzing GEOGRAPHY

Answers:
1. St. Louis
2. the Rio Grande and the Brazos River

Hands-On Chapter Project
Step 3

Presidential Customs

Step 3: The Presidency Today Students will research the procedures and customs of the presidency today.

Directions Divide the class into the small groups established in previous steps of the Chapter project. Groups will divide research topics among their members. For example, one group member may research the procedures and customs of presidents in the area of foreign policy; another may research presidential customs in the area of organizing the executive department, and so on.

Comparing and Contrasting Students will gather with the results of their independent research to compare notes. They should compare the customs and procedures of the presidency today with the actions taken by the nation's first president. **OL**

(Chapter Project continued on page 177)

D Differentiated Instruction

Kinesthetic Have interested students work alone or with a partner to learn more about one of the expeditions mentioned in this section. After they conduct their research, have students create a poster illustrating the highlights of the expedition. Encourage students to find and include excerpts from the explorers' journals. Finally, have them make a presentation to the class about the expedition. OL

W Writing Support

Narrative Writing Have students research the Hamilton-Burr duel and then write the script for a television news special report about the event. Tell them to include background information on both Hamilton and Burr and to describe the context of the duel. Encourage volunteers to read aloud all or part of what they have written and solicit feedback. AL

Reading Check

Answer:
to shift control of the federal judiciary away from the Federalists

Additional Support

In May 1804 the "Corps of Discovery," as the expedition was called, headed west up the Missouri River. Along the way they met **Sacagawea,** a Shoshone woman who joined the expedition as a guide and interpreter. The expedition found a path through the Rocky Mountains and eventually traced the Columbia River to the Pacific Ocean. The expedition also gave the United States a claim to the Oregon territory along the coast.

D **The Pike Expedition** Lewis and Clark's expedition was not the only one exploring the Louisiana Purchase. In 1805 Zebulon Pike mapped much of the upper Mississippi, and in 1806 he headed west to find the headwaters of the Arkansas River. Pike traveled to Colorado, where he charted the mountain now known as Pikes Peak. He also mapped part of the Rio Grande and traveled across northern Mexico and what is now southern Texas. Pike provided Americans with detailed description of the Great Plains and the Rocky Mountains.

The Essex Junto The Louisiana Purchase alarmed New England Federalists. It meant that, eventually, their region would lose its influence in national affairs while the South and West gained political strength through new states. In Massachusetts, a small group of Federalists known as the Essex Junto drafted a plan to take New England out of the Union.

Hoping to expand their movement, they persuaded Vice President Aaron Burr to run for governor of New York in 1804. During the campaign, Alexander Hamilton called Burr "a dangerous man, and one who ought not be trusted with the reins of government." W Offended, Burr challenged Hamilton to a duel. When the two met on July 11, 1804, though, Hamilton refused to fire. Burr shot and killed his foe. In 1807, Burr was accused of plotting to create his own country in the western U.S. He was charged with treason but acquitted.

An Independent Judiciary

At the end of their term, the Federalist majority in Congress enacted the Judiciary Act of 1801. This act created 16 new federal judges. President Adams then appointed Federalists to these positions. These judges were nicknamed "midnight judges" because Adams supposedly stayed up signing appointments until midnight on his last day in office.

Republicans in Congress were not pleased that the Federalists controlled the courts. One of the first acts of Congress after Jefferson took office was to repeal the Judiciary Act of 1801, thereby doing away with the "midnight judges" by abolishing their offices.

Impeaching Judges The Republicans then tried to remove other Federalists from the judiciary by impeachment. Republican leaders believed that the impeachment power was one of the checks and balances in the Constitution. Congress could impeach and remove judges for arbitrary or unfair decisions, not just for criminal behavior.

In 1804, the House impeached Supreme Court Justice Samuel Chase. During one trial, Chase had ordered Democratic-Republicans removed from the jury. He had also denounced Jefferson to another jury. The Senate, however, did not convict Chase. Many senators did not think he was guilty of "treason, bribery, or other high crimes and misdemeanors" that the Constitution required for his removal. The impeachment of Justice Chase established that judges could be removed only for criminal behavior, not simply because Congress disagreed with their decisions.

John Marshall and *Marbury* v. *Madison* The most important judicial appointment President Adams made before leaving office was the choice of **John Marshall** as Chief Justice of the United States. Marshall served as Chief Justice for 34 years. He was more responsible than any other justice for making the Supreme Court into a powerful, independent branch of the federal government.

Marshall increased the power of the Supreme Court in 1803 with the decision in *Marbury* v. *Madison*. In this case, the Supreme Court ruled part of the Judiciary Act of 1789 to be unconstitutional. The decision marked the first time the Supreme Court asserted the power of **judicial review**—the power to decide whether laws passed by Congress were constitutional and to strike down those that were not. Although the Supreme Court would not strike down another federal law until the case of *Dred Scott* v. *Sandford* 54 years later, the power to do so had been established.

Reading Check **Explaining** Why did Congress repeal the Judiciary Act of 1801?

Extending the Content

Voyage of Discovery Since many of the plants and animals that Lewis and Clark encountered were unknown to them, they collected and preserved many specimens including prairie dog, jackrabbit, black-tailed deer, pronghorn, and mountain sheep. Huge grizzly bears were a common threat to the expedition. They also found some huge bones that may have been from a dinosaur. As an avid collector of mastodon bone (the word *dinosaur* was not coined until 1840), Thomas Jefferson sent William Clark in search of more bones to add to his collection.

Should the Supreme Court Have the Power of Judicial Review?

★ *Marbury* v. *Madison*, 1803

Background to the Case

William Marbury had been appointed a justice of the peace shortly before President Adams left office. Adams had signed Marbury's appointment, but the documents had not been delivered when Adams left office. The new secretary of state, James Madison, was supposed to deliver the documents, but President Jefferson told him to hold them, hoping Marbury would quit and allow Jefferson to appoint someone else. Marbury then asked the Supreme Court to issue a court order telling Madison to deliver the documents.

How the Court Ruled

Marbury based his request for a court order on the Judiciary Act of 1789, which said that requests for federal court orders go directly to the Supreme Court. In *Marbury* v. *Madison*, the Supreme Court decided that part of the Judiciary Act was unconstitutional and thus invalid. The Constitution specifies which cases can go directly to the Supreme Court, and court orders are not mentioned. The decision established the Court's power to declare laws unconstitutional and invalid.

▲ *Chief Justice John Marshall (1755–1835) established many precedents that helped to make the judiciary branch powerful enough to check and balance the other two branches of the federal government.*

PRIMARY SOURCE

The Court's Opinion

"It is emphatically the province and duty of the judicial department to say what the law is. Those who apply the rule to particular cases must of necessity expound and interpret that rule. If two laws conflict with each other, the courts must decide on the operation of each.

So, if a law be in opposition to the Constitution; if both the law and the Constitution apply to a particular case, so that the court must either decide that case conformably to the law, disregarding the Constitution, or conformably to the Constitution, disregarding the law, the court must determine which of these conflicting rules governs the case. This is of the very essence of judicial duty."

—Chief Justice John Marshall in *Marbury* v. *Madison*

PRIMARY SOURCE

Federalist No. 78 and the Court's Decision

Some scholars argue that the Court was wrong to claim the power of judicial review, but no one who helped write the Constitution objected. In Federalist No. 78, *Alexander Hamilton implies that judicial review is to be expected:*

"The interpretation of the laws is the proper and peculiar province of the courts. A constitution is in fact, and must be, regarded by the judges as a fundamental law. It therefore belongs to them to ascertain its meaning as well as the meaning of any particular act proceeding from the legislative body. If there should happen to be an irreconcilable variance between the two, that which has the superior obligation and validity ought of course to be preferred; or in other words, the constitution ought to be preferred to the statute. . ."

—from *Federalist No. 78*

DBQ Document-Based Questions

1. **Identifying** What does Chief Justice John Marshall say is the main duty of the judiciary?
2. **Describing** How does Alexander Hamilton uphold the principle of judicial review?
3. **Contrasting** On what point do Marshall and Hamilton disagree?

Teach

More About the Case

John Marshall had long been influential in U.S. politics, when he was appointed chief justice of the Supreme Court by Adams in 1801. He held this position until his death in 1835.

During Marshall's 34 years on the court, he wrote more than 500 decisions, firmly grounding the principle of judicial review and establishing American legal precedents still cited today.

DBQ Document Based Questions

Answers:

1. to say what the law is
2. He says that the interpretation of the law is the job of the judiciary and that the Constitution is the fundamental law.
3. Marshall says that judges must determine which law is valid—the new law or the Constitution—in a given situation, while Hamilton says that a constitution "ought to be preferred" over any other law.

Differentiated Instruction

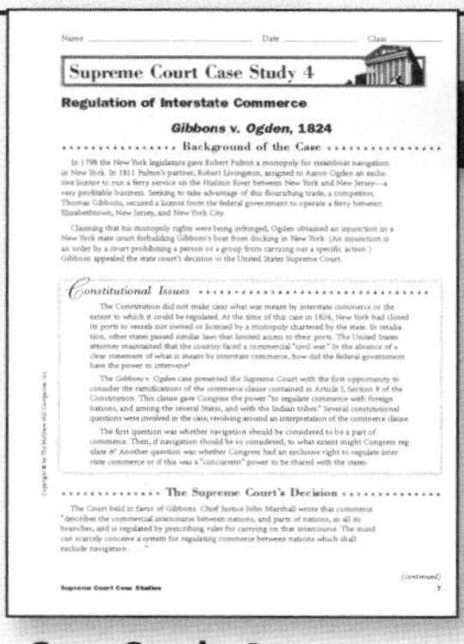

Supreme Court Case Study 4

Regulation of Interstate Commerce

Gibbons v. *Ogden*, 1824

Background of the Case

Constitutional Issues

The Supreme Court's Decision

Case Study 4: *Gibbons* v. *Ogden*, p. 7

Analyzing a Supreme Court Decision: *Gibbons* v. *Ogden*

Objective: Learn how judicial review was applied to a significant Supreme Court case.

Focus: Identify the central issue of the case.

Teach: Discuss the Court's opinion.

Assess: Explain the importance of the case (broad interpretation of Congressional power).

Close: Write a paragraph summarizing the case.

Differentiated Instruction Strategies

- **BL** Create a chart to list the issue before the Court and the Court's opinion.
- **OL** Write a summary of the case.
- **AL** Role-play lawyers and justices.
- **ELL** Illustrate a map of the steamboat route from New York City to New Jersey and list the businesses located in the area.

S Skill Practice

Using Geography Skills Help students identify the Barbary States on a map and point out the number of countries with coastlines on the Mediterranean Sea. **Ask:** **Which bodies of water did these states control access to?** *(the Mediterranean, the Atlantic Ocean, the Black Sea)* Challenge interested students to learn more about European and American trade routes and to create a map showing these routes. **OL**

Analyzing VISUALS

Answers:

1. King George is threatening to hurt Jefferson, while Napoleon is demanding money.
2. British and French seem to be in control, while Jefferson surrenders. Cartoon expresses American anger over Jefferson's embargo policy that hurt American trade and did not fight British and French interference with U.S. trade.

Differentiated Instruction

Rising International Tensions

MAIN Idea To avoid getting drawn into the war between France and England, Jefferson banned trade with other countries.

HISTORY AND YOU Jefferson used a trade embargo as a tool of diplomacy. Are there countries today with which the U.S. does not trade?

In addition to acquiring Louisiana from the French, Jefferson had to contend with pirate raids against American ships traveling in the Mediterranean. Then, during his second term, he also had to focus his efforts on keeping the United States out of the war between Britain and France.

The Barbary Pirates

S For years, the Barbary States on the North African coast—Morocco, Algiers, Tunis, and Tripoli—had menaced Mediterranean shipping. European nations had routinely paid "tribute" to these countries so that their ships would be undisturbed, believing that it was less expensive than fighting. In 1795 the United States paid nearly $1 million to the ruler of Algiers for the release of a ship and its crew.

S Jefferson refused to continue such payments. In 1801 Tripoli declared war on the United States and, in turn, Jefferson sent a naval squadron into the Mediterranean. For four years the United States fought its first foreign military conflict. In 1805 an American threat to force a coup in Tripoli ended hostilities. It took a second conflict with the Barbary States in 1815, however, to finally end American tribute payments.

Economic Warfare

In mid-1803, Napoleon's armies surged out of France and headed east. France and Britain were at war again. At first, the war actually benefited American merchants. As the British seized French ships, American merchants began trad-

POLITICAL CARTOONS PRIMARY SOURCE
Economic Pressure on Britain and France

▲ *This 1809 cartoon expresses anger at Jefferson's embargo policy, which hurt American trade but did not stop the British and French from seizing American ships.*

Analyzing VISUALS

1. **Identifying** In the cartoon, what are King George and Napoleon doing?
2. **Explaining** What is the figurative meaning of this cartoon?

Leveled Activities

BL Reinforcing Skills Activity, URB p. 31

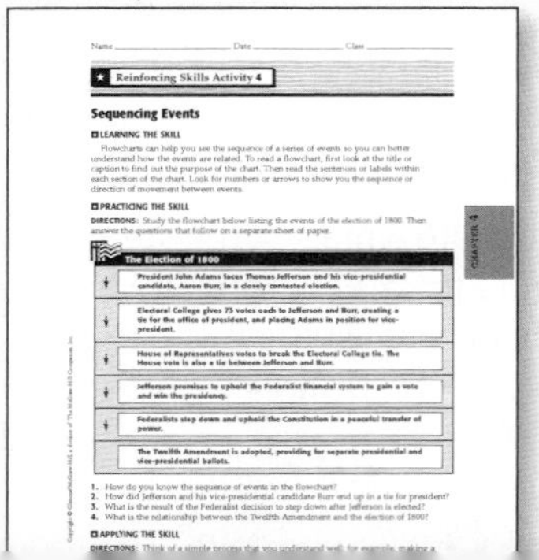

OL American Art and Music Activity, URB p. 39

AL Enrichment Activity, URB p. 44

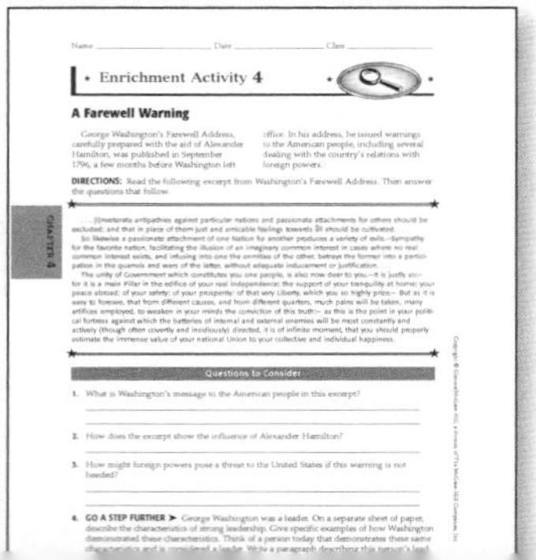

ELL English Learner Activity, URB p. 26

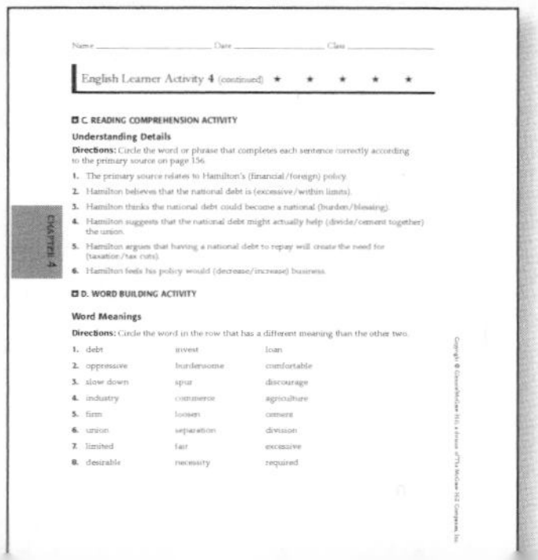

ing with French colonies. The British left the American ships alone because the United States had proclaimed neutrality.

In 1806 Britain issued regulations known as the Orders in Council. These declared that all ships going to Europe needed British **licenses** and would be searched for contraband. In response, Napoleon declared that merchants who obeyed the British system would have their goods confiscated when they reached Europe. American merchants were caught in the middle. No matter whom they obeyed, they were going to lose their goods.

Impressment The British navy was short of recruits because of low pay and terrible shipboard conditions. British sailors often deserted to American vessels. Britain tried to solve this problem by impressment, a legalized form of kidnapping that forced people into military service. Britain claimed the right to stop American ships and search for deserters. On many occasions they impressed American citizens into service as well.

In June 1807 these tensions reached the boiling point when the British warship *Leopard* stopped the American warship *Chesapeake* to search for British deserters. When the captain of the *Chesapeake* refused to comply, the *Leopard* opened fire, killing three Americans. After the Americans surrendered, the British went aboard and seized four sailors.

The Embargo of 1807 The attack on the *Chesapeake* enraged the public, and American newspapers clamored for war. Like Washington and Adams before him, however, President Jefferson did not want to entangle the United States in the affairs of Europe. Instead of going to war, he asked Congress to pass the Embargo Act of 1807, halting all trade between the United States and Europe.

The **embargo,** a government ban on trade with other countries, wound up hurting the United States more than France or Britain. In the Northeast, the shipping business came to a standstill. Farmers in the South and West saw the demand for their crops plummet. In Congress, Maryland's Philip Barton Key railed against the embargo:

PRIMARY SOURCE

"In a commercial point of view, it has annihilated our trade. In an agricultural point of view. it has paralised [sic] industry. . . . Our most fertile lands are reduced to sterility, so far as it respects our surplus product. . . . [I]t will drive (if continued) our seamen into foreign employ, and our fishermen to foreign sand banks. In a financial point of view, it has dried up our revenue."

—from *The National Intelligencer and Washington Advertiser,* May 27, 1808

Realizing the embargo was not working, Congress repealed it in March 1809, shortly before Jefferson left office. After his second term, President Jefferson gladly retired to his estate, Monticello, in Virginia. While the embargo made Jefferson unpopular, his administration had reversed the Federalist course by limiting the power of the federal government. It had also acquired a vast new territory in the West.

Reading Check **Examining** Why did Jefferson have Congress pass the Embargo Act?

Section 3 REVIEW

Vocabulary

1. **Explain** the significance of: Louisiana Purchase, Meriwether Lewis, William Clark, Sacagawea, John Marshall, judicial review, embargo.

Main Ideas

2. **Explaining** Why did Napoleon sell Louisiana to the United States?

3. **Determining Cause and Effect** What led to the war with the Barbary States?

Critical Thinking

4. **Big Ideas** How did the Supreme Court decision in *Marbury* v. *Madison* strengthen the federal judiciary?

5. **Organizing** Use a graphic organizer similar to the one below to list the causes and effects of the Embargo Act of 1807.

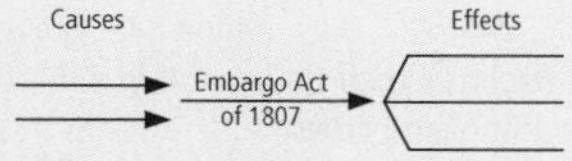

6. **Analyzing Visuals** Study the map of the Louisiana Purchase on page 169. In what territories did Lewis and Clark make their winter camps during their expedition?

Writing About History

7. **Descriptive Writing** Suppose that you are a member of the Lewis and Clark or Zebulon Pike expedition. Write a journal entry describing what you have done or seen on your trip.

History ONLINE
Study Central™ To review this section, go to glencoe.com and click on Study Central.

173

Reading Check

Answer:
He thought that if the United States ended trade with all European nations, it would not become entangled in the war between Britain and France.

Assess

History ONLINE

Study Central™ provides summaries, interactive games, and online graphic organizers to help students review content.

Close

Summarizing Ask: What were two major accomplishments of the Jefferson administration? *(possible answers: territorial expansion through the Louisiana Purchase, trying to keep the United States out of war)* OL

Section 3 REVIEW

Answers

1. All definitions can be found in the section and the Glossary.
2. France needed the money, and Napoleon did not want the United States and Great Britain to form an alliance.
3. Once president, Jefferson refused to keep making tribute payments to the Barbary States, and Tripoli declared war. In response, Jefferson sent a naval squadron.
4. It established the Supreme Court's power of judicial review.
5. Causes: blockades and impressments; Effects: halted trade between the United States and Europe, greatly harmed the U.S. economy
6. Louisiana Territory and the Oregon Territory
7. Students' journal entries will vary. Journal entries should focus on what a member of the expedition might have done or seen.

Focus

Tell students that President Jefferson charged the explorers with the task of observing, taking notes, and making sketches. Two copies of information were to be made on birch bark, which was less likely than paper to be damaged by damp conditions. William Clark produced 60 maps, and, in addition to Lewis and Clark's writings, seven men kept journals of the trip, six of which have been located. The journals include drawings and descriptive writings.

Teach

R Reading Strategy

Activating Prior Knowledge Invite students to recall how this vast region came into the possession of the United States. *(France sold the land, known as the Louisiana Purchase, because it needed money to finance wars in Europe.)* **OL**

Additional Support

NATIONAL GEOGRAPHIC

GEOGRAPHY & HISTORY

The Lewis and Clark Expedition

R When Thomas Jefferson asked Congress to fund an expedition to explore the Louisiana Territory, his goal was to find a water route—the fabled "Northwest Passage"—to the Pacific Ocean. The Corps of Discovery set out in May 1804. It was led by Captain Meriwether Lewis and Captain William Clark and included some 40 people—36 soldiers, 2 civilian employees, and 2 dependents.

After sailing up the Missouri River into the Great Plains, the expedition spent the winter with the Mandan people. In the spring of 1805, they headed into the Rocky Mountains. The group spent a month carrying their boats and supplies 18 miles around Great Falls. Then, as the river grew shallow, they abandoned their boats, obtained horses from the Shoshone, and crossed the Rockies in the fall of 1805. Once across the mountains, they built dugout canoes and headed down the Columbia River to the Pacific Coast where they waited for the winter to pass. They then headed back across the Rockies, down the Missouri and home.

What Was Learned About the West's Geography?

The Lewis and Clark expedition recorded 178 new species of plant life and 122 previously unknown species of animal life. Numerous specimens and sketches were brought back, and to this day, the expedition's journals remain a vital source of information about the region in the early 1800s. The expedition found a route from the Missouri through the Rockies to the Pacific, and demonstrated that no Northwest Passage existed because the Rocky Mountains divided the continent.

Analyzing GEOGRAPHY

1. **Movement** How did the geography of the route followed by the Corps of Discovery make movement difficult for the explorers?
2. **Human-Environment Interaction** How did the explorers adapt to the physical barriers they faced?

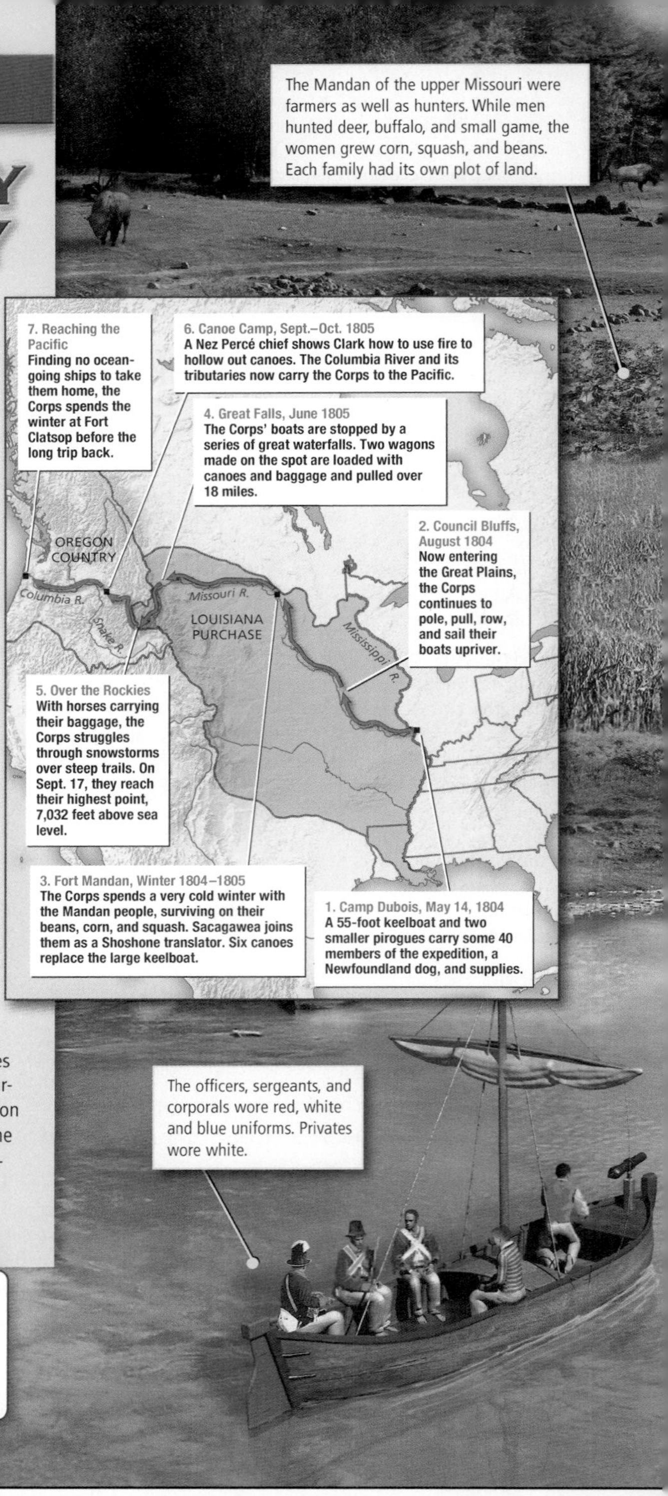

Extending the Content

York and Sacagawea York was William Clark's enslaved African. Not only was he an excellent trapper, hunter, and swimmer, but he also struck awe in the Native Americans. Many of them had never seen a black person, especially one more than six feet tall. Native American warriors often used charcoal to paint their bodies as a sign of battle success. Seeing charcoal-colored York inspired them to believe him among the mightiest of men. Despite his services to the expedition, when York requested his freedom after the trip ended, Clark refused.

Sacagawea had been kidnapped from the Shoshone tribe as a child. When the Shoshone came to the camp, reluctant to sell horses to the expedition, Sacagawea recognized that the leader was her brother. The Shoshone then sold the horses that the expedition needed.

GEOGRAPHY & HISTORY

Assess/Close

Ask students to identify the challenges that members of the expedition faced. *(potentially hostile Native Americans, winter, insufficient food, danger from the terrain itself, weather, illness)* **OL**

Analyzing GEOGRAPHY

Answers:

1. They were traveling upriver for the first part of the journey, and so going against the current.
2. They replaced the large keelboat with smaller canoes. They made wagons to carry their supplies overland; they also bought horses to carry baggage over the mountains. They learned to survive on corn, beans, and squash during a difficult winter.

Additional Support

Activity: Economics Connection

Financing Explorations Organize the class into small groups and have them use library and Internet resources to research what it might cost to outfit an expedition of 40 explorers today. Challenge students to identify the types of supplies, including food, clothing, equipment, and transportation, needed for a one-year geographic exploration covering more than 7,000 miles (11,265 km). Remind students to have accurate figures for their calculations. Ask groups to share their findings and calculations. Discuss similarities and differences as a class. **OL**

Focus

Bellringer

Daily Focus Transparency 4-4

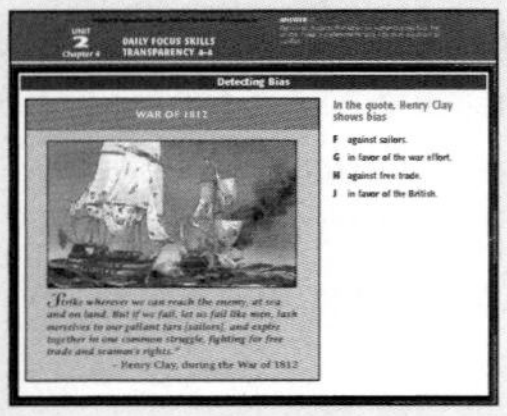

Guide to Reading

Answers may include: British impressment of American sailors, British seizure of American cargoes, British trade restrictions angered southern planters and frontier farmers, failure of U.S. negotiations to lift British trade restrictions, suspicions about British role in Native American attacks on frontier settlers

Section Spotlight Video

To generate student interest and provide a springboard for class discussion, access the Chapter 4, Section 4 video at glencoe.com or on the video DVD.

Section 4 — Section Audio — Spotlight Video

The War of 1812

Guide to Reading

Big Ideas

Individual Action Military leaders, including William Henry Harrison, Tecumseh, Oliver Perry, and Andrew Jackson, contributed to the outcome of the War of 1812.

Content Vocabulary
- nationalism *(p. 181)*

Academic Vocabulary
- overseas *(p. 177)*
- enable *(p. 178)*

People and Events to Identify
- Non-Intercourse Act *(p. 176)*
- War Hawks *(p. 177)*
- Tecumseh *(p. 178)*
- William Henry Harrison *(p. 178)*
- Oliver Perry *(p. 179)*
- Hartford Convention *(p. 181)*
- Treaty of Ghent *(p. 181)*

Reading Strategy

Organizing Complete a graphic organizer similar to the one below by listing the causes of the War of 1812.

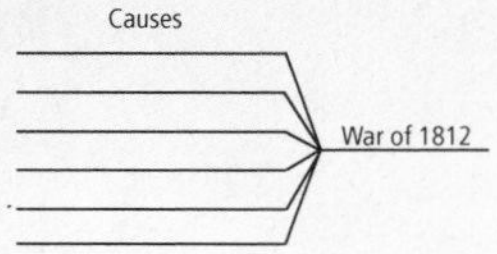

The War of 1812 was the second major clash between the United States and Britain in North America. Although neither side won a clear victory, the war gave Americans a strong sense of national pride.

The Decision for War

MAIN Idea Trade restrictions and the belief that the British encouraged Native American attacks on Americans led to war.

HISTORY AND YOU Do you remember reading about Pontiac's rebellion? Read how conflicts in western territories influenced the decision to go to war.

After Thomas Jefferson announced that he would not run again for president in 1808, the Republican Party nominated James Madison. The Federalists nominated Charles Pinckney. Despite some lingering anger about the Embargo Act of 1807, Madison won the election easily. He assumed office in the midst of an international crisis. Tensions between the United States and Britain were rising, and it would fall to Madison to decide whether or not to lead the United States into its first full-scale war since the Revolution.

Economic Pressures

Like Jefferson, Madison wanted to avoid war. To force the British to stop seizing American ships, he asked Congress to pass the **Non-Intercourse Act.** This act forbade trade with France and Britain while authorizing the president to reopen trade with whichever country removed its trade restrictions first. The idea was to play France and Britain against each other, but the plan failed.

In May 1810, Congress took a different approach with a plan drafted by Nathaniel Macon of North Carolina. The plan, called Macon's Bill Number Two, reopened trade with both Britain and France, but stated that if either nation dropped its restrictions on trade, the United States would stop importing goods from the other nation. Soon afterward, Napoleon announced that France would no longer restrict American trade, although his statement still allowed for the seizure of American ships. Madison accepted Napoleon's statement, despite its conditions, hoping to pressure the British into dropping their trade restrictions, as well. When the British refused, Congress passed a non-importation act against Britain in early 1811.

Madison's strategy eventually worked. By early 1812, the refusal of the United States to buy British goods had begun to hurt the British economy. British merchants began to pressure their government to repeal its restrictions on trade. Finally, in June 1812, Britain ended all

Resource Manager

R Reading Strategies	C Critical Thinking	D Differentiated Instruction	W Writing Support	S Skill Practice
Teacher Edition • Outlining, p. 177 • Making Connections, p. 177 **Additional Resources** • American Lit. Reading, URB p. 13 • Guide Read. Act., URB p. 49	**Teacher Edition** • Det. Cause and Effect, p. 178 **Additional Resources** • Linking Past/Present, URB p. 34 • Auth. Assess, p. 13 • Quizzes and Tests, p. 54	**Teacher Edition** • Visual/Spatial, p. 180 **Additional Resources** • Reteach. Act., URB p. 43	**Additional Resources** • Am. Art and Music Act., URB p. 39	**Teacher Edition** • Using Geo. Skills, p. 179 **Additional Resources** • Read. Essen., p. 47

PRIMARY SOURCE

The Causes of the War of 1812

The War of 1812 had four main causes: the British policy of intercepting U.S. ships trading with France; British impressments of American sailors; problems with Native Americans on the frontier; and a group of Congressmen from the South and West who strongly pushed for war.

NATIVE AMERICAN ATTACKS

▲ *Americans blamed the British for tensions with Native Americans that led to confrontations such as the Battle of Tippecanoe in 1811 (above).*

THE WAR HAWKS

"Has not Congress solemnly pledged itself to the world not to surrender our rights? And has not the nation . . . resolved to maintain at all hazards our maritime independence?

. . . No man in the nation wants peace more than I: but I prefer the troubled ocean of war, demanded by the honor and independence of the country, with all its calamities and desolation, to the tranquil and putrescent pool of ignominious peace. . . . Britain stands preeminent in her outrage on us, by her violation of the sacred personal rights of American freemen, in the arbitrary and lawless imprisonment of our seamen, the attack on the *Chesapeake*—the murder, sir."

—Henry Clay, speech before the Senate, February 22, 1810

▲ *Henry Clay*

▲ *John C. Calhoun*

R1

IMPRESSMENT

▶ *British impressment of American sailors angered many Americans.*

DBQ Document-Based Questions

1. **Paraphrasing** What does Clay say that war with Great Britain is "demanded by"?
2. **Summarizing** According to Clay, why does "Britain stand pre-eminent in her outrage on" the United States?

restrictions on American trade, but it was too late. Two days later, the British learned that the United States had declared war.

The War Hawks

R2 Although it seemed that Britain's actions had hurt Eastern merchants, most members of Congress who wanted war came from the South and West. Nicknamed the **War Hawks** by their opponents, they were led by Henry Clay of Kentucky, John C. Calhoun of South Carolina, and Felix Grundy of Tennessee. The War Hawks believed economic pressure had failed and the nation's reputation was in danger if it did not go to war to stop the British from seizing American sailors.

Americans in the South and West wanted war for two more reasons. British trade restrictions had hurt Southern planters and Western farmers, who earned much of their income by shipping tobacco, rice, wheat, and cotton **overseas.** Eastern merchants could still make a profit despite British restrictions because they passed the cost of losing their ships and goods onto the farmers. R2

Teach

R1 Reading Strategy

Outlining As students read the section, have them create an outline showing the main events that occurred during the War of 1812, including important dates, people, and locations. OL

R2 Reading Strategy

Making Connections Review the pro-war opinions of people in the eastern, southern, and western regions of the United States. **Ask:** What regional conflicts exist in the United States today? *(possible response: the argument about restricting immigration from Mexico and South America, which has a much more immediate effect on people living near the border with Mexico)* OL

DBQ Document Based Questions

Answers:

1. the honor and independence of the United States
2. Britain has violated the rights of Americans through impressment and murder.

Hands-On Chapter Project Step 4

Presidential Customs

Step 4: The Presidency Then and Now Students will work in the groups established from Steps 2 and 3 to present their research.

Directions Divide students into the groups from Step 2. Students will synthesize the information they have gathered by preparing a presentation. Their presentations should relate the presidency today to Washington's presidency. Students should illustrate how certain procedures and functions taken by our current president are the result of actions or decisions taken by Washington. Encourage students to include a chart or other visual organizers and images in their presentations.

Synthesizing Students will use the information they have gathered during the chapter project, summarize it, and clearly present the main points relating to the topic. OL

(Chapter Project continued on the Visual Summary page)

C Critical Thinking

Determining Cause and Effect Remind students about the Northwest Ordinance of 1787, which they learned about in Chapter 3. Challenge students to explain the cause-and-effect relationship between the Northwest Ordinance and the events in Canada during the War of 1812. *(The Northwest Ordinance had attracted large numbers of settlers to the Northwest Territory, displacing many Native Americans in the region. Many of them went to Canada, and some allied with the British against the United States.)* **AL**

Reading Check

Answer:
British trade restrictions hurt Southern planters and frontier farmers because they earned much of their income from selling crops overseas. Western farmers and settlers also blamed the British for supporting Native American efforts against them along the frontier.

Westerners also blamed the British for clashes with Native Americans along the frontier. In the early 1800s, settlers had begun moving past the line established by the Treaty of Greenville. As clashes with Native Americans increased, many settlers accused the British in Canada of arming the Native Americans and encouraging them to attack American settlements.

Tecumseh and Tippecanoe

Although western settlers blamed the British for their problems with the Native Americans, it was the increasing demands of speculators and settlers that sparked Native American resistance. **Tecumseh,** a Shawnee leader, believed that Native Americans needed to unite to protect their lands.

While Tecumseh worked for political union, his brother Tenskwatawa (known as "the Prophet") called for a spiritual rebirth of Native American cultures. His followers lived in Prophetstown on the Tippecanoe River in Indiana, where they tried to practice traditional Native American ways of living.

Aware that Tecumseh's movement was gaining strength, **William Henry Harrison,** governor of the Indiana Territory, prepared to stamp it out. In November 1811, after learning that Tecumseh had gone south to recruit more followers, Harrison gathered troops and marched toward Prophetstown. Tenskwatawa sent fighters to intercept Harrison near the Tippecanoe River. The Battle of Tippecanoe left nearly 200 of Harrison's troops dead or wounded, but it shattered Native American confidence in the Prophet. Many, including Tecumseh, fled to Canada.

Tecumseh's flight to Canada seemed to prove that the British were supporting the Native Americans, as did the British-made rifles his forces left behind on the battlefield. Many western farmers argued that war with Britain would **enable** the United States to seize Canada and end Native American attacks. In June 1812, President Madison gave in to the pressure and asked Congress to declare war. The vote in Congress split along regional lines. The South and West generally voted for war; the Northeast did not.

Reading Check **Examining** Why did Americans in the South and West favor war with Great Britain?

The Invasion of Canada

MAIN Idea Americans attacked British Canada at several points along the border and fought for control of the Great Lakes.

HISTORY AND YOU Can you think of any war that has deeply divided Americans? Read how Americans disagreed about the War of 1812.

Although the Republican-led Congress had called for war, the nation was not ready to fight. The army had fewer than 7,000 troops and little equipment. The navy had only 16 ships. Also, Americans were deeply divided over the war. Many people in New York and New England called it "Mr. Madison's War," implying that it was a private fight that did not deserve the nation's support.

Paying for the war also posed a problem. **C** The year before the war, Republicans had shut down the Bank of the United States by refusing to renew its charter. This made it difficult for the government to borrow money because most private bankers were located in the Northeast. They opposed the war and would not lend money to the government. Despite the nation's military and financial weaknesses, President Madison ordered the military to invade Canada.

Three Strikes Against Canada

American military leaders planned to attack Canada from three directions—from Detroit, from Niagara Falls, and up the Hudson River valley toward Montreal. All three attacks failed. The British navy on Lake Erie rapidly shuttled troops to Detroit and forced the American commander, General William Hull, to surrender.

The British then shifted their troops to the Niagara peninsula, where they took up positions on Queenston Heights along the Niagara River. From there, they easily drove off some 600 American troops who had landed on the Canadian side of the Niagara River. The American force would have been larger, except that the New York militia, many of whom opposed the war, refused to cross the river. They argued that the terms of their military service did not require them to leave the country.

Additional Support

Extending the Content

Tecumseh Tecumseh (c. 1768–1813) was a Shawnee chief born near present-day Springfield, Ohio. Tecumseh urged all Native Americans to unite. They were all one people, he said, and should cooperate in a confederacy to control their destiny. He was furious when the Delaware and Potawatomi agreed to cede about 3 million acres (1.2 million ha) to the United States. The land belonged to all Native Americans, Tecumseh argued. How could one group give it up?

In the end, Tecumseh saw no choice but to fight. During the War of 1812, he allied himself with the British. A superb commander, he met his end at the Battle of the Thames River, near Chatham, Ontario, in October 1813. There, 300 British troops commanded by General Henry Proctor and about 1,000 Native Americans led by Tecumseh fought some 3,000 American troops led by General William Henry Harrison. During the battle, the British broke ranks and fled, leaving Tecumseh's men to face the American forces alone. After Tecumseh's death, his confederacy collapsed.

The War of 1812

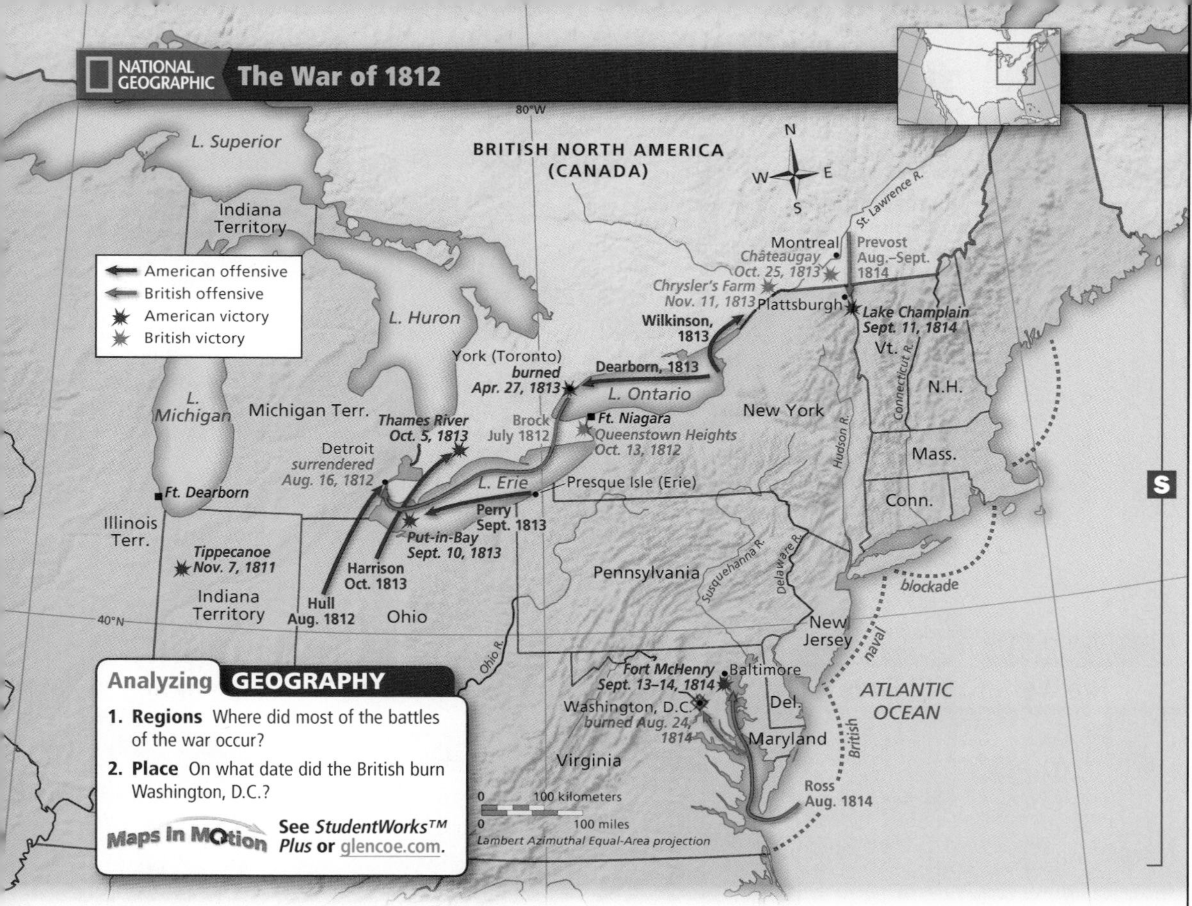

Analyzing GEOGRAPHY

1. **Regions** Where did most of the battles of the war occur?
2. **Place** On what date did the British burn Washington, D.C.?

Maps In MOtion See *StudentWorks™ Plus* or glencoe.com.

The third American attack fared no better than the first two. General Henry Dearborn, marching up the Hudson River toward Montreal, called off the attack after the militia refused to cross the border.

Perry's Victory on Lake Erie

The following year, the United States had more success after Commodore **Oliver Perry** secretly arranged for the construction of a fleet on the coast of Lake Erie in Ohio. On September 10, 1813, Perry's fleet attacked the British fleet on Lake Erie near Put-in-Bay. When his own ship was no longer able to fight, Perry rowed to another vessel. After a grueling four-hour battle, the British surrendered.

Perry's victory gave the Americans control of Lake Erie. It also enabled General Harrison to recover Detroit and march into Canada, where he defeated a combined force of British troops and Native Americans at the Battle of the Thames River.

Harrison's troops from the west were supposed to meet up with American troops from Niagara Falls in the east. British troops and Canadian militia, however, stopped the American attack from the east at the Battle of Stony Creek. When Harrison learned of the defeat, he retreated to Detroit. By the end of 1813, the United States still had not conquered any territory in Canada.

Reading Check **Explaining** Why was conquering Canada an important American goal in the War of 1812?

S Skill Practice

Using Geography Skills Point out that nearly all of the fighting during the war of 1812 took place on or near bodies of water. Remind students of the conflict between the United States and the Barbary pirates in the Mediterranean. **Ask:** Why are waterways strategically important? *(Waterways are key to trade; many settlements are built near water.)* BL

Analyzing GEOGRAPHY

Answers:
1. along the Great Lakes and the border between British North America and the United States
2. August 24, 1814

Reading Check

Answer:
Many Americans believed that controlling Canada would end British support for Native Americans and thus end Native American attacks on the frontier.

Additional Support

Activity: Interdisciplinary Connection

Language Arts Have students read a novel set during the War of 1812. Sample titles include: *A Question of Respect,* by Robert L. Worley; *Danger at Niagara,* by Margaret Goff Clark; *1812,* by David Nevin; and *The Captain From Connecticut,* by C.S. Forester. Have them write brief reports and share details of the novel they have read with other students. Encourage them to discuss what they have learned about the period and how literature can reveal details and perspectives that other sources cannot. OL

D Differentiated Instruction

Visual/Spatial Have students create a graphic organizer to explain strategies employed by the United States and Britain during the War of 1812. *(Possible entries: U.S. strategies: invade Canada, attack British on Lake Erie; British strategies: raid coastal cities, isolate New England, and seize New Orleans)* OL

Analyzing VISUALS

Answers:

1. It greatly weakened the Federalist Party.
2. Possible response: Because the United States did not lose the war to Britain, the British probably had more respect for the United States and did not want to fight over the border, and were, therefore, willing to seek a diplomatic solution.

The War Ends

MAIN Idea After more than two years of fighting, the war ended with a treaty that left boundaries the same and did not address the causes of the war.

HISTORY AND YOU When was the last time you heard the national anthem, "The Star-Spangled Banner"? Read about the attack on Fort McHenry that inspired the lyrics by Francis Scott Key.

In 1814 Napoleon's empire collapsed. With the war against France over, the British were able to send much of their navy and many more troops to deal with the United States. The British strategy for the war had three parts. **D** First, the British navy would raid American cities along the coast. Second, they would march south into New York from Montreal, cutting New England off from the rest of the country. Third, they would seize New Orleans and close the Mississippi River to western farmers. The British believed this strategy would force the United States to make peace.

British Forces Attack Washington and Baltimore

With attention focused on Canada, in August 1814, a British fleet sailed into Chesapeake Bay and landed troops within marching distance of Washington, D.C. The British easily dispersed the poorly trained militia defending the capital and entered the city unopposed. Madison and other government officials hastily fled. The British set fire to the White House and the Capitol. They then prepared to attack Baltimore.

Unlike Washington, D.C., Baltimore was ready for the British. The city militia inflicted heavy casualties on the British troops that went ashore. After bombarding Fort McHenry throughout the night of September 13, the

PRIMARY SOURCE
The War of 1812 Ends

▼ *Although it took place after the peace treaty had been signed in Ghent, the Battle of New Orleans made future president Andrew Jackson a national hero, easing his entrance into politics.*

The Battle of New Orleans, 1815

The Effects of the War of 1812

- Increased the prestige of the United States
- Generated a new spirit of patriotism among Americans
- Fostered national unity
- Greatly weakened the Federalist Party

Analyzing VISUALS

1. **Explaining** How did the War of 1812 affect national politics?
2. **Determining Cause and Effect** In 1818 Britain and the United States reached an agreement on the border between Canada and the United States. How might the outcome of the war have helped them reach agreement?

Additional Support

Teacher Tip

Collaborative Learning This activity allows students at different levels to work together. As you form groups, consider the needed skills and choose students accordingly.

Activity: Interdisciplinary Connection

Music Have students work in small groups to write a fifth verse for "The Star-Spangled Banner." The verse should be written following the same meter and rhyming pattern as the other verses. Encourage students to locate the words to all known verses of the national anthem and listen to recordings of the song to help them understand the rhythm. Invite groups to perform their verses for the class. OL

British abandoned their attack on the city. Francis Scott Key, a young lawyer held aboard a British ship during the shelling, was elated to see the American flag still flying above the fort at dawn. On the back of a letter, he scribbled a poem about the battle that would later become the national anthem of the United States. The final lines of the poem evoke the powerful symbolism of the flag: "O say does that Star-Spangled Banner yet wave / O'er the land of the free and the home of the brave?"

The same month the British attacked Washington and Baltimore, they sent a force of 15,000 well-trained British soldiers south from Montreal into New York. The key to the British advance was control of Lake Champlain. On September 11, 1814, the American fleet on the lake defeated the British fleet; realizing that the Americans could use their control of the lake to surround them, the British abandoned the attack and retreated to Montreal.

Events in New England and New Orleans

The British offensive increased New England's opposition to the war. In December 1814, Federalists from the region met in Hartford, Connecticut, to discuss what they could do independently of the United States. Although members of the Essex Junto urged New England to secede, moderate delegates refused to support such extreme action. Instead, the **Hartford Convention** called for several constitutional amendments to increase the region's political power.

Less than a month after the Hartford Convention began, an American victory in the South put a stop to Federalist complaints. In January 1815, a British fleet with some 7,500 men landed near New Orleans. The American commander, General Andrew Jackson, quickly improvised a defense using cotton bales. The thick bales absorbed the British bullets, while the British advancing in the open provided easy targets for the American troops. The fighting ended in a decisive American victory.

The Battle of New Orleans made Andrew Jackson a national hero. It also helped to destroy the Federalist Party. As **nationalism,** or feelings of strong patriotism, surged, the Federalists at the Hartford Convention appeared divisive and unpatriotic. They never recovered nationally, and within a few years the party ceased to exist.

Peace negotiations began in the Belgian city of Ghent even before the major battles of 1814. On December 24, 1814, the negotiators signed the **Treaty of Ghent,** ending the War of 1812. The treaty restored prewar boundaries but did not mention neutral rights or impressment, and no territory changed hands. Still, the War of 1812 increased the nation's prestige overseas and generated a new spirit of patriotism and national unity.

Four years later in the Convention of 1818, the United States and Great Britain set the U.S.-Canadian border from what is now Minnesota to the Rocky Mountains at 49° north latitude. The countries also agreed to claim jointly for the next ten years a region farther west known as the Oregon Country.

Reading Check **Examining** What were the effects of the Battle of New Orleans?

Section 4 REVIEW

Vocabulary

1. **Explain** the significance of: Non-Intercourse Act, War Hawks, Tecumseh, William Henry Harrison, Oliver Perry, Hartford Convention, Treaty of Ghent.

Main Ideas

2. **Explaining** What was the significance of the Battle of Tippecanoe?
3. **Determining Cause and Effect** What was the outcome of Oliver Perry's attack on the British on Lake Erie?
4. **Identifying** What happened in 1814 that enabled the British to focus on the war with the United States?

Critical Thinking

5. **Big Ideas** How did the Battle of Tippecanoe affect the Native Americans of the Northwest Territory?
6. **Organizing** Use a graphic organizer similar to the one below to list how Americans in different regions felt about war with Great Britain.

Section of U.S.	Position on War	Reason for War Position
West		
South		
North		

7. **Analyzing Visuals** Study the map about the War of 1812 on page 179. Which battle of the war was fought furthest north, and which side had the victory?

Writing About History

8. **Descriptive Writing** Suppose you are an American citizen at the beginning of the War of 1812. Write a letter to a friend describing how the idea of the war makes you feel.

History ONLINE
Study Central™ To review this section, go to glencoe.com and click on Study Central.

Reading Check

Answer:
It made Andrew Jackson a hero, caused a surge in nationalism, and helped destroy the Federalist Party.

Assess

History ONLINE

Study Central™ provides summaries, interactive games, and online graphic organizers to help students review content.

Close

Summarizing Ask: What was the outcome of the War of 1812? *(The Treaty of Ghent, which restored prewar boundaries, was signed in 1814; the U.S. gained prestige and gained a new sense of patriotism.)* OL

Section 4 REVIEW

Answers

1. All definitions can be found in the section and the Glossary.
2. It shattered Native American confidence in the Prophet and forced Tecumseh and others to flee to Canada, which, additionally, seemed to confirm American suspicions that the British were supporting Native American attacks on frontier settlers.
3. It gave the United States control of Lake Erie and enabled Harrison to recover Detroit and march into Canada.
4. Napoleon's empire collapsed when he was defeated and captured by the British.
5. The battle shattered Native American confidence in the Prophet and caused many, including Tecumseh, to flee to Canada.
6. West: favored war, wanted to lift trade barriers and stop Native American attacks; South: favored war, wanted to lift trade barriers; North: against war, still made money despite British trade restrictions
7. Châteaugay; the British
8. Students' letters should focus on feelings about the war.

Identifying Central Issues
Ask: Which three events listed under "Organizing the Government and Expanding the Nation" do you think will, in the long run, have the greatest impact on the United States? *(Students should give reasons for their answers.)* Encourage students to debate this question. AL

Visual/Spatial Have students create a flowchart showing the causes of the War of 1812. OL

Chapter 4 VISUAL SUMMARY

STUDY TO GO You can study anywhere, anytime by downloading quizzes and flashcards to your PDA from glencoe.com.

Organizing the Government and Expanding the Nation

- Washington creates the first cabinet: a secretary of war, a secretary of the treasury, a secretary of state, and an attorney general.
- Congress passes the Judiciary Act, establishing federal courts, including the Supreme Court.
- The Bill of Rights is added to the Constitution.
- To finance the new government, Alexander Hamilton proposes a national tariff, excise taxes, a Bank of the United States, and redeeming Revolutionary War bonds at full value.
- In *Marbury* v. *Madison,* the Supreme Court asserts the power of judicial review.
- The Louisiana Purchase nearly doubles the size of the United States. Lewis and Clark, and Zebulon Pike explore the territory.
- Jay's Treaty improves trade relations with the British Empire.
- Pickney's Treaty secures use of the lower Mississippi River from Spain.
- The debate over Hamilton's plans leads to the emergence of the first two political parties—the Federalists, supported by artisans and merchants in the Northeast, and the Democratic-Republicans, supported by farmers in the South and the West.
- Jay's Treaty with Britain angers Republicans.
- France's attacks on American ships leads to the Quasi-War, and Federalists try to limit political criticism with the Alien and Sedition Acts.

▲ *Washington's first cabinet, from left to right: Secretary of War Henry Knox, Secretary of State Thomas Jefferson, Attorney General Edmund Randolph, and Secretary of the Treasury Alexander Hamilton.*

▲ *In one of the most spectacular American victories of the War of 1812, the USS* Constitution *defeated the British HMS* Guerriere.

Causes of the War of 1812

- The French Revolution leads to a war between Britain and France; the British and French start seizing merchant ships—including American ships—headed to each other's ports. The war increases party divisions; the Federalists support Britain and the Republicans support France.
- When the Republicans gain control of Congress and the presidency, tensions with Britain grow worse.
- British impressment of American sailors angers Americans.
- British support of Native Americans, including Tecumseh, angers settlers in the West.
- British trade restrictions and seizure of merchant cargo heading to France angers Southern planters and frontier farmers.
- An American embargo fails to convince the British to change their policies.
- A group of congressmen, known as War Hawks, call for war, both to avenge Britain's violations of American sovereignty and to protect the interests of the South and the West.

Hands-On Chapter Project
Step 5: Wrap Up

Presidential Customs

Step 5: Wrap Up Students will write a brief essay summarizing the chapter project.

Directions After all of the groups have presented, have students write a brief essay. In their essay, students should select one presidential custom or procedure still in place today and explain Washington's legacy in relation to that precedent. Students should describe why the precedent is important.

Drawing Conclusions Students will explain their conclusions on why certain presidential procedures or customs are important to the nation today. OL

Chapter 4 ASSESSMENT

Reviewing Vocabulary

Directions: Choose the word or words that best complete the sentence.

1. President Washington set a precedent when he met regularly with his
- **A** secretary.
- **B** speculators.
- **C** cabinet.
- **D** generals.

2. The Constitution's "necessary and proper" clause created ________. These powers expanded the potential power of the federal government.
- **A** implied powers
- **B** speculator powers
- **C** enumerated powers
- **D** creditor powers

3. Under the theory of ________, the states could declare a federal law invalid.
- **A** republicanism
- **B** agrarianism
- **C** interposition
- **D** nullification

4. In the early 1800s, the United States protested British ________ of American sailors.
- **A** impressment
- **B** enlistment
- **C** execution
- **D** embargoes

5. After the War of 1812, there was an upsurge of ________ in the United States.
- **A** internationalism
- **B** nationalism
- **C** agrarianism
- **D** republicanism

Reviewing Main Ideas

Directions: Choose the best answer for each of the following questions.

Section 1 *(pp. 154–159)*

6. One of the most important acts of the first U.S. Congress under the Constitution was to
- **A** elect George Washington as the first president.
- **B** establish a federal banking system.
- **C** pass the Tariff of 1789.
- **D** add a Bill of Rights to the Constitution.

7. The Democratic-Republican Party was started mainly to oppose the ideas of
- **A** Thomas Jefferson.
- **B** John Adams.
- **C** Alexander Hamilton.
- **D** George Washington.

Section 2 *(pp. 162–167)*

8. In 1795 Pinckney's Treaty granted the United States the right to which of the following?
- **A** take over British forts in the Northwest Territory
- **B** navigate the Mississippi River
- **C** impress British sailors
- **D** remain neutral between Britain and France

9. The Convention of 1800 ended which conflict?
- **A** Little Turtle's War
- **B** the War of 1812
- **C** the Franco-British War
- **D** the Quasi-War

TEST-TAKING TIP

Often it is helpful to identify the key term in a question and then locate its synonym in an answer choice to identify the correct answer.

Need Extra Help?

If You Missed Questions . . .	1	2	3	4	5	6	7	8	9
Go to Page . . .	154–155	157	167	173	181	154–155	158–159	164	164–165

GO ON

Answers and Analyses
Reviewing Vocabulary

1. C Washington's cabinet consisted of the heads of the Departments of State, Treasury, and War and the office of the Attorney General. This tradition continues today, although the cabinet has expanded over the years.

2. A The Constitution does not mention speculator powers or creditor powers. It describes enumerated powers, which are clearly listed in the document. Implied powers are suggested in the description of powers but are not clearly mentioned.

3. D Discuss with students the root "null" in nullification, which comes from the Anglo-French *nul*, which means "not any." Null means invalid or having no value, and often has a legal connotation. To nullify is to legally invalidate. Introduce students to the phrase "null and void."

4. A The British began the practice of impressment in response to its difficulty in keeping sailors. Students can focus on the word "press" in impressment, to help remember that these men were illegally pressed, or forced, into service.

5. B Nationalism is intense pride in one's nation, or patriotism. Make a comparison between the feelings of nationalism that swept the nation at the conclusion of the American Revolution and the feelings of nationalism after the War of 1812. In both cases, uniting against a common enemy instilled a feeling of unity among Americans.

Reviewing Main Ideas

6. D Remind students of the Federalist v. Anti-Federalist debate regarding ratification of the Constitution. The Anti-Federalists were convinced to support ratification on the condition that a bill of rights be added to the Constitution.

7. C Alexander Hamilton caused quite a bit of controversy when he proposed the creation of a national bank. The Democratic-Republican Party had an agrarian base, in favor of agriculture over trade and commerce and against the National Bank.

8. B It is not likely a treaty would include the right to impressment, and treaties usually end fighting rather than confirming neutrality eliminating *C* and *D*. It was in Jay's Treaty that Britain agreed to give up its forts, eliminating *A*.

9. D Quasi means "almost" or "not quite." The war that took place between the U.S. and France, which involved the XYZ affair, was an undeclared war. If students remember that the two parties involved were the U.S. and France, they should be able to eliminate *A* and *C*. *B* is not a realistic answer; a convention to end a conflict in 1812 could not have taken place twelve years earlier, in 1800.

10. B The United States won its independence in 1783, so *A* does not make sense. *B* is correct; Washington, afraid to damage relations with both nations, chose to remain neutral in the conflict. *C* is a tempting distractor, because the U.S. had agreed to help defend French colonies in the Caribbean, but Washington ultimately chose neutrality.

11. A An easy way to remember that Lewis and Clark explored the Louisiana Territory is to use alliteration: **L**ewis = **L**ouisiana. Two of the United States's most famous explorers, Lewis and Clark reached the Pacific Ocean in 1806.

12. A Here, students may become confused by choice *D*, because *Marbury* v. *Madison* established judicial review, or the review of the constitutionality of laws. It is vital that students grasp the concept of judicial review, which was born out of the system of checks and balances.

13. C This is another place students can use alliteration as a mnemonic device: **T**ippecanoe = **T**ecumseh and Tenskwatawa. The Battle of Tippecanoe took place in 1811. Little Turtle was a Miami chief who clashed with white settlers in 1790.

14. D The Hartford Convention took place in response to the War of 1812 due to New England's opposition to the war. In light of this, *B* and *C* do not make sense. *A* does not make sense either; the two nations were already at war. It was members of the Essex Junto that urged New England to secede. Junto (sometimes spelled Junta) means "faction."

Chapter 4 Assessment

10. How did President George Washington react to the conflict between France and England in 1793?

- **A** He used the opportunity to begin the war for American independence.
- **B** He declared the neutrality of the United States.
- **C** He aided the French because they had supported the American Revolution.
- **D** He negotiated a peace settlement between the warring nations.

Section 3 *(pp. 168–173)*

11. In 1804 Lewis and Clark set off to explore

- **A** the Louisiana Territory.
- **B** the Colorado Territory.
- **C** Spanish Florida.
- **D** the Mississippi River.

12. The Supreme Court decision in *Marbury* v. *Madison* established the principle of

- **A** judicial review.
- **B** democratic republicanism.
- **C** nullification.
- **D** constitutionality.

Section 4 *(pp. 176–181)*

13. In the Battle of Tippecanoe, U.S. General William Henry Harrison defeated the forces of

- **A** Little Turtle.
- **B** Great Britain.
- **C** Tecumseh and Tenskwatawa.
- **D** Napoleon.

14. At the Hartford Convention in 1814, some delegates urged New England to

- **A** boycott British goods.
- **B** fight against the national bank.
- **C** establish a whiskey tax.
- **D** secede from the United States.

Critical Thinking

Base your answers to questions 15 and 16 on the map below and on your knowledge of Chapter 4.

15. In the Treaty of Greenville, Native Americans gave up most of which present-day state?

- **A** Ohio
- **B** Pennsylvania
- **C** Kentucky
- **D** Virginia

16. The new territory acquired by this treaty gave the United States access to which of the following?

- **A** Lake Michigan
- **B** the Atlantic Ocean
- **C** Lake Erie
- **D** the Mississippi River

Need Extra Help?

If You Missed Questions . . .	10	11	12	13	14	15	16
Go to Page . . .	162	169	171	178	181	184	184

GO ON

Critical Thinking

15. A Study the map with students. Point out that the title is "Treaty of Greenville," therefore, the contents of the map will all relate to the treaty. Students must use their knowledge of U.S. geography to determine the present-day state. Show students who have trouble with this question a present-day map to compare with this one.

16. C Here, students should compare the shaded territory to the listed bodies of water. Only Lake Erie makes sense. The territory does not border Lake Michigan or the Mississippi River. The U.S. already had access to the Atlantic Ocean. Remind students that map questions often combine the visual with prior knowledge.

17. Why did James Madison argue that Congress could not establish a national bank?

A Congress could establish only state banks.

B Establishing a bank was not one of the federal government's enumerated powers.

C The power to establish a bank was explicitly given to the judicial branch.

D Congress had the power to do only what was necessary and proper.

Analyze the cartoon and answer the question that follows. Base your answer on the cartoon and on your knowledge of Chapter 4.

18. This cartoon, in which French leaders harass a woman symbolizing the United States, was created in response to the

A Essex Junto.

B XYZ Affair.

C Hartford Convention.

D Hamilton-Burr Duel.

---

19. What was one way Jefferson limited the power of the federal government? Which of the following is one action he took to achieve this goal?

A increasing the size of the army

B renewing the Alien and Sedition Acts

C dissolving the Republican Party to eliminate conflict

D cutting the federal budget

Document-Based Questions

Directions: Analyze the document and answer the short-answer questions that follow the document.

At a town meeting in Brewster, Massachusetts, on July 20, 1812, the residents wrote a petition to President Madison. In it they stated the reasons they opposed the war:

> "In attending to the *reasons* for the present states of warfare as exhibited to our view by public documents, we lament that they do not furnish to our minds satisfactory evidence of its prosperity. . . .
>
> We ask leave in conclusion to state that about three fourths of our townsmen depend on the sea for means of subsistence for themselves and families. By the recent declaration of war more than one half of that proportion is liable to fall into the hands of the enemy with a large proportion of their property, and many of their wives and children may thereby be reduced to extreme poverty. We would be permitted to further remark that out of this large proportion of [seamen] belonging to this town, we have but *four* detained by foreign nations. . . ."
>
> —from *The Repertory and General Advertiser,* July 31, 1812

20. What reasons do the residents give for opposing the war?

21. Were the residents of Brewster worried more about losing townsmen and property to impressment or to fighting the British?

Extended Response

22. Each of the first three presidents under the new Constitution experienced both successes and failures. Write an essay discussing the highest and lowest points of the presidencies of Washington, Adams, and Jefferson. Your essay should include an introduction and three paragraphs using evidence from the chapter to support your ideas.

STOP

History ONLINE

For additional test practice, use Self-Check Quizzes—Chapter 4 at glencoe.com.

Need Extra Help?

If You Missed Questions . . .	17	18	19	20	21	22
Go to Page . . .	156–157	164–165	168	185	185	154–181

17. B Choice *A* is not true; it is a state power. *C* does not make sense. There is no reason the judicial branch would be involved in setting up a national bank. *D* may be distracting to students, because it mentions "necessary and proper." However, the question asks why Madison argued *against* the bank. Those who supported the bank (loose constructionists) believed that Congress had the power to establish it *because of* the necessary and proper clause. Therefore, this could not be Madison's argument against it.

18. B Remind students that the XYZ Affair involved France. The Essex Junto and the Hartford Convention dealt with war opposition. Help students relate the cartoon to the XYZ affair. Explain the parallel between French leaders harassing the U.S. by trying to extort money to meet with U.S. leaders and the leaders in the cartoon harassing the woman.

19. D The only answer that makes sense is *D*. By cutting the federal budget, the federal government would have less money to spend on programs and on itself. Choices *A* and *B* would actually increase the power of the federal government. *C* is not legal. A president could not dissolve a political party.

Document-Based Questions

20. They felt the reasons given for the war were insufficient. Direct students to the first paragraph, where it states "...we lament that they do not furnish to our minds satisfactory evidence of its prosperity." Help students translate this into simpler language, "we are sad that they do not supply to us acceptable evidence of the war's potential for success."

21. They were more worried about losses that could occur if the war broke out with Britain, as they had lost only four men to impressments so far. They felt many more would be lost during the war. Again, review the source and help students break it down into simpler language.

Extended Response

22. Students' essays will vary, but should identify what they think is the greatest success and greatest failure of each president. They should provide support in the form of logical reasoning and use details from the chapter.

History ONLINE

Have students visit the Web site at glencoe.com to review Chapter 4 and take the Self-Check Quiz.

Need Extra Help?

Have students refer to the pages listed if they miss any of the questions.

Chapter 5 Planning Guide

Key to Ability Levels

- **BL** Below Level
- **OL** On Level
- **AL** Above Level
- **ELL** English Language Learners

Key to Teaching Resources

- Print Material
- CD-ROM or DVD
- Transparency

Levels				Resources	Chapter Opener	Section 1	Section 2	Section 3	Section 4	Chapter Assess
BL	OL	AL	ELL							
FOCUS										
BL	OL	AL	ELL	Daily Focus Skills Transparencies		5-1	5-2	5-3	5-4	
TEACH										
BL	OL		ELL	Reading Essentials and Note-Taking Guide*		p. 50	p. 53	p. 56	p. 59	
	OL			Historical Analysis Skills Activity, URB					p. 54	
BL	OL		ELL	Guided Reading Activities, URB*		p. 78	p. 79	p. 80	p. 81	
BL	OL	AL	ELL	Content Vocabulary Activity, URB*	p. 59					
BL	OL	AL	ELL	Academic Vocabulary Activity, URB	p. 61					
	OL	AL		Critical Thinking Skills Activity, URB		p. 64				
BL	OL		ELL	Reading Skills Activity, URB			p. 53			
BL			ELL	English Learner Activity, URB	p. 57					
	OL	AL		Reinforcing Skills Activity, URB				p. 63		
BL	OL	AL	ELL	Differentiated Instruction Activity, URB				p. 55		
BL	OL		ELL	Time Line Activity, URB			p. 65			
	OL			Linking Past and Present Activity, URB			p. 66			
BL	OL	AL	ELL	American Art and Music Activity, URB				p. 71		
BL	OL	AL	ELL	Interpreting Political Cartoons Activity, URB				p. 73		
	OL	AL		Economics and History Activity, URB		p. 7				
		AL		Enrichment Activity, URB		p. 76				
BL	OL	AL	ELL	American Biographies			✓			
BL	OL	AL	ELL	Primary Source Reading, URB		p. 69	p. 67			
BL	OL	AL	ELL	The Living Constitution*	✓	✓	✓	✓	✓	✓
	OL	AL		American History Primary Source Documents Library	✓	✓	✓	✓	✓	✓
BL	OL	AL	ELL	Unit Map Overlay Transparencies	✓	✓	✓	✓	✓	✓
BL	OL	AL	ELL	Differentiated Instruction for the American History Classroom	✓	✓	✓	✓	✓	✓
BL	OL	AL	ELL	StudentWorks™ Plus	✓	✓	✓	✓	✓	✓

Note: Please refer to the *Unit 2 Resource Book* for this chapter's URB materials.

* Also available in Spanish

TeacherWorks Plus
All-In-One Planner and Resource Center

- Interactive Lesson Planner
- Interactive Teacher Edition
- Fully editable blackline masters
- Section Spotlight Videos Launch
- Differentiated Lesson Plans
- Printable reports of daily assignments
- Standards Tracking System

Levels: BL	OL	AL	ELL		Resources	Chapter Opener	Section 1	Section 2	Section 3	Section 4	Chapter Assess
					TEACH *(continued)*						
BL	OL	AL	ELL	CD	American Music Hits Through History CD	✓	✓	✓	✓	✓	✓
BL	OL	AL	ELL	Folder	Unit Time Line Transparencies and Activities	✓	✓	✓	✓	✓	✓
BL	OL	AL	ELL	Folder	Cause and Effect Transparencies, Strategies, and Activities	✓	✓	✓	✓	✓	✓
BL	OL	AL	ELL	Folder	Why It Matters Transparencies, Strategies, and Activities	✓	✓	✓	✓	✓	✓
BL	OL	AL	ELL	Folder	American Issues	✓	✓	✓	✓	✓	✓
	OL	AL	ELL	Folder	American Art and Architecture Transparencies, Strategies, and Activities	✓	✓	✓	✓	✓	✓
BL	OL	AL		Folder	High School American History Literature Library	✓	✓	✓	✓	✓	✓
BL	OL	AL	ELL	CD	*The American Vision* Video Program	✓	✓	✓	✓	✓	✓
Teacher Resources				Folder	Strategies for Success	✓	✓	✓	✓	✓	✓
Teacher Resources				Folder	Success with English Learner	✓	✓	✓	✓	✓	✓
Teacher Resources				Folder	Reading Strategies and Activities for the Social Studies Classroom	✓	✓	✓	✓	✓	✓
Teacher Resources				CD	Presentation Plus! with MindJogger CheckPoint	✓	✓	✓	✓	✓	✓
					ASSESS						
BL	OL	AL	ELL	Folder	Section Quizzes and Chapter Tests*		p. 63	p. 64	p. 65	p. 66	p. 67
BL	OL	AL	ELL	Folder	Authentic Assessment With Rubrics						p. 15
BL	OL	AL	ELL	Folder	Standardized Test Practice Workbook						p. 9
BL	OL	AL	ELL	CD	*ExamView® Assessment Suite*		5-1	5-2	5-3	5-4	Ch. 5
					CLOSE						
BL			ELL	Folder	Reteaching Activity, URB						p. 75
BL	OL		ELL	Folder	Reading and Study Skills Foldables™	p. 52					

✓ Chapter- or unit-based activities applicable to all sections in this chapter.

Using StudentWorks™ Plus Online

Teach With Technology

What is StudentWorks™ Plus Online?
StudentWorks™ Plus Online is a powerful learning and teaching tool that offers the entire textbook online in an interactive, searchable format. It provides links to student workbooks, audio recordings of the textbook, audio summaries in Spanish, In Motion animations, and links to Section Spotlight Videos.

How can StudentWorks™ Plus Online help my students and me?
StudentWorks™ Plus Online helps students learn and master the material in the textbook. Students can go to a specific chapter and read the text, listen to audio of the text, and type and print their answers on workbook pages. While reading about a topic, students can quickly search the entire text and the glossary for a key term. You can project StudentWorks™ Plus Online during a classroom lecture and launch Section Spotlight Videos directly.

Visit glencoe.com and enter a ***QuickPass***™ code to go to StudentWorks™ Plus Online.

History ONLINE
Visit glencoe.com and enter ***QuickPass***™ code TAV9399c5T for Chapter 5 resources.

You can easily launch a wide range of digital products from your computer's desktop with the McGraw-Hill Social Studies widget.

	Student	Teacher	Parent
Media Library			
• Section Audio	●		●
• Spanish Audio Summaries	●		●
• Section Spotlight Videos	●	●	●
***The American Vision* Online Learning Center (Web Site)**			
• StudentWorks™ Plus Online	●	●	●
• Multilingual Glossary	●	●	●
• Study-to-Go	●	●	●
• Chapter Overviews	●	●	●
• Self-Check Quizzes	●	●	●
• Student Web Activities	●	●	●
• ePuzzles and Games	●	●	●
• Vocabulary eFlashcards	●	●	●
• In Motion Animations	●	●	●
• Study Central™	●	●	●
• Web Activity Lesson Plans		●	
• Vocabulary PuzzleMaker	●	●	●
• Historical Thinking Activities		●	
• Beyond the Textbook	●	●	●

Reading Support From Jamestown Education

- **Timed Readings Plus in Social Studies** helps students increase their reading rate and fluency while maintaining comprehension. The 400-word passages are similar to those found on state and national assessments.
- **Reading in the Content Area: Social Studies** concentrates on six essential reading skills that help students better comprehend what they read. The book includes 75 high-interest nonfiction passages written at increasing levels of difficulty.
- **Reading Social Studies** includes strategic reading instruction and vocabulary support in Social Studies content for both ELLs and native speakers of English.

www.jamestowneducation.com

Biography / A&E Home Video / The History Channel

The following videotape programs are available from Glencoe as supplements to this chapter:

- Railroads That Tamed The West (ISBN 0-76-700033-1)
- The Erie Canal (ISBN 0-76-703154-7)

To order, call Glencoe at 1-800-334-7344. To find classroom resources to accompany many of these videos, check the following home pages:

A&E Television: www.aetv.com
The History Channel: www.historychannel.com

Reading List Generator CD-ROM — Glencoe BookLink 3

Use this database to search more than 30,000 titles to create a customized reading list for your students.

- Reading lists can be organized by students' reading level, author, genre, theme, or area of interest.
- The database provides Degrees of Reading Power™ (DRP) and Lexile™ readability scores for all selections.
- A brief summary of each selection is included.

Leveled reading suggestions for this chapter:

For students at a Grade 8 reading level:
- ***James Monroe***, by Anne Welsbacher

For students at a Grade 9 reading level:
- ***Many Thousand Gone: African-Americans from Slavery to Freedom***, by Virginia Hamilton

For students at a Grade 10 reading level:
- ***Eli Whitney: Cotton Gin Genius***, by Kaye Patchett

For students at a Grade 11 reading level:
- ***Life of a Slave on a Southern Plantation***, by Stephen Currie

For students at a Grade 12 reading level:
- ***The Confessions of Nat Turner***, by William Styron

National Geographic

Index to National Geographic Magazine:

The following articles relate to this chapter:

- "America's First Highway" by William R. Newcott, March 1998.
- "Erie Canal: Living Link to our Past" by Joel L. Swerdlow and Bob Sacha, November 1990.

National Geographic Society Products To order the following, call National Geographic at 1-800-368-2728:

- *ZipZapMap! USA* (ZipZapMap!)

Access National Geographic's new, dynamic MapMachine Web site and other geography resources at:

www.nationalgeographic.com
www.nationalgeographic.com/maps

Introducing
Chapter 5

Focus

MAKING CONNECTIONS

Can Economies Shape Politics?

Ask students to suggest ways the economy can shape politics and policies. Students may suggest the condition of the economy, whether strong or weak, can affect the policies and issues on which politicians concentrate. A weak economy with many people out of work would be cause for politicians to concentrate on job creation and welfare issues. A strong economy would open the door for infrastructure improvements like roads. **OL**

Teach

The Big Ideas

As students study the chapter, remind them to consider the section-based Big Ideas included in each section's Guide to Reading. The **Essential Questions** in the activities below tie in to the Big Ideas and help students think about and understand important chapter concepts. In addition, the Hands-on Chapter Projects with their culminating activities relate the content from each section to the Big Ideas. These activities build on each other as students progress through the chapter. Section activities culminate in the wrap-up activity on the Visual Summary page.

Chapter 5

Growth and Division

1816–1832

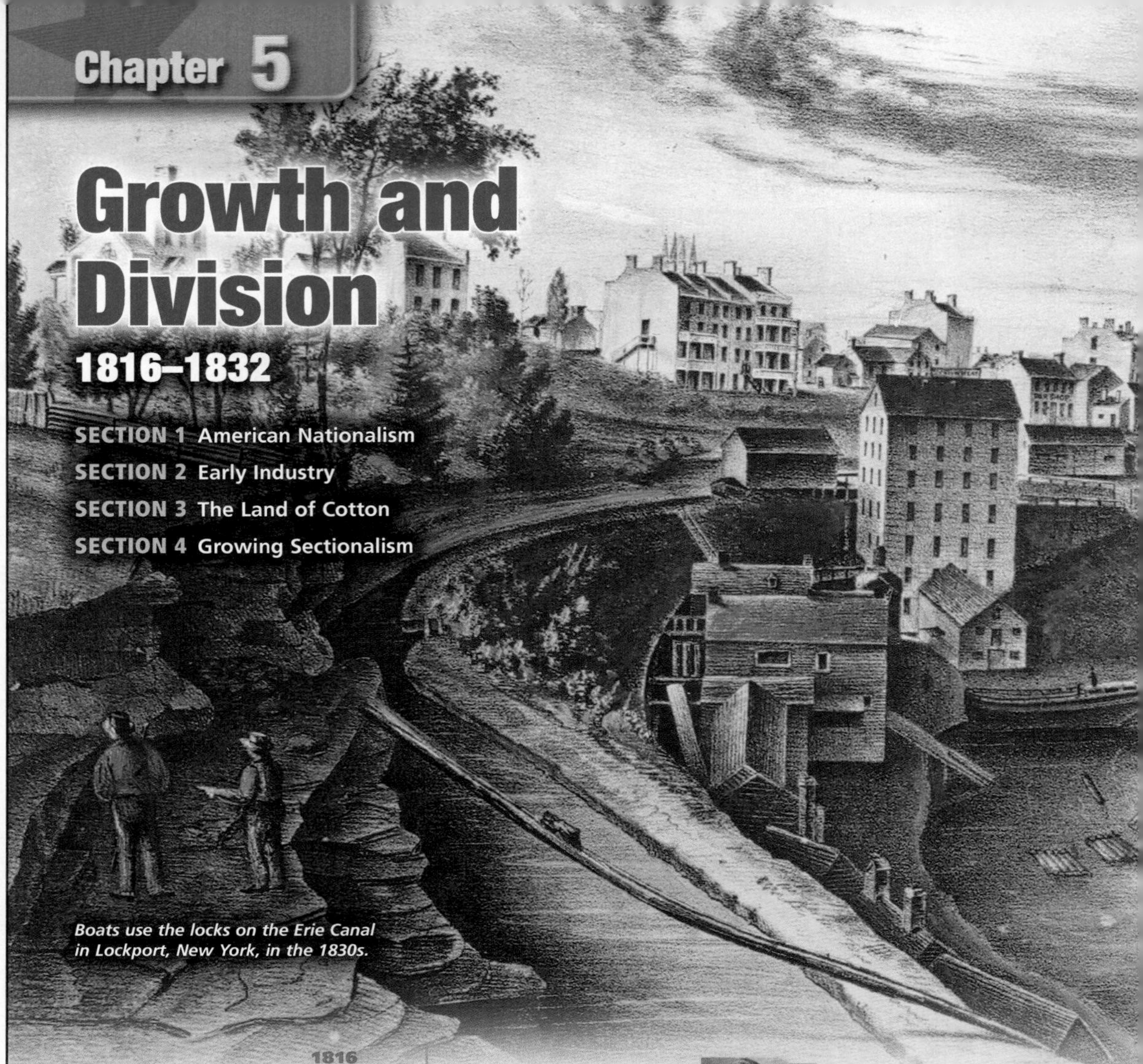

Boats use the locks on the Erie Canal in Lockport, New York, in the 1830s.

U.S. PRESIDENTS
Madison 1809–1817
Monroe 1817–1825

U.S. EVENTS
- **1816** • Congress establishes Second Bank of the United States
- **1819** • Spain cedes Florida to the United States
- **1820** • Henry Clay guides the Missouri Compromise through Congress
- **1823** • Monroe Doctrine declared

1815 — 1820

WORLD EVENTS
- **1815** • Napoleon is defeated at Battle of Waterloo
- **1817** • Exploration of Australia's interior begins
- **1821** • Mexico declares independence from Spain
- **1822** • Greece declares independence from the Ottoman Empire

186 **Chapter 5** Growth and Division

Section 1

American Nationalism

Essential Question: Nationalism affected what three aspects of U.S. government? *(the economy, by giving the national bank power; the judicial system, by giving federal courts more power; foreign affairs, by expanding U.S. borders)* Point out that in Section 1 students will learn that nationalism strengthened federal power. Ask students if nationalism is dangerous to a country made up of individual states. **OL**

Section 2

Early Industry

Essential Question: What technologies contributed to early industry in America? *(Possible answers: transportation: roads and turnpikes, canals and steamboats, railroads and trains; industry: factories, interchangeable parts, cotton gin and telegraph)* Point out that in Section 2 students will learn about the technologies that fueled and were a result of the Industrial Revolution. **OL**

Chapter Audio

MAKING CONNECTIONS

Can Economics Shape Politics?

After the War of 1812, a new spirit of nationalism took hold in American society. New roads and canals helped connect the country. Industry developed in the North, while agriculture based on slave labor grew strong in the South. By the 1830s, the two regions were increasingly at odds with each other.

- ***Why do you think roads and canals helped build nationalism?***
- ***How did the economic differences between North and South cause tensions?***

FOLDABLES

Describing Innovations Create a Three-Tab Book Foldable that describes the advances and innovations in transportation for the following: roads, railroads, and travel by water. Describe the location and routes and list the relevant dates, legislation, and building projects for each category.

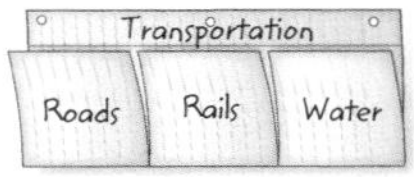

1825 • Erie Canal opens

J. Q. Adams 1825–1829

1828 • Jackson defeats Adams's reelection bid

Jackson 1829–1837

1831 • Nat Turner slave rebellion

1825 — 1830

1829 • Slavery abolished in Mexico

1830 • French seize control of Algiers

History ONLINE Visit glencoe.com and enter ***QuickPass***™ code TAV9846c5 for Chapter 5 resources.

More About the Photo

Visual Literacy Canal builders (seen far left) chip away at the Niagara Escarpment, the sheer cliff of rocks that became the future home of five mechanical locks in Lockport, New York. Lockport entrepreneur Jesse Hawley's seemingly impossible dream, to provide an inland waterway from New York to Buffalo, found favor with New York Governor Dewitt Clinton. The amazing locks were completed on October 26, 1825.

FOLDABLES Study Organizer Dinah Zike's Foldables

Dinah Zike's Foldables are three-dimensional, interactive graphic organizers that help students practice basic writing skills, review vocabulary terms, and identify main ideas. Instructions for creating and using Foldables can be found in the Appendix at the end of this book and in the *Dinah Zike's Reading and Study Skills Foldables* booklet.

Section 3

The Land of Cotton

Essential Question: What were the major industries of the South? *(The South depended on farming and cash crops, such as cotton, rice, tobacco, and sugarcane.)* Point out that in Section 3 students will learn that the economy and society of the Southern states differed from the economy and society of the Northern states. Discuss with students the results of slavery on the Southern economy and society. Ask students how Southern society differed from Northern society. **OL**

Section 4

Growing Sectionalism

Essential Question: How did the Missouri Compromise address growing sectionalism? *(The Missouri Compromise sought to restore the balance of power in Congress by admitting Missouri to the Union as a slave state.)* Point out that in Section 4 students will learn about the issues that lead to sectional disputes over slavery. Challenge students to activate prior knowledge about the effects of nationalism and how it contributed to sectionalism. **OL**

History ONLINE

Visit glencoe.com and enter ***QuickPass***™ code TAV9399c5T for Chapter 5 resources, including a Chapter Overview, Study Central™, Study-to-Go, Student Web Activity, Self-Check Quiz, and other materials.

Focus

Bellringer

Daily Focus Transparency 5-1

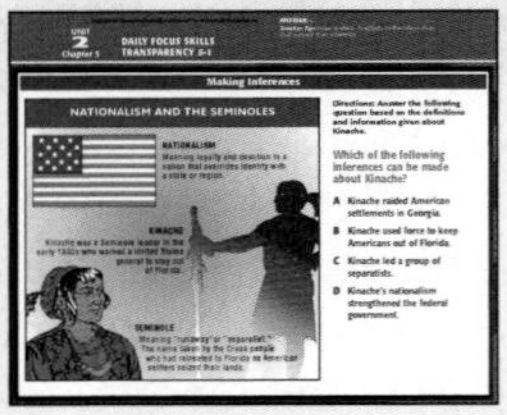

Guide to Reading

Answers: Actions: creation of new national bank, imposition of protective tariff, decisions by Supreme Court established dominance of the nation over states, proclamation of the Monroe Doctrine

Section Spotlight Video

To generate student interest and provide a springboard for class discussion, access the Chapter 5, Section 1 video at glencoe.com or on the video DVD.

Section 1

Section Audio | Spotlight Video

American Nationalism

Guide to Reading

Big Ideas

Past and Present Increased national pride marked the years following the War of 1812.

Content Vocabulary
- revenue tariff *(p. 189)*
- protective tariff *(p. 189)*

Academic Vocabulary
- interpret *(p. 190)*
- finalize *(p. 193)*

People and Events to Identify
- Era of Good Feelings *(p. 188)*
- John C. Calhoun *(p. 189)*
- Seminoles *(p. 192)*
- Adams-Onís Treaty *(p. 193)*
- Monroe Doctrine *(p. 193)*

Reading Strategy

Organizing Complete a graphic organizer similar to the one below by listing actions that strengthened the federal government after the War of 1812.

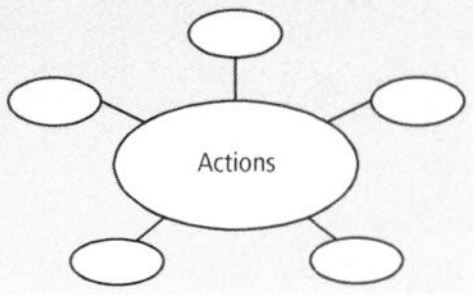

The United States entered an "Era of Good Feelings" after the War of 1812. The federal government began building the national road, defended its authority to regulate interstate commerce, and declared the Western Hemisphere off-limits for future colonization.

Economic Nationalism

MAIN Idea The surge of nationalism and the survival of only one political party created an atmosphere in which some economic proposals of the Federalists were enacted.

HISTORY AND YOU Do you think the government should place tariffs on imports or practice free trade? Read how tariffs became a bitterly debated issue in the early republic.

After the War of 1812, a strong sense of national pride swept the United States. The *Columbian Centinel,* a Boston newspaper, called this time the **"Era of Good Feelings."** The name came to describe the period of James Monroe's presidency.

During the last two years of James Madison's second term, American leaders launched an ambitious program to bind the nation together. The program included creating a new national bank, protecting American manufacturers from foreign competition, and building new canals and roads to improve transportation and link the country together.

Partisan infighting had largely ended in national politics because only one major political party—the Republicans—remained. The Federalist Party rapidly lost political influence after the War of 1812, in part because of public disapproval of the Hartford Convention. At the same time, the war taught Republican leaders that a stronger federal government was necessary. This new perspective allowed many who might have been Federalists to join the Republicans instead. James Monroe won the presidency in 1816 with 83 percent of the electoral vote. By the election of 1820, the Federalist Party was gone. All the presidential candidates were Republicans.

The Second Bank

Republicans traditionally had opposed the idea of a national bank. They had blocked the charter renewal of the First Bank of the United States in 1811 and offered nothing in its place. The results were disastrous. State-chartered banks and other private banks greatly expanded their lending with bank notes that were used as money. Without a national bank to regulate currency, prices rose rapidly

Resource Manager

R Reading Strategies	C Critical Thinking	D Differentiated Instruction	W Writing Support	S Skill Practice
Teacher Edition • Organizing Info., p. 193 **Additional Resources** • Prim. Source Reading, URB p. 69 • Guided Reading, URB p. 78	**Teacher Edition** • Analyzing Information, p. 190 **Additional Resources** • Econ. and History, URB p. 7 • Crit. Think. Skills Act., URB p. 64 • Quizzes and Tests, p. 63	**Additional Resources** • Enrich. Act., URB p. 76	**Teacher Edition** • Persuasive Writing, p. 191 • Narrative Writing, p. 192 **Additional Resources** • Academic Vocab. Act., URB p. 61	**Teacher Edition** • Using Geography Skills, p. 189 • Interp. Maps, p. 192 **Additional Resources** • Read. Essen., p. 50

NATIONAL GEOGRAPHIC **Building the National Road, 1811–1838**

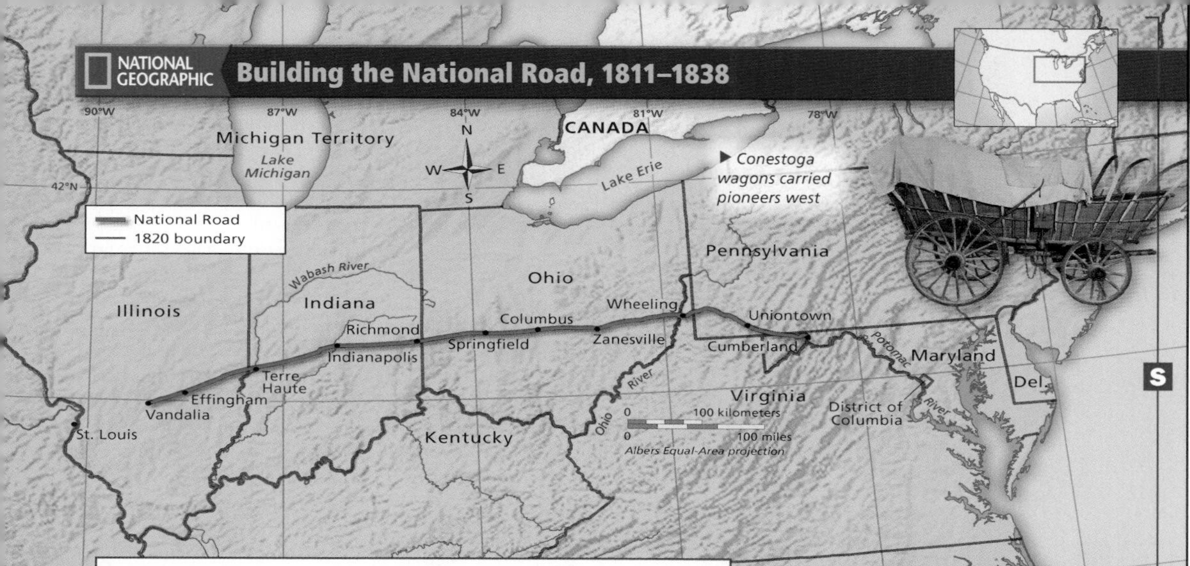

In 1806 Congress funded the building of a major east-west highway to connect the eastern United States to St. Louis and the Missouri River, the gateway to the territory of the new Louisiana Purchase. In 1811 laborers started cutting the roadbed westward from Cumberland, Maryland. The 32-foot-wide bed had a surface of sand and gravel. By the 1820s the National Road was a heavily traveled superhighway for its time. It was completed to Vandalia, Illinois, when funding ceased. The National Road turned out to be the only great federally funded transportation project of its time. President Madison vetoed a bill to fund further roads and canals. He did not think the Constitution gave the federal government the authority to make "internal improvements."

Analyzing GEOGRAPHY

1. **Location** Where did the National Road begin and end?
2. **Movement** How long was the stretch of National Road that was federally funded?

during the War of 1812. When the government borrowed money to pay for the war, it had to pay high interest rates on the loans.

Because of these problems, many Republicans changed their minds after the war. In 1816 Representative **John C. Calhoun** of South Carolina introduced a bill proposing the Second Bank of the United States. With the support of Henry Clay of Kentucky and Daniel Webster of Massachusetts, the bill passed in 1816. This legislation gave the bank the power to issue notes that would serve as a national currency and to control state banks.

Tariffs and Transportation

Protection of manufacturers was another part of the Republican program. Because an embargo had prevented Americans from buying British goods during the War of 1812, American manufacturers had increased their output to meet the demand. Once the war was over, however, British goods flowed into the United States at such low prices that they threatened to put American manufacturers out of business.

Congress responded with the Tariff of 1816. Unlike earlier **revenue tariffs,** which provided income for the federal government, this tariff was a **protective tariff,** designed to protect American manufacturers by taxing imports to drive up their prices. New England shippers and Southern farmers opposed the tariff and the higher prices it caused, but they could not block its passage.

The Republicans also wanted to improve the nation's transportation system. In 1816 Calhoun sponsored a federal internal improvement plan, but President Madison vetoed it, arguing that spending money to improve transportation was not expressly granted in the Constitution. Nevertheless, road and canal construction soon began, with private businesses and state and local governments funding much of the work.

Reading Check **Summarizing** What are three examples of economic nationalism after the War of 1812?

Teach

S Skill Practice

Using Geography Skills

Ask: How do you think the rural landscape changed with the building of the National Road? *(Possible answers: farmland was lost, forests had to be cut down, more people passing though created more noise and pollution, new towns sprung up)* OL

Analyzing GEOGRAPHY

Answers:

1. The National Road began in Cumberland, Maryland, and ended in Vandalia, Illinois.
2. About 600 miles.

Reading Check

Answer:
a national bank, protective tariffs, and internal improvements

Hands-On Chapter Project
Step 1

Making a Map

Step 1: Plan a Steamboat Trip In Step 1, students will take an outline map of the United States circa 1850 and plan a steamboat trip from Wheeling, West Virginia, to New Orleans, Louisiana.

Directions Instruct students to draw in the major rivers and state borders and locate the major cities along the route.

Ask: What is the most direct water route from West Virginia to the Gulf of Mexico? *(Ohio River to the Mississippi River to the Gulf of Mexico)*

Problem Solving Organize students into small groups. Using information from the chapter as well as library or Internet resources, have students plot out their trip and estimate how many days it will take to reach various interim destinations. OL

(Chapter Project continued on page 197)

C Critical Thinking

Analyzing Information

Ask: How did Chief Justice John Marshall strengthen the Supreme Court? *(Marshall's judicial philosophy and influence over the decisions of the Supreme Court, between 1816 and 1824, strengthened the power of the federal government over the power of the state governments.)* **OL**

Reading Check

Answer:
Martin v. *Hunter's Lessee* established the Supreme Court as the court of final appeal. *McCulloch* v. *Maryland* prohibited states from interfering with agencies of the federal government exercising its specific constitutional powers within a state's borders. *Gibbons* v. *Ogden* defined interstate commerce broadly and granted control of it to the federal government.

Additional Support

Judicial Nationalism

MAIN Idea Under Chief Justice John Marshall, the Supreme Court issued decisions that helped strengthen the national government.

HISTORY AND YOU Do you recall the earlier debate over the meaning of the "necessary and proper" clause in the Constitution? Read on to find out how the Supreme Court interpreted its meaning.

C The judicial philosophy of Chief Justice John Marshall boosted the forces helping to unify the nation after the war. Between 1816 and 1824, the Supreme Court issued rulings that established the dominance of the nation over the states.

For further information on the cases of *Martin* v. *Hunter's Lessee* and *Gibbons* v. *Ogden*, see page R59 in **Supreme Court Case Summaries.**

Martin v. *Hunter's Lessee*

In 1816 the Court decided in *Martin* v. *Hunter's Lessee* that it had the authority to hear all appeals of state court decisions in cases involving federal statutes and treaties. In this case, Denny Martin, a British subject, tried to sell land in Virginia inherited from his uncle, Lord Fairfax, a British Loyalist during the war. However, Virginia law stated that no "enemy" could inherit land. The Supreme Court upheld Martin's case, ruling that Virginia's law conflicted with Jay's Treaty, which stated that land belonging to Loyalists before the war was still theirs. This historic decision helped establish the Supreme Court as the nation's court of final appeal.

McCulloch v. *Maryland*

This 1819 case concerned Maryland's attempt to tax the Second Bank of the United States. Before addressing Maryland's right to tax the national bank, the Supreme Court ruled on the federal government's right to create a national bank in the first place. In the Court's opinion, written by Marshall, the bank was constitutional, even though the Constitution did not specifically give Congress the power to create one.

As had been the case during the struggle to establish the first national bank, the conflict over the second centered on the "necessary and proper" clause. Marshall observed that the Constitution gave the federal government the power to collect taxes, to borrow money, to regulate commerce, and to raise armies and navies. He noted that the national bank helped the federal government exercise these powers. He concluded that the Constitution's "necessary and proper" clause allowed the federal government to create a bank.

Opponents argued that the "necessary and proper" clause meant the government could only do things absolutely necessary, but Marshall rejected that idea. Instead, he held that "necessary and proper" meant the government could use any method that was convenient for carrying out its powers as long as the method was not expressly forbidden.

Marshall then argued that the federal government was "supreme in its own sphere of action." This meant that a state government could not interfere with an agency of the federal government exercising its specific constitutional powers within a state's borders. Taxing the national bank was a form of interference and, therefore, unconstitutional.

Gibbons v. *Ogden*

This 1824 case involved a company that had been granted a monopoly by the state of New York to control all steamboat traffic in New York waters. When the company tried to expand its monopoly to New Jersey, the matter went to court. The Supreme Court declared the monopoly unconstitutional. Marshall noted that the Constitution gave the federal government control over interstate commerce, which the Court **interpreted** to include all trade along the coast or on waterways dividing the states.

In writing the Supreme Court's decision, Marshall defined interstate commerce in a way that went beyond the exchange of goods between states. The Court ensured that federal law would take precedence over state law in interstate transportation.

All these cases strengthened the power of the federal government at the expense of the states. Although defenders of states' rights bitterly attacked Marshall's opinions, his views helped make the "necessary and proper" clause and the interstate commerce clause major vehicles for expanding federal power.

Reading Check **Identifying** How did the Supreme Court establish and expand federal power over the states?

Activity: Collaborative Learning

Preparing a Presentation Have students work in small groups to prepare a presentation on one of the Supreme Court decisions listed to the right. Each presentation should include a brief explanation of the circumstances of the case, the issue before the court, and the impact of the decision. **OL**

Marbury v. *Madison*
Fletcher v. *Pack*
Martin v. *Hunter's Lessee*
Trustees of Dartmouth College v. *Woodward*
Sturges v. *Crowninshield*
McCulloch v. *Maryland*
Cohens v. *Virginia*
Gibbons v. *Ogden*

ANALYZING SUPREME COURT CASES

What Does "Necessary and Proper" Mean?

★ ***McCulloch* v. *Maryland*, 1819**

Background to the Case

In 1816, President James Madison and Congress worked to establish the Second Bank of the United States. Two years later, the state of Maryland passed legislation imposing a tax on the Second Bank. The cashier at the Second Bank's branch in Baltimore, Maryland, James McCulloch, refused to pay the tax, and the matter went to the Supreme Court.

How the Court Ruled

In a unanimous decision the Court found that, under the "necessary and proper" clause, the federal government did have the unenumerated power to establish a national bank and that, while the states had the power to tax, they could not interfere with instruments of the federal government, and the tax was construed to be interference. This established the supremacy of the federal government over the governments of the states.

▲ *The Second Bank of the United States was located in Philadelphia. The Supreme Court held with the* McCulloch v. Maryland *ruling that the federal government had the right to establish a national bank and that the states could not tax it or otherwise interfere in any federal enterprise.*

PRIMARY SOURCE

The Court's Opinion

Can the Federal Government Create a Bank?

". . . Although, among the enumerated powers of government, we do not find the word 'bank' or 'incorporation,' we find the great powers, to lay and collect taxes; to borrow money; to regulate commerce; to declare and conduct a war; and to raise and support armies and navies. . . . But it may with great reason be contended, that a government, entrusted with such ample powers . . . must also be entrusted with ample means for their execution.

. . . To its enumeration of powers is added, that of making 'all laws which shall be necessary and proper, for carrying into execution the foregoing powers, and all other powers vested by this constitution, in the government of the United States, or in any department thereof.'. . . [I]t is the unanimous and decided opinion of this Court, that the act to incorporate the Bank of the United States is . . . constitutional."

Can a State Tax a Federal Agency or Activity?

". . . the power to tax involves the power to destroy. . . . If the states may tax one instrument, employed by the government . . . they may tax all the means employed by the government, to an excess which would defeat all the ends of government. . . . The result is a conviction that the states have no power, by taxation or otherwise, to retard, impede, burden, or in any manner control, the operations of the constitutional laws enacted by congress to carry into execution the powers vested in the general government. This is, we think, the unavoidable consequence of that supremacy which the constitution has declared."

—Chief Justice John Marshall writing for the Court in *McCulloch* v. *Maryland*

DBQ Document-Based Questions

1. **Specifying** What two questions did the decision in *McCulloch* v. *Maryland* address?
2. **Describing** How did Marshall interpret the "necessary and proper" clause in this case?
3. **Summarizing** How did Marshall's decision establish the authority of the federal government over the states?

SUPREME COURT CASES

More About the Case This ruling established the basis for the expansive authority of Congress. The Supreme Court held that the necessary and proper clause allows Congress to do more than the Constitution specifically authorizes it to do. **AL**

DBQ Document Based Questions

Answers:

1. Does the federal government have the power to establish a national bank? Do the states have the authority to interfere in the operations of the federal government?
2. He interpreted "necessary and proper" to mean whatever may be convenient to fulfill the functions of the federal government.
3. It established the supremacy of the federal government over the states by recognizing the federal government's power to establish a national bank under the "necessary and proper" clause and by stating that states could not interfere with instruments of the federal government.

Additional Support

Activity: Collaborative Learning

Arguing Sides Have students work in pairs to recreate the arguments of one of the cases in this section. Have the pairs work together to decide which side of the issue each of them will present. Have them research the case and present a summary of the arguments to the class. Encourage the pairs to pretend that they are arguing their case before the Supreme Court. Allow the class, acting as the Court, to ask questions of each person. **OL**

W Writing Support

Narrative Writing Have students assume the role of Seminole leader Kinache during the time Jackson invaded Florida. Then ask students to write a narrative from Kinache's perspective about that time that will be passed down to younger tribe members. **OL**

S Skill Practice

Interpreting Maps Have students use the map to determine the European country that occupied what is now southwestern United States and Mexico. *(Spain)* **OL**

DBQ Document Based Questions

Answers:

1. any attempts by European nations to retake colonies that have gained independence or to create any new colonies in the Western Hemisphere
2. It will not interfere in existing colonies.

Nationalist Diplomacy

MAIN Idea The surge of national pride and confidence after the War of 1812 led the United States to push to expand its borders.

HISTORY AND YOU Can you think of a time when success at one endeavor gave you confidence to stretch yourself in other ways? Read on to find out how the young United States began to assert itself in foreign affairs.

Read the Monroe Doctrine on page R48 in **Documents in American History.**

The wave of nationalism within Congress and among voters influenced the nation's foreign affairs, too. Led by President Monroe, the United States expanded its borders and asserted itself internationally.

Jackson Invades Florida

W In the early 1800s, Spanish-held Florida was a source of anger and frustration for Southerners. Many runaway slaves fled there, knowing that Americans had no authority to capture them in Spanish territory. Similarly, many Creek groups had retreated to Florida as American settlers seized their lands. These peoples united with escaped slaves and other Native Americans and took a new name for themselves—*Seminole,* meaning "runaway." The **Seminoles** in Spanish Florida and Americans in Georgia staged raids against each other. Spain was unable to control the border, and many Americans clamored for the United States government to step in. **W** As tensions heightened in the region, the Seminole leader Kinache warned an American general to stay out of Florida:

PRIMARY SOURCE

"You charge me with killing your people, stealing your cattle and burning your houses; it is I that have cause to complain of the Americans. . . . I shall use force to stop any armed Americans from passing my towns or my lands."

—quoted in *The Seminoles of Florida*

PRIMARY SOURCE

Nationalism and Diplomacy, 1818–1823

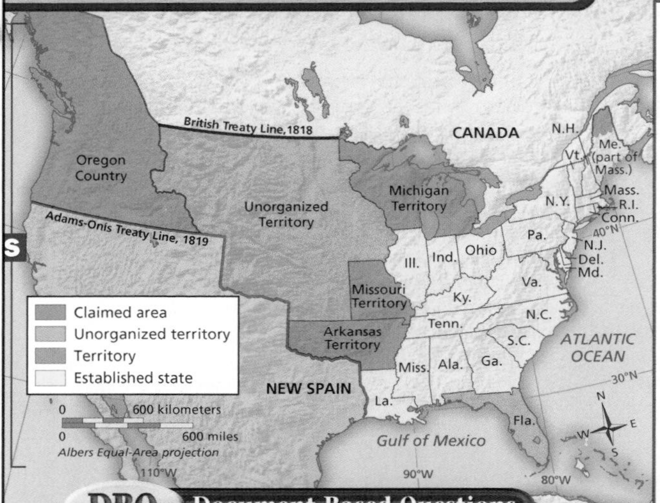

PRIMARY SOURCE

"[T]he occasion has been judged proper for asserting . . . that the American continents . . . are henceforth not to be considered as subjects for future colonization by any European powers . . .

. . . In the wars of the European powers in matters relating to themselves we have never taken any part. . . . With the movements in this hemisphere we are of necessity more immediately connected. . . . We owe it, therefore, to candor and to the amicable relations existing between the United States and those powers to declare, that we should consider any attempt on their part to extend their system to any portion of this hemisphere as dangerous to our peace and safety. With the existing colonies or dependencies of any European power we have not interfered and shall not interfere. But, with the Governments who have declared their independence, and maintained it . . . we could not view any interposition for the purpose of oppressing them, or controlling, in any other manner, their destiny, by any European power, in any other light than as the manifestation of an unfriendly disposition toward the United States."

—from President Monroe's message to Congress, December 2, 1823

DBQ Document-Based Questions

1. **Identifying Central Issues** What does the Monroe Doctrine prohibit?
2. **Analyzing** According to the Monroe Doctrine, what is the United States position on existing colonies?

Additional Support

Activity: Collaborative Learning

Seminole Wars The United States government and the Seminoles fought a series of three wars between 1817 and 1858. The First Seminole War began with U.S. forces attempting to recapture escaped African American slaves living with the Seminoles in Florida. The second war resulted from the refusal of Seminoles to leave Florida and move west forfeiting their reservation lands to white Americans wishing to settle in Florida. Eventually, most did leave. The third and final war was undertaken to convince those Seminoles who did not leave Florida after the Second Seminole War to move west. The Third Seminole War ended with the U.S. government paying the most resistant band of Seminole to abandon their land.

The warning fell on deaf ears. In 1818 former member of Congress, John C. Calhoun, now secretary of war, ordered U.S. troops under the command of General Andrew Jackson into Florida to stop the Seminole raids. After destroying several Seminole villages, Jackson disobeyed orders and seized the Spanish settlements of St. Marks and Pensacola. He then removed the Spanish governor of Florida from power.

Furious, Spanish officials demanded that Jackson be punished. Secretary of State John Quincy Adams, however, defended Jackson and argued that the cause of the dispute was Spain's failure to keep order in Florida. Adams used this incident to put pressure on Spain during the ongoing negotiations to settle the border. Occupied with problems throughout its Latin American empire, Spain gave in and ceded all of Florida to the United States in the **Adams-Onís Treaty** of 1819. The treaty also **finalized** the western border of the Louisiana Purchase, which now lay along the Sabine, Red, and Arkansas Rivers to the Rocky Mountains and then followed the 42nd parallel west to the Pacific Ocean.

The Monroe Doctrine

In 1809 rebellions began to erupt in Spain's colonies. By 1824, all of Spain's colonies on the American mainland had declared independence. Spain's once vast empire had been reduced to three islands: Cuba, Puerto Rico, and Santo Domingo.

Meanwhile, a group of European countries—Great Britain, Austria, Prussia, and Russia (later joined by France)—formed the Quadruple Alliance in an effort to suppress movements against monarchies in Europe. Over Britain's objection, in 1822 the alliance raised the possibility of helping Spain regain control of its overseas colonies. Great Britain and the United States made a great deal of money trading with Latin America and did not want the Spanish to reassert control. In August 1823, British officials suggested that the two nations issue a joint statement supporting the independence of the new Latin American countries. R

At the same time, Russia's growing presence on North America's Pacific Coast also worried the American government. Russia already claimed Alaska, and in 1821 it announced that its empire extended south into the Oregon Country between Russian Alaska and the western United States.

Secretary Adams urged Monroe to avoid working with the British when dealing with Spain and Russia. He did not want the United States to be regarded as Britain's junior partner. Monroe agreed, and in 1823, without consulting the British, he declared that the American continents were "henceforth not to be considered as subjects for future colonization by any European power."

The president's proclamation, later called the **Monroe Doctrine,** marked the beginning of a long-term American policy of trying to prevent European powers from interfering in Latin American political affairs. The Monroe Doctrine upheld Washington's policy of avoiding entanglements in European power struggles.

Reading Check **Examining** In what ways did U.S. foreign policy become more assertive in the early 1800s?

Section 1 REVIEW

Vocabulary

1. **Explain** the significance of: Era of Good Feelings, John C. Calhoun, revenue tariff, protective tariff, Seminoles, Adams-Onís Treaty, Monroe Doctrine.

Main Ideas

2. **Contrasting** How was the Tariff of 1816 different from previous tariffs?
3. **Summarizing** What did the Marshall Court interpret the "necessary and proper" clause to mean?
4. **Determining Cause and Effect** What caused the United States to send Andrew Jackson into Spanish Florida?

Critical Thinking

5. **Big Ideas** How did the Monroe Doctrine reinforce President Washington's ideas about foreign policy?
6. **Categorizing** Use a graphic organizer to list examples of nationalism in the United States after the War of 1812.

Examples of Nationalism		
Economic	Judicial	Diplomatic

7. **Analyzing Visuals** Study the map on page 192. What areas of the present-day United States were in dispute or held by another nation at this time?

Writing About History

8. **Persuasive Writing** Suppose you are a newspaper publisher in Georgia in 1818. Write an editorial in which you defend Andrew Jackson's actions in seizing Spanish settlements in Florida.

History ONLINE
Study Central™ To review this section, go to glencoe.com and click on Study Central.

R Reading Strategy

Organizing Information
Have students use a graphic organizer to identify the members of the Quadruple Alliance. *(Austria, Great Britain, Prussia, and Russia)* ELL

Reading Check

Answer:
invasion of Florida and the Monroe Doctrine

Assess

History ONLINE

Study Central™ provides summaries, interactive games, and online graphic organizers to help students review content.

Close

Summarizing Ask students to explain how nationalism strengthened the federal government. OL

Section 1 REVIEW

Answers

1. All definitions can be found in the section and the Glossary.
2. Earlier tariffs had been revenue tariffs, while the Tariff of 1816 was a protective tariff to help U.S. manufacturers compete with British goods.
3. It held that the "necessary and proper" clause meant that the government could use any method that was convenient for carrying out its powers, as long as the method was not expressly forbidden by the Constitution.
4. U.S. government sent Jackson to control the raids at the Georgia/Florida border between the Seminoles in Spanish Florida and Americans in Georgia when the Spanish failed to control the situation.
5. It reduced somewhat the possibility that the United States would become involved in European affairs, and Washington had warned against foreign entanglements.
6. economic: national bank, protective tariffs; judicial: Supreme Court authority grew along with the authority of the nation over the states; diplomatic: invasion of Florida and Monroe Doctrine
7. Florida and the southwestern United States
8. Editorials will vary, but should use persuasive language and include details from the section.

Focus

Bellringer

Daily Focus Transparency 5-2

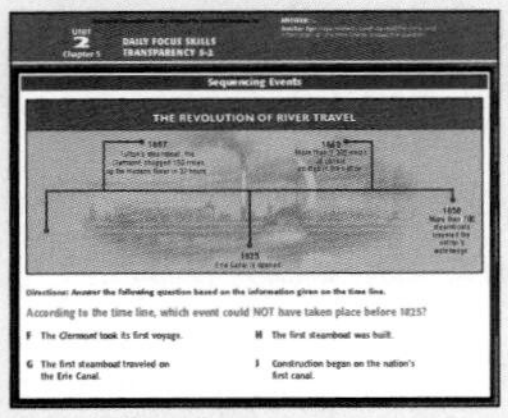

Guide to Reading

Answers: Transportation: 1807, Clermont; 1811, National Road; 1825, Erie Canal; 1830, first locomotive; Industrialization: 1789, water frame; 1814, textile mill; 1832, telegraph and Morse code; 1844, first long-distance telegraph lines.

Section Spotlight Video

To generate student interest and provide a springboard for class discussion, access the Chapter 5, Section 2 video at glencoe.com or on the video DVD.

Section 2

Section Audio   Spotlight Video

Early Industry

Guide to Reading

Big Ideas

Science and Technology New manufacturing techniques reshaped the way Americans worked.

Content Vocabulary

- free enterprise system *(p. 197)*
- interchangeable parts *(p. 198)*
- labor union *(p. 199)*
- strike *(p. 199)*

Academic Vocabulary

- transportation *(p. 194)*
- extraction *(p. 196)*

People and Events to Identify

- Erie Canal *(p. 194)*
- National Road *(p. 194)*
- Robert Fulton *(p. 196)*
- Industrial Revolution *(p. 197)*
- Francis C. Lowell *(p. 198)*
- Eli Whitney *(p. 198)*
- Samuel F. B. Morse *(p. 199)*

Reading Strategy

Categorizing Complete a graphic organizer by listing the major milestones in transportation and industrialization that occurred in the United States in the early 1800s.

Transportation	Industrialization

A technological revolution in transportation and industry swept through the North. This revolution led to dramatic social and economic changes. Early industrialization also led to the growth of towns and cities in the North.

A Revolution in Transportation

MAIN Idea New modes of transportation unified the nation and strengthened its economy.

HISTORY AND YOU How do you think life would be without highways, trains, and other ways to move people and goods quickly? Read on to learn how new forms of transportation developed in the United States.

In the summer of 1817, explosions suddenly began disturbing the peace and quiet of rural upstate New York. What had started was not a war but a great engineering challenge: a canal 40 feet (12.2 m) wide and 4 feet (1.2 m) deep, connecting the Hudson River at Albany to Lake Erie at Buffalo. The longest canal in the nation at that time was almost 28 miles (45 km) long. The new **Erie Canal** would span a colossal 363 miles (584.1 km).

Building the canal was difficult and dangerous. Canal beds collapsed, burying diggers. Blasting accidents killed other workers. In 1819 alone more than 1,000 men were stricken with diseases contracted in the swamps through which they dug. Despite the dangers they faced, the canal workers pressed on and completed the immense project in 1825. The Erie Canal was a striking example of a revolution in **transportation** that swept through the Northern states in the early 1800s. This revolution led to dramatic social and economic changes.

Roads and Turnpikes

As early as 1806, the nation took the first steps toward a transportation revolution when Congress funded the building of a major east–west highway, the **National Road.** In 1811 laborers started cutting the roadbed westward from the Potomac River at Cumberland, Maryland. By 1818, the roadway had reached Wheeling, Virginia (now West Virginia), on the Ohio River. The route was almost parallel to the military road George Washington helped open in 1754. Conestoga wagons drawn by teams of oxen or mules carried migrating pioneers west on this road, while livestock and wagonloads of farm produce traveled the opposite way, toward the markets of the East.

Rather than marking the start of a federal campaign to improve transportation, the National Road turned out to be the only great

Resource Manager

R Reading Strategies	C Critical Thinking	D Differentiated Instruction	W Writing Support	S Skill Practice
Teacher Edition • Reading Maps, p. 195 • Monitoring, p. 197 • Using Word Parts, p. 198 • Listing, p. 199 **Additional Resources** • Prim. Source Reading, URB p. 67 • Guided Reading, URB p. 79	**Teacher Edition** • Making Generalizations, p. 200 **Additional Resources** • Linking Past and Present Activity, URB p. 66 • Quizzes and Tests, p. 64	**Teacher Edition** • Visual/Spatial, p. 199	**Teacher Edition** • Descriptive Writing, p. 196	**Additional Resources** • Read. Skills Act., URB p. 53 • Time Line Act., URB p. 65 • Read. Essen., p. 53

The Transportation Revolution, 1810–1840

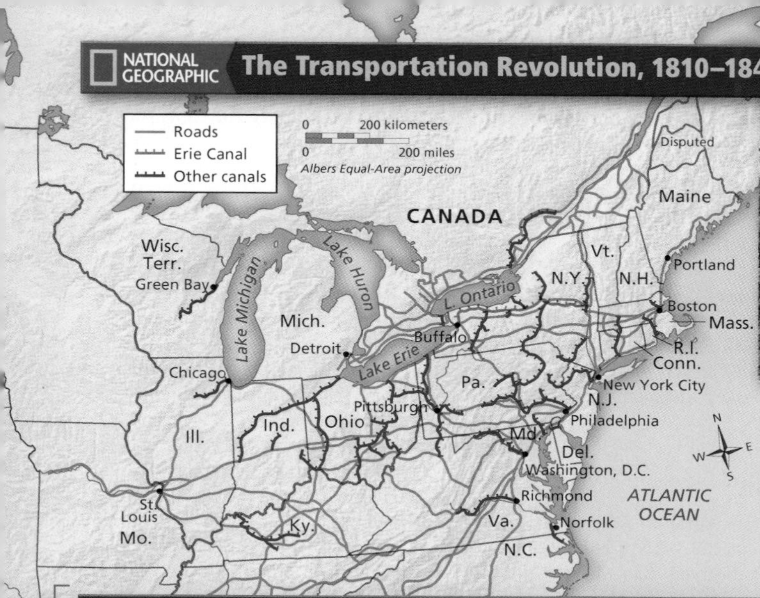

▲ *Locks at Lockport, New York, on the Erie Canal*

Travel Time From New York, 1800 and 1857

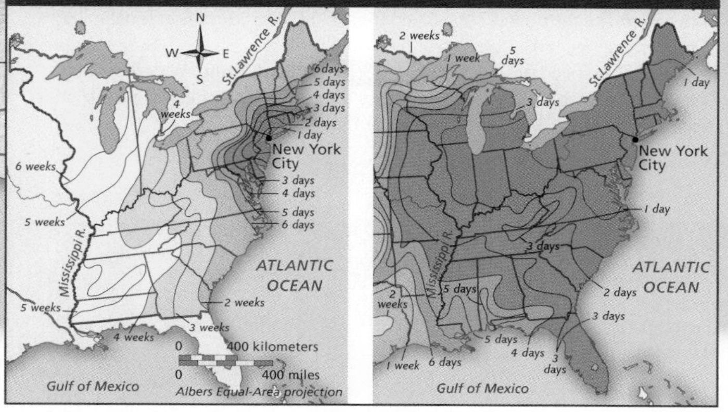

◀ *In a little over 50 years, the transportation revolution changed the nature of travel in the United States. For example, the journey from New York to the Mississippi River went from being a month-long expedition to a relatively short trip of just a few days.*

Analyzing GEOGRAPHY

1. **Movement** How did travel time between New York City and Washington, D.C., change between 1800 and 1857?
2. **Location** In 1800, what was the furthest west that a person could travel from New York City in one week? In 1857?

federally funded transportation project of its time. Madison and his successors believed in a strict interpretation of the Constitution and doubted that the federal government had the power to fund roads and other "internal improvements."

Instead, states, localities, and private businesses took the initiative. Private companies laid down hundreds of miles of toll roads. By 1821 some 4,000 miles (6,400 km) of toll roads had been built, mainly to connect Eastern cities, where heavy traffic made the roads extremely profitable. Even so, major roads going west had also been built, connecting Pittsburgh, Pennsylvania, and Buffalo, New York, to Eastern markets.

Steamboats and Canals

Rivers offered a far faster, more efficient, and cheaper way to move goods than did roads, which were often little more than wide paths. A barge could hold many wagonloads of grain or coal. Loaded boats and barges, however, could usually travel only downstream, as moving against the current with heavy cargoes proved difficult.

Teach

R Reading Strategy

Reading Maps Ask students to use the Travel Time from New York in 1800 map and information in the Infographic to determine the travel time from New York City to the following cities: Portland, Maine *(5 days);* Norfolk, Virginia *(6 days),* Chicago, Illinois *(6 weeks);* and Washington, D.C. *(4 days).* As a class, discuss how much travel times to the same places improved by 1857. **AL**

Analyzing GEOGRAPHY

Answers:

1. Travel time decreased from about 4 days to less than 1 day.
2. A person could travel to eastern Ohio from New York City in a week's time; western Iowa, Minnesota; eastern Texas

Additional Support

Activity: Collaborative Learning

Creating a Thematic Map Organize students into groups of two. Provide students with an outline map of the United States that does not show state borders. Instruct students to draw the Ohio River and Mississippi River and the major tributaries of each. Tell students to imagine they are planning a steamboat trip in 1850 from Wheeling, West Virginia, to New Orleans, Louisiana. Have students draw in the state borders that surround their route of travel and locate and label the major cities along the route. **BL** **ELL**

W Writing Support

Descriptive Writing Ask interested students to use the library and Internet sources to write a one-page essay describing how Robert Fulton's steamboat changed travel and commerce along the nation's waterways. Encourage students to save their essays on a class database so other students can access and view them. **OL**

Reading Check

Answer:
Trains moved much faster than other modes of transportation and they could go anywhere track could be laid.

W The steamboat changed all that. In 1807 **Robert Fulton** and Robert R. Livingston stunned the nation when the *Clermont* chugged 150 miles up the Hudson River from New York City to Albany in just 32 hours. The steamboat made river travel more reliable and upstream travel easier. By 1850 over 700 steamboats, also called riverboats, traveled along the nation's waterways.

History ONLINE
Student Web Activity Visit glencoe.com and complete the activity on the Erie Canal.

The growth of river travel—and the success of the Erie Canal—spurred a wave of canal building throughout the country. By 1840 more than 3,300 miles of canals snaked through the nation, increasing trade and stimulating new economic growth.

The "Iron Horse"

Another mode of transportation—the railroad—also developed in the early 1800s. A wealthy, self-educated industrialist named Peter Cooper built an American engine based on the ones developed in Great Britain. In 1830 Cooper's tiny but powerful locomotive, *Tom Thumb*, pulled the nation's first load of train passengers. Forty people traveled at the then incredible speed of 10 miles per hour along 13 miles of track between Baltimore and Ellicott City, Maryland.

The new machines did not win universal favor. Some said they were not only dangerous and uncomfortable, but dirty and ugly as well. "It is the Devil's own invention," declared one critic, "compounded of fire, smoke, soot, and dirt, spreading its infernal poison throughout the fair countryside."

The advantages of train travel, however, soon became apparent to almost everyone. Trains traveled much faster than stagecoaches or wagons, and, unlike steamboats, they could go nearly anywhere track was laid. More than any other form of transportation, railroads sped the settlement of the American West and expanded trade.

As railroads expanded, they created national markets for many goods by making transportation cheaper. They increased the demand for iron and coal even more directly. Between 1830 and 1861, the United States laid more than 30,000 miles of railroad track—so it needed more than 60,000 miles of iron rail. Since mills used coal to make iron, the need for rails added to the increasing demand for coal. Coal **extraction** shot up from 50,000 tons in 1820 to 14 million tons in 1860.

Reading Check **Evaluating** What were two advantages of trains over other kinds of transportation in the 1800s?

TECHNOLOGY & HISTORY

New technologies developed in the North revolutionized transportation and communications, and helped begin the transformation of the United States from an agricultural to an industrial nation.

▲ **The Steamboat**
Paddle-wheeled steamboats, such as Robert Fulton's *Clermont*, made river travel easier and more reliable.

▲ **The Railroad Locomotive**
The *Tom Thumb* was the first American locomotive. Railroads transformed the nation, allowing people and goods to move quickly from city to city and helping to encourage settlement in the West.

Differentiated Instruction

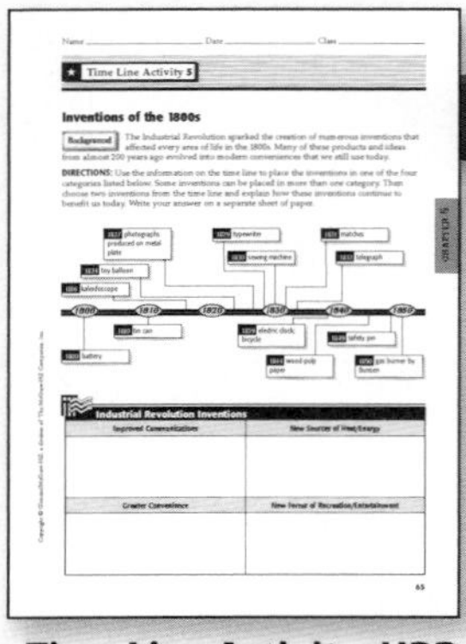

Time Line Activity, URB p. 65

Reading a Time Line

Objective: Read a time line of numerous inventions during the Industrial Revolution.

Focus: Categorize inventions according to how they affected life.

Teach: Explain how these inventions affected Americans' lives.

Assess: Describe how two of these inventions were important in American history.

Close: Discuss whether any of the inventions are still used today.

Differentiated Instruction Strategies

BL Describe two of the inventions listed.

AL Create a flowchart that starts with an invention and describes the evolution of the invention to today.

ELL Choose two inventions. Summarize their importance.

A New System of Production

MAIN Idea A revolution in manufacturing—the Industrial Revolution—dramatically changed the American economy and way of life.

HISTORY AND YOU How would your life be different without instant electronic communication? Read how one man developed the first method of communicating instantly over long distances.

Along with dramatic changes in transportation, a revolution occurred in business and industry. The **Industrial Revolution,** which began in Great Britain in the mid-1700s, consisted of several basic developments. Manufacturing shifted from hand tools to large, complex machines. Skilled artisans gave way to workers, organized by specific tasks, and often unskilled. Factories, some housing hundreds of machines and workers, replaced home-based workshops. Manufacturers sold their wares nationwide or abroad instead of just locally.

Industry developed quickly in the United States in the early 1800s for several reasons. Perhaps the most important factor was the American **free enterprise system** based on private property rights. Individuals could acquire capital and decide how to use it without strict government controls.

The free enterprise system also encouraged industrialization because companies in competition with each other were always willing to experiment with new technologies to make goods cheaper and to transport them more quickly. The era's low taxes also meant that entrepreneurs had more money to invest.

Beginning in the 1830s, many states encouraged industrialization by passing general incorporation laws. These laws allowed companies to become corporations and to raise money by issuing stock without having to obtain a charter from the state legislature. These laws also limited investor liability. If a person bought stock in a company and it went bankrupt, the person risked losing his or her investment but was not responsible for the company's debts. By limiting liability, the new state laws encouraged people to invest money, spurring economic growth.

Industrialization began in the Northeast, where many streams and rivers could provide mills with waterpower. The region was also home to many entrepreneurs who were willing to invest in British industrial techniques.

◀ **The Water Frame**
The water frame allowed cotton fibers to be easily spun into cotton thread.

▲ **The Telegraph**
The first modern breakthrough in communications was the telegraph and Morse code. Suddenly, news and other information could be sent via telegraph keys over long distances nearly instantly.

Sewing Machines ▶
By the mid 1840s, mass-produced cloth could be sewn into mass-produced clothing with sewing machines invented by Elias Howe.

Analyzing VISUALS

1. **Making Connections** How were the inventions of the water frame and the sewing machine connected?
2. **Discussing** Which invention do you think was the most significant? Why?

R Reading Strategy

Monitoring Tell students that some text selections will be more difficult to read than others. They can check their understanding and read at a slower pace when they encounter difficult concepts or words. For example, the concept of the stock market and its relationship to business is difficult for many people to understand. Encourage students to turn to other sources, such as dictionaries and encyclopedias, or the Internet for help. **ELL** **BL**

Analyzing VISUALS

Answers:

1. The water frame enabled people to easily create cotton thread. The sewing machine allowed people to mass produce clothing (using the cotton threads).
2. Students' answers will vary. They should support their choices.

Hands-On Chapter Project
Step 2

Making a Map

Step 2: Writing an Essay Students will write an informative and descriptive essay.

Directions Returning to their groups established in Step 1, have students research a city (Louisville, Kentucky, Memphis, Tennessee, or Vicksburg, Mississippi) along their path and write an essay explaining how the river shaped its history.

Describing Have volunteers from each group explain the history of the city and describe its major landmarks. **OL**

(Chapter Project continued on page 203)

R Reading Strategy

Using Word Parts Write on the board the word *interchangeable*. Underline the root word *change*. **Ask:** What does the root word *change* mean? *(to make or become different or to alter)* What does the prefix *inter* mean? *(between)* What does the suffix *able* mean? *(able, can do)* How do the prefix and the suffix alter the meaning of the root word? *(to put each in place of another)* Discuss with students the value of the revolution of interchangeable parts. OL ELL

DBQ Document Based Questions

Answers:

1. because the daylight lasts for shorter hours in the winter, so there is less light to work by if the mill is not lit artificially
2. rest up for the next day of grueling work

PRIMARY SOURCE

Working at the Lowell Mills

Primary Source

In 1846 a visitor to the Lowell mills described the employees' work schedule:

"The operatives work *thirteen hours* a day in the summer time, and *from daylight to dark* in the winter. At half past four in the morning the factory bell rings, and at five the girls must be in the mills. . . . At seven the girls are allowed thirty minutes for breakfast, and at noon thirty minutes more for dinner. . . . But within this time they must hurry to their boarding-houses and return to the factory. . . . At seven o'clock in the evening the factory bell sounds the close of the day's work.

. . . So fatigued . . . are numbers of the girls, that they go to bed soon after their evening meal and endeavor . . . to resuscitate their weakened frames for the toils of the coming day."

—from *The Harbinger*, November 14, 1846

DBQ Document-Based Questions

1. **Drawing Conclusions** Why are working days shorter in the mills during the winter?
2. **Making Inferences** What does the writer mean by "resuscitate their weakened frames"?

Importing British technology was not easy. Britain had passed strict laws making it illegal to share industrial technology with foreigners. A young English textile worker named Samuel Slater was willing to take the risk. In 1789 he moved to Rhode Island, where he received funding from Moses Brown, a wealthy merchant who had been trying to duplicate British technology. Slater built a British water frame from memory. The frame stretched and spun raw cotton fiber into cotton thread.

The American textile industry took a huge step forward when entrepreneur **Francis C. Lowell** began opening a series of mills in northeastern Massachusetts in 1814. Using machinery he had built after touring British textile mills, Lowell introduced mass production of cotton cloth to the United States. In Waltham, Massachusetts, the site of the first mill, his Boston Manufacturing Company built residences for workers. The company employed thousands of workers—mostly women and children, who would work for lower wages than men. By 1840 dozens of textile mills had been built in the Northeast. Industrialists also began applying factory techniques to the production of lumber, shoes, leather, wagons, and other products.

Technological Advances

A wave of inventions and technological innovations further spurred the nation's industrial growth. An ingenious young New Englander named **Eli Whitney**—perhaps most famous for inventing the cotton gin—also popularized the concept of **interchangeable parts,** transforming gun-making from a one-by-one process into a factory process. R Using this process, machines turned out large quantities of identical pieces that workers assembled into finished weapons.

Additional Support

Activity: Interdisciplinary Connection

Science Organize students into small groups. Have the groups use the library and Internet resources to research how a lock in a canal works. Have groups use their findings to build a working model of a lock. Encourage students to create drawings and select appropriate materials for the model. A brief written explanation of how the model works should accompany the model. Ask groups to show and explain their models to the class. AL

Communications improved as well. American inventor **Samuel F. B. Morse** began work on the telegraph in 1832 and developed the Morse code for sending messages. By 1844 the first long-distance telegraph line connected Washington, D.C., and Baltimore. Morse publicly demonstrated the device, tapping out in code the words "What hath God wrought?" From Baltimore came a reply: "What is the news from Washington?"

R

Journalists saw the telegraph as a tool for speedy transmission of the news. In 1848 a group of newspapers pooled their resources to collect and share news over the telegraph wires. This organization was the Associated Press. Spurred by the demands of journalists and other businesses that needed quick reliable communications with distant markets, more than 50,000 miles of telegraph wire connected most parts of the country by 1860.

The Rise of Large Cities

The industrialization of the United States drew thousands of people from farms and villages to towns in search of factory jobs with higher wages. Many city populations doubled or tripled. In 1820 only one American city boasted more than 100,000 residents. By 1860, eight cities had reached that size.

D

New York City became the country's largest city in the 1820s. The success of the Erie Canal started this growth, which continued with the expanding railroad network of the 1840s. These new transportation methods gave Midwestern farmers two cheaper means of transporting goods to markets. New York City's growing importance as a business center also increased its financial network. This led to the expansion of the financial district on Wall Street and the creation of the New York Stock Exchange. In this manner, New York's importance as the nation's business hub grew alongside its population. By the mid-1870s, New York City had become the first American city to reach a population of more than one million people.

The growing cities provided opportunities for many different occupations. One group was printers and publishers, who shared the goal of keeping the public informed. America had always claimed a high literacy rate, and by 1840, over 75 percent of the total population and over 90 percent of the white population could read.

Many of the early writers, editors, and teachers were educated women. Sarah Buell Hale and Lydia Howard Huntley Sigourney were leading editors and literary figures of their day. Unlike women who worked in factories, women in publishing generally came from the nation's growing middle class.

Workers Begin to Organize

The industrial boom created a new kind of laborer, the factory worker, whose ranks swelled to 1.3 million by 1860. Although the owners of early factory mills expressed a paternalistic concern for their workers, the relationship between management and labor became more strained whenever prices slumped and wages dropped.

Hoping to help improve working conditions, some workers began to join together in **labor unions.** During the late 1820s and early 1830s, about 300,000 men and women belonged to some form of union. Most of the organizations were local and focused on a single trade, such as printing or shoemaking. Although these unions worked separately, they began pushing for similar changes, such as higher wages or a shorter, 10-hour workday.

During this time, unions had little success. Most employers refused to recognize or bargain with them. Unions also had little power or money to support **strikes,** or work stoppages, to achieve their goals. The courts often ruled against these early unions, seeing them as unlawful conspiracies that limited free enterprise. "Competition is the life of trade," a New York court declared in an 1835 case involving a union's demand that its workers be paid at least one dollar to make a pair of shoes. "If the defendants cannot make coarse boots for less than one dollar per pair, let them refuse to do so: but let them not directly or indirectly undertake to say that others shall not do the same work for less price."

Unions did make some gains, however. In 1840 President Martin Van Buren showed his gratitude for labor's political support by reducing the workday for federal employees to 10 hours. Two years later, in *Commonwealth* v. *Hunt,* the Massachusetts Supreme Court ruled that union strikes were legal.

✓Reading Check **Explaining** What was life like for a factory worker in the early 1820s?

R Reading Strategy

Listing Have students list the major changes in the communications industry that occurred between 1800 and 1850. *(the telegraph, and Morse code)* **BL**

D Differentiated Instruction

Visual/Spatial Have students work in small groups to create posters from the perspective of a factory owner looking for more workers. The posters should convince rural Americans to move to large cities. Display the posters around the classroom. Have students vote on which ones are the most convincing and explain why they think so. **ELL**

✓Reading Check

Answer:
Hours were long and the machines were loud and dangerous.

Additional Support

Activity: Collaborative Learning

Analyzing Tell students that America enjoyed one of the highest literacy rates in the world in the early 1800s. As a class, discuss the role that literacy played in the growth of industry and in the growth of the middle class, beginning in the nineteenth century. Have students list their ideas on the board. Then have students create a graphic organizer showing the cause-and-effect relationship between literacy and economic growth. Ask students to provide examples of this relationship. **OL**

C Critical Thinking

Making Generalizations
Have students work together to make generalizations about life for the majority of citizens in the North. After students read Life in the North, ask the following.
Ask: Why might people continue to reside in Northern cities despite the problems they faced? *(lack of money to afford to better their situation; lack of economic mobility; lack of education)* OL

Analyzing VISUALS

Answers:
1. Answers may include: People are happy, content, and well-to-do.
2. the middle class

Life in the North

MAIN Idea The rise of industrialization and the growth of cities led to change and reform in American society.

HISTORY AND YOU What is life like in your community? Read on to find out how people lived in the North in the early 1800s.

C Most of the cities in the North were still relatively small before the Civil War, compared to the expansion that would come later. They had, however, begun to suffer some of the negative results of growth: crime, overcrowding, and public health problems. Immigration from Europe also added to the growing population and its problems.

Life in Northern Cities

The population growth in urban centers provided many challenges to city leaders. To combat rising crime and frequent labor riots, many cities established police departments. Fire, which had long been a concern in crowded conditions when many structures were still made of wood, was also a major urban danger. Volunteer or loosely organized fire departments that had existed since colonial times in cities such as Boston, New York, and Philadelphia, were professionalized during this period.

Crime and fire were not the only dangers in early nineteenth-century cities—they were also extremely unsanitary. Transportation was horse-based, making animal waste an enormous problem, along with human waste, in the era before sewer systems. Additionally, people and industries dumped waste and garbage into public water supplies, such as local rivers. Diseases such as cholera, typhoid, and yellow fever raged through urban areas. Water supplies were made safe only after medical advances in the latter nineteenth century.

Families in the growing cities retained the same structure as they had in the country or in the lands they emigrated from. In general, a family consisted of two parents, often with many children. Infant mortality remained commonplace. Men worked and were expected to

PRIMARY SOURCE

Life in the North, 1820–1860

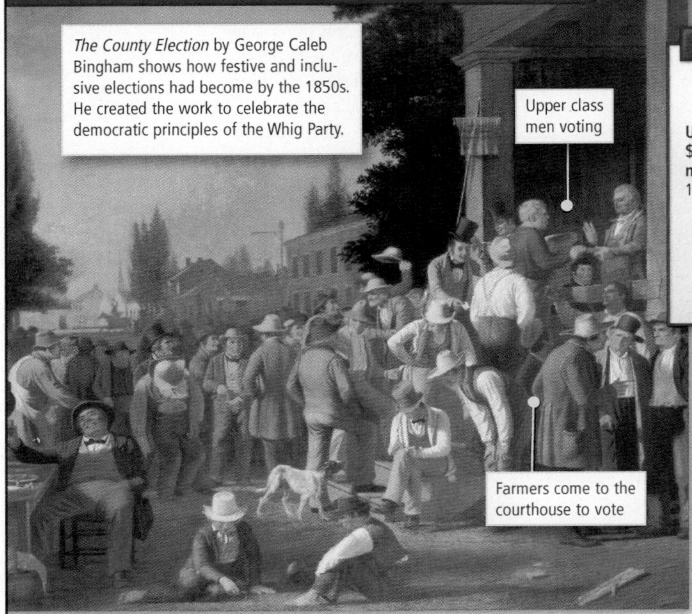

The County Election by George Caleb Bingham shows how festive and inclusive elections had become by the 1850s. He created the work to celebrate the democratic principles of the Whig Party.

Wealth Distribution in Boston, 1833

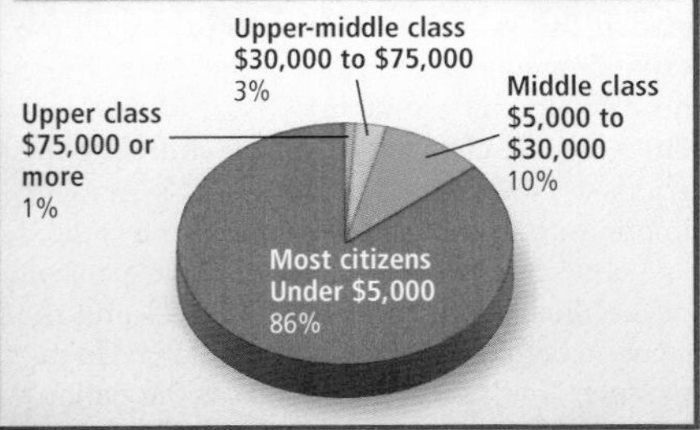

▲ *In 1833, most people in the Northeast were farmers who made a moderate or low income.*

Analyzing VISUALS

1. **Expressing** What is the overall tone of this painting?
2. **Specifying** What income group was the second-largest in 1833 in the North?

Additional Support

Activity: Collaborative Learning

Writing a Script Organize students into small groups. Have the groups research the lives of children who worked in the textile mills. Based on their research, have the groups write a script of an event that might have occurred in the life of such a child. Examples include an encounter between a foreman and a worker who has fallen asleep, a dialogue with another worker as they are on the way home from a day's work, or a monologue of the child's thoughts as he or she walks to work on a hot summer day. Encourage groups to perform the script for the class. OL rule their families. If they did not share in running a family business, women, especially in the middle class, were expected to remain at home to create an orderly, nurturing environment. In towns, women found that bakeries, butcher shops, clothiers, and candle shops offered goods that women once had to labor long hours to produce at home. Institutions of higher education were not available to women until the 1830s, and even then few had the prior education or resources to attend college.

Until the 1850s, public schools did not exist in many cities, or attendance was not mandatory. Before that time, middle-class boys generally finished high school and the wealthy might attend college. Their sisters went to "academies" for young ladies, if they were not tutored at home. Working-class boys might attend school briefly before joining the workforce; working-class girls had to be taught at home if they were to learn to read at all.

Northern cities became havens for runaway slaves as well as free African Americans, but most African Americans remained poor. Many African American women worked as domestic servants, as maids and laundresses. Many African American men found work in New England's shipping industry, as sailors or dock workers. In cities with larger African American populations, such as New York and Philadelphia, a small African American middle class emerged, including carpenters, shoemakers, schoolteachers, and ministers.

Life on the Farm

Even though industry and cities expanded in the Northeast during the first half of the nineteenth century, agriculture remained the country's leading economic activity. On most farms, the entire family shared the work. Fields had to be planted, tended, and plowed. Cows, pigs, and chickens had to be cared for. In the winter months, men and boys made repairs and cut wood for the fire while women spun thread into yarn and wove cloth for clothing. Until late in the century, farming employed more people and produced more wealth than any other kind of work.

A reporter traveling through Ohio in 1851 described a scene that resembled much of the North at that time:

> "As far as the eye can stretch in the distance nothing but corn and wheat fields are to be seen; and on some points in the Scioto Valley as high as a thousand acres of corn may be seen in adjoining fields, belonging to some eight or ten different proprietors."
>
> —from *The Cultivator*, September 1851

Northern farmers produced enough to sell their surplus in the growing Eastern cities and towns. The farmers' labors not only helped feed the population but also nourished the region's economy. As parts of the North began concentrating on manufacturing, the South continued to tie its fortunes to agriculture—and to the institution of slavery.

Reading Check **Comparing** Why was farming more important in the South than in the North?

Section 2 REVIEW

Vocabulary

1. **Explain** the significance of: Erie Canal, National Road, Robert Fulton, Industrial Revolution, free enterprise system, Francis C. Lowell, Eli Whitney, interchangeable parts, Samuel F. B. Morse, labor union, strike.

Main Ideas

2. **Describing** How did the building of canals and railways boost the U.S. economy?
3. **Summarizing** What factors contributed to the development of industry in the North?
4. **Identifying** What was the leading economic activity in the United States in the early 1800s?

Critical Thinking

5. **Big Ideas** How did interchangeable parts revolutionize the manufacturing process?
6. **Organizing** Use a graphic organizer to list the effects of some of the technological advances of the early 1800s.

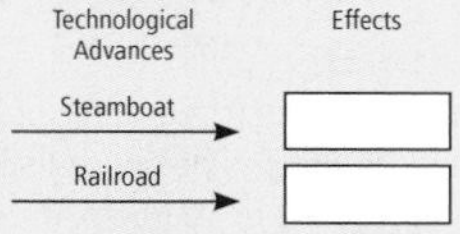

7. **Analyzing Visuals** Study the maps on page 195. What inventions helped to decrease the amount of time required to travel from New York City?

Writing About History

8. **Descriptive Writing** Suppose that you are a teenager working in a textile factory in the early 1800s. Write a letter to your family describing what your life is like there.

History ONLINE
Study Central™ To review this section, go to glencoe.com and click on Study Central.

Assess

History ONLINE

Study Central™ provides summaries, interactive games, and online graphic organizers to help students review content.

Reading Check

Answer:
The South had fewer cities and less industry and had an economy based on enslaved labor.

Close

Synthesizing Ask students to discuss how the Industrial Revolution changed life in America. **OL**

Section 2 REVIEW

Answers

1. All definitions can be found in the section and the Glossary.
2. These new ways of transporting goods increased trade, created national markets because shipping goods was now cheaper, and the railroads increased the demand for iron and coal.
3. the free enterprise system, low taxes, incorporation laws, access to swift-flowing streams to power mills, the presence of entrepreneurs
4. farming
5. allowed complex products to be made in stages by unskilled workers
6. Steamboat: made river transportation reliable and extended the range of transportation in both directions; Railroad: helped settle the West, created national markets, and expanded trade among the nation's regions
7. roads and canals
8. Students' letters will vary, but should include descriptive language and be from a teenage worker's point of view.

Focus

Bellringer
Daily Focus Transparency 5-3

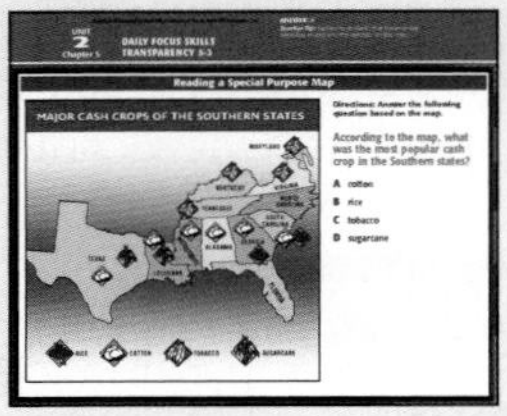

Guide to Reading

Answers: From top to bottom: planter elite, urban professionals, yeoman farmers, white rural poor, free African Americans, enslaved African Americans

Section Spotlight Video

To generate student interest and provide a springboard for class discussion, access the Chapter 5, Section 3 video at glencoe.com or on the video DVD.

Section 3

Section Audio   Spotlight Video

The Land of Cotton

Guide to Reading

Big Ideas

Science and Technology The invention of the cotton gin made cotton a key part of the South's economy and ensured that slavery continued to shape the South's society and culture.

Content Vocabulary
- cotton gin *(p. 202)*
- yeoman farmer *(p. 205)*
- task system *(p. 206)*

Academic Vocabulary
- annual *(p. 202)*
- ambiguous *(p. 208)*

People and Events to Identify
- Frederick Douglass *(p. 207)*
- Gabriel Prosser *(p. 209)*
- Nat Turner *(p. 209)*

Reading Strategy

Organizing Complete a graphic organizer similar to the one below by listing the main categories of Southern society.

Southern Society

Highest ______________________

____

____

Lowest ______________________

The economy of the South was based on the production of cash crops, including tobacco, rice, and cotton, for export. Southern society had a distinct class system made up of the planter elite, yeoman farmers, and enslaved people.

The Southern Economy

MAIN Idea The cotton gin made cotton the most important cash crop in the South and deepened the region's dependency on enslaved labor.

HISTORY AND YOU Do you know how the clothing you wear is made? What is the cloth made from? Read on to learn how the invention of the cotton gin transformed the economy and society of the South.

The South thrived on the production of several major cash crops. In the upper Southern states—Maryland, Virginia, Kentucky, and Tennessee—farmers grew tobacco. Rice paddies dominated the coastal regions of South Carolina and Georgia. In Louisiana and parts of eastern Texas, fields of sugarcane stretched for miles. No crop, however, played a greater role in the South's fortunes than cotton. It was grown in a wide belt stretching from inland South Carolina, west through Georgia, Alabama, and Mississippi, and into eastern Texas.

During a visit to the South in 1793, Eli Whitney, the inventive young New Englander, noticed that removing cotton seeds by hand from the fluffy bolls was so tedious that it took a worker an entire day to separate a pound of cotton lint. An acquaintance knew of Whitney's mechanical ingenuity and suggested that he try building a machine to pick out the seeds. In only ten days, Whitney built a simple **cotton gin**—*gin* being short for *engine*—that quickly and efficiently combed the seeds out of cotton bolls. The machine pulled the cotton through a rotating cylinder with openings that were too small for the seeds to pass through.

The invention of the cotton gin happened at the same time that textile mills were expanding in Europe. Mills in England and France clamored for all the cotton they could get. In 1792, the year before Whitney invented his cotton gin, the South produced about 6,000 bales of cotton. By 1801, **annual** production reached 100,000 bales.

Cotton Becomes King

Cotton soon dominated the region. By the late 1840s, Southerners were producing more than 2 million bales of cotton annually, and in 1860 production reached almost 4 million bales.

Resource Manager

R Reading Strategies	C Critical Thinking	D Differentiated Instruction	W Writing Support	S Skill Practice
Teacher Edition • Comparing and Contrasting, p. 203 • Activating Prior Knowl., p. 204 • Inferring, p. 209 **Additional Resources** • Guided Reading, URB p. 80	**Teacher Edition** • Predicting Consequences, p. 206 • Drawing Conclusions, p. 207 **Additional Resources** • Interpreting Political Cartoons Activity, URB p. 73 • Quizzes and Tests, p. 65	**Teacher Edition** • English Learners, p. 205 **Additional Resources** • Differentiated Instruction Activity, URB p. 55 • Am. Art and Music Act., URB p. 71	**Teacher Edition** • Persuasive Writing, p. 208	**Additional Resources** • Reinf. Skills Act., URB p. 63 • Read. Essen., p. 56

TECHNOLOGY & HISTORY

The Cotton Gin

In 1793 Eli Whitney built a device that removed the seeds of the "green-seed" cotton. Whitney's "gin" combed the seeds out of the cotton. The cotton gin was easy to mass produce, and quickly increased the profitability of cotton, which, in turn, increased the size and number of plantations and the need for enslaved laborers.

◀ *Eli Whitney*

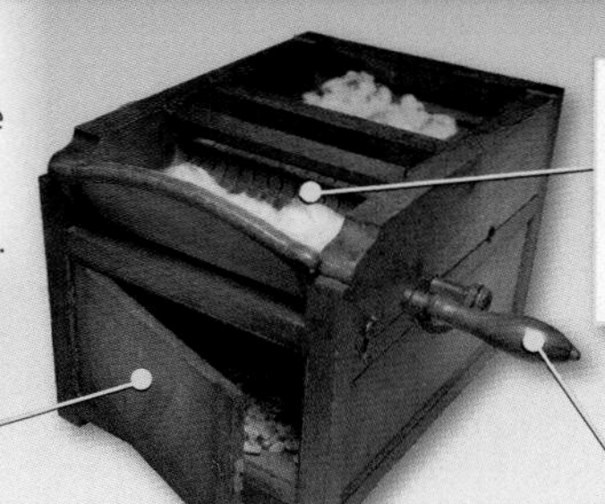

Cotton Production in the South

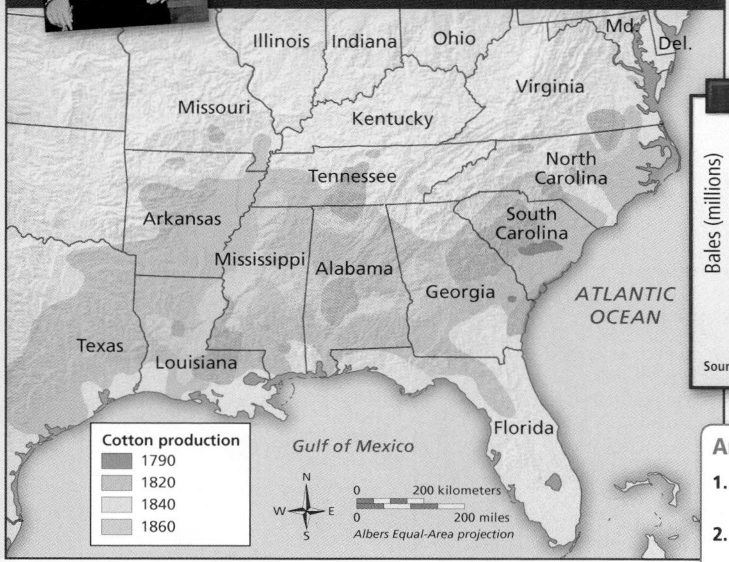

Cotton Production, 1790–1860

Source: *Historical Statistics of the United States.*

Analyzing VISUALS

1. **Explaining** How did the cotton gin affect slavery in the South?
2. **Identifying** Where did cotton production spread most widely between 1820 and 1840?

In that year, Southern cotton sold for a total of $191 million in European markets—nearly two-thirds of the total export trade of the United States. Southerners began saying, "Cotton is King."

"The whole interior of the Southern states was languishing," observed one Southern judge, but Whitney's invention changed everything. "Individuals who were depressed with poverty, and sunk with idleness, have suddenly risen to wealth and respectability. Our debts have been paid off, our capitals increased; and our lands are treble [triple] in value." **R**

While the cotton gin made some Southern planters rich, it also strengthened the institution of slavery. The spread of cotton plantations across the Deep South made the demand for slave labor skyrocket. Congress had outlawed the foreign slave trade in 1808, but a high birthrate among enslaved women—encouraged by slaveholders eager to sell new laborers at high prices—meant that the enslaved population kept growing. Between 1820 and 1850, the number of people who were enslaved in the South rose from about 1.5 million to nearly 4 million. **R**

Teach

R Reading Strategy

Comparing and Contrasting Remind students of their early reading about the economy of the North. Have students compare and contrast the economies of the North and South during this period in history. *(Possible answers: North: birthplace of American Industrial Revolution, large cities, paid labor, technological advances in communications and transportation, free-enterprise. South: cash crops and farming, little industrialization, rural villages and plantations, slave labor, invention of the cotton gin.)* **OL**

Analyzing VISUALS

Answers:

1. The cotton gin increased the profitability of cotton, so it increased the need for enslaved labor.
2. Deep South; Georgia, South Carolina, Alabama, Mississippi, Louisiana

Hands-On Chapter Project
Step 3

Making a Map

Step 3: Labeling Maps Students will research the canals that connected rivers.

Directions Returning to their groups, have students research which canals connected to the Ohio and Mississippi Rivers. Students should use library resources and/or Internet resources.

Labeling Have students label the canals on their map and indicate towns and cities that benefited from them. Students should label those towns on the map. **OL**

(Chapter Project continued on page 213)

R Reading Strategy

Activating Prior Knowledge
Explain that the rigid, clearly defined society of the South was similar to the societal confines many European immigrants sought to escape. In the North, people were divided into class by the amount of money they earned. **Ask:** Which system is the better one? *(Answers may vary.)* Discuss as a class the issues of class and fairness. Remind students of the Bill of Rights in the U.S. Constitution.
Ask: What does it say about the rights of American citizens? How does our justice system secure the rights of American citizens? *(Answers may vary.)* **OL**

Reading Check

Answer:
The need for slave labor increased enormously.

Additional Support

Industry Lags

Although the South became prosperous from agriculture, it did not industrialize as quickly as the North. For the most part, the South remained a region of rural villages and plantations, with only three large cities: Baltimore, Charleston, and New Orleans.

The South did have some industry. Coal, iron, salt, and copper mines, as well as ironworks and textile mills, could be found there. The region still relied heavily on imported goods, however, which worried some people. As one Southerner noted, "For what have we not looked to our Northern friends? From them we get not only our clothes, carriages, saddles, hats, shoes, flour, potatoes, but even our onions and horn buttons." At this time, in 1860, manufacturing in the South accounted for only 16 percent of the nation's manufacturing total. Most Southerners were content to rely on agriculture.

Reading Check **Synthesizing** What effect did the cotton gin have on slavery in the South?

Society in the South

MAIN Idea In contrast to the North, the South had a rigid social class system dominated by a planter elite.

HISTORY AND YOU What mental images do you have of the Old South? What are they based on? Read on to learn more about how Southern society was organized.

R The economy of the South resulted in a society with rigid and clearly defined class structure. At the top of Southern society was the planter elite, who owned the larger plantations. The 1850 census showed that in a Southern white population of just over 6 million, a total of 347,725 families were slaveholders. Of this number, around 37,000 were planters, defined as those who held 20 or more enslaved people. Fewer than 8,000 planters held 50 or more people in slavery; only 11 held 500 or more.

A very small percentage of Southern slaveholders lived a life of gentility in grand

PRIMARY SOURCE
Life in the Old South

Many enslaved African Americans worked on cotton plantations during the early 1800s. Cotton was the main cash crop for the South and required large amounts of manual labor to harvest. Cotton plantations located near rivers, similar to the one below, would transport bales of cotton to the docks to be sent to markets in the North or in Europe.

Slaveholding in the South

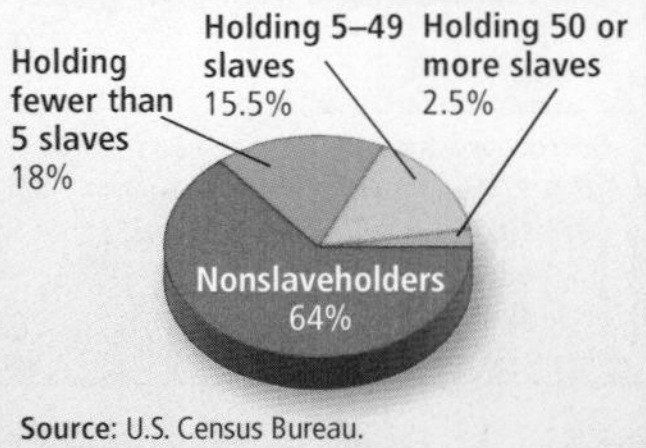

Source: U.S. Census Bureau.

Activity: Interdisciplinary Connection

Music Have interested students use library or Internet sources to research the music of the African Americans who lived enslaved in the South. Ask them to share examples of the music, lyrics, and tune with the class. Students may either perform the music or bring recordings. Have students explain the meaning of the lyrics of the songs they have chosen. Discuss common themes reflected in the lyrics. **BL**

mansions. Many planter mansions were little more than cottages with newly built facades.

Although wealthy planters made up a tiny group—representing less than half of one percent of white Southern families and slightly over two percent of slaveholding families—they dominated the region's economy and its political system.

Ordinary farmers—often called **yeoman farmers**—and their families made up the vast majority of the white population. They may have held four or fewer enslaved persons, though most held none at all, and they worked on the land themselves. In his novel *Huckleberry Finn* author Mark Twain gives his impressions of a typical small Southern farm: **D**

PRIMARY SOURCE

"A rail fence around a two-acre yard . . . big double log house for the white folks—hewed logs, with the chinks stopped up with mud or mortar . . . outside of the fence a garden; . . . then the cotton fields begin; and after the fields, the woods."

—from *Huckleberry Finn*

Near the bottom of the social ladder stood the white, rural poor. This group, made up mostly of families living on land too barren for successful farming, scratched a meager existence from hunting and fishing, vegetable gardening, and raising a few half-wild hogs and chickens. They made up less than 10 percent of the white population.

At the bottom of society were African Americans, 93 percent of them enslaved. In 1850 nearly 3.6 million African Americans lived in the South—about 37 percent of the total Southern population.

Rounding out Southern society was a small urban class of lawyers, doctors, merchants, and other professionals. Agriculture's influence was so great that even many of these city dwellers invested in or owned farms. As one observer noted, "No matter how one might begin, as lawyer, physician, clergyman, mechanic, or merchant, he ended, if prosperous, as proprietor of a rice or cotton plantation."

Reading Check **Identifying** What classes made up the South's social structure?

THE PLANTER CLASS

◀ *The planter elite lived extremely comfortable lives of wealth, leisure, and privilege.*

THE YEOMAN CLASS

▲ *Yeoman farmers did not have the wealth or power of the planter elite but lived comfortably. They may have held enslaved persons, though most held none.*

THE ENSLAVED

◀ *Most enslaved people lived hard lives as either field hands or house servants.*

Analyzing VISUALS

1. **Specifying** What percentage of Southerners held 50 or more slaves?
2. **Explaining** If most Southern whites did not hold slaves, why do you think that most Southerners still defended the institution?

D Differentiated Instruction

English Learners Have students work in pairs to find other meanings for the word *yeoman*. **Ask:** **Why might the word *yeoman* have been used to describe ordinary farmers in the South?** *(South held on to some aspects of European life, like strict class system; plantation owners were similar in many ways to European landowners and nobles.)* **ELL**

Analyzing VISUALS

Answers:

1. 2.5%
2. Southern economy relied on agriculture, which in turn relied on enslaved labor.

Reading Check

Answer:
planter elite, urban professionals, yeoman farmers, white rural poor, free African Americans, enslaved African Americans

Additional Support

Activity: Interdisciplinary Connection

Math Provide students with the population data shown on the right and ask students to create a line graph. Discuss with the class the population trends shown in the data. **AL**

Year	Total Pop. of the U.S. (in mill.)	Slave Pop. of the U.S. (in mill.)
1800	5.1	0.9
1810	6.8	1.1
1820	10.0	1.5
1830	12.8	2.0
1840	17.0	2.5
1850	23.0	3.2
1860	31.0	4.0

C Critical Thinking

Predicting Consequences Remind students that enslaved African Americans had very few rights. **Ask:** **What rights were denied enslaved African Americans at this time?** *(Enslaved African Americans were forbidden to own property or leave the slaveholder's property without permission, could not bring a lawsuit or sign a contract, could not possess firearms, could not testify in court against a white person, and were banned by law from learning to read and write.)* Have students write a one-page essay predicting what might have happened to the South and to enslaved African Americans had slavery never been abolished. Have students share their essays with the class. **AL**

Slavery

MAIN Idea Enslaved African Americans had no legal rights; resistance and rebellion were two ways of coping with enslavement.

HISTORY AND YOU Do you remember reading about the Stono Rebellion? Read on to learn about slave revolts and attempted revolts in the 1800s.

The rice and cotton plantations depended on enslaved labor for their existence. The overwhelming majority of enslaved African Americans toiled in the South's fields. Some, however, worked in the region's few industrial plants or as skilled workers, such as blacksmiths, carpenters, and coopers. Others became house servants.

C Enslaved people had few legal rights. State slave codes forbade enslaved men and women from owning property or leaving a slaveholder's premises without permission. They could not bring a lawsuit or sign a contract. They could not possess firearms or testify in court against a white person. Laws banned them from learning to read and write. Society viewed enslaved persons as property.

Plantation Life

Enslaved African Americans working in the fields were organized using two basic labor systems. On farms and small plantations that held few enslaved people, the **task system** was used. Under this system, workers were given a specific set of jobs to accomplish every day. After completing their tasks, they were allowed to spend the remainder of the day as they chose. Some enslaved people earned money through their skills as artisans. Others cultivated personal gardens for extra food.

In the 1800s, as cotton production became more common and slavery more widespread, slaveholders who owned large plantations adopted the gang system of labor. Under this system, enslaved people were organized into work gangs that labored from sunup to sundown—plowing, planting, cultivating, or picking, depending on the season.

INFOGRAPHIC

Slavery in America, 1800–1860

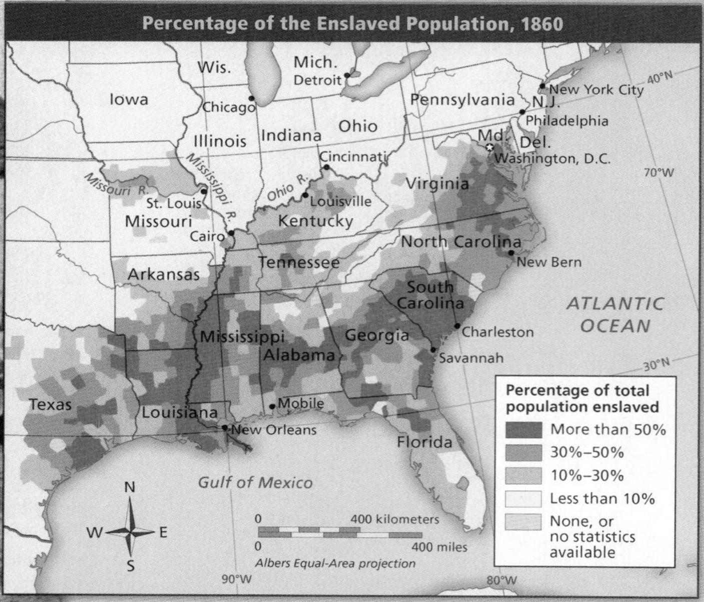

◄ *Enslaved African Americans on a Southern plantation*

Additional Support

Activity: Collaborative Learning

Comparing Systems Have students work in groups to research the two systems used to organize slave labor in the South, the task system and the gang system. Instruct students to use the Internet or library resources to find additional information about these two systems. Have each group create a chart that compares the systems from the point of view of either the landowner or the enslaved person. Display the charts in the classroom. **OL**

A driver acted as the director of a work gang. Often these individuals were enslaved people themselves, chosen for their loyalty or willingness to cooperate. They ensured that the workers labored continuously. No matter which labor system was used, slavery was a degrading experience. **Frederick Douglass,** who rose from slavery to become a prominent leader of the antislavery movement, recalled how life as an enslaved person affected him:

C

PRIMARY SOURCE

"My natural elasticity was crushed; my intellect languished; the disposition to read departed; the cheerful spark that lingered about my eye died; the dark night of slavery closed in upon me, and behold a man transformed to a brute."

—from *Narrative of the Life of Frederick Douglass*

Enslaved Women and Children

African American women did not have an easier time than men as enslaved people. They worked long, hard days in the fields or in the plantation house, where they served as maids, nannies, or cooks. These jobs may have seemed less arduous than fieldwork, but the responsibilities were greater and the demands were constant, as was the scrutiny of the master or mistress of the house. On larger plantations, older enslaved women cared for the babies of other enslaved women in nurseries while they worked. Where family relationships were allowed, they also cooked and cared for their own families.

Young enslaved children might be allowed to play, often with the plantation owner's own children, but as soon as they were able, they were given chores. They were not allowed to attend school, although there were rare occasions when some children learned to read.

Free African Americans

Although most African Americans of the time lived in slavery, some did not. By 1850, some 225,000 free African Americans resided in the South. Most lived in the cities, especially in Maryland and Virginia.

C Critical Thinking

Drawing Conclusions Explain to students that enslaved African American and abolitionist Frederick Douglass was born Frederick Augustus Washington Bailey. After escaping slavery, he headed north and eventually settled in New Bedford, Massachusetts. **Ask:** What reasons might Douglass have had for changing his name? *(to avoid capture by slave hunters; to establish a new life with a new identity; to have a fresh start in the North)* **OL**

Analyzing GEOGRAPHY

Answers:

1. South Carolina, Louisiana, Alabama, Mississippi, Georgia
2. The economies of the states with the greatest percentages of enslaved people in their populations are those states with economies centered around cotton.

NATIONAL GEOGRAPHIC **An Economy Built on Enslaved Labor, c. 1850**

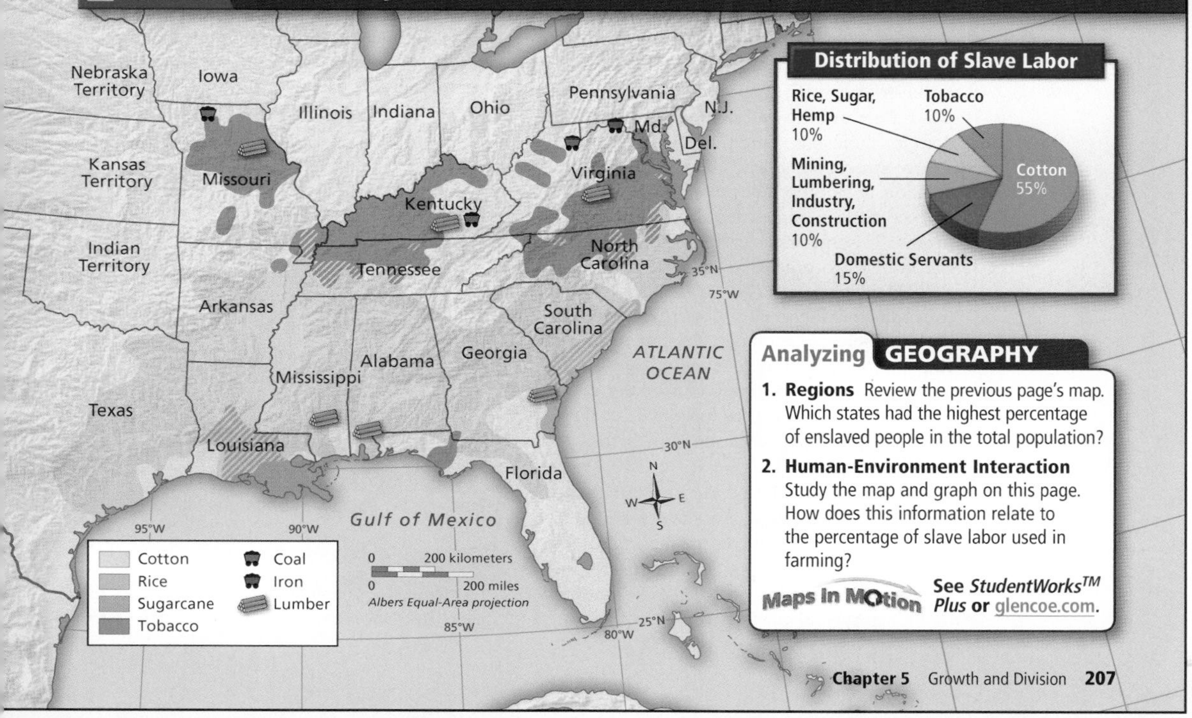

Analyzing GEOGRAPHY

1. **Regions** Review the previous page's map. Which states had the highest percentage of enslaved people in the total population?
2. **Human-Environment Interaction** Study the map and graph on this page. How does this information relate to the percentage of slave labor used in farming?

Maps In MOtion See *StudentWorks*™ *Plus* or glencoe.com.

Additional Support

Activity: Collaborative Learning

Creating an Annotated Map Provide students with an outline map of the Southern states that shows state boundaries. Have students list the crops grown in each state. Work with students to explain the reason that certain crops grow better in certain states. Students may need to consult outside resources. **OL**

People IN HISTORY

Answer:
Many states adopted even harsher restrictions on both enslaved and free African Americans.

W Writing Support

Persuasive Writing Ask students to find books in the library or use Internet resources to find out about the lives of enslaved African Americans in the 1800s. Have them use information from the books to assume the point of view of an adolescent enslaved African American, who has been taught to read and write by the sympathetic child of the plantation owner. Have students write a letter to a free-born cousin living in the North, telling him or her about the life of an enslaved person. The letter should persuade the cousin to help him or her escape to the North. Encourage students to share their letters with the class. OL

Additional Support

People IN HISTORY

Nat Turner
1800–1831

The man who led the nation's best-known slave revolt believed from an early age—through his mother's encouragement—that he was divinely inspired. "I was intended for some great purpose," he once declared.

Although many considered Nat Turner a religious fanatic—he claimed to take his directions from mysterious voices and the movements of heavenly bodies—others knew he had a sharp mind. "He certainly never had the advantages of education," said the man appointed to be his lawyer, "but he can read and write . . . and for natural intelligence and quickness of apprehension is surpassed by few men I have ever seen."

As he awaited execution, Turner reportedly showed little remorse for his deeds, certain that he had acted in the name of God to free his people. "I am here loaded with chains and willing to suffer the fate that awaits me," he said.

Turner's revolt sent a wave of terror through the South and heightened fears of future uprisings. As a result, many states adopted even harsher restrictions on both enslaved and free African Americans.

What was the result of Turner's revolt?

▲ *Nat Turner, an enslaved minister, led a group of African Americans in an armed uprising in August 1831.*

A few enslaved persons were descended from Africans brought to the United States as indentured servants in the 1700s, before the slave system became universal. Some had earned their freedom fighting in the American Revolution, and still others were the half-white children of slaveholders, who had granted them freedom. There were also some formerly enslaved persons whose slaveholders had freed them or who had managed to buy freedom for themselves and their families.

W Free African Americans had an **ambiguous** position in Southern society. The experiences of freed African Americans differed from state to state. In some states they had to obtain special licenses to preach or to own firearms. In cities like Charleston and New Orleans, some were successful enough to become slaveholders themselves. One such African American was Cecee McCarty, who amassed a fortune in New Orleans by retailing imported dry goods. She eventually had a sales force of 32 enslaved African Americans who she sent across the state to sell her wares.

Another 196,000 free African Americans lived in the North, where slavery had been outlawed, but they were not accepted into white society. African American educator and minister Samuel Ward of New York lamented that racial prejudice was "ever at my elbow":

PRIMARY SOURCE

"As a servant, it denied me a seat at the table with my white fellow servants . . . along the streets it ever pursued, ever ridiculed, ever abused me. If I sought redress, the very complexion I wore was pointed out as the best reason for my seeking it in vain; if I desired to turn to account a little learning, in the way of earning a living by it, the idea of employing a black clerk was preposterous—too absurd to be seriously entertained."

—from *Autobiography of a Fugitive Negro*

Still, free African Americans could organize their own churches and voluntary associations, and publish newspapers, as well as earn money from the jobs they held.

One African American who not only kept his wages but also multiplied them many times over was James Forten of Philadelphia. He went to sea in his teens as a powder monkey—the person on board a warship who handled explosives. Later, he worked as a sailmaker. By the age of 32, he owned a thriving sail factory employing 40 African American and white workers. He devoted much of his wealth to the cause of abolishing slavery.

Coping With Enslavement

African Americans dealt with the horrors of slavery in a variety of ways. From language to

Activity: Collaborative Learning

Writing a Diary Entry Organize the class into small groups. Assign each student one of the following: a planter, a yeoman farmer, an enslaved person, or a free African American. Have each student write his or her reaction to the uprising led by Nat Turner in the form of a diary entry. Then have students share their entries with the group. As a group, discuss how and why the viewpoints of the uprising varied. OL music to religion, they developed a culture that provided them with a sense of mutual support.

African American Culture Songs were important to many enslaved people. Field-workers often used songs to pass the long workdays. Some songs were more provocative than most plantation owners knew, using subtle language and secret meanings to lament the singers' bondage and to express a continuing hope for freedom.

Songs also played a key role in one of the most important aspects of African American culture: religion. By the early 1800s, large numbers of African Americans were Christians. The religious services enslaved people held often centered on praying about their particular concern—their dreams of freedom or a better life in the next world.

Resistance and Rebellion Many enslaved men and women found ways to oppose the dreadful lives forced on them. Some quietly staged work slowdowns. Others broke tools or set fire to houses and barns. Still others risked beatings or mutilations to run away. Some African Americans turned on their slaveholders and killed them. On occasion, enslaved people also plotted uprisings.

The first major slave uprising in the United States occurred in 1800. It was organized by an enslaved man named **Gabriel Prosser.** Prosser learned to read and grew deeply religious. Inspired by the Biblical story of the Israelite struggle for freedom from their enslavement in Egypt, Prosser began to organize those among the enslaved who were willing to revolt. They made their own weapons and ammunition and planned to capture Richmond, kill all whites living there, except for French people, Methodists, and Quakers—groups whom Prosser felt were against slavery—and establish a separate African American nation.

On the night of August 30, 1800, about 1,000 armed enslaved **R** people approached Richmond but in the end were forced to turn back due to a heavy storm. The plot, however, was exposed, and Governor James Monroe then sent out the state militia, who eventually captured Prosser. He, along with 34 other leaders of the revolt, was shortly hanged.

In 1822 Denmark Vesey, a free African American who operated a woodworking shop in Charleston, South Carolina, was accused of planning an armed revolt to free the region's slaves. Whether or not Vesey actually planned an uprising is not known. The Charleston authorities claimed to have learned of the plot from an informer, and in 1822 Vesey was tried, convicted, and hanged.

A group of African Americans in Virginia did carry out an armed uprising on August 22, 1831. Leading the attack was **Nat Turner,** an enslaved minister who believed God had chosen him to bring his people out of bondage. Turner and his followers killed more than 50 white men, women, and children before state and local troops put down the uprising.

Reading Check **Describing** What was life like for African Americans in the 1800s?

Section 3 REVIEW

Vocabulary

1. **Explain** the significance of: cotton gin, yeoman farmer, task system, Frederick Douglass, Gabriel Prosser, Nat Turner.

Main Ideas

2. **Analyzing** What happened at the same time as the invention of the cotton gin to increase the importance of cotton in the South?
3. **Identifying** Which class in the South during the early 1800s made up the largest percentage of the white population?
4. **Discussing** How was working within the task system different than working within the gang system?

Critical Thinking

5. **Big Ideas** How did the cotton gin and cotton farming change the South?
6. **Organizing** Complete a graphic organizer by listing the provisions of some slave codes.

Slave Codes

7. **Analyzing Visuals** Study the graph about slave labor on page 207. After those who worked to produce cotton, what was the next-largest group of enslaved workers?

Writing About History

8. **Expository Writing** Suppose you are a European visitor to the South in 1830. Write a newspaper article explaining your impressions of life in this region.

History ONLINE
Study Central™ To review this section, go to glencoe.com and click on Study Central.

R Reading Strategy

Inferring Ask: What long-term impact do you think the slave revolts had on the lives of enslaved people? *(Possible answers: may have helped crystallize opposition to slavery, may have given enslaved people a ray of hope for the future)* **OL**

Reading Check

Answer:
Most were enslaved, treated poorly, and had few legal rights.

Assess

History ONLINE

Study Central™ provides summaries, interactive games, and online graphic organizers to help students review content.

Close

Summarizing Have students explain how the South's economy led to a reliance on slave labor. **OL**

Section 3 REVIEW

Answers

1. All definitions can be found in the section and the Glossary.
2. Textile mills were expanding in England and France, creating a huge increase in the demand for cotton.
3. yeoman farmers
4. Although they were still enslaved, but under task system they were assigned one type of task and, when their work was done, they could do what they wished with their time. In gang system, enslaved workers worked sunup to sundown with no free time.
5. Increased emphasis on cotton, and the ability now to process it more quickly led to larger plantations and an increase in enslaved labor. Urban growth and industrialization continued to be slow.
6. Enslaved people could not own property, leave the premises without permission, possess firearms, testify against a white person, or learn to read and write.
7. domestic servants
8. Students' articles will vary, but should include descriptive language and details from the section.

ANALYZING PRIMARY SOURCES

Focus

Analyzing Primary Sources Have students examine the advertisement in Source 2. **Ask:** What other items are to be sold the same day as the three slaves? *(ten slaves for rent, rice, gram, paddy, books, muslins, needles, pins, ribbons, and a celebrated English horse called Blucher)* What does this advertisement show about the way slaves were treated? *(They were sold like crops, goods, and animals.)* What else do you notice about the advertisement? *(The slaves were listed by their first names only, and some of the goods to be sold were of interest to women.)* **OL**

Teach

Synthesizing Ask: Why might song have been an important part of the enslaved African American culture? *(Songs helped pass time during the workday, provided enjoyment, express their hopes and desire for freedom, and were used in religious services.)* **OL**

Additional Support

ANALYZING PRIMARY SOURCES

Living Under Slavery

Enslaved persons were not free. That fundamental fact meant they could be sold and separated from their families. They could not legally marry or leave their slaveholder's property without permission. Slaveholders held such power that they controlled access to basic life necessities and could physically punish, even kill, the people they held in slavery without breaking the law.

Study these primary sources and answer the questions that follow.

PRIMARY SOURCE 1

Autobiography, 1845

"The men and women slaves received, as their monthly allowance of food, eight pounds of pork, or its equivalent in fish, and one bushel of corn meal. Their yearly clothing consisted of two coarse linen shirts, one pair of linen trousers, like the shirts, one jacket, one pair of trousers for winter, made of coarse negro cloth, one pair of stockings, and one pair of shoes; the whole of which could not have cost more than seven dollars. The allowance of the slave children was given to their mothers, or the old women having the care of them. The children unable to work in the field had neither shoes, stockings, jackets, nor trousers, given to them; their clothing consisted of two coarse linen shirts per year. When these failed them, they went naked until the next allowance-day. Children from seven to ten years old, of both sexes, almost naked, might be seen at all seasons of the year.

There were no beds given the slaves, unless one coarse blanket be considered such, and none but the men and women had these. This, however, is not considered a very great privation. They find less difficulty from the want of beds, than from the want of time to sleep; for when their day's work in the field is done, the most of them having their washing, mending, and cooking to do, and having few or none of the ordinary facilities for doing either of these, very many of their sleeping hours are consumed in preparing for the field the coming day; and when this is done, old and young, male and female, married and single, drop down side by side, on one common bed,—the cold, damp floor,—each covering himself or herself with their miserable blankets; and here they sleep till they are summoned to the field by the driver's horn."

—from *Narrative of the Life of Frederick Douglass, an American Slave*

PRIMARY SOURCE 2

Advertisement, 1829

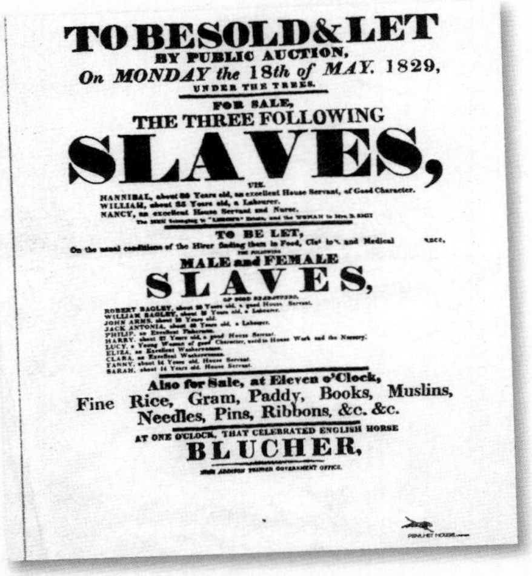

PRIMARY SOURCE 3

Photograph, 1863

▼ *Gordon escaped from his slaveholder in Mississippi during the Civil War. In this photograph, he shows the scars from a brutal whipping.*

Extending the Content

Celebrations Enslaved persons broke the monotony of their everyday lives by holding occasional celebrations on weekends and special holidays. These "parties" usually included a meal followed by singing, dancing, and storytelling. Some planters tried to stop these parties, but others encouraged them. As Frederick Douglass noted, the "parties were among the most effective means in the hands of the slaveholders of keeping down the spirit of insurrection among the slaves." Without this outlet, Douglass continued, "the slave would have been forced to a dangerous desperation."

Primary Source 4

Autobiography, 1861

"I once saw two beautiful children playing together. One was a fair white child; the other was her slave, and also her sister. When I saw them embracing each other, and heard their joyous laughter, I turned sadly away from the lovely sight. I foresaw the inevitable blight that would fall on the little slave's heart. I knew how soon her laughter would be changed to sighs. The fair child grew up to be a still fairer woman. From childhood to womanhood her pathway was blooming with flowers, and overarched by a sunny sky. Scarcely one day of her life had been clouded when the sun rose on her happy bridal morning.

How had those years dealt with her slave sister, the little playmate of her childhood? She, also, was very beautiful; but the flowers and sunshine of love were not for her. She drank the cup of sin, and shame, and misery, whereof her persecuted race are compelled to drink."

—from *Incidents in the Life of a Slave Girl*

Primary Source 5

Painting, c. 1852

Slave Auction of African Family

Primary Source 6

Photograph, 1858

► *Louisa, an enslaved teenager from St. Louis, Missouri, is shown photographed with her slaveholders' son.*

DBQ Document-Based Questions

1. **Analyzing** What does Source 1 reveal about the daily lives of enslaved persons?
2. **Interpreting** Examine Sources 2 and 3. What do these images demonstrate about the status and treatment of enslaved persons?
3. **Comparing and Contrasting** Read Source 4. How were the lives of the two girls similar when they were young but different when they became young women?
4. **Analyzing Visuals** Look at Source 5 and examine the people in the painting. Write a paragraph describing what you see going on in this scene.
5. **Speculating** Study Source 6. How do you think Louisa felt about taking care of this young boy? How might slavery complicate personal relationships?

Assess/Close

Visual/Spatial Have students take on the role of an African American artist from the 1800s. Ask them to create artwork showing what it was like to be enslaved. They may draw, paint, sculpt, or use any other means to express themselves. Encourage students to share their creations with the class. **BL** **ELL**

DBQ Document Based Questions

Answers:

1. Daily life was harsh. They lacked sufficient clothing and food. There were no beds and poor blankets. They worked for endless hours in the fields.
2. They were bought and sold like property and were subject to whatever punishment the slaveholder gave out. Slaves were not protected from abuse by laws.
3. Both seemed to enjoy a happy childhood together. However, the enslaved child faced an adulthood of sin, shame, and misery while the white child's happiness continued into adulthood.
4. An African American family is being sold at an auction attended by well-dressed plantation owners. Most likely, the family will be separated and never see one another again.
5. Louisa's feelings about taking care of the boy may depend on how well she is treated by the child's parents. Louisa may love the boy like her own, because her own children may have been sold away. She may see the boy she loved as a child grow up to reject her because of her place in society.

Focus

Bellringer

Daily Focus Transparency 5-4

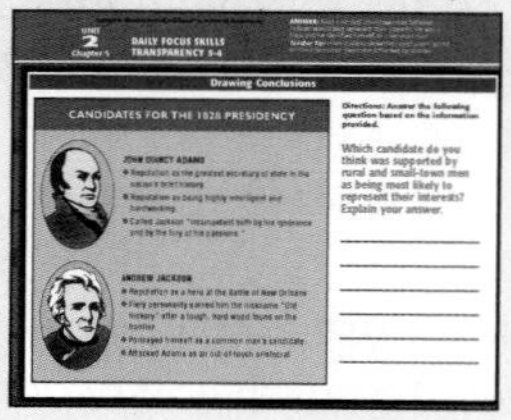

Guide to Reading

Answers: slavery, states' rights, interpretation of the Constitution, national bank, tariffs

Section Spotlight Video

To generate student interest and provide a springboard for class discussion, access the Chapter 5, Section 4 video at glencoe.com or on the video DVD.

Section 4

Section Audio   Spotlight Video

Growing Sectionalism

Guide to Reading

Big Ideas

Government and Society The rise of a new political party represented a disagreement between those who wanted to expand federal power and those who wanted to limit it.

Content Vocabulary

- favorite son *(p. 214)*
- corrupt bargain *(p. 215)*
- mudslinging *(p. 215)*

Academic Vocabulary

- controversy *(p. 213)*
- ignorance *(p. 215)*

People and Events to Identify

- Missouri Compromise *(p. 213)*
- Henry Clay *(p. 213)*
- William Crawford *(p. 214)*
- American System *(p. 214)*

Reading Strategy

Organizing Complete a graphic organizer similar to the one below by listing the divisive issues of the 1820s.

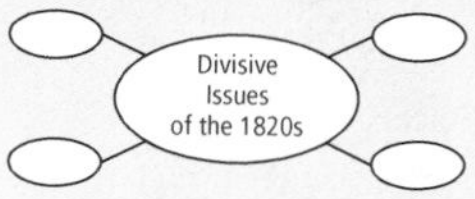

Sectional disputes over slavery and its westward spread eroded the spirit of nationalism that swept the nation after the War of 1812. The one-party political system—dominated by the Democratic-Republicans—began to unravel in the 1820s.

The Missouri Compromise

MAIN Idea The Missouri Compromise tried to resolve, at least temporarily, the growing disagreement between Northern and Southern states over the issue of slavery.

HISTORY AND YOU Have you ever used compromise to solve a dispute with a friend? Read on to find out how Congress established a compromise that maintained a political balance of power.

The Monroe administration's Era of Good Feelings could not ward off the nation's growing sectional disputes and the passionately differing opinions over slavery. Tensions rose to the boiling point in 1819, when Missouri's application for statehood stirred up the country's most divisive issue: whether slavery should expand westward.

In 1819 the Union consisted of 11 free and 11 slave states. While the House of Representatives already had a majority of Northerners, admitting any new state, either slave or free, would upset the balance in the Senate and touch off a bitter struggle over political power.

Missouri's territorial government requested admission into the Union as a slave state in 1819. Acting for slavery's opponents, Congressman James Tallmadge, Jr., of New York proposed a resolution that prohibited slaveholders from bringing new slaves into Missouri. The resolution also called for all enslaved children currently living in Missouri to be freed at age 25. The House accepted the proposal, but the Senate rejected it. Most Senators and members of the House of Representatives from the South voted against the ban, while most from the North voted in favor of it.

Finally, a solution emerged when Maine, which for decades had been part of Massachusetts, requested admission to the Union as a separate state. The Senate decided to combine Maine's request with Missouri's, and it voted to admit Maine as a free state and Missouri as a slave state. This solution preserved the balance in the Senate. Senator Jesse Thomas of Illinois then proposed an amendment that would prohibit slavery in the Louisiana Purchase territory north of Missouri's southern border. This would allow slavery to expand into Arkansas territory south of Missouri, but it would keep it out of the rest of the Louisiana Purchase.

Resource Manager

R Reading Strategies	C Critical Thinking	D Differentiated Instruction	W Writing Support	S Skill Practice
Teacher Edition • Making Connections, p. 215 **Additional Resources** • Guided Reading, URB p. 81	**Additional Resources** • Hist. Analysis Skills Act., URB p. 54 • Quizzes and Tests, p. 66	**Additional Resources** • Reteaching Act., URB p. 75	**Teacher Edition** • Narrative Writing, p. 214 **Additional Resources** • Authentic Assessment, p. 45	**Teacher Edition** • Creating a Map, p. 213 • Creating a Table, p. 214 **Additional Resources** • Read. Essen., p. 59

The Missouri Compromise

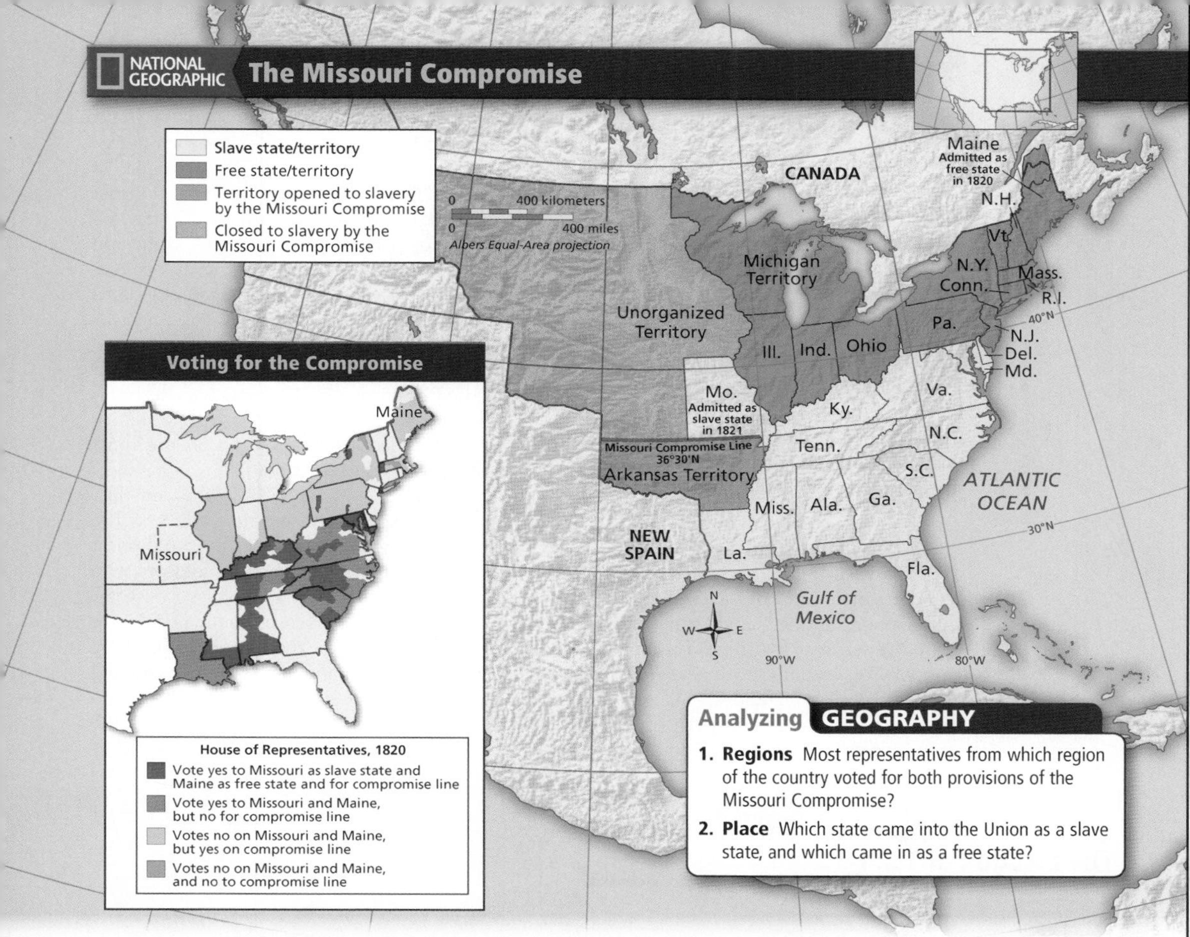

Analyzing GEOGRAPHY

1. **Regions** Most representatives from which region of the country voted for both provisions of the Missouri Compromise?
2. **Place** Which state came into the Union as a slave state, and which came in as a free state?

Since many people at the time thought the Great Plains area north of Missouri was not suitable for farming, it appeared that this **Missouri Compromise** benefited the South. By a very close vote, carefully man- **S** aged by **Henry Clay** of Kentucky, the House of Representatives voted to accept the Compromise. The Compromise held out the hope that pairing the admission of free and slave states together would quiet the dispute over the expansion of slavery.

Once the issue was settled, however, a new problem developed. Pro-slavery members of the Missouri constitutional convention added a clause to the proposed state constitution prohibiting free African Americans from entering the state. This new **controversy** threatened final approval of Missouri's admission to the Union. Clay again engineered a solution by getting the Missouri legislature to state that they would not honor the spirit of the clause's wording.

Despite Clay's efforts, many leaders feared that the Missouri Compromise was only a temporary solution. "I take it for granted," John Quincy Adams wrote, "that the present question is a mere preamble—a title page to a great tragic volume." The Compromise merely postponed a debate over the future of slavery.

Reading Check **Examining** Why was the Missouri Compromise proposed?

Teach

Analyzing GEOGRAPHY

Answers:
1. the South
2. Missouri entered as a slave state; Maine as a free state

S Skill Practice

Creating a Map Have students work in small groups to create annotated maps showing slave and free states before and after the Missouri Compromise. Have them annotate the maps showing the number of seats in the House of Representatives for each state. Show the total representatives from slave and free states in a chart beside the maps. **BL**

Reading Check

Answer:
to keep the Senate balanced between slave and non-slave states

Hands-On Chapter Project
Step 4

Making a Map

Step 4: Primary Source Annotations Students will annotate their map using primary sources.

Directions Returning to their groups, have students research steamboat travel between the Ohio and Mississippi Rivers. Students should collect images and accounts of steamboat travel. Then students will annotate their maps with these images and callouts. Students should use pointers to connect the images and callouts to the relevant location.

Synthesizing Students should collect a variety of information. They should determine which pieces of information are most relevant to the map and most interesting to include as a map annotation. **OL**

(Chapter Project continued on the Visual Summary page)

S Skill Practice

Creating a Table Have students create a table of the four main candidates for president in 1824. Tables should include the candidates' names, party affiliations, home states, and positions on issues. **Ask:** Are the political issues faced then different from the issues we face today? Explain. *(Yes, society is different and more complex today. We have to deal not only with local, state, and national issues but with global issues as well.)* **OL**

W Writing Support

Narrative Writing Have students use library or Internet resources to find out about Andrew Jackson's life before he ran for president in 1824. Have them present their findings in a one-page report. **OL**

Analyzing VISUALS

Answers:
1. Clay seems confused as to whether the race has started. (He won the least number of votes.)
2. The cartoon shows who the cartoonist believed would win.

Differentiated Instruction

The Elections of 1824 and 1828

MAIN Idea The presidential elections of 1824 and 1828 highlighted the growing sectionalism in the nation.

HISTORY AND YOU Do you recall the divisions that led to the creation of the Federalist Party and the Democratic-Republican Party? Read on to learn how the Democratic-Republican Party split over issues in the 1820s.

Politics reflected the sectional tensions of the day. Although the Republicans had supporters throughout the nation, the presidential campaigns of 1824 and 1828 showed how deeply the party was torn along regional lines.

A Battle of Favorite Sons

S Four candidates ran for president in 1824. All belonged to the Republican Party and all were **"favorite sons,"** men who enjoyed the support of leaders from their own state and region. Two candidates, Henry Clay of Kentucky and Andrew Jackson of Tennessee, represented the West. John Quincy Adams, the Massachusetts son of John Adams, who was serving as President Monroe's secretary of state, was New England's favorite son. **William Crawford** of Georgia represented the South.

Crawford ran on the original principles of Jefferson's party—states' rights and strict interpretation of the Constitution. Clay favored the national bank, the protective tariff, and nationwide internal improvements—collectively known as the **American System.** Adams also favored internal improvements but was W less enthusiastic about tariffs. Jackson avoided taking a stand on specific issues. His campaign focused on his leadership qualities and heroism at the Battle of New Orleans.

On Election Day, Jackson won the most popular votes, but no candidate won a majority in the Electoral College. Following constitutional procedure, the election went to the House of Representatives, which would select the president from the three candidates who had received the most electoral votes. Clay, who had placed fourth, was eliminated.

As the Speaker of the House, Henry Clay had tremendous influence, and few doubted whom he would support. Clay and Jackson had been rivals for political leadership in the West. Clay once described Jackson as "igno-

POLITICAL CARTOON PRIMARY SOURCE
The Election of 1824

Analyzing VISUALS
1. **Explaining** Why is Clay scratching his head over the race?
2. **Summarizing** Why is Jackson shown running in third place?

Leveled Activities

BL Content Vocabulary Activity, URB p. 59

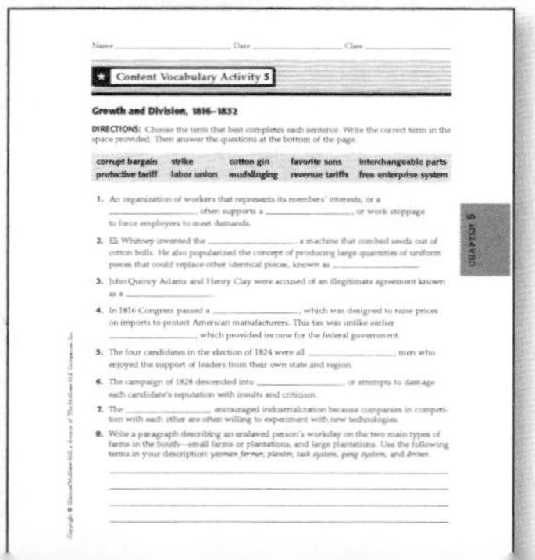

OL Reading Skills Activity, URB p. 53

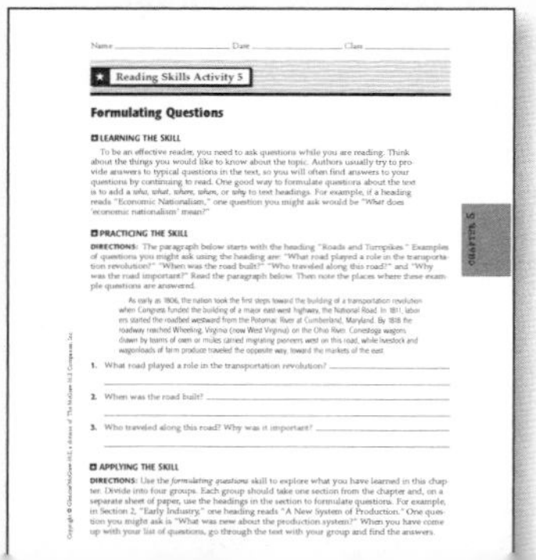

AL Interpreting Political Cartoons, URB p. 73

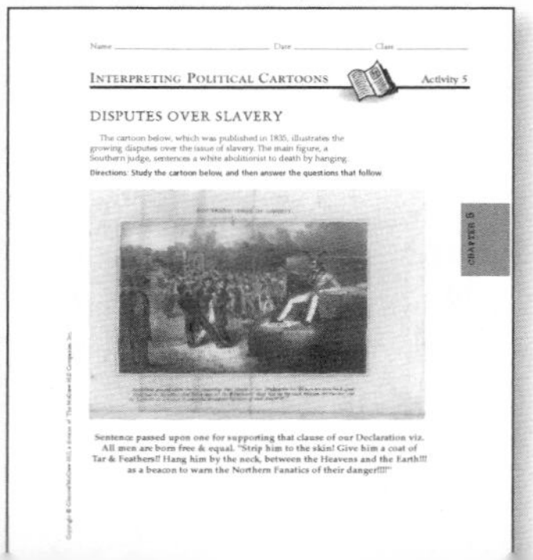

ELL English Learner Activity, URB p. 57

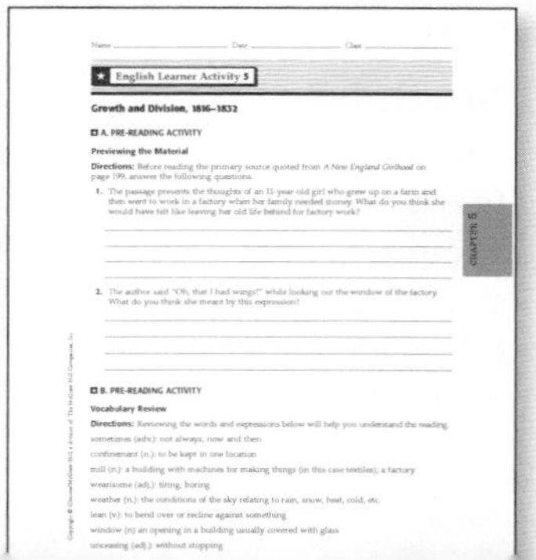

rant, passionate, hypocritical, [and] corrupt." Jackson referred to Clay as the "meanest scoundrel that ever disgraced the image of his god."

On a snowy February 9, 1825, the representatives met to make their choice. As expected, Clay threw his support behind Adams, and he won the House election easily. Adams received 13 votes, while Jackson won 7, and Crawford won 4. Many Jackson supporters accused Clay of arranging votes for Adams in return for a cabinet post. When Adams took office, he did indeed name Clay as his secretary of state, and Jackson's supporters accused Adams and Clay of striking a **"corrupt bargain."** Adams and Clay denied any wrongdoing, but the incident split the party. Jackson's supporters began referring to themselves as Democrats, while Henry Clay and his supporters formed a new party called the National Republicans.

John Quincy Adams Takes Office

In his first message to Congress, John Quincy Adams announced an ambitious program of nationalist legislation that exceeded even Clay's American System. In addition to standard internal improvements, Adams urged that federal revenue also be used to build a national university and astronomical observatories, and to fund scientific research. His proposals, however, struck many legislators as a return to Federalist ideas. His opponents in Congress argued that it was a waste of taxpayers' money.

In the end, Congress granted the president funds for improving rivers and harbors and for extending the National Road westward, but this was far less than he had wanted. The repeated rebuffs he suffered in Congress set the stage for Adams's defeat in 1828.

The Election of 1828

The election of 1828 pitted John Quincy Adams against Andrew Jackson. Jackson fought to achieve a victory that his supporters believed had been unjustly denied him four years earlier. Both candidates engaged in **mudslinging,** criticizing each other's personalities and morals. Adams called his opponent "incompetent both by his **ignorance** and by the fury of his passions." Jackson portrayed himself as the candidate of the common man and attacked Adams as an out-of-touch aristocrat. Jackson also revived the alleged "corrupt bargain" between Adams and Clay to show that the president was untrustworthy. R

When the results came in, Jackson had 56 percent of the popular vote and 178 of the 261 electoral votes, a clear victory. Many of the voters who supported Jackson were from the West and the South, rural and small-town men who saw Jackson as the candidate most likely to represent their interests. The man whose fiery personality had earned him the nickname "Old Hickory," after a tough, hard wood found on the frontier, finally had reached the White House.

Reading Check **Identifying** What did John Quincy Adams hope to accomplish during his presidency?

Section 4 REVIEW

Vocabulary

1. **Explain** the significance of: Missouri Compromise, Henry Clay, favorite son, William Crawford, American System, corrupt bargain, mudslinging.

Main Ideas

2. **Explaining** How did the Missouri Compromise maintain the balance of power in the Senate?
3. **Describing** What events helped John Quincy Adams win the presidency in 1824?

Critical Thinking

4. **Big Ideas** Why was the Democratic Party formed after the election of 1824?
5. **Organizing** Use a graphic organizer similar to the one below to list the terms of the Missouri Compromise.

Missouri Compromise

6. **Analyzing Visuals** Study the maps on page 213. Why was the Missouri Compromise only a temporary measure?

Writing About History

7. **Expository Writing** Suppose that you are a voter in the election of 1828. Write a letter to a family member explaining which presidential candidate you support and why.

History ONLINE
Study Central™ To review this section, go to glencoe.com and click on Study Central.

R Reading Strategy

Making Connections Point out the term *mudslinging* and discuss how *mudslinging* is a term still used today. **Ask:** How is mudslinging in political campaigns today different from the mudslinging in the 1820s? *(Most mudslinging today is used to attack a politician's personal beliefs or stance on an issue, such as taxes or healthcare.)* OL

Reading Check

Answer:
additional internal improvements, including funds for scientific research

Assess

History ONLINE

Study Central provides summaries, interactive games, and online graphic organizers to help students review content.

Close

Explaining Ask students to explain how nationalism gave way to sectionalism. OL

Section 4 REVIEW

Answers

1. All definitions can be found in the section and the Glossary.
2. It allowed a slave state and a non-slave state to enter the Union at the same time keeping Senate representation equal between slave and non-slave states.
3. In the election, no candidate won a mâjority of electoral votes, so the vote went to the House of Representatives who voted to elect Adams. Clay was eliminated from the election because he had come in fourth; however, he was Speaker of the House and hated Andrew Jackson, so worked to make sure that Adams won. Some people said he did it as part of a "corrupt bargain" with Adams in exchange for a cabinet post.
4. Jackson's supporters wished to stress their differences from John Quincy Adams and Henry Clay.
5. Maine admitted to the Union as a free state; Missouri admitted to the Union as a slave state; slavery prohibited in the Louisiana Territory above Missouri's southern border
6. The Missouri Compromise calmed the debate over the future of slavery only temporarily. More debate would come as more territories applied for statehood.
7. Letters will vary, but should indicate at least one reason for supporting the chosen candidate.

Analyzing Information
Ask: How did the effects of nationalism set the stage for sectionalism? *(Nationalism set the interests of the nation above the states. As the Northern and Southern states developed differently—industry in the North and agriculture supported by slavery in the South—their interests were no longer the same. As the North became increasingly hostile toward slavery, the South felt that it had to protect its interests from the rest of the nation. Slavery became one of the issues that led to sectionalism.)* **OL**

Chapter 5 VISUAL SUMMARY

STUDY TO GO You can study anywhere, anytime by downloading quizzes and flashcards to your PDA from glencoe.com.

Effects of Nationalism

Economic Nationalism

- Second Bank of the United States is created.
- Tariff of 1816 is passed to protect the nation's industries.
- The federal government funds the National Road, and states fund other roads and canals, helping to tie the nation together.

Judicial Nationalism

- In *Martin* v. *Hunter's Lessee,* Supreme Court asserts right to hear appeals from state courts in cases involving federal law.
- In *McCulloch* v. *Maryland,* Supreme Court establishes that the "necessary and proper" clause has broad meaning and that the federal government is supreme in its own sphere.
- In *Gibbons* v. *Ogden,* the Supreme Court gives the federal government broad power to regulate interstate commerce.

Nationalism in Foreign Policy

- Andrew Jackson invades Florida; Spain cedes the territory to the United States in 1819.
- The United States issues the Monroe Doctrine, telling Europeans they may no longer colonize the Americas.

▲ *The Erie Canal was one of several developments in transportation that changed the economy and society of the United States in the first half of the nineteenth century.*

▲ *The invention of the cotton gin and an increase in demand in the market led to the spread of cotton plantations and a further entrenchment of slavery as an institution in the South.*

Causes of Sectionalism

Life in the North

- Construction of canals, roads, and railroads is widespread.
- Development of steam engine leads to the first railroads and extensive use of steamboats.
- Industrialization begins, and factories begin to be built to manufacture textiles and other goods.
- Large cities develop as does an urban working class.
- Northern farmers live on individual family farms.

Life in the South

- Eli Whitney's cotton gin makes cotton production with slave labor feasible; cotton becomes main product of the South.
- Southern society is generally divided into elite planters, yeoman farmers, and enslaved African Americans.
- Enslaved Americans generally live on plantations helping to plant and harvest cotton, rice, and sugarcane, although some are employed in other industries.
- A distinct African American culture develops among the enslaved who develop many strategies to cope with and resist slavery.

Hands-On Chapter Project
Step 5: Wrap Up

Making a Map

Step 5: Map Review Teams will present their maps and review them.

Directions Invite team leaders to present their maps. With the class, teams should discuss their maps and why they chose to annotate them in the way that they did. Then members of each team should complete an evaluation of the project. The evaluation should include the following:

- What did I learn from this project?
- What was the most difficult part of this project? Why?
- How could I improve the map?

Evaluating Students will provide a written response to the entire project. **OL**

Chapter 5 ASSESSMENT

Reviewing Vocabulary

Directions: Choose the word or words that best complete the sentence.

1. Unlike earlier measures, the Tariff of 1816 was a

A promotional tariff.
B protective tariff.
C revenue tariff.
D state tariff.

2. The system of ________ changed how factories produced complex products.

A checks and balances
B mill work
C interchangeable parts
D free enterprise

3. Factory workers used work stoppages, or ________, to improve their working conditions during this era of increasing industrialization.

A free enterprise
B extraction
C privatization
D strikes

4. As cotton production increased and slavery spread, plantation owners developed the ________ to organize the work of enslaved people.

A American system
B free enterprise system
C task system
D gang system

5. Some people accused John Quincy Adams of having made a ________ to win the presidency in 1824.

A compromise
B corrupt bargain
C fair deal
D gentleman's agreement

Reviewing Main Ideas

Directions: Choose the best answer for each of the following questions.

Section 1 *(pp. 188–193)*

6. Which of the following cases established the Supreme Court as the final court of appeal?

A *Commonwealth* v. *Hunt*
B *Martin* v. *Hunter's Lessee*
C *McCulloch* v. *Maryland*
D *Gibbons* v. *Ogden*

7. What began the United States' long-term policy of opposing European intervention in Latin America?

A Monroe Doctrine
B Adams-Onís Treaty
C the Missouri Compromise
D the "corrupt bargain"

Section 2 *(pp. 194–201)*

8. The Erie Canal connected Lake Erie to

A the Missouri River.
B the Hudson River.
C the St. Lawrence River.
D the Mississippi River.

9. In 1814 Francis Lowell introduced

A interchangeable parts in the production of weapons.
B mass-produced textiles into the United States.
C the idea of a Second Bank of the United States in Congress.
D a bill to complete the National Road.

TEST-TAKING TIP

As you read a question, underline key phrases so that you can easily refer to them as you review the answer choices.

Need Extra Help?

If You Missed Questions . . .	1	2	3	4	5	6	7	8	9
Go to Page . . .	189	198	199	206	215	190	193	194	198

GO ON

Answers and Analyses
Reviewing Vocabulary

1. B The Tariff of 1816 was instated in order to *protect* American businesses by placing a tax on imported goods. Import taxes raise the prices of foreign goods, which causes consumers to buy the less expensive, American-made goods.

2. C The Constitution includes a system of checks and balances to balance the power of the government. Mills are factories. Free enterprise is an economic principle. Interchangeable parts revolutionized factories. This system allowed unskilled workers to do work that could formerly only be done by skilled craftsmen.

3. D Factory workers did not have any government-granted protections from the actions of their employers. They turned to strikes to halt production and make their voices heard.

4. D The gang system and the task system were both systems of slave labor, so students may have trouble choosing between the two. Reinforce the definitions of each. Under the task system, each enslaved person had a specific job to perform each day, and could rest when the job was done. Under the gang system, enslaved Africans were put into groups that worked all day, regardless of task.

5. B Have students who have trouble with this question review each answer choice carefully and consider similarities and differences in answer choices. Choices *A*, *C*, and *D* all imply a positive arrangement of some sort. Only *B* is negative. When one answer is in direct opposition to all of the other answers, it is usually correct.

Reviewing Main Ideas

6. B As chapters progress, students may have trouble remembering more Supreme Court cases. Encourage students to make a chart or flashcards of all the Supreme Court cases they encounter in reading. These will serve as an effective study aid. In this case, students may be distracted by choice *A*, so reinforce the importance of remembering the names of each case.

7. A President Monroe's statement that the Americas were "henceforth not to be considered as subjects for future colonization by any European powers" became known as the Monroe Doctrine. Explain that this doctrine would provide a basis for foreign relations regarding the Americas well into the future.

8. B Use a map to help students who have trouble with this question. Point out Lake Erie and the Hudson River. The Erie Canal was meant to connect the two bodies of water to increase commerce and travel.

9. B Students should hopefully be able to relate Francis Lowell to the textile industry. Lowell created the first factory town in the U.S., Lowell, MA. It included factories and living quarters for the girls who worked there.

10. B Planters were wealthy landowners who owned large plantations. They held the majority of wealth in the South, but represented a small portion of the population. Yeoman farmers were ordinary farmers. Urban professionals existed, but were a very small group. Some merchants may have been wealthy, but wealthy merchants were more associated with the North.

11. A The invention of the cotton gin revolutionized the South. The technology led to the spread of cotton plantations, leading to increased demand for enslaved Africans.

12. D The key words in the question are *balance of power.* The only answer choice that includes any kind of balance is *D*, one free state and one slave state were added. The other answer choices are all in favor of either free or slave states.

13. A It may be easy for students to remember that the Democratic-Republican Party split into two parties, one with Democrat in the name and the other with Republican in the name. This may lead some students to incorrectly choose *C*. Remind students that these political parties are not the same as the parties today. This may help them remember "National Republican" is correct, not Republican.

Chapter 5 Assessment

Section 3 *(pp. 202–209)*

10. In the social class system of the South, which of the following groups was at the top?

A yeoman farmers
B planters
C urban professionals
D merchants

11. In the early 1800s, slavery expanded in the South because

A the cotton gin was invented.
B industry flourished in the North.
C Spain ceded Florida.
D Gabriel Prosser's rebellion was discovered.

Section 4 *(pp. 212–215)*

12. The Missouri Compromise maintained a balance of power between the North and South in the Senate by

A allowing slavery in all new states that joined the Union.
B splitting Massachusetts into two free states.
C allowing slavery in no portion of the Louisiana Territory.
D adding a slave state and a free state to the Union simultaneously.

13. After the election of 1824, the Democratic-Republican Party split into which two new parties?

A National Republicans and Democrats
B Democratic-Republicans and Federalists
C Democrats and Republicans
D Federalists and Republicans

Critical Thinking

Directions: Choose the best answers to the following questions.

14. The Era of Good Feelings was characterized by

A a decrease in national pride.
B a one-party political system.
C a decrease in urban populations.
D an increase in state power.

Base your answers to questions 15 and 16 on the map below and your knowledge of Chapter 5.

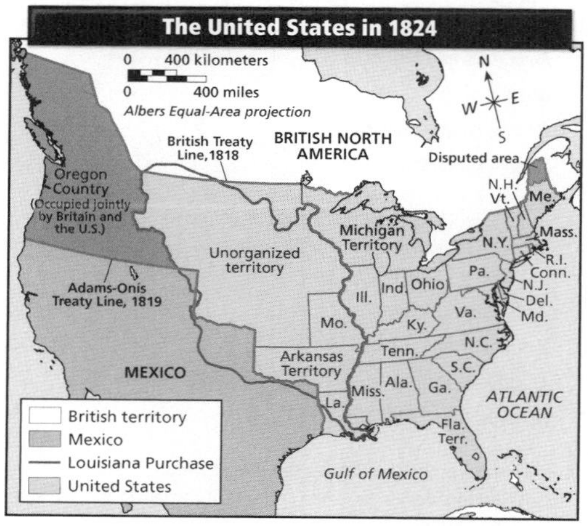

15. Which future state was jointly occupied by Britain and the U.S. in 1824?

A Texas
B Oregon
C Michigan
D Arkansas

16. According to the map, there was a border dispute between British North America and

A Mexico.
B New York.
C Michigan Territory.
D Maine.

Need Extra Help?

If You Missed Questions . . .	10	11	12	13	14	15	16
Go to Page . . .	204	203	212	214	188	R15	R15

GO ON

Critical Thinking

14. B Part of the reason for the "good feelings" was a decrease in political disagreement, due to the fact that only the Republican Party was still intact. There was no competing party, so partisan politics were suspended for a bit. The Era of Good Feelings occurred during a time of increased nationalism, which resulted in the strengthening of federal power over state power, so *A* and *D* would not apply. Urban populations in the North increased during this time.

15. B The map indicates that Oregon Country was jointly occupied by Britain and the United States. Oregon Country was later divided between the two nations, and the U.S. portion became the state of Oregon.

16. D The map is titled "The United States in 1824," so students must look for the disputed boundary. It is marked "Disputed area."

Chapter 5 Assessment

17. During his administration, President John Quincy Adams called for Congress to provide the funds for

A the Second Bank of the United States.
B the fulfillment of the Adams-Onís Treaty.
C a national university.
D the building of the Erie Canal.

Analyze the image and answer the question that follows. Base your answer on the image and on your knowledge of Chapter 5.

18. What is the artist implying about slavery?

A Slavery separates individuals from their families.
B Southern slaveholders only enslaved males.
C Most slaveholders kept families together.
D Enslaved males were more important than females.

Document-Based Questions

Directions: Analyze the document and answer the short-answer questions that follow the document.

In her 1861 memoir, Harriet Ann Jacobs recounted life under enslavement including circumstances endured by her enslaved maternal grandmother:

> "She was the daughter of a planter . . . who, at his death, left her mother and his three children free, with money to go to St. Augustine. . . . It was during the Revolutionary War; and they were captured. . . . She was a little girl when she was captured and sold to the keeper of a large hotel. . . . But as she grew older she evinced so much intelligence, and was so faithful, that her master and mistress could not help seeing it was for their interest to take care of such a valuable piece of property. She became an indispensable personage in the household, officiating in all capacities, from cook and wet nurse to seamstress. She was much praised for her cooking. . . . In consequence of numerous requests . . . she asked permission of her mistress to bake crackers at night, after all the household work was done; and she obtained leave to do it, provided she would clothe herself and her children from the profits."
>
> —from *Incidents in the Life of a Slave Girl*

19. In what ways was Jacobs's grandmother treated like property and not a person?

20. Why is the grandmother allowed to bake crackers?

Extended Response

21. In an essay, explore the state of the Southern economy before the cotton boom, explain why cotton became "king" in the South, and then describe the effects, in the South and in the nation as a whole, of that development. Your essay should include an introduction, at least three paragraphs, and supporting details from the chapter.

STOP

History ONLINE
For additional test practice, use Self-Check Quizzes—Chapter 5 at glencoe.com.

Need Extra Help?

If You Missed Questions . . .	17	18	19	20	21
Go to Page . . .	215	R18	219	219	202–209

20. The mistress would lose nothing by giving her permission, since the grandmother baked on her own time. Since the grandmother would pay for her own and her children's clothes with the money she earned, it was one less expense for the mistress.

Extended Response

21. Students' answers will vary, but should explain how and why cotton rose to become the main cash crop in the South and the various effects it had on the region, including the spread of slavery, and on the nation, such as the development of sectionalism. Essays must include relevant details from the chapter.

17. C Adams' desire for a national university was part of an ambitious plan that included national observatories and scientific funding. His internal improvement ideas were accepted by Congress, but his other ideas were not, including the national university.

18. A In the cartoon, a task-master stands between an enslaved woman and baby and her husband. They are physically being kept apart. For enslaved Africans, keeping their families together was extremely difficult. *B* is untrue; both men and women were enslaved.

Document-Based Questions

19. Jacobs' grandmother was given her freedom, and then captured and sold as a child. She had to work at various tasks for her master and mistress. She had to ask permission to earn extra money. She had to use the money she made to buy clothes for herself and her enslaved family.

History ONLINE
Have students visit the Web site at glencoe.com to review Chapter 5 and take the Self-Check Quiz.

Need Extra Help?
Have students refer to the pages listed if they miss any of the questions.

Chapter 6 Planning Guide

Key to Ability Levels	
BL Below Level	AL Above Level
OL On Level	ELL English Language Learners

Key to Teaching Resources	
Print Material	Transparency
CD-ROM or DVD	

BL	OL	AL	ELL		Resources	Chapter Opener	Section 1	Section 2	Section 3	Section 4	Chapter Assess
					FOCUS						
BL	OL	AL	ELL	Transparency	Daily Focus Transparencies		6-1	6-2	6-3	6-4	
					TEACH						
BL	OL		ELL	Print	Guided Reading Activity, URB*		p. 112	p. 113	p. 114	p. 115	
BL	OL		ELL	Print	Reading Skills Activity, URB					p. 85	
	OL			Print	Historical Analysis Skills Activity, URB			p. 86			
BL	OL	AL	ELL	Print	Reading Essentials and Note-Taking Guide*		p. 62	p. 66	p. 69	p. 72	
BL	OL	AL	ELL	Print	Differentiated Instruction Activity, URB			p. 87			
BL	OL		ELL	Print	English Learner Activity, URB	p. 89					
BL	OL	AL	ELL	Print	Content Vocabulary Activity, URB*	p. 91					
BL	OL	AL	ELL	Print	Academic Vocabulary Activity, URB	p. 93					
	OL	AL		Print	Reinforcing Skills Activity, URB		p. 95				
	OL	AL		Print	Critical Thinking Skills Activity, URB			p. 96			
BL	OL		ELL	Print	Time Line Activity, URB				p. 97		
	OL			Print	Linking Past and Present Activity, URB		p. 98				
BL	OL	AL	ELL	Print	Primary Source Reading, URB				p. 101	p. 99	
BL	OL	AL	ELL	Print	American Art and Music Activity, URB			p. 103			
BL	OL	AL	ELL	Print	Interpreting Political Cartoons Activity, URB		p. 105				
		AL		Print	Enrichment Activity, URB		p. 109				
BL	OL	AL	ELL	Print	Differentiated Instruction for the American History Classroom	✓	✓	✓	✓	✓	✓
BL	OL	AL	ELL	Transparency	Unit Map Overlay Transparencies	✓	✓	✓	✓	✓	✓
BL	OL	AL	ELL	Print	Unit Time Line Transparencies, Strategies, and Activities	✓	✓	✓	✓	✓	✓
BL	OL	AL	ELL	Print	Cause and Effect Transparencies, Strategies, and Activities	✓	✓	✓	✓	✓	✓
BL	OL	AL	ELL	Print	Why It Matters Chapter Transparencies, Strategies, and Activities	✓	✓	✓	✓	✓	✓
BL	OL	AL	ELL	Print	American Biographies		✓	✓		✓	

Note: Please refer to the *Unit 2 Resource Book* for this chapter's URB materials.

* Also available in Spanish

TeacherWorks Plus
All-In-One Planner and Resource Center

- Interactive Lesson Planner
- Interactive Teacher Edition
- Fully editable blackline masters
- Section Spotlight Videos Launch
- Differentiated Lesson Plans
- Printable reports of daily assignments
- Standards Tracking System

Levels					Resources	Chapter Opener	Section 1	Section 2	Section 3	Section 4	Chapter Assess
BL	OL	AL	ELL								
TEACH *(continued)*											
BL	OL	AL			**Supreme Court Case Studies**		p. 9				
BL	OL	AL	ELL		**The Living Constitution**	✓	✓	✓	✓	✓	✓
BL	OL	AL	ELL		**American Issues**	✓	✓	✓	✓	✓	✓
	OL	AL	ELL		**American Art and Architecture Transparencies, Strategies, and Activities**	✓	✓	✓	✓	✓	✓
BL	OL	AL			**High School American History Literature Library**	✓	✓	✓	✓	✓	✓
	OL	AL			**American History Primary Source Documents Library**	✓	✓	✓	✓	✓	✓
BL	OL	AL	ELL		**American Music: Hits Through History CD**	✓	✓	✓	✓	✓	✓
BL	OL	AL	ELL		**StudentWorks™ Plus**	✓	✓	✓	✓	✓	✓
BL	OL	AL	ELL		***The American Vision* Video Program**	✓	✓	✓	✓	✓	✓
Teacher Resources					**Reading Strategies and Activities for the Social Studies Classroom**	✓	✓	✓	✓	✓	✓
					Strategies for Success	✓	✓	✓	✓	✓	✓
					Presentation Plus! with MindJogger CheckPoint	✓	✓	✓	✓	✓	✓
					Success With English Learners	✓	✓	✓	✓	✓	✓
ASSESS											
BL	OL	AL	ELL		**Section Quizzes and Chapter Tests***		p. 75	p. 76	p. 77	p. 78	p. 79
BL	OL	AL	ELL		**Authentic Assessment With Rubrics**						p. 17
BL	OL	AL	ELL		**Standardized Test Practice Workbook**						p. 11
BL	OL	AL	ELL		***ExamView® Assessment Suite***		6-1	6-2	6-3	6-4	Ch. 6
CLOSE											
BL			ELL		**Reteaching Activity, URB**						p. 107
BL	OL		ELL		**Reading and Study Skills Foldables™**	p. 53, p. 68					
BL	OL	AL	ELL		**American History in Graphic Novel**				p. 15		

✓ Chapter- or unit-based activities applicable to all sections in this chapter.

Using ExamView® Assessment Suite

Teach With Technology

What is *ExamView® Assessment Suite?*

Glencoe's *ExamView® Assessment Suite* is a powerful assessment tool that enables you to create and customize tests for your students. Tests can be either printed or administered online.

How can *ExamView® Assessment Suite* help me?

ExamView® allows you to create your own test questions or choose from existing, fully editable banks of questions customized for this book. Question formats include true/false, multiple choice, completion, matching, short answer, and essay, and many questions are based on documents, maps, or graphs. Each question includes reteach information where students can go for more help on the topic. The flexibility of *ExamView®* allows you to develop testing materials that:

- focus on specific skills or competencies
- address state or national standards
- are leveled for different abilities
- can be translated to Spanish in one click

ExamView® Assessment Suite is one of Glencoe's technology resources available for teachers.

History ONLINE
Visit glencoe.com and enter ***QuickPass***™ code TAV9399c6T for Chapter 6 resources.

You can easily launch a wide range of digital products from your computer's desktop with the McGraw-Hill Social Studies widget.

	Student	Teacher	Parent
Media Library			
• Section Audio	●		●
• Spanish Audio Summaries	●		●
• Section Spotlight Videos	●	●	●
***The American Vision* Online Learning Center (Web Site)**			
• StudentWorks™ Plus Online	●	●	●
• Multilingual Glossary	●	●	●
• Study-to-Go	●	●	●
• Chapter Overviews	●	●	●
• Self-Check Quizzes	●	●	●
• Student Web Activities	●	●	●
• ePuzzles and Games	●	●	●
• Vocabulary eFlashcards	●	●	●
• In Motion Animations	●	●	●
• Study Central™	●	●	●
• Web Activity Lesson Plans		●	
• Vocabulary PuzzleMaker	●	●	●
• Historical Thinking Activities		●	
• Beyond the Textbook	●	●	●

Reading Support From Jamestown Education

- **Timed Readings Plus in Social Studies** helps students increase their reading rate and fluency while maintaining comprehension. The 400-word passages are similar to those found on state and national assessments.
- **Reading in the Content Area: Social Studies** concentrates on six essential reading skills that help students better comprehend what they read. The book includes 75 high-interest nonfiction passages written at increasing levels of difficulty.
- **Reading Social Studies** includes strategic reading instruction and vocabulary support in Social Studies content for both ELLs and native speakers of English.

www.jamestowneducation.com

Biography / A&E Home Video / The History Channel

The following videotape programs are available from Glencoe as supplements to this chapter:

- Andrew Jackson: A Man for the People (ISBN 1-56-501647-5)
- Underground Railroad (ISBN 0-76-701679-3)

To order, call Glencoe at 1–800–334–7344. To find classroom resources to accompany many of these videos, check the following home pages:

A&E Television: www.aetv.com
The History Channel: www.historychannel.com

National Geographic

Index to National Geographic Magazine:

The following articles relate to this chapter:

- "America's Poet: Walt Whitman" by Joel L. Swerdlow and Maria Stenzel, December 1994.
- "Escape from Slavery: The Underground Railroad" by Charles L. Blockson and Louis Psihoyos, July 1984.

National Geographic Society Products To order the following, call National Geographic at 1-800-368-2728:

- *Immigration* (CD-ROM)

Access National Geographic's new dynamic MapMachine Web site and other geography resources at:
www.nationalgeographic.com
www.nationalgeographic.com/maps

Reading List Generator CD-ROM — Glencoe BookLink 3

Use this database to search more than 30,000 titles to create a customized reading list for your students.

- ***Reading lists can be organized by students' reading level***, author, genre, theme, or area of interest.
- ***The database provides Degrees of Reading Power™ (DRP) and Lexile™ readability scores for all selections.***
- ***A brief summary of each selection is included.***

Leveled reading suggestions for this chapter:

For students at a Grade 8 reading level:
- ***Narrative of the Life of Frederick Douglass [Adapted],*** by Frederick Douglass

For students at a Grade 9 reading level:
- ***Andrew Jackson: Frontier Patriot,*** by Louis Sabin

For students at a Grade 10 reading level:
- ***Frederick Douglass: The Black Lion,*** by Patricia McKissack & Frederick McKissack

For students at a Grade 11 reading level:
- ***Narrative of the Life of Frederick Douglass,*** by Frederick Douglass

For students at a Grade 12 reading level:
- ***Frederick Douglass and the Fight for Freedom,*** by Douglas T. Miller

Focus

MAKING CONNECTIONS

Can Average Citizens Change Society?

Discuss with students why social change is often difficult to achieve. Activate students' prior knowledge about social reform by asking what they recall about social movements of the past, such as the civil rights movement or the feminist movement. Students may recall that most people are very resistant to change and that large-scale advancements take time and perseverance. Sometimes violence occurs. Have students suggest what they think are the best ways to make reforms acceptable to society. Lastly, ask students to predict how they think the movement to end slavery will affect relations between the North and the South.

Teach

The Big Ideas

As students study the chapter, remind them to consider the section-based Big Ideas included in each section's Guide to Reading. The **Essential Question** in the activities below tie in to the Big Ideas and help students think about and understand important chapter concepts. In addition, the Hands-on Chapter Projects with their culminating activities relate the content from each section to the Big Ideas. These activities build on each other as students progress through the chapter. Section activities culminate in the wrap-up activity on the Visual Summary page.

Chapter 6

The Spirit of Reform

1828–1845

Town members listen to a local politician in the early 1800s.

U.S. PRESIDENTS

Jackson 1829–1837

Van Buren 1837–1841

U.S. EVENTS

1828
- North-South rift develops over tariff

1830
- Mormon religion officially organizes

1832
- Democrats hold their first presidential nominating convention

1833
- American Anti-slavery Society is founded by William Lloyd Garrison

1825 — 1830 — 1835

WORLD EVENTS

1826
- First railway tunnel built in England

1829
- Mexico abolishes slavery

1835
- Fairy tales of Hans Christian Andersen are published

1837
- Queen Victoria ascends to English throne

Section 1

Essential Question: How did democracy expand in the United States during Andrew Jackson's presidency? *(Voting rights expanded, presidential candidates were selected in conventions, Jackson supported the spoils system and destroyed the Second Bank of the United States because he believed it was unconstitutional.)* Point out that in Section 1 students will learn how the nation's political system became more democratic in the early to mid-1800s. **OL**

Section 2

Essential Question: What contributed to changes in American culture in the first half of the nineteenth century? *(Large waves of immigrants, the Second Great Awakening, and a cultural renaissance.)* Explain that in Section 2, students will learn how immigration, a new religious movement, and a new creative period in the arts changed American culture in the first half of the nineteenth century. **OL**

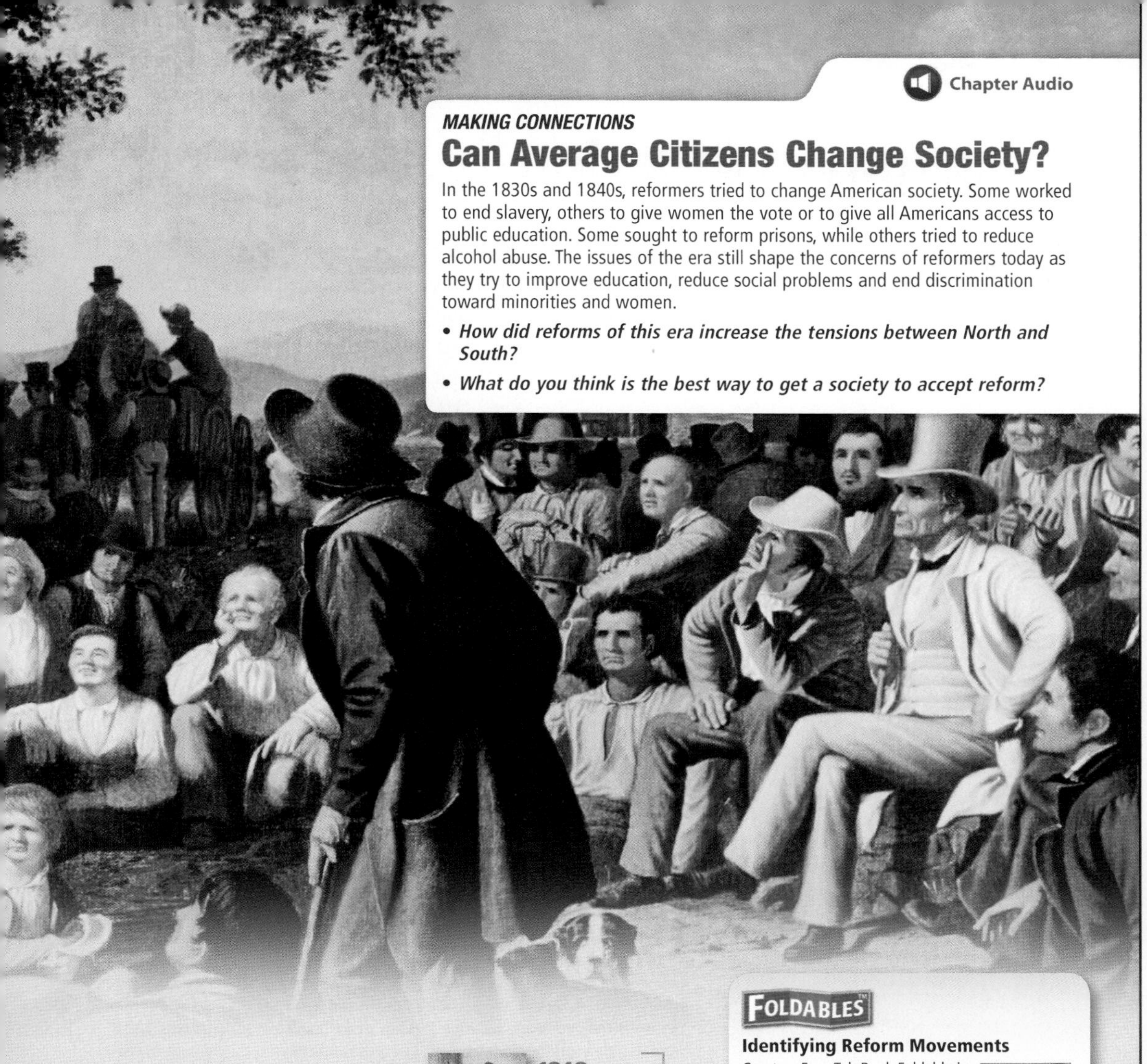

Chapter Audio

MAKING CONNECTIONS

Can Average Citizens Change Society?

In the 1830s and 1840s, reformers tried to change American society. Some worked to end slavery, others to give women the vote or to give all Americans access to public education. Some sought to reform prisons, while others tried to reduce alcohol abuse. The issues of the era still shape the concerns of reformers today as they try to improve education, reduce social problems and end discrimination toward minorities and women.

- ***How did reforms of this era increase the tensions between North and South?***
- ***What do you think is the best way to get a society to accept reform?***

1838
- Cherokee embark on the Trail of Tears

W. Harrison 1841

Tyler 1841–1845

1848
- Women's rights convention is held at Seneca Falls, New York

1840

1845

1839
- Slave revolt occurs aboard the *Amistad*

1842
- China is opened by force to foreign trade

1845
- The Great Irish Famine begins

FOLDABLES

Identifying Reform Movements

Create a Four-Tab Book Foldable in order to identify the major reform movements in American society in the early nineteenth century. For each reform movement, list when it began, its causes, its leadership, and its accomplishments.

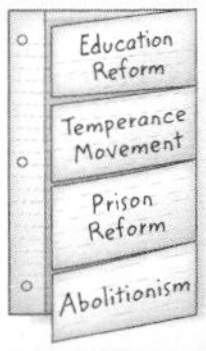

History ONLINE Visit glencoe.com and enter *QuickPass*™ code TAV9846c6 for Chapter 6 resources.

Section 3

Essential Question: What were some of the main areas of society targeted for reform in the first half of the 1800s? *(Answers include: temperance, mental illness, urban poverty, prisons, education, and women's rights.)* Point out that in Section 3 students will learn how the ideals of the Second Great Awakening led to reforms in so many areas of society. **OL**

Section 4

Essential Question: What were the effects of the abolitionist movement on the relationship between the North and the South? *(The abolitionist movement increased tensions enormously between the North and the South, particularly over the regional division of power in Congress.)* Tell students that they will learn in Section 4 how the abolitionist movement in the United States developed and its effects on the nation's society and politics. **OL**

Introducing **Chapter 6**

More About the Photo

Visual Literacy Tell students that this painting, titled *Stump Speaking* (1856), by George Caleb Bingham, depicts an American politician in the 1850s giving a speech on "the stump," or campaign tour. Discuss with students other details in the scene, such as the man in the center of page 221, who is either asking the candidate a question or arguing with him. Ask students how political events have changed or remained the same since the time of this painting.

FOLDABLES™ Study Organizer **Dinah Zike's Foldables**

Dinah Zike's Foldables are three-dimensional, interactive graphic organizers that help students practice basic writing skills, review vocabulary terms, and identify main ideas. Instructions for creating and using Foldables can be found in the Appendix at the end of this book and in the *Dinah Zike's Reading and Study Skills Foldables* booklet.

History ONLINE

Visit glencoe.com and enter *QuickPass*™ code TAV9399c6T for Chapter 6 resources, including a Chapter Overview, Study Central™, Study-to-Go, Student Web Activity, Self-Check Quiz, and other materials.

Focus

Bellringer

Daily Focus Transparency 6-1

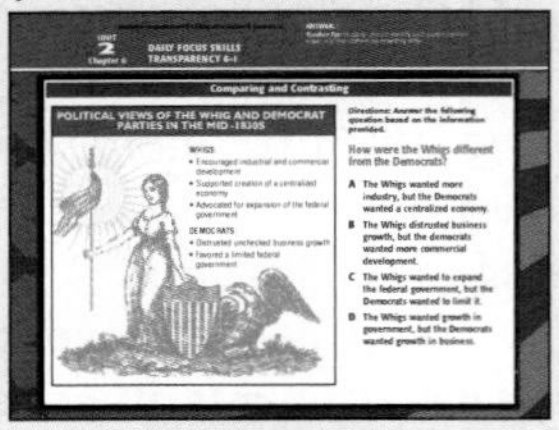

Guide to Reading

Answers to the Graphic:
Jackson's position: states cannot nullify federal laws if the Union is to hold together; Calhoun's position: states have the right to declare a federal law invalid because they created the Union

Section Spotlight Video

To generate student interest and provide a springboard for class discussion, access the Chapter 6, Section 1 video at glencoe.com or on the video DVD.

Section 1 — Section Audio — Spotlight Video

Jacksonian America

Guide to Reading

Big Ideas

Government and Society The American political system became more democratic during the Jacksonian era.

Content Vocabulary
- suffrage *(p. 223)*
- spoils system *(p. 224)*
- caucus system *(p. 224)*
- secede *(p. 225)*

Academic Vocabulary
- evident *(p. 223)*
- exposure *(p. 227)*

People and Events to Identify
- Tariff of Abominations *(p. 225)*
- Daniel Webster *(p. 225)*
- Force Bill *(p. 226)*
- Indian Removal Act *(p. 226)*
- Trail of Tears *(p. 227)*
- Panic of 1837 *(p. 229)*

Reading Strategy

Organizing Complete a graphic organizer, similar to the one below, listing the positions of Jackson and Calhoun during the nullification crisis.

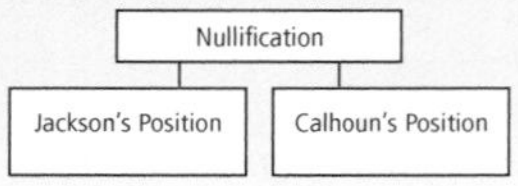

Andrew Jackson was elected with wide popular support. As president, he stood up for federal authority, tried to move Native Americans to the West, and fatally undermined the Bank of the United States. A new party, the Whigs, emerged to oppose him.

A New Era in Politics

MAIN Idea States expanded voting rights in the late 1820s, making the nation more democratic, which in turn helped Andrew Jackson win election. As president, Jackson opposed South Carolina's nullification vote, supported the Indian Removal Act, and closed the Bank of the United States.

HISTORY AND YOU Have you ever felt that someone "played favorites"? Read how Andrew Jackson used the "spoils system" to reward his political supporters.

Margaret Bayard Smith was one of the thousands of Americans who attended the presidential inauguration of Andrew Jackson in 1829. She later wrote to a friend about how much the atmosphere in Washington, D.C., impressed her. "Thousands and thousands of people, without distinction of rank, collected in an immense mass around the Capitol, silent, orderly and tranquil," she explained.

On that day, President Jackson broke a long tradition by inviting the public to his reception. When Smith later attended the White House gala, however, she quickly formed a different opinion about the crowd she had so admired just hours before.

PRIMARY SOURCE

"The *Majesty of the People* had disappeared, and a rabble, a mob, of boys, . . . women, children—[were] scrambling, fighting romping. . . . The President, after having been *literally* nearly pressed to death and almost suffocated and torn to pieces by the people in their eagerness to shake hands with Old Hickory, had retreated through the back way. . . . Cut glass and china to the amount of several thousand dollars had been broken in the struggle to get refreshments. . . . Ladies and gentlemen, only had been expected at this Levee [reception], not the people en masse. But it was the People's day, and the People's President, and the People would rule."

—from *The First Forty Years of Washington Society*

The citizens who had turned the normally dignified inauguration reception into a boisterous affair represented a new class of American voters and a new era in American politics. Beginning in the early 1800s and continuing through the presidency of Andrew Jackson, the nation's political system became more democratic, and ordinary citizens became a greater political force.

Resource Manager

R Reading Strategies	C Critical Thinking	D Differentiated Instruction	W Writing Support	S Skill Practice
Teacher Edition • Summarizing, p. 226 **Additional Resources** • Guide Read Act., URB p. 112	**Teacher Edition** • Ident. Cent. Issues, p. 224 • Making Inferences, p. 226 • Drawing Con., p. 228 **Additional Resources** • Quizzes and Tests, p. 75 • Linking Past and Present, URB p. 98 • Interpreting Political Cartoons, URB p. 105 • Supreme Court Case Studies, p. 9	**Teacher Edition** • English Learners, p. 225 **Additional Resources** • Enrich. Act., URB p. 109		**Teacher Edition** • Using Geo. Skills, p. 227 **Additional Resources** • Reinf. Skills Act., URB p. 95 • Read Essen., p. 62

Turning Point

The Election of 1828

More than three times the number of voters turned out for the election of 1828 than had participated in the presidential election four years earlier. This surge had two sources. First, Andrew Jackson's supporters encouraged high voter turnout by using tactics to appeal to average citizens—parades, speeches, barbecues, and even a popular campaign song. Second, and more important, more men were eligible to vote in 1828. Most states had lowered or eliminated property requirements for voters, allowing many more white men to vote. These new voters heavily favored Andrew Jackson.

ANALYZING HISTORY **Do you think that the election of 1828 indicated a change in the way government worked? Write a brief essay to explain your opinion.**

▲ *Excited that a western war hero of humble origins had made it to the White House, crowds flocked to see Andrew Jackson as he traveled to his inauguration as president in 1829.*

The Election of 1828

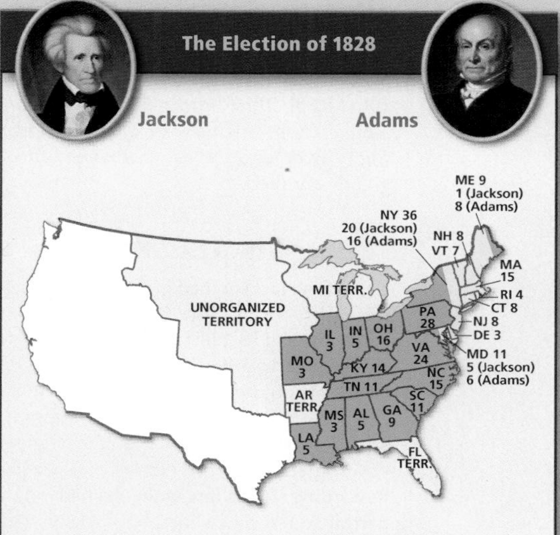

Presidential Candidate	Popular Vote	% of Popular Vote	Electoral Vote
Jackson	647,286	56.03%	178
Adams	508,064	43.97%	83

Voter Participation

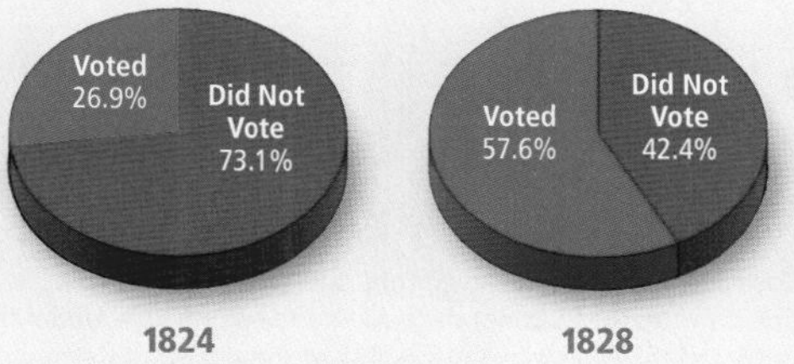

Source: *Historical Statistics of the United States.*

States Expand Voting Rights

In the early 1800s, hundreds of thousands of Americans, mostly white men, gained the right to vote. This happened because many states lowered or eliminated property ownership as a voting qualification. In addition, as cities and towns grew, the percentage of working people who did not own property increased. These people paid taxes and had an interest in political affairs—and they too wanted a greater voice in electing those who represented them.

The expansion of **suffrage**—the right to vote—was **evident** in the turnout for the presidential election of 1828. In 1824 about 355,000 Americans had voted for president. Four years later, more than 1.1 million citizens cast a ballot in the presidential election. Eventually every state made its voting qualifications more democratic, and by 1840, over 2 million Americans voted in the presidential election.

Teach

Turning Point

Background Andrew Jackson's personality also made him an attractive candidate to many Americans. Jackson once killed a man in a duel, an acceptable way to settle disputes in his day. When he considered something a matter of honor, he refused to compromise. Have students study the political campaign poster in this feature. **Ask:** How is Jackson described in this poster? *(He is described as a man of the people and a hero of two wars. His nickname, "Old Hickory," is included, which reminds voters of his toughness and refusal to compromise.)*

Answers:
Students' essays will vary, but opinions should be logically argued and supported with facts from the feature and the section content.

Hands-On Chapter Project Step 1

Creating a Pamphlet

Step 1: Understanding the Significance of Reform Working in small groups, students will skim the chapter looking for the different reforms and reform movements that occurred in the United States during the early to mid-1800s.

Directions Hold a class discussion in which you discuss the different reforms that occurred in the United States during the early to mid-1800s. On the board create a chart that has the headings: social, political, cultural, and economic reform. Have the students help you decide in which category to place each reform. Have each group choose one of the reforms or reform movements listed in the chart.

Identifying Information As reforms and reform movements are added to the chart, students should discuss the importance each has played in the history of the United States. **OL** *(Chapter Project continued on page 231)*

C Critical Thinking

Identifying Central Issues Discuss the spoils system with students. **Ask:** Do you think that the spoils system still exists? What is your opinion of the fairness of the system? *(Answers will vary; students should use logical reasoning in expressing their opinions.)* Discuss the advantages and disadvantages of the spoils system and if people today would think it was democratic or not. OL

Reading Check

Answer: More people had the right to vote, ordinary citizens held government jobs through the spoils system, and Democrats held a national convention to choose the party's presidential candidate.

Additional Support

In 1828 Andrew Jackson benefited from the large number of new voters, many of whom lived on the frontier. Many of the citizens who voted for the first time in 1828 saw in Jackson a man whose origins were little different from their own, and whose achievements they greatly admired.

The Spoils System

Andrew Jackson had great confidence in the capability and intelligence of average Americans. He believed that the majority should rule in a democracy and that ordinary citizens should play a role in government.

C These beliefs led Jackson to support the **spoils system**—the practice of giving people government jobs on the basis of party loyalty. Rewarding supporters with jobs had long been part of American politics, but Jackson was the first president to fire a large number of federal employees so as to appoint his own followers. A shocked John Quincy Adams warned that the policy would make government "a perpetual . . . scramble for office."

Jackson considered the spoils system to be democratic because it put an end to a permanent, nonelected office-holding class. Because government jobs were "so plain and simple," in his opinion, they could easily be rotated at will and given to supporters.

From Caucus to Convention

Jackson's supporters also changed the way presidential candidates were chosen. At that time, political parties used the caucus system to select presidential candidates. Members of the party who served in Congress, known as the party caucus, would meet to choose the nominee for president. Jackson's supporters believed that the **caucus system** restricted nominations to the elite and well-connected.

The Jacksonians replaced the caucus with a national nominating convention. At nominating conventions, delegates from the states gathered to decide on the party's presidential nominee. Supporters believed that conventions allowed the people, not the elite, to decide on party nominees. In 1832 the Democrats held a convention and renominated Andrew Jackson for president.

Reading Check **Examining** In what ways did the United States become more democratic in the early 1800s?

PAST & PRESENT

Choosing a President

Today, nearly all American citizens age 18 and older are eligible to vote. This was not the case in the early 1800s. Under the state constitutions adopted at the time of the American Revolution, the right to vote was usually limited to white males who owned property. Over the next few decades, however, states began lowering or eliminating property requirements for voters. Women could not vote, nor could the overwhelming majority of African American men, even those living in the North who met other requirements for voting. Still, changes in the Jacksonian era meant many more Americans could participate in presidential elections.

The rise of national nominating conventions also changed the process of choosing a president. Rather than congressional party leaders deciding on the party's candidate, delegates from the states could participate in the decision at a nominating convention.

Today, parties still hold national conventions in presidential election years, but voting to choose the party's nominee for president has become largely symbolic. The party's nominee has generally been decided in advance, through state primaries and state caucuses.

1844

▲ *Men crowd around the ballot boxes at a New York City polling station, waiting for their chance to vote in the presidential election of 1844.*

Activity: Technology Connection

Mathematics Have students use the data in the table at the right to create a line or bar graph showing the change in the number of voters in presidential elections between 1824 and 1848. **Ask:** Along with a lowering of voting restrictions, what other reasons might account for the increase in cast votes? *(Possible answers: immigrants becoming citizens, new voters coming of age)*

Challenge interested students to research U.S. population statistics from the period—for example, for census years 1820, 1830, 1840, and 1850—to compare the number of white, male citizens to the number of votes cast. OL

Election Year	Approximate Number of Votes Cast
1824	364,000
1828	1,152,000
1832	1,278,000
1836	1,502,000
1840	2,409,000
1844	2,672,000
1848	2,878,000

The Nullification Crisis

MAIN Idea Resentment about high tariffs led Southern states to claim that states could declare a federal law null or void.

HISTORY AND YOU Have you ever felt so strongly about an issue that you wrote a letter of complaint? Read how Southern states were outraged about tariff rates.

Jackson had not been in office long before he had to focus on a national crisis. It centered on South Carolina, but it also highlighted the growing rift between the nation's Northern and Southern regions.

The Debate Over Nullification

In the early 1800s, South Carolina's economy began to decline. Many of the state's residents blamed this situation on the nation's tariffs. Because it had few industries, South Carolina purchased many of its manufactured goods, such as cooking utensils and tools, from England, but tariffs made them extremely expensive. When Congress levied yet another new tariff in 1828—which critics called the **Tariff of Abominations**—many South Carolinians threatened to **secede,** or withdraw, from the Union. **D**

The growing turmoil troubled one politician in particular: John C. Calhoun, the nation's vice president and a resident of South Carolina. Calhoun felt torn between upholding the country's policies and helping his fellow South Carolinians. Rather than support secession, Calhoun put forth the idea of nullification to defuse the situation. He explained this idea in an anonymously published work, *The South Carolina Exposition and Protest,* which argued that states had the right to declare a federal law null, or not valid. Calhoun theorized that the states had this right because they had created the federal Union.

The issue continued to simmer beneath the surface until January 1830, when Robert Hayne of South Carolina and **Daniel Webster** of Massachusetts confronted each other on the floor of the Senate. The debate consisted of several speeches delivered for over a week. Webster, perhaps the greatest orator of his day, was a ferocious defender of the Union. Hayne was an eloquent champion of the right of states to chart their own course.

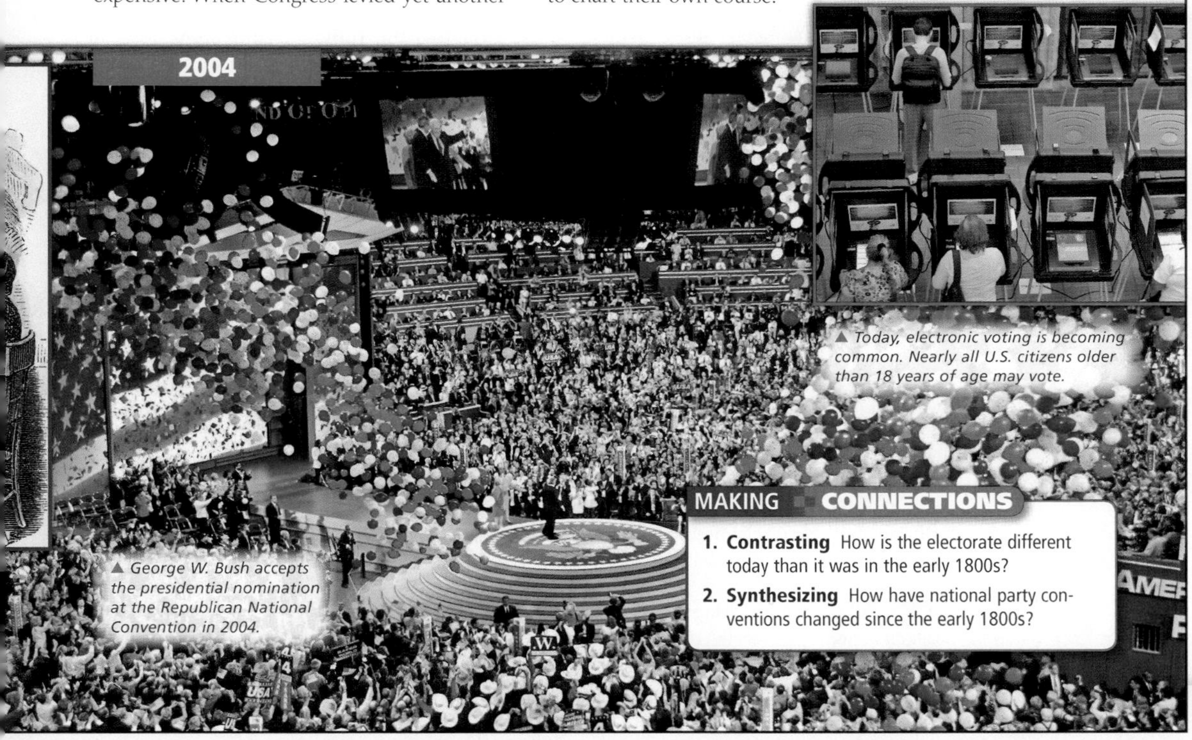

▲ George W. Bush accepts the presidential nomination at the Republican National Convention in 2004.

▲ Today, electronic voting is becoming common. Nearly all U.S. citizens older than 18 years of age may vote.

MAKING CONNECTIONS

1. **Contrasting** How is the electorate different today than it was in the early 1800s?
2. **Synthesizing** How have national party conventions changed since the early 1800s?

D Differentiated Instruction

English Learners Point out to students the content vocabulary term *secede* on this page. Clarify for them that the term means "to withdraw or to leave a group." Tell students that this term will appear frequently in the next few chapters. Explain that students will also read a related word, *secession*, and that this word is the noun form of the verb *secede.* **Ask:** If *secession* is the noun form of the verb *secede,* what do you think it means? *(the leaving or withdrawal from something)* **ELL**

MAKING CONNECTIONS

Answers:

1. Today it includes all American citizens over the age of 18, including women and African Americans.
2. In the 1830s, they actually determined who the party's candidates would be. Today, they confirm and celebrate the selection that is usually made through primary elections and states caucuses.

Additional Support

Activity: Interdisciplinary Connection

Government Discuss the spoils system with students. **Ask:** What are the possible positive aspects of the system? What are the possible negative aspects of the system? *(Positive: helps job of president to have loyal workers, cooperation makes it easier to get things accomplished; Negative: people could be given jobs on the basis of their support rather than on their qualifications and abilities; experienced workers would be replaced with people new to the job.)* **OL** **AL**

R Reading Strategy

Summarizing Have students use a flowchart-style graphic organizer to list the steps in the nullification crisis between the federal government and South Carolina. Then have students use the information they recorded to write a paragraph to summarize the events. BL

C Critical Thinking

Making Inferences Discuss with students the reasons why the United States government was interested in pushing remaining Native American groups in the east off their lands. **Ask:** For what reasons do you think Americans were anxious to relocate Native Americans? *(Possible answer: They wanted their lands for settlement and for farming and they were prejudiced against the Native Americans.)*

Reading Check

Answer:
the imposition of tariffs that hurt an already struggling South Carolina economy

Additional Support

Hayne asserted that the Union was no more than a voluntary association of states and advocated the motto, "Liberty first and Union afterward." Webster countered that liberty depended on the strength of the Union:

PRIMARY SOURCE

"I have not allowed myself, sir, to look beyond the Union, to see what might lie hidden in the dark recess behind. I have not coolly weighed the chances of preserving liberty when the bonds that unite us together shall be broken asunder. I have not accustomed myself to hang over the precipice of disunion, to see whether, with my short sight, I can fathom the depth of the abyss below. . . . Liberty and Union, now and for ever, one and inseparable!"

—from *The Writings and Speeches of Daniel Webster*

Jackson Defends the Union

Several months after the Webster-Hayne debate, President Jackson let everyone know his position on the issue. During a political dinner, Jackson stood to make a toast. Looking directly at John Calhoun, he said, "Our federal Union—it must be preserved." Calhoun's hand shook, but he rose to counter with, "The Union—next to our liberty, most dear."

The war of words erupted into a full confrontation in 1832, when Congress passed yet another tariff law. At President Jackson's request, the new law cut tariffs significantly, but South Carolinians were not satisfied. The state legislature asked South Carolina voters to R elect a special state convention. In November 1832 the convention adopted an ordinance of nullification declaring the tariffs of 1828 and 1832 to be unconstitutional.

Jackson considered the nullification ordinance an act of treason, and he sent a warship to Charleston. In 1833 Congress passed the **Force Bill,** authorizing the president to use the military to enforce acts of Congress. As tensions rose, Senator Henry Clay pushed through Congress a bill that would lower the nation's tariffs gradually until 1842. In response, South Carolina repealed its nullification of the tariff law. Both sides claimed victory, and the issue was laid to rest—at least temporarily.

Reading Check **Summarizing** What caused the nullification crisis?

Policies Toward Native Americans

MAIN Idea During Andrew Jackson's administration Native American groups were forced to relocate onto western reservations.

HISTORY AND YOU Do you know a family that was forced to move from their home by the government? Read on to learn how Native Americans reacted to the Indian Removal Act.

Andrew Jackson's commitment to extending democracy did not benefit everyone. His attitude toward Native Americans reflected the views of many westerners at that time. Jackson had fought the Creek and Seminole people in Georgia and Florida, and in his inaugural address he declared his intention to move all Native Americans to the Great Plains.

This idea had been gaining support in the United States since the Louisiana Purchase. C John C. Calhoun had formally proposed it in 1823, when he was secretary of war. Many Americans believed that the Great Plains was a wasteland that would never be settled. They thought that if they moved Native Americans to that region, the nation's conflict with them would be over. In 1830 Jackson pushed through Congress the **Indian Removal Act,** which provided money for relocating Native Americans.

Most Native Americans eventually gave in and resettled on the Great Plains, but not the Cherokee of Georgia. Over the years, this Native American group had adopted many aspects of white culture. The Cherokee had adopted a written language, drawn up a written constitution modeled on the United States Constitution, and sent many of their children to schools established by white missionaries.

The Cherokee hired lawyers to sue the state of Georgia in order to challenge the state's attempt to extend its authority over Cherokee lands. Their case, *Worcester* v. *Georgia,* eventually reached the Supreme Court. In 1832 Chief Justice John Marshall ordered state officials to honor Cherokee property rights. Jackson refused to support the decision. "Marshall has made his opinion," the president reportedly said, "now let him enforce it."

Most Cherokee resisted the government's offers of western land. Jackson's successor, Martin Van Buren, sent in the army to end the

Extending the Content

Relative and Absolute Dates The South Carolina Ordinance of Nullification was passed on November 24, 1832. The last paragraph of the Ordinance recorded the date in two ways—the actual and the relative dates. First, it gave the actual date, "the twenty-fourth of November, in the year of our Lord one thousand eight hundred and thirty-two." Then it gave a relative date—"the fifty-seventh year of the Declaration of Independence of the United States of America."

conflict in 1838. The army forced the remaining people from their homes and marched them to what is now Oklahoma. About 2,000 Cherokee died in camps while waiting for the relocation to begin. Roughly 2,000 more died of starvation, disease, and **exposure** on the journey, which became known as the **Trail of Tears.**

By 1838, most Native Americans living east of the Mississippi had been moved to reservations. Most American citizens supported the removal policies. Only a few denounced the harsh treatment of Native Americans. Nonsupporters included some National Republicans and a few religious denominations, especially the Quakers and Methodists.

✓Reading Check **Interpreting** What was the Trail of Tears?

Jackson Battles the National Bank

MAIN Idea Jackson deliberately destroyed the national bank; his opponents formed a new political party.

HISTORY AND YOU Do you know of any political parties other than the Democratic and Republican parties? Read how the Whigs fared in the 1836 presidential election.

One of the biggest controversies of Jackson's presidency was his campaign against the Second Bank of the United States. Like most Westerners, and many working people in the East, Jackson regarded the Bank as a monopoly that benefited the wealthy elite.

NATIONAL GEOGRAPHIC Effects of the Indian Removal Act, 1831–1842

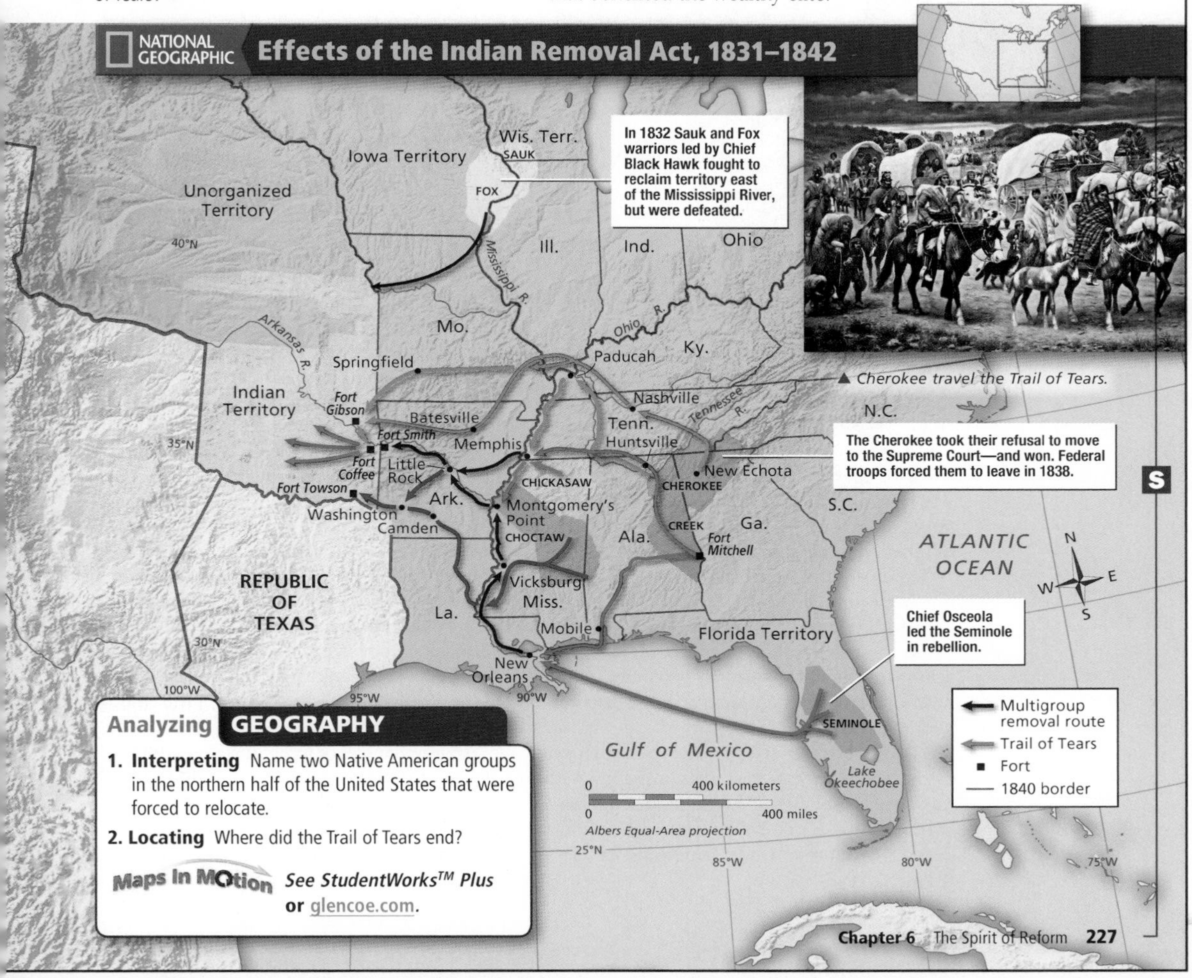

Analyzing GEOGRAPHY

1. **Interpreting** Name two Native American groups in the northern half of the United States that were forced to relocate.
2. **Locating** Where did the Trail of Tears end?

Maps In MOtion *See StudentWorks™ Plus or glencoe.com.*

S Skill Practice

Using Geography Skills

Discuss with students the removal of the Cherokee from Georgia to what is now Oklahoma. **Ask:** **How is the geography of Oklahoma different from the geography of Georgia and how do you think the differences affected Cherokee culture after the relocation?** *(Possible answer: Not only did the Cherokee suffer being torn from homelands they had occupied for centuries, they also had to leave a landscape of forested hills with streams for one of flat, arid plains. This probably destroyed many of their traditional methods of producing food and other ways of life.)* **AL**

Reading Check

Answer: the name given to the forced relocation route of the Cherokee from Georgia to Indian Territory in what is now Oklahoma

Analyzing GEOGRAPHY

Answers:

1. Sauk, Fox
2. in the new Indian Territory north of the Republic of Texas (modern-day Oklahoma)

Differentiated Instruction

Leveled Activities

BL Reinforcing Skills Activity, URB p. 95

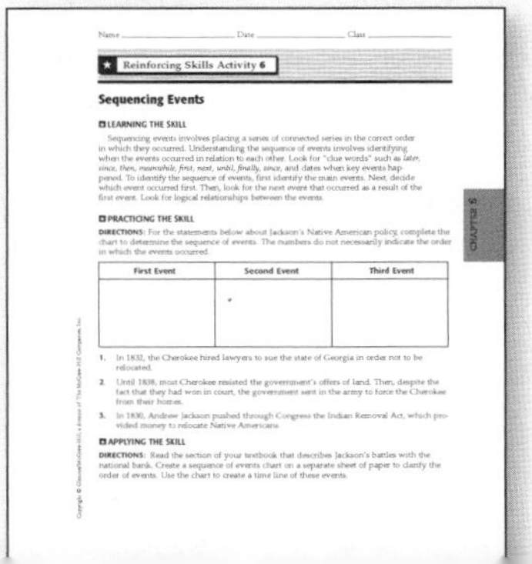

OL Linking Past and Present Activity, p. 98

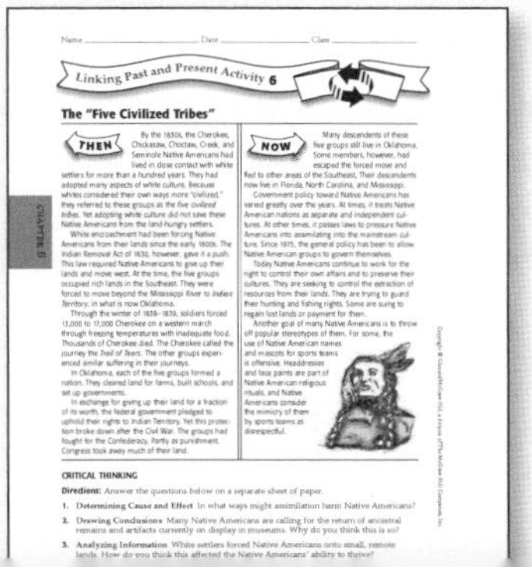

AL Enrichment Activity, URB p. 109

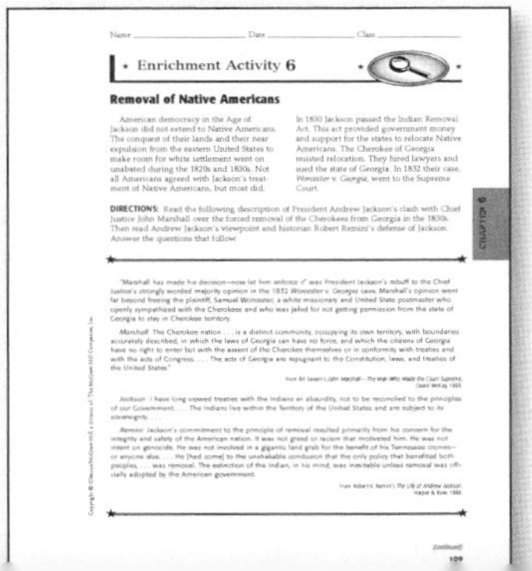

ELL English Learner Activity, URB p. 89

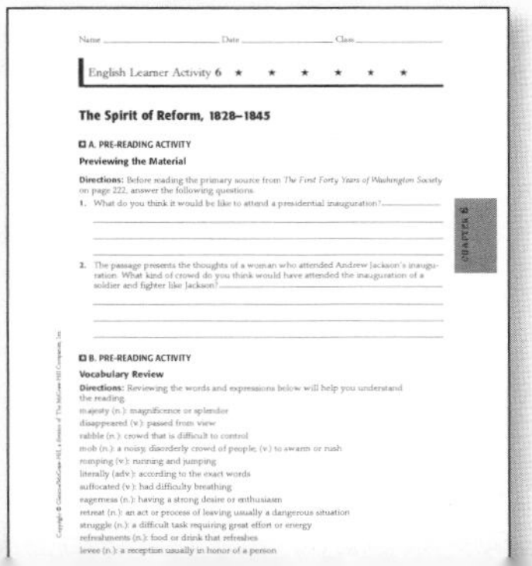

C Critical Thinking

Drawing Conclusions Discuss with students Jackson's issues with the Second Bank of the United States. **Ask:** Why was President Jackson against the Second Bank? *(He believed that the Bank was a financial monopoly controlled by the wealthy elite, and was therefore harmful to regular citizens and undemocratic.)* How did Jackson go about virtually destroying the Bank even though its charter did not expire until 1836? *(He removed the government's deposits and redistributed them among the state banks. This greatly weakened the Bank and essentially killed it.)* **OL**

Analyzing VISUALS

Answers:

1. The cartoon on the right; he is shown standing tall and powerful, bringing down the Bank and causing "smaller men," to run away in fear.
2. That cartoonist thinks that their plans to destroy the Bank are harming the nation, personified by Uncle Sam and the eagle.

Additional Support

POLITICAL CARTOONS PRIMARY SOURCE

Jackson Battles the Bank

▲ *Democrats Andrew Jackson, Thomas Hart Benton, and Martin Van Buren are depicted as quack doctors trying to cure Uncle Sam of his economic ills. Uncle Sam complains that their remedies are making him worse.*

▲ *Jackson holds up an order removing federal deposits from the National Bank. The Bank begins to collapse. The tiny figures scurrying away are newspaper publishers, bankers, and other Bank supporters.*

Analyzing VISUALS

1. **Interpreting Points of View** Which cartoon is pro-Jackson? Why do you think so?
2. **Analyzing** What does the artist of the cartoon on the left think of Jackson and the Democrats' plans for the bank?

Despite its reputation, the Bank played an important role in keeping the money supply of the United States stable. At the time, most paper money consisted of bank notes issued by private state banks. State banks promised that the notes could always be turned in for "hard" money—gold or silver coins. The state banks, however, would often issue more paper money than they could redeem in gold or silver. This allowed them to make more loans at lower interest rates, but it created the danger of inflation—that money might lose its value.

To prevent the state banks from lending too much money, the Bank of the United States regularly collected bank notes and asked state banks to redeem them for gold and silver. This action forced state banks to be careful about how much money they loaned, and it also limited inflation.

C Many western settlers, who needed easy credit to run their farms, were unhappy with the Bank's policies. President Jackson also believed the Bank to be unconstitutional, despite the Supreme Court's ruling in *McCulloch v. Maryland.*

To make the Bank an issue in the 1832 election, Jackson's opponents in Congress introduced a bill extending the Bank's charter for another 20 years. Congress passed the bill, but Jackson vetoed it. It quickly became clear that most Americans supported Jackson as he easily went on to win a second term.

Jackson took his reelection as a directive from the people to destroy the Bank at once, even though its charter did not run out until 1836. He removed the government's deposits from the Bank and placed them in state banks. The removal of the deposits greatly weakened the bank, leading to a slow death. Jackson had won a major political victory by attacking the Bank. Later, however, critics would charge that destroying the Bank contributed significantly to the financial woes that plagued the country in the years ahead.

Andrew Jackson's forceful style earned him plenty of detractors, and by the mid-1830s a new party had emerged to oppose him. The group named itself the Whigs after the party in England that had worked to limit the king's power. The Whigs advocated a stronger federal

Activity: Economics Connection

Federal Reserve System Explain to students that over time it became apparent to the nation's financial and political leaders that a central bank or banking system was necessary for the economic well-being of the country. Have students write a report on the roots, structure, and main functions of the Federal Reserve System. In their reports, students should compare the Federal Reserve to the Second Bank of the United States. **Ask:** How is the Federal Reserve System today the same as and different from the Second Bank of the United States? *(Answers will vary, but may include keeping the money supply stable and preventing inflation.)* **OL**

government and support for industrial and commercial development. Jackson's Democrats, on the other hand, continued to favor a limited federal government.

Martin Van Buren

The Whigs were united in opposing Jackson, but they were unable to settle on a leader. During the 1836 presidential election, Jackson's popularity and the nation's continuing prosperity helped Democrat Martin Van Buren defeat the Whigs, who ran three candidates for president.

The new president had little time to savor his victory. Shortly after Van Buren took office, a crippling economic crisis hit the nation. During this **Panic of 1837,** as the crisis was called, many banks and businesses failed. Thousands of farmers lost their land, and unemployment soared among eastern factory workers. Van Buren, a firm believer in his party's philosophy of a limited federal government, did little to ease the crisis.

"Tippecanoe and Tyler Too"

With the nation experiencing hard times, the Whigs looked forward to ousting the Democrats in the presidential election of 1840. They nominated General William Henry Harrison, who was regarded as a hero for his role in the Battle of Tippecanoe and in the War of 1812. John Tyler, a Southerner and former Democrat who had left his party in protest over the nullification issue, joined the ticket as the vice presidential candidate. Adopting the campaign slogan "Tippecanoe and Tyler too," the Whigs blamed Van Buren for the economic depression and presented Harrison, a man born to wealth and privilege, as a simple frontiersman.

The strategy worked. Harrison won a decisive victory—234 electoral votes to 60, although the popular vote was much closer. On March 4, 1841, Harrison delivered his inauguration speech. The weather that day was bitterly cold, but Harrison insisted on delivering his nearly two-hour address without a hat or coat. He came down with pneumonia and died 32 days later, thereby serving the shortest term of any American president. Vice President John Tyler then became president.

Tyler's rise to the presidency shocked Whig leaders. Tyler actually opposed many Whig policies, and party leaders had placed him on the ticket mainly to attract Southern voters. The Whigs in Congress tried to push through their agenda anyway, including a Third Bank of the United States and a higher tariff, but Tyler sided with the Democrats on these key issues.

Foreign relations occupied the country's attention during much of Tyler's administration, especially relations with Great Britain. Disputes over the Maine-Canadian border, and other issues, resulted in the 1842 Webster-Ashburton Treaty, which established the border between the United States and Canada from Maine to Minnesota.

Reading Check **Identifying** What new political party won the presidential election of 1840?

Section 1 REVIEW

Vocabulary

1. **Explain** the significance of: suffrage, spoils system, caucus system, Tariff of Abominations, secede, Daniel Webster, Force Bill, Indian Removal Act, Trail of Tears, Panic of 1837.

Main Ideas

2. **Explaining** Why did President Jackson support the spoils system?
3. **Describing** How was the nullification crisis resolved?
4. **Summarizing** How did the system of checks and balances in the federal government fail during the struggle over the Indian Removal Act?
5. **Organizing** Use a graphic organizer, similar to the one below, to list the policies of the Whigs and Jacksonian Democrats.

Party	Policies
Whigs	
Democrats	

Critical Thinking

6. **Big Ideas** In what ways did the United States become more democratic during Jackson's administration?
7. **Analyzing Visuals** Study the circle graphs on page 223. How much had voter participation increased in 1828 over 1824?

Writing About History

8. **Persuasive Writing** Suppose that you are a Native American living in the United States during Andrew Jackson's presidency. Write an essay giving your opinion of the Indian Removal Act.

History ONLINE
Study Central™ To review this section, go to glencoe.com and click on Study Central.

Reading Check

Answer:
the Whig Party

Assess

History ONLINE

Study Central™ provides summaries, interactive games, and online graphic organizers to help students review content.

Close

Summarizing Ask: What was the significance of Andrew Jackson's election to the presidency? *(He was considered a frontiersman and a military hero and appealed to middle- and working-class voters. Once he was elected, he made changes to the democratic process that expanded participation.)* OL

Section 1 REVIEW

Answers

1. All definitions can be found in the section and the Glossary.
2. He felt it was more democratic than having a professional class of bureaucrats running the government.
3. Henry Clay pushed through Congress a bill that would lower the nation's tariffs gradually until 1842. In response, South Carolina repealed its nullification of the tariff law.
4. President Jackson refused to use his executive power to uphold a decision of the Supreme Court because he did not agree with it.
5. Whigs advocated expanding federal government, encouraging industrial and commercial development, and creating a central economy. Democrats favored limited federal government.
6. More white males, regardless of wealth or class, participated in government through voting and government jobs.
7. It had more than doubled from 26.9% to 57.6%.
8. Students' letters will vary, but should reflect the situation before the forced location began.

Focus

Bellringer
Daily Focus Transparency 6-2

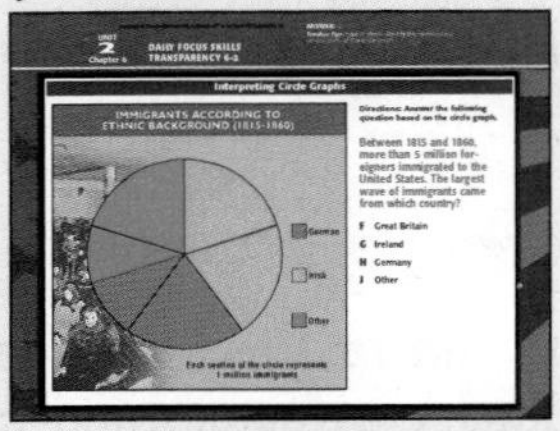

Guide to Reading
Answers to the Graphic:
Unitarians: Believe Jesus was a great teacher, not the Son of God. Believe God is a unity, not a trinity; Universalists: Believe in universal salvation and reject the idea of hell; Mormons: Followers of Joseph Smith believe that God is coming and that they need to build a kingdom on Earth to receive him; Shakers: Believe in communal life. Because they did not marry or have children, their group could only grow through converts.

Section Spotlight Video
To generate student interest and provide a springboard for class discussion, access the Chapter 6, Section 2 video at glencoe.com or on the video DVD.

Resource Manager

Section 2 — Section Audio — Spotlight Video

A Changing Culture

Guide to Reading

Big Ideas
Group Action The Second Great Awakening increased membership in many religious groups in the United States.

Content Vocabulary
- nativism *(p. 232)*
- utopia *(p. 234)*
- romanticism *(p. 234)*
- transcendentalism *(p. 234)*

Academic Vocabulary
- predominantly *(p. 232)*
- philosopher *(p. 234)*

People and Events to Identify
- Know-Nothings *(p. 232)*
- Second Great Awakening *(p. 232)*
- Charles Grandison Finney *(p. 233)*
- Joseph Smith *(p. 233)*

Reading Strategy
Categorizing Complete a graphic organizer, similar to the one below, by listing the beliefs of religious groups during the Second Great Awakening.

Religious Groups	Beliefs

Between 1815 and 1860, over 5 million immigrants arrived in the United States. Most of these newcomers found opportunity and a fresh start, but some also found discrimination and prejudice. At the same time, a new religious movement began to change American society.

The New Wave of Immigrants

MAIN Idea In the early 1800s, millions of Irish and Germans immigrated to the United States. The many Catholics among them encountered religious prejudice.

HISTORY AND YOU Recall what you may have read about conflicts between Protestants and Catholics in Europe. During the 1800s, many Protestant Americans disliked the large numbers of Catholics coming into the country. Read on to learn about nativism in the early 1800s in the United States.

In June 1850 Daniel Guiney decided to leave his impoverished town in Ireland and move to the United States. Ireland was suffering a devastating famine. Tens of thousands of citizens were dying of starvation, while many more were fleeing the country. By August, Guiney had moved to Buffalo, New York. After settling in, Guiney wrote home about the wondrous land where he now resided:

PRIMARY SOURCE

"We mean to let you know our situation at present. . . . We arrived here about five o'clock in the afternoon of yesterday, fourteen of us together, where we were received with the greatest kindness of respectability. . . . When we came to the house we could not state to you how we were treated. We had potatoes, meat, butter, bread, and tea for dinner. . . . If you were to see Denis Reen when Daniel Danihy dressed him with clothes suitable for this country, you would think him to be a boss or steward, so that we have scarcely words to state to you how happy we felt at present."

—from *Out of Ireland*

Daniel Guiney was just one of the millions of immigrants who came to the United States in search of a better life in the mid-1800s. Between 1815 and 1860, the United States experienced a massive influx of immigrants, mostly from Europe. Many had fled violence and political turmoil at home, while others sought to escape starvation and poverty. Although immigrants provided a large source of labor for America's industries, many citizens feared the influence of so many foreigners.

R Reading Strategies	C Critical Thinking	D Differentiated Instruction	W Writing Support	S Skill Practice
Teacher Edition • Act. Prior Know., p. 232 • Summarizing, p. 233 **Additional Resources** • Guide Read Act., URB p. 113	**Teacher Edition** • Det. Cause/Effect, p. 231 **Additional Resources** • Crit. Think. Skills, URB p. 96 • Quizzes and Tests, p. 75	**Additional Resources** • Diff. Instr., URB p. 87	**Teacher Edition** • Expository Writing, p. 233 **Additional Resources** • Amer. Art/Music, URB p. 103	**Additional Resources** • Hist. Analysis Skills, URB p. 86 • Read. Essen., p. 66

PRIMARY SOURCE

The Irish Famine and Immigration to America

▲ Starving peasants try to break into a workhouse during the Great Irish Famine of 1846-47.

Irish Population Decline, 1841–1851

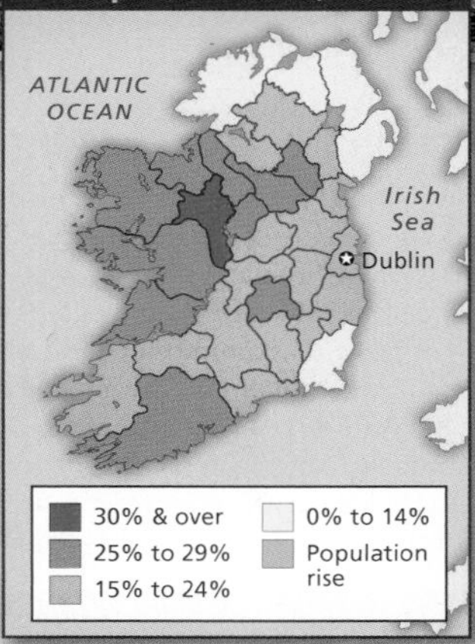

Irish Immigration to the U. S., 1830–1860

Source: *Historical Statistics of the United States: Colonial Times to 1970.*

▲ Irish immigrants arrive in New York in 1847. Economic opportunities brought the Irish to America. Irish men worked in factories, helped build railroads, and took part in other construction projects. Irish women took jobs in factories and as domestic servants in the homes of the growing middle and upper classes.

Analyzing VISUALS

1. **Interpreting** In what year did Irish immigration to the United States peak? Why might it have declined afterward?
2. **Explaining** What was the main pull factor that brought Irish immigrants to the United States?

Germans and Irish Arrive

The largest wave of immigrants, almost two million, came from Ireland. The Irish were fleeing a famine that began in 1845, when a fungus destroyed much of the nation's potato crop—a mainstay of the Irish diet. Most Irish immigrants arrived with no money and few skills. They generally settled in the industrialized cities of the Northeast, where many worked as unskilled laborers and servants.

Germans were the second-largest group of immigrants to arrive. At the time, Germany was divided into many states and, in 1848, revolutionaries across Germany tried and failed to impose reforms. The ensuing violence and repression convinced many Germans to emigrate. By 1860, over 1.5 million had arrived in the United States. Most had enough money to buy land and settle in Ohio and Pennsylvania, where they became farmers or went into business. **C**

Teach

C Critical Thinking

Determining Cause and Effect Discuss with students the reasons for Irish and German immigration in this period. **Ask:** Why did so many Irish and German immigrants come to the United States at this time? *(The Irish were in the midst of a terrible famine and the Germans came to escape revolution and the resulting repression in the German states. Both groups also came hoping to improve their economic status.)* Have students predict the effects of these waves of immigrants on American society. **OL**

Analyzing VISUALS

Answers:

1. in about 1851; because conditions improved in Ireland or there were no more Irish who could afford the journey or who wanted to make it
2. economic opportunities

Hands-On Chapter Project
Step 2

Creating a Pamphlet

Step 2: Researching Selected Reforms Each group will do research on the reform movement selected in Step 1.

Directions Have students use the library, Internet, and other resources to learn more about the reform movement chosen. Groups should write a persuasive essay encouraging support for the reform movement.

Identifying Central Issues Students must identify the most important information about the selected reform movement and develop those important pieces of information into a persuasive essay. **OL**

(Chapter Project continued on page 237)

R Reading Strategy

Activating Prior Knowledge Ask students to recall what they learned about the first Great Awakening. Remind them that it occurred in the United States in colonial times and its leaders included Jonathan Edwards and George Whitefield. **Ask:** How was the Second Great Awakening similar to and different from the first Great Awakening? *(The first Great Awakening developed in reaction to a perceived loss of religious zeal. It featured fiery sermons that promised that sinners would go to hell for eternity. The Second Great Awakening also grew out of a perception that Americans were losing their faith, however, sermons, while emotional, were geared more to creating emotional outpourings of faith, rather than great fear.)* **OL**

Reading Check

Answer:
The influx of immigrants with different languages, religions, and cultural backgrounds led to this hostility toward foreigners.

Additional Support

Nativism

While immigrants often found a new sense of freedom in the United States, some encountered discrimination. The presence of people from different cultures, with different languages and different religions, produced feelings of **nativism,** or hostility toward foreigners.

In the 1800s, many Americans were anti-Catholic. Many Protestant ministers preached anti-Catholic sermons and, occasionally, anti-Catholic riots erupted. The arrival of millions of **predominantly** Catholic Irish and German immigrants led to the rise of several nativist groups, such as the Supreme Order of the Star-Spangled Banner, founded in 1849. These groups pledged never to vote for a Catholic and pushed for laws banning immigrants and Catholics from holding public office. In July 1854 delegates from these groups formed the American Party. Membership in the party was secret, and those questioned about it were obliged to answer, "I know nothing." The **Know-Nothings,** as the party was nicknamed, built a large following in the 1850s.

Reading Check **Analyzing** Why did nativism become so strong in the mid-1800s?

A Religious Revival

MAIN Idea During the Second Great Awakening, many revivals were held, and new religious denominations formed.

HISTORY AND YOU Have you ever been inspired by a gifted speaker? Read on to learn how ministers used emotional sermons to reach their audiences.

While immigrants added to the diversity of society, Americans were transforming society in their own ways. One important change occurred in religious life, where Protestantism experienced a dramatic revival, and new forms of worship emerged.

R The Second Great Awakening

By the end of the 1700s, many church leaders had grown concerned that Americans' commitment to the Christian faith was weakening. In the early 1800s, ministers began an effort to revive people's commitment to religion. The resulting movement came to be called the **Second Great Awakening.** It began in Kentucky among frontier farmers and spread to the rest of the country. Leaders of various Protestant denominations—most

PRIMARY SOURCE
The Second Great Awakening

▲ *Charles Grandison Finney (above) was a founder of modern revivalism. Finney's emotional sermons helped launch the Second Great Awakening, which was spread across the nation at outdoor camp meetings (left).*

Activity: Collaborative Learning

Group Activity The early 1800s saw many new social and cultural movements emerge. One of these was the Second Great Awakening. Organize the class into small groups. Have each group discuss and speculate how the Second Great Awakening might have affected different social groups in different parts of the United States. Each member of the group should contribute to the discussion. As a class, have students discuss their group's ideas and speculations.

often Methodists, Baptists, and Presbyterians—held camp meetings that attracted thousands of followers for several days of song, prayer, and emotional outpourings of faith.

The basic message of the Second Great Awakening was that individuals must re-admit God and Jesus into their daily lives. The new revivalism rejected the traditional Calvinist idea that only a chosen few were predestined for salvation. Instead, ministers preached that all people could attain grace through faith.

One of the most prominent advocates of this new message was a Presbyterian minister named **Charles Grandison Finney.** Finney preached that each person contained within himself or herself the capacity for spiritual rebirth and salvation. Finney helped found modern revivalism. His camp meetings were carefully planned and rehearsed to create as much emotion as possible. He compared his methods to those used by politicians and salespeople, and he used emotion to focus people's attention on his message.

Finney began preaching in upstate New York, where he launched a series of revivals in towns along the Erie Canal. He then took his message to the cities of the Northeast. Finney warned against using politics to change society. He believed that if Christian ideas reformed people from within, society would become better, but if people remained selfish and immoral, political reforms would not make any difference.

▲ *Finney's success enabled him to build the Broadway Tabernacle in New York City. The church opened in 1836 and held 2,400 people.*

Analyzing VISUALS

1. **Interpreting** Study the picture on page 232. How is the audience reacting?
2. **Theorizing** Why do you think revivalism was effective in spreading Christian ideas?

New Religious Groups

A number of new religious groups also emerged during the Second Great Awakening. Many Americans were looking for spiritual answers to the problems in their lives but chose to look to new religious ideas rather than return to traditional Protestant beliefs.

Unitarians and Universalists Two groups that grew rapidly in the 1830s were the Unitarians and Universalists. Unitarians reject the idea that Jesus was the son of God, arguing instead that he was a great teacher. Their name comes from the belief that God is a unity, rather than a trinity of Father, Son, and Holy Spirit. Universalists believe in the universal salvation of souls. They reject the idea of hell and believe that God intends to save everyone.

The Mormons Another group that began during this period was the Church of Jesus Christ of Latter-day Saints, whose followers are commonly known as Mormons. **Joseph Smith,** a New Englander living in western New York, began preaching Mormon ideas in 1830 after claiming to have been called to restore the Christian church to its original form. Smith published *The Book of Mormon* in that year, saying it was a translation of words inscribed on golden plates he had received from an angel. The text told of the coming of God and the need to build a kingdom on Earth. Smith made hundreds of converts across New England and the Midwest.

After enduring harassment in Ohio, Missouri, and elsewhere, Mormons moved to Commerce, Illinois, in 1839. They bought the town and renamed it Nauvoo. The group prospered in the Midwest, and Nauvoo grew to about 15,000 by 1844. Persecution continued, however, and that same year local residents murdered Smith. Brigham Young then became the leader of the Church. The Mormons left Illinois and headed west to Utah Territory, where they established permanent roots.

R Reading Strategy

Summarizing Have students write a sentence that summarizes the main goals of each group active in the Second Great Awakening. BL ELL

W Writing Support

Expository Writing Instruct students to locate a sermon from the period of the Second Great Awakening. Ask them to analyze the text and identify ways in which the speaker used emotion to focus attention on the point being made. Have students list at least three specific phrases in the work that indicate an emotional appeal or attempt at persuasion. Then have students write an essay about the three phrases, explaining what likely effect each had on an audience listening to the sermon. AL

Analyzing VISUALS

Answers:

1. Many of the audience members are overcome with emotion or even appear to have fainted.
2. Answers will vary, but should address the question logically.

Differentiated Instruction

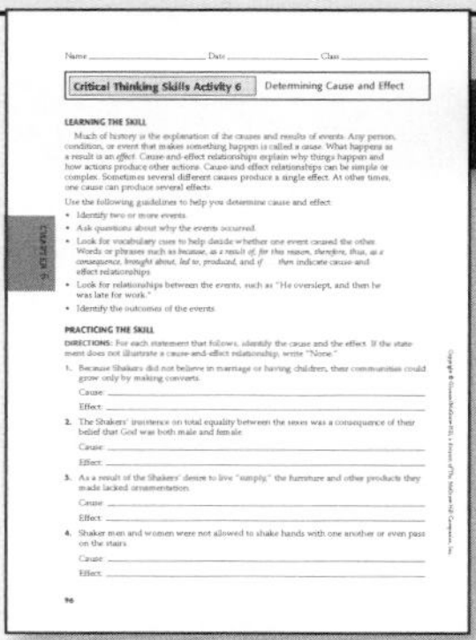
Critical Thinking Skills Activity 6 Determining Cause and Effect

Critical Thinking Skills Activity 6, URB p. 96

Determining Cause and Effect

Objective: Distinguish between cause and effect.

Focus: Read the statements about Shaker culture.

Teach: Make a list of the different aspects of Shaker culture that you learned from the statements.

Assess: Choose one aspect of Shaker culture and write a few sentences describing how it would affect your daily life.

Close: Imagine you are a Shaker. Write a few paragraphs describing your daily activities.

Differentiated Instruction Strategies

- **BL** Draw a design for Shaker furniture.
- **AL** Research a Shaker community and write a detailed description of it.
- **ELL** For each statement, write words or phrases that identify the cultural aspects described. For example, for Statement 1, you might write: "did not believe in marriage or having children."

People IN HISTORY

Ask: Why might Thoreau and Fuller have been controversial in their lifetimes? *(Possible answer: Thoreau was seemingly anti-social, a failure at conventional life, and advocated protesting against the government. Fuller led a life that was largely unconventional for a woman in the early 1800s and many of her ideas were contrary to what was generally acceptable at the time.)*

Henry David Thoreau

Answer: He wanted to live close to nature, to find out for himself what the point of living is.

Margaret Fuller

Answer: She was a philosopher and women's rights advocate, magazine publisher, and foreign-war correspondent.

Reading Check

Answer:
Individuals must re-admit God and Christ into their daily lives.

Additional Support

For an excerpt of Emerson's writing, see pages R66–67 in **American Literature Library.**

Utopian Communities

Some Americans in the 1830s concluded that society had corrupted human nature. They decided that the solution was to separate from society and form a **utopia,** or ideal society. Cooperative living and the absence of private property characterized these communities. Perhaps the best known were Brook Farm, a cooperative community in Massachusetts, and the Oneida Community, a religious society in upstate New York.

The Shakers were a religious group that established utopian communities. The group got its name from a ritual "shaking" dance its members performed. The society believed in social and spiritual equality for all of its members. The first Shaker communities had been founded in the 1780s. They peaked with some 6,000 members before their numbers began to decline. Since they did not believe in marrying or having children, the group could only expand by making converts.

Reading Check **Summarizing** What was the basic message of the Second Great Awakening?

Cultural Renaissance

MAIN Idea Nationalism and sectionalism gave rise to a creative period for American writers and artists.

HISTORY AND YOU Do you read a newspaper regularly? Read on to learn how the "penny press" made newspapers affordable for average people.

The optimism of the Second Great Awakening also influenced **philosophers** and writers. Many leading thinkers of the day adopted the tenets of **romanticism,** a movement that began in Europe in the late 1700s. Romanticism advocated feeling over reason, inner spirituality over external rules, the individual above society, and nature over environments created by humans.

One notable expression of American romanticism came from New England writers and philosophers, who were known as the transcendentalists. **Transcendentalism** urged people to transcend, or overcome, the limits of their minds and let their souls reach out to embrace the beauty of the universe.

People IN HISTORY

Henry David Thoreau
1817–1862

One of America's most admired thinkers, Henry David Thoreau lived in Concord, Massachusetts, and became a protégé of transcendentalist Ralph Waldo Emerson. Thoreau is particularly famous for his experiment in living the transcendentalist life. In one of his most popular works, *Walden*, he recounts his feelings and experiences during a two-year period in which he lived in a shack by Walden Pond outside Concord.

He said of his stay there, "I went to the woods because I wished to live deliberately, to front only the essential facts of life, and see if I could not learn what it had to teach, and not, when I came to die, discover that I had not lived."

In 1849 Thoreau published "Civil Disobedience." In this influential essay, he discussed issues of personal conscience versus the demands of the government. Thoreau was inspired to write the essay after he spent a night in jail for refusing to pay a tax. He felt the tax supported an immoral government that condoned slavery and was fighting what he believed was an imperialist war with Mexico. The ideas in "Civil Disobedience" would influence future civil rights leaders, such as Mahatma Gandhi and Martin Luther King, Jr.

How did Thoreau's purpose for living on Walden Pond reflect transcendentalist ideas?

Margaret Fuller
1810–1850

As a young woman, Margaret Fuller was another member of the prominent group of New England writers and philosophers who developed transcendentalism. In 1840, with the help of Ralph Waldo Emerson, she founded the magazine *The Dial*, in which she published writings of the transcendentalist movement.

Fuller also organized groups of Boston women to promote their educational and intellectual development. These meetings convinced her to write the book *Women in the Nineteenth Century*, in which she argued that women deserve equal political rights.

Fuller's success in editing *The Dial* caught the eye of Horace Greeley, the famous editor of the *New York Tribune*, and in 1844 he hired Fuller to be the *Tribune's* literary critic. In 1846 Greeley sent Fuller to Europe to cover reform efforts there. While in Italy, Fuller married Giovanni Angelo Ossoli, a revolutionary fighting to unite Italy. Fuller sent home reports about the Italian revolution of 1848, becoming the first American woman foreign-war correspondent. Tragically, in 1850, on a trip to the United States, Fuller, Ossoli, and their young son were drowned when their ship sank as it approached New York.

How was Fuller unusual among the women of her time?

Activity: Interdisciplinary Connection

Language Arts Divide class into small groups. Provide each student with a copy of the folowing excerpt from *Walden*:

"I went to the woods because I wished to live deliberately, to front only the essential facts of life, and see if I could not learn what it had to teach, and not, when I came to die, to discover that I had not lived. I did not wish to live what was not life, living is so dear; nor did I wish to practice resignation, unless it was quite necessary. I wanted to live deep and suck out all the marrow of life, to live so sturdily and Spartan-like as to put to rout all that was not life, to cut a broad swath and shave close, to drive life into a corner, and reduce it to its lowest terms, and, if it proved to be mean, why then to get the whole and genuine meanness of it, and publish its meanness to the world; or if it were sublime, to know it by experience, and to be able to give a true account of it in my next excursion."

Ask each group to rewrite the paragraph using contemporary English. Have groups compare their final results. **AL**

American Writers Emerge

The most influential transcendentalist was Ralph Waldo Emerson. In his 1836 essay "Nature," Emerson wrote that those who wanted fulfillment should try to commune with nature. Emerson influenced other writers, including Margaret Fuller and Henry David Thoreau. Thoreau believed that individuals must fight the pressure to conform. "If a man does not keep pace with his companions, perhaps it is because he hears a different drummer," he wrote. "Let him step to the music which he hears, however measured or far away."

Emerson and Thoreau were only two of many writers who set out to create uniquely American works. Washington Irving, famous for writing "The Legend of Sleepy Hollow" (1819), became the first internationally prominent American writer. James Fenimore Cooper romanticized Native Americans and frontier explorers in his Leatherstocking Tales, the most famous being *The Last of the Mohicans* (1826). Nathaniel Hawthorne, a New England customs official and resident of Brook Farm, wrote more than 100 short stories and novels. His novel *The Scarlet Letter* (1850), with its Puritan setting, explored the persecution and psychological suffering that may result from sin. Herman Melville, another New Englander, wrote the great *Moby Dick* (1851). Edgar Allan Poe, a poet and short story writer, achieved fame as a writer of terror and mystery. Perhaps the era's most important poet was Walt Whitman, who published *Leaves of Grass* in 1855. Whitman loved nature, the common people, and American democracy, and his famous work reflects these passions. Another major poet of the era, Emily Dickinson, wrote unconventional, mystical, and deeply personal works.

The Penny Press

Another important development of the early 1800s was the rise of the mass distribution newspaper. Before the 1800s, most newspapers catered to well-educated readers. They were typically published once a week and cost around six cents—too much for the average worker.

As more Americans learned to read and gained the right to vote, publishers began producing inexpensive newspapers, known as penny papers, which provided the kind of content most people wanted. Reports of fires, crimes, marriages, gossip, politics, and other local news made the papers an instant success with a mass audience.

General interest magazines that catered to a more specialized readership also emerged around this time. In 1830 Louis A. Godey founded *Godey's Lady's Book*, the first American magazine for women. The poet James Russell Lowell launched *Atlantic Monthly*, another magazine for the well educated, in 1857, while *Harper's Weekly* covered everything from book reviews to news reports.

Reading Check **Evaluating** What were the main themes of American writers in the early 1800s?

Section 2 REVIEW

Vocabulary

1. **Explain** the significance of: nativism, Know-Nothings, Second Great Awakening, Charles Grandison Finney, Joseph Smith, utopia, romanticism, transcendentalism.

Main Ideas

2. **Explaining** What pushed Irish and German people to immigrate to the United States in the mid-1800s?
3. **Specifying** What new religious group formed in the 1830s?
4. **Identifying** What was the penny press?

Critical Thinking

5. **Big Ideas** Which religious denominations increased their influence in the Second Great Awakening?
6. **Organizing** Use a graphic organizer, similar to the one below, to list American cultural movements in the mid-1800s.

7. **Analyzing Visuals** Study the map on page 231. What level of population decrease did most of Ireland experience?

Writing About History

8. **Expository Writing** Suppose you are an Irish or German immigrant to the United States in the mid-1800s. Write an article to be published in your home country that contrasts your new life in the United States with how your life was in your home country.

History ONLINE
Study Central™ To review this section, go to glencoe.com and click on Study Central.

235

Reading Check

Answer:
Romantic writers advocated feelings over reason, inner spirituality over external rules, the individual over society, and nature over human-made environments. Transcendentalist writers focused on overcoming the limits of the human mind and embracing the beauty of the universe.

Assess

History ONLINE

Study Central™ provides summaries, interactive games, and online graphic organizers to help students review content.

Close

Summarizing Ask: What brought about changes in American culture and society in the mid-1800s? *(Mass immigration of non-Protestant, non-English speakers, the Second Great Awakening, and new intellectual movements, such as transcendentalism all contributed to changing American culture and society in the mid-1800s.)* **OL**

Section 2 REVIEW

Answers

1. All definitions can be found in the section and the Glossary.
2. Irish people were escaping famine and poverty, while German people were escaping chaos, violence, and repression.
3. the Mormons
4. inexpensive newspapers that printed local news for a mass audience
5. Protestant denominations such as Methodists, Baptists, Presbyterians
6. nativism, revivalism, romanticism, transcendentalism, utopian communities
7. between 15% and 29%
8. Students' articles will vary, but should focus on the differences between life in the United States and life in either Ireland or the German states.

Focus

Bellringer

Daily Focus Transparency 6-3

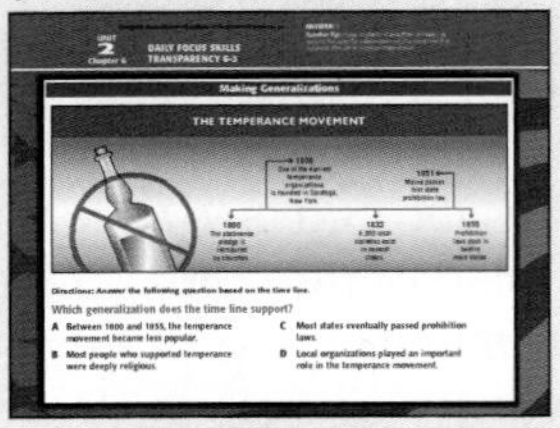

Guide to Reading

Answers to the Graphic:

I. The Reform Spirit
  A. The Temperance Movement
  B. Prison Reform
  C. Educational Reform
  D. Women's Education
II. The Early Women's Movement
  E. "True Womanhood"
  F. Women Seek Greater Equality

Section Spotlight Video

To generate student interest and provide a springboard for class discussion, access the Chapter 6, Section 3 video at glencoe.com or on the video DVD.

Section 3

Section Audio · Spotlight Video

Reforming Society

Guide to Reading

Big Ideas

Past and Present Reform movements sought to change American society in ways that upheld American values and ideals.

Content Vocabulary
- benevolent society *(p. 237)*
- temperance *(p. 238)*
- penitentiary *(p. 238)*

Academic Vocabulary
- institution *(p. 236)*
- imposition *(p. 238)*

People and Events to Identify
- Dorothea Dix *(p. 236)*
- Lyman Beecher *(p. 236)*
- Horace Mann *(p. 238)*
- Elizabeth Cady Stanton *(p. 241)*
- Seneca Falls Convention *(p. 241)*

Reading Strategy

Organizing Use the major headings in Section 3 to create an outline, similar to the one below, about American reform efforts in the first half of the nineteenth century.

Reforming Society
I. The Reform Spirit
  A.
  B.
  C.
  D.
II.

The Second Great Awakening created an environment for social change. Spurred on by this revival of religion, as well as a heightened belief in the power of individuals to improve society and themselves, Americans engaged in reform movements.

The Reform Spirit

MAIN Idea Inspired by the Second Great Awakening, reformers tried to tackle many problems in society.

HISTORY AND YOU Identify a local, national, or world issue that you believe citizens and lawmakers need to address. Why is this issue important to you? Read on to learn about reformers during the mid-1800s.

In 1841 a clergyman asked schoolteacher **Dorothea Dix** to lead a Sunday school class at a local prison. What Dix saw there appalled her. Mentally ill persons lay neglected in dirty, unheated rooms. Putting aside her teaching career, she began a crusade to improve conditions for the mentally ill and to provide them with the facilities and treatment they needed.

In 1843 Dix composed a letter to the Massachusetts legislature, calling for a new approach to mental illness. She gave the history of a local woman as evidence that more humane treatment might help many of the mentally ill: "Some may say these things cannot be remedied . . . I know they can. . . . A young woman, a pauper . . . was for years a raging maniac. A cage, chains, and the whip were the agents for controlling her, united with harsh tones and profane language." Dix explained that a local couple took the woman in and treated her with care and respect. "They are careful of her diet. They keep her very clean. She calls them 'father' and 'mother.' Go there now, and you will find her 'clothed,' and though not perfectly in her 'right mind,' so far restored as to be a safe and comfortable inmate."

Largely through the efforts of Dorothea Dix, more than a dozen states enacted sweeping prison reforms that created special **institutions,** often referred to as asylums, for the mentally ill. As influential as she was, Dix was just one of many citizens who worked to reform various aspects of American society in the mid 1800s.

The reform movements of the mid-1800s stemmed in large part from the revival of religious fervor. Revivalists preached the power of individuals to improve themselves and the world. **Lyman Beecher,** a prominent minister, insisted that it was the nation's citizenry, more than its government, that should take charge of building a better society. True reform, he said, could take place only through "the voluntary energies of the nation itself."

Resource Manager

R Reading Strategies	C Critical Thinking	D Differentiated Instruction	W Writing Support	S Skill Practice
Teacher Edition • Visualizing, p. 238 **Additional Resources** • Pri. Source Read., URB p. 101 • Guide Read. Act., URB p. 114 • American History in Graphic Novel, p. 15	**Teacher Edition** • Ident. Cent. Issues, p. 238 • Pred. Consequences, p. 239 **Additional Resources** • Quizzes and Tests, p. 77	**Teacher Edition** • English Learners, p. 240 **Additional Resources** • Time Line Act., URB p. 97		**Teacher Edition** • Using Ref. Tools, p. 237 **Additional Resources** • Read. Essen., p. 69

PRIMARY SOURCE

The Beechers: A Family of Reformers

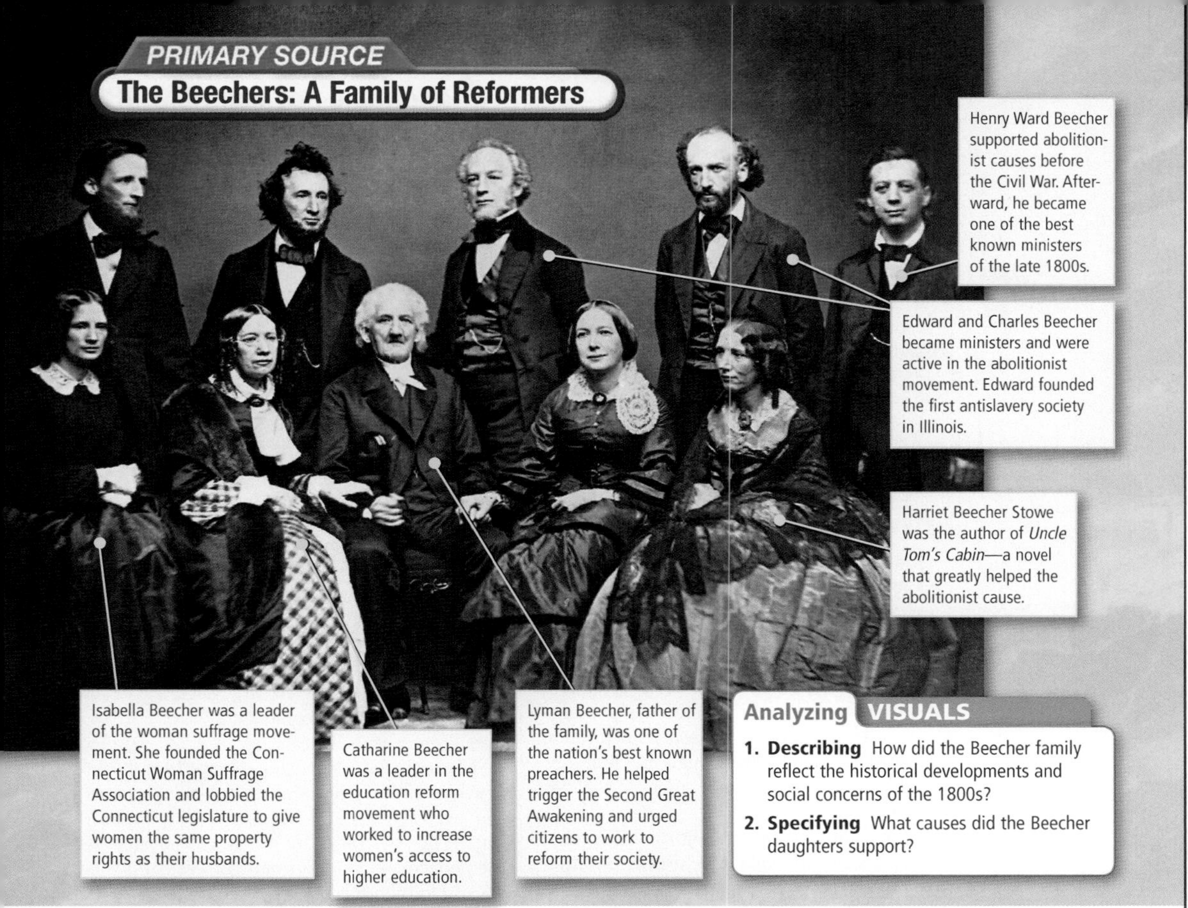

Analyzing VISUALS

1. **Describing** How did the Beecher family reflect the historical developments and social concerns of the 1800s?
2. **Specifying** What causes did the Beecher daughters support?

Under the guidance of Beecher and other religious leaders, associations known as **benevolent societies** sprang up in cities and towns across the country. At first, they focused on spreading the word of God and attempting to convert nonbelievers. Soon, however, they sought to combat a number of social problems.

One striking feature of the reform effort was the overwhelming presence of women. Young women in particular had joined the revivalist movement in much larger numbers than men. One reason was that many unmarried women with uncertain futures discovered in religion a foundation on which to build their lives.

As more women turned to the church, many also joined religious-based reform groups. These reform groups targeted aspects of American society they considered in dire need of change. Among these issues were excessive consumption of alcohol, prisons, and education.

The Temperance Movement S

Many reformers argued that no behavior caused more crime, disorder, and poverty than the abuse of alcohol. Men who drank too much, they argued, spent their money on liquor rather than necessities for their families, and they sometimes abused their wives and children. While not everyone agreed, no one doubted that alcoholism was widespread in the early 1800s. In small towns throughout the West, citizens drank to ease the isolation and loneliness of rural life, while in the pubs and saloons in Eastern cities, drinking was the main leisure activity for many workers.

Teach

S Skill Practice

Using Reference Tools Point out the word *temperance* in the heading on this page and in the text on the next page. Ask students to use a dictionary or Internet resources to find as many words as they can with the root *temper,* and to record the words and their definitions in a table or chart. Then have students analyze all the words' meanings and histories to write a summary explaining how the words are related. **AL**

Analyzing VISUALS

Answers:

1. The father was an active reformer and minister of the Second Great Awakening, as were several of his sons. Most of Lyman's children were activists in women's rights or abolition.
2. Isabella and Catharine worked in the area of women's rights and women's education, while Harriet wrote works, such as *Uncle Tom's Cabin,* against slavery.

Hands-On Chapter Project
Step 3

Creating a Pamphlet

Step 3: Illustrating the Issue Each group will research images, cartoons, and posters that were produced to support the reform movement chosen in Step 1.

Directions Have students use the library, Internet, and other resources for examples of images, cartoons and posters from the period that support the group's topic. Students should combine these images or images of their own creation with the essay written in Step 2 to create a pamphlet supporting the group's reform movement.

Synthesizing Information Students will work in their groups to organize the information and determine the best way to present the topic to an audience in order to gain their support. **OL**

(Chapter Project continued on page 243)

R Reading Strategy

Visualizing Invite students to share what they know or ideas they may have about what elementary and high school education was like in the early 1800s, before reform. **Ask:** What would a schoolroom look like in this period? What would it feel like to be a student at this time? *(Answers will vary; encourage students to use descriptive words in their responses.)* Discuss the fact that, although reformers' goals were to improve society at large, changes in education benefited individual children and improved their lives. Have students compare their own educational experiences with what they think education was like before the reforms of the 1830s. **OL**

C Critical Thinking

Identifying Central Issues Discuss with students the ideas in the primary source quotation about the goals of education on this page. Ask volunteers to paraphrase the quotation. **Ask:** What is the main point of this quotation? *(The main point is that a republic must have educated citizens to continue to exist; if citizens are ignorant and cannot think critically, then that could spell the end of the republican government.)* **BL**

Although advocates of **temperance,** or moderation in the consumption of alcohol, had been active since the late 1700s, the new reformers energized the campaign. Across the country, temperance groups began preaching the evils of alcohol and persuading heavy drinkers to give up liquor. In 1833 several of the groups united to form the American Temperance Union.

Temperance societies also pushed for laws prohibiting the sale of liquor. In 1851 Maine passed the first state prohibition law, an example followed by a dozen other states by 1855. Other states passed "local option" laws, which allowed towns and villages to prohibit liquor sales within their boundaries.

Prison Reform

The spirit of reform also prompted some people to try to improve the prison system. Inmates of all kinds, from violent offenders to debtors and the mentally ill, were often indiscriminately crowded together in jails and prisons, which were literally holes in the ground in some cases. One jail in Connecticut, for example, was an abandoned mineshaft. Beginning around 1816, many states began building new facilities to provide a better environment for inmates.

Underlying the prison reform movement was a belief in rehabilitating prisoners rather than merely locking them up. Officials imposed rigid discipline to rid criminals of the "laxness" they believed had led them astray. Solitary confinement and the **imposition** of silence on work crews were meant to give prisoners the chance to meditate and think about their wrongdoing. The name of these new prisons, **penitentiaries,** expressed the idea that they were places where prisoners would work to achieve penitence, or remorse.

Educational Reform

R In the early 1800s, many reformers sought to establish a system of public education—government-funded schools open to all citizens. The increase in the number of voters in the 1820s and 1830s and the arrival of millions of new immigrants convinced many people of the need for public education. Most American leaders and social reformers believed that a democratic republic could only survive if the electorate was well educated.

Massachusetts legislator **Horace Mann** was a leader of the movement for public education. As president of the Massachusetts Senate, Mann pressed for more public education and helped create a state board of education in 1837. He then left the state senate to serve as secretary of the new board. During his 12 years in that post, he doubled teachers' salaries, opened 50 new high schools, and established training schools for teachers. Massachusetts quickly became a model for other states. As he wrote in one report, Mann was convinced the nation needed public education to survive:

Primary Source

C "The establishment of a republican government, without well-appointed and efficient means for the universal education of the people, is the most rash and foolhardy experiment ever tried by man. . . . It may be an easy thing to make a republic, but it is a very laborious thing to make republicans; and woe to the republic that rests upon no better foundations than ignorance, selfishness and passion!"

—from "Report of the Massachusetts Board of Education," 1848

PRIMARY SOURCE

Reforming Society, 1830–1860

Reformers of the mid-1800s saw it as their Christian duty to improve society. They wanted to alleviate suffering in society.

▲ *Reformers in the 1800s pushed for more education for women. The Emerson School for Girls in Boston (above) was an early example of a girls' school.*

Additional Support

Teacher Tip

Collaborative Learning Before groups begin work, ask them to discuss and mutually agree on group members' roles, such as manager, artist(s), presenter, and so on. If necessary, break up the project into discrete tasks, such as research, planning, and presenting.

Activity: Collaborative Learning

Making a Poster Have students work in groups of at least three to create a poster advocating reform in one of the areas mentioned in this section. **Ask:** How did reformers focus attention on their causes? *(Answers will vary.)* Encourage students to use library and Internet resources to learn more about their selected reform issue and to study actual materials from the time related to it, such as leaflets, broadsides, and posters. When students have completed their posters, have a presenter from each group explain elements of the posters to the class. Display finished posters in the classroom. **OL** **BL** **ELL**

▲ Sing Sing prison, built in 1828 in New York, was an example of the new approach favored by reformers. This woodcut shows prisoners arriving at the dining room, marching in hand-on-shoulder lockstep. They were required to eat in silence.

▲ Temperance groups used images such as the one above, entitled "The Drunkard's Progress," to warn people about drinking. The image shows the progress from taking one drink to a ruined life of poverty and crime. Below, a wife and child weep at the loss of their husband and father.

Analyzing VISUALS

1. **Synthesizing** In the image of Sing Sing prison, how would you describe the environment? What was the goal of creating such a prison environment?
2. **Analyzing** From "The Drunkard's Progress," what indicates that women were often temperance supporters?

In 1852 Massachusetts passed the first mandatory school attendance law; New York passed a similar measure the next year. Reformers focused on creating elementary schools to teach all children the basics of reading, writing, and arithmetic, and to instill a work ethic. These schools were open to all and supported by local and state taxes and tuition.

By the 1850s, tax-supported elementary schools had gained widespread support in the northeastern states and had begun to spread to the rest of the country. Rural areas responded more slowly because children were needed to help with planting and harvesting for large portions of the year.

In the South, reformer Calvin Wiley played a similar role in North Carolina to that of Horace Mann in Massachusetts. In 1839 North Carolina began providing aid to local communities that established taxpayer-funded schools. Wiley traveled throughout the state, building support for public education. By 1860, about two-thirds of North Carolina's white children attended school for part of the year. The South as a whole responded less quickly, and only about one-third of white children were enrolled by 1860. African American children were excluded almost entirely. C

Women's Education

When officials talked about educating voters, they had men in mind, as women were still not allowed to vote in the early 1800s. Nonetheless, women reformers, such as Catharine Beecher, seized the opportunity to push for more educational opportunities for girls and women.

Emma Willard, who founded a girls' school in Vermont in 1814, was another educational pioneer. Her school covered the usual subjects for young women, such as cooking and etiquette, but it also taught academic subjects, such as history, math, and literature, which were rarely taught to women. In 1837 another educator, Mary Lyon, opened Mount Holyoke Female Seminary in Massachusetts, the first institution of higher education for women only.

In 1849 new opportunities for higher education enabled Elizabeth Blackwell to become the first woman to earn a medical degree. In 1857 she founded the New York Infirmary for Women and Children—a hospital staffed entirely by women.

Reading Check **Identifying** What three areas of social reform did reformers target?

C Critical Thinking

Predicting Consequences

Have students compare the education reforms in the South to those in the North. **Ask:** What do you think might be the consequences of the South's slower response to education reform? *(The South's economy will lag behind the North's and the two regions will also grow further apart as northern citizens become more educated.)* **OL**

Analyzing VISUALS

Answers:

1. It is very neat, regular, and orderly. The goal was probably to keep prisoners in check but also to provide them a quiet, safe, and orderly place to reform themselves.
2. A woman and child are depicted as victims of intemperance. As victims, women would be likely to support the movement.

Reading Check

Answer: temperance, prison reform, education reform

Additional Support

Activity: Interdisciplinary Connection

Sociology Invite a professor or women's activist to speak to your class about issues that face women in today's society in the United States and other countries. The presentation should include social and economic issues. Ask the speaker to address topics that are appropriate for the adolescent audience. Have the speaker work with the students to compare today's reform movements with those of the early and mid-1800s. **OL**

D Differentiated Instruction

English Learners Discuss with students how the Industrial Revolution affected the roles of men and women. **Ask:** How did the idea of "true womanhood" develop and what were its main traits? *(It developed during the Industrial Revolution when men went off to work in factories and women began to stay home alone to care for the home and children. True womanhood meant that women should stay in the home, be the moral centers of their families, and work to build the characters of their children.)* Ask students to make a concept web for "true womanhood" and record words and phrases about it as they read the information under the heading. **BL** **ELL**

DBQ Document Based Questions

Answers:

1. to achieve their right to vote
2. to promote every righteous cause by every righteous means

Additional Support

The Early Women's Movement

MAIN Idea Women were generally expected to be homemakers and models for their children, but some began demanding greater rights.

HISTORY AND YOU How did you think the lives of women changed from the colonial period to the mid-1800s? Read on to learn about the early women's movement.

For the text of the Seneca Falls Declaration, see page R48 in **Documents in American History.**

In the early 1800s, the Industrial Revolution began to change the economic roles of men and women. In the 1700s, most economic activity took place in or near the home because most Americans lived and worked in a rural farm setting. Although husbands and wives had distinct chores, maintaining the farm was the focus of their efforts. By the mid-1800s, these circumstances had started to change, especially in the northeastern states. The development of factories and other work centers separated the home from the workplace. Men now often left home to go to work, while women tended the house and children. In time, this development led to the emergence of the first women's movement.

"True Womanhood"

D As the nature of work changed, many Americans began to divide life into two spheres of activity—the home and the workplace. Many believed the home to be the proper sphere for women, partly because the outside world was seen as corrupt and dangerous, and partly because of popular ideas about the family.

The Christian revivalism of the 1820s and 1830s greatly influenced the American family. For many parents, raising children was treated as a solemn responsibility because it prepared young people for a disciplined Christian life.

PRIMARY SOURCE

The Seneca Falls Declaration

PRIMARY SOURCE

Declaration of Sentiments

". . . We hold these truths to be self-evident: that all men and women are created equal; that they are endowed by their Creator with certain inalienable rights. . . .

The history of mankind is a history of repeated injuries and usurpations on the part of man toward woman, having in direct object the establishment of an absolute tyranny over her. . . .

Resolutions

Resolved, That all laws which prevent woman from occupying such a station in society as her conscience shall dictate, or which place her in a position inferior to that of man, are contrary to the great precept of nature, and therefore of no force or authority.

Resolved, That woman is man's equal—was intended to be so by the Creator, and the highest good of the race demands that she should be recognized as such.

. . . *Resolved,* That it is the duty of women of this country to secure to themselves their sacred right to the elective franchise.

. . . *Resolved,* therefore, That, being invested by the Creator with the same capabilities, and the same consciousness of responsibility for their exercise, it is demonstrably the right and duty of woman, equally with man, to promote every righteous cause by every righteous means . . . both in private and in public, by writing and by speaking, by any instrumentalities proper to be used, and in any assemblies proper to be held. . . ."

—from The Seneca Falls Declaration

▲ *Susan B. Anthony (left) and Elizabeth Cady Stanton (right) were two of the most prominent women's suffrage advocates. Stanton attended the Seneca Falls Convention that issued the Declaration of Sentiments.*

DBQ Document-Based Questions

1. **Identifying** According to the third resolution, what is the duty of American women?
2. **Paraphrasing** What does the Declaration ask all women to do?

Activity: Collaborative Learning

Text Comparison Refer students to the full text of the Declaration of Sentiments on page R48. Explain that it was written by Elizabeth Cady Stanton based on the Declaration of Independence. Divide the class into groups and ask them to analyze the two texts. **Ask:** Why do you think that Stanton modeled the Declaration of Sentiments on the Declaration of Independence? *(Possible answer: Stanton wanted to equate the struggle of women to achieve their natural rights from men with the colonists' struggle to achieve their natural rights from Great Britain. It also underscored the irony of the fact that the United States was founded on principles of equality and liberty when half the population still had few civil rights.)* **OL**

Women often were viewed as more moral and charitable than men, and they were expected to be models of piety and virtue to their children and husbands.

The idea that women should be homemakers and should take responsibility for developing their children's characters evolved into a set of ideas known as "true womanhood." Magazine articles and novels aimed at women reinforced the value of their role at home. In 1841 Catharine Beecher, a daughter of minister and reformer Lyman Beecher, wrote a book called *A Treatise on Domestic Economy*. The popular volume argued that women could find fulfillment at home and gave instruction on childcare, cooking, and health matters.

Women Seek Greater Rights

Many women did not believe the ideas of true womanhood were limiting. Instead, the new ideas implied that wives were now partners with their husbands and in some ways were morally superior to them. Women were held up as the conscience of the home and society.

The idea that women had an important role to play in building a virtuous home was soon extended to making society more virtuous. As women became involved in the great moral crusades of the era, some began to argue that they needed greater political rights to promote their ideas.

An advocate of this idea was Margaret Fuller. Fuller argued that every woman had her own relationship with God and needed "as a soul to live freely and unimpeded." She declared, "We would have every arbitrary barrier thrown down and every path laid open to women as freely as to men." Fuller believed that if men and women, whom she called the "two sides" of human nature, were treated equally, it would end injustice in society.

In 1848 Lucretia Mott and **Elizabeth Cady Stanton,** two women active in the antislavery movement, organized the **Seneca Falls Convention.** This gathering of women reformers marked the beginning of an organized women's movement. The convention issued a "Declaration of Sentiments and Resolutions" that began with words expanding the Declaration of Independence: "We hold these truths to be self-evident: that all men and women are created equal. . . ." Stanton shocked many of the women present by proposing that they focus on gaining the right to vote. Nevertheless, the Seneca Falls Convention is considered by many to be the unofficial beginning of the struggle for women's voting rights.

Throughout the 1850s, women continued to organize conventions to gain greater rights for themselves. The conventions did meet with some success. By 1860, for example, reformers had convinced 15 states to pass laws permitting married women to retain their property if their husbands died. Above all, these conventions drew attention to their cause and paved the way for a stronger women's movement to emerge after the Civil War.

✓Reading Check **Examining** What events of the mid-1800s sparked the first women's movement?

Section 3 REVIEW

Vocabulary

1. **Explain** the significance of: Dorothea Dix, Lyman Beecher, benevolent society, temperance, penitentiary, Horace Mann, Elizabeth Cady Stanton, Seneca Falls Convention.

Main Ideas

2. **Explaining** What principle was the basis for the drive for public education?
3. **Specifying** On what document did the Seneca Falls Convention base the "Declaration of Sentiments"?

Critical Thinking

4. **Big Ideas** How did the Second Great Awakening affect the reform movements of the mid-1800s?
5. **Organizing** Use a graphic organizer, similar to the one below, to list the major areas of reform in the mid-1800s.

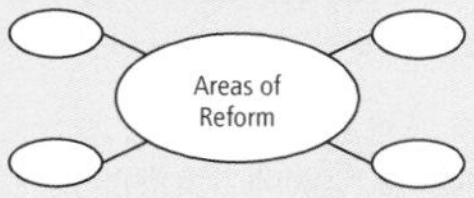

6. **Analyzing Visuals** Study the photograph of the classroom on page 238. How is your classroom similar to or different from this one?

Writing About History

7. **Persuasive Writing** Think of one social reform that you believe is needed today. Write a letter to a legislator explaining why you believe the reform is needed and how it might be achieved. Give examples of specific problems in your community or state to support your argument.

History ONLINE

Study Central™ To review this section, go to glencoe.com and click on Study Central.

✓Reading Check

Answer:
the Industrial Revolution, Christian revivalism, women's involvement in antislavery and other reform movements, the Seneca Falls Convention

Assess

History ONLINE

Study Central™ provides summaries, interactive games, and online graphic organizers to help students review content.

Close

Summarizing Ask: In what areas did reformers work to improve society? *(They worked in mental healthcare reform, for temperance, prison reform, education reform, and women's rights.)* **OL**

Section 3 REVIEW

Answers

1. All definitions can be found in the section and the Glossary.
2. the idea that a republic needs well-educated citizens to survive
3. the Declaration of Independence
4. It encouraged people to work to improve themselves and society and also brought women into the reform movement via their involvement with religion.
5. reform in the care of mentally ill people, the temperance movement, prison reform, education reform
6. Answers will vary; accept all reasonable responses.
7. Students' letters will vary, but should focus on a problem that has an impact on your state or community today.

Focus

Bellringer
Daily Focus Transparency 6-4

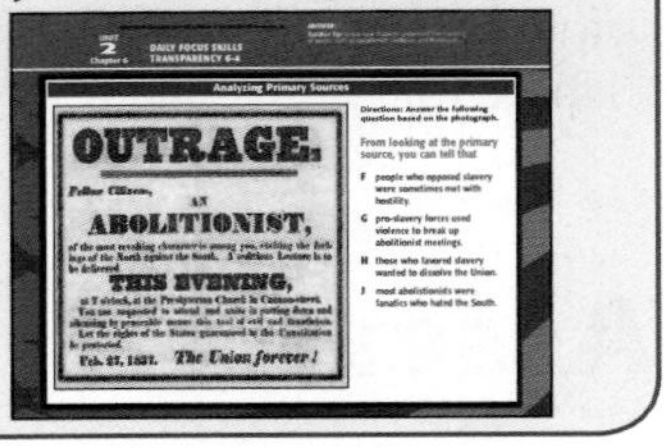

Guide to Reading
Answers to the Graphic:

1790s: First antislavery societies
1816: American Colonization Society (ACS) is founded
1821: ACS acquires land in West Africa
1831: William Lloyd Garrison begins publishing The Liberator
1832: New England Anti-Slavery Society is founded
1833: American Anti-Slavery Society is founded
1840s: Sojourner Truth's eloquent speeches draw huge crowds

Section Spotlight Video

To generate student interest and provide a springboard for class discussion, access the Chapter 6, Section 4 video at glencoe.com or on the video DVD.

Resource Manager

R Reading Strategies	C Critical Thinking	D Differentiated Instruction	W Writing Support	S Skill Practice
Teacher Edition • Outlining, p. 247 **Additional Resources** • Read. Skills Act., URB p. 85 • Pri. Source Read., URB p. 99 • Guide. Read., URB p. 115	**Teacher Edition** • Drawing Con., p. 244 **Additional Resources** • Quizzes and Tests, p. 78	**Teacher Edition** • Verbal/Linguistic, p. 244 **Additional Resources** • Reteaching Activity, URB p. 107	**Teacher Edition** • Persuasive Writing, p. 245 **Additional Resources** • Authentic Assessment, p. 17	**Teacher Edition** • Visual Literacy, p. 246 **Additional Resources** • Read. Essen., p. 72

Section 4

Section Audio | Spotlight Video

The Abolitionist Movement

Guide to Reading

Big Ideas
Individual Action Abolitionists challenged the morality and legality of slavery in the United States.

Content Vocabulary
- gradualism *(p. 242)*
- abolition *(p. 243)*
- emancipation *(p. 244)*

Academic Vocabulary
- compensate *(p. 242)*
- demonstration *(p. 245)*

People and Events to Identify
- American Colonization Society *(p. 243)*
- William Lloyd Garrison *(p. 244)*
- American Anti-Slavery Society *(p. 244)*
- Frederick Douglass *(p. 245)*
- Sojourner Truth *(p. 246)*

Reading Strategy
Sequencing Complete a time line similar to the one below to record early events of the abolitionist movement.

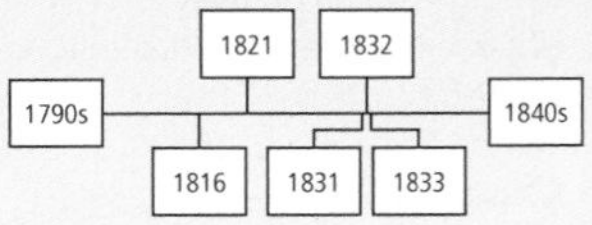

In the early and mid-1800s, some Americans, mainly in the North, embarked on a crusade to abolish slavery in the United States. As the country became more polarized about the issue, the work of abolitionists created controversy and sometimes led to violence.

The New Abolitionists

MAIN Idea In the early years of the United States, some religious groups proposed ending slavery gradually, but by the 1830s, a new generation of abolitionists demanded an immediate end to slavery.

HISTORY AND YOU Have you ever tried to do something slowly to make it less difficult? Is it better to do something difficult quickly to get it over with? What is the best approach when the choice affects human lives? Read to learn about the different proposals for ending slavery.

In the 1830s a growing number of Americans had begun to demand an immediate end to slavery in the South. Of all the reform movements that began in the early 1800s, the movement to end slavery was the most divisive. By pitting North against South, it polarized the nation and helped bring about the Civil War.

Early Opposition to Slavery

From the earliest days of the Republic, many Americans had opposed slavery. Many of the country's founders knew that a nation based on the principles of liberty and equality would have difficulty remaining true to its ideals if it continued to enslave human beings. Quakers and Baptists in both the North and South had long argued that slavery was a sin. After the Revolution, Baptists in Virginia called for "every legal measure to [wipe out] this horrid evil from the land."

Gradualism Early antislavery societies generally supported an approach known as **gradualism,** or the belief that slavery had to be ended gradually. First they would stop slave traders from bringing new slaves into the country. Then they would phase out slavery in the North and the Upper South before finally ending slavery in the Lower South. Slaveholders would also be **compensated** for their loss. Supporters of gradualism believed it would give the South's economy time to adjust to the loss of enslaved labor.

Colonization The first antislavery societies also believed that ending slavery would not end racism in the United States. Many thought that the best solution was to send African Americans back to their ancestral homelands in Africa. In December 1816, antislavery reformers founded

Turning Point

The Abolitionist Movement Begins

Since colonial times, many Americans had believed slavery was immoral. The Second Great Awakening and the general spirit of reform in the 1830s, however, created an environment in which abolitionism began to gain widespread support. William Lloyd Garrison sparked the movement by publishing the *Liberator*, through which he spread his ideas, and by founding the American Anti-Slavery Society. Garrison's energy, moral certitude, and strong rhetoric attracted fellow activists, as well as new converts, and gave the movement momentum on a national scale.

ANALYZING HISTORY How did William Lloyd Garrison start the abolitionist movement of the 1830s?

▲ *William Lloyd Garrison, editor of the Liberator, supported the immediate abolition of slavery.*

◀ *The Philadelphia Anti-Slavery Society was one example of the abolitionist groups that formed in the North in the 1830s. Lucretia Mott, also a supporter of women's suffrage, is in the front row, second from right.*

the **American Colonization Society** (ACS) to move African Americans to Africa. The society had the support of many prominent Americans, including James Madison, James Monroe, Henry Clay, Daniel Webster, and John Marshall.

By 1821 the ACS had acquired land in West Africa. The following year, free African Americans began boarding ships chartered by the society to take them to Africa. There they established a colony that eventually became the country of Liberia. It declared its independence as a republic in 1847 and adopted a constitution based on the U.S. Constitution. The capital, Monrovia, was named for President Monroe.

Colonization was never a realistic solution to racism. The cost of transportation to Africa was high, and the ACS had to depend on donations. Moving roughly 1.5 million African Americans from the United States to Africa was nearly impossible. Furthermore, most African Americans regarded the United States as their home and did not want to move to another continent. Only an estimated 12,000 African Americans moved to Africa between 1821 and 1860.

Abolitionism

Gradualism and colonization remained the main goals of antislavery groups until the 1830s, when a new idea, **abolition,** began to gain ground. Abolitionists argued that enslaved African Americans should be freed immediately, without gradual measures or compensation to former slaveholders.

Abolitionism began to gain support in the 1830s for several reasons. As with other reform movements of the era, it drew its strength from the Second Great Awakening, with its focus on sin and repentance. In the eyes of abolitionists, slavery was an enormous evil for which the country needed to repent.

History ONLINE Student Web Activity Visit glencoe.com and complete the activity on abolitionism.

Teach

Turning Point

Background Abolitionists used a wide variety of media to create support for the cause. For example, William Lloyd Garrison not only published the *Liberator*, but wrote this stanza to the traditional melody of "Auld Lang Syne."

I am an abolitionist!
I glory in the name;
Though now by Slavery's
minions hiss'd,
And covered o'er with shame;
It is a spell of light and power—
The watchword of the free:—
Who spurns it in this trial-hour,
A craven soul is he!

Ask: **What tools did Garrison use to fight for the abolition of slavery?** *(He published the* Liberator, *he began the American Anti-Slavery Society, and he wrote other abolitionist materials.)*

Answer: Students should cite examples from the feature and the text to describe Garrison's role in starting the abolitionist movement of the 1830s.

Hands-On Chapter Project
Step 4

Creating a Pamphlet

Step 4: Creating a Commercial Each group will write a commercial as a tool to further persuade others to support their reform movement.

Directions Have the groups write a script for their commercial. Groups can choose to perform their commercial in front of the class or prerecord the commercial, either audio or visual, and play it for the class.

Justifying Students will use facts to justify their argument in a persuasive audio or visual format. **OL**

(Chapter Project continued on the Visual Summary page)

D Differentiated Instruction

Verbal/Linguistic Have students prepare a short oral presentation about one of the abolitionists mentioned in this section. Encourage students to use library and Internet resources to learn more about their subjects. OL

C Critical Thinking

Drawing Conclusions Point out to students that the Constitution allowed slavery, that it was against the law to help enslaved African Americans to escape, and that the law required runaway enslaved people to be returned to their owners. Give students five minutes to write about the following: Are there some situations in which breaking the law is an acceptable form of protest? Then have students use the thoughts they wrote to participate in a class discussion about whether abolitionists should have broken the law to help enslaved people escape. Extend the discussion, if appropriate, to include other situations in which it might be acceptable to break the law as a form of protest. OL

PRIMARY SOURCE

The Abolitionist Movement

In the 1830s a vigorous movement to end slavery developed, mainly in the North. The abolitionist movement began a fight to end slavery.

▲ *Minister Theodore Weld, his wife Angelina Grimké, and her sister Sarah were radical activists in the abolitionist movement. The Grimké sisters had grown up in the South and witnessed slavery firsthand. In the course of their activism, Angelina Grimké became the first woman to address the Massachusetts legislature. The three wrote regularly for abolitionist newspapers, such as the* Liberator, *and worked together on the influential book* Slavery As It Is: Testimony of a Thousand Witnesses *(1839).*

D

◄ *In 1850 a convention was held in Cazenovia, New York, to oppose the Fugitive Slave Law. Many abolitionist leaders attended. Frederick Douglass is seated left of the table; Theodore Weld is in front.*

The first well-known advocate of abolition was a free African American from North Carolina named David Walker, who published *Appeal to the Colored Citizens of the World.* In this pamphlet, Walker advocated violence and rebellion as the only way to end slavery. Although Walker's ideas were influential, the rapid development of a large national abolitionist movement in the 1830s was largely due to the efforts of **William Lloyd Garrison.**

William Lloyd Garrison In 1829 Garrison became an assistant to Benjamin Lundy, the Quaker publisher of the Baltimore antislavery newspaper *Genius of Universal Emancipation.* Garrison admired Lundy but grew impatient with his gradualist approach. In 1831 Garrison moved to Boston where he founded the antislavery newspaper, the *Liberator.* C

In the pages of the *Liberator,* Garrison published caustic attacks on slavery and called for an immediate end to it. He condemned colonization and attacked the Constitution because it did not ban slavery. To those who objected to his fiery language, he responded that the time for moderation was over:

PRIMARY SOURCE

"I am aware that many object to the severity of my language; but is there not cause for severity? I *will be* as harsh as truth and as uncompromising as justice. On this subject, I do not wish to think, or speak, or write, with moderation. No! No! Tell a man whose house is on fire, to give a moderate alarm; tell him to moderately rescue his wife from the hands of the ravisher; tell the mother to gradually [remove] her babe from the fire into which it has fallen—but urge me not to use moderation in a cause like the present. I am in earnest—I will not equivocate—I will not excuse—I will not retreat a single inch—AND I WILL BE HEARD."

—from the *Liberator,* January 1, 1831

In Garrison's opinion, the situation was clear: Slavery was immoral and slaveholders were evil. The only option was immediate and complete **emancipation,** or the freeing of all enslaved people. In 1833 Garrison founded the **American Anti-Slavery Society.** Membership grew quickly. By the mid-1830s, there were hundreds of society chapters, and by 1838, there were more than 1,350 chapters and over 250,000 members.

Additional Support

Activity: Interdisciplinary Connection

Language Arts Have students explore the significance of the slave narrative, as a source of history and as a literary genre, by selecting one to read and report on to the class. Explain that narratives were published as early as the mid-1700s. Many narratives were dictated to abolitionists who encouraged enslaved people to tell their stories to call attention to the evils of slavery. Over 2,000 first-person accounts of life in enslavement were collected as part of the Federal Writers' Project of the Works Progress Administration during the 1930s. After students share their reports, discuss the genre as a class. **Ask:** How do you think people in the mid-1800s reacted to slave narratives? *(Answers will vary, but may include the South seeing these narratives as personal attacks. In the North, the response may have been outrage and joining of antislavery cause.)* OL

▲ *Frederick Douglass was a powerful advocate for the abolitionist movement. His autobiography (above) helped build support for the abolition of slavery.*

In 1852 abolitionist and former slave Frederick Douglass gave a speech at the Fourth of July celebration in Rochester, New York:

PRIMARY SOURCE

"What, to the American slave, is your 4th of July? I answer; a day that reveals to him, more than all other days in the year, the gross injustice and cruelty to which he is the constant victim. To him, your celebration is a sham; your boasted liberty, an unholy license; your national greatness, swelling vanity; your sounds of rejoicing are empty and heartless; . . . a thin veil to cover up crimes which would disgrace a nation of savages. There is not a nation on the earth guilty of practices more shocking and bloody than are the people of the United States, at this very hour."

—from *The Frederick Douglass Papers*

DBQ Document-Based Questions

1. **Making Inferences** Why do you think Douglass was invited to speak on the Fourth of July?
2. **Summarizing** How does Douglass characterize the Fourth of July celebrations from the viewpoint of an enslaved person?

Other Abolitionist Leaders Garrison was not the only leader of the abolitionist movement. Theodore Weld, a disciple of the evangelist Charles Grandison Finney, was one of the most effective leaders, recruiting and training many abolitionists for the American Anti-Slavery Society. Arthur and Lewis Tappan, two devout and wealthy brothers from New York City, helped to finance the movement. The orator Wendell Phillips, the poet John Greenleaf Whittier, and many others became active in the cause as well.

Many women also gave their efforts to the abolitionist movement. Prudence Crandall worked as a teacher and an abolitionist in Connecticut, and Lucretia Mott—the women's rights advocate—often spoke out in favor of abolitionism as well. Some Southern women also joined the crusade. Among the earliest were Sarah and Angelina Grimké, South Carolina sisters who moved north to work openly against slavery.

African American Abolitionists Not surprisingly, free African Americans played a prominent role in the abolitionist movement. African Americans in the North, who numbered over 190,000 by 1850, endured much prejudice, but they cherished their freedom nonetheless. Even before Garrison launched his movement, African Americans had established at least 50 abolitionist societies in the North. When Garrison launched his newspaper, African Americans rushed to his support, not only buying the paper but also helping to sell it. Many began writing and speaking out against slavery and taking part in protests and **demonstrations**.

W **Frederick Douglass** was one of the most prominent African Americans in the abolitionist movement. In 1838 Douglass had escaped from slavery in Maryland by posing as a free African American sailor. "I appear before the immense assembly this evening as a thief and a robber," he told one Massachusetts group in 1842. "I stole this head, these limbs, this body from my master, and ran off with them." Douglass published his own antislavery newspaper, the *North Star*, and wrote an autobiography, *Narrative of the Life of Frederick Douglass*, which quickly sold 4,500 copies after its publication in 1845.

W Writing Support

Persuasive Writing Have students take on the role of a nineteenth-century abolitionist and write a speech or pamphlet arguing for abolition. Encourage students to give their speeches or read their pamphlets to the class. **OL**

DBQ Document Based Questions

Answers:

1. Possible answer: The Fourth of July is the anniversary of the signing of the Declaration of Independence, a founding document of the United States that argues for equality and liberty. Abolitionists believed that it was hypocritical of the nation to maintain legal slavery when it supposedly stood for liberty, equality, and justice.
2. as bombast, fraud, deception, impiety, and hypocrisy

Differentiated Instruction

Leveled Activities

BL Reading Skills Activity, URB, p. 85

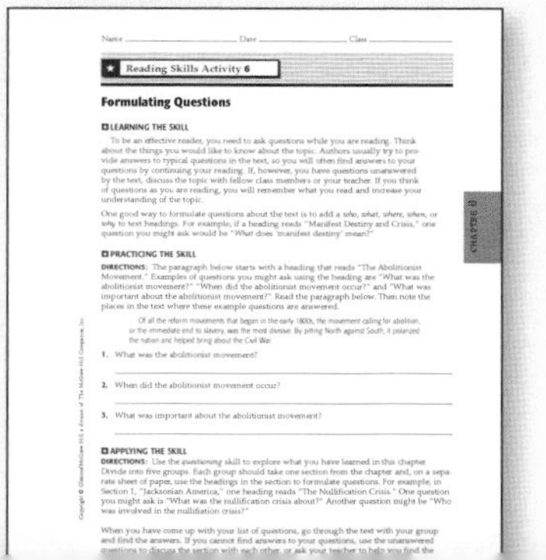

OL Guided Reading Activity, URB, p. 115

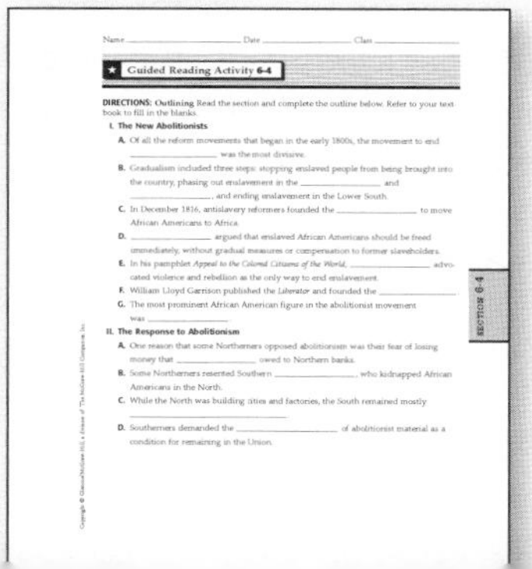

AL Content Vocabulary Activity, URB, p. 91

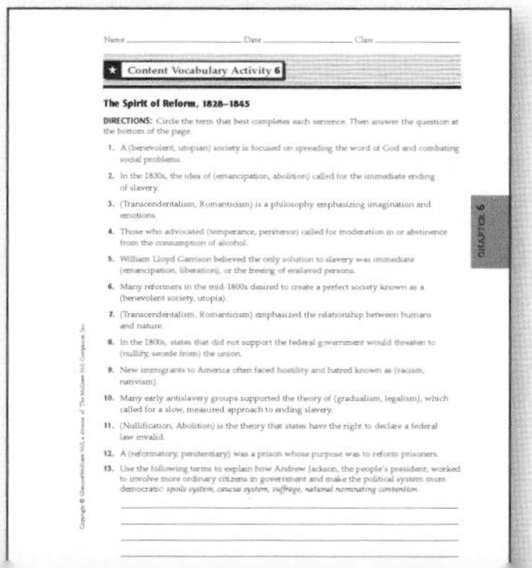

ELL English Language Learner Activity, p. 89

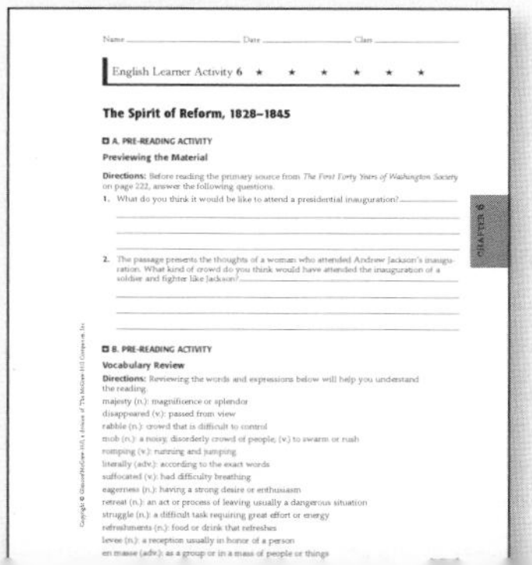

S Skill Practice

Visual Literacy Refer students to the political cartoons on this page. Discuss the meanings of the symbols used in each cartoon. **Ask:** Which cartoon do you think is most effective at conveying an abolitionist message? *(Accept all reasonable responses; students may feel that the cartoon on the left is more effective as it uses stronger and more dramatic symbolic images than the cartoon on the right.)* OL

Analyzing VISUALS

Answers:

1. the North; they are very critical of Southerners so it is unlikely that they were created in the South.
2. They are inflammatory images and the first one is extremely angry in its tone. Both depict Southerners as lawless and savage.

Reading Check

Answer: He founded the New England Anti-Slavery Society and American Anti-Slavery Society, and published the antislavery newspaper, the *Liberator*.

Additional Support

Another important African American abolitionist was **Sojourner Truth.** She gained freedom in 1827 when New York freed all remaining enslaved people in the state. In the 1840s her antislavery speeches—eloquent, joyous, and deeply religious—drew huge crowds. Though lacking a formal education, Truth enthralled listeners with her folksy wit, engaging stories, contagious singing, and strong message:

PRIMARY SOURCE

> "I have had five children and never could take one of them up and say, 'My child' or 'My children,' unless it was when no one could see me. . . . I was forty years a slave but I did not know how dear to me was my posterity."
>
> —from the *Anti-Slavery Bugle*, 1856

Reading Check **Summarizing** How did William Lloyd Garrison work to end slavery?

The Response to Abolitionism

MAIN Idea Many people in both the North and the South opposed abolitionism for economic, political, and cultural reasons.

HISTORY AND YOU Would you be willing to go to jail to defend a principle? Read on to learn the risks taken by abolitionists to defend their position.

Abolitionism was a powerful force, and it provoked a powerful public response. In the North, citizens looked upon the abolitionist movement with views ranging from support to indifference to opposition. In the South, many residents feared that their entire way of life was under attack. They rushed to defend the institution of slavery, which they saw as the key to the region's economy.

POLITICAL CARTOONS PRIMARY SOURCE
Should Slavery Be Abolished?

S

▲ *This cartoon, titled "Southern Ideas of Liberty," denounces southern attempts to suppress abolitionism. A judge with donkey ears and whip sits on bales of cotton with his feet on the Constitution and condemns an abolitionist to be lynched.*

▲ *This cartoon shows pro-slavery forces raiding a post office in Charleston, South Carolina, and destroying abolitionist materials, including copies of the Liberator. The reward sign refers to Arthur Tappan, president of the American Anti-Slavery Society.*

Analyzing VISUALS

1. **Identifying Points of View** In what region of the country do you think these cartoons were created? Why?
2. **Interpreting** How do these cartoons reflect the seriousness of sectional tensions?

Activity: Collaborative Learning

Dramatizing Escape Organize the class into small groups for this activity. Have each group first do research to learn more about what it was like to live under slavery and the dangers African Americans faced if they attempted to escape. Then, have groups create an escape episode to dramatize. Stories can be about people fleeing via the Underground Railroad or attempting to escape independently. Some students should do the research, while others write dialogue, make props and costumes, or play roles in the dramatization. OL ELL

Reaction in the North

While many Northerners disapproved of slavery, some opposed abolitionism even more. They viewed the movement as a threat to the existing social system. Some whites, including many prominent businesspeople, warned it would lead to war between the North and the South. Others feared it might create an influx of freed African Americans to the North, overwhelming the labor and housing markets. Many in the North also had no desire to see the South's economy crumble. If that happened, they might lose the money Southern planters owed to Northern banks, as well as the cotton that fed Northern textile mills.

Given such attitudes, it was not surprising that mobs in Northern cities also attacked abolitionists. A mob in Boston stoned and almost hanged Garrison, and Weld was frequently attacked following his public speeches. Arthur Tappan's home was sacked by a New York mob in 1834, and in 1837 abolitionist publisher Reverend Elijah P. Lovejoy was killed trying to protect his printing press. Yet Northerners also resented Southern slave-catchers, who kidnapped African American runaways in the North and hauled them back south. In response, several states in the North passed personal liberty laws restricting slave recapture.

Reaction in the South

To most Southerners, slavery was a "peculiar institution" vital to Southern life. While the North was building factories, the South remained agricultural, tied to cotton and the enslaved people who harvested it. Southerners responded to criticisms of slavery by defending the institution. South Carolina's governor called it a "national benefit," while Thomas Dew, a leading Southern academic, claimed that most slaves had no desire for freedom because of their close relationship with their slaveholders. "[T]hroughout the whole slaveholding country," he declared, "the slaves of good [slaveholders] are his warmest, most constant, and most devoted friends."

Eight months after Garrison first printed the *Liberator* in 1831, Nat Turner, an enslaved preacher, led a revolt that killed over 50 Virginians. Many Southerners thought papers like the *Liberator* sparked the rebellion. Garrison's paper did not even circulate in the South, but furious Southerners demanded the suppression of abolitionist material as a condition for remaining in the Union. Southern postal workers refused to deliver abolitionist newspapers. In 1836, under Southern pressure, the House of Representatives passed a gag rule providing that all abolitionist petitions be shelved without debate.

For all the uproar it caused, the abolitionist movement remained small. Few people accepted the idea that slavery should be immediately eliminated. The crusade that William Lloyd Garrison started, however, and that thousands of men and women struggled to keep alive, became a powerful reminder that the institution of slavery fundamentally divided the nation.

Reading Check **Evaluating** How did Northerners and Southerners view abolitionism differently?

Section 4 REVIEW

Vocabulary

1. **Explain** the significance of: gradualism, American Colonization Society, abolition, William Lloyd Garrison, emancipation, American Anti-Slavery Society, Frederick Douglass, Sojourner Truth.

Main Ideas

2. **Identifying** What were two early proposals for ending slavery in the early 1800s?
3. **Describing** How did Congress react to the growing conflict over slavery?

Critical Thinking

4. **Big Ideas** Which individuals helped to build support for abolition, and what did they do to gain that support?
5. **Organizing** Use a graphic organizer, similar to the one below, to list the reasons why many Northerners opposed extreme abolitionism.

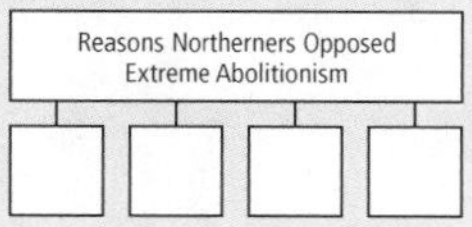

6. **Analyzing Visuals** Examine the cartoon on the left on page 246. What is the meaning of the judge having his feet on the Constitution?

Writing About History

7. **Descriptive Writing** Suppose you are writing for the *Liberator* in the 1830s. Write a letter to a friend describing what you hope to accomplish as a member of the staff of an abolitionist newspaper. Be sure to explain why you sought the job.

History ONLINE
Study Central™ To review this section, go to glencoe.com and click on Study Central.

R Reading Strategy

Outlining Have students use the headings in this section to create an outline to review the content of the section. BL ELL

Reading Check

Answer:
In the North, some people supported abolitionism, some were violently opposed to it, and others were indifferent. In the South, abolition was widely opposed.

Assess

History ONLINE

Study Central™ provides summaries, interactive games, and online graphic organizers to help students review content.

Close

Summarizing Ask: How did abolitionists begin the fight to end slavery? *(They began to publish abolitionist newspapers, held rallies, gave speeches, and formed abolitionist societies.)* OL

Section 4 REVIEW

Answers

1. All definitions can be found in the section and the Glossary.
2. Some people worked for gradualism and others thought that African Americans needed to go to live in Africa and made attempts to achieve that end.
3. In the House of Representatives, a gag rule was passed to shelve all debates on abolition.
4. Key individuals include David Walker, William Lloyd Garrison, Theodore Weld, Sarah and Angelina Grimké, Arthur and Lewis Tappan, Frederick Douglass, and Sojourner Truth. They gave speeches, organized followers, and published antislavery material.
5. (1) threat to existing order; (2) might cause civil war; (3) would take jobs away from Northern whites; (4) could hurt those with investments in the South
6. It implies a disregard for the law and disrespect for the Constitution, and probably for the government of the federal Union.
7. Letters will vary, but should describe the students' goals and what they hope to accomplish.

Questioning Discuss with students the information provided in the Visual Summary. **Ask:** **What information does it provide?** *(It provides a summary of the causes and effects of the chapter content focus, social, cultural, and political change and reform in the early 1800s.)* Have students use the items in the Visual Summary to write questions and answers for a chapter quiz. Then have them exchange quizzes with a partner to check their knowledge of the chapter content. **OL**

Visual/Spatial Have students use the information in the Visual Summary as a basis for designing a collage that represents many of the causes and effects of social change during the period covered in the chapter. Students should use varied materials, including images and type from old magazines and newspapers. Encourage students to be creative and to include words as well as images in their collages. Display completed collages in the classroom. **OL**

Chapter 6 Visual Summary

STUDY TO GO You can study anywhere, anytime by downloading quizzes and flashcards to your PDA from glencoe.com.

Causes of Social Change and Reform in the 1830s and 1840s

Political Change

- States expand voting rights for white males by lowering or eliminating property qualifications.
- Andrew Jackson wins the presidency in the 1828 election.

Social Change

- Large numbers of Irish and German immigrants enter the United States.
- A religious revival—the Second Great Awakening—sweeps the country.
- New religious ideas and philosophies, such as romanticism, transcendentalism, and utopianism, gain support.
- Newspapers become cheap and are widely read, helping create a common popular culture.

▲ *Painter George Caleb Bingham depicts the bustle and energy of a county election in the early 1800s. The painting shows that elections in America involved all social classes.*

▲ *An anti-Catholic mob battles militia during a riot in Philadelphia in 1844. Nativism became strong in the 1840s as people objected to the arrival of Irish Catholic immigrants.*

▶ *An abolitionist poster from 1835*

Effects of Social Change and Reform in the 1830s and 1840s

Political Effects

- Andrew Jackson wins the presidency and supports the spoils system.
- Political parties begin using the convention to nominate candidates instead of the caucus system.
- Government becomes more responsive to public opinion.
- Jackson blocks South Carolina's attempts at nullification, pulls funds from the unpopular Bank of the United States, and supports the Indian Removal Act.
- Women begin demanding more political rights. Susan B. Anthony, Elizabeth Cady Stanton, and others organize the woman suffrage movement and issue the Declaration of Sentiments and Resolutions.

Social Effects

- Nativism gains support, leading to the creation of the anti-immigrant American Party—the "Know-Nothings."
- New American literature is written, including works by Emerson, Thoreau, Irving, Hawthorne, Melville, Poe, Whitman, and Dickinson.
- Religious enthusiasm helps trigger a series of new reform movements, including efforts to reform prisons, mental institutions, and schools, and to reduce the consumption of alcohol.
- Efforts to end slavery gradually and through colonization give way to a rising abolition movement led by William Lloyd Garrison, Frederick Douglass, and others.

Hands-On Chapter Project
Step 5: Wrap Up

Creating a Pamphlet

Step 5: Writing an Informed Response Have students respond to one of the pamphlets created by a group other than their own.

Directions Students should write an essay describing why they did or did not find the pamphlet persuasive. For example, did it influence them to support the reform or turn them against it?

Comparing and Contrasting As a group compare and contrast all of the pamphlets created by the class. Use this comparison to argue which of the reforms were most influential in United States history. **OL**

Chapter 6 Assessment

Reviewing Vocabulary

Directions: Choose the word or words that best complete the sentence.

1. As president, Andrew Jackson used which method of giving out government jobs?
- **A** the caucus system
- **B** the spoils system
- **C** the nullification system
- **D** the American system

2. The philosophy of ________ encouraged people to let their souls reach out to embrace the beauty in the universe.
- **A** romanticism
- **B** revivalism
- **C** nativism
- **D** transcendentalism

3. Under the guidance of religious leaders, associations known as ________ began to address social problems.
- **A** benevolent societies
- **B** penitentiaries
- **C** asylums
- **D** seminaries

4. The ________ movement grew in popularity during the 1830s by rejecting efforts to gradually end slavery.
- **A** compensation
- **B** demonstration
- **C** abolition
- **D** nullification

5. In his newspaper, the *Liberator*, William Lloyd Garrison called for the immediate ________ of enslaved people.
- **A** colonization
- **B** abolition
- **C** emancipation
- **D** incarceration

Reviewing Main Ideas

Directions: Choose the best answer for each of the following questions.

Section 1 *(pp. 222–229)*

6. In 1828 passage of which piece of legislation caused South Carolinians to threaten to secede from the Union?
- **A** the charter for the Second Bank of the United States
- **B** the Tariff of Abominations
- **C** the Force Bill
- **D** the Indian Removal Act

7. Which Whig candidate won the presidential election in 1840?
- **A** William Henry Harrison
- **B** John Tyler
- **C** Andrew Jackson
- **D** John C. Calhoun

Section 2 *(pp. 230–235)*

8. In the early 1800s, the Know-Nothings developed in reaction to
- **A** Andrew Jackson's push for expanded democracy.
- **B** the Second Great Awakening.
- **C** the transcendentalists.
- **D** a huge influx of immigrants.

9. The teachings of the Second Great Awakening differed from earlier Protestant teachings in which way?
- **A** Its ministers preached that all people could attain salvation.
- **B** Its ministers preached that God was a trinity.
- **C** Its ministers preached that women could belong to the church.
- **D** Its ministers preached the idea of nativism.

TEST-TAKING TIP

Unless you are sure you know the answer, always try to narrow down answer choices to at least two before making a final selection.

Need Extra Help?

If You Missed Questions . . .	1	2	3	4	5	6	7	8	9
Go to Page . . .	224	234	237	243	244	225–226	229	232	232–234

GO ON

Answers and Analyses Reviewing Vocabulary

1. B The spoils system rewarded loyal party members in politics by appointing them to government positions. The name developed out of the saying "to the victor belong the spoils [of war]." Students may be tempted to choose *A*, which is also a vocabulary term in Section 1, but remind them that the caucus system was the method political parties used to choose candidates.

2. D Transcendentalism, practiced by artists and writers in New England, was a form of romanticism. Revivalism is not a movement. Nativism was a reaction against immigration.

3. A Tell students that benevolent means kind or compassionate. So, a compassionate society would care for others and try to improve society. Penitentiaries are prisons. Asylums housed the mentally ill. Seminaries are religious schools.

4. C The abolition movement gained supporters after gradualism and colonialism failed to provide a workable end to slavery in the United States. Abolitionists argued that the federal government should outlaw slavery immediately.

5. C To liberate is to free. To emancipate is to free. Students should connect the *Liberator* with freedom and abolition. William Lloyd Garrison was a prominent abolitionist. Students may be confused by *B*, abolition, which means to end, but in this case, it is not the *best* answer to the question, given the context of the chapter.

Reviewing Main Ideas

6. B To remember that the Tariff of Abominations caused South Carolina to threaten to secede, tell students that abominations are outrages or atrocities. It makes sense that something atrocious would have to happen to force a state to do something as drastic as threatening to secede from the U.S.

7. A William Henry Harrison defeated Martin Van Buren in the 1840 election. His vice president was John Tyler. The slogan "Tippecanoe and Tyler, Too" should help students remember this.

8. D Know-Nothings were members of the secret American Party, composed of nativists, those who discriminated against immigrants. Members when questioned said they "knew nothing" of the party.

9. A Ministers of the Second Great Awakening rejected the Calvinist idea that only a chosen few were predestined for salvation. All Christian groups preached the trinity and women had always been members of the churches, so *B* and *C* are incorrect. *D* is simply untrue.

10. C Dorothea Dix championed the cause of the mentally ill. She was appalled at the fact that mentally ill people were housed in awful conditions in prisons, and fought for the establishment of adequate mental health facilities.

11. B The Seneca Falls Convention was focused on women's rights and is considered the beginning of the women's rights movement. Stanton did propose that women should fight for the vote.

12. B Students must first connect the American Colonization Society with African Americans. The society was founded with the goal of moving free African Americans to Liberia, in West Africa. It acquired the land that became Liberia. However, the movement was not very successful.

13. D This question may be confusing to students, because three of the answer choices are partially correct; they include Frederick Douglass and Sojourner Truth. However, David Walker had not been enslaved. He was born free because his mother was free. The Grimké sisters were prominent white abolitionists. Benjamin Lundy was a Quaker who published an antislavery paper.

Critical Thinking

14. B Americans' attitudes, as a whole, toward Native Americans changed little from colonial days. People wanted the land the Native Americans occupied. Therefore, the removal of Native Americans from the Southeast benefited Americans who wanted the land. *A* is not true; the East was not too crowded. American attitudes had not shifted so much that guilt was a prevailing feeling at the time. *D* is a contradiction of the correct answer.

Chapter 6 Assessment

Section 3 *(pp. 236–241)*

10. In the 1840s, Dorothea Dix became the foremost reformer in the area of
- **A** woman suffrage.
- **B** temperance.
- **C** mental illness.
- **D** education.

11. At the Seneca Falls Convention in 1848, attendees were shocked when Elizabeth Cady Stanton
- **A** wore pants to all the meetings.
- **B** proposed that women seek the right to vote.
- **C** insisted that African Americans be admitted.
- **D** announced that she would run for Congress.

Section 4 *(pp. 242–247)*

12. The goal of the American Colonization Society was to move
- **A** all enslaved people to the West.
- **B** free African Americans to West Africa.
- **C** free Africans to Canada.
- **D** formerly enslaved and free African Americans to the North.

13. Which of the following people were former slaves who fought hard for abolition in the mid-1800s?
- **A** David Walker and Frederick Douglass
- **B** Angelina Grimké and Sarah Grimké
- **C** Sojourner Truth and Benjamin Lundy
- **D** Frederick Douglass and Sojourner Truth

Critical Thinking

Directions: Choose the best answers to the following questions.

14. One reason many Americans were in favor of the Indian Removal Act was that they
- **A** thought the East had become too crowded.
- **B** wanted remaining Native American lands in the Southeast.
- **C** felt guilty about earlier treatment of Native Americans.
- **D** wanted to expand democracy to include Native Americans.

Base your answers to questions 15 and 16 on the chart below and your knowledge of Chapter 6.

Major American Political Parties Since 1789

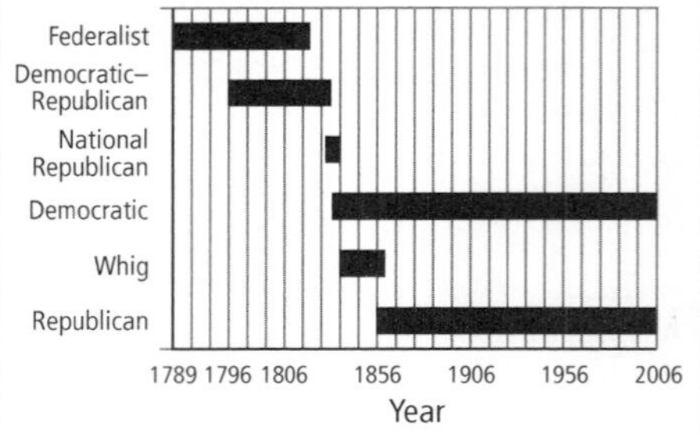

Source: *Government by Consent.*

15. Which party shown had the shortest life span?
- **A** Federalist
- **B** Democratic-Republican
- **C** Whig
- **D** National Republican

16. Which party emerged to oppose Andrew Jackson and his policies?
- **A** Democratic
- **B** Federalist
- **C** Whig
- **D** Republican

Need Extra Help?

If You Missed Questions . . .	10	11	12	13	14	15	16
Go to Page . . .	236	240–241	243	245–246	226	250	228–229

GO ON

15. D Reading the graph, the bar that represents the National Republican Party is by far the shortest on the graph.

16. C The Whigs, formed in opposition to Jackson, were not successful in defeating his successor, Martin van Buren, in 1836, but they did succeed in 1840 when William Henry Harrison won the election.

Chapter 6 Assessment

17. American education reformers believed that free public education was

A important to create a skilled workforce.

B a risky experiment that could fail.

C the only way to prevent civil unrest.

D necessary to maintain a democratic republic.

Analyze the cartoon and answer the question that follows. Base your answer on the cartoon and on your knowledge of Chapter 6.

18. What does Jackson appear to be trampling underfoot?

A Presidential veto orders

B Declaration of Independence

C Articles of Confederation

D United States Constitution

Document-Based Questions

Directions: Analyze the document and answer the short-answer questions that follow the document.

Some people did not support free public education in the early 1800s. In the Raleigh Register of November 9, 1829, the following editorial appeared, addressed to members of the North Carolina legislature:

> *"Common schools indeed! Money is very scarce, and the times are unusually hard. . . . Gentlemen, it appears to me that schools are sufficiently plenty, and that the people have no desire they should be increased. Those now in operation are not filled, and it is very doubtful if they are productive or of much real benefit. Would it not redound as much to the advantage of young persons, and to the honour of the State, if they should pass their days in the cotton patch, or at the plow, or in the cornfield, instead of being [confined] in a school house, where they are earning nothing?"*
>
> —from the *Raleigh Register*, November 9, 1829

19. What reasons does the author give for opposing free public education?

20. Do you think that the author's arguments are valid? Explain your answer.

Extended Response

21. In the 1800s several important themes developed among America's writers and philosophers. Do you think that their writings influenced the reform movements in the United States during the early to mid-1800s? Write an essay in which you discuss the possible influences of romanticism and transcendentalism on reforms of the time. In your essay include an introduction, at least three paragraphs, and supporting details from the chapter.

STOP

History ONLINE

For additional test practice, use Self-Check Quizzes—Chapter 6 at glencoe.com.

Need Extra Help?

If You Missed Questions . . .	17	18	19	20	21
Go to Page . . .	238–239	227–229	251	251	230–241

Extended Response

21. Essays will vary, but must include a discussion of romanticism and transcendentalism, and how the two are related. Students should take a position either for or against how these movements influenced reform movements, using details from the text.

17. D Reformers reasoned that educated people were needed to carry on the U.S. Educated citizens make better voting decisions. They were not concerned with creating a skilled workforce. *B* does not make sense; reformers believed they would succeed, not fail.

18. D Study the cartoon with students. Under Jackson's right foot is a piece of paper that says "Constitution of the United States." He is holding the veto in his hand, not stepping on it.

Document-Based Questions

19. The author's reasons include scarcity of money, existence of plenty of schools that are not even full, questionable benefits of schooling, and lack of ability for children to earn money while in school.

20. Students' responses will vary. Accept all well-reasoned answers.

History ONLINE

Have students visit the Web site at glencoe.com to review Chapter 6 and take the Self-Check Quiz.

Need Extra Help?

Have students refer to the pages listed if they miss any of the questions.

Chapter 7 Planning Guide

Key to Ability Levels

BL Below Level
OL On Level
AL Above Level
ELL English Language Learners

Key to Teaching Resources

Print Material
CD-ROM or DVD
Transparency

BL	OL	AL	ELL		Resources	Chapter Opener	Section 1	Section 2	Section 3	Section 4	Chapter Assess
					FOCUS						
BL	OL	AL	ELL	Transparency	**Daily Focus Skills Transparencies**		7-1	7-2	7-3	7-4	
					TEACH						
BL		AL		Print Material	**Geography and History, URB**			p. 3			
	OL	AL		Print Material	**History Simulations and Problem Solving, URB**						p. 7
BL	OL		ELL	Print Material	**Reading Essentials and Note-Taking Guide***		p. 75	p. 78	p. 81	p. 84	
	OL			Print Material	**Historical Analysis Skills Activity, URB**		p. 120				
BL	OL		ELL	Print Material	**Guided Reading Activities, URB***		p. 144	p. 145	p. 146	p. 147	
BL	OL	AL	ELL	Print Material	**Content Vocabulary Activity, URB***	p. 125					
BL	OL	AL	ELL	Print Material	**Academic Vocabulary Activity, URB**	p. 127					
	OL	AL		Print Material	**Critical Thinking Skills Activity, URB**					p. 130	
BL	OL		ELL	Print Material	**Reading Skills Activity, URB**			p. 119			
BL			ELL	Print Material	**English Learner Activity, URB**	p. 123					
	OL	AL		Print Material	**Reinforcing Skills Activity, URB**				p. 129		
BL	OL	AL	ELL	Print Material	**Differentiated Instruction Activity, URB**		p. 121				
BL	OL		ELL	Print Material	**Time Line Activity, URB**		p. 131				
	OL			Print Material	**Linking Past and Present Activity, URB**		p. 132				
BL	OL	AL	ELL	Print Material	**American Art and Music Activity, URB**						p. 137
BL	OL	AL	ELL	Print Material	**Interpreting Political Cartoons Activity, URB**		p. 139				
		AL		Print Material	**Enrichment Activity, URB**						p. 142
BL	OL	AL	ELL	Print Material	**Primary Source Reading, URB**		pp. 133, 135				
BL	OL	AL	ELL	Print Material	**The Living Constitution***	✓	✓	✓	✓	✓	✓
	OL	AL		CD-ROM or DVD	**American History Primary Source Documents Library**	✓	✓	✓	✓	✓	✓
BL	OL	AL	ELL	Transparency	**Unit Map Overlay Transparencies**	✓	✓	✓	✓	✓	✓
BL	OL	AL	ELL	Print Material	**Differentiated Instruction for the American History Classroom**	✓	✓	✓	✓	✓	✓
BL	OL	AL	ELL	CD-ROM or DVD	**StudentWorks™ Plus**	✓	✓	✓	✓	✓	✓

Note: Please refer to the *Unit 2 Resource Book* for this chapter's URB materials.

* Also available in Spanish

TeacherWorks Plus
All-In-One Planner and Resource Center

- Interactive Lesson Planner
- Interactive Teacher Edition
- Fully editable blackline masters
- Section Spotlight Videos Launch
- Differentiated Lesson Plans
- Printable reports of daily assignments
- Standards Tracking System

Levels BL	OL	AL	ELL		Resources	Chapter Opener	Section 1	Section 2	Section 3	Section 4	Chapter Assess
					TEACH *(continued)*						
BL	OL	AL	ELL	CD	American Music Hits Through History CD	✓	✓	✓	✓	✓	✓
BL	OL	AL	ELL	Folder	Unit Time Line Transparencies and Activities	✓	✓	✓	✓	✓	✓
BL	OL	AL	ELL	Folder	Cause and Effect Transparencies, Strategies, and Activities	✓	✓	✓	✓	✓	✓
BL	OL	AL	ELL	Folder	Why It Matters Transparencies, Strategies, and Activities	✓	✓	✓	✓	✓	✓
BL	OL	AL	ELL	Folder	American Issues	✓	✓	✓	✓	✓	✓
	OL	AL	ELL	Folder	American Art and Architecture Transparencies, Strategies, and Activities	✓	✓	✓	✓	✓	✓
BL	OL	AL		Folder	High School American History Literature Library	✓	✓	✓	✓	✓	✓
BL	OL	AL	ELL	CD	*The American Vision* Video Program	✓	✓	✓	✓	✓	✓
Teacher Resources				Folder	Strategies for Success	✓	✓	✓	✓	✓	✓
				Folder	Success with English Learner	✓	✓	✓	✓	✓	✓
				Folder	Reading Strategies and Activities for the Social Studies Classroom	✓	✓	✓	✓	✓	✓
				CD	Presentation Plus! with MindJogger CheckPoint	✓	✓	✓	✓	✓	✓
					ASSESS						
BL	OL	AL	ELL	Folder	Section Quizzes and Chapter Tests*		p. 87	p. 88	p. 89	p. 90	p. 91
BL	OL	AL	ELL	Folder	Authentic Assessment With Rubrics						p. 19
BL	OL	AL	ELL	Folder	Standardized Test Practice Workbook						p. 13
BL	OL	AL	ELL	CD	*ExamView® Assessment Suite*		7-1	7-2	7-3	7-4	Ch. 7
					CLOSE						
BL			ELL	Folder	Reteaching Activity, URB						p. 141
BL	OL		ELL	Folder	Reading and Study Skills Foldables™	p. 54					
BL	OL	AL	ELL	Folder	*American History* in Graphic Novel		p. 23				

✓ Chapter- or unit-based activities applicable to all sections in this chapter.

Using Section Spotlight Videos

Teach With Technology

What are Section Spotlight Videos?

Section Spotlight Videos are one of the digital media associated with your textbook and present a topic specific to each section of the textbook.

How can Section Spotlight Videos help my students?

Section Spotlight Videos generate student interest and provide a springboard for classroom discussion. Students can watch videos from their classroom computer screen or review for a test while on their home computer.

Visit glencoe.com to access the Media Library, and enter a ***QuickPass***™ code to go to Section Spotlight Videos. These videos can also be launched from StudentWorks ™ Plus Online or PresentationPlus! with MindJogger CheckPoint.

History ONLINE
Visit glencoe.com and enter ***QuickPass***™ code TAV9399c7T for Chapter 7 resources.

TeacherWorks

You can easily launch a wide range of digital products from your computer's desktop with the McGraw-Hill Social Studies widget.

	Student	Teacher	Parent
Media Library			
• Section Audio	●		●
• Spanish Audio Summaries	●		●
• Section Spotlight Videos	●	●	●
***The American Vision* Online Learning Center (Web Site)**			
• StudentWorks™ Plus Online	●	●	●
• Multilingual Glossary	●	●	●
• Study-to-Go	●	●	●
• Chapter Overviews	●	●	●
• Self-Check Quizzes	●	●	●
• Student Web Activities	●	●	●
• ePuzzles and Games	●	●	●
• Vocabulary eFlashcards	●	●	●
• In Motion Animations	●	●	●
• Study Central™	●	●	●
• Web Activity Lesson Plans		●	
• Vocabulary PuzzleMaker	●	●	●
• Historical Thinking Activities		●	
• Beyond the Textbook	●	●	●

Reading Support From Jamestown Education

- **Timed Readings Plus in Social Studies** helps students increase their reading rate and fluency while maintaining comprehension. The 400-word passages are similar to those found on state and national assessments.
- **Reading in the Content Area: Social Studies** concentrates on six essential reading skills that help students better comprehend what they read. The book includes 75 high-interest nonfiction passages written at increasing levels of difficulty.
- **Reading Social Studies** includes strategic reading instruction and vocabulary support in Social Studies content for both ELLs and native speakers of English.

www.jamestowneducation.com

National Geographic

Index to National Geographic Magazine:

The following articles relate to this chapter:

- "Along the Santa Fe Trail," February 1989
- "The American Prairie: Roots of the Sky," October 1993
- "The Cherokee," May 1995
- "Life and Death on the Oregon Trail: The Itch to Move West," August 1986
- "Tex-Mex Border," February 1996
- "The Way West," September 2000

Access National Geographic's new, dynamic MapMachine Web site and other geography resources at:

www.nationalgeographic.com
www.nationalgeographic.com/maps

Biography · A&E Home Video · The History Channel

The following videotape programs are available from Glencoe as supplements to this chapter:

- The Alamo (Two Video Set) (ISBN 1-56-501784-6)

To order, call Glencoe at 1-800-334-7344. To find classroom resources to accompany many of these videos, check the following home pages:

A&E Television: www.aetv.com
The History Channel: www.historychannel.com

Reading List Generator CD-ROM — Glencoe BookLink 3

Use this database to search more than 30,000 titles to create a customized reading list for your students.

- Reading lists can be organized by students' reading level, author, genre, theme, or area of interest.
- The database provides Degrees of Reading Power™ (DRP) and Lexile™ readability scores for all selections.
- A brief summary of each selection is included.

Leveled reading suggestions for this chapter:

For students at a Grade 8 reading level:
- ***James K. Polk***, by Anne Welsbacher

For students at a Grade 9 reading level:
- ***Make Way for Sam Houston***, by Jean Fritz

For students at a Grade 10 reading level:
- ***Texas History***, by Mary Dodson Wade

For students at a Grade 11 reading level:
- ***James K. Polk: 11th President of the United States***, by Miriam Greenblatt

For students at a Grade 12 reading level:
- ***The Mexican War: "Mr. Polk's War,"*** by Charles W. Carey

Introducing
Chapter 7

Focus

MAKING CONNECTIONS
Why Did People Migrate West?

Discuss with students the two questions posed on page 253. Ask students what they know about the westward migration and encourage them to speculate about how their lives would be different if it had never happened. To give students a sense of the scope of the westward migration, ask them to imagine what it would be like to travel for days and days and see only travelers like themselves, and to imagine how, once they had arrived at their destination, they would need to be wholly self-sufficient. Point out that Americans continue to be a restless people, seeking better lives for themselves and their children. Like the early settlers of the West, they too take risks. **OL**

Teach

The Big Ideas

As students study the chapter, remind them to consider the section-based Big Ideas included in each section's Guide to Reading. The **Essential Questions** in the activities below tie in to the Big Ideas and help students think about and understand important chapter concepts. In addition, the Hands-on Chapter Projects with their culminating activities relate the content from each section to the Big Ideas. These activities build on each other as students progress through the chapter. Section activities culminate in the wrap-up activity on the Visual Summary page.

Chapter 7

Manifest Destiny
1820–1848

Settlers head west in covered wagons, carrying all their belongings with them.

U.S. PRESIDENTS
Van Buren 1837–1841
W. Harrison 1841
Tyler 1841–1845

U.S. EVENTS

1836
- Texas wins independence from Mexico

1841
- President Harrison becomes first president to die in office

WORLD EVENTS

1839
- First pedal-propelled bicycle is designed by Kirkpatrick MacMillan of Scotland

1842
- China cedes Hong Kong to Britain

1836 · 1839 · 1842

Section 1

The Western Pioneers

Essential Question: How did the idea of Manifest Destiny influence the settlement of the West? *(People felt that it was their God-given right to settle western lands.)* Point out that in Section 1 students will learn about the early settlement of the West. **OL**

Section 2

The Hispanic Southwest

Essential Question: How did American settlement of the Southwest cause tensions with Mexico? *(The Mexican borderlands drew many settlers from the East. They resisted Mexican authority by refusing to convert to Catholicism. American influence in the area grew quickly.)* Point out that in Section 2 students will learn about the settlement of the Mexican borderlands. **OL**

Chapter Audio

MAKING CONNECTIONS

Why Did People Migrate West?

Beginning in the 1820s, Americans began moving in large numbers west across the Great Plains. They headed south to Texas and west to Oregon, Utah, and California. By 1848, the United States had taken the Southwest from Mexico and divided Oregon with Great Britain.

- *Why do you think Americans wanted to move west in the 1800s?*
- *How do you think westward migration affected America's relationship with other countries and native peoples?*

1845
- Congress votes to annex Republic of Texas

Polk 1845–1849

1846
- Great Britain and U.S. divide Oregon Territory at 49th parallel
- United States begins war with Mexico

1848
- Treaty of Guadalupe Hidalgo ends war with Mexico

1845 — 1848

1843
- Charles Dickens's *A Christmas Carol* is published

1845
- Irish potato famine begins

1848
- Karl Marx and Frederick Engels publish *The Communist Manifesto*
- Numerous revolutions sweep Europe

FOLDABLES

Organizing Create a Four-Door Book Foldable that helps in researching the development of early transportation routes. Record key facts about each route in the Four-Door Book under *What, When, Where,* and *Why.*

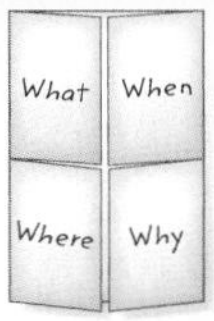

History ONLINE Visit glencoe.com and enter *QuickPass*™ code TAV9846c7 for Chapter 7 resources.

More About the Painting

Visual Literacy The idea of Manifest Destiny captivated not only the westward bound settlers but also the artists of the era. The painting *Wild West* by Frances F. Palmer (1812–1876) shows a romantic view of the West that was popular in art at the time—the epic, peaceful occupation of an empty continent. None of the forbidding dangers of the journey are represented. The wagon train is following the banks of a gentle stream in a lush setting, while benevolent Native Americans watch from the far bank.

FOLDABLES Study Organizer **Dinah Zike's Foldables**

Dinah Zike's Foldables are three-dimensional, interactive graphic organizers that help students practice basic writing skills, review vocabulary terms, and identify main ideas. Instructions for creating and using Foldables can be found in the Appendix at the end of this book and in the *Dinah Zike's Reading and Study Skills Foldables* booklet.

History ONLINE

Visit glencoe.com and enter *QuickPass*™ code TAV9399c7T for Chapter 7 resources, including a Chapter Overview, Study Central™, Study-to-Go, Student Web Activity, Self-Check Quiz, and other materials.

Section 3

Independence for Texas

Essential Question: How did Texas gain its independence? *(Texans rebelled against the Mexican government, fought many battles, and finally defeated Mexico at the Battle of San Jacinto.)* Point out that in Section 3 students will learn about the Texas defeat of Mexican forces and the formation of a new republic. **OL**

Section 4

The War with Mexico

Essential Question: What resulted from the annexation of Texas and the war with Mexico? *(After defeating Mexico, annexing Texas, and reaching an agreement with Britain about the Oregon Territory, the United States gained so much land that it stretched across the entire continent.)* Point out that in Section 4 students will learn about how the United States was transformed by the war with Mexico. **OL**

Focus

Bellringer

Daily Focus Transparency 7-1

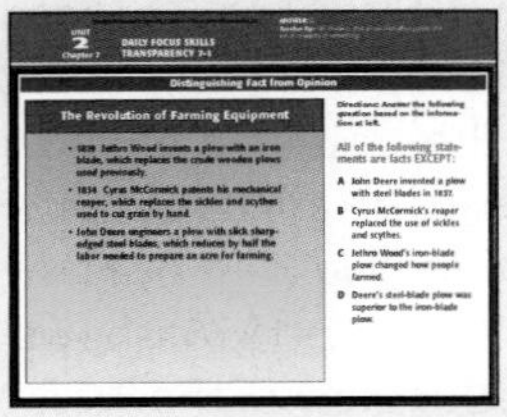

Guide to Reading

Answers Include:
Oregon Trail, California Trail, Santa Fe Trail, Mormon Trail, Old Spanish Trail, Butterfield Overland Mail Trail, Pony Express Trail

Section Spotlight Video

To generate student interest and provide a springboard for class discussion, access the Chapter 7, Section 1 video at glencoe.com or on the video DVD.

Section 1

Section Audio   Spotlight Video

The Western Pioneers

Guide to Reading

Big Ideas
Science and Technology Several inventions in the early 1800s helped make it possible to settle the West.

Content Vocabulary
- squatter *(p. 254)*
- overlander *(p. 256)*

Academic Vocabulary
- guarantee *(p. 254)*
- convert *(p. 255)*

People and Events to Identify
- Manifest Destiny *(p. 254)*
- Jethro Wood *(p. 255)*
- John Deere *(p. 255)*
- Cyrus McCormick *(p. 255)*
- Kit Carson *(p. 256)*

Reading Strategy
Organizing Use a graphic organizer, like the one below, to list the trails to the West used by settlers in the 1840s.

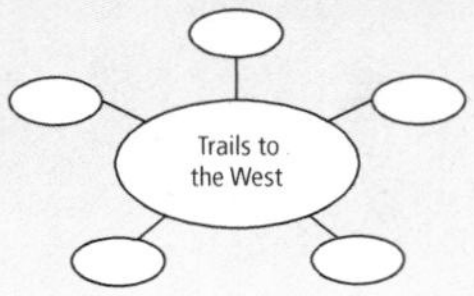

In the 1840s, Americans made the grueling trek west to the frontier states of the Midwest and the rich lands of the Oregon Country. The invention of new farming equipment made it easier to clear and cultivate new land, thus encouraging settlement of the Midwest.

Settling New Lands

MAIN Idea Americans moved westward and established new farms in the Midwest; later settlers traveled in wagon trains to the Pacific Coast.

HISTORY AND YOU Have you ever packed for a long trip? What things did you take with you? Read on to learn how settlers faced difficult times on the trail west.

In 1800 only around 387,000 white settlers lived west of the Appalachian Mountains. By 1820, that number had grown to more than 2.4 million, and the numbers continued to rise rapidly. By the time the Civil War began, more Americans lived west of the Appalachians than lived in states along the Atlantic Coast.

Some Americans headed west for religious reasons. Others were lured by the chance to own their own farms. While most settled east of the Mississippi River, more than 250,000 Americans continued farther west, across the Great Plains and Rocky Mountains to California and the Pacific Northwest.

In 1845 a magazine editor named John Louis O'Sullivan declared that it was the "manifest destiny" of Americans "to overspread the continent allotted by Providence." Many Americans believed in this concept of **Manifest Destiny**—the idea that God had given the entire continent to Americans and wanted them to settle western land.

Farming the New Lands

Early settlers marked out farms on the rich river bottom land. Others occupied fertile woodlands. These pioneers became known as **squatters,** because they settled on lands they did not own. The federal government intended to survey the land and then sell large parcels to real estate companies, but squatters wanted to buy the land they occupied directly from the government.

Bowing to public pressure, Congress passed the Preemption Act of 1830, a renewable law made permanent in 1841. This law protected squatters by **guaranteeing** them the right to claim land before it was surveyed and the right to buy up to 160 acres at the government's minimum price of $1.25 per acre.

Resource Manager

R Reading Strategies	C Critical Thinking	D Differentiated Instruction	W Writing Support	S Skill Practice
Additional Resources • Prim. Source Read., URB pp. 133, 135 • Guid. Read. Act., URB p. 144 • Am. Hist. in Graphic Novel, p. 23	**Teacher Edition** • Making Generalizations, p. 257 **Additional Resources** • Hist. Analysis Act., URB p. 120 • Link. Past/Present, URB p. 132 • Quizzes and Tests, p. 83	**Teacher Edition** • Kinesthetic, p. 255 **Additional Resources** • Diff. Instr. Act., URB p. 121 • Eng. Learner Act., URB p. 123 • Acad. Vocab. Act., URB p. 127	**Teacher Edition** • Descriptive Writing, p. 256 **Additional Resources** • Content Vocab. Act., URB p. 125	**Teacher Edition** • Using Geo. Skills, URB p. 256 **Additional Resources** • Time Line Act., URB p. 131 • Int. Pol. Cartoons Act, URB, p. 139 • Read. Essen., p. 75

PRIMARY SOURCE
The Idea of Manifest Destiny

▲ *Entitled "American Progress," this famous painting of the idea of Manifest Destiny depicts America as a woman, leading the country into the West. She carries a book, which represents American enlightenment and is laying a telegraph wire.*

PRIMARY SOURCE

Although John L. O'Sullivan did not use the phrase "manifest destiny" until 1845, as early as 1839 he was declaring that it was America's destiny to spread its ideas to the world:

". . . our national birth was the beginning of a new history. . . . [W]e are the nation of progress, of individual freedom, of universal enfranchisement. . . . We must onward to the fulfilment [sic] of our mission—to the entire development of the principle of our organization—freedom of conscience, freedom of person, freedom of trade and business pursuits, universality of freedom and equality. This is our high destiny. . . . For this blessed mission to the nations of the world . . . has America been chosen; and her high example shall smite unto death the tyranny of kings, hierarchs, and oligarchs. . . ."

—from "The Great Nation of Futurity," *The United States Democratic Review*

DBQ Document-Based Questions

1. **Analyzing** What symbolizes progress in the painting? Why is the left portion of the painting darker than the right?
2. **Paraphrasing** For what does O'Sullivan say that the United States has been chosen?

Plows and Reapers

A few decades earlier, farmers had only wooden plows to break the grass cover and roots of Midwestern sod. **Jethro Wood** patented an iron-bladed plow in 1819, and in 1837 **John Deere** engineered a plow with sharp-edged steel blades that cut cleanly through the sod. This reduced, by half, the labor needed to prepare an acre for farming.

D

Midwestern agriculture also received a boost from the mechanical reaper, which **Cyrus McCormick** patented in 1834. For centuries farmers had cut grain by hand, using a sickle or a scythe—exhausting and time-consuming work. Switching from a sickle to a McCormick reaper pulled by horses or mules, farmers could harvest far more grain with far less effort.

Settling the Pacific Coast

Latecomers to the Midwest set their sights on the Pacific Coast, partly because emigrants assumed that the treeless Great Plains had poor land for farming. The United States and Great Britain—as well as Native Americans—laid claim to Oregon Country, a region that included present-day Oregon, Washington, and British Columbia. In 1818 Britain and the United States had agreed to occupy the land jointly. In the 1830s, American missionaries began arriving in Oregon to **convert** Native Americans. These missionaries spread the word about Oregon and persuaded others to come to the lush Willamette Valley.

History ONLINE
Student Web Activity Visit glencoe.com and complete the activity on the Oregon Trail.

Reading Check **Describing** How did Congress help squatters attain land in the West?

Teach

D Differentiated Instruction

Kinesthetic Encourage students to learn about the inventions of the period, including the plow, the reaper, the telegraph, and the steam locomotive, and prepare an oral presentation about how these inventions contributed to the settlement of the west. **OL**

DBQ Document Based Questions

Answers:

1. The floating woman—representing Manifest Destiny—is stringing telegraph wire; the suggestion is that the settlers are bringing light into the darkness.
2. to develop the American way of life based on freedom

Reading Check

Answer:
Congress passed the Preemption Act of 1830, a law that gave squatters the right to claim land before it was surveyed and buy up to 160 acres at the price of $1.25 per acre.

Hands-On Chapter Project Step 1

Creating a Thematic Map

Step 1: The United States in 1820 Students will research and collect information on the states and territories of the United States in 1820.

Directions Have students research the population of the states and territories that were part of the United States in 1820. Have students use an outline map of the United States and create a map key that represents areas. For example, students may use one color to represent states, territories, unorganized territories, and claims.

Creating and Reading Maps Students will interpret information from their textbooks and other sources to create their own maps of the United States in 1820. **OL**

(Chapter Project continued on page 262)

Westward Migration

MAIN Idea Emigrant groups followed specific trails through territory belonging to Native Americans.

HISTORY AND YOU Do you remember which religious groups came to America to escape religious persecution? Read on to learn why the Mormons left the United States to practice their religion freely.

Much of the terrain from the edge of the frontier to the Pacific was difficult. A small number of trailblazers—mountain men like **Kit Carson** and Jim Bridger—made their living by trapping beaver and selling the furs to traders. At the same time, they gained a thorough knowledge of the territory and the local Native Americans.

By the 1840s, the mountain men had carved out several East-to-West trails that helped settlers travel. The most popular route was the Oregon Trail. Others included the California Trail and the Santa Fe Trail.

Emigrants made the journey in groups of covered wagons called wagon trains. Before starting out, the trains assembled at staging areas outside a frontier town. There, families exchanged information about routes, bought supplies, trained oxen, and practiced steering the cumbersome wagons, which new drivers were apt to tip over.

The first wagon trains hired mountain men to guide them. Once the trails became well worn, most of the travelers—known as **overlanders**—found their own way with the help of guidebooks. Sometimes the guidebooks were wrong, leading to tragedy. In 1846 a group of 87 overlanders known as the Donner Party, after the two brothers who led them, were trapped by winter snows high up in the Sierra Nevada. After 41 died of starvation, those still alive resorted to cannibalism in order to survive.

NATIONAL GEOGRAPHIC Overland Trails West, 1840–1860

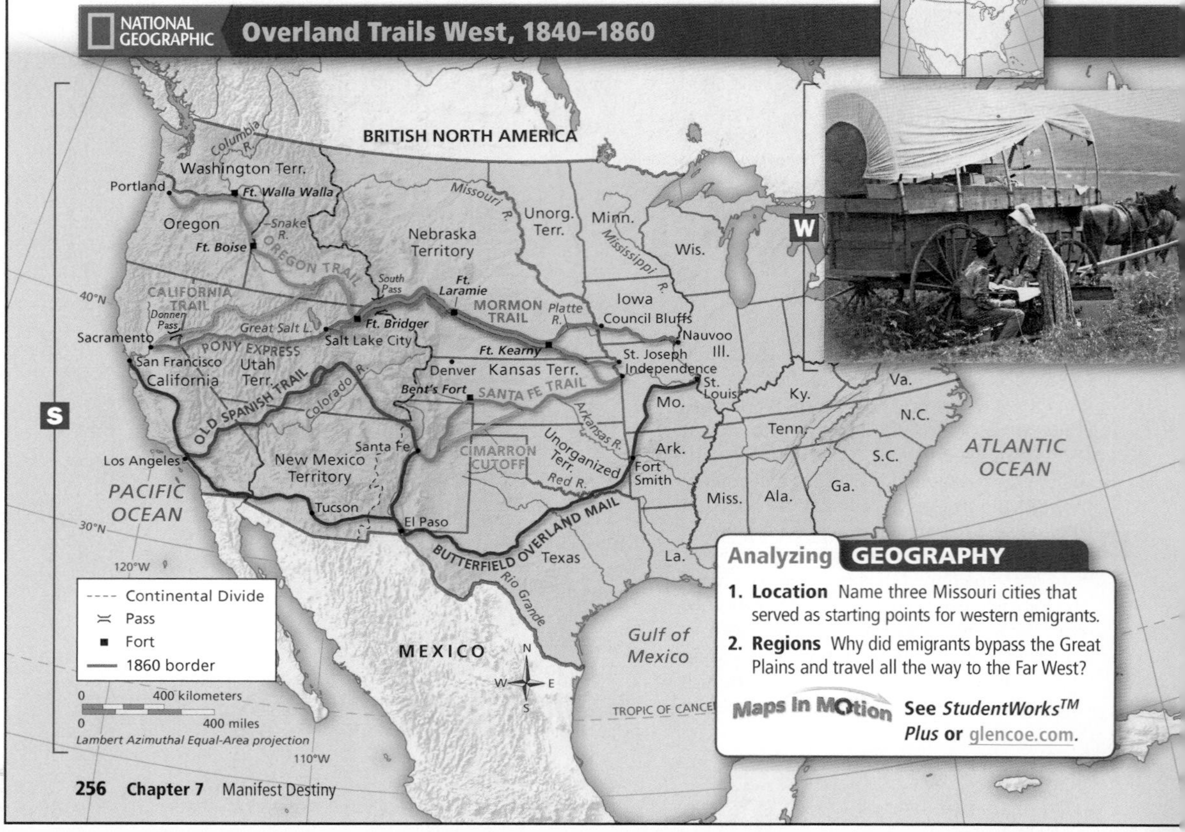

Analyzing GEOGRAPHY

1. **Location** Name three Missouri cities that served as starting points for western emigrants.
2. **Regions** Why did emigrants bypass the Great Plains and travel all the way to the Far West?

Maps In MOtion See *StudentWorks™ Plus* or glencoe.com.

S Skill Practice

Using Geography Skills Have students use a current map of the United States to follow one of the trails shown on the map on page 256. Instruct students to name the current states and major geographic landmarks along the trail. **ELL**

W Writing Support

Descriptive Writing Have students research the daily lives of people heading west. Then have them write a monologue about the woman in the photograph—either to be delivered by her or an observer. The monologue should contain details about the journey so far and her excitement and worry about the future. **OL**

Analyzing GEOGRAPHY

Answers:

1. St. Louis, St. Joseph, Independence
2. They assumed that the land was not good for farming and feared encounters with Native Americans.

Differentiated Instruction

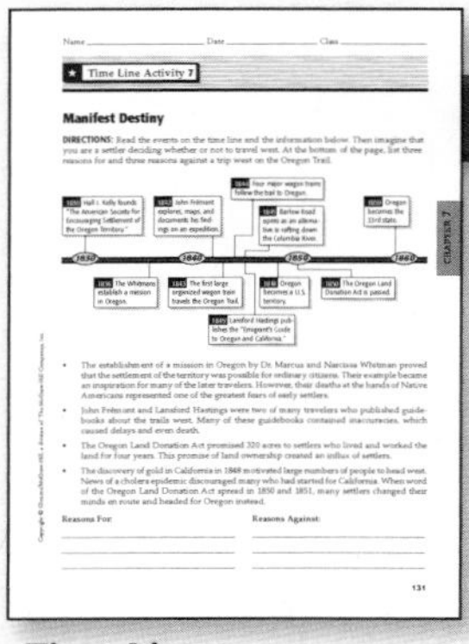

Time Line Activity 7, URB p. 131

Determining the Risks and Rewards of Emigration

Objective: Read to evaluate information about the risks and rewards of moving west.

Focus: Read the information on the risks of the trip.

Teach: Make a list of the risks and rewards of moving.

Assess: Decide whether the risks outweigh the rewards or if the trip is too dangerous to make. Write a few paragraphs outlining your decision.

Close: Make a poster either as a company encouraging people to move west or as a community leader encouraging people to stay.

Differentiated Instruction Strategies

BL Identify the Oregon Trail on a map. Determine the distance that travelers had to go to reach their destination.

AL Write a description of a wagon train. Include information on the different members and their roles.

ELL Illustrate a map of Oregon with land formations and natural resources.

The typical trip west took five to six months, with the wagon trains progressing about 15 miles (24 km) per day. Generally, men drove the wagons, hunted game, and fed and cared for the animals at night, while women looked after the children, cooked the meals, cleaned the camp, and laundered the clothes. As Elizabeth Geer recounts, the journey was exhausting and difficult:

C

PRIMARY SOURCE

"I carry my babe and lead, or rather carry, another through snow, mud, and water, almost to my knees. It is the worst road. . . . [T]here was not one dry thread on one of us—not even my babe. . . . I have not told you half we suffered. I am not adequate to the task."

—quoted in *Women's Diaries of the Westward Journey*

Native Americans

Early travelers feared attacks by Native American warriors, but such encounters were rare. By one estimate, only 362 emigrants died due to Native American attacks between 1840 and 1860, while emigrants killed 426 Native Americans in the same period. In fact, Native Americans often gave emigrants gifts of food, as well as helpful information about routes, edible plants, and sources of water. They often traded fresh horses for items such as cotton clothing and ammunition.

As the overland traffic increased, Native Americans on the Great Plains became concerned and angry over the threat this influx of people posed to their way of life. The Sioux, Cheyenne, Arapaho, and other groups relied on buffalo for food, shelter, clothing, tools, and countless other necessities of everyday life. Now they feared that the age-old wanderings of the buffalo herds would be disrupted.

Hoping to ensure peace, the federal government negotiated the Treaty of Fort Laramie in 1851. In that document, the United States promised eight Native American groups that specific territories in the region of the Great Plains would belong to them as long as they allowed settlers to pass through peacefully. The government also agreed to make payments to the groups.

The Mormon Migration

Unlike those bound for the West in search of land, the Mormons followed a deeply rooted American tradition—the quest for religious freedom. The Mormons, however, had to seek that freedom by leaving the Eastern states, instead of coming to them.

In 1844, after a mob murdered their leader, Joseph Smith, the church's new leader, Brigham Young, took his people west to escape further persecution. Several thousand Mormons forged their way along a path that became known as the Mormon Trail. It served as a valuable route into the western United States. In 1847 the Mormons stopped at the Great Salt Lake in what is now Utah. Undeterred by the wildness of the area, they staked a claim on the land they called "Deseret."

✓ Reading Check **Describing** What difficulties did settlers face in the American West?

Section 1 REVIEW

Vocabulary

1. **Explain** the significance of: Manifest Destiny, squatters, Jethro Wood, John Deere, Cyrus McCormick, Kit Carson, overlander.

Main Ideas

2. **Specifying** Who encouraged settlers to emigrate to the Oregon Territory?
3. **Describing** What was the purpose of the 1851 Treaty of Fort Laramie, and what were its main points?

Critical Thinking

4. **Big Ideas** What two inventions made it easier to farm on the frontier?
5. **Organizing** Use a graphic organizer, similar to the one below, to list the reasons that Americans emigrated to the West.

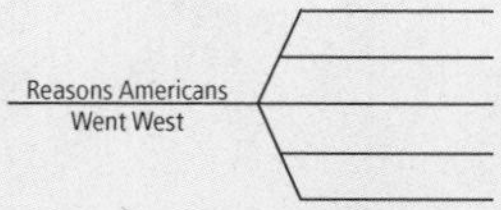

6. **Analyzing Visuals** Study the map of overland trails to the West on page 256. Where did the Old Spanish Trail begin, and where did it end?

Writing About History

7. **Descriptive Writing** Suppose that you emigrated from the East to a frontier farm in the West. Write a journal entry describing a day in your journey.

History ONLINE
Study Central™ To review this section, go to glencoe.com and click on Study Central.

C Critical Thinking

Making Generalizations Have students locate and read excerpts from diaries written by people who traveled West between 1820 and 1860. Have students make generalizations about daily life during that time. **OL**

✓ Reading Check

Answer: difficult terrain, bad weather, attacks by Native Americans

Assess

History ONLINE

Study Central™ provides summaries, interactive games, and online graphic organizers to help students review content.

Close

Summarizing Ask: Why were people willing to leave their homes in the East and head West? *(They moved for religious reasons, or for the chance to own their own farms. Many were drawn by the ideal of Manifest Destiny.)* **OL**

Section 1 REVIEW

Answers

1. All definitions can be found in the section and the Glossary.
2. American Christian missionaries who went to the Oregon Territory to convert Native Americans
3. Its purpose was to ensure peace with Native Americans on the Great Plains so that settlers could travel to the West. In the treaty, the United States agreed that if they allowed to let settlers pass through the Great Plains peacefully, the Native Americans could have specific territories in the region; the United States also agreed to make payments to the Native Americans.
4. steel-bladed plow, mechanical reaper
5. religious freedom, opportunity to own their own farms, to fulfill the principle of Manifest Destiny, to convert Native Americans to Christianity, to trap for furs, to act as trailblazers
6. It began in Santa Fe and ended in Los Angeles.
7. Students' journals will vary, but should contain specific details about the journey.

Focus

Have students read Chief Joseph's eulogy for his father. **Ask:** What did Old Joseph say Chief Joseph's responsibility was? *(to guide his people and to never sell or give away his land.)* **Ask:** Why do you think Old Joseph told his son to stop his ears when asked to sign a treaty? *(Answers may vary. He suggests that the terms of the treaty might sound good and reasonable, but that his son should not even listen to the white man nor sell the land.)* Help students connect this speech to what they have read about the westward migration of white settlers and to consider how this wave of migration might have concerned the Native Americans already residing in the country.

Teach

R Reading Strategy

Making Connections Have students compare these rules of baseball to the modern rules for the game. **Ask:** Which rules are still part of the game of baseball? *(Accept all reasonable answers.)* OL

Additional Support

TIME NOTEBOOK

EDWARD S. CURTIS/CORBIS

Eulogy

CHIEF JOSEPH *(above), a leader of the Nez Perce of the Wallowa Valley in eastern Oregon, remembers his father, Old Joseph. The Nez Perce were forced to leave the Wallowa Valley less than a decade after Old Joseph's death.*

MY FATHER SENT FOR ME. I SAW HE WAS DYING. I TOOK HIS HAND IN MINE. He said, "My son, my body is returning to my mother earth, and my spirit is going very soon to see the Great Spirit Chief. When I am gone, think of your country. You are the chief of these people. They look to you to guide them. Always remember that your father never sold his country. You must stop your ears whenever you are asked to sign a treaty selling your home. A few years more, and white men will be all around you. They have their eyes on this land. My son, never forget my dying words. This country holds your father's body. Never sell the bones of your father and your mother."

I pressed my father's hand and told him I would protect his grave with my life. My father smiled and passed to the spirit land.

I buried him in that beautiful valley of winding rivers. I love that land more than all the rest of the world. A man who would not love his father's grave is worse than a wild animal.

Baseball for Beginners

Thinking of taking up the new game of baseball? Watch out! The rules keep changing!

1845

- Canvas bases will be set 90 feet apart in a diamond shape.
- Only nine men will play on each side.
- Pitches are to be thrown underhanded.
- A ball caught on the first bounce is an out. R

1846

- At first base, a fielder can tag the bag before the runner reaches it and so make an out.

1847

- Players may no longer throw the ball at a runner to put him out.

These changes may be coming:

- A poor pitch is a ball; nine balls gives the runner first base, a walk.
- A ball caught on the first bounce is no longer an out.

O. PIERRE HAVENS/CORBIS

An early New York baseball team

Extending the Content

Dangers on the Oregon Trail Many of the people who emigrated along the Oregon Trail during the mid-1800s feared attacks by Native Americans. It was certainly a dangerous journey, but of the estimated 20,000 to 30,000 deaths along the trail, fewer than one percent were due to altercations with Native Americans. Disease, particularly cholera, was the primary cause of death along the trail.

WESTERN WORD PLAY

Word Watch

Can you talk Western? Match the word to its meaning.

1. maverick
2. Hangtown fry
3. grubstake
4. bonanza
5. palo alto
6. pard or rawwheel

a. gold rush favorite, made of eggs, bacon, and oysters
b. inexperienced '49er, Eastern type not used to wearing boots
c. a lucky discovery of gold; a source of sudden wealth
d. a style of hat worn by gold rush miners
e. a lone dissenter who takes an independent stand, from the name of a Texas cattleman who left his herd unbranded
f. food provided by an investor to a gold prospector in exchange for a share of whatever gold he finds

answers: 1.e; 2.a; 3.f; 4.c; 5.d; 6.b

Milestones

SETTLED, 1847. THE VALLEY OF THE GREAT SALT LAKE, by Brigham Young, leader of the Mormons, and a party of 143, to escape hostility toward their group in Illinois. Young plans to return to Council Bluffs, Iowa, and lead the rest of the members of his faith to a permanent home in Utah.

MOVED, 1845. HENRY DAVID THOREAU, writer, to Walden Pond, Concord, Massachusetts. Thoreau intends to build his own house on the shore of the pond and earn his living by the labor of his hands only. "Many of the so-called comforts of life," writes Thoreau, "are not only not indispensable, but positive hindrances to the elevation of mankind."

AILING, 1847. EDGAR ALLAN POE, in Baltimore, following the death of his wife, Virginia. Other than a poem on death, Poe has written little this year, devoting his dwindling energies to plagiarism suits against other authors.

LIBRARY OF CONGRESS/CORBIS

Frederick Douglass

EMIGRATED, 1845. FREDERICK DOUGLASS, former slave, author, and abolitionist leader, to England to escape the danger of re-enslavement in reaction to his autobiography, *Narrative of the Life of Frederick Douglass.* On his 1845 trip across the Atlantic, Douglass was not permitted cabin accommodations. After a lecture during the crossing, some passengers threatened to throw him overboard.

NUMBERS

18,000 Miles from New York to California by sea route around Cape Horn

90,000 People arriving in California in 1849, half by sea, half by overland route

BETTMANN/CORBIS

Panning for gold

$20 Average earned per day by California gold miners in 1849

$435 Value of miners' average daily earnings in 2006 dollars

50 Number of years after the signing of the Declaration of Independence that Thomas Jefferson and John Adams die—within hours of each other.

17,069,453 U.S. population in 1840

55,000 Number of emigrants moving west along the Oregon Trail in 1850

CRITICAL THINKING

1. ***Categorizing*** As a leader, Old Joseph combined spiritual beliefs with practical politics. Give examples of each.

2. ***Identifying Points of View*** Thoreau believed that the basics in life rather than the extra comforts made people better human beings. Do you agree or disagree with his view? Why?

Assess/Close

Summarizing Ask: What general statement can you make about the period? *(Possible response: It was a time of change and the movement of large groups of people.)*

CRITICAL THINKING

Answers:

1. Spiritual beliefs: At death, our bodies return to mother earth and our spirits go to see the Great Spirit Chief; Practical politics: In spite of pressure from encroaching settlers, he doesn't sell his country or sign treaties; he guides and supports his people.
2. Responses will vary. Students should give reasons to support their beliefs.

Visit the TIME Web site at www.time.com for up-to-date news, weekly magazine articles, editorials, online polls, and an archive of past magazine and Web articles.

Additional Support

Activity: Collaborative Learning

Determining Cause and Effect Remind students that the ambition to acquire land, both for individuals and for the nation, was a driving force between many of the events during the first half of the 1800s. Lead a class discussion about attitudes toward land and property in the United States today. **Ask:** For what purposes do people hope to acquire land today? *(for development, for housing, for recreation, for business construction, and so on)* **Ask:** How does this ambition shape the economy and politics of the United States today? *(Some students may mention property taxes and disputes over industrial access to national parks.)* **OL**

Focus

Bellringer

Daily Focus Transparency 7-2

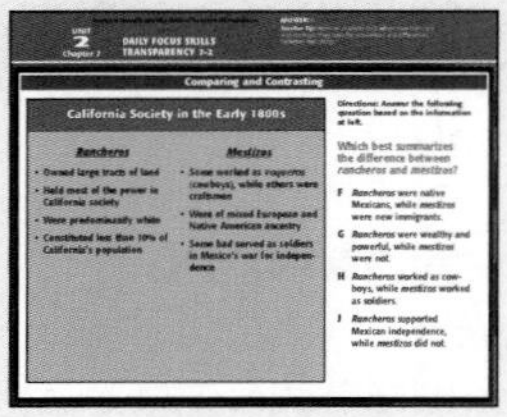

Guide to Reading

Answers:
California: Hispanic elite rancheros at the top of society, followed by mestizos, and then Native Americans; missions secularized; some tension between Americans and Mexican government; New Mexico: rural; sheep ranching; some farming; suffered attacks from Native Americans; revolt of settlers; Texas: sparsely populated; recurring Native American raids; Americans allowed to settle, and flood in.

Section Spotlight Video

To generate student interest and provide a springboard for class discussion, access the Chapter 7, Section 2 video at glencoe.com or on the video DVD.

Resource Manager

Section 2

Section Audio   Spotlight Video

The Hispanic Southwest

Guide to Reading

Big Ideas

Trade, War, and Migration
Americans began to settle in the Mexican borderlands, leading to conflict with the Mexican government.

Content Vocabulary
- secularize *(p. 261)*
- mestizo *(p. 262)*
- vaqueros *(p. 262)*

Academic Vocabulary
- civil *(p. 261)*
- ultimately *(p. 263)*

People and Events to Identify
- John Sutter *(p. 263)*
- William Becknell *(p. 263)*
- Santa Fe Trail *(p. 263)*
- *Tejano (p. 263)*

Reading Strategy

Categorizing Use a graphic organizer, similar to the one below, to list features of each Mexican territory after Mexico gained independence.

Territory	Features
California	
New Mexico	
Texas	

Mexico won its independence from Spain in 1821. For the next quarter century, the Mexican government neglected its far northern territories. American influence grew as more Americans settled in the region.

Mexican Independence and the Borderlands

MAIN Idea Far from Mexico City, the Mexican borderlands were sparsely populated; the region's economy centered on cattle and sheep ranching.

HISTORY AND YOU Have you ever visited or seen pictures of an old Spanish mission in the Southwest? Read on to learn about the purpose of the missions, the way they functioned, and why they were abandoned after Mexican independence.

In 1821, after more than a decade of fighting, Mexico won its independence from Spain. During the decades that followed, Mexico experienced great turmoil and political chaos. The far northern territories of California, New Mexico, and Texas remained part of Mexico, although their great distance from the capital, Mexico City, allowed for considerable political independence. As the young Mexican republic struggled to establish a stable national government, it neglected its northern borderlands.

Located more than 1,000 miles from Mexico City, this region was sparsely populated by Native Americans and Hispanic settlers. Thus, the Mexican frontier was threatened on several fronts. Settlements in Texas and New Mexico faced attacks by Apaches, Comanches, and other Native American groups. In addition, the under-populated northern territories were threatened by the westward expansion of the United States and the southward expansion of Russian settlements along the Pacific Coast. (Russia had begun colonizing Alaska in the 1780s.)

The Spanish had expanded the territory of New Spain by establishing missions on the northern frontier. The purpose of the state-financed missions was to spread the Christian faith and Spanish culture to Native Americans. Missions controlled vast tracts of land on which grazed cattle, sheep, and horses. Native Americans tended to the livestock and did other work at the missions under conditions of near slavery.

By the early 1800s, the mission system was in decline. By the time Mexico became independent, it had nearly collapsed, having received little financial support during the struggle for independence. In 1821

R Reading Strategies	C Critical Thinking	D Differentiated Instruction	W Writing Support	S Skill Practice
Additional Resources • Guided Reading Act., URB p. 145	**Teacher Edition** • Drawing Conclusions, p. 261 **Additional Resources** • Geo. and History, URB p. 3 • Quizzes and Tests, p. 88	**Teacher Edition** • Visual/Spatial, p. 262	**Teacher Edition** • Expository Writing, p. 261	**Additional Resources** • Reading Skills Act., URB p. 119 • Read. Essen., p. 78

INFOGRAPHIC
Spanish Missions

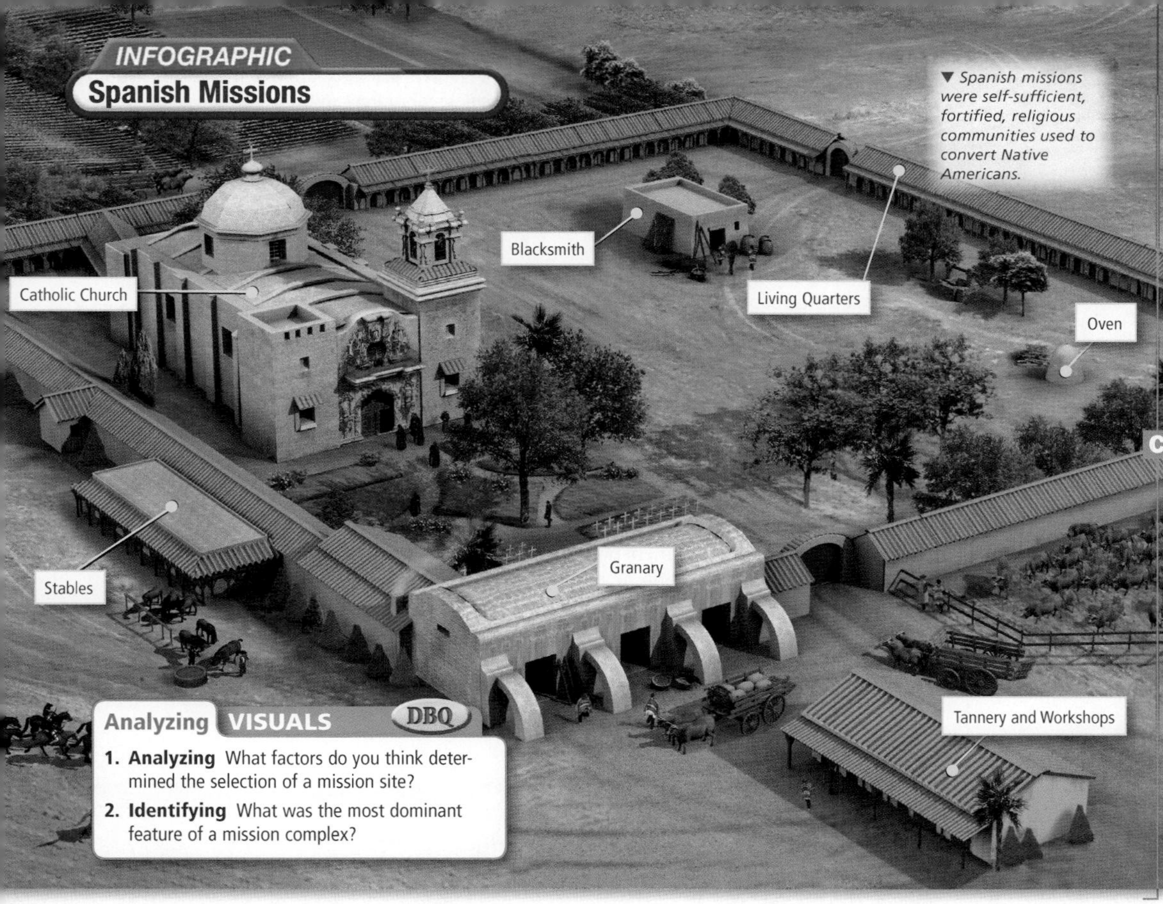

▼ *Spanish missions were self-sufficient, fortified, religious communities used to convert Native Americans.*

Analyzing VISUALS DBQ

1. **Analyzing** What factors do you think determined the selection of a mission site?
2. **Identifying** What was the most dominant feature of a mission complex?

California had only 36 Franciscan friars to run 21 missions.

Many Mexicans believed that maintaining state-supported religious institutions was not appropriate for a republic. In 1834 the Mexican government **secularized**—or transferred from religious control to **civil** control—the missions and then transferred the land to private ownership. Although the goal of reformers was to divide mission lands among Native Americans, most land ended up in the hands of cattle ranchers who then relied on Native Americans for labor. The frontier presidios, or forts, established by the Spanish similarly became weak due to labor shortages and reduced funding. This left frontier settlers vulnerable to attack.

In the borderlands, political chaos followed Mexican independence. In 1837 a visitor described conditions in frontier California:

PRIMARY SOURCE

"The old monastic order is destroyed and nothing seems to have replaced it except anarchy. The official power is weak and flutters irresolutely in the hands of its holders. Doubtless a new political order will arise out of this chaos but while waiting for it the country is badly administered, society is without ties, without guarantees, and the people are wretched."

—quoted in *The Mexican Frontier 1821–1846*

California

In the 1810s and 1820s, most of the approximately 3,200 Hispanic Californians took no direct role in Mexico's struggle for independence. Secularization of the missions had a tremendous impact on life in California, because it freed up land for cattle ranching, which became the mainstay of the economy.

Teach

W Writing Support

Expository Writing Many of the events in the region were affected by the outcome of the Mexican Wars for Independence. Have interested students research the Mexican struggle for independence and write a summary of its main causes, major battles, and outcome. **AL**

C Critical Thinking

Drawing Conclusions Ask: According to the information in this illustration, were the missions self-sufficient? Why would this be important? *(Yes, because they raised food, had wells for water, and were protected by soldiers; the missions were often isolated and could not depend on the Spanish government for support or protection.)* **BL**

Analyzing VISUALS

Answers:
1. the availability of wood, water, and arable land
2. a Catholic church

Additional Support

Extending the Content

Spanish Missions and Native Americans Thousands of Native Americans were lured to the missions by gifts and by the prospect of finding safety and food. They were instructed in Catholicism and Spanish and put to work. Women wove cloth and cooked; men labored at handicrafts or in the fields. In addition to the native beans and corn, the converts planted crops introduced by the Spaniards such as wheat, oats, oranges, olives, and grapes.

Some of the missions would not allow the Native Americans to leave without permission once they had entered the community. Making this transition to a regimented life was difficult, and escapes were common. To enforce order and hunt down runaways, many missions had a small detachment of soldiers. The soldiers rode on horses, which the Spaniards brought to the Southwest.

The Spaniards also brought measles and smallpox—devastating diseases against which the Native Americans had no natural immunity. Mission cemeteries often held the bones of thousands of Native Americans who died of these European diseases.

D Differentiated Instruction

Visual/Spatial Have students create a pyramid showing the following: elite (rancheros), middle class (mestizos), and Native Americans. Challenge them to research these classes and to supplement their pyramids with illustrations showing distinct features of each class's lifestyle. BL

DBQ Document Based Questions

Answers:

1. There were so many that they had to be destroyed and perhaps they could not feed them all.
2. The ranchers in the painting are on horseback and obviously used horses in their work; the primary source mentions that people traveled mainly on horseback, fast and beautiful horses were prized

Reading Check

Answer:
rancheros, mestizos, Native Americans

Rancheros, or ranchers, owned sprawling tracts of land. These predominantly white "Spanish Dons" and their families constituted less than 10 percent of California's population but dominated California society.

Beneath these elites was a class of **mestizos** (persons of mixed European and Native American ancestry). Some of this middle class worked as **vaqueros** (cowboys), but many were skilled craftspeople. D

At the bottom of society were Native Americans. They had suffered high mortality rates under Spanish rule. After Mexican independence, their situation improved little. Although freed from the missions, they were often exploited by the new class of rancheros. Many escaped to live among the independent Native Americans on the edges of the California frontier.

In the California territory, men played a powerful role in the family, and only men could vote or hold elective office. Yet women, especially upper-class women, had rights and privileges as well. Unlike American women of the era, Hispanic women retained control over their own property after marriage and could seek legal redress in the courts.

New Mexico

As in California, Mexican independence brought little immediate change to New Mexico (which included present-day Arizona). New Mexico remained largely rural. Sheep ranching thrived in the region's dry climate. Large ranches were established south of Santa Fe. North of Santa Fe, Hispanic settlers focused more on farming.

In the 1820s, when the Navajo and Apache launched a series of attacks on New Mexico, the Mexican government was unable to provide protection. This fed a growing dissatisfaction with the national government. Finally, in 1837, Pueblo people and Hispanic settlers north of Santa Fe launched a rebellion and killed the unpopular territorial governor and 16 other government officials.

Reading Check **Identifying** What were the major social classes in California?

PRIMARY SOURCE

Life on the California Frontier

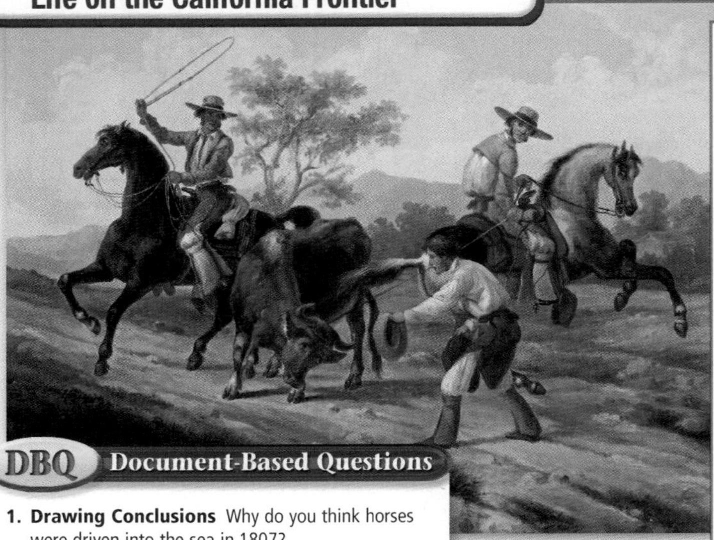

▲ *The painting* Los Californios *depicts three California ranchers of Hispanic descent, known as* los Californios, *lassoing a steer.*

PRIMARY SOURCE

"In the old days every one seemed to live out-doors. There was much gaiety and social life, even though people were widely scattered. We traveled as much as possible on horseback. . . . Young men would ride from one ranch to another for parties, and whoever found his horse tired would let him go and catch another. In 1806 there were so many horses in the valleys about San José that seven or eight thousand were killed. Nearly as many were driven into the sea at Santa Barbara in 1807, and the same thing was done at Monterey in 1810. Horses were given to the runaway sailors, and to trappers and hunters who came over the mountains, for common horses were plenty, but fast and beautiful horses were never more prized in any country than in California, and each young man had his favorites."

—from Guadalupe Vallejo, "Ranch and Mission Days in Alta California," *Century Magazine* (December 1890)

DBQ Document-Based Questions

1. **Drawing Conclusions** Why do you think horses were driven into the sea in 1807?
2. **Analyzing Visuals** How can you tell that the horse was important on the California frontier?

Hands-On Chapter Project Step 2

Creating a Thematic Map

Step 2: The Spanish Borderlands Students will research and collect information on the borderlands of the Southwest after Mexico gained its independence.

Directions After Mexico claimed its independence in 1821, many changes began to take place in the Southwest of the United States. Have students annotate their maps created in Section 1 by indicating the borderlands of the Southwest. Students should also write a small callout for their map of the changes that were taking place in the borderlands at this time.

Summarizing Information Students will need to identify the borderlands of the Southwest and summarize the changes occurring there in a brief callout. OL

(Chapter Project continued on page 265)

Americans Arrive in the Borderlands

MAIN Idea Trade between the borderlands and the United States increased after Mexican independence; Americans began to settle in the Southwest.

HISTORY AND YOU What can you recall about how trade restrictions imposed by Britain angered American colonists? Read to learn how trade with foreign nations grew after Mexico became independent from Spain.

After Mexican independence, American influence in the borderlands increased. Americans had begun moving into California before Mexican independence, and immigration increased after 1821. Trade with California rose significantly once Mexico was no longer part of Spain's empire. Traders from the United States, Russia, and other countries arrived in California ports to exchange manufactured goods for sea otter skins and hides and tallow derived from cattle.

In 1839, hoping to attract more settlers, Juan Bautista Alvarado, governor of California, granted 50,000 acres in the Sacramento Valley to **John Sutter,** a Swiss immigrant from Germany. There, Sutter built a trading post and cattle ranch. "Sutter's Fort" was often the first stopping point for Americans reaching California. As more Americans arrived, the differences between California and southern Mexico increased. This fueled political tensions between frontier leaders and the Mexican national government. The American population, however, was still small. Only about 700 Americans lived in California in 1845.

During the Spanish colonial period, New Mexicans received most manufactured goods from traders who came north from the state of Chihuahua. This began to change in 1821, the year of Mexican independence, when an American trader named **William Becknell** arrived in Santa Fe. He opened the **Santa Fe Trail,** which became a major trade route connecting Santa Fe with Independence, Missouri. Caravan wagons brought American manufactured goods to New Mexico and exchanged them for silver, mules, and furs. As trade increased, a small American population settled in Santa Fe.

East of New Mexico, Texas had long served as a buffer territory between the United States and the rest of Mexico. Texas was a sparsely populated region where settlers faced recurring raids by the Comanche and Apache. Most of the 2,500 Spanish-speaking ***Tejanos*** were concentrated in the towns of San Antonio and Goliad (then called La Bahía). Just before Mexican independence, Spain began allowing foreigners to settle in Texas. Mexico continued this policy, and Americans soon began to flood into that territory.

The decision to invite Americans to settle led, **ultimately,** to a revolt against Mexican rule and independence for Texas. California and New Mexico remained Mexican territory for 25 years after Mexican independence. Texas—where Americans soon vastly outnumbered *Tejanos*—broke away after fifteen years.

Reading Check **Summarizing** In what ways did Americans have an influence in the Mexican borderlands?

Section 2 REVIEW

Vocabulary

1. **Explain** the significance of: secularize, mestizo, vaquero, John Sutter, William Becknell, Santa Fe Trail, *Tejano.*

Main Ideas

2. **Describing** What happened to the mission system in California after Mexican independence?

3. **Determining Cause and Effect** What caused Americans to settle in Santa Fe?

Critical Thinking

4. **Big Ideas** Why do you think the conflict in Texas between American settlers and the Mexican government was more serious than the conflict in California?

5. **Organizing** Use a time line, similar to the one below, to list some events that occurred in Mexican territories after Mexico achieved independence.

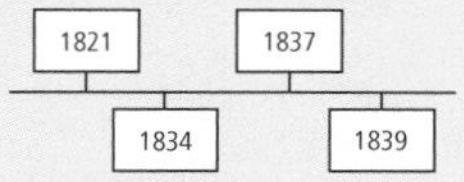

6. **Analyzing Visuals** Study the image of the mission on page 261. Why do you think the missions had troops stationed within them? Why would they have been built with the living quarters all facing inward?

Writing About History

7. **Expository Writing** Review the section and then write a short essay to summarize the state of the Mexican borderlands in the period after Mexico achieved independence.

History ONLINE
Study Central™ To review this section, go to glencoe.com and click on Study Central.

Reading Check

Answer:
John Sutter established Sutter's Fort and William Becknell established the Santa Fe Trail, bringing in trade and encouraging Americans to settle there. Increasing numbers of Americans in California and later in Texas led to conflict with the Mexican government.

Assess

History ONLINE

Study Central™ provides summaries, interactive games, and online graphic organizers to help students review content.

Close

Summarizing **Ask:** How did Mexico lose control over its borderlands? *(Its mission and presidio systems declined, and large numbers of American settlers, some invited by Spain, began to have more influence.)* **OL**

Section 2 REVIEW

Answers

1. All definitions can be found in the section and the Glossary.
2. The Mexican government secularized the system; the government took control of the missions and then sold the land to private owners.
3. In 1821, William Becknell went to Santa Fe and established the Santa Fe Trail, connecting the city with Independence, Missouri. This caused a growth in trade and encouraged Americans to settle in Santa Fe.
4. In California, the population of American settlers was much smaller than the Hispanic population, whereas in Texas, American settlers soon outnumbered the *Tejanos*.
5. 1821: Mexico wins independence; William Becknell arrives in Santa Fe, establishes the Santa Fe Trail; 1834: Mexico secularizes the missions; 1837: Pueblo and Hispanic settlers north of Santa Fe rebel; 1839: Alvarado, governor of California, grants John Sutter 50,000 acres in the Sacramento Valley
6. Possible response: The priests and others in the mission probably needed troops to keep the peace and to protect them from attacks by Native Americans; because the church was located on the inside.
7. Essays will vary, but students should summarize the main issues and events in the Mexican borderlands of California, New Mexico, and Texas after Mexican independence based on what they learned in the section.

Focus

Bellringer

Daily Focus Transparency 7-3

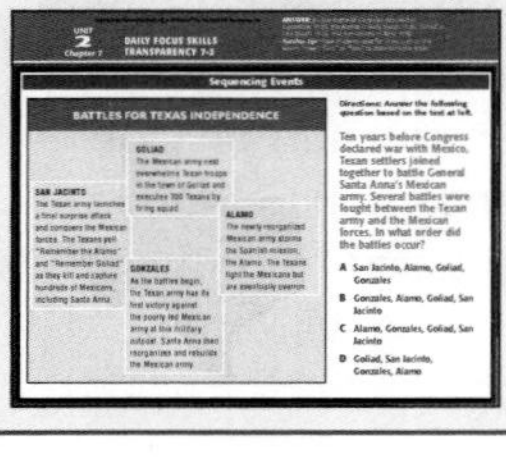

Guide to Reading

Answers:
Gonzales: Mexicans retreat; Alamo: Texans defeated but hold off Mexicans and inflict serious casualties; San Jacinto: Texans defeat the Mexicans decisively and capture Santa Anna, forcing him to sign a treaty recognizing the Republic of Texas.

Section Spotlight Video

To generate student interest and provide a springboard for class discussion, access the Chapter 7, Section 3 video at glencoe.com or on the video DVD.

Section 3 — Section Audio — Spotlight Video

Independence for Texas

Guide to Reading

Big Ideas
Culture and Beliefs Americans in Texas hoped to transplant American institutions to their new homeland.

Content Vocabulary
- *empresario* (p. 264)
- annexation (p. 269)

Academic Vocabulary
- convention (p. 266)
- reinforcement (p. 268)

People and Events to Identify
- National Colonization Act (p. 264)
- Washington-on-the-Brazos (p. 265)
- Antonio López de Santa Anna (p. 266)
- Sam Houston (p. 267)
- Alamo (p. 267)
- William B. Travis (p. 267)

Reading Strategy
Categorizing Complete a graphic organizer, similar to the one below, by filling in the major battles of the Texas war for independence and the outcome of each battle.

Major Battle	Outcome

Americans who settled in Texas did not assimilate as the Mexican government had hoped. The struggle over control of that border territory resulted in rebellion and, after some dramatic military encounters, independence for Texas.

Opening Texas to Americans

MAIN Idea Mexico invited Americans to settle in Texas but insisted that they adopt local customs, obey Mexican law, and convert to Catholicism.

HISTORY AND YOU Why do you think Mexico required Americans to become Mexican citizens? Read on to learn how *empresarios* brought American settlers to Texas.

In July 1821 Stephen F. Austin set off from Louisiana for the Texas territory in the northeastern corner of Mexico. The Spanish government had promised to give his father, Moses, a huge tract of Texas land if the elder Austin settled 300 American families there. Moses died before he could fulfill his end of the deal. On his deathbed, he asked Stephen to take his place in Texas.

When Austin settled in Texas, it was not a wild and empty land. Spanish-speaking *Tejanos* had established such settlements as San Antonio de Bexar and Hidalgo in the southern portion of the region. The land north of these settlements was the territory of the Apache, Comanche, and other Native American groups. In 1824 Texas was joined with Coahuila to become part of the Mexican state of Coahuila y Texas.

Unable to persuade its own citizens to settle on this frontier, Mexico decided to continue Spanish policy and allow foreigners to settle there. Between 1823 and 1825, Mexico passed three colonization laws, which offered cheap land to nearly anyone willing to come. The last law granted new immigrants a ten-year exemption from paying taxes but required that they become Mexican citizens, abide by Mexican law, and convert to Roman Catholicism.

Empresarios and Settlers

Although some American emigrants headed to Texas on their own, most came at the encouragement of ***empresarios,*** a Spanish word meaning "agents" or "contractors." Under the **National Colonization Act,** Mexico gave 26 *empresarios* large grants of Texas land. In exchange, the *empresarios* promised to fill it with a certain number of settlers. The *empresarios* assigned a plot to each family and governed the colonies they established.

Resource Manager

R Reading Strategies	C Critical Thinking	D Differentiated Instruction	W Writing Support	S Skill Practice
Teacher Edition • Activating Prior Knowledge, p. 265 **Additional Resources** • Guided Reading Act., URB p. 146	**Additional Resources** • Quizzes and Tests, p. 89	**Teacher Edition** • Auditory/Musical, p. 267 • Verbal/Linguistic, p. 268 • English Learners, p. 269	**Teacher Edition** • Persuasive Writing, p. 266	**Teacher Edition** • Reading a Time Line, p. 266 **Additional Resources** • Reinforcing Skills Act., URB p. 129 • Read. Essen., p. 81

NATIONAL GEOGRAPHIC **American Settlement of Texas**

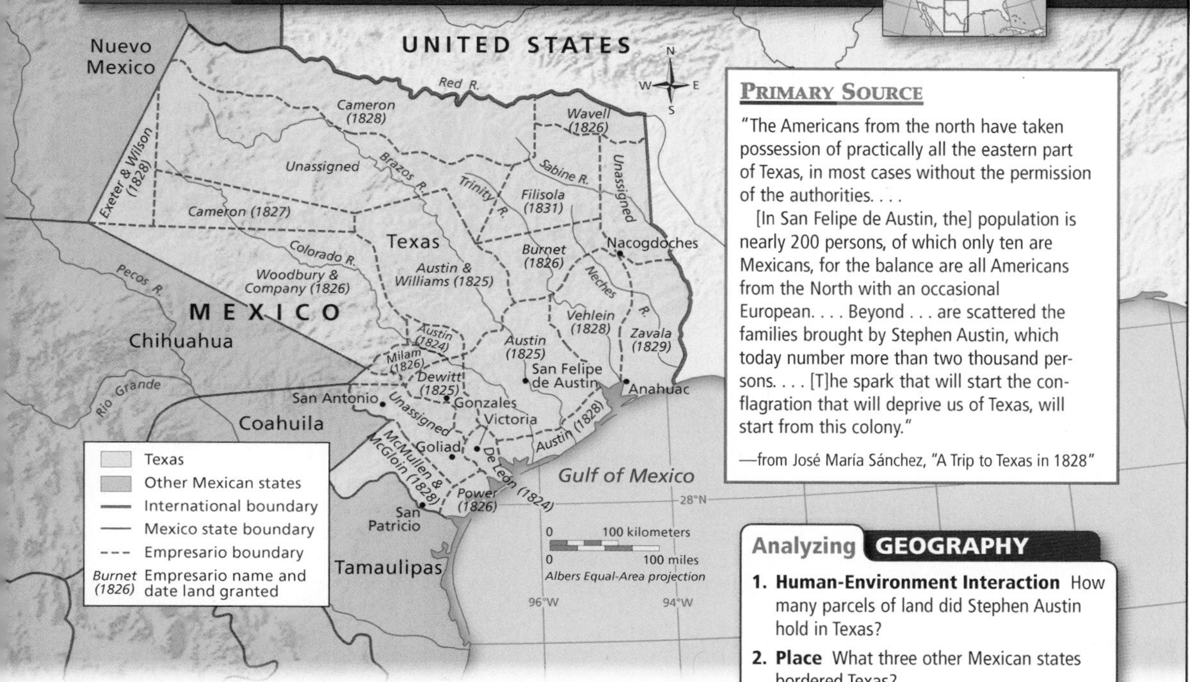

Primary Source

"The Americans from the north have taken possession of practically all the eastern part of Texas, in most cases without the permission of the authorities. . . .

[In San Felipe de Austin, the] population is nearly 200 persons, of which only ten are Mexicans, for the balance are all Americans from the North with an occasional European. . . . Beyond . . . are scattered the families brought by Stephen Austin, which today number more than two thousand persons. . . . [T]he spark that will start the conflagration that will deprive us of Texas, will start from this colony."

—from José María Sánchez, "A Trip to Texas in 1828"

Analyzing GEOGRAPHY

1. **Human-Environment Interaction** How many parcels of land did Stephen Austin hold in Texas?
2. **Place** What three other Mexican states bordered Texas?

Stephen Austin was the most successful *empresario*. He founded the town **Washington-on-the-Brazos** and, by the mid-1830s, had persuaded 1,500 American families to immigrate.

Americanizing Texas

Americans in Texas initially accepted Mexican citizenship. The government assumed they would adopt Mexican customs and come to see Mexico as their own country, but few did. Mexican customs and the Roman Catholic Church were alien to most American settlers.

Many Mexicans, in turn, distrusted the settlers because of their American lifestyle and rejection of Mexican ways. Mexicans' unease increased in 1826, when Benjamin Edwards, the brother of *empresario* Haden Edwards, led a rebellion against Mexican authority. Angry over disputes about whether Mexico or the *empresario* ruled the region, Edwards declared that the settlements of Americans in Texas now constituted the independent nation of Fredonia. When threatened by Mexican troops and a party of *Tejanos* led by Stephen Austin, the rebels dispersed.

Although most settlers ignored Edwards's call for revolution, the Mexican government feared it signaled an American plot to acquire Texas. In 1830 Mexico closed its borders to further immigration by Americans and banned the import of enslaved labor. It also taxed goods imported from foreign countries, hoping to discourage trade with the United States. **R**

These new laws infuriated the settlers. Without immigration their settlements could not grow. The import tax meant higher prices for goods they were accustomed to purchasing from the United States. Perhaps worst of all, the Mexican government was making rules for them. They saw no reason to obey a government they hardly considered their own.

Reading Check **Examining** What did Mexico's colonization laws offer settlers in northern Texas, and what did the laws require of these settlers?

Teach

R Reading Strategy

Activating Prior Knowledge
Remind students of the colonists' revolt against Great Britain before the American Revolution. **Ask:** What similarities does the tension between the settlers and the Mexican government have in common with the earlier conflict? *(Both conflicts were sparked by unreasonable taxation and rebellion against unfair government that they didn't consider to have much authority.)* **OL**

Analyzing GEOGRAPHY

Answers:
1. 4
2. Chihuahua, Coahuila, Tamaulipas

Reading Check

Answers:
offer: cheap land and a ten-year tax exemption; requirement: settlers had to become Mexican citizens, follow Mexican law, and convert to Roman Catholicism

Hands-On Chapter Project
Step 3

Creating a Thematic Map

Step 3: The United States in 1850 Students will research and collect information on the states and territories of the country in 1850.

Directions Have students research the population of the states and territories that were part of the United States in 1850. Also have them find the population of these states using the last census figures.

Comparing and Contrasting Ask students to find the answers to the following questions: Which states and territories were most populous in 1850? How has the population shifted today? *(northeast, south; large concentration in west and midwest)* **OL**

(Chapter Project continued on page 271)

W Writing Support

Persuasive Writing Have students write an invitation from Stephen F. Austin to the settlers, urging them to attend the conventions held in San Felipe. The invitation should summarize the events that have led to the convention and express a desire for a specific outcome. Suggest that students include in the invitation an argument to convince uneasy settlers how it will be to their benefit to attend the convention. AL

S Skill Practice

Reading a Time Line For which events is Stephen F. Austin mentioned in the time line, and when did those events occur? *(He arrived in San Antonio in 1821, and he was arrested for writing a letter calling for a separate state of Texas in 1834.)* BL

Texas Goes to War

MAIN Idea When Mexico tried to enforce its laws, American settlers rebelled and established an independent state.

HISTORY AND YOU Have you heard the motto "Remember the Alamo"? Read on to learn how Texas became an independent nation.

With tensions simmering, settlers met at two **conventions** in the Texas town of San Felipe in 1832 and 1833. At the first convention, settlers chose Stephen Austin to be the convention's president. The convention asked Mexico to reopen Texas to American immigrants and to loosen the taxes on imports. The second convention recommended separating Texas from Coahuila and creating a new Mexican state. The convention also created a constitution for the new state and designated Austin to travel to Mexico City to negotiate with the Mexican government.

In the fall of 1833 negotiations stalled. An irritated Austin sent a letter to *Tejano* leaders in San Antonio, suggesting that Texas start peacefully organizing its own state government. Then he visited Mexican President **Antonio López de Santa Anna** in Mexico City and persuaded him to agree to several demands, including lifting the hated ban on immigration.

As Austin was returning home, he was arrested on January 3, 1834, by Mexican officials, who had intercepted his letter to the *Tejanos*. He was taken back to Mexico City and imprisoned for treason, without trial. Shortly afterward, in April 1834, President Santa Anna denounced Mexico's constitution of 1824 and declared himself dictator.

Austin was released from prison in July 1835. Even he saw that further negotiation with Santa Anna was pointless and, in September, he urged Texans to organize an army, which they quickly did.

The Early Battles

The Mexican army had serious problems. Continuing political instability in Mexico City had denied the army sound leadership, training, and support. Against this handicapped

History of Texas, 1819–1836

1819
Spain and the United States sign the Adams-Onís Treaty recognizing Spanish sovereignty over Texas

1824
The new Mexican government establishes the state of Coahuila y Texas, combining Texas with Coahuila to the south

1827
New constitution of the State of Coahuila y Texas declares that from this point forward no one born in the state can be born into slavery and bans the importation of enslaved persons after six months

1819 · 1821 · 1823 · 1825 · 1827 · 1829

1821
Stephen F. Austin arrives in San Antonio

1826–1827
American settlers Haden and Benjamin Edwards lead a revolt against Mexican rule; the brothers briefly declare an independent state called "Fredonia"; the rebellion falls apart without any violence

1828
Mexican General Manuel de Mier y Terán reports *Tejanos* are still importing slaves and ignoring Mexican law; warns Texas is likely to revolt

Additional Support

Extending the Content

Texas Flags Texans of the time proudly flew their Lone Star flag—a blue, five-pointed star on a white background with the inscription "Liberty or Death." Johanna Troutman of Georgia designed it for volunteers from her state who were fighting in Texas. When independence was declared, Texans raised a flag designed by Texan Sarah Dodson. With squares of red, white, and blue and a white star in the blue square, it looked very much like the modern flag of Texas.

force, the Texan army enjoyed its first taste of victory at the military post of Gonzales, about 75 miles east of San Antonio. There, Mexican soldiers ordered the Texans to surrender their arms. In response, the rebels pointed a cannon at the Mexican force and held up a cloth sign painted with the taunt, "Come and Take It." Having no orders to attack, the Mexicans retreated to San Antonio, and the Texans followed them. The rebels, numbering only about 350, drove the much larger Mexican force out of San Antonio in December 1835.

On March 2, 1836, Texas declared its independence from Mexico. Shortly thereafter, the Texans drafted a new constitution that drew heavily from the U.S. Constitution and specifically protected slavery.

The Alamo

Few of the Texas rebels had any military training, and at first, no one could agree on who should lead them. Finally, a former governor of Tennessee and proven military leader named **Sam Houston** took command. In the meantime, Santa Anna organized a force of about 6,000 troops to put down the rebellion.

When Santa Anna's forces arrived at San Antonio in February 1836, they found over 180 Texas rebels holed up in an abandoned Catholic mission called the **Alamo.** Under the command of Lieutenant Colonel **William B. Travis,** the small force sought to delay Santa Anna and give Houston's army more time to prepare. From within the mission, Travis dispatched a courier with a plea to fellow Texans and U.S. citizens for help:

PRIMARY SOURCE

"I am besieged with a thousand or more of the Mexicans under Santa Anna. . . . I shall never surrender or retreat. Then, I call on you in the name of Liberty, of patriotism, and of everything dear to the American character, to come to our aid with all dispatch. . . . If this call is neglected, I am determined to sustain myself as long as possible, and die like a soldier who never forgets what is due to his own honor and that of his country. VICTORY OR DEATH!"

—quoted in *Lone Star*

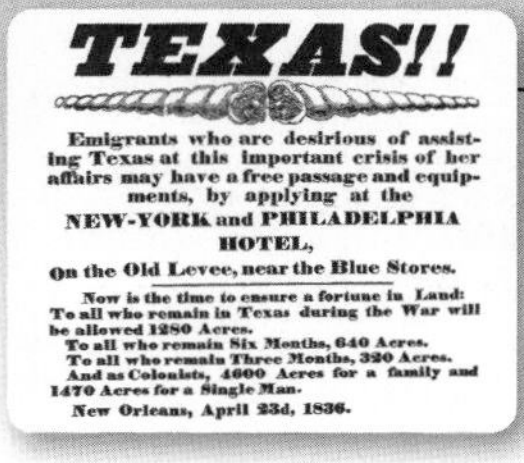
TEXAS!!

Emigrants who are desirious of assisting Texas at this important crisis of her affairs may have a free passage and equipments, by applying at the

NEW-YORK and PHILADELPHIA HOTEL,

On the Old Levee, near the Blue Stores.

Now is the time to ensure a fortune in Land: To all who remain in Texas during the War will be allowed 1280 Acres.

To all who remain Six Months, 640 Acres.

To all who remain Three Months, 320 Acres.

And as Colonists, 4600 Acres for a family and 1470 Acres for a Single Man.

New Orleans, April 23d, 1836.

1834
Stephen F. Austin is arrested for writing a letter that calls for establishing a separate Mexican state of Texas

1835
At Gonzales and San Antonio, Texas rebels force Mexican military to retreat

April 1836
Santa Anna surrenders to Texans after defeat at the Battle of San Jacinto

D

1831 1833 1835 1837

1830
Mexico passes law barring Americans from immigration to Texas, increasing military forces in Texas, and forbidding the importation of slaves

February 1836
Alamo falls to Santa Anna

Analyzing TIME LINES

1. **Specifying** What event occurred in 1827, and what was the result?
2. **Identifying** In what year did Texas achieve independence?

D Differentiated Instruction

Auditory/Musical Have students write a ballad describing one of the battles described in this section. Explain that a ballad is a kind of narrative song, with short stanzas, rhyming words, and repeating lines. Have them research one of the battles to find more details about the participants as well as the turning point of each battle. When they have written the ballad, encourage students to set it to music. Encourage volunteers to perform their ballads before the class. AL

Analyzing TIME LINES

Answers:

1. A new constitution of the state of Coahuila y Texas banned the importation of slaves after six months and declared that no one could be born into slavery in the state; when this law wasn't followed, Mexican General Manuel de Mier y Terán warned that Texas was likely to revolt.
2. 1836

Additional Support

Extending the Content

Sam Houston Standing over six feet tall, Sam Houston seemed larger than life. A military hero in the Creek wars, he had a brief political career in Tennessee before heading to Texas in 1832. He soon revived his military career and led the army of the Republic of Texas to victory over Mexico at the Battle of San Jacinto. Texans elected him president of the Republic.

When Texas jointed the Union, Houston served as a U.S. senator. A position he held from 1846 until 1859. Despite being a slaveholder himself, while in Congress, Houston voted consistently against the expansion of slavery into new territories. He also was adamantly against secession.

In 1859, the people of Texas elected Houston governor. When Texas voted to secede in 1861, Houston refused to swear allegiance to the Confederacy and was removed from office. He died in 1863 on his farm in Texas.

D Differentiated Instruction

Verbal/Linguistic Challenge students to think about the battles for Texas independence from the Mexican perspective, and then to write a dialogue between two Mexican soldiers as they prepare for one of the battles described in this section. **OL**

Did You Know?

In 1960, John Wayne portrayed Davy Crockett in *The Alamo*. A 2004 remake of the movie starred Billy Bob Thornton as Davy Crockett and Dennis Quaid as Sam Houston.

Analyzing VISUALS

Answers:

1. the Rio Grande
2. first: Gonzales, October 2, 1835; last: San Jacinto, April 21, 1836

NATIONAL GEOGRAPHIC The Texas War for Independence, 1835–1836

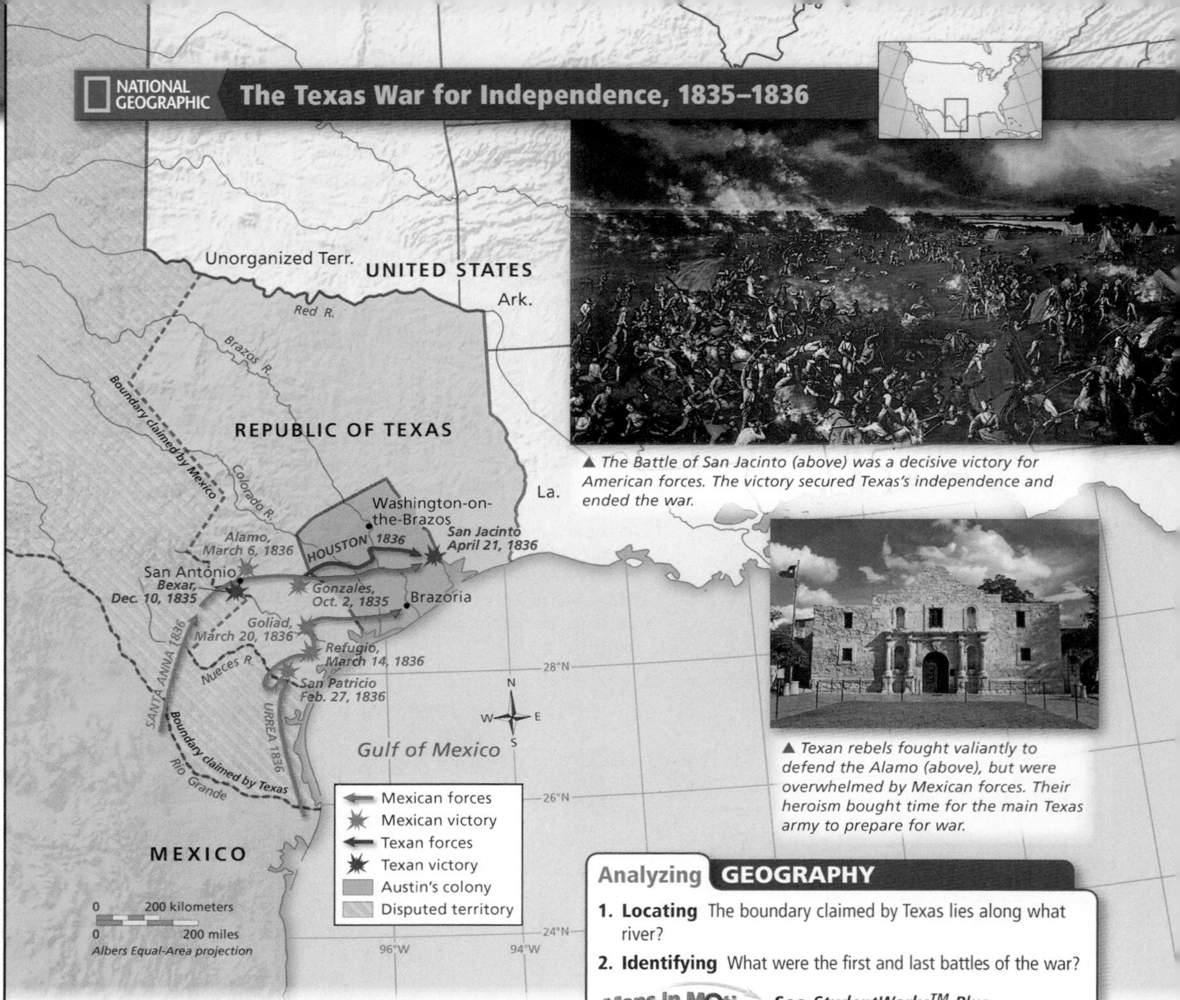

▲ *The Battle of San Jacinto (above) was a decisive victory for American forces. The victory secured Texas's independence and ended the war.*

▲ *Texan rebels fought valiantly to defend the Alamo (above), but were overwhelmed by Mexican forces. Their heroism bought time for the main Texas army to prepare for war.*

Analyzing GEOGRAPHY

1. **Locating** The boundary claimed by Texas lies along what river?
2. **Identifying** What were the first and last battles of the war?

Maps In MOtion See *StudentWorks™ Plus* or glencoe.com.

D The call for **reinforcements** went almost unanswered. Only 32 settlers from Gonzales, deciding on their own to join the fight, made it into the Alamo. Running low on ammunition and gunpowder, the Texans held off Santa Anna's besieging army for 13 days. It was during the standoff that the new Texas government met at Washington-on-the-Brazos and formally declared independence.

On March 6, 1836, Santa Anna's army stormed the Alamo. The Texans fought off the attackers for six hours, killing or wounding about 600 before being overrun. Although the defenders of the Alamo had been defeated, they had bought Houston's army nearly two extra weeks to organize.

Goliad

Two weeks later the Mexican army overwhelmed Texan troops led by James W. Fannin at Goliad, a town southeast of San Antonio near the Gulf Coast. Fannin and his men surrendered, hoping that the Mexicans would disarm them and expel them from Texas. Though the Mexican field general at Goliad wrote to

Additional Support

Activity: Interdisciplinary Connection

Government Explain to students that Texas draws on a rich history that includes having been a part of Mexico. Have students conduct research using library or Internet sources to learn about the various flags that have flown over Texas throughout its history. Have students use their findings to prepare displays showing each flag, and explain when and why it was used. Ask students to share their displays with the class. **BL**

Santa Anna requesting clemency, Santa Anna demanded execution. At dawn on March 27, 1836, a firing squad executed more than 300 men. The losses at the Alamo and Goliad devastated Texans but also united them in support of their new country.

The Battle of San Jacinto

With the Texan army in disarray, Sam Houston desperately needed more time to recruit fresh volunteers and to train the soldiers who remained. Rather than fight, he chose to retreat, heading east toward Louisiana.

Houston was biding his time. Up against a larger, more disciplined army, he decided to wait for Santa Anna to make a mistake. The mistake occurred on April 21, when both armies were encamped along the San Jacinto River near what is now the city of Houston. Santa Anna no longer saw Houston's army as a threat, so he allowed his men to sleep in the afternoon, confident that Houston would wait until the next day to launch an attack.

Eager for a fight, Houston's soldiers convinced the officers to launch an afternoon assault. Shielded from sight by a hill, Houston's troops crept up on Santa Anna's sleeping soldiers and charged. The surprise attack threw the Mexican soldiers into a panic.

The Battle of San Jacinto lasted less than 20 minutes, but the killing continued for hours. Yelling "Remember the Alamo" and "Remember Goliad," Houston's men attacked the Mexican troops with guns, knives, and clubs. In addition to the hundreds killed, over 700 members of Santa Anna's force were taken captive. The Texans suffered only 9 killed and 34 wounded.

Among the captured troops was Santa Anna himself. Houston forced Santa Anna to order his army out of Texas and sign a treaty recognizing independence for the Republic of Texas. The Mexican Congress refused to accept the treaty, but it was unwilling to launch another military campaign. Texas had won the war. **D**

The Republic of Texas

In September 1836 the newly independent republic called its citizens to the polls. They elected Sam Houston as their first president and voted 3,277 to 91 in favor of **annexation,** or becoming part of the United States.

Given that Americans had enthusiastically supported the war, most Texans assumed the United States would want to annex the republic. Many northern members of Congress, however, opposed admitting Texas as a slave state.

President Andrew Jackson did not want to increase North-South tensions or risk a costly war with Mexico, which continued to claim ownership of Texas. Jackson made no move toward annexation, although on his last day in office he did sign a resolution officially recognizing Texas as an independent nation.

Reading Check **Summarizing** What difficulties did the Texans face in their war against Mexico?

Section 3 REVIEW

Vocabulary

1. **Explain** the significance of: *empresario,* National Colonization Act, Washington-on-the-Brazos, Antonio López de Santa Anna, Sam Houston, Alamo, William B. Travis, annexation.

Main Ideas

2. **Identifying** What was Fredonia?
3. **Stating** What was the military contribution of the soldiers defending the Alamo during the Texas war for independence?

Critical Thinking

4. **Big Ideas** What aspects of their culture did American settlers in Texas refuse to change?
5. **Organizing** Use a graphic organizer, similar to the one below, to list the reasons that Texans did not wish to become Mexican citizens.

Reasons Texans Opposed Mexican Citizenship

6. **Analyzing Visuals** Examine the time line on pages 266–267. How many years after Stephen Austin arrived in Texas did the Texans win the Battle of San Jacinto?

Writing About History

7. **Persuasive Writing** Suppose you live in Texas in the late 1830s. Write a letter to the U.S. Congress to persuade them to vote for or against the annexation of Texas.

History ONLINE
Study Central™ To review this section, go to glencoe.com and click on Study Central.

D Differentiated Instruction

English Learners Have students create a time line of the life of Stephen F. Austin or Santa Anna. **BL**

Reading Check

Answer:
Few men had military training, there was no clear leader at first, and the Texans were outnumbered.

Assess

History ONLINE

Study Central™ provides summaries, interactive games, and online graphic organizers to help students review content.

Close

Summarizing Ask: Why did Texans fight for independence from Mexico? *(Texans became unhappy with high taxes and limits on immigration. There was also a lack of understanding between cultures.)* **OL**

Section 3 REVIEW

Answers

1. All definitions can be found in the section and the Glossary.
2. the name given by rebel Benjamin Edwards to the American settlements in Texas, which he declared to be an independent nation, during his rebellion in 1826
3. They delayed the Mexican army long enough to give Sam Houston some time to prepare his troops for battle. They also killed or wounded 600 Mexican soldiers before being overrun by Santa Anna's army.
4. They did not become Catholic
5. did not want to adopt Mexican customs, did not see Mexico as their own country, did not want to adopt the Catholic religion
6. 15 years
7. Students' letters will vary, but should express appropriate reasons for or against annexation.

Focus

Bellringer

Daily Focus Transparency 7-4

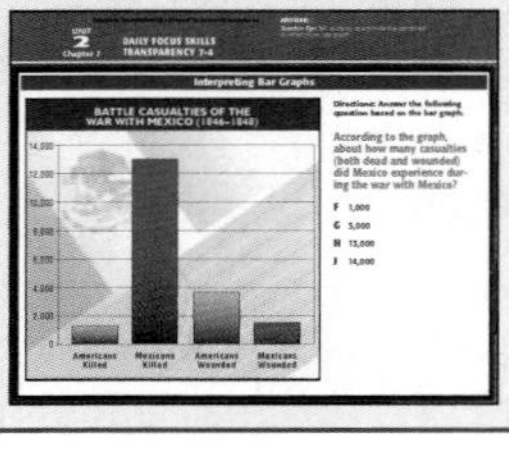

Guide to Reading

Answers:

The War With Mexico
I. The Lingering Question of Texas
A. Texas and Oregon Enter the Union
a. The Election of 1844
b. The Oregon Question
c. The Annexation of Texas
II. The War with Mexico
A. Calling All Volunteers
B. The Fighting Begins
C. To Mexico City
D. The Peace Treaty

Section Spotlight Video

To generate student interest and provide a springboard for class discussion, access the Chapter 7, Section 4 video at glencoe.com or on the video DVD.

Section 4 — Section Audio — Spotlight Video

The War With Mexico

Guide to Reading

Big Ideas
Trade, War, and Migration War with Mexico brought new territories under the control of the United States.

Content Vocabulary
- envoy *(p. 272)*
- cede *(p. 275)*

Academic Vocabulary
- resolution *(p. 272)*
- secure *(p. 275)*

People and Events to Identify
- James K. Polk *(p. 271)*
- "Fifty-four Forty or Fight" *(p. 272)*
- Zachary Taylor *(p. 272)*
- John C. Frémont *(p. 275)*
- Bear Flag Republic *(p. 275)*
- Winfield Scott *(p. 275)*
- Treaty of Guadalupe Hidalgo *(p. 275)*

Reading Strategy
Taking Notes As you read about the war with Mexico, use the major headings of the section to complete the outline started below.

The War With Mexico
I. The Lingering Question of Texas
A.
a.

By 1844, control of Oregon and the annexation of Texas had become major political issues. After the annexation of Texas, the border between the United States and Mexico was in dispute. The United States declared war on Mexico and took Mexico's northern territories.

The Lingering Question of Texas

MAIN Idea In 1844 James K. Polk was elected president and promised to annex Texas and Oregon and to buy California from Mexico.

HISTORY AND YOU Can you remember a slogan from a recent election campaign? Find out what "Fifty-four Forty or Fight" referred to and why it is still remembered.

Territorial disputes between the United States and Mexico began as far back as 1803, when the United States claimed Texas as part of the Louisiana Purchase. The United States renounced that claim in the Adams-Onís Treaty of 1819, but the idea of Manifest Destiny and of acquiring Mexican territory had strong popular support.

Tensions increased during the administration of John Tyler, who hoped to bring Texas into the Union. Because Texas already had a large population of Southerners who had taken slaves into Texas, Texans were certain to support the cause of slavery. Antislavery leaders in Congress, therefore, opposed annexation. Moreover, Mexico had never recognized the independence of Texas. Although militarily unable to regain control over Texas, Mexico still regarded the Republic of Texas as Mexican territory.

Texas and Oregon Enter the Union

In early 1844, after spearheading a publicity campaign in favor of annexation, President Tyler brought the matter before the Senate. He blundered, however, by including in the supporting documents a letter written by Secretary of State John C. Calhoun that contained a fierce defense of slavery. Outraged Northerners pointed to the letter as evidence that annexation was nothing but a pro-slavery plot, and by a count of 35 to 16, the Senate voted against annexation. The maneuver that Tyler believed would win him a second term instead destroyed his chances of retaining the presidency.

The Election of 1844 As the presidential race began later that year, the front-runners for the nomination were Whig Senator Henry Clay and former Democratic president Martin Van Buren. Although

Resource Manager

R Reading Strategies	C Critical Thinking	D Differentiated Instruction	W Writing Support	S Skill Practice
Teacher Edition • Identifying, p. 272 **Additional Resources** • Guided Read. Act., URB p. 147	**Additional Resources** • Hist. Simulations, URB p. 7 • Quizzes and Tests, p. 90	**Teacher Edition** • Visual/Spatial, p. 271 • English Learners, p. 274 **Additional Resources** • Am. Art and Music Act., URB p. 137 • Enrich. Act., URB p. 142 • Reteach. Act., URB p. 141 • Authentic Assess., p. 19	**Teacher Edition** • Expository Writing, pp. 272, 274 • Descriptive Writing, p. 275	**Additional Resources** • Critical Think. Skills Act., URB p. 130 • Read. Essen., p. 84

POLITICAL CARTOONS PRIMARY SOURCE
The Election of 1844

Presidential Candidate	Popular Vote	% of Popular Vote	Electoral Vote
Polk (D)	1,337,243	49.55%	170
Clay (R)	1,299,062	48.14%	105
Birney (L)	62,300	2.31%	0

▲ *A ship symbolizing Texas carries James K. Polk to victory as it enters the Union. Henry Clay, and other Whigs who oppose Texas's annexation, are pulled into Salt River. In the 1800s, if someone "fell into Salt River," it meant the person had ruined his political career.*

▲ *James K. Polk's bridge across Salt River collapses under the weight of his pack, labeled Texas Annexation. Meanwhile, Henry Clay safely crosses "The People's Bridge" to the presidential chair.*

Analyzing VISUALS DBQ

1. **Comparing and Contrasting** How are the two cartoons alike and how are they different?
2. **Identifying** Which states did Clay win in the election of 1844?

politicians on both sides of the annexation issue pressed the candidates to state their positions, both responded cautiously to avoid losing supporters.

Van Buren's indecision cost him the Democratic nomination. His party instead **D** chose **James K. Polk,** a former member of Congress and governor of Tennessee. Polk promised to annex not only Texas but also the contested Oregon Territory in the Northwest. In addition, he vowed to buy California from Mexico. This ambitious platform appealed to both Northerners and Southerners because it expanded the country while promising to maintain the delicate balance between free and slave states.

The Democrats' unity on annexation caused Clay to backpedal. Reversing a statement made in the spring of 1844 against immediate annexation, Clay now supported annexation **D** of Texas as long as it was done without causing war with Mexico. This so angered antislavery Whigs in his party that they threw their support to the Liberty Party—a small third party that supported abolition. With the Whig vote split, Polk won the election.

Teach

D Differentiated Instruction

Visual/Spatial Have students reread the passage "The Election of 1844" on pages 270–271. Then ask them to create a flowchart documenting events during the presidential campaign of 1844. The flowchart should begin with the start of the campaign and end with the election of James Polk. **BL**

Analyzing VISUALS

Answers:

1. Both cartoons use a bridge metaphor, but the first uses it to predict the successful Democrat-supported annexation, while the second uses the bridge metaphor to indicate that Whig Henry Clay might swiftly and easily win the presidency because the Democrats' bridge is flimsy and breaks under the weight of annexation.
2. Vermont, Massachusetts, Rhode Island, Connecticut, New Jersey, Maryland, Delaware, Ohio, Kentucky, Tennessee, North Carolina

Hands-On Chapter Project
Step 4

Creating a Thematic Map

Step 4: Mapping the United States in 1850 Students will use the information they researched in Section 3 to create another map of the United States.

Directions Tell students to use an outline map of the United States to shade the states that were part of the Union in 1850 and label them with the name of the state, its population in 1850, and its population in the last census.

Drawing Conclusions Ask students to write a brief statement summarizing the population of the United States in 1850. Students should write the statement using their completed maps from the Chapter Project. **OL**

(Chapter Project continued on the Visual Summary page)

R Reading Strategy

Identifying President Polk's desire to provoke Mexico resulted in Zachary Taylor leading American soldiers south of the Nueces River into disputed territory. **Ask:** What geographical feature did the United States claim as the boundary between the United States and Mexico? *(the Rio Grande)* **Ask:** What geographical feature did Mexico claim as the border? *(the Nueces River)*

W Writing Support

Expository Writing Have students write short essays on the concept of Manifest Destiny. In the essays, students should analyze the concept from a personal point of view, considering how their lives would be different if Americans had not embraced the concept of Manifest Destiny. Tell them to give examples to support their point of view. OL

Reading Check

Answer:
He promised to annex Texas and secure the contested Oregon territory in the Northwest.

Additional Support

The Oregon Question Polk took a strong stance on what came to be known as the Oregon Question. Despite British claims to the region, which had been established in the Convention of 1818, Polk and the Democrats held that the United States had a "clear and unquestionable" right to *all* of the Oregon Country, including the region north of the 49th parallel that is today known as British Columbia. Their rallying cry, **"Fifty-four Forty or Fight,"** declared that the United States should control all of Oregon below the line of 54° 40′ north latitude.

Despite such slogans, few Americans wanted to fight the British to gain control of Oregon. After lengthy debates in Congress, Polk agreed to use diplomatic negotiations to settle the Oregon Question. In June 1846, as the United States fought with Mexico, and Great Britain was dealing with problems in Ireland, the two nations negotiated the Oregon Treaty to settle the dispute. In this agreement, the United States received all of Oregon south of 49° north latitude and west of the Rocky Mountains, except for the southern tip of Vancouver Island. In exchange, the British were guaranteed navigation rights on the Columbia River.

The Annexation of Texas Even before Polk took office, outgoing President Tyler pushed an annexation **resolution** through Congress in February 1845, and Texas joined the Union that year. As predicted, Mexico was outraged and broke diplomatic relations with the United States government. Matters worsened when the two countries disputed the location of Texas's southwestern border. Mexico said it was at the Nueces River. Texans, and then the United States, claimed the Rio Grande, about 150 miles (240 km) farther west and south, as the boundary. The Texas–United States claim covered far more territory than the Mexican claim.

Polk's intentions in California added to the growing strife with Mexico. In November 1845 he sent John Slidell as a special **envoy,** or representative, to Mexico City to try to purchase the territory. Mexico's new president, José Joaquín Herrera, refused even to meet with Slidell.

Reading Check **Examining** What did James Polk promise to do if elected president?

The War With Mexico

MAIN Idea Hostilities over the southwestern boundary of Texas led to war with Mexico.

HISTORY AND YOU Have you ever thought that someone took something that did not belong to him or her? Read on to learn Mexico's reaction to the United States's annexation of Texas.

Herrera's snub ended any realistic chance of a diplomatic solution. Polk ordered troops led by General **Zachary Taylor** to cross the Nueces River—in Mexico's view, an invasion of its territory. Polk wanted Mexican soldiers to fire the first shot. If he could say that Mexico was the aggressor, he could more easily win popular support for a war.

Finally, on May 9, 1846, news reached him that a force of Mexicans had attacked Taylor's

Debates IN HISTORY

Should the United States Go to War With Mexico?

Although many Americans supported war with Mexico for personal or political gain or because they subscribed to the principle of Manifest Destiny, many were against it. Debates raged between citizens, in newspapers, and in Congress over President Polk's motives and the tactics he had used to force a declaration of war against America's southern neighbor. While Polk insisted that Mexico had been the aggressor, many thought that the United States had purposefully incited the war to gain more land or, as Frederick Douglass believed, to extend slavery into new territory.

Activity: Interdisciplinary Connection

Sociology Between 1812 and 1845, a number of states—Louisiana, Alabama, Mississippi, Missouri, Arkansas, Florida, and Texas—had entered the Union as slave states. The demand for cotton grew rapidly as textile manufacturing expanded during the Industrial Revolution. Slave labor was used in the large scale cultivation of cotton, and also tobacco. But over time this intense cultivation exhausted the soil, reducing production and encouraging the spread of slavery to the West. **Ask:** What likely effect did the spread of slavery have upon the abolitionist movement? *(Possible answers may include: cause it to gain strength, have more power, influence)* men. In an address to Congress, Polk declared that the United States was at war "by the act of Mexico herself." Hoping to incite the public's indignation, he added that "American blood has been shed on the American soil!"

Many Whigs opposed the war as yet another plot to extend slavery. Most Washington politicians, though, recognized that, no matter how questionable Polk's actions were, the United States was committed to war. On May 13 the Senate voted 40 to 2 and the House voted 174 to 14 in favor of war. Critics quickly dubbed the conflict "Mr. Polk's War."

Calling All Volunteers

Polk and his advisers developed a three-pronged military strategy. Taylor's troops would continue to move south, crossing the Rio Grande near the Gulf of Mexico. A separate force to the northwest would capture Santa Fe, an important trading center and now the capital of New Mexico, and then march west to take control of California with the help of the American navy. Finally, U.S. forces would advance on Mexico City and force Mexico to surrender.

To implement the ambitious plan, the United States needed to expand its army. Congress authorized the president to call for 50,000 volunteers, and men from all over the country rushed to enlist. Almost 73,000 answered the call.

Undisciplined and unruly, the volunteers proved to be less than ideal soldiers. As one officer observed, "They will do well enough to defend their own firesides, but they can not endure the fatigue incident to an invading army."

YES

James K. Polk
U.S. President

PRIMARY SOURCE

"Upon the pretext that Texas, a nation as independent as [Mexico], thought proper to unite its destinies with our own, [Mexico] has affected to believe that we have severed her rightful territory, and in official proclamations and manifestoes has repeatedly threatened to make war upon us for the purpose of reconquering Texas. In the meantime we have tried every effort at reconciliation. . . . But now, after reiterated menaces, Mexico has . . . invaded our territory and shed American blood upon the American soil. . . .

As war exists, and, notwithstanding all our efforts to avoid it, exists by the act of Mexico herself, we are called upon by every consideration of duty and patriotism to vindicate with decision the honor, the rights, and the interests of our country."

—from *The Congressional Globe,* May 11, 1846

NO

Frederick Douglass
American Abolitionist

PRIMARY SOURCE

"The war . . . was [begun] with no higher or holier motive than that of upholding and propagating slavery. In 1829 Mexico . . . had declared the entire abolition of slavery in her territories. The consequence was a decrease in the value of slaves in the border states of America, . . . What was the desperate purpose of the United States? . . . [T]hey stirred up a revolt against Mexico in Texas, which, . . . ultimately severed from the mother country. Their next step was kindly to recognise the independence of Texas, and in 1844 it was annexed to the Union. An army of men was sent to protect the Texians [sic]; . . . and the Mexicans firing at the invaders, the United States at once recognised a war, . . ."

—from *The Frederick Douglass Papers*

DBQ Document-Based Questions

1. **Paraphrasing** According to President Polk, what was the United States's attitude toward war with Mexico before Mexican forces attacked?
2. **Specifying** What reasons does Polk give for declaring war on Mexico?
3. **Summarizing** According to Frederick Douglass, what steps did the United States take to incite the war?
4. **Identifying Central Issues** What does Douglass say is the true reason for the war with Mexico?

Debates IN HISTORY

DBQ Document Based Questions

Answers:

1. Polk implies that the United States had tried in every way to avoid war with Mexico, despite the fact that Mexico had repeatedly threatened the United States.
2. He says that Mexico killed Americans on American soil and that it is, therefore, the patriotic duty of the United States to defend its rights.
3. Douglass says that the United States connived with emigrants in Texas in their rebellion against Mexico, then recognized Texan independence, and then worked to annex the territory. Finally, in the name of protecting Texan citizens, the United States sent troops over what Mexico considered the border, causing Mexican forces to fire on the Americans
4. to extend and perpetuate slavery

Additional Support

Teacher Tip

Collaborative Learning This activity allows students at different levels to work together. Help students divide responsibility for the project. Check in to make sure all students are making contributions to the project.

Activity: Collaborative Learning

Taking a Stand Form small groups, and tell students that they are going to work together to develop, write, and perform a play about the Mexican War. The students will need to decide if the play should have a small group of characters or a large cast. While some students develop a script, others can design costumes and sets. Finally, have students perform the play. AL

W Writing Support

Expository Writing Have students research historical documents and writings of the era. Then have them write a newspaper editorial evaluating the progress of the war and the conduct of the American and Mexican armies. AL

Did You Know?

When California settlers declared independence, they raised a flag with a white background, a single star, a red bar, and a grizzly bear. The bear flag officially became the state flag in 1911.

Analyzing GEOGRAPHY

Answers:

1. Sloat, Kearny, and Frémont
2. Veracruz

Differentiated Instruction

NATIONAL GEOGRAPHIC **The War With Mexico, 1846–1848**

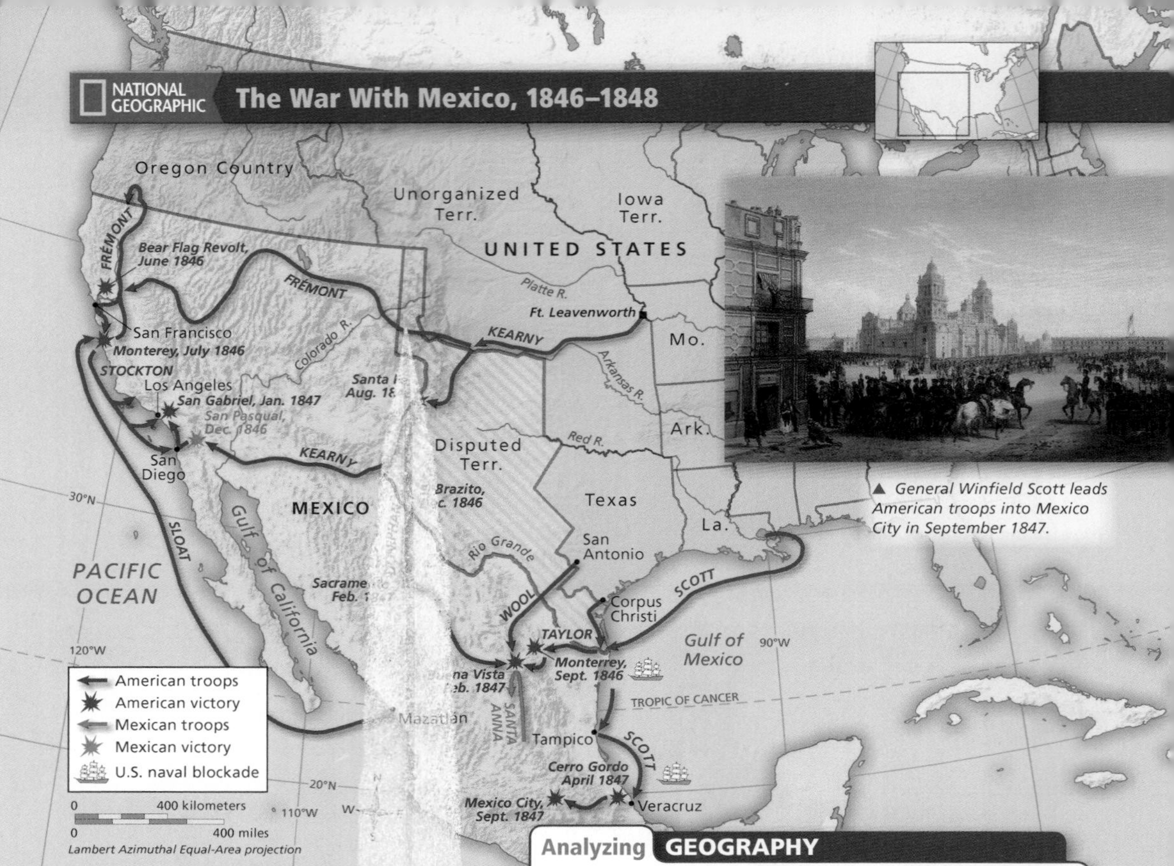

▲ General Winfield Scott leads American troops into Mexico City in September 1847.

Analyzing GEOGRAPHY

1. **Movement** Which commanders led the invasion of California?
2. **Location** At what city did Scott's troops land to begin their march to capture Mexico City?

Maps In MOtion See *StudentWorks™ Plus* or glencoe.com.

Other officers saw similar problems. One bemoaned in a half-comical way that the green recruits constantly demanded his attention:

PRIMARY SOURCE

"[O]ne wanted me to read a letter he had just received; another wanted me to write one for him; another wanted me to send his money home; another wanted me to keep it for him. . . . [O]ne complained that his uniform was too large, another that his was too small."

—From *Memoirs of a Maryland Volunteer*

The Fighting Begins

In early May, several days before Polk signed the declaration of war, Taylor's troops defeated Mexican forces, first at Palo Alto and then at Resaca de la Palma. Taylor then moved south, defeating Mexican forces at Matamoros. By late September, he had marched about 200 miles (322 km) west from the coast of the Gulf of Mexico and captured Monterrey. W

In the meantime, Colonel Stephen W. Kearny led troops from Fort Leavenworth, west of Missouri, toward Santa Fe. The march through the dry countryside was brutal, but

Leveled Activities

BL Reteaching Activity, URB p. 141

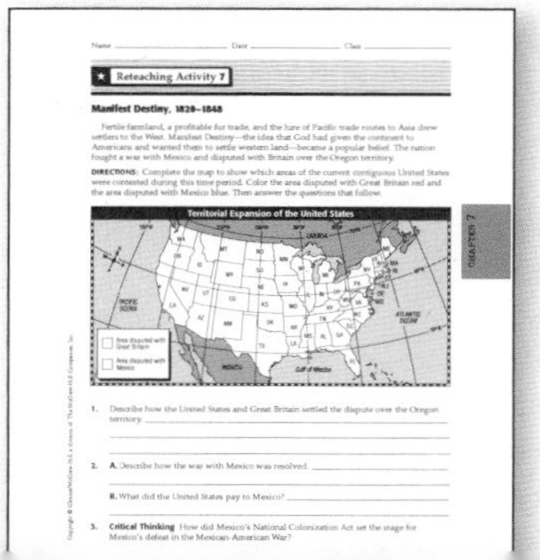

OL Time Line Activity, URB p. 131

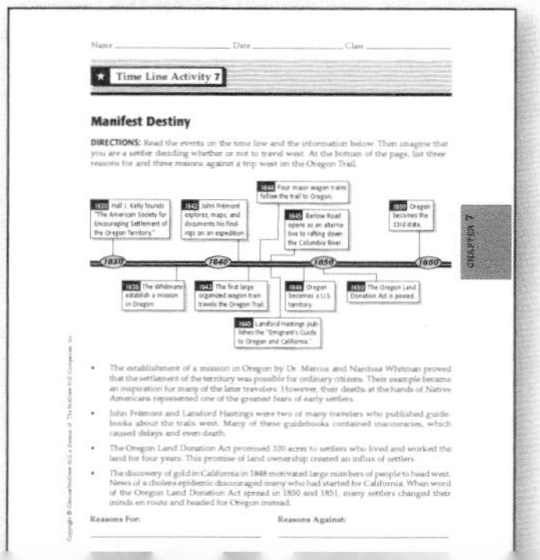

AL Enrichment Activity, URB p. 142

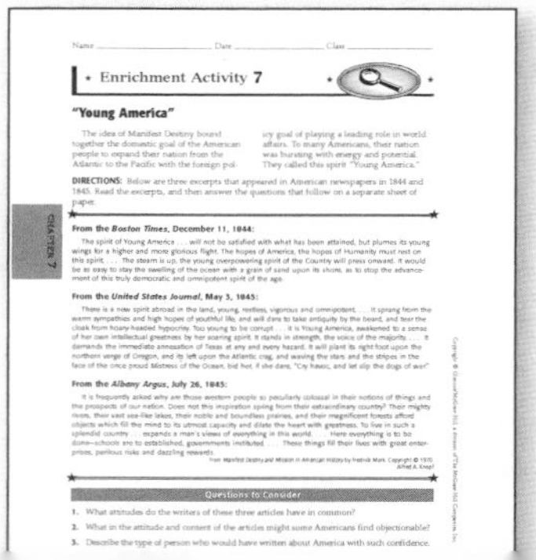

ELL English Learner Activity, URB p. 123

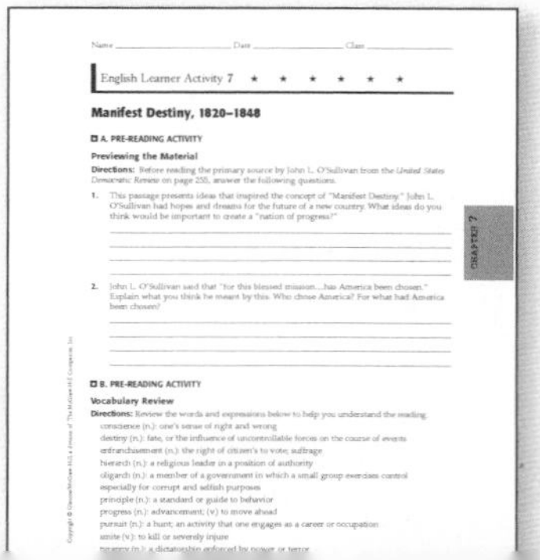

when Kearny's men reached the city in August, the Mexican force there had already fled. With Santa Fe **secured,** Kearny led a small U.S. force into California.

Before Kearny arrived, and even before war with Mexico was officially declared, settlers in northern California led by American General **John C. Frémont** had begun an uprising. The official Mexican presence in the territory had never been strong, and the settlers had little trouble overcoming it. On June 14, 1846, they declared California independent of Mexico and renamed the region the **Bear Flag Republic.** A few weeks later, the Bear Flag Republic came to an end when American naval forces arrived and took possession of California for the United States.

To Mexico City

Despite having lost vast territories, Mexico's leaders refused to surrender. Polk decided to force things to a conclusion by sending soldiers on ships to the Mexican port of Veracruz. From there they would march west and capture the Mexican capital, Mexico City.

Polk, seeing Taylor as a potential rival in the 1848 election, eased him out of the war by placing General **Winfield Scott,** a member of the Whig Party, in command of this campaign. In March 1847 Scott's force landed at Veracruz, which his forces took after a three-week siege. Having taken control of this strategic port, the American troops then headed for Mexico City, fighting vicious and bloody battles with Mexican forces along the way. On September 14, after storming Chapultepec Castle, which guarded the city, they finally captured the capital after a hard fight at the city gates. With the Americans in control of the capital, a group of city leaders finally surrendered to General Scott unconditionally. American forces went on to establish a formal occupation of Mexico.

The Peace Treaty

On February 2, 1848, Mexican leaders signed the **Treaty of Guadalupe Hidalgo.** In the agreement, Mexico **ceded,** or gave up, more than 500,000 square miles (1,295,000 sq. km) of territory to the United States. Mexico also accepted the Rio Grande as the southern border of Texas. In exchange, the United States paid Mexico $15 million and agreed to take over $3.25 million in debts Mexico owed to American citizens.

With Oregon and the former Mexican territories now under the American flag, the dream of Manifest Destiny was finally realized: the United States now stretched from ocean to ocean. Valuable ports on the West Coast opened up new markets to the Pacific nations of Asia. The question of whether the new lands should allow slavery, however, would soon lead the country into a bloody civil war. The experience that such men as Robert E. Lee and Ulysses S. Grant gained during the war with Mexico would soon be used to lead Americans in battle against each other. **W**

Reading Check **Summarizing** What was President Polk's military strategy in the war with Mexico?

Section 4 REVIEW

Vocabulary

1. **Explain** the significance of: James K. Polk, "Fifty-four Forty or Fight," envoy, Zachary Taylor, John C. Frémont, Bear Flag Republic, Winfield Scott, Treaty of Guadalupe Hidalgo, cede.

Main Ideas

2. **Specifying** What were the provisions of the Oregon Treaty?

3. **Explaining** What brought an end to the Bear Flag Republic?

Critical Thinking

4. **Big Ideas** The idea of Manifest Destiny was realized as a result of the war with Mexico. What new problem did the additional territories cause for the United States?

5. **Organizing** Use a graphic organizer, similar to the one below, to list the provisions of the Treaty of Guadalupe Hidalgo.

Treaty of Guadalupe Hidalgo
- Mexico's Provisions
- United States's Provisions

6. **Analyzing Visuals** Study the painting of Scott's entry into Mexico City on page 274. How does the artist depict the event? How might the real event have differed from the painting?

Writing About History

7. **Expository Writing** Suppose you are James K. Polk, the Democratic candidate for president in 1844. Write a speech in which you explain your platform.

History ONLINE
Study Central™ To review this section, go to glencoe.com and click on Study Central.

275

W Writing Support

Descriptive Writing Have students write an essay explaining what life would be like in the southwestern United States had the land remained a part of Mexico. **OL**

Reading Check

Answer:
move south across the Rio Grande, capture Santa Fe and march west to take California, and capture Mexico City

Assess

History ONLINE

Study Central™ provides summaries, interactive games, and online graphic organizers to help students review content.

Close

Summarizing Ask: Why did the United States annex Texas and fight a war with Mexico? *(to fulfill Manifest Destiny and expand the United States's territory; also, some argued, to extend slavery)* **OL**

Section 4 REVIEW

Answers

1. All definitions can be found in the section and the Glossary.
2. the United States received all of Oregon south of 49° north latitude and west of the Rocky Mountains, except for the southern tip of Vancouver Island; in exchange, the British were guaranteed navigation rights on the Columbia River
3. Naval forces of the United States came and took possession of California for the United States.
4. It raised the question of whether the new lands should allow slavery. This debate would lead the country into a civil war.
5. Mexico: ceded over 500,000 square miles (1,295,000 sq. km) of territory, accepted Rio Grande as Southern Texas border; United States: paid Mexico $15 million and claimed $3.25 million in Mexican debt to American citizens
6. They are not resisting the Americans' arrival; student answers may vary. Some may suggest that Mexicans may have shown some resistance.
7. Students' speeches will vary, but should include information on Polk's platform from the section.

Descriptive Writing Challenge students to write a poem that addresses some of the themes in the chapter. As a starting point, students might begin by describing one of the illustrations on this page. AL

Predicting Consequences
Ask: What do you think will happen now that the United States has achieved Manifest Destiny and reached the Pacific Ocean? *(Students may say that the United States will continue to grow in economic and political power, and that the conflict over slavery will probably come to a boil.)* OL

Chapter 7 Visual Summary

STUDY TO GO You can study anywhere, anytime by downloading quizzes and flashcards to your PDA from glencoe.com.

Causes of Western Expansion

- The idea of Manifest Destiny influences many political leaders who believe the nation is destined to expand across the continent.
- The Preemption Act of 1830 gives settlers the right to claim land.
- New technology, including plows and reapers, enables settlers to farm the Midwest.
- Lush soil and moderate climate lures settlers to Oregon Territory and northern California.
- Christian beliefs lead missionaries to head west to try to convert Native Americans.
- Trailblazers map paths across the plains and mountains, making it easier for settlers to head west safely in long wagon trains.
- Treaty of Fort Laramie limits attacks by Native Americans on settlers and wagon trains heading west.
- Religious persecution leads Mormons to migrate west to Utah, where they can practice their religion freely.
- Mission system had already brought Spanish to the Southwest in the 1600s and 1700s.
- Hispanics move to California to establish large ranches.
- Mexico lures settlers to Texas with the National Colonization Act, giving large tracts of cheap land to *empresarios* and granting settlers exemption from taxes for 10 years.

▲ *Astoria (above) was the first permanent settlement in the Oregon Territory.*

▶ *Vaqueros rest outside Santa Inez mission in California. Ranching and missionary work brought many Spanish settlers to the region.*

▲ *American troops land at Monterey in Mexico in 1846. The War with Mexico ended with the United States in control of much of the Southwest.*

Effects of Western Expansion

- Texas becomes American in culture, and Texans grow frustrated with Mexican laws, specifically the tariffs on trade with the United States, the ban on slavery, and the requirement that settlers become Catholic.
- Led by Stephen Austin and Sam Houston, Texans rebel against Mexico, declare independence, and defeat the Mexican forces led by Santa Anna.
- Americans in Texas and Oregon want to join the United States.
- The debate over Texas triggers a sectional crisis—Northerners believe the South wants Texas in order to expand slavery.
- James K. Polk campaigns, promising to get both Texas and Oregon, and wins the presidency.
- Britain and the United States agree to divide the Oregon territory.
- Congress approves the annexation of Texas.
- After fighting begins between American and Mexican forces on the Texas border, the United States declares war and invades Mexico.
- In the peace treaty, Mexico cedes much of its northern territory to the United States, including California and the American Southwest.

Hands-On Chapter Project
Step 5: Wrap Up

Creating a Thematic Map

Step 5: Wrap Up Students will use the maps created in the Chapter Project to compare the United States of 1850 with the United States today.

Directions Have students identify the least populous states and territories in 1850 and compare them to the least populous states today.

Comparing and Contrasting Have student volunteers take turns answering the following question: What characteristics are common among the least populous states? *(Answers will vary.)* OL

Chapter 7 Assessment

Reviewing Vocabulary

Directions: Choose the word or words that best complete the sentence.

1. By the 1840s, travelers known as ________ were moving in wagon trains along the trails to the West.

A squatters
B mountain men
C overlanders
D *Tejanos*

2. In 1834 Mexico moved to ________ the missions, bringing them under civil control.

A annex
B cede
C expand
D secularize

3. Under the National Colonization Act, Mexico gave ________ large grants of Texas land.

A mestizos
B *empresarios*
C vaqueros
D *Tejanos*

4. The war with the United States caused Mexico to ________ what became areas of the American Southwest.

A cede
B annex
C conquer
D sell

5. In the Mexican territories of the Southwest, ________, or cowboys, worked on large ranches.

A rancheros
B vaqueros
C mestizos
D dons

Reviewing Main Ideas

Directions: Choose the best answer for each of the following questions.

Section 1 *(pp. 254–257)*

6. The term "Manifest Destiny" describes the idea that

A European nations have no right to establish new colonies in the Western Hemisphere.
B Protestantism should be the official religion of the United States.
C God wants the United States to control all of North America.
D Native Americans should be allowed to retain all their original lands.

7. Which group left the United States to establish a settlement called Deseret in the West?

A Mormons
B *empresarios*
C Seminoles
D mountain men

Section 2 *(pp. 260–263)*

8. In the early 1800s, California society was dominated by which group?

A mestizos
B vaqueros
C rancheros
D *empresarios*

TEST-TAKING TIP

Be sure to examine carefully statements that contain the words *always, not,* and *never.* These are strong words that give clues to the incorrect answer.

Need Extra Help?

If You Missed Questions . . .	1	2	3	4	5	6	7	8
Go to Page . . .	256	261	264	275	262	254	257	262

GO ON

Answers and Analyses
Reviewing Vocabulary

1. C To help remember this, students should think about the fact that wagon trains moved *over (or on) land.* Hence, overlanders. Squatters are people who illegally occupy a place. Mountain men were western fur trappers. *Tejanos* were Spanish-speaking people in Texas.

2. D Secular means not religious or controlled by a religious body. To secularize is to change something from religious to civil control. Missions were religious institutions. Students may be tempted to choose *A*, annex. Although to annex something means to add it or bring it under control, it does not denote a change from religious to civil.

3. B *Empresarios* tried to attract settlers by offering land to families who settled in their territory, or colony. Mestizos are people of Spanish and Native American ancestry. Vaqueros are cowboys.

4. A To cede means to give up or transfer. Annex means the opposite: to add. *C* does not make sense. *D* is incorrect, because sell implies that Mexico was given money in return in a voluntary transaction, which was not the case.

5. B Rancheros were the owners of the large ranches; mestizos were Mexicans of mixed European and Native American ancestry; don was an informal title applied to wealthy landowners in the Hispanic Southwest.

Reviewing Main Ideas

6. C The concept of Manifest Destiny is uniquely applied to the expansion of the United States. This should help students eliminate *A* and *B*. *D* is incorrect. The wishes of Native Americans were not considered as part of Manifest Destiny.

7. A Mormons traveled west to escape religious persecution. They eventually settled in Utah, which was then not a part of the United States.

8. C Rancheros owned large parcels of land. To help students remember this, they should focus on *ranch* in rancheros. A ranch is a large farm.

9. A Here, only *A* makes sense. Make sure students relate the Santa Fe Trail with commerce and trade. It is not likely that a department store would open in a border territory.

10. B For this type of question, remind students that they are looking for the answer choice that is *not true*. In this case, although settlers were required to become Mexican citizens, they were not banned from ever returning to the United States.

11. C Students may have trouble choosing between *A* and *C*. If necessary, review a map with students and point out San Jacinto River, in Texas, near Houston.

12. D James Polk ran during a time of interest in western expansion and Manifest Destiny. Therefore, it is logical that promises to add new territory would be a part of Polk's platform. In this context, the other answer choices do not make sense.

13. B The Treaty of Guadalupe Hidalgo ended the war with Mexico. It required Mexico to cede more than 500,000 square miles of territory and accept the Rio Grande as the southern border of Texas. Making a connection between the Spanish in the treaty name and Mexico may help students remember this.

Chapter 7 Assessment

9. In 1821 William Becknell arrived in New Mexico and opened up trade in that border territory by

A establishing the Santa Fe Trail.
B starting the first American department store.
C building a railroad line from Missouri.
D leading a revolt against Mexico.

Section 3 *(pp. 264–269)*

10. Which of the following was not a condition set by Mexico for American emigrants to Texas?

A They received a ten-year exemption from paying taxes.
B They could never return to live in the United States.
C They were required to become Mexican citizens.
D They were required to convert to the Roman Catholic faith.

11. The result of the Battle of San Jacinto was that

A California became an independent republic.
B the Cherokee were forced to leave the Southeast.
C Texas became an independent republic.
D the Mormons were forced to leave Ohio.

Section 4 *(pp. 270–275)*

12. As part of his platform in the 1844 presidential election, James Polk promised to

A extend American power around the world.
B create a large, standing army.
C remove all Native Americans from the Midwest.
D annex Texas and Oregon.

13. The war with Mexico was officially ended by which of the following events?

A the signing of the Oregon Treaty
B the signing of the Treaty of Guadalupe Hidalgo
C the annexation of Texas
D the establishment of the Bear Flag Republic

Critical Thinking

Directions: Choose the best answers to the following questions.

14. The invention of the McCormick reaper encouraged

A settlement of the Great Plains.
B trade with New Mexico.
C mountain men to create trails to California.
D the expansion of slavery into new territories.

Base your answers to question 15 on the map below and your knowledge of Chapter 7.

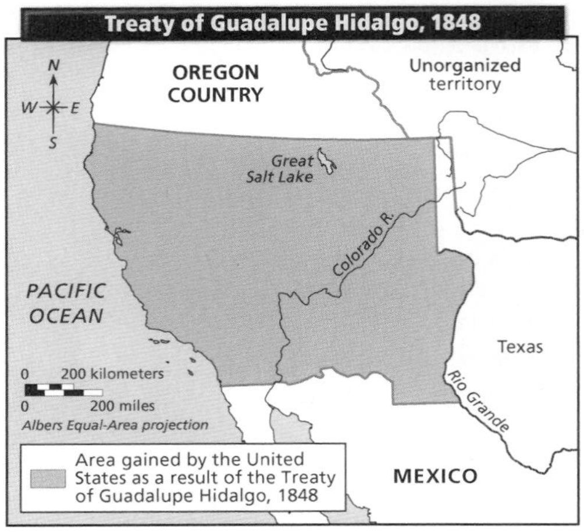

15. Which of the following states now include territory acquired as a result of the war with Mexico?

A Oregon and Washington
B Montana and Idaho
C California and Nevada
D Texas and Oklahoma

Need Extra Help?							
If You Missed Questions . . .	9	10	11	12	13	14	15
Go to Page . . .	263	264	269	271	275	255	278

GO ON

14. A The McCormick reaper, pulled by animals, harvested grain. It revolutionized farming, which led to greater settlement of the Great Plains. Students should equate the reaper with farming, therefore eliminating the other answer choices, none of which concern farming.

15. C The dark-shaded area on the map represents lands the U.S. gained as a result of the treaty that ended the war with Mexico. While knowledge of the locations of present-day California and Nevada is helpful, the other answers can be eliminated by the non-shaded areas.

16. In retrospect, the invitation to Americans to settle in Texas was a mistake for Mexico because the Mexican government
   - **A** failed to set aside enough land for settlement.
   - **B** overestimated the settlers' willingness to assimilate.
   - **C** did not realize that most of the settlers were criminals.
   - **D** was too eager for Texas to become independent.

17. Whom did Texans choose to lead them in the rebellion against Mexico?
   - **A** William B. Travis
   - **B** James K. Polk
   - **C** Sam Houston
   - **D** General Santa Anna

18. What did the saying "Fifty-four Forty or Fight" refer to?
   - **A** the large number of Americans seeking farmland in California
   - **B** the war with Mexico over boundary disputes at the Rio Grande
   - **C** the area of land Polk supporters wanted in Oregon
   - **D** the annexation of Texas and the battle at the Alamo

19. Who was Brigham Young?
   - **A** a mountain man
   - **B** a squatter
   - **C** an overlander
   - **D** a leader of the Mormons

Document-Based Questions

Directions: Analyze the document and answer the short-answer questions that follow the document.

In April 1847 future U.S. Senator Charles Sumner presented his views on the causes of the war with Mexico in his "Report on the War With Mexico" to the Commonwealth of Massachusetts. The excerpt below is from that report:

> "It can no longer be doubted that this is a war of conquest. . . . In a letter to Commodore Sloat, . . . the Secretary [of War] says, 'You will take such measures as will render that vast region [California] a desirable place of residence for emigrants from our soil.' In a letter to Colonel Kearny . . . he says: 'Should you conquer and take possession of New Mexico and Upper California, you will establish civil governments therein. You may assure the people of these provinces that it is the wish of the United States to provide for them a free government with the least possible delay. . . .'"
>
> —quoted in *Readings in American History*

20. According to Charles Sumner, why did the United States become involved in a war with Mexico?
21. What evidence does Sumner provide to show that this was the U.S. government's intention?

Extended Response

22. Even at the time, many Americans questioned the motives and goals of the war with Mexico, while others felt it was necessary to fulfill America's Manifest Destiny and the needs of the developing nation. Do you think that the war was justified or not? Choose to either support or oppose the United States's war with Mexico. Write a persuasive essay that includes an introduction and at least three paragraphs that support your position, using information from Chapter 7.

STOP

History ONLINE
For additional test practice, use Self-Check Quizzes—Chapter 7 at glencoe.com.

Need Extra Help?

If You Missed Questions . . .	16	17	18	19	20	21	22
Go to Page . . .	265	267	272	257	279	279	270–275

Document-Based Questions

20. According to Sumner, the United States set out to acquire new lands. Sumner calls it a "war of conquest."

21. According to Sumner, the secretary of war gave the generals the task of making newly acquired territories ready for new settlers, including the formation of civil governments.

Extended Response

22. Students' essays will vary, but should provide a clear and reasoned argument to support the viewpoint they choose. Students should not waver from their chosen viewpoint. Essays must follow the format of a persuasive essay and include sufficient support from the text.

16. B To answer this question, students should consider the rebellion of American settlers against Mexico. The Mexican government felt that Americans would move to Texas and gain an allegiance to Mexico and consider themselves Mexicans. This was not the case and had dire consequences for Mexico in terms of retaining Texas.

17. C To help students remember this, simply remind them to think of Houston, Texas. James K. Polk was a U.S. president. General Santa Anna was a Mexican general. William B. Travis was the commander of Texan forces at the Alamo.

18. C Polk supporters wanted the U.S. to control all of the land in Oregon south of the line of 54° 40′ north latitude. To help students who have trouble visualizing this, use a map to point out 54° 40′.

19. D Brigham Young led the Mormons after the death of Joseph Smith. Young led the Mormons further west, to Salt Lake. Brigham Young University bears his name.

History ONLINE
Have students visit the Web site at glencoe.com to review Chapter 7 and take the Self-Check Quiz.

Need Extra Help?
Have students refer to the pages listed if they miss any of the questions.

Unit 3 Planning Guide

UNIT PACING CHART					
	Unit 3	Chapter 8	Chapter 9	Chapter 10	Unit 3
Day 1	Unit Opener,	Chapter 8 Opener, Section 1	Chapter 9 Opener, Section 1	Chapter 10 Opener, Section 1	Wrap-Up/Project, Unit Assessment
Day 2		Section 2	Section 2	Section 2	
Day 3		Section 3	Section 3	Section 3	
Day 4		Chapter Assessment	Section 4	Chapter Assessment	
Day 5			Section 5		
Day 6			Chapter Assessment		

Teacher to Teacher

James Gill
Binghamton High School
Binghamton, NY

Four-Way Socratic Seminar This is my favorite Socratic Seminar/class discussion exercise. It works with any unit of study, and is a 1 and ½ period exercise. The best example to use it in is the Slavery/Civil War unit. Count off the students in the class by groups of 1, 2, 3, and 4. Each group gets a different reading. In the case of the slavery issue, two groups would get pro-abolitionist readings (William Lloyd Garrison, Frederick Douglass) while two groups would get two pro-slavery readings. Have students read their own readings for homework. The next day, have the four groups meet to share ideas and notes on their readings. After about 10 to 15 minutes into the class, go to each group and separate the members into groups A, B, C, and D. If there are extras in each group that is fine, exact numbering is not important. Split all of the various As, Bs, Cs, and Ds around the classroom, and have them each teach their new group members about their own readings. After about 20 minutes, bring the whole class back to a Socratic Seminar circle, and review all four readings, making sure that all themes and important points were clearly covered. Grading rubrics are easy for Socratic Seminars. If you listen, do not interrupt, discuss a few details about your reading, and take notes you get an easy 10 out of 10 grade. If you talk or are disruptive, each time I have to ask you to focus, I take 1 point off. It works great, I get an assessment and four readings completed in 1 and ½ class periods.

Author Note

Dear American History Teacher,

It would be impossible to exaggerate the impact of the Civil War on America. The 620,000 soldiers who lost their lives in that war constituted 2 percent of the American population. If the same percentage of Americans were to be killed in a war fought today, the number of American dead would be more than six million. The war also devastated and impoverished the South. Two big questions arise: How and why did the Civil War happen? Were the results worth the cost? These are the overarching questions addressed in this unit. From the time of the Constitutional Convention in 1787 the issue of slavery in this new nation supposedly founded on a charter of liberty split the American polity. That division became stronger as the slave states evolved into a planter-dominated society whose economy rested on slavery and staple-crop agriculture while the free states evolved into a dynamic free-labor economy diversified into agricultural, commercial, and industrial sectors. Each of these socioeconomic systems generated an ideology that rationalized its own social order and portrayed the other as a threat. The contest between them for expansion into the vast new territories acquired by the United States in 1845 and 1848 generated the conflict that provoked most slave states to secede in 1861, after Abraham Lincoln was elected on a platform pledged to contain the further expansion of slavery. The Lincoln Administration refused to acquiesce in the legitimacy of secession. And the war came.

The question whether the results of Union victory were worth the cost is a subjective one on which opinions might differ. What can be said, however, is that the war resolved two festering issues left unresolved by the Revolution of 1776 and Constitution of 1787. Until 1865 it remained uncertain whether the United States would survive as one nation, indivisible, and whether the House Divided would remain half slave and half free. Appomattox resolved those questions definitively. The Reconstruction Amendments to the Constitution (14th and 15th Amendments) mandated equal civil and political rights for all Americans. Imperfectly enforced at the time and partially abandoned after 1877, they remained in the Constitution and became the legal basis of the civil rights movement in the second half of the 20th century.

James M. McPherson

Senior Author

Introducing Unit 3

Focus

Why It Matters

Have students consider the issues of racism and civil rights in the United States today and conduct a class discussion focusing on those issues' impacts on American society. Then have them make generalizations about how the problems of America's past contribute to the issues faced by citizens today. **OL**

Connecting to Past Learning

Have students recall some of the major differences between the North and the South prior to the Civil War. **Ask:** **Why was compromise between the two regions not possible?** *(The differences had become too great; the South felt that the North threatened its way of life.)* Tell students that in this unit they will learn about the immediate causes of the Civil War, how both sides planned to win the war, and the war's social and economic impacts on the nation. **OL**

Unit Launch Activity

Discuss with students what they know about the causes of the Civil War. For example, they may know that slavery was a root cause of the war, but the firing on Fort Sumter marked the beginning of the armed conflict. Tell students that President Lincoln did not enter the war with the intention of ending slavery in the South. Ask them if they can recall any other issues that fueled the sectional conflict. **OL**

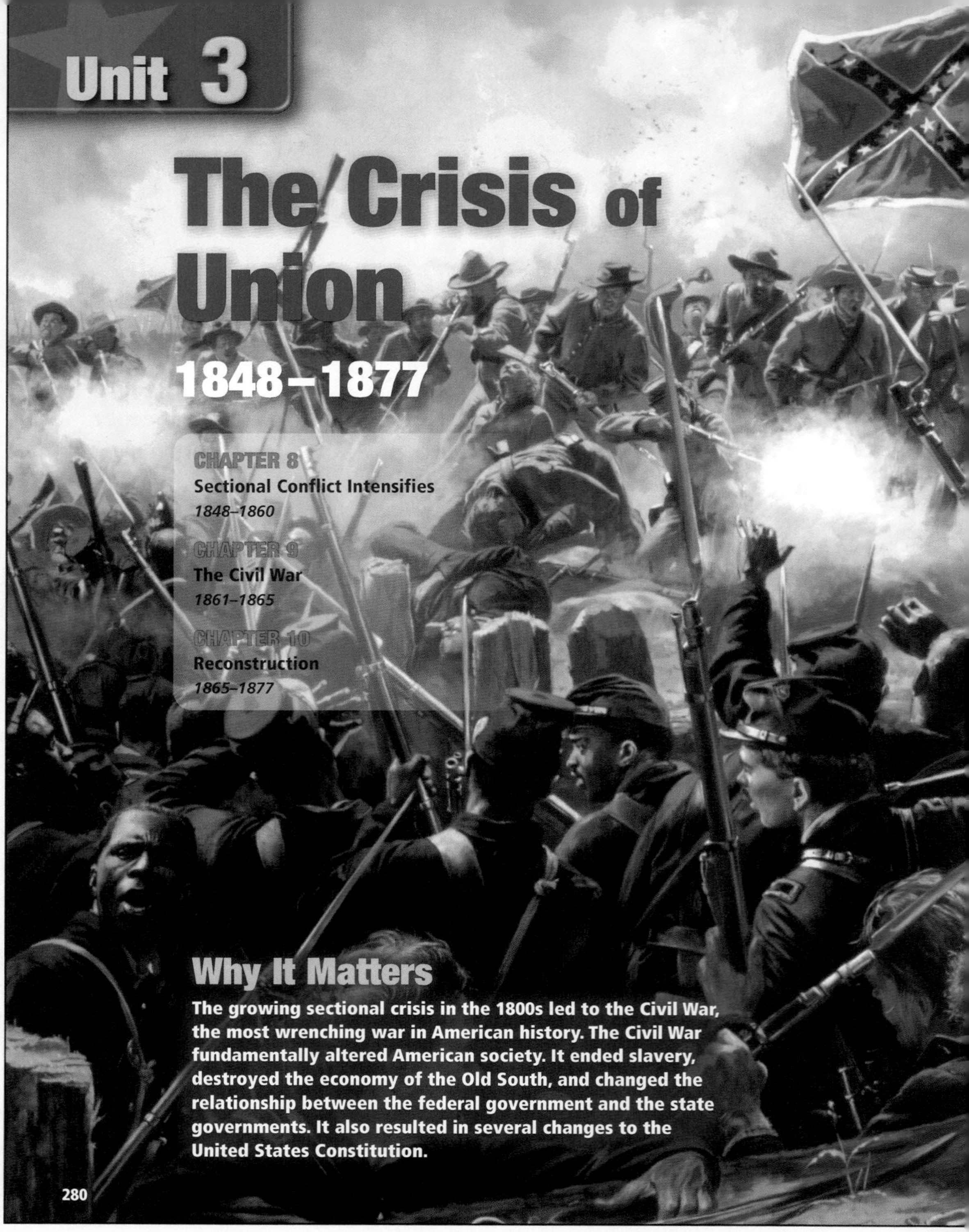

Unit 3

The Crisis of Union

1848–1877

Why It Matters

The growing sectional crisis in the 1800s led to the Civil War, the most wrenching war in American history. The Civil War fundamentally altered American society. It ended slavery, destroyed the economy of the Old South, and changed the relationship between the federal government and the state governments. It also resulted in several changes to the United States Constitution.

280

Team Teaching Activity

Language Arts Have the language arts teacher discuss the personal accounts of the Civil War contained in letters between soldiers and their families. As a class, discuss the role that bias plays in firsthand accounts of events. Have the language arts teacher point out examples of bias and personal opinions in a letter. Then have students work in groups to review other letters from the Civil War and identify bias in them. **OL**

Confederate soldiers of the 6th Virginia Infantry charge troops of the Union 9th Corps at the Battle of the Crater in Petersburg, Virginia, 1864.

Teach

Skill Practice

Analyzing Visuals Ask students to study the painting and then write a one-paragraph essay describing the scene it depicts. Students' essays should note that while the Confederate troops are all white, the Union troops in the battle are mostly African American. In addition, students should note that the Union soldiers are fighting from inside the crater, below ground level. **OL**

Skill Practice

Identifying Points of View Inform students that the battle depicted on this page occurred in the last year of the war. **Ask:** **Why did African Americans enlist to serve in the Union army?** *(Answers will vary, but should note that Lincoln had issued the Emancipation Proclamation, freeing people from slavery.)* **BL**

More About the Painting

Visual Literacy Fought on July 30, 1864, the Battle of the Crater, depicted here, was a part of the Siege of Petersburg in Virginia. Confederate General Robert E. Lee commanded the Army of Northern Virginia, and Major General George Meade commanded the Army of the Potomac. After the battle, the South claimed losses of more than 1,000 men; the North lost about 5,300 in a stunning defeat. The battle site is now a part of the Petersburg National Battlefield Park, established on July 3, 1926.

NCLB — No Child Left Behind

Teaching Tip The NCLB Act emphasizes reading. Ask students to write down events and people they will encounter in this unit and keep the list with them as they read. When students find a person or item on the list, they should note the page number and write a brief summary. Students can use this list while studying.

Chapter 8 Planning Guide

Key to Ability Levels	
BL Below Level	AL Above Level
OL On Level	ELL English Language Learners

Key to Teaching Resources	
Print Material	Transparency
CD-ROM or DVD	

BL	OL	AL	ELL		Resources	Chapter Opener	Section 1	Section 2	Section 3	Chapter Assess
					FOCUS					
BL	OL	AL	ELL	Transparency	Daily Focus Transparencies		8-1	8-2	8-3	
					TEACH					
BL	OL	AL		Print Material	Economics and History Activity, URB		p. 7			
		AL		Print Material	American Literature Reading, URB				p. 13	
BL	OL	AL	ELL	Print Material	Reading Essentials and Note-Taking Guide*		p. 87	p. 90	p. 93	
BL	OL		ELL	Print Material	Reading Skills Activity, URB		p. 21			
	OL			Print Material	Historical Analysis Skills Activity, URB	p. 22				
BL	OL		ELL	Print Material	Guided Reading Activity, URB*		p. 46	p. 47	p. 48	
BL	OL	AL	ELL	Print Material	Differentiated Instruction Activity, URB			p. 23		
BL	OL		ELL	Print Material	English Learner Activity, URB	p. 25				
BL	OL	AL	ELL	Print Material	Content Vocabulary Activity, URB*	p. 27				
BL	OL	AL	ELL	Print Material	Academic Vocabulary Activity, URB	p. 29				
	OL	AL		Print Material	Reinforcing Skills Activity, URB		p. 31			
	OL	AL		Print Material	Critical Thinking Skills Activity, URB		p. 32			
BL	OL		ELL	Print Material	Time Line Activity, URB		p. 33			
	OL			Print Material	Linking Past and Present Activity, URB					p. 34
BL	OL	AL	ELL	Print Material	Primary Source Reading, URB		p. 35	p. 37		
BL	OL	AL	ELL	Print Material	American Art and Music Activity, URB					p. 39
BL	OL	AL	ELL	Print Material	Interpreting Political Cartoons Activity, URB				p. 41	
		AL		Print Material	Enrichment Activity, URB			p. 44		
BL	OL	AL	ELL	Print Material	Differentiated Instruction for the American History Classroom	✓	✓	✓	✓	✓
BL	OL	AL	ELL	Transparency	Unit Map Overlay Transparencies	✓	✓	✓	✓	✓
BL	OL	AL	ELL	Print Material	Unit Time Line Transparencies, Strategies, and Activities	✓	✓	✓	✓	✓
BL	OL	AL	ELL	Print Material	Cause and Effect Transparencies, Strategies, and Activities	✓	✓	✓	✓	✓
BL	OL	AL	ELL	Print Material	Why It Matters Chapter Transparencies, Strategies, and Activities	✓	✓	✓	✓	✓
BL	OL	AL	ELL	Print Material	American Biographies		✓			

Note: Please refer to the *Unit 3 Resource Book* for this chapter's URB materials.

* Also available in Spanish

TeacherWorks Plus
All-In-One Planner and Resource Center

- Interactive Lesson Planner
- Interactive Teacher Edition
- Fully editable blackline masters
- Section Spotlight Videos Launch
- Differentiated Lesson Plans
- Printable reports of daily assignments
- Standards Tracking System

Levels BL	OL	AL	ELL		Resources	Chapter Opener	Section 1	Section 2	Section 3	Chapter Assess
					TEACH *(continued)*					
BL	OL	AL			Supreme Court Case Studies			p. 11		✓
BL	OL	AL	ELL		The Living Constitution	✓	✓	✓	✓	✓
BL	OL	AL	ELL		American Issues	✓	✓	✓	✓	✓
	OL	AL	ELL		American Art and Architecture Transparencies, Strategies, and Activities	✓	✓	✓	✓	✓
BL	OL	AL			High School American History Literature Library	✓	✓	✓	✓	✓
	OL	AL			American History Primary Source Documents Library	✓	✓	✓	✓	✓
BL	OL	AL	ELL		American Music: Hits Through History CD	✓	✓	✓	✓	✓
BL	OL	AL	ELL		StudentWorks™ Plus	✓	✓	✓	✓	✓
BL	OL	AL	ELL		*The American Vision* Video Program	✓	✓	✓	✓	✓
Teacher Resources					Reading Strategies and Activities for the Social Studies Classroom	✓	✓	✓	✓	✓
Teacher Resources					Strategies for Success	✓	✓	✓	✓	✓
Teacher Resources					Presentation Plus! with MindJogger CheckPoint	✓	✓	✓	✓	✓
Teacher Resources					Success With English Learners	✓	✓	✓	✓	✓
					ASSESS					
BL	OL	AL	ELL		Section Quizzes and Chapter Tests*		p. 107	p. 108	p. 109	p. 111
BL	OL	AL	ELL		Authentic Assessment With Rubrics					p. 21
BL	OL	AL	ELL		Standardized Test Practice Workbook					p. 15
BL	OL	AL	ELL		*ExamView® Assessment Suite*		8-1	8-2	8-3	Ch. 8
					CLOSE					
BL			ELL		Reteaching Activity, URB					p. 43
BL	OL		ELL		Reading and Study Skills Foldables™	p. 55				
BL	OL	AL	ELL		American History in Graphic Novel				p. 31	

✓ Chapter- or unit-based activities applicable to all sections.

Using Self-Check Quizzes

Teach With Technology

What is a Self-Check Quiz?

A Self-Check Quiz is a set of 10 or more multiple-choice questions that assess student comprehension of the chapter.

How can a Self-Check Quiz help my students?

A Self-Check Quiz is a quick and easy way for students to check how much they have learned and identify areas needing improvement. It allows students to:

- view their results immediately
- view the correct answers
- e-mail their results to you or themselves
- receive feedback on each question for where students can go to review topics they missed or had trouble answering

Visit glencoe.com and enter a ***QuickPass***™ code to go to a Self-Check Quiz.

History ONLINE
Visit glencoe.com and enter ***QuickPass***™ code TAV9399c8T for Chapter 8 resources.

You can easily launch a wide range of digital products from your computer's desktop with the McGraw-Hill Social Studies widget.

TeacherWorks

	Student	Teacher	Parent
Media Library			
• Section Audio	●		●
• Spanish Audio Summaries	●		●
• Section Spotlight Videos	●	●	●
***The American Vision* Online Learning Center (Web Site)**			
• StudentWorks™ Plus Online	●	●	●
• Multilingual Glossary	●	●	●
• Study-to-Go	●	●	●
• Chapter Overviews	●	●	●
• Self-Check Quizzes	●	●	●
• Student Web Activities	●	●	●
• ePuzzles and Games	●	●	●
• Vocabulary eFlashcards	●	●	●
• In Motion Animations	●	●	●
• Study Central™	●	●	●
• Web Activity Lesson Plans		●	
• Vocabulary PuzzleMaker	●	●	●
• Historical Thinking Activities		●	
• Beyond the Textbook	●	●	●

Reading Support From Jamestown Education

- **Timed Readings Plus in Social Studies** helps students increase their reading rate and fluency while maintaining comprehension. The 400-word passages are similar to those found on state and national assessments.
- **Reading in the Content Area: Social Studies** concentrates on six essential reading skills that help students better comprehend what they read. The book includes 75 high-interest nonfiction passages written at increasing levels of difficulty.
- **Reading Social Studies** includes strategic reading instruction and vocabulary support in Social Studies content for both ELLs and native speakers of English.

www.jamestowneducation.com

Biography / A&E Home Video / The History Channel

The following videotape programs are available from Glencoe as supplements to this chapter:

- Civil War Battlefields (ISBN 0-76-704083-X)
- Civil War Journal (Six Video Set) (ISBN 1-56-501326-3)

To order, call Glencoe at 1-800-334-7344. To find classroom resources to accompany many of these videos, check the following home pages:

A&E Television: www.aetv.com
The History Channel: www.historychannel.com

Reading List Generator CD-ROM — Glencoe BookLink 3

Use this database to search more than 30,000 titles to create a customized reading list for your students.

- Reading lists can be organized by students' reading level, author, genre, theme, or area of interest.
- The database provides Degrees of Reading Power™ (DRP) and Lexile™ readability scores for all selections.
- A brief summary of each selection is included.

Leveled reading suggestions for this chapter:

For students at a Grade 8 reading level:
- ***Gentle Annie: The True Story of a Civil War Nurse,*** by Mary Francis Shura

For students at a Grade 9 reading level:
- ***Virginia's General: Robert E. Lee and the Civil War,*** by Albert Marrin

For students at a Grade 10 reading level:
- ***The Civil War for Kids,*** by Janis Herbert

For students at a Grade 11 reading level:
- ***Civil War Ghosts,*** by Daniel Cohen

For students at a Grade 12 reading level:
- ***Mathew Brady: Civil War Photographer,*** by Elizabeth Van Steenwyk

National Geographic

Index to National Geographic Magazine:

The following articles relate to this chapter:

- "Fields of Honor: Pivotal Battles of the Civil War" By Thomson Gale, June 2006.
- "The Real Story: Diamonds" By Andrew Cockburn, March 2002.

National Geographic Society Products To order the following, call National Geographic at 1-800-368-2728:

- *The Civil War* (CD-ROM)

Access National Geographic's new dynamic MapMachine Web site and other geography resources at:
www.nationalgeographic.com
www.nationalgeographic.com/maps

Introducing Chapter 8

Focus

MAKING CONNECTIONS

What Keeps Nations United?

What can the leaders of nations do to keep their nations united? When nations suffer internal strife, it can erupt into civil war. Discuss with students the reasons why a nation might divide. Students might suggest that a country would divide across ethnic lines, such as in the breakup of Yugoslavia. **OL**

Teach

Big Ideas

As students study the chapter, remind them to consider the section-based Big Ideas included in each section's Guide to Reading. The **Essential Questions** in the activities below tie in to the Big Ideas and help students think about and understand important chapter concepts. In addition, the Hands-on Chapter Projects with their culminating activities relate the content from each section to the Big Ideas. These activities build on each other as students progress through the chapter. Section activities culminate in the wrap-up activity on the Visual Summary page.

Chapter 8

Sectional Conflict Intensifies

1848–1860

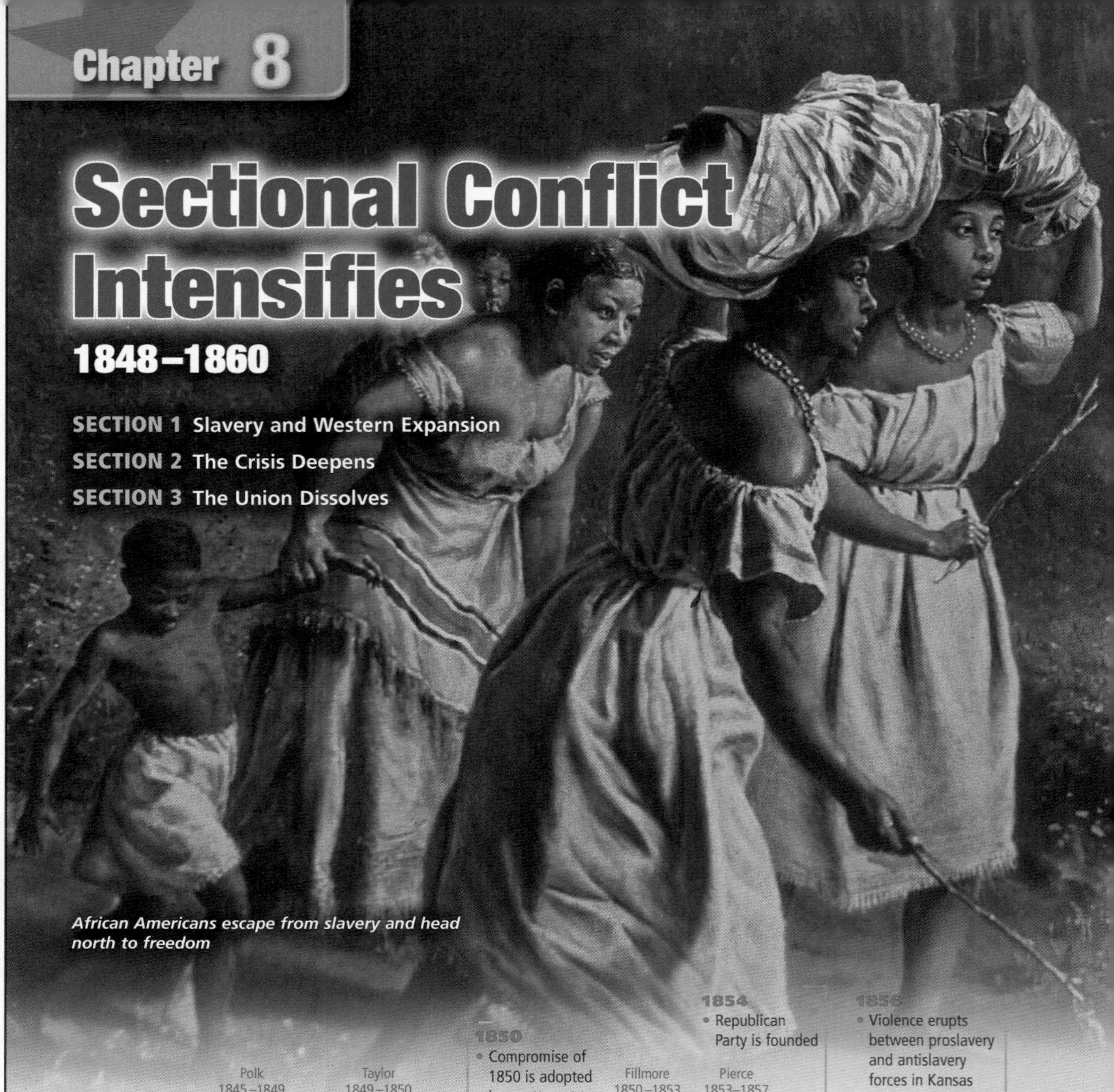

African Americans escape from slavery and head north to freedom

U.S. PRESIDENTS

Polk 1845–1849

Taylor 1849–1850

Fillmore 1850–1853

Pierce 1853–1857

U.S. EVENTS

1850
- Compromise of 1850 is adopted in an attempt to ease sectional tensions

1854
- Republican Party is founded

1856
- Violence erupts between proslavery and antislavery forces in Kansas

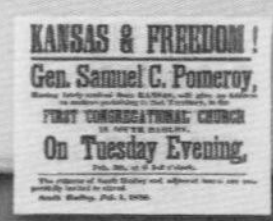

1848 — 1850 — 1852 — 1854 — 1856

WORLD EVENTS

1847
- Working hours in Britain are limited

1848
- Serfdom is abolished in Austrian Empire

1852
- Livingstone explores Africa's Zambezi River

1853
- Crimean War begins, pitting Russia against Great Britain and Turkey

Section 1

Slavery and Western Expansion

Essential Question: How did western expansion cause the North and South to confront the issue of slavery? *(The new territories or states gained after the Mexican War had to decide whether they would be free or slave.)* Point out that in Section 1 students will learn how political leaders sought to hold together the Union through legislative compromise. **OL**

Section 2

The Crisis Deepens

Essential Question: How did the controversy over slavery break up and create new political parties? *(The Kansas-Nebraska Act upset the agreement ironed out in the Missouri Compromise. Political parties with members from both the North and the South became increasingly divided over the slavery issue.)* Point out that in Section 2 students will learn about the growing division in the country over the issue of slavery. **OL**

Chapter Audio

MAKING CONNECTIONS

What Keeps Nations United?

From the days of the Constitutional Convention until the late 1840s, people in the North and South had made compromises to keep the nation united. That began to change in the 1850s as the nation expanded westward rapidly and the controversy over slavery in the new territories intensified.

- ***Why do you think Northerners and Southerners became less willing to compromise in the 1850s?***
- ***Was the Civil War inevitable?***

Buchanan 1857–1861

1859
- John Brown raids the federal arsenal at Harpers Ferry, Virginia

1860
- South Carolina secedes from the Union

CHARLESTON MERCURY EXTRA: UNION DISSOLVED!

Lincoln 1861–1865

1861
- Fort Sumter is bombarded by Confederate forces; the Civil War begins

1858 1860

1858
- First transatlantic telegraph cable laid between Europe and North America

1859
- Darwin's *Origin of Species* is published

FOLDABLES™

Analyzing Events Create a Trifold Book Foldable about one of the following events: the Fugitive Slave Act, the *Dred Scott* decision, the Lincoln-Douglas debates, the Missouri Compromise, the Kansas-Nebraska Act, or John Brown's raid. Describe the event, how it influenced events leading to the Civil War, and what might have happened if the event had turned out differently.

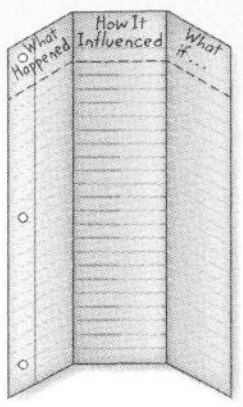

History ONLINE Visit glencoe.com and enter **QuickPass™** code **TAV9846c8** for **Chapter 8 resources.**

Section 3

The Union Dissolves

Essential Question: What is the final outcome of the national split over the slavery issue? *(the American Civil War)* Point out that in Section 3 students will learn about the outcome of an election in 1860 that was a precursor to America's Civil War. **OL**

More About the Photo

Visual Literacy The Underground Railroad assisted fugitive slaves to freedom. It employed terms much like the steam railroads. "Conductors" led fleeing slaves to safe places, "stations" or "depots," to eat and rest. Stations were run by "stationmasters." People who contributed money or goods to the cause were called "stockholders." Between the years 1810 and 1850, the South lost 100,000 slaves with the help of the Underground Railroad.

FOLDABLES™ Study Organizer **Dinah Zike's Foldables**

Dinah Zike's Foldables are three-dimensional, interactive graphic organizers that help students practice basic writing skills, review vocabulary terms, and identify main ideas. Instructions for creating and using Foldables can be found in the Appendix at the end of this book and in the *Dinah Zike's Reading and Study Skills Foldables* booklet.

History ONLINE

Visit glencoe.com and enter **QuickPass™** code TAV9399c8T for Chapter 8 resources, including a Chapter Overview, Study Central™, Study-to-Go, Student Web Activity, Self-Check Quiz, and other materials.

Focus

Bellringer

Daily Focus Transparency 8-1

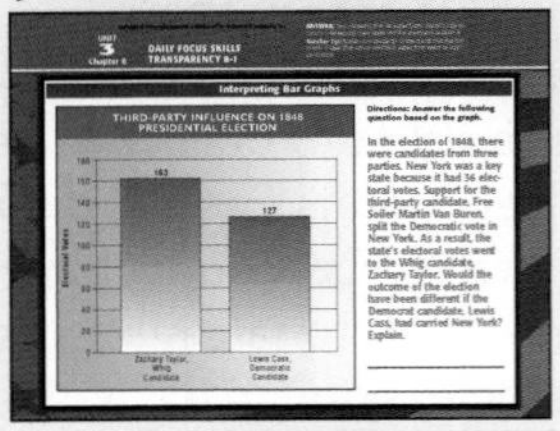

Guide to Reading

Answers: Democrat Lewis Cass supported popular sovereignty; Free Soiler Martin Van Buren opposed slavery in the West; Whig Zachary Taylor did not express a position.

Section Spotlight Video

To generate student interest and provide a springboard for class discussion, access the Chapter 8, Section 1 video at glencoe.com or on the video DVD.

Section 1

Section Audio   Spotlight Video

Slavery and Western Expansion

Guide to Reading

Big Ideas

Struggles for Rights As sectional tensions rose, some Americans openly defied laws they thought were unjust.

Content Vocabulary

- popular sovereignty *(p. 285)*
- secession *(p. 287)*
- transcontinental railroad *(p. 291)*

Academic Vocabulary

- survival *(p. 286)*
- perception *(p. 291)*

People and Events to Identify

- Wilmot Proviso *(p. 284)*
- Free-Soil Party *(p. 285)*
- "Forty-Niners" *(p. 286)*
- Compromise of 1850 *(p. 288)*
- Fugitive Slave Act *(p. 288)*
- Underground Railroad *(p. 289)*
- Harriet Tubman *(p. 289)*
- *Uncle Tom's Cabin* *(p. 291)*
- Gadsden Purchase *(p. 291)*
- Kansas-Nebraska Act *(p. 292)*

Reading Strategy

Categorizing Complete a graphic organizer similar to the one below by pairing the presidential candidates of 1848 with their positions on slavery in the West.

Candidate	Position

The spread of slavery into new territory became the overriding political issue of the 1850s. Admitting new slave states or new free states would upset the balance of power between Northern states and Southern states in the national government.

The Search for Compromise

MAIN Idea Continuing disagreements over the westward expansion of slavery increased sectional tensions between the North and South.

HISTORY AND YOU What do you recall about the compromise Henry Clay previously negotiated between Northerners and Southerners? Read on to learn about the Great Compromise of 1850 and how it allowed California to be admitted to the Union.

As many people in both the North and South had anticipated, the Mexican War greatly increased sectional tensions. The war had opened vast new lands to American settlers raising, once again, the divisive issue of whether slavery should be allowed to spread westward into the new lands. As part of the debate over the new western territories, Southerners also demanded new laws to help them retrieve slaves who escaped to free states.

The Wilmot Proviso

In August 1846 Representative David Wilmot, a Democrat from Pennsylvania, proposed an addition to a war appropriations bill. His amendment, known as the **Wilmot Proviso,** proposed that in any territory that the United States gained from Mexico "neither slavery nor involuntary servitude shall ever exist."

Wilmot's proposal outraged Southerners. They believed that any antislavery decision about the territories would threaten slavery everywhere. Despite fierce Southern opposition, a coalition of Northern Democrats and Whigs passed the Wilmot Proviso in the House of Representatives. The Senate, however, refused to vote on it. During the debate, Senator John C. Calhoun of South Carolina prepared a series of resolutions to counter the Wilmot Proviso. The Calhoun Resolutions never came to a vote, but they demonstrated the growing anger of many Southerners.

In the resolutions, Calhoun argued that the states owned the territories of the United States in common, and that Congress had no right to ban slavery in them. Calhoun warned somberly that "political revolution, anarchy, [and] civil war" would surely erupt if the North failed to heed Southern concerns.

Resource Manager

R Reading Strategies	C Critical Thinking	D Differentiated Instruction	W Writing Support	S Skill Practice
Teacher Edition • Inferring, p. 286 • Sequencing Info., p. 290 • Making Connections, p. 293 **Additional Resources** • Read. Skills Act., URB p. 21 • Content Vocab. Act., URB p. 27 • Prim. Source Read., URB p. 35 • Guided Read., URB p. 46	**Teacher Edition** • Determining Cause/Effect, p. 285 • Identify. Central Issues, p. 288 **Additional Resources** • Economics and History, URB p. 7 • Critical Thinking Skills, URB p. 32 • Quizzes and Tests, p. 107	**Additional Resources** • Eng. Learner Act., URB p. 25	**Teacher Edition** • Expository Writing, p. 287 **Additional Resources** • Academic Vocab. Act., URB p. 29	**Teacher Edition** • Creating a Time Line, pp. 286, 292 • Using Geo. Skills, p. 289 • Creating a Pol. Cartoon, p. 291 **Additional Resources** • Hist. Analysis Skills Act., URB p. 22 • Reinforcing Skills, URB p. 31 • Time Line Act., URB p. 33 • Read. Essen., p. 87

POLITICAL CARTOONS PRIMARY SOURCE

Debating Popular Sovereignty

In the nineteenth century, farmers would sometimes burn down their barns to kill all the rats. Democrats who supported free soil—many of whom, like Martin Van Buren, came from New York—were nicknamed Barn Burners. They opposed the nomination of Lewis Cass for president and supported the Wilmot Proviso.

Analyzing VISUALS DBQ

1. **Finding the Main Idea** What is the main idea of this cartoon?
2. **Identifying Central Issues** Is the cartoon supporting free soil or popular sovereignty? How do you know?

Popular Sovereignty

With the country increasingly divided along sectional lines over the issue of slavery's expansion in the territories, many moderates began searching for a solution that would spare Congress from having to deal with the issue. Senator Lewis Cass of Michigan proposed one solution. Cass suggested that the citizens of each new territory should be allowed to decide for themselves whether or not they wanted to permit slavery. This idea came to be called **popular sovereignty.**

Popular sovereignty appealed to many members of Congress because it removed the slavery issue from national politics. It also appeared democratic since settlers themselves would make the decision. Abolitionists argued that it denied African Americans their right to freedom, but many Northerners supported the idea because they believed Northerners would settle most of the new territory and then ban slavery there.

The Free-Soil Party Emerges With the 1848 election approaching, the Whigs chose Zachary Taylor, hero of the war with Mexico, to run for president. The Whig Party in the North was split. Many Northern Whigs, known as Conscience Whigs, opposed slavery. They also opposed Taylor, a large slaveholder, because they believed he wanted to expand slavery westward. Other Northern Whigs supported Taylor and voted with the Southern Whigs to nominate him. These Northern Whigs were known as Cotton Whigs because many of them were linked to Northern textile manufacturers who needed Southern cotton. C

The decision to nominate Taylor convinced many Conscience Whigs to quit the party. They then joined antislavery Democrats from New York, who were frustrated that their party had nominated Lewis Cass instead of Martin Van Buren. These two groups then joined members of the abolitionist Liberty Party to form the **Free-Soil Party,** which opposed slavery in the "free soil" of western territories.

Teach

Analyzing VISUALS

Answers:

1. that popular sovereignty, and Lewis Cass who developed and supported the idea, was a danger to the Union
2. It is supporting free soil over popular sovereignty, because Lewis Cass is freeing the rats which Martin Van Buren is trying to burn out of the "barn," which probably stands for the United States.

C Critical Thinking

Determining Cause and Effect To help students organize the information under the subhead "The Free-Soil Party Emerges," have them illustrate in a flowchart the cause-and-effect chain that shows how the Free-Soil Party developed. **Ask:** What caused the development of the Free-Soil Party? *(The Whig decision to nominate Taylor led Conscience Whigs to join antislavery Democrats from New York who were frustrated with the nomination of Cass over Van Buren.)* BL OL

Hands-On Chapter Project Step 1

Mapping Events of the Mid-1800s

Step 1: Laying the Foundation Students will create an outline map of the United States and determine which events from Section 1 to represent on the map.

Directions Students should work in small groups or as a class for this activity. Students can either copy an outline map (and enlarge it) or draw an outline map of the United States. Each group should select one major topic from Section 1 to illustrate on the map, such as the Underground Railroad, the Kansas-Nebraska Act, or the transcontinental railroad. Groups should depict the topic on the map using images. They should also include captions that explain the importance of the topic.

Locating and Labeling Students will determine where on the U.S. map to illustrate their topic. Students should use symbols and map keys to clearly label the map. OL

(Chapter Project continued on page 299)

S Skill Practice

Creating a Time Line Have students use library and Internet resources to create a time line of the events of the California Gold Rush from 1848 to 1855. **BL**

R Reading Strategy

Inferring Have students look at the art in the Primary Source feature of the Compromise of 1850. **Ask:** How do Daniel Webster and John Calhoun appear to be responding to Henry Clay's speech? *(Students' answers will vary and depend on their knowledge of the event. They may note that Webster looks thoughtful and attentive, while Calhoun looks frustrated or angry.)* **ELL** **OL**

Although some Free-Soilers condemned slavery as immoral, most simply wanted to preserve the western territories for white farmers. They believed that allowing slavery to expand would make it difficult for free men to find work. The Free-Soil Party's slogan summed up their views: "Free soil, free speech, free labor, and free men."

Candidates from three parties campaigned for the presidency in 1848. Democrat Lewis Cass supported popular sovereignty, although this support was not mentioned in the South. His promise to veto the Wilmot Proviso, should Congress pass it, however, was often reported. Former president Martin Van Buren led the Free-Soil Party, which took a strong position against slavery in the territories and backed the Wilmot Proviso. General Zachary Taylor, the Whig candidate, avoided the whole issue. On Election Day, support for the Free-Soilers split the Democratic vote in New York. This enabled Taylor to win the state, and with it, enough electoral votes to win the election.

The Forty-Niners Head to California S Within a year of Taylor's inauguration, the issue of slavery again took center stage. In 1848 gold was discovered in California, and thousands of people headed west, hoping to become rich. By the end of 1849, more than 80,000 **"Forty-Niners"** had arrived to look for gold—more than enough people for California to apply for statehood. Congress had to decide whether California would enter the Union as a free state or a slave state.

Before leaving office, President Polk had urged Congress to create territorial governments for California and New Mexico, but Congress had not been able to agree on whether to allow slavery in these territories. Although President Taylor was himself a slaveholder, he did not think slavery's **survival** depended on its expansion westward. He believed that the way to avoid a fight in Congress was to have Californians make their own decision about slavery. With Taylor's encouragement, California applied for admission as a free state in late 1849. Thus, the Gold Rush had forced the nation once again to confront the divisive issue of slavery.

The Great Debate Begins

If California became a free state, the slaveholding states would be in the minority in the Senate. Southerners dreaded this, fearing it

PRIMARY SOURCE

R The Compromise of 1850

Leaders in the California Territory submitted their request to become a state in 1849. Debate in Congress over California's entry into the Union as a free state ended in the Compromise of 1850. California joined the Union in September 1850 as part of the Compromise.

◀ *As word of the discovery of gold in California spread through the nation, Americans rushed to the mountains in search of gold.*

PRIMARY SOURCE

"... [I]t is this circumstance, Sir, the prohibition of slavery ... which has contributed to raise ... the dispute as to the propriety of the admission of California into the Union under this constitution."

—Daniel Webster, speech in the Senate, March 7, 1850

▶ *Daniel Webster, Henry Clay, and John Calhoun were the main participants in the 1850 debate over the slavery issue and California's entry into the Union.*

Additional Support

Activity: Collaborative Learning

Making an Oral Presentation Organize the class into eight groups. Read the following quote made by Sidney George Fisher, a Philadelphia lawyer, in 1844: "Every day the difference between the North and the South is becoming more prominent and apparent. The difference exists in everything which forms the life of the people—in institutions, laws, opinions, manners, feelings, education, pursuits, climate, and soil." Assign each group one thing which "forms the life of the people" to prepare a brief oral presentation about the growing differences between the North and South. **OL**

might result in limits on slavery and states' rights. A few Southern leaders began to talk openly of **secession**—of taking their states out of the Union.

Clay's Proposal In early 1850 one of the most senior and influential leaders in the Senate, Henry Clay of Kentucky, tried to find a compromise that would enable California to join the Union. Clay—nicknamed "The Great Compromiser" because of his role in promoting the Missouri Compromise in 1820 and solving the nullification crisis in 1833—proposed eight resolutions to solve the crisis.

Clay grouped the resolutions in pairs, offering concessions to both sides. The first pair allowed California to come in as a free state but organized the rest of the Mexican cession without any restrictions on slavery. The second pair settled the border between New Mexico and Texas in favor of New Mexico but compensated Texas by having the federal government take on its debts. This would win Southern votes because many Southerners held Texas bonds.

Clay's third pair of resolutions outlawed the slave trade in the District of Columbia but did not outlaw slavery itself. The final two resolutions were concessions to the South. Congress would be prohibited from interfering with the slave trade and would pass a new fugitive slave act to help Southerners recover enslaved African Americans who had fled to the North. These concessions were intended to reassure the South that after California joined the Union, the North would not use its control of the Senate to abolish slavery.

Clay's proposals triggered a massive debate. Any compromise would need the approval of Senator John C. Calhoun, the great defender of the South's rights. Calhoun was too ill to address the Senate. He wrote a speech and then sat, hollow-eyed and shrouded in flannel blankets, as another senator read it aloud.

Calhoun's Response Calhoun's address was brutally frank. It asserted flatly that Northern agitation against slavery threatened to destroy the South. He did not think Clay's compromise would save the Union. The South needed an acceptance of its rights, the return of fugitive slaves, and a guarantee of a balance of power between the sections. If the Southern states could not live in safety within the Union, Calhoun darkly predicted, secession was the only honorable solution.

PRIMARY SOURCE

"[T]he equilibrium between [the North and the South] . . . has been destroyed. . . . [o]ne section has the exclusive power of controlling the government, which leaves the other without any adequate means of protecting itself against its encroachment and oppression."

—John C. Calhoun, speech in the Senate, March 4, 1850

PRIMARY SOURCE

"California, with suitable boundaries, ought, upon her application, to be admitted as one of the States of this Union, without the imposition by Congress of any restriction in respect to the exclusion or introduction of slavery within those boundaries."

—Henry Clay's resolution, January 29, 1850

The Compromise of 1850

- California admitted to the Union as a free state
- Popular sovereignty to determine slavery issue in Utah and New Mexico territories
- Texas border dispute with New Mexico resolved
- Texas receives $10 million
- Slave trade, but not slavery itself, abolished in the District of Columbia
- New, stringent Fugitive Slave Law adopted

W

DBQ Document-Based Questions

1. **Summarizing** How does Clay think slavery should be treated in California?
2. **Finding Main Ideas** What is Calhoun's concern about adding California to the Union?
3. **Generalizing** Do you think the North or the South achieved more of its goals in the Compromise of 1850? Why?

W Writing Support

Expository Writing Have students select a person mentioned in this section and do research to write a biography of him or her. You may want to encourage students to work in groups and to plan and write their biographies so that there is no duplication. Then have students create a class booklet or a Website showcasing their work.

DBQ Document Based Questions

Answers:

1. He thought California should be admitted without the burden of accepting or rejecting slavery.
2. He feels that it will now give the North complete control of the government, and over the South.
3. Answers will vary, but students should give reasons for their opinions based on the text and the information in the feature.

Additional Support

Activity: Collaborative Learning

Verbal/Linguistic Sometimes inattention is caused by the difficulty of the material. Have students preview Section 1 with a partner to list and assess components that they might find difficult. Ask volunteers to share items from their lists. Then, discuss with students the factors that might affect their ability to maintain attention. For example, ask the following questions: In which subsection is it easier for you to maintain attention, "The Search for Compromise" or "The Fugitive Slave Act"? Why? BL ELL

C Critical Thinking

Identifying Central Issues
Discuss with students the Fugitive Slave Act of 1850. **Ask:** What were the results of the Fugitive Slave Act in the Northern states? *(Neither fugitive African Americans nor free African Americans were safe even in the North. The testimony of a white witness held more weight than that of an African American. Federal commissioners who judged the cases were paid to rule in favor of the slaveholder.)* **OL**

Reading Check

Answer:
California's population increased rapidly with the Gold Rush, which allowed it to qualify for statehood. The decision to admit California as a slave or free state created a heated debate in Congress.

Additional Support

Three days later, Senator Daniel Webster of Massachusetts rose to respond to Calhoun's talk of secession. Calling on the Senate to put national unity above sectional loyalties, Webster voiced his support for Clay's plan, claiming that it was the only hope for preserving the Union. Although he sought conciliation, Senator Webster did not back away from speaking bluntly—and with chilling foresight:

PRIMARY SOURCE

"I wish to speak to-day, not as a Massachusetts man, nor as a Northern man, but as an American. . . . I speak to-day for the preservation of the Union. 'Hear me for my cause'. . . . There can be no such thing as a peaceable secession. Peaceable secession is an utter impossibility. . . . I see as plainly as I see the sun in heaven what that disruption itself must produce; I see that it must produce war, and such a war as I will not describe."

—from the *Congressional Globe*

The Compromise of 1850

At first, Congress did not pass Clay's bill, in part because President Taylor opposed it. Then, unexpectedly, Taylor died in office that summer. Vice President Millard Fillmore succeeded him and quickly threw his support behind the compromise.

By the end of summer, Calhoun was dead, Webster had accepted the position of secretary of state, and Clay was exhausted, leaving leadership of the Senate to younger men. Thirty-seven-year-old Stephen A. Douglas of Illinois took charge of the effort to resolve the crisis. Douglas divided the large compromise initiative into several smaller bills. This allowed his colleagues from different sections to abstain or vote against whatever parts they disliked while supporting the rest. By fall, Congress had passed all the parts of the original proposal as Clay had envisioned it, and President Fillmore had signed them into law.

Fillmore called the compromise a "final settlement" between the North and South. For a short time, the **Compromise of 1850** did ease the tensions over slavery. In the next few years, however, more conflicts arose, and the hope of a permanent solution through compromise would begin to fade.

Reading Check **Summarizing** How did the Gold Rush affect the issue of slavery?

The Fugitive Slave Act C

MAIN Idea Many Northerners opposed the Fugitive Slave Act and vowed to disobey it.

HISTORY AND YOU Under what circumstances, if any, do you believe citizens should disobey a law? Read to learn how some Northerners responded to the Fugitive Slave Act of 1850.

Although Henry Clay had conceived the **Fugitive Slave Act** as a benefit to slaveholders, it actually hurt the Southern cause by creating active hostility toward slavery among many Northerners who had been indifferent.

Northern Resistance Grows

Under the Fugitive Slave Act of 1850, a person claiming that an African American had escaped from slavery had only to point out that person as a runaway to take him or her into custody. The accused then would be brought before a federal commissioner. With no right to testify on their own behalf, African Americans had no way to prove their cases. An affidavit asserting that the captive had escaped from a slaveholder or testimony by white witnesses was all a court needed to order the person sent south. Furthermore, federal commissioners had an incentive to rule in favor of the slaveholder; such judgments earned the commissioner a $10 fee, but judgments in favor of the accused paid only $5.

The law also required federal marshals to assist slave catchers, and it authorized marshals to deputize citizens on the spot to help capture fugitives. A citizen who refused to cooperate could be jailed.

Newspaper accounts of the unjust seizure of African Americans fueled Northern indignation. One Northern newspaper proclaimed that "almost no colored man is safe in our streets." As outraged as Northerners were over such seizures, they were even angrier over the requirement that ordinary citizens help capture runaways. This provision drove many into active defiance. Frederick Douglass emphasized this part of the law over and over again in his speeches. A powerful orator, Douglass would paint an emotional picture of an African American fleeing kidnappers. Then he would ask his audience whether they would give the runaway over to the "pursuing bloodhounds." "No!" the crowd would roar.

Activity: Interdisciplinary Connection

Political Science Conduct a class discussion about the reasons senators from the North and the South disagreed on the Compromise of 1850. List the reasons on the board under the headings "North" and "South." Tell students that much of the reasoning was the result of differences over states' rights. Ask students to describe examples of such differences. Conclude the discussion by emphasizing the differences between the politics of the North and the South. **AL**

NATIONAL GEOGRAPHIC Slavery and the Underground Railroad, 1830–1860

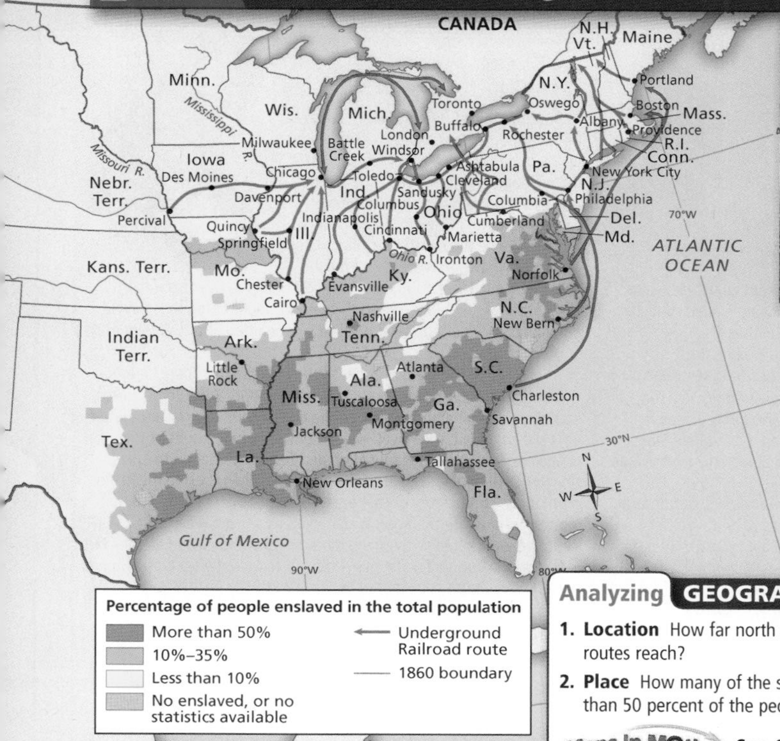

▲ *Courageous "conductors" led thousands of enslaved people out of the South to freedom along routes of the Underground Railroad.*

Analyzing GEOGRAPHY

1. **Location** How far north did many Underground Railroad routes reach?
2. **Place** How many of the states shown had areas where more than 50 percent of the people were enslaved?

Maps In MOtion See *StudentWorks™ Plus* or glencoe.com.

The Underground Railroad

Antislavery activists often used the words of writer Henry David Thoreau to justify defying the Fugitive Slave Act. In his 1849 essay, "Civil Disobedience," Thoreau advocated disobeying laws on moral grounds. "Unjust laws exist," he wrote. "Shall we be content to obey them, or shall we endeavor to amend them, and obey them until we have succeeded, or shall we transgress them at once?" For many, the answer was to disobey them without delay.

Although the Fugitive Slave Act included heavy fines and prison terms for helping a runaway, whites and free African Americans continued their work with the **Underground Railroad.** This informal but well-organized system was legendary during the 1840s and 1850s and helped thousands of enslaved persons escape. Members, called "conductors," transported runaways north in secret, gave them shelter and food along the way, and saw them to freedom in the Northern states or in Canada, with some money for a fresh start.

Dedicated people, many of them African Americans, made dangerous trips into the South to guide enslaved persons along the Underground Railroad to freedom. The most famous of these conductors was **Harriet Tubman,** herself a runaway. She risked many trips to the South, even after slaveholders offered a large reward for her capture.

In Des Moines, Iowa, Isaac Brandt used secret signals to communicate with conductors on the Underground Railroad—a hand lifted palm outwards, for example, or a certain kind of tug at the ear. "I do not know how these signs or signals originated," he later remembered, "but they had become well understood. Without them the operation of the system of running slaves into free territory would not have been possible."

Analyzing GEOGRAPHY

Answers:

1. to Canada
2. 13 (although Maryland, Kentucky, and Tennessee had relatively few enslaved people, they had areas in which more than 50% of the population was enslaved)

S Skill Practice

Using Geography Skills Have students study the map "Slavery and the Underground Railroad, 1830–1860." **Ask:** Which route appears to be the quickest way from the South for fugitive enslaved people to make it to freedom in the North? *(Routes along the Ohio River and into Ohio.)*

Additional Support

Activity: Collaborative Learning

Writing a Screenplay Organize the class into small groups for this activity. Have groups use library resources and the Internet to learn more about the Underground Railroad. Then have each group write a screenplay that accurately depicts the experiences of either an enslaved person escaping north or a conductor helping runaways.

People IN HISTORY

Answers:

1. Answers will vary. Tubman may have meant that she felt that freedom had transformed her so that she was not sure she was still the same person
2. It further hardened the positions of the abolitionists and slaveholders, helping to bring on the Civil War.

Did You Know?

Defending Her Work In response to criticism of her work, Harriet Beecher Stowe published *A Key to Uncle Tom's Cabin* in 1853. This volume contained documents and testimonies that supported the picture of slavery she had painted in *Uncle Tom's Cabin.*

People IN HISTORY

Harriet Tubman
1820–1913

Known as "Moses" for her courage in leading enslaved people to freedom as Moses had led the Hebrews out of slavery in Egypt, Harriet Tubman was a heroine of the antislavery movement. Tubman was born into slavery in Maryland and struggled early against the system's brutality. At age 13, she tried to save another enslaved person from punishment, and an overseer fractured her skull. Miraculously, she recovered, but she suffered from occasional blackouts for the rest of her life.

Tubman escaped to freedom in 1849. About crossing into Pennsylvania, she later wrote, "I looked at my hands to see if I was the same person. There was such a glory over everything. The sun came up like gold through the trees, and I felt like I was in Heaven."

Her joy inspired others. After Congress passed the Fugitive Slave Act, Tubman returned to the South 19 times to guide enslaved people along the Underground Railroad to freedom.

Tubman became notorious in the eyes of slaveholders, but despite a large reward offered for her capture, no one ever betrayed her whereabouts. Furthermore, in all her rescues, she never lost a "passenger." Tubman's bravery and determination made her one of the most important figures in the antislavery movement.

What do you think Tubman meant when she wrote, "I looked at my hands to see if I was the same person?"

Harriet Beecher Stowe
1811–1896

Daughter of reformer-minister Lyman Beecher, Harriet Beecher Stowe was born into a family of high achievers. Unlike many young women of the time, Stowe received a good education, including teacher training in Hartford, Connecticut. In 1832 Stowe moved to Cincinnati, Ohio. There, Stowe began writing and teaching. She spent 18 years in Ohio—right across the river from the slave state of Kentucky. During this period, she met fugitive slaves, employed a former enslaved woman, and learned about slavery from Southern friends.

In 1850 Stowe moved with her husband to Maine. There, in reaction to the Fugitive Slave Law, she began writing *Uncle Tom's Cabin*, based on what she had learned while in Ohio and antislavery materials she had read. The novel, which humanized the plight of the enslaved, was an instant sensation and further hardened the positions of both abolitionists and slaveholders. When President Lincoln met Stowe, so the story goes, he exclaimed, "So you're the little woman who wrote the book that started this Great War!"

Stowe went on to write many more novels, stories, and articles but is today best known for the novel that so fanned the sectional flames over slavery that it contributed to the start of the Civil War.

What was the effect of Uncle Tom's Cabin on the slavery debate?

Levi Coffin was born to a Quaker family in North Carolina. As a boy, he witnessed a group of African Americans in chains being led to an auction. The incident deeply affected him, and years later, he allowed escaped African Americans to stay at his home in Indiana, where three Underground Railroad routes from the South converged.

To read an excerpt from **Uncle Tom's Cabin**, see page R68 in **American Literature Library.**

PRIMARY SOURCE

"We knew not what night or what hour of the night we would be roused from slumber by a gentle rap at the door. . . . Outside in the cold or rain, there would be a two-horse wagon loaded with fugitives, perhaps the greater part of them women and children. I would invite them, in a low tone, to come in, and they would follow me into the darkened house without a word, for we knew not who might be watching and listening."

—quoted in *The Underground Railroad*

An estimated 2,000 African Americans stopped at Coffin's Indiana house on their way to freedom. Coffin later moved to Cincinnati, Ohio, where he assisted another 1,300 African Americans who had crossed the river from Kentucky to freedom. A thorn in the side of slaveholders, the Underground Railroad deepened Southern mistrust of Northern intentions.

Uncle Tom's Cabin

One evening in 1851, the well-educated, deeply religious Stowe family sat in their parlor in Brunswick, Maine, listening to a letter being read aloud. The letter was from Harriet Beecher Stowe's sister, Isabella, in Boston.

The new Fugitive Slave Act, part of the Compromise of 1850, had gone into effect, Isabella reported, and slave catchers prowled the streets. They pounced on African Americans without warning, breaking into their houses, destroying their shops, and carrying them off. Isabella described daily attacks. She also told of outraged Bostonians, white and African American alike, who rallied to resist the kidnappers.

Activity: Collaborative Learning

Creating a Thematic Map Organize students into small groups to create a thematic map showing the major Underground Railroad routes. Have students use library and Internet sources to learn more about the extensive network of routes traveled by African Americans as they escaped slavery. Maps should include a title, a map key, and a compass rose. Make arrangements to display the maps. **OL**

Harriet Beecher Stowe listened with growing despair. She had lived for many years in Cincinnati, across the Ohio River from the slave state of Kentucky. There, she had met many runaways from slavery and heard their tragic tales. She had also visited Kentucky and witnessed slavery firsthand.

As the reading of her sister's letter continued, Stowe, who was an accomplished author, received a challenge. "Now Hattie," Isabella wrote, "if I could use a pen as you can, I would write something that would make this whole **R** nation feel what an accursed thing slavery is." Stowe suddenly rose from her chair and announced, "I will write something. I will if I live." That year, she began writing sketches for a book called ***Uncle Tom's Cabin.***

After running as a serial in an antislavery newspaper, *Uncle Tom's Cabin* came out in book form in 1852 and sold 300,000 copies in its first year—an astounding number for the time. Today, the writing may seem overly sentimental, but to Stowe's original readers, mostly Northerners, it was powerful. Her depiction of the enslaved hero Tom and the villainous overseer Simon Legree changed Northern **perceptions** of African Americans and slavery.

Stowe presented African Americans as real people imprisoned in dreadful circumstances. Because she saw herself as a painter of slavery's horrors rather than an abstract debater, Stowe was able to evoke pity and outrage even in readers who were unmoved by rational arguments.

Theatrical dramatizations of *Uncle Tom's Cabin* increased the story's appeal. The plays reached a wider audience than the novel and specifically attracted the working class, which tended to ignore abolitionism.

Southerners tried unsuccessfully to have the novel banned and attacked its portrayal of slavery, accusing Stowe of writing "distortions" and "falsehoods." One Southern editor said he wanted a review of *Uncle Tom's Cabin* to be "as hot as hellfire, blasting and searing the reputation of the vile wretch in petticoats."

Despite Southern outrage, the book eventually sold millions of copies. It had such a dramatic impact on public opinion that many historians consider it one of the causes of the Civil War.

Reading Check **Examining** What was an unintended consequence of the Fugitive Slave Act?

The Kansas-Nebraska Act

MAIN Idea In the 1850s the debate over the spread of slavery became increasingly heated and sometimes turned violent.

HISTORY AND YOU Have you ever watched Congress on television? Do you think politicians behave differently when they know the public is watching? Read on to find out how debate gave way to a physical assault on the Senate floor in 1856.

The opening of Oregon and the admission of California to the Union had convinced Americans that a **transcontinental railroad** should be built to connect the West Coast to the rest of the country. In the 1850s getting to the West Coast required many grueling weeks of travel overland or a long sea voyage around the tip of South America. A transcontinental railroad would reduce the journey to four relatively easy days, while promoting further settlement and growth in the territories along the route.

Debating the Route of the Transcontinental Railroad

The transcontinental railroad had broad appeal, but the choice of its eastern starting point became a new element in the sectional conflict. Two routes were initially proposed—a northern route and a southern route.

Many Southerners preferred a southern route from New Orleans, but the geography of the Southwest required the railroad to pass through northern Mexico. Secretary of War Jefferson Davis, a supporter of the South's interests, convinced President Franklin Pierce to send James Gadsden, a South Carolina politician and railroad promoter, to buy the land **S** from Mexico. In 1853 Mexico accepted $10 million for the **Gadsden Purchase**—a 30,000-square-mile strip of land that today is part of southern Arizona and New Mexico.

Meanwhile, Senator Stephen A. Douglas of Illinois, the head of the Senate committee on territories, had his own ideas for a transcontinental railroad. Douglas wanted the eastern terminus to be in Chicago, but he knew that northern route required Congress to organize the unsettled lands west of Missouri and Iowa.

R Reading Strategy

Sequencing Information

Ask: What experiences helped Harriet Beecher Stowe write *Uncle Tom's Cabin*? *(During Stowe's years in Ohio, she met many runaways from slavery. She visited Kentucky and witnessed slavery firsthand.)* **OL**

S Skill Practice

Creating a Political Cartoon

Have students create their own political cartoon expressing their point of view about the debate over the starting point of the Transcontinental Railroad. Encourage students to share their cartoons with the class. Discuss how each student approached the debate. **AL**

Reading Check

Answer:
It created active hostility toward slavery and slaveholders in the North where there had been little before. It also led Harriet Beecher Stowe to write *Uncle Tom's Cabin*, which created sympathy for enslaved people.

Additional Support

Activity: Technology Connection

Verbal/Linguistic Have students select one of the people mentioned in the section on the Transcontinental Railroad. Have them prepare a speech that could have been given by that person expressing his or her views on the railroad, its proposed route, and its purpose. Students may need to use library or Internet sources to learn more about the Transcontinental Railroad and the people involved with it. Have students present their speeches to the class. **OL**

S Skill Practice

Creating a Time Line Have students use the map on this page to create a time line of "Bleeding Kansas." Encourage them to add other information to their time lines. They can find the information in the textbook and other library and Internet sources. **BL**

Analyzing VISUALS

Answers:

1. two
2. The cartoonist was on the side of the North. He shows Sumner armed only with a pen while he is being beaten with a cane by Brooks. Also the caption says, "Southern Chivalry," which seems sarcastic and critical of a Southern gentleman who would strike another, unarmed person.

Additional Support

NATIONAL GEOGRAPHIC **"Bleeding Kansas," 1855–1856**

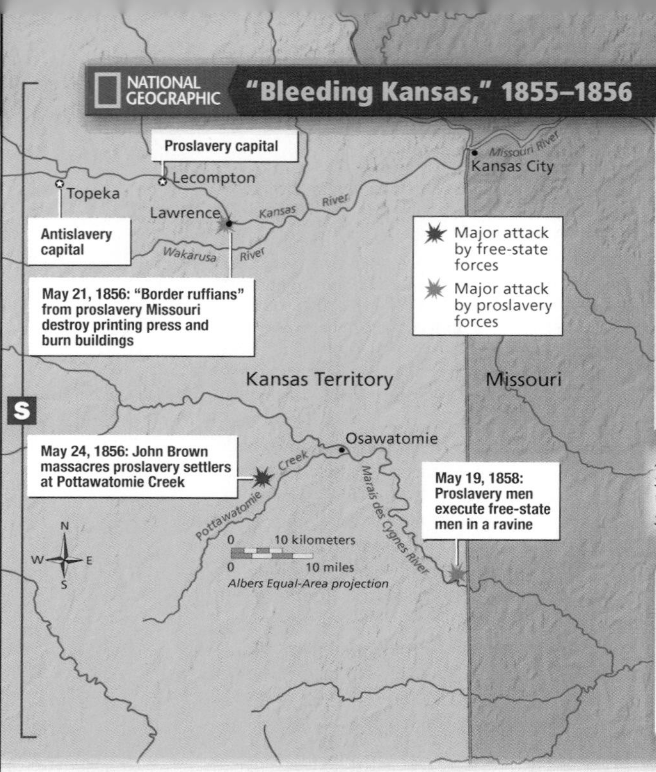

▲ *Representative Preston Brooks beat Senator Charles Sumner for criticizing Brooks's cousin, Senator Andrew Butler. While many Northerners were outraged over the incident, Southerners voiced their approval by sending Brooks canes.*

Analyzing VISUALS

1. **Interpreting** According to the map, how many governments were in the Kansas Territory in 1856?
2. **Analyzing** In the cartoon shown above depicting the beating of Charles Sumner, which side do you think the cartoonist favored? Explain.

In 1853 Douglas prepared a bill to organize the region into a new territory to be called Nebraska. Although the House of Representatives passed the bill quickly, Southern senators who controlled key committees refused to go along, and they prevented the bill from coming to a vote. These senators made it clear to Douglas that if he wanted Nebraska organized, he needed to work to repeal the Missouri Compromise and allow slavery in the new territory.

History ONLINE
Student Web Activity Visit glencoe.com and complete the activity on Bleeding Kansas.

Repealing the Missouri Compromise

Douglas knew that any attempt to repeal the Missouri Compromise would divide the country. Nevertheless, he wanted to open the northern Great Plains to settlement. At first he tried to dodge the issue and gain Southern support for his bill by saying that any states organized in the new Nebraska territory would be allowed to exercise popular sovereignty, deciding for themselves whether to allow slavery.

Southern leaders in the Senate were not fooled. If the Missouri Compromise remained in place while the region was settled, slaveholders would not move there. As a result, the states formed in the region would naturally become free states. Determined to get the territory organized, Douglas's next version of the bill proposed to undo the Missouri Compromise and allow slavery in the region. He also proposed dividing the region into two territories. Nebraska would be to the north, adjacent to the free state of Iowa, and Kansas would be to the south, west of the slave state of Missouri. This looked like Nebraska was intended to be free territory, while Kansas was intended for slavery.

Douglas's bill outraged Northern Democrats and Whigs. Free-Soilers and antislavery Democrats called the act an "atrocious plot." They claimed abandoning the Missouri Compromise broke a solemn promise to limit the spread of slavery. Despite this opposition, the leaders of the Democrats in Congress won enough support to pass the **Kansas-Nebraska Act** in May 1854.

Activity: Collaborative Learning

Recognizing Cause and Effect Copy the following headings on the board:

CAUSES → EVENT → EFFECTS

Under "Event," write *Kansas-Nebraska Act, 1854.* Then call on students to complete the chain by adding the causes and effects related to passage of the Kansas-Nebraska Act. *(Causes: desire to organize new territories; desire to resolve the issue of expanding slavery; Effects: Northern anger over the spread of slavery to "free" land; outbreak of violence in Kansas.)* **OL**

"Bleeding Kansas"

Kansas became the first battleground between those favoring the extension of slavery and those opposing it. Since eastern Kansas offered the same climate and rich soil as the slave state of Missouri, settlers moving there from Missouri were likely to bring enslaved persons with them and claim Kansas for the South. Northerners responded by hurrying into the territory themselves, intent on creating an antislavery majority. Northern settlers could count on the support of the New England Emigrant Aid Society, an abolitionist group founded to recruit and outfit antislavery settlers bound for Kansas. Carrying supplies and rifles, hordes of Northerners headed for the new territory.

Pro-slavery Senator David Atchison of Missouri responded by calling on men from his state to storm into Kansas. In the spring of 1855, thousands of Missourians—called "border ruffians" in the press—voted illegally in Kansas, helping to elect a proslavery legislature. Antislavery settlers countered by holding a convention in Topeka and drafting their own constitution that banned slavery. By March 1856, Kansas had two governments. **R**

On May 21, 1856, border ruffians, worked up by the arrival of more Northerners, attacked the town of Lawrence, a stronghold of antislavery settlers. The attackers wrecked newspaper presses, plundered shops and homes, and burned a hotel and the home of the elected free-state governor.

"Bleeding Kansas," as newspapers dubbed the territory, became the scene of a territorial civil war between pro-slavery and antislavery settlers. By the end of 1856, 200 people had died in the fighting and $2 million worth of property had been destroyed.

The Caning of Charles Sumner

While bullets flew and blood ran in Kansas, the Senate hotly debated the future of the western territories. In mid-May 1856, Senator Charles Sumner of Massachusetts, a fiery abolitionist, delivered a speech accusing pro-slavery senators of forcing Kansas into the ranks of slave states. He singled out Senator Andrew P. Butler of South Carolina, saying Butler had "chosen a mistress . . . the harlot, Slavery."

Several days later, Butler's second cousin, Representative Preston Brooks, approached Sumner at his desk in the Senate chamber. Brooks shouted that Sumner's speech had been "a libel on South Carolina, and Mr. Butler, who is a relative of mine." Before Sumner could respond, Brooks raised a gold-handled cane and beat him savagely, leaving the senator severely injured.

Many Southerners considered Brooks a hero. Some sent him canes inscribed "Hit Him Again." Shocked by the attack and outraged by the flood of Southern support for Brooks, Northerners strengthened their determination to resist the "barbarism of slavery." One New York clergyman wrote in his journal that "no way is left for the North, but to strike back, or be slaves."

Reading Check **Describing** Why did Stephen Douglas propose repealing the Missouri Compromise?

Section 1 REVIEW

Vocabulary

1. **Explain** the significance of: Wilmot Proviso, popular sovereignty, Free-Soil Party, "Forty-Niners," secession, Compromise of 1850, Fugitive Slave Act, Underground Railroad, Harriet Tubman, *Uncle Tom's Cabin*, transcontinental railroad, Gadsden Purchase, Kansas-Nebraska Act.

Main Ideas

2. **Describing** How did Stephen Douglas achieve passage of the Compromise of 1850?
3. **Explaining** How could *Uncle Tom's Cabin* be considered a cause of the Civil War?
4. **Summarizing** How did the Kansas Territory become an arena of civil war?

Critical Thinking

5. **Big Ideas** How did antislavery activists justify disobeying the Fugitive Slave Act?
6. **Organizing** Use a graphic organizer similar to the one below to list the main elements of the Compromise of 1850.

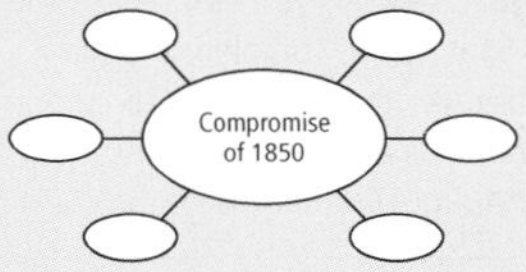

7. **Analyzing Visuals** Study the photo on page 286. What does the photo reveal about the people who traveled to California to find gold?

Writing About History

8. **Expository Writing** Suppose you are a reporter for a Southern or a Northern newspaper in the 1850s. Write an article on public reaction to *Uncle Tom's Cabin*.

History ONLINE
Study Central™ To review this section, go to glencoe.com and click on Study Central.

R Reading Strategy

Making Connections Ask: How is the voting process today protected against the type of illegal voting that occurred in Kansas in 1855? *(Today, you must be registered to vote in the precinct assigned to you.)* **OL**

Reading Check

Answer: He needed Southern support to organize the Nebraska territory, pass the Kansas-Nebraska Act.

Assess

History ONLINE

Study Central™ provides summaries, interactive games, and online graphic organizers to help students review content.

Close

Evaluating Ask students to evaluate how the Fugitive Slave Act and the Underground Railroad heightened sectional tensions.

Section 1 REVIEW

Answers

1. All definitions can be found in the section and the Glossary.
2. He broke it up into separate bills so that Congress members could vote for, against, or abstain on various parts.
3. The book was widely read and had a dramatic impact on public opinion in the North by evoking outrage and pity for the plight of enslaved people.
4. Proslavery and antislavery settlers tried to establish a majority to ensure that they could control the future of slavery in Kansas. Tensions soon turned into armed conflict.
5. They followed the principle of civil disobedience—that it is immoral to support or follow an immoral law.
6. Answers should include: California entered the Union as free state, the rest of the Mexican cession did not have any slavery restrictions, the border between New Mexico and Texas was settled in favor of New Mexico, the federal government would take Texas's debts, the slave trade was outlawed in the District of Columbia, Congress could not interfere in the slave trade, and a new fugitive slave law was passed.
7. Answers will vary.
8. Students' articles should be well organized with a clear outline, introduction, body, and conclusion.

Focus

Bellringer

Daily Focus Transparency 8-2

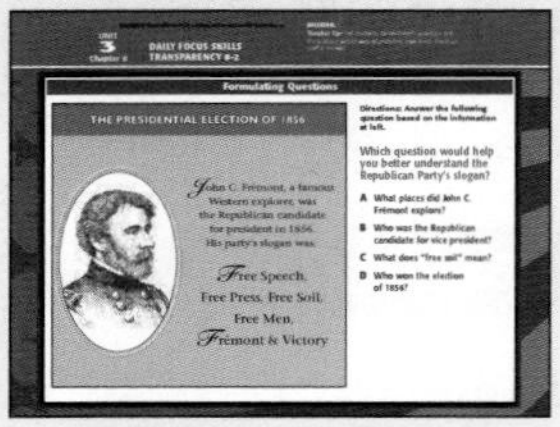

Guide to Reading

Answers:

Executive: Buchanan elected in 1856

Legislative: Kansas' Lecompton constitution authorized slavery in the territory

Judicial: *Dred Scott* decision

Nongovernmental: John Brown's raid on the Harpers Ferry federal arsenal.

Section Spotlight Video

To generate student interest and provide a springboard for class discussion, access the Chapter 8, Section 2 video at glencoe.com or on the video DVD.

Resource Manager

R Reading Strategies	**C** Critical Thinking	**D** Differentiated Instruction	**W** Writing Support	**S** Skill Practice
• Making Connections, p. 295 • Academic Vocab., p. 298 • Identifying, p. 298 • Activate Prior Knowl., p. 301 **Additional Resources** • Prim. Source Read., URB p. 37 • Guided Read., URB p. 47	**Teacher Edition** • Drawing Concl., p. 299 **Additional Resources** • Supreme Court Case Studies, p. 11 • Quizzes and Tests, p. 108	**Additional Resources** • Diff. Instruction Act., URB p. 23 • Enrich. Act., URB p. 44		**Teacher Edition** • Explain. a Quote, p. 296 • Analyz. Visuals, p. 300 **Additional Resources** • Read. Essen., p. 90

Section 2

Section Audio   Spotlight Video

The Crisis Deepens

Guide to Reading

Big Ideas

Group Action Due to differing opinions within established parties, Americans forged new political alliances in the 1850s.

Content Vocabulary
- referendum *(p. 298)*
- insurrection *(p. 301)*

Academic Vocabulary
- correspondence *(p. 294)*
- formulate *(p. 300)*

People and Events to Identify
- Republican Party *(p. 294)*
- Dred Scott *(p. 296)*
- Lecompton constitution *(p. 298)*
- Freeport Doctrine *(p. 300)*
- John Brown *(p. 301)*

Reading Strategy

Categorizing As you read about the North-South split, complete a graphic organizer like the one below to categorize events as executive, legislative, judicial, or nongovernmental.

Executive	
Legislative	
Judicial	
Nongovernmental	

The controversy over slavery accelerated the breakdown of the major political parties and the formation of new ones, including the party of future president Abraham Lincoln. Friction intensified until the North and South became unable to compromise any further.

The Birth of the Republican Party

MAIN Idea Continuing disagreements over the expansion of slavery—most notably the Kansas-Nebraska Act—led to the formation of the Republican Party.

HISTORY AND YOU Do you know of any foreign governments that are controlled by a coalition of political parties? Read on to learn how the Republican Party was formed by a coalition of political parties.

When the Kansas-Nebraska Act repealed the Missouri Compromise, it had a dramatic effect on the political system. Proslavery Southern Whigs and antislavery Northern Whigs had long battled for control of their party, but the Kansas-Nebraska Act finally split the party. Every Northern Whig in Congress had voted against the bill, while most Southern Whigs had voted for it. "We Whigs of the North," wrote one member from Connecticut, "are unalterably determined never to have even the slightest political **correspondence** or connexion" with the Southern Whigs.

Anger over the Kansas-Nebraska Act convinced former Whigs, members of the Free-Soil Party, and a few antislavery Democrats to work together during the congressional elections of 1854. Their coalitions took many different names, including the Anti-Nebraska Party, the Fusion Party, the People's Party, and the Independent Party. The most popular name was the **Republican Party.**

Republicans Organize

At a convention in Michigan in July 1854, the Republican Party was officially organized. In choosing the same name as Thomas Jefferson's original party, the Republicans declared their intention to revive the spirit of the American Revolution. Just as Jefferson had chosen the name because he wanted to prevent the United States from becoming a monarchy, the new Republicans chose their name because they feared that the Southern planters were becoming an aristocracy that controlled the federal government.

Republicans did not agree on whether slavery should be abolished in the Southern states, but they did agree that it had to be kept out of the territories. A large majority of Northern voters seemed to agree,

POLITICAL CARTOONS PRIMARY SOURCE

The Politics and Election of 1856

In 1856 three candidates ran for president: James Buchanan for the Democrats, John Frémont for the Republicans, and Millard Fillmore for the American Party. None of them had wide support because of their position for or against abolition. The fractured electorate chose Buchanan. **R**

▲ The cartoon above shows Buchanan as a "buck"—a play on his name—winning the presidential race. Fillmore is shown as an underfed horse that has collapsed. Frémont is shown trying to win by riding two horses—a wooly nag labeled "abolitionism" and a horse with Horace Greeley's face. Greeley was editor of the New York Tribune—a very popular paper that supported antislavery causes.

▼ Fremont pulls ahead in the presidential race. Buchanan has crashed into the Democratic platform and blames the slavery plank in the platform for scaring his mount and causing the crash. Fillmore rides a goose and holds a Know-Nothing lantern. He warns that if he loses, the Union will be dissolved. Spectators note that the goose has a curved spine—with no back bone.

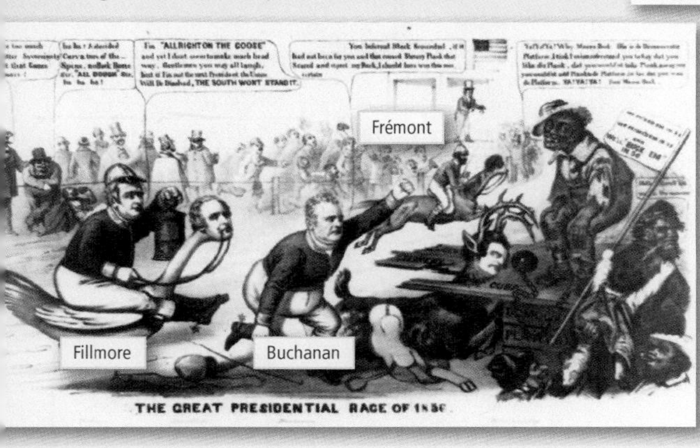

Analyzing VISUALS

1. **Making Inferences** Why do you think that both cartoons are so critical of Fillmore?
2. **Identifying Points of View** Which cartoon do you think might have appeared in the North and which in the South? Why?

enabling the Republicans and the other antislavery parties to make great strides in the elections of 1854.

The Know-Nothings

At the same time, Northern anger against the Democrats enabled the American Party—also known as the Know-Nothings—to make gains, particularly in the Northeast. The American Party was an anti-Catholic and nativist party. It opposed immigration, especially Catholic immigration. Prejudice, and fear that immigrants would take away jobs, enabled the American Party to win many seats in Congress and state legislatures in 1854.

Soon after the election, the Know-Nothings suffered the same fate as the Whigs. Many Know-Nothings had been elected from the Upper South, particularly Maryland, Tennessee, and Kentucky. They quickly split with Know-Nothings from the North over their support for the Kansas-Nebraska Act. Furthermore, the violence in Kansas and the beating of Charles Sumner made slavery a far more important issue to most Americans than immigration. Eventually, the Republican Party absorbed most Northern Know-Nothings.

The Election of 1856

To gain the widest possible support in the 1856 campaign, Republicans nominated John C. Frémont, a famous Western explorer nicknamed "The Pathfinder." Frémont had spoken in favor of Kansas becoming a free state. He had little political experience but also no embarrassing record to defend.

Teach

R Reading Strategy

Making Connections

Tell students: The American Party was a party that opposed immigration. **Ask:** How is the issue of immigration different or the same today as it was in 1856? *(Answers will vary.)* **OL**

Analyzing VISUALS

Answers:

1. Fillmore's party was divided over the Kansas-Nebraska Act and he had no chance of winning.
2. Possible answer: The one on the right would most likely be from a Southern paper because it shows the Democrat and Southern sympathizer Buchanan in the lead and pokes fun at Frémont, while the one on the left shows the Republican Frémont in the lead and Buchanan crashing into the Democrats' slavery platform.

Additional Support

Activity: Collaborative Learning

Forming a Hypothesis To review the *Dred Scott* decision, organize the class into groups of four. Have each student present one aspect of the event to the rest of the group. Use the following aspects: President Buchanan's reasons for letting the Supreme Court decide the issue of slavery in the territories, the reasons for the Supreme Court's decision, reaction in the North, and reaction in the South. Based on discussion, have each group form a hypothesis stating what might have happened had Northerners not challenged the Court's decision. **AL**

S Skill Practice

Explaining a Quote Ask students to explain the words of Robert Purvis that are quoted on this page. Encourage students to look up the meaning of unfamiliar words, such as *sublimity* and *impudence*. ELL OL

Reading Check

Answer:
Instead of removing slavery as an issue, the decision itself became a political issue by stating that the concept of free soil was unconstitutional because the Court stated that the federal government had no right to prohibit slavery in a territory.

Additional Support

The Democrats nominated James Buchanan. Buchanan had served in Congress for 20 years and had been the American ambassador to Russia and then to Great Britain. He had been in Great Britain during the debate over the Kansas-Nebraska Act and had not taken a stand on the issue, but his record in Congress showed that he believed the best way to save the Union was to make concessions to the South.

The American Party tried to reunite its Northern and Southern members at its convention, but most of the Northern delegates walked out when the party refused to call for the repeal of the Kansas-Nebraska Act. The rest of the convention then chose former president Millard Fillmore to represent the American Party, hoping to attract the vote of former Whigs.

The campaign was really two separate contests: Buchanan against Frémont in the North, and Buchanan against Fillmore in the South. Buchanan had solid support in the South and only needed his home state of Pennsylvania and one other state to win the presidency. Democrats campaigned on the idea that only Buchanan could save the Union and that the election of Frémont would cause the South to secede. When the votes were counted, Buchanan had won.

The *Dred Scott* Decision

In his March 1857 inaugural address, James Buchanan suggested that the nation let the Supreme Court decide the question of slavery in the territories. Most people who listened to the address did not know that Buchanan had contacted members of the Supreme Court and therefore knew that a decision was imminent.

Many Southern members of Congress had quietly pressured the Supreme Court justices to issue a ruling on slavery in the territories. They expected the Southern majority on the court to rule in favor of the South. They were not disappointed. Two days after the inauguration, the Court released its opinion in the case of *Dred Scott* v. *Sandford*.

Dred Scott was an enslaved man whose Missouri slaveholder had taken him to live in free territory before returning to Missouri. Assisted by abolitionists, Scott sued to end his slavery, arguing that the time he had spent in free territory meant he was free.

Scott's case went all the way to the Supreme Court. On March 6, 1857, Chief Justice Roger B. Taney delivered the majority opinion in the case. Taney ruled against Scott because, he claimed, African Americans were not citizens and therefore could not sue in the courts. Taney then addressed the Missouri Compromise's ban on slavery in territory north of Missouri's southern border:

PRIMARY SOURCE

"[I]t is the opinion of the court that the act of Congress which prohibited a citizen from holding and owning [enslaved persons] in the territory of the United States north of the line therein mentioned is not warranted by the Constitution and is therefore void."

—from *Dred Scott* v. *Sandford*

Instead of removing the issue of slavery in the territories from politics, the *Dred Scott* decision itself became a political issue that further intensified the sectional conflict. The Supreme Court had said that the federal government could not prohibit slavery in the territories. Free soil, one of the basic ideas uniting Republicans, was unconstitutional.

Democrats cheered the decision, but Republicans claimed it was not binding. They argued that it was an *obiter dictum*, an incidental opinion not called for by the circumstances of the case. Southerners, on the other hand, called on Northerners to obey the decision if they wanted the South to remain in the Union.

Many African Americans, among them Philadelphia activist Robert Purvis, publicly declared contempt for any government that could produce such an edict:

PRIMARY SOURCE

"Mr. Chairman, look at the facts—here, in a country with a sublimity of impudence that knows no parallel, setting itself up before the world as a free country, a land of liberty!, 'the land of the free, and the home of the brave,' the 'freest country in all the world' . . . and yet here are millions of men and women . . . bought and sold, whipped, manacled, killed all the day long." **S**

—quoted in *Witness for Freedom*

Reading Check **Explaining** How did the *Dred Scott* decision contribute to the growing split between North and South?

Activity: Technology Connection

Auditory/Musical Have interested students write a script for a "You Are There" radio program on the reaction to the *Dred Scott* decision. Suggest that the scripts include an introduction that provides background information and interviews with lawyers, Dred Scott, John F. A. Sandford, other eyewitnesses at the court, and various experts on the Supreme Court. Encourage students to "broadcast" their scripts for the rest of the class on the Internet, DVDs, or other presentation tools. OL

ANALYZING SUPREME COURT CASES

Can the Government Ban Slavery in Territories?

★ ***Dred Scott* v. *Sandford*, 1857**

Background to the Case

Between 1833 and 1843, enslaved African American Dred Scott and his wife Harriet had lived in the free state of Illinois and in the part of the Louisiana Territory that was considered free under the Missouri Compromise. When he was returned to Missouri, Scott sued his slaveholder, John Sanford, based on the idea that he was free because he had lived in free areas, and won. That decision was reversed by the Missouri Supreme Court, and Scott's case went to the U.S. Supreme Court.

How the Court Ruled

The 7-2 decision enraged many Northerners, and delighted many in the South. In his lengthy opinion for the Court, Chief Justice Roger B. Taney found that enslaved descendants of enslaved Africans were property, could not be citizens of the United States, or of a state, and that therefore Scott had no rights under the Constitution and no right to sue Sanford. Further, Taney decreed that Congress did not have the authority to prohibit slavery in the territories. This made the Missouri Compromise unconstitutional.

▲ Chief Justice Roger B. Taney (above, right) delivered the Supreme Court's ruling in the *Dred Scott* case. The decision made Scott and his family a topic for the nation's press.

PRIMARY SOURCE

The Court's Opinion

"[T]he right of property in a slave is distinctly and expressly affirmed in the Constitution. . . . And no word can be found in the Constitution which gives Congress a greater power over slave property, or which entitles property of that kind to less protection than property of any other description. . . . Upon these considerations, it is the opinion of the court that the act of Congress which prohibited a citizen from holding and owning property of this kind in the territory of the United States north of the line therein mentioned, is not warranted by the Constitution, and is therefore void; and that neither Dred Scott himself, nor any of his family, were made free by being carried into this territory."

—Chief Justice Roger B. Taney, writing for the Court in *Dred Scott* v. *Sandford*

PRIMARY SOURCE

Dissenting Views

"The prohibition of slavery north of thirty-six degrees thirty minutes, and of the State of Missouri . . . was passed by a vote of 134, in the House of Representatives, to 42. Before [President] Monroe signed the act, it was submitted by him to his Cabinet, and they held the restriction of slavery in a Territory to be within the constitutional powers of Congress. It would be singular, if in 1804 Congress had power to prohibit the introduction of slaves in Orleans Territory [the future state of Louisiana] from any other part of the Union, under the penalty of freedom to the slave, if the same power, embodied in the Missouri compromise, could not be exercised in 1820."

—Justice John McLean, dissenting in *Dred Scott* v. *Sandford*

DBQ Document-Based Questions

1. **Finding the Main Idea** What is the main idea of Chief Justice Roger B. Taney's opinion in *Dred Scott* v. *Sandford*?
2. **Summarizing** What argument does Justice John McLean offer in favor of Congress's right to prohibit slavery in the territories?
3. **Expressing** Which argument do you feel is stronger? Explain.

More About the Case

Tell students that in this case, the Supreme Court held that an enslaved person was property, not a citizen, and thus had no rights under the Constitution. Point out that this decision was a prime factor leading to the Civil War.

DBQ Document Based Questions

Answers:

1. Taney argues that the Constitution protects property, that slaves are property, and that therefore Congress has no right to prohibit the ownership of this "property"—enslaved people—anywhere in the territories.
2. McLean argues that Congress prohibited the introduction of slaves in the Orleans Territory, so therefore, Congress obviously has that right under the Constitution.
3. Answers will vary, but students should express a reasoned argument in support of one side or the other.

Additional Support

Activity: Collaborative Learning

Analyzing Information Have students work in pairs to analyze the effects of the growth of slavery. Tell them that in 1790, there were about 698,000 enslaved persons in the United States. By 1860, there were almost 4 million enslaved persons in the South. Ask each pair to list reasons why political compromise over the slavery question might have been easier right after the American Revolution than during the 1850s. *(Possible reasons: the economy of the South did not yet depend entirely on slavery and a better political climate for compromise may have existed after the Revolution.)* Discuss student responses with the class. **OL**

R1 Reading Strategy

Academic Vocabulary Have students locate and read the sentence that includes the vocabulary word *referendum.* **Ask:** What is a synonym for the word referendum? Encourage students to use the thesaurus. Ask volunteers to use the word referendum in a sentence of their own. ELL OL

R2 Reading Strategy

Identifying Ask: Where did the name *Lecompton* in the Lecompton Constitution come from? *(the town of Lecompton, Kansas)* Encourage students to use the library and Internet sources to find the answer. Ask for a volunteer to locate Lecompton on a map of Kansas. BL

Additional Support

The Emergence of Abraham Lincoln

MAIN Idea Stephen Douglas took positions on Kansas and the *Dred Scott* case that reduced his popularity while Abraham Lincoln gained a reputation within the Republican Party.

HISTORY AND YOU What do you know about Abraham Lincoln? Read on to find out how he rose to national prominence in the 1850s through a series of famous debates.

After losing in 1856, Republicans realized they needed a candidate who could win every Northern state. They also knew that Senator Stephen Douglas of Illinois was a rising star in the Democratic Party and a Northerner whom the South might trust with the presidency in order to stop a Republican victory. To win, Republicans needed a candidate who could defeat Douglas in his home state of Illinois. They also needed Douglas to take unpopular positions on the issues under consideration.

By late 1858, both conditions had been fulfilled. Douglas had taken positions on Kansas and the *Dred Scott* case that made him less popular in both the North and the South. At the same time, Republicans had found a candidate from Illinois who might be able to challenge Douglass—a relatively unknown politician named Abraham Lincoln.

Kansas's Constitution

Douglas began to lose popularity in the South because of events in Kansas. Hoping to end the troubles there, President Buchanan urged the territory to apply for statehood. The proslavery legislature scheduled an election for delegates to a constitutional convention, but antislavery Kansans boycotted it, claiming it was rigged. The resulting constitution, drafted in the town of Lecompton in 1857, legalized slavery in the territory.

R1 Each side then held its own **referendum,** or popular vote, on the constitution. Antislavery forces voted down the constitution; proslavery forces approved it. Buchanan accepted the proslavery vote and asked Congress to admit R2 Kansas as a slave state. The Senate quickly voted to accept the **Lecompton constitution,** but the House of Representatives blocked it. Many members of Congress became so angry during the debates that fistfights broke out. Southern leaders were stunned when even Stephen Douglas refused to support them. Many had thought that Douglas was one of the few Northern leaders who understood the South's concerns and would be willing to compromise.

Finally, to get the votes they needed, Southern leaders in Congress agreed to allow Kansas to hold another referendum on the constitution. Southern leaders expected to win this referendum. If settlers in Kansas rejected the Lecompton constitution, they would delay statehood for Kansas for at least two more years. Despite these conditions, the settlers in Kansas voted overwhelmingly in 1858 to reject the Lecompton constitution. They did not want slavery in their state. As a result, Kansas did not become a state until 1861.

Debates IN HISTORY

Can Slavery be Prohibited in the Western Territories?

In the 1850s, much of the political debate over slavery centered on the spread of slavery into the western territories. The *Dred Scott* decision held that the federal government could not ban slavery in the territories. Opponents of slavery then debated whether residents of a territory could ban slavery. This became a central issue in the Lincoln-Douglas debates of 1858.

Activity: Interdisciplinary Connection

Language Arts Encourage students to act as news reporters attending the Lincoln-Douglas debates. Ask them to write a news story on the debates, detailing the major issues raised and the exchanges between Lincoln and Douglas. Recommend that students review recent news articles to help them understand the style used in good news reporting. Ask volunteers to read their news stories to the class. OL

Lincoln and Douglas

In 1858 Illinois Republicans chose Abraham Lincoln to run for the Senate against the Democratic incumbent, Stephen A. Douglas. Lincoln launched his campaign in June with a memorable speech, in which he declared:

PRIMARY SOURCE

"A house divided against itself cannot stand. I believe this Government cannot endure, permanently half *slave* and half *free.* I do not expect the Union to be dissolved—I do not expect the house to *fall*—but I *do* expect it will cease to be divided. It will become *all* one thing or *all* the other."

—from *Abraham Lincoln, Slavery, and the Civil War*

The nationally prominent Douglas, a short, stocky man nicknamed "The Little Giant," regularly drew large crowds on the campaign trail. Seeking to overcome Douglas's fame, Lincoln proposed a series of debates between the candidates, which would expose him to larger audiences than he could attract on his own. Douglas confidently accepted.

Although not an abolitionist, Lincoln believed slavery to be morally wrong and opposed its spread into western territories. Douglas, by contrast, supported popular sovereignty. During a debate in Freeport, Lincoln asked Douglas if the people of a territory could legally exclude slavery before achieving statehood. If Douglas said yes, he would appear to be opposing the *Dred Scott* ruling, which would cost him Southern support. If he said no, it would make it seem as if he had abandoned popular sovereignty, the principle on which he had built his following in the North.

YES

Stephen Douglas
United States Senator

PRIMARY SOURCE

"It matters not what way the Supreme Court may hereafter decide as to the abstract question whether slavery may or may not go into a territory under the constitution, the people have the lawful means to introduce it or exclude it as they please, for the reason that slavery cannot exist a day or an hour anywhere, unless it is supported by local police regulations. Those police regulations can only be established by the local legislature, and if the people are opposed to slavery they will elect representatives to that body who will by unfriendly legislation effectually prevent the introduction of it into their midst. If, on the contrary, they are for it, their legislation will favor its extension."

—speech delivered August 27, 1858

NO

Abraham Lincoln
Former Congressman

PRIMARY SOURCE

"What is Popular Sovereignty? Is it the right of the people to have Slavery or not have it, as they see fit, in the territories? I will state . . . my understanding is that Popular Sovereignty, as now applied to the question of Slavery, does allow the people of a Territory to have Slavery if they want to, but does not allow them not to have it if they do not want it. I do not mean that if this vast concourse of people were in a Territory of the United States, any one of them would be obliged to have a slave if he did not want one; but I do say that, as I understand the Dred Scott decision, if any one man wants slaves, all the rest have no way of keeping that one man from holding them."

—speech delivered August 21, 1858

C

DBQ Document-Based Questions

1. **Finding the Main Idea** According to Abraham Lincoln, why could territorial residents *not* ban slavery through popular sovereignty?
2. **Comparing** Why does Stephen Douglas think popular sovereignty can effectively limit slavery?
3. **Speculating** After reading both points of view, which author do you think had a more realistic assessment of the effectiveness of popular sovereignty to stop the spread of slavery?

C Critical Thinking

Drawing Conclusions Have students read the speeches of Lincoln and Douglas on this page, examine their photos, and read the text describing the candidates. **Ask:** How might the Lincoln-Douglas debates play out on modern television? *(Answers will vary, but could include that Lincoln could have the advantage over Douglas in height, but maybe not in appearance.)*

DBQ Document Based Questions

Answers:

1. Because the *Dred Scott* decision said that slavery could not be banned from a territory.
2. Douglas stated that the *Dred Scott* decision does not really matter, and that a territory will determine on its own by what type of policing it establishes whether or not it will have slavery or be free.
3. Answers will vary, but students should demonstrate an understanding of both points of view.

Hands-On Chapter Project
Step 2

Mapping Events of the Mid-1800s

Step 2: Mapping a Debate Students will select an event from Section 2 and illustrate it on their outline map of the United States.

Directions Students should work in small groups. Each group will select an event from Section 2 to illustrate on the map. Students will choose an image, for example of the people involved in the event. Students will also color code the map as needed, to portray territories, for example. Students should then create text/caption boxes or images to show each side of the debate. For example, students may show Stephen Douglas's and Abraham Lincoln's views on whether slavery should be allowed in western territories.

Summarizing Information Students will determine the main points of each side in a debate and summarize those points succinctly for inclusion on the map. OL

(Chapter Project continued on page 306)

Analyzing VISUALS

Answers:

1. He is portrayed as a kind, dignified, wronged martyr.
2. The cartoonist is implying that justice was denied to Brown when he was executed.

S Skill Practice

Analyzing Visuals Have students examine the political cartoon on this page and read each of the boxes. **Ask:** **What does the number "76" on the tricornered hat symbolize?** *(The founding year of the United States—1776.)* **OL**

Reading Check

Answer:
Douglas supported popular sovereignty. Although Lincoln was not an abolitionist, he believed that slavery was morally wrong and opposed its spread into western territories.

Additional Support

POLITICAL CARTOONS PRIMARY SOURCE

John Brown Becomes a Martyr

Issued in the North in 1863, in the middle of the Civil War, this print depicts John Brown being led to his execution. The symbols in the print show how John Brown had become a martyr to many Northerners.

S A figure wearing a tri-cornered hat of the American Revolution with the number *76* emblazoned on it looks on with concern.

A statue of Justice is shown with her arms and scales broken.

The flag says *Sic Semper Tyrannis*—Latin for "as always with tyrants" and refers to the idea that tyrants must be killed.

Brown is shown standing upright, unhurt, and uncowed as he is led to his death.

Brown's jailers look malevolent, with angry snarls and hands on weapons.

According to tradition, Brown kissed an enslaved child as he was led to the scaffold. This enslaved child and its mother are portrayed in a way that would remind viewers of paintings of Jesus and his mother Mary.

Analyzing VISUALS

1. **Identifying Central Issues** How is John Brown portrayed in this image?
2. **Drawing Conclusions** Why do you think that the statue of Justice is depicted as broken?

Douglas tried to avoid the dilemma, **formulating** an answer that became known as the **Freeport Doctrine.** He replied that he accepted the *Dred Scott* ruling, but he argued that people could still keep slavery out by refusing to pass the laws needed to regulate and enforce it. "Slavery cannot exist . . . anywhere," argued Douglas, "unless it is supported by local police regulations." Douglas's response pleased Illinois voters but angered Southerners.

Lincoln also attacked Douglas's claim that he "cared not" whether Kansans voted for or against slavery. Denouncing "the modern Democratic idea that slavery is as good as freedom," Lincoln called on voters to elect Republicans, "whose hearts are in the work, who do care for the result":

PRIMARY SOURCE

"Has any thing ever threatened the existence of this Union save and except this very institution of Slavery? What is it that we hold most dear amongst us? Our own liberty and prosperity. What has ever threatened our liberty and prosperity save and except this institution of Slavery? If this is true, how do you propose to improve the condition of things by enlarging Slavery—by spreading it out and making it bigger? You may have a wen [sore] or cancer upon your person and not be able to cut it out lest you bleed to death; but surely it is no way to cure it, to engraft it and spread it over your whole body. That is no proper way of treating what you regard a wrong."

—from *Abraham Lincoln, Slavery, and the Civil War*

Douglas won the election, but Lincoln did not come away empty-handed. He had used the debates to make clear the principles of the Republican Party. He had also established a national reputation for himself as a man of clear, insightful thinking who could argue with force and eloquence. Within a year, however, national attention shifted to another figure, a man who opposed slavery not with well-crafted phrases, but with a gun.

Reading Check **Examining** What were the positions of Stephen Douglas and Abraham Lincoln on slavery?

Extending the Content

Political Science Edmund Ruffin, a Southern publisher and a strident supporter of slavery and secession, predicted in his diary that no Southerner could win enough support in the North to be elected president. Part of his August 28, 1858, diary entry reads: "Nothing can be done until after the nomination & election of 1860. Then these southern leaders, blinded now by their ambition, will all be disappointed, & may understand the truth that no southern man can be made president, or as a candidate, receive the support of the northern democrats."

John Brown's Raid

MAIN Idea Abolitionist John Brown planned to free and arm enslaved African Americans to stage a rebellion against slaveholders.

HISTORY AND YOU Do you recall a previous time in American history when citizens revolted against what they believed was an unfair government? Read on to learn about John Brown's raid at Harpers Ferry.

John Brown was a fervent abolitionist who believed, as one minister who knew him in Kansas said, "that God had raised him up on purpose to break the jaws of the wicked." In 1859 he developed a plan to seize the federal arsenal at Harpers Ferry, Virginia (today in West Virginia), free and arm the enslaved people in the area, and begin an **insurrection,** or rebellion, against slaveholders.

On the night of October 16, 1859, Brown and 18 followers seized the arsenal. To the terrified night watchman, he announced, "I have possession now of the United States armory, and if the citizens interfere with me I must only burn the town and have blood." R

Soon, however, Brown was facing a contingent of U.S. Marines, rushed to Harpers Ferry from Washington, D.C., under the command of Colonel Robert E. Lee. Just 36 hours after it had begun, Brown's attempt to start a slave insurrection ended with his capture. A Virginia court tried and convicted him and sentenced him to death. In his last words to the court, Brown, repenting nothing, declared:

PRIMARY SOURCE

"I believe that to have interfered as I have done, as I have always freely admitted I have done in behalf of [God's] despised poor, I did no wrong, but right. Now if it is deemed necessary that I should forfeit my life for the furtherance of the ends of justice and mingle my blood . . . with the blood of millions in this slave country whose rights are disregarded by wicked, cruel and unjust enactments, I say, let it be done!"

—from *The Life and Letters of Captain John Brown*

On December 2, the day of his execution, Brown handed one of his jailers a prophetic note: "I, John Brown, am now quite certain that the crimes of this guilty land will never be purged away but with Blood. I had as I now think vainly flattered myself that without very much bloodshed it might be done."

Many Northerners viewed Brown as a martyr in a noble cause. The execution, Henry David Thoreau predicted, would strengthen abolitionist feeling in the North. "He is not old Brown any longer," Thoreau declared, "he is an angel of light."

For most Southerners, however, Brown's raid offered all the proof they needed that Northerners were actively plotting the murder of slaveholders. "Defend yourselves!" cried Georgia Senator Robert Toombs. "The enemy is at your door!"

Reading Check **Evaluating** In what ways might a Northerner and a Southerner view John Brown's action differently?

Section 2 REVIEW

Vocabulary

1. **Explain** the significance of: Republican Party, Dred Scott, referendum, Lecompton constitution, Freeport Doctrine, John Brown, insurrection.

Main Ideas

2. **Listing** What were the two rulings in *Dred Scott* v. *Sandford* that increased sectional divisiveness?
3. **Explaining** What was the ultimate fate of the Lecompton constitution?
4. **Synthesizing** How did Americans react to John Brown's raid?

Critical Thinking

5. **Big Ideas** What were the main goals of the Republican and American parties?
6. **Organizing** Use a graphic organizer similar to the one below to list causes of the growing tensions between the North and South.

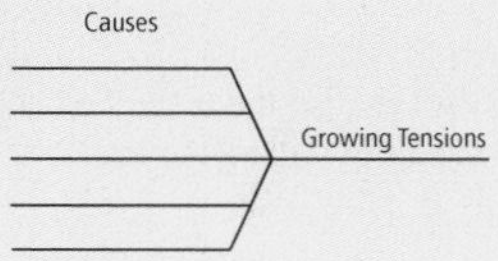

7. **Analyzing Visuals** Study the image of John Brown's martyrdom on page 300. What do you think is the signficance of the figure in the tri-cornered hat?

Writing About History

8. **Expository Writing** Suppose that you have just read the Supreme Court's ruling in the *Dred Scott* case. Write a letter to the editor explaining your reaction to the decision.

History ONLINE
Study Central™ To review this section, go to glencoe.com and click on Study Central.

R Reading Strategy

Activating Prior Knowledge Review the details of the Boston Tea Party. **Ask:** How does John Brown's raid differ from the Boston Tea Party? *(No one was physically harmed at the Boston Tea Party.)*

Reading Check

Answer: Many Northerners viewed Brown as a martyr for the cause of abolition, while Southerners saw his raid as a direct threat of attack by Northerners.

Assess

History ONLINE

Study Central™ provides summaries, interactive games, and online graphic organizers to help students review content.

Close

Analyzing Ask students to identify and write one sentence about each of the events that increased sectional tensions in the late 1850s.

Section 2 REVIEW

Answers

1. All definitions can be found in the section and the Glossary.
2. African Americans could not sue in courts because they were not citizens and the prohibition of slavery established by the Missouri Compromise was unconstitutional.
3. The settlers in Kansas voted overwhelmingly in 1858 to reject the Lecompton constitution because they did not want a constitution that allowed slavery.
4. Many Northerners saw Brown's act as heroic, while Southerners saw it as terrifying and threatening.
5. Republican Party: limit the influence of Southern planters and keep slavery out of the territories; American Party: oppose immigration
6. Kansas-Nebraska Act, *Dred Scott* decision, Lecompton constitution, John Brown's raid
7. The figure represents the founding ideals of the nation and freedom from tyranny.
8. Students' letters will vary, but should express a clear Northern or Southern point of view on the *Dred Scott* decision.

Focus

Bellringer

Daily Focus Transparency 8-3

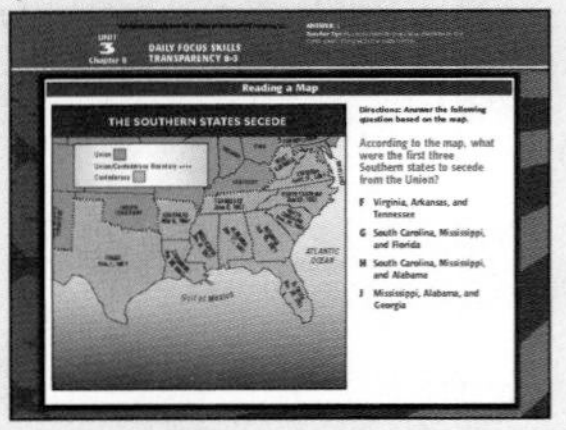

Guide to Reading

Answers to the Graphic:

The Union Dissolves
I. The Election of 1860
A. The Democrats Split
B. Lincoln Is Elected
C. Secession Begins
D. Founding the Confederacy
II. The Civil War Begins
A. Fort Sumter Falls
B. The Upper South Secedes
C. Hanging On to the Border States

Section Spotlight Video

To generate student interest and provide a springboard for class discussion, access the Chapter 8, Section 3 video at glencoe.com or on the video DVD.

Resource Manager

R Reading Strategies	C Critical Thinking	D Differentiated Instruction	W Writing Support	S Skill Practice
Teacher Edition • Activate Prior Knowl., p. 304 **Additional Resources** • Guided Read., URB p. 48	**Teacher Edition** • Am. Lit. Reading, URB p. 306 • Drawing Concl., p. 307 **Additional Resources** • Link. Past and Present, URB p. 34 • Inter. Pol. Cartoons, URB p. 41 • Quizzes and Tests, p. 109	**Additional Resources** • Am. Lit. Reading, URB p. 13 • Reteaching Act., URB p. 43 • Authentic Assess., p. 21 • Am. Hist. in Graphic Novel, p. 31	**Teacher Edition** • Descriptive Writing, p. 306	**Teacher Edition** • Creating a Circle Graph, p. 303 • Creating a Thematic Map, p. 305 **Additional Resources** • Read. Essen., p. 93

Section 3

Section Audio   Spotlight Video

The Union Dissolves

Guide to Reading

Big Ideas

Struggles for Rights After Lincoln's election to the presidency, many Southerners placed state loyalty above loyalty to the Union.

Content Vocabulary

- martial law *(p. 307)*

Academic Vocabulary

- commitment *(p. 306)*
- impose *(p. 307)*

People and Events to Identify

- John C. Breckinridge *(p. 303)*
- John Bell *(p. 303)*
- Fort Sumter *(p. 304)*
- Crittenden's Compromise *(p. 305)*
- Confederacy *(p. 305)*
- Jefferson Davis *(p. 305)*

Reading Strategy

Taking Notes Use the major headings of this section to outline the events that led to the U.S. Civil War.

The Union Dissolves
I. The Election of 1860
A.
B.
C.
D.
II.

In the end, all attempts at compromise between the North and South over slavery failed to end the sectional differences. Finally, the outcome of the 1860 election triggered a showdown and the first shots of the long, bloody Civil War.

The Election of 1860

MAIN Idea The election of Abraham Lincoln led the Southern states to secede from the Union.

HISTORY AND YOU Is it always important to give someone a chance to keep a promise? Lincoln had promised not to free slaves in the Southern states. Read on to learn how South Carolina decided to secede anyway.

John Brown's raid on Harpers Ferry was a turning point for the South. The possibility of a slave uprising had long haunted many Southerners, but they were frightened and angered by the idea that Northerners would deliberately try to arm enslaved people and encourage them to rebel.

Although the Republican leaders quickly denounced Brown's raid, many Southerners blamed Republicans. To them, the key point was that both the Republicans and John Brown opposed slavery. As one Atlanta newspaper noted: "We regard every man who does not boldly declare that he believes African slavery to be a social, moral, and political blessing as an enemy to the institutions of the South."

In the Senate, Robert Toombs of Georgia warned that the South would "never permit this Federal government to pass into the traitorous hands of the Black Republican party." In April 1860, with the South in an uproar, Democrats headed to Charleston, South Carolina, to choose their nominee for president.

The Democrats Split

In 1860 the debate over slavery in the western territories finally tore the Democratic Party apart. Their first presidential nominating convention ended in dispute. Northern delegates wanted to support popular sovereignty, while Southern delegates wanted the party to uphold the *Dred Scott* decision and endorse a federal slave code for the territories. Stephen Douglas was not able to get the votes needed to be nominated for president, but neither was anyone else.

In June 1860 the Democrats met again, this time in Baltimore, to select their candidate. Douglas's supporters in the South had organized rival delegations to ensure Douglas's endorsement. The original Southern delegations objected to these rival delegates and again

POLITICAL CARTOONS PRIMARY SOURCE

The Election of 1860

After the slavery issue split the Democratic Party, the election of 1860 evolved into a four-way race. In the cartoon, the artist implies that Lincoln won because he had the best bat, which is labeled "equal rights and free territories," while the other candidates were for compromise or the extension of slavery.

Stephen Douglas holds a bat labeled "Non-intervention" and blames Lincoln's rail for his loss.

John Breckinridge's bat is labeled "slavery extension" and his belt says Disunion Club.

John Bell's bat is labeled "Fusion" and his belt says Union Club.

Abraham Lincoln, the winner, stands on home base holding a rail labeled "Equal Rights and Free Territory."

NATIONAL GEOGRAPHIC Election of 1860

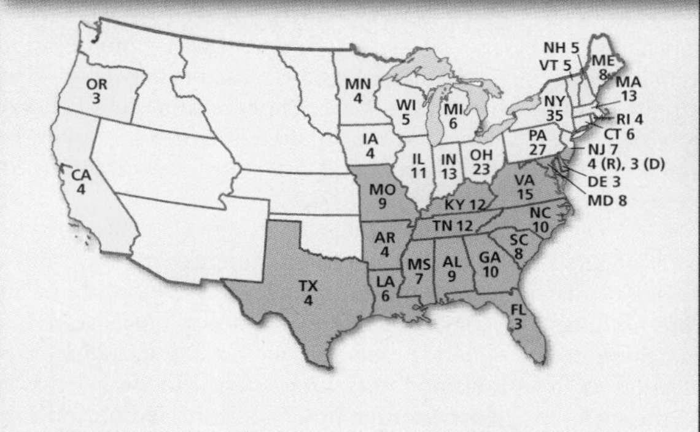

Presidential Candidate	Political Party	Popular Votes	% of Popular Vote	Electoral Votes
Lincoln	Republican	1,866,452	39.83%	180
Breckinridge	Southern Democratic	847,953	18.10%	72
Bell	Constitutional Union	590,901	12.61%	39
Douglas	Democratic	1,380,202	29.46%	12

S

Analyzing VISUALS DBQ

1. **Interpreting** How does the map show that Lincoln was a sectional candidate?
2. **Identifying Points of View** Do you think that the artist was sympathetic to abolition or not? Explain.

walked out. The remaining Democrats then chose Douglas to run for president.

The Southern Democrats who had walked out organized their own convention and nominated the current vice president, **John C. Breckinridge** of Kentucky, for president. Breckinridge supported the *Dred Scott* decision and agreed to endorse the idea of a federal slave code for the western territories.

The split in the Democratic Party greatly improved Republican prospects, which was what some of the more radical Southern delegates had intended all along. They hoped that a Republican victory would be the final straw that would convince the Southern states to secede.

Other people, including many former Whigs, were greatly alarmed at the danger to the Union. They created another new party, the Constitutional Union Party, and chose former Tennessee senator **John Bell** as their candidate. The Constitutional Unionists campaigned on a position of upholding both the Constitution and the Union.

Teach

S Skill Practice

Creating a Circle Graph Have students use the column "% of Popular Vote" from the map "Election of 1860" to create a circle graph. Encourage students to use a computer program to present the information and also to include a title and key. **OL**

Analyzing VISUALS

Answers:

1. He won no states south of the Ohio River.
2. Possible answer: The artist labels Lincoln's larger "bat" with the words "equal rights and free territory," and adds the words "wide awake" on Lincoln's belt. Also, Lincoln is saying that you need a "good bat," to hit a "fair ball." All these words are positive. Also Lincoln is standing tall, while the others look somewhat ridiculous.

Differentiated Instruction

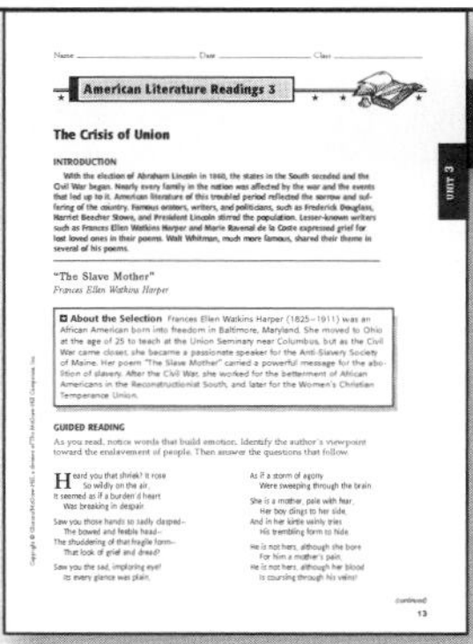

American Literature Reading, URB pp. 13–18

Investigating Literary Perspective

Objective: Read literature that expresses personal emotions during wartime.

Focus: Read three selections and note the emotions expressed, and why.

Teach: Summarize each writer's perspective.

Assess: Describe a possible setting for each reading using fictional characters.

Close: Ask: What emotions do all three writers share? Why?

Differentiated Instruction Strategies

BL Identify the emotions that are expressed in each selection.

AL Choose one selection and paraphrase it for another student.

ELL Choose a reading or poem in your native language that expresses similar emotions as the selections in this activity. Paraphrase it for the class.

R Reading Strategy

Activating Prior Knowledge
After reading the second paragraph under the subhead "Lincoln is Elected," review with students the vision of Jefferson and the Democrat-Republicans and review the creation of the new Republican Party in Section 2 of this chapter. **Tell students:** The new Republican Party formed in 1854 declared that it would revive the spirit of Thomas Jefferson and the Democrat-Republican Party. **Ask:** Was the new Republican Party vision anything like Jefferson's? *(The new Republican Party supported higher tariffs and was formed in the North, but did oppose the Southern aristocracy that controlled the federal government. The Democrat-Republican Party was against tariffs and believed the United States should be a nation of self-sufficient yeomen farmers.)* **OL**

Lincoln Is Elected

With no chance of winning electoral votes in the South, the Republican candidate had to sweep the North. The most prominent Republican at the time was Senator William Seward from New York. Delegates at the Republican convention in Chicago did not think Seward had a wide enough appeal. Instead they nominated Abraham Lincoln, whose debates with Douglas had made him very popular in the North.

R During the campaign, the Republicans tried to persuade voters they were more than just an antislavery party. They denounced John Brown's raid and reaffirmed the right of the Southern states to preserve slavery within their borders. They also supported higher tariffs, a new homestead law for western settlers, and a transcontinental railroad.

The Republican proposals greatly angered many Southerners. However, with Democratic votes split between Douglas and Breckinridge, Lincoln won the election without Southern support. For the South, the election of a Republican president represented the victory of the abolitionists. The survival of Southern society and culture seemed to be at stake. For many, there was now no choice but to secede.

Secession Begins

The dissolution of the Union began with South Carolina, where anti-Northern, secessionist sentiment had long been intense. Shortly after Lincoln's election, the state legislature called for a convention. The convention unanimously voted for the Ordinance of Secession. By February 1, 1861, six more states in the Lower South—Mississippi, Florida, Alabama, Georgia, Louisiana, and Texas—had voted to secede. Many Southerners believed secession was in the tradition of the American Revolution and that they were fighting for their rights.

As the states of the Lower South seceded one after another, Congress tried to find a compromise to save the Union. Ignoring Congress's efforts, the secessionists seized all federal property in their states, including arsenals and forts. Only the island strongholds of **Fort Sumter** in Charleston Harbor and Fort

Steps to Civil War, 1846–1860

▲ David Wilmot

1846
Wilmot Proviso proposing to ban slavery in Mexican cession enrages Southerners

1847
Vice President George Dallas proposes popular sovereignty; Democrat Lewis Cass popularizes the idea, angering Northern antislavery Democrats

1848
Free-Soil Party is founded by Northern antislavery Whigs, Democrats, and members of the Liberty Party

1849
California Gold Rush brings flood of settlers; California applies for statehood

1850
Compromise of 1850 allows California to enter Union as a free state, giving free states a Senate majority, but the new Fugitive Slave law enrages Northerners

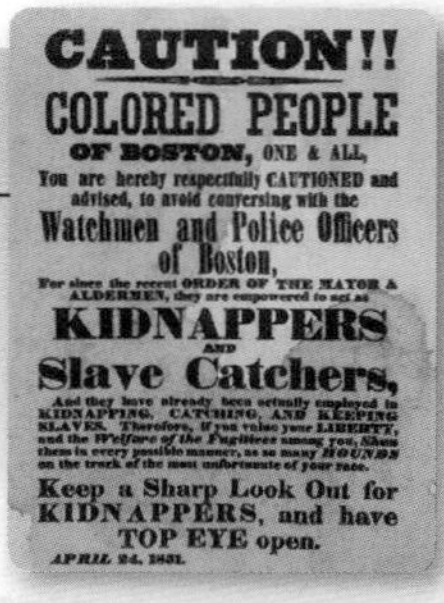

1852
Uncle Tom's Cabin is published

1846 1848 1850 1852

Leveled Activities

BL Reading Skills Activity, URB p. 21

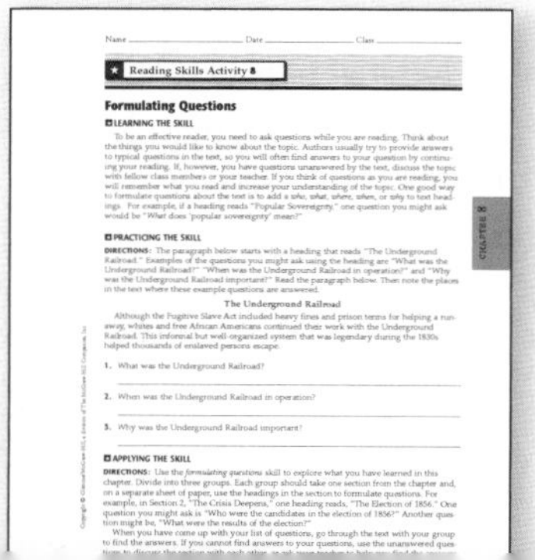

OL Academic Vocabulary Activity, URB p. 29

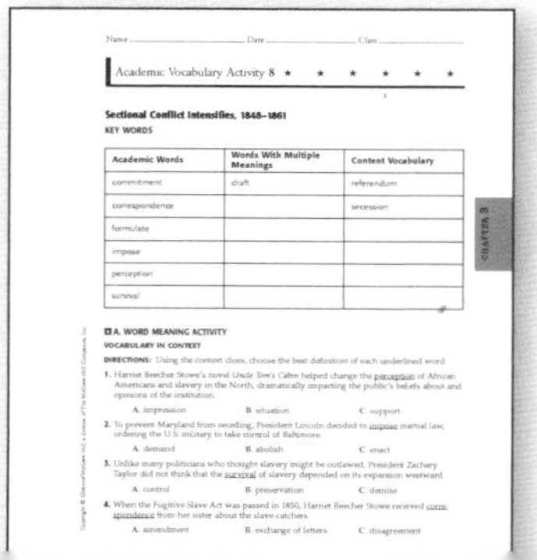

AL Critical Thinking Skills Activity, URB p. 32

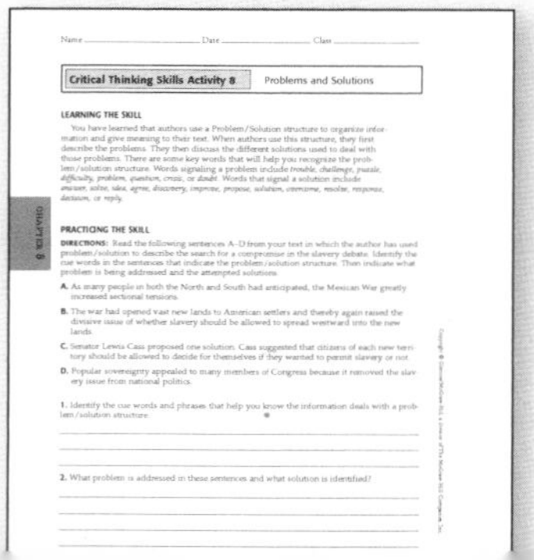

ELL English Learner Activity, URB p. 25

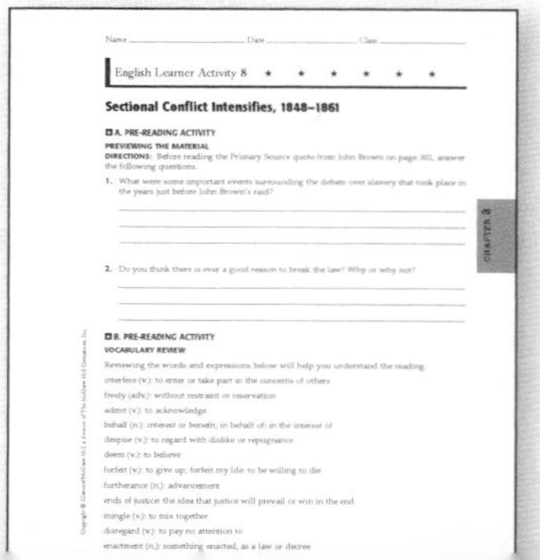

Pickens in Pensacola Harbor, as well as a few other islands off the coast of Florida, remained out of Southern hands.

Although horrified at the seizure of federal property by the secessionists, many members of Congress were still willing to compromise to avoid civil war. To that end, Kentucky senator John J. Crittenden proposed several amendments to the Constitution. One would guarantee slavery where it already existed. Another would also reinstate the Missouri Compromise line, extending it to the California border. Slavery would be prohibited north of the line and protected south of it. Lincoln, however, asked congressional Republicans to stand firm, and **Crittenden's Compromise** did not pass.

Virginia—a slave state but still in the Union—then proposed a peace conference. Delegates from 21 states attended the conference in Washington, D.C. The majority came from Northern and border states. None came from the secessionist states. The delegates met for three weeks, but came up with little more than a modified version of Crittenden's Compromise. When presented to Congress, the plan went down in defeat.

Founding the Confederacy

On the same day the peace conference met, delegates from the seceding states met in Montgomery, Alabama. There, in early February, they declared themselves to be a new nation—the Confederate States of America—or the **Confederacy,** as it became known. The convention then drafted a constitution based largely on the U.S. Constitution but with some important changes. It declared that each state was independent and guaranteed the existence of slavery in Confederate territory. It did ban the import of slaves from other countries. It also banned protective tariffs and limited the presidency to a single six-year term.

The delegates to the convention chose **Jefferson Davis,** a former senator from Mississippi, as president of the Confederate States of America. In his inaugural address, Davis declared, "The time for compromise has now passed. The South is determined to . . . make all who oppose her smell Southern powder and feel Southern steel."

Reading Check **Identifying** What main event triggered the secession of Southern states?

1854 Kansas-Nebraska Act crafted by Stephen Douglas repeals Missouri Compromise; Republican Party is founded

1856 Charles Sumner is caned in the Senate

1858 Abraham Lincoln wins national attention during Lincoln-Douglas debates

1859 John Brown raids Harpers Ferry

1860 Lincoln is elected; secession begins

1854 1856 1858 1860

▲ *Antislavery settlers in Kansas*

1856 Border ruffians attack antislavery settlers in Lawrence, Kansas; John Brown leads attack on pro-slavery settlers in Pottawatomie Creek, Kansas

1857 *Dred Scott* decision allowing slavery in all federal territories enrages Northerners

Analyzing TIME LINES

1. **Specifying** How many years elapsed between the Compromise of 1850 and the beginning of the Civil War?
2. **Identifying** Which came first—the *Dred Scott* decision or the Wilmot Proviso?

S Skill Practice

Creating a Thematic Map Have students create a map that John J. Crittenden could have used as a visual aid when he presented his compromise to Congress. **BL**

Reading Check

Answer:
the election of Abraham Lincoln, a Republican, to the presidency

Analyzing TIME LINES

Answers:
1. 10 years until Lincoln is elected; 11 years until the first shots are fired
2. the Wilmot Proviso

Additional Support

Activity: Interdisciplinary Connection

Geography Provide students with an outline map of the United States that shows the current state boundaries. Have students create a thematic map by first labeling and shading in one color all the states that were part of the Union on June 10, 1861. Next, have students use a different color to label and shade all the states that had seceded. Finally, have students use a third color to shade the remaining area and label it "Territories." **OL**

W Writing Support

Descriptive Writing Have students write an announcement of the attack on Fort Sumter from either the Northern or Southern perspective. The announcement should include all the details of the attack. It should demonstrate knowledge of the event as well as an understanding of the Northern or Southern perspective.

C Critical Thinking

Analyzing Ask students to select five states that seceded. Have them identify the specific reasons these states gave for seceding. Have students consider what, if anything, might have been done to prevent their secession. Students should share their research findings with the class. OL

Turning Point

Answer:
because the shelling and fall of Fort Sumter began the Civil War, which was a test of the strength of the Union

The Civil War Begins

MAIN Idea The plan to resupply Fort Sumter triggered the beginning of the Civil War.

HISTORY AND YOU Do you think it is ever appropriate for the government to declare martial law? Why or why not? Read to learn how Lincoln used martial law to keep Maryland from seceding.

In his inaugural address on March 4, 1861, Lincoln spoke directly to the seceding states. He repeated his **commitment** not to interfere with slavery where it existed but insisted that C "the Union of these States is perpetual." Lincoln did not threaten the seceded states, but he said he intended to "hold, occupy, and possess" federal property in those states. Lincoln also encouraged reconciliation:

PRIMARY SOURCE

"In your hands, my dissatisfied countrymen, and not in mine is the momentous issue of civil war. The government will not assail you. You can have no conflict, without yourselves being the aggressors. . . . We are not enemies, but friends. We must not be enemies. Though passion may have strained, it must not break our bonds of affection."

—from Lincoln's first Inaugural Address

Fort Sumter Falls

In April Lincoln announced that he would resupply Fort Sumter. Confederate President Jefferson Davis now faced a dilemma. Leaving federal troops in the South's most vital harbor was unacceptable if the Confederacy was to be an independent nation. Firing on the supply ship, however, would undoubtedly lead to war with the United States.

Davis decided to capture Fort Sumter before the supply ship arrived. If he was successful, peace might be preserved. Confederate leaders sent a note to Major Robert Anderson, the fort's commander, demanding Fort Sumter's surrender by the morning of April 12, 1861.

Anderson stood fast. The fateful hour came and went, and cannon fire suddenly shook the

Turning Point

The Fall of Fort Sumter

When the Confederacy took Fort Sumter, it fired the first shots of the American Civil War. The Civil War was the most serious test of the strength of the Union up to that point, or since. The North, led by President W Lincoln, was determined to preserve the United States as a whole, while the South, led by Jefferson Davis and Robert E. Lee, was determined to start a new nation of its own to preserve the institution of slavery.

ANALYZING HISTORY Why was the shelling of Fort Sumter a turning point in American history?

◀ The attack on Fort Sumter sparked the Civil War.

Hands-on Chapter Project: Step 3

Mapping Events of the Mid-1800s

Step 3: Secession and the Confederacy Students will represent the division of the Union on their map.

Directions Students will represent the seceding states and border states. Students should include a time line of events leading to secession on the side of their maps.

Representing Information Students will need to show the events for Step 3 in a way that does not interfere with the images, colors, and text that they have already placed on it. They will have to label information clearly and concisely. OL

(Chaper Project continued on Visual Summary page)

air. Confederate forces bombarded Fort Sumter for 33 hours, wrecking the fort but killing no one, until Anderson and his exhausted men finally surrendered. The Civil War had begun.

The Upper South Secedes

After the fall of Fort Sumter, President Lincoln called for 75,000 volunteers to serve in the military for 90 days. The call for troops created a crisis in the Upper South. Many people there did not want to secede, but faced with the prospect of civil war, they believed they had no choice but to leave the Union. Virginia acted first, passing an Ordinance of Secession on April 17, 1861. The Confederate Congress responded by moving the capital of the Confederacy to Richmond, Virginia. By early June of 1861, Arkansas, North Carolina, and Tennessee had also seceded.

Hanging On to the Border States

With the upper South gone, Lincoln was determined to keep the slaveholding border states from seceding. Delaware seemed safe, but Lincoln worried about Kentucky, Missouri, and Maryland. Virginia's secession had placed a Confederate state across the Potomac River from the nation's capital. If Maryland seceded, Washington would be surrounded by Confederate territory.

To prevent Maryland's secession, Lincoln **imposed martial law** in Baltimore, where mobs had already attacked federal troops. Under martial law, the military takes control of an area, replaces civilian authorities, and suspends many civil rights. Fearing that Confederate agents in Washington, D.C., were plotting against the Union government, Lincoln suspended the right of habeas corpus, which protects citizens from illegal imprisonment without evidence. Union Army officers imprisoned dozens of suspected secessionist leaders and held them without trial. Chief Justice Roger Taney ruled that Lincoln had wrongly denied the right of habeas corpus, but Lincoln ignored this in the face of impending war. C

Kentucky stayed neutral until September 1861, when Confederate forces occupied part of the state, prompting Union troops to move in as well. The Confederate invasion angered many in the Kentucky legislature, which now voted to fight the Confederacy. This led other Kentuckians who supported the Confederacy to create a rival government and secede.

The third border state Lincoln worried about was Missouri. Although many people in the state sympathized strongly with the Confederacy, its convention voted almost unanimously against secession. A struggle then broke out between the convention and pro-secession forces led by Governor Claiborne F. Jackson. In the end, Missouri stayed with the Union with the support of federal forces. From the very beginning of the Civil War, Lincoln had been willing to take political, even constitutional, risks to preserve the Union. The issue of its preservation now shifted to the battlefield.

Reading Check **Describing** Why were the border states of Maryland and Kentucky important to the Union?

Section 3 REVIEW

Vocabulary

1. **Explain** the significance of: John C. Breckinridge, John Bell, Fort Sumter, Crittenden's Compromise, Confederacy, Jefferson Davis, martial law.

Main Ideas

2. **Explaining** How did problems in the Democratic Party help Abraham Lincoln win the 1860 election?
3. **Identifying** Where and under what circumstances did the American Civil War begin?

Critical Thinking

4. **Big Ideas** How did Lincoln prevent Kentucky, Missouri, and Maryland from seceding? Was Lincoln justified in his actions? Why or why not?
5. **Categorizing** Use a graphic organizer similar to the one below to list the various parties' candidates and political positions in the 1860 election.

Party	Candidate	Position
Northern Democrat		
Southern Democrat		
Constitutional Unionist		
Republican		

6. **Analyzing Visuals** Examine the map on the election of 1860 on page 303. Explain why Douglas won only one state.

Writing About History

7. **Persuasive Writing** Suppose you are an adviser to President Lincoln and have just heard about the firing on Fort Sumter. Write a brief report for the president, advising him on what steps to take next.

History ONLINE
Study Central™ To review this section, go to glencoe.com and click on Study Central.

C Critical Thinking

Drawing Conclusions
Ask: How does martial law restrict the civil rights of citizens? *(Answers will vary but should include some aspect of personal freedoms being restricted.)* OL

Reading Check

Answers:
If Maryland seceded, Washington, D.C., would be surrounded by Confederate states. Kentucky was important for its control of the southern bank of the Ohio River.

Assess

History ONLINE
Study Central™ provides summaries, interactive games, and online graphic organizers to help students review content.

Close

Explaining Ask students to briefly explain how and why the Civil War began.

Section 3 REVIEW

Answers

1. All definitions can be found in the section and the Glossary.
2. The Democratic Party split over slavery, and supported two candidates. The split Democratic vote allowed Lincoln, a Republican, to win the election.
3. The Confederacy attacked Fort Sumter in Charleston Harbor, forcing the Union troops there to surrender.
4. He declared martial law in Maryland, promised to leave Kentucky alone as long as the Confederacy did the same, and sent federal forces into Missouri. Students' responses should be supported with reasoned arguments.
5. Northern Democrat: Stephen Douglas, support popular sovereignty; Southern Democrat: John C. Breckinridge, uphold the *Dred Scott* decision and endorse a federal slave code for the territories; Constitutional Unionist: John Bell, preserve the Union and the Constitution; Republican: Abraham Lincoln, right of Southern states to preserve slavery within their borders, supporter higher tariffs, a new homestead law, and a transcontinental railroad
6. The Democratic Party had split over the issue of popular sovereignty.
7. Students' reports will vary, but should include a summary of the Confederate actions against Fort Sumter, the results, and include recommendations for future action.

Narrative Writing Have students select one cause, effect, or visual in the Visual Summary as a short story starter for a piece of realistic fiction. Encourage students to do additional research to find historical details that will enrich their work. Encourage students to read their stories to the class. **OL**

Chapter 8 Visual Summary

STUDY TO GO You can study anywhere, anytime by downloading quizzes and flashcards to your PDA from glencoe.com.

Causes of Sectional Tensions

- Disagreement continues over the legality, morality, and politics of slavery.
- Congressman David Wilmot proposes the Wilmot Proviso to ban slavery in territory acquired from Mexico.
- The concept of popular sovereignty—that local settlers can decide whether their state will be a free state or slave state—is popularized.
- The California Gold Rush leads to Californians applying for statehood as a free state, creating the possibility of more free states than slave states in the Senate.
- The Compromise of 1850 leads to the Fugitive Slave Law.
- Harriet Beecher Stowe publishes *Uncle Tom's Cabin* in 1852.
- The Kansas-Nebraska Act repeals the Missouri Compromise.
- The *Dred Scott* case results in the Supreme Court declaring the Missouri Compromise unconstitutional.
- John Brown launches a raid on Harpers Ferry, hoping to incite a slave rebellion.
- Lincoln wins the presidency in 1860.

▲ *The Dred Scott decision and the publication of Uncle Tom's Cabin fueled the bitter sectional struggle over slavery.*

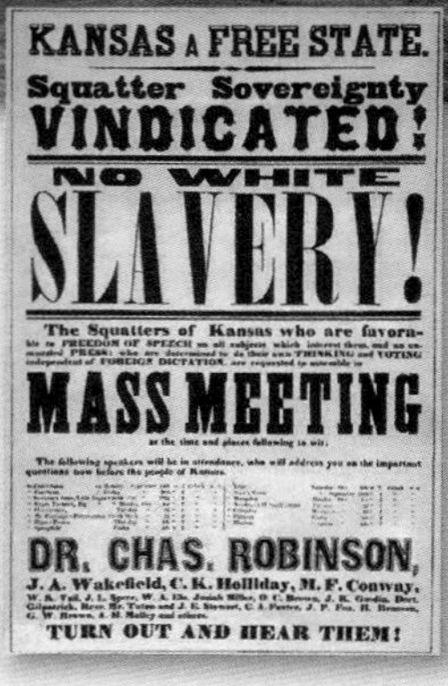

◄ *When Northern settlers organized to stop slavery from spreading into Kansas (left), their efforts were met with a violent response by Southerners. Ultimately, the struggle over slavery led to Civil War, when the Confederacy fired on Fort Sumter (above)*

Effects of Sectional Tensions

- The Free-Soil Party, seeking to stop the spread of slavery into western territories, is formed.
- The Republican Party is formed by antislavery Whigs, Democrats, Free-Soilers, and members of the abolitionist Liberty Party.
- Some Northerners actively resist the Fugitive Slave Law and help escaped slaves; the Underground Railroad moves runaway slaves from the South to freedom in Canada.
- Violence erupts between proslavery and antislavery settlers in Kansas.
- John Brown and *Uncle Tom's Cabin* polarized the North and South.
- Missouri Compromise is found unconstitutional by the Supreme Court in *Dred Scott* v. *Sandford*.
- John Brown's raid convinces many Southerners that secession is necessary to keep the South safe.
- Lincoln's election is the final straw. Several Southern states secede from the Union and form the Confederacy.
- Confederates attack Fort Sumter in South Carolina and take it.
- Lincoln calls for troops to put down the rebellion; the Civil War begins.

308 Chapter 8 Sectional Conflict Intensifies

Hands-On Chapter Project
Step 4: Wrap Up

Mapping Events of the Mid-1800s

Step 4: Wrap Up Student groups will summarize the chapter's content by presenting the map to the rest of the class.

Directions Divide students into groups. Each group will prepare a presentation of the map. Each presentation should include the main topics illustrated on the map. Student presentations should include not only a listing of facts and events, but also explanations of the causes and effects of the events.

Putting It Together Students will analyze the causes and effects of sectional conflict and present them during their oral presentations to the class. **OL**

Chapter 8 Assessment

Reviewing Vocabulary

Directions: Choose the word or words that best complete the sentence.

1. To spare Congress from further arguments over slavery, Senator Lewis Cass proposed the idea of ________, which would allow each territory to decide if it wanted to allow slavery or not.

A martial law
B popular sovereignty
C abolition
D insurrection

2. John C. Calhoun warned that Southern states might agree upon ________, to break away from the national Union, if their way of life was not protected by the federal government.

A ratification
B imposition
C secession
D composition

3. In Kansas, antislavery supporters voted in a ________ against the Lecompton constitution.

A committee
B convention
C proviso
D referendum

4. To keep Maryland in the Union, Abraham Lincoln declared ________ in Baltimore.

A martial law
B abolition
C secession
D popular sovereignty

5. John Brown was executed for his attack on Harpers Ferry and a plan to lead a slave ________ against slaveholders.

A demonstration
B referendum
C insurrection
D revolution

Reviewing Main Ideas

Directions: Choose the best answer for each of the following questions.

Section 1 *(pp. 284–293)*

6. The Wilmot Proviso declared that there would be no

A more slavery in the United States.
B slavery in the lands won from Mexico.
C further territorial acquisitions.
D new states added to the Union.

7. Which of the following was an effect of the Fugitive Slave Law?

A Southerners had no more problems with escaped enslaved people.
B Enslaved people could now leave slavery whenever they wished.
C California was brought into the Union as a free state.
D Northerners who had been neutral about slavery were now outraged.

8. Which of the following was not an element of the Compromise of 1850?

A The Fugitive Slave Act was passed.
B California was admitted as a state.
C The slave trade was ended in Washington, D.C.
D Slavery was permitted in Texas.

Section 2 *(pp. 294–301)*

9. In the *Dred Scott* decision, the Supreme Court determined that it was unconstitutional to

A allow slavery in the territories.
B prohibit slavery in the territories.
C free slaves in the United States.
D bring enslaved people from one state to another.

TEST-TAKING TIP

When a question contains a negative, try to reword the sentence or phrase to make it positive.

Need Extra Help?

If You Missed Questions . . .	1	2	3	4	5	6	7	8	9
Go to Page . . .	285	287	298	307	301	284	288	288	296

GO ON

Answers and Analyses
Reviewing Vocabulary

1. B Popular means "of the public" and sovereignty means "freedom from external control." The concept of popular sovereignty means people can determine for themselves how they are ruled. Rather than the government deciding whether or not slavery was allowed, the territories would decide for themselves.

2. C Calhoun wanted Southern states' rights to be guaranteed, a return of fugitive slaves, and a balance of power between slaveholding states and free states.

3. D Referendum is the only answer choice that is by definition a vote. Choices *A* and *C* are types of meetings or groups. A proviso is a clause that introduces a condition (as in a contract).

4. A Martial law is when the military takes over for local government. The military acts as an agent for the federal government, and people's civil rights are suspended. Declaring martial law is a drastic action. Abolition is to end something, and does not make sense. Martial law was declared in response to secession.

5. C An insurrection is a rebellion. Students may be confused by *D,* revolution. Although revolution is a type of rebellion, revolution implies an attempt to overthrow a government or to make a drastic change. It is on a much larger scale than an insurrection.

Reviewing Main Ideas

6. B The Wilmot Proviso was suggested as an add-on to a military appropriations bill. Its proposal angered Southerners who felt it would lead to an end to slavery. *A* is the most likely distractor, but it suggests that the Proviso banned all slavery, which is incorrect. *C* and *D* do not make sense, because the U.S. was actively interested in adding new territories.

7. D Use the process of elimination to help students arrive at the correct answer. The Fugitive Slave Act did not stop enslaved people from trying to escape. *B* is the opposite of the act. The admission of California and the Fugitive Slave Act were both parts of the Compromise of 1850, so one did not cause the other.

8. D As stated above, both the admission of California and the Fugitive Slave Act were part of the Compromise of 1850. In addition, the slave trade was ended in Washington, D.C.

9. B The Supreme Court decision said that Congress could not bar slaveholders from taking their slave "property" into the territories.

10. D Know-Nothings were nativists. They were against immigration. Their formation was in reaction to the wave of new immigrants, especially Irish people, who were Catholic.

11. B The Kansas-Nebraska Act split the Whig party, and the antislavery faction joined members of the Free-Soil Party and formed the Republican Party, a turning point in American party politics. Lincoln would run as the Republican candidate in the 1860 election.

12. C Lincoln represented the Republican Party, which was seen as antislavery. Therefore, his victory was seen as a victory for abolitionists. *A* is the opposite of the correct answer. *B* does not make sense; from the Southern, proslavery point of view, Lincoln's election would not benefit the South in any way.

13. B Students can approach this question in a chronological way. Fort Sumter fell before the events in the other answer choices happened. Virginia seceded right after Sumter fell. Army officers imprisoned suspected secessionists during martial law in Maryland. Shortly after that, Lincoln refused to send troops into Kentucky.

14. C Lincoln first and foremost wanted to preserve the Union. His declaration of martial law showed that he would go to great lengths to achieve this. The declaration of martial law was a risk, because it could backfire and cause greater anger, which it did.

Critical Thinking

15. C The slave states that did not secede are shaded in solid dark gray. The only one listed in the answer choices is Missouri.

16. D States that seceded after the Fort Sumter attack are striped. Help students locate these states on the map.

Chapter 8 ASSESSMENT

10. Which of the following best describes the party called the Know-Nothings?

- **A** proslavery and antigovernment
- **B** antislavery and pro-immigration
- **C** pro-Catholic and pro-immigration
- **D** anti-immigration and anti-Catholic

11. Anger over the Kansas-Nebraska Act brought about the formation of which party?

- **A** the American Party
- **B** the Republican Party
- **C** the Cotton Whig Party
- **D** the Free-Soil Party

Section 3 *(pp. 302–307)*

12. The South saw the election of Abraham Lincoln in 1860 as a

- **A** political victory for proslavery supporters.
- **B** chance to take over Congress.
- **C** victory for the abolitionists.
- **D** good opportunity to end years of sectionalism.

13. The Civil War began when

- **A** Lincoln refused to send troops into Kentucky.
- **B** Fort Sumter fell to the Confederacy.
- **C** Virginia seceded from the Union.
- **D** army officers imprisoned many suspected secessionists.

14. Lincoln's actions in Missouri at the start of the Civil War signaled his

- **A** desperate desire to end slavery.
- **B** deep disappointment at Claiborne F. Jackson.
- **C** willingness to take risks to save the Union.
- **D** desire to accommodate the South.

Critical Thinking

Directions: Choose the best answers to the following questions.

Base your answers to questions 15 and 16 on the map below and on your knowledge of Chapter 8.

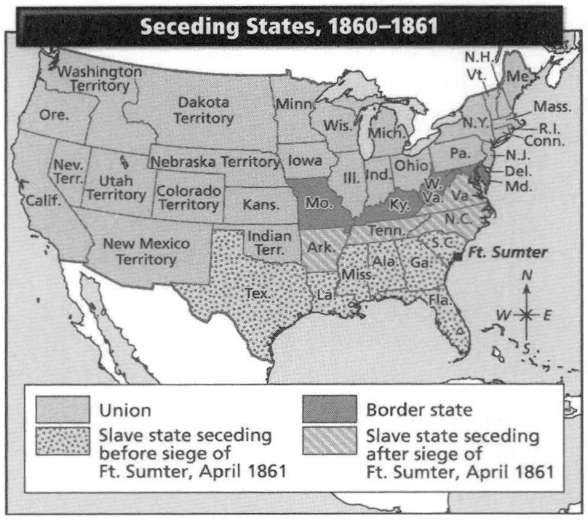

15. Which slave state remained in the Union after the Fort Sumter attack?

- **A** Arkansas
- **B** Virginia
- **C** Missouri
- **D** Texas

16. Which states did not secede until after the Fort Sumter attack?

- **A** North Carolina, South Carolina, and Virginia
- **B** Arkansas, Tennessee, and Kentucky
- **C** Alabama, Georgia, and South Carolina
- **D** Tennessee, North Carolina, and Virginia

Need Extra Help?

If You Missed Questions . . .	10	11	12	13	14	15	16
Go to Page . . .	295	294	304	306	307	307	307

GO ON

17. "A house divided against itself cannot stand. . . . I do not expect the Union to be dissolved; I do not expect the house to fall; but I do expect it will cease to be divided. It will become all one thing, or all the other. . . ."

—Abraham Lincoln, 1858

The "divided house" referred to in this speech was caused primarily by

A expansionism.

B war with Mexico.

C slavery.

D the suffrage movement.

Analyze the cartoon and answer the question that follows. Base your answer on the cartoon and on your knowledge of Chapter 8.

18. What do you think this cartoon is satirizing?

A the Wilmot Proviso

B the presidential election of 1856

C the presidential election of 1860

D the formation of the Republican Party

Document-Based Questions

Directions: Analyze the document and answer the short-answer questions that follow the document.

Edward A. Pollard of Virginia was the editor of the *Daily Richmond Examiner* during the Civil War. He wrote a book, *The Lost Cause,* about the Civil War from the Southern point of view. In this excerpt from the book, Pollard gives his view of the causes of the Civil War:

> *"In the ante-revolutionary period, the differences between the populations of the Northern and Southern colonies had already been strongly developed. The early colonists did not bear with them from the mother-country to the shores of the New World any greater degree of congeniality than existed among them at home. They had come not only from different stocks of population, but from different feuds in religion and politics. There could be no congeniality between . . . New England, and the South. . . ."*
>
> —from *The Lost Cause*

19. According to Pollard, when did differences between the North and South begin?

20. What did he believe caused the differences between the people of the North and the South?

Extended Response

21. John Brown's goal in seizing the arsenal at Harpers Ferry was to begin a rebellion against slaveholders. Write a persuasive essay expressing your opinion that either John Brown should have or should not have been executed for his action. In your essay, include an introduction and at least three paragraphs with details from the chapter to support your opinion.

STOP

History ONLINE

For additional test practice, use Self-Check Quizzes—Chapter 8 at glencoe.com.

Need Extra Help?

If You Missed Questions . . .	17	18	19	20	21
Go to Page . . .	302	302	311	311	294–301

Extended Response

21. Essays will vary, but must be written in a persuasive format. Students must take a definitive position on the issue and support it fully with details and examples from the text.

17. C The United States was divided, in part, over the issue of slavery. Expansionism (including lands won in the war with Mexico) brought the issue of slavery to a head, but did not cause the divide. The suffrage movement is irrelevant to the cause of the split between North and South.

18. C The cartoon includes politicians tearing apart a map of the United States. The Election of 1860 illustrated the deep national divide.

Document-Based Questions

19. According to Pollard, the differences began before settlers even arrived in the colonies. Explain to students that ante- means before. The ante-revolutionary period is the period before the American Revolution. Pollard speaks of the attitudes these settlers brought with them to the colonies.

20. He believed the differences were caused by differences in religious and political backgrounds.

History ONLINE

Have students visit the Web site at glencoe.com to review Chapter 8 and take the Self-Check Quiz.

Need Extra Help?

Have students refer to the pages listed if they miss any of the questions.

Chapter 9 Planning Guide

Key to Ability Levels	
BL Below Level	AL Above Level
OL On Level	ELL English Language Learners

Key to Teaching Resources: Print Material · CD-ROM or DVD · Transparency

BL	OL	AL	ELL	Resources	Chapter Opener	Section 1	Section 2	Section 3	Section 4	Section 5	Chapter Assess
				FOCUS							
BL	OL	AL	ELL	Daily Focus Skills Transparencies		9-1	9-2	9-3	9-4	9-5	
				TEACH							
	OL	AL		Geography and History, URB					p. 3		
	OL	AL		History Simulations and Problem Solving, URB					p. 9		
BL	OL		ELL	Reading Essentials and Note-Taking Guide*		p. 96	p. 99	p. 102	p. 105	p. 108	
	OL			Historical Analysis Skills Activity, URB		p. 52					
BL	OL		ELL	Guided Reading Activities, URB*		p. 78	p. 79	p. 80	p. 81	p. 82	
BL	OL	AL	ELL	Content Vocabulary Activity, URB*	p. 57						
BL	OL	AL	ELL	Academic Vocabulary Activity, URB	p. 59						
	OL	AL		Critical Thinking Skills Activity, URB				p. 62			
BL	OL		ELL	Reading Skills Activity, URB		p. 51					
BL			ELL	English Learner Activity, URB	p. 55						
	OL	AL		Reinforcing Skills Activity, URB							p. 61
BL	OL	AL	ELL	Differentiated Instruction Activity, URB				p. 53			
BL	OL		ELL	Time Line Activity, URB							p. 63
	OL			Linking Past and Present Activity, URB			p. 64				
BL	OL	AL	ELL	American Art and Music Activity, URB					p. 69		
BL	OL	AL	ELL	Interpreting Political Cartoons Activity, URB	p. 71						
		AL		Enrichment Activity, URB					p. 75		
BL	OL	AL	ELL	American Biographies	✓	✓	✓	✓	✓	✓	✓
BL	OL	AL	ELL	Primary Source Reading, URB		p. 65		p. 67			
BL	OL	AL	ELL	Supreme Court Case Studies							p. 13
BL	OL	AL	ELL	The Living Constitution*	✓	✓	✓	✓	✓	✓	✓
	OL	AL		American History Primary Source Documents Library	✓	✓	✓	✓	✓	✓	✓
BL	OL	AL	ELL	Unit Map Overlay Transparencies	✓	✓	✓	✓	✓	✓	✓

Note: Please refer to the *Unit 3 Resource Book* for this chapter's URB materials.

* Also available in Spanish

TeacherWorks Plus
All-In-One Planner and Resource Center

- Interactive Lesson Planner
- Interactive Teacher Edition
- Fully editable blackline masters
- Section Spotlight Videos Launch
- Differentiated Lesson Plans
- Printable reports of daily assignments
- Standards Tracking System

Levels: BL	OL	AL	ELL	Resources	Chapter Opener	Section 1	Section 2	Section 3	Section 4	Section 5	Chapter Assess
				TEACH *(continued)*							
BL	OL	AL	ELL	Differentiated Instruction for the American History Classroom	✓	✓	✓	✓	✓	✓	✓
BL	OL	AL	ELL	StudentWorks™ Plus	✓	✓	✓	✓	✓	✓	✓
BL	OL	AL	ELL	American Music Hits Through History CD	✓	✓	✓	✓	✓	✓	✓
BL	OL	AL	ELL	Unit Time Line Transparencies and Activities	✓	✓	✓	✓	✓	✓	✓
BL	OL	AL	ELL	Cause and Effect Transparencies, Strategies, and Activities	✓	✓	✓	✓	✓	✓	✓
BL	OL	AL	ELL	Why It Matters Transparencies, Strategies, and Activities	✓	✓	✓	✓	✓	✓	✓
BL	OL	AL	ELL	American Issues	✓	✓	✓	✓	✓	✓	✓
	OL	AL	ELL	American Art and Architecture Transparencies, Strategies, and Activities	✓	✓	✓	✓	✓	✓	✓
BL	OL	AL		High School American History Literature Library	✓	✓	✓	✓	✓	✓	✓
BL	OL	AL	ELL	*The American Vision* Video Program	✓	✓	✓	✓	✓	✓	✓
Teacher Resources				Strategies for Success	✓	✓	✓	✓	✓	✓	✓
Teacher Resources				Success with English Learner	✓	✓	✓	✓	✓	✓	✓
Teacher Resources				Reading Strategies and Activities for the Social Studies Classroom	✓	✓	✓	✓	✓	✓	✓
Teacher Resources				Presentation Plus! with MindJogger CheckPoint	✓	✓	✓	✓	✓	✓	✓
				ASSESS							
BL	OL	AL	ELL	Section Quizzes and Chapter Tests*		p. 119	p. 120	p. 121	p. 122	p. 123	p. 125
BL	OL	AL	ELL	Authentic Assessment With Rubrics							p. 23
BL	OL	AL	ELL	Standardized Test Practice Workbook							p. 17
BL	OL	AL	ELL	*ExamView® Assessment Suite*		9-1	9-2	9-3	9-4	9-5	CH. 9
				CLOSE							
BL			ELL	Reteaching Activity, URB							p. 73
BL	OL		ELL	Reading and Study Skills Foldables™	p. 56						

✓ Chapter- or unit-based activities applicable to all sections in this chapter.

Using Study Central™

Teach With Technology

What is Study Central™?

Study Central™ is an interactive, online tool that helps students understand and remember content section-by-section. It can be used alongside lessons or before a test.

How can Study Central™ help my students?

Study Central™ contains fun activities that students can use to review important content and reinforce effective study habits. Using the format of the Guide to Reading that opens each section in the textbook, Study Central™ has students write main idea statements as questions, review academic and content vocabulary, and take notes using online graphic organizers. Students can also read section summaries, take multiple-choice quizzes, and find Web links for more information.

Visit glencoe.com and enter a ***QuickPass***™ code to go to Study Central™.

History ONLINE
Visit glencoe.com and enter ***QuickPass***™ code TAV9399c9T for Chapter 9 resources.

You can easily launch a wide range of digital products from your computer's desktop with the McGraw-Hill Social Studies widget.

	Student	Teacher	Parent
Media Library			
• Section Audio	●		●
• Spanish Audio Summaries	●		●
• Section Spotlight Videos	●	●	●
The American Vision **Online Learning Center (Web Site)**			
• StudentWorks™ Plus Online	●	●	●
• Multilingual Glossary	●	●	●
• Study-to-Go	●	●	●
• Chapter Overviews	●	●	●
• Self-Check Quizzes	●	●	●
• Student Web Activities	●	●	●
• ePuzzles and Games	●	●	●
• Vocabulary eFlashcards	●	●	●
• In Motion Animations	●	●	●
• Study Central™	●	●	●
• Web Activity Lesson Plans		●	
• Vocabulary PuzzleMaker	●	●	●
• Historical Thinking Activities		●	
• Beyond the Textbook	●	●	●

Reading Support From JAMESTOWN EDUCATION

- **Timed Readings Plus in Social Studies** helps students increase their reading rate and fluency while maintaining comprehension. The 400-word passages are similar to those found on state and national assessments.
- **Reading in the Content Area: Social Studies** concentrates on six essential reading skills that help students better comprehend what they read. The book includes 75 high-interest nonfiction passages written at increasing levels of difficulty.
- **Reading Social Studies** includes strategic reading instruction and vocabulary support in Social Studies content for both ELLs and native speakers of English.

www.jamestowneducation.com

NATIONAL GEOGRAPHIC

Index to National Geographic Magazine:

The following articles relate to this chapter:

- "Civil War Battlefields: Saving the Landscapes of America's Deadliest War" By Adam Goodheart, April 2005.
- "The Wreck of the C.S.S. Alabama: Avenging Angel of the Confederacy" By Max Guerout and Rod M. Farb, December 1994.

National Geographic Society Products To order the following, call National Geographic at 1-800-368-2728:

- *The Civil War* (CD-ROM)

Access National Geographic's new dynamic MapMachine Web site and other geography resources at:
www.nationalgeographic.com
www.nationalgeographic.com/maps

Biography A&E Home Video THE HISTORY CHANNEL

The following videotape programs are available from Glencoe as supplements to this chapter:

- Civil War Journal (Set) (Six Video Set) (ISBN 1-56-501326-3)
- Abraham Lincoln: Preserving the Union (ISBN 0-76-700034-X)

To order, call Glencoe at 1-800-334-7344. To find classroom resources to accompany many of these videos, check the following home pages:

A&E Television: www.aetv.com
The History Channel: www.historychannel.com

Reading List Generator CD-ROM

GLENCOE BOOKLINK 3

Use this database to search more than 30,000 titles to create a customized reading list for your students.

- Reading lists can be organized by students' reading level, author, genre, theme, or area of interest.
- The database provides Degrees of Reading Power™ (DRP) and Lexile™ readability scores for all selections.
- A brief summary of each selection is included.

Leveled reading suggestions for this chapter:

For students at a Grade 8 reading level:
- ***Private Captain: A Story of Gettysburg***, by Marty Crisp

For students at a Grade 9 reading level:
- ***The Battle of Gettysburg: Turning Point of the Civil War***, by Gina DeAngelis

For students at a Grade 10 reading level:
- ***A Yankee Girl at Gettysburg,*** by Alice Turner Curtis

For students at a Grade 11 reading level:
- ***To Hold this Ground: A Desperate Battle at Gettysburg,*** by Susan Provost Beller

For students at a Grade 12 reading level:
- ***Outrageous Women of Civil War Times,*** by Mary Rodd Furbee

Focus

MAKING CONNECTIONS

How is Modern Warfare Different?

Ask students to recall how the battles of the Revolutionary War were fought. Then, activate prior knowledge by asking them about what battle was like in the Civil War. Students may recall the massive casualties of major battles, the horrors of medical amputations, and trench warfare. **OL**

Teach

The Big Ideas

As students study the chapter, remind them to consider the section-based Big Ideas included in each section's Guide to Reading. The **Essential Questions** in the activities below tie in to the Big Ideas and help students think about and understand important chapter concepts. In addition, the Hands-on Chapter Projects with their culminating activities relate the content from each section to the Big Ideas. These activities build on each other as students progress through the chapter. Section activities culminate in the wrap-up activity on the Visual Summary page.

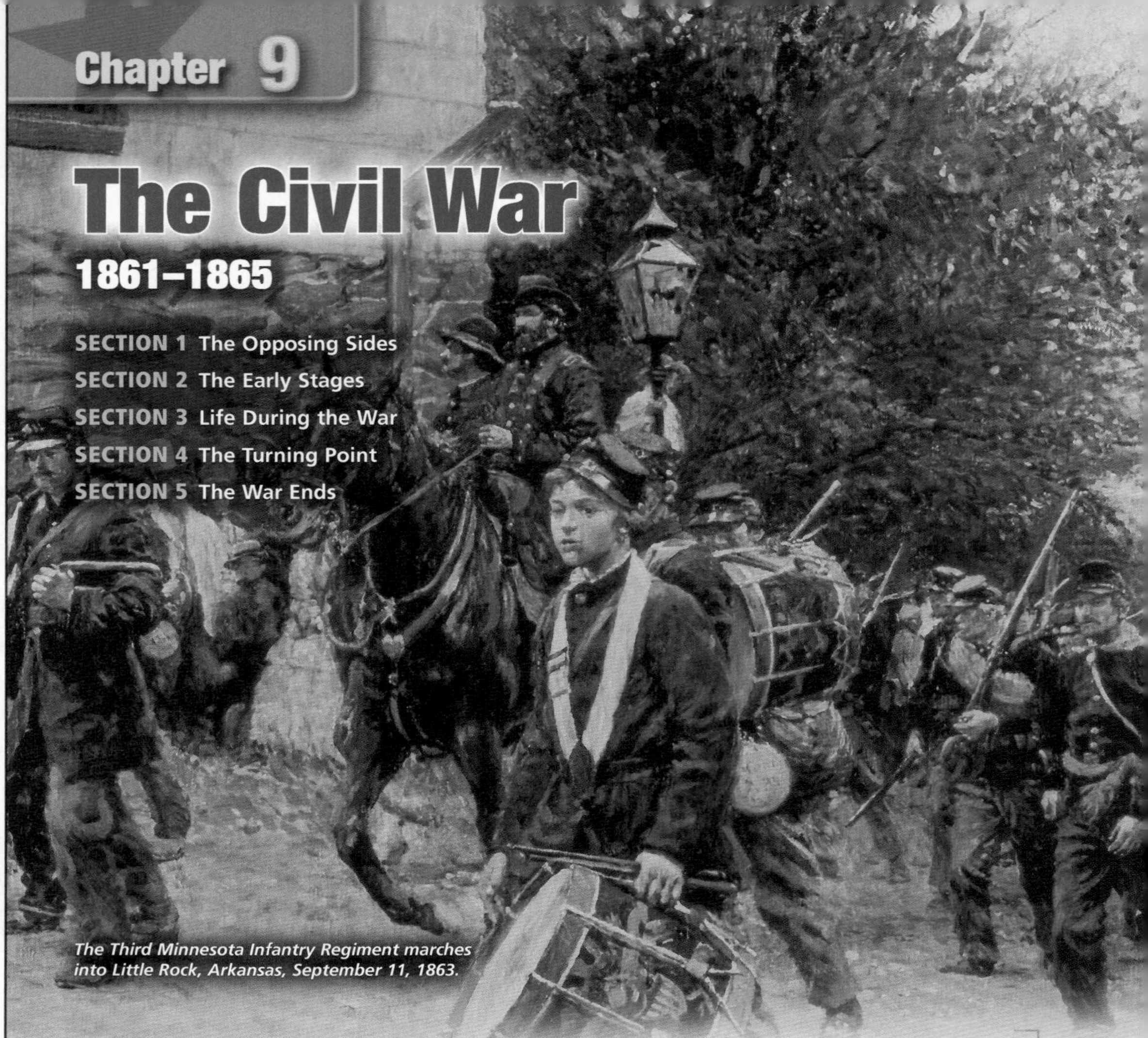

Chapter 9

The Civil War

1861–1865

The Third Minnesota Infantry Regiment marches into Little Rock, Arkansas, September 11, 1863.

U.S. PRESIDENTS

U.S. EVENTS

1859
- John Brown leads raid on federal arsenal at Harpers Ferry, Virginia

1861
- Fort Sumter attacked
- First Battle of Bull Run

Lincoln 1861–1865

1862
- Battle of Antietam halts Lee's invasion
- Lincoln presents Emancipation Proclamation

1860 · 1861 · 1862

WORLD EVENTS

1859
- Work on the Suez Canal begins in Egypt

1861
- Russian serfs emancipated by Czar Alexander II

1862
- British firm builds Confederate warship *Alabama* which begins sinking Union shipping

Section 1

The Opposing Sides

Essential Question: What advantages and disadvantages did the North and the South have at the start of the Civil War? *(The North had a better transportation network, more factories, and a larger population; the South had valuable export crops and many top military leaders.)* Point out that in Section 1 students will learn about how the Civil War began and how the fighting differed from earlier wars. **OL**

Section 2

The Early Stages

Essential Question: How did the Emancipation Proclamation change the Civil War? *(By putting the abolition of slavery at the heart of the Union war effort, the Emancipation Proclamation gave the Union effort a new moral dimension.)* Point out that in Section 2 students will learn about the naval war, Lee's invasion of the North, and the Emancipation Proclamation. **OL**

Chapter Audio

MAKING CONNECTIONS

How Is Modern Warfare Different?

The Civil War was in many respects the first modern war. Both sides fielded large armies equipped with mass-produced weapons. Railroads and the telegraph ensured rapid communications and troop movements. Hundreds of thousands of soldiers were killed.

- ***Why was the North able to defeat the South?***
- ***How did specific battles affect President Lincoln's political decisions?***

1863
- Battle of Gettysburg
- Vicksburg is captured

1864
- Atlanta falls; Sherman begins march to the sea
- Grant battles Lee in Virginia

1865
- Lee surrenders to Grant
- Abraham Lincoln assassinated

A. Johnson 1865–1869

1863 — 1864 — 1865

1863
- French troops occupy Mexico City

1864
- Karl Marx founds First International Workingmen's Association to promote socialism

FOLDABLES™

Outlining Compromise Efforts Create a Half Book Foldable that lists the failure of compromise efforts before the Civil War. Complete the chart by showing the series of compromises attempted. Describe each compromise effort in the left-hand column. In the right-hand column, describe the outcome of each compromise.

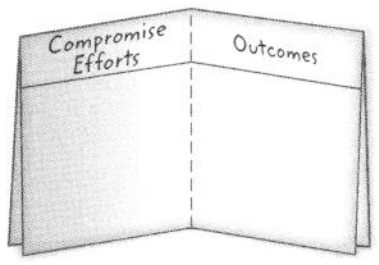

History ONLINE Visit glencoe.com and enter ***QuickPass***™ code TAV9846c9 for Chapter 9 resources.

Introducing

Chapter 9

More About the Photo

Visual Literacy The Third Minnesota Infantry Regiment put down an uprising among the Sioux in Minnesota, known as the Dakota War of 1862. This painting depicts the unit in September 1863, in the campaign against the Confederacy.

FOLDABLES™ Study Organizer **Dinah Zike's Foldables**

Dinah Zike's Foldables are three-dimensional, interactive graphic organizers that help students practice basic writing skills, review vocabulary terms, and identify main ideas. Instructions for creating and using Foldables can be found in the Appendix at the end of this book and in the *Dinah Zike's Reading and Study Skills Foldables* booklet.

History ONLINE

Visit glencoe.com and enter ***QuickPass***™ code TAV9399c9T for Chapter 9 resources, including a Chapter Overview, Study Central™, Study-to-Go, Student Web Activity, Self-Check Quiz, and other materials.

Section 3

Life During the War

Essential Question: What was life like for soldiers and nurses during the Civil War? *(For soldiers, food was often inadequate and medical care was primitive; many women served as nurses during the war and tried to make conditions in hospitals and camps more sanitary.)* Point out that in Section 3 students will learn how riots broke out in the North and the South during the war. **OL**

Section 4

The Turning Point

Essential Question: Why was 1863 the pivotal year of the Civil War? *(The fall of Vicksburg gave Union forces control of the Mississippi River and divided the South; the Union victory at Gettysburg marked the last Confederate invasion of the North.)* Point out that in Section 4 students will learn about the largest battle ever to take place in the Western Hemisphere. **OL**

Section 5

The War Ends

Essential Question: Why did the Union army wage "total war" against the South? *(To force the Confederacy to surrender, Union military leaders believed that the entire Southern population, not just the Confederate military, had to share in the war's suffering and deprivation.)* Point out that in Section 5 students will learn about Sherman's destructive "march to the sea." **OL**

Focus

Bellringer

Daily Focus Transparency 9-1

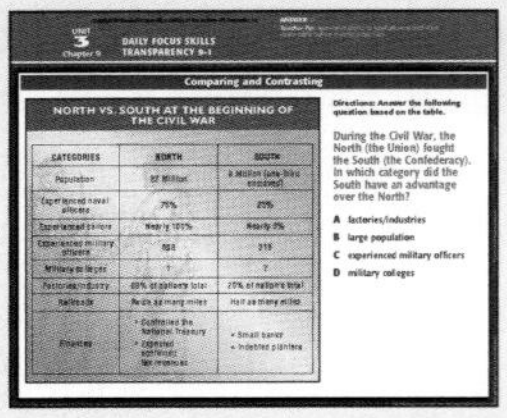

Guide to Reading

Answers:

Students' outlines should include the following points:

I. Choosing Sides
  A. The Opposing Economies
  B. Financing the War
  C. Party Politics in the North
  D. Weak Southern Government
  E. The Diplomatic Challenge
II. The First Modern War
  A. Military Technology
  B. The South's Strategy
  C. The Union's Anaconda Plan

Section Spotlight Video

To generate student interest and provide a springboard for class discussion, access the Chapter 9, Section 1 video at glencoe.com or on the video DVD.

Resource Manager

Section 1 — Section Audio — Spotlight Video

The Opposing Sides

Guide to Reading

Big Ideas

Government and Society The Confederacy's weak central government had difficulty coordinating the war effort.

Content Vocabulary
- greenback *(p. 315)*
- conscription *(p. 316)*
- habeas corpus *(p. 316)*
- attrition *(p. 319)*

Academic Vocabulary
- sufficient *(p. 316)*
- implement *(p. 319)*

People and Events to Identify
- Robert E. Lee *(p. 314)*
- Copperheads *(p. 316)*
- James Mason *(p. 317)*
- John Slidell *(p. 317)*
- *Trent* Affair *(p. 317)*
- Anaconda Plan *(p. 319)*

Reading Strategy

Taking Notes Use the major headings in this section to create an outline similar to the one below, to record the advantages and disadvantages of the North and the South at the start of the Civil War.

I. The Opposing Sides
  A.
  B.
  C.
  D.
  E.
II.

At the start of the Civil War, the North and South each had distinct advantages and disadvantages. Both sides expected the conflict to end quickly. Instead, the Civil War became a long, bloody, and bitter struggle in which neither side won an easy triumph.

Choosing Sides

MAIN Idea The Union had economic advantages at the start of the Civil War, but was politically divided; if the Confederacy could gain European support and wear down the North, it had a chance at victory.

HISTORY AND YOU Do you believe the government should limit civil liberties during wartime? Read on to learn how President Lincoln decided to suspend writs of habeas corpus during the Civil War.

On the same day that he learned his home state of Virginia had voted to secede from the Union, **Robert E. Lee**—one of the most respected senior officers in the United States Army—received an offer from General Winfield Scott to command the Union's troops. Although Lee had spoken against secession and considered slavery "a moral and political evil," he wrote, "I cannot raise my hand against my birthplace, my home, my children." Instead, he resigned from the army and offered his services to the Confederacy.

Lee was only one of hundreds of military officers who had to choose whether to support the Union or the Confederacy. Eventually 313 officers, or about one-third of the total, resigned to join the Confederacy. The South had a strong military tradition. In 1860 the United States had eight military colleges, and seven of them were in the South. These colleges provided the South with a large number of trained officers to lead its armies.

Just as the South had a strong military tradition, the North had a strong naval tradition. More than three-quarters of the United States Navy's officers came from the North. Perhaps even more important, most of the navy's warships and all but one of the country's shipyards remained under Union control.

The Opposing Economies

Although the South had many experienced officers to lead its troops in battle, the North had several economic advantages. In 1860 the population of the North was about 22 million, while the South had about 9 million people, more than one-third of whom were enslaved. The North's larger population gave it a great advantage in raising an army and in supporting the war effort. The North's

R Reading Strategies	C Critical Thinking	D Differentiated Instruction	W Writing Support	S Skill Practice
Teacher Edition • Simulating, p. 315 • Drawing Concl., p. 318 **Additional Resources** • Guided Reading, URB p. 78 • Prim. Source Read, URB p. 65	**Additional Resources** • Hist. Analysis Skills Act., URB p. 52 • Quizzes and Tests, p. 119	**Teacher Edition** • Verbal/Linguistic, p. 316 **Additional Resources** • Eng. Learner Act., URB p. 55	**Additional Resources** • Content Vocab. Act., URB p. 57 • Academic Vocab. Act., URB p. 59	**Teacher Edition** • Public Speaking, p. 319 **Additional Resources** • Reading Skills Act., URB p. 51 • Reading Essen., p. 94

INFOGRAPHIC

The Opposing Sides

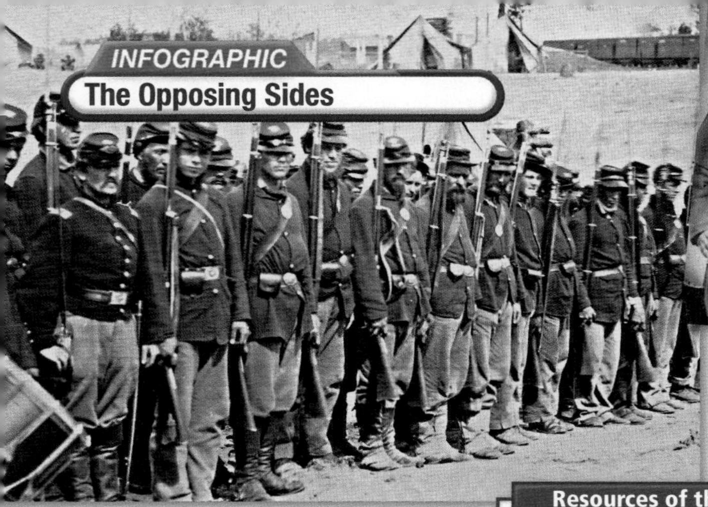

▲ Men of the 110th Pennsylvania Infantry Regiment at Falmouth, Virginia, April 1863. Union troops were generally better equipped than Confederate forces.

▲ Confederate soldiers of the 3rd Georgia Infantry (above) fought under Lee's command during the Peninsula campaign. The Confederacy had fewer soldiers but many of the nation's best officers.

Resources of the Union and of the Confederacy

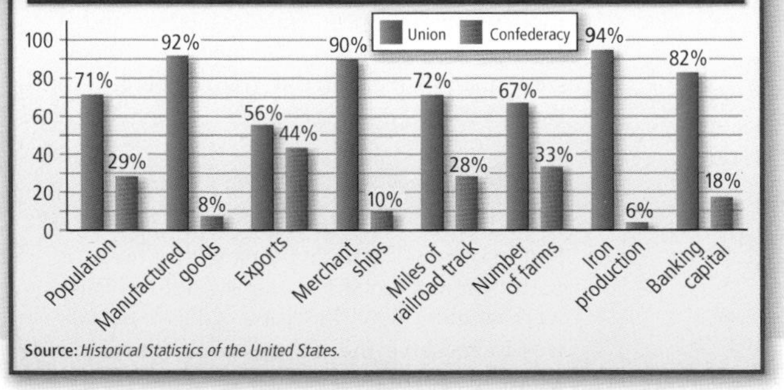

Source: *Historical Statistics of the United States.*

Analyzing VISUALS

1. **Interpreting** Based on the graph, what were the North's greatest advantages over the South?
2. **Assessing** Which of the North's advantages do you think were most important in winning the war? Why?

industries gave the region an important economic advantage over the South as well. In 1860 almost 90 percent of the nation's factories were in the North. They produced more than 90 percent of the country's clothing, boots, and shoes, and 94 percent of its pig iron (unrefined iron), vital for manufacturing weapons and equipment.

Both sides were able to produce the food they needed. Although much of the South's fertile land was used for the production of cash crops, such as cotton and tobacco, Southern farmers also grew rice and great quantities of corn. The problem facing the South was not its ability to produce food, but its ability to distribute it once the war began. It had only half as many miles of railroad track as the North and had only one line—from Memphis to Chattanooga—connecting the western states of the Confederacy to the east. This made it much easier for Northern forces to disrupt the movement of food and troops.

Financing the War

Both the North and the South had to act quickly to raise money for the war. The North enjoyed several financial advantages. In addition to controlling the national treasury, the Union could expect continued revenue from tariffs. Many Northern banks also held large reserves of cash, which they lent the government by purchasing bonds.

Concern about the North's ability to win the war caused many people to withdraw gold and silver from the banks. Without gold and silver, the banks could not buy government bonds, and without the gold and silver from the sale of bonds, the government could not pay its suppliers and troops. To solve this problem, Congress passed the Legal Tender Act in February 1862. This act created a national currency and allowed the government to issue paper money. These paper bills came to be known as **greenbacks** because of their color.

Teach

R Reading Strategy

Simulating Make the following announcement to your students: "Wanted: Soldiers to fight for the Union! Skilled soldiers needed for the 9th regiment of Boston. Volunteers sign up today!" Based on the announcement, have students take on the role of an army recruiter addressing potential soldiers. Using the format of a newspaper article, have students explain five reasons to enlist in the Union Army. OL

Analyzing VISUALS

Answers:

1. The North produced 94% of the nation's iron and 92% of manufactured goods; it also possessed 90% of the nation's merchant ships.
2. Possible answers include its banking capital and population, which gave the North an advantage in financing the war and replacing wounded or killed soldiers.

Hands-On Chapter Project

Step 1

Chronicling the Lives of Southerners and Northerners

Step 1: Choosing Sides Essential Question: **Why did Americans choose their sides at the start of the Civil War?** Write the essential question on the board to focus students' research. Students will complete research throughout the chapter to chronicle the changing lives of Southerners and Northerners during the Civil War.

Directions At the start of the war, many Americans, especially those of the border states, had to choose which side to support. Divide the class into two teams. One team will research the lives of Southerners during the class project. The other team will research the lives of Northerners. Have each team determine which aspects of life to research. Then the team will divide up research responsibilities.

Synthesizing Information Students will synthesize their research by creating 1 to 3 pages of a Civil War diary. Encourage students to research primary sources, images, narratives, and other sources of information. Note that each team will create their own pages—those for Southerners and those for Northerners. OL

(Chapter Project continued on page 321)

Did You Know?

Copperheads The Republicans referred to Peace Democrats as *Copperheads,* but the derivation of the term is less certain. They might have been thinking of the copperhead snake when they coined the term. The snake is poisonous and known for its sneak attacks. Both attributes described the Republicans' view of the Peace Democrats. Another theory suggests that the term was derived from buttons, made from copper coins, worn by Peace Democrats.

D Differentiated Instruction

Verbal/Linguistic Have students look up the word *conscription* in the dictionary. After they know the meaning of the word, ask students to offer synonyms. Write these words on the board. OL BL

Additional Support

In contrast to the Union, the Confederacy's financial situation was poor, and it became worse over time. Most Southern planters were in debt and unable to buy bonds. At the same time, Southern banks were small and had few cash reserves. As a result, they could not buy many bonds.

The best hope for the South to raise money was by taxing trade. Shortly after the war began, however, the Union Navy blockaded Southern ports, which reduced trade and revenue. The Confederacy then imposed new taxes on property and farm products, but many Southerners refused to pay.

Lacking **sufficient** money from taxes or bonds, the Confederacy was forced to print paper money to pay its bills. This caused rapid inflation in the South. Confederate paper money became almost worthless. By the end of the war, the South had experienced 9,000 percent inflation, compared to only 80 percent in the North.

Party Politics in the North

As the Civil War began, President Lincoln had to contend with divisions within his own party. Many members of the Republican Party were abolitionists. Lincoln's goal, however, was to preserve the Union, even if it meant allowing slavery to continue.

The president also had to contend with the Democrats. One faction, known as the War Democrats, supported a war to restore the Union but opposed ending slavery. Another faction, known as the Peace Democrats, opposed the war and called for reuniting the states through negotiation. Many Republicans viewed them as traitors and referred to them as **Copperheads,** after the poisonous snake.

D One major disagreement between Republicans and Democrats concerned the use of **conscription,** or forcing people into military service. In 1862 Congress passed a militia law requiring states to use conscription if they could not recruit enough volunteers. Many Democrats opposed the law, and riots erupted in several strongly Democratic districts in Indiana, Ohio, Pennsylvania, and Wisconsin.

To enforce the militia law, Lincoln suspended writs of **habeas corpus.** Habeas corpus refers to a person's right not to be imprisoned unless charged with a crime and given a trial. A writ of habeas corpus is a court order that requires the government either to charge an imprisoned person with a crime or let the person go free. When writs of habeas corpus are suspended, a person can be imprisoned indefinitely without trial. In this case, President Lincoln suspended the writ for anyone who openly supported the rebels or encouraged others to resist the militia draft. Lincoln justified imposing limits on speech in wartime: "Must I shoot a simple-minded soldier boy who deserts," the president asked, "while I must not touch a hair of a wily agitator who induces him to desert?"

Weak Southern Government

Although the South had no organized opposition party, President Jefferson Davis still faced many problems. The Confederate constitution emphasized states' rights and limited the central government's power. This commitment to states' rights often interfered with Davis's ability to conduct the war.

Although many Southern leaders supported the war, some opposed Jefferson Davis when he supported conscription and established martial law early in 1862. Leaders from North Carolina and Georgia, including Davis's vice president, Alexander Stephens, were among those who dissented. They objected to the Confederacy forcing people to join the army and opposed Davis's decision to suspend writs of habeas corpus.

The Diplomatic Challenge

The outbreak of the Civil War put the major governments of Europe in a difficult position. The United States did not want the Europeans interfering in the war and expected them to respect the North's blockade of Southern ports. Confederate leaders, on the other hand, wanted the Europeans, particularly the British, to recognize the Confederate States of America as an independent country, and to provide military assistance to the South. Southern leaders knew that British and French textile factories depended on Southern cotton. To pressure these nations, Southern planters stopped selling their cotton to them until they recognized the Confederacy.

The British and French met informally with Confederate representatives in May 1861. The French promised to recognize the Confederacy

Activity: Connecting with the United States

Comparing and Contrasting Provide students with a copy of the Constitution of the Confederate States of America (available on-line from the Library of Congress at http://memory.loc.gov/ammem/amlaw/lwcc.html) and ask them to compare it to the Constitution of the United States of America in their textbook. Have students prepare an outline that lists the points upon which the two documents agree and disagree. **Ask:** On which points do the two documents agree? On which points are the two documents different? *(Similarities: Students should note that the basic framework for government is the same and presented in the same order. Direct students to Article I, Section 9 and Article 6, Section 5 of the Confederate Constitution and ask them to compare these sections to the Bill of Rights.*

Differences: In addition to replacing "United States" with "Confederate States," the Constitution of the Confederacy uses the term slave while the U.S. Constitution uses "other persons." Direct students to examine closely those sections of the Confederate Constitution that deal with slavery and the rights of slaveholders.) AL

POLITICAL CARTOONS PRIMARY SOURCE

The Politics of the Civil War

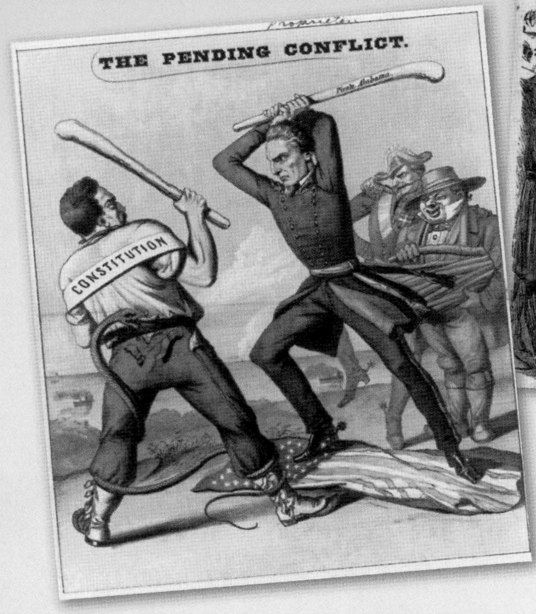

▲ *The cartoon above shows "Union" fighting "Secession." Union's feet are entangled by a copperhead snake, and his arms are bound by the Constitution. Secession tramples the flag, and holds a club labeled Pirate Alabama—referring to a Southern warship the British let the South build in Britain. Behind the fighters are two men—one representing France and the other Britain. The British figure is handing clubs to Secession to help him beat Union.*

▲ *The cartoon above is entitled "The Copperhead Plan for Subjugating the South." It shows Peace Democrats meeting with a Southerner (possibly Jefferson Davis). The Peace Democrats are saying: "Please come back" and "We will do anything you want." The Southerner is saying, "Oh Dear, I can't stand this much longer."*

Analyzing VISUALS DBQ

1. **Making Inferences** Do you think the cartoon on the left was created by a Northerner or a Southerner? Why?
2. **Identifying Points of View** What opinion of the Peace Democrats does the cartoon on the right express?

if the British did so, as well. British leaders, however, were not ready to risk war with the United States. Until the Confederacy won decisive victories on the battlefield and proved it would survive and eventually win the war, the British would not risk recognizing it.

In late 1861, the Confederacy decided to send **James Mason** of Virginia to Britain, and **John Slidell** of Louisiana, to France. The two men were to negotiate on behalf of the Confederacy. Mason and Slidell traveled to Havana, Cuba, and boarded the *Trent*, a British ship. When the *Trent* left Havana, it was intercepted by the Union warship *San Jacinto*.

The British were furious the United States had stopped one of their ships. They sent an ultimatum to the United States, demanding the release of the two Confederates. Britain then sent troops to Canada and strengthened its Atlantic fleet. After a few tense weeks, Lincoln freed Mason and Slidell, commenting, "One war at a time."

After being freed, the diplomats continued on their journey to seek Confederate allies. Although the arrest of Mason and Slidell in the so-called ***Trent* Affair** had excited interest worldwide, their diplomatic mission failed to gain the support the South wanted.

Reading Check **Explaining** How would British and French recognition of the Confederacy have helped the South to overcome the North's advantages in the war?

Analyzing VISUALS

Answers:

1. The cartoon on the left was probably created by a Northerner, since it depicts the Union wrapped in the Constitution, while the Secession figure attacks with help from Britain and France and treads on the American flag.
2. The cartoon on the right expresses the opinion that the Peace Democrats were nearly traitors in offering to do anything necessary to get the South back in the Union. The tone is very sarcastic about any fear or hardship they may be causing to the South in the person of Davis.

Reading Check

Answer:
British and French recognition of the Confederacy would have given the South powerful allies with money and resources and this might have enabled the South to overpower the North.

Additional Support

Activity: Collaborative Learning

Creating a Graphic Organizer Have students work in groups of four to create a graphic organizer about the strengths and weaknesses of the North and the South. They should scan the section for information on strengths and weaknesses and cooperatively categorize each strength and weakness into the following categories: cultural, social, economic, and political factors. As a group, students should decide which type of graphic organizer they want to use. Then have each student decide which category to depict on the graphic organizer. Finally, each student should illustrate the information in his or her specific category on the graphic organizer. **OL**

R Reading Strategy

Drawing Conclusions Have students recall fighting methods during the Revolutionary War and compare these methods to those in the Civil War. **Ask:** How did new weapons change warfare? *(Answers may include new and improved weapons were more accurate, so new methods of warfare, including the use of trenches and barricades, were used for the first time.)* **OL**

Analyzing VISUALS

Answers:

1. Hot air balloons made it possible to get an aerial view of the surrounding countryside and observe the location of the enemy's troops. Since they had more accurate information about the enemy, military leaders could plan more elaborate strategies for attack.
2. The telegraph allowed generals to learn of the results of battles, respond to such information, and transmit orders long distance more quickly.

Additional Support

The First Modern War

MAIN Idea Unlike previous wars, the Civil War was fought with huge, mostly volunteer armies equipped with new technologies.

HISTORY AND YOU Do you know what types of weapons and other gear soldiers carry today? Read on to learn about the weapons and supplies available to soldiers in the Civil War.

The economic and political situation in the North and South was very important to the outcome of the war because, in many respects, the Civil War was the first "modern" war. Unlike most of the wars fought in Europe during the previous two centuries, the Civil War was not fought by small disciplined armies with limited goals. It involved huge armies, made up mostly of civilian volunteers, that required vast quantities of supplies and equipment.

Military Technology

Many of the top officers who led the Union and Confederate troops had studied Napoleon's campaigns and had fought in the war with Mexico in the 1840s. They believed that the best way to win a battle was to organize troops into tight columns and march toward the enemy, firing in massed volleys. When the troops got close enough, they would charge the enemy and attack with bayonets. These tactics had been necessary in the early 1800s because soldiers used smooth bore muskets firing round metal balls. They were very inaccurate except at close range.

By the 1850s, French and American inventors had developed a new, inexpensive conoidal—or cone-shaped—bullet for rifles. Rifles firing conoidal bullets were accurate at much greater ranges. This meant that troops would be fired on several more times while charging enemy lines.

TECHNOLOGY & HISTORY

Civil War Technology Military conflict often leads to the use of new technologies. The Civil War was no exception. New weapons, ships and means of communication greatly changed the nature of warfare.

▲ **Conoidal Bullets**

These new bullets made gunfire more accurate at greater ranges and increased the number of casualties.

▲ **Telegraph**

Invented before the war, the telegraph let generals learn the results of battles almost immediately, and change their strategy and give new orders quickly.

▲ **Balloons**

The Civil War marked the first time aerial reconnaissance was used in war. Both sides used balloons to observe enemy troops.

◀ **Ironclads**

To operate on enemy rivers and coastlines guarded by shore-based cannon, both sides built armor-plated steamships. Ironclads marked the beginning of the shift from wooden ships to steel ships.

Analyzing VISUALS

1. **Explaining** How did balloons change warfare?
2. **Describing** How did the telegraph help both sides fight the war?

Activity: Technology Connection

Synthesizing Have students consider how the Civil War would have been reported using modern communications methods. **Ask:** Do you think modern reporting might have gained the South the international diplomatic support it sought? Why or why not? Have students consider how the Civil War might be covered today in forms such as international satellite broadcasts, instant electronic communications, and Internet blogs. Then, ask students to predict whether more intense international coverage of the war would have won more or less support for the Confederate cause. *(Answers will vary.)* **OL**

The Civil War also marked the first time that troops defending their positions protected themselves with trenches and barricades instead of standing upright in a line. By combining rifles firing conoidal bullets with the protection of trenches, defenders were able to inflict very high casualties on attacking forces. High casualties meant that armies had to keep replacing their soldiers. **Attrition**—the wearing down of one side by the other through exhaustion of soldiers and resources—played a critical role as the war dragged on. The North, with its large population, could replace its troops much more easily than the South.

The South's Strategy

Early in the war, Jefferson Davis imagined a struggle similar to the Revolutionary War. His generals would pick their battles carefully, attacking and retreating when necessary and avoiding large battles that might risk heavy losses. Davis believed that if **S** the South waged a defensive war of attrition in this manner, it would force the Union to spend its resources until it became tired of the war and agreed to negotiate.

The idea of a defensive war of attrition, however, outraged many Southerners. Believing themselves superior fighters, they scorned the idea of defensive warfare. "The idea of waiting for blows, instead of inflicting them, is altogether unsuited to the genius of our people," declared the *Richmond Examiner* in 1861.

The Southern disdain for remaining on the defensive meant that when battles occurred, Southern troops often went on the offensive, charging enemy lines and suffering very high casualties. In 1862 and 1863, Confederate armies fought nine large battles. In six of them, they went on the offensive, and they suffered 20,000 more casualties than the Union forces.

The Union's Anaconda Plan

Early in the war, the general in chief of the United States, Winfield Scott, proposed a strategy for defeating the South. Scott suggested that the Union blockade Confederate ports and send gunboats down the Mississippi to divide the Confederacy. The South, thus separated, would gradually run out of resources and surrender. The plan would take time, Scott admitted, but it would defeat the South with the least amount of bloodshed.

Many Northerners rejected the plan as too slow and indirect for certain victory. Northern newspapers referred to the strategy as the **Anaconda Plan,** after the snake that slowly strangles its prey to death. Opponents argued that a rapid and massive invasion of the South would bring victory more quickly. Although Lincoln agreed to **implement** Scott's suggestions, and imposed a blockade of Southern ports, he hoped that a quick victory over the Southern forces massing in Virginia might discredit the secessionists and bring an end to the crisis. Ultimately, he and other Union leaders realized that only a long war that focused on destroying the South's armies had any chance of success.

Reading Check **Describing** What war strategy did Jefferson Davis develop for the South?

Section 1 REVIEW

Vocabulary

1. **Explain** the significance of: Robert E. Lee, greenback, Copperheads, conscription, habeas corpus, James Mason, John Slidell, *Trent* Affair, attrition, Anaconda Plan.

Main Ideas

2. **Explaining** Why did some members of Lincoln's own Republican Party disagree with him over the war?
3. **Describing** How did Southern pride and tradition interfere with the South's ability to win the war?

Critical Thinking

4. **Big Ideas** How did the belief in states' rights hamper the Confederate government during the war?
5. **Organizing** Using a graphic organizer similar to the one below, list the military innovations of the Civil War era.

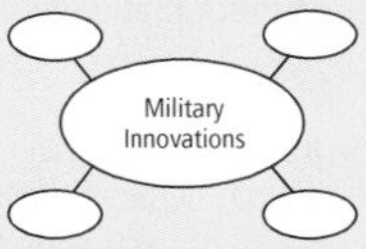

6. **Analyzing Visuals** Examine the conoidal bullets shown on page 318. How did conoidal bullets affect the war effort? What other innovations made the Civil War the first "modern" war?

Writing About History

7. **Descriptive Writing** Suppose that you are living in one of the border states at the beginning of the Civil War. Write a letter to a relative explaining why you are planning to join either the Union or the Confederate army.

History ONLINE
Study Central™ To review this section, go to glencoe.com and click on Study Central.

S Skill Practice

Public Speaking Invite students to prepare a two-minute oral presentation on Jefferson Davis's plan for war. Have students use resources from the library and the Internet to learn more about the plan and why it was opposed by many Southerners. **OL**

Reading Check

Answer:
a defensive war of attrition

Assess

History ONLINE

Study Central™ provides summaries, interactive games, and online graphic organizers to help students review content.

Close

Contrasting Have students contrast the effects of the war on the economies of the North and the South. **OL**

Section 1 REVIEW

Answers

1. All definitions can be found in the section and the Glossary.
2. They were abolitionists and wanted the war to be fought to end slavery, while Lincoln was fighting the war to preserve the Union, even if slavery continued.
3. Many Southerners were outraged by Jefferson Davis's strategy of a defensive war of attrition because they believed that they were excellent fighters who should take the offensive in the war.
4. The South lacked a strong central government needed to coordinate the war effort.
5. huge armies, civilian volunteers, conoidal bullets, trenches and barricades
6. Conoidal bullets caused high casualty rates; other innovations included quick-loading rifles and new defensive strategies such as trenches and barricades.
7. Students' letters will vary, but should offer plausible scenarios about the decision to join one side or the other.

Focus

Bellringer

Daily Focus Transparency 9-2

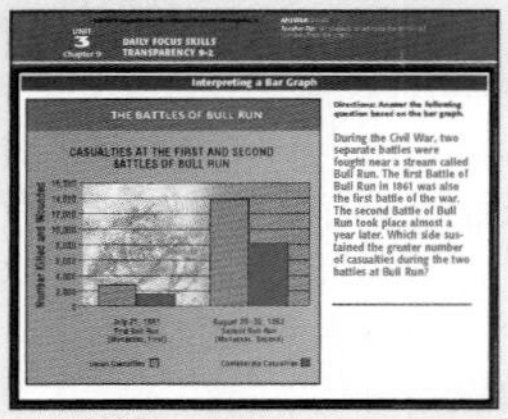

Guide to Reading

First Battle of Bull Run	Confederate victory
Battle of Shiloh	Union victory, both sides suffered high casualties
Battle of Murfreesboro	no decisive victory, Union retreated
Seven Days' Battle	no decisive victory, heavy casualties, Union retreated
Second Battle of Bull Run	Confederate victory, invasion of Maryland

Section Spotlight Video

To generate student interest and provide a springboard for class discussion, access the Chapter 9, Section 2 video at glencoe.com or on the video DVD.

Resource Manager

Section 2 — Section Audio — Spotlight Video

The Early Stages

Guide to Reading

Big Ideas

Geography and History The Union hoped to seize the Mississippi River valley and cut the Confederacy in two.

Content Vocabulary

- bounty *(p. 321)*
- blockade runner *(p. 322)*

Academic Vocabulary

- assemble *(p. 324)*
- crucial *(p. 326)*

People and Events to Identify

- "Stonewall" Jackson *(p. 320)*
- David G. Farragut *(p. 322)*
- Ulysses S. Grant *(p. 323)*
- George B. McClellan *(p. 324)*
- Emancipation Proclamation *(p. 327)*

Reading Strategy

Categorizing Complete a graphic organizer similar to the one below by filling in the results of each early Civil War battle listed.

Battle	Results
First Battle of Bull Run	
Battle of Shiloh	
Battle of Murfreesboro	
Seven Days' Battle	
Second Battle of Bull Run	

Both the North and the South developed strategies to win the Civil War. Both sides, however, experienced military setbacks and high casualties early in the war. President Lincoln issued the Emancipation Proclamation and put ending slavery at the heart of the Union war effort.

Mobilizing the Troops

MAIN Idea To fight the war successfully, it became clear to leaders on both sides that they would need conscription to ensure the necessary numbers of troops.

HISTORY AND YOU Do you know anyone who was drafted into military service? Read on to find out how the Union had to draft men into service during the Civil War.

In the first months of the Civil War, President Lincoln was under great pressure to strike quickly against the South. Confederate troops, led by General P.G.T. Beauregard, were gathering 25 miles (40 km) south of Washington, D.C., along the Bull Run River near Manassas Junction, an important railroad center in northern Virginia. Lincoln approved an assault on these forces, hoping that a Union victory would lead to a quick end to the conflict.

Expecting a short exciting fight, hundreds of spectators from Washington, D.C., picnicked a few miles away to watch the battle. They were soon horrified and dismayed by the chaos and death that they witnessed. At first, the attack went well for the Union. Its forces slowly pushed the Confederates back from their positions behind the Bull Run. During the fighting, Confederate reinforcements from Virginia, led by Thomas J. Jackson, moved into the line. As Confederate troops retreated past Jackson, their commander yelled: "There is Jackson standing like a stone wall! Rally behind the Virginians!" Afterward, Jackson became known as **"Stonewall" Jackson,** and went on to become one of the most effective commanders in the Confederate army.

As Confederate reinforcements arrived, Union commander General Irwin McDowell decided to fall back. The retreat quickly turned into a panic, although the exhausted Confederate troops did not pursue the Union forces very far. The Union defeat at the First Battle of Bull Run made it clear that the North would need a large, well-trained army to defeat the South. Lincoln had originally called for 75,000 men to serve for three months. The day after Bull Run, he signed another bill for the enlistment of 500,000 men for three years.

At first, excitement about the war inspired many men to enlist on both sides, swamping recruitment offices and training camps. As the

R Reading Strategies	C Critical Thinking	D Differentiated Instruction	W Writing Support	S Skill Practice
Additional Resources • Guided Reading, URB p. 79	**Additional Resources** • Linking Past/Present, URB p. 64 • Quizzes and Tests, p. 120	**Teacher Edition** • Gifted and Talented, p. 321 • Verbal/Linguistic, p. 327		**Teacher Edition** • Visual Literacy, p. 325 **Additional Resources** • Read. Essen., p. 99

PRIMARY SOURCE
The Naval War

An important element in the Union's success in the Civil War was its ability to blockade most of the Confederacy's ports. Because of the blockade, trade goods became very scarce in the South, which hurt morale.

▲ *Admiral David Farragut's daring and successful capture of New Orleans gave the North control of the most important port in the South and control of the lower part of the Mississippi River.*

▲ *The Civil War witnessed the first use of metal warships, known as ironclads, because they were covered in sloped iron plates. The most famous battle of ironclads took place in March 1862, when the South tried to break the Union blockade of Virginia using an ironclad built from the captured Union ship* Merrimack. *Renamed the* Virginia, *the ironclad sank two Union ships. The next day, the Union's newly built ironclad, the* Monitor, *challenged the* Virginia. *The ships battled for hours, but neither was able to sink the other. The* Monitor's *presence, however, kept the* Virginia *from breaking the blockade.*

Analyzing VISUALS DBQ

1. **Describing** How did the *Virginia* and the *Monitor* represent a new type of war technology?
2. **Explaining** What was the significance of Farragut's capture of New Orleans?

war dragged on and casualties rose, however, fewer young men volunteered, forcing both governments to resort to conscription. The South introduced conscription in April 1862 for all white men between the ages of 18 and 35. The draft, however, exempted certain people, including key government workers, teachers, and after 1862, planters who held at least 20 enslaved African Americans.

The North at first tried to encourage voluntary enlistment by offering a **bounty**—a sum of money given as a bonus—to individuals who promised to serve three years in the military. Congress also passed the Militia Act in July 1862, giving Lincoln the authority to call state militias, which included drafted troops, into federal service. Finally, after these measures failed to meet military needs, Congress introduced a national draft in 1863 to raise the necessary troops.

Reading Check **Summarizing** What was the significance of the First Battle of Bull Run?

The Naval War

MAIN Idea Although the Union had experienced setbacks on land, its naval forces successfully blockaded Southern ports and took control of the mouth of the Mississippi River.

HISTORY AND YOU Is there a military leader from a recent war that you consider to be a "hero"? Read on to find out how a Southerner became a naval hero in the North during the Civil War.

While the Union and Confederacy mobilized their armies, the Union navy began operations against the South. In April 1861, President Lincoln proclaimed a blockade of all Confederate ports. By the spring of 1862, the Union navy had sealed off every major Southern harbor along the Atlantic coast, except for Charleston, South Carolina, and Wilmington, North Carolina. Lincoln intended to hurt the South's economy as much as possible by cutting its trade with the world.

Teach

D Differentiated Instruction

Gifted and Talented Have students create a multimedia presentation that shows David G. Farragut's capture of New Orleans, beginning with the bombardment of the Confederate forts and ending with Benjamin Butler's capture of the city. OL

Analyzing VISUALS

Answers:

1. They had ironclad hulls so were able to withstand cannon fire.
2. The capture of New Orleans gave the North control over a major Southern port and control of the lower Mississippi River.

Reading Check

Answer:
It became clear that the North would need a large, well-trained army to defeat the South.

Hands-On Chapter Project
Step 2

Chronicling the Lives of Southerners and Northerners

Step 2: The Early Years of the War

Essential Question: How did Southerners and Northerners react to news from the battlefield in the early part of the war? Write the essential question on the board to help students focus their research.

Directions Divide the class into the teams determined in Step 1. Each team will meet to develop a plan and divide up research responsibilities. Teams will research how news from early battles affected the populations of the North and the South. They will also describe the reactions to the Emancipation Proclamation.

Synthesizing Information Students will synthesize their research by creating 1 to 3 pages of a Civil War diary. Note that each team will be creating their own pages—those for Southerners and those for Northerners. OL

(Chapter Project continued on page 329)

Did You Know?

The Union Blockade
Historians disagree over whether or not the Union blockade of the Confederacy was a success. Although it has been estimated that between 1861 and 1865 approximately five out of six blockade runners made it through the blockade, their impact on the war's outcome remains questionable. By the end of the war, the Confederacy was suffering from a lack of supplies, weakening its ability to continue fighting. The supply shortage was due, in part, to the fact that the blockade runners that did slip through were designed to be fast and maneuverable and, therefore, were limited in the amount of supplies they could carry.

Reading Check

Answer:
They tried to break the blockade by using small, fast vessels known as blockade runners to slip past Union ships at night.

Additional Support

The Blockade

Although the Union blockade became increasingly effective as the war dragged on, Union vessels were thinly spread and found it difficult to stop all of the **blockade runners**—small, fast vessels the South used to smuggle goods past the blockade, usually under cover of night. By using blockade runners, the South could ship at least some of its cotton to Europe in exchange for shoes, rifles, and other supplies. The amount of material that made it through the blockade, however, was much less than the amount that had been shipped before the war.

At the same time, Confederate ships operating out of foreign ports attacked Northern merchant ships at sea. Two of the most famous Confederate raiders were the warships *Alabama* and *Florida,* both of which the Confederacy had built in Great Britain. The *Alabama* captured 64 ships before a Union warship sank it off the coast of France in 1864. The *Florida* destroyed 38 merchant ships before being captured at a harbor in Brazil.

The damage done by these two ships strained relations between the United States and Great Britain. Union officials did not think Great Britain should have allowed the ships to be built, and they demanded Britain pay damages for the losses the Union suffered.

Farragut Seizes New Orleans

While the Union navy fought to seal off the Confederacy's Atlantic ports, it also began preparations to seize New Orleans and gain control of the lower Mississippi River. In February 1862, **David G. Farragut** took command of a Union force of 42 warships and 15,000 soldiers led by General Benjamin Butler.

At the time, Farragut was 60 years old. He had gone to sea at age 9 and was a veteran of the War of 1812 and the war with Mexico. His father had moved to the United States from Spain in 1776 and had fought in the Revolutionary War and served as governor of the Mississippi Territory. Although he was born in Tennessee, Farragut was a staunch supporter of the Union.

Farragut's actions at the battle for New Orleans made him a hero in the North. In early April, his fleet began bombarding Confederate forts defending the lower Mississippi River. When the attack failed to destroy the forts, Farragut made a daring decision. At 2:00 A.M. on April 24, 1862, his ships headed upriver past the forts in single file, exposing themselves to attack. The forts opened fire with more than 80 guns, while Confederate gunboats tried to ram the fleet and tugboats placed flaming rafts in front of the Union ships. Remarkably, all but four of Farragut's ships survived the battle and continued upriver.

On April 25, 1862, Farragut arrived at New Orleans. Six days later, General Butler's troops took control of the city. The South's largest city, and a center of the cotton trade, was now in Union hands.

Reading Check **Explaining** How did the Confederates try to break the Union blockade?

NATIONAL GEOGRAPHIC

▲ *At the battle of Shiloh, one of the bloodiest battles in American history with 20,000 casualties, the North forced the South to retreat.*

▲ *The warships* Essex *(above), and* Richmond *(right), helped Admiral Farragut capture New Orleans and establish Union control over the Mississippi River.*

Activity: Collaborative Learning

Sequencing Hang poster board or a large sheet of paper in the classroom with a time line marked 1861 through 1865. Organize the class into five groups and ask each group to be responsible for filling in dates in one year of the time line. Above the line students should mark Civil War battles, summarizing their significance and listing the number of casualties on both sides of the battle. Below the line other group members should mark significant socio-economic and political developments, such as the founding of the American Red Cross or the issuing of the Emancipation Proclamation. **OL**

The War in the West

MAIN Idea After the Union victory at Shiloh, the Union took control of eastern Tennessee.

HISTORY AND YOU Do you know someone with great perseverance? Read on to learn how General Grant demonstrated his worth to President Lincoln with his actions at the Battle of Shiloh.

In February 1862, as Farragut prepared for his attack on New Orleans, Union general **Ulysses S. Grant** began a campaign to seize control of the Cumberland and Tennessee Rivers. Control of these rivers would cut Tennessee in two and provide the Union with a river route deep into the Confederacy.

Backed by armored gunboats, Grant seized Fort Henry, the Confederacy's main fort on the Tennessee River. He then marched his troops east and surrounded Fort Donelson on the Cumberland River, forcing its garrison to surrender. With the fall of Fort Donelson and Fort Henry, all of Kentucky and most of western Tennessee came under Union control.

Shiloh

Next, Grant led his troops up the Tennessee River to attack Corinth, Mississippi. Seizing Corinth would cut the Confederacy's only rail line connecting Mississippi and western Tennessee. Determined to stop the Union advance, Confederate forces launched a surprise attack on Grant's troops early on April 6, 1862. The battle took place about 20 miles (32 km) north of Corinth near a small church named Shiloh.

Did You Know?

Shiloh As the Union troops were driven back at the Battle of Shiloh, they established a line along an area known as the Sunken Road. The Union forces withstood 12 attacks against this position. The area became known as the Hornets' Nest because of the intensity of the gunfire and the grazing of bullets. Southern troops organized 62 artillery pieces to fire on the Hornets' Nest, the largest concentration of artillery yet assembled in the war. The shells splintered trees and boulders. After six hours, the Union soldiers surrendered.

The War in the West, 1862–1863

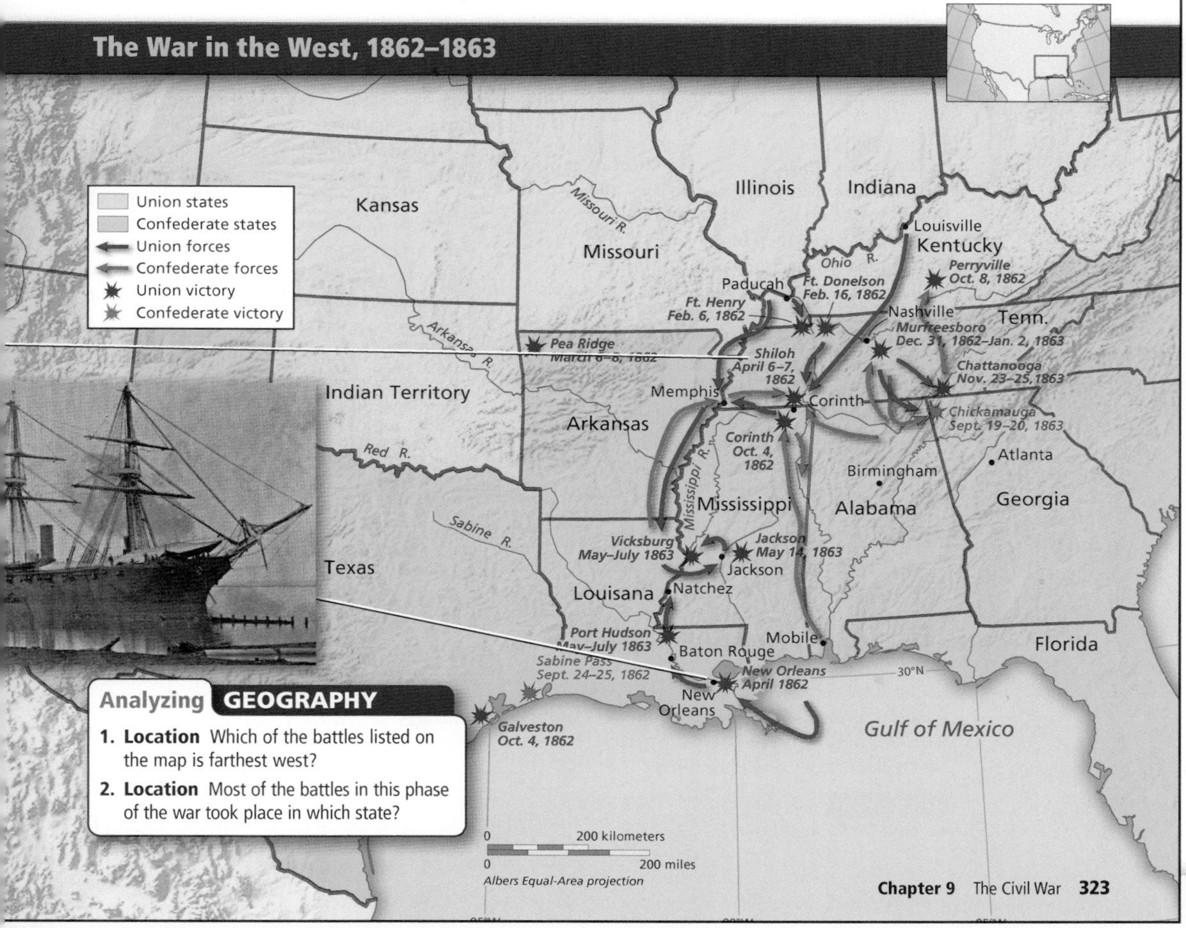

Analyzing GEOGRAPHY

1. **Location** Which of the battles listed on the map is farthest west?
2. **Location** Most of the battles in this phase of the war took place in which state?

Analyzing GEOGRAPHY

Answers:
1. Galveston
2. Tennessee

Additional Support

Activity: Interdisciplinary Connection

Geography Explore with students the important role that physical geography played in Civil War battles. Have students work in groups to build a model of the Battle of Shiloh. Students can use paper, poster board, modeling clay, craft sticks, or any other materials necessary to make their models as realistic as possible. As a starting point for researching information about the battle, have students visit the National Park Service's Web site about the battle at http://www.nps.gov/shil. Have each group present and explain its model to the class. Then, as a class, compare and contrast the groups' models. **OL**

Did You Know?

George B. McClellan (1826–1885) A veteran of the war with Mexico, George B. McClellan returned to military service in the Civil War. Early in the conflict, he was placed in command of what later became the Army of the Potomac. Despite some victories, General McClellan was criticized for being overly cautious in pursuing Lee's army and President Lincoln removed him from command on November 7, 1862. McClellan ran for president on the Democratic ticket in 1864, denouncing the war as a failure. He won 45 percent of the popular vote, compared to Lincoln's 55 percent.

Reading Check

Answer:
Union forces cut the only railroad lines connecting Mississippi and western Tennessee; both sides suffered high casualties, but Grant proved his willingness to fight hard.

Additional Support

Hearing the attack, Grant raced from his headquarters to the battle. Although the Union troops were forced back, Grant rushed around the battlefield and managed to **assemble** a defensive line that held off repeated Southern attacks. The next morning, knowing reinforcements were coming, Grant went on the offensive, surprising the Confederates and forcing General Beauregard, their commander, to order a retreat.

The Battle of Shiloh stunned people in both the North and the South. Twenty thousand troops were killed or wounded, more than in any other battle up to that point. When newspapers demanded Grant be fired because of the high casualties, Lincoln refused, saying, "I can't spare this man; he fights."

Murfreesboro

Grant's victory at Shiloh cheered Lincoln, but the fighting was not over. Confederate troops evacuated Corinth and quickly moved east by railroad to Chattanooga, Tennessee, where they were placed under the command of General Braxton Bragg.

Bragg took his troops into Kentucky, hoping the Union armies would follow. He also hoped that his invasion of Kentucky would lead to an uprising of pro-Confederate supporters in the state. Bragg's invasion failed. Union troops led by General Don Carlos Buell stopped Bragg's forces at the Battle of Perryville.

After Bragg retreated, Lincoln ordered Buell to seize Chattanooga and cut the railroad lines that passed through the city. Lincoln knew that eastern Tennessee was home to many Union sympathizers, and he wanted it under Union control. He also knew that cutting the rail lines would deprive the Confederacy of "hogs and hominy"—vital supplies of meat and corn that the South needed.

Frustrated at Buell's slow advance, Lincoln fired him and put General William Rosecrans in command. As Rosecrans's forces headed south, Bragg's forces attacked them west of the Stones River near Murfreesboro. Although the Union lines fell back, they did not break, and the battle ended inconclusively. Four days later, with Union reinforcements arriving from Nashville, Bragg decided to retreat.

Reading Check **Evaluating** What was the significance of the Battle of Shiloh?

The War in the East

MAIN Idea After the Union defeated Lee at Antietam, Britain decided to stay out of the conflict and Lincoln issued a proclamation to end slavery.

HISTORY AND YOU Can you think of a point in your life when things suddenly improved? Read how victory at Antietam improved Northern morale and made the war more challenging for the South.

While Union and Confederate troops were struggling for control of Tennessee and the Mississippi River, another major campaign was being waged in the east to capture Richmond, Virginia. After General McDowell's failure at the First Battle of Bull Run, President Lincoln ordered General **George B. McClellan** to lead the Union army in the east.

The Peninsula Campaign

After taking several months to prepare his forces, McClellan began transporting the troops by ship to the mouth of the James River, southeast of Yorktown, Virginia. From there, he intended to march up the peninsula formed by the James and York Rivers toward Richmond, only 70 miles (113 km) away.

Although popular with the troops, McClellan proved overly cautious and unwilling to attack unless he had overwhelming strength. He took 30 days to capture Yorktown, giving the Confederates time to move their troops into position near Richmond.

As McClellan advanced toward Richmond, he made another mistake. He allowed his forces to become divided by the Chickahominy River. Seizing this opportunity, the Confederate commander, General Joseph E. Johnston, attacked McClellan's army, inflicting heavy casualties. After Johnston was wounded in the battle, General Robert E. Lee was placed in command.

In late June of 1862, Lee began a series of attacks on McClellan's army that became known collectively as the Seven Days' Battle. Although Lee was unable to decisively defeat the Union army, he inflicted heavy casualties and forced McClellan to retreat to the James River. Together, the two sides suffered more than 30,000 casualties. Despite McClellan's protests, Lincoln ordered him to withdraw

Activity: Collaborative Learning

Problem Solving Organize students into two groups and ask them to develop strategies for either side in the Civil War. Groups may need to use library or Internet sources to learn more about military strategies during the Civil War. Suggest that each group create its own maps of the United States and territories at the time of the war. Groups should also create a diagram showing a step-by-step plan that might lead to a speedy victory. Have each group share its strategy for victory. Then have a class discussion about why fighting a defensive war might become a disadvantage for the South. Ask students to explain which side faced the more difficult task and why. **OL**

NATIONAL GEOGRAPHIC The War in the East, 1862–1863

▲ Union troops lay a pontoon bridge across the Rappahannock River in preparation for the assault on Fredericksburg. The battle was a major victory for the South.

▲ The soldiers of the Union Army sit above their encampment at Cumberland Landing during the Peninsula Campaign.

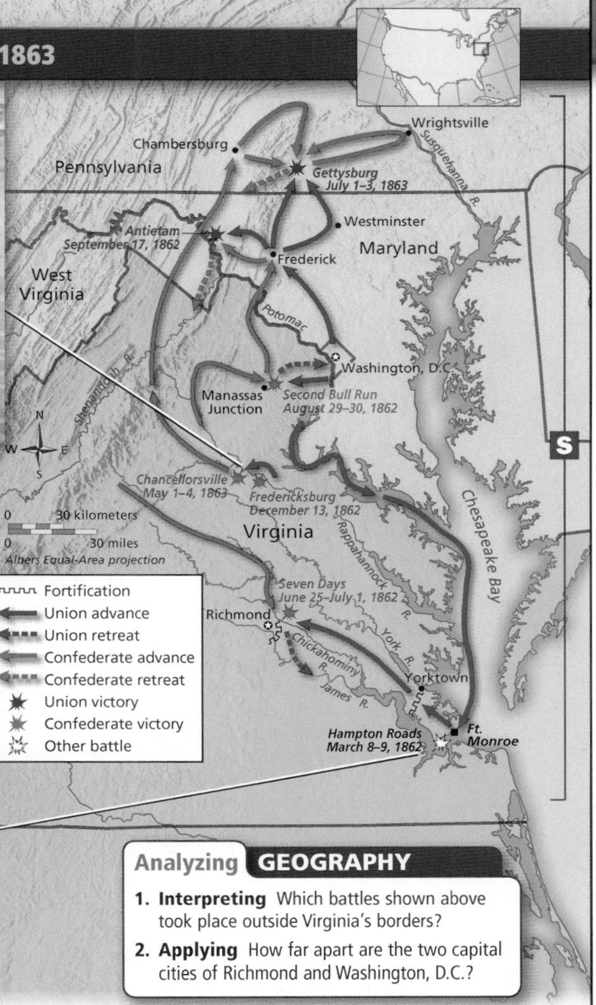

Analyzing GEOGRAPHY

1. **Interpreting** Which battles shown above took place outside Virginia's borders?
2. **Applying** How far apart are the two capital cities of Richmond and Washington, D.C.?

from the peninsula and bring his troops back to Washington.

As McClellan's troops withdrew, Lee decided to attack the Union forces that were defending Washington. The maneuvers by the two sides led to another battle at Bull Run, near Manassas Junction—the site of the first major battle of the war. Again, the South forced the North to retreat, leaving the Confederate forces only 20 miles (32 km) from Washington. Soon after, word arrived at the White House that Lee's forces had crossed into Maryland and begun an invasion of the North.

The Battle of Antietam

Lee decided to invade Maryland for several reasons. Both he and Jefferson Davis believed that an invasion might convince the North to accept the South's independence. They also thought that a victory on Northern soil might help the South win recognition from the British and help the Peace Democrats gain control of Congress in the upcoming elections. By heading north, Lee could also feed his troops from Northern farms and draw Union troops out of Virginia during harvest season.

S Skill Practice

Visual Literacy Have students examine Civil War photographs, sketches, and paintings. Ask them to select an image they find particularly moving. Students can write descriptive paragraphs or poems about the mood or atmosphere of the image. The Library of Congress maintains a Web site containing photographs from the Civil War at http://memory.loc.gov/ammem/cwphtml/cwphome.html. **OL** **BL**

Analyzing GEOGRAPHY

Answers:
1. Gettysburg and Antietam
2. about 100 miles (about 161 km)

Additional Support

Activity: Interdisciplinary Connection

Mathematics Write the following typical organizational structure of Civil War infantry units on the chalkboard: company = 100 soldiers; regiment = 10 companies; brigade = 5 regiments; division = 3 brigades; corps = 3 divisions. **Ask:** How many soldiers make up each military unit (regiment, brigade, division, corps)? How many companies are in a brigade? How many regiments are in a division? How many companies are in a corps? *(regiment = 1,000 soldiers; brigade = 5,000 soldiers; division = 15,000 soldiers; corps = 45,000 soldiers; brigade = 50 companies; division = 15 regiments; corps = 450 companies)* **OL**

Did You Know?

William McKinley
(1843–1901) Future president William McKinley joined the Twenty-Third Ohio Volunteer Infantry when the Civil War broke out. Within a year, he had been promoted to the rank of commissary sergeant (that is, he was in charge of supplying troops with food provisions). During the Battle of Antietam, nineteen-year-old McKinley dodged bullets on the battlefield to take hot coffee and rations to his fellow soldiers. For his courage, he was promoted to the rank of second lieutenant.

Turning Point

Answer:
Students' answers will vary, but students should generally mention that emancipation gave the Union cause an important moral dimension.

Turning Point

▲ *President Lincoln meets General George McClellan (left center, facing Lincoln) after the battle of Antietam.*

◀ *With their backs to Antietam Creek, Union troops under the command of General McClellan attack Confederate positions, September 17, 1862.*

The Battle of Antietam and the Emancipation Proclamation

The Battle of Antietam marked an important turning point in the war. The Union's victory kept Britain from recognizing the Confederacy as a separate nation. If Britain had taken this action, the balance in the struggle might have tipped in favor of the Confederacy. Also, the victory at Antietam and the terribly high casualties brought President Lincoln to the decision that the time had come to end slavery in the South by issuing the Emancipation Proclamation. The Proclamation was the first step toward finally outlawing slavery throughout the United States.

ANALYZING HISTORY How did emancipation change the war? Write a brief essay explaining your opinion.

▲ *Lincoln reads the Emancipation Proclamation to members of his cabinet. Left of Lincoln are Secretary of War Edwin M. Stanton and Secretary of the Treasury Salmon P. Chase. In front of the table sits Secretary of State William Seward.*

For the text of the Emancipation Proclamation, see page R49 in **Documents in American History.**

When he learned that McClellan had been sent after him, Lee ordered his troops to congregate near Sharpsburg, Maryland. Meanwhile, McClellan's troops took positions along Antietam (an•TEE•tuhm) Creek, east of Lee. On September 17, 1862, McClellan ordered his troops to attack.

The Battle of Antietam, the bloodiest one-day battle in the war and in American history, ended with over 6,000 men killed and 16,000 wounded. Although McClellan did not break Lee's lines, he inflicted so many casualties that Lee decided to retreat to Virginia.

The Battle of Antietam was a **crucial** victory for the Union. The British government had been ready to intervene in the war as a mediator if Lee's invasion had succeeded. It had also begun making plans to recognize the Confederacy in the event the North rejected mediation. Lee's defeat at Antietam changed everything. The British decided once again to wait and see how the war progressed, and with this decision the South lost its best chance at gaining international recognition and support. The South's defeat at Antietam had an even greater political impact in the United States. It

Differentiated Instruction

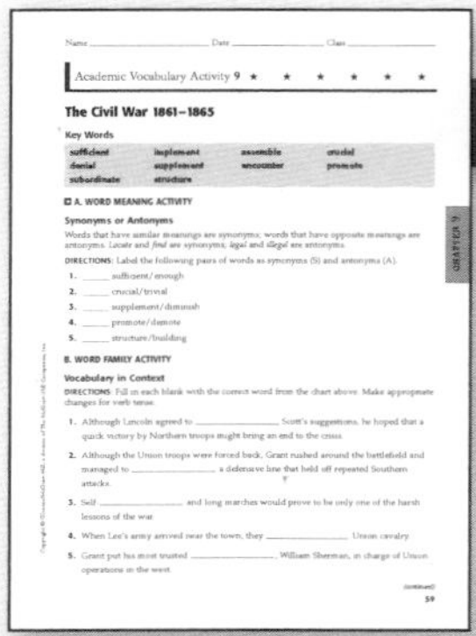

Academic Vocabulary Activity, URB pp. 59–60

The Civil War

Objective: Become familiar with key vocabulary terms.

Focus: Have student volunteers point out how each of the terms listed relates to the Civil War.

Teach: Have students guess the meaning of each term. Have them write their definitions down.

Assess: Students should choose one of the following activities for each key term: create a diagram or image, write a sentence using the term, or "teach" the term to another student.

Close: Revisit students' definitions of the terms.

Differentiated Instruction Strategies

BL Working in pairs, have one student recite the term, while the other writes it correctly.

AL Write a paragraph, *not* about the Civil War, using six of the key terms.

ELL Working with partners who share the same native language, state the key term and its definition in both the native language and English.

convinced Lincoln that the time had come to end slavery in the South.

The Emancipation Proclamation

Although most Democrats opposed any move to end slavery, Republicans were divided on the issue. Many Republicans were strong abolitionists, but others, like Lincoln, did not want to risk losing the loyalty of the slaveholding border states that had chosen to remain in the Union. During the first year of the war, Lincoln had described the conflict as a war to preserve the Union, never as a battle against slavery. In August 1861, for example, General John C. Frémont had declared that all enslaved African Americans who worked for rebels in his region were now free. Worried that Frémont's policy would cost the Union support in border states, such as Kentucky, Lincoln overturned the order and insisted that Union officers could only seize enslaved African Americans who worked directly for Confederate troops.

A year later, however, with Northern casualties rising to staggering levels, many Northerners, including the president, began to conclude that slavery had to end—in part to punish the South and in part to make the soldiers' sacrifices worthwhile. George Julian, a Republican from Indiana, summed up the argument for freeing the slaves in an important speech delivered early in 1862:

PRIMARY SOURCE

"When I say that this rebellion has its source and life in slavery, I only repeat a simple truism. . . . The mere suppression of the rebellion will be an empty mockery of our sufferings and sacrifices, if slavery shall be spared to canker the heart of the nation anew, and repeat its diabolical misdeeds."

—quoted in *Battle Cry of Freedom*

D

As Lee's forces marched toward Antietam, Lincoln said that if the Union could drive those forces from Northern soil, he would issue a proclamation ending slavery. On September 22, 1862, just five days after the battle, Lincoln publicly announced that he would issue the **Emancipation Proclamation**—a decree freeing all enslaved persons in states still in rebellion after January 1, 1863. The Proclamation freed enslaved African Americans only in states at war with the Union. It did not address slavery in the border states. Short of a constitutional amendment, however, Lincoln could not end slavery in the border states, nor did he want to risk losing their loyalty.

The proclamation, by its very existence, transformed the conflict from a war to preserve the Union to a war of liberation. "We shout for joy that we live to record this righteous decree," exulted Frederick Douglass. Abolitionists rejoiced at the announcement, and looked forward to new energy among Union forces. "We were no longer merely the soldiers of a political controversy," recalled Union officer Regis de Trobiand. "We were now the missionaries of a great work of redemption, the armed liberators of millions."

Reading Check **Examining** Why did Lincoln issue the Emancipation Proclamation and what events affected the timing of the proclamation?

Section 2 REVIEW

Vocabulary

1. **Explain** the significance of: "Stonewall" Jackson, bounty, blockade runner, David G. Farragut, Ulysses S. Grant, George B. McClellan, Emancipation Proclamation.

Main Ideas

2. **Explaining** Why did both sides begin to use conscription early in the war?
3. **Paraphrasing** Why did Lincoln refuse to fire Grant after the Battle of Shiloh?
4. **Identifying Central Issues** What was the significance of the Battle of Antietam?

Critical Thinking

5. **Big Ideas** Why was seizing control of the Mississippi River an important strategy of the Union Navy?
6. **Organizing** Use a graphic organizer similar to the one below to explain President Lincoln's reasons for issuing the Emancipation Proclamation and the effects it had on the war.

Reasons for		Emancipation Proclamation		Effect on War
	→		→	

7. **Analyzing Visuals** Examine the painting of the battle between the *Monitor* and the *Virginia* on page 321. What made these vessels superior to regular warships?

Writing About History

8. **Persuasive Writing** Suppose that you are asked to advise President Lincoln about issuing the Emancipation Proclamation. Write a short paper in which you advise him on whether or not to issue it and explain the reasons for your position.

History ONLINE

Study Central™ To review this section, go to glencoe.com and click on Study Central.

D Differentiated Instruction

Verbal/Linguistic Make available to students a copy of the Emancipation Proclamation. Working in pairs, students should choose the portion of the proclamation they think is the most important and rewrite it in their own words. BL ELL

Reading Check

Answer:
Abraham Lincoln began to believe that slavery had to be ended and he wanted to help justify the growing war casualties.

Assess

History ONLINE

Study Central™ provides summaries, interactive games, and online graphic organizers to help students review content.

Close

Assessing Ask students to explain the immediate impact of the Emancipation Proclamation in the North and in the South.

Section 2 REVIEW

Answers

1. All definitions can be found in the section and the Glossary.
2. They both realized that they would need more permanent and better-trained soldiers to fight the war.
3. Possible answer: His statement that Grant "fights" and so could not be spared shows that Lincoln admired Grant for his persistence and hard work.
4. It kept Great Britain from joining the Confederacy at that time when it was poised to do so, and also the Emancipation Proclamation set free all enslaved people in rebel states.
5. It would divide the Confederacy and hurt the cotton trade.
6. Reasons: to help justify the war's sacrifices, to help end slavery. Effects: transformed the war from a conflict over preservation of the Union into a war of liberation.
7. Ironclad vessels were resistant to regular cannon fire and less likely to burn.
8. Students' essays will vary, but should offer specific advice, including a rationale.

Focus

Bellringer

Daily Focus Transparency 9-3

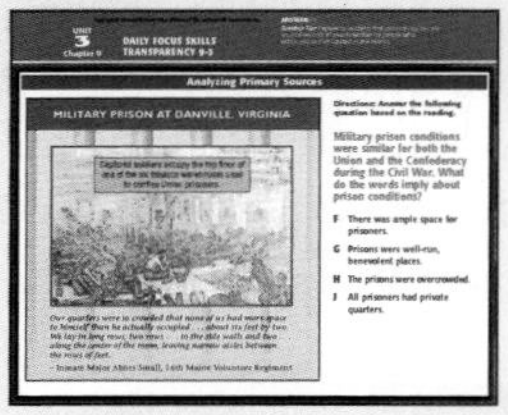

Guide to Reading

Answers:

industry supplied troops with uniforms, munitions, other necessities; innovations in agriculture minimized the effect of the loss of labor as men went off to fight; women filled labor shortages; new sewing machines increased productivity

Section Spotlight Video

To generate student interest and provide a springboard for class discussion, access the Chapter 9, Section 3 video at glencoe.com or on the video DVD.

Section 3

Section Audio | Spotlight Video

Life During the War

Guide to Reading

Big Ideas

Trade, War, and Migration The Civil War brought great suffering and widespread changes to civilians, as well as soldiers, on both sides of the conflict.

Content Vocabulary

- hardtack *(p. 331)*
- prisoner of war *(p. 333)*

Academic Vocabulary

- denial *(p. 331)*
- supplement *(p. 331)*

People and Events to Identify

- 54th Massachusetts *(p. 330)*
- Elizabeth Blackwell *(p. 332)*
- United States Sanitary Commission *(p. 332)*
- Clara Barton *(p. 333)*

Reading Strategy

Organizing Complete a graphic organizer similar to the one below to list the reasons that the North experienced a wartime economic boom.

Reason for North's Economic Boom

While the economic hardships of the Civil War began to wear down the morale of Southerners, the North experienced an economic boom. Life for soldiers in the field was difficult; medical treatment was primitive, and conditions in prison camps were horrific.

The Wartime Economies

MAIN Idea While the South suffered inflation and food shortages, the North prospered during the war.

HISTORY AND YOU Do you know anyone who experienced rationing during World War II? Read on to learn how the South struggled to produce enough food.

Pressed by the costs of the war, both the North and the South struggled to keep their economies working. The South, with few financial resources and little industry, suffered more from wartime inflation and critical shortages. In contrast, the North, supported by banks and industries, responded quickly to the demands of the war.

Southern Shortages, Falling Morale

By the end of 1862, the South's economy had begun to suffer from the war. The collapse of the South's transportation system, the blockade of Southern ports, and the presence of Union troops in several important agricultural regions led to severe food shortages during the winter of 1862–1863.

Southerners began to question the sacrifices they were being called upon to make—or to demand of others. Hearing of the hardships faced by their families, many Confederate soldiers deserted and returned home to help.

In the spring of 1863, Southern food shortages led to riots. In several communities, mobs of women armed with knives and guns marched into shops to seize food. In the Confederate capital, Richmond, several hundred women broke into shops, yelling, "Bread! Bread!" and then began to loot the stores for food, clothing, shoes, and other goods. The riot finally ended when Jefferson Davis sent troops to confront the mob and order the rioters to disperse.

The Union's War Boom

In contrast, the North experienced an economic boom because of the war. Its growing industries supplied the troops with uniforms, munitions, and other necessities.

Resource Manager

R Reading Strategies	C Critical Thinking	D Differentiated Instruction	W Writing Support	S Skill Practice
Teacher Edition • Interpreting, p. 330 **Additional Resources** • Pri. Source Read., URB p. 67 • Guided Reading, URB p. 80	**Additional Resources** • Crit. Think. Skills Act., URB p. 62 • Quizzes and Tests, p. 121	**Additional Resources** • Diff. Instr. Act., URB p. 53	**Teacher Edition** • Descriptive Writing, p. 331	**Teacher Edition** • Drawing a Graph, p. 330 **Additional Resources** • Read. Essen., p. 102

PRIMARY SOURCE

Life on the Home Front

The Civil War affected people other than soldiers. It changed the economy for people on the home front, required women to take on new jobs, and led to civil unrest as well.

▲ *The Union Army's requirements led to an economic boom in the North. These factory workers were hired by the Union to make wagon wheels.*

▲ *Opposition to the draft led to riots in New York in July 1863. Local military police fired on the rioters to stop the violence.*

▲ *Women helped produce goods needed for the war effort. While most worked on their farms, others went to work in factories to produce goods for the war effort. Above, women work in a munitions factory in Massachusetts.*

Analyzing VISUALS

1. **Explaining** How did the war help the economy of the North?
2. **Describing** What kinds of social changes did the war cause?

The expanded use of mechanized reapers and mowers made farming possible with fewer workers, many of whom were women. One missionary in Iowa in late 1862 commented that he "met more women driving teams on the road and saw more at work in the fields than men."

Women also filled labor shortages in various industries. New sewing machines greatly increased the productivity of seamstresses. As more women entered the textile industry, the North produced an abundance of uniforms for its soldiers.

The North, however, also experienced episodes of mob violence. In 1863 riots broke out across the North over the Union's new conscription legislation. In March of that year, Congress had passed the Union Conscription Act, making all healthy males aged 20 to 45 eligible for military service. However, if a man could find a replacement or pay a $300 fee, he did not have to serve. This meant that wealthy men were able to buy their way out of fighting in the war. In New York City, the most infamous of the draft riots occurred over four days in July. Rioters, mainly recent immigrants from Ireland and Germany, killed about 100 people and destroyed over $1 million worth of property. Militia regiments had to be called away from the war to restore order.

History ONLINE
Student Web Activity Visit glencoe.com and complete the activity on Civil War letters.

Reading Check **Explaining** What were the effects of food shortages on the South?

Teach

Analyzing VISUALS

Answers:
1. The needs of the Union army for supplies created increased demand for goods and provided many jobs.
2. The war led to unrest as riots occurred over the draft, but it also provided new opportunities for women to work in positions that had been closed to them previously.

Reading Check

Answer:
Food shortages hurt morale as people began to question the sacrifices they were being asked to make and caused desertions as soldiers wanted to return home to help their families survive.

Hands-On Chapter Project
Step 3

Chronicling the Lives of Southerners and Northerners

Step 3: War Societies Essential Question: What was life like for Northerners or Southerners during the war? Write the essential question on the board to help students focus their research.

Directions Divide the class into the teams determined in Step 1. Each team will meet to develop a plan and divide up research responsibilities. Teams will research the lives of ordinary Southerners or Northerners during the war. Students should focus on the economy, the morale of the population, and daily life.

Synthesizing Information Students will synthesize their research by creating 1 to 3 pages of a Civil War diary. Note that each team will create their own pages—those for Southerners and those for Northerners. **OL** *(Chapter Project continued on page 337)*

R Reading Strategy

Interpreting Have students closely read the quote from Frederick Douglass on page 330. **Ask:** How does this quote relate to the Dred Scott decision? *(According to the Supreme Court's ruling in* Dred Scott v. Sandford *(1857), African Americans were not citizens of the United States and, thus, had no rights under the U.S. Constitution.)* **OL**

S Skill Practice

Drawing a Graph Have students draw a pair of circle graphs showing the percentage of African Americans in the Union army and Union navy. **BL** **ELL**

Reading Check

Answer:
Answers will vary. A possible answer is that African Americans saw volunteering to fight in the war as a way to ensure their freedom from enslavement.

Additional Support

African Americans in the Military

MAIN Idea Many African Americans eagerly enlisted in the Union war effort.

HISTORY AND YOU Do you know anyone who joined the military after September 11, 2001? Read how the Emancipation Proclamation inspired African Americans to join the Union forces.

The Emancipation Proclamation officially permitted African Americans to enlist in the Union forces. Almost immediately, thousands of African Americans, including Frederick Douglass's two sons, Charles and Lewis, rushed to join the military. Douglass approved; he believed serving in the military would help African Americans overcome discrimination:

PRIMARY SOURCE

R "Once let the black man get upon his person the brass letters U.S.; let him get an eagle on his button, and a musket on his shoulder and bullets in his pocket, and there is no power on earth which can deny that he has earned the right to citizenship."

—quoted in *Battle Cry of Freedom*

About 180,000 African Americans served in the Union army during the Civil War, roughly 9 percent of the army's total soldiers. Another 10,000 to 15,000 served in the Union navy. S

Among the first African American regiments organized in the North was the **54th Massachusetts.** The regiment fought valiantly at Fort Wagner near Charleston Harbor in July 1863, losing nearly half of its soldiers in the battle. "Men all around me would fall and roll down the slope into the ditch," remembered Lewis Douglass. "Swept down like chaff, still our men went on and on." The *New York Tribune* applauded the regiment's achievement:

PRIMARY SOURCE

". . . if this Massachusetts Fifty-Fourth had faltered when its trial came, two hundred thousand [African Americans] for whom it was a pioneer would never have been put into the field. . . . But it did not falter. It made Fort Wagner such a name to [African Americans] as Bunker Hill has been for ninety years to white Yankees."

—from *Like Men of War*

Reading Check **Analyzing** Why might African Americans have wanted to fight in the Civil War?

PRIMARY SOURCE
African Americans Fight for the Union

The bravery of African American units, such as the 54th Massachusetts Regiment, demonstrated that they could fight as well as white soldiers, and, in the long term, it may have helped to overcome discrimination.

African American servicemen, such as the sailors of the USS Vermont (above) and the members of Fourth Colored Regiment (left), fought bravely for the Union. African Americans made up about 9 percent of the Union army and nearly 12 percent of the Union navy.

330 Chapter 9 The Civil War

Activity: Interdisciplinary Connection

Daily Life Have students conduct research using library or Internet resources to find primary sources such as letters, diary entries, or contemporary newspaper and magazine articles that shed light on what life was like in the army and navy for African Americans during the Civil War. Direct students to share what they find in class in short oral summaries. You may want to ask student volunteers to read excerpts from the primary sources they found. Use the information as a springboard for a class discussion about the pros and cons of serving under such circumstances. **OL** **AL**

Military Life

MAIN Idea Soldiers suffered physical hardship and women provided medical assistance.

HISTORY AND YOU You probably know that it is important to clean and sanitize a wound. Read to learn how doctors performed surgery during the Civil War.

Early in the war, General Irwin McDowell's troops stopped to pick berries and foolishly wasted water from their canteens to wash them. "They were not used to denying themselves much; they were not used to journeys on foot," McDowell later reflected. Self-**denial** and long marches would prove to be only the first of the harsh realities of the war.

The Soldiers in the Field

Union and Confederate soldiers suffered many hardships during the long days and weeks between battles. Some Southern soldiers had to sleep without blankets and tramp the roads shoeless. Union soldier Elisha Rhodes wrote home that "all that we have to eat is the cattle killed by the way. No bread or salt in the Regiment and I am most starved."

For the Union soldier, meals often consisted of **hardtack** (a hard biscuit made of wheat flour), potatoes, and beans, flavored at times with dried salt pork (pork fat cured in salty brine). Confederate bread was usually made of cornmeal instead of wheat. Whenever possible, soldiers **supplemented** their diet with fruit or vegetables seized or purchased from farms they passed.

Battlefield Medicine

When Americans went to war in 1861, most were not prepared for the horrors of battle. "The sights and smells that assailed us were simply indescribable," wrote one Southern soldier. "Corpses were swollen to twice their size, some actually burst asunder. . . . The odors were so deadly that in a short time we all sickened [and] . . . most of us [were] vomiting profusely."

The Civil War produced huge numbers of casualties, and doctors struggled to tend to the wounded. In the mid-1800s doctors had little understanding of infection and germs. They used the same unsterilized instruments on all patients and, as a result, infection spread quickly in the field hospitals.

The Battle of Fort Wagner

On July 18 the Union tried to capture Fort Wagner with the 54th Massachusetts, one of the first African American regiments. Although they did not capture the fort, their valor and willingness to die for the Union underscored the worth of African American soldiers to the Union.

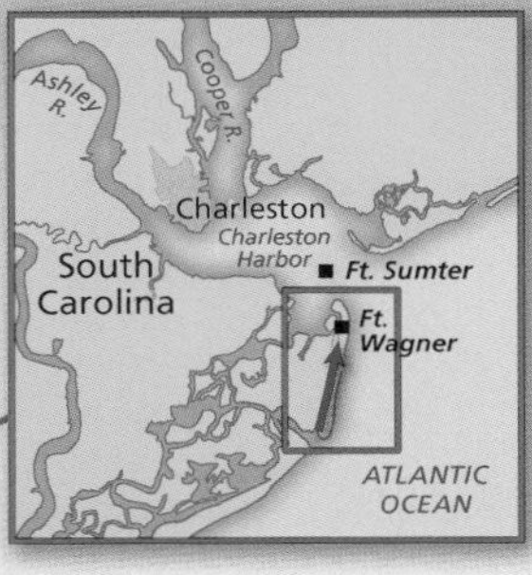

Analyzing VISUALS

1. **Identifying** Who mainly made up the 54th Massachusetts?
2. **Explaining** How did African American troops contribute to the success of the Union in the Civil War?

W

W Writing Support

Descriptive Writing Have students imagine themselves as a soldier in the 54th Massachusetts regiment. **Ask:** What does it mean to you to participate in the war? What are your goals as a soldier and free African American? *(Students' answers will vary.)* OL

Did You Know?

Medical Schools Prior to the Civil War, there were only a few medical schools in the United States. Many doctors served only an apprenticeship and those who attended medical school trained for less than two years.

Analyzing VISUALS

Answers:

1. free African American volunteers
2. Units proved the worth of African American troops to the Union cause, and they volunteered in large numbers, which gave the Union a further advantage in troop numbers over the South.

Additional Support

Activity: Interdisciplinary Connection

Health Ask a health care professional to speak to the class about first aid and infection prevention. Have students recall what they have learned, and describe to the professional some of the unsanitary conditions that existed in battlefield hospitals during the Civil War. Then ask the health care professional to describe how modern facilities and techniques would have prevented many of the diseases and infections (and amputations and deaths) that occurred during the Civil War. OL BL

Did You Know?

Mary Ann Bickerdyke (1817–1901) Ohio native Mary Ann Bickerdyke took the lead in improving conditions and care for injured and sick soldiers. Under her direction, about 300 field hospitals were built. In her tireless fight to improve sanitary conditions, she earned the respect of Generals Grant and Sherman, as well as common soldiers.

Analyzing VISUALS

Answers:

1. Hospitals were dirty, crowded, and unsanitary. Disease and infections spread easily, leading to more deaths and amputations.
2. Women took a direct role in caring for the sick and wounded as nurses. Elizabeth Blackwell established the U.S. Sanitary Commission to provide medical assistance and supplies to hospitals.

Additional Support

PRIMARY SOURCE

Nurses and Field Hospitals

▲ *Soldiers wounded at the Battle of the Wilderness in 1864 rest at a Fredericksburg hospital.*

▲ *Nurses and doctors of the U.S. Sanitary Commission stand outside their hospital in Fredericksburg, Virginia, 1864. The Commission was started by Dr. Elizabeth Blackwell.*

▲ *Thousands of women, such as Union nurse Anne Bell, volunteered to care for wounded soldiers during the war.*

Analyzing VISUALS DBQ

1. **Explaining** What were the conditions in Civil War field hospitals?
2. **Describing** What medical role did women play during the war?

Disease was one of the greatest threats facing Civil War soldiers. In many cases, regiments lost half their men to illness. Crowded together in army camps, drinking from unsanitary water supplies, many soldiers became sick. Smallpox, dysentery, typhoid, and pneumonia killed thousands of soldiers.

Battlefield physicians also used extreme measures in treating casualties. Faced with appalling wounds, doctors often amputated arms and legs to prevent gangrene and other infections from spreading. General Carl Schurz described the scene in a field hospital:

PRIMARY SOURCE

"As a wounded man was lifted on the table, often shrieking with pain . . . the surgeon quickly examined the wound and resolved upon cutting off the wounded limb. Some ether was administered. . . . The surgeon snatched the knife from between his teeth, where it had been while his hands were busy, wiped it rapidly once or twice across his blood-stained apron, and the cutting began. The operation accomplished, the surgeon would look around with a deep sigh, and then—'Next!'"

—quoted in *The Civil War*

Women Serve As Nurses

Women helped the war effort at home by managing family farms and businesses. On the battlefield, women made dramatic contributions to the Civil War by serving as nurses. Before the war, most army nurses had been men. Inspired by the famous British nurse Florence Nightingale, American women took on many of the nursing tasks in Civil War army hospitals.

In 1861 **Elizabeth Blackwell,** the first female physician in the United States, started the nation's first training program for nurses. Her work led to the creation of the **United States Sanitary Commission,** an organization that provided medical assistance and supplies to army camps and hospitals. Tens of thousands of women

Activity: Technology Connection

Identifying Points of View The Internet provides access to an abundance of primary material related to the Civil War, including personal diaries and letters. Direct students to explore the primary sources available at the Library of Congress's Web site at http://www.loc.gov/exhibits/treasures/tr11b.html#civil. Ask students to select one letter or diary passage and write a one-page expository essay explaining that individual's attitude toward the war and experiences during wartime. Have students share their essays with the class. AL volunteered to work for the Commission, and raised money to send bandages, medicine, clothing, and food to army camps.

Not all women helping at the front lines were members of the Sanitary Commission. On her own, **Clara Barton** left her job in a patent office to nurse soldiers on the battlefield. With her face sometimes bluish with gunpowder, Barton fed the sick, bandaged the wounded, and even dug out bullets with her own small knife.

Although Southern women were encouraged to stay at home and support the troops by making bandages and other supplies, many founded small hospitals or braved the horrors of the battlefield. Kate Cumming of Mobile, Alabama, served as a nurse following the Battle of Shiloh. In her diary she vividly described a makeshift hospital:

PRIMARY SOURCE

"Nothing that I had ever heard or read had given me the faintest idea of the horrors witnessed here. . . . The men are lying all over the house. . . . The foul air from this mass of human beings at first made me giddy and sick, but I soon got over it. . . . "

—quoted in *Battle Cry of Freedom*

The Civil War was a turning point for the nursing profession. The courage and energy of the women also helped to break down the belief that women were weaker than men.

Military Prisons

The horrors of the battlefield and danger of disease were not the only hardships endured by soldiers during the Civil War. **Prisoners of war**—soldiers captured by the enemy in battle—also suffered terribly during the conflict.

Early in the war, the United States and the Confederacy held formal prisoner exchanges. After Lincoln issued the Emancipation Proclamation, however, the Confederacy announced that it would not exchange freed African Americans for Southern white prisoners. Instead, it would either re-enslave or execute all African American troops captured in battle.

In response to the South's treatment of African American troops, Lincoln stopped all prisoner exchanges. As a result, both the North and the South found themselves with large and growing numbers of prisoners of war. Taking care of them proved difficult, especially in the South. While conditions were bad in Northern prisons, the South could not even feed their prisoners adequately because of food shortages.

The most infamous prison in the South, Andersonville in Georgia, had no shade or shelter. Exposure, overcrowding, lack of food, and disease killed more than 100 men per day during the sweltering summer of 1864. In all, 13,000 of the 45,000 prisoners sent to Andersonville died there. After the war, Henry Wirz, Andersonville's commandant, became the only person executed for war crimes during the Civil War.

Reading Check **Summarizing** What medical problems did Union and Confederate soldiers face?

Section 3 REVIEW

Vocabulary

1. **Explain** the significance of: 54th Massachusetts, hardtack, Elizabeth Blackwell, United States Sanitary Commission, Clara Barton, prisoner of war.

Main Ideas

2. **Determining Cause and Effect** What was the cause of rioting in the North during the Civil War?
3. **Explaining** Why was the performance of the 54th Massachusetts significant for African Americans?
4. **Organizing** Complete a graphic organizer similar to the one below by listing the contributions of women during the Civil War.

Critical Thinking

5. **Big Ideas** How did the Emancipation Proclamation affect African Americans in the military?
6. **Analyzing Visuals** Examine the photographs of battlefield hospitals on page 332. Why do you think infections spread so easily in these hospitals, resulting in numerous deaths from disease, rather than from battle wounds?

Writing About History

7. **Descriptive Writing** Suppose that you are a nurse on one of the battlefields during the Civil War. Write a journal entry describing the conditions of the soldiers and your reaction to the situation.

History ONLINE
Study Central™ To review this section, go to glencoe.com and click on Study Central.

Reading Check

Answer:
infections, small pox, dysentery, typhoid, pneumonia, and amputations when limbs might have been saved to prevent gangrene

Assess

History ONLINE

Study Central™ provides summaries, interactive games, and online graphic organizers to help students review content.

Close

Drawing Conclusions Point out that the Civil War was the bloodiest conflict in United States history, resulting in the most American casualties. **Ask:** Why were American casualties so high? *(Americans fought against Americans; primitive medical care and facilities.)* **OL**

Section 3 REVIEW

Answers

1. All definitions can be found in the section and the Glossary.
2. unfair draft legislation passed by Congress in 1863
3. If the 54th had performed badly, then it is possible that African Americans would not have been allowed to participate in combat, but their heroic behavior made it clear that African Americans could make good soldiers.
4. worked as battlefield nurses, managed farms and businesses, volunteered, raised money
5. It officially permitted African Americans to enlist in the Union's armed forces.
6. Doctors had little understanding of infectious germs and they used the same unsterilized instruments on patient after patient. Also, conditions were crowded, nutrition was poor, and water supplies were unclean.
7. Students' entries will vary, but should include descriptions and reactions.

ANALYZING PRIMARY SOURCES

Focus

When Abraham Lincoln ran for president in 1860, he promised he would not interfere with the institution of slavery in the Southern states. Rather the political debate centered on the *spread* of slavery into western territories. Although he believed slavery was morally wrong, he questioned whether he had the legal authority to deprive Southern slaveholders of their "property" without compensation or due process.

Teach

C Critical Thinking

Interpreting Have students read the text of the Emancipation Proclamation located on page R49 in Documents in American History. **Ask:** **Why did the proclamation not immediately end slavery in the South?** *(The proclamation did not affect slavery in the loyal border states and had little immediate impact on slavery in Southern states that were outside of Union control.)* OL

Additional Support

ANALYZING PRIMARY SOURCES

The Emancipation Proclamation

The secession of the Southern states was prompted by fears that the institution of slavery was under attack. The Civil War, however, began as a battle over the question of the right of the Southern states to secede. When Abraham Lincoln decided to issue the Emancipation Proclamation, he put ending slavery at the heart of the Union effort. In doing so, he changed the meaning of the war. The proclamation was the first bold step in the abolition of slavery throughout the nation.

Study these primary sources and answer the questions that follow.

PRIMARY SOURCE 1

Political Speech, 1861

"[The Confederate States of America's] constitution has put at rest, *forever*, all the agitating questions relating to our peculiar institution—African slavery as it exists among us—the proper *status* of the negro in our form of civilization. . . . The prevailing ideas entertained by . . . most of the leading statesmen at the time of the formation of the old constitution, were that the enslavement of the African was in violation of the laws of nature; that it was wrong in *principle*, socially, morally, and politically. . . .

Our new government is founded upon exactly the opposite idea; its foundations are laid, its corner-stone rests, upon the great truth that the negro is not equal to the white man; that slavery—subordination to the superior race—is his natural and normal condition."

—Alexander H. Stephens, vice president of the Confederate States of America, March 21, 1861

PRIMARY SOURCE 2

Political Cartoon, 1864

▼ "Lincoln Writing the Emancipation Proclamation," by Adalbert J. Volck

PRIMARY SOURCE 3

Political Speech, 1862

"Mr. Speaker . . . the people of the loyal States . . . know that slavery lies at the bottom of all our troubles. They know that but for this curse this horrid revolt against liberty and law would not have occurred. They know that all the unutterable agonies of our many battle-fields, all the terrible sorrows which rend so many thousands of loving hearts, all the ravages and desolation of this stupendous conflict, are to be charged to slavery. They know that its barbarism has molded the leaders of this rebellion into the most atrocious scoundrels of the nineteenth century. . . . What I said on this floor in January last, I repeat now, that the mere suppression of this rebellion will be an empty mockery of our sufferings and sacrifices, if slavery shall be spared to canker the heart of the nation anew, and repeat its diabolical deeds."

—Representative George W. Julian of Indiana in the U.S. House of Representatives, May 23, 1862

Activity: Collaborative Learning

Defending Points of View Organize students into two groups. Have students read Greeley's letter and Lincoln's response in Primary Source 4. Discuss with students Lincoln's purpose with regards to slavery and the Union. Then discuss why, according to Greeley, you cannot preserve the Union without striking down slavery. Instruct one group to come up with arguments in support of Greeley's position. The other group will develop a set of arguments to support Lincoln's position. Students may need to use the textbook or library or Internet resources to learn more about the issue. Once both groups are ready, have them defend their position in a class debate. OL

PRIMARY SOURCE 4

Letters, 1862

"To Abraham Lincoln, president of the United States:

". . . On the face of this wide earth, Mr. President, there is not one disinterested, determined, intelligent champion of the Union cause who does not feel that all attempts to put down the Rebellion, and at the same time uphold its inciting cause, are preposterous and futile—that the Rebellion, if crushed out tomorrow, would be renewed within a year if Slavery were left in full vigor—that Army officers who remain to this day devoted to Slavery can at best be but halfway loyal to the Union—and that every hour of deference to Slavery is an hour of added and deepened peril to the Union."

—Horace Greeley, editor of the *New York Tribune*, August, 19, 1862

"Dear Sir—

". . . If there be those who would not save the Union unless they could at the same time save slavery, I do not agree with them—If there be those who would not save the Union unless they could at the same time destroy slavery, I do not agree with them.

"My paramount object in this struggle is to save the Union, and is not either to save or destroy slavery—If I could save the Union without freeing any slave, I would do it; and if I could save it by freeing all the slaves, I would do it; and if I could do it by freeing some and leaving others alone, I would also do that."

—Abraham Lincoln's response, August 22, 1862

PRIMARY SOURCE 5

Political Cartoon, 1864

▼ "President Lincoln Writing the Proclamation of Freedom," by Daniel G. Blythe

PRIMARY SOURCE 6

Letter, 1863

"My dear Sir—

". . . After the commencement of hostilities I struggled nearly a year and a half to get along without touching the 'institution' [of slavery]; and when finally I conditionally determined to touch it, I gave a hundred days fair notice of my purpose, to all the States and people, within which time they could have turned it wholly aside, by simply again becoming good citizens of the United States. They chose to disregard it, and I made the peremptory proclamation on what appeared to me to be a military necessity. And being made, it must stand. As to the States not included in it, of course they can have their rights in the Union as of old. Even the people of the states included, if they choose, need not to be hurt by it. Let them adopt systems of apprenticeship . . . conforming substantially to the most approved plans of gradual emancipation; and, with the aid they can have from the general government, they may be nearly as well off, in this respect, as if the present trouble had not occurred, and much better off than they can possibly be if the contest continues persistently."

—Abraham Lincoln, letter to Major General John A. McClernand, January 8, 1863

W

DBQ Document-Based Questions

1. **Summarizing** According to Alexander H. Stephens's speech in Source 1, how does the government of the Confederacy differ from that of the Union?
2. **Contrasting** Study the images in Sources 2 and 5. What views of the Emancipation Proclamation do they present? How is Abraham Lincoln portrayed?
3. **Assessing** In Source 3, why does Representative George W. Julian believe the war must put an end to slavery?
4. **Contrasting** Read the letters in Source 4 and Source 6. How do the positions of Horace Greeley and Abraham Lincoln toward ending slavery differ? How does Lincoln's position change over time?

W Writing Support

Expository Writing Invite students to write a short essay about public reactions to the Emancipation Proclamation. Have students use library and Internet resources to locate primary sources such as newspaper articles, journal entries, or letters written in late 1862 and early 1863. Encourage them to include quotations from these primary sources in their essay. AL

Assess

Assign the Document-Based Questions as homework or as an in-class activity and then discuss student responses as a group.

Close

Discuss the following statement made by American historian Henry Adams while he was in London in 1863: "The Emancipation Proclamation has done more for us here than all our former victories and all our diplomacy. It is creating an almost convulsive reaction in our favor." OL

DBQ Document Based Questions

Answers:

1. U.S. constitution avoids issue of slavery because the Founders thought it was wrong. Confederacy is based on slavery and the belief that the enslavement of African Americans is "natural and normal."
2. Source 2: Lincoln surrounded by evil symbols, looks possessed/maniacal, stepping on book, possibly a law book. Picture of a slave riot is in background. Source 5: Lincoln is in room with Bible and Constitution at hand. Flag is in the background; bust of Andrew Jackson (strong unionist) on mantle and bust of James Buchanan (weak leader preceding Civil War) hanging in background.
3. Slavery is the underlying cause of the war; to end the war without ending slavery will mean lives lost were wasted and the country will end up getting into another war on same unresolved issue.
4. Greeley: ending the war without ending slavery will be a worthless victory. Lincoln: saving the Union is the most important issue, the decision whether to leave slavery alone or end slavery matters only so far as it would help or hinder the decision to save the Union. According to the letter, Lincoln's attitude really did not change, he issued the proclamation as a "military necessity" to undermine the Confederacy.

Focus

Bellringer

Daily Focus Transparency 9-4

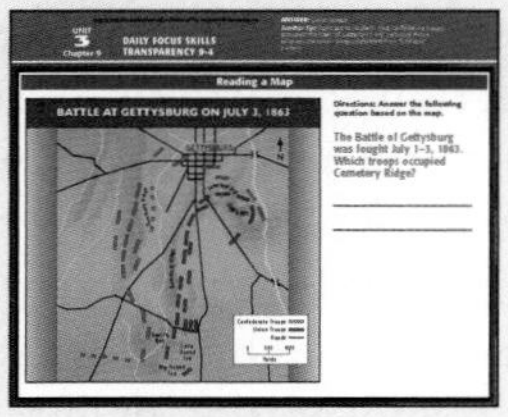

Guide to Reading

Answers:

Vicksburg	Union victory cut South in two
Chancellorsville	Confederate victory
Gettysburg	Union victory and turning point of the war
Chickamauga Creek	Confederate victory
Missionary Ridge	Union victory, fall of Chattanooga

Section Spotlight Video

To generate student interest and provide a springboard for class discussion, access the Chapter 9, Section 4 video at glencoe.com or on the video DVD.

Resource Manager

Section 4 — Section Audio — Spotlight Video

The Turning Point

Guide to Reading

Big Ideas

Geography and History The Union victory at Vicksburg cut the Confederacy in two.

Content Vocabulary

- forage *(p. 337)*
- siege *(p. 337)*

Academic Vocabulary

- encounter *(p. 339)*
- promote *(p. 341)*

People and Events to Identify

- Ambrose Burnside *(p. 338)*
- Joseph Hooker *(p. 338)*
- George Meade *(p. 339)*
- Gettysburg *(p. 339)*
- Pickett's Charge *(p. 339)*
- William Tecumseh Sherman *(p. 341)*

Reading Strategy

Categorizing Complete a graphic organizer to record the results of the listed battles that shaped the Union victory.

Battle	Results
Vicksburg	
Chancellorsville	
Gettysburg	
Chickamauga Creek	
Missionary Ridge	

For a while, the North floundered under a series of generals who were overly cautious or intimidated by the reputation of General Robert E. Lee. The tide of the war began to turn after the North won pivotal victories at Vicksburg and Gettysburg.

Vicksburg Falls

MAIN Idea General Grant captured Vicksburg, thus gaining control of the Mississippi River and dividing the South.

HISTORY AND YOU How long do you think you could go hungry to defend a cause? Read how Confederate soldiers surrendered after their food supply was cut off.

In April 1862, Admiral David G. Farragut captured New Orleans and secured control of the Mississippi River delta for the Union. Later that year, General Ulysses S. Grant seized control of the river as far south as Memphis after his victory at Shiloh. Despite these successes, there remained one major Confederate stronghold on the river—Vicksburg, Mississippi.

"Vicksburg is the key," Lincoln said. "The war can never be brought to a close until the key is in our pocket." If Grant could take Vicksburg, the Confederacy would be cut in two. If not, as Lincoln commented, the earlier victories in the west would make little difference: "We can take all the northern ports of the Confederacy, and they can still defy us from Vicksburg. It means hog and hominy without limit, fresh troops from the States of the far South, and a cotton country where they can raise the staple without interference."

Grierson's Raid

The city of Vicksburg was located on the east bank of the Mississippi River. At first, Grant tried to approach the city from the north, but the land was too swampy, and the rivers in the area were covered with vegetation and blocked by trees. To get at Vicksburg, Grant decided to move his troops across the Mississippi to the west bank and then march south. Once he was past the city, he intended to cross back to the east bank and attack the city from the south.

To distract the Confederates while he carried out this difficult maneuver, Grant ordered Colonel Benjamin Grierson to take 1,700 cavalry troops on a raid through Mississippi. Grierson's forces traveled 600 miles (965 km) in two weeks, tearing up railroads, burning depots, and fighting skirmishes. His raid enabled Grant to move his troops south of the city.

R Reading Strategies	C Critical Thinking	D Differentiated Instruction	W Writing Support	S Skill Practice
Teacher Edition • Outlining, p. 338 • Determining Importance, p. 341 **Additional Resources** • Guided Reading, URB p. 81	**Additional Resources** • History Simulations, URB p. 9 • Quizzes and Tests, p. 121	**Additional Resources** • Am. Art & Music Act., URB p. 69 • Enrich. Act., URB p. 75	**Additional Resources** • Geo and History, URB p. 3	**Teacher Edition** • Visual Literacy, p. 337 • Using Geography Skills, p. 339 **Additional Resources** • Read. Essen., p. 105

PRIMARY SOURCE

The Siege of Vicksburg

▲ *Union ironclads commanded by Rear Admiral David Porter sealed off Vicksburg's access to the Mississippi and bombarded the city's defenses.*

During the siege of Vicksburg, Union troops dug 13 "approach trenches" along their lines, allowing them to get close to the Confederate fortifications. In the meantime, the gunboats bombarded the city. The city was unable to receive food and other supplies. The city surrendered on July 4, 1863.

Grant Closes in on Vicksburg, March–July 1863

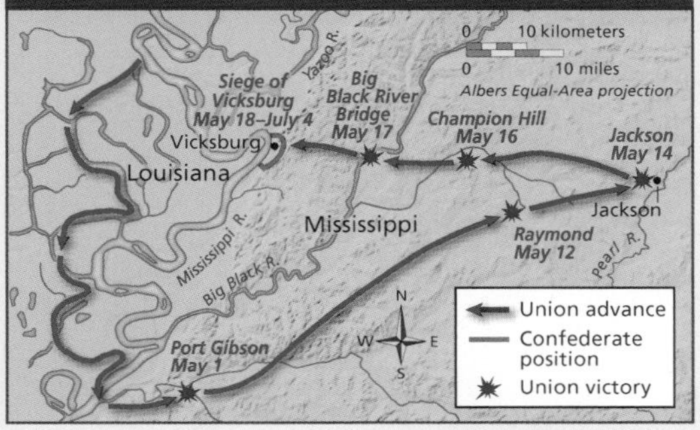

Analyzing VISUALS DBQ

1. **Describing** How did the Union work to break down the defenses at Vicksburg?
2. **Making Inferences** At Vicksburg, the siege was successful, but under what circumstances might a siege be risky for the attackers?

The Siege of Vicksburg

After returning to the east bank of the Mississippi River, Grant embarked on a daring march east, ordering his troops to live off the country. **Foraging**—or searching and raiding for food—as they marched, Grant's troops headed east into Mississippi. They captured the town of Jackson before turning back west toward Vicksburg. Grant's troops marched an astonishing 180 miles (290 km) in 17 days, fought 5 battles, and inflicted 7,200 casualties on the Confederates. The march ended by driving the Confederate forces back into their defenses at Vicksburg.

In May 1863 Grant launched two assaults on Vicksburg, but the city's defenders repulsed both attacks and inflicted high casualties. Grant decided that the only way to take the city was to put it under **siege**—to cut off its food and supplies and bombard it until its defenders gave up. The siege of Vicksburg lasted for six weeks, with Confederate troops and the city's residents facing near-starvation. On July 4, 1863, the Confederate commander at Vicksburg surrendered. The Union victory had cut the Confederacy in two.

Reading Check **Explaining** Why did President Lincoln want the Union army to capture Vicksburg?

Teach

S

S Skill Practice

Visual Literacy Have students study the two paintings of the siege of Vicksburg. Ask students to write a brief descriptive essay based upon the images and explain how Union troops forced Vicksburg to surrender. AL

Analyzing VISUALS

Answers:

1. The Union surrounded Vicksburg, dug approach trenches and bombarded the city.
2. If a siege takes too long, it is possible for enemy troops to come to the city's rescue and attack the besiegers from the rear. The troops outside may have to abandon a siege to fight elsewhere.

Reading Check

Answer:
to cut the South in two and control the Mississippi River

Hands-On Chapter Project Step 4

Chronicling the Lives of Southerners and Northerners

Step 4: Later Battles of the War
Essential Question: How did life change for Southerners and Northerners in the final days of the war? Write the essential question on the board to help students focus their research.

Directions Divide the class into the teams determined in Step 1. Each team will meet to develop a plan and divide up research responsibilities. Teams will research how the lives of Southerners and Northerners changed during the final months of the war. Students may choose to focus on either the lives of civilians or the lives of soldiers.

Synthesizing Information Students will synthesize their research by creating 1 to 3 pages of a Civil War diary. Note that each team will create their own pages—those for Southerners and those for Northerners. OL *(Chapter Project continued on page 345)*

R Reading Strategy

Outlining As students read The Road to Gettysburg, have them take notes using the headings found in the text. Students may want to use an outline to help them organize the information. Remind students that although they do not have to write complete sentences, they should be able to understand what they have written. After students read the section, ask questions about what they have read. Students should use their notes to help answer the questions. **BL** **ELL**

Did You Know?

Military Terms The Civil War was the first war in which strictly military terms were passed into widespread usage. Many of these terms are still used in common speech today, including: *K.P.* (kitchen police), *AWOL* (absent without leave), *pup tents* (originally known as dog tents), and *shoddy* (uniforms made from recycled woolen fibers known as shoddy, which came to denote any article of inferior quality.)

R The Road to Gettysburg

MAIN Idea Gettysburg was the bloodiest battle of the war and the last time the Confederates invaded the North.

HISTORY AND YOU Have you read the Gettysburg Address? Read on to learn about the battle that inspired one of the greatest speeches in American history.

Shortly after General McClellan's victory at Antietam, Lincoln became frustrated with him. At Antietam, McClellan might have destroyed Lee's army, but he let it slip away. He then moved so slowly after the battle that Lee was able to recover and block McClellan's advance on Richmond. On November 7, 1862, Lincoln fired McClellan and gave command of the army to General **Ambrose Burnside.**

Lincoln wanted a general who was not intimidated by Lee's reputation. He urged Burnside to push south into Virginia and destroy Lee's army. Lincoln did not know that the turning point in the east would come not in Virginia but to the north, in Pennsylvania.

Fredericksburg and Chancellorsville

On December 13, 1862, Burnside ordered a series of assaults against Lee's Confederate troops entrenched in the hills south of Fredericksburg, Virginia. The Union troops suffered over 12,000 casualties, more than twice the loss suffered by the Confederates. Faced with complaints about Burnside from other officers, Lincoln replaced him with General **Joseph Hooker.**

General Hooker devised a plan to get at Lee's troops on the hills near Fredericksburg. First, he left a large part of his army at Fredericksburg to keep Lee's troops from moving. He then took the rest of the army west to

PRIMARY SOURCE

The Gettysburg Address

The bloody victory at Gettysburg was a major turning point in the Civil War. It kept Britain out of the war, inflicted serious losses on the Confederacy and helped restore Union morale. In November 1863 Lincoln went to Gettysburg to dedicate part of the battlefield as a cemetery. His speech, the Gettysburg Address, became one of the best-known orations in American history.

▼ *On July 3, 1863, the Confederate forces launched an attack known later as Pickett's Charge. Charging up Cemetery Ridge into withering cannon fire, the Confederates suffered nearly 7000 casualties in less than two hours. Soon after the attack failed, General Lee ordered Southern forces to withdraw.*

Differentiated Instruction

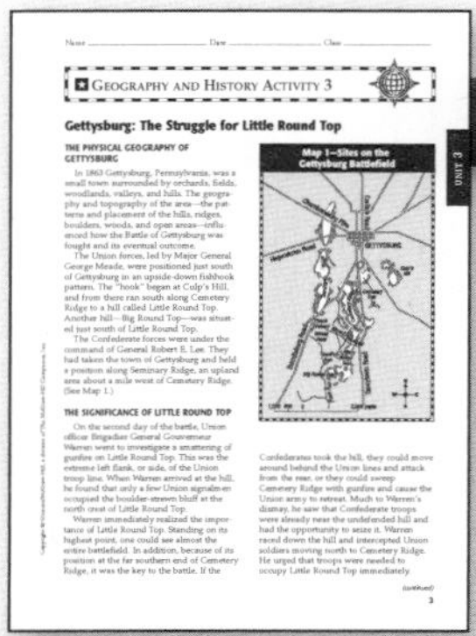

Geography and History Activity, URB p. 3

Gettysburg: The Struggle for Little Round Top

Objective: Understand how geography influenced battles.

Focus: Read a description of the battle for Little Round Top at Gettysburg.

Teach: Have students annotate the three maps on the activity pages with notes describing the battle.

Assess: Have students generalize to answer: Why is geography important on the battlefield?

Close: Ask: Which side won this struggle? Why?

Differentiated Instruction Strategies

- **BL** Recreate or enlarge one map. Explain what the map shows.
- **AL** Compare the role geography played in Pickett's Charge to its role in the battle for Little Round Top.
- **ELL** Create a time line of the battle for Little Round Top.

circle around behind Lee's troops and attack them from the rear. Realizing what was going on, Lee also divided his forces. He left a small force at Fredericksburg and headed west with most of his troops to stop Hooker.

On May 2, 1863, Lee's troops attacked Hooker's in dense woods known as the Wilderness near Chancellorsville, Virginia. Although outnumbered two to one, Lee's forces repeatedly defeated the Union troops. On May 5, Hooker decided to retreat.

The Battle of Gettysburg

S

Having weakened the Union forces at Chancellorsville, Lee decided to invade the North again. In June 1863, he marched into Pennsylvania. After Hooker failed to stop Lee, Lincoln removed him from command and appointed General **George Meade** as his replacement. Meade immediately headed north to intercept Lee.

At the end of June, as Lee's army foraged in the Pennsylvania countryside, some of his troops headed into the town of **Gettysburg,** to scout for the enemy. When they arrived near the town, however, they **encountered** Union cavalry. On July 1, 1863, the Confederates pushed the Union troops out of the town into the hills to the south. At the same time, the main forces of both armies hurried to the scene of the fighting.

On July 2, Lee attacked, but the Union troops held their ground. The following day, he ordered nearly 15,000 men under the command of General George E. Pickett and General A.P. Hill to undertake a massive assault. The attack came to be known as **Pickett's Charge.** A mile-wide line of Confederate troops marched across open farmland toward Union positions on Cemetery Ridge. Union cannons and guns opened fire, inflicting 7,000 casualties in less than half an hour of fighting.

S

Primary Source

"Four score and seven years ago our fathers brought forth on this continent, a new nation, conceived in Liberty, and dedicated to the proposition that all men are created equal.

Now we are engaged in a great civil war, testing whether that nation, or any nation so conceived and so dedicated, can long endure. We are met on a great battle-field of that war. We have come to dedicate a portion of that field, as a final resting place for those who here gave their lives that that nation might live. It is altogether fitting and proper that we should do this.

But, in a larger sense, we cannot dedicate—we cannot consecrate—we cannot hallow—this ground. The brave men, living and dead, who struggled here, have consecrated it, far above our poor power to add or detract. The world will little note, nor long remember what we say here, but it can never forget what they did here. It is for us the living, rather, to be dedicated here to the unfinished work which they who fought here have thus far so nobly advanced. It is rather for us to be here dedicated to the great task remaining before us—that from these honored dead we take increased devotion to that cause for which they gave the last full measure of devotion—that we here highly resolve that these dead shall not have died in vain—that this nation, under God, shall have a new birth of freedom—and that government of the people, by the people, for the people, shall not perish from the earth."

—The Gettysburg Address, November 19, 1863

▲ *More than 50,000 Americans were killed or wounded during the battle of Gettysburg.*

DBQ Document-Based Questions

1. **Specifying** To what event is Lincoln referring that occurred "fourscore and seven years ago"?
2. **Identifying Central Issues** What does Lincoln say is the main purpose of the Civil War and the reason for the sacrifices at Gettysburg?

S Skill Practice

Using Geography Skills Have students work in groups to create a relief map depicting one day at Gettysburg. Each student should be assigned the role of researcher, designer, or artist. Researchers find information about the day's battles; designers create plans for the maps, which the artists can use to create the maps. **OL** **AL**

DBQ Document Based Questions

Answers:

1. the issuing of the Declaration of Independence in 1776
2. He says that the main purpose of the war is to restore the Union and preserve the republic, which is a unique "government of the people, by the people, for the people."

Additional Support

Activity: Interdisciplinary Connection

Art Although Mathew Brady revolutionized the artistic documentation of the Civil War through his photography, many artists of the time captured this historic era through fine art. For example, Winslow Homer's paintings *Veteran in a New Field* and *Prisoners from the Front* were completed from sketches he drew from the field. Have students use library or Internet sources to research a painting that stirs up personal feelings about the Civil War. Then ask students to present and explain the painting to the class. **OL** **BL** **ELL**

People IN HISTORY

On April 7, 1865, Grant wrote Lee the following: "I . . . regard it as my duty to shift from myself the responsibility of any further effusion of blood, by asking of you [to] surrender . . ." Lee replied: "I reciprocate your desire to avoid useless effusion of blood, and therefore, before considering your proposition, ask the terms you will offer on condition of its surrender."

Answers:
Grant: His relentless drive and willingness to sustain high casualties provided the push needed to defeat the South.
Lee: He renewed his allegiance to the United States after the war, setting an example for many other former Confederate officers, and encouraged his students to put the war behind them and act as responsible citizens.

Reading Check

Answer:
It failed to break Union lines and resulted in heavy casualties.

Additional Support

The Aftermath

Fewer than 5,000 Confederate troops made it up the ridge, and Union troops quickly overwhelmed those who did. Lee then quickly rallied his troops and began a retreat to Virginia on a rainy July 4. Confederate forces soon became trapped between a swollen Potomac River and pursuing Union troops, but General Meade, with his army depleted by the battle, decided not to attack the defenses put up by the retreating Confederate forces.

At Gettysburg, Confederate forces lost approximately 28,000 killed or wounded. This amounted to over one-third of Lee's entire force. The Union army suffered about 23,000 casualties, but could better afford the losses.

Gettysburg proved to be the turning point of the war. The Union's victory strengthened the Republicans politically and ensured that Britain would not recognize the Confederacy. For the rest of the war, Lee's forces fought on the defensive, slowly giving ground.

Reading Check **Summarizing** What was the result of Pickett's Charge?

Battle for Tennessee

MAIN Idea After Grant won control of Tennessee, Lincoln appointed him general in chief.

HISTORY AND YOU Have you ever planned a strategy to win a game? Read on to learn how Grant's planned assault on Chattanooga was even more successful than expected.

After the Union's major victories at Vicksburg and Gettysburg, fierce fighting erupted in Tennessee near Chattanooga. Chattanooga was a vital railroad junction. Both sides knew that if the Union forces captured Chattanooga, they would control a major railroad running south to Atlanta.

Chickamauga

During the summer of 1863, Union General William Rosecrans outmaneuvered Confederate General Braxton Bragg. In early September, Rosecrans forced the Confederates to evacuate Chattanooga without a fight. Bragg did not retreat far, however. When Rosecrans advanced

People IN HISTORY

Ulysses S. Grant
1822–1885

Before his victories in Kentucky and Tennessee, Ulysses S. Grant had been an average West Point cadet, a failed businessman, and had served in the Mexican War. More than any other Union commander, however, Grant changed the strategy—and the outcome—of the Civil War. Grant's restless urge for offensive fighting and his insistence on "unconditional surrender" at Fort Donelson convinced Lincoln to place the general in command of all Union troops in 1864. Lincoln's confidence was not misplaced. Despite mounting casualties and accusations that he was a "butcher," Grant pushed relentlessly until Lee finally surrendered at Appomattox.

The Union's enthusiasm for its victorious general made Grant a two-term president after the war, although scandals in his administration marred his reputation. The Civil War had been the high point of Grant's life, the challenge that brought out his abilities as a leader.

How did Grant change the outcome of the Civil War?

Robert E. Lee
1807–1870

The son of a distinguished—though not wealthy—Virginia family, Robert E. Lee was raised in the socially exclusive world of the aristocratic South. From the beginning, he seemed marked by fate for brilliant success. At West Point he excelled in both his studies and his social life, impressing teachers and fellow cadets with his talent and good nature. As an army officer in the war with Mexico, he performed with brilliance and courage.

Offered command of Union troops at the beginning of the Civil War, Lee refused, unable to oppose his fellow Virginians. A hero to Southerners during the war, Lee felt a responsibility to set an example of Southern honor in defeat. His swearing of renewed allegiance to the United States after the war inspired thousands of former Confederate soldiers to do the same. As president of Washington College in Virginia (later renamed Washington and Lee), Lee encouraged his students to put the war behind them and to behave as responsible citizens.

How did Lee work to heal the wounds of the Civil War?

Activity: Interdisciplinary Connection

Language Arts Tell students that Stephen Crane's novel *The Red Badge of Courage* presents a realistic view of the war. Select a few passages from the book that demonstrate how Crane paints a picture of the war. Then tell students that Crane did not actually fight in the Civil War. He based his book on war stories told by veterans and on the photographs taken by Mathew Brady, a famous Civil War photographer. Discuss with students the difference between participating in an event and having the event described by others. **OL** **BL**

into Georgia, Bragg launched an assault against him at Chickamauga Creek on September 19, 1863. Bragg soon smashed through part of the Union defenses, and Rosecrans ordered his troops to fall back to Chattanooga, where he found himself almost completely surrounded by Bragg's forces.

The Battle of Chattanooga

In an effort to save the Union troops in Chattanooga, Lincoln decided to send some of Meade's forces to help Rosecrans. Dozens of trains were assembled, and 11 days later 20,000 men with their artillery, horses, and equipment arrived near Chattanooga after traveling more than 1,200 miles (1,930 km).

Lincoln also decided to reorganize the military leadership in the west, and he placed Grant in overall command. Grant then hurried to Chattanooga to take charge of the coming battle. In late November, he ordered his troops to attack Confederate positions on Lookout Mountain. Charging uphill through swirling fog, the Union forces quickly drove the Confederate troops off the mountain.

Confederate soldiers retreating from Lookout Mountain hurried to join other Confederate forces at Missionary Ridge east of Chattanooga. The Confederates were outnumbered, but they awaited a Union attack, secure on a high rugged position, just as the Union troops had been at Cemetery Ridge near Gettysburg. R

Grant did not intend to storm Missionary Ridge. He believed an all-out assault would be suicidal. Instead, he ordered General **William Tecumseh Sherman** to attack Confederate positions on the north end of the ridge. When Sherman failed to break through, Grant ordered 23,000 men under General George Thomas to launch a limited attack against the Confederates in front of Missionary Ridge as a diversion.

To Grant's astonishment, Thomas's troops overran the Confederate trenches and charged up the steep slope of Missionary Ridge itself. "They shouted 'Chickamauga,'" one Confederate remembered, "as though the word itself were a weapon." The rapid charge scattered the surprised Confederates, who retreated in panic, leaving Missionary Ridge—and Chattanooga—to the Union army.

Grant Becomes General in Chief

By the spring of 1864, Grant had accomplished two crucial objectives for the Union. His capture of Vicksburg had given the Union control of the Mississippi River, while his victory at Chattanooga had secured eastern Tennessee and cleared the way for an invasion of Georgia. Lincoln rewarded Grant by appointing him general in chief of the Union forces and **promoting** him to lieutenant general, a rank no one had held since George Washington. When the president met Grant in March 1864 he told him, "I wish to express my satisfaction with what you have done. . . . The particulars of your plan I neither know nor seek to know." The president had finally found a general he trusted to win the war.

✓ Reading Check **Examining** Why was capturing Chattanooga important to the Union?

Section 4 REVIEW

Vocabulary

1. **Explain** the significance of: forage, siege, Ambrose Burnside, Joseph Hooker, George Meade, Gettysburg, Pickett's Charge, William Tecumseh Sherman.

Main Ideas

2. **Explaining** What was the purpose of Grierson's Raid?
3. **Identifying Central Issues** How was Gettysburg a turning point in the war?
4. **Summarizing** Why did Lincoln make Grant general in chief of the army?

Critical Thinking

5. **Big Ideas** Why was capturing Vicksburg important to the Union?
6. **Organizing** Using a graphic organizer, list the results of the Battle of Gettysburg. Consider both the Union and the Confederacy.

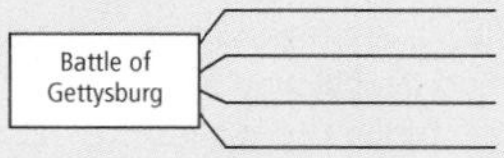

7. **Analyzing Visuals** Study the map of Grant's approach to Vicksburg on page 337. Why do you think he fought several battles outside Vicksburg before he laid siege to the city itself?

Writing About History

8. **Descriptive Writing** Take on the role of a Confederate soldier at the Battle of Gettysburg. Write a letter to your family describing the battle and your feelings about its result.

History ONLINE
Study Central™ To review this section, go to glencoe.com and click on Study Central.

R Reading Strategy

Determining Importance
Have students explain how battles in Tennessee began turning the war in favor of the Union. OL

✓ Reading Check

Answer:
The Union could control the major railroad line running to Atlanta.

Assess

History ONLINE

Study Central™ provides summaries, interactive games, and online graphic organizers to help students review content.

Close

Analyzing Have students describe the events at Vicksburg and Gettysburg and explain why these two battles were pivotal. OL

Answers

1. All definitions can be found in the section and the Glossary.
2. to distract Confederate forces while Grant moved his army across the Mississippi River, then south, and then back across the river to attack Vicksburg.
3. The Union victory strengthened the Republicans politically and ensured that the British would not recognize the Confederacy.
4. Grant had accomplished two crucial objectives for the Union by capturing Vicksburg and Chattanooga. Also, Lincoln probably felt he could depend on and trust Grant.
5. It gave the Union control of the Mississippi River and made it difficult for the South to get supplies.
6. strengthened Republicans politically, very high casualties, put Confederacy on the defensive, ended the South's hope for help from Britain
7. Possible answer: to destroy any Confederate forces that might come up behind him before he started the siege
8. Students' entries will vary, but should describe some details of the battle and their feelings about it.

GEOGRAPHY & HISTORY

Focus

Thirty years after the war ended, Congress made Gettysburg a National Military Park in tribute to the armies that fought there. Each summer, historical reenactors have recreated the battle. Today National Park Service rangers also provide information to visitors.

Teach

C Critical Thinking

Comparing and Contrasting Tell students that the Union and Confederate armies were similar in many ways. For example, both armies used similar weapons. Have students use the library or Internet resources to identify other ways in which the two armies were alike and different. You may recommend the National Parks Service Web site as a starting point for their research. **OL**

Additional Support

NATIONAL GEOGRAPHIC

GEOGRAPHY & HISTORY

The Battle of Gettysburg

The Confederate invasion of the North in 1863 was a bold stroke. By moving north, General Robert E. Lee gained access to the rich farms and other resources of Pennsylvania. When his troops arrived in Gettysburg on July 1, they forced Union troops to flee to the hills south of the town. Had Confederate forces attacked the Union troops in the hills immediately, they might have won. The decision not to attack enabled Union troops to reinforce their position and build a formidable defensive line.

How Did Geography Shape the Battle?

The Union line stretched from Culp's Hill and Cemetery Hill in the north, south along Cemetery Ridge to another hill called Little Round Top. The Union forces controlled the high ground and were deployed in such a way that troops could easily be moved from one part of the line to another depending on where the enemy attacked.

On July 2, Lee tried to seize Little Round Top. Controlling the hill would have let his artillery fire down the length of the Union line. After savage fighting, his attack was repulsed, but Lee believed the Union had shifted so many troops south to hold Little Round Top that it had left its line on Cemetery Ridge vulnerable to attack.

C On July 3, Lee ordered some 12,500 troops to attack Cemetery Ridge in what became known as Pickett's Charge. Union artillery ripped holes in the Confederate line as it advanced. When the Confederates neared the crest of the ridge, Union troops, protected by trenches and barricades they had built, unleashed volley after volley. Firing at point-blank rage, stabbing with bayonets, and battering with rifle butts, the Union soldiers drove the Confederates back. Lee knew he had been beaten. The next day he began his retreat to Virginia.

Analyzing GEOGRAPHY

1. **Place** Why was the Union army in such a strong position in the Battle of Gettysburg?
2. **Movement** What made Pickett's charge so difficult? Why did Lee think it would succeed?

Extending the Content

The Hero of Little Round Top The extreme left flank of the Union lines at Gettysburg—a hill called Little Round Top—was commanded by Colonel Joshua Lawrence Chamberlain, a college professor who had taken leave from teaching to fight in the war. Chamberlain knew that if the Confederates took Little Round Top, they would have a view of the whole Union line. Although greatly outnumbered, Chamberlain's forces withstood numerous attacks. Finally, Chamberlain led his troops in a bayonet charge that drove the Confederates from the field. Chamberlain received the Medal of Honor for his bravery at Gettysburg.

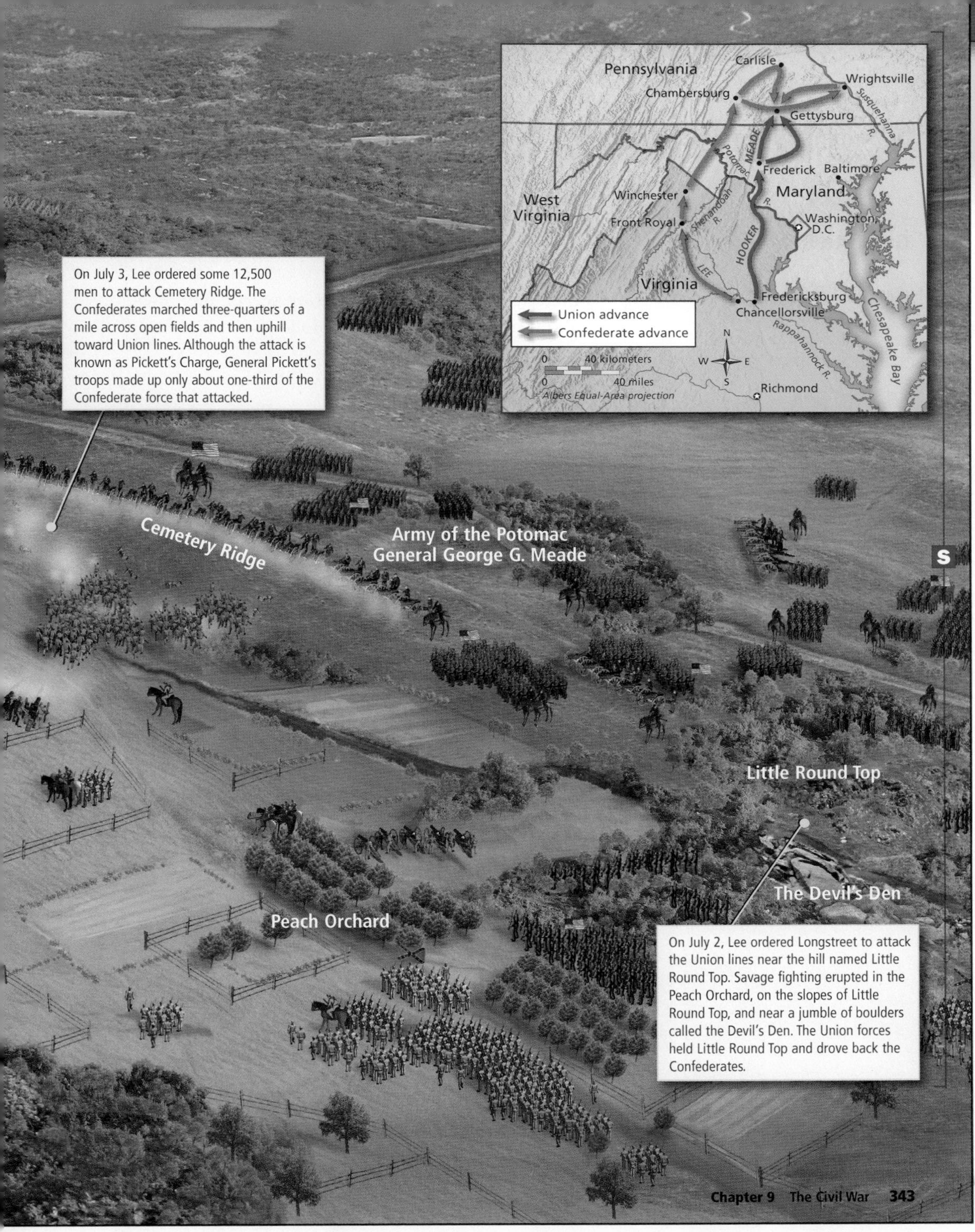

GEOGRAPHY & HISTORY

Assess/Close

S Skill Practice

Reading Maps Have students identify the landforms on the image and explain how the armies used those landforms. **OL**

Analyzing GEOGRAPHY

Answers:

1. The Union army controlled high ground, allowing them to fire down on Confederate troops, and they could move troops easily from one part of the line to another.
2. Pickett's Charge was difficult because the Union troops were protected by barricades and trenches and could fire at the Confederate soldiers as they advanced. Lee believed it would succeed because he thought the Union army had shifted most of the troops to hold Little Round Top, leaving Cemetery Ridge vulnerable.

Additional Support

Activity: Collaborative Learning

Newspaper Page Organize the class into groups to create a newspaper page highlighting the details from the Battle of Gettysburg. Have each group choose whether to describe the Northern or Southern view of the battle. Have students research the Battle of Gettysburg using their book, the Internet, and other sources. Groups should illustrate their newspaper page with drawings depicting a scene from the battle. Have each group compose its newspaper page on a computer using desktop publishing software.

Focus

Bellringer

Daily Focus Transparency 9-5

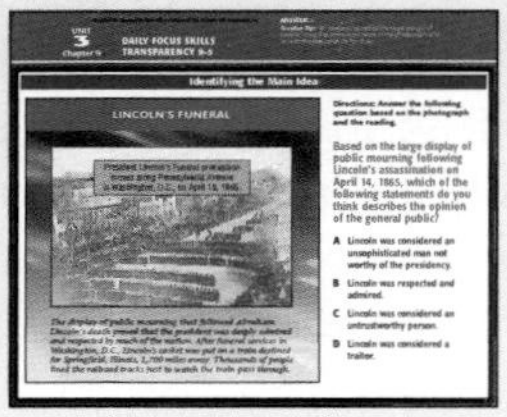

Guide to Reading

Answers:
May: Wilderness (inconclusive battle)
June: Cold Harbor (Confederate victory)
August: Mobile Bay (Union victory)
September: Atlanta falls (Union victory)
November: March to the Sea (Union victory)
December: Savannah falls (Union victory)

Section Spotlight Video

To generate student interest and provide a springboard for class discussion, access the Chapter 9, Section 5 video at glencoe.com or on the video DVD.

Resource Manager

R Reading Strategies	C Critical Thinking	D Differentiated Instruction	W Writing Support	S Skill Practice
Additional Resources • Guided Read., URB p. 82	**Teacher Edition** • Drawing Conclusions, p. 347 • Analyzing Information, p. 348 • Evaluating, p. 349 **Additional Resources** • Quizzes and Tests, p. 123	**Additional Resources** • Reteach. Act., URB p. 73 • Authentic Assessment, p. 23	**Teacher Edition** • Expository Writing, p. 348	**Teacher Edition** • Using Geography Skills, p. 345 **Additional Resources** • Reinforcing Skills Act., URB p. 61 • Read. Essen., p. 108

Section 5 — Section Audio — Spotlight Video

The War Ends

Guide to Reading

Big Ideas
Individual Action In the final year of the Civil War, General Ulysses S. Grant refused to take the pressure off General Robert E. Lee's weary troops.

Content Vocabulary
- pillage *(p. 347)*
- mandate *(p. 348)*

Academic Vocabulary
- subordinate *(p. 344)*
- structure *(p. 346)*

People and Events to Identify
- Philip Sheridan *(p. 345)*
- "Sherman neckties" *(p. 346)*
- March to the Sea *(p. 346)*
- Thirteenth Amendment *(p. 348)*
- Appomattox Courthouse *(p. 349)*

Reading Strategy
Sequencing Complete a time line similar to the one below to record the final battles of the Civil War and their results.

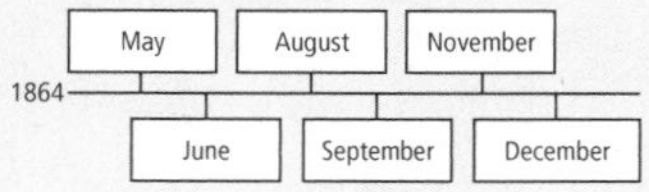

After four bloody years of fighting, Union forces began to wear down the Confederate army. As the war neared its conclusion, however, the assassination of President Lincoln left the nation with many questions about how to reunite the Union.

Grant Versus Lee

MAIN Idea During the final year of the war, Grant's forces battled Lee's forces for control of Virginia.

HISTORY AND YOU Have you read about trench warfare during World War I? Read to learn how the Confederate Army used trenches to defend Petersburg, Virginia.

In the spring of 1864, the most successful general of the Union Army faced the most renowned Confederate commander. Grant put his most trusted **subordinate,** William Tecumseh Sherman, in charge of operations in the west. He then headed to Washington, D.C., to take command of the Union troops facing Lee.

From the Wilderness to Cold Harbor

"Whatever happens, there will be no turning back," Grant promised Lincoln. He was determined to march southward, attacking Lee's forces relentlessly, until the South surrendered.

The first battle of Grant's campaign erupted in the Wilderness, a densely forested area near Fredericksburg, Virginia. The battle lasted for two days, continuing even after the woods caught fire, blinding and choking the combatants. Despite suffering heavy casualties, Grant attacked again near Spotsylvania Courthouse. First in terrible heat and then in pouring rain, the two armies battled for 11 days, often in bloody hand-to-hand combat that left many traumatized.

Unlike past campaigns, in which several weeks of reinforcing and resupplying followed battles, warfare now continued without pause. Savage combat, advances and retreats, and the digging of defensive trenches filled most days and nights. One Union officer noted that the men "had grown thin and haggard. The experience . . . seemed to have added twenty years to their age."

Unable to break Lee's lines at Spotsylvania, Grant headed toward Cold Harbor, a strategic crossroads northeast of Richmond. Convinced that his relentless attacks had weakened and demoralized Lee's troops, Grant decided to launch an all-out assault at Cold Harbor. The attack cost his army 7,000 casualties, compared to 1,500 for the South.

NATIONAL GEOGRAPHIC **Grant v. Lee, 1864–1865**

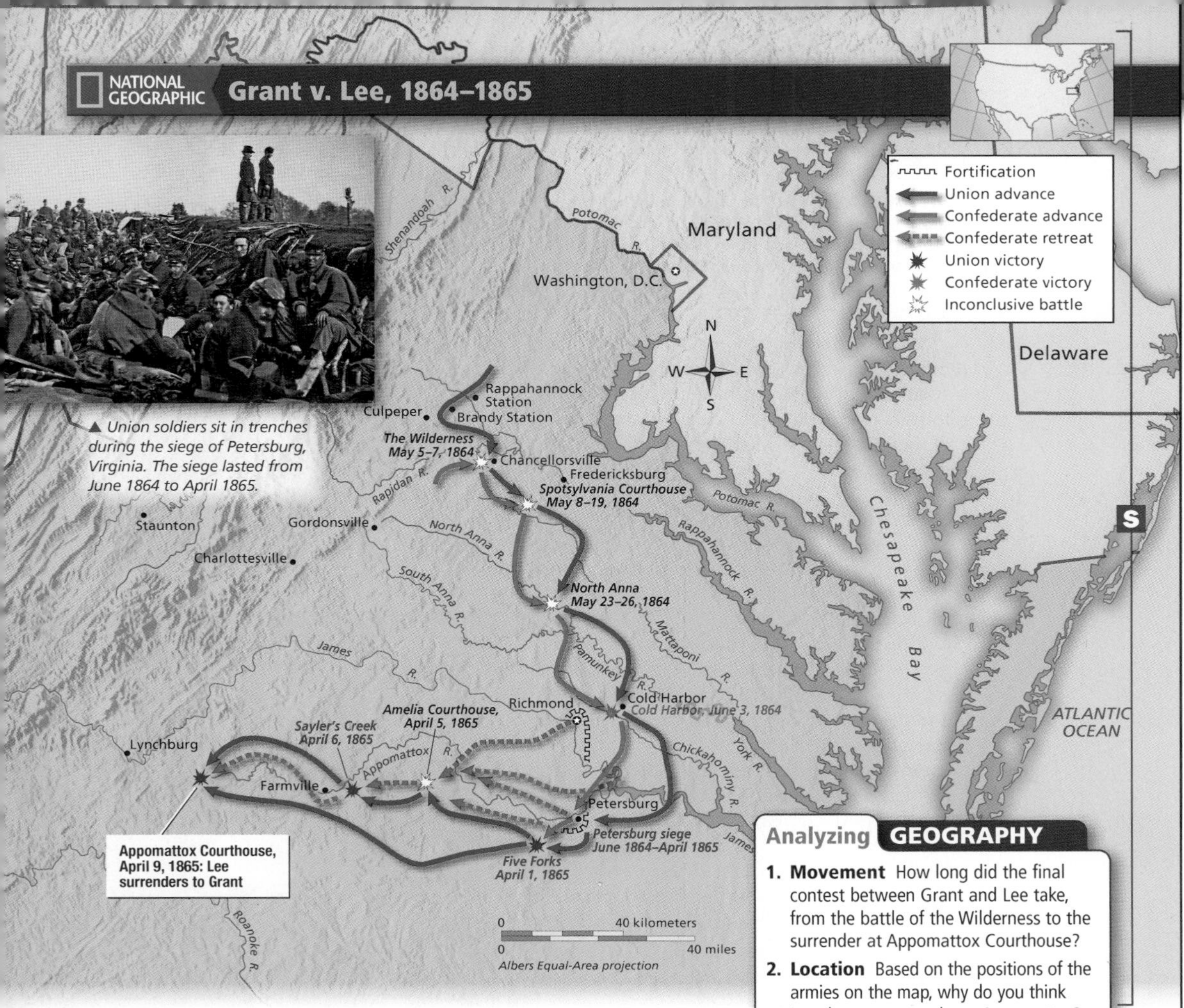

▲ *Union soldiers sit in trenches during the siege of Petersburg, Virginia. The siege lasted from June 1864 to April 1865.*

Analyzing GEOGRAPHY

1. **Movement** How long did the final contest between Grant and Lee take, from the battle of the Wilderness to the surrender at Appomattox Courthouse?
2. **Location** Based on the positions of the armies on the map, why do you think Lee chose to surrender at Appomattox?

The Siege of Petersburg

Stopped by Lee at Cold Harbor, Grant tried another plan similar to the one he had used near Vicksburg. He ordered General **Philip Sheridan** to stage a cavalry raid north and west of Richmond. While Sheridan's troops distracted Lee, Grant headed southeast, crossed the James River, and then turned west toward Petersburg. Capturing Petersburg would cut the only railroad line into Richmond.

When the first Union troops reached the outskirts of Petersburg, they paused. The city was defended by miles of barricades 20 feet (7 m) thick. In front of the Confederate trenches were ditches up to 15 feet (4.6 m) deep to slow down attackers. Carefully positioned cannons supported Confederate lines.

The strength of the defenses the Confederates had erected at Petersburg intimidated the Union troops, who were already exhausted. Realizing a full-scale frontal assault would be suicidal, Grant ordered his troops to put the city under siege.

Reading Check **Summarizing** Why did General Grant decide to capture Petersburg?

S Skill Practice

Using Geographic Skills Have students read the map on this page. **Ask:** Of the battles shown on the map, how many were won by the North? By the South? How many were inconclusive? *(3; 1; 4)* **OL** **BL** **ELL**

Analyzing GEOGRAPHY

Answers:
1. about 11 months
2. Possible answer: Because Grant had Lee surrounded at Appomattox Courthouse.

Reading Check

Answer:
It would cut the only rail line into Richmond, the Confederate capital.

Hands-On Chapter Project Step 5

Chronicling the Lives of Southerners and Northerners

Step 5: After the War Essential Question: How did the surrender of the South (immediately) affect the lives of Northerners and Southerners? Write the essential question on the board to help students focus their research.

Directions Divide the class into the teams determined in Step 1. Each team will meet to develop a plan and divide up research responsibilities. Teams will research and describe the lives of Southerners and Northerners immediately upon the surrender of the South. Students should focus on how people reacted to the news of the surrender.

Synthesizing Information Students will synthesize their research by creating 1 to 3 pages of a Civil War diary. Note that each team will create its own pages—those for Southerners and those for Northerners. **OL**

(Chapter Project continued on the Visual Summary page)

Did You Know?

Sherman's March to the Sea In December 1864, Sherman's troops left Savannah and headed for South Carolina. One phase of Sherman's plan of total war called for a demoralization of Confederate soldiers in the field by attacks on the home front. Sherman wrote, "The simple fact that a man's home has been visited by the enemy makes a soldier in Lee's or Johnston's army very, very, anxious to get home." North Carolina Governor Zebulon Vance received letters from soldiers stating their concern for their homes and families. They asked him to do something to prevent the desertion of those who felt the need to leave the army to protect their families. Governor Vance, however, could do little to stop the Union troops.

The Union Advances

MAIN Idea After the fall of Atlanta, General Sherman led his troops across the state of Georgia, causing mass destruction along the way.

HISTORY AND YOU Do you think that armies should treat civilians differently from soldiers during a war? Read on to learn how General Sherman treated Southerners during his March to the Sea.

While Grant fought Lee, General Sherman marched his army from Chattanooga toward Atlanta and the Union navy prepared to seal the last major port on the Gulf of Mexico east of the Mississippi—Mobile, Alabama.

Farragut Attacks Mobile

On August 5, 1864, Admiral Farragut took 18 ships past the three Confederate forts defending Mobile Bay. As the fleet headed into the bay, a mine—which in the 1860s was called a torpedo—blew up a Union ship. The explosion brought the fleet to a halt, right in front of a fort's guns. "Damn the torpedoes! Full speed ahead!" cried Farragut, whose ship led the way through the minefield.

After getting past the Confederate forts, Farragut's ships destroyed a Confederate fleet defending Mobile Bay. Although Farragut did not capture Mobile, he did seal off the bay. Blockade runners moving goods in and out of the Deep South east of the Mississippi could no longer use any port on the Gulf of Mexico.

Sherman's March to the Sea

In late August 1864, Sherman sent his troops south around Atlanta to cut the roads and railways leading into the city. His troops destroyed the rail lines by heating the rails and twisting them into snarls of steel nicknamed **"Sherman neckties."** To avoid being trapped in the city, Confederate General John B. Hood ordered his troops to evacuate Atlanta on September 1, 1864.

After occupying Atlanta, Sherman proposed to march across Georgia. "I could cut a swath to the sea," he explained, "and divide the Confederacy in two." The march would be "a demonstration to the world . . . that we have a power that Davis cannot resist. I can make the march, and make Georgia howl!"

Sherman ordered all civilians to leave Atlanta. He explained to the city's mayor that he was "not only fighting hostile armies, but a hostile people." To end the war, he believed, he had no choice but to "make old and young, rich and poor, feel the hard hand of war." Sherman then ordered his troops to destroy everything of military value, including mills, warehouses, factories, railroads, and machine shops. Sherman's troops set fires to destroy these **structures,** but the fires quickly spread, burning down more than one-third of the city.

On November 15, 1864, Sherman began his **March to the Sea.** His troops cut a path of destruction through Georgia that was, in places, 60 miles (97 km) wide. They ransacked houses, burned crops, and killed cattle. By December 21, 1864, they had reached the coast and seized the city of Savannah.

NATIONAL GEOGRAPHIC

Sherman's forces destroyed anything that might help the Confederate war effort, such as the Atlanta train depot (above) and railroad tracks (below).

Additional Support

Activity: Collaborative Learning

Analyzing Maps Divide the class into groups of three students each. Each member of the group will have a specific role. One member of the group will describe the movements of the Union army, using the map on page 347. Another member of the group will describe the movements of the Confederate army. These two group members will alternate narration. Their narration should include the battle location (for example Chancellorsville), the date of the battle, the result of the battle, and then the direction that the army headed next. The third member of the group will confirm the narrator's descriptions against the map, correcting the members as needed and filling in missing information. **AL**

After reaching the sea, Sherman ordered his troops to turn north and head into South Carolina—the state that many people believed had started the Civil War. "The whole army," Sherman wrote, "is burning with an insatiable desire to wreak vengeance upon South Carolina." As one Union soldier declared, "Here is where treason began and . . . here is where it shall end."

As the troops marched north, they burned and **pillaged,** or looted, nearly everything in front of them. At least 12 towns were set on fire, including Columbia, the state capital. The march demoralized Southerners. As one South Carolinian wrote, "All is gloom, despondency and inactivity. Our army is demoralized and the people panic stricken . . . to fight longer seems madness."

Reading Check **Examining** Why did General Sherman march his army through Georgia?

The South Surrenders

MAIN Idea After Lee surrendered, Lincoln was assassinated before the country had agreed on the future of former slaves and the defeated South.

HISTORY AND YOU When do you think disloyalty amounts to treason? Read on to learn why Grant promised not to prosecute Confederate soldiers for taking up arms against the government.

When Sherman and Grant began their campaigns in the spring of 1864, Lincoln knew that his own reelection depended on their success. By summer, sensing the public's anger over the costly war, Lincoln confided to an army officer, "I am going to be beaten." He did not know, however, that the war was nearly over. Only a few months later, the Confederacy was on the verge of collapse.

Sherman's March to the Sea

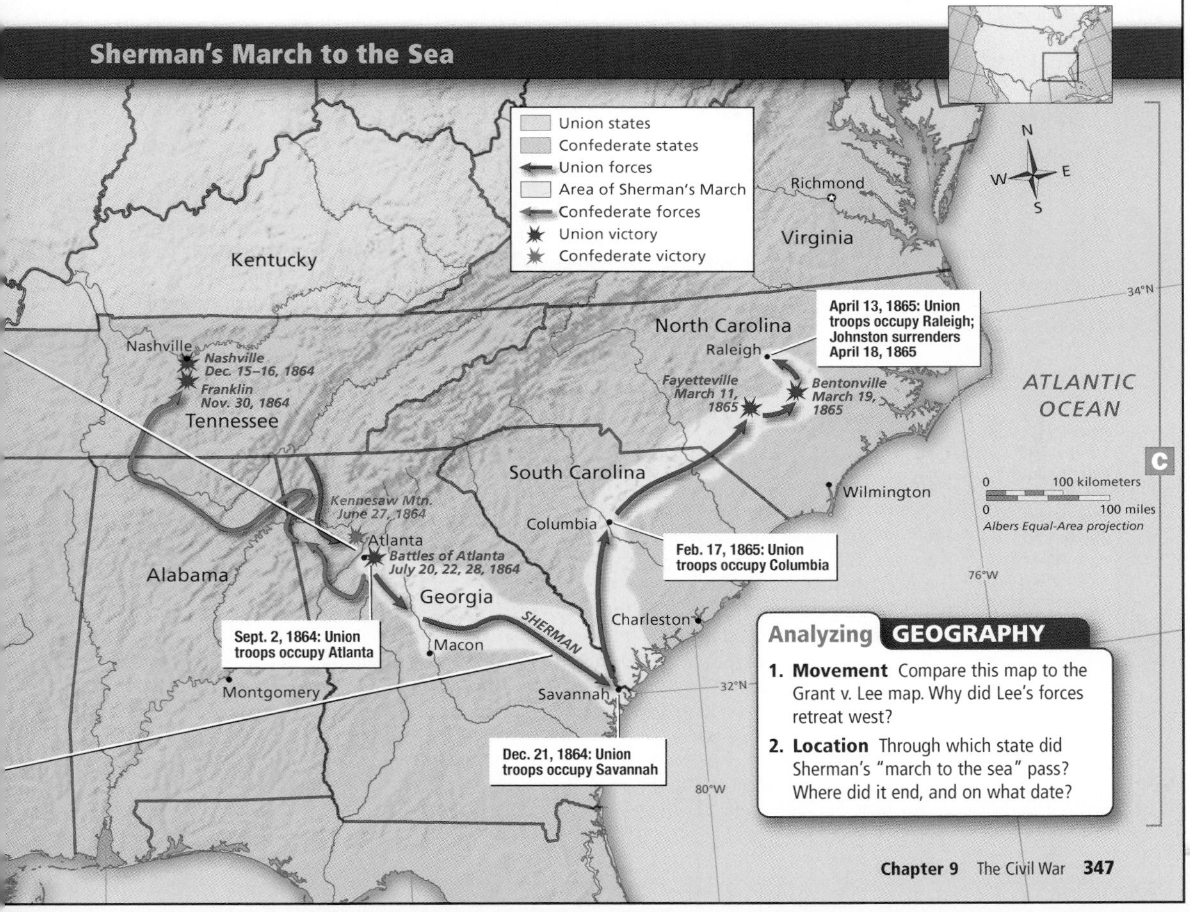

Analyzing GEOGRAPHY

1. **Movement** Compare this map to the Grant v. Lee map. Why did Lee's forces retreat west?
2. **Location** Through which state did Sherman's "march to the sea" pass? Where did it end, and on what date?

C Critical Thinking

Drawing Conclusions Discuss the methods used during "Sherman's March." **Ask:** How might civilians along Sherman's path have reacted to the methods of the Union army? *(Answers may include fear, anger, attacks against soldiers, running away. Accept all reasonable answers.)*

Reading Check

Answer:
to convince Southern civilians to give up the struggle; to divide the Confederacy in two

Analyzing GEOGRAPHY

Answers:
1. Because he would have run into Sherman's troops moving north.
2. Georgia; Savannah, December 21, 1864

Differentiated Instruction

Leveled Activities

BL Reteaching Activity, URB p. 73

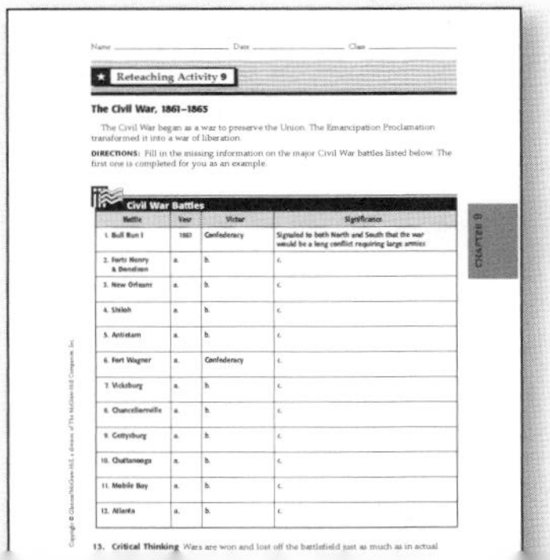

OL Historical Analysis Skills Activity, URB p. 52

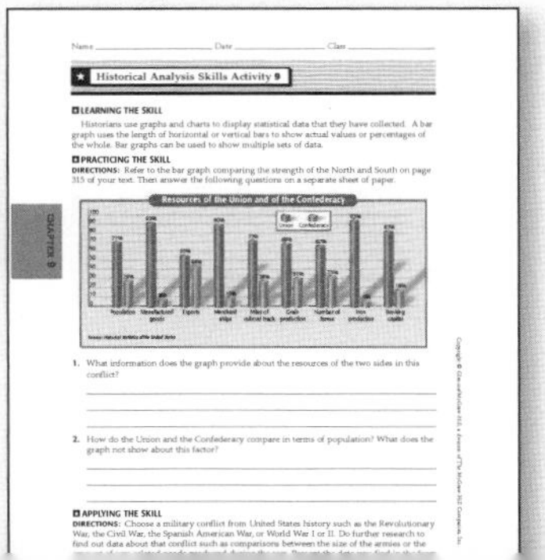

AL Economics and History Activity, URB p. 7

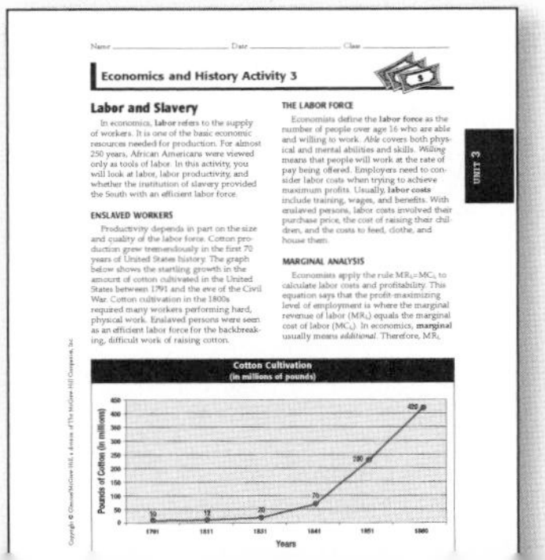

ELL Content Vocabulary Activity, URB p. 57

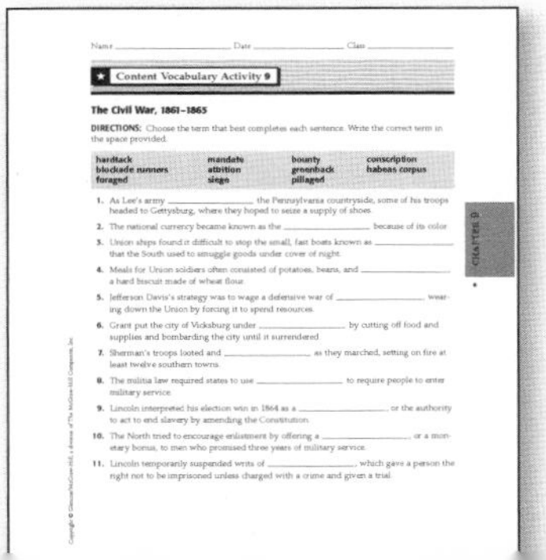

W Writing Support

Expository Writing Have students analyze Lincoln's second Inaugural Address. Students should write a one-page essay that explains Lincoln's ideas about union, liberty, equality, and the responsibility of government. **OL** **AL**

C Critical Thinking

Analyzing Information

Votes Cast in General Election

1860	4,689,568
1864	4,010,725

Votes Cast in Electoral College

1860	303
1864	233

Ask: What explains the difference in the number of popular votes and electoral votes cast in the 1860 and 1864 presidential elections? *(In 1864, only Northern voters participated and only Northern electors cast a ballot.)* **OL**

Analyzing VISUALS

Answers:
1. World War I and World War II
2. the North

Additional Support

PRIMARY SOURCE

The Cost of the Civil War

▲ Robert E. Lee surrenders to General Grant at Appomattox Courthouse on April 9, 1865.

▲ The war devastated the South. Hundreds of thousands of people were dead, and several major cities, including Richmond (above), lay in ruins.

Casualties of the Civil War

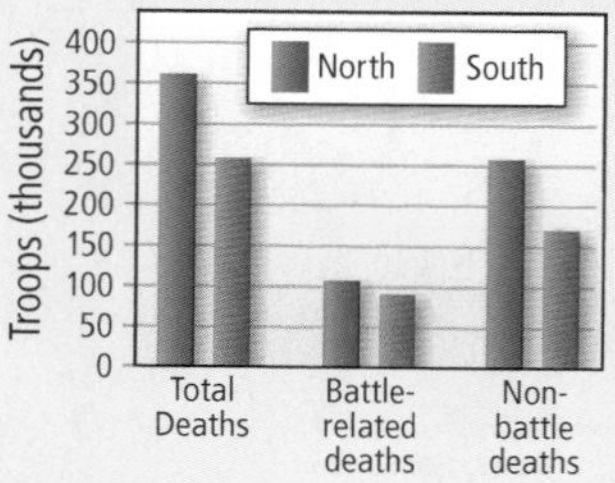

Source: *For the Common Defense.*

American War Deaths*

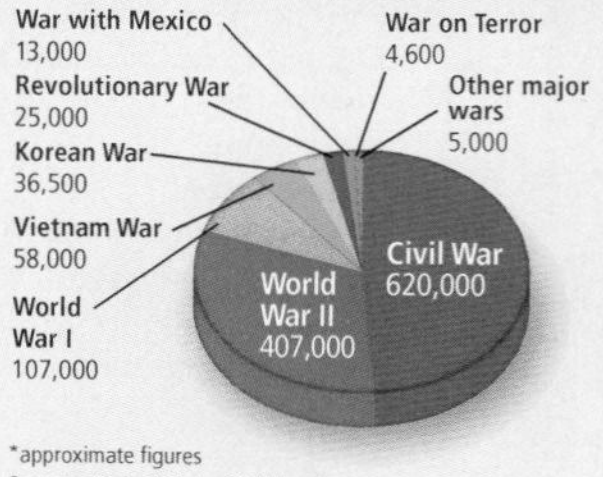

*approximate figures

Sources: United States Civil War Center; *For the Common Defense*

Analyzing VISUALS

1. **Identifying** The Civil War cost more American lives than any other conflict. What were the next two most deadly wars?
2. **Specifying** Which region suffered the highest number of battle-related deaths?

History ONLINE
Student Skill Activity To learn how to create and modify spreadsheets, visit glencoe.com and complete the Skill activity.

The Election of 1864 W C

To oppose Lincoln in the 1864 election, the Democrats nominated General George B. McClellan, whose popularity had remained high despite his dismissal earlier in the war. Knowing the country was growing weary of the war, McClellan promised to stop the hostilities and open negotiations with the South to restore the Union peaceably.

The capture of Atlanta came just in time to revitalize Northern support for the war and for Lincoln himself. The president won reelection with 55 percent of the popular vote. Lincoln interpreted his reelection as a **mandate,** or a command from the voters, to end slavery permanently by amending the Constitution. To get the amendment through Congress, Republicans asked Democrats who were against slavery to help them. On January 31, 1865, the **Thirteenth Amendment** to the Constitution, banning slavery in the United States, narrowly passed the House of Representatives and was sent to the states for ratification.

Surrender

Meanwhile, in the trenches near Petersburg, Lee knew that time was running out. On April 1, 1865, Union troops led by Sheridan cut the last railroad line into Petersburg at the Battle of Five Forks. The following night, Lee's troops withdrew from their positions near the city and raced west.

Activity: Technology Connection

Inventions and Innovations Tell students that many innovations occurred during the battles of the Civil War. For example, ironclads first battled in the seas, the Medal of Honor was bestowed on servicemen, and it was the first time that battles were documented through photography. Have students work in pairs or individually to research other Civil War "firsts." Students should identify the "first" and describe it and its importance. Students should also note whether the technology or "first" is still in use or practice today. **OL**

Lee's desperate attempt to escape Grant's forces failed when Sheridan's cavalry got ahead of Lee's troops and blocked the road at **Appomattox Courthouse.** When his troops failed to break through, Lee sadly observed, "There is nothing left for me to do but go and see General Grant, and I would rather die a thousand deaths." With his ragged and battered troops surrounded and outnumbered, Lee surrendered to Grant at Appomattox Courthouse on April 9, 1865.

Grant's generous terms of surrender guaranteed that the United States would not prosecute Confederate soldiers for treason. When Grant agreed to let Confederates take their horses home "to put in a crop to carry themselves and their families through the next winter," Lee thanked him, adding that the kindness would "do much toward conciliating our people." As Lee left, he shook hands with Ely Parker, a Senecan who served as Grant's secretary. "I am glad to see a real American here," Lee told the Native American. Parker replied, "We are all Americans."

Lincoln's Assassination

With the war over, Lincoln described his plan to restore the Southern states to the Union. In the speech, he mentioned including African Americans in Southern state governments. One listener, the actor John Wilkes Booth, sneered to a friend, "That is the last speech he will ever make." The president's advisers repeatedly warned him not to appear unescorted in public. Nevertheless, on the evening of April 14, 1865, Lincoln went to Ford's Theatre with his wife to see a play. During the third act, Booth slipped quietly behind him and shot the president in the back of the head. C

Lincoln's death shocked the nation. Once viewed as a rustic, unsophisticated man not suited for the presidency, Lincoln had become the Union's greatest champion. The usually stern General Grant wept openly as Lincoln's body lay in state at the White House. Tens of thousands of men, women, and children lined railroad tracks across the nation as Lincoln's body was transported back to Springfield, Illinois, for burial.

Aftermath of the Civil War

The North's victory in the Civil War strengthened the power of the federal government over the states. It also transformed American society by finally ending the enslavement of millions of African Americans. At the same time, it left the South socially and economically devastated.

Following the war, many questions remained unresolved. When would the Southern states be permitted back into the Union? Under what conditions would that occur? What would be the status of newly freed African Americans? Americans from the North and the South tried to answer these questions in the years following the Civil War—an era known as Reconstruction.

Reading Check **Explaining** Why did President Lincoln doubt he could win the 1864 election?

Section 5 REVIEW

Vocabulary

1. **Explain** the significance of: Philip Sheridan, "Sherman neckties," March to the Sea, pillage, mandate, Thirteenth Amendment, Appomattox Courthouse.

Main Ideas

2. **Describing** What was the fighting like at Spotsylvania?
3. **Analyzing** What was the effect of Farragut's blockade of Mobile Bay?
4. **Listing** What were three short-term consequences of the Civil War?

Critical Thinking

5. **Big Ideas** How did Northern military strategy change after Ulysses S. Grant took command of the Union Army?
6. **Organizing** Complete a graphic organizer that lists the purposes of the Union march on Atlanta and the effects of the city's capture on both sides.

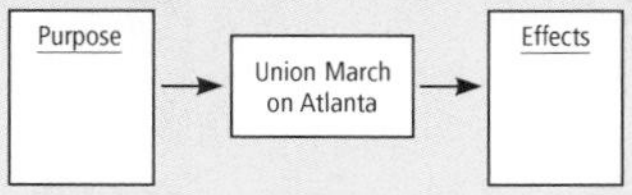

7. **Analyzing Visuals** Examine the graphs of war deaths on page 348. Create a spreadsheet of battles, and for each, list the outcome and number of lives lost to analyze the overall outcome of the Civil War.

Writing About History

8. **Descriptive Writing** Take on the role of a reporter living in Georgia during Sherman's March. Write a brief article describing the Union's actions and their effects on the people of Georgia.

History ONLINE
Study Central™ To review this section, go to glencoe.com and click on Study Central.

C Critical Thinking

Evaluating Have students search the Web for articles about Abraham Lincoln's assassination. Ask them to print out the page of each site and write a brief explanation of whether or not they rate the site as authoritative. OL

Reading Check

Answer:
He believed that his successful reelection depended on the successes of Sherman and Grant.

Assess

History ONLINE

Study Central™ provides summaries, interactive games, and online graphic organizers to help students review content.

Close

Explaining Ask students to explain the importance of Union victories in Virginia and the Deep South. OL

Section 5 REVIEW

Answers

1. All definitions can be found in the section and the Glossary.
2. Unlike in previous campaigns, warfare now continued without pause. Savage combat, advances and retreats, and the digging of defensive trenches filled most days and nights.
3. It closed the last port in the Gulf of Mexico to Confederate blockade runners.
4. It strengthened the power of the federal government over the states, began the process of ending slavery, and devastated the South socially and economically.
5. It became focused on relentlessly attacking the Confederate troops and making life very difficult for Southern civilians.
6. Purpose: to gain access to the heart of Southern territory and destroy Southern railroads; Effect: crippled Southern morale and helped Lincoln win re-election, which led to the introduction of the Thirteenth Amendment.
7. Students should prepare a spreadsheet with the appropriate information.
8. Students' articles will vary, but should be based on facts, not on the writer's opinion.

Analyzing Have students research the point of view that someone in one of the following groups might have had about the war: Southern farmers, Southern shopkeepers, Southern merchant ship owners, Northern farmers, free Northern African American laborers, or Northern textile mill owners. Tell students to then write an essay explaining how such a person might have felt about the war once it was over and why. Have students share their essays in class, and have classmates evaluate whether each essay accurately portrays the point of view of that type of person. **AL**

Chapter 9 VISUAL SUMMARY

STUDY TO GO You can study anywhere, anytime by downloading quizzes and flashcards to your PDA from glencoe.com.

▲ *Jefferson Davis meets with his cabinet and General Lee.*

North v. South

1861

- Lincoln orders a blockade of Southern ports.
- The Confederacy organizes its government.
- The South wins the First Battle of Bull Run.
- Both sides begin building up their forces.

▼ *The capture of New Orleans (below) gave the Union control of the mouth of the Mississippi River.*

1862

- Farragut captures New Orleans.
- After the Battles of Shiloh and Murfreesboro, the Union gains control of western Tennessee.
- Led by McClellan, Union troops land in Virginia to begin the Peninsula Campaign; after a series of battles with Lee's forces, McClellan's forces withdraw.
- Lee invades the North, but is defeated at the Battle of Antietam.

▲ *After the Battle of Antietam (above), Lincoln issued the Emancipation Proclamation.*

1863: The Turning Point

- Lincoln issues the Emancipation Proclamation.
- Grant captures Vicksburg after a long siege and cuts the Confederacy in two.
- After winning the battles of Fredericksburg and Chancellorsville, Lee invades the north but is defeated at the Battle of Gettysburg.
- After losing the Battle of Chickamauga, Union forces drive back Southern forces at the Battle of Chattanooga.
- Grant is given command of all Union forces.

▼ *The failure of Pickett's Charge convinced Lee to withdraw from Gettysburg. It was the turning point of the war.*

▲ *Grant's forces wore down Lee's troops in a series of battles in northern Virginia. At Cold Harbor (above), the Union suffered heavy losses.*

1864

- Grant battles Lee's forces in northern Virginia; Lee retreats into Petersburg, which Grant puts under siege.
- Sherman captures Atlanta, then begins his March to the Sea across Georgia.

1865

- Lee attempts to escape from Petersburg but is surrounded by Grant's forces and surrenders at Appomattox Courthouse; other Confederate forces surrender as well.
- Lincoln is assassinated.

▼ *Mourners surround Lincoln's hearse in Philadelphia in April 1865.*

Hands-On Chapter Project
Step 6: Wrap Up

Chronicling the Lives of Southerners and Northerners

Step 6: Wrap Up The two teams will come together as a class to put together the Civil War diary.

Directions Bring the class together to review the pages made by each team. The class will determine how to arrange the pages to best tell the story of the Civil War. Students might also decide to create new "transition" pages to help tell the story from one part of the war to another. Students from the teams may give suggestions to improve pages already created.

Synthesizing Information Students will synthesize their research by creating a complete Civil War diary. The diary will chronicle the lives of Northerners and Southerners during the Civil War. **OL**

Reviewing Vocabulary

Directions: Choose the word or words that best complete the sentence.

1. During the Civil War, the Union was forced to resort to _________ to raise enough troops for the large armies needed to win.
   A attrition
   B habeas corpus
   C emancipation
   D conscription

2. Because of the effectiveness of the Union navy, the Confederacy often used _________ to get supplies.
   A ironclads
   B blockade runners
   C cavalry
   D British warships

3. Union soldiers survived on beans and _________, while Confederate soldiers ate bread made of cornmeal.
   A hardtack
   B molasses
   C hominy
   D tomatoes

4. General Ulysses S. Grant employed a strategy known as a _________ to capture the city of Vicksburg.
   A battle
   B blockade
   C siege
   D charge

5. Union General Sherman claimed he would "make old and young, rich and poor, feel the hard hand of war." He accomplished this during his March to the Sea as his soldiers _________, or looted, nearly everything in their path.
   A mandated
   B pillaged
   C foraged
   D conscripted

Reviewing Main Ideas

Directions: Choose the best answer for each of the following questions.

Section 1 *(pp. 314–319)*

6. At the beginning of the Civil War, which of the following was an advantage held by the South?
   A It had 90 percent of the nation's factories.
   B It had most of the experienced army officers.
   C It had twice as many miles of railroad track.
   D It had most of the shipbuilding facilities.

7. Which of the following was part of the Union's Anaconda Plan for defeating the Confederacy?
   A a blockade of Southern ports
   B a quick ground offensive
   C the assassination of Jefferson Davis
   D a defensive war of attrition

Section 2 *(pp. 320–327)*

8. The damage done by the *Alabama* and the *Florida* created tension between the Union and Great Britain because
   A it helped the Confederacy to nearly win the war.
   B Great Britain had joined the war on the side of the Confederacy.
   C the ships initially had been promised to the Union.
   D Great Britain had allowed the ships to be built in Britain by the Confederacy.

TEST-TAKING TIP

Be sure to read each question carefully to identify any key words that may help you either to choose the correct answer choice or eliminate incorrect answer choices.

Need Extra Help?

If You Missed Questions . . .	1	2	3	4	5	6	7	8
Go to Page . . .	316	322	331	337	347	314	319	322

GO ON

Answers and Analyses
Reviewing Vocabulary

1. D Attrition means a wearing away, and does not work in the blank. Habeas corpus protects citizens from unlawful imprisonment. Emancipation is the freeing of enslaved peoples. Only *D* works. To conscript is to enlist by compulsion, or draft.

2. B Three of the answers are types of ships, which may confuse students. However, the Union navy was successful in instituting blockades, which means they sealed off Southern harbors and cut them off to trade. Blockade runners literally ran (moved) through the blockades to smuggle supplies.

3. A Hardtack was a *hard* biscuit made of wheat flour. The mention of the type of bread that Confederate soldiers ate should tip students off that the answer is also a type of bread. Even if students do not remember the definition of hardtack, the other answer choices are definitely not bread and can be eliminated.

4. C Students should think of a siege as an all-out attack. Grant cut off food supply and troops bombarded the city. *Battle* and *charge* are too general to work in the blank. A *blockade* cuts off food and supplies, but does not involve a coordinated attack to devastate a city.

5. B A mandate is an authorization to act. Foraging, or searching for food, was done by soldiers, but it is not the proper answer in this case. Conscription is a method of forcing people into military service, but it also does not fit in this case.

Reviewing Main Ideas

6. B Choices *A*, *C*, and *D* were all advantages held by the industrial North. The South had the most experienced officers, such as General Lee.

7. A Remind students that an anaconda is a snake that kills its prey by strangulation. The Anaconda Plan included a blockade, *A*, in addition to splitting the Confederacy by taking the Mississippi. This would slowly "strangle" the South.

8. D The *Alabama* and the *Florida* were Confederate ships. This should be easy for students to remember, because Alabama and Florida were Confederate, Southern states. Tension was caused because the Union did not believe that Great Britain should have allowed the ships to be built in Britain.

9. D Make sure students carefully read each answer choice. Choices *A*, *B*, and *C* are untrue. Direct students who have trouble with this question to reread "Battlefield Medicine" on pages 331–332.

10. A Students hopefully eliminate *D* immediately, because it is not closely related enough to war contributions. Women were not allowed to be soldiers and did not serve as reporters. Remind students to always keep in mind the time frame. Many women acted as nurses on the battlefield, including Clara Barton.

11. B Here, students may have trouble choosing between *A* and *B*, because they both mention the Confederacy. Gettysburg, the turning point in the war, was a Union victory. This victory cemented the Union politically, so Great Britain would not recognize the weakened Confederacy as a separate nation.

12. D Grant's capture of Vicksburg and victory at Chattanooga proved his military skill and leadership.

13. B If students have trouble with this question, review "From the Wilderness to Cold Harbor" on page 344. The third paragraph discusses the change to continuous fighting. *A* and *C* are untrue, and the introduction of new technology took place earlier, rather than later, in the war.

Critical Thinking

14. B Choices *A*, *C*, and *D* are untrue. The largest weapons factories were in the North. It cannot be said that most people in the country agreed with the Southern states, given the amount of states that stayed with the Union. The Confederacy failed in its efforts to gain support from Great Britain and France.

Chapter 9 Assessment

Section 3 *(pp. 328–333)*

9. Why were war deaths so high during the Civil War?

- **A** Doctors were hesitant to amputate damaged limbs.
- **B** There was little medical care available.
- **C** Women refused to work on the battlefields as nurses.
- **D** Doctors knew little about infectious germs.

10. In the Civil War, women made huge contributions as

- **A** nurses.
- **B** soldiers.
- **C** reporters.
- **D** teachers.

Section 4 *(pp. 336–341)*

11. What was one outcome of the Battle of Gettysburg?

- **A** The British began to support the Confederacy.
- **B** The British decided not to support the Confederacy.
- **C** The British wanted to support the Union.
- **D** The British decided to sell ships to the Union.

12. After the successful capture of Chattanooga, Lincoln

- **A** recalled General Sherman to Washington, D.C.
- **B** issued the Emancipation Proclamation.
- **C** began negotiations for peace with the Confederacy.
- **D** made General Grant general in chief of the army.

Section 5 *(pp. 344–349)*

13. By 1864, when Grant faced Lee at Spotsylvania, the nature of the war had changed in which of the following ways?

- **A** It had been fought mostly in the South and was now fought mostly in the North.
- **B** Where there had been long breaks between battles, there was now continuous fighting.
- **C** The Confederacy, not the Union, now began to win most of the battles.
- **D** Both sides now introduced new technologies, such as ironclads and conoidal bullets.

Critical Thinking

Directions: Choose the best answers to the following questions.

14. One advantage that the Confederacy held during the Civil War was that

- **A** it received military and financial support from the British and the French.
- **B** many battles occurred on lands with which Southerners were more familiar.
- **C** the largest weapons factories were located in the South.
- **D** most people in the country agreed with the position of the Southern states.

Base your answers to questions 15 and 16 on the map below and on your knowledge of Chapter 9.

Peninsula Campaign, April–May 1862

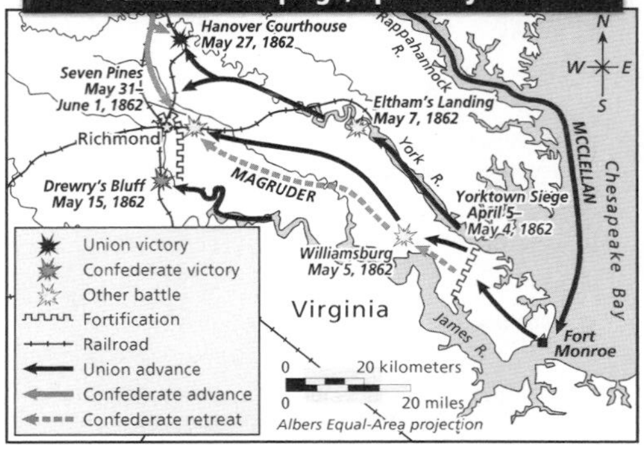

15. How did General McClellan move his troops to Virginia?

- **A** railroad
- **B** wagon
- **C** land
- **D** water

16. The object of the Peninsula Campaign for the Union was to

- **A** capture Richmond.
- **B** capture Yorktown.
- **C** outrace Magruder to Fredericksburg.
- **D** blockade Chesapeake Bay.

Need Extra Help?								
If You Missed Questions . . .	9	10	11	12	13	14	15	16
Go to Page . . .	331–332	332	340	341	344	314–317	352	352

GO ON

15. D General McClellan was a Union general. Have students trace the black arrow, which according to the key represents the Union advance. Have students trace their finger along the line. It begins by running down the Chesapeake Bay, although some parts of it continue on land, a good portion of the line then travels up the York River, and another Union advance traveled up the James River. There is more water travel evident than there is land travel. There is no evidence to support *A* and *B*.

16. A Even without knowledge from the chapter, it is evident from the map that all of the Union and Confederate paths move toward a convergence at Richmond.

17. One result of the Battle of Antietam was that
- **A** Lincoln decided to issue the Emancipation Proclamation.
- **B** the Confederacy was split in two.
- **C** Great Britain decided to support the Confederacy.
- **D** David Farragut became a hero in the North.

18. The Union blockade of Southern ports helped to win the war by
- **A** forcing Jefferson Davis to resign as president of the Confederacy.
- **B** destroying Southern morale through food and supply shortages.
- **C** making heroes out of the blockade runners.
- **D** making it easier for enslaved people to escape to the North.

Analyze the cartoon and answer the question that follows. Base your answer on the cartoon and on your knowledge of Chapter 9.

19. What was the main idea of this cartoon, which features Peace Democrats, called "Copperheads?"
- **A** Peace Democrats are helpful to the Union cause.
- **B** Peace Democrats are a threat to the Union cause.
- **C** Peace Democrats are frightening to many people.
- **D** Peace Democrats are peaceful and caring.

Document-Based Questions

Directions: Analyze the document and answer the short-answer questions that follow the document.

At the beginning of the Civil War, Robert E. Lee wrote a letter to his sister, Anne Marshall, explaining his decision to resign from the U.S. Army. Below is an excerpt from that letter:

> *"My Dear Sister:*
>
> *. . . With all my devotion to the Union and the feeling of loyalty and duty of an American citizen, I have not been able to make up my mind to raise my hand against my relatives, my children, my home. I have, therefore, resigned my commission in the Army, and, save in defense of my native state . . . I hope I may never be called on to draw my sword. I know you will blame me; but you must think as kindly of me as you can. . . ."*
>
> —from *Personal Reminiscences, Anecdotes, and Letters of General Robert E. Lee*

20. Why did Robert E. Lee think it was necessary to resign from the U.S. Army at the start of the war?

21. What do you think Lee's feelings were about the war?

Extended Response

22. President Lincoln suspended writs of habeas corpus during the Civil War. In a persuasive essay, explain your views on the suspension of civil liberties under this circumstance and in general. Do you think that the suspension of civil liberties is justified in some situations? Be sure to include an introduction and at least three paragraphs using details to support your views.

STOP

History ONLINE

For additional test practice, use Self-Check Quizzes—Chapter 9 at glencoe.com.

Need Extra Help?

If You Missed Questions . . .	17	18	19	20	21	22
Go to Page . . .	326	328	316	353	353	314–317

Document-Based Questions

20. Lee did not want to stay in the Union army and fight fellow Virginians. Lee, like hundreds of other Southern military men, did not want to break up the Union, but his loyalty to his "countrymen" would not permit him to take up arms against them.

21. Answers will vary. Possible answer: He probably thought it was a terrible tragedy, and he could not fight a war against his own family.

Extended Response

22. Students' essays must present a clear position, either for or against the suspension of habeas corpus during war and in other circumstances. Argument must be focused and well-reasoned. Essay must include supporting details from the text, as well as an introduction, conclusion, and at least three body paragraphs.

17. A Lincoln had not emancipated enslaved African Americans at the beginning of the war, for fear of alienating border states. However, after Antietam, the issuance of the Proclamation added a new motivation to the war: freeing enslaved people.

18. B The blockade of southern ports caused food shortages in the South and the ensuing hardship lowered morale.

19. B Help students analyze the cartoon. The woman, carrying a shield that says "Union" represents the Union. This is a play on the traditional Lady Liberty figure. The Copperheads are clearly advancing on the woman in a threatening way. *A* and *D* do not fit with the threatening nature of the Copperheads. *C* is too general to describe the cartoon.

History ONLINE

Have students visit the Web site at glencoe.com to review Chapter 9 and take the Self-Check Quiz.

Need Extra Help?

Have students refer to the pages listed if they miss any of the questions.

Chapter 10 Planning Guide

Key to Ability Levels	
BL Below Level	AL Above Level
OL On Level	ELL English Language Learners

Key to Teaching Resources	
Print Material	Transparency
CD-ROM or DVD	

Levels: BL	OL	AL	ELL		Resources	Chapter Opener	Section 1	Section 2	Section 3	Chapter Assess
					FOCUS					
BL	OL	AL	ELL	Transparency	**Daily Focus Skills Transparencies**		10-1	10-2	10-3	
					TEACH					
BL	OL		ELL	Print Material	**Reading Essentials and Note-Taking Guide***		p. 111	p. 114	p. 117	
	OL			Print Material	**Historical Analysis Skills Activity, URB**		p. 86			
BL	OL		ELL	Print Material	**Guided Reading Activities, URB***		p. 112	p. 113	p. 114	
BL	OL	AL	ELL	Print Material	**Content Vocabulary Activity, URB***	p. 91				
BL	OL	AL	ELL	Print Material	**Academic Vocabulary Activity, URB**	p. 93				
	OL	AL		Print Material	**Critical Thinking Skills Activity, URB**					p. 96
BL	OL		ELL	Print Material	**Reading Skills Activity, URB**		p. 85			
BL			ELL	Print Material	**English Learner Activity, URB**	p. 89				
	OL	AL		Print Material	**Reinforcing Skills Activity, URB**		p. 95			
BL	OL	AL	ELL	Print Material	**Differentiated Instruction Activity, URB**			p. 87		
BL	OL		ELL	Print Material	**Time Line Activity, URB**		p. 97			
	OL			Print Material	**Linking Past and Present Activity, URB**		p. 98			
BL	OL	AL	ELL	Print Material	**American Art and Music Activity, URB**					p. 103
BL	OL	AL	ELL	Print Material	**Interpreting Political Cartoons Activity, URB**			p. 105		
		AL		Print Material	**Enrichment Activity, URB**			p. 109		
BL	OL	AL	ELL	Print Material	**American Biographies**		✓	✓		
BL	OL	AL	ELL	Print Material	**Primary Source Reading, URB**		p. 99	p. 101		
BL	OL	AL	ELL	Print Material	**The Living Constitution***	✓	✓	✓	✓	✓
	OL	AL		CD-ROM or DVD	**American History Primary Source Documents Library**	✓	✓	✓	✓	✓
BL	OL	AL	ELL	Transparency	**Unit Map Overlay Transparencies**	✓	✓	✓	✓	✓
BL	OL	AL	ELL	Print Material	**Differentiated Instruction for the American History Classroom**	✓	✓	✓	✓	✓
BL	OL	AL	ELL	CD-ROM or DVD	**StudentWorks™ Plus**	✓	✓	✓	✓	✓
BL	OL	AL	ELL	CD-ROM or DVD	**American Music Hits Through History CD**	✓	✓	✓	✓	✓
BL	OL	AL	ELL	Print Material	**Unit Time Line Transparencies and Activities**	✓	✓	✓	✓	✓

Note: Please refer to the *Unit 3 Resource Book* for this chapter's URB materials.

* Also available in Spanish

TeacherWorks Plus
All-In-One Planner and Resource Center

- Interactive Lesson Planner
- Interactive Teacher Edition
- Fully editable blackline masters
- Section Spotlight Videos Launch
- Differentiated Lesson Plans
- Printable reports of daily assignments
- Standards Tracking System

BL	OL	AL	ELL		Resources	Chapter Opener	Section 1	Section 2	Section 3	Chapter Assess
					TEACH *(continued)*					
BL	OL	AL	ELL		Cause and Effect Transparencies, Strategies, and Activities	✓	✓	✓	✓	✓
BL	OL	AL	ELL		Why It Matters Transparencies, Strategies, and Activities	✓	✓	✓	✓	✓
BL	OL	AL	ELL		American Issues	✓	✓	✓	✓	✓
	OL	AL	ELL		American Art and Architecture Transparencies, Strategies, and Activities	✓	✓	✓	✓	✓
BL	OL	AL			High School American History Literature Library	✓	✓	✓	✓	✓
BL	OL	AL	ELL		*The American Vision* Video Program	✓	✓	✓	✓	✓
Teacher Resources					Strategies for Success	✓	✓	✓	✓	✓
					Success with English Learner	✓	✓	✓	✓	✓
					Reading Strategies and Activities for the Social Studies Classroom	✓	✓	✓	✓	✓
					Presentation Plus! with MindJogger CheckPoint	✓	✓	✓	✓	✓
					ASSESS					
BL	OL	AL	ELL		Section Quizzes and Chapter Tests*		p. 133	p. 134	p. 135	p. 137
BL	OL	AL	ELL		Authentic Assessment With Rubrics					p. 25
BL	OL	AL	ELL		Standardized Test Practice Workbook					p. 20
BL	OL	AL	ELL		*ExamView® Assessment Suite*		10-1	10-2	10-3	CH. 10
					CLOSE					
BL			ELL		Reteaching Activity, URB					p. 107
BL	OL		ELL		Reading and Study Skills Foldables™	p. 57				

✓ Chapter- or unit-based activities applicable to all sections in this chapter.

Using Section Audio

Teach With Technology

What is Section Audio?

Section Audio is a recording of each section of the textbook and helps students learn the content in the textbook.

How can Section Audio help my students?

Section Audio allows students to:

- read and listen simultaneously to improve content comprehension
- practice reading skills
- review important concepts for struggling readers
- improve listening comprehension

Visit glencoe.com to access the Media Library, and enter a ***QuickPass***™ code to go to Section Audio recordings.

History ONLINE
Visit glencoe.com and enter ***QuickPass***™ code TAV9399c10T for Chapter 10 resources.

You can easily launch a wide range of digital products from your computer's desktop with the McGraw-Hill Social Studies widget.

TeacherWorks

	Student	Teacher	Parent
Media Library			
• Section Audio	●		●
• Spanish Audio Summaries	●		●
• Section Spotlight Videos	●	●	●
***The American Vision* Online Learning Center (Web Site)**			
• StudentWorks™ Plus Online	●	●	●
• Multilingual Glossary	●	●	●
• Study-to-Go	●	●	●
• Chapter Overviews	●	●	●
• Self-Check Quizzes	●	●	●
• Student Web Activities	●	●	●
• ePuzzles and Games	●	●	●
• Vocabulary eFlashcards	●	●	●
• In Motion Animations	●	●	●
• Study Central™	●	●	●
• Web Activity Lesson Plans		●	
• Vocabulary PuzzleMaker	●	●	●
• Historical Thinking Activities		●	
• Beyond the Textbook	●	●	●

Reading Support From Jamestown Education

- **Timed Readings Plus in Social Studies** helps students increase their reading rate and fluency while maintaining comprehension. The 400-word passages are similar to those found on state and national assessments.
- **Reading in the Content Area: Social Studies** concentrates on six essential reading skills that help students better comprehend what they read. The book includes 75 high-interest nonfiction passages written at increasing levels of difficulty.
- **Reading Social Studies** includes strategic reading instruction and vocabulary support in Social Studies content for both ELLs and native speakers of English.

www.jamestowneducation.com

Biography · A&E Home Video · The History Channel

The following videotape programs are available from Glencoe as supplements to this chapter:

- Ku Klux Klan: A Secret History (ISBN 0-76-700878-2)
- Frederick Douglass (ISBN 0-76-700120-6)

To order, call Glencoe at 1-800-334-7344. To find classroom resources to accompany many of these videos, check the following home pages:

A&E Television: www.aetv.com
The History Channel: www.historychannel.com

National Geographic

Index to National Geographic Magazine:

The following articles relate to this chapter:

"Lost Gold: Bounty From a Civil War Ship" By Priit J. Vesilind

National Geographic Society Products To order the following, call National Geographic at 1-800-368-2728:

- *ZipZapMap! USA* (ZipZapMap!)

Access National Geographic's new dynamic MapMachine Web site and other geography resources at:
www.nationalgeographic.com
www.nationalgeographic.com/maps

Reading List Generator CD-ROM — Glencoe BookLink 3

Use this database to search more than 30,000 titles to create a customized reading list for your students.

- Reading lists can be organized by students' reading level, author, genre, theme, or area of interest.
- The database provides Degrees of Reading Power™ (DRP) and Lexile™ readability scores for all selections.
- A brief summary of each selection is included.

Leveled reading suggestions for this chapter:

For students at a Grade 8 reading level:
- ***Tancy***, by Belinda Hurmence

For students at a Grade 9 reading level:
- ***Voices—and Stories—From the Past***, by Kathryn Satterfield

For students at a Grade 10 reading level:
- ***Ulysses S. Grant: 18th President of the United States***, by Lucille Falkof

For students at a Grade 11 reading level:
- ***Up from Slavery***, by Booker T. Washington

For students at a Grade 12 reading level:
- ***Andrew Johnson: 17th President of the United States***, by Rita Stevens

Introducing Chapter 10

Focus

MAKING CONNECTIONS

How Do Nations Recover From War?

Ask students to suggest issues that must be settled after a war. Activate their prior knowledge by asking them to discuss what had to be done after the American Revolution. Remind them of the need to form state governments and reconcile people who fought on different sides, as well as physical issues such as rebuilding infrastructure, replenishing food supplies, and so forth. **OL**

Teach

The Big Ideas

As students study the chapter, remind them to consider the section-based Big Ideas included in each section's Guide to Reading. The **Essential Questions** in the activities below tie in to the Big Ideas and help students think about and understand important chapter concepts. In addition, the Hands-on Chapter Projects with their culminating activities relate the content from each section to the Big Ideas. These activities build on each other as students progress through the chapter. Section activities culminate in the wrap-up activity on the Visual Summary page.

Chapter 10

Reconstruction

1865–1877

Richmond, Virginia, lies in ruins after the city falls to Union troops in April 1865.

U.S. PRESIDENTS

A. Johnson 1865–1869

Grant 1869–1877

U.S. EVENTS

1865
- Freedmen's Bureau is founded
- Lincoln is assassinated

1866
- Congress passes the Fourteenth Amendment

1867
- Radical Republicans take control of Congress

1870
- Fifteenth Amendment ratified

1871
- Congress passes the Ku Klux Klan Act

1865 — 1867 — 1869 — 1871

WORLD EVENTS

1866
- Transatlantic cable is completed

1868
- Meiji Restoration begins Japanese modernization

1869
- First ships pass through Suez Canal

1871
- Germany is unified; German Empire is proclaimed

Section 1

The Debate Over Reconstruction

Essential Question: What key issues caused disagreements about how Reconstruction should take place? *(Under what conditions Southern states could organize state governments; oaths of loyalty; amnesty for high-ranking Confederates; protection of formerly enslaved African Americans' rights.)* Tell students that in this section they will learn about three plans for handling these issues, over which there was much debate. **OL**

Section 2

Republican Rule

Essential Question: How did the politics of Reconstruction affect African Americans? *(Corruption; influx of Northerners; community prominence of African American churches; rise of African American politicians; Ku Klux Klan)* Tell students that in this section they will learn about the role African Americans played in Reconstruction. **OL**

Chapter Audio

MAKING CONNECTIONS

How Do Nations Recover From War?

After war devastates a country, it needs to feed and house refugees, repair damage, create jobs, and get the economy growing again. The United States faced all of these problems after the Civil War, but it also had to find a way to reconcile Northerners and Southerners and protect the rights of the formerly enslaved.

- ***What did the United States do to reconstruct the South?***
- ***Considering both the short term and the long term, was Reconstruction a success or a failure?***

FOLDABLES

Contrasting Before and After Collect information about life in the South before and after the Civil War. List the most important facts in a Two-Tab Foldable. Include information about all levels of Southern society—rich and poor, white and African American, native-born and immigrant—and how conditions changed for each group.

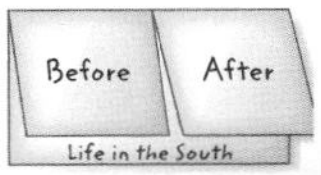

1875
- "Whiskey Ring" scandal breaks

Hayes 1877–1881

1877
- Compromise of 1877 ends Reconstruction efforts

1873 — 1875 — 1877

1874
- First Impressionist art exhibit opens in Paris

History ONLINE Visit glencoe.com and enter *QuickPass*™ code TAV9846c10 for Chapter 10 resources.

Section 3

Reconstruction Collapses

Essential Question: What problems hindered rebuilding of the Southern economy? *(Political scandals and corruption; terrorist groups; Panic of 1873; lack of industry)* Tell students that in this section they will learn about the problems that besieged the Grant and Hayes administrations and the attempts to create a "New South." **OL**

Introducing
Chapter 10

More About the Photo

Visual Literacy Many panoramic photos were taken of Richmond in 1865. Instead of today's panoramic technique of rotating the camera to take a continuous image, these photos were taken by exposing one plate, moving the camera, then taking another plate. The plates were physically joined in the studio.

FOLDABLES Study Organizer **Dinah Zike's Foldables**

Dinah Zike's Foldables are three-dimensional, interactive graphic organizers that help students practice basic writing skills, review vocabulary terms, and identify main ideas. Instructions for creating and using Foldables can be found in the Appendix at the end of this book and in the *Dinah Zike's Reading and Study Skills Foldables* booklet.

History ONLINE
Visit glencoe.com and enter *QuickPass*™ code TAV9399c10T for Chapter 10 resources, including a Chapter Overview, Study Central™, Study-to-Go, Student Web Activity, Self-Check Quiz, and other materials.

Focus

Bellringer

Daily Focus Transparency 10-1

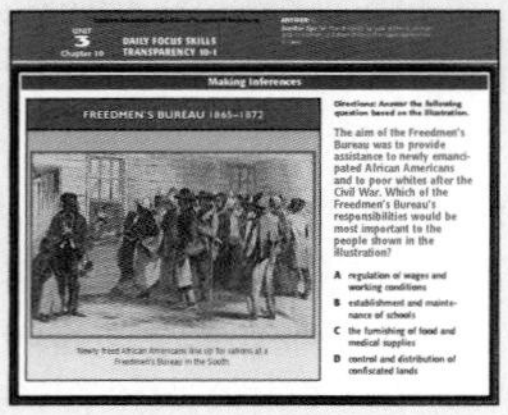

Guide to Reading

Answers:

Legislation	Effect
black codes	Severely limited African Americans' rights
Civil Rights Act of 1866	Granted citizenship; allowed African Americans to own property and to sue
Fourteenth Amendment	Granted equal protection/ due process
Fifteenth Amendment	suffrage

Section Spotlight Video

To generate interest and provide a springboard for class discussion, access the Chapter 10, Section 1 video at glencoe.com or on the video DVD.

Section 1

Section Audio   Spotlight Video

The Debate Over Reconstruction

Guide to Reading

Big Ideas

Group Action Northerners disagreed about which policies would best rebuild the South and safeguard the rights of African Americans.

Content Vocabulary

- amnesty *(p. 356)*
- pocket veto *(p. 358)*
- black codes *(p. 360)*
- impeach *(p. 363)*

Academic Vocabulary

- requirement *(p. 362)*
- precedent *(p. 363)*

People and Events to Identify

- Radical Republicans *(p. 357)*
- Wade-Davis Bill *(p. 358)*
- Freedmen's Bureau *(p. 358)*
- Civil Rights Act of 1866 *(p. 361)*
- Fourteenth Amendment *(p. 361)*
- Fifteenth Amendment *(p. 363)*

Reading Strategy

Organizing Complete a graphic organizer similar to the one below to explain how each listed piece of legislation affected African Americans.

Legislation	Effect
black codes	
Civil Rights Act of 1866	
Fourteenth Amendment	
Fifteenth Amendment	

In the months after the Civil War ended, the nation began to rebuild and reunite. Almost immediately, fierce struggles began over how long it should take to restore the Southern states to the Union and how punitive Reconstruction should be.

The Reconstruction Battle Begins

MAIN Idea Presidents Lincoln and Johnson, as well as Radical Republicans in Congress, put forward different plans for reconstructing the Union.

HISTORY AND YOU Think of another war that you have studied. What were the peace terms, and who benefited? Read on to learn about different plans for peace following the American Civil War.

By 1865, large areas of the former Confederacy lay in ruins, and the South's economy was in a state of collapse. The value of land had fallen significantly. Confederate money was worthless. Roughly two-thirds of the transportation system no longer functioned, with dozens of bridges destroyed and miles of railroad twisted and rendered useless. Most dramatically of all, the emancipation of African Americans had thrown the agricultural system into chaos. Until the South developed a new system to replace enslaved labor, it could not maintain its agricultural output.

While some Southerners felt bitter over the Union's military victory, for many the more important struggle was rebuilding their land and their lives. Meanwhile, the president and Congress grappled with the difficult task of Reconstruction, or rebuilding after the war.

Lincoln's Plan

In December 1863 President Lincoln offered a general **amnesty,** or pardon, to all Southerners who took an oath of loyalty to the United States and accepted the Union's proclamations concerning slavery. When 10 percent of a state's voters in the 1860 presidential election had taken this oath, they could organize a new state government. Certain people, such as officials, Confederate government, and military officers could not take the oath or be pardoned. In March 1865, in his Second Inaugural Address, President Lincoln spoke of ending the war "with malice toward none, with charity for all." Therefore, President Lincoln wanted a moderate policy to reconcile the South with the Union, instead of punishing it for treason.

Resource Manager

R Reading Strategies	C Critical Thinking	D Differentiated Instruction	W Writing Support	S Skill Practice
Teacher Edition • Organizing, p. 358 • Outlining, p. 360 • Questioning, p. 363 **Additional Resources** • Content Vocab. Act, URB p. 91 • Guided Read. Act., URB p. 112 • Prim. Source Read., URB p. 99	**Teacher Edition** • Contrasting, p. 357 • Drawing Conclusions., pp. 359, 361 • Analyzing, p. 362 **Additional Resources** • Hist. Analysis Skills Act., URB p. 86 • Quizzes/Tests, p. 133 • Linking Past/Present Act., URB p. 98	**Additional Resources** • English Learner Act., URB p. 89	**Teacher Edition** • Persuasive Writing, p. 357 **Additional Resources** • Academic Vocab. Act., URB p. 93	**Teacher Edition** • Reading Maps, p. 362 **Additional Resources** • Reading Skills, URB p. 85 • Reinforcing Skills, URB p. 95 • Time Line Act., URB p. 97 • Read. Essen., p. 111

C

INFOGRAPHIC

Three Plans for Reconstruction

After the Civil War, three plans were proposed to restore the South to the Union. The political struggle that resulted revealed that sectional tensions had not ended with the Civil War.

1. Lincoln's Plan for Reconstruction

- Amnesty to all but a few Southerners who took an oath of loyalty to the United States and accepted its proclamations concerning slavery
- When 10 percent of a state's voters in the 1860 presidential election had taken the oath, they could organize a new state government
- Members of the former Confederate government, officers of the Confederate army, and former federal judges, members of Congress, and military officers who had left their posts to help the Confederacy would not receive amnesty

2. Congressional Reconstruction

- Passed the Fourteenth and Fifteenth Amendments
- Military Reconstruction Act divided the South into five military districts
- New state constitutions required to guarantee voting rights
- Military rule protected voting rights for African Americans
- Empowered African Americans in government and supported their education

▲ *Thaddeus Stevens*

▶ *Charles Sumner*

3. Johnson's Plan for Reconstruction

- Amnesty for those taking an oath of loyalty to the United States; excluded high-ranking Confederates and those with property over $20,000, but they could apply for pardons individually
- Required states to ratify the Thirteenth Amendment abolishing slavery

W

Analyzing VISUALS

1. **Identifying** Which plan made the most provisions for formerly enslaved African Americans?
2. **Specifying** Which plan was most forgiving of former Confederate political and military leaders?

The Radical Republicans

Resistance to Lincoln's plan surfaced at once among the more radical Republicans in Congress. Led by Representative Thaddeus Stevens of Pennsylvania and Senator Charles Sumner of Massachusetts, the radicals did not want to reconcile with the South. They wanted, in Stevens's words, to "revolutionize Southern institutions, habits, and manners."

The **Radical Republicans** had three main goals. First, they wanted to prevent the leaders of the Confederacy from returning to power after the war. Second, they wanted the Republican Party to become a powerful institution in the South. Third, they wanted the federal government to help African Americans achieve political equality by guaranteeing their right to vote in the South.

Republicans knew that, once the South was restored to the Union, it would gain about 15 seats in the House of Representatives. Before the Civil War, the number of Southern seats in the House was based on the Three-Fifths Compromise in the Constitution. According to this compromise, only three-fifths of the enslaved population counted toward representation. The abolition of slavery entitled the South to more seats in the House. This would endanger Republican control of Congress, unless Republicans could find a way to protect African Americans' voting rights.

Teach

W Writing Support

Persuasive Writing Have students assume the role of a former Confederate officer and write a letter to the president requesting a pardon. Remind students that those receiving amnesty must sign a loyalty oath. **OL**

C Critical Thinking

Contrasting Have students review the three plans for Reconstruction. **Ask:** How do the three plans differ? *(Answers may include: amnesty eligibility, voting rights, requirements for forming state governments, abolition)*

Analyzing VISUALS

Answers:
1. the Congressional plan
2. Johnson's plan

Hands-On Chapter Project
Step 1

Reconstruction Correspondence

Step 1: Understanding Reconstruction from a Northern Point of View Working in small groups, students will study the different approaches toward Reconstruction addressed in Section 1.

Directions Hold a class discussion in which you discuss with students the different approaches toward Reconstruction in the South. On the board, write the components of the Military Reconstruction Act passed by Congress.

Analyzing Instruct groups to analyze the information and decide whether they support or oppose the Military Reconstruction Act. Have them assume the role of a Northerner during Reconstruction and write a letter to Congress expressing their views. **OL** *(Chapter Project continued on page 367)*

R Reading Strategy

Organizing Have students complete a graphic organizer like the one below showing what the Wade-Davis Bill would have required of Southern states. **BL**

Wade-Davis Bill →
- Abolish slavery
- Reject Confederate debts
- No suffrage or offices for former Confederate officers or officials

Reading Check

Answer:
Lincoln wanted to reconcile Southerners with the Union rather than punish them for treason.

Additional Support

Although Radical Republicans knew that giving African American men in the South the right to vote would help their party win elections, most were not acting cynically. Many had been abolitionists before the Civil War and had pushed Lincoln into making emancipation a goal of the war. They believed in a right to political equality for all men, regardless of race. Senator Henry Wilson of Massachusetts summarized their position:

PRIMARY SOURCE

"[Congress] must see to it that the man made free by the Constitution . . . is a freeman indeed; that he can go where he pleases, work when and for whom he pleases . . . go into schools and educate himself and his children; that the rights and guarantees of the good old common law are his, and that he walks the earth, proud and erect in the conscious dignity of a free man."

—from the *Congressional Globe*, December 21, 1865

History ONLINE Student Web Activity Visit glencoe.com and complete the activity on Southern Reconstruction.

The Wade-Davis Bill

Caught between Lincoln and the Radical Republicans were a large number of moderate Republicans. The moderates thought Lincoln was too lenient but that the radicals were going too far in supporting African Americans.

By the summer of 1864, the moderates and radicals had agreed on an alternative plan to Lincoln's and introduced it in Congress as the **Wade-Davis Bill.** This bill required the majority of the adult white males in a former Confederate state to take an oath of allegiance to the Union. The state could then hold a constitutional convention to create a new state government. Each state's convention would then have to abolish slavery, reject all debts the state had acquired as part of the Confederacy, and deprive all former Confederate government officials and military officers of the right to vote or hold office.

Although Congress passed the Wade-Davis Bill, Lincoln blocked it with a **pocket veto**—that is, he let the session of Congress expire without signing the legislation. He thought that imposing a harsh peace would be counterproductive. The president wanted "no persecution, no bloody work."

Reading Check **Summarizing** Why did President Lincoln favor a lenient policy toward the South?

Freedmen's Bureau

MAIN Idea The Freedmen's Bureau helped newly freed African Americans obtain food, find work, and get an education.

HISTORY AND YOU Do you remember the slave codes that denied African Americans basic rights, including an education? Read on to learn how the Freedmen's Bureau tried to help former slaves start their new lives.

After considering different approaches to restoring the Southern states to the Union, Lincoln decided that harsh terms would only alienate many whites in the South. The devastation of the war and the collapse of the economy had left hundreds of thousands of people unemployed, homeless, and hungry. At the same time, the victorious Union armies had to contend with the thousands of African Americans who had fled to Union lines as the war progressed. As Sherman marched through Georgia and South Carolina, thousands of freed African Americans—now known as freedmen—began following his troops, seeking food and shelter.

To help the freedmen feed themselves, Sherman reserved all abandoned plantation land within 30 miles of the coast from Charleston, South Carolina, to Jacksonville, Florida, for the use of freed African Americans. Over the next few months, Union troops settled more than 40,000 African Americans on roughly half a million acres of land in South Carolina and Georgia.

The refugee crisis prompted Congress to establish the Bureau of Refugees, Freedmen, and Abandoned Lands—better known as the **Freedmen's Bureau.** It was given the task of feeding and clothing war refugees in the South using surplus army supplies. Beginning in September 1865, the bureau provided nearly 30,000 rations a day for the next year and helped prevent mass starvation in the South.

The Bureau also helped formerly enslaved people find work on plantations. It negotiated labor contracts with planters, specifying the amount of pay workers would receive and the number of hours they had to work. It also established special courts to deal with grievances between workers and planters.

Although many Northerners backed the Bureau, some argued that freedmen should be given "forty acres and a mule" to support

Activity: Collaborative Learning

Reading Support Immediately after students read this section, lead a discussion about the various Reconstruction plans. Tell students that you will be using some important terms from the text. Have students write down each term they hear that also appeared in the text. Suggested terms include: *Reconstruction, amnesty, Radical Republicans,* and *pocket veto.* Then ask students to work with a partner to write a brief summary of the plans for Reconstruction using the terms they listed. **OL** **ELL**

themselves. These people urged the federal government to seize Confederate land and distribute it to emancipated slaves. To others, however, taking land from plantation owners was wrong because it violated individual property rights. Ultimately, Congress rejected land confiscation.

The Freedmen's Bureau made an important contribution in the field of education. The Bureau worked closely with Northern charities to educate formerly enslaved African Americans. It provided buildings for schools, paid teachers, and helped to establish colleges for training African American teachers. Morehouse College, originally known as Augusta Institute, was founded in 1867. It benefited from these educational efforts and has graduated figures such as Martin Luther King, Jr., and filmmaker Spike Lee.

Reading Check **Explaining** What were the purposes of the Freedmen's Bureau?

Johnson Takes Office

MAIN Idea President Johnson wanted to readmit Southern states on generous terms; meanwhile, Southern states passed laws restricting the rights of African Americans.

HISTORY AND YOU Have you ever had a dispute with a longtime friend? After it was over, did the situation improve? Read to learn how Southern states passed laws to limit African Americans' rights.

Lincoln's assassination drastically changed the politics of Reconstruction. Lincoln's vice president, Andrew Johnson, now became president. Johnson had been a Southern Democrat before the Civil War. A resident of Tennessee, he had served as a mayor and state legislator before being elected to the United States Senate. When Tennessee seceded, Johnson remained loyal and stayed in the Senate, making him a hero in the North.

PRIMARY SOURCE

The Freedmen's Bureau in Action

The Freedmen's Bureau was established by the Union to help formerly enslaved people make new lives for themselves. Headed by Union General Oliver Otis Howard, the Bureau provided food, clothing, and medical care. It also helped African Americans to build and manage many schools, such as those pictured here, throughout the South.

▲ *Schools funded by the Freedmen's Bureau, such as the one above, led to a dramatic increase in literacy among African Americans. By 1870, more than 1,000 new schools had been established.* C

▲ *Formerly enslaved African Americans await the distribution of food at office of the Freedmen's Bureau in South Carolina in 1865.*

Analyzing VISUALS

1. **Specifying** Aside from basic relief efforts, what other services did the Freedmen's Bureau provide?
2. **Explaining** Why do you think education was a priority for formerly enslaved people?

C Critical Thinking

Drawing Conclusions

Ask: Why do you think plantation owners in the South did not want enslaved African Americans to be educated? What did the government do about it? *(Students should note that the plantation owners wanted to maintain the status quo of slavery. Through the Freedmen's Bureau, the government provided educational services.)* **OL**

Analyzing VISUALS

Answers:
1. education, food, land, work, labor courts
2. They had not been allowed education while enslaved and would need it to find better jobs.

Reading Check

Answer:
Its purpose was to help newly freed African Americans obtain food, find work, and get an education.

Additional Support

Activity: Technology Connection

Analyzing Information Have interested students work in groups to research African American colleges founded in the nineteenth century. Students should use Internet resources to conduct their research. Groups should then prepare a one-page description of each school—including current and historical information—for presentation to the class. They also should bring in historical photos, if available. Students descriptions should answer the following questions. Who founded the school? What is its history, in brief, including any illustrious alumni? How many students does it currently have and does it have an educational focus? What other information about the school is important? **OL** **AL**

Turning Point

Answer:
The Fourteenth Amendment expanded federal power over the states; its equal protection clause has been used to extend civil rights.

R Reading Strategy

Outlining Have students outline the section "Johnson's Plan," using the paragraph indents as keys to organizing the outline. BL

Reading Check

Answer:
He blamed the rich planter elite in the South.

As Union troops advanced into Tennessee in 1862, Lincoln appointed Johnson military governor of the state. The president then approved Johnson's nomination as vice president in 1864, hoping to convince some Democrats to vote Republican. Johnson was hot-tempered and stubborn at times, but, like Lincoln, he believed that a moderate policy was needed to bring the South back into the Union and to win Southern loyalty.

R Johnson's Plan

In the summer of 1865, with Congress in recess, Johnson initiated what he called his restoration program, which closely resembled Lincoln's plan. In late May 1865, he issued an amnesty proclamation to supplement the one Lincoln had issued earlier. Johnson offered to pardon all former citizens of the Confederacy who took an oath of loyalty to the Union and to return their property. He excluded from the pardon former Confederate officers and officials, as well as former Confederates who owned property worth more than $20,000. These were the people—the rich planter elite—who Johnson believed had caused the Civil War. Those who were excluded could apply individually for a pardon.

On the same day that he issued the pardon, Johnson issued another proclamation for North Carolina. This became a model of how he wanted to restore the South to the Union. Under it, each former Confederate state had to call a constitutional convention to revoke its ordinance of secession, ratify the Thirteenth Amendment, and reject all Civil War debts.

The former Confederate states, for the most part, met Johnson's conditions. While they organized their new governments and elected members to Congress, Johnson began granting pardons to thousands of Southerners.

By the time Congress gathered for its next session in December 1865, Johnson's plan was well under way. Many members of Congress were astonished and angered when they realized that Southern voters had elected to Congress many former Confederate officers and political leaders, including Alexander Stephens, the former vice president of the Confederacy. Many Republicans found this unacceptable and voted to reject the new Southern members of Congress.

Black Codes

The election of former Confederate leaders to Congress was not the only development that angered congressional Republicans. The new Southern state legislatures also passed a series of laws known as **black codes,** which severely limited African Americans' rights.

The black codes varied from state to state, but they all seemed intended to keep African Americans in a condition similar to slavery. African Americans were generally required to enter into annual labor contracts. Their children had to accept apprenticeships in some states and could be whipped or beaten while serving in these apprenticeships. Several state codes set specific work hours for African Americans and required them to get licenses to work in nonagricultural jobs.

The black codes enraged many Northerners. Gideon Welles, the secretary of the navy, warned, "The entire South seem to be stupid and vindictive, know not their friends, and are pursuing just the course which their opponents, the Radicals, desire."

Reading Check **Summarizing** Whom did President Johnson blame for the Civil War?

Turning Point

The Fourteenth Amendment

The passage of the Fourteenth Amendment was a turning point in American political and legal history. Since its ratification, the amendment has been used to expand federal power over the states and to extend civil rights through its equal protection clause. It also provided the foundation for the doctrine of incorporation—the concept that the rights and protections in the Bill of Rights apply to the states. This doctrine was first upheld by the Supreme Court in *Gitlow* v. *New York* in 1925. In the 1950s and 1960s, the Warren Court used the clause extensively to extend civil rights in cases such as *Brown* v. *Board of Education*, *Gideon* v. *Wainwright*, and *Reynolds* v. *Sims*, among others.

ANALYZING HISTORY What is significant about the ratification of the Fourteenth Amendment? Write a brief essay to explain your answer.

Additional Support

Activity: Interdisciplinary Connection

Political Science Have students use library and Internet resources to research the harsh restrictions placed on African Americans by the black codes. Then ask students to work in pairs, using their research to create a political cartoon that expresses their reaction to these laws. Encourage students to share their completed cartoons with the class and have others interpret their meaning. Ask students to find present-day political cartoons that represent their feelings on a social issue. Have students share these cartoons with the class. OL ELL

Radical Republicans Take Control

MAIN Idea Radical Republicans, angered by President Johnson's actions, designed their own policies to reconstruct the South.

HISTORY AND YOU If you disagree with a political decision, what can you do to change it? Read how Republicans responded to Johnson's plan.

The election of former Confederate leaders to Congress and the introduction of the black codes convinced many moderate Republicans to join the Radicals. In late 1865, House and Senate Republicans created a Joint Committee on Reconstruction. Their goal was to develop their own program for rebuilding the Union.

The Fourteenth Amendment

In an effort to override the black codes, Congress passed the **Civil Rights Act of 1866.** The act granted citizenship to all persons born in the United States except Native Americans. It allowed African Americans to own property and stated that they were to be treated equally in court. It also gave the federal government the power to sue people who violated those rights.

Worried that the Supreme Court might overturn the Civil Rights Act, the Republicans then introduced the **Fourteenth Amendment** to the Constitution. This amendment granted citizenship to all persons born or naturalized in the United States and declared that no state could deprive any person of life, liberty, or property "without due process of law." It also declared that no state could deny any person "equal protection of the laws."

Increasing violence in the South convinced moderates to support the amendment. The most dramatic incident occurred in Memphis, Tennessee, in May 1866, when white mobs killed 46 African Americans and burned hundreds of their homes, churches, and schools. Congress passed the amendment in June and sent it to the states for ratification.

President Johnson attacked the amendment and made it the major issue of the 1866 congressional elections. He hoped voters would reject the Radical Republicans and elect a new majority in Congress that would support his plan for Reconstruction instead.

The Fourteenth Amendment

"No State shall make or enforce any law which shall abridge the privileges or immunities of citizens of the United States; nor shall any State deprive any person of life, liberty, or property, without due process of law; nor deny to any person within its jurisdiction the equal protection of the laws."

▲ *In 1964, in* Reynolds v. Sims, *the Court used the Fourteenth Amendment's equal protection clause to ensure that state voting districts were of equal size.*

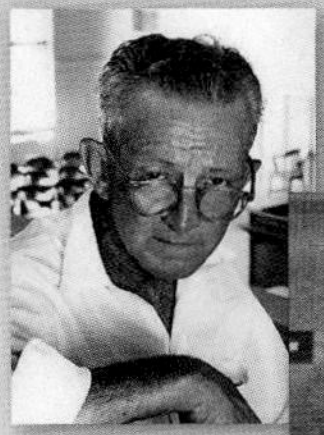

◀ *Clarence Gideon*

▶ *Ernesto Miranda*

▲ *In two major cases,* Gideon v. Wainwright *in 1963 and* Miranda v. Arizona *in 1966, the Court clarified that the Fifth and Sixth Amendments of the Bill of Rights had to be upheld by the states.*

▶ *In 1925, in* Gitlow v. New York, *the Supreme Court began using the Fourteenth Amendment to apply the Bill of Rights to the states. In this case, it held that state laws had to protect free speech.*

▲ *Benjamin Gitlow*

◀ *In 1954 the Supreme Court based its decision ending school segregation,* Brown v. Board of Education, *on the Fourteenth Amendment's equal protection clause.*

C

C Critical Thinking

Drawing Conclusions Have students review the Turning Point feature on the Fourteenth Amendment. **Ask:** On what part of the Fourteenth Amendment did the Supreme Court base the Brown v. Board of Education decision? *(the equal protection clause)* OL

Additional Support

Teacher Tip

Suggesting that one group choose the presidential election of 2000 as an example for the activity may produce an interesting class discussion of contemporary application of the Fourteenth Amendment.

Activity: Collaborative Learning

Explaining Divide the class into three groups. Have each group research a Supreme Court case based on the Fourteenth Amendment. They may use one of the cases mentioned on page 361 or any other case they find. Students will assume the role of attorneys arguing the case before the Court—in this case, the rest of the class. One member of the group should present a brief background of the case. The rest of the group should be divided into two teams—one for each side of the argument. Each of the members should present one point for or against the plaintiff's case. After the presentations, the class should render a decision for each case. OL

C Critical Thinking

Analyzing After students read the "Military Reconstruction" section, have them consider the reasons behind Southern resistance to the Fourteenth Amendment and to African American suffrage. **Ask:** Why did so many Southern states resist ratifying the Fourteenth Amendment and suffrage for all men? *(Students should note that the Southern states had large populations of African Americans, who with voting rights, could be a powerful influence.)* **OL**

S Skill Practice

Reading Maps Ask: Which state was readmitted to the Union first? *(Tennessee)* **ELL**

Analyzing GEOGRAPHY

Answers:
1. Tennessee
2. Five years after the end of the war, the last Southern state was readmitted to the Union.

Additional Support

NATIONAL GEOGRAPHIC **Military Reconstruction, 1867**

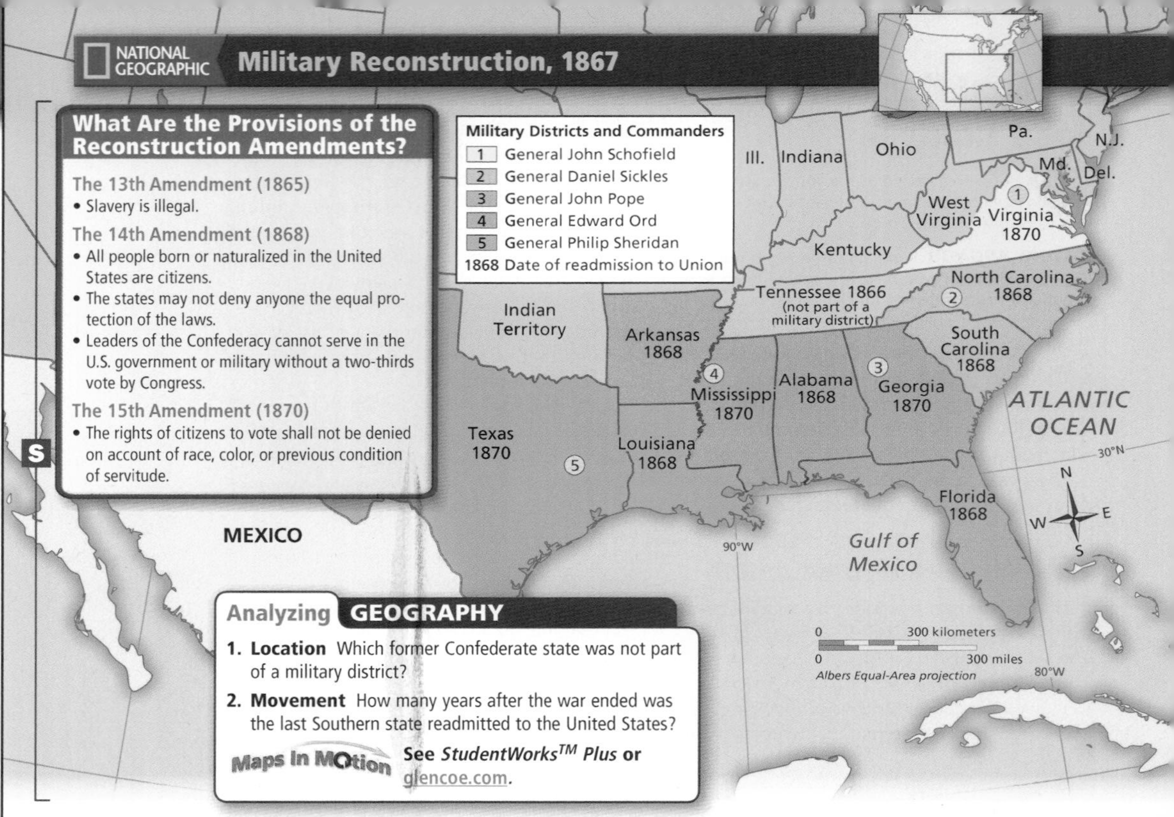

What Are the Provisions of the Reconstruction Amendments?

The 13th Amendment (1865)
- Slavery is illegal.

The 14th Amendment (1868)
- All people born or naturalized in the United States are citizens.
- The states may not deny anyone the equal protection of the laws.
- Leaders of the Confederacy cannot serve in the U.S. government or military without a two-thirds vote by Congress.

The 15th Amendment (1870)
- The rights of citizens to vote shall not be denied on account of race, color, or previous condition of servitude.

Analyzing GEOGRAPHY

1. **Location** Which former Confederate state was not part of a military district?
2. **Movement** How many years after the war ended was the last Southern state readmitted to the United States?

Maps In MOtion See *StudentWorks™ Plus* or glencoe.com.

As the election campaign got under way, more violence erupted in the South. In July 1866, a white mob attacked delegates to a convention in New Orleans that supported African American voting rights. As Johnson attacked Radical Republicans, Republicans responded by accusing Democrats of being traitors and starting the Civil War. When the votes were counted, the Republicans had won a roughly three-to-one majority in Congress. The Fourteenth Amendment was ratified by the states in 1868.

Military Reconstruction

In March 1867 congressional Republicans passed the Military Reconstruction Act, which essentially wiped out Johnson's programs. The act divided the former Confederacy, except for Tennessee—which had ratified the Fourteenth Amendment in 1866—into five military districts. A Union general was placed in charge of each district.

In the meantime, each former Confederate state had to hold another constitutional convention. The new state constitutions had to give the right to vote to all adult male citizens, regardless of their race. After a state had ratified its new constitution, it had to ratify the Fourteenth Amendment before it would be allowed to elect members to Congress.

With military officers supervising voter registration, the Southern states began holding elections and organizing constitutional conventions. By the end of 1868, six former Confederate states—North Carolina, South Carolina, Florida, Alabama, Louisiana, and Arkansas—had met all the **requirements** and were readmitted to the Union.

Johnson Is Impeached The Republicans knew that they had the votes to override any veto of their policies, but they also knew that President Johnson could interfere with their plans by refusing to enforce the laws they

Activity: Collaborative Learning

Defending Divide the class into four groups and have them use library and Internet sources to research the attitudes of various groups toward the exclusion of women from the suffrage granted to African American men by the Fifteenth Amendment. Remind students that education of African Americans had been illegal under slavery, so newly enfranchised African American men had little or no education. Each group should prepare an argument for presentation to the class defending the views of one of these constituents: educated white suffragists, such as Elizabeth Cady Stanton; uneducated, formerly enslaved African American women; educated white men; uneducated African American men. Once groups have presented their arguments, have a class discussion to compare and contrast arguments. **OL** **AL**

passed. Although they distrusted Johnson, Republicans in Congress knew that Secretary of War Edwin M. Stanton agreed with their program and would enforce it. They also trusted General Ulysses S. Grant, the head of the army, to support their policies.

To prevent Johnson from bypassing Grant or firing Stanton, Congress passed the Command of the Army Act and the Tenure of Office Act. The Command of the Army Act required all orders from the president to go through the headquarters of the general of the army—Grant's headquarters. The Tenure of Office Act required the Senate to approve the removal of any government official whose appointment had required the Senate's consent.

Determined to challenge the Tenure of Office Act, Johnson fired Stanton on February 21, 1868. Stanton barricaded himself inside his office and refused to leave. Three days later, the House of Representatives voted to **impeach** Johnson, meaning that they charged him with "high crimes and misdemeanors" in office. The main charge against Johnson was that he had broken the law by refusing to uphold the Tenure of Office Act. **R**

As provided in the Constitution, the Senate put the president on trial. If two-thirds of the senators found the president guilty, he would be removed from office. On May 16, 1868, the Senate voted 35 to 19 that Johnson was guilty—one vote short of conviction. Seven Republicans joined the Democrats in refusing to convict Johnson. These senators believed that it would set a dangerous **precedent** to impeach a president simply because he did not agree with congressional policies.

Although Johnson remained in office, he finished his term quietly and did not run for reelection in 1868. That year the Republicans nominated General Grant to run for president. During the campaign, ongoing violence in the South convinced many Northern voters that the Southern states could not be trusted to reorganize their governments without military supervision. At the same time, the presence of Union troops in the South enabled African Americans to vote in large numbers. As a result, Grant won six Southern states and most of the Northern states. The Republicans retained large majorities in both houses of Congress.

The Fifteenth Amendment With their majority secure and a trusted president in office, Republicans moved to expand their Reconstruction program. Realizing the importance of African American voters, Congress passed the **Fifteenth Amendment** to the Constitution. This amendment declared that the right to vote "shall not be denied . . . on account of race, color, or previous condition of servitude." By March 1870, enough states had ratified the amendment to make it part of the Constitution.

Radical Reconstruction had a dramatic impact on the South, particularly in the short term. It changed Southern politics by bringing hundreds of thousands of African Americans into the political process for the first time. It also began to change Southern society. This angered many white Southerners, who began to fight back against the federal government's policies.

Reading Check **Identifying** What two laws did the Radical Republicans pass to reduce presidential power?

Section 1 REVIEW

Vocabulary

1. **Explain** the significance of: amnesty, Radical Republicans, Wade-Davis Bill, pocket veto, Freedmen's Bureau, black codes, Civil Rights Act of 1866, Fourteenth Amendment, impeach, Fifteenth Amendment.

Main Ideas

2. **Identifying** What were the three main goals of the Radical Republicans?
3. **Specifying** In what area did the Freedmen's Bureau have the most impact?
4. **Explaining** Under what circumstances did Andrew Johnson become president?
5. **Listing** What were the main provisions of the Military Reconstruction Act?

Critical Thinking

6. **Big Ideas** What services did the Freedmen's Bureau provide?
7. **Listing** Use a graphic organizer to list the effects of the Civil War on the South.

I. Johnson Takes Office
  A.
  B.
  C.
II.
  A.
  B.
  C.

8. **Analyzing Visuals** Review the images on page 361. How has the Fourteenth Amendment changed over time?

Writing About History

9. **Descriptive Writing** Take on the role of a Southerner after the Civil War. Write a journal entry describing the postwar South and what you hope the future will hold for the region.

History ONLINE
Study Central™ To review this section, go to glencoe.com and click on Study Central.

R Reading Strategy

Questioning Ask: For what offenses do you think a president should be impeached? *(Students should support their opinions.)* **OL**

Reading Check

Answer: the Command of the Army Act and the Tenure of Office Act

Assess

History ONLINE

Study Central provides summaries, interactive games, and online graphic organizers to help students review content.

Close

Summarizing Ask: What were the successes and the failures that occurred at the end of Reconstruction? *(Answers will vary. Students may note that the rights granted to African Americans were successes and states were readmitted to the Union. Failures may include the violence and anger that erupted in the South.)* **OL**

Section 1 REVIEW

Answers

1. All definitions can be found in the section and the Glossary.
2. They wanted to prevent Confederate leaders from returning to power, to gain power for the Republican Party in the South, and to help African Americans achieve political equality via suffrage.
3. education
4. In 1862 Lincoln appointed Johnson military governor of Tennessee and then in 1864 approved his nomination as vice president. When Lincoln was assassinated, Johnson then became president.
5. divided the former Confederate states, except Tennessee, into five military districts under command of a Union general; required states to hold new constitutional convention to write a constitution that included voting rights for all adult males, regardless of race; required states to ratify the new constitution and ratify the Fourteenth Amendment to be readmitted to the Union.
6. It provided food, clothing, education, work, and courts to resolve grievances between workers and planters.
7. Students should list the following in their outlines: cities in ruins; transportation system destroyed; money worthless; agricultural system in chaos.
8. The Fourteenth Amendment has been applied to a wide range of issues.
9. Entries will vary, but should express the view of a Southerner whose world has been drastically changed.

Focus

Tell students that Edmund Ross was the senator who cast the deciding vote not to impeach Andrew Johnson. Some historians view him as courageous; others see him as politically expedient.

Teach

C Critical Thinking

Evaluating Divide the class into small groups and assign them to research Edmund Ross and his decision to vote against impeachment. Assign half the groups to write editorials expressing the opinion that Ross was a courageous man. Assign the other half to write editorials expressing the opinion that he was a scoundrel using his vote for political favors. "Publish" the editorials on photocopied sheets with a banner that sounds like the name of a newspaper. Distribute the sheets to the class. As a class, discuss how our understanding of events is influenced by the opinions of contemporary writers and historians. OL

Additional Support

TIME NOTEBOOK

PHOTOWORLD/FPG

WILLIAM H. CROOKE *served as a bodyguard for President Andrew Johnson and witnessed the decisive vote by Edmund Ross during the impeachment trial in the Senate on Saturday, May 16, 1868. Here, Crooke recalls the scene:*

The tension grew. There was a weary number of names before that of Ross was reached. When the clerk called it, and Ross [senator from Kansas] stood forth, the crowd held its breath.

'Not guilty,' called the senator from Kansas. It was like the babbling [sic] over of a caldron. The Radical Senators, who had been laboring with Ross only a short time before, turned to him in rage; all over the house people began to stir. The rest of the roll-call was listened to with lessened interest. . . . When it was over, and the result—35 to 19—was announced, there was a wild outburst, chiefly groans of anger and disappointment, for the friends of the president were in the minority.

It was all over in a moment, and Mr. Johnson was ordering some whiskey from the cellar. [President Johnson was not convicted.]

C

VERBATIM

"If the South is ever to be made a safe Republic, let her lands be cultivated by the toil of the owners, or the free labor of intelligent citizens."
THADDEUS STEVENS,
arguing for land redistribution in the South during Reconstruction

"In the South, the [Civil] war is what A.D. is elsewhere; they date from it."
MARK TWAIN,
from Life on the Mississippi

"For we colored people did not know how to be free and the white people did not know how to have a free colored person about them."
HOUSTON HARTSFIELD HOLLOWAY,
freedman, on the problem of Reconstruction

"As in the war, freedom was the keynote of victory, so now is universal suffrage the keynote of Reconstruction."
ELIZABETH CADY STANTON,
arguing for universal suffrage, 1867

"We thought we was goin' to be richer than the white folks, 'cause we was stronger and knowed how to work, and the whites didn't and they didn't have us to work for them anymore. But it didn't turn out that way. We soon found out that freedom could make folks proud but it didn't make 'em rich."
FELIX HAYWOOD,
former slave

PRESIDENTIAL SUPERLATIVES

Andrew Johnson

BETTMANN/CORBIS

While he was neither "first in war, first in peace" nor "first in the hearts of his countrymen," President Andrew Johnson left his mark on history:

- First to have never attended school
- First to be impeached
- First to be elected to the Senate both before and after being president
- First to host a queen at the White House
- First tailor/president who made his own clothes
- Last not to attend successor's inauguration
- Most vetoes overridden
- Father of the Homestead Act

Cooperative Learning Activity

Creating a Display Organize the class into groups of four or five. Have each group select one of the following periods: 1860–1865, 1866–1870, or 1871–1872. Have each group create a display relating to the period selected, including a time line. Encourage students to be creative with the elements of the display and to include such items as photos, quotations from primary sources, artifacts, and drawings. Then have students select one U.S. president and create a list of interesting facts and firsts about his term in office or special accomplishments before taking office. Compile the lists, placing them in sequential order beneath a photo of each chosen president, and add them to the time line. OL

(Re)inventing America

Patents awarded to African American inventors during the Reconstruction period:

BETTMANN/CORBIS

Refrigerators keep foods cool.

ALEXANDER ASHBOURNE biscuit cutter

LANDROW BELL locomotive smokestack

LEWIS HOWARD LATIMER water closets (toilets) for railway cars, electric lamp with cotton filament, dough kneader

THOMAS ELKINS refrigerator with cooling coils

THOMAS J. MARTIN fire extinguisher

ELIJAH MCCOY automatic oil cup and 57 other devices and machine parts, including an ironing board and lawn sprinkler

Milestones

REEXAMINED, 1870. THE ROMANTIC STORY OF POCAHONTAS, based on the written account of Captain John Smith. *The London Spectator,* reporting on the work of Mr. E. Neils, debunks Smith's tale of the young Pocahontas flinging herself between him and her father's club. The young girl was captured and held prisoner on board a British ship and then forcibly married to Mr. John Rolfe. Comments *Appleton's Journal* in 1870: "All that is heroic, picturesque, or romantic in history seems to be rapidly disappearing under the microscopic scrutiny of modern critics."

FOUNDED, 1877. NICODEMUS, KANSAS, by six African American and two white Kansans. On the high, arid plains of Graham County, the founders hope to establish a community of homesteading former slaves.

TOPPED, 1875. THE ONE MILLION MARK FOR POPULATION, by New York City. New York is the ninth city in the history of the world to achieve a population level of more than one million. The first was Rome in 133 B.C.

MPI/HULTON GETTY PICTURE LIBRARY/LIAISON

Pocahontas

EXTINGUISHED, 1871. THE PESHTIGO FOREST FIRE in Wisconsin. The conflagration caused 2,682 deaths. The Peshtigo tragedy has been overshadowed by the Great Chicago Fire of the same year, which killed 300.

PUBLISHED, 1865. *DRUM TAPS,* by Walt Whitman. Based on his experiences as a hospital volunteer, Whitman's new poems chronicle the horrors of the Civil War.

NUMBERS

$7,200,000 Purchase price paid by U.S. to Russia for Alaska in 1867

2¢ Price paid per acre for Alaska

$30 Boarding and tuition, per quarter in 1870, at Saint Frances Academy, boarding school for African American girls in Baltimore, Maryland. Students come from states as distant as Florida and Missouri for an education "productive of the happiest effects among individuals and in society."

$5 Extra charge for instruction in embroidery

$25 Extra charge for instruction in making wax fruit

$3 Tuition, per quarter, for local "day scholars"

5,407 Number of pupils in Mississippi Freedmen's schools in 1866

50 Number of schools established for freed African Americans in Mississippi in 1866

20% Percentage of state income of Mississippi spent on artificial arms and legs for war veterans in 1866

CRITICAL THINKING

1. ***Theorizing*** Do you think the quote from *Appleton's Journal* can be applied to events in America today? Explain your thinking.
2. ***Comparing*** What do the quotes by Felix Haywood and Houston Hartsfield Holloway reveal about the views of African Americans during Reconstruction?

Assess/Close

Summarizing Ask: What general statement can you make about the period? *(Possible answers include: a time of change and recovery after a devastating civil war; a period of innovation and growth.)*

CRITICAL THINKING Answers:

1. Answers will vary. Students should defend their answers.
2. Although originally optimistic freed slaves soon realized that they still faced many challenges.

Visit the TIME Web site at www.time.com for up-to-date news, weekly magazine articles, editorials, online polls, and an archive of past magazine and Web articles.

Additional Support

Extending the Content

Reconstruction Refugees Between 1866 and 1885, approximately 4,000 Confederates fled the Deep South rather than live under Reconstruction. Unable to accept the changes in their lives wrought by the war and Reconstruction, they emigrated to Brazil. They were drawn by promises of cheap land, a booming cotton industry, and the existence of slavery, which was tolerated in Brazil until 1888. Although some of the refugees succeeded there, many were driven back to the United States by drought, tropical diseases, and the remoteness of their settlements. The largest settlement came to be called Americana. Today, descendants of some of the Reconstruction refugees are members of the Fraternity of American Descendants. These descendants travel to Brazil several times a year to remember their ancestors and renew friendships. Interested students might want to research the topic and present their findings to the class.

Focus

Bellringer

Daily Focus Transparency 10-2

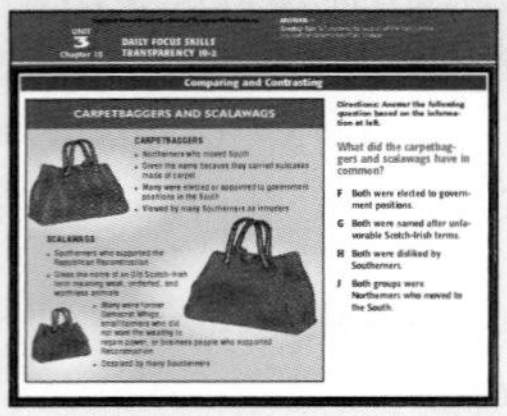

Guide to Reading

Answers:

State convention delegates
State legislators
Local officials
Church leaders

Section Spotlight Video

To generate interest and provide a springboard for class discussion, access the Chapter 10, Section 2 video at glencoe.com or on the video DVD.

Section 2

Section Audio   Spotlight Video

Republican Rule

Guide to Reading

Big Ideas

Group Action Despite opposition, African Americans took active roles in politics during Reconstruction.

Content Vocabulary

- carpetbagger *(p. 366)*
- scalawag *(p. 366)*
- graft *(p. 368)*

Academic Vocabulary

- commissioner *(p. 368)*
- comprehensive *(p. 369)*

People and Events to Identify

- Ku Klux Klan Act *(p. 371)*

Reading Strategy

Organizing Complete a graphic organizer similar to the one below to identify how African Americans helped to govern the South during Reconstruction.

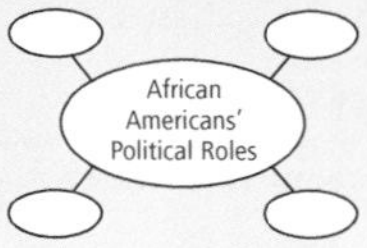

Under the Republican-controlled Congress, the South began to rebuild. During this time, African Americans gained some new opportunities, particularly in politics, while some white Southerners organized to resist the changes that were occurring.

Republican Rule in the South

MAIN Idea During Reconstruction, African Americans organized politically and took part in governing the South.

HISTORY AND YOU What are the factors that help you decide to support a political party? Read on to learn why the Republican Party won the support of African Americans during Reconstruction.

By late 1870, all the former Confederate states had rejoined the Union under the congressional Reconstruction plan. Throughout the South, the Republican Party took power and introduced major reforms. Most white Southerners scorned the Republicans, however, partly because the party included Northerners and African Americans. Southerners also believed that the Union Army had forced the new Republican governments on them.

Carpetbaggers and Scalawags

As Reconstruction began, many Northerners moved to the South. Quite a few were eventually elected or appointed to positions in the South's new state governments. Southerners, particularly Democratic Party supporters, referred to these newcomers as **carpetbaggers** because some arrived with suitcases made of carpet fabric. Many local residents viewed the Northerners as intruders seeking to exploit the South.

Some carpetbaggers did seek to take advantage of the war-torn region, and corruption plagued parts of the South. Others, however, hoped to find more opportunities than existed for them in the North or the West. Some simply wanted to help. Many Northern schoolteachers, for example, moved south to help educate whites and African Americans.

While many Southerners despised carpetbaggers, they also disliked white Southerners who worked with the Republicans and supported Reconstruction. They called these people **scalawags**—an old Scotch-Irish term for weak, underfed, worthless animals.

The scalawags were a diverse group. Some were former Whigs who had grudgingly joined the Democratic Party before the war. Many were owners of small farms who did not want the wealthy

Resource Manager

R Reading Strategies	C Critical Thinking	D Differentiated Instruction	W Writing Support	S Skill Practice
Teacher Edition • Setting a Purpose, p. 368 **Additional Resources** • Primary Source Reading, URB p. 101 • Guided Reading Act., URB p. 113	**Teacher Edition** • Inferring, p. 367 • Drawing Conclusions, p. 369 **Additional Resources** • Interpret. Political Cartoons, URB p. 105 • Quizzes/Tests, p. 134	**Additional Resources** • Differ. Instruction Act., URB p. 87 • Enrichment Act., URB p. 109	**Teacher Edition** • Expository Writing, p. 368 • Narrative Writing, p. 370	**Teacher Edition** • Problem Solving, p. 369 **Additional Resources** • Read. Essen., p. 114

PRIMARY SOURCE

African Americans Enter Politics

Reconstruction provided African Americans with new opportunities to participate in politics. Many took part in the state constitutional conventions and were elected to state legislatures—achieving a majority in South Carolina's state assembly—and to local offices.

▲ This sketch from 1868 shows African Americans campaigning. African Americans were excited to participate in politics. The sketch shows women and children as well, suggesting that the entire community regarded political issues as important, even though only adult males could vote.

C

▲ This drawing from 1867 depicts the primary groups that became political leaders of the South's African American community—artisans (shown with tools), the middle class, and Union soldiers.

▲ The sketch above from the 1870s shows South Carolina's legislature—the only state legislature with an African American majority during Reconstruction.

Analyzing VISUALS

1. **Identifying Central Issues** Why do you think African Americans were so enthusiastic about participating in politics?
2. **Explaining** What about the illustration above indicates the political position of women?

planters to regain power. Still others were business people who favored Republican plans for developing the South's economy.

African Americans in Politics

The Fifteenth Amendment allowed many freedmen to take part in governing the South. With the right to vote, African American men could organize politically. "You never saw a people more excited on the subject of politics than are the [African Americans] of the South," wrote one plantation manager.

At first, the leadership of the African American community came from among those individuals who had been educated before the war. These included artisans, shopkeepers, and ministers. Many had lived in the North and fought in the Union Army. Aided by the Republican Party, these leaders delivered speeches to former plantation workers, drawing them into politics. Within a few remarkable years, many African Americans went from enslaved laborers to legislators and administrators working in nearly all levels of government.

Teach

C Critical Thinking

Inferring Have students study the sketch on the left. **Ask:** What do you think the presence of women and children at this political meeting implies about the importance of politics to Southern African Americans during Reconstruction? *(Answers may include that Southern African Americans saw it as so important that all people were included, even though only men could vote. Some students may note that the women, although included, were not at the center of the conversation because they did not have the right to vote.)*

Analyzing VISUALS

Answers:

1. Under slavery, they had had no power to control their own lives. Voting and holding public office gave them political power.
2. Women are either not present or are on the side or in back of the men, showing that the political power belonged only to the men.

Hands-On Chapter Project
Step 2

Reconstruction Correspondence

Step 2: Understanding Reconstruction from a Southern Point of View Each group should discuss the Southern reaction to the Military Reconstruction Act discussed in Step 1.

Directions As a class discuss the reactions of white Southerners and former enslaved African Americans to the Military Reconstruction Act. Have groups choose a role to take—either white Southerner or former enslaved African American—and research that group's viewpoint using their book, the Internet, and the library. The information gathered should be used to write a letter to a friend or family member expressing their view of Reconstruction.

Summarizing Students will summarize the positive and/or negative effects of Reconstruction on either white or African American citizens in the South. OL

(Chapter Project continued on page 374)

W Writing Support

Expository Writing Have interested students research prominent leaders of African American churches, either during Reconstruction or at any time up to the present. Ask them to write a one-page biography of the person they choose and to read it to the class. **AL**

R Reading Strategy

Setting a Purpose Write two column heads on the board: "Positive" and "Negative." Ask students to review the section "Republican Reforms" and then complete both lists. **BL**

Reading Check

Answer:
African American men, poor white farmers, and other white Southerners

Additional Support

Hundreds of formerly enslaved men served as delegates to state constitutional conventions. They also won election to numerous local offices, from mayor to police chief to school **commissioner.** Dozens of African Americans served in Southern state legislatures, while 14 were elected to the U.S. House of Representatives, and two, Hiram Revels and Blanche K. Bruce, were elected to the Senate.

R Republican Reforms

With formerly enslaved men making such political gains, many Southerners claimed that "Black Republicanism" ruled the South. Such claims, however, were greatly exaggerated. No African American was ever elected governor. In South Carolina, African Americans did gain control of the legislature, but were able to hold power for only one term.

The Republican Party took power in the South because it also had the support of a large number of white Southerners. Poor white farmers, who resented the planters and the Democratic Party that dominated the South before the Civil War, often joined with African American voters to elect Republicans.

The newly elected Republican governments instituted a number of reforms. They repealed the black codes and made many more state offices elective. They established state hospitals and institutions for orphans, the mentally ill, and the hearing and visually impaired. They rebuilt roads, railways, and bridges, and funded the construction of new railroads and industries in the South. They also established a system of public schools.

The Republican reforms did not come without cost. Many state governments were forced to borrow money and to impose high property taxes to pay for the repairs and new programs. Many property owners, unable to pay these new taxes, lost their land.

Although many Republicans wanted to help the South, others were corrupt. One Republican governor accepted more than $40,000 in bribes. **Graft,** or gaining money illegally through politics, was common in the South, just as it was in the North at the time, but it gave Democrats another issue that would help them regain power in the 1870s.

Reading Check **Summarizing** Which groups helped elect Republicans in the South during Reconstruction?

PAST & PRESENT

The African American Church

Since colonial times, churches have been important to African Americans as both religious and social institutions. After Reconstruction ended, churches became the only institution that remained under their control once they lost voting rights and segregation was imposed. African American ministers were community leaders in places where political leaders did not exist. Later, during the civil rights struggles of the 1950s and 1960s, the churches and their ministers took W the lead in organizing the community for political action. For example, Martin Luther King, Jr., was one of a long line of pastors who worked to help protect and advance their communities. His Dexter Avenue Baptist Church in Montgomery, Alabama, became the headquarters for the famous bus boycott in that city in 1955.

An African American congregation (above) listens as their minister preaches in a Washington, D.C. church in 1876. Henry Turner (left) was a bishop of the African Methodist Episcopalian (AME) Church. He and others helped make black churches places of social and religious leadership.

Extending the Content

Henry McNeal Turner As a young boy, Turner dreamed of becoming a teacher, but it was illegal in his home state of South Carolina to educate African Americans when Turner was a child. It was not until he worked as a janitor in a law firm at age 15 that he learned to read and write. Soon thereafter, he became a licensed preacher, married Eliza Ann Preacher, and moved to Baltimore. The couple eventually had 14 children, only two of whom survived. Turner joined the lobbying effort to convince Lincoln to allow freedmen to enlist in the Union army. In 1863, he became the army's first African American chaplain. After the war, he was elected to the Georgia legislature, but all African American officials were ousted by the white legislators. Turning his back on the political process, Turner then became a bishop in the American Methodist Episcopal Church and focused on the political potential of the African American church.

African American Communities

MAIN Idea Reconstruction governments expanded public education to all children, and African Americans built their own churches.

HISTORY AND YOU Do you remember how Horace Mann started a movement for public education? Read on to learn how new schools were built in the South during Reconstruction.

In addition to entering politics, African Americans worked to improve their lives in other ways during Reconstruction. Many sought to establish their own thriving communities and to gain an education.

African American Churches

Religion had long played a central role in the lives of many African Americans, and with the shackles of slavery now gone, formerly enslaved people across the South began building their own churches. Churches frequently became the center of African American communities, as they housed schools and hosted social events and political gatherings. In rural areas, church picnics, festivals, and other activities provided residents with many of their recreational and social opportunities. In many communities, churches acted as unofficial courts by promoting social values, settling disputes among residents, and disciplining individuals for improper behavior.

A Desire to Learn

Once freed, many African Americans immediately sought an education. In the first years of Reconstruction, the Freedmen's Bureau, with the help of Northern charities, established schools for African Americans across the South. By 1870, some 4,000 schools and 9,000 teachers—roughly half of them African American—taught 200,000 formerly enslaved people of all ages. In the 1870s Reconstruction governments built a **comprehensive** public school system in the South, and by 1876, about 40 percent of all African American children (roughly 600,000 students) attended school. C S

2000s

▼ Churches played a key role in the struggle for civil rights and have produced many prominent African American leaders. They still play an important role in the African American community today.

MAKING CONNECTIONS

1. **Describing** What role did churches take in the lives of African Americans after Reconstruction?
2. **Explaining** How have African American churches expanded their role in modern times?

C Critical Thinking

Drawing Conclusions Discuss how eagerly African Americans set about building schools during Reconstruction. **Ask:** What do you think your life would be like if you had no opportunity to get an education? *(Students may note that they may not be able to easily progress and could not get the information they need to take action if needed.)* OL AL

S Skill Practice

Problem Solving Have students pretend they are newly appointed school administrators in the South in 1867. **Ask:** What would be the first things you would do? List their answers on the board. Then have the class prioritize the tasks. OL

MAKING CONNECTIONS

Answers:

1. Churches became the center of society. Schools, social events, and political gatherings were held at the church.
2. Churches still serve as center of life providing a center of communication, socializing, and education in modern life.

Differentiated Instruction

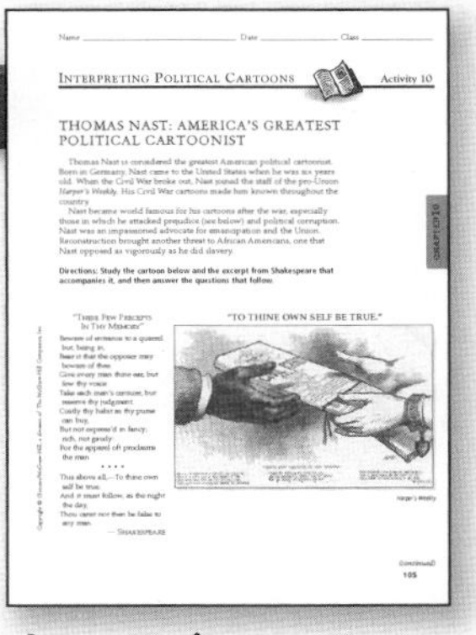
INTERPRETING POLITICAL CARTOONS Activity 10

THOMAS NAST: AMERICA'S GREATEST POLITICAL CARTOONIST

Interpreting Political Cartoons, URB p. 105

Interpreting Political Cartoons

Objective: Interpret a political cartoon and a Shakespearean excerpt.

Focus: Determine the message of the cartoon in terms of civil rights.

Teach: Read the excerpt aloud, then discuss it and its relation to the cartoon.

Assess: Ask: What advice might Nast give to legislators and those in authority?

Close: Ask: How might the message of the cartoon relate to your life today?

Differentiated Instruction Strategies

BL Explain the cartoon title in your own words.

AL Name another situation in which the advice given in the excerpt can be applied.

ELL Work with a partner to together interpret the cartoon.

W Writing Support

Narrative Writing Have interested students research a prominent graduate of an African American college or university and write a one-page biography of the person. **OL**

Analyzing VISUALS

Answers:

1. terrorism and intimidation
2. Answers may vary, but students should consider violence and voter intimidation.

Reading Check

Answer:
Under slavery, it was illegal for African Americans to be educated. During Reconstruction, thousands of schools and colleges were established to provide basic and advanced education, as well as vocational training.

POLITICAL CARTOONS Primary Source

The White League and Ku Klux Klan

▲ *This cartoon from 1874 reads "Everything points to a Democratic victory this fall" and shows members of the White League—a group similar to the Ku Klux Klan—denying African Americans the right to vote.*

▲ *Ku Klux Klansmen (top) disguised their identities. The cartoon says that White Leagues and the KKK made life worse for African Americans than it had been under slavery.*

Analyzing VISUALS

1. **Summarizing** What methods did the White League and the Ku Klux Klan use to deny African Americans their civil rights?
2. **Expressing** Do you think the cartoon on the right is correct in its assumption? Why or why not?

Several African American academies were established in the South. These academies grew into an important network of African American colleges and universities, including Fisk University in Tennessee and Atlanta University and Morehouse College in Georgia. The institution that would become Howard University was founded in 1867 in Washington, D.C., by a group of Congregationalists who wanted to establish a seminary for African American ministers. Soon the idea expanded to the creation of an entire university, named for one of the founders and head of the Freedmen's Bureau, General Oliver Howard. Howard University quickly expanded to include the first law school, established in 1869, for African Americans.

The Hampton Institute was started in 1868 in Virginia to teach African Americans a trade or agricultural techniques. In 1881, after Reconstruction, Spelman College—the first college for African American women—and the Tuskegee Institute, now Tuskegee University, were founded. The first teacher at Tuskegee was Booker T. Washington, who later became an important African American leader.

African Americans also established thousands of other organizations to support each other. These organizations ranged from burial societies and debating clubs to drama societies and trade associations.

Reading Check **Examining** How did education for African Americans change during Reconstruction?

Additional Support

Activity: Collaborative Learning

Writing a Family History Tell students that many families separated by slavery sought to reunite after emancipation and the war's end. African Americans used a family record to keep track of births, deaths, and marriages after emancipation. Ask students to create a record of their own families. It should include the following information for every family member for whom it is available: name, birth date, marriage date and to whom, death date. Discuss the difficulties in trying to recreate this information from memory. Students should discuss completed records. **BL** **OL** **ELL**

The Ku Klux Klan Forms

MAIN Idea Some Southerners hated the "Black Republican" governments and started groups such as the Ku Klux Klan that terrorized African Americans.

HISTORY AND YOU Have you heard of recent activities of the Ku Klux Klan? Read on to learn when and why the organization was founded.

At the same time as these changes were taking place, African Americans faced intense resentment from many Southern whites. Many Southerners also despised the "Black Republican" governments, which they believed vindictive Northerners had forced upon them.

Unable to strike openly at the Republicans running their states, some Southerners organized secret societies. The largest of these groups was the Ku Klux Klan. Started in 1866 by former Confederate soldiers in Pulaski, Tennessee, the Klan grew rapidly throughout the South. Its goal was to drive out the carpetbaggers and intimidate African American voters so as to regain control of the South for the Democratic Party.

Hooded, white-robed Klan members rode in bands at night, terrorizing supporters of the Republican governments. They broke up Republican meetings, drove Freedmen's Bureau officials out of their communities, burned African American homes, schools, and churches, and attempted to keep African Americans and white Republicans from voting.

Some Republicans and African Americans formed their own militia groups and fought back. As the violence perpetrated by both sides increased, one African American organization sent a report to the federal government asking for help:

PRIMARY SOURCE

"We believe you are not familiar with the description of the Ku Klux Klan's riding nightly over the country, going from county to county, and in the county towns spreading terror wherever they go by robbing, whipping, ravishing, and killing our people without provocation, compelling colored people to break the ice and bathe in the chilly waters of the Kentucky River. . . . We pray you will take some steps to remedy these evils."

—from a petition to Congress, March 25, 1871, National Archives

The Ku Klux Klan's activities outraged President Ulysses S. Grant and congressional Republicans. In 1870 and 1871, Congress passed three Enforcement Acts to combat the acts of violence in the South. The first act made it a federal crime to interfere with a citizen's right to vote. The second put federal elections under the supervision of federal marshals. The third act, also known as the **Ku Klux Klan Act,** outlawed the activities of the Klan. Local authorities and federal agents, acting under the Enforcement Acts, arrested more than 3,000 Klan members throughout the South. Southern juries, however, convicted only about 600, and fewer still served any time in prison.

Reading Check **Describing** Why did Congress pass the Enforcement Acts?

Section 2 REVIEW

Vocabulary

1. **Explain** the significance of: carpetbagger, scalawag, graft, Ku Klux Klan Act.

Main Ideas

2. **Identifying** In what state did African Americans gain control of the legislature for a time, and why did this occur?
3. **Specifying** Where and when was the first law school for African Americans established?
4. **Explaining** What were the three main provisions of the Enforcement Acts?

Critical Thinking

5. **Big Idea** How did the establishment of schools, churches, and social organizations benefit African Americans during Reconstruction?
6. **Categorizing** Use a graphic organizer to identify both the negative and positive aspects of carpetbagger rule.

Carpetbagger Rule	
Positives	Negatives

7. **Analyzing Visuals** Study the images on page 367. What do they suggest about the African American community in the South after the Civil War?

Writing About History

8. **Descriptive Writing** Suppose you are a Northerner who has recently moved to the Reconstruction South. Write a letter to a friend describing your life in the South at this time.

History ONLINE
Study Central™ To review this section, go to glencoe.com and click on Study Central.

Reading Check

Answer:
The Enforcement Acts were passed to combat acts of violence in the South.

Assess

History ONLINE

Study Central provides summaries, interactive games, and online graphic organizers to help students review content.

Close

Comparing Ask students how conditions changed for African Americans in the South from before the war to after Reconstruction. *(They were free, but rights gained at the beginning of Reconstruction were lost at its end.)* **OL**

Section 2 REVIEW

Answers

1. All definitions can be found in the section and the Glossary.
2. South Carolina; they made up the majority of the population.
3. Washington, D.C. in 1869 (Howard University)
4. The first act made it a federal crime to interfere with a citizen's right to vote. The second put federal elections under the supervision of federal marshals. The third (Ku Klux Klan Act) outlawed the activities of the Klan.
5. Schools provided African Americans with an education so that they could lead richer lives, take part in politics, and learn a trade or profession to improve their financial status. Churches served as community centers, political organizing centers, and unofficial courts. Social organizations helped African Americans to support one another.
6. **positives:** provided an influx of capital, educated whites and African Americans; **negatives:** exploited the South's postwar turmoil for personal gain; some were corrupt
7. Answers will vary, but should mention that African Americans took advantage of the opportunities Reconstruction provided for participation in government.
8. Letters should describe specific conditions of life in the South, such as resentment of Northerners by white Southerners.

Focus

Bellringer

Daily Focus Transparency 10-3

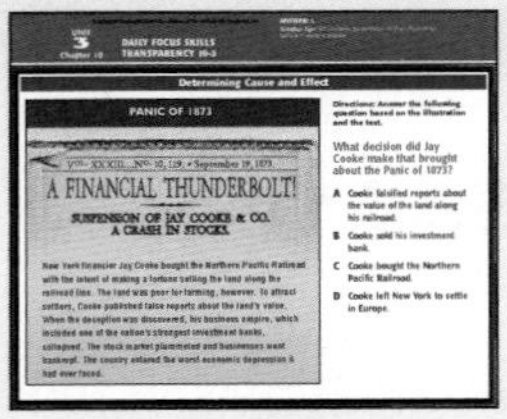

Guide to Reading

Answers:

I. The Grant Administration
  A. The Republicans Split
  B. Panic of 1873
  C. Bribery scandals
II. Reconstruction Ends
  A. "Redeeming" the South
  B. Compromise of 1877
III. A "New South" Arises

Section Spotlight Video

To generate interest and provide a springboard for class discussion, access the Chapter 10, Section 3 video at glencoe.com or on the video DVD.

Resource Manager

Section 3 — Section Audio — Spotlight Video

Reconstruction Collapses

Guide to Reading

Big Ideas

Economics and Society After Reconstruction the South tried to build a new economy but problems lingered.

Content Vocabulary

- "sin tax" *(p. 372)*
- tenant farmer *(p. 377)*
- sharecropper *(p. 377)*
- crop lien *(p. 377)*
- debt peonage *(p. 377)*

Academic Vocabulary

- outcome *(p. 375)*
- circumstance *(p. 377)*

People and Events to Identify

- Horace Greeley *(p. 373)*
- "Whiskey Ring" *(p. 373)*
- Panic of 1873 *(p. 374)*
- Compromise of 1877 *(p. 375)*
- "New South" *(p. 377)*

Reading Strategy

Taking Notes Use the major headings of Section 3 to create an outline listing the major events of the Grant administration and the end of Reconstruction.

I. The Grant Administration
  A.
  B.
II.
  A.

As Reconstruction came to an end in the late 1870s, the gains made by African Americans after the Civil War were steadily eroded by Southern whites as they reclaimed control of state legislatures. In the meantime, Southerners were developing strategies for a rebirth of the region's economy.

The Grant Administration

MAIN Idea Political scandals and an economic depression tarnished Grant's presidency.

HISTORY AND YOU Can you think of any recent political scandals? Read on to learn how bribery and corruption hurt the Grant administration.

As commander of the Union forces, Ulysses S. Grant had led the North to victory in the Civil War. His reputation had then carried him into the White House in the election of 1868. Unfortunately, Grant had little experience in politics. He believed that the president's role was to carry out the laws and leave the development of policy to Congress. This approach pleased the Radical Republicans in Congress, but it left the president weak and ineffective when dealing with other issues. Eventually, Grant's lack of political experience helped to divide the Republican Party and to undermine public support for Reconstruction.

The Republicans Split

During Grant's first term in office, the Republican-controlled Congress continued to enforce Reconstruction. At the same time, it expanded the programs it had introduced during the Civil War to promote commerce and industry. It kept tariffs high, tightened banking regulations, promised to repay its debts with gold—not paper money—and increased federal spending on railroads, port facilities, and the national postal system.

The Republican Congress also kept in place the taxes on alcohol and tobacco that had been introduced as emergency measures during the war. These taxes, nicknamed **"sin taxes,"** helped the government pay off the bonds that had been issued to pay for the Civil War.

Democrats attacked these Republican economic policies, arguing that they benefited the wealthy, such as government bondholders, at the expense of the poor, who paid most of the sin taxes. They argued that wealthy Americans were gaining too much influence in Grant's administration.

R Reading Strategies	C Critical Thinking	D Differentiated Instruction	W Writing Support	S Skill Practice
Additional Resources • Guided Reading Act., URB p. 114	**Teacher Edition** • Analyzing, p. 375 **Additional Resources** • Critical Thinking Act., URB p. 96 • Authentic Assess., p. 25 • Quizzes/Tests, p. 135	**Additional Resources** • Reteaching Act., URB p. 107	**Teacher Edition** • Expository Writing, pp. 373, 374 • Personal Writing, p. 376	**Teacher Edition** • Debating, p. 374 • Sequencing Information, p. 375 **Additional Resources** • Read. Essen., p. 117

POLITICAL CARTOONS **PRIMARY SOURCE**

The Scandals of the Grant Administration

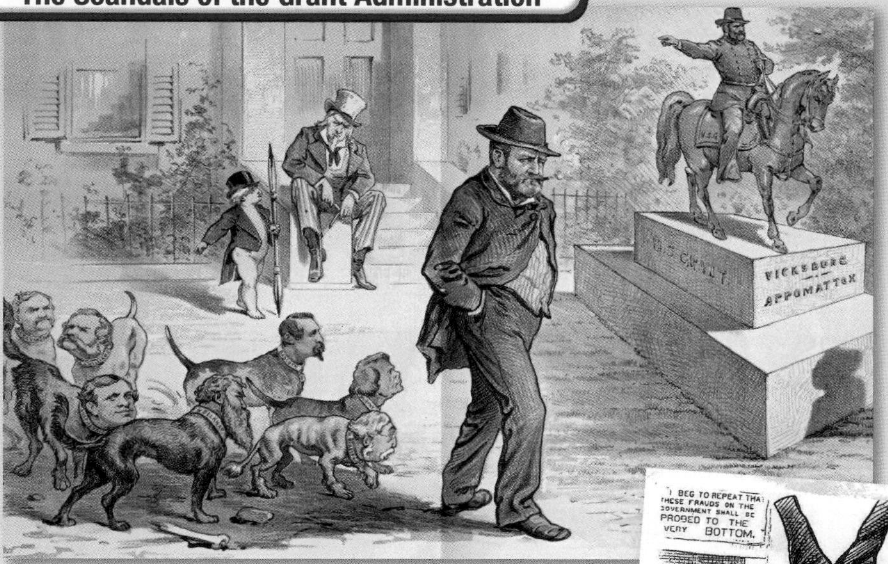

▲ *In this cartoon, Grant, the Civil War hero of Vicksburg and Appomattox Courthouse, is "dogged" by the men in his administration who have been involved in various scandals.*

▼ *This cartoonist shows the Grant administration looking for those guilty of fraud in a whiskey barrel—symbol of the "Whiskey Ring."*

Analyzing VISUALS

1. **Interpreting** What is Uncle Sam's mood in the cartoon above, and why do you think he has this attitude?
2. **Making Inferences** In the cartoon on the right, how far does the cartoonist suggest that the corruption in government has spread?

Some Republicans, known as Liberal Republicans, agreed with the Democrats. They were concerned that men who were in office to make money and sell influence were beginning to dominate the Republican Party. The Liberal Republicans tried to prevent Grant's renomination in 1872. When that failed, they left the Republican Party and nominated their own candidate, **Horace Greeley,** the influential newspaper publisher.

To attract Southern support, the Liberal Republicans promised to pardon nearly all former Confederates and to remove Union troops from the South. As a result, the Democratic Party, believing that only a united effort would defeat Grant, also nominated Greeley. Despite the split in his own party and Greeley's passionate campaigning, Grant won the election easily.

During Grant's second term, a series of scandals hurt the reputation of his administration. Grant's secretary of war, William Belknap, had accepted bribes from merchants operating at army posts in the West. He was impeached but resigned before the Senate could try him. Then, in 1875, the **"Whiskey Ring"** scandal broke. A group of government officials and distillers in St. Louis, Missouri, cheated the government out of millions of dollars by filing false tax reports. Reportedly, Orville E. Babcock, Grant's private secretary, was involved, although this was never proved. **W**

Teach

W Writing Support

Expository Writing Have students make lists of some specific types of corruption that can plague an administration. Some of the examples on their lists should be from the Grant administration; others may be more current. Then ask students to assume the role of a television news anchor. Each student should choose one scandal, research it, and write a press release exposing the scandal to the public. Students should also bring to class a relevant photo and read their press releases to the class as though they were television news anchors.

Analyzing VISUALS

Answers:

1. He looks annoyed and dejected because the president is not dealing with the corruption perpetrated by his appointees.
2. Corruption has spread to all levels of government—from federal to city wards.

Differentiated Instruction

Leveled Activities

BL Reading Skills Activity, URB p. 85

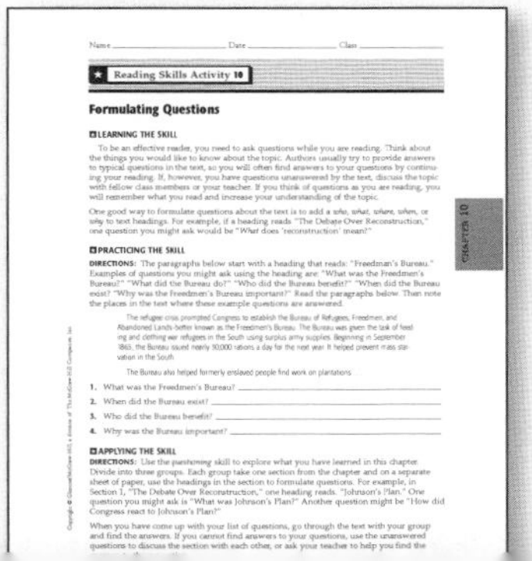

OL Historical Analysis Skills Activity, URB p. 86

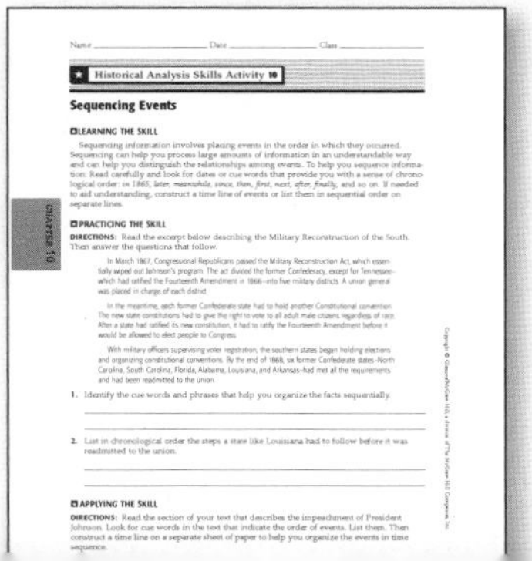

AL Primary Source Reading, URB p. 99

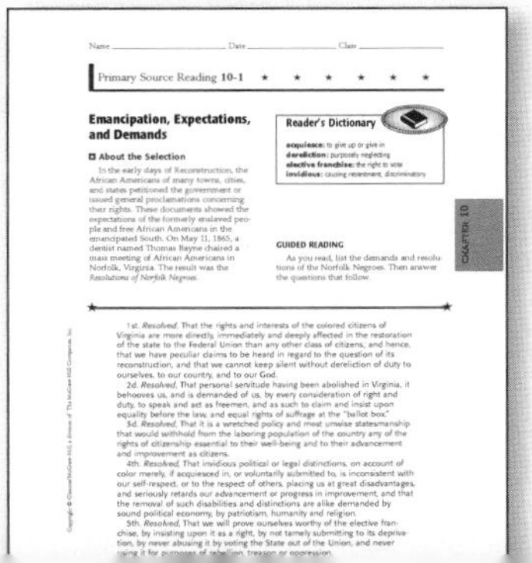

ELL Content Vocabulary Activity, p. 91

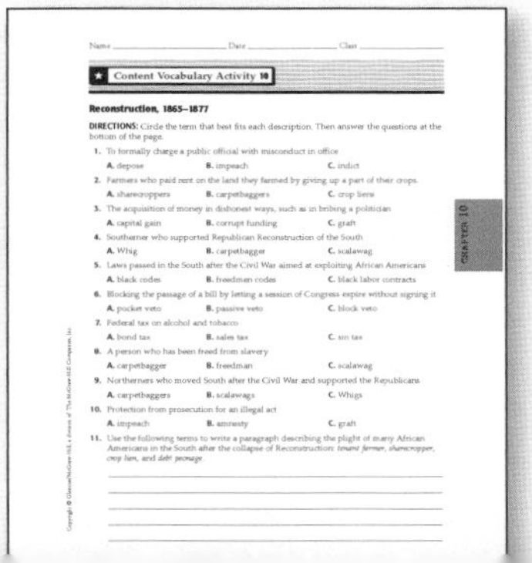

W Writing Support

Expository Writing Have students research Ulysses S. Grant's background. **Ask:** How did Grant's background improve or deter his effectiveness as president? *(Answers will vary.)* Have students write a brief essay responding to this question. **OL**

S Skill Practice

Debating Call students' attention to the map of the 1877 election, which shows that Tilden won the popular vote but lost the election. Divide the class into two teams and ask them to do research on the Electoral College. Then have them debate the topic "The Electoral College Should Be Abolished." In making the assignment, mention the concept of One Person, One Vote. **OL** **AL**

Reading Check

Answer:
They thought the wealthy and big business were gaining too much power in the Republican Party.

The Panic of 1873

In addition to the political scandals of Grant's second term, the nation endured a severe economic crisis. The turmoil started in 1873, when a series of bad railroad investments forced the powerful banking firm of Jay Cooke and Company to declare bankruptcy. A wave of fear known as the **Panic of 1873** quickly spread through the financial community. Dozens of smaller banks closed, and the stock market plummeted. Thousands of businesses shut down, and unemployment soared.

The scandals in the Grant administration and the deepening economic depression hurt the Republicans politically. In the 1874 midterm elections, the Democrats won control of the House of Representatives and made gains in the Senate.

Reading Check **Explaining** Why did the Liberal Republicans oppose President Grant?

Reconstruction Ends

MAIN Idea After Republican Rutherford B. Hayes became president in a disputed election, he removed the last federal troops from the South.

HISTORY AND YOU What is the process by which presidents are elected? Read on to learn how contested returns in three states created a political crisis in 1876.

The rising power of the Democrats made enforcing Reconstruction more difficult. At the same time, many Northerners were more concerned with their own economic problems than with the political situation in the South.

"Redeeming" the South

In the 1870s, Southern Democrats had worked to regain control of their state and local governments from Republicans. Southern

POLITICAL CARTOONS PRIMARY SOURCE

The Compromise of 1877

Presidential Candidate	Popular Votes	% of Popular Vote	Electoral Votes
Hayes	4,036,298	47.98%	185
Tilden	4,300,590	51.12%	184

The South's economy lies in ruins.

President Grant rides a carpetbag propped up by Union troops.

The South struggles under the weight of the carpetbag.

▲ *In the 1876 presidential election, 20 electoral votes were in dispute. They were eventually awarded to Hayes, and many believed he made a deal with Southern Democrats in Congress to win the presidency. Whether or not this was true, Hayes's election signified the end of Reconstruction.*

Hands-On Chapter Project Step 3

Reconstruction Correspondence

Step 3: Describing the "New South" Have students choose a role to take—either an African American or white citizen from the South. Students will research the effect the collapse of Reconstruction had on that group including the advantages and disadvantages experienced by that group in the "New South."

Directions As either an African American or white citizen from the South, students will write a letter to a friend or family member detailing how their life has changed since the collapse of Reconstruction and the type of life they perceive for themselves in the "New South."

Making Generalizations Students will use the information gained to generalize about the lives of either African American or white citizens of the South after Reconstruction. **OL**

(Chapter Project continued on the Visual Summary page)

terrorist groups, such as the Ku Klux Klan and Knights of the White Camellia, intimidated African American and white Republican voters, while some Democrats resorted to various forms of election fraud, such as stuffing ballot boxes, bribing vote counters, and stealing ballot boxes in Republican precincts. Southern Democrats also called on all whites to help "redeem"—or save—the South from "Black Republican" rule.

By appealing to white racism and defining elections as a struggle between whites and African Americans, Democrats were able to win back the support of white owners of small farms who had supported Republicans. By 1876, the Democrats had taken control of all Southern state legislatures except those of Louisiana, South Carolina, and Florida. In those states, the large number of African American voters, protected by Union troops, was able to keep the Republicans in power.

Analyzing VISUALS

1. **Identifying Points of View** Which government did the cartoonist approve of more? How can you tell?
2. **Identifying Central Issues** What criticism of Hayes is the cartoonist responding to with this cartoon?

The Compromise of 1877 S

With Grant's reputation damaged by scandals, the Republicans decided not to nominate him for a third term in 1876. Instead, they nominated Rutherford B. Hayes, a former governor of Ohio. Many Americans regarded Hayes as a moral man untainted by scandal. Hayes wanted to end Radical Reconstruction.

The Democrats responded by nominating Samuel Tilden, a wealthy corporate lawyer and former governor of New York who had tried to end the corruption in New York City's government. On Election Day, Tilden clearly won 184 electoral votes, 1 short of a majority. Hayes clearly won 165 electoral votes, leaving 20 votes in dispute. Nineteen of the votes were in the three Southern states Republicans still controlled: Louisiana, South Carolina, and Florida. There had been so much election fraud on both sides that no one could tell which candidate had won.

To resolve the situation, Congress appointed a 15-person commission made up equally of members of the House, the Senate, and the Supreme Court. The commission had 8 Republicans and 7 Democrats, and eventually voted along party lines, 8 to 7, to give the votes to Hayes. The commission's recommendations, however, were not binding if either house of Congress rejected them.

After much debate, several Southern Democrats joined with Republicans in the Democrat-controlled House of Representatives and voted to accept the commission's findings. This gave the election to Hayes. Noting that Hayes could not have won without the support of Southern Democrats, many people concluded that a deal had been made. This is why the **outcome** of the election is known as the **Compromise of 1877.** C

Historians are not sure if a deal was actually made or, if so, what its exact terms were. The Compromise of 1877 reportedly included a promise by the Republicans to pull federal troops out of the South if Hayes were elected, and that is, in fact, what happened within a month of Hayes taking office. It is also true, however, that the nation was tired of the politics of Reconstruction and that even Republican leaders were ready to put an end to it. Indeed, President Grant pulled troops out of Florida even before Hayes took office, so it is possible that no deal was actually made.

S Skill Practice

Sequencing Information
Have students reread the section on the Compromise of 1877. Ask them to create a time line listing the events leading to the compromise. **BL**

C Critical Thinking

Analyzing Have students recall examples from their lives when a compromise was needed.
Ask: Was the compromise that was reached effective? Why or why not? **OL**

Analyzing VISUALS

Answers:

1. The cartoonist approves of Hayes' policy of leaving the South to run its own affairs. Even though the title of the cartoon on the previous page is "The 'Strong' Government," the cartoonist is showing that Grant's policy is only strong if supported by armed troops.
2. Hayes was criticized for having allegedly striking the Compromise of 1877, by which federal troops were pulled out of the South.

Additional Support

Teacher Tip

Tell students that, in a later chapter, they will learn how the Panic of 1873 affected the building of the Panama Canal.

Activity: Economics Connection

Analyzing Have students use what they may already know about other economic crises, as well as library or Internet research, to create a table. The table should list at least three economic crises, their dates, and causes. Possible choices include Panic of 1857, Panic of 1873, Panic of 1893, Financial Crisis of 1914, stock market crash of 1929, Black Monday 1987. *(Tables may include causes such as overuse of credit, loss of confidence in banks, widened gap between the rich and the poor, currency not backed by gold, a sudden rise in short-term interest rates plus widening yield differences between safe and risky assets).* **AL**

W Writing Support

Personal Writing Ask: What background and personal qualities do you think a president should have? Have each student write a half-page essay expressing one personal quality and one type of professional experience they consider the most important for a president. **OL** **BL**

Analyzing VISUALS

Answers:

1. North Carolina, South Carolina, Georgia
2. Possible answer: The South still had land that was good for planting, the know-how to do it, and the labor force, in the form of African Americans who, while technically free, were still available, and with sharecropping could be forced to farm the land as they had done under slavery.

Reading Check

Answer:
the presidential election of 1876

Additional Support

PRIMARY SOURCE

The New South

The New South was a blend of the old and the new. Industry began to develop, but agriculture remained vital to the economy. By the 1890s, the South was exporting more cotton, rice, and tobacco than before the Civil War. Although slavery had ended, many African Americans were poor sharecroppers who harvested crops for landowners.

▲ *The industry of the "New South" was still driven by agricultural products, such as tobacco. The workers shown above are processing tobacco in a Richmond tobacco factory in 1899.*

Sharecropping in the South, 1880

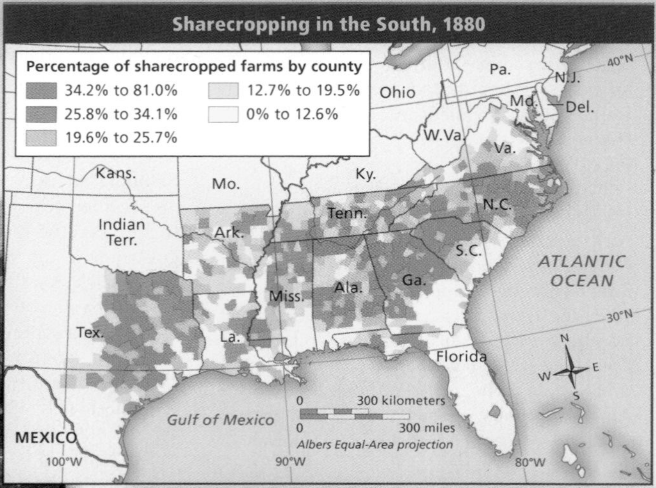

▲ *Sharecroppers harvest cotton in Georgia in 1898.*

Analyzing VISUALS

1. **Specifying** In which three states was sharecropping most common?
2. **Explaining** Why do you think the South's economy remained so dependent on agriculture after Reconstruction?

W During his inaugural speech on March 5, 1877, President Hayes expressed his desire to move the country beyond the quarrelsome years of Reconstruction:

PRIMARY SOURCE

"Let me assure my countrymen of the Southern States that it is my earnest desire to regard and promote their truest interests—the interests of the white and colored people both equally—and to put forth my best efforts in behalf of a civil policy which will forever wipe out . . . the distinction between North and South, . . . that we may have not merely a united North or a united South, but a united country."

—quoted in *The Life of Rutherford Birchard Hayes*

Whether the speech expressed Hayes's real thoughts is unknown, but in April 1877 he pulled federal troops out of the South. Without soldiers to support them, the last Republican governments in South Carolina and Louisiana collapsed. The Democrats had "redeemed" the South. Reconstruction was now over.

Reading Check **Explaining** What major issue was settled by the Compromise of 1877?

Activity: Collaborative Learning

Reconstruction Display Organize the class into small groups, each of which should develop an exhibit to illustrate Reconstruction. Groups may focus on an important person; an important event such as the impeachment of President Johnson; the culture of the period, such as hair and clothing styles, songs, and available reading material; or an important idea, such as what people expected of a Reconstruction policy. Exhibits should include illustrations, short written descriptions, and primary sources. **OL**

A "New South" Arises

MAIN Idea The postwar South developed more industry, but most people still worked in agriculture.

HISTORY AND YOU What do you recall about the disadvantages of the South during the Civil War? Read on to learn how the region tried to industrialize in the postwar period.

Many Southern leaders realized that the South could never return to the pre–Civil War agricultural economy once dominated by the planter elite. Instead, they called for the creation of a **"New South"**—a phrase coined by Henry W. Grady, editor of the *Atlanta Constitution*. They believed the region had to develop a strong industrial economy.

Powerful white Southerners and Northern financiers brought great economic changes to parts of the South. Northern capital helped to build railroads, and by 1890 almost 40,000 miles of track crisscrossed the South. Southern industry also grew. A thriving iron and steel industry developed around Birmingham, Alabama. In North Carolina, tobacco processing became big business, and cotton mills appeared in numerous small towns.

In other ways, the South changed little. Despite its industrial growth, the region remained agrarian. As late as 1900, only 6 percent of the Southern labor force worked in manufacturing. For many African Americans, the end of Reconstruction meant a return to the "Old South," where they had little political power and were forced to labor under difficult and unfair conditions.

The collapse of Reconstruction ended African Americans' hopes of being granted their own land in the South. Instead, many returned to plantations owned by whites, where they either worked for wages or became **tenant farmers,** paying rent for the land they farmed. Most tenant farmers eventually became **sharecroppers.** Sharecroppers did not pay their rent in cash. Instead, they paid a share of their crops—often as much as one-half to two-thirds.

Many sharecroppers also needed more seed and other supplies than their landlords could provide. As a result, country stores and local suppliers provided them with the supplies they needed on credit and at interest rates often as high as 40 percent. To make sure that sharecroppers paid their debts, laws allowed merchants to put liens on their crops. These **crop liens** meant that the merchants could take crops to cover the debts.

The crop-lien system and high interest rates led many sharecroppers into a financial condition called **debt peonage.** Debt peonage trapped sharecroppers on the land because they could not make enough money to pay off their debts and leave, nor could they declare bankruptcy. Failure to pay off debts could lead to imprisonment or forced labor. The Civil War had ended slavery, but the failure of Reconstruction trapped many African Americans in economic **circumstances** that severely limited their newly gained freedom.

Reading Check **Summarizing** What factors brought about an economic rebuilding of the South?

Section 3 REVIEW

Vocabulary

1. **Explain** the significance of: "sin tax," Horace Greeley, "Whiskey Ring," Panic of 1873, Compromise of 1877, "New South," tenant farmer, sharecropper, crop lien, debt peonage.

Main Ideas

2. **Analyzing** What caused the Panic of 1873?
3. **Explaining** How did Reconstruction end?
4. **Describing** How did conditions for African Americans in the post-Reconstruction South resemble conditions before the Civil War?

Critical Thinking

5. **Big Ideas** What factors contributed to the improving economy of the South after Reconstruction?
6. **Organizing** Use a graphic organizer to identify the problems faced by Grant's administration.

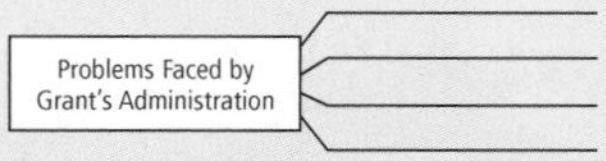

7. **Analyzing Visuals** Study the map of the election of 1876 on page 374. Which candidate won the popular vote?

Writing About History

8. **Expository Writing** Write a short essay explaining what you consider to be the three most important events of the Reconstruction period. Explain why you chose those events.

History ONLINE
Study Central™ To review this section, go to glencoe.com and click on Study Central.

377

Reading Check

Answer:
Powerful white Southern and Northern financiers invested in the South because they believed the region had to develop a strong industrial economy.

Assess

History ONLINE

Study Central provides summaries, interactive games, and online graphic organizers to help students review content.

Close

Comparing Ask students to describe the South after Reconstruction. *(Slavery was abolished, more industry developed, but the South remained dependent on agriculture.)*

Section 3 REVIEW

Answers

1. All definitions can be found in the section and the Glossary.
2. Fear within the financial community sparked by the bankruptcy of Jay Cooke and Company bank due to bad railroad investments
3. After Rutherford Hayes became president as a result of the Compromise of 1877, he pulled all federal troops out of the South, ending Reconstruction.
4. The collapse of Reconstruction ended African Americans' hopes of being granted their own land in the South. They still had little political power and were forced to labor under difficult and unfair conditions for the plantation elite, with little hope for future success.
5. acceptance that things were never going to be as they were before the Civil War, investment by Northerners, growth of industry
6. perception that wealthy Americans had too much influence, Belknap scandal, "Whiskey Ring" scandal, Panic of 1873
7. Tilden
8. Essays should include three events and an explanation for each.

Visual/Spatial Ask students to research the percentages of eligible voters who actually voted in four presidential elections in different decades. Have them create circle graphs or bar graphs showing the percentages. Discuss their findings, including their ideas about why some people don't vote. **OL**

Interested students may also want to find breakdowns of voter participation by income, location, ethnicity, and age. **AL**

Analyzing Have students review "The Events of Reconstruction." **Ask:** **Which event do you think was the most important?** *(Answers may include rights for African Americans and the vote for African American males; industrialization of South)* Write their answers on the board and have students explain their choices. Then ask the class to vote on the event they consider the most important. **OL**

Chapter 10 Visual Summary

STUDY TO GO You can study anywhere, anytime by downloading quizzes and flashcards to your PDA from glencoe.com.

Plans for Reconstruction

Lincoln's Plan

- Amnesty for all Southerners who take an oath of loyalty and accept the end of slavery, excluding former Confederate officials
- Once 10 percent had taken the oath, new state governments could be formed

Congressional Plan—The Wade-Davis Bill

- A majority of Southerners must take an oath of loyalty in order for new state governments to form
- Each state must hold a convention to abolish slavery, reject Confederate debts, and deprive former Confederate officials and officers of the right to vote or hold office

Johnson's Plan

- Amnesty for all Southerners who take an oath of loyalty, excluding former Confederate officers and owners of large amounts of property
- Each Confederate state must hold a convention to revoke secession ordinance and ratify the 13th Amendment

▲ *During Reconstruction, many African American men held elected offices, some as state senators and representatives.*

▲ *After the Civil War, the South's agricultural economy revived, and many African Americans found themselves doing much the same work they had when enslaved. Many became sharecroppers, trapped on the land because of the high debts they were forced to accumulate.*

The Events of Reconstruction

The White Southern Response

- The South elects many former Confederate officials to Congress
- Southern states introduce black codes to restrict African American freedom and force them into labor contracts
- White mobs riot and attack African Americans
- Militant groups, such as the Ku Klux Klan, organize to oppose reconstruction and prevent African Americans from voting
- Southern Democrats slowly regain power by using racism to bring poor white voters back to the Democratic party

Congress

- Congress passes the Civil Rights Act of 1866 and the Fourteenth Amendment
- Congress imposes Military Reconstruction, requiring former Confederate states to give the right to vote to all adult males
- Congress passes the Fifteenth Amendment

African Americans

- Freedmen's Bureau and Reconstruction governments build schools enabling formerly enslaved African Americans to get an education
- During Reconstruction, African Americans enter politics in large numbers, holding many political offices in the South
- As Reconstruction ends and the South's agrarian economy revives, many African Americans become sharecroppers

Hands-On Chapter Project
Step 4: Wrap Up

Reconstruction Correspondence

Step 4: The Other Side of the Story Have students review the letters they have written for this project. They will take on the opposing role and respond to the letters.

Directions Students should write a brief response to each of their letters from the opposing point of view. For example, have students write a letter reacting to Reconstruction from the point of view of a white citizen of the South rather than the African American point of view.

Comparing and Contrasting As a class, have students compare and contrast all of the different views about Reconstruction (Northern, Southern white, African American, etc.). Use this discussion to debate the successes and failures of Reconstruction of the South. **OL**

Reviewing Vocabulary

Directions: Choose the word or words that best complete the sentence.

1. Part of President Lincoln's plan for Reconstruction was to offer ________ to Southerners who would take an oath of loyalty to the United States.

A imprisonment
B amnesty
C debt peonage
D exile

2. A Northerner who came to the South during Reconstruction, or a ________, was often there to exploit the South's misfortune.

A scalawag
B sharecropper
C carpetbagger
D furnishing merchant

3. During Reconstruction, the Republican Congress maintained ________ to pay its debts.

A sin taxes
B crop liens
C debt peonage
D black codes

4. A type of corruption called ________ among the Republicans in Congress gave the Democrats an issue to help them regain power in the 1870s.

A scandal mongering
B graft
C welching
D thievery

5. Even though the Civil War ended slavery, many freed African American farmers faced ________, a set of financial circumstances that confined them to the land because they could not make enough money to get out of debt.

A the "New South"
B debt peonage
C black codes
D amnesty

Reviewing Main Ideas

Directions: Choose the best answer for each of the following questions.

Section 1 *(pp. 356–363)*

6. Which provision was part of the Wade-Davis Bill?

A The majority of white men in the state had to take an oath of allegiance to the United States.
B States could not hold a constitutional convention.
C All former Confederate political and military leaders would be given the right to vote.
D Freed African Americans had to be provided with "forty acres and a mule."

7. The Freedmen's Bureau made the most lasting impact in

A education.
B land redistribution.
C voter registration.
D labor negotiations.

Section 2 *(pp. 366–371)*

8. The first African American leaders who emerged during Reconstruction came from which group?

A scalawags who wanted to strengthen the Republican Party
B those who had been educated before the Civil War
C those who had just been freed from enslavement
D former Confederate political leaders

9. The third Enforcement Act was passed by Congress in 1871 to

A divide the Confederacy into five military districts.
B provide all adult males with the right to vote.
C outlaw the activities of the Ku Klux Klan.
D establish the Freedmen's Bureau.

TEST-TAKING TIP

Be sure to evaluate each possible answer before you make your final choice. Do not just choose the first one that you think is correct.

Need Extra Help?

If You Missed Questions . . .	1	2	3	4	5	6	7	8	9
Go to Page . . .	356	366	372	368	377	359	359	367	371

GO ON

Answers and Analyses
Reviewing Vocabulary

1. B A good strategy for fill-in-the-blank questions is for students to fill in the blank themselves before looking at the answer choices. The answer choice that most closely matches the word they chose is most likely correct. Amnesty is the only answer choice that is a positive, and based on the question, it is likely that Lincoln offered something positive in return for a loyalty oath.

2. C Carpetbaggers were called so because of their bags made of carpet remnants. A scalawag was a white Southerner that supported Reconstruction. Furnishing merchant is a distractor based on similarity to "carpet."

3. A Sin taxes were taxes on alcohol and tobacco. Explain to students that taxes are how the government generates revenue. Crop liens and debt patronage would not be used by the government to raise money. Black codes were discriminatory Southern laws.

4. B A graft is cheating by someone who is corrupt or can also mean money obtained through corruption. Welching, thieving, and scandal mongering are all negative things, but graft is more clearly connected with corruption.

5. B The financial circumstances that created debt peonage included liens that reduced the profitability of crops harvested and the high interest rates that made it difficult for farmers to get out of debt.

Reviewing Main Ideas

6. A This question can be answered using the process of elimination. *A* is correct. *B* is incorrect, because under the Bill, once all white men in the state had taken an oath of allegiance, they could then hold a constitutional convention. *C* is the opposite of one of the provisions, which stated the constitutions must ban all former Confederate leaders from voting.

7. A Many members of the Freedmen's Bureau recognized the importance of education. The Bureau did not make nearly as large strides in the areas listed in the other choices.

8. B African American leaders educated before the war would logically emerge as leaders after the war. *A* is incorrect, because scalawags were white Southerners, not African American leaders. *C* would not make sense, because most recently freed enslaved Africans did not have enough knowledge or education. Confederate leaders would not have been African American.

9. C A good way to help students remember that the third Enforcement Act was passed to outlaw the Ku Klux Klan is to focus on the number 3. It was the **third** Enforcement Act, and there are **three Ks** in Ku Klux Klan.

10. B As discussed in previous answers, scalawags were white Southerners, which eliminates *A* and *C*. Scalawags supported Reconstruction, which eliminates *D*.

11. B It is important that students understand what motivated the Southern Democrats. Just because the Union had remained intact, did not mean that the North and South had healed or experienced any fundamental change in beliefs. Therefore, Southern Democrats wanted to redeem the South.

12. D Choice *A* is untrue. *B* is incorrect, because Reconstruction was not the cause of the scandal in Grant's administration. Democrats did not gain complete control of every level of government; *C* is too broad. Reconstruction failed because African Americans, although freed from slavery, faced massive discrimination and economic hardship.

13. D The Compromise of 1877 was the name given to the election of Hayes. Although the details of a compromise, if there indeed was one, are murky, it was said that Hayes promised to remove federal troops from the South. Federal troops were removed from the South shortly after Hayes became president, which confirmed for some that a compromise had taken place.

Critical Thinking

14. C The culture of the South during Reconstruction makes choices *A*, *B*, and *D* highly unlikely. The Reconstruction South was not kind to African Americans. Black codes limited the rights of southern African Americans.

Chapter 10 Assessment

10. Which of the following groups was among the scalawags during Reconstruction?

- **A** formerly enslaved African Americans
- **B** Southern whites who owned small farms
- **C** Northern Radical Republicans
- **D** members of the Ku Klux Klan

Section 3 *(pp. 372–377)*

11. The concept of "redeeming" the South was an appeal to

- **A** Northern capitalists to help rebuild the Southern economy.
- **B** white racists to rid the region of "Black Republican" governments.
- **C** Radical Republicans to bring an end to Reconstruction.
- **D** former Confederates to officially apologize for starting the Civil War.

12. One way in which Reconstruction failed was that, in the end, it

- **A** did not reunite the Confederate states with the Union.
- **B** led to much corruption in the Grant administration.
- **C** gave the Democrats complete control of every level of government.
- **D** allowed African Americans to lose many of their new rights.

13. In the Compromise of 1877, what did Rutherford B. Hayes supposedly promise to do as president?

- **A** free all enslaved African Americans in the Southern states
- **B** ensure the passage of the Enforcement Acts
- **C** pardon members of President Grant's administration
- **D** remove all federal troops from the Southern states

Critical Thinking

Directions: Choose the best answers to the following questions.

14. Following the Civil War, many Southern states enacted black codes to

- **A** provide free farmland for African Americans.
- **B** guarantee equal civil rights for African Americans.
- **C** restrict the rights of formerly enslaved persons.
- **D** support the creation of the Freedmen's Bureau.

Base your answers to questions 15 and 16 on the map below and your knowledge of Chapter 10.

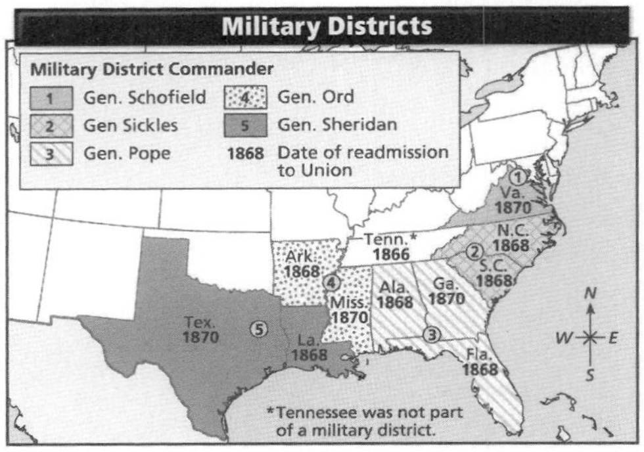

15. Which general commanded a district comprised only of states that had been readmitted to the Union in 1868?

- **A** General Sickles
- **B** General Pope
- **C** General Ord
- **D** General Sheridan

16. What were three of the last states to be readmitted to the Union?

- **A** Arkansas, Louisiana, Alabama
- **B** Texas, Mississippi, Georgia
- **C** North Carolina, South Carolina, Virginia
- **D** Virginia, Texas, Arkansas

Need Extra Help?

If You Missed Questions . . .	10	11	12	13	14	15	16
Go to Page . . .	366	375	377	375	360	380	380

GO ON

15. A To answer correctly, students must understand the map key and read the map carefully. General Sickles's district is marked with a crosshatch pattern. In addition, the key tells students that the boldface date is the date of readmission to the Union. Each state with the crosshatch pattern was readmitted in 1868.

16. B Looking at the boldface dates, Texas, Mississippi, and Georgia were all readmitted to the Union in 1870. All of the other answer choices include at least one state readmitted in 1868.

Chapter 10 ASSESSMENT

17. What effect did the system of sharecropping have on the South after the Civil War?

A It kept formerly enslaved persons economically dependent.

B It brought investment capital to the South.

C It encouraged Northerners to migrate South.

D It provided for a fairer distribution of farm profits.

Analyze the cartoon and answer the question that follows. Base your answer on the cartoon and on your knowledge of Chapter 10.

18. What does the trapeze act that Ulysses S. Grant is performing represent?

A economic hardship

B a split Republican party

C a scandal-ridden administration

D controversial sin taxes

Document-Based Questions

Directions: Analyze the document and answer the short-answer questions that follow the document.

In 1867, a speech was read for Radical Republican Thaddeus Stevens who was ill. He argued in favor of confiscating the land of former Confederates and putting it to a new use.

> *"Four million of persons [former slaves] have just been freed from a condition of dependence, . . . Make them independent of their old masters, so that they may not be compelled to work for them upon unfair terms, which can only be done by giving them a small tract of land to cultivate for themselves, . . . Nothing is so likely to make a man a good citizen as to make him a freeholder. Nothing will so multiply the productions of the South as to divide it into small farms. Nothing will make men so industrious and moral as to let them feel that they are above want and are the owners of the soil which they till. . . . How is it possible for them to cultivate their lands if these people were expelled? If Moses should lead or drive them into exile, or carry out the absurd idea of colonizing them, the South would become a barren waste."*

—from the *Congressional Globe,* speech to House of Representatives, March 19, 1867

19. What was Stevens arguing the federal government should do?

20. What does Stevens suggest would happen to the South if all the formerly enslaved African Americans left the region?

Extended Response

21. In your opinion, who had the best plan for Reconstruction—Lincoln, Johnson, or Congress? Write a persuasive essay that includes an introduction and at least three paragraphs that explain and support your position.

STOP

History ONLINE

For additional test practice, use Self-Check Quizzes—Chapter 10 at glencoe.com.

Need Extra Help?

If You Missed Questions . . .	17	18	19	20	21
Go to Page . . .	377	381	381	381	356–363

Document-Based Questions

19. Stevens wanted Confederate lands to be redistributed to former enslaved African Americans in the form of small farms. Stevens believes that being a freeholder (landholder) is the best way to make a man a good citizen.

20. Stevens suggests it would become a barren waste. Have students reread the last sentence if they have trouble with this question. Discuss with students why they think Stevens held this belief.

Extended Response

21. Essays will vary, but students should provide a clear and reasoned argument to support their choice of the most appropriate Reconstruction plan (Lincoln's plan, Radical Reconstruction, etc.,) and include supporting details from the chapter. Students should remain focused on the argument they choose, and follow the guidelines for writing a persuasive essay.

17. A The word *share* in sharecropping should help students remember that sharecroppers did not own their own land; in essence, they "shared" it (albeit to their economic disadvantage). Sharecroppers were tied to the land because they were constantly working to pay off debts that could never be repaid; they were essentially economically enslaved.

18. C In the cartoon, Grant is swinging from a trapeze, holding a lower trapeze in his mouth. Have students study the words written on the various parts of the trapeze and on the men's belts, like *corruption* and *whiskey.*

History ONLINE

Have students visit the Web site at glencoe.com to review Chapter 10 and take the Self-Check Quiz.

Need Extra Help?

Have students refer to the pages listed if they miss any of the questions.

UNIT PACING CHART					
	Unit 4	Chapter 11	Chapter 12	Chapter 13	Unit 4
Day 1	Unit Opener	Chapter 11 Opener, Section 1	Chapter 12 Opener, Section 1	Chapter 13 Opener, Section 1	Wrap-Up/Project, Unit Assessment
Day 2		Sections 2 & 3	Section 2	Section 2	
Day 3		Chapter Assessment	Section 3	Section 3	
Day 4			Section 4	Section 4	
Day 5			Chapter Assessment	Section 5	
Day 6				Chapter Assessment	

Teacher to Teacher

Teresa Squires Osborne
Reynolds High School
Troutdale, OR

Immigration Panel Create a panel of students, from your class and/or from the school, made up of first and second generation immigrants to the United States. After panel members have shown their country of origin on a map, have the student panel address the following information:

1. What is the story of your family's arrival here? Where and when did you or your parents arrive in the United States?
2. Why did your family choose to leave your native country?
3. What is different or similar about life in the United States compared to your family's native country?
4. How would your life be different if you or your parents had remained?

Have students compare the answers of the panel with the experiences of earlier immigrant groups.

Author Note

Dear American History Teacher,

Each of the chapters in this unit focuses on one of the three major developments in the United States during the generation after the Civil War. The Union victory removed the conflict between slavery and freedom that had entangled westward expansion before 1861, and loosened dynamic forces of expansion that filled up a million square miles of the West and brought 10 new states into the Union. Five transcontinental railroads built during these years connected the western half of the country to the rest in a continental economy of unprecedented proportions. Cattle ranching and mining became dominant features of this new West. But if for white Americans (and some African Americans) the West represented frontiers of opportunity, for Native Americans these decades spelled the doom of their once vital independent culture as they were squeezed onto smaller and smaller reservations.

All kinds of industry grew exponentially after the Civil War. A distant second to Britain in world industrial production in 1860, the United States surpassed Britain in the 1880s and, by 1900, American factories produced as much as those of Britain and Germany combined. But this growth produced a widening gap between rich and poor and violent conflict between capital and labor that at times seemed to threaten the very fabric of American society.

So did the growth of American cities, fed by large-scale immigration. The United States became a multi-ethnic and multi-cultural nation where various nationalities and languages co-existed uneasily in burgeoning cities whose institutions and infrastructures failed to keep pace with this rapid growth.

At the local, state, and national levels, government seemed unable to cope with these multiple dimensions of spatial, industrial, and population growth. All of these developments climaxed in what historians have described as "the crisis of the 1890s." Not until the post-1890s generation would the American polity begin to get a grip on these problems.

James M. McPherson

Senior Author

Introducing **Unit 4**

Focus

Why It Matters

Have students consider the changes that have occurred in their lifetimes as a result of technological advances. Then have them make generalizations about the effects of technological change on peoples' lives. **OL**

Connecting to Past Learning

Have students recall social and economic conditions after the Civil War. **Ask:** How were conditions in the North different from conditions in the South? *(The infrastructure of the North was intact and manufacturing industries were growing; the South was in ruins.)* Tell students that in this unit they will learn about the rapid industrialization that took place after the Civil War, as well as reform movements that developed in response to industrialization. **OL**

Unit Launch Activity

Making Connections Have students brainstorm a list of inventions or new technologies that they did not have five or ten years ago. List students' answers on the board. **Ask:** How is your life different with these inventions or new technologies? *(Answers will vary, but students might note that communication is faster; downloading music or video is easier.)* Discuss with the class how inventions and new technologies changed the lives of the people living after the Civil War. **OL**

Unit 4

The Birth of Modern America

1865–1901

CHAPTER 11
Settling the West
1865–1890

CHAPTER 12
Industrialization
1865–1901

CHAPTER 13
Urban America
1865–1896

Why It Matters

Following the turmoil of the Civil War and Reconstruction, the United States began its transformation from a rural nation to an industrial, urban nation linked together by railroads. New inventions and scientific discoveries fundamentally altered how Americans lived and worked. New factories employed thousands of workers; cities grew dramatically in size, and tens of millions of new immigrants flooded into the country.

382

Team Teaching Activity

Economics Have the economics teacher compare and contrast small, entrepreneurial businesses with big businesses, and family farms with large agricultural enterprises. After the presentation, have a class discussion using the following questions: How are workers treated differently in different types of enterprises? How is family life affected by various enterprises? How does the type of enterprise in which your family is involved affect where and how you live? What effect do economic changes such as recessions have on these types of enterprises? **OL**

Wabash Avenue and the elevated railroad in downtown Chicago, 1900.

383

Introducing
Unit 4

Teach

Skill Practice

Visual Literacy Have students study the unit photograph. **Ask:** What types of transportation are shown in the photograph? *(elevated rail lines, horse-drawn-cart)* Based on the photograph, have students make a generalization about Chicagoans' lives at the time. *(Answers will vary, but students should note that it was a time of great change.)* BL

Skill Practice

Describing Have students again review the unit photograph. **Ask:** Based on the photograph, what concerns or issues might some citizens have? *(Answers might include overcrowding, noise pollution, air pollution, unsanitary conditions.)* Given the list of issues, have students describe what concerned citizens might do. *(Organize reform movements.)* OL

More About the Photo

Visual Literacy Because of its location, Chicago grew to be a transportation hub. To help the city's growing population move around, the city built elevated commuter rail lines, which have become known as the "L." The first line was completed in 1888.

NCLB — NO CHILD LEFT BEHIND

Teaching Tip The NCLB Act emphasizes reading. Ask students to write down events and people they will encounter in this unit and keep the list with them as they read. When students find a person or item on the list, they should note the page number and write a brief summary. Students can use this list while studying.

Chapter 11 Planning Guide

Key to Ability Levels	
BL Below Level	AL Above Level
OL On Level	ELL English Language Learners

Key to Teaching Resources	
Print Material	Transparency
CD-ROM or DVD	

Levels					Resources	Chapter Opener	Section 1	Section 2	Section 3	Chapter Assess
BL	OL	AL	ELL							
					FOCUS					
BL	OL	AL	ELL	Transparency	**Daily Focus Transparencies**		11-1	11-2	11-3	
					TEACH					
BL	OL		ELL	Print Material	**Reading Skills Activity, URB**			p. 21		
	OL			Print Material	**Historical Analysis Skills Activity, URB**		p. 22			
BL	OL	AL	ELL	Print Material	**Differentiated Instruction Activity, URB**		p. 23			
BL			ELL	Print Material	**English Learner Activity, URB**	p. 25				
BL	OL	AL	ELL	Print Material	**Content Vocabulary Activity, URB***	p. 27				
BL	OL	AL	ELL	Print Material	**Academic Vocabulary Activity, URB**	p. 29				
	OL	AL		Print Material	**Reinforcing Skills Activity, URB**			p. 31		
	OL	AL		Print Material	**Critical Thinking Skills Activity, URB**				p. 32	
BL	OL		ELL	Print Material	**Time Line Activity, URB**				p. 33	
	OL			Print Material	**Linking Past and Present Activity, URB**		p. 34			
BL	OL	AL	ELL	Print Material	**Primary Source Reading, URB**				p. 35, 37	
BL	OL	AL	ELL	Print Material	**American Art and Music Activity, URB**					p. 39
BL	OL	AL	ELL	Print Material	**Interpreting Political Cartoons Activity, URB**				p. 41	
		AL		Print Material	**Enrichment Activity, URB**				p. 45	
BL	OL		ELL	Print Material	**Guided Reading Activity, URB***		p. 48	p. 49	p. 50	
BL	OL	AL	ELL	Print Material	**Reading Essentials and Note-Taking Guide***		p. 120	p. 123	p. 126	
BL	OL	AL	ELL	Print Material	**Differentiated Instruction for the American History Classroom**	✓	✓	✓	✓	✓
BL	OL	AL	ELL	Transparency	**Unit Map Overlay Transparencies**	✓	✓	✓	✓	✓
BL	OL	AL	ELL	Print Material	**Unit Time Line Transparencies, Strategies, and Activities**	✓	✓	✓	✓	✓
BL	OL	AL	ELL	Print Material	**Cause and Effect Transparencies, Strategies, and Activities**	✓	✓	✓	✓	✓
BL	OL	AL	ELL	Print Material	**Why It Matters Chapter Transparencies, Strategies, and Activities**	✓	✓	✓	✓	✓

Note: Please refer to the *Unit 4 Resource Book* for this chapter's URB materials.

* Also available in Spanish

TeacherWorks Plus — All-In-One Planner and Resource Center

- Interactive Lesson Planner
- Interactive Teacher Edition
- Fully editable blackline masters
- Section Spotlight Videos Launch
- Differentiated Lesson Plans
- Printable reports of daily assignments
- Standards Tracking System

BL	OL	AL	ELL	Resources	Chapter Opener	Section 1	Section 2	Section 3	Chapter Assess
				TEACH *(continued)*					
BL	OL	AL	ELL	American Biographies				✓	
BL	OL	AL	ELL	The Living Constitution	✓	✓	✓	✓	✓
BL	OL	AL	ELL	American Issues	✓	✓	✓	✓	✓
	OL	AL	ELL	American Art and Architecture Transparencies, Strategies, and Activities	✓	✓	✓	✓	✓
BL	OL	AL		High School American History Literature Library	✓	✓	✓	✓	✓
	OL	AL		American History Primary Source Documents Library	✓	✓	✓	✓	✓
BL	OL	AL	ELL	American Music: Hits Through History CD	✓	✓	✓	✓	✓
BL	OL	AL	ELL	StudentWorks™ Plus	✓	✓	✓	✓	✓
BL	OL	AL	ELL	*The American Vision* Video Program	✓	✓	✓	✓	✓
Teacher Resources				Reading Strategies and Activities for the Social Studies Classroom	✓	✓	✓	✓	✓
Teacher Resources				Strategies for Success	✓	✓	✓	✓	✓
Teacher Resources				Presentation Plus! with MindJogger CheckPoint	✓	✓	✓	✓	✓
Teacher Resources				Success With English Learners	✓	✓	✓	✓	✓
				ASSESS					
BL	OL	AL	ELL	Section Quizzes and Chapter Tests*		p. 153	p. 154	p. 155	p. 157
BL	OL	AL	ELL	Authentic Assessment With Rubrics					p. 27
BL	OL	AL	ELL	Standardized Test Practice Workbook					p. 22
BL	OL	AL	ELL	*ExamView® Assessment Suite*		11-1	11-2	11-3	Ch. 11
				CLOSE					
BL			ELL	Reteaching Activity, URB					p. 43
BL	OL		ELL	Reading and Study Skills Foldables™		p. 59			
BL	OL	AL	ELL	*American History* in Graphic Novel		p. 23			

✓ Chapter- or unit-based activities applicable to all sections in this chapter.

Chapter 11 Integrating Technology

Using Chapter Overviews

Teach With Technology

What is a Chapter Overview?

A Chapter Overview provides an online section-by-section summary of the content of each chapter. It can help students review—or preview—chapter content to increase comprehension of main ideas.

How can a Chapter Overview help my students and me?

A Chapter Overview helps you and your students review the main points from each chapter section-by-section. It can help:

- students preview chapter content
- students focus on the main ideas
- students review chapter content
- students practice reading and comprehension skills
- you devise discussion points
- you summarize the chapter for your students

Visit glencoe.com and enter a ***QuickPass***™ code to go to a Chapter Overview.

History ONLINE
Visit glencoe.com and enter ***QuickPass***™ code TAV9399c11T for Chapter 11 resources.

You can easily launch a wide range of digital products from your computer's desktop with the McGraw-Hill Social Studies widget.

TeacherWorks

	Student	Teacher	Parent
Media Library			
• Section Audio	●		●
• Spanish Audio Summaries	●		●
• Section Spotlight Videos	●	●	●
The American Vision **Online Learning Center (Web Site)**			
• StudentWorks™ Plus Online	●	●	●
• Multilingual Glossary	●	●	●
• Study-to-Go	●	●	●
• Chapter Overviews	●	●	●
• Self-Check Quizzes	●	●	●
• Student Web Activities	●	●	●
• ePuzzles and Games	●	●	●
• Vocabulary eFlashcards	●	●	●
• In Motion Animations	●	●	●
• Study Central™	●	●	●
• Web Activity Lesson Plans		●	
• Vocabulary PuzzleMaker	●	●	●
• Historical Thinking Activities		●	
• Beyond the Textbook	●	●	●

Reading Support from Jamestown Education

- **Timed Readings Plus in Social Studies** helps students increase their reading rate and fluency while maintaining comprehension. The 400-word passages are similar to those found on state and national assessments.
- **Reading in the Content Area: Social Studies** concentrates on six essential reading skills that help students better comprehend what they read. The book includes 75 high-interest nonfiction passages written at increasing levels of difficulty.
- **Reading Social Studies** includes strategic reading instruction and vocabulary support in Social Studies content for both ELLs and native speakers of English.

www.jamestowneducation.com

National Geographic

Index to National Geographic Magazine:

The following articles relate to this chapter:

- "The American Prairie: Roots of the Sky," by Douglas H. Chadwick and Jim Brandenbur, October 1993.
- "Custer and the warriors of the plains; Ghosts on the Little Bighorn. (George Armstrong Custer)," by Robert Paul Jordan, December 1986.

National Geographic Society Products To order the following, call National Geographic at 1-800-368-2728:

- *The Westward Movement* (CD-ROM).

Access National Geographic's new dynamic MapMachine Web site and other geography resources at:
www.nationalgeographic.com
www.nationalgeographic.com/maps

Biography · A&E Home Video · The History Channel

The following videotape programs are available from Glencoe as supplements to this chapter:

- Buffalo Bill: Showman of the West (ISBN 1-56-501940-7)
- Sitting Bull: Chief of the Lakota Nation (ISBN 1-56-501684-X)

To order, call Glencoe at 1-800-334-7344. To find classroom resources to accompany many of these videos, check the following home pages:

A&E Television: www.aetv.com
The History Channel: www.historychannel.com

Reading List Generator CD-ROM — Glencoe BookLink 3

Use this database to search more than 30,000 titles to create a customized reading list for your students.

- Reading lists can be organized by students' reading level, author, genre, theme, or area of interest.
- The database provides Degrees of Reading Power™ (DRP) and Lexile™ readability scores for all selections.
- A brief summary of each selection is included.

Leveled reading suggestions for this chapter:

For students at a Grade 8 reading level:
- ***Laura Ingalls Wilder: Young Pioneer,*** by Beatrice Gormley

For students at a Grade 9 reading level:
- ***The Story of the Little Bighorn,*** by R. Conrad Stein

For students at a Grade 10 reading level:
- ***Wild West,*** by Mike Stotter

For students at a Grade 11 reading level:
- ***Sod Houses on the Great Plains,*** by Glen Rounds

For students at a Grade 12 reading level:
- ***In the Days of the Vaqueros: America's First True Cowboys,*** by Russell Freedman

Introducing Chapter 11

Focus

MAKING CONNECTIONS

Why Did Settlers Move West? Ask: For what reasons might Americans have wanted to move west after the Civil War? Might the reasons have been different for white Americans and for African Americans? *(Possible answer: Students might conclude that both white Americans and African Americans sought new lives and new economic opportunities. White settlers, however, had not been enslaved, while many formerly enslaved African American settlers moved west to escape from the sharecropping system that developed in the South after the Civil War.)* **OL**

Teach

Big Ideas

As students study the chapter, remind them to consider the section-based Big Ideas included in each section's Guide to Reading. Focusing on these ideas will help them understand the important concepts in each section and in the chapter as a whole. In addition, the Hands-on Chapter Projects with their culminating activities relate the content from each section to the Big Ideas. These activities build on each other as students progress through the chapter. Section activities culminate in the wrap-up activity on the Visual Summary page.

Chapter 11

Settling the West

1865–1890

Cattle ranching in the American West has changed little in 140 years. Here an Apache cowboy herds cattle into a corral during spring roundup on an Arizona ranch.

U.S. PRESIDENTS

Johnson 1865–1869

Grant 1869–1877

Hayes 1877–1881

Garfield 1881

U.S. EVENTS

1862 • Homestead Act makes cheap land available to settlers

1864 • Sand Creek Massacre takes place

1867 • Chisholm Trail cattle drive begins

1876 • Battle of the Little Bighorn

1860 — 1870 — 1880

WORLD EVENTS

1867 • British colonies unite to form Canada

1871 • Prussia unites German states to create Germany

1876 • Porfirio Diaz becomes dictator of Mexico

1879 • Zulu launch war against British settlers

Section 1

Miners and Ranchers

Ask: What economic opportunities did miners and ranchers seek? *(Miners sought to strike it rich quickly; ranchers saw their ranches as a long-term economic investment.)* Point out that in Section 1 students will learn about the impact of miners and ranchers on Western settlement. **OL**

Section 2

Farming the Plains

Ask: What difficulties might farmers have faced as they worked the new land? *(hard soil that was difficult to plow; lack of rain; few trees from which to build cabins for shelter)* Point out that in Section 2 students will learn how land once called "The Great American Desert" became the most productive farmland in the world. **OL**

Chapter Audio

MAKING CONNECTIONS

Why Did Settlers Move West?

After the Civil War, many American settlers continued migrating to the western frontier. The lives of western miners, farmers, and ranchers were filled with hardships.

- ***Why do you think settlers continued migrating west when life on the Great Plains was so difficult?***
- ***When the frontier closed, what effect do you think this had on American society?***

Arthur 1881–1885

1887
- Dawes Act eliminates communal ownership of Native American reservations

Cleveland 1885–1889

Harrison 1889–1893

Cleveland 1893–1897

McKinley 1897–1901

1890

1900

1886
- Gold is discovered in South Africa

1891
- Russia begins Trans-Siberian railway and many settlers head east to Siberia

FOLDABLES

Summarizing Displacement Make a Sentence Strips Foldable to represent how the arrival of settlers changed the American West. Choose an event and create a flip book. On the front of each strip write the event and its location. Write a brief explanation of how the event changed the West.

History ONLINE **Visit** glencoe.com **and enter *QuickPass*™ code TAV9846c11 for Chapter 11 resources.**

Section 3

Native Americans

Ask: **Why did conflicts arise between Native Americans and the settlers?** *(Miners, ranchers, and farmers took Native Americans' land and destroyed their sources of food.)* Point out that in Section 3 students will learn about how the American government tried to settle the conflicts between the Native Americans and the settlers. **OL**

More About the Photo

Visual Literacy Despite the success of ranching in the late 1800s, cowboys received little of the profits. Cattle hands who endured the grueling 800 mile drive from Texas to Kansas earned only $30 dollars a month. Because of this, most cowboys were young men looking for temporary work. Many other drivers were African Americans, who were barred from other types of jobs and found a sense of freedom on the trails.

FOLDABLES Study Organizer Dinah Zike's Foldables

Dinah Zike's Foldables are three-dimensional, interactive graphic organizers that help students practice basic writing skills, review vocabulary terms, and identify main ideas. Instructions for creating and using Foldables can be found in the Appendix at the end of this book and in the Dinah Zike's Reading and Study Skills Foldables booklet.

History ONLINE

Visit glencoe.com and enter ***QuickPass***™ code TAV9399c11T for Chapter 11 resources, including a Chapter Overview, Study Central™, Study-to-Go, Student Web Activity, Self-Check Quiz, and other materials.

Focus

Bellringer

Daily Focus Transparency 11-1

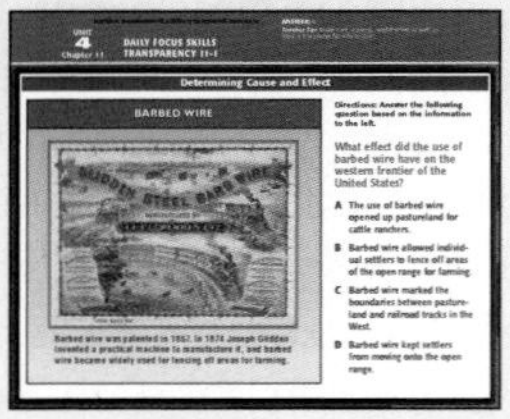

Guide to Reading

Answers may include: silver in Nevada (Comstock Lode), lead and silver in Leadville, Colorado, gold in Colorado, gold in Dakota Territory, copper in Montana, copper in Arizona

Section Spotlight Video

To generate student interest and provide a springboard for class discussion, access the Chapter 11, Section 1 video at glencoe.com or on the video DVD.

Section 1

Section Audio   Spotlight Video

Miners and Ranchers

Guide to Reading

Big Ideas

Geography and History Miners and ranchers settled large areas of the West.

Content Vocabulary

- vigilance committee *(p. 387)*
- hydraulic mining *(p. 389)*
- open range *(p. 390)*
- long drive *(p. 391)*
- hacienda *(p. 392)*
- barrios *(p. 393)*

Academic Vocabulary

- extract *(p. 388)*
- adapt *(p. 390)*
- prior *(p. 390)*

People and Events to Identify

- Henry Comstock *(p. 386)*
- boomtown *(p. 386)*

Reading Strategy

Organizing As you read about the development of the mining industry, complete a graphic organizer listing the locations of mining booms and the discoveries made there.

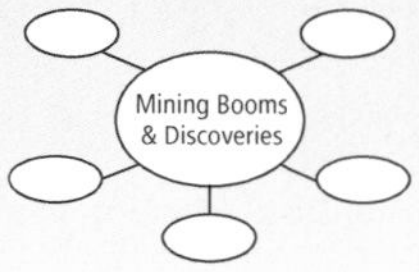

Mining and ranching attracted settlers to western territories that soon had populations large enough to qualify for statehood. People mined for gold, silver, and lead, or shipped longhorn cattle to the East.

Growth of the Mining Industry

MAIN Idea The discovery of gold, silver, and other minerals attracted thousands of settlers who established new states on the frontier.

HISTORY AND YOU Do you remember reading about the 1849 California gold rush? Read on to learn how mineral discoveries shaped the settlement of the West.

Mining played an important role in the settling of the American West. Beginning with the California gold rush, and continuing throughout the late 1800s, wave after wave of prospectors came to the region hoping to strike it rich mining gold, silver, and other minerals. Demand for minerals rose dramatically after the Civil War as the United States changed from a farming nation to an industrial nation. Mining in the West also encouraged the building of railroads to connect the mines to factories back east.

Boomtowns

In 1859 a prospector named **Henry Comstock** staked a claim in Six-Mile Canyon, near Virginia City, Nevada. Frustrated by his failure to find any gold, Comstock sold his claim a few months later. He had not realized that the sticky, blue-gray clay that made mining in the area difficult was in fact nearly pure silver ore.

News of the Comstock Lode, as the strike came to be called, brought a flood of eager prospectors to Virginia City. So many people arrived that, in 1864, Nevada was admitted as the 36th state. The Comstock Lode generated more than $230 million and helped the Union finance the Civil War.

The story of the Comstock Lode was replayed many times in the American West. News of a mineral strike would start a stampede of prospectors. Almost overnight, tiny frontier towns were transformed into small cities. Virginia City, for example, grew from a town of a few hundred people to nearly 30,000 in just a few months. It had an opera house, shops with furniture and fashions from Europe, several newspapers, and a six-story hotel.

These quickly growing towns were called **boomtowns.** Using the word "boom" this way began in the late 1800s. It refers to a time of rapid economic growth.

Resource Manager

R Reading Strategies	C Critical Thinking	D Differentiated Instruction	W Writing Support	S Skill Practice
Teacher Edition • Using Context Clues, p. 390 • Read Prim. Sources, p. 392 **Additional Resources** • Guided Read. Act., URB p. 48 • Am. History in Graphic Novel, p. 23	**Teacher Edition** • Making Gen., p. 388 • Identify. Central Issues, p. 391 • Predict. Conseq., p. 392 **Additional Resources** • Link. Past and Present, URB p. 34 • Quizzes and Tests, p. 153	**Teacher Edition** • Visual/Spatial, p. 388 • Kinesthetic, p. 393 **Additional Resources** • Diff. Instruction Act., URB p. 23 • Eng. Learner Act., URB p. 25 • Foldables, p. 59	**Teacher Edition** • Descrip. Writing, pp. 389, 390 **Additional Resources** • Content Vocab. Act., URB p. 27 • Acad. Vocab. Act., URB p. 29	**Teacher Edition** • Reading a Graph, p. 387 **Additional Resources** • Hist. Analysis Skills Act., URB p. 22 • Read. Essen., p. 120

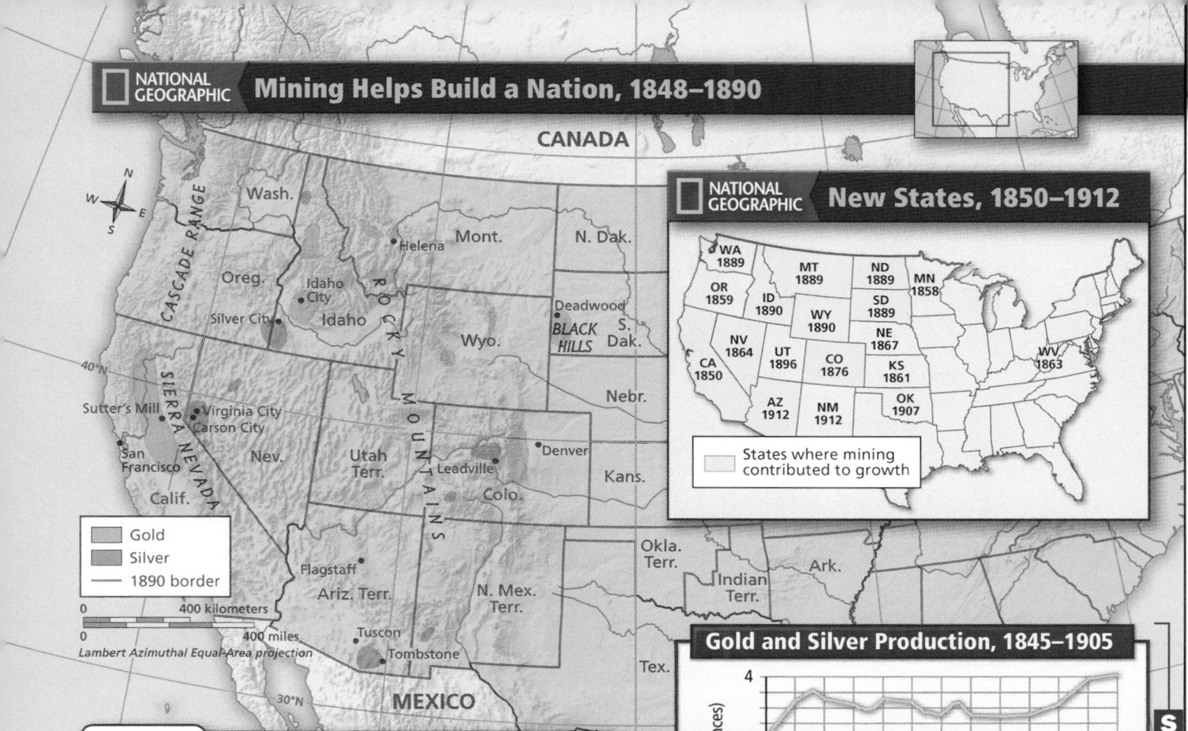

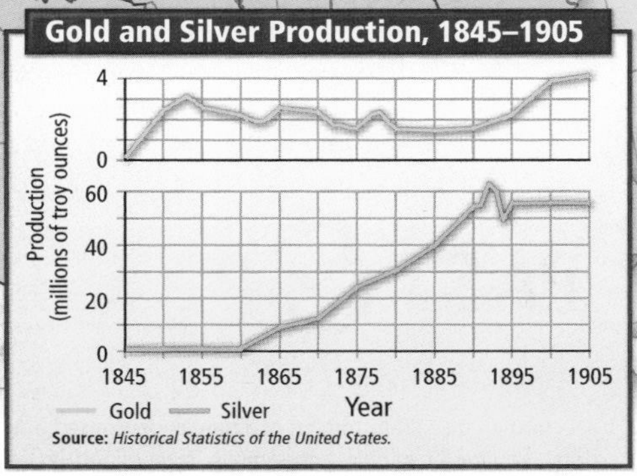

Analyzing GEOGRAPHY

1. **Location** In which states or territories were the four largest silver deposits located?
2. **Region** Which territories were the last to enter as states? Why might this have been so?
3. **Human-Environment Interaction** What happened to gold production after 1895?

Maps In MOtion See *StudentWorks™ Plus* or glencoe.com.

Boomtowns were rowdy places. Prospectors fought over claims, and thieves haunted the streets and trails. Often, "law and order" was enforced by **vigilance committees**—self-appointed volunteers who would track down and punish wrongdoers. In some cases, they punished the innocent or let the guilty go free, but most people respected the law and tried to deal firmly but fairly with the accused.

Men were usually first to arrive at a mining site, but women soon followed. Many found work in laundries or as cooks. Others worked at "hurdy-gurdy" houses (named after the mechanical violin), where they waited on tables and danced with men for the price of a drink. Some women became property owners and community leaders.

Boomtowns could not last forever because, eventually, the mines that supported the economy would be used up. A few boomtowns were able to survive when the mines closed, but many did not. Instead, they went "bust"—a term borrowed from card games that refers to players losing all of their money. In Virginia City, for example, the mines were exhausted by the late 1870s, and the economy collapsed. Most residents moved on; by 1930, Virginia City had only 500 residents. Other towns were completely abandoned, becoming "ghost-towns."

Teach

S Skill Practice

Reading a Graph Ask: Compare the number of troy ounces of gold produced in 1885 with the number of troy ounces of silver in that same year. How do you think the differing outputs affected the value of the two metals? *(About 1.5 million troy ounces of gold were produced in 1885; about 40 million troy ounces of silver were produced the same year. Gold was more scarce than silver and was thus much more valuable.)* **AL**

Analyzing GEOGRAPHY

Answers:

1. Nevada, Idaho, Arizona Territory, Colorado
2. Arizona and New Mexico; Answers will vary but may include climate, location of deposits near border with Mexico, in the case of New Mexico few deposits would have attracted fewer settlers.
3. It increased

Hands-On Chapter Project
Step 1

Making the Move West

Step 1: Planning your Move Pairs of students will make a list of items to take with them as they prepare to move to the Great Plains to begin a new farm.

Essential Question What resources, types of soil, weather, and people will be encountered on the Great Plains?

Directions Write the Big Idea on the board and ask pairs of students to assume the role of small farmers living in upstate New York. They have decided to sell their farm to seek new opportunities on the Great Plains.

First, each pair of students should use the maps in this chapter, as well as library or Internet resources, to determine exactly where they will move. Remind students to consider the climate and geography of the region under consideration. Students should also plan what type or types of transportation they will need to get to their new farm, and at what cities and towns they will stop as they move west. After each pair of students has made their decisions, they should plot their route on an outline map of the United States, labeling the cities and towns along the way and the distances between each place.

Summarizing Allow time for pairs to share their decisions and what they have learned about their destination as well as the places along their route. Students may also include pictures of the places where they will stop along the way. **OL**

(Chapter Project continued on page 167)

C Critical Thinking

Making Generalizations Have students reread this paragraph. Note that it states that unsuccessful miners "headed home." Have them think about what other actions unsuccessful miners might have taken. Have students write a paragraph describing an alternate action. OL

D Differentiated Instruction

Visual/Spatial Have students work in small groups to create a thematic map showing important mining towns in Colorado, the Dakota Territory, and Montana. Encourage students to use library and Internet resources to locate the information needed to construct their maps. Display the maps throughout the classroom. OL

Mining Leads to Statehood

C Mining also spurred the development of Colorado, Arizona, the Dakotas, and Montana. After gold was discovered in 1858 in Colorado near Pikes Peak, miners rushed to the area, declaring "Pikes Peak or Bust." Many panned for gold without success and headed home, complaining of a "Pikes Peak hoax."

In truth, the Colorado mountains contained plenty of gold and silver, although much of it was hidden beneath the surface and hard to **extract.** Deep deposits of lead mixed with silver were found at Leadville in the 1870s. News of the strike attracted as many as 1,000 newcomers a week, making Leadville one of the West's most famous boomtowns.

D Operations at Leadville and other mining towns in Colorado yielded more than $1 billion worth of silver and gold (many billions in today's money). This bonanza spurred the building of railroads through the Rocky Mountains and transformed Denver, the supply point for the mining areas, into the second largest city in the West, after San Francisco.

Three railroads, the Denver and Rio Grande Western, the South Park and Pacific, and the Colorado Midland all made stops at towns in the mining region.

The discovery of gold in the Black Hills of the Dakota Territory and copper in Montana drew miners to the region in the 1870s. When the railroads were completed, many farmers and ranchers settled the area. In 1889 Congress admitted three new states: North Dakota, South Dakota, and Montana.

In the Southwest, the Arizona Territory followed a similar pattern. Miners had already begun moving to Arizona in the 1860s and 1870s to work one of the nation's largest copper deposits. When silver was found at the town of Tombstone in 1877, however, it set off a boom that attracted a huge wave of prospectors to the territory.

The boom lasted less than 10 years, but in that time, Tombstone became famous for its lawlessness. Marshall Wyatt Earp and his brothers gained their reputations during the famous gunfight at the O. K. Corral there in 1881. Although Arizona did not grow as quickly as Colorado, Nevada, or Montana, by 1912 it had enough people to apply for statehood, as did the neighboring territory of New Mexico.

PAST & PRESENT

New Mining Technology

In the late 1800s, mining companies developed a new technology—hydraulic mining—to remove large quantities of earth and process it for minerals. Miners generated a high-pressure spray by directing water from nearby rivers into narrower and narrower channels, through a large canvas hose and out a giant iron nozzle called a monitor. Using a powerful high-pressure blast of water, "a handful of men," as one journalist wrote, "took out the very heart of a mountain."

Although hydraulic mining is no longer used in the United States, the invention of earth-moving machines such as bulldozers and excavators has made it possible to continue to dig for minerals by removing large quantities of earth. This kind of mining is called open-pit mining or strip mining. It has many of the same problems faced by hydraulic miners. Specifically, something has to be done with the leftovers. The processed ore is usually pumped to a pond, where the water evaporates. These ponds can often be toxic because of the chemicals and minerals that are left after the ore is removed.

▲ *The high-pressure water washed the loose earth into large sluices, or ditches that carried the water and earth into riffle boxes. The boxes agitated the water, causing the silver or gold to settle out. The leftover debris, called tailings or "slickens," was then washed into a nearby stream.*

388 Chapter 11 Settling the West

Additional Support

Activity: Collaborative Learning

Constructing a Plan Organize students into several groups and ask groups to construct a plan for a late-1800s Western town. Students should use their book, the Internet, and other sources to find examples of how towns were organized in the West and the types of buildings and amenities that were located in towns. Suggest that groups consider the following points in preparing their plans: the buildings they will include and their location; the building materials, energy sources, and landscaping they want to use; and the public facilities they will include. Have each group draw a pictorial map of their town and accompany it with a short report explaining the choices they made in planning.

Mining Technology

Extracting minerals from the rugged mountains of the American West required ingenuity and patience. Early prospectors extracted shallow deposits of ore in a process called placer mining, using simple tools like picks, shovels, and pans.

Other prospectors used sluice mining. Sluices were used to search riverbeds more quickly than the panning method. A sluice diverted the current of a river into trenches. The water was directed to a box with metal "riffle" bars that caused heavier minerals to settle to the bottom of the box. A screen at the end of the box prevented the minerals from escaping with the water and sediment.

When deposits near the surface ran out, miners began **hydraulic mining** to remove large quantities of earth and process it for minerals. Miners sprayed water at very high pressure against the hill or mountain they were mining. The water pressure washed away the dirt, gravel, and rock, and exposed the minerals beneath the surface.

Hydraulic mining began in California, near Nevada City. It effectively removed large quantities of minerals and generated a lot of tax money for local and state governments. Unfortunately, it also had a devastating effect on the local environment. Millions of tons of silt, sand, and gravel were washed into local rivers. The sediment raised the riverbed, and the rivers began overflowing their banks, causing major floods that wrecked fences, destroyed orchards, and deposited rocks and gravel on what had been good farm soil.

In the 1880s farmers fought back by suing the mining companies. In 1884 federal judge Lorenzo Sawyer ruled in favor of the farmers. He declared hydraulic mining a "public and private nuisance" and issued an injunction stopping the practice.

Congress eventually passed a law in 1893 allowing hydraulic mining if the mining company created a place to store the sediment. By then most mining companies had moved to quartz mining—the kind of mining familiar to people today—in which deep mine shafts are dug, and miners go underground to extract the minerals. **W**

Reading Check **Explaining** What role did mining play in the development of the American West?

August 1995

▼ *Mining is still very important to the western economy. The Kennecott Copper Mine in Bingham Canyon, Utah, is the largest human-made excavation in the world. The mine is 2½ miles wide and ¾ mile deep. It supplies approximately 15% of all copper used in the United States.*

▲ *An example of the problems of open-pit mining can be seen at the Berkeley Pit copper mine in Montana (above). When the mine closed, groundwater flooded the pit. The water passed through mineral deposits and became very acidic and contaminated with chemicals. Cleanup is scheduled for 2018 once a treatment plant has been built.*

MAKING CONNECTIONS

1. **Comparing** How was mining in the 1880s similar to mining today?
2. **Problem-Solving** How might mining companies avoid damaging the environment and still extract the minerals they need?

Activity: Collaborative Learning

Creating a Thematic Map Ask: What effects did the mining industry have upon the West? *(Possible answers: populated the West, led to statehood for western territories)* Divide students into small groups. Have the groups create thematic maps showing the locations mentioned under the heading "Growth of the Mining Industry." Some of the locations that should be included are: Virginia City, NV; Leadville, CO; Black Hills, Dakota Territory; Montana; Arizona Territory. **OL**

W Writing Support

Descriptive Writing Invite students to use library and Internet resources to write a one-page essay describing the process of quartz mining; students should describe the method and note how it differs from hydraulic mining. Encourage students to share their essays with the class. **OL**

MAKING CONNECTIONS

Answers:

1. Both kinds of mining damage Earth and create the problem of what to do with the byproducts. Both then and now, mining was and is important to the economy.
2. Students' answers will vary but may mention reclamation projects

Reading Check

Answer:
Prospectors and others came to the area, giving it enough people to apply for statehood.

Additional Support

R Reading Strategy

Using Context Clues Have students reread the first two paragraphs on this page. Using clue words and phrases such as "cattle from the East could not survive" and "these cattle had been allowed to run wild and, slowly, a new breed—the longhorn—emerged," ask students to define the term *adapted.* Students should note that the term means, "to change to fit a new purpose." BL

W Writing Support

Descriptive Writing Ask students to find books in the library about the long drives. Then have students write letters describing to family members their experiences during a cattle drive. Students should include details such as daily routines, problems they had to solve, and wildlife they may have encountered. OL

Additional Support

Ranching and Cattle Drives

MAIN Idea Ranchers built vast cattle ranches on the Great Plains and shipped their cattle on railroads to eastern markets.

HISTORY AND YOU What images come to mind when you think of cowboys? Read on to learn about the realities of life as a cowboy in the West.

While many Americans headed to the Rocky Mountains to mine gold and silver, others began herding cattle on the Great Plains. Americans had long believed it was impossible to raise cattle in the region. Water was scarce, and cattle from the East could not survive on the tough prairie grasses. R In Texas, however, lived a breed of cattle that had **adapted** to the Great Plains—the Texas longhorn.

The longhorn was descended from Spanish cattle introduced two centuries earlier. These cattle had been allowed to run wild and, slowly, a new breed—the longhorn—had emerged. Lean and rangy, the longhorn could easily survive the harsh climate of the Plains. By 1865, some 5 million roamed the Texas grasslands.

Cattle ranching also prospered on the Plains because of the **open range,** a vast area of grassland that the federal government owned. The open range covered much of the Great Plains and provided land where ranchers could graze their herds free of charge and unrestricted by private property.

The Long Drive Begins

Prior to the Civil War, ranchers had little incentive to round up the longhorns. Beef prices were low, and moving cattle to eastern markets was not practical. The Civil War and the coming of the railroads changed this situation. During the Civil War, eastern cattle were slaughtered in huge numbers to feed the armies of the Union and the Confederacy. After the war, beef prices soared and ranchers looked for a way to round up the longhorns and sell them to eastern businesses.

W

NATIONAL GEOGRAPHIC **Cattle Ranching and the Long Drive, c. 1870**

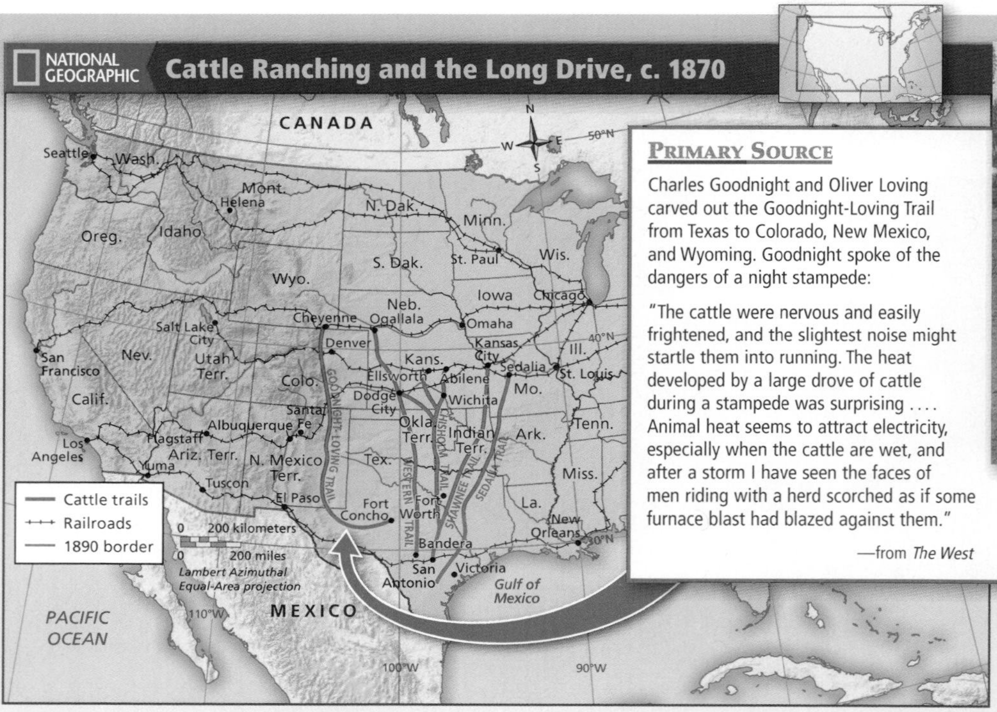

Primary Source

Charles Goodnight and Oliver Loving carved out the Goodnight-Loving Trail from Texas to Colorado, New Mexico, and Wyoming. Goodnight spoke of the dangers of a night stampede:

"The cattle were nervous and easily frightened, and the slightest noise might startle them into running. The heat developed by a large drove of cattle during a stampede was surprising . . . . Animal heat seems to attract electricity, especially when the cattle are wet, and after a storm I have seen the faces of men riding with a herd scorched as if some furnace blast had blazed against them."

—from *The West*

Activity: Interdisciplinary Connection

Mathematics: Longhorns, Long Drives, Long Distances To make a profit, the ranchers of South Texas had to get their huge herds of cattle to market. This lengthy process included the long drive—taking herds of cattle north to be loaded onto railway cars and then shipping the cattle to slaughterhouses in cities such as Chicago. Using the map key on the map on this page, have students calculate the approximate distance from Fort Concho to Cheyenne and then from Cheyenne to Chicago. *(800 miles (approximately 1287 km); 800 miles (approximately 1287 km))* Then have students determine the approximate distance of the Shawnee Trail and then the approximate distance from Kansas City to Chicago. (600 miles (approximately 965 km); just less than 400 miles (approximately 644 km)) **Ask:** Why might ranchers choose one route over another? *(Answers may include: Ranchers would have started the long drive from near their ranch; some routes may have been less likely to be attacked by Native Americans.)* OL

By the 1860s, railroads had reached the Great Plains. Lines ended at Abilene and Dodge City in Kansas and at Sedalia in Missouri. Ranchers and livestock dealers realized that if they could move the cattle as far as the railroad, the longhorns could be sold for a huge profit and shipped east to market.

In 1866 ranchers began rounding up the longhorns and drove about 260,000 of them to Sedalia, Missouri. Most of the cattle did not survive this first **long drive,** but those that survived sold for 10 times the price they would have brought in Texas. Other trails soon opened. The route to Abilene, Kansas, became the major route north. Between 1867 and 1871, cowboys drove nearly 1.5 million head of cattle up the Chisholm Trail from southern Texas to Abilene. As the railroads expanded in the West, other trails reached from Texas to more towns in Kansas, Nebraska, Montana, and Wyoming.

A long drive was a spectacular sight. In the spring, ranchers met with their cowboys to round up cattle from the open range. Stock from many different owners made up these herds. Cowboys from major ranches went north with the herds. The only way to tell them apart was by the brands burned onto their hides by branding irons. Stray calves without brands were called mavericks. These were divided and branded. The herds could number anywhere from 2,000 to 5,000 cattle.

▼ *Women help rope and brand cattle at the J. W. Lough ranch in Kansas, 1891.*

Analyzing VISUALS DBQ

1. **Explaining** What were two by-products of a cattle stampede?
2. **Analyzing** Why did the cattle trails north stop where they did?

Ranching Becomes Big Business

Cowboys drove millions of cattle north from Texas to Kansas and points beyond. Some of the longhorns went straight to slaughterhouses, but others were sold to ranchers who were building up herds in Wyoming, Montana, and other territories. Sheep herders moved their flocks onto the range and farmers settled there, blocking the trails. "Range wars" broke out among groups competing for land. Eventually, after much loss of life, hundreds of square miles were fenced cheaply and easily with a new invention—barbed wire. C

At first, ranchers did not want to abandon open grazing and complained when farmers put up barriers that prevented the ranchers' livestock from roaming. Soon, however, ranchers used barbed wire to shut out those competing with them for land and to keep their animals closer to sources of food and water. For cowboys, however, barbed wire ended the adventure of the long cattle drive.

The fencing of the range was not the only reason the long drives ended. Investors from the East and from Britain had poured money into the booming cattle business, causing an oversupply of animals on the market. Prices plummeted in the mid-1880s and many ranchers went bankrupt. Then, in the winter of 1886–1887, blizzards buried the Plains in deep snow, and temperatures dropped as low as 40 degrees below zero. Massive numbers of cattle froze or starved to death.

The cattle industry survived this terrible blow, but it was changed forever. The day of the open range had ended. From that point on, herds were raised on fenced-in ranches. New European breeds replaced longhorns, and the cowboy became a ranch hand.

Reading Check **Analyzing** How did heavy investment in the cattle industry affect the industry as a whole?

C Critical Thinking

Identifying Central Issues
Ask students to review the conflict between the ranchers and the farmers on the Western plains.
Ask: What is the main issue at the root of the conflict between these two groups? *(The two groups wanted to use the land for different purposes and did not see a means of compromise.)* OL

Analyzing VISUALS DBQ

Answers:

1. animal heat and the apparent attraction of electricity to wet cattle
2. They all stopped at main railroad lines to ship cattle east.

Reading Check

Answer:
It caused an oversupply of cattle, which drove prices down. Many ranchers went bankrupt.

Additional Support

Activity: Interdisciplinary Connection

Economics Explain the basic principles of supply and demand in a free market economy. Have students formulate generalizations on the impact of supply and demand on the boom and bust in the cattle industry. *(Possible examples: Because of a large supply of cattle and a huge demand for meat, profits in the cattle industry increased. Profits decreased when the supply of meat was greater than the demand for it.)* Discuss students' generalizations and use the generalizations to construct a basic supply-and-demand graph. OL

C Critical Thinking

Predicting Consequences
Remind students that thousands of Mexicans became American citizens when the United States acquired the Mexican Cession in 1848. **Ask:** What were some of the characteristics of these new citizens? *(spoke Spanish, were Roman Catholic)* Have students write an essay predicting how these new citizens might interact with the English-speaking settlers who moved into these lands. AL

R Reading Strategy

Reading Primary Sources
Have students reread the primary source on this page and summarize the skills of the vaquero. OL

Analyzing VISUALS

Answers:
1. He may be a performer. His colorful, decorated clothing is not suitable for ranching.
2. All ages/families worked farms; all had to work to support the family because as white settlers moved in, the status of Mexican Americans fell.

Additional Support

Settling the Hispanic Southwest

MAIN Idea The arrival of new settlers changed life for Hispanics in the Southwest.

HISTORY AND YOU Do you remember reading about New Spain? Read on to learn how the Hispanic community changed when the Southwest became part of the United States.

For centuries, much of what is today the American Southwest belonged to Spain's empire. After Mexico won its independence, the region became the northern territories of the Republic of Mexico. When the United States defeated Mexico in 1848 and took control of the region, it acquired the Spanish-speaking population living there. According to the Treaty of Guadalupe Hidalgo ending the war, the region's residents retained their property rights and became American citizens. C

In California, the Spanish mission system had collapsed by the early 1800s. In its place, a society dominated by a landholding elite had emerged. These landowners owned vast **haciendas**—huge ranches that covered thousands of acres. The heavy influx of "Forty-Niners" during the California gold rush, however, changed this society dramatically. California's population grew from 14,000 to 100,000 in two years. Suddenly, Hispanic Californians were vastly outnumbered.

Some Hispanic Californians welcomed the newcomers and the economic growth that resulted. Others distrusted the English-speaking prospectors, who tried to exclude them from the mines. When California achieved statehood in 1850, Hispanics served in many state and local offices. Increasingly, however, the original Hispanic population found their status diminished and, frequently, they were relegated to lower-paying and less desirable jobs.

As they had done with Native Americans, settlers from the East clashed with Mexican Americans over land. Across the region, many Hispanics lost their land to the new settlers.

PRIMARY SOURCE
Hispanics in the Southwest

In the mid-19th century, most Hispanics in the Southwest lived on large haciendas where they worked in the fields harvesting crops or helped tend cattle.

A fancily dressed vaquero, known as a *charro*, poses for a photo in 1890.

▲ *Hispanic farmworkers harvest grapes in southern California in 1905.*

PRIMARY SOURCE

"As a horseman, [the vaquero] has no superiors, and it is mounted that he operates with such sure effect against the wild animals. The sport of 'lassoing' wild bulls and other cattle is highly exciting, and one of which all Spanish Americans are passionately fond. To catch the animal by his horns or neck requires much skill, yet to seize him with certainty by the leg, when at the top of his speed, requires greater practice and dexterity." R

—from *Gleason's Pictorial Drawing-Room Companion*, 1852

Analyzing VISUALS

1. **Making Generalizations** Based on the appearance of the vaquero in the photo at left, what generalizations can you make about the man?
2. **Analyzing** What do you notice about the types of people who were farmworkers? Why might this be so?

Activity: Collaborative Learning

Land Ownership In the Treaty of Guadalupe Hidalgo, the United States promised that Hispanics living on the territory the United States gained could retain their property and became American citizens. As settlers moved into the area, they also claimed territory. American courts frequently sided with settlers and revoked Mexican American property rights. **Ask:** How might the Hispanics living in the western territories have reacted to becoming American citizens? *(Possible Answers: some may have been happy, others frightened or angry)* Have students split into small groups. Have each group use library or Internet resources to find out how life changed for Mexican Americans living in the West. Pretending they are Mexican Americans whose property rights have been revoked, students should write a persuasive letter to the president requesting that their property rights be reinstated. AL

Mexican American claims to the land often dated back to Spanish land grants. These grants were hundreds of years old and defined the boundaries of property in vague terms. When ownership of a property was claimed by more than one person, American courts frequently held that the old land grants were insufficient proof of ownership. This allowed others to stake claim to the property. In some instances, outright fraud was used to take land illegally from Mexican Americans.

The cattle boom of the 1870s and 1880s had a tremendous impact on Hispanics in the Southwest, where many had long worked as vaqueros (the Spanish word for "cowboys"). Vaqueros developed the tools and techniques for managing cattle. They taught American cowboys their trade and enriched the English language with words of Spanish origin, including "lariat," "lasso," and "stampede."

With the increasing demand for beef in the eastern United States, English-speaking ranchers wanted to expand their herds and claimed large tracts of land of Mexican origin. In some cases, the Hispanic population fought back. In New Mexico, residents of the town of Las Vegas were outraged when English-speaking ranchers tried to fence in land that had long been used by the community to graze livestock. In 1889 a group of Hispanic New Mexicans calling themselves *Las Gorras Blancas* (white caps) raided ranches owned by English-speakers, tore down their fences, and burned their barns and houses. The raids finally ended in 1890 when the governor threatened to call in federal troops.

Despite the influx of English-speaking settlers, Hispanics in New Mexico remained more influential in public affairs than did their counterparts in California and Texas. Hispanics remained the majority, both in population and in the territorial legislature. In addition, a Hispanic frequently served as New Mexico's territorial delegate to Congress.

As more railroads were built in the 1880s and 1890s, the population of the Southwest continued to swell. The region not only attracted Americans and European immigrants, but also immigrants from Mexico. Mexican immigrants worked mainly in agriculture and on the railroads. In the growing cities of the Southwest—such as El Paso, Albuquerque, and Los Angeles— **D** Hispanics settled in neighborhoods called **barrios.** Barrios had Spanish-speaking businesses and Spanish-language newspapers and they helped keep Hispanic cultural and religious traditions alive. As native Californian Mariano Guadalupe Vallejo explained in 1890:

PRIMARY SOURCE

"No class of American citizens is more loyal than the Spanish Californians, but we shall always be especially proud . . . to honor the founders of our ancient families, and the saints and heroes of our history since the days when Father Junipero planted the cross at Monterey."

—quoted in *Foreigners in Their Native Land*

Reading Check **Describing** How did vaqueros contribute to the cattle industry in the West?

Section 1 REVIEW

Vocabulary

1. **Explain** the significance of: Henry Comstock, boomtown, vigilance committee, hydraulic mining, open range, long drive, hacienda, barrios.

Main Ideas

2. **Explaining** How did hydraulic mining affect the environment?
3. **Stating** What caused the decline of the cattle business in the late 1800s?
4. **Describing** How did the gold rush change society in California?

Critical Thinking

5. **Big Ideas** How did mining contribute to the development of the West?
6. **Organizing** Use a graphic organizer similar to the one below to list the ways barbed wire was used and the result of using barbed wire on the Great Plains.

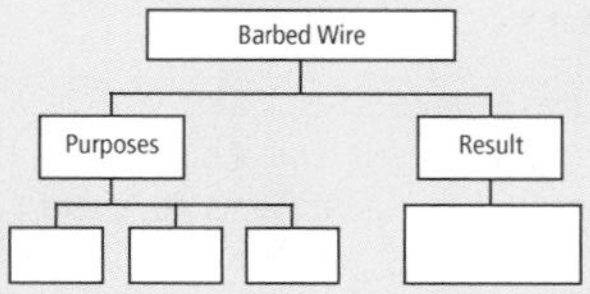

7. **Analyzing Visuals** Sketch a map of the western cattle trails. Then compare your map to the one on page 390, and list the differences between the two maps.

Writing About History

8. **Descriptive Writing** Write a summary for a story line for a Hollywood movie. Your script should realistically portray the life of either a miner or rancher in the West in the mid- to late 1800s.

History ONLINE
Study Central™ To review this section, go to glencoe.com and click on Study Central.

393

D Differentiated Instruction

Kinesthetic Have students create a map of the Southwestern United States today, showing present-day state boundaries. Students should find out the current percentage of the Hispanic population of each state and display this data on the map. **BL**

Reading Check

Answer:
developed tools and techniques for managing cattle

Assess

History ONLINE

Study Central™ provides summaries, interactive games, and online graphic organizers to help students review content.

Close

Summarizing **Ask:** Why did miners and ranchers move to the Great Plains? *(They sought new economic opportunities.)* **OL**

Section 1 REVIEW

Answers

1. All definitions can be found in the section and the Glossary.
2. Millions of tons of silt, sand, and gravel were washed into local rivers.
3. An oversupply of cattle drove down prices, and the winter of 1886 to 1887 killed a large number of cattle.
4. More settlers moved into the state. Spanish-speaking people became the minority, and their status diminished.
5. People moved west, towns sprung up, and railroads expanded.
6.

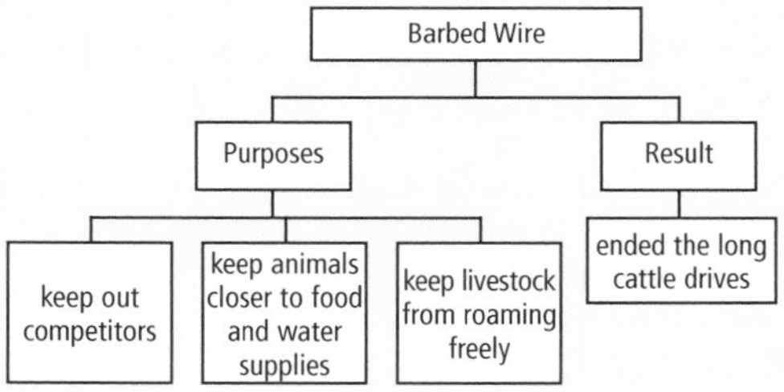

7. Maps should include rail lines, towns, and trails. Students' list should correctly note any differences.
8. Students' summaries will vary but should reflect facts found in the section.

Focus

Bellringer

Daily Focus Transparency 11-2

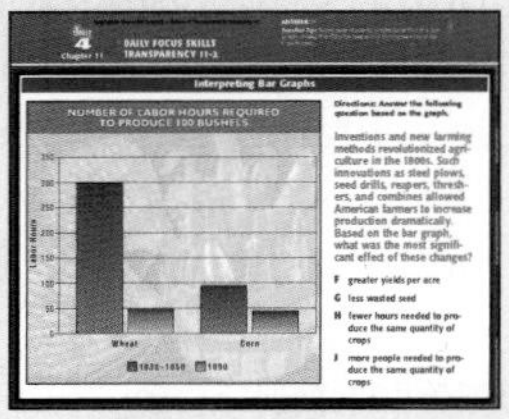

Guide to Reading

Answers:

offered 160 acres of land to settlers under Homestead Act; later legislation increased size of land given to settlers; opened Oklahoma Territory for settlement

Section Spotlight Video

To generate student interest and provide a springboard for class discussion, access the Chapter 11, Section 2 video at glencoe.com or on the video DVD.

Section 2

Section Audio   Spotlight Video

Farming the Plains

Guide to Reading

Big Ideas

Group Action After 1865 settlers staked out homesteads and began farming the Great Plains.

Content Vocabulary

- homestead *(p. 395)*
- dry farming *(p. 396)*
- sodbuster *(p. 396)*
- bonanza farm *(p. 397)*

Academic Vocabulary

- prospective *(p. 394)*
- innovation *(p. 396)*

People and Events to Identify

- Great Plains *(p. 394)*
- Stephen Long *(p. 394)*
- Homestead Act *(p. 395)*
- Wheat Belt *(p. 397)*

Reading Strategy

Organizing As you read about the settlement of the Great Plains, complete a graphic organizer similar to the one below by listing the ways the government encouraged settlement.

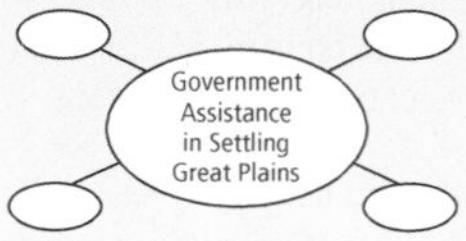

The Homestead Act encouraged settlers to move to the Great Plains. Although life was difficult, settlers discovered that wheat could be grown on the Great Plains using new technologies. By 1890 there was no longer a true frontier in the United States.

The Beginnings of Settlement

MAIN Idea Settlers staked out homesteads and began farming the region.

HISTORY AND YOU Would you move to a region with extreme weather such as drought and blizzards? Read on to learn how settlers coped with the harsh environment of the Great Plains.

The population of the **Great Plains** grew steadily in the decades after the Civil War. Land once thought to be worthless for farming was transformed into America's wheat belt. Homesteaders faced many challenges. Without trees to use as timber, many early settlers built their homes from chunks of sod, densely packed soil held together by grass roots. To obtain water, they had to drill wells more than 100 feet deep and operate the pump by hand. Nothing was wasted. Homesteader Charley O'Kieffe recalled eating weeds from the garden, as well as the vegetables, joking that he was obeying the rule, "If you can't beat 'em, eat 'em."

O'Kieffe and his neighbors were early settlers on the Great Plains. This region extends westward to the Rocky Mountains from around the 100th meridian—a line of longitude running north and south from the central Dakotas through western Texas. It is dry grassland where trees grow naturally only along rivers and streams. For centuries this open country had been home to vast herds of buffalo that grazed on the prairie grasses. Nomadic Native American groups had hunted the buffalo for food and used buffalo hides for clothing and shelter.

Major **Stephen Long,** who explored the region with an army expedition in 1819, called it the "Great American Desert" and concluded that it was "almost wholly unfit for cultivation." He predicted that the scarcity of wood and water would prove to be "an insuperable obstacle in . . . settling the country."

During the late 1800s, several developments undermined the assumption that the region was uninhabitable. One important factor was the construction of the railroads. Railroad companies sold land along the rail lines at low prices and provided credit to **prospective** settlers. Pamphlets and posters spread the news to city dwellers across Europe and America that cheap farm land was theirs to claim if they were willing to move.

Resource Manager

R Reading Strategies	C Critical Thinking	D Differentiated Instruction	W Writing Support	S Skill Practice
Additional Resources • Read. Skills Act., URB p. 21 • Guided Read. Act., URB p. 49	**Teacher Edition** • Draw. Concl., p. 397 **Additional Resources** • Quizzes and Tests, p. 154	**Teacher Edition** • English Learners, p. 395	**Teacher Edition** • Expository Writing, p. 396 • Persuasive Writing, p. 396	**Additional Resources** • Reinforcing Skills Act., URB p. 31 • Read. Essen., p. 123

NATIONAL GEOGRAPHIC Farming the American West, 1870–1900

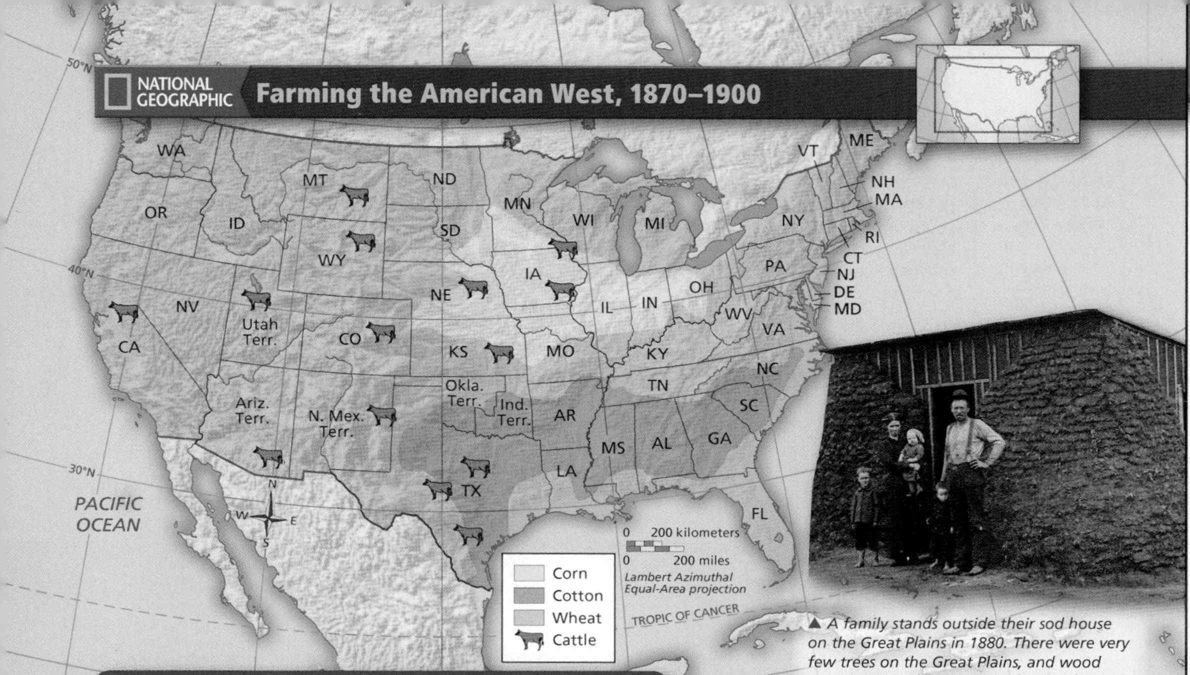

▲ *A family stands outside their sod house on the Great Plains in 1880. There were very few trees on the Great Plains, and wood was expensive because it had to be shipped to the region. So settlers cut chunks of earth from the ground to build their homes.*

What Was the Homestead Act?

The Homestead Act of 1862 created a procedure for people who wanted to settle on federal land in the West.

Requirements of the Act

- Settlers had to be 21 years of age.
- Settlers had to be head of a household.
- Settlers had to pay a $10 filing fee and $2 commission to the land agent to be given 160 acres of land.
- To gain title to the land, settlers had to live on it for five years, and make improvements such as building a house and clearing land for farming.
- Alternatively, settlers could buy the land for $1.25 per acre after six months.

Analyzing GEOGRAPHY

1. **Human-Environment Interaction** What were the similarities and differences in land use between Iowa and California?
2. **Region** In what region of the country were both cattle raised and cotton grown?

A Nebraskan coined the slogan "Rain follows the plow" to sell the idea that cultivating the Plains would increase rainfall. The weather seemed to cooperate. For more than a decade beginning in the 1870s, rainfall on the Plains was well above average. The lush green of the plains contradicted assertions that the region was a desert.

In 1862 the government encouraged settlement on the Great Plains by passing the **Homestead Act.** For a $10 registration fee, an individual could file for a **homestead**—a tract of public land available for settlement. A homesteader could claim up to 160 acres of land and could receive title to that land after living there for five years. Later government legislation increased the size of the tracts available. With their property rights assured, more settlers moved to the Plains. **D**

Settlers often found life very difficult on the Plains. In addition to building sod houses and drilling deep wells for water, they faced summer temperatures greater than 100°F. Prairie fires were a frequent danger. Sometimes swarms of grasshoppers swept over farms and destroyed the crops. In winter there were terrible blizzards and extreme cold. Despite these challenges and hardships, most homesteaders persisted and gradually learned how to live in the difficult environment.

Reading Check **Analyzing** What is the relationship between private property rights and the settlement of the Great Plains?

Teach

D Differentiated Instruction

English Learners Have students work together in small groups to create posters or pamphlets convincing Americans to move to the Great Plains. Display the pamphlets and posters around the classroom. Have students vote on which ones are most convincing and explain why they think so. **BL**

Analyzing GEOGRAPHY

Answers:

1. Both raised cattle. Iowa also grew corn.
2. Texas

Reading Check

Answer:
The government promised land to settlers who stayed for five years, thus encouraging settlers to come to the Great Plains.

Hands-On Chapter Project
Step 2

Making the Move West

Step 2: Preparing for the Trip Pairs of students continue to plan their trip west to begin a new farm on the Great Plains.

Directions Write the Big Idea on the board. Tell the pairs of students that they will make a list of the items they will need to take with them as they move west. Based on the information in the text, as well as library and Internet sources, students should first identify the items needed for survival in the Great Plains. Remind students to consider what resources they might find in their new locale as well as weather conditions. Next have pairs review their chosen route and the methods of transportation they will use. Have the pairs review their lists to determine if all the items can be taken with them given their proposed methods of transportation. Remind students that, in addition to personal items such as clothing, they will likely need to bring tools and farm implements. They may also consider bringing some livestock or other farm animals with them. Have students consider the weight, bulk, and portability of the items on their list. Also, have them consider if any items on their list will spoil during the trip west. Pairs should prepare a final list based on their research.

Putting it Together Ask volunteers to explain what they are going to pack and why. Next have pairs share what they have learned about the Big Idea while preparing for the trip. **OL**

(Chapter Project continued on page 399)

W1 Writing Support

Expository Writing Have students find out details about the process of dry farming, and write a one-page essay describing the process. **OL**

W2 Writing Support

Persuasive Writing Ask students to find books in the library about the lives of farmers in the Great Plains between the 1860s and 1890s. Have them use information from their books to assume the point of view of a settler and write a persuasive letter to a family member back East. The letter should encourage the family member to move to the Great Plains and should describe the settler's daily life, challenges, and successes. **OL**

Analyzing VISUALS

Answers:
1. wind
2. horses

The Wheat Belt

MAIN Idea As a result of new farming methods and machinery, settlers on the Great Plains were able to produce large amounts of wheat.

HISTORY AND YOU Do you remember learning about the way the cotton gin changed Southern life? Read on to learn how agricultural practices changed life on the Plains.

History ONLINE Student Web Activity Visit glencoe.com and complete the activity on settling the West.

Many new farming methods and inventions in the nineteenth century revolutionized agriculture. One approach, called **dry farming,** W1 was to plant seeds deep in the ground, where there was enough moisture for them to grow. By the 1860s farmers on the Plains were using plows, seed drills, reapers, and threshing machines. These new steel machines made dry farming possible. Unfortunately, soil on the plains could blow away during a dry season. Many **sodbusters,** as those who plowed the Plains were called, eventually lost their homesteads through the combined effects of drought, wind erosion, and overuse of the land.

Large landholders could invest in mechanical reapers and steam tractors that made it easier to harvest a large crop. Threshing machines knocked kernels loose from the stalks. Mechanical binders tied the stalks into bundles for collection. These **innovations** were well suited for harvesting wheat, a crop that could endure the dry conditions of the Great Plains.

W2 During the 1880s many farmers from the Midwest moved to the Great Plains to take advantage of the inexpensive land and the new

TECHNOLOGY & HISTORY

Farm Machinery Farmers are indebted to the inventions of John Deere and Cyrus McCormick. Deere's steel plow broke through the hard ground. McCormick's mechanical reaper did the work of five men. Later inventions included a mechanical harrow to help prepare the ground for seeds and a grain drill to plant seeds.

▼ *Windmills were vital to settling the Great Plains where farmers faced one major problem: a lack of water. There were few rivers, and it rarely rained. To get water, settlers drilled deep wells and used windmills to pump the water to the surface. The strong winds on the flat, treeless plains were an ideal power source.*

▼ *Technology made farming the vast open plains of America feasible. Here, horse-drawn binders are being used to gather hay in the late 1800s.*

Analyzing VISUALS

1. **Identifying** What was used to power the windmill?
2. **Analyzing Visuals** In addition to field hands, what else did farmers using mechanical harvesting machines need?

Differentiated Instruction

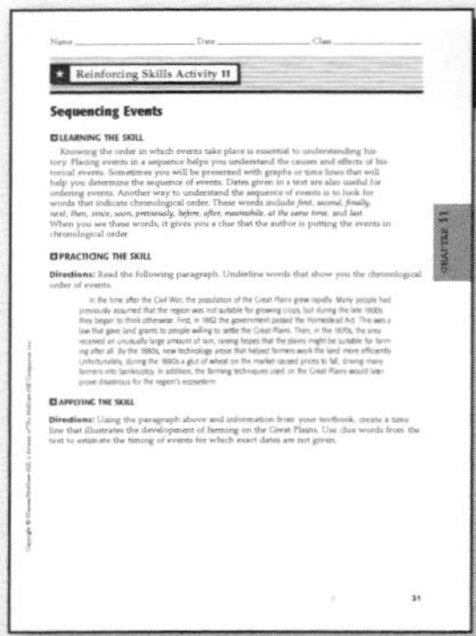

Reinforcing Skills Activity 11, URB p. 31

Organizing Information: Sequencing Events

Objective: Read a newspaper article and outline the sequence of events described.

Focus: Choose an article from a recent newspaper or newsmagazine. Read the article.

Teach: Circle words that show the chronological structure of the event or events described.

Assess: Make a list of circled words. Discuss what each word tells about the order of events.

Close: Draw a time line or diagram and order the event or events from the article.

Differentiated Instruction Strategies

BL Read the news article and determine words that show chronological order.

AL Write a short essay predicting why the farming techniques used on the Great Plains were harmful to the region's ecosystem.

ELL Write a few sentences about your daily activities. Use as many words that indicate chronological order as you can.

farming technology. The **Wheat Belt** began at the eastern edge of the Great Plains and encompassed much of the Dakotas and parts of Nebraska and Kansas. The new machines allowed a single family to bring in a substantial harvest on a wheat farm covering several hundred acres. Some wheat farms covered up to 50,000 acres. These were called **bonanza farms** because they yielded big profits. Like mine owners, bonanza farmers formed companies, invested in property and equipment, and hired laborers as needed.

Farmers Fall on Hard Times

The bountiful harvests in the Wheat Belt helped the United States become the world's leading exporter of wheat by the 1880s. Then things began to go wrong. A severe drought struck the Plains in the late 1880s, destroying crops and turning the soil to dust. In addition, competition from farmers in other countries began to increase. By the 1890s a glut of wheat on the world market caused prices to drop. Some farmers tried to make it through these difficult times by mortgaging their land—that is, they borrowed money based on the value of their land. If they failed to meet their mortgage payments, they forfeited the land to the bank. Some who lost their land continued to work it as tenant farmers, renting the land from its new owners. By 1900 tenants cultivated about one-third of the farms on the Plains.

Closing the Frontier

On April 22, 1889, the government opened one of the last large territories for settlement. Within hours, more than 10,000 people raced to stake claims in an event known as the Oklahoma Land Rush. The next year, the Census Bureau reported that there was no longer a true frontier left in America. In reality, there was still a lot of unoccupied land, and new settlement continued into the 1900s, but the "closing of the frontier" marked the end of an era. It worried many people, including historian Frederick Jackson Turner. Turner believed that the frontier had provided a "safety-valve of social discontent." It was a place where Americans could always make a fresh start.

Most settlers did indeed make a fresh start, adapting to the difficult environment of the Plains. Water from their deep wells enabled them to plant trees and gardens. Railroads brought lumber and brick to replace sod as a building material, as well as coal for fuel. They also brought manufactured goods from the East, such as clothes and household goods. Small-scale farmers rarely became wealthy, but they could be self-sufficient. Typical homesteaders raised cattle, chickens, and a few crops. The real story of the West was not one of limitless opportunity, nor one in which heroes rode off into the sunset. It was about ordinary people who settled down and built homes and communities through great effort. C

Reading Check **Identifying** What technological innovations helped farmers cultivate the Plains?

Section 2 REVIEW

Vocabulary

1. **Explain** the significance of: Great Plains, Stephen Long, Homestead Act, homestead, dry farming, sodbuster, Wheat Belt, bonanza farm.

Main Ideas

2. **Identifying** How did the Homestead Act encourage settlement of the Plains?
3. **Explaining** What factors contributed to the making of the Wheat Belt in the Great Plains and then to troubled times for wheat farmers in the 1890s?

Critical Thinking

4. **Big Ideas** What challenges did Plains farmers face?
5. **Organizing** Make a graphic organizer similar to the one below that lists the effects of technology on farming in the Great Plains.

Invention	Advantage for Farmers

6. **Analyzing Visuals** Examine the photograph on page 396 of farmers using machinery. Based on the terrain and the type of work they needed to do, what other types of technology would have helped farmers on the Plains?

Writing About History

7. **Persuasive Writing** Write an advertisement to persuade people from the East and Europe to establish homesteads on the Great Plains.

History ONLINE
Study Central™ To review this section, go to glencoe.com and click on Study Central.

C Critical Thinking

Drawing Conclusions Historian Frederick Jackson Turner believed the spirit of the United States was tied to westward expansion. When the frontier closed, he concluded that the period that had fostered individualism and economic opportunity had ended. Have students write an essay defending or refuting Turner's ideas. AL

Reading Check

Answer:
the mechanical reaper, steam tractor, threshing machines

Assess

History ONLINE

Study Central™ provides summaries, interactive games, and online graphic organizers to help students review content.

Close

Summarizing Ask: What caused economic hardship for farmers? *(severe drought, a wheat glut, and competition from foreign countries)* OL

Section 2 REVIEW

Answers

1. All definitions can be found in the section and the Glossary.
2. Individuals could file for 160 acres of public land and would receive the title after living and making improvements on the land for five years.
3. the Homestead Act, new farming techniques and equipment; good harvests and world competition led to a glut that caused prices to drop
4. difficult climate: hot summers and harsh cold winters; lack of wood for homes; had to dig deep wells for water; drought; grasshoppers; prairie fires
5.

Invention	Advantage for Farmers
mechanical reapers	speeded harvesting
mechanical binders	tied stalks
threshing machines	knocked kernels loose

6. Answers may include telegraph for communication.
7. Advertisements will vary but should reflect information presented in the section.

Focus

Bellringer

Daily Focus Transparency 11-3

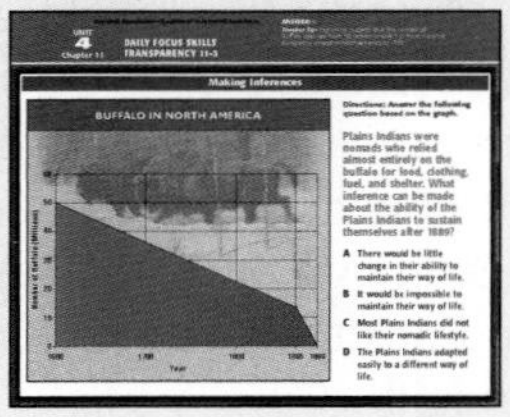

Guide to Reading

1862-Dakota Sioux Uprising: deaths of settlers and Native Americans
1864-Sand Creek Massacre: formation of the Indian Peace Commission
1866-Fetterman's Massacre: U.S. Army defeat
1876-Battle of Little Big Horn: Native American victory
1890-Wounded Knee: about 200 Lakota died

Section Spotlight Video

To generate student interest and provide a springboard for class discussion, access the Chapter 11, Section 3 video at glencoe.com or on the video DVD.

Section 3

Section Audio | Spotlight Video

Native Americans

Guide to Reading

Big Ideas

Culture and Beliefs Settling the West dramatically changed the way of life of the Plains Indians.

Content Vocabulary
- nomad *(p. 398)*
- annuity *(p. 398)*
- assimilate *(p. 403)*
- allotment *(p. 403)*

Academic Vocabulary
- relocate *(p. 398)*
- ensure *(p. 400)*
- approximately *(p. 403)*

People and Events to Identify
- Sand Creek Massacre *(p. 400)*
- Indian Peace Commission *(p. 400)*
- George A. Custer *(p. 401)*
- Chief Joseph *(p. 402)*
- Dawes Act *(p. 403)*

Reading Strategy

Sequencing As you read about the crises facing Native Americans during the late 1800s, complete a time line to record the battles between Native Americans and the United States government and the results of each.

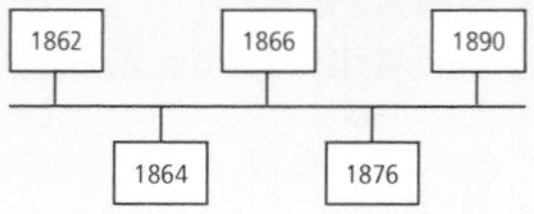

As settlers entered Native American lands on the Great Plains, clashes grew more common. Conflicts continued as the government tried to force Native Americans onto reservations and encouraged them to assimilate into the culture of the United States.

Struggles of the Plains Indians

MAIN Idea The settlement of the West dramatically altered the way of life of the Plains Indians.

HISTORY AND YOU Can you recall a situation in which someone broke a promise to you? Do you remember your reaction? Read on to learn how Native Americans responded when the federal government broke treaties.

For centuries the Great Plains were home to many groups of Native Americans. Some lived in communities as farmers and hunters, but many were **nomads** who roamed vast distances, following their main source of food—the buffalo.

The groups of Plains Indians were similar in many ways. Plains Indian nations were divided into bands consisting of up to 500 people. A governing council headed each band, but most members participated in making decisions. Most lived in extended family groups and believed in the spiritual power of the natural world.

The ranchers, miners, and farmers who moved onto the Plains deprived Native Americans of their hunting grounds, broke treaties guaranteeing certain lands to the Plains Indians, and often forced them to **relocate** to new territory. Native Americans resisted by attacking wagon trains, stagecoaches, and ranches. Occasionally, an entire group would go to war against nearby settlers and troops.

The Dakota Sioux Uprising

The first major clash began in 1862, when the Dakota people (also known as the Sioux) launched a major uprising in Minnesota. The Sioux had agreed to live on a reservation in exchange for **annuities,** or annual payments from the government. The annuities, however, frequently got caught up in bureaucracy and corruption and never reached them. By 1862 many lived in desperate poverty and faced possible starvation. When Chief Little Crow asked local traders to provide food on credit, one replied, "If they are hungry, let them eat grass or their own dung." Two weeks later, when the Dakota took up arms, that trader was found dead with his mouth stuffed with grass.

Little Crow reluctantly agreed to lead this uprising. He wanted to wage war against soldiers, not civilians, but he was unable to keep

Resource Manager

R Reading Strategies	C Critical Thinking	D Differentiated Instruction	W Writing Support	S Skill Practice
Additional Resources • Guided Read. Act., URB p. 50	**Teacher Edition** • Draw. Concl., p. 401 • Analy. Info., p. 402 • Comparing, p. 403 **Additional Resources** • Interp. Pol. Cartoons, URB p. 41 • Authentic Assess. p. 27 • Quizzes and Tests, p. 155	**Teacher Edition** • Advanced Learners, p. 399 • Visual/Spatial, p. 400 **Additional Resources** • Am. Art and Music Act., URB p. 39 • Reteach. Act., URB p. 43 • Enrich. Act., URB p. 45	**Teacher Edition** • Narrative Writing, p. 399 • Persuasive Writing, p. 400 • Descriptive Writing, p. 401	**Additional Resources** • Critical Thinking Skills Act., URB p. 32 • Time Line Act., URB p. 33 • Read. Essen., p. 126

Native American Battles and Reservations, 1860–1890

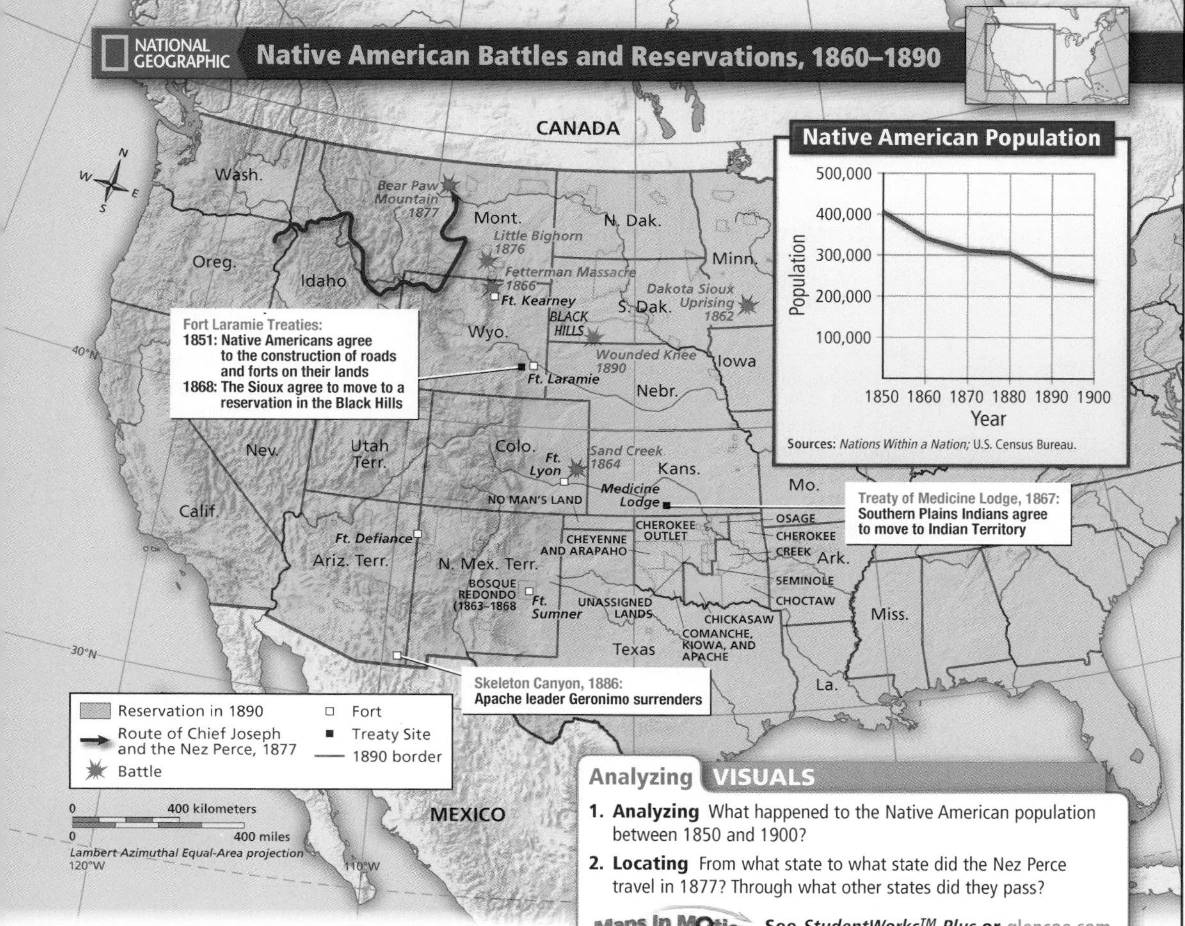

Analyzing VISUALS

1. **Analyzing** What happened to the Native American population between 1850 and 1900?
2. **Locating** From what state to what state did the Nez Perce travel in 1877? Through what other states did they pass?

Maps in MOtion See *StudentWorks™ Plus* or glencoe.com.

angry Dakota from slaughtering hundreds of settlers in the area.

After the rebellion was suppressed, a military tribunal sentenced 307 Dakota to death. After reviewing the evidence, President Lincoln reduced the number to 38. Others fled the reservation when federal troops arrived and became exiles in a region that bore their name—the Dakota Territory.

Red Cloud's War

The Dakota Territory was home to another Sioux tribe, the Lakota. The Lakota were a nomadic tribe who fought hard to keep control of their hunting grounds, which extended from the Black Hills westward to the Bighorn Mountains. They had battled rival groups for this country and did not intend to let settlers have it. Leading them were chiefs Red Cloud, Crazy Horse, and Sitting Bull. **W** **D**

The army suffered a major defeat during "Red Cloud's War" of 1866–1868. The army was constructing forts along the Bozeman Trail, the path used to reach the Montana gold mines. In December 1866, Crazy Horse, a religious leader and war chief, tricked the fort's commander into sending Captain William Fetterman and about 80 soldiers out to pursue what they thought was a small raiding party.

Teach

D Differentiated Instruction

Advanced Learners Have students research the geography and mineral resources of the Black Hills. Have students use their findings to write a one-page essay explaining why white settlers wanted to remove Native Americans from the Black Hills. **AL**

W Writing Support

Narrative Writing Have students find out about one leading Native American chief, such as Red Cloud, Crazy Horse, or Sitting Bull. Have students write a brief narrative describing the life of the leader chosen. **BL**

Analyzing VISUALS

Answers:
1. declined dramatically
2. Oregon to Montana; Idaho and Wyoming

Hands-On Chapter Project
Step 3

Making the Move West

Step 3: Take the Trip Students will describe the various people they will likely meet on their journey westward.

Directions Write the Big Idea on the board. Have the pairs of students refer to the map they created in Step 1. Using information from the textbook, as well as library or Internet resources, students should research the types of people they will likely encounter on their trip westward. For example, as they move through towns and cities, they might meet merchants, innkeepers, and bankers. As they pass through established farmland, they might meet other small farmers. Finally, as they approach their destination, they might encounter native peoples. Based on their research, students should create brief personal profiles of five different individuals that they will likely meet along the way. Remind pairs to provide a physical description of the people, identify their occupations, and describe their daily lives. Students should also include how they interacted with each of the five people they profiled.

Putting it Together Ask volunteers to describe the people they have met on their journey westward. **OL**

(Chapter Project continued on the Visual Summary page)

W Writing Support

Persuasive Writing Have interested students assume the role of an assistant to territorial governor John Evans and write a letter to Cheyenne Chief Black Kettle attempting to persuade him to go to Fort Lyon. Remind students to provide solid and compelling reasons to Chief Black Kettle. OL

D Differentiated Instruction

Visual/Spatial Have students use their textbooks and library and Internet resources to create two maps of Native American reservations. One map should show the reservations before the formation of the Indian Peace Commission and the other should show the reservations after the Commission. Use the maps to discuss how the federal government tried to gain authority over Native Americans in the Great Plains. AL

Reading Check

Answer:
creating two large reservations for the Sioux and for the Southern Plains Indians

Additional Support

Teacher Tip

Collaborative Learning This activity requires students to do research, write, and illustrate. The activity allows students with different levels to work together. As you form groups, consider the needed skills and choose students accordingly.

Hundreds of warriors were waiting in ambush and wiped out the entire unit (an event that became known as Fetterman's Massacre). The Sioux continued to resist any military presence in the region, and in 1868 the army abandoned its posts along the trail.

Sand Creek

In the 1860s tensions began to rise between the miners coming into Colorado in search of silver and gold and the Cheyenne and Arapaho who already lived there. As the number of settlers increased, bands of Native Americans began raiding wagon trains and stealing cattle and horses from ranches. By the summer of W 1864, trade had come to a standstill, dozens of homes had been burned, and an estimated 200 settlers had been killed. The territorial governor, John Evans, ordered the Native Americans to surrender at Fort Lyon, where he said they would be given food and protection. Those who failed to report would be subject to attack.

Although several hundred Native Americans surrendered at the fort, many others did not. In November 1864, Chief Black Kettle brought several hundred Cheyenne to the fort, not to surrender but to negotiate a peace deal. The fort's commander did not have the authority to negotiate, and he told Black Kettle to make camp at Sand Creek while he waited for orders. Shortly afterward, Colonel John Chivington of the Colorado Volunteers was ordered to attack the Cheyenne at Sand Creek.

When Chivington stopped at Fort Lyon, he was told that the Native Americans at Sand Creek were waiting to negotiate. Chivington replied that, since the Cheyenne had been attacking settlers, including women and children, there could be no peace. The events that followed became known as the **Sand Creek Massacre.**

What actually happened at Sand Creek is unclear. Some witnesses stated afterward that Black Kettle had been flying both an American flag and a white flag of truce, which Chivington ignored. Others reported that the American troops fired on the unsuspecting Native Americans and then brutally murdered hundreds of women and children. Still others described a savage battle in which both sides fought ferociously for two days. Fourteen soldiers died, but the number of Native Americans reported killed varied from 69 to 600. One general later called Chivington's attack "the foulest and most unjustifiable crime in the annals of America." The truth of what really happened is still debated.

A Doomed Plan for Peace

In light of escalating conflict with Native Americans on the Great Plains, Congress took action. In 1867 Congress formed an **Indian Peace Commission,** which proposed creating two large reservations on the Plains, one for D the Sioux and another for Native Americans of the southern Plains. Agents from the federal government's Bureau of Indian Affairs would run the reservations. The army would deal with any groups that refused to report or remain there.

Reservations were not a new idea. Both Puritan and Jesuit missionaries had used them in colonial days to separate Native American nations from one another. The reservations were also intended to encourage Native Americans to adopt white culture. After the American Revolution, the Iroquois (who called themselves the Haudenosaunee) were placed on reservations in western New York. These reservations, however, existed to separate Native Americans and citizens of the United States. Nearly a century later, reservations were based exclusively on keeping the Native Americans separate from American citizens.

The reservation system was again tested after the California gold rush. California, Oregon, and Washington all tried reservations as a way to minimize conflicts between Native Americans and settlers.

The Indian Peace Commission's plan was doomed to failure. Pressuring Native American leaders into signing treaties, as negotiators did at Medicine Lodge Creek in 1867, did not **ensure** that chiefs or their followers would abide by them, nor could they prevent settlers from violating their terms. Those who did move to reservations faced much the same conditions that drove the Dakota Sioux to violence—poverty, despair, and the corrupt practices of American traders.

Reading Check **Explaining** What proposal did the Indian Peace Commission present to the Plains Indians?

Activity: Collaborative Learning

Conflicting Evidence Ask: Why are the details of the Sand Creek Massacre still being debated? *(Historians have received conflicting eyewitness accounts; reports of the massacre may have been tarnished by the observers' personal biases.)* Organize the class into small groups. Have each group use library or Internet resources to find different primary sources, eyewitness accounts, or secondary sources of the fateful events surrounding the Sand Creek Massacre. Have each group analyze its findings and write a report on its conclusions. Each group should also illustrate its findings with maps, drawings, or dioramas. OL

The Last Native American Wars

MAIN Idea Settlers and Native Americans fought for land and cultural traditions.

HISTORY AND YOU Can you identify parts of the world where development is destroying local cultures? Read how the destruction of the buffalo changed some Native American cultures.

By the 1870s many Native Americans on the southern Plains had left the reservations in disgust. They preferred hunting buffalo on the open plains, so they joined others who had also shunned the reservations. Buffalo, however, were rapidly disappearing as settlers killed off thousands of the animals.

C

Following the Civil War, professional buffalo hunters invaded the area, seeking buffalo hides for markets in the East. Other hunters killed merely for sport, leaving carcasses to rot. Then railroad companies hired sharpshooters to kill large numbers of buffalo that were obstructing rail traffic and used them to feed the workers. The army, determined to force Native Americans onto reservations, encouraged buffalo killing. By 1889 very few of the animals remained.

Battle of the Little Bighorn

In 1876 prospectors overran the Lakota Sioux reservation in the Dakota Territory to mine gold in the Black Hills. The Lakota saw no reason they should abide by a treaty that American settlers were violating, so many left the reservation that spring to hunt near the Bighorn Mountains in southeastern Montana.

W

The government responded by sending an expedition commanded by General Alfred H. Terry. Lieutenant Colonel **George A. Custer** and the Seventh Cavalry were with the expedition. Custer underestimated the fighting capabilities of the Lakota and Cheyenne. On June 25, 1876, ignoring orders, and acting on his own initiative, he launched a three-pronged attack in broad daylight on one of the largest groups of Native American warriors ever assembled on the Great Plains.

POLITICAL CARTOONS — PRIMARY SOURCE
Government Native American Policies

▲ *This cartoon from 1878 shows Secretary of the Interior Carl Schurz investigating the Indian "bureau."*

▲ *This cartoon is labeled "The Reason of the Indian Outbreak" and quotes General Miles who said the "Indians are starved into rebellion."*

Analyzing VISUALS DBQ

1. **Examining** Who does the cartoon on the right blame for the problems of Native Americans?
2. **Analyzing** According to the cartoon on the left, why was the Indian Bureau unable to help Native Americans?

C Critical Thinking

Drawing Conclusions The buffalo of the Great Plains were slaughtered for many reasons. **Ask:** What was the main reason the U.S. army sought to eliminate the buffalo? *(to force Native Americans onto reservations)* Have students find out more about the slaughter of the buffalo in the late 1800s. Then have them write a brief essay explaining their findings. **AL**

W Writing Support

Descriptive Writing Have students find more about the Battle of Little Bighorn. Then have students write a one-page essay describing the battle from the viewpoint of either the Native Americans or the American cavalry. **OL**

Analyzing VISUALS

Answers:
1. General Miles and the Bureau of Indian Affairs
2. Agents were fraudulent, dishonest, and corrupt.

Additional Support

Activity: Collaborative Activity

Newspaper Page Organize the class into groups to create a newspaper page highlighting details from the Battle of Little Bighorn. Have each group choose whether to describe the Native Americans' or the American soldiers' view of the battle. Have students research the Battle of Little Bighorn using their book, the Internet, and other sources. Groups should illustrate their newspaper page with drawings depicting a scene from the battle. Have each group compose their newspaper page on a computer using desktop publishing software.

People IN HISTORY

Answer:
Custer: Custer might persevere despite overwhelming odds
Sitting Bull: Sitting Bull wanted it to be remembered that he was the last Lakota to surrender his rifle.

C Critical Thinking

Analyzing Information
Remind students that the army forced the Nez Perce to move to Oklahoma. **Ask:** How did this action by the U.S. government affect the rights of these Native Americans? *(It denied them basic rights guaranteed under the Constitution.)*

Additional Support

People IN HISTORY

George Custer
1839–1876

George Custer, who graduated at the bottom of his West Point class, became an unlikely hero during the Civil War. During the many cavalry charges he led, 11 horses were shot out from under him. At the age of 23, he became the youngest Union Army general. When Custer later commanded the Seventh Cavalry in the West, the Cheyenne called him "Yellow Hair," because he wore his curly blond hair to his shoulders. Custer wore buckskins for battle, though he wore velveteen uniforms in the camp. He spent many hours studying military tactics and reading military history. He risked his own career to testify against the corruption of the Indian Bureau. In anger at his testimony, President Grant removed him from command. However, the public outcry in favor of Custer led to his return to command, a decision that cost the lives of Custer and all his troops.

How did Custer's actions in the Civil War indicate what he might do in other combat situations?

Sitting Bull
c. 1831–1890

The great Lakota chief Sitting Bull faced his first battle at age 14, in a raid against the Crow tribe. As a young man he joined two groups, a warrior society known as Strong Heart and a group that worked for tribal welfare, Silent Eaters. Sitting Bull became chief when he was 37 years old. A holy man as well as a warrior, Sitting Bull led Native Americans in sun dances and prayers to the Great Spirit. After his victory at the Little Bighorn, Sitting Bull led his people to Canada to avoid the reservation system. In 1881, with his people facing starvation, Sitting Bull led them to Montana. He asked his son to hand the commanding officer of Fort Buford his rifle, hoping to show that "he has become a friend of the Americans." Sitting Bull also asked it to be remembered that "I was the last man of my tribe to surrender my rifle." Four years later, he briefly joined Buffalo Bill's Wild West show. He was killed by a Lakota, as he had seen in a vision five years before: A Lakota policeman shot him in a scuffle trying to keep the great chief from joining a Ghost Dance, which had been outlawed.

How did Sitting Bull wish to be remembered?

The Native American forces first repulsed a cavalry charge from the south. Then they turned on Custer and his 210 soldiers and killed all but one of them. One Lakota warrior recalled the scene afterward: "The soldiers were piled one on top of another, dead, with here and there, an Indian among the soldiers. Horses lay on top of men, and men on top of horses."

Newspaper accounts portraying Custer as a victim of a massacre produced a public outcry in the East, and the army stepped up its campaign against Native Americans on the Plains. Sitting Bull fled with his followers to Canada, but the other Lakota were forced to return to the reservation and give up the Black Hills.

Flight of the Nez Perce

Farther west, the Nez Perce people, led by **Chief Joseph,** refused to be moved to a smaller reservation in Idaho in 1877. When the army came to relocate them, they fled their homes **C** and embarked on a journey of more than 1,300 miles. Finally, in October 1877, Chief Joseph surrendered, and he and his followers were exiled to Oklahoma. His speech summarized the hopelessness of their cause:

PRIMARY SOURCE

"Our chiefs are killed. . . . The little children are freezing to death. My people . . . have no blankets, no food. . . . Hear me, my chiefs; I am tired; my heart is sick and sad. From where the sun now stands I will fight no more forever."

—quoted in *Bury My Heart at Wounded Knee*

Tragedy at Wounded Knee

Native American resistance came to a final and tragic end on the Lakota Sioux reservation in 1890. Defying the orders of the government, the Lakota continued to perform the Ghost Dance, a ritual that celebrated a hoped-for day of reckoning when settlers would disappear, the buffalo would return, and Native Americans would reunite with their dead ancestors.

Federal authorities had banned the ceremony fearing it would lead to violence. They blamed the latest defiance on Chief Sitting Bull, who had returned from Canada, and sent police to arrest the chief. Sitting Bull's supporters tried to stop the arrest. In the exchange of gunfire that followed, the chief himself was killed.

Leveled Activities

BL Reading Skills Activity, URB p. 21

Reading Skills Activity 11

Identifying the Main Idea

OL Linking Past and Present Activity, URB p. 34

Linking Past and Present Activity 11

Grabbing the Gold

AL Enrichment Activity, URB p. 45

Enrichment Activity 11

Two Views on Native Americans

ELL Content Vocabulary Activity, URB p. 27

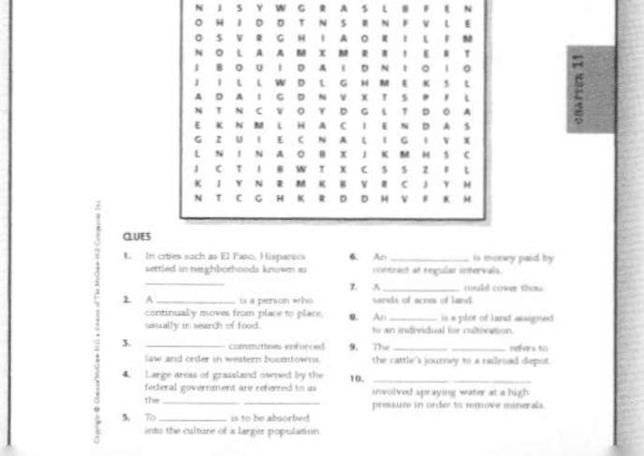

Content Vocabulary Activity 11

A group of Ghost Dancers then fled the reservation, and the army went after them. On December 29, 1890, as troops tried to disarm them at Wounded Knee Creek, gunfire broke out. A deadly battle ensued, taking the lives of 25 U.S. soldiers and **approximately** 200 Lakota men, women, and children.

The Dawes Act

Some Americans had long opposed the treatment of Native Americans. In her 1881 book *A Century of Dishonor*, Helen Hunt Jackson detailed the years of broken promises and injustices. Her descriptions of events such as the massacre at Sand Creek sparked new debate on the issue. Some Americans believed the solution was to encourage Native Americans to **assimilate,** or be absorbed, into American society as landowners and citizens. This meant dividing reservations into individual **allotments,** where families could become self-supporting.

This policy became law in 1887 when Congress passed the **Dawes Act.** This act allotted to each head of household 160 acres of reservation land for farming; single adults received 80 acres, and 40 acres were allotted for children. The land that remained after all members had received allotments would be sold to American settlers, with the proceeds going into a trust for Native Americans.

This plan failed to achieve its goals. Some Native Americans succeeded as farmers or ranchers, but many had little training or enthusiasm for either pursuit. Like homesteaders, they often found their allotments too small to be profitable, so they sold them. Some Native American groups had grown attached to their reservations and hated to see them transformed into homesteads for settlers as well as Native Americans.

In the end, the assimilation policy proved a dismal failure. No legislation could provide a satisfactory solution to the Native American issue, because there was no entirely satisfactory solution to be had. The Native Americans were doomed because they were dependent on buffalo for food, clothing, fuel, and shelter. When the herds were wiped out, Native Americans on the Plains had no way to sustain their way of life, and few adopted American settlers' lifestyles in place of their traditional cultures. C

The Dawes Act granted citizenship to Native Americans who stayed on their allotments for 25 years. Few qualified, and it was not until 1924 that Congress passed the Citizenship Act, granting all Native Americans citizenship. Some states—Arizona, Maine, and New Mexico—did not grant Native Americans the right to vote until after World War II.

Under Franklin Roosevelt's New Deal, the policies of assimilation and allotments finally ended in 1934. The Indian Reorganization Act reversed the Dawes Act's policy of assimilation. It restored some reservation lands, gave Native American tribes control over those lands, and permitted them to elect tribal governments.

✔ Reading Check **Cause and Effect** What effect did Helen Hunt Jackson's book *A Century of Dishonor* have?

Section 3 REVIEW

Vocabulary

1. **Explain** the significance of: nomad, annuity, Sand Creek Massacre, Indian Peace Commission, George A. Custer, Chief Joseph, assimilate, allotment, Dawes Act.

Main Ideas

2. **Comparing** In what ways were the different groups of the Plains Indians similar?
3. **Discussing** Why do you think the government's policy of assimilation of Native Americans was a failure?

Critical Thinking

4. **Big Ideas** How did Native Americans respond to the loss of land from white settlement of the Great Plains?
5. **Organizing** Use a graphic organizer similar to the one below to list the reasons the government's plans to move the Plains Indians onto reservations failed.

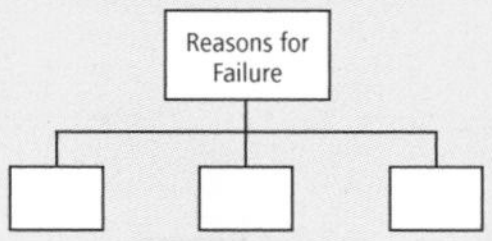

6. **Analyzing Visuals** Examine the map of battle sites and reservations on page 399. Then, from the point of view of a historian, explain the actions taken against Native Americans within the historical context of the time.

Writing About History

7. **Descriptive Writing** Assume the role of a Plains Indian. Write a journal entry describing how you feel about the Dawes Act and how it has affected your life.

History ONLINE
Study Central™ To review this section, go to glencoe.com and click on Study Central.

C Critical Thinking

Comparing Have students use library or Internet resources to find more information about the Dawes Act and the Indian Reorganization Act. Have students create a bulletin board display comparing the two laws. BL

Assess

History ONLINE

Study Central™ provides summaries, interactive games, and online graphic organizers to help students review content.

Close

Summarizing Ask: Why did settlers and Native Americans come into conflict? *(Native Americans sought to maintain traditional ways of life, while settlers wanted their land)* OL

✔ Reading Check

Answer: It sparked debate on the treatment of Native Americans.

Section 3 REVIEW

Answers

1. All definitions can be found in the section and the Glossary.
2. many were nomadic, divided into bands with a governing council heading each band, lived in extended family groups, believed in spiritual power of natural world
3. Answers may include: Native Americans were unwilling or unable to change their way of life. They received no training in farming and their allotments were too small to be profitable.
4. Some attacked wagon trains and ranches, going to war against nearby settlers and troops
5.

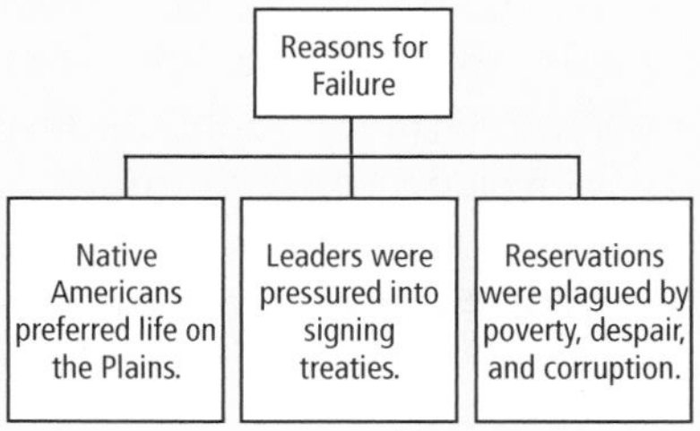

6. Answers may vary. Accept different viewpoints as long as the reasoning is sound and based on facts.
7. Students' journal entries will vary. Entries should be written from the perspective of a Native American.

Determining Cause and Effect The Visual Summary lists the causes and effects of settlers moving west to the Great Plains. Have students use the information provided to create a cause-and-effect flow chart illustrating these events. **BL**

Descriptive Writing Have students select one of the three major occupations that affected the settlement of the Great Plains—mining, ranching, or farming—and write a paragraph describing why a settler might move west to pursue one of those ways of life. **OL**

Chapter 11 Visual Summary

STUDY TO GO You can study anywhere, anytime by downloading quizzes and flashcards to your PDA from glencoe.com.

Causes of Settlers Moving West to the Great Plains

Mining

- Deposits of gold, silver, and copper are discovered.
- New technologies, such as hydraulic mining, make it possible to remove vast quantities of ore.

Ranching

- Wild longhorn cattle, found to survive well on the Plains, are available in large numbers to be rounded up.
- Railroads provide an easy way to ship cattle to eastern markets.

Farming

- Congress passes the Homestead Act in 1862.
- New farming technologies, including new plows, reapers, and drills, make it possible to farm on the Plains.
- Railroads advertise for settlers and bring necessities such as lumber and coal to the Plains.

▶ *Tens of thousands of settlers headed west, lured by the possibility of striking it rich mining gold or silver. This photo shows miners standing beside a stack of silver ingots in Leadville, Colorado, c. 1880.*

▶ *A Plains family stands atop their reaper on their Nebraska farm in the 1890s. Technology such as the reaper made farming the Great Plains practical.*

▲ *Although the Dawes Act was intended to assimilate Native Americans, traditional ways of life persisted. Above, a Cheyenne woman uses a stone mortar and pestle to grind wild cherries outside her home in the 1890s.*

Effects of Settling the Great Plains

- Miners arrive in such large numbers that Colorado, the Dakotas, Nevada, and Montana are able to become states.
- Hydraulic mining damages the environment in some areas and interferes with farming.
- The Great Plains becomes the nation's Wheat Belt, growing tens of thousands of acres of wheat.
- The arrival of miners, ranchers, and farmers leads to conflict with Native Americans.
- The federal government fights several wars with the Native Americans, establishes reservations, and passes the Dawes Act to assimilate Native Americans.

Hands-On Chapter Project
Step 4: Wrap Up

Making the Move West

Step 4: Describing the Trip Students will synthesize what they have learned in Steps 1, 2, and 3.

Directions Write the Essential Question on the board. Have students refer to their maps, their lists, and the personal profiles of the people they encountered on the trip westward. Using this information and what they have learned, students should write a brief paragraph describing the most difficult part of moving westward. Ask volunteers to share their observations and list them on the board. Discuss their thoughts and observations.

Putting It Together Next, have students write a letter to a neighbor left behind in upstate New York. Students should describe how they decided where to move, what items they took with them, what route they traveled, and who they met along the way. Students should also describe difficulties they encountered along the way. Finally, they should conclude their letter—either recommending that their neighbor should join them on the Great Plains or recommending that the neighbor stay in upstate New York. **OL**

Reviewing Vocabulary

Directions: Choose the word or words that best completes the sentence.

1. Cattle ranching developed on the Great Plains as a result of the __________, which was a vast area of grassland owned by the government.

A open range
B long drive
C barbed wire
D Chisholm Trail

2. The government promoted settlement in the Great Plains by allowing individuals to file for a __________, which let people claim public land as their own.

A bonanza farm
B mine permit
C homestead
D reservation

3. The challenges of farming on the Great Plains led to new agricultural techniques and technologies. __________ required the invention of seed drills to place crop seeds deep in the ground where moisture was more plentiful.

A Sodbusting
B Bonanza farming
C Reservations
D Dry farming

4. __________ were yearly payments made by the United States government to Native Americans on reservations.

A Nomads
B Allotments
C Sodbusters
D Annuities

5. In the early 1800s, society in California was dominated by landowners who lived on large

A barrios.
B haciendas.
C bonanza farms.
D homesteads.

Reviewing Main Ideas

Directions: Choose the best answers to the following questions.

Section 1 *(pp. 386–393)*

6. In 1889 the discovery of gold and copper led to the rapid development of the northern Great Plains with the following states being formed:

A Montana, North Dakota, South Dakota.
B Montana, Wyoming, Idaho.
C North Dakota, South Dakota, Iowa.
D North Dakota, South Dakota, Nebraska.

7. The open range was closed to grazing with the use of

A the long drive.
B barbed wire.
C hydraulic mining.
D placer mining.

8. Why did *Las Gorras Blancas* carry out night raids in New Mexico?

A The English-speaking ranchers claimed land used by the community to graze livestock.
B Vaqueros were outlawed by the English-speaking ranchers.
C The English-speaking majority in the legislature closed the barrios.
D The Hispanic minority did not want New Mexico to join the United States.

TEST-TAKING TIP

Look at each question to find clues to support your answer. Try not to get confused by the wording of the question. Then look for an answer that best fits the question.

Need Extra Help?

If You Missed Questions . . .	1	2	3	4	5	6	7	8
Go to Page . . .	390–391	394–395	396	398	392	388	390–391	392–393

GO ON

Answers and Analyses
Reviewing Vocabulary

1. A Students who are unsure of the answer should look for the answer that is closest in meaning to "vast area of grassland." *B* and *C* are incorrect because neither describes a place. Long drive refers to cattle drives, and barbed wire is an object. The Chisholm Trail was not a vast area of grassland. Only open range makes sense.

2. C Choice *A* is a distracter that may confuse students. Bonanza farms were large wheat farms that made large profits. Homesteads were tracts of land. A homesteader's $10 registration fee could allow them to claim up to 160 acres of land. Thinking about this "purchase" as settlers "buying a home" may help students remember the definition of homestead.

3. D A lack of steady rain on the Great Plains encouraged the dry farming techniques and the new agricultural inventions that made farming in this climate more likely to be successful.

4. D Students who have trouble answering this question will most likely have trouble choosing between "allotments" and "annuities." Remind these students that annuities are yearly, or annual, payments. The shared word root may help them retain the definition of annuities.

5. B Choice *A* is incorrect. *Barrios* are Spanish-speaking neighborhoods. Bonanza farms and homesteads were on the Great Plains, not California. Haciendas were huge ranches in California. If students have trouble with this question, have them review "Settling the Hispanic Southwest" on page 392.

Reviewing Main Ideas

6. A North Dakota, South Dakota, and Montana were admitted as states in 1889. Developing a rhyme or acrostic can help students remember facts like this one. Consider pairing up students to create rhymes or acrostics to share with the class.

7. B A careful reading of the question should lead students to the correct answer. The key words in the question are "closed to grazing." Barbed wire literally fenced in, or closed, the open range.

8. A English-speaking ranchers began fencing in community land, causing *Las Gorras Blancos* to raid their homes. Students may be tempted to choose *B*, which also mentions English-speaking ranchers. It is important that students read each answer choice carefully to avoid choosing a similar sounding, but incorrect, answer.

9. C Using the process of elimination can help lead students to the correct answer. *A* is incorrect; long cattle drives were a result of settlement, not a cause. The Great Plains do not get large amounts of rainfall, so *B* can be eliminated. It is unlikely that dry, windy weather would provide an incentive to farm. *C* is correct. The Homestead Act allowed people the opportunity to own land and contributed to the expansion of the Plains.

10. D Wind is not a factor that affects growing crops. Students should eliminate *B* and *C* based on what they have learned about the geography of the Plains. Review innovations such as mechanical reapers and steam tractors that helped make wheat farming suitable.

11. B It is important that students understand what the frontier represented to Americans: a place of opportunity that offered the chance of a fresh start. For many, the frontier also represented the ideas of freedom and adventure.

12. C The two proposed reservations were for the Sioux and the Southern Plains Indians. Students should remember that the reservations were based on keeping Native Americans separate from American citizens to keep the peace.

13. D In this question, the correct choice is the one that is opposite the three other choices. *A, B,* and *C* would be positive and respectful to Native Americans. However, the American government was not respectful of Native American lands and culture. White Americans felt superior to Native Americans, and sought to make Native Americans more like Americans of European descent with actions such as the passage of the Dawes Act.

Chapter 11 ASSESSMENT

Section 2 *(pp. 394–397)*

9. Which of the following factors provided an incentive for people to farm the Great Plains?

A long cattle drives
B large amounts of rainfall
C the Homestead Act
D dry, windy weather

10. Why was wheat a suitable crop to grow on the Great Plains?

A The environment was windy.
B Wheat needs more water than corn.
C Wheat requires large amounts of rainfall.
D New innovations were suited for harvesting wheat.

11. Why were some Americans concerned about the closing of the frontier?

A People were worried that Native Americans might revolt.
B People were worried that the idea of Americans traveling west to make a new start had come to an end.
C Some farmers wanted more land to increase their political power with the federal government.
D Settlers worried about the cost of supplies with the increased number of homesteaders.

Section 3 *(pp. 398–403)*

12. The Indian Peace Commission was formed to end the conflict with Native Americans on the Great Plains. They proposed

A a treaty to end the Battle of the Little Bighorn.
B federal regulations for hunting buffalo.
C creating two large reservations for the Plains Indians.
D removing Sitting Bull from power.

13. The aim of the Dawes Act of 1887 was to

A restore previously taken land to Native American tribes.
B maintain traditional Native American cultures.
C end all governmental contact with Native Americans.
D assimilate Native Americans into American culture.

Critical Thinking

Directions: Choose the best answers to the following questions.

14. The Native American wars that occurred between 1860 and 1890 were mainly the result of

A disputes over the spread of slavery.
B conflict with Mexico over Texas and California.
C the search for gold in California.
D the movement of settlers onto the Great Plains.

Base your answers to questions 15 and 16 on the chart below and your knowledge of Chapter 11.

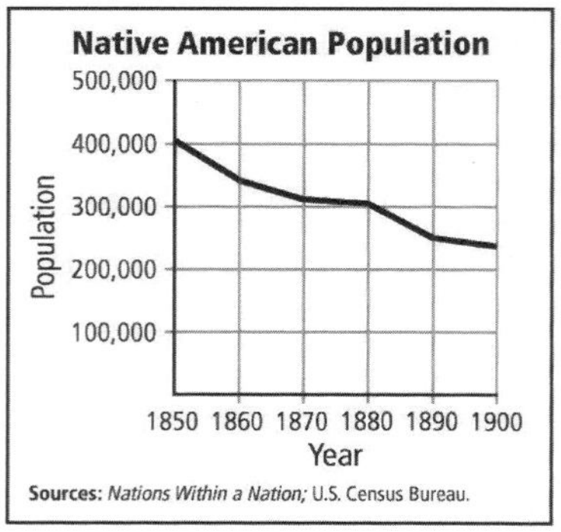

15. What does the graph indicate about the Native American population between 1850 and 1900?

A The Native American population was over 400,000 in 1860.
B The Native American population increased over 50 years.
C The Native American population declined between 1840 and 1850.
D The Native American population was less than 300,000 in 1890.

16. What factor caused the Native American population to decline sharply between 1880 and 1890?

A increase in reservation land
B conflict with American settlers from the East
C increase in the number of wild buffalo
D conflict with Hispanic settlers

Need Extra Help?

If You Missed Questions . . .	9	10	11	12	13	14	15	16
Go to Page . . .	394–395	396–397	397	400	402–403	401–403	398–403	401–403

GO ON

Critical Thinking

14. D Only choice *D* relates to Native Americans. Point out to students that careful reading of the answer choices reveals that the first three involve disputes or events that had little if nothing to do with Native Americans. The movement of settlers onto the Great Plains displaced the Native Americans who lived there.

15. D Students should examine each choice and compare each one to the graph. The Native American population was between 200,000 and 300,000 according to the graph, so *D* is correct.

16. B Although the graph does show a decline in the Native American population, it does not explain reasons for this decline. Therefore, students must rely on their knowledge of the chapter. *B* is the only choice that makes sense, based on the chapter.

17. Placer mining is a process by which
   - **A** deep mine shafts are dug and miners go underground to extract the minerals.
   - **B** miners use simple tools like picks, shovels, and pans to extract shallow deposits of minerals.
   - **C** a number of men use a high-pressure blast of water to loosen large quantities of earth and remove the minerals.
   - **D** earth-moving machines remove large quantities of earth to remove the minerals.

18. Vigilance committees performed what function?
   - **A** found new lodes
   - **B** ensured that mining companies did not harm the environment
   - **C** supervised the building of western railroads
   - **D** enforced law and order in boomtowns

19. What type of mining allowed sediment into the local rivers, causing them to overflow and flood the area?
   - **A** placer mining
   - **B** quartz mining
   - **C** hydraulic mining
   - **D** panning mining

20. Why did the Dakota Sioux clash with local traders and settlers in 1862?
   - **A** Annuity payments never reached them, resulting in poverty.
   - **B** Other Native American tribes claimed the area as their own.
   - **C** Settlers began to increase in the area, disregarding the local treaties.
   - **D** Buffalo hunters invaded the area and killed the remaining buffalo.

Document-Based Questions

Directions: Analyze the document and answer the short-answer questions that follow the document.

In the late 1860s, the U.S. government adopted a policy of forcing Native Americans onto small reservations. Many Native Americans refused to move and fought to maintain their traditional way of life. In the excerpt that follows, Satanta, a chief of the Kiowa, responds to the government's policy:

> *"I have heard that you intend to settle us on a reservation near the mountains. I don't want to settle. I love to roam over the prairies. There I feel free and happy, but when we settle down we grow pale and die. I have laid aside my lance, bow, and shield, and yet I feel safe in your presence. I have told you the truth. I have no little lies hid about me, but I don't know how it is with the commissioners. Are they as clear as I am? A long time ago this land belonged to our fathers; but when I go up to the river I see camps of soldiers on its banks. These soldiers cut down my timber; they kill my buffalo; and when I see that, my heart feels like bursting; I feel sorry. . . . Has the white man become a child that he should recklessly kill and not eat? When the red men slay game, they do so that they may live and not starve."*
>
> —quoted in *Bury My Heart at Wounded Knee*

21. What reasons does Satanta give for not wanting to settle on a reservation?

22. How does Satanta view the white settlers' approach to the land and the resources on it?

Extended Response

23. Write an essay comparing two different perspectives of the settlement of the West. Analyze how the views of Native Americans and white settlers differed on settling the Great Plains. How did each group view the government's involvement and the environment? The essay should include an introduction, at least three paragraphs, and a conclusion that supports your position.

STOP

History ONLINE
For additional test practice, use Self-Check Quizzes—Chapter 11 at glencoe.com.

Need Extra Help?

If You Missed Questions . . .	17	18	19	20	21	22	23
Go to Page . . .	388–389	387	388–389	398–399	407	R19	394–403

20. A The Dakota Sioux experienced poverty and starvation because their annuities never reached them. They did not clash with other Native American tribes. Local traders refused to help the Sioux, resulting in harsh feelings.

Document-Based Questions

21. Students should state that Satanta enjoyed his nomadic life. Point students to the beginning of the passage, in which he states, "I do not want to settle. I love to roam over the prairies."

22. Students' answers should include: Satanta thinks the white man does not respect his land. He says the white men kill buffalo recklessly.

Extended Response

23. Students' responses will vary, but their answers must address the different views of white settlers and Native Americans. Students must provide adequate support for their claims, as well.

17. B Review the section on Mining Technology on page 161 with students. Placer mining is described in the first paragraph as mining with simple tools. Placer mining was only useful for mining on the surface, however. The other answer choices differ from the correct answer in that they describe more advanced mining techniques.

18. D Remind students that vigilance means "watchfulness." Vigilance committees watched over boomtowns, enforcing law and order. *B* is a distracter, but students should be aware that there was no concern for the environment involved in early mining.

19. C The root hydra- is used for water, which may help students recall that hydraulic mining uses water to remove quantities of earth, which students should relate to flooding.

History ONLINE
Have students visit the Web site at glencoe.com to review Chapter 11 and take the Self-Check Quiz.

Need Extra Help?
Have students refer to the pages listed if they miss any of the questions.

Chapter 12 Planning Guide

Key to Ability Levels	
BL Below Level	AL Above Level
OL On Level	ELL English Language Learners

Key to Teaching Resources	
Print Material	Transparency
CD-ROM or DVD	

Levels BL	OL	AL	ELL		Resources	Chapter Opener	Section 1	Section 2	Section 3	Section 4	Chapter Assess
					FOCUS						
BL	OL	AL	ELL	Transparency	**Daily Focus Transparencies**		12-1	12-2	12-3	12-4	Ch. 12
					TEACH						
BL	OL	AL		Print	**Economics and History Activity, URB**		p. 7				
BL	OL	AL	ELL	Print	**Reading Essentials and Note-Taking Guide***		p. 129	p. 132	p. 135	p. 138	
BL	OL		ELL	Print	**Reading Skills Activity, URB**				p. 53		
	OL			Print	**Historical Analysis Skills Activity, URB**			p. 54			
BL	OL		ELL	Print	**Guided Reading Activity, URB***		p. 80	p. 81	p. 82	p. 83	
BL	OL	AL	ELL	Print	**Differentiated Instruction Activity, URB**					p. 55	
BL	OL		ELL	Print	**English Learner Activity, URB**	p. 57					
BL	OL	AL	ELL	Print	**Content Vocabulary Activity, URB***	p. 59					
BL	OL	AL	ELL	Print	**Academic Vocabulary Activity, URB**	p. 61					
	OL	AL		Print	**Reinforcing Skills Activity, URB**		p. 63				
	OL	AL		Print	**Critical Thinking Skills Activity, URB**					p. 64	
BL	OL		ELL	Print	**Time Line Activity, URB**		p. 65				
	OL			Print	**Linking Past and Present Activity, URB**		p. 66				
BL	OL	AL	ELL	Print	**Primary Source Reading, URB**		p. 67	p. 69		pp. 67, 69	
BL	OL	AL	ELL	Print	**American Art and Music Activity, URB**						p. 71
BL	OL	AL	ELL	Print	**Interpreting Political Cartoons Activity, URB**				p. 73		
		AL		Print	**Enrichment Activity, URB**		p. 77				
BL	OL	AL	ELL	Print	**Differentiated Instruction for the American History Classroom**	✓	✓	✓	✓	✓	✓
BL	OL	AL	ELL	Transparency	**Unit Map Overlay Transparencies**	✓	✓	✓	✓	✓	✓
BL	OL	AL	ELL	Print	**Unit Time Line Transparencies, Strategies, and Activities**	✓	✓	✓	✓	✓	✓
BL	OL	AL	ELL	Print	**Cause and Effect Transparencies, Strategies, and Activities**	✓	✓	✓	✓	✓	✓
BL	OL	AL	ELL	Print	**Why It Matters Chapter Transparencies, Strategies, and Activities**	✓	✓	✓	✓	✓	✓
BL	OL	AL	ELL	Print	**American Biographies**					✓	

Note: Please refer to the *Unit 4 Resource Book* for this chapter's URB materials.

* Also available in Spanish

TeacherWorks Plus
All-In-One Planner and Resource Center

- Interactive Lesson Planner
- Interactive Teacher Edition
- Fully editable blackline masters
- Section Spotlight Videos Launch
- Differentiated Lesson Plans
- Printable reports of daily assignments
- Standards Tracking System

Levels BL	OL	AL	ELL	Resources	Chapter Opener	Section 1	Section 2	Section 3	Section 4	Chapter Assess
				TEACH *(continued)*						
BL	OL	AL		Supreme Court Case Studies			p. 21	p. 29	p. 25	
BL	OL	AL	ELL	The Living Constitution	✓	✓	✓	✓	✓	✓
BL	OL	AL	ELL	American Issues	✓	✓	✓	✓	✓	✓
	OL	AL	ELL	American Art and Architecure Transparencies, Strategies, and Activities	✓	✓	✓	✓	✓	✓
BL	OL	AL		High School American History Literature Library	✓	✓	✓	✓	✓	✓
	OL	AL		American History Primary Source Documents Library	✓	✓	✓	✓	✓	✓
BL	OL	AL	ELL	American Music: Hits Through History CD	✓	✓	✓	✓	✓	✓
BL	OL	AL	ELL	StudentWorks™ Plus	✓	✓	✓	✓	✓	✓
BL	OL	AL	ELL	*The American Vision* Video Program	✓	✓	✓	✓	✓	✓
Teacher Resources				Reading Strategies and Activities for the Social Studies Classroom	✓	✓	✓	✓	✓	✓
Teacher Resources				Strategies for Success	✓	✓	✓	✓	✓	✓
Teacher Resources				Presentation Plus! with MindJogger CheckPoint	✓	✓	✓	✓	✓	✓
Teacher Resources				Success With English Learners	✓	✓	✓	✓	✓	✓
				ASSESS						
BL	OL	AL	ELL	Section Quizzes and Chapter Tests*		p. 165	p. 166	p. 167	p. 168	p. 169
BL	OL	AL	ELL	Authentic Assessment With Rubrics						p. 29
BL	OL	AL	ELL	Standardized Test Practice Workbook						p. 24
BL	OL	AL	ELL	*ExamView® Assessment Suite*		12-1	12-2	12-3	12-4	Ch. 12
				CLOSE						
BL			ELL	Reteaching Activity, URB						p. 75
BL	OL		ELL	Reading and Study Skills Foldables™	p. 60					

✓ Chapter- or unit-based activities applicable to all sections in this chapter.

Using StudentWorks™ Plus Online

Teach With Technology

What is StudentWorks™ Plus Online?

StudentWorks™ Plus Online is a powerful learning and teaching tool that offers the entire textbook online in an interactive, searchable format. It provides links to student workbooks, audio recordings of the textbook, audio summaries in Spanish, In Motion animations, and links to Section Spotlight Videos.

How can StudentWorks™ Plus Online help my students and me?

StudentWorks™ Plus Online helps students learn and master the material in the textbook. Students can go to a specific chapter and read the text, listen to audio of the text, and type and print their answers on workbook pages. While reading about a topic, students can quickly search the entire text and the glossary for a key term. You can project StudentWorks™ Plus Online during a classroom lecture and launch Section Spotlight Videos directly.

Visit glencoe.com and enter a ***QuickPass***™ code to go to StudentWorks™ Plus Online.

History ONLINE
Visit glencoe.com and enter ***QuickPass***™ code TAV9399c12T for Chapter 12 resources.

You can easily launch a wide range of digital products from your computer's desktop with the McGraw-Hill Social Studies widget.

TeacherWorks

	Student	Teacher	Parent
Media Library			
• Section Audio	●		●
• Spanish Audio Summaries	●		●
• Section Spotlight Videos	●	●	●
***The American Vision* Online Learning Center (Web Site)**			
• StudentWorks™ Plus Online	●	●	●
• Multilingual Glossary	●	●	●
• Study-to-Go	●	●	●
• Chapter Overviews	●	●	●
• Self-Check Quizzes	●	●	●
• Student Web Activities	●	●	●
• ePuzzles and Games	●	●	●
• Vocabulary eFlashcards	●	●	●
• In Motion Animations	●	●	●
• Study Central™	●	●	●
• Web Activity Lesson Plans		●	
• Vocabulary PuzzleMaker	●	●	●
• Historical Thinking Activities		●	
• Beyond the Textbook	●	●	●

Reading Support From Jamestown Education

- **Timed Readings Plus in Social Studies** helps students increase their reading rate and fluency while maintaining comprehension. The 400-word passages are similar to those found on state and national assessments.
- **Reading in the Content Area: Social Studies** concentrates on six essential reading skills that help students better comprehend what they read. The book includes 75 high-interest nonfiction passages written at increasing levels of difficulty.
- **Reading Social Studies** includes strategic reading instruction and vocabulary support in Social Studies content for both ELLs and native speakers of English.

www.jamestowneducation.com

Biography / A&E Home Video / The History Channel

The following videotape programs are available from Glencoe as supplements to this chapter:

- The Transcontinental Railroad (ISBN 1-56-501731-5)
- Legacy of King Coal: Empires of American Industry (ISBN 0-76-700621-6)

To order, call Glencoe at 1-800-334-7344. To find classroom resources to accompany many of these videos, check the following home pages:

A&E Television: www.aetv.com
The History Channel: www.historychannel.com

Reading List Generator CD-ROM — Glencoe BookLink 3

Use this database to search more than 30,000 titles to create a customized reading list for your students.

- Reading lists can be organized by students' reading level, author, genre, theme, or area of interest.
- The database provides Degrees of Reading Power™ (DRP) and Lexile™ readability scores for all selections.
- A brief summary of each selection is included.

Leveled reading suggestions for this chapter:

For students at a Grade 8 reading level:
- ***The Wright Brothers: The Birth of Modern Aviation,*** by Anna Sproule

For students at a Grade 9 reading level:
- ***The Story of Thomas Alva Edison,*** by Margaret Cousins

For students at a Grade 10 reading level:
- ***Mother Jones: Fierce Fighter for Workers' Rights,*** by Judith Pinkerton Josephson

For students at a Grade 11 reading level:
- ***Telephones,*** by Elaine Marie Alphin

For students at a Grade 12 reading level:
- ***The Wright Brothers: How They Invented the Airplane,*** by Russell Freedman

National Geographic

Index to National Geographic Magazine:

The following articles relate to this chapter:

- "Alexander Graham Bell," by Robert V. Bruce and Ira Block, September 1988.
- "Pittsburgh–Stronger than Steel," by Peter Miller, December 1991.

National Geographic Society Products To order the following, call National Geographic at 1-800-368-2728:

- *ZipZapMap! USA Windows* (ZipZapMap! USA)

Access National Geographic's new, dynamic MapMachine Web site and other geography resources at:

www.nationalgeographic.com
www.nationalgeographic.com/maps

Introducing
Chapter 12

Focus

MAKING CONNECTIONS

Did Industry Improve Society?

Ask students to give suggestions as to the ways they think industry has improved society. Students may cite improvements in manufacturing processes, transportation, communication, entertainment, or trade. Activate students' prior knowledge by asking them to name various inventions with which they are familiar. Students may identify a wide variety of items. Discuss how different their lives would be if the items they identified had not been produced by American industries. **OL**

Teach

The Big Ideas

As students study the chapter, remind them to consider the section-based Big Ideas included in each section's Guide to Reading. The **Essential Questions** in the activities below tie in to the Big Ideas and help students think about and understand important chapter concepts. In addition, the Hands-on Chapter Projects with their culminating activities relate the content from each section to the Big Ideas. These activities build on each other as students progress through the chapter.

Chapter 12

Industrialization

1865–1901

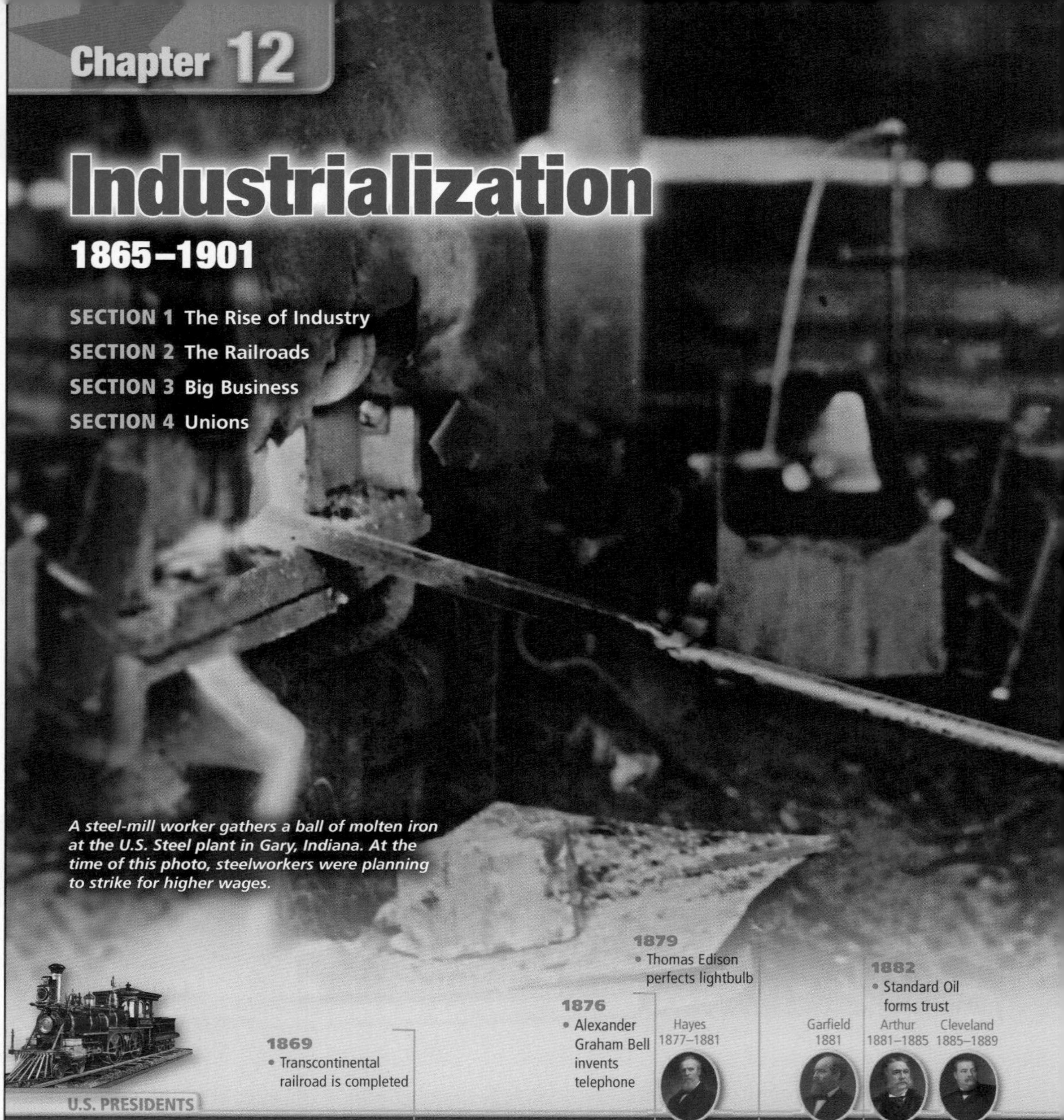

A steel-mill worker gathers a ball of molten iron at the U.S. Steel plant in Gary, Indiana. At the time of this photo, steelworkers were planning to strike for higher wages.

U.S. PRESIDENTS: Hayes 1877–1881; Garfield 1881; Arthur 1881–1885; Cleveland 1885–1889

U.S. EVENTS

- **1869** • Transcontinental railroad is completed
- **1876** • Alexander Graham Bell invents telephone
- **1879** • Thomas Edison perfects lightbulb
- **1882** • Standard Oil forms trust

1865 — 1875 — 1885

WORLD EVENTS

- **1865** • Dmitri Mendeleyev creates periodic table of elements
- **1876** • Nicholas Otto builds first practical gasoline engine
- **1880** • John Milne develops seismograph
- **1885** • Canada's transcontinental railway is completed

Section 1

The Rise of Industry

Essential Question: What economic policies allowed industries to expand after the Civil War? *(Laissez-faire, or "hands-off," economic policies allowed industries to grow rapidly because there was no government interference to restrict growth.)* Point out that in Section 1 students will learn about laissez-faire and other factors that led to the rapid growth of industry in the United States. **OL**

Section 2

The Railroads

Essential Question: How did the railroads encourage the settlement of the Plains and the West? *(The railroads brought settlers and goods west; they transported goods east. Railroads make travel and shipping of goods fast and cheap.)* Point out that in Section 2 students will learn how the railroads accelerated the settlement of the Plains and the West. **OL**

MAKING CONNECTIONS

Did Industry Improve Society?

Many factors promoted industrialization, including cheap labor, new inventions and technology, and plentiful raw materials. Railroads rapidly expanded, while government policies encouraged economic growth.

- ***What changes in lifestyle do you think occurred because of industrialization?***
- ***How do you think industrialization changed American politics?***

1886
- Haymarket riot occurs

1892
- Homestead strike occurs

B. Harrison 1889–1893

Cleveland 1893–1897

1894
- Pullman strike begins

McKinley 1897–1901

1901
- J.P. Morgan forms U.S. Steel

1895

1892
- Rudolf Diesel patents diesel engine

1895
- Louis and Auguste Lumière introduce motion pictures

FOLDABLES™

Analyzing Organizations Make a Three-Tab Book Foldable to help you analyze how the Civil War transformed the nature of industry. As you read the chapter, write details under the corresponding tab.

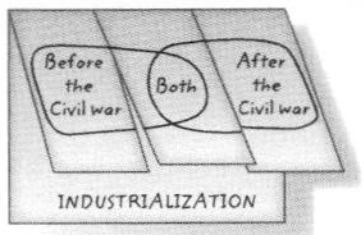

History ONLINE Visit glencoe.com and enter ***QuickPass***™ code TAV9846c12 for Chapter 12 resources.

Section 3

Big Business

Essential Question: Why did captains of industry such as Andrew Carnegie expand their businesses through new ways of organization? *(They sought to control all aspects of their respective businesses to keep costs low and profits high. They also sought to eliminate competition.)* Point out that in Section 3 students will learn about how big businesses became monopolies. **OL**

Section 4

Unions

Essential Question: Why did workers form unions? *(Workers wanted to form unions because unionization allowed workers to join forces. Forming unions was the only tool available after requests for better wages and working conditions failed.)* Point out that in Section 4 students will learn about how unions were organized and the social and political opposition to unions that prevented them from success. **OL**

Introducing **Chapter 12**

More About the Photo

Visual Literacy Working in a steel mill was dirty. Work conditions were often hazardous, and there was no compensation in case of death or injury. Strikes were often the only tool available to workers as they sought better wages and working conditions.

FOLDABLES™ Study Organizer **Dinah Zike's Foldables**

Dinah Zike's Foldables are three-dimensional, interactive graphic organizers that help students practice basic writing skills, review vocabulary terms, and identify main ideas. Instructions for creating and using Foldables can be found in the Appendix at the end of this book and in the *Dinah Zike's Reading and Study Skills Foldables* booklet.

History ONLINE

Visit glencoe.com and enter ***QuickPass***™ code TAV9399c12T for Chapter 12 resources, including a Chapter Overview, Study Central™, Study-to-Go, Student Web Activity, Self-Check Quiz, and other materials.

Focus

Bellringer

Daily Focus Transparency 12-1

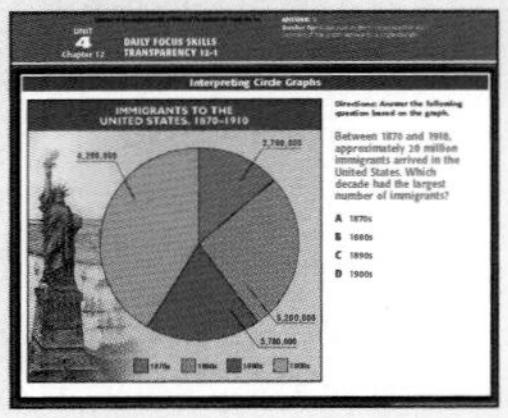

Guide to Reading

Answer: abundance of raw materials; oil production; population increase; free enterprise system; large free trade area; new inventions

Section Spotlight Video

To generate student interest and provide a springboard for class discussion, access the Chapter 12, Section 1 video at glencoe.com or on the video DVD.

Resource Manager

Section 1 — Section Audio — Spotlight Video

The Rise of Industry

Guide to Reading

Big Ideas

Government and Society The United States government adopted a policy of laissez-faire economics, allowing business to expand.

Content Vocabulary

- gross national product *(p. 410)*
- laissez-faire *(p. 414)*
- entrepreneur *(p. 415)*

Academic Vocabulary

- resource *(p. 410)*
- practice *(p. 415)*

People and Events to Identify

- Edwin Drake *(p. 410)*
- Alexander Graham Bell *(p. 412)*
- Thomas Alva Edison *(p. 412)*
- Morrill Tariff *(p. 415)*

Reading Strategy

Organizing As you read about the changes brought about by industrialization, complete a graphic organizer similar to the one below, listing the causes of industrialization.

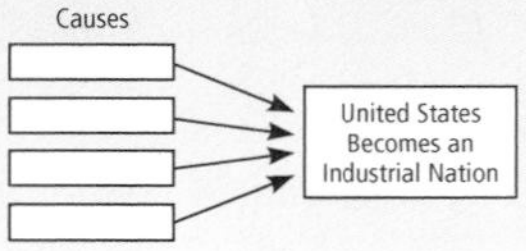

American business and industry grew rapidly after the end of the Civil War. Industrialization changed the way people lived and worked.

The United States Industrializes

MAIN Idea Natural resources and a large labor force allowed the United States to industrialize rapidly.

HISTORY AND YOU What natural resources are located in your area? Read to learn how the availability of raw materials encouraged industrialization.

Although the Industrial Revolution reached the United States in the early 1800s, most Americans still lived on farms. Out of a population of over 30 million, only 1.3 million Americans worked in industry when the Civil War began in 1861. After the war, industry rapidly expanded, and millions of Americans left their farms to work in mines and factories. Factories began to replace smaller workshops as complex machinery began to substitute for simpler hand tools.

By the late 1800s, the United States was the world's leading industrial nation. By 1914 the nation's **gross national product** (GNP)—the total value of all goods and services that a country produces—was eight times greater than it had been in 1865 when the Civil War came to an end.

Natural Resources

An abundance of raw materials was one reason for the nation's industrial success. The United States had vast natural **resources,** including timber, coal, iron, and copper. This meant that American companies could obtain them cheaply and did not have to import them from other countries. Many of these resources were located in the American West. The settlement of this region helped accelerate industrialization, as did the transcontinental railroad. Railroads took settlers and miners to the region and carried resources back to factories in the East.

At the same time, people began using a new resource, petroleum. Even before the automotive age, petroleum was in high demand because it could be turned into kerosene. The American oil industry was built on the demand for kerosene, a fuel used in lanterns and stoves. The industry began in western Pennsylvania, where residents had long noticed oil bubbling to the surface of area springs and streams. In 1859 **Edwin Drake** drilled the first oil well near Titusville, Pennsylvania. By 1900 oil fields from Pennsylvania to Texas had been drilled. As oil production rose, it led to economic expansion.

R Reading Strategies	C Critical Thinking	D Differentiated Instruction	W Writing Support	S Skill Practice
Teacher Edition • Seq. Info., p. 412 **Additional Resources** • Content Vocab., URB p. 59 • Guided Read., URB p. 80	**Teacher Edition** • Analyzing Info., p. 415 **Additional Resources** • Economics and Hist. Act., URB p. 7 • Linking Past/Present, URB p. 66 • Quizzes/Tests, p. 165	**Additional Resources** • English Learner, URB p. 57 • Enrichment Act., URB p. 77	**Teacher Edition** • Descrip. Writing, pp. 412, 413, 414 **Additional Resources** • Academic Vocab., URB p. 61	**Teacher Edition** • Analyzing, p. 411 • Explaining, p. 412 **Additional Resources** • Reinforc. Skills, URB p. 63 • Time Line Act., URB p. 65 • RENTG, p. 129

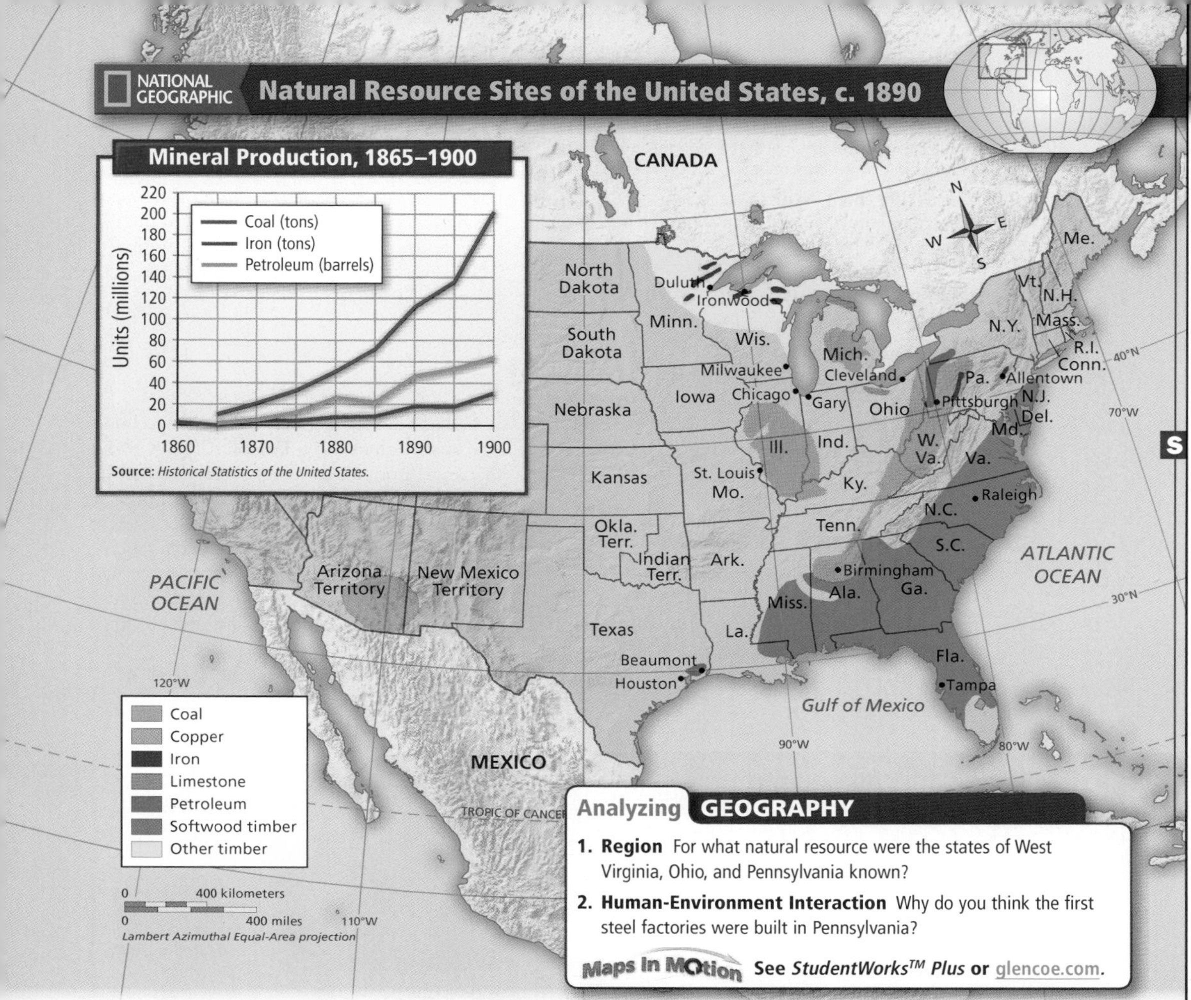

Analyzing GEOGRAPHY

1. **Region** For what natural resource were the states of West Virginia, Ohio, and Pennsylvania known?
2. **Human-Environment Interaction** Why do you think the first steel factories were built in Pennsylvania?

Maps In MOtion See *StudentWorks™ Plus* or glencoe.com.

A Large Workforce

The human resources available to American industry were as important as natural resources in enabling the nation to industrialize rapidly. Between 1860 and 1910 the population of the United States nearly tripled. This population growth provided industry with an abundant workforce and also created greater demand for the consumer goods manufactured by factories.

Population growth stemmed from two causes—large families and a flood of immigrants. Because of better living conditions, more children survived and grew to adulthood. American industry began to grow at a time when social and economic conditions in eastern Europe and China convinced many people to immigrate to the United States in search of a better life. Many were also seeking to escape oppressive governments and religious persecution. Between 1870 and 1910, more than 17 million immigrants arrived in the United States. These multitudes entered the growing industrial workforce, helped factories increase production, and became consumers of industrial products.

Reading Check **Explaining** How did oil production affect the American economy?

Teach

S Skill Practice

Analyzing Ask: In what region of the United States was most softwood timber harvested? What role might the climate and geography have played? *(the southeast; the rich soil and warm climate of this region were essential to the growth of softwood timber.)* BL

Analyzing GEOGRAPHY

Answers:
1. coal
2. The nearby coal mines provided coal to fuel the smelting process.

Reading Check

Answer:
It increased economic expansion.

Hands-On Chapter Project
Step 1

Starting a Business

Step 1: Planning Your Business Working in small groups, students will determine what business they would like to start and how to organize it to be successful.

Essential Question What resources will the business require to be successful?

Directions Organize students into small groups. Have them assume the role of entrepreneurs. Using information from the chapter as well as library or Internet resources, each group of students should first determine what their business will be.

Students should then make a list of the resources they will need for their business. Remind students to consider labor or human resources, natural resources, and financial resources, as well as machinery, factories, processing plants, and so on. Using library or Internet resources, students should determine how much capital will be needed to acquire the resources the group identified.

Next, students should create a flowchart illustrating the processes that will likely be followed in their business. The flowchart should identify where in the process each resource identified by the group will be utilized or consumed.

Summarizing Allow time for groups to share their decisions, what they have learned about their businesses, and the costs of the businesses. Students may also include pictures of the resources or of the processes used in the business. OL

(Chapter Project continued on page 417)

R Reading Strategy

Sequencing Information Have students research one of the inventions of the late 1800s. Instruct students to create time lines for significant events related to their chosen invention. For example, a time line for the telephone might include the dates for the invention of the telephone keypad, the cordless telephone, and the cell phone. **OL**

W Writing Support

Descriptive Writing Have students write a paragraph describing how one of the inventions shown on the time line has changed the way people work. Encourage students to share their paragraphs with the class. **BL**

S Skill Practice

Explaining Have interested students research to find out the processes that Bell, Edison, or Westinghouse used when developing their inventions. Encourage students to share their findings with the class. **AL**

Additional Support

New Inventions

MAIN Idea During the late 1800s, inventions such as the telephone and the lightbulb spurred economic development.

HISTORY AND YOU What invention has most changed your daily life? Read about the new inventions of the late 1800s.

Natural resources and labor were essential to America's economic development, but new inventions and technology were important as well. New technology increased the nation's productivity and improved transportation and communications networks. New inventions also resulted in new industries, which in turn produced more wealth and jobs.

Bell and the Telephone

In 1874 a Scottish immigrant named **Alexander Graham Bell** suggested the idea of a telephone to his assistant, Thomas Watson. Watson recalled, "He had an idea by which he believed it would be possible to talk by telegraph." Bell began experimenting with ways to transmit sound via an electrical current of varying intensity. In 1876 he succeeded. Picking up the crude telephone, he placed a call to the next room, saying, "Come here, Watson, I want you." Watson heard and came. The telephone revolutionized business and personal communication. In 1877 Bell organized the Bell Telephone Company, which eventually became the American Telephone and Telegraph Company (AT&T).

Edison, Westinghouse, and Electricity

Perhaps the leading pioneer in new technology was **Thomas Alva Edison.** Curious about the world from an early age, he learned all he could about the mechanical workings of objects. His laboratory at Menlo Park, New Jersey, was the forerunner of the modern research laboratory. Edison set up his lab with money he earned by improving the telegraph system for Western Union. He referred to it as an "invention factory." During the first five years Menlo Park existed, Edison patented an invention almost every

American Inventions, 1865–1895

1870 · 1875 · 1880 · 1885

1872 Elijah McCoy invents automatic lubricator for steam engines, allowing trains to run faster with less maintenance

1873 Christopher Sholes develops typewriter and sells it to Remington and Sons

1876 Alexander Graham Bell invents telephone

▲ Alexander Graham Bell

1877 Thomas Edison develops phonograph

▲ Early Edison phonograph

▲ Bell's first telephone

1882 Lewis Latimer invents the carbon filament for lightbulbs, allowing them to last much longer

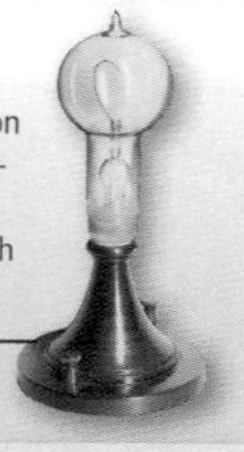

▲ Edison's first commercial lightbulb

1886 Josephine Cochrane develops automatic dishwasher; its basic design is still used today

Activity: Interdisciplinary Connections

Science Invite a science teacher or a representative of a telephone company to demonstrate the science behind the invention of the telephone and discuss the science involved in cellular communications. Encourage students to ask questions. After the presentation, discuss how the standard telephone and cellular telephone have changed the way people communicate with one another. List the advantages and disadvantages of telephone communications. **OL**

month. By the time he died, Edison held more than one thousand patents.

Edison first achieved international fame in 1877 with the invention of the phonograph. Two years later he perfected the electric generator and the lightbulb. Although Edison had expected to produce an inexpensive lightbulb in six weeks, the task took more than a year. His laboratory then went on to invent or improve several other major devices, including the battery, the dictaphone, and the motion picture.

An Edison company began to transform American society in 1882 when it started supplying electric power to New York City. In 1889 several Edison companies merged to form the Edison General Electric Company (today known as GE).

Engineer and industrialist George Westinghouse invented an air-brake system for railroads. Unlike earlier manual systems that required brakes to be applied to each car, Westinghouse's invention provided a continuous braking system, so that all the cars' brakes were applied at the same time. Because the trains could brake rapidly and smoothly, they could safely travel at higher speeds.

Westinghouse also developed an alternating current (AC) system to distribute electricity using transformers and generators. Working with inventor Nikola Tesla, Westinghouse further improved his system. His Westinghouse Electric Company lit Chicago's Columbia Exhibition in 1893. It was also the first to use the hydroelectric power of Niagara Falls to generate electricity for streetcars and lights in Buffalo, New York, 22 miles away.

Technology's Impact

In ways big and small, technology changed the way people lived. Shortly after the Civil War, Thaddeus Lowe invented the ice machine, the basis of the refrigerator. In the early 1870s Gustavus Swift, founder of Swift Meatpacking, hired an engineer to develop a refrigerated railroad car. Swift shipped the first refrigerated **W** load of fresh meat in 1877. The widespread use of refrigeration kept food fresh longer and reduced the risk of food poisoning.

W Writing Support

Descriptive Writing Invite students to use library and Internet resources to write a one-page essay describing the process of how a refrigerated railroad car worked in the 1870s and how it differs today. Encourage students to share their essays with the class. **OL**

Analyzing TIME LINES

Answers:

1. The invention of the phonograph came after the invention of the typewriter.
2. 10 years
3. the automatic dishwasher

1893
Charles and Frank Duryea invent gasoline-powered automobile

▲ *The Wright Flyer lifts off, December 17, 1903.*

1903
Wilbur and Orville Wright make first successful powered flight at Kitty Hawk, North Carolina

1890 — 1895 — 1900 — 1905

1888
George Eastman patents first hand-held camera, the Kodak

Analyzing TIME LINES

1. **Sequencing** Did the invention of the phonograph occur before or after the invention of the typewriter?
2. **Calculating** How much time elapsed between the invention of a gasoline-powered automobile and the first flight of the Wright brothers?
3. **Identifying** For what invention is Josephine Cochrane known?

Differentiated Instruction

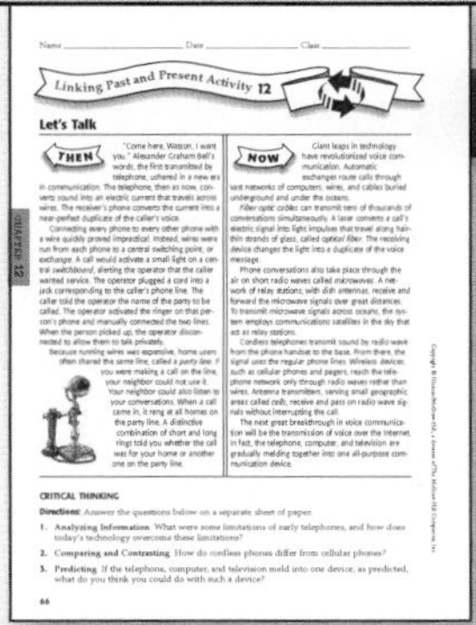

Linking Past and Present Activity, URB p. 66

The Telephone: Past and Present

Objective: To link technological innovations in the late 1800s to technology today.

Focus: Have students relate how Alexander Graham Bell's telephone has impacted their lives today.

Teach: Explain Bell's invention and how it changed Americans' lives.

Assess: Create a time line describing the history of the telephone.

Close: Discuss other inventions from the 1800s and 1900s that have greatly affected our lives today.

Differentiated Instruction Strategies

BL Explain how technology like the telephone improves people's lives.

AL Create a flowchart illustrating how another invention from this period influenced today's technology.

ELL Create a list of all new or unfamiliar terms in the reading. First, guess at the meanings. Then look up the words.

W Writing Support

Descriptive Writing Ask students to find books in the library about the laying of the Atlantic cable. Then have students write a telegram to family members in Europe describing their experiences using one "new" invention of the 1860s or 1870s. Students should include details such as how the invention works and how it affects their daily routines. **OL**

Analyzing VISUALS

Answers:

1. They are being washed away by a flood of foreign goods.
2. In the absence of free trade, the consumer faces higher (inflated) costs.

Reading Check

Answer:
It revolutionized business by opening up entirely new markets for inventions and goods to sell.

Additional Support

The textile industry had long depended on machines to turn fibers into cloth. By the mid-1800s, the introduction of the Northrop automatic loom allowed cloth to be made at a much faster rate. Bobbins, which had to be changed by hand, could now be changed automatically.

Changes also took place in the clothing industry. Standard sizes were used in making ready-made clothes. Power-driven sewing machines and cloth cutters rapidly moved the clothing business from small tailor shops to large factories. Similar changes took place in shoemaking. By 1900 cobblers had nearly disappeared.

W Technology's impact also included improved communications. Cyrus Field laid a telegraph cable across the Atlantic Ocean in 1866. This cable provided instant contact between the United States and Europe.

Reading Check **Explaining** How did the use of electric power affect economic development?

Free Enterprise

MAIN Idea Laissez-faire economics promoted industrialization, but tariffs protected American companies from competition.

HISTORY AND YOU Do you remember how Americans objected to British taxes on trade before the American Revolution? Read how tariffs affected American industries in the late 1800s.

Another important reason the United States was able to industrialize rapidly was its free enterprise system. In the late 1800s, many Americans embraced the idea of **laissez-faire** (leh•say•FARE), a French phrase meaning "let people do as they choose." Supporters of laissez-faire believe the government should not interfere in the economy other than to protect private property rights and maintain peace. They argue that if the government regulates the economy, it increases costs and eventually hurts society more than it helps.

POLITICAL CARTOONS PRIMARY SOURCE
Should Government Regulate the Economy?

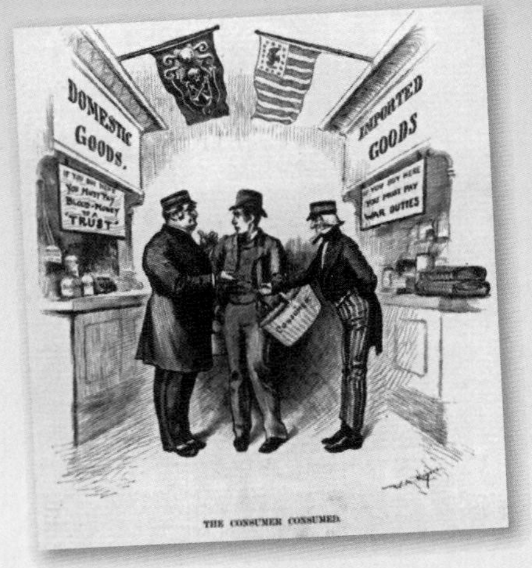

◀ *Entitled "The Consumer Consumed," this cartoon shows a shopper being told that if he buys domestic goods, he has to pay extra money to trusts (monopolies), and if he buys foreign goods, he has to pay extra money (duties) to the government.*

The gate is labeled "Protection." The flood is labeled "European manufactures."

Several buildings are labeled "American factory."

▲ *The original caption for this cartoon read "Goods will be so much cheaper—Democratic argument. But what will happen to all the American factories?"*

Analyzing VISUALS DBQ

1. **Interpreting** What is happening to American factories after the protection gate is opened?
2. **Analyzing** What argument does the cartoon on the left give in favor of free trade?

Activity: Collaborative Learning

Survey Divide students into groups. Have each group develop a list of the electrical equipment he or she uses during a typical week. Then have the groups survey one adult between 30 and 40 years old, a second between 40 and 50 years old, and a third between 60 and 70 years old about the electrical equipment they used as teenagers. Have students compare what is the same and different about the lists from each group. Ask students what these lists reflect about changes in technology.

Laissez-faire relies on supply and demand, rather than the government, to regulate wages and prices. Supporters believe a free market with competing companies leads to greater efficiency and creates more wealth for everyone. Laissez-faire advocates also support low taxes and limited government debt to ensure that private individuals, not the government, will make most of the decisions about how the nation's wealth is spent.

In the late 1800s, the profit motive attracted many capable and ambitious people into business. **Entrepreneurs**—people who risk their capital to organize and run businesses—were attracted by the prospect of making money in manufacturing and transportation. Many entrepreneurs from New England, who had accumulated money by investing in trade, fishing, and textile mills, now invested in factories and railroads. An equally important source of private capital was Europe, especially Great Britain. Foreign investors saw great opportunities for profit in the United States. C

In many ways, the United States **practiced** laissez-faire economics in the late 1800s. State and federal governments kept taxes and spending low. They did not impose costly regulations on industry or try to control wages and prices. In other ways, however, the government went beyond laissez-faire and introduced policies intended to promote business.

Since the early 1800s, leaders in the Northeast and the South had different ideas about the proper role of the government in the economy. Northern leaders wanted high tariffs to protect manufacturers from foreign competition and also supported federal subsidies for companies building roads, canals, and railroads. Southern leaders opposed subsidies and favored low tariffs to promote trade and to keep the cost of imported goods low.

The Civil War ended the debate. After the Southern states seceded, the Republican-controlled Congress passed the **Morrill Tariff,** which greatly increased tariff rates. By 1865 tariffs had nearly tripled. Congress also gave vast tracts of Western land and nearly $65 million in loans to Western railroads, and sold public lands with mineral resources for much less than their market value.

In the late 1800s, the United States was one of the largest free trade areas in the world. The Constitution bans states from imposing tariffs, and there were few regulations on commerce or immigration. Supporters of laissez-faire say these factors played a major role in the country's tremendous economic growth.

High tariffs, however, contradicted laissez-faire ideas. When the nation raised tariffs on foreign goods, other countries raised their tariffs on American goods. This hurt American companies trying to sell goods abroad, particularly farmers who sold their products overseas. Despite these problems, many business leaders and members of Congress believed tariffs were necessary. Few believed that new American industries could compete with established European factories without tariffs to protect them. Later, in the early 1900s, after American companies had become large and efficient, business leaders began to push for free trade. They believed they could now compete internationally and win sales in foreign markets.

Reading Check **Analyzing** Do you think government policies at this time helped or hindered industrialization? Why?

Section 1 REVIEW

Vocabulary

1. **Explain** the significance of: gross national product, Edwin Drake, Alexander Graham Bell, Thomas Alva Edison, laissez-faire, entrepreneur, Morrill Tariff.

Main Ideas

2. **Explaining** How did an abundance of natural resources contribute to economic growth in the United States in the late 1800s?

3. **Organizing** Use a graphic organizer similar to the one below to indicate how the inventions listed affected the nature of American work and business.

Invention	Effects
telephone	
lightbulb	
automatic loom	

4. **Describing** How did the principles of the free enterprise system, laissez-faire, and profit motive encourage the rise of industry?

Critical Thinking

5. **Big Ideas** What role did the federal government play in increasing industrialization after the Civil War?

6. **Analyzing Visuals** Examine the time line on pages 412–413. Choose one invention and explain how it changed society.

Writing About History

7. **Descriptive Writing** Imagine you are a young person living in this country in the late 1800s. Choose one of the inventions discussed in the section and write a journal entry describing its impact on your life.

History ONLINE
Study Central™ To review this section, go to glencoe.com and click on Study Central.

C Critical Thinking

Analyzing Information Ask interested students to use library or Internet resources to find out more about the roles of entrepreneurs in the free enterprise system. **Ask:** Who are entrepreneurs in the United States today? **AL**

Assess

History ONLINE

Study Central™ provides summaries, interactive games, and online graphic organizers to help students review content.

Close

Summarizing Ask: In what ways did the federal government encourage industrialization in the late 1800s? *(Laissez-faire policies; grants to railroads)* **OL**

Reading Check

Answer:
Students might mention that while higher tariffs hurt consumers, they spurred industrialization.

Section 1 REVIEW

Answers

1. All definitions can be found in the section and the Glossary.
2. Americans did not have to import resources from other countries, saving resources for internal growth.
3. telephone: better communications; lightbulb: cheap lighting; automatic loom: made cloth faster
4. They put development in the hands of entrepreneurs rather than in the hands of the government.
5. Congress subsidized railroads and sold land for below market value.
6. Answers will vary depending on which invention students select.
7. Students' journal entries will vary. Students should describe the invention and its impact from a firsthand perspective.

Focus

Bellringer
Daily Focus Transparency 12-2

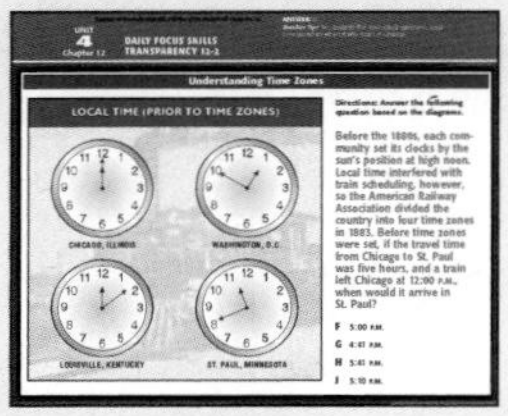

Guide to Reading

Answers: development of time zones; sped long-distance transportation; longer and heavier trains used; rate per mile declined; united America's regions; promoted a national market

Section Spotlight Video

To generate student interest and provide a springboard for class discussion, access the Chapter 12, Section 2 video at glencoe.com or on the video DVD.

Section 2 — Section Audio — Spotlight Video

The Railroads

Guide to Reading

Big Ideas

Science and Technology The growth of railroads encouraged development of the Plains and Western regions.

Content Vocabulary
- time zone *(p. 419)*
- land grant *(p. 420)*

Academic Vocabulary
- integrate *(p. 419)*
- investor *(p. 420)*

People and Events to Identify
- Pacific Railway Act *(p. 416)*
- Grenville Dodge *(p. 416)*
- Leland Stanford *(p. 417)*
- Cornelius Vanderbilt *(p. 419)*
- Jay Gould *(p. 420)*
- Crédit Mobilier *(p. 421)*
- James J. Hill *(p. 421)*

Reading Strategy

Organizing As you read about the development of a nationwide rail network, complete a graphic organizer similar to the one below, listing the effects of this rail network on the nation.

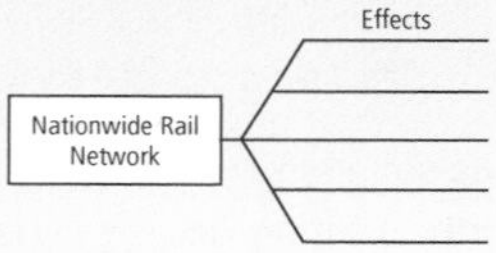

Major railroads, including the transcontinental railroad, were constructed rapidly after the Civil War ended. Railroads required major capital investment and government land grants. The huge profits to be made, however, led to some corruption as well.

Linking the Nation

MAIN Idea After the Civil War, the rapid construction of railroads accelerated the nation's industrialization and linked the country together.

HISTORY AND YOU How has technology helped unify the United States in recent years? Read to learn how railroads helped connect the nation.

In 1865 the United States had about 35,000 miles of railroad track, almost all of it east of the Mississippi River. After the Civil War, railroad construction expanded dramatically, linking the distant regions of the nation in a transportation network. By 1900 the United States, now a booming industrial power, had more than 200,000 miles of track.

The Transcontinental Railroad

The railroad boom began in 1862, when President Abraham Lincoln signed the **Pacific Railway Act.** This act provided for the construction of a transcontinental railroad by two corporations. To encourage rapid construction, the government offered each company land along its right-of-way. A competition between the two companies developed, as each raced to obtain as much land and money as possible.

The Union Pacific Under the direction of engineer **Grenville Dodge,** a former Union general, the Union Pacific began pushing westward from Omaha, Nebraska, in 1865. The laborers faced blizzards in the mountains, scorching heat in the desert, and, sometimes, angry Native Americans. Labor, money, and engineering problems plagued the supervisors of the project. As Dodge observed:

PRIMARY SOURCE

"Everything—rails, ties, bridging, fastenings, all railway supplies, fuel for locomotives and trains, and supplies for men and animals on the entire work—had to be transported from the Missouri River."

—quoted in *The Growth of the American Republic*

The railroad workers of the Union Pacific included Civil War veterans, newly recruited Irish immigrants, frustrated miners and farmers, cooks, adventurers, and ex-convicts. At the height of the project, the Union

Resource Manager

R Reading Strategies	C Critical Thinking	D Differentiated Instruction	W Writing Support	S Skill Practice
Teacher Edition • Using Context Clues, p. 419 **Additional Resources** • Guided Read., URB p. 81	**Teacher Edition** • Drawing Concl., p. 421 **Additional Resources** • Historical Analysis Skills, URB p. 54 • Supreme Court Case Studies, p. 21	**Teacher Edition** • Visual/Spatial, p. 420	**Teacher Edition** • Narr. Writing, p. 417 • Descrip. Writing, p. 418	**Teacher Edition** • Kinesthetic, p. 417 **Additional Resources** • RENTG, p. 132 • Quizzes/Tests, p. 166

HISTORY AND GEOGRAPHY

The Transcontinental Railroad Connects the Nation

▲ Led by Grenville Dodge (top right), workers built the Union Pacific Railroad from Omaha, across the Great Plains, to Utah. Many Irish immigrants worked on the railroad.

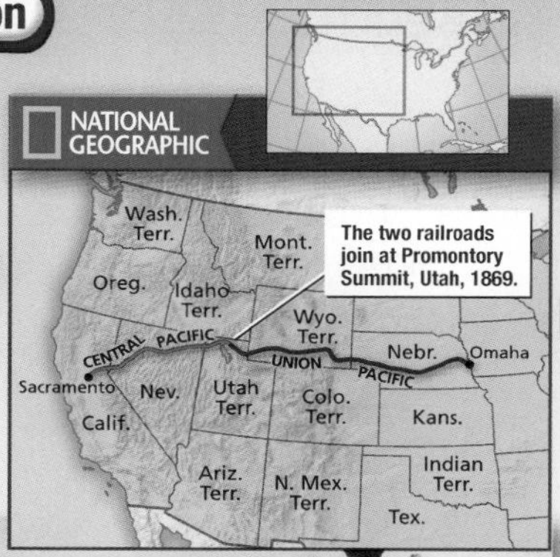

▲ The Union Pacific and Central Pacific met in Utah, where a ceremonial gold spike was driven, joining the two lines.

▲ Led by Theodore Judah (above, left), workers built the Central Pacific Railroad eastward from Sacramento, through the Rocky Mountains to Utah. Many Chinese immigrants worked on the railroad.

Analyzing VISUALS

1. **Analyzing** Based on the map and photos, why do you think Union Pacific workers were able to lay so many more miles of track than Central Pacific workers?
2. **Describing** Based on the photos, why do you think life as a railroad worker was so difficult?

Pacific employed about 10,000 workers. Camp life was rough, dirty, and dangerous, with lots of gambling, hard drinking, and fighting.

The Central Pacific The Central Pacific Railroad began as the dream of engineer Theodore Judah. He sold stock in his fledgling Central Pacific Railroad Company to four Sacramento merchants: grocer **Leland Stanford,** shop owner Charley Crocker, and hardware store owners Mark Hopkins and Collis P. Huntington. These "Big Four" eventually made huge fortunes, and Stanford became governor of California, served as a United States senator, and founded Stanford University.

Because of a shortage of labor in California, the Central Pacific Railroad hired about 10,000 workers from China and paid them about $1.00 a day. All the equipment—rails, cars, locomotives, and machinery—was shipped from the eastern United States, either around Cape Horn at the tip of South America or over the isthmus of Panama in Central America.

Teach

S Skill Practice

Kinesthetic Have students create a map of the western United States today, showing the routes of the Transcontinental Railroad, state boundaries, and capital cities. Students should then locate major cities along the route of the railroad. Have students draw conclusions about the impact of the railroad on the settlement of the West. BL

W Writing Support

Narrative Writing Have students research the life of a railroad worker. Using their findings, students should write a letter to family members back home describing one day at work. OL

Analyzing VISUALS

Answers:

1. The land where the Union Pacific workers laid track was much flatter.
2. little or no shelter from the elements; no conveniences; workers moved as the track was laid

Hands-On Chapter Project
Step 2

Starting a Business

Step 2: Obtaining the Capital

Directions Returning to their groups, students should review the plans, lists, and flowcharts for their business. Using their textbook as well as library or Internet resources, students should find out how business leaders obtain the money necessary to start a business. Students may want to look ahead and refer to the table on page 423. Remind students that a sole proprietorship is usually a small business owned by one person and that a partnership is owned by two or more people who usually invest their own money in the business. Larger businesses, however, require huge amounts of money, or capital. Two of the most common ways businesses obtain the large amounts of capital required are bank loans and the selling of stocks to investors, who then own part of the business. Each group should prepare a chart showing the advantages and disadvantages of these two options. After the charts are complete, a representative from each group should share the group's chart and findings with the class. Next, have students return to their groups and decide the best way for their business to obtain the needed capital.

Putting It Together Have volunteers from each group explain how the group plans to obtain the required capital and why the group chose that particular option. Discuss with the class the likelihood of each business's success in obtaining the necessary capital. OL

(Chapter Project continued on page 423)

W Writing Support

Descriptive Writing Have students find out more about the celebratory events at Promontory Summit, Utah, on May 10, 1869. Then have students use that information to create a newspaper article describing the celebrations for their hometown paper back East. OL

Did You Know?

Nearly 50 years after the United States completed its transcontinental railroad, the Russians hammered the final spike into their own cross-country rail line. Begun in 1891 and completed in 1916, the Trans-Siberian Railroad was the longest in the world, running nearly 5,800 miles (9,330 km) from Moscow in the west to Vladivostok on the Sea of Japan (East Sea) in the east. Like the American railroads, the Trans-Siberian line opened up the way for trade and settlement throughout Russia's frontier. A passenger train takes seven days to travel between Moscow to Vladivostok.

TECHNOLOGY & HISTORY

Railroads and the Economy Building the railroad system led to the creation of new technologies and jobs. Economists refer to this as the "multiplier effect." Whenever a new technology becomes widely used, it creates many new jobs in other industries that are needed to support it.

Building railroad engines and cars created many jobs in other industries. For example, textile workers made fabric for seats in passenger cars, glassworkers made the lenses for the lamps, and metalworkers cast the bronze bells.

Railroads greatly increased the demand for coal, both to power locomotives and to melt iron in steel refineries. This created a huge coal-mining industry in Pennsylvania and West Virginia. In 1860, some 36,000 people were coal miners; by 1889, there were more than 290,000.

Railroads created many new jobs. Engineers, firemen, and brakemen were needed to run the trains; mechanics, machinists, oilers, dispatchers, track workers, loaders, and many others were needed to keep the railway running. By 1900, more than 1 million people worked for the railroads.

In 1860 the nation had 30,000 miles of railroad track. By 1890, another 130,000 miles had been laid. Track-laying crews employed thousands of workers. In addition, the lumber industry needed tens of thousands of workers to make railroad ties. Thousands of others worked in iron mines and in the steel industry, helping make rails, engine boilers, and other steel components.

The Last Spike Workers completed the Transcontinental Railroad in only four years, despite the physical challenges. Each mile of track required 400 rails; each rail took 10 spikes. The Central Pacific, starting from the west, laid a total of 688 miles of track. The Union Pacific laid 1,086 miles.

W On May 10, 1869, hundreds of spectators gathered at Promontory Summit, Utah, to watch dignitaries hammer five gold and silver spikes into the final rails that would join the Union Pacific and Central Pacific. General Grenville Dodge was at the ceremony:

PRIMARY SOURCE

"The trains pulled up facing each other, each crowded with workmen. . . . The officers and invited guests formed on each side of the track. . . . Prayer was offered; a number of spikes were driven in the two adjoining rails . . . and thus the two roads were welded into one great trunk line from the Atlantic to the Pacific."

—from *Mine Eyes Have Seen*

After Leland Stanford hammered in the last spike, telegraph operators sent the news across the nation. Cannons blasted in New York City, Chicago held a parade, and citizens in Philadelphia rang the Liberty Bell.

Railroads Spur Growth

The transcontinental railroad was the first of many lines that began crisscrossing the nation after the Civil War. By linking the nation, railroads increased the markets for many products, spurring American industrial growth. Railroads also stimulated the economy by spending huge amounts of money on steel, coal, timber, and other materials.

Hundreds of small, unconnected railroads had been built before the Civil War. Gradually, however, large rail lines took them over. By 1890, for example, the Pennsylvania Railroad had consolidated 73 smaller companies. Eventually, seven giant systems with terminals in major cities and scores of branches

Additional Support

Interdisciplinary Activity: Language Arts

Tell students that most large industries have their own specialized terms that are used on the job. Have interested students create a lexicon of terms used by railroad workers. Tell them that the lexicon should include the pronunciation and solid working definitions for each term. For at least two of the terms, students should also include a drawing or diagram for further explanation. OL

NATIONAL GEOGRAPHIC **Federal Land Grants to Railroads, 1870**

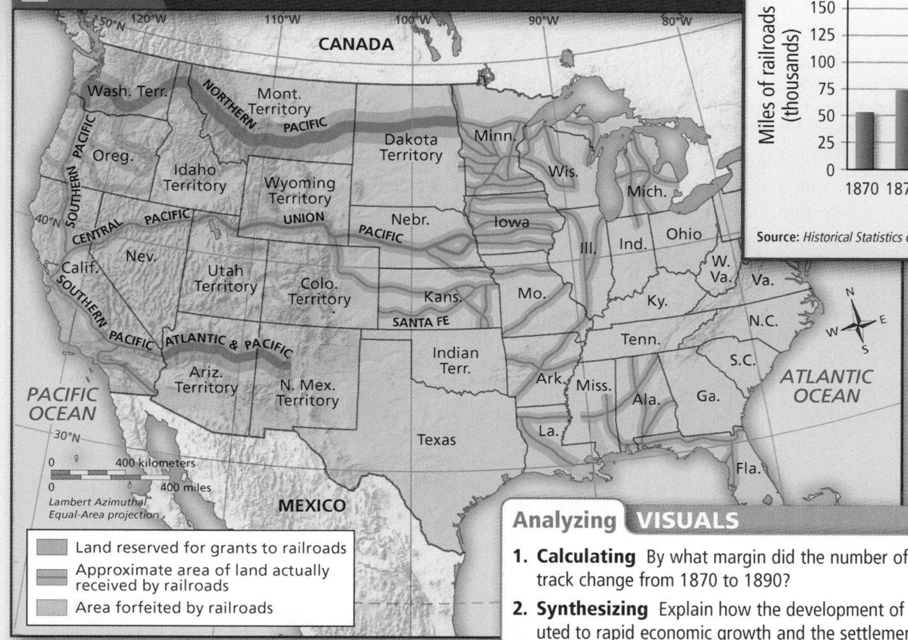

Miles of Track, 1870–1890

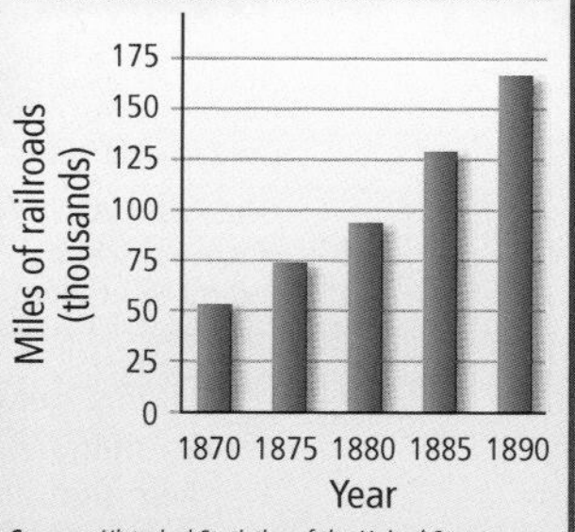

Source: *Historical Statistics of the United States.*

Analyzing VISUALS

1. **Calculating** By what margin did the number of miles of laid track change from 1870 to 1890?
2. **Synthesizing** Explain how the development of railroads contributed to rapid economic growth and the settlement of the West.

reaching into the countryside controlled most rail traffic.

One of the most successful railroad consolidators was **Cornelius Vanderbilt.** By 1869, Vanderbilt had purchased and merged three short New York railroads to form the New York Central, running from New York City to Buffalo. Within four years he had extended his control over lines all the way to Chicago, which enabled him to offer the first direct rail service between New York City and Chicago. In 1871 Vanderbilt began building New York's Grand Central Terminal.

Before the 1880s each community set its clocks by the sun's position at noon. Having many local time zones interfered with train scheduling, however, and at times even threatened passenger safety. When two trains traveled on the same track, collisions could result from scheduling errors caused by variations in time. To make rail service safer and more reliable, the American Railway Association divided the country into four **time zones** in 1883. The federal government ratified this change in 1918.

Meanwhile, new locomotive technology and the invention of air brakes enabled railroads to put longer and heavier trains on their lines. When combined with large, **integrated** railroad systems, operations became so efficient that the average rate per mile for a ton of freight dropped from two cents in 1860 to three-quarters of a cent in 1900. R

The nationwide rail network also helped unite Americans in different regions. The *Omaha Daily Republican* observed in 1883 that railroads had "made the people of the country homogeneous, breaking through the peculiarities and provincialisms which marked separate and unmingling sections." This was a bit of an overstatement, but it recognized that railroads were changing American society.

Reading Check **Explaining** Why was the country divided into four time zones?

R Reading Strategy

Using Context Clues Have students reread the first full paragraph in column two on this page. Using clue words and phrases such as "combined" and "railroad systems," ask students to define the term *integrated.* Students should note that the term means "to join together" or "to unify." BL

Analyzing VISUALS

Answers:

1. about 110,000
2. Railroads brought settlers and goods west cheaply and efficiently.

Reading Check

Answer:
to make rail service safer and more reliable

Additional Support

Extending the Content

Time Zones Opponents of standard time called local time "God's time" because it was based on the laws of nature—the sun's position in the sky—rather than on human criteria. They referred to standard time as "railroad time," and blocked attempts to create time zones. Not until 1918 was Congress able to pass a law that standardized time zones.

D Differentiated Instruction

Visual/Spatial Have interested students use library or Internet resources to research an entrepreneur of today. Have the students use their findings to create a political cartoon satirizing or supporting the entrepreneur's efforts. Display the cartoons in the classroom. OL

Analyzing VISUALS

Answers:

1. Banker, inexperienced investor, small operator, and stockbroker; it implies that Gould has manipulated stock prices, which hurt small investors and businesses.
2. The four robber barons are enjoying themselves as they carve up the United States.

Robber Barons

MAIN Idea The government helped finance railroad construction by providing land grants, but this system also led to corruption.

HISTORY AND YOU Have you heard of any recent financial scandals? Read to learn how government grants led to large-scale corruption.

Building railroad lines often required more money than most private **investors** could raise on their own. To encourage railroad construction across the Great Plains, the federal government gave **land grants** to many railroad companies. The railroads then sold the land to settlers, real estate companies, and other businesses to raise money to build the railroad.

During the 1850s and 1860s, the federal land grant system gave railroad companies more than 120 million acres of public land, an area larger than New England, New York, and Pennsylvania combined. Several railroads, including the Union Pacific and Central Pacific, received enough land to cover most of the cost of building their lines.

The great wealth many railroad entrepreneurs acquired in the late 1800s led to accusations that they had built their fortunes by swindling investors and taxpayers, bribing officials, and cheating on their contracts and debts. Infamous for manipulating stock, **Jay Gould** was the most notoriously corrupt railroad owner.

Bribery occurred frequently, partly because government helped fund the railroads. Some investors quickly discovered that they could make more money by acquiring government land grants than by operating a railroad. To get more grants, some investors began bribing members of Congress.

POLITICAL CARTOONS PRIMARY SOURCE
The Robber Barons

D

▲ *Jay Gould bowls on Wall Street with balls labeled "Trickery," and "False Reports." The pins are labeled "Banker," "Inexperienced Investor," "Small Operator," and "Stock Broker."*

▲ *Railroad owners Jay Gould (lower left), Cornelius Vanderbilt (upper left), Russell Sage (upper right), and Cyrus W. Field (lower right) carve up the United States. The figure in back is lowering an envelope to European royalty labeled "Sealed proposals for the purchase of Europe."*

Analyzing VISUALS DBQ

1. **Analyzing Visuals** What "pins" has Jay Gould managed to knock down, and what does this suggest?
2. **Interpreting** What do the faces and actions of the five men in the cartoon suggest?

Additional Support

Activity: Collaborative Learning

Illustrated Time Lines Organize students into groups. Assign each group one of the following subjects: the development of the steam locomotive in the United States, custom Pullman cars, or the architecture of railroad terminals. Have groups use the Internet and library resources to do research and create an illustrated time line that details important events in the development of their assigned topic. Display the illustrated time lines in the classroom.

The Crédit Mobilier Scandal

Corruption in the railroad industry became public in 1872, when the **Crédit Mobilier** scandal erupted. Crédit Mobilier was a construction company set up by several stockholders of the Union Pacific Railroad, including Oakes Ames, a member of Congress. Acting for both the Union Pacific and Crédit Mobilier, the investors signed contracts with themselves. Crédit Mobilier greatly overcharged Union Pacific and added miles to the railroad construction. Because the same investors controlled both companies, the railroad agreed to pay the inflated bills without questions.

By the time the Union Pacific railroad was completed, these investors had made millions of dollars, but the railroad itself had used up its federal grants and was almost bankrupt. To convince Congress to give the railroad more grants, Ames sold other members of Congress shares in the Union Pacific at a price well below their market value.

C During the election campaign of 1872, an angry associate of Ames sent a letter to the *New York Sun* listing the members of Congress who had accepted shares. The scandal led to an investigation that implicated several members of Congress, including Speaker of the House James G. Blaine and Representative James Garfield, who later became president. It also revealed that Vice President Schuyler Colfax had accepted stock from the railroad. Neither criminal nor civil charges were filed against anyone involved with Crédit Mobilier, however, nor did the scandal affect the outcome of the elections.

The Great Northern Railroad

The Crédit Mobilier scandal created the impression that all railroad entrepreneurs were "robber barons"—people who loot an industry and give nothing back. Some, like Jay Gould, deserved this reputation, but others did not.

James J. Hill was clearly no robber baron. Hill built and operated the Great Northern Railroad from Wisconsin and Minnesota in the East to Washington in the West, without any federal land grants or subsidies. He had carefully planned the railroad's route to pass close to established towns in the region.

To increase business, he offered low fares to settlers who homesteaded along his route. Later, he sold homesteads to the Norwegian and Swedish immigrants coming to the region. He then identified American products that were in demand in China, including cotton, textiles, and flour, and arranged to haul those goods to Washington for shipment to Asia. This enabled the railroad to earn money by hauling goods both east and west, instead of simply sending lumber and farm products east and coming back empty, as many other railroads did at that time. The Great Northern became the most successful transcontinental railroad and the only one that was not eventually forced into bankruptcy.

Reading Check **Describing** How was the Great Northern different from other railroads of its time?

Section 2 REVIEW

Vocabulary

1. **Explain** the significance of: Pacific Railway Act, Grenville Dodge, Leland Stanford, Cornelius Vanderbilt, time zone, land grant, Jay Gould, Crédit Mobilier, James J. Hill.

Main Ideas

2. **Describing** How did Grenville Dodge contribute to the economic growth of the United States in the late 1800s?
3. **Listing** Use a graphic organizer similar to the one below to list the different ways by which railroads were financed.

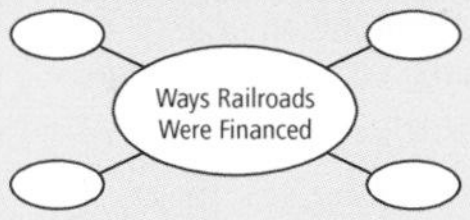

Critical Thinking

4. **Big Ideas** How did railroad expansion lead to industrial growth?
5. **Theorizing** Why might politicians be tempted to accept gifts of railroad stock? Why did Crédit Mobilier become a scandal?
6. **Analyzing Visuals** Examine the map and graph on page 419. Then make up a quiz of at least five questions based on the information presented.

Writing About History

7. **Persuasive Writing** Take on the role of an employee of a major railroad corporation. Your job is to write an advertisement to recruit workers for your corporation. After writing the advertisement, present it to your class.

History ONLINE
Study Central™ To review this section, go to glencoe.com and click on Study Central.

421

C Critical Thinking

Drawing Conclusions Remind students that the Crédit Mobilier scandal did not affect the outcome of the 1872 election. Have students recall more recent political scandals such as Watergate, Iran-Contra, or Whitewater. **Ask:** Do you think political scandals affect election outcomes? *(Answers will vary.)* **AL**

Assess

History ONLINE

Study Central™ provides summaries, interactive games, and online graphic organizers to help students review content.

Close

Summarizing Ask: What roles did "robber barons" play in the industrialization of the United States? *(Although many "robber barons" were ruthless in their tactics, they greatly expanded the nation's industry.)* **OL**

Reading Check

Answer:
It shipped goods both ways, operated without aid, and was a financial success.

Section 2 REVIEW

Answers

1. All definitions can be found in the section and the Glossary.
2. He supervised the Union Pacific's westward expansion.
3. land grants; private investment; gifts of public land to railroads; money generated by running the railroads
4. Railroads increased the markets for many products and great amounts of money were spent on resources.
5. to gain money and influence; It was a scandal because investors made millions of dollars, but the railroad was nearly bankrupt. To receive further grants from Congress, members of Congress were bribed with shares of the Union Pacific at below market value.
6. Students' questions will vary but should relate to the map and graph on page 419.
7. Students' advertisements will vary but should include a list of benefits for workers.

Focus

Bellringer

Daily Focus Transparency 12-3

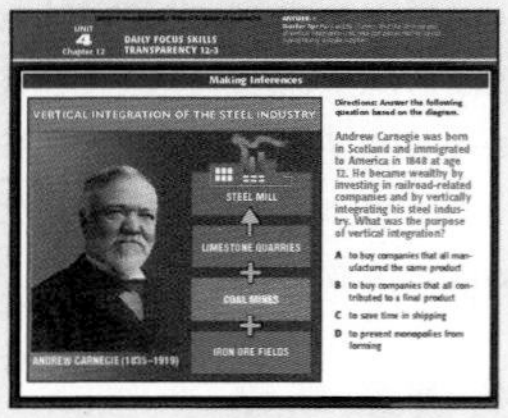

Guide to Reading

Answer: pools; vertical and horizontal integration; holding companies; trusts

Section Spotlight Video

To generate student interest and provide a springboard for class discussion, access the Chapter 12, Section 3 video at glencoe.com or on the video DVD.

Resource Manager

Section 3

Section Audio Spotlight Video

Big Business

Guide to Reading

Big Ideas

Economics and Society Business people such as Andrew Carnegie developed new ways to expand business.

Content Vocabulary

- corporation *(p. 422)*
- stock *(p. 422)*
- economies of scale *(p. 422)*
- pool *(p. 424)*
- vertical integration *(p. 425)*
- horizontal integration *(p. 425)*
- monopoly *(p. 425)*
- trust *(p. 426)*
- holding company *(p. 426)*

Academic Vocabulary

- distribution *(p. 422)*
- consumer *(p. 424)*

People and Events to Identify

- Andrew Carnegie *(p. 424)*
- John D. Rockefeller *(p. 425)*

Reading Strategy

Organizing As you read about the rise of corporations in the United States, complete a graphic organizer showing the steps large business owners took to weaken or eliminate competition.

Slashed prices temporarily → [ ] → [ ] → [ ]

Following the Civil War, large corporations developed that could consolidate various business functions and produce goods more efficiently. Retail stores began using advertising and mail-order catalogs to attract new consumers.

The Rise of Big Business

MAIN Idea Corporations could produce goods more efficiently, which allowed the rise of big business.

HISTORY AND YOU Do you own stock in a corporation or know someone who does? Read to learn why corporations issue stock.

Before the Civil War, most manufacturing enterprises were owned by just a few people working in partnership. Everything had changed by 1900. Big businesses dominated the economy, operating vast complexes of factories, warehouses, and **distribution** facilities.

Big business would not have been possible without the **corporation.** A corporation is an organization owned by many people but treated by law as though it were a person. It can own property, pay taxes, make contracts, and sue and be sued. The people who own the corporation are called stockholders because they own shares of ownership called **stock.** Issuing stock allows a corporation to raise large amounts of money for big projects while spreading out the financial risk.

Before the 1830s there were few corporations, because entrepreneurs had to convince a state legislature to issue them a charter. In the 1830s, however, states began passing general incorporation laws, allowing companies to become corporations and issue stock without charters from the legislature.

With the money they raised from the sale of stock, corporations could invest in new technologies, hire large workforces, and purchase many machines, greatly increasing their efficiency. This enabled them to achieve **economies of scale:** the cost of manufacturing is decreased by producing goods quickly in large quantities.

All businesses have two kinds of costs, fixed costs and operating costs. Fixed costs are costs a company has to pay, whether or not it is operating. For example, a company has to pay its loans, mortgages, and taxes, regardless of whether it is operating. Operating costs are costs that occur when running a company, such as paying wages and shipping costs and buying raw materials and supplies.

The small manufacturers that were common before the Civil War usually had low fixed costs but high operating costs. If sales dropped, it was cheaper to shut down temporarily. Big manufacturers,

R Reading Strategies	C Critical Thinking	D Differentiated Instruction	W Writing Support	S Skill Practice
Additional Resources • Guided Read., URB p. 82	**Teacher Edition** • Identify Issues, p. 424 • Draw Concl., p. 426 • Analyze Info., p. 427 **Additional Resources** • Interp. Political Cartoons, URB p. 73	**Additional Resources** • Reading Skills Act., URB p. 53	**Teacher Edition** • Descrip. Writing, p. 423 • Persuas. Writing, pp. 424, 425 **Additional Resources** • Supreme Court Case Studies, p. 29	**Additional Resources** • RENTG, p. 135 • Quizzes/Tests, p. 167

INFOGRAPHIC

Types of Business Organizations

	Sole proprietorship	Partnership	Corporation
Who owns the business?	One person owns the business and often manages it	Two or more people own and manage the business	All investors who own its stock; managers are hired
How is money raised?	Owner uses savings and borrows money from a bank	Partners each invest some of their own money and borrow money from a bank	Shares of stock are sold to finance business; bank loans are also used
Advantages	Easy to start Low fixed costs, as facilities are usually small and inexpensive to maintain	Partners share responsibility for running the business Low fixed costs	Limited liability for investors Low operating costs; can stay open if economy slows
Disadvantages	Difficult to raise money; limited opportunities for growth; owner has unlimited liability; high operating costs may force business to shut down if the economy is weak	Partners may disagree on direction the company should take; owners have unlimited liability High operating costs	Often have high fixed costs because of size of facilities and equipment needed

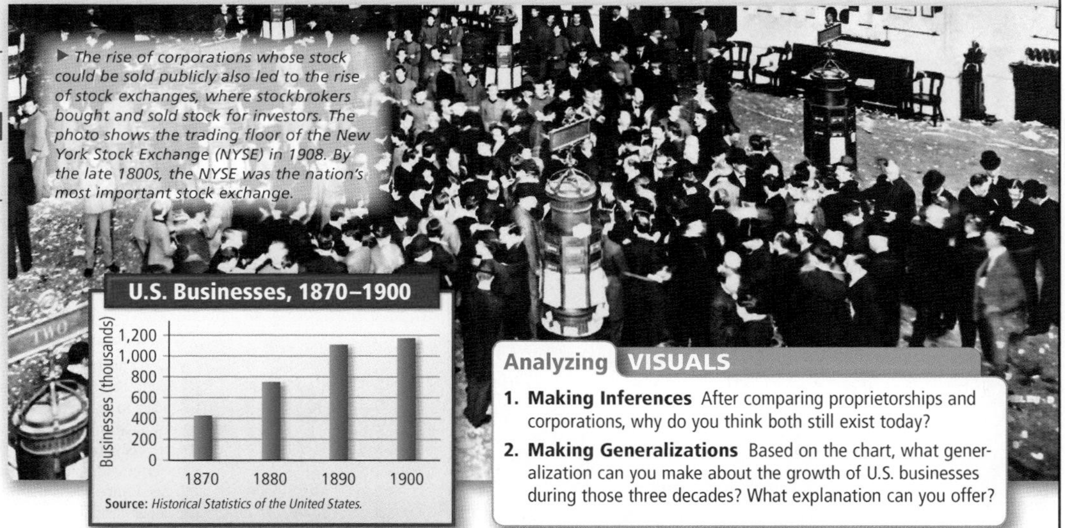

▶ The rise of corporations whose stock could be sold publicly also led to the rise of stock exchanges, where stockbrokers bought and sold stock for investors. The photo shows the trading floor of the New York Stock Exchange (NYSE) in 1908. By the late 1800s, the NYSE was the nation's most important stock exchange.

Source: *Historical Statistics of the United States.*

Analyzing VISUALS

1. **Making Inferences** After comparing proprietorships and corporations, why do you think both still exist today?
2. **Making Generalizations** Based on the chart, what generalization can you make about the growth of U.S. businesses during those three decades? What explanation can you offer?

however, had the high fixed costs of building and maintaining a factory. Compared to their fixed costs, the operating costs of big businesses were low. Operating costs, such as wages, were such a small part of a corporation's costs that it made sense to continue operating, even in a recession.

In these circumstances, big corporations had several advantages. They could produce more goods cheaply and efficiently. They could continue to operate in poor economic times by cutting prices to increase sales rather than shutting down. Many were also able to negotiate rebates from the railroads, further lowering their operating costs.

Small businesses with high operating costs found it difficult to compete with large corporations, and many were forced out of business. At the time, many people criticized corporations for cutting prices and negotiating rebates. They believed the corporations were behaving unethically by driving small companies out of business. In many cases, it was the changing nature of business organization and the new importance of fixed costs that caused competition to become so severe and led to so many small companies going out of business.

✓ Reading Check **Describing** What factors led to the rise of big business in the United States?

Teach

W Writing Support

Descriptive Writing Have students find out about the New York Stock Exchange. Have students write two paragraphs describing the activities on the floor of the exchange. Encourage students to share their descriptions with the class. BL

Analyzing VISUALS

Answers:

1. Both sole proprietorships and corporations are viable ways of organizing a business, and each fills a different purpose in the nation's economy.
2. The number of businesses grew quickly between 1870 and 1890, but then the rate of increase slowed. Explanations may include that new restrictions were placed on businesses at the turn of the last century.

✓ **Reading Check**

Answer:
general incorporation laws and economies of scale

Hands-On Chapter Project
Step 3

Starting a Business

Step 3: Expanding the Business

Directions Returning to their groups, students should review the plans, lists, and flowcharts for their business. They should also assume that they have received the necessary capital and that, so far, their business is successful. Given their business's success, each group of business leaders now wants to expand the business by becoming more efficient, keeping costs low, and eliminating competition.

Using their textbook as well as library or Internet resources, each group should research what steps might be taken to expand or improve the business. For example, the group might decide that vertical or horizontal integration might be a useful way to expand the business. Alternatively, the group may decide to expand the business by building more factories and hiring more workers. Each group should make a final recommendation based on members' research.

Putting It Together Have volunteers from each group present the group's recommendation to the class. Discuss with the class the pros and cons of the various recommendations. Have the class hypothesize which recommendations are likely to be the most successful. OL

(Chapter Project continued on page 429)

C Critical Thinking

Identifying Central Issues Remind students that the pools received no support from state legislatures and no protection from American courts. **Ask:** Why did legislatures and the courts see pools as suspect? *(Because pools interfered with competition and property rights)* **AL**

W Writing Support

Persuasive Writing Have students assume the role of an assistant to Andrew Carnegie and write a memo to Carnegie attempting to persuade him to adopt the Bessemer process. **OL**

Did You Know?

Steel Output In 1898, although Carnegie's steel output had increased threefold over the previous few years, the number of workers needed to produce the steel had decreased by 400. The use of electricity to drive machinery was largely responsible for the decline in the workforce.

Additional Support

Consolidating Industry

MAIN Idea Business leaders devised new and larger forms of business organizations and new ways to promote their products.

HISTORY AND YOU How does advertising reach you today? How has technology created new ways to market and sell goods? Read to learn how an increase in new products led to new selling methods.

Many business leaders did not like the intense competition that had been forced on them. Although falling prices benefited **consumers,** they cut into profits. To stop prices from falling, many companies organized **pools,** or agreements, to keep prices at a certain level.

American courts and legislatures were suspicious of pools because they interfered with competition and property rights. As a result, companies that formed pools had no legal protection and could not enforce their agreements in court. Pools generally did not last long anyway. They broke apart whenever one member cut prices to steal the market share from another. By the 1870s, competition had reduced many industries to a few large and highly efficient corporations.

W Andrew Carnegie and Steel

The remarkable life of **Andrew Carnegie** illustrates many of the factors that led to the rise of big business in the United States. Born in Scotland, Carnegie was the son of a poor hand weaver who moved to the United States in 1848. At age 12, Carnegie went to work as a bobbin boy in a textile factory earning $1.20 per week. After two years, he became a messenger in a telegraph office, then worked as secretary to Thomas Scott, a superintendent and, later, president of the Pennsylvania Railroad. Carnegie's energy impressed Scott, and when Scott was promoted, Carnegie became the new superintendent.

As a railroad supervisor, Carnegie knew that he could make a lot of money by investing in companies that served the railroad industry. He bought shares in iron mills and factories that made sleeping cars and locomotives. He also invested in a company that built railroad bridges. By his early 30s, he was earning $50,000 per year and decided to quit his job to concentrate on his own business investments.

As part of his business activities, Carnegie frequently traveled to Europe. On one trip, he

INFOGRAPHIC
The Rise of the Steel Industry

Activity: Interdisicplinary Connection

Debate Divide students into groups. Have the groups form opinions as to whether big business should or should not be allowed to function without restraints on size, competition, hiring policies, ways of obtaining investment capital, and so on. Have groups do additional research using library sources and the Internet to support the chosen opinion. Have students from opposing sides debate. As a class, decide which group presented the more convincing argument.

met Sir Henry Bessemer, who had invented a new process for making high-quality steel efficiently and cheaply. After meeting Bessemer, Carnegie opened a steel company in Pittsburgh in 1875 and began using the Bessemer process. Carnegie often boasted about how cheaply he could produce steel:

PRIMARY SOURCE

"Two pounds of iron stone mined upon Lake Superior and transported nine hundred miles to Pittsburgh; one pound and one-half of coal mined and manufactured into coke, and transported to Pittsburgh; one-half pound of lime, mined and transported to Pittsburgh; a small amount of manganese ore mined in Virginia and brought to Pittsburgh—and these four pounds of materials manufactured into one pound of steel, for which the consumer pays one cent."

—quoted in *The Growth of the American Republic*

To make his company more efficient, Carnegie began the **vertical integration** of the steel industry. A vertically integrated company owns all of the different businesses on which it depends for its operation. Instead of paying companies for coal, lime, and iron, Carnegie's steel company bought coal mines, limestone quarries, and iron ore fields. Vertical integration saved money and enabled many companies to become even bigger.

Rockefeller and Standard Oil W

Successful business leaders also pushed for **horizontal integration,** or combining firms in the same business into one large corporation. Horizontal integration took place as companies competed. When a company began to lose market share, it would often sell out to competitors to create a larger organization.

Perhaps the most famous industrialist who achieved almost complete horizontal integration of his industry is **John D. Rockefeller.** When oil was discovered in Pennsylvania, many entrepreneurs started drilling for oil, hoping to strike it rich. Rockefeller decided to build oil refineries instead. By 1870, his company, Standard Oil, was the nation's largest oil refiner. He then began buying out his competitors. By 1880, the company controlled about 90 percent of the oil-refining industry in the United States. When a single company achieves control of an entire market, it becomes a **monopoly.**

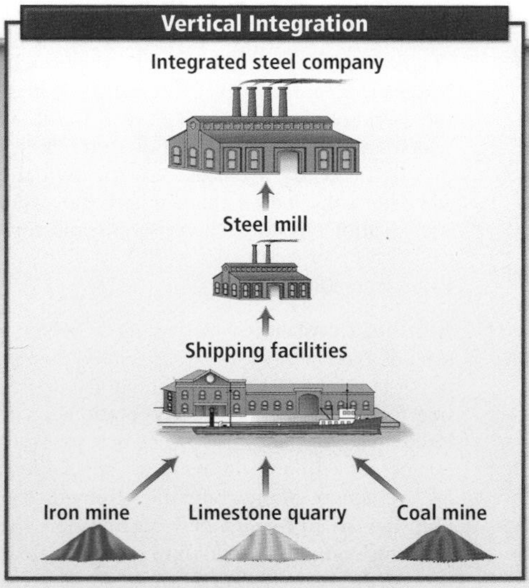

▲ *In a vertically integrated industry, a company owns all parts of the industrial process. In this case, a steel company owns the iron and coal mines, the limestone quarries, and the ships and trains that move the materials, as well as the steel mills.*

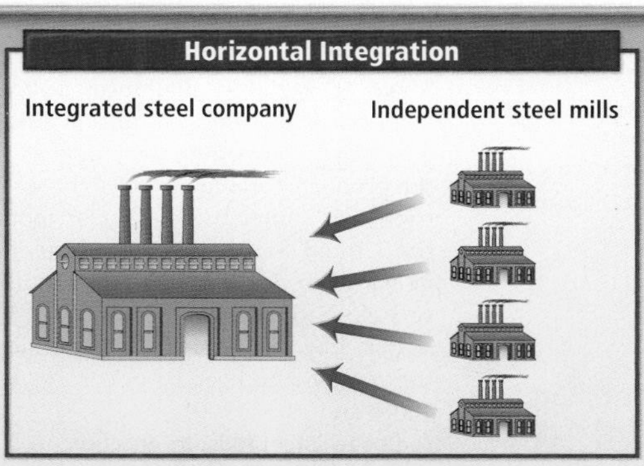

▲ *When one company grows by buying up its competitors, it is using horizontal integration to expand.*

Analyzing VISUALS

1. **Analyzing Visuals** What enabled entrepreneurs such as Andrew Carnegie to build large steel factories?
2. **Explaining** Why did business owners want to vertically integrate their companies?

W Writing Support

Persuasive Writing Have interested students use library or Internet resources to find out more information about Standard Oil. Then have students write a one-page letter to John D. Rockefeller attempting to persuade him to sell off parts of Standard Oil. Remind students to be persuasive in their reasoning. Encourage students to share their letters with the class. **OL**

Analyzing VISUALS

Answers:

1. Carnegie grew rich from his businesses and thus had the capital to buy his competitors.
2. They could control all aspects of the business and thus keep costs low.

Additional Support

Teacher Tip

Collaborative Learning This activity requires students to do research, write, and illustrate. The activity allows students with different levels of academic skill to work together. As you form groups, consider the needed skills and choose students accordingly.

Activity: Collaborative Learning

Conflicting Evidence Ask: Are monopolies bad for consumers? *(Answers will vary, but students should support their viewpoints with examples.)* Organize the class into small groups. Have each group use library or Internet resources to find out more information about monopolies or near monopolies that have existed in American business. Have each group analyze its findings and write a report on its conclusions. Each group should also illustrate its findings with maps, drawings, or dioramas. **OL**

C Critical Thinking

Drawing Conclusions Trusts and holding companies became widespread ways of business organization in the 1880s.

Ask: Are trusts and holding companies good for America's consumers? Have students use library or Internet resources to find out more information about trusts and holding companies. Then have them write a brief essay explaining their findings. Remind students that their essay should reach a conclusion supporting their viewpoint. **AL**

People IN HISTORY

Answers:

Rockefeller: Rockefeller invested in the newest, most efficient refining methods; he used ruthless business tactics; he organized the Standard Oil Trust.

Morgan: Morgan tried to make the railroad industry more efficient.

Additional Support

People IN HISTORY

John D. Rockefeller
1839–1937

John Davison Rockefeller was one of the foremost industrialists of the late 1800s. Born in upstate New York, Rockefeller moved with his family to Cleveland, Ohio, as a teenager. As a young man, he established a grain and livestock business that made huge profits during the Civil War.

Meanwhile, Cleveland had emerged as a center for refining the oil extracted from the oil fields of western Pennsylvania. In 1863 Rockefeller used his wartime profits to start an oil-refining company. He then began buying up other oil refineries. In 1870 Rockefeller and some associates founded the Standard Oil Company. Rockefeller invested in the newest and most efficient refining technology. He also became known for using ruthless tactics to get preferential shipping rates from railroad companies and acquire competing oil refineries.

By the early 1880s, Rockefeller had created the Standard Oil Trust. With a near-monopoly on American oil refining, Standard Oil made Rockefeller one of the richest men in the world. Rockefeller later donated much of his wealth to philanthropic causes, most notably funding colleges and universities.

What made Standard Oil so successful?

J. P. Morgan
1837–1913

John Pierpont Morgan, the most powerful and influential financier of his era, built a financial empire that became known as the "House of Morgan." The son of a successful Boston banker, Morgan began his career working in the New York City branch of his father's bank.

Morgan soon developed a reputation for shrewd business sense. He specialized in financing railroads, an industry plagued by cut-throat competition and instability. Before Morgan would agree to rescue a troubled railroad company, he insisted the company reorganize to become more efficient, combine smaller railway lines to create a larger coordinated railroad system, and agree to have a representative from Morgan's firm oversee future decisions.

During the depression of the 1890s, Morgan used his immense fortune to finance a bond to rescue the federal government's depleted gold reserve. In 1901 Morgan made history when he organized the first billion-dollar corporation, U.S. Steel, by merging the Carnegie Steel Company and several other steel companies.

How did Morgan try to help the railroad industry?

New Business Organizations

Many Americans feared monopolies because they believed that a monopoly could charge whatever it wanted for its products. Others, however, believed that monopolies had to keep prices low because raising prices would encourage competitors to reappear and offer the products for a lower price. In some industries, one company had a near-monopoly in the United States but was competing on a global scale. Standard Oil, for example, came very close to having a monopoly in the United States, but international competition forced the company to keep its prices low in the late 1800s and early 1900s.

In the late 1800s, in an effort to stop horizontal integration and the rise of monopolies, many states made it illegal for one company to own stock in another company. It did not take long, however, for companies to discover ways around the laws.

Trusts In 1882 Standard Oil formed the first **trust,** a new way of merging businesses that did not violate such laws. A trust is a legal arrangement that allows one person to manage another person's property. The person who manages that property is called a trustee.

Instead of buying a company outright, Standard Oil had stockholders give their stocks to a group of Standard Oil trustees. In exchange, the stockholders received shares in the trust, which entitled them to a portion of the trust's profits. Since the trustees did not own the stock but were merely managing it, they were not violating any laws. The trustees could control a group of companies as if they were one large, merged company.

Holding Companies Beginning in 1889, the state of New Jersey further accelerated the rise of big business with a new general incorporation law. This law allowed corporations chartered in New Jersey to own stock in other businesses without any need for special legislative action. Many companies immediately used the law to create a new organization, the **holding company.** A holding company does not produce anything itself. Instead, it owns the stock of companies that do produce goods. The holding company manages the companies it owns, effectively merging them into one large enterprise.

Activity: Interdisciplinary Connection

Economics Invite a representative from the Small Business Administration to speak to the class about the impact of small businesses on the community. Ask the speaker to address the basics of how one goes about setting up a small business. As a class, discuss the various ways to finance a business.

Investment Banking Another increase in the size of corporations began in the mid-1890s, when investment bankers began to help put new holding companies together. Perhaps the most famous and successful investment banker of the era was J. P. Morgan. John Pierpont Morgan began his career in 1857 as an agent for his father's banking company in New York, America's financial capital. Investment bankers like Morgan specialized in helping companies issue stock. Companies would sell large blocks of stock to investment bankers at a discount. The bankers would then find people willing to buy the stock and sell it for a profit.

In the mid-1890s, investment bankers became interested in selling stock in holding companies that merged many of America's already large corporations. In 1901, J. P. Morgan bought out Andrew Carnegie. Morgan then merged Carnegie Steel with other large steel companies into an enormous holding company called the United States Steel Company. U.S. Steel, worth $1.4 billion, was the first billion-dollar company in American history. By 1904, the United States had 318 holding companies. Together, these giant corporations controlled over 5,300 factories and were worth more than $7 billion.

Selling the Product

The creation of giant manufacturing companies in the United States forced retailers—companies that sell products directly to consumers—to expand in size as well. The vast array of products that American industries produced led retailers to look for new ways to attract consumers. N. W. Ayer and Son, the first advertising company, began creating large illustrated ads instead of relying on the old small print line ads previously used in newspapers. By 1900, retailers were spending over $90 million a year on advertising in newspapers and magazines.

Advertising attracted readers to the newest retail business, the department store. In 1877 advertisements billed John Wanamaker's new Philadelphia department store, the Grand Depot, as the "largest space in the world devoted to retail selling on a single floor." When it opened, only a handful of department stores existed in the United States; soon hundreds sprang up. Department stores provided a huge selection of products in one large, elegant building. The store atmosphere made shopping seem glamorous and exciting.

Chain stores, a group of retail outlets owned by the same company, first appeared in the mid-1800s. In contrast to department stores, which offered many services, chain stores focused on offering low prices. Woolworth's, which opened in 1879, became one of the most successful retail chains in American history. **C**

To reach the millions of people who lived in rural areas far from chain stores or department stores, retailers began issuing mail-order catalogs. Two of the largest mail-order retailers were Montgomery Ward and Sears, Roebuck and Co. Their huge catalogs, widely distributed through the mail, used attractive illustrations and appealing descriptions to advertise thousands of items for sale.

Reading Check **Explaining** What techniques did corporations use to consolidate their industries?

Section 3 REVIEW

Vocabulary

1. **Explain** the significance of: corporation, stock, economies of scale, pool, Andrew Carnegie, vertical integration, horizontal integration, John D. Rockefeller, monopoly, trust, holding company.

Main Ideas

2. **Stating** Why did the number of corporations increase in the late 1800s?
3. **Comparing** Use a graphic organizer to list ways business leaders in the 1800s tried to eliminate competition.

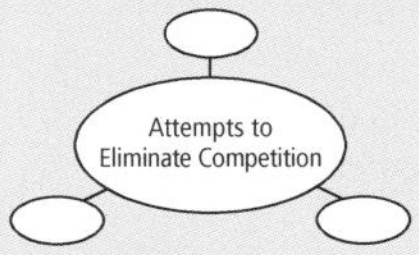

Critical Thinking

4. **Big Ideas** What techniques were used by Carnegie and others to consolidate their industries? How did state governments respond?
5. **Forming an Opinion** Do you think an individual today can rise from "rags to riches" like Andrew Carnegie did? Why or why not?
6. **Analyzing Visuals** Look again at the chart on page 423. During which decade did the number of U.S. businesses increase the most? By how many?

Writing About History

7. **Expository Writing** Write a newspaper editorial in which you explain why entrepreneurs were a positive or a negative force on the U.S. economy in the late 1800s.

History ONLINE
Study Central™ To review this section, go to glencoe.com and click on Study Central.

C Critical Thinking

Analyzing Information Have students name chain stores and describe the types of items available for sale in those stores. **Ask:** How do chain stores serve consumers in their community? *(Chain stores provide a wide variety of goods in one location.)* **OL**

Reading Check

Answer:
pools, vertical and horizontal integration, monopolies, trusts, and holding companies

Assess

History ONLINE

Study Central™ provides summaries, interactive games, and online graphic organizers to help students review content.

Close

Identifying Central Issues As a class, discuss how large corporations came to dominate American business. Have students write an essay in which they address whether large corporations have helped or hindered the American economy.

Section 3 REVIEW

Answers

1. All definitions can be found in the section and the Glossary.
2. Companies were allowed to incorporate without getting a state charter; companies sold stock and, with the profits, were able to achieve economies of scale that smaller companies could not.
3. pools; trusts; monopolies; vertical and horizontal integration
4. Pools, trusts, monopolies, vertical and horizontal integration; many states made it illegal for one company to own stock in another company.
5. Students' answers will vary but should be supported.
6. during the 1870s; about 27,000
7. Editorials should incorporate clear arguments.

Focus

Bellringer

Daily Focus Transparency 12-4

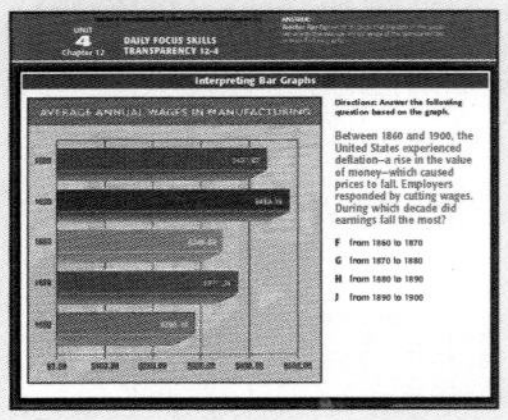

Guide to Reading

Answers:
1877—Great Railroad Strike: involves 80,000 workers; police, state militias, and federal troops break up strike; millions of dollars in damage; more than 100 people killed
1886—Haymarket Riot: weakens the Knights of Labor
1894—Pullman Strike: nearly paralyzes the economy; federal troops force end to strike; federal court issued an injunction to halt the boycott

Section Spotlight Video

To generate student interest and provide a springboard for class discussion, access the Chapter 12, Section 4 video at glencoe.com or on the video DVD.

Resource Manager

R Reading Strategies	C Critical Thinking	D Differentiated Instruction	W Writing Support	S Skill Practice
Additional Resources • Pri. Source Reading, URB pp. 67, 69 • Guided Read., URB p. 83 • Supreme Court Cases, p. 25	**Teacher Edition** • Compare/Contrast, pp. 430, 434 • Analyz. Pri. Sources, p. 431 • Make Inferences, p. 432 • Analyz. Info., p. 433 • Drawing Concl., p. 435 **Additional Resources** • Critical Thinking Skills, URB p. 64	**Teacher Edition** • Visual/Spatial, p. 429 **Additional Resources** • Diff. Instruction, URB p. 55 • Reteaching Act., URB p. 75	**Teacher Edition** • Descrip. Writing, pp. 429, 432, 433, 434 • Persuas. Writing, pp. 431, 435	**Additional Resources** • Authentic Assess., p. 29 • RENTG, p. 138 • Quizzes/Tests, p. 168

Section 4

Section Audio   Spotlight Video

Unions

Guide to Reading

Big Ideas
Struggles for Rights Unions grew and labor unrest intensified as workers fought for more rights.

Content Vocabulary
- deflation *(p. 428)*
- trade union *(p. 429)*
- industrial union *(p. 429)*
- blacklist *(p. 429)*
- lockout *(p. 430)*
- arbitration *(p. 432)*
- injunction *(p. 433)*
- closed shop *(p. 434)*

Academic Vocabulary
- restraint *(p. 430)*
- constitute *(p. 435)*

People and Events to Identify
- Marxism *(p. 430)*
- Knights of Labor *(p. 432)*
- American Federation of Labor *(p. 434)*
- Samuel Gompers *(p. 434)*

Reading Strategy
Sequencing As you read about the increase of American labor unions in the late 1800s, complete a time line similar to the one below by filling in the incidents of labor unrest discussed and the results of each incident.

Workers tried to form unions in the late 1800s, hoping to improve wages, hours, and working conditions. Business leaders were willing to deal with some trade unions but generally opposed industrial unions. Many strikes in this era led to violence, which hurt the image of unions and slowed their growth.

Working in the United States

MAIN Idea Low wages, long hours, and difficult working conditions caused resentment among workers and led to efforts to organize unions.

HISTORY AND YOU Have you ever felt that you were underpaid for an after-school job? Read about the conditions that made workers want to organize.

Life for workers in industrial America was difficult. Many workers had to perform dull, repetitive tasks in working conditions that were often unhealthy and dangerous. Workers breathed in lint, dust, and toxic fumes. Heavy machines lacking safety devices caused many injuries. Despite the difficult working conditions, industrialism led to a dramatic rise in the standard of living. The average worker's wages rose by 50 percent between 1860 and 1890. Nonetheless, the uneven division of income between the wealthy and the working class caused resentment among workers. In 1900 the average industrial worker made 22¢ per hour and worked 59 hours per week.

Deflation, or a rise in the value of money, added to tensions between workers and employers. Between 1865 and 1897, deflation caused prices to fall, which increased the buying power of workers' wages. Although companies cut wages regularly in the late 1800s, prices fell even faster, so that wages were actually still going up in buying power. Workers, however, resented getting less money. Eventually, many concluded that they needed a union to bargain for them in order to get higher wages and better working conditions.

Early Unions

There were two basic types of industrial workers in the United States in the 1800s—craft workers and common laborers. Craft workers had special skills and training. They included machinists, iron molders, stonecutters, shoemakers, printers, and many others. Craft workers received higher wages and had more control over how they organized their time. Common laborers had few skills and received lower wages.

PRIMARY SOURCE

Why Did Workers Want to Organize?

In 1893 a recession hit the United States; by 1894, millions of workers were unemployed and over 750,000 were on strike. A former quarry foreman named Jacob Coxey organized unemployed workers and began a march on Washington to demand jobs on public works projects. The marchers were known as "Coxey's Army."

▲ Whether they were working in Western silver mines (top photo) or handling hot steel at a Pittsburgh foundry (above), workers toiled in unsafe conditions for very little money.

Annual Nonfarm Earnings

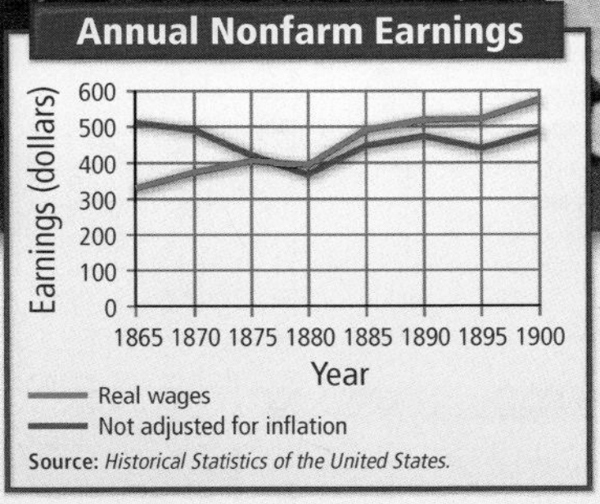

Source: *Historical Statistics of the United States.*

Analyzing VISUALS

1. **Analyzing** What do you observe about the working conditions and equipment of the men in both of the inset photos?
2. **Contrasting** What happened to real wages and those not adjusted for inflation between 1865 and 1900? Given this fact, why do you think workers wanted to organize?

In the 1830s, as industrialization began to spread, craft workers began to form **trade unions.** By 1873 there were 32 national trade unions in the United States. Among the largest and most successful were the Iron Molders' International Union, the International Typographical Union, and the Knights of St. Crispin—the shoemakers' union.

Industry Opposes Unions Employers often had to negotiate with trade unions because they represented workers whose skills they needed. However, employers generally viewed unions as conspiracies that interfered with property rights. Business leaders particularly opposed **industrial unions,** which united all workers in a particular industry.

Companies used several techniques to stop workers from forming unions. They required workers to take oaths or sign contracts promising not to join a union. They hired detectives to identify union organizers. Workers who tried to organize a union or strike were fired and placed on a **blacklist**—a list of "troublemakers"—so that no company would hire them. W

Teach

D Differentiated Instruction

Visual/Spatial Organize students into groups of four and have each group create a collage of workers today. They should show how working conditions are different or similar to working conditions in the late 1800s. OL

W Writing Support

Descriptive Writing Have students find out more about the practices that industries used against unionized workers. Then have students write a letter to the editor explaining why they believe that being blacklisted is unfair. OL

Analyzing VISUALS

Answers:

1. Working conditions are poor.
2. Real wages increased even though actual wages decreased. Workers wanted to organize because they were being paid less.

Hands-On Chapter Project
Step 4

Starting a Business

Step 4: Negotiating With a Union

Directions Have students return to their groups. Each group should assume that their business is successful and that the business owners are making a good profit. The business's workers have joined a union and are now asking for improvements such as better benefits, a shorter work week, and higher wages.

Using their textbook as well as library or Internet resources, have each group make a list of their workers' specific demands. Groups should include a rationale from the workers' viewpoint for each request.

Next, each group should review and evaluate the list of the workers' demands; have the group determine if the business will accept, reject, or attempt to compromise on each point. Remind the groups that each worker's demand will likely cost money, thus reducing the profitability of the business. The group should also provide a rationale for each of the business's decisions.

Putting It Together Have a volunteer from each group present to the class the list of workers' demands and the business's responses. Discuss what might happen if a compromise between the business and the workers cannot be reached. After the class discussion, groups may want to reconvene to reevaluate the business's decisions.

(Chapter Project continued on the Visual Summary page.)

C Critical Thinking

Comparing and Contrasting Organize students into pairs. Have one student in each pair use library and Internet resources to find out more information about Karl Marx and his views on communism; have the second student in each pair find out more about Adam Smith and capitalism. Have students create a chart comparing and contrasting the differences of each man's philosophy. Have pairs of students present their charts to the class. AL

Reading Check

Answer:
They associated unions with immigrants, revolution, and anarchy.

When workers formed a union, companies used **"lockouts"** to break it. They locked workers out of the property and refused to pay them. If the union called a strike, employers would hire replacements, or strikebreakers.

Political and Social Opposition Efforts to break unions often succeeded because there were no laws giving workers the right to form unions or requiring owners to negotiate with them. Courts frequently ruled that strikes were "conspiracies in **restraint** of trade," for which labor leaders might be fined or jailed.

Unions also suffered from the perception that they were un-American. In the 1800s, the ideas of Karl Marx, called **Marxism,** became very influential in Europe. Marx argued that the basic force shaping capitalist society was the class struggle between workers and owners. He believed that workers would eventually revolt, seize control of the factories, and overthrow the government.

Marxists claimed that after the revolution the government would seize all private property and create a socialist society where wealth was evenly divided. Eventually, Marx thought, the state would disappear, leaving a communist society where classes did not exist.

While many labor supporters agreed with Marx, a few supported anarchism. Anarchists believe that society does not need any government. At the time, some believed that with only a few acts of violence they could ignite a revolution to topple the government. In the late 1800s, anarchists assassinated government officials and set off bombs all across Europe, hoping to trigger a revolution.

During the same period, tens of thousands of European immigrants headed to America. Anti-immigrant feelings were already strong in the United States and, as people began to associate immigrant workers with radical ideas, they became suspicious of unions. These fears, and concerns for law and order, often led officials to use the courts, the police, and even the army to crush strikes and break up unions.

Reading Check **Identifying** Why were some Americans suspicious of unions?

INFOGRAPHIC

Working in the United States, 1870–1900

The status of the American economy played an important role in the development of unions. Although union membership rose dramatically by 1900, the willingness of people to join unions at any given time varied depending on how well the economy was doing.

Sources: *New Estimates of Union Membership; The Growth of American Trade Unions.*

Source: *The Great Republic.*

Leveled Activities

BL Guided Reading Activity, URB p. 83

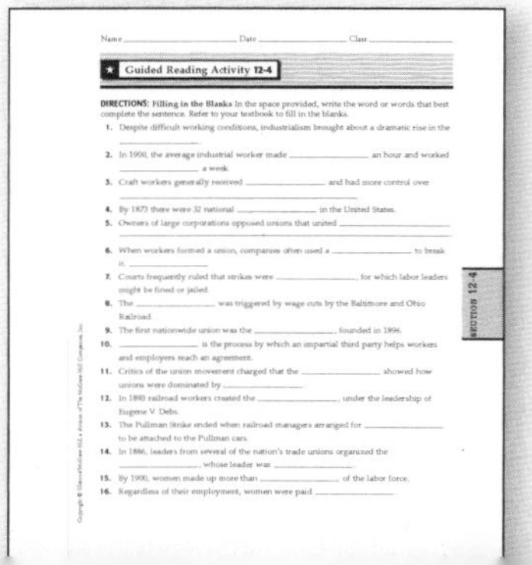

OL Critical Thinking Skills Activity, URB p. 64

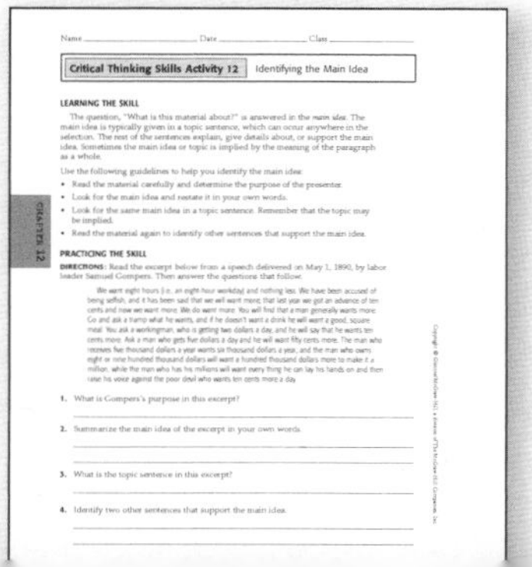

AL Primary Source Reading, URB pp. 67–70

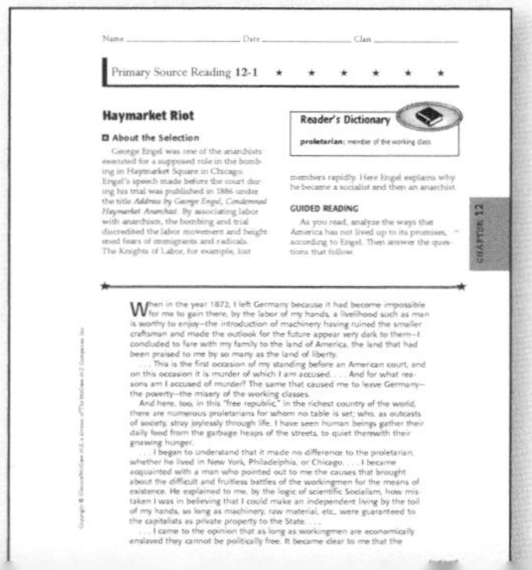

ELL Reading Essentials and Note-Taking Guide, p. 138

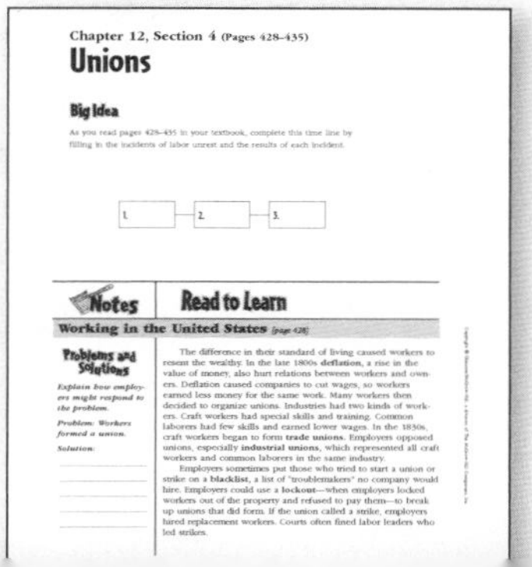

Struggling to Organize

MAIN Idea Workers began to form unions to fight for better wages and working conditions but had few successes.

HISTORY AND YOU Do you sometimes feel that you spend too many hours a day in school? Read to learn how workers sought an eight-hour workday.

Although workers attempted on many occasions to create large industrial unions, they rarely succeeded. In many cases the confrontations with owners and the government led to violence and bloodshed. In 1868 William Sylvis, president of the Iron Molders' Union, wrote to Karl Marx in support of his work and to express his own beliefs:

PRIMARY SOURCE

C "... monied power is fast eating up the substance of the people. We have made war upon it, and we mean to win it. If we can we will win through the ballot box; if not, we will resort to sterner means. A little bloodletting is sometimes necessary in desperate causes."

—quoted in *Industrialism and the American Worker*

The Great Railroad Strike W

The panic of 1873 was a severe recession that struck the American economy and forced many companies to cut wages. The economy had still not recovered when, in July 1877, the Baltimore and Ohio Railroad announced it was cutting wages, for the third time. In Martinsburg, West Virginia, workers walked off the job and blocked the tracks.

As word spread, railroad workers across the country walked off the job. The strike eventually involved 80,000 railroad workers and affected two-thirds of the nation's railways. Angry strikers smashed equipment, tore up tracks, and blocked rail service in New York, Baltimore, Pittsburgh, St. Louis, and Chicago. The governors of several states called out their militias. In many places, gun battles erupted between the militia and the strikers.

Declaring a state of "insurrection," President Hayes sent federal troops to Martinsburg, Baltimore, Pittsburgh, and elsewhere. It took 12 bloody days for police, state militias, and

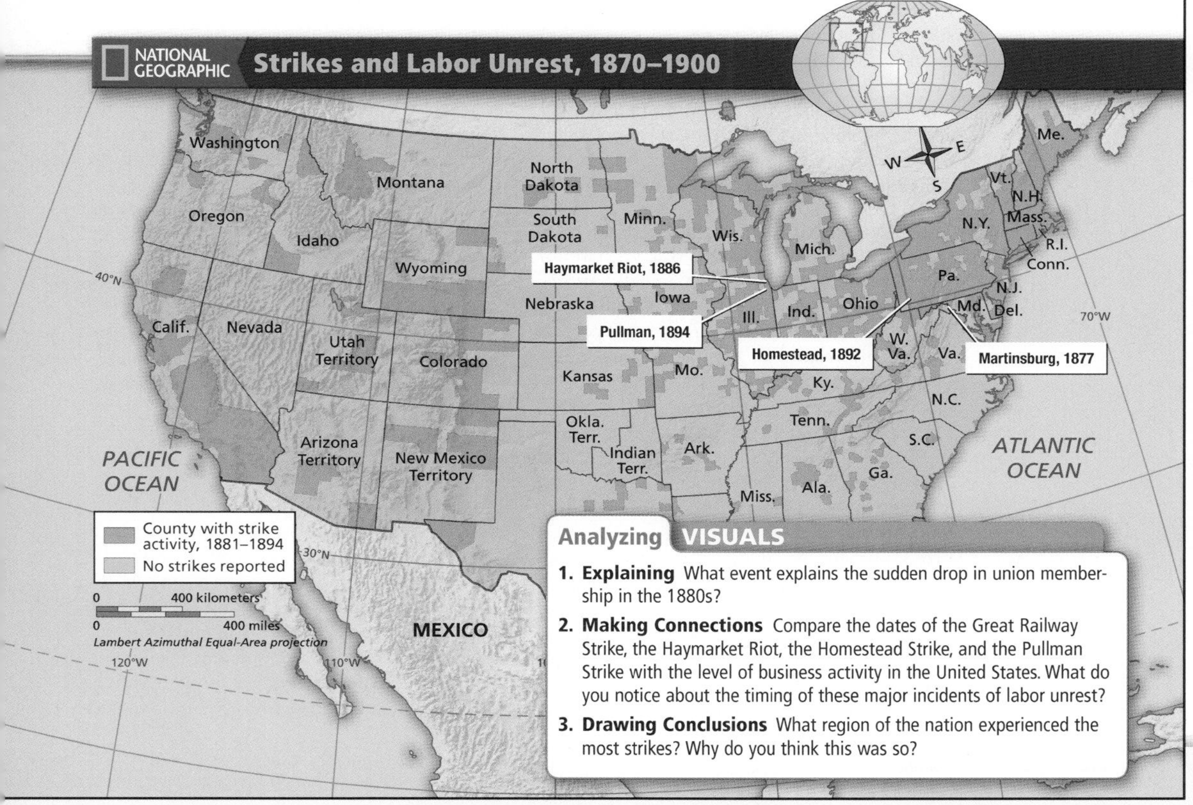

Analyzing VISUALS

1. **Explaining** What event explains the sudden drop in union membership in the 1880s?
2. **Making Connections** Compare the dates of the Great Railway Strike, the Haymarket Riot, the Homestead Strike, and the Pullman Strike with the level of business activity in the United States. What do you notice about the timing of these major incidents of labor unrest?
3. **Drawing Conclusions** What region of the nation experienced the most strikes? Why do you think this was so?

C Critical Thinking

Analyzing Primary Sources Have students reread the primary source on this page. **Ask:** What methods does Karl Marx indicate that his followers will use to defeat the "monied power?" *(first the ballot, then revolution)* **OL**

W Writing Support

Persuasive Writing Have interested students assume the role of a striking railroad worker and write a one-paragraph letter to the editor of their local newspaper calling on other unionized workers to strike as a show of sympathy. The letters should provide solid reasons why other workers should join the strike. Encourage students to read their letters to the class. **BL**

Analyzing VISUALS

Answers:
1. the Haymarket Riot
2. Labor unrest increased during economic downturns.
3. the Northeast; because it was the most industrialized

Interdisciplinary Activity: Economics

Union Membership Have interested students use library or Internet resources to research the history of union membership from 1870 to the present day. Students should determine union membership at five-year intervals, beginning with 1870. Students should then make a bar graph using their data. Next have students choose one year shown on the graph; using additional resources, have students determine the state of the U.S. economy in that year. **Ask:** Does there seem to be a relationship between union membership and the state of the economy? *(Answers will vary, but in general, union membership tended to increase during times of economic hardship.)* **AL**

C Critical Thinking

Making Inferences Remind students that the Knights of Labor welcomed African American and female workers into its ranks. **Ask:** Why might the Knights of Labor and other early unions include all workers among its members? *(Early unions were looking for support from all workers.)* AL

W Writing Support

Descriptive Writing Have interested students use library or Internet resources to find out more about the Haymarket Riot, the Homestead Strike, or the Pullman Strike. Then have students write a one-page essay describing the conditions that caused the workers to strike. OL

Additional Support

federal troops to restore order. By the time the strike collapsed, more than 100 people lay dead, and over $10 million in railroad property had been destroyed. The violence of this strike alarmed many Americans and pointed to the need for more peaceful means to settle labor disputes.

The Knights of Labor

The **Knights of Labor,** founded in 1869, took a different approach to labor issues. Its leader, Terence Powderly, opposed strikes, preferring to use boycotts to pressure employers. The Knights of Labor also supported **arbitration,** a process in which a third party helps workers and employers reach an agreement. The Knights called for an eight-hour workday and supported equal pay for women, the abolition of child labor, and the creation of worker-owned factories. Unlike many organizations of the era, the Knights welcomed women and African Americans as members.

History ONLINE **Student Web Activity** Visit glencoe.com and complete the activity on the Homestead Strike.

Early Successes In the early 1880s, the Knights began to use strikes and were initially successful. After they convinced one of Jay Gould's railroads to reverse wage cuts in 1885, membership in the union soared. In less than one year, the Knights grew from 100,000 to 700,000 members. Then, in the spring of 1886, an event known as the Haymarket Riot undermined the Knights' reputation.

The Haymarket Riot In 1886 supporters of the eight-hour workday called for a nationwide strike on May 1st. On that date, strikes took place in many cities. In Chicago, the local Knights of Labor led a march of 80,000 people through the center of the city on that date. Over the next few days, nearly 70,000 workers went on strike across the city.

On May 3, police intervened to stop a fight on the picket line at the McCormick Harvesting Machine Company. The incident turned violent and police fired on the strikers, killing four. Afterward, a local anarchist group organized a meeting in Chicago's Haymarket Square to protest the shooting of the strikers.

On the evening of May 4, about 3,000 people gathered to hear the speeches. As the meeting began to break up, the police moved in to keep order. Someone threw a bomb, killing one officer and wounding six others. The police opened fire, and workers shot back. About 100 people, including nearly 70 police officers, were injured.

The police arrested eight people for the bombing. Seven were German immigrants and advocates of anarchism. The incident horrified people across the country. Although the evidence was weak, all eight men were convicted, and four were executed.

Critics long opposed to the union movement pointed to the Haymarket riot to claim that unions were dominated by dangerous radicals. One of the men arrested was a member of the Knights of Labor. This association hurt the Knights' reputation and, coupled with lost strikes, led to a steady decline in membership and influence.

The Homestead Strike

In the summer of 1892, another labor dispute led to bloodshed. A steel mill owned by Andrew Carnegie in Homestead, Pennsylvania, was managed by an anti-union business partner, Henry Clay Frick. The mill's employees belonged to the Amalgamated Association of Iron, Steel, and Tin Workers, the largest craft union in the country. When the union's contract was about to expire, Frick proposed to cut wages by 20 percent. He then locked employees out of the plant and arranged for the Pinkerton Detective Agency to bring in replacement workers.

When the Pinkertons and strikebreakers approached the plant on barges, the strikers refused to let them land. Gunfire followed. After 14 hours, several Pinkertons and strikers were dead, and dozens more were injured. The governor of Pennsylvania then ordered the militia to take control and protect the replacement workers. After four months, the strike collapsed.

The Pullman Strike

Under the leadership of Eugene V. Debs, railroad employees organized the American Railway Union (ARU) in 1893. As an industrial union, the ARU tried to organize all employees of the railroad industry. Among the workers the union organized were the employees of the Pullman Palace Car Company. The owner, George Pullman, had built a company town, Pullman, just outside of Chicago and required

Activity: Collaborative Learning

Debate For and Against Unions Divide students into two groups. Ask one group to act as the employers and have the group discuss what they would tell employees to keep them from joining a union. Ask the other group to act as union organizers and have the group discuss what they would tell workers about the advantages of joining a union. Have students from each group present their arguments. After the debates, discuss as a class the long-range economic and social effects of unions in the United States. OL

INFOGRAPHIC

Comparing Major Strikes

	Homestead Steel Strike, 1892	Pullman Railroad Strike, 1894	Lawrence Textile Strike, 1912
Conditions	Seeking to break the union, the Carnegie Steel Company rejects wage increase and proposes a 20% wage cut	Deep wage cuts without cuts in rent and food prices at company housing and company stores	Very low wages; high mortality among workers (many workers are young girls); extreme poverty among workers; strike begins after new wage cuts
Union	Amalgamated Association of Iron, Steel, and Tin Workers	American Railway Union	International Workers of the World (IWW); strikers mostly female, immigrant textile workers
Tactics	**Workers:** Surround factory with pickets and armed workers to keep it shut down and keep strikebreakers out **Employer:** Locks workers out of the plant; hires Pinkertons to break strike	**Workers:** Refuse to handle any railcars built by Pullman; railroads are tied up nationwide **Employer:** Locks workers out of factory	**Workers:** Picketing; union provides food and money to strikers; gains support by touring child workers around country **Employer:** Uses firehoses on picketing workers
Role of Government	State government sends in militia to end violence between strikers and Pinkertons	Federal government gets court injunction to end strike because it interferes with shipment of U.S. mail; federal troops end strike	Local police and state and local militia make mass arrests, attack picketers; after attack on women and children, strike is publicized; Congress and President Taft investigate
Outcome	Company hires strikebreakers; strike collapses after anarchist tries to kill plant manager	ARU leaders are jailed, strike ends unsuccessfully; ARU membership declines	Employers give in, grant workers' demands

W

Analyzing VISUALS

1. **Contrasting** How does the Lawrence Textile Strike differ from the others?
2. **Analyzing Visuals** In which instance do federal troops break the strike, and on what grounds?

his workers to live there and to buy goods from company stores. In 1893 the Pullman Company laid off workers and slashed wages. The wage cuts made it difficult for workers to pay their rent and the high prices at the company stores. After the company refused to discuss workers' grievances, a strike began on May 11, 1894. To show support for the Pullman strikers, other ARU members across the United States refused to handle Pullman cars. C

This boycott tied up the railroads and threatened to paralyze the economy. Determined to break the strike, railroad managers arranged for U.S. mail cars to be attached to the Pullman cars. If the strikers refused to handle the Pullman cars, they would be interfering with the U.S. mail, a violation of federal law. President Grover Cleveland then sent in troops, claiming it was his responsibility to keep the mail running. Then a federal court issued an **injunction,** or formal court order, directing the union to halt the boycott. Debs went to jail for violating the injunction, but both the strike at Pullman and the ARU strike collapsed. In the case *In re Debs* (1895), the Supreme Court upheld the right to issue such an injunction. This gave business a powerful tool for dealing with labor unrest.

✓ Reading Check **Summarizing** Why was it difficult for unions to succeed in the 1800s?

W Writing Support

Descriptive Writing Have students find out more about one of the major strikes and describe the conditions that led to the strike. BL

C Critical Thinking

Analyzing Information

Ask: What are the advantages and disadvantages of living in a company town? *(advantages might include the convenience of living near work; disadvantages might include being too dependent on one's employer.)* OL

Analyzing VISUALS

Answers:

1. the employers give in and grant the workers' demands
2. the Pullman Railroad strike because the strike stopped the delivery of the U.S. mail

✓ Reading Check

Answer:
People lost faith in unions after frequent strikes and interference by the authorities.

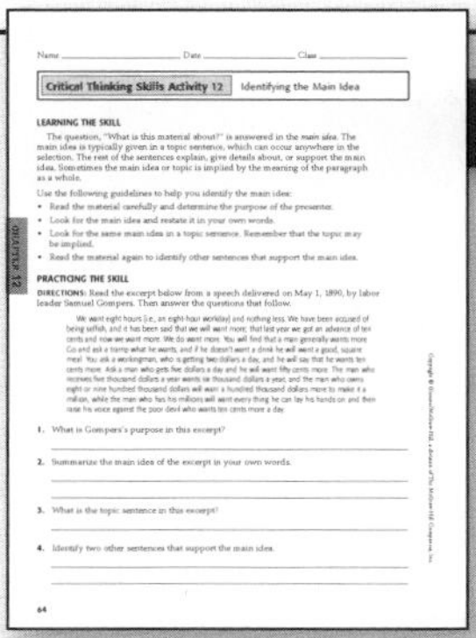

Critical Thinking Skills Activity, URB p. 64

Identifying the Main Idea

Objective: Identify the main idea from the excerpt of a speech.

Focus: What is Samuel Gompers' message in this speech?

Teach: The main idea of a reading or speech is the "big idea" of the material.

Assess: Paraphrase the excerpt, that is, restate the speech, but in your own words. Is the main idea the same?

Close: Ask: Why did Gompers give this speech?

Differentiated Instruction Strategies

BL Explain how to find the main idea in a paragraph from the textbook.

AL Bring an excerpt to class from a newsmagazine, the newspaper, or from an online source. Summarize the article, then state the main idea.

ELL Write the steps to finding a main idea in a flowchart.

C Critical Thinking

Comparing Have interested students find out more about the lives of Gompers and Debs.
Ask: What were the similarities and differences between their approaches to union activity? *(Gompers stuck to major issues and tried not to get political; Debs was very politically oriented.)* OL

W Writing Support

Descriptive Writing Have students use library or Internet resources to determine the difference between a closed shop and an open shop. Have students write a brief paragraph describing the difference between the two. BL

People IN HISTORY

Answers:
Gompers: Students' responses should be supported.
Debs: Students should note that Debs was a member of the Socialist Party, while Gompers distrusted socialism.

New Unions Emerge

MAIN Idea The AFL fought for skilled workers; new unions tried to organize unskilled workers.

HISTORY AND YOU Do you know anyone who belongs to a union? Read on to learn about the different types of unions and how they tried to help their members.

Although workers often shared the same complaints about wage rates and working hours, unions took very different approaches to how they tried to improve workers' lives. Trade unions remained the most common type of labor organization. Of course, most workers were unskilled and unrepresented by trade unions. Thus, new types of unions emerged that tried to reach out to those workers and had different ideas about how to help them.

The Rise of the AFL

The **American Federation of Labor** (AFL) was the dominant union of the late 1800s. In 1886 leaders of several national trade unions came together to create the AFL. From its beginning, the AFL focused on promoting the interests of skilled workers.

Samuel Gompers was the first president of the AFL, a position he held until 1924 (with the exception of one year). While other unions became involved in politics, Gompers tried to steer away from controversy and stay focused on "pure and simple" unionism. That is, he thought it best that the AFL stay focused on "bread and butter" issues—wages, working hours, and working conditions. He was willing to use the strike but preferred to negotiate.

W The AFL had three main goals. First, it tried to convince companies to recognize unions and to agree to collective bargaining. Second, it pushed for **closed shops,** meaning that companies could only hire union members. Third, it promoted an eight-hour workday.

The AFL grew slowly, but by 1900 it was the biggest union in the country, with over 500,000 members. Still, at that time, the AFL represented less than 15 percent of all nonfarm workers. Most AFL members were white men, because the unions discriminated against African Americans, and only a few would admit women.

The IWW

In 1905 a group of labor radicals, many of them socialists, created the Industrial

People IN HISTORY

Samuel Gompers
1850–1924

Samuel Gompers was the longest-serving president of the American Federation of Labor. Born in London to a Dutch Jewish family, Gompers quit school at 10 to earn money for his family, working as a cigarmaker. He and his family moved to the United States in 1863.

C In 1877 Gompers became president of the Cigarmakers' Union. In 1886 he persuaded other craft unions to form the American Federation of Labor and became its first president. Within four years, the AFL had a quarter of a million members. That number grew to one million during the next two years.

A practical man who distrusted socialism, Gompers avoided political ideas and concentrated on improving working conditions. He believed that a just society was built on a fair labor policy. "Show me the country in which there are no strikes and I will show you that country in which there is no liberty," he said.

Do you agree that a union can try to improve working conditions without becoming involved in politics? Explain your answer.

Eugene V. Debs
1855–1926

Eugene Victor Debs was a prominent labor leader and member of the American Socialist Party. Born in Terre Haute, Indiana, Debs went to work at age 15 as a railroad fireman. He helped found the Brotherhood of Locomotive Firemen.

In 1893 Debs helped organize the American Railway Union (ARU). At the time, railway engineers, firemen, conductors, and switchmen all had separate unions. The ARU tried to organize all railroad employees into one union. Debs was arrested for interfering with the U.S. mail during the ARU's unsuccessful Pullman strike. While in prison, Debs read works by Karl Marx and became very critical of capitalism.

Debs ran for president five times between 1900 and 1920 as the nominee of the American Socialist Party. He waged his last campaign from prison while serving time for speaking against America's involvement in World War I.

What did Debs think about combining politics with union activities? How does this differ from Gompers's approach?

Additional Support

Activity: Collaborative Learning

Strike Negotiation Organize students into groups of four. Have each group write a skit and role-play the pre-strike negotiations among a company representative, two union workers, and a union representative. The dialogue should reflect the attitudes of the characters and should include the vocabulary in the section. Each group member should write the dialogue for his or her character. Have groups present their skits. OL

Workers of the World (IWW). Nicknamed "the Wobblies," the IWW wanted to organize all workers according to industry, without making distinctions between skilled and unskilled workers. The IWW endorsed using strikes and believed "The working class and the employing class have nothing in common."

The IWW believed all workers should be organized into "One Big Union." In particular, the IWW tried to organize the unskilled workers who were ignored by most unions.

In 1912 the IWW led a successful strike of textile workers in Lawrence, Massachusetts. After textile companies cut wages, 25,000 workers went on strike. During the strike, the children of strikers were sent out of town—in case things became violent. The companies reversed the wage cuts after ten weeks. The Lawrence strike was the IWW's greatest victory. Most IWW strikes failed.

The IWW never gained a large membership, but its radical philosophy and controversial strikes led many to condemn the organization as subversive.

Working Women

After the Civil War, the number of women wage earners began to increase. By 1900 women made up more than 18 percent of the labor force. The type of jobs women did outside the home reflected society's ideas about what **constituted** "women's work." About one-third of women wage earners worked as domestic servants. Another third worked as teachers, nurses, and sales clerks. The remaining third were industrial workers. Many worked in the garment industry and food-processing plants.

Regardless of the job, women were paid less than men even when they performed the same jobs. It was assumed that a woman had a man helping to support her, and that a man needed higher wages to support a family. Most unions excluded women.

One of the most famous labor leaders of the era was Mary Harris Jones, also known as "Mother Jones." An Irish immigrant, Jones began as a labor organizer for the Knights of Labor, then helped to organize mine workers. Her persuasiveness as a public speaker made her a very successful organizer, leading John D. Rockefeller to label her "the most dangerous woman in America."

In 1900 Jewish and Italian immigrants who worked in the clothing business in New York City founded the International Ladies' Garment Workers Union. The membership, composed mostly of female workers, expanded rapidly in a few years. In 1909 a strike of 20,000 garment workers won union recognition in the industry and better wages and benefits for employees.

In 1903 Mary Kenney O'Sullivan and Leonora O'Reilly decided to establish a separate union for women. With the help of Jane Addams and Lillian Wald, they established the Women's Trade Union League (WTUL), the first national association dedicated to promoting women's labor issues. The WTUL pushed for an eight-hour workday, the creation of a minimum wage, an end to evening work for women, and the abolition of child labor.

Reading Check **Comparing** How were female industrial workers treated differently from male workers in the late 1800s?

Section 4 REVIEW

Vocabulary

1. **Explain** the significance of: deflation, trade union, industrial unions, blacklist, lockout, Marxism, Knights of Labor, arbitration, injunction, American Federation of Labor, Samuel Gompers, closed shop.

Main Ideas

2. **Identifying** Use a graphic organizer similar to the one below to list the factors that led to an increase in unions in the late 1800s.

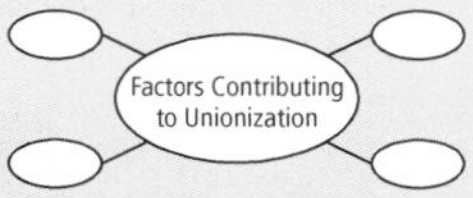

3. **Describing** What groups of workers were represented by the Knights of Labor?
4. **Discussing** How did employers and unions treat women differently from men? What reasons were given for the differences?

Critical Thinking

5. **Big Ideas** Why did industrial unions frequently fail in the late 1800s?
6. **Determining Cause and Effect** Why do you think the rise of unions might have led to increased opposition to immigrants in the United States?
7. **Analyzing Visuals** Look at the map on page 431. In what state did two major disturbances occur? How do you explain this?

Writing About History

8. **Persuasive Writing** Imagine that you are an American worker living in one of the nation's large cities. Write a letter to a friend explaining why you support or oppose the work of labor unions.

History ONLINE
Study Central™ To review this section, go to glencoe.com and click on Study Central.

C Critical Thinking

Drawing Conclusions Review with students the information about the IWW. **Ask:** What is the advantage of organizing workers into "One Big Union?" *(Workers would have more power against businesses than if they were organized into many smaller unions.)*

W Writing Support

Persuasive Writing Have interested students use library or Internet resources to find out more about the Women's Trade Union League (WTUL). Then have students write a persuasive letter to a colleague encouraging him or her to join the league. Encourage students to share their letters with the class. **AL**

Reading Check

Answer:
They were excluded from unions, paid less than men for the same job, and worked in jobs considered appropriate for women.

Section 4 REVIEW

Answers

1. All definitions can be found in the section and the Glossary.
2. concern for working conditions; concern for pay; concern for job security; economic challenges such as deflation
3. industrial workers, trade workers
4. Women were paid less because it was assumed that they were being supported by a man's salary. Women were thought to be good at domestic tasks, so often they did "women's work," which paid less. Most unions excluded women, assuming that a father or husband would express the woman's concerns.
5. confrontations led to violence, courts ruled against them, there were frequent strikes, they fought for many things all at the same time, and blacklisting
6. Many of those in the unions were immigrants and were associated with fears of anarchy and revolution.
7. Illinois; the Chicago area was heavily industrialized and had a large immigrant population.
8. Students' letters will vary but should express and support a point of view.

Determining Cause and Effect The Visual Summary lists causes of industrialization and the growth of big business, as well as the effects on the workplace. Ask students to use the information on the page to create a time line of the era's events. Students should color code "causes" in blue and "events" in red. Display the time lines in the classroom. OL

Chapter 12 Visual Summary

STUDY TO GO You can study anywhere, anytime by downloading quizzes and flashcards to your PDA from glencoe.com.

Causes of Industrialization

- Abundant natural resources
- Cheap immigrant labor force
- High tariffs reduce the import of foreign goods
- National transportation and communication networks

▶ The Central Pacific Railroad Company changed the way companies did business and helped link the nation together.

▲ Blast furnaces of a U.S. Steel plant line the Monongahela River east of Pittsburgh in Braddock, Pennsylvania, in 1905. New technology and new forms of business organization made possible the rise of large-scale industrial factories in the late 1800s.

Causes of the Growth of Big Business

- Little or no government intervention
- Development of pools, trusts, holding companies, and monopolies
- Small businesses could not compete with economies of scale of larger businesses
- Practices of some big businesses sometimes limited competition

Effects on the Workplace

- Rural migration and immigration created large, concentrated workforce
- Low wages, long hours, and dangerous working conditions were common in large-scale industries
- First large unions formed but had little bargaining power against larger companies

▶ Workers fill molds with molten steel at a foundry in 1905. Working conditions of the era led to many industrial accidents and contributed to the rise of unions.

Hands-On Chapter Project
Step 5: Wrap Up

Starting a Business

Step 5: Being an Entrepreneur Students will synthesize what they have learned in Steps 1, 2, 3, and 4.

Directions Have the groups of students review their business, its cost, its growth, and its relationship with its workers. Have students determine which of the general aspects of starting the business was the most difficult. Have each group try to reach a consensus. Have a volunteer from each group share the group's decision with the class. Discuss with the class the difficulty of being a business leader, or entrepreneur. OL

Reviewing Vocabulary

Directions: Choose the word or words that best completes the sentence.

1. ________ are formed by a legal agreement in which one person manages another person's property.

A Trusts
B Pools
C Corporations
D Monopolies

2. The American Railway Association created ________ to make the railroads run more safely and more reliably.

A fixed costs
B time zones
C land grants
D holding companies

3. ________ united all craft workers and common laborers in a particular industry.

A Closed shops
B Trade unions
C Industrial unions
D Blacklists

4. Costs a company has to pay, such as loans, mortgages, and taxes, whether or not it is operating, are called

A investment funds.
B economies of scale.
C fixed costs.
D operating costs.

5. Supporters of ________ believe that the government should not interfere in the economy other than to protect private property rights.

A high tariffs
B laissez-faire
C industrial regulations
D high taxes for private individuals

Reviewing Main Ideas

Directions: Choose the best answers to the following questions.

Section 1 *(pp. 410–415)*

6. What factors contributed to industrialization?

A lack of natural resources
B free enterprise system
C limited workforce
D deteriorating railroad system

7. Laissez-faire relies on

A the government to regulate wages and prices.
B high taxes and government debt to fund businesses.
C high tariffs on foreign goods.
D supply and demand to regulate wages and prices.

Section 2 *(pp. 416–421)*

8. How did the federal government aid railroad construction in the 1850s and 1860s?

A advertised overseas to attract immigrants to help build tracks
B used tax dollars to fund many railroad projects
C passed laws to legalize railroad monopolies
D granted public lands to railroads to sell to raise funds

9. The Pacific Railway Act provided for the construction of a railway

A by offering right-of-way land grants to railroad companies.
B along the Pacific coast from California north to Canada.
C solely by the Union Pacific Railroad company.
D solely by the Central Pacific Railroad company.

TEST-TAKING TIP

Be sure to pay close attention to specific words in a question. Words can change the meaning of the sentence and of the correct answer.

Need Extra Help?

If You Missed Questions . . .	1	2	3	4	5	6	7	8	9
Go to Page . . .	426	419	429–430	422–423	414–415	414–415	414–415	420	416

GO ON

Answers and Analyses Reviewing Vocabulary

1. A The formation of trusts allowed big businesses to skirt anti-monopoly laws while maintaining monopolistic control of their respective industries. A good method to remember the definition of *trusts* is to think of one business *trusts* another to manage its business.

2. B The nation was divided into four time zones to systematize train arrival and departure across the country. This avoided situations wherein two trains using the same track might collide.

3. C Closed shops and blacklists were tactics used by management and labor unions in labor disputes. Tell struggling students that the key words are "united craft workers and *common laborers*." Trade unions united skilled workers in the same trade. Industrial unions united all workers in the same *industry*, regardless of skill.

4. C Point out to students who are confused by choice *D* that the question specifies costs a company has to pay "whether or not it is *operating*." Operating costs pay for the running, or operating, of a company. Fixed costs are *always present*.

5. B Students should realize that one answer choice, *B*, is in opposition to the other answer choices. The other choices all imply government interference or regulation in business. It is government that would impose tariffs, regulations, and taxes.

Reviewing Main Ideas

6. B Choices *A*, *C*, and *D* are the negatives of factors that contributed to industrialization. Students must read the choices carefully to answer correctly.

7. D This question presents a good opportunity to reinforce the definition of *laissez-faire*. An understanding of the free enterprise system will help students learn about other economic systems, such as socialism.

8. D Although immigrants helped build the railroad tracks, the business did not advertise overseas for help, so *A* is not correct. The Pacific Railway Act provided for two corporations to build the Transcontinental Railroad, so the government would not need tax dollars to fund it. The government did not pass laws to legalize any monopolies, so students should eliminate *C*. Review "The Transcontinental Railroad" on page 416 with students who have trouble with this question.

9. A Review the Pacific Railway Act with students who have trouble with this question. Despite the name "Pacific," the act provided for a *transcontinental* railroad. A misunderstanding of this may lead some students to select *B*. The act provided for *two* corporations to build the railroad, so *C* and *D* are incorrect.

10. B Any business can receive federal funds or have a monopoly (until the government breaks it up, at any rate). These are not characteristics limited to corporations. A corporation earns money for its stockholders, not its workers (unless the workers hold stock). Corporations do sell stock, however. A corporation is owned by a number of people, but acts as a single entity.

11. D A discussion of the board game Monopoly® can help reinforce the concept of a monopoly. Remind students that the point of the game is to own all of a certain color or all of the railroads, which *eliminates competition* from the other players. The winner of the game is the person who owns the most "monopolies" and makes the most money. Explain that the other answer choices are all related to labor unions, not business strategies.

12. B Students should eliminate *A,* which suggests that unions help *owners,* not labor. Explain that although unions did fight to prevent lockouts, this is not the reason they were *formed.*

13. C Review the section on the Knights of Labor on page 432 and the Haymarket Riot on page 432, which explain that the Haymarket Riot contributed to the decline of the organization. Those who were opposed to unions used the riot to undermine the reputation of unions and their leaders.

14. B As the United States industrialized, business grew, spurring the growth of a middle class. New industries required workers. Meanwhile, businesses sought to preserve competition by establishing trusts. The lives of workers under large corporations became difficult, leading to the creation of labor unions.

Chapter 12 Assessment

Section 3 *(pp. 422–427)*

10. Corporations are organizations that
- **A** receive federal funding.
- **B** sell stock to the public.
- **C** have a monopoly on a product or service.
- **D** earn profits for their workers.

11. In the late 1800s, which of the following helped business leaders eliminate competition?
- **A** strikes
- **B** labor unions
- **C** closed shops
- **D** monopolies

Section 4 *(pp. 428–435)*

12. Labor unions were formed to
- **A** protect factory owners and improve workers' wages.
- **B** improve workers' wages and make factories safer.
- **C** make factories safer and prevent lockouts.
- **D** prevent lockouts and fight deflation.

13. Which of the following events reduced membership in the Knights of Labor?
- **A** the Pullman Strike
- **B** the panic of 1873
- **C** the Haymarket Riot
- **D** the Great Railroad Strike of 1877

14. In the last half of the 1800s, which development led to the other three?
- **A** expansion of the middle class
- **B** growth of industrialization
- **C** formation of trusts
- **D** creation of labor unions

Critical Thinking

Directions: Choose the best answers to the following questions.

15. The slogan "Eight hours for work, eight hours for sleep, eight hours for what we will" was used in the late 1800s to promote a major goal of
- **A** farmers.
- **B** politicians.
- **C** industrialists.
- **D** organized labor.

Base your answers to questions 16 and 17 on the chart below and your knowledge of Chapter 12.

Steel Production, 1865–1895

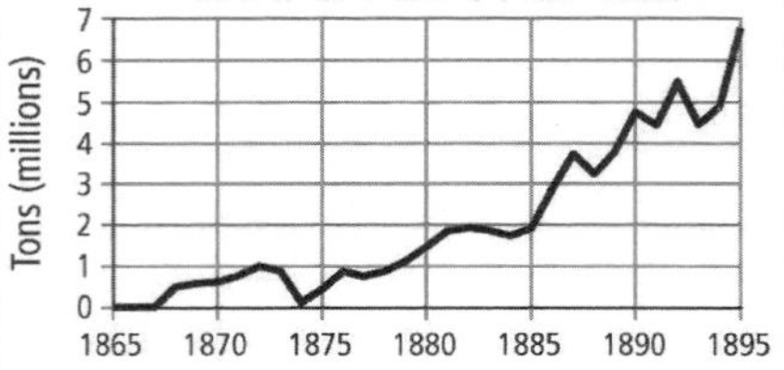

Source: *Historical Statistics of the United States.*

16. Between what years did steel production increase the most?
- **A** 1865–1870
- **B** 1885–1890
- **C** 1890–1895
- **D** 1895–1900

17. How did increased steel production contribute to American industrialization?
- **A** decreased the number of jobs available for workers
- **B** discouraged the consolidation of industry
- **C** improved transportation methods such as railroads
- **D** encouraged immigration by providing a safe work environment

Need Extra Help?								
If You Missed Questions . . .	10	11	12	13	14	15	16	17
Go to Page . . .	422	425–427	428–430	432	428–432	428–435	422–427	424–425

GO ON

Critical Thinking

15. D Organized labor sought better working conditions and pay, among other reforms in industry. Farmers' workdays and working conditions were dictated by nature. Politicians did not need regulation of their working hours. The slogan was directed at industrialists from members of organized labor. The gist of the slogan is the limiting of the workday to 8 hours.

16. B Between the years of 1885 and 1890, steel production jumped by 3 million tons.

17. C The question asks how steel production *contributed* to industrialization, so students should look for the answer choice that had a *positive effect* on industrialization. Improved transportation allowed industry to grow by providing more efficient and less expensive means of moving goods.

18. Which of the following statements about labor unions in the late 1800s is accurate?
   - **A** Strikes by labor unions usually gained public support.
   - **B** Labor union activities were frequently opposed by the government.
   - **C** Demands by labor unions were usually met.
   - **D** Arbitration was commonly used to end labor unrest.

19. The immigrants who came to the United States between 1870 and 1910 came primarily from
   - **A** eastern Europe and China.
   - **B** northern and western Europe.
   - **C** East Asia.
   - **D** Latin America.

Analyze the cartoon and answer the question that follows. Base your answer on the cartoon and on your knowledge of Chapter 12.

Source: Bernhard Gillam, *Puck*, February 7, 1883

20. What does this cartoon say about Gould and Vanderbilt?
   - **A** They are giving money to the hard-working laborers.
   - **B** They are getting rich at the expense of others' back-breaking work.
   - **C** The ship is slowly crumbling like their empires.
   - **D** The workers are determined to overthrow them.

Document-Based Questions

Directions: Analyze the document and answer the short-answer questions that follow the document.

In the following excerpt from *History of the Standard Oil Company*, Ida Tarbell warns of the effects of Rockefeller's business practices on the nation's morality. Read the excerpt and answer the questions that follow:

> *"Very often people who admit the facts, who are willing to see that Mr. Rockefeller has employed force and fraud to secure his ends, justify him by declaring, 'It's business.' That is, 'It's business' has come to be a legitimate excuse for hard dealing, sly tricks, special privileges. It is a common enough thing to hear men arguing that the ordinary laws of morality do not apply in business.*
>
> *As for the ethical side, there is no cure but in an increasing scorn of unfair play. . . . When the businessman who fights to secure special privileges, to crowd his competitor off the track by other than fair competitive methods, receives the same summary disdainful ostracism by his fellows that the doctor or lawyer who is 'unprofessional,' . . . we shall have gone a long way toward making commerce a fit pursuit for our young men."*
>
> —from *History of the Standard Oil Company*

21. According to Tarbell, what practices had Rockefeller used to establish Standard Oil Company?

22. In what way did Tarbell believe the attitudes of the American people contributed to Rockefeller's business practices?

Extended Response

23. Identify labor unions formed during the late 1800s and early 1900s. Discuss the different views, goals, and activities of each organization. How were these organizations similar to or different from each other? What roles did unions and union members play in industrialization? Write an expository essay that supports your position with relevant facts and details.

STOP

History ONLINE

For additional test practice, use Self-Check Quizzes—Chapter 12 at glencoe.com.

Need Extra Help?

If You Missed Questions . . .	18	19	20	21	22	23
Go to Page . . .	429–435	410–415	425–427	439	439	428–435

Document-Based Questions

21. According to Tarbell, Rockefeller used "force and fraud" to establish Standard Oil. This answer can be found in the first sentence of the first paragraph. Tarbell then explains that his excuse was that it was "just business."

22. Tarbell believed that the attitude that "it's just business" was held by the American people, and contributed to Rockefeller's practices. She speaks here of a pervasive attitude that creates an environment of acceptance of Rockefeller's tactics of "force and fraud."

Extended Response

23. Students' essays will vary, but must follow the guidelines for an expository essay. Each essay should include an introduction, body, and a conclusion. Essays should identify at least two labor unions and provide a well thought out comparison of the organizations. A complete essay will also discuss the contributions of unions to industrialization.

18. B This is another question in which one answer choice is the opposite of the others. As students read, labor unions struggled to gain the support of the government, the public, and industry. Strikes did not often have public support, and often contributed to a negative public opinion. Demands of unions were often not met, and arbitration was not commonly used in the 1800s. Government opposition in the 1800s, however, was a large obstacle to labor unions.

19. A As a result of social and economic conditions in eastern Europe and China, many people immigrated to the United States in search of a better life.

20. B In the cartoon, laborers are bent over in what looks like painful positions, holding up the ship on their backs. Captains of industry sit on top of the ship. They are not giving money to anyone. There is no evidence that the ship is crumbling.

History ONLINE

Have students visit the Web site at glencoe.com to review Chapter 12 and take the Self-Check Quiz.

Need Extra Help?

Have students refer to the pages listed if they miss any of the questions.

Chapter 13 Planning Guide

Key to Ability Levels

- **BL** Below Level
- **OL** On Level
- **AL** Above Level
- **ELL** English Language Learners

Key to Teaching Resources

- Print Material
- CD-ROM or DVD
- Transparency

Levels				Resources	Chapter Opener	Section 1	Section 2	Section 3	Section 4	Section 5	Chapter Assess
BL	OL	AL	ELL								
				FOCUS							
BL	OL	AL	ELL	Daily Focus Transparencies		13-1	13-2	13-3	13-4	13-5	
				TEACH							
	OL	AL		Geography and History, URB			p. 3				
	OL	AL		History Simulations and Problem Solving, URB				p. 9			
BL	OL	AL	ELL	Reading Essentials and Note-Taking Guide		p. 141	p. 144	p. 147	p. 150	p. 153	
		AL		American Literature Reading, URB		p. 13					
BL	OL		ELL	Reading Skills Activity, URB							p. 87
	OL			Historical Analysis Skills Activity, URB	p. 88						
BL	OL		ELL	Guided Reading Activity, URB		p. 114	p. 115	p. 116	p. 117	p. 118	
BL	OL	AL	ELL	Differentiated Instruction Activity, URB		p. 89					
BL	OL		ELL	English Learner Activity, URB		p. 91					
BL	OL	AL	ELL	Content Vocabulary Activity, URB	p. 93						
BL	OL	AL	ELL	Academic Vocabulary Activity, URB	p. 95						
	OL	AL		Reinforcing Skills Activity, URB		p. 97					
	OL	AL		Critical Thinking Skills Activity, URB						p. 98	
BL	OL		ELL	Time Line Activity, URB			p. 99				
	OL			Linking Past and Present Activity, URB		p. 100					
BL	OL	AL	ELL	Primary Source Reading, URB			p. 101		p. 103		
BL	OL	AL	ELL	American Art and Music Activity, URB				p. 105			
BL	OL	AL	ELL	Interpreting Political Cartoons Activity, URB							p. 107
		AL		Enrichment Activity, URB			p. 111				
BL	OL	AL	ELL	Differentiated Instruction for the American History Classroom	✓	✓	✓	✓	✓	✓	✓
BL	OL	AL	ELL	Unit Map Overlay Transparencies	✓	✓	✓	✓	✓	✓	✓
BL	OL	AL	ELL	Unit Time Line Transparencies and Activities	✓	✓	✓	✓	✓	✓	✓
BL	OL	AL	ELL	Cause and Effect Transparencies, Strategies, and Activities	✓	✓	✓	✓	✓	✓	✓

Note: Please refer to the *Unit 4 Resource Book* for this chapter's URB materials.

* Also available in Spanish

Planning Guide | Chapter 13

TeacherWorks Plus — All-In-One Planner and Resource Center

- Interactive Lesson Planner
- Interactive Teacher Edition
- Fully editable blackline masters
- Section Spotlight Videos Launch
- Differentiated Lesson Plans
- Printable reports of daily assignments
- Standards Tracking System

Levels: BL	OL	AL	ELL	Resources	Chapter Opener	Section 1	Section 2	Section 3	Section 4	Section 5	Chapter Assess
				TEACH *(continued)*							
BL	OL	AL	ELL	Why It Matters Transparencies, Strategies, and Activities	✓	✓	✓	✓	✓	✓	✓
BL	OL	AL	ELL	American Biographies			✓	✓	✓	✓	
BL	OL	AL		Supreme Court Case Studies				p. 23	p. 15	p. 27	
BL	OL	AL	ELL	The Living Constitution	✓	✓	✓	✓	✓	✓	✓
BL	OL	AL	ELL	American Issues	✓	✓	✓	✓	✓	✓	✓
	OL	AL	ELL	American Art and Architecture Transparencies, Strategies, and Activities	✓	✓	✓	✓	✓	✓	✓
BL	OL	AL		High School American History Literature Library	✓	✓	✓	✓	✓	✓	✓
	OL	AL		American History Primary Source Documents Library	✓	✓	✓	✓	✓	✓	✓
BL	OL	AL	ELL	American Music: Hits Through History CD	✓	✓	✓	✓	✓	✓	✓
BL	OL	AL	ELL	StudentWorks™ Plus	✓	✓	✓	✓	✓	✓	✓
BL	OL	AL	ELL	*The American Vision* Video Program	✓	✓	✓	✓	✓	✓	✓
Teacher Resources				Strategies for Success	✓	✓	✓	✓	✓	✓	✓
				Presentation Plus! with MindJogger CheckPoint	✓	✓	✓	✓	✓	✓	✓
				Success With English Learners	✓	✓	✓	✓	✓	✓	✓
				ASSESS							
BL	OL	AL	ELL	Section Quizzes and Chapter Tests		p. 177	p. 178	p. 179	p. 180	p. 181	p. 183
BL	OL	AL	ELL	Authentic Assessment With Rubrics							p. 31
BL	OL	AL	ELL	Standardized Test Practice Workbook							p. 26
BL	OL	AL	ELL	*ExamView® Assessment Suite*		13-1	13-2	13-3	13-4	13-5	Ch. 13
				CLOSE							
BL			ELL	Reteaching Activity, URB							p. 109
BL	OL		ELL	Reading and Study Skills Foldables™	pp. 58, 61, 63						

✓ Chapter- or unit-based activities applicable to all sections in this chapter.

Using *ExamView®* Assessment Suite

Teach With Technology

What is *ExamView®* *Assessment Suite?*

Glencoe's *ExamView® Assessment Suite* is a powerful assessment tool that enables you to create and customize tests for your students. Tests can be either printed or administered online.

How can *ExamView® Assessment Suite* help me?

ExamView® allows you to create your own test questions or choose from existing, fully editable banks of questions customized for this book. Question formats include true/false, multiple choice, completion, matching, short answer, and essay, and many questions are based on documents, maps, or graphs. Each question includes reteach information where students can go for more help on the topic. The flexibility of *ExamView®* allows you to develop testing materials that:

- focus on specific skills or competencies
- address state or national standards
- are leveled for different abilities
- can be translated to Spanish in one click

ExamView® Assessment Suite is one of Glencoe's technology resources available for teachers.

History ONLINE
Visit glencoe.com and enter ***QuickPass***™ code TAV9399c13T for Chapter 13 resources.

You can easily launch a wide range of digital products from your computer's desktop with the McGraw-Hill Social Studies widget.

TeacherWorks

	Student	Teacher	Parent
Media Library			
• Section Audio	●		●
• Spanish Audio Summaries	●		●
• Section Spotlight Videos	●	●	●
The American Vision **Online Learning Center (Web Site)**			
• StudentWorks™ Plus Online	●	●	●
• Multilingual Glossary	●	●	●
• Study-to-Go	●	●	●
• Chapter Overviews	●	●	●
• Self-Check Quizzes	●	●	●
• Student Web Activities	●	●	●
• ePuzzles and Games	●	●	●
• Vocabulary eFlashcards	●	●	●
• In Motion Animations	●	●	●
• Study Central™	●	●	●
• Web Activity Lesson Plans		●	
• Vocabulary PuzzleMaker	●	●	●
• Historical Thinking Activities		●	
• Beyond the Textbook	●	●	●

Reading Support From Jamestown Education

- **Timed Readings Plus in Social Studies** helps students increase their reading rate and fluency while maintaining comprehension. The 400-word passages are similar to those found on state and national assessments.
- **Reading in the Content Area: Social Studies** concentrates on six essential reading skills that help students better comprehend what they read. The book includes 75 high-interest nonfiction passages written at increasing levels of difficulty.
- **Reading Social Studies** includes strategic reading instruction and vocabulary support in Social Studies content for both ELLs and native speakers of English.

www.jamestowneducation.com

Biography / A&E Home Video / The History Channel

The following videotape programs are available from Glencoe as supplements to this chapter:

- Ellis Island (ISBN 0-76-700005-6)
- Ellis Island DVD (ISBN 0-76-704451-7)

To order, call Glencoe at 1-800-334-7344. To find classroom resources to accompany many of these videos, check the following home pages:

A&E Television: www.aetv.com
The History Channel: www.historychannel.com

National Geographic

Index to National Geographic Magazine:

The following articles relate to this chapter:

- "New Life for Ellis Island," by Alice J. Hall, September 1990.
- "Boston's North Enders," by Erla Zwingle, October 2000.

National Geographic Society Products To order the following, call National Geographic at 1-800-368-2728:

- *Immigration* (CD-ROM)

Access National Geographic's new, dynamic MapMachine Web site and other geography resources at:
www.nationalgeographic.com
www.nationalgeographic.com/maps

Reading List Generator CD-ROM — Glencoe BookLink 3

Use this database to search more than 30,000 titles to create a customized reading list for your students.

- Reading lists can be organized by students' reading level, author, genre, theme, or area of interest.
- The database provides Degrees of Reading Power™ (DRP) and Lexile™ readability scores for all selections.
- A brief summary of each selection is included.

Leveled reading suggestions for this chapter:

For students at a Grade 8 reading level:
- ***The Great Wheel,*** by Robert Lawson

For students at a Grade 9 reading level:
- ***If Your Name Was Changed at Ellis Island,*** by Ellen Levine

For students at a Grade 10 reading level:
- ***My Antonia,*** by Willa Cather

For students at a Grade 11 reading level:
- ***Irish Immigrants: 1840–1920,*** by Megan O'Hara

For students at a Grade 12 reading level:
- ***We Are Americans: Voices of the Immigrant Experience,*** by Dorothy Hoobler and Thomas Hoobler

Introducing Chapter 13

Focus

MAKING CONNECTIONS
Why Do People Migrate?

Have students brainstorm the reasons people move to other countries and list their answers on the chalkboard. Discuss with students the reasons, if any, for which they might move to another country. Then discuss how they think life would be different in a new country. **OL** **BL**

Teach

The Big Ideas

As students study the chapter, remind them to consider the section-based Big Ideas included in each section's Guide to Reading. The **Essential Questions** in the activities below tie in to the Big Ideas and help students think about and understand important chapter concepts. In addition, the Hands-on Chapter Projects with their culminating activities relate the content from each section to the Big Ideas. These activities build on each other as students progress through the chapter. Section activities culminate in the wrap-up activity on the Visual Summary page.

Chapter 13

Urban America

1865–1896

SECTION 1 Immigration
SECTION 2 Urbanization
SECTION 3 The Gilded Age
SECTION 4 Populism
SECTION 5 The Rise of Segregation

Immigrants look toward New York City while waiting on a dock at Ellis Island in the early 1900s.

U.S. PRESIDENTS

Hayes 1877–1881

Garfield 1881

Arthur 1881–1885

Cleveland 1885–1889

U.S. EVENTS

1870
- Fifteenth Amendment ratified
- Farmers' Alliance founded

1881
- President Garfield assassinated

1883
- Brooklyn Bridge completed
- Civil Service Act adopted

1870 — 1875 — 1880 — 1885

WORLD EVENTS

1872
- Ballot Act makes voting secret in Britain

1876
- Porfirio Diaz becomes dictator of Mexico

1881
- Anti-Jewish pogroms erupt in Russia

1884
- First subway in London opens

Section 1

Immigration

Essential Question: Why did Europeans come to America in the late 1900s? *(better economic opportunities, new freedoms, peace)* Tell students that in this section they will learn why millions of people came to the United States and how they changed America. **OL**

Section 2

Urbanization

Essential Question: What are some of the characteristics of cities? *(Answers might include large populations, density of buildings, noise, pollution, traffic, cultural amenities, access to public services.)* Tell students that this section will focus on how the growth of cities changed the United States. **OL**

Section 3

The Gilded Age

Essential Question: What were the characteristics of the Gilded Age? *(growth of big business, the idea of individualism, new social reforms)* Tell students that in Section 3 they will learn about the Gilded Age in the United States, as well as how society and culture changed during that time. **OL**

Chapter Audio

MAKING CONNECTIONS

Why Do People Migrate?

European and Asian immigrants arrived in the United States in great numbers during the late 1800s. Providing cheap labor, they made rapid industrial growth possible. They also helped populate the growing cities.

- ***How do you think life in big cities was different from life on farms and in small towns?***
- ***How do you think the immigrants of the late 1800s changed American society?***

FOLDABLES™

Analyzing Information Make a Folded Table Foldable to clarify your understanding of how immigration and urbanization are related. As you read the chapter, list the causes and effects of immigration and urbanization. In each cell, list as many causes and effects as possible and include approximate dates where appropriate.

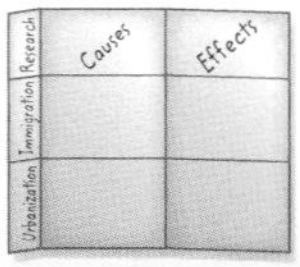

1888
- First electric trolley line opens in Richmond, Virginia

Harrison 1889–1893

1890
- Sherman Antitrust Act passed

1895
- Booker T. Washington gives Atlanta Compromise speech

Cleveland 1893–1897

1896
- *Plessy* v. *Ferguson* establishes "separate but equal" doctrine

1890 — 1895

1888
- Brazil ends slavery

1889
- Eiffel Tower completed for Paris World Exhibit

1896
- Athens hosts first modern Olympic games

History ONLINE Visit glencoe.com and enter ***QuickPass***™ code TAV9846c13 for Chapter 13 resources.

Section 4

Populism

Essential Question: What is populism and how did it affect the United States? *(A reform movement that started with the nation's farmers; the movement brought attention to the plight of farmers, and farmers organized to increase their political power.)* Tell students that this section will cover the rise of the Populist Movement and its impact on the nation. **OL**

Section 5

The Rise of Segregation

Essential Question: What is racial segregation? Why is it inherently wrong? *(Separation of racial groups based on skin color; it is wrong because it violates the founding principles of the United States.)* Tell students that this section will focus on the increase of racial segregation in the late 1800s and the passing of laws that legalized racial separation. **OL**

Introducing

Chapter 13

More About the Photo

Visual Literacy More than 12 million immigrants passed through the Ellis Island Immigration Station between 1892 and 1954, and the vast majority of them were allowed to enter the United States. Most immigrants were poor and traveled in steerage, one of the lowest decks on a ship. Steerage lacked privacy and toilet facilities were limited.

FOLDABLES™ Study Organizer **Dinah Zike's Foldables**

Dinah Zike's Foldables are three-dimensional, interactive graphic organizers that help students practice basic writing skills, review vocabulary terms, and identify main ideas. Instructions for creating and using Foldables can be found in the Appendix at the end of this book and in the Dinah Zike's Reading and Study Skills Foldables booklet.

History ONLINE

Visit glencoe.com and enter ***QuickPass***™ code TAV9399c13T for Chapter 13 resources, including a Chapter Overview, Study Central™, Study-to-Go, Student Web Activity, Self-Check Quiz, and other materials.

Focus

Bellringer

Daily Focus Transparency 13-1

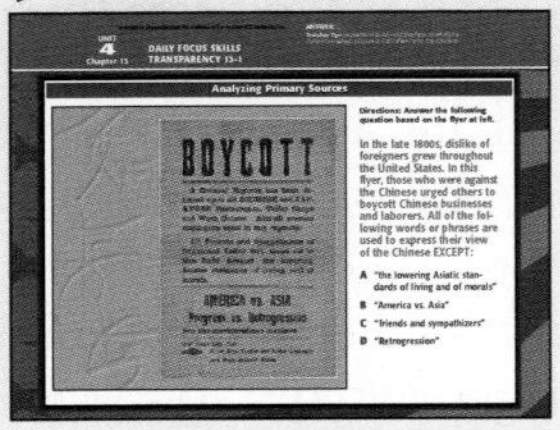

Guide to Reading

Answers to Graphic:

Reasons for Immigrating	
Push Factors	**Pull Factors**
Farm poverty and worker uncertainty	Plenty of land and plenty of work
Wars and compulsory military service	Higher standard of living
Political tyranny	Democratic political system
Religious oppression	Opportunity for social advancement
Population pressure	

Section Spotlight Video

To generate student interest and provide a springboard for class discussion, access the Chapter 13, Section 1 video at glencoe.com or on the video DVD.

Resource Manager

R Reading Strategies	C Critical Thinking	D Differentiated Instruction	W Writing Support	S Skill Practice
Teacher Edition • Using Word Parts, p. 446 **Additional Resources** • American Lit. Read.,URB p. 13 • Acad. Vocab, URB p. 95 • Guide Read, URB p. 114	**Teacher Edition** • Determining Cause and Effect, p. 443 • Contrasting, p. 445 • Assessing, p. 446 **Additional Resources** • Link. Past and Present, URB p. 100 • Quizzes and Tests, p. 177	**Teacher Edition** • Interpersonal, p. 444 **Additional Resources** • Diff Instruction Act., URB p. 89 • English Learner Act., URB p. 91	**Teacher Edition** • Personal Writing, p. 444 **Additional Resources** • Cont. Vocab, URB p. 93	**Teacher Edition** • Analyzing Visuals, p. 443 • Reading Charts, p. 445 **Additional Resources** • Historical Analysis Skills Act., URB p. 88 • Reinforce Skills Act., URB p. 97 • Read. Essen., p. 141

Section 1

Section Audio — Spotlight Video

Immigration

Guide to Reading

Big Ideas

Trade, War, and Migration Many people from Europe came to the United States to escape war, famine, or persecution or to find better jobs.

Content Vocabulary

- steerage *(p. 443)*
- nativism *(p. 446)*

Academic Vocabulary

- immigrant *(p. 442)*
- ethnic *(p. 444)*

People and Events to Identify

- Ellis Island *(p. 443)*
- Jacob Riis *(p. 444)*
- Angel Island *(p. 445)*
- Chinese Exclusion Act *(p. 447)*

Reading Strategy

Categorizing Complete a graphic organizer similar to the one below by filling in the reasons people left their homelands to immigrate to the United States.

Reasons for Immigrating	
Push Factors	Pull Factors

In the late nineteenth century, a major wave of immigration began. Most immigrants settled in cities, where distinctive ethnic neighborhoods emerged. Some Americans, however, feared that the new immigrants would not adapt to American culture or might be harmful to American society.

Europeans Flood Into America

MAIN Idea Immigrants from Europe came to the United States for many reasons and entered the country through Ellis Island.

HISTORY AND YOU Have you ever been to an ethnic neighborhood where residents have re-created aspects of their homeland? Read on to learn how immigrants adjusted to life in the United States.

Between 1865—the year the Civil War ended—and 1914—the year World War I began—nearly 25 million Europeans immigrated to the United States. By the late 1890s, more than half of all **immigrants** in the United States were from eastern and southern Europe, including Italy, Greece, Austria-Hungary, Russia, and Serbia. This period of immigration is known as "new" immigration. The "old" immigration, which occurred before 1890, had been primarily of people from northern and western Europe. More than 70 percent of these new immigrants were men; they were working either to be able to afford to purchase land in Europe or to bring family members to America.

Europeans immigrated to the United States for many reasons. Many came because American industries had plenty of jobs available. Europe's industrial cities, however, also offered plenty of jobs, so economic factors do not entirely explain why people migrated. Many came in the hope of finding better jobs that would let them escape poverty and the restrictions of social class in Europe. Some moved to avoid forced military service, which in some nations lasted for many years. In some cases, as in Italy, high food prices encouraged people to leave. In Poland and Russia, population pressure led to emigration. Others, especially Jews living in Russia and the Austro-Hungarian Empire, fled to escape religious persecution.

In addition, most European states had made moving to the United States easy. Immigrants were allowed to take their savings with them, and most countries had repealed old laws forcing peasants to stay in their villages and banning skilled workers from leaving the country. At the same time, moving to the United States offered a chance to break away from Europe's class system and move to a democratic nation where people had the opportunity to move up the social ladder.

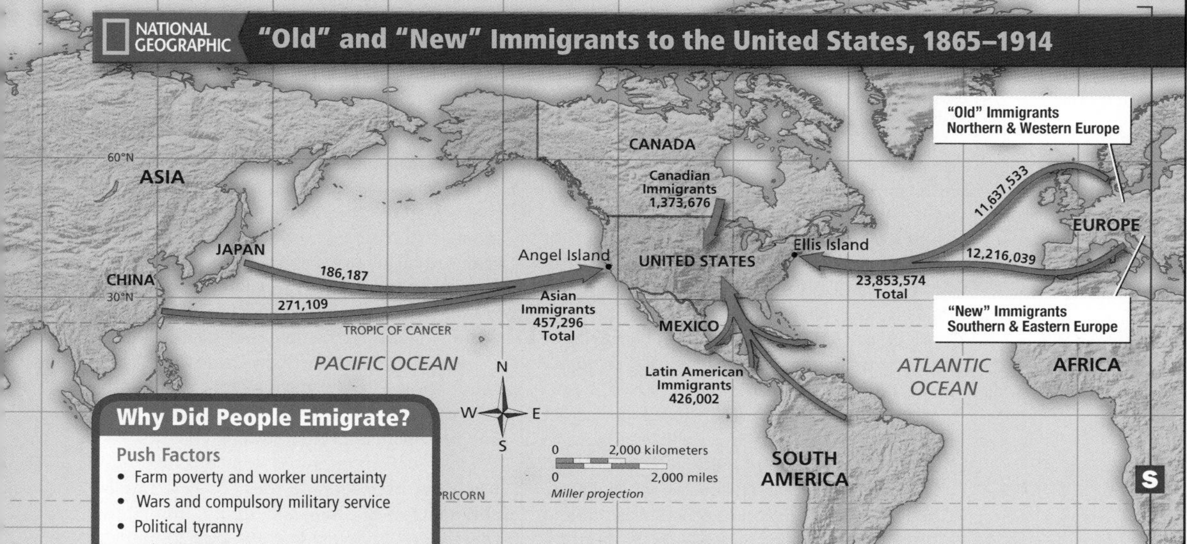

Why Did People Emigrate?

Push Factors
- Farm poverty and worker uncertainty
- Wars and compulsory military service
- Political tyranny
- Religious oppression
- Population pressure

Pull Factors
- Plenty of land and plenty of work
- Higher standard of living
- Democratic political system
- Opportunity for social advancement

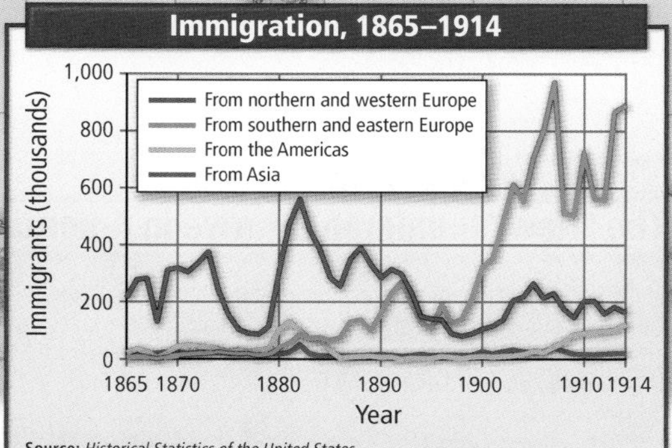

Source: *Historical Statistics of the United States.*

Analyzing VISUALS

1. **Describing** When was the level of immigration from the different regions of Europe roughly equal? How did it later change?
2. **Analyzing** Did more immigrants come from Canada or Latin America?

S

The Atlantic Voyage

The voyage to the United States was often very difficult. Most immigrants booked passage in **steerage,** the cheapest accommodations on a steamship. Edward Steiner, an Iowa clergyman who posed as an immigrant in order to write a book on immigration, described the miserable quarters: C

Primary Source

"Narrow, steep and slippery stairways lead to it. Crowds everywhere, ill smelling bunks, uninviting washrooms—this is steerage. The odors of scattered orange peelings, tobacco, garlic and disinfectants meeting but not blending. No lounge or chairs for comfort, and a continual babble of tongues—this is steerage. The food, which is miserable, is dealt out of huge kettles into the dinner pails provided by the steamship company."

—quoted in *World of Our Fathers*

At the end of a 14-day journey, the passengers usually disembarked at **Ellis Island,** a tiny island in New York Harbor. There, a huge three-story building served as the processing center for many of the immigrants arriving from Europe after 1892.

Teach

S Skill Practice

Analyzing Visuals Ask: From 1865 to 1914, which region experienced the highest level of immigration to the United States? *(Europe)* ELL BL

C Critical Thinking

Determining Cause and Effect Ask: What negative effects might steerage conditions have had on passengers? *(Answers may vary but could include illness and quarrels.)* OL

Analyzing VISUALS

Answers:

1. around 1895; southern and eastern European immigration rose.
2. Canada

Additional Support

Activity: Technology Connection

Sea Travel Today Ask: Why were passengers allowed to travel in the steerage sections of ships in the 1800s? *(There were little or no regulations in place that monitored passenger safety or ship conditions.)* Explain that the International Maritime Organization (IMO) was created as a special agency of the United Nations in 1948. Its purpose has been to ensure safe shipping practices throughout the world. Have students work with a partner to research current regulations on passenger ships. Students can find this information on the IMO Internet site at www.imo.org/. Ask students to create charts showing five protective measures that the IMO requires of all passenger ships in the first column. Using their knowledge of current safety provisions, have students reread the text and cite violations of current practices that were present in the steerage sections in which many immigrants traveled. OL

W Writing Support

Personal Writing Explain that immigrants were sometimes denied entrance, which separated families. People then had to decide whether all would return to their homeland or some would remain. Have students write a personal response to the inspection process. AL

D Differentiated Instruction

Interpersonal Ask: How did ethnic neighborhoods both help and hinder immigrants? *(Answers will vary. Possible response: People could communicate more easily and feel more comfortable; however, this comfort may have made some less willing to learn new customs, language, and ideas.)* BL

Reading Check

Answer:
The population became more ethnically diverse, especially in the urban areas.

Additional Support

Ellis Island

Most immigrants passed through Ellis Island in about a day. They would not soon forget their hectic introduction to the United States. A medical examiner who worked there later described how "hour after hour, ship load after ship load . . . the stream of human beings with its kaleidoscopic variations was . . . hurried through Ellis Island by the equivalent of 'step lively' in every language of the earth." About 12 million immigrants passed through Ellis Island between 1892 and 1954.

In Ellis Island's enormous hall, crowds of immigrants filed past the doctor for an initial inspection. "Whenever a case aroused suspicion," an inspector wrote, "the alien was set aside in a cage apart from the rest . . . and his coat lapel or shirt marked with colored chalk" to indicate the reason for the isolation. About one out of five newcomers was marked with an "H" for heart problems, "K" for hernias, "Sc" for scalp problems, or "X" for mental disability. Newcomers who failed the inspection might be separated from their families and returned to Europe.

Ethnic Cities

Many of those who passed these inspections settled in the nation's cities. By the 1890s, immigrants made up a large percentage of the population of major cities, including New York, Chicago, Milwaukee, and Detroit. **Jacob Riis,** a Danish-born journalist, observed in 1890 that a map of New York City, "colored to designate nationalities, would show more stripes than on the skin of a zebra."

In the cities, immigrants lived in neighborhoods that were often separated into **ethnic** groups, such as "Little Italy" or the Jewish "Lower East Side" in New York City. There they spoke their native languages and re-created the churches, synagogues, clubs, and newspapers of their homelands.

How well immigrants adjusted depended partly on how quickly they learned English and adapted to American culture. Immigrants also tended to adjust well if they had marketable skills or money, or if they settled among members of their own ethnic group.

Reading Check **Explaining** How did immigration affect demographics in the United States?

PRIMARY SOURCE

The "New" Immigrants Arrive in America

In the late 1800s, the number of immigrants coming from northwest Europe began to decline, while "new immigrants," fleeing war, poverty, and persecution, began to arrive in large numbers from southern and eastern Europe, and from Asia.

▲ *Many Italian immigrants took jobs as construction workers, bricklayers, and dockworkers in urban areas, but this group is building a railroad, c. 1900.*

▲ *Jewish people migrated to the United States from all across Europe seeking an opportunity to better their lives. Many Jews from Eastern Europe (such as those above) were also fleeing religious persecution.*

◄ *Many Chinese came to America to escape poverty and civil war. Many helped build railroads. Others set up small businesses. These children were photographed in San Francisco's Chinatown, c. 1900.*

Activity: Interdisciplinary Connection

Civics Ask: How did you become a United States citizen? *(Answers will vary. Some students may respond that they were born in the United States. Others may say they were born abroad but to American parents. Others may volunteer that they have undergone the naturalization process.)* Have students work with a partner to list the requirements immigrants must meet before they can apply for U.S. citizenship. Students can obtain this information by taking the U.S. Immigration Service online quiz at www.uscitizenship.info/en_US/citizenship/home.html. Then ask partners to research the naturalization process on the Internet at www.uscitizenship.info/ins-citizenship-process.htm. Have partners create a poster that could be displayed in your community, informing immigrants of the application requirements and naturalization process. Display the posters in your school. OL

Asian Immigration

MAIN Idea Asian immigrants arrived on the West Coast, where they settled mainly in cities.

HISTORY AND YOU Do you know someone who has moved to the United States from Asia? What motivated that person to come here? Read on to learn about the experiences of earlier generations of Asian immigrants.

In the mid-1800s, China's population reached about 430 million, and the country was suffering from severe unemployment, poverty, and famine. Then, in 1850, the Taiping Rebellion erupted in China. This insurrection caused such suffering that thousands of Chinese left for the United States. In the early 1860s, as construction began on the Central Pacific Railroad, the demand for railroad workers led to further Chinese immigration.

Chinese immigrants settled mainly in western cities, where they often worked as laborers or servants or in skilled trades. Others became merchants. Because native-born Americans kept them out of many businesses, some Chinese immigrants opened their own.

Japanese also began immigrating to the United States. Although some came earlier, the number of Japanese immigrants soared upward between 1900 and 1910. As Japan industrialized, economic problems caused many Japanese to leave their homeland for new economic opportunities.

Until 1910 Asian immigrants arriving in San Francisco first stopped at a two-story shed at the wharf. As many as 500 people at a time were often squeezed into this structure, which Chinese immigrants from Canton called *muk uk*, or "wooden house." In January 1910 California opened a barracks on **Angel Island** C for Asian immigrants. Most were young men in their teens or twenties, who nervously awaited the results of their immigration hearings. The wait could last for months. On the walls of the barracks, several immigrants wrote anonymous poems in pencil or ink.

Reading Check **Making Generalizations** Why did Chinese immigrants come to the United States?

NATIONAL GEOGRAPHIC Immigration Settlement Patterns

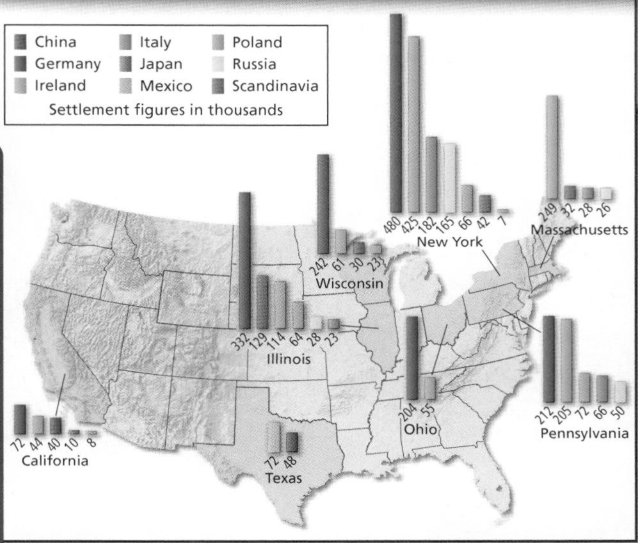

S

Why Did Immigrants Come to America?	Typical Occupations in America
Italians • cholera epidemic in 1880s • land shortage for peasants; landlords charge high rent • food shortages • poverty, unemployment	**Italians** • unskilled labor—dock work, construction, railroads • some skilled labor, such as bricklayers, stonemasons, and other trades
East Europeans • Russians, Poles: land shortages for peasants, unemployment, high taxes; long military draft • Jews: discrimination, poverty, and recurring pogroms	**East Europeans** • Poles: farmers, coal miners, steel and textile millworkers; meatpacking • Jews: laborers, garment workers, merchants
Chinese • famine • land shortage for peasants • civil war (Taiping rebellion)	**Chinese** • railroad and construction workers; some skilled labor • merchants, small businesses

Analyzing VISUALS

1. **Analyzing Visuals** To which state did most Russian immigrants come to live?
2. **Contrasting** How would you contrast the immigration settlement patterns of Texas and Ohio?

S Skill Practice

Reading Charts **Ask:** What push factor did the three groups of immigrants have in common? *(land shortage for peasants)* **ELL**

C Critical Thinking

Contrasting **Ask:** How did the immigration process at Angel Island differ from that at Ellis Island? *(Immigrants had to wait longer at Angel Island.)* **OL**

Analyzing VISUALS

1. New York
2. Unlike the two fairly equal groups in Texas, one immigrant group far outnumbered the other in Ohio.

Reading Check

Answer:
high unemployment; poverty and famine in China; Taiping Rebellion; availability of railroad jobs in the United States

Extending the Content

Chinese Immigration During the 1906 San Francisco earthquake, most immigration records in the city burned. This helped the Chinese bring others from China into America. Because no records were available, the Chinese already living in the United States could claim they were born here, which automatically made them citizens. This entitled them to bring their children from China. As children of citizens, they too were automatically citizens.

R Reading Strategies

Using Word Parts Ask: What base word helps define *nativism*? *(native)* BL

C Critical Thinking

Assessing Explain that irony is when the opposite of the expected happens. **Ask:** Why was nativism ironic? *(The ancestors of most native-born Americans were immigrants.)* OL

DBQ Document Based Questions

Answers:

1. Catholic beliefs; school funding
2. priests shown as beasts who prey on children; funding Catholic schools takes money from public schools

Nativism Resurges

MAIN Idea Economic concerns and religious and ethnic prejudices led some Americans to push for laws restricting immigration.

HISTORY AND YOU In what ways does immigration affect the area in which you live? Read on to learn why nativists tried to stop immigration.

C R Eventually the wave of immigration led to increased feelings of nativism on the part of many Americans. **Nativism** is an extreme dislike of immigrants by native-born people. It had surfaced during the heavy wave of Irish immigration in the 1840s and 1850s. In the late 1800s, anti-immigrant feelings focused mainly on Asians, Jews, and eastern Europeans.

Nativists opposed immigration for many reasons. Some feared that the influx of Catholics from countries such as Ireland, Italy, and Poland would swamp the mostly Protestant United States. Many labor unions also opposed immigration, arguing that immigrants undermined American workers because they would work for low wages and accept jobs as strikebreakers.

Prejudice Against Catholics

Increased feelings of nativism led to the founding of anti-immigrant organizations. The American Protective Association, founded by Henry Bowers in 1887, was an anti-Catholic organization. Its members vowed not to hire or vote for Catholics.

The Irish were among the immigrants who suffered most from the anti-Catholic feeling. Arriving to escape famine and other hardships, many were illiterate and found only the lowest-paying work as miners, dockhands, ditch-diggers, and factory workers. Irish women worked as cooks, servants, and millworkers. The dominant Protestant, British culture in America, which considered Irish poverty to be the result of laziness, superstition, and ignorance, had no use for the Catholic Irish.

Although several presidents vetoed legislation that would have limited immigration, prejudice

POLITICAL CARTOONS Primary Source

Prejudice Against Catholic Immigrants

Anti-Catholic prejudice was strong in the United States for most of the 1800s. Many Americans tried to prevent Catholic immigration to the United States, fearing Catholic beliefs were incompatible with American values.

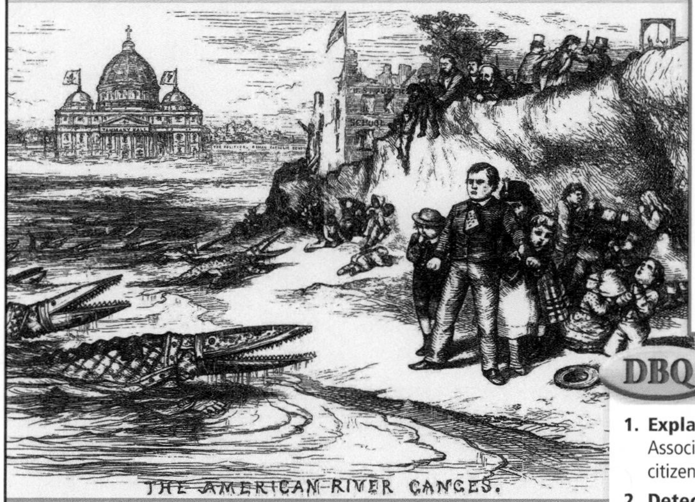

▲ *Catholic priests crawl ashore as children are tossed to them by New York politicians in this 1871 cartoon criticizing New York's decision to fund Catholic schools.*

Primary Source

"We unite to protect our country and its free institutions against the secret, intolerant, and aggressive efforts . . . by a certain religious political organization to control the government of the United States. . . .

. . . We have men born in several countries remote from this that are as loyal as any native, but they are not Romanists [Catholics]. American loyalty consists in devotion to our Constitution, laws, institutions, flag, and, above all, our public schools, for without intelligence this representative republic will go to pieces. . . . We are opposed to priests and prelates as such 'taking part in elections' and voting their laity as a unit in the interests of a foreign corporation . . ."

—from the platform of the American Protective Association, 1894

DBQ Document-Based Questions

1. **Explaining** What does the American Protective Association believe is incompatible with American citizenship? To what power does the statement refer?
2. **Detecting Bias** How does the cartoon express hostility toward Catholicism? Why might the cartoonist have depicted the public school on the hill in ruins?

Hands-On Chapter Project Step 1

Researching Immigration and Political Ads

Step 1: Researching German and Irish Immigration, 1815–1860

Essential Question: When did Irish and German immigrate in this period and where did they settle?

Directions Explain to students that they will create a poster display of the dominant groups that immigrated in this period. Students should research historical census figures using library books and the Internet. Student teams can focus on different elements for the final product: numbers of German and Irish immigrants by decade or half-decade; maps of their migration routes (even narrowing in on the area of the "home country" if possible) and copies of art or visuals that represent the time period, immigrants' backgrounds, and so on.

Putting It Together When the teams meet, they can sift through their data and determine how to best display it on a white board or poster. German and Irish immigrant information might be presented in a side-by-side format if the data is comparable, or on separate posters. OL

(Chapter Project continued on page 454)

against immigrants stimulated the passage of a new federal law. Enacted in 1882, the law banned convicts, paupers, and the mentally disabled from immigrating to the United States. The law also placed a 50¢ per head tax on each newcomer.

Restrictions on Asian Immigration

In the West, anti-Chinese sentiment sometimes led to racial violence. Denis Kearney, himself an Irish immigrant, organized the Workingman's Party of California in the 1870s to fight Chinese immigration. The party won seats in California's legislature and pushed to cut off Chinese immigration.

In 1882 Congress passed the **Chinese Exclusion Act.** The law barred Chinese immigration for 10 years and prevented the Chinese already in the country from becoming citizens. The Chinese in the United States organized letter-writing campaigns, petitioned the president, and even filed suit in federal court, but their efforts failed. Congress renewed the law in 1892 and made it permanent in 1902. It was not repealed until 1943.

On October 11, 1906, in response to rising Japanese immigration, the San Francisco Board of Education ordered "all Chinese, Japanese and Korean children" to attend the racially segregated "Oriental School" in the city's Chinatown neighborhood. (Students of Chinese heritage had been forced to attend racially segregated schools since 1859.) The directive caused an international incident. Japan took great offense at the insulting treatment of its people.

In response, Theodore Roosevelt invited school board leaders to the White House. He proposed a deal. He would limit Japanese immigration, if the school board would rescind its segregation order. Roosevelt then carried out his end of the deal. He began talks with Japan, and negotiated an agreement whereby Japan agreed to curtail the emigration of Japanese to the continental United States. The San Francisco school board then revoked its segregation order. This deal became known as the "Gentleman's Agreement" because it was not a formal treaty and depended on the leaders of both countries to uphold the agreement.

The Literacy Debate

In 1905 Theodore Roosevelt commissioned a study on how immigrants were admitted to the nation. The commission recommended an English literacy test. Two years later, another commission suggested literacy tests—in any language—for immigration. These recommendations reflected the bias of people against the "new immigrants," who were thought to be less intelligent than the "old immigrants." Although Presidents Taft and Wilson both vetoed legislation to require literacy from immigrants, the legislation eventually passed in 1917 over Wilson's second veto. The purpose of the law was to reduce immigration from southeastern European nations.

Reading Check **Explaining** Why did the federal government pass the Chinese Exclusion Act?

Section 1 REVIEW

Vocabulary

1. **Explain** the significance of: steerage, Ellis Island, Jacob Riis, Angel Island, nativism, Chinese Exclusion Act.

Main Ideas

2. **Listing** Why did European immigrants come to the United States?
3. **Describing** What caused the increase in Chinese immigration in the 1860s?
4. **Organizing** Complete a graphic organizer by listing the reasons nativists opposed immigration to the United States.

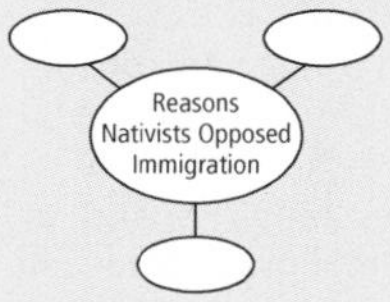

Critical Thinking

5. **Big Ideas** Where did most immigrants settle in the late 1800s? How did this benefit ethnic groups?
6. **Interpreting** Why did some Americans blame immigrants for the nation's problems?
7. **Analyzing Visuals** Select one of the people featured in any photo in this section. Write a journal entry about his or her experience, based on what you see in the photo.

Writing About History

8. **Descriptive Writing** Imagine that you are an immigrant who arrived in the United States in the 1800s. Write a letter to a relative in your home country describing your feelings during processing at either Ellis Island or Angel Island.

History ONLINE
Study Central™ To review this section, go to glencoe.com and click on Study Central.

Reading Check

Answer:
to limit Chinese immigration; It was a reaction to violence against Chinese immigrants in California and a reflection of the era's prejudice.

Assess

History ONLINE

Study Central™ provides summaries, interactive games, and online graphic organizers to help students review content.

Close

Identifying Ask: What government actions limited Asian immigration? *(Chinese Exclusion Act, Gentleman's Agreement, required literacy tests)* OL

Section 1 REVIEW

Answers

1. Significant terms, people, and events are boldfaced and highlighted in the section.
2. The United States had few immigration restrictions. There were plenty of available jobs. It was a way to escape poverty, forced military service, and religious persecution.
3. severe unemployment, poverty, famine, war, job opportunities
4.

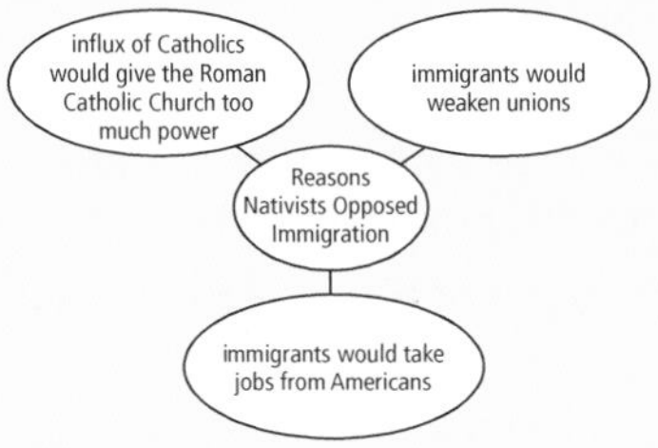

5. large cities; more available jobs, easier access to transportation, and greater ability to be part of a community
6. Answers will vary. Possible responses: Immigrants took jobs from native-born Americans. The large influx of immigrants caused cities to spend money to upgrade public utilities and law enforcement.
7. Journals will vary but should accurately reflect the experience of one of the individuals pictured in this section.
8. Letters will vary but should incorporate details from the text about the Ellis and Angel Island processing centers.

ANALYZING PRIMARY SOURCES

Focus

Chinese immigrants who could prove they were children of American fathers were automatically American citizens. Because "paper sons and daughters" bought false documents to claim citizenship, all were carefully questioned before being admitted. **Ask:** How might this have affected processing at Angel Island? *(slowed the process)*

Teach

S Skill Practice

Visual Literacy Ask: According to the cartoon, what push factors drew immigrants to the United States? *(no oppressive taxes, no expensive kings, no compulsory military service, no knouts or dungeons)* **BL**

C Critical Thinking

Predicting Consequences
Ask: What may have happened as a result of the eye examinations? *(Answers will vary but could include that immigrants received eye injuries and infections from the examinations.)* **OL**

ANALYZING PRIMARY SOURCES

Immigration

The United States is a nation of immigrants. In the late nineteenth century, more immigrants arrived on American shores than ever before. Some came from places such as the British Isles and Germany, from which many earlier immigrants had arrived. Others came from southern and eastern Europe, Asia, and other parts of the Americas. As the United States welcomed this mixture of ethnicities, religions, and languages, immigration became a subject of heated political debate.

Study these primary sources and answer the questions that follow.

PRIMARY SOURCE 1

Political Cartoon, 1880

▼ *"Welcome to All," by J. Keppler,* Puck *(1880)*

S

PRIMARY SOURCE 2

Photograph, 1905

▼ *Immigrants are checked for trachoma and other contagious eye diseases at Ellis Island. The inspector is using a buttonhook, normally used to fasten ladies' gloves, to lift this woman's eyelid. The instrument was "cleaned" between inspections by wiping it on the towel hanging nearby.*

C

PRIMARY SOURCE 3

Memoir Reflecting on Arrival at Ellis Island

"A group of Slovenian immigrants, of which this writer was one, arrived in New York from . . . Austria. . . . It was a beautiful morning in May 1906. After leaving the French ship LA TOURAINE, we were transported to Ellis Island for landing and inspection. There we were 'sorted out' as to the country we came from and placed in a 'stall' with the letter 'A' above us. ('A' was for Austria.)

There were at least a hundred Slovenian immigrants. We separated ourselves, as was the custom at home—men on the right and women and children on the left. All of us were waiting to leave for all parts of the United States.

The day was warm and we were very thirsty. An English-speaking immigrant asked the near-by guard where we could get a drink of water. The guard withdrew and returned shortly with a pail of water, which he set before the group of women. Some men stepped forward quickly to have a drink, but the guard pushed them back saying: 'Ladies first!' When the women learned what the guard had said, they were dumbfounded, for in Slovenia . . . women always were second to men. . . . Happy at the sudden turn of events, one elderly lady stepped forward, holding a dipper of water, and proposed this toast:

'Živijo Amerika, kjer so ženske prve!'
(Long live America, where women are first!)"

—Marie Priesland, recalling her arrival in the United States

Differentiated Instruction

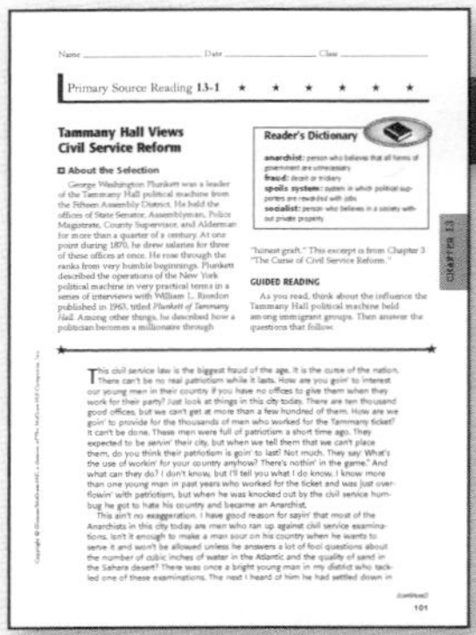
Name ________ Date ________ Class ________

Primary Source Reading 13-1

Tammany Hall Views Civil Service Reform

About the Selection

George Washington Plunkitt was a leader of the Tammany Hall political machine from the Fifteen Assembly District. He held the offices of State Senator, Assemblyman, Police Magistrate, County Supervisor, and Alderman for more than a quarter of a century. At one point during 1870, he drew salaries for three of these offices at once. He rose through the ranks from very humble beginnings. Plunkitt described the operations of the New York political machine in very practical terms in a series of interviews with William L. Riordon published in 1963, titled *Plunkitt of Tammany Hall.* Among other things, he described how a politician becomes a millionaire through "honest graft." This excerpt is from Chapter 3 "The Curse of Civil Service Reform."

Reader's Dictionary

anarchist: person who believes that all forms of government are unnecessary
fraud: deceit or trickery
spoils system: system in which political supporters are rewarded with jobs
socialist: person who believes in a society without private property

GUIDED READING

As you read, think about the influence the Tammany Hall political machine held among immigrant groups. Then answer the questions that follow.

This civil service law is the biggest fraud of the age. It is the curse of the nation. There can't be no real patriotism while it lasts. How are you goin' to interest our young men in their country if you have no offices to give them when they work for their party? Just look at things in this city today. There are ten thousand good offices, but we can't get at more than a few hundred of them. How are we goin' to provide for the thousands of men who worked for the Tammany ticket? It can't be done. These men were full of patriotism a short time ago. They expected to be servin' their city, but when we tell them that we can't place them, do you think their patriotism is goin' to last? Not much. They say: What's the use of workin' for your country anyhow? There's nothin' in the game." And what can they do? I don't know, but I'll tell you what I do know. I know more than one young man in past years who worked for the ticket and was just overflowin' with patriotism, but when he was knocked out by the civil service humbug he got to hate his country and became an Anarchist.

This ain't no exaggeration. I have good reason for sayin' that most of the Anarchists in this city today are men who ran up against civil service examinations. Isn't it enough to make a man sour on his country when he wants to serve it and won't be allowed unless he answers a lot of fool questions about the number of cubic inches of water in the Atlantic and the quality of sand in the Sahara desert? There was once a bright young man in my district who tackled one of these examinations. The next I heard of him he had settled down in

(continued)

101

Primary Source Reading, URB p. 101

Primary Source Reading

Objective: Read to learn why political machines like Tammany Hall appealed to immigrants.

Focus: Discern why the civil service system is inefficient according to this political machine leader.

Assess: Summarize the content of this excerpt in 2 to 3 sentences.

Close: Create an advertisement aimed at recruiting workers to the political machine.

Differentiated Learning Strategies

BL Describe what's wrong with the civil service law according to Plunkett.

AL Write a brief counterpoint to Plunkett's argument.

ELL Work with a partner to paraphrase the excerpt (using your own words.)

PRIMARY SOURCE 4

Magazine Article, 1903

"When I went to work for that American family I could not speak a word of English, and I did not know anything about housework. The family consisted of husband, wife and two children. They were very good to me and paid me $3.50 a week, of which I could save $3.

"I did not understand what the lady said to me, but she showed me how to cook, wash, iron, sweep, dust, make beds, wash dishes, clean windows, paint and brass, polish the knives and forks, etc., by doing the things herself and then overseeing my efforts to imitate her. . . . In six months I had learned how to do the work of our house quite well, and . . . I had also learned English. . . . I worked for two years as a servant . . . . and I was now ready to start in business."

—Chinese immigrant Lee Chew, reflecting on his first years in America

PRIMARY SOURCE 6

Political Cartoon, 1896

"The Immigrant: The Stranger at Our Gate," The Ram's Horn *(April 25, 1896)*
Emigrant: "Can I come in?"
Uncle Sam: "I 'spose you can; there's no law to keep you out."

THE STRANGER AT OUR GATE.
EMIGRANT.—Can I come in? UNCLE SAM.—I 'spose you can; there's no law to keep you out.

PRIMARY SOURCE 5

Questions Asked Immigrants, c. 1907

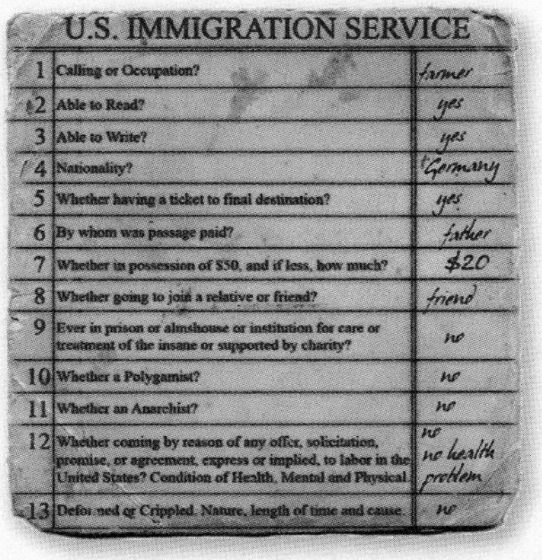
U.S. IMMIGRATION SERVICE

1	Calling or Occupation?	farmer
2	Able to Read?	yes
3	Able to Write?	yes
4	Nationality?	Germany
5	Whether having a ticket to final destination?	yes
6	By whom was passage paid?	father
7	Whether in possession of $50, and if less, how much?	$20
8	Whether going to join a relative or friend?	friend
9	Ever in prison or almshouse or institution for care or treatment of the insane or supported by charity?	no
10	Whether a Polygamist?	no
11	Whether an Anarchist?	no
12	Whether coming by reason of any offer, solicitation, promise, or agreement, express or implied, to labor in the United States? Condition of Health, Mental and Physical	no no health problem
13	Deformed or Crippled. Nature, length of time and cause.	no

DBQ Document-Based Questions

1. **Analyzing Visuals** Compare the political cartoons in Sources 1 and 6. How do the two depictions differ on the reasons why immigrants left their homeland and why they came to the United States?
2. **Making Inferences** Why did immigrants have to undergo health inspections? What do you suppose happened when an immigrant was found to have a contagious illness?
3. **Interpreting** Why do you think the author of Source 3 remembered Ellis Island so clearly decades later?
4. **Evaluating** According to Lee Chew in Source 4, what were some factors that helped him adapt as an immigrant and become a small business owner?
5. **Making Inferences** Study the questions listed in Source 5. Why do you think immigrants were required to answer these questions?

Assess/Close

Have students work in pairs to research the symbolism of the Statue of Liberty. Ask students to draw a new statue to attract immigrants in the twenty-first century.

DBQ Document Based Questions

Answers:

1. Source 1: a U.S. free from the problems of immigrants' homelands, eager to welcome them; Source 6: reluctance to accept immigrants who brought with them poverty, disease, and different religious and political beliefs.
2. Some came from homelands where disease was epidemic, such as Italy. Most of the sick were denied entrance.
3. Answers will vary. Perhaps coming to America meant a great deal to her, especially since the author is a woman.
4. He was able to save a large portion of his wages, learn skills and English.
5. The idea that a healthy, literate immigrant could be self-supporting.

Additional Support

Activity: Collaborative Learning

Immigration Skit Ask: Were all immigrants glad they had moved to the United States? *(Responses may vary. Explain that a number of immigrants regretted leaving their homelands and moved back.)* **Ask:** Why did immigrants have different views of their new homeland? *(Responses may vary, but should include age, gender, and personal experiences.)* Have the students form "family" groups consisting of a grandparent, two parents, a daughter, and a son. Suggest that students choose one of the homelands discussed in this chapter. Have the groups discuss how age, gender, and experiences influenced how immigrants felt about living in the United States. Have each group perform a skit in which family members evaluate their decision to move to the United States. Encourage students to include details from the text about problems that "pushed" the family from its homeland. **OL ELL**

Focus

Bellringer

Daily Focus Transparency 13-2

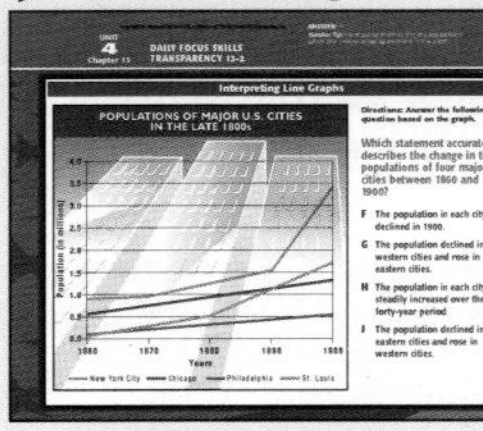

Guide to Reading

Answers to Graphic: crime, violence, disease, pollution, fire

Section Spotlight Video

To generate student interest and provide a springboard for class discussion, access the Chapter 13, Section 2 video at glencoe.com or on the video DVD.

Section 2 — Section Audio — Spotlight Video

Urbanization

Guide to Reading

Big Ideas

Government and Society The growth of and problems in major cities led to political machines that controlled local politics.

Content Vocabulary
- skyscraper *(p. 450)*
- tenement *(p. 453)*
- political machine *(p. 455)*
- party boss *(p. 455)*
- graft *(p. 455)*

Academic Vocabulary
- incentive *(p. 450)*
- trigger *(p. 455)*

People and Events to Identify
- Louis Sullivan *(p. 451)*
- George Plunkitt *(p. 455)*
- William "Boss" Tweed *(p. 455)*

Reading Strategy

Organizing As you read about urbanization in the United States in the late 1800s, complete a graphic organizer similar to the one below by filling in the problems the nation's cities faced.

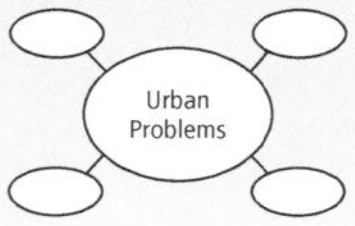

Native-born Americans and immigrants were drawn to cities by the jobs available in America's growing industries. The new, modern cities had skyscrapers, public transportation systems, and neighborhoods divided by social class. In many cities, political machines controlled city government.

Americans Migrate to the Cities

MAIN Idea Rural Americans and immigrants moved to the cities where skyscrapers and mass transit were developed to deal with congestion.

HISTORY AND YOU Have you ever ridden the bus, subway, or railway system? How do you think your ride to school or the store would be different without mass transportation? Read on to learn why cities developed mass transportation systems.

After the Civil War, the urban population of the United States grew from around 10 million in 1870 to more than 30 million in 1900. New York City, which had more than 800,000 inhabitants in 1860, grew to almost 3.5 million by 1900. During the same period, Chicago swelled from 109,000 residents to more than 1.6 million. The United States had only 131 cities with populations of 2,500 or more residents in 1840; by 1900, there were more than 1,700 such urban areas.

Most of the immigrants who poured into the United States in the late 1800s lacked both the money to buy farms and the education to obtain higher-paying jobs. Thus, they settled in the nation's growing cities, where they toiled long hours for little pay in the rapidly expanding factories of the United States. Despite the harshness of their new lives, most immigrants found that the move had improved their standard of living.

Rural Americans also began moving to the cities at this time. Farmers moved to cities because urban areas offered more and better-paying jobs than did rural areas. Cities had much to offer, too—bright lights, running water, and modern plumbing, plus attractions such as museums, libraries, and theaters.

The physical appearance of cities also changed dramatically. As city populations grew, demand raised the price of land, creating the **incentive** to build upward rather than outward. Soon, tall, steel frame buildings called **skyscrapers** began to appear. Chicago's ten-story Home Insurance Building, built in 1885, was the first skyscraper, but other buildings quickly dwarfed it. New York City, with its business district on the narrow island of Manhattan, boasted more skyscrapers than any other city in the world. With limited space, New Yorkers had to build up, not out.

Resource Manager

R Reading Strategies	C Critical Thinking	D Differentiated Instruction	W Writing Support	S Skill Practice
Teacher Edition • Making Connections, p. 454 • Organizing, p. 455 **Additional Resources** • Prim. Source Read., URB p. 101 • Guide Reading Act., URB p. 115	**Teacher Edition** • Contrasting, p. 451 • Drawing Conclusions, p. 452 • Speculating, p. 453 • Making Inferences, p. 454 **Additional Resources** • Geog. And Hist., URB p. 3 • Quizzes and Tests, p. 177	**Teacher Edition** • Visual/ Spatial, p. 452 • Kinesthetic, p. 453 **Additional Resources** • Enrichment Act., URB p. 111	**Teacher Edition** • Persuasive Writing, p. 452	**Additional Resources** • Time Line Act., URB p. 99 • Read. Essen., p. 144

TECHNOLOGY & HISTORY

The Technology of Urbanization

Before the mid-1800s, few buildings exceeded four or five stories. To make wooden and stone buildings taller required enormously thick walls in the lower levels. This changed when steel companies began mass-producing cheap steel girders and steel cable.

▲ **Steel Cable**

Steel also changed the way bridges were built. Engineers could now suspend bridges from steel towers using thick steel cables. Using this technique, engineer John Roebling designed New York's Brooklyn Bridge—the world's largest suspension bridge at the time. It was completed in 1883.

Completed in 1913, the Woolworth Building is 792 feet high. It was the tallest building in the world until 1930.

A steel frame carries the weight, allowing the building to be much taller than stone or wood structures.

With steel beams instead of walls supporting the building, windows could be larger.

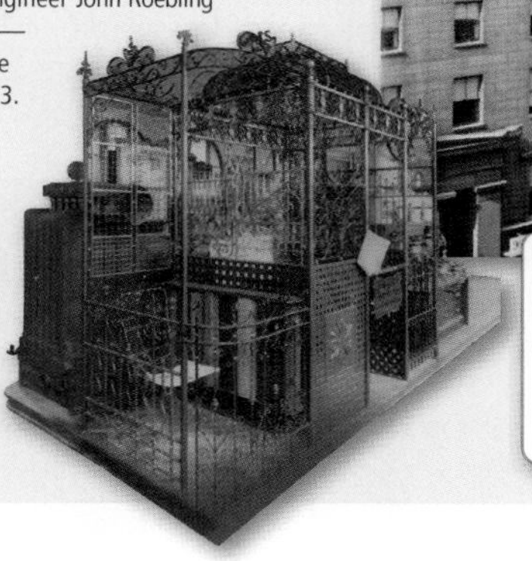

▶ **Elevators**

Elisha Otis invented the safety elevator in 1852. By the late 1880s, the first electric elevators had been installed, making tall buildings practical.

Analyzing VISUALS

1. **Theorizing** What other technologies were necessary in order to build modern skyscrapers?
2. **Predicting** What long-term effects do you think the new building technologies had on cities?

No one contributed more to the design of skyscrapers than Chicago's **Louis Sullivan.** "What people are within, the buildings express without," explained Sullivan, whose lofty structures featured simple lines and spacious windows using new, durable plate glass.

To move people around cities quickly, various kinds of mass transit developed. At first, almost all cities relied on the horsecar, a railroad car pulled by horses. In 1890 horsecars moved about 70 percent of urban traffic in the United States.

More than 20 cities, beginning with San Francisco in 1873, installed cable cars, which were pulled along tracks by underground cables. Then, in 1887, engineer Frank J. Sprague developed the electric trolley car. The country's first electric trolley line opened the following year in Richmond, Virginia.

In the largest cities, congestion became so bad that engineers began looking for ways to move mass transit off the streets. Chicago responded by building an elevated railroad, while Boston, followed by New York, built the first subway systems. C

Reading Check **Summarizing** What new technologies helped people in the late 1800s get to and from work?

Teach

C Critical Thinking

Contrasting Ask: How did Chicago's and Boston's mass transit systems differ? *(Chicago's is aboveground; Boston's is underground.)* BL

Analyzing VISUALS

Answers:
1. mass production of steel; elevators; durable plate glass
2. Answers will vary but could include the idea of unlimited future expansion.

Reading Check

Answer:
cable cars, electric trolley cars, elevated railroads, subways

Differentiated Instruction

Leveled Activities

BL Academic Vocabulary Activity 13, pp. 95–96

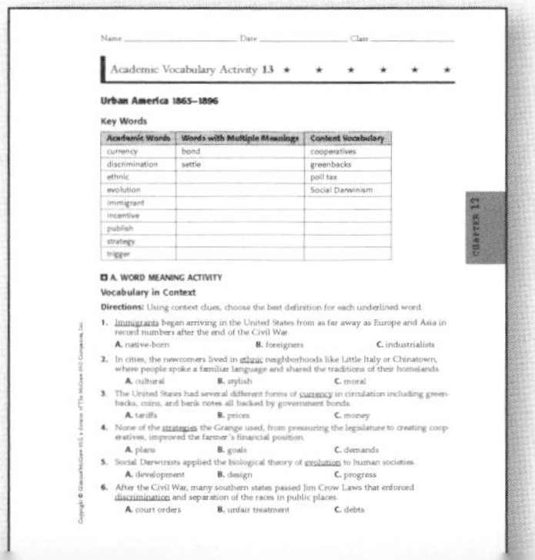

OL Time Line Activity 13, p. 99

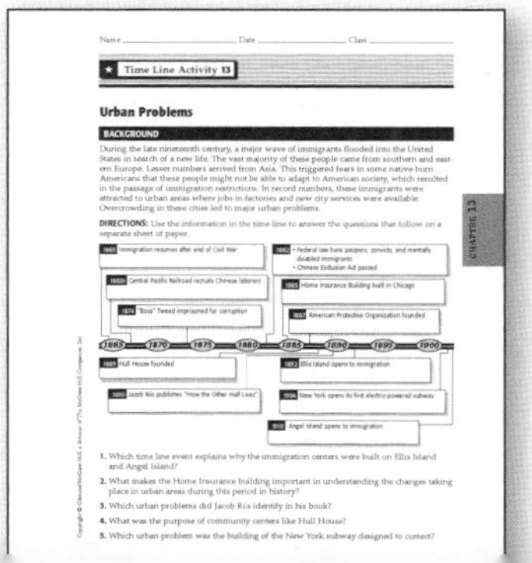

AL Enrichment Activity 13, p. 111

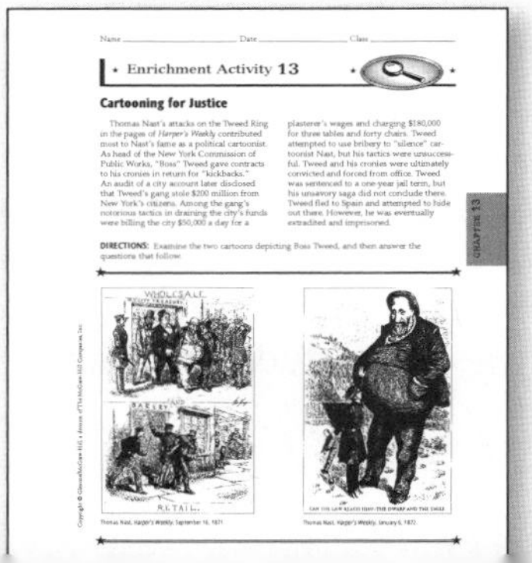

ELL Content Vocabulary Activity 13, p. 93

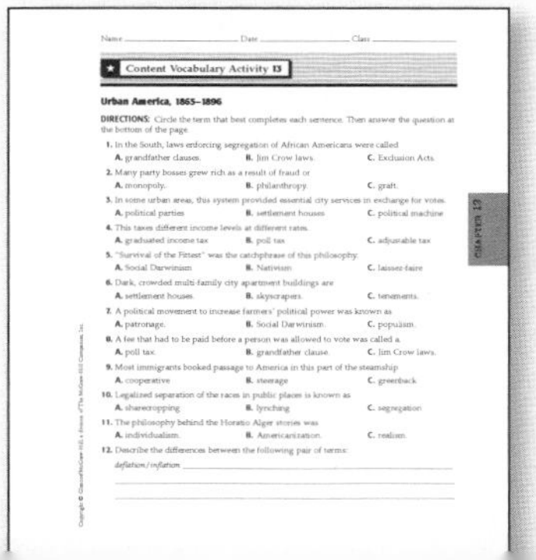

W Writing Support

Persuasive Writing Ask students to write newspaper editorials defending or criticizing the right of the wealthy to spend money as they chose despite the harsh living conditions of an impoverished working class. **AL**

D Differentiated Instruction

Visual/Spatial Have students work in pairs to research housing styles described in the text. Ask students to draw, paint, or construct a model of one of the styles. **ELL**

C Critical Thinking

Drawing Conclusions Ask: Why did the middle class choose to move away from the central city? *(to escape the crime and pollution of the city)* **BL**

Separation by Class

MAIN Idea In the cities, society was separated by classes, with the upper, middle, and working classes living in different neighborhoods.

HISTORY AND YOU Do you know the history of certain neighborhoods in your city or town? Can you see where the classes were divided? Read on to learn how each class lived in the cities.

In the growing cities, the wealthy people and the working class lived in different parts of town. So, too, did members of the middle class. The boundaries between neighborhoods were quite definite and can still be seen in many American cities today.

High Society

During the last half of the 1800s, the wealthiest families established fashionable districts in the heart of a city. Americans with enough money could choose to construct homes in the style of a feudal castle, an English manor house, a French château, a Tuscan villa, or a Persian pavilion. In Chicago, merchant and real estate developer Potter Palmer chose a castle. In New York, Cornelius Vanderbilt's grandson commissioned a $3 million French château with a two-story dining room, a gymnasium, and a marble bathroom.

As their homes grew larger, wealthy women managed an increasing number of servants, such as cooks, maids, butlers, coachmen, nannies, and chauffeurs, and spent a great deal of money on social activities. In an age in which many New Yorkers lived on $500 a year, socialite hostess Cornelia Sherman Martin spent $360,000 on a dance.

Middle-Class Gentility

American industrialization also helped expand the middle class. The nation's rising middle class included doctors, lawyers, engineers, managers, social workers, architects, and teachers. Many people in the middle class moved away from the central city so as to escape the crime and pollution and be able to afford larger homes. Some took advantage of the new commuter rail lines to move to "streetcar suburbs."

PRIMARY SOURCE

Urban Society

Urban industrial society in the late 1800s was divided into social classes. The upper class and middle class lived well, but conditions for the working class and poor were often abysmal.

THE UPPER CLASS

▲ *The upper class could afford elaborate mansions and many servants. Men typically owned or managed large businesses. Women almost never worked. Clothing was elaborate and expensive. Events, such as afternoon tea in their garden (above), required formal dress and shows they had substantial leisure time.*

THE MIDDLE CLASS

▲ *Middle class families could generally afford their own homes and better quality clothing. Women rarely worked—and if they did it was usually because they wanted a career, not out of necessity. Many families had at least one servant (shown above in back holding the baby) and enough money left over to buy luxuries, such as the new gramophone shown above.*

Additional Support

Activity: Technology Connection

Analyzing High Society Ask: Are homes built by the wealthy in the last half of 1800s still standing today? Assign groups of students a major U.S. city such as New York, Chicago, or Philadelphia. Have groups use the Internet to research the historic homes in these cities that have been preserved. Groups should find images of these homes and make a list of their different styles. Have students create posters with drawing or prints of some of the homes in their cities and present them to the class. **OL**

In the late nineteenth century, most middle class families had at least one live-in servant. This gave the woman of the house more time to pursue activities outside the home. "Women's clubs" became popular. At first, these clubs focused on social and educational activities. Over time, however, "club women" became very active in charitable and reform activities. In Chicago, for example, the Women's Club helped establish juvenile courts and exposed the terrible conditions at the Cook County Insane Asylum.

The Working Class

Few families in the urban working class could hope to own a home. Most spent their lives in crowded **tenements,** or apartment buildings. The first tenement in the United States was built in 1839. In New York, three out of four residents squeezed into tenements, dark and crowded multi-family apartments. To supplement the average industrial worker's annual income of $445, many families rented precious space to a boarder. Zalmen Yoffeh, a journalist, lived in a New York tenement as a child. He recalled:

PRIMARY SOURCE

"With . . . one dollar a day [our mother] fed and clothed an ever-growing family. She took in boarders. Sometimes this helped; at other times it added to the burden of living. Boarders were often out of work and penniless; how could one turn a hungry man out? She made all our clothes. She walked blocks to reach a place where meat was a penny cheaper, where bread was a half cent less. She collected boxes and old wood to burn in the stove."

—quoted in *How We Lived*

History ONLINE
Student Web Activity Visit glencoe.com and complete the activity on tenement life.

The Family Economy

Within the working class, some people were better off than others. White native-born men earned higher wages than African American men, immigrants, and women.

One economist estimated that 64 percent of working class families relied on more than one wage earner in 1900. In some cases, the whole family worked, including the children. The dangerous working conditions faced by child workers, and the fact that they were not in school, alarmed many reformers.

THE WORKING CLASS

▲ *Most working class families lived in apartments, often only a single room in size. They had no servants, and often husbands and wives both had to work.*

WORKING WOMEN

▶ *Many young women, such as this one making a straw hat in a factory, worked long hours for little pay.*

URBAN POVERTY

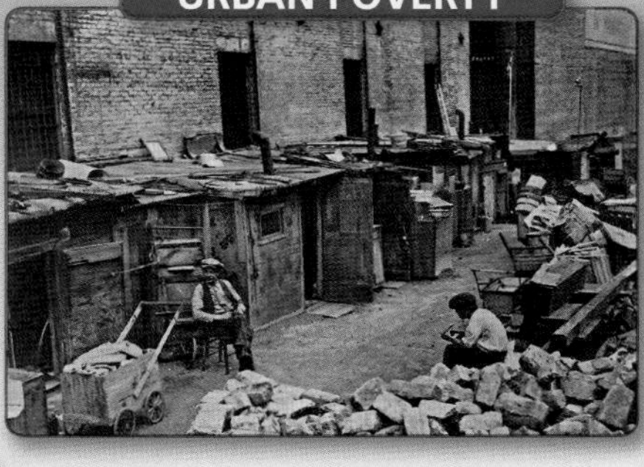

▲ *Unable to afford homes, the urban poor slept on the street or built shacks in back alleys like these in New York City in the early 1900s.*

Analyzing VISUALS

1. **Comparing and Contrasting** What do the upper class and middle class have in common compared to the working class and poor?
2. **Drawing Conclusions** How effective was industrial society at meeting people's needs?

D Differentiated Instruction

Kinesthetic Have students form "families" of eight. Block window light. Have students cooking, playing, studying, and sleeping in a small area. Have "families" describe their reactions to "tenement life." **BL**

C Critical Thinking

Speculating Ask: Why did the woman accept nonpaying boarders? *(Answers will vary but may assert that the woman knew how poverty felt.)* **OL**

Analyzing VISUALS

Answers:
1. The upper and middle classes owned homes; the working class rented apartments, and the poor were homeless.
2. Most students will answer that the needs of only the top two classes were met.

Additional Support

Activity: Economics Connection

Budgeting Ask: What factors do you consider before buying something? *(Answers may include the price, affordability, or need for an item.)* Have students work in pairs to develop a household budget. Allow class time for partners to compare their itemized budgets and add expenditures they had not considered. Then ask partners to interview a family member or other adult about the costs of each budget item for a family of four. Have students calculate the income of two working adults, assuming 40-hour workweeks at minimum wage. Ask partners to calculate the shortfall between income and expenses and then list ways in which their shortfall can be addressed (such as deleting recreational and luxury items, working additional jobs, and so on). As a class, discuss the challenges of "making ends meet" and the emotional repercussions of not being able to meet the needs of the family. **OL**

C Critical Thinking

Making Inferences Ask: Why do you think social isolation was a result of domestic service? *(The upper and middle classes regarded domestic servants as social inferiors and did not associate with them.)* **AL**

R Reading Strategies

Making Connections Remind students that there was no compensation for maimed or killed workers during this time period. **Ask:** How are disabled or injured workers or families of killed workers protected today? *(Worker's compensation, disability and work-related life insurance.)* **OL**

DBQ Document Based Questions

Answers:

1. His men notify him.
2. Plunkitt receives their votes.

Reading Check

Answer:
doctors, lawyers, engineers, managers, social workers, teachers; streetcar suburbs

A growing number of women took jobs outside the home. Native-born white women typically had more years of education than other women. Thus, many used their literacy to work as teachers or do clerical work.

The largest source of employment for women, however, remained domestic service. Immigrant women often worked as domestic **C** servants in the North; African American women usually worked as domestic servants in the South. Such work involved long hours, low wages, and social isolation.

When people were physically unable to work, they had to rely on family members or charity. When a worker was maimed or killed on the job, there was usually no compensation. **R** Most older Americans lived with family members. Nearly 70 percent of those 65 or older lived with their grown children. A growing number, however, lived independently or in homes for the aged.

Reading Check **Explaining** Who was in the "middle class" in the late 1800s? Where did they live?

Urban Problems

MAIN Idea Major problems plagued the cities; political machines provided help for some residents but were frequently corrupt.

HISTORY AND YOU What kinds of programs are used in your area to deal with urban problems? Read about political machines and how they ran city government.

City living posed the risks of crime, violence, fire, disease, and pollution. The rapid growth of cities only made these problems worse and complicated the ability of urban governments to respond to these problems.

Crime and Pollution

Crime was a growing problem in American cities. Minor criminals, such as pickpockets, swindlers, and thieves, thrived in crowded urban living conditions. Major crimes multiplied as well. From 1880 to 1900, the murder rate jumped sharply from 25 per million people to more than 100 per million people.

POLITICAL CARTOONS PRIMARY SOURCE

Were Political Machines Bad for Cities?

Critics of political machines said that they took bribes and gave contracts to friends, robbing cities of resources. Defenders argued that they provided services and kept the city running.

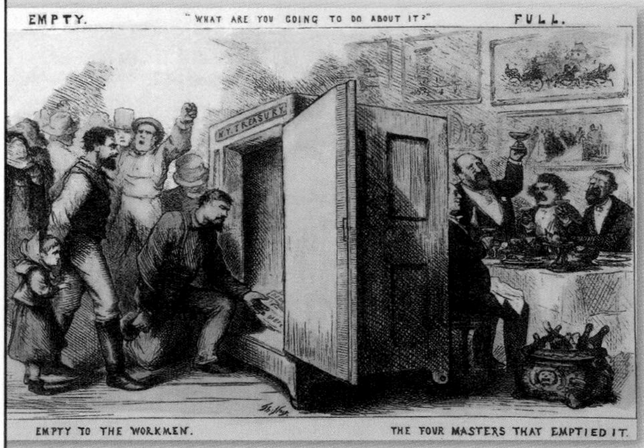

▲ *Workers in New York find the city treasury empty, while behind the scenes, Boss Tweed and other city politicians enjoy a sumptuous feast.*

PRIMARY SOURCE

New York "Boss" George W. Plunkitt explains the benefits of the political machines:

"The poor are the most grateful people in the world, and, let me tell you, they have more friends in their neighborhoods than the rich have in theirs.

If there's a family in my district in want I know it before the charitable societies do, and me and my men are first on the ground.... The consequence is that the poor look up to George W. Plunkitt ... and don't forget him on election day.

Another thing, I can always get a job for a deservin' man.... I know every big employer in the district and in the whole city, for that matter, and they ain't in the habit of sayin' no to me when I ask them for a job."

—quoted in William L. Riordan, *Plunkitt of Tammany Hall*

DBQ Document-Based Questions

1. **Analyzing Primary Sources** How does Plunkitt say he learns of people in need in his district?
2. **Determining Cause and Effect** What is the result of Plunkitt's care for the needy in his district?

Hands-On Chapter Project Step 2

Researching Immigration and Political Ads

Step 2: Compiling Data on Hispanic Immigration, 1960–2005 Essential Question: When did Hispanic groups immigrate in this period to the United States and where did they settle?

Directions Explain to students that they will create a poster display of Hispanic immigration to the United States in recent decades. They can use figures and graphs from their textbook, historical census figures, library books and the Internet. Student teams can focus on different elements for the final product: numbers of immigrants by decade or half-decade; maps of their migration route (even targeting the area of their home country, if possible) and copies of art or visuals that illustrate important points; e.g., the class background of most immigrants.

Putting It Together When the teams meet they can sift through their data and determine how to best display it on a white board or poster. Information and visuals might include other text to explain any particular forces impelling emigration from Mexico and Central and South America. **OL**

(Chapter Project continued on page 464)

Alcohol contributed to violent crime, both inside and outside the home. Danish immigrant Jacob Riis, who documented slum life in his 1890 book *How the Other Half Lives,* accused saloons of "breeding poverty," corrupting politics, bringing suffering to the wives and children of drunkards, and fostering "the corruption of the child" by selling beer to minors.

Disease and pollution posed even bigger threats. Improper sewage disposal contaminated city drinking water and **triggered** epidemics of typhoid fever and cholera. Though flush toilets and sewer systems existed in the 1870s, pollution remained a severe problem as horse manure was left in the streets, smoke belched from chimneys, and soot and ash accumulated from coal and wood fires. R

Machine Politics

The **political machine,** an informal political group designed to gain and keep power, came about partly because cities had grown much faster than their governments. New city dwellers needed jobs, housing, food, heat, and police protection. In exchange for votes, political machines and the **party bosses** who ran them eagerly provided these necessities.

Graft and Fraud The party bosses who ran the political machines also controlled the city's finances. Many machine politicians grew rich as the result of fraud or **graft**—getting money through dishonest or questionable means. **George Plunkitt,** one of New York City's most powerful party bosses, defended what he called "honest graft." For example, a politician might find out in advance where a new park was to be built and buy the land near the site. The politician would then sell the land to the city for a profit. As Plunkitt stated, "I see my opportunity, and I take it."

Outright fraud occurred when party bosses accepted bribes from contractors who were supposed to compete fairly to win contracts to build streets, sewers, and buildings. Corrupt bosses also sold permits to their friends to operate public utilities, such as railroads, waterworks, and power systems.

Tammany Hall Tammany Hall, the New York City Democratic political machine, was the most infamous such organization. **William "Boss" Tweed** was its leader during the 1860s and 1870s. Tweed's corruptness led to a prison sentence in 1874.

City machines often controlled all the city services, including the police department. In St. Louis, the "boss" never feared arrest when he called out to his supporters at the police-supervised voting booth, "Are there any more repeaters out here that want to vote again?"

Opponents of political machines, such as political cartoonist Thomas Nast, blasted bosses for their corruption. Defenders, though, argued that machines provided necessary services and helped to assimilate the masses of new city dwellers.

Reading Check **Evaluating** Why did political machines help city dwellers in the late 1800s?

Section 2 REVIEW

Vocabulary

1. **Explain** the significance of: skyscraper, Louis Sullivan, tenement, political machine, party boss, graft, George Plunkitt, William "Boss" Tweed.

Main Ideas

2. **Identifying** What technologies made the building of skyscrapers possible?
3. **Comparing** How did the living conditions of the upper, middle, and the working classes in the late 1800s compare?
4. **Organizing** Complete the graphic organizer below by listing the effects of many Americans moving from rural to urban areas in the late 1800s.

Migration → Effects: ____ / ____ / ____

Critical Thinking

5. **Big Ideas** How did political machines respond to the needs of the people?
6. **Synthesizing** Why were pollution and sewage a problem in American cities in the late 1800s?
7. **Analyzing Visuals** Look at the photos on pages 452–453. How did industrialization affect the class structure in the United States?

Writing About History

8. **Persuasive Writing** Take on the role of an urban planner in a major city in the late 1800s. Write a letter to members of the city government listing specific reasons for the importance of setting aside city land for parks and recreational areas.

History ONLINE
Study Central™ To review this section, go to glencoe.com and click on Study Central.

R Reading Strategies

Organizing Have students draw a 3-part organizer to show the chain of events that leads to cholera. BL

Reading Check

Answer:
to gain immigrant votes and, thus, retain political power

Assess

History ONLINE

Study Central™ provides summaries, interactive games, and online graphic organizers to help students review content.

Close

Describing Ask: How did immigration challenge American cities? *(Cities were unprepared for sudden population growth and struggled to provide services.)* OL

Section 2 REVIEW

Answers

1. Significant terms, places, and people are boldfaced and highlighted in the section.
2. steel frames, elevators, durable plate glass
3. The wealthy lived in grand homes in fashionable areas, the middle class lived in comfortable homes in streetcar suburbs, and the working class lived in tenements.
4. Migration → Effects: larger urban population / more disease / growth of political machines
5. Political machines provided jobs, housing, food, heat, and police protection.
6. They contaminated drinking water and triggered epidemics of typhoid fever and cholera, as well as other health problems.
7. Answers will vary but may include: expanded the middle class; separated classes into distinctly different neighborhoods.
8. Letters will vary but should include specific reasons for parks and recreational areas.

GEOGRAPHY & HISTORY

Focus

Tell students that the first settlement house was founded in New York City in 1886. Settlement houses helped immigrants adjust to life in America. Italians coming to the United States would be able to learn English, send their children to school, enjoy recreational activities, and have access to health services.

Teach

R Reading Strategy

Reading Maps Ask: What other ethnic group had a large presence in New York City? *(Chinese, in Chinatown)* **BL**

C Critical Thinking

Drawing Conclusions Ask: Why did people from different parts of Italy live on different New York City streets? *(Dialects and customs changed from village to village in Italy and people were more likely to live near those they have connections with.)* **OL**

Additional Support

NATIONAL GEOGRAPHIC

GEOGRAPHY & HISTORY

Italian Immigration to America

Italians from southern Italy were among the largest group of the "new immigrants"—the peoples who flooded American shores between 1880 and 1920. In Italy, most were poor peasants who worked for absentee landlords and lived in extreme poverty. They were often illiterate and had never traveled even as far as the next village. Leaving for America was daunting. "Make yourself courage"—those were the last words one boy heard his father say as they said goodbye in Naples. **R**

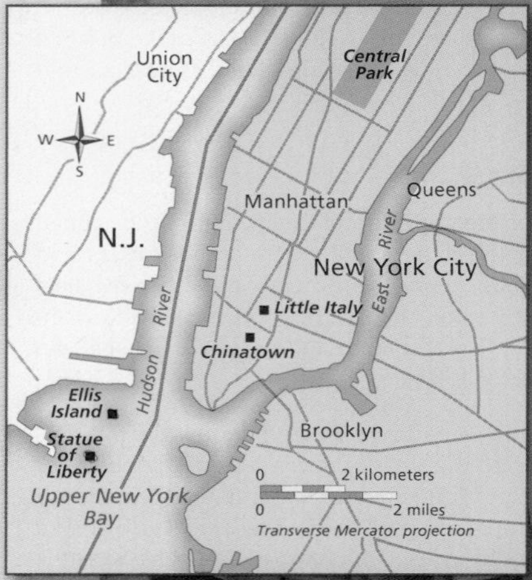

How Did Geography Shape Urban Life?

In New York City, these peasant-immigrants congregated in Little Italy in lower Manhattan. They would find an apartment on the street where people from their village in Italy lived. In 1910, as many as 40,000 people were packed in a 17-block area of Little Italy. As they mingled with other Italians, they began thinking of themselves as Italians, not Neapolitans (from Naples) or Sicilians (from Sicily).

C New York's Little Italy bustled with peddlers, bakers, and laborers, but also with immigrants moving in or out of the area. Italian families were hardworking and thrifty. As soon as possible, they moved to cleaner, sunnier places, such as Brooklyn or Long Island. By 1914, one reformer said there were at least 1500 lawyers, 500 physicians, and a growing number of merchants, bankers, and businessmen in New York City who were of Italian heritage. It was a very American success story.

Women worked long hours. They went out once or even twice a day to shop from pushcarts for their meals. They often cooked and did the washing for their family and for male boarders, too.

Analyzing GEOGRAPHY

1. **Place** What drew Italian immigrants to specific areas of New York City?
2. **Movement** What years represented the peak period for the new immigrants to the United States?

Activity: Collaborative Learning

Learn About Little Italy Divide the class into small groups. Ask each group to select a major city in the United States known to have a Little Italy or other ethnic neighborhood. (San Diego, San Francisco, Cleveland, and Chicago all have a Little Italy.) Have each group use library or Internet resources to research that city's unique contributions. Ask each group to use its findings to prepare a presentation for the class. Presentations should include visual elements such as photographs, maps, and illustrations. **OL**

GEOGRAPHY & HISTORY

Assess/Close

Have students assume the role of the young person whose father told him to "Make yourself courage." Have them write a letter back to their family in Italy telling them about life in New York's Little Italy. **OL**

Analyzing GEOGRAPHY

Answers:

1. Italian immigrants moved to neighborhoods in New York where other people from their home villages lived.
2. between 1880 and 1920

Additional Support

Activity: Economics Connection

Migrant Workers and the Law The young Italian males who came to the United States often intended to work for one or two seasons before returning to Italy. They generally did not speak English, and relied on labor bosses to find them jobs in construction. The padrones, as they were called, sometimes cheated the young workers. Have students find contemporary examples of similar situations that migrant workers or other immigrants face. Lead a discussion of how this justice issue might be resolved. **OL**

Focus

Bellringer

Daily Focus Transparency 13-3

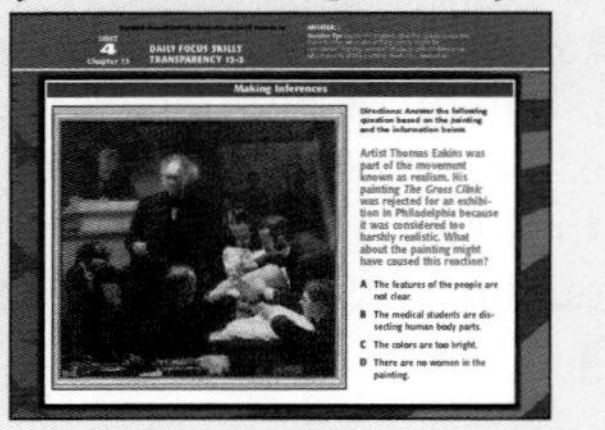

Guide to Reading

Answers To Graphic:

Theory or Movement	Main Idea
Social Darwinism	survival of the fittest
Laissez-faire	no government interference in business
Gospel of Wealth	the wealthy use philanthropy to create conditions that help people help themselves
Realism	portray the world realistically

Section Spotlight Video

To generate student interest and provide a springboard for class discussion, access the Chapter 13, Section 3 video at glencoe.com or on the video DVD.

Section 3

Section Audio · Spotlight Video

The Gilded Age

Guide to Reading

Big Ideas

Past and Present Ideas about wealth during the last part of the 1800s continue to affect society today.

Content Vocabulary

- individualism *(p. 458)*
- Social Darwinism *(p. 459)*
- philanthropy *(p. 460)*
- settlement house *(p. 467)*
- Americanization *(p. 467)*

Academic Vocabulary

- evolution *(p. 459)*
- publish *(p. 461)*

People and Events to Identify

- Gilded Age *(p. 458)*
- Gospel of Wealth *(p. 460)*
- Mark Twain *(p. 461)*
- Social Gospel *(p. 466)*
- Jane Addams *(p. 467)*

Reading Strategy

Categorizing Complete a graphic organizer similar to the one below by filling in the main idea of each of the theories and movements listed.

Theory or Movement	Main Idea
Social Darwinism	
Laissez-Faire	
Gospel of Wealth	
Realism	

The industrialization of the United States led to new art and literature and new ideas about government's role in society. Social Darwinists believed society developed through "survival of the fittest." Other Americans thought steps needed to be taken to help the less fortunate.

Social Darwinism

MAIN Idea Individualism and Social Darwinism shaped Americans' attitudes toward industrial society.

HISTORY AND YOU Do you think each individual person should be left on his or her own to succeed, or should people help those who fall behind? Read to learn about people who applied the notion of "survival of the fittest" to human society.

In 1873 Mark Twain and Charles Warner wrote a novel entitled *The Gilded Age: A Tale of Today*. Historians later adopted the term and applied it to the era in American history that began about 1870 and ended around 1900. The era was in many ways a time of marvels. Amazing new inventions led to rapid industrial growth. Cities expanded to sizes never seen before. Masses of workers thronged the streets. Skyscrapers reached to the sky, electric lights banished the darkness, and wealthy entrepreneurs built spectacular mansions.

By calling this era the **Gilded Age,** Twain and Warner were sounding an alarm. Something is gilded if it is covered with gold on the outside but made of cheaper material inside. A gilded age might appear to sparkle, but critics pointed to corruption, poverty, crime, and great disparities in wealth between the rich and the poor.

Whether the era was golden or merely gilded, it was certainly a time of great cultural activity. Industrialism and urbanization altered the way Americans looked at themselves and their society, and these changes gave rise to new values, new art, and new entertainment.

The Idea of Individualism

One of the strongest beliefs of the era—and one that remains strong today—was the idea of **individualism.** Many Americans firmly believed that no matter how humble their origins, they could rise in society and go as far as their talents and commitment would take them. No one expressed the idea of individualism better than Horatio Alger, who wrote more than 100 "rags-to-riches" novels. In his books, a poor person goes to the big city and, through a combination of hard work and luck,

Resource Manager

R Reading Strategies	C Critical Thinking	D Differentiated Instruction	W Writing Support	S Skill Practice
Teacher Edition • Academic Vocab., p. 460 • Using Context Clues, p. 462 • Activ. Prior Knowledge, pp. 463, 464, 466 • Paraphrasing, p. 465 **Additional Resources** • Guided Reading Act., URB p. 116	**Teacher Edition** • Predicting Consequences, p. 462 • Making Inferences, p. 461 • Cause/Effect, p. 463 • Explaining, p. 464 **Additional Resources** • History Simulations, URB p. 9 • Quizzes and Tests, p. 179	**Teacher Edition** • Auditory/Musical, p. 460 **Additional Resources** • Art and Music Act., URB p. 105	**Teacher Edition** • Personal Writing, pp. 459, 466 **Additional Resources** • Supreme Court Case Studies, p. 23	**Teacher Edition** • Analyzing Visuals, p. 461 **Additional Resources** • Read. Essen., p. 147

PRIMARY SOURCE

Social Darwinism and Society

PRIMARY SOURCE

The Gospel of Wealth

"In bestowing charity, the main consideration should be to help those who will help themselves; to provide part of the means by which those who desire to improve may do so; to give those who desire to rise the aids by which they may rise; to assist, but rarely or never to do all. Neither the individual nor the race is improved by almsgiving. Those worthy of assistance, except in rare cases, seldom require assistance. The really valuable men of the race never do, except in cases of accident or sudden change.... He is the only true reformer who is as careful and as anxious not to aid the unworthy as he is to aid the worthy, and, perhaps, even more so, for in almsgiving more injury is probably done by rewarding vice than by relieving virtue.... "

—Andrew Carnegie, quoted in *The North American Review*, June 1889

W

PRIMARY SOURCE

"Robert was very different. He inherited from his father an unusual amount of courage and self-reliance, and if one avenue was closed to him, he at once set out to find another. It is of this class that successful men are made, and we have hopes that Robert will develop into a prosperous and successful man."

—from Horatio Alger, *Brave and Bold*

DBQ Document-Based Questions

1. **Analyzing Primary Sources** What does Carnegie believe is the way to dignify the lives of rich people?
2. **Describing** On what does Alger base Robert's chances of success? Do you agree with his criteria? Why or why not?

becomes successful. His popular books convinced many young people that no matter how many obstacles they faced, success was possible.

Social Darwinism

Another powerful idea of the era was **Social Darwinism.** This philosophy, loosely derived from Darwin's theories, strongly reinforced the idea of individualism.

Herbert Spencer British philosopher Herbert Spencer applied Charles Darwin's theory of **evolution** and natural selection to human society. In his 1859 book *On the Origin of Species by Means of Natural Selection,* Darwin argued that plant and animal life had evolved over the years by a process he called natural selection. In this process, those species that cannot adapt to the environment in which they live gradually die out, while those that do adapt thrive and live on.

Spencer took this theory intended to explain developments over millions of years and argued that human society also evolved through competition and natural selection. He argued that society progressed and became better because only the fittest people survived. Spencer and others, such as American scholar William Graham Sumner, who shared his views, became known as Social Darwinists, and their ideas became known as Social Darwinism. "Survival of the fittest" became the catchphrase of their philosophy.

Social Darwinism also paralleled the economic doctrine of laissez-faire that opposed any government programs that interfered with business. Not surprisingly, industrial leaders heartily embraced the theory. John D. Rockefeller maintained that survival of the fittest, as demonstrated by the growth of huge businesses like his own Standard Oil, was "merely the working out of the law of nature and the law of God."

Teach

W Writing Support

Personal Writing Have students write letters to Andrew Carnegie, agreeing or disagreeing with his philosophy. OL

DBQ Document Based Questions

Answers:

1. using their power to help others
2. courage, self-reliance, and perseverance; Answers will vary but should contain supporting evidence for the opinion.

Additional Support

Activity: Interdisciplinary Connection

Science Ask: In the natural world, which animals survive and which do not? *(Answers may include that the physically weak, sick, injured, or small animals may not survive predation or environmental factors, such as extreme climate and drought.)* Invite a science teacher to talk with students about "survival of the fittest" in the animal world. Ask the teacher to describe how animals adapt to improve their chances of survival. After the presentation, have students form groups to list ways in which immigrants adapt to improve their chances of physical, economic, and social survival. Have groups create a "Tips for Survival" poster that will help a new immigrant succeed in today's United States. Display the posters and discuss them as a class. **Ask:** Does adapting to fit into American society threaten an immigrant's chances of retaining his or her cultural heritage? Can an individual live successfully within two cultures? OL

R Reading Strategy

Academic Vocabulary Explain that the Greek *philos* means "loving" and *anthropos* means "human being." **Ask:** From these word parts, what is philanthropy? *(a desire to help humanity, especially through charitable activities)* OL

D Differentiated Instruction

Auditory/Musical Read aloud the excerpt from *Huckleberry Finn.* **Ask:** What conclusions can you reach about Huck by listening to him speak? *(Answers will vary but may include that he is poorly educated and lives in a different time or place.)* BL

Reading Check

Answer:
Human society evolves through competition and natural selection, or survival of the fittest.

Additional Support

Darwinism and the Church For many devout Christians, however, Darwin's conclusions were upsetting and offensive. They rejected the theory of evolution because they believed it contradicted the Bible's account of creation. Some ministers, however, concluded that evolution may have been God's way of creating the world. One of the most famous ministers of the era, Henry Ward Beecher, called himself a "Christian evolutionist."

Carnegie's Gospel of Wealth Andrew Carnegie advocated a gentler version of Social Darwinism that he called the **Gospel of Wealth.** This philosophy held that wealthy Americans should engage in **philanthropy** and use their great fortunes to create the conditions that would help people help themselves. Building schools and hospitals, for example, was better than giving handouts to the poor. Carnegie himself helped fund the creation of public libraries in cities across the nation because libraries provided the information people needed to get ahead in life.

Reading Check **Summarizing** What was the main idea of Social Darwinism?

A Changing Culture

MAIN Idea Artists and writers began portraying life in America more realistically, and cities offered new forms of entertainment.

HISTORY AND YOU Have you read Mark Twain's *The Adventures of Huckleberry Finn*? Read to learn about how Twain portrayed American life in a realistic way.

The late 1800s was a period of great cultural change for writers and artists, and for many urban Americans who sought new forms of entertainment.

Realism

A new movement in art and literature called realism began in the 1800s. Just as Darwin tried to explain the natural world scientifically, artists and writers tried to portray the world realistically. European realists included Edgar Degas and Edouard Manet. Perhaps the best known American realist painter was Thomas Eakins. In realistic detail, he painted young men rowing and athletes playing baseball, and he showed surgeons and scientists in action.

PRIMARY SOURCE

Realism in Art and Literature

Realist writers and artists did not want to portray people and the world idealistically. Instead they sought to present things as accurately as possible.

PRIMARY SOURCE

"'Say, who is you? Whar is you? Dog my cats ef I didn' hear sumf'n. Well, I know what I's gwyne to do: I's gwyne to set down here and listen tell I hears it agin.'"

So he set down on the ground betwixt me and Tom. He leaned his back up against a tree, and stretched his legs out till one of them most touched one of mine. My nose begun to itch. It itched till the tears come into my eyes. But I dasn't scratch. Then it begun to itch on the inside. Next I got to itching underneath. I didn't know how I was going to set still. This miserableness went on as much as six or seven minutes; but it seemed a sight longer than that."

—from *The Adventures of Huckleberry Finn* by Mark Twain

▲ *Realist painters did not generally choose heroic or historical topics for their art. Instead they preferred to depict ordinary people doing ordinary things. Thomas Eakins, perhaps the best-known American realist, depicted various aspects of American life, including a carriage ride by the wealthy (above) or a professional baseball game (right).*

Activity: Technology Connection

Using Technology to Create Realist Art Ask: What images would you choose to realistically portray American life to a prospective immigrant? *(Students may name game systems, popular foods, sports teams, and so on.)* Have students work in pairs with a computer presentation program to create a slide show of images that realistically represent various facets of American life today, such as home life, school, work, recreation, communities, politics, and organizations. Encourage students to use their imaginations. Suggest that they incorporate music into their presentations. Have partners present their slide shows to the class. During the presentations, ask class members to note particularly effective and realistic images. At the end of the presentations, discuss memorable images with the class. **Ask:** Did some presentations give conflicting views of American life? Why might one person's "reality" differ from another's? OL

Writers also attempted to capture the world as they saw it. In several novels, William Dean Howells presented realistic descriptions of American life. For example, his novel *The Rise of Silas Lapham* (1885) described the attempts of a self-made man to enter Boston society. Also an influential literary critic, Howells was the first to declare **Mark Twain** an incomparable American genius.

Twain, whose real name was Samuel Clemens, **published** his masterpiece, *The Adventures of Huckleberry Finn*, in 1884. In this novel, the title character and his friend Jim, an escaped slave, float down the Mississippi River on a raft. Twain wrote in local dialect with a lively sense of humor. He had written a true American novel, in which the setting, subject, characters, and style were clearly American.

Popular Culture

Popular culture changed considerably in the late 1800s. Industrialization improved the standard of living for many people, enabling them to spend money on entertainment and recreation. Increasingly, urban Americans divided their lives into separate units—that of work and that of home. People began "going out" to public entertainment.

The Saloon In cities, saloons often outnumbered groceries and meat markets. As a place for social gathering, saloons played a major role in the lives of male workers. Saloons offered drinks, free toilets, water for horses, and free newspapers for customers. They even offered the first "free lunch": salty food that made patrons thirsty and eager to drink more. Saloons also served as political centers and saloonkeepers were often key figures in political machines.

Amusement Parks and Sports Working-class families and single adults could find entertainment at new amusement parks such as New York's Coney Island. Amusements such as water slides and railroad rides cost only a nickel or dime.

Watching professional sports also became popular during the late 1800s. Formed in 1869, the first professional baseball team was the Cincinnati Red Stockings. Other cities soon fielded their own teams. In 1903 the first official World Series was played between the Boston Red Sox and the Pittsburgh Pirates. Football also gained in popularity and by the late 1800s had spread to public colleges.

As work became less strenuous, many people looked for activities involving physical exercise. Tennis, golf, and croquet became popular. In 1891 James Naismith, athletic director for a college in Massachusetts, invented a new indoor game called basketball.

S **Vaudeville and Ragtime** Adapted from French theater, vaudeville took on an American flavor in the early 1880s with its hodgepodge of animal acts, acrobats, and dancers. The fast-paced shows went on continuously all day and night.

Like vaudeville, ragtime music echoed the hectic pace of city life. Its syncopated rhythms **C** grew out of the music of riverside honky-tonks, saloon pianists, and banjo players, using the patterns of African American music. Scott Joplin, one of the most important African American ragtime composers, became known as the "King of Ragtime." He wrote his most famous piece, "The Maple Leaf Rag," in 1899.

Reading Check **Describing** What was the importance of the saloon in city life?

For examples of literature from the Gilded Age, read excerpts from the writings of Mark Twain and Carl Sandburg on pages R70–71 in **American Literature Library.**

Analyzing VISUALS DBQ

1. **Analyzing** How does Twain's writing reflect a realist approach to writing?
2. **Making Inferences** Why might Realist art have become popular in the late 1800s?

S Skill Practice

Analyzing Visuals Ask: Why is this a realist painting? *(It shows players and surroundings as they are, without romanticizing them.)* **OL**

C Critical Thinking

Making Inferences Ask: Why might vaudeville shows have run continuously day and night? *(to accommodate shift workers)* **OL** **AL**

Analyzing VISUALS

1. Twain used realistic characters, setting, dialect, subject, and style.
2. Answers will vary but may suggest that some Realist artists and writers sought to show the lives of ordinary Americans as they faced the challenges of an industrializing society.

Reading Check

Answer:
It served as a community and political center for male workers.

Additional Support

Activity: Collaborative Learning

Social Classes in the Gilded Age Ask: How does personal wealth affect your daily life? *(Answers will vary but could include that wealth dictates what is purchased, what activities are pursued, and the amount of leisure time people have.)* Divide students into six groups. Assign two groups to the wealthy class, two to the middle class, and two to the working class. Have groups use the Internet to obtain more information about everyday life in the Gilded Age, such as recreational opportunities, social groups, and types of vocations. Then ask groups to write a daily activity log for one week, describing activities and tasks people in their assigned class might perform. Have groups share their logs with the class. **OL**

R Reading Strategies

Using Context Clues

Ask: Which words of the text define *patronage*? *(the power to reward supporters by giving them government jobs)* **ELL**

C Critical Thinking

Predicting Consequences

Ask: What positive consequence resulted from the creation of civil service positions? *(Jobs were performed better because workers were better qualified; reduced corruption because continued employment no longer relied on political support.)* **OL**

Additional Support

Politics in Washington

MAIN Idea The two major parties were closely competitive in the late 1800s; tariff rates and big business regulation were hotly debated political issues.

HISTORY AND YOU Have you ever considered getting a job working for the government once you graduate? Read to learn why you will have to take an examination if you want a government job.

After President James A. Garfield was elected in 1880, many of his supporters tried to claim the "spoils of office"—the government jobs that are handed out following an election victory. President Garfield did not believe in the spoils system. One of these job seekers made daily trips to the White House in the spring of 1881 asking for a job. He was repeatedly rejected. Reasoning that he would have a better chance for a job if Vice President Chester A. Arthur were president, this man shot President Garfield on July 2, 1881. Weeks later, Garfield died from his wounds.

Civil Service Reform

For many, Garfield's assassination highlighted the need to reform the political system. Traditionally, under the spoils system, elected politicians extended patronage—the power to reward supporters by giving them government jobs. Many Americans believed the system made government inefficient and corrupt. In the late 1870s, reformers had begun pushing him for an end to patronage.

When Rutherford B. Hayes became president in 1877, he tried to end patronage by firing officials who had been given their jobs because of their support of the party and replacing them with reformers. His actions divided the Republican Party between "Stalwarts" (who supported patronage) and the "Halfbreeds" (who opposed it), and no reforms were passed. In 1880 the Republicans nominated James Garfield, a "Halfbreed," for president and Chester A. Arthur, a "Stalwart," for vice president. Despite the internal feud over patronage, the Republicans managed to win the election, only to have Garfield assassinated a few months later.

Garfield's assassination turned public opinion against the spoils system. In 1883 Congress responded by passing the Pendleton Act. This law required that some jobs be filled by competitive written examinations, rather than through patronage. This marked the beginning of professional civil service—a system where most government workers are given jobs based on their qualifications rather than on their political affiliation. Although only about 10 percent of federal jobs were made civil service positions in 1883, the percentage steadily increased over time.

The Election of 1884

In 1884 the Democratic Party nominated Grover Cleveland, the governor of New York, for president. Cleveland was a reformer with a reputation for honesty. The Republican Party nominated James G. Blaine, a former Speaker of the House rumored to have accepted bribes. Some Republican reformers were so unhappy with Blaine that they supported Cleveland. They became known as "Mugwumps," from an Algonquian word meaning "great chief." If Blaine was their party's candidate, declared the Mugwumps, they would vote for Cleveland, "an honest Democrat."

Blaine hoped to make up for the loss of the Mugwumps by courting Catholic voters. Shortly before the election, however, Blaine met with a Protestant minister who denounced the Democrats for having ties to Catholicism. When Blaine was slow to condemn the remark, he lost many Catholic votes. Cleveland narrowly won the election.

As the first elected Democratic president since 1856, Grover Cleveland faced a horde of supporters who expected him to reward them with jobs. Mugwumps, on the other hand, expected him to increase the number of jobs protected by the civil service system. Cleveland chose a middle course and angered both sides. Economic issues, however, soon replaced the debate about patronage reform.

The Interstate Commerce Commission

Many Americans were concerned by the power of large corporations. Small businesses and farmers had become particularly angry at the railroads. While large corporations such as Standard Oil were able to negotiate rebates and lower rates because of the volume of goods they shipped, others were forced to pay much higher rates. Although the high fixed costs and low operating costs of railroads caused much

Activity: Economics Connection

National Budget Divide the class into groups. Have each group research the nation's budget surpluses and deficits since 1860. Based on the information, groups should create a line graph showing the changing trends. At each point where the trend shows a change of direction, identify the events that might have brought about the change. Have students write a paragraph stating how political leaders have contributed to surpluses and deficits and whether their decisions have helped or hurt the country. **OL AL**

POLITICAL CARTOONS PRIMARY SOURCE
Political Debates of the Gilded Age

▲ Senator Pendleton is congratulated for his civil service bill; behind him a trash bin overflows with papers saying reform is impossible.

▲ John Bull, symbol of Britain, thanks Grover Cleveland for free trade because it keeps British workers employed even if everyone else starves.

Analyzing VISUALS

1. **Analyzing** Does the cartoon on the right say free trade is a good idea? How do you know?
2. **Explaining** Did the artist who drew the cartoon on the left favor civil service reform? How does he indicate his opinion?

of this problem, many Americans believed railroads were gouging customers.

Neither party moved quickly at the federal level to address these problems. Both believed that government should not interfere with corporations' property rights, which courts had held to be the same as those of individuals. Many states, however, passed laws regulating railroad rates; in 1886 the Supreme Court ruled in the case of *Wabash, St. Louis, and Pacific Railway* v. *Illinois* that states could not regulate railroad rates for traffic between states because only the federal government could regulate interstate commerce.

R Public pressure forced Congress to respond to the Wabash ruling. In 1887 Cleveland signed the Interstate Commerce Act. This act, which created the Interstate Commerce Commission (ICC), was the first federal law to regulate interstate commerce. The legislation limited railroad rates to what was "reasonable and just," forbade rebates to high-volume users, and made it illegal to charge higher rates for shorter hauls. The commission was not very C effective in regulating the industry, however, because it had to rely on the courts to enforce its rulings.

Debating Tariffs Another major economic issue concerned tariffs. Many Democrats thought that Congress should cut tariffs because these taxes had the effect of raising the price of manufactured goods. Although it may have made sense to protect weak domestic manufacturing after the Civil War, many questioned the need to maintain high tariffs in the 1880s, when large American companies were fully capable of competing internationally. High tariffs also forced other nations to respond in kind, making it difficult for farmers to export their surpluses.

In December 1887 President Cleveland proposed lowering tariffs. The House, with a Democratic majority, passed moderate tariff reductions, but the Republican-controlled Senate rejected the bill. With Congress deadlocked, tariff reduction became a major issue in the election of 1888.

R Reading Strategies

Activating Prior Knowledge
Ask: Why does Congress respond to public pressure? *(They want people to vote for them when they are up for reelection.)* OL

C Critical Thinking

Determining Cause and Effect Ask: What might have made the ICC more effective? *(Answers will vary but could include the ability to assess fines and shut down railroad operations.)* AL

Analyzing VISUALS

1. No; Lifting tariffs let foreign companies more ably compete and take business away from American businesses. John Bull, or England, thanks the president for free trade.
2. Yes; Senator Pendleton is congratulated for helping the civil service bill pass despite the papers around him that say it's impossible.

Additional Support

Activity: Economics Connection

Tariffs Ask: What imported goods do you buy? *(Answers will vary.)* Explain that tariffs affect the prices of imported items. Ask students to work in groups to list five imported goods they or their family have purchased, and the prices they paid. Ask groups to discuss the following questions: *If the government were to place a tariff on these goods, would you still buy them? At what price would you look for a domestically produced item instead? Are there some imported items that you would buy regardless of price? Why?* Have groups share their lists and the answers to the questions with the class. OL

R Reading Strategies

Activating Prior Knowledge Remind students that Harrison won the electoral vote, but not the popular vote. **Ask:** Why was Harrison ruled the winner of the 1888 election if he did not receive the majority of the popular vote? *(The electoral vote, not the popular vote, decides the presidency.)* **OL**

C Critical Thinking

Explaining Ask: Why were trusts powerful? *(Trusts consolidated similar businesses, giving them monopolies; without competition, they could set prices as high as they wished.)* **OL**

Reading Check

Answer: created the Interstate Commerce Commission and passed the Sherman Antitrust Act

Republicans Regain Power

R The Republicans and their presidential candidate, Benjamin Harrison, received large campaign contributions in 1888 from industrialists who benefited from high tariffs. Cleveland and the Democrats campaigned against high tariff rates. In one of the closest races in American history, Harrison lost the popular vote but won the electoral vote.

The McKinley Tariff The election of 1888 gave the Republicans control of both houses of Congress as well as the White House. Using this power, the party passed legislation to address points of national concern. In 1890 Representative William McKinley of Ohio pushed through a tariff bill that cut tobacco taxes and tariff rates on raw sugar but greatly increased rates on other goods, such as textiles, to discourage people from buying those imports.

The McKinley Tariff was intended to protect American industry from foreign competition and encourage consumers to buy American goods. Instead, it helped to trigger a steep rise in the price of all goods that angered many Americans and may have contributed to President Harrison's defeat in the 1892 election.

The Sherman Antitrust Act Congress also responded to popular pressure to do something about the power of the large business combinations known as trusts. In 1890 Congress passed the Sherman Antitrust Act, which prohibited any "combination . . . or conspiracy, in restraint of trade or commerce among the several States." The law, however, was vaguely worded, poorly enforced, and C weakened by judicial interpretation. Most significantly, the Supreme Court ruled the law did not apply to manufacturing, holding that manufacturing was not interstate commerce. Thus the law had little impact. In the 1890s businesses formed trusts and combinations at a great rate. Like the ICC, the Sherman Antitrust Act was more important for establishing a precedent than for its immediate impact.

Reading Check **Summarizing** What actions did Congress take to regulate big business?

The Rebirth of Reform

MAIN Idea Reformers developed new methods and philosophies for helping the urban poor.

HISTORY AND YOU Have you ever been to a YMCA? What activities can you do there? Read on to find out the origin of the YMCA and other community centers.

The tremendous changes that industrialism and urbanization brought triggered a debate over how best to address society's problems. While many Americans embraced the ideas of individualism and Social Darwinism, others disagreed, arguing that society's problems could be fixed only if Americans and their government began to take a more active role in regulating the economy and helping those in need.

Debates IN HISTORY

Is Social Darwinism the Best Approach for Ensuring Progress and Economic Growth?

The social problems that came with industrialization led to a debate over government's role in the economy. Some believed that government should intervene to help the poor and solve problems while others argued that leaving things alone was the best solution.

Hands-on Chapter Project Step 3

Researching Immigration and Political Ads

Step 3: Comparing Immigration in 19th and 20th Centuries Essential Question: Has immigration differed in basic ways in the past nearly 200 years?

Directions Students can compare their work from Steps 1 and 2 and formulate questions that will focus on what may differ. For example: Are the numbers vastly different? Have the reasons for migration changed? Students may find that their earlier research is helpful here, even if it was not reflected on the poster. Encourage students to consider the political and social conditions in both the home countries and in the United States in, say 1860 compared to 2000.

Putting It Together Students may want to create a bulleted list or another poster to illustrate their comparative findings with charts, tables, or other visuals. **OL**

(Chapter Project continued on page 472)

Challenging Social Darwinism

In 1879 journalist Henry George published *Progress and Poverty,* a discussion of the American economy that quickly became a national bestseller. In his book George observed, "The present century has been marked by a prodigious increase in wealth-producing power." This should, he asserted, have made poverty "a thing of the past." Instead, he claimed, the "gulf between the employed and the employer is growing wider; social contrasts are becoming sharper." In other words, laissez-faire economics was making society worse—the opposite of what Social Darwinists believed.

Most economists now argue that George's analysis was flawed. Industrialism did make some Americans very wealthy, but it also improved the standard of living for most others as well. At the time, however, in the midst of poverty, crime, and harsh working conditions, many Americans did not believe things were improving. George's economic theories encouraged other reformers to challenge the assumptions of the era.

Lester Frank Ward In 1883 Lester Frank Ward published *Dynamic Sociology,* in which he argued that humans were different from animals because they had the ability to make plans to produce the future outcomes they desired.

Ward's ideas came to be known as Reform Darwinism. People, he insisted, had succeeded in the world because of their ability to cooperate; competition was wasteful and time-consuming. Government, he argued, could regulate the economy, cure poverty, and promote education more efficiently than competition in the marketplace could. **R**

YES

William Graham Sumner
Professor

PRIMARY SOURCE

"The moment that government provided work for one, it would have to provide work for all, and there would be no end whatever possible. Society does not owe any man a living. In all the cases that I have ever known of young men who claimed that society owed them a living, it has turned out that society paid them—in the State prison . . . The fact that a man is here is no demand upon other people that they shall keep him alive and sustain him. He has got to fight the battle with nature as every other man has; and if he fights it with the same energy and enterprise and skill and industry as any other man, I cannot imagine his failing—that is, misfortune apart."

—testimony before the U.S. House of Representatives, 1879

NO

Lester Frank Ward
Sociologist

PRIMARY SOURCE

"The actions of men are a reflex of their mental characteristics. Where these differ so widely the acts of their possessors will correspondingly differ. Instead of all doing the same thing they will do a thousand different things. The natural and necessary effect of this is to give breadth to human activity. Every subject will be looked at from all conceivable points of view, and no aspect will be overlooked or neglected. It is due to this multiplicity of viewpoints, growing out of natural inequalities in the minds of men, that civilization and culture have moved forward along so many lines and swept the whole field of possible achievement."

—from "Social Classes in the Light of Modern Sociological Theory," 1908

DBQ Document-Based Questions

1. **Summarizing** What argument does Professor Sumner make against government assisting people?
2. **Paraphrasing** How does Professor Ward believe that different abilities aid society?
3. **Contrasting** How can you contrast the ideas of the two men?
4. **Evaluating** Which opinion do you agree with? Write a brief essay explaining your ideas.

R Reading Strategies

Paraphrasing Ask: In your own words, what was the main idea of Ward's *Dynamic Sociology?* *(Government is better able to fix social and economic problems because it represents a cooperative effort on the part of everyone.)* **AL**

Debates IN HISTORY

Answers:

1. There would be no end to government assistance; society does not owe people a living.
2. Because people look at things differently, civilization and culture will advance.
3. the need for personal struggle vs. the creation of a society in which each person can develop his or her own talents
4. Answers should contain supporting evidence.

Additional Support

Activity: Interdisciplinary Connection

Civics A supporter of *laissez-faire,* William Graham Sumner objected to government regulation of the economy, social legislation, and trade unions. When asked by a congressman whether government could hire workers who had lost their jobs to mechanization, Sumner said the worker must make the best of the situation and rely on his own resourcefulness. In contrast, Ward felt that a kind government could meet the needs of its citizens. He believed in equality for all, regardless of class, race, or gender. Universal education, Ward thought, was the key to establishing full equality. **Ask:** In what way are both men's ideas similar? *(Both believed people are capable of examining a situation and taking action.)* **OL**

R Reading Strategy

Activating Prior Knowledge
Ask: How does twentieth century history prove that Bellamy's fictional society is not realistic? *(The Soviet Union collapsed under the weight of economic problems due to socialism.)* **AL**

W Writing Support

Personal Writing Have students write a journal entry describing a personal experience in which they either made choices to improve their situation or suffered through no fault of their own. **BL**

People IN HISTORY

Answer: Hull House provided day care, kindergartens, libraries, an art gallery, an employment agency, and a union meeting place.

People IN HISTORY

Jane Addams
1860–1935

After visiting a settlement house in London, England, Jane Addams decided to open Hull House in 1889 to assist poor immigrants in Chicago.

That assistance took on many forms: day care, kindergartens, libraries, an art gallery, an employment agency, and a meeting place for trade unions. The women who worked at Hull House, many of them college-educated in social work, pushed for protective legislation for children and women, which was enacted first in Illinois and then nationally.

Addams wrote books about her experiences at Hull House, giving an example to many others throughout the nation who also founded settlement houses. She favored woman suffrage and supported the founding of the American Civil Liberties Union and the National Association for the Advancement of Colored People. She was active in the peace movement, serving as first president of the organization that became the Women's International League for Peace and Freedom. For her efforts, she was awarded the Nobel Peace Prize in 1931.

What kind of assistance did Hull House provide immigrants?

▲ *Children stand in front of Hull House in 1905.*

Looking Backward Writer Edward Bellamy promoted another alternative to Social Darwinism and laissez-faire economics. In 1888 he published *Looking Backward,* a novel about a man who falls asleep in 1887 and awakens in the year 2000 to find that the nation has become a perfect society with no crime, poverty, or politics. In this fictional society, the government owns all industry and shares the wealth equally with all Americans. Bellamy's ideas were essentially a form of socialism. His book became a bestseller and helped to shape the thinking of some American reformers.

Naturalism in Literature Criticism of industrial society also appeared in literature in a new style of writing known as naturalism. Social Darwinists argued that people could make choices to improve their situation. Naturalists challenged this idea by suggesting that some people failed in life simply because they were caught up in circumstances they could not control. Sometimes people's lives were destroyed through no fault of their own.

Among the most prominent naturalist writers were Stephen Crane, Jack London, and Theodore Dreiser. Stephen Crane's novel *Maggie, A Girl of the Streets* (1893), told the story of a girl's descent into prostitution and death. Jack London's tales of the Alaskan wilderness demonstrated the power of nature over civilization. Theodore Dreiser's novels, such as *Sister Carrie* (1900), painted a world where people sinned without punishment and where the pursuit of wealth and power often destroyed their character.

Helping the Urban Poor

The plight of the urban poor prompted some reformers to find new ways to help. Their efforts gave rise to the Social Gospel movement, the Salvation Army, the YMCA, and settlement houses.

The Social Gospel The **Social Gospel** movement worked to better conditions in cities according to the biblical ideals of charity and justice. Washington Gladden, a minister, was an early advocate who popularized the movement in writings such as *Applied Christianity* (1887). Walter Rauschenbusch, a Baptist minister from New York, became the leading voice in the Social Gospel movement.

Additional Support

Activity: Interdisciplinary Connection

Sociology The eighth of nine children in a prosperous family, Jane Addams was valedictorian of her college graduating class. Although she attempted to study medicine, poor health forced her to stop. Upon recovery, Addams toured Europe with her friend Ellen G. Starr. There they visited Toynbee Hall, a settlement house in London's East End. Convinced they could open a similar place in the United States, Addams and Starr leased a large house in Chicago, made speeches to raise money, convinced young women of wealthy families to volunteer their time and services, took care of children, nursed the sick, and listened to the troubles of people who came for help. By its second year, Hull House saw over 2,000 people every week. **Ask:** Would Jane Addams have been as successful today? *(Answers will vary but should be supported with sound reasoning.)* **OL**

The Church, he argued, must "demand protection for the moral safety of the people." The Social Gospel movement inspired many churches to take on new community functions. Some churches built gyms and provided social programs and child care. Others focused exclusively on helping the poor.

The Salvation Army and the YMCA The Salvation Army and the YMCA also combined faith and an interest in reform. The Salvation Army offered practical aid and religious counseling to the urban poor. The Young Men's Christian Association (YMCA) tried to help industrial workers and the urban poor by organizing Bible studies, citizenship training, and group activities. YMCAs, or "Ys," offered libraries, gymnasiums, auditoriums, and low-cost hotel rooms available on a temporary basis to those in need.

The head of the Chicago YMCA, Dwight L. Moody, was a gifted preacher who founded his own church, today known as Moody Memorial Church. By 1867, Moody had begun to organize revival meetings in other American cities, which drew thousands of people. Moody rejected both the Social Gospel and Social Darwinism. He believed the way to help the poor was not by providing them with services but by redeeming their souls and reforming their character.

The Settlement House Movement The **settlement house** movement began as an offshoot of the Social Gospel movement. In the late 1800s idealistic reformers—including many college-educated women—established settlement houses in poor, often heavily immigrant neighborhoods. A settlement house was a community center where reformers resided and offered everything from medical care and English classes to kindergartens and recreational programs. **Jane Addams** opened the famous Hull House in Chicago in 1889. Her work inspired others. Jewish reformer Lillian Wald founded the Henry Street Settlement in New York City.

Public Education As the United States became increasingly industrialized and urbanized, it needed more workers who were trained and educated. The number of public schools increased dramatically after the Civil War. The number of children attending school rose from 6,500,000 in 1870 to 17,300,000 in 1900. Public schools were often crucial to the success of immigrant children. At public schools, immigrant children were taught English and learned about American history and culture, a process known as **Americanization.**

Schools also tried to instill discipline and a strong work ethic. Grammar schools divided students into grades and drilled them in punctuality, neatness, and efficiency—necessary habits for the workplace. At the same time, vocational education in high schools taught skills required in specific trades.

Not everyone had access to school. Cities were far ahead of rural areas. Many African Americans also did not have equal educational opportunities. Some African Americans started their own schools, following the example of Booker T. Washington, who founded the Tuskegee Institute in 1881.

Reading Check **Explaining** What was the purpose of a settlement house?

Section 3 REVIEW

Vocabulary

1. **Explain** the significance of Gilded Age, individualism, Social Darwinism, Gospel of Wealth, philanthropy, Mark Twain, Social Gospel, settlement house, Jane Addams, Americanization.

Main Ideas

2. **Defining** What were the defining characteristics of the Gilded Age?
3. **Describing** How did changes in art and literature reflect the issues and characteristics of the late 1800s?
4. **Explaining** Why was the Sherman Antitrust Act ineffective?
5. **Categorizing** Complete a chart like the one below by listing the names and goals of reform movements that arose in the late 1800s to help the urban poor.

Reform Movement	Goals

Critical Thinking

6. **Big Ideas** Do you think the idea of the Gospel of Wealth is still alive today? Why or why not?
7. **Analyzing Visuals** Look at the cartoon on the right on page 463. What do the figures in the background suggest?

Writing About History

8. **Descriptive Writing** Imagine that you are a newspaper editor in the late 1800s. Write an editorial in which you support or oppose the philosophy of Social Darwinism.

History ONLINE
Study Central™ To review this section, go to glencoe.com and click on Study Central.

467

Reading Check

Answer: a community center where reformers offered medical care, English classes, kindergartens, and recreational programs

Assess

History ONLINE

Study Central™ provides summaries, interactive games, and online graphic organizers to help students review content.

Close

Determining Importance

Ask: Why were reformers important in the Gilded Age? *(They exposed and worked to cure social ills, such as poverty and illiteracy which were otherwise ignored by a society experiencing newly increasing wealth.)*

Section 3 REVIEW

Answers

1. Significant terms are boldfaced and highlighted throughout the section.
2. individualism; urbanization; new values, art, and forms of entertainment
3. Art and literature became more realistic as artists and writers depicted the changing values of industrializing America.
4. The enforcing courts judged the legislation too vague and refused to rule against big companies.
5.

Reform Movement	Goals
Social Gospel	better conditions in cities according to biblical ideals of charity and justice
Revivalism	help the poor by redeeming their souls
Settlement house	improve living conditions of the poor

6. Answers will vary but should be backed up by examples of and/or statistics on philanthropy of wealthy individuals.
7. disgruntled, out-of-work Americans whose factory is no longer producing, while the British factory continues to operate
8. Editorials will vary but should accurately express the philosophy of Social Darwinism.

Focus

Ask: Why is the author appalled at the number of children? *(Answers may vary but may include the idea that tenements were unsafe for children.)* What is the irony in the water and beer reference? *(While the second floor of the tenement has no running water, immigrants spend their money on beer.)*

Teach

C Critical Thinking

Assessing Ask: The author says the immigrant is *sullen*, or resentful. Does the immigrant have any choices? *(Answers will vary but could reflect that the immigrant does not have to buy beer.)* **OL**

S Skill Practice

Calculating Ask: What percentage of monthly income is spent on charitable donations? *(just under 2%)* **AL**

Additional Support

TIME NOTEBOOK

BROWN BROTHERS

In his exposé of urban poverty, How the Other Half Lives *(1890),* **JACOB RIIS** *documented the living conditions in New York City tenements:*

C "The statement once made a sensation that between seventy and eighty children had been found in one tenement. It no longer excites even passing attention, when the sanitary police report counting 101 adults and 91 children in a Crosby Street house, one of twins, built together. The children in the others, if I am not mistaken, numbered 89, a total of 180 for two tenements! Or when midnight inspection in Mulberry Street unearths a hundred and fifty "lodgers" sleeping on filthy floors in two buildings. In spite of brown-stone fittings, plate-glass and mosaic vestibule floors, the water does not rise in summer to the second story, while the beer flows unchecked to the all-night picnics on the roof. The saloon with the side-door and the landlord divide the prosperity of the place between them, and the tenant, in sullen submission, foots the bill."

VERBATIM

"Tell 'em quick, and tell 'em often."

WILLIAM WRIGLEY,
soap salesman and promoter of chewing gum, on his marketing philosophy

"A pushing, energetic, ingenious person, always awake and trying to get ahead of his neighbors."

HENRY ADAMS,
historian, describing the average New Yorker or Chicagoan

"We cannot all live in cities, yet nearly all seem determined to do so."

HORACE GREELEY,
newspaper editor

INDICATORS:

Livin' in the City

Moving off the farm for a factory job? Sharpen your pencil. You'll need to budget carefully to buy all you will need.

Here are the numbers for a Georgia family of four in 1890. The husband is a textile worker, and the wife works at home. There is one child, age 4, and a boarder. They share a two-room, wood-heated, oil-lighted apartment.

INCOME: (annual)	
husband's income	$312.00
boarder's rent	10.00
TOTAL INCOME	**$322.00**

S

EXPENSES: (annual)	
medical	$65.00
furniture	46.90
clothing	46.00
rent	21.00
flour/meal	25.00
hog products	17.00
other meat	13.00
vegetables	13.00
lard	6.50
potatoes	6.40
butter	5.00
sugar	4.00
charitable donations	6.10
vacation	3.25
alcohol	3.25
tobacco	3.00
molasses	2.00
other food	27.80
miscellaneous	68.20
TOTAL EXPENSES	**$382.40**

Extending the Content

The Woman Suffrage Movement Years before Susan B. Anthony began her suffrage work, President John Adams' wife, Abigail, reminded him to "remember the ladies" as he and others met to write the Declaration of Independence in 1776. Sarah Grimké lent her speaking talent to the cause of both women's suffrage and abolition. In 1848, the first women's rights convention was held in Seneca Falls, New York. Another dynamic speaker, former slave Sojourner Truth delivered her famous "Ain't I a Woman" speech at a similar convention in Ohio in 1851. Anthony became more vocal as she and Elizabeth Cady Stanton formed the American Equal Rights Association with both male and female membership. At the same time Anthony was jailed in New York, Sojourner Truth was denied a ballot at a polling booth in Michigan. It wasn't until 1912 that the first political party—Teddy Roosevelt's Bullmoose Party—supported women's suffrage. Although World War I slowed down suffrage efforts, the 19th Amendment was finally ratified in 1920, marking almost 150 years of effort.

Milestones

ON THE RUN, 1881. THE JESSE JAMES GANG, after robbing a Chicago, Rock Island, and Pacific train near Winston, Missouri, and killing the conductor and a passenger.

OVERTURNED, 1878. BY THE SUPREME COURT, a Louisiana court decision that awarded damages to an African American woman who had been refused admission to a steamship stateroom reserved for whites.

PLAGUED BY GRASSHOPPERS, 1874. THE AMERICAN GREAT PLAINS. Insect swarms a mile wide blot out the midday sun. Two inches deep on the ground, they leave "nothing but the mortgage," as one farmer put it.

CELEBRATED IN EUROPE, 1887. ANNIE OAKLEY, star of Buffalo Bill's Wild West Show. Oakley shot a cigarette from the lips of Crown Prince Wilhelm of Germany. Years later, when the U.S. goes to war against Kaiser Wilhelm, Oakley will quip: "I wish I'd missed that day!"

BROWN BROTHERS

Jesse James

REMOVED, 1884. IDA B. WELLS, journalist and former slave, from a ladies coach on a train. Wells refused to move to the smoking car where African Americans were to be seated.

ARRESTED, 1872. SUSAN B. ANTHONY, for casting a ballot in Rochester, New York. Anthony argued that the Fourteenth and Fifteenth Amendments applied to women.

R

BROWN BROTHERS

Susan B. Anthony

NUMBERS

1 in 12 **Americans living in cities of 100,000 or more in 1865**

BROWN BROTHERS

A crowded New York City street

1 in 5 **Americans living in cities in 1896**

522 **Inhabitants in a one-acre area in the Bowery, New York City**

$2 **Daily wage for a farm laborer, New York, 1869**

C

$4 **Daily wage for a plumber, New York City, 1869**

50¢ **Price of a pair of boy's knee pants, a parasol, button boots, or a necktie (1870s)**

$8 **Price of a "Fine All-Wool Suit," 1875**

25¢ **Admission to "Barnum's American Museum" (featuring the smallest pair of human beings ever seen!), 1896**

CRITICAL THINKING

1. ***Analyzing Visuals*** Look at the Jacob Riis photo of an urban family and the photo of a New York City street. What do the pictures tell you about urban life in the 1890s?

2. ***Comparing*** What character traits do you think Ida B. Wells and Susan B. Anthony may have shared?

R Reading Strategies

Identifying Ask: Whose civil rights did Wells and Anthony work to establish? *(The rights of African Americans and women)* ELL

C Critical Thinking

Inferring Ask: Why do you think plumbers were paid twice as much as farm laborers in 1889? *(With the rapid growth of cities, plumbers were in demand. There was no shortage of farm laborers.)* OL

Assess/Close

Have students explain the connection between Greeley's comment and the tenement conditions described by Riis.

Critical Thinking Answers:

1. Urban life was crowded and filled with poverty.
2. determination, courage, a sense of justice.

Visit the TIME Web site at www.time.com for up-to-date news, weekly magazine articles, editorials, online polls, and an archive of past magazine and Web articles.

Additional Support

Activity: Collaborative Activity

Congressional Debate Ask: Why is it important that all Americans have the right to vote? *(Answers will vary but may include the ideas that all citizens should have a voice in their government, that universal suffrage lends varied perspectives and a balanced approach to decision-making, and that crucial legislation affecting women and minority groups may not have passed without universal suffrage.)* Tell students they are members of the House of Representatives and are considering a bill that would require women, as well as men, to register for the draft. Have students form groups of four or five by gender (all male, all female) and list the merits or disadvantages of the bill. Ask groups to share their lists while you note their points on the board. Place a star by comments proffered by females. Ask students to volunteer how perspectives might differ because of gender. As a class, vote on the bill. OL

Focus

Bellringer

Daily Focus Transparency 13-4

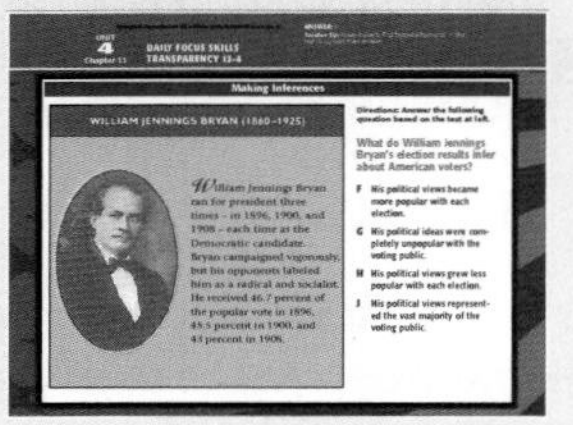

Guide to Reading

Answers to Graphic:

Populism
- I. Unrest in Rural America
  - A. The Money Supply
  - B. The Grange Takes Action
  - C. The Farmers' Alliance
- II. The Rise of Populism
  - A. The Subtreasury Plan
  - B. A Populist Runs for President
- III. The Election of 1896
  - A. Bryan's Campaign
  - B. The Front Porch Campaign

Section Spotlight Video

To generate student interest and provide a springboard for class discussion, access the Chapter 13, Section 4 video at glencoe.com or on the video DVD.

Resource Manager

Section 4

Section Audio   Spotlight Video

Populism

Guide to Reading

Big Ideas

Economics and Society The Populist movement and its presidential candidate William Jennings Bryan strongly supported silver as the basis for currency.

Content Vocabulary
- populism *(p. 470)*
- greenbacks *(p. 470)*
- inflation *(p. 470)*
- deflation *(p. 470)*
- cooperatives *(p. 471)*
- graduated income tax *(p. 473)*

Academic Vocabulary
- bond *(p. 470)*
- currency *(p. 471)*
- strategy *(p. 472)*

People and Events to Identify
- Farmers' Alliance *(p. 472)*
- People's Party *(p. 473)*
- William Jennings Bryan *(p. 474)*
- William McKinley *(p. 475)*

Reading Strategy

Taking Notes As you read about the emergence of populism in the 1890s, use the major headings of the section to create an outline similar to the one below.

Populism
I. Unrest in Rural America
A.
B.
C.
II.
A.
B.

After the Civil War, falling crop prices and deflation made it hard for farmers to make a living. Farmers tried to overcome these problems by forming organizations such as the Grange and the Farmers' Alliance. In the 1890s, many farmers joined the Populist Party.

Unrest in Rural America

MAIN Idea Deflation, low crop prices, and tariffs hurt farmers economically.

HISTORY AND YOU What can you buy for a dollar today? Read on to learn how the value of a dollar has changed over time.

Populism was a movement to increase farmers' political power and to work for legislation in their interest. Farmers joined the Populist movement because they were in the midst of an economic crisis. New technology enabled farmers to produce more crops, but the greater supply had caused prices to fall. High tariffs also made it hard for farmers to sell their goods overseas. Farmers also felt they were victimized by large and faraway entities: the banks from which they obtained loans and the railroads that set their shipping rates.

The Money Supply

Some farmers thought adjusting the money supply would solve their economic problems. During the Civil War, the federal government had expanded the money supply by issuing millions of dollars in **greenbacks**—paper currency that could not be exchanged for gold or silver coins. This increase in the money supply without an increase in goods for sale caused **inflation,** or a decline in the value of money. As the paper money lost value, the prices of goods soared.

After the Civil War ended, the United States had three types of currency in circulation—greenbacks, gold and silver coins, and national bank notes backed by government **bonds.** To get inflation under control, the federal government stopped printing greenbacks and began paying off its bonds. In 1873 Congress also decided to stop making silver into coins. These decisions meant that the money supply was not large enough for the country's growing economy. In 1865, for example, there was about $30 in circulation for each person. By 1895, there was only about $23. As the economy expanded, **deflation**—or an increase in the value of money and a decrease in prices—began. As money increased in value, prices fell.

Deflation hit farmers especially hard. Most farmers had to borrow money for seed and other supplies to plant their crops. Because

R Reading Strategies	C Critical Thinking	D Differentiated Instruction	W Writing Support	S Skill Practice
Teacher Edition • Using Word Parts, p. 471 • Using Context Clues, p. 472 • Sequencing Info, p. 474 **Additional Resources** • Pri. Source Reading, URB p. 103 • Guide Reading Act., URB p. 117	**Teacher Edition** • Det. Cause/Effect, p. 472 • Explaining, p. 473 **Additional Resources** • Quizzes and Tests, p. 180	**Teacher Edition** • Logical/Math., p. 473	**Additional Resources** • Supreme Court Case Stud., p. 15	**Teacher Edition** • Reading Graphs, p. 471 • Analyzing Maps, p. 474 **Additional Resources** • Read. Essen., p. 150

PRIMARY SOURCE

Why Were Farmers Having Problems?

New technology, such as this McCormick grain binder, allowed more land to be farmed, but more food on the market drove down prices and profits.

Farmers had to buy seed and supplies and pay railroads to ship their harvest. They also had to pay their mortgage. As food prices fell and interest rates stayed high, farmers were caught in the middle.

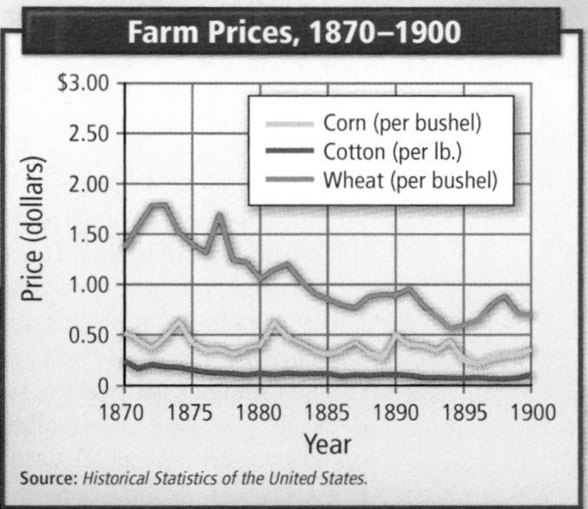

Source: *Historical Statistics of the United States.*

Analyzing VISUALS

1. **Analyzing** Which crop declined in price the most by 1900? Which region would be most affected by this decline?
2. **Explaining** How did technology contribute to the decline in farm prices?

money was in short supply, interest rates began to rise, which increased the amount farmers owed. Rising interest rates also made mortgages more expensive, but falling prices meant the farmers sold their crops for less, and they still had to make the same mortgage payments to the banks.

Realizing that their problems were partly caused by a shortage of **currency,** many farmers concluded that Eastern bankers had pressured Congress into reducing the money supply. Some farmers called for the printing of more greenbacks. Others, particularly those in the West where new silver mines had been found, wanted the government to mint silver coins. They referred to the decision to stop minting silver as "The Crime of '73."

The Grange Takes Action

In 1866 the Department of Agriculture sent Oliver H. Kelley to tour the rural South and report on the condition of the region's farmers. Realizing how isolated farmers were from each other, Kelley founded the first national farm organization, the Patrons of Husbandry, better known as the Grange, in 1867.

At first Grangers met largely for social and educational purposes. Then, in 1873, the nation plunged into a severe recession, and farm income fell sharply. Farmers looking for help joined the Grange in large numbers. By 1874, the Grange had between 800,000 and 1.5 million members.

Grangers responded to the crisis by pressuring state legislatures to regulate railroad and warehouse rates. They also tried to create **cooperatives**—marketing organizations that try to increase prices and lower costs for their members.

One of the reasons farmers could not charge higher prices for their crops was that there were so many farmers in competition. If a farmer raised prices, a buyer could always go elsewhere and pay less. Cooperatives pooled farmers' crops and held them off the market in order to force up prices. Because a cooperative controlled a large quantity of farm products, it could also negotiate better shipping rates with the railroads.

Teach

S Skill Practice

Reading Graphs Ask: Which crop price was least affected by technology? *(wheat)* **ELL**

R Reading Strategies

Using Word Parts Ask: How does the base word in *cooperatives* explain how these organizations work? *(Members cooperate to improve the profits for all.)* **BL**

Analyzing VISUALS

Answers:

1. wheat; Great Plains
2. Technology enhanced production. Overproduction created surpluses, which lowered prices.

Differentiated Instruction

Primary Source Reading, URB pp. 103–104

The Farmers' Plight

Objective: Interpret a primary source to determine the concerns of farmers in the late 1800s.

Focus: Students should underline or circle all of the causes of suffering by the farmers.

Teach: Summarize the farmers' plight in one sentence.

Assess: Create a Problem-Solution chart (graphic organizer) by listing the problems and the proposed solutions.

Close: Draft a (legislative) bill that would address the farmers' concerns raised in this excerpt.

Differentiated Instruction Strategies

BL Characterize this excerpt. Is it a positive or negative message? Why do you think so?

AL Compare the plight of the farmers of the late 1800s with the plight of farmers today. Do any similarities exist?

ELL Two words are defined in the Reader's Dictionary. Add at least three other words to this list and definitions.

None of the **strategies** the Grangers employed improved farmers' economic conditions. Several Western states passed "Granger laws" that set maximum rates and prohibited railroads from charging more for short hauls than for long ones. The railroads fought back by cutting services and refusing to lay new track. Then, in 1886, the Supreme Court ruled in *Wabash* v. *Illinois* that states could not regulate railroads or any commerce that crossed state lines.

The Grange's cooperatives also failed, partly because they were too small to have any effect on prices, and partly because Eastern businesses and railroads considered them to be similar to unions—illegitimate conspiracies that restricted trade—so they refused to do business with them. By the late 1870s, farmers began to leave the Grange for organizations they hoped would address their problems.

The Farmers' Alliance

As the Grange began to fall apart, a new organization, known as the **Farmers' Alliance,** began to form. By 1890, the Alliance had between 1.5 and 3 million members, with strong support in the South and on the Great Plains, particularly in Kansas, Nebraska, North Dakota, and South Dakota.

R When Charles W. Macune became the leader of the Alliance, he announced a plan to organize very large cooperatives, which he called exchanges. Macune hoped these exchanges would be big enough to force farm prices up and to make loans to farmers at low interest rates. The exchanges had some success. The Texas Exchange successfully marketed cotton at prices slightly higher than those paid to individual farmers, while the Illinois Exchange negotiated slightly better railroad rates for wheat farmers.

Ultimately, the large cooperatives failed. C Many overextended themselves by lending too much money at low interest rates that was never repaid. In many cases, wholesalers, railroads, and bankers discriminated against them, making it difficult for them to stay in business. They also failed because they were still too small to affect world prices for farm products.

Reading Check **Explaining** How did the Farmers' Alliance try to help farmers?

POLITICAL CARTOONS Primary Source
Who Is to Blame for Farmers' Problems?

▲ A farmer wearing a Granger hat tries to warn people about the railroad.

▲ A thin farmer is an unwelcome guest at the Congressional kitchen, where businessmen are enjoying their meals.

Analyzing VISUALS

1. **Analyzing** What is the cartoon on the left implying about the railroad's relationship to farmers?
2. **Explaining** Who does the cartoon on the right blame for the problems facing farmers?

R Reading Strategies

Using Context Clues Ask: Which words from the text explain exchanges? *(very large cooperatives)* **ELL**

C Critical Thinking

Determining Cause and Effect Ask: What caused wholesalers, railroads, and bankers to discriminate against exchanges? *(Exchanges would have lowered their profits, so they discriminated against them to run them out of business.)* **BL**

Analyzing VISUALS

Answers:
1. Farmers suffer while railroads prosper.
2. big business and Congress

Reading Check

Answer:
by forming large cooperatives to force prices up and to make low-interest loans to farmers

Hands-on Chapter Project
Step 4

Researching Immigration and Political Ads

Step 4: Determining the Winning Messages in the 1896 Election
Essential question: What turned the tide in the historic 1896 election?

Directions Explain to students that they will use their imagination for this project, pretending that McKinley and Bryan, the Republican and Democratic candidates, had access to television campaigning. Two teams will be working, one for the Democrats and one for the Republicans. Their product will be the scripts and ideas for visuals for three short TV ads directed at different groups of voters.

Putting It Together Each team must research the planks of their respective candidate and what part of the body politic he needed to persuade. At the end of this stage, they can meet to share their information and refine it. **OL**

(Chapter Project continued on page 480)

The Rise of Populism

MAIN Idea Farmers started the People's Party to fight for their interests and attracted many supporters when a depression hit in the 1890s.

HISTORY AND YOU Do you remember reading about the creation of the Republican Party in the 1850s? Read how another new party, the Populists, shook up politics in the 1890s.

By 1890 the Alliance's lack of success had started a debate in the organization. Some Alliance leaders, particularly in the western states, wanted to form a new party and push for political reforms. Members of the Kansas Alliance formed the **People's Party,** also known as the Populists, and nominated candidates to run for Congress and the state legislature. Alliances in Nebraska, South Dakota, and Minnesota quickly followed Kansas's example.

Most Southern leaders of the Alliance opposed the idea of a third party. They did not want to undermine the Democrats' control of the South. Instead, they suggested that the Alliance produce a list of demands and promise to vote for candidates who supported those demands. They hoped this would force Democrats to adopt the Alliance program.

The Subtreasury Plan

To get Southern Democrats to support the Alliance, Charles Macune introduced the subtreasury plan, which called for the government to set up warehouses called subtreasuries. Farmers would store their crops in the warehouses, and the government would provide low-interest loans to the farmers.

Macune believed the plan would enable farmers to hold their crops off the market in large enough quantities to force prices up. The Alliance also called for the free coinage of silver, an end to protective tariffs and national banks, tighter regulation of the railroads, and direct election of senators by voters. **D**

Macune's strategy seemed to work at first. In 1890 the South elected four governors, all Democrats, who had pledged to support the Alliance program. Several Southern legislatures now had pro-Alliance majorities, and more than 40 Democrats who supported the Alliance program were elected to Congress.

A Populist Runs for President

Meanwhile, the new People's Party did equally well in the West. Populists took control of the Kansas and Nebraska legislatures. Populists also held the balance of power in Minnesota and South Dakota. Eight Populist representatives and two Populist senators were elected to the United States Congress.

At first, Southern members of the Alliance were excited over their success in electing so many pro-Alliance Democrats to Congress and to Southern state legislatures, but over the next two years, their excitement turned into frustration. Despite their promises, few Democrats followed through in their support of the Alliance program.

In May 1891 Western populists met with some labor and reform groups in Cincinnati. There, they endorsed the creation of a new national People's Party to run candidates for president. The following year, many Southern farmers had reached the point where they were willing to break with the Democratic Party and join the People's Party.

In July 1892 the People's Party held its first national convention in Omaha, Nebraska. James B. Weaver was nominated to run for president. The Omaha convention endorsed a platform that denounced the government's refusal to coin silver as a "vast conspiracy against mankind" and called for a return to unlimited coinage of silver at a ratio that gave 16 ounces of silver the same value as one ounce of gold. It also called for federal ownership of railroads and a **graduated income tax,** one that taxed higher earnings more heavily.

Populists also adopted proposals designed to appeal to organized labor. The Omaha platform also called for an eight-hour workday and immigration restrictions, but workers found it hard to identify with a party focused on rural problems and the coinage of silver. The Populists had close ties to the Knights of Labor, but that organization was in decline, and the fast-growing American Federation of Labor had steered clear of an alliance with them. As a result, most urban workers continued to vote for the Democrats, whose candidate, Grover Cleveland, won the election. **C**

Reading Check **Summarizing** What was the main outcome of the Populist campaign in the elections of 1892?

D Differentiated Instruction

Logical/Mathematical

Ask: Why would keeping crops off the market drive prices up? *(People are willing to pay more for goods that are scarce.)* **BL**

C Critical Thinking

Explaining Ask: What impact did immigration restrictions have on labor unions? *(Fewer immigrants meant fewer workers willing to work for low wages which, in turn, boosted unions' bargaining power.)* **OL**

Reading Check

Answer:
The Populist candidate lost the election.

Additional Support

Activity: Economics Connection

Scarcity and Choice Ask: How do you determine what you are willing to pay for an item while you're shopping? *(Answers will vary but may include an evaluation of need or want, item availability, and price.)* Discuss each consideration and relate them to the situation in which crop farmers found themselves in the 1890s. Have students work in pairs to design an item they wish to "sell" to classmates. Allow student partners to decide quantity and price (ranging from $5 to $25). Reconvene the class, giving each student $25 in play money. Ask each student pair to auction their item after providing a verbal description of what they are selling. When the auction concludes, ask students why they purchased particular items. **Ask:** Which items appealed to you because supply was limited? **OL**

R Reading Strategies

Sequencing Information

Ask: In what order were the 1896 political party conventions held? *(Republicans, Democrats, Populists)* **BL**

S Skill Practice

Analyzing Maps Ask: How does the map show the influence of the Populists on the election? *(All the states where populism was popular voted the same way.)* **AL**

Turning Point

Answer:

Essays will vary but should accurately compare a recent election to the election of 1896.

Additional Support

The Election of 1896

MAIN Idea Although William Jennings Bryan had the support of the Populists and the Democrats, Republican William McKinley defeated him.

HISTORY AND YOU What was the best speech you have ever heard? How did the speaker draw you in? Read on to learn how a powerful speech won the presidential nomination for William Jennings Bryan.

As the election of 1896 approached, leaders of the People's Party decided to make the free coinage of silver the focus of their campaign. They also decided to hold their convention after the Republican and Democratic conventions. They believed the Republicans would **R** endorse a gold standard, and they did. They also expected the Democrats to nominate Grover Cleveland, even though Cleveland also strongly favored a gold standard. The People's Party hoped that when they endorsed silver, pro-silver Democrats would abandon their party and vote for the Populists.

Unfortunately for the Populists, their strategy failed. The Democrats did not waiver on the silver issue. Instead, they nominated **William Jennings Bryan,** a strong supporter of silver. When the Populists gathered in St. Louis for their own convention, they faced a difficult choice: endorse Bryan and risk undermining their identity as a separate party, or nominate their own candidate and risk splitting the silver vote. They eventually decided to support Bryan as well.

Bryan's Campaign

William Jennings Bryan, a former member of Congress from Nebraska, was only 36 years old when the Democrats and the Populists nominated him for president. Bryan had served in Congress as a representative from Nebraska. He was a powerful speaker and he won the Democratic nomination by delivering an electrifying address in defense of silver—one of the most famous in American political history.

Turning Point

The Election of 1896

Before the Civil War, farmers of the West and the South determined the outcome of elections. As industrialization caused Eastern cities to grow, the balance of political power shifted. From the 1870s to the 1890s, elections became very close, and power swung back and forth between the parties. The election of 1896 marked a turning point. Political power shifted from voters in the rural parts of the country to those in urban areas in the Northeast and industrial Midwest. Never again would farm votes determine the winner of a presidential election. The South and West did not regain their political importance until their urban areas grew to match those in the Northeast and Midwest.

MAKING CONNECTIONS Does the pattern of 1896's election resemble recent elections? Write an essay comparing a recent election to the 1896 election.

◀ *For many, the campaign to elect William Jennings Bryan was viewed as both a crusade and a revolution, as the symbols and slogans on this 1896 poster show.*

Election of 1896

McKinley

Bryan

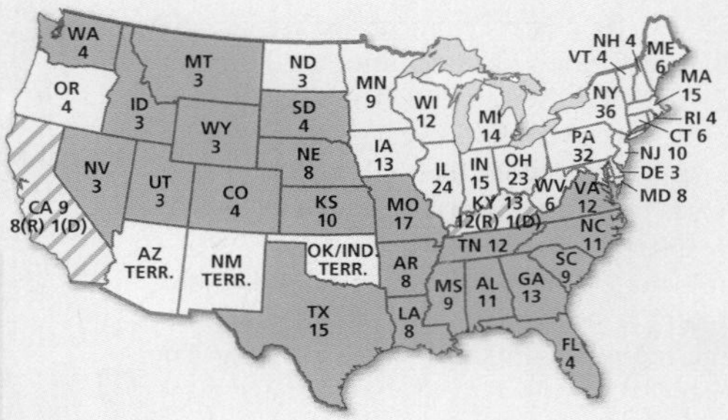

Presidential Candidate	Popular Vote	% of Popular Vote	Electoral Vote
McKinley (R)	7,104,779	51.03%	271
Bryan (D)	6,502,925	46.71%	176

S

Activity: Economics Connection

Campaign Spending Reluctant to leave his sick wife and refusing to compete with Bryan, McKinley talked to a total of 750,000 people from the front porch of his home. His campaign was well-managed by a close friend and wealthy businessman, Marcus Hanna. The first campaign to hand out walking sticks, campaign buttons, umbrellas, ribbons, and other memorabilia, it raised $3.5 million, largely from leading industrialists. Known as a defender of farmers and laborers, Bryan was nicknamed the "Great Commoner" because of his concern for the common people. Bryan's campaign, while garnering great support in the South and West, raised far less money. At the end of the campaign, McKinley had outspent Bryan 20 to 1. **Ask:** How might campaign spending affect the outcome of an election? *(Students will most likely answer that well-financed campaigns more thoroughly promote their candidates.)* **Ask:** Are presidential campaigns financed in the same way today? *(Although campaigns still raise money from businesses and individuals, contribution limits and disclosure requirements have now been imposed.)* **AL**

With a few well-chosen words, Bryan transformed the campaign for silver into a crusade:

PRIMARY SOURCE

"Having behind us the producing masses of this nation and the world, supported by the commercial interests, the laboring interests and the toilers everywhere, we will answer their demand for a gold standard by saying to them: You shall not press down upon the brow of labor this crown of thorns; you shall not crucify mankind upon a cross of gold."

—quoted in *America in the Gilded Age*

Bryan waged an energetic campaign, traveling thousands of miles and delivering 600 speeches in 14 weeks. Some found his relentless campaigning undignified, and Catholic immigrants and other city dwellers cared little for the silver issue. They did not like Bryan's speaking style either. It reminded them of rural Protestant preachers, who were sometimes anti-Catholic. Republicans knew that Democrats and Populists would be hard to beat in the South and the West. To regain the White House, they had to sweep the Northeast and the Midwest. They decided on **William McKinley,** the governor of Ohio, as their candidate.

The Front Porch Campaign

Unlike Bryan, McKinley launched a "Front Porch Campaign," greeting delegates who came to his home in Canton, Ohio. The Republicans campaigned against the Democrats by promising workers that McKinley would provide a "full dinner pail." This meant more to urban workers than the issue of silver money because the economy was in a severe recession following the Panic of 1893. At the same time, most business leaders supported the Republicans, convinced that unlimited silver coinage would ruin the country. Many employers warned workers that if Bryan won, businesses would fail and unemployment would rise further.

McKinley's reputation as a moderate on labor issues and as tolerant toward ethnic groups helped improve the Republican Party's image with urban workers and immigrants. When the votes were counted, McKinley had won with a decisive victory. He captured 51 percent of the popular vote and had a winning margin of 95 electoral votes—hefty numbers in an era of tight elections. As expected, Bryan won the South and most of the West, but few of the states he carried had large populations or delivered many electoral votes. By embracing populism and its rural base, Bryan and the Democrats lost the northeastern industrial areas, where votes were concentrated.

The Populist Party declined after 1896. Their efforts to ease the economic hardships of farmers and to regulate big business had not worked. Some of the reforms they favored, including the graduated income tax and some governmental regulation of the economy—however, came about in the subsequent decades.

Reading Check **Evaluating** What were the results of the 1896 presidential election?

Section 4 REVIEW

Vocabulary

1. **Explain** the significance of: populism, greenbacks, inflation, deflation, cooperatives, Farmers' Alliance, People's Party, graduated income tax, William Jennings Bryan, William McKinley.

Main Ideas

2. **Organizing** Use a graphic organizer that lists the factors that contributed to and the results of farmers' unrest in the 1890s.

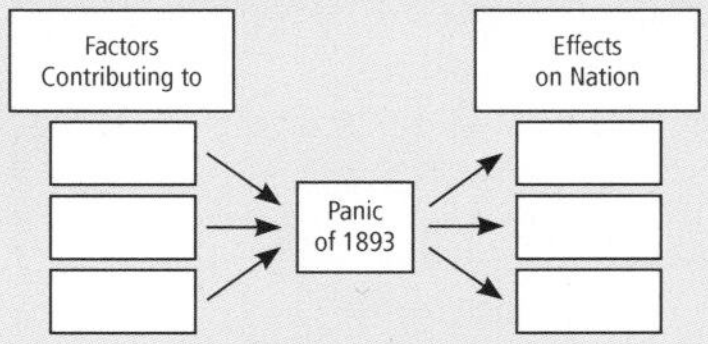

3. **Describing** What economic factors caused farmers to support populism?

4. **Listing** What issues did the Democrats endorse in the 1896 presidential election?

Critical Thinking

5. **Big Ideas** Why did the Populists support William Jennings Bryan?

6. **Synthesizing** How did the Farmers' Alliance contribute to the rise of a new political party?

7. **Analyzing Visuals** Look at the campaign poster on page 474. Choose one of the symbols or slogans and explain its meaning to Bryan's campaign.

Writing About History

8. **Persuasive Writing** Imagine you support the Populist Party and that you have been asked to write copy for a campaign poster. Include a slogan that provides reasons for people to support the Populists.

History ONLINE
Study Central™ To review this section, go to glencoe.com and click on Study Central.

Reading Check

Answer:
McKinley won and the Populist Party waned.

Assess

History ONLINE

Study Central™ provides summaries, interactive games, and online graphic organizers to help students review content.

Close

Summarizing **Ask:** What was the main issue in the election of 1896? *(free coinage of silver vs. currency backed by reserve gold)* **OL**

Section 4 REVIEW

Answers

1. Significant terms, persons, and places are boldfaced and highlighted in the section.
2. Factors: deflation, falling crop prices, high railroad shipping rates; Effects: crop prices fell, farmers borrowed money, farmers joined cooperatives
3. economic depression, little influence on railroads
4. free coinage of silver, aiding the plight of farmers
5. They did not want to split the silver vote.
6. Some Alliance members wanted to form a new party to get their programs passed.
7. Answers will vary but should accurately connect one of the symbols or slogans to Bryan's campaign platform.
8. Posters will vary but should accurately reflect the goals of the Populist Party. Posters should include a slogan suggesting why people should support the party.

Focus

Bellringer

Daily Focus Transparency 13-5

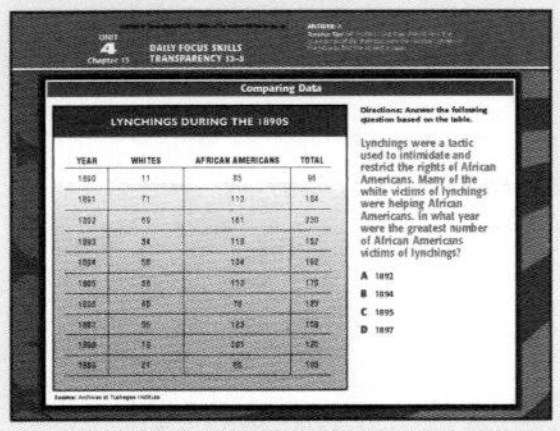

Guide to Reading

Answers to Graphic: poll tax, literacy test, grandfather clause, Jim Crow laws

Section Spotlight Video

To generate student interest and provide a springboard for class discussion, access the Chapter 13, Section 5 video at glencoe.com or on the video DVD.

Section 5

Section Audio | Spotlight Video

The Rise of Segregation

Guide to Reading

Big Ideas

Individual Action Several prominent African Americans led the fight against racial discrimination.

Content Vocabulary

- poll tax *(p. 478)*
- segregation *(p. 478)*
- Jim Crow laws *(p. 478)*
- lynching *(p. 480)*

Academic Vocabulary

- discrimination *(p. 478)*

People and Events to Identify

- Ida B. Wells *(p. 480)*
- Booker T. Washington *(p. 481)*
- W. E. B. Du Bois *(p. 481)*

Reading Strategy

Organizing As you read, complete a web diagram listing ways that states disenfranchised African Americans and legalized discrimination.

After Reconstruction ended, Southern states began passing laws that eroded the rights of African Americans by introducing segregation and denying voting rights. African American leaders struggled to protect civil rights and improve quality of life but could not always agree on the most effective strategy.

Resistance and Repression

MAIN Idea Many African Americans fled the South, but some stayed and joined the Populist Party.

HISTORY AND YOU Do you remember reading about the rise of sharecropping after the Civil War? Read how African American farmers tried to work together in the late 1800s.

After Reconstruction, many African Americans in the rural South lived in conditions of grinding poverty. Most were sharecroppers, landless farmers who gave their landlords a large portion of their crops as rent, rather than paying cash. Sharecropping usually left farmers in chronic debt. Many eventually left farming and sought jobs in Southern towns or headed west to claim homesteads.

The Exodusters Head to Kansas

In the mid-1870s, Benjamin "Pap" Singleton, a former slave, became convinced that African Americans would never be given a chance to get ahead in the South. He began urging African Americans to move west, specifically to Kansas, and form their own independent communities where they could help each other get ahead. His ideas soon set in motion a mass migration. In the spring of 1879, African American communities in Louisiana, Mississippi, and Texas were swept with a religious enthusiasm for moving to Kansas—seeing it as a new promised land. In less than two months, approximately 6,000 African Americans left their homes in the rural South and headed to Kansas. The newspapers called it "an Exodus," like the Hebrews' escape from Egyptian bondage. The migrants themselves came to be known as "Exodusters."

One of the migrants to Kansas later explained why they went: "The whole South—every State in the South—had got into the hands of the very men that held us as slaves." The first Exodusters, many possessing little more than hope and the clothes on their backs, arrived in Kansas in the spring of 1879. A journalist named Henry King described the scene:

Resource Manager

R Reading Strategies	C Critical Thinking	D Differentiated Instruction	W Writing Support	S Skill Practice
Teacher Edition • Summarizing, p. 477 • Activ. Prior Knowledge, p. 480 • Academic Vocab., p. 478 **Additional Resources** • Guide Reading Act., URB p. 118	**Teacher Edition** • Predict Consequences, p. 478 • Speculating, p. 480 **Additional Resources** • Critical Thinking Skills Act., URB p. 98 • Interpreting Polit. Cartoons, URB p. 107 • Quizzes and Tests, p. 181	**Additional Resources** • Reteaching Act., URB p. 109 • Auth. Assess, p. 31	**Additional Resources** • Supreme Court Case Stud., p. 27	**Teacher Edition** • Reading Maps, p. 477 **Additional Resources** • Reading Skills Act., URB p. 87 • Read. Essen., p. 153

PRIMARY SOURCE

The Exodusters

▲ *In 1879, soon after Reconstruction ended, an estimated 6,000–15,000 African Americans left the rural South and headed to Kansas where they hoped to build a better life for themselves.*

NATIONAL GEOGRAPHIC **The Exodus to Kansas**

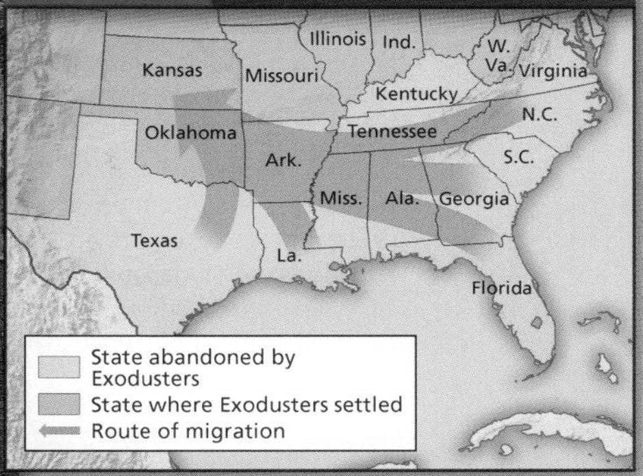

S

Analyzing VISUALS

1. **Analyzing** According to the map, which states were departure points for the Exodusters?
2. **Making Connections** What earlier events in American history would have made the Exodusters think Kansas was a good place to settle?

PRIMARY SOURCE

"One morning in April, 1879, a Missouri steamboat arrived at Wyandotte, Kansas, and discharged a load of negro men, women and children, with . . . barrels, boxes, and bundles of household effects. . . . [T]heir garments were incredibly patched and tattered . . . and there was not probably a dollar in money in the pockets of the entire party. . . . They looked like persons coming out of a dream. And, indeed, such they were . . . . for this was the advance guard of the Exodus."

—quoted in *Eyewitness: The Negro in History*

Forming a Separate Alliance

While some African Americans fled the South, others joined with poor white farmers who had created the Farmers' Alliance. Alliance leaders urged African Americans to form a similar organization. In 1886 African American farmers established the Colored Farmers' National Alliance. By 1890, the organization had about 1.2 million members.

When the Populist Party formed in 1891, many African American farmers joined the new organization. This posed a major challenge to the Democratic Party in the South. If poor whites left the party and joined with African Americans in voting for the Populists, the coalition might be unbeatable.

To win back the poor white vote, Democratic leaders began appealing to racism, warning whites that support for Populism would return the South to "Black Republican" rule, similar to Reconstruction. In addition, election officials began using various methods to make it harder and harder for African Americans to vote. As one Democratic leader in the South told a reporter, "Some of our people, some editors especially, deny that [African Americans] are hindered from voting; but what is the good of lying? They are interfered with, and we are obliged to do it, and we may as well tell the truth." R

✓Reading Check **Examining** Who were the Exodusters, and why did they migrate to Kansas?

Teach

S Skill Practice

Reading Maps Ask: Where did the Exodusters settle? *(Kansas)* **ELL**

R Reading Strategies

Summarizing Ask: What tactics did Democrats use to win the vote of poor whites in the South? *(appeals to racism; conjuring memories, fear, and anger associated with Reconstruction)* **OL**

Analyzing VISUALS

Answers:

1. North Carolina, Georgia, Louisiana, Texas, Florida
2. "Bleeding Kansas" was an antislavery battleground.

✓Reading Check

Answers:

African Americans who migrated from the rural South to Kansas; to escape discrimination

Additional Support

Extending the Content

Exodusters Benjamin Singleton's association—the Edgefield Real Estate and Homestead Association in Tennessee—had scouted out land and had carefully planned the movement, but by 1879, the sheer number of African Americans heading to Kansas overwhelmed his efforts. In total, more than 20,000 African American migrants headed for Kansas between 1877 and 1879.

C Critical Thinking

Predicting Consequences **Ask:** What results when a group of people are denied the vote? *(Answers will vary but may include that they are denied rights; have no one to represent them and their rights and interests.)* OL

R Reading Strategies

Academic Vocabulary **Ask:** What synonym can be used for *poll* in the term *poll tax*? *(voting)* OL

Reading Check

Answers:
It upheld segregation and expressed a new legal doctrine endorsing "separate but equal" facilities for African Americans.

Additional Support

Imposing Segregation

MAIN Idea Southern states passed laws that imposed segregation and denied African American men their voting rights.

HISTORY AND YOU Can you think of a rule that is unfairly or unevenly enforced? Read about the tactics used to disfranchise African Americans.

After Reconstruction ended in 1877, the rights of African Americans were gradually undermined. Attempts to unify whites and African Americans politically and economically failed. Instead, a movement to diminish the civil rights of African Americans gained momentum as the century ended.

Taking Away the Vote

The Fifteenth Amendment prohibits states from denying citizens the right to vote on the basis of "race, color, or previous condition of servitude," but it does not bar states from denying the right to vote on other grounds. In the late 1800s, Southern states began imposing restrictions that, while not mentioning race, were designed to make it difficult or impossible for African Americans to vote.

R C In 1890 Mississippi began requiring all citizens registering to vote to pay a **poll tax** of $2, a sum beyond the means of most poor African Americans. Mississippi also instituted a literacy test, requiring voters to read and understand the state constitution. Few African Americans born after the Civil War had been able to attend school and those who had grown up under slavery were largely illiterate. Even those who knew how to read often failed the test because officials deliberately picked passages that few people could understand.

Other Southern states adopted similar restrictions. In Louisiana the number of African Americans registered to vote fell from about 130,000 in 1890 to around 5,300 in 1900. In Alabama the number fell from about 181,000 to about 3,700.

Election officials were far less strict in applying the poll tax and literacy requirements to whites, but the number of white voters also fell significantly. To let more whites vote, Louisiana introduced the "grandfather clause," which allowed any man to vote if he had an ancestor who could vote in 1867. This provision, which C was adopted in several Southern states, exempted most whites from voting restrictions such as literacy tests.

Legalizing Segregation

African Americans in the North were often barred from public places, but **segregation,** or the separation of the races, was different in the South. Southern states passed laws that enforced **discrimination**. These laws became known as **Jim Crow laws.** The term probably refers to the song "Jump Jim Crow," which was popular in minstrel shows of the day.

Civil Rights Cases In 1883 the Supreme Court set the stage for legalized segregation when it overturned the Civil Rights Act of 1875. That law had prohibited keeping people out of public places on the basis of race and barred racial **discrimination** in selecting jurors. The 1883 Supreme Court decision, however, said that the Fourteenth Amendment provided only that "no state" could deny citizens equal protection under the law. Private organizations—such as hotels, theaters, and railroads—were free to practice segregation.

Encouraged by the Supreme Court's ruling and by the decline of congressional support for civil rights, Southern states passed a series of laws that established racial segregation in virtually all public places. Southern whites and African Americans could no longer ride together in the same railroad cars, eat in the same dining halls, or even drink from the same fountains.

Plessy* v. *Ferguson In 1892 an African American named Homer Plessy challenged a Louisiana law that forced him to ride in a separate railroad car from whites. He was arrested for riding in a "whites-only" car. In 1896 the Supreme Court, in *Plessy* v. *Ferguson*, upheld the Louisiana law and set out a new doctrine of "separate but equal" facilities for African Americans. The ruling established the legal basis for discrimination in the South for more than 50 years. While public facilities for African Americans in the South were always separate, they were far from equal. In many cases, they were inferior.

Reading Check **Summarizing** How did the Supreme Court help to legalize segregation?

Activity: Collaborative Learning

Recognizing Bias **Ask:** What required tests do Americans take in order to gain the right to do something? *(Answers will vary but may include driver's tests, blood tests for marriage licenses, drug tests for employment, and so on.)* Remind students that literacy tests required of African Americans in the South were designed to ensure failure so African Americans could not vote. Have students form groups. Tell students for the purpose of this exercise that the school now requires students to pass a test in order to attend dances, athletic events, and other extracurricular activities. Have groups decide what qualifications students should meet in order to be allowed to attend these events. Ask them to use these qualifications to design a screening test. Ask groups to share their tests with the class. Discuss differences and similarities and the fairness of criteria and questions. OL

Do states have the right to segregate citizens by race?

★ ***Plessy* v. *Ferguson*, 1896**

Background to the Case

When Homer Adolph Plessy, a light-skinned man who was one-eighth African American, took a seat in the whites-only section of an East Louisiana Railway train and refused to move, he was arrested. Convicted of breaking a Louisiana law enacted in 1890, Plessy appealed his case to the Louisiana Supreme Court, then to federal Supreme Court. The incident was planned in advance to test the statute, using Plessy, who appeared to be white, to show the folly of the law. Although the words "separate but equal" do not appear in the court responses, the term came to describe a condition that persisted until 1954.

How the Court Ruled

The Court upheld the right of states to make laws that sustained segregation. The majority of justices wanted to distinguish between political rights guaranteed by the Fourteenth and Fifteenth Amendments and social rights.

▲ *A conductor orders Homer Plessy to leave the white section of the railroad car.*

PRIMARY SOURCE

The Court's Opinion

"The object of the [Fourteenth] amendment was undoubtedly to enforce the absolute equality of the two races before the law, but . . . it could not have been intended to abolish distinctions based upon color, or to enforce social, as distinguished from political equality, or a commingling of the two races upon terms unsatisfactory to either. Laws permitting, and even requiring, their separation in places where they are liable to be brought into contact do not necessarily imply the inferiority of either race to the other . . . We cannot say that a law which authorizes or even requires the separation of the two races in public conveyances is unreasonable."

—Justice Henry Billings Brown writing for the Court in *Plessy* v. *Ferguson*

PRIMARY SOURCE

Other Views

"Our constitution is color-blind, and neither knows nor tolerates classes among citizens. In respect of civil rights, all citizens are equal before the law. . . . We boast of the freedom enjoyed by our people above all other peoples. But it is difficult to reconcile that boast with a state of law which, practically, puts the brand of servitude and degradation upon a large class of our fellow citizens—our equals before the law. The thin disguise of 'equal' accommodations for passengers in railroad coaches will not mislead any one, nor atone for the wrong this day done."

—Justice John Marshall Harlan writing the lone dissent in *Plessy* v. *Ferguson*

DBQ Document-Based Questions

1. **Analyzing Primary Sources** What distinction does Justice Brown make about the rights of citizens?
2. **Identifying Points of View** How does Justice Harlan regard the Court's decision?
3. **Evaluating** What rights do you think all states should extend to their citizens? Why do you think so?

Supreme Court Cases

More About the Case

What arguments did Homer Plessy make to the courts?

- He said the Separate Car Act violated his civil rights under the 13th and 14th Amendments.
- He said that, since he was only one-eighth black and looked white, he should have a white man's rights.

The three lower courts upheld the Act, since equal accommodations were available. Although the Supreme Court agreed, it found the issue of Plessy's race important but not properly placed in this case.

DBQ Document Based Questions

Answers:

1. He distinguishes between civil/political and social rights.
2. He sees it as wrong and argues that the Constitution is color-blind.
3. Answers will vary but should support choices.

Differentiated Instruction

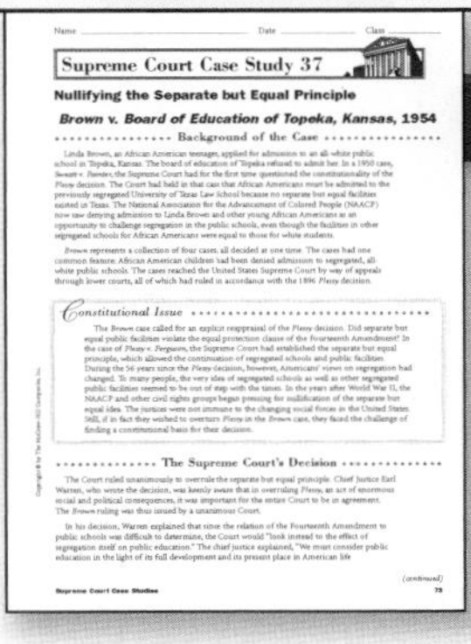

Name ________ Date ________ Class ________

Supreme Court Case Study 37

Nullifying the Separate but Equal Principle

***Brown* v. *Board of Education of Topeka, Kansas*, 1954**

Background of the Case

Linda Brown, an African American teenager, applied for admission to an all-white public school in Topeka, Kansas. The board of education of Topeka refused to admit her. In a 1950 case, *Sweatt* v. *Painter*, the Supreme Court had for the first time questioned the constitutionality of the *Plessy* decision. The Court had held in that case that African Americans must be admitted to the previously segregated University of Texas Law School because no separate but equal facilities existed in Texas. The National Association for the Advancement of Colored People (NAACP) now saw denying admission to Linda Brown and other young African Americans as an opportunity to challenge segregation in the public schools, even though the facilities in other segregated schools for African Americans were equal to those for white students.

Brown represents a collection of four cases, all decided at one time. The cases had one common feature: African American children had been denied admission to segregated, all-white public schools. The cases reached the United States Supreme Court by way of appeals through lower courts, all of which had ruled in accordance with the 1896 *Plessy* decision.

Constitutional Issue

The *Brown* case called for an explicit reappraisal of the *Plessy* decision. Did separate but equal public facilities violate the equal protection clause of the Fourteenth Amendment? In the case of *Plessy* v. *Ferguson*, the Supreme Court had established the separate but equal principle, which allowed the continuation of segregated schools and public facilities. During the 56 years since the *Plessy* decision, however, Americans' views on segregation had changed. To many people, the very idea of segregated schools as well as other segregated public facilities seemed to be out of step with the times. In the years after World War II, the NAACP and other civil rights groups began pressing for nullification of the separate but equal idea. The justices were not immune to the changing social forces in the United States. Still, if in fact they wished to overturn *Plessy* in the *Brown* case, they faced the challenge of finding a constitutional basis for their decision.

The Supreme Court's Decision

The Court ruled unanimously to overrule the separate but equal principle. Chief Justice Earl Warren, who wrote the decision, was keenly aware that in overruling *Plessy*, an act of enormous social and political consequences, it was important for the entire Court to be in agreement. The *Brown* ruling was thus issued by a unanimous Court.

In his decision, Warren explained that since the relation of the Fourteenth Amendment to public schools was difficult to determine, the Court would "look instead to the effect of segregation itself on public education." The chief justice explained, "We must consider public education in the light of its full development and its present place in American life

(continued)

Supreme Court Case Studies 73

Case Study 37: *Brown* v. *Board of Education of Topeka, KS*, p. 73

Analyzing a Supreme Court Case

Objective: Learn why "separate but equal" was ruled to be unconstitutional.

Focus: Identify the central issue of the case.

Teach: Discuss the Court's opinion.

Assess: Explain the importance of the case (segregation was outlawed).

Close: Write a paragraph summarizing the case.

Differentiated Instruction Strategies

BL List two methods people use to fight discrimination.

AL Create a time line that shows the impact of the *Brown* decision.

ELL Explain the difference between the *Plessy* decision and the *Brown* decision.

R Reading Strategies

Activating Prior Knowledge
Ask: Which Bill of Rights amendment supports Wells' demand? *(Fifth)* **OL**

C Critical Thinking

Speculating Ask: Why do you think Harrison was unwilling to publicly condemn lynching? *(Answers will vary but may include the idea that he would lose voter support in the South.)* **BL**

People IN HISTORY

Answers:
Washington: He founded the Tuskegee Institute, and organized the Negro Business League.
Du Bois: He focused on legal and voting rights while Washington promoted economic gains.

The African American Response

MAIN Idea Some African American leaders focused on practical vocational education, while others pushed for full civil rights and educational opportunities.

HISTORY AND YOU How would your life be different without an education? Read on to learn why some early civil rights leaders focused on access to education.

The African American community responded to violence and discrimination in several ways. Ida B. Wells used the press to end violence, while Mary Church Terrell worked in education. Booker T. Washington proposed that African Americans focus on achieving economic goals, rather than political goals. W. E. B. Du Bois argued African Americans should demand equal rights immediately.

Ida B. Wells

In the late 1800s, mob violence increased in the United States, particularly in the South. Between 1890 and 1899, there was an average of 187 **lynchings**—hangings without proper court proceedings—each year.

In 1892 **Ida B. Wells,** a fiery young African American woman from Tennessee, launched a fearless crusade against lynching. After a mob drove Wells out of town, she settled in Chicago and continued her campaign. In 1895 she published a book denouncing mob violence and demanding "a fair trial by law for those accused of crime, and punishment by law after honest conviction." Although Congress rejected an anti-lynching bill, the number of lynchings decreased significantly in the 1900s, due in great part to the efforts of activists such as Wells.

Mary Church Terrell

One lynching victim had been a close friend of Mary Church Terrell, a college-educated woman who'd been born during the Civil War. This death, and President Harrison's refusal to publicly condemn lynching, started Terrell on her lifelong battle against lynching, racism, and sexism.

Terrell also worked with woman suffrage workers such as Jane Addams and Susan B. Anthony. In addition to helping found the

People IN HISTORY

Booker T. Washington
1856–1915

Born into slavery on a plantation in Virginia, Booker T. Washington spent his childhood working in the coal mines of West Virginia. At age 16, he heard about the Hampton Institute in Virginia, where African Americans could learn farming or a trade. With little money in his pockets, Washington left home and walked nearly 500 miles to the school, where he was able to work as a janitor to pay for his education.

When the Alabama legislature decided in 1881 to begin a school to train black leaders, Washington was recommended for the job. He borrowed money to buy an abandoned plantation; the students built classrooms, a chapel, and dormitories. The Tuskegee Institute became well-known, attracting prominent scholars such as George Washington Carver to the faculty.

Washington used his influence with white businessmen to raise money for the school. He encouraged the development of black-owned businesses, and he organized the National Negro Business League in 1900. He was a nationally known spokesperson for the African American community and advised presidents William Howard Taft and Theodore Roosevelt on political appointments.

What were Booker T. Washington's most important achievements?

W.E.B. Du Bois
1868–1963

W. E. B. Du Bois was born in Massachusetts a few years after the end of the Civil War. After graduating from Fisk University, Du Bois earned a Ph.D. from Harvard. As a professor at Atlanta University, Du Bois focused his research on race relations in the United States.

The Souls of Black Folk, Du Bois's 1903 collection of essays, had a major impact on its readers. In them, Du Bois directly criticized Booker T. Washington for being too cautious and conservative on civil rights issues. Du Bois believed African Americans needed to insist upon equal treatment and voting rights. He also helped to found the Niagara Movement, the forerunner of the NAACP. In 1910 he began publishing *The Crisis*, the official magazine of the NAACP.

In his later years, Du Bois turned to socialism and became active in the peace movement. This led to political censure and the State Department's refusal to allow Du Bois to travel outside the country. When he was permitted to leave, he went to Ghana, where he became a citizen the year he died.

How did W. E. B. Du Bois's approach to civil rights differ from Washington's approach?

Hands-on Chapter Project: Step 5

Researching Immigration and Political Ads

Step 5: Comparing Campaigns
Essential Question: Are today's presidential campaigns less substantive and more sensationalized than nineteenth-century and early twentieth-century campaigns?

Directions Each team should review what they learned about the McKinley-Bryan campaign in Step 4, as well as previous campaigns they have studied. Then ask the teams to conduct research on recent presidential elections and compare and contrast these aspects of the candidates' campaigns: the types of communication used, major issues stressed, voter segments they tried to reach, and campaign strategies that defeated the losing candidate or won the White House. **OL**

(Chapter Project continued on the Visual Summary page)

National Association of Colored Women and the National Association for the Advancement of Colored People, Terrell formed the Women Wage-Earners Association, which assisted African American nurses, waitresses, and domestic workers.

Terrell led a boycott against department stores in Washington, D.C., that refused to serve African Americans. In an address to the National American Women's Suffrage Association Terrell said, "With courage, born of success achieved in the past, with a keen sense of the responsibility which we shall continue to assume, we look forward to a future large with promise and hope. Seeking no favors because of our color, nor patronage because of our needs, we knock at the bar of justice, asking an equal chance."

Calls for Compromise

The most famous African American of the late nineteenth century was the influential educator **Booker T. Washington.** He proposed that African Americans concentrate on achieving economic goals rather than political ones. In 1895 Washington summed up his views in a speech before a mostly white audience in Atlanta. Known as the Atlanta Compromise, the speech urged African Americans to postpone the fight for civil rights and instead concentrate on preparing themselves educationally and vocationally for full equality:

PRIMARY SOURCE

"The wisest among my race understand that the agitation of questions of social equality is the extremest folly, and that the enjoyment of all the privileges that will come to us must be the result of severe and constant struggle rather than of artificial forcing. . . . It is important and right that all privileges of the law be ours, but it is vastly more important that we be prepared for the exercise of these privileges. The opportunity to earn a dollar in a factory just now is worth infinitely more than the opportunity to spend a dollar in an opera-house."

—adapted from *Up From Slavery*

Du Bois Rejects Compromise

The Atlanta Compromise speech provoked a strong challenge from **W. E. B. Du Bois,** the leader of a new generation of African American activists. In his 1903 book *The Souls of Black Folk,* Du Bois explained why he saw no advantage in giving up civil rights, even temporarily. He was particularly concerned with protecting and exercising voting rights. "Negroes must insist continually, in season and out of season," he wrote, "that voting is necessary to proper manhood, that color discrimination is barbarism." In the years that followed, many African Americans worked to win the vote and end discrimination. The struggle, however, would prove to be a long one.

Reading Check **Describing** How did Ida B. Wells try to stop the practice of lynching?

Section 5 REVIEW

Vocabulary

1. **Explain** the significance of: poll tax, segregation, Jim Crow laws, lynching, Ida B. Wells, Booker T. Washington, W. E. B. Du Bois.

Main Ideas

2. **Describing** Under what kind of conditions did many African Americans in the South live in after Reconstruction?
3. **Identifying** How did Southern states restrict African American voting in the 1890s?
4. **Organizing** Use a graphic organizer similar to the one below to list the responses of some prominent African Americans to racial discrimination.

African American	Response to Discrimination
Ida B. Wells	
Booker T. Washington	
W.E.B. Du Bois	

Critical Thinking

5. **Big Ideas** How did Booker T. Washington's answer to racial discrimination differ from that of W. E. B. Du Bois?
6. **Analyzing Visuals** Look at the cartoon on page 479. How does the cartoonist play into white fears?

Writing About History

7. **Expository Writing** Imagine that you are living in the 1890s. Write a letter to the editor of the local newspaper explaining your view of the Supreme Court ruling in *Plessy* v. *Ferguson*.

History ONLINE
Study Central™ To review this section, go to glencoe.com and click on Study Central.

Reading Check

Answer:
She wrote newspaper articles and a book denouncing lynching.

Assess

History ONLINE

Study Central™ provides summaries, interactive games, and online graphic organizers to help students review content.

Close

Summarizing Ask: How did African Americans work to end violence and discrimination? *(They wrote news articles and books, formed associations such as the NAACP and NACW, and worked to educate others about the evils of prejudice.)* OL

Section 5 REVIEW

Answers

1. Sentences should use vocabulary words according to their definitions in the section and in the Glossary.
2. Conditions were little better than slavery because African Americans owned no property and gained little or no economic freedom as sharecroppers.
3. poll taxes, literacy tests, grandfather clause
4.

African American	Response to Discrimination
Ida B. Wells	wrote against lynching
Booker T. Washington	urged African Americans to prepare educationally and vocationally for equality
W.E.B. Du Bois	campaigned for civil and voting rights and helped found the Niagara Movement

5. Washington concentrated on achieving economic goals rather than legal and political ones. Du Bois was concerned with protecting legal and voting rights.
6. By portraying a prosperous African American sitting while a white woman stands, the cartoonist suggests that African Americans are usurping the social, economic, and political power of whites.
7. Letters will vary but should clearly state a position on the *Plessy v. Ferguson* ruling with logical supporting evidence.

Assessing **Ask:** How might political machines have done more good than harm? *(Answers will vary but may include that, although machines manipulated voters for the selfish motives of party bosses and their associates, the practical help they gave new immigrants made it possible for immigrants to survive in their new homeland.)*

In what way are today's voters similar to those of the late nineteenth century? *(Answers will vary but may include that voters often choose candidates who promise programs and legislation that benefit their constituents.)* **OL**

Synthesizing **Ask:** Why were artistic realism and naturalism natural outcomes of the times? *(Answers will vary but could include the fact that the American experience was rapidly changing and that artists wanted to capture the reality of those changes. Writers and artists also wanted to depict the problems that arose with industrialization.)* **AL**

Chapter 13 VISUAL SUMMARY

STUDY TO GO You can study anywhere, anytime by downloading quizzes and flashcards to your PDA from glencoe.com.

Effects of Industrialization:

1. Immigration and Urbanization

- Rise of large factories greatly increases the demand for labor in the United States, encouraging immigrants to move to America in large numbers.
- The increase in industrial jobs encourages large numbers of Americans and immigrants to settle in cities.
- As cities grow large, pollution, crime, disease, and fire become serious problems.
- New industrial technology allows cities to grow even larger with the development of the skyscraper, the elevator, and the trolley car.
- Large urban areas change the nature of politics creating corrupt urban political "machines" such as Tammany Hall in New York.

▲ *A crowded immigrant community in New York in the early 1900s*

Effects of Industrialization:

2. Farm Problems

- Industrialization and new technology increases farm production and creates the ability to ship farm products across the country.
- Farmers produce huge surpluses, driving down food prices, while a money shortage leads to high interest rates; farmers grow deeper in debt while income falls.
- High railroad rates in the West combine with high rents for tenant farmers in the South to create a crisis for farmers.
- Farmers form the Grange, the Alliance, and the Populist Party to help address their concerns.

▲ *Sharecroppers in the South were often trapped in poverty and debt.*

Effects of Industrialization:

3. Changes in Culture

- Industrial society initially leads to a strong belief in individualism; Social Darwinism emerges as the idea that government should not interfere in society.
- Ongoing social problems caused by industrialization lead to Reform Darwinism and the emergence of reformers who want to use government to help solve society's problems and regulate the economy.
- New forms of realist and naturalist art and literature depict industrial life in serious and realistic ways.

▲ *Settlement houses, such as Hull House (above), helped poor immigrants educate their children and adapt to life in the United States.*

482 **Chapter 13** Urban America

Hands-On Chapter Project Step 6:

Researching Immigration and Political Ads

Step 6: Creating the Ads **Essential Question:** In a 60-90 second television time-slot, what will get a candidate's message across to a specific group?

Directions Students may have new ideas about campaign strategies after completing Step 5. In Step 6 they should review the scripts they began earlier. They will probably need to throw out some of their ideas as they realize that a message to one group might result in a negative reaction from another group. Their final product of 3 short ads can be in different forms—a written script and sketches of visuals, digital camera shots—whatever a given class can access.

Putting It Together The Democratic and Republican teams can meet to review the work of the other team, comparing notes about the process and offering ideas for improvement or revision. **OL**

Reviewing Vocabulary

Directions: Choose the word or words that best completes the sentence.

1. ________ was a philosophy that believed wealthy Americans bore the responsibility of using their fortunes to further social progress.
A Social Darwinism
B Realism
C Gospel of Wealth
D Individualism

2. Immigrant children became knowledgeable about American culture at public schools—a process known as
A Americanization.
B nativism.
C Social Darwinism.
D individualism.

3. The rapid increase in the money supply without an increase in the amount of goods for sale caused ________, or the decline in the value of money.
A goldbugs
B silverites
C deflation
D inflation

4. The ________ was an informal political group that provided city services in return for votes and political power.
A party bosses
B political machine
C Populists
D Grange

5. The ________ was one method of segregation used in the South after the Civil War.
A cooperative
B poll tax
C tenement
D graft

Reviewing Main Ideas

Directions: Choose the best answers to the following questions.

Section 1 *(pp. 442–447)*

6. In the late nineteenth century, many labor unions opposed immigration, arguing that immigrants
A would work for higher wages.
B eased financial drains on social services.
C assimilated into American culture.
D would accept jobs as strikebreakers.

7. What was the major reason for Chinese immigration to the United States in the early nineteenth century?
A Many Chinese were escaping severe unemployment and famine.
B Many Chinese were escaping religious persecution.
C Many Chinese left to avoid required military service.
D Many Chinese left to escape the class system and move up the social ladder.

Section 2 *(pp. 450–455)*

8. Working class individuals residing in cities usually lived
A in the streetcar suburbs.
B in tenements.
C in fashionable downtown districts.
D away from the central city.

9. Who was the leader of Tammany Hall during the 1860s and 1870s?
A Thomas Nast
B James Pendergast
C William Tweed
D Thomas Pendergast

TEST-TAKING TIP

Read the questions carefully. From the wording of each question, you can see that some have two or three concepts in common. Find the one choice that best answers each question.

Need Extra Help?

If You Missed Questions . . .	1	2	3	4	5	6	7	8	9
Go to Page . . .	459–460	467	470–471	455	478	446	445	453	455

GO ON

Answers and Analyses
Reviewing Vocabulary

1. C Social Darwinism was the application of survival of the fittest to society. Realism was an artistic movement. Individualism was a philosophy that prized success by individual effort. The Gospel of Wealth was coined by Andrew Carnegie. He believed those who had money should use it to help people help themselves.

2. A This is a good place to discuss the suffix *–ization*, which means a process or the result of making something. So, Americanization means the process of making someone American.

3. D Students may have trouble choosing between inflation and deflation. An **in**crease in the money supply leads to **in**flation. (A decrease in the money supply can lead to **de**flation.) Goldbugs and silverites are not economic terms.

4. B Party bosses, such as the infamous Boss Tweed in New York, "ran" political machines. The Populists grew out of the Grange movement, and both are associated with democratic ideals, not corruption.

5. B Cooperatives were stores where farmers bought products from each other. A tenement was a multifamily apartment. Graft is the dishonest collection of money.

Reviewing Main Ideas

6. D *A, B,* and *C* are incorrect, because they inaccurately represent the feelings of many labor unions toward immigrants. In reality, immigrants' willingness to work for *lower* wages worried unions. In addition, increased immigration placed increasing strains on social services. Immigrants did not immediately assimilate into American culture, which caused prejudice against them.

7. A The answer choices all list push factors that cause immigration, but only one applies to Chinese immigrants. Review the chart "Why Did Immigrants Come to America?" on page 445.

8. B Students will hopefully eliminate A, since suburbs are not cities. Immigrants were poor, so they would not live in the fashionable district downtown; they lived in the inner city. The term *inner city* is still used today to describe economically depressed urban areas. Tenement buildings housed working-class people in cities in extremely tight quarters.

9. C William "Boss" Tweed led Tammany Hall. Thomas Nast was a cartoonist who opposed political machines. James Pendergast ran a huge political machine in Kansas City, MO. Thomas was his brother.

10. C Each answer choice describes a nineteenth-century philosophy. Students should connect Social Darwinism with Darwin's theory of survival of the fittest, which is described in *C*. *A* describes socialism. *B* and *D* describe communism.

11. D The federal government began regulating the railroads due to the type of problems described in the first three answer choices.

12. C The Populist Party was closely tied to economic goals and principles, so C makes the most sense.

13. C *Plessy* v. *Ferguson* established the concept of "separate but equal" facilities for whites and African Americans. This concept was based on the Fourteenth Amendment.

Critical Thinking

14. A The People's Party originated with farmers, and the subtreasury plan was introduced by Charles Macune to help farmers raise crop prices. The other answer choices were opposite of Populist goals.

15. D Wheat prices decreased significantly during this ten-year period, while cotton prices decreased gradually.

Chapter 13 ASSESSMENT

Section 3 *(pp. 458–467)*

10. The nineteenth-century philosophy of Social Darwinism maintained that

A the government should have control over the means of production and the marketplace.

B all social class distinctions in American society should be eliminated.

C economic success comes to those who are the hardest working and most competent.

D wealth and income should be more equally distributed.

11. The Interstate Commerce Act (1887) was designed to regulate interstate commerce by requiring

A railroads to increase rebates to high-volume users.

B railroads to charge higher rates for short hauls.

C states to regulate interstate railroad traffic.

D the federal government to regulate railroad rates.

Section 4 *(pp. 470–475)*

12. Populists supported federal ownership of railroads because they thought the government would

A increase access to railroads in rural areas.

B make the trains run on time.

C manage the railroads in the public interest.

D collect enough revenue to allow it to eliminate the graduated income tax.

Section 5 *(pp. 476–481)*

13. The ruling from *Plessy* v. *Ferguson* (1896) was based on the Supreme Court's interpretation of the

A necessary and proper clause from Article I, Section 8 of the U.S. Constitution.

B free speech provision of the First Amendment.

C equal protection clause in the Fourteenth Amendment.

D voting rights provision in the Fifteenth Amendment.

Critical Thinking

Directions: Choose the best answers to the following questions.

14. In 1890 the Populists formed the People's Party and supported

A the subtreasury plan where farmers could store crops in warehouses to force prices up.

B limited governmental regulations for the railroad companies.

C the election of senators by state legislatures.

D the free coinage of gold.

Base your answer to question 15 on the chart below and your knowledge of Chapter 13.

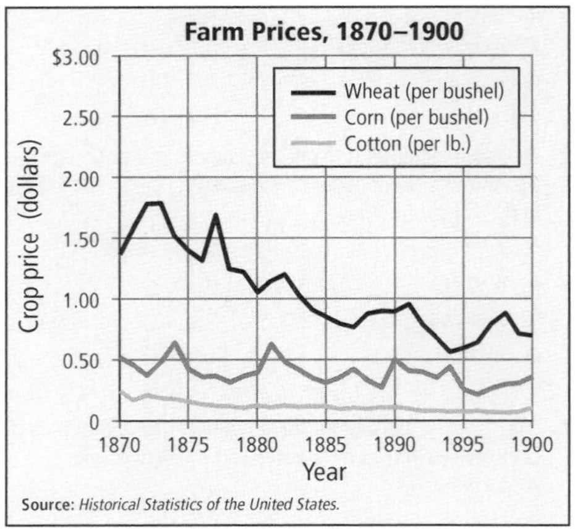

15. What happened to crop prices between 1870 and 1880?

A The price of cotton increased as the price of wheat and corn decreased.

B The price of wheat, corn, and cotton increased.

C The price of cotton, wheat, and corn stayed the same following an initial increase.

D The price of wheat significantly decreased as the price of cotton decreased steadily.

Need Extra Help?						
If You Missed Questions . . .	10	11	12	13	14	15
Go to Page . . .	458–459	462–463	473	478	473	471

GO ON

16. Which of the following concepts is associated with the Gospel of Wealth?
   - **A** survival of the fittest
   - **B** laissez-faire
   - **C** unregulated competition
   - **D** philanthropy

Analyze the cartoon and answer the question that follows. Base your answer on the cartoon and on your knowledge of Chapter 13.

17. What does the cartoon express about immigrants coming to the United States?
   - **A** Immigrants were welcome to the United States.
   - **B** Immigrants had to pass by dogs to gain entry.
   - **C** Anarchists, Socialists, and Communists were welcome.
   - **D** Anarchists, Socialists, and Communists were not welcome.

18. The "new immigrants" to the United States between 1890 and 1915 came primarily from
   - **A** southern and eastern Europe.
   - **B** northern and western Europe.
   - **C** East Asia.
   - **D** Latin America.

Document-Based Questions

Directions: Analyze the document and answer the short-answer questions that follow the document.

Reaction in the United States to "old" immigration was generally more favorable than reaction to "new" immigration. The following excerpt from an 1882 editorial in the *Commercial and Financial Chronicle* addresses the effects of immigration on the nation:

> *"In the very act of coming and traveling to reach his destination, he [the immigrant] adds . . . to the immediate prosperity and success of certain lines of business. Not only do the ocean steamers . . . get very large returns in carrying passengers of this description, but in forwarding them to the places chosen by the immigrants as their future homes the railroad companies also derive great benefit and their passenger traffic is greatly swelled. . . .*
>
> *. . . These immigrants not only produce largely, . . . but, having wants which they cannot supply themselves, create a demand for outside supplies. . . . Thus it is that the Eastern manufacturer finds the call upon him for his wares and goods growing more urgent all the time, thus the consumption of coal keeps on expanding notwithstanding the check to new railroad enterprises, and thus there is a more active and larger interchange of all commodities."*
>
> —from *Commercial and Financial Chronicle*

19. According to the editorial, what effect did immigration have on the nation's economy?

20. How is the editorial's view of the effects of immigration different from that of the nativists?

Extended Response

21. Identify how events during the late 1800s and early 1900s, such as urbanization and immigration, influenced social change, and evaluate the extent to which reform movements were successful in bringing about change. Write an expository essay that supports your answer with relevant facts, examples, and details.

STOP

History ONLINE

For additional test practice, use Self-Check Quizzes—Chapter 13 at glencoe.com.

Need Extra Help?

If You Missed Questions . . .	16	17	18	19	20	21
Go to Page . . .	459–460	458–461	442–443	485	446–447	464–467

Document-Based Questions

19. Immigration had a positive effect by increasing prosperity for ocean steamers, railroads, and manufacturing. The editorial states that "by the very act of coming and traveling [to the U.S.]" immigrants lend success to certain businesses.

20. The editorial views immigration in a positive light and focuses on the economic benefits. Nativists opposed immigration and worried about cultural and economic threats they thought immigration presented.

Extended Response

21. Responses will vary. Answers must address and evaluate the effectiveness of the different reform movements during the period. Essays should include Social Darwinism, nativist response, populism, and changes in cities.

16. D Philanthropy was associated with the Gospel of Wealth, but not with survival of the fittest—a central Social Darwinist theory. Unregulated competition is a feature of laissez-faire.

17. D In the cartoon, Lady Liberty is signaling figures representing Anarchists, Communists, and Socialists to halt by holding up her hand. In addition, she is holding guard dogs to help keep them at bay.

18. A Have students who incorrectly answer this question refer to the map on page 443. Although it covers a longer time period, it should help students in answering the question.

History ONLINE

Have students visit the Web site at glencoe.com to review Chapter 13 and take the Self-Check Quiz.

Need Extra Help?

Have students refer to the pages listed if they miss any of the questions.

Unit 5 Planning Guide

UNIT PACING CHART					
	Unit 5	Chapter 14	Chapter 15	Chapter 16	Unit 5
Day 1	Unit Opener	Chapter 14 Opener, Section 1	Chapter 15 Opener, Section 1	Chapter 16 Opener, Section 1	Wrap-Up/Project, Unit Assessment
Day 2		Section 2	Section 2	Section 2	
Day 3		Section 3	Section 3	Section 3	
Day 4		Chapter Assessment	Chapter Assessment	Section 4	
Day 5				Chapter Assessment	

Teacher to Teacher

Lee Weber
Price Laboratory School
Cedar Falls, IA

U.S. Entrance into World War I Place the following "Causes of American Entrance into World War I" on an overhead transparency:

- Loss of innocent lives
- Loss of trade
- Historical/cultural ties to British/French
- Defense of democracy against dictatorship
- Freedom of the seas
- The Zimmermann Note

Ask students to individually rank the causes from most important to least important. Then randomly group students and have them try to reach consensus. The interrelated nature of the six causes makes the task extremely difficult. If time permits repeat the process and make a hypothetical change in the historical facts. For instance, suggest that Germany had a large surface navy and Britain developed unrestricted submarine warfare. How would U.S. policy have changed? Or, what if Germany were our major trading partner, not England and its allies?

Author Note

Dear American History Teacher:

The great industrial development of the United States in the second half of the nineteenth century transformed the character of the nation. It also produced new pressures and new problems that shaped the era that began with the depression of 1893 and led ultimately to America's entry into World War I.

The rapidly expanding economic growth of the industrial era led America to look for new sources of raw materials and new markets for the nation's goods. The United States began its search for international influence not through traditional imperialism, but through aggressive engagement in international trade (accompanied by a strong missionary movement that attempted to spread both Christianity and western knowledge and values into distant lands). American imperialism was in many ways different from the imperialism practiced by European nations, but it had similar goals—economic growth—and encountered similar problems—resistance, sometimes violent, from native peoples.

Industrial growth changed not only America's role in the world but the character of life and politics within the United States. The factory system gave birth to a new kind of working class; it led to the growth of cities and industrial towns and to substantial population growth; and it produced new conflicts and crises that alarmed many Americans and helped create a series of reform efforts that came to be known, collectively, as progressivism. Progressivism took so many different forms and embraced so many various, and sometimes contradictory values that some scholars have argued that "progressivism" has little or no meaning. But Americans in the early twentieth century believed that progressivism was filled with meaning, and one of the challenges of teaching this period is explaining what that meaning was. The progressive era helped produce a series of questions and beliefs that shaped the whole of the twentieth century and continue to evoke both interest and controversy even today.

Introducing Unit 5

Focus

Why It Matters

Tell students that today many people consider the United States the world's only superpower. Ask students if they agree with that assessment and why or why not. **OL**

Connecting to Past Learning

Have students identify nations that they think are powerful. **Ask:** What makes a nation powerful? *(Answers might include a strong military, a robust economy, industry, and political influence.)* Tell students that in this unit they will learn about how the United States became a world power and became increasingly involved in world events. **OL**

Unit Launch Activity

Making Connections Have students brainstorm a list of weapons used in warfare today. List students' answers on the board. **Ask:** Which of these weapons existed at the beginning of the twentieth century? *(Answers will vary.)* Discuss with the class how new weaponry has changed warfare since the early 1900s. **OL**

Unit 5

Imperialism and Progressivism

1890–1920

Why It Matters

Between 1890 and 1920 two very important developments took place in American history. First, the United States began its rise to the global superpower it is today. Second, reformers began changing the government to solve problems caused by industrialism. Government became more involved in society than ever before.

Team Teaching Activity

Sociology Read to the students the following lines written by poet Sarah Cleghorn in the early 1900s: "The golf links lie so near the mill/That almost every day/The laboring children can look out/And see the men at play." **Ask:** What do you think this quote tells you about the economic and social conditions in the United States in 1900? *(There were no child labor laws; children worked in factories; wealthy men played golf.)* Have the economics teacher come and explain the evolution of child labor laws and their impact on the business world. **OL**

U.S. warships battle the Spanish off the coast of Cuba, 1898.

487

More About the Photo

The U.S. fleet set out for Havana Harbor during the Spanish-American War. The quick American victory in that war made the nation an imperialist power.

Teach

S1 Skill Practice

Visual Literacy Have students study the unit painting.
Ask: What impression or feeling is the artist trying to convey in this painting? *(The United States is militarily strong; the Spanish fleet is weak.)* **BL**

S2 Skill Practice

Concluding Have students again review the unit painting.
Ask: What is the topic of the painting? *(America's military power)* Discuss with the class why reformers might be opposed to the nation's growing military power at the beginning of the twentieth century. **OL**

NCLB No Child Left Behind

Teaching Tip The NCLB Act emphasizes reading. Have students make a time line that begins with 1872 and ends with 1919. Have them keep the time line with them and add key events as they read the unit. Students can use the time line while studying to help understand the sequence of events.

Chapter 14 Planning Guide

Key to Ability Levels	
BL Below Level	AL Above Level
OL On Level	ELL English Language Learners

Key to Teaching Resources	
Print Material	Transparency
CD-ROM or DVD	

BL	OL	AL	ELL	Resources	Chapter Opener	Section 1	Section 2	Section 3	Chapter Assess
				FOCUS					
BL	OL	AL	ELL	Daily Focus Skills Transparencies		14-1	14-2	14-3	
				TEACH					
BL	OL		ELL	Reading Essentials and Note-Taking Guide*		p. 156	p. 159	p. 162	
	OL			Historical Analysis Skills Activity, URB				p. 20	
BL	OL		ELL	Guided Reading Activities, URB*		p. 46	p. 47	p. 48	
BL	OL	AL	ELL	Content Vocabulary Activity, URB*		p. 25			
BL	OL	AL	ELL	Academic Vocabulary Activity, URB		p. 27			
	OL	AL		Critical Thinking Skills Activity, URB				p. 30	
BL	OL		ELL	Reading Skills Activity, URB		p. 19			
BL			ELL	English Learner Activity, URB			p. 23		
	OL	AL		Reinforcing Skills Activity, URB			p. 29		
BL	OL	AL	ELL	Differentiated Instruction Activity, URB				p. 21	
BL	OL		ELL	Time Line Activity, URB				p. 31	
	OL			Linking Past and Present Activity, URB		p. 32			
BL	OL	AL	ELL	American Art and Music Activity, URB			p. 37		
BL	OL	AL	ELL	Interpreting Political Cartoons Activity, URB				p. 39	
		AL		Enrichment Activity, URB			p. 43		
BL	OL	AL	ELL	American Biographies			✓		
BL	OL	AL	ELL	Primary Source Reading, URB		p. 35	p. 33		
BL	OL	AL	ELL	The Living Constitution*	✓	✓	✓	✓	✓
	OL	AL		American History Primary Source Documents Library	✓	✓	✓	✓	✓
BL	OL	AL	ELL	Unit Map Overlay Transparencies	✓	✓	✓	✓	✓
BL	OL	AL	ELL	Differentiated Instruction for the American History Classroom	✓	✓	✓	✓	✓
BL	OL	AL	ELL	StudentWorks™ Plus	✓	✓	✓	✓	✓

Note: Please refer to the *Unit 5 Resource Book* for this chapter's URB materials.

* Also available in Spanish

TeacherWorks Plus
All-In-One Planner and Resource Center

- Interactive Lesson Planner
- Interactive Teacher Edition
- Fully editable blackline masters
- Section Spotlight Videos Launch
- Differentiated Lesson Plans
- Printable reports of daily assignments
- Standards Tracking System

Levels					Resources	Chapter Opener	Section 1	Section 2	Section 3	Chapter Assess
BL	OL	AL	ELL							
TEACH *(continued)*										
BL	OL	AL	ELL		American Music Hits Through History CD	✓	✓	✓	✓	✓
BL	OL	AL	ELL		Unit Time Line Transparencies and Activities	✓	✓	✓	✓	✓
BL	OL	AL	ELL		Cause and Effect Transparencies, Strategies, and Activities	✓	✓	✓	✓	✓
BL	OL	AL	ELL		Why It Matters Transparencies, Strategies, and Activities	✓	✓	✓	✓	✓
BL	OL	AL	ELL		American Issues	✓	✓	✓	✓	✓
	OL	AL	ELL		American Art and Architecture Transparencies, Strategies, and Activities	✓	✓	✓	✓	✓
BL	OL	AL			High School American History Literature Library	✓	✓	✓	✓	✓
BL	OL	AL	ELL		*The American Vision* Video Program	✓	✓	✓	✓	✓
Teacher Resources					Strategies for Success	✓	✓	✓	✓	✓
					Success with English Learners	✓	✓	✓	✓	✓
					Reading Strategies and Activities for the Social Studies Classroom	✓	✓	✓	✓	✓
					Presentation Plus! with MindJogger CheckPoint	✓	✓	✓	✓	✓
ASSESS										
BL	OL	AL	ELL		Section Quizzes and Chapter Tests*		p. 199	p. 200	p. 201	p. 203
BL	OL	AL	ELL		Authentic Assessment With Rubrics					p. 33
BL	OL	AL	ELL		Standardized Test Practice Workbook					p. 31
BL	OL	AL	ELL		*ExamView® Assessment Suite*		14-1	14-2	14-3	CH. 14
CLOSE										
BL			ELL		Reteaching Activity, URB					p. 41
BL	OL		ELL		Reading and Study Skills Foldables™	p. 64				

✓ Chapter- or unit-based activities applicable to all sections in this chapter.

Using Section Spotlight Videos

Teach With Technology

What are Section Spotlight Videos?

Section Spotlight Videos are one of the digital media associated with your textbook and present a topic specific to each section of the textbook.

How can Section Spotlight Videos help my students?

Section Spotlight Videos generate student interest and provide a springboard for classroom discussion. Students can watch videos from their classroom computer screen or review for a test while on their home computer.

Visit glencoe.com to access the Media Library, and enter a *QuickPass*™ code to go to Section Spotlight Videos. These videos can also be launched from StudentWorks™ Plus Online or PresentationPlus! with MindJogger CheckPoint.

History ONLINE
Visit glencoe.com and enter *QuickPass*™ code TAV9399c14T for Chapter 14 resources.

You can easily launch a wide range of digital products from your computer's desktop with the McGraw-Hill Social Studies widget.

TeacherWorks

	Student	Teacher	Parent
Media Library			
• Section Audio	●		●
• Spanish Audio Summaries	●		●
• Section Spotlight Videos	●	●	●
***The American Vision* Online Learning Center (Web Site)**			
• StudentWorks™ Plus Online	●	●	●
• Multilingual Glossary	●	●	●
• Study-to-Go	●	●	●
• Chapter Overviews	●	●	●
• Self-Check Quizzes	●	●	●
• Student Web Activities	●	●	●
• ePuzzles and Games	●	●	●
• Vocabulary eFlashcards	●	●	●
• In Motion Animations	●	●	●
• Study Central™	●	●	●
• Web Activity Lesson Plans		●	
• Vocabulary PuzzleMaker	●	●	●
• Historical Thinking Activities		●	
• Beyond the Textbook	●	●	●

Reading Support From Jamestown Education

- **Timed Readings Plus in Social Studies** helps students increase their reading rate and fluency while maintaining comprehension. The 400-word passages are similar to those found on state and national assessments.
- **Reading in the Content Area: Social Studies** concentrates on six essential reading skills that help students better comprehend what they read. The book includes 75 high-interest nonfiction passages written at increasing levels of difficulty.
- **Reading Social Studies** includes strategic reading instruction and vocabulary support in Social Studies content for both ELLs and native speakers of English.

www.jamestowneducation.com

Biography / A&E Home Video / The History Channel

The following videotape programs are available from Glencoe as supplements to this chapter:

- The Panama Canal (ISBN 1-56-501243-7)
- Teddy Roosevelt: An American Lion (0-76-705176-9)

To order, call Glencoe at 1-800-334-7344. To find classroom resources to accompany many of these videos, check the following home pages:

A&E Television: www.aetv.com

The History Channel: www.historychannel.com

National Geographic

Index to National Geographic Magazine:

The following articles relate to this chapter:

- "Remember the *Maine*," by Thomas B. Allen, February 1998
- "Panama's rite of passage. (Panama receives control of the Panama Canal Zone from the US)," by Lewis M. Simons. November, 1999.

National Geographic Society Products To order the following, call National Geographic at 1-800-368-2728:

- *ZipZapMap! USA* (ZipZapMap!)

Access National Geographic's new, dynamic MapMachine Web site and other geography resources at:
www.nationalgeographic.com
www.nationalgeographic.com/maps

Reading List Generator CD-ROM — Glencoe BookLink 3

Use this database to search more than 30,000 titles to create a customized reading list for your students.

- Reading lists can be organized by students' reading level, author, genre, theme, or area of interest.
- The database provides Degrees of Reading Power™ (DRP) and Lexile™ readability scores for all selections.
- A brief summary of each selection is included.

Leveled reading suggestions for this chapter:

For students at a Grade 8 reading level:
- ***Theodore Roosevelt,*** by Clara Ingram Judson

For students at a Grade 9 reading level:
- ***Bully for You, Teddy Roosevelt,*** by Jean Fritz

For students at a Grade 10 reading level:
- ***The Spanish-American War,*** by Kerry A. Graves

For students at a Grade 11 reading level:
- ***The Panama Canal,*** by Lesley A. DuTemple

For students at a Grade 12 reading level:
- ***Mornings on Horseback,*** by David McCullough

Introducing Chapter 14

Focus

MAKING CONNECTIONS
How Are Empires Built?

Essential Question: What geographic considerations might have played a role in where the United States built its empire? *(Latin America was located just to the south of the United States; East Asia, located due west across the Pacific Ocean, was also being exploited by European powers. Both areas were accessible to the U.S. Navy.)* **Essential Question:** Why do some experts say that today the United States is the world's sole superpower? *(Today, the United States is one of the world's richest nations; it has more military power than any other nation.)* OL

Teach

Big Ideas

As students study the chapter, remind them to consider the Big Ideas presented at the beginning of each section. The **Essential Questions** in the activities below tie in to the Big Ideas and help students think about and understand important chapter concepts. In addition, the Hands-on Chapter Project relates the content from each section to the Big Ideas. The steps in each section build on each other and culminate in the Wrap-up activity on the Visual Summary page.

Chapter 14

Becoming a World Power

1872–1917

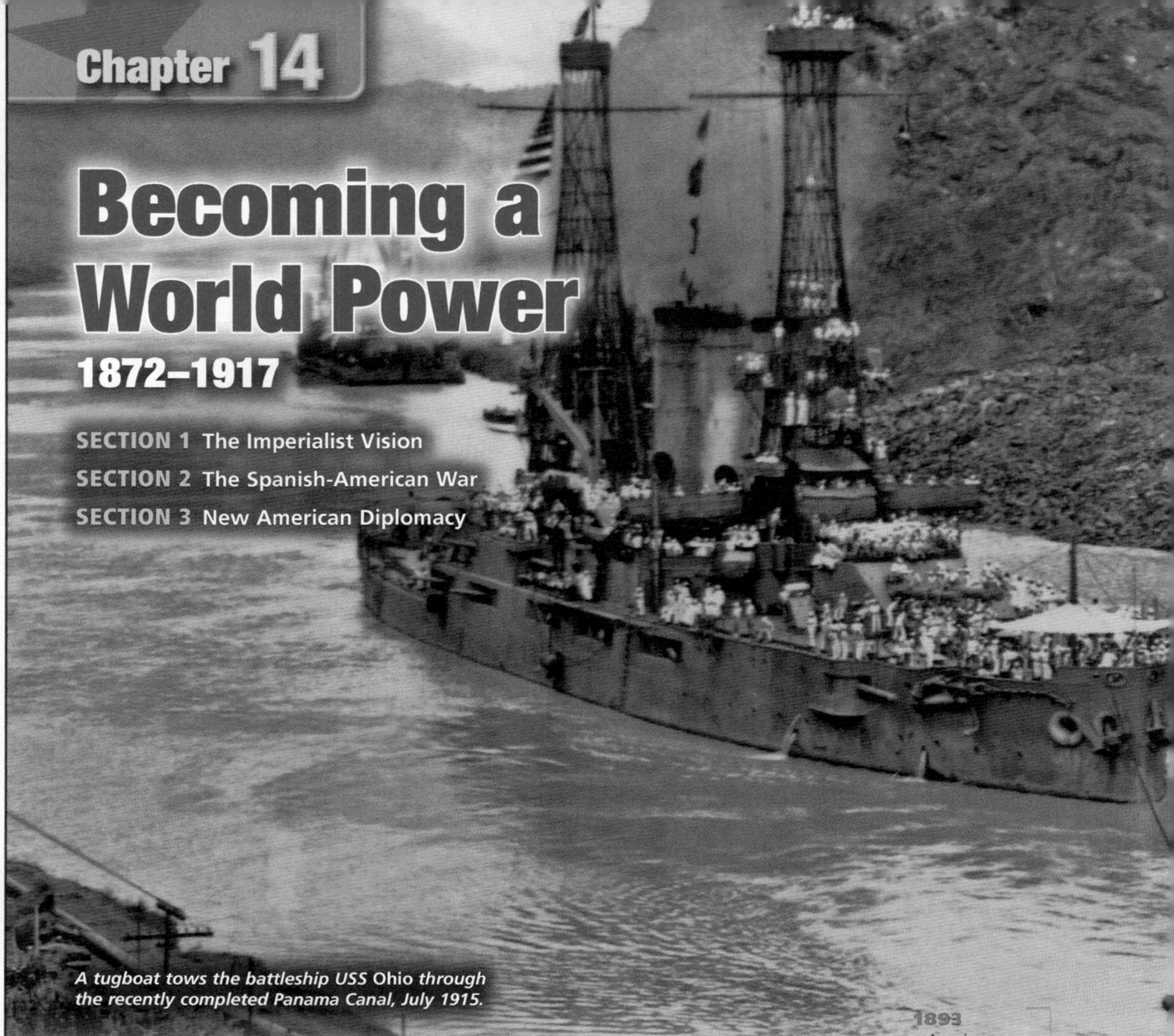

A tugboat tows the battleship USS Ohio through the recently completed Panama Canal, July 1915.

U.S. PRESIDENTS

- Hayes 1877–1881
- Garfield 1881
- Arthur 1881–1885
- Cleveland 1885–1889
- B. Harrison 1889–1893
- Cleveland 1893–1897

U.S. EVENTS

- **1878** • U.S. signs treaty with Samoa to use Pago Pago harbor
- **1893** • Americans overthrow Queen Liliuokalani of Hawaii

1872 — 1882 — 1892

WORLD EVENTS

- **1874** • Britain annexes Fiji Islands
- **1882** • Germany, Austria, and Italy form Triple Alliance
- **1889** • First Pan-American conference is held
- **1894** • Sino-Japanese War breaks out

Section 1

The Imperial Vision

Essential Question: Why did the United States seek to become an imperialist power? *(National pride; an extension of Manifest Destiny; businesses sought new markets for their products)* Point out that in Section 1 students will learn about why the United States began an imperialist foreign policy. OL

Section 2

The Spanish-American War

Essential Question: Was sympathy for the Cuban people or economic expansion the major reason why the United States declared war on Spain? *(Students' answers will vary, but they should point out that the causes of the war were intertwined.)* Point out that in Section 2 students will learn the causes of the Spanish-American War. OL

Chapter Audio

MAKING CONNECTIONS

How Are Empires Built?

International economic and military competition convinced the United States it must become a world power. In the late 1800s, the United States increased its trade and military presence in East Asia and Latin America, and by the early 1900s, it had created an American empire.

- *Why do you think the United States focused on East Asia and Latin America?*
- *What factors make a nation a world power?*

1898
- U.S. declares war on Spain

McKinley 1897–1901

T. Roosevelt 1901–1909

1904
- Panama Canal construction begins
- Roosevelt Corollary is issued

Taft 1909–1913

1902

1912

1899
- John Hay sends Open Door notes

1900
- Boxer Rebellion begins in China

1904
- Russo-Japanese War begins

FOLDABLES™

Taking Notes Create a Concept-Map Book Foldable to help you take basic notes about the relationship between economic and military power. As you read the chapter, write details under each tab and be careful to note the years in which events and developments occurred.

U.S. Expansion / Economic Power / Military Power

History ONLINE Visit glencoe.com and enter QuickPass™ code TAV9846c14 for Chapter 14 resources.

Introducing **Chapter 14**

More About the Photo

Visual Literacy The chapter opening photograph was taken on July 16, 1915. It shows the tugboat *Tavernela* towing the battleship USS *Ohio* through the Gaillard Cut of the Panama Canal.

FOLDABLES™ Study Organizer Dinah Zike's Foldables

Dinah Zike's Foldables are three-dimensional, interactive graphic organizers that help students practice basic writing skills, review vocabulary terms, and identify main ideas. Instructions for creating and using Foldables can be found in the Appendix at the end of this book and in the *Dinah Zike's Reading and Study Skills Foldables* booklet.

History ONLINE

Visit glencoe.com and enter QuickPass™ code TAV9399c14T for Chapter 14 resources, including a Chapter Overview, Study Central™, Study-to-Go, Student Web Activity, Self-Check Quiz, and other materials.

Section 3

New American Diplomacy

Essential Question: Why did the United States use diplomacy to achieve its economic objectives in Asia? *(Diplomacy, rather than war, allowed the United States as well as the European powers access to Asian markets.)* Point out that in Section 3 students will learn about the success of the Open Door Policy in Asia. **OL**

Focus

Bellringer

Daily Focus Transparency 14-1

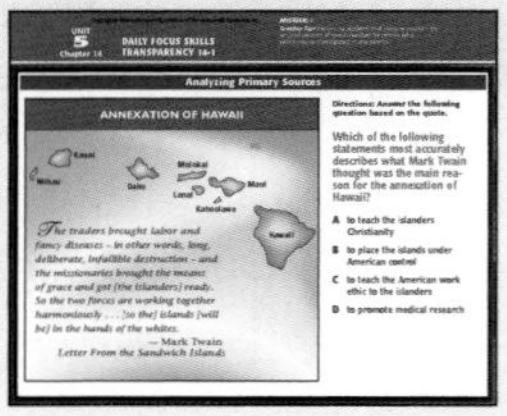

Guide to Reading

Answers:

I. Building Support for Imperialism
  A. A Desire for New Markets
  B. A Feeling of Superiority
  C. Building a Modern Navy
II. American Expansion in the Pacific
  A. Perry Opens Japan
  B. Annexing Hawaii
III. Diplomacy in Latin America

Section Spotlight Video

To generate student interest and provide a springboard for class discussion, access the Chapter 14, Section 1 video at glencoe.com or on the video DVD.

Resource Manager

Section 1 — Section Audio — Spotlight Video

The Imperialist Vision

Guide to Reading

Big Ideas

Economics and Society In the late 1800s, many Americans wanted the United States to expand its military and economic power overseas.

Content Vocabulary
- imperialism *(p. 490)*
- protectorate *(p. 490)*

Academic Vocabulary
- expansion *(p. 491)*
- conference *(p. 495)*

People and Events to Identify
- Anglo-Saxonism *(p. 492)*
- Matthew C. Perry *(p. 493)*
- Queen Liliuokalani *(p. 494)*
- Pan-Americanism *(p. 495)*

Reading Strategy

Organizing As you read about the development of the United States as a world power, use the major headings of the section to create an outline similar to the one below.

The Imperialist Vision
I. Building Support for Imperialism
  A.
  B.
  C.
II.
  A.
  B.

During the late 1800s, the desire to find new markets, increase trade, and build a powerful navy caused the United States to become more involved in international affairs.

Building Support for Imperialism

MAIN Idea A desire for world markets and belief in the superiority of Anglo-Saxon culture led the United States to assert itself as a world power.

HISTORY AND YOU Do you remember what role George Washington thought the United States should play in world affairs? Read to learn why Americans' opinions changed in the 1880s.

In the years immediately following the Civil War, most Americans showed little interest in expanding their nation's territory outside the United States or increasing its international influence. Instead, they focused on reconstructing the South, building up the nation's industries, and settling the West. Beginning in the 1880s, however, economic and military competition from other nations, as well as a growing feeling of cultural superiority, convinced many Americans that the United States should become a world power.

A Desire for New Markets

Several European nations were already expanding overseas, a development known as the New Imperialism. **Imperialism** is the economic and political domination of a strong nation over weaker ones. Europeans expanded their power overseas for many reasons. Factories depended on raw materials from all over the world. No country had all of the resources its economy needed. In addition, by the late 1800s, most industrialized countries had placed high tariffs against each other. These tariffs were intended to protect a nation's industries from foreign competition. The tariffs reduced trade between industrialized countries, forcing companies to look for other markets overseas.

At the same time, the growth of investment opportunities in Western Europe had slowed. Most of the factories, railroads, and mines that Europe's economy needed had been built. Increasingly, Europeans began looking overseas for places to invest their capital. They started to invest in industries located in other countries, particularly in Africa and Asia.

To protect their investments, European nations began exerting control over those territories. Some areas became colonies. Many others became protectorates. In a **protectorate,** the imperial power

R Reading Strategies	C Critical Thinking	D Differentiated Instruction	W Writing Support	S Skill Practice
Additional Resources • Guided Read. Act., URB p. 46 • Content Vocab. Act., URB p. 25 • Prim. Source Read., URB p. 35 • Reading Skills Act., p. 19	**Teacher Edition** • Draw. Concl., p. 492 • Identify. Central Issues, p. 494 **Additional Resources** • Link. Past/Present, URB p. 32 • Quizzes and Tests, p. 199	**Additional Resources** • Foldables, p. 64 • Academic Vocab. Act., URB p. 27	**Teacher Edition** • Persuas. Writing, pp. 491, 492 • Descrip. Writing, p. 493	**Teacher Edition** • Inferring, p. 491 **Additional Resources** • Read. Essen., p. 156

PRIMARY SOURCE

Causes of American Imperialism

American imperialism had three main causes:

1. The belief in the superiority of American culture
2. The belief that the nation needed a large navy for security, with bases overseas
3. The belief that the economy needed overseas markets

1. ANGLO-SAXONISM

"The work which the English race began when it colonized North America is destined to go on until every land . . . that is not already the seat of an old civilization shall become English in its language, in its religion, in political habits and traditions, and to a predominant extent in the blood of its people."
—John Fiske, quoted in *The Expansionists of 1898*

2. MILITARY BASES

". . . [T]he ships of war of the United States, in war, will be like land birds, unable to fly far from their own shores. To provide resting-places for them, where they can coal and repair, would be one of the first duties of a government proposing to itself the development of the power of the nation at sea."
—Alfred Thayer Mahan, *The Influence of Sea Power Upon History*

3. OVERSEAS MARKETS

"[W]e are raising more than we can consume, . . . making more than we can use. Therefore we must find new markets for our produce. . ."
—Albert Beveridge, quoted in *The Meaning of the Times and Other Speeches*

Exports and Imports, 1865–1900

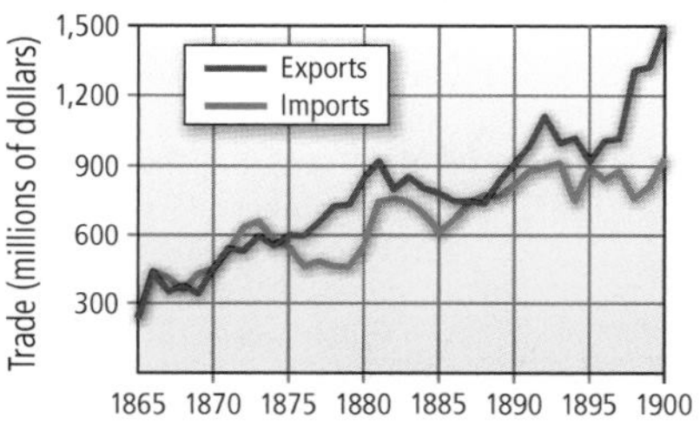

Source: *Historical Statistics of the United States.*

DBQ Document-Based Questions

1. **Interpreting** Based on the quote above, how do you think Albert Beveridge would use the data shown in the graph to support his argument?
2. **Comparing** What is the difference between Fiske's support for expanding American power overseas and Mahan's support for establishing military bases overseas?

allowed the local rulers to stay in control and protected them against rebellions and invasion. In exchange, the local rulers usually had to accept advice from the Europeans on how to govern their countries.

The United States noticed the **expansion** of European power overseas. As the United States industrialized, many Americans took an interest in the new imperialism. Until the late 1800s, the United States had expanded by settling more territory in North America. Now, with settlers finally filling up the western frontier, many Americans concluded that the nation needed new overseas markets to keep its economy strong.

A Feeling of Superiority

In addition to economic concerns, certain other key ideas convinced many Americans to encourage their nation's expansion overseas. Many supporters of Social Darwinism argued that nations competed with each other politically, economically, and militarily, and that only the strongest would survive. To them, this idea justified increasing American influence abroad.

Teach

S Skill Practice

Inferring Ask: Based on the quotation by John Fiske, what can you infer about his views of other cultures and peoples? *(Fiske believed that English-speaking white Christians were superior to all others.)* **AL**

DBQ Document Based Questions

Answers:

1. Exports were growing rapidly.
2. Fiske supports imperialism to bring American culture and civilization to other parts of the world; Mahan is interested in building military bases so that warships can be refueled or repaired.

W Writing Support

Persuasive Writing Invite interested students to write an essay supporting or opposing Social Darwinism as justification for the United States to pursue its imperialist foreign policy. **AL**

Hands-On Chapter Project Step 1

Preparing a Multimedia Presentation

Step 1: Research American Areas of Interest

Directions Divide the class into small groups, assigning each group one of the following categories: Cuba, China, Japan, the Philippines, Puerto Rico, and Guam. Have students use Internet and library resources, as well as their textbooks, to locate and analyze information about the reasons for and the effects of imperialism in their assigned country. Encourage students to use both primary and secondary resources in their research.

Tell students to focus on the following causes and effects of imperialism: economics, naval power, national pride, Manifest Destiny, loss of autonomy, increased development, and war and other conflicts.

Putting It Together Give students a tutorial on the software they will be using to develop their presentations. Encourage students to ask questions about aspects of the program they find confusing. If necessary, pair students who have experience using the program with those who do not. **OL**

(Chapter Project continued on page 497)

C Critical Thinking

Drawing Conclusions Ask: How might a strong navy support Fiske's idea of Anglo-Saxonism? *(A strong navy would militarily support the spread of Anglo-Saxonism to other places.)* OL

W Writing Support

Persuasive Writing Have interested students write a letter to Senator Lodge or Senator Beveridge advocating or opposing a big navy. Encourage students to share their essays with the class. BL

Reading Check

Answer: More people believed it was America's destiny to spread its civilization overseas.

Many Americans, such as the well-known writer and historian John Fiske, took this idea even further. Fiske argued that English-speaking nations had superior character, ideas, and systems of government.

C Fiske's ideas, known as **Anglo-Saxonism,** were popular in Britain and the United States. Many Americans linked it with the idea of Manifest Destiny. They believed the nation's destiny had been to expand westward to the Pacific Ocean. Now they believed the United States was destined to expand overseas and spread its civilization to other people.

Another influential advocate of Anglo-Saxonism was Josiah Strong, a popular American minister in the late 1800s. Strong linked Anglo-Saxonism to Christian missionary ideas. His ideas influenced many Americans. "The Anglo-Saxon," Strong declared, "[is] divinely commissioned to be, in a peculiar sense, his brother's keeper." By linking missionary work with Anglo-Saxonism, Strong convinced many Americans to support an expansion of American power overseas.

Building a Modern Navy

As imperialism and Anglo-Saxonism gained support, the United States became increasingly assertive in foreign affairs. Three international crises illustrated this new approach. In 1888 the country risked war to prevent Germany from taking control of Samoa in the South Pacific. Three years later, when a mob in Chile attacked American sailors in the port of Valparaíso, the United States threatened to go to war unless Chile paid reparations. Then, in 1895, the United States backed Venezuela against Great Britain in a border dispute with British Guiana. After Britain rejected an American ultimatum, many newspapers and members of Congress called for war. All three crises were eventually resolved peacefully.

As Americans became increasingly willing to risk war to defend American interests overseas, support for building a large modern navy began to grow. Supporters argued that if the United States did not build up its navy and acquire bases overseas, European nations would shut it out of foreign markets.

Captain Alfred T. Mahan, an officer in the U.S. Navy who taught at the Naval War College, best expressed this argument. In 1890 Mahan published his lectures in a book called *The Influence of Sea Power upon History, 1660–1783.* In this book Mahan pointed out that many prosperous peoples in the past, such as the British and Dutch, had built large fleets of merchant ships to trade with the world. He then suggested that a nation also needed a large navy to protect its merchant ships and to defend its right to trade with other countries.

W Mahan's book became a best-seller, helping to build public support for a big navy. Two powerful senators, Henry Cabot Lodge and Albert J. Beveridge, pushed for constructing a new navy. In the executive branch, Benjamin Tracy, secretary of the navy under President Harrison, and John D. Long, secretary of the navy under President McKinley, strongly supported Mahan's ideas.

By the 1890s, several different ideas had come together in the United States. Business leaders wanted new markets overseas. Anglo-Saxonism had convinced many Americans of their destiny to dominate the world. Growing European imperialism threatened America's security. Combined with Mahan's theories, these ideas convinced Congress to authorize the construction of a large, modern navy.

Reading Check **Summarizing** How did Americans' opinions about overseas expansion change in the late 1800s?

PRIMARY SOURCE

Perry Arrives in Japan

In 1853 Japan was a closed society. Its rulers had deliberately ended contact with the outside world, permitting only a small amount of trade with the Dutch and the Chinese. They were largely unaware of the changes the industrial revolution had brought to Europe and the United States. Perry's black steamships, belching smoke, and moving without any visible sails, were something the Japanese had never seen before.

The Japanese had cannons and guns, but Perry's ships carried 65 large cannons—a staggering number that represented immense power—and a direct threat to Japan's many coastal castles and towns. Perry's arrival carried different meanings for people living in the two countries, as shown in the two images to the right—one from Japan and the other from the United States.

Additional Support

Activity: Technology Connection

Shipbuilding Organize interested students into two groups. Have one group use library or Internet resources to find out more information about the Great White Fleet. Students should find out at what shipyards the ships were built; the size, length, and displacement of the ships; and how the ships were powered. Have the other group find out the same types of information about recently built ships. Each group should make posters detailing their findings. Have a spokesperson from each group present their findings to the class. Then ask the entire class to write a brief paragraph comparing one aspect of shipbuilding in the early 1900s with modern-day shipbuilding. OL

American Expansion in the Pacific

MAIN Idea The desire for new markets led to trade with Japan and the annexation of Hawaii.

HISTORY AND YOU What products do you use that are made in Japan? Read how the United States and Japan first became trading partners.

From the earliest days of the Republic, Americans had expanded their nation by moving westward. When Americans began looking overseas for new markets in the 1800s, therefore, they naturally tended to look toward the Pacific. Even before imperialist ideas became popular, American businesses had begun sending ships to trade in East Asia.

Perry Opens Japan

Many American business leaders believed that the United States would benefit from trade with Japan, as well as with China. Japan's rulers, however, who believed that excessive contact with the West would destroy their culture, allowed only the Chinese and Dutch to trade with their nation. In 1852, after receiving several petitions from Congress, President Millard Fillmore decided to force Japan to trade with the United States. He ordered Commodore **Matthew C. Perry** to take a naval expedition to Japan to negotiate a trade treaty.

On July 8, 1853, four American warships under Perry's command entered Edo Bay (today known as Tokyo Bay). The display of American technology and firepower impressed the Japanese, who had never before seen steamships. Realizing that they could not resist modern Western technology and weapons, the Japanese agreed to sign the Treaty of Kanagawa. In addition to granting the United States permission to trade at two ports in Japan, the treaty called for peace between the two countries; promised help for any American ships and sailors shipwrecked off the Japanese coast; and gave American ships permission to buy supplies such as wood, water, food, and coal in the Japanese ports.

The American decision forcing Japan to open trade played an important role in Japanese history. Japanese leaders concluded that it was time to remake their society. They adopted Western technology and launched their own industrial revolution. By the 1890s, the Japanese had a powerful navy and had begun building their own empire in Asia.

W

▶ *American painter James Evans entitled his work "Commodore Perry Carrying the Gospel of God to the Heathen, 1853."*

▼ *This Japanese color print depicts one artist's perspective of Perry's "black ships" that arrived in Japan in 1853.*

Analyzing VISUALS

1. **Comparing** What elements did both the American and Japanese artists depict the same way? Which were different?
2. **Making Inferences** What impression of the Americans does the Japanese image convey? What is the American painting communicating about Perry's mission?

W Writing Support

Descriptive Writing Have students compare the two paintings of Commodore Perry's ships shown on this page. Then have students write a paragraph describing how the two artists portrayed the ships. Encourage students to share their essays with the class. BL

Analyzing VISUALS

Answers:

1. same: smoke, smokestacks, sails, waves; different: shape of the ship, Asian elements on the Japanese print are not shown on the American painting
2. The Japanese print makes the Americans look aggressive and threatening; the American painting makes the ship appear majestic and the mission divinely inspired.

Differentiated Instruction

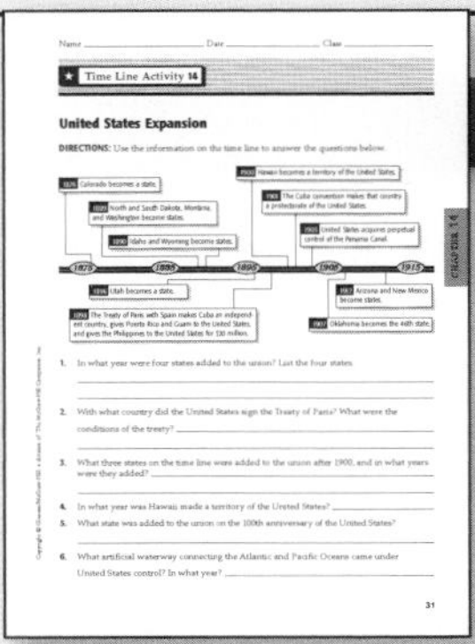

Time Line Activity 14, URB p. 31

Illustrating Expansion: Make a Map

Objective: Create a map to show the expansion of U.S. territory from 1872–1912.

Focus: Give each student a copy of a world map.

Teach: Make a list of the states, countries, and territories that were involved in events that led to U.S. expansion.

Assess: Identify which areas became new parts of the U.S.

Close: Draw a new map or color the world map to show the expansion of U.S. territory.

Differentiated Instruction Strategies

BL Write a list of the states that joined the Union from 1872 to 1912.

AL Research each of the states that joined the Union from 1872 to 1912. Find out their size and determine in square miles how much territory was added during this time period.

ELL Based on the time line, make a list of the years in which new states were added to the Union.

People IN HISTORY

Answer:
Planters revolted against Liliuokalani because they wanted Hawaii to become part of the United States.

C Critical Thinking

Identifying Central Issues
Ask students to review the conflict between the Hawaiian rulers and the planters. **Ask:** What is the main issue at the root of the conflict between these two groups? *(who would be the ruler of the Hawaiian Islands)* **OL**

Reading Check

Answer:
It led them to annex Hawaii and to open trade with Japan.

Additional Support

People IN HISTORY

Queen Liliuokalani
1838–1917

Queen Liliuokalani was the last ruling monarch of the Hawaiian Islands. A group of white sugar planters had forced her predecessor to accept a new constitution that minimized the power of the monarchy, gave voting rights to Americans and Europeans, and denied voting rights to most Hawaiians and all Asians.

As queen, Liliuokalani was determined to regain royal power and reduce the power of foreigners. On January 14, 1893, she issued a new constitution, which restored the power of the monarchy and the rights of the Hawaiian people. In response, a group of planters led by Sanford B. Dole launched a revolt. Under protest, Liliuokalani surrendered her throne on January 17. After supporters led a revolt in an attempt to restore her to power in 1895, Liliuokalani was placed under house arrest for several months. After her release, she lived out her days in Washington Place in Honolulu.

Why did sugar planters lead a revolt against Queen Liliuokalani?

▲ *Sanford B. Dole gives Hawaii, represented as the bride, to Uncle Sam.*

For an example of American views on annexing Hawaii read "President Harrison on Hawaiian Annexation" on page R51 in **Documents in American History.**

Annexing Hawaii

As trade with Asia grew during the 1800s, Americans began seeking ports where they could refuel and resupply while crossing the Pacific Ocean. Pago Pago, in the Samoan Islands, had one of the finest harbors in the South Pacific. In 1878 the United States negotiated permission to open a base there.

More important was Hawaii. Whaling ships and merchant vessels crossing the Pacific often stopped there to rest and to take on supplies. In 1820 missionaries from New England arrived in Hawaii. American settlers found that sugarcane grew well in Hawaii's climate and soil. By the mid-1800s, businessmen had established many plantations on the islands.

A severe recession struck Hawaii in 1872. Three years later, worried that the economic crisis might force the Hawaiians to turn to the British or French for help, the United States signed a treaty exempting Hawaiian sugar from tariffs. When the treaty came up for renewal several years later, the Senate insisted that Hawaii grant the United States exclusive rights to a naval base at Pearl Harbor.

The treaty led to a boom in the Hawaiian sugar industry and wealth for the planters. In 1887 prominent planters pressured the Hawaiian king into accepting a constitution that limited the king's authority. As tensions mounted between the planters and Hawaiians, Congress passed a new tariff in 1890 that gave subsidies to sugar producers in the United States. The subsidies made Hawaiian sugar more expensive than American sugar. Unable to sell much sugar, planters concluded that the only way to increase sales was to have Hawaii become part of the United States.

In 1891 **Queen Liliuokalani** ascended the Hawaiian throne. Liliuokalani disliked the influence that American settlers had gained in Hawaii. In January 1893 she tried to impose a new constitution reasserting her authority as ruler of Hawaii. In response, a group of planters tried to overthrow the monarchy. Supported by the marines from the *USS Boston*, they forced the queen to step down. Then they set up a provisional government and asked the United States to annex Hawaii. **C**

President Cleveland strongly opposed imperialism. He withdrew the annexation treaty from the Senate and tried to return Liliuokalani to power. Hawaii's new leaders refused to restore the queen and decided to wait until Cleveland left office. Five years later, the United States annexed Hawaii.

Reading Check **Explaining** How did the search for new markets push the United States to become a world power?

Extending the Content

American Samoa In the mid-nineteenth century, islands across the Pacific attracted the interest of imperialist nations. In the South Pacific, the Samoan Islands drew the attention of Germany, Britain, and the United States, all of which laid claim to parts of Samoa. The Samoan Islands attracted attention because the islands lay in a strategic position in the Pacific, could serve as coaling stations to refuel ships, and offered new markets for imperialist powers. The United States signed a "treaty of friendship and commerce" with Samoa in 1878 that granted the U.S. a coaling and naval station in the port of Pago Pago. In 1899 Germany and the United States signed the Treaty of Berlin, by which the United States annexed the eastern islands of Samoa and Germany annexed the western islands. Today the residents of American Samoa elect one nonvoting congressperson to the U.S. House of Representatives.

Diplomacy in Latin America

MAIN Idea The United States worked to increase trade with Latin America.

HISTORY AND YOU What products have you used that come from Latin America? Read to learn how the United States tried to expand its trade relations with Latin America.

The Pacific was not the only region where the United States sought to increase its influence in the 1800s. It also focused on Latin America. Although the United States bought raw materials from this region, Latin Americans bought most of their manufactured goods from Europe. American business leaders and government officials wanted to increase the sale of American products to the region. They also wanted the Europeans to understand that the United States was the dominant power in the region.

James G. Blaine, who served as secretary of state in three administrations in the 1880s, led early efforts to expand American influence in Latin America. "What we want," Blaine explained, "are the markets of these neighbors of ours that lie to the south of us. . . . With these markets secured new life would be given to our manufacturers, the product of the western farmer would be in demand, the reasons for and inducements to strikers, with all their attendant evils, would cease." Blaine proposed that the United States invite the Latin American nations to a **conference** in Washington, D.C. The conference would discuss ways in which the American nations could work together to support peace and to increase trade. The idea that the United States and Latin America should work together came to be called **Pan-Americanism.**

On October 2, 1889, Washington, D.C., hosted the first modern Pan-American conference, which all Latin American nations except the Dominican Republic attended. Blaine had two goals for the conference. First, he wanted to create a customs union between Latin America and the United States. He also wanted to create a system for American nations to work out their disputes peacefully.

A customs union would require all of the American nations to reduce their tariffs against each other and to treat each other equally in trade. Blaine hoped that a customs union would turn the Latin Americans away from European products and toward American products. He also hoped that a common system for settling disputes would keep the Europeans from meddling in American affairs.

Although the warm reception they received in the United States impressed the Latin American delegates to the conference, they rejected both of Blaine's ideas. They did agree, however, to create the Commercial Bureau of the American Republics, an organization that worked to promote cooperation among the nations of the Western Hemisphere. In 1902 the name was changed to the International Bureau of the American Republics. This organization was later known as the Pan-American Union and is today called the Organization of American States (OAS).

Reading Check **Summarizing** How did Secretary of State Blaine attempt to increase American influence in Latin America?

Section 1 REVIEW

Vocabulary

1. **Explain** the significance of: imperialism, protectorate, Anglo-Saxonism, Matthew C. Perry, Queen Liliuokalani, Pan-Americanism.

Main Ideas

2. **Listing** Use a graphic organizer to list the factors that led the United States to adopt an imperialist policy in the 1890s.

3. **Describing** Why and how did the Americans force the Japanese to trade with the United States?
4. **Explaining** Why did Secretary of State James G. Blaine convene the Pan-American conference in 1889?

Critical Thinking

5. **Big Ideas** Do you think the United States should have supported the planters in their attempt to overthrow Queen Liliuokalani of Hawaii? Why or why not?
6. **Evaluating** How did trade with the United States change Japanese society?
7. **Analyzing Visuals** Study the two images of Perry's ship on page 493. How do the artists' perspectives vary? Do you think the artists show any bias in their representations? Why or why not?

Writing About History

8. **Persuasive Writing** Imagine that you are living in the United States in the 1890s. Write a letter to the president persuading him to support or oppose an imperialist policy for the United States.

History ONLINE
Study Central™ To review this section, go to glencoe.com and click on Study Central.

Reading Check

Answer:
He wanted to create a customs union between Latin America and the United States. He also wanted to create a system for American nations to work out their disputes peacefully.

Assess

History ONLINE

Study Central™ provides summaries, interactive games, and online graphic organizers to help students review content.

Close

Summarizing **Ask:** Why did the United States become an imperial power? *(to spread American culture and civilization; to find new economic opportunities and markets; to compete with European powers)* **OL**

Section 1 REVIEW

Answers

1. All definitions can be found in the section and the Glossary.
2. feeling of superiority, interest in expanding trade, need for strategic military bases, European competition
3. Pressured by Congress, which in turn had been pressured by American businessmen, President Millard Fillmore sent Matthew C. Perry and a naval expedition to Tokyo to open Japan. The Japanese were impressed by modern ships and technology, against which they could not compete.
4. He convened the conference to support peace and increase trade among the nations in the Americas.
5. Students' answers will vary. Students should be able to defend their points of view.
6. Many Japanese leaders determined that it was time to remake and modernize their society. They launched an industrial revolution and built a navy, and then they began to build an empire.
7. Each artist depicts the ship from his own point of view. Both artists are biased in their representations because each is expressing the viewpoint of his or her nation.
8. Letters should express a clear point of view.

Focus

Bellringer

Daily Focus Transparency 14-2

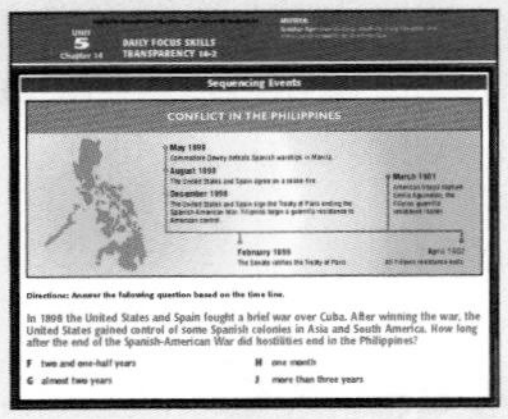

Guide to Reading

Answers to Graphic Organizer: sinking of the *Maine*; sympathy for Cuban revolution; need to protect American investments in Cuba

Section Spotlight Video

To generate student interest and provide a springboard for class discussion, access the Chapter 14, Section 2 video at glencoe.com or on the video DVD.

Resource Manager

R Reading Strategies	C Critical Thinking	D Differentiated Instruction	W Writing Support	S Skill Practice
Teacher Edition • Using Contxt. Clues, p. 498 • Inferring, p. 502 **Additional Resources** • Guided Read. Act., URB p. 47 • Prim. Source Read., URB p. 33	**Teacher Edition** • Analy. Prim. Sources, p. 497 • Making Infer., p. 499 • Draw. Concl., p. 500 • Comparing, p. 502 **Additional Resources** • Hist. Analysis Skills Act., URB p. 20 • Quizzes and Tests, p. 200	**Teacher Edition** • Visual/Spatial, p. 498 **Additional Resources** • Am. Art and Music Act., URB p. 37 • Enrich. Act., URB p. 43 • English Learner Act., URB p. 23	**Teacher Edition** • Persuasive Writing, pp. 497, 501	**Additional Resources** • Read. Essen., p. 159 • Reinforcing Skills Act., URB p. 29

Section 2

Section Audio

Spotlight Video

The Spanish-American War

Guide to Reading

Big Ideas

Trade, War, and Migration The United States defeated Spain in a war, acquired new overseas territories, and became an imperial power.

Content Vocabulary

- yellow journalism *(p. 497)*
- autonomy *(p. 498)*
- jingoism *(p. 499)*

Academic Vocabulary

- intervene *(p. 498)*
- volunteer *(p. 500)*

People and Events to Identify

- José Martí *(p. 496)*
- William Randolph Hearst *(p. 497)*
- Joseph Pulitzer *(p. 497)*
- Emilio Aguinaldo *(p. 500)*
- Platt Amendment *(p. 502)*
- Foraker Act *(p. 503)*

Reading Strategy

Organizing As you read about the Spanish-American War, complete a graphic organizer like the one below by listing the circumstances that contributed to war with Spain.

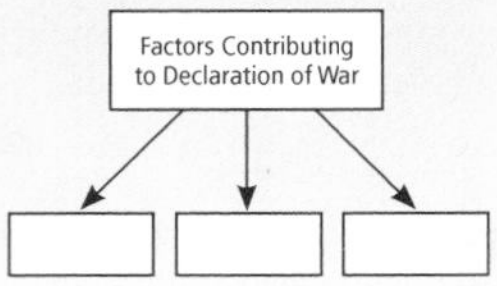

During the Spanish-American War, the United States defeated Spanish troops in Cuba and the Philippines. Afterward, the United States annexed the Philippines and became an imperial power.

The Coming of War

MAIN Idea In support of the Cuban rebellion and in retaliation for the loss of the USS *Maine*, the United States declared war on Spain.

HISTORY AND YOU Do you remember what led the American colonists to declare their independence from Britain? Read about another colony that fought for independence from a colonial ruler.

By 1898 Cuba and Puerto Rico were Spain's last remaining colonies in the Western Hemisphere. Cubans had periodically revolted against Spanish rule, and many Americans regarded the Spanish as tyrants. Ultimately, the United States issued a declaration of war. Although the fighting lasted only a few months, the "splendid little war," as Secretary of State John Hay described it, dramatically altered the position of the United States on the world stage.

The Cuban Rebellion Begins

Cuba was one of Spain's oldest colonies in the Americas. Its sugarcane plantations generated considerable wealth for Spain and produced nearly one-third of the world's sugar in the mid-1800s. Until Spain abolished slavery in 1886, about one-third of the Cuban population was enslaved and forced to work for wealthy landowners on the plantations.

In 1868 Cuban rebels declared independence and launched a guerrilla war against Spanish authorities. Lacking internal support, the rebellion collapsed a decade later. Many Cuban rebels then fled to the United States. One of the exiled leaders was **José Martí,** a writer and poet. While living in New York City in the 1880s, Martí brought together Cuban exile groups living in the United States. The groups raised funds, purchased weapons, and trained troops in preparation for an invasion of Cuba.

By the early 1890s, the United States and Cuba had become closely linked economically. Cuba exported much of its sugar to the United States, and Americans had invested approximately $50 million in Cuba's sugar plantations, mines, and railroads. These economic ties created a crisis in 1894, when the United States imposed a new tariff on sugar that devastated Cuba's economy. With Cuba in financial

PRIMARY SOURCE
Causes of the Spanish-American War

The Spanish-American War had four main causes:

1. The Cuban Rebellion against Spain
2. American desire to protect its investments in Cuba
3. Yellow journalism that intensified public anger at Spain
4. The explosion of the USS *Maine*

YELLOW JOURNALISM

NEW YORK JOURNAL
AND ADVERTISER.

DESTRUCTION OF THE WAR SHIP MAINE WAS THE WORK OF AN ENEMY

$50,000!
$50,000 REWARD! For the Detection of the Perpetrator of the Maine Outrage!

Assistant Secretary Roosevelt Convinced the Explosion of the War Ship Was Not an Accident.

The Journal Offers $50,000 Reward for the Conviction of the Criminals Who Sent 258 American Sailors to Their Death. Naval Officers Unanimous That the Ship Was Destroyed

$50,000!
$50,000 REWARD! For the Detection of the Perpetrator of the Maine Outrage!

▲ *Dramatic and emotional stories in newspapers owned by Hearst and Pulitzer described Spanish atrocities in Cuba and enraged the American people, some of whom began to call for war.*

CUBANS REBEL AGAINST SPAIN

◀ *Spanish oppression of the Cuban people triggered a rebellion that earned the sympathy of many Americans, some of whom began providing arms and money to the rebels.*

THE *MAINE* EXPLODES, 1898

▲ *President McKinley sent the battleship Maine to Cuba to help Americans evacuate. When the ship exploded, an enraged nation blamed Spain, and "Remember the Maine!" became the battle cry for war.*

U.S. Investment in Cuba, 1897

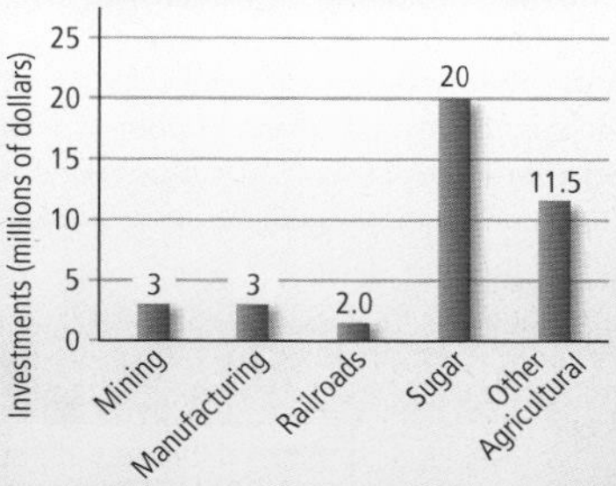

Source: *America's Stake in International Investments.*

◀ *With $30 to $50 million invested in Cuba and nearly $100 million in annual trade, American business leaders wanted Spain out of Cuba and an end to the rebellion.*

C

Analyzing VISUALS

1. **Interpreting** What do you think contributed to American sympathy with the Cubans?
2. **Identifying Central Issues** What role did economics play in the lead-up to war with Spain?

distress, Martí's followers launched a new rebellion in February 1895. Although Martí died during the fighting, the rebels seized control of eastern Cuba, declared independence, and formally established the Republic of Cuba in September 1895.

America Supports Cuba

When the uprising in Cuba began, President Grover Cleveland declared the United States neutral. Outside the White House, however, many people openly supported the rebels. Some citizens compared the Cubans' struggle to the American Revolution. A few sympathetic Americans even began smuggling guns from Florida to the Cuban rebels.

What caused most Americans to support the rebels were the stories of Spanish atrocities reported in two of the nation's major newspapers, the *New York Journal* and the *New York World*. The *Journal*, owned by **William Randolph Hearst,** and *The World*, owned by **Joseph Pulitzer,** competed with each other to increase their circulation. The *Journal* reported outrageous stories of the Spanish feeding Cuban prisoners to sharks and dogs. Not to be outdone, *The World* described Cuba as a place with "blood on the roadsides, blood in the fields, blood on the doorsteps, blood, blood, blood!" This kind of sensationalist reporting, in which writers often exaggerated and even made up stories to attract readers, became known as **yellow journalism.**

W

Teach

C Critical Thinking

Analyzing Primary Sources Have students study the Primary Source feature on this page.

Ask: What events caused American public opinion to favor the Cubans? What event caused the United States to declare war on Spain? *(the Cuban revolution, yellow journalism, and U.S. economic involvement; the sinking of the* Maine*)*

Analyzing VISUALS

Answers:

1. the oppression of the Cuban people by the Spanish
2. The United States had money invested in Cuba in the late 1890s and sought to protect those economic interests.

W Writing Support

Persuasive Writing Have students write a letter to the editor of the *New York Journal* supporting or opposing the newspaper's views on the uprising in Cuba. BL

Hands-On Chapter Project
Step 2

Preparing a Multimedia Presentation

Step 2: Organizing Information on the Presentation Groups begin to create and organize their presentations.

Directions Have students meet in their groups with the notes they have taken on their assigned country. Have groups discuss how they want to organize the information they've gathered. Suggest the options of chronology, cause-and-effect, or organization by subcategory.

Once groups have determined the format, have them begin assembling the information they want to include in their presentations. Encourage students to use primary source quotes, informational text, diagrams, photographs, or even drawings they've created. Students may also use propaganda from the period.

Putting It Together Have students review their presentation once they have entered their information to verify the accuracy of the information and to make sure nothing has been left out. OL

(Chapter Project continued on page 505)

R Reading Strategy

Using Context Clues Have students reread the first paragraph under "Calls for War" on this page. Using clue words and phrases such as "believing it would cost too many lives," "hurt the economy," and "asked the Spanish if the United States could help negotiate an end to the conflict," ask students to define the term *intervene*. Students should note that the term means "to get involved or to interfere." BL

D Differentiated Instruction

Visual/Spatial Have interested students create a map of Cuba. Using library or Internet resources, students should show the location of the battles that occurred during the Spanish-American War and the position of the American navy around the island. Display the maps in the classroom. BL

Although the press invented sensational stories, Cubans indeed suffered horribly. The Spanish sent nearly 200,000 troops to the island to put down the rebellion and appointed General Valeriano Weyler as governor. Weyler's harsh policies quickly earned him the nickname *"El Carnicero"* ("The Butcher").

The Cuban rebels staged hit-and-run raids, burned plantations and sugar mills, tore up railroad tracks, and attacked supply depots. Knowing that many American businesses had investments in Cuba, the rebels hoped that the destruction of American property would lead to American intervention in the war.

To prevent Cuban villagers from helping the rebels, Weyler herded hundreds of thousands of rural men, women, and children into "reconcentration camps," where tens of thousands died of starvation and disease. News reports of these camps enraged Americans.

Calls for War

R In 1897 Republican William McKinley became president of the United States. The new president did not want to **intervene** in the war, believing it would cost too many lives and hurt the economy. In September 1897, he asked the Spanish if the United States could help negotiate an end to the conflict. He made it clear that if the war did not end soon, the United States might have to intervene. R

Spain removed Weyler from power and offered the Cubans **autonomy**—the right to their own government—but only if Cuba remained part of the Spanish empire. The Cuban rebels refused to negotiate.

Spain's concessions enraged many Spanish loyalists in Cuba. In January 1898, the loyalists rioted in Havana. Worried that Americans in Cuba might be attacked, McKinley sent the battleship USS *Maine* to Havana in case the Americans had to be evacuated.

On February 9, 1898, the *New York Journal* printed a letter intercepted by a Cuban agent. Written by Enrique Dupuy de Lôme, the Spanish ambassador to the United States, the letter described McKinley as "weak and a bidder for the admiration of the crowd." The nation erupted in fury over the insult.

Then, on the evening of February 15, 1898, while the *Maine* sat in Havana Harbor, it was ripped apart by an explosion and sank. No one is sure why the *Maine* exploded. An investigation

PRIMARY SOURCE

The Spanish-American War

When the United States declared war on Spain, the U.S. Army had approximately 25,000 soldiers. Spain had roughly 200,000 in Cuba alone. To expand its forces, the government called into service soldiers from the state militias and also enlisted some 180,000 volunteers in the army. Among those volunteers was the First Volunteer Cavalry, nicknamed the Rough Riders, under the command of Colonels Leonard Wood and Theodore Roosevelt.

U.S. Deaths in the Spanish-American War

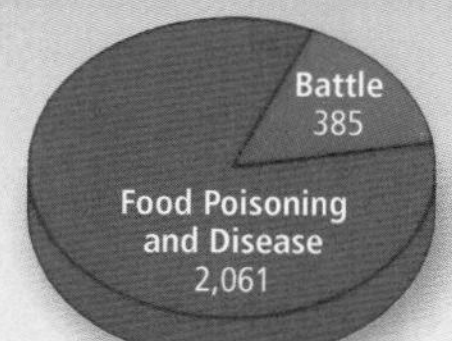

Source: *The Nystrom Atlas of United States History.*

NATIONAL GEOGRAPHIC **The Battle for Cuba, 1898**

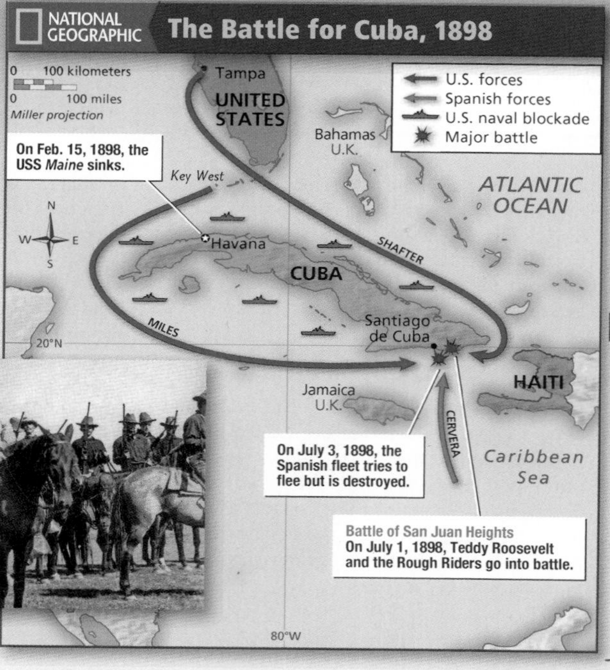

D

Additional Support

Extending the Content

The Rough Riders When Congress called for raising three cavalry units, Assistant Secretary of the Navy Theodore Roosevelt leapt at the opportunity to recruit his diverse acquaintances. The background of these recruits reflected Roosevelt's affluent background and interests as an outdoorsman and hunter, as he later recounted:

"We drew recruits from Harvard, Yale, Princeton . . . from clubs like the Somerset, of Boston, and Knickerbocker, of New York . . . Four of the policemen who had served under me while I was President of the New York Police Board . . . the high jumper . . . the football players . . . the steeple-chase rider . . . the crack polo player . . . the cowboy, the hunter, and the mining prospector . . . From the Indian Territory there came a number of Indians—Cherokees, Chickasaws, Choctaws, and Creeks."

in the 1970s suggested that the spontaneous combustion of a coal bunker aboard the ship caused the explosion, but a study in the 1990s concluded that a mine could have done the damage. In 1898, however, many Americans believed it was an act of sabotage by Spanish agents. "Remember the *Maine*!" became the rallying cry for those demanding a declaration of war against Spain.

C In response, Congress authorized McKinley to spend $50 million for war preparations. McKinley faced tremendous pressure to go to war. Within the Republican Party, **jingoism**—aggressive nationalism—was very strong. Many Democrats also demanded war, and Republicans feared that if McKinley did not go to war, the Democrats would win the elections in 1900. Finally, on April 11, 1898, McKinley asked Congress to authorize the use of force.

On April 19, Congress proclaimed Cuba independent, demanded that Spain withdraw from the island, and authorized the president to use armed force if necessary. In response, on April 24, Spain declared war on the United States. For the first time in 50 years, the United States was at war with another nation.

Reading Check **Examining** What conditions led to the Cuban rebellion in 1895?

A War on Two Fronts

MAIN Idea The United States fought and defeated Spain in both the Caribbean and the Pacific.

HISTORY AND YOU Have you ever had to plan a trip or an event? Read to learn about the problems American troops encountered in the war of 1898.

The United States Navy was ready for war with Spain. The navy's North Atlantic Squadron blockaded Cuba, and Commodore George Dewey, commander of the American naval squadron based in Hong Kong, was ordered to attack the Spanish fleet based in the Philippines. The Philippines was a Spanish colony, and American naval planners wanted to prevent the Spanish fleet based there from sailing east to attack the United States.

The Battle of Manila Bay

A short time after midnight, on May 1, 1898, Dewey's squadron entered Manila Bay in the Philippines. As dawn broke, four American ships in the squadron opened fire and rapidly destroyed all eight of the severely outgunned Spanish warships.

NATIONAL GEOGRAPHIC **The Battle for the Philippines**

▲ *U.S. soldiers fight near Manila while Emilio Aguinaldo, to the right, leads a revolt against the Spanish.*

Analyzing GEOGRAPHY

1. **Location** Where did the major battle take place?
2. **Human-Environment Interaction** How are the geography of Cuba and the Philippines similar? How did this help the Americans?

Maps in MOtion See ***StudentWorks™ Plus*** **or** glencoe.com.

C Critical Thinking

Making Inferences Point out to students that, at first, President McKinley was reluctant to go to war with Spain but eventually asked Congress for a declaration of war. **Ask:** **Did McKinley yield to political pressure when he asked Congress to declare war on Spain?** *(Students might infer that because many Republicans and some Democrats favored war, McKinley felt he had no choice but to ask Congress for war.)* **OL**

Reading Check

Answer:
Spanish oppression, Spanish economic exploitation

Analyzing GEOGRAPHY

Answers:
1. near Santiago and Manila
2. Both are islands, and the American navy was much stronger than the Spanish navy.

Additional Support

Activity: Collaborative Learning

Writing a Feature Article Organize the students into groups of four. Have each student in the group write a feature article about the causes of the Spanish-American War from one of the following points of view: a U.S. soldier, a yellow journalist, a wife of a crew member of the USS *Maine*, or a Cuban who had been forced to live in a reconcentration camp. Have the group review and critique each feature article. Then have the groups combine the articles into a small newspaper. Encourage students to share their newspapers with others in the class. **OL**

C Critical Thinking

Drawing Conclusions The text states that both the Spanish and American militaries believed that the war would be decided at sea. **Ask:** What factors would lead military planners to that conclusion? *(The Americans did not have a large navy at the beginning of the war, but they still needed to send troops to Cuba or other Spanish-controlled areas. The Spanish fleet, however, was old; yet the Spanish needed to send new troops to Cuba to reinforce those already there, who were tired and strained from fighting the Cuban rebels.)* **AL**

Reading Check

Answer:
Although at first poorly prepared in comparison to the U.S. Navy, the U.S. Army created a plan to attack around Santiago, frightening the Spanish fleet out of the harbor and into battle with the American navy.

Dewey's quick victory took McKinley and his advisers by surprise. The army was not yet ready to send troops to help Dewey. Hastily, the army assembled 20,000 troops to sail from San Francisco to the Philippines. On the way, the Americans also seized the island of Guam, another Spanish possession in the Pacific.

While waiting for the American troops to arrive, Dewey contacted **Emilio Aguinaldo,** a Filipino revolutionary leader who had staged an unsuccessful uprising against the Spanish in 1896. Aguinaldo quickly launched a new rebellion against the Spanish. While the rebels took control of most of the islands, American troops seized the Philippine capital of Manila.

American Forces in Cuba

The Spanish in Cuba were not prepared for war. Tropical diseases and months of fighting rebels had weakened their soldiers. Their warships were old and their crews poorly trained. **C** Both sides knew that the war would ultimately be decided at sea. If the United States could defeat the Spanish fleet, Spain would not be able to supply its troops in Cuba. Eventually, they would have to surrender.

The United States Army was not prepared for war either. Although there were many **volunteers,** the army lacked the resources to train and equip them. In many training camps, conditions were so unsanitary that epidemics broke out, and hundreds died—far more than would be killed in battle with the Spanish.

Finally, on June 22, 1898, a force of about 17,000 troops landed east of the city of Santiago, Cuba. The Spanish fleet, well-protected by powerful shore-based guns, occupied Santiago Harbor. American military planners wanted to capture those guns to drive the Spanish fleet out of the harbor and into battle with the American fleet waiting nearby.

Among the American troops advancing toward Santiago was a volunteer cavalry unit from the American west. They were a flamboyant mix of cowboys, miners, and law officers known as the "Rough Riders." Colonel Leonard Wood commanded them. Theodore Roosevelt was second in command.

On July 1, American troops attacked the village of El Caney northeast of Santiago. Another force attacked the San Juan Heights. While one group of soldiers attacked San Juan Hill, the Rough Riders attacked Kettle Hill. After seizing Kettle Hill, Roosevelt and his men assisted in the capture of San Juan Hill.

The all-black 9th and 10th Cavalry Regiments accompanied the Rough Riders up Kettle Hill. Roughly one-fourth of the American troops fighting in Cuba were African Americans, four of whom received the Medal of Honor for their bravery during the war.

The Spanish commander in Santiago panicked after the American victories at El Caney and the San Juan Heights and ordered the Spanish fleet in the harbor to flee. As they exited the harbor on July 3, American warships attacked them, sinking or beaching every Spanish vessel. Two weeks later, the Spanish troops in Santiago surrendered. Soon afterwards, American troops occupied the nearby Spanish colony of Puerto Rico as well.

Reading Check **Comparing** How prepared was the U.S. Army as compared to the U.S. Navy to fight a war against Spain?

Debates IN HISTORY

Should the United States Annex the Philippines?

In the Treaty of Paris of 1898, Spain ceded control of the Philippine Islands to the United States. Americans were divided over whether the United States should give the Filipinos their independence or become an imperial power by annexing the Philippines. Supporters of annexation argued the United States would benefit economically and the Filipinos would benefit from exposure to American values and principles. Opponents, however, considered it hypocritical for the United States, with its own colonial past, to become an imperial nation.

Differentiated Instruction

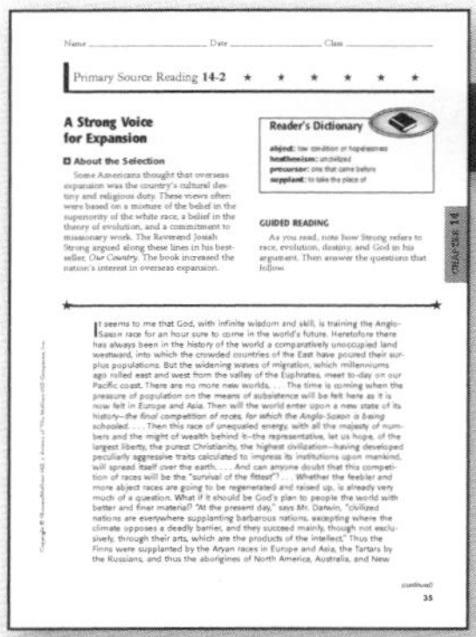

Primary Source Reading, URB pp. 35–36

Primary Source Readings: Recognizing Bias

Objective: Read to identify bias in primary sources.

Focus: Read the primary source in support of expansionism.

Teach: Define bias and discuss how it can affect students' understanding of history.

Assess: Identify instances of bias in the selection and highlight the passages.

Differentiated Instruction Strategies

BL Identify two instances of bias in the selection.

AL Search magazines and newspapers for articles that show bias. Discuss how the bias influences the information presented in the article.

ELL Define each vocabulary word in the selection using glossaries or dictionaries.

An American Empire

MAIN Idea In defeating Spain, the United States acquired an overseas empire.

HISTORY AND YOU Do you think Puerto Rico should become the 51st state? Read how Puerto Rico became an American territory.

As American and Spanish leaders met to discuss the terms for a peace treaty, Americans debated what to do about their newly acquired lands. Cuba would receive its independence as promised, and Spain had agreed to the U.S. annexation of Guam and Puerto Rico. The big question was what to do with the Philippines. The United States faced a difficult choice—remain true to its republican ideals or become an imperial power that ruled a foreign country without the consent of its people. The issue sparked an intense political debate.

The Debate Over Annexation

Many people who supported annexing the Philippines emphasized the economic and military benefits of taking the islands. They would provide the United States with another Pacific naval base, a stopover on the way to China, and a large market for American goods.

Other supporters believed America had a duty to help "less civilized" peoples. "Surely this Spanish war has not been a grab for empire," **W** commented a New England minister, "but a heroic effort [to] free the oppressed and to teach the millions of ignorant, debased human beings thus freed how to live."

Not all Americans supported annexation. Anti-imperialists included William Jennings Bryan, industrialist Andrew Carnegie, social worker Jane Addams, writer Samuel Clemens (Mark Twain), and Samuel Gompers, leader of the American Federation of Labor.

W Writing Support

Persuasive Writing Invite students to assume the perspective of a citizen who opposes annexation of the Philippines. Have them write a letter to the editor of a newspaper persuading readers to write letters to President McKinley in support of their view. Remind students to use library or Internet resources to obtain information to support their position. Encourage students to share their letters with the class. **OL**

Debates IN HISTORY

YES

Albert J. Beveridge
United States Senator

PRIMARY SOURCE

"The Opposition tells us that we ought not to govern a people without their consent. I answer, The rule of liberty that all just government derives its authority from the consent of the governed, applies only to those who are capable of self-government. We govern the Indians without their consent, we govern our territories without their consent, we govern our children without their consent. . . . Would not the people of the Philippines prefer the just, humane, civilizing government of this Republic to the savage, bloody rule of pillage and extortion from which we have rescued them?"

—from *The Meaning of the Times*

NO

William Jennings Bryan
Presidential Candidate

PRIMARY SOURCE

"It is not necessary to own people in order to trade with them. We carry on trade today with every part of the world, and our commerce has expanded more rapidly than the commerce of any European empire. . . . A harbor and coaling station in the Philippines would answer every trade and military necessity and such a concession could have been secured at any time without difficulty.

. . . Imperialism finds no warrant in the Bible. The command 'Go ye into all the world and preach the gospel to every creature' has no Gatling gun attachment. . . .

—from *Speeches of William Jennings Bryan*

DBQ Document-Based Questions

1. **Making Inferences** According to Albert Beveridge, why is annexation of the Philippines an honorable decision?
2. **Recognizing Bias** What does Beveridge think of the people of the Philippines?
3. **Analyzing** What are William Jennings Bryan's two main criticisms of imperialism?
4. **Drawing Conclusions** After studying both sides of the issue, who do you think was right? Explain.

Answers:

1. because annexation would provide a just, humane, and civilizing government for the Filipinos
2. He believes that they are uncivilized and childlike.
3. It is not necessary to own people to trade with them; imperialism is not in the Bible.
4. Answers will vary, but students should support their viewpoints with information from the text.

Additional Support

Activity: Technology Connection

Preparing a Multimedia Presentation Divide students into groups and have them use library or Internet resources to learn more about the debate over annexation of the Philippines. Have students create a computer-based multimedia presentation to portray both sides of the debate. Groups should depict the views of one imperialist and one anti-imperialist. Encourage students to include quotes from their chosen debaters as well as background information on their lives. Have groups conclude their presentations by imagining the reaction of both parties to McKinley's decision to annex the islands. **AL**

R Reading Strategy

Inferring Have students reread the Primary Source quote from President McKinley. **Ask:** What can you infer about McKinley's views of the Filipino people? *(He thought they were not Christians, when in fact, most Filipinos were Catholic.)* OL

C Critical Thinking

Comparing Review with students the status of the Philippines and Cuba after the 1898 peace treaty and the passage of the Platt Amendment. **Ask:** How did the status of the Philippines and Cuba differ? *(The Philippines were a territory of the United States; Cuba was nominally independent.)* OL

Analyzing VISUALS

Answers:

1. McKinley is supporting imperialism while Bryan is attacking imperialism.
2. Uncle Sam is going to choose several items from the "menu." Uncle Sam states that he can't decide which to order first.

Differentiated Instruction

POLITICAL CARTOONS PRIMARY SOURCE

The Debate Over Empire

▲ President McKinley raises the American flag over the Philippines while William Jennings Bryan tries to chop it down.

▲ *President McKinley (the waiter) prepares to take Uncle Sam's order. The menu posted on the wall shows three regions of choice: the Cuba steak, the Porto [Puerto] Rico pig; and the Philippines and Sandwich Islands (Hawaii) in the Pacific.*

Analyzing VISUALS

1. **Identifying Central Issues** Based on the cartoon on the left, what do you think McKinley is trying to accomplish? What about Bryan?
2. **Making Inferences** What does the cartoon on the right suggest that Uncle Sam is going to do? On what basis do you infer that?

History ONLINE **Student Web Activity** Visit glencoe.com and complete the activity on American imperialism.

Andrew Carnegie argued that the cost of an empire far outweighed the economic benefits it provided. Gompers worried that competition from cheap Filipino labor would drive down American wages. Addams, Clemens, and others believed imperialism violated American principles. Despite the objections of the anti-imperialists, President McKinley ultimately decided to annex the islands. He later explained his reasoning as follows:

PRIMARY SOURCE

R "And one night late it came to me this way. . . (1) that we could not give them back to Spain—that would be cowardly and dishonorable; (2) that we could not turn them over to France or Germany. . . that would be bad for business and discreditable; (3) that we could not leave them to themselves—they were unfit for self-government. . . and (4) that there was nothing left for us to do but to take them all, and to educate the Filipinos, and uplift and civilize and Christianize them."

—*A Diplomatic History of the American People*

On December 10, 1898, the United States and Spain signed the Treaty of Paris. Under the treaty, Cuba became an independent nation, and the United States acquired Puerto Rico and Guam and agreed to pay Spain $20 million for the Philippines. After an intense debate, the Senate ratified the treaty in February 1899. The United States had become an imperial power.

The Platt Amendment

Although the United States had promised to grant Cuba its independence, President McKinley took steps to ensure that Cuba would remain tied to the United States. He allowed the Cubans to prepare a new constitution for their country but attached conditions. The **Platt Amendment,** submitted by Senator Orville Platt, specified the following: (1) Cuba could not make any treaty with another nation that would weaken its independence; (2) Cuba had to allow the United States to buy or lease naval stations in Cuba; (3) Cuba's debts had to be kept low to prevent foreign countries from landing troops to enforce payment; and (4) the United States would have the right to intervene to protect Cuban independence and keep order. C

Leveled Activities

BL Guided Reading Activity, URB p. 47

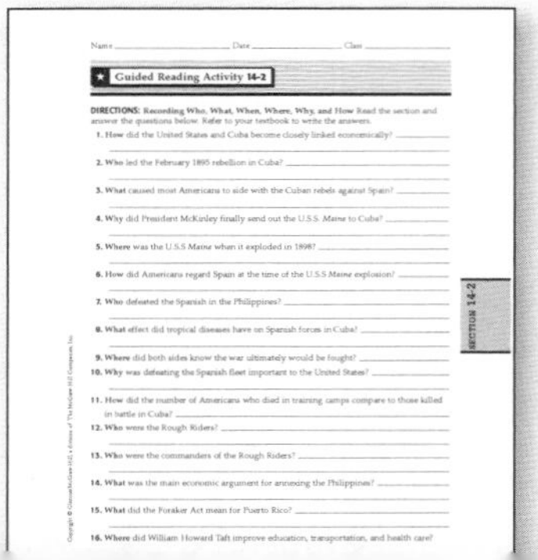

OL American Art and Music, URB p. 37

AL Enrichment Activity, URB p. 43

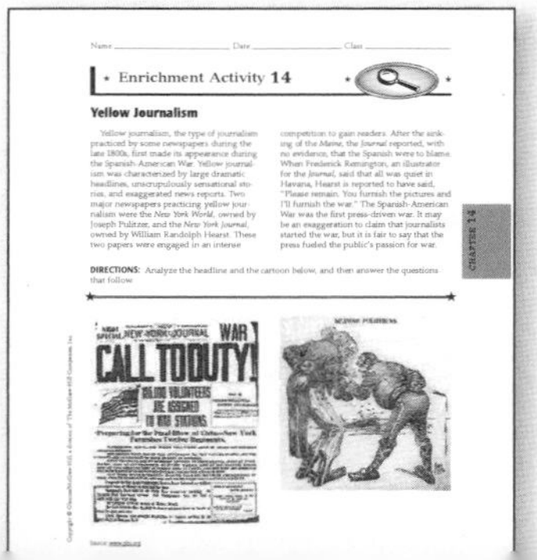

ELL Reading Essentials and Note-Taking Guide, URB p. 159

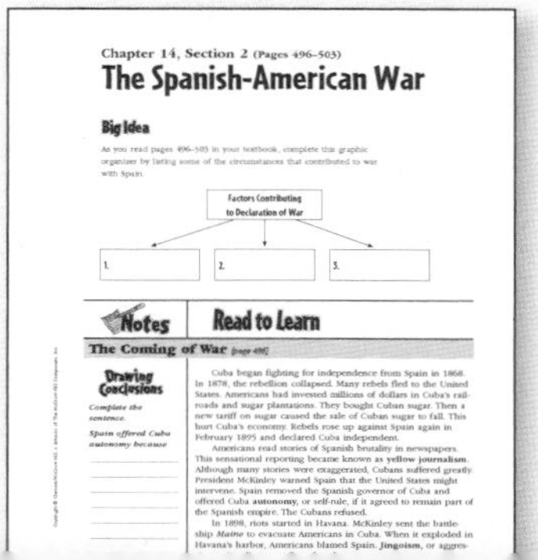

Reluctantly, the Cubans added the amendment to their constitution. The Platt Amendment, which effectively made Cuba an American protectorate, remained in effect until its repeal in 1934.

Governing Puerto Rico

Another pressing question was how to govern Puerto Rico. In 1900 Congress passed the **Foraker Act,** establishing a civil government for the island. The law provided for an elected legislature, but also called for a governor and executive council, to be appointed by the president, who held final authority. Supreme Court rulings subsequently held that Puerto Ricans were not American citizens and so did not possess the constitutional rights of citizens.

Congress gradually allowed Puerto Ricans greater self-government. In 1917 it granted Puerto Ricans American citizenship. Thirty years later, islanders were allowed to elect their own governor. At this time a debate began over whether Puerto Rico should become a state, become independent, or continue as a self-governing commonwealth of the United States. This debate over Puerto Rico's status continues today.

Rebellion in the Philippines

The United States quickly learned that controlling its new empire would not be easy. Emilio Aguinaldo called the American decision to annex his homeland a "violent and aggressive seizure" and ordered his troops to attack American soldiers. The Philippine-American war, or Philippine Insurrection as it was referred to at the time, lasted for more than three years. Approximately 126,000 American soldiers were sent to the Philippines to fight the insurgency. More than 4,300 American soldiers died, either from combat or disease, as did an estimated 50,000–200,000 Filipinos.

To fight the Filipino guerrillas, the United States military adopted many of the same policies that America had condemned Spain for using in Cuba. Reconcentration camps were established to separate Filipino guerrillas from civilians. Consequently, thousands of people died from disease and starvation, just as they had in Cuba.

While American troops fought the guerrillas, the first U.S. civilian governor of the islands, William Howard Taft, tried to win over the Filipinos by improving education, transportation, and health care. Railroads and bridges were built. Public schools were set up, and new health-care policies virtually eliminated diseases such as cholera and smallpox. These reforms slowly reduced Filipino hostility.

In March 1901, American troops captured Aguinaldo. A month later, Aguinaldo called on the guerrillas to surrender. On July 4, 1902, the United States declared the war over. Eventually the United States allowed the Filipinos a greater role in governing their own country. By the mid-1930s, they were permitted to elect their own congress and president. Finally, in 1946, the United States granted independence to the Philippines.

Reading Check **Explaining** What were the arguments for and against establishing an American empire?

Section 2 REVIEW

Vocabulary

1. **Explain** the significance of: José Martí, William Randolph Hearst, Joseph Pulitzer, yellow journalism, autonomy, jingoism, Emilio Aguinaldo, Platt Amendment, Foraker Act.

Main Ideas

2. **Explaining** Why did many Americans blame Spain for the explosion of the USS *Maine*?
3. **Identifying** How did the U.S. fight the Spanish-American War on two fronts?
4. **Categorizing** Complete the table by summarizing the effects of the United States annexing lands obtained after the Spanish-American War.

Lands Annexed	Effects

Critical Thinking

5. **Big Ideas** How has the government of Puerto Rico changed since the Foraker Act was passed in 1900?
6. **Evaluating** Why did Filipinos feel betrayed by the U.S. government after the Spanish-American War?
7. **Analyzing Visuals** Study the circle graph on page 498. What caused the most casualties during the war? Explain.

Writing About History

8. **Descriptive Writing** Imagine that you are a Filipino living during the time of the U.S. annexation of the Philippine Islands. Write a journal entry in which you describe your feelings about American control of the islands.

History ONLINE
Study Central™ To review this section, go to glencoe.com and click on Study Central.

Reading Check

Answer:
for: a naval base in Asia and a market for American goods, a chance to teach people who were regarded as less fortunate; against: cost, competition, violated American principles, cheap labor might drive down American wages

Assess

History ONLINE

Study Central™ provides summaries, interactive games, and online graphic organizers to help students review content.

Close

Summarizing **Ask:** Why did the United States go to war with Spain? *(public opinion favored Cuban uprising; to protect American economic interests in Cuba; public swayed by yellow journalism; sinking of the battleship USS* Maine*)* OL

Section 2 REVIEW

Answers

1. All definitions can be found in the section and the Glossary.
2. Cuba was fighting Spain for its independence, and many Americans saw the Spanish as tyrants.
3. The navy's North Atlantic Squadron blockaded Cuba. The American fleet based in Hong Kong attacked the Spanish fleet in the Philippines to prevent the ships from sailing east to attack the United States. While waiting for the army to arrive with reinforcements, the navy cooperated with Filipino revolutionaries.
4. Puerto Rico: U.S. control of its government, Puerto Ricans become U.S. citizens after 1917; Philippines: some improvements in Filipino schools, roads, and healthcare.
5. Under the Foraker Act, Puerto Ricans had no constitutional rights or power of self-government. Over time, Puerto Ricans were made citizens and allowed to elect their own governor. Debate continues over whether the commonwealth should become a state, become an independent nation, or remain as it is.
6. The Filipinos believed that the United States was helping them achieve independence from Spain, and so they were disappointed to be made part of an empire. The United States attempted to gain support by improving education, transportation, and health care. These efforts were somewhat successful.
7. Food poisoning and disease caused the most deaths. Sanitary conditions were poor.
8. Journal entries will vary but should express a Filipino's point of view.

Focus

Bellringer

Daily Focus Transparency 14-3

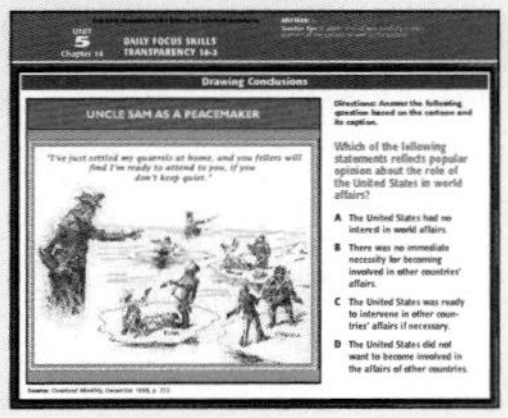

Guide to Reading

Answers to Graphic Organizer: save time, save money, help the United States remain a world power

Section Spotlight Video

To generate student interest and provide a springboard for class discussion, access the Chapter 14, Section 3 video at glencoe.com or on the video DVD.

Section 3

Section Audio | Spotlight Video

New American Diplomacy

Guide to Reading

Big Ideas

Trade, War, and Migration Under President Theodore Roosevelt, the United States increased its power on the world stage.

Content Vocabulary

- sphere of influence *(p. 504)*
- Open Door policy *(p. 505)*
- dollar diplomacy *(p. 509)*
- guerrilla *(p. 511)*

Academic Vocabulary

- access *(p. 505)*
- tension *(p. 508)*

People and Events to Identify

- Boxer Rebellion *(p. 506)*
- Hay-Pauncefote Treaty *(p. 508)*
- Roosevelt Corollary *(p. 508)*
- Victoriano Huerta *(p. 511)*
- Pancho Villa *(p. 511)*

Reading Strategy

Organizing As you read about American diplomacy complete a graphic organizer by listing the reasons the U.S. wanted a canal through Central America.

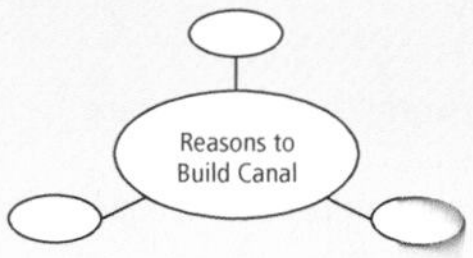

Succeeding President McKinley, President Theodore Roosevelt mediated disputes in Asia and Latin America and acquired the Panama Canal Zone. Presidents Taft and Wilson worked to increase American trade and influence in Latin America.

American Diplomacy in Asia

MAIN Idea The United States pursued an Open Door policy to allow all nations access to China's markets.

HISTORY AND YOU Do you remember reading about a trade agreement with Japan in the 1850s? Read to learn about America's efforts to keep trade open with China in the 1900s.

In 1899 the United States was a major power in Asia, with naval bases all across the Pacific. Operating from those bases, the United States Navy—by then the third-largest navy in the world—could exert American power anywhere in East Asia. The nation's primary interest in Asia, however, was not conquest but commerce. Between 1895 and 1900, American exports to China increased fourfold. Although China bought only about two percent of American exports, the vast Chinese markets excited American business leaders, especially those in the textile, oil, and steel industries.

The Open Door Policy

In 1894 war erupted between China and Japan over Korea, which at that time was a client state of China. Western observers were astonished when Japan easily defeated China's massive military. In the peace treaty, China recognized the independence of Korea and gave Japan territory in Manchuria. The war showed that Japan had mastered Western technology and industry. It also demonstrated that China was far weaker than anyone had thought.

The Russians were concerned about Japan's rising power. They did not want Japan to acquire the territory in Manchuria, because it bordered Russia. Backed by France and Germany, Russia forced Japan to return the Manchurian territory it had acquired. Then, in 1898, Russia demanded China lease the territory to Russia instead.

Leasing a territory meant that it would still belong to China, even though a foreign government would maintain overall control. Soon Germany, France, and Britain demanded "leaseholds" in China as well. Each "leasehold" became the center of a country's **sphere of influence,** an area where a foreign nation controlled economic development such as railroad construction and mining.

Resource Manager

R Reading Strategies	C Critical Thinking	D Differentiated Instruction	W Writing Support	S Skill Practice
Teacher Edition • Inferring, p. 505 **Additional Resources** • Guided Read. Act., URB p. 48 • Critical Thinking Act., URB p. 30	**Teacher Edition** • Comparing, p. 507 • Identify. Central Issues, p. 507 • Draw. Concl., p. 508 • Analyz. Info., p. 509 **Additional Resources** • Inter. Pol. Cartoons Act., URB p. 39 • Quizzes and Tests, p. 201	**Teacher Edition** • Visual/Spatial, pp. 506, 508 • Advanced Learners, p. 510 **Additional Resources** • Diff. Instr. Act., URB p. 21 • Authentic Assess., p. 33 • Reteach. Act., URB p. 41 • Historical Analysis Skills Act., URB p. 20	**Teacher Edition** • Persuasive Writing, pp. 505, 509 • Descrip. Writing, p. 511	**Additional Resources** • Read. Essen., p. 162 • Time Line Act., URB p. 31

NATIONAL GEOGRAPHIC The Open Door Policy and the Boxer Rebellion

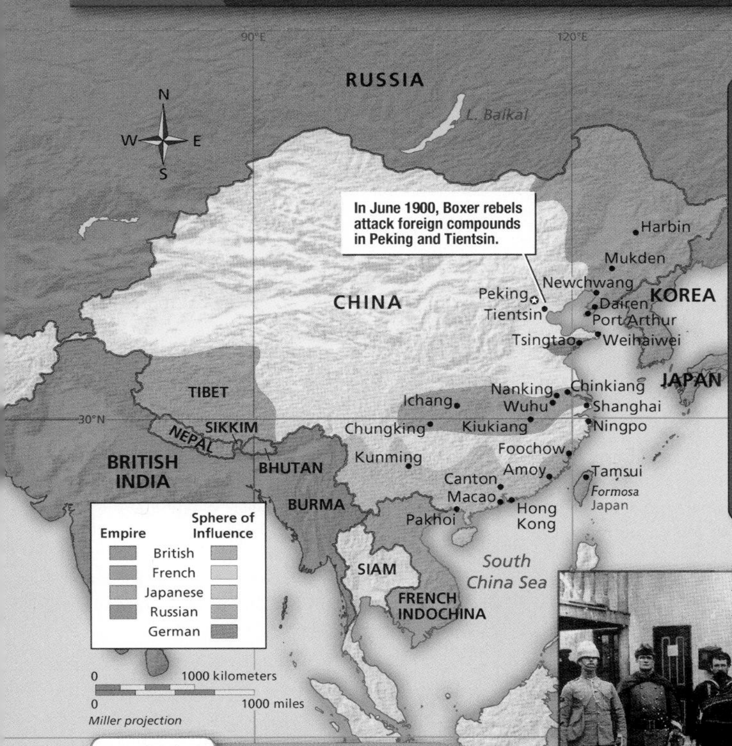

What Was the Open Door Policy?

1. Within its sphere of influence, each power agreed not to interfere with any existing business interests or port treaties of other powers.
2. Existing Chinese tariffs would remain unchanged in all spheres of influence and would be collected by the Chinese government.
3. Within each sphere of influence, harbor fees and railroad charges would be the same for all countries, giving no special rates to the countries whose businesses owned and operated the harbors and railroads.

▲ *Secretary of State John Hay*

W

Analyzing VISUALS

1. **Interpreting** What do you think Britain was attempting with the locations of their spheres of influence?
2. **Analyzing** Based on the map, which country do you believe had the most influence?

▲ *International soldiers pose in Tianjin after rescuing their besieged delegations during the Boxer Rebellion. The American is second from left.*

R

Politicians and businessmen in the United States worried about these events. President McKinley and Secretary of State John Hay both supported what they called an **Open Door policy,** in which all countries would be allowed to trade with China. In 1899 Hay sent notes to countries with leaseholds in China asking them not to discriminate against other nations wanting to do business in their sphere of influence. Each of the nations responded by saying they accepted the Open Door policy but would not act on it unless all of the others agreed. Once Hay had received assurances from all of the nations with leaseholds, he declared that the United States expected the other powers to uphold the policy. R

The Boxer Rebellion

While foreign countries debated **access** to China's market, secret Chinese societies organized to fight foreign control. Westerners referred to one such group, the Society of Harmonious Fists, as the Boxers. In 1900 the group decided to destroy both the "foreign devils" and their Chinese Christian converts, whom they believed were corrupting Chinese society.

Teach

R Reading Strategy

Inferring Ask: Based on the text, what was the United States's motivation for putting forth the Open Door Policy? *(The United States wanted access to all of China's markets.)* **OL**

W Writing Support

Persuasive Writing Ask interested students to write a letter to the governments of Great Britain, France, Germany, and Russia persuading them to accept the Open Door Policy. **AL**

Analyzing VISUALS

Answers:
1. keep the French sphere of influence from expanding
2. Students may say Britain or Russia because of the amount of territory they control bordering China and the size of their spheres of influence.

Hands-On Chapter Project Step 3

Preparing a Multimedia Presentation

Step 3: Editing the Presentation Groups will edit their presentations for accuracy, content, and mechanics.

Directions Have groups run through their presentations to make sure that links to other pages are working properly and that all information is displayed correctly. Students should also edit their presentations for grammar, punctuation, and sentence structure. Encourage students to pair up with another group and review each other's presentations. Tell students that presentations should be coherent and easily understood.

Putting It Together Once students have reviewed their presentations, they should make any necessary changes, additions, or corrections. **OL**

(Chapter Project continued on the Visual Summary page)

D Differentiated Instruction

Visual/Spatial Have interested students locate the parts of Beijing and Tianjin that were under siege by the Boxers. Then have the students create maps of the cities showing the areas of fighting. **OL**

Reading Check

Answer:
to ensure that all nations had access to China's markets

In what became known as the **Boxer Rebellion,** the Boxers, supported by some Chinese troops, besieged foreign embassies in Peking and Tientsin, killing more than 200 foreigners and taking others prisoner. After the German ambassador to China was killed, eight **D** nations—Germany, Austria-Hungary, Britain, France, Italy, Japan, Russia, and the United States—decided to intervene. A large international force of nearly 50,000 troops, including 3,400 Americans, landed in China to rescue the foreigners and smash the rebellion.

During the crisis, Secretary of State John Hay worked with British diplomats to persuade the other powers not to partition China. In a second set of Open Door notes, Hay convinced the participating powers to accept compensation from China for damages caused by the rebellion. After some discussion, the powers agreed not to break up China into European-controlled colonies. The United States retained access to China's lucrative trade in tea, spices, and silk and maintained an increasingly larger market for its own goods.

Reading Check **Explaining** What was the purpose of the Open Door policy?

Roosevelt's Diplomacy

MAIN Idea Presidents Roosevelt and Taft continued to support a policy of expanding United States influence in foreign countries.

HISTORY AND YOU Do you know of a country that is trying to expand its influence today? Read to find out about expansion of United States influence in the early 1900s.

The election of 1900 once again pitted President McKinley against William Jennings Bryan. Bryan, an anti-imperialist, attacked the Republicans for their support of imperialism in Asia. McKinley, who chose war hero Theodore Roosevelt as his running mate, focused on the country's increased prosperity and ran on the slogan "Four Years More of the Full Dinner Pail." He won the election by a wide margin.

On September 6, 1901, while visiting Buffalo, New York, President McKinley was attacked by Leon Czolgosz, an anarchist who opposed all forms of government. Czolgosz fired two shots and hit the president. A few days later, McKinley died from his wounds. Theodore Roosevelt took over the presidency.

PAST & PRESENT

The Great White Fleet

In 1907 President Theodore Roosevelt sent 16 new battleships on a voyage around the world to showcase the nation's ability to project power to any place in the world. Painted white, the ships became known as the "Great White Fleet." The tour made a stop in Japan to demonstrate that the United States would uphold its interests in Asia. The visit did not help ease the growing tensions between the United States and Japan.

The use of naval power to send a diplomatic message continues today. Just as the battleship symbolized naval power in 1900, so too today does the aircraft carrier symbolize the power and global reach of the United States Navy. In March 1996, for example, a strike force led by the aircraft carrier *Kitty Hawk* was sent to the Taiwan Straits. This show of force came after China tested missiles in the area. The carrier sent the message to China that the United States would protect Taiwan from aggression.

▲ *The Great White Fleet gets underway in December 1907.*

Great White Fleet

◀ *The Great White Fleet circumnavigated the globe.*

Activity: Economics Connection

The Open Door Policy Ask students to use library and Internet resources to identify the products that were traded between countries involved with China. Have students use what they learn to create a chart showing the trading relationships among the various nations. Then ask students to write a position paper supporting or opposing the Open Door Policy. Discuss students' positions on the Open Door Policy. **AL**

Additional Support

Theodore Roosevelt, just 42 years old at the time, was the youngest person ever to become president. Republican leaders had asked him to run for vice president because his charisma and status as a war hero would win votes, but they had hoped the relatively powerless position of vice president would keep him from causing political problems. Now they cringed at the thought of him in the White House. Ohio Republican senator Mark Hanna exclaimed, "Now look, that . . . cowboy is president of the United States!"

Roosevelt favored increasing American power on the world stage. He warned Americans not to become "an assemblage of well-to-do hucksters who care nothing for what happens beyond." Roosevelt also accepted some of Anglo-Saxonism's ideas. He believed that the United States had a duty to shape the "less civilized" corners of the earth.

Balancing Power in East Asia

As president, Theodore Roosevelt supported the Open Door policy in China and worked to prevent any single nation from monopolizing trade there. This concern prompted Roosevelt to help negotiate an end to the war between Japan and Russia that had broken out in 1905. At a peace conference in Portsmouth, New Hampshire, Roosevelt convinced the Russians to recognize Japan's territorial gains and persuaded the Japanese to stop fighting and to seek no further territory. For his efforts in ending the war, Roosevelt won the Nobel Peace Prize in 1906.

In the years after the peace treaty, relations between the United States and Japan grew steadily worse. As the two nations vied for greater influence in Asia, they held each other in check through a series of agreements. They pledged to respect each other's territorial possessions, to uphold the Open Door policy, and to support China's independence.

The Panama Canal

Theodore Roosevelt believed in a strong global military presence. He insisted that displaying American power to the world would make nations think twice about fighting, and thus promote peace. He often expressed this belief with a West African saying, "Speak softly and carry a big stick."

2003

▼ *The aircraft carrier USS* Kitty Hawk *leaves Yokosuka Naval Base in Japan en route to monitor North Korea.*

MAKING CONNECTIONS

1. **Comparing** In what ways are the missions of the Great White Fleet and a modern carrier force similar?
2. **Making Generalizations** Do you think a large navy is a useful tool in diplomacy? Explain your answer. What problems can it cause? What benefits does it bring?

C1 Critical Thinking

Comparing Have students find out more information about the political careers of McKinley and Roosevelt. Have students create a bulletin board display comparing the careers of these two presidents. **BL**

C2 Critical Thinking

Identifying Central Issues Review with the class President Roosevelt's role in settling the Russo-Japanese War. **Ask:** What reasons might Roosevelt have had to intervene in the Russo-Japanese War? *(increase prestige of the United States; help further the United States's economic interests; limit Japanese expansion in Asia)* **OL**

MAKING CONNECTIONS

Answers:

1. The missions are similar in that the presence of the ships can reinforce America's interests; the ships also carry weaponry and can thus attack if ordered to do so.
2. Students should note that while a large navy indicates power and prestige, it is also very expensive.

Additional Support

Activity: Interdisciplinary Connection

Geography Provide students with a world map. Have them trace the water route from San Francisco to New York City around Cape Horn, using the map's scale to calculate the approximate distance. *(about 13,000 miles)* Next, have students trace the route by ship from San Francisco to New York City via the Panama Canal and calculate that distance. *(about 5,200 miles)* Ask students to write a sentence explaining how the Panama Canal improved United States trade and business. **OL**

D Differentiated Instruction

Visual/Spatial Provide students with a world map. Have them trace the water route from San Francisco to New York City around Cape Horn, using the map's scale to calculate the approximate distance. *(about 13,000 miles)* Next have students trace the route by ship from San Francisco to New York City via the Panama Canal and calculate the distance. *(about 5,200 miles)* Have students write a paragraph explaining how the Panama Canal improved United States trade and business. **OL**

C Critical Thinking

Drawing Conclusions Tell students that President Roosevelt bragged, "I took the Canal Zone and let Congress debate; and while the debate goes on, the canal does also." **Ask:** Were President Roosevelt's actions in the Panama revolt justified? *(Answers will vary, but students should defend their opinions.)* **AL**

Differentiated Instruction

D Roosevelt's "big stick" policy was perhaps most evident in the Caribbean. There the world witnessed one of the most dramatic acts of his presidency—the acquisition and construction of the Panama Canal. Roosevelt and others believed that having a canal through Central America was vital to American power in the world. A canal would save time and money for both commercial and military shipping.

Acquiring the Canal Zone As early as 1850, the United States and Great Britain had agreed not to build a canal without the other's participation. In 1901 the United States and Great Britain signed the **Hay-Pauncefote Treaty,** which gave the United States the exclusive right to build any proposed canal through Central America.

A French company had begun digging a canal through Panama in 1881. By 1889, however, it abandoned its efforts because of bankruptcy and terrible losses from disease among the workers. The company was reorganized in 1894, but it hoped only to sell its rights to dig the canal.

The United States had long considered two possible canal sites, one through Nicaragua and one through Panama. The French company eased this choice by offering to sell its rights and property in Panama to the United States.

In 1903 Panama was Colombia's most northern province. Secretary of State Hay offered Colombia $10 million and a yearly rent of $250,000 for the right to construct the canal and to control a narrow strip of land on either side of it. Considering the price too low and afraid of losing control of Panama, the Colombian government refused the offer.

Panama Revolts Some Panamanians feared losing the commercial benefits of the canal. Panama had opposed Colombian rule since the mid-1800s, and the canal issue added to the **tension.** In addition, the French company remained concerned that the United States would build the canal in Nicaragua instead. The French company's agent, Philippe Bunau-Varilla, and Panamanian officials decided that the only way to ensure the canal would be built was to make their own deal with the United States. Bunau-Varilla arranged for a small army to stage an uprising in Panama. Meanwhile, to prevent Colombian interference, President Roosevelt ordered U.S. warships to the area.

On November 3, 1903, with ten U.S. warships looming offshore, Bunau-Varilla's forces revolted. Within a few days, the United States recognized Panama's independence, and the two nations soon signed a treaty allowing the canal to be built.

C Protesters in the United States and throughout Latin America condemned Roosevelt's actions as unjustifiable aggression. The president countered that he had advanced "the needs of collective civilization" by building a canal that shortened the distance between the Atlantic and the Pacific by about 8,000 nautical miles (14,816 km).

The Roosevelt Corollary

By the early 1900s, American officials had become very concerned about the size of the debts Latin American nations owed to European banks. In 1902, after Venezuela defaulted on its debts, Great Britain, Germany, and Italy blockaded Venezuelan ports. The crisis was resolved peacefully after the United States intervened and put pressure on both sides to reach an agreement.

To address the problem, Roosevelt gave an address to Congress in which he declared what came to be known as the **Roosevelt Corollary** to the Monroe Doctrine. The corollary stated that the United States would intervene in Latin American affairs when necessary to maintain economic and political stability in the Western Hemisphere:

PRIMARY SOURCE

"Chronic wrongdoing . . . may, in America, as elsewhere, ultimately require intervention by some civilized nation, and in the Western Hemisphere the adherence of the United States to the Monroe Doctrine may force the United States, however reluctantly, in flagrant cases of such wrongdoing or impotence, to the exercise of an international police power."

—quoted in *The Growth of the United States*

The goal of the Roosevelt Corollary was to prevent European powers from using the debt problems of Latin America to justify intervening in the region. The United States first applied the Roosevelt Corollary in the

Leveled Activities

BL Guided Reading Activity, URB p. 48

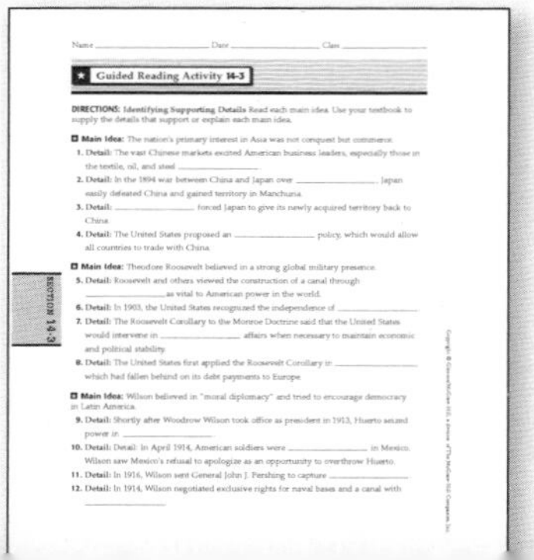

OL Differentiated Instruction, URB p. 21

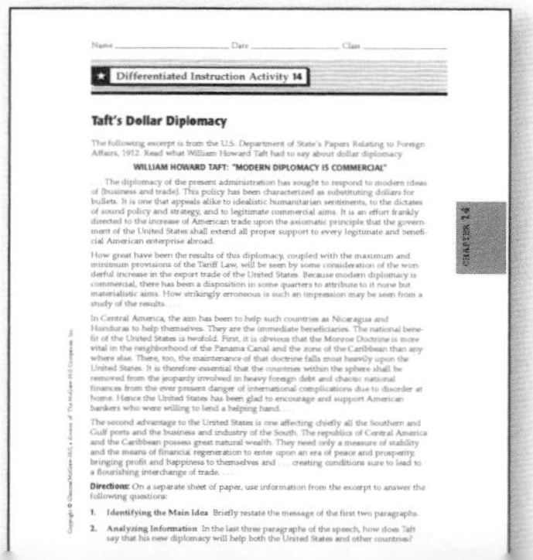

AL Interpreting Political Cartoons, URB p. 39

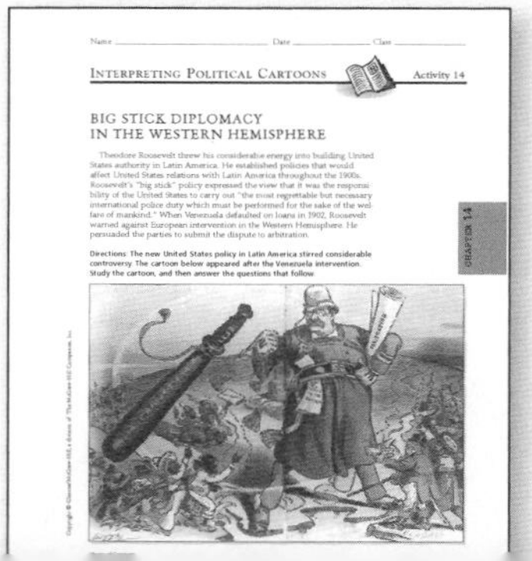

ELL Reading Essentials and Note-Taking Guide, URB p. 162

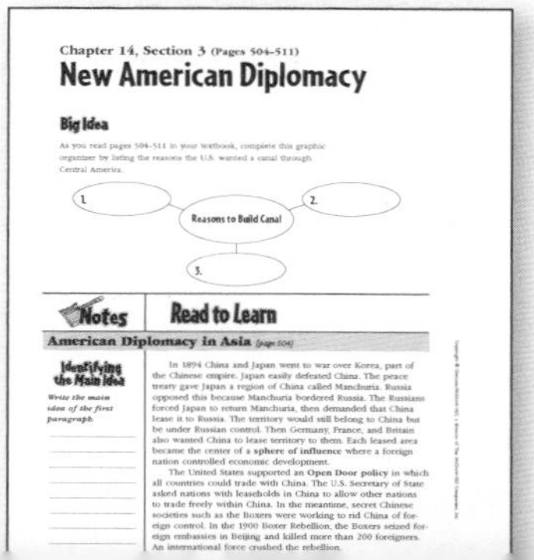

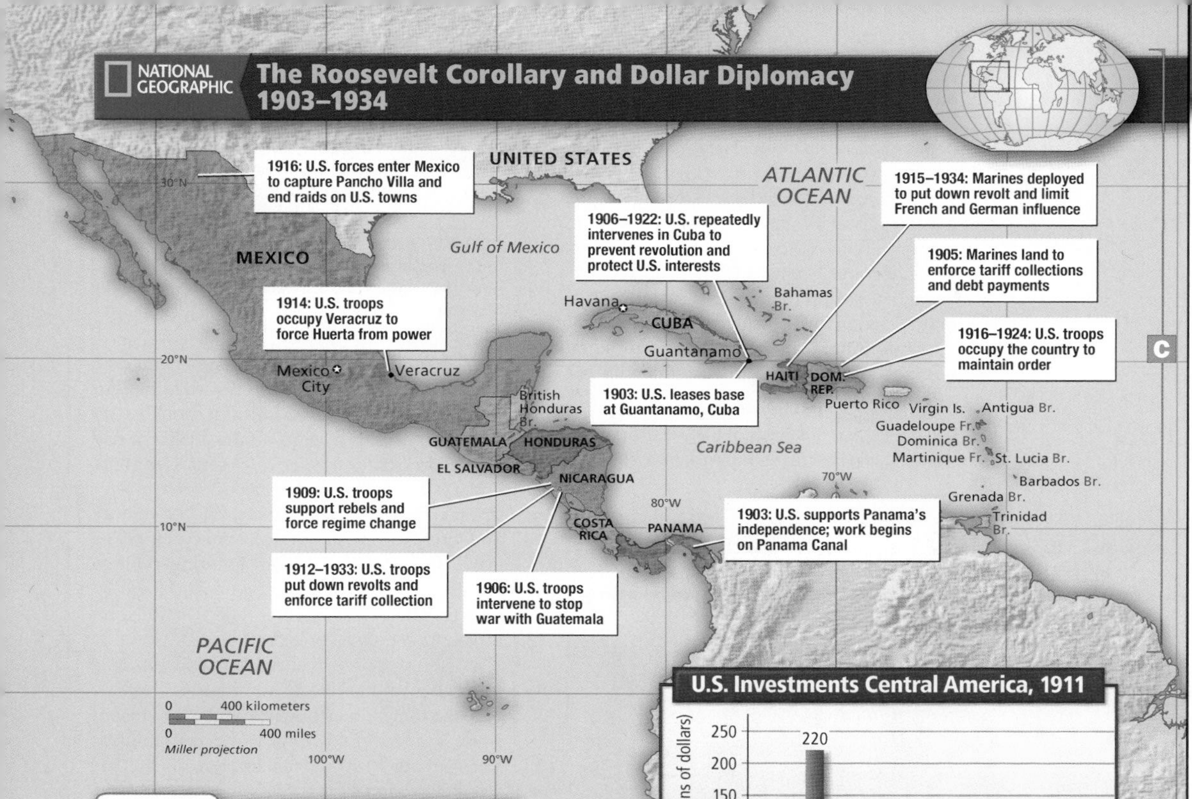

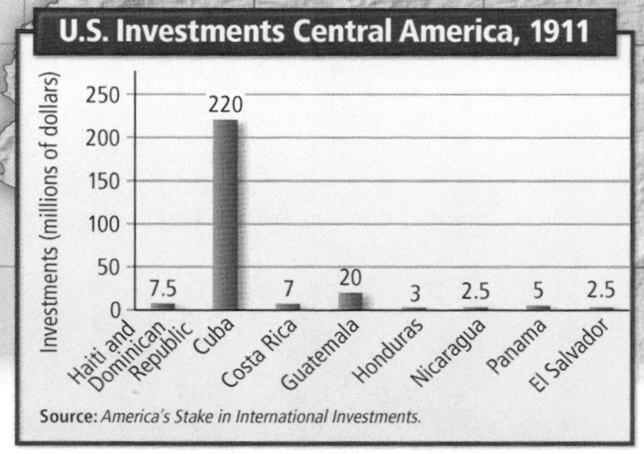

Analyzing VISUALS

1. **Analyzing** Based on the map, what are the main reasons the United States intervened in Latin American states?
2. **Inferring** Where did the United States invest the most money in Latin America? Why do you think this happened?

Dominican Republic, which had fallen behind on its debt payments to European nations. In 1905 the United States assumed the responsibility of collecting customs tariffs in the Dominican Republic, using the United States Marine Corps as its agent.

Dollar Diplomacy

W Latin American nations resented the growing American influence in the region, but Roosevelt's successor, William Howard Taft, continued his policies. Taft placed much less emphasis on military force and more on helping Latin American industry. He believed that if American business leaders supported Latin American development, everyone would benefit. American businesses would increase their trade and profits, and countries in Latin America would rise out of poverty and social disorder. Taft's policy came to be called **dollar diplomacy.**

Administration officials also worked hard W to replace European loans with loans from American banks. The goal of this policy was to give the Europeans fewer reasons to intervene in Latin American affairs. During Taft's administration, American bankers took over debts that Honduras owed to Britain and took control of Haiti's national bank.

W Writing Support

Persuasive Writing Have students imagine they are President Taft. Ask them to write a speech to persuade the American people that dollar diplomacy is in the best interests of the United States. Then organize students into groups of four or five to critique each other's speeches. **OL**

C Critical Thinking

Analyzing Information Have students study the map on this page, looking closely at the nations to which the United States sent troops. **Ask:** Did the United States violate the sovereignty of those nations by intervening? *(Answers will vary.)*

Analyzing VISUALS

Answers:

1. to protect its economic interests and to keep European powers from meddling in the region
2. Cuba, because the United States had long-standing investments in the island and because of the island's proximity to the United States

Additional Support

Activity: Interdisciplinary Connection

Civics Ask students to search through current newspapers and journals for articles about recent U.S. involvement with Latin American nations. Have them consider whether the information they learned demonstrates that the United States remains committed to the Roosevelt Corollary, or if it shows that the United States has abandoned that principle. **Ask:** Is the United States still committed to maintaining stability in the Western Hemisphere? Have students respond by writing an editorial in which they defend their position and incorporate the information they learned in their research. **OL** **AL**

D Differentiated Instruction

Advanced Learners Have students determine the level of education achieved by U.S. presidents. Then have students find out how historians have rated the presidents. Based on the information, they should write a paper analyzing the relationship between education and success in the presidency. **AL**

Analyzing VISUALS

Answers:

1. The cartoonist is indicating that Wilson believes he is smarter than the leaders of the Latin American countries.
2. The cartoon implies that Mexico favors revolution and may be spreading it to other countries.

Reading Check

Answer:
"Speak softly and carry a big stick." Using diplomacy to settle problems, while openly displaying U.S. military might.

Additional Support

Although Taft described his brand of diplomacy as "substituting dollars for bullets," in Nicaragua he used both. American bankers began making loans to Nicaragua to support its shaky government in 1911. The following year, civil unrest forced the Nicaraguan president to appeal for greater assistance. American marines entered the country, replaced the collector of customs with an American agent, and formed a committee of two Americans and one Nicaraguan to control the customs commissions. American troops stayed to support both the government and customs until 1925.

Reading Check **Summarizing** What was Roosevelt's view of the role of the United States in the world and how did he implement it?

POLITICAL CARTOONS PRIMARY SOURCE

Wilson and Mexico

▲ *President Wilson (who had a Ph.D.) is shown teaching Venezuela, Nicaragua, and Mexico that revolution for personal gain is wrong, while Mexico is shown hiding a note labeled "How to create a revolution."*

Analyzing VISUALS

1. **Analyzing** In what ways is the cartoon making fun of President Wilson?
2. **Inferring** What is the cartoon implying about Mexico?

Woodrow Wilson's Diplomacy in Mexico

MAIN Idea Wilson believed in "moral diplomacy" and tried to encourage democracy in Latin America.

HISTORY AND YOU Can you think of a country today that is going through a long civil war? Read how the United States became involved in the Mexican Revolution.

"It would be the irony of fate," remarked Woodrow Wilson just before he was inaugurated in 1913, "if my administration had to deal chiefly with foreign affairs." Wilson had written books on state government, Congress, and George Washington, as well as a five-volume history of the nation. His experience and interest were in domestic policy. He was a university professor before entering politics. He also was a committed progressive. However, foreign affairs did absorb much of Wilson's time and energy as president. **D**

Wilson opposed imperialism and resolved to "strike a new note in international affairs" and see that "sheer honesty and even unselfishness . . . should prevail over nationalistic self-seeking in American foreign policy." He also believed that democracy was essential to a nation's stability and prosperity. To ensure a world free of revolution and war, the United States should promote democracy. During Wilson's presidency, however, other forces frustrated his hope to lead the world by moral example. In fact, Wilson's first international crisis was awaiting him when he took office.

The Mexican Revolution

For more than 30 years, Porfirio Díaz ruled Mexico as a dictator. During his reign, Mexico became much more industrialized, but foreign investors owned and financed the new railroads and factories that were built. Most Mexican citizens remained poor and landless. In 1911 widespread discontent erupted into revolution.

Francisco Madero, a reformer who appeared to support democracy, constitutional government, and land reform, led the revolution. Madero, however, proved to be an unskilled administrator. Worried about Madero's plans for land reform, conservative forces plotted

Extending the Content

Eyewitness to Revolution On the night of April 21, 1914, Edith O'Shaughnessy wrote of her fears of a pending U.S.-Mexican conflict in her diary, later published as *A Diplomat's Wife in Mexico*:

"I can't sleep. National and personal potentialities are surging through my brain. Three stalwart railroad men came to the Embassy this evening. They brought reports of a plan for the massacre of Americans in the street to-night, but, strange and wonderful thing, a heavy rain is falling. It is my only experience of a midnight rain in Mexico ... rain is as potent as shell-fire in clearing the streets ... Providence seems to keep an occasional unnatural shower on hand for Mexican crises."

Neither the rain shower nor Providence could stop what O'Shaughnessy feared. On April 21, she recorded: "We are at war. American and Mexican blood flowed in the streets of Vera Cruz to-day."

against him. In February 1913, General **Victoriano Huerta** seized power; Madero was murdered, presumably on Huerta's orders.

Huerta's brutality repulsed Wilson, who refused to recognize the new government. Instead, Wilson announced a new policy. Groups that seized power in Latin America would have to set up "a just government based upon law, not upon arbitrary or irregular force," in order to win American recognition. Wilson was convinced that, without the support of the United States, Huerta soon would be overthrown. Meanwhile, Wilson ordered the navy to intercept arms shipments to Huerta's government. He also permitted Americans to arm Huerta's opponents.

Wilson Sends Troops Into Mexico

In April 1914, American sailors visiting the city of Tampico were arrested after entering a restricted area. Although they were quickly released, their American commander demanded an apology. The Mexicans refused. Wilson saw the refusal as an opportunity to overthrow Huerta. He asked Congress to authorize the use of force, and shortly after Congress passed the resolution, he learned that a German ship was unloading weapons at the Mexican port of Veracruz. Wilson immediately ordered American warships to shell the Veracruz harbor and then sent marines to seize the city.

Although the president expected the Mexican people to welcome his action, anti-American riots broke out. Wilson then accepted international mediation to settle the dispute. Venustiano Carranza, whose forces had acquired arms from the United States, became Mexico's president.

W

Mexican forces opposed to Carranza were not appeased, and they conducted raids into the United States, hoping to force Wilson to intervene. In March 1916, **Pancho Villa** (VEE•yah) and a group of **guerrillas**—an armed band that uses surprise attacks and sabotage rather than open warfare—burned the town of Columbus, New Mexico, and killed 16 Americans. Wilson responded by sending 6,000 troops under General John J. Pershing across the border to find and capture Villa. The expedition dragged on with no success. Wilson's growing concern over the war raging in Europe finally caused him to recall Pershing's troops in 1917.

Wilson's Mexican policy damaged U.S. foreign relations. The British ridiculed the president's attempt to "shoot the Mexicans into self-government." Latin Americans regarded his "moral imperialism" as no improvement over Theodore Roosevelt's "big stick" diplomacy. In fact, Wilson followed Roosevelt's example in the Caribbean. In 1914 he negotiated exclusive rights for naval bases and a canal with Nicaragua. In 1915 he sent marines into Haiti to put down a rebellion. The marines remained there until 1934. In 1916 he sent troops into the Dominican Republic to preserve order and to set up a government he hoped would be more stable and democratic than the current regime.

Reading Check **Examining** Why did President Wilson intervene in Mexico?

Section 3 REVIEW

Vocabulary

1. **Explain** the significance of: sphere of influence, Open Door policy, Boxer Rebellion, Hay-Pauncefote Treaty, Roosevelt Corollary, dollar diplomacy, Victoriano Huerta, Pancho Villa, guerrilla.

Main Ideas

2. **Summarizing** Use a graphic organizer to list the results of the Open Door policy.

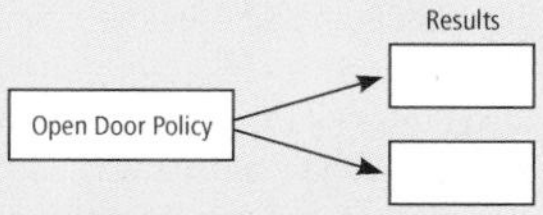

3. **Identifying** Why did President Theodore Roosevelt want to increase U.S. influence overseas?
4. **Specifying** How did Latin Americans view Wilson's "moral imperialism"?

Critical Thinking

5. **Big Ideas** Why did the United States decide to build a canal through Panama? How did Roosevelt assist Panama in becoming independent?
6. **Analyzing** How did the Roosevelt Corollary and dollar diplomacy affect U.S. relations with other countries?
7. **Analyzing Visuals** Study the map on page 509. To which countries did the U.S. send troops most often?

Writing About History

8. **Expository Writing** Imagine that you are a Mexican citizen during Wilson's presidency. Write a radio news broadcast expressing your feelings about American actions in Mexico.

History ONLINE
Study Central™ To review this section, go to glencoe.com and click on Study Central.

W Writing Support

Descriptive Writing Have students find out more information about the American occupation of Veracruz. Then have students write an essay describing the Americans' actions and the response of the people of Veracruz. **OL**

Reading Check

Answer:
first to help support the overthrow of Huerta; later to suppress Villa

Assess

History ONLINE

Study Central™ provides summaries, interactive games, and online graphic organizers to help students review content.

Close

Summarizing Ask: How did America's diplomacy affect its role as a world power? *(America's diplomacy required it to build up its power.)* **OL**

Section 3 REVIEW

Answers

1. All definitions can be found in the section and the Glossary.
2. all countries could trade with China; prevented warfare among competing nations
3. He felt the United States should become involved in world events and become a world power. Believing in some of the ideas of Anglo-Saxonism, he also felt it was the United States's duty to help other "less fortunate" nations.
4. Students' answers will vary. Possible answers: The Latin-American nations wanted the right of self-determination. They knew that America would act in its own interests, not in the interests of Latin-American countries.
5. A canal would save time and money in commercial and military shipping. Panama was chosen over Nicaragua because a French company sold its rights and property in Panama. Roosevelt sent ships to Panama and recognized that nation's independence from Colombia.
6. Many nations resented America's policies.
7. Nicaragua, Cuba
8. Students' broadcasts will vary. Broadcasts should be based on information from the chapter.

GEOGRAPHY & HISTORY

Focus

Tell students that the Spanish, as early as the 1500s, were the first to imagine a canal to connect the Atlantic and Pacific Oceans. The American interest in such a waterway developed only after the Civil War. Businessman Cornelius Vanderbilt attempted to build a canal through Nicaragua, but without success. During the 1840s both Britain and the United States wanted to build the canal, but it was the same French company that built the Suez Canal that actually began the work. The attempt bankrupted the company.

Teach

R Reading Strategy

Activating Prior Knowledge Ask students to identify some historical events that might have motivated interest in a canal through Central America. *(Students may suggest the California Gold Rush, Civil War battles, or the Spanish American War.)* **OL**

Additional Support

NATIONAL GEOGRAPHIC

GEOGRAPHY & HISTORY

The Panama Canal

The idea of a canal connecting the Atlantic and Pacific oceans had been around for a long time before a French company began digging a canal across Panama in 1882. Disease and mud slides killed more than 20,000 workers before financial setbacks halted construction. **R** In the early 1900s, the United States negotiated rights to build the canal with Colombia (Panama was part of Colombia at that time), but Colombia's Senate refused to ratify the treaty. With the support of the United States, Panama declared independence from Colombia and signed a treaty giving the United States a perpetual lease on the canal site in exchange for $10 million and annual payments. Construction resumed in 1904, and the canal was opened in 1914.

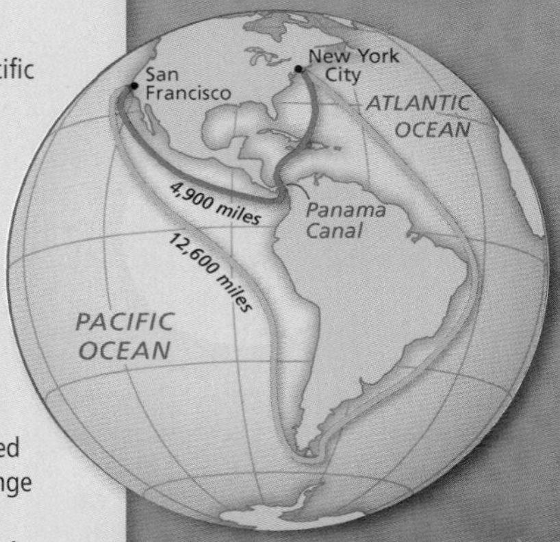

How Does Geography Affect the Canal?

Before the canal opened, ships sailing from New York to San Francisco traveled 12,600 miles (20,277 km) around the treacherous tip of South America. Afterwards, the trip was only 4,900 miles (7,886 km) and could be completed in less than half the time. Panama's geography made building the canal a challenge because the center of the country was much higher than sea level. Engineers built a series of lakes and concrete locks to raise and lower ships as they traveled the 51-mile canal. In each chamber of the locks, some 26 million gallons of water are pumped in or drained out in only 7 minutes to raise or lower a ship. At the artificial Gatun Lake, a dam generates electricity that powers the locks while gravity adjusts the water level.

Ships transit the canal more than 14,000 times each year, generating over $1 billion in tolls.

Analyzing GEOGRAPHY

1. **Human-Environment Interaction** How were the geographical features of Panama used or overcome in order to build the canal?
2. **Location** Why do you think the Panama site was ultimately selected for the canal?

Interdisciplinary Connection

Health About 6,000 workers died while the United States built the canal. Many of them succumbed to yellow fever or malaria, diseases carried by mosquitoes. Ask students to find out more about the challenges due to diseases that Panama Canal workers faced and how those challenges were met. Have them present their findings to the class as a radio or newscast. **OL**

▲ *The Miraflores locks (above) are one of three sets of locks on the Panama Canal, and the first set for ships entering from the Pacific. After a ship enters a lock chamber, water is pumped in raising the ship up 27 feet to the next level. The ship then moves to the next chamber and is raised another 27 feet.*

GEOGRAPHY & HISTORY

Assess/Close

D Differentiated Instruction

Visual/Spatial Invite students to make a sketch or a three-dimensional model of the three locks that allow passage through the Panama Canal. **OL**

Analyzing GEOGRAPHY

Answers:

1. The center of the country was higher than sea level, so engineers built a series of locks and canals to raise and lower ships going through the 51-mile canal.
2. Panama offered the shortest distance across Central America.

Technology Connection

Investigate Primary Sources Several Web sites offer extensive information and primary resources on the building of the Panama Canal. Ask students to select three articles from different sites and summarize their contents. The following sites are possible starting points:

Smithsonian Institute, Make the Dirt Fly!
PBS's American Experience
American Treasures of the Library of Congress

Creating a Time Line The Visual Summary lists the causes of American imperialism, the effects of the Spanish-American War, and the events in which the United States demonstrated its might as a world power. Have students choose six events from the Visual Summary and create a time line, placing the events in the correct chronological order. **BL**

Chapter 14 Visual Summary

STUDY TO GO You can study anywhere, anytime by downloading quizzes and flashcards to your PDA from glencoe.com.

Causes of American Imperialism

- The United States wanted new markets for its products, particularly its manufactured goods.
- Many Americans believed it was the destiny of the United States to spread its power and civilization to other parts of the world.
- American leaders believed that having a powerful navy and controlling trade were key to being a world power.

▶ *USS Texas docks in port in 1896*

▲ *American soldiers in Cuba cheer the news that the city of Santiago, Cuba, has surrendered during the Spanish-American War, 1898.*

Effects of the Spanish-American War

- Cuba officially became an independent nation, although the United States claimed control over its foreign relations and exerted influence over internal politics.
- The United States acquired Puerto Rico, Guam, and the Philippines.
- Americans debated the morality and wisdom of becoming an imperial nation.
- The United States fought a three-year war to secure control over the Philippines.

The United States Acts As a World Power

- The United States used diplomatic means to establish the Open Door policy in China.
- President Theodore Roosevelt negotiated a peace agreement between Russia and Japan.
- The United States completed construction of the Panama Canal.
- The United States intervened, with the intent to provide stability, in the affairs of several Caribbean nations.
- The United States twice intervened in the lengthy Mexican Revolution.

▲ *After supporting a revolution in Panama, the United States begins construction of the Panama Canal.*

Hands-On Chapter Project
Step 4: Wrap Up

Preparing a Multimedia Presentation

Step 4: Sharing the Presentation Groups will share their presentations with the class.

Directions Tell students to develop a narrative to go along with their presentations. The narrative should compliment their presentations and explain the causes and effects of imperialism in their assigned nation. Once all groups have presented, encourage students to individually take a closer look at any of the presentations that intrigued them.

Next have students critique the presentations on quality of information, ease of use, and creativity. Encourage students to share aspects of their own presentations they found interesting or challenging.

Putting It Together Have students discuss each of the six countries presented: Cuba, China, Japan, the Philippines, Puerto Rico, and Guam. Ask students to draw a conclusion about the effects of imperialism on other nations. **Ask:** Was imperialism beneficial or harmful for these nations? **OL**

Chapter 14 Assessment

Reviewing Vocabulary

Directions: Choose the word or words that best complete the sentence.

1. The major European powers each had a(n) ________ in China.
- **A** protectorate
- **B** sphere of influence
- **C** Open Door policy
- **D** tariff policy

2. Taft's policies in Latin America were called
- **A** "big stick" diplomacy.
- **B** open door diplomacy.
- **C** missionary diplomacy.
- **D** dollar diplomacy.

3. Congress's authorization of $50 million for war preparation after the destruction of the U.S.S. *Maine* was an example of
- **A** Anglo-Saxonism.
- **B** imperialism.
- **C** jingoism.
- **D** dollar diplomacy.

4. Support for the war against Spain came in part from the ________ practiced by some newspapers.
- **A** anti-Americanism
- **B** objectivity
- **C** yellow journalism
- **D** sphere of influence

5. Local rulers are permitted to retain some power in a
- **A** protectorate.
- **B** monarchy.
- **C** republic.
- **D** dictatorship.

Reviewing Main Ideas

Directions: Choose the best answers to the following questions.

Section 1 *(pp. 490–495)*

6. Which of the following was a major contributor to the growth of American imperialism in the late 1800s?
- **A** curiosity about other cultures
- **B** need for spices from the East Indies
- **C** the end of the Civil War
- **D** desire for new markets for American goods

7. What effect did Commodore Matthew C. Perry have on Japan?
- **A** Japan began building an army.
- **B** Japan began to westernize.
- **C** Japan ended its trade with China.
- **D** Japan refused to negotiate with the United States.

8. A major goal of the Pan-American conference in 1889 was to
- **A** create a customs union for nations in the Americas.
- **B** end trade with the nations of Europe.
- **C** free Cuba from Spanish control.
- **D** decide on a route for a canal through Central America.

Section 2 *(pp. 496–503)*

9. The effect of yellow journalism on the Cuban rebellion was
- **A** unimportant to people in the United States.
- **B** helpful in changing McKinley's mind about going to war with Spain.
- **C** critical to raising public support for war against Spain.
- **D** harmful to American businesses in Cuba.

TEST-TAKING TIP

Note that in some cases you are asked to choose the BEST answer. This means that in some instances there will be more than one possible answer. Be sure to read all the choices carefully before selecting your answer.

Need Extra Help?

If You Missed Questions . . .	1	2	3	4	5	6	7	8	9
Go to Page . . .	504	509	499	497	490–491	490–492	493	495	497

GO ON

Answers and Analyses
Reviewing Vocabulary

1. B A sphere of influence was an area in China in which a foreign nation controlled economic development. These spheres were held by the major European powers, and worried the U.S. A protectorate was a territory that maintained local rulers, but was protected by and had to take advice from other nations. The Open Door Policy was instated as a reaction to spheres of influence.

2. D Taft's policies in Latin America were a form of economic imperialism. This allowed the U.S. to control events without creating protectorates or colonies. These economic policies were called dollar diplomacy. They may have been economically unfair, but this is not what they were called.

3. C Jingoism is defined as extreme nationalism marked by aggressive foreign policy.

4. C Yellow journalism was sensationalist reporting, which often used exaggeration and untruths to provoke an emotional response. The response provoked helped rally Americans to support a war against Spain.

5. A A monarchy is a system of government ruled by monarchs, or a royal family. A republic is a system of representative government. A dictatorship is a form of government in which one person holds all of the power. In a protectorate, a nation allows another nation to influence its policies in exchange for protection.

Reviewing Main Ideas

6. D The Industrial Revolution led to a massive increase in manufacturing. Leaders soon realized that more money could be made if there were expanded markets for goods. Remind students who are distracted by choice *B* that the need for spices motivated European exploration in the 15th century.

7. B Commodore Matthew Perry's visit to Japan caused Japan to modernize, because Japan realized the need to compete with Western technology. Therefore, Japan began to Westernize. This led to cooperation between the two nations. However, remind students that before Perry and the American warships arrived in Japan, Japan had refused contact. The U.S. forced contact by sending Perry.

8. A This is a good opportunity to discuss *pan* as a prefix from the Greek that means "all." Although the Pan-American conference did not include Canada, this information should help students remember that only nations in the Americas would be involved in the Pan-American conference.

9. C The fact that journalism is intended to reach the masses should help students figure out this answer. Increased public support for the war was a direct consequence of yellow journalism.

10. D Review the section "American Forces in Cuba" if students have trouble with this question. San Juan Hill and Kettle Hill were both captured by the U.S. in battle, but this happened before the surrender. Guam is a different island from Cuba. It may be helpful to have students create a time line of events of the war.

11. A If students read each answer choice carefully, only *A* makes sense. Sugarcane production was an issue in Hawaii. Students may be tempted to choose *C* because they relate an amendment with the Bill of Rights. However, remind students that the Bill of Rights only applies to American citizens and (now) citizens of Puerto Rico. It would not make sense for the U.S. to allow European nations to buy or lease naval stations in Cuba, since it is so close to the U.S.

12. D To remember that the Open Door Policy ensured trading rights for all nations, students should think of an open door as allowing everything through. Leaseholds were what created spheres of influence. However, spheres of influence are what *caused* the U.S. to push for the Open Door Policy: to combat the Europeans' spheres of influence. The Boxer Rebellion was a response to the Open Door Policy. A cause-and-effect chart might help students understand this chain of events.

13. C The Monroe Doctrine informed Europe that the Americas were no longer open to European colonization. If students remember this, it is not a stretch to remember that the Roosevelt Corollary was basically an extension of this: its purpose was to protect American interests in Latin America. Instead of ending colonization, however, it banned European interference in Latin American affairs.

Chapter 14 ASSESSMENT

10. Spanish resistance in Cuba ended with the surrender of
- **A** San Juan Hill.
- **B** Kettle Hill.
- **C** Guam.
- **D** Santiago.

11. What effect did the Platt Amendment have on Cuba?
- **A** It made Cuba a virtual protectorate of the United States.
- **B** It cut sugarcane production so Cuba could not compete with production in the United States.
- **C** It guaranteed all the freedoms of the Bill of Rights to Cubans.
- **D** It gave Cuba the right to allow European countries to buy or lease naval stations in Cuba.

Section 3 *(pp. 504–511)*

12. The purpose of the Open Door policy in China was to
- **A** end the Boxer Rebellion.
- **B** gain leaseholds.
- **C** establish spheres of influence.
- **D** ensure trading rights for all nations.

13. What was the Roosevelt Corollary to the Monroe Doctrine?
- **A** It provided for the purchase of land to build a canal across Panama.
- **B** It warned the nations of Europe not to impose high tariffs on goods from the Americas.
- **C** It stated that the United States would intervene in Latin American affairs as needed for political and economic stability.
- **D** It reinforced the policy of isolationism of the United States in world affairs.

Critical Thinking

Directions: Choose the best answers to the following questions.

Base your answers to questions 14 and 15 on the map below and your knowledge of Chapter 14.

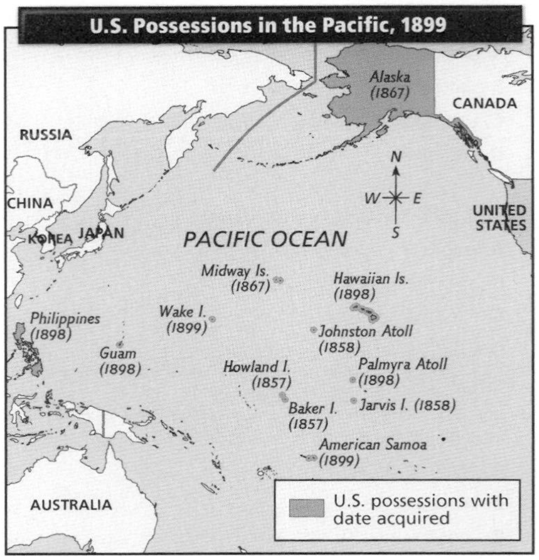

14. Which of the following became a U.S. possession before the Spanish-American War?
- **A** Wake Island
- **B** Howland Island
- **C** American Samoa
- **D** Guam

15. Which U.S. possession are the Philippines nearest to?
- **A** Alaska
- **B** Hawaii
- **C** Midway Islands
- **D** Guam

Need Extra Help?						
If You Missed Questions . . .	10	11	12	13	14	15
Go to Page . . .	500	502–503	504–505	508–509	499–502	499–502

GO ON

Critical Thinking

14. B The U.S. acquired Howland Island in 1857.

15. D Students should be able to answer this question by simply glancing at the map. Among the choices given, Guam is clearly the closest to the Philippines. Midway is the next closest but is between Guam and Hawaii.

16. The "big stick" policy and dollar diplomacy were attempts to

A increase the United States's power in Latin America.

B contain the spread of communism in eastern Europe.

C protect free trade on the Asian continent.

D strengthen political ties with Western Europe.

Analyze the cartoon and answer the question that follows. Base your answer on the cartoon and on your knowledge of chapter 14.

17. What does the cartoon demonstrate?

A It disagrees with Taft's dollar diplomacy.

B It shows Theodore Roosevelt's "big stick" policy in the Caribbean.

C It shows the effect of John Jay's Open Door policy.

D It demonstrates the difficulty of finding land for a canal.

18. The sugarcane planters in Hawaii revolted against Queen Liliuokalani because

A she taxed the sugarcane plantations too heavily.

B she wanted a constitution that returned her to power as the ruler of Hawaii.

C they wanted to overturn the McKinley Tariff.

D they hoped to open Asian markets to sugarcane from Hawaii.

Document-Based Questions

Directions: Analyze the document and answer the short-answer questions that follow the document.

After the Spanish-American War, Carl Schurz, the leader of the liberal wing of the Republican Party, opposed American expansion abroad. In the following excerpt, Schurz attacks the arguments for taking over the Philippine Islands:

> *"Many imperialists admit that our trade with the Philippines themselves will not nearly be worth its cost; but they say that we must have the Philippines as a foothold, a sort of power station, for the expansion of our trade on the Asiatic continent, especially in China. Admitting this, for argument's sake, I ask what kind of a foothold we should really need. Coaling stations and docks for our fleet, and facilities for the establishment of commercial houses and depots. That is all. And now I ask further, whether we could not easily have had these things if we had, instead of making war upon the Filipinos, favored the independence of the islands. Everybody knows that we could. We might have those things now for the mere asking if we stopped the war and came to a friendly understanding with the Filipinos tomorrow. . . ."*
>
> —quoted in *The Policy of Imperialism*

19. What does Schurz believe is necessary to establish a foothold in trade with Asia?

20. What action other than annexation does Schurz suggest the United States could have taken to obtain trade with Asia?

Extended Response

21. Discuss U.S. foreign policy during the late 1800s and early 1900s. How were the various countries and regions of the world changed by the policies of the United States? Write an expository essay that includes an introduction, several paragraphs, and a conclusion that supports your position.

STOP

History ONLINE

For additional test practice, use Self-Check Quizzes—Chapter 14 at glencoe.com.

Need Extra Help?

If You Missed Questions . . .	16	17	18	19	20	21
Go to Page . . .	504–511	506–509	494	517	517	490–511

Document-Based Questions

19. Schurz believes coaling stations, docks, and facilities for commercial houses and depots are all that is necessary to establish a foothold in trade with Asia. Schurz is arguing against war with the Philippines. He believes these few needs could have been met by supporting Philippine independence.

20. Schurz believes the U.S. could have supported Philippine independence and kept open communication. He does not argue against the benefits of having strategic footholds in the Philippines, but he doesn't feel force was needed in achieving this goal.

Extended Response

21. Students' essays will vary, but must demonstrate a strong grasp of the imperialist policies of the United States. Essays should describe the effects of these policies on the people and the lands that were affected by U.S. imperialism. Students may discuss, for example, the Panama Canal, the Spanish-American War, the annexation of Hawaii, or relations with Asian nations. Essays must include an introduction and a conclusion.

16. A It is important that students understand the motivations behind the "big stick" policy and dollar diplomacy and can relate them to Latin America. The United States practiced economic imperialism in Latin America—these policies did not concern Europe or Asia.

17. B Students should be able to identify the figure of Theodore Roosevelt in this cartoon by his uniform, glasses, and mustache. He is striding over the islands of Latin America, and he carries a big stick that actually says "Big Stick" on it. From these clues, *C* is the obvious choice. Make sure students are comfortable analyzing images.

18. B The sugarcane planters in Hawaii were not native Hawaiians; they were American businessmen. Therefore, their best interest would be served if Hawaii were part of the United States. If the Queen reasserted her power, this would not happen, so the planters revolted.

History ONLINE

Have students visit the Web site at glencoe.com to review Chapter 14 and take the Self-Check Quiz.

Need Extra Help?

Have students refer to the pages listed if they miss any of the questions.

Chapter 15 Planning Guide

Key to Ability Levels

BL Below Level
OL On Level
AL Above Level
ELL English Language Learners

Key to Teaching Resources

Print Material
CD-ROM or DVD
Transparency

BL	OL	AL	ELL	Resources	Chapter Opener	Section 1	Section 2	Section 3	Chapter Assess
				FOCUS					
BL	OL	AL	ELL	**Daily Focus Skills Transparencies**		15-1	15-2	15-3	
				TEACH					
		AL		**American Literature Reading, URB**		p. 13			
	OL	AL		**Geography and History, URB**			p. 3		
	OL	AL		**History Simulations and Problem Solving, URB**		p. 9			
BL	OL		ELL	**Reading Essentials and Note-Taking Guide***		p. 165	p. 168	p. 171	
	OL			**Historical Analysis Skills Activity, URB**			p. 52		
BL	OL		ELL	**Guided Reading Activities, URB***		p. 78	p. 79	p. 80	
BL	OL	AL	ELL	**Content Vocabulary Activity, URB***		p. 57			
BL	OL	AL	ELL	**Academic Vocabulary Activity, URB**		p. 59			
	OL	AL		**Critical Thinking Skills Activity, URB**		p. 62	p. 62		
BL	OL		ELL	**Reading Skills Activity, URB**	p. 51				
BL			ELL	**English Learner Activity, URB**		p. 55			
	OL	AL		**Reinforcing Skills Activity, URB**		p. 61			
BL	OL	AL	ELL	**Differentiated Instruction Activity, URB**		p. 53			
BL	OL		ELL	**Time Line Activity, URB**		p. 63			
	OL			**Linking Past and Present Activity, URB**			p. 64		
BL	OL	AL	ELL	**American Art and Music Activity**				p. 69	
BL	OL	AL	ELL	**Interpreting Political Cartoons Activity, URB**		p. 71			
BL	OL	AL		**Economics and History Activity, URB**			p. 7		
		AL		**Enrichment Activity, URB**				p. 75	
BL	OL	AL	ELL	**American Biographies**		✓	✓		
BL	OL	AL	ELL	**Primary Source Reading, URB**		p. 65	p. 67		
BL	OL	AL	ELL	**Supreme Court Case Studies**		p. 33	p. 29		
BL	OL	AL	ELL	**The Living Constitution***	✓	✓	✓	✓	✓
	OL	AL		**American History Primary Source Documents Library**	✓	✓	✓	✓	✓
BL	OL	AL	ELL	**Unit Map Overlay Transparencies**	✓	✓	✓	✓	✓

Note: Please refer to the *Unit 5 Resource Book* for this chapter's URB materials.

* Also available in Spanish

TeacherWorks Plus
All-In-One Planner and Resource Center

- Interactive Lesson Planner
- Interactive Teacher Edition
- Fully editable blackline masters
- Section Spotlight Videos Launch
- Differentiated Lesson Plans
- Printable reports of daily assignments
- Standards Tracking System

Levels				Resources	Chapter Opener	Section 1	Section 2	Section 3	Chapter Assess
BL	OL	AL	ELL						
TEACH *(continued)*									
BL	OL	AL	ELL	Differentiated Instruction for the American History Classroom	✓	✓	✓	✓	✓
BL	OL	AL	ELL	StudentWorks™ Plus	✓	✓	✓	✓	✓
BL	OL	AL	ELL	American Music Hits Through History CD	✓	✓	✓	✓	✓
BL	OL	AL	ELL	Unit Time Line Transparencies and Activities	✓	✓	✓	✓	✓
BL	OL	AL	ELL	Cause and Effect Transparencies, Strategies, and Activities	✓	✓	✓	✓	✓
BL	OL	AL	ELL	Why It Matters Transparencies, Strategies, and Activities	✓	✓	✓	✓	✓
BL	OL	AL	ELL	American Issues	✓	✓	✓	✓	✓
	OL	AL	ELL	American Art and Architecture Transparencies, Strategies, and Activities	✓	✓	✓	✓	✓
BL	OL	AL		High School American History Literature Library	✓	✓	✓	✓	✓
BL	OL	AL	ELL	*The American Vision* Video Program	✓	✓	✓	✓	✓
Teacher Resources				Strategies for Success	✓	✓	✓	✓	✓
Teacher Resources				Success with English Learners	✓	✓	✓	✓	✓
Teacher Resources				Reading Strategies and Activities for the Social Studies Classroom	✓	✓	✓	✓	✓
Teacher Resources				Presentation Plus! with MindJogger CheckPoint	✓	✓	✓	✓	✓
ASSESS									
BL	OL	AL	ELL	Section Quizzes and Chapter Tests*		p. 211	p. 212	p. 213	p. 215
BL	OL	AL	ELL	Authentic Assessment With Rubrics					p. 35
BL	OL	AL	ELL	Standardized Test Practice Workbook					p. 33
BL	OL	AL	ELL	*ExamView® Assessment Suite*		15-1	15-2	15-3	CH. 15
CLOSE									
BL			ELL	Reteaching Activity, URB					p. 73
BL	OL		ELL	Reading and Study Skills Foldables™	pp. 65–66				
BL	OL	AL	ELL	*American History* in Graphic Novel		p. 15			

✓ Chapter- or unit-based activities applicable to all sections in this chapter.

Using Self-Check Quizzes

Teach With Technology

What is a Self-Check Quiz?

A Self-Check Quiz is a set of 10 or more multiple-choice questions that assess student comprehension of the chapter.

How can a Self-Check Quiz help my students?

A Self-Check Quiz is a quick and easy way for students to check how much they have learned and identify areas needing improvement. It allows students to:

- view their results immediately
- view the correct answers
- e-mail their results to you or themselves
- receive feedback on each question for where students can go to review topics they missed or had trouble answering

Visit glencoe.com and enter a QuickPass™ code to go to a Self-Check Quiz.

History ONLINE
Visit glencoe.com and enter QuickPass™ code TAV9399c15T for Chapter 15 resources.

You can easily launch a wide range of digital products from your computer's desktop with the McGraw-Hill Social Studies widget.

TeacherWorks

	Student	Teacher	Parent
Media Library			
• Section Audio	●		●
• Spanish Audio Summaries	●		●
• Section Spotlight Videos	●	●	●
***The American Vision* Online Learning Center (Web Site)**			
• StudentWorks™ Plus Online	●	●	●
• Multilingual Glossary	●	●	●
• Study-to-Go	●	●	●
• Chapter Overviews	●	●	●
• Self-Check Quizzes	●	●	●
• Student Web Activities	●	●	●
• ePuzzles and Games	●	●	●
• Vocabulary eFlashcards	●	●	●
• In Motion Animations	●	●	●
• Study Central™	●	●	●
• Web Activity Lesson Plans		●	
• Vocabulary PuzzleMaker	●	●	●
• Historical Thinking Activities		●	
• Beyond the Textbook	●	●	●

Reading Support From Jamestown Education

- **Timed Readings Plus in Social Studies** helps students increase their reading rate and fluency while maintaining comprehension. The 400-word passages are similar to those found on state and national assessments.
- **Reading in the Content Area: Social Studies** concentrates on six essential reading skills that help students better comprehend what they read. The book includes 75 high-interest nonfiction passages written at increasing levels of difficulty.
- **Reading Social Studies** includes strategic reading instruction and vocabulary support in Social Studies content for both ELLs and native speakers of English.

www.jamestowneducation.com

Biography · A&E Home Video · The History Channel

The following videotape programs are available from Glencoe as supplements to this chapter:

- Susan B. Anthony: Rebel for the Cause (ISBN 1-56-501646-7)
- Woodrow Wilson: Reluctant Warrior (ISBN 0-76-700101-X)

To order, call Glencoe at 1-800-334-7344. To find classroom resources to accompany many of these videos, check the following home pages:

A&E Television: www.aetv.com

The History Channel: www.historychannel.com

National Geographic

Index to National Geographic Magazine:

The following articles relate to this chapter:

- "Roosevelt country: T.R.'s wilderness legacy," by John L. Eliot and Farrell Grehan, September 1982.
- "Time Machine: Yosemite in Photos Then and Now," by Claire Stanford, October 2005.

National Geographic Society Products To order the following, call National Geographic at 1-800-368-2728:

- *ZipZapMap! USA* (ZipZapMap!)

Access National Geographic's new, dynamic MapMachine Web site and other geography resources at:

www.nationalgeographic.com

www.nationalgeographic.com/maps

Reading List Generator CD-ROM — Glencoe BookLink 3

Use this database to search more than 30,000 titles to create a customized reading list for your students.

- Reading lists can be organized by students' reading level, author, genre, theme, or area of interest.
- The database provides Degrees of Reading Power™ (DRP) and Lexile™ readability scores for all selections.
- A brief summary of each selection is included.

Leveled reading suggestions for this chapter:

For students at a Grade 8 reading level:
- ***Alice Paul***, by Elizabeth Raum

For students at a Grade 9 reading level:
- ***The Story of Susan B. Anthony***, by Susan Clinton

For students at a Grade 10 reading level:
- ***Susan B. Anthony: Daring to Vote***, by Barbara Keevil Parker

For students at a Grade 11 reading level:
- ***Forward into Light: The Struggle for Woman's Suffrage***, by Madeleine Meyers

For students at a Grade 12 reading level:
- ***Failure Is Impossible: Susan B. Anthony in Her Own Words***, by Lynn Sherr

Introducing Chapter 15

Focus

MAKING CONNECTIONS

Can Politics Fix Social Problems?

Ask students to suggest ways that they think today's society might be improved and list their suggestions on the board. Discuss how these suggestions could be implemented and who would be responsible for them. **OL**

Teach

The Big Ideas

As students study the chapter, remind them to consider the section-based Big Ideas included in each section's Guide to Reading. The **Essential Questions** in the activities below tie in to the Big Ideas and help students think about and understand important chapter concepts. In addition, the Hands-on Chapter Projects with their culminating activities relate the content from each section to the Big Ideas. These activities build on each other as students progress through the chapter. Section activities culminate in the wrap-up activity on the Visual Summary page.

Chapter 15

The Progressive Movement

1890–1920

SECTION 1 The Roots of Progressivism

SECTION 2 Roosevelt and Taft

SECTION 3 The Wilson Years

Women wearing academic dress march in a New York City parade for woman suffrage in 1910.

U.S. PRESIDENTS

B. Harrison 1889–1893

Cleveland 1893–1897

McKinley 1897–1901

T. Roosevelt 1901–1909

U.S. EVENTS

1889
- Hull House opens in Chicago

1890
- Jacob Riis's *How the Other Half Lives* is published

1902
- Maryland passes first U.S. workers' compensation laws

1906
- Pure Food and Drug Act passed

1890 | 1900

WORLD EVENTS

1884
- Toynbee Hall, first settlement house, is established in London

1903
- Russian Bolshevik Party is established by Lenin

1906
- British pass workers' compensation law

Section 1

The Roots of Progressivism

Essential Question: Why did many citizens call for reforms? *(Some citizens wanted to restrict the power of big business; others wanted to improve living conditions in the cities; women sought the right to vote; others wanted to improve society overall.)* Tell students that in this section they will learn about the social reforms that were carried out in the early 1900s. **OL**

Section 2

Roosevelt and Taft

Essential Question: What were the policies and achievements of the Roosevelt and Taft presidencies? *(Answers might include the breaking up of the trusts, increased consumer protection, and better conservation of resources.)* Tell students that this section will focus on the reforms achieved during the Roosevelt and Taft administrations. **OL**

Chapter Audio

MAKING CONNECTIONS

Can Politics Fix Social Problems?

Industrialization changed American society. Cities were crowded, working conditions were often bad, and the old political system was breaking down. These conditions gave rise to the Progressive movement. Progressives campaigned for both political and social reforms.

- ***What reforms do you think progressives wanted to achieve?***
- ***Which of these reforms can you see in today's society?***

Taft 1909–1913

Wilson 1913–1921

1910
- Mann-Elkins Act passed

1913
- Seventeenth Amendment requires direct election of senators

1920
- Nineteenth Amendment gives women voting rights

1910 | 1920

1908
- Germany limits working hours for children and women

1911
- British create national health insurance program

1914
- World War I begins in Europe

1917
- Russian Revolution begins

FOLDABLES™

Analyzing Reform Programs Create a Pocket Book Foldable that divides the Progressive agenda into political reforms and social reforms. Take notes on a wide range of reforms, placing each one in the proper column of the Foldable.

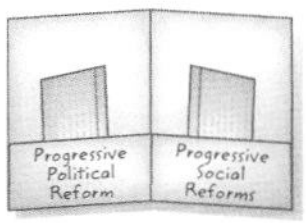

History ONLINE Visit glencoe.com and enter *QuickPass*™ code TAV9846c15 for Chapter 15 resources.

Introducing
Chapter 15

More About the Photo

Visual Literacy Before the ratification of the Nineteenth Amendment in 1920, women's voting rights varied by state. Most Western states had already granted full suffrage to women. In many Midwestern states, women could vote for some political offices—such as president, city mayor, or school board members—but not all. Most Southern and Eastern states had not yet granted voting rights to women. In this 1910 photograph, members of the Collegiate Equal Suffrage League, wearing caps and gowns, participate in a suffrage demonstration in New York City. In 1917 New York granted full suffrage to women.

FOLDABLES™ Study Organizer **Dinah Zike's Foldables**

Dinah Zike's Foldables are three-dimensional, interactive graphic organizers that help students practice basic writing skills, review vocabulary terms, and identify main ideas. Instructions for creating and using Foldables can be found in the Appendix at the end of this book and in the *Dinah Zike's Reading and Study Skills Foldables* booklet.

Section 3

The Wilson Years

Essential Question: What reforms did President Wilson undertake? *(tariff reforms, antitrust actions, and new business regulations)* Tell students that in Section 3 they will learn about President Wilson's policies during the first part of his administration. **OL**

History ONLINE

Visit glencoe.com and enter *QuickPass*™ code TAV9399c15T for Chapter 15 resources, including a Chapter Overview, Study Central™, Study-to-Go, Student Web Activity, Self-Check Quiz, and other materials.

Focus

Bellringer

Daily Focus Transparency 15-1

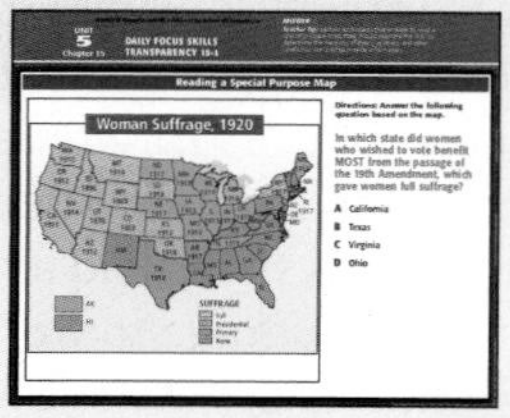

Guide to Reading

Answers:
Progressive Beliefs:
Industrialization and urbanization created social problems; Free market unable to fix social problems; Government should address social problems; Government should be reformed; Business should be regulated; Scientific principles useful in fixing social problems

Section Spotlight Video

To generate student interest and provide a springboard for discussion, access the Chapter 15, Section 1 video at glencoe.com or on the video DVD.

Section 1

Section Audio Spotlight Video

The Roots of Progressivism

Guide to Reading

Big Ideas
Group Action The progressives sought to improve life in the United States with social, economic, and political reforms.

Content Vocabulary
- muckraker *(p. 521)*
- direct primary *(p. 522)*
- initiative *(p. 523)*
- referendum *(p. 523)*
- recall *(p. 523)*
- suffrage *(p. 524)*
- prohibition *(p. 527)*

Academic Vocabulary
- legislation *(p. 523)*
- advocate *(p. 527)*

People and Events to Identify
- Jacob Riis *(p. 521)*
- Robert M. La Follette *(p. 522)*
- Carrie Chapman Catt *(p. 525)*

Reading Strategy
Organizing As you read about the beginnings of progressivism, complete a graphic organizer similar to the one below by filling in the beliefs of progressives.

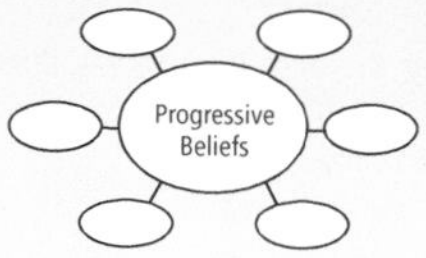

The Progressive Era was a time when many Americans tried to improve their society. They tried to make government honest, efficient, and more democratic. The movement for women's suffrage gained more support, as did efforts to limit child labor and reduce alcohol abuse.

The Rise of Progressivism

MAIN Idea Progressives tried to solve the social problems that arose as the United States became an urban, industrialized nation.

HISTORY AND YOU What areas of public life do you believe need to be reformed? Read on to learn about a movement that tried to fix many of society's problems.

Progressivism was a collection of different ideas and activities. It was not a tightly organized political movement with a specific set of reforms. Rather, it was a series of responses to problems in American society that had emerged from the growth of industry. Progressives had many different ideas about how to fix the problems they saw in American society.

Who Were the Progressives?

Progressivism was partly a reaction against laissez-faire economics and its emphasis on an unregulated market. Progressives generally believed that industrialization and urbanization had created many social problems. After seeing the poverty of the working class and the filth and crime of urban society, reformers began doubting the free market's ability to address those problems.

Progressives belonged to both major political parties. Most were urban, educated, middle-class Americans. Among their leaders were journalists, social workers, educators, politicians, and members of the clergy. Most agreed that government should take a more active role in solving society's problems. At the same time, they doubted that the government in its present form could fix those problems. They concluded that government had to be fixed before it could be used to fix other problems.

One reason progressives thought they could improve society was their strong faith in science and technology. The application of scientific knowledge had produced the lightbulb, the telephone, and the automobile. It had built skyscrapers and railroads. Science and technology had benefited people; thus, progressives believed using scientific principles could also produce solutions for society.

Resource Manager

R Reading Strategies	C Critical Thinking	D Differentiated Instruction	W Writing Support	S Skill Practice
Teacher Edition • Organizing Info p. 521 • Setting Purpose p. 522 • Monitoring p. 526 • Summarizing p. 526 **Additional Resources** • Guided Read., URB p. 78 • Prim. Source, URB p. 65 • Am. History in Graphic Novel, p. 15	**Teacher Edition** • Making Inferences p. 522 • Pred. Consequences p. 524 **Additional Resources** • Hist. Sim., URB p. 9 • Inter. Pol. Cartoons, URB p. 71 • Quizzes and Tests, p. 211	**Teacher Edition** • Gifted Talented pp. 523, 527 **Additional Resources** • Diff. Instr., URB p. 53 • Academic Vocab. Act., URB p. 59 • Eng. Learner Act., URB p. 55 • Foldables, pp. 65–66	**Teacher Edition** • Personal Writing p. 524 **Additional Resources** • Supreme Court Case Studies, p. 33 • Econ. and History Act., URB p. 7 • Content Vocab. Act., URB p. 57	**Teacher Edition** • Reading a Time Line p. 525 **Additional Resources** • Read. Essen., p. 165 • Reinf. Skills Act., URB p. 61 • Read. Skills Act., URB p. 51 • Time Line Act., URB p. 63

PRIMARY SOURCE

The Photojournalism of Jacob Riis

Photography offered a new tool in combating injustice. One of the most famous early photojournalists was Jacob Riis, whose book, *How the Other Half Lives*, helped stir progressives to action:

PRIMARY SOURCE

"Look into any of these houses, everywhere the same piles of rags, of malodorous bones and musty paper. . . . Here is a 'flat' or 'parlor' and two pitch-dark coops called bedrooms. Truly, the bed is all there is room for. The family teakettle is on the stove, doing duty for the time being as a wash-boiler. By night it will have returned to its proper use again, a practical illustration of how poverty in 'the Bend' makes both ends meet. One, two, three beds are there, if the old boxes and heaps of foul straw can be called by that name; a broken stove with crazy pipe from which the smoke leaks at every joint, a table of rough boards propped up on boxes, piles of rubbish in the corner. The closeness and smell are appalling. How many people sleep here? The woman with the red bandanna shakes her head sullenly, but the bare-legged girl with the bright face counts on her fingers—five, six!"

—from *How the Other Half Lives*

▲ New York slum dwellers in this Jacob Riis photograph, taken about 1890, lived in wooden shacks in a city alley.

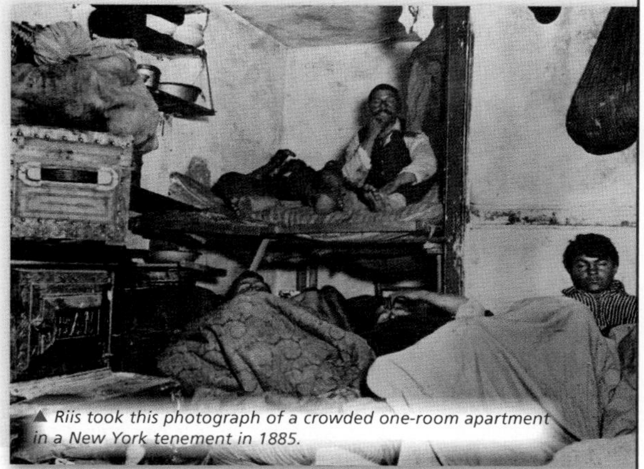

▲ Riis took this photograph of a crowded one-room apartment in a New York tenement in 1885.

DBQ Document-Based Questions

1. **Analyzing Visuals** What effect do Riis's photos convey?
2. **Making Inferences** Based on the quotation above, how could you summarize Riis's views on changing life in the slums?

The Muckrakers

Among the first people to articulate progressive ideas was a group of crusading journalists who investigated social conditions and political corruption. President Theodore Roosevelt nicknamed these writers "**muckrakers.**" The term referred to a character in John Bunyan's book *Pilgrim's Progress*, who
R single-mindedly scraped up the filth on the ground, ignoring everything else. These journalists, according to Roosevelt, were obsessed with scandal and corruption. Widely circulated, cheap newspapers and magazines helped to spread the muckrakers' ideas.

Muckrakers uncovered corruption in many areas. Some concentrated on exposing the unfair practices of large corporations. In *Everybody's Magazine*, Charles Edward Russell attacked the beef industry. In *McClure's*, Ida Tarbell published a series of articles critical of the Standard Oil Company. Other muckrakers targeted government and social problems. Lincoln Steffens reported on vote stealing and other corrupt practices of urban political machines. These articles were later collected into a book, *The Shame of the Cities*.

Still other muckrakers concentrated on social problems. In his influential book, *How the Other Half Lives* (1890), **Jacob Riis** published photographs and descriptions of the poverty, disease, and crime that afflicted many immigrant neighborhoods in New York City. By raising public awareness of these problems, the muckrakers stimulated calls for reform.

Read literature from the era on pages R72–R73 in the **American Literature Library.**

Reading Check **Describing** How did the muckrakers help spark the Progressive movement?

Teach

R Reading Strategy

Organizing Information
Have students create a chart listing progressive actions discussed in this section, the social causes they represented, and their approaches to solving the problems. OL

DBQ Document Based Questions

Answers:
1. the hardships of poverty
2. Slums are filthy, appalling places that are unfit for people to live in and society must find a way to improve living conditions in poor neighborhoods.

Reading Check

Answer:
Muckrakers raised awareness about corruption and social problems through their writing.

Hands-On Chapter Project
Step 1

Learning how Government Affects People's Lives

Step 1: Becoming a Progressive In the first of four activities for this chapter, students will relate their knowledge of the problems the progressives addressed to contemporary community issues. They will identify a community problem and suggest a solution.

Directions Have students review Section 1, noting the types of issues reformers tackled. Each student will then identify a problem in his or her community that affects citizens' lives today.

Identifying Problems and Solutions Students will either present to the class or write an analysis of the problem that includes these points: problem description, explanation of why they think the problem exists, and a statement about whether or how they believe government should go about solving the problem. If they believe the problem should not or cannot be solved by government, students should explain why and what other resources should be used. OL

(Project continued on page 534)

R Reading Strategy

Setting a Purpose Tell students that reading texts with a specific question in mind can provide a focus to help them better understand what they are reading. As they read the section titled "Making Government Efficient," have students ask themselves how progressives attempted to combat corruption and inefficiency in municipal government. **BL**

C Critical Thinking

Making Inferences Ask: Why was "laboratory of democracy" a good nickname for La Follette's Wisconsin? *(Wisconsin reformed the way political candidates were chosen. The direct primary gave political power to many instead of a few.)* **OL**

Additional Support

History ONLINE Student Web Activity Visit glencoe.com and complete the activity on the Progressive movement.

Reforming Government

MAIN Idea Progressives tried to make government more efficient and more responsive to citizens.

HISTORY AND YOU How do you use your time and resources wisely? Read on to learn how progressives tried to make the government more efficient.

Progressivism included a wide range of reform activities. Different issues led to different approaches, and progressives even took opposing positions on how to address some problems. They condemned corruption in government but did not always agree on the best way to fix the problem.

Making Government Efficient

One group of progressives focused on making government more efficient by using ideas from business. Theories of business efficiency first became popular in the 1890s. Books such as Frederick W. Taylor's *The Principles of Scientific Management* (1911) described how a company could increase efficiency by managing time, breaking tasks down into small parts, and using standardized tools. In his book, Taylor argued that this "scientific method" of managing businesses optimized productivity and provided more job opportunities for unskilled workers. Many progressives argued that managing a modern city required the use of business management techniques.

R Progressives saw corruption and inefficiency in municipal government where, in most cities, the mayor or city council chose the heads of city departments. Traditionally, they gave these jobs to political supporters and friends, who often knew little about managing city services.

Progressives supported two proposals to reform city government. The first, a commission plan, divided city government into several departments, each one under an expert commissioner's control. The second approach was a council-manager system. The city council would hire a city manager to run the city instead of the mayor. In both systems, experts play a major role in managing the city. Galveston, Texas, adopted the commission system in 1901. Other cities soon followed.

Democratic Reforms

Another group of progressives focused on making the political system more democratic and more responsive to citizens. Many believed that the key to improving government was to make elected officials more responsive and accountable to the voters.

La Follette's Laboratory of Democracy Led by Republican governor **Robert M. La Follette,** Wisconsin became a model of progressive reform. La Follette attacked the way political parties ran their conventions. Party bosses controlled the selection of convention delegates, which meant they also controlled the C nomination of candidates. La Follette pressured the state legislature to pass a law requiring parties to hold a **direct primary,** in which all party members could vote for a candidate to run in the general election. This and other successes earned Wisconsin a reputation as the "laboratory of democracy." La Follette later recalled:

PRIMARY SOURCE

New Types of Government

The most deadly hurricane in United States history slammed into Galveston, Texas, on September 8, 1900, killing about 6,000 people. Because the political machine running the city was incapable of responding to the disaster, local business leaders convinced the state to allow them to take control. The following April, Galveston introduced the commission system of local government, which replaced the mayor and city council with five commissioners. Sometimes referred to as the Galveston Plan, its constitutionality was confirmed and took effect.

Four of those commissioners were local business leaders. Reformers in other cities were impressed by the city's rapid recovery. Clearly, the city benefited from dividing the government into departments under the supervision of an expert commissioner. Soon, other cities adopted either the commission or council-manager systems of government.

▶ *A house sits on its side after a hurricane ripped through Galveston, Texas, in September 1900.*

Activity: Collaborative Learning

Making Decisions Divide students into groups of four or five. Students will work together to plan the most efficient way to perform a task. **Ask:** What is the most efficient way for your group to prepare thirty bag lunches? Tell students the bag lunches will contain: peanut butter and jam sandwiches, cleaned and sliced carrot sticks, and a piece of fruit. Remind students to consider the management techniques of: managing time, breaking tasks into small parts, and using standardized tools. Ask groups to present their efficiency plans to the class. Then create a class plan. Encourage students to pick and choose the most efficient techniques from each group to create the overall plan. **BL** **OL**

Primary Source

"It was clear to me that the only way to beat boss and ring rule was to keep the people thoroughly informed. Machine control is based upon misrepresentation and ignorance. Democracy is based upon knowledge. It is of first importance that the people shall know about their government and the work of their public servants."

—from La Follette's *Autobiography*

Wisconsin's use of the direct primary soon spread to other states, but to force legislators to listen to the voters, progressives also pushed for three additional reforms: the initiative, the referendum, and the recall. The **initiative** permitted a group of citizens to introduce **legislation** and required the legislature to vote on it. The **referendum** allowed citizens to vote on proposed laws directly without going to the legislature. The **recall** provided voters an option to demand a special election to remove an elected official from office before his or her term had expired.

D

Direct Election of Senators Progressives also targeted the Senate. As originally written, the federal constitution directed each state legislature to elect two senators. Political machines and business interests often influenced these elections. Some senators, once elected, repaid their supporters with federal contracts and jobs.

To counter Senate corruption, progressives called for direct election of senators by the state's voters. In 1912, Congress passed a direct-election amendment. Although the direct election of senators was intended to end corruption, it also removed one of the state legislatures' checks on federal power. In 1913 the amendment was ratified and became the Seventeenth Amendment to the Constitution.

Reading Check **Evaluating** What was the impact of the Seventeenth Amendment? What problem was it intended to solve?

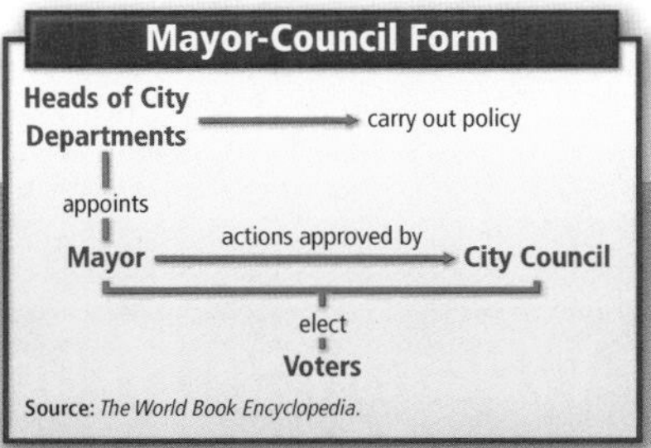

Source: *The World Book Encyclopedia*.

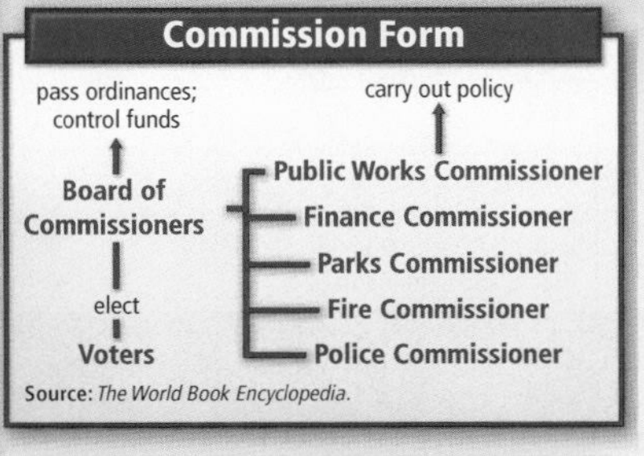

Source: *The World Book Encyclopedia*.

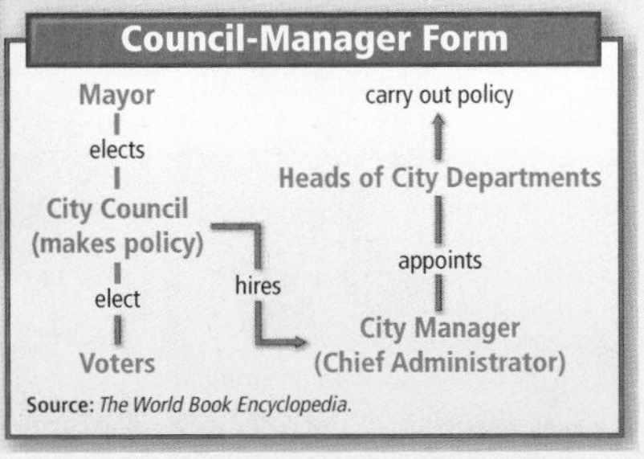

Source: *The World Book Encyclopedia*.

Analyzing VISUALS

1. **Differentiating** In what forms of government do voters elect the City Council?
2. **Analyzing** In a mayor-council form of government, who is responsible to carry out policy?

D Differentiated Instruction

Gifted and Talented Have students research and write a report about a referendum issue. They should describe the referendum, present both sides of the issue, and report on the result of the vote. **AL**

Reading Check

Answer:
It led to the direct election of senators and was intended to counter Senate corruption.

Analyzing VISUALS

Answers:

1. Mayor-Council and Council-Manager forms
2. Heads of city departments

Additional Support

Activity: Collaborative Learning

Drafting an Initiative Divide the class into groups of three or four students and have the students work to identify a social or political problem they wish the legislature to address. After identifying a problem, the group should develop a proposal for the problem's solution. Next, have group members write the text of their initiative, as it would be presented to legislators. Have groups read their initiatives to the class. Encourage the class to discuss how effective the initiatives might be in addressing the problems they seek to solve. **Ask:** How does an initiative differ from a referendum? *(An initiative is presented to legislators to be voted on, referendums are voted on directly by citizens.)* **OL**

W Writing Support

Personal Writing Ask students to write a few paragraphs about whether abolition should have been given a higher priority than woman suffrage. Have students explain their reasoning. **OL**

C Critical Thinking

Predicting Consequences
Ask: Do you think American women might have gained suffrage sooner if the group agreed on a strategy? *(Students' answers will vary.)* **OL**

For an example of the early woman suffrage movement read "The Seneca Falls Declaration" on page R48 in **Documents in American History.**

Suffrage

MAIN Idea Many progressives joined the movement to win voting rights for women.

HISTORY AND YOU Do you remember reading about the Seneca Falls Convention in 1848? Read about the momentum of the women's rights movement in the 1910s.

At the first women's rights convention in Seneca Falls, New York, in 1848, Elizabeth Cady Stanton convinced the delegates that their first priority should be the right to vote. Decades later, universal woman **suffrage**—the right to vote—still had not been granted. It became a major goal for women progressives.

Early Problems

W The woman suffrage movement got off to a slow start. Some people threatened women suffragists and said they were unfeminine and immoral. Many of its supporters were abolitionists, as well. In the years before the Civil War, abolishing slavery took priority.

After the Civil War, Congress introduced the Fourteenth and Fifteenth Amendments to grant citizenship to African Americans and voting rights to African American men. Leaders of the woman suffrage movement wanted these amendments to give women the right to vote, as well. They were disappointed when Republicans refused.

The debate over the Fourteenth and Fifteenth Amendments split the suffrage movement into two groups: the New York City–based National Woman Suffrage Association, which Elizabeth Cady Stanton and Susan B. Anthony founded in 1869, and the Boston-based American Woman Suffrage Association, which Lucy Stone and Julia Ward Howe led.

C The first group wanted to focus on passing a constitutional amendment. The second group believed that the best strategy was convincing state governments to give women voting rights before trying to amend the Constitution. This split weakened the movement, and by 1900 only Wyoming, Idaho, Utah, and Colorado had granted women full voting rights.

THE Woman Suffrage Movement

1848
The first women's rights convention is held in Seneca Falls, New York, and issues a "Declaration of Rights and Sentiments"

1872
Susan B. Anthony votes illegally in the presidential election in Rochester, New York, claiming the Fourteenth Amendment gives her that right; she is arrested and found guilty

▲ Susan B. Anthony

1850 1870 1890

▲ Women voting in Cheyenne, Wyoming, 1869

1869
Territory of Wyoming becomes the first state or territory to grant women the right to vote

▲ Elizabeth Cady Stanton

1890
Elizabeth Cady Stanton becomes president of the National American Woman Suffrage Association

Additional Support

Activity: Collaborative Learning

Analyzing Primary Sources Have students work in groups to search the Internet for primary documents concerning woman suffrage. For each event on the Woman Suffrage Movement time line, have student groups find a pertinent quote from a primary source such as a speech, article, book, or song. Have each group recreate the time line using the quotes they selected for each date. Remind students to identify the speaker and source of each quote on their time line. Have groups present their time lines and compare the quotes they selected. **Ask:** What do the quotes tell you about attitudes toward woman suffrage? **OL**

Building Support

In 1890 the two groups united to form the National American Woman Suffrage Association (NAWSA) but still had trouble convincing women to become politically active. As the Progressive movement gained momentum, however, many middle-class women concluded that they needed the vote to promote the reforms they favored. Many working-class women also wanted the vote to pass labor laws protecting women.

As the movement grew, women began lobbying lawmakers, organizing marches, and delivering speeches on street corners. On March 3, 1913, the day before President Wilson's inauguration, suffragists marched on Washington, D.C.

Alice Paul, a Quaker social worker who headed NAWSA's congressional committee, had organized the march. Paul wanted to use protests to confront Wilson on suffrage. Other members of NAWSA who wanted to negotiate with Wilson were alarmed. Paul left NAWSA and formed the National Woman's Party. Her supporters picketed the White House, blocked sidewalks, chained themselves to lampposts, and went on hunger strikes if arrested.

In 1915 **Carrie Chapman Catt** became NAWSA's leader and tried to mobilize the suffrage movement in one final nationwide push. She also threw NAWSA's support behind Wilson's reelection campaign.

As more states granted women the right to vote, Congress began to favor a constitutional amendment. In 1918 the House of Representatives passed a women's suffrage amendment. The Senate voted on the amendment, but it failed by two votes.

During the midterm elections of 1918, Catt used NAWSA's resources to defeat two antisuffrage senators. In June 1919 the Senate passed the amendment by slightly more than the two-thirds vote needed. On August 26, 1920, after three-fourths of the states had ratified it, the Nineteenth Amendment, guaranteeing women the right to vote, went into effect.

Reading Check **Evaluating** How successful were women in lobbying for the Nineteenth Amendment?

▲ *Women and children march in a 1912 suffrage parade in New York City.*

1910 — 1920

1913
Alice Paul and Lucy Burns found the Congressional Union for Woman Suffrage (later the National Woman's Party), which uses civil disobedience to promote women's suffrage

1920
Nineteenth Amendment, granting women the right to vote, is ratified

Woman Suffrage, 1869–1920

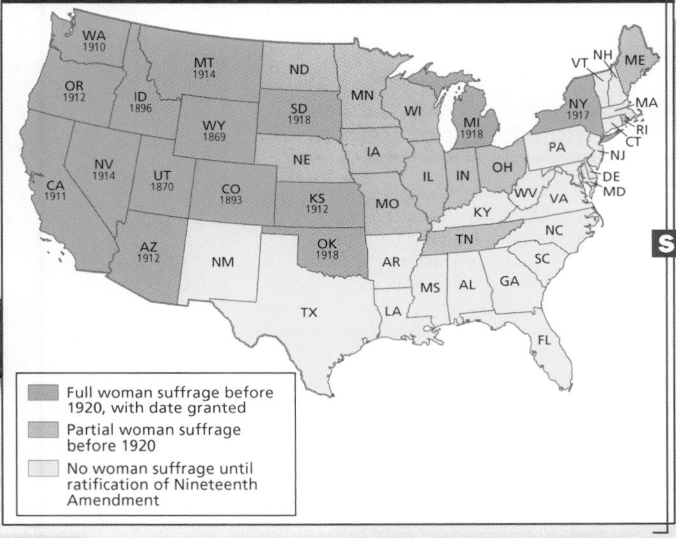

S

Analyzing TIME LINES

1. **Identifying** In what state or territory were women first granted the right to vote?
2. **Analyzing** What region of the nation seemed most willing to grant woman suffrage without a national amendment?

S Skill Practice

Reading a Time Line Have students use the time line to determine the different tactics suffragists used to gain the right to vote. *(holding conventions, attempting to vote, marching, civil disobedience)* OL

Reading Check

Answer:
In 1920 the Nineteenth Amendment was ratified.

Analyzing TIME LINES

Answers:
1. Wyoming
2. the West

Additional Support

Activity: Interdisciplinary Connection

Art Tell students that the 1913 suffrage parade in Washington, D.C., was filled with posters and pageantry. Gowned women rode horseback, and young girls carried posters with slogans such as "Votes for us when we are women!" Have students work in groups to research photographs of the parade. Then have each group create their own suffrage posters inspired by images they found through their research. **Ask:** Which symbols convey the most powerful message? Have groups share their posters with the class. BL OL

R1 Reading Strategy

Monitoring Ask: What influenced states to pass child labor laws? *(books such as* The Bitter Cry of the Children*)* **BL**

R2 Reading Strategy

Summarizing Have students write a short summary of adult working conditions and the influence of progressives and unions on labor laws. **OL**

Analyzing VISUALS

Answers:

1. Students may note that the spray from fire hoses barely reaches top floor and people are trapped in the building looking for help.
2. the protest signs mention Hebrew trades, some of the background signs are in other languages.

Reforming Society

MAIN Idea Many progressives focused on social welfare problems such as child labor, unsafe working conditions, and alcohol abuse.

HISTORY AND YOU Have you heard of companies using "sweatshop" labor in foreign countries? Read on to learn how progressives tried to ban child labor and make factories safer for workers.

History ONLINE Student Skill Activity To learn how to create and modify a database, visit glencoe.com and complete the skill activity.

While many progressives focused on reforming the political system, others focused on social problems. These social-welfare progressives created charities to help the poor and disadvantaged. They also pushed for new laws they hoped would fix social problems.

Child Labor

R1 Probably the most emotional progressive issue was the campaign against child labor. Children had always worked on family farms, but mines and factories presented more dangerous and unhealthy working conditions. Muckraker John Spargo's 1906 book, *The Bitter Cry of the Children,* presented detailed evidence of child labor conditions. It told of coal mines that hired thousands of 9- or 10-year-old "breaker boys" to pick slag out of coal, paying them 60 cents for a 10-hour day. It described the way that the work bent their backs permanently and often crippled their hands. R1

Reports like these convinced states to pass laws that set a minimum age for employment and established other limits on child labor, such as maximum hours children could work.

Health and Safety Codes

Many adult workers also labored in difficult conditions. When workers were injured or killed on the job, they and their families received little or no compensation. Progressives joined union leaders to pressure states for workers' compensation laws. These laws established insurance funds that employers financed. Workers injured in accidents received payments from the funds. R2

In two cases, *Lochner* v. *New York* (1905) and *Muller* v. *Oregon* (1908), the Supreme Court addressed government's authority to regulate business to protect workers. In the Lochner case, the Court ruled that a New York law forbidding bakers to work more than 10 hours a day was unconstitutional. The state did not have the right to interfere with the liberty of

PRIMARY SOURCE

A Tragedy Brings Reform

Fire broke out on the top floors of the Triangle Shirtwaist Company on March 25, 1911. Young women struggled against locked doors to escape. A few women managed to get out using the fire escape before it collapsed. The single elevator stopped running. Some women jumped from windows on the ninth floor to their death, while others died in the fire. Nearly 150 of the 500 employees lost their lives in the blaze.

The Triangle factory was a nonunion shop. Health and safety issues were a major concern for unions. The disaster illustrated that fire precautions and inspections were inadequate. Exit doors were kept locked, supposedly to prevent theft. As a result of the fire and loss of life, New York created a Factory Investigating Commission. Between 1911 and 1914, the state passed 36 new laws reforming the labor code.

▲ *Firemen fight Triangle Shirtwaist fire, March 25, 1911.*

▲ *Trade union members march in support of the women who died.*

Analyzing VISUALS

1. **Analyzing** What do you observe about the efforts at fighting the fire in the photo at left?
2. **Interpreting** What clues in the photo at right suggest that at least some of the women who died were immigrants?

Additional Support

Activity: Technology Connection

Discussing Working Conditions Divide students into groups of 4 or 5. Have them use the Internet to research industrial accidents and unsafe conditions in such cases as the Wal-Mart Lock-Ins, 2003; Imperial Foods Fire, 1991; and the Kader Industrial Fire, 1993. Ask groups to write a report summarizing the accident or working conditions they researched. Have students include in their report the impact, if any, of the incident on labor laws and working conditions. Students should share their reports with the class. **Ask:** What basic rights and working conditions do you think workers should be guaranteed? **OL AL**

employers and employees. In the case of women working in laundries in Oregon, however, the Court upheld the state's right to limit hours. The different judgments were based on gender differences. The Court stated that healthy mothers were the state's concern and, therefore, the limits on women's working hours did not violate their Fourteenth Amendment rights.

Some progressives also favored zoning laws as a method of protecting the public. These laws divided a town or city into zones for commercial, residential, or other development, thereby regulating how land and buildings could be used. Building codes set minimum standards for light, air, room size, and sanitation, and required buildings to have fire escapes. Health codes required restaurants and other facilities to maintain clean environments for their patrons.

The Prohibition Movement

Many progressives believed alcohol explained many of society's problems. Settlement house workers knew that hard-earned wages were often spent on alcohol and that drunkenness often led to physical abuse and sickness. Some employers believed drinking hurt workers' efficiency. The temperance movement—which **advocated** that people stop, or at least moderate, their alcohol consumption—emerged from these concerns.

For the most part, women led the temperance movement. In 1874 a group of women formed the Woman's Christian Temperance Union (WCTU). By 1911 the WCTU had nearly 250,000 members. In 1893 evangelical Protestant ministers formed another group, the Anti-Saloon League. When the temperance movement began, it concentrated on reducing alcohol consumption. Later it pressed for **prohibition**—laws banning the manufacture, sale, and consumption of alcohol.

Progressives Versus Big Business

Many progressives agreed that big business needed regulation. Some believed the government should break up big companies to restore competition. This led to the Sherman Antitrust Act in 1890. Others argued that big business was the most efficient way to organize the economy. They pushed for government to regulate big companies and prevent them from abusing their power. The Interstate Commerce Commission (ICC), created in 1887, was an early example of this kind of thinking.

Some progressives went even further and advocated socialism—the idea that the government should own and operate industry for the community. They wanted the government to buy up large companies, especially industries that affected everyone, such as utilities. At its peak, socialism had some national support. Eugene V. Debs, the former American Railway Union leader, won nearly a million votes as the American Socialist Party candidate for president in 1912. Most progressives and most Americans, however, believed the American system of free enterprise was superior.

Reading Check **Comparing** In what ways were progressive efforts to end child labor and impose safety codes similar?

Section 1 REVIEW

Vocabulary

1. **Explain** the significance of: muckraker, Jacob Riis, Robert M. La Follette, direct primary, initiative, referendum, recall, suffrage, Carrie Chapman Catt, prohibition.

Main Ideas

2. **Organizing** Use a graphic organizer similar to the one below to list the kinds of problems that muckrakers exposed.

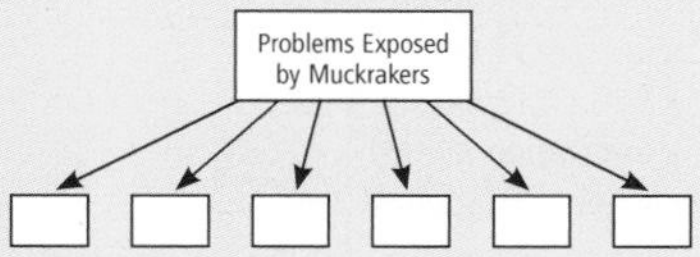

3. **Summarizing** How did initiative, referendum, and recall change democracy in the United States?
4. **Stating** What key provision did the Nineteenth Amendment make?
5. **Describing** Explain the various zoning laws and codes favored by progressives.

Critical Thinking

6. **Big Ideas** Identify the different social issues associated with progressives. How do these ideals influence society today?
7. **Analyzing Visuals** Study the charts on page 523. Which system gives voters the most control over department heads? How?

Writing About History

8. **Expository Writing** Create a database of progressive ideas of the period. Then write a one-page report using a word processor to summarize the progressive ideals.

History ONLINE
Study Central™ To review this section, go to glencoe.com and click on Study Central.

527

D Differentiated Instruction

Gifted and Talented Have students prepare a report on the Sherman Antitrust Act of 1890. Have them describe the conditions that contributed to the act, the support and opposition it faced, and what resulted from its enactment. AL

Assess

History ONLINE

Study Central™ provides summaries, interactive games, and online graphic organizers to help students review content.

Close

Summarizing Have students summarize the influences progressives had on society during this period in history.

Reading Check

Answer:
Women formed suffrage and temperance organizations to push their agendas.

Section 1 REVIEW

Answers

1. Definitions for the vocabulary terms are found in the section and the Glossary.
2. Problems Exposed by Muckrakers: unfair practices by big business, corrupt government, inefficient government, poverty, child labor practices, adult labor conditions.
3. Initiatives permitted citizens to introduce legislation that lawmakers were required to vote on. Referendums allowed citizens to vote directly on proposed laws. Recall provided voters with a way to remove politicians from office before their terms ended.
4. The Nineteenth Amendment granted women the right to vote.
5. Zoning laws divided areas into commercial or residential areas to regulate building and land use. Building codes regulated room size and required fire escapes.
6. Progressives were concerned with issues of social justice including poverty, fair labor practices, and reigning in big business. These concerns are still with us today and are major topics of public debate.
7. The commission form of government gives voters the most control over department heads because voters elect them directly.
8. Letters will vary but should give reasons for a clearly stated position.

Focus

Bellringer

Daily Focus Transparency 15-2

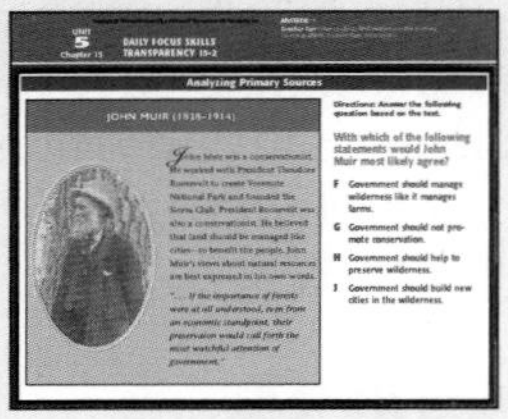

Guide to Reading

Answers:

Roosevelt and Taft

1. Roosevelt Revives the Presidency
- A. Roosevelt Takes on the Trusts
- B. The Coal Strike of 1902
- C. Regulating Big Business
- D. Consumer Protection

II. Conservation
- A. Western Land Development
- B. Gifford Pinchot
- C. Roosevelt's Legacy

Section Spotlight Video

To generate student interest and provide a springboard for discussion, access the Chapter 15, Section 2 video at glencoe.com or on the video DVD.

Resource Manager

R Reading Strategies	C Critical Thinking	D Differentiated Instruction	W Writing Support	S Skill Practice
Teacher Edition • Monitoring p. 533 • Det. Importance p. 534 • Academic Vocab. p. 535 **Additional Resources** • Guided Reading, URB p. 79 • Prim. Source Read., URB p. 67	**Teacher Edition** • Det. Cause/Effect p. 529 • Drawing Con. pp. 530, 532 **Additional Resources** • Quizzes and Tests, p. 212 • Crit. Think. Skills Act., URB p. 62 • Linking Past/Present, URB p. 64	**Teacher Edition** • Gifted/Talented p. 530	**Teacher Edition** • Persuasive Writing p. 532 **Additional Resources** • Geo. and History, URB p. 3 • Supreme Court Case Studies, p. 29 • Econ. and History Act., URB p. 7	**Teacher Edition** • Visual Literacy p. 529 **Additional Resources** • Read Essen., p. 168 • Hist. Analysis Skills Act., URB p. 52

Section 2

Section Audio   Spotlight Video

Roosevelt and Taft

Guide to Reading

Big Ideas

Individual Action Presidents Theodore Roosevelt and William Taft worked to improve labor conditions, control big business, and support conservation.

Content Vocabulary
- Social Darwinism *(p. 528)*
- arbitration *(p. 529)*
- insubordination *(p. 535)*

Academic Vocabulary
- regulate *(p. 530)*
- environmental *(p. 532)*

People and Events to Identify
- Square Deal *(p. 528)*
- United Mine Workers *(p. 529)*
- Hepburn Act *(p. 530)*
- Upton Sinclair *(p. 530)*
- Meat Inspection Act *(p. 530)*
- Pure Food and Drug Act *(p. 530)*
- Gifford Pinchot *(p. 532)*
- Richard A. Ballinger *(p. 534)*
- Children's Bureau *(p. 535)*

Reading Strategy

Notes As you read about the Roosevelt and Taft administrations, use the headings of the section to create an outline similar to the one below.

Roosevelt and Taft
I. Roosevelt Revives the Presidency
A.
B.
C.
D.
II.

As president, Theodore Roosevelt extended the federal government's ability to curb the power of big business and to conserve natural resources. His successor, William Howard Taft, was less popular with progressives.

Roosevelt Revives the Presidency

MAIN Idea Theodore Roosevelt, who believed in progressive ideals for the nation, took on big business.

HISTORY AND YOU How much do you think a president's personal beliefs should shape national policy? Read on to learn how Theodore Roosevelt used his ideas to change trusts and big business.

Theodore Roosevelt became president at age 42—the youngest person ever to take office. Roosevelt was intensely competitive, strong-willed, and extremely energetic. In international affairs, Roosevelt was a Social Darwinist. He believed the United States was in competition with the other nations of the world and that only the fittest would survive. Domestically, however, Roosevelt was a committed progressive, who believed that government should actively balance the needs of competing groups in American society.

"I shall see to it," Roosevelt declared in 1904, "that every man has a square deal, no less and no more." His reform programs soon became known as the **Square Deal.** To Roosevelt, it was not inconsistent to believe in **Social Darwinism** and progressivism at the same time.

Roosevelt Takes on the Trusts

Roosevelt believed that trusts and other large business organizations were very efficient and part of the reason for America's prosperity. Yet Roosevelt remained concerned that the monopoly power of some trusts hurt the public interest. His goal was to ensure that trusts did not abuse their power. When the *New York Sun* declared that Roosevelt was "bringing wealth to its knees," the president disagreed. "We draw the line against misconduct," he declared, "not against wealth."

Roosevelt decided to make an example out of major trusts that he believed were abusing their power. His first target was J. P. Morgan's railroad holding company, Northern Securities. Established in 1901, the company proposed, through an exchange of stock, to merge existing railroad systems to create a monopoly on railroad traffic in the Northwest. As a monopoly, Northern Securities would have no competition. Farmers and business owners feared it would raise rates and hurt their profits. In 1902 the president ordered the attorney

POLITICAL CARTOONS Primary Source

Roosevelt Versus the Trusts

Jay Gould was a well-known railroad speculator who had been involved in many scandals. At one point, he controlled the four largest western railroads, including the Union Pacific.

James J. Hill, founder of the Great Northern Railway Company and a partner with J. P. Morgan in Northern Securities

Theodore Roosevelt, shown standing in the middle of Wall Street carrying a sword labeled "Public Service"

John D. Rockefeller, founder of Standard Oil, which controlled most oil production in the United States

J. P. Morgan controlled a huge banking and financial empire. He also created the U.S. Steel Corporation and helped finance several railroads.

Analyzing VISUALS DBQ

1. **Inferring** Why do you think the scene is set on Wall Street?
2. **Analyzing** What do the giants represent?

general to file suit under the Sherman Antitrust Act, charging the company was a "combination in restraint of trade."

Roosevelt's action baffled J. P. Morgan. Expecting to resolve the suit without legal action, he inquired what could be done to "fix it up." Unmoved, Roosevelt proceeded with the case. In 1904, in *Northern Securities* v. *United States,* the Supreme Court ruled that Northern Securities had indeed violated the Sherman Antitrust Act. Roosevelt proclaimed, "The most powerful men in the country were held to accountability before the law." Newspapers hailed Roosevelt as a "trustbuster," and his popularity with the American public soared.

The Coal Strike of 1902

As president, Roosevelt regarded himself as the nation's head manager. He believed it was his job to keep society operating efficiently by mediating conflicts between different groups and their interests. In the fall of 1902, he put these beliefs into practice.

The previous spring, the **United Mine Workers** (UMW) had launched a strike by the anthracite (hard coal) miners of eastern Pennsylvania. Nearly 150,000 workers walked out, demanding increased pay, reduced work hours, and union recognition. Coal prices began to rise. Roosevelt viewed it as another example of groups pursuing their private interests at the nation's expense. If the strike dragged on too long, the country would face a coal shortage that could shut down factories and leave many homes unheated.

Roosevelt urged the union and the owners to accept **arbitration**—a settlement negotiated by an outside party. The union agreed; the mine owners did not. The mine owners' stubbornness infuriated Roosevelt, as well as the public. Roosevelt threatened to order the army to run the mines. Fearful of this, the mine owners finally accepted arbitration. By intervening in the dispute, Roosevelt took the first step toward establishing the federal government as an honest broker between powerful groups in society.

Teach

S Skill Practice

Visual Literacy What is the cartoonist saying by picturing Roosevelt battling giants? *(He is facing powerful forces.)* **OL**

C Critical Thinking

Determining Cause and Effect **Ask:** Why did the mine owners finally agree to arbitration? *(Roosevelt threatened to order the army to run the mines.)* **OL**

Analyzing VISUALS

Answers:
1. Wall Street is the home of the stock market.
2. the trusts

Additional Support

Activity: Interdisciplinary Connection

Literature Have student groups select a passage from *The Jungle* to present as a reading to the class. Ask groups to select a section in which there is both description and characters speaking dialogue. Have each group select a student to be the narrator and read descriptions; assign the characters to other students. Have each group practice reading their sections clearly and with feeling. When groups are ready, have them present their readings to the class. Encourage the class to discuss their reactions to the novel. **Ask:** If you wanted to influence changes in today's society, what would you write about? **AL**

C Critical Thinking

Drawing Conclusions
Ask: When the ICC limited competition among railroads and began setting rates to ensure industry profits, was it betraying its original mission? Why or why not? *(Student responses will vary.)* **OL** **AL**

D Differentiated Instruction

Gifted and Talented Have students research early 20th century ads for patent medicines and compare them to ads for present-day medicines. How are they similar and different? **AL**

Reading Check

Answer:
Roosevelt's policies were called a "Square Deal." This term was accurate because he attempted to protect all Americans through industry regulation.

Additional Support

Regulating Big Business

Despite his lawsuit against Northern Securities and his role in the coal strike, Roosevelt believed most trusts benefited the economy and that breaking them up would do more harm than good. Instead, he proposed creating a new federal agency to investigate corporations and publicize the results. He believed the most effective way to keep big business from abusing its power was to keep the public informed.

In 1903 Roosevelt convinced Congress to create the Department of Commerce and Labor. The following year, this department began investigating U.S. Steel, a gigantic holding company that had been created in 1901. Worried about a possible antitrust lawsuit, the company's leaders met privately with Roosevelt and offered a deal. They would open their account books and records for examination. In exchange, if any problems were found, the company would be advised privately and allowed to correct them without having to go to court.

Roosevelt accepted this "gentlemen's agreement," as he called it, and soon made similar deals with other companies. These arrangements gave Roosevelt the ability to **regulate** big business without having to sacrifice economic efficiency by breaking up the trusts.

In keeping with his belief in regulation, Roosevelt pushed the **Hepburn Act** through Congress in 1906. This act was intended to strengthen the Interstate Commerce Commission (ICC) by giving it the power to set railroad rates. At first, railroad companies were suspicious of the ICC and tied up its decisions by challenging them in court. Eventually, **C** the railroads realized that they could work with the ICC to set rates and regulations that limited competition and prevented new competitors from entering the industry. Over time, the ICC became a supporter of the railroads' interests, and by 1920 it had begun setting rates at levels intended to ensure the industry's profits.

Consumer Protection

By 1905 consumer protection had become a national issue. That year, a journalist named Samuel Hopkins Adams published a series of articles in *Collier's* magazine describing the patent medicine business.

Many companies patented and marketed potions they claimed would cure a variety of ills. Many of these medicines were little more than alcohol, colored water, and sugar. Others contained caffeine, opium, cocaine, and other dangerous compounds. Consumers had no way to know what they were taking, nor did they receive any assurance that the medicines worked as claimed. Adams's articles pointed out that these supposed cures could cause health problems. The articles in *Collier's* outraged many Americans. **D**

Many Americans were equally concerned about the food they ate. Dr. W. H. Wiley, chief chemist at the United States Department of Agriculture, had issued reports documenting the dangerous preservatives being used in what he called "embalmed meat." Then, in 1906, **Upton Sinclair** published his novel *The Jungle*. Based on Sinclair's close observations of the slaughterhouses of Chicago, the powerful book featured appalling descriptions of conditions in the meatpacking industry:

PRIMARY SOURCE

"[T]here would come all the way back from Europe old sausage that had been rejected, and that was [moldy] and white—it would be dosed with borax and glycerine, and dumped into the hoppers, and made over again for home consumption. . . . There would be meat stored in great piles in rooms; and the water from leaky roofs would drip over it, and thousands of rats would race about [upon] it."

—from *The Jungle*

Sinclair's book was a best-seller. It made consumers ill—and angry. Many became vegetarians after reading the book. Roosevelt and Congress responded with the **Meat Inspection Act,** passed in 1906. It required federal inspection of meat sold through interstate commerce and required the Agriculture Department to set standards of cleanliness in meatpacking plants. The **Pure Food and Drug Act,** passed on the same day in 1906, prohibited the manufacture, sale, or shipment of impure or falsely labeled food and drugs.

Reading Check **Identifying** What term was used to describe Roosevelt's policies and how accurate was it?

Activity: Collaborative Learning

Comparing and Contrasting National Parks Divide students into small groups. Have each group research and create a guide for a national park. Guides should include a general history of the park, the park's mission, and points of interest. Ask students to include photographs of the park in their guides. Students may produce their guides as a pamphlet, slide show, or live presentation. Encourage groups to share their guides with the class. Ask students to compare the features of various parks. **Ask:** In what ways are the parks similar and different? **BL** **OL**

Analyzing Supreme Court Cases

Can Government Regulate Business Activity?

★ ***Northern Securities* v. *United States*, 1904**

Background to the Case

In 1901 three powerful businessmen, J. P. Morgan, James J. Hill, and Edward H. Harriman, created Northern Securities—a holding company that owned the majority of the stock in several major railroads. The government sued the company for violating the Sherman Antitrust Act, and a court ordered the company broken up.

How the Court Ruled

The Constitution gives the federal government the power to regulate interstate commerce—but did "commerce" mean all business activity, or just the movement of goods across state lines? The owners of Northern Securities argued that their company was a holding company set up to buy stock. It had been created legally under New Jersey law, and federal laws should not apply because the company itself did not engage in interstate commerce. In a 5-4 decision, the Court concluded that the commerce clause allows the federal government to regulate the ownership of companies.

NO MOLLY-CODDLING HERE

▲ *President Roosevelt once said "Speak softly and carry a big stick." This cartoon shows Roosevelt swinging his stick and knocking down the trusts—and everything else, as well.*

PRIMARY SOURCE

The Court's Opinion

"No state can, by merely creating a corporation . . . project its authority into other states, and across the continent, so as to prevent Congress from exerting the power it possesses under the Constitution over interstate and international commerce. . . .

. . . Every corporation created by a state is necessarily subject to the supreme law of the land. . . . In short, the court may make any order necessary to bring about the dissolution or suppression of an illegal combination that restrains interstate commerce. All this can be done without infringing in any degree upon the just authority of the states.

—Justice John Marshall Harlan, writing for the Court

PRIMARY SOURCE

Dissenting Views

"Commerce depends upon population, but Congress could not, on that ground, undertake to regulate marriage and divorce. If the act before us is to be carried out according to what seems to me the logic of the argument . . . I can see no part of the conduct of life with which . . . Congress might not interfere.

. . . This act is construed by the Government to affect the purchasers of shares in two railroad companies because of the effect it may have . . . upon the competition of these roads. If such a remote result of the exercise of an ordinary incident of property and personal freedom is enough to make that exercise unlawful, there is hardly any transaction concerning commerce between the States that may not be made a crime by the finding of a jury or a court."

—Justice Oliver Wendell Holmes, dissenting

DBQ Document-Based Questions

1. **Interpreting** How does Justice Harlan view the rights of states and the authority of Congress?
2. **Defining** How does Justice Harlan refer to the Sherman Antitrust Act?
3. **Analyzing** What does Justice Holmes fear in narrowly applying a law?

Supreme Court Cases

Teach

Five months into his presidency, Roosevelt took on the richest man in the country, J. Pierpont Morgan. Morgan was an international investment banker who made his money from the many trusts he ran. He used his wealth to support and influence politicians. When Roosevelt brought suit against his railroad company, Northern Securities, Morgan was surprised and furious. Morgan wanted to settle things quietly between himself and the president. Roosevelt said no because he believed the public interest had to be protected.

DBQ Document Based Questions

Answers:

1. The authority of Congress supercedes the rights of states.
2. as a Constitutional power
3. Congress could interfere in all areas of life.

Differentiated Instruction

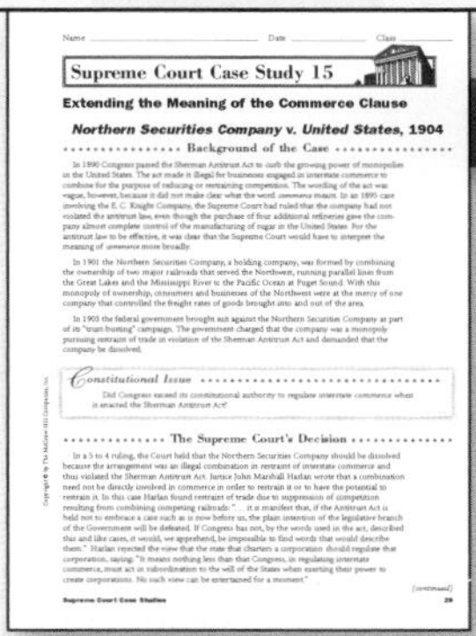
Supreme Court Case Study 15

Extending the Meaning of the Commerce Clause

Northern Securities Company v. United States, 1904

Background of the Case

Constitutional Issue

The Supreme Court's Decision

Case Study 15: *Northern Securities v. United States*, p. 29

Analyzing a Supreme Court Decision

Objective: Learn how the Constitution is applied to a Supreme Court case.

Focus: Identify the central issue of the case.

Teach: Discuss the Court's opinion.

Assess: Explain the importance of the case (broad interpretation of Congressional power).

Close: Write a paragraph summarizing the case.

Differentiated Instruction Strategies

BL Restate the constitutional issue at stake in your own words.

AL According to the decision, Congress was allowed and not allowed to take certain actions. Create a graphic organizer that details this.

ELL Explain to a partner the issue that brought the case to the Supreme Court and its resolution.

C Critical Thinking

Drawing Conclusions

Ask: How did Roosevelt's personal experience influence his environmental policies? *(As an enthusiastic outdoorsman, he placed a great value on protecting the environment.)* **OL**

W Writing Support

Persuasive Writing Write a paragraph that supports or disputes the idea that because it is in the best interest of lumber companies to conserve forests, the government should stay out of regulating forest conservation. Use facts to support your position. **OL** **AL**

Conservation

MAIN Idea New legislation gave the federal government the power to conserve natural resources.

HISTORY AND YOU Have you ever visited a national park or forest? Read on to find out how Roosevelt made some national parks and forests possible.

Roosevelt put his stamp on the presidency most clearly in the area of **environmental** conservation. Realizing that the nation's bountiful natural resources were being used up at an alarming rate, Roosevelt urged Americans to conserve those resources.

C An enthusiastic outdoorsman, Roosevelt valued the country's minerals, animals, and rugged terrain. He cautioned against unregulated exploitation of public lands and believed in conservation to manage the nation's resources. Roosevelt argued that the government must distinguish "between the man who skins the land and the man who develops the country. I am going to work with, and only with, the man who develops the country."

Western Land Development

Roosevelt quickly applied his philosophy in the dry Western states, where farmers and city dwellers competed for scarce water. In 1902 Roosevelt supported passage of the Newlands Reclamation Act, authorizing the use of federal funds from public land sales to pay for irrigation and land development projects. The federal government thus began transforming the West's landscape and economy on a large scale.

Gifford Pinchot

Roosevelt also backed efforts to save the nation's forests through careful management of the timber resources of the West. He appointed his close friend **Gifford Pinchot** to head the United States Forest Service established in 1905. "The natural resources," Pinchot said, "must be developed and preserved for the benefit of the many and not merely for the profit of a few."

As progressives, Roosevelt and Pinchot both believed that trained experts in forestry and resource management should apply the same scientific standards to the landscape that others were applying to managing cities and industry. They rejected the laissez-faire argument that the best way to preserve public land was to sell it to lumber companies, who would then carefully conserve it because it was the source of their profits. With the president's **W** support, Pinchot's department drew up regulations controlling lumbering on federal lands. Roosevelt also added over 100 million acres to the protected national forests and established five new national parks and 51 federal wildlife reservations.

Roosevelt's Legacy

President Theodore Roosevelt changed the role of the federal government and the nature of the presidency. He used his power in the

Debates IN HISTORY

Should Resources Be Preserved?

The origins of the environmentalist movement can be traced back to the Progressive Era. Then, as now, people disagreed over the best approach to the environment. Their disagreements were represented in the differing views of John Muir, founder of the Sierra Club, who worked with Roosevelt to create Yosemite National Park, and Gifford Pinchot, head of the U.S. Forest Service under Theodore Roosevelt. Muir was a preservationist, hoping that wild places could be left as they were. Pinchot was a conservationist who believed in managing the use of land for the benefit of the nation's citizens.

Differentiated Instruction

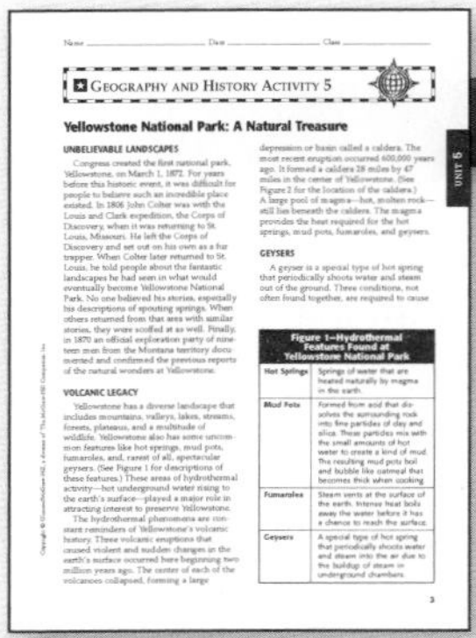
Geography and History Activity 5
Yellowstone National Park: A Natural Treasure

Geography and History Activity, URB p. 3

Yellowstone National Park: A Natural Treasure

Objective: Understand a result of the conservation movement.

Focus: Describe the features of Yellowstone National Park and why it has been preserved.

Teach: Explain how Yellowstone National Park set a precedent for future national parks.

Assess: Explain why conservation is important.

Close: Cite other examples of "national treasures."

Differentiated Instruction Strategies

- **BL** Research to find or draw diagrams of the hydrothermal features found at Yellowstone National Park.
- **AL** Describe a scenario in which Yellowstone is not a national park.
- **ELL** Research to find a "Did You Know" fun fact about Yellowstone National Park.

White House to present his views, calling it his "bully pulpit." Increasingly, Americans began looking to the federal government to solve the nation's economic and social problems.

R Under Roosevelt, the power of the executive branch of government had dramatically increased. The Hepburn Act gave the Interstate Commerce Commission the power to set rates, the Meat Inspection Act stated that the Agriculture Department could inspect food, the Department of Commerce and Labor could monitor business, the Bureau of Corporations could investigate corporations and issue reports, and the attorney general could rapidly bring antitrust lawsuits under the Expedition Act.

Reading Check **Examining** How did Roosevelt's policies help the conservation of natural resources?

Taft's Reforms

MAIN Idea William Howard Taft broke with progressives on tariff and conservation issues.

HISTORY AND YOU Have you ever been judged in comparison with the accomplishments of a sibling or friend? Read on to learn how Taft had to deal with comparisons with Roosevelt.

Roosevelt believed William Howard Taft to be the ideal person to continue his policies. Taft had worked closely with Roosevelt. He had served as a judge, as governor of the Philippines, and as Roosevelt's secretary of war. Taft easily received his party's nomination. His victory in the general election in November 1908 was a foregone conclusion. The Democratic candidate, William Jennings Bryan, lost for a third time.

YES

John Muir
Sierra Club Founder

PRIMARY SOURCE

"The making of gardens and parks goes on with civilization all over the world, and they increase both in size and number as their value is recognized.

Everybody needs beauty as well as bread, places to play in and pray in, where Nature may heal and cheer and give strength to body and soul alike. . . . Nevertheless, like anything else worth while . . . they have always been subject to attack by despoiling gainseekers . . . eagerly trying to make everything immediately and selfishly commercial, with schemes disguised in smug-smiling philanthropy, industriously, shampiously crying, 'Conservation, conservation, panutilization,' that man and beast may be fed and the dear Nation made great."

—from *The Yosemite*

NO

Gifford Pinchot
Chief of U.S. Forest Service

PRIMARY SOURCE

"The first principle of conservation is development, the use of the natural resources now existing on this continent for the benefit of the people who live here now. There may be just as much waste in neglecting the development and use of certain natural resources as there is in their destruction. . . .

Conservation stands emphatically for the development and use of water-power now, without delay. It stands for the immediate construction of navigable waterways . . . as assistants to the railroads. . . .

In addition . . . natural resources must be developed and preserved for the benefit of the many, and not merely for the profit of the few."

—from *The Fight for Conservation*

DBQ Document-Based Questions

1. **Contrasting** How do the two men differ in their views about nature?
2. **Making Connections** Which view do you think is more common today? Why do you think so?
3. **Speculating** Which viewpoint do you think was more likely to be held by ranchers and farmers in California in the early twentieth century?

R Reading Strategy

Monitoring Ask: During Roosevelt's presidency, which bureau was charged with inspecting food? *(the Agriculture Department)* BL

Reading Check

Answer:
He regulated use of public lands and supported conservation acts such as the Newlands Reclamation Act.

Debates IN HISTORY

Answers:
1. Muir believed that wild places should be left as they are. Pinchot believed in managing the use of land to benefit citizens.
2. Students should back up their positions.
3. Most students will say that ranchers and farmers would likely support the idea of managing natural resources because their livelihoods depended on access to land and water.

Additional Support

Extending the Content

Conservationists Gifford Pinchot and John Muir were friends who shared a love of nature. But their friendship ended in a bitter disagreement over Yosemite National Park in the Sierra Nevada mountains of California.

The dispute focused on the desire of some to dam a river in the park to supply drinking water for San Francisco, California. Muir argued that it was the right of all Americans to enjoy the undisturbed beauty of nature. Pinchot felt that natural resources should be used wisely to meet the needs of people. In 1913 Congress decided the issue by passing the Raker Act, which allowed the dam to be built.

R Reading Strategy

Determining Importance

Ask: What did progressives suspect when Ballinger attempted to make public forests and mineral reserves available for private development? *(He was more loyal to business than to a progressive agenda.)* **OL**

Analyzing VISUALS

Answers:

1. One of the boys is barefoot.
2. Student answers will vary but might include that people felt sorry for the boy and wanted to make sure the same thing did not happen to others.

PRIMARY SOURCE

Campaigning Against Child Labor

In 1900, 18 percent of children were employed. Mary Harris Jones, "Mother" Jones, as she was called, campaigned against child labor. After working with children in an Alabama cotton mill, she wrote, "Little girls and boys . . . reaching thin little hands into the machinery to repair snapped threads. They replaced spindles all day long; all night through . . . six-year-olds with faces of sixty did an eight-hour shift for ten cents a day . . ."

Using posters like the one shown at right to build public support, the campaign against child labor made steady progress. Between 1880 and 1910, 36 states passed laws on the minimum age for manufacturing workers.

▲ *At a Georgia cotton mill in 1909, two boys keep a spinning machine running by repairing broken thread and replacing bobbins as they are filled.*

Analyzing VISUALS

1. **Analyzing** What in the photo indicates that the children could easily be injured?
2. **Hypothesizing** What effect do you think the images on the inset poster may have had on people in the early 1900s?

The Payne-Aldrich Tariff

Like many progressives, Taft believed high tariffs limited competition, hurt consumers, and protected trusts. Roosevelt had warned him to stay away from tariff reform because it would divide the Republican Party. Taft, however, called Congress into special session to lower tariff rates.

As Roosevelt predicted, the tariff debate divided progressives, who favored tariff reduction, and conservative Republicans who wanted to maintain high tariffs. In the prolonged negotiations on the bill, Taft's support for tariff reductions wavered, and then collapsed. In the end, Taft signed into law the Payne-Aldrich Tariff, which cut tariffs hardly at all and actually raised them on some goods.

Progressives felt outraged by Taft's decision: "I knew the fire had gone out of [the progressive movement]," recalled the head of the U.S. Forest Service, Gifford Pinchot, after Roosevelt left office. "Washington was a dead town. Its leader was gone, and in his place [was] a man whose fundamental desire was to keep out of trouble."

Ballinger Versus Pinchot

With Taft's standing among Republican progressives deteriorating, a sensational controversy broke out late in 1909 that helped permanently destroy Taft's popularity with reformers. Many progressives were unhappy when Taft replaced Roosevelt's secretary of the interior, James R. Garfield, an aggressive conservationist, with **Richard A. Ballinger,** a more conservative corporate lawyer. Suspicion of Ballinger grew when he tried to make nearly a million acres of public forests and mineral reserves available for private development.

In the midst of this mounting concern, Gifford Pinchot charged the new secretary with having once plotted to turn over valuable public lands in Alaska to a private business group for personal profit. Taft's attorney general investigated the charges and decided they R

Hands-On Chapter Project Step 2

Learning how Government Affects People's Lives

Step 2: Create a Conservation Poster To reinforce the ways in which government's conservation efforts affect people's lives, each student will choose a conserved area of the country, such as Yellowstone National Park (or a local one), and create an annotated poster.

Directions Have students use library or Internet resources to trace or copy a map of their chosen conserved area. They will then draw or paste pictures of the plant and animal life it protects, and any recreation it provides.

Analyzing Special-Purpose Maps In a box on the poster, students should add and complete these bulleted items: Date Preserved, Reason for Preservation (value to society), Conservation Authority (legislation or other action that protected the area), and Recent Action (efforts to expand or develop the site, legal action, and so on). Display the posters in the classroom or somewhere else in the school. **OL**

(Project continued on page 537)

R were groundless. Not satisfied, Pinchot leaked the story to the press and asked Congress to investigate. Taft fired Pinchot for **insubordination,** or disobedience to authority. The congressional investigation cleared Ballinger.

By the second half of his term of office, many Americans believed that Taft had "sold the Square Deal down the river." Popular indignation was so great that the congressional elections of 1910 resulted in a sweeping Democratic victory, with Democrats taking the majority in the House, and Democrats and progressive Republicans grabbing control of the Senate from conservative Republicans.

Taft's Achievements

Despite his political problems, Taft also had several successes. Although Roosevelt was nicknamed the "trustbuster," Taft was a strong opponent of monopoly and actually brought twice as many antitrust cases in four years as his predecessor had in seven. In other areas, too, Taft pursued progressive policies. Taft established the **Children's Bureau** in 1912, an agency that investigated and publicized the problems of child labor. The agency exists today, and deals with issues such as child abuse prevention, adoption, and foster care.

The Ballinger-Pinchot controversy aside, Taft was also a dedicated conservationist. His contributions in this area actually equaled or surpassed those of Roosevelt. He set up the Bureau of Mines in 1910 to monitor the activities of mining companies, expand the national forests, and protect waterpower sites from private development. Most of the new and emerging technologies in the minerals field were partly made possible by the existence of the Bureau of Mines.

After Taft took office in 1909, Roosevelt left for a big-game hunt in Africa, followed by a tour of Europe. He did not return to the United States until June 1910. Although disturbed by stories of Taft's "betrayal" of progressivism, Roosevelt at first refused to criticize the president.

In October 1911 Taft announced an antitrust lawsuit against U.S. Steel, claiming that the company's decision to buy the Tennessee Coal and Iron Company in 1907 had violated the Sherman Antitrust Act. The lawsuit was the final straw for Roosevelt. As president, he had approved U.S. Steel's plan to buy the company.

Roosevelt believed Taft's focus on breaking up trusts was destroying the carefully crafted system of cooperation and regulation that Roosevelt had established with big business. In November 1911 Roosevelt publicly criticized Taft's decision. Roosevelt argued that the best way to deal with the trusts was to allow them to exist while continuing to regulate them.

After Roosevelt broke with Taft, it was only a matter of time before progressives convinced him to reenter politics. In late February 1912, Roosevelt announced that he would enter the presidential campaign of 1912 and attempt to replace Taft as the Republican nominee for president.

Reading Check **Evaluating** How did Taft's accomplishments regarding conservation and trust-busting compare to Roosevelt's?

Section 2 REVIEW

Vocabulary

1. **Explain** the significance of: Square Deal, Social Darwinism, United Mine Workers, arbitration, Hepburn Act, Upton Sinclair, Meat Inspection Act, Pure Food and Drug Act, Gifford Pinchot, Richard A. Ballinger, insubordination, Children's Bureau.

Main Ideas

2. **Explaining** What was the intent of the Hepburn Act?
3. **Describing** How did Roosevelt's policies change the Western landscape?
4. **Discussing** How did Taft help conservation efforts and child labor problems?

Critical Thinking

5. **Big Ideas** How did Upton Sinclair contribute to involving the federal government in protecting consumers?
6. **Organizing** Use a graphic organizer to list Taft's progressive reforms.

Taft's Progressive Reforms

7. **Analyzing Visuals** Study the photo on page 534. Could this photo be used to rally the cause against child labor? Explain the dangerous elements of the job.

Writing About History

8. **Expository Writing** Suppose that you are living in the early 1900s and have just read Sinclair's *The Jungle*. Write a letter to a friend summarizing the plot and how it characterizes the Progressive Era.

History ONLINE
Study Central™ To review this section, go to glencoe.com and click on Study Central.

R Reading Strategy

Academic Vocabulary Have students demonstrate their understanding of the word *insubordination* by using it correctly in a sentence. OL

Reading Check

Answer:
Taft brought more antitrust cases than Roosevelt, and his conservation efforts at least equaled those of Roosevelt.

Assess

History ONLINE

Study Central™ provides summaries, interactive games, and online graphic organizers to help students review content.

Close

Summarizing Ask: What was the response of progressives to presidents Roosevelt and Taft? *(Roosevelt was very popular with progressives. Taft was not popular with progressives despite his accomplishments regarding antitrust and conservation.)* OL

Section 2 REVIEW

Answers

1. Definitions for the vocabulary terms are found in the section and the Glossary.
2. It was intended to strengthen the Interstate Commerce Commission by giving it the authority to set railroad rates.
3. Roosevelt supported passage of the Newland Reclamation Act, which authorized use of federal funds from sale of public lands for irrigation and land development projects.
4. Taft set up the Bureau of Mines to monitor mining companies, expanded national forests, and protected waterpower sites. He established the Children's Bureau to investigate and publicize problems of child labor.
5. He wrote a novel about the meatpacking industry called *The Jungle*. It publicized disgusting industry practices.
6. Taft's Progressive Reforms: Children's Bureau, Bureau of Mines, antitrust lawsuit against U.S. Steel
7. This photo could be used to rally against child labor. Children could easily get hurt on the job because their small hands were used to fix machines. Also, child laborers worked long hours with little pay.
8. Writing will vary but should explain that Sinclair's investigation of the meatpacking industry spurred people to work for change.

Focus

Bellringer

Daily Focus Transparency 15-3

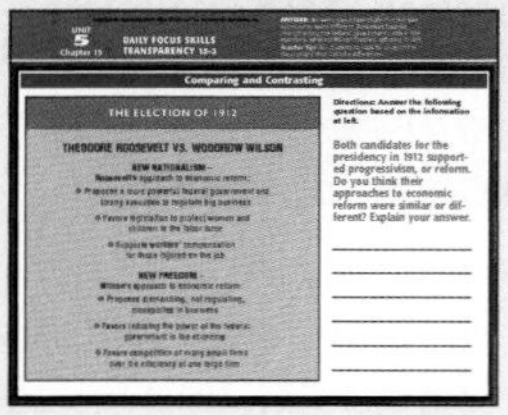

Guide to Reading

Answers:

Economic Reforms

Lowered tariffs

Taxed earnings

Established federal reserve system

Created Federal Trade Commission

Social Reforms

Attempted to regulate child labor

Established 8-hour day for railroad workers

Provided farmers with low-interest loans

Section Spotlight Video

To generate student interest and provide a springboard for discussion, access the Chapter 15, Section 3 video at glencoe.com or on the video DVD.

Section 3

Section Audio | Spotlight Video

The Wilson Years

Guide to Reading

Big Ideas

Individual Action Woodrow Wilson increased the control of the government over business.

Content Vocabulary

- income tax *(p. 538)*
- unfair trade practices *(p. 539)*

Academic Vocabulary

- academic *(p. 536)*
- unconstitutional *(p. 540)*

People and Events to Identify

- Progressive Party *(p. 536)*
- New Nationalism *(p. 537)*
- New Freedom *(p. 537)*
- Federal Reserve Act *(p. 539)*
- Federal Trade Commission *(p. 539)*
- Clayton Antitrust Act *(p. 539)*
- National Association for the Advancement of Colored People *(p. 541)*

Reading Strategy

Organizing As you read about progressivism during the Wilson administration, complete a chart similar to the one below by listing Wilson's progressive economic and social reforms.

Economic Reforms	Social Reforms

Woodrow Wilson, a progressive Democrat, won the election of 1912. While in office, he supported lower tariffs, more regulation of business, and creation of a federal reserve banking system.

The Election of 1912

MAIN Idea Woodrow Wilson was elected after Republican voters split between Taft and Roosevelt.

HISTORY AND YOU Do you remember a catchy slogan from a political campaign? Read about the competing slogans and platforms in the 1912 election.

The 1912 presidential campaign featured a current president, a former president, and an **academic** who had entered politics only two years earlier. The election's outcome determined the path of the Progressive movement.

Picking the Candidates

Believing that President Taft had failed to live up to progressive ideals, Theodore Roosevelt informed seven state governors that he was willing to accept the Republican nomination. "My hat is in the ring!" he declared. "The fight is on."

The struggle for control of the Republican Party reached its climax at the national convention in Chicago in June 1912. Conservatives rallied behind Taft. Most of the progressives supported Roosevelt. When it became clear that Taft's delegates controlled the nomination, Roosevelt decided to leave the party and campaign as an independent.

Declaring himself "fit as a bull moose," Roosevelt became the presidential candidate for the newly formed **Progressive Party,** which quickly became known as the Bull Moose Party. Because Taft had alienated so many groups, the election of 1912 became a contest between two progressives: Roosevelt and the Democratic candidate, Woodrow Wilson.

After a university teaching career that ended in his becoming the president of Princeton University, Woodrow Wilson entered politics as a firm progressive. As governor of New Jersey, he pushed through one progressive reform after another. He signed laws that introduced the direct primary, established utility regulatory boards, and allowed cities to adopt the commissioner form of government. In less than two years, New Jersey became a model of progressive reform.

Resource Manager

R Reading Strategies	C Critical Thinking	D Differentiated Instruction	W Writing Support	S Skill Practice
Teacher Edition • Skimming, p. 538 • Monitoring, p. 539 • Identifying, p. 540 **Additional Resources** • Guided Reading, URB p. 80	**Teacher Edition** • Det. Cause/Effect p. 538 **Additional Resources** • Quizzes and Tests, p. 213	**Teacher Edition** • Gifted/Talented p. 539 **Additional Resources** • Enrich. Act., URB p. 75 • Amer. Art/Music, URB p. 69 • Authentic Assessment, p. 35 • Reteaching Act., URB p. 73	**Teacher Edition** • Expository Writing p. 541	**Teacher Edition** • Reading a Chart, p. 537 **Additional Resources** • Read Essen., p. 171

PRIMARY SOURCE

New Nationalism Versus New Freedom

Presidential Election of 1912

Presidential Candidate	Popular Votes	% of Popular Vote	Electoral Votes
Wilson	6,293,454	41.86%	435
Roosevelt	4,119,207	27.40%	88
Taft	3,483,922	23.17%	8

*Eleven voters in California voted for Roosevelt and two for Wilson.

WILSON'S NEW FREEDOM

"I am perfectly willing that [a business] should beat any competitor by fair means . . . But there must be no squeezing out the beginner . . . no secret arrangements against him. All the fair competition you choose, but no unfair competition of any kind. . . . A trust is an arrangement to get rid of competition. . . . A trust does not bring efficiency . . . it *buys efficiency out of business*. I am for big business, and I am against the trusts . . . any man who can put others out of business by making the thing cheaper to the consumer . . . I take off my hat to . . ."

—from *The New Freedom*

ROOSEVELT'S NEW NATIONALISM

"Combinations in industry [trusts] are the result of an imperative economic law which cannot be repealed by political legislation. . . . The way out lies, not in attempting to prevent such combinations, but in completely controlling them in the interest of the public welfare. . . . The absence of an effective state, and, especially national, restraint upon unfair money getting has tended to create a small class of enormously wealthy and economically powerful men. . . . The prime need is to change the conditions which enable these men to accumulate power."

—from *The New Nationalism*

DBQ Document-Based Questions

1. **Analyzing Visuals** From which state did Roosevelt gain the most Electoral College votes?
2. **Analyzing Primary Sources** How do Wilson and Roosevelt differ on trusts?
3. **Making Generalizations** What can you generalize about the two men based solely on their appearance in giving a speech?

Maps In MOtion See *StudentWorks™ Plus* or glencoe.com.

Wilson Versus Roosevelt

The election of 1912 was a contest between two progressives with different approaches to reform. Roosevelt accepted the large trusts as a fact of life and set out proposals to increase regulation. Roosevelt also outlined a complete program of reforms. He favored legislation to protect women and children in the labor force and supported workers' compensation for those injured on the job. Roosevelt called his program the **New Nationalism.**

Wilson countered with what he called the **New Freedom.** He criticized Roosevelt's New Nationalism for supporting "regulated monopoly." Monopolies, he believed, should be destroyed, not regulated. Wilson argued that Roosevelt's approach gave the federal government too much power in the economy and did nothing to restore competition. Freedom, in Wilson's opinion, was more important than efficiency. "The history of liberty," Wilson declared, "is the history of the limitation of governmental power. . . . If America is not to have free enterprise, then she can have freedom of no sort whatever."

As expected, Roosevelt and Taft split the Republican voters, enabling Wilson to win the Electoral College with 435 votes and the election, even though he received less than 42 percent of the popular vote.

Reading Check **Summarizing** Who were the major candidates in the election of 1912?

Teach

S Skill Practice

Reading a Chart Ask: Did most of the electorate vote for Woodrow Wilson or for other candidates? *(Though Wilson received the most votes [6,294,345 votes], most of the electorate voted for the other two candidates [a total of 7,603,129 votes])* **BL** **OL**

DBQ Document Based Questions

Answers:

1. Pennsylvania
2. Wilson is completely against trusts; Roosevelt wants to control them.
3. Wilson is more reserved while Roosevelt is larger than life.

Reading Check

Summarizing
William Howard Taft, Theodore Roosevelt, and Woodrow Wilson

Hands-On Chapter Project Step 3

Learning how Government Affects People's Lives

Step 3: Presentations Students will work in groups to present the community problem they researched or their conservation posters.

Directions Have students work together as a team to present a community problem and its resolution to the class. Students may also choose to present their conservation posters.

Representing Information Give students time to prepare for their presentations. They may role play or use media other than their posters to present the information. Encourage students to state the topic clearly, describe it, and summarize the information. **OL**

(Project continued on the Visual Summary page)

R Reading Strategy

Skimming Have students glance at the text under the heading "Wilson's Reforms." **Ask:** About what key issues do you expect to learn? *(tariff and tax reform)* **BL**

C Critical Thinking

Determining Cause and Effect Ask: What effect did Wilson believe lowering tariffs would produce? *(improved products and lower prices)* **OL**

Wilson's Reforms

MAIN Idea President Wilson reformed tariffs and banks and oversaw the creation of the Federal Trade Commission.

HISTORY AND YOU Are you aware of recent economic concerns and presidential responses to them? Read to learn of Wilson's economic actions after his election.

R The new chief executive lost no time in embarking on his program of reform. "The president is at liberty, both in law and conscience, to be as big a man as he can," Wilson had once written. "His capacity will set the limit." During his eight years as president, Wilson demonstrated his executive power as he crafted reforms affecting tariffs, the banking system, trusts, and workers' rights.

Reforming Tariffs

Five weeks after taking office, Wilson appeared before Congress, the first president to do so since John Adams. He had come to present his bill to reduce tariffs. Wilson personally lobbied members of Congress to support the tariff reduction bill. Not even Roosevelt had taken such an active role in promoting legislation.

Wilson believed that lowering tariffs would benefit both American consumers and manufacturers. If tariff rates were lowered, he reasoned, the pressure of foreign competition would lead American manufacturers to improve their products and lower their prices. In the long term, businesses would benefit from the "constant necessity to be efficient, economical, and enterprising." C

In 1913 Congress passed the Underwood Tariff, and Wilson signed it into law. This law reduced the average tariff on imported goods to about 30 percent of the value of the goods, or about half the tariff rate of the 1890s.

An important section of the Underwood Tariff Act provided for levying an **income tax,** or a direct tax on the earnings of individuals. The Constitution originally prohibited direct taxes on individuals. Ratification of the Sixteenth Amendment in 1913, however, gave the federal government the power to tax the income of individuals directly.

INFOGRAPHIC

Progressives Reform the Economic System

During Wilson's presidency, Congress passed several major reforms affecting the nation's economy. The Federal Reserve and the Federal Trade Commission were created, federal income tax was introduced, and unions were legalized.

The Federal Reserve

Why Was the Federal Reserve Created?
- to create national supervision of the banking industry
- to decentralize banking institutions and access to credit
- to prevent recurring "panics," such as the Panic of 1907
- to allow the demands of business to control the expanding and contracting of currency

What Does the Federal Reserve Do?
- controls the money supply and credit policies
- raises interest rates to member banks in times of plenty so that people won't borrow or spend too much money
- lowers interest rates to member banks during recessions so that people can more easily obtain needed credit
- supervises and supports Federal Reserve banks in twelve regions
- buys and sells government bonds and other securities

NATIONAL GEOGRAPHIC **Federal Reserve System**

Activity: Economics Connection

Analyzing the Federal Reserve Have students find a current news article about the Federal Reserve. Ask them to write a brief summary of the news story. Then have students list actions taken by the Federal Reserve in the news story. Have students match those actions with the functions of the Federal Reserve listed in the infographic "Progressives Reform the Economic System." Encourage volunteers to share their summaries and action lists. **Ask:** What are the intended consequences of the actions taken by the Federal Reserve? **OL AL**

Additional Support

Reforming the Banks

The United States had not had a central bank since the 1830s. During the economic depressions that hit the country periodically after that time, hundreds of small banks collapsed, wiping out the life savings of many of their customers.

R To restore public confidence in the banking system, President Wilson supported the establishment of a federal reserve system. Banks would have to keep a portion of their deposits in a regional reserve bank, which would provide a financial cushion against unanticipated losses. The **Federal Reserve Act** of 1913 created 12 regional banks to be supervised by a Board of Governors, appointed by the president. This allowed national supervision of the banking system. The Board could set the interest rates the reserve banks charged other banks, thereby indirectly controlling the interest rates of the entire nation and the amount of money in circulation. The Federal Reserve Act became one of the most significant pieces of legislation in American history.

Other Reforms

Why Was the Federal Trade Commission Created?

- to advise business people on the legality of their actions
- to protect consumers from false advertising
- to investigate unfair trade practices

What Was the Clayton Antitrust Act?

- outlawed unfair trade practices
- made it illegal for a company to hold stock in another, if by doing so, it reduced competition
- made owners and directors of businesses guilty of violating antitrust laws criminally liable
- allowed private parties who had been injured by trusts to collect any damages in legal suits
- banned use of injunctions against strikes
- farm and labor organizations could no longer be considered illegal combinations in restraint of trade

Analyzing VISUALS

1. **Analyzing** What do the Federal Trade Commission and the Clayton Antitrust Act have in common?
2. **Identifying** What do you notice about the Western states and the locations of the Federal Reserve Banks? Why do you think this pattern exists?

Antitrust Action

During his campaign, Wilson had promised to restore competition to the economy by breaking up monopolies. Roosevelt had argued this was unrealistic, because big businesses were more efficient and unlikely to be replaced by smaller, more competitive firms. Once in office, Wilson's opinion shifted and he came to agree with Roosevelt. Progressives in Congress, however, continued to demand action against big business.

In the summer of 1914, at Wilson's request, Congress created the **Federal Trade Commission** (FTC) to monitor American business. The FTC had the power to investigate companies and issue "cease and desist" orders against companies engaging in **unfair trade practices,** or those that hurt competition. The FTC could be taken to court if a business disagreed with its rulings.

Wilson did not want the FTC to break up big business. Instead, it was to work toward limiting business activities that unfairly limited competition. He deliberately appointed conservative business leaders to serve as the FTC's first commissioners.

D Unsatisfied by Wilson's approach, progressives in Congress responded by passing the **Clayton Antitrust Act** in 1914. The act outlawed certain practices that restricted competition. For example, it forbade agreements that required retailers who bought from one company to stop selling a competitor's products. It also banned price discrimination. Businesses could not charge different customers different prices. Manufacturers could no longer give discounts to some retailers who bought a large volume of goods, but not to others. Farm and labor organizations could no longer be considered illegal combinations in restraint of trade. The passing of the Clayton Antitrust Act corrected deficiencies in the Sherman Antitrust Act of 1890, which was the first federal antitrust law.

Before the Clayton act passed, labor unions lobbied Congress to exempt unions from antitrust legislation. The Clayton Antitrust Act specifically declared that its provisions did not apply to labor organizations or agricultural organizations. When the bill became law, Samuel Gompers, the head of the American Federation of Labor, called the act the workers' "Magna Carta" because it gave unions the right to exist.

R Reading Strategy

Monitoring Ask: Why did the Federal Reserve Act require banks to keep a portion of their deposits in a regional reserve bank? *(to provide a financial cushion against unanticipated losses)* BL OL

D Differentiated Instruction

Gifted and Talented Have students research the Clayton Antitrust Act and the Sherman Antitrust Act and list their similarities and differences. AL

Analyzing VISUALS

Answers:

1. They regulate big business to promote fair competition.
2. There are fewer Federal Reserve Banks in the West (District 12) because the West had a smaller population.

Additional Support

Activity: Collaborative Learning

Locating Information Tell students that Samuel Gompers was one of the founders of the American Federation of Labor. Gompers was also active in the effort to persuade Congress to exempt unions from antitrust legislation. Break the class up into groups and have them research Gompers' life. Assign groups areas of research including: Gompers' early life, his work with the Cigar Makers' Union, formation of the American Federation of Labor, his political involvement with the Democratic Party, and his death and legacy. Have groups prepare a short report from their research and present it to the class. OL AL

R Reading Strategy

Identifying Ask: Why did the Supreme Court declare the Keating-Owen Child Labor Act unconstitutional? *(Child labor was not interstate commerce and therefore only states could regulate it.)* BL OL

Reading Check

Answer:
The Sixteenth Amendment made it legal for the federal government to directly tax individual income.

DBQ Document Based Questions

Answers:
1. The magazine took the name "The Crisis" to reflect that it was a critical time in history.
2. One of peace and goodwill among all races

Regulating Business

Despite his accomplishments, Wilson was not guaranteed reelection. In the congressional elections of 1914, Democrats suffered major losses. The Republican Party was also not likely to be divided as it had been in the election of 1912.

In 1916 Wilson signed the first federal law regulating child labor. The Keating-Owen Child Labor Act prohibited the employment of children under the age of 14 in factories producing goods for interstate commerce. In 1918 R the Supreme Court declared the law **unconstitutional** on the grounds that child labor was not interstate commerce and therefore only states could regulate it. Wilson's effort, however, helped his reputation with progressive voters. Wilson also supported the Adamson Act, which established the eight-hour workday for railroad workers, and the Federal Farm Loan Act, which helped provide farmers with loans at low interest rates.

Reading Check **Evaluating** What was the impact of the passage of the Sixteenth Amendment?

Progressivism's Legacy and Limits

MAIN Idea Progressivism changed many people's ideas about the government's role in social issues.

HISTORY AND YOU Do you believe that groups of people have been left out of "the American dream"? Read on to find out about progressivism's failures and successes.

During his presidency, Wilson had built upon Roosevelt's foundation. He expanded the role of the federal government and the power of the president.

A New Kind of Government

Progressivism made important changes in the political life of the United States. Before this era, most Americans did not expect the government to pass laws protecting workers or regulating big business. In fact, many courts had previously ruled the passage of such laws unconstitutional.

PRIMARY SOURCE

Founding of the NAACP

W.E.B. Du Bois was one of six founders of the NAACP. In *The Crisis*, the journal of the NAACP, Du Bois wrote:

PRIMARY SOURCE

"The object of this publication is to set forth those facts and arguments which show the danger of race prejudice. . . . It takes its name from the fact that the editors believe that this is a critical time in the history. . . . Catholicity and tolerance, reason and forbearance can today make the world-old dream of human brotherhood approach realization: while bigotry and prejudice, emphasized race consciousness and force can repeat the awful history of the contact of nations and groups in the past. We strive for this higher and broader vision of Peace and Good Will."

—from *The Crisis*, November 1910

▲ *W.E.B. Du Bois works with his staff in the office of* The Crisis.

▲ *The first issue of* The Crisis, *November 1910*

DBQ Document-Based Questions

1. **Analyzing** According to Du Bois, why was the magazine given its name?
2. **Analyzing Primary Sources** What "vision" does Du Bois recommend to his readers?

Differentiated Instruction

Leveled Activities

BL Reading Skills Activity, URB p. 51

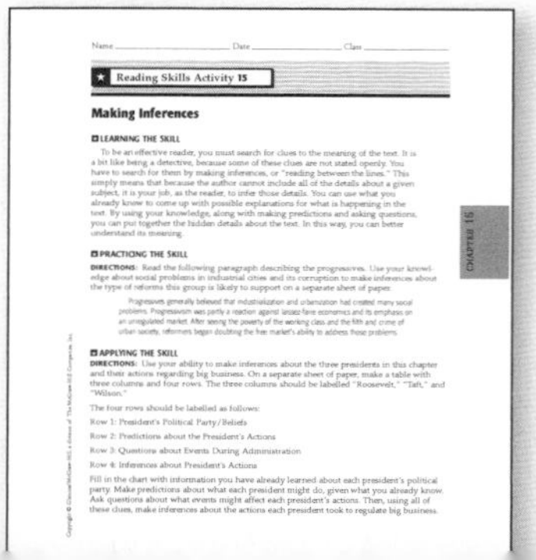

OL American Literature Reading, URB pp. 13–14

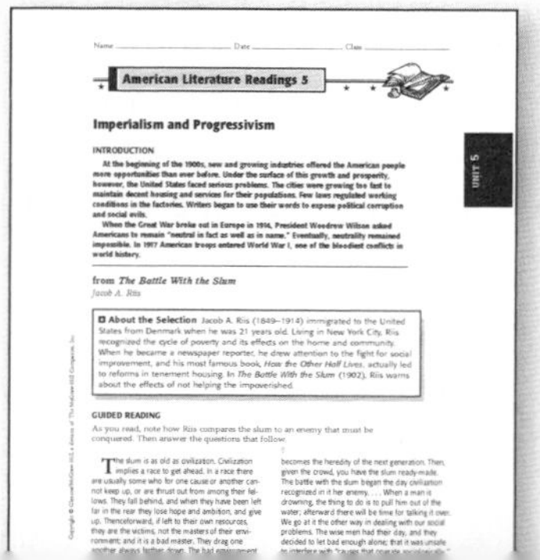

AL Economics and History Activity, URB pp. 7–8

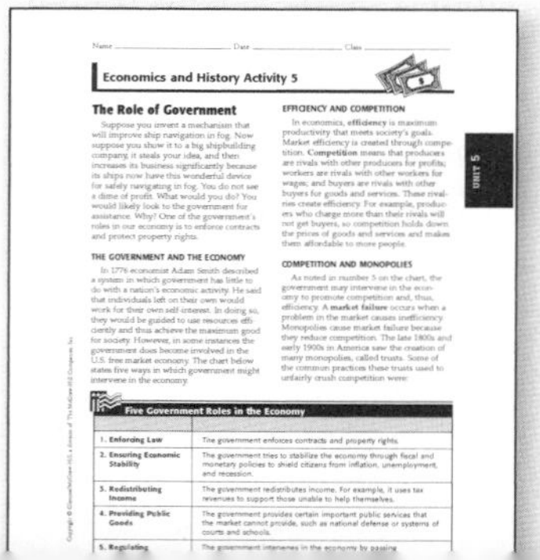

ELL English Learner Activity, URB pp. 55–56

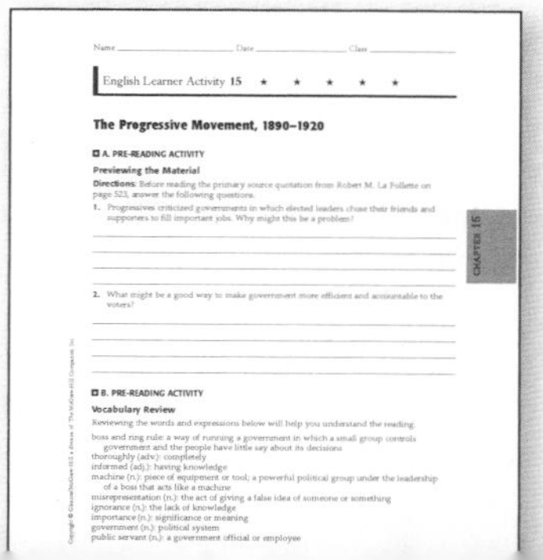

By the end of the Progressive Era, however, both legal and public opinion had shifted. Increasingly, Americans expected the government, particularly the federal government, to play a more active role in regulating the economy and solving social problems.

The Limits of Progressivism

The most conspicuous limit to progressivism was its failure to address racial and religious discrimination. African Americans themselves, however, were absorbing the reform spirit, which fueled their longstanding desire for advancement.

In 1905 W.E.B. Du Bois and 28 other African American leaders met at Niagara Falls to demand full rights for African Americans. They met on the Canadian side of the falls because no hotel on the American side would accept them. There, they launched what became known as the Niagara Movement. This meeting was one of many steps leading to the founding of the **National Association for the Advancement of Colored People** (NAACP) in 1909. Du Bois and other NAACP founders believed that voting rights were essential to end lynching and racial discrimination. "The power of the ballot we need in sheer self-defense," Du Bois said, "else what shall save us from a second slavery? Freedom too, the long-sought we still seek,—the freedom of life and limb, the freedom to work and think, the freedom to love and aspire. Work, culture, liberty,—all these we need, not singly, but together."

In 1908 race riots in Springfield, Illinois, shocked many people, including Mary White Ovington, a settlement house worker. She had been studying African Americans in New York, determined to do something to improve their situation. Other progressives, including Jane Addams of Hull House, and muckrakers Ida Wells-Barnett and Lincoln Steffens, joined Ovington in calling for change. Capitalizing on Springfield as Lincoln's hometown and his centennial birthday on February 12, 1909, they organized a national conference to take stock of the progress in emancipation. At a second conference the following year, the NAACP was born. Through Du Bois, the members learned of the Niagara Movement, and the two groups eventually merged.

W

African Americans were not the only minority group facing discrimination. Jewish people also lived in fear of mob violence. In 1913 Leo Frank, a Jew being tried in Atlanta for a murder he did not commit, was sentenced to death. Although his sentence was changed to life imprisonment, a mob lynched him two years later.

In this context, lawyer Sigmund Livingston started the Anti-Defamation League (ADL) to combat stereotypes and discrimination. The ADL worked to remove negative portrayals of Jews in movies, in print, and on stage. For example, the League protested an army manual published during World War I that targeted Jews as likely to pretend to be sick to escape work or battle. When the ADL complained, President Wilson had the manual recalled.

✓ Reading Check **Evaluating** How did progressivism change American beliefs about the federal government?

Section 3 REVIEW

Vocabulary

1. **Explain** the significance of: Progressive Party, New Nationalism, New Freedom, income tax, Federal Reserve Act, Federal Trade Commission, unfair trade practices, Clayton Antitrust Act, National Association for the Advancement of Colored People.

Main Ideas

2. **Discussing** Explain how Wilson won the presidency without winning the popular vote.
3. **Identifying** Why did Wilson propose the Federal Reserve system?
4. **Organizing** Use a graphic organizer similar to the one below to list the effects progressivism had on American society.

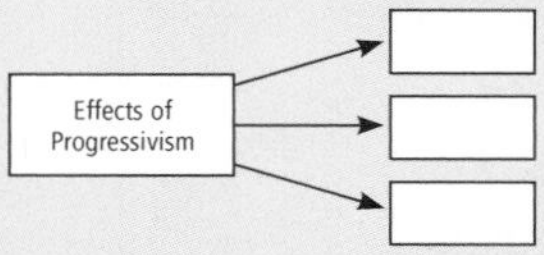

Critical Thinking

5. **Big Ideas** What new federal agencies increased the government's power to regulate the economy?
6. **Forming an Opinion** Which of Wilson's reforms do you consider to be most important? Why?
7. **Analyzing Visuals** Study the chart on page 538. What was the purpose of the Federal Reserve?

Writing About History

8. **Expository Writing** Suppose that you are a newspaper editor during Wilson's administration. Write an article about the failure of Progressives to address African American reform issues.

History ONLINE
Study Central™ To review this section, go to glencoe.com and click on Study Central.

W Writing Support

Expository Writing Have students research a progressive figure (such as Jane Addams, Lincoln Steffens, or Sigmund Livingston) and write a short report on their life and accomplishments.
OL AL

✓ Reading Check

Answer:
expanded democracy and raised expectations of the federal government's role in the economy and society

Assess

History ONLINE

Study Central™ provides summaries, interactive games, and online graphic organizers to help students review content.

Close

Summarizing Ask: What economic reforms did President Wilson institute? *(Wilson lowered tariffs, created the Federal Reserve and the Federal Trade Commission.)*
OL

Section 3 REVIEW

Answers

1. Definitions for the vocabulary terms are found in the section and the Glossary.
2. Although Wilson did not win a majority of the popular vote, he won in the Electoral College.
3. to restore public confidence in the banking system
4. expanded democracy, improved quality of life, expanded role of government, increased regulation of business and banking
5. Federal Reserve System, Federal Trade Commission
6. Students' answers will vary but should include a reasonable argument.
7. The purpose of the Federal Reserve was to require banks to set aside a portion of their deposits in a regional bank to protect against unanticipated losses.
8. Students' editorials will vary but should point out specific shortcomings and suggest ways that the progressives could have addressed these social problems.

Summarizing Ask: Which progressive reforms were attempts to lessen problems from laissez-faire economic practices? *(labor laws, health and safety codes, antitrust laws, government oversight agencies, consumer protection laws, conservation efforts, tariff reforms)* OL

Expository Writing The Children's Bureau was established in 1912 by President Taft. The agency is still in existence. Research the agency and write a short report of its history.
Ask: How has the mission of the Children's Bureau changed since it was established in 1912? OL AL

Chapter 15 Visual Summary

STUDY TO GO You can study anywhere, anytime by downloading quizzes and flashcards to your PDA from glencoe.com.

Causes of the Progressive Movement

- People thought progress in science and knowledge could improve society.
- People thought immigration, urbanization, and industrialization had created social problems.
- People thought laissez-faire economics and an unregulated market led to social problems and that government could fix them.
- Political corruption prevented the government from helping its citizens.

▶ *In 1910 a young boy works in a glass factory, an example of the type of child labor progressive reformers wanted to end.*

▲ *Trade unions begin their march honoring victims of the Triangle Shirtwaist Factory fire.*

Effects on Business and Society

- Interstate Commerce Commission is strengthened.
- Consumer protection laws are passed.
- Federal Trade Commission is created.
- Federal Reserve System is created to regulate the money supply.
- Clayton Antitrust Act grants labor unions more rights.
- Zoning laws and building codes improve urban housing.
- Child labor laws are passed, regulating time and conditions for minors to work.
- Workers' compensation laws are passed.
- Temperance movement begins seeking limitations on the production and consumption of alcohol.

Effects on Politics

- Cities begin adopting commission and city-manager forms of government.
- States begin to adopt the direct primary system, allowing voters to choose candidates for office.
- States begin to allow initiatives, referendums, and recall votes.
- Seventeenth Amendment is ratified, requiring direct election of senators.
- Nineteenth Amendment is ratified, guaranteeing women the right to vote.

▶ *Women march in 1916 in support of Woodrow Wilson's efforts to grant women the right to vote.*

Hands-On Chapter Project
Step 4: Wrap Up

Learning how Government Affects People's Lives

Step 4: Wrap Up This activity will synthesize the causes of the Progressive Movement and its effects on people's lives by personalizing the issues.

Directions Divide the class into six teams. Each team should select one presenter to take on the role of an individual whose life was affected by the Progressive Movement (such as a former child laborer now enrolled in school, a woman voting for the first time, and so on). To avoid duplication among the teams, have each team announce which role their presenter will play. If there are duplicates, assign another role to one of the teams. Be sure at least one team covers the effects of progressivism on some aspect of business, society, and politics.

Analyzing Information Team members will collaboratively write a journal page from the perspective of the presenter. Each journal page should describe vividly the person's life before and after the reform resulting from progressives' efforts. It should also mention the legislation or other action that made the reform possible. Presenters will read the group's journal page to the class. The rest of the class may want to ask the presenters questions. To make the presentations more lively and memorable, presenters may wish to carry relevant signs, dress in costumes, or hold up photos. OL

Chapter 15 Assessment

Reviewing Vocabulary

Directions: Choose the word or words that best complete each sentence.

1. The term "muckraker" was used in the early 1900s to describe
   - **A** street sweepers.
   - **B** investigative journalists.
   - **C** farmers.
   - **D** garden designers.

2. Women spent more than 70 years actively seeking ________, or the right to vote.
   - **A** initiative
   - **B** petition
   - **C** recall
   - **D** suffrage

3. The temperance movement was linked to the ________ of alcohol.
   - **A** prohibition
   - **B** production
   - **C** reduction
   - **D** requisition

4. When Gifford Pinchot leaked a story to the press against William Taft's will, the president fired him for
   - **A** arbitration.
   - **B** prohibition.
   - **C** insubordination.
   - **D** initiation.

5. The Federal Trade Commission was created to combat monopolies and trusts. It did this, in part, by preventing
   - **A** unfair trade practices.
   - **B** Social Darwinism.
   - **C** insubordination.
   - **D** regulation.

Reviewing Main Ideas

Directions: Choose the best answers to the following questions.

Section 1 *(pp. 520–527)*

6. Progressivism used the principles of science to solve problems resulting from
   - **A** industrialization and urbanization.
   - **B** global warming and fossil fuel use.
   - **C** the outbreak of war and proliferation of weapons.
   - **D** epidemic diseases and plagues.

7. Which of the following allowed proposed legislation to be placed on the ballot for voter approval?
   - **A** direct primary
   - **B** referendum
   - **C** initiative
   - **D** veto

8. What did the Nineteenth Amendment accomplish?
   - **A** It required colleges to accept women.
   - **B** It guaranteed child care for workers' children.
   - **C** It granted women the right to vote.
   - **D** It guaranteed equal pay for equal work.

Section 2 *(pp. 528–535)*

9. Theodore Roosevelt became known as a trustbuster for his actions against
   - **A** the Northern Securities company.
   - **B** the United Mine Workers.
   - **C** the automobile industry.
   - **D** national parks.

TEST-TAKING TIP

You can eliminate some answers by using your own knowledge and common sense. Read through each option and decide if it fits with what you know; if it does not, discard it.

Need Extra Help?

If You Missed Questions . . .	1	2	3	4	5	6	7	8	9
Go to Page . . .	521	524–525	527	534–535	539	532	523	524–525	528–529

GO ON

Answers and Analyses
Reviewing Vocabulary

1. B Muckrakers brought to light urban and social problems by writing about them in newspapers, magazines, and books. They were called muckrakers by President Roosevelt. Muck is another word for dirt. These writers exposed the dirt and corruption.

2. D Suffrage is the right to vote. Initiative, petition, and recall are political ways that people can affect legislation or remove elected officials from office.

3. A It is important that students connect the temperance movement with the prohibition of alcohol. Temperance means restraint. Those in favor of temperance did not just want to reduce alcohol, they wanted to eliminate it. Production is the opposite of the correct answer. Requisition is to acquire something.

4. C A subordinate is someone of lower status than someone else. For example, an employee is a subordinate of a boss. Insubordination is when a subordinate rebels against the superior. In this case, Taft, the boss, fired Pinchot, the subordinate, for disobeying orders.

5. A Unfair trade practices are actions that hurt competition. The FTC worked to prevent unfair competition rather than breaking up big businesses.

Reviewing Main Ideas

6. A Progressives sought to make social *progress*. That means they wanted to solve problems, as the question states. During the late nineteenth century, industrialization and urbanization were the driving forces behind society's problems.

7. B Review with students these important political terms. The direct primary allows all members of a political party to vote for candidates to run in the general election. Referendum allows proposed legislation to be submitted to the voters, initiative allowed citizens to introduce legislation that the legislature was required to vote on, and veto is the power to reject a bill.

8. C The Nineteenth Amendment granted women the right to vote.

9. A To answer this question, students should be aware of the dominance of the railroad industry at the time. Roosevelt's busting of J.P. Morgan's Northern Securities led newspapers to hail him as a trustbuster.

10. B The easiest way for students to remember that *The Jungle* dealt with the meatpacking industry is to remember that there are animals in the jungle, and animals are used for meat. None of the other answer choices deal with animals.

11. D Taft was warned by Roosevelt to stay away from tariff reform, because of the problems it would cause, but Taft did not listen and it hurt him politically.

12. A The establishment of the Federal Reserve System had far-reaching significance. This is a good opportunity to discuss the role the Federal Reserve took in regulating the economy, and to discuss the role it plays today in setting monetary policy.

13. C The NAACP believed voting rights were essential, because if African Americans could not vote and take part in government, how could they change it? Discuss with students how this was similar to the colonists wanting the right to vote and have a say in legislation governing them.

Critical Thinking

14. B La Follette's requiring political parties to hold direct primaries caused a monumental change in party politics.

15. C Students should locate the state in each answer choice and make note of the date listed. Reformers came to power in Washington in 1889.

16. A States in which reformers controlled state legislatures are shaded in the lightest gray. These states are concentrated in the Pacific Northwest, Great Plains, and South.

Chapter 15 Assessment

10. Upton Sinclair's novel *The Jungle* was instrumental in exposing which industry?

A steel
B meatpacking
C oil
D alcohol

11. President Taft broke with Roosevelt and progressives over

A unions.
B child labor.
C trust-busting.
D tariffs.

Section 3 *(pp. 536–541)*

12. How did President Wilson attempt to reform the banking industry?

A He created the Federal Reserve System.
B He vetoed the Underwood Tariff Act.
C He opposed the Sixteenth Amendment.
D He refused to break up monopolies.

13. What did Du Bois and other NAACP founders believe was essential to end racial violence?

A establishment of African American colleges
B higher-paying jobs for low-income citizens
C voting rights for African Americans
D private schools for African American children

Critical Thinking

Directions: Choose the best answers to the following questions.

14. How did Wisconsin governor Robert M. La Follette help to expand democracy in the United States?

A by favoring women's suffrage
B by requiring political parties to hold a direct primary
C by allowing recall elections to remove elected officials from office before the end of his or her term
D by providing for absentee ballots to voters

Base your answers to questions 15 and 16 on the map below and on your knowledge of Chapter 15.

Progressives and State Governments, 1889–1912

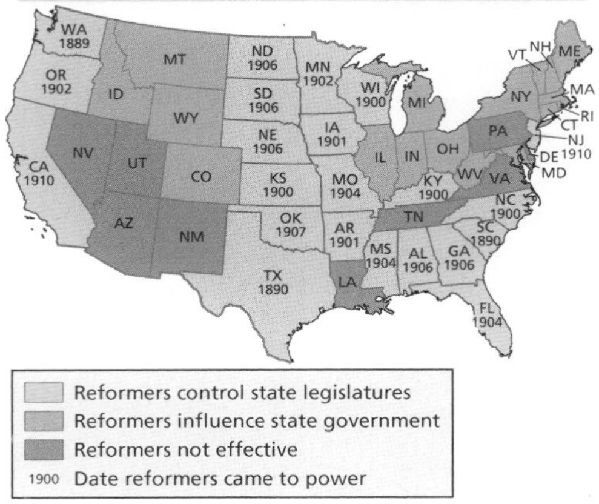

15. Which state came under the control of reformers before Wisconsin?

A Florida
B Oregon
C Washington
D Nebraska

16. According to the map, what generalization can you make about progressives in state governments?

A Progressives were most active in the Pacific Northwest, the Great Plains, and the South.
B They had no influence in the New England states.
C Reformers controlled few state legislatures by 1910.
D Reformers had little success in the Deep South.

Need Extra Help?

If You Missed Questions . . .	10	11	12	13	14	15	16
Go to Page . . .	530	534	539	541	522–523	522–523	522–523

GO ON

17. The Progressive movement strengthened the cause of women's suffrage by

- **A** drawing attention to child labor.
- **B** encouraging trustbusting.
- **C** making government more efficient.
- **D** showing women they needed the vote to get the reforms they wanted.

Analyze the cartoon and answer the question that follows. Base your answer on the cartoon and on your knowledge of Chapter 15.

Source: S.D. Ehrhart, *Puck*, February 24, 1909

18. How does the cartoon portray William Howard Taft?

- **A** as eager to see Roosevelt leave the White House
- **B** as Roosevelt's equal in every way
- **C** as a servant walking off with Roosevelt's big stick
- **D** as a nursemaid to the baby, Roosevelt's policies

Document-Based Questions

Directions: Analyze the document and answer the short-answer questions that follow the document.

Lucy Haessler writes of her childhood memories surrounding the woman suffrage movement:

> *"The suffragettes had a big headquarters in downtown Washington. My mother would take me up there on Saturdays when she volunteered to help out with mailings. The backbone of the suffrage movement was composed of well-to-do, middle-class women, both Republicans and Democrats. There weren't many working-class women in the movement. . . .*
>
> *The suffragettes organized pickets and marches and rallies. I was only ten years old the first time I went to a march with my mother. She told me, 'Oh, you're too young, you can't go.' But I said, 'I am going, because you're going to win the right to vote and I'm going to vote when I'm grown-up.' So she let me march. . . . The more marches that were held, the more you could feel the movement just building and building. . . ."*
>
> —quoted in *The Century for Young People*

19. Who does Haessler say were the backbone of the movement? Why do you think working-class women were not involved?

20. Why did Haessler want to march when she was only ten years old?

Extended Response

21. Upton Sinclair and other muckrakers took on the social ills of their day, forcing passage of legislation such as the Pure Food and Drug Act. Select one social problem of modern life and write a persuasive essay that suggests legislation to address the issue. The essay should include an introduction, several paragraphs, and a conclusion that supports your position.

STOP

History ONLINE

For additional test practice, use Self-Check Quizzes—Chapter 15 at glencoe.com.

Need Extra Help?

If You Missed Questions . . .	17	18	19	20	21
Go to Page . . .	522–525	533–535	524–525	524–525	521–527

Extended Response

21. Answers will vary. Students must select and focus on one social problem. Essays must follow proper format for a persuasive essay and include support from the text. Some possible social problems are global warming, poverty, education inequalities, and racism. Accept any problem a student chooses to write about that is appropriate and pertains to the topic.

17. D Showing women they needed the vote to get the reforms they wanted.

18. D Review the cartoon with students. Roosevelt is standing on the steps, smiling and taking the baby (with a blanket titled "my policies") from Taft. The baby represents Roosevelt's policies. Taft is dressed as a nursemaid (note the frilly cap and apron). Taft is the nursemaid to Roosevelt's policies.

Document Based Questions

19. The backbone of the movement was well-to-do, middle-class women. Working-class women may have lacked the time to get involved and may have been less educated about political issues.

20. She wants to march because she expects her mother and the suffragettes to succeed and looks forward to being able to vote herself.

History ONLINE

Have students visit the Web site at glencoe.com to review Chapter 15 and take the Self-Check Quiz.

Need Extra Help?

Have students refer to the pages listed if they miss any of the questions.

Chapter 16 Planning Guide

Key to Ability Levels	
BL Below Level	AL Above Level
OL On Level	ELL English Language Learners

Key to Teaching Resources	
Print Material	Transparency
CD-ROM or DVD	

BL	OL	AL	ELL		Resources	Chapter Opener	Section 1	Section 2	Section 3	Section 4	Chapter Assess
					FOCUS						
BL	OL	AL	ELL	Transparency	Daily Focus Transparencies		16-1	16-2	16-3	16-4	
					TEACH						
BL	OL		ELL	Print	Reading Skills Activity, URB			p. 83			
	OL			Print	Historical Analysis Skills Activity, URB			p. 84			
BL	OL	AL	ELL	Print	Differentiated Instruction Activity, URB			p. 85			
BL	OL		ELL	Print	English Learner Activity, URB		p. 87				
BL	OL	AL	ELL	Print	Content Vocabulary Activity, URB*		p. 89				
BL	OL	AL	ELL	Print	Academic Vocabulary Activity, URB		p. 91				
	OL	AL		Print	Reinforcing Skills Activity, URB					p. 93	
	OL	AL		Print	Critical Thinking Skills Activity, URB		p. 94				
BL	OL		ELL	Print	Time Line Activity, URB				p. 95		
	OL			Print	Linking Past and Present Activity, URB			p. 96			
BL	OL	AL	ELL	Print	Primary Source Reading, URB			p. 97		p. 99	
BL	OL	AL	ELL	Print	American Art and Music Activity, URB			p. 101			
BL	OL	AL	ELL	Print	Interpreting Political Cartoons Activity, URB					p. 103	
		AL		Print	Enrichment Activity, URB			p. 106			
BL	OL		ELL	Print	Guided Reading Activity, URB*		p. 108	p. 109	p. 110	p. 111	
BL	OL	AL	ELL	Print	Reading Essentials and Note-Taking Guide*		p. 174	p. 177	p. 180	p. 183	
BL	OL	AL	ELL	Print	Differentiated Instruction for the American History Classroom	✓	✓	✓	✓	✓	✓
BL	OL	AL	ELL	Transparency	Unit Map Overlay Transparencies	✓	✓	✓	✓	✓	✓
BL	OL	AL	ELL	Print	Unit Time Line Transparencies, Strategies, and Activities	✓	✓	✓	✓	✓	✓
BL	OL	AL	ELL	Print	Cause and Effect Transparencies, Strategies, and Activities	✓	✓	✓	✓	✓	✓
BL	OL	AL	ELL	Print	Why It Matters Chapter Transparencies, Strategies, and Activities	✓	✓	✓	✓	✓	✓
BL	OL	AL	ELL	Print	American Biographies		✓	✓	✓		

Note: Please refer to the *Unit 5 Resource Book* for this chapter's URB materials.

* Also available in Spanish

TeacherWorks Plus
All-In-One Planner and Resource Center

- Interactive Lesson Planner
- Interactive Teacher Edition
- Fully editable blackline masters
- Section Spotlight Videos Launch
- Differentiated Lesson Plans
- Printable reports of daily assignments
- Standards Tracking System

Levels BL	OL	AL	ELL	Resources	Chapter Opener	Section 1	Section 2	Section 3	Section 4	Chapter Assess
				TEACH *(continued)*						
BL	OL	AL		**Supreme Court Case Studies**			p. 37			
BL	OL	AL	ELL	**The Living Constitution**	✓	✓	✓	✓	✓	✓
BL	OL	AL	ELL	**American Issues**	✓	✓	✓	✓	✓	✓
	OL	AL	ELL	**American Art and Architecture Transparencies, Strategies, and Activities**	✓	✓	✓	✓	✓	✓
BL	OL	AL		**High School American History Literature Library**	✓	✓	✓	✓	✓	✓
	OL	AL		**American History Primary Source Documents Library**	✓	✓	✓	✓	✓	✓
BL	OL	AL	ELL	**American Music: Hits Through History CD**	✓	✓	✓	✓	✓	✓
BL	OL	AL	ELL	**StudentWorks™ Plus**	✓	✓	✓	✓	✓	✓
BL	OL	AL	ELL	***The American Vision* Video Program**	✓	✓	✓	✓	✓	✓
Teacher Resources				**Reading Strategies and Activities for the Social Studies Classroom**	✓	✓	✓	✓	✓	✓
				Strategies for Success	✓	✓	✓	✓	✓	✓
				Presentation Plus! with MindJogger CheckPoint	✓	✓	✓	✓	✓	✓
				Success With English Learners	✓	✓	✓	✓	✓	✓
				ASSESS						
BL	OL	AL	ELL	**Section Quizzes and Chapter Tests***		p. 223	p. 224	p. 225	p. 226	p. 227
BL	OL	AL	ELL	**Authentic Assessment With Rubrics**						p. 37
BL	OL	AL	ELL	**Standardized Test Practice Workbook**						p. 36
BL	OL	AL	ELL	***ExamView® Assessment Suite***		16-1	16-2	16-3	16-4	Ch. 16
				CLOSE						
BL			ELL	**Reteaching Activity, URB**						p. 105
BL	OL		ELL	**Reading and Study Skills Foldables™**	p. 67					
BL	OL	AL	ELL	***American History* in Graphic Novel**			p. 45			

✓ Chapter- or unit-based activities applicable to all sections in this chapter.

Using Study Central™

Teach With Technology

What is Study Central™?

Study Central™ is an interactive, online tool that helps students understand and remember content section-by-section. It can be used alongside lessons or before a test.

How can Study Central™ help my students?

Study Central™ contains fun activities that students can use to review important content and reinforce effective study habits. Using the format of the Guide to Reading that opens each section in the textbook, Study Central™ has students write main idea statements as questions, review academic and content vocabulary, and take notes using online graphic organizers. Students can also read section summaries, take multiple-choice quizzes, and find Web links for more information.

Visit glencoe.com and enter a QuickPass™ code to go to Study Central™.

History ONLINE
Visit glencoe.com and enter QuickPass™ code TAV9399c16T for Chapter 16 resources.

You can easily launch a wide range of digital products from your computer's desktop with the McGraw-Hill Social Studies widget.

TeacherWorks

	Student	Teacher	Parent
Media Library			
• Section Audio	●		●
• Spanish Audio Summaries	●		●
• Section Spotlight Videos	●	●	●
***The American Vision* Online Learning Center (Web Site)**			
• StudentWorks™ Plus Online	●	●	●
• Multilingual Glossary	●	●	●
• Study-to-Go	●	●	●
• Chapter Overviews	●	●	●
• Self-Check Quizzes	●	●	●
• Student Web Activities	●	●	●
• ePuzzles and Games	●	●	●
• Vocabulary eFlashcards	●	●	●
• In Motion Animations	●	●	●
• Study Central™	●	●	●
• Web Activity Lesson Plans		●	
• Vocabulary PuzzleMaker	●	●	●
• Historical Thinking Activities		●	
• Beyond the Textbook	●	●	●

Reading Support From Jamestown Education

- **Timed Readings Plus in Social Studies** helps students increase their reading rate and fluency while maintaining comprehension. The 400-word passages are similar to those found on state and national assessments.
- **Reading in the Content Area: Social Studies** concentrates on six essential reading skills that help students better comprehend what they read. The book includes 75 high-interest nonfiction passages written at increasing levels of difficulty.
- **Reading Social Studies** includes strategic reading instruction and vocabulary support in Social Studies content for both ELLs and native speakers of English.

www.jamestowneducation.com

National Geographic

Index to National Geographic Magazine:

The following articles relate to this chapter:

- "Riddle of the *Lusitania*," by Robert D. Ballard, April 1994.
- "The American Red Cross: A Century of Service," by Louise Levathes and Annie Griffiths, June 1981.

National Geographic Society Products To order the following, call National Geographic at 1-800-368-2728:

- *World War I Era* (PicturePack Transparencies)

Access National Geographic's new dynamic MapMachine Web site and other geography resources at:
www.nationalgeographic.com
www.nationalgeographic.com/maps

Biography A&E Home Video The History Channel

The following videotape programs are available from Glencoe as supplements to this chapter:

- Secrets of the Romanovs (ISBN 0-76-700231-8)
- The Red Baron: Master of the Air (ISBN 1-56-501582-7)

To order, call Glencoe at 1-800-334-7344. To find classroom resources to accompany many of these videos, check the following home pages:

A&E Television: www.aetv.com
The History Channel: www.historychannel.com

Reading List Generator CD-ROM — Glencoe BookLink 3

Use this database to search more than 30,000 titles to create a customized reading list for your students.

- Reading lists can be organized by students' reading level, author, genre, theme, or area of interest.
- The database provides Degrees of Reading Power™ (DRP) and Lexile™ readability scores for all selections.
- A brief summary of each selection is included.

Leveled reading suggestions for this chapter:

For students at a Grade 8 reading level:
- ***First Woman in Congress: Jeannette Rankin,*** by Florence Meiman White

For students at a Grade 9 reading level:
- ***Anastasia's Album,*** by Hugh Brewster

For students at a Grade 10 reading level:
- ***World War I,*** by Gail B. Stewart

For students at a Grade 11 reading level:
- ***Remember the Lusitania!,*** by Diana Preston

For students at a Grade 12 reading level:
- ***World War I,*** by Virginia Schomp

Introducing Chapter 16

Focus

MAKING CONNECTIONS

Why Do Nations Go to War?

Have students brainstorm the reasons nations go to war and list their answers on the chalkboard. Discuss with students if they think any of the reasons listed are valid and have them consider if the reasons might be different today than they were in 1914. **OL**

Teach

The Big Ideas

As students study the chapter, remind them to consider the section-based Big Ideas included in each section's Guide to Reading. The **Essential Questions** in the activities below tie in to the Big Ideas and help students think about and understand important chapter concepts. In addition, the Hands-on Chapter Projects with their culminating activities relate the content from each section to the Big Ideas. These activities build on each other as students progress through the chapter. Section activities culminate in the wrap-up activity on the Visual Summary page.

Chapter 16

World War I and Its Aftermath

1914–1920

SECTION 1 The United States Enters World War I

SECTION 2 The Home Front

SECTION 3 A Bloody Conflict

SECTION 4 The War's Impact

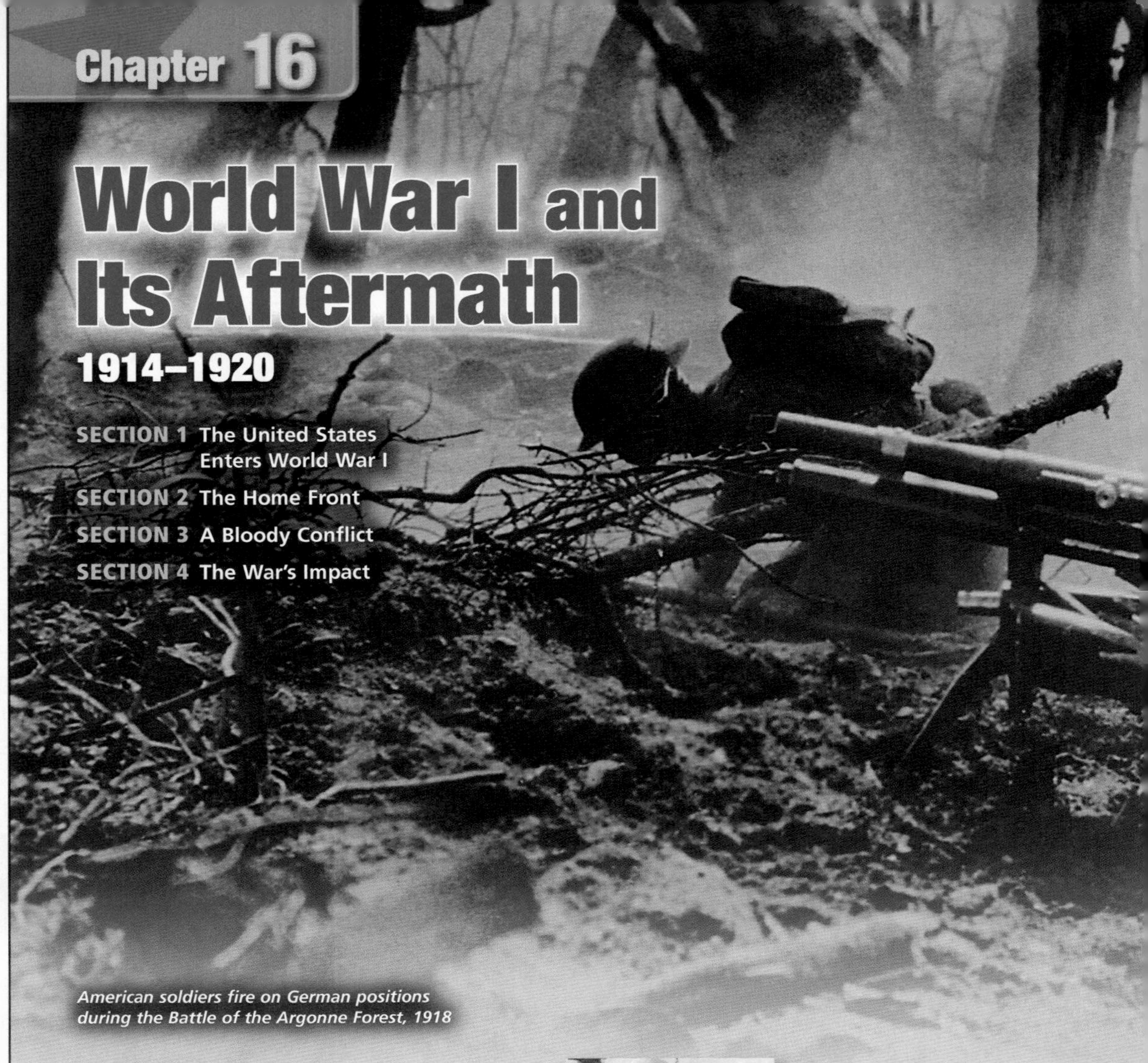

American soldiers fire on German positions during the Battle of the Argonne Forest, 1918

U.S. PRESIDENTS

Wilson 1913–1921

U.S. EVENTS

1915
- German submarine sinks the *Lusitania*

1917
- U.S. enters the war
- Selective Service Act passed

WORLD EVENTS

1914 — 1916

1914
- Franz Ferdinand assassinated; war begins in Europe

1916
- Battle of Verdun begins in February
- Battle of the Somme begins in July

1917
- Bolshevik Revolution begins in October

Section 1

The United States Enters World War I

Essential Question: What is neutrality? *(supporting neither side in a quarrel or war)* When would you remain neutral in a conflict with friends, and what would cause you to intervene? Tell students that in this section they will learn how the United States attempted to remain neutral in World War I and the events that finally led to U.S. involvement. **OL**

Section 2

The Home Front

Essential Question: If the United States were currently preparing for war, what needs would be different from its needs in preparing for World War I? What needs would be the same? *(Answers will vary, but students should support their answers with examples.)* Have students discuss what a country would need in order to be prepared for war. Tell them that this section will focus on how the United States mobilized for World War I. **OL**

Chapter Audio

MAKING CONNECTIONS

Why Do Nations Go to War?

World War I was the first time in American history that the United States sent troops to fight in Europe. This decision ended the long-standing policy of remaining neutral in Europe's wars.

- ***Why do you think the United States changed its policy and sent troops to Europe?***
- ***Do you think it was a difficult decision?***

FOLDABLES™

Organizing Information As you read the chapter, write information under each tab, listing which country is in the alliance, why it joined the alliance, or what reasons it had for disagreeing with the countries in the opposing alliance.

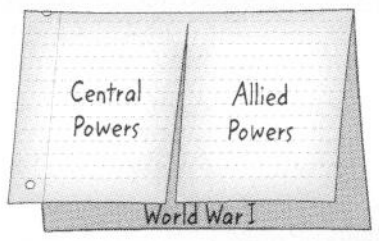

1918
- Congress passes Sedition Act
- Armistice ends fighting on November 11

1919
- Race riots and strikes take place in Northern cities

1920
- Red Scare and Palmer Raids

1918 — 1920

1918
- Treaty of Brest-Litovsk ends Russian-German war

1919
- Versailles Peace Conference begins

History ONLINE Visit glencoe.com and enter ***QuickPass***™ code TAV9846c16 for Chapter 16 resources.

Section 3

A Bloody Conflict

Essential Question: What are some synonyms for *reparations*? *(compensation, restitution, amends)* In what situations are people required to make reparations? *(replacing a damaged item, paying for repairs when causing a car accident, court cases)* Tell students that in Section 3 they will learn about the reparations Germany was forced to make after World War I. **OL**

Section 4

The War's Impact

Essential Question: How does a strike affect consumers? *(services become unavailable, costs rise)* Have students discuss reasons that workers go on strike. *(poor working conditions, lack of benefits, low wages)* Tell students that this section will cover some of the strikes that resulted from the economic upheaval following World War I. **OL**

Introducing

Chapter 16

More About the Photo

Visual Literacy The 23rd Infantry participated in six campaigns during World War I: Aisne, Lorraine, Île de France, Aisne-Marne, St. Mihiel, and Meuse-Argonne.

FOLDABLES™ Study Organizer **Dinah Zike's Foldables**

Dinah Zike's Foldables are three-dimensional, interactive graphic organizers that help students practice basic writing skills, review vocabulary terms, and identify main ideas. Instructions for creating and using Foldables can be found in the Appendix at the end of this book and in the *Dinah Zike's Reading and Study Skills Foldables* booklet.

History ONLINE

Visit glencoe.com and enter ***QuickPass***™ code TAV9399c16T for Chapter 16 resources, including a Chapter Overview, Study Central™, Study-to-Go, Student Web Activity, Self-Check Quiz, and other materials.

Focus

Bellringer

Daily Focus Transparency 16-1

Guide to Reading

Answers may include: Balkan crisis, alliance system, naval race, assassination of Franz Ferdinand

Section Spotlight Video

To generate student interest and provide a springboard for class discussion, access the Chapter 16, Section 1 video at glencoe.com or on the video DVD.

Resource Manager

R Reading Strategies	C Critical Thinking	D Differentiated Instruction	W Writing Support	S Skill Practice
Teacher Edition • Predicting, p. 552 • Setting a Purpose, p. 552 • Act. Prior Know., p. 554 • Using Word Parts, p. 554 • Sequencing Info., p. 555 **Additional Resources** • Guid. Read. Act, URB p. 108	**Teacher Edition** • Drawing Con., p. 550 **Additional Resources** • Crit. Think. Skills Act., URB p. 94 • Quizzes and Tests, p. 223	**Teacher Edition** • Visual/Spatial, p. 554 **Additional Resources** • Eng. Learner Act., URB p. 87 • Foldables, p. 67	**Teacher Edition** • Persuasive Writing, pp. 549, 552, 553 • Narrative Writing, p. 550 **Additional Resources** • Content Vocab. Act., URB p. 89 • Academic Vocab. Act., URB p. 91	**Teacher Edition** • Analyzing Visuals, p. 549 • Using Geo. Skills, p. 551 **Additional Resources** • Read. Essen., p. 174

Section 1 Section Audio Spotlight Video

The United States Enters World War I

Guide to Reading

Big Ideas

Trade, War, and Migration Although the United States tried to stay neutral, events pushed the nation into war.

Content Vocabulary
- militarism *(p. 549)*
- nationalism *(p. 550)*
- propaganda *(p. 552)*
- contraband *(p. 554)*

Academic Vocabulary
- emphasis *(p. 550)*
- erode *(p. 554)*

People and Events to Identify
- Balkans *(p. 550)*
- Franz Ferdinand *(p. 550)*
- Sussex pledge *(p. 555)*
- Zimmermann telegram *(p. 555)*

Reading Strategy

Organizing Complete the graphic organizer shown below by identifying the factors that contributed to the conflict.

Militarism, alliances, imperialism, and nationalism led to World War I in Europe. Attacks on U.S. ships and American support for the Allies eventually caused the United States to enter the war.

World War I Begins

MAIN Idea Old alliances and nationalist sentiments among European nations set the stage for World War I.

HISTORY AND YOU Does your school have a long-standing rivalry with another school? Read how European nations formed political alliances that brought most of the continent into war.

Despite more than 40 years of general peace, tensions among European nations were building in 1914. Throughout the late 1800s and early 1900s, a number of factors created problems among the powers of Europe and set the stage for a monumental war.

Militarism and Alliances

The roots of World War I date back to the 1860s. In 1864, while Americans fought the Civil War, the German kingdom of Prussia launched the first of a series of wars to unite the various German states into one nation. By 1871 Prussia had united Germany and proclaimed the birth of the German Empire. The new German nation rapidly industrialized and quickly became one of the most powerful nations in the world.

The creation of Germany transformed European politics. In 1870, as part of their plan to unify Germany, the Prussians had attacked and defeated France. They then forced the French to give up territory along the German border. From that point forward, France and Germany were enemies. To protect itself, Germany signed alliances with Italy and with Austria-Hungary, a huge empire that controlled much of southeastern Europe. This became known as the Triple Alliance.

The new alliance alarmed Russian leaders, who feared that Germany intended to expand eastward into Russia. Russia and Austria-Hungary were also competing for influence in southeastern Europe. Many of the people of southeastern Europe were Slavs—the same ethnic group as the Russians—and the Russians wanted to support them against Austria-Hungary. As a result, Russia and France had a common interest in opposing Germany and Austria-Hungary. In 1894 they signed the Franco-Russian Alliance, promising to come to each other's aid in a war with the Triple Alliance.

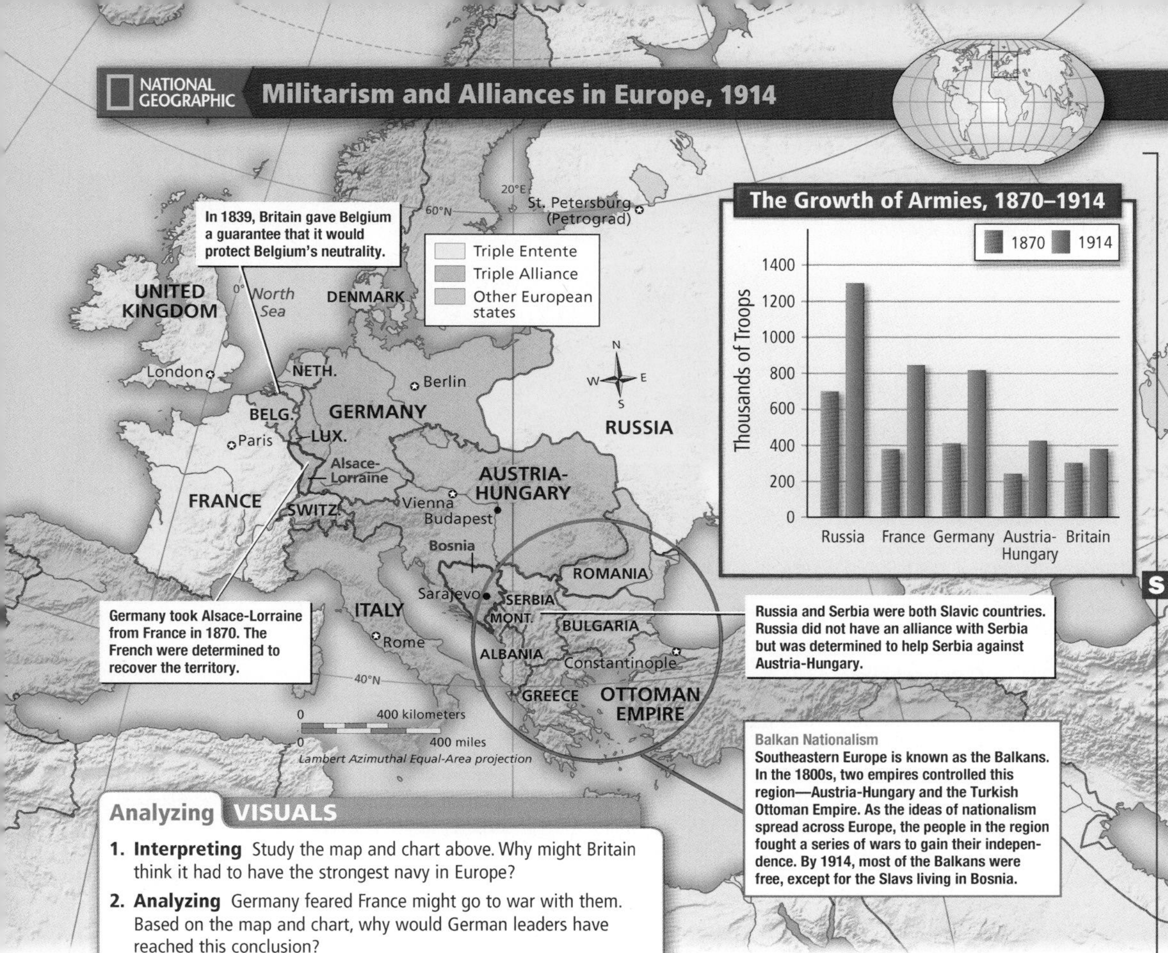

Analyzing VISUALS

1. **Interpreting** Study the map and chart above. Why might Britain think it had to have the strongest navy in Europe?
2. **Analyzing** Germany feared France might go to war with them. Based on the map and chart, why would German leaders have reached this conclusion?

Maps In MOtion See *StudentWorks™ Plus* or glencoe.com.

The system of alliances in Europe encouraged **militarism**—the aggressive build-up of armed forces to intimidate and threaten other nations. German militarism eventually forced Britain to become involved in the alliance system. Britain's policy was to support weaker countries against stronger ones so as to make sure no country conquered all of Europe. By the late 1800s, it was clear that Germany had become the strongest nation in Europe.

In 1898 Germany began building a large modern navy as well. A strong German navy threatened the British, who depended on their naval strength to protect their island from invasion. By the early 1900s, an arms race had begun between Great Britain and Germany, as both nations raced to build warships.

The naval race greatly increased tensions between Germany and Britain and convinced the British to establish closer relations with France and Russia. The British still refused to sign a formal alliance, so their new relationship with the French and Russians became known as an entente cordiale—a friendly understanding. Britain, France, and Russia became known as the Triple Entente.

Teach

S Skill Practice

Analyzing Visuals Ask: Why might Balkan nationalism have been a factor in causing World War I? *(Nationalism instilled pride in people and led them to want self-government.)* OL

W Writing Support

Persuasive Writing Invite students to write a letter to the German emperor advising him of the risks of alliances and the growth of militarism in Europe. Students should use library or Internet resources to find out more about the European alliances. OL

Analyzing VISUALS

Answers:

1. Britain is an island nation and a navy would be essential to its defense.
2. Germany feared that France would attempt to regain Alsace-Lorraine; France and Germany appear to be in competition building up their armies.

Hands-On Chapter Project
Step 1

Presenting World War I

Step 1: Presenting the United States's Entry into the War Ask: Why did the United States enter World War I?

Directions Explain to students that they will create one to three multimedia slides or screens to explain why the United States entered World War I. Divide students into two teams. The first team should focus on the root causes of the war. The second team should focus on American neutrality and how and why it changed. (In both groups, further division might be made between those responsible for boiling down the literal explanation and those finding graphic/visual elements.)

Putting It Together When the two teams meet to finalize the choices for the slides or screens, they will have to think critically to summarize these topics into a few slides. OL *(Chapter Project continued on page 557)*

R Reading Strategy

Making Connections Write the terms *nationalism* and *imperialism* on the board. Then have students list the ways in which the ideas of nationalism and imperialism were opposed to each other. Discuss with students the roles that these opposing ideas played in World War I. AL

W Writing Support

Narrative Writing Have students write a newspaper article from the point of view of a reporter who witnessed the assassination of Archduke Franz Ferdinand. Instruct students to use narrative and descriptive techniques in their articles. Encourage students to share their articles with the class. BL

C Critical Thinking

Drawing Conclusions Have students list the peoples who were pushing for independence before World War I. Have students choose one of these groups and, using library or Internet resources, write a history of that group from World War I to the present. Have volunteers share their findings with the class.

PRIMARY SOURCE

Causes of World War I

Use the acronym MAIN to remember the four main causes of World War I: Militarism, Alliances, Imperialism, Nationalism.

MILITARISM

▲ *Warships of the German Imperial fleet are shown anchored near Kiel, Germany in 1911. The naval race between Britain and Germany caused tension in Europe prior to World War I.*

ALLIANCES

▲ *An 1883 British cartoon illustrates the Triple Alliance.*

IMPERIALISM

▲ *Franz Joseph, Emperor of Austria-Hungary, and Wilhelm II, Emperor of Germany, salute during a parade in Berlin in 1889.*

Imperialism and Nationalism

By the late 1800s, **nationalism,** or a feeling of intense pride in one's homeland, had become a powerful idea in Europe. Nationalists place primary **emphasis** on promoting their homeland's culture and interests above those of other countries. Nationalism was one of the reasons for the tensions among the European powers. Each nation viewed the others as competitors, and many people were willing to go to war to expand their nation at the expense of others.

R One of the basic ideas of nationalism is the right to self-determination—the idea that people who share a national identity should have their own country and government. In the 1800s nationalism led to a crisis in southeastern Europe in the region known as the **Balkans.** Historically, the Ottoman Empire and the Austro-Hungarian Empire had ruled the Balkans. Both of these empires were made up of many different nations.

Imperialism—the idea that a country can increase its power and wealth by controlling other peoples—had convinced the major European powers to build empires in the 1700s and 1800s. Nationalism ran counter to imperialism. As the idea of nationalism spread in the late 1800s and early 1900s, the different national groups within Europe's empires began to press for independence.

Among the groups pushing for independence were the Serbs, Bosnians, Croats, and Slovenes. These people all spoke similar languages and had come to see themselves as one people. They called themselves South Slavs, or Yugoslavs. The first of these people to obtain independence were the Serbs, who formed a nation called Serbia between the Ottoman and Austro-Hungarian Empires. Serbs believed their nation's mission was to unite the South Slavs. C

Russia supported the Serbs, while Austria-Hungary did what it could to limit Serbia's growth. In 1908 Austria-Hungary annexed Bosnia, which had belonged to the Ottoman Empire. The Serbs were furious. They wanted Bosnia to be part of their nation. The annexation demonstrated to the Serbs that Austria-Hungary had no intention of letting the Slavic people in its empire become independent.

A Terrorist Attack Brings War

In late June 1914 the heir to the Austro-Hungarian throne, the Archduke **Franz Ferdinand,** visited the Bosnian capital of Sarajevo. As he and his wife rode through the city, a Bosnian revolutionary named Gavrilo W

Differentiated Instruction

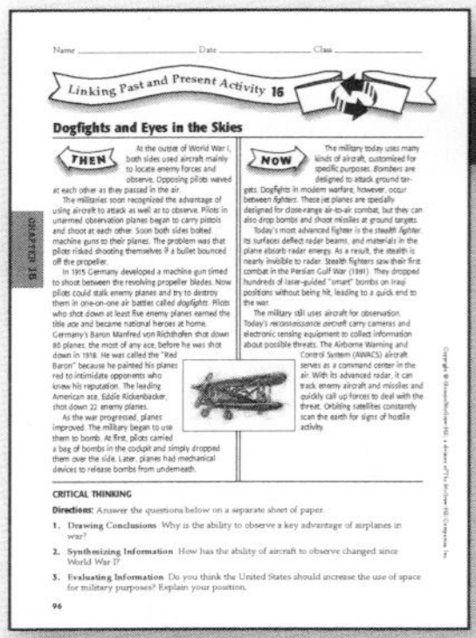

Linking Past and Present Activity 19, URB p. 96

Writing a Narrative Essay

Objective: Make decisions on budget priorities.

Focus: Discuss how budgets require decision-makers to prioritize needs and wants.

Teach: List rounded prices for each type of aircraft mentioned in the reading. Give a set amount to spend on aircraft.

Assess: List how many of each kind of aircraft to purchase. Make sure to stay within the budget.

Close: Write a paragraph explaining the decisions made in spending the budget.

Differentiated Instruction Strategies

- **BL** With a partner, make a time line that shows the progression of the ways aircraft were used in World War I.
- **AL** Choose one part of the most recent U.S. budget and explain the priorities of that particular department.
- **ELL** Write the definition of each of the italicized words in the reading using context clues and other resources.

NATIONALISM

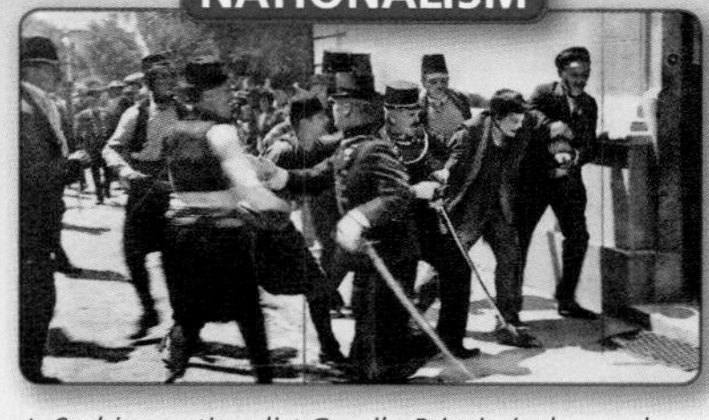

▲ *Serbian nationalist Gavrilo Princip is dragged into police headquarters in Sarajevo shortly after killing Archduke Franz Ferdinand, heir to the Austro-Hungarian throne.*

Analyzing VISUALS

1. **Interpreting** What point is the cartoonist trying to make about the Triple Alliance?
2. **Explaining** How did Austrian imperialism and Balkan nationalism contribute to the outbreak of World War I?

Princip rushed their open car and shot the couple to death. The assassin was a member of a Serbian nationalist group nicknamed the "Black Hand." The assassination took place with the knowledge of Serbian officials who hoped to start a war that would bring down the Austro-Hungarian Empire.

The Alliances Are Triggered The Austro-Hungarian government blamed Serbia for the attack and decided the time had come to crush Serbia in order to prevent Slavic nationalism from undermining its empire. Knowing an attack on Serbia might trigger a war with Russia, the Austrians asked their German allies for support. Germany promised to support Austria-Hungary if war erupted.

Austria-Hungary then issued an ultimatum to the Serbian government. The Serbs counted on Russia to back them up, and the Russians, in turn, counted on France. French leaders were worried that they might someday be caught alone in a war with Germany, so they promised to support Russia if war began.

On July 28 Austria-Hungary declared war on Serbia. Russia immediately mobilized its army, including troops stationed on the German border. On August 1 Germany declared war on Russia. Two days later, it declared war on France. World War I had begun.

Germany's Plan Fails Germany had long been prepared for war against France and Russia. It immediately launched a massive invasion of France, hoping to knock the French out of the war. It would then be able to send its troops east to deal with the Russians.

The German plan had one major problem. **S** It required the German forces to advance through neutral Belgium in order to encircle the French troops. The British had guaranteed Belgium's neutrality. When German troops crossed the Belgian frontier, Britain declared war on Germany.

Those fighting for the Triple Entente were called the Allies. France, Russia, and Great Britain formed the backbone of the Allies along with Italy, which joined them in 1915 after the other Allies promised to cede Austro-Hungarian territory to Italy after the war. What remained of the Triple Alliance—Germany and Austria-Hungary—joined with the Ottoman Empire and Bulgaria to form the Central Powers.

The German plan seemed to work at first. German troops swept through Belgium and headed into France, driving back the French and British forces. Then, to the great surprise of the Germans, Russian troops invaded Germany. The Germans had not expected Russia to mobilize so quickly. They were forced to pull some of their troops away from the attack on France and send them east to stop the Russians. This weakened the German forces just enough to give the Allies a chance to stop them. The Germans drove to within 30 miles (48 km) of Paris, but stubborn resistance by British and French troops at the Battle of the Marne finally stopped the German advance. Because the swift German attack had failed to defeat the French, both sides became locked in a bloody stalemate along hundreds of miles of trenches that would barely change position for the next three years.

The Central Powers had greater success on the Eastern Front. German and Austro-Hungarian forces stopped the Russian attack and then went on the offensive. They swept across hundreds of miles of territory and took hundreds of thousands of prisoners. Russia suffered 2 million killed, wounded, or captured in 1915 alone, but it kept fighting.

Reading Check **Explaining** What incident triggered the beginning of World War I?

S Skill Practice

Using Geography Skills

Provide students with a topographical map of Europe. Instruct them to research the path Germany hoped to take through Belgium and eventually to Paris. Have students trace the path and then mark the location where British and French troops stopped the German advance. **OL**

Analyzing VISUALS

Answers:

1. The Triple Alliance is poised to attack France.
2. Austria was determined to maintain its influence and control in the Balkans; the people of the Balkans were just as determined to establish independent nations and rule themselves.

Reading Check

Answer:
the assassination of Austrian Archduke Franz Ferdinand, the heir to the Austro-Hungarian throne

Additional Support

Activity: Collaborative Learning

Explaining Causes Write the following terms on the chalkboard: *imperialism, nationalism, militarism,* and *balance of power.* Have students define each term. Using the text and additional research, ask them to explain how each contributed to the war in Europe. Ask if students think that any one nation or group of nations was primarily responsible for World War I. Ask each student to present evidence to support his or her opinion. **OL**

R1 Reading Strategy

Predicting While war enveloped Europe, American politicians attempted to remain uninvolved in the global conflict. **Ask:** As foreign tensions escalate, do you think it will be possible for President Wilson to maintain his neutral stance? Why or why not? *(Students may state that it will not be possible as the United States becomes more directly affected by events overseas.)* OL

W Writing Support

Persuasive Writing Have interested students find out more information about the preparedness debate before the nation's entry into World War I. Have them use their findings to decide whether they favor preparedness or not. Then have them write a letter to President Wilson persuading him to support their point of view. OL

R2 Reading Strategy

Setting a Purpose Have students discuss how news reporting, propaganda, and advertising differed. Ask students to identify the purpose and value of each. AL

Additional Support

America Declares War

MAIN Idea British propaganda and business interests led most Americans to a pro-British stance on the war.

HISTORY AND YOU Do you recall a time when you tried to remain neutral in a fight between friends? Read how the United States tried to stay out of World War I.

R1 When the fighting began, President Wilson was determined to keep the country out of a European war. He immediately declared the United States to be neutral in the conflict. "We must be impartial in thought as well as in action," Wilson stated. For many Americans that proved difficult to do.

Americans Take Sides

Despite the president's plea, many Americans supported one side or the other. Many of the country's 8 million German Americans, for example, supported their homeland. Many of the nation's 4.5 million Irish Americans, whose homeland endured centuries of British rule, also sympathized with the Central Powers.

In general, however, American public opinion favored the Allied cause. Many Americans valued the heritage, language, and political ideals they shared with Britain. Others treasured America's links with France, a great friend to America during the Revolutionary War.

W For more than two years, the United States officially remained neutral. During this time a great debate began over whether the United States should prepare for war. Supporters of the "preparedness" movement believed that preparing for war was the best way to stay out of the conflict. They also argued that if the United States was pulled into the war, it was better to be prepared.

Other Americans disagreed. In 1915 Carrie Chapman Catt and Jane Addams—leaders of the woman suffrage movement—founded the Women's Peace Party (later known as the International League for Peace and Freedom). This organization, along with others such as the League to Limit Armament, worked to keep America out of the war by urging the president not to build up the military.

Government Officials Back Britain One select group of Americans was decidedly pro-British: President Wilson's cabinet. Only Secretary of State William Jennings Bryan favored neutrality. The other cabinet members, as well as Bryan's chief adviser, Robert Lansing, and Walter Hines Page, the American ambassador to London, argued forcefully on behalf of Britain. Many American military leaders also backed the British. They believed that an Allied victory was the only way to preserve the international balance of power.

British officials worked diligently to win American support. One method they used was **propaganda,** or information designed to influence opinion. Both sides used propaganda, but German propaganda was mostly anti-Russian and did not appeal to most Americans. British propaganda, on the other hand, was extremely skillful. R2

Debates IN HISTORY

Should America Stay Neutral in World War I?

Americans were deeply divided about whether the United States should remain neutral in World War I. Despite President Wilson's pronouncement that Americans should remain neutral in thought as well as action, many Americans, including those working for the government, had very definite opinions as to whether or not the United States should enter the war.

Activity: Collaborative Learning

Making Inferences Remind students that to infer means to draw a conclusion based on facts and on what is known about the usual outcome of similar situations. Then ask students to make an inference about the Americans who wanted the United States to remain neutral. Discuss and list the various reasons these citizens had for not entering World War I. Ask students to write a paragraph giving their opinions about whether or not a nation should require citizens to fight in a war even if they do not understand its causes or they disagree with its causes. OL

To control the flow of news to the United States, the British cut the transatlantic telegraph cable from Europe to the United States. This meant that most war news would be based on British reports. The American ambassador to Britain, Walter Hines Page, himself strongly pro-British, gave the reports legitimacy by endorsing many of them. When stories arrived describing German atrocities, enough Americans believed them to help sway American support in favor of the Allies.

Business Supports Britain American business interests also leaned toward the Allies. Companies in the United States, particularly on the East Coast, had strong ties with businesses in the Allied countries. As business leader Thomas W. Lamont stated, "Our firm had never for one moment been neutral: we did not know how to be. From the very start we did everything that we could to contribute to the cause of the Allies."

Many American banks began to invest heavily in an Allied victory. American loans to the cash-hungry Allies skyrocketed. By 1917 such loans would total over $2 billion. Other American banks, particularly in the Midwest, where pro-German feelings were strongest, also lent some $27 million to Germany.

More money might have been lent to Germany, but most foreign loans required the approval of William McAdoo, the secretary of the Treasury. McAdoo was strongly pro-British and did what he could to limit loans to Germany. As a result, the country's prosperity was intertwined with the military fortunes of Britain, France, and Russia. If the Allies won, the money would be paid back; if not, the money might be lost forever. **W**

YES

John Works
Civil War Veteran and U.S. Senator

PRIMARY SOURCE

"Germany is not moving against this country. She has not been guilty of any aggression against us. She has taken the lives of a few of our citizens, because they got in the way when she was prosecuting a war against another nation and fighting to preserve her existence. If the German Government should make aggressive warfare against the United States you would not need any exhortation in the Senate of the United States to arouse the patriotism of the American people. You would not be holding open your enlisting stations without getting any soldiers."

—from *The Congressional Record,* March 4, 1917

NO

Robert Lansing
Secretary of State

PRIMARY SOURCE

"I have come to the conclusion that the German Government is utterly hostile to all nations with democratic institutions because those who compose it see in democracy a menace to absolutism and the defeat of the German ambition for world domination. . . .

. . . Germany must not be permitted to win this war and to break even, though to prevent it this country is forced to take an active part. This ultimate necessity must be constantly in our minds in all our controversies with the belligerents. American public opinion must be prepared for the time, which may come, when we will have to cast aside our neutrality and become one of the champions of democracy."

—from *War Memoirs of Robert Lansing*

DBQ Document-Based Questions

1. **Summarizing** When does Senator Works believe war is justified?
2. **Explaining** Why does Secretary of State Lansing believe Germany is a threat to the United States?
3. **Comparing** Based on these sources, what is the focus of the neutrality debate? What is not being discussed?
4. **Evaluating** Which position do you agree with? Write an essay explaining why the other side is wrong.

W Writing Support

Persuasive Writing Organize students into pairs and ask them to write a letter to Secretary of the Treasury William McAdoo either supporting or opposing his pro-British stance concerning foreign loans. Encourage students to use library or Internet resources to find out more about McAdoo and the nation's loans to the Allies during World War I. Have pairs take turns presenting their letters to the class. **AL**

Debates IN HISTORY

Answers:

1. when a nation makes aggressive warfare against the United States
2. because Germany is hostile to all nations with democratic institutions
3. whether Germany poses a threat to the United States; not being debated is the preparedness issue
4. Answers will vary, but students should support their opinions with facts.

Activity: Collaborative Learning

American Neutrality Have students brainstorm to analyze the United States's dilemma over whether to enter the war. They should consider the principles that guided the foreign policy of the time, moral and idealistic beliefs, and emotional and economic interests. Remind students that the war occurred at a time when the United States had a large population of European immigrants who had close ties to their native countries. Ask students to write a personal essay in response to the following question: Is it possible for a nation to become involved in war because it desires a peaceful world? **OL**

R1 Reading Strategy

Activating Prior Knowledge
Point out to students the desire of many Americans to remain neutral. **Ask:** Why did many Americans want to avoid involvement? *(history of neutrality and avoiding entangling alliances)* **OL**

R2 Reading Strategy

Using Word Parts Sometimes an unfamiliar word can be separated into its different parts to help students understand its meaning. **Ask:** What does the prefix contra mean? (*against*) What are some other words that use this prefix and what do they mean? (contrary: *opposed to*; contradict: *to deny a statement*) **OL**

D Differentiated Instruction

Visual/Spatial Have students find a picture of a German U-boat in library or Internet resources, and write a description of it. **BL**

Turning Point

Answer:
Students should use the text to support their opinions.

Additional Support

Moving Toward War

R1 Although most Americans supported the Allies and hoped for their victory, they did not want to join the conflict. However, a series of events gradually **eroded** American neutrality and drew the nation into the war.

German Submarines Go Into Action

R2 Shortly after the war began, the British declared a blockade of German ports and began intercepting neutral merchant ships sailing to Europe. They forced the ships to land at British ports where they were inspected for **contraband,** or goods prohibited from shipment to Germany and its allies.

D Although Britain's decision to intercept neutral ships, including American ships, led to protests from the U.S. government, the German response angered Americans even more. Britain and France depended on food, equipment, and other supplies from both the United States and their overseas empires. To stop those shipments, Germany deployed submarines known as U-boats—from the German word *Unterseeboot* ("underwater boat"). In February 1915, the Germans announced that they would sink without warning any ship they found in the waters around Britain.

Germany's announcement triggered outrage in the United States and elsewhere. Germany had signed an international treaty that banned attacks on civilian ships without warning. The Germans claimed that their U-boats would be placed at great risk if they had to surface and give a warning before firing.

The Germans Sink the *Lusitania* The issue reached a crisis on May 7, 1915, when the British passenger ship *Lusitania* entered the war zone. A German submarine sunk the ship, killing nearly 1,200 passengers—including 128 Americans. The attack outraged Americans who saw the sinking as a terrorist attack on civilians, including women and children, not as a legitimate act of war.

Wilson tried to defuse the crisis. He refused to threaten Germany with war saying that the United States was "too proud to fight." Instead, he sent several official protests to Germany insisting that it stop endangering the lives of noncombatants in the war zone.

Late in March 1916, Wilson's policy was tested when a U-boat torpedoed the French passenger ship *Sussex*, injuring several Americans on board. Although Wilson's closest advisers favored breaking off diplomatic relations with Germany, the president chose

Turning Points

The Sinking of the *Lusitania*

When World War I began, many Americans supported one side or the other, but most agreed the United States should stay out of the war. Eight months later, when the German submarine U-20 sank the *Lusitania*, killing 1,195 people, including 128 Americans, attitudes began to shift.

The attack seemed to prove that Germany was acting in an uncivilized way and it gave credibility to British propaganda. Even though the United States would not enter the war for nearly two more years, the attack on the *Lusitania* marked a turning point in the war because it changed American attitudes and set the stage for the American entry into the war.

ANALYZING HISTORY Do you think the use of submarines in World War I was justified? Write a brief essay explaining your opinion.

The New York Times. EXTRA

LUSITANIA SUNK BY A SUBMARINE, PROBABLY 1,260 DEAD; TWICE TORPEDOED OFF IRISH COAST; SINKS IN 15 MINUTES; CAPT. TURNER SAVED, FROHMAN AND VANDERBILT MISSING; WASHINGTON BELIEVES THAT A GRAVE CRISIS IS

▲ *A mass funeral for Lusitania victims was held in Queenston, Ireland, on May 23, 1915.* **How do you think people reacted when they saw photos like this in the newspaper?**

▲ *After the sinking, the Boston Committee of Public Safety issued this poster showing a drowning woman and baby and urging Americans to prepare for war by building up the military.*

Activity: Collaborative Learning

Creating a Newsmagazine Have students create a special issue of a magazine that reports United States foreign policy from Wilson's inauguration on March 4, 1913 to his war message to Congress on April 2, 1917. Students might include news articles, news analyses, news features, editorials, and political cartoons. Advise students to determine specific tasks for each individual. Suggest that they elect an editor-in-chief to help organize the selection of topics so that the end product contains varied and accurate coverage of the foreign policy of the period. **AL**

to issue one last warning. He demanded that the German government abandon its methods of submarine warfare or risk war with the United States.

Germany did not want to strengthen the Allies by drawing the United States into the war. It promised with certain conditions to sink no more merchant ships without warning. The **Sussex Pledge,** as it was called, met the foreign-policy goals of both Germany and President Wilson by keeping the United States out of the war a little longer.

Wilson's efforts to keep American soldiers at home played an important part in his reelection bid in 1916. Campaigning as the "peace" candidate, his campaign slogan, "He kept us out of the war," helped Wilson win a narrow victory over the Republican nominee, Charles Evans Hughes.

The United States Declares War

Following Wilson's reelection, events quickly brought the country to the brink of war. In January 1917, a German official named Arthur Zimmermann sent a telegram to the German ambassador in Mexico asking him to make an offer to the Mexican government: If Mexico agreed to become an ally of Germany in a war with the United States, Germany promised Mexico would regain its "lost territory in Texas, New Mexico, and Arizona" after the war. British intelligence intercepted the **Zimmermann telegram.** Shortly afterward, it was leaked to American newspapers. Furious, many Americans now concluded war with Germany was necessary.

R

Then, on February 1, 1917, Germany resumed unrestricted submarine warfare. German military leaders believed that they could starve Britain into submission in four to six months if their U-boats began sinking all ships on sight. Although they knew this decision might draw the United States into the war, they did not believe the Americans could raise an army and transport it to Europe in time. Between February 3 and March 21, German U-boats sank six American ships. Finally roused to action, President Wilson appeared before a special session of Congress on April 2, 1917. Declaring that "the world must be made safe for democracy," Wilson asked Congress to declare war on Germany.

PRIMARY SOURCE

"It is a fearful thing to lead this great peaceful people into war. . . . But the right is more precious than peace, and we shall fight for the things which we have always carried nearest to our hearts—for democracy, for the right of those who submit to authority to have a voice in their own governments, for the rights and liberties of small nations. . . ."

—quoted in the Congressional Record, 1917

After a debate, the Senate passed the resolution on April 4 by a vote of 82 to 6. The House concurred 373 to 50 on April 6, and Wilson signed the resolution. America was at war.

Reading Check **Summarizing** How did Germany's use of unrestricted submarine warfare bring America into World War I?

Section 1 REVIEW

Vocabulary

1. **Explain** the significance of: militarism, nationalism, Balkans, Franz Ferdinand, propaganda, contraband, Sussex Pledge, Zimmermann telegram.

Main Ideas

2. **Identifying** Name the two alliances in Europe at the start of World War I, and list the members of each alliance.

3. **Explaining** Why did many Americans support the British in the war even though the United States was officially neutral?

Critical Thinking

4. **Big Ideas** How did trade and economics contribute to America's entry into World War I?

5. **Organizing** Use a graphic organizer similar to the one below to identify the events that led the United States to enter World War I.

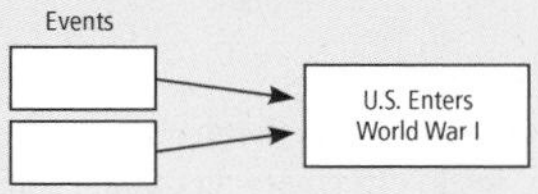

6. **Analyzing Visuals** Examine the images on page 554. How did images like these contribute to America's eventual entry into the war?

Writing About History

7. **Expository Writing** Imagine you are an American survivor of the sinking of the *Lusitania.* Write a letter to President Wilson about what you think he should do.

History ONLINE
Study Central™ To review this section, go to glencoe.com and click on Study Central.

R Reading Strategy

Sequencing Information Have students create a time line that highlights the events that led the United States to enter World War I. Display the time lines in the classroom. OL

Assess

History ONLINE

Study Central™ provides summaries, interactive games, and online graphic organizers to help students review content.

Close

Summarizing Ask: What were the main causes of World War I? *(militarism, alliances, imperialism, and nationalism)* OL

Reading Check

Answer:
With the resumption of unrestricted submarine warfare, German U-boats sank six American ships between February 3 and March 21. Wilson asked Congress to declare war.

Section 1 REVIEW

Answers

1. All definitions can be found in the section and the Glossary.
2. Triple Alliance: Germany, Austria-Hungary, Italy; Triple Entente: France, Great Britain, Russia
3. They believed that Allied victory was the only way to preserve the international balance of power, had greater financial and business ties to the Alliance countries, and they cited the close historical ties with Great Britain and France.
4. The economy of the United States was deeply intertwined with the economies of the Allies.
5. unrestricted submarine warfare; the Zimmermann telegram
6. images turned public opinion against Germany
7. Letters will vary, but students should use information from the textbook in their letters.

Focus

Bellringer

Daily Focus Transparency 16-2

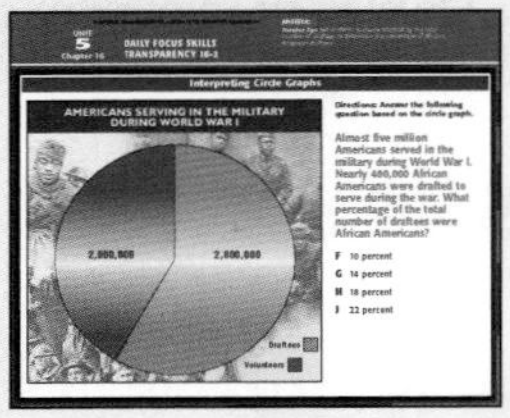

Guide to Reading

Answers:

The Home Front
I. Organizing the Economy
  A. Wartime Agencies
  B. Mobilizing the Workforce
  C. Shaping Public Opinion
II. Building the Military

Students should complete the outline by using all the heads in this section.

Section Spotlight Video

To generate student interest and provide a springboard for class discussion, access the Chapter 16, Section 2 video at glencoe.com or on the video DVD.

Resource Manager

Section 2 — Section Audio — Spotlight Video

The Home Front

Guide to Reading

Big Ideas
Government and Society To successfully fight the war, the United States government had to mobilize the entire nation.

Content Vocabulary
- victory garden *(p. 556)*
- espionage *(p. 558)*

Academic Vocabulary
- migrate *(p. 558)*
- draft *(p. 560)*

People and Events to Identify
- War Industries Board *(p. 556)*
- National War Labor Board *(p. 557)*
- Committee on Public Information *(p. 558)*
- selective service *(p. 560)*

Reading Strategy
Taking Notes Use the major headings of this section to create an outline similar to the one below.

The Home Front
I. Organizing the Economy
  A.
  B.
  C.
II.
  A.
  B.

To fight World War I, the American government used progressive ideas and new government agencies to mobilize the population and organize the economy.

Organizing the Economy

MAIN Idea The government used progressive ideas to manage the economy and pay for the war.

HISTORY AND YOU How do you help conserve food or fuel resources? Read how Americans made sacrifices to aid the war effort.

When the United States entered the war in April 1917, progressives controlled the federal government. Rather than abandon their ideas during wartime, they applied progressive ideas to fighting the war. Their ideas about planning and scientific management shaped how the American government organized the war effort.

Wartime Agencies

To efficiently manage the relationship between the federal government and private companies, Congress created new agencies to coordinate mobilization and ensure the efficient use of national resources. These agencies emphasized cooperation between big business and government, not direct government control. Business executives, managers, and government officials staffed the new agencies.

Managing the Economy Perhaps the most important of the new agencies was the **War Industries Board** (WIB), established in July 1917 to coordinate the production of war materials. At first, the WIB's authority was limited, but problems with production convinced Wilson to expand its powers and appoint Bernard Baruch, a Wall Street stockbroker, to run it. The WIB told manufacturers what they could produce, allocated raw materials, ordered the construction of new factories, and, in a few instances, set prices.

Perhaps the most successful agency was the Food Administration, run by Herbert Hoover. This agency was responsible for increasing food production while reducing civilian consumption. Using the slogan "Food Will Win the War—Don't Waste It," it encouraged families to conserve food and grow their own vegetables in **victory gardens.** By having Wheatless Mondays, Meatless Tuesdays, and Porkless Thursdays, families would leave more food for the troops.

While Hoover managed food production, the Fuel Administration, run by Harry Garfield, tried to manage the nation's use of coal and oil.

R Reading Strategies	C Critical Thinking	D Differentiated Instruction	W Writing Support	S Skill Practice
Teacher Edition • Understanding Vocab., p. 560 **Additional Resources** • Prim. Source Read., URB p. 97 • Guid. Read. Act., URB p. 109 • Am. History in Graphic Novel, p. 45 • Reading Skills Act., URB p. 83	**Additional Resources** • Enrichment Act., URB p. 106 • Linking Past and Present, URB p. 96 • Supreme Court Case Studies, p. 37 • Quizzes and Tests, p. 224	**Teacher Edition** • Special Ed., p. 558 • Verbal/Ling., p. 560 **Additional Resources** • Diff. Instr. Act., URB p. 85 • Am. Art and Music Act., URB p. 101	**Teacher Edition** • Narrative Writing, p. 561 **Additional Resources** • Enrichment Act., URB p. 106	**Teacher Edition** • Making Conn., p. 557 • Using Geo. Skills, p. 558 **Additional Resources** • Hist. Analysis Skills Act., URB p. 84 • Read. Essen., p. 177

PRIMARY SOURCE

Raising Money for World War I

▶ *The actor Douglas Fairbanks urges Americans to buy Liberty Bonds at a rally held in New York City in 1918.*

Analyzing VISUALS

To pay for World War I, the U.S. government increased taxes and issued bonds. Progressives liked bonds because they were voluntary and Americans could buy them based on their financial situation. Officials worried, however, that the war had so divided Americans that few would buy them. To get people to buy bonds, the government printed posters, organized parades, and asked movie stars to promote them.

1. **Analyzing** What was the total revenue raised by loans? What percentage of the cost of the war was paid by taxes?
2. **Interpreting** What point is the poster for the 2nd Liberty Loan making? What group of people does the poster for the 3rd Liberty Loan address?

To conserve energy, Garfield introduced daylight savings time and shortened workweeks for factories that did not make war materials. He also encouraged Americans to observe Heatless Mondays.

Paying for the War By the end of the war, the United States had spent about $32 billion. To fund the war effort, Congress raised income tax rates, placed new taxes on corporate profits, and imposed an extra tax on the profits of arms factories.

Taxes, however, did not cover the entire cost of the war. The government also borrowed over $20 billion through the sale of Liberty Bonds and Victory Bonds. Americans who bought bonds were lending money to the government that would be repaid with interest in a specified number of years.

Mobilizing the Workforce

The success of the war effort also required the cooperation of workers. To prevent strikes from disrupting the war effort, the government established the **National War Labor Board** (NWLB) in March 1918. Chaired by William Howard Taft and Frank Walsh, a prominent labor attorney, the NWLB attempted to mediate labor disputes that might otherwise lead to strikes.

The NWLB often pressured industry to improve wages, adopt an eight-hour workday, and allow unions the right to organize and bargain collectively. In exchange, labor leaders agreed not to disrupt war production with strikes or other disturbances. As a result, membership in unions increased by just over one million between 1917 and 1919.

History ONLINE
Student Web Activity Visit glencoe.com and complete the activity on wartime propaganda.

Teach

S Skill Practice

Making Connections Have students review the photograph, posters, and chart on this page.
Ask: In what way are they connected? *(The photograph and the posters are appeals for money to support the war; the chart illustrates the results of those appeals.)*
Ask: How does national unity help a nation win a war? *(National unity helps direct all the nation's resources to the common goal of winning the war.)* OL

Analyzing VISUALS

Answers:
1. about $25 billion; about 23% came from taxes
2. The poster for 2nd Liberty Loan appeals to Americans to make sure there are enough funds to equip and support soldiers properly. The poster for 3rd Liberty Loan appeals to immigrants who recently came to the United States.

Hands-On Chapter Project
Step 2

Presenting World War I

Step 2: Presenting the Home Front at the Start of the War Ask: What actions did the United States take to mobilize for the war?

Directions Explain to students that they will create one to three multimedia slides or screens to explain the actions the United States took to mobilize for war. Divide students into two teams. The first team should focus on the mobilization of the military. The second team should focus on the mobilization of industry and the workforce. (In both groups, further division might be made between those responsible for boiling down the literal explanation and those finding graphic/visual elements.)

Putting It Together When the two teams meet to finalize the choices for the slides, they will determine how the selected slides demonstrate the preparations of the United States for war. OL

(Chapter Project continued on page 565)

S Skill Practice

Using Geography Skills Provide students with a map of the United States and have them locate the major cities affected by the Great Migration. **Ask:** Why do you think these cities attracted so many African Americans? *(the cities offered job opportunities and less discrimination)* OL

D Differentiated Instruction

Special Education Listening in class to several World War I songs, such as "Over There," "Pack Up Your Troubles in Your Old Kit Bag," and "Keep the Home Fires Burning," may provide an opportunity to engage students who have difficulty relating to the content in more traditional ways. Have students listen to the songs and prompt them to discuss their understanding of the lyrics. BL

Reading Check

Answer:
to make it illegal to interfere with the war effort

Differentiated Instruction

For an example of government efforts to promote patriotism, read "The American's Creed" on page R51 in **Documents in American History.**

Women Support Industry With large numbers of men in the military, employers were willing to hire women for jobs that had traditionally been limited to men. Some one million women joined the workforce for the first time during the war, and another 8 million switched to higher paying industrial jobs. Women worked in factories, shipyards, and railroad yards and served as police officers, mail carriers, and train engineers.

The wartime changes in female employment were not permanent. When the war ended, most women returned to their previous jobs or stopped working. Although the changes were temporary, they demonstrated that women were capable of holding jobs that many had believed only men could do.

The Great Migration Begins Women were not the only group in American society to benefit economically. Desperate for workers, Henry Ford sent company agents to the South to recruit African Americans. Other companies quickly followed Ford's example. Their promises of high wages and plentiful work convinced between 300,000 and 500,000 African Americans to leave the South and move to northern cities.

S This massive population movement became known as the "Great Migration." It greatly altered the racial makeup of such cities as Chicago, New York, Cleveland, and Detroit. It would also, eventually, change American politics. In the South, African Americans were generally denied the right to vote, but in the northern cities they were able to vote and affect the policies of northern politicians.

Mexican Americans Head North The war also encouraged other groups to **migrate.** Continuing political turmoil in Mexico and the wartime labor shortage in the United States convinced many Mexicans to head north. Between 1917 and 1920, over 100,000 Mexicans migrated into the Southwest, providing labor for farmers and ranchers.

Meanwhile, Mexican Americans found new opportunities in factory jobs in Chicago, St. Louis, Omaha, and other cities. Many faced hostility and discrimination when they arrived in American cities. Like other immigrant groups before them, they tended to settle in their own separate neighborhoods, called barrios, where they could support each other.

Shaping Public Opinion

Progressives did not think that organizing the economy was enough to ensure the success of the war effort. They also believed the government needed to shape public opinion.

D **Selling the War** Eleven days after asking Congress to declare war, President Wilson created the **Committee on Public Information** (CPI) to "sell" the war to the American people. Headed by George Creel, a journalist, the CPI recruited advertising executives, artists, authors, songwriters, entertainers, public speakers, and motion picture companies to help sway public opinion in favor of the war.

The CPI distributed pamphlets and arranged for thousands of short patriotic talks, called "four-minute speeches," to be delivered at movie theaters and other public places. Some 75,000 speakers, known as Four-Minute Men, urged audiences to support the war in various ways, from buying war bonds to reporting draft dodgers to the authorities.

Civil Liberties Curtailed Besides using propaganda, the government also passed legislation to limit opposition to the war and fight **espionage,** or spying to acquire government information. The Espionage Act of 1917 made it illegal to aid the enemy, give false reports, or interfere with the war effort. The Sedition Act of 1918 made it illegal to speak against the war publicly. In practice, it allowed officials to prosecute anyone who criticized the government. These two laws led to over 1,000 convictions.

Wartime fears also led to attacks on German Americans, labor activists, socialists, and pacifists. Ads urged Americans to monitor their fellow citizens. Americans even formed private groups, such as the American Protective League and the Boy Spies of America, to spy on neighbors and coworkers.

Despite protests, the Espionage and Sedition Acts were upheld in court. Although the First Amendment specifically states that "Congress shall make no law . . . abridging the freedom of speech, or of the press," the Supreme Court departed from a strict literal interpretation of the Constitution. The Court ruled that the government could restrict speech when the words constitute a "clear and present danger."

Reading Check **Explaining** Why did Congress pass the Espionage Act in 1917?

Leveled Activities

BL **Time Line Activity, URB p. 95**

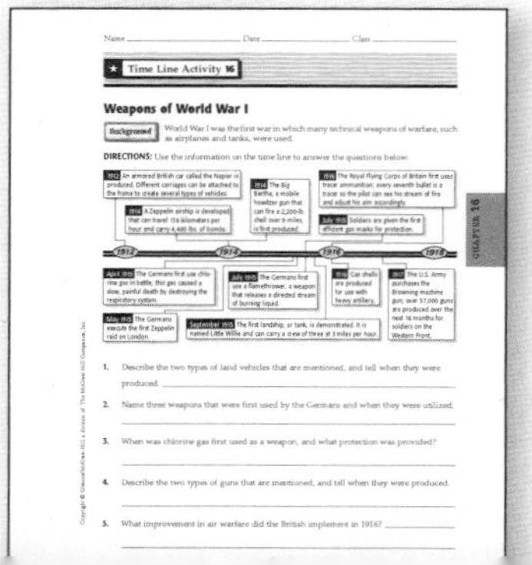

OL **Reinforcing Skills Activity, URB p. 93**

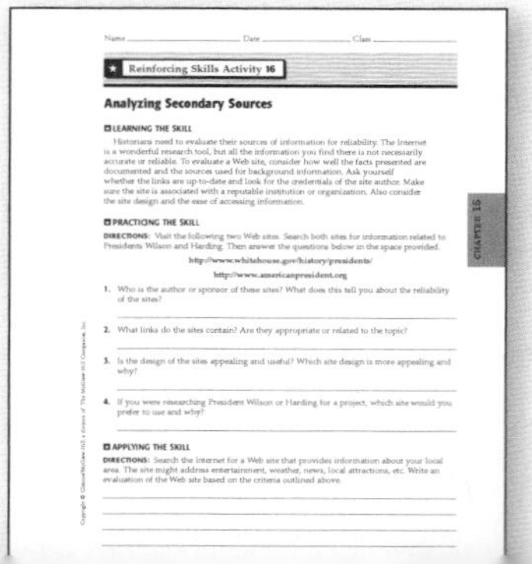

AL **Historical Analysis Skills Activity, URB p. 84**

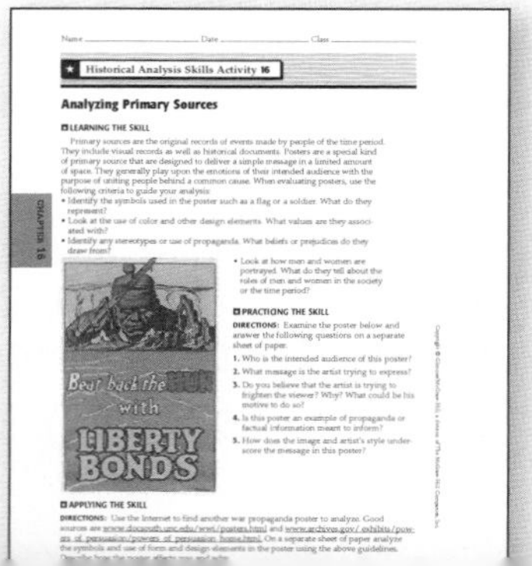

ELL **Content Vocabulary Activity, URB p. 89**

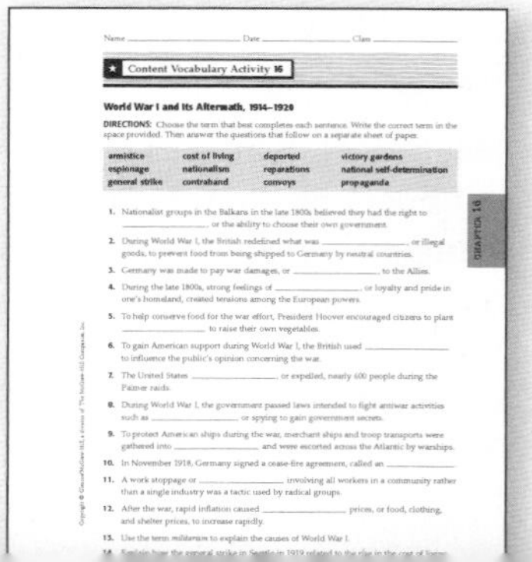

ANALYZING SUPREME COURT CASES

Can Government Limit Free Speech?

★ *Schenck* v. *United States,* 1919
★ *Abrams* v. *United States,* 1919

Background to the Cases

In the fall of 1917, Charles Schenck mailed pamphlets to draftees telling them the draft was wrong and urging them to write protest letters. In August 1918, Jacob Abrams wrote pamphlets denouncing the war and criticizing the decision to send troops to Russia to fight communist forces. Both men were convicted of violating the Espionage Act. Both appealed their convictions all the way to the Supreme Court.

How the Court Ruled

The Schenck and Abrams cases raised the question: Are there some circumstances in which the First Amendment's protection of free speech no longer applies? In both cases, the Supreme Court upheld the Espionage Act, concluding that under certain circumstances, the government can indeed limit free speech. In the Schenck case, the Supreme Court decision was unanimous, but in the Abrams case, the Court split 7-2 in their decision.

▲ Eugene Debs, leader of the American Socialist Party, delivers a speech protesting the war in Canton, Ohio, in 1918. Debs was arrested for making the speech and convicted under the Espionage Act. He appealed to the Supreme Court, but the Court upheld his conviction, citing the *Schenck* case as the precedent.

PRIMARY SOURCE

The Court's Opinion

"The most stringent protection of free speech would not protect a man in falsely shouting fire in a theatre and causing a panic. . . . The question in every case is whether the words used are used in such circumstances and are of such a nature as to create a clear and present danger that they will bring about the substantive evils that Congress has a right to prevent. It is a question of proximity and degree. When a nation is at war, many things that might be said in time of peace are such a hindrance to its effort that their utterance will not be endured so long as men fight, and that no Court could regard them as protected by any constitutional right."

—Justice Oliver Wendell Holmes writing for the Court in *Schenck* v. *U.S.*

PRIMARY SOURCE

Dissenting Views

"It is only the present danger of immediate evil or an intent to bring it about that warrants Congress in setting a limit to the expression of opinion where private rights are not concerned. . . . Now nobody can suppose that the surreptitious publishing of a silly leaflet by an unknown man, without more, would present any immediate danger that its opinions would hinder the success of the government arms. . . .

. . . the ultimate good desired is better reached by free trade in ideas—that the best test of truth is the power of the thought to get itself accepted in the competition of the market . . ."

—Justice Oliver Wendell Holmes dissenting in *Abrams* v. *U.S.*

DBQ Document-Based Questions

1. **Explaining** When does Holmes think the government can restrict speech?
2. **Analyzing** What does Holmes mean by referring to the "free trade in ideas?" Do you think the government should ever be allowed to restrict free speech? Why or why not?
3. **Making Inferences** Why do you think Holmes regarded *Schenck* as a much more immediate danger than *Abrams*? What was the difference between their actions?

SUPREME COURT CASES

Teach

Use the library or Internet to find a copy of the speech delivered by Eugene V. Debs that led to his arrest and conviction under the Espionage Act. Make copies and distribute them to students. Ask students to read the speech and highlight the passages that they think might have been considered to be in violation of the Espionage Act. Then, ask students to write an essay explaining whether or not they believe Debs broke the law.

DBQ Document Based Questions

Answers:

1. when the nation is at war
2. Being able to discuss ideas and opinions openly; answers will vary.
3. Schenck's pamphlets were a direct attempt to undermine the American war effort; Abrams was expressing his opinions of the war and criticizing a government decision.

Extending the Content

Defending Free Speech Not all Americans were caught up in the wartime frenzy. Some spoke out against the espionage and sedition laws and what they considered violations of free speech. Senator Robert La Follette and Professor Zechariah Chafee, Jr., of Harvard Law School, openly defended Americans' rights to exercise freedom of speech with regard to war. The newly formed Civil Liberties Union assisted pacifists and conscientious objectors who had been subjected to ridicule and abuse. Professor Chafee explained that he believed that the Framers of the First Amendment intended "to wipe out the common law of sedition, and make further prosecutions for criticism of the government, without any incitement to law breaking, forever impossible in the United States of America." Most Americans, however, gave little thought to restrictions on speech and supported the war without questioning the rights they were giving up.

R Reading Strategy

Understanding Vocabulary Have students paraphrase their understanding of *conscription.* **Ask:** Do you believe it is the responsibility of all able-bodied individuals to serve in the military, or should they have a choice to abstain? *(Students' answers will vary.)* OL

D Differentiated Instruction

Verbal/Linguistic Instruct students to write a three-minute speech persuading young men to enlist in the army in 1917. Students can use patriotic music, posters, emotionally charged rhetoric, and symbolism to make their speeches convincing. OL

Analyzing VISUALS

Answers:

1. The French do not have the same history of segregation as the United States.
2. Lincoln freed enslaved African Americans and saved the Union.

Additional Support

Building the Military

MAIN Idea The United States instituted a draft for military service, and African Americans and women took on new roles.

HISTORY AND YOU Describe a time you were required to do something that you might not have done otherwise. Read on to learn about the selective service system.

Progressives did not abandon their ideas when it came to building up the military. Instead, they applied their ideas and developed a new system for recruiting a large army.

Volunteers and Conscripts

When the United States entered the war in 1917, the army and National Guard together had slightly more than 300,000 troops. Many men volunteered after war was declared, but many more were still needed.

R **Selective Service** Many progressives believed that conscription—forced military service—was a violation of democratic and republican principles. Believing a **draft** was necessary, however, Congress, with Wilson's support, created a new conscription system called **selective service.**

Instead of having the military run the draft from Washington, D.C., the Selective Service Act of 1917 required all men between 21 and 30 to register for the draft. A lottery randomly determined the order in which they were called before a local draft board in charge of selecting or exempting people from military service.

The thousands of local boards were the heart of the system. The members of the draft boards were civilians from local communities. Progressives believed local people, understanding community needs, would know which men to draft and would do a far better job than a centralized government bureaucracy. Eventually about 2.8 million Americans were drafted.

Volunteers for War Not all American soldiers were drafted. Approximately 2 million men volunteered for military service. Some had heard stories of German atrocities and wanted to fight back. Others believed democracy was at stake. Many believed they had a duty to respond to their nation's call. They had D

PRIMARY SOURCE
African Americans in World War I

During World War I, the U.S. Army kept most African American soldiers out of combat, assigning them to work as cooks, laborers, and laundrymen. The 369th Regiment, however, was assigned to the French Army and was sent to frontline trenches almost immediately. Nicknamed the "Harlem Hell-Fighters," the entire 369th was awarded the French Croix de Guerre ("war cross"), for gallantry in combat. The regiment spent 191 days in the trenches, much longer than many other units, and suffered 1,500 casualties.

▼ African American soldiers march near Verdun, France, November 1918.

▲ A 1918 poster commemorates the 369th Regiment—the first Americans to see combat in World War I.

Analyzing VISUALS

1. **Theorizing** Why do you think the French were willing to use African Americans in combat?
2. **Analyzing** Why do you think the poster includes a quote from Abraham Lincoln?

Activity: Collaborative Learning

Planning Promotional Campaigns Organize students into four groups. Have one group create a plan to promote conscription; another group plan to promote food conservation; a third group to rouse support for the war effort among business and labor organizations; and a fourth group to plan to promote pacifism or opposition to the war. Have each group research its topic and then choose a spokesperson to present the plan. Make sure students find an appropriate way to divide and complete the work. OL BL grown up listening to stories of the Civil War and the Spanish-American War. They saw World War I as a great adventure and wanted to fight for their country.

Although the horrors of war soon became apparent to the American troops, their morale remained high, helping to ensure victory. More than 50,000 Americans died in combat and over 200,000 were wounded. Another 60,000 soldiers died from disease, mostly from the influenza epidemic of 1918 and 1919.

The flu epidemic was not limited to the battlefield. It spread around the world and made more than a quarter of all Americans sick. The disease killed an estimated 25–50 million people worldwide, including more than 500,000 Americans.

African Americans in the War Of the nearly 400,000 African Americans who were drafted, about 42,000 served overseas as combat troops. African American soldiers encountered discrimination and prejudice in the army, where they served in racially segregated units, almost always under the supervision of white officers.

Despite these challenges, many African American soldiers fought with distinction. For example, the African American 92nd and 93rd Infantry Divisions fought in bitter battles along the Western Front. Many of them won praise from both the French commander, Marshal Henri Pétain, and the United States commander, General John Pershing.

Women Join the Military

World War I was the first war in which women officially served in the armed forces, although only in noncombat positions. As the military prepared for war in 1917, it faced a severe shortage of clerical workers because so many men were assigned to active duty. Early in 1917, the navy authorized the enlistment of women to meet its clerical needs.

Women serving in the navy wore a standard uniform and were assigned the rank of yeoman. By the end of the war, over 11,000 women had served in the navy. Although most performed clerical duties, others served as radio operators, electricians, pharmacists, chemists, and photographers.

Unlike the navy, the army refused to enlist women. Instead, it began hiring women as temporary employees to fill clerical jobs. The only women to actually serve in the army were in the Army Nursing Corps.

W Women nurses had served in both the army and navy since the early 1900s, but as auxiliaries. They were not assigned ranks, and were not technically enlisted in the army or navy. Army nurses were the only women in the military sent overseas during the war. More than 20,000 nurses served in the Army Nursing Corps during the war, including more than 10,000 overseas.

Reading Check **Describing** How did Congress ensure that the United States would have enough troops to serve in World War I?

Section 2 REVIEW

Vocabulary

1. **Explain** the significance of: War Industries Board, victory gardens, National War Labor Board, Committee on Public Information, espionage, selective service.

Main Ideas

2. **Examining** How did government efforts to ensure public support for the war conflict with ideas about civil rights?

3. **Describing** What were the contributions of African Americans during the war?

Critical Thinking

4. **Big Ideas** How did progressives use their ideas to mobilize both the economy and the American people during the war?

5. **Organizing** Use a graphic organizer similar to the one below to identify the effects of the war on the American workforce.

U.S. Groups	Effects
Women	
African Americans	
Hispanics	

6. **Analyzing Visuals** Examine the graph on page 557. How much did World War I cost? Do you think the government should rely on taxes or loans to fund a war? Explain.

Writing About History

7. **Persuasive Writing** Imagine that you are working for the Committee on Public Information. Write text for an advertisement or lyrics to a song in which you attempt to sway public opinion in favor of the war.

History ONLINE
Study Central™ To review this section, go to glencoe.com and click on Study Central.

W Writing Support

Narrative Writing Have students write a one-page paper that describes the gains for women due to World War I and the limitations they still faced. **OL**

Assess

History ONLINE

Study Central™ provides summaries, interactive games, and online graphic organizers to help students review content.

Close

Summarizing **Ask:** How did World War I affect America on the home front? *(the government managed the economy; civil liberties were curtailed; African Americans moved to northern cities; many Mexicans migrated to the United States)* **OL**

Reading Check

Answer:
The United States initiated the draft.

Section 2 REVIEW

Answers

1. All definitions can be found in the section and the Glossary.
2. The government passed the Espionage and Sedition Acts. These acts made it illegal to print information opposed to the war or speak against the war publicly. These provisions curtailed First Amendment freedoms.
3. Most African Americans served in support services, but some served alongside French troops against the Germans. At home, African Americans supported the war effort by working in factories.
4. Progressives established agencies such as the War Industries Board and the National War Labor Board and created the Committee on Public Information to sell the war.
5. women: worked in jobs that had been traditionally held by men, joined the navy, served as army nurses; African Americans: moved to Northern cities for more opportunities, served in the military; Hispanics: migrated to the United States and Mexican Americans moved to industrial cities.
6. About $32 billion; answers will vary, but students should support their opinions with examples.
7. Students' advertisements or lyrics will vary.

ANALYZING PRIMARY SOURCES

Focus

Propaganda is defined as material disseminated by the advocates or opponents of a doctrine or cause, such as *wartime propaganda*. During World War I, both sides used propaganda to increase support for the war.

Teach

C Critical Thinking

Analyzing Primary Sources Have students study Primary Source 1. **Ask:** What connection is the poster attempting to make? *(It compares Pershing's army to the Crusaders of the Middle Ages.)* OL

R Reading Strategy

Inferring Have students read Primary Source 3. **Ask:** What clear distinction is the author making between "Germans, and a German"? *(The Germans, as a nation, are the enemy, but individual Germans are human beings with feelings and families, not much different from Americans.)* OL

ANALYZING PRIMARY SOURCES

Propaganda in World War I

All of the warring nations in World War I used propaganda to boost support for their side. Many Americans believed the propaganda coming from Europe, particularly from the British government and press. When the United States entered the war, the American government also began using propaganda in an attempt to unite Americans behind the war effort.

Read the passages and study the posters. Then answer the questions that follow.

PRIMARY SOURCE 1

Movie Poster, 1918

C

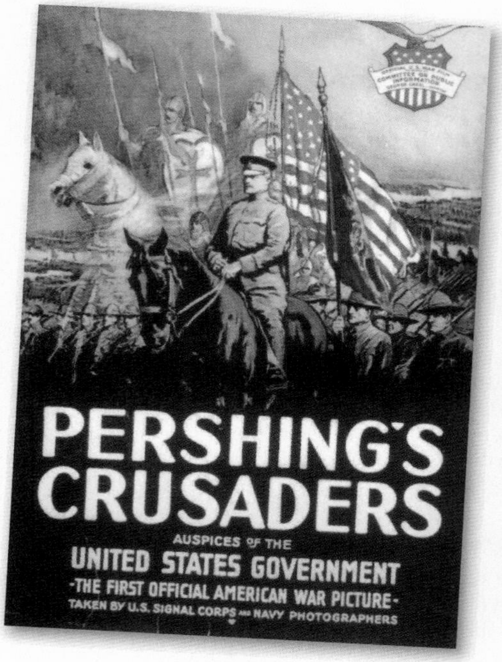

PRIMARY SOURCE 2

Government War Bond Advertisement, 1918

PRIMARY SOURCE 3

American Soldier's Diary, 1918

"Germans, and a German—so different. Fishing through the poor torn pockets of shabby German body, drooped over wreck of machine gun, to find well-thumbed photograph of woman and little boy and little girl—so like one's own . . . impossible to hate what had been that body.

Nothing so revolting as bitter, pitiless cruelty of those who know nothing of reality of it all. Those . . . Germano-baiters at home, so much more cruel than those who have the right—and are not."

—Diary of Lieutenant Howard V. O'Brien, October 6, 1918

R

Differentiated Instruction

Differentiated Instruction Activity 16, URB pp. 85–86

Analyzing Propaganda: Support for World War I

Objective: To analyze propaganda.

Focus: Discuss how propaganda is used to sway public opinion.

Teach: Explain the propaganda techniques used on this page and in the activity.

Assess: Ask students whether they think propaganda is an appropriate way to influence opinion.

Close: Discuss how propaganda is still used today and give recent examples.

Differentiated Instruction Strategies

- **BL** Explain the purpose of each piece of propaganda on pages 562–563 and in the activity.
- **AL** Research Axis propaganda used in World War I. How is it different from Allied propaganda? Focus on symbolism and ideology.
- **ELL** Describe the pictures used in the posters. What effect do they produce?

PRIMARY SOURCE 4

Newspaper Column, *New York Times*, May 1915

▼ *Great Britain established the Bryce Committee to investigate German atrocities in Belgium. Its findings, released just five days after the sinking of the* Lusitania, *increased anti-German sentiment in the United States. Investigations after the war, however, found that many of the stories were false or gross exaggerations.*

GERMAN ATROCITIES ARE PROVED, FINDS BRYCE COMMITTEE

Not Only Individual Crimes, but Premeditated Slaughter in Belgium.

YOUNG AND OLD MUTILATED

Women Attacked, Children Brutally Slain, Arson and Pillage Systematic.

COUNTENANCED BY OFFICERS

Wanton Firing on Red Cross and White Flag; Prisoners and Wounded Shot.

CIVILIANS USED AS SHIELDS

Proof That Belgians Did Not Fire on Germans at Louvain—Germans Received Kindness.

R

PRIMARY SOURCE 5

U.S. Government Pamphlet, 1918

"Fear, perhaps, is rather an important element to be bred in the civilian population. It is difficult to unite a people by talking only on the highest ethical plane. To fight for an ideal, perhaps, must be coupled with thoughts of self-preservation. So a truthful appeal to the fear of men, the recognition of the terrible things that would happen if the German Government were permitted to retain its prestige, may be necessary in order that all people unite in the support of the needed sacrifices."

—Pamphlet for speakers from the Committee on Public Information, quoted in the *New York Times*, February 4, 1918

C

PRIMARY SOURCE 6

American Red Cross Poster

R

DBQ Document-Based Questions

1. **Explaining** Examine Primary Source 1. What is the underlying message behind the poster for "Pershing's Crusaders"?
2. **Identifying** What images of the Germans do Primary Sources 2 and 6 promote?
3. **Analyzing** Study Primary Source 4. How do you think stories of German atrocities affected American neutrality?
4. **Making Connections** Read Primary Sources 3 and 5. Why do you think the government used propaganda? Do you think propaganda is a good idea in wartime?
5. **Evaluating** According to Primary Sources 2, 5, and 6, what is at stake in the war? What should citizens do to help the war effort?

Assess/Close

C Critical Thinking

Drawing Conclusions Have students read Primary Source 5. **Ask:** What message is being given by this pamphlet excerpt? *(that fear is to be used to turn public opinion against the Germans and keep the public united in supporting the war)* **OL**

R Reading Strategy

Summarizing Have students review Primary Sources 4 and 6. **Ask:** What is the common message of these primary sources? *(That the Germans are willing to ruin the lives of civilians to achieve their military goals.)* **OL**

Document Based Questions

Answers

DBQ Document Based Questions

1. The fight against the Germans is righteous.
2. The Germans are barbarians.
3. The stories of German atrocities made it difficult, if not impossible, to remain neutral.
4. to sway public opinion in favor of the war; answers will vary
5. German barbarism would dominate the world; citizens should support the war, buy war bonds, and give blood.

Focus

Bellringer

Daily Focus Transparency 16-3

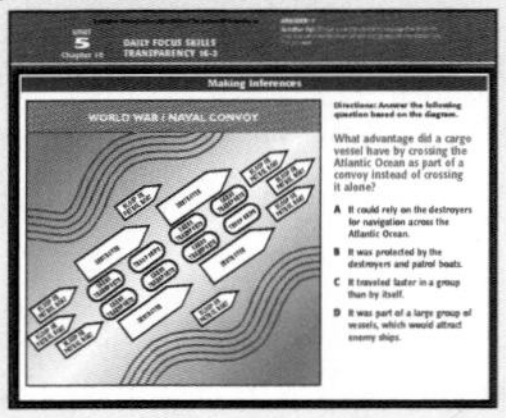

Guide to Reading

Answers may include: airplanes, poison gas, machine guns, trenches, tanks

Section Spotlight Video

To generate student interest and provide a springboard for class discussion, access the Chapter 16, Section 3 video at glencoe.com or on the video DVD.

Section 3 — Section Audio — Spotlight Video

A Bloody Conflict

Guide to Reading

Big Ideas

Individual Action American troops played a major role in helping end the war.

Content Vocabulary

- convoy *(p. 567)*
- armistice *(p. 569)*
- national self-determination *(p. 570)*
- reparations *(p. 572)*

Academic Vocabulary

- network *(p. 564)*
- adequately *(p. 567)*
- resolve *(p. 570)*

People and Events to Identify

- no-man's-land *(p. 564)*
- John J. Pershing *(p. 568)*
- Treaty of Versailles *(p. 570)*
- Fourteen Points *(p. 570)*
- League of Nations *(p. 571)*

Reading Strategy

Organizing Complete a graphic organizer similar to the one below by listing the kinds of warfare and technology used in the fighting.

Technology caused both sides to lose millions of men during World War I. The arrival of American troops helped the Allies win, but the peace treaty set the stage for another war to come.

Combat in World War I

MAIN Idea New technologies made World War I the first modern war.

HISTORY AND YOU What new technologies have been developed or proposed in your lifetime? Read on to learn about the weapons that World War I personnel faced.

By the spring of 1917, World War I had devastated Europe. Old-fashioned strategies and new technologies resulted in terrible destruction. Many Americans believed, however, that their troops would make a difference and quickly bring the war to an end.

Trench Warfare

Early offensives in 1914 demonstrated that warfare had changed. Powerful artillery guns were placed several miles behind the front lines. From there, they hurled huge explosive shells onto the battlefield. More people were killed by artillery fire than by any other weapon in World War I. Artillery fire produced horrific scenes of death and destruction, as one American noted in his diary:

Primary Source

"Many dead Germans along the road. One heap on a manure pile. . . . Devastation everywhere. Our barrage has rooted up the entire territory like a ploughed field. Dead horses galore, many of them have a hind quarter cut off—the Huns [Germans] need food. Dead men here and there."

—quoted in *The American Spirit*

To protect themselves from artillery, troops began digging trenches. On the Western Front—where German troops confronted French, British, and Belgian forces—the troops dug a **network** of trenches that stretched from the English Channel to the Swiss border. To prevent the enemy from overrunning the trenches, troops relied upon a new weapon, the machine gun, to hold off the attackers. The space between opposing trenches was called **no-man's-land.** It was a rough barren landscape filled with craters from artillery fire. To prevent troops from crossing no-man's-land, both sides built barbed wire entanglements and obstacles in front of their trenches.

Resource Manager

R Reading Strategies	C Critical Thinking	D Differentiated Instruction	W Writing Support	S Skill Practice
Teacher Edition • Analyzing, p. 565 • Analyzing Text Structure, p. 566 **Additional Resources** • Guid. Read. Act., URB p. 110	**Teacher Edition** • Drawing Conclusions, p. 572 • Det. Cause and Effect, p. 567 • Making Inferences, pp. 568, 570, 572 **Additional Resources** • Quizzes and Tests, p. 225	**Teacher Edition** • Visual/Spatial, p. 571	**Teacher Edition** • Narrative Writing, p. 569 • Descriptive Writing, pp. 566, 568, 571 • Expository Writing, pp. 567, 570	**Teacher Edition** • Visual Literacy, p. 568 • Ident. Point of View, p. 573 **Additional Resources** • Time Line Act., URB p. 95 • Read. Essen., p. 180

NATIONAL GEOGRAPHIC The War in the Trenches, 1914–1916

Trench Warfare

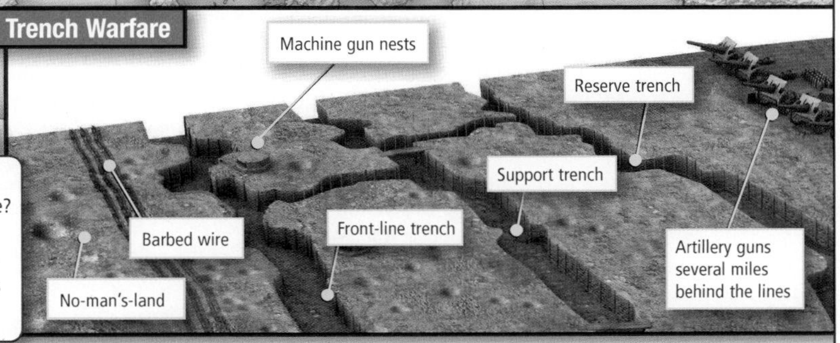

Analyzing GEOGRAPHY

1. **Location** Along what nations' boundaries did the Western Front lie?
2. **Human-Environment Interaction** In addition to weapons, what other dangers did troops in the trenches face?

R To break through enemy lines, the attacker would begin with a massive artillery barrage. Soldiers would then scramble out of their trenches, race across no-man's-land while enemy machine guns fired at them, and try to capture the enemy's trenches.

Before charging enemy trenches, troops fixed bayonets—long knives—to their rifles. For those troops that made it across no-man's-land, fighting in the trenches was brutal. Troops threw grenades—small bombs—at each other, and used bayonets, rifle butts, knives, axes, pistols and even rocks and fists to kill the enemy.

The results of this kind of warfare were horrific. In major battles, both sides often lost hundreds of thousands of men, yet neither side was able to break through the other's lines.

New Technology

New technologies were needed to break through enemy lines. In April 1915, the Germans first used poison gas near Ypres. The fumes caused vomiting, blindness, and suffocation. Soon afterward the Allies also began using poison gas. To counter gas attacks, both sides developed gas masks.

In late 1915, the British introduced the armored tank into battle. These tanks were slow and mechanically unreliable, but they could crush barbed wire and cross trenches. Unfortunately, there were not enough of them. The tanks could support the troops, but they did not revolutionize warfare in World War I. By the time World War II broke out, however, tanks had replaced cavalry in most modern armies and made trench warfare obsolete.

Teach

R Reading Strategy

Analyzing Tell students to read the description of trench warfare. **Ask:** Why were casualty rates so high in World War I? *(Troops crossing the open spaces between trenches known as "no-man's land" were easily gunned down by enemy fire.)* **BL**

Did You Know?

Corpses left in trenches, as well as food scraps, attracted many rats. Since rats propagate rapidly (one pair of rats can produce 880 offspring in a year), the trenches soon became infested. The rats became large and bold and would even eat a wounded man if he could not defend himself.

Analyzing GEOGRAPHY

Answers:

1. France, Germany, and Belgium
2. disease; poor sanitary conditions; weather exposure

Hands-On Chapter Project
Step 3

Presenting World War I

Step 3: Presenting the Battles and Victories of World War I

Ask: What were the crucial factors that led to a victory in the war?

Directions Explain to students that they will create one to three multimedia slides or screens to describe the factors that led to an Allied victory in the war. Divide students into two teams. The first team should focus on the battles and the factors that led to military victories. The second team should focus on the victory and the peace that followed. (In both groups, further division might be made between those responsible for boiling down the literal explanation and those finding graphic/visual elements.)

Putting It Together When the two teams meet to finalize the choices for the slides, they will determine how to illustrate the battles of the war and the peace that followed. **OL** *(Chapter Project continued on page 577)*

W Writing Support

Descriptive Writing Have students use library or Internet resources to find out more about one of the weapons first used in World War I. Then have students write a paragraph describing this weapon in use as if they are seeing it for the first time. **BL**

R Reading Strategy

Analyzing Text Structures Ask students to define the word *convoy* as both a noun and a verb. (noun: a group of cars, trucks, or ships traveling together; verb: to escort or guide) **Ask:** Where do you typically see convoys today? *(trucks traveling together on the highway)* **BL**

World War I also marked the first use of aircraft in war. In addition, it was the first and last time that zeppelins were used in combat. Zeppelins are giant rigid balloons, also known as blimps or dirigibles. Early in the war, the Germans sent squadrons of zeppelins to drop bombs on British warships in the North Sea.

At first, airplanes were used as scouts. They flew over enemy territory, as well as the English Channel and the North Sea, spying on enemy troops and ships. Before long, however, the Allies equipped them with machine guns to attack the German zeppelin fleet. The machine guns were timed to fire through the aircraft's propeller as it spun so that the bullets did not hit the propeller. A few airplanes even carried rockets to destroy the zeppelins. Others carried small bombs to drop on enemy lines.

As technology advanced, aircraft were used to shoot down other aircraft. Battles between aircraft became known as dogfights. Early military aircraft were difficult to fly and easy to destroy. The wings and body frame were covered in cloth and easily caught fire. Pilots did not carry parachutes. The average life expectancy of a combat pilot in World War I was about two weeks.

✓Reading Check **Describing** What new technologies were introduced in World War I?

The Americans Arrive

MAIN Idea The arrival of Americans changed the course of the war and helped the Allies win.

HISTORY AND YOU Have you ever had to boost someone's morale? Read on to learn about Americans who helped the Allies win World War I.

Waves of American troops marched into this bloody stalemate—nearly 2 million before the war's end. Although the "doughboys," as American soldiers were nicknamed, were inexperienced, they were fresh and eager to fight. Their presence boosted the morale of Allied forces. It also demoralized the German soldiers, who now faced large numbers of fresh troops. As the Americans began to arrive, many in Germany concluded that the war was lost.

Winning the War at Sea

No American troopships were sunk on their way to Europe thanks to the efforts of American Admiral William S. Sims. The British preferred to fight German submarines by sending warships to find them, while merchant ships would race across the Atlantic individually. This approach enabled German submarines to inflict heavy losses on British shipping. Sims

TECHNOLOGY & HISTORY

New Weapons World War I is often called the first modern war because troops used new technology that is still widely used in warfare today. Much of this new technology developed in response to trench warfare.

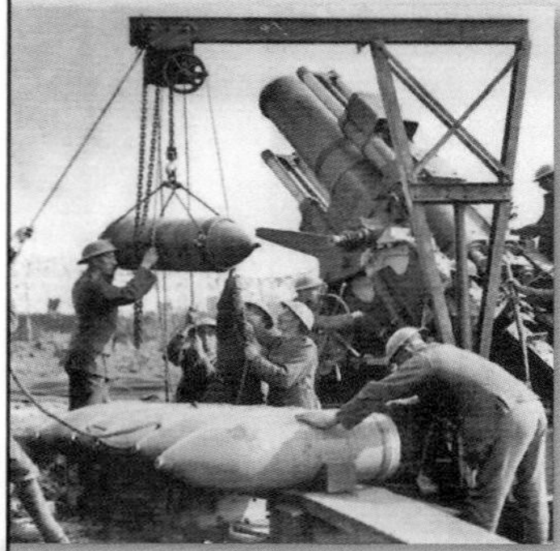

Australian War Memorial Negative Number, E00921

◀ **Artillery Forces Troops into Trenches** Australian soldiers load an artillery shell during the Battle of Passchendaele in 1917. Powerful long-range artillery fire from guns like this forced troops to build trenches for protection.

▲ **Machine Guns Defend Trenches** Machine guns made it very difficult to capture enemy trenches. They could fire thousands of bullets per minute. A small team with a machine gun could down hundreds of troops crossing open terrain. This photo shows a German machine gun crew.

Additional Support

Extending the Content

Flying Aces Three pilots who flew bombers in World War I were among the best-known fighters of the war. American Eddie Rickenbacker shot down 22 planes during the war. Using a daring method, Rickenbacker flew extremely close to enemy planes before firing his guns. He often returned from dogfights with his own plane riddled with bullets. After the war, Rickenbacker settled into the automobile industry and started the Rickenbacker Motor Company.

Flying aces from other countries also became famous. Manfred von Richthofen of Germany, known as the "Red Baron," was credited with 80 victories. As von Richthofen's fame spread he increasingly became the target of Allied warplanes, and on April 21, 1918, he was shot down and killed. His body was recovered by British forces, who buried him with full military honors.

Frenchman René Fonck was credited with 75 victories in World War I. He closely studied the methods of enemy pilots and strictly conserved ammunition during fights—tactics that aided him in his victories. After the war, Fonck worked as a demonstration pilot and an inspector of fighter aviation within the French Air Force.

proposed that merchant ships and troop transports be gathered into groups, called **convoys.** Small highly maneuverable warships called destroyers would protect and escort the convoys across the Atlantic.

Convoys also saved lives. If a ship was sunk, other ships in the convoy could rescue survivors. The system worked. Convoys greatly reduced shipping losses and ensured that a large number of American troops arrived safely in Europe in time to help stop Germany's last great offensive on the Western Front.

Russia Leaves the War

In March 1917, riots broke out in Russia over the government's handling of the war and the scarcity of food and fuel. Czar Nicholas II, the leader of the Russian Empire, abdicated his throne. This marked the beginning of the Russian Revolution.

C W Political leadership in Russia passed to a provisional, or temporary, government. The leaders of the provisional government wanted Russia to stay in the war. However, the government was unable to deal **adequately** with the major problems afflicting the nation, such as food shortages. The Bolshevik Party, led by Vladimir Lenin, overthrew the provisional government and established a Communist government in November 1917.

Germany's military fortunes improved with the Bolshevik takeover of Russia. Lenin's first act after seizing power was to pull Russia out of the war and concentrate on establishing a Communist state. Lenin agreed to the Treaty of Brest-Litovsk with Germany on March 3, 1918. Under this treaty, Russia lost substantial territory. It gave up the Ukraine, its Polish and Baltic territories, and Finland.

With the Eastern Front settled, Germany could now concentrate its forces in the west. German leaders knew this was their last chance to win. If the troops transferred from Russia could not break Allied lines, it was only a matter of time before Germany would have to surrender.

Americans Enter Combat

At the time World War I began, many Americans knew that the French had helped the United States during the American Revolution. American school children still learned the story of the Marquis de Lafayette, who had brought French officers to America to help train American soldiers and who had served on George Washington's staff during the Revolutionary War. Many Americans regarded the French people as friends and believed the nation owed the French a debt for their help in the revolution.

◀ **Poison Gas vs. Trenches**
To break through trench lines, both sides began using poison gas. To protect against gas attacks, troops were forced to carry gas masks similar to those shown here worn by American soldiers in France in 1917.

▲ **Airplanes Bomb Trenches**
Airplanes offered both sides a way to counter trench warfare. Several types of aircraft, including the British Sopwith Camel shown above, could carry 4–5 small bombs to drop on enemy artillery and trenches. They also attacked troops using their machine guns.

Tanks vs. Trenches ▶
To help capture trenches, the Allies built tanks that were immune to machine gun fire and able to smash through barbed wire. Tanks had tracks instead of wheels, enabling them to cross the mud and craters of no-man's-land.

Analyzing VISUALS

1. **Analyzing** Modern militaries do not use trench warfare. Which weapons pictured eventually ended the use of trenches?
2. **Synthesizing** Explain how the different technologies of World War I worked together to kill so many people.

W Writing Support

Expository Writing Using library or Internet resources, have students write a biographical report on Vladimir Lenin, focusing on his Communist beliefs and his leadership philosophies. **OL**

C Critical Thinking

Determining Cause and Effect Have students reread the section "Russia Leaves the War."
Ask: How did the Russian Revolution help the German war effort? *(Students should note that with peace on the Eastern Front, Germany could move all its troops and weapons to the Western Front to fight against the Allies.)* **OL**

Analyzing VISUALS

Answers:
1. tanks and airplanes
2. All the new weapons were able to cause death on a scale previously unknown; also, as these technologies were new, inventions to repel or fight against them had not been invented.

Additional Support

Extending the Content

Gas Masks During World War I, soldiers were equipped with gas masks to protect them against poison gas attacks. So, too, were their horses. In his war diary, Lieutenant Robert Casey of the 124th Field Artillery described his experience:

"The horses wear gas masks also. . . . Neat little bundle perched atop the nose and soaked every time the animal takes a drink. A horse without a gas mask can live about five minutes. With a gas mask he can live about five minutes. It takes only about eleven minutes to convince the horse that he ought to wear the gas mask. And there you are."

C Critical Thinking

Making Inferences Remind students that almost all American troops who fought in World War I remained under American, rather than foreign, command. **Ask:** Why was it important for American troops to answer to American generals during the war? *(Answers will vary, but students might note that it helped build public support at home and gave U.S. commanders independence.)* **AL**

W Writing Support

Descriptive Writing Have students use library or Internet resources to find out more information about the Battle of Cantigny. Then have students assume the role of a newspaper reporter and write an article about the battle. **OL**

S Skill Practice

Visual Literacy Have students refer back to the photo of the Argonne Forest on pages 546 and 547. **Ask:** What conditions do you observe that would make fighting difficult? *(Answers might include fog, mud, and lack of cover.)* **OL**

Additional Support

When General **John J. Pershing,** commander of the American Expeditionary Force (AEF), arrived in Paris on July 4, 1917, he and his officers headed to Picpus Cemetery where Lafayette was buried. One of Pershing's officers, Colonel Charles E. Stanton, raised his hand in salute and proclaimed, "Lafayette, we are here!" France had helped the United States gain its freedom. Now American soldiers would help the French to preserve theirs.

When American troops began arriving in France, the British and French commanders wanted to integrate them into their armies under British and French command. Pershing refused, and President Wilson supported him. Pershing insisted that American soldiers fight in American units under American command.

Despite French and British pleas that they needed American soldiers to replace their own losses, Pershing held firm with one exception. The 93rd Infantry Division—an African American unit—was transferred to the French. Its soldiers became the first Americans to enter combat.

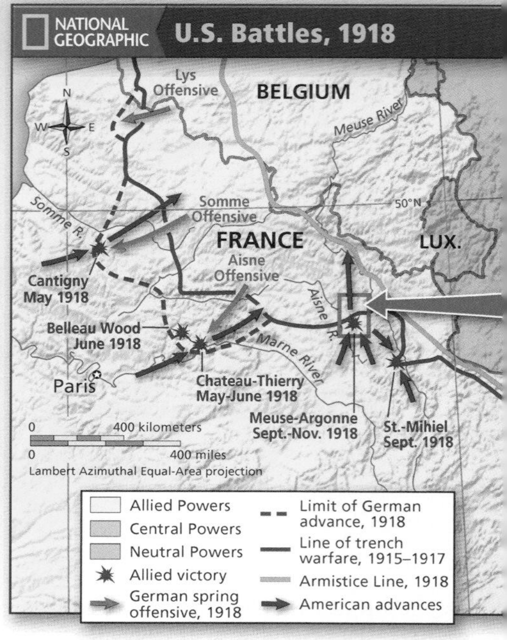

Germany's Last Offensive On March 21, 1918, the Germans launched a massive attack along the Western Front, beginning with gas attacks and a huge artillery bombardment. German forces, strengthened by reinforcements from the Russian front, pushed deep into Allied lines. By early June, they were less than 40 miles (64 km) from Paris.

American troops played an important role in containing the German offensive. In late May, as the German offensive continued, the Americans launched their first major attack, quickly capturing the village of Cantigny. On June 1, American and French troops blocked the German drive on Paris at the town of Château-Thierry. On July 15, the Germans launched one last massive attack in an attempt to take Paris, but American and French troops held their ground.

The Battle of the Argonne Forest With the German drive stalled, French Marshal Ferdinand Foch, supreme commander of the Allied forces, ordered massive counterattacks. In mid-September, American troops drove back German forces at the battle of Saint-Mihiel. Next, an American offensive was launched in the region between the Meuse River and the Argonne Forest. General Pershing assembled over 600,000 American troops, 40,000 tons of supplies, and roughly 4,000 artillery pieces for the most massive attack in American history.

The attack began on September 26, 1918. German positions slowly fell to the advancing American troops. The Germans inflicted heavy casualties, but by early November the Americans had shattered German defenses and opened a hole on the eastern flank of the German lines. Soon after, all across the Western Front, the Germans began to retreat.

American Heroes

Although the brutal trench warfare of World War I led to many acts of astonishing bravery, the actions of two Americans, Corporal Alvin York and Captain Eddie Rickenbacker, captured the nation's imagination.

Alvin York Born in 1887, Alvin York grew up poor in the mountains of Tennessee, where he learned to shoot by hunting wild game. Opposed to war, he initially tried to avoid the draft as a conscientious objector—a person who refuses to obey the law because of his moral or religious beliefs. As a Christian, York

Activity: Interdisciplinary Connection

Literature Explain that German author Erich Maria Remarque (1898–1970) served in the front line trenches during the Great War. In his 1929 novel *All Quiet on the Western Front,* he wrote of the devastation and cruelty of the war and life in the trenches. Have students read the following quote and ask them to paraphrase Remarque's words. **OL**

"The sun goes down, night comes, the shells whine, life is at an end.

Still the little piece of convulsed earth in which we lie is held. We have yielded no more than a few hundred yards of it as a prize to the enemy. But on every yard there lies a dead man."

PRIMARY SOURCE

Alvin York and the Battle of the Argonne Forest

October 8th 1918, Argonne Forest, France.

"So on the morning of the 8th, just before daylight, we started for the hill of Chattel Chehery. So before we got there it got light, and the Germans sent over a heavy barrage and also gas, and we put on our gas masks and just pressed right on through those shells and got to the top of hill 223. . . . [A]t the zero hour . . . we done went over the top. . . . The Germans . . . jes stopped us in our tracks. Their machine guns were up there on the heights overlooking us and well hidden, and we couldn't tell for certain where the terrible heavy fire was coming from. . . . So we decided to try and get them by a surprise attack in the rear. . . . So there was 17 of us boys went around on the left flank to see if we couldn't put those guns out of action."

—from *Sergeant York*

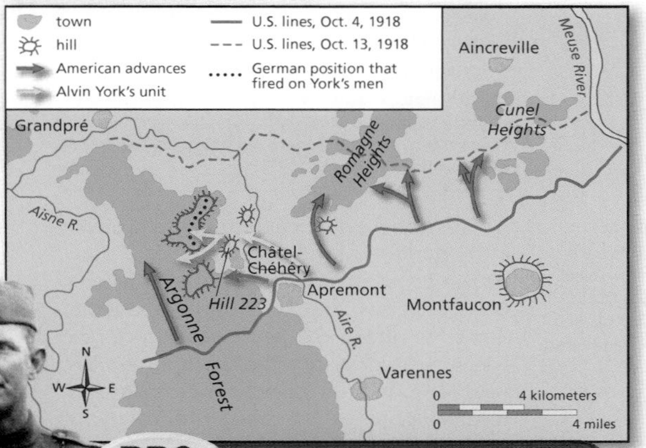

DBQ Document-Based Questions

1. **Extrapolating** Why was the American victory in the Argonne Forest important?
2. **Explaining** What made capturing enemy positions in the Argonne Forest so difficult?

Maps In MOtion See *StudentWorks™ Plus* or glencoe.com.

believed he was not allowed to kill anyone. Eventually, he decided that he could fight in a war if the cause was just.

On October 8, 1918, during the Battle of the Argonne Forest, German machine guns on a fortified hill fired on York's platoon and killed nine men. York took command and charged the machine guns. By the end of the battle, York had killed between 9 and 25 Germans, captured the machine guns, and taken 132 prisoners. For his actions, he received the Medal of Honor and the French Croix de Guerre. After returning home, he used his fame to raise money for the Alvin York Institute—a school for poor Tennessee children.

Eddie Rickenbacker Born in Columbus, Ohio, Eddie Rickenbacker was a famous race car driver before the war. Rickenbacker's car-racing reflexes served him well as a combat pilot. He was named commander of the 94th Aero Squadron, the first all-American squadron to enter combat. In all, he fought in 134 air battles and shot down 26 aircraft, becoming the top American combat pilot. In one battle, he single-handedly fought seven German aircraft—a feat for which he was later awarded the Congressional Medal of Honor.

The War Ends

While fighting raged along the Western Front, a revolution engulfed Austria-Hungary. In October 1918, Poland, Hungary, and Czechoslovakia declared independence. By early November, the governments of the Austro-Hungarian Empire and the Ottoman Empire had surrendered to the allies.

On November 3, sailors in Kiel, the main base of the German fleet, mutinied. Within days, groups of workers and soldiers seized power in other German towns. As the revolution spread, the German emperor decided to step down. On November 9, Germany became a republic. Two days later the government signed an **armistice**—a truce, or an agreement to stop fighting. At the 11th hour on the 11th day of the 11th month, 1918, the fighting stopped. W

Reading Check **Interpreting** Why would Pershing want to keep U.S. soldiers in their own units?

W Writing Support

Narrative Writing Have interested students use library or Internet resources to find out more information about the abdication of the German emperor. Then have them write a one-page paper telling why he stepped down and fled to the Netherlands. Encourage volunteers to read their papers to the class. OL

DBQ Document Based Questions

Answers:

1. It caused the Germans to begin their final retreat.
2. The land was hilly and the forest was thick; the Germans also used gas.

Reading Check

Answer:
to be sure the troops were following American commanders' orders

Additional Support

Extending the Content

Veterans Day The holiday that is now celebrated as Veterans Day originated in efforts to commemorate the armistice of November 11, 1918 that ended World War I. The first Armistice Day was observed the following year. On November 11, 1919, President Woodrow Wilson delivered the following address:

"The war showed us the strength of great nations acting together for high purposes, and the victory of arms foretells the enduring conquests which can be made in peace when nations act justly and in furtherance of the common interests of men. To us in America, the reflections of Armistice Day will be filled with solemn pride in the heroism of those who died in the country's service and with gratitude for the victory, both because of the thing from which it has freed us and because of the opportunity it has given America to show her sympathy with peace and justice in the councils of the nations."

Most states designated November 11 as a legal holiday. In 1938, Armistice Day became a federal holiday. To extend recognition to the veterans of World War II and the Korean War, President Eisenhower signed into law a bill in 1954 that changed the name of the holiday to Veterans Day.

W Writing Support

Expository Writing Have interested students use library or Internet resources to create a database of the four leaders of the Allied nations. Instruct students to include the number of years each served as leader and any information on other international conflicts in which they were involved. Have students use the facts they gather to write a paragraph about the leader they feel was the most experienced. AL

C Critical Thinking

Making Inferences Have students define, in their own words, the idea of national self-determination. Discuss with the class how national self-determination played a role in Wilson's Fourteen Points and in the treaties that ended World War I. **Ask:** **What groups today seek national self-determination?** *(Answers will vary, but students might note the Kurds, Palestinians, Basques, Taiwanese, and the people of Kosovo.)* OL

A Flawed Peace

MAIN Idea The United States Senate refused to ratify the Treaty of Versailles and rejected the League of Nations.

HISTORY AND YOU How might your feelings toward a peace plan differ if you lived in a defeated country compared to a victorious country? Read on to learn why the U.S. Senate did not ratify the Treaty of Versailles.

Read Wilson's "Fourteen Points" on page R52 in **Documents in American History.**

Although the fighting stopped in November 1918, World War I was not over. A peace treaty had to be negotiated and signed. In January 1919, delegates from 27 countries traveled to France to attend the peace conference. The conference took place at the Palace of Versailles, near Paris, and the treaty with Germany that resulted came to be called the **Treaty of Versailles.** The conference also negotiated the Treaty of Saint-Germain, ending the war with Austria-Hungary.

W Negotiations on the Treaty of Versailles lasted five months. The most important participants were the so-called "Big Four" of the Allies: President Wilson of the United States, British Prime Minister David Lloyd George, French Premier Georges Clemenceau, and Italian Prime Minister Vittorio Orlando.

Representatives from Russia were not invited to the conference. Wilson and the other Allied leaders refused to recognize Lenin's government as legitimate. At the time of the peace conference, a civil war was raging in Russia between communist and non-communist forces. In mid-1918, the United States, Great Britain, and Japan had sent troops to Russia to help the anti-communist forces. Nearly 15,000 American troops remained in Russia—which had been renamed the Soviet Union by the Bolsheviks—until the spring of 1920. By that time, it had become clear that the Bolsheviks had won the civil war.

The Fourteen Points

When President Wilson arrived in Paris in January 1919, he brought with him a peace plan known as the **Fourteen Points.** Wilson had presented the plan to Congress in January 1918 to explain the goals of the United States in the war. The president believed that if the Fourteen Points were implemented, they would establish the conditions for a lasting peace in Europe.

INFOGRAPHIC

The Paris Peace Conference

What Did President Wilson Want?

The Fourteen Points

1. End secret treaties and secret diplomacy among nations.
2. Guarantee freedom of navigation on the seas for all nations.
3. Create free trade among nations.
4. Reduce armed forces as much as possible consistent with domestic safety.
5. Settle all colonial claims fairly taking into account the views of both the colonial peoples and the imperial nations.
6. Evacuate German troops from Russia and restore all conquered territory.
7. Restore Belgium's independence.
8. Restore all French territory occupied by Germany, including Alsace-Lorraine.
9. Adjust Italy's borders based on where Italians live.
10. Divide Austria-Hungary into new nations for each ethnic group.
11. Base borders of the Balkan states on nationality.
12. Break up the Ottoman Empire and make Turkey a separate country.
13. Create an independent Poland.
14. Create a League of Nations.

The Fourteen Points were based on "the principle of justice to all peoples and nationalities." In the first five points, Wilson proposed to eliminate the causes of the war through free trade, freedom of the seas, disarmament, an impartial adjustment of colonial claims, and open diplomacy instead of secret agreements.

The next eight points addressed the right of **national self-determination.** This is the idea that the borders of countries should be based on ethnicity and national identity. A group of people who feel that they are a nation should be allowed to have their own country. Wilson and other supporters of national self-determination believed that when borders are not based on national identity, border disputes will occur C and nations are more likely to go to war to **resolve** them.

The principle of national self-determination also meant that no nation should be allowed to keep territory taken from another nation. Wilson's Fourteen Points required the Central Powers to evacuate all of the countries invaded during the war. Wilson also wanted the territory

Additional Support

Activity: Collaborative Learning

Negotiating Have students hold a peace conference. Organize the class into four groups. Each group should participate as one of the Big Four nations. Structure the negotiations around Woodrow Wilson's Fourteen Points (see page R52). Tell students that they have the power to accept, amend, or reject each point and should confer within their group before negotiating with the other groups' members. OL

What Did the Allies Agree to Do?

Treaty of Versailles (peace with Germany)
- German troops will return all captured territory to Belgium, Russia, and France.
- Germany will be divided in two; some German territory will be given to Denmark, France, Poland, Czechoslovakia, and Belgium.
- Germany will be held responsible for all wartime losses and must pay reparations.
- Germany's army and navy will be limited in size. Germany cannot have an air force, and cannot have military forces west of the Rhine.

Treaty of Saint-Germain (peace with Austria)
- The Austro-Hungarian Empire is dissolved and replaced by the nation of Austria.
- Four new nations are recognized: Czechoslovakia, Hungary, Poland, and Yugoslavia.
- Austria may not unite with Germany; its army is limited to 30,000 men.

The Covenant of the League of Nations (included in both peace treaties above)
- Members agree to reduce armaments.
- Members agree to protect each other against aggression.
- Colonies of the Central Powers will now be supervised by League members.
- Parts of the Ottoman Empire will be made independent under League supervision.

NATIONAL GEOGRAPHIC Changes in Europe, 1919

Analyzing VISUALS

1. **Comparing** How many of the Fourteen Points were accepted at the Paris Peace Conference?
2. **Analyzing** What nations received territory from the Austro-Hungarian Empire?

Maps In MOtion See *StudentWorks™ Plus* or glencoe.com.

of Alsace-Lorraine that Germany had taken in 1871 restored to France.

The fourteenth point was most important to Wilson. It called for the creation of a "general association of nations" that would later be called the **League of Nations.** The League's member nations would help preserve peace by pledging to respect and protect each other's territory and political independence. Wilson was so determined to get agreement on the League of Nations that he was willing to give up other goals in the Fourteen Points in exchange for support for the League.

The Treaty of Versailles

Wilson received an enthusiastic reception from crowds in Paris and other national capitals that he visited. Wilson's popularity in Europe put W him in a strong negotiating position. He was delighted when the peace conference decided to use the Fourteen Points as the basis for negotiations.

Not everyone was impressed by President Wilson's ideas. Premier Clemenceau of France and British Prime Minister Lloyd George wanted the Germans punished for the suffering they had inflicted on the rest of Europe. Additionally, Great Britain refused to give up its sizable naval advantage by agreeing to Wilson's call for freedom of the seas. Clemenceau, in particular, was determined to end the German threat once and for all. Other Allied governments tended to agree.

Despite Wilson's hopes, the peace terms were harsh. The Treaty of Versailles, reluctantly signed by Germany on June 28, 1919, included many terms designed to punish and weaken Germany. Germany's armed forces were greatly reduced in size and Germany was not allowed to put troops west of the Rhine River—the region near the French border. The treaty also specifically blamed Germany for the war, stating that it had been caused by "the aggression of Germany."

W Writing Support

Descriptive Writing Have students find out more about the Treaty of Versailles. Ask students to use what they have learned to write one paragraph describing the terms of the treaty. Encourage students to include whether they believe the terms are fair or not. **BL**

D Differentiated Instruction

Visual/Spatial Distribute two outline maps of Europe to each member of the class. On one map, have students draw the boundaries of European nations in 1914, before World War I, and on the other map have students draw the boundaries in 1919, after the Treaty of Versailles. After students have completed their maps, discuss the changes in the borders. **AL**

Analyzing VISUALS

Answers:
1. nine
2. Austria, Hungary, Czechoslovakia, Poland, Romania, Yugoslavia, and Italy

Additional Support

Activity: Interdisciplinary Connection

Literature Ask interested students to use library and Internet resources to learn more about Wilson's trip to Paris in 1919 and the triumphant greeting he received. Be sure students identify the people who accompanied Wilson on this trip. Based on this information, students may write a one-act play depicting Wilson's arrival in Paris. After the play is complete, have students enact the play. **AL**

C1 Critical Thinking

Drawing Conclusions Review with students the new nations that were created after World War I. **Ask:** **Is it important for all people of one ethnic group to have their own country?** *(Students might note that having common customs, traditions, religion, and language help unify people and prevent dissent.)* **OL**

C2 Critical Thinking

Making Inferences Remind students that Wilson was not successful in getting the Allies to include freedom of the seas or free trade in the Treaty of Versailles. **Ask:** **Given Wilson's position at the peace conference, could he have pushed to get these issues addressed?** *(Answers will vary.)* **AL**

Analyzing VISUALS

Answers:

1. The Treaty of Versailles was beaten up and defeated.
2. International agreement will help maintain peace.

When the German government signed the treaty, it, in effect, acknowledged that Germany was guilty of causing the war. This allowed the Allies to demand that Germany pay **reparations**—monetary compensation for all of the war damage it had caused. A commission set up after the treaty was signed decided that Germany owed the Allies approximately $33 billion. This sum was far more than Germany could pay all at once and was intended to keep Germany's economy weak for a long time.

C1 Wilson had somewhat better success in promoting national self-determination. Four empires were dismantled as a result of World War I and the peace negotiations: the Austro-Hungarian Empire, the Russian Empire, the German Empire, and the Ottoman Empire. The various peace treaties signed after the war created nine new nations in Europe: Austria, Czechoslovakia, Estonia, Finland, Hungary, Latvia, Lithuania, Poland and Yugoslavia. In general, the majority of people in these new countries were from one ethnic group.

National self-determination was not, however, applied to Germany. Both Poland and Czechoslovakia were given territory where the majority of the people were German. Germany was even split in two in order to give Poland access to the Baltic Sea. By leaving a large number of Germans living outside Germany, the Treaty of Versailles helped set the stage for a new series of crises in the 1930s.

The Treaty of Versailles did not address several of Wilson's Fourteen Points. It did not mention freedom of the seas or free trade. It also ignored Wilson's goal of a fair settlement of colonial claims. No colonial people in Asia or Africa were granted independence. Germany's colonies in Africa and the Middle East were placed under the supervision of Britain and France. Japan was given responsibility for Germany's colonies in East Asia. C2

The treaty also stated that new countries were to be created from the Ottoman Empire. In 1920 the Ottoman Empire was divided into the state of Turkey, the French Mandate of Syria and Lebanon, and the British Mandates of Iraq and Palestine. In 1921 the Palestine Mandate was divided to create the kingdom of Transjordan.

Although disappointed with many parts of the Treaty of Versailles, Wilson achieved his

POLITICAL CARTOONS PRIMARY SOURCE

Debating the Treaty of Versailles

◀ *In the original caption of this cartoon, President Wilson is saying: "Build your house up there where it can't be washed away."*

◀ *Senator Henry Cabot Lodge escorts the peace treaty out of the Senate.*

Analyzing VISUALS DBQ

1. **Identifying** What point is the cartoon on the right trying to make?
2. **Interpreting** Why does the cartoon on the left suggest that international agreement on a peace treaty is important?

Additional Support

Activity: Interdisciplinary Connection

Art Have interested students use library and Internet resources to find other political cartoons about the Treaty of Versailles and have them make a poster collage of the cartoons—highlighting either the "Irreconcilable" or the "Reservationist" point of view. Then have students draw their own political cartoon to include in the collage. Be sure students write a caption describing their poster. Display the posters in the classroom. **AL**

primary goal. The treaty called for the creation of a League of Nations. League members promised to reduce armaments, to submit all disputes that endangered the peace to arbitration, and to come to the aid of any member who was threatened with aggression by another state.

The U.S. Senate Rejects the Treaty

President Wilson was confident the American people would support the Treaty of Versailles, but he had badly underestimated the opposition in Congress. All treaties signed by the United States must be ratified by two-thirds of the Senate, and in November 1918, the Democratic Party had lost control of the Senate. Even though he needed Republican support to ratify the treaty, Wilson refused to take any Republican leaders with him to the peace conference. This ensured that Wilson's views prevailed, but it also meant that Republican concerns were not addressed.

S

Opposition in the Senate focused on the League of Nations. One group of senators, nicknamed the "Irreconcilables," refused to support the treaty under any circumstances. They assailed the League as the kind of "entangling alliance" that the Founders had warned against. A larger group of senators, known as the "Reservationists," was led by the powerful chairman of the Foreign Relations committee, Henry Cabot Lodge. The Reservationists were willing to support the treaty if certain amendments were made to the League of Nations.

The Reservationists pointed out that the Constitution requires Congress to declare war. Yet the League of Nations could require member states to aid any member who was attacked. The Reservationists argued that this might force the United States into a war without Congressional approval. They agreed to ratify the treaty if it was amended to say that any military action by the United States required the approval of Congress. Wilson refused, fearing the change would undermine the League's effectiveness.

To overcome Senate opposition, Wilson decided to take his case directly to the American people. If public support for the treaty was strong enough, the senators would back down. Starting in September 1919, Wilson traveled 8,000 miles and made over 30 major speeches in three weeks. On September 25, the president collapsed from the physical strain and soon afterward suffered a stroke. Bedridden, Wilson ignored the advice of his wife and Democratic leaders and refused to compromise on the treaty.

The Senate finally voted in November 1919. It voted again in March 1920. Both times it refused to ratify the treaty. After Wilson left office in 1921, the United States negotiated separate peace treaties with each of the Central Powers. The League of Nations, the foundation of President Wilson's plan for lasting world peace, took shape without the United States.

Reading Check **Examining** What was national self-determination and why did Wilson think it would help prevent war?

Section 3 REVIEW

Vocabulary

1. **Explain** the significance of: no-man's-land, convoy, John J. Pershing, armistice, Treaty of Versailles, Fourteen Points, national self-determination, League of Nations, reparations.

Main Ideas

2. **Explaining** How did technology change the way World War I was fought?
3. **Analyzing** What impact did John J. Pershing and the Battle of the Argonne Forest have on World War I?
4. **Organizing** Use a graphic organizer to list the results of World War I.

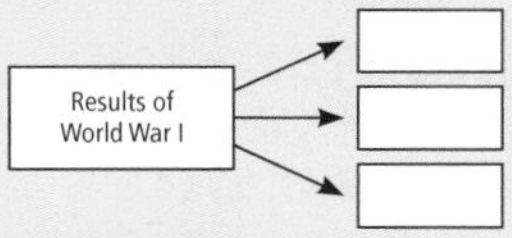

Critical Thinking

5. **Big Ideas** Why did President Wilson propose his Fourteen Points?
6. **Analyzing** What countries were involved in the Paris peace conference in 1919? Which country was not invited to participate? Why?
7. **Analyzing Maps and Charts** Examine the map and chart on page 571. Prepare a quiz with questions based on information from both. Give the quiz to some of your classmates.

Writing About History

8. **Descriptive Writing** Imagine that you are an American soldier fighting in Europe during World War I. Write a letter home describing your situation and how you feel about fighting there.

History ONLINE
Study Central™ To review this section, go to glencoe.com and click on Study Central.

S Skill Practice

Identifying Point of View
Ask students to summarize the opinions of the "Irreconcilables" and "Reservationists" toward the Treaty of Versailles. OL

Assess

History ONLINE

Study Central™ provides summaries, interactive games, and online graphic organizers to help students review content.

Close

Summarizing Ask: Was World War I the "war to end all wars?" *(No; in fact the peace terms ending World War I laid the foundation for World War II.)* OL

Reading Check

Answer:
each group of people, or nation, should govern itself, Wilson believed it would lessen border disputes and international conflict

Section 3 REVIEW

Answers

1. All definitions can be found in the section and the Glossary.
2. Tanks could crush barbed wire and roll over trenches; poison gas was used by both sides, killing troops or rendering them unable to fight; airplanes were used as scouts and later battles took place in the air.
3. General Pershing directed the AEF attack which broke through German lines.
4. answers may include: League of Nations, dissolution of four empires, nine new European countries, Germany pays reparations
5. He wanted to prevent future wars.
6. the United States, Great Britain, France, and Italy; Russia was not invited because the allies refused to recognize Lenin's government
7. Answers will vary; quizzes should be accurate.
8. Answers will vary; students should use descriptive terms in their letters.

Focus

Ask: After reading the information on these pages, what do you think were the major issues or topics of the era? *(World War I; communism)* **Ask:** Why is Jeannette Rankin pictured? *(She was the first woman elected to Congress.)* **Ask:** What items does a doughboy need and how much is the cost? How does the cost then likely compare to the cost of outfitting a soldier today? *(A doughboy required 107 pieces of fighting equipment, 50 articles of clothing, eating utensils, and 11 cooking implements, which cost $156.30. Today the cost of outfitting a soldier is likely to run into the thousands of dollars.)* **OL**

Teach

C Critical Thinking

Analyzing Primary Sources
Have students read the quote by Woodrow Wilson. **Ask:** Why does Wilson think applauding his speech is odd? *(because his request for war against Germany will result in the deaths of thousands of young American soldiers)* **AL**

Additional Support

TIME NOTEBOOK

BROWN BROTHERS (5)

American soldiers set sail for Europe.

World War Firsts

Human ingenuity goes to work in the service of war:

AERIAL COMBAT, 1914. War takes to the air. Two Allied aircraft chase two German planes across Britain.

GAS ATTACKS, 1915. The German High Command admits to using chlorine gas bombs and shells on the field of combat. Deadly mustard gas is used in 1917.

GAS MASKS. Issued to Allied soldiers in 1915.

DONKEY'S EARS. A new trench periscope enables soldiers to observe the battleground from the relative safety of a trench without risking sniper fire.

BIG BERTHA. Enormous howitzer gun bombards Paris. "Big Bertha," named after the wife of its manufacturer, is thought to be located nearly 63 miles behind German lines. Moving at night on railroad tracks, the gun is difficult for the Allies to locate.

Color My World

Some bright spots in a dark decade:

- Color newspaper supplements (1914)
- 3-D films (1915)
- Nail polish (1916)
- Three-color traffic lights (1918)
- Color photography introduced by Eastman Kodak (1914)

One of the first color photographs

LEON GIMPEL/SOCIETE FRANCAISE DE PHOTOGRAPHIE/LIFE

VERBATIM

"My message was one of death for young men. How odd to applaud that." C
WOODROW WILSON,
on returning to the White House after asking Congress for a declaration of war, 1917

"Food is Ammunition—Don't Waste It"
POSTER FROM U.S. FOOD ADMINISTRATION,
administered by Herbert Hoover

"I have had a hard time getting over this war. My old world died."
RAY STANNARD BAKER,
journalist

"Let us, while this war lasts, forget our special grievances and close our ranks shoulder to shoulder with our own white fellow citizens and the allied nations that are fighting for democracy."
W.E.B. DU BOIS,
African American scholar and leader, 1918

"America has at one bound become a world power in a sense she never was before."
BRITISH PRIME MINISTER DAVID LLOYD GEORGE,
on the U.S. entry into World War I, 1917

"In the camps I saw barrels mounted on sticks on which zealous captains were endeavoring to teach their men how to ride a horse."
THEODORE ROOSEVELT,
on touring U.S. military training facilities, 1917

"The war was over, and it seemed as if everything in the world were possible, and everything was new, and that peace was going to be all we dreamed about."
FLORENCE HARRIMAN,
Red Cross volunteer, in Paris on Armistice Day, 1918

Background

Stars and Stripes *Stars and Stripes,* the armed forces newspaper staffed entirely by soldiers, was first published in 1918. In addition to being a source of information and morale for soldiers, it provided many young journalists and cartoonists with their first jobs. Two well-known cartoonists whose work appeared in *Stars and Stripes* were Milt Caniff ("Terry and the Pirates") and Bill Mauldin, who won the Pulitzer Prize in 1945 for his "Willie" and "GI Joe" cartoons.

How to Make a Doughboy

Take one American infantryman.

1. Arm with 107 pieces of fighting equipment, including:
   - rifle
   - rifle cartridges
   - cartridge belt
   - steel helmet
   - clubs
   - knives
   - gas mask
   - wire cutters
   - trench tool
   - bayonet and scabbard
   - grenades
2. Add 50 articles of clothing, including 3 wool blankets and a bedsack.
3. Equip with eating utensils and 11 cooking implements.
4. Train well.

TOTAL COST: $156.30

(not including training and transportation to Europe)

Milestones

W **SHOT DOWN AND KILLED, APRIL 22, 1918. "THE RED BARON,"** Manfred von Richthofen, Germany's ace pilot. Von Richthofen destroyed more than 80 Allied aircraft. The English fighter pilot Edward Mannock said, "I hope he roasted all the way down."

Vladimir Lenin

REPATRIATED, APRIL 10, 1917. VLADIMIR ILYICH LENIN, to Russia, after an 11-year absence. The leader of the leftist Bolshevik party hopes to reorganize his revolutionary group.

Jeannette Rankin

ELECTED, NOVEMBER 7, 1916. JEANNETTE RANKIN of Montana, to the U.S. Congress. The first woman congressional representative explained her victory by saying that women "got the vote in Montana because the spirit of pioneer days was still alive."

NUMBERS 1915

$1,040 Average annual income for workers in finance, insurance, and real estate

$687 Average income for industrial workers (higher for union workers, lower for nonunion workers)

$510 Average income for retail trade workers

$355 Average income for farm laborers

$342 Average income for domestic servants

$328 Average income for public school teachers

$11.95 Cost of a bicycle

$1.15 Cost of a baseball

$1 Average cost of a hotel room

39¢ Cost of one dozen eggs

5¢ Cost of a glass of cola

7¢ Cost of a large roll of toilet paper

CRITICAL THINKING

1. ***Analyzing*** What pioneer qualities was Jeannette Rankin referring to when she said women "got the vote in Montana because the spirit of pioneer days was still alive"?

2. ***Drawing Conclusions*** How do you think the inventions in "Color My World" kept up spirits on the home front during World War I? Why was this important?

W Writing Support

Narrative Writing Have students reread the Milestone concerning "The Red Baron." Then have students use library or Internet resources to find out more about "The Red Baron" and his role in World War I. Using what they have learned, have students write a British newspaper article announcing the Baron's death. OL

Assess/Close

Have students select an item listed under Numbers and find a correlating statistic from today.

Visit the Time Web site at www.time.com for up-to-date news, weekly magazine articles, editorials, online polls, and an archive of past magazines and Web articles.

Critical Thinking Answers:

1. individualism, freedom, ruggedness, the desire to explore
2. New inventions meant progress and something to look forward to, good morale on the home front was essential to winning the war.

Additional Support

Activity: Technology Connection

Comparing and Contrasting Have students review the information presented in the TIME Notebook and have students use library or Internet resources to find out more about the topics presented. Then have them make a list of items, issues, or inventions from the World War I era that are still relevant today. **Ask:** How do you think the events, issues, or inventions from the World War I era affect your life today? What inventions are still useful today? Which inventions have been improved upon? What political issues or ideas are still relevant today? *(Answers will vary, but students should cite data from the TIME Notebook and their research to support their ideas.)* OL

Focus

Bellringer

Daily Focus Transparency 16-4

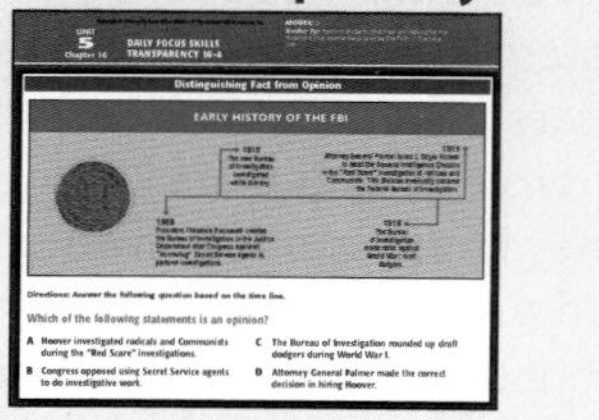

Guide to Reading

Answers:

Effects of World War I on Economy → rapid inflation
Effects of World War I on Economy → mass demand for goods
Effects of World War I on Economy → strikes

Section Spotlight Video

To generate student interest and provide a springboard for class discussion, access the Chapter 16, Section 4 video at glencoe.com or on the video DVD.

Resource Manager

Section 4

Section Audio   Spotlight Video

The War's Impact

Guide to Reading

Big Ideas

Economics and Society The change from wartime to peacetime caused many economic and social problems.

Content Vocabulary

- cost of living *(p. 576)*
- general strike *(p. 577)*
- deport *(p. 580)*

Academic Vocabulary

- widespread *(p. 577)*
- authorities *(p. 580)*

People and Events to Identify

- Calvin Coolidge *(p. 577)*
- Red Scare *(p. 579)*
- A. Mitchell Palmer *(p. 579)*
- J. Edgar Hoover *(p. 580)*

Reading Strategy

Organizing Complete a graphic organizer similar to the one below to list the effects of the end of World War I on the American economy.

Effects of World War I on Economy → [ ] [ ] [ ]

America's victory overseas led to turmoil at home. The end of the wartime economy led to a depression and fears of communism, as strikes, riots, and bombings took place.

An Economy in Turmoil

MAIN Idea The country suffered economic uncertainty, strikes, and riots in the year after the war.

HISTORY AND YOU Do you know anyone who has participated in a strike? Read why millions of workers went on strike in 1919.

With the war over, Americans welcomed the soldiers back as heroes. Parades were thrown in their honor, and a new organization, the American Legion, was created to support the veterans. But their arrival home was also bittersweet. Two million men now needed to find jobs in an economy that was shutting down its production of war materials and sliding into recession.

When the war ended, government agencies removed their controls from the economy. People raced to buy goods that had been rationed, while businesses rapidly raised prices they had been forced to keep low during the war. The result was rapid inflation. In 1919 prices rose more than 15 percent. Inflation greatly increased the **cost of living**—the cost of food, clothing, shelter, and other essentials that people need to survive. Orders for war materials evaporated, so factories laid off workers. Soldiers returned home looking for civilian employment but found jobs scarce. In short, 1919 was a year of economic turmoil.

Inflation Leads to Strikes

Many companies had been forced to raise wages during the war, but inflation now threatened to wipe out the gains workers had made. While workers wanted higher wages to keep up with inflation, companies resisted because inflation was also driving up their operating costs.

During the war, the number of workers in unions had increased dramatically. By the time the war ended, workers were better organized and much more capable of implementing strikes. Many business leaders, on the other hand, were determined to break the power of the unions and roll back the gains labor had made. These circumstances led to an enormous wave of strikes in 1919. By the end of the year, more than 3,600 strikes involving more than 4 million workers had taken place.

R Reading Strategies	C Critical Thinking	D Differentiated Instruction	W Writing Support	S Skill Practice
Teacher Edition • Categorizing Info., p. 577 • Act. Prior Know., p. 579 **Additional Resources** • Guid. Read. Act., URB p. 111 • Prim. Source Read., URB p. 99	**Teacher Edition** • Drawing Conclusions, p. 579 • Analyzing Prim. Sources, p. 581 **Additional Resources** • Interp. Pol. Cartoons, URB p. 103 • Quizzes and Tests, p. 226 • Auth. Assess., p. 37	**Teacher Edition** • Visual/Spatial, p. 577 **Additional Resources** • English Learner Act., URB p. 87 • Reteach. Act., URB p. 105	**Teacher Edition** • Narrative Writing, pp. 578, 580 • Persuasive Writing, p. 580 **Additional Resources** • American Art and Music, URB p. 101	**Additional Resources** • Read. Skills Act., URB p. 83 • Reinforcing Skills Act., URB p. 93 • Read. Essen., p. 183

PRIMARY SOURCE

The Strikes of 1919

▲ National Guard troops get rioting under control in Boston during the Police Strike of 1919

Workers on Strike, 1916–1921

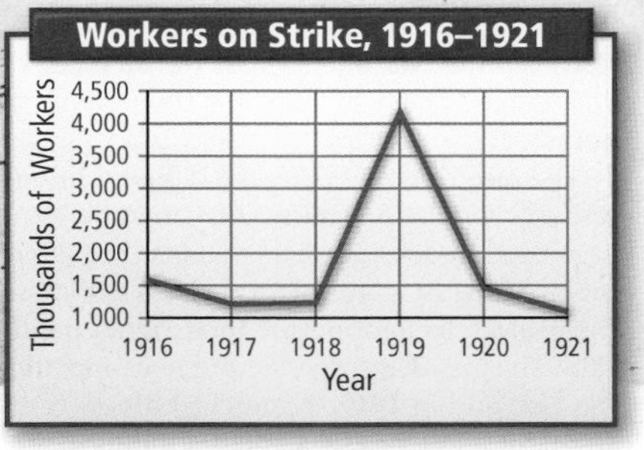

Analyzing VISUALS

1. **Evaluating** Why do you think strikes in 1919 worried the government more than strikes in previous years?
2. **Making Inferences** Why do you think the Boston Police Strike received so much attention? Why were officials willing to use military force in Boston so quickly?

The Seattle General Strike The first major strike took place in Seattle, where some 35,000 shipyard workers walked off the job demanding higher wages and shorter hours. Other unions in Seattle soon joined the shipyard workers and organized a general strike.

A **general strike** is a strike that involves all workers in a community, not just workers in a particular industry. The Seattle general strike involved more than 60,000 people and paralyzed the city for five days. Although the strikers returned to work without making any gains, their actions worried many Americans because R the general strike was a common tactic used in Europe by communists and other radical groups.

The Boston Police Strike Perhaps the most famous strike of 1919 took place in Boston, where roughly 75 percent of the police force walked off the job. Riots and looting soon erupted in the city, forcing the governor, **Calvin Coolidge,** to call in the National Guard. When the strikers tried to return to work, the police commissioner then fired the strikers and hired a new police force instead.

Despite protests, Coolidge agreed that the men should be fired, declaring: "There is no right to strike against the public safety by anybody, anywhere, anytime." Coolidge's response earned him **widespread** public support and convinced the Republicans to make him their vice presidential candidate in the 1920 election.

The Steel Strike Shortly after the police strike ended, one of the largest strikes in American history began when an estimated 350,000 steelworkers went on strike for higher pay, shorter hours, and recognition of their union. Elbert H. Gary, the head of U.S. Steel, refused even to talk to union leaders. Instead, he set out to break the union by using anti-immigrant feelings to divide the workers.

Many steelworkers were immigrants. The company blamed the strike on foreign radicals D and called for loyal Americans to return to work. Meanwhile, to keep the mills running, the company hired African Americans and Mexicans as replacement workers. Clashes between company guards and strikers were frequent. In Gary, Indiana, a riot left 18 strikers dead. The strike collapsed in early 1920 and its failure set back the union cause in the steel industry. Steel workers remained unorganized until 1941.

Teach

R Reading Strategy

Categorizing Information Have students create a graphic organizer with five columns labeled "Who," "What," "Where," "How Many," and "Results." Label the rows with the three major strikes in this section. As students read, have them use this graphic organizer to compare the strikes. OL

D Differentiated Instruction

Visual/Spatial Have students create signs that steel workers could have carried during the 1919 strike. Signs can exhibit any effective use of language. BL

Analyzing VISUALS

Answers:

1. Many believed communists were behind the strikes.
2. Public officials were not supposed to strike; to prevent further disruption in the city and to keep the peace.

Hands-On Chapter Project Step 4

Presenting World War I

Step 4: Post-War America Ask: How did the war influence the economy and society of the United States?

Directions Explain to students that they will create one to three multimedia slides or screens to describe the effect of the war on the United States. Divide students into two teams. The first team should focus on the economy of post-war United States. The second team should focus on the American society after the war. (In both groups, further division might be made between those responsible for boiling down the literal explanation and those finding graphic/visual elements.)

Putting It Together When the two teams meet to finalize the choices for the slides, they will determine not only how to illustrate the post-war economy and society, but also how to explain why the war impacted the economy and society. OL

(Chapter Project continued on the Visual Summary page)

W Writing Support

Narrative Writing Have half of the class write an eyewitness account of an African American viewing the Chicago riot while the other half of the students write the account from the point of view of a newspaper reporter describing the event. Have volunteers read the narratives in class. OL

Reading Check

Answer:
Soldiers returning from the war found it hard to get jobs and blamed African Americans for their economic hardships.

Racial Unrest

The economic turmoil after the war also contributed to widespread racial unrest. Many African Americans had moved north during the war to take factory jobs. As people began to be laid off and returning soldiers found it hard to find work and affordable housing, many gave in to feelings of racism and blamed African Americans for taking their jobs. Frustration and racism combined to produce violence.

In the summer of 1919, 25 race riots broke out across the nation. African American leader James Weldon Johnson called the summer of 1919, "the red summer" because of the amount of blood that was spilled. The riots began in July, when a mob of angry white people burned shops and homes in an African American neighborhood in Longview, Texas. A week later, in Washington, D.C., gangs of African Americans and whites fought each other for four days before troops got the riots under control.

W The worst violence occurred in Chicago. On a hot July day, African Americans went to a whites-only beach. Both sides began throwing stones at each other. Whites also threw stones at an African American teenager swimming near the beach to prevent him from coming ashore, and he drowned. A full-scale riot then erupted in the city.

Angry African Americans attacked white neighborhoods while whites attacked African American neighborhoods. The Chicago riot lasted for almost two weeks and the government was forced to send in National Guard troops to impose order. By the time the rioting ended, 38 people had been killed—15 white and 23 black—and over 500 had been injured.

The race riots of 1919 disillusioned some African Americans who felt their wartime contributions had been for nothing. For others, however, the wartime struggle for democracy encouraged them to fight for their rights at home.

The race riots of 1919 were different in one respect. For the first time, African Americans organized and fought back against the white mobs. Many African Americans also dedicated themselves to fighting for their rights politically. The NAACP surged in membership after the war, and in 1919, it launched a new campaign for a federal law against lynching.

Reading Check **Analyzing** Why did the end of the war lead to race riots?

PAST & PRESENT

Terrorists Attack America

When terrorists attacked the United States on September 11, 2001, many Americans believed the United States was experiencing something new—multiple attacks by a terrorist organization.

It is almost forgotten by the American people that in June 1919, eight bombs exploded in eight American cities within minutes of each other, and another 30 bombs sent through the mail were intercepted before they exploded. In September 1920 an even larger bomb exploded in New York. As it did after 9/11, the United States government created a new federal agency to protect the American people. In 1919 the government created the General Intelligence Division, headed by Herbert Hoover, who later headed the FBI. In 2002 the government created the Department of Homeland Security.

June 1919 Bombings

September, 1920

▲ *In September 1920, a bomb made of 100 lbs. of dynamite and 500 lbs. of steel fragments exploded in New York City, killing 38 people and injuring 300 others.*

Additional Support

Activity: Interdisciplinary Connection

Literature American writer John Dos Passos published his trilogy *U.S.A.* between 1930 and 1936. The second novel in the series, simply titled *1919,* is set during the tumultuous year that followed World War I. In the trilogy, Dos Passos experimented with unconventional techniques. He interwove the fictional story of his characters with sections that included headlines, news stories, and brief biographies of important or notorious figures from the era. Provide students with excerpts from *1919* and then ask them to compose an essay in Dos Passos's style in which they present the material from this section of Chapter 16. AL

The Red Scare

MAIN Idea Fear of a Communist revolution caused a nationwide panic.

HISTORY AND YOU Many Americans believed the country was in danger in 1919. Read on to see similarities with today's concerns about security.

The wave of strikes in 1919 helped to fuel fears that Communists were conspiring to start a revolution in the United States. Americans had been stunned when Communists seized power in Russia and negotiated a separate peace agreement with Germany. Many Americans viewed this as a betrayal, and hostility toward Communists increased. Communism became associated with disloyalty and treachery.

Americans had long been suspicious of communist ideas. Since the late 1800s, many Americans had accused immigrants of importing radical socialist and communist ideas and blamed them for labor unrest and violence. Events in Russia seemed to justify fears of a Communist revolution. The Soviet establishment of the Communist International in 1919—an organization for coordinating Communist parties in other countries—appeared to be further proof of a growing threat.

The strikes of 1919 fueled fears that Communists, or "reds," as they were called, might seize power. This led to a nationwide panic known as the **Red Scare.** Many people were particularly concerned about workers using strikes to start a revolution. Seattle's mayor, Ole Hanson, for example, claimed that the Seattle general strike was part of an attempt to "take possession of our American government and try to duplicate the anarchy of Russia."

In April, the postal service intercepted more than 30 parcels containing homemade bombs addressed to prominent Americans. In May, union members, socialists, and communists organized a parade in Cleveland to protest the jailing of American Socialist Party leader Eugene Debs. The parade turned into a series of riots. By the time police and army units got the violence under control, two people were dead and another 40 were injured.

In June, eight bombs in eight cities exploded within minutes of one another, suggesting a nationwide conspiracy. One of them damaged the home of United States Attorney General **A. Mitchell Palmer.** Most people believed the bombings were the work of radicals trying to destroy the American way of life.

September, 2001

▼ *Firefighters search for victims in the rubble of the World Trade Center in September 2001.*

MAKING CONNECTIONS

1. **Comparing** How was the government's response to the 1919 and 1920 attacks similar to its response to the attacks of September 11, 2001? How was it different?
2. **Synthesizing** How do you think the government should have responded to the bombings of 1919 and 1920? In what ways were the government's policies inappropriate?

R Reading Strategy

Activating Prior Knowledge Discuss with students any existing understanding they have of communism. Reinforce their understanding by having students use library or Internet resources to help write a summary of the basic principles of communism. **BL**

C Critical Thinking

Drawing Conclusions Remind students that the Red Scare targeted Communists. **Ask:** Why did Americans fear Communists and blame them for violence in America? *(They had long associated communism with unionization efforts and thus blamed recent violence on these ties.)* **OL**

MAKING CONNECTIONS

Answers:

1. In 1919 the government created the FBI, and in 2002 it created the Department of Homeland Security; the response to 9/11 was different in that the United States launched a war on terror.
2. Students' answers will vary, but they should support their answers using the text.

Activity: Interdisciplinary Connection

Music Have students work in small groups to write a song describing the turmoil of the early 1900s. Ask each group to chose an existing melody, or write their own, and then write lyrics that relate to one of the topics: fear of radicalism, racial strife, or labor unrest. Encourage students to use the names of people, places, and events mentioned in this section. Invite students to perform their songs for the class. **OL**

W1 Writing Support

Narrative Writing Have interested students use library or Internet resources to research and write a five-page paper on the early history of the General Intelligence Division. AL

W2 Writing Support

Persuasive Writing Have students imagine that they are the defense attorney for a citizen falsely accused during the Palmer raids. Instruct students to write an argument describing their client's rights that have been violated and why their client should be released. OL

Analyzing GEOGRAPHY

Answers:

1. the South; the Northeast
2. The West because the people of the West were more opposed to the nation's involvement in international affairs; answers will vary.

HISTORY AND GEOGRAPHY

The End of Progressivism?

Presidential Candidate	Popular Vote	% of Popular Vote	Electoral Vote
Wilson	9,126,868	49.24%	277
Hughes	8,548,728	46.12%	254

* Seven electors in West Virginia voted for Hughes and one for Wilson.

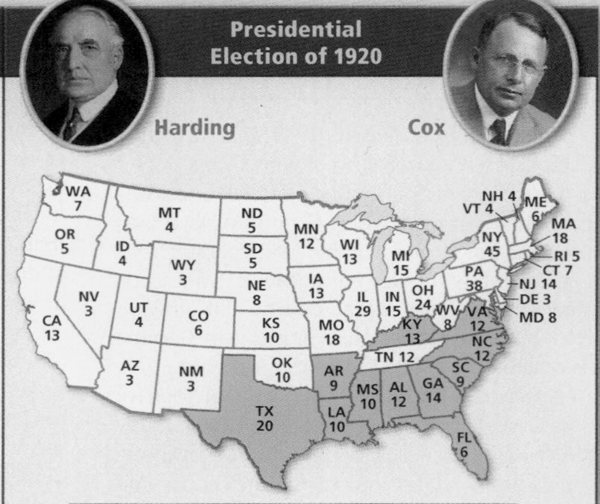

Presidential Candidate	Popular Vote	% of Popular Vote	Electoral Vote
Harding	16,144,093	60.32%	404
Cox	3,139,661	34.15%	127

Many political historians used to think of the election of 1920 as the end of the Progressive Era. It is true that the 1920 election represented a dramatic shift from the progressive Woodrow Wilson to the much more traditionally conservative Warren Harding. But did the election really show a great change in voting habits throughout the country?

Analyzing GEOGRAPHY

1. **Region** Which region voted for the Democrats in both elections? Which region voted Republican in both elections?
2. **Region** What region of the country changed its vote between 1916 and 1920? Why do you think this happened? Does this change suggest people's views of progressivism had changed?

The Palmer Raids

W1 Declaring that a "blaze of revolution" was "burning up the foundations of society," Palmer took action. He established a special division within the Justice Department, the General Intelligence Division. This division, headed by **J. Edgar Hoover,** eventually became the Federal Bureau of Investigation (FBI).

Although evidence pointed to no single group as the bombers, Palmer's agents targeted the foreign-born. On November 7, 1919, Palmer ordered a series of raids on offices of the Union of Russian Workers in 12 cities. Less than seven weeks later, a transport ship left New York for Russia carrying 249 immigrants who had been deported, or expelled from the country.

W2 In January 1920, Palmer ordered another series of raids, this time on the headquarters of various radical organizations. Nearly 6,000 people were arrested. That same month, the New York state legislature expelled five members of the Socialist Party who had been elected to the legislature. Over the next few months, 32 states passed sedition laws making it illegal to join groups advocating revolution. Palmer's raids continued until the spring of 1920. **Authorities** detained thousands of suspects and nearly 600 people were **deported.**

Additional Support

Activity: Interdisciplinary Connection

Language Arts Remind students that the Palmer raids took place at the same time that several major strikes were taking place. Have students discuss what daily life was like for industrial workers and the effect a major strike might have on businesses and the public. Help students recognize that each major strike caused elements of the public to be less tolerant of strikers, and to blame communist influences. Even though strikers only wanted safer working conditions, public fear of violence and revolution overrode the real strike issues. Finally, have students write a letter from a young steelworker to a parent explaining the situation. OL BL

Palmer's agents often ignored the civil liberties of the suspects. Officers entered homes and offices without search warrants. People were mistreated. Some were jailed for indefinite periods of time and were not allowed to talk to their attorneys. Many of the immigrants who were deported were never granted a court hearing to challenge the evidence against them or to contest the deportation order.

For a while, Palmer was regarded as a national hero. His raids, however, failed to turn up any hard evidence of revolutionary conspiracy. When his prediction that violence would rock the nation on May Day 1920—a celebration of workers in Europe—proved wrong, Palmer lost much of his credibility and support.

The Red Scare greatly influenced people's attitudes during the 1920s. Americans often linked radicalism with immigrants, and that attitude led to a call for Congress to limit immigration.

The Election of 1920

Economic problems, labor unrest, and racial tensions, as well as the fresh memories of World War I, all combined to create a general sense of disillusionment in the United States. By 1920 Americans wanted an end to the upheaval.

During the 1920 campaign, Ohio governor James M. Cox and his running mate, Assistant Secretary of the Navy Franklin D. Roosevelt, ran on a platform of progressive ideals. President Wilson tried to convince the Democrats to make the campaign a referendum on the Treaty of Versailles and the League of Nations, but the party chose not to take a strong stand on the issue for fear of alienating voters.

The Republican candidate, Warren G. Harding, called for a return to "normalcy." His vice-presidential running mate, Calvin Coolidge, was chosen because people admired the way he had handled the Boston police strike. Harding argued that what the United States needed was a return to simpler days before the Progressive Era reforms:

PRIMARY SOURCE

C

"[Our] present need is not heroics, but healing; not nostrums, but normalcy; not revolution, but [bold] restoration; not agitation, but adjustment; not surgery, but serenity; not the dramatic, but the dispassionate; . . . not submergence in internationality, but sustainment in triumphant nationality."

—quoted in *Portrait of a Nation*

Harding's sentiments struck a chord with voters, and he won the election by a landslide margin of over 7 million votes. Many Americans were weary of more crusades to reform society and the world. They hoped to put the country's racial and labor unrest and economic troubles behind them and build a more prosperous and stable society.

Reading Check **Examining** After World War I, why were Americans suspicious of some union leaders?

Section 4 REVIEW

Vocabulary

1. **Explain** the significance of: cost of living, general strike, Calvin Coolidge, Red Scare, A. Mitchell Palmer, J. Edgar Hoover, deport.

Main Ideas

2. **Identifying** Use a chart like the one below to list the various causes of labor unrest in 1919.

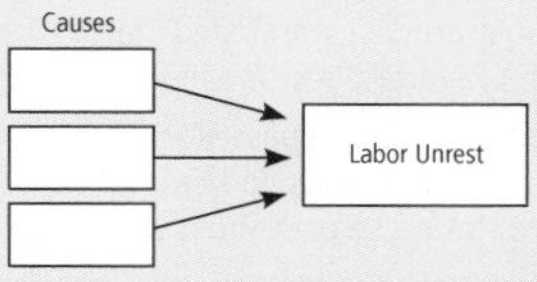

3. **Describing** What events made many Americans believe a revolution was imminent in 1919?

Critical Thinking

4. **Big Ideas** Why did the end of World War I bring such turmoil to the United States?

5. **Analyzing** Provide evidence to explain whether or not the Palmer raids deprived some people of their civil rights.

6. **Analyzing Visuals** Examine the photograph on page 577. What do you notice about the rioters? What does this tell you about the riots?

Writing About History

7. **Persuasive Writing** Imagine that you are a European immigrant working in a factory in the United States in 1919. Write a letter to a relative in Europe describing the feelings of Americans toward you and other immigrants.

History ONLINE
Study Central™ To review this section, go to glencoe.com and click on Study Central.

581

C Critical Thinking

Analyzing Primary Sources Have students read the quote from candidate Warren G. Harding on this page. **Ask:** What message is the candidate giving? *(The nation needs a period of peace.)* **OL**

Assess

History ONLINE

Study Central™ provides summaries, interactive games, and online graphic organizers to help students review content.

Close

Summarizing **Ask:** How did the end of World War I affect the United States? *(Conversion to a peacetime economy led to strikes and race riots; people grew fearful of communism.)* **OL**

Reading Check

Answer:
They blamed union leaders for causing social unrest through strikes and thought unions were dominated by radicals.

Section 4 REVIEW

Answers

1. All definitions can be found in the section and the Glossary.
2. answers may include: conversion to peacetime economy, inflation, layoffs, lowered wages
3. strikes, race riots, protests, the 1917 Russian Revolution
4. soldiers returned home from the war; shift from a wartime to a peacetime economy; pent-up demand for higher wages to purchase new consumer goods; adjusting to new social climate after the Great Migration
5. Answers will vary, but most students will likely note that the raids did deprive some people of their civil rights.
6. The rioters were mostly white men; they were unarmed. Violence may not have been imminent.
7. Students' letters will vary.

Determining Cause and Effect The Visual Summary lists causes of America's entry into World War I and its social and cultural effects. Ask students to use the information on the page to create a time line of the era's events. Display the time lines in the classroom. **OL**

Descriptive Writing Have students select the one effect or event that they believe has had the most impact on the United States today. Have students write a letter describing their chosen effect or event to a friend, describing its impact on today's America. Remind students to use descriptive words and terms in their letters. Have volunteers share their letters with the class. **OL**

Chapter 16 VISUAL SUMMARY

STUDY TO GO — You can study anywhere, anytime by downloading quizzes and flashcards to your PDA from glencoe.com.

Causes of America's Entry Into World War I

- Americans hear stories of German atrocities and many become anti-German.
- Many of President Wilson's advisors support the Allies.
- American banks lend the Allies large amounts of money and American companies sell the Allies food, weapons, and military supplies.
- Germany angers the United States by ordering submarines to attack neutral ships carrying goods to the Allies.
- Germany sinks the passenger ships *Lusitania* and *Sussex*, enraging Americans. To keep America out of the war, Germany stops sinking ships without warning in 1916.
- Germany tries to make an alliance with Mexico, further angering Americans.
- In a last attempt to win the war, Germany orders submarines to attack ships without warning in 1917; six American ships are sunk.
- The United States declares war, April 1917.

EIGHTH EDITION NEW YORK JOURNAL EIGHTH EDITION

House by a Vote of 373 to 50 Passes Joint Resolution

WAR IS DECLARED BY U.S.

Interned German Ships Seized by Customs Authorities

Washington, April 6.—After a debate of nearly seventeen hours, the House early to-day passed the resolution previously adopted in the Senate, declaring a state of war against the Government of Germany. The vote was 373 to 50.

The resolution now goes to Vice-President Marshall, who must sign it in formal session of the

▶ *German U-boats helped cause the United States to enter the war.*

▲ *World War I enabled women to take jobs traditionally reserved for men.*

Social and Cultural Effects of World War I

- Northern factories recruit African Americans from the rural South; African Americans migrate to northern cities in large numbers, improving their standard of living and changing politics in northern cities.
- In search of workers, companies also hire large numbers of women for jobs traditionally reserved for men.
- Labor shortages cause many Mexicans to migrate north to take work in the United States. Many Hispanic Americans leave farmwork for factory work.
- Laws limiting civil rights in wartime are upheld by the Supreme Court in the cases of *Schenck* v. *U.S.* and *Abrams* v. *U.S.*
- During the war, anti-German feelings are widespread.
- The end of the war leads to economic and social tensions; many workers go on strike; race riots erupt in many cities.
- After the war, many Americans become anti-immigrant, anti-communist, and anti-union.

Hands-On Chapter Project
Step 5: Wrap Up

Presenting World War I

Step 5: Wrap Up Students will divide into teams to complete their presentations.

Directions Divide the class into two teams. Each team will complete the presentation by placing all the slides created in Sections 1, 2, 3, and 4 into a unified presentation. Students will need to provide logical transitions between topics, as well as edit the slides prior to presentation day.

Putting It Together Set aside class time for each team to give their presentations. Allow time for a discussion after all presentations have been given. Ask students the following questions:

- What were the main points of the presentation?
- Did the presentation present World War I clearly?
- Were the transitions clear?
- What were the good (and bad) parts of the presentation? How could it be improved? **OL**

Reviewing Vocabulary

Directions: Choose the word or words that best complete the sentence.

1. The British used ________ to convince Americans to support the Allied war effort.
   - **A** espionage
   - **B** armistice
   - **C** conscription
   - **D** propaganda

2. The ________ system ensured that American troops arrived safely in Europe.
   - **A** nationalism
   - **B** convoy
   - **C** reparations
   - **D** cost of living

3. British officials ordered a naval blockade to prevent ________, or prohibited materials, from entering Germany.
   - **A** contraband
   - **B** cost of living
   - **C** conscription
   - **D** self-determination

4. Soldiers in World War I dug a complex ________ of trenches to protect themselves.
   - **A** emphasis
   - **B** stability
   - **C** restoration
   - **D** network

5. During the war, the federal government tried to shape opinions about the war and to prevent ________, spying to acquire government information.
   - **A** espionage
   - **B** propaganda
   - **C** reparations
   - **D** militarism

Reviewing Main Ideas

Directions: Choose the best answers to the following questions.

Section 1 *(pp. 548–555)*

6. Which of the following was one of the primary causes of World War I?
   - **A** a complex set of alliances among European nations
   - **B** the exile of Mexican General Victoriano Huerta
   - **C** the dissatisfaction of Russian peasants
   - **D** the breakup of the Austro-Hungarian Empire

7. The event that triggered the American entry into World War I was
   - **A** the sinking of the *Lusitania*.
   - **B** the resumption of unrestricted submarine warfare.
   - **C** the invasion of neutral Belgium.
   - **D** the interception of the Zimmermann telegram.

Section 2 *(pp. 556–561)*

8. During World War I, which federal mobilization agency introduced daylight savings time and shortened the work week for some factories?
   - **A** War Industries Board
   - **B** Committee on Public Information
   - **C** National War Labor Board
   - **D** Fuel Administration

9. Both the Espionage Act and the Sedition Act of 1918 were designed to
   - **A** provide plans for rebuilding Germany after the war.
   - **B** help the British and French economies during the war.
   - **C** limit opposition to the war in the United States.
   - **D** protect the rights of German Americans.

TEST-TAKING TIP

Eliminate answers that do not make sense. For instance, if an answer refers to World War II, you know it cannot be correct.

Need Extra Help?

If You Missed Questions . . .	1	2	3	4	5	6	7	8	9
Go to Page . . .	552	566–567	554	564	558	548–550	554–555	556–557	558

GO ON

Answers and Analyses
Reviewing Vocabulary

1. D One strategy to employ with vocabulary questions is to substitute the definition of each answer choice into the blank to find the one that makes the most sense. Propaganda is information that is meant to influence someone's position. The other choices do not fit. Espionage is spying. Armistice is a cease-fire. Conscription is drafting a person into military service.

2. B In a convoy, cargo ships and ships carrying troops were protected by destroyers. Convoy means "fleet" or "procession." Nationalism is feelings of intense national pride. Reparations are payments for damages. Cost of living is an economic term.

3. A Contra- as a prefix means "against" or "contrary." This should help students remember that contraband is goods that are prohibited (*against* the law/rules).

4. D Only *D* makes sense. A network is a system or complex. *A* and *B* do not make sense. Soldiers did not "restore" trenches, they dug new trenches.

5. A Propaganda was the information that the government used to influence opinion; reparations were monetary payments demanded for war damages; militarism was the aggressive buildup of armed forces that led to war.

Reviewing Main Ideas

6. A European nations developed a system of complex alliances in response to the actions taken during the creation/uniting of Germany and also to the spread of nationalism in Europe. Because of these alliances, one act of aggression triggered many nations to be at odds.

7. B There is never a single cause for a nation entering a war, but there is often a "final straw," that triggers a nation's involvement. Choices *A* and *D* both contributed to American support of going to war, but it was Germany's resumption of unrestricted warfare that finally drew the U.S. into war.

8. D Discuss the purposes/benefits of daylight savings with students. It allows more work to be done during daylight. This, in turn, saves energy. The Fuel Administration is the most likely organization listed to want to conserve energy.

9. C Espionage is spying. Sedition is subversion or treason. The passage of these acts suppressed war opposition. They did not protect rights, they suspended them.

Chapter 16 Assessment

Section 3 *(pp. 564–573)*

10. Which of the following technologies was first used during World War I?
- **A** tanks
- **B** cannons
- **C** aircraft carriers
- **D** hot air balloons

11. Why did the Senate reject the Treaty of Versailles?
- **A** to keep the United States free from foreign entanglements
- **B** to express opposition to the harsh sanctions imposed on Germany
- **C** to avoid the dues for membership in the League of Nations
- **D** to reduce United States military forces in Europe

Section 4 *(pp. 576–581)*

12. The Red Scare was a fear that
- **A** nuclear power would result in widespread destruction in the United States.
- **B** Communists would seize power in the United States.
- **C** fire would spread quickly through overcrowded American cities.
- **D** the Soviet Union would develop an atomic bomb.

13. The organization that eventually became the Federal Bureau of Investigation was originally formed to
- **A** uncover German spies during World War I.
- **B** spread propaganda within the United States in support of World War I.
- **C** infiltrate unions to head off strikes.
- **D** raid the headquarters of radical organizations in order to look for evidence of a Communist conspiracy.

Critical Thinking

Directions: Choose the best answers to the following questions.

14. How did Congress ensure that the United States would have enough troops to serve in World War I?
- **A** Congress allowed women to serve in the armed forces.
- **B** The Selective Service Act of 1917 required all men ages 21 to 30 to register for the draft.
- **C** Congress allowed African Americans to serve in the armed forces.
- **D** Congress offered a free education and cheap land to anyone willing to serve.

Base your answer to question 15 on the map below and your knowledge of Chapter 16.

Europe after WWI

15. Which countries lost territory as a result of World War I?
- **A** Germany, Russia, France
- **B** Germany, France, England
- **C** Germany, Italy, Austria-Hungary
- **D** Germany, Austria-Hungary, Russia

Need Extra Help?

If You Missed Questions . . .	10	11	12	13	14	15
Go to Page . . .	565–567	571–573	579	580	560–561	570–571

GO ON

10. A The use of cannons far predates the use of tanks. Remind students that cannons were used during the Revolutionary War. Aircraft carriers were developed in the early 1900s, but were not used in combat until after WWI. Hot air balloons were developed in eighteenth century.

11. A Remind students of the desire to return to isolationist ways and retreat from world affairs expressed by many at the close of WWI. The Treaty of Versailles was rejected because of the inclusion of the League of Nations. Members of Congress thought the agreement would entangle the U.S. in world affairs.

12. B Communists were called "reds." The Red Scare was a fear of communism that swept through the nation in the years following WWI. Nuclear power was not invented until the WWII era, so *A* and *D* can be eliminated. *C* is not likely.

13. D The General Intelligence Division was formed during the Red Scare in response to a series of bombings that many believed to be the acts of subversives, Communists in particular. Damage to the home of the Attorney General prompted him to form the Division, which later became the FBI. The organization was formed after WWI, so *A* and *B* can be eliminated. Although many believed that unions were involved with communism, the organization was not intended to head off strikes.

Critical Thinking

14. B Women did not serve in combat positions, so *A* can be eliminated. African Americans did serve in the armed forces; but only a small number served in combat. The Selective Service Act required men to sign up for the draft, and the draft ensured that the U.S. would have a large pool of possible troops.

15. D Examine the map with students. Explain that there were three empires broken up at the end of the war: the German Empire, the Russian Empire, and the Austro-Hungarian Empire. France, Italy, and England were part of the "Big Four" present at the Peace Conference. Any answer containing these countries can be eliminated as they were unlikely to lose any territory in the war.

16. President Wilson's Fourteen Points plan called for

A Germany to pay war reparations to the Allies.

B Germany to acknowledge guilt for the outbreak of World War I.

C the creation of the United Nations.

D the creation of the League of Nations.

Analyze the cartoon and answer the question that follows. Base your answers on the cartoon and on your knowledge of Chapter 16.

17. The cartoonist is expressing the opinion that

A England's blockade of Germany was beneficial for neutral shipping.

B England's blockade of the United States hurt neutral shipping.

C England's blockade of the United States hurt American shipping.

D England's blockade of Germany hurt American shipping.

Document-Based Questions

Directions: Analyze the document and answer the short-answer questions that follow the document.

On September 12, 1918, Socialist leader Eugene V. Debs was convicted of violating the Espionage Act. Debs later spoke to the court at his sentencing. The document below is an excerpt from that speech:

> *"I look upon the Espionage laws as a despotic enactment in flagrant conflict with democratic principles and with the spirit of free institutions. . . . I am opposed to the social system in which we live. . . . I believe in fundamental change, but if possible by peaceful and orderly means. . . .*
>
> *I am thinking this morning of the men in the mills and factories, . . . of the women who for a paltry wage are compelled to work out their barren lives; of the little children who in this system are robbed of their childhood and . . . forced into industrial dungeons. . . . In this high noon of our twentieth century Christian civilization, money is still so much more important than the flesh and blood of childhood. In very truth gold is god: . . . "*
>
> —from Eugene Debs in *Echoes of Distant Thunder*

18. According to Debs, what were some problems in American society at this time? How did he believe change should be brought about?

19. How did Debs seem to feel about the Espionage Act? Do you agree with him? Why or why not?

Extended Response

20. After World War I, the United States Senate refused to ratify the Treaty of Versailles despite the intense efforts of Woodrow Wilson to convince Americans that ratification would help ensure that the peace would be an enduring one. Choose to either support or oppose the United States's ratification of the Treaty of Versailles. Write a persuasive essay that includes an introduction and at least three paragraphs that support your position.

STOP

History ONLINE

For additional test practice, use Self-Check Quizzes—Chapter 16 at glencoe.com.

Need Extra Help?

If You Missed Questions . . .	16	17	18	19	20
Go to Page . . .	570–571	552–555	585	R19	570–573

Document-Based Questions

18. Debs said the problems in American society were the espionage acts, unfair working conditions, and the importance of profit over peoples' lives.

19. Debs felt the espionage laws went against the democratic principles upon which the nation was founded. Answers to the second question will vary. Accept all well-reasoned and relevant answers.

Extended Response

20. Students' essays will vary, but must demonstrate an understanding of the purpose of the League of Nations and of the motivations behind those who opposed it. Essays should take a position for or against the rejection of the Treaty of Versailles and present a balanced argument using information from the chapter as support. Essays should follow proper guidelines for writing a persuasive essay.

16. D Direct students who have trouble with this question to review the chart on page 570 that lists the Fourteen Points. Students should relate President Wilson with the creation of the League of Nations, even if the U.S. eventually failed to join. The United Nations was created at the end of WWII.

17. D Study the cartoon with students. Uncle Sam is chastising England for interfering with those who have the right to trade on the seas, namely, neutral commerce and American shipping, represented by crying children. England is trying to "hit" Germany with the blockade (see writing on the stick/bat). England blockaded Germany, not the United States, so B and C can be eliminated. The children are unhappy about England's actions toward Germany, eliminating choice A.

History ONLINE

Have students visit the Web site at glencoe.com to review Chapter 16 and take the Self-Check Quiz.

Need Extra Help?

Have students refer to the pages listed if they miss any of the questions.

Unit 6 Planning Guide

UNIT PACING CHART					
	Unit 6	Chapter 17	Chapter 18	Chapter 19	Unit 6
Day 1	Unit Opener	Chapter 17 Opener, Section 1	Chapter 18 Opener, Section 1	Chapter 19 Opener, Section 1	Wrap-Up/Project, Unit Assessment
Day 2		Section 2	Section 2	Section 2	
Day 3		Sections 3 & 4	Section 3	Section 3	
Day 4		Section 5	Chapter Assessment	Chapter Assessment	
Day 5		Chapter Assessment			

Teacher to Teacher

Jennifer G. Lange
Forest Hills High School
Forest Hills, NY

The Culture of Slang Provide the students with a list of slang expressions from the Jazz Age. Do not give them the explanations of the slang. Ask students to try to decide what the words mean (some of the expressions we still use today). Ask students to explain how the new vocabulary reflected the culture of the Jazz Age. Ask students to describe the role that slang plays in their lives today. Some slang terms that developed in the period include:

- cat's meow (or cat's pajamas)—something fantastic
- crush—an infatuation with someone
- gatecrasher—someone who "crashes" a party
- blind date—dating someone you never met
- big cheese—the boss
- bump off—murder or kill
- goofy—silly
- gams—a woman's legs
- heebie jeebies—jitters
- high-hat—snub
- flapper—the "new woman" of the 1920s
- gyp—cheat
- darb—something truly wonderful
- gin mill—a speakeasy

Author Note

Dear American History Teacher:

When I teach the period covered in this unit, I try to convey to students the extraordinary character of this period in American history—an economic boom that transformed the nation's landscape and culture, and a catastrophic economic collapse that destabilized not just the United States but much of the world.

The Great Depression of the 1930s was a direct result of some of the economic changes of the 1920s, and of the weaknesses those changes helped to produce. Indeed, the real beginning of the Great Depression came not in the aftermath of the stock market crash of 1929, but with an agricultural depression that had begun several years earlier. And the response to the Great Depression—first by Herbert Hoover and later by Franklin Roosevelt—drew heavily from ideas about the economy that the 1920s boom helped create.

Looming behind the domestic issues that preoccupied the nation during much of the period between the two world wars was a continuing global crisis. The settlement of World War I had not stabilized the international system. On the contrary, the aftermath of the war unleashed new regimes and new ideologies—most notably communism and fascism—that slowly eroded the peace and led to the outbreak of war in China in the mid-1930s, in Europe in 1939, and in the United States in 1941.

The period between the two wars was in many ways a catastrophic time for the world, unleashing forces that produced the greatest and most terrible war in human history. This period marked a fundamental break in history. The United States was ultimately drawn into the war too, but despite the many sacrifices Americans made in World War II, America emerged from the conflict stronger and more stable than it had been in decades.

It is important to introduce students to the contrasts and crises of this period, and to the continuities in American life that tied these years together.

Senior Author

Introducing
Unit 6

Focus

Why It Matters

Write these terms on the board: *Roaring '20s, Great Depression, New Deal.* Have students describe what images come to mind when they see or hear these terms. Then have them make generalizations about what their lives would be like during each of the time periods described by those terms. **OL**

Connecting to Past Learning

Remind students that in the previous unit they learned about the development of the United States after the Civil War era. **Ask:** **What challenges from the recent past might people in the 1920s, 1930s, and 1940s have continued to face?** *(Answers may include economic challenges, social change, and racial prejudice.)* Tell students that in this unit they will learn about the Boom and Bust cycles the United States experienced from 1920 until 1941. **OL**

Unit Launch Activity

Making Connections Point out to students that the early part of this unit's time span was a carefree time, seen by some as a decadent period prior to the hardships of economic depression and war. **Ask:** **Why do you think the 1920s was a decade of great cultural change?** *(Answers will vary, but students might note that new inventions and new styles of music, art, and literature all affected the nation.)* **OL**

Unit 6

Boom and Bust
1920–1941

Why It Matters

In the 1920s, new technology, including automobiles, airplanes, radios, and electric appliances helped create a booming economy with rising stock prices and increased consumer spending. In 1929, economic problems triggered the Great Depression. This led to increased federal regulation of the economy and several new programs, such as Social Security as the federal government took on the task of protecting people from economic hardship.

586

Team Teaching Activity

Art Invite the art teacher to your class to explain the Art Deco style and show classic examples of the style. Then have students research your local community for examples of Art Deco architecture, art, and design. If possible, have students take photographs of the examples to present to the class. Have students point out why the samples they have chosen illustrate Art Deco style. **OL**

The Great White Way, Times Square, New York, 1925

Teach

S1 Skill Practice

Visual Literacy Have students study the image on the page.
Ask: What time of day is shown in the painting? *(night)* What do you think the bright colors shown on the buildings indicate to people who view the painting? *(There is much to see and do in New York at night.)* **BL**

S2 Skill Practice

Describing Have students again review the unit painting.
Ask: What feelings or emotions was the artist attempting to evoke from people who view the painting? *(Answers will vary, but students might note that the artist is depicting an exuberant, carefree, lively nightlife in New York's Times Square.)* Why do you think the artist titled his painting *The Great White Way, Times Square, 1925?* *(The bright lights from all the billboards lit up the street at night.)* **OL**

More About the Painting

Howard Thain Although he was a Texas native, Howard Thain's favorite subject was his adopted home, New York City. Originally an impressionist, he became a modernist painter of urban scenes and portraits. *The Great White Way* (1925) captures the energy of Times Square at night. Obsessed with light, Thain conveys the glitz and excitement of urban nightlife during the period when electric lights first became more common than kerosene lamps and cities became nighttime playgrounds for urbanites with disposable income. Many of his paintings depict the frenzied pursuit of pleasure and diversion associated with the Roaring Twenties.

NCLB No Child Left Behind

Teaching Tip The NCLB Act emphasizes reading. Ask students to make a time line that begins with 1920 and ends with 1941. Have them keep the time line with them as they read and add people and events to the time line, as well as note the page number on which they encountered the person or event. Students can use this time line while studying.

Chapter 17 Planning Guide

Key to Ability Levels	
BL Below Level	AL Above Level
OL On Level	ELL English Language Learners

Key to Teaching Resources	
Print Material	Transparency
CD-ROM or DVD	

Levels				Resources		Chapter Opener	Section 1	Section 2	Section 3	Section 4	Section 5	Chapter Assess
BL	OL	AL	ELL									
FOCUS												
BL	OL	AL	ELL	Transparency	**Daily Focus Skills Transparencies**		17-1	17-2	17-3	17-4	17-5	
TEACH												
	OL	AL		Print Material	**History Simulations and Problem Solving, URB**					p. 9		
		AL		Print Material	**American Literature Reading, URB**					p. 15	p. 13	
BL	OL		ELL	Print Material	**Reading Essentials and Note-Taking Guide***		p. 186	p. 189	p. 192	p. 195	p. 198	
	OL			Print Material	**Historical Analysis Skills Activity, URB**			p. 22				
BL	OL		ELL	Print Material	**Guided Reading Activities, URB***		p. 46	p. 47	p. 48	p. 49	p. 50	
BL	OL	AL	ELL	Print Material	**Content Vocabulary Activity, URB***			p. 27				
BL	OL	AL	ELL	Print Material	**Academic Vocabulary Activity, URB**			p. 29				
	OL	AL		Print Material	**Critical Thinking Skills Activity, URB**				p. 32			
BL	OL		ELL	Print Material	**Reading Skills Activity, URB**					p. 21		
BL			ELL	Print Material	**English Learner Activity, URB**			p. 25				
	OL	AL		Print Material	**Reinforcing Skills Activity, URB**		p. 31					
BL	OL	AL	ELL	Print Material	**Differentiated Instruction Activity, URB**				p. 23			
BL	OL		ELL	Print Material	**Time Line Activity, URB**			p. 33				
	OL			Print Material	**Linking Past and Present Activity, URB**			p. 34				
BL	OL	AL	ELL	Print Material	**American Art and Music Activity, URB**						p. 39	
BL	OL	AL	ELL	Print Material	**Interpreting Political Cartoons Activity, URB**				p. 41			
		AL		Print Material	**Enrichment Activity, URB**						p. 44	
BL	OL	AL	ELL	Print Material	**American Biographies**				✓	✓	✓	
BL	OL	AL	ELL	Print Material	**Primary Source Reading, URB**				p. 35		p. 37	
BL	OL	AL	ELL	Print Material	**Supreme Court Case Studies**				p. 43			
BL	OL	AL	ELL	Print Material	**The Living Constitution***	✓	✓	✓	✓	✓	✓	✓
	OL	AL		CD-ROM or DVD	**American History Primary Source Documents Library**	✓	✓	✓	✓	✓	✓	✓
BL	OL	AL	ELL	Transparency	**Unit Map Overlay Transparencies**	✓	✓	✓	✓	✓	✓	✓

Note: Please refer to the *Unit 6 Resource Book* for this chapter's URB materials.

* Also available in Spanish

TeacherWorks Plus
All-In-One Planner and Resource Center

- Interactive Lesson Planner
- Interactive Teacher Edition
- Fully editable blackline masters
- Section Spotlight Videos Launch
- Differentiated Lesson Plans
- Printable reports of daily assignments
- Standards Tracking System

Levels BL	OL	AL	ELL	Resources	Chapter Opener	Section 1	Section 2	Section 3	Section 4	Section 5	Chapter Assess
				TEACH *(continued)*							
BL	OL	AL	ELL	Differentiated Instruction for the American History Classroom	✓	✓	✓	✓	✓	✓	✓
BL	OL	AL	ELL	StudentWorks™ Plus	✓	✓	✓	✓	✓	✓	✓
BL	OL	AL	ELL	American Music Hits Through History CD	✓	✓	✓	✓	✓	✓	✓
BL	OL	AL	ELL	Unit Time Line Transparencies and Activities	✓	✓	✓	✓	✓	✓	✓
BL	OL	AL	ELL	Cause and Effect Transparencies, Strategies, and Activities	✓	✓	✓	✓	✓	✓	✓
BL	OL	AL	ELL	Why It Matters Transparencies, Strategies, and Activities	✓	✓	✓	✓	✓	✓	✓
BL	OL	AL	ELL	American Issues	✓	✓	✓	✓	✓	✓	✓
	OL	AL	ELL	American Art and Architecture Transparencies, Strategies, and Activities	✓	✓	✓	✓	✓	✓	✓
BL	OL	AL		High School American History Literature Library	✓	✓	✓	✓	✓	✓	✓
BL	OL	AL	ELL	*The American Vision* Video Program	✓	✓	✓	✓	✓	✓	✓
Teacher Resources				Strategies for Success	✓	✓	✓	✓	✓	✓	✓
				Success with English Learners	✓	✓	✓	✓	✓	✓	✓
				Reading Strategies and Activities for the Social Studies Classroom	✓	✓	✓	✓	✓	✓	✓
				Presentation Plus! with MindJogger CheckPoint	✓	✓	✓	✓	✓	✓	✓
				ASSESS							
BL	OL	AL	ELL	Section Quizzes and Chapter Tests*		p. 243	p. 244	p. 245	p. 246	p. 247	p. 249
BL	OL	AL	ELL	Authentic Assessment With Rubrics							p. 39
BL	OL	AL	ELL	Standardized Test Practice Workbook							p. 38
BL	OL	AL	ELL	*ExamView® Assessment Suite*		17-1	17-2	17-3	17-4	17-5	Ch. 17
				CLOSE							
BL			ELL	Reteaching Activity, URB							p. 43
BL	OL		ELL	Reading and Study Skills Foldables™	pp. 68–70						

✓ Chapter- or unit-based activities applicable to all sections in this chapter.

Chapter 17 Integrating Technology

Using Section Audio

Teach With Technology

What is Section Audio?

Section Audio is a recording of each section of the textbook and helps students learn the content in the textbook.

How can Section Audio help my students?

Section Audio allows students to:

- read and listen simultaneously to improve content comprehension
- practice reading skills
- review important concepts for struggling readers
- improve listening comprehension

Visit glencoe.com to access the Media Library, and enter a ***QuickPass***™ code to go to Section Audio recordings.

History ONLINE
Visit glencoe.com and enter ***QuickPass***™ code TAV9399c17T for Chapter 17 resources.

You can easily launch a wide range of digital products from your computer's desktop with the McGraw-Hill Social Studies widget.

	Student	Teacher	Parent
Media Library			
• Section Audio	●		●
• Spanish Audio Summaries	●		●
• Section Spotlight Videos	●	●	●
***The American Vision* Online Learning Center (Web Site)**			
• StudentWorks™ Plus Online	●	●	●
• Multilingual Glossary	●	●	●
• Study-to-Go	●	●	●
• Chapter Overviews	●	●	●
• Self-Check Quizzes	●	●	●
• Student Web Activities	●	●	●
• ePuzzles and Games	●	●	●
• Vocabulary eFlashcards	●	●	●
• In Motion Animations	●	●	●
• Study Central™	●	●	●
• Web Activity Lesson Plans		●	
• Vocabulary PuzzleMaker	●	●	●
• Historical Thinking Activities		●	
• Beyond the Textbook	●	●	●

READING SUPPORT FROM JAMESTOWN EDUCATION

- **Timed Readings Plus in Social Studies** helps students increase their reading rate and fluency while maintaining comprehension. The 400-word passages are similar to those found on state and national assessments.
- **Reading in the Content Area: Social Studies** concentrates on six essential reading skills that help students better comprehend what they read. The book includes 75 high-interest nonfiction passages written at increasing levels of difficulty.
- **Reading Social Studies** includes strategic reading instruction and vocabulary support in Social Studies content for both ELLs and native speakers of English.

www.jamestowneducation.com

NATIONAL GEOGRAPHIC

Index to National Geographic Magazine:

The following articles relate to this chapter:

- "Growing up in East Harlem," by Jere Van Dyk, May 1990.
- "Traveling the Blues Highway," by Charles E. Cobb, Jr., April 1999.

National Geographic Society Products To order the following, call National Geographic at 1-800-368-2728:

- ZipZapMap! USA (ZipZapMap!)

Access National Geographic's new, dynamic MapMachine Web site and other geography resources at:

www.nationalgeographic.com
www.nationalgeographic.com/maps

Biography A&E HOME VIDEO THE HISTORY CHANNEL

The following videotape programs are available from Glencoe as supplements to this chapter:

- The Prohibition Era (ISBN 0-76-700179-6)
- The Monkey Trial, In Search of History (ISBN 0-76-700609-7)

To order, call Glencoe at 1-800-334-7344. To find classroom resources to accompany many of these videos, check the following home pages:

A&E Television: www.aetv.com
The History Channel: www.historychannel.com

Reading List Generator CD-ROM

GLENCOE BOOKLINK 3

Use this database to search more than 30,000 titles to create a customized reading list for your students.

- Reading lists can be organized by students' reading level, author, genre, theme, or area of interest.
- The database provides Degrees of Reading Power™ (DRP) and Lexile™ readability scores for all selections.
- A brief summary of each selection is included.

Leveled reading suggestions for this chapter:

For students at a Grade 8 reading level:
- ***Giants of Jazz***, by Studs Terkel

For students at a Grade 9 reading level:
- ***Great African Americans in Jazz***, by Carlotta Hacker

For students at a Grade 10 reading level:
- ***Jazz and Blues***, by Roger Thomas

For students at a Grade 11 reading level:
- ***Jazz: An American Saga***, by James Lincoln Collier

For students at a Grade 12 reading level:
- ***When the Negro Was in Vogue***, by Langston Hughes

Introducing Chapter 17

Focus

MAKING CONNECTIONS

Why Does Culture Change?

Ask students to explain what their culture is like today. Then ask them how it was different ten years ago. Students may point out that the latest technologies did not exist ten years earlier. Activate students' prior knowledge by asking them to name aspects of their present-day culture that did not exist in the time of their parents' or caregivers' youth. Students may note that cell phones were not common, mp3 players did not exist, and so on. Discuss with students how watching movies or listening to music has changed since the 1920s. BL ELL

Teach

The Big Ideas

As students study the chapter, remind them to consider the section-based Big Ideas included in each section's Guide to Reading. The **Essential Questions** in the activities below tie in to the Big Ideas and help students think about and understand important chapter concepts. In addition, the Hands-on Chapter Projects with their culminating activities relate the content from each section to the Big Ideas. These activities build on each other as students progress through the chapter. Section activities culminate in the wrap-up activity on the Visual Summary page.

Chapter 17

The Jazz Age

1921–1929

Joe "King" Oliver's jazz band plays in San Francisco in 1921, with singer Lil Hardin.

U.S. PRESIDENTS

Harding 1921–1923

Coolidge 1923–1929

U.S. EVENTS

- **1921** • Washington Conference convenes
- **1922** • Claude McKay's *Harlem Shadows* is published

- **1923** • Teapot Dome scandal erupts
- **1924** • Congress passes National Origins Act
- **1925** • Scopes trial begins

1921 1923 1925

WORLD EVENTS

- **1921** • Ireland becomes independent country
- **1922** • Mussolini and Fascists take power in Italy
- **1923** • France invades Ruhr • Hitler writes *Mein Kampf*
- **1924** • Vladimir Lenin dies

Section 1

The Politics of the 1920s

Essential Question: Why did the American people want life to return to the way it was before World War I? *(People wanted to put the suffering of the war behind them; they were eager to buy new goods that were not available during the war.)* Point out that in Section 1 students will learn about the scandals of the Harding administration and the successes of the Coolidge Administration. OL

Section 2

A Growing Economy

Essential Question: How did new industries contribute to economic growth? *(New industries such as the automobile industry and the airline industry required vast amounts of material from other industries, including the steel, oil, rubber, and glass industries.)* Point out that in Section 2 students will learn how the new industries accelerated economic growth in the 1920s. OL

Chapter Audio

Making Connections

Why Does Culture Change?

In the 1920s, technology spurred economic growth and cultural change. Although not everyone approved, young people adopted new styles of dress, listened to jazz music, and had more independence than earlier generations.

- ***What technologies changed life in the 1920s?***
- ***How do you think the invention of radio and movies changed popular culture?***

FOLDABLES™

Categorizing the Harlem Renaissance
Create a Trifold Book Foldable to present a brief biography, with artistic works, of major figures in the Harlem Renaissance under the category of writers, poets, and musicians. You may want to expand on your entries by using the Internet.

1927
- Lindbergh completes first solo transatlantic flight

1928
- Kellogg-Briand Pact signed

Hoover 1929–1933

1927 1929

1926
- British General Strike paralyzes British economy

1927
- Stalin gains control of Soviet Union

1928
- Chiang Kai-shek becomes leader of China

History ONLINE Visit glencoe.com and enter *QuickPass*™ code TAV9846c17 for Chapter 17 resources.

Introducing
Chapter 17

More About the Photo

Visual Literacy Joe "King" Oliver began his musical career in New Orleans. He settled in Chicago in 1919, and then spent time performing in California. In 1921 he returned to Chicago and formed King Oliver's Creole Jazz Band, which Louis Armstrong later joined.

FOLDABLES™ Study Organizer **Dinah Zike's Foldables**

Dinah Zike's Foldables are three-dimensional, interactive graphic organizers that help students practice basic writing skills, review vocabulary terms, and identify main ideas. Instructions for creating and using Foldables can be found in the Appendix at the end of this book and in the *Dinah Zike's Reading and Study Skills Foldables* booklet.

History ONLINE
Visit glencoe.com and enter *QuickPass*™ code TAV9399c17T for Chapter 17 resources, including a Chapter Overview, Study Central™, Study-to-Go, Student Web Activity, Self-Check Quiz, and other materials.

Section 3

A Clash of Values
Essential Question: Why did the modern culture of the 1920s cause some people to think that traditional society and morality were under attack? *(Many people were afraid of new beliefs and ways of doing things. In addition, some people were fearful of immigrants.)* Point out that in Section 3 students will learn how some Americans reacted to the culture of the 1920s. **OL**

Section 4

Cultural Innovations
Essential Question: How did popular culture, the arts, and literature change in the 1920s? *(More Americans used their increased leisure time to enjoy popular culture; artists and writers expressed the exuberance as well as the loneliness of the decade.)* Point out that in Section 4 students will learn how popular culture and the arts reflected the moods of the 1920s. **OL**

Section 5

African American Culture
Essential Question: How did African Americans affect American society in the 1920s? *(The Harlem Renaissance led to new African American literature, music, and art; the influx of African Americans to northern cities made them a powerful political voice.)* Point out that in Section 5 students will learn about the contributions of African Americans in the 1920s. **OL**

Focus

Bellringer

Daily Focus Transparency 17-1

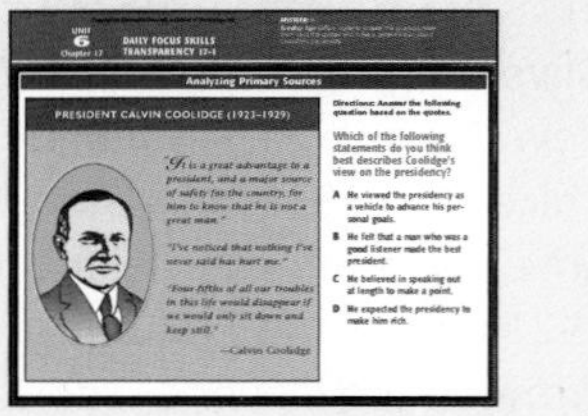

Guide to Reading

Answers may include:

Presidential Politics

I. The Harding Administration

 A. Teapot Dome and Other Scandals

 B. "Silent Cal" Takes Over

Students should complete the outline by including all the heads in the section.

Section Spotlight Video

To generate student interest and provide a springboard for class discussion, access the Chapter 17, Section 1 video at glencoe.com or on the video DVD.

Section 1 — Section Audio — Spotlight Video

The Politics of the 1920s

Guide to Reading

Big Ideas

Economics and Society Government policies helped create prosperity in the 1920s.

Content Vocabulary

- supply-side economics *(p. 593)*
- cooperative individualism *(p. 593)*
- isolationism *(p. 594)*

Academic Vocabulary

- investigation *(p. 591)*
- revelation *(p. 592)*

People and Events to Identify

- Teapot Dome *(p. 591)*
- Charles G. Dawes *(p. 595)*
- Charles Evans Hughes *(p. 595)*
- Kellogg-Briand Pact *(p. 595)*

Reading Strategy

Taking Notes As you read about Presidents Harding and Coolidge, create an outline similar to the one below.

The Politics of the 1920s
I. The Harding Administration
 A.
 B.
II.
III.
 A.
 B.

Warren G. Harding's administration suffered from corruption and scandals. His successor, Calvin Coolidge, worked hard to restore the American public's faith in their government and to promote a healthy economy.

The Harding Administration

MAIN Idea President Harding staffed his administration with political friends from Ohio; his presidency was marred by many scandals.

HISTORY AND YOU If you were choosing teammates, would you pick a friend or a better player? Read on to learn about the problems Harding created by making poor choices for government appointments.

Warren G. Harding was born in 1865 in Corsica, Ohio. In 1898 voters elected Harding to the Ohio General Assembly, where he fit in comfortably with the powerful Ohio Republican political machine. Voters elected him as Ohio's lieutenant governor in 1903 and United States senator in 1914. After serving one term in the Senate, Harding ran for and won the presidency in 1920.

Harding's political philosophy fit in well with the times. In his campaign, he had promised "a return to normalcy," by which he meant "normal" life after the war. His charm and genial manner endeared him to the nation, and people applauded when the open, easygoing atmosphere of the Harding administration replaced the quiet gloom of President Wilson's last years.

Teapot Dome and Other Scandals

Harding made several distinguished appointments to the cabinet, including former Supreme Court Justice Charles Evans Hughes as secretary of state, former Food Administrator Herbert Hoover as secretary of commerce, and business tycoon Andrew Mellon as secretary of the treasury. All three men would play an important role in supporting and shaping the economic prosperity of the 1920s.

Many of Harding's other appointments, however, were disastrous. He gave cabinet posts and other high-level jobs to friends and political allies from Ohio. Harding named Harry M. Daugherty, his campaign manager and boss of the Ohio Republican Party, attorney general. He made his boyhood friend Daniel Crissinger chairman of the Federal Reserve Board and selected Colonel Charles R. Forbes—another Ohio acquaintance—to head the Veterans Bureau.

Harding felt more comfortable among his old poker-playing friends, known as the Ohio Gang, than he did around such sober and

Resource Manager

R Reading Strategies	C Critical Thinking	D Differentiated Instruction	W Writing Support	S Skill Practice
Additional Resources • Guide Read, URB p. 46	**Teacher Edition** • Analyzing Prim. Sources, p. 591 • Making Comparisons, p. 593 • Making Inferences, p. 594 • Analyze Info., p. 595 **Additional Resources** • Quizzes and Tests, p. 243	**Teacher Edition** • Visual/Spatial, p. 594 **Additional Resources** • Foldables, pp. 68–70	**Teacher Edition** • Persuasive Writing, p. 592 **Additional Resources** • Supreme Court Case Stud., p. 43	**Teacher Edition** • Analyzing, p. 591 **Additional Resources** • Read Essen, p. 186 • Reinf. Skills Act., URB p. 31

POLITICAL CARTOONS PRIMARY SOURCE

An Administration Plagued by Scandal

▲ This cartoon shows politicians on the slippery "White House Highway" trying to outrun the scandal of Teapot Dome.

▲ "Bargain Day in Washington" shows the U.S. Capitol, the Washington Monument, the army, the White House, and the navy as having been "sold" to the highest bidder.

Analyzing VISUALS DBQ

1. **Drawing Conclusions** What does the cartoon on the left suggest about politicians?
2. **Analyzing** What does the cartoon on the right imply about corruption in the federal government?

serious people as Herbert Hoover. According to Alice Roosevelt Longworth, the White House study resembled a speakeasy.

PRIMARY SOURCE

"The air [would be] heavy with tobacco smoke, trays with bottles containing every imaginable brand of whiskey . . . cards and poker chips at hand—a general atmosphere of waistcoat unbuttoned, feet on desk, and spittoons alongside."

—quoted in *The Perils of Prosperity, 1914–1932*

The Ohio Gang did more than drink, smoke, and play poker with the president. Some members used their positions to sell government jobs, pardons, and protection from prosecution. Forbes sold scarce medical supplies from veterans' hospitals and kept the money for himself, costing the taxpayers about $250 million. When Harding learned what was going on, he complained privately that he had been betrayed. He said that he had no troubles with his enemies, but his friends were a different story: "They're the ones that keep me walking the floor nights!"

In June 1923 Harding left to tour the West. En route from Alaska to California, he became ill with what was probably a heart attack. He died in San Francisco on August 2, shortly before the news of the Forbes scandal broke. Early the next morning, the vice president, Calvin Coolidge, took the oath of office and became president.

The Forbes scandal was only the latest in a series of scandals and accusations that had marked the Harding administration. The most famous scandal, known as **Teapot Dome,** began in early 1922 when Harding's secretary of the interior, Albert B. Fall, secretly allowed private interests to lease lands containing U.S. Navy oil reserves at Teapot Dome, Wyoming, and Elk Hills, California. In return, Fall received bribes from these private interests totaling more than $300,000.

After the *Wall Street Journal* broke the story, the Senate launched an **investigation** that took most of the 1920s to complete. Trials followed; the Supreme Court invalidated the leases in 1927, and in 1929 Secretary Fall became the first cabinet officer in American history to go to prison.

Teach

S Skill Practice

Analyzing Have students study the political cartoons. **Ask:** Why are politicians fearful of scandals? Why do politicians worry about how their actions are perceived in their home districts? *(The hint of scandal or the perception that they are not responsible to their constituents may make them lose the next election.)* **OL**

C Critical Thinking

Analyzing Primary Sources Have students reread the primary source excerpt on this page. **Ask:** What impression does the excerpt describe? *(The excerpt describes a very relaxed, laid-back, casual atmosphere—hardly indicative of leadership.)* **BL**

Analyzing VISUALS

Answers:

1. They are fearful that the scandal will hurt their careers.
2. The government is for sale to the highest bidder.

Hands-On Chapter Project Step 1

Creating a Memory Book

Step 1: Selecting Memorable Participants Students will skim the chapter and choose a person who played a role in the events of this chapter. Students may choose people mentioned in the chapter or research other people not mentioned, but involved in the events of this period. Students will learn more about him or her in order to contribute a page to a class memory book.

Directions Make a scrapbook with the title "Memories of the Jazz Age" on the cover, and write the title on the board. Ask students to list on the board the names of people they may already know who played active roles in this period, such as Calvin Coolidge, Henry Ford, John T. Scopes, Mary Pickford, or Duke Elliington. Have students read ahead or do research to add as many names to the list as there are class members. Then have each student choose one name from the list.

Analyzing Information Students will identify the role played by each person added to the list. **OL**

(Chapter Project continued on page 369)

W Writing Support

Persuasive Writing Have students write a letter to a friend in Europe explaining why they agree or disagree with President Coolidge's views on Americans and business. Encourage students to share their letters with the class. BL

Reading Check

Answer:
They demonstrate poor judgment on the part of the president in choosing government officials.

Another Harding administration scandal involved Attorney General Harry Daugherty. During World War I, the federal government had seized a German-owned company in the United States as enemy property. To acquire the company and its valuable chemical patents, a German agent bribed a "go-between" politician, and a portion of the bribe ended up in a bank account that Daugherty controlled.

Under investigation by his own Justice Department, Daugherty refused to turn over requested files and bank records. He also refused to testify under oath, claiming immunity, or freedom from prosecution, on the grounds that he had had confidential dealings with the president. Daugherty's actions disgusted the new president, Calvin Coolidge, who demanded his resignation.

"Silent Cal" Takes Over

Calvin Coolidge was very different from Harding. Harding had enjoyed the easy conversation and company of old friends. Coolidge, joked a critic, could be "silent in five languages." Although he quickly distanced himself from the Harding administration, Coolidge asked the most capable cabinet members—Hughes, Mellon, and Hoover—to remain in the cabinet. Coolidge's philosophy of government was simple. He believed that prosperity rested on business leadership and that part of his job as president was to make sure that government interfered with business and industry as little as possible.

In the year following Harding's death and the **revelations** of the scandals, Coolidge avoided crises and adopted policies to help keep the nation prosperous. He easily won the Republican nomination for president in 1924.

The Republicans campaigned using the slogan "Keep Cool with Coolidge." They promised the American people that the policies that had brought prosperity would continue. Coolidge won the election easily, winning more than half the popular vote and 382 electoral votes.

Reading Check **Analyzing** What do the scandals of the Harding administration have in common with each other?

PRIMARY SOURCE

Coolidge and Prosperity

Critics have accused Calvin Coolidge of catering to big business and cite his comment that the "business of the American people is business." This quote comes from his 1925 speech to the American Society of Newspaper Editors. Examine the graphs and the speech to assess if his policies benefited business at the expense of the public.

PRIMARY SOURCE

"After all, the chief business of the American people is business. They are profoundly concerned with producing, buying, selling, investing and prospering in the world. . . . In all experience, the accumulation of wealth means the multiplication of schools, the increase of knowledge, the dissemination of intelligence, the encouragement of science, the broadening of outlook, the expansion of liberties, the widening of culture. . . . We make no concealment of the fact that we want wealth, but there are many other things that we want very much more. We want peace and honor, and that charity which is so strong an element of all civilization.

The chief ideal of the American people is idealism. I cannot repeat too often that America is a nation of idealists."

—*New York Times,* January 18, 1925

W

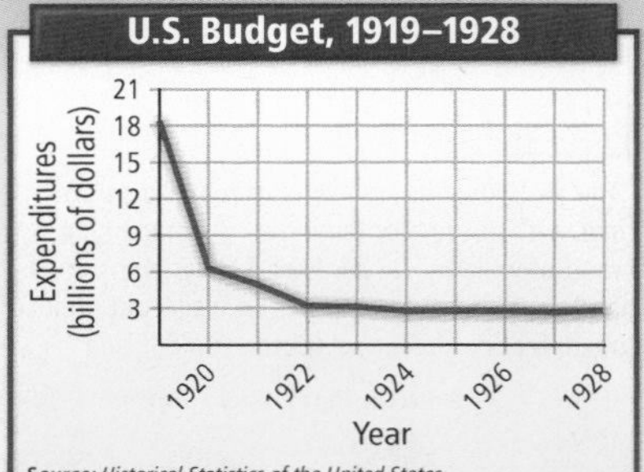

Source: *Historical Statistics of the United States.*

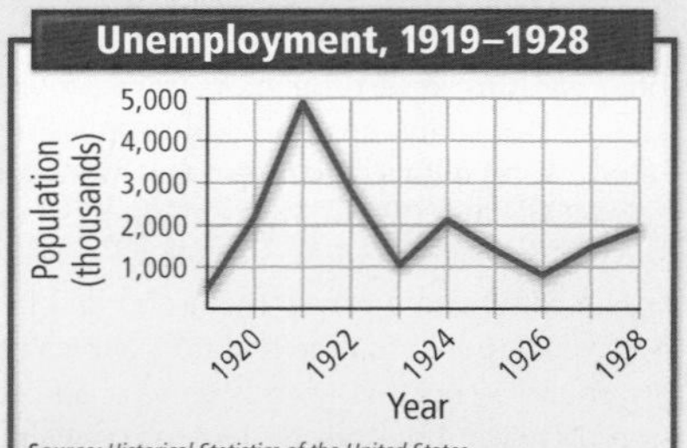

Source: *Historical Statistics of the United States.*

Additional Support

Extending the Content

Calvin Coolidge In August 1923, Vice President Calvin Coolidge was taking a short vacation at his family's homestead in Vermont. The straitlaced Coolidge went to bed at 9:00 as usual on August 2, but at 2:30 A.M., his father woke him. "I noticed that his voice trembled," Coolidge later wrote. "I knew that something of the gravest nature had occurred." After learning that President Harding was dead, Coolidge dressed hurriedly and went downstairs. Shortly afterward, in a small, sparsely furnished room lit by a flickering kerosene lamp, the elder Coolidge, a farmer and justice of the peace, got out the family Bible and administered the presidential oath of office to his son.

Later, while painting a portrait of the new president, artist Charles Hopkinson asked, "Mr. Coolidge, what was the first thought that came into your mind when you were told that Mr. Harding was dead and the presidency was yours?" Coolidge replied, "I thought I could swing it."

Policies of Prosperity

MAIN Idea During the 1920s, the government cut taxes and spending to encourage economic growth.

HISTORY AND YOU Do you have a sales tax in your state? Do you think taxes are too high? How do you know? Read to learn about changes to American taxes in the 1920s.

Although Harding gave many corrupt friends government jobs, he also selected several highly qualified individuals for his cabinet. Among them were Andrew Mellon and Herbert Hoover. Both of these men were responsible for policies that contributed to the economic growth and prosperity of the 1920s.

At the beginning of the 1920s, the nation had a large national debt, and many people were worried that it would not recover from the postwar recession. Harding chose Andrew Mellon, a successful banker and industrialist, to be secretary of the treasury. Mellon became the chief architect of economic policy and served as secretary of the treasury for three Republican presidents.

U.S. Income Tax Receipts

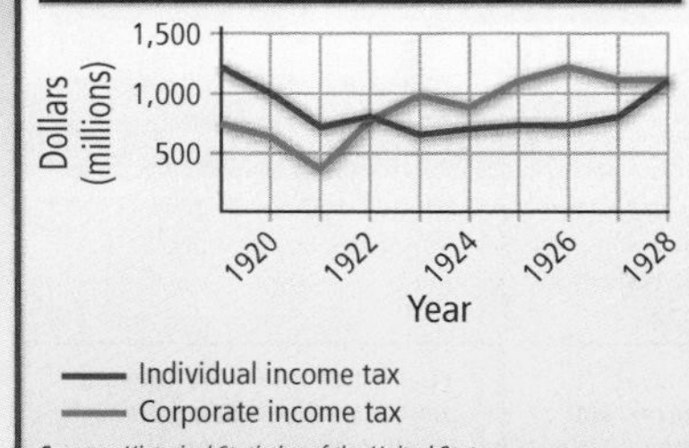

Source: *Historical Statistics of the United States.*

Analyzing VISUALS DBQ

1. **Analyzing Primary Sources** What does Coolidge believe is the point of accumulating wealth? Do you believe that the United States has achieved Coolidge's goals? Explain.
2. **Evaluating** Based on the graphs, what did Coolidge's economic policies achieve in the 1920s?

When Mellon took office, he had three major goals: to balance the budget, to reduce the government's debt, and to cut taxes. He was convinced these policies would promote economic growth and prosperity. He also firmly believed that the government should apply business principles to its operations.

In 1921 Mellon convinced Congress to create both the Bureau of the Budget to prepare a unified federal budget, and the General Accounting Office to track spending. He then began cutting spending. The federal budget fell from $6.4 billion to less than $3 billion in seven years. He also cut tax rates.

Mellon argued that high tax rates actually reduced the amount of tax money the government collected. If taxes were lower, businesses and consumers would spend and invest their extra money, causing the economy to grow. As the economy grew, Americans would earn more money, and the government would actually collect more taxes at a lower rate than it would if it kept tax rates high. This idea is known today as **supply-side economics,** or "trickle-down" economics. C

At Mellon's urging, Congress dramatically reduced tax rates. When Mellon took office, most taxpayers paid 4 percent federal income tax, while wealthy Americans in the highest bracket paid 73 percent. By 1928, Congress had reduced the rate most Americans paid to 0.5 percent and cut the rate for the wealthiest Americans to 25 percent.

Secretary of Commerce Herbert Hoover also sought to promote economic growth. He tried to balance government regulation with his own philosophy of **cooperative individualism.** This idea involved encouraging businesses to form trade associations that would voluntarily share information with the federal government. Hoover believed this system would reduce costs and promote economic efficiency.

To assist businesses, Hoover directed the Bureau of Foreign and Domestic Commerce to find new markets for companies. He also established the Bureau of Aviation to regulate and promote the growth of the airline industry and the Federal Radio Commission to help the young radio industry by regulating radio frequencies and the power of transmitters.

Reading Check **Summarizing** What strategies did Mellon use to promote economic growth?

C Critical Thinking

Making Comparisons Have students find out Americans' tax rates today. **Ask:** How do the tax rates that Andrew Mellon recommended compare with tax rates today? Why might this be so? *(Rates today are higher overall. Students might point out that the government today pays for many goods and services that it did not in 1928.)* **OL**

DBQ Document Based Questions

Answers:

1. More schools, more knowledge, greater intelligence, development of science, a broadened outlook, expanded liberties, and widened culture; students' responses will vary but should be supported.
2. He increased the government's revenue from taxes.

Reading Check

Answer:
He balanced the budget, reduced the government's debt, and cut taxes.

Differentiated Instruction

Activity: Collaborative Learning

Debate Have students work in groups to research the financial philosophy of Andrew Mellon using their book, the Internet, and library resources. Remind students that Mellon believed that the wealthy should not be penalized in the form of taxes on excess profits, inheritances, and large incomes because such taxes would discourage investment. Hold a class debate in which students discuss whether they agree or disagree with Mellon's philosophy. Students' arguments should be supported by facts gained in their research of Mellon's philosophy.

D Differentiated Instruction

Visual/Spatial Have students use library or Internet resources to find political cartoons about isolationism in the 1920s to create a bulletin board display either favoring or opposing an isolationist foreign policy. OL

C Critical Thinking

Making Inferences Have students review the Infographic on this page. **Ask:** What were these three treaties designed to accomplish? Were the treaties successful? *(The treaties were designed to prevent war; the treaties were not successful.)* Conduct a class discussion focusing on why these treaties were not successful. AL

Analyzing VISUALS

Answers:
1. the United States, Great Britain, France, Japan, and Italy
2. The western powers were trying to restrain Japan's aggressive foreign policy and to keep China open to trade.

Additional Support

Trade and Arms Control

MAIN Idea During the 1920s, the United States tried to promote peace and stability through economic policies and arms control agreements.

HISTORY AND YOU Do you remember reading about the Treaty of Versailles and how the United States never ratified it? Read to learn how America initiated other treaties in the 1920s.

Before World War I the United States was a debtor nation. By the end of the war, the situation was reversed. Wartime allies owed the United States more than $10 billion in war debts. By the 1920s, the United States was the dominant economic power in the world. Under the leadership of Secretary of State Charles Evan Hughes, the nation tried to use its economic power to promote peace and stability.

The Myth of Isolationism

D The majority of Americans—tired of being entangled in the baffling, hostile, and dangerous politics of Europe—favored **isolationism.** This is the idea that the United States will be safer and more prosperous if it stays out of world affairs.

To many people at the time, it appeared that the United States had become isolationist. The United States had not ratified the Treaty of Versailles and had not joined the League of Nations. The Permanent Court of International Justice, better known as the World Court, opened in 1921, but the United States refused to join it as well. D

Despite appearances, the United States was too powerful and too interconnected with other countries economically to be truly isolationist. Instead of relying on armed force and the collective security of the League of Nations, the United States tried to promote peace by using economic policies and arms control agreements.

The Dawes Plan

America's former allies had difficulty making the payments on their immense war debts. High American tariffs hampered their economic

INFOGRAPHIC

The Washington Conference, November 1921–February 1922

C

Treaty	Signers	Terms	Weaknesses
Four-Power Treaty	United States, Great Britain, France, Japan	• All agreed to respect the others' territory in the Pacific • Full and open negotiations in the event of disagreements	• Mutual defense of other co-signers not specified
Five-Power Treaty	United States, Great Britain, France, Japan, Italy	• All agreed to freeze naval production at 1921 levels and halt production of large warships for 10 years • U.S. and Great Britain agreed not to build new naval bases in the western Pacific	• No restrictions on the construction of smaller battle craft such as submarines and naval destroyers • Did not place restrictions on the ground forces
Nine-Power Treaty	United States, Great Britain, France, Japan, Italy, Belgium, China, the Netherlands, Portugal	• All agreed to preserve equal commercial rights to China—a reassertion of the Open Door policy	• No enforcement of the terms of the Open Door policy specified

Analyzing VISUALS

1. **Interpreting Charts** Which countries signed the Five-Power Treaty?
2. **Analyzing** Why do you think the terms of the treaties focused on the Pacific region?

Extending the Content

The Washington Naval Conference A major American goal at the Washington Naval Conference was to limit Japanese expansion in East Asia. For this reason, the American delegation proposed that the United States be allowed to have 10 major warships for every 6 that Japan had. The Japanese accepted the proposal but in return the United States had to agree not to fortify its bases in the Philippines or Guam. This decision shifted the balance of power in East Asia. Without fortified bases in the region, the United States had no hope of stopping a Japanese attack. When war erupted in 1941, the Philippines and Guam fell quickly to the Japanese forces, and the United States was forced to begin its campaign against Japan from much further east.

recovery by making it difficult to sell their products in the United States. This meant they could not acquire the money to pay off their war debts. These countries also were receiving reparations—huge cash payments Germany was required to make as punishment for starting the war. These payments, however, were crippling the German economy.

It was vital for the United States that European economies be healthy so that the Europeans could buy American exports and repay their debts. Thus, in 1924, American diplomat **Charles G. Dawes** negotiated an agreement with France, Britain, and Germany by which American banks would make loans to Germany that would enable it to make reparations payments. In exchange, Britain and France would accept less in reparations and pay back more on their war debts.

The Washington Conference

Despite their debts, the major powers were involved in a costly postwar naval arms race. To end the weapons race, the United States invited representatives from eight major countries—Great Britain, France, Italy, China, Japan, Belgium, the Netherlands, and Portugal—to Washington, D.C., to discuss disarmament. The Washington Conference opened on November 12, 1921.

In his address to the delegates, Secretary of State **Charles Evans Hughes** proposed a 10-year moratorium, or halt, on the construction of new warships. He also proposed a list of warships in each country's navy to be destroyed, beginning with some American battleships. The discussions that followed produced the Five-Power Naval Limitation Treaty in which Britain, France, Italy, Japan, and the United States essentially formalized Hughes's proposal.

As a long-term effort to prevent war, the conference had some serious shortcomings. It did nothing to limit land forces. It also angered the Japanese because it required Japan to maintain a smaller navy than either the United States or Great Britain. It did, however, give Americans cause to look forward to a period of peace, recovery, and prosperity.

Abolishing War

The apparent success of the Washington Conference boosted hopes that written agreements could end war altogether. Perhaps the highest expression of that idea occurred when U.S. Secretary of State Frank Kellogg and French Foreign Minister Aristide Briand proposed a treaty to outlaw war. On August 27, 1928, the C United States and 14 other nations signed the **Kellogg-Briand Pact.** Although it had no binding force, the pact was hailed as a victory for peace. It stated that all signing nations agreed to abandon war and to settle all disputes by peaceful means. The Kellogg-Briand Pact and the Dawes Plan were perhaps the most notable foreign policy achievements of the Coolidge administration.

Reading Check **Identifying** What problem was the Dawes Plan intended to solve?

Section 1 REVIEW

Vocabulary

1. **Explain** the significance of: Teapot Dome, supply-side economics, cooperative individualism, isolationism, Charles G. Dawes, Charles Evans Hughes, Kellogg-Briand Pact.

Main Ideas

2. **Summarizing** What scandals marred Harding's presidency?
3. **Explaining** What strategies did Andrew Mellon and Herbert Hoover use to stimulate economic growth?
4. **Describing** In what two ways did the United States try to promote peace during the 1920s?

Critical Thinking

5. **Big Ideas** What efforts did the United States make to promote worldwide economic recovery?
6. **Categorizing** Use a graphic organizer like the one below to list the major terms of the treaties resulting from the Washington Conference.

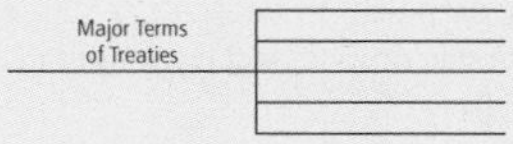

7. **Analyzing Visuals** Examine the charts on page 592. What explanation can you offer for the drop in the United States's budget from 1919 to 1928?

Writing About History

8. **Persuasive Writing** Imagine that you are an American business owner or farmer in the 1920s. Write a letter to your representatives in Congress explaining why you think cutting taxes is a good or bad idea.

History ONLINE
Study Central™ To review this section, go to glencoe.com and click on Study Central.

C Critical Thinking

Analyzing Information Ask students to find out more about the Kellogg-Briand Pact. **Ask:** Is it possible to outlaw war? *(Students should support their opinions.)* AL

Reading Check

Answer:
the problem of former Allied nations being unable to pay their war debts and to purchase American-made goods

Assess

History ONLINE
Study Central™ provides summaries, interactive games, and online graphic organizers to help students review content.

Close

Summarizing Ask: In what ways did the federal government encourage a return to "normalcy" in the 1920s? *(decrease of government spending; support for business; attempts to prevent another war)* OL

Section 1 REVIEW

Answers

1. All definitions can be found in the section and the Glossary.
2. The Ohio Gang members sold medicine intended for the Veterans Bureau and kept the money, Albert Fall leased private lands to oil interests for a bribe in the Teapot Dome scandal, and Daugherty was accused of accepting bribes.
3. balanced federal budget, reduced government debts, cut taxes, encouraged the development of trade associations to share information with the government to reduce costs and promote efficiency
4. economic policies and arms control agreements
5. Students' answers should reflect analysis of text information, including the Dawes Plan and the Washington Conference.
6. respect the other nations' territories in the Pacific; full and open negotiations in the event of disagreements; agreed to freeze naval production at 1921 levels and halt production of large warships for 10 years; the U.S. and Great Britain agreed not to build new naval bases in the western Pacific; agreed to preserve equal commercial rights to China—a reassertion of the Open Door Policy
7. The government was not spending money on war equipment and supplies.
8. Letters should be written from the point of view of a business owner or farmer.

Focus

Bellringer

Daily Focus Transparency 17-2

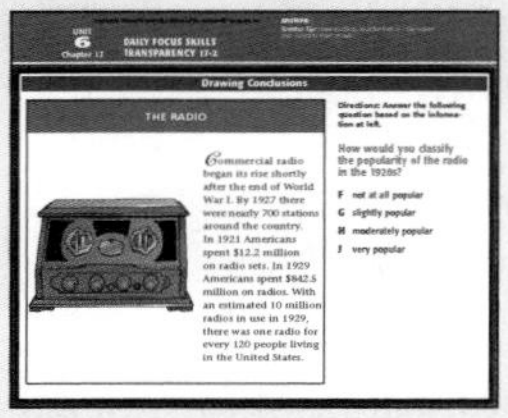

Guide to Reading

Answers: Industry: air travel, automobiles, consumer goods, radio; Society: consumer-oriented credit, workers shifting from farming to industry, labor-saving devices, growing mobility

Section Spotlight Video

To generate student interest and provide a springboard for class discussion, access the Chapter 17, Section 2 video at glencoe.com or on the video DVD.

Resource Manager

Section 2

Section Audio | Spotlight Video

A Growing Economy

Guide to Reading

Big Ideas

Economics and Society The United States experienced stunning economic growth during the 1920s.

Content Vocabulary

- mass production *(p. 596)*
- assembly line *(p. 596)*
- Model T *(p. 596)*
- welfare capitalism *(p. 602)*
- open shop *(p. 602)*

Academic Vocabulary

- disposable *(p. 598)*
- credit *(p. 600)*

People and Events to Identify

- Charles Lindbergh *(p. 600)*

Reading Strategy

Organizing As you read about the booming era of the 1920s, complete a graphic organizer to analyze the causes of economic growth and prosperity in the 1920s.

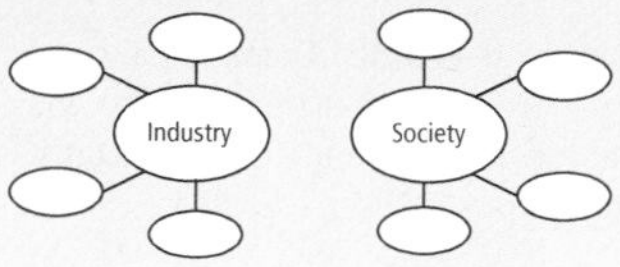

In the 1920s widespread ownership of automobiles, radios, and other innovations changed how Americans lived. The Coolidge administration encouraged business growth and tried to promote stability in international affairs.

The Rise of New Industries

MAIN Idea Mass production and the assembly line allowed new industries, such as automobile and airplane manufacturing, to grow.

HISTORY AND YOU How would businesses, governments, and your family be affected if air travel did not exist? Read to learn how the transportation industry changed during the 1920s and 1930s.

By the 1920s, the automobile had become an accepted part of American life. In a 1925 survey conducted in Muncie, Indiana, 21 out of 26 families who owned cars did not have bathtubs with running water. When asked why her family decided a car was more important than indoor plumbing, a farm wife explained, "You can't ride to town in a bathtub."

The automobile was just one part of a rising standard of living that Americans experienced in the 1920s. Real per capita earnings soared 22 percent between 1923 and 1929. Meanwhile, as Americans' wages increased, their work hours decreased. In 1923 U.S. Steel cut its daily work shift from 12 hours to 8 hours. In 1926 Henry Ford cut the workweek for his employees from six days to five, and International Harvester, a maker of farm machinery, instituted an annual two-week paid vacation for employees. These changes took place because **mass production,** or large-scale manufacturing done with machinery, increased supply and reduced costs. Workers could be paid more and the consumer goods they bought cost less.

The Assembly Line and the Model T

First adopted by carmaker Henry Ford, the moving **assembly line** divided operations into simple tasks and cut unnecessary motion to a minimum. In 1913 Ford installed the first moving assembly line at his plant in Highland Park, Michigan. By the following year, workers were building an automobile every 93 minutes. Before, the task had taken 12 hours. By 1925 a Ford car was rolling off the line every 10 seconds.

Ford's assembly-line product, the **Model T**—affectionately called the "Tin Lizzie" or "Flivver"—demonstrated the economic concept of elasticity, or how sensitive product demand is to price. In 1908, the

R Reading Strategies	C Critical Thinking	D Differentiated Instruction	W Writing Support	S Skill Practice
Teacher Edition • Categorizing Info., p. 599 • Act. Prior Know., p. 602 **Additional Resources** • Guide Read, URB p. 47 • Acad Vocab, URB p. 29	**Teacher Edition** • Ident. Cent. Issues, p. 598 • Det. Cause and Effect, p. 600 **Additional Resources** • Quizzes and Tests, p. 244 • Linking Past and Present Act., URB p. 34	**Teacher Edition** • Visual/Spatial, p. 601 • Verbal/Linguistic, p. 600 **Additional Resources** • Eng Learner Act, URB p. 25	**Teacher Edition** • Narrative Writing, p. 597 • Descriptive Writing, p. 598 **Additional Resources** • Content Vocab, URB p. 27	**Teacher Edition** • Chronological Thinking, p. 603 **Additional Resources** • Read Essen, p. 189 • Hist. Analysis Skills Act., URB p. 22 • Time Line Act., URB p. 33

INFOGRAPHIC
The Car Changes America

Many industries that were needed to build cars prospered. Car manufacturers needed steel for the car body, glass for the windows, and rubber for the tires. The automobile also led to changes in society. People moved to the suburbs, but were less isolated from the benefits of the city. At the same time, there was a decline in mass transportation such as railroads and trolleys.

▲ Cars greatly increased the demand for oil, leading to a boom in the oil business, as shown by the forest of oil wells in Signal Hills, California in 1930. To keep cars refueled, roadside gas stations sprang up across the country.

▲ Cars allowed people greater mobility and freedom. These young women drove to the country to have a picnic.

W ▶ The auto industry spurred a boom in other industries, as well. These workers at Goodyear Tire and Rubber in Akron, Ohio, are removing car tires from curing pits.

▲ The car let people live further out in the suburbs and commute to jobs in the city.

Analyzing VISUALS DBQ

1. **Determining Cause and Effect** How did the automobile help other industries grow? Which industries were most affected?
2. **Drawing Conclusions** Based on the images above, how did the car change people's lives?

Model T's first year, it sold for $850. In 1914 mass production reduced the price to $490. Three years later, improved assembly-line methods and a high volume of sales brought the price down to $360. By 1924 Model Ts were selling for $295, and Ford sold millions of them. His business philosophy was: lower the cost per car and thereby increase the volume of sales.

The low prices made possible by Ford's mass-production methods not only created an immense market for his cars but also spawned imitators. By the mid-1920s, other car manufacturers, notably General Motors and Chrysler, competed successfully with Ford. The auto industry also spurred growth in other industries, such as rubber, plate glass, nickel, and lead. The auto industry alone consumed 15 percent of the nation's steel and led to a huge expansion of the petroleum industry.

High Wages for Workers Ford also increased his workers' wages in 1914 to $5 a day (doubling their pay) and reduced the workday to eight-hour shifts. Ford took these dramatic steps to build up workers' loyalty and to undercut union organizers.

Teach

W Writing Support

Narrative Writing Have students use library or Internet sources to find out information about the life of a worker in a rubber factory, such as Goodyear Tire and Rubber in Akron, Ohio. Using their findings, students should write a letter to family members back home describing one day at work. Remind students to use details to bring their letters to life. Encourage students to share their letters with the class. OL

Analyzing VISUALS

Answers:

1. The automobile industry helped the steel, rubber, glass, and oil industries grow. Answers will vary, but students will likely identify the oil and steel industries.
2. People had more mobility; they could live farther away from where they worked; they used the automobile for leisure activities.

Hands-On Chapter Project Step 2

Creating a Memory Book

Step 2: Researching Selected Names Each student will do research on the name chosen in Step 1.

Directions Have students use library, Internet, or family resources to learn more about the person whose name they chose. They should write a short biography of the person, and select a quotation or short paragraph written by the person, if possible.

Evaluating Information To decide which information to include, students will gain practice in evaluating the reliability of sources and the relevance of the information to the project. OL

(Chapter Project continued on page 605)

C Critical Thinking

Identifying Central Issues Tell students to imagine that their school has instituted a new policy of home visitations. Explain that you will be coming by their homes regularly to make sure they are eating properly, getting enough sleep, and doing their homework. **Ask:** What do you think of this policy? Is it necessary or worthwhile? *(Answers will vary, but students will likely view such visits as an invasion of their privacy.)* After some discussion, read the paragraph about Ford's Sociological Department. Ask the class to discuss circumstances that made this policy possible. OL

W Writing Support

Descriptive Writing Have students reread the paragraph "The Social Impact of the Automobile." Then have them write a paragraph describing how their own lives would be different if the automobile had not been invented. Encourage students to share their paragraphs. BL

Additional Support

C There were strings attached, however. Ford created a "Sociological Department," which set requirements workers had to meet. For example, renting space in one's home to nonfamily members was strictly forbidden. Investigators visited employees' homes to verify their eligibility and workers who broke the rules could be disqualified from extra pay, suspended, or even fired.

W **The Social Impact of the Automobile** Cars revolutionized American life. They eased the isolation of rural life and enabled more people to live farther from work. An entirely new kind of worker, the auto commuter, appeared. Since commuters could drive from their homes in suburbia to their workplaces, other forms of urban transportation, such as the trolley, became less popular.

Consumer Goods

In response to rising **disposable** income, many other new goods came on the market. Americans bought such innovations as electric razors, facial tissues, frozen foods, and home hair color.

Companies created many new products for the home. As indoor plumbing became more common, Americans' concern for hygiene led to the development of numerous household cleaning products. By appealing to people's health concerns, advertisers convinced homemakers to buy cleansers in hopes of protecting their families from disease.

New appliances advertised as labor-savers changed the home. Electric irons, vacuum cleaners, washing machines, and refrigerators changed the way people cleaned their homes and prepared meals.

Another lucrative category of consumer products focused on Americans' concern with fashion and youthful appearance. Mouthwash, deodorants, cosmetics, and perfumes became popular products in the 1920s.

Birth of the Airline Industry

In the early 1900s, many people were trying to build the first powered airplane that could

TECHNOLOGY & HISTORY

Labor- and Time-saving Machines The technology of the 1920s changed the way many people lived. Applying electric motors to items such as washers, dryers, food mixers, and refrigerators revolutionized household tasks. Improved technology helped raise many Americans' standard of living.

◀ **Assembly Lines Reduce Prices**
The moving assembly line and standardized parts made auto assembly fast, efficient and cheap. As a result, most Americans could afford to buy a car.

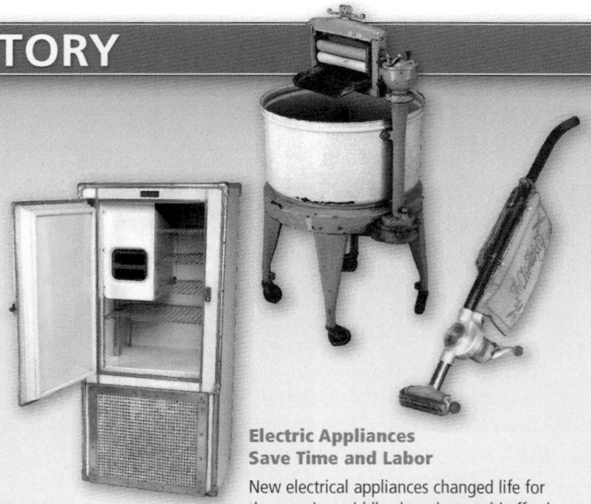

Electric Appliances Save Time and Labor
New electrical appliances changed life for the growing middle class that could afford them. Refrigerators, such as the 1926 Kelvinator (above left) made it practical to buy and store larger quantities of food. The electric washer with hand wringer (above center) and the vacuum cleaner saved cleaning time. The Air-Way Sanitizor vacuum cleaner (above right) was the first to have a disposable bag.

Activity: Interdisciplinary Activity

Language Arts Explain to students that many new words were developed to better describe the societal changes that came about because of the automobile. Tell students that a lexicon is a list of words and their meanings. Have interested students create a lexicon of terms that developed in the early 1900s after the automobile was invented and became popular. Tell them that the lexicon should include the pronunciation and solid working definitions for each term. For at least two of the terms, students should also include a drawing or diagram for further explanation. OL carry a human being. Samuel Langley, secretary of the Smithsonian Institution, was perhaps best known for his attempts at the time. Langley had built small model airplanes powered by steam engines, and the War Department had awarded him $50,000 to build an airplane that could carry a person. On December 8, 1903, Langley demonstrated his plane to government officials in Washington, D.C. Unfortunately, his plane broke apart on takeoff and crashed into the Potomac River.

The War Department, in its final report on the Langley project, concluded that "[W]e are still far from the ultimate goal, and it would seem as if years of constant work and study by experts, together with the expenditure of thousands of dollars, would still be necessary before we can hope to produce an apparatus of practical utility on these lines."

Nine days later, Wilbur and Orville Wright, two inventors from Dayton, Ohio, tested the airplane they had built using only $1,000 of their personal savings. The Wright brothers had carefully studied the problems of earlier airplanes and had designed one with better wings, a more efficient propeller, and a strong but very light engine. On December 17, 1903, at Kitty Hawk, North Carolina, Orville made the first crewed, powered flight in history.

After the Wright brothers' successful flight, the aviation industry began developing rapidly. Leading the way was American inventor Glenn Curtiss. Curtiss owned a motorcycle company in Hammondsport, New York. Fascinated by airplanes, he agreed in 1907 to become director of experiments at the Aerial Experiment Association, an organization that Alexander Graham Bell founded. Within a year, Curtiss had invented ailerons—surfaces attached to wings that can be tilted to steer the plane. Ailerons made it possible to build rigid wings and much larger aircraft. They are still used today.

Curtiss's company began building aircraft and sold the first airplanes in the United States. The company grew from a single factory to a huge industrial enterprise during World War I, as orders for his biplanes and engines flooded in from Allied governments. Although Curtiss retired in 1920, his inventions made possible the airline industry that emerged in the 1920s.

Radio Links the Nation Together ▶

Commercial radio grew rapidly in the 1920s. It helped create a national community as people across the country could listen to the same music, sports, news, and entertainment programs. The technicians shown at right are preparing for the first NBC radio show, which was broadcast in 1926.

Airlines Speed Travel

The aviation industry developed quickly after the Wright brothers' first successful flight in 1903 (above). Below, passengers are shown boarding a Northwest Orient Airlines Ford Tri-motor. Although seating was cramped (right), passenger airlines carried increasing numbers of people in the 1920s.

Analyzing VISUALS DBQ

1. **Making Connections** Which of the inventions pictured is most important to your life? Which do you think is most important to the nation as a whole?
2. **Making Generalizations** How have advances in transportation and communication changed life in the United States in the past 100 years?

R Reading Strategy

Categorizing Information Have students research the economic impact of the airline industry in the United States during the 1900s. Tell them that they can focus on the revenues generated by the industry or on the number of people employed in the industry. Have students create tables or charts to show the growth of the airline industry and its effects on the American economy. **Ask:** **Based on the information and trends identified, can you predict what will happen to the airline industry in the first half of the twenty-first century?** *(Answers will vary, depending upon how students have interpreted their data.)* **OL**

Analyzing VISUALS

Answers:
1. Answers will vary, but students should support their responses with examples.
2. Transportation and communication have become faster, more efficient, and cheaper.

Additional Support

Extending the Content

The *Wright Flyer* The Wright brother's aircraft flown at Kitty Hawk was named the *Wright Flyer*. It was a wood-and-muslin fabric aircraft. After the initial success of the first flight on December 17, 1903, at Kitty Hawk, the Wright brothers continued to improve the designs of their aircraft. The Wright brothers' first planes were difficult to control and frequently crashed.

The *Wright Flyer III* made its first flight at Huffman Prairie in Dayton, Ohio, in 1905. This plane could be steered, make turns, and be controlled in a gust of wind. Soon, the plane was modified to hold a passenger. Later versions of the *Wright Flyer III* reached speeds of 45 miles per hour (72 km/h), soared to an altitude of 360 feet (107.9 m), and covered a distance of 77 miles (124 km).

The *Wright Flyer III* was taken apart and its parts were displayed in many locations. Finally, in 1947, with direction from Orville Wright, the plane was reassembled, although some new parts had to be created. The original *Wright Flyer*, which flew at Kitty Hawk, hangs in the Smithsonian Air and Space Museum in Washington, D.C. The *Wright Flyer III* is on display in Wright Hall at Dayton's Carillon Park.

D Differentiated Instruction

Verbal/Linguistic Invite students to research the development of CBS and NBC from radio broadcasting companies to multimedia corporations. Ask them to prepare written reports that focus on this transformation, and then have them share their findings in a class presentation. **OL**

C Critical Thinking

Determining Cause and Effect The use of credit is commonplace among consumers today, but misuse of this purchasing power remains a problem. **Ask:** How can consumers get into trouble when they buy things on credit? *(Answers may include that consumers may be encouraged to buy more things than they need and borrow more from creditors than they can afford to repay. Remind students to withhold personal details.)* **OL**

Reading Check

Answer:
It allowed people to live further from work and eased rural isolation.

Additional Support

After Curtiss and other entrepreneurs started building practical aircraft, the federal government began to support the airline industry. President Wilson's postmaster general introduced the world's first regular airmail service in 1918 by hiring pilots to fly mail between Washington, D.C., and New York. In 1919 the Post Office expanded airmail service across the continent.

The aviation industry received an economic boost in 1925 when Congress passed the Kelly Act, authorizing postal officials to contract with private airplane operators to carry mail. The following year Congress passed the Air Commerce Act, which provided federal aid for building airports. Former airmail pilot **Charles Lindbergh** made an amazing transatlantic solo flight in 1927, showing the possibilities of commercial aviation. By the end of 1928, 48 airlines were serving 355 American cities.

The Radio Industry

In 1913 Edwin Armstrong, an American engineer, invented a special circuit that made it practical to transmit sound via long-range radio. The radio industry began a few years later. In November 1920 the Westinghouse Company broadcast the news of Harding's landslide election victory from station KDKA in Pittsburgh—one of the first public broadcasts in history. That success persuaded Westinghouse to open other stations.

In 1926 the National Broadcasting Company (NBC) set up a network of stations to broadcast daily programs. By 1927, almost 700 stations dotted the country. Sales of radio equipment grew from $12.2 million in 1921 to $842.5 million in 1929, by which time 10 million radios were in use across the country.

D In 1928 the Columbia Broadcasting System (CBS) assembled a coast-to-coast network of stations to rival NBC. The two networks sold advertising time and hired musicians, actors, and comedians from vaudeville, movies, and the nightclub circuit to appear on their shows. Americans experienced the first presidential election campaign to use radio broadcasts in 1928, when the radio networks sold more than $1 million in advertising time to the Republican and Democratic Parties.

Reading Check **Analyzing** How did the automobile change the way people lived?

The Consumer Society

MAIN Idea Consumer credit and advertising helped to create a nation of consumers.

HISTORY AND YOU Have you ever purchased something on credit or bought an item because of advertising? Read to discover the beginnings of the widespread consumer culture in America.

Higher wages and shorter workdays resulted in a decade-long buying spree that kept the economy booming. Shifting from traditional attitudes of thrift and prudence, Americans in the 1920s enthusiastically accepted their new role as consumers.

Easy Consumer Credit

One notable aspect of the economic boom was the growth of individual borrowing. **Credit** had been available before the 1920s, but most Americans had considered debt shameful. Now, however, attitudes toward debt started changing as people began believing in their ability to pay their debts over time. Many

PRIMARY SOURCE
Advertising to Consumers

C The early advertising age used techniques that continue to persuade consumers today. Easy credit terms and installment plans, envy of peers and neighbors, and the link of a product with a famous, attractive person all convinced people that they needed the flood of newly available consumer goods.

Extending the Content

Air Travel In the 1920s, airlines attracted an elite group of travelers. Forced to compete with comfortable, affordable rail service and highway travel, early airlines survived on mail delivery, splitting up a few lucrative government contracts. The airmail boom of the early 1930s led to improved airstrips and air traffic control. Meanwhile, the search began for a plane large enough, safe enough, and comfortable enough to attract a profitable number of passengers. The plane would also have to be inexpensive to run and maintain. Aeronautical engineer Donald Douglas set his designers to work on a large, two engine plane that would fly even if an engine, a set of instruments, or the landing gear failed. The result was the DC-1 in 1932 and the improved DC-2 in 1933. In 1935, the new DC-3 became the first profitable plane, carrying passengers for Transcontinental and Western Air (TWA).

listened to the sales pitch "Buy now and pay in easy installments," and racked up debts. Americans bought 75 percent of their radios and 60 percent of their automobiles on the installment plan. Some started buying on credit at a faster rate than their incomes increased.

Mass Advertising

When inventor Otto Rohwedder developed a commercial bread slicer in 1928, he faced a problem common to new inventions: the invention—sliced bread—was something no one knew was needed. To attract consumers, manufacturers turned to advertising, another **D** booming industry in the 1920s.

Advertisers linked products with qualities associated with the modern era, such as progress, convenience, leisure, success, and style. In a 1924 magazine advertisement for deodorant, the headline read, "Flappers they may be—but they know the art of feminine appeal!" An advertisement for a spaghetti product told homemakers that heating is the same as cooking: "Just one thing to do and it's ready to serve." Advertisers also preyed on consumers' fears and anxieties, such as jarred nerves due **D** to the hectic pace of modern life or insecurities about one's status or weight.

The Managerial Revolution

By the early 1920s, many industries had begun to create modern organizational structures. Companies were split into divisions with different functions, such as sales, marketing, and accounting. To run these divisions, businesses needed to hire managers. Managers freed executives and owners from the day-to-day running of the companies.

The managerial revolution in companies created a new career—the professional manager. The large numbers of new managers helped expand the size of the middle class, which in turn added to the nation's prosperity. Similarly, so many companies relied on new technology that engineers were also in very high demand. They, too, joined the ranks of the growing middle class.

By promising long-term savings and offering 30-day free trials, advertisers were often able to get consumers to try their products.

Easy credit terms and installment payment plans encouraged consumers to purchase goods, and often put them further into debt than they could afford.

Growth of Consumer Debt, 1920–1933

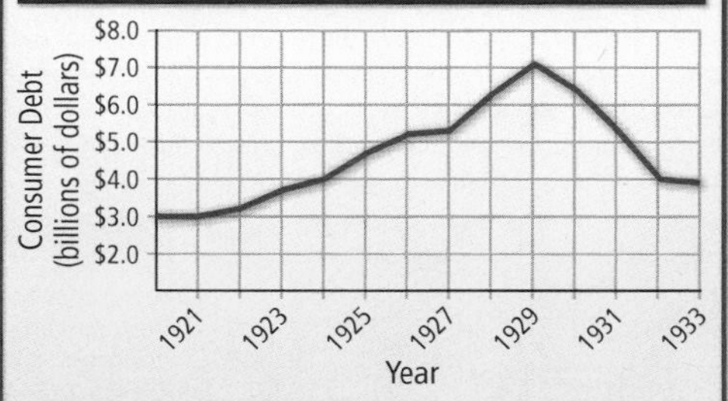

Source: *Historical Statistics of the United States.*

This 1928 advertisement appeals to "expert opinion" to sell the product. It also shows that 1920s advertisers believed ironing to be a woman's job.

Analyzing VISUALS

1. **Making Connections** What techniques do advertisers use today to sell automobiles?
2. **Analyzing Visuals** What happened to consumer debt between 1921 and 1929? Why might this have happened?

D Differentiated Instruction

Visual/Spatial A great deal of study has been done about the techniques of advertising. **Ask:** What kinds of print and media ads have you noticed lately? Do you think they have an effect on your buying habits? Tell students to keep a diary of advertisements they encounter for three days, along with any impressions or thoughts they have while viewing the ads. Ask students to present their findings at the end to the class. **OL**

Analyzing VISUALS

Answers:

1. television, radio, print ads, the Internet
2. Consumer debt increased by about $4 billion; retailers and businesses freely extended credit to consumers.

Additional Support

Activity: Economics Connection

Advertising Ask students to create an advertisement with pictures and text promoting a refrigerator, radio, or labor-saving device that was new in the 1920s. Students will have to research one of these developments, think about the potential market for the product, and write accompanying text that rings true for both product and audience. They may also want to research period illustrations and design styles as they create the pictures. Encourage students to present their advertisements on a class Web page. **OL**

R Reading Strategy

Activating Prior Knowledge Remind students that they have studied the terms *welfare*, *capitalist*, and *open shop* in earlier chapters. Review the meanings of these terms and then ask students to apply that knowledge as they determine the meanings of new terms found on this page. **OL**

Analyzing VISUALS

Answers:
1. the South
2. The wages of farm employees remained consistently lower than the wages of non-farm employees.

Reading Check

Answer:
preyed on consumers' fears and anxieties; linked products to progress and success

Additional Support

Welfare Capitalism

Middle-class Americans were not the only members of the new consumer society. Industrial workers also had more disposable income, partly due to rising wages and partly because many corporations introduced what came to be called **welfare capitalism.** Companies allowed workers to buy stock, participate in profit sharing, and receive medical care and pensions.

R **The Decline of Unions** Benefits programs also made unions seem unnecessary to many workers. During the 1920s, unions lost both influence and membership. Employers promoted the **open shop**—a workplace where employees were not required to join a union. With benefits covering some of their basic needs, workers were able to spend more of their income to improve their quality of life. Many purchased consumer goods they previously could not afford.

Uneven Prosperity Not all Americans shared in this economic boom. Thousands of African Americans had factory jobs during World War I. When servicemen returned from the war, they replaced both African Americans and women.

Native Americans were also excluded from prosperity. Although granted citizenship in 1924, they were often isolated on reservations, where there was little productive work.

The majority of immigrants to the United States continued to come from Europe. Even these people often found it difficult to find work; most of them were farmers and factory workers whose wages were pitifully low.

Many people in the Deep South were also left out of the economic boom. The traditional agricultural economic base eroded after the war ended. Farmers in general failed to benefit from the growing economy.

Reading Check **Analyzing** How did advertisers try to convince Americans to buy their products?

PRIMARY SOURCE
Prosperity for Whom?

Although many people benefited from the economic boom of the 1920s, several groups did not share in the general prosperity, nor did all regions of the country. Members of minority groups, newly arrived immigrants, and farmers often struggled economically. During the 1920s, for example, laborers in manufacturing not only outnumbered farmers but also acquired three times more actual wealth.

▼ For many African Americans, including this family in rural Georgia, the 1920s was a time of poverty, not prosperity.

Average Hourly Earnings, 1929

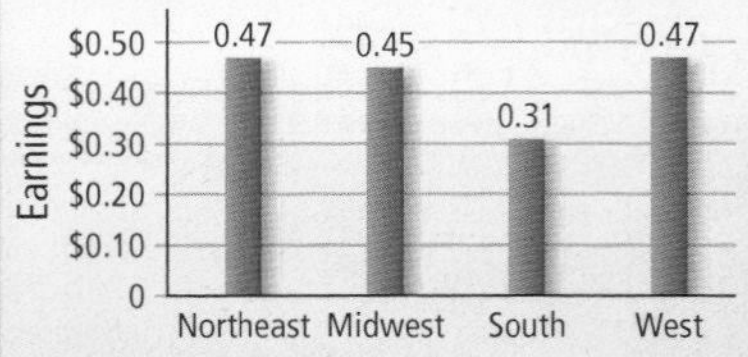

Source: *Manpower in Economic Growth.*

Annual Earnings, 1920–1930

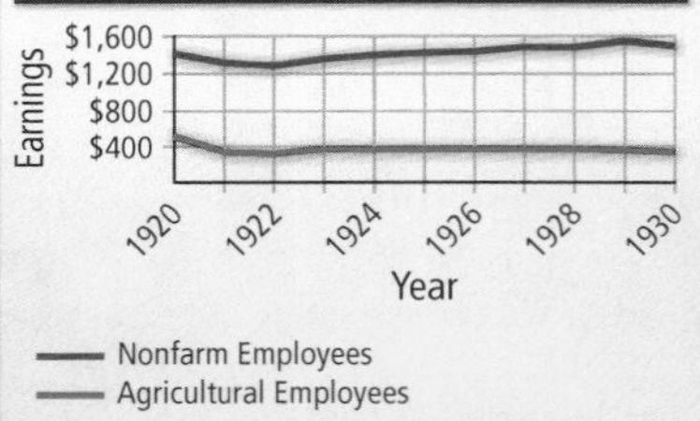

Source: *Manpower in Economic Growth.*

Analyzing VISUALS

1. **Identifying** In what region of the nation were hourly wages lowest in 1929?
2. **Analyzing** What pattern characterizes the gap between wages of farm and nonfarm employees during the 1920s?

Activity: Interdisciplinary Connection

Sociology Have interested students select one group who was left out of the prosperity of the 1920s—African Americans, Native Americans, or farmers—and use library or Internet resources to find out more about the group and why they were excluded. Have students use their findings to write a two-page report describing the group's situation. Tell students to consider the following question as they prepare their reports: **Might prejudice and racism have been a factor in determining who enjoyed prosperity and who did not?** *(Answers will vary, but students should base their answers on their research findings.)* After students have completed their reports, conduct a class discussion about the connection of prejudice and racism to economic success and prosperity in the United States today. Ask students to provide examples of this connection. **AL**

S The Farm Crisis

MAIN Idea Increases in farm productivity and decreases in foreign markets led to lower prices for farmers.

HISTORY AND YOU Do you remember reading about the platform of the Populist Party in the 1890s? Read to learn about farmers' troubles in the 1920s.

American farmers did not share in the prosperity of the 1920s. On average, they earned less than one-third of the income of workers in the rest of the economy. Technological advances in fertilizers, seed varieties, and farm machinery allowed them to produce more, but higher yields without a corresponding increase in demand meant that they received lower prices. Between 1920 and 1921, corn prices dropped almost 19 percent, and wheat went from $1.83 a bushel to $1.03. The cost of the improved farming technology, meanwhile, continued to increase.

Changing Market Conditions

Many factors contributed to this "quiet depression" in American agriculture. During the war, the government had urged farmers to produce more to meet the great need for food supplies in Europe. Many farmers borrowed heavily to buy new land and new machinery to raise more crops. Sales were strong, prices were high, and farmers prospered. After the war, however, European farm output rose, and the debt-ridden countries of Europe had little money to spend on American farm products. Congress had unintentionally made matters worse when it passed the Fordney-McCumber Act in 1922. This act raised tariffs dramatically in an effort to protect American industry from foreign competition. By dampening the American market for foreign goods, however, it provoked a reaction in foreign markets against American agricultural products. Farmers in the United States could no longer sell as much of their crops overseas, and prices tumbled.

Helping Farmers

Some members of Congress tried to help the farmers sell their surplus. Every year from 1924 to 1928, Senator Charles McNary of Oregon and Representative Gilbert Haugen of Iowa proposed the McNary-Haugen Bill, a plan in which the government would boost farm prices by buying up surpluses and selling them, at a loss, overseas.

Congress passed the bill twice, but President Coolidge vetoed it both times. He argued that with money flowing to farmers under this law, they would be encouraged to produce even greater surpluses. American farmers remained mired in a recession throughout the 1920s.

Reading Check **Synthesizing** What factors led to the growing economic crisis in farming?

Section 2 REVIEW

Vocabulary

1. **Explain** the significance of: mass production, assembly line, Model T, Charles Lindbergh, welfare capitalism, open shop.

Main Ideas

2. **Evaluating** How did the automobile affect American society?
3. **Summarizing** What factors led to the new consumer society in the United States during the 1920s?
4. **Analyzing** What conditions contributed to the tough times farmers faced in the early 1920s?

Critical Thinking

5. **Big Ideas** How did the availability of credit change society?
6. **Organizing** Use a graphic organizer like the one below to list some of the new industries that grew in importance during the 1920s.

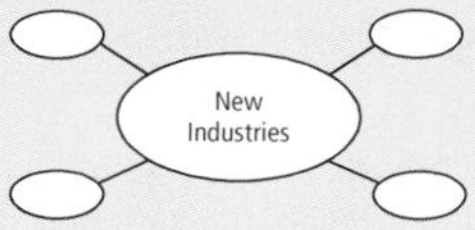

7. **Analyzing Visuals** Study the Technology & History on pages 598–599. How do appliances, cars, and airplanes differ today? How do you think new products change society today?

Writing About History

8. Write an article for a contemporary newspaper analyzing the impact of Charles Lindbergh's transatlantic flight on the development of aviation in the United States and the world.

History ONLINE
Study Central™ To review this section, go to glencoe.com and click on Study Central.

603

S Skill Practice

Chronological Thinking Ask students to create a time line that shows the various economic difficulties that farmers faced and the solutions they found before the 1920s. **OL**

Assess

History ONLINE

Study Central™ provides summaries, interactive games, and online graphic organizers to help students review content.

Close

Summarizing **Ask:** Who benefited and who did not from the growing economy of the 1920s? *(Most consumers benefited from new inventions, new industries, and easy credit; African Americans, Native Americans, and farmers in general did not enjoy the prosperity of the 1920s.)* **OL**

Reading Check

Answer:
a decline in foreign markets and increased productivity

Section 2 REVIEW

Answers

1. All definitions can be found in the section and the Glossary.
2. eased rural isolation, allowed workers to live farther away from work
3. mass production, mass advertising, easy credit, and economic prosperity
4. Higher crop yields led to lower prices, and European markets stopped buying at the same level.
5. Consumers were able to purchase large-ticket items sooner because they did not need to save money for the purchases. Financial institutions made money by offering credit to consumers.
6. airline, automobile, consumer goods, radio
7. Appliances today are more efficient, faster, and use less energy. New products often save time and labor.
8. Students' articles will vary but should include factual information.

Focus

Bellringer

Daily Focus Transparency 17-3

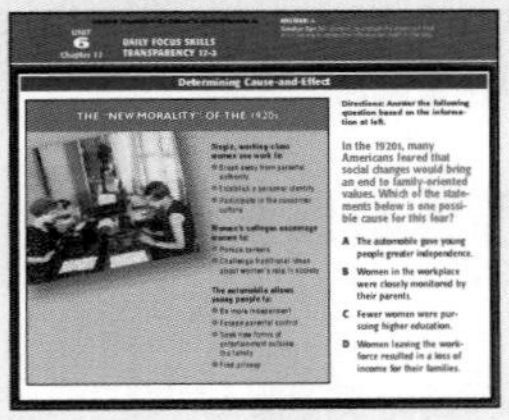

Guide to Reading

Answers may include: Causes: job competition, European immigrant influx, eugenics, economic recession; Effects: return of KKK, Sacco-Vanzetti case, governmental control of immigration

Section Spotlight Video

To generate student interest and provide a springboard for class discussion, access the Chapter 17, Section 3 video at glencoe.com or on the video DVD.

Resource Manager

Section 3 — Section Audio — Spotlight Video

A Clash of Values

Guide to Reading

Big Ideas

Past and Present The struggles of the 1920s regarding immigration and proper behavior continue to affect current events.

Content Vocabulary

- nativism *(p. 604)*
- anarchist *(p. 604)*
- evolution *(p. 608)*
- creationism *(p. 608)*
- speakeasy *(p. 609)*

Academic Vocabulary

- source *(p. 606)*
- deny *(p. 608)*

People and Events to Identify

- Emergency Quota Act *(p. 606)*
- National Origins Act *(p. 606)*
- Fundamentalism *(p. 608)*

Reading Strategy

Organizing As you read about Americans' reactions to immigrants during the 1920s, complete a graphic organizer similar to the one below by filling in the causes and effects of anti-immigrant prejudices.

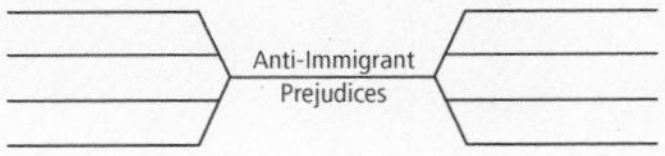

The 1920s are often called the "Roaring Twenties" because to many the decade seemed to be one long party. Urban Americans celebrated the new "modern" culture, but not everyone agreed that the new trends were a good thing. Rural Americans believed traditional society and morality were under attack.

Nativism Resurges

MAIN Idea Nativism and racism increased in the 1920s and led to changes in immigration laws.

HISTORY AND YOU In your school, is there a limit to the number of students in each class? Read to learn why the United States imposed new rules in the 1920s limiting the number of immigrants admitted each year.

The 1920s was a time of economic growth, but it was also a time of cultural turmoil. When the 1920s began, an economic recession, an influx of immigrants, and cultural tensions combined to create an atmosphere of disillusionment and intolerance. The fear and prejudice many felt toward Germans and communists during and after World War I expanded to include all immigrants. This triggered a general rise in racism and **nativism**—a belief that one's native land needs to be protected against immigrants.

During World War I, immigration to the United States had dropped sharply. By 1921, however, it had returned to prewar levels, with the majority of immigrants coming from southern and eastern Europe. Many Americans reacted to the bombings, strikes, and recession of the postwar years by blaming immigrants. Many believed immigrants were taking jobs that would otherwise have gone to soldiers returning home from the war.

The Sacco-Vanzetti Case

The controversial Sacco-Vanzetti case reflected the prejudices and fears of the era. On April 15, 1920, two men robbed and murdered two employees of a shoe factory in Massachusetts. Police subsequently arrested two Italian immigrants, Nicola Sacco and Bartolomeo Vanzetti, for the crime.

The case created a furor when newspapers revealed that the two men were **anarchists,** or people who oppose all forms of government. They also reported that Sacco owned a gun similar to the murder weapon and that the bullets used in the murders matched those in Sacco's gun. The evidence was questionable, but the fact that the accused men were anarchists and foreigners led many people to assume they were guilty, including the jury. On July 14, 1921,

R Reading Strategies	C Critical Thinking	D Differentiated Instruction	W Writing Support	S Skill Practice
Additional Resources • Guide Read, URB p. 48 • Read Essen., URB p. 190 • Guide Read. Act., URB p. 48 • Prim. Source Read., URB p. 35	**Teacher Edition** • Analyzing Info., p. 606 • Making Generalizations, p. 608 • Making Inferences, p. 609 **Additional Resources** • Quizzes and Tests, p. 245 • Crit. Thinking Skills Act., URB p. 32 • Hist. Simulations, URB p. 9	**Teacher Edition** • Visual/Spatial, p. 607 **Additional Resources** • Diff. Inst., URB p. 23	**Teacher Edition** • Persuasive Writing, p. 605	**Additional Resources** • Read Essen, p. 192 • Interpret. Pol. Cartoons, URB p. 41

POLITICAL CARTOONS PRIMARY SOURCE

Hostility Toward Immigrants

In the 1920s, many Americans believed that immigrants from southern and eastern Europe would not assimilate into American culture. These concerns led to the rise of a new Ku Klux Klan and efforts in Congress to pass legislation that would keep "undesirable" immigrants out.

Men, women, and children participate in a Klan march in Cincinnati, Ohio, in 1925 (left). Membership in the KKK soared in the early 1920s because of its opposition to immigrants. Not everyone agreed with the klan, however; the cartoon above mocks a proposal to impose a literacy test on immigrants.

European Immigration, 1900–1924

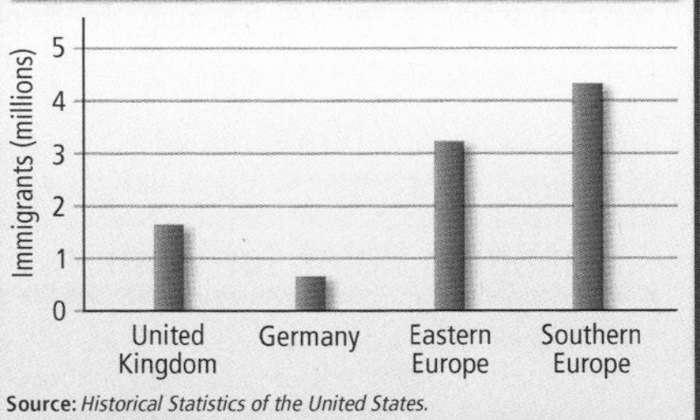

Source: *Historical Statistics of the United States.*

Analyzing VISUALS DBQ

1. **Making Inferences** What does the presence and membership of children in the Klan suggest to others?
2. **Analyzing Visuals** What is the "wall" made of in the cartoon?
3. **Making Connections** From which two regions did the majority of immigrants come? Why were so many people from these regions willing to leave their homelands and come to the United States?

Sacco and Vanzetti were found guilty and sentenced to death. After six years of appeals, Sacco and Vanzetti were executed on August 23, 1927.

Return of the Ku Klux Klan

W At the forefront of the movement to restrict immigration was the Ku Klux Klan, or KKK. The old KKK had flourished in the South after the Civil War and used threats and violence to intimidate newly freed African Americans. The new Klan had other targets as well: Catholics, Jews, immigrants, and other groups said to be "un-American." In the 1920s, the Klan claimed it was fighting for "Americanism."

William J. Simmons founded the new Ku Klux Klan in Georgia, in 1915. A former preacher, Simmons pledged to preserve America's white, Protestant civilization. The Klan attracted few members until 1920, when Simmons began using professional promoters to sell Klan memberships. By 1924 membership had reached nearly 4 million as it spread beyond the South into Northern cities. W

The Klan began to decline in the late 1920s, however, largely as a result of scandals and power struggles between its leaders. Membership shrank, and politicians backed by the Klan were voted out of office. In addition, new restrictions on immigration deprived the Klan of one of its major issues.

Read "Sacco and Vanzetti Must Die" by John Dos Passos on pages R74–R75 of the **American Literature Library.**

Teach

W Writing Support

Persuasive Writing Have interested students use library or Internet resources to find out more about the rise of the Ku Klux Klan in the early 1900s, as well as the terror tactics it employed against minorities. Have students use their findings to write a persuasive letter to their member of Congress encouraging him or her to pass legislation to curb or outlaw the Klan's activities. Encourage volunteers to share their letters with the class. **AL**

Analyzing VISUALS

Answers:

1. Their parents are teaching them bigotry and intolerance.
2. a literacy test with pens
3. Most immigrants came from southern and eastern Europe. They were looking for new economic opportunities and trying to escape war, revolution, religious persecution, and poor economic conditions.

Hands-On Chapter Project
Step 3

Creating a Memory Book

Step 3: Researching Images for Selected Persons Ask students to gather photos and information about the person's background, motivation, and his or her role in the history of this period.

Directions Students will illustrate the biography of the person by finding photographs, related images, or drawing diagrams related to the person. Students should annotate all images with captions or explanations.

Identifying Central Issues Students must identify the central role played by the selected person, and illustrate the biography with images that relate to this role. **OL**

(Chapter Project continued on page 611)

C Critical Thinking

Analyzing Information Have students use library or Internet resources to locate historical immigration statistics for 1890, 1900, 1910, 1920, and 1930. Tell them to select two countries, one from Western Europe and one from Eastern Europe. Have students use the data to construct an immigration chart that shows the effects of the immigration laws of 1921 and 1924. Ask students to write a brief explanation of the significance of their findings. OL

Reading Check

Answer:
The Klan of the 1920s targeted Jews, Catholics, immigrants, and anyone else they thought had "un-American" values, as well as the African American community that the earlier Klan had targeted.

Additional Support

Controlling Immigration

American immigration policies changed in response to the postwar recession and nativist pleas to "Keep America American." Even some business leaders, who had favored immigration as a **source** of cheap labor, now saw the new immigrants as radicals.

In 1921 President Harding signed the **Emergency Quota Act.** The act restricted annual admission to the United States to only 3 percent of the total number of people in any ethnic group already living in the nation. Ethnic identity and national origin thus determined admission to the United States. C

In 1924 the **National Origins Act** made immigration restriction a permanent policy. The law set quotas at 2 percent of each national group represented in the U.S. Census of 1890. Thus, immigration quotas were based on the ethnic composition of the country more than 30 years earlier—before the heavy wave of immigration from southern and eastern Europe. The new quotas deliberately favored immigrants from northwestern Europe. Although subsequent legislation made some changes in immigration laws, the National Origins Act set the framework for immigration for the next four decades.

Hispanic Immigration

While workers and unions rejoiced at the reduction in competition with European immigrants for jobs, employers desperately needed laborers for agriculture, mining, and railroad work. Mexican immigrants were able to fill this need because the National Origins Act of 1924 exempted natives of the Western Hemisphere from the quota system.

Large numbers of Mexican immigrants had already begun moving to the United States after the passage of the Newlands Reclamation Act of 1902. The act funded irrigation projects in the Southwest and led to the creation of large factory farms that needed thousands of farmworkers. As the demand for cheap farm labor steadily increased, Mexican immigrants crossed the border in record numbers. By the end of the 1920s, nearly 700,000 had migrated to the United States.

Reading Check **Explaining** How was the Ku Klux Klan of the 1920s different from the earlier Klan?

A Clash of Cultures

MAIN Idea Supporters of the new morality in the 1920s clashed with those who supported more traditional values.

HISTORY AND YOU How do you think older generations view your generation? Read about the changes in morality during the 1920s.

Many groups that wanted to restrict immigration also wanted to preserve what they considered to be traditional values. They feared that a "new morality" was taking over the nation. Challenging traditional ways of behaving, the new morality glorified youth and personal freedom and changed American society—particularly the status of women.

Women in the 1920s

Having won the right to vote in 1920, many women sought to break free of the traditional roles and behaviors that were expected of them. Attitudes toward marriage—popularized by magazines and other media—changed considerably. As the loving and emotional aspects of marriage grew in importance, the

PRIMARY SOURCE
Changing Roles for Women

As women achieved greater independence, access to higher education, and professional opportunities in the 1920s, they adopted new clothing styles that expressed their identities.

▶ *Many young women adopted the flapper style in the 1920s. They stopped wearing corsets, bobbed their hair, and wore short skirts, high heels, and rounded hats with almost no brim. The style expressed the sense of freedom many women felt in the 1920s.*

Extending the Content

Women Voters After 1869, when the Territory of Wyoming granted women the right to vote, woman suffrage expanded unevenly across the nation. By 1920, some states had granted women full voting rights, others had granted women the right to vote for some, but not all, political offices, and other states did not allow women to vote for any political office.

When the Nineteenth Amendment (1920) went into effect, it dramatically expanded the electorate. Many Americans predicted that the addition of so many female voters would transform American politics. They anticipated that women would support progressive candidates who would push for social and labor reform legislation. The 1920s, however, proved to be an era dominated by political conservatives. As it turned out, factors such as income, ethnicity, and religion influenced the political allegiances of female voters just as much as they influenced those of male voters.

ideas of romance, pleasure, and friendship became linked to successful marriages.

The popularizing of Sigmund Freud's psychological theories also changed people's ideas about relationships. Freudian psychology emphasized human sexuality and his theories (often oversimplified) became acceptable subjects of public conversation.

The automobile played a role in encouraging the new morality. Cars allowed young people to escape the careful watch of their parents. Instead of socializing at home with the family, many youths could now use cars to "go out" with their friends.

Women in the workforce began to define the new morality. Many working-class women took jobs because they or their families needed the wages but for some young, single women, work was a way to break away from parental authority and establish financial independence. **D** Earning money also allowed women to participate in the consumer culture.

Fashion, too, changed during the 1920s, particularly for women, who "bobbed," or shortened, their hair, wore flesh-colored silk stockings, and copied the glamorous look of movie stars. The flapper personified these changes, even though she was not typical of most women. The flapper smoked cigarettes, drank prohibited liquor, and wore makeup and sleeveless dresses with short skirts.

Women who attended college in the 1920s often found support for their emerging sense of independence. Women's colleges, in particular, encouraged their students to pursue careers and to challenge traditional ideas about women's role in society.

Many professional women made major contributions in science, medicine, law, and literature in the 1920s. In medicine, Florence Sabin's research led to a dramatic drop in death **D** rates from tuberculosis while Edith Wharton, Willa Cather, and Edna Ferber each won a Pulitzer Prize in fiction for their novels.

Public health nurse Margaret Sanger believed that families could improve their standard of living by limiting the number of children they had. She founded the American Birth Control League in 1921 to promote knowledge about birth control. This organization became Planned Parenthood in the 1940s. During the 1920s and 1930s, the use of birth control increased dramatically, particularly among middle-class couples.

◀ *Educational opportunities for women increased in the 1920s, and with education came new professional opportunities. A 1922 magazine cover depicts a college girl. Below is Judge Florence E. Allen, in her judge's chambers in Ohio. In 1920 she became the first woman elected to a state supreme court.*

Women Earning College Degrees

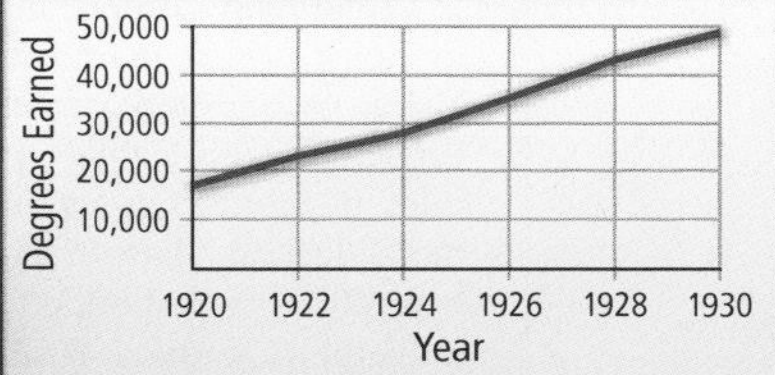

Source: *Historical Statistics of the United States.*

Analyzing VISUALS

1. **Speculating** Clothing is often used to create a specific impression or to convey social status. What image or attitude does each of these women convey with her attire?
2. **Analyzing Visuals** What happened to the number of women earning college degrees during the 1920s?

D Differentiated Instruction

Visual/Spatial Have students make a table showing areas where women's roles changed in the 1920s. Ask them to include visuals and examples for each area on the chart. Display the charts in the classroom. **OL**

Analyzing VISUALS

Answers:

1. The flappers are dressed to look free and fun loving; the student is dressed to look smart and sophisticated; the judge is dressed to appear thoughtful and authoritative.
2. increased from about 18,000 to almost 50,000 annually

Additional Support

Activity: Interdisciplinary Connection

Civics Organize the class into teams of two. Have student pairs use library or Internet resources to learn more about Florence Sabin, Edith Wharton, Willa Cather, Edna Ferber, or Margaret Sanger and their contributions to their respective field. Students will use their findings to prepare an oral report for the class. Remind students to incorporate visual aids, such as photos and posters into their presentations. Once all student pairs have completed their oral reports, conduct a class discussion. **Ask:** **What effect do the contributions of these women have on women of the twenty-first century?** *(Answers will vary, but students should note that the contributions of these women paved the way for successful women since their time.)* **OL**

C Critical Thinking

Making Generalizations

Initiate a class discussion about the attempts to control the use of alcohol. **Ask:** What sorts of attempts have been made to limit alcohol consumption in recent years? *(raising the minimum legal age for alcohol purchase, restrictions on hard liquor advertisements on television, warning labels on alcohol products, high alcohol taxes, education programs, MADD, SADD)* Discuss whether students think these attempts have been successful and whether other initiatives should be considered. **OL**

Analyzing VISUALS

Answers:

1. Opponents of Prohibition might have pointed out a connection between the rise of organized crime and the murder rate. Other reasons for the increase in the murder rate might include the economic conditions resulting from the Great Depression.
2. The mother and child are being overshadowed by the alcohol bottle.

Additional Support

PRIMARY SOURCE

The War Against Alcohol

Prohibition supporters argued that it reduced violence, illness, and poverty. Critics argued that it increased violence because gangs fought to control the sale of illegal alcohol, and that it led to illness because many people drank unsafe "moonshine."

▲ *Supporters of Prohibition portrayed the sale of alcohol as a danger to mothers and children.*

◀ *Prohibition led to the creation of a special federal bureau charged with stopping the sale of illegal alcohol. In this photo, a federal agent cracks open barrels of illegal rum in San Francisco in 1927.*

Murder Rate, 1920–1940

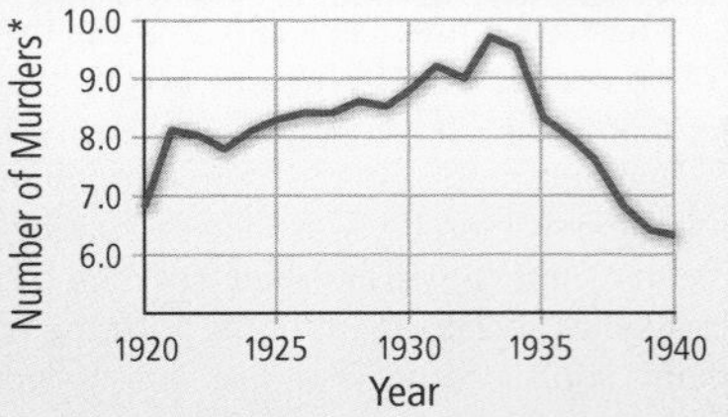

*per 100,000 residents

Source: *Historical Statistics of the United States.*

Analyzing VISUALS DBQ

1. **Theorizing** How might opponents of Prohibition use the murder rate in the 1920s and 1930s to support their argument? Can you think of other reasons the murder rate might have fallen in the 1930s?
2. **Analyzing Visuals** How does the poster use emotional appeal to strengthen its argument?

Fundamentalism

While many Americans embraced the new morality, others feared that the country was losing its traditional values. They viewed the consumer culture, relaxed ethics, and changing roles of women as evidence of the nation's moral decline. Many of these people, especially in rural towns, responded by joining a religious movement known as **Fundamentalism,** a name derived from a series of Christian religious pamphlets titled "The Fundamentals."

Fundamentalist Beliefs Fundamentalists believed that the Bible was literally true and without error. They rejected the idea that human beings derived their moral behavior from society and nature, not God. In particular, they rejected Charles Darwin's theory of **evolution,** which said that human beings had developed from lower forms of life over the course of millions of years. Instead, they believed in **creationism**—the belief that God created the world as described in the Bible.

Two popular preachers, Billy Sunday and Aimee Semple McPherson, stirred supporters by preaching in very nontraditional ways. Sunday, a former professional baseball player, drew huge crowds with his showmanship and rapid-fire sermons. McPherson conducted her revivals and faith healings in Los Angeles in a flamboyant theatrical style, using stage sets and costumes that expressed the themes of her highly emotional sermons.

The Scopes Trial In 1925 Tennessee outlawed any teaching that **denied** "the story of the Divine Creation of man as taught in the Bible," or taught that "man descended from a lower order of animals." The American Civil Liberties Union (ACLU) advertised for a teacher willing to be arrested for teaching evolution. John T. Scopes, a biology teacher in Dayton, Tennessee, volunteered. He taught evolution and was arrested.

The trial took place in the summer of 1925. William Jennings Bryan, a three-time presidential candidate, was the prosecutor who

Extending the Content

Agents of Prohibition Isador Einstein, known as Izzy, and his partner Moe Smith worked as a team to trap lawbreakers during Prohibition. Masters of disguise, they were a flamboyant pair who used any number of methods to enforce the law. Izzy was particularly adept at going through diverse neighborhoods because he spoke five languages. He once seized an unsuspecting speakeasy owner by disguising himself as a pickle salesman. Together, Izzy and Moe made some 4,000 arrests and hauled in around $15 million worth of alcohol.

represented the creationists. Clarence Darrow, one of the country's most celebrated trial lawyers, defended Scopes. After eight days of trial, Scopes was found guilty and fined $100, although the conviction was later overturned on a technicality. The trial had been broadcast over the radio, and Darrow's blistering cross-examination of Bryan hurt the Fundamentalist cause. Increasingly, Fundamentalists felt isolated and their commitment to political activism declined.

Prohibition

The movement to ban alcohol grew stronger in the early 1900s. People supported the prohibition of alcohol sales for many reasons. Some opposed alcohol consumption for religious reasons; others thought prohibition would reduce unemployment, domestic violence, and poverty. Prohibition supporters achieved their goal when the Eighteenth Amendment went into effect in January 1920.

C Congress passed the Volstead Act, making the U.S. Treasury Department responsible for enforcing Prohibition. Treasury agents had enforced federal tax laws for many years, but police powers—a government's power to control people and property in the interest of public safety, health, welfare, and morals—had generally been reserved for state governments. The Eighteenth Amendment granted federal and state governments the power to enforce Prohibition, marking a dramatic increase in federal police powers.

The Treasury Department struggled to enforce Prohibition. During the 1920s, treasury agents made more than 540,000 arrests, but Americans persisted in blatantly ignoring the law. People flocked to secret bars called **speakeasies,** where they could purchase alcohol. In New York City alone, an estimated 32,000 speakeasies sold liquor illegally. Liquor also was readily available in rural areas, where bootlegging—the illegal production and distribution of liquor—was common.

Organized crime thrived on the illegal trade in alcohol. Huge profits could be made smuggling liquor from Canada and the Caribbean. Crime became big business, and some gangsters had enough money to corrupt local politicians. Al Capone, one of the most successful and violent gangsters of the era, had many police officers, judges, and other officials on his payroll. Capone dominated organized crime in Chicago. Finally, Eliot Ness, the leader of a special Treasury Department task force, brought Capone to justice. More than 70 federal agents were killed while enforcing Prohibition in the 1920s.

The battle to repeal Prohibition began almost as soon as the Eighteenth Amendment was ratified. The Twenty-first Amendment, ratified in 1933, repealed the Eighteenth Amendment and ended Prohibition. Prohibition had reduced alcohol consumption, but it had not improved society in the ways its supporters had hoped.

Reading Check **Identifying** What political, social, and economic contributions did women make to American society in the 1920s?

Section 3 REVIEW

Vocabulary

1. **Explain** the significance of: nativism, anarchist, Emergency Quota Act, National Origins Act, Fundamentalism, evolution, creationism, speakeasy.

Main Ideas

2. **Identifying** What two factors influenced the limits on immigration?
3. **Summarizing** What issues caused clashes between traditional and new moralities?

Critical Thinking

4. **Big Ideas** Why did many Americans oppose immigration after World War I? What connections can you make with immigration policies today?
5. **Categorizing** Use a graphic organizer similar to the one below to list the provisions of the immigration acts passed in the 1920s.

Act	Provisions

6. **Analyzing Visuals** Look at the chart on page 605 showing European immigration. How would these figures have affected someone who was a nativist? Why?

Writing About History

7. **Persuasive Writing** Imagine it is the 1920s. Write a letter to your senator persuading him or her either to continue supporting Prohibition or to work for its repeal.

History ONLINE
Study Central™ To review this section, go to glencoe.com and click on Study Central.

C Critical Thinking

Making Inferences Have students find out more about the Volstead Act and write a one-page summary of their findings. OL

Reading Check

Answer:
Some pursued social freedoms, some entered the workforce, and some contributed to medicine, literature, and science.

Assess

History ONLINE

Study Central™ provides summaries, interactive games, and online graphic organizers to help students review content.

Close

Summarizing Ask: Why did some Americans reject the new morality and embrace traditional values? *(They were afraid that consumer culture, relaxed ethics, and growing urbanism symbolized the nation's moral decline.)* OL

Section 3 REVIEW

Answers

1. All definitions can be found in the section and the Glossary.
2. post-World War I recession and nativism
3. behavior of women, drinking alcohol, beliefs about the creation of the world
4. People feared immigrants as radicals and as a threat to job security. Students may suggest similar fears exist today, leading to new attempts to secure the border with Mexico.
5. 1921 Emergency Quota Act: limited the number of immigrants to 3 percent of the existing immigrant population based on the 1910 census; 1924 National Origins Act: limited the number of immigrants to 2 percent of the existing immigrant population based on the 1890 census
6. A nativist would be upset because of the large number of immigrants from eastern and southern Europe.
7. Letters should clearly express a point of view.

Focus

Bellringer

Daily Focus Transparency 17-4

Guide to Reading

Answers: Art: diverse, individual expression influenced by European art movement; Literature: various styles and subject matter, themes of disillusionment and emptiness; Popular Culture: sports heroes, Hollywood allure, radio shows, jazz, and blues

Section Spotlight Video

To generate student interest and provide a springboard for class discussion, access the Chapter 17, Section 4 video at glencoe.com or on the video DVD.

Resource Manager

Section 4

Section Audio   Spotlight Video

Cultural Innovations

Guide to Reading

Big Ideas

Culture and Beliefs Through sharing in the arts and sports of the time, Americans embraced new ways of thinking.

Content Vocabulary

- bohemian *(p. 610)*
- mass media *(p. 613)*

Academic Vocabulary

- diverse *(p. 610)*
- unify *(p. 613)*

People and Events to Identify

- Carl Sandburg *(p. 611)*
- Willa Cather *(p. 611)*
- Ernest Hemingway *(p. 612)*
- F. Scott Fitzgerald *(p. 612)*
- Edith Wharton *(p. 612)*

Reading Strategy

Organizing As you read about the 1920s, complete a graphic organizer like the one below by filling in the main characteristics of art, literature, and popular culture that reflect the era.

Cultural Movement	Main Characteristics
Art	
Literature	
Popular Culture	

The 1920s was an era of great artistic innovation. Artists and writers experimented with new techniques. Popular culture also changed. Broadcast radio introduced Americans around the country to the latest trends in music and entertainment, and motion pictures became a major leisure-time activity.

Art and Literature

MAIN Idea New York City's Greenwich Village and Chicago's South Side became known as centers for new artistic work.

HISTORY AND YOU Is there a neighborhood with many art galleries in your community? Read about the flowering of the arts during the 1920s in the United States.

During the 1920s, American artists and writers challenged traditional ideas. These artists explored what it meant to be "modern," and they searched for meaning in the emerging challenges of the modern world. Many artists, writers, and intellectuals of the era flocked to Manhattan's Greenwich Village and Chicago's South Side. The artistic and unconventional, or **bohemian,** lifestyle of these neighborhoods allowed young artists, musicians, and writers greater freedom to express themselves.

Modern American Art

European art movements greatly influenced the modernists of American art. Perhaps most striking was the **diverse** range of artistic styles, each attempting to express the individual, modern experience. American painter John Marin drew on nature as well as the urban dynamics of New York for inspiration, explaining, "the whole city is alive; buildings, people, all are alive; and the more they move me the more I feel them to be alive." Painter Charles Scheeler applied the influences of photography and the geometric forms of Cubism to urban and rural American landscapes. Edward Hopper revived the visual accuracy of realism in his haunting scenes. His paintings conveyed a modern sense of disenchantment and isolation. Georgia O'Keeffe's landscapes and flowers were admired in many museums throughout her long life.

Poets and Writers

Poets and writers of the 1920s varied greatly in their styles and subject matter. Chicago poet, historian, folklorist, and novelist **Carl**

R Reading Strategies	C Critical Thinking	D Differentiated Instruction	W Writing Support	S Skill Practice
Additional Resources • Guide Read Act., URB p. 49 • Read. Skills Act., URB p. 21 • Am. Lit. Read., URB p. 15	**Additional Resources** • Quizzes and Tests, p. 142	**Additional Resources** • Differentiated Instruction Act., URB p. 23	**Teacher Edition** • Descriptive Writing, pp. 611, 612	**Additional Resources** • Read Essen, p. 109

PRIMARY SOURCE

Ashcan Realists and the Lost Generation

Many artists and writers focused on the isolation and alienation of modern society. A group of artists who painted urban life became known as the Ashcan Realists. The writers who described modern life as spiritually empty and materialistic became known as the "Lost Generation."

Excerpt from
"The Hollow Men" (1925)
by T.S. Eliot

We are the hollow men
We are the stuffed men
Leaning together
Headpiece filled with straw. Alas!
Our dried voices, when
We whisper together
Are quiet and meaningless
As wind in dry grass
Or rats' feet over broken glass
In our dry cellar
Shape without form, shade without colour,
Paralysed force, gesture without motion;
Those who have crossed
With direct eyes, to death's other Kingdom
Remember us—if at all—not as lost
Violent souls, but only
As the hollow men
The stuffed men.

◀ *Edward Hopper studied with one of the founders of the Ashcan Realist movement. His painting,* Automat, *(left) expresses the loneliness and isolation many young people felt during the 1920s. An automat was a place where a person could buy food or drinks from vending machines.*

Excerpt from *The Great Gatsby* (1925)
by F. Scott Fitzgerald

"They were careless people, Tom and Daisy—they smashed up things and creatures and then retreated back into their money or their vast carelessness, or whatever it was that kept them together, and let other people clean up the mess they had made. . . .

I shook hands with him; it seemed silly not to, for I felt suddenly as though I were talking to a child. Then he went into the jewelry store to buy a pearl necklace—or perhaps only a pair of cuff buttons—rid of my provincial squeamishness forever."

DBQ Document-Based Questions

1. **Analyzing Primary Sources** How does Fitzgerald characterize Tom and Daisy? What does their attitude say about the culture of the 1920s?
2. **Explaining** Eliot uses the adjectives *hollow* and *stuffed* to describe contemporary people. How can both be true?
3. **Analyzing Primary Sources** How is Hopper's painting similar to Eliot's poem and Fitzgerald's novel?

Sandburg used common speech to glorify the Midwest, as did Pulitzer Prize–winner **Willa Cather,** who wrote about life on the Great Plains. In Greenwich Village, another Pulitzer Prize winner, Edna St. Vincent Millay, expressed women's equality and praised a life intensely lived.

Several poets had an important impact on the literary culture. Gertrude Stein, an avant-garde poet of the era, was a mentor to many writers, including Ernest Hemingway. Some poets, including Ezra Pound, Amy Lowell, and William Carlos Williams, used clear, concise images to express moments in time. Others concentrated on portraying what they perceived to be the negative effects of modernism. In "The Hollow Men," for example, T.S. Eliot described a world filled with empty dreams that would end "not with a bang but a whimper."

Among playwrights, one of the most innovative was Eugene O'Neill. His plays, filled with bold artistry and modern themes, portrayed realistic characters and situations, offering a vision of life that sometimes touched on the tragic.

Teach

W Writing Support

Descriptive Writing Have interested students read a work by one of the authors or playwrights mentioned in this section. Have them write a one-page essay describing the main idea of the work. Encourage students to read their essays to the class. OL

DBQ Document Based Questions

Answers:

1. Tom and Daisy were careless and rich; they did not care about other people. Their attitude symbolizes the carefree spirit of the 1920s.
2. The men Eliot describes are hollow and unfeeling; they are filled only with dead straw.
3. All three reflect the materialistic nature of the 1920s and the loneliness and desertion felt by many people.

Hands-On Chapter Project
Step 4

Creating a Memory Book

Step 4: Selecting and Researching a Cultural Innovation Ask students to choose a cultural innovation discussed in Section 4. Students will work in teams to design and create a memory page centered on the innovation selected.

Directions Have students either take turns stating their selected topic or write their topics on a class sheet of paper. Then have students divide into groups of two or three to create the memory page.

Analyzing Information Students will need to determine how to illustrate their topic using both images and text. Students will summarize the importance of the innovation through their page design. OL

(Chapter Project continued on page 617)

W Writing Support

Descriptive Writing Have students use library or Internet resources to find out more about how people spent their leisure time in the 1920s. Have students write a one-page essay that describes leisure time in the 1920s. Discuss with the class the differences and similarities between how leisure time was spent in the 1920s and how it is spent now. **OL**

Analyzing VISUALS

Answers:

1. There are no live musicians at movies today; moviegoers do not dress up.
2. The crowd appears to be all male; most are wearing suits with jackets, ties, and caps.

Reading Check

Answer:
It offered freedom from the conformity to old ideas.

Additional Support

Many American writers wrote about their disillusionment with World War I. Some, known as the "Lost Generation," moved to Paris or other cities in Europe. There, they often wrote about "heroic antiheroes"—flawed individuals who still had heroic qualities. **Ernest Hemingway** was one such writer. In direct simple prose, he described the experience of war in such novels as *For Whom the Bell Tolls* and *A Farewell to Arms*.

Sinclair Lewis wrote about the absurdities of small-town life in *Main Street* and *Babbitt*. **F. Scott Fitzgerald's** colorful characters chased futile dreams in *The Great Gatsby*, a novel critical of modern society's superficiality. Similarly, **Edith Wharton** used irony and humor to criticize upper-class ignorance and pretensions. Her 1920 novel, *The Age of Innocence*, won the Pulitzer Prize.

Reading Check **Examining** Why did many creative people flock to Greenwich Village during the 1920s?

Popular Culture

MAIN Idea Broadcast radio and "talking" pictures were new forms of popular entertainment.

HISTORY AND YOU What forms of entertainment make up today's popular culture? Read how Americans spent their leisure time in the 1920s.

The economic prosperity of the 1920s provided many Americans with more leisure time and more spending money, which they devoted to making their lives more enjoyable. Millions of Americans eagerly watched sports and enjoyed music, theater, and other forms of popular entertainment. They also fell in love with motion pictures and radio programs.

Movies and Radio Shows

For many Americans in the 1920s, nothing quite matched the allure of motion pictures. Before technology made sound possible in

PRIMARY SOURCE

Entertainment Brings Americans Together

Part of what made the 1920s feel "new" and "modern" was the rise of mass culture. Popular entertainment—whether movies or sports—brought Americans together in a shared experience.

W

Movies were very popular in the 1920s. Note the live musicians playing music to accompany the silent film. On screen is actress Clara Bow. At left are actors Douglas Fairbanks, Sr., Mary Pickford, Charlie Chaplin, and director D. W. Griffith. They founded the United Artists movie studio in 1919.

Professional sports drew huge crowds in the 1920s. Top players such as Babe Ruth (left) and Ty Cobb (above) became celebrities and were among the first to be paid to endorse products in advertisements.

Analyzing VISUALS

1. **Making Connections** How does the experience of seeing a movie today compare or contrast with what you observe in the photograph of early filmgoers?
2. **Analyzing** What do you observe about the crowds at the baseball games?

Extending the Content

Nickelodeons and Cinemas Tiny halls and converted shops where motion pictures were projected on a screen were first called nickelodeons because they charged an entrance fee of five cents. By 1907 it was estimated that there were 3,000 nickelodeons in the United States. As larger cinemas were built, however, the older and ill-equipped nickelodeons were replaced. By the mid-1920s the picture palace, with its plush décor and white-gloved ushers, was an accepted and cherished part of American life. Theater openings and movie premiers drew crowds. By the late 1920s, the number of cinemas had grown from about 15,000 in 1915 to more than 20,000. The introduction of sound caused an immediate reduction in the number of buildings, for it proved uneconomic to convert many of the older and more dilapidated silent cinemas.

films, theaters hired piano players to provide music during the feature, while subtitles explained the plot. Audiences thronged to see such stars as Mary Pickford, Charlie Chaplin, Tom Mix, Douglas Fairbanks, Sr., Rudolph Valentino, and Clara Bow. In 1927 the golden age of Hollywood began when the first "talking" picture—*The Jazz Singer*—was produced.

Irving Berlin was one of the famous songwriters of the 1920s. He worked in an area of New York City known as Tin Pan Alley, where composers wrote the popular music of the era. Berlin's famous songs include "Puttin' on the Ritz" and "White Christmas." Radio broadcasts such as *The Eveready Hour* offered everything from classical music to comedy. In one of the most popular shows, *Amos 'n' Andy*, the troubles of two African American characters (portrayed by white actors) captured the nation's attention every evening.

The **mass media**—radio, movies, newspapers, and magazines aimed at a broad audience—did more than just entertain. Their easy availability to millions helped break down patterns of provincialism, or narrow focus on local interests. They fostered a sense of shared experience that helped **unify** the nation and spread new ideas and attitudes.

Sports

Thanks to motion pictures and radio, sports such as baseball and boxing reached new heights of popularity in the 1920s. Baseball star Babe Ruth became a national hero, famous for hitting hundreds of home runs. As one broadcaster remarked, "He wasn't a baseball player. He was a worldwide celebrity, an international star, the likes of which baseball has never seen since."

Sports fans also idolized boxer Jack Dempsey. Dempsey held the title of world heavyweight champion from 1919 until 1926, when he lost it to Gene Tunney. When Dempsey attempted to win back the title in 1927, fans' enthusiasm for the rematch reached such a frenzy that one store sold $90,000 worth of radios—an incredible sum at that time—in the two weeks before the event.

Americans eagerly followed other sports and sports figures, too. Newspaper coverage helped generate enthusiasm for college football. One of the most famous players of the 1920s was Red Grange of the University of Illinois. Grange was known as the "Galloping Ghost" because of his speed and ability to evade members of opposing teams.

The triumphs of Bobby Jones, the best golfer of the decade, and tennis players Bill Tilden and Helen Wills, who dominated world tennis, also thrilled sports fans. In 1926 Jones became the first golfer to win the U.S. Open and the British Open in the same year. When swimmer Gertrude Ederle shattered records by swimming the English Channel in a little over 14 hours in 1927, Americans were enchanted.

✓Reading Check **Summarizing** How did the economy of the 1920s affect popular culture?

Section 4 REVIEW

Vocabulary

1. **Explain** the significance of: bohemian, Carl Sandburg, Willa Cather, Ernest Hemingway, F. Scott Fitzgerald, Edith Wharton, mass media.

Main Ideas

2. **Describing** What were the main themes of artists and writers during the 1920s?
3. **Discussing** How did Americans enjoy their leisure time in the 1920s? What made these activities possible?

Critical Thinking

4. **Big Ideas** How did writers, artists, and popular culture of the 1920s affect traditional ideas in the United States?
5. **Organizing** Use a graphic organizer similar to the one below to list the effects of mass media on American culture.

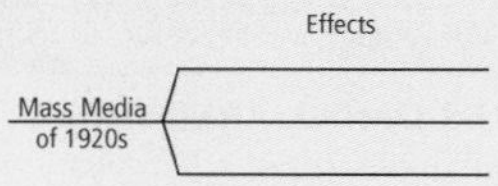

6. **Analyzing Visuals** Look at the painting on page 611. How does Edward Hopper create a sense of alienation in this painting?

Writing About History

7. **Descriptive Writing** Imagine that you have moved to New York's Greenwich Village in the 1920s. Write a letter to a friend describing the atmosphere in your neighborhood.

History ONLINE
Study Central™ To review this section, go to glencoe.com and click on Study Central.

613

✓Reading Check

Answer:
Economic prosperity allowed Americans more leisure time and more spending money to pursue different kinds of popular culture.

Assess

History ONLINE

Study Central™ provides summaries, interactive games, and online graphic organizers to help students review content.

Close

Summarizing Ask: How did the cultural innovations of the 1920s reflect the spirit and mood of the era? *(The art and literature reflected the exuberance of the era as well as the desperation and loneliness that some Americans experienced. The increase in leisure time allowed more people to attend sports events and movie theaters.)*

Section 4 REVIEW

Answers

1. All definitions can be found in the section and the Glossary.
2. disenchantment, isolation, disillusionment, and emptiness
3. They enjoyed movies, radio, and sporting events. The increase in income and leisure time made this possible.
4. They helped create a national culture as they broke down local patterns of narrow interest.
5. broke down patterns of provincialism, unified Americans through shared national experience, spread new ideas and attitudes
6. The woman is seated alone, staring at her coffee cup; the background is dark.
7. Letters will vary but should include descriptive details.

Focus

Ask: After reading the information on these pages, what do you think were the major issues or topics of the era? *(jazz, isolationism vs. internationalism; new inventions)* **Ask:** Why is Santa Claus pictured? *(He was being marketed heavily in the 1920s.)* **Ask:** Why is Charles Lindbergh pictured? In what way is he symbolic of the era? *(Lindbergh was the first man to fly solo across the Atlantic Ocean. He became a worldwide celebrity. To many people, he symbolized the 1920s because of his bravery and daring achievement.)*

Teach

R Reading Strategy

Recognizing Bias Have students reread the excerpt from *Pravda*. **Ask:** Do you think the author was fair in his observations? Why or why not? *(Most likely, the writer was biased against America even before his observations in New York City.)* OL

Additional Support

BETTMANN/CORBIS

LOUIS DANIEL ARMSTRONG *Writer Stanley Crouch remembers Louis Armstrong, a Jazz Age great.*

Pops. Sweet Papa Dip. Satchmo. He had perfect pitch and perfect rhythm. His improvised melodies and singing could be as lofty as a moon flight or as low-down as the blood drops of a street thug dying in the gutter. The extent of his influence across jazz and across American music continues to this day.

Not only do we hear Armstrong in trumpet players who represent the present renaissance in jazz, we can also detect his influence in certain rhythms that sweep from country-and-western music to rap.

Louis Daniel Armstrong was born in New Orleans on August 4, 1901. It was at a home for troubled kids that young Louis first put his lips to the mouthpiece of a cornet and, later, a trumpet.

In 1922 Armstrong went to Chicago, where he joined King Oliver and his Creole Jazz Band. The band brought out the people and all the musicians, black and white, who wanted to know how it was truly done.

When he first played in New York City in 1924, his improvisations set the city on its head. The stiff rhythms of the time were slashed away by his combination of the percussive and the soaring. He soon returned to Chicago, perfected what he was doing, and made one record after another.

Louis Armstrong was so much, in fact, that every school of jazz since has had to address how he interpreted the basics of the idiom—swing, blues, ballads, and Afro-Hispanic rhythms. His freedom, his wit, and his discipline give his music a perpetual position in the wave of the future that is the station of all great art.

VERBATIM

"The great creators of the government . . . thought of America as a light to the world, as created to lead the world in the assertion of the right of peoples and the rights of free nations."

WOODROW WILSON,
in defense of the League of Nations, 1920

"We seek no part in directing the destinies of the Old World."

WARREN G. HARDING,
Inaugural Address, 1921

"Here was a new generation, . . . dedicated more than the last to the fear of poverty and the worship of success; grown up to find . . . all wars fought, all faiths in man shaken."

CULVER PICTURES

F. Scott Fitzgerald

F. SCOTT FITZGERALD,
author, This Side of Paradise

"There has been a change for the worse during the past year in feminine dress, dancing, manners and general moral standards. [One should] realize the serious ethical consequences of immodesty in girls' dress."

from the **PITTSBURGH OBSERVER,** *1922*

"[In New York] I saw 7,000,000 two-legged animals penned in an evil smelling cage, . . . streets as unkempt as a Russian steppe, . . . rubbish, waste paper, cigar butts. . . . One glance and you know no master hand directs." R

article in Soviet newspaper **PRAVDA**
describing New York City in 1925

Extending the Content

Flapper Style In 1922 psychologist G. Stanley Hall wrote an article for the *Atlantic Monthly* in which he described a typical flapper:

"[H]er gait was swagger and superior. . . . She wore a knitted hat, with hardly any brim, of a flame or bonfire hue; a henna scarf; two strings of Betty beads, of different colors, twisted together; an open short coat, with ample pockets; a skirt with vertical stripes. . . . On her wrist were several bangles; on her left, of course, a wrist watch. Her shoes were oxfords, with a low broad heel. Her stockings were woolen and of brilliant hue. But most noticeable of all were her high overshoes or galoshes. One seemed to be turned down at the top and entirely unbuckled, while the other was fastened below and flapped about her trim ankle in a way that compelled attention. . . . She was out to see the world and, incidentally, to be seen of it . . ."

TIME NOTEBOOK

WHAT'S NEW

Invented This Decade

How did we live without . . .

BROWN BROTHERS

- push-button elevators
- neon signs
- oven thermostats
- electric razors
- tissues
- spiral-bound notebooks
- motels
- dry ice
- zippers
- pop-up toasters
- flavored yogurt
- car radios
- adhesive tape
- food disposals
- water skiing
- automatic potato peeler
- self-winding wristwatch

Milestones

EMBARRASSED, 1920. TEXAS SENATOR MORRIS SHEPPARD, a leading proponent of the Eighteenth Amendment, when a large whiskey still is found on his farm.

ERASED, 1922. THE WORD "OBEY," from the Episcopal marriage ceremony, by a vote of American Episcopal bishops.

C **DIED, 1923. HOMER MOREHOUSE,** 27, in the 87th hour of a record-setting 90-hour, 10-minute dance marathon.

EXONERATED, 1921. EIGHT CHICAGO WHITE SOX PLAYERS charged with taking bribes to throw the 1919 World Series. The players were found "not guilty" when grand jury testimony disappeared. Newly appointed commissioner of baseball Kenesaw Mountain Landis banned the "Black Sox" from baseball.

MAKING A COMEBACK, 1926. SANTA CLAUS, after falling into low favor in the last decade. Aiming at children, advertisers are marketing St. Nick heavily.

CULVER PICTURES

NUMBERS

60,000
Families with radios in 1922

9,000,000
Motor vehicles registered in U.S. in 1920

33.5 **Number of hours Charles Lindbergh spent in his nonstop flight from New York to Paris on May 20, 1927**

1,800 **Tons of ticker tape and shredded paper dropped on Charles Lindbergh in his parade in New York City**

$16,000 **Cost of cleaning up after the parade**

7,000 **Job offers received by Lindbergh**

3.5 million
Number of letters received by Lindbergh

BROWN BROTHERS

Charles Lindbergh

CRITICAL THINKING

1. ***Recognizing Bias*** How does the communist newspaper *Pravda* describe New York City? Why do you think the writer described the city in such negative terms?

2. ***Making Connections*** Why do you think Charles Lindbergh's flight caused such excitement among Americans in 1927?

C Critical Thinking

Comparing and Contrasting Have students create two political cartoons, one expressing the popular sentiment about Prohibition and one expressing the concerns over alcohol consumption today. **AL**

Critical Thinking Answers:

1. The city is described as a dirty, out-of-control cage. The writer was hoping to make Russian cities seem more desirable.
2. His bravery and can-do spirit appealed to Americans at this happy time.

Assess/Close

Have students select an item listed under Numbers and find a correlating statistic today.

TIME Visit the Time Web site at www.time.com for up-to-date news, weekly magazine articles, editorials, online polls, and an archive of past magazines and Web articles.

Additional Support

Activity: Technology Connection

Comparing and Contrasting Have students review the information presented in the TIME Notebook and have students use library or Internet resources to find out more about the topics presented. Then have them make a list of items, issues, or inventions from the 1920s that are still relevant today. **Ask:** How do you think the events, issues, or inventions of the 1920s affect your life today? What 1920s inventions are still useful today? Which inventions have been improved upon? What political issues or ideas are still relevant today? *(Answers will vary, but students should cite data from the TIME Notebook and their research to support their ideas.)* **OL**

Focus

Bellringer

Daily Focus Transparency 17-5

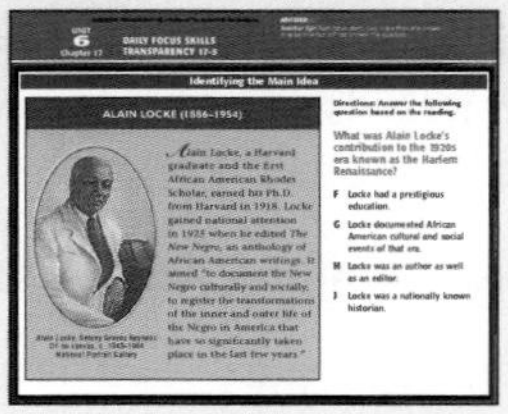

Guide to Reading

Answers may include: Causes: Great Migration and racial pride; Effects: important African American writers, jazz, blues, theater, sparked political change

Section Spotlight Video

To generate student interest and provide a springboard for class discussion, access the Chapter 17, Section 5 video at glencoe.com or on the video DVD.

Resource Manager

R Reading Strategies	C Critical Thinking	D Differentiated Instruction	W Writing Support	S Skill Practice
Teacher Edition • Act. Prior Know., p. 617 **Additional Resources** • Guide Read, URB p. 50 • Prim. Source Read., URB p. 37 • Am. Lit. Read., p. 13	**Teacher Edition** • Making Inferences, pp. 618, 620 **Additional Resources** • Quizzes and Tests, p. 247 • Auth Assess, p. 39	**Teacher Edition** • Auditory/Musical, p. 618 **Additional Resources** • Enrich Act, p. 44 • Reteaching Act., URB p. 43 • Am. Art and Music Act., URB p. 39	**Teacher Edition** • Narrative Writing, pp. 619, 620 • Persuasive Writing, p. 621	**Additional Resources** • Read Essen, p. 198

Section 5

Section Audio   Spotlight Video

African American Culture

Guide to Reading

Big Ideas

Group Action The artistic and political contributions of African Americans changed American society.

Content Vocabulary
- jazz *(p. 617)*
- blues *(p. 618)*

Academic Vocabulary
- symbolize *(p. 618)*
- impact *(p. 620)*
- ongoing *(p. 621)*

People and Events to Identify
- Great Migration *(p. 616)*
- Harlem Renaissance *(p. 616)*
- Claude McKay *(p. 616)*
- Langston Hughes *(p. 616)*
- Zora Neale Hurston *(p. 616)*
- Cotton Club *(p. 618)*
- Marcus Garvey *(p. 621)*

Reading Strategy

Organizing As you read about the African American experience in the 1920s, complete a graphic organizer similar to the one below by filling in the causes and effects of the Harlem Renaissance.

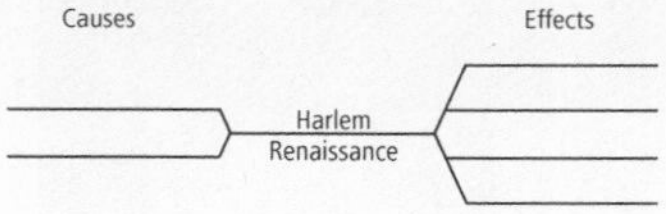

The Harlem Renaissance was a creative era for African American artists and writers. The growing African American population in the North meant an increasing number of African Americans had meaningful political power to continue the struggle for civil rights.

The Harlem Renaissance

MAIN Idea The Harlem Renaissance sparked new trends in literature, music, and art.

HISTORY AND YOU Can you think of any examples of integrating different cultures in today's music and visual arts? Read to learn about the contributions of African Americans to the arts during the 1920s.

During World War I and the 1920s, hundreds of thousands of African Americans joined in the **Great Migration** from the rural South to industrial cities in the North. By moving north, African Americans sought to escape Southern segregation, find economic opportunities, and build better lives. Although job discrimination and economic inequality remained the norm in Northern cities, the North still offered much greater economic opportunities for African Americans compared to the South. After World War I, African American populations swelled in large Northern cities. The cities were full of nightclubs and music, particularly in the New York City neighborhood of Harlem—the heart and soul of the African American renaissance. It was there that African American artistic development, racial pride, and political organization thrived. The result was a flowering of African American arts that became known as the **Harlem Renaissance.**

The Writers

Claude McKay was the first important writer of the Harlem Renaissance. McKay translated the shock of American racism into *Harlem Shadows,* a collection of poetry published in 1922. In such poems as "The Lynching" and "If We Must Die," McKay's eloquent verse expressed a proud defiance and bitter contempt of racism—two striking characteristics of Harlem Renaissance writing. **Langston Hughes** was a prolific, original, and versatile writer. He became a leading voice of the African American experience in America.

Another important Harlem Renaissance author was **Zora Neale Hurston.** Hurston published her first novels, *Jonah's Gourd Vine* and *Their Eyes Were Watching God,* in the 1930s. Hurston's personal and spirited portrayals of rural African American culture were also the

PRIMARY SOURCE

Voices From the Harlem Renaissance

▲ Zora Neale Hurston

Excerpt from
Dust Tracks on a Road
by Zora Neale Hurston

"I can look back and see sharp shadows, high lights, and smudgy inbetweens. I have been in Sorrow's kitchen and licked out all the pots. Then I have stood on the peaky mountain wrapped in rainbows, with a harp and a sword in my hands.

"What I had to swallow in the kitchen has not made me less glad to have lived, nor made me want to low-rate the human race . . . It is the graceless acknowledgment of defeat . . . I am in the struggle with the sword in my hands, and I don't intend to run until you run me [away]."

R

I, Too, Sing America
by Langston Hughes

I, too, sing America.

I am the darker brother.
They send me to eat in the kitchen
When company comes,
But I laugh,
And eat well,
And grow strong.

Tomorrow,
I'll be at the table
When company comes.
Nobody'll dare
Say to me,
"Eat in the kitchen,"
Then.

Besides,
They'll see how
beautiful I am
And be ashamed—

I, too, am America.

▲ Langston Hughes stressed racial pride in his poetry. He reminded African Americans that they had their own history and achievements which were in every way as worthy of celebration as those of white people.

If We Must Die
By Claude McKay

If we must die—let it not be like hogs
Hunted and penned in an inglorious spot,
While round us bark the mad and hungry
dogs,Making their mock at our accursed
lot. If we must die—oh, let us nobly die,
So that our precious blood may not be shed
In vain; then even the monsters we defy
Shall be constrained to honor us though dead!
Oh, Kinsmen! We must meet the common foe;
Though far outnumbered, let us show us brave,
And for their thousand blows deal one deathblow!
What though before us lies the open grave?
Like men we'll face the murderous, cowardly pack,
Pressed to the wall, dying, but fighting back!

◀ Originally from Jamaica, Claude McKay wrote both poems and novels. "If We Must Die" was written shortly after World War I when race riots were erupting across the nation.

DBQ Document-Based Questions

1. **Speculating** What might have been some of the "pots" in Sorrow's kitchen for a woman in the Harlem Renaissance?
2. **Comparing and Contrasting** What does McKay's poem have in common with Hurston's excerpt and the poem by Hughes?

first major stories featuring African American women as central characters. Other notable writers of the Harlem Renaissance include Countee Cullen, Alain Locke, Dorothy West, and Nella Larsen.

Jazz, Blues, and the Theater

When New Orleans native Louis Armstrong moved to Chicago in 1922, he introduced an improvisational early form of **jazz,** a style of music influenced by Dixieland blues and ragtime, with its syncopated rhythms and improvisational elements. Three years later, Armstrong awed fellow musicians with a series of recordings made with his group, the Hot Five. In these recordings, especially in the song "Cornet Chop Suey," Armstrong broke away from the New Orleans tradition of ensemble or group playing by performing highly imaginative solos. He became the first great cornet and trumpet soloist in jazz music. The artistic freedom of Chicago's South Side gave Armstrong the courage to create his own type of jazz.

History ONLINE
Student Web Activity Visit glencoe.com and complete the activity on the Jazz Age.

Teach

R Reading Strategy

Activating Prior Knowledge Before students begin to take in any new knowledge, prepare them by bringing to mind what they already know about the topic they are about to study. Before beginning this section, ask students what they know about the Harlem Renaissance, including whom it involved and where it began. Use the ideas generated to encourage students to think about the topic in more detail and to share more ideas. As students read the section, point out where the ideas they generated can be found in the text. BL

DBQ Document Based Questions

Answers:

1. Answers will vary, but should focus on the discrimination blacks experienced even in northern cities.
2. All reflect African American pride.

Hands-On Chapter Project
Step 5

Creating a Memory Book

Step 5: Design a Class Memory Page Students will collaborate as a class to plan, design, and create a memory page focused on the content of Section 5—African American Culture.

Directions Divide the class into four groups. Each group will sketch a storyboard that depicts, using both images and text, the African American culture of this historical period. After the groups have created their storyboards, bring the class into one discussion. Have group representatives present their ideas, and then decide on a class presentation of the topic. The class will then determine roles for each group to build the memory page.

Synthesizing Information Students will collect information from each group and determine the best way to present the topic using all the ideas presented. OL *(Chapter Project continued on Visual Summary page)*

D Differentiated Instruction

Auditory/Musical Have interested students create a presentation titled "Introduction to Jazz." Encourage students to create a multimedia presentation that provides a musical overview of the patterns and themes common in jazz. **OL**

C Critical Thinking

Making Inferences Have interested students research why the Cotton Club, which featured African American performers and was located in the Harlem area of New York City, served only white customers. **Ask:** Based on what you have learned, what can you infer about the racial attitudes and prejudices of the 1920s? *(Answers will vary, but students will likely point out that racial segregation was still the norm at the time.)* **AL**

Ragtime also influenced the composer, pianist, and bandleader Edward "Duke" Ellington, who listened as a teenager to ragtime piano players in Washington, D.C. In 1923 Ellington, also known simply as "Duke," formed a small band, moved to New York, and began playing in speakeasies and clubs. He soon created his own sound, a blend of improvisation and orchestration using different combinations of instruments. In fact, Ellington often did not like to use the word "jazz," since he believed it put a restriction on the general concept of his music. The Ellington style appeared in such hits as "Mood Indigo" and "Sophisticated Lady." **D** Ellington, who had to be forced to practice piano as a child, eventually composed nearly 6,000 musical pieces, about a third of them jazz numbers. He also wrote religious music, the scores for five movies, and a ballet.

Like many other African American entertainers, Ellington got his start at the **Cotton Club,** **C** the most famous nightclub in Harlem (but one that served only white customers). Years later, reflecting on the music of this era, Ellington said, "Everything, and I repeat, everything had to swing. And that was just it, those cats really had it; they had that soul. And you know you can't just play some of this music without soul. Soul is very important." **C**

Bessie Smith seemed to **symbolize** soul. Her emotional singing style and commanding voice earned her the title "the Empress of the Blues." Smith sang of unfulfilled love, poverty, and oppression—the classic themes of the **blues,** a soulful style of music that evolved from African American spirituals. Born in Tennessee, Smith started performing in tent shows, saloons, and small theaters in the South. Discovered by Ma Rainey, one of the early great blues singers, Smith later performed with many of the greatest jazz bands of the era, including those of Louis Armstrong, Fletcher Henderson, and Benny Goodman. Her first recorded song, "Down Hearted Blues," became a major hit in 1923.

While jazz and blues filled the air during the Harlem Renaissance, the theater arts were also flourishing. *Shuffle Along,* the first musical written, produced, and performed by African Americans, made its Broadway debut in 1921. The show's success helped launch a number of

PRIMARY SOURCE
Scenes From the Harlem Renaissance

The Harlem Renaissance made both jazz and blues music popular and enabled African American entertainers to reach a wide audience.

▲ *Many famous acts got their start at Harlem's Cotton Club. Patrons flocked there to hear the latest jazz music—African American music played by African American musicians—but the audience was limited to whites.*

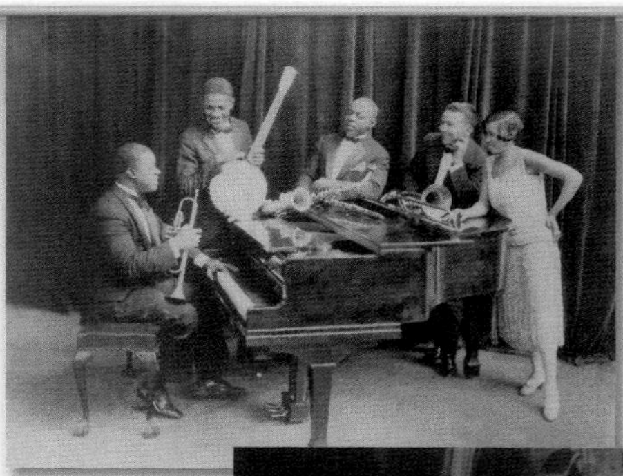

▲ *Louis Armstrong and his band, the Hot Five*

▶ *Duke Ellington and his band at a Chicago nightclub*

Additional Support

Activity: Interdisciplinary Connection

Music Have interested students listen to recordings of jazz and blues performances by popular artists from the 1920s, such as Duke Ellington or Bessie Smith. Instruct students to use library or Internet resources to learn more about the performer they have selected. Then have students prepare a profile of the life of their chosen performer. Encourage students to include information about their music and their personal lives. Invite students to share their profiles with the class. If possible, arrange to play clips of music from the various jazz and blues performers. **OL**

careers, including those of Florence Mills and Paul Robeson.

Robeson first gained recognition as an athlete at Rutgers University, where he was valedictorian of his class. After graduating from law school, he focused on an acting career. A celebrated singer and actor, Robeson received wide acclaim in the title role of a 1924 New York production of *Emperor Jones,* a play by Eugene O'Neill. Four years later, Robeson gained fame for his work in the musical, *Show Boat.* He also often appeared at the Apollo Theater, another famous club in Harlem.

Perhaps the most daring performer of the era, Josephine Baker transformed a childhood knack for flamboyance into a career as a well-known singer and dancer. Baker performed on Broadway but later moved to Paris and launched an international career.

The Harlem Renaissance succeeded in bringing international fame to African American arts. It also sparked a political transformation in the United States.

Reading Check **Analyzing** How did African Americans help shape the national identity through the use of music?

African Americans and 1920s Politics

MAIN Idea While the NAACP pursued racial equality through the courts, black nationalists supported independence and separation from whites.

HISTORY AND YOU How does a sense of positive self-esteem help you perform better? Read how African Americans developed a new sense of pride.

In 1919, 1,300 African American veterans of World War I marched through Manhattan to Harlem. The march symbolized the new aspirations of African Americans in the 1920s. W. E. B. Du Bois captured the new sense of dignity and defiance of African Americans:

PRIMARY SOURCE

"We return. We return from fighting. We return fighting. Make way for democracy! We saved it in France, and by the Great Jehovah, we will save it in the United States of America, or know the reason why."

—quoted in *When Harlem Was in Vogue*

Excerpt from Bessie Smith's first hit song, 1923

Down Hearted Blues

Gee, but it's hard to love someone when that someone don't love you!

I'm so disgusted, heart-broken, too; I've got those down-hearted blues;

Once I was crazy 'bout a man; he mistreated me all the time,

The next man I get has got to promise me to be mine, all mine!

Trouble, trouble, I've had it all my days,

Trouble, trouble, I've had it all my days;

It seems like trouble going to follow me to my grave.

◀ *Bessie Smith was one of the earliest and most famous women blues singers.*

▲ *Singer and actor Paul Robeson created a sensation in a 1925 production of Eugene O'Neill's play* Emperor Jones.

▶ *Dancer Josephine Baker*

Analyzing VISUALS

1. **Hypothesizing** Why do you think many African American performers of the 1920s dressed so formally?
2. **Speculating** How might the Harlem Renaissance have helped overcome racism in American society?

W Writing Support

Narrative Writing Have interested students use library or Internet resources to find out more about the life of Paul Robeson. Have students write a narrative of his life, highlighting the many aspects of his career. Encourage volunteers to share their essays with the class. **OL**

Analyzing VISUALS

Answers:

1. Performers—African Americans included—dressed in more formal or glamorous styles in the 1920s than performers typically wear today.
2. The Harlem Renaissance showcased the many talents of African American authors, playwrights, singers, musicians, and poets.

Reading Check

Answer:
They developed the rhythms and sound of jazz and the blues.

Additional Support

Extending the Content

Black Swan Records African American musicians were rarely recorded in the early twentieth century. White record companies would buy songs written by African Americans for white singers to record. In 1921 Harry Herbert Pace formed Black Swan Records, the first major African American owned recording company. During its existence, the company, which Pace first ran from his basement in Harlem, recorded for and marketed to African American consumers. During its heyday, Black Swan Records produced and sold some 7,000 recordings daily.

C Critical Thinking

Making Inferences Have students find out more about the Great Migration of the 1920s. **Ask:** How did the influx of large numbers of African Americans affect northern cities? *(Answers will vary, but students should support their answers with findings from their research. They may note that racial tensions increased in some cities as workers competed for jobs. Students may also note that African Americans were able to vote as a bloc, thus gaining political power.)* **AL**

W Writing Support

Narrative Writing Have students use library or Internet resources to find out more about Oscar DePriest. Have students write a one-page narrative of his career, including his early life and his efforts in Congress. **OL**

Analyzing GEOGRAPHY

Answers:

1. St. Louis, Chicago, and Detroit
2. New York and Philadelphia

Additional Support

NATIONAL GEOGRAPHIC The Great Migration, 1917–1930

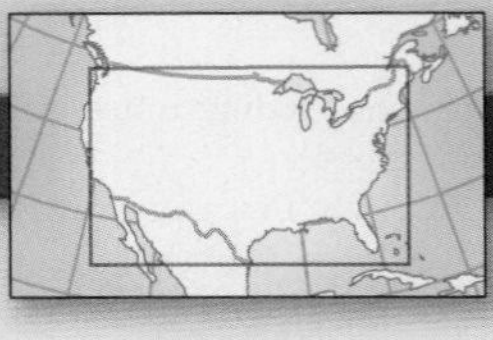

During World War I, thousands of African Americans began the Great Migration from the rural South to the industrial cities of the North. Many African American neighborhoods, including Harlem in New York City, developed at this time.

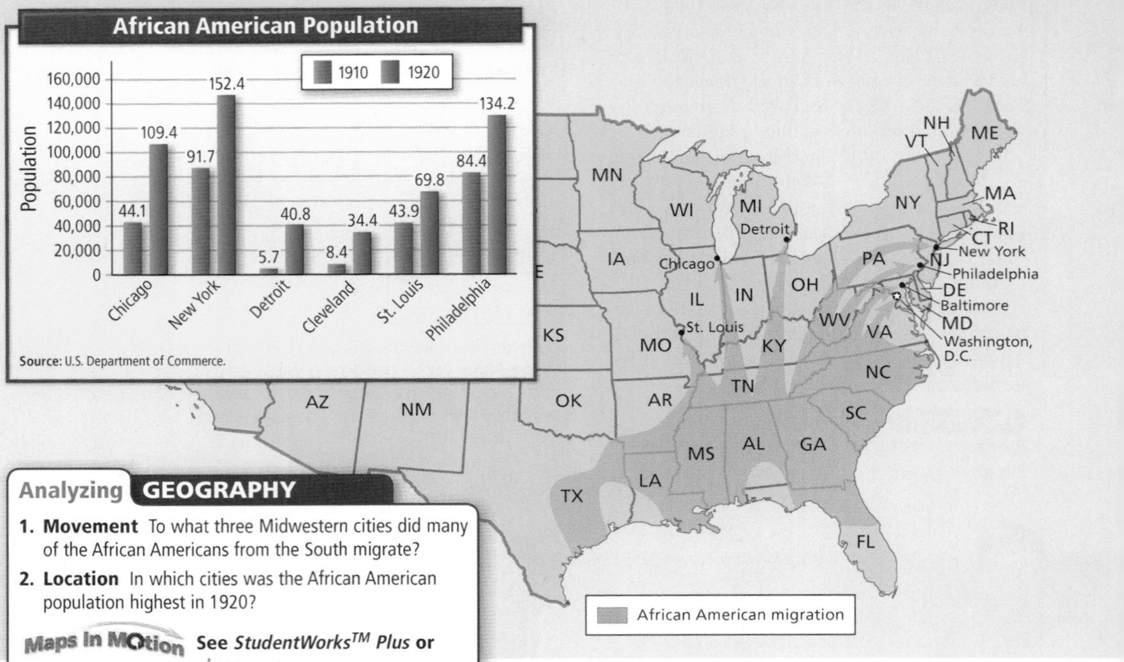

Analyzing GEOGRAPHY

1. **Movement** To what three Midwestern cities did many of the African Americans from the South migrate?
2. **Location** In which cities was the African American population highest in 1920?

Maps In MOtion See *StudentWorks™ Plus* or glencoe.com.

The Black Vote in the North

World War I set the stage for African Americans to reenter federal politics in the United States, although perhaps not in the way many expected. The Great Migration of African Americans to the North to take jobs in the war factories had a significant **impact** on the political power of African Americans in the United States as well. As their numbers grew in city neighborhoods, African Americans became a powerful voting bloc that could sometimes sway the outcome of elections.

At election time, most African American voters in the North cast their votes for Republicans, the party of Abraham Lincoln. In 1928 African American voters in Chicago achieved a significant political breakthrough. Voting as a bloc, they helped elect Oscar DePriest, the first African American representative in Congress from a Northern state. During his three terms in Congress, DePriest introduced laws to oppose racial discrimination and make lynching a federal crime.

The NAACP Battles Injustice

The National Association for the Advancement of Colored People (NAACP) battled valiantly—but often unsuccessfully—against segregation and discrimination against African Americans. Its efforts focused primarily on lobbying public officials and working through the court system.

The NAACP also lobbied and protested against the horrors of lynching. The NAACP's

Activity: Economics Connection

The NAACP Have interested students find out more information about the NAACP today. Students should also find out how the NAACP uses its organization to boycott cities or states that allegedly discriminate against minorities. **Ask:** Based on your findings, are the NAACP's economic boycotts successful? What financial impact do the boycotts have on the targeted area? *(Answers will vary, but students should note that the purchasing power of the African American community, especially if a boycott attracts widespread support, could have a major economic impact on an area.)* **OL**

persistent efforts led to the passage of antilynching legislation in the House of Representatives in 1922. The Senate defeated the bill, but the NAACP continued the fight. Its **ongoing** efforts to end lynching kept the issue in the news and probably helped to reduce the number of lynchings that took place.

One of the NAACP's greatest political triumphs occurred in 1930 with the defeat of Judge John J. Parker's nomination to the U.S. Supreme Court. The NAACP joined with labor unions to launch a highly organized national campaign against the North Carolina judge, who allegedly was racist and antilabor. By a narrow margin, the Senate refused to confirm Parker's nomination. His defeat demonstrated that African American voters and lobby groups had finally achieved enough influence to affect national politics and change decisions in Congress.

Black Nationalism and Marcus Garvey

While the NAACP fought for integration and improvement in the economic and political position of African Americans, other groups began to emphasize black nationalism and black pride. Eventually, some began calling for black separation from white society.

W A dynamic black leader from Jamaica, **Marcus Garvey,** captured the imagination of millions of African Americans with his "Negro Nationalism," which glorified the black culture and traditions. Inspired by Booker T. Washington's call for self-reliance, Garvey founded the Universal Negro Improvement Association (UNIA), an organization aimed at promoting black pride and unity. The central message of Garvey's Harlem-based movement was that African Americans could gain economic and political power by educating themselves. Garvey also advocated separation and independence from whites. In 1920, at the height of his power, Garvey told his followers they would never find justice or freedom in America, and he proposed leading them to Africa.

The emerging African American middle class and intellectuals distanced themselves from Garvey and his push for racial separation. FBI officials saw UNIA as a dangerous catalyst for black uprisings in urban areas. Garvey also alienated key figures in the Harlem Renaissance by characterizing them as "weak-kneed and cringing . . . [flatterers of] the white man." Convicted of mail fraud in 1923, Garvey served time in prison. In 1927 President Coolidge commuted Garvey's sentence and used Garvey's immigrant status to have him deported to Jamaica.

Despite Garvey's failure to keep his movement alive, he instilled millions of African Americans with a sense of pride in their heritage and inspired hope for the future. That sense of pride and hope survived long after Garvey and his "back to Africa" movement was gone. This pride and hope reemerged strongly during the 1950s and played a vital role in the civil rights movement of the 1960s.

✓Reading Check **Summarizing** How did World War I change attitudes among African Americans toward themselves and their country?

Section 5 REVIEW

Vocabulary

1. **Explain** the significance of: Great Migration, Harlem Renaissance, Claude McKay, Langston Hughes, Zora Neale Hurston, jazz, Cotton Club, blues, Marcus Garvey.

Main Ideas

2. **Analyzing** What musical style did Duke Ellington create? How was it different from other styles of music?
3. **Synthesizing** How did the Great Migration affect the political power of African Americans in the North?

Critical Thinking

4. **Big Ideas** What actions did the NAACP take to expand political rights for African Americans?
5. **Organizing** Use a graphic organizer similar to the one below to describe the impact of the Harlem Renaissance on U.S. society.

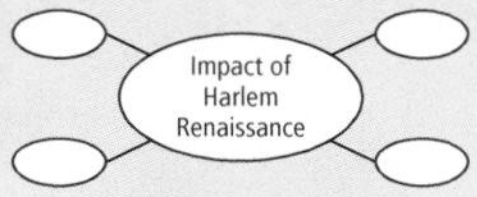

6. **Analyzing Visuals** Look at the photographs of Harlem Renaissance writers on page 617. Select one person and write a description of him or her, based only on what you see in the photo.

Writing About History

7. **Descriptive Writing** Imagine that you witnessed the African American men of the 369th Infantry, who had come back from the war, march through Manhattan and home to Harlem. Write a paragraph describing your feelings upon seeing these men.

History ONLINE
Study Central™ To review this section, go to glencoe.com and click on Study Central.

W Writing Support

Persuasive Writing Have students find out more about Marcus Garvey and the "Back to Africa" movement and write a letter to President Coolidge giving an opinion about Garvey. OL

✓Reading Check

Answer:
They saw themselves as entitled to all the rights of citizens.

Assess

History ONLINE

Study Central™ provides summaries, interactive games, and online graphic organizers to help students review content.

Close

Summarizing Ask: How did African Americans influence American society in the 1920s? *(They contributed to the arts and gained political power as they moved to northern cities.)* OL

Section 5 REVIEW

Answers

1. All definitions can be found in the section and the Glossary.
2. distinctive orchestration and improvisation; Ellington's music had "soul"
3. created a strong voting bloc
4. lobbied and worked through the courts
5. literature, new styles of music, theater, political influence
6. Answers will vary, but descriptions should accurately reflect the image.
7. Students' paragraphs should focus on emotional responses.

Determining Cause and Effect The Visual Summary lists causes of prosperity and its effects on society. Ask students to use the information on the page to create a time line of the era's events. Display the time lines in the classroom. OL

Descriptive Writing Have students select the one characteristic or event that they believe is symbolic of the 1920s. Examples may include Prohibition, the rise of the automobile, jazz, the Harlem Renaissance, Lindbergh's flight, and the arts and literature of the era. Have students write a letter describing their chosen event or characteristic to a friend. Remind students to use descriptive words and terms in their letters. Have volunteers share their letters with the class. OL

Chapter 17 Visual Summary

STUDY TO GO — You can study anywhere, anytime by downloading quizzes and flashcards to your PDA from glencoe.com.

Causes of Prosperity

Government's Role

- Limits interference with business
- Cuts taxes, debt, and government spending
- Imposes higher tariffs to protect young industries

Business Innovation and Technology

- Mass production creates a wide range of consumer goods sold at low prices.
- Technology such as autos, airplanes, and radio leads to new industries and economic growth.
- Business pays high wages.

New Consumer Society

- People have more disposable income and leisure time
- Credit is more readily available
- Mass advertising begins

▲ *The moving assembly line, pioneered by Henry Ford, made building automobiles efficient and greatly reduced prices.*

▲ *Joe "King" Oliver's band, with Louis Armstrong on slide trumpet, performs in Chicago in 1923, introducing the sound of jazz to America.*

A Changing Society

Cultural Changes

- A new youth culture with a "new morality" develops.
- Young people and women gain more independence.
- The working class enjoys more leisure time.
- New mass media in radio, movies, and sports develops.

Changes for African Americans

- Harlem Renaissance begins.
- Literature reveals racial pride and contempt of racism.
- Jazz and blues are popularized.
- Great Migration during the war creates strong African American voting blocs in Northern cities.
- First African American from the North is elected to Congress.
- NAACP battles segregation and discrimination.

Opposition to Change

- Nativists and a new Ku Klux Klan target immigrants, Catholics, Jews, and African Americans.
- Government imposes new quotas on immigration.
- Fundamentalists push for traditional values.
- Prohibition is implemented.

◀ *A federal agent enforces Prohibition by dumping barrels of illegal alcohol as neighborhood children watch.*

622 **Chapter 17** The Jazz Age

Hands-On Chapter Project
Step 6: Wrap Up

Creating a Memory Book

Step 6: Wrap Up Students will use their prior knowledge and the materials they researched to edit and revise the pages of the memory book.

Directions Give each student a page of the memory book. Each student will edit and revise the page as needed to create an attractive, informative page. They may wish to decorate the pages with other appropriate images, as well. The complete book may be used by the class to review the chapter and then displayed in the school.

Analyzing Information Students will determine the main topics presented and clarify the information to best represent the main ideas of the topic. OL

Chapter 17 Assessment

Reviewing Vocabulary

Directions: Choose the word or words that best complete each sentence.

1. What economic philosophy encouraged businesses to form trade associations?
   - **A** monopolies
   - **B** cooperative individualism
   - **C** moratorium
   - **D** supply-side economics

2. Companies introduced ________, which were programs that benefited workers by allowing them to participate in profit-sharing and to receive health benefits and pensions.
   - **A** normalcy
   - **B** open shop system
   - **C** supply-side economics
   - **D** welfare capitalism

3. Sacco and Vanzetti were ________, or people who opposed all forms of government.
   - **A** anarchists
   - **B** Communists
   - **C** bohemians
   - **D** creationists

4. Prohibition led to an increase in ________, or bars where people sold liquor illegally.
   - **A** mass media
   - **B** speakeasies
   - **C** police powers
   - **D** bootlegging

5. The artistic and unconventional, or ________ lifestyles of some urban neighborhoods spurred 1920s cultural innovations.
   - **A** bohemian
   - **B** anarchistic
   - **C** nativist
   - **D** open shop

Reviewing Main Ideas

Directions: Choose the best answers to the following questions.

Section 1 *(pp. 590–595)*

6. Teapot Dome is an example of a scandal during the administration of
   - **A** Calvin Coolidge.
   - **B** Warren G. Harding.
   - **C** Woodrow Wilson.
   - **D** William Howard Taft.

7. What agreement involved American banks giving loans to Germany to pay war reparations to France and Britain?
   - **A** the Washington Conference
   - **B** Kellogg-Briand Pact
   - **C** the Dawes Plan
   - **D** Four-Power Treaty

Section 2 *(pp. 596–603)*

8. Henry Ford's contribution to manufacturing was the
   - **A** expansion of the petroleum industry.
   - **B** requirement of open shop.
   - **C** idea of mass marketing.
   - **D** adoption of the assembly line.

9. The change in Americans' ideas about ________ resulted in more spending on what had once been luxury goods.
   - **A** mass production
   - **B** consumer credit
   - **C** advertising
   - **D** welfare capitalism

TEST-TAKING TIP

Make sure that you can define the chapter's vocabulary terms. You will see these words in questions on standardized tests. By understanding their meanings you can omit incorrect answers through the process of elimination.

Need Extra Help?

If You Missed Questions . . .	1	2	3	4	5	6	7	8	9
Go to Page . . .	593	602	604–605	609	610	590–592	594–595	596–598	600–601

GO ON

Answers and Analyses Reviewing Vocabulary

1. B In a trade association, businesses interact and "cooperate" with each other. A monopoly is a type of business, not a philosophy. A moratorium is an action taken. Supply-side economics is a philosophy, which may throw students off, so make sure students understand the difference between the two philosophies.

2. D Welfare means "benefit" or "well-being." Therefore, welfare capitalism provides benefits to workers. Help students who have trouble with this question connect welfare with the concept of helping people make improvements.

3. A For students who have trouble with this question, review the definitions of the answer choices. Communists believed in a classless society in which people would share wealth equally, but they did not oppose all forms of government. Creationists are people who believe in the creation story as told in the book of Genesis in the Bible. Bohemians are either people from Bohemia, or, in the context of the chapter, people who lived an unconventional lifestyle.

4. B Students who read the question carefully will have no trouble selecting the correct answer. The question specifies that the missing word is another word for a type of bar. A bar is a place. Choices *A*, *C*, and *D* are not places. Students who do not carefully read the question may select bootlegging as the correct answer, as it is related to Prohibition.

5. A Anarchists were opposed to government, while nativists were opposed to immigrants. Open shops referred to workplaces that did not require union membership.

Reviewing Main Ideas

6. B Warren G. Harding's administration was plagued with scandal. Harding was from Ohio, which may help students remember his connection with the Ohio Gang.

7. C The Washington Conference was a meeting, not an agreement. It is unlikely that a treaty would involve loans. The Kellogg-Briand Pact outlawed war. The Dawes Plan is correct. It was suggested by a diplomat named Charles G. Dawes.

8. D Remind students that the assembly line led to the mass production of the Model-T, the first automobile to be accessible to the masses. The use of the assembly line helped Ford keep the cost of the final product down.

9. B Only *B* makes sense in the context of the sentence. The rise in consumer credit resulted from changing American ideals, as a whole. In the past, being in debt was dishonorable. This change in attitude was reflected in the number of Americans using consumer credit to pay off luxury items over time.

10. A The Eighteenth Amendment, ratified in 1920, prohibited the sale or consumption of alcohol.

11. B Students may have trouble choosing between the two immigration acts listed in the answer choices: the Emergency Quota Act and the National Origins Act. However, the question asks which act restricted "each *national* group." This should clue students in to the correct answer—the National Origins Act.

12. A As two of the nation's largest cities, Chicago and New York were, of course, centers of industry, politics, and banking. However, the question does not ask about the cities, it asks about neighborhoods within the cities. These neighborhoods provided a nurturing environment for artists, writers, and musicians.

13. D To help students remember this, briefly review the Renaissance with them, explaining the artistic and social strides made in that period. Also explain that a renaissance of any kind is a revitalization or a revival. The Harlem Renaissance was a revival of African American culture. While the other answer choices are related to African Americans during that time period, none is broad enough to encompass all artistic developments of African Americans in the 1920s.

14. B Black nationalism differed from other African American movements in that it supported pride in African American culture, including independence from whites. Integration and political improvement was an idea of the NAACP. Marcus Garvey supported the "back to Africa" idea, not back to Jamaica. He was deported to Jamaica.

Chapter 17 Assessment

Section 3 *(pp. 604–609)*

10. The passage of the Eighteenth Amendment was seen as a victory for

- **A** opponents of alcohol consumption.
- **B** supporters of women's suffrage.
- **C** nativists.
- **D** Sacco and Vanzetti.

11. What act restricted immigration to 2 percent of each national group represented in the 1890 U.S. Census?

- **A** Emergency Quota Act
- **B** National Origins Act
- **C** Reclamation Act
- **D** Clayton Antitrust Act

Section 4 *(pp. 610–613)*

12. Chicago's South Side and New York's Greenwich Village were centers for

- **A** the arts.
- **B** industry.
- **C** politics.
- **D** banking.

Section 5 *(pp. 616–621)*

13. The artistic developments of African Americans in the 1920s were known as the

- **A** Great Migration.
- **B** Saint Louis blues.
- **C** New Orleans sound.
- **D** Harlem Renaissance.

14. What was an idea of black nationalism?

- **A** integration and political improvement in society
- **B** separation and independence from whites
- **C** emigration from the United States to Jamaica
- **D** support for the arts as a way to improve African American society

Critical Thinking

Directions: Choose the best answers to the following questions.

15. What effect did greater education and job opportunities for women create?

- **A** Many women began earning as much money as men did.
- **B** Women contributed to both scientific and artistic knowledge.
- **C** More women preferred to remain at home.
- **D** Most women working outside the home gained leadership positions.

Base your answer to question 16 on the map below and on your knowledge of Chapter 17.

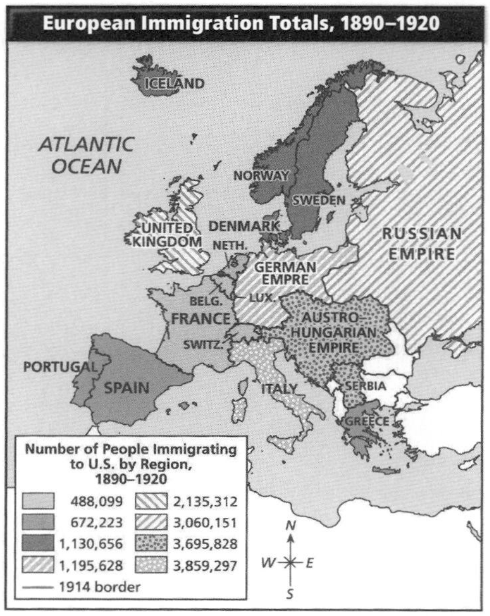

16. Which nation or empire sent the greatest number of immigrants to the United States between 1890 and 1920?

- **A** Italy
- **B** Russian Empire
- **C** German Empire
- **D** Spain

Need Extra Help?							
If You Missed Questions . . .	10	11	12	13	14	15	16
Go to Page . . .	609	606	610–612	616	621	606–607	605–606

GO ON

Critical Thinking

15. B Students should approach this question as a cause-and-effect question. Although women had greater education and job opportunities, it did not lead to equality with men in the workplace. Therefore, most women working outside the home did not achieve leadership positions. By the same token, women did not earn as much as men. It does not make sense that greater opportunity would cause more women to remain at home. However, these opportunities allowed women to make scientific and artistic contributions.

16. A Using the key, students should first find the color or pattern that represents the greatest number of immigrants: 3,859,297. They should then find this area on the map. Italy is correct.

17. What written agreement declared war illegal?

- **A** the Washington Conference
- **B** the Dawes Plan
- **C** the Kellogg-Briand Pact
- **D** the League of Nations Charter

18. What was a principal reason for rapid economic growth in the United States during the 1920s?

- **A** prosperity of American agriculture
- **B** increase of American imports
- **C** development of many new consumer goods
- **D** increased spending on defense

Analyze the cartoon and answer the question that follows. Base your answer on the cartoon and your knowledge of Chapter 17.

19. What does the cartoon imply about Coolidge?

- **A** He was trying to select which party to support in the next election.
- **B** He wanted to control the congressional leadership.
- **C** He wanted to cut back on unnecessary government expenditures.
- **D** He wanted to increase taxes and government spending.

Document-Based Questions

Directions: Analyze the document and answer the short-answer questions that follow the document.

Charles Lindbergh, who made the first transatlantic flight from New York to Paris in 1927, later wrote a book about the experience. He titled the book after the plane he flew, *The Spirit of St. Louis.* The following excerpt is from that book:

> *"What endless hours I worked over this chart in California, measuring, drawing, rechecking each 100-mile segment of its great-circle route, each theoretical hour of my flight. . . . A few lines and figures on a strip of paper, a few ounces of weight, this [map] strip is my key to Europe. With it, I can fly the ocean. With it, that black dot at the other end marked 'Paris' will turn into a famous French city with an aerodrome where I can land. But without this chart, all my years of training, all that went into preparing for this flight, no matter how perfectly the engine runs or how long the fuel lasts, all would be as directionless as those columns of smoke in the New England valleys behind me."*
>
> —from *The Spirit of St. Louis*

20. What does Lindbergh believe is the most valuable tool he has?

21. What conclusions can you draw about Lindbergh as a person, based on this excerpt?

Extended Response

22. The Harding and Coolidge administrations promoted economic prosperity and world peace. Consider how both administrations attempted this difficult task. Write an essay that explains the methods used to accomplish the goal of economic and political stability worldwide. How successful was each administration? Your essay should include an introduction, several paragraphs, and a conclusion. Use relevant facts and details to support your conclusion.

STOP

History ONLINE
For additional test practice, use Self-Check Quizzes—Chapter 17 at glencoe.com.

Need Extra Help?						
If You Missed Questions . . .	17	18	19	20	21	22
Go to Page . . .	595	595–600	R18	625	R19	590–593

Document-Based Questions

20. Lindbergh believes his most valuable tool is the map strips of his journey that he has so carefully drawn and checked. Lindbergh writes that "this map strip is my key to Europe."

21. Lindbergh is careful, detail-oriented, and patient. If students have trouble with this conclusion, read the passage aloud to class, and ask student to brainstorm their impressions and give reasons for them.

Extended Response

22. Students' essays will vary, but must include discussion of both Harding's and Coolidge's administrations and should stay focused on economic improvement and international diplomacy. Students should provide well-reasoned assessments of the success of each administration.

17. C The Washington Conference was the impetus for the Kellogg-Briand Pact, which outlawed war. The Dawes Plan was related to helping Germany repay war debts. The League of Nations charter set up the League, but it did not outlaw war.

18. C The development of new goods helped spur growth by raising wages and encouraging consumption. *A*, *B* and *D* were not factors for growth.

19. C In the cartoon, Coolidge is making elephants and donkeys jump through hoops labeled economy. *A* and *B* don't make sense as they don't deal with economic issues. *D* doesn't work because jumping through hoops usually implies making something harder, in this case government action. So *C* is the correct answer.

History ONLINE
Have students visit the Web site at glencoe.com to review Chapter 17 and take the Self-Check Quiz.

Need Extra Help?
Have students refer to the pages listed if they miss any of the questions.

Chapter 18 Planning Guide

Key to Ability Levels	
BL Below Level	**AL** Above Level
OL On Level	**ELL** English Language Learners

Key to Teaching Resources	
Print Material	Transparency
CD-ROM or DVD	

Levels				Resources	Chapter Opener	Section 1	Section 2	Section 3	Chapter Assess
BL	OL	AL	ELL						
FOCUS									
BL	OL	AL	ELL	**Daily Focus Skills Transparencies**		18-1	18-2	18-3	
TEACH									
	OL	AL		**Geography and History, URB**				p. 3	
BL	OL		ELL	**Reading Essentials and Note-Taking Guide***		p. 201	p. 204	p. 207	
	OL			**Historical Analysis Skills Activity, URB**		p. 54			
BL	OL		ELL	**Guided Reading Activities, URB***		p. 78	p. 79	p. 80	
BL	OL	AL	ELL	**Content Vocabulary Activity, URB***			p. 59		
BL	OL	AL	ELL	**Academic Vocabulary Activity, URB**		p. 61			
	OL	AL		**Critical Thinking Skills Activity, URB**			p. 64		
BL	OL		ELL	**Reading Skills Activity, URB**			p. 53		
BL			ELL	**English Learner Activity, URB**			p. 57		
	OL	AL		**Reinforcing Skills Activity, URB**		p. 63			
BL	OL	AL	ELL	**Differentiated Instruction Activity, URB**			p. 55		
BL	OL		ELL	**Time Line Activity, URB**				p. 65	
	OL			**Linking Past and Present Activity, URB**			p. 66		
BL	OL	AL	ELL	**American Art and Music Activity, URB**			p. 71		
BL	OL	AL	ELL	**Interpreting Political Cartoons Activity, URB**		p. 73			
BL	OL	AL		**Economics and History Activity, URB**			p. 7		
		AL		**Enrichment Activity, URB**				p. 76	
BL	OL	AL	ELL	**American Biographies**			✓		
BL	OL	AL	ELL	**Primary Source Reading, URB**		p. 67	p. 69		
BL	OL	AL	ELL	**The Living Constitution***	✓	✓	✓	✓	✓
	OL	AL		**American History Primary Source Documents Library**	✓	✓	✓	✓	✓
BL	OL	AL	ELL	**Unit Map Overlay Transparencies**	✓	✓	✓	✓	✓
BL	OL	AL	ELL	**Differentiated Instruction for the American History Classroom**	✓	✓	✓	✓	✓
BL	OL	AL	ELL	**StudentWorks™ Plus**	✓	✓	✓	✓	✓

Note: Please refer to the *Unit 6 Resource Book* for this chapter's URB materials.

* Also available in Spanish

TeacherWorks Plus
All-In-One Planner and Resource Center

- Interactive Lesson Planner
- Interactive Teacher Edition
- Fully editable blackline masters
- Section Spotlight Videos Launch
- Differentiated Lesson Plans
- Printable reports of daily assignments
- Standards Tracking System

Levels BL	OL	AL	ELL		Resources	Chapter Opener	Section 1	Section 2	Section 3	Chapter Assess
					TEACH *(continued)*					
BL	OL	AL	ELL	CD	American Music Hits Through History CD	✓	✓	✓	✓	✓
BL	OL	AL	ELL	Print	Unit Time Line Transparencies and Activities	✓	✓	✓	✓	✓
BL	OL	AL	ELL	Print	Cause and Effect Transparencies, Strategies, and Activities	✓	✓	✓	✓	✓
BL	OL	AL	ELL	Print	Why It Matters Transparencies, Strategies, and Activities	✓	✓	✓	✓	✓
BL	OL	AL	ELL	Print	American Issues	✓	✓	✓	✓	✓
	OL	AL	ELL	Print	American Art and Architecture Transparencies, Strategies, and Activities	✓	✓	✓	✓	✓
BL	OL	AL		Print	High School American History Literature Library	✓	✓	✓	✓	✓
BL	OL	AL	ELL	CD	*The American Vision* Video Program	✓	✓	✓	✓	✓
Teacher Resources				Print	Strategies for Success	✓	✓	✓	✓	✓
Teacher Resources				Print	Success with English Learners	✓	✓	✓	✓	✓
Teacher Resources				Print	Reading Strategies and Activities for the Social Studies Classroom	✓	✓	✓	✓	✓
Teacher Resources				CD	Presentation Plus! with MindJogger CheckPoint	✓	✓	✓	✓	✓
					ASSESS					
BL	OL	AL	ELL	Print	Section Quizzes and Chapter Tests*		p. 257	p. 258	p. 259	p. 261
BL	OL	AL	ELL	Print	Authentic Assessment With Rubrics					p. 41
BL	OL	AL	ELL	Print	Standardized Test Practice Workbook					p. 40
BL	OL	AL	ELL	CD	*ExamView® Assessment Suite*		18-1	18-2	18-3	Ch. 18
					CLOSE					
BL			ELL	Print	Reteaching Activity, URB					p. 75
BL	OL		ELL	Print	Reading and Study Skills Foldables™	p. 71				

✓ Chapter- or unit-based activities applicable to all sections in this chapter.

Using the Lesson Planner

Teach With Technology

What is the Lesson Planner?

The TeacherWorks™ Plus Lesson Planner is a practical tool for creating and organizing daily lesson plans using an interactive calendar.

How can the Lesson Planner help me?

The Lesson Planner makes it easy to see, at a glance, the resources you have chosen to use for each class on any given day. Using a simple drag-and-drop format, you can generate lesson plans using any number of ancillary titles included in the TeacherWorks™ Plus software, as well as Internet links, documents, files, and programs of your choosing. Once a lesson plan is created, the Lesson Planner serves as a launching point for these resources.

The Lesson Planner is a feature of TeacherWorks™ Plus.

History ONLINE
Visit glencoe.com and enter ***QuickPass***™ code TAV9399c18T for Chapter 18 resources.

You can easily launch a wide range of digital products from your computer's desktop with the McGraw-Hill Social Studies widget.

	Student	Teacher	Parent
Media Library			
• Section Audio	●		●
• Spanish Audio Summaries	●		●
• Section Spotlight Videos	●	●	●
***The American Vision* Online Learning Center (Web Site)**			
• StudentWorks™ Plus Online	●	●	●
• Multilingual Glossary	●	●	●
• Study-to-Go	●	●	●
• Chapter Overviews	●	●	●
• Self-Check Quizzes	●	●	●
• Student Web Activities	●	●	●
• ePuzzles and Games	●	●	●
• Vocabulary eFlashcards	●	●	●
• In Motion Animations	●	●	●
• Study Central™	●	●	●
• Web Activity Lesson Plans		●	
• Vocabulary PuzzleMaker	●	●	●
• Historical Thinking Activities		●	
• Beyond the Textbook	●	●	●

Reading Support From Jamestown Education

- **Timed Readings Plus in Social Studies** helps students increase their reading rate and fluency while maintaining comprehension. The 400-word passages are similar to those found on state and national assessments.
- **Reading in the Content Area: Social Studies** concentrates on six essential reading skills that help students better comprehend what they read. The book includes 75 high-interest nonfiction passages written at increasing levels of difficulty.
- **Reading Social Studies** includes strategic reading instruction and vocabulary support in Social Studies content for both ELLs and native speakers of English.

www.jamestowneducation.com

Biography / A&E Home Video / The History Channel

The following videotape programs are available from Glencoe as supplements to this chapter:

- The Stock Exchange (ISBN 0-76-700562-7)
- The Great Depression (ISBN 0-76-700859-6)

To order, call Glencoe at 1-800-334-7344. To find classroom resources to accompany many of these videos, check the following home pages:

A&E Television: www.aetv.com
The History Channel: www.historychannel.com

National Geographic

Index to National Geographic Magazine:

The following articles relate to this chapter:

- "The Okies—Beyond the Dust Bowl," by William Howarth, September 1984.
- "Nary a Drop to Spare: Drought Grips the West," by Chris Carroll, July 2005.

National Geographic Society Products To order the following, call National Geographic at 1-800-368-2728:

- ZipZapMap! USA (ZipZapMap!)

Access National Geographic's new, dynamic MapMachine Web site and other geography resources at:
www.nationalgeographic.com
www.nationalgeographic.com/maps

Reading List Generator CD-ROM — Glencoe BookLink 3

Use this database to search more than 30,000 titles to create a customized reading list for your students.

- Reading lists can be organized by students' reading level, author, genre, theme, or area of interest.
- The database provides Degrees of Reading Power™ (DRP) and Lexile™ readability scores for all selections.
- A brief summary of each selection is included.

Leveled reading suggestions for this chapter:

For students at a Grade 8 reading level:
- ***Cat Running,*** by Zilpha Keatley Snyder

For students at a Grade 9 reading level:
- ***A Renaissance in Harlem: Lost Voices of an American Community,*** by Lionel C. Bascom

For students at a Grade 10 reading level:
- ***Seabiscuit: An American Legend,*** by Laura Hillenbrand

For students at a Grade 11 reading level:
- ***Children of the Dust Bowl: The True Story of the School at Weedpatch Camp,*** by Jerry Stanley

For students at a Grade 12 reading level:
- ***Herbert Hoover,*** by David M. Holford

Introducing
Chapter 18

Focus

MAKING CONNECTIONS
What Causes Depressions?
Discuss with students the two questions posed on p. 399. If you live in or near a region of the country where many traditional, manufacturing jobs have been lost, use that experience to enhance discussion and give students a sense of the scope of the Great Depression. Invite students to imagine life in their community if one in every four people lost his or her job. **OL** **ELL**

Teach

The Big Ideas

As students study the chapter, remind them to consider the section-based Big Ideas included in each section's Guide to Reading. The **Essential Questions** in the activities below tie in to the Big Ideas and help students think about and understand important chapter concepts. In addition, the Hands-on Chapter Projects, with their culminating activities, relate the content from each section to the Big Ideas. These activities build on each other as students progress through the chapter. Section activities culminate in the wrap-up activity on the Visual Summary page.

Chapter 18

The Great Depression Begins

1929–1932

Women and children wait in a bread line at New York City's New Hope Mission in the early 1930s.

U.S. PRESIDENTS

Hoover 1929–1933

U.S. EVENTS

1929
- Stock market crashes on Black Tuesday

1930
- Congress passes Hawley-Smoot Tariff

1929 — 1930 — 1931

WORLD EVENTS

1928
- Soviets introduce First Five-Year Plan to industrialize the country

1929
- Mexico passes 8-hour day, right to strike, and unemployment insurance

1930
- France creates a health and old age insurance plan

1931
- Collapse of large Austrian bank triggers bank failures across Europe

626 **Chapter 18** The Great Depression Begins

Section 1

The Causes of the Great Depression

Essential Question: What factors led to the Great Depression? *(inflated stock prices, overproduction, high tariffs, and mistakes by the Federal Reserve Board)* Point out that in Section 1 students will learn about the root causes of the Great Depression. **OL**

Section 2

Life During the Depression

Essential Question: How did people cope with life's struggles during the Great Depression? *(They escaped through movies and popular culture. Some, especially farmers living in the Dust Bowl, went west to seek better jobs.)* Tell students that in Section 2 they will learn about the increased problems during the Depression and how people struggled to survive. **OL**

Chapter Audio

Making Connections

What Causes Depressions?

In the 1930s, the Great Depression caused high unemployment, business failures, and farm foreclosures. Many people lost their homes and savings and became willing to vote for politicians who offered new approaches to solving the crisis.

- ***What kind of political and social problems do you think depressions cause?***
- ***Why do you think the Great Depression was worse than other economic slowdowns?***

1931
- National Credit Corporation is created

1932
- Drought begins on Great Plains
- Bonus Marchers arrive in Washington, D.C.

Franklin D. Roosevelt 1933–1945

1932

1933

1931
- Japan invades Manchuria

1932
- Government-induced famine begins in USSR, killing millions
- Unemployment in Germany reaches 6 million

FOLDABLES

Analyzing Popular Culture Create a Two-Tab Book Foldable to research the way people coped with adversity during the Depression. As you read the chapter, list examples of the hardships people endured in real life and the kinds of entertainment that flourished.

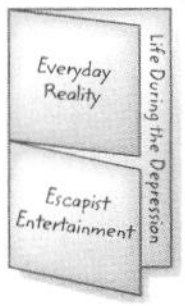

History ONLINE Visit glencoe.com and enter *QuickPass*™ code TAV9846c18 for Chapter 18 resources.

Section 3

Hoover Responds to the Depression

Essential Question: How did Hoover's policies attempt to lessen the Great Depression? *(He organized a series of conferences with business leaders and increased funding for public works. He created the National Credit Corporation after the Federal Reserve Board refused his request to put more money into circulation. He set up the Reconstruction Finance Corporation to offer businesses loans.)* Tell students that in Section 3 they will learn about Hoover's strategies for ending the Great Depression and why they failed. **OL**

Introducing **Chapter**

More About the Photo

Visual Literacy The lyrics to "Brother, Can You Spare a Dime?" were written by E.Y. Harburg in the early 1930s. First recorded by crooner Rudy Vallee in 1932, the song became the signature song of the Great Depression:

"They used to tell me I was building a dream
With peace and glory ahead.
Why should I be standing in line
Just waiting for bread?

"Once I built a railroad, made it run,
Made it race against time.
Once I built a railroad, now it's done,
Brother, can you spare a dime?"

FOLDABLES Study Organizer **Dinah Zike's Foldables**

Dinah Zike's Foldables are three-dimensional, interactive graphic organizers that help students practice basic writing skills, review vocabulary terms, and identify main ideas. Instructions for creating and using Foldables can be found in the Appendix at the end of this book and in the *Dinah Zike's Reading and Study Skills Foldables* booklet.

History ONLINE

Visit glencoe.com and enter *QuickPass*™ code TAV9399c18T for Chapter 18 resources, including a Chapter Overview, Study Central™, Study-to-Go, Student Web Activity, Self-Check Quiz, and other materials.

Focus

Bellringer

Daily Focus Transparency 18-1

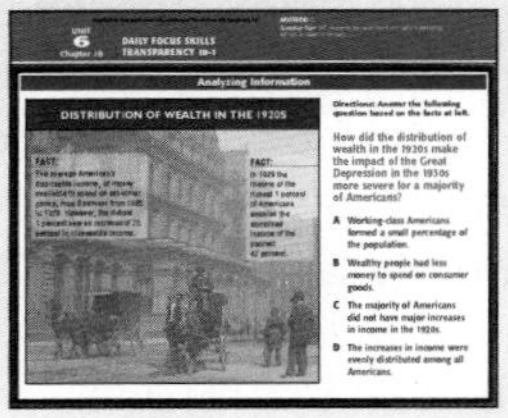

Guide to Reading

Answers: Hoover: Republican, Quaker, engineer, secretary of commerce; Issues: prosperity Smith: Democrat, Catholic, four-time governor of New York; Issues: Catholicism

Section Spotlight Video

To generate student interest and provide a springboard for class discussion, access the Chapter 18, Section 1 video at glencoe.com or on the video DVD.

Section 1

Section Audio   Spotlight Video

The Causes of the Great Depression

Guide to Reading

Big Ideas

Economics and Society Stock speculation on an unregulated stock market put investors and banks at risk in the 1920s.

Content Vocabulary
- stock market *(p. 628)*
- bull market *(p. 629)*
- margin *(p. 629)*
- margin call *(p. 629)*
- speculation *(p. 629)*
- bank run *(p. 631)*
- installment *(p. 633)*

Academic Vocabulary
- collapse *(p. 628)*
- invest *(p. 629)*
- sum *(p. 631)*

People and Events to Identify
- Alfred E. Smith *(p. 628)*
- Black Tuesday *(p. 630)*
- Hawley-Smoot Tariff *(p. 633)*

Reading Strategy

Categorizing As you read about the election of 1928, complete a graphic organizer similar to the one below comparing the backgrounds and issues of the presidential candidates.

1928 Presidential Campaign		
Candidate	Background	Issues

Although the 1920s were prosperous, speculation in the stock market, risky lending policies, overproduction, and uneven income distribution eventually undermined the economy and led to the Great Depression.

The Long Bull Market

MAIN Idea A strong economy helped Herbert Hoover win the 1928 election, but increasing speculation in the stock market set the stage for a crash.

HISTORY AND YOU Have you ever taken a risk while playing a game or sport? How did you decide if the risk was worth it? Read on to learn about the risks people were willing to take in the stock market in the 1920s.

The economic **collapse** that began in 1929 seemed unimaginable only a year earlier. In the 1928 election, both presidential candidates tried to paint a rosy picture of the future. Republican Herbert Hoover declared, "We are nearer to the final triumph over poverty than ever before in the history of any land."

The Election of 1928

When Calvin Coolidge declined to run for reelection in 1928, the Republicans nominated his secretary of commerce, Herbert Hoover. Hoover was well-known to Americans because he had run the Food Administration during World War I. The Democrats chose **Alfred E. Smith,** four-time governor of New York. Smith was the first Roman Catholic to win a major party's nomination for president.

Smith's beliefs became a campaign issue. Some Protestants claimed that the Catholic Church financed the Democratic Party and would rule the United States if Smith became president. These slurs embarrassed Hoover, a Quaker, and he tried to quash them, but the charges damaged Smith's candidacy.

Smith's biggest challenge, however, was the prosperity of the 1920s, for which the Republicans took full credit. Hoover defeated Smith by more than 6 million votes and won the Electoral College in a landslide, 444 to 87. On March 4, 1929, an audience of 50,000 stood in the rain to hear Hoover's inaugural speech. "I have no fears for the future of our country," Hoover said. "It is bright with hope."

The Stock Market Soars

The optimism that swept Hoover into the White House also drove stock prices to new highs. Sometimes the **stock market** experiences

Resource Manager

R Reading Strategies	C Critical Thinking	D Differentiated Instruction	W Writing Support	S Skill Practice
Teacher Edition • Predicting, p. 630 • Analyzing Text Structure, p. 631 • Making Connections, p. 632 • Act. Prior Know., p. 633 **Additional Resources** • Guid. Read. Act., URB p. 78	**Teacher Edition** • Analyzing Prim. Sources, p. 630 **Additional Resources** • Prim. Source Read., URB p. 67 • Intr. Polit. Cartoon, URB p. 73 • Quizzes and Tests, p. 257	**Teacher Edition** • Special Ed., p. 632	**Additional Resources** • Academic Vocab. Act., URB p. 61	**Teacher Edition** • Analyzing Maps, p. 629 • Reading Graphs, p. 631 **Additional Resources** • Hist. Analysis Skills, URB p. 54 • Reinforcing Skills Act., URB p. 63 • Read. Essen., p. 201

PRIMARY SOURCE

Hoover and "Rugged Individualism"

S

Presidential Candidate	Popular Vote	% of Popular Vote	Electoral Vote
Hoover	21,392,190	58.18%	444
Smith	15,016,443	40.84%	87

PRIMARY SOURCE

"We were challenged with a peacetime choice between the American system of rugged individualism and a European philosophy of diametrically opposed doctrines—doctrines of paternalism and state socialism. . . . [T]hese ideas would have meant the destruction of self-government through centralization of government. It would have meant the undermining of . . . individual initiative and enterprise . . .

". . . You cannot extend the mastery of the government over the daily working life of a people without at the same time making it the master of the people's souls and thoughts. . . . Free speech does not live many hours after free industry and free commerce die. . . . Every step of bureaucratizing of the business of our country poisons the very roots of liberalism—that is, political equality, free speech, free assembly, free press, and equality of opportunity. It is the road not to more liberty, but to less liberty."

—Herbert Hoover, speech delivered October 22, 1928

DBQ Document-Based Questions

1. **Contrasting** Against what other system does Hoover contrast "rugged individualism"?
2. **Analyzing Primary Sources** What does Hoover believe is at stake if free industry and free commerce die? Do you agree or disagree? Explain your position.

a long period of rising stock prices, or a **bull market.** In the late 1920s a prolonged bull market convinced many people to **invest** in stocks. By 1929 approximately 10 percent of American households owned stocks.

As the market continued to soar, many investors began buying stocks on **margin,** making only a small cash down payment (as low as 10 percent of the price). With $1,000, an investor could buy $10,000 worth of stock. The other $9,000 would come as a loan from a stockbroker, who earned both a commission on the sale and interest on the loan. The broker held the stock as collateral.

If the price of the stock kept rising, the investor could make a profit. For example, the investor who borrowed to buy $10,000 worth of stock had only to wait for it to rise to $11,000 in value. The investor could then sell the stock, repay the loan, and make $1,000 in profit. The problem came if the stock price began to fall. To protect the loan, a broker could issue a **margin call,** demanding the investor repay the loan at once. As a result, many investors were very sensitive to any fall in stock prices. If prices fell, they had to sell quickly, or they might not be able to repay their loans.

Before the late 1920s, the prices investors paid for stocks had generally reflected the stocks' true value. If a company made a profit or had good future sales prospects, its stock price rose; prices fell when earnings dropped. In the late 1920s, however, many investors bid prices up without considering a company's earnings and profits. Buyers, hoping for a quick windfall, engaged in **speculation.** They bet the market would continue to climb, thus enabling them to sell the stock and make money quickly.

Reading Check **Summarizing** What was the stock market like in the 1920s?

Teach

S Skill Practice

Analyzing Maps Point out the 1928 election map in the Primary Source. **Ask:** What section of the nation supported Smith? Why might this be surprising? *(The South supported Smith, which might be surprising because Smith was Catholic, and the Ku Klux Klan, much of which centered in the South, was anti-Catholic.)* OL

DBQ Document Based Questions

Answers:

1. European paternalism and state socialism
2. Free speech and the other freedoms of the Bill of Rights: free assembly, free press, political equality and equality of opportunity; students' opinions will vary but should be supported.

Reading Check

Answer: The stock market was a bull market, a long period of rising stock prices that fueled speculation.

Hands-On Chapter Project Step 1

Making a Storyboard

Step 1: "Seeing" the Story Have small groups work together to create storyboards for the chapter content.

Essential Question Ask: What was life like during the Depression?

Directions Divide the class into small groups. Tell students that they will be presenting section content in storyboard format, as if they are going to make a short film. Students can create a character who is an omniscient narrator or one who is part of the story and responds to events as they occur. Students can also incorporate historical figures mentioned in the text. Remind students as they read Section 1 to look for events or ideas that can be illustrated.

Putting It Together Suggest that students divide the work according to their skills, with one student doing the drawing, another writing captions, and so on. OL

(Chapter Project continued on page 635)

R Reading Strategy

Predicting Invite students to predict how the stockbroker and Groucho Marx fared in the Great Depression. *(Students may suggest that a film star would have new opportunities to make another fortune, but a stockbroker during a financial depression would probably not fare well.)* **OL**

C Critical Thinking

Analyzing Primary Sources Have a volunteer read aloud the Primary Source quotation. **Ask:** What descriptions show the stockbroker's despair? *(He is sitting with his head in his hands; the floor is messy with ticker tape.)* **BL**

Turning Point

Answer:
Students' answers will vary. Students should note that many cities and people needed help, but had nowhere to go for help.

The Great Crash

MAIN Idea Rising stock prices led to risky investment practices; when the stock market crashed, banks were in trouble.

HISTORY AND YOU Have you ever paid more for something than it was worth? Read on to learn why the stock market collapsed in 1929.

The bull market lasted only as long as investors continued putting new money into it. By the latter half of 1929, the market was running out of new customers. In September, professional investors sensed danger and began to sell off their holdings. Prices slipped. Other investors sold shares to pay the interest on their brokerage loans. Prices fell further.

The Stock Market Crash

R On Monday, October 21, 1929, the comedian Groucho Marx was awakened by a telephone call from his broker. "You'd better get down here with some cash to cover your margin," the broker said. The stock market had plunged. The dazed comedian had to pay back the money he had borrowed to buy stocks, which were now selling for far less than he had paid for them. Other brokers made similar margin calls. Nervous customers put their stocks up for sale at a frenzied pace, driving the market into a tailspin.

On October 24, a day that came to be called Black Thursday, the market plummeted further. Marx was wiped out. He had earned a small fortune from plays and films, but now it was gone, and he was deeply in debt. His son recalled his final visit to the brokerage firm, as Groucho spotted his broker: R

PRIMARY SOURCE

"He was sitting in front of the now-stilled ticker-tape machine, with his head buried in his hands. Ticker tape was strewn around him on the floor, and the place . . . looked as if it hadn't been swept out in a week. Groucho tapped [him] on the shoulder and said, 'Aren't you the fellow who said nothing could go wrong?' 'I guess I made a mistake,' the broker wearily replied. 'No, I'm the one who made a mistake,' snapped Groucho. 'I listened to you.'" C

—quoted in *1929: The Year of the Great Crash*

The following week, on October 29, a day that was later dubbed **Black Tuesday,** prices took the steepest dive yet. That day, almost 16 million shares of stock were sold; the stock

Turning Point

A Crash Becomes a Depression

When the stock market crashed in October 1929, it exposed many weaknesses in the American economy. By 1932 over 25 percent of American workers were unemployed. Charities could not help all who were in need. Many cities had gone bankrupt and newly created state relief agencies had insufficient funds to help.

The Great Depression prompted major political changes. When Franklin D. Roosevelt ran for president in 1932, he had offered few details about how he would save the economy. Once in office, however, he launched a massive program to rescue the banking system, stabilize industry, and aid the unemployed. By the late 1930s, the federal government had taken on huge new responsibilities for the health of the economy and welfare of American families.

ANALYZING HISTORY Do you think the Great Depression required government intervention to resolve? Write a brief essay explaining your opinion.

Stock Prices, 1920–1932

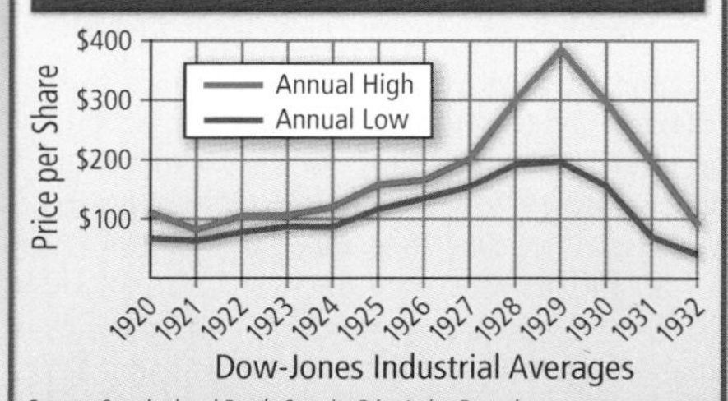

Source: Standard and Poor's *Security Price Index Record.*

▼ *Mayhem erupts on Wall Street after the stock market crash.*

Additional Support

Activity: Economics Connection

Evaluating Businesses wanting to expand during the prosperous 1920s increased the number of stock shares available to the public, feeding the buying frenzy. The number of stockholders of American Telephone and Telegraph (AT&T) increased dramatically. In 1920, there were 139,000 stockholders; ten years later, the number had grown to 567,000. Speculation inflated stocks' value. In 1925 stocks were valued at $27 billion. That figure increased to more than $87 billion by October 1929.

The problems on Wall Street after the crash affected both the unemployed and the employed. Between 1929 and 1931, average working hours per week had dropped from 48 to 38 hours. In addition, wages continued to fall. In 1929 the average weekly salary was $28.50. It fell to $18.46 in 1932. **Ask:** Could government regulation of the stock market have prevented the Wall Street crash? *(Students may say that the economy was headed for a fall, regardless of what the government did.)* **OL** market lost between $10 billion and $15 billion in value. By mid-November, stock prices had dropped by more than one-third. Some $30 billion was lost, a **sum** roughly equal to the total wages Americans earned in 1929. Although the stock market crash was not the major cause of the Great Depression, it undermined the economy's ability to overcome other weaknesses.

Banks Begin to Close

R The market crash severely weakened the nation's banks in two ways. First, by 1929 banks had loaned nearly $6 billion to stock speculators. Second, many banks had invested depositors' money in the stock market, hoping for higher returns than they could get by using the money for loans.

When stock values collapsed, banks lost money on their investments, and speculators defaulted on their loans. Having suffered serious losses, many banks cut back drastically on the loans they made. With less credit available, consumers and businesses were not able to borrow as much money. This helped to send the economy into a recession.

Some banks could not absorb the losses they suffered and were forced to close. The government did not insure bank deposits, so if a bank collapsed, customers, including those who did not invest in the stock market, lost their savings. Bank failures in 1929 and 1930 created a crisis of confidence in the banking system.

News of bank failures worried Americans. Some depositors made runs on banks, causing the banks to collapse. A **bank run** takes place when many depositors decide to withdraw their money at one time, usually because of fear that the bank is going to collapse.

Most banks make a profit by lending money received from depositors and collecting interest on the loans. The bank keeps only a fraction of depositors' money in reserve to cover daily business and withdrawals. Usually, that reserve is enough to meet the bank's needs. If too many people withdraw their money, however, the bank will collapse. More than 10 percent of the nation's banks—nearly 3,500—had closed by 1932.

Reading Check **Determining Cause and Effect** What chain of events led to the economic crash of 1929?

S

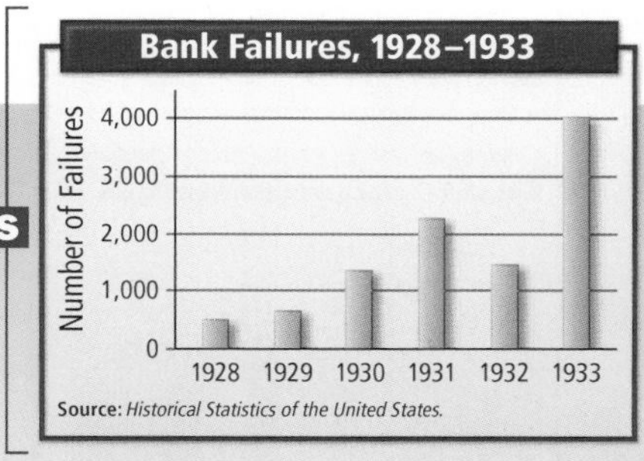

▼ *The homeless lived in shacks in shantytowns known as Hoovervilles.*

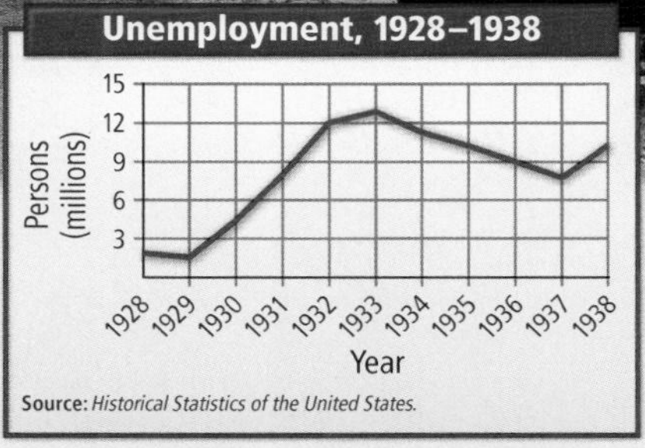

◀ *Depositors at a New York bank line up to withdraw their money in 1930.*

R Reading Strategy

Analyzing Text Structure Have students read the first paragraph under "Banks Begin to Close." Discuss how the text makes the information understandable and clear. *(The text says there are two ways the nation's banks were weakened. The next two sentences begin with the words* First *and* Second.*)* **OL**

S Skill Practice

Reading Graphs Ask students to look at the graph showing bank failures. **Ask:** Which two years had nearly similar numbers of closings? *(1928 and 1929; 1930 and 1932)* **Ask:** Based on these statistics, why might people have been hopeful in 1932? *(The number of bank closings decreased from 1931 to 1932.)* **BL**

Reading Check

Answer:
Fewer investors entered the market, professional investors sold off their stock holdings, prices fell, others sold shares to pay interest on brokerage loans, prices fell again, market collapsed on Black Thursday and Black Tuesday, and banks collapsed.

Additional Support

Activity: Collaborative Learning

The Stock Market Stock market profits began rising in 1924, gradually at first. The wild bull market did not begin until 1927. Stocks began to double and triple in value, some doing so nearly overnight. Leaders in business and government, as well as economics professors, believed this trend would continue, bringing a golden age of prosperity to all. **As a class discuss the question:** What is a sensible way to invest in the stock market? *(research the company's background and growth before buying stock; invest broadly in several types of companies)* **OL**

D Differentiated Instruction

Special Education Students with reading difficulties may benefit from making an outline of this section. Have them copy the main heading and subheadings into their notebooks, with room under each head for taking notes about the key events and concepts. Remind students to use the chapter time lines to preview events they will read about. **BL**

R Reading Strategy

Making Connections Have students find out the current statistics on distribution of wealth and disposable income in the United States. Ask them to compare their findings to the information presented for 1929. **AL**

Analyzing VISUALS

1. There was less demand for steel, causing lower wages and unemployment.
2. 1929 and 1930

Additional Support

D The Roots of the Great Depression

MAIN Idea An uneven distribution of income, tariff policies, and the Federal Reserve Board's mistakes contributed to the Great Depression.

HISTORY AND YOU How evenly is wealth distributed in your community? Read about the uneven distribution of income in the late 1920s.

The stock market crash played a major role in putting the economy into a recession. Yet the crash would not have led to a long-lasting depression if other forces had not been at work. The roots of the Great Depression were deeply entangled in the economy of the 1920s.

The Uneven Distribution of Income

Overproduction was one factor contributing to the onset of the Great Depression. More efficient machinery increased the production capacity of both factories and farms. Most Americans, however, did not earn enough to buy up the flood of goods they helped produce. While manufacturing output per person-hour rose 32 percent, the average worker's wage increased only 8 percent. In 1929 the top 5 percent of all American households earned 30 percent of the nation's income. In contrast, about two-thirds of families earned less than $2,500 a year, leaving them with little disposable income. **R**

INFOGRAPHIC

Causes of the Great Depression

What Caused the Economy to Collapse?

- **Low Interest Rates** Federal Reserve kept interest rates low; companies borrowed money and expanded more than necessary.
- **Overproduction** Companies made more goods than could be sold.
- **Uneven Distribution of Wealth** Not everyone who wanted consumer goods could afford them.
- **High Tariffs** Tariffs restricted foreign demand for American goods.
- **Falling Demand** With too many goods unsold, production was cut back and employees were laid off.
- **Stock Market Speculation** Low interest rates encouraged borrowing money to speculate, endangering bank solvency.

Cyclical Effect

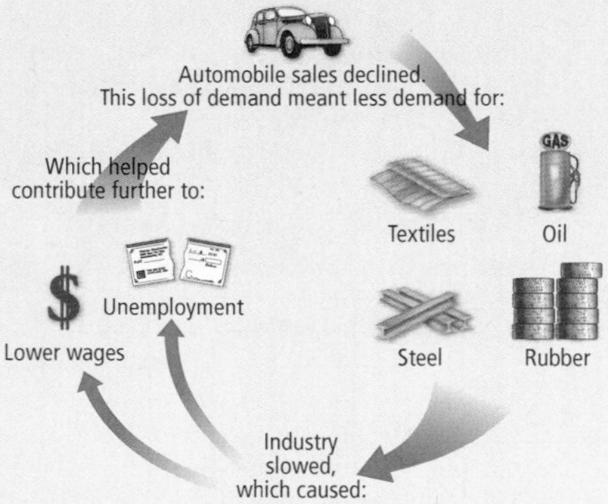

Income and Spending

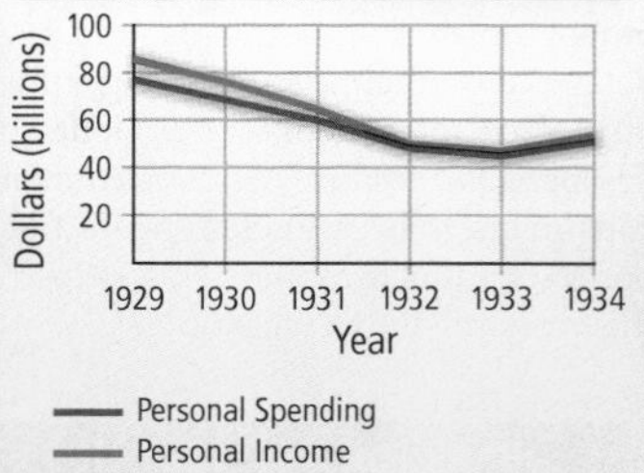

Source: *Historical Statistics of the United States.*

Value of Exports, 1929–1932

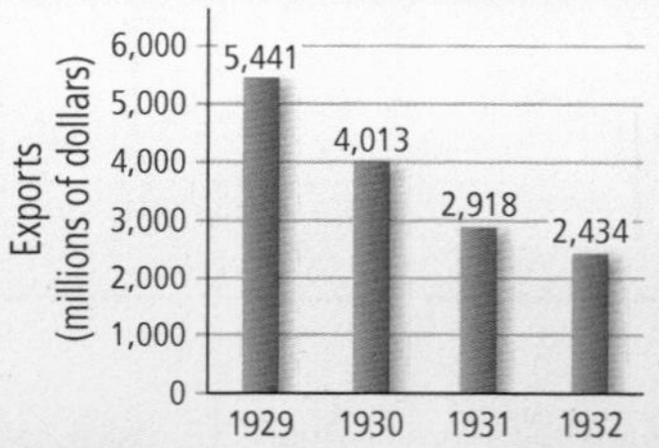

Source: *Historical Statistics of the United States.*

Analyzing VISUALS DBQ

1. **Analyzing** What effect did the decline in automobile sales have on the steel industry?
2. **Calculating** Between what two years was the decrease in the value of exports the greatest?

Activity: Interdisciplinary Connection

Economics Invite an economics teacher or economist to speak to the class about the safeguards now in place to help prevent a depression as serious as the one during the 1920s and 1930s. Ask the speaker to look at other drops in the market and how these safeguards have worked at these times. Ask the speaker to provide an activity or pretest that the students can complete before he or she comes to speak. **OL**

During the 1920s many Americans had purchased high-cost items, such as refrigerators and cars, on the **installment** plan. Purchasers could make small down payments and pay the remainder of the item's price in monthly installments. Paying off such debts eventually forced some buyers to stop making new purchases. Because of the decrease in sales, manufacturers in turn cut production and laid off employees.

The slowdown in retail sales reverberated throughout the economy. When radio sales slumped, for example, makers cut back on orders for copper wire, wood cabinets, and glass radio tubes. Montana copper miners, Minnesota lumberjacks, and Ohio glassworkers, in turn, lost their jobs. Jobless workers cut back on purchases, further cutting sales. This kind of chain reaction put more and more Americans out of work. Many families had little or no savings. They had nothing to support themselves when they lost their jobs. In 1930 alone, about 26,000 businesses collapsed.

The Loss of Export Sales

Many jobs might have been saved if American manufacturers had sold more goods abroad. As the bull market of the 1920s sped up, U.S. banks made loans to speculators rather than loans to foreign companies. Foreign countries were also facing a recession after World War I. Many nations did not have the money to buy American-manufactured goods or crops.

In 1929 Hoover wanted to encourage overseas trade by lowering tariffs. Conservative Republicans, however, wanted to protect American industry from foreign competition by raising tariffs. The resulting legislation, the **Hawley-Smoot Tariff,** raised the average tariff rate to the highest level in American history. In the end, it failed to help American businesses, because foreign countries responded by raising their own tariffs. This meant fewer American products were sold overseas. By 1932 exports had fallen to about one-fifth of what they had been in 1929, which hurt both American companies and farmers.

Mistakes by the Federal Reserve

Just as consumers were able to buy more goods on credit, access to easy money propelled the stock market. Instead of raising interest rates to curb excessive speculation, the Federal Reserve Board kept its rates very low throughout the 1920s.

The Board's failure to raise interest rates significantly helped cause the Depression in two ways. First, by keeping rates low, it encouraged member banks to make risky loans. Second, its low interest rates led business leaders to think the economy was still expanding. As a result, they borrowed more money to expand production, a serious mistake because it led to overproduction when sales were falling. When the Depression finally hit, companies had to lay off workers to cut costs. Then the Federal Reserve made another mistake. It raised interest rates, tightening credit. The economy continued to spiral downward.

Reading Check **Listing** What were three factors that contributed to the Great Depression?

Section 1 REVIEW

Vocabulary

1. **Explain** the significance of: Alfred E. Smith, stock market, bull market, margin, margin call, speculation, Black Tuesday, bank run, installment, Hawley-Smoot Tariff.

Main Ideas

2. **Identifying** What factors contributed to Herbert Hoover's election in 1928?
3. **Examining** How did the stock market collapse affect banks?
4. **Explaining** What effect did tariff policies have on the Great Depression?

Critical Thinking

5. **Big Ideas** How did the practice of buying on margin and speculation cause the stock market to rise?
6. **Organizing** Use a graphic organizer similar to the one below to list the causes of the Great Depression.

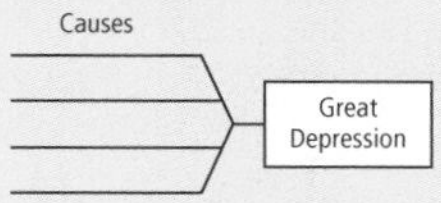

7. **Analyzing Visuals** Look at the graph on page 630. What generalization can you make about the variation in highs and lows of the stock market from 1920 to 1932?

Writing About History

8. **Expository Writing** Write an article for a financial magazine explaining the stock market's rapid decline in 1929 and the reasons for the crash on Black Tuesday.

History ONLINE
Study Central™ To review this section, go to glencoe.com and click on Study Central.

633

R Reading Strategy

Activating Prior Knowledge Ask students to recall the terms of reparations after World War I and which country might be facing the most severe recession. *(Heavy reparations were placed on Germany.)* **OL**

Reading Check

Answer: uneven distribution of income, loss of export sales, and mistakes by the Federal Reserve

Assess

History ONLINE

Study Central™ provides summaries, interactive games, and online graphic organizers to help students review content.

Close

Summarizing Ask: How did the stock market crash lead to bank failures? *(Banks lost money when speculators could not repay the money they borrowed to buy stock. Banks had also invested depositors' money in the stock market. Many depositors withdrew their funds.)* **OL**

Section 1 REVIEW

Answers

1. All definitions can be found in the section and the Glossary.
2. apparently strong economy and rising stock market prices
3. Banks had lent money to investors, who lost everything and couldn't repay it; they had also invested depositors' money in the stock market. They lost money on their investments, and debtors defaulted on loans. Some banks had to close and this further eroded consumer confidence.
4. They led to a decrease in export trade, which further hurt the economy.
5. Buying on margin meant that an investor could make a small down payment and borrow the rest of the stocks' cost from the broker. Many people bought stocks on speculation, hoping that the market would continue climbing.
6. uneven distribution of wealth, decline in sales, mistakes by the Federal Reserve
7. The gap between the two wasn't so large until highs began to spike in 1928. The gap remained large until 1932, when highs and lows returned to the distance level of 1920.
8. Students' articles will vary but should include appropriate vocabulary.

Focus

Bellringer

Daily Focus Transparency 18-2

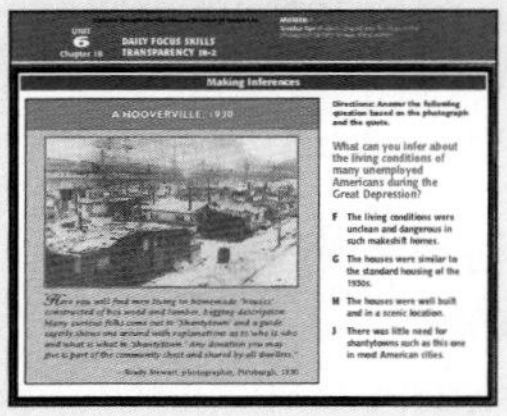

Guide to Reading

Answers:

I. The Depression Worsens
  A. Struggling to Get By
  B. The Dust Bowl
II. Art and Entertainment
  A. Hollywood
  B. On the Air
  C. Literature and Art

Section Spotlight Video

To generate student interest and provide a springboard for class discussion, access the Chapter 18, Section 2 video at glencoe.com or on the video DVD.

Section 2 — Section Audio — Spotlight Video

Life During the Depression

Guide to Reading

Big Ideas

Past and Present As the Great Depression and the drought worsened, thousands of people tried to find work and shelter in other places.

Content Vocabulary

- bailiff *(p. 634)*
- hobo *(p. 634)*
- soap opera *(p. 637)*

Academic Vocabulary

- suspend *(p. 634)*
- colleague *(p. 636)*
- technique *(p. 637)*

People and Events to Identify

- Dust Bowl *(p. 635)*
- Walt Disney *(p. 636)*
- John Steinbeck *(p. 637)*
- William Faulkner *(p. 637)*
- Grant Wood *(p. 637)*

Reading Strategy

Taking Notes As you read about life in the United States during the Great Depression, use the major headings of the section to create an outline similar to the one below.

Life During the Depression
I. The Depression Worsens
  A.
  B.
II.

The Great Depression caused large numbers of people to lose their jobs and property. To help people escape their misery, popular entertainment offered humorous and optimistic movies and radio programs. Novelists and photographers created more realistic portrayals of American life.

The Depression Worsens

MAIN Idea Hunger and homelessness became severe problems by the early 1930s; then, a terrible drought devastated the Great Plains.

HISTORY AND YOU Have you ever been caught outside in a thunderstorm? Read about the deadly dust storms of the 1930s.

The Depression grew steadily worse during Hoover's administration. In 1930, 1,352 banks **suspended** operations across the nation, more than twice the number of bank failures in 1929. More than 9,000 banks had failed by 1933. In 1932 alone, some 30,000 companies went out of business. By 1933 more than 12 million workers, or roughly one-fourth of the workforce, were unemployed.

Struggling to Get By

People without jobs often went hungry. Whenever possible they stood in bread lines—sometimes blocks long—for free food or lined up outside soup kitchens, which private organizations set up to give the poor meals. New York City's YMCA fed up to 12,000 people daily.

Families or individuals who could not pay their rent or mortgage lost their homes. Some of them, paralyzed by fear and humiliation over their sudden misfortune, simply would not or could not move. Their landlord would then ask the court for an eviction notice. Court officers known as **bailiffs** then ejected the nonpaying tenants, piling their belongings in the street.

Throughout the country, newly homeless people put up shacks on unused or public lands, forming communities called shantytowns. Blaming the president for their plight, people referred to such places as Hoovervilles.

In search of work or a better life, many homeless and unemployed Americans began to wander around the country—walking, hitchhiking, or, most often, "riding the rails." These wanderers, called **hobos,** would sneak past railroad police to slip into open boxcars on freight trains. Hundreds of thousands of people, mostly boys and young men, wandered from place to place in this fashion.

Resource Manager

R Reading Strategies	C Critical Thinking	D Differentiated Instruction	W Writing Support	S Skill Practice
Teacher Edition • Making Connections, p. 636 **Additional Resources** • Guid. Read. Act., URB p. 79	**Teacher Edition** • Det. Cause/Effect, p. 635 **Additional Resources** • Econ. and Hist., URB p. 7 • Critical Thinking Skills, URB p. 64 • Prim. Source Read., URB p. 69 • Quizzes and Tests, p. 258 • Linking Past and Present, URB p. 66	**Teacher Edition** • Logical/Math., p. 636 **Additional Resources** • Differentiated Instr., URB p. 55 • American Art and Music Act., URB p. 71 • Econ. and History Act., URB p. 7 • English Learner Act., URB p. 57	**Additional Resources** • Cont. Vocab. Act., URB p. 59	**Additional Resources** • Read. Essen., p. 204 • Reading Skills Act., URB p. 53

PRIMARY SOURCE

Fleeing the Dustbowl

The fierce dust storms of the 1930s destroyed farms and caused many to flee the Great Plains. Below, girls pump water during a dust storm in Springfield, Colorado.

About 40 percent of migrant farmers who fled the Dust Bowl went to California's San Joaquin Valley to pick cotton and grapes. In his novel *The Grapes of Wrath*, John Steinbeck describes what these migrants found when they arrived to harvest crops:

PRIMARY SOURCE

"Maybe he [the owner of the fields] needs two hunderd men, so he talks to five hunderd, an' they tell other folks, an' when you get to the place, they's a thousan' men. This here fella says, 'I'm payin' twenty cents an hour.' An' maybe half the men walk off. But they's still five hunderd that's so . . . hungry they'll work for nothin' but biscuits. Well, this here fella's got a contract to pick them peaches or—chop that cotton. You see now? The more fellas he can get, an' the hungrier, less he's gonna pay. An' he'll get a fella with kids if he can."

—from *The Grapes of Wrath*

DBQ Document-Based Questions

1. **Analyzing Primary Sources** What advantage does the owner of the fields have when it comes to paying people to work?
2. **Drawing Conclusions** Why might the owners of the fields prefer to get "a fella with kids"?

The Dust Bowl

Farmers soon faced a new disaster. Since homesteading had begun on the Great Plains, farmers' plows had uprooted the wild grasses that held the soil's moisture. When crop prices dropped in the 1920s, farmers left many of their fields uncultivated. Then, a terrible drought struck the Great Plains. With neither grass nor wheat to hold the scant rainfall, the soil dried to dust. From the Dakotas to Texas, America's wheat fields became a vast **"Dust Bowl."**

C Winds whipped the arid earth, blowing it aloft and blackening the sky for hundreds of miles. When the dust settled, it buried crops and livestock. Humans and animals caught outdoors sometimes died of suffocation when the dust filled their lungs. The number of yearly dust storms grew, from 22 in 1934 to 72 in 1937. Will and Carolyn Henderson farmed in western Oklahoma. Carolyn wrote a series of articles for the *Atlantic Monthly* about their life during the drought.

PRIMARY SOURCE

"At the little country store, after one of the worst of these storms, the candies in the show case all looked alike and equally brown. Dust to eat and dust to breathe and dust to drink. Dust in the beds and in the flour bin, on dishes and walls and windows, in hair and eyes and ears and teeth and throats. . . ."

—from *Dust to Eat: Drought and Depression in the 1930s*

History ONLINE Student Web Activity Visit glencoe.com and complete the activity on hobo life during the Depression.

Some Great Plains farmers managed to hold on to their land, but many had no chance. If their withered fields were mortgaged, they had to turn them over to the banks. Then, nearly penniless, many families headed west, hoping for a better life in California. Because many migrants were from Oklahoma, they became known as "Okies." In California, they lived in roadside camps and remained homeless and impoverished.

Reading Check **Explaining** What chain of events turned the once-fertile Great Plains into the Dust Bowl?

Teach

C Critical Thinking

Determining Cause and Effect Ask students to read the first column on this page. Have them create graphic organizers showing the cause-and-effect nature of events that led to the Dust Bowl. **BL**

DBQ Document Based Questions

Answers:

1. People are so hungry they will work for food only.
2. If someone with kids is hired, the children will work in the fields too.

Reading Check

Answer:
uprooting the wild grasses, a drop in prices left fields uncultivated, and terrible drought

Hands-On Chapter Project
Step 2

Making a Storyboard

Step 2: Begin Making Drawings

Directions Have students begin making their storyboard drawings based on what they have learned in Section 1. Remind them that working on the drawings as they read can help them comprehend the material. Section 2 is particularly suited for this activity. Encourage students to have fun while using the material in the text as the topics of their drawings.

Putting It Together Allow time for students to share preliminary drawings. Discuss ideas for any key elements in Section 1 they found difficult to illustrate. **OL**

(Chapter Project continued on page 641)

R Reading Strategy

Making Connections Draw students' attention to the comment about the beginning of the "superhero" genre of comic books. Ask students to discuss why this period of time might have produced the genre. *(Students may suggest that in a time of national crisis, a superhero brought hope and a diversion from troubles.)* BL

D Differentiated Instruction

Logical/Mathematical Invite students to find out the U.S. population in 1930 and the U.S. population according to the most recent census. Then have them use library or Internet resources to find out rates of movie attendance in 1930 and today. Have students graph the percentages of movie attendance for both periods of time. OL

People IN HISTORY

Answer:
She was the first woman to photograph combat; she did not photograph happy subjects but tried to show life as it was.

Additional Support

Art and Entertainment

MAIN Idea Movies and radio shows were very popular during the 1930s, a period that also produced new art and literature.

HISTORY AND YOU Has a movie ever helped you get through a difficult time? Read to learn ways that people coped with the Great Depression.

R The hard times of the 1930s led many Americans to prefer entertainment that let them escape their worries. For this reason, movies and radio plays grew increasingly popular. Also, in the 1930s, comic books grew rapidly in popularity. The first comic books cheered people by reprinting newspaper comics, but in the late 1930s, the "superhero" genre was born with the printing of the first tales of *Superman* in 1938 and *Batman* in 1939.

Hollywood

D During the 1930s more than 60 million Americans went to the movies each week. Child stars such as Shirley Temple and Jackie Coogan delighted viewers. Groucho Marx wisecracked while his brothers amused audiences in such films as *Animal Crackers,* and comedies became very popular because they provided a release from daily worries.

King Kong, first released in 1933, showcased new special effects. Moviegoers also loved cartoons. **Walt Disney,** who brought Mickey Mouse to life in 1928, produced the first feature-length animated film, *Snow White and the Seven Dwarfs,* in 1937.

Even serious films were optimistic. In *Mr. Smith Goes to Washington,* Jimmy Stewart played a naïve scout leader who becomes a senator. He exposes the corruption of some of his **colleagues** and calls upon senators to view American government as a high achievement.

In 1939 MGM produced *The Wizard of Oz,* a colorful musical that lifted viewers' spirits. That same year, Vivien Leigh and Clark Gable thrilled audiences in *Gone with the Wind,* a Civil War epic that won nine Academy Awards. Hattie McDaniel, who won the award for Best Supporting Actress, was the first African American to win an Academy Award.

On the Air

While movies captured the imagination, radio offered information and entertainment as near as the living room. Tens of millions of people listened to the radio daily, and radio comedians such as Jack Benny, George Burns, and Gracie Allen were popular, as were the radio adventures of superheroes such as the Green Hornet and the Lone Ranger.

People IN HISTORY

Margaret Bourke-White
1904–1971

While a student at Columbia University, Margaret Bourke-White took a course on photography. She went on to become one of the leading photographers of her time.

In 1927 she began photographing architectural and industrial subjects. Her originality led to jobs at major magazines such as *Fortune* and *Life.*

During World War II she became the first woman photographer attached to the U.S. armed forces. She covered the Italian campaign and the siege of Moscow. She was among those who photographed concentration camp survivors. Bourke-White traveled to India after the war to document Gandhi's efforts to gain that nation's independence from Great Britain. During the Korean War, she traveled with South Korean troops.

What made Margaret Bourke-White's career and photography unusual for the time?

▲ *African American flood victims wait for food and clothing from the Red Cross in 1937 in one of Margaret Bourke-White's most famous photos. The people contrast sharply with the billboard.*

Extending the Content

Female Photographer Margaret Bourke-White began her career as a commercial photographer, and her work reflects the importance of American industry. Part of Bourke-White's success was her fearlessness. When photographing steel mills in Cleveland, Ohio, she got so close to the metal being poured that her face turned red and her camera's finish blistered. She climbed on top of New York City's Chrysler Building, perching on a gargoyle to get a shot. She hung out of bomber airplanes. She was the only woman on staff at the launch of *Life* magazine, and a photo of hers was used on the cover of the premiere issue. Bourke-White invented the photographic essay.

Daytime radio dramas carried over their story lines from day to day. Programs such as *The Guiding Light* presented middle-class families confronting illness, conflict, and other problems. The shows' sponsors were often makers of laundry soaps, so the shows were nicknamed **soap operas.** Radio created a new type of community. Even strangers found common ground in discussing the lives of radio characters.

Literature and Art

Literature and art also flourished during the 1930s. Writers and artists tried to portray life around them, using the homeless and unemployed as their subjects in stories and pictures.

Novelist **John Steinbeck** added flesh and blood to journalists' reports of poverty and misfortune. His writing evoked both sympathy for his characters and indignation at social injustice. In *The Grapes of Wrath* (1939), which was awarded the Pulitzer Prize and was made into a movie, Steinbeck tells the story of the Joad family fleeing the Dust Bowl to find a new life in California after losing their farm. The novel was based on Steinbeck's visits to migrant camps and his interviews with migrant families. In one article he described typical housing for the migrants, for which they paid the growers as much as $2.00 daily:

PRIMARY SOURCE

"[They have] one-room shacks usually about 10 by 12 feet, have no rug, no water, no bed. In one corner there is a little iron wood stove. Water must be carried from the faucet at the end of the street."

—from *Dust to Eat: Drought and Depression*

Other novelists developed new writing techniques. In *The Sound and the Fury,* **William Faulkner,** who later won the Nobel Prize for Literature, shows what his characters are thinking and feeling before they speak. Using this stream of consciousness **technique,** he exposes hidden attitudes of Southern whites and African Americans in a fictional Mississippi county.

Although written words remained powerful, images were growing more influential. Photographers roamed the nation with the new 35-millimeter cameras, seeking new subjects. In 1936, *Time* magazine publisher Henry Luce introduced *Life,* a weekly photojournalism magazine that enjoyed instant success. The striking pictures of photojournalists Dorothea Lange and Margaret Bourke-White showed how the Great Depression had affected average Americans.

Painters in the 1930s included Thomas Hart Benton and **Grant Wood,** whose styles were referred to as the regionalist school. Their work emphasized traditional American values, especially those of the rural Midwest and South. Wood's painting that is best-known today is *American Gothic.* The portrait pays tribute to no-nonsense Midwesterners while gently making fun of their severity.

✓Reading Check **Examining** What subjects did artists, photographers, and writers emphasize during the 1930s?

Section 2 REVIEW

Vocabulary

1. **Explain** the significance of: bailiff, hobo, Dust Bowl, Walt Disney, soap opera, John Steinbeck, William Faulkner, Grant Wood.

Main Ideas

2. **Analyzing** What environmental event of the 1930s worsened the Great Depression?
3. **Explaining** How did people try to escape the realities of life during the Great Depression?

Critical Thinking

4. **Big Ideas** How did some Great Plains farmers respond to the loss of their fields to the banks?
5. **Organizing** Use a graphic organizer such as the one below to identify the effects of the Great Depression.

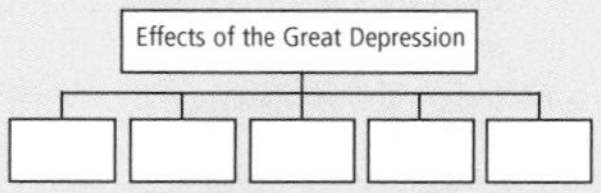

6. **Analyzing Visuals** Look at the photo on page 635. What details indicate that this is a severe dust storm?

Writing About History

7. **Descriptive Writing** Imagine you are writing the catalogue for an art show of photographs by Dorothea Lange or Margaret Bourke-White. Write a paragraph describing one of the images in this section or discussing their photographic skill.

History ONLINE
Study Central™ To review this section, go to glencoe.com and click on Study Central.

✓Reading Check

Answer:
Some work, such as Disney's cartoons, was escapist; other artists focused on the plight of those most clearly affected by the Great Depression and Dust Bowl.

Assess

History ONLINE

Study Central™ provides summaries, interactive games, and online graphic organizers to help students review content.

Close

Summarizing Ask: What forms of entertainment were popular during the Great Depression? *(reading comic books, going to the movies, listening to radio shows and soap operas)* **BL**

Section 2 REVIEW

Answers

1. All definitions can be found in the section and the Glossary.
2. drought and resulting crop failure
3. movies and radio
4. Many farmers headed west, hoping for a better life in California.
5. bank failures, unemployment, hunger, homelessness, and a terrible drought
6. They hold handkerchiefs to cover their mouths and noses. They are wearing hats; one has on a coat to protect herself. The girl holding the cup has it close to the faucet so no sand will blow into it. The wind is whipping their skirts.
7. Students' paragraphs will vary but should focus on one photo in the chapter.

GEOGRAPHY & HISTORY

Focus

Tell students that more than 325 dust storms hit between 1930 and 1941. A May, 1934 storm moved perhaps a third of a billion tons of topsoil, dropping it in Boston, Washington, D.C., and on ships hundreds of miles in the Atlantic.

Teach

D Differentiated Instruction

Naturalist Invite students to find out about measures that the government took to conserve the soil and improve farming practices during the Dust Bowl years. Have them take on the role of a worker from the Soil Conservation Service explaining options to the class. **OL**

C Critical Thinking

Predicting Consequences Ask students to imagine what might happen to the land when farmers left for California or other places to find work. *(Possible answer: it reverted back to uninhabited plains)* **OL**

Additional Support

NATIONAL GEOGRAPHIC

GEOGRAPHY & HISTORY

The Dust Bowl

In the late nineteenth century, settlers on the Great Plains turned the semiarid region into the bread-basket of America, growing vast fields of wheat and other crops. Intensive farming destroyed the region's native grasses and loosened the soil. At first, this was not a problem, as the Great Plains experienced higher than normal rainfall in the late 1800s. Over time, however, farmers exhausted the soil. When rainfall began
D C to decline and temperatures rose in the 1920s, the soil began to dry out. In 1932, a full-scale drought hit. The fierce heat dried the exhausted soil into fine dustlike particles. The high winds of the open plains easily lifted the dirt into the air creating "dust storms." In 1932 alone, 14 dust storms struck the Great Plains. These storms carried the soil of the Great Plains hundreds of miles. In May 1934, a huge storm dumped piles of dirt in Chicago. Further east, silt from the storm collected on the windows of the White House.

How Did the Dust Bowl Affect Americans?

The "Dust Bowl" is sometimes called a human-made natural disaster. The drought and rising temperatures of the 1930s were a natural disaster. But the dust storms were human-made, the result of decades of overcultivation. These "black blizzards" scoured and buried homes, ruined vehicle engines, and diminished visibility. The blowing dirt could injure eyes and damage lungs; it even suffocated people. As the drought destroyed their livelihood, and the dust storms destroyed their belongings, many farmers abandoned the land, packed up their families, and fled the region in search of work elsewhere.

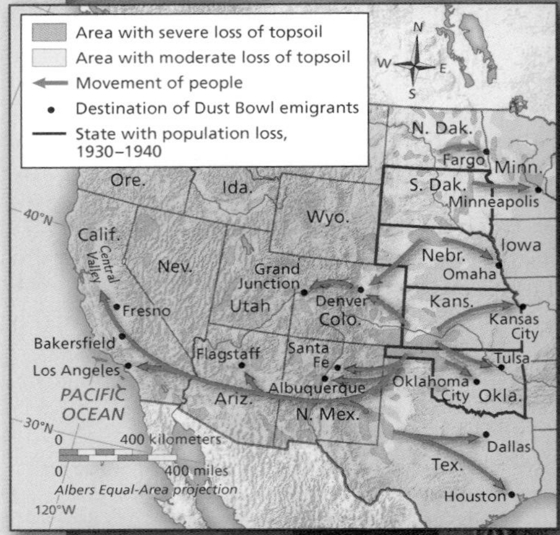

The drought on the Great Plains in the 1930s was the worst ever recorded in U.S. history. Summer temperatures soared above 110 degrees in many locations, setting records that still stand. The lack of water and fierce heat dried the soil to a fine dust. An estimated 200 million acres of land lost some or all of its topsoil.

Analyzing GEOGRAPHY

1. **Movement** Which states lost population in the 1930s? In which direction did most people fleeing the Dust Bowl move?
2. **Human-Environment Interaction** Study the image at right. What problems and dangers does the dust storm create?

Extending the Content

Drought Conditions The Dust Bowl of the 1930s was not the only drought in the United States during the 20th century. A drought occurred in Great Plains states and Texas from 1951 until 1956. By 1953, three-quarters of Texas reported below normal amounts of rainfall. By 1957, when the spring rains ended the drought, 244 of Texas's 254 counties had been declared federal drought disaster areas. More than a third of the United States was affected by the drought of 1987 to 1989. There were catastrophic fires in 1988, such as the ones that burned in Yellowstone National Park. During the early years of the 21st century, the Plains states again suffered years of drought.

▲ *Many farmers in the Dust Bowl, such as Elmer Thomas and his family of Muskogee, Oklahoma (above), decided to leave the region. Many became migrant workers, traveling from across the west in search of short-term employment.*

GEOGRAPHY & HISTORY

Assess/Close

R Reading Skill

Making Connections Have students find out about the Green Belt Movement, in which Nobel Prize winner Wangari Maathai began to counter the threat of drought in Africa as a result of deforestation and soil erosion. Allow time for them to report their findings to the class.

Analyzing GEOGRAPHY

Answers:

1. North Dakota, South Dakota, Nebraska, and Kansas all lost population. Most people headed west to California.
2. Dust storms cause a loss of topsoil; create breathing problems, particularly for the aged and children; cause a loss of visibility, and damage equipment such as engines.

Interdisciplinary Connection

Language Arts

Hold a Debate Global warming continues to be a topic of concern to farmers and others. Have students debate the possible solutions to this problem and the role that the United States might take.

Focus

Bellringer

Daily Focus Transparency 18-3

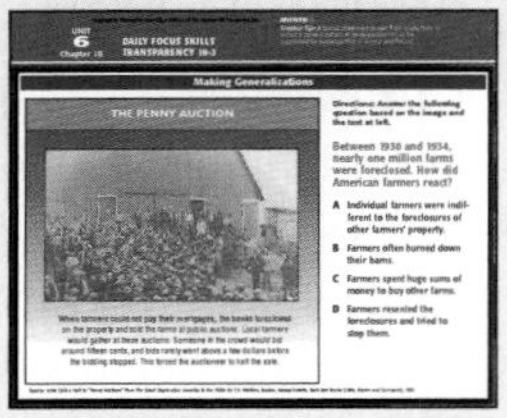

Guide to Reading

Answers: Initiative: Industry was to keep factories open and stop slashing wages; Result: business leaders did not follow through; Initiative: Hoover wanted to increase public works; Result: this had little effect; Initiative: to pump money into the economy; Result: this was too limited and could not reverse the accelerating collapse

Section Spotlight Video

To generate student interest and provide a springboard for class discussion, access the Chapter 18, Section 3 video at glencoe.com or on the video DVD.

Resource Manager

Section 3

Section Audio Spotlight Video

Hoover Responds to the Depression

Guide to Reading

Big Ideas

Government and Society President Hoover's ideas about government shaped his response to the Great Depression, making the government slow to respond.

Content Vocabulary
- public works *(p. 640)*
- relief *(p. 642)*
- foreclose *(p. 643)*

Academic Vocabulary
- series *(p. 640)*
- community *(p. 641)*

People and Events to Identify
- Reconstruction Finance Corporation *(p. 641)*
- Bonus Army *(p. 643)*

Reading Strategy

Categorizing As you read about Herbert Hoover's response to the Depression, create a graphic organizer listing his major initiatives and their results.

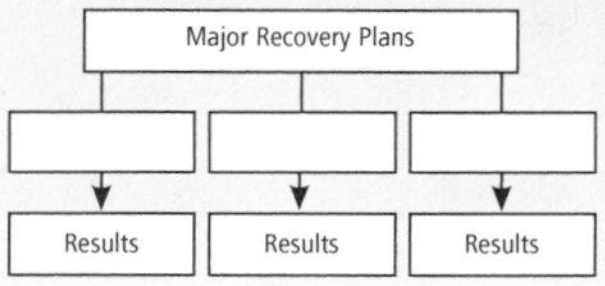

President Hoover tried to fix the economy by providing loans to banks and corporations and by starting public works projects. Later, he reluctantly supported direct aid to impoverished families. By the early 1930s, more Americans were demanding the government's help.

Promoting Recovery

MAIN Idea Hoover encouraged businesses to stop laying off workers and created public works projects.

HISTORY AND YOU What efforts would you have taken to help the economy if you had been president? Read about the public works efforts of the early 1930s.

On Friday, October 25, 1929, the day after Black Thursday, President Herbert Hoover declared that "the fundamental business of the country . . . is on a sound and prosperous basis." On March 7, 1930, he told the press that "the worst effects of the crash upon employment will have passed during the next sixty days." Critics derided his optimism as conditions worsened. Hoover, however, hoped to downplay the public's fears. He wanted to avoid more bank runs and layoffs by urging consumers and business leaders to make rational decisions. In the end, Hoover's efforts failed to inspire the public's confidence, and the economy continued its downward slide.

President Hoover believed that the American system of "rugged individualism" would keep the economy moving. He felt that the government should not step in to help individuals out. After World War I, many European countries had implemented a form of socialism, which Hoover felt contributed to their lack of economic recovery. In 1922 Hoover had written a book, *American Individualism,* which presented arguments for why the American system of individualism was the best social, political, spiritual, and economic system in the world. Thus, it was difficult for Hoover to propose policies that had the government taking more control.

Despite his public statements that the economy was not in trouble, Hoover was worried. To devise strategies for improving the economy, he organized a **series** of conferences, bringing together the heads of banks, railroads, and other big businesses, as well as labor leaders and government officials.

Industry leaders pledged to keep factories open and to stop slashing wages. By 1931, however, they had broken those pledges. Hoover then increased the funding for **public works,** or government-financed building projects. The resulting construction jobs were intended to replace some of those lost in the private sector.

R Reading Strategies	C Critical Thinking	D Differentiated Instruction	W Writing Support	S Skill Practice
Teacher Edition • Analyzing Text Structure, p. 641 **Additional Resources** • Guid. Read. Act., URB p. 80 • RENTG, p. 207 • Reteaching Act., URB p. 75	**Additional Resources** • Quizzes and Tests, p. 259 • Auth. Assess, p. 41	**Teacher Edition** • Visual/Spatial, p. 641 **Additional Resources** • Geography and Hist., URB p. 3 • Enrichment Act., URB p. 76	**Teacher Edition** • Persuasive Writing, p. 642	**Additional Resources** • Interp. Pol. Cartoons, URB p. 73 • Time Line Act., URB p. 65

POLITICAL CARTOONS — PRIMARY SOURCE
Can Hoover Fight the Depression?

▲ While the Democratic Party donkey marches outside singing old songs, Hoover tries to deal with economic problems caused by high tariffs, depression and drought.

▲ Herbert Hoover reassures a farmer his scarecrow labeled farm relief will help.

Analyzing VISUALS DBQ

1. **Analyzing** What does the cartoon on the right suggest about Hoover's plan to help farmers?
2. **Analyzing** How are Hoover and the Democrats portrayed in the cartoon on the left?

Public works projects did create some jobs but for only a small fraction of the millions who were unemployed. The government could create enough new jobs only by massively increasing government spending, which Hoover refused to do.

R Someone had to pay for public works projects. If the government raised taxes to pay for them, consumers would have less money to spend, further hurting already struggling businesses. If the government kept taxes low and ran a budget deficit instead—spending more money than it collected in taxes—it would have to borrow the money. Borrowing would mean less money available for businesses to expand and for consumer loans. Hoover feared that deficit spending would actually delay an economic recovery.

As the 1930 congressional elections approached, most Americans felt threatened by rising unemployment. Citizens blamed the party in power for the ailing economy. The Republicans lost 49 seats and their majority in the House of Representatives; they held on to the Senate by a single vote.

Trying to Rescue the Banks

To get the economy growing again, Hoover focused on expanding the money supply. The government, he believed, had to help banks make loans to corporations, which could then expand production and rehire workers.

The president asked the Federal Reserve Board to put more currency into circulation, but the Board refused. In an attempt to ease the money shortage, Hoover set up the National Credit Corporation (NCC) in October 1931. The NCC created a pool of money that allowed troubled banks to continue lending money in their **communities.** This program, however, failed to meet the nation's needs. **D**

In 1932 Hoover requested Congress to set up the **Reconstruction Finance Corporation** (RFC) to make loans to businesses. By early 1932 the RFC had lent about $238 million to approximately 160 banks, 60 railroads, and 18 building-and-loan organizations. The RFC was overly cautious, however. It failed to increase its lending sufficiently to meet the need, and the economy continued its decline.

Teach

R Reading Strategy

Analyzing Text Structure Draw students' attention to the second paragraph. Ask them to develop flowcharts showing the options for paying for public works projects. OL

D Differentiated Instruction

Visual/Spatial Invite students to create time lines showing the efforts Hoover made to try to keep disaster from occurring. BL

Analyzing VISUALS

Answers:

1. The cartoonist pictures Hoover's farm relief as a scarecrow, trying to scare off the birds labeled "hard times."
2. Hoover is shown as a nursemaid trying to quiet the various unhappy "babies," or problems his administration faces. The Democrats are shown as loudly singing about the problems.

Hands-On Chapter Project Step 3

Making a Storyboard

Step 3: Peer Review Groups will exchange storyboards completed to this point.

Directions Have the groups exchange storyboard projects completed thus far. Ask each group to honestly and fairly evaluate whether the storyboard captures the most important material in Sections 1 and 2. Comments should be constructive and helpful and should be limited to content, rather than focusing on the quality of the drawings.

Putting It Together Have students incorporate the suggestions they have received for improving their storyboards.

(Chapter Project continued on the Visual Summary page)

W Writing Support

Persuasive Writing Ask students to suppose they are living in 1931 when President Hoover refused to extend federal assistance to those in need. Ask them to write editorials to the local newspaper persuading a local Congressperson to support direct relief to the citizens. Remind them to use facts and reasons to support their argument. **OL**

Analyzing VISUALS

Answers:
1. They had no weapons.
2. Students may suggest they would be dismayed at the loss of good food.

Reading Check

Answer:
He felt that only state and city governments should provide relief.

Direct Help for Citizens

W From the start, Hoover strongly opposed the federal government's participation in **relief**—money given directly to impoverished families. He believed that only state and local governments should dole out relief. Any other needs should be met by private charity, not by the federal government. By the spring of 1932, however, state and local governments were running out of money, and private charities lacked the resources to handle the crisis.

That year, political support for a federal relief measure increased, and Congress passed the Emergency Relief and Construction Act in July. Reluctantly, Hoover signed the bill. The new act called for $1.5 billion for public works and $300 million in emergency loans to the states for direct relief. For the first time in United States history, the federal government was supplying direct relief funds, although governors of the states had to apply for the loans. By this time, however, the new program could not reverse the accelerating collapse.

Reading Check **Summarizing** Why did Hoover oppose a federal relief program?

In an Angry Mood

MAIN Idea Farmers, veterans, and others who were suffering grew frustrated and demanded the government do something to help.

HISTORY AND YOU Have you ever felt strongly enough about an issue to take part in a protest? Read what happened when veterans of World War I demonstrated in Washington, D.C., in 1932.

In the months after the Wall Street crash, most Americans were resigned to bad economic news. By 1931, however, many people were becoming increasingly discontent.

Hunger Marches and Protests by Farmers

In January 1931 about 500 residents of Oklahoma City looted a grocery store. Crowds began showing up at rallies and "hunger marches" organized by the American Communist Party. On December 5, 1932, in Washington, D.C., a group of about 1,200 hunger marchers chanted, "Feed the hungry, tax the rich." Police herded them into a cul-de-sac

PRIMARY SOURCE

An Angry Nation

◄ *Hunger marchers march through White Plains, New York, on their way to the nation's capital in 1932.*

◄ *On July 29, 1932, armed guards use tear gas and clubs to move Bonus Army marchers.*

▲ *Angry at low prices, dairy farmers dump milk in an attempt to drive up prices and draw attention to their problems.*

Analyzing VISUALS DBQ

1. **Analyzing Visuals** What do you observe about the Bonus Army's attempt to defend itself?
2. **Speculating** How do you think poor and hungry people would have responded to the photo at top right?

Additional Support

Activity: Interdisciplinary Connection

Language Arts Point out to students that selfless activity is a survival mechanism for groups. Often the most selfless people are those who have the least in terms of material possessions. In *The Grapes of Wrath,* for example, Ma Joad declares, "If you're in trouble or hurt or need—go to poor people. They're the only ones that'll help." Ask students to analyze this statement and then write a paragraph discussing why they feel that acting selflessly might be a group survival mechanism. Have students support their analyses with examples. **AL**

and denied them food and water, until some members of Congress insisted on the marchers' right to petition their government. They were then permitted to march to Capitol Hill.

The hungry poor were not the only people who began to protest conditions during the Depression. During World War I's agricultural boom, many farmers had heavily mortgaged their land to pay for seed, feed, and equipment. After the war, prices sank so low that farmers began losing money. Creditors **foreclosed** on nearly one million farms between 1930 and 1934, taking ownership of the land and evicting the families. Some farmers began destroying their crops, desperately trying to raise prices by reducing the supply. In Nebraska, farmers burned corn to heat their homes. Georgia dairy farmers blocked highways and stopped milk trucks, dumping the milk into ditches.

The Bonus Marchers

After World War I, Congress had enacted a $1,000 bonus for each veteran, to be distributed in 1945. In 1931 Texas congressman Wright Patman introduced a bill that would authorize early payment of these bonuses. In May 1932 several hundred Oregon veterans began marching to Washington to lobby for passage of the legislation. As they moved east, other veterans joined them until they numbered about 1,000. Wearing ragged military uniforms, they trudged along the highways or rode the rails, singing old war songs. The press termed the marchers the **"Bonus Army."**

Once in Washington, the marchers camped in Hoovervilles. More veterans joined them until the Bonus Army swelled to 15,000. President Hoover acknowledged the veterans' right to petition but refused to meet with them. When the Senate voted down the bonus bill, veterans outside the Capitol began to grumble. Many returned home, but some marchers stayed on. Some squatted in vacant buildings downtown.

In late July, Hoover ordered the buildings cleared. The police tried, but when an officer panicked and fired into a crowd, killing two veterans, the city government called in the army. General Douglas MacArthur ignored Hoover's orders to clear the buildings but to leave the camps alone. MacArthur sent in cavalry, infantry, and tanks to clear the camps.

Soon unarmed veterans were running away, pursued by 700 soldiers. The soldiers tear-gassed stragglers and burned the shacks. National press coverage of troops assaulting veterans further harmed Hoover's reputation and hounded the president throughout the 1932 campaign.

Although Hoover failed to resolve the economic crisis, he did more than any prior president to expand the federal government's economic role. The Reconstruction Finance Corporation was the first federal agency created to stimulate the economy during peacetime. The rout of the Bonus Army marchers and the lingering Depression, however, tarnished Hoover's public image.

Reading Check **Evaluating** How did Americans react as the Depression continued?

Section 3 REVIEW

Vocabulary

1. **Explain** the significance of: public works, Reconstruction Finance Corporation, relief, foreclose, Bonus Army.

Main Ideas

2. **Identifying** What two major strategies did President Hoover use to promote economic recovery?
3. **Explaining** What did World War I veterans do to try to get their service bonuses early?

Critical Thinking

4. **Big Ideas** How did President Hoover's philosophy of government guide his response to the Depression?
5. **Organizing** Use a graphic organizer similar to the one below to list American reactions to the Great Depression.

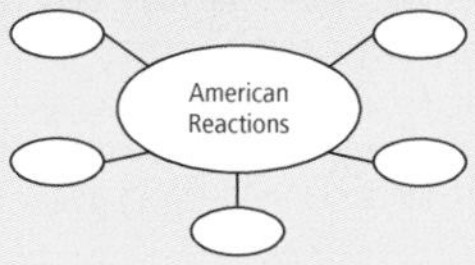

6. **Analyzing Visuals** Look at the photo of the Hunger Marchers on page 642. How would you compare their approach and style to protestors today?

Writing About History

7. **Persuasive Writing** Imagine that you are a World War I veteran in 1931. Write a persuasive letter to your congressperson explaining why you need your bonus now, not in 1945.

History ONLINE
Study Central™ To review this section, go to glencoe.com and click on Study Central.

Reading Check

Answer:
Reactions included hunger marches, farmers' revolts, and the Bonus Army's march attempting to receive their bonuses early.

Assess

History ONLINE

Study Central™ provides summaries, interactive games, and online graphic organizers to help students review content.

Close

Summarizing Ask: What were some of the main events during the Great Depression that led to Hoover's decline in popularity? *(the suffering economy, hunger marchers petitioning the government, protests by farmers, and the Bonus Marchers being assaulted)* **OL**

Answers

1. All definitions can be found in the section and the Glossary.
2. He encouraged businesses to stop laying off workers and he created public works projects.
3. They marched to Washington to lobby and camped in Hoovervilles. They stayed outside the Capitol and squatted in vacant buildings.
4. Because he believed in the role of state and local government to assist those in need, he delayed federal intervention until the crisis became enormous.
5. Possible answers include: bonus marchers, discontent, farmers' revolts, hunger marches, squatting, escaping through entertainment
6. The marchers are all men; they are dressed formally in suits, hats, ties, and white shirts; today's protestors are not dressed so formally, but like the Hunger Marchers they carry signs to advocate their demands.
7. Students' letters will vary but should be written from the perspective of a World War I veteran and include reasons for receiving a bonus at that time.

Auditory/Musical Play for students a recording of one of the songs popular during the Depression era. Many of these are available online, as well as at libraries. Then invite students to compose a song with lyrics focusing on one of the effects of the Depression. Suggest they use a tune they are already familiar with or compose an alternative tune. **AL**

Descriptive Writing Have students select one of the photographs on this page. Ask them to focus on the elements of the photo and to describe them in such a way that someone who had not seen the photo would understand its impact. **BL**

Chapter 18 VISUAL SUMMARY

STUDY TO GO You can study anywhere, anytime by downloading quizzes and flashcards to your PDA from glencoe.com.

Causes of the Depression

Long-Range Causes

- Uneven distribution of wealth ensures that many consumers do not have enough income to purchase the goods being produced.
- Interest rates are kept too low by the Federal Reserve, which encourages businesses to borrow money and to expand production beyond market demand.
- Overproduction by business eventually floods the market with goods that cannot be sold. Businesses begin laying off workers and shutting down production.

Immediate Causes

- People and businesses borrow money to invest in the stock market; speculation drives stock prices too high and when they collapse, many people lose all of their money, and many banks collapse when loans are not repaid.
- As companies lay off workers, demand for goods falls as workers lack the income to purchase goods being produced. This in turn causes even more layoffs and a cyclical effect sets in, driving up unemployment.
- In order to protect American companies from competition, Congress raises tariffs. When other countries respond in kind, foreign demand for American goods falls, further hurting American companies.

▲ *A New York paper trumpets the stock crash. To raise cash to pay their stock debts, people began selling anything of value, including this car.*

▲ *Shantytowns appeared in many cities during the Depression as homelessness and unemployment rose.*

Effects of the Depression

- Unemployment rises to record levels.
- Many people, unable to pay their debts, lose their homes and farms; the homeless create shantytowns, nicknamed Hoovervilles, on the edges of cities.
- Hunger marches, protests by farmers, and marches by veterans seeking their bonuses indicate growing anger among the population at economic conditions.
- The Republican Party rapidly loses political support, enabling the Democrats to take control of Congress.
- The federal government, for the first time, begins providing direct relief to citizens in need.
- Forms of entertainment, including movies, radio shows, and comic books, focus on distracting people from their daily lives.

Hands-On Chapter Project

Step 4: Wrap Up

Making a Storyboard

Step 4: Complete the Storyboards Groups finalize the drawings and captions of their storyboards for the chapter.

Directions Have students complete the final frames of the storyboard for Section 3 materials. Allow time for students to present their storyboards to the class. **OL**

Chapter 18 ASSESSMENT

Reviewing Vocabulary

Directions: Choose the word or words that best complete the sentence.

1. In the late 1920s, many investors engaged in speculation, or purchasing stock
- **A** after considering a company's earnings and profits.
- **B** and quickly selling the stock for a profit.
- **C** by borrowing money from a stockbroker.
- **D** to invest long-term in the future of the company.

2. The Democratic Party's first Roman Catholic candidate for president was
- **A** Alfred E. Smith.
- **B** Franklin Delano Roosevelt.
- **C** Herbert Hoover.
- **D** Calvin Coolidge.

3. A ________ most often traveled by hopping a railroad car.
- **A** photographer
- **B** journalist
- **C** novelist
- **D** hobo

4. Which popular radio style of the 1930s gained its description from its sponsor?
- **A** *Amos 'n' Andy*
- **B** soap operas
- **C** *Animal Crackers*
- **D** *American Gothic*

5. President Hoover opposed ________, or giving money directly to needy families.
- **A** foreclosure
- **B** relief
- **C** public works
- **D** unionization

Reviewing Main Ideas

Directions: Choose the best answers to the following questions.

Section 1 *(pp. 628–633)*

6. One of the major problems with the stock market in the late 1920s was the number of people who bought stocks
- **A** on margin, with borrowed money.
- **B** in companies that they supported.
- **C** only after carefully studying a company's history.
- **D** without knowing their stockbroker's reputation.

7. Which of the following was a root cause of the Great Depression?
- **A** prohibiting the sale of alcohol
- **B** giving women the right to vote
- **C** uneven distribution of income
- **D** the end of federal control of banks

8. Herbert Hoover won the 1928 election in a landslide, in part because of
- **A** fears of another world war.
- **B** prosperity under Calvin Coolidge.
- **C** having been vice president.
- **D** his support for unions.

Section 2 *(pp. 634–637)*

9. Drought and ________ brought about the conditions that caused the Dust Bowl.
- **A** overgrazing at large cattle farms
- **B** the near-extinction of the buffalo
- **C** famine
- **D** poor farming practices

TEST-TAKING TIP

If you are not sure of the answer, try to narrow the options. First, eliminate any choices that you know are clearly wrong. Then, if necessary, make a guess among the remaining choices.

Need Extra Help?

If You Missed Questions . . .	1	2	3	4	5	6	7	8	9
Go to Page . . .	629	628	634	637	642	628–629	632–633	628	635

GO ON

Answers and Analyses

Reviewing Vocabulary

1. B Many students may choose *C*, because borrowing money from a stockbroker was a common practice before the Depression. Remind them this is called buying on the margin. *A* and *D* represent good stock-buying strategies and so can be easily dismissed.

2. A This question requires students to recall either the religious affiliations of the candidates mentioned or the attacks on Smith during the 1928 election.

3. D The term *hopping* should be a major clue for students. Most passengers *board* a train; *hopping* denotes a way around tickets and authority, which only a hobo without money would need to do.

4. B Soap operas were usually sponsored by laundry soap companies. *Amos 'n' Andy* was the name of a favorite radio program; *Animal Crackers* was a popular Marx Brothers movie; *American Gothic* was a famous painting.

5. B Students may associate the other meaning of *relief* to answer this question correctly. Needy families receiving money would feel relief that their basic needs can be met. *Public works* is the next best answer, but it gives job opportunities rather than money directly.

Reviewing Main Ideas

6. A In analyzing this question, students should focus on the term *major problem.* Doing so eliminates both *B* and *C* as choices. The stockbroker's reputation could have been a problem, but it was not the major problem.

7. C The term *root cause* is the essential part of the question. Students should remember the great disparity in incomes during the 1920s and correctly identify the answer.

8. B The 1928 election followed a period of postwar prosperity. Students should recall that World War I had ended in 1919 and Americans had returned to isolationism.

9. D None of the other distractors were the issue during the 1930s. The removal of native grasses from the prairies to plant domestic crops, among other practices, hastened the drought.

10. A Students can associate Hoover, president during the beginning of the Depression, with Hoovervilles to determine the correct answer.

11. C Students should note that the major reason for high movie attendance was that movies provided a temporary escape from daily worries.

12. B To find the correct response, students should recall that social welfare programs are costly. Hoover, a conservative, opposed deficit spending, though he supported public works funded by state and local groups and private charities.

13. D Only two of the responses could be possible. Unhappy voters do not reelect their leaders, nor do they avoid the polls, their only means of expressing displeasure.

14. B Because three of the options are positive actions, the correct answer stands out. Remind students to use this strategy to eliminate distractors.

Critical Thinking

15. D Remind students to look carefully at the map. Although each body of water listed as a possible answer is marked, the dam clearly spans only the Colorado River.

16. B Careful attention to the map is all that is needed to answer this correctly. Utah is easily eliminated, because the map shows no benefit to it. The other two states gained less than half the power that California did.

Chapter 18 Assessment

10. The people who lost their homes in the Great Depression sometimes lived

- **A** in shantytowns.
- **B** in roadside motels.
- **C** on the lawn of the U.S. Capitol.
- **D** in public libraries opened to them.

11. Despite the poverty of the 1930s, more than 60 million people went to the movies weekly. Why were movies so popular?

- **A** The special effects used in movies then were amazing.
- **B** People could not get over the fact that actors talked.
- **C** Movies offered an escape from viewers' hard lives.
- **D** Theaters were air conditioned and offered free popcorn.

Section 3 *(pp. 640–643)*

12. Hoover was slow to respond to the economic crisis because he opposed

- **A** all public works projects.
- **B** deficit spending.
- **C** investing in stocks.
- **D** private charities.

13. How did American citizens respond to the Great Depression in the 1930 midterm election?

- **A** by reelecting Hoover
- **B** by electing socialist candidates
- **C** by staying away from the polls
- **D** by electing Democrats

14. What was Hoover's response to the Bonus Army marchers who came to Washington, D.C.?

- **A** He ordered them to be paid their bonuses.
- **B** He had the army remove them.
- **C** He visited them and listened to them.
- **D** He set up soup kitchens to feed them.

Critical Thinking

Base your answers to questions 15 and 16 on the map below and on your knowledge of Chapter 18.

The Flow of Electricity

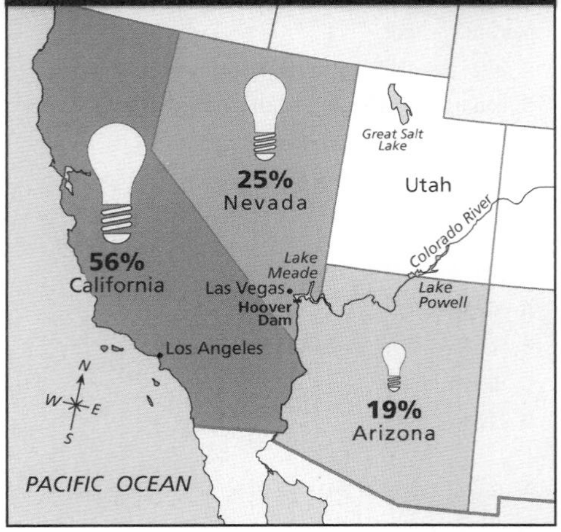

Directions: Choose the best answers to the following questions.

15. The federal government began building Hoover Dam in 1931. What body of water was it designed to control?

- **A** the Pacific Ocean
- **B** Lake Powell
- **C** the Great Salt Lake
- **D** the Colorado River

16. Which state benefited most from the hydroelectric power of Hoover Dam?

- **A** Utah
- **B** California
- **C** Nevada
- **D** Arizona

Need Extra Help?

If You Missed Questions . . .	10	11	12	13	14	15	16
Go to Page . . .	634	636–637	641	641	643	R15	R15

GO ON

17. Why did writers such as John Steinbeck use fiction to draw attention to the Great Depression?
   - **A** Readers could be sympathetic to the characters' situations.
   - **B** Writing fiction meant the authors didn't have to do any research.
   - **C** Nonfiction sales had dropped during the 1920s.
   - **D** Publishers weren't interested in true accounts of national events.

Analyze the cartoon and answer the question that follows. Base your answer on the cartoon and on your knowledge of Chapter 18.

18. What does the cartoon reveal about the character?
   - **A** The man was careless with his money.
   - **B** He saved his money so it would be there in hard times but lost it through no fault of his own.
   - **C** The man should have purchased stocks and bonds rather than put his money in the bank.
   - **D** The man should be more prepared by storing his money under his mattress.

Document-Based Questions

Directions: Analyze the document and answer the short-answer questions that follow the document.

Gordon Parks, who later became a famous photographer, was a young man when the stock market crashed in 1929:

> "The newspapers were full of it, and I read everything I could get my hands on, gathering in the full meaning of such terms as Black Thursday, deflation and depression. I couldn't imagine such financial disaster touching my small world; it surely concerned only the rich. But by the first week of November I too knew differently; along with millions of others across the nation, I was without a job. All that next week I searched for any kind of work that would prevent my leaving school. Again it was, 'We're firing, not hiring.' 'Sorry, sonny, nothing doing here.' Finally, on the seventh of November I went to school and cleaned out my locker, knowing it was impossible to stay on. A piercing chill was in the air as I walked back to the rooming house. The hawk had come. I could already feel his wings shadowing me."
>
> —from *A Choice of Weapons*

19. Why did Parks at first think he was safe from the effects of the stock market crash? What changed his mind?

20. Why do you think Parks used the image of a hawk to express his feelings about the Great Depression?

Extended Response

21. Write an essay that analyzes the following quote from John Steinbeck's novel *The Grapes of Wrath*. "If you're in trouble or hurt or need—go to poor people. They're the only ones that'll help." Based on your knowledge of the Great Depression, indicate whether you believe the quote to be true or false and why. Support your answer with relevant facts and details.

STOP

History ONLINE
For additional test practice, use Self-Check Quizzes—Chapter 18 at glencoe.com.

Need Extra Help?

If You Missed Questions . . .	17	18	19	20	21
Go to Page . . .	637	R18	647	R19	634–637

Extended Response

21. Students may say that poor people will help because they understand the need and have learned compassion from dealing with their own problems.

17. A Students need only recall books or films they have seen to know the power of empathy with a fictionalized character.

18. B The label on the man indicates he had done the "right" thing by placing his money in a bank for savings. The other possible answers were not wise choices to prepare for the future.

Document-Based Questions

19. He wasn't one of the wealthy people who owned stocks, but a struggling student. He learned differently when he lost his job.

20. Possible answer: Hawks are large birds of prey; they connote the ideas of death and feeding on carrion.

History ONLINE
Have students visit the Web site at glencoe.com to review Chapter 18 and take the Self-Check Quiz.

Need Extra Help?
Have students refer to the pages listed if they miss any of the questions.

Chapter 19 Planning Guide

Key to Ability Levels	
BL Below Level	AL Above Level
OL On Level	ELL English Language Learners

Key to Teaching Resources	
Print Material	Transparency
CD-ROM or DVD	

Levels					Resources	Chapter Opener	Section 1	Section 2	Section 3	Chapter Assess
BL	OL	AL	ELL							
FOCUS										
BL	OL	AL	ELL		**Daily Focus Skills Transparencies**		19-1	19-2	19-3	
TEACH										
BL	OL		ELL		**Reading Essentials and Note-Taking Guide***		p. 210	p. 214	p. 217	
	OL				**Historical Analysis Skills Activity, URB**		p. 84			
BL	OL		ELL		**Guided Reading Activities, URB***		p. 110	p. 111	p. 112	
BL	OL	AL	ELL		**Content Vocabulary Activity, URB***			p. 89		
BL	OL	AL	ELL		**Academic Vocabulary Activity, URB**			p. 91		
	OL	AL			**Critical Thinking Skills Activity, URB**		p. 94			
BL	OL		ELL		**Reading Skills Activity, URB**		p. 83			
BL			ELL		**English Learner Activity, URB**		p. 87			
	OL	AL			**Reinforcing Skills Activity, URB**			p. 93		
BL	OL	AL	ELL		**Differentiated Instruction Activity, URB**			p. 85		
BL	OL		ELL		**Time Line Activity, URB**				p. 95	
	OL				**Linking Past and Present Activity, URB**		p. 96			
BL	OL	AL	ELL		**American Art and Music Activity, URB**			p. 101		
BL	OL	AL	ELL		**Interpreting Political Cartoons Activity, URB**			p. 103		
		AL			**Enrichment Activity, URB**			p. 107		
BL	OL	AL	ELL		**American Biographies**		✓		✓	
BL	OL	AL	ELL		**Primary Source Reading, URB**			p. 97	p. 99	
BL	OL	AL	ELL		**Supreme Court Case Studies**				p. 49	
BL	OL	AL	ELL		**The Living Constitution***	✓	✓	✓	✓	✓
	OL	AL			**American History Primary Source Documents Library**	✓	✓	✓	✓	✓
BL	OL	AL	ELL		**Unit Map Overlay Transparencies**	✓	✓	✓	✓	✓
BL	OL	AL	ELL		**Differentiated Instruction for the American History Classroom**	✓	✓	✓	✓	✓
BL	OL	AL	ELL		**StudentWorks™ Plus**	✓	✓	✓	✓	✓

Note: Please refer to the *Unit 6 Resource Book* for this chapter's URB materials.

* Also available in Spanish

TeacherWorks Plus
All-In-One Planner and Resource Center

- Interactive Lesson Planner
- Interactive Teacher Edition
- Fully editable blackline masters
- Section Spotlight Videos Launch
- Differentiated Lesson Plans
- Printable reports of daily assignments
- Standards Tracking System

Levels				Resources	Chapter Opener	Section 1	Section 2	Section 3	Chapter Assess
BL	OL	AL	ELL						
				TEACH *(continued)*					
BL	OL	AL	ELL	American Music Hits Through History CD	✓	✓	✓	✓	✓
BL	OL	AL	ELL	Unit Time Line Transparencies and Activities	✓	✓	✓	✓	✓
BL	OL	AL	ELL	Cause and Effect Transparencies, Strategies, and Activities	✓	✓	✓	✓	✓
BL	OL	AL	ELL	Why It Matters Transparencies, Strategies, and Activities	✓	✓	✓	✓	✓
BL	OL	AL	ELL	American Issues	✓	✓	✓	✓	✓
	OL	AL	ELL	American Art and Architecture Transparencies, Strategies, and Activities	✓	✓	✓	✓	✓
BL	OL	AL		High School American History Literature Library	✓	✓	✓	✓	✓
BL	OL	AL	ELL	*The American Vision* Video Program	✓	✓	✓	✓	✓
Teacher Resources				Strategies for Success	✓	✓	✓	✓	✓
Teacher Resources				Success with English Learners	✓	✓	✓	✓	✓
Teacher Resources				Reading Strategies and Activities for the Social Studies Classroom	✓	✓	✓	✓	✓
Teacher Resources				Presentation Plus! with MindJogger CheckPoint	✓	✓	✓	✓	✓
				ASSESS					
BL	OL	AL	ELL	Section Quizzes and Chapter Tests*		p. 269	p. 270	p. 271	p. 253
BL	OL	AL	ELL	Authentic Assessment With Rubrics					p. 43
BL	OL	AL	ELL	Standardized Test Practice Workbook					p. 43
BL	OL	AL	ELL	*ExamView® Assessment Suite*		19-1	19-2	19-3	Ch. 19
				CLOSE					
BL			ELL	Reteaching Activity, URB					p. 105
BL	OL		ELL	Reading and Study Skills Foldables™	p. 72				
BL	OL	AL	ELL	*American History* in Graphic Novel		p. 49			

✓ Chapter- or unit-based activities applicable to all sections in this chapter.

Using Glencoe's Vocabulary Tools

Teach With Technology

What Glencoe technology products improve students' vocabulary?

Vocabulary eFlashcards, **ePuzzles and Games**, and **Vocabulary PuzzleMaker** all build students' vocabulary and help students understand key words and concepts from the textbook.

How can these products help my students?

Vocabulary eFlashcards help students review and test their recall of content vocabulary, academic vocabulary, and people, places, and events for each chapter. **ePuzzles and Games** are an entertaining way for students to study the key facts, concepts, and vocabulary introduced in each chapter. The **Vocabulary PuzzleMaker** lets you quickly create word searches, crosswords, and jumbles that students can use to practice vocabulary from each chapter.

For **Vocabulary eFlashcards** and **ePuzzles and Games**, visit glencoe.com and enter a student *QuickPass*™ code to go directly to student resources for the chapter. For **Vocabulary PuzzleMaker**, enter a teacher code to go to teacher resources.

History ONLINE
Visit glencoe.com and enter *QuickPass*™ code TAV9399c19T for Chapter 19 resources.

You can easily launch a wide range of digital products from your computer's desktop with the McGraw-Hill Social Studies widget.

	Student	Teacher	Parent
Media Library			
• Section Audio	●		●
• Spanish Audio Summaries	●		●
• Section Spotlight Videos	●	●	●
***The American Vision* Online Learning Center (Web Site)**			
• StudentWorks™ Plus Online	●	●	●
• Multilingual Glossary	●	●	●
• Study-to-Go	●	●	●
• Chapter Overviews	●	●	●
• Self-Check Quizzes	●	●	●
• Student Web Activities	●	●	●
• ePuzzles and Games	●	●	●
• Vocabulary eFlashcards	●	●	●
• In Motion Animations	●	●	●
• Study Central™	●	●	●
• Web Activity Lesson Plans		●	
• Vocabulary PuzzleMaker	●	●	●
• Historical Thinking Activities		●	
• Beyond the Textbook	●	●	●

READING SUPPORT FROM JAMESTOWN EDUCATION

- **Timed Readings Plus in Social Studies** helps students increase their reading rate and fluency while maintaining comprehension. The 400-word passages are similar to those found on state and national assessments.
- **Reading in the Content Area: Social Studies** concentrates on six essential reading skills that help students better comprehend what they read. The book includes 75 high-interest nonfiction passages written at increasing levels of difficulty.
- **Reading Social Studies** includes strategic reading instruction and vocabulary support in Social Studies content for both ELLs and native speakers of English.

www.jamestowneducation.com

NATIONAL GEOGRAPHIC
Index to National Geographic Magazine:

The following article relates to this chapter:

- "The Okies—Beyond the Dust Bowl," by William Howarth, September 1984.

National Geographic Society Products To order the following, call National Geographic at 1-800-368-2728:

- ZipZapMap! USA (ZipZapMap!)

Access National Geographic's new, dynamic MapMachine Web site and other geography resources at:

www.nationalgeographic.com
www.nationalgeographic.com/maps

Biography A&E HOME VIDEO THE HISTORY CHANNEL

The following videotape programs are available from Glencoe as supplements to this chapter:

- The Tennessee Valley Authority (ISBN 0-76-700031-5)
- Eleanor Roosevelt: A Restless Spirit (ISBN 1-56-501405-7)

To order, call Glencoe at 1-800-334-7344. To find classroom resources to accompany many of these videos, check the following home pages:

A&E Television: www.aetv.com
The History Channel: www.historychannel.com

Reading List Generator CD-ROM

GLENCOE BOOKLINK 3

Use this database to search more than 30,000 titles to create a customized reading list for your students.

- Reading lists can be organized by students' reading level, author, genre, theme, or area of interest.
- The database provides Degrees of Reading Power™ (DRP) and Lexile™ readability scores for all selections.
- A brief summary of each selection is included.

Leveled reading suggestions for this chapter:

For students at a Grade 8 reading level:
- ***Franklin D. Roosevelt***, by Steve Potts

For students at a Grade 9 reading level:
- ***Franklin D. Roosevelt***, by Michael Burgan

For students at a Grade 10 reading level:
- ***Empire State Building***, by Elizabeth Mann

For students at a Grade 11 reading level:
- ***Eleanor Roosevelt: First Lady of the World***, by Doris Faber

For students at a Grade 12 reading level:
- ***Eleanor Roosevelt: A Life of Discovery***, by Russell Freedman

Introducing Chapter 19

Focus

MAKING CONNECTIONS

Can Government Fix the Economy?

Ask students to give examples of some of the ways that government tries to fix the economy, such as the Federal Reserve Board's regulation of interest rates. Discuss with students the questions listed on p. 649. Challenge students to activate prior knowledge of regulation of any of the economic sectors mentioned. **AL**

Teach

The Big Ideas

As students study the chapter, remind them to consider the section-based Big Ideas included in each section's Guide to Reading. The **Essential Questions** in the activities below tie in to the Big Ideas and help students think about and understand important chapter concepts. In addition, the Hands-on Chapter Projects with their culminating activities relate the content from each section to the Big Ideas. These activities build on each other as students progress through the chapter. Section activities culminate in the wrap-up activity on the Visual Summary page.

Chapter 19

Roosevelt and the New Deal

1933–1941

SECTION 1 The First New Deal
SECTION 2 The Second New Deal
SECTION 3 The New Deal Coalition

During the 1932 presidential campaign, New York governor Franklin D. Roosevelt greets a coal miner in West Virginia.

Hoover 1929–1933

Franklin D. Roosevelt 1933–1945

U.S. PRESIDENTS

U.S. EVENTS

WORLD EVENTS

1931 — 1933 — 1935

1933
- Unemployment peaks at 24.9%
- FDR's "100 Days" results in 9 new federal programs

1934
- Securities and Exchange Commission is created

1935
- Social Security Act and Wagner Act are passed
- Supreme Court strikes down NIRA

1933
- Hitler becomes German chancellor
- World Economic Conference fails to reduce tariffs

1935
- Hitler denounces Treaty of Versailles
- Canada creates minimum wage and unemployment insurance

Section 1

The First New Deal

Essential Question: In what areas did the New Deal attempt to make major economic improvements? *(The New Deal targeted banks [FDIC], the stock market [SEC], debt relief for home owners [HOLC], farms [FCA and AAA], industry [NRA], and public works programs to aid the unemployed [CCC, PWA, CWA].)* Tell students that in Section 1 they will learn about many programs that were developed to stimulate the economy. **OL**

Section 2

The Second New Deal

Essential Question: How did the Second New Deal assist unions, the elderly, and the unemployed? *(The Wagner Act gave workers the right to organize in unions. The Social Security Act benefited both the elderly workers and the unemployed.)* Inform students that in this section they will study programs that still exist. **OL**

Chapter Audio

MAKING CONNECTIONS

Can Government Fix the Economy?

During the 1930s, New Deal programs increased government regulation of banking, industry, and farming; gave greater rights to workers; and provided government aid to the unemployed and senior citizens.

- ***What kind of problems do you think government can solve?***
- ***What difficulties can result when the government tries to regulate the economy?***

FOLDABLES

Analyzing Long-Term Effects Make a Folded Chart Foldable showing major New Deal programs and their long-term effects. In one column, describe the program's original purpose. In the second column, identify how those programs still influence government and society today.

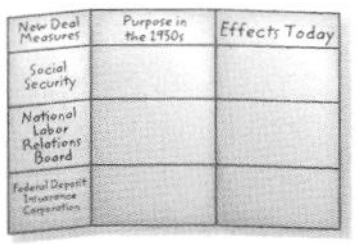

1936
- "Court-packing" plan creates controversy

1937
- Sit-down strikes force General Motors to recognize UAW

1938
- Fair Labor Standards Act sets minimum wage and 40-hour workweek

1937

1939

1936
- Wave of sit-down strikes in France leads to 40-hour workweek
- Spanish Civil War begins

1938
- Germany annexes Austria
- Mexico takes control of U.S. oil companies in Mexico

1939
- World War II begins

History ONLINE Visit glencoe.com and enter *QuickPass*™ code TAV9846c19 for Chapter 19 resources.

Section 3

The New Deal Coalition

Essential Question: What was the legacy of the New Deal? *(New Deal programs gave many people a stronger sense of stability and security by creating a safety net. It positioned the federal government as conflict mediator in a broker state.)* Tell students that in Section 3 they will learn about the lasting effects of the New Deal. **OL**

Introducing
Chapter 19

More About the Photo

Visual Literacy After becoming disabled, Roosevelt had a special Model A Ford with hand controls built for his use. Driving that car, he could feel physically independent. During campaigning, however, he often used a driver to free him for greeting voters. During his first campaign, he delivered almost 60 speeches, 27 of them major addresses, to allay fears that he was not physically strong enough to endure the strain of the presidency.

FOLDABLES™ Study Organizer **Dinah Zike's Foldables**

Dinah Zike's Foldables are three-dimensional, interactive graphic organizers that help students practice basic writing skills, review vocabulary terms, and identify main ideas. Instructions for creating and using Foldables can be found in the Appendix at the end of this book and in the *Dinah Zike's Reading and Study Skills Foldables* booklet.

History ONLINE

Visit glencoe.com and enter *QuickPass*™ code TAV9399c19T for Chapter 19 resources, including a Chapter Overview, Study Central™, Study-to-Go, Student Web Activity, Self-Check Quiz, and other materials.

Focus

Bellringer

Daily Focus Transparency 19-1

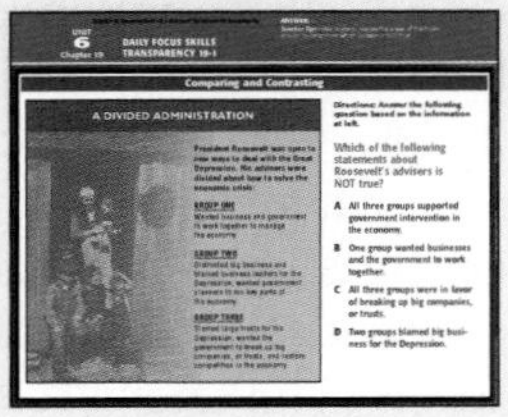

Guide to Reading

Answer: Major problems addressed include bank runs, unprotected bank deposits, stock fraud, and the plight of farmers.

Section Spotlight Video

To generate student interest and provide a springboard for class discussion, access the Chapter 19, Section 1 video at glencoe.com or on the video DVD.

Section 1 — Section Audio — Spotlight Video

The First New Deal

Guide to Reading

Big Ideas

Individual Action Franklin Delano Roosevelt's character and experiences prepared him for the presidency.

Content Vocabulary
- polio *(p. 650)*
- gold standard *(p. 652)*
- bank holiday *(p. 652)*
- fireside chats *(p. 653)*

Academic Vocabulary
- apparent *(p. 651)*
- ideology *(p. 652)*
- fundamental *(p. 658)*

People and Events to Identify
- New Deal *(p. 651)*
- Hundred Days *(p. 652)*
- Civilian Conservation Corps *(p. 658)*

Reading Strategy

Sequencing As you read about Roosevelt's first three months in office, complete a time line to record the major problems he addressed during this time.

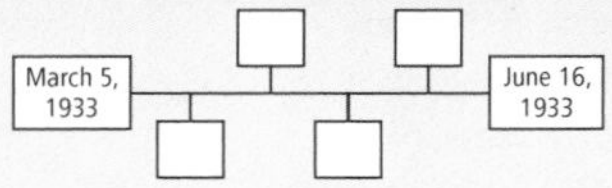

Franklin Delano Roosevelt was elected president in 1932, following his promise of a "new deal" for Americans. In his first 100 days in office, he let loose a flood of legislation designed to rescue banks, industry, and agriculture and provide jobs for the unemployed.

Roosevelt's Rise to Power

MAIN Idea Franklin D. Roosevelt was governor of New York when he was elected president in 1932, promising a New Deal for the American people.

HISTORY AND YOU Do you believe your past experiences can make you stronger? Read how FDR's experiences helped prepare him to be president.

A distant cousin of Theodore Roosevelt, Franklin Delano Roosevelt grew up in Hyde Park, New York. In his youth he learned to hunt, ride horses, and sail; he also developed a lifelong commitment to conservation and a love of rural America. Roosevelt was educated at Harvard and Columbia Law School. While at Harvard, he became friends with Theodore Roosevelt's niece Eleanor, whom he later married.

Intensely competitive, Roosevelt liked to be in control. He also liked being around people. His charming personality, deep rich voice, and wide smile expressed confidence and optimism. In short, his personality seemed made for a life in politics.

Roosevelt began his political career in 1910, when he was elected to the New York State Senate. Three years later, having earned a reputation as a progressive reformer, he became assistant secretary of the navy in the Wilson administration. In 1920 his reputation (and famous surname) helped him win the vice presidential nomination on the unsuccessful Democratic ticket.

After losing the election, Roosevelt temporarily withdrew from politics. The next year he caught the dreaded paralyzing disease **polio.** Although there was no cure, Roosevelt refused to give in. He began a vigorous exercise program to restore muscle control. Eventually, by wearing heavy steel braces on his legs, he was able to walk short distances by leaning on a cane and someone's arm and swinging his legs forward from his hips.

While recovering from polio, Roosevelt depended on his wife and his aide Louis Howe to keep his name prominent in the New York Democratic Party. Eleanor Roosevelt became an effective public speaker, and her efforts kept her husband's political career alive.

By the mid-1920s, Roosevelt was again active in the Democratic Party. In 1928 he ran for governor of New York. He campaigned hard

Resource Manager

R Reading Strategies	C Critical Thinking	D Differentiated Instruction	W Writing Support	S Skill Practice
Teacher Edition • Taking Notes, p. 652 • Predicting, p. 658 • Act. Prior Know., p. 659 **Additional Resources** • Read Skills Act., URB p. 83 • Guid. Read. Act., URB p. 110 • Prim. Source Read., URB p. 97 • Foldables, p. 72	**Teacher Edition** • Ident. Central Issues, p. 651 • Compare/Contrast, p. 652 • Det. Cause/Effect, p. 654 • Predict. Conseq., p. 656 • Analyzing Info, p. 657 • Making Gen., p. 658 **Additional Resources** • Interp. Pol. Cartoons, URB p. 103 • Quizzes and Tests, p. 269	**Teacher Edition** • Advanced Learners, p. 653 • Logical/Math., p. 655 **Additional Resources** • English Learner Act., URB p. 87 • Am. History in Graphic Novel, p. 49	**Teacher Edition** • Persuasive Writing, p. 656 **Additional Resources** • Supreme Court Case Studies, p. 49	**Teacher Edition** • Reading a Time Line, p. 654 **Additional Resources** • Read. Essen., p. 210 • Historical Analy., URB p. 84 • Past & Present, URB p. 96 • Crit. Think. Skills, URB p. 94

PRIMARY SOURCE

Roosevelt's First Inaugural Address

March 4, 1933

"This is preeminently the time to speak the truth, the whole truth, frankly and boldly. Nor need we shrink from honestly facing conditions in our country today. This great Nation will endure as it has endured, will revive and will prosper. So, first of all, let me assert my firm belief that the only thing we have to fear is fear itself—nameless, unreasoning, unjustified terror which paralyzes needed efforts to convert retreat into advance.

. . . Restoration calls, however, not for changes in ethics alone. This Nation asks for action, and action now.

. . . Our greatest primary task is to put people to work. This is no unsolvable problem if we face it wisely and courageously. It can be accomplished in part by direct recruiting by the Government itself, treating the task as we would treat the emergency of a war.

. . . Action in this image and to this end is feasible under the form of government which we have inherited from our ancestors. Our Constitution is so simple and practical that it is possible always to meet extraordinary needs by changes in emphasis and arrangement without loss of essential form.

We do not distrust the future of essential democracy. The people of the United States have not failed. In their need they have registered a mandate that they want direct, vigorous action."

—from *The Public Papers and Addresses of Franklin D. Roosevelt*

▲ *Franklin Roosevelt delivers his First Inaugural Address.*

DBQ Document-Based Questions

1. **Analyzing Primary Sources** Why does Roosevelt think that "nameless, unreasoning, unjustified terror" is such a big problem?
2. **Identifying Central Issues** What unspoken fear does Roosevelt address in the final two paragraphs?

to demonstrate that his illness had not slowed him down, and he narrowly won the election. Two years later he was reelected in a landslide. As governor, Roosevelt oversaw the creation of the first state relief agency to aid the unemployed.

Roosevelt's popularity in New York paved the way for his presidential nomination in 1932. Americans saw in him an energy and optimism that gave them hope despite the tough economic times. After Roosevelt became president, his serenity and confidence amazed people. When one aide commented on his attitude, Roosevelt replied, "If you had spent two years in bed trying to wiggle your big toe, after that anything else would seem easy."

In mid-June 1932, with the country deep in the Depression, Republicans gathered in Chicago and nominated Herbert Hoover to run for a second term as president. Later that month, the Democrats also held their national convention in Chicago. When Roosevelt won the nomination, he broke with tradition by flying to Chicago to accept it in person. His speech set the tone for his campaign:

PRIMARY SOURCE

"Let it be from now on the task of our Party to break foolish traditions. . . . It is inevitable that the main issue of this campaign should revolve about . . . a depression so deep that it is without precedent. . . . Republican leaders not only have failed in material things, they have failed in national vision, because in disaster they have held out no hope. . . . I pledge you, I pledge myself, to a new deal for the American people."

—from *The Public Papers and Addresses of Franklin D. Roosevelt*

From that point forward, Roosevelt's policies for ending the Depression became known as the **New Deal.** Roosevelt's confidence that he could make things better contrasted sharply with Herbert Hoover's **apparent** failure to do anything effective. On Election Day, Roosevelt won in a landslide, receiving the electoral vote of all but six states.

Reading Check **Interpreting** What events in Roosevelt's life shaped his ideas and character?

Teach

C Critical Thinking

Identifying Central Issues

Ask students to read the Primary Source quotation. **Ask:** What did Roosevelt consider to be the failure of the Republican leaders? *(They failed in national vision and in holding out hope.)* **OL**

DBQ Document Based Questions

Answers:

1. It keeps people from taking action to tackle the Depression.
2. that by taking action, the government will somehow overstep its rights given in the Constitution and the nation will lose democracy

Reading Check

Answer:

privileged upbringing, love of outdoors, good marriage, polio, experiences as a state senator, assistant secretary of the Navy, and a governor

Hands-On Chapter Project

Step 1

Writing a Newspaper

Step 1: Identifying American Groups to Watch Small groups of students receive their assignments.

Directions Divide the class into five groups, assigning each group one of the following groups of Americans: women, children, African Americans, Native Americans, and Hispanic Americans. Tell students that they will create a newspaper from the viewpoint of their assigned group during the 1930s. The newspaper will include news stories, editorials, and cartoons. Encourage students to begin a separate section of their notebooks to take notes on the chapter from their assigned viewpoint and to record findings from additional research in the library or on the Internet.

Putting It Together Make sure that students have in-class access to copies of local and national newspapers as a model on which to base their own newspapers. **OL**

(Chapter Project continued on page 663)

C Critical Thinking

Comparing and Contrasting Ask students to think about the question: How was the New Deal a continuation of the Progressive era? Tell students to write down ways in which the two were alike and different as they read the section. At the end of the section, debate the question. AL

R Reading Strategy

Taking Notes Have students create graphic organizers to take notes on the section "A Divided Administration." Suggest they use a three-column chart to jot down the ideas of the three groups within FDR's administration. BL

Reading Check

Answer:
One group wanted joint government-business cooperation, another wanted government control of business, and a third group wanted more competition.

The Hundred Days

MAIN Idea Upon taking office, FDR launched the New Deal by sending 15 major pieces of legislation to Congress.

HISTORY AND YOU Do you remember reading about the "New Nationalism" and "New Freedom"? Read how those ideas influenced New Deal legislation.

Although Roosevelt won the presidency in November 1932, the country's unemployed and homeless had to endure another winter as they waited for his inauguration on March 4, 1933. All through the winter, unemployment continued to rise and bank runs increased, further threatening the banking system.

Some of the bank runs occurred because people feared that Roosevelt would abandon the **gold standard** and reduce the value of the dollar in order to fight the Depression. Under the gold standard, one ounce of gold equaled a set number of dollars. To reduce the value of the dollar, the United States would have to stop exchanging dollars for gold. Many Americans, and many foreign investors with deposits in American banks, decided to take their money out of the banks and convert it to gold before it lost its value.

Across the nation, people stood in long lines with paper bags and suitcases, waiting to withdraw their money from banks. By March 1933, more than 4,000 banks had collapsed, wiping out nine million savings accounts. In 38 states, governors declared **bank holidays**—closing the remaining banks before bank runs could put them out of business.

By the day of Roosevelt's inauguration, most of the nation's banks were closed. One in four workers was unemployed. The economy seemed paralyzed. Roosevelt knew he had to restore the nation's confidence. "First of all," the president declared in his Inaugural Address, "let me assert my firm belief that the only thing we have to fear is fear itself. . . . This nation asks for action, and action now!"

The New Deal Begins

Roosevelt and his advisers, sometimes called the "brain trust," came into office bursting with ideas about how to end the Depression. Roosevelt had no clear agenda, nor did he have a strong political **ideology.** The previous spring, during his campaign for the presidential nomination, Roosevelt had revealed the approach he would take as president. "The country needs," Roosevelt explained, "bold, persistent experimentation . . . . Above all, try something."

The new president began to send bill after bill to Congress. Between March 9 and June 16, 1933—which came to be called the **Hundred Days**—Congress passed 15 major acts to resolve the economic crisis, setting a pace for new legislation that has never been equaled. Together, these programs made up what would later be called the First New Deal. **C**

A Divided Administration

To generate new ideas and programs, Roosevelt deliberately chose advisers who disagreed with each other. He wanted to hear many different points of view, and by setting his advisers against one another, Roosevelt ensured that he alone made the final decision on what policies to pursue.

Despite their disagreements, Roosevelt's advisers generally favored some form of government intervention in the economy—although they disagreed over what the government's role should be.

One influential group during the early years of Roosevelt's administration supported the "New Nationalism" of Theodore Roosevelt. These advisers believed that if government agencies worked with businesses to regulate wages, prices, and production, they could lift the economy out of the Depression. **R**

A second group of Roosevelt's advisers went even further. They distrusted big business and blamed business leaders for causing the Depression. These advisers wanted government planners to run key parts of the economy.

A third group in Roosevelt's administration supported the "New Freedom" of Woodrow Wilson. These advisers wanted Roosevelt to support "trust busting" by breaking up big companies and allowing competition to set wages, prices, and production levels. They also thought the government should impose regulations to keep economic competition fair.

Reading Check **Summarizing** What ideas did Roosevelt's advisers support?

Additional Support

Teacher Tip

At the time of the Great Depression, the United States did not have any social programs in place for its citizens. Suggest students use the Internet to find current programs that assist those in need. The government Web site for HUD, for example, offers information on housing.

Activity: Collaborative Learning

Making a Plan Before students begin reading about actual New Deal programs, divide the class into small groups of four or five. Ask each student within each group to concentrate on one of the issues facing Roosevelt: safeguarding bank deposits, providing emergency relief, bolstering business, or creating jobs. Have members of the groups review and refine each other's ideas. Allow time for groups to present their ideas to the class. OL

People IN HISTORY

Eleanor Roosevelt
1884–1962

Orphaned at age 10, Eleanor Roosevelt was raised by relatives and later attended boarding school in England. When she returned home as a young woman, she devoted time to a settlement house on Manhattan's Lower East Side. During this time, she became engaged to Franklin D. Roosevelt, a distant cousin. They were married in 1905. At their wedding, Eleanor's uncle, President Theodore Roosevelt, gave her away.

During FDR's presidency, Eleanor Roosevelt transformed the role of First Lady. Rather than restricting herself to traditional hostess functions, she became an important figure in his administration. She traveled extensively, toured factories and coal mines, and met with factory workers and farmers. She then told her husband what people were thinking. In doing so, she became FDR's "eyes and ears" when his disability made travel difficult.

Eleanor was also a strong supporter of civil rights and prodded her husband to stop discrimination in New Deal programs. When the Daughters of the American Revolution barred African American singer Marian Anderson from performing in its auditorium, Eleanor intervened and arranged for Anderson to perform at the Lincoln Memorial instead.

After FDR's death, Eleanor remained politically active. She continued to write her syndicated newspaper column, "My Day," which she began in 1936, and became a delegate to the United Nations where she helped draft the Universal Declaration of Human Rights.

How might Franklin Roosevelt's political career have been different if Eleanor had not been his wife?

▲ *In this 1935 photo, Eleanor Roosevelt speaks to Geraldine Walker, a five-year-old from Detroit, Michigan, as slums in that city were about to be cleared.*

Banks and Debt Relief

MAIN Idea President Roosevelt took steps to strengthen banks and the stock market and to help farmers and homeowners keep their property.

HISTORY AND YOU Have you ever watched a presidential address? Read about Roosevelt's "fireside chats" and how they encouraged optimism that the economy would get better.

As the debate over policies and programs swirled around him, President Roosevelt took office with one thing clear in his mind. Very few of the proposed solutions would work as long as the nation's banks remained closed. The first thing he had to do was restore confidence in the banking system.

D On his very first night in office, Roosevelt told Secretary of the Treasury William H. Woodin that he wanted an emergency banking bill ready for Congress in less than five days. The following afternoon, Roosevelt declared a national bank holiday, temporarily closing all banks, and called Congress into a special session scheduled to begin on March 9, 1933.

When Congress convened, the House of Representatives unanimously passed the Emergency Banking Relief Act after only 38 minutes of debate. The Senate approved the bill that evening, and Roosevelt signed it into law shortly afterward. The new law required federal examiners to survey the nation's banks and issue Treasury Department licenses to those that were financially sound.

On March 12 President Roosevelt addressed the nation by radio. Sixty million people listened to this first of many "**fireside chats,**" direct talks in which Roosevelt let the American people know what he was trying to accomplish. He told people that their money would be secure if they put it back into the banks: "I assure you that it is safer to keep your money in a reopened bank than under the mattress." When banks opened the day after the speech, deposits far outweighed withdrawals. The banking crisis was over.

D Differentiated Instruction

Advanced Learners Invite students to find out the usual amount of time it takes for present-day Congresses to write and pass a bill. Then have them compare that to FDR's request for a banking bill in less than five days, perhaps using a chart to explain their findings to the class. **AL**

People IN HISTORY

Answer: If Eleanor Roosevelt had not been Franklin's wife, his political career may well have ended when he contracted polio. His effectiveness as president would have been less without her unannounced eyewitness observations.

Additional Support

Extending the Content

Eleanor Roosevelt Not used to public speaking, Eleanor Roosevelt experienced stage fright when confronted with an audience. Her knees shook, but she soon became one of the most successful speakers of her time. She was also the first First Lady to hold her own regular press conferences, which offered female reporters the opportunity to find out White House information. When the Second Bonus Army marched on Washington, D.C., Eleanor went down to visit the veterans, who were using an army camp the president had offered them. Even though the bonuses were still not paid, veterans were offered food, medical care, and a navy band. One said, "Hoover sent the army. Roosevelt sent his wife." Eleanor traveled to check on so many government projects that the Secret Service gave her the code name "Rover."

C Critical Thinking

Determining Cause and Effect Have students read the section on the FDIC and SEC. Ask them to identify the causes for each provision of the Securities Act and Glass-Steagall Act. *(Securities Act: required companies selling stocks and bonds to give complete and truthful information to investors, because many investors during the 1920s had no reliable information about companies. Glass-Steagall Act: separated commercial and investment banking firms because banks had lent money to play the stock market, putting depositors' funds at risk. It also created the FDIC to insure deposited funds.)* OL

S Skill Practice

Reading a Time Line **Ask:** On what days did two major events occur and what were they? *(May 12: Agricultural Adjustment Act signed and Federal Emergency Relief Administration begins making grants to the states; June 16: PWA begins and the NRA begins setting codes for industry)* OL

Additional Support

C The FDIC and SEC

Although President Roosevelt had restored confidence in the banking system, many of his advisers urged him to go further. They pushed for new regulations for both banks and the stock market. Roosevelt agreed with their ideas and supported the Securities Act of 1933 and the Glass-Steagall Banking Act.

The Securities Act required companies that sold stocks and bonds to provide complete and truthful information to investors. The following year, Congress created a government agency, the Securities and Exchange Commission (SEC), to regulate the stock market and prevent fraud.

The Glass-Steagall Act separated commercial banking from investment banking. Commercial banks handle everyday transactions. They take deposits, pay interest, cash checks, and lend money for mortgages. Under the Glass-Steagall Act, these banks were no longer allowed to risk depositors' money by using it to speculate on the stock market.

To further protect depositors, the Glass-Steagall Act also created the Federal Deposit Insurance Corporation (FDIC) to provide government insurance for bank deposits up to a certain amount. By protecting depositors in this way, the FDIC greatly increased public confidence in the banking system.

Mortgage and Debt Relief

While some of Roosevelt's advisers believed low prices had caused the Depression, others believed that debt was the main obstacle to economic recovery. With incomes falling, people had to use most of their money to pay their debts and had little left over to buy goods or services. Many Americans, terrified of losing their homes and farms, cut back on their spending to make sure they could pay their mortgages. Roosevelt responded to the crisis by introducing several policies intended to assist Americans with their debts.

The Home Owners' Loan Corporation To help homeowners make their mortgage payments, Roosevelt asked Congress to establish the Home Owners' Loan Corporation (HOLC). The HOLC bought the mortgages of many

THE First Hundred Days

March 9
Roosevelt signs the Emergency Banking Relief Act and 3 days later delivers his first fireside chat

▲ Farmers in Texas receive their AAA checks.

May 12
The Agricultural Adjustment Act is signed, and farmers soon begin receiving payments to destroy their crops in an effort to push up prices

April 1933 — May 1933

S

March 31
The Civilian Conservation Corps is created and soon afterward begins hiring 3 million young men to work in the nation's forests

May 12
The Federal Emergency Relief Administration begins making grants to states to help the unemployed

Activity: Economics Connection

Personal Debt Americans generally have high debt levels and low savings levels. Ask students to use library or Internet resources to find the latest figures on individual and national credit debt. Then have them find recommendations for wise use of credit. Ask them to share their findings with the class via a poster presentation. **Ask:** How can a young person establish credit wisely? *(Students may suggest limiting the number of credit cards and paying off balances each month, as well as choosing cards with low interest rates.)* OL homeowners who were behind in their payments. It then restructured them with longer terms of repayment and lower interest rates. Roughly 10 percent of homeowners received HOLC loans.

The HOLC did not help everyone. It made loans only to homeowners who were not farm owners and who were still employed. When **D** people lost their jobs and could no longer make their mortgage payments, the HOLC foreclosed on their property, just as a bank would have done. Between 1933 and 1936, the three years during which it functioned as a loan source, the HOLC made loans to cover one million mortgages—one out of every ten in the United States.

The Farm Credit Administration Three days after Congress authorized the creation of the HOLC, it authorized the Farm Credit Administration (FCA) to help farmers refinance their mortgages. Over the next seven months, the FCA lent four times as much money to farmers as the entire banking system had the year before. It was also able to push interest rates substantially lower. These loans saved millions of farms from foreclosure.

Although FCA loans helped many farmers in the short term, their long-term value can be questioned. FCA loans helped less efficient farmers keep their land, but giving loans to poor farmers meant that the money was not available to lend to more efficient businesses in the economy. Although FCA loans may have slowed the overall economic recovery, they did help many desperate and impoverished people hold onto their land.

Reading Check **Explaining** How did the government restore confidence in the banking system?

▲ *Workers of the Grand Coulee Dam in Washington.*

May 18
Congress creates the Tennessee Valley Authority

June 13
The Home Owners' Loan Corporation is authorized to make low interest mortgage loans to homeowners

June 16
The Public Works Administration is created. Under the leadership of Harold Ickes, it begins spending over $3 billion on public works such as new highways, dams, and public buildings. The agency begins spending.

June 1933

June 16
The National Recovery Administration is authorized to begin setting codes and regulations for industry

Analyzing TIME LINES

1. **Analyzing** What groups of people were targeted for help in the first hundred days of Roosevelt's first term?
2. **Drawing Conclusions** What was Roosevelt's first act after becoming president? Why do you think he chose this as a first step?

D Differentiated Instruction

Logical/Mathematical
Invite students to create bar or circle graphs that show the scope of the Home Owners' Loan Corporation. **AL**

Analyzing TIME LINES

Answers:
1. the unemployed, farmers, home owners
2. His first act was to sign the Emergency Banking Relief Act, then to deliver a fireside chat three days later. He wanted to restore confidence in the banks and to reassure people that things were getting better.

Reading Check

Answer:
Roosevelt ordered a bank holiday, signed the Emergency Banking Relief Act into law, and addressed the nation in a "fireside chat." He also supported the Glass-Steagall Act, which created the FDIC to provide government insurance for bank deposits.

Additional Support

Activity: Interdisciplinary Connection

Language Arts Have students listen to a recording of one of Roosevelt's fireside chats, which are available at libraries and on the Internet. Then have them view an address by the current president. Discuss how the speeches and delivery compare and contrast. **Ask:** How do the styles of speaking reflect the people in office and the events going on at the time of the speech? *(Answers will vary depending on the speeches that students hear.)* **AL**

C Critical Thinking

Predicting Consequences Have students read only the first paragraph of the section "The AAA." Then ask them to predict what would happen to prices after farmers followed the advice of the AAA. *(They would rise.)* **BL**

W Writing Support

Persuasive Writing Ask students to write a newspaper editorial in favor of or opposed to the policy of slaughtering animals and taking fields out of production during a time of hunger. Remind them to support their ideas with facts. **OL**

Farms and Industry

MAIN Idea New Deal legislation tried to raise crop prices and stabilize industry.

HISTORY AND YOU Can you think of a product that gets more expensive when less of it is available? Read to learn how some New Deal programs tried to raise prices.

Many of Roosevelt's advisers believed that both farmers and businesses were suffering because prices were too low and production too high. Several advisers believed competition was inefficient and bad for the economy. They favored creating federal agencies to manage the economy.

The AAA

To further help the nation's farmers, Secretary of Agriculture Henry Wallace drafted the Agricultural Adjustment Act. President Roosevelt asked Congress to pass the act. This legislation was based on a simple idea—that prices for farm goods were low because farmers grew too much food. Under Roosevelt's program, the government would pay some farmers *not* to raise certain livestock, and *not* to grow certain crops. Some farmers were also asked *not* to produce dairy products. As the program went into effect, farmers slaughtered 6 million piglets and 200,000 sows and plowed under 10 million acres of cotton—all in an effort to raise prices. The program was administered by the Agricultural Adjustment Administration (AAA).

Over the next two years, farmers withdrew millions more acres from cultivation and received more than $1 billion in support payments. The program accomplished its goal: the farm surplus fell greatly by 1936. Food prices then rose, as did total farm income, which quickly increased by more than 50 percent.

In a nation caught in a Depression, however, raising food prices drew harsh criticism. Furthermore, not all farmers benefited. Large commercial farmers who concentrated on one crop profited more than smaller farmers who raised several products. Worse, thousands of poor tenant farmers, many of them African Americans, became homeless and jobless when landlords took their fields out of production.

PAST & PRESENT

The TVA

The Tennessee Valley Authority (TVA) was a New Deal project that produced visible benefits. The TVA built dams to control floods, conserve forest lands, and bring electricity to rural areas.

Today, TVA power facilities include 17,000 miles of transmission lines, 29 hydroelectric dams, 11 fossil-fuel plants, 4 combustion-turbine plants, 3 nuclear power plants, and a pumped-storage facility. These combine to bring power to nearly 8 million people in a seven-state region.

Since 1998, the TVA has been working to reduce air pollution. Projects are designed to cut harmful emissions released into the air. The TVA is committed to developing programs that protect the environment.

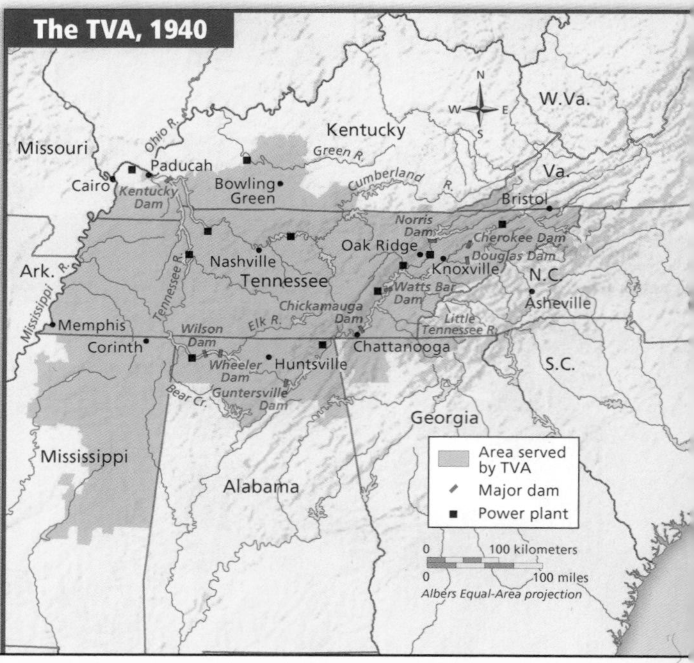

Additional Support

Activity: Economics Connection

Supply and Demand Remind students of the economic law of supply and demand in establishing prices. Discuss any current situation in which this law is affecting their lives. For example, bad weather in California or Florida affects the availability of fresh, inexpensive produce. **Ask:** Do you believe it is right to keep fields out of production when people are hungry in order to drive up prices? *(Students' opinions will vary, but may suggest that feeding people is more important than making a profit.)* **OL**

The NRA

The government turned its attention to manufacturing in June 1933, when Roosevelt and Congress enacted the National Industrial Recovery Act (NIRA). The NIRA suspended antitrust laws and allowed business, labor, and government to cooperate in setting up voluntary rules for each industry.

These rules were known as codes of fair competition. Some codes set prices, established minimum wages, and limited factories to two shifts per day so that production could be spread to as many firms as possible. Other codes shortened workers' hours, with the goal of creating additional jobs. Another provision in the law guaranteed workers the right to form unions. The codes also helped businesses develop codes of fair competition within industries.

Under the leadership of Hugh Johnson, the National Recovery Administration (NRA) ran the entire program. Business owners who signed code agreements received signs displaying the National Recovery Administration's symbol—a blue eagle—and the slogan, "We Do Our Part." The NRA had limited power to enforce the codes, but urged consumers to buy goods only from companies that displayed the blue eagle.

The NRA did revive a few American industries, but its gains proved short-lived. Small companies complained, justifiably, that large corporations wrote the codes to favor themselves. American employers disliked codes that gave workers the right to form unions and bargain collectively over wages and hours. They also argued that paying high minimum wages forced them to charge higher prices to cover their costs.

C

The codes were also difficult to administer, and business leaders often ignored them. Furthermore, businesses could choose not to sign code agreements and thus not be bound by their rules. It became obvious that the NRA was failing when industrial production actually fell after the organization was established. By the time the Supreme Court declared the NRA unconstitutional in 1935, it had already lost much of its political support.

Reading Check **Examining** What were the goals of the Agricultural Adjustment Act and the National Industrial Recovery Act?

2006

This photo shows the completed Cherokee Hydroelectric Dam.

Tennessee's Cherokee Dam is today part of the TVA. Workers (upper right) built it in the late 1930s.

MAKING CONNECTIONS

1. **Listing** Look at the map on the previous page. What states other than Tennessee benefited from the TVA projects?
2. **Examining** Where were most of the projects located?

Maps In MOtion See *StudentWorks™ Plus* or glencoe.com.

C Critical Thinking

Analyzing Information Ask students to analyze why the National Recovery Administration largely failed in its task. Tell them to find at least three reasons for the failure. *(Large companies wrote the codes to favor their interests, employers disliked unions and paying higher wages, and rules were difficult to administer and voluntary.)* **OL**

MAKING CONNECTIONS

Answers:
1. Kentucky, Alabama, Virginia, North Carolina, Georgia, and Mississippi
2. eastern Tennessee

Reading Check

Answer:
to improve the lot of farmers, set cooperative codes of fair competition, and improve the economy

Additional Support

Extending the Content

The National Industrial Recovery Act The NIRA was influenced by the work of the War Industries Board that functioned during World War I. Labor and business leaders also offered suggestions. The primary writers of the legislation were General Hugh S. Johnson, who had served on the War Industries Board, and New York senator Robert F. Wagner, later to be known for the act that bears his name. The NIRA also established the Public Works Administration, funding it with $3.3 billion.

R Reading Strategy

Predicting Ask students if they think that young people today would be interested in working in a group similar to the Civilian Conservation Corps. Have students explain their reasoning. **BL**

C Critical Thinking

Making Generalizations Invite students to generalize the CCC's effect on the morale of each of the groups of workers mentioned in the final paragraph. Ask them to imagine as well the effect on the families of those men. **OL**

Analyzing VISUALS

1. People are tossing quack solutions to Uncle Sam, the dock is collapsing, and pieces of it are hitting Uncle Sam.
2. Congress, shown as a nurse to ailing Uncle Sam

Additional Support

Relief Programs

MAIN Idea Programs such as the CCC, the PWA, and the WPA provided jobs for some unemployed workers.

HISTORY AND YOU Do you know who built your school, post office, or playground? Read about the projects completed by the New Deal workers.

History ONLINE Student Skill Activity To learn how to use a word processor, visit glencoe.com and complete the Skill activity.

While many of President Roosevelt's advisers emphasized tinkering with prices and providing debt relief to solve the Depression, others maintained that its **fundamental** cause was low consumption. They thought getting money into the hands of needy individuals would be the fastest remedy. Because neither Roosevelt nor his advisers wanted simply to give money to the unemployed, they supported work programs for the unemployed.

The CCC

R The most highly praised New Deal work relief program was the **Civilian Conservation Corps** (CCC). The CCC offered unemployed young men 18 to 25 years old the opportunity to work under the direction of the forestry service planting trees, fighting forest fires, and building reservoirs. To prevent a repeat of the Dust Bowl, the workers planted a line of more than 200 million trees, known as a Shelter Belt, from north Texas to North Dakota. R

The young men lived in camps near their work areas and earned $30 a month, $25 of which was sent directly to their families. The average CCC worker returned home after six to twelve months, better nourished and with greater self-respect. CCC programs also taught more than 40,000 of its recruits to read and write. By the time the CCC closed down in 1942, it had put 3 million young men to work outdoors—including 80,000 Native Americans, who helped to reclaim land they had once owned. After a second Bonus Army March on Washington in 1933, Roosevelt added some 250,000 veterans to the CCC as well. C

FERA and the PWA

A few weeks after authorizing the CCC, Congress established the Federal Emergency Relief Administration (FERA). Roosevelt chose

POLITICAL CARTOONS PRIMARY SOURCE
Did the New Deal Help Americans?

▲ This cartoon, entitled "How Much More Do We Need?" shows Uncle Sam grasping New Deal lifesavers to stay afloat.

▶ This 1935 cartoon shows FDR as a doctor with a variety of medicines to help ailing Uncle Sam.

Analyzing VISUALS DBQ

1. **Interpeting** In the cartoon at the left, what is happening to the dock, and why?
2. **Analyzing** With whom is President Roosevelt conferring in the cartoon at right?

Activity: Interdisciplinary Connection

Science Have interested students use library or Internet resources to find out about current conservation efforts by government agencies. For example, the United States Forestry Service, a division of the Department of Agriculture, manages 193 million acres (78 million ha) of national grasslands and forests. Students may want to start their research by visiting the Forest Service Web site at www.fs.fed.us. Ask students to share their findings with the class during a class discussion. **OL**

Harry Hopkins, a former social worker, to run the agency. FERA did not initially create projects for the unemployed. Instead, it channeled money to state and local agencies to fund their relief projects.

Half an hour after meeting with Roosevelt to discuss his new job, Hopkins set up a desk in the hallway outside of his office. In the next two hours, he spent $5 million on relief projects. When critics charged that some of the projects did not make sense in the long run, Hopkins replied, "People don't eat in the long run—they eat every day."

In June 1933 Congress authorized another relief agency, the Public Works Administration (PWA). One-third of the nation's unemployed were in the construction industry. To put them back to work, the PWA began building highways, dams, sewer systems, schools, and other government facilities. In most cases, the PWA did not hire workers directly but instead awarded contracts to construction companies. By insisting that contractors not discriminate against African Americans, the agency broke down some of the long-standing racial barriers in the construction trades.

The CWA

By the fall of 1933 neither FERA nor the PWA had reduced unemployment significantly. Hopkins realized that unless the federal government acted quickly, a huge number of unemployed citizens would be in severe distress once winter began. After Hopkins explained the situation, President Roosevelt authorized him to set up the Civil Works Administration (CWA).

R Unlike the PWA, the CWA hired workers directly. That winter the CWA employed 4 million people, including 300,000 women. Under Hopkins's direction, the agency built or improved 1,000 airports, 500,000 miles of roads, 40,000 school buildings, and 3,500 playgrounds and parks. The cost of the CWA was huge—the program spent nearly $1 billion in just five months.

Although the CWA helped many people get through the winter, President Roosevelt was alarmed by how quickly the agency was spending money. He did not want Americans to get used to the federal government providing them with jobs. Warning that the CWA would "become a habit with the country," Roosevelt insisted that it be shut down the following spring.

Success of the First New Deal

During his first year in office, Roosevelt convinced Congress to pass an astonishing array of legislation. The programs enacted during the first New Deal did not restore prosperity, but they reflected Roosevelt's zeal for action and his willingness to experiment. Banks were reopened, many more people retained their homes and farms, and more people were employed. Perhaps the most important result of the first New Deal was a noticeable change in the spirit of the American people. Roosevelt's actions had inspired hope and restored Americans' faith in their nation.

✓ Reading Check **Identifying** What types of projects did public works programs undertake?

Section 1 REVIEW

Vocabulary

1. **Explain** the significance of: polio, New Deal, gold standard, bank holiday, Hundred Days, fireside chats, Civilian Conservation Corps.

Main Ideas

2. **Describing** What actions did Roosevelt take during the Hundred Days?
3. **Explaining** How did government regulate banks and the stock market in the first Roosevelt administration?
4. **Interpreting** How did the AAA affect farm prices?
5. **Organizing** Use a graphic organizer to list the major organizations of the First New Deal.

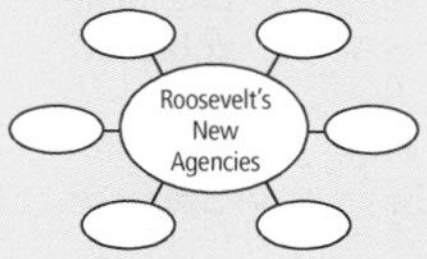

Critical Thinking

6. **Big Ideas** In what ways did FDR's early experiences shape his political ideology?
7. **Analyzing Charts** Look at the time line on pages 654–655. How did the various agencies listed change the role of government?

Writing About History

8. **Expository Writing** Interview a member of your community who lived during the Great Depression. How did the New Deal programs affect your community? Create a one-page report using a word processor to summarize your findings.

History ONLINE
Study Central™ To review this section, go to glencoe.com and click on Study Central.

R Reading Strategy

Activating Prior Knowledge Invite students to recall another example of women being included in a major national effort. *(Women gained new roles during World War I.)* **AL**

✓ Reading Check

Answer:
conservation and construction

Assess

History ONLINE

Study Central™ provides summaries, interactive games, and online graphic organizers to help students review content.

Close

Summarizing Ask students what they can infer was a secondary goal of the relief programs of the New Deal. *(to end racial discrimination)* **Ask:** What other example of this goal have you read about in this section? *(Eleanor Roosevelt's support of civil rights, particularly in the case of Marian Anderson)* **AL**

Section 1 REVIEW

Answers

1. All definitions can be found in the section and the Glossary.
2. FDR began to fix the banks and stock market, help farmers and the unemployed, and assist industry, as well as provide debt relief.
3. Congress created the Securities and Exchange Commission and the Federal Deposit Insurance Corporation.
4. It increased farm prices by providing an incentive to plant and raise less.
5. Answers may include the following: Major organizations: HOLC (Home Owners' Loan Corporation); FCA (Farm Credit Administration); AAA (Agricultural Adjustment Administration); NRA (National Recovery Administration); CCC (Civilian Conservation Corps); FERA (Federal Emergency Relief Administration); PWA (Public Works Administration); CWA (Civil Works Administration); TVA (Tennessee Valley Authority).
6. FDR's privileged upbringing, love of outdoors, good marriage, polio, and various political offices shaped his political ideology.
7. Answers should match text information.
8. Students' journal entries will vary but should reflect a working day for a member of one of the relief agencies.

ANALYZING PRIMARY SOURCES

Focus

Tell students that prior to the New Deal, most Americans had very little contact with the federal government or federal agencies because the government was much smaller. Before the 1930s, the only federal agency with which most Americans had regular contact was the U.S. Postal Service. Ask students to name some federal agencies that individual citizens may come into contact with today.

Teach

R Reading Strategy

Predicting Ask students to read carefully the last paragraph in Source 1. **Ask:** To what other sort of national crisis does President Roosevelt compare the challenge of solving the Depression? *(war)* Based on his speech, what would you expect him to do next? *(take immediate action to solve the nation's economic problems, commit huge government resources and money to the task)* OL AL

ANALYZING PRIMARY SOURCES

The First New Deal

When FDR took office in 1933, the economy had been getting worse for more than three years. During the first one hundred days of his presidency, he oversaw 15 major pieces of legislation that attempted to revive the nation's economy and provide relief to the unemployed. Never before had the federal government intervened so directly in the economy. Key to stopping the economic downslide was FDR's ability to inspire confidence that the nation's economic problems could be solved.

Study these primary sources and answer the questions that follow.

PRIMARY SOURCE 1

Inaugural Address, 1933

"I am certain that my fellow Americans expect that on my induction into the Presidency I will address them with a candor and a decision which the present situation of our nation impels. This is pre-eminently the time to speak the truth, the whole truth, frankly and boldly. . . .

"So, first of all, let me assert my firm belief that the only thing we have to fear is fear itself—nameless, unreasoning, unjustified terror which paralyzes needed efforts to convert retreat into advance. In every dark hour of our national life a leadership of frankness and vigor has met with that understanding and support of the people themselves which is essential to victory. I am convinced that you will again give that support to leadership in these critical days. . . .

"This Nation asks for action, and action now.

R "Our greatest primary task is to put people to work. This is no unsolvable problem if we face it wisely and courageously. It can be accomplished in part by direct recruiting by the Government itself, treating the task as we would treat the emergency of a war, but at the same time, through this employment, accomplishing greatly needed projects to stimulate and reorganize the use of our natural resources."

—President Franklin D. Roosevelt, first inaugural address, delivered March 4, 1933

Excerpted from *The Public Papers and Addresses of Franklin D. Roosevelt*

PRIMARY SOURCE 2

Oral History Interview

"During the whole '33 one-hundred days' Congress, people didn't know what was going on, the public. Couldn't understand these things that were being passed so fast. They knew something was happening, something good for them. They began investing and working and hoping again. . . .

"A Depression is much like a run on a bank. It's a crisis of confidence. People panic and grab their money."

—Raymond Moley, original member of FDR's "brains trust"

Excerpted from *Hard Times: An Oral History of the Great Depression (1970)*

PRIMARY SOURCE 3

Magazine Cover, 1933

► *"The Faces of Victory and Defeat," portrayal of Herbert Hoover and Roosevelt on inauguration day, March 4, 1933*

Additional Support

Activity: Interdisciplinary Connection

Political Science Unlike most Western European nations, the United States did not have any national system of unemployment insurance or retirement benefits before the 1930s. Today, most Americans do not question the need to have at least a basic system of social insurance (for retirees, unemployed workers, persons with disabilities, impoverished children). Using library or Internet sources, have students compare the system of social insurance created by the New Deal with similar programs that existed in the 1930s in another country (suggest Canada, Britain, or Germany). Then, ask them to compare the social policies and programs in their chosen country today with those that exist in the United States today. AL

PRIMARY SOURCE 4

New Deal poster for the CCC, c. 1935 ▼

PRIMARY SOURCE 5

Oral History Interview

"What Roosevelt and the New Deal did was to turn about and face the realities. . . . A hundred years from now, when historians look back on it, they will say a big corner was turned. People agreed that old things didn't work. What ran through the whole New Deal was finding a way to make things work.

"Before that, Hoover would loan money to farmers to keep their mules alive, but wouldn't loan money to keep their children alive. This was perfectly right within the framework of classical thinking. If an individual couldn't get enough to eat, it was because he wasn't on the ball. It was his responsibility. The New Deal said: Anybody who is unemployed isn't necessarily unemployed because he's shiftless."

—Economist Gardiner C. Means,
economic adviser in the Roosevelt administration

Excerpted from *Hard Times: An Oral History of the Great Depression (1970)*

PRIMARY SOURCE 7

Political Cartoon, 1933

▶ *President Roosevelt tries to "prime" the economic pump with government spending.*

PRIMARY SOURCE 6

Contemporary Book, 1934

"Even if the government conduct of business could give us the maximum of efficiency instead of least efficiency, it would be purchased at the cost of freedom. It would increase rather than decrease abuse and corruption, stifle initiative and invention, undermine the development of leadership, cripple the mental and spiritual energies of our people and the forces which make progress."

—Former president Herbert Hoover in his book,
The Challenge to Liberty (1934)

Excerpted from *The Era of Franklin D. Roosevelt, 1933–1945*

DBQ Document-Based Questions

1. **Evaluating** What themes did Roosevelt emphasize in his inaugural address? How would you have responded to this speech if you had been an unemployed worker?
2. **Explaining** Study Sources 2 and 3. How did FDR inspire confidence and optimism? What effect did this have on the economy?
3. **Describing** In Source 4, the poster highlights four opportunities offered by the CCC. Describe some specific ways the CCC provided such opportunities.
4. **Paraphrasing** In Source 5, how does the author define Roosevelt's attitude toward unemployment and Hoover's approach to unemployment?
5. **Evaluating** In Source 6, why does Herbert Hoover object to the New Deal? What programs do you think he found most objectionable?
6. **Speculating** Study the picture in Source 7. How does the artist feel about the New Deal? What symbols are used to convey that message?

D Differentiated Instruction

English Learners Ask students to study Source 5 and then write a paragraph that paraphrases its main points. Help students with words or idioms (such as "on the ball") with which they may be unfamiliar. **ELL**

W Writing Support

Persuasive Writing Ask students to write an essay in which they agree or disagree with the ideas of President Hoover as expressed in Source 6. In their essays, they should critique at least one New Deal program as an example to bolster their argument. **OL**

Assess/Close

Ask students to name some programs, agencies, or policies that were introduced during the First New Deal. Then, as a class, discuss whether they were a success, a failure, or moderately effective. Which ones are still around today?

Review

Answers

DBQ Document Based Questions

Answers:

1. Themes include truth and honesty, confidence, taking action, using the government to get people back to work. Answers will vary, but should note that most unemployed workers would respond positively to his message of hope.
2. Exerting a positive attitude (compare grinning FDR to dour Hoover) and getting legislation enacted inspired confidence. When people felt more confidence about the economy they were willing to invest and place money in banks again.
3. Answers will vary. Students may draw on examples from the previous section of the chapter.
4. Hoover's approach assumed direct aid, "the dole," to the poor would be bad for their personal character. Roosevelt's New Deal approach recognized farmers and unemployed workers were living in hardship due to forces beyond their control.
5. New Deal gives too much power to government, takes away personal freedom, and is less efficient than letting the free market solve economic problems. NRA and AAA are two good examples of programs that were attacked by conservatives.
6. The artist thinks the New Deal is failing to end the Depression and that the New Deal is too expensive. Despite the buckets of water (representing taxes) taken from the people, the New Deal pump leaks water in every direction (wasting taxpayer money).

Focus

Bellringer

Daily Focus Transparency 19-2

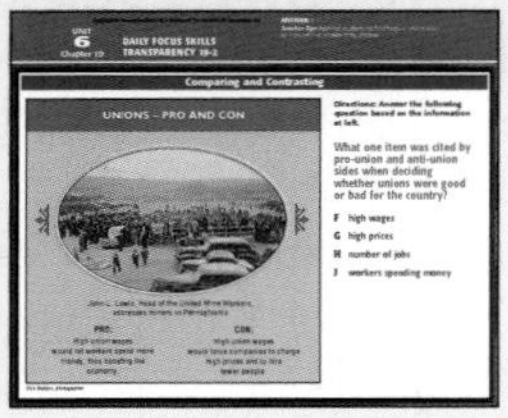

Guide to Reading

Answers may include the following: Legislation: Wagner Act; Provision: Workers had right to organize and to collective bargaining; Legislation: Social Security Act; Provision: security for retired workers, who received monthly checks beginning at age 65, unemployment insurance, and aid for people with certain disabilities and impoverished mothers with dependent children

Section Spotlight Video

To generate student interest and provide a springboard for class discussion, access the Chapter 19, Section 2 video at glencoe.com or on the video DVD.

Section 2 — Section Audio — Spotlight Video

The Second New Deal

Guide to Reading

Big Ideas

Economics and Society In 1935 Roosevelt introduced new programs to help unions, senior citizens, and the unemployed.

Content Vocabulary

- deficit spending *(p. 662)*
- binding arbitration *(p. 666)*
- sit-down strike *(p. 666)*

Academic Vocabulary

- benefit *(p. 663)*
- finance *(p. 664)*
- thereby *(p. 665)*

People and Events to Identify

- American Liberty League *(p. 663)*
- Works Progress Administration *(p. 664)*
- National Labor Relations Board *(p. 665)*
- Congress of Industrial Organizations *(p. 667)*
- Social Security Act *(p. 667)*

Reading Strategy

Organizing As you read about President Roosevelt's Second New Deal, complete a graphic organizer similar to the one below by filling in his main legislative successes during this period.

Legislation	Provisions

In response to criticisms of the New Deal, President Roosevelt introduced several major pieces of legislation in 1935. These laws created the Works Progress Administration, the National Labor Relations Board, and the Social Security Administration.

Launching the Second New Deal

MAIN Idea By 1935, the New Deal faced political and legal challenges, as well as growing concern that it was not ending the Depression.

HISTORY AND YOU Do you know anyone who can easily convince others to follow his or her ideas? Read about several people who used this power against Roosevelt and his New Deal policies.

Harry Hopkins, head of the Federal Emergency Relief Administration, worked long hours in his Washington office, a bare, dingy room with exposed water pipes. Hopkins also took to the road to explain the New Deal. Once in Iowa, where he was discussing spending programs, someone called out, "Who's going to pay for it?" Hopkins peeled off his jacket, loosened his tie, and rolled up his sleeves, before roaring his response: "You are!"

President Roosevelt appreciated Harry Hopkins's feistiness. He needed effective speakers who were willing to contend with his adversaries. Although Roosevelt had been tremendously popular during his first two years in office, opposition to his policies had begun to grow.

The economy had shown only a slight improvement, even though the New Deal had been in effect for two years. Although the programs had created more than 2 million new jobs, more than 10 million workers remained unemployed, and the nation's total income was about half of what it had been in 1929.

Criticism From Left and Right

Hostility toward Roosevelt came from both the political right and the left. People on the right generally believed the New Deal regulated business too tightly. The right wing also included many Southern Democrats who believed the New Deal had expanded the federal government's power at the expense of states' rights.

The right wing, which had opposed the New Deal from the beginning, increased that opposition by late 1934. To pay for his programs, Roosevelt had started **deficit spending,** abandoning a balanced budget and borrowing money. Many business leaders became greatly alarmed at the government's growing deficit.

Resource Manager

R Reading Strategies	C Critical Thinking	D Differentiated Instruction	W Writing Support	S Skill Practice
Teacher Edition • Academic Vocabulary, p. 663 • Act. Prior Know., p. 666 **Additional Resources** • Guid. Read. Act., URB p. 111 • Prim. Source Read., URB p. 99	**Teacher Edition** • Ident. Cent. Issues, p. 665 • Analyzing Prim. Sources, p. 666 **Additional Resources** • Interp. Political Cartoons, URB p. 103 • Supreme Court Case Studies, p. 51 • Quizzes and Tests, p. 270	**Teacher Edition** • Logical/Math, p. 664 **Additional Resources** • American Art and Music, URB p. 101 • Enrichment Act., URB p. 107 • Differentiated Instruct. Act., URB p. 85	**Teacher Edition** • Expository Writing, p. 664 **Additional Resources** • Content Vocab. Act., URB p. 89 • Academic Vocab. Act., URB p. 91	**Additional Resources** • Reinforcing Skills Act., URB p. 93 • Read. Essen., p. 214

PRIMARY SOURCE

Opposition to the New Deal

By 1935 some Americans had grown impatient with the New Deal economic recovery. They believed that the reforms did not go far enough and called for wider-ranging change.

◀ *Dr. Francis Townsend explains his ideas to offer pensions to business leaders at a 1936 luncheon in Philadelphia.*

▲ *Father Coughlin speaks to a crowd of 6,000 members of the National Union for Social Justice at the Hippodrome in Detroit shortly after the stock market collapse in 1929. By the mid-1930s, Coughlin favored massive taxes.*

▶ *Huey Long, who served Louisiana in the U.S. Senate, looked for ways to redistribute wealth.*

Analyzing VISUALS

1. **Comparing and Contrasting** What strikes you as the same and different about these three men?
2. **Assessing** Which man do you think would have the largest audience, and why?

In August 1934 business leaders and anti–New Deal politicians from both parties joined together to create the **American Liberty League.** Its purpose was to organize opposition to the New Deal and "teach the necessity of respect for the rights of person and property."

While criticisms from the right threatened to split the Democratic Party and reduce business support for Roosevelt, another serious challenge to the New Deal came from the political left. People on the left believed Roosevelt had not gone far enough. They wanted even more dramatic government economic intervention to shift wealth from the rich to middle-income and poor Americans.

Huey Long Perhaps the most serious threat came from Huey Long of Louisiana. As governor of Louisiana, Long had championed the poor and downtrodden. He had improved schools, colleges, and hospitals, and built roads and bridges. These **benefits** made Long popular, enabling him to build a powerful—but corrupt—political machine. In 1930 Long was elected to the U.S. Senate.

R

Long's attacks on the rich were popular in the midst of the Great Depression. He captivated audiences with folksy humor and fiery oratory. By 1934, he had established a national organization, the Share Our Wealth Society, to promote his plan for massive redistribution of wealth. Long announced he would run for president in 1936.

Father Coughlin Roosevelt also faced a challenge from Father Charles Coughlin, a Catholic priest in Detroit. About 30 to 45 million listeners heard his weekly radio show.

Originally an ardent New Deal supporter, Coughlin had become impatient with its moderate reforms. He called instead for inflating the currency and nationalizing the banking system. In 1935 Coughlin organized the National Union for Social Justice, which some Democrats feared would become a new political party.

History ONLINE Student Web Activity Visit glencoe.com and complete the activity on the New Deal.

Teach

R Reading Strategy

Academic Vocabulary Point out the term *benefits* near the end of the first column. Tell students that the Latin root *bene* means "well." Ask students to brainstorm other words that incorporate this root. *(beneficiary, benevolent, benediction)* **OL**

Analyzing VISUALS

Answers:

1. Students' responses will vary but may mention the more cheerful appearance of Father Coughlin and the different means each man used to spread his message. Each offered specific solutions to the nation's problems.
2. Students may say that Father Coughlin had the largest audience because he used the modern medium of radio rather than the more personal approach Townsend used.

Hands-On Chapter Project
Step 2

Writing a Newspaper

Step 2: Write and Plan Newspaper Copy Students begin to write articles and editorials and to draw cartoons based on the content of Section 1.

Directions Remind students to include the basic facts in news stories and to support opinions in editorials and letters to the editor. Have them plan the length of their newspaper and begin to write to fit that length. Encourage students to find templates online or in word processing software that can help them place copy in newspaper format.

Putting It Together Invite a teacher familiar with word processing programs to class to offer a tutorial for students unfamiliar with the software and how to use it.

(Chapter Project continued on page 669)

D Differentiated Instruction

Logical/Mathematical Invite students to depict the information on the WPA's achievements in graph form. Suggest they use a bar or circle graph. OL

W Writing Support

Expository Writing Have students use library or Internet resources to find out more about the women and men supported through Federal Number One. Ask students to use their findings to write a short essay describing the artists or their works. OL

Reading Check

Answer:
The economy did not improve quickly after two years. Right wing critics of the New Deal felt that it regulated business too tightly. Southern Democrats feared the expansion of the federal government. Business leaders opposed Roosevelt's deficit spending. Critics on the left felt the New Deal had not gone far enough.

Additional Support

The Townsend Plan A third challenge came from Francis Townsend, a California physician. Townsend proposed that the federal government pay citizens over age 60 a pension of $200 a month. Recipients would have to retire and spend their entire pension check each month. He believed the plan would increase spending and remove people from the workforce, freeing up jobs for the unemployed.

Townsend's proposal attracted millions of supporters, especially among older Americans, who mobilized as a political force for the first time. Townsend's program was particularly popular in the West. When combined with Long's support in the Midwest and South, and Coughlin's support among urban Catholics in the Northeast, Roosevelt faced the possibility of a coalition that would draw enough votes to prevent his reelection.

The WPA

Roosevelt was also disturbed by the failure of the New Deal to generate a rapid economic recovery. In 1935 he launched a series of programs now known as the Second New Deal.

D Among these new programs was the **Works Progress Administration** (WPA). Headed by Harry Hopkins, the WPA was the largest public works program of the New Deal. Between 1935 and 1941, the WPA spent $11 billion. Its 8.5 million workers constructed about 650,000 miles of highways, roads, and streets, 125,000 public buildings, and more than 8,000 parks. It built or improved more than 124,000 bridges and 853 airports.

W The WPA's most controversial program was Federal Number One, a program for artists, musicians, theater people, and writers. The artists created thousands of murals and sculptures for public buildings. Musicians established 30 symphony orchestras, as well as hundreds of smaller musical groups. The Federal Theater Project **financed** playwrights, actors, and directors. It also funded writers who recorded the stories of former slaves and others whose voices were not often heard.

The Supreme Court's Role

In May 1935, in *Schechter Poultry Company* v. *United States*, the Supreme Court unanimously struck down the authority of the National Recovery Administration. The Schechter brothers had been convicted of violating the NRA's poultry code.

The Court ruled that the Constitution did not allow Congress to delegate its legislative powers to the executive branch. Thus, it declared the NRA's codes unconstitutional. Although relieved to be rid of that "awful headache," the NRA, Roosevelt still worried about the ruling. It suggested that the Court could strike down the rest of the New Deal.

Roosevelt knew he needed a new series of programs to keep voters' support. He called congressional leaders to a White House conference. Pounding his desk, he thundered that Congress could not go home until it passed his new bills. That summer, Congress worked busily to pass Roosevelt's programs.

Reading Check **Identifying Points of View** What criticisms prompted the Second New Deal?

Debates IN HISTORY

Was the New Deal Socialistic?

Franklin Roosevelt took extraordinary measures to stimulate the economy with his New Deal programs. Many Americans were divided on the issue of increased government intervention in the economy. Some claimed the New Deal was socialistic and a violation of American values. Others thought the New Deal did not do enough to help Americans.

Extending the Content

Federal Writers' Project The Federal Writers' Project was one of four segments of Federal One, which also included components in music, theater, and art. To avoid the controversy that might come from allowing writers to produce works of the imagination, the Federal Writers' Project asked authors to focus on nonfiction. A series of popular guidebooks, the American Guide series, was produced for each state, as well as major counties and cities, interstate highway routes, and areas of the nation. Interviews and oral histories of formerly enslaved persons, farm and mill owners, and others published in *These Are Our Lives* gave new dimensions to American history. At its peak in 1936, the Federal Writers' Project employed 6,700 writers. Some 10,000 writers gained employment through the program, producing more than 1,000 publications.

Reforms for Workers and Senior Citizens

MAIN Idea Roosevelt asked Congress to pass the Wagner Act and Social Security to build support among workers and older Americans.

HISTORY AND YOU Do you have an older relative who has retired from his or her job? Read about benefits created by the Social Security Act.

When the Supreme Court struck down the NRA, it also invalidated the section of the NIRA that gave workers the right to organize. President Roosevelt and the Democrats in Congress knew that the working-class vote was very important in winning reelection in 1936. They also believed that unions could help end the Depression. They thought that high union wages would give workers more money to spend, **thereby** boosting the economy. Opponents disagreed, arguing that high wages forced companies to charge higher prices and hire fewer people. Despite these concerns, Congress pushed ahead with new labor legislation.

The Wagner Act

In July 1935 Congress passed the National Labor Relations Act (also called the Wagner Act after its author, Senator Robert Wagner of New York). The act guaranteed workers the right to organize unions and to bargain collectively. It also set up the **National Labor Relations Board** (NLRB), which organized factory elections by secret ballot to determine whether workers wanted a union. C

Debates IN HISTORY

YES

Alfred E. Smith
Former Democratic Candidate

PRIMARY SOURCE

"Now what would I have my party do? I would have them re-declare the principles that they put forth in that 1932 platform [reduce the size of government, balance the federal budget] . . .

Just get the platform of the Democratic party and get the platform of the Socialist party and . . . make your mind up to pick up the platform that more nearly squares with the record, and you will have your hand on the Socialist platform. . . .

[I]t is all right with me, if they want to disguise themselves as Karl Marx or Lenin or any of the rest of that bunch, but I won't stand for their allowing them to march under the banner of Jackson or Cleveland."

—speech delivered January 25, 1936

NO

Norman Thomas
Socialist Party Candidate

PRIMARY SOURCE

"All of these leaders or would-be leaders out of our wilderness, however they may abuse one another, however loosely they may fling around the charge of socialism or communism—still accept the basic institutions and loyalties of the present system. A true Socialist is resolved to replace that system. . . .

The New Deal did not say, as socialism would have said, 'Here are so many millions of American people who need to be well fed and well clothed. How much food and cotton do we require?' We should require more, not less. What Mr. Roosevelt said was 'How much food and cotton can be produced for which the exploited masses must pay a higher price?'"

—speech delivered February 2, 1936

DBQ Document-Based Questions

1. **Distinguishing Fact From Opinion** Compare Smith's attack on the New Deal with what you have read about it elsewhere. Does he make any valid points?
2. **Contrasting** According to Thomas, how are the principles of the New Deal and those of the Socialist Party different?
3. **Evaluating** Which speaker do you find more persuasive? Why?
4. **Hypothesizing** Do you think either speaker would be able to persuade someone who did not agree with him to reconsider his or her attitudes?

C Critical Thinking

Identifying Central Issues Have students create word webs to record the provisions of the Wagner Act. Remind them to use these graphic organizers as study aids. **BL**

Debates IN HISTORY

Answers:

1. Students may say that Smith's call for a balanced budget, which was part of the 1932 platform, seems valid.
2. The New Deal accepts the basic institutions and loyalties of the present system, while the Socialist Party wants to replace the system.
3. Students' answers will vary.
4. Students' answers will vary.

Additional Support

Activity: Interdisciplinary Connection

Language Arts The question of whether the New Deal was socialistic in nature began in light of disillusionment with Roosevelt's policies. The conservatives charged that Roosevelt was considering a fascist dictatorship and later changed their rhetoric to suggest the administration was proposing "absolute communism." The debate grew louder as the 1934 elections approached and has continued among historians to this day. **Ask:** How does word choice influence the nature of a debate? *(Students may note that name calling and labeling inflame opinions but do not clarify issues.)* If the United States had not vigorously opposed communism and socialism, would labeling something socialistic provoke such intense feelings? *(Students may suggest that these terms gained power to generate intense feelings primarily based on the Red Scare of 1919. Had the United States not given much attention to the movement, words such as socialism would not be likely to create such intense feelings.)* **OL**

R Reading Skill

Activating Prior Knowledge

Ask: How had unions generally been organized before the Committee for Industrial Organization? *(They were established for workers of each trade.)* AL

C Critical Thinking

Analyzing Primary Sources

Invite a volunteer to read the Primary Source quotation in the second column. Ask students what most impressed the journalist being quoted. *(The fact that no General Motors property had been damaged or destroyed.)* OL

Analyzing VISUALS

Answers:

1. They have reading material and are seated comfortably on seats intended for the cars they are not assembling.
2. Between 1936 and 1937; the Wagner Act gave workers new rights and the CIO started organizing industrial workers.

The Wagner Act also set up a process called **binding arbitration** whereby dissatisfied union members could take their complaints to a neutral party who would listen to both sides and decide on the issues. The NLRB could investigate employers' actions and stop unfair practices, such as spying on workers.

The CIO Is Formed The Wagner Act led to a burst of labor activity. John L. Lewis led the United Mine Workers union. He worked with several other unions to organize industrial workers. They formed the Committee for Industrial Organization (CIO) in 1935.

The CIO set out to organize unions that included all workers, skilled and unskilled, in a particular industry. It focused first on the automobile and steel industries—two of the largest industries in which workers were not yet unionized.

Sit-Down Strikes Union organizers used new tactics, such as the **sit-down strike,** in which employees stopped work inside the factory and refused to leave. (This technique prevented management from sending in replacement workers.) First used effectively to organize rubber workers, the sit-down strike became a common CIO tactic for several years.

The United Auto Workers (UAW), a CIO union, initiated a series of sit-down strikes against General Motors. On December 31, 1936, the workers at General Motor's plant in Flint, Michigan, began a sit-down strike. The UAW strikers held the factory for weeks, while spouses, friends, and other supporters passed them food and other provisions through windows. A journalist who was allowed to enter the plant reported on conditions in the factory:

PRIMARY SOURCE

"Beds were made up on the floor of each car, the seats being removed if necessary. . . . I could not see—and I looked for it carefully—the slightest damage done anywhere to the General Motors Corporation. The nearly completed car bodies, for example, were as clean as they would be in the salesroom, their glass and metal shining."

—quoted in *The Great Depression*

Violence broke out in Flint when police launched a tear gas assault on one of the plants. The police wounded 13 strikers, but the strike held. On February 11, 1937, the company gave in and recognized the UAW as its employees' sole bargaining agent. The UAW became one of the most powerful unions in the United States.

PRIMARY SOURCE

The CIO Uses Sit-Down Strikes

▲ *Sit-down strikers at the GM Fisher Body plant in Flint, Michigan, take over the plant on December 30, 1936. Their action led to a national strike that lasted until February 11, 1937.*

Union Membership, 1933–1940

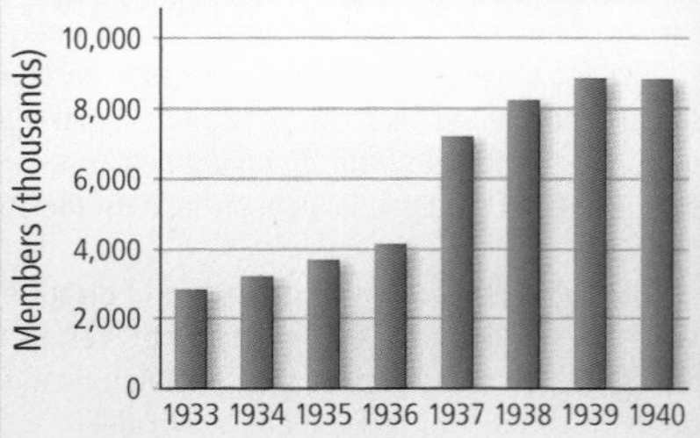

Source: *Historical Statistics of the United States.*

Analyzing VISUALS

1. **Analyzing** How can you tell from the men's appearance and activities that they intend to stay?
2. **Summarizing** When did union membership increase the most? How can you account for this jump?

Additional Support

Activity: Interdisciplinary Connection

Civics Explain to students that sit-down strikes were a form of nonviolent protest that would be used extensively during the Civil Rights Movement of the 1960s. Invite students to use library or Internet resources to find other instances of the technique as well as the 1930s Supreme Court rulings on the legality of the strikes. Ask students to write a brief summary or create a time line to show their findings. Invite volunteers to share their finished work with the class. AL

U.S. Steel, the nation's largest steel producer and a longstanding opponent of unionizing, decided it did not want to repeat the General Motors experience. In March 1937 the company recognized the CIO's steelworkers union. Smaller steel producers did not follow suit and suffered bitter strikes. By 1941, however, the steelworkers union had won contracts throughout the industry.

In the late 1930s, workers in other industries worked hard to gain union recognition from their employers. Union membership tripled from roughly 3 million in 1933 to about 9 million in 1939. In 1938 the CIO changed its name to the **Congress of Industrial Organizations** and became a federation of industrial unions.

Social Security

After passing the Wagner Act, Congress began work on one of America's most important pieces of legislation. This was the **Social Security Act.** Its major goal was to provide some security for older Americans and unemployed workers.

Roosevelt and his advisers spent months preparing the bill, which they viewed primarily as an insurance measure. Workers earned the right to receive benefits because they paid premiums, just as they did in buying a life insurance policy. The premiums were a tax paid to the federal government. The legislation also provided modest welfare payments to other needy people, including those with disabilities and poor mothers with dependent children.

The core of Social Security was the monthly retirement benefit, which people could collect when they stopped working at age 65. Another important benefit, unemployment insurance, supplied a temporary income to unemployed workers looking for new jobs. Some critics did not like the fact that the money came from payroll taxes imposed on workers and employers, but to Roosevelt these taxes were crucial: "We put those payroll contributions there so as to give the contributors a legal, moral, and political right to collect their pensions and their unemployment benefits."

Since the people receiving benefits had already paid for them, he explained, "no . . . politician can ever scrap my social security program." What Roosevelt did not anticipate was that, in the future, Congress would borrow money from the Social Security fund to pay for other programs while failing to raise payroll deductions enough to pay for the benefits.

Although Social Security helped many people, initially it left out many of the neediest—farm and domestic workers. Some 65 percent of all African American workers in the 1930s fell into these two categories. Nevertheless, Social Security established the principle that the federal government should be responsible for those who, through no fault of their own, were unable to work.

Reading Check **Explaining** How did the Social Security Act protect workers?

Section 2 REVIEW

Vocabulary

1. **Explain** the significance of: deficit spending, American Liberty League, Works Progress Administration, National Labor Relations Board, binding arbitration, sit-down strike, Congress of Industrial Organizations, Social Security Act.

Main Ideas

2. **Summarizing** How did the ideas of Father Coughlin, Senator Long, and Dr. Townsend differ?
3. **Analyzing** Why was the Social Security Act an important piece of legislation?

Critical Thinking

4. **Big Ideas** How did the New Deal contribute to the growth of industrial unions?
5. **Organizing** Use a graphic organizer similar to the one below to list the political challenges Roosevelt faced in his first term.

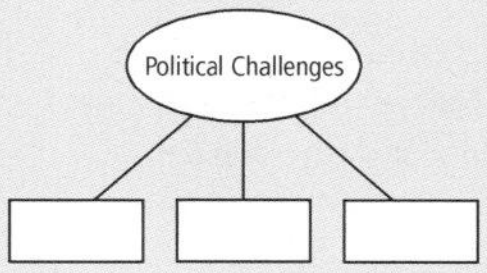

6. **Analyzing Visuals** Look again at the photo of Dr. Townsend on page 663. How does he intend to prevent economic chaos?

Writing About History

7. **Persuasive Writing** Choose one of the figures who criticized the New Deal. Write an editorial to the local newspaper expressing why people should be in favor of or opposed to that person's ideas.

History ONLINE
Study Central™ To review this section, go to glencoe.com and click on Study Central.

667

Reading Check

Answer:
It provided temporary income to unemployed workers looking for new jobs and a small pension for retired workers.

Assess

History ONLINE

Study Central™ provides summaries, interactive games, and online graphic organizers to help students review content.

Close

Summarizing Ask: What were some of the criticisms of the New Deal? *(Some detractors thought that Roosevelt was not doing enough to help the American people, while others feared the plan resembled socialism and did not align with American values. There was also great concern about the growing deficit.)* OL

Section 2 REVIEW

Answers

1. All definitions can be found in the section and the Glossary.
2. Coughlin: tax the rich and nationalize the banking system; Long: share the wealth; Townsend: pensions for the elderly
3. It provided a basic social safety net for the elderly, the unemployed, and other vulnerable groups.
4. The Wagner Act encouraged workers to organize unions and set up a process to protect unions as they developed.
5. American Liberty League, left-wing Democrats, the Depression had not ended
6. by putting control of credit in the hands of the people by giving $200 a month to those over 60
7. Students' editorials will vary but should express an opinion and support it.

Focus

Bellringer
Daily Focus Transparency 19-3

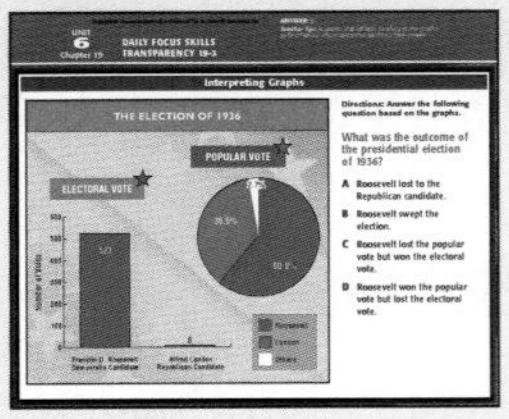

Guide to Reading

The New Deal Coalition
I. Roosevelt's Second Term
  A. The Election of 1936
  B. The Court-Packing Plan
  C. The Recession of 1937
II. The New Deal Ends
  A. The Last New Deal Reforms
  B. The New Deal's Legacy

Section Spotlight Video

To generate student interest and provide a springboard for class discussion, access the Chapter 19, Section 3 video at glencoe.com or on the video DVD.

Section 3 — Section Audio — Spotlight Video

The New Deal Coalition

Guide to Reading

Big Ideas
Group Action Backed by a new coalition of voters FDR easily won reelection, but conservative opposition prevented the passage of additional reforms.

Content Vocabulary
- court-packing *(p. 670)*
- broker state *(p. 673)*
- safety net *(p. 673)*

Academic Vocabulary
- recovery *(p. 670)*
- mediate *(p. 673)*

People and Events to Identify
- Frances Perkins *(p. 669)*
- Henry Morgenthau *(p. 670)*
- John Maynard Keynes *(p. 670)*

Reading Strategy
Taking Notes As you read, create an outline similar to the one below.

The New Deal Coalition
I. Roosevelt's Second Term
  A.
  B.
  C.
II.
  A.
  B.

President Roosevelt won a landslide reelection victory in 1936. Early in his second term, however, his court-packing plan and a new recession hurt him politically. The Fair Labor Standards Act, the last significant piece of New Deal legislation, provided new protections for workers.

Roosevelt's Second Term

MAIN Idea Roosevelt was easily reelected, but the New Deal lost momentum during his second term due to his court-packing plan and a new recession.

HISTORY AND YOU Does your family rent or own your home? Read how the New Deal started programs that tried to make home ownership more affordable.

Since the Civil War, African Americans had been reliable Republican voters. The Republican Party was the party of both Abraham Lincoln and emancipation. In the 1930s, however, this allegiance unraveled. The Great Depression had hit African Americans hard, and the Republican Party had done little to help. To many African Americans, it seemed their votes were taken for granted. That was certainly the sentiment of Robert L. Vann, editor of the *Pittsburgh Courier,* Pennsylvania's leading African American newspaper. Vann decided it was time for a change and started a campaign to persuade African Americans to join the Democratic Party. "My friends, go turn Lincoln's picture to the wall," he told audiences. "That debt has been paid in full."

The dramatic shift in party allegiance by African Americans was part of a historic political realignment the New Deal triggered. As the election of 1936 approached, millions of voters owed their jobs, mortgages, and bank accounts to the New Deal, and they knew it.

The white South, which had been the core of the Democratic Party, now became just one part of a new coalition that included farmers, industrial workers, African Americans, new immigrants, ethnic minorities, women, progressives, and intellectuals. First Lady Eleanor Roosevelt helped bring about the change in the African American and women's vote. She had demonstrated strong sympathies toward African Americans in her many tours of the country. She recounted her experiences to her husband and persuaded him to address at least some of their problems in his New Deal programs.

African Americans made some modest gains during the New Deal. The president appointed several African Americans to positions in his administration, where they informally became known as the Black Cabinet. FDR also tried to see that public works projects included African Americans.

Resource Manager

R Reading Strategies	C Critical Thinking	D Differentiated Instruction	W Writing Support	S Skill Practice
Teacher Edition • Act. Prior Know., p. 670 • Read. Prim. Sources, p. 672 • Academic Vocab., p. 673 **Additional Resources** • Guid. Read. Act., URB p. 112	**Teacher Edition** • Drawing Con., p. 670 • Analyzing Info., p. 672 **Additional Resources** • Quizzes and Tests, p. 271	**Teacher Edition** • Visual/Spatial, p. 669 **Additional Resources** • Auth Assess., p. 43 • Reteach. Act., URB p. 105	**Teacher Edition** • Expository Writing, p. 669	**Additional Resources** • Read. Essen., p. 217 • Time Line Act., URB p. 95

PRIMARY SOURCE

Building the New Deal Coalition

By creating programs that addressed the needs of different groups in American society, the New Deal created a new voting coalition: African Americans, women, and laborers.

▲ ***New Deal Raises African American Hopes***
Mary McLeod Bethune, shown with Eleanor Roosevelt, was appointed in 1936 as director of the Office of Minority Affairs within the National Youth Association. Bethune became the first black woman to head a federal agency. Roosevelt also relied on an informal advisory group, the "Black Cabinet," also known as the "Black Brain Trust." FDR failed in some areas of civil rights, such as not opposing poll taxes for fear of causing Southern Democrats to block New Deal programs.

▲ ***Appealing to Women and Workers***
The appointment of Secretary of Labor Frances Perkins, shown surveying work on the Golden Gate Bridge in 1935, was one example of Roosevelt's effort to bring women voters into the New Deal coalition. Perkins headed the team that designed the Social Security program and the Fair Labor Standards Act. Social Security, along with the New Deal's labor programs, helped bring many workers into the New Deal coalition.

▲ ***A New Deal for Native Americans***
Commissioner of Indian Affairs John Collier, shown here consulting with Native American leaders in South Dakota, helped create the Indian Reorganization Act of 1934. The act reversed the Dawes Act's policy of assimilation. It restored some reservation lands, gave Native Americans control over those lands, and permitted them to elect their own governments.

Analyzing VISUALS

1. **Analyzing** Look at the photo of Frances Perkins and the workers. What clues do you get that she took her job seriously?
2. **Evaluating** What mood does the photograph of Mary McLeod Bethune and Eleanor Roosevelt convey?

W A similar policy guided FDR's approach to women. He appointed the first woman to a cabinet post, Secretary of Labor **Frances Perkins,** and appointed many other women to lower-level posts. He also appointed two female diplomats and a female federal judge. Despite these gains, New Deal programs paid women lower wages than men.

D The Election of 1936

To challenge President Roosevelt's reelection bid, the Republicans nominated Alfred Landon, the governor of Kansas. Although Landon favored some New Deal policies, he declared it was time "to unshackle initiative and free the spirit of American enterprise." Landon was unable to convince the majority of American voters it was time for a change. Roosevelt and the New Deal that he represented remained very popular, and on Election Day, Roosevelt swept to victory in one of the largest landslides in American history. He won more than 60 percent of the popular vote and carried every state except Maine and Vermont.

Teach

W Writing Support

Expository Writing Invite students to find out more about the women whom Roosevelt appointed to government posts. Suggest that students focus on one woman or on one arena, such as federal judges or diplomats. Have students write a one-page summary of their findings. OL

D Differentiated Instruction

Visual/Spatial Ask students to create election maps of the 1932 and 1936 elections. Remind them to make a key. Ask them to compare the results and report their findings to the class. OL

Analyzing VISUALS

Answers:

1. She is wearing a hard hat, intending to be on the construction site rather than just reading or hearing about it.
2. Both are laughing, as is one of the men in the background. There is a sense of a pleasant meeting of friends.

Hands-On Chapter Project
Step 3

Writing a Newspaper

Step 3: Copyedit and Content Edit the Paper Students submit their articles to designated "editors" who evaluate both the content and the grammar of the pieces.

Directions Ask each group to choose a person to be the editor. Then have groups exchange their articles so that an objective, outside reader sees each one. Then have students revise according to the feedback they receive.

Putting It Together Remind students that careful editing involves an attention to detail and to factual accuracy. Encourage editors to find positive comments to make about each piece they edit.

(Chapter Project continued on the Visual Summary page)

C Critical Thinking

Drawing Conclusions

Ask: What have you already learned about Roosevelt that prepares you to read that he was "furious" that the Supreme Court declared the Agricultural Adjustment Act unconstitutional? *(He was intensely competitive; he had held executive office before on the state level and was used to command and power)* Ask students what other steps might Roosevelt have taken instead of his court-packing plan. *(He might have gone to the members individually and talked with them.)* **OL**

R Reading Strategy

Activating Prior Knowledge

Ask students how a house of Congress can "kill" a bill. *(Bills can die in committee or never be brought to the floor for a vote.)* **OL**

Reading Check

Answer: court-packing plan and recession

Additional Support

The Court-Packing Plan

Although many people supported the New Deal, the Supreme Court saw things differently. In January 1936, in *United States* v. *Butler,* the Court had declared the Agricultural Adjustment Act unconstitutional. With cases pending on Social Security and the Wagner Act, it was possible that the Court would strike down most of the major New Deal programs.

C Roosevelt was furious that a handful of jurists, "nine old men" as he called them, were blocking the wishes of a majority of the people. After winning reelection, he decided to try to change the political balance on the Court. In March 1937 he sent Congress a bill to increase the number of justices. It proposed that if any justice had served for 10 years and did not retire within six months after reaching the age of 70, the president could appoint an additional justice to the Court. Since four justices were in their 70s and two more were in their late 60s, the bill, if passed, would allow Roosevelt to quickly appoint as many as six new justices.

The **court-packing** plan, as the press called it, was Roosevelt's first serious political mistake. Although Congress had the power to change the Court's size, the scheme created the impression that the president was trying to undermine the Court's independence.

The issue split the Democratic Party. Many Southern Democrats feared Roosevelt's plan would put justices on the Court who would overturn segregation. At the same time, African American leaders worried that once Roosevelt set the precedent of changing the Court's makeup, a future president might pack the Court with justices opposed to civil rights. Many Americans believed the plan would give the president too much power.

Despite the uproar, Roosevelt's actions appeared to force the Supreme Court to back down. In April 1937, the Court upheld the constitutionality of the Wagner Act by a vote of 5-4 in the case *National Labor Relations Board* v. *Jones and Laughlin Steel Corporation.* In May the Court narrowly upheld the Social Security Act in *Steward Machine Company* v. *Davis.* Shortly afterward, a conservative justice resigned, enabling Roosevelt to appoint a New Deal supporter to the Court.

R In mid-July the Senate quietly killed the court-packing bill without bringing it to a vote. Roosevelt achieved his goal of changing the Court's view of the New Deal. The fight over the court-packing plan, however, hurt his reputation and encouraged conservative Democrats to work with Republicans to block any further New Deal proposals.

The Recession of 1937

In late 1937 Roosevelt's reputation again suffered when unemployment suddenly surged. Early in the year, the economy had seemed on the verge of full **recovery.** Industrial output was almost back to pre-Depression levels, and many people believed the worst was over. Roosevelt decided it was time to balance the budget. Concerned about the dangers of too much debt, Roosevelt ordered the WPA and the PWA to be cut significantly. Unfortunately, Roosevelt cut spending just as the first Social Security payroll taxes removed $2 billion from the economy, which plummeted. By the end of 1937, about 2 million people had been thrown out of work.

The recession of 1937 led to a debate inside Roosevelt's administration. Treasury Secretary **Henry Morgenthau** favored balancing the budget and cutting spending. This would encourage business leaders to invest in the economy. Harry Hopkins, head of the WPA, and Harold Ickes, head of the PWA, both disagreed. They pushed for more government spending using a new theory called Keynesianism to support their arguments.

Keynesianism was based on the theories of an influential British economist named **John Maynard Keynes.** In 1936 Keynes published a book arguing that government should spend heavily in a recession, even if it required deficit spending, to jump-start the economy.

According to Keynesian economics, Roosevelt had done the wrong thing when he cut back programs in 1937. At first, Roosevelt was reluctant to begin deficit spending again. Many critics believed the recession proved the public was becoming too dependent on government spending. Finally, in the spring of 1938, with no recovery in sight, Roosevelt asked Congress for $3.75 billion for the PWA, the WPA, and other programs.

Reading Check **Summarizing** What events weakened Roosevelt's reputation in 1937?

Activity: Economics Connection

Keynesian Economics Invite students to use library or Internet resources to find out more about Keynesian theory and how it affected the New Deal. Suggest that students use charts and graphs to show the economic changes between 1932 and 1941, when the war economy effectively ended the Great Depression. Ask students to determine how effective they believe Keynesian theory was during Roosevelt's time and if it is a valid theory. Have them record their thoughts in a brief essay. **AL**

ANALYZING SUPREME COURT CASES

Can Government Regulate Business?

★ ***Schechter Poultry* v. *United States* (1935)**
★ ***NLRB* v. *Jones & Laughlin Steel Corp.* (1937)**

Background to the Cases

These two cases look at the federal government's right to regulate interstate commerce. In the *Schechter* case, the Court overturned the NIRA and the industrial codes that regulated business. In the *Jones & Laughlin* case, Chief Justice Hughes switched sides from the *Schechter* case and upheld the Wagner Act's labor regulations. The case marks the Supreme Court's shift toward upholding New Deal legislation.

How the Court Ruled

Both cases addressed the question of federal power to regulate interstate commerce. In the *Schechter* case, the Court ruled that the federal government could regulate only business activity that was *directly* related to interstate commerce. In the *NLRB* case, the Court extended congressional power to regulate commerce and upheld the constitutionality of the Wagner Act.

▲ *In this 1937 cartoon, the donkey, a symbol of the Democratic Party, kicks up a storm and the dove of peace flies off, dropping the olive branch, in response to FDR's court-packing plan.*

PRIMARY SOURCE

The Court's Opinion

"The persons employed in slaughtering and selling in local trade are not employed in interstate commerce. Their hours and wages have no direct relation to interstate commerce. The question of how many hours these employees should work and what they should be paid differs in no essential respect from similar questions in other local businesses which handle commodities brought into a state and there dealt in as a part of its internal commerce. . . .

On both the grounds we have discussed, the attempted delegation of legislative power and the attempted regulation of intrastate transactions which affect interstate commerce only indirectly, we hold the code provisions here in question to be invalid."

—Chief Justice Charles E. Hughes
writing for the Court in *Schechter* v. *U.S.*

PRIMARY SOURCE

Dissenting Views

"The fundamental principle is that the power to regulate commerce is the power to enact 'all appropriate legislation' for its 'protection or advancement' . . . Although activities may be intrastate in character when separately considered, if they have such a close and substantial relation to interstate commerce that their control is essential or appropriate to protect that commerce from burdens and obstructions, Congress cannot be denied the power to exercise that control.

When industries organize themselves on a national scale . . . . how can it be maintained that their industrial labor relations constitute a forbidden field into which Congress may not enter when it is necessary to protect interstate commerce from the paralyzing consequences of industrial war?"

—Chief Justice Charles E. Hughes
writing for the Court in *NLRB* v. *Jones & Laughlin Steel Corporation*

DBQ Document-Based Questions

1. **Explaining** In *Schechter,* why does the Court assert that poultry workers are not engaged in interstate commerce?
2. **Analyzing** In the *NLRB* decision, how has the Court's reasoning changed?
3. **Drawing Conclusions** How would you explain the shift in the Court's attitude toward federal labor regulations?

SUPREME COURT CASES

Teach

Sometimes termed the "Sick Chicken Case," *Schechter Poultry* v. *U.S.* brought down the NIRA. Chief Justice Hughes made three arguments against the NIRA:

1. The NIRA gave legislative power to the executive branch.
2. There was no constitutional authority for the legislation.
3. Businesses that were intrastate in nature could not be subjected to federal regulation.

DBQ Document Based Questions

Answers:

1. Their hours and wages have no direct relations to interstate commerce.
2. It decides that because industries organize themselves nationally, industrial labor relations are not a field forbidden to Congress.
3. Students may suggest that the Court had adopted a broader interpretation of the commerce clause or the Court was afraid to knock down a popular New Deal program.

Differentiated Instruction

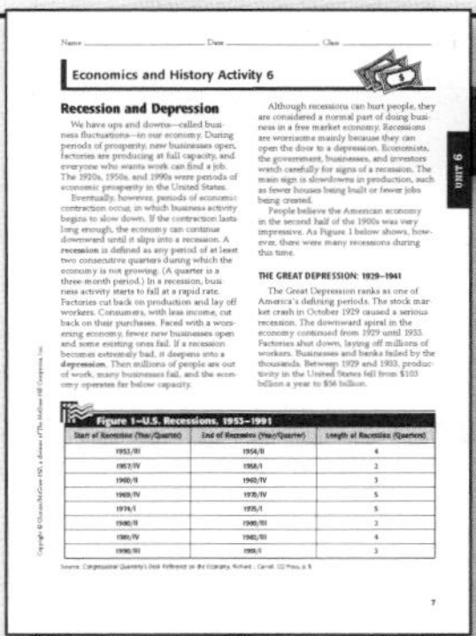

Economics and History Activity 6, URB p. 7–8

Identifying Cause-and-Effect: Recession and Depression

Objective: Identify the causes and effects of recessions and depressions.

Focus: Read the information on recessions and depressions.

Teach: Define *recession* and *depression* and list the causes and effects of each.

Assess: Make a list of the things that will need to happen to lift the economy out of a recession or depression.

Close: Create a poster illustrating an economic cycle from boom to recession.

Differentiated Instruction Strategies

BL Identify two causes of recession and the resulting effects on businesses.

AL Research unemployment rates during the recession periods and write a short report of the results.

ELL Underline any words that are unclear. Use a dictionary or develop a definition for each word.

R Reading Strategy

Reading Primary Sources
Ask: What does Roosevelt say is the test of progress? *(whether we provide enough for those who have too little)* **OL**

C Critical Thinking

Analyzing Information Ask students to create graphic organizers to note the three final New Deal reforms as they read. *(National Housing Act, Farm Security Administration, Fair Labor Standards Act)* **BL**

Analyzing VISUALS

Answers:
1. the Securities and Exchange Commission
2. Department of Housing and Urban Development

The New Deal Ends

MAIN Idea The New Deal expanded federal power over the economy and established a social safety net.

HISTORY AND YOU Do you think the government should help those in need? Read how people felt about the government as the New Deal came to an end.

In his second Inaugural Address, Roosevelt had pointed out that despite the nation's progress in climbing out of the Depression, many Americans were still poor:

PRIMARY SOURCE

"I see one-third of a nation ill-housed, ill-clad, ill-nourished. . . . The test of our progress is not whether we add more to the abundance of those who have much; it is whether we provide enough for those who have too little." R

—from *The Public Papers and Addresses of Franklin D. Roosevelt*

The Last New Deal Reforms

One of the president's goals for his second term was to provide better housing for the nation's poor. Eleanor Roosevelt, who had toured poverty-stricken Appalachia and the rural South, strongly urged the president to do something. Roosevelt responded with the National Housing Act, establishing the United States Housing Authority. This organization received $500 million to subsidize loans for builders willing to provide low-cost housing. C

Roosevelt also sought to help the nation's tenant farmers. Before being shut down, the AAA had paid farmers to take land out of production. In doing so, it had inadvertently hurt tenant farmers. Landowners had expelled tenants from the land to take it out of production. As a result, some 150,000 white and 195,000 African American tenants left farming during the 1930s. To stop this trend, Congress created the Farm Security Administration to give loans to tenants so they could purchase farms.

INFOGRAPHIC
What New Deal Programs Still Exist Today?

▲ All workers are required to have a Social Security card, printed on bank paper to decrease forgeries.

FDIC
FEDERAL DEPOSIT INSURANCE CORPORATION

▶ The Federal Deposit Insurance Corporation sign is posted at most banks.

Program	Purpose Today
Social Security	The Social Security Administration provides old age pensions, unemployment insurance, and disability insurance.
National Labor Relations Board	The NLRB oversees union elections, investigates complaints of unfair labor practices, and mediates labor disputes.
Securities and Exchange Commission	The SEC regulates and polices the stock market.
Federal Deposit Insurance Corporation	The FDIC insures deposits up to $100,000.
Tennessee Valley Authority	The TVA provides electrical power to more than 8 million consumers.
Federal Housing Authority	Renamed the Department of Housing and Urban Development (HUD) in 1965, it insures mortgage loans, assists low-income renters, and fights housing discrimination.

Your Door to FHA HOMEOWNERSHIP

◀ The Federal Housing Administration Web site uses this logo.

Analyzing VISUALS

1. **Identifying** Which organization regulates and oversees the stock market policies?
2. **Listing** What is the new name for the Federal Housing Authority?

Additional Support

Activity: Collaborative Learning

Analyze Roosevelt's Inaugural Addresses Divide the class into four groups, assigning each group one of the four inaugural addresses that Roosevelt gave. Have students look for key thoughts in the speech and determine how Roosevelt fostered hope and vision during difficult times. **Ask:** To what extent did the inaugural address set forth an agenda, or blueprint, to be followed? *(Students' responses will vary depending on the inaugural address they studied.)* **OL**

To further help workers, Roosevelt pushed through Congress the Fair Labor Standards Act, which abolished child labor, limited the workweek to 44 hours for most workers, and set the first federal minimum wage at 25 cents an hour. The Fair Labor Standards Act was the last major piece of New Deal legislation. The recession of 1937 enabled the Republicans to win seats in Congress in the midterm elections of 1938. Together with conservative Southern Democrats, they began blocking further New Deal legislation. By 1939, the New Deal era had come to an end.

The New Deal's Legacy

The New Deal had only limited success in ending the Depression. Unemployment remained high, and economic recovery was not complete until after World War II. Even so, the New Deal gave many Americans a stronger sense of security and stability.

As a whole, the New Deal tended to balance competing economic interests. Business leaders, farmers, workers, homeowners, and others now looked to government to protect their interests. The federal government's ability to take on this new role was enhanced by two important Supreme Court decisions. In 1937, in *NLRB* v. *Jones and Laughlin Steel,* the Court ruled that the federal government had the authority to regulate production within a state. Later, in 1942, in *Wickard* v. *Filburn,* the Court used a similar argument to allow the federal government to regulate consumption in the states. These decisions increased federal power over the economy and allowed it to **mediate** between competing groups.

R

In taking on this mediating role, the New Deal established what some have called the **broker state,** in which the government works out conflicts among different interests. This broker role has continued under the administrations of both parties ever since. The New Deal also brought about a new public attitude toward government. Roosevelt's programs had succeeded in creating a **safety net** for Americans—safeguards and relief programs that protected them against economic disaster. By the end of the 1930s, many Americans felt that the government had a duty to maintain this safety net, even though doing so required a larger, more expensive federal government.

Critics continue to argue that the New Deal made the government too powerful. Thus, another legacy of the New Deal is a continuing debate over how much the government should intervene in the economy or support the disadvantaged. Throughout the hard times of the Depression, most Americans maintained a surprising degree of confidence in the American system. Journalist Dorothy Thompson expressed this feeling in 1940:

PRIMARY SOURCE

"We have behind us eight terrible years of a crisis. . . . Here we are, and our basic institutions are still intact, our people relatively prosperous and most important of all, our society relatively affectionate. . . . No country is so well off."

—from the *Washington Post*, October 9, 1940

Reading Check **Summarizing** What was the legacy of Roosevelt's New Deal?

Section 3 REVIEW

Vocabulary

1. **Explain** the significance of: Frances Perkins, court-packing, Henry Morgenthau, John Maynard Keynes, broker state, safety net.

Main Ideas

2. What caused a recession early in Roosevelt's second term?
3. How did the New Deal expand federal power over the economy?

Critical Thinking

4. **Big Ideas** What groups made up the New Deal coalition?
5. **Organizing** Use a chart like the one below to list the achievements and defeats of Roosevelt's second term.

Achievements	Defeats

6. **Analyzing Visuals** Choose one of the photos on page 669 and write a brief account of the day's activities from the viewpoint of one of the people in the photograph.

Writing About History

7. **Persuasive Writing** Imagine that you are a staff member in Roosevelt's cabinet. Write a short paper criticizing or defending FDR's court-packing plan.

History ONLINE
Study Central™ To review this section, go to glencoe.com and click on Study Central.

R Reading Strategy

Academic Vocabulary Tell students that the Latin root word used in *mediate* means "middle." Ask them for other words that use this same root. *(intermediary, intermediate, medium)* OL

Reading Check

Answer:
It increased the government's role and fostered the attitude that the government was responsible for a safety net.

Assess

History ONLINE

Study Central™ provides summaries, interactive games, and online graphic organizers to help students review content.

Close

Summarizing Ask: At the end of Roosevelt's second term, how did Americans view the effects of the New Deal? *(Many felt it was a positive plan that provided a safety net against economic disaster.)* OL

Section 3 REVIEW

Answers

1. All definitions can be found in the section and the Glossary.
2. The recession was created when Social Security began making payments just as WPA and PWA programs were cut.
3. The New Deal introduced federal regulations in agriculture, industry, banking, and the stock market. It also established a minimum wage.
4. African Americans, farmers, labor, minorities, new immigrants, women, intellectuals, and progressives
5. Achievements: court upholds reforms, National Housing Act, Fair Labor Standards Act; Defeats: Great Depression continued, court-packing plan
6. Students' responses will vary but should be consistent with text material.
7. Students' papers will vary but should take a position on the court-packing plan and defend it.

Determining Cause and Effect Invite students to write at least one cause-and-effect statement for each of the four areas covered by the Visual Summary. **Ask:** What was the overall effect of the New Deal? *(Although the New Deal assisted many people, it did not end the Depression. It did, however, expand the role of the federal government and offered a social safety net.)* **OL**

Expository Writing Have students select one of the four categories and write a one-page summary of the provisions and effects of the New Deal in that area. **Ask:** In which area do you think the New Deal had the most lasting and important effect? *(Students' responses will vary but should be supported by reasons.)* **OL**

Chapter 19 VISUAL SUMMARY

STUDY TO GO — You can study anywhere, anytime by downloading quizzes and flashcards to your PDA from glencoe.com.

The New Deal in Action

Banking and Finances

- Emergency Banking Relief Act regulated banks.
- Federal Deposit Insurance Corporation insured bank deposits.
- Farm Credit Administration refinanced farm mortgages.
- Home Owners' Loan Corporation financed homeowners' mortgages.

▲ *A steel worker labors on the Grand Coulee Dam on the Columbia River in eastern Washington.*

Agriculture and Industry

- Agricultural Adjustment Administration paid farmers to limit surplus production.
- National Industrial Recovery Act limited industrial production and set prices.
- National Labor Relations Act gave workers the right to organize unions and bargain collectively.
- Tennessee Valley Authority financed rural electrification and helped develop the economy of a seven-state region.

Work and Relief

- Civilian Conservation Corps created forestry jobs for young men.
- Federal Emergency Relief Administration funded city and state relief programs.
- Public Works Administration created work programs to build public projects, such as roads, bridges, and schools.

◄ *A Civilian Conservation Corps member plants trees.*

Social "Safety Net"

- Social Security Act provided
  - income for senior citizens, handicapped, and unemployed
  - monthly retirement benefit for people over 65

► *In 1935 President Roosevelt signs the Social Security Bill while Secretary of Labor Perkins and legislators observe.*

Hands-On Chapter Project
Step 4: Wrap Up
Writing a Newspaper

Step 4: Produce and Distribute the Paper Have students make enough copies of their newspaper for the class. Allow time for students to read and comment on each other's completed work. Display the completed papers in the classroom.

Putting It Together Use the newspapers as the basis of a classroom display or bulletin board. Enhance the display with photos and maps. **OL**

Reviewing Vocabulary

Directions: Choose the word or words that best complete the sentence.

1. The purpose of a ________ was to prevent banks from being closed completely because of bank runs.

A New Deal
B bank holiday
C gold standard
D fireside chat

2. The period of intense congressional activity after FDR took office was known as the

A Square Deal.
B Securities and Exchange Commission.
C New Deal.
D Hundred Days.

3. ________ involves borrowing money to pay for programs.

A Deficit spending
B The gold standard
C States' rights
D Binding arbitration

4. Roosevelt ran into major opposition to his ________ plan.

A broker state
B gold standard
C recovery
D court-packing

5. The New Deal created a new public attitude toward government, by imagining the federal government used a ________ to protect citizens from economic disasters.

A broker state
B deficit nation
C safety net
D gold standard

Reviewing Main Ideas

Directions: Choose the best answers to the following questions.

Section 1 *(pp. 650–659)*

6. One of the ways in which Franklin Roosevelt gained political experience before being president was by serving as the

A U.S. senator for Maine.
B mayor of Boston.
C governor of New York.
D congressional representative from Connecticut.

7. The ________ was created to protect bank deposits.

A Agricultural Adjustment Act
B Home Owners' Loan Corporation
C Securities and Exchange Commission
D Federal Deposit Insurance Corporation

8. To ________, the Agricultural Adjustment Act paid farmers not to grow certain crops.

A raise farm prices
B lower farm prices
C feed the homeless
D let farmers relax

9. The ________ provided work for unemployed young men, who planted trees and built reservoirs.

A Civil Works Administration
B Public Works Administration
C Civilian Conservation Corps
D Federal Emergency Relief Administration

TEST-TAKING TIP

Questions sometimes ask for the exception, rather than the one right answer. Be sure to read through the question carefully, as well as each response, to see which one does not fit.

Need Extra Help?

If You Missed Questions . . .	1	2	3	4	5	6	7	8	9
Go to Page . . .	652	652	662–663	670	673	650–651	654	656	658

GO ON

Answers and Analyses
Reviewing Vocabulary

1. B Although all the terms given as possible answers to this question do relate to the New Deal, only *bank holiday* fully answers the question. The New Deal itself was larger than a bank holiday and not designed only to prevent bank closings. The fear that Roosevelt would take the nation off the gold standard actually provoked some bank runs. The fireside chats were intended to calm the nation in general and to give listeners a sense that they had a friend in the White House.

2. D The Square Deal can be easily eliminated, as it refers to Theodore Roosevelt's agenda. The word *commission* does not refer to a time period; the Securities and Exchange Commission was created to control the activities of Wall Street. The New Deal was a series of broad programs designed to help the nation's economic recovery.

3. A The gold standard demanded that an ounce of gold equaled a certain amount of dollars. States' rights was the insistence on the right of individual states to conduct business without the interference of the federal government. In binding arbitration, two sides in a dispute agree to accept the decision of a neutral party.

4. D By defining each term, students can eliminate distractors.

5. C The network of safeguards and relief programs that the New Deal represented made the federal government highly involved in guiding people's choices and possibilities.

Reviewing Main Ideas

6. C This question asks students to differentiate from among political offices and locations. They need to remember that Roosevelt was from New York.

7. D Although all the possible answers have to do with programs that the New Deal created, only "the FDIC" completely answers the question. The Agricultural Adjustment Act provided a way to raise farm prices. The Home Owners' Loan Corporation was designed to help homeowners with their mortgage payments. The SEC regulated stock market activities.

8. A The key term in the name of this act is *Adjustment*. Students should recall that farm prices were already very low. Also, remind students that generally in tests, when two possible answers directly contradict each other, one of them is the correct answer and the other distractors can be ignored.

9. C This question asks students to select among various New Deal programs to find the correct answer. The term *conservation* in the correct response should be a clue.

10. D This question requires students to place events in sequence and to recall that 1935 was the year before the 1936 presidential election. Knowing that FDR wanted a second term and that the failure to end the Great Depression stood in his way can help students find the correct response.

11. C The term *benefits* can be a key to finding the right answer to this question. Students can link the word *Security* in the correct response with *benefit* and thus eliminate the other programs mentioned.

12. A Students may recall the cartoon showing the Democratic donkey kicking the fence and thereby remember the uproar created by Roosevelt's court-packing plan.

13. B The possible answers offer a preliminary choice between two options: was the New Deal a state or federal program? Then students must decide if the federal expansion was over economy or the Constitution.

14. D To answer this question, students can frame it as a then/now issue. By doing so, they can see that the major issue was that of providing a safety net for retired or disabled workers, who had suffered deeply during the Great Depression.

Critical Thinking

15. C By correctly identifying the lighter-colored region on the map as the Northeast, students can answer this question.

16. A Remind students to look carefully at the map to be sure they have not overlooked any state before they answer.

Chapter 19 Assessment

Section 2 *(pp. 662–667)*

10. By 1935 the New Deal was criticized because it
- **A** had created too many new programs.
- **B** was focusing only on the Midwest.
- **C** had spent too much money on the stock market.
- **D** had not ended the Great Depression.

11. Benefits for older Americans were guaranteed by the
- **A** Congress of Industrial Organizations.
- **B** Works Progress Administration.
- **C** Social Security Act.
- **D** Wagner Act.

Section 3 *(pp. 668–673)*

12. Roosevelt split his own party by suggesting the need to
- **A** appoint additional Supreme Court judges.
- **B** include African Americans in New Deal programs.
- **C** appoint women to his cabinet.
- **D** follow Keynesian economics.

13. Part of the New Deal's legacy was an expansion of
- **A** state power over the courts.
- **B** federal power over the economy.
- **C** federal power over the Constitution.
- **D** state power over social safety nets.

14. The New Deal changed American attitudes toward government and
- **A** the desire for easy wealth.
- **B** the challenge of unionization.
- **C** the duty to regulate industry.
- **D** the need to provide a safety net.

Critical Thinking

Directions: Choose the best answers to the following questions.

Base your answers to questions 15 and 16 on the map below and on your knowledge of Chapter 19.

Presidential Election of 1932

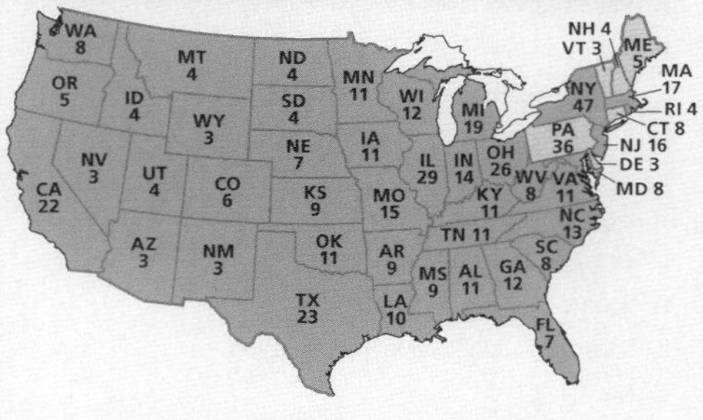

Presidential Candidate	Popular Votes	% of Popular Vote	Electoral Votes
Roosevelt	22,821,857	57.43%	472
Hoover	15,761,841	39.66%	59

15. Which of the following regions remained supportive of Republican President Hoover?
- **A** Midwest
- **B** South
- **C** Northeast
- **D** West

16. Which state gave Hoover the largest number of votes in the Electoral College?
- **A** Pennsylvania
- **B** New York
- **C** Connecticut
- **D** Texas

Need Extra Help?							
If You Missed Questions . . .	10	11	12	13	14	15	16
Go to Page . . .	662–664	667	670	673	668–672	R15	R15

GO ON

17. Social Security was an important piece of legislation because it
   - **A** provided monthly retirement benefits.
   - **B** encouraged state governments to improve schools.
   - **C** forced the federal government to hire the unemployed.
   - **D** mandated that workers be issued safety equipment.

Analyze the cartoon and answer the question that follows. Base your answer on the cartoon and your knowledge of Chapter 19.

18. This cartoon was published just after FDR took office. What message does it send?
   - **A** Republicans are not very happy about the new legislation.
   - **B** Congress is slow and stubborn as a donkey.
   - **C** The new president is not slowed down by being in a wheelchair.
   - **D** The Congress and many people are happy to follow Roosevelt.

Document-Based Questions

Directions: Analyze the document and answer the short-answer questions that follow the document.

Eleanor Roosevelt wrote in her autobiography of her experiences with people around the country:

> *"This trip to the mining areas was my first contact with the work being done by the Quakers. I liked the idea of trying to put people to work to help themselves. The men were started on projects and taught to use their abilities to develop new skills. The women were encouraged to revive any household arts they might once have known but which they had neglected in the drab life of the mining village.*
>
> *This was only the first of many trips into the mining districts but it was the one that started the homestead idea [placing people in communities with homes, farms, and jobs] . . . . It was all experimental work, but it was designed to get people off relief, to put them to work building their own homes and to give them enough land to start growing food."*
>
> —from *The Autobiography of Eleanor Roosevelt*

19. Why did Eleanor Roosevelt like the Quaker project?

20. Based on this excerpt, how do you think Eleanor Roosevelt felt about New Deal programs? Explain your answer.

Extended Response

21. Review the various New Deal programs discussed in the chapter. Select one that you think could be used or adapted to a current situation. Explain what group or groups it would help and how it would do so.

STOP

History ONLINE
For additional test practice, use Self-Check Quizzes—Chapter 19 at glencoe.com.

Need Extra Help?

If You Missed Questions . . .	17	18	19	20	21
Go to Page . . .	667	R18	677	R19	650–659

17. A Social Security provided monthly retirement checks.

18. D A careful look at the cartoon shows people for as far as the horizon extends, following FDR. Congress is leading the pack. All other distractors are incorrect.

Document-Based Questions

19. It emphasized individual initiative in improving the lives of the miners.

20. She supported the New Deal programs; this is clear because she advised FDR on peoples' needs and visited projects.

Extended Response

21. Answers will vary. Students' answers should involve one specific New Deal program and one current situation to which it might be adapted.

History ONLINE
Have students visit the Web site at glencoe.com to review Chapter 19 and take the Self-Check Quiz.

Need Extra Help?
Have students refer to the pages listed if they miss any of the questions.

Unit 7 Planning Guide

UNIT PACING CHART						
	Unit 7	Chapter 20	Chapter 21	Chapter 22	Chapter 23	Unit 7
Day 1	Unit Opener	Chapter 20 Opener, Section 1	Chapter 21 Opener, Section 1	Chapter 22 Opener, Section 1	Chapter 23 Opener, Section 1	Wrap-Up/Project, Unit Assessment
Day 2		Section 2	Section 2	Section 2	Section 2	
Day 3		Section 3	Section 3	Section 3	Sections 3 & 4	
Day 4		Section 4	Section 4	Section 4	Chapter Assessment	
Day 5		Chapter Assessment	Section 5	Chapter Assessment		
Day 6			Chapter Assessment			

Teacher to Teacher

Peter DeWolf
First Colonial High School
Virginia Beach, Virginia

A-Bomb Shelters Divide the students into groups. Each group must come up with a list of items to stock a 12′ x 12′ bomb shelter with everything a family of four would need to survive for four weeks. Ask the groups to prioritize their list by categories. Upon list completion, each group will share its list with the class. Then the class will discuss how each group made decisions about prioritizing.

- Why did they rank some categories higher than others?
- Did they include provisions for personal hygiene, nutrition, comfort, entertainment, and medical care? Why or why not?
- Why aren't all the lists and the categories the same?

Conclude the activity by discussing:

1. What was the hardest thing about supplying the shelter?
2. How would students feel about spending four weeks in the shelter they had supplied?

Explain that the Cold War forced people to deal with unusual situations that they were not accustomed to. This added to the fear of what may happen. Students should have obtained some awareness and insight into that uncomfortable position by completing this activity.

Author Note

Dear American History Teacher:

As you begin to teach this unit, there are themes that recur throughout the chapters that you will want to point out to students.

In this unit, students will monitor a debate between those Americans who wanted the U.S. to stay out of another war, and those who felt that the U.S. had a responsibility to resist the spread of tyranny. That debate took place in the halls of Congress, on the pages of the newspapers, and in mass public rallies. It ended when Japan attacked Pearl Harbor.

World War II became a total war that affected every citizen. My father was among the millions of Americans who responded to the call to defend their nation. He stood in a long line of recruits whom military personnel were sending, seemingly at random, through different doors. The door that he entered put him in the Coast Guard. Vast numbers of American volunteers and conscripts fought in Africa, Europe, and across the Pacific, while civilians mobilized on the home front. New opportunities opened for women and minorities in the defense industries. Yet Japanese Americans suffered grievous restrictions of their civil liberties.

Victory in World War II was followed closely by a prolonged Cold War in which the United States and its allies confronted the Communist bloc nations. International tensions, especially the anxiety over the threat of nuclear war, spurred investigations of Communist subversion within the United States. For those of us in school at the time, the nuclear threat meant "duck and cover" exercises under our desks and in the hallways. Such drills brought home to us the significance that world events had within our own communities.

By studying these events, your students will be able to consider the links between U.S. foreign policy and its domestic politics, as well as between international affairs and the everyday lives of individuals.

Donald A. Ritchie

Senior Author

Focus

Why It Matters

Have a volunteer read the *Why It Matters* paragraph on this page. Ask students to identify the three results of the United States's involvement in the war. *(emerged as a global power, abandoned isolationism, and began building alliances)* Then have students suggest current examples illustrating each of those results. *(Answers may include leading other nations in fighting terrorism or United Nations and NATO membership.)* **OL**

Connecting to Past Learning

Challenge students to recall the reasons for **both** World War I and the involvement of the United States in that war. *(Germany's military build-up, forming of alliances, assassination of Archduke Ferdinand; the United States entered the war in 1917 because of German submarine attacks on American ships, and growing anti-German sentiment in Wilson's administration and among the public.)*

Unit Launch Activity

Fact Finding Mission Place students in three groups, one for each decade represented in the unit. Challenge the groups to recall or find five facts about their assigned decade within a short period of time. Allow them to skim their textbooks for facts. **OL**

Unit 7

Global Struggles 1931–1960

Why It Matters

The rise of dictatorships in the 1930s led to World War II, the most destructive war in world history. The United States played a major role in the war, fighting in Europe, Africa, and Asia. Afterwards, the United States emerged as a global superpower, abandoned isolationism, and began building alliances around the world. Confrontation with the Soviet Union led to the Cold War, as the United States sought to contain the spread of communism.

678

Team Teaching Activity

Economics Explain to students that the booming postwar economy affected millions of Americans and continues to ripple through today's economy. Cold War military spending, new home construction, and demand for consumer goods each played a role in the healthy U.S. economy. Work with the economics teacher to coordinate the study of the economic trends of postwar America. Then invite the economics teacher to teach a lesson on the topic to your history class. Encourage students to participate in the discussion. **OL**

Despite the fog, American soldiers march in Belgium during the winter of 1944–1945.

679

Introducing
Unit 7

Teach

Differentiated Instruction

Auditory/Musical Play for students recorded samples of popular music from each decade covered in the unit. Ask students to jot down impressions of the way life must have been during each decade as they listen to the songs. BL

Skill Practice

Using Geography Skills Use a large classroom map to pinpoint places of war and conflict between 1941 and 1960. Invite students to place flags or other markers on the locations you mention so that students can visualize the truly global nature of the wars. OL

More About the Photo

Visual Literacy In December 1944, as Allied forces marched through Belgium and northern France toward the German border, Adolf Hitler ordered a massive counterattack. German forces smashed into American lines in Belgium with the goal of splitting Allied forces in two and capturing the city of Antwerp. The attack caught the Americans by surprise, but their lines did not break. Instead, as American forces fell back, the front line "bulged" outward on the map. This is why the engagement became known as the Battle of the Bulge. The troops had to fight in heavy snow in sub-zero conditions. Snowstorms reduced visibility and prevented aircraft from aiding the troops. Some 19,000 Americans were killed during the Battle of the Bulge, making it the deadliest engagement of the war for Americans.

NCLB NO CHILD LEFT BEHIND

Teaching Tip The NCLB Act places an emphasis on reading skills. Review with students the skills of scanning and skimming and when each would be useful in studying this unit.

Chapter 20 Planning Guide

Key to Ability Levels	
BL Below Level	AL Above Level
OL On Level	ELL English Language Learners

Key to Teaching Resources	
Print Material	Transparency
CD-ROM or DVD	

Levels					Resources	Chapter Opener	Section 1	Section 2	Section 3	Section 4	Chapter Assess
BL	OL	AL	ELL								
FOCUS											
BL	OL	AL	ELL	Transparency	**Daily Focus Transparencies**		20-1	20-2	20-3	20-4	
TEACH											
BL	OL		ELL	Print Material	**Reading Skills Activity, URB**		p. 21				
	OL			Print Material	**Historical Analysis Skills Activity, URB**		p. 22				
BL	OL	AL	ELL	Print Material	**Differentiated Instruction Activity, URB**					p. 23	
BL	OL		ELL	Print Material	**English Learner Activity, URB**		p. 25				
BL	OL	AL	ELL	Print Material	**Content Vocabulary Activity, URB***		p. 27				
BL	OL	AL	ELL	Print Material	**Academic Vocabulary Activity, URB**		p. 29				
	OL	AL		Print Material	**Reinforcing Skills Activity, URB**		p. 31				
	OL	AL		Print Material	**Critical Thinking Skills Activity, URB**		p. 32				
BL	OL		ELL	Print Material	**Time Line Activity, URB**				p. 33		
	OL			Print Material	**Linking Past and Present Activity, URB**		p. 34				
BL	OL	AL	ELL	Print Material	**Primary Source Reading, URB**		p. 35			p. 37	
BL	OL	AL	ELL	Print Material	**American Art and Music Activity, URB**		p. 39				
BL	OL	AL	ELL	Print Material	**Interpreting Political Cartoons Activity, URB**					p. 41	
		AL		Print Material	**Enrichment Activity, URB**					p. 45	
BL	OL		ELL	Print Material	**Guided Reading Activity, URB***		p. 48	p. 49	p. 50	p. 51	
BL	OL	AL	ELL	Print Material	**Reading Essentials and Note-Taking Guide***		p. 220	p. 223	p. 226	p. 229	
BL	OL	AL	ELL	Print Material	**Differentiated Instruction for the American History Classroom**	✓	✓	✓	✓	✓	✓
BL	OL	AL	ELL	Transparency	**Unit Map Overlay Transparencies**	✓	✓	✓	✓	✓	✓
BL	OL	AL	ELL	Print Material	**Unit Time Line Transparencies, Strategies, and Activities**	✓	✓	✓	✓	✓	✓
BL	OL	AL	ELL	Print Material	**Cause and Effect Transparencies, Strategies, and Activities**	✓	✓	✓	✓	✓	✓
BL	OL	AL	ELL	Print Material	**Why It Matters Chapter Transparencies, Strategies, and Activities**	✓	✓	✓	✓	✓	✓
BL	OL	AL	ELL	Print Material	**American Biographies**				✓		

Note: Please refer to the *Unit 7 Resource Book* for this chapter's URB materials.

* Also available in Spanish

TeacherWorks Plus
All-In-One Planner and Resource Center

- Interactive Lesson Planner
- Interactive Teacher Edition
- Fully editable blackline masters
- Section Spotlight Videos Launch
- Differentiated Lesson Plans
- Printable reports of daily assignments
- Standards Tracking System

Levels				Resources	Chapter Opener	Section 1	Section 2	Section 3	Section 4	Chapter Assess
BL	OL	AL	ELL							
TEACH *(continued)*										
BL	OL	AL	ELL	The Living Constitution	✓	✓	✓	✓	✓	✓
BL	OL	AL	ELL	American Issues	✓	✓	✓	✓	✓	✓
	OL	AL	ELL	American Art and Architecture Transparencies, Strategies, and Activities	✓	✓	✓	✓	✓	✓
BL	OL	AL		High School American History Literature Library	✓	✓	✓	✓	✓	✓
	OL	AL		American History Primary Source Documents Library	✓	✓	✓	✓	✓	✓
BL	OL	AL	ELL	American Music: Hits Through History CD	✓	✓	✓	✓	✓	✓
BL	OL	AL	ELL	StudentWorks™ Plus	✓	✓	✓	✓	✓	✓
BL	OL	AL	ELL	*The American Vision* Video Program	✓	✓	✓	✓	✓	✓
Teacher Resources				Reading Strategies and Activities for the Social Studies Classroom	✓	✓	✓	✓	✓	✓
Teacher Resources				Strategies for Success	✓	✓	✓	✓	✓	✓
Teacher Resources				Presentation Plus! with MindJogger CheckPoint	✓	✓	✓	✓	✓	✓
Teacher Resources				Success With English Learners	✓	✓	✓	✓	✓	✓
ASSESS										
BL	OL	AL	ELL	Section Quizzes and Chapter Tests*		p. 289	p. 290	p. 291	p. 292	p. 293
BL	OL	AL	ELL	Authentic Assessment With Rubrics						p. 45
BL	OL	AL	ELL	Standardized Test Practice Workbook						p. 45
BL	OL	AL	ELL	*ExamView® Assessment Suite*		20-1	20-2	20-3	20-4	Ch. 20
CLOSE										
BL			ELL	Reteaching Activity, URB						p. 43

✓ Chapter- or unit-based activities applicable to all sections in this chapter.

Using the Media Library

Teach With Technology

What is the Media Library?

The Media Library is an all-in-one online resource center that provides students with access to digital media associated with the textbook.

How can the Media Library help my students?

The Media Library contains Section Audio and Section Spotlight Videos. Section Audio can help struggling readers and English Language Learners better comprehend the textbook. Section Spotlight Videos engage visual learners and generate student interest. Students can download audio to their digital media player or listen from their computer screen.

Visit glencoe.com and enter a QuickPass™ code to go to the Media Library.

History ONLINE
Visit glencoe.com and enter QuickPass™ code TAV9399c20T for Chapter 20 resources.

You can easily launch a wide range of digital products from your computer's desktop with the McGraw-Hill Social Studies widget.

	Student	Teacher	Parent
Media Library			
• Section Audio	●		●
• Spanish Audio Summaries	●		●
• Section Spotlight Videos	●	●	●
***The American Vision* Online Learning Center (Web Site)**			
• StudentWorks™ Plus Online	●	●	●
• Multilingual Glossary	●	●	●
• Study-to-Go	●	●	●
• Chapter Overviews	●	●	●
• Self-Check Quizzes	●	●	●
• Student Web Activities	●	●	●
• ePuzzles and Games	●	●	●
• Vocabulary eFlashcards	●	●	●
• In Motion Animations	●	●	●
• Study Central™	●	●	●
• Web Activity Lesson Plans		●	
• Vocabulary PuzzleMaker	●	●	●
• Historical Thinking Activities		●	
• Beyond the Textbook	●	●	●

Reading Support From Jamestown Education

- **Timed Readings Plus in Social Studies** helps students increase their reading rate and fluency while maintaining comprehension. The 400-word passages are similar to those found on state and national assessments.
- **Reading in the Content Area: Social Studies** concentrates on six essential reading skills that help students better comprehend what they read. The book includes 75 high-interest nonfiction passages written at increasing levels of difficulty.
- **Reading Social Studies** includes strategic reading instruction and vocabulary support in Social Studies content for both ELLs and native speakers of English. www.jamestowneducation.com

Biography / A&E Home Video / The History Channel

The following videotape programs are available from Glencoe as supplements to this chapter:

- FDR: The War Years (ISBN 1-56-501458-8)
- Anne Frank (ISBN 0-76-701409-X)

To order, call Glencoe at 1-800-334-7344. To find classroom resources to accompany many of these videos, check the following home pages:

A&E Television: www.aetv.com

The History Channel: www.historychannel.com

Reading List Generator CD-ROM — Glencoe BookLink 3

Use this database to search more than 30,000 titles to create a customized reading list for your students.

- Reading lists can be organized by students' reading level, author, genre, theme, or area of interest.
- The database provides Degrees of Reading Power™ (DRP) and Lexile™ readability scores for all selections.
- A brief summary of each selection is included.

Leveled reading suggestions for this chapter:

For students at a Grade 8 reading level:
- ***Edith's Story,*** by Edith Velmans

For students at a Grade 9 reading level:
- ***Anne Frank: The Diary of a Young Girl,*** by Anne Frank

For students at a Grade 10 reading level:
- ***The Painted Bird,*** by Jerzy Kosinski

For students at a Grade 11 reading level:
- ***Never to Forget: The Jews of the Holocaust,*** by Milton Meltzer

For students at a Grade 12 reading level:
- ***The Hidden Children,*** by Howard Greenfeld

National Geographic

Index to National Geographic Magazine:

The following articles relate to this chapter:

- "Pearl Harbor: A Return to the Day of Infamy," by Thomas B. Allen, December 1991.
- "Remembering the Blitz," by Cameron Thomas, July 1991.

National Geographic Society Products To order the following, call National Geographic at 1-800-368-2728:

- World War II Era (PicturePack Transparencies).

Access National Geographic's new, dynamic MapMachine Web site and other geography resources at:

www.nationalgeographic.com
www.nationalgeographic.com/maps

Introducing **Chapter 20**

Focus

MAKING CONNECTIONS

Could World War II Have Been Prevented?

Use the two questions as the basis for a class discussion about the inevitability of a second world war. Elicit from students the terms of the Treaty of Versailles, including reparations and land partitions, that might contribute to bad feelings among the nations that lost World War I. Students should also comment on the United States's refusal to join the League of Nations as Wilson requested. **OL**

Teach

The Big Ideas

As students study the chapter, remind them to consider the section-based Big Ideas included in each section's Guide to Reading. The **Essential Questions** in the activities below tie in to the Big Ideas and help students think about and understand important chapter concepts. In addition, the Hands-on Chapter Projects with their culminating activities relate the content from each section to the Big Ideas. These activities build on each other as students progress through the chapter. Section activities culminate in the wrap-up activity on the Visual Summary page.

Chapter 20

A World in Flames

1931–1941

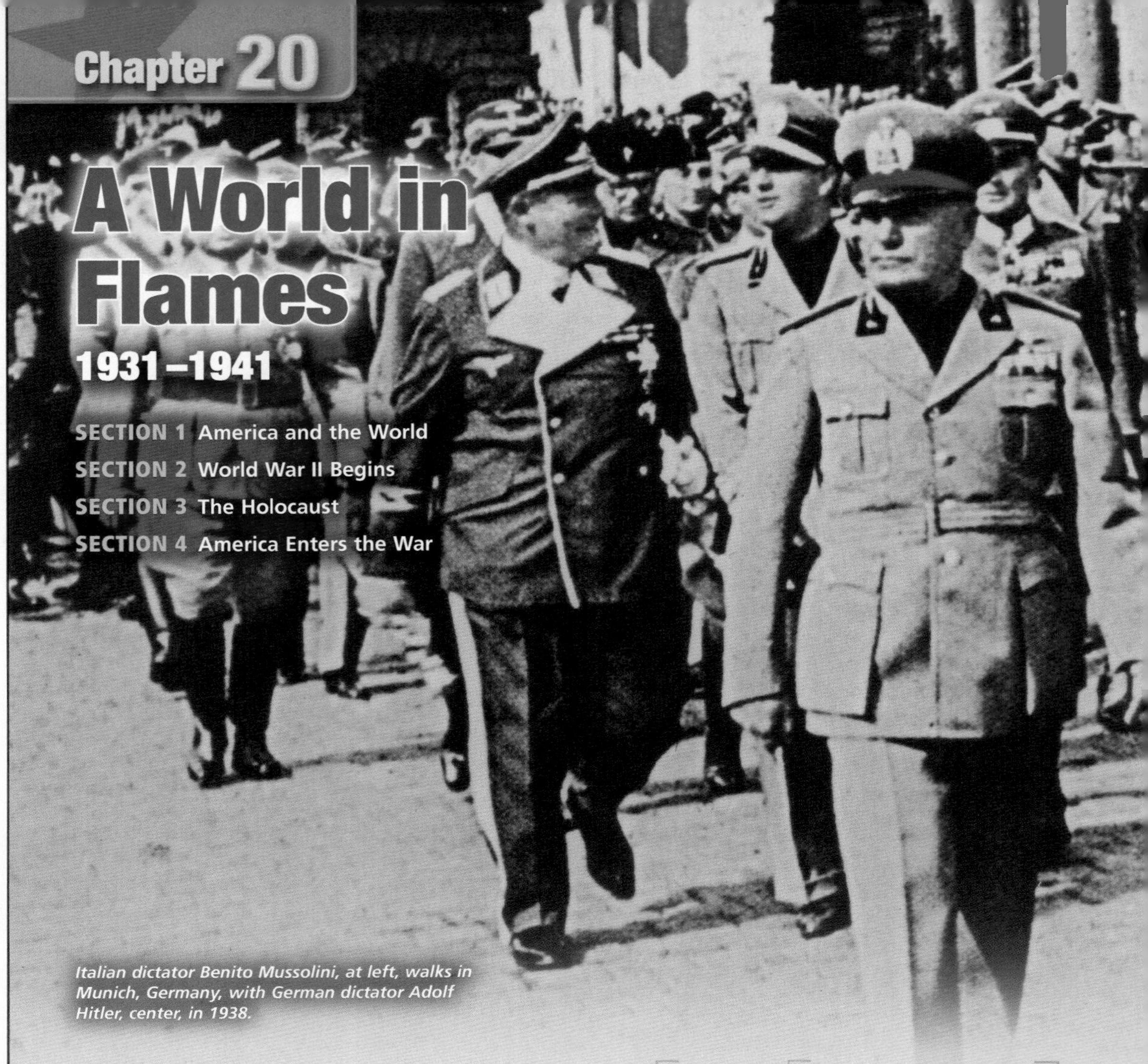

Italian dictator Benito Mussolini, at left, walks in Munich, Germany, with German dictator Adolf Hitler, center, in 1938.

U.S. PRESIDENTS

Roosevelt 1933–1945

U.S. EVENTS

1934
- Nye Committee holds hearings on causes of World War I

1935
- First Neutrality Act bars sale of weapons to warring nations

1937
- Neutrality Act limits trade with all warring nations

1931 · 1933 · 1935 · 1937

WORLD EVENTS

1931
- Japan invades Manchuria

1933
- Hitler becomes chancellor of Germany

1935
- Hitler denounces Treaty of Versailles
- Italy invades Ethiopia

1936
- Spanish Civil War begins
- Hitler reoccupies the Rhineland

1937
- Japan invades China

Section 1

America and the World

Essential Question: How did events after WWI lead to dictatorships and American neutrality? *(Many nations were dissatisfied with the Treaty of Versailles, and worldwide financial depression made people desperate. Americans wanted to avoid another war.)* Tell students that in Section 1 they will learn about events around the world that led to dictatorships even as America retreated into isolation. **OL**

Section 2

World War II Begins

Essential Question: What steps led to war in Europe in the late 1930s? *(Hitler violated the Versailles Treaty, rebuilt Germany's forces, occupied Austria, demanded the Sudetanland from Czechoslovakia. Britain and France tried to appease Hitler but Hitler occupied Czechoslovakia, then invaded Poland.)* Inform students that in this section they will be learning about how World War II began in Europe. **OL**

Chapter Audio

MAKING CONNECTIONS

Could World War II Have Been Prevented?

In the 1930s, global economic problems brought dictators to power in Europe and Japan, and another world war erupted. Many Americans, disillusioned by World War I, wanted to remain neutral, but when Japan attacked Pearl Harbor, the United States was forced to join the war.

- ***What problems do you think World War I created that contributed to the outbreak of World War II?***
- ***Do you think different American policies in the 1920s and 1930s could have prevented World War II?***

FOLDABLES

Comparing Totalitarian Dictators Make a Trifold Book Foldable to compare and contrast the dictatorships of Benito Mussolini, Joseph Stalin, and Adolf Hitler. As you read the chapter, add details about each ruler under his name. Use your list as a helpful study guide on their differences and similarities.

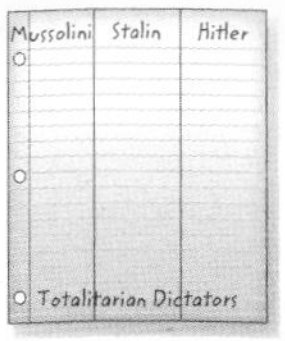

1938
- Munich Conference gives Sudetenland to Hitler

1939
- United States denies SS *St. Louis* permission to dock

1939
- Poland invaded; World War II begins

1940
- Roosevelt makes "destroyers-for-bases" deal with Britain

1940
- France surrenders to Germany; Britain wins Battle of Britain

1941
- Congress passes Lend Lease Act
- Japan attacks Pearl Harbor

1939 — 1941

History ONLINE Visit glencoe.com and enter QuickPass™ code TAV9846c20 for Chapter 20 resources.

Section 3

The Holocaust

Essential Question: How did the Nazis persecute the Jewish people? *(Nuremberg Laws, Kristallnacht, concentration and extermination camps)* Tell students that in this section they will learn about Hitler's attempts to destroy the Jewish people. **OL**

Section 4

America Enters the War

Essential Question: How did the United States become involved in World War II? *(supporting Britain through the Lend-Lease Act and the hemispheric defense zone, embargoing Japan, responding to the attack on Pearl Harbor)* Inform students that in this section they will learn about America's response to and involvement in the war. **OL**

More About the Photo

Visual Literacy In the 1930s, Germany and Italy established a military alliance on May 22, 1939, with the Pact of Steel, an agreement that committed both countries to support the other in the event of war. War came on September 1, 1939, when Nazi Germany invaded Poland. Italy joined the war on June 10, 1940, by declaring war against France and Great Britain. In September 1940, Italy attacked British forces in Egypt, spreading the war to North Africa.

FOLDABLES Study Organizer Dinah Zike's Foldables

Dinah Zike's Foldables are three-dimensional, interactive graphic organizers that help students practice basic writing skills, review vocabulary terms, and identify main ideas. Instructions for creating and using Foldables can be found in the Appendix at the end of this book and in the *Dinah Zike's Reading and Study Skills Foldables* booklet.

History ONLINE

Visit glencoe.com and enter QuickPass™ code TAV9399c20T for Chapter 20 resources, including a Chapter Overview, Study Central™, Study-to-Go, Student Web Activity, Self-Check Quiz, and other materials.

Focus

Bellringer

Daily Focus Transparency 20-1

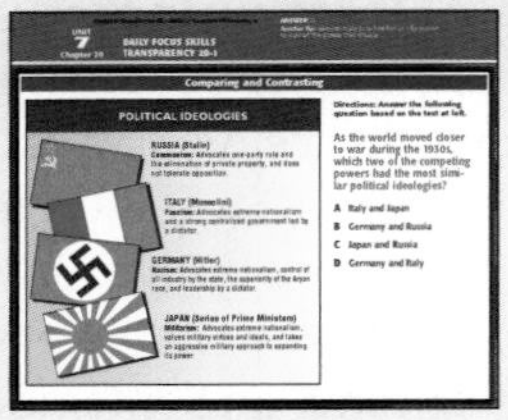

Guide to Reading

Answers may include:

America and the World
I. The Rise of Dictators
  A. Mussolini and Fascism in Italy
  B. Stalin Takes Over the USSR
  C. Hitler and Nazi Germany
  D. Militarists Control Japan
II. American Neutrality
  A. The Nye Committee
  B. Legislating Neutrality
  C. Roosevelt's Internationalism

Section Spotlight Video

To generate student interest and provide a springboard for class discussion, access the Chapter 20, Section 1 video at glencoe.com or on the video DVD.

Resource Manager

Section 1 | Section Audio | Spotlight Video

America and the World

Guide to Reading

Big Ideas

Government and Society In the years following World War I, aggressive and expansionistic governments took power in both Europe and Asia.

Content Vocabulary
- fascism *(p. 682)*
- collective *(p. 683)*
- internationalism *(p. 687)*

Academic Vocabulary
- exploit *(p. 682)*
- dominate *(p. 685)*

People and Events to Identify
- Benito Mussolini *(p. 682)*
- Vladimir Lenin *(p. 683)*
- Joseph Stalin *(p. 683)*
- Adolf Hitler *(p. 684)*
- Manchuria *(p. 685)*
- Neutrality Act of 1935 *(p. 686)*
- Axis Powers *(p. 687)*

Reading Strategy

Taking Notes As you read about the events in Europe and Asia after World War I, use the major headings of the section to create an outline similar to the one below.

America and the World
I. The Rise of Dictators
  A.
  B.
  C.
  D.
II.

In the years following World War I, aggressive and expansionist governments took power in Europe and Asia. Meanwhile, most Americans did not want to get involved in another foreign war.

The Rise of Dictators

MAIN Idea Dictators took control of the governments of Italy, the Soviet Union, Germany, and Japan.

HISTORY AND YOU Can you think of a country today that is ruled by a dictator? Read about the repressive governments that arose during the 1920s and 1930s.

When World War I ended, President Wilson had hoped that the United States could "aid in the establishment of just democracy throughout the world." Instead, the treaty that ended the war, along with the economic depression that followed, contributed to the rise of antidemocratic governments in both Europe and Asia.

Mussolini and Fascism in Italy

One of Europe's first dictatorships arose in Italy. In 1919 **Benito Mussolini** founded Italy's Fascist Party. **Fascism** was an aggressive nationalistic movement that considered the nation more important than the individual. Fascists believed that order in society would come only through a dictator who led a strong government. They also thought nations became great by building an empire.

Fascism was also strongly anticommunist. After the Russian Revolution, many Europeans feared that communists, allied with labor unions, were trying to bring down their governments. Mussolini **exploited** these fears by portraying fascism as a bulwark against communism. Fascism began to stand for the protection of private property and the middle class. Mussolini also promised the working class full employment and social security. He pledged to return Italy to the glories of the Roman Empire.

Backed by the Fascist militia known as the Blackshirts, Mussolini threatened to march on Rome in 1922, claiming he was coming to defend Italy against a communist revolution. Liberal members of the Italian parliament insisted that the king declare martial law. When he refused, the cabinet resigned. Conservative advisers then persuaded the king to appoint Mussolini as the premier.

Once in office, Mussolini worked quickly to set up a dictatorship. Weary of strikes and riots, many Italians welcomed Mussolini's leadership. With the support of industrialists, landowners, and the Roman

R Reading Strategies	C Critical Thinking	D Differentiated Instruction	W Writing Support	S Skill Practice
Teacher Edition • Organizing, p. 684 • Taking Notes, p. 686 **Additional Resources** • Read. Skills Act., URB p. 21 • Guid. Read. Act., URB p. 48 • Prim. Source Read., URB p. 35	**Teacher Edition** • Comp. & Cont., p. 684 • Ident. Cent. Iss., p. 685 **Additional Resources** • Crit. Think. Skills, URB p. 32 • Quizzes and Tests, p. 289	**Teacher Edition** • Advanced Learners, p. 683 • Visual/Spatial, p. 686 **Additional Resources** • English Learn. Act., URB p. 25 • Foldables, p. 73 • American Art and Music, URB p. 39	**Additional Resources** • Cont. Vocab. Act., URB p. 27 • Academic Vocab. Act., URB p. 29 • Linking Past and Present, URB p.34	**Teacher Edition** • Using Geography Skills, p. 683 **Additional Resources** • Reinforcing Skills Act., URB p. 31 • Hist. Analysis Skills, URB p. 22 • Read. Essen., p. 220

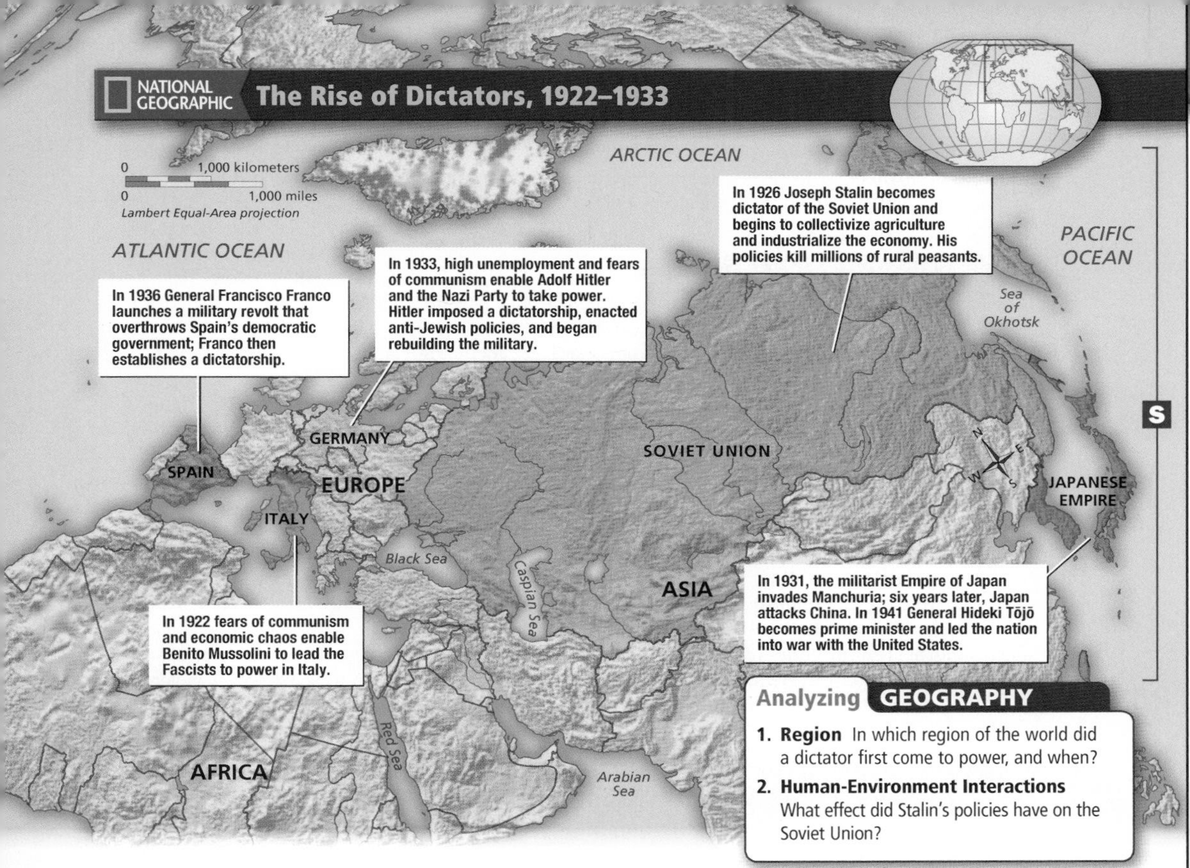

Analyzing GEOGRAPHY

1. **Region** In which region of the world did a dictator first come to power, and when?
2. **Human-Environment Interactions** What effect did Stalin's policies have on the Soviet Union?

Catholic Church, Mussolini—who took the title of Il Duce, or "The Leader"—embarked on an ambitious program of bringing order to Italy.

Stalin Takes Over the USSR

After the Russian Revolution, the Communist Party, led by **Vladimir Lenin,** established communist governments throughout the Russian Empire. In 1922 they renamed these territories the Union of Soviet Socialist Republics (USSR). The Communists instituted one-party rule, suppressed individual liberties, and punished opponents. **D**

After Lenin died in 1924, a power struggle began between Leon Trotsky and **Joseph Stalin.** Born with the surname of Dzuhgashvili, Stalin replaced his last name with the Russian word *stal,* meaning "steel." Between 1902 and 1913, he had been imprisoned or exiled seven times, but he always escaped.

By 1926, Stalin had become the new Soviet dictator. He began a massive effort to industrialize his country, using Five-Year Plans. During the first two of these Five-Year Plans, from 1928 to 1937, steel production increased from 4 million to 18 million tons (3.628 to 16.326 million t). At the same time, however, industrial wages declined by 43 percent from 1928 to 1940. Family farms were combined and turned into **collectives,** or government-owned farms. Peasants who resisted by killing livestock or hoarding crops faced show trials or death from starvation. As many as 10 million peasants died in famines during 1932 and 1933.

Stalin tolerated no opposition, targeting not only political enemies but also artists and intellectuals. During the late 1930s, the USSR was a nation of internal terrorism, with public trials that featured forced confessions. A new constitution, passed in 1936, promised many freedoms but was never enforced.

Teach

D Differentiated Instruction

Advanced Learners Invite students to learn more about the power struggles that ensued after Lenin's death and Trotsky's fate. Suggest they present their findings to the class as a play or radio drama. **AL**

S Skill Practice

Using Geography Skills Ask students to look at the map and identify what they see as likely difficulties in governing the USSR. *(Students may suggest that the nation's great size would make effective government difficult, especially in the 1920s and 1930s, before improvements in both telecommunications and transportation.)* **OL**

Analyzing GEOGRAPHY

Answers:
1. Italy, 1922
2. farms and factories belonged to the state; millions died

Hands-On Chapter Project Step 1

Creating a World War II Memory Book

Step 1: Selecting Memorable People

Ask: What famous people can you name who were in World War II?

Directions Ask students to list on the board the names of people who played a role in the war. Have students read ahead or do research to add as many names to the list as there are class members. Tell students to choose a name from the list and learn more about him or her in order to contribute a page to a class memory book. Make a scrapbook with the title "Memories of World War II" on the cover.

Putting It Together Students will identify the role played by each person added to the list. When dictators are chosen, students will discuss what conditions in each country allowed the dictators to gain power. **OL**
(Chapter Project continued on page 689)

R Reading Strategy

Organizing Have students create word webs or other graphic organizers to note the beliefs of postwar Germany's Nazi Party. Remind students that these graphic organizers can be helpful study aids. BL

C Critical Thinking

Comparing and Contrasting Have students compare Hitler's ideology to the ideas of Stalin and Mussolini. Ask them to identify elements that are similar and elements that are unique to Nazism. *(Hitler, Stalin, and Mussolini all created one-party states ruled by one strong leader; all three used violence to control political opponents; only Hitler had a specific racial component to his ideology)* OL

Stalin also used concentration camps; by 1935 some 2 million people were in camps, most of which were located in the Arctic. Prisoners were used as slave labor. Between 8 and 10 million people died as a result of Stalin's rule, which lasted until his death in 1953.

Hitler and Nazi Germany

Adolf Hitler was a fervent anticommunist and an admirer of Mussolini. A native Austrian, Hitler had fought for Germany in World War I. Germany's surrender and the subsequent Treaty of Versailles caused him and many other Germans to hate both the victorious Allies and the German government that had accepted the peace terms. R

Postwar Germany's political and economic chaos led to the rise of new political parties. One of these was the National Socialist German Workers' Party, or the Nazi Party. The party was nationalistic and anticommunist, calling for Germany to expand its territory and not abide by the terms of the Treaty of Versailles. It also was anti-Semitic. Using the words *Socialist* and *Workers* in its name, the party hoped to attract unhappy workers. Adolf Hitler was one of the party's first recruits.

In November 1923, the Nazis tried to seize power by marching on city hall in Munich, Germany. Hitler intended to seize power locally and then march on Berlin, the German capital, but the plan failed. The Nazi Party was banned for a time, and Hitler was arrested.

While in prison, Hitler wrote *Mein Kampf* ("My Struggle"), in which he called for the unification of all Germans under one government. He claimed that Germans, particularly blond, blue-eyed Germans, belonged to a "master race" called Aryans. He argued that Germans needed more space and called for Germany to expand east into Poland and Russia. According to Hitler, the Slavic peoples of eastern Europe belonged to an inferior race, which Germans should enslave. Hitler's racism was strongest, however, toward Jews. Hitler blamed the Jews for many of the world's problems, especially for Germany's defeat in World War I. C

After his release, Hitler changed his tactics. Instead of trying to seize power violently, he focused on getting Nazis elected to the

NATIONAL GEOGRAPHIC War and Civil War in the 1930s

▼ *Japanese officers targeted resource-rich Manchuria as the first goal in their drive to build an empire.*

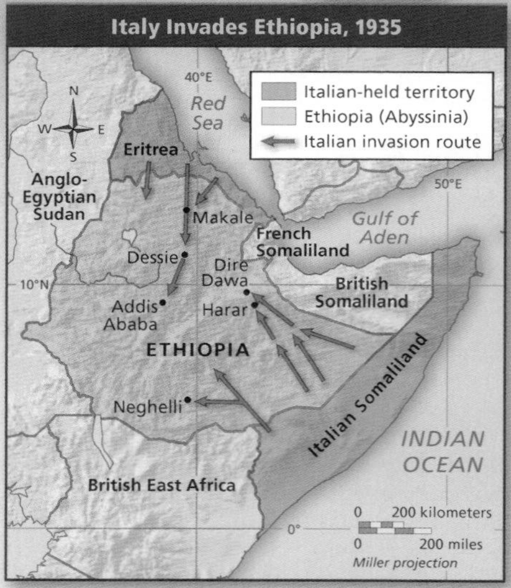

▲ *Mussolini, the dictator of Italy, wanted to build a new Roman Empire in Africa. In 1935 the Italian army invaded Ethiopia, then known as Abyssinia. The emperor, Haile Selassie, went into exile.*

Additional Support

Extending the Content

Inflation Remind students that inflation occurs when the cost of goods and services goes up and the value of money declines. One of the reasons for Germany's despair and willingness to accept Hitler as a leader can be attributed to the experience Germans had with inflation ten years earlier. In October 1922 the exchange rate was 4,500 German marks for one United States dollar. Eleven months later, the rate was 4.2 trillion marks per dollar. In 1923 a Hershey chocolate bar that sold for five cents in the United States cost 150,000 German marks or almost 33 dollars. Children used bundles of German marks to make building blocks; women used them to light fires. Although Germany got inflation under control, many people lost their savings and lost faith in the government. When the Great Depression hit in the 1930s, many Germans were willing to support Hitler and the Nazi Party because they recalled how badly the government had handled the economy during the time of inflation.

Reichstag, the lower house of the German parliament. When the Great Depression struck Germany, many desperate Germans began to vote for radical parties, including the Nazis and Communists. By 1932, the Nazis were the largest party in the Reichstag. The following year, the German president appointed Hitler as chancellor, or prime minister.

After taking office, Hitler called for new elections. He then ordered the police to crack down on the Socialist and Communist Parties. Storm troopers, as the Nazi paramilitary units were called, began intimidating voters. After the election, the Reichstag, dominated by the Nazis and other right-wing parties, voted to give Hitler dictatorial powers. In 1934 Hitler became president, which gave him control of the army. He then gave himself the new title of Der Führer, or "The Leader."

Militarists Control Japan

In Japan, as in Germany, difficult economic times helped undermine the political system. Japanese industries had to import nearly all of the resources they needed to produce goods. During the 1920s Japan did not earn enough money from its exports to pay for its imports, which limited economic growth. When the Depression struck, other countries raised their tariffs. This made the situation even worse.

Many Japanese military officers blamed the country's problems on corrupt politicians. Most officers believed that Japan was destined to **dominate** East Asia and saw democracy as "un-Japanese" and bad for the country.

Japanese military leaders and their civilian supporters argued that seizing territory was **C** the only way Japan could get the resources it needed. In September 1931, the Japanese army invaded **Manchuria,** a resource-rich region of northern China. When the Japanese prime minister tried to stop the war by negotiating with China, officers assassinated him. From that point forward, the military controlled the country. Japan's civilian government supported the nationalist policy of expanding the empire and appointed a military officer to serve as prime minister.

Reading Check **Examining** How did postwar conditions contribute to the rise of dictatorships in Europe?

The Spanish Civil War, 1936–1939

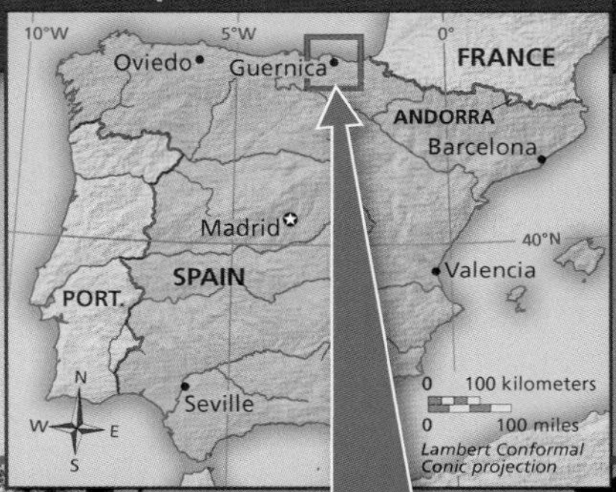

In 1936 a civil war broke out in Spain when Fascist General Francisco Franco attempted a military coup. With aid from Hitler and Mussolini, Spain became a testing ground for new military ideas such as air strikes. On April 26, 1937, planes released 100,000 pounds of bombs, destroying 70% of Guernica, shown at left after the bombing. A mere 15 days after the bombing, the artist Pablo Picasso began painting Guernica (above).

Analyzing VISUALS

1. **Comparing** In what way were the three wars shown on the map all a prelude to World War II?
2. **Analyzing** How does Picasso show the terror of the Guernica bombing?

C Critical Thinking

Identifying Central Issues As students read this section, ask them to point out reasons why nations went to war. *(Japan wanted resources to produce goods, and Germany wanted land to expand. Italy wanted a return to former glory.)* **OL**

Analyzing VISUALS

Answers:

1. The wars involved fascist leadership and expansion—both of which were causes of WWII.
2. severed limbs, mouths open as if screaming

Reading Check

Answer: Postwar inequalities caused by the Versailles Treaty fueled nationalism. Economic depression and social unrest created desperation for new, stronger leadership. Dictators were able to capitalize on these feelings to seize control of governments.

Additional Support

Extending the Content

Japan and China Japan had dominated Manchuria since 1905, when Japan defeated both Russia and China. Japan at that time also controlled Korea and Taiwan, then known as Formosa. Japan was the strongest military power in the region and expanded industrially, only to face major losses due to the worldwide economic depression. During the mid-1930s, the Chinese were fighting a civil war between communists and nationalists. The two sides agreed, however, to join forces to defeat Japan. In spite of China's resistance, by 1938 Japan controlled much of eastern China, with puppet governments in both Nanjing and Beijing. The war between these two Asian nations continued until the end of World War II.

R Reading Strategy

Taking Notes Ask students to design a graphic organizer focusing on the events of 1934 that led to the Neutrality Act of 1935. **OL**

D Differentiated Instruction

Visual/Spatial Invite students to use color-coded index cards to record the provisions of the Neutrality Acts discussed in the Primary Source material. Each Act should have a different color card or ink to help students recall the information. **BL**

Analyzing VISUALS

1. Americans felt the country should have stayed out of World War I.
2. They wanted to avoid another war.

American Neutrality

MAIN Idea Most Americans did not want to get involved in another European war, despite Franklin Roosevelt's emphasis on internationalism.

HISTORY AND YOU Do you think the United States should become involved in the wars of other nations even when it is not under attack? Read to learn about American attitudes during the 1930s.

The rise of dictatorships and militarism discouraged many Americans. The sacrifices they had made during World War I seemed pointless. Once again, Americans began supporting isolationism and trying to avoid involvement in international conflicts.

The Nye Committee

Isolationist ideas became stronger in the early 1930s for two reasons. When the Depression began, many European nations found it difficult to repay money they had borrowed during World War I. In 1934 all of the debtor nations except Finland announced they would no longer repay their war debts.

Meanwhile, dozens of books and articles appeared arguing that arms manufacturers had tricked the United States into entering World War I. In 1934 Senator Gerald P. Nye of North Dakota held hearings to investigate these allegations. The Nye Committee documented the huge profits that arms factories had made during the war. The report created the impression that these businesses influenced the decision to go to war. Coupled with the European refusal to repay their loans, the Nye Committee's findings turned even more Americans toward isolationism.

Legislating Neutrality

R Italian and German aggression increased under Mussolini and Hitler. Worried that the actions of these nations might lead to war, Congress passed the **Neutrality Act of 1935.** This legislation—reflecting the belief that arms sales had helped bring the United States into World War I—made it illegal for Americans to sell arms to any country at war.

In 1936 a rebellion erupted in Spain after voters elected a coalition of Republicans, Socialists, and Communists. General Francisco Franco led the rebellion, backed by Spanish Fascists, army officers, landowners, and Catholic Church leaders. The revolt became a civil war and attracted

D

INFOGRAPHIC

The Neutrality Acts, 1935–1937

Causes	Act
• Nye Senate Committee report suggesting that the American arms industry had pushed the nation into World War I for its own profit • growing belief that America should have stayed out of World War I	**The Neutrality Act of 1935** • mandatory embargo on selling or exporting arms, ammunition, or implements of war to nations at war • discretionary travel restrictions • set to expire after 6 months
• Italy's invasion of Ethiopia; FDR encourages a moral embargo against Italy, which he could not enforce	**The Neutrality Act of 1936** • arms embargo with countries at war • discretionary travel restrictions • ban on loans to nations fighting, but short-term credits exempted • republics in the Americas exempted
• Spanish Civil War • sale of aviation parts to rebels in Spain, which FDR thought unpatriotic • agreements creating the Axis alliance	**The Neutrality Act of 1937** • arms embargo against nations at war • travel ban on warring nations' ships • trade with countries at war on a cash-and-carry basis allowed if goods were not contraband or sent on foreign ships

▲ *Republican Senator Gerald Nye headed the Senate Munitions Committee, whose findings convinced many that arms makers were "merchants of death" and that the United States should remain neutral.*

Analyzing VISUALS

1. **Analyzing** What impact did the Nye Committee's findings have on public opinion?
2. **Evaluating** Why did so many Americans support neutrality?

Additional Support

Activity: Collaborative Learning

Write a Résumé Have students work together in pairs to create a résumé for one of the major leaders of this period. Tell them to include the leader's education, career experience, political offices held, and major events in which the person participated. Also ask them to include any skills, activities, and memberships that might present a fuller picture. Possible subjects include Adolf Hitler, Benito Mussolini, Joseph Stalin, Hideki Tojo, Winston Churchill, and Franklin Roosevelt. **OL**

worldwide attention. Congress passed a second neutrality act, banning the sale of arms to either side in a civil war.

Shortly after the Spanish Civil War began, Hitler and Mussolini pledged to cooperate on several international issues. Mussolini termed this new relationship the Rome-Berlin Axis. The following month, Japan aligned itself with Germany and Italy when it signed the Anti-Comintern Pact with Germany. The pact required the two countries to exchange information about communist groups. Together, Germany, Italy, and Japan became known as the **Axis Powers,** although they did not formally become military allies until September 1940.

With tensions in Europe worsening, Congress passed the Neutrality Act of 1937. This act not only continued the ban on selling arms to warring nations, but also required them to buy all nonmilitary supplies from the United States on a "cash-and-carry" basis. Countries at war had to send their own ships to the United States to pick up the goods, and they had to pay cash. Loans were not allowed. Isolationists knew that attacks on American ships carrying supplies to Europe had helped bring the country into World War I. They wanted to prevent such attacks from involving the nation in another European war.

Roosevelt's Internationalism

When he took office in 1933, President Roosevelt knew that ending the Great Depression was his first priority. He was not, however, an isolationist. He supported **internationalism,** the idea that trade between nations creates prosperity and helps prevent war. Internationalists also believed that the United States should try to preserve peace in the world. Roosevelt warned that the neutrality acts "might drag us into war instead of keeping us out," but he did not veto the bills.

In July 1937, Japanese forces in Manchuria launched a full-scale attack on China. Roosevelt decided to help the Chinese. Because neither China nor Japan had actually declared war, Roosevelt claimed the Neutrality Act of 1937 did not apply, and he authorized the sale of weapons to China. He warned that the nation should not stand by and let an "epidemic of lawlessness" infect the world:

PRIMARY SOURCE

"When an epidemic of physical disease starts to spread, the community . . . joins in a quarantine of the patients in order to protect the health of the community against the spread of the disease. . . . War is a contagion, whether it be declared or undeclared. . . . There is no escape through mere isolation or neutrality. . . . "

—quoted in *Freedom From Fear*

Despite his words, Americans were still not willing to risk another war. "It is a terrible thing," the president said, "to look over your shoulder when you are trying to lead—and find no one there."

Reading Check **Evaluating** Why did many Americans support isolationism?

Section 1 REVIEW

Vocabulary

1. **Explain** the significance of: Benito Mussolini, fascism, Vladimir Lenin, Joseph Stalin, collectives, Adolf Hitler, Manchuria, Neutrality Act of 1935, Axis Powers, internationalism.

Main Ideas

2. **Identifying** Which nations did dictators govern during the years after World War I?
3. **Analyzing** What events caused Roosevelt to become more of an internationalist?

Critical Thinking

4. **Big Ideas** Why did antidemocratic governments rise to power in postwar Europe and Asia?
5. **Organizing** Use a graphic organizer similar to the one below to compare the governments opposed to democracy in Europe and Asia.

Country	Dictator	Ideology

6. **Analyzing Visuals** Look at the photograph on page 685 of Guernica after it was destroyed. How might both isolationists and internationalists have used the image to win support for their cause?

Writing About History

7. **Persuasive Writing** Write a newspaper editorial supporting either isolationism or internationalism after World War I. Include reasons that support your ideas and that help convince others to embrace your position.

History ONLINE
Study Central™ To review this section, go to glencoe.com and click on Study Central.

Assess

History ONLINE

Study Central™ provides summaries, interactive games, and online graphic organizers to help students review content.

Close

Summarizing Ask: How did World War I influence the political destinies of both European nations and the United States? *(In European nations, many were faced with heavy reparations, unemployment, and economic depression and grew desperate for powerful leadership, even at the loss of personal liberties. In the United States, a feeling of betrayal and a return to isolationism produced an unwillingness to become involved in Europe's difficulties.)* **OL**

Reading Check

Answer: They felt that remaining apart from European conflicts would avoid another war.

Section 1 REVIEW

Answers

1. All definitions can be found in the section and the Glossary.
2. Italy, the USSR, and Germany
3. Japanese invasion of China
4. unhappiness with Treaty of Versailles terms, worldwide economic depression
5. Italy: Mussolini, Fascism; USSR: Stalin, Communism; Germany: Hitler, Nazism; Japan: Japanese military, Japanese militarism
6. Students' responses will vary but students may suggest that isolationists would have depicted the destruction as a reason to stay out of war, while internationalists may have emphasized growing fascism as a reason to increase involvement.
7. Answers will vary but should include text material.

Focus

Bellringer

Daily Focus Transparency 20-2

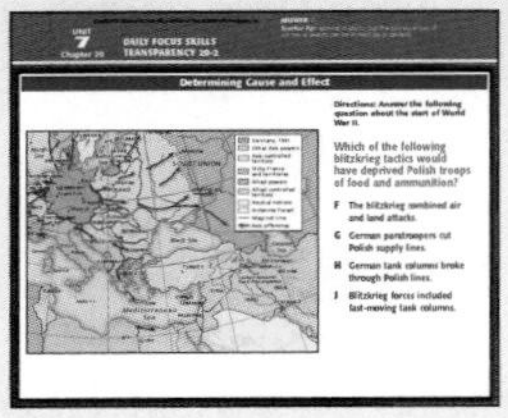

Guide to Reading

Answers:
1937: Hitler calls for German unity; February 1938: Hitler threatens to invade Austria; March 1938: the *Anschluss*; September 1938: Germany claims Sudetenland; October 1938 Germany demands return of Danzig; March 1939: Germany annexes Czechoslovakia; May 1939 Germany invades Poland; August 1939: Nazi-Soviet Nonaggression Pact

Section Spotlight Video

To generate student interest and provide a springboard for class discussion, access the Chapter 20, Section 2 video at glencoe.com or on the video DVD.

Section 2

Section Audio Spotlight Video

World War II Begins

Guide to Reading

Big Ideas

Trade, War, and Migration World War II officially began with the Nazi invasion of Poland and the French and British declarations of war on Germany in September 1939.

Content Vocabulary
- appeasement *(p. 689)*
- blitzkrieg *(p. 690)*

Academic Vocabulary
- violation *(p. 688)*
- regime *(p. 688)*
- concentrate *(p. 690)*
- transport *(p. 693)*

People and Events to Identify
- *Anschluss (p. 688)*
- Munich Conference *(p. 689)*
- Maginot Line *(p. 690)*
- Winston Churchill *(p. 693)*
- Battle of Britain *(p. 693)*

Reading Strategy

Sequencing As you read about the events leading up to World War II, record them by completing a time line similar to the one below.

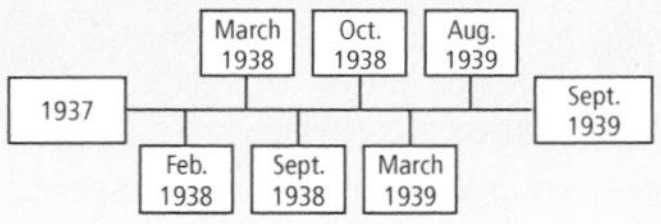

The shadow of World War I loomed large in the minds of European leaders in the late 1930s. Although Nazi Germany appeared increasingly aggressive, Britain and France wanted to avoid another bloody conflict. Efforts to negotiate peaceful agreements with Nazi Germany ultimately failed.

Path to War

MAIN Idea European nations tried to prevent war by giving in to Adolf Hitler's demands.

HISTORY AND YOU Do you remember reading how Europe was divided after World War I? Read to learn how German demands for more territory started World War II.

In 1935 Hitler began to defy the Treaty of Versailles that had ended World War I. He announced that Germany would build a new air force and begin a military draft that would greatly expand its army—actions in direct **violation** of the treaty. Rather than enforce the treaty by going to war, European leaders tried to negotiate with Hitler. At the time, the Nazi **regime** was weaker than it later would become. If European leaders had responded more aggressively, could war have been avoided? Historians still debate this question today.

Europe's leaders had several reasons for believing—or wanting to believe—that a deal could be reached with Hitler and that war could be avoided. First, they wanted to avoid a repeat of the bloodshed of World War I. Second, some thought most of Hitler's demands were reasonable, including his demand that all German-speaking regions be united. Third, many people assumed that the Nazis would be more interested in peace once they gained more territory.

The Austrian *Anschluss*

In late 1937 Hitler again called for the unification of all German-speaking people, including those in Austria and Czechoslovakia. He believed that Germany could expand its territory only by "resort[ing] to force with its attendant risks."

In February 1938 Hitler threatened to invade German-speaking Austria unless Austrian Nazis were given important government posts. Austria's chancellor gave in to this demand, but then tried to put the matter of unification with Germany to a democratic vote. Fearing the outcome, Hitler sent troops into Austria in March and announced the ***Anschluss***, or unification, of Austria and Germany.

Resource Manager

R Reading Strategies	C Critical Thinking	D Differentiated Instruction	W Writing Support	S Skill Practice
Teacher Edition • Using Word Parts, p. 689 **Additional Resources** • Guid. Read. Act., URB p. 49	**Teacher Edition** • Making Inferences, p. 689 • Drawing Con., p. 690 • Analyzing Info., p. 692 • Det. Cause/Effect, p. 693 **Additional Resources** • Quizzes and Tests, p. 290	**Teacher Edition** • Verbal/Linguistic, p. 691	**Additional Resources** • Content Vocabulary Act., URB p. 61	**Additional Resources** • Read. Essen., p. 223

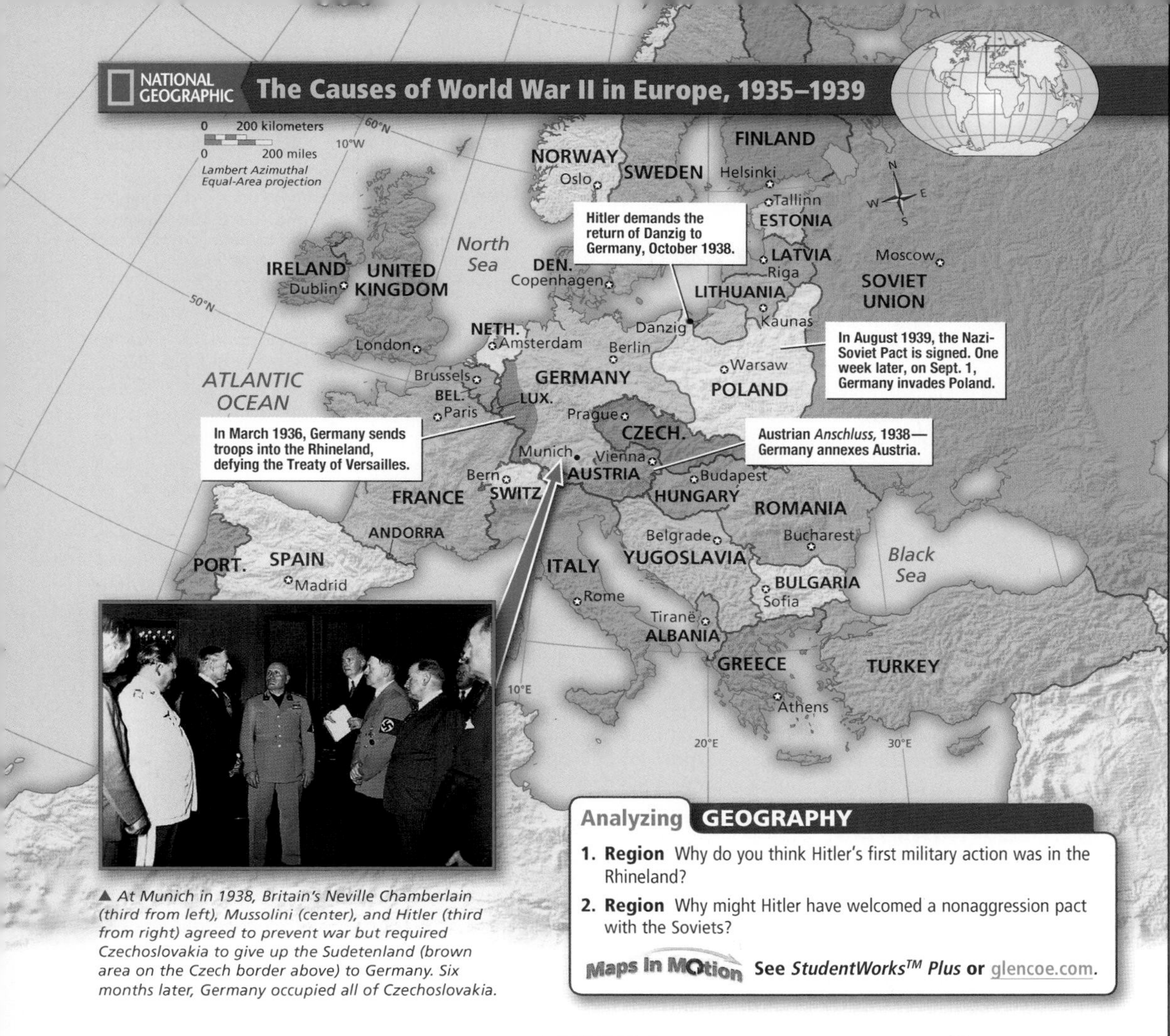

▲ *At Munich in 1938, Britain's Neville Chamberlain (third from left), Mussolini (center), and Hitler (third from right) agreed to prevent war but required Czechoslovakia to give up the Sudetenland (brown area on the Czech border above) to Germany. Six months later, Germany occupied all of Czechoslovakia.*

Analyzing GEOGRAPHY

1. **Region** Why do you think Hitler's first military action was in the Rhineland?
2. **Region** Why might Hitler have welcomed a nonaggression pact with the Soviets?

Maps in Motion See *StudentWorks™ Plus* **or** glencoe.com.

The Munich Crisis

Hitler next announced German claims to the Sudetenland, an area of Czechoslovakia with a large German-speaking population. The Czechs strongly resisted Germany's demands for the Sudetenland. France threatened to fight if Germany attacked Czechoslovakia, and the Soviet Union also promised aid. Prime Minister Neville Chamberlain pledged Britain's support to France, its ally.

Representatives of Britain, France, Italy, and Germany agreed to meet in Munich to decide Czechoslovakia's fate. At the **Munich Conference,** on September 29, 1938, Britain and France agreed to Hitler's demands, a policy that came to be known as **appeasement.** In other words, they made concessions in exchange for peace. Supporters of appeasement believed that Hitler had a few limited demands. They felt that if they gave him what he wanted, they could avoid war. Czechoslovakia was told to give up the Sudetenland or fight Germany on its own. When Chamberlain returned home, he promised "a peace with honor . . . peace in our time," but he also began to speed up British rearmament—in case appeasement failed. R C

Teach

R Reading Strategy

Using Word Parts Ask students to identify the root and the suffix in *appeasement.* (*appease* is the root; *-ment* is the suffix) Remind students that the suffix *-ment* means "process or action." EL

C Critical Thinking

Making Inferences Point out the final sentence of text on this page. **Ask:** How do you know that Chamberlain did not trust Hitler? *(He began rearming Britain at a faster pace.)* OL

Analyzing GEOGRAPHY

Answers:

1. the Rhineland was part of Germany so it was harder to object to his actions there
2. Hitler wanted to free himself for war against Western countries by making sure the Soviets would not halt his expansionism.

Hands-On Chapter Project
Step 2

Creating a World War II Memory Book

Step 2: Researching Selected Names Each student will do research on the name chosen in Step 1.

Directions Have students use library, Internet, or family resources to learn more about the person whose name they chose. Ask students to gather photos and information about the person's background, motivation, and his or her role in the war. They should also select a quotation or short paragraph written by the person, if possible.

Evaluating Information To decide which information to include, students will gain practice in evaluating the reliability of sources and the relevance of the information to the project. OL

(Project continued on page 695)

Did You Know?

The Baltic city of Gdansk (or Danzig in German) has historically been politically free and part of either Poland or German-speaking Prussia. It was part of Prussia until the Treaty of Versailles, when it became free. Identification with Germany has been strong, however; in the 1930s, Nazi officials were voted into the majority of the city assembly.

C Critical Thinking

Drawing Conclusions

Ask: What did Germany and the USSR each stand to gain by this treaty? *(They both would gain some of Poland and other Eastern European lands. Germany would not have to fight on two fronts and could concentrate on defeating Britain and France. The USSR would be safe from German attack.)* **OL**

Reading Check

Answer: Austria, Czechoslovakia, Danzig, Poland

Additional Support

Appeasement did fail to preserve the fragile peace. In March 1939 Germany sent troops into Czechoslovakia and divided the country. Slovakia became independent in name, but it was actually under German control. The Czech lands became a German protectorate.

Hitler Demands Danzig

A month after the Munich Conference, Hitler demanded that the city of Danzig be returned to German control. Although Danzig was more than 90 percent German, it had been part of Poland since World War I. Hitler also requested a highway and railroad across the Polish Corridor, an area that separated western Germany from the German state of East Prussia.

Hitler's new demands convinced Britain and France that war was inevitable. On March 31, 1939, Britain announced that if Poland went to war to defend its territory, Britain and France would come to its aid. This declaration encouraged Poland to refuse Hitler's demands. In May 1939, Hitler ordered the German army to prepare to invade Poland. He also ordered his foreign minister to begin negotiations with the USSR. If Germany was going to fight Britain and France, Hitler did not want to have to fight the Soviets, too.

The Nazi-Soviet Pact

When German officials proposed a nonaggression treaty to the Soviets, Stalin agreed. He believed the best way to protect the USSR was to turn the capitalist nations against each other. If the treaty worked, Germany would go to war against Britain and France, and the USSR would be safe.

C The nonaggression pact, signed by Germany and the USSR on August 23, 1939, shocked the world. Communism and Nazism were supposed to be totally opposed to each other. Leaders in Britain and France understood, however, that Hitler had made the deal to free himself for war against their countries and Poland. They did not know that the treaty also contained a secret deal to divide Poland between Germany and the Soviet Union.

Reading Check **Identifying** What regions did Hitler take or demand in the lead-up to the war?

The War Begins

MAIN Idea After Poland and France fell to the Nazis, the British evacuated thousands of trapped troops from Dunkirk.

HISTORY AND YOU Can you think of a contemporary situation in which people acted heroically to save others in danger? Read to learn about the heroism of civilians and soldiers in World War II.

On September 1, 1939, Germany invaded Poland. Two days later, Britain and France declared war on Germany. World War II had begun.

Poland resisted, but its army was outdated. The Polish army rode horses and carried lances against German tanks. The Germans used a new type of warfare called **blitzkrieg,** or "lightning war." Blitzkrieg used large numbers of massed tanks to break through and encircle enemy positions. To support the tanks, waves of aircraft bombed enemy positions and dropped paratroopers to cut their supply lines. Warsaw, the Polish capital, fell to the Germans on September 27. By October 5, 1939, the Germans had defeated the Polish military.

The Fall of France

Meanwhile, western Europe remained eerily quiet. The British had sent troops to France, and both countries remained on the defensive, waiting for the Germans to attack.

After World War I, the French had built a line of concrete bunkers and fortifications called the **Maginot Line** along the German border. The French preferred to wait behind the Maginot Line for the Germans to approach. This decision proved to be disastrous for two reasons. First, it allowed Germany to **concentrate** on Poland first before facing the British and French. Second, Hitler decided to go around the Maginot Line, which protected France's border with Germany but not France's border with Belgium.

On May 10, Hitler launched a new blitzkrieg. While German troops parachuted into the Netherlands, tanks rolled into Belgium and Luxembourg. Expecting the attack, British and French forces raced north into Belgium. This was a mistake. Instead of sending their tanks through the open countryside of central Belgium, the Germans sent their main force

Activity: Cooperative Learning

Prepare a News Broadcast Divide the class into six small groups. Assign each group one of the following events: the Austrian Anschluss, the Munich Conference, the Nazi-Soviet Nonaggression Pact, the invasion of Poland, the invasion of France, or the evacuation of Dunkirk. Have each group create a brief television newscast covering the event. If possible, allow students to videotape their stories in chronological order and then play the videotape for the class. **OL**

through the Ardennes Mountains of Luxembourg and eastern Belgium. The French did not think that large numbers of tanks could move through the mountains, and had left only a few troops to defend that part of the border. The Germans smashed through the French lines, and then turned west across northern France to the English Channel. The British and French armies could not move back into France quickly enough and were trapped in Belgium.

The Miracle at Dunkirk

After trapping the Allied forces in Belgium, the Germans began to drive them toward the English Channel. The only hope for Britain and France was to evacuate their surviving troops by sea, but the Germans had captured all but one port, Dunkirk, in northern France near the Belgian border.

As German forces closed in on Dunkirk, Hitler suddenly ordered them to stop. No one is sure why he gave this order. Historians know that Hitler was nervous about risking his tank forces, and he wanted to wait until more infantry arrived. Hermann Goering, the head of the German air force, also assured Hitler that aircraft alone could destroy the trapped soldiers.

Whatever Hitler's reasons, his order provided a three-day delay. This gave the British time to strengthen their lines and begin the evacuation. Some 850 ships of all sizes—from navy warships to small sailboats operated by civilian volunteers—headed to Dunkirk from

TECHNOLOGY & HISTORY

Blitzkrieg In 1939 Germany unleashed blitzkrieg—lightning war—on Europe. Blitzkrieg combined several technologies—aircraft, tanks, parachutes, and radios—to produce a highly mobile, fast-moving army that could coordinate multiple attacks, break through lines, and rapidly encircle enemy positions.

▲ German tanks rolled into Poland in 1939, ahead of the infantry, which followed to end any resistance. The bombers supported the swift-moving tanks from the air. The armored tanks, known as Panzers, often moved so rapidly that they had to wait for the infantry to catch up.

◀ A superior air force led to Germany's defeat of western Europe by summer 1940. The aircraft could drop paratroopers behind enemy lines as well as bomb targets.

Analyzing VISUALS

1. **Drawing Conclusions** What do you observe about the advance of the Panzer tanks in the photo on the left?
2. **Evaluating** What dangers do you think the paratroopers in the center photo may have faced?

D Differentiated Instruction

Verbal/Linguistic Invite students to read Paul Gallico's short story "The Snow Goose," which is about a disabled man in England who helps with the invasion of Dunkirk. Ask them to take notes as they read and prepare a response summarizing the story and describing why they think that so many citizens wanted to contribute to the war effort. OL

C Critical Thinking

Analyzing Information Tell students to discuss assumed reasons for Hitler's delay in attacking Dunkirk. Ask students to evaluate each reason and determine its validity. OL

Analyzing VISUALS

Answers:

1. Students may point out the long line of tanks, the isolated countryside, or the lack of any resistance.
2. Students may suggest snipers, land mines, or other forms of enemy attack, in addition to risk of parachutes not opening.

Additional Support

Extending the Content

Winston Churchill British Prime Minister Neville Chamberlain resigned in May 1940. Winston Churchill, heading a coalition government, took office on May 11. Less than a month later, the evacuation of Dunkirk began. Although the successful evacuation raised morale, Churchill warned members of Parliament that, "Wars are not won by evacuations." The son of an American mother and a British lord, Churchill had attended the British equivalent of West Point and had seen fighting in Cuba, India, Sudan, and South Africa before his service in France during World War I. He was among the first to sense the danger of the Nazi Party.

W Writing Strategy

Expository Writing Have students investigate Charles de Gaulle's role as leader of the Free French resistance during World War II. Ask them to present their findings. **OL**

Reading Check

Answer: by use of the blitzkrieg, using large numbers of tanks, infantry, and air power in a coordinated attack

DBQ Document Based Questions

Answers:

1. None; they are going to fight and defend the island regardless of Nazi successes elsewhere.
2. their confidence and their strength in the air
3. Students' responses will vary but may suggest that it gave his audience determination and hope.

England, many of them making the 48-mile trip multiple times. French, Dutch, and Belgian ships joined British ones in "Operation Dynamo." The British had hoped to rescue about 45,000 troops. Instead, when the evacuation ended on June 4, an estimated 338,000 British and French troops had been saved. This became known as the "Miracle at Dunkirk."

The evacuation had its price, however. Almost all of the British army's equipment remained at Dunkirk—90,000 rifles, 7,000 tons of ammunition, and 120,000 vehicles. If Hitler invaded Britain, it would be almost impossible to stop him from conquering the country.

Three weeks later, on June 22, 1940, Hitler accepted the French surrender in the same railway car in which the Germans had surrendered at the end of World War I. Germany now occupied much of northern France and its Atlantic coastline. To govern the rest of France, Germany installed a puppet government at the town of Vichy and made Marshal Philippe Pétain the new government's figurehead leader. Though Vichy France was officially a neutral party in the war, its powerless leaders collaborated with the Nazis to repress the people of France.

During the war, the United States recognized Vichy France as the official French government, but General Charles de Gaulle and his Free French resistance forces challenged the legitimacy of Vichy France. De Gaulle argued that he represented the continuity of the pre-invasion French government, that the Vichy government was illegal, and that the Vichy government leadership were traitors. From England and the French colony of Algiers, **W** de Gaulle cooperated with Allied political leaders to fight against the Germans and to bring about the liberation of France. De Gaulle refused to concede the defeat of France. Similarly, the leaders and citizens of Great Britain were not ready to give up the fight against Germany's advancing troops.

Reading Check **Explaining** By what means did Hitler overtake both Poland and France?

PRIMARY SOURCE

The Battle of Britain, 1940

During the Battle of Britain, bombs fell around London's St. Paul's Cathedral, a famous architectural treasure as well as a place of worship. Some of the subways no longer ran but were converted to air-raid shelters where people could sleep.

PRIMARY SOURCE

▲ *Winston Churchill*

"Even though large tracts of Europe and many old and famous States have fallen or may fall into the grip of the Gestapo and all the odious apparatus of Nazi rule, we shall not flag or fail, we shall go on to the end, we shall fight in France, we shall fight on the seas and oceans, we shall fight with growing confidence and growing strength in the air, we shall defend our island, whatever the cost may be, we shall fight on the beaches, we shall fight on the landing grounds, we shall fight in the fields and in the streets, we shall fight in the hills; we shall never surrender. . . ."

—Winston Churchill, Speech to Parliament, June 4, 1940

DBQ Document-Based Questions

1. **Identifying Points of View** What effect does Churchill suggest the fall of other European states will have on Britain?
2. **Analyzing Primary Sources** What does Churchill expect to grow as the Allied forces fight the Nazis?
3. **Hypothesizing** What effect do you think Churchill's words had on those who heard or read the speech?

Differentiated Instruction

Leveled Activities

BL **Critical Thinking Skills Activity, URB p. 32**

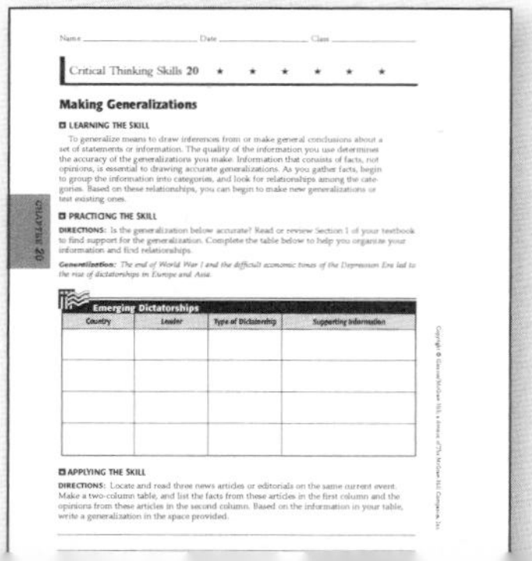

OL **American Art and Music Activity, URB p. 40**

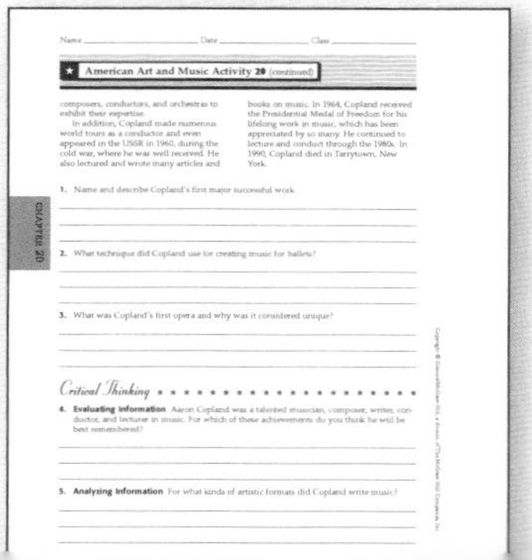

AL **Enrichment Activity, URB p. 46**

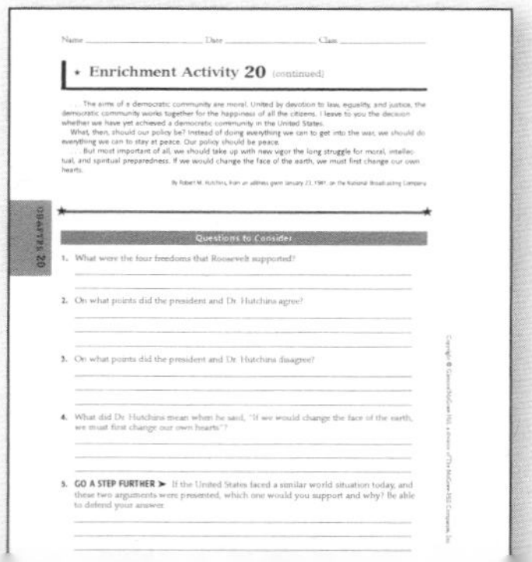

ELL **Primary Source Reading Activity, URB p. 35**

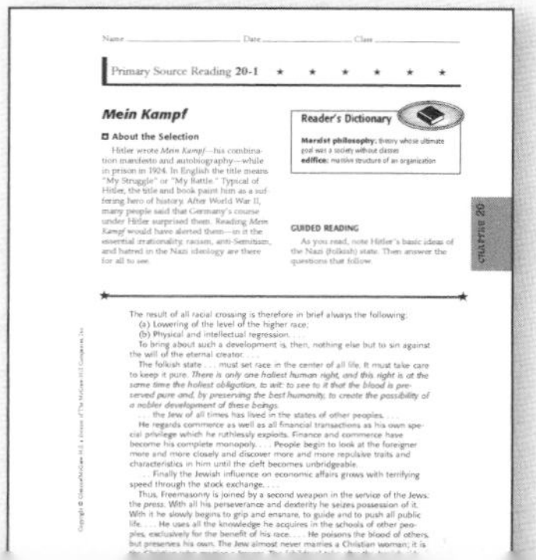

Britain Remains Defiant C

MAIN Idea Despite the bombing of London and other major cities, Britain's Winston Churchill stood firm against the threat of Nazi invasion.

HISTORY AND YOU Think of a time when the odds were against you. How did you react? Read about British resolve when faced with Nazi air raids.

Neither Pétain nor Hitler anticipated the bravery of the British people or the spirit of their leader, **Winston Churchill,** who had replaced Neville Chamberlain as prime minister. Hitler expected Britain to negotiate peace after France surrendered, but on June 4, 1940, Churchill delivered a defiant speech in Parliament, vowing that Britain would never surrender. The speech was intended to rally the British people and to alert the isolationist United States to Britain's plight.

Realizing Britain would not surrender, Hitler ordered his commanders to prepare to invade. Getting across the English Channel, however, posed a major challenge. Germany had few **transport** ships, and the British air force would sink them if they tried to land troops in England. To invade, therefore, Germany first had to defeat the British Royal Air Force.

In June 1940, the German air force, called the *Luftwaffe,* began to attack British shipping in the English Channel. Then, in mid-August, the *Luftwaffe* launched an all-out air battle to destroy the Royal Air Force. This air battle, which lasted into the fall of 1940, became known as the **Battle of Britain.**

On August 23, German bombers accidentally bombed London, the British capital. This attack on civilians enraged the British, who responded by bombing Berlin the following night. For the first time in the war, bombs fell on the German capital. Infuriated, Hitler ordered the *Luftwaffe* to stop its attacks on British military targets and to concentrate on bombing London.

Hitler's goal was to terrorize the British people into surrendering. The British endured, however, taking refuge in cellars and subway stations whenever German bombers appeared.

Although the Royal Air Force was greatly outnumbered, the British had one major advantage. They had developed a new technology called radar. Using radar stations placed along their coast, the British were able to detect incoming German aircraft and direct British fighters to intercept them.

Day after day, the British fighters inflicted more losses on the Germans than they suffered. During the long battle, Germany lost 1,733 aircraft while the British lost 915 fighter planes, along with 449 pilots. The skill of more than 2,000 British and 500 foreign pilots—including many Poles, Canadians, Frenchmen, and a few Americans—successfully thwarted Hitler's plan to invade Britain. These pilots flew as often as five times a day. Praising them, Churchill told Parliament, "Never in the field of human conflict was so much owed by so many to so few." On October 12, 1940, Hitler canceled the invasion of Britain.

Reading Check **Evaluating** How was Britain able to resist Hitler and the Nazis?

Section 2 REVIEW

Vocabulary

1. **Explain** the significance of: *Anschluss,* Munich Conference, appeasement, blitzkrieg, Maginot Line, Winston Churchill, Battle of Britain.

Main Ideas

2. **Explaining** Why did Europe's leaders first try to deal with Hitler through appeasement?
3. **Analyzing** Why was the decision to leave French forces behind the Maginot Line disastrous for Europe?
4. **Summarizing** In what ways did Winston Churchill prove to be an effective leader for Britain as the war began?

Critical Thinking

5. **Big Ideas** What was the new type of warfare used by Germany against Poland? Explain the technique.
6. **Organizing** Use a graphic organizer similar to the one below to list early events of the war in Poland and western Europe.

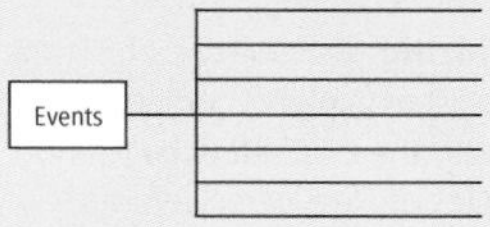

7. **Analyzing Visuals** Look again at the photograph on page 689. What do you observe about the participants at the Munich Conference?

Writing About History

8. **Expository Writing** Choose one dramatic incident from the beginnings of World War II and write a news story explaining what happened.

History ONLINE

Study Central™ To review this section, go to glencoe.com and click on Study Central.

693

C Critical Thinking

Determining Cause and Effect Ask students to read the material under the subheading "Britain Remains Defiant." Have them make cause-and-effect graphic organizers and use them to show the interaction between Britain and Germany in 1940. OL

Assess

History ONLINE

Study Central™ provides summaries, interactive games, and online graphic organizers to help students review content.

Close

Summarizing Ask: What factor encouraged Hitler's aggression in Europe? *(the reluctance of France and Britain to fight another war)* OL

Reading Check

Answer: Germany had few transport ships to send troops across the English Channel; the British had developed radar.

Section 2 REVIEW

Answers

1. All definitions can be found in the section and the Glossary.
2. They believed that Hitler had few demands and that by giving in they could prevent another war.
3. It allowed Germany to concentrate on Poland first; when Germany went around the line, troops were trapped in Belgium.
4. Churchill was determined to prevent the Germans from controlling Britain.
5. The Germans used blitzkrieg, a lightning war in which tanks on the ground supported airstrikes.
6. Answers may include the following: Germany and Soviets invade Poland; Britain and France enter the war; Germany invades Norway, Denmark, Belgium, the Netherlands, Luxembourg, and France
7. No one looks pleased or relaxed, despite the apparent progress in preventing war.
8. Students' news stories will vary but should center on a single event at the beginning of World War II and be written in journalistic style.

Focus

Bellringer

Daily Focus Transparency 20-3

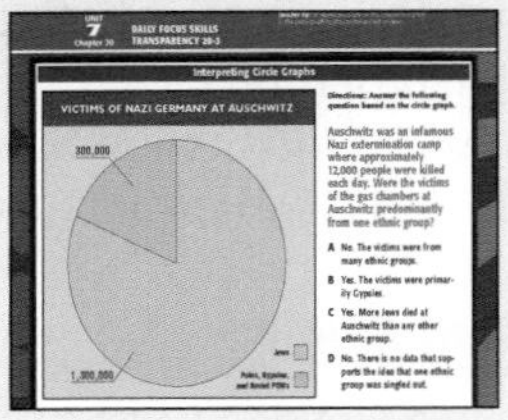

Guide to Reading

Answers:

Answers may include the following: segregated from the rest of the population, lost their jobs, stripped of citizenship, prohibited from voting or holding office, had identifying mark placed on passport, confined to concentration camps, killed in extermination camps

Section Spotlight Video

To generate student interest and provide a springboard for class discussion, access the Chapter 20, Section 3 video at glencoe.com or on the video DVD.

Section 3 | Section Audio | Spotlight Video

The Holocaust

Guide to Reading

Big Ideas

Group Action The Nazis believed Jews to be subhuman. They steadily increased their persecution of Jews and eventually set up death camps and tried to kill all the Jews in Europe.

Content Vocabulary

- concentration camp *(p. 698)*
- extermination camp *(p. 698)*

Academic Vocabulary

- prohibit *(p. 694)*
- assume *(p. 696)*
- virtually *(p. 699)*

People and Events to Identify

- *Shoah (p. 694)*
- Nuremberg Laws *(p. 694)*
- Gestapo *(p. 696)*
- Wannsee Conference *(p. 698)*

Reading Strategy

Organizing As you read about the Holocaust, complete a graphic organizer similar to the one below by listing examples of Nazi persecution of European Jews.

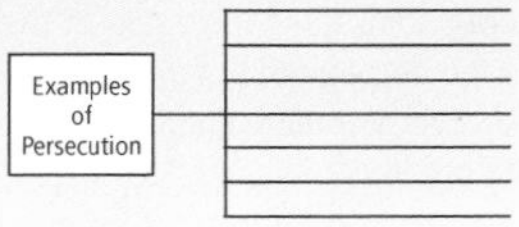

Nazis first acted upon their racist ideology when they imposed restrictions on Jews and stripped them of basic rights. Eventually, Nazi Germany created concentration camps and systematically attempted to kill all European Jews.

Nazi Persecution of the Jews

MAIN Idea Nazi laws stripped Jews of their citizenship and rights; immigration restrictions in other countries made leaving Germany difficult.

HISTORY AND YOU Do you know anyone who came to the United States as a refugee? Read how Jewish refugees were turned away in the late 1930s.

During the Holocaust, the Nazis killed nearly 6 million European Jews. The Nazis also killed millions of people from other groups they considered inferior. The Hebrew term for the Holocaust is ***Shoah.*** The basic meaning of the word is "catastrophe," but its most common current usage is as a specific designation of the Nazi campaign to exterminate the Jews during World War II.

The Nuremberg Laws

Although the Nazis persecuted anyone who dared oppose them, as well as the disabled, Gypsies, homosexuals, and Slavic peoples, they reserved their strongest hatred for the Jews. This loathing went far beyond the European anti-Semitism that was common at the time. Over the centuries, people who were prejudiced against Jews had discriminated against them in many ways. For example, Jews had sometimes been segregated in ghettos or **prohibited** from owning land.

After the Nazis took power, they quickly moved to deprive German Jews of many established rights. In September 1935, the **Nuremberg Laws** took citizenship away from Jewish Germans and banned marriage between Jews and other Germans. Two months later, another decree defined a Jew as a person with at least one Jewish grandparent and barred Jews from holding public office or voting. Another law compelled Jews with German-sounding names to adopt "Jewish" names. Soon the passports of Jews were marked with a red *J* to identify them as Jewish.

By the summer of 1936, at least half of Germany's Jews were jobless, having lost the right to work as civil servants, journalists, farmers, teachers, and actors. In 1938 the Nazis also banned Jews from practicing law and medicine and from operating businesses. With no source of income, life became very difficult.

Resource Manager

R Reading Strategies	C Critical Thinking	D Differentiated Instruction	W Writing Support	S Skill Practice
Teacher Edition • Summarizing, p. 695 • Act. Prior Know., p. 697 • Inferring, p. 697 • Using Word Parts, p. 698 • Using Context Clues, p. 698 **Additional Resources** • Guid. Read. Act., URB p. 50	**Teacher Edition** • Analyzing Prim. Sources, p. 695 **Additional Resources** • Quizzes and Tests, p. 291	**Teacher Edition** • Verbal/Linguistic, p. 696	**Additional Resources** • Time Line Act., URB p. 33	**Teacher Edition** • Creating Charts, p. 696 **Additional Resources** • Read. Essen., p. 226

PRIMARY SOURCE
The Persecution Begins, 1935–1938

▼ Nazi storm troopers place warning signs encouraging a boycott on Jewish-owned businesses in 1933.

▲ On Kristallnacht, November 9, 1938, roaming bands of Nazi storm troopers destroyed Jewish property and terrorized Jewish families across the Third Reich.

Analyzing VISUALS

1. **Hypothesizing** What effect do you think the signs might have had on the woman in the photograph on the left?
2. **Making Connections** How do you think publication of the photograph of the synagogue would have affected world opinion toward the Nazis?

Despite worsening conditions, many Jews chose to remain in Germany during the early years of Nazi rule. Well integrated into German society before this time, they were reluctant to leave and give up the lives they had built there. Many also thought that conditions would surely improve after a time. In fact, conditions soon became worse.

Kristallnacht

On November 7, 1938, a young Jewish refugee named Herschel Grynszpan shot and killed a German diplomat in Paris. Grynszpan's father and 10,000 other Jews had been deported **R** from Germany to Poland, and the distraught young man was seeking revenge for this act and for the persecution of the Jews in general.

In retaliation, an infuriated Hitler ordered his minister of propaganda, Joseph Goebbels, to stage attacks against the Jews that would seem like a spontaneous popular reaction to news of the murder. On the night of November 9, this plan played out in a spree of destruction. In Vienna, a Jewish child named Frederic Morton watched in terror that night as Nazi storm troopers broke into his family's apartment:

PRIMARY SOURCE

"They yanked out every drawer in every one of our chests and cupboards, and tossed each in the air. They let the cutlery jangle across the floor, the clothes scatter, and stepped over the mess to fling the next drawer. . . . 'We might be back,' the leader **C** said. On the way out he threw our mother-of-pearl ashtray over his shoulder, like confetti. We did not speak or move or breathe until we heard their boots against the pavement."

—quoted in *Facing History and Ourselves*

Teach

R Reading Strategy

Summarizing Have students write one-paragraph summaries of the events of *Kristallnacht*. Then place students in pairs to have them proofread each other's summaries. **OL**

C Critical Thinking

Analyzing Primary Sources Draw students' attention to the quotation by Frederic Morton. **Ask:** How did the storm troopers make sure that the family would not rest after they left? (Not only did they create disorder, but they also threatened to return.) **OL**

Analyzing VISUALS

Answers:

1. Students' responses will vary but may suggest that the signs would prevent her from shopping in that store.
2. Students' responses will vary but may suggest that further evidence of aggression would have turned world opinion even more strongly against the Nazis.

Hands-On Chapter Project
Step 3

Creating a World War II Memory Book

Step 3: Researching the Holocaust Students will work in groups to create a page in the Memory Book dedicated to Holocaust survivors.

Directions Have students use library, Internet, or family resources to learn more about the Holocaust and the survivors. Ask students to gather information about how they survived the war and lived their lives after the war. Students may choose to include primary sources on these pages of the Memory Book.

Putting It Together To decide which information to include, students will gain practice in finding relevant sources and synthesizing information from many sources. **OL** *(Project continued on page 703)*

D Differentiated Instruction

Verbal/Linguistic Albert Einstein was only one of many scientists who left Nazi Germany. Ask students to find out more about these scientists and their contributions to the Allied war effort. Have them present their findings to the class in the character of the scientist, telling his or her own story. **AL**

S Skill Practice

Creating Charts Have students use the information presented in this section to create a chart illustrating the following facts: the number of Jews who fled Germany from 1933 to 1939, the number of immigrants allowed to enter the United States each year, the number of Jews killed at Auschwitz, and the total number of Jews killed in Europe. **OL**

The anti-Jewish violence that erupted throughout Germany and Austria that night came to be called *Kristallnacht,* or "night of broken glass," because broken glass littered the streets afterward. By the following morning, more than 90 Jews were dead, hundreds were badly injured, and thousands more were terrorized. The Nazis had forbidden police to interfere while roving bands of thugs destroyed 7,500 Jewish businesses and hundreds of synagogues.

The lawlessness of *Kristallnacht* persisted. Following that night of violence, the **Gestapo,** the government's secret police, arrested about 30,000 Jewish men, releasing them only if they agreed to emigrate and surrender all their possessions. The state also confiscated insurance payments owed to Jewish owners of ruined businesses.

Jewish Refugees Try to Flee

Kristallnacht and its aftermath marked a significant escalation of Nazi persecution against the Jews. Many Jews, including Frederic Morton's family, decided that it was time to leave and fled to the United States. Between 1933, when Hitler took power, and the start of World War II in 1939, some 350,000 Jews escaped Nazi-controlled Germany. These emigrants included prominent scientists, such as Albert Einstein, and business owners like Otto Frank, who resettled his family in Amsterdam in 1933. Otto's daughter Anne kept a diary of her family's life in hiding after the Nazis overran the Netherlands. The "secret annex," as she called their hiding place, has become a museum.

Limits on Jewish Immigration By 1938, one American consulate in Germany had a backlog of more than 100,000 visa applications from Jews trying to leave for the United States. Following the Nazi *Anschluss,* some 3,000 Austrian Jews applied for American visas each day. Most never received visas to the United States or to the other countries where they applied. As a result, millions of Jews remained trapped in Nazi-dominated Europe.

Several factors limited Jewish immigration to the United States. Nazi orders prohibited Jews from taking more than about four dollars out of Germany. American immigration law, however, forbade granting a visa to anyone "likely to become a public charge." Customs officials tended to **assume** that this description

PRIMARY SOURCE

The Holocaust

▼ *After World War II broke out, the Nazis imposed anti-Jewish policies on the nations Germany conquered, often confining Jews to overcrowded ghettos. After weeks of fierce resistance, Jews in the Warsaw ghetto in Poland (below) were rounded up for deportation to concentration camps in May 1943.*

▲ *Shortly after Germany invaded the Soviet Union in 1941, the Nazis implemented plans to exterminate the Jews. Roving units called Einsatzgruppen began killing Jews in Soviet territory. In Poland, death camps were built and the system of ghettos was abandoned in favor of herding men, women, and children onto cattle cars for transport to the death camps.*

Additional Support

Activity: Interdisciplinary Connection

Language Arts Invite students from a drama class to perform one or two scenes from the play based on *The Diary of Anne Frank*, dramatized by Frances Goodrich and Albert Hackett. After the performance, have students discuss the scenes, including their initial impression and the social and historical importance of the play. **OL**

applied to Jews, because Germany had forced them to leave behind any wealth. High unemployment rates in the 1930s also made immigration unpopular. Few Americans wanted to raise immigration quotas, even to accommodate European refugees. Others did not want to admit Jews because they held anti-Semitic attitudes. The existing immigration policy **R1** allowed only 150,000 immigrants annually, with a fixed quota from each country. The law permitted no exceptions for refugees or victims of persecution.

International Response At an international conference on refugees in 1938, several European countries, the United States, and Latin America stated their regret that they could not take in more of Germany's Jews without raising their immigration quotas. Meanwhile, Nazi propaganda chief Joseph Goebbels announced that "if there is any country that believes it has not enough Jews, I shall gladly turn over to it all our Jews." Hitler also **R2** declared himself "ready to put all these criminals at the disposal of these countries . . . even on luxury ships."

As war loomed in 1939, many ships departed from Germany crammed with Jews desperate to escape. Some of their visas, however, had been forged or sold illegally, and Mexico, Paraguay, Argentina, and Costa Rica all denied access to Jews with such documents. So, too, did the United States.

The *St. Louis* Affair On May 27, 1939, the SS *St. Louis* entered the harbor in Havana, Cuba, with 930 Jewish refugees on board. Most of these passengers hoped to go to the United States eventually, but they had certificates improperly issued by Cuba's director of immigration giving them permission to land in Cuba. When the ships arrived in Havana, the Cuban government revoked the certificates and refused to let the refugees come ashore. For several days, the ship's captain steered his ship in circles off the coast of Florida, awaiting official permission to dock at an American port. Denied permission, the ship turned back toward Europe. The passengers finally disembarked in France, Holland, Belgium, and Great Britain. Within two years, the first three of these countries fell under Nazi domination. Many of the refugees brought to these countries perished in the Nazis' "final solution."

Reading Check **Analyzing** Why did many Jews stay in Germany despite being persecuted?

To read more of *Night* by Elie Wiesel, see page R76 in the **American Literature Library.**

In 1944 Elie Wiesel was taken to a concentration camp. In the excerpt below, he describes his wait during a move from one camp to another in 1944:

PRIMARY SOURCE

"The snow fell thickly. We were forbidden to sit down or even to move. The snow began to form a thick layer over our blankets. They brought us bread—the usual ration. We threw ourselves upon it. Someone had the idea of appeasing his thirst by eating the snow. Soon the others were imitating him. As we were not allowed to bend down, everyone took out his spoon and ate the accumulated snow off his neighbor's back. A mouthful of bread and a spoonful of snow. The SS [guards] who were watching laughed at the spectacle."

—Elie Wiesel, *Night*

▲ *When the war ended, Allied troops managed to liberate the few surviving inmates of the death camps—many of whom were too shocked to believe they were being freed.*

DBQ Document-Based Questions

1. **Explaining** How did the prisoners in Weisel's account try to quench their thirst?
2. **Describing** How did the guards react?

R1 Reading Strategy

Activating Prior Knowledge Ask students why the strict immigration laws had been passed in the United States. *(A resurgence of nativism during the 1920s led to tighter quotas.)* **OL**

R2 Reading Strategy

Inferring Point out the comments by Goebbels and Hitler concerning their willingness to send Jews to other nations.

Ask: What effect are these men's words intended to convey? *(that Jewish people are worthless and criminals)* **OL**

DBQ Document Based Questions

Answers:

1. by eating the snow off each others' backs
2. They laughed.

Reading Check

Answer: restrictions on immigration to other countries, they thought conditions would improve, Germany was their home, or they had no money

Additional Support

Activity: Collaborative Learning

Researching Historical Events Divide the class into small groups, assigning each group one of the following topics: *Kristallnacht*, the Warsaw ghetto, German use of slave labor, or stolen artwork, which Germany stole from occupied nations and from the Jews. Have each group present their findings to the class as a panel discussion. **Ask:** What is acceptable behavior in situations of war? *(Students may suggest that basic human rights should be preserved even in conditions of war.)* **OL**

R1 Reading Strategy

Using Word Parts Point out the terms *concentration* and *extermination*. Ask students to identify the suffix (*-tion*). Remind them that the suffix means "process or act." **BL**

R2 Reading Strategy

Using Context Clues Draw students' attention to the word *concentration*. Ask them to give multiple meanings for the word. *(a liquid made stronger and thicker by removing water from it; to focus attention or thoughts; to come together in a single place)* Remind students that when faced with an unfamiliar term, they can use the context of the sentence or paragraph to determine the meaning of the word. **OL**

Analyzing GEOGRAPHY

Answers:

1. Poland
2. Poland, Ukrainian SSR, Hungary

Additional Support

The Final Solution

MAIN Idea The Nazis planned and to a large degree carried out what they called "the final solution," the systematic extermination of Europe's Jews.

HISTORY AND YOU Can you think of a conflict today where violence is motivated by ethnic or religious hatred? Read to learn how prejudice led to mass murder in Nazi Germany.

On January 20, 1942, Nazi leaders met at the **Wannsee Conference** to determine the "final solution of the Jewish question." Previous "solutions" had included rounding up Jews, Gypsies, Slavs, and others from conquered areas, shooting them, and piling them into mass graves. Another method forced Jews and other "undesirables" into trucks and then piped in exhaust fumes to kill them. These methods, however, had proven too slow and inefficient for the Nazis.

R1 At Wannsee, the Nazis made plans to round up Jews from the vast areas of Nazi-controlled Europe and take them to detention centers known as **concentration camps.** There, healthy R2 individuals would work as slave laborers until they dropped dead of exhaustion, disease, or malnutrition. Most others, including the elderly, the infirm, and young children, would be sent to **extermination camps,** attached to many of the concentration camps, to be executed in massive gas chambers.

NATIONAL GEOGRAPHIC **The Holocaust, 1939–1945**

Jewish Losses, 1939–1945

Baltic States	228,000
Belgium	40,000
Bulgaria	14,000
Byelorusian SSR	245,000
Czechoslovakia	155,000
Denmark	500
France	90,000
Germany and Austria	210,000
Greece	54,000
Hungary	450,000
Italy	8,000
Netherlands	195,000
Poland	3,000,000
Romania	300,000
Russian SSR	107,000
Ukrainian SSR	900,000
Yugoslavia	26,000

◀ *A survivor of the Buchenwald camp drinks water outside the camp barracks, April 1945*

Analyzing GEOGRAPHY

1. **Place** Where were most of the extermination camps located?
2. **Region** Which three nations had the highest number of Jewish losses?

Maps In MOtion See *StudentWorks™ Plus* or glencoe.com.

Activity: Interdisciplinary Connection

Civics Have students work in pairs to create charts that compare the U.S. Bill of Rights with the rights that Nazis denied to the Jews. Students may need to conduct outside research to complete their charts. Use the charts as a basis for a class discussion on civil liberties. **Ask:** What effects did Nazi rule have on Jewish civil liberties? *(Jewish civil liberties effectively ceased to exist under the Nazis.)* **OL**

Concentration Camps

The Nazis had established their first concentration camps in 1933 to jail political opponents. After the war began, the Nazis built concentration camps throughout Europe.

Buchenwald, one of the largest concentration camps, was built near the town of Weimar in Germany in 1937. During its operation, more than 200,000 prisoners worked 12-hour shifts as slave laborers in nearby factories. Although Buchenwald had no gas chambers, hundreds of prisoners died there every month from exhaustion and horrible living conditions.

Leon Bass, an American soldier, saw Buchenwald at the end of the war. A room built for 50 people had housed more than 150, with bunk beds built almost to the ceiling. Bass recalled:

PRIMARY SOURCE

"I looked at a bottom bunk and there I saw one man. He was too weak to get up; he could just barely turn his head. He was skin and bones. He looked like a skeleton; and his eyes were deep set. He didn't utter a sound; he just looked at me with those eyes, and they still haunt me today."

—quoted in *Facing History and Ourselves*

Extermination Camps

In late 1941, the Nazis built extermination facilities at the Chelmno and Auschwitz concentration camps in western Poland and began murdering Jews living in the region. After the Wannsee Conference, extermination facilities were built at four other camps in Poland as well. At these camps, including the infamous Treblinka and Auschwitz, Jews were the Nazis' main victims. Auschwitz alone housed about 100,000 people in 300 prison barracks. Its gas chambers, built to kill 2,000 people at a time, sometimes gassed 12,000 people in a day. Of the estimated 1,600,000 people who died at Auschwitz, about 1,300,000 were Jews. The other 300,000 were Poles, Soviet prisoners of war, and Gypsies.

Upon arrival at Auschwitz, healthy prisoners were selected for slave labor. Elderly or disabled people, the sick, and mothers and children went immediately to the gas chambers, after which their bodies were burned in giant crematoriums.

In only a few years, Jewish culture, which had existed in Europe for over 1,000 years, had been **virtually** obliterated by the Nazis in the lands they conquered. Despite exhaustive debate, there is still great controversy about why and how an event so horrifying as the Holocaust could have occurred. No consensus has been reached, but most historians point to a number of factors: the German people's sense of injury after World War I; severe economic problems; Hitler's control over the German nation; the lack of a strong tradition of representative government in Germany; German fear of Hitler's secret police; and a long history of anti-Jewish prejudice and discrimination in Europe.

Reading Check **Summarizing** How did Hitler try to exterminate Europe's Jewish population?

Section 3 REVIEW

Vocabulary

1. **Explain** the significance of: *Shoah*, Nuremberg Laws, Gestapo, Wannsee Conference, concentration camp, extermination camp.

Main Ideas

2. **Listing** What early steps did Germany take in persecution of Jewish people?

3. **Analyzing** What was the purpose of the Wannsee Conference?

Critical Thinking

4. **Big Ideas** Do you think the German people or other nations could have prevented the Holocaust? Why or why not?

5. **Organizing** Use a graphic organizer similar to the one below to list the methods the Nazis used to try to destroy the Jewish population.

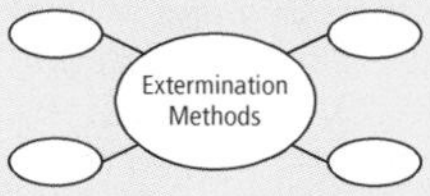

6. **Analyzing Visuals** Study the photos on pages 695–696. How do the images show the destruction of Jewish life?

Writing About History

7. **Persuasive Writing** Imagine that you are living in the United States during the 1930s. You believe that more Jewish immigrants should be allowed to come into the country. Write a letter to your representative or senator in Congress to express your point of view.

History ONLINE
Study Central™ To review this section, go to glencoe.com and click on Study Central.

Assess

History ONLINE

Study Central™ provides summaries, interactive games, and online graphic organizers to help students review content.

Close

Summarizing Ask: Do you think that greater American involvement in Europe could have prevented or limited the effects of Nazi persecution? *(Responses will vary but may suggest that Hitler was determined and had a powerful army at his disposal to enforce his desires.)* **OL**

Reading Check

Answer: In extermination camps, Jews were immediately killed in gas chambers. In concentration camps, they were worked until they died of disease, starvation, or exhaustion.

Section 3 REVIEW

Answers

1. All definitions can be found in the section and the Glossary.
2. required them to live in ghettos, deprived them of citizenship and the right to vote, identified in passports and through yellow stars as Jewish, and *Kristallnacht*, the destruction of Jewish areas
3. to determine a "final solution of the Jewish question"
4. Students' answers will vary but should be supported by reasons.
5. gas chambers, malnutrition and starvation, untreated disease, worked to death
6. They show stages of Hitler's campaign, from civil discrimination and violence to deportation to camps.
7. Students' letters will vary, but should use information from the section.

ANALYZING PRIMARY SOURCES

Focus

When people arrived at a concentration camp, their heads were shaved, their clothing and belongings removed, and, at Auschwitz, identification numbers were tattooed on their arms. Those able to work did so 12 hours a day, with little food. Some Nazi officers took pleasure in abusing inmates; the infamous Dr. Josef Mengele conducted experiments on both dead and living prisoners.

Teach

C Critical Thinking

Analyzing Primary Sources
Invite students to read the first Primary Source. Ask them to identify the ways in which both the Nazis and the prisoners were described. (Nazis were brutes, barbarians; prisoners were hordes of people, poor innocents)
Ask: What effect does this word choice have on the account? *(Students may say the descriptions make it very clear who is the villain and who is the victim.)* OL

ANALYZING PRIMARY SOURCES

The Holocaust

As the Allies liberated areas from German control in the spring of 1945, they discovered horrifying scenes in Nazi concentration camps. The Nazi regime had systematically murdered six million Jews and killed another six million Poles, Slavs, Gypsies, homosexuals, communists, and mentally disabled persons. Photographs of the newly liberated camps shocked the American public, although the Roosevelt administration and the State Department had evidence of the death camps as early as 1942.

Study these primary sources and answer the questions that follow.

PRIMARY SOURCE 1

Eyewitness Account

C "[There] were two barracks: the men stood on one side, the women on the other. They were addressed in a very polite and friendly way: 'You have been on a journey. You are dirty. You will take a bath. Get undressed quickly.' Towels and soap were handed out, and then suddenly the brutes woke up and showed their true faces: this horde of people, these men and women were driven outside with hard blows and forced both summer and winters to go the few hundred metres to the 'Shower Room.' Above the entry door was the word 'Shower'. One could even see shower heads on the ceiling which were cemented in but never had water flowing through them.

These poor innocents were crammed together, pressed against each other. Then panic broke out, for at last they realized the fate in store for them. But blows with rifle butts and revolver shots soon restored order and finally they all entered the death chamber. The doors were shut and, ten minutes later, the temperature was high enough to facilitate the condensation of the hydrogen cyanide for the condemned were gassed with hydrogen cyanide. This was the so-called 'Zyklon B' . . . which was used by the German barbarians. . . . One could hear fearful screams, but a few moments later there was complete silence."

—André Lettich, Jewish prisoner assigned to remove bodies from the gas chambers at Birkenau
from *Nazism 1919–1945, Volume 3: Foreign Policy, War and Racial Extermination—A Documentary Reader*

PRIMARY SOURCE 2

Photograph, 1945

▼ *Newly liberated survivors at Dachau concentration camp, May 4, 1945*

PRIMARY SOURCE 3

Nazi Decree, 1941

I (1) Jews over six years of age are prohibited from appearing in public without wearing a Jewish star.
(2) The Jewish star is a yellow piece of cloth with a black border, in the form of a six-pointed star the size of the palm of the hand. The inscription reads "JEW" in black letters. It shall be worn visibly, sewn on the left chest side of the garment.

II Jews are forbidden:
(a) to leave their area of residence without written permission of the local police, carried on their person.
(b) to wear medals, decorations or other insignia.

—Nazi decree issued September 1, 1941
from *Nazism 1919–1945, Volume 3: Foreign Policy, War and Racial Extermination—A Documentary Reader*

Differentiated Instruction

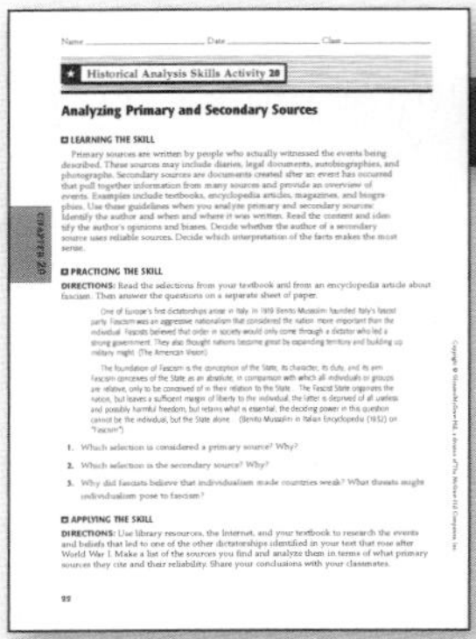

Historical Analysis Activity 20, URB p. 22

Identifying Facts and Opinions: Primary and Secondary Sources

Objective: Read to identify facts and opinions in primary and secondary sources.
Focus: Read the selections from the textbook and from an encyclopedia article on p. 22.
Teach: Define fact and opinion.
Assess: Identify the facts in the selections by underlining them. Identify the opinions by circling them.
Close: Write one or two factual sentences about fascism and one or two opinion sentences.

Differentiated Instruction Strategies

- **BL** Identify one fact and one opinion in each selection.
- **AL** Choose an op-ed piece from a newspaper, and identify the facts and opinions. Discuss how the writer used facts to support his or her opinions.
- **ELL** Flip through the textbook and identify as many primary sources as possible.

Primary Source 4

American Soldier's Diary, 1945

"One thousand Weimar citizens toured the Buchenwald camp in groups of 100. They saw blackened skeletons and skulls in the ovens of the crematorium. In the yard outside, they saw a heap of white human ashes and bones. . . .

The living actually looked worse than the dead. Those who lived wore striped uniforms, with the stripes running up and down. Those who were dead were stripped of their clothing and lay naked, many stacked like cordwood waiting to be burned in the crematory. At one time, 5,000 had been stacked on the vacant lot next to the crematory.

Often . . . the SS wished to make an example of someone in killing him. They hung him on the lot adjacent to the crematory, and all the three sections of the camp witnessed the sight—some 30,000 prisoners. They used what I call hay hooks, catching him under the chin and the other in the back of his neck. He hung in this manner until he died."

—diary of Captain Luther D. Fletcher, from *World War II: From the Battle Front to the Home Front*

Primary Source 5

Photograph, April 17, 1945

American soldiers force German civilians to view bodies after the liberation of the Buchenwald concentration camp.

Primary Source 6

Painting

Unable to Work, by Auschwitz survivor David Olère

DBQ Document-Based Questions

1. **Speculating** How do you suppose soldiers could participate in such barbaric acts?
2. **Analyzing Visuals** What does the appearance of these survivors tell you about conditions in the camps?
3. **Drawing Conclusions** What purpose did the restrictions listed in Source 3 serve?
4. **Drawing Conclusions** Study Sources 5 and 6. How do you think American troops reacted to the horrifying scenes they found in the concentration camps? Why do you think American troops made Germans tour the liberated concentration camps?
5. **Analyzing Visuals** Study the painting in Source 6. What symbols does the artist use to illustrate the fate of those too weak to work?

Assess/Close

Have students read Primary Source 4. Discuss with students the historical value of Primary Source accounts such as diaries and letters written at the time, rather than written after the fact. *(The accounts are not edited nor impressions blurred by the passage of time.)*

Encourage students who have not read Anne Frank's diary to do so, noting that Anne actually kept two accounts, one meant to be public and the other her own.

Document Based Questions

Answers

1. Student answers will vary but may suggest that the soldiers saw these acts as part of their jobs.
2. The extreme thinness of the survivors indicates that life was hard and food was scarce.
3. The restrictions made Jews easily identifiable and served to make life more difficult for them.
4. American troops probably reacted with horror. They wanted Germans to tour the camps to try to get them to see the evil that had been done while they did nothing to stop it.
5. A skeletal figure hovers over the weak ones, indicating coming death.

Focus

Bellringer

Daily Focus Transparency 20-4

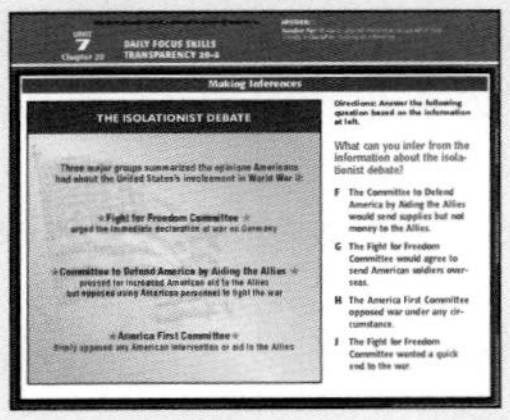

Guide to Reading

Answers:
Britain's struggle with Germany; Japan's attack on Pearl Harbor

Section Spotlight Video

To generate student interest and provide a springboard for class discussion, access the Chapter 20, Section 4 video at glencoe.com or on the video DVD.

Section 4 — Section Audio — Spotlight Video

America Enters the War

Guide to Reading

Big Ideas

Government and Society After World War II began, the United States attempted to continue its prewar policy of neutrality.

Content Vocabulary
- hemispheric defense zone *(p. 704)*
- strategic materials *(p. 706)*

Academic Vocabulary
- revise *(p. 702)*
- purchase *(p. 702)*
- underestimate *(p. 707)*

People and Events to Identify
- America First Committee *(p. 703)*
- Lend-Lease Act *(p. 704)*
- Atlantic Charter *(p. 705)*

Reading Strategy

Organizing As you read about America's efforts to stay neutral, complete a graphic organizer similar to the one below by naming events that shifted American opinion toward helping the Allies.

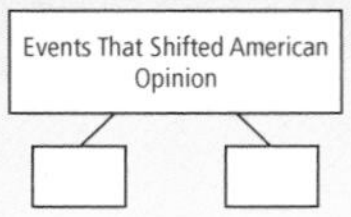

As World War II began, the United States remained officially neutral but aided Great Britain considerably in its fight against Germany. In the Pacific, Japan's territorial expansion led to growing tensions with the United States, which peaked when Japan attacked Pearl Harbor.

FDR Supports England

MAIN Idea President Roosevelt favored changes in American neutrality laws, although Americans remained divided about the war and American involvement.

HISTORY AND YOU Have you ever been drawn into an argument when you just wanted to be left alone? Read about the increasing difficulties that the United States faced in trying to stay out of World War II.

President Roosevelt officially proclaimed the United States neutral two days after Britain and France declared war on Germany. Despite this proclamation, however, he was determined to help the two countries as much as possible in their struggle against Hitler.

Destroyers-for-Bases Deal

Soon after the war began, Roosevelt called Congress into a special session to **revise** the neutrality laws. He asked Congress to eliminate the ban on arms sales to nations at war. Public opinion strongly supported the president. Congress passed the new law, but isolationists demanded a price for the revision. Under the Neutrality Act of 1939, warring nations could buy weapons from the United States only on a "cash-and-carry" basis. This law was similar to the 1937 Neutrality Act governing the sale of nonmilitary items to countries that were at war.

In the spring of 1940, the United States faced its first test in remaining neutral. In May, Prime Minister Winston Churchill asked Roosevelt to transfer old American destroyers to Britain, which had lost nearly half its destroyers. To protect its cargo ships from German submarines and to block any German attempt to invade Britain, the nation needed more destroyers.

Determined to give Churchill the destroyers, Roosevelt used a loophole in the neutrality act that required cash for **purchases.** In exchange for the right to build American bases on British-controlled Newfoundland, Bermuda, and islands in the Caribbean, Roosevelt sent 50 old American destroyers to Britain. Because the deal did not involve an actual sale, the neutrality act did not apply.

Resource Manager

R Reading Strategies	C Critical Thinking	D Differentiated Instruction	W Writing Support	S Skill Practice
Teacher Edition • Act. Prior Know., p. 704 • Inferring, p. 705 • Taking Notes, p. 706 **Additional Resources** • Guid. Read. Act., URB p. 51 • Prim. Source Read., URB p. 37	**Teacher Edition** • Making Generalizations, p. 703 • Analyzing Prim. Sources, p. 704 • Comparing, p. 706 **Additional Resources** • Quizzes and Tests, p. 292 • Auth Assess, p. 45 • Interpret. Pol. Cartoons, URB p. 41	**Additional Resources** • Differentiated Intsr., URB p. 23 • Reteaching Act., URB p. 43	**Teacher Edition** • Expository Writing, p. 707 **Additional Resources** • Enrichment Act., URB p. 45	**Teacher Edition** • Using Geo. Skills, p. 705 **Additional Resources** • Read. Essen., p. 229

POLITICAL CARTOONS PRIMARY SOURCE

Should America Stay Neutral in World War II?

▲ *This 1939 cartoon shows Uncle Sam standing guard over Democracy, whose only refuge is America.*

▲ *Nazi bullets whiz past Uncle Sam and his isolationist policies.*

Analyzing VISUALS DBQ

1. **Analyzing Visuals** According to the cartoon at left, what message is Democracy sending to Uncle Sam?
2. **Analyzing Visuals** What do you observe about Uncle Sam's perch in the cartoon above?

The Isolationist Debate

Widespread acceptance of the destroyers-for-bases deal reflected a change in public opinion. By July 1940, most Americans favored offering limited aid to the Allies. That spirit was hardly unanimous, however. In fact, people who wanted greater American involvement in the war and those who felt that the United States should remain neutral began debating the issue in the spring of 1940.

At one extreme was the Fight for Freedom Committee, a group that urged the repeal of all neutrality laws and stronger action against Germany. At the other extreme was the **America First Committee.** It was a staunchly isolationist group opposed to any American intervention or aid to the Allies. The committee's members included aviator Charles Lindbergh and Senator Gerald Nye.

C

Closer to the center, the Committee to Defend America by Aiding the Allies, which journalist William Allen White headed, pressed for increased American aid to the Allies but opposed armed intervention.

The heated neutrality debate took place during the 1940 presidential election campaign. For months, Americans had wondered whether President Roosevelt would follow the tradition George Washington had set and retire after a second term. With the United States in a precarious position, however, many believed a change of leaders might not be in the country's best interest. Roosevelt decided to run for an unprecedented third term.

During the campaign, FDR steered a careful course between neutrality and intervention. The Republican nominee, Wendell Willkie, did the same, promising he too would assist the Allies but stay out of the war. The voters reelected Roosevelt by a wide margin, preferring to keep a president they knew during this crisis period.

✓ Reading Check **Identifying** Identify different groups and their positions on U.S. neutrality in the late 1930s.

Teach

C Critical Thinking

Making Generalizations

Ask: What effect do you think it had on people to realize that famous men such as Lindbergh and Nye were part of this group? *(Students may say that men of their fame and stature might sway the opinions of people.)* **OL**

Analyzing VISUALS

Answers:

1. Uncle Sam should stay out of European conflicts.
2. It seems very unsteady and unsafe.

✓ **Reading Check**

Answer: The America First Committee was isolationist. The Committee to Defend America by Aiding the Allies opposed armed intervention but wanted to aid the Allies. The Fight for Freedom Committee wanted repeal of all neutrality laws.

Hands-On Chapter Project
Step 4

Creating a World War II Memory Book

Step 4: Debating the War Students will create a page in their Memory Book that documents the debate over whether the United States should remain neutral.

Directions Have students use library or Internet sources to find arguments for and against the United States's neutrality in 1940. Students will build a page in the Memory Book that illustrates this debate.

Putting It Together Students will select quotations or summarize arguments for and against neutrality. **OL**

(Project continued on the Visual Summary page)

R **Reading Strategy**

Activating Prior Knowledge Draw students' attention to the "Four Freedoms" Roosevelt identifies. **Ask:** In what American document can the first two Freedoms be found? *(the First Amendment in the Bill of Rights in the United States Constitution)* **OL**

C **Critical Thinking**

Analyzing Primary Sources Invite a volunteer to read aloud the fourth freedom that Roosevelt addresses. **Ask:** How much progress do you think the world has made toward this goal since the end of 1945? *(Students' answers will vary but may suggest that nuclear arms and the arms race have not allowed this goal to be accomplished.)* **OL**

Additional Support

Edging Toward War

MAIN Idea In 1940 and 1941, the United States took more steps to provide aid to Great Britain.

HISTORY AND YOU What kinds of aid does America provide other countries today? Why? Read why FDR thought it was important to "lend" Britain some help.

Read "The Four Freedoms" on page R53 in **Documents in American History.**

With the election over, Roosevelt expanded the nation's role in the war. Britain was fighting for democracy, he said, and the United States had to help. Speaking to Congress, he listed the "Four Freedoms" for which both the United States and Britain stood: freedom of speech, freedom of worship, freedom from want, and freedom from fear.

The Lend-Lease Act

By December 1940, Great Britain had run out of funds to wage its war against Germany. Roosevelt came up with a way to remove the cash requirement of the most recent neutrality act. He proposed the **Lend-Lease Act,** which allowed the United States to lend or lease arms to any country considered "vital to the defense of the United States." The act allowed Roosevelt to send weapons to Britain if the British government promised to return or pay rent for them after the war.

Roosevelt warned that, if Britain fell, an "unholy alliance" of Germany, Japan, and Italy would keep trying to conquer the world. The president argued that the United States should become the "great arsenal of democracy" to keep the British fighting and make it unnecessary for Americans to go to war.

The America First Committee disagreed, but Congress passed the Lend-Lease Act by a wide margin. By the time the program ended, the United States had "lent" more than $40 billion in weapons, vehicles, and other supplies to the Allied war effort.

While shipments of supplies to Britain began at once, lend-lease aid eventually went to the Soviet Union, as well. In June 1941, violating the Nazi-Soviet pact, Hitler invaded the Soviet Union. Although Churchill detested communism and considered Stalin a harsh dictator, he vowed that any person or state "who fights against Nazism will have our aid." Roosevelt, too, supported this policy.

A Hemispheric Defense Zone

Congressional approval of the Lend-Lease Act did not solve the problem of getting American arms and supplies to Britain. German submarines patrolling the Atlantic Ocean were sinking hundreds of thousands of tons of shipments each month; the British Navy did not have enough ships to stop them.

Because the United States was still technically neutral, Roosevelt could not order the U.S. Navy to protect British cargo ships. Instead, he developed the idea of a **hemispheric defense zone.** Roosevelt declared that the entire western half of the Atlantic was part of the Western Hemisphere and, therefore, neutral. He then ordered the U.S. Navy to patrol the western Atlantic and reveal the location of German submarines to the British.

The Atlantic Charter

In August 1941, Roosevelt and Churchill met on board American and British warships anchored near Newfoundland. During these meetings, the two men agreed on the text of

PRIMARY SOURCE

Aiding Britain, 1939–1941

The Four Freedoms

"In the future days, which we seek to make secure, we look forward to a world founded upon four essential human freedoms.

The first is freedom of speech and expression—everywhere in the world.

The second is freedom of every person to worship God in his own way—everywhere in the world.

The third is freedom from want—which . . . will secure to every nation a healthy peacetime life for its inhabitants—everywhere in the world.

The fourth is freedom from fear—which, translated into world terms, means a world-wide reduction of armaments to such a point and in such a thorough fashion that no nation will be in a position to commit an act of physical aggression against any neighbor—anywhere in the world."

—Address to Congress, January 6, 1941

Activity: Collaborative Learning

Analyzing Propaganda Divide the class into three groups. Have each group analyze the propaganda used by both the Axis powers and the Allied powers during World War II. Assign each member of the group one of the following tasks: researching the information, writing descriptions of the information, or analyzing the propaganda. Have group members combine their efforts to make an in-class presentation. **OL**

the **Atlantic Charter.** This agreement committed both nations to a postwar world of democracy, nonaggression, free trade, economic advancement, and freedom of the seas. By late September, an additional 15 anti-Axis nations had signed the charter. Churchill later said that FDR pledged to "force an 'incident' . . . which would justify him in opening hostilities" with Germany.

An incident quickly presented itself. In early September, a German submarine, or U-boat, fired on an American destroyer that had been radioing the U-boat's position to the British. Roosevelt promptly responded by ordering American ships to follow a "shoot-on-sight" policy toward German submarines.

The Germans escalated hostilities the following month, targeting two American destroyers. One of them, the *Reuben James,* sank after being torpedoed, killing 115 sailors. As the end of 1941 drew near, Germany and the United States continued a tense standoff.

Reading Check **Evaluating** How did the Lend-Lease Act help the Allied war effort?

Japan Attacks

MAIN Idea The Japanese attack on Pearl Harbor led the United States to declare war on Japan.

HISTORY AND YOU Do you remember how the United States acquired territory in the Pacific? Read about the threats to American interests as Japan expanded its empire.

Despite the growing tensions in the Atlantic, the Japanese attack on Pearl Harbor finally brought the United States into World War II. Ironically, Roosevelt's efforts to help Britain fight Germany resulted in Japan's decision to attack the United States.

America Embargoes Japan

Roosevelt knew that Britain needed much of its navy in Asia to protect its territories there from Japanese attack. As German submarines sank British ships in the Atlantic, however, the British began moving warships from Southeast Asia, leaving India and other colonial possessions vulnerable.

How Did FDR Help Britain While the U.S. Remained Neutral?

- Neutrality Act of 1939 allowed warring nations to buy weapons from the United States if they paid cash and transported arms on their own ships
- Destroyers-for-bases provided old American destroyers in exchange for the right to build U.S. defense bases in British-controlled Bermuda, Caribbean Islands, and Newfoundland
- Lend-Lease Act permitted U.S. to lend or lease arms to any country "vital to the defense of the United States"
- Hemispheric defense zone established the entire western half of the Atlantic as part of the Western Hemisphere and, therefore, neutral

NATIONAL GEOGRAPHIC Sending Aid to Britain, 1939–1941

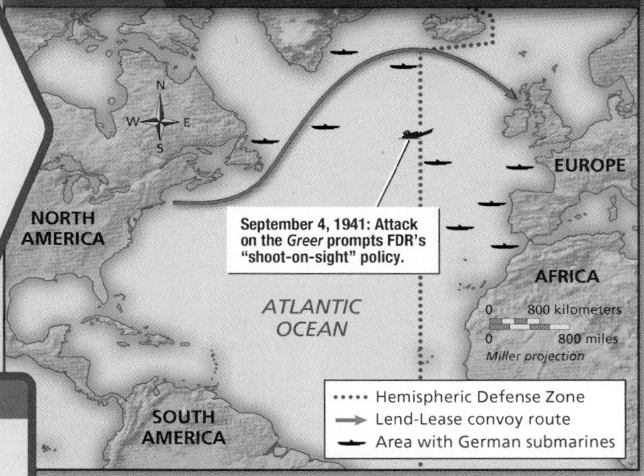

What Did the Atlantic Charter Declare?

1. The U.S. and Britain do not seek to expand their territories.
2. Neither seeks territorial changes against the wishes of the people involved.
3. Both respect people's right to select their own government.
4. All nations should have access to trade and raw materials.
5. Improved labor standards and economic advances are vital.
6. Both nations hope people will be free from want and fear.
7. Everyone should be able to freely travel the high seas.
8. All nations must abandon the use of force; disarmament is necessary after the war.

DBQ Document-Based Questions

1. **Drawing Conclusions** Why do you think it was important to begin the Atlantic Charter with the first three points?
2. **Analyzing Primary Sources** How does the Atlantic Charter echo FDR's Four Freedoms speech?

R Reading Strategy

Inferring Draw students' attention to the quotation by Churchill. **Ask:** What does this information tell you about Roosevelt? *(He was committed to assisting Britain and fighting against Germany.)* **OL**

S Skill Practice

Using Geography Skills Have students look at the map titled "Sending Aid to Britain, 1939–1941." **Ask:** Where was the largest concentration of German submarines? *(off the coasts of Europe and Africa)* **BL**

DBQ Document Based Questions

Answers:

1. Students' responses will vary but may suggest that the Allies wanted to reassure the world that they were not seeking additional territory.
2. It repeats the need for freedom from want and fear.

Reading Check

Answer: It helped by getting arms to the Allies.

Additional Support

Extending the Content

Great Britain was not the only country to receive aid under the Lend-Lease Act of 1941. The Soviet Union, which prior to World War II had little trade with the United States, received over $11 billion dollars in war materials between 1941 and 1945. The Allies wanted to keep the Soviet Union fighting against Germany on the Eastern Front. Aid to civilians in the Soviet Union came through the Red Cross and the U.S. Russian War Relief (a private, nonprofit organization).

Joseph Stalin never told his people how much Lend-Lease and the private aid helped the USSR survive the war. However, at the Yalta Conference at the end of the war he said, "Lend-Lease is one of Franklin Roosevelt's most remarkable and vital achievements in the formation of the anti-Hitler alliance."

R Reading Strategy

Taking Notes Have students create a graphic organizer listing the three actions Roosevelt took in response to the Japanese sending troops to southern Indochina. *(He froze all Japanese assets in the United States, reduced the amount of oil being shipped to Japan, and sent General Douglas MacArthur to the Philippines to build up American defenses there.)* **BL**

C Critical Thinking

Comparing Remind students of the embargo Roosevelt ordered in 1940 against exports of scrap metal to Japan, which later extended to other products that had military uses. Discuss the embargoes or sanctions currently in effect. Discuss whether these are effective in preventing war or accomplishing the goals established by the nations that impose them. **AL**

Turning Point

Answer: Students' responses will vary but should be supported with reasons.

Additional Support

Turning Point

Japan Attacks Pearl Harbor

Pearl Harbor was an important turning point because it not only brought the United States into the war but also decisively marked an end to U.S. isolationism. After the war ended, the nation did not withdraw from its role in international affairs, as it had done following World War I. Involvement in the war signaled the beginning of a global role for the United States that has continued to the present day. With the decision to support the United Nations and efforts to rebuild Europe, the nation became actively involved in international events.

HYPOTHESIZING Do you believe the United States would have entered the war regardless of the attack on Pearl Harbor? Support your ideas with reasons.

▲ *Rescue boats approach the burning USS* West Virginia *and USS* Tennessee*, which were hit by enemy fire on December 7, 1941. In the photo to the right, President Roosevelt addresses Congress the following day.*

◀ *Although ideas to create a memorial of Pearl Harbor were put forth as early as 1946, not until 1958 did President Eisenhower sign the bill that authorized this memorial, a bridge built over the sunken USS Arizona. The completed memorial was dedicated in 1962.*

History ONLINE Student Web Activity Visit glencoe.com and complete the activity on Pearl Harbor.

History ONLINE Student Skill Activity To learn how to create multimedia presentations, visit glencoe.com and complete the skill activity.

To hinder Japanese aggression, Roosevelt began applying economic pressure. Japan depended on the United States for many key materials, including scrap iron, steel, and especially oil. At that time, the United States supplied roughly 80 percent of Japan's oil. In July 1940 Congress gave the president the power to restrict the sale of **strategic materials** (materials important for fighting a war). Roosevelt immediately blocked the sale of airplane fuel and scrap iron to Japan. Furious, the Japanese signed an alliance with Germany and Italy, becoming a member of the Axis.

In 1941 Roosevelt began sending lend-lease aid to China. Japan, which had invaded China in 1937, controlled much of the Chinese coast by 1941. Roosevelt hoped that lend-lease aid would enable the Chinese to tie down the Japanese and prevent them from attacking elsewhere. The strategy failed. By July 1941, Japan had sent military forces into southern Indochina, posing a direct threat to the British Empire.

R Roosevelt responded. He froze all Japanese assets in the United States, reduced the amount of oil being shipped to Japan, and sent General Douglas MacArthur to the Philippines to build up American defenses there.

C Roosevelt made it clear that the oil embargo would end only if Japan withdrew from Indochina and made peace with China. With its war against China in jeopardy because of a lack of oil and other resources, the Japanese military planned to attack the resource-rich British and Dutch colonies in Southeast Asia. They also decided to seize the Philippines and to attack the American fleet at Pearl Harbor. While the Japanese prepared for war, negotiations with the Americans continued, but neither side would back down. In late November

Extending the Content

Attack on Pearl Harbor Japanese pilots began training for the attack on Pearl Harbor in the spring of 1941. The commander of the Japanese fleet devised a plan that used naval aviation and aircraft carriers on a large scale. Six aircraft carriers and 24 supporting vessels coordinated the attack in addition to submarines intended to sink any warships that survived the attack. The first wave of the surprise attack involved 181 planes. A second wave of 170 planes took off half an hour later. In addition to hitting the fleet anchored in Pearl Harbor, the Japanese also hit two Navy air bases, a Marine air field, and three Army Air Corps fields. By hitting these additional sites, the Japanese hoped to prevent American planes from intercepting the Japanese force. The attack lasted less than two hours. More than 90 percent of the attacking planes survived and returned to the Japanese aircraft carriers.

1941, six Japanese aircraft carriers, two battleships, and several other warships set out for Hawaii.

Japan Attacks Pearl Harbor

The Japanese government appeared to be continuing negotiations with the United States in good faith. American intelligence, however, had decoded Japanese communications that made it clear that Japan was preparing to go to war against the United States.

On November 27, American commanders at the Pearl Harbor naval base received a war warning from Washington, but it did not mention Hawaii as a possible target. Because of the great distance from Japan to Hawaii, officials doubted that Japan would attempt such a long-range attack.

The U.S. military's inability to correctly interpret the information they were receiving left Pearl Harbor an open target. The result was devastating. Japan's surprise attack on December 7, 1941, sank or damaged eight battleships, three cruisers, four destroyers, and six other vessels. The attack also destroyed 188 airplanes and killed 2,403 Americans. Another 1,178 were injured. **W**

That night, a gray-faced Roosevelt met with his cabinet, telling them the country faced the most serious crisis since the Civil War. The next day, he asked Congress to declare war:

PRIMARY SOURCE

"Yesterday, December 7, 1941—a date which will live in infamy—the United States of America was suddenly and deliberately attacked by naval and air forces of the Empire of Japan. . . . No matter how long it may take us . . . the American people in their righteous might will win through to absolute victory."

—from *The Public Papers and Addresses of Franklin D. Roosevelt*

The Senate voted 82 to 0 and the House 388 to 1 to declare war on Japan.

Germany Declares War

Although Japan and Germany were allies, Hitler was not bound to declare war against the United States. The terms of the alliance specified that Germany had to come to Japan's aid only if Japan was attacked, not if it attacked another country. Hitler had grown frustrated with the American navy's attacks on German submarines, however, and he believed the time had come to declare war.

Hitler greatly **underestimated** the strength of the United States. He expected the Japanese to easily defeat the Americans in the Pacific. By helping Japan, he hoped for Japanese support against the Soviet Union after they had defeated the Americans. On December 11, Germany and Italy both declared war on the United States.

Reading Check **Examining** Why did military officials not expect an attack on Pearl Harbor?

Section 4 REVIEW

Vocabulary

1. **Explain** the significance of: America First Committee, Lend-Lease Act, hemispheric defense zone, Atlantic Charter, strategic materials.

Main Ideas

2. **Analyzing** What early efforts did Roosevelt make to help the British?
3. **Explaining** What was the hemispheric defense zone? Why was it developed?
4. **Summarizing** Why was the United States unprepared for Japan's attack on Pearl Harbor?

Critical Thinking

5. **Big Ideas** After Roosevelt's efforts to help Britain, some people accused him of being a dictator. Do you agree or disagree with this label? Explain your answer.
6. **Organizing** Use a graphic organizer similar to the one below to show how Roosevelt helped Britain while remaining officially neutral.

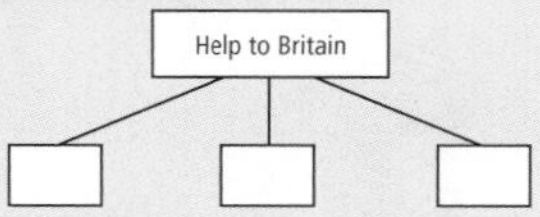

7. **Analyzing Visuals** Study the images on page 706. Then create a multimedia presentation that traces the Japanese attack on Pearl Harbor.

Writing About History

8. **Expository Writing** Write a letter to the editor of your newspaper explaining why you think the United States should either remain neutral or become involved in World War II.

History ONLINE
Study Central™ To review this section, go to glencoe.com and click on Study Central.

W Writing Strategy

Expository Writing Have students investigate the Pearl Harbor Memorial and other efforts to preserve the history of the attack. Ask them to present their findings. **OL**

Assess

History ONLINE

Study Central™ provides summaries, interactive games, and online graphic organizers to help students review content.

Close

Summarizing Ask: How did Americans slowly leave their position of staying out of Europe's wars? *(offered aid to Allies, responded to Japanese aggression, signed agreements such as the Atlantic Charter)* **OL**

Reading Check

Answer: They did not think that the Japanese would attempt an attack at such a distance.

Section 4 REVIEW

Answers

1. All definitions can be found in the section and the Glossary.
2. destroyers for bases deal, Lend-Lease Act, hemispheric defense zone
3. The hemispheric defense zone was an imaginary division of the Atlantic Ocean to justify patroling for German submarines that were disrupting British shipping.
4. The United States did not expect Japan to attack a target at such a distance. It also failed to correctly interpret military information.
5. Students may say it was important to stop Germany; others will say that Roosevelt violated the Neutrality Act.
6. destroyers for bases deal, Lend-Lease Act, hemispheric defense zone
7. Students' presentations should note that isolationism failed to prevent the attack. Presentations should also contain accurate accounts of the attack.
8. Students' letters will vary but should express a clear and reasoned opinion.

Organizing Divide the class into three groups, assigning each group one of the three nations listed under "Causes of the Rise of Dictators." Invite students to create graphic organizers that link the causes that pertain to their countries to particular effects.

Special Education Help students organize events by having them make a four-column chart. Ask them to label the columns Allied Powers, Axis Powers, Axis-controlled Countries, and Neutral Countries. Students then can use the text and maps to identify and list the countries under the appropriate headings.

Chapter 20 VISUAL SUMMARY

STUDY TO GO You can study anywhere, anytime by downloading quizzes and flashcards to your PDA from glencoe.com.

Causes of the Rise of Dictators

Italy
- Mussolini's Fascist Party believed in the supreme power of the state.
- In 1922 Mussolini threatened to march on Rome; the king appointed Mussolini as the premier.

Germany
- Hitler's Nazi Party believed in an all-powerful state, territorial expansion, and ethnic purity.
- Hitler believed that Germans needed more living space and called for Germany to expand east into Poland and Russia.
- Germany invaded Poland in 1939, France in 1940, and the USSR in 1941.

Japan
- Military leaders pushed for territorial expansion.
- Japan attacked Manchuria in 1931.
- Japan invaded China in 1937.
- Japan attacked Pearl Harbor in 1941.

▲ *German tanks move down a highway near Soissons, France in May 1940.*

▲ *These survivors of Buchenwald, liberated in 1945, show the horrifying conditions under which they lived.*

Effects

Holocaust
- During the Holocaust, the Nazis killed an estimated 6 million Jews.
- Jews were targeted and sent to concentration or extermination camps throughout Europe.

World War II
- Leaders of France and Britain tried to appease Hitler by allowing territorial growth.
- Britain and France declared war on Germany following the invasion of Poland.
- The United States sent aid to the Allied forces through the lend-lease program and cash-and-carry provision.
- France was defeated by the Nazis, who occupied the country in 1940.
- The United States declared war on Japan in 1941, after the bombing of Pearl Harbor.

Hands-On Chapter Project Step 5

Creating a World War II Memory Book

Step 5: Wrap Up Students will use their prior knowledge and the materials they researched to complete the pages of the memory book.

Directions Give each student a page of the memory book and ask them to use the photos and information they researched to create an attractive, informative page. They may wish to decorate the pages with other appropriate images, as well. The complete book may be used by the class to review the chapter and then displayed in the school or donated to a local VFW chapter or other group. **OL**

Chapter 20 Assessment

Reviewing Vocabulary

Directions: Choose the word or words that best complete the sentence.

1. What type of government considered the nation more important than the individual?
- **A** dictatorship
- **B** monarchy
- **C** fascism
- **D** democracy

2. What did Hitler call Germany's quick air strikes?
- **A** blitzkrieg
- **B** *Kristallnacht*
- **C** *Anschluss*
- **D** gestapo

3. What were the Nuremberg Laws?
- **A** regulations passed by Congress that explained when the United States could go to war against Germany
- **B** regulations passed by Congress that restricted the number of Jewish immigrants allowed into the U.S.
- **C** regulations passed by the United Nations that outlawed World War II
- **D** regulations passed by Germany that deprived German Jews of certain rights such as citizenship

4. Buchenwald was a ________ built in 1937. Throughout its years of operation, over 200,000 prisoners worked there to the point of exhaustion and death.
- **A** ghetto
- **B** appeasement
- **C** Gestapo
- **D** concentration camp

5. ________, such as oil, steel, and iron supplies, were used by the United States to put pressure on Japan.
- **A** Rationed items
- **B** Strategic materials
- **C** Lend-Lease goods
- **D** Cash-and-carry materials

Reviewing Main Ideas

Directions: Choose the best answers to the following questions.

Section 1 *(pp. 682–687)*

6. Which factor encouraged an American policy of neutrality during the 1930s?
- **A** disillusionment with World War I and its results
- **B** decline in the military readiness of other nations
- **C** repeal of Prohibition
- **D** economic prosperity of the period

7. In the 1930s the United States responded to the rise of fascism in Europe by
- **A** invading Germany and Italy.
- **B** forming military alliances.
- **C** passing a series of neutrality laws.
- **D** joining the League of Nations.

Section 2 *(pp. 688–693)*

8. What term refers to the German annexation of Austria?
- **A** *Kristallnacht*
- **B** *Anschluss*
- **C** Munich Conference
- **D** Nazi-Soviet Nonaggression Pact

9. When France fell to the Nazis, the French and British evacuated thousands of troops from
- **A** Dunkirk.
- **B** Danzig.
- **C** Buchenwald.
- **D** Poland.

TEST-TAKING TIP

Look at each question to find clues to support your answer. Try not to get confused by the wording of the question. Then look for an answer that best fits the question.

Need Extra Help?

If You Missed Questions . . .	1	2	3	4	5	6	7	8	9
Go to Page . . .	682	690	694	698–699	706	686–687	686	688	690–692

GO ON

Answers and Analyses Reviewing Vocabulary

1. C The main distractor for students will likely be *A,* because dictatorships and fascism are sometimes associated. Remind students that not all dictatorships are within fascist states, nor do all dictatorships consider the nation of supreme importance.

2. A This question can be confusing because of the number of foreign terms. Point out the key term, *quick,* and help students associate it with *blitz.*

3. D Only one response assigns the laws to Germany. Students may associate Nuremberg with the German city to reach the correct answer.

4. D While ghettos were areas of cities where Jews lived, these areas were not wartime creations.

5. B By recalling that the last two options were directed toward Britain, students can eliminate answers *C* and *D.* No mention has yet been made of rationing, so *B* is the correct answer.

Reviewing Main Ideas

6. A Students may be confused by the distractor *B.* The responses *C* and *D* are clearly irrelevant or false. By recalling that all of the Axis nations were building up their militaries, students can see that *A* is the correct answer.

7. C The key to this question is the date given. Responses *B* and *D* are similar in nature and can be eliminated. Invasions did not occur before Pearl Harbor, so *A* is also false.

8. B Students can eliminate *C* and *D,* because conferences and pacts have nothing to do with invasions. They are left with two German words; it may help to have them associate the letter *A* with the nation, the act of annexing, and the term *Anschluss.*

9. A This question asks students to recall geography and locations. The key to the question is the mention of France. Students may be able to eliminate all distractors simply by analyzing the words as unlikely to be connected to France.

10. B Suggest that students observe the words *extermination* and *final* to identify the correct response. Camps deprived Jews of any sort of justice, so *A* can be eliminated. Students should also note that *B* is the only answer choice contained in quotations. The question asks the *name* of the Nazi policy, so students should deduce that the correct answer would contain quotation marks.

11. A The key to this question is the date given, 1939, and the term *immediate*, thus eliminating *B*. Because *A* is in contrast to *C*, logically only one of them is the correct response.

12. A The hemispheric defense zone established an imaginary line in the Atlantic Ocean. The western half of the Atlantic was declared neutral to allow U.S. ships to patrol for German subs. Students should remember that the Wannsee Conference was held by Germany and concerned the "final solution," while the Munich Conference was held to appease Hitler. The America First Committee was an isolationist group and thus would not be interested in aiding Britain.

13. B Students should recognize that Pearl Harbor is part of the United States and therefore the bombing demanded a response. Both *A* and *C* involved other nations. They can also eliminate *D*, which occurred in World War I.

Chapter 20 Assessment

Section 3 *(pp. 694–699)*

10. Concentration camps and extermination camps were part of what Nazis called
- **A** justice for all.
- **B** the "final solution."
- **C** population control.
- **D** the last straw.

Section 4 *(pp. 702–707)*

11. In 1939 the immediate response of the United States to the start of World War II in Europe was to
- **A** modify its neutrality policy by providing aid to the Allies.
- **B** declare war on Germany and Italy.
- **C** strengthen its isolationist position by ending trade with Britain.
- **D** send troops to the Allied nations to act as advisers.

12. What was one step that America took to aid Great Britain?
- **A** created a hemispheric defense zone
- **B** founded the America First Committee
- **C** called for the Wannsee Conference
- **D** attended the Munich Conference

13. Why did the United States enter the war in 1941?
- **A** blitzkrieg over Poland
- **B** bombing of Pearl Harbor
- **C** embargo on Japan
- **D** sinking of the *Lusitania*

Critical Thinking

Directions: Choose the best answers to the following questions.

14. When Roosevelt signed the Lend-Lease Act, he said America must become the "arsenal of democracy" in order to
- **A** end the Depression.
- **B** help the Axis Powers.
- **C** remain neutral.
- **D** help Britain.

Base your answers to questions 15 and 16 on the map below and on your knowledge of Chapter 20.

Nazi Concentration and Extermination Camps

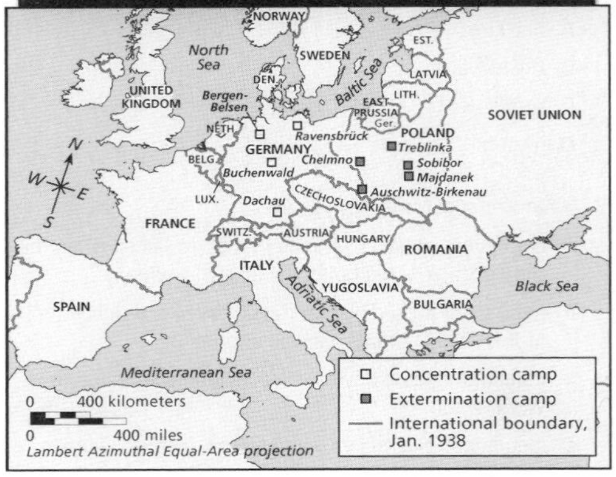

15. In which two countries were most of the concentration and extermination camps located?
- **A** Germany and France
- **B** Germany and Poland
- **C** Germany and the Soviet Union
- **D** Germany and Austria

16. What can you conclude about the extent of the Nazis' concentration and extermination camps?
- **A** The Nazis constructed camps in every European country.
- **B** The Nazis constructed camps in countries that Germany conquered.
- **C** The Nazis constructed camps in Britain.
- **D** The Nazis constructed camps in the Soviet Union.

Need Extra Help?

If You Missed Questions . . .	10	11	12	13	14	15	16
Go to Page . . .	698–699	702–704	704–705	705–707	704	R15	R15

GO ON

Critical Thinking

14. D Students should focus on the word "arsenal" to help them answer this question. If they think of weapons in connection with Lend-Lease, they should be able to narrow the choices to *B* and *D*. Students should then recognize that America was against the Axis Powers, leaving only *D* as the correct response.

15. B Remind students to look carefully at the map in answering this question. Although all responses include Germany, the second part of the answer is determinative.

16. B Students should use the map to help them answer the question. The map shows many European countries without concentration camps, so *A* can be eliminated. The map also shows that no camps existed in Britain or the Soviet Union, eliminating *C* and *D*.

17. Why were the British able to prevent the Germans from invading their country?

A The United States joined the Allied forces.

B Germany could not penetrate the Maginot Line.

C France defeated Germany and pushed them back into Belgium.

D Britain had developed radar stations to detect German aircraft.

Analyze the cartoon and answer the question that follows. Base your answer on the cartoon and on your knowledge of Chapter 20.

18. According to the cartoon, how did Americans feel about assisting the Allies?

A They sent troops to help make the world safe for democracy.

B Many Americans were willing to help the British but did not want to sell them arms.

C Many Americans did not want to help the British fight the Germans.

D The United States sold arms to Britain and France.

Document-Based Questions

Directions: Analyze the document and answer the short-answer questions that follow the document.

Daniel Inouye earned a Medal of Honor for his service in World War II and later became a United States senator. In 1941, however, he was a teenager living in Hawaii. This is his account of Pearl Harbor:

> *"As soon as I finished brushing my teeth and pulled on my trousers, I automatically clicked on the little radio that stood on the shelf above my bed. I remember that I was buttoning my shirt and looking out the window . . . when the hum of the warming set gave way to a frenzied voice. 'This is no test,' the voice cried out. 'Pearl Harbor is being bombed by the Japanese!'"*
>
> *[The family ran outside to look toward the naval base at Pearl Harbor.]*
>
> *"And then we saw the planes. They came zooming up out of that sea of gray smoke, flying north toward where we stood and climbing into the bluest part of the sky, and they came in twos and threes, in neat formations, and if it hadn't been for that red ball on their wings, the rising sun of the Japanese Empire, you could easily believe that they were Americans, flying over in precise military salute."*
>
> —quoted in *Eyewitness to America*

19. How did Inouye find out about the attack on Pearl Harbor?

20. What made him certain that the planes were Japanese, not American?

Extended Response

21. Could the Holocaust have been avoided if the Allies had intervened? Write an essay that takes a position and defends it. Your essay should include an introduction, several paragraphs, and a conclusion. Use relevant facts and details to support your conclusion.

STOP

History ONLINE
For additional test practice, use Self-Check Quizzes—Chapter 20 at glencoe.com.

Need Extra Help?

If You Missed Questions . . .	17	18	19	20	21
Go to Page . . .	693	R18	711	711	R6

Extended Response

21. Students' essays will vary but should take a position and support it with relevant facts and details. Essays should include an introduction, multiple paragraphs, and a conclusion.

17. D Students may need to focus on order of events to answer this question correctly. The United States did not join the Allies until after Germany's attempt to invade Britain. Germany went around the Maginot Line. *C* is clearly false, because Germany defeated France.

18. B Careful examination of the cartoon indicates that Americans wanted only to honor long friendship and ties with Britain, not to provide troops or arms.

Document-Based Questions

19. over the radio

20. the red ball painted on the wings of the planes, representing the rising sun of the Japanese Empire

History ONLINE
Have students visit the Web site at glencoe.com to review Chapter 20 and take the Self-Check Quiz.

Need Extra Help?
Have students refer to the pages listed if they miss any of the questions.

Chapter 21 Planning Guide

Key to Ability Levels	
BL Below Level	AL Above Level
OL On Level	ELL English Language Learners

Key to Teaching Resources	
Print Material	Transparency
CD-ROM or DVD	

Levels BL	OL	AL	ELL	Resources	Chapter Opener	Section 1	Section 2	Section 3	Section 4	Section 5	Chapter Assess
FOCUS											
BL	OL	AL	ELL	**Daily Focus Skills Transparencies**		21-1	21-2	21-3	21-4	21-5	
TEACH											
	OL	AL		**Geography and History Activity, URB**					p. 3		
	OL	AL		**American Literature Reading, URB**		p. 13		p. 15			
BL	OL		ELL	**Reading Essentials and Note-Taking Guide***		p. 232	p. 235	p. 238	p. 241	p. 244	
	OL			**Historical Analysis Skills Activity, URB**		p. 56					
BL	OL		ELL	**Guided Reading Activities, URB***		p. 82	p. 83	p. 84	p. 85	p. 86	
BL	OL	AL	ELL	**Content Vocabulary Activity, URB***		p. 61					
BL	OL	AL	ELL	**Academic Vocabulary Activity, URB**		p. 63					
	OL	AL		**Critical Thinking Skills Activity, URB**						p. 66	
BL	OL		ELL	**Reading Skills Activity, URB**		p. 55					
BL			ELL	**English Learner Activity, URB**						p. 59	
	OL	AL		**Reinforcing Skills Activity, URB**					p. 65		
BL	OL	AL	ELL	**Differentiated Instruction Activity, URB**				p. 57			
BL	OL		ELL	**Time Line Activity, URB**						p. 67	
	OL			**Linking Past and Present Activity, URB**		p. 68					
BL	OL	AL	ELL	**American Art and Music Activity, URB**					p. 73		
BL	OL	AL	ELL	**Interpreting Political Cartoons Activity, URB**			p. 75				
		AL		**Enrichment Activity, URB**				p. 79			
BL	OL	AL	ELL	**American Biographies**		✓		✓			
BL	OL	AL	ELL	**Primary Source Reading, URB**			p. 69	p. 71			
BL	OL	AL	ELL	**Supreme Court Case Studies**				p. 61			
BL	OL	AL	ELL	**The Living Constitution***	✓	✓	✓	✓	✓	✓	✓
	OL	AL		**American History Primary Source Documents Library**	✓	✓	✓	✓	✓	✓	✓
BL	OL	AL	ELL	**Unit Map Overlay Transparencies**	✓	✓	✓	✓	✓	✓	✓
BL	OL	AL	ELL	**Differentiated Instruction for the American History Classroom**	✓	✓	✓	✓	✓	✓	✓

Note: Please refer to the *Unit 7 Resource Book* for this chapter's URB materials.

* Also available in Spanish

TeacherWorks Plus All-In-One Planner and Resource Center

- Interactive Lesson Planner
- Interactive Teacher Edition
- Fully editable blackline masters
- Section Spotlight Videos Launch
- Differentiated Lesson Plans
- Printable reports of daily assignments
- Standards Tracking System

Levels BL	OL	AL	ELL		Resources	Chapter Opener	Section 1	Section 2	Section 3	Section 4	Section 5	Chapter Assess
					TEACH *(continued)*							
BL	OL	AL	ELL	CD	**StudentWorks™ Plus**	✓	✓	✓	✓	✓	✓	✓
BL	OL	AL	ELL	CD	**American Music Hits Through History CD**	✓	✓	✓	✓	✓	✓	✓
BL	OL	AL	ELL	Folder	**Unit Time Line Transparencies and Activities**	✓	✓	✓	✓	✓	✓	✓
BL	OL	AL	ELL	Folder	**Cause and Effect Transparencies, Strategies, and Activities**	✓	✓	✓	✓	✓	✓	✓
BL	OL	AL	ELL	Folder	**Why It Matters Transparencies, Strategies, and Activities**	✓	✓	✓	✓	✓	✓	✓
BL	OL	AL	ELL	Folder	**American Issues**	✓	✓	✓	✓	✓	✓	✓
	OL	AL	ELL	Folder	**American Art and Architecture Transparencies, Strategies, and Activities**	✓	✓	✓	✓	✓	✓	✓
BL	OL	AL		Folder	**High School American History Literature Library**	✓	✓	✓	✓	✓	✓	✓
BL	OL	AL	ELL	CD	***The American Vision* Video Program**	✓	✓	✓	✓	✓	✓	✓
Teacher Resources				Folder	**Strategies for Success**	✓	✓	✓	✓	✓	✓	✓
Teacher Resources				Folder	**Success with English Learners**	✓	✓	✓	✓	✓	✓	✓
Teacher Resources				Folder	**Reading Strategies and Activities for the Social Studies Classroom**	✓	✓	✓	✓	✓	✓	✓
Teacher Resources				CD	**Presentation Plus! with MindJogger CheckPoint**	✓	✓	✓	✓	✓	✓	✓
					ASSESS							
BL	OL	AL	ELL	Folder	**Section Quizzes and Chapter Tests***		p. 301	p. 302	p. 303	p. 304	p. 305	p. 307
BL	OL	AL	ELL	Folder	**Authentic Assessment With Rubrics**							p. 47
BL	OL	AL	ELL	Folder	**Standardized Test Practice Workbook**							p. 47
BL	OL	AL	ELL	CD	***ExamView® Assessment Suite***		21-1	21-2	21-3	21-4	21-5	Ch. 21
					CLOSE							
BL			ELL	Folder	**Reteaching Activity, URB**							p. 77
BL	OL		ELL	Folder	**Reading and Study Skills Foldables™**	p. 74						

✓ Chapter- or unit-based activities applicable to all sections in this chapter.

Using PresentationPlus!

Teach With Technology

What is PresentationPlus! with MindJogger CheckPoint?
Glencoe's PresentationPlus! with MindJogger CheckPoint offers ready-made presentations and review activities for each chapter or section in the textbook.

How can PresentationPlus! help me?

PresentationPlus! allows you to create your presentations quickly and includes links to glencoe.com, In Motion Animations (maps, graphs, and charts), and a selection of transparencies that enhance the classroom discussion. Additionally, MindJogger CheckPoint offers entertaining ask-the-audience games that review content and generate student interest.

PresentationPlus! with MindJogger CheckPoint is one of Glencoe's technology resources available for teachers.

History ONLINE
Visit glencoe.com and enter ***QuickPass***™ code TAV9399c21T for Chapter 21 resources.

You can easily launch a wide range of digital products from your computer's desktop with the McGraw-Hill Social Studies widget.

TeacherWorks

	Student	Teacher	Parent
Media Library			
• Section Audio	●		●
• Spanish Audio Summaries	●		●
• Section Spotlight Videos	●	●	●
***The American Vision* Online Learning Center (Web Site)**			
• StudentWorks™ Plus Online	●	●	●
• Multilingual Glossary	●	●	●
• Study-to-Go	●	●	●
• Chapter Overviews	●	●	●
• Self-Check Quizzes	●	●	●
• Student Web Activities	●	●	●
• ePuzzles and Games	●	●	●
• Vocabulary eFlashcards	●	●	●
• In Motion Animations	●	●	●
• Study Central™	●	●	●
• Web Activity Lesson Plans		●	
• Vocabulary PuzzleMaker	●	●	●
• Historical Thinking Activities		●	
• Beyond the Textbook	●	●	●

Reading Support From Jamestown Education

- **Timed Readings Plus in Social Studies** helps students increase their reading rate and fluency while maintaining comprehension. The 400-word passages are similar to those found on state and national assessments.
- **Reading in the Content Area: Social Studies** concentrates on six essential reading skills that help students better comprehend what they read. The book includes 75 high-interest nonfiction passages written at increasing levels of difficulty.
- **Reading Social Studies** includes strategic reading instruction and vocabulary support in Social Studies content for both ELLs and native speakers of English.

www.jamestowneducation.com

Biography / A&E Home Video / The History Channel

The following videotape programs are available from Glencoe as supplements to this chapter:

- The Last Days of World War II (ISBN 1-56-501536-3)
- D-Day: The Total Story (ISBN 0-76-700606-2)

To order, call Glencoe at 1-800-334-7344. To find classroom resources to accompany many of these videos, check the following home pages:

A&E Television: www.aetv.com
The History Channel: www.historychannel.com

National Geographic

Index to National Geographic Magazine:

The following articles relate to this chapter:

- "The Wings of War: How the Yanks of the Eighth Air Force Helped Turn the Tide in World War II," by Thomas B. Allen, March 1994.
- "Remembering the Blitz," by Cameron Thomas, July 1991.

National Geographic Society Products To order the following, call National Geographic at 1-800-368-2728:

- *World War II Era CD-ROM* (CD-ROM)

Access National Geographic's new, dynamic MapMachine Web site and other geography resources at:

www.nationalgeographic.com
www.nationalgeographic.com/maps

Reading List Generator CD-ROM — Glencoe BookLink 3

Use this database to search more than 30,000 titles to create a customized reading list for your students.

- Reading lists can be organized by students' reading level, author, genre, theme, or area of interest.
- The database provides Degrees of Reading Power™ (DRP) and Lexile™ readability scores for all selections.
- A brief summary of each selection is included.

Leveled reading suggestions for this chapter:

For students at a Grade 8 reading level:
- ***Summer of My German Soldier***, by Bette Greene

For students at a Grade 9 reading level:
- ***The Winds of War***, by Herman Wouk

For students at a Grade 10 reading level:
- ***Flags of Our Fathers***, by James Bradley and Ron Powers

For students at a Grade 11 reading level:
- ***Never to Forget: The Jews of the Holocaust***, by Milton Meltzer

For students at a Grade 12 reading level:
- ***America in World War II: 1945***, by Edward F. Dolan

Introducing Chapter 21

Focus

MAKING CONNECTIONS

What Kind of Sacrifices Does War Require?
Ask students what kind of sacrifices they would be willing to make for their country. Lead a discussion regarding citizens' roles at home during wartime. Discuss different attitudes people have about supporting war. Encourage students to state why World War II inspired patriotism throughout the country. **BL** **OL**

Teach

The Big Ideas

As students study the chapter, remind them to consider the section-based Big Ideas included in each section's Guide to Reading. The **Essential Questions** in the activities below tie in to the Big Ideas and help students think about and understand important chapter concepts. In addition, the Hands-on Chapter Projects with the culminating activities relate the content from each section to the Big Ideas. These activities build on each other as students progress through the chapter. Section activities culminate in the wrap-up activity on the Visual Summary page.

Chapter 21

America and World War II

1941–1945

Allied troops land in Normandy on D-Day, 1944.

U.S. PRESIDENTS

Franklin D. Roosevelt 1933–1945

U.S. EVENTS

1941
- United States enters World War II
- Roosevelt bans discrimination in defense industries

1942
- Women's Army Auxiliary Corps established
- Japanese American relocation ordered

1943
- Detroit race riots
- Zoot-suit riots in Los Angeles

1941 — 1942 — 1943

WORLD EVENTS

1941
- Japan attacks Pearl Harbor

1942
- Japan captures the Philippines
- Americans win Battle of Midway

1943
- Germans defeated at Stalingrad
- Allied forces land in Italy

Section 1

Mobilizing for War

Essential Question: How could the United States increase its productivity in a short period of time? *(Workers must be motivated to work long hours. Materials must be readily available to allow for faster production.)* Tell students that Section 1 describes how Roosevelt and business leaders rapidly mobilized the economy to ensure success in the war. **OL**

Section 2

The Early Battles

Essential Question: What unique decisions did the United States face as a result of fighting a war on two fronts? *(whether to fight both wars with equal strength or to emphasize one front and one enemy over the other)* Inform students that Section 2 will highlight how the U.S. balanced operations against Japan and Germany. **OL**

Section 3

Life on the Home Front

Essential Question: How do you think women and African Americans responded to the war? *(They took factory jobs typically held by white men. Some may have protested the war.)* Explain that in Section 3, students will learn about how these groups responded to new opportunities, prejudices, and restrictions. **OL**

Chapter Audio

MAKING CONNECTIONS

What Kinds of Sacrifices Does War Require?

During World War II, millions of Americans enlisted in the armed forces, risking their lives in the struggle. On the home front, Americans also helped the war effort by giving up goods needed by the military and buying war bonds.

- ***Why do you think so many Americans volunteered to fight in World War II?***
- ***Should civilians have to make sacrifices in wartime?***

1944
- Supreme Court rules in *Korematsu* v. *United States* that Japanese American relocation is constitutional

Harry Truman 1945–1953

1945
- Franklin Roosevelt dies in office; Harry S. Truman becomes president

1944 — 1945

1944
- Eisenhower leads D-Day invasion
- MacArthur's forces land in the Philippines

1945
- U.S. Marines capture Iwo Jima
- United States drops atomic bomb on Japan

FOLDABLES

Summarizing American Life During World War II Make a Pocket Book Foldable to summarize various aspects of daily life that World War II affected. Label the two pockets as Economic and Social. Include general effects as well as specific programs under each pocket.

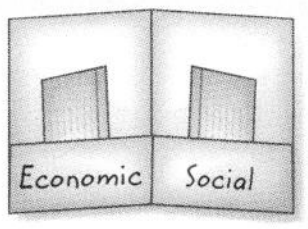

History ONLINE Visit glencoe.com and enter ***QuickPass***™ code TAV9846c21 for Chapter 21 resources.

Section 4

Pushing Back the Axis

Essential Question: Why were Americans still willing to fight a war with so many American casualties? *(Responses may include the desire to protect America from Hitler, stop the Holocaust, seek revenge for Pearl Harbor.)* Tell students that in Section 4, they will learn about the strategic battles of the war and the large number of casualties. **OL**

Section 5

The War Ends

Essential Question: Why do you think America used atomic weapons against Japan? *(Responses may include to bring about the end of the war with Japan; save the lives of American soldiers fighting in Pacific.)* As you lead a discussion, remind students that this question continues to be debated. Section 5 will cover some of the debate. **OL**

Introducing
Chapter 21

More About the Photo

Visual Literacy On June 6, 1944, American, British, and Canadian troops assaulted five different beach heads in Normandy, France. Known as D-Day, the invasion included nearly 7,000 ships, including battleships and landing craft. Allied troops stormed the beaches in the early morning. Though they suffered heavy losses, with the heaviest casualties at Omaha Beach, they succeeded at pushing the German troops inland.

FOLDABLES™ Study Organizer **Dinah Zike's Foldables**

Dinah Zike's Foldables are three-dimensional, interactive graphic organizers that help students practice basic writing skills, review vocabulary terms, and identify main ideas. Instructions for creating and using Foldables can be found in the Appendix at the end of this book and in the *Dinah Zike's Reading and Study Skills Foldables* booklet.

History ONLINE
Visit glencoe.com and enter ***QuickPass***™ code TAV9399c21T for Chapter 21 resources, including a Chapter Overview, Study Central™, Study-to-Go, Student Web Activity, Self-Check Quiz, and other materials.

Focus

Bellringer

Daily Focus Transparency 21-1

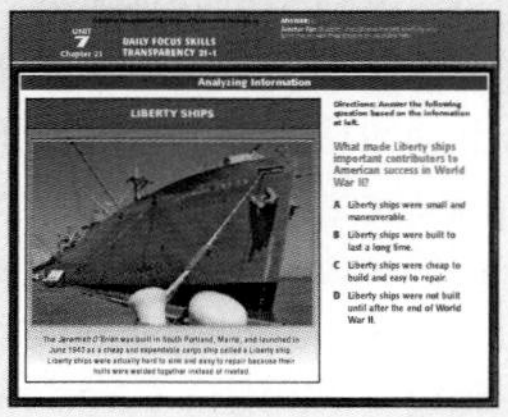

Guide to Reading

Answers:

Government Agencies Created to Mobilize the Economy:
National Defense Advisory Committee
Reconstruction Finance Corporation
War Production Board
Office of War Mobilization

Section Spotlight Video

To generate student interest and provide a springboard for class discussion, access the Chapter 21, Section 1 video at glencoe.com or on the video DVD.

Resource Manager

R Reading Strategies	C Critical Thinking	D Differentiated Instruction	W Writing Support	S Skill Practice
Teacher Edition • Inferring, pp. 715, 718 • Academic Vocab., p. 718 • Paraphrasing, p. 721 **Additional Resources** • Guide. Reading, URB p. 82 • Reading Skills Act., URB p. 55	**Teacher Edition** • Det. Cause/Effect, p. 715 • Hypothesizing, p. 717 • Evaluating, p. 719 • Making Inf., p. 720 **Additional Resources** • Historical Analysis Skills Act, URB p. 56 • Quizzes and Tests, p. 301 • Linking Past and Present, URB p. 68	**Teacher Edition** • Visual/Spatial, pp. 716, 717 **Additional Resources** • Acad. Vocab. Act., URB p. 63 • Foldables, p. 74	**Teacher Edition** • Persuasive Writing, p. 720 **Additional Resources** • Content Vocab. Act., URB p. 61	**Teacher Edition** • Interpreting a Chart, p. 718 **Additional Resources** • Read. Essen., p. 232

Section 1

Section Audio Spotlight Video

Mobilizing for War

Guide to Reading

Big Ideas

Economics and Society Americans quickly converted to a wartime economy to support the war effort.

Content Vocabulary
- cost-plus *(p. 716)*
- disenfranchised *(p. 719)*

Academic Vocabulary
- vehicle *(p. 717)*
- draft *(p. 718)*

People and Events to Identify
- War Production Board *(p. 717)*
- Office of War Mobilization *(p. 717)*
- "Double V" campaign *(p. 720)*
- Tuskegee Airmen *(p. 720)*
- Oveta Culp Hobby *(p. 721)*
- Women's Army Corps *(p. 721)*

Reading Strategy

Organizing Complete a graphic organizer similar to the one below by filling in the agencies that the U.S. government created to mobilize the nation for war.

After World War I, America returned to isolationism. When the nation entered World War II in 1941, its armed forces ranked nineteenth in might, behind the tiny European nation of Belgium. Three years later, the United States was producing 40 percent of the world's arms.

Converting the Economy

MAIN Idea The United States quickly mobilized the economy to fight the war.

HISTORY AND YOU Have you ever changed the way you performed a task in order to do it faster or more efficiently? What steps did you take to speed things up? Read on to learn how the United States changed the way factories produced goods during World War II.

Shortly after 1:30 P.M. on December 7, 1941, Secretary of the Navy Frank Knox phoned President Roosevelt at the White House. "Mr. President," Knox said, "it looks like the Japanese have attacked Pearl Harbor." A few minutes later, Admiral Harold Stark, chief of naval operations, phoned and confirmed the attack.

Although President Roosevelt remained calm when he heard the news, he later expressed his concerns to his wife Eleanor: "I never wanted to have to fight this war on two fronts. We haven't got the Navy to fight in both the Atlantic and Pacific. . . . We will have to build up the Navy and the Air Force and that will mean we will have to take a good many defeats before we can have a victory."

Although the difficulties of fighting a global war troubled the president, British prime minister Winston Churchill was not worried. Churchill knew that victory in modern war depended on a nation's industrial power. He compared the American economy to a gigantic boiler: "Once the fire is lighted under it there is no limit to the power it can generate."

Churchill was right. The industrial output of the United States during the war astounded the rest of the world. American workers were twice as productive as German workers and five times more productive than Japanese workers. In 1943 the Soviet leader Joseph Stalin toasted "American production, without which this war would have been lost." American war production turned the tide in favor of the Allies. In less than four years, the United States and its allies achieved what no other group of nations had ever done—they fought and won a two-front war against two powerful military empires, forcing each to surrender.

PRIMARY SOURCE

The Arsenal of Democracy

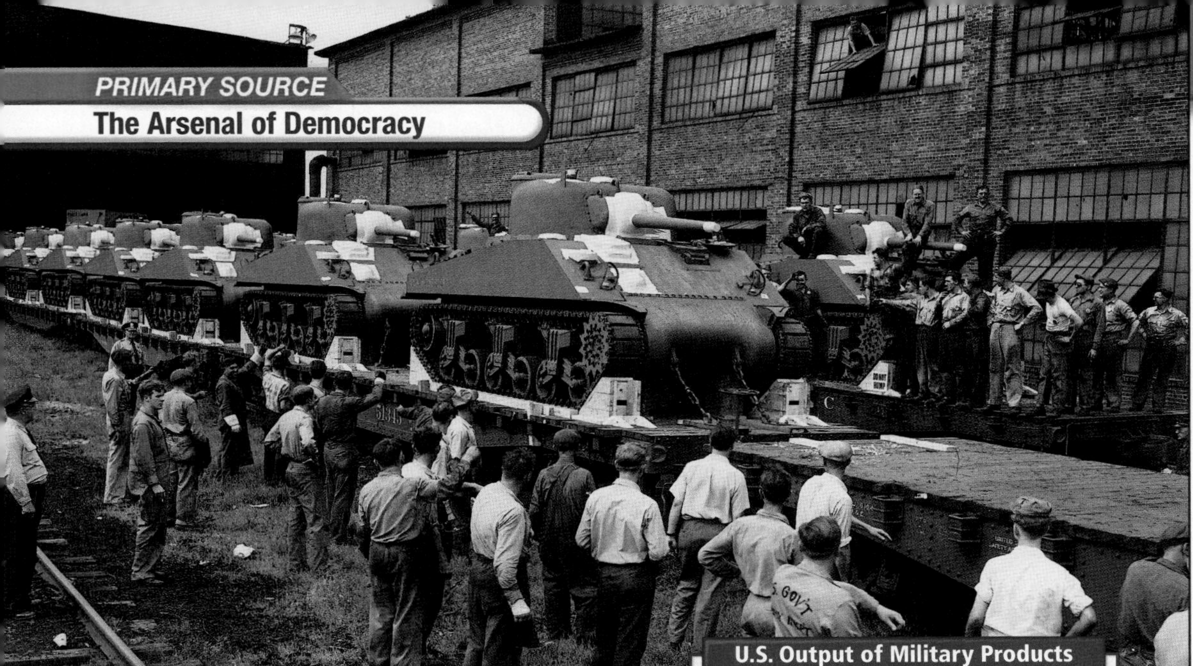

U.S. Output of Military Products

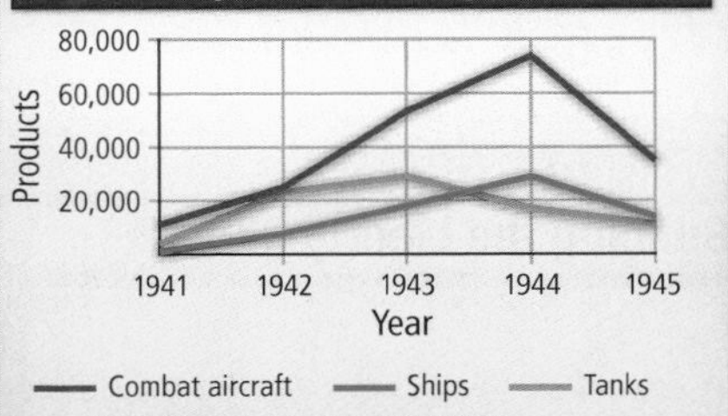

Source: *The Big 'L': American Logistics in World War II.*

Analyzing VISUALS

1. **Determining Cause and Effect** When did tank production begin to drop? Why might this be so?
2. **Making Connections** How do you think the workers felt as they watched the tanks rolling out of the factory?

The United States rapidly increased its war production after the attack on Pearl Harbor. The expansion was possible in part because the government had already begun mobilizing the economy before the country entered the war. When the German blitzkrieg swept into France in May 1940, President Roosevelt declared a national emergency and announced a plan to build 50,000 warplanes a year. Two months later he asked Congress for $4 billion to build a "Two-Ocean" Navy.

Shocked by the success of the German attack, many Americans were willing to build up the country's defenses. By October 1940, Congress had increased the defense budget to more than $17 billion. The Army-Navy Munitions Board—the military agency in charge of buying equipment—began signing contracts with American companies for new aircraft, ships, and equipment.

Roosevelt believed that government and business had to work together to prepare for war. He created the National Defense Advisory Committee to help mobilize the economy and asked several business leaders to serve on the committee. The president and his advisers believed that giving industry an incentive to move quickly was the best way to rapidly mobilize the economy. As Henry Stimson, the new secretary of war, wrote in his diary: "If you are going to try and go to war, or to prepare for war, in a capitalist country, you have got to let business make money out of the process or business won't work."

Teach

Reading Strategy

Inferring Ask: Why were Americans eager to increase production? *(Answers may include shock at German success; national pride; a desire to build up U.S. defenses.)* **OL**

Critical Thinking

Determining Cause and Effect Ask: Why did Roosevelt provide incentives to businesses that would aid in the war? *(He knew that businesses were better equipped than the government. If they made money, they would work harder.)* **OL**

Analyzing VISUALS

Answers:

1. after 1943; Answers may include steady growth in tank production over 2 years lessened the need for production
2. proud to be helping with the war effort

Additional Support

Activity: Technology Connection

Analyzing Technology Assign students to small groups and have them research new technology that was being used in American tanks and fighter planes in the 1940s (for example, Sherman tanks, Wildcat, Hellcat, and Mustang fighters). Direct them to read about the reasoning for utilizing the new technology, about production information, and about how the tanks and planes fared in actual warfare. Students should write a short report and include photos or other visuals to support their findings. **OL**

D Differentiated Instruction

Visual/Spatial Have students work in pairs to create posters that illustrate information about unemployment, production figures for several industries, and other economic indications from before the war and then again after mobilization. OL

Reading Check

Answer:
The cost-plus program encouraged companies to make many products quickly. The RFC made loans to help companies convert to war production.

DBQ Document Based Questions

Answers:
1. to protect herself from getting burned
2. She had to fill in the seams of the ship with hot lead before the welders came in.

Normally when the government needed military equipment, it would ask companies to bid for the contract, but that system was too slow in wartime. Instead of asking for bids, the government signed **cost-plus** contracts. The government agreed to pay a company whatever it cost to make a product plus a guaranteed percentage of the costs as profit.

Under the cost-plus system, the more a company produced and the faster it did the work, the more money it would make. The system was not cheap, but it did get war materials produced quickly and in quantity.

Cost-plus convinced many companies to convert to war production. Other firms, however, could not afford to reequip their factories to make military goods. To convince more companies to convert, Congress gave new authority to the Reconstruction Finance Corporation (RFC). That government agency, set up during the Depression, could make loans to companies wanting to convert their factories to war production.

Reading Check **Analyzing** What government policies helped American industry to produce large quantities of war materials?

American Industry Gets the Job Done

MAIN Idea Factories built tanks, airplanes, trucks, and jeeps for military use, as well as safer ships.

HISTORY AND YOU Has a coach or an instructor ever challenged you to improve your speed or efficiency at a task? Read on to learn how American industry helped the war effort.

By the fall of 1941, much had already been done to prepare the economy for war, but it was still only partially mobilized. Although many companies were producing military equipment, most still preferred to make consumer goods. The Great Depression was ending, demand was up, and sales were rising. The Japanese attack on Pearl Harbor, however, changed everything. A flood of orders by the government for war materials began, and by the summer of 1942, almost all major industries and some 200,000 companies had converted to war production. Together they made the nation's wartime "miracle" possible.

PRIMARY SOURCE
Building the Liberty Ships

▲ In this 1942 photograph, workers construct a Liberty ship in San Francisco.

PRIMARY SOURCE

"I took classes on how to weld. I had leather gloves, leather pants, a big hood, goggles and a leather jacket. . . . They put me forty feet down in the bottom of the ship to be a tacker. I filled the long seams of the cracks in the ship corners full of hot lead and then brushed them good and you could see how pretty it was. The welders would come along and weld it so it would take the strong waves and deep water and heavy weight."

—Katie Grant, World War II riveter at Kaiser Richmond Shipyard, California

DBQ Document-Based Questions

1. **Interpreting** Why would Katie Grant have had to wear leather clothing?
2. **Summarizing** What was her job?

Hands-On Chapter Project Step 1

An Interview with a World War II Veteran

Step 1: Finding a Veteran to Interview and Shaping the Questions
Essential Question: What can we learn from a World War II veteran?

Directions Explain to students that they will document an interview with a World War II veteran (using a CD or DVD). Students should begin by thinking about what they might learn from a veteran. For example, students could learn American attitudes in that person's community toward the war, where he or she served, what he or she knew at the time about Europe, how service affected his or her political views. The next and crucial task is to find a veteran to interview. A local VFW group can be helpful (asking other community organizations or churches is also a possibility.) Students may write a letter or phone the veteran to ask for his/her participation.

Putting It Together Once students know the basics about their interviewee (such as the branch of the military and theater of the war involved), they should write out the questions they will ask in a question-and-answer format, organizing the questions in a logical fashion (the person's life before the war, mission during the war, and so on). OL

(Chapter Project continued on page 724)

Tanks Replace Cars

The automobile industry was uniquely suited to the mass production of military equipment. Automobile factories began producing trucks, jeeps, and tanks. Mass production was critical in modern warfare, because the country that could move troops and supplies most quickly usually won the battle. As General George C. Marshall, chief of staff for the United States Army, observed:

PRIMARY SOURCE

"The greatest advantage . . . the United States enjoyed on the ground in the fighting was . . . the jeep and the two-and-a-half ton truck. These are the instruments that moved and supplied United States troops in battle, while the German army . . . depended heavily on animal transport. . . . The United States, profiting from the mass production achievements of its automotive industry . . . had mobility that completely outclassed the enemy."

—quoted in *Miracle of World War II*

Automobile factories did not just produce **vehicles.** They also built artillery, rifles, mines, helmets, pontoon bridges, and dozens of other pieces of military equipment. Henry Ford created an assembly line for the enormous B-24 bomber known as the "Liberator" at Willow Run Airport near Detroit. By the end of the war, the factory had built more than 8,600 aircraft. Overall, the auto industry produced nearly one-third of all military equipment manufactured during the war. **D**

Building the Liberty Ships

Ford's remarkable achievement in aircraft production was more than matched by Henry Kaiser's shipyards. Henry Kaiser started in the construction industry, but when World War II began, Kaiser shifted from the construction industry to shipbuilding.

German submarines were sinking American cargo ships at a terrifying rate. The United States had to find a way to build cargo ships as quickly as possible. Kaiser believed that speed was more important than quality and that cost was less important than results. He spent whatever it took to get the job done quickly. To save time, he applied techniques from the construction industry to shipbuilding. Instead of building an entire ship in one place from the keel up, parts were prefabricated and brought to the shipyard for assembly.

Kaiser's shipyards built many different kinds of ships, but they were best known for Liberty ships. The Liberty ship was the basic cargo ship used during the war. Liberty ships were welded instead of riveted. Although welded ships tended to crack, Vice Admiral Emory Land, head of the U.S. Maritime Commission, preferred the Liberty ships:

PRIMARY SOURCE

"Every time a riveted ship goes into dock you have a lot of repairs to do. You do not have them in welded ships. . . . On combat damage, comparing the welded Liberty ships and others, everything is in favor of the Liberty. . . . riveted ships are apt to go to the bottom if they are bombed or mined or torpedoed. . . . Never mind about the fractures or the cracks—[the Liberty ships] get into port."

—quoted in *Miracle of World War II*

When the war began, it took 244 days to build the first Liberty ship. After Kaiser shipyards applied their mass-production techniques, average production time dropped to 41 days. Kaiser's shipyards built 30 percent of all American ships constructed during the war, including nearly 3,000 Liberty ships.

The War Production Board

As American companies converted to war production, many business leaders became frustrated with the mobilization process. Government agencies argued constantly about supplies and contracts and whose orders had the highest priority.

After Pearl Harbor, President Roosevelt tried to improve the system by creating the **War Production Board** (WPB). He gave the WPB the authority to set priorities and production goals and to control the distribution of raw materials and supplies. Almost immediately, the WPB clashed with the military. Military agencies continued to sign contracts without consulting with the WPB. Finally, in 1943, Roosevelt established the **Office of War Mobilization** (OWM) to settle arguments among the different agencies. **C**

Reading Check **Explaining** What military need led to the production of Liberty ships?

D Differentiated Instruction

Visual/Spatial Tell students they are on a committee to design a stamp commemorating the World War II mobilization effort. They must choose between Henry Ford and Henry Kaiser. Have each student draw a picture of their stamp and explain their design. **BL**

C Critical Thinking

Hypothesizing Have students theorize why government agencies and private businesses argued over supplies. *(Students may suggest that government officials may have had previous business relations with companies that they did not want to offend.)* **OL**

Reading Check

Answer:
The Germans had been sinking cargo ships regularly, keeping important cargo from reaching U.S. ports. New ships that were cheap, easy to build, and fast were in great demand.

Additional Support

Teacher Tip

Collaborative Learning This activity requires students to research, write, and illustrate. As you form groups, allow students with different levels of academic skills to work together. Assist groups by assigning tasks based on each student's strengths.

Activity: Collaborative Learning

Identifying Central Issues Assign students to small groups. Students will work together to research the Liberty ships. Encourage them to use the Internet to find information as well as photographs of the ships. **Ask:** How important were the ships to the Allied victory in World War II? *(Students may suggest that ships were important in supplying and transporting troops.)* Each group should prepare a report to answer the question. Have groups present their reports and photographs to the class. Discuss students' findings following the presentations. **OL**

R1 Reading Strategy

Academic Vocabulary Have students use context clues and prior knowledge to define the word *draft.* *(choosing individuals for compulsory military service)* **OL**

R2 Reading Strategy

Inferring Lead students in a discussion about current U.S. policy regarding military preparedness and reinstating the draft. **Ask:** Under what circumstances, if any, do you think the United States should reinstate the draft? *(Answers may include a need for more soldiers in time of war; for national defense in time of war.)* Write a list of pros and cons of reinstating the draft on the board. **OL**

S Skill Practice

Interpreting a Chart Have students look at the chart. **Ask:** In which year were the armed forces at a peak? *(1945)* at a low? *(1939–40)* **BL**

Building an Army

MAIN Idea Minorities and women played an important role in the United States armed forces during World War II.

HISTORY AND YOU Do you think the United States should have a military draft? Read to learn about the first peacetime draft in American history.

Converting factories to war production was only part of the mobilization process. To fight and win the war, the United States also needed to build up its armed forces.

Creating an Army

Within days of Germany's attack on Poland in 1939, President Roosevelt expanded the army to 227,000 soldiers. Before the spring of 1940, college students, unions, isolationists, and most members of Congress had opposed a peacetime **draft**. Opinions changed after France surrendered to Germany in June 1940. Two members of Congress introduced the Selective Service and Training Act, a plan for the first peacetime draft in American history. In September, Congress approved the draft by a wide margin.

You're in the Army Now

More than 60,000 men enlisted in the month after the attack on Pearl Harbor. At first, the flood of recruits overwhelmed the army's training facilities. Many recruits had to live in tents rather than barracks. The army also experienced equipment shortages. Troops carried sticks representing guns, threw stones simulating grenades, and practiced maneuvers with trucks labeled "TANK."

New recruits were initially sent to a reception center, where they were given physical exams and injections against smallpox and typhoid. The draftees were then issued uniforms, boots, and whatever equipment was available. The clothing bore the label "G.I.," meaning "Government Issue," which is why American soldiers were called GIs.

After taking aptitude tests, recruits went to basic training for eight weeks. They learned

PRIMARY SOURCE
Creating an American Army

▲ *Soldiers from a Mexican-American platoon train at Fort Benning in 1943.*

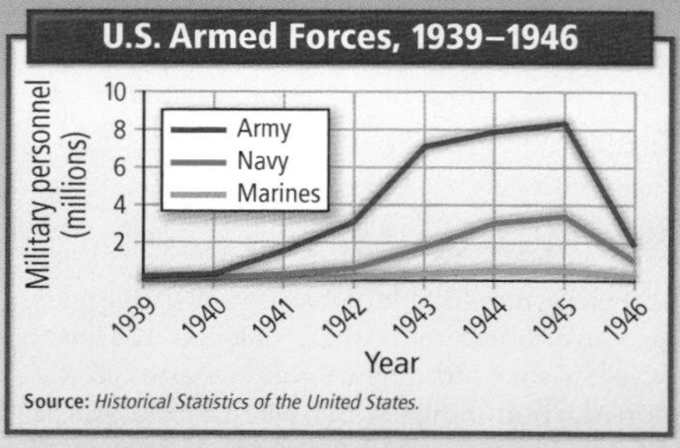

PRIMARY SOURCE

For many Americans, entering the army changed their perspective, as historian Carl Degler recalls:

"Entrance into the Army in August, 1942, widened my horizons literally as well as experientially: for the first time I travelled beyond a 200 mile radius from Newark. I marvelled at the flatness of the prairie in Illinois . . . . Stops at posts in Miami Beach, Florida, and Richmond, Virginia, were my introduction to the American South."

—from *The History Teacher,* vol. 23, 1990

Additional Support

Activity: Collaborative Learning

Diagramming the Draft From 1948 until 1973, during both peacetimes and periods of conflict, men were drafted to fill vacancies in the armed forces that could not be filled through voluntary means. The draft ended in 1973, toward the close of the Vietnam War, and the United States converted to an all-volunteer military. **Ask:** Who had to sign up for the draft? Where did they sign up? What happened when they went to sign up? When was the lottery introduced? How were numbers picked? Have students use the Internet and interview people who were drafted to get answers to these questions. Have students work together to create a flow chart that illustrates the draft process. **OL**

how to handle weapons, load backpacks, read maps, pitch tents, and dig trenches. Trainees drilled and exercised constantly and learned how to work as a team.

Basic training helped to break down barriers between soldiers. Recruits came from all over the country, and training together created a "special sense of kinship," as one soldier noted. "The reason you storm the beaches is not patriotism or bravery. It's that sense of not wanting to fail your buddies."

A Segregated Army

Although basic training promoted unity, most recruits did not encounter Americans from every part of society. At the start of the war, the U.S. military was segregated. White recruits did not train alongside African Americans. African Americans had separate barracks, latrines, mess halls, and recreational facilities. Once trained, African Americans were organized into their own military units, but white officers generally commanded them. Most military leaders also wanted to keep African American soldiers out of combat and assigned them to construction and supply units.

Some African Americans did not want to support the war. As one student at a black college noted: "The Army Jim Crows us. . . . Employers and labor unions shut us out. Lynchings continue. We are **disenfranchised** . . . and spat upon. What more could Hitler do to us than that?" Despite the bitterness, most African Americans agreed with African American writer Saunders Redding that they should support their country:

PRIMARY SOURCE

"There are many things about this war that I do not like . . . yet I believe in the war. . . . [W]e know that whatever the mad logic of [Hitler's] New Order there is no hope for us under it. The ethnic theories of the Hitler 'master folk' admit of no chance of freedom. . . . This is a war to keep [people] free. The struggle to broaden and lengthen the road of freedom—our own private and important war to enlarge freedom here in America—will come later. . . . I believe in this war because I believe in America. I believe in what America professes to stand for."

—from "A Negro Looks at This War"

C

A Segregated Army

Although the U.S. armed forces were segregated, discrimination did not prevent minority groups from performing with courage. Two of the best-known examples are the Tuskegee Airmen (right), comprised of African American volunteers, and the 442nd Regimental Combat Team (below), made up of Japanese American volunteers. The 450 Tuskegee Airmen fought in North Africa, Sicily, and Italy. The 442nd Regimental Combat Team became the most decorated unit in U.S. history.

Analyzing VISUALS

1. **Identifying** In what year did the army experience the most rapid growth? Why do you think that is the case?
2. **Evaluating** What do the expressions on the faces of the Tuskegee Airmen convey?

C Critical Thinking

Evaluating Point out to students that segregation was a common practice during the 1940s. **Ask:** Do you agree with Redding that African Americans had a duty to support their country despite the discrimination they faced at home? Why or why not? *(Answers will vary.)* Write major points on the board. **OL**

Analyzing VISUALS

Answers:

1. 1942; because it was the first year of the war and the period following the December 7, 1941, Japanese attack.
2. bravery, devotion to the cause, seriousness

Additional Support

Activity: Collaborative Learning

Making Connections Assign students to small groups. Have them read about the Tuskegee Airmen. The Tuskegee Airmen were the fighter pilots who opened the door for African American pilots and helped integrate the army. After students have completed their reading, have them create a worksheet about the Tuskegee Airmen with short answer questions, a crossword puzzle, a trivia game, and so on. Have groups exchange and complete each other's worksheets. Then have a class discussion about what students have learned. Encourage volunteers to share worksheet elements they found creative or interesting. **OL**

C Critical Thinking

Making Inferences Partly in response to the Double V campaign, President Roosevelt ordered recruitment of African Americans for combat.

Ask: How do you think both whites and African Americans responded to Roosevelt's new policies toward African American soldiers? *(Answers will vary, but students should note the racial discrimination of the 1940s.)* **OL**

W Writing Support

Persuasive Writing Direct students to write letters to the editor supporting racial integration of the U.S. armed forces during World War II. Have students share their letters with the class. **OL**

Analyzing VISUALS

Answers:

1. Answers may include that they felt women lacked necessary skills and physical strength
2. lacked necessary supplies; overcrowded

History ONLINE Student Skill Activity To learn how to conduct an interview, visit glencoe.com and complete the Skill activity.

Pushing for "Double V" Many African American leaders combined patriotism with protest. In 1941 the National Urban League asked its members to encourage African Americans to join the war effort. It also asked them to make plans for building a better society in the United States after the war. The *Pittsburgh Courier,* a leading African American newspaper, launched the **"Double V" campaign.** The campaign urged African Americans to support the war to achieve a double victory—over both Hitler's racism abroad and the racism at home.

C **African Americans in Combat** Under pressure from African American leaders, President Roosevelt ordered the army, air force, navy, and marines to recruit African Americans, and he told the army to put African Americans into combat. He also promoted Colonel Benjamin O. Davis, Sr., the highest-ranking African American officer, to the rank of brigadier general.

In early 1941 the air force created its first African American unit, the 99th Pursuit Squadron. The pilots trained in Tuskegee, Alabama, and became known as the **Tuskegee Airmen.** In April 1943, after General Davis urged the military to put African Americans into combat as soon as possible, the squadron was sent to the Mediterranean. Lieutenant Colonel Benjamin O. Davis, Jr., General Davis's son, commanded the squadron and helped win the battle of Anzio in Italy. W

In late 1943 Colonel Davis took command of three new squadrons that had trained at Tuskegee. Known as the 332nd Fighter Group, these squadrons were ordered to protect American bombers as they flew to their targets. The 332nd Fighter Group flew 200 such missions and did not lose a single member to enemy aircraft.

African Americans also performed well in the army. The all–African American 761st Tank Battalion was commended for its service during the Battle of the Bulge. Although the

PRIMARY SOURCE
Women in World War II

About 400,000 American women played a major role in the military side of the war effort, if not in direct combat. Sixteen American women were awarded the Purple Heart for being injured as a result of enemy action. More than 400 American military women lost their lives.

◀ *In this 1943 photo, Nancy Nesbit checks with the control tower from her plane at Avenger Field in Sweetwater, Texas, where the Women's Auxiliary Ferrying Squadron of the U.S. Army trained.*

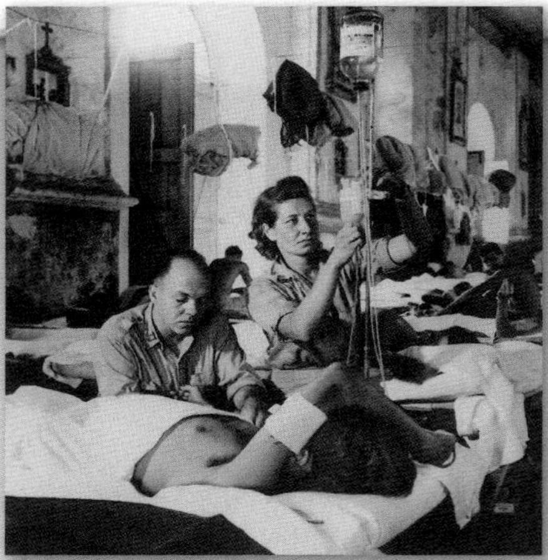

▲ *A doctor and an army nurse tend to a patient at a U.S. Army hospital in Leyte in the Philippines.*

Analyzing VISUALS

1. **Inferring** Why might the military have been reluctant to allow women in combat?
2. **Evaluating** What does the photo above suggest about conditions in military hospitals?

Differentiated Instruction

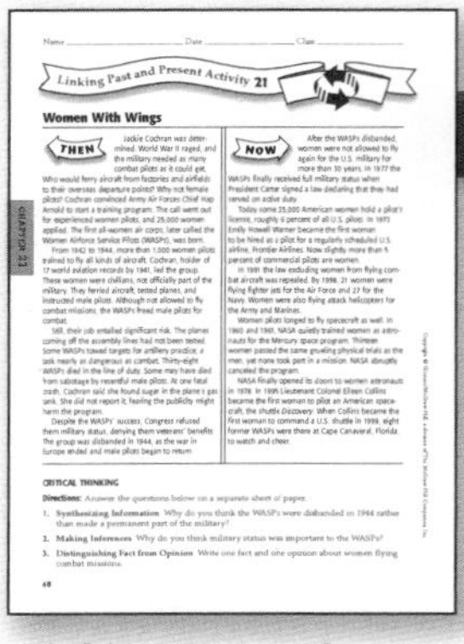

Linking Past and Present Activity, URB p. 68

Women With Wings

Objective: Compare the roles of women in the military in World War II with the roles of women in the military today.

Focus: Determine how the necessities of war granted female pilots an opportunity to participate.

Teach: In a bulleted list, describe the risks that female pilots faced during World War II.

Assess: Use a graphic organizer to compare female pilots then and now.

Close: Have students read ahead and list other ways the war enabled women to progress.

Differentiated Instruction Strategies

BL Write a short letter as Jackie Cochran attempting to convince the army chief to start a female pilot training program.

AL Find other instances of women's accounts of their actions in World War II. Share what you find with the class.

ELL Create a list of unfamiliar terms in the reading. Then define the terms.

military did not end all segregation during the war, it did integrate military bases in 1943 and steadily expanded the role of African Americans within the armed forces. These successes paved the way for President Truman's decision to fully integrate the military in 1948.

Other Minorities in the Military Japanese Americans were not allowed to serve in the military at first. As the war progressed, however, second-generation Japanese Americans served in the 100th Infantry Battalion and the 442nd Regimental Combat Team. Almost half had been in internment camps in the American Southwest. Together these units became the most decorated in the history of the United States military. Many Mexican Americans had joined the National Guard during the 1930s and served on the front lines. Most minorities were allowed only in noncombat positions, such as kitchen workers. Native Americans, who were regarded as fierce warriors, were an exception to that policy. One-third of all healthy Native American men aged 18–50 served during the war.

Women Join the Armed Forces

Women joined the armed forces, as they had done during World War I. The army enlisted women for the first time, although they were barred from combat. Many jobs in the army were administrative and clerical. Assigning women to these jobs made more men available for combat.

Congress first allowed women in the military in May 1942, when it established the Women's Army Auxiliary Corps (WAAC) and appointed **Oveta Culp Hobby,** an official with the War Department, to serve as its first director. Although pleased about the establishment of the WAAC, many women were unhappy that it was an auxiliary corps and not part of the regular army. A little over a year later, the army replaced the WAAC with the **Women's Army Corps** (WAC). Director Hobby was assigned the rank of colonel. "You have a debt and a date," Hobby explained to those training to be the nation's first women officers. "A debt to democracy, a date with destiny."

R

As early as 1939, pilot Jackie Cochran had written to Eleanor Roosevelt suggesting that women pilots could aid the war effort. The following year, Nancy Love wrote to army officials to suggest that women be allowed to deliver planes. (The air force was not yet a separate branch of the military.) Training programs began in 1942; the Women Airforce Service Pilots (WASPs) began the next year. Although the WASPs were no longer needed after 1944, about 300 women pilots made more than 12,000 deliveries of 77 different kinds of planes.

The Coast Guard, the navy, and the marines quickly followed the army and set up their own women's units. In addition to serving in these new organizations, another 68,000 women served as nurses in the army and navy.

Reading Check **Summarizing** How did the status of women and African Americans in the armed forces change during the war?

Section 1 REVIEW

Vocabulary

1. **Explain** the significance of: cost-plus, War Production Board, Office of War Mobilization, disenfranchised, "Double V" campaign, Tuskegee Airmen, Oveta Culp Hobby, Women's Army Corps.

Main Ideas

2. **Describing** How did Congress support factories that converted to war production?
3. **Analyzing** What role did the OWM play in the war production effort?
4. **Explaining** How were minorities discriminated against in the military?

Critical Thinking

5. **Big Ideas** How did American industry rally behind the war effort?
6. **Organizing** Use a graphic organizer like the one below to list the challenges facing the United States as it mobilized for war.

7. **Analyzing Visuals** Look again at the photograph on page 716. What do you observe about the construction process?

Writing About History

8. **Expository Writing** Interview a World War II veteran or research your community during the war. How did industry rally behind the war effort? Write a one-page report to summarize your findings.

History ONLINE
Study Central™ To review this section, go to glencoe.com and click on Study Central.

R Reading Strategy

Paraphrasing Have students reread the quote by Director Hobby. **Ask:** What did Oveta Culp Hobby mean when she said that women had a date with destiny? *(By serving, they expanded women's equality.)* **OL**

Reading Check

Answer:
Each received more and new roles.

Assess

History ONLINE

Study Central™ provides summaries, interactive games, and online graphic organizers to help students review content.

Close

Summarizing Have students create two columns: businesses and minorities. Have them make a bulleted list of how these groups assisted in war mobilization. **OL**

Section 1 REVIEW

Answers

1. All definitions can be found in the section and in the Glossary.
2. It supported them financially by allowing the Reconstruction Finance Corporation to make loans to companies who wanted to covert their factories to war production.
3. The OWM served as a mediator between different government agencies.
4. Minorities were placed in segregated units, with segregated barracks, mess halls, latrines, and recreational facilities. They were often assigned to non-combat duties such as construction and supply units.
5. Major industries started to rapidly produce trucks, jeeps, tanks, and ships.
6.

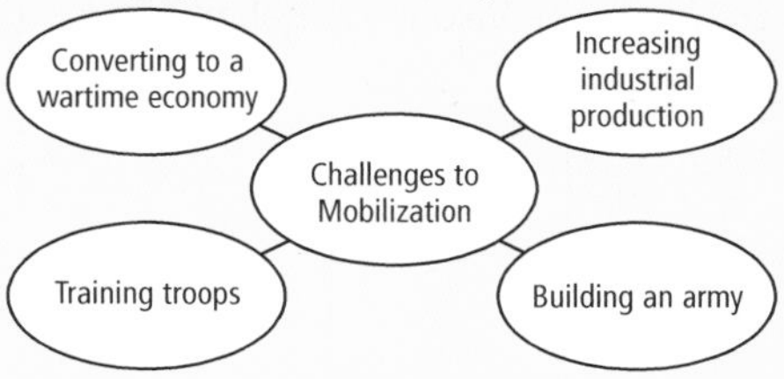

7. The construction appears to take place in stages, like an assembly line. It took a lot of workers to get the job done.
8. Students' reports will vary but should provide factual information about industry's support of the war effort.

Focus

Bellringer

Daily Focus Transparency 21-2

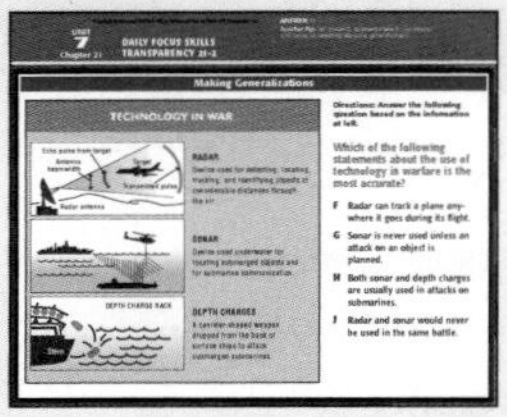

Guide to Reading

Answers:

April 1942 Doolittle Raid, Allies
April 1942 Philippines, Axis
May 1942 Coral Sea, Allies
June 1942 Midway, Allies
February 1943 Stalingrad, Allies
May 1943 North Africa, Allies

Section Spotlight Video

To generate student interest and provide a springboard for class discussion, access the Chapter 21, Section 2 video at glencoe.com or on the video DVD.

Section 2

Section Audio   Spotlight Video

The Early Battles

Guide to Reading

Big Ideas

Individual Action Several key people made decisions that changed the course of the war.

Content Vocabulary
- periphery *(p. 725)*
- convoy system *(p. 727)*

Academic Vocabulary
- code *(p. 724)*
- target *(p. 726)*

People and Events to Identify
- Chester Nimitz *(p. 722)*
- Douglas MacArthur *(p. 722)*
- Bataan Death March *(p. 723)*
- Corregidor *(p. 723)*
- James Doolittle *(p. 723)*

Reading Strategy

Organizing Complete a time line similar to the one below to record the major battles discussed and the victor in each.

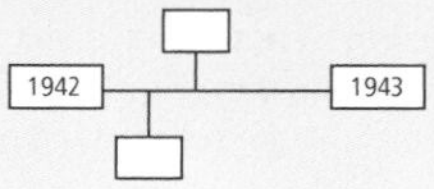

The early battles of the war on both fronts required changes in strategy from all sides. In the Pacific, the Battle of Midway was a major turning point against the Japanese, while the Battle of the Atlantic and the Battle of Stalingrad made it clear that Germany would not win the war.

Holding the Line Against Japan

MAIN Idea The Japanese continued to win victories in the Pacific until the Battle of Midway.

HISTORY AND YOU Have you ever continued toward a goal even though the odds were against you? Read on to learn about the early battles in the Pacific.

Admiral **Chester Nimitz,** the commander of the United States Navy in the Pacific, began planning operations against the Japanese Navy. Although the Japanese had badly damaged the American fleet at Pearl Harbor, the American aircraft carriers, which were on a mission at sea, were safe. The United States had several carriers in the Pacific, and Nimitz was determined to use them. In the days just after Pearl Harbor, however, he could do little to stop Japan's advance into Southeast Asia.

The Fall of the Philippines

A few hours after bombing Pearl Harbor, the Japanese attacked American airfields in the Philippines. Two days later, they landed troops. The American and Filipino forces defending the Philippines were badly outnumbered. Their commander, General **Douglas MacArthur,** retreated to the Bataan Peninsula. Using the peninsula's rugged terrain, the troops held out for more than three months.

By March, in desperation, the troops ate cavalry horses and mules. The lack of food and supplies, along with diseases such as malaria, scurvy, and dysentery, took their toll. The women of the Army Nurse Corps worked on Bataan in primitive conditions. Patients slept in the open air. One nurse, Rose Meier, reported, "If we needed more room, we got our axes and chopped some bamboo trees down."

Realizing MacArthur's capture would demoralize the American people, President Roosevelt ordered the general to evacuate to Australia. MacArthur promised, "I came through, and I shall return."

On April 9, 1942, the weary defenders of the Bataan Peninsula finally surrendered. Nearly 78,000 prisoners of war were forced

Resource Manager

R Reading Strategies	C Critical Thinking	D Differentiated Instruction	W Writing Support	S Skill Practice
Additional Resources • Primary Source Reading, URB p. 69 • Guide. Reading, URB p. 83	**Teacher Edition** • Problem-Solving, p. 723 • Contrasting, p. 725 • Drawing Con., p. 727 **Additional Resources** • Quizzes and Tests, p. 302 • Interpreting Pol. Cartoons, URB p. 75	**Teacher Edition** • Gifted and Talented, p. 724 • Visual/Spatial, p. 726	**Teacher Edition** • Expository Writing, p. 723 • Descriptive Writing, p. 726	**Teacher Edition** • Visual Literacy, p. 724 **Additional Resources** • Time Line Act., URB p. 67 • Read. Essen., p. 235

PRIMARY SOURCE
The Bataan Death March, April 1942

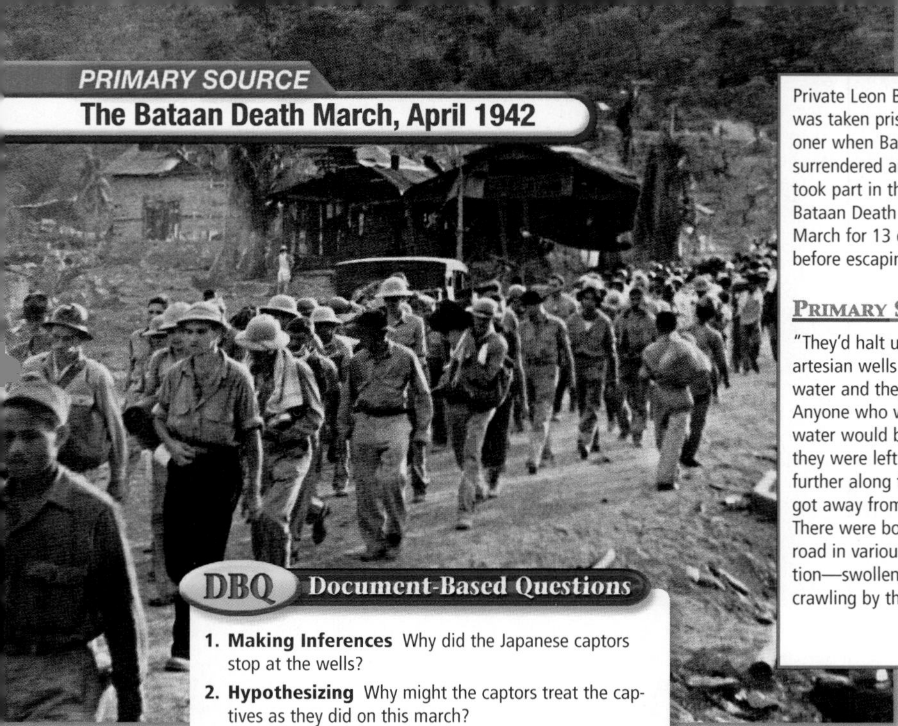

Private Leon Beck was taken prisoner when Bataan surrendered and took part in the Bataan Death March for 13 days before escaping:

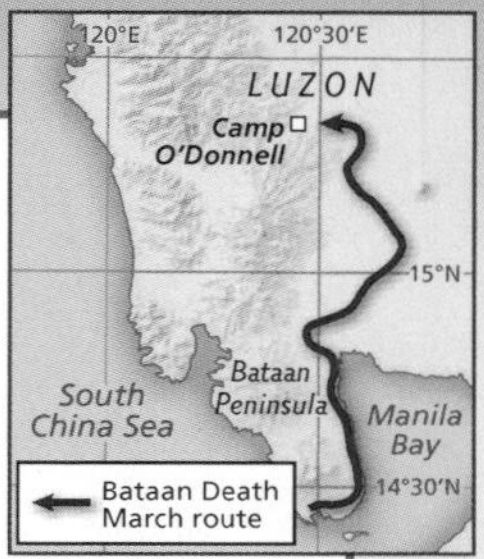

PRIMARY SOURCE

"They'd halt us in front of these big artesian wells . . . so we could see the water and they wouldn't let us have any. Anyone who would make a break for water would be shot or bayoneted. Then they were left there. Finally, it got so bad further along the road that you never got away from the stench of death. There were bodies laying all along the road in various degrees of decomposition—swollen, burst open, maggots crawling by the thousands. . . ."

—from *Death March: The Survivors of Bataan*

DBQ Document-Based Questions

1. **Making Inferences** Why did the Japanese captors stop at the wells?
2. **Hypothesizing** Why might the captors treat the captives as they did on this march?

to march—sick, exhausted, and starving—65 miles (105 km) to a Japanese prison camp. Almost ten thousand troops died on this march, which was later called the **Bataan Death March.** Sixty-six women nurses were also captured and sent to the University of Santo Tomas in Manila. They remained there—with 11 navy nurses and some 3,000 Allied civilians—until early in 1945.

Although the troops in the Bataan Peninsula surrendered, a small force held out on the island of **Corregidor** in Manila Bay. Finally, in May 1942, Corregidor surrendered. The Philippines had fallen to the Japanese.

The Doolittle Raid on Tokyo

Even before the Philippines fell, President Roosevelt was searching for a way to raise the morale of the American people. He wanted to bomb Tokyo, but American planes could reach Tokyo only if an aircraft carrier brought them close enough. Unfortunately, Japanese ships in the North Pacific prevented carriers from getting near Japan.

In early 1942, a military planner suggested replacing the carrier's usual short-range bombers with long-range B-25 bombers that could attack from farther away. The only problem was that, although B-25s could take off from a carrier, the bombers could not land on its short deck. After attacking Japan, they would have to land in China. C

President Roosevelt put Lieutenant Colonel **James Doolittle** in command of the mission to bomb Tokyo. At the end of March, a crane loaded sixteen B-25s onto the aircraft carrier *Hornet.* The next day, the *Hornet* headed west across the Pacific. On April 18, American bombs fell on Japan for the first time. W

Japan Changes Strategy

While Americans rejoiced in the air force's success, Japanese leaders were aghast at the raid. Those bombs could have killed the emperor, who was revered as a god. The Doolittle raid convinced Japanese leaders to change their strategy.

Teach

C Critical Thinking

Problem-Solving Have students create a graphic, stating the problem the military had attacking Japan in one box and their solution in another box. *(Problem: could not get planes over Japan for air attack; Solution: used long range bombers (B-25s) instead of short-range bombers; B-25's could reach target)* **OL**

W Writing Support

Expository Writing Have students prepare a one-page report about Lieutenant Colonel James Doolittle. The reports should address how Doolittle contributed to the war effort, the events of the Doolittle Raid, and what he did later in his career. **OL**

DBQ Document Based Questions

Answers:

1. It was a form of torture. Prisoners could see the water, but were not allowed to have any.
2. to demoralize the troops and the civilians back home

Additional Support

Extending the Content

Bataan Death March Of the 78,000 Allied prisoners of war who began the six-day march from Bataan, only 54,000 survived. The Bataan Death March began on April 10, 1942. Any troops who fell behind were executed. Soldiers were beaten, denied food and water, and were forced to sit in the sun. Those who asked for water were executed. Survivors of the March faced starvation and disease as they were transported on "hell ships" to Japan. Prisoners were released after Japan's formal surrender.

D Differentiated Instruction

Gifted and Talented Have students research how the Japanese code was broken. Ask students to discuss the importance of using codes during war, the job code-breakers have, and how code is deciphered in present times. **AL**

S Skill Practice

Visual Literacy Have students organize the information from the map into a time line. Based on their time lines, ask them to identify the point in which the battle seemed to shift toward an Allied victory. *(Answers will vary. Students should note the sinking of three Japanese ships as a significant event.)* **OL**

Before the raid, the Japanese navy had disagreed about the next step. The officers in charge of the navy's planning wanted to cut American supply lines to Australia by capturing the south coast of New Guinea. The commander of the fleet, Admiral Yamamoto, wanted to attack Midway Island—the last American base in the North Pacific west of Hawaii. Yamamoto believed that attacking Midway would lure the American fleet into battle and enable his fleet to destroy it.

After Doolittle's raid, the Japanese war planners dropped their opposition to Yamamoto's idea. The American fleet had to be destroyed to protect Tokyo from bombing. The attack on New Guinea would still go ahead, but only three aircraft carriers were assigned to the mission. All of the other carriers were ordered to assault Midway.

The Battle of the Coral Sea

D The Japanese believed that they could safely proceed with two attacks at once because they thought their operations were secret. What the Japanese did not know was that an American team of code breakers based in Hawaii had already broken the Japanese navy's secret **code** for conducting operations.

In March 1942, decoded Japanese messages alerted the United States to the Japanese attack on New Guinea. In response, Admiral Nimitz sent two carriers, the *Yorktown* and the *Lexington*, to intercept the Japanese in the Coral Sea. There, in early May, carriers from both sides launched all-out airstrikes against each other. Although the Japanese sank the *Lexington* and badly damaged the *Yorktown*, the American attacks prevented the Japanese from landing on New Guinea's south coast and kept the supply lines to Australia open.

The Battle of Midway

Back at Pearl Harbor, the code-breaking team now learned of the plan to attack Midway. With so many ships at sea, Admiral Yamamoto transmitted the plans for the Midway attack by radio, using the same code the Americans had already cracked.

Admiral Nimitz had been waiting for the opportunity to ambush the Japanese fleet. He

NATIONAL GEOGRAPHIC **The Battle of Midway, 1942**

S

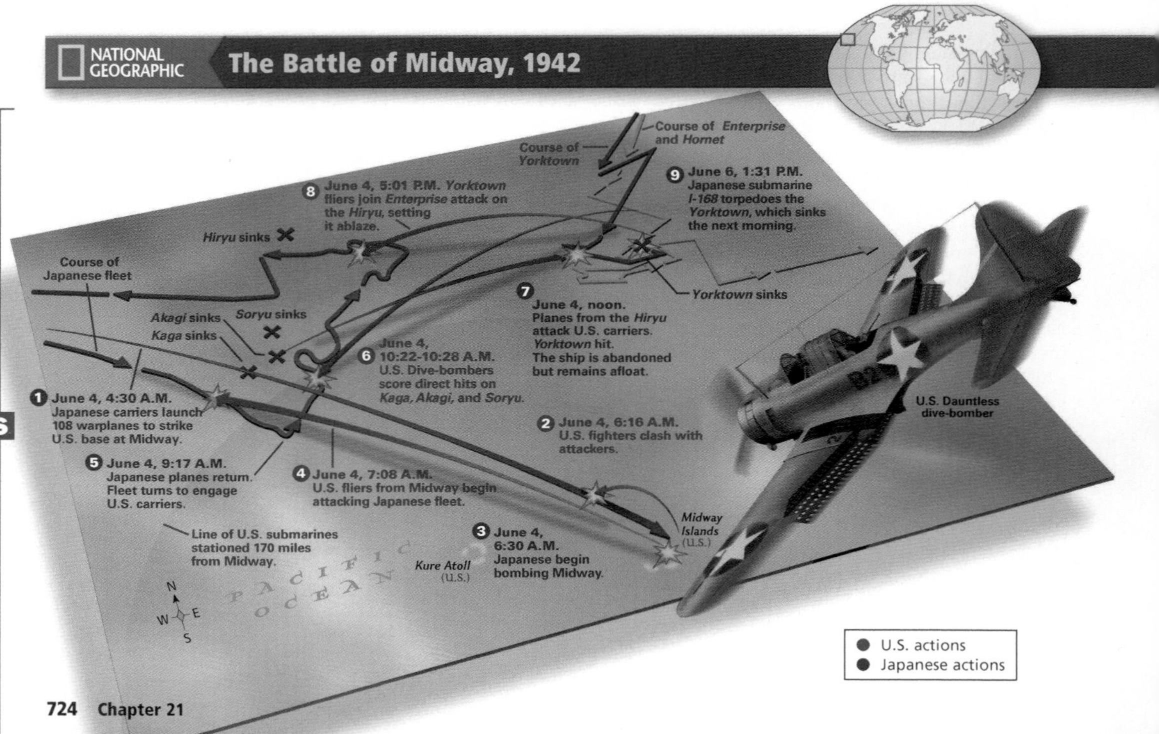

Hands-On Chapter Project
Step 2

An Interview with a World War II Veteran

Step 2: Practicing the Interview
Essential Question: What is the most important information to get?

Directions Students should use the list of questions that they created in Step 1 to conduct mock interviews to get practice in interviewing (especially in being alert to follow up a question when a discussion gets off the script) and to help decide on the interviewing team. One to two students should be present at the interview. Students should select a location that is informal, yet quiet enough to conduct the interview without disturbances.

Putting It Together As students practice, they should refine their list of questions. Students should note the content of their questions. (Are they getting the information they want?) They should also note the length of their questions and question list. (Are there enough questions? Are there too many questions?) The interview should not take longer than one hour. **OL**

(Chapter Project continued on page 730)

immediately ordered carriers to take up positions near Midway. Unaware that they were heading into an ambush, the Japanese launched their aircraft against Midway on June 4, 1942. The Americans were ready. The Japanese ran into a blizzard of antiaircraft fire, and 38 planes were shot down. As the Japanese prepared a second wave to attack Midway, aircraft from the American carriers *Hornet, Yorktown,* and *Enterprise* then launched a counterattack. The American planes caught the Japanese carriers with fuel, bombs, and aircraft exposed on their flight decks. Within minutes, three Japanese carriers were reduced to burning wrecks. A fourth was sunk a few hours later, and Admiral Yamamoto ordered his remaining ships to retreat.

The Battle of Midway was a turning point in the war. The Japanese navy lost four large carriers—the heart of its fleet. Just six months after Pearl Harbor, the United States had stopped the Japanese advance. The victory was not without cost, however. The battle killed 362 Americans and 3,057 Japanese.

✓ Reading Check **Explaining** Why was the United States able to ambush the Japanese at Midway?

▼ *Japanese aircraft bomb the USS Yorktown near Midway, June 1942.*

Analyzing VISUALS

1. **Interpreting** When did Japan launch the attack on Midway?
2. **Drawing Conclusions** Why were aircraft carriers so vital to the war in the Pacific?

Maps In MOtion See *StudentWorks™ Plus* or glencoe.com.

Stopping the Germans

MAIN Idea The Allies defeated Germany in Africa and in the Atlantic. The Soviet victory at Stalingrad was a turning point of the war.

HISTORY AND YOU Have you ever tried something simple before attempting a more challenging problem? Read on to learn about the Allied strategy for attacking the Germans.

In 1942 Allied forces began to win victories in Europe as well. Almost from the moment the United States declared war in 1941, Joseph Stalin, the leader of the Soviet Union, urged President Roosevelt to open a second front in Europe. Stalin appreciated the lend-lease supplies that the United States had sent, but the Soviets were doing most of the fighting. If British and American troops opened a second front against Germany, it would take pressure off the Soviet Union.

Since 1940, U.S. military strategists had discussed with President Roosevelt the pressures of a two-front war. "Plan Dog" argued that the European theater must be the main focus because losing Great Britain would severely weaken any chance of regaining lost European territory. The shocking reality of Pearl Harbor put an end to theory. The United States carried out a two-front war, fighting both in the Pacific and in Europe.

Roosevelt wanted to get U.S. troops into battle in Europe, but Prime Minister Churchill did not believe the United States and Great Britain were ready to invade Europe. Instead, Churchill wanted to attack the **periphery,** or edges, of the German empire. Roosevelt agreed, and in July 1942, he ordered the invasion of Morocco and Algeria—two French territories indirectly under German control. C

The Battle for North Africa

Roosevelt decided to invade Morocco and Algeria for two reasons. The invasion would give the army some experience without requiring a lot of troops. More important, it would help the British troops fight the Germans in Egypt. Great Britain needed Egypt because the Suez Canal was located there. Most of Britain's empire, including India, Hong Kong, Singapore, Malaya, and Australia, sent supplies to Britain through the canal.

History ONLINE **Student Web Activity** Visit glencoe.com and complete the activity on America and World War II.

C Critical Thinking

Contrasting Discuss the opposing views of Roosevelt and Churchill regarding a European invasion. **Ask:** Why might Roosevelt have decided to support Churchill's cautious approach? *(Students may suggest that Roosevelt did not want to confront Churchill or perhaps he realized fighting two fronts called for a more guarded approach.)* **OL**

Analyzing VISUALS

Answers:

1. June 4, 1942, 4:30 A.M.
2. reduced distance planes had to fly; reduced amount of fuel they consumed; supplied fuel

✓ **Reading Check**

Answer:
The U.S. had broken the Japanese code and knew their attack plans.

Additional Support

Activity: Collaborative Learning

Contrasting Assign half the class to research Fleet Admiral Chester W. Nimitz. The other half will research Admiral Isoroku Yamamoto. Have students research details of their education, their commands, major victories in battle, and an overview of their military careers. In addition, students should provide a statement of each man's philosophy. Encourage students to find visuals to use in their reports. Have volunteers share their reports with the class. Then create a Venn diagram for the class to compare the two men. **OL**

D Differentiated Instruction

Visual/Spatial Have students draw a map of Africa and use colored pens to show the direction of the separate American forces who tried to trap Rommel. OL

W Writing Support

Descriptive Writing Have students imagine they had to dim their lights every evening to protect American ships. Ask students to write how they might feel if they lived in an area that was close to enemy submarines. Ask students to reflect on what they would be willing to give up in order to protect the United States. OL

Analyzing VISUALS

Answers:

1. El Alamein was a desert. The terrain was rough, and there was no cover for soldiers. Stalingrad was brutally cold.
2. These two battles were major defeats for the Germans. They also gave confidence to Allied forces.

Additional Support

PRIMARY SOURCE

El Alamein and Stalingrad, November 1942

Just as the Battle of Midway was a turning point in the war in the Pacific, so too were the battles of El Alamein in North Africa and Stalingrad in Europe. The British victory over German General Rommel at El Alamein secured the Suez Canal and kept the Germans away from the oil resources of the Middle East. Germany's defeat at the Battle of Stalingrad was a major turning point by ending Hitler's plans to dominate Europe.

◄ *A British tank successfully navigates a wide ditch outside a town in North Africa.*

▲ *A Soviet gun crew fights against Nazi forces in Stalingrad. Only one day after the Nazis publicly boasted that the city would fall to them, the Red Army turned the tide of battle.*

Analyzing VISUALS

1. **Assessing** How do you think the environment made combat at El Alamein and Stalingrad challenging?
2. **Evaluating** Why were the battles shown so important to the Allies?

D General Erwin Rommel, whose success earned him the nickname "Desert Fox," commanded the "Afrika Korps." Although the British forced him to retreat in November 1942, after a 12-day battle against the coastal city of El Alamein, German forces remained a serious threat. Later that month, Americans commanded by General Dwight D. Eisenhower invaded North Africa. American general George Patton's forces in Morocco captured the city of Casablanca, while those in Algeria seized the cities of Oran and Algiers. The Americans then headed east into Tunisia, while British forces headed west into Libya.

When the American troops advanced into the mountains of western Tunisia, they had to fight the German army for the first time. At the Battle of Kasserine Pass, the Americans were outmaneuvered and outfought. They suffered roughly 7,000 casualties and lost nearly 200 tanks. Eisenhower fired the general who led the attack and put Patton in command. Together, the American and British forces finally pushed the Germans back. On May 13, 1943, the last German troops in North Africa surrendered.

The Battle of the Atlantic

As American and British troops fought the German army in North Africa, the war against German submarines in the Atlantic Ocean intensified. After Germany declared war on the United States, German submarines entered American coastal waters. American cargo ships were easy **targets,** especially at night when the glow from the cities in the night sky silhouetted the vessels. To protect the ships, cities on the East Coast dimmed their lights every evening. People also put up special "blackout curtains" and, if they had to drive at night, did so with their headlights off. W

Activity: Collaborative Activity

Sequencing Assign students to small groups and have them research the Allied pursuit of Rommel and the Germans in North Africa. Students should use the Internet, library resources, and their book to make a list of significant events that occurred, including the Allied capture of cities in North Africa such as El Alamein, Casablanca, Oran, and Algiers. Allied losses such as the American defeat at the Battle of Kasserine Pass in Tunisia should also be recorded. Using the information collected, students should create a time line complete with photos, quotes, and other primary sources.

By August 1942, German submarines had sunk about 360 American ships along the East Coast. So many oil tankers were sunk that gasoline and fuel oil had to be rationed. To keep oil flowing, the government built the first long-distance oil pipeline, stretching some 1,250 miles (2,010 km) from Texas to Pennsylvania.

The loss of so many ships convinced the U.S. Navy to set up a **convoy system.** Under this system, cargo ships traveled in groups escorted by navy warships. The convoy system improved the situation dramatically. It made it much more difficult for a submarine to torpedo a cargo ship and escape without being attacked.

The spring of 1942 marked the high point of the German submarine campaign. In May and June alone, over 1.2 million tons of shipping were sunk. Yet in those same two months, American and British shipyards built more than 1.1 million tons of new shipping. From July 1942 onward, American shipyards produced more ships than German submarines managed to sink. At the same time, American airplanes and warships began to use new technology, including radar, sonar, and depth charges, to locate and attack submarines. As the new technology began to take its toll on German submarines, the Battle of the Atlantic turned in favor of the Allies.

The Battle of Stalingrad

In the spring of 1942, before the Battle of the Atlantic turned against Germany, Adolf Hitler was very confident that he would win the war. The German army was ready to launch a new offensive to knock the Soviets out of the war.

Hitler was convinced that only by destroying the Soviet economy could he defeat the Soviet Union. In May 1942, he ordered his army to capture strategic oil fields, factories, and farmlands in southern Russia and Ukraine. The city of Stalingrad, which controlled the Volga River and was a major railroad junction, was the key to the attack. If the German army captured Stalingrad, they would cut off the Soviets from the resources they needed to stay in the war.

When German troops entered Stalingrad in mid-September, Stalin ordered his troops to hold the city at all costs. Retreat was forbidden. The Germans were forced to fight from house to house, C losing thousands of soldiers in the process. They were not equipped to fight in the bitter cold, but Soviet troops had quilted undersuits, felt boots, fur hats, and white camouflaged oversuits.

On November 23, Soviet reinforcements arrived and surrounded Stalingrad, trapping almost 250,000 German troops. When the battle ended in February 1943, some 91,000 Germans had surrendered, although only 5,000 of them survived the Soviet prison camps and returned home after the war. Each side lost nearly half a million soldiers. The Battle of Stalingrad was a major turning point in the war. Just as the Battle of Midway put the Japanese on the defensive for the rest of the war, the Battle of Stalingrad put the Germans on the defensive as well.

Reading Check **Describing** How did the United States begin winning the Battle of the Atlantic?

Section 2 REVIEW

Vocabulary

1. **Explain** the significance of: Chester Nimitz, Douglas MacArthur, Bataan Death March, Corregidor, James Doolittle, periphery, convoy system.

Main Ideas

2. **Explaining** Briefly explain the causes and effects of the effort to defeat the Japanese in 1942.
3. **Analyzing** Why did Churchill want to defeat the Germans in Africa before staging a European invasion?

Critical Thinking

4. **Big Ideas** Explain the significance of one person whose actions made a difference in the war.
5. **Organizing** Use a graphic organizer like the one below to list the reasons that the Battle of Midway is considered a turning point of the war.

Battle of Midway

6. **Analyzing Visuals** Look again at the map on page 724. How long did the Battle of Midway last?

Writing About History

7. **Expository Writing** Much of the course of wars is determined by the need for supply lines to remain open. Write a brief essay explaining how this need shaped early battles in which the United States was involved.

History ONLINE
Study Central™ To review this section, go to glencoe.com and click on Study Central.

727

Chapter 21 • Section 2

C Critical Thinking

Drawing Conclusions Ask: Why did the Soviet army need to hold the city of Stalingrad? *(to keep their supply lines opened.)* What was the result of the Battle of Stalingrad? *(It put the Germans on the defensive.)* OL

Reading Check

Answer:
They started using a convoy system to protect the cargo ships, and they started using new technology to locate and attack German submarines.

Assess

History ONLINE
Study Central™ provides summaries, interactive games, and online graphic organizers to help students review content.

Close

Summarizing Have students work in groups and review their battle time lines. Have each group take notes while discussing the importance of each battle. OL

Section 2 REVIEW

Answers

1. All definitions can be found in the section and in the Glossary.
2. U.S. bombing of Tokyo led to Japanese attack on Midway. The Battle of Midway resulted in a U.S. victory that stopped the Japanese advance.
3. Churchill did not believe the Allied forces were ready to launch a full-scale invasion of Europe.
4. Student choices will vary. Students should support their choice by using specific details from the text.
5. Battle of Midway: Japanese lost four carriers; Stopped Japanese advance in the Pacific; Ended Japanese offensive
6. June 4 to June 6
7. Essays will vary but should explain the importance of supply lines.

Focus

Bellringer
Daily Focus Transparency 21-3

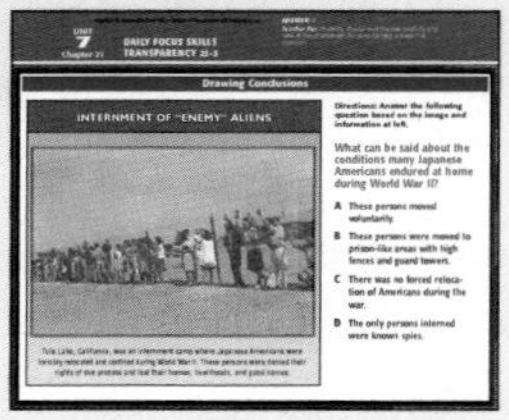

Guide to Reading
Answers:

	Women	African Americans
Before War	few job opportunities, low pay	few opportunities
After War	better job selection	Fair Employment Practices oversight
Still Needed	Answers will vary	Answers will vary

Section Spotlight Video
To generate student interest and provide a springboard for class discussion, access the Chapter 21, Section 3 video at glencoe.com or on the video DVD.

Resource Manager

Section 3
Section Audio · Spotlight Video

Life on the Home Front

Guide to Reading

Big Ideas
Trade, War, and Migration During World War II, Americans faced demands and new challenges at home.

Content Vocabulary
- Sunbelt *(p. 730)*
- zoot suit *(p. 732)*
- victory suit *(p. 732)*
- rationing *(p. 734)*
- victory garden *(p. 735)*

Academic Vocabulary
- coordinate *(p. 731)*
- justify *(p. 732)*

People and Events to Identify
- A. Philip Randolph *(p. 730)*
- Bracero Program *(p. 730)*
- Great Migration *(p. 731)*
- Office of Price Administration *(p. 734)*

Reading Strategy
Organizing Complete a graphic organizer listing opportunities for women and African Americans before and after the war. Evaluate what progress was still needed after the war.

Opportunities

	Before War	After War	Still Needed
Women			
African Americans			

Although women and African Americans gained new work opportunities, Latinos and Japanese Americans faced violence in American cities. To assist with the war effort, the government controlled wages and prices, rationed goods, encouraged recycling, and sold bonds.

Women and Minorities Gain Ground

MAIN Idea With many men on active military duty, women and minorities found factory and other jobs open to them.

HISTORY AND YOU Do you remember reading about the unequal treatment of African American soldiers in World War I? Read on to learn how desegregation of the military began in World War II.

As American troops fought their first battles against the Germans and Japanese, the war began dramatically changing American society at home. In contrast to the devastation that large parts of Europe and Asia experienced, American society gained some benefits from World War II. The war finally ended the Great Depression. Mobilizing the economy created almost 19 million new jobs and nearly doubled the average family's income. For Robert Montgomery, a worker at an Ohio machine tool plant, "one of the most important things that came out of World War II was the arrival of the working class at a new status level in this society. . . . The war integrated into the mainstream a whole chunk of society that had been living on the edge."

The improvement in the economy did not come without cost. American families had to move to where the defense factories were located. Housing conditions were terrible. The pressures and prejudices of the era led to strikes, race riots, and rising juvenile delinquency. Goods were rationed and taxes were higher than ever before. Workers were earning more money, but they were also working an average of 90 hours per week. Despite the hardships, James Covert, whose mother owned a grocery store during the war, was probably right when he said that the war "changed our lifestyle and more important, our outlook. . . . There was a feeling toward the end of the war that we were moving into a new age of prosperity."

When the war began, American defense factories wanted to hire white men. With so many men in the military, however, there simply were not enough white men to fill all of the jobs. Under pressure to produce, employers began to recruit women and minorities.

R Reading Strategies	**C** Critical Thinking	**D** Differentiated Instruction	**W** Writing Support	**S** Skill Practice
Teacher Edition • Act. Prior Know., p. 730 **Additional Resources** • Guide. Reading, URB p. 84 • Prim. Source Read., URB p. 71	**Teacher Edition** • Compare/Contrast, p. 729 • Recognizing Bias, p. 730 • Det. Cause & Effect, p. 731 • Defending, p. 734 **Additional Resources** • Quizzes and Tests, p. 303	**Teacher Edition** • Interpersonal, p. 731 • Visual/Spatial, p. 732 • Logical/Math, p. 734 • Differentiated Instruct. Act., URB p. 57 • Enrichment Act., URB p. 79	**Teacher Edition** • Descriptive Writing, p. 729 • Persuasive Writing, p. 732	**Additional Resources** • Read. Essen., p. 238

PRIMARY SOURCE

Women Working in the Defense Plants

At left, a riveter works on a bomber in Fort Worth, Texas. Posters such as those above and to the right encouraged women to participate in the war effort.

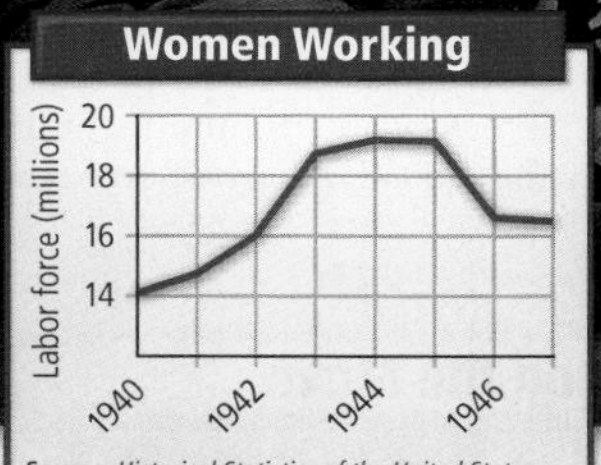

Source: *Historical Statistics of the United States.*

Analyzing VISUALS

1. **Listing** During what years did women's employment outside the home hit its highest levels?
2. **Analyzing** How are the women portrayed in the posters?

Women in the Defense Plants

C During the Great Depression, many people believed married women should not work outside the home, especially if they took jobs that could go to men trying to support their families. Most working women were young, single, and employed in traditional female jobs such as domestic work or teaching. The wartime labor shortage, however, forced factories to recruit married women for industrial jobs traditionally reserved for men.

Although the government hired nearly 4 million women, primarily for clerical jobs, the women working in the factories captured the public's imagination. The great symbol of the campaign to hire women was "Rosie the Riveter," a character from a popular song by the Four Vagabonds. The lyrics told of Rosie, who worked in a factory while her boyfriend served in the marines. Images of Rosie appeared on posters, in newspapers, and in magazines. Eventually 2.5 million women worked in shipyards, aircraft factories, and other manufacturing plants. Working in a factory changed the perspectives of many middle-class women like Inez Sauer:

PRIMARY SOURCE

W "I learned that just because you're a woman and have never worked is no reason you can't learn. The job really broadened me. . . . I had always been in a shell; I'd always been protected. But at Boeing I found a freedom and an independence I had never known. After the war I could never go back to playing bridge again, being a club woman. . . . when I knew there were things you could use your mind for. The war changed my life completely."

—quoted in *The Homefront*

C Critical Thinking

Comparing and Contrasting Draw a Venn diagram on the board. Label one circle World War II and the other Today. Have students make observations about the changes in women's roles in the workplace since World War II. **OL**

W Writing Support

Descriptive Writing Have students review the quote from Inez Sauer. **Ask:** Based on the passage, how did some women spend their days before the war? How did the war change that? *(doing recreational tasks; they wanted to join the workforce)* Have students write a descriptive paragraph on how holding a job changed many women's self image. **OL**

Analyzing VISUALS

Answers:
1. 1944–1945
2. strong, capable, independent

Additional Support

Activity: Interdisciplinary Connection

Art When millions of men took up the uniform, women were recruited to work in factories, performing "men's work." Many women worked in shipyards, especially those owned by Henry Kaiser. This was not work for the weak! Rosie the Riveter was used as a propaganda technique to lure women into these tough industrial jobs. She was tough, loyal, efficient, and of course, patriotic. Rosie the Riveter was also a response to Tokyo Rose and Axis Sally, enemy characters who broadcast anti-Allied propaganda over the radio in the Pacific and in Europe. Have students find the music to the song, "Rosie the Riveter." Then have students work in groups to either sing the song in its original version, perform a new musical rendition of the song, write a poem based on the song lyrics, or create a new Rosie poster. The poster should reflect the strength of the women who worked in shipyards. **OL**

R Reading Strategy

Activating Prior Knowledge
After students read the section "African Americans Demand War Work," ask them to identify other times in which a crisis has provided opportunity for minorities to gain social and economic opportunities. *(Students might mention the slight gains African Americans and women made after World War I and the gains industrial workers gained during the Great Depression.)* **OL**

C Critical Thinking

Recognizing Bias Have students gather more details about the Bracero Program. Have students write a one-page report describing the living conditions of the migrant workers, the pay they received, and what happened to them after the war. **OL**

Reading Check

Answer:
Mobilizing the economy for war production created nearly 19 million new jobs and nearly doubled the average income.

By the end of the war, the number of working women had increased from 12.9 million to 18.8 million. Although most women were laid off or left their jobs voluntarily after the war, their success permanently changed American attitudes about women in the workplace.

African Americans Demand War Work

Although factories were hiring women, they resisted hiring African Americans. Frustrated by the situation, **A. Philip Randolph,** the head of the Brotherhood of Sleeping Car Porters—a major union for African American railroad workers—decided to take action. He informed President Roosevelt that he was organizing "from ten to fifty thousand [African Americans] to march on Washington **R** in the interest of securing jobs . . . in national defense and . . . integration into the military and naval forces."

In response, Roosevelt issued Executive Order 8802, on June 25, 1941. The order declared, "there shall be no discrimination in the employment of workers in defense industries or government because of race, creed, color, or national origin." To enforce the order, the president created the Fair Employment Practices Commission—the first civil rights agency the federal government had established since the Reconstruction Era.

Mexican Farmworkers

American citizens were not the only ones who gained in the wartime economy. In 1942 the federal government arranged for Mexican farmworkers to help with the harvest in the Southwest. The laborers were part of the **Bracero Program.** *Bracero* is a Spanish **C** word meaning "worker." More than 200,000 Mexicans came to help harvest fruit and vegetables. Many also helped to build and maintain railroads. The Bracero Program continued until 1964. Migrant farmworkers thus became an important part of the Southwest's agricultural system.

Reading Check **Describing** How did mobilizing the economy help end the Depression?

A Nation on the Move

MAIN Idea Millions of Americans relocated during the war to take factory jobs or to settle in less prejudiced areas.

HISTORY AND YOU Has someone in your family moved because of a job transfer? Read on to find out about relocations that resulted from the war.

The wartime economy created millions of new jobs, but the Americans who wanted these jobs did not always live near the factories. To get to the jobs, 15 million Americans moved during the war. The Midwest assembly plants and Northeast and Northwest shipyards attracted many workers. Most Americans, however, headed west and south in search of jobs.

The growth of southern California and the expansion of cities in the Deep South created a new industrial region—the **Sunbelt.** For the first time since the Industrial Revolution began

PRIMARY SOURCE

A Nation on the Move

During the war, millions of Americans flocked to the cities to work in factories. Many immigrants stayed on after the war to become citizens. As a result, the populations of Northern cities became more ethnically diverse, and these cities remained more populous after the war.

▼ *Workers at an Iowa arms plant lived in this trailer camp in 1942.*

Hands-On Chapter Project
Step 3

An Interview with a World War II Veteran

Step 3: Conducting the Interview
Essential Question: What is the goal of this interview? What information am I trying to get?

Directions Explain to students that only one or at most two people can actually meet with the subject (the second person may want to take notes). It is also a good idea to record the interview. Students should obtain permission to record from the subject. No more than one hour of the interviewee's time should be taken. The interview can be conducted in a home or at school (wherever a computer with a microphone hook-up is available).

Putting It Together After the interview, students should meet to review what happened and discuss it. Was anything missed? Are any answers ambiguous? Are there gaps in what the script had covered? This information will prepare students for Step 4. **OL**

(Chapter Project continued on page 738)

in the United States, the South and West led the way in manufacturing and urbanization.

The Housing Crisis

C The most difficult task facing cities with war industries was where to put the thousands of workers arriving in their communities. Tent cities and parks filled with tiny trailers sprang up. Anticipating the housing crisis, Congress had passed the Lanham Act in 1940. The act provided $150 million for housing. In 1942 President Roosevelt created the National Housing Agency (NHA) to **coordinate** all government housing programs. By 1943, those programs had been allocated over $1.2 billion. Although prefabricated public housing had tiny rooms, thin walls, poor heating, and almost no privacy, it was better than no housing at all. Nearly 2 million people lived in government-built housing during the war.

Racism Leads to Violence

African Americans left the South in large numbers during World War I in what became known to historians as the "**Great Migration.**" The migration slowed during the Great Depression but resumed when jobs in war factories opened up for African Americans during World War II. In the crowded cities of the North and West, however, African Americans were often met with suspicion and intolerance.

D The worst racial violence of the war erupted in Detroit on Sunday, June 20, 1943. Nearly 100,000 people crowded into Belle Isle, a park on the Detroit River, to cool off. Gangs of white and African American teenage girls began fighting. These fights triggered others, and a riot erupted across the city. Twenty-five African Americans and 9 whites were killed.

The Zoot Suit Riots

Wartime prejudice boiled over elsewhere as well. In southern California, racial tensions became entangled with juvenile delinquency. Across the nation, the number of crimes committed by young people rose dramatically. In Los Angeles, racism against Mexican Americans and the fear of juvenile crime became linked because of the "zoot suit."

Major Cities, 1940 and 1947

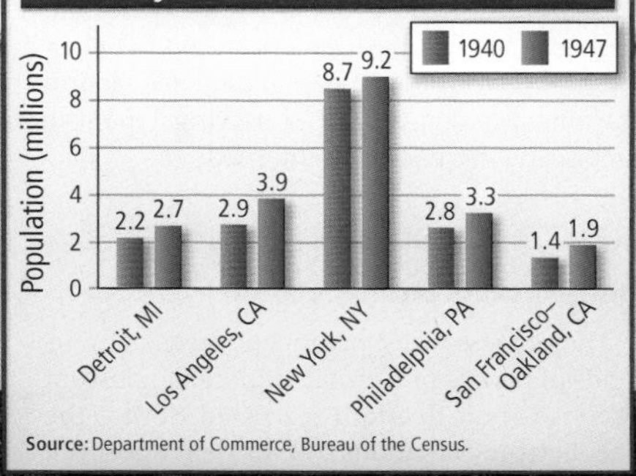

Source: Department of Commerce, Bureau of the Census.

NATIONAL GEOGRAPHIC **Migration in the United States, 1940–1950**

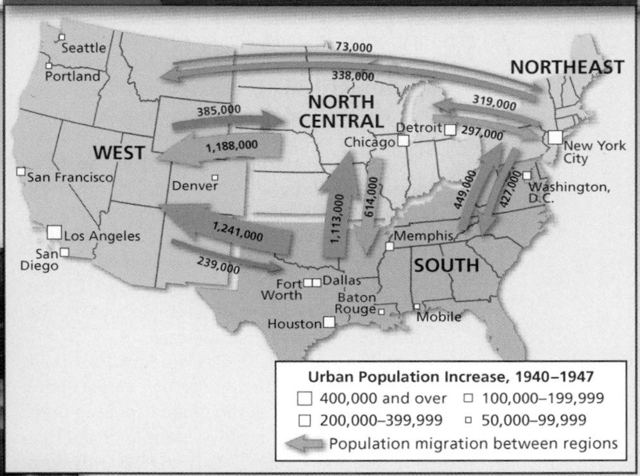

Analyzing GEOGRAPHY

1. **Movement** What region of the nation had the most total population gain?
2. **Movement** What region of the nation had the largest population loss?

C Critical Thinking

Determining Cause and Effect Ask: Why did workers have to create tent cities? *(The new locations did not have enough lodging built to house the influx of new workers.)* What was Roosevelt's solution to this problem? *(He set up the National Housing Agency to build inexpensive government housing.)* **OL**

D Differentiated Instruction

Intrapersonal Discuss how wartime crisis can sometimes create unrest at home. Ask students to provide examples of racial unrest due to present day conflicts. Invite students to discuss how tensions can be avoided. **OL**

Analyzing GEOGRAPHY

Answers:
1. the West
2. the South

Additional Support

Activity: Technology Connection

Identifying Central Issues Assign students to small groups and have them research the 1943 Detroit race riot. Remind students to use reliable sources on the Internet and encourage them to find old newspapers from the library. Have students create their own newspaper, complete with headlines, several articles, photos, captions, editorials, and a small advertisement, perhaps something to do with the war effort. Invite students to present their newspapers to the class. **OL**

D Differentiated Instruction

Visual/Spatial Have students use the library or Internet to find photographs of the zoot suit and victory suit. Challenge them to find other fashions worn during World War II. Have students create posters with the photos they found and display them in the room. **Ask:** Why was it patriotic to wear a victory suit? *(They saved fabric for the war.)* OL

W Writing Support

Persuasive Writing Have students research Japanese-American internment camps and Executive Order 9066. Encourage them to read personal narratives during their research. Then have students write a one-page editorial, voicing their opinions about internment camps. AL

Reading Check

Answer:
They were looking for job opportunities in factories.

Additional Support

A **zoot suit** had very baggy, pleated pants and an overstuffed, knee-length jacket with wide lapels, and sometimes a wide-brimmed hat. In order to save fabric for the war, most men wore a "**victory suit**"—a suit with no vest, no cuffs, a short jacket, and narrow lapels.

In California, Mexican American teenagers adopted the zoot suit. In June 1943, after hearing rumors that zoot-suiters had attacked several sailors, some 2,500 soldiers and sailors attacked Mexican American neighborhoods in Los Angeles. The police did not intervene, and the violence continued for several days.

Racial hostility against Mexican Americans did not deter them from joining the war effort. Approximately 500,000 Hispanic Americans served in the armed forces during the war. Most—about 400,000—were Mexican American. Another 65,000 were from Puerto Rico. By the end of the war, 17 Mexican Americans had received the Medal of Honor.

Japanese American Relocation

When Japan attacked Pearl Harbor, many Americans living on the West Coast turned their anger against Japanese immigrants and Japanese Americans. Mobs attacked their businesses and homes. Banks would not cash their checks, and grocers refused to sell them food.

Newspapers printed rumors about Japanese spies in the Japanese American community. Members of Congress, mayors, and many business and labor leaders demanded that all people of Japanese ancestry be removed from the West Coast. They did not believe that Japanese Americans would remain loyal to the United States in the war with Japan.

On February 19, 1942, President Roosevelt signed an order allowing the War Department to declare any part of the United States a military zone and to remove people from that zone. He must have felt **justified** only four days later, when a Japanese submarine surfaced north of Santa Barbara, California, and shelled an oil refinery, or in September of that year, when Japanese bombers twice dropped bombs on an Oregon forest. Secretary of War Henry Stimson declared most of the West Coast a military zone and ordered all people of Japanese ancestry to evacuate to 10 internment camps further inland.

Not all Japanese Americans accepted the relocation without protest. Fred Korematsu argued that his rights had been violated and took his case to the Supreme Court. In December 1944, in *Korematsu* v. *United States*, the Supreme Court ruled that the relocation was constitutional because it was based not on race, but on "military urgency." Shortly afterward, the Court did rule in *Ex parte Endo* that loyal American citizens could not be held against their will. In early 1945, therefore, the government began to release the Japanese Americans from the camps.

Despite the fears and rumors, no Japanese American was ever tried for espionage or sabotage. Japanese Americans served as translators for the army during the war in the Pacific. The all-Japanese 100th Battalion, later integrated into the 442nd Regimental Combat Team, was the most highly decorated unit in World War II.

After the war, the Japanese American Citizens League (JACL) tried to help Japanese Americans who had lost property during the relocation. In 1988 President Ronald Reagan apologized to Japanese Americans on behalf of the U.S. government and signed legislation granting $20,000 to each surviving Japanese American who had been interned.

Italian American and German American Relocation

Though less well-known, hundreds of thousands of people of German and Italian descent also had their freedom restricted during the war. Two proclamations by President Roosevelt on December 8, 1941, stated that all unnaturalized residents of German and Italian descent, fourteen years of age or over, were designated as enemy aliens and were subject to government regulations such as travel restrictions, being forced to carry identification cards, and the seizure of personal property. Over 5000 were arrested and forced to live in military internment camps, primarily in Montana and North Dakota.

Reading Check **Comparing** Why did millions of people relocate during the war?

Activity: Interdisciplinary Connection

Literature Have students read one of the many personal narratives about the Japanese internment camps. Suggested readings include *The Cross on Castle Rock: A Childhood Memoir* by George Nakagawa, *Looking Like the Enemy* by Mary Matsuda Gruenewald, and *Farewell to Manzanar* by Jeanne Houston. Then have students work in small groups to create short plays about daily life in the internment camps during the war. Have groups present their plays to the rest of the class. As a class, discuss what students have learned about internment camps and their reactions to them. AL

Can the Government Limit Civil Liberties in Wartime?

Korematsu v. *United States*, 1944

Background to the Case

During World War II, President Roosevelt's Executive Order 9066 and other legislation gave the military the power to exclude people of Japanese descent from areas that were deemed important to U.S. national defense and security. In 1942, Toyosaburo Korematsu refused to leave San Leandro, California, which had been designated as a "military area," based on Executive Order 9066. Korematsu was found guilty in federal district court of violating Civilian Exclusion Order No. 34. Korematsu petitioned the Supreme Court to review the federal court's decision.

How the Court Ruled

In their decision, the majority of the Supreme Court, with three dissenting, found that, although exclusion orders based on race are constitutionally suspect, the government is justified in time of "emergency and peril" to suspend citizens' civil rights. A request for a rehearing of the case in 1945 was denied.

▲ *Japanese American women and their children talk together at the Heart Mountain Relocation Camp.*

PRIMARY SOURCE

The Court's Opinion

"It should be noted, to begin with, that all legal restrictions which curtail the civil rights of a single racial group are immediately suspect. That is not to say that all such restrictions are unconstitutional. It is to say that courts must subject them to the most rigid scrutiny. Pressing public necessity may sometimes justify the existence of such restrictions; racial antagonism never can. . . . Korematsu was not excluded from the Military Area because of hostility to him or his race. He was excluded because . . . the properly constituted military authorities feared an invasion of our West Coast [by Japan] and felt constrained to take proper security measures, because they decided that the military urgency of the situation demanded that all citizens of Japanese ancestry be segregated from the West Coast temporarily, and finally, because Congress . . . determined that they should have the power to do just this."

—Justice Hugo Black writing for the court in *Korematsu* v. *United States*

PRIMARY SOURCE

Dissenting View

"I dissent, because I think the indisputable facts exhibit a clear violation of Constitutional rights. This is not . . . a case of temporary exclusion of a citizen from an area for his own safety or that of the community, nor a case of offering him an opportunity to go temporarily out of an area where his presence might cause danger to himself or to his fellows. On the contrary, it is the case of convicting a citizen as a punishment for not submitting to imprisonment in a concentration camp, based on his ancestry, and solely because of his ancestry, without evidence or inquiry concerning his loyalty and good disposition towards the United States. If this be a correct statement of the facts disclosed by this record, and facts of which we take judicial notice, I need hardly labor the conclusion that Constitutional rights have been violated."

—Justice Owen J. Roberts, dissenting in *Korematsu* v. *United States*

DBQ Document-Based Questions

1. **Explaining** Why did the Supreme Court find in favor of the government in this case, even though the justices were suspicious of exclusion based on race?
2. **Contrasting** Why did Justice Roberts disagree with the majority opinion?
3. **Analyzing** Under what circumstances, if any, do you think the government should be able to suspend civil liberties of all or specific groups of American citizens?

Teach

In March 1942, U.S. General John DeWitt, acting under War Department orders, began the evacuation of all persons of Japanese descent from the western parts of Washington, Oregon, and California and the southern part of Arizona. Most of the evacuees had been born in the United States. DeWitt, however, explained the evacuation by saying, "It makes no difference whether a Japanese is theoretically a citizen. He is still Japanese. . . ."

DBQ Document Based Questions

Answers:

1. The majority felt that Korematsu was relocated not due to his race but rather that the United States was in danger of being attacked.
2. He felt the confinements were unconstitutional. He believed it was a clear case of racial discrimination.
3. Answers will vary. Students should support their opinions.

Differentiated Instruction

Case Study 32: *Korematsu* v. *United States*, p. 63

Analyzing a Supreme Court Decision

Objective: Learn how the Supreme Court determined whether the relocation program was constitutional.

Focus: Identify the central issue of the case.

Teach: Discuss the Court's opinion.

Assess: Explain the importance of the case (interpretation of War Relocation Authority).

Close: Write a paragraph summarizing the case.

Differentiated Instruction Strategies

BL Explain how the *Korematsu* and *Endo* decisions are similar or different.

AL Paraphrase the Court's decision. Read your version to the class.

ELL Explain what a relocation camp was.

D Differentiated Instruction

Logical/Mathematical Assign students to small groups and have them explore the effects of inflation on consumer prices. Have the groups research the way in which inflation is measured, in particular the Consumer Price Index (CPI). Ask groups to prepare displays showing the effects of inflation from 1900 to 1999. Encourage groups to link inflation to political and social events. **AL**

C Critical Thinking

Defending Roosevelt used the federal government to regulate wages and prices on certain products. **Ask:** Do you think the government should have such authority? *(Students may suggest the world was different then, but now, such a move by the government would not be acceptable.)* **OL**

Analyzing VISUALS

Answers:

1. They encourage people to act heroically and help them believe they can win.
2. They boosted morale and made the enemy less frightening.

Additional Support

Daily Life in Wartime

MAIN Idea The federal government took steps to stabilize wages and prices, as well as to prevent strikes. Americans supported the war through rationing, growing food, recycling, and buying bonds.

HISTORY AND YOU Have you ever given up something you enjoyed for a short period of time to gain something greater? Read on to learn how Americans sacrificed during the war.

Housing shortages and racial tensions were serious difficulties during the war, but mobilization strained society in other ways as well. Prices rose, materials were in short supply, and the question of how to pay for the war loomed ominously over the war effort.

Wage and Price Controls

D Both wages and prices began to rise quickly during the war because of the high demand for workers and raw materials. The president worried about inflation. To stabilize both wages and prices, Roosevelt created the C **Office of Price Administration** (OPA) and the Office of Economic Stabilization (OES). The OES regulated wages and the price of farm products. The OPA regulated all other prices. Despite some problems with labor unions, the OPA and OES kept inflation under control. At the end of the war, prices had risen only about half as much as they had during World War I.

While the OPA and OES worked to control inflation, the War Labor Board (WLB) tried to prevent strikes. In support, most American unions issued a "no strike pledge." Instead of striking, unions asked the WLB to mediate wage disputes. By the end of the war, the WLB had helped to settle more than 17,000 disputes involving more than 12 million workers.

Blue Points, Red Points

The demand for raw materials and supplies created shortages. The OPA began **rationing,** or limiting the purchase of, many products to make sure enough were available for military use. Meat and sugar were rationed. Gasoline was rationed, driving distances were restricted, and the speed limit was set at 35 miles per hour to save gas and rubber.

PRIMARY SOURCE

Hollywood Goes to War

In 1942 President Roosevelt created the Office of War Information (OWI). The OWI's role was to improve the public's understanding of the war and to act as a liaison office with the various media. The OWI established detailed guidelines for filmmakers, including a set of questions to be considered before making a movie, such as, "Will this picture help win the war?"

▲ *Movies ranged from a comic Donald Duck cartoon to a serious portrayal of a bombing raid on Germany.*

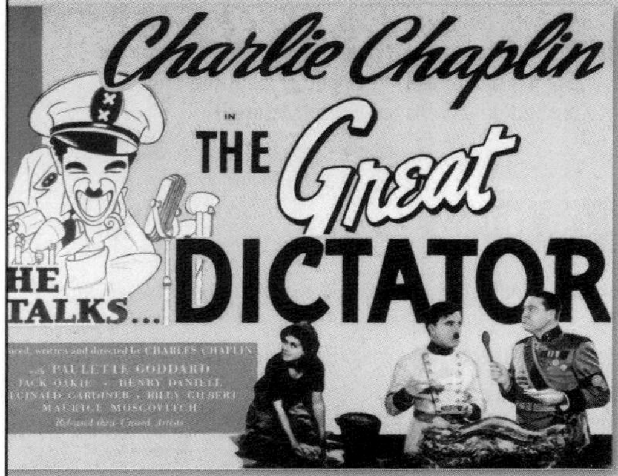

◀ *Chaplin, noted as a comic and a director, made this movie in 1940, before the United States entered the war.*

Analyzing VISUALS

1. **Interpreting** How would heroic movies like *The Memphis Belle* help win the war?
2. **Analyzing** Why do you think so many movies about Hitler were comedies?

Activity: Interdisciplinary Connection

Daily Life Tell students that women painted seams on their legs to make it look as though they were wearing stockings. During the war, silk was needed to make parachutes, not stockings. Have students pair up and use Internet or library resources to research other items that were rationed. Encourage students to interview family members or community members to get first-hand accounts of rationing. Finally, have students create a pamphlet that describes and illustrates the information they found. Ask students to present their pamphlets to the class. **OL**

A person from each household picked up a book of ration coupons every month. Blue coupons, called blue points, controlled processed foods. Red coupons, or red points, controlled meats, fats, and oils. Other coupons controlled items such as coffee, shoes, and sugar. Thirteen rationing programs were in effect at the height of the program. When people bought food, they also had to give enough coupon points to cover their purchases. Most rationing ended before the war was over. Sugar and rubber rationing continued after the war; sugar was rationed until 1947.

Victory Gardens and Scrap Drives

Americans also planted gardens to produce more food for the war effort. Any area of land might become a garden—backyards, school yards, city parks, and empty lots. The government encouraged **victory gardens** by praising them in film reels, pamphlets, and official statements.

Certain raw materials were so vital to the war effort that the government organized scrap drives. Volunteers collected spare rubber, tin, aluminum, and steel. They donated pots, tires, tin cans, car bumpers, broken radiators, and rusting bicycles. Oils and fats were so important to the production of explosives that the WPB set up fat-collecting stations. Americans would exchange bacon grease and meat drippings for extra ration coupons. The scrap drives boosted morale and did contribute to the success of American industry during the war.

Paying for the War

The federal government spent more than $300 billion during World War II—more money than it had spent from Washington's administration to the end of Franklin Roosevelt's second term. To raise money, the government raised taxes. Because most Americans opposed large tax increases, Congress refused to raise taxes as high as Roosevelt requested. As a result, the extra taxes collected covered only 45 percent of the war's cost.

The government issued war bonds to make up the difference between what was needed and what taxes supplied. Buying bonds is a way to lend money to the government. In exchange for the money, the government promises to repay the bonds' purchase price plus interest at some future date. The most common bonds during World War II were E bonds, which sold for $18.75 and could be redeemed for $25.00 after 10 years. Individuals bought nearly $50 billion worth of war bonds. Banks, insurance companies, and other financial institutions bought the rest—more than $100 billion worth of bonds.

Despite the hardships, the overwhelming majority of Americans believed the war had to be fought. Although the war brought many changes to the United States, most Americans remained united behind one goal—winning the war.

Reading Check **Evaluating** How did rationing affect daily life in the United States? How did it affect the economy?

Section 3 REVIEW

Vocabulary

1. **Explain** the significance of: A. Philip Randolph, Bracero Program, Sunbelt, Great Migration, zoot suit, victory suit, Office of Price Administration, rationing, victory garden.

Main Ideas

2. **Assessing** Why were jobs suddenly available to women and minorities?
3. **Evaluating** For what reasons did Americans relocate during the war?
4. **Explaining** How did the federal government control the economy during the war?

Critical Thinking

5. **Big Ideas** What challenges did Americans at home face during the war?
6. **Organizing** Use a graphic organizer like the one below to list the results of increased racial tensions during the war.

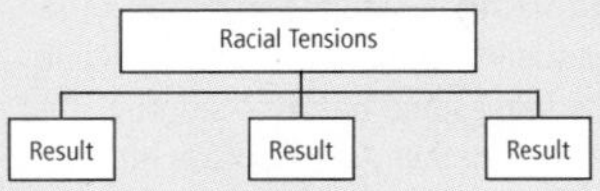

7. **Analyzing Visuals** Look again at the photograph on pages 730–731. How does the photographer capture the feeling of people settling into a new area?

Writing About History

8. **Persuasive Writing** Write a newspaper editorial urging fellow citizens to conserve resources so that those resources can be used in the war effort.

History ONLINE
Study Central™ To review this section, go to glencoe.com and click on Study Central.

Reading Check

Answer:
Rationing limited access to many products allowing people to buy them in limited supply. It helped control inflation and ensure there were goods for citizens and military.

Assess

History ONLINE

Study Central™ provides summaries, interactive games, and online graphic organizers to help students review content.

Close

Identifying Central Issues
Have students break into groups and discuss prejudices in society, in the 1940s and today. Have students create two lists: one that shows how people worked together in the 1940s, the other showing modern examples of American unity. **OL**

Section 3 REVIEW

Answers

1. All definitions can be found in the section and in the Glossary.
2. Many of the white men had enlisted in the armed forces. They were fighting the war.
3. to find work in factories; to escape prejudice
4. The government controlled the economy through wage and price controls, rationing, and the selling of bonds to pay for the war.
5. They had to accept rationing, growing their own gardens, living in government housing, recycling of scrap materials, paying higher taxes, and learning to work with minorities.
6.

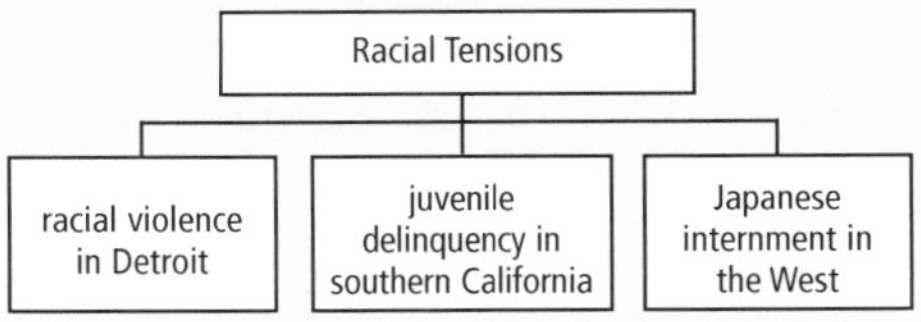

7. The photographer captures how make-shift and temporary the housing was.
8. Editorials will vary but should reflect positive, persuasive techniques.

Focus

Bellringer

Daily Focus Transparency 21-4

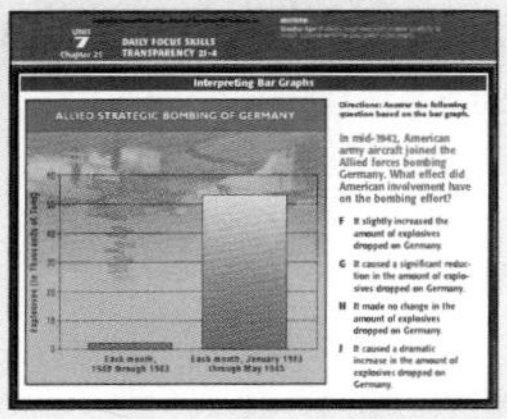

Guide to Reading

Answers:
Pacific: Tarawa Atoll, Gilbert Islands, Allies
Kwajalein Atoll, Marshall Islands, Allies
Guam, Mariana Islands, Allies
Europe: Sicily, Allies
Northern Italy, Allies
D-Day June 1944, Allies

Section Spotlight Video

To generate student interest and provide a springboard for class discussion, access the Chapter 21, Section 4 video at glencoe.com or on the video DVD.

Section 4 — Section Audio — Spotlight Video

Pushing Back the Axis

Guide to Reading

Big Ideas

Geography and History The Allies slowly pushed back the German and Japanese forces during 1943 and 1944.

Content Vocabulary
- amphtrac (p. 742)
- kamikaze (p. 743)

Academic Vocabulary
- briefly (p. 740)
- intense (p. 740)

People and Events to Identify
- Casablanca Conference (p. 736)
- D-Day (p. 740)
- Omar Bradley (p. 740)
- Guadalcanal (p. 743)

Reading Strategy

Organizing Complete a graphic organizer similar to the one below by filling in the names and battles fought. Indicate whether Allied or Axis forces won the battle.

After British and American troops won victories over the Axis in North Africa and Italy, Allied leaders made plans for an invasion of Europe. Led by Admiral Nimitz and General MacArthur, American forces steadily advanced across the Pacific.

Striking Germany and Italy

MAIN Idea The Allies stepped up bombing of Germany and invaded Sicily and Italy.

HISTORY AND YOU Have you ever talked over your ideas with a good friend whose opinion you value? Read on to learn about FDR's meetings with Churchill and Stalin.

The Allied invasion of North Africa in November 1942 had shown that a large-scale invasion from the sea was possible. The success of the landings convinced Roosevelt to meet again with Churchill to plan the next stage of the war. In January 1943, FDR headed to Casablanca, Morocco, to meet the prime minister.

At the **Casablanca Conference,** Roosevelt and Churchill agreed to step up the bombing of Germany. The goal of this new campaign was "the progressive destruction of the German military, industrial, and economic system, and the undermining of the morale of the German people." The Allies also agreed to attack the Axis on the island of Sicily. Churchill called Italy the "soft underbelly" of Europe. He was convinced that the Italians would quit the war if the Allies invaded their homeland.

Strategic Bombing

The Allies had been bombing Germany even before the Casablanca Conference. Britain's Royal Air Force had dropped an average of 2,300 tons (2,093 t) of explosives on Germany every month for more than three years. The United States Eighth Army Air Force had dropped an additional 1,500 tons (1,365 t) of bombs during the last six months of 1942. These numbers were small, however, compared to the massive new campaign. Between January 1943 and May 1945, the Royal Air Force and the United States Eighth Army Air Force dropped approximately 53,000 tons (48,230 t) of explosives on Germany every month.

The bombing campaign did not destroy Germany's economy or undermine German morale, but it did cause a severe oil shortage and wrecked the railroad system. It also destroyed so many aircraft factories that Germany's air force could not replace its losses. By the time

Resource Manager

R Reading Strategies	C Critical Thinking	D Differentiated Instruction	W Writing Support	S Skill Practice
Teacher Edition • Identifying, p. 737 • Det. Importance, pp. 738, 742 • Listing, p. 739 • Explaining, p. 741 **Additional Resources** • Guide. Reading, URB p. 85	**Teacher Edition** • Pred. Consequences, p. 738 • Making Decisions, p. 740 • Making Inferences, p. 742 **Additional Resources** • Quizzes and Tests, p. 304	**Teacher Edition** • Visual/Spatial, pp. 740, 741 **Additional Resources** • Am. Art and Music Act., URB p. 73	**Teacher Edition** • Descriptive Writing, p. 743	**Teacher Edition** • Using Geo. Skills, p. 739 **Additional Resources** • Read. Essen., p. 241 • Reinforcing Skills Act., URB p. 65

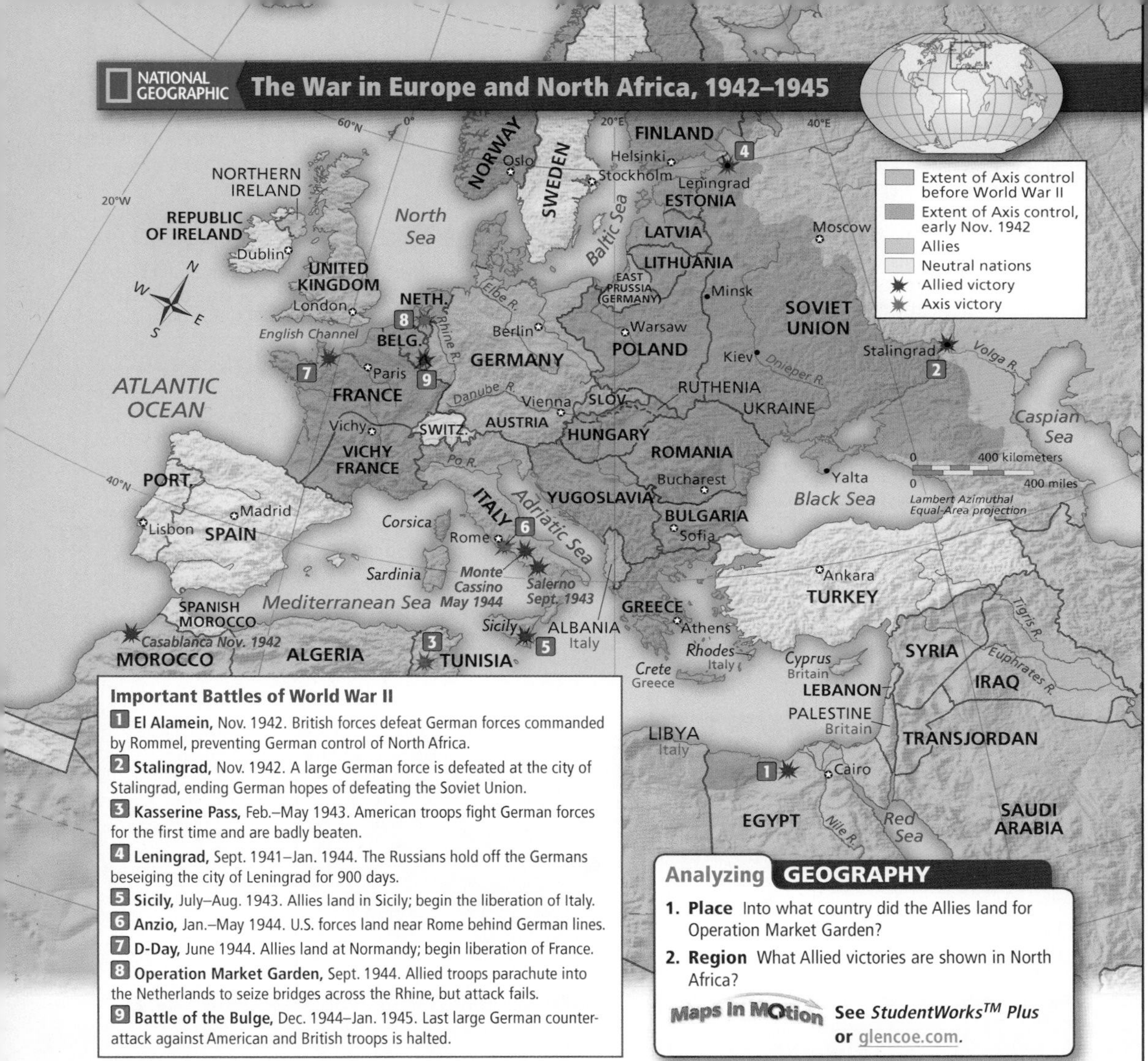

Important Battles of World War II

1 **El Alamein,** Nov. 1942. British forces defeat German forces commanded by Rommel, preventing German control of North Africa.

2 **Stalingrad,** Nov. 1942. A large German force is defeated at the city of Stalingrad, ending German hopes of defeating the Soviet Union.

3 **Kasserine Pass,** Feb.–May 1943. American troops fight German forces for the first time and are badly beaten.

4 **Leningrad,** Sept. 1941–Jan. 1944. The Russians hold off the Germans beseiging the city of Leningrad for 900 days.

5 **Sicily,** July–Aug. 1943. Allies land in Sicily; begin the liberation of Italy.

6 **Anzio,** Jan.–May 1944. U.S. forces land near Rome behind German lines.

7 **D-Day,** June 1944. Allies land at Normandy; begin liberation of France.

8 **Operation Market Garden,** Sept. 1944. Allied troops parachute into the Netherlands to seize bridges across the Rhine, but attack fails.

9 **Battle of the Bulge,** Dec. 1944–Jan. 1945. Last large German counter-attack against American and British troops is halted.

Analyzing GEOGRAPHY

1. **Place** Into what country did the Allies land for Operation Market Garden?
2. **Region** What Allied victories are shown in North Africa?

Maps in MOtion See *StudentWorks™ Plus* or glencoe.com.

the Allies landed in France, they had control of the air, ensuring that their troops would not be bombed.

Striking the Soft Underbelly

R As the bombing campaign against Germany intensified, plans to invade Sicily also moved ahead. General Dwight D. Eisenhower commanded the invasion, with General Patton and the British General Bernard Montgomery heading the ground forces. The invasion began before dawn on July 10, 1943. Despite bad weather, the Allied troops made it ashore with few casualties. A new amphibious truck delivered supplies and artillery to the soldiers on the beach.

Eight days after the troops came ashore, American tanks smashed through enemy lines and captured the western half of the island. Patton's troops then headed east, while the British attacked from the south. By August 18, the Germans had evacuated the island.

Teach

R Reading Strategy

Identifying Ask: Why did the Allies decide to attack Italy first? *(They thought the Italians would surrender more quickly than the Germans.)* How long did it take Allied troops to take over Sicily? *(about 1 month)* **OL**

Did You Know?

Leaflets signed by Roosevelt and Churchill were dropped onto Rome from Allied planes on June 7, 1943. They read, "The time has come for you, the Italian people, to decide whether Italians should die for Mussolini and Hitler—or live for Italy and civilization."

Analyzing GEOGRAPHY

Answers:
1. the Netherlands
2. Casablanca, El Alamein

Differentiated Instruction

Leveled Activities

BL Reteaching Activity, URB p. 77

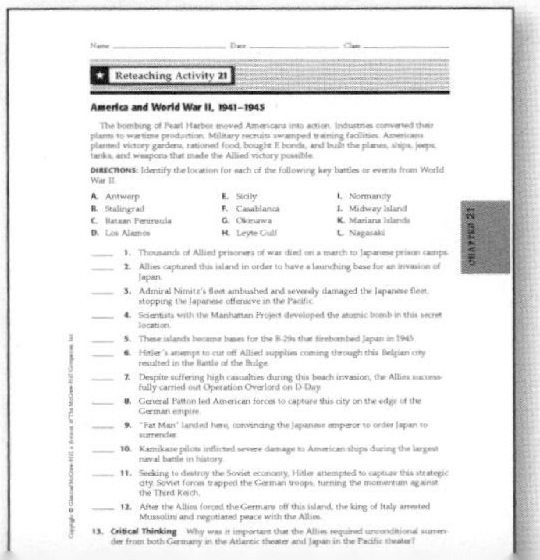

OL Primary Source Reading, URB pp. 67–72

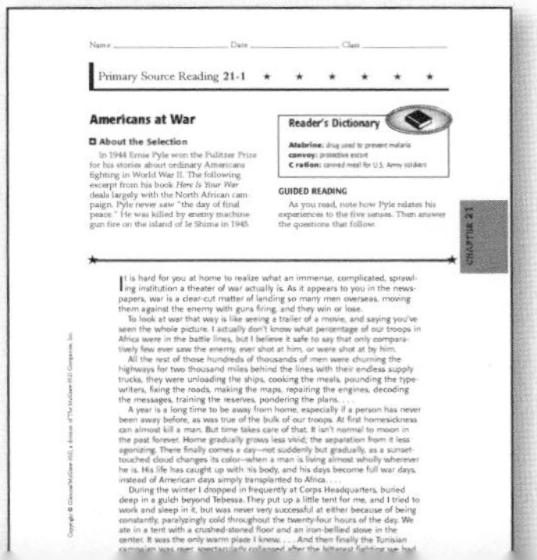

AL Interpreting Political Cartoons, URB pp. 75–76

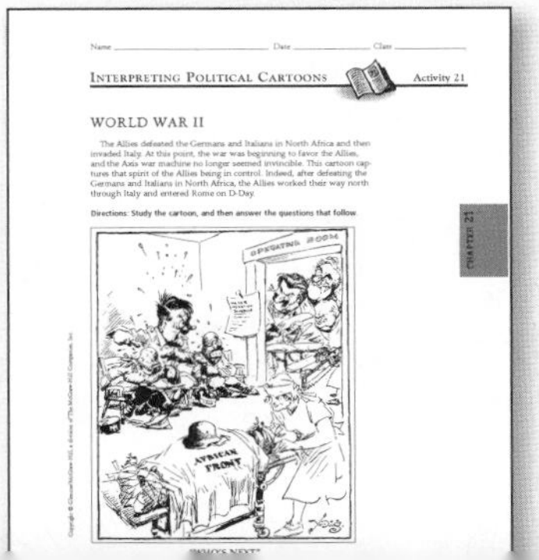

ELL Time Line Activity, URB p. 67

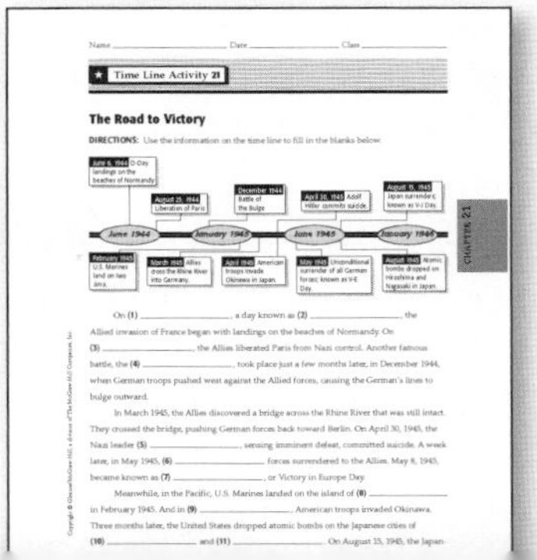

C Critical Thinking

Predicting Consequences
Remind students that Russia and the United States had different political and economic structures. Ask students to speculate on what kind of differences would arise after the war, regardless of promises. **OL**

R Reading Strategy

Determining Importance
Have students explain the significance of the promises Stalin made at the Tehran Conference. *(Stalin made two promises to Roosevelt. He promised to aid U.S. forces against Japan after Germany's defeat and to join Roosevelt's proposed peacekeeping organization. These worked to strengthen the relationship between the two countries.)* **OL**

Reading Check

Answer:
It created a crisis; Mussolini was briefly deposed. The Italian government began surrender negotiations, but Germany intervened.

The attack on Sicily created a crisis within the Italian government. The king of Italy, Victor Emmanuel, and a group of Italian generals decided that it was time to depose Mussolini. On July 25, 1943, the king invited the dictator to his palace. "My dear Duce," the king began, "it's no longer any good. Italy has gone to bits. The soldiers don't want to fight anymore. At this moment, you are the most hated man in Italy." The king then arrested Mussolini, and the new Italian government began negotiating a surrender to the Allies.

Following Italy's surrender, however, German troops seized control of northern Italy, including Rome, and returned Mussolini to power. The Germans then took up positions near the heavily fortified town of Cassino. The terrain near Cassino was steep, barren, and rocky. Rather than attack such difficult terrain, the Allies landed at Anzio, behind German lines. Instead of retreating, however, as the Allies had hoped, the Germans surrounded the Allied troops near Anzio.

It took the Allies five months to break through the German lines at Cassino and Anzio. Finally, in late May 1944, the Germans retreated. Less than two weeks later, the Allies captured Rome. Fighting in Italy continued, however, for another year. The Italian campaign was one of the bloodiest in the war, with more than 300,000 Allied casualties.

The Tehran Conference

Roosevelt wanted to meet with Stalin before the Allies invaded France. In late 1943, Stalin agreed, proposing that Roosevelt and Churchill meet him in Tehran, Iran.

The leaders reached several agreements. Stalin promised to launch a full-scale offensive against the Germans when the Allies invaded France in 1944. Roosevelt and Stalin then agreed to divide Germany after the war so that it would never again threaten world peace. **C** Stalin promised that once Germany was defeated, the Soviet Union would help the United States against Japan. He also accepted Roosevelt's proposal of an international peacekeeping organization after the war. **R**

Reading Check **Explaining** What effect did the Allied victory in Sicily have on Italy?

Driving Back the Germans, 1943–1944

January 1943
The British and American air forces begin massive strategic bombing of German industry and infrastructure

November 28, 1943
Stalin, Roosevelt, and Churchill meet at the Tehran Conference

Jan. 1943 | March 1943 | July 1943 | Dec. 1943

July 10, 1943
Patton and Montgomery land forces on Sicily, beginning the invasion of Italy

July 25, 1943
The king of Italy puts Mussolini under arrest and the new Italian government negotiates surrender with the Allies

December 4–6, 1943
Roosevelt and Churchill meet in Cairo to plan D-Day. Roosevelt selects Eisenhower to command the invasion

Hands-On Chapter Project Step 4

An Interview with a World War II Veteran

Step 4: Burning the CD/DVD **Essential Question:** What is the essential core of the interview to be preserved and what introduction and conclusion needs to be added to it?

Directions Students will probably need to edit the material for the final product. They will also want to collectively write an introduction and conclusion for the final product. The tasks involved can be divided among the students according to their interests and skills. Then students should do a final edit on the interview by asking themselves:

- Did I give a good introduction?
- Are the questions and answers clear to my audience?
- What conclusions should be drawn from the information given?
- Did I close the interview with a summary or closing statement?

Putting It Together The teams can meet to burn the final version onto a CD. Students can review each other's work to create a final, polished product. **OL**

(Chapter Project continued on page 748)

Landing in France

MAIN Idea The Allies landed a massive force on France's beaches on June 6, 1944, known as D-Day.

HISTORY AND YOU What has been the biggest surprise you ever planned? Read on to find out how the Allies made a surprise landing in France.

After the conference in Tehran, Roosevelt headed to Cairo, Egypt, where he and Churchill continued planning the invasion of France. One major decision still had to be made. The president had to choose the commander for Operation Overlord—the code name for the invasion. Roosevelt selected General Eisenhower.

Planning Operation Overlord

Hitler had fortified the French coast along the English Channel, but he did not know when or where the Allies would land. The Germans believed the landing would be in Pas-de-Calais—the area of France closest to Britain. The Allies encouraged this belief by placing dummy equipment along the coast across from Calais. The real target was further south, a 60-mile stretch of five beaches along the Normandy coast.

Planners also discussed who should lead France after the invasion. General Eisenhower had informed Charles de Gaulle that the French Resistance forces would assist in the liberation of Paris, but President Roosevelt was not sure he trusted de Gaulle and refused to recognize him as the official French leader.

By the spring of 1944, more than 1.5 million American soldiers, 12,000 airplanes, and 5 million tons (4.6 million t) of equipment had been sent to England. Only setting the invasion date and giving the command to go remained. The invasion had to begin at night to hide the ships crossing the English Channel. The ships had to arrive at low tide so that they could see the beach obstacles. The low tide had to come at dawn so that gunners bombarding the coast could see their targets. Paratroopers, who would be dropped behind enemy lines, needed a moonlit night to see where to land. Perhaps most important of all, was good weather. A storm would ground the airplanes, and high waves would swamp landing craft.

March 4, 1944
The Allies make their first major daylight bombing raid on Berlin

June 6, 1944
Over 130,000 American, British, and Canadian troops land in Normandy on D-Day, beginning the liberation of France

Jan. 1944 — **June 1944**

January 1944
American forces attack Monte Cassino and land at Anzio in an attempt to break through German lines and capture Rome

Analyzing TIME LINES

1. **Identifying** On what date did Allied forces land at Normandy to begin liberating France, and what is the date known as?
2. **Determining Cause and Effect** What effect did the successful Allied invasion of Sicily have on politics in Italy?

S Skill Practice

Using Geography Skills Have students locate the coast of Normandy on a map. **Ask:** Why did the Allies choose to land at Normandy rather than at Pas-de-Calais? *(Students may note the element of surprise, the geography of the beaches, and so on.)* **OL**

R Reading Strategy

Listing Have students create two columns: *conditions* and *reasons*. Have students list the conditions required for the invasion and why they were required. *(begin at night—to conceal ships; low tide—to see obstacles; moonlit night—paratroopers could see where to land; good weather—bad weather could ground airplanes and high waves would swamp landing craft.)* **OL**

Analyzing TIME LINES

Answers:
1. June 6, 1944; D-Day
2. Mussolini was arrested, and a new government negotiated with the Allies.

Additional Support

Activity: Technology Connection

Creating a Radio Broadcast Have students work in small groups to prepare a radio broadcast of the D-Day invasion. Remind students that the operation was secretive, so the landing would have been quite a shock. Tell students they can broadcast from the point of view of an Allied radio station or an Axis one. Make sure students include some synthesis of the event. The broadcaster should describe what the invasion means for their side. Students may add music or sound effects, if they choose. Have students enact or perform their broadcasts in class. **OL**

C Critical Thinking

Making Decisions Eisenhower had a difficult decision to make: Should he launch D-Day on June 6 or wait another month? Have students work in pairs and make two lists of reasons: one that supports the launch and the other to postpone it. Ask students what advice they would give Eisenhower if they were on his advisory committee. **OL**

D Differentiated Instruction

Visual/Spatial Have students research and create a chart that documents the number of ships, troops, and aircraft used at each of the five beaches. Have them include number of casualties as well. **OL**

Reading Check

Answer:
The invasion had to begin at night; the ships had to arrive at low tide; and the weather had to be relatively good.

Additional Support

Given all these requirements, there were only a few days each month to begin the invasion. The first opportunity was from June 5 to 7, 1944. Eisenhower's planning staff referred to the day any operation began by the letter *D*. The invasion date, therefore, came to be known as **D-Day.** Heavy cloud cover, strong winds, **C** and high waves made landing on June 5 impossible. The weather was forecast to improve **briefly** a day later. The Channel would still be rough, but the landing ships and aircraft could operate. After looking at forecasts one last time, shortly after midnight on June 6, 1944, Eisenhower gave the final order: "OK, we'll go."

The Longest Day

Nearly 7,000 ships carrying more than 100,000 soldiers headed for Normandy's coast. At the same time, 23,000 paratroopers were dropped inland, east and west of the beaches. **D** Allied fighter-bombers raced up and down the coast, hitting bridges, bunkers, and radar sites. At dawn, Allied warships began a tremendous barrage. Thousands of shells rained down on the beaches, code-named "Utah," "Omaha," "Gold," "Sword," and "Juno."

The American landing at Utah Beach went well. The German defenses were weak, and in less than three hours the troops had captured the beach and moved inland, suffering fewer than 200 casualties. On the eastern flank, the British and Canadian landings also went well. By the end of the day, British and Canadian forces were several miles inland. Omaha Beach, however, was a different story. Under **intense** German fire, the American assault almost disintegrated. Lieutenant John Bentz Carroll was in the first wave that went ashore:

PRIMARY SOURCE

"Two hundred yards out, we took a direct hit. . . . Somehow or other, the ramp door opened up . . . and the men in front were being struck by machine-gun fire. Everyone started to jump off into the water. . . . The tide was moving us so rapidly. . . . We would grab out on some of those underwater obstructions and mines built on telephone poles and girders, and hang on. We'd take cover, then make a dash through the surf to the next one, fifty feet beyond."

—from *D-Day: Piercing the Atlantic Wall*

General **Omar Bradley,** commander of the American forces landing at Omaha and Utah, began making plans to evacuate. Slowly, however, the American troops began to knock out the German defenses. More landing craft arrived, ramming their way through the obstacles to get to the beach. Nearly 2,500 Americans were either killed or wounded on Omaha, but by early afternoon, Bradley received this message: "Troops formerly pinned down on beaches . . . [are] advancing up heights behind beaches." By the end of the day, nearly 35,000 American troops had landed at Omaha, and another 23,000 had landed at Utah. More than 75,000 British and Canadian troops were on shore as well. The invasion—the largest amphibious operation in history—had succeeded.

Reading Check **Summarizing** What conditions had to be met before Eisenhower could order D-Day to begin?

PRIMARY SOURCE

The United States began island-hopping across the Pacific with the Battle of Tarawa in November 1943. Reporter Robert Sherrod witnessed the savage hand-to-hand fighting:

"A Marine jumped over the seawall and began throwing blocks of fused TNT into a coconut-log pillbox. . . . Two more Marines scaled the seawall, one of them carrying a twin-cylindered tank strapped to their shoulders, the other holding the nozzle of the flame thrower. As another charge of TNT boomed inside the pillbox, causing smoke and dust to billow out, a khaki-clad figure ran out the side entrance. The flame thrower, waiting for him, caught him in its withering stream of intense fire. As soon as it touched him, the [Japanese soldier] flared up like a piece of celluloid. He was dead instantly . . . charred almost to nothingness."

—from *Tarawa: The Story of a Battle*

Activity: Interdisciplinary Connection

Art Storming the Normandy beaches was no small feat. Troops on the ground and in the air had to be prepared. They were going to be exposed to enemy attack on open beachheads. Many soldiers were laden with 70 pounds of gear and had to jump in neck-deep water. **Ask:** **What was the typical D-Day soldier carrying when he landed in Normandy?** Have students use the Internet and library resources to find the answer to this question. Have students sketch the typical battle gear of the Allied soldiers during the D-Day invasion. Have students write paragraphs to accompany each sketch that describes each item and how they were used during the invasion. Display students' work in class. **BL**

Driving Japan Back

MAIN Idea American troops slowly regained islands in the Pacific that the Japanese had captured.

HISTORY AND YOU Have you ever had to do a project over? Read to learn about American forces that took back Pacific islands from the Japanese.

While the buildup for invading France was taking place in Britain, American military leaders were also developing a strategy to defeat Japan. **R** The American plan called for a two-pronged attack. The Pacific Fleet, commanded by Admiral Nimitz, would advance through the central Pacific by "hopping" from one island to the next, closer and closer to Japan. Meanwhile, General MacArthur's troops would advance through the Solomon Islands, capture the north coast of New Guinea, and then launch an invasion to retake the Philippines.

Island-Hopping in the Pacific

By the fall of 1943, the navy was ready to launch its island-hopping campaign, but the geography of the central Pacific posed a problem. Many of the islands were coral reef atolls. **D** The water over the coral reef was not always deep enough to allow landing craft to get to the shore. If the landing craft ran aground on the reef, the troops would have to wade to the beach. As some 5,000 United States Marines learned at Tarawa Atoll, wading ashore could cause very high casualties. Tarawa, part of the Gilbert Islands, was the navy's first objective. The Japanese base there had to be captured in order to put air bases in the nearby Marshall Islands.

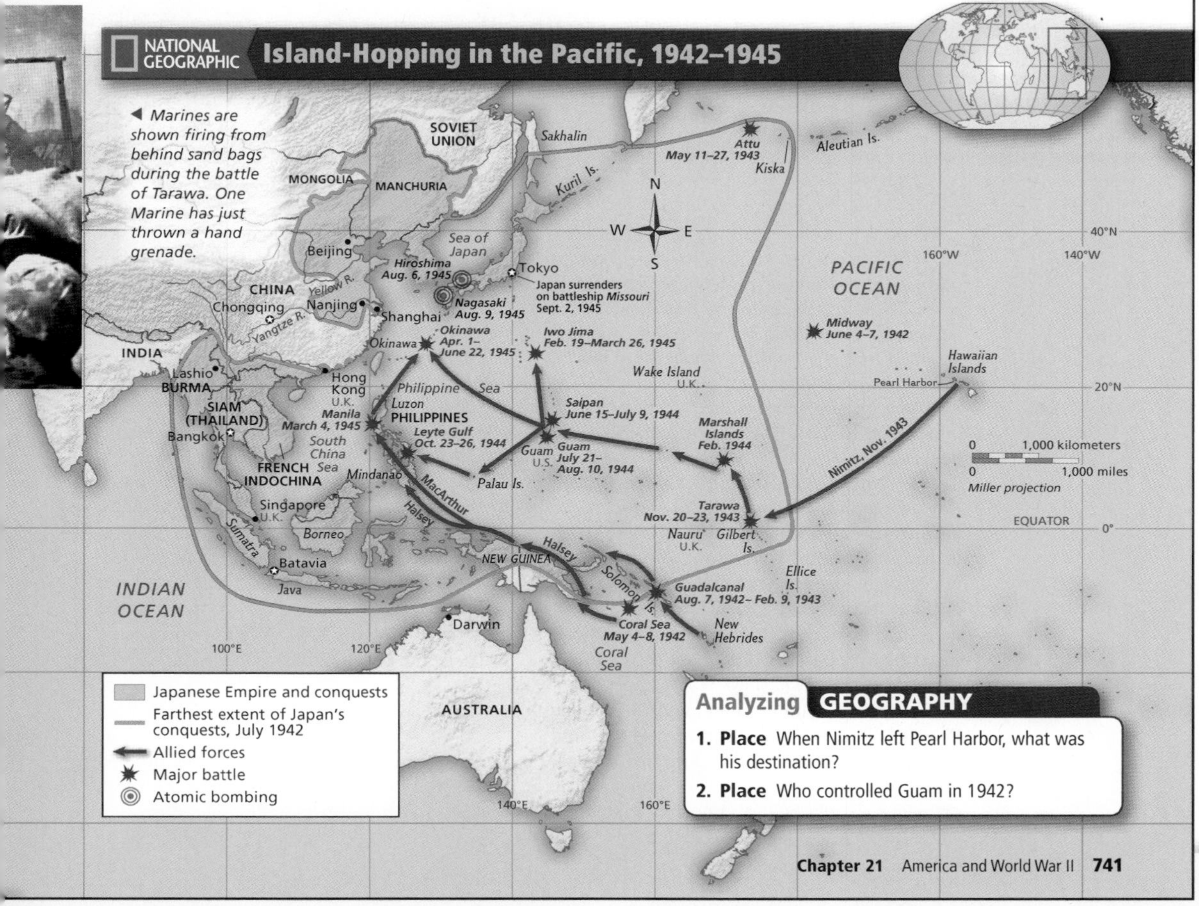

Analyzing GEOGRAPHY

1. **Place** When Nimitz left Pearl Harbor, what was his destination?
2. **Place** Who controlled Guam in 1942?

R Reading Strategy

Explaining Ask: What was the purpose of "island-hopping" in the Pacific? *(to take over islands in the Pacific, one at a time, in order to establish bases as close as possible to Japan)* **BL**

D Differentiated Instruction

Visual/Spatial Have students find photos of coral reef atolls or draw them. Have them explain why these reefs proved difficult for armed forces. **OL**

Analyzing GEOGRAPHY

Answers:

1. Tarawa, part of the Gilbert Islands
2. the Japanese

Additional Support

Activity: Collaborative Learning

Summarizing Have partners create a map similar to the one on page 513. Assign pairs major battles in the Pacific. **Ask:** Was there a change in control of an island in the battle you have been assigned during the war? Have each pair discuss their battle and use their maps to show military movement and changes. They may also include a drawing that depicts the battle on their island. After students have finished their maps, make a class list that summarizes the changes on the Pacific islands during the course of the war. **OL**

C Critical Thinking

Making Inferences Ask: After receiving the shocking news about Tarawa, why were so many Americans willing to continue to support a war that had such negative consequences? *(Student answers will vary. Have them think about the political and social issues during World War II to help them develop an answer.)* **AL**

R Reading Strategy

Determining Importance
Ask: Why was securing the Mariana Islands so important to the military? *(The islands were close enough to Japan to allow bomber runs. They wanted to build airstrips on these islands.)* **BL**

People IN HISTORY

Answer:
They could send and receive sensitive information easily and quickly without having it decoded by the enemy.

People IN HISTORY

The Navajo Code Talkers

When American marines stormed an enemy beach, they used radios to communicate. Using radios, however, meant that the Japanese could intercept and translate the messages. In the midst of the battle, however, there was no time to use a code-machine. Acting upon the suggestion of Philip Johnston, an engineer who had lived on a Navajo reservation as a child, the marines recruited Navajos to serve as "code talkers."

The Navajo language had no written alphabet and was known only to the Navajo and a few missionaries and anthropologists. The Navajo recruits developed code words, using their own language, that stood for military terms. For example, the Navajo word *jay-sho*, or "buzzard," was code for *bomber; lotso*, or "whale," meant *battleship;* and *na-ma-si*, or "potatoes," stood for *grenades.*

Code talkers proved invaluable in combat. They could relay a message in minutes that would have taken a code-machine operator hours to encipher and transmit. At the battle of Iwo Jima, code talkers transmitted more than 800 messages during the first 48 hours as the marines struggled to get ashore under intense bombardment. More than 400 Navajo served in the marine corps as code talkers. Sworn to secrecy, their mission was not revealed until 1971. In 2001 Congress awarded the code talkers the Congressional Gold Medal for their unique contribution during the war.

What advantage did the code talkers provide over traditional forms of communication?

▲ *These Navajo code talkers assigned to a Pacific-based marine regiment relay orders using a field radio.*

When the landing craft hit the reef, at least 20 ships ran aground. The marines had to plunge into shoulder-high water and wade several hundred yards to the beach. Raked by Japanese fire, only one marine in three made it ashore. Once the marines reached the beach, the battle was still far from over.

Although many troops died wading ashore, one vehicle had been able to cross the reef and deliver its troops onto the beaches. The vehicle was a boat with tank tracks, nicknamed the "Alligator." This amphibious tractor, or **amphtrac,** had been invented in the late 1930s to rescue people in Florida swamps. It had never been used in combat, and the navy decided to buy only 200 of them in 1941. If more had been available at Tarawa, American casualties probably would have been much lower.

C More than 1,000 marines died on Tarawa. Photos of bodies lying crumpled next to burning landing craft shocked Americans back home. Many people began to wonder how many lives would be lost in defeating Japan.

The next assault—Kwajalein Atoll in the Marshall Islands—went much more smoothly. This time all of the troops went ashore in amphtracs. Although the Japanese resisted fiercely, the marines captured Kwajalein and nearby Eniwetok with far fewer casualties.

After the Marshall Islands, the navy targeted the Mariana Islands. American military planners wanted to use the Marianas as a base for a new heavy bomber, the B-29 Superfortress. The B-29 could fly farther than any other plane in the world. From airfields in the Marianas, B-29s could bomb Japan. Admiral Nimitz R decided to invade three of the Mariana Islands: Saipan, Tinian, and Guam. Despite strong Japanese resistance, American troops captured all three by August 1944. A few months later, B-29s began bombing Japan.

MacArthur Returns

As the forces under Admiral Nimitz hopped across the central Pacific, General Douglas MacArthur's troops began their own campaign

Additional Support

Activity: Interdisciplinary Connection

Art and Literature Ask: Why was Douglas MacArthur so important to the war effort? Have students draw a picture of MacArthur, with his famed corncob pipe. Students may either write a brief biography of his life or a poem about him, describing why he is admired and considered a great leader. Have students use library or Internet sources to learn more about his views concerning the use of atomic weapons, as well. **BL**

in the southwest Pacific. The campaign began by invading **Guadalcanal** in the Solomon Islands, east of New Guinea, in August 1942. It continued until early 1944, when MacArthur's troops finally captured enough islands to surround the main Japanese base in the region. In response, the Japanese withdrew their ships and aircraft from the base, although they left 100,000 troops behind to hold the island.

Worried that the navy's advance across the central Pacific was leaving him behind, MacArthur ordered his forces to leap nearly 600 miles (966 km) to capture the Japanese base at Hollandia on the north coast of New Guinea. Shortly after securing New Guinea, MacArthur's troops seized the island of Morotai—the last stop before the Philippines.

To take back the Philippines, the United States assembled an enormous invasion force. In October 1944, more than 700 ships carrying more than 160,000 troops sailed for Leyte Gulf in the Philippines. On October 20, the troops began to land on Leyte, an island on the eastern side of the Philippines. A few hours after the invasion began, MacArthur headed to the beach. Upon reaching the shore, he strode to a radio and spoke into the microphone: "People of the Philippines, I have returned. By the grace of Almighty God, our forces stand again on Philippine soil."

To stop the American invasion, the Japanese sent four aircraft carriers toward the Philippines from the north and secretly dispatched another fleet to the west. Believing the Japanese carriers were leading the main attack, most of the American carriers protecting the invasion left Leyte Gulf and headed north to stop them. Seizing their chance, the Japanese warships to the west raced through the Philippine Islands into Leyte Gulf and ambushed the remaining American ships.

W The Battle of Leyte Gulf was the largest naval battle in history. It was also the first time that the Japanese used **kamikaze** attacks. *Kamikaze* means "divine wind" in Japanese. It refers to the great storm that destroyed the Mongol fleet during its invasion of Japan in the thirteenth century. Kamikaze pilots would deliberately crash their planes into American ships, killing themselves but also inflicting severe damage. Luckily for the Americans, just as their situation was becoming desperate, the Japanese commander, believing more American ships were on the way, ordered a retreat.

Although the Japanese fleet had retreated, the campaign to recapture the Philippines from the Japanese was long and grueling. More than 80,000 Japanese were killed; fewer than 1,000 surrendered. MacArthur's troops did not capture Manila until March 1945. The battle left the city in ruins and more than 100,000 Filipino civilians dead. The remaining Japanese retreated into the rugged terrain north of Manila; they were still fighting in August 1945 when word came that Japan had surrendered.

Reading Check **Describing** What strategy did the United States Navy use to advance across the Pacific?

Section 4 REVIEW

Vocabulary

1. **Explain** the significance of: Casablanca Conference, D-Day, Omar Bradley, amphtrac, Guadalcanal, kamikaze.

Main Ideas

2. **Determining Cause and Effect** What event prompted Italy to surrender?
3. **Describing** Why was D-Day's success so vital to an Allied victory?
4. **Summarizing** What was the military goal in the Pacific?

Critical Thinking

5. **Big Ideas** How did the geography of the Pacific affect American strategy?
6. **Organizing** Use a graphic organizer like the one below to explain the importance of each leader listed in the text.

Leader	Significance
Dwight Eisenhower	
George Patton	
George Marshall	
Omar Bradley	
Douglas MacArthur	

7. **Analyzing Visuals** Look at the photo on page 739 of the D-Day landing. What do you observe about the manner of the landing?

Writing About History

8. **Persuasive Writing** Imagine that you are living in Florida and see the potential for the amphtrac in the war. Write a letter to a member of Congress detailing reasons why it would be a good purchase for the marines.

History ONLINE
Study Central™ To review this section, go to glencoe.com and click on Study Central.

W Writing Support

Descriptive Writing Have students research Kamikaze pilots. Then have students write a poem that compares the pilots to the storm. **OL**

Reading Check

Answer:
island-hopping

Assess

History ONLINE

Study Central™ provides summaries, interactive games, and online graphic organizers to help students review content.

Close

Summarizing Have groups create five posters that describe five important events that happened between 1941–1945. Students should note how the events affected U.S. and foreign policy. **OL**

Section 4 REVIEW

Answers

1. All definitions can be found in the section and in the Glossary.
2. the successful Allied invasion of Sicily
3. It would force the Germans to fight on two fronts.
4. to move from island to island, recapturing islands that had earlier been lost to the Japanese, to stop the Japanese offensive, and to slowly advance toward Japan
5. Coral reefs around the atolls made it difficult for landing craft to land. They began using amphtracs to land soldiers.
6.

Leader	Significance
Dwight Eisenhower	commanded invasion of Italy and D-Day operations
George Patton	led ground forces in Africa and Italy
George Marshall	planned Operation Overlord
Omar Bradley	commander at Omaha and Utah beaches
Douglas MacArthur	took back the Philippines from the Japanese

7. It looks as though a lot of men had to be landed quickly. For such a large operation, it had to be orchestrated very precisely.
8. Letters will vary but should be persuasive in nature.

GEOGRAPHY & HISTORY

Focus

Highlight for students the incredible drama and significance of D-Day, June 6, 1944. Tell them that the Russians had been pressing their American and British allies for a second front since 1942.

Teach

S Skill Practice

Using Geography Skills Have students study the geography of western Europe. Discuss with students why a seaborne attack on western Europe was so difficult and how the Nazis used geography as a defense. **AL**

Analyzing GEOGRAPHY

Answers:

1. firm, flat beaches within range of Allied planes and enough roads and paths to move troops.
2. cliffs and bluff overlooking the beach gave the Germans great defense advantages

Additional Support

NATIONAL GEOGRAPHIC

GEOGRAPHY & HISTORY

The Battle for Omaha Beach

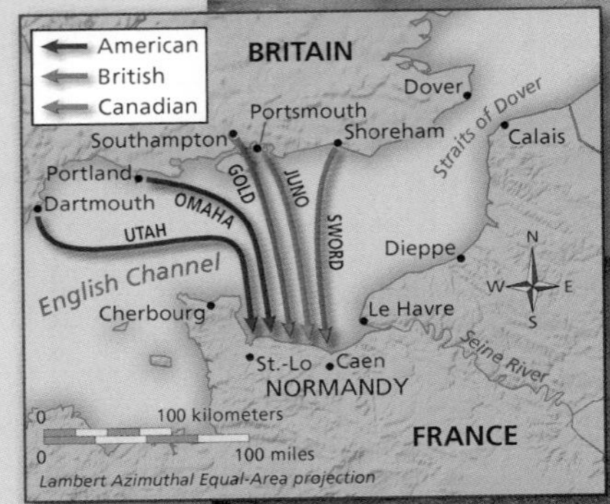

The selection of a site for the largest amphibious landing in history was one of the biggest decisions of World War II. Allied planners considered coastlines from Denmark to Portugal in search of a sheltered location with firm flat beaches within range of friendly fighter planes in England. There also had to be enough roads and paths to move jeeps and trucks off the beaches and to accommodate the hundreds of thousands of American, Canadian, and British troops set to stream ashore following the invasion. An airfield and a seaport that the Allies could use were also needed. Most important was a reasonable expectation of achieving the element of surprise.

How Did Geography Shape the Battle?

Surrounded at both ends by cliffs that rose wall-like from the sea, Omaha Beach was only four miles long. The entire beach was overlooked by a 150-foot high bluff and there were only five ravines leading from the beach to **S** the top of the bluff.

The Germans made full use of the geographic advantage the 150-foot bluff gave them. They dug trenches and built concrete bunkers for machine guns at the top of the cliffs and positioned them to guard the ravines leading to the beach.

Once ashore they had to cross 300 yards of open beach to the base of the bluff.

The men had to jump into the water and wade ashore against a strong tide in water that was nearly over their heads.

Analyzing GEOGRAPHY

1. **Location** Why did the Allies choose Normandy as the invasion site?
2. **Human-Environment Interaction** How did geography make the invasion of Omaha Beach difficult?

Extending the Content

"Ducks" on D-Day Photos of the D-Day landing invariably feature the DUKW, the square-shaped vehicle the Allied troops used to land on Omaha Beach. The nickname "duck" came from soldiers, a take-off from the technical name of DUKW (a code acronym that identified that it was amphibian and had front and rear wheel drive). The DUKW was developed by General Motors to withstand difficult amphibious operations. It was first used in 1943 for the Allied invasion of Sicily.

American troops were carried to Omaha Beach in landing craft. Many of the landing craft came under such intense fire that they opened their front ramp doors early.

C

GEOGRAPHY & HISTORY

C Critical Thinking

Comparing Help students learn more about D-Day by comparing it to other military campaigns or battles. Students might choose a battle or campaign from a historic war—the Revolutionary War, the Civil War, or World War I. Once they have chosen a battle or campaign, have students make a list of points to compare it with D-Day. Students' criteria may include: How important was each battle to each war? How did strategy differ? Were a large number of troops involved? Have students discuss their findings. **OL**

Assess/Close

Summarizing Ask: **What might have happened if the Allies had attacked the Germans from the west sooner than June 1944?** *(Students might suggest that the Allied assault would not have been so massive and may have failed. Others might say that it would have been successful.)*

Additional Support

Extending the Content

Taking Pointe du Hoc Pointe du Hoc was a piece of land held by the Germans that allowed them to observe the Omaha and Utah beaches. With huge cannons in their heavily reinforced bunkers, the Germans could hit either beach with artillery shells. For that reason, the Allies bombarded the Pointe du Hoc bunkers for weeks before D-Day. They ceased fire when 225 men of the 2nd Ranger Battalion were due to land. Navigational problems and tidal currents made them late, and once they scaled the cliffs with ropes and grappling hooks, the Germans were waiting. The fighting was fierce, and the surviving rangers had to fend off further attack once they took the Pointe, but their determined action played a key role in the events of D-Day.

Focus

Bellringer

Daily Focus Transparency 21-5

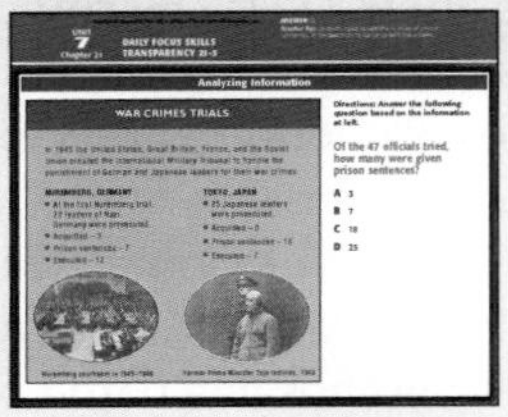

Guide to Reading

Answers:
Students should complete the outline by including all headings in the section.

Section Spotlight Video

To generate student interest and provide a springboard for class discussion, access the Chapter 21, Section 5 video at glencoe.com or on the video DVD.

Section 5 — Section Audio — Spotlight Video

The War Ends

Guide to Reading

Big Ideas
Individual Action After fierce military campaigns, President Harry S. Truman decided to use atomic weapons against Japan.

Content Vocabulary
- hedgerow *(p. 746)*
- napalm *(p. 749)*
- charter *(p. 753)*

Academic Vocabulary
- despite *(p. 748)*
- nuclear *(p. 751)*

People and Events to Identify
- Battle of the Bulge *(p. 746)*
- V-E Day *(p. 747)*
- Harry S. Truman *(p. 748)*
- Iwo Jima *(p. 748)*
- Manhattan Project *(p. 751)*
- V-J Day *(p. 752)*
- United Nations *(p. 752)*
- Nuremberg Trials *(p. 753)*

Reading Strategy
Create an outline of the section, using the major headings as the main points. Follow the structure shown below.

The War Ends
I. The Third Reich Collapses
 A.
 B.
II.
 A.
 B.

Fierce fighting in both Europe and the Pacific during 1945 led to the defeat of the Axis powers. The Allies began war crimes trials and set up a peacekeeping organization to prevent another global war.

The Third Reich Collapses

MAIN Idea The war in Europe ended in spring 1945 after major battles, as the Allies moved west toward Germany.

HISTORY AND YOU Have you ever been in a competition in which you persevered, despite fatigue, to win? Read to learn how the Allies fought in Europe to defeat Germany.

Although D-Day had been a success, it was only the beginning. Surrounding many fields in Normandy were **hedgerows**—dirt walls, several feet thick, covered in shrubbery. The hedgerows had been built to fence in cattle and crops, but they also enabled the Germans to fiercely defend their positions. The battle of the hedgerows ended on July 25, 1944, when 2,500 American bombers blew a hole in the German lines, enabling American tanks to race through the gap.

As the Allies broke out of Normandy, the French Resistance—French civilians who had secretly organized to resist the German occupation of their country—staged a rebellion in Paris. When the Allied forces liberated Paris on August 25, they found the streets filled with French citizens celebrating their victory.

The Battle of the Bulge

As the Allies advanced toward the German border, Hitler decided to stage one last desperate offensive. His goal was to cut off Allied supplies coming through the port of Antwerp, Belgium. The attack began just before dawn on December 16, 1944. Six inches (15 cm) of snow covered the ground, and the weather was bitterly cold. Moving rapidly, the Germans caught the American defenders by surprise. As the German troops raced west, their lines bulged outward, and the attack became known as the **Battle of the Bulge.**

Shortly after the Germans surrounded the Americans, Eisenhower ordered General Patton to rescue them. Three days later, faster than anyone expected in the midst of a snowstorm, Patton's troops slammed into the German lines. As the weather cleared, Allied aircraft began hitting German fuel depots.

On Christmas Eve, out of fuel and weakened by heavy losses, the German troops driving toward Antwerp were forced to halt. Two days later, Patton's troops broke through to the German line. Although

Resource Manager

R Reading Strategies	C Critical Thinking	D Differentiated Instruction	W Writing Support	S Skill Practice
Teacher Edition • Paraphrasing, p. 748 • Identifying, p. 750 **Additional Resources** • English Learner Act., URB p. 59 • Guide. Reading, URB p. 86	**Teacher Edition** • Defending, p. 749 • Contrasting, p. 750 • Evaluating, p. 752 • Speculating, p. 752 **Additional Resources** • Crit. Think. Skills Act., URB p. 66 • Supreme Court Case Studies, p. 61 • Quizzes and Tests, p. 305	**Teacher Edition** • Gifted and Talented, p. 748 • Naturalist, p. 751 **Additional Resources** • Reteach Act., URB p. 77 • Authentic Assess., p. 47 • English Learner Act., URB p. 59	**Teacher Edition** • Expository Writing, p. 747 • Descriptive Writing, p. 749	**Additional Resources** • Read. Essen., p. 244 • Time Line Act., URB p. 67

INFOGRAPHIC

The War Ends in Europe, 1945

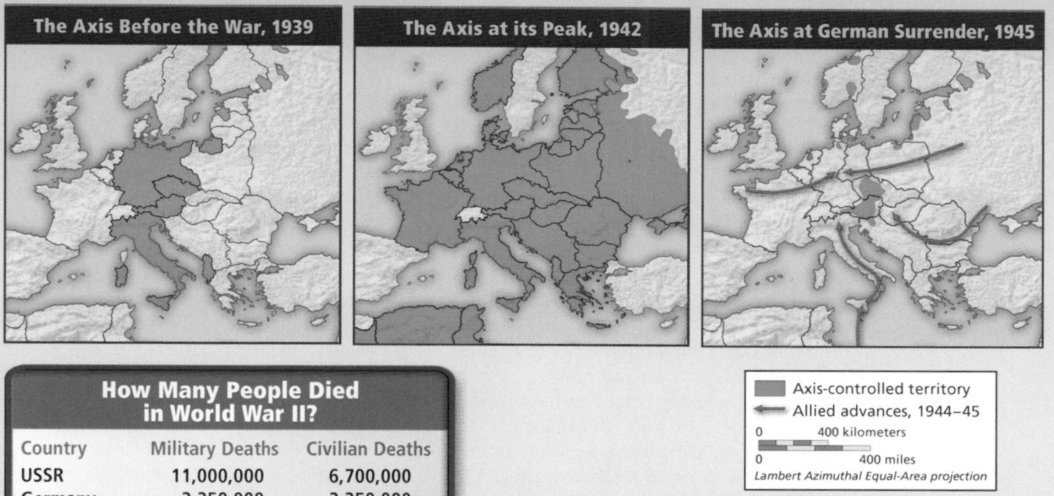

How Many People Died in World War II?

Country	Military Deaths	Civilian Deaths
USSR	11,000,000	6,700,000
Germany	3,250,000	2,350,000
Japan	1,740,000	393,000
China	1,400,000	8,000,000
Poland	110,000	5,300,000
United States	405,000	2,000
Great Britain	306,000	61,000
Italy	227,000	60,000
France	122,000	470,000

Analyzing VISUALS

1. **Comparing** Which nation had the greatest number of civilian casualties?
2. **Analyzing** Why did the United States have so few civilian deaths?

fighting continued for three weeks, the United States had won the Battle of the Bulge. On January 8, the Germans began to withdraw. **W** They had suffered more than 100,000 casualties and lost many tanks and aircraft. They had very few resources left to prevent the Allies from entering Germany.

The War Ends in Europe

While American and British forces fought to liberate France, the Soviets began a massive attack on German troops in Russia. By the time the Battle of the Bulge ended, the Soviets had driven Hitler's forces out of Russia and back across Poland. By February 1945, Soviet troops were only 35 miles (56 km) from Berlin.

As the Soviets crossed Germany's eastern border, American forces attacked Germany's western border. By the end of February 1945, American troops had fought their way to the Rhine River, Germany's last major line of defense in the west. On March 7, American tanks crossed the Rhine.

As German defenses crumbled, American troops raced east to within 70 miles (113 km) of Berlin. On April 16, Soviet troops finally smashed through the German defenses and reached the outskirts of Berlin five days later.

Deep in his Berlin bunker, Adolf Hitler knew the end was near. On April 30, 1945, he committed suicide. Before killing himself, Hitler chose Grand Admiral Karl Doenitz as his successor. Doenitz tried to surrender to the Americans and British while continuing to fight the Soviets, but Eisenhower insisted on unconditional surrender. On May 7, 1945, Germany accepted the terms. The next day—May 8, 1945—was proclaimed **V-E Day,** for "Victory in Europe."

Reading Check **Explaining** Why was the Battle of the Bulge such a disastrous defeat for Germany?

Teach

W Writing Support

Expository Writing Have students research the movements of the Allied and Axis forces at the Battle of the Bulge. Have them write a two-page report. The first page should identify the good and bad strategic moves related to the battle. Encourage students to include a map that shows the movement. The second page will highlight General Patton's contribution. **OL**

Reading Check

Answer:
The Germans lost over 100,000 troops and lost many of their tanks and aircraft. They had little left to keep the Allies out of Germany.

Analyzing VISUALS

Answers:
1. China
2. The war was not fought on U.S. soil.

Additional Support

Extending the Content

German Surrender Germany accepted unconditional surrender on May 7, 1945, at a small schoolhouse in France. In Moscow, gigantic rays of light were projected in the air to celebrate. In the United States, the Washington Monument, the Capitol dome, and the Statue of Liberty were lit the very first time since the bombing of Pearl Harbor. After less than a month in office, President Truman reflected on this triumph when he addressed the nation by saying, "This is a solemn but glorious hour. I only wish FDR had lived to witness this day."

R Reading Strategy

Paraphrasing Ask students to offer their interpretation of Truman's words about President Roosevelt. *(Most students will say that Truman was overwhelmed with grief. It seemed as though nothing was right—everything was out of order. Truman had a great weight (the war) to deal with.)* **OL**

D Differentiated Instruction

Gifted and Talented The Battle of Iwo Jima was a heroic victory. The famous photograph boosted American morale. A monument based on this photo was sculpted and stands in the Arlington National Cemetery. Have students research the photographer, the men in the photograph, and the sculptor and create their own montage that symbolizes the importance of this battle. **AL**

Japan Is Defeated

MAIN Idea The United States decided to end the war with Japan by using napalm and atomic bombs.

HISTORY AND YOU When was the last time you had to make a difficult decision, with no really good choice? Read to learn about the decision President Truman made in 1945.

Unfortunately, President Roosevelt did not live to see the defeat of Germany. On April 12, 1945, while vacationing in Warm Springs, Georgia, he died of a stroke. His vice president, **Harry S. Truman,** became president during this difficult time.

R The next day, Truman told reporters: "Boys, if you ever pray, pray for me now. . . . When they told me yesterday what had happened, I felt like the moon, the stars, and all the planets had fallen on me." **Despite** his feelings, Truman began at once to make decisions about the war. Although Germany surrendered a few weeks later, the war with Japan continued, and Truman was forced to make some of the most difficult decisions of the war during his first six months in office.

The Battle of Iwo Jima

D On November 24, 1944, bombs fell on Tokyo. Above the city flew 80 B-29 Superfortress bombers that had traveled more than 1,500 miles (2,414 km) from new American bases in the Mariana Islands.

At first the B-29s did little damage because they kept missing their targets. By the time the B-29s reached Japan, they did not have enough fuel left to fix their navigational errors or to adjust for high winds. The pilots needed an island closer to Japan so the B-29s could refuel. American military planners decided to invade **Iwo Jima.**

Iwo Jima was perfectly located, roughly halfway between the Marianas and Japan, but its geography was formidable. At its southern tip was a dormant volcano. The terrain was rugged, with rocky cliffs, jagged ravines, and

Winning the War Against Japan, 1944–1945

March 9, 1945 Firebombing destroys most of Tokyo

April 1, 1945 American troops land on Okinawa

Feb. 1945 — April 1945 — June 1945

October 23–24, 1944 Victory in the Battle of Leyte Gulf enables MacArthur to return to the Philippines

February 19, 1945 U.S. Marines land on Iwo Jima; over 6,800 marines are killed before the island is captured

Hands-On Chapter Project Step 5

An Interview with a World War II Veteran

Step 5: Presenting the Interview
Essential Question: How should the interview be presented?

Directions Students will determine the final format of the interview presentation. For example, should it be a video presented to the class? Should it be part of a large Web page or presentation? Students should integrate the interview into the final presentation. Set class time aside for students to present their interviews. Students may also present it to a community group and, certainly, to the veteran who was the subject.

Putting It Together Presenters should be prepared for follow-up questions from their audience. They should be sure that they have researched the topics covered in the interview and are familiar with those mentioned by the subject. **OL**

(Chapter Project continued on the Visual Summary page)

dozens of caves. Volcanic ash covered the ground. Even worse, the Japanese had built a vast network of concrete bunkers connected by miles of tunnels.

On February 19, 1945, some 60,000 Marines landed on Iwo Jima. As the troops leapt from the amphtracs, they sank up to their ankles in the soft ash. Meanwhile, Japanese artillery began to pound the invaders.

W The marines crawled inland, using flamethrowers and explosives to attack the Japanese bunkers. More than 6,800 marines were killed capturing the island. Admiral Nimitz later wrote that, on Iwo Jima, "uncommon valor was a common virtue."

Firebombing Japan

C While American engineers prepared airfields on Iwo Jima, General Curtis LeMay, commander of the B-29s based in the Marianas, decided to change strategy. To help the B-29s hit their targets, he ordered them to drop bombs filled with **napalm**—a kind of jellied gasoline. The bombs were designed not only to explode but also to start fires. Even if the B-29s missed their targets, the fires they started would spread to the intended targets.

The use of firebombs was very controversial because the fires would also kill civilians; however, LeMay could think of no other way to destroy Japan's war production quickly. Loaded with firebombs, B-29s attacked Tokyo on March 9, 1945. As strong winds fanned the flames, the firestorm grew so intense that it sucked the oxygen out of the air, asphyxiating thousands. As one survivor later recalled:

PRIMARY SOURCE

"The fires were incredible . . . with flames leaping hundreds of feet into the air. . . . With every passing moment the air became more foul. . . the noise was a continuing crashing roar. . . . Fire-winds filled with burning particles rushed up and down the streets. I watched people . . . running for their lives. . . . The flames raced after them like living things, striking them down. . . . Wherever I turned my eyes, I saw people . . . seeking air to breathe."

—quoted in *New History of World War II*

August 9, 1945
A second atomic bomb is dropped on Japan, destroying the city of Nagasaki

September 2, 1945
The Japanese delegation boards the battleship USS *Missouri* in Tokyo Bay for the official surrender ceremony

August 1945

August 6, 1945
An atomic bomb destroys the Japanese city of Hiroshima

Analyzing TIME LINES

1. **Listing** When was Tokyo destroyed?
2. **Sequencing** How many days lapsed between the dropping of the first and second atomic bombs?

W Writing Support

Descriptive Writing Have students use the details from the text and what they have seen in the movies to write a description of the landing at Iwo Jima from a news reporter's point of view. Allow students to work in groups. **OL**

C Critical Thinking

Defending The military started using weapons that were designed to destroy more than military targets. Civilians would be killed. Using napalm was controversial, both in World War II and Vietnam. Have a student read the Primary Source aloud. Then, lead a discussion about the use of such weapons. Write major ideas on the board. **OL**

Analyzing TIME LINES

Answers:
1. March 9, 1945
2. three days

Additional Support

Activity: Interdisciplinary Connection

Science The B-29s that attacked Tokyo dropped almost 2,000 tons of incendiaries. Large portions of the city were destroyed and nearly 100,000 civilians died. Since many residential areas were constructed from wood, the fires spread quickly. The air filled with lethal gases, superheating the atmosphere, and the firestorm that occurred was like a hurricane of fire. Ten square miles of Tokyo was completely destroyed. Have students write a report that describes the physics behind this phenomenon. Encourage students to use a visual graphic. **AL**

R Reading Strategy

Identifying Ask: How long did it take to capture Okinawa? *(almost three months)* Why was the fighting difficult? *(the terrain was rugged, Japanese troops hid in caves and bunkers)* **BL**

C Critical Thinking

Contrasting Ask: What were the American terms for surrender in Japan? *(an unconditional surrender)* What condition did the Japanese request in exchange for surrender? *(to allow the emperor to stay in power)* Why did Truman reject this condition? *(Most Americans blamed the emperor for the war and wanted him removed from power.)* **OL**

Additional Support

The Tokyo firebombing killed more than 80,000 people and destroyed more than 250,000 buildings. By the end of June 1945, Japan's six most important industrial cities had been firebombed, destroying almost half of their total urban area. By the end of the war, the B-29s had firebombed 67 Japanese cities.

The Invasion of Okinawa

Despite the massive damage the firebombing caused, there were few signs in the spring of 1945 that Japan was ready to quit. Many American officials believed the Japanese would not surrender until Japan had been invaded. To prepare for the invasion, the United States needed a base near Japan to stockpile supplies and build up troops. Iwo Jima was small and still too far away. Military planners chose Okinawa—only 350 miles (563 km) from Japan.

R American troops landed on Okinawa on April 1, 1945. Instead of defending the beaches, the Japanese troops took up positions in the island's rugged mountains. To dig the Japanese out of their caves and bunkers, the Americans had to fight their way up steep slopes against constant machine gun and artillery fire. More than 12,000 American soldiers, sailors, and marines died during the fighting, but by June 22, 1945, Okinawa had finally been captured.

The Terms for Surrender

Shortly after the United States captured Okinawa, the Japanese emperor urged his government to find a way to end the war. The biggest problem was the American demand for unconditional surrender. Many Japanese leaders were willing to surrender, but on one condition: the emperor had to stay in power.

C American officials knew that the fate of the emperor was the most important issue for the Japanese. Most Americans, however, blamed the emperor for the war and wanted him removed from power. President Truman was reluctant to go against public opinion. Furthermore, he knew the United States was almost ready to test a new weapon that might force Japan to surrender without any conditions. The new weapon was the atomic bomb.

The Manhattan Project

In 1939 Leo Szilard, a Jewish physicist who had fled Nazi persecution, learned that the Germans had split the uranium atom. Szilard had been the first scientist to suggest that splitting the atom might release enormous energy. Worried that the Nazis were working on an atomic bomb, Szilard convinced the world's best-known physicist, Albert Einstein, to sign a letter Szilard had drafted and send it to President Roosevelt. In the letter, Einstein warned that by using uranium, "extremely powerful bombs of a new type may . . . be constructed."

Roosevelt responded by setting up a scientific committee to study the issue. The committee remained skeptical until 1941, when they met with British scientists who were already working on an atomic bomb. The British research so impressed the Americans that they

Debates IN HISTORY

Should America Drop the Atomic Bomb on Japan?

More than 60 years later, people continue to debate what some historians have called the most important event of the twentieth century—President Truman's order to drop atomic bombs on Japan. Did his momentous decision shorten the war and save American lives, as Truman contended, or was it a barbaric and unnecessary show of superior military technology designed to keep the Soviet Union out of Japan?

Extending the Content

The Bombing of Hiroshima Historians continue this debate, more than 60 years after the bombing. Some historians say the bombing was avoidable and find its use similar to Nazi war crimes. Their argument is that the U.S. could have used blockades, conventional bombing, and waited for the Soviet Union to declare war on the Japanese to force the Japanese to surrender.

On the other side, historians feel that the use of the bomb was a necessary choice. They claim that if the Americans had to invade Japan, the number of American casualties would have been higher than those who died at Hiroshima. Another argument was that the second bomb wasn't necessary. Truman should have waited a few days longer to allow the Japanese to surrender.

convinced Roosevelt to begin a program to build an atomic bomb.

The secret American program to build an atomic bomb was code-named the **Manhattan Project** and was headed by General Leslie R. Groves. The first breakthrough came in 1942, when Szilard and Enrico Fermi, another physicist, built the world's first **nuclear** reactor at the University of Chicago. Groves then organized a team of engineers and scientists to build an atomic bomb at a secret laboratory in Los Alamos, New Mexico. J. Robert **D** Oppenheimer led the team. On July 16, 1945, they detonated the world's first atomic bomb in New Mexico.

Hiroshima and Nagasaki

Even before the bomb was tested, American officials began debating how to use it. Admiral William Leahy, chairman of the Joint Chiefs of Staff, opposed using the bomb because it killed civilians indiscriminately. He believed an economic blockade and conventional bombing would convince Japan to surrender. Secretary of War Henry Stimson wanted to warn the Japanese about the bomb while at the same time telling them that they could keep the emperor if they surrendered. Secretary of State James Byrnes, however, wanted to drop the bomb without any warning to shock Japan into surrendering.

President Truman later wrote that he "regarded the bomb as a military weapon and never had any doubts that it should be used." His advisers had warned him to expect massive casualties if the United States invaded Japan. Truman believed it was his duty as president to use every weapon available to save American lives.

YES

Harry S. Truman
President of the United States

PRIMARY SOURCE

"The world will note that the first atomic bomb was dropped on Hiroshima, a military base. . . . If Japan does not surrender, bombs will have to be dropped on her war industries and, unfortunately, thousands of civilian lives will be lost. . . .

Having found the bomb we have used it. We have used it against those who attacked us without warning at Pearl Harbor, against those who have starved and beaten and executed American prisoners of war, against those who have abandoned all pretense of obeying international laws of warfare. We have used it in order to shorten the agony of war, in order to save the lives of thousands and thousands of young Americans."

—from *Public Papers of the Presidents*

NO

William Leahy
Chairman of the Joint Chiefs of Staff

PRIMARY SOURCE

"It is my opinion that the use of this barbarous weapon at Hiroshima and Nagasaki was of no material assistance in our war against Japan. The Japanese were already defeated and ready to surrender because of the effective sea blockade and the successful bombing with conventional weapons. . . .

The lethal possibilities of atomic warfare in the future are frightening. My own feeling was that in being the first to use it, we had adopted an ethical standard common to the barbarians of the Dark Ages. I was not taught to make war in that fashion, and wars cannot be won by destroying women and children."

—from *I Was There*

DBQ Document-Based Questions

1. **Explaining** What reasons does Truman offer to justify the use of the atomic bomb?
2. **Summarizing** Why does Leahy say he was against using the bomb?
3. **Evaluating** Whom do you think makes the more persuasive argument? Explain your answer.

D Differentiated Instruction

Naturalist In July, 1945, atomic tests were also conducted on Bikini Island in the Pacific Ocean. Have students research atomic testing at Bikini Island and create a poster that describes the effects the bomb had on the environment. **OL**

Debates IN HISTORY

Answers:

1. recompense for the Japanese attacking Pearl Harbor without warning; starving and executing American prisoners of war; refusing to obey international laws of warfare. He also said it would save thousands of American lives.
2. He said the Japanese were already defeated and ready to surrender and that such a lethal weapon is barbaric. It is not honorable for warriors to use such weapons.
3. Responses will vary.

Additional Support

Activity: Collaborative Learning

Summarizing Once the atomic bombs were dropped on Hiroshima and Nagasaki, it was obvious that international controls on atomic weapons and energy were necessary. Who would be able to objectively monitor atomic weapons? In 1946, the United States, who at the time held the secret to atomic bombs, asked the United Nations to establish these controls. Have students work in small groups to research the decision the United Nations made to call for an elimination of atomic weapons and weapons of mass destruction. **Ask:** **How was the arms control decision received by the nations, particulary the United States and Russia?** Have students write a summary of the UN's resolution, and have them speculate on why no atomic bombs have been used since Hiroshima and Nagasaki. **OL**

C1 Critical Thinking

Evaluating Ask students if they, like Truman, would have threatened to use the bomb. **Ask:** How far would you have gone to end the war in the Pacific? **OL**

C2 Critical Thinking

Speculating Ask: When the Japanese saw the power of the atomic bomb, why do you think they did not surrender? *(Students may suggest that they thought it might be a one-time incident, or perhaps they were so shocked, they could not respond.)* **OL**

Reading Check

Answer:
the potentially massive casualties involved in a ground invasion of Japan and his duty to save American lives

DBQ Document Based Questions

Answers:
1. 21
2. Without the basic human rights listed earlier, an education is worthless.
3. Responses will vary.

Additional Support

The Allies threatened Japan with "prompt and utter destruction" if the nation did not surrender, but the Japanese did not reply. Truman then ordered the military to drop the bomb. On August 6, 1945, a B-29 bomber named *Enola Gay* dropped an atomic bomb, code-named "Little Boy," on Hiroshima, an important industrial city.

C1 The bomb destroyed about 63 percent of the city. Between 80,000 and 120,000 people died instantly, and thousands more died later from burns and radiation sickness. Three days later, on August 9, the Soviet Union declared war on Japan. Later that day, the United States dropped another atomic bomb, code-named "Fat Man," on the city of Nagasaki, killing between 35,000 and 74,000 people.

Faced with such massive destruction and the shock of the Soviets joining the war, the C2 Japanese emperor ordered his government to surrender. On August 15, 1945—**V-J Day**—Japan surrendered. The long war was over.

Reading Check **Analyzing** What arguments did Truman consider when deciding whether to use the atomic bomb?

Building a New World

MAIN Idea The victorious Allies tried to create an organization to prevent future wars.

HISTORY AND YOU What are some of your most noble goals? Read to learn about the goals of the Allied forces after the war.

Well before the war ended, President Roosevelt had begun thinking about what the world would be like after the war. The president had wanted to ensure that war would never again engulf the world.

Creating the United Nations

President Roosevelt believed that a new international political organization could prevent another world war. In 1944, at the Dumbarton Oaks estate in Washington, D.C., delegates from 39 countries met to discuss the new organization, which was to be called the **United Nations** (UN). The delegates at the conference agreed that the UN would have a General Assembly, in which every member

PRIMARY SOURCE

Plans for a Better World

▲ The Nuremberg trials

The Universal Declaration of Human Rights

Issued by the United Nations, December 10, 1948

1. All human beings are born free and equal in dignity and rights.
3. Everyone has the right to life, liberty, and security of person.
4. No one shall be held in slavery or servitude . . .
5. No one shall be subjected to torture or to cruel, inhuman or degrading treatment or punishment.
7. All are equal before the law and are entitled without any discrimination to equal protection of the law.
11. Everyone charged with a penal offense has the right to be presumed innocent until proved guilty . . .
13. Everyone has the right to freedom of movement . . .
16. Men and women . . . are entitled to equal rights as to marriage, during marriage and at its dissolution . . .
17. Everyone has the right to own property . . .
18. Everyone has the right to freedom of thought, conscience and religion . . .
19. Everyone has the right to freedom of opinion and expression . . .
20. Everyone has the right to freedom of peaceful assembly and association.
21. The will of the people . . . shall be expressed in periodic and genuine elections which shall be by universal and equal suffrage . . .
23. Everyone has the right to work . . .
25. Everyone has the right to a standard of living adequate for the health and well-being of himself and of his family, including food, clothing, housing and medical care and necessary social services, and the right to security in the event of unemployment, sickness, disability, widowhood, old age or other lack of livelihood . . .
26. Everyone has the right to education . . .

DBQ Document-Based Questions

1. **Identifying** Which right relates to free elections?
2. **Speculating** Why do you think that the right to an education might be so far down on the list?
3. **Evaluating** Which five of the human rights included in the Declaration do you feel are the most important today? Why?

Activity: Interdisciplinary Connection

Health Assign students to small groups. Have them use the library or Internet to research the kind of short- and long-term heath problems the Japanese people suffered after the atomic bomb was dropped. Students should research the different kinds of radiation sickness and how long the effects lasted. Students may also include information about how food, especially crops and livestock, were affected and the consequences of eating contaminated food. **OL**

nation in the world would have one vote. The UN would also have a Security Council with 11 members. Five countries would be permanent members of the Security Council: Britain, France, China, the Soviet Union, and the United States—the five big powers that had led the fight against the Axis. These five permanent members would each have veto power.

On April 25, 1945, representatives from 50 countries came to San Francisco to officially organize the United Nations and design its **charter,** or constitution. The General Assembly was given the power to vote on resolutions, to choose the non-permanent members of the Security Council, and to vote on the UN's budget. The Security Council was responsible for international peace and security. It could investigate any international problem and propose settlements. It could also take action to preserve the peace, including asking its members to use military force to uphold a UN resolution.

Soon after its founding, the UN created a Commission on Human Rights and chose Eleanor Roosevelt to serve as its first chair. The Commission drafted the Universal Declaration of Human Rights, and the UN issued it in 1948. The document strongly reflects the ideas and principles that Eleanor Roosevelt espoused during her life. It lists 30 rights that are said to be universally applicable to all human beings in all societies.

Putting the Enemy on Trial

Although the Allies had declared their intention to punish German and Japanese leaders for war crimes, they did not work out the details until the summer of 1945. In August, the United States, Britain, France, and the Soviet Union created the International Military Tribunal (IMT). The Tribunal held trials in Nuremberg, Germany, where Hitler had staged Nazi Party rallies.

Twenty-two leaders of Nazi Germany were prosecuted at the **Nuremberg Trials.** Three were acquitted and seven were given prison sentences. The remaining 12 were sentenced to death. Trials of lower-ranking officials and military officers continued until April 1949. Those trials led to the execution of 24 more German leaders. Another 107 were given prison sentences.

Similar trials were held in Tokyo. The IMT for the Far East charged 25 Japanese leaders with war crimes. Significantly, the Allies did not indict the Japanese emperor. They feared that any attempt to put him on trial would lead to an uprising by the Japanese people. Eighteen Japanese defendants were sentenced to prison. The rest were sentenced to death by hanging.

The war crimes trials punished many of the people responsible for World War II and the Holocaust, but they were also part of the American plan for building a better world. As Robert Jackson, chief counsel for the United States at Nuremberg, observed in his opening statement to the court: "The wrongs we seek to condemn and punish have been so calculated, so malignant and so devastating, that civilization cannot tolerate their being ignored because it cannot survive their being repeated."

✓ Reading Check **Describing** How is the United Nations organized?

Section 5 REVIEW

Vocabulary

1. **Explain** the significance of: hedgerow, Battle of the Bulge, V-E Day, Harry S. Truman, Iwo Jima, napalm, Manhattan Project, V-J Day, United Nations, charter, Nuremberg Trials.

Main Ideas

2. **Explaining** What was the significance of the Battle of the Bulge?
3. **Identifying** What was the advantage of using napalm bombs?
4. **Synthesizing** How was the United Nations designed to prevent global wars?

Critical Thinking

5. **Big Ideas** If you had been a member of President Truman's cabinet, what advice would you have given him about dropping the atomic bomb?
6. **Organizing** Using a graphic organizer like the one below, indicate the steps to victory in Europe and over Japan. Add boxes as needed.

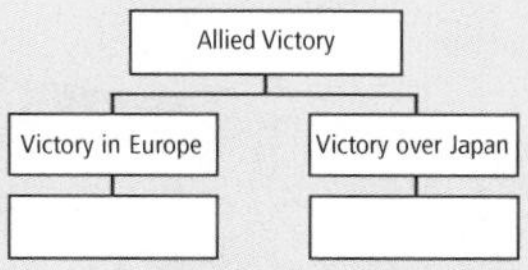

7. **Analyzing Visuals** Look at the photo of the Japanese delegation on page 749. What do you observe about the scene?

Writing About History

8. **Descriptive Writing** Imagine that you are in a large American city when news of victory over Japan comes. Describe the celebrations and the mood of the people.

History ONLINE
Study Central™ To review this section, go to glencoe.com and click on Study Central.

✓ Reading Check

Answer:
a General Assembly of all member nations and an 11-member Security Council with five permanent members, each of whom has veto power over UN actions

Assess

History ONLINE

Study Central™ provides summaries, interactive games, and online graphic organizers to help students review content.

Close

Identifying Central Issues
Have students work in groups to create a collage that illustrates the major battles that ended World War II. Then have them write several paragraphs that explain the images on their collage. **OL**

Section 5 REVIEW

Answers

1. All definitions can be found in the section and in the Glossary.
2. It weakened the German military enough to allow the Allies to enter Germany.
3. The bombs did not have to hit exact targets. The fires would spread and cause general destruction.
4. If all nations were under the surveillance of an international organization, a country would be less likely to start a war. The Security Council can investigate international problems, propose settlements, and send military forces to uphold a resolution.
5. Answers will vary but should be defensible.
6.

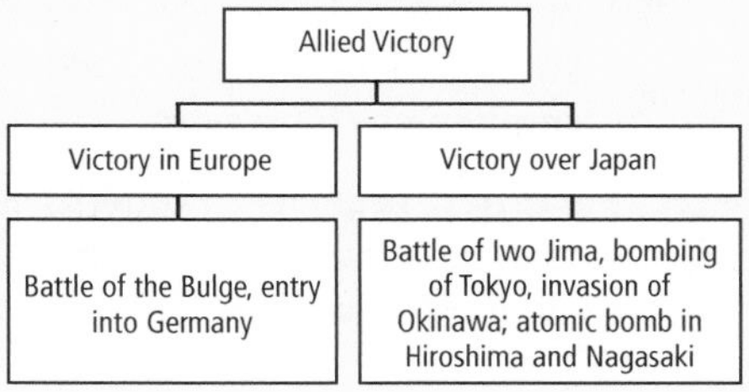

7. The Japanese look proud but also somber and defeated. The scene looks very formal.
8. Descriptions will vary but should reflect the exuberance and relief of the people.

Categorizing Have students create a cluster diagram to list the major campaigns the United States fought in the Pacific and in Europe. **OL**

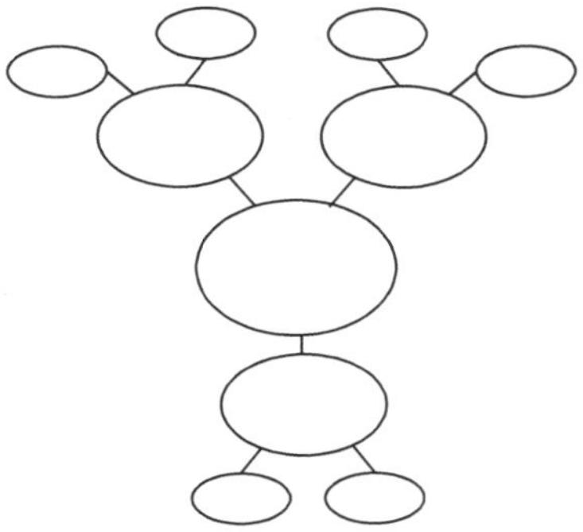

Cause and Effect Have students list and describe five effects World War II had on the social lives of Americans. Then have them list and describe three effects the war had on the economy. **AL**

Chapter 21 VISUAL SUMMARY

STUDY TO GO You can study anywhere, anytime by downloading quizzes and flashcards to your PDA from glencoe.com.

The Pacific

1941
- Japan attacks Pearl Harbor, Dec. 7

1942
- The United States defeats Japan in the Battles of the Coral Sea and Midway

1943
- The United States begins its island-hopping campaign

1944
- The United States retakes the Philippines

1945
- The United States drops the atomic bomb; Japan surrenders on August 15

Europe and North Africa

1941
- Germany invades the Soviet Union

1942
- The Allies turn the tide in the Battle of the Atlantic

1943
- The Allies invade Italy; German forces in North Africa and Stalingrad surrender to Allies

1944
- The Allies invade Normandy on June 6

1945
- Germany surrenders unconditionally on May 7

The Home Front

1941
- President Roosevelt forbids race discrimination in defense industries

1942
- Congress establishes WAAC; War Department relocates Japanese Americans to internment camps

1943
- Race riots occur in Detroit and Los Angeles; Roosevelt establishes OWM

1944
- Supreme Court hears case of *Korematsu* v. *United States*

1945
- Nearly 40 nations sign the United Nations charter

▼ *A convoy of Allied M-3 tanks moves forward.*

▼ *Fire erupts on the USS* Bunker Hill *after a kamikaze attack, May 1945.*

754 **Chapter 21** America and World War II

Hands-On Chapter Project
Step 6: Wrap Up

An Interview with a World War II Veteran

Step 6: Wrap Up Students will review the presentations and provide an evaluation of their work.

Directions Students follow up their presentations with a self-evaluation of both the project and their work on it. Students should write a brief essay that answers the questions to the right.

- What was the most difficult part of this project? Why?
- What was the best part of this project? Why?
- What could be done to improve the presentation?
- What did I learn about World War II by completing this project?

Putting It Together Students should provide clear essays and succinct answers to each question above. **OL**

Chapter 21 Assessment

Reviewing Vocabulary

Directions: Choose the word or words that best complete the sentence.

1. One complaint of African Americans at the beginning of World War II was that they were

A integrated.
B employed.
C empowered.
D disenfranchised.

2. Winston Churchill wanted to attack the ______, or edges, of the German Empire.

A eastern front
B periphery
C left flank
D western front

3. To aid in the war effort, American citizens accepted the ______ of some items.

A rationing
B disappearance
C abundance
D commandeering

4. Japanese suicide pilots were known as ______ pilots.

A Shinto
B Samurai
C kamikaze
D amphtrac

5. Germans fiercely resisted the Allied invasion of France by hiding behind thick, shrubbery-covered dirt walls called ______ that surrounded the fields of Normandy.

A napalm
B hedgerows
C amphtracs
D guadalcanals

Reviewing Main Ideas

Directions: Choose the best answers to the following questions.

Section 1 *(pp. 714–721)*

6. The Liberty ship was superior to many warships because it was

A welded instead of riveted.
B riveted instead of welded.
C painted in camouflage colors.
D painted red, white, and blue.

7. African Americans pushed for a ______ victory in the war effort.

A Tuskegee
B Triple C
C Double V
D Carver

Section 2 *(pp. 722–727)*

8. The Japanese were determined to destroy the American fleet in the Pacific after

A they were successful at Pearl Harbor.
B the Americans surrendered at Bataan.
C the crew of the *Enola Gay* dropped an atomic bomb on Hiroshima.
D James Doolittle dropped bombs on Tokyo.

9. To prevent huge shipping losses in the Atlantic, Americans used

A antisubmarine devices.
B a convoy system.
C an air force escort.
D minesweepers.

TEST-TAKING TIP

Look at each question to find clues to support your answer. Try not to get confused by the wording of the question. Then look for an answer that best fits the question.

Need Extra Help?

If You Missed Questions . . .	1	2	3	4	5	6	7	8	9
Go to Page . . .	719	725	734	743	746	717	720	723–724	727

GO ON

Answers and Analyses
Reviewing Vocabulary

1. D Enfranchised means "given the right to vote." The prefix dis- means absence of, deprived of, or not. Therefore, disenfranchised means deprived of the right to vote.

2. B Periphery means edges. Help students remember this by discussing or explaining peripheral vision. Make sure students read vocabulary questions carefully, because often, as in this case, the definition is given in the question.

3. A *C* does not make sense. Students may be distracted by *B,* by equating disappearing with scarcity. Items were not taken over, they were just not available in abundance. Ration means to distribute or allocate. In this case, scarce items were rationed so as not to waste them and so everyone, theoretically, could have some.

4. C Shinto is a religion. Samurai are Japanese warriors who lived by the code of Bushido. They are not pilots. Amphtracs were military vehicles involved in Pacific invasions.

5. B These earthen walls were made to fence in cattle and crops. The battle of the hedgerows lasted from early June until July 25.

Reviewing Main Ideas

6. A *C* and *D* do not make sense; how a ship is painted would not make it superior to other ships. Welding is the melding of metals with heat. Welded ships required fewer repairs.

7. C Students may be confused by choice *B*. An easy way for students to remember double V is to relate the two As in African American to the double (two) in double V.

8. D If students have trouble with this question, review "Japan Changes Strategy" on page 723. The Japanese decided to destroy the American fleet after they realized the bombs dropped on Tokyo might have killed the emperor. The other answer choices do not make sense, chronologically.

9. B In a convoy, cargo ships traveled with warships, which cut down on losses. It is important that students read the question carefully. The key words in the question are shipping losses.

10. B One meaning of drive, as a noun, is a collection effort. Students are probably familiar with clothing and food drives. Victory gardens, rationing, and war bonds were all ways that citizens could support the war effort, but none involved collecting materials.

11. A Study a map with students who have trouble with this question. Only Sicily is near Italy. Have students identify each answer choice on the map so they can see that, clearly, invading Sicily would most help move troops into Italy.

12. C The D-Day invasion involved amphibious landings on the beaches of the French coastline. Therefore, weather was a huge concern.

13. A This code name is something students must simply commit to memory. Thinking of the building of the bomb as a science project may help trigger students' memories. In addition, the other answer choices all describe military action. Only *A* implies a plan to build something, rather than attack something.

14. C The five permanent members of the Security Council were Great Britain, France, China, the Soviet Union, and the United States.

Critical Thinking

15. B By process of elimination, only *B* can be correct. The Soviet Union had already been involved. *C* is too broad; it is not likely that this was the first successful invasion by sea in all of history. Geographically, *D* does not make sense.

Chapter 21 Assessment

Section 3 *(pp. 728–735)*

10. During the war, Americans ________ to collect materials that could be used for the war effort.
- **A** planted victory gardens
- **B** held scrap drives
- **C** conserved energy
- **D** sold war bonds

Section 4 *(pp. 736–743)*

11. Where did the Allies begin their invasion of Italy?
- **A** Sicily
- **B** Casablanca
- **C** Tehran
- **D** Normandy

12. Planning for D-Day was complicated by concerns for the
- **A** German army.
- **B** amphtracs.
- **C** weather.
- **D** air forces.

Section 5 *(pp. 746–753)*

13. What was the code name for the plan to build the atomic bomb?
- **A** Manhattan Project
- **B** Doolittle Raid
- **C** Operation Overlord
- **D** V-J Day

14. Which UN body has five permanent members with veto power?
- **A** General Assembly
- **B** Commision on Human Rights
- **C** Security Council
- **D** International Military Tribunal

Critical Thinking

Directions: Choose the best answers to the following questions.

15. The invasion of Normandy was important because it
- **A** brought the Soviet Union into the war.
- **B** forced the Germans to fight a two-front war.
- **C** marked the first successful invasion by sea.
- **D** protected the Pacific fleet.

Base your answer to question 16 on the map below and your knowledge of Chapter 21.

Relocation Camps, 1942–1946

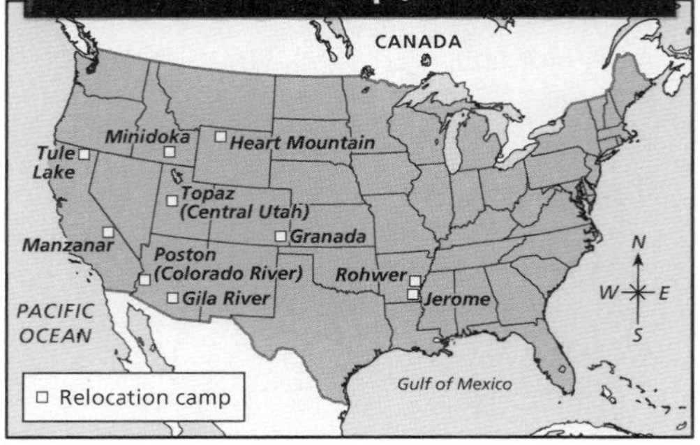

16. Most of the relocation camps were located in what region of the United States?
- **A** the West
- **B** the Southeast
- **C** the Deep South
- **D** the Midwest

17. What was the purpose of the Japanese American Citizens League?
- **A** to fight the Japanese invasion of California
- **B** to fight Roosevelt's order to declare the western United States a military zone
- **C** to help Japanese Americans recover lost property from the relocation
- **D** to encourage Japanese Americans to join the U.S. armed forces

Need Extra Help?

If You Missed Questions . . .	10	11	12	13	14	15	16	17
Go to Page . . .	735	737–738	739–740	750–751	753	738	R15	732

GO ON

16. A Examine the map with students. The relocation camps are marked by white boxes. It is clear that the majority of the centers were located in the West.

17. C Hopefully, students are able to immediately eliminate *A*, which never took place. The JACL helped Japanese Americans who had been held at the centers get back the property they had owned.

18. Women were able to serve in noncombat positions in the military and in factories at home because

A there were not enough men to fill the positions.

B no one else wanted the jobs.

C people realized it was unfair to keep them out.

D women organized, as they did to win the vote.

Analyze the cartoon and answer the question that follows. Base your answer on the cartoon and on your knowledge of Chapter 21.

19. According to the cartoon, why were Americans encouraged to turn out their lights?

A The British could use the lights to create a blockade.

B The lights prevented American ships from seeing the British ships.

C The lights provided a silhouette for ships, making them targets for German submarines.

D The lights used too much electricity, creating city-wide blackouts.

Document-Based Questions

Directions: Analyze the document and answer the short-answer questions that follow the document.

Many historians believe that the civil rights movement of the 1950s and 1960s had its roots in the "Double V" campaign and the march on Washington. Alexander Allen, a member of the Urban League during the war, believed that World War II was a turning point for African Americans.

> *"Up to that point the doors to industrial and economic opportunity were largely closed. Under the pressure of war, the pressures of government policy, the pressures of world opinion, the pressures of blacks themselves and their allies, all this began to change. . . .The war forced the federal government to take a stronger position with reference to discrimination, and things began to change as a result. There was a tremendous attitudinal change that grew out of the war. There had been a new experience for blacks, and many weren't willing to go back to the way it was before."*
>
> —quoted in *Wartime America*

20. How did the war change the status of African Americans in American society?

21. Why do you think the war forced the government to take a stronger position on discrimination in the workplace?

Extended Response

22. World War II was a complex historical event involving nations, people, and decisions from around the world. Write an essay that traces the progress of the war, making sure to include major events and leaders. In the essay, make note of the war's turning points and the use of the atomic bomb. Discuss major decisions of Franklin D. Roosevelt, Winston Churchill, Joseph Stalin, and Charles de Gaulle. To assist you in organizing this essay, construct a time line that includes the battles of Midway, Iwo Jima, Okinawa, the Normandy Invasion, and the Battle of the Bulge.

STOP

History ONLINE

For additional test practice, use Self-Check Quizzes—Chapter 21 at glencoe.com.

Need Extra Help?

If You Missed Questions . . .	18	19	20	21	22
Go to Page . . .	729	R18	757	R19	712–713

Document-Based Questions

20. The new positions and roles African Americans played in industry and the military changed attitudes about African Americans and caused the federal government to take a stronger position on discrimination. The experiences of African Americans made many unwilling to go back to life as it was before the war.

21. Answers will vary. Accept any reasonable, focused answer.

Extended Response

22. Essays must demonstrate a clear, organized grasp of the war's progress. Essays should focus on the important events and personalities listed in the question. The roles and agreements of each person should be clearly stated in each essay.

18. A When men left for war, they left behind many open positions that needed to be filled. So many men were away at war, that women had to take their places in the workforce. After the war, women lost their jobs as returning men took them over.

19. C In the foreground, a submarine can be seen with its periscope pointed toward the New York skyline (it can be identified by the flag). The glowing lights of the city illuminate the American ships, so the submarine could attack the ships. The message is, "Turn out your lights to keep us safe."

History ONLINE

Have students visit the Web site at glencoe.com to review Chapter 21 and take the Self-Check Quiz.

Need Extra Help?

Have students refer to the pages listed if they miss any of the questions.

Chapter 22 Planning Guide

Key to Ability Levels	
BL Below Level	**AL** Above Level
OL On Level	**ELL** English Language Learners

Key to Teaching Resources	
Print Material	Transparency
CD-ROM or DVD	

Levels				Resources	Chapter Opener	Section 1	Section 2	Section 3	Section 4	Chapter Assess
BL	OL	AL	ELL							
FOCUS										
BL	OL	AL	ELL	**Daily Focus Transparencies**		22-1	22-2	22-3	22-4	
TEACH										
	OL	AL		**History Simulations and Problem Solving, URB**		p. 9				
BL	OL		ELL	**Reading Skills Activity, URB**			p. 89			
	OL			**Historical Analysis Skills Activity, URB**				p. 90		
BL	OL	AL	ELL	**Differentiated Instruction Activity, URB**			p. 91			
BL	OL		ELL	**English Learner Activity, URB**			p. 93			
BL	OL	AL	ELL	**Content Vocabulary Activity, URB***		p. 95				
BL	OL	AL	ELL	**Academic Vocabulary Activity, URB**		p. 97				
	OL	AL		**Reinforcing Skills Activity, URB**			p. 99			
	OL	AL		**Critical Thinking Skills Activity, URB**		p. 100				
BL	OL		ELL	**Time Line Activity, URB**					p. 101	
	OL			**Linking Past and Present Activity, URB**				p. 102		
BL	OL	AL	ELL	**Primary Source Reading, URB**				p. 105	p. 103	
BL	OL	AL	ELL	**American Art and Music Activity, URB**					p. 107	
BL	OL	AL	ELL	**Interpreting Political Cartoons Activity, URB**				p. 109		
		AL		**Enrichment Activity, URB**					p. 113	
BL	OL		ELL	**Guided Reading Activity, URB***		p. 116	p. 117	p. 118	p. 119	
BL	OL	AL	ELL	**Reading Essentials and Note-Taking Guide***		p. 247	p. 250	p. 253	p. 256	
BL	OL	AL	ELL	**Differentiated Instruction for the American History Classroom**	✓	✓	✓	✓	✓	✓
BL	OL	AL	ELL	**Unit Map Overlay Transparencies**	✓	✓	✓	✓	✓	✓
BL	OL	AL	ELL	**Unit Time Line Transparencies, Strategies, and Activities**	✓	✓	✓	✓	✓	✓
BL	OL	AL	ELL	**Cause and Effect Transparencies, Strategies, and Activities**	✓	✓	✓	✓	✓	✓
BL	OL	AL	ELL	**Why It Matters Chapter Transparencies, Strategies, and Activities**	✓	✓	✓	✓	✓	✓

Note: Please refer to the *Unit 7 Resource Book* for this chapter's URB materials.

* Also available in Spanish

TeacherWorks Plus
All-In-One Planner and Resource Center

- Interactive Lesson Planner
- Interactive Teacher Edition
- Fully editable blackline masters
- Section Spotlight Videos Launch
- Differentiated Lesson Plans
- Printable reports of daily assignments
- Standards Tracking System

Levels: BL	OL	AL	ELL	Resources	Chapter Opener	Section 1	Section 2	Section 3	Section 4	Chapter Assess
TEACH *(continued)*										
BL	OL	AL		**Supreme Court Case Studies**				p. 69	p. 77	
BL	OL	AL	ELL	**The Living Constitution**	✓	✓	✓	✓	✓	✓
BL	OL	AL	ELL	**American Issues**	✓	✓	✓	✓	✓	✓
	OL	AL	ELL	**American Art and Architecture Transparencies, Strategies, and Activities**	✓	✓	✓	✓	✓	✓
BL	OL	AL		**High School American History Literature Library**	✓	✓	✓	✓	✓	✓
	OL	AL		**American History Primary Source Documents Library**	✓	✓	✓	✓	✓	✓
BL	OL	AL	ELL	**American Music: Hits Through History CD**	✓	✓	✓	✓	✓	✓
BL	OL	AL	ELL	**StudentWorks™ Plus**	✓	✓	✓	✓	✓	✓
BL	OL	AL	ELL	***The American Vision* Video Program**	✓	✓	✓	✓	✓	✓
Teacher Resources				**Reading Strategies and Activities for the Social Studies Classroom**	✓	✓	✓	✓	✓	✓
				Strategies for Success	✓	✓	✓	✓	✓	✓
				Presentation Plus! with MindJogger CheckPoint	✓	✓	✓	✓	✓	✓
				Success With English Learners	✓	✓	✓	✓	✓	✓
ASSESS										
BL	OL	AL	ELL	**Section Quizzes and Chapter Tests***		p. 315	p. 316	p. 317	p. 318	p. 319
BL	OL	AL	ELL	**Authentic Assessment With Rubrics**						p. 49
BL	OL	AL	ELL	**Standardized Test Practice Workbook**						p. 49
BL	OL	AL	ELL	***ExamView® Assessment Suite***		22-1	22-2	22-3	22-4	Ch. 22
CLOSE										
BL			ELL	**Reteaching Activity, URB**						p. 111
BL	OL		ELL	**Reading and Study Skills Foldables™**	pp. 75–76					
BL	OL	AL	ELL	***American History* in Graphic Novel**					p. 57	

✓ Chapter- or unit-based activities applicable to all sections in this chapter.

Using Student Web Activities

Teach With Technology

What is a Student Web Activity?
A Student Web Activity uses the Internet to enrich chapter content. It also helps students to enhance their online research skills.

How can a Student Web Activity help my students?
A Student Web Activity can teach students how to conduct research online and extends the content provided in the textbook. Features include:

- a research topic based on the chapter
- links to Web sites with more information on the topics
- short answer questions to assess comprehension
- a form to e-mail answers to you or to themselves

Visit glencoe.com and enter a *QuickPass*™ code to go to a Student Web Activity.

History ONLINE
Visit glencoe.com and enter *QuickPass*™ code TAV9399c22T for Chapter 22 resources.

You can easily launch a wide range of digital products from your computer's desktop with the McGraw-Hill Social Studies widget.

TeacherWorks

	Student	Teacher	Parent
Media Library			
• Section Audio	●		●
• Spanish Audio Summaries	●		●
• Section Spotlight Videos	●	●	●
***The American Vision* Online Learning Center (Web Site)**			
• StudentWorks™ Plus Online	●	●	●
• Multilingual Glossary	●	●	●
• Study-to-Go	●	●	●
• Chapter Overviews	●	●	●
• Self-Check Quizzes	●	●	●
• Student Web Activities	●	●	●
• ePuzzles and Games	●	●	●
• Vocabulary eFlashcards	●	●	●
• In Motion Animations	●	●	●
• Study Central™	●	●	●
• Web Activity Lesson Plans		●	
• Vocabulary PuzzleMaker	●	●	●
• Historical Thinking Activities		●	
• Beyond the Textbook	●	●	●

Reading Support From Jamestown Education

- **Timed Readings Plus in Social Studies** helps students increase their reading rate and fluency while maintaining comprehension. The 400-word passages are similar to those found on state and national assessments.
- **Reading in the Content Area: Social Studies** concentrates on six essential reading skills that help students better comprehend what they read. The book includes 75 high-interest nonfiction passages written at increasing levels of difficulty.
- **Reading Social Studies** includes strategic reading instruction and vocabulary support in Social Studies content for both ELLs and native speakers of English.

www.jamestowneducation.com

Biography · A&E Home Video · The History Channel

The following videotape programs are available from Glencoe as supplements to this chapter:

- Berlin Airlift: The First Battle of the Cold War (ISBN 0-76-701166-X)
- Harry S. Truman: A New View (ISBN 1-56-501449)

To order, call Glencoe at 1-800-334-7344. To find classroom resources to accompany many of these videos, check the following home pages:

A&E Television: www.aetv.com
The History Channel: www.historychannel.com

Reading List Generator CD-ROM — Glencoe BookLink 3

Use this database to search more than 30,000 titles to create a customized reading list for your students.

- Reading lists can be organized by students' reading level, author, genre, theme, or area of interest.
- The database provides Degrees of Reading Power™ (DRP) and Lexile™ readability scores for all selections.
- A brief summary of each selection is included.

Leveled reading suggestions for this chapter:

For students at a Grade 8 reading level:
- ***Joseph McCarthy and the Cold War,*** by Victoria Sherrow

For students at a Grade 9 reading level:
- ***I Remember Korea: Veterans Tell Their Stories of the Korean War, 1950–53,*** by Linda Granfield

For students at a Grade 10 reading level:
- ***The Emperor's General: A Novel,*** by James Webb

For students at a Grade 11 reading level:
- ***Wild Swans: Three Daughters of China,*** by Jung Chang

For students at a Grade 12 reading level:
- ***Spectacular Space Travelers,*** by Jason Richie

National Geographic

Index to National Geographic Magazine:

The following articles relate to this chapter:

- "DMZ: Korea's Dangerous Divide," by Tom O'Neill, July 2003.
- "Douglas MacArthur: An American Soldier," by Geoffrey C. Ward and Cary Wolinsky, March 1992.

National Geographic Society Products To order the following, call National Geographic at 1-800-368-2728:

- *ZipZapMap! USA Windows* (ZipZapMap! USA).

Access National Geographic's new dynamic MapMachine Web site and other geography resources at:
www.nationalgeographic.com
www.nationalgeographic.com/maps

Introducing **Chapter 22**

Focus

MAKING CONNECTIONS

How Did the Atomic Bomb Change the World?

Ask students to imagine that a new, powerful weapon has been invented by an enemy nation. This new weapon is so powerful that no one, not even its inventor, knows the extent of the damage that the new weapon might cause. Have students explain what feelings they might have about the use of such a weapon and list them on the board. Explain that many Americans grew fearful of the power of the atomic bomb, especially after the Soviet Union developed a bomb of its own. **OL**

The Big Ideas

As students study the chapter, remind them to consider the section-based Big Ideas included in each section's Guide to Reading. The **Essential Questions** in the activities below tie in to the Big Ideas and help students think about and understand important chapter concepts. In addition, the Hands-on Chapter Projects with their culminating activities relate the content from each section to the Big Ideas. These activities build on each other as students progress through the chapter. Section activities culminate in the wrap-up activity on the Visual Summary page.

Chapter 22

The Cold War Begins

1945–1960

The world's first nuclear artillery shell is test fired on May 25, 1953. Such tests were common during the early cold war.

U.S. PRESIDENTS

Truman 1945–1953

Eisenhower 1953–1961

U.S. EVENTS

1945
- Franklin Roosevelt dies

1947
- Truman Doctrine is declared

1948
- Berlin airlift begins

1950
- McCarthy charges that Communists staff the U.S. State Department
- Korean War begins

1953
- Armistice agreement is reached in Korea

1945 — 1950

WORLD EVENTS

March 1945
- Yalta Conference is held to plan postwar world

July 1945
- Potsdam Conference partitions Germany

1948
- State of Israel is created

1949
- Communists take power in China

Section 1

The Origins of the Cold War

Essential Question: How did the Cold War emerge after World War II? *(Relations between the Soviet Union and the other Allies soured as the Soviets set up Communist governments in Eastern Europe.)* Tell students that in this section they will learn how the Cold War began and how it affected American foreign policy. **OL**

Section 2

The Early Cold War Years

Essential Question: How did President Truman attempt to deter Communism? *(Truman authorized billions of dollars of American aid to devastated European nations as well as to the Allies' former enemies, Germany and Japan.)* Tell students that this section will focus on how American policies controlled the spread of Communism during the Cold War. **OL**

Chapter Audio

MAKING CONNECTIONS

How Did the Atomic Bomb Change the World?

The destructiveness of the atomic bomb raised the stakes in military conflicts. Growing tensions between the United States and the Soviet Union after World War II led to a constant threat of nuclear war.

- *How did the atomic bomb change relations between nations?*
- *Do you think the invention of the atomic bomb made the world safer?*

1955 — **1960**

1956
- Hungarians rebel against the Communist government

1957
- Soviet Union launches Sputnik

1960
- U-2 incident occurs

FOLDABLES

Analyzing Causes Make a Two-Tab Book Foldable that lists the long-term and short-term causes of the Cold War. List the information as you read and review the chapter.

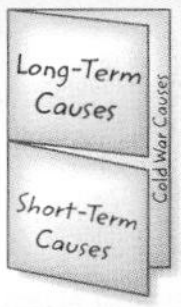

History ONLINE Visit glencoe.com and enter *QuickPass*™ code TAV9846c22 for Chapter 22 resources.

Section 3

The Cold War and American Society

Essential Question: How did the Cold War change the nation at home? *(People grew fearful of the possibility of Communists infiltrating the U.S. government; others were afraid that the Soviet Union would attack the United States with nuclear weapons).* Tell students that in Section 3 they will learn about how the Cold War affected all parts of American society. **OL**

Section 4

Eisenhower's Cold War Policies

Essential Question: How did Eisenhower's policies address Cold War issues? *(Eisenhower believed the United States needed a strong economy as well as a strong military; he also used covert operations to prevent Soviet expansion.)* Tell students that in Section 4 they will learn about how President Eisenhower confronted the Soviet Union during the Cold War. **OL**

Introducing **Chapter 22**

More About the Photo

Visual Literacy In the 1950s, nuclear tests were regularly carried out above ground. People did not fully understand the dangerous side effects of nuclear fallout. The United States alone has conducted more than 1,000 nuclear tests, some above ground and some below ground. The Test Ban Treaty of 1963 prohibits nuclear weapons tests "or any other nuclear explosion" in the atmosphere, in outer space, and under water. The treaty does not ban underground testing.

FOLDABLES™ Study Organizer **Dinah Zike's Foldables**

Dinah Zike's Foldables are three-dimensional, interactive graphic organizers that help students practice basic writing skills, review vocabulary terms, and identify main ideas. Instructions for creating and using Foldables can be found in the Appendix at the end of this book and in the *Dinah Zike's Reading and Study Skills Foldables* booklet.

History ONLINE

Visit glencoe.com and enter *QuickPass*™ code TAV9399c22T for Chapter 22 resources, including a Chapter Overview, Study Central™, Study-to-Go, Student Web Activity, Self-Check Quiz, and other materials.

Focus

Bellringer

Daily Focus Transparency 22-1

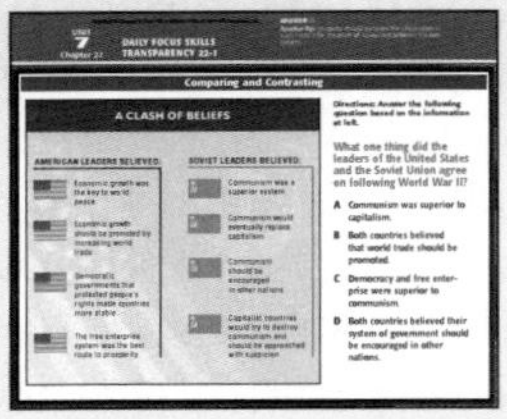

Guide to Reading

Answers:

Conferences	Outcomes
Yalta Conference	Poland's government recognized, free elections for Poland, Declaration of Liberated Europe, Germany divided, German reparations set
Potsdam Conference	German-Polish border established, German reparations to the Soviets reconstructed

Section Spotlight Video

To generate student interest and provide a springboard for class discussion, access the Chapter 22, Section 1 video at glencoe.com or on the video DVD.

Section 1

Section Audio | Spotlight Video

The Origins of the Cold War

Guide to Reading

Big Ideas

Government and Society Although World War II was nearly over, personal and political differences among Allied leaders and the peoples they represented led to new global challenges.

Content Vocabulary
- satellite nations *(p. 765)*
- Iron Curtain *(p. 765)*

Academic Vocabulary
- liberate *(p. 760)*
- equipment *(p. 762)*

People and Events to Identify
- Yalta *(p. 760)*
- Cold War *(p. 762)*
- Potsdam *(p. 764)*

Reading Strategy

Categorizing Complete a graphic organizer similar to the one below by filling in the names of the conferences held among the "Big Three" Allies and the outcomes of each.

Conferences	Outcomes

After the war ended, tensions continued to rise over the amount of freedom the Soviets were going to allow the nations they controlled. Leaders of Britain, the United States, and the Soviet Union held conferences but could not resolve this issue.

The Yalta Conference

MAIN Idea Roosevelt, Churchill, and Stalin met at Yalta to discuss Poland, Germany, and the rights of liberated Europe.

HISTORY AND YOU Do you remember Wilson's idealistic Fourteen Points and how they were changed during negotiations after World War I? Read on to learn how negotiations during and after World War II led to results different from what Roosevelt and Truman wanted.

In February 1945, with the war in Europe almost over, Roosevelt, Churchill, and Stalin met at **Yalta**—a Soviet resort on the Black Sea—to plan the postwar world. Although the conference seemed to go well, several agreements reached at Yalta later played an important role in causing the Cold War.

Poland

The first issue discussed at Yalta was what to do about Poland. Shortly after the Germans invaded Poland, the Polish government fled to Britain. In 1944, however, Soviet troops drove back the Germans and entered Poland. As they **liberated** Poland from German control, the Soviets encouraged Polish Communists to set up a new government. This meant there were now two governments claiming the right to govern Poland: one Communist and one non-Communist.

President Roosevelt and Prime Minister Churchill both argued that the Poles should be free to choose their own government. "This is what we went to war against Germany for," Churchill explained, "that Poland should be free and sovereign."

Stalin quickly responded to Churchill's comments. According to Stalin, because Poland was on the Soviet Union's western border, the need for its government to be friendly was a matter of "life and death" from the Soviet point of view. Every time invaders had entered Russia from the west, they had come through Poland. Eventually, the three leaders compromised. Roosevelt and Churchill agreed to recognize the Polish government set up by the Soviets. Stalin agreed that the government would include members of the prewar Polish government and that free elections would be held as soon as possible.

Resource Manager

R Reading Strategies	C Critical Thinking	D Differentiated Instruction	W Writing Support	S Skill Practice
Teacher Edition • Identifying, p. 762 • Det. Importance, p. 764 **Additional Resources** • Academic Vocab. Act., URB p. 97 • Guided Read., URB p. 116	**Teacher Edition** • Pred. Consequences, p. 761 • Contrasting, p. 762 • Hypothesizing, p. 763 **Additional Resources** • History Simulations, URB p. 9 • Critical Thinking Skills Act., URB p. 100 • Quizzes/Tests, p. 315	**Teacher Edition** • Visual/Spatial, p. 765 **Additional Resources** • Foldables, pp. 75–76	**Teacher Edition** • Personal Writing, p. 762 **Additional Resources** • Content Vocab. Act., p. 95	**Teacher Edition** • Interpreting a Map, p. 764 **Additional Resources** • Read. Essen., p. 247

PRIMARY SOURCE
The Yalta Conference, 1945

▲ Churchill, Roosevelt, and Stalin at Yalta

The Declaration of Liberated Europe

At Yalta, the Allies issued the Declaration of Liberated Europe. The Soviet Union's failure to uphold the Declaration contributed to the coming of the Cold War. The Declaration contained the following commitments:

- The peoples of Europe will be allowed to create democratic institutions of their own choice, but must destroy all remaining aspects of Nazism and fascism in their societies.
- The United States, Great Britain, and the Soviet Union will help the peoples of Europe to do the following:
  1. Establish peace in their country
  2. Provide aid to people in distress
  3. Form temporary governments that represent all democratic elements of the society and hold free elections to choose a government that responds to the will of the people
- The United States, Great Britain, and the Soviet Union will continue to support the principles expressed in the Atlantic Charter.

NATIONAL GEOGRAPHIC **The Division of Germany, 1945**

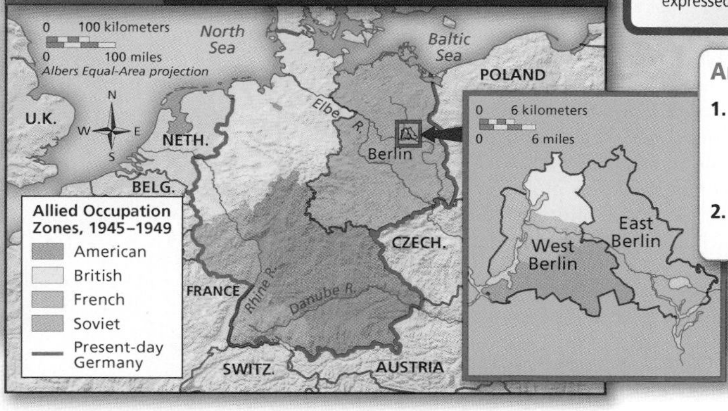

Analyzing VISUALS

1. **Specifying** In the Declaration of Liberated Europe, what three things did the Big Three promise to help the peoples of Europe do?
2. **Locating** In what zone in the divided Germany was Berlin located?

The Declaration of Liberated Europe C

After reaching a compromise on Poland, Roosevelt, Churchill, and Stalin agreed to issue the Declaration of Liberated Europe. The declaration asserted "the right of all people to choose the form of government under which they will live."

The Allies promised that the people of Europe would be allowed "to create democratic institutions of their own choice." They also promised to create temporary governments that represented "all democratic elements" and pledged "the earliest possible establishment through free elections of governments responsive to the will of the people."

Dividing Germany

After discussing Poland and agreeing to a set of principles for liberating Europe, the conference focused on Germany. Roosevelt, Churchill, and Stalin agreed to divide Germany into four zones. Great Britain, the United States, the Soviet Union, and France would each control one zone. The same four countries would also divide the German capital city of Berlin into four zones, even though it was in the Soviet zone.

Teach

C Critical Thinking

Predicting Consequences

Ask: What compromise did Roosevelt, Churchill, and Stalin, reach about Poland? *(Roosevelt and Churchill agreed to accept the Communist government Stalin had set up, and Stalin promised free elections for Poland as soon as possible.)* Based on Stalin's actions, do you think he would honor his word about a liberated Europe? *(probably not; He saw the situation from a "Soviet point of view.")* **OL**

Analyzing VISUALS

Answers:

1. to establish peace in their countries, to provide aid to people in distress, and to form temporary, free governments until a government elected by the people could be formed
2. in the Soviet zone

Additional Support

Activity: Economics Connection

Making Connections Explain to students that after World War II, millions of people were uprooted. After six years of fighting, they had fled their countries, hoping to find a place of refuge. Many large cities were completely devastated, or left in ruins. Have students use library or Internet resources to research the ways in which the United States and Great Britain provided aid to these people in distress. Organize students into three groups to conduct research on the Marshall Plan, the American Red Cross, and UNICEF. Have groups present their findings in a chart showing the main goals of each organization, how aid was given, and the effectiveness of each organization. **OL**

W Writing Support

Personal Writing The Soviets promised that Poland would have free elections, then refused to let the Poles vote. Have students write a journal entry about how they would feel to learn that their country was not liberated and their right to vote was suddenly gone. **OL**

R Reading Strategy

Identifying Ask: What was the Cold War? *(a silent war of hostility and competition between the United States and the Soviet Union.)* **OL**

C Critical Thinking

Contrasting Have students create a T-chart. On one side, have students list Soviet goals after World War II *(to keep Germany weak, to encourage communism in other countries)* and U.S goals on the other side *(to repair the economies of European countries, to avoid future wars)* **OL**

Although pleased with the decision to divide Germany, Stalin also demanded that Germany pay heavy reparations for the war damage it had caused. Roosevelt agreed, but he insisted reparations be based on Germany's ability to pay. He also suggested, and Stalin agreed, that Germany pay reparations with trade goods and products instead of cash. The Allies would also be allowed to remove industrial machinery, railroad cars, and other **equipment** from Germany as reparations. This decision did not resolve the issue. Over the next few years, arguments about German reparations greatly increased tensions between the United States and the Soviet Union.

Tensions Begin to Rise

The Yalta decisions shaped the expectations of the United States. Two weeks after Yalta, the Soviets pressured the king of Romania into appointing a Communist government. The United States accused the Soviets of violating the Declaration of Liberated Europe.

Soon afterward, the Soviets refused to allow more than three non-Communist Poles to serve in the 18-member Polish government. There was also no indication that they intended to hold free elections in Poland as promised. On April 1, President Roosevelt informed the Soviets that their actions in Poland were not acceptable.

Yalta marked a turning point in Soviet-American relations. President Roosevelt had hoped that an Allied victory and the creation of the United Nations would lead to a more peaceful world. Instead, as the war came to an end, the United States and the Soviet Union became increasingly hostile toward each other. This led to an era of confrontation and competition between the two nations that lasted from about 1946 to 1990. This era became known as the **Cold War.**

Soviet Security Concerns

The tensions between the United States and the Soviet Union led to the Cold War because the two sides had different goals. As the war ended, Soviet leaders became concerned about security. They wanted to keep Germany weak and make sure that the countries between Germany and the Soviet Union were under Soviet control.

Although security concerns influenced their thinking, Soviet leaders were also communists. They believed that communism was a superior economic system that would eventually replace capitalism, and that the Soviet Union should encourage communism in other nations. Soviet leaders also accepted Lenin's theory that capitalist countries would eventually try to destroy communism. This made them suspicious of capitalist nations.

American Economic Issues

While Soviet leaders focused on securing their borders, American leaders focused on economic problems. Many American officials believed that the Depression had caused World War II. Without it, Hitler would never have come to power, and Japan would not have wanted to expand its empire.

Debates IN HISTORY

Did the Soviet Union Cause the Cold War?

Many people have debated who was responsible for the Cold War. Most Americans, including diplomat George Kennan who had served in Russia, believed that it was Soviet ideology and insecurity that brought on the Cold War. On the other side, communist leaders, such as Stalin's adviser Andrei Zhdanov, believed that capitalism and imperialism caused the Cold War.

Additional Support

Activity: Interdisciplinary Connection

Geography Tell students that several nations in Eastern Europe have a long history of being overrun by more powerful nations. Organize students into small groups. Give each group a blank outline map of Eastern Europe today and several overhead transparencies. Have the groups research to show how the boundaries of these countries have changed by creating a series of overlays for the map. Suggest that students show the boundaries at the turn of each century or on other significant dates from 1500 to the present. **OL**

American advisers also thought that the Depression became so severe because nations reduced trade. They believed that when nations stop trading, they are forced into war to get resources. By 1945, Roosevelt and his advisers were convinced that economic growth was the key to peace. They wanted to promote economic growth by increasing world trade.

Similar reasoning convinced American leaders to promote democracy and free enterprise. They believed that democratic governments with protections for people's rights made countries more stable and peaceful. They also thought that the free enterprise system, with private property rights and limited government intervention in the economy, was the best route to prosperity. **C**

✓ Reading Check **Identifying** What did the Allies decide at Yalta?

Truman Takes Control

MAIN Idea Although President Truman took a firm stand against Soviet aggression, Europe remained divided after the war.

HISTORY AND YOU Have you ever had to say no to someone or insist they do something? Read to learn about President Truman's actions at Potsdam.

Eleven days after confronting the Soviets on Poland, President Roosevelt died and Harry S. Truman became president. Truman was strongly anti-Communist. He also believed that World War II had begun because Britain had tried to appease Hitler. He did not intend to make the same mistake with Stalin. "We must stand up to the Russians," he told Secretary of State Edward Stettinius the day after taking office.

YES

George F. Kennan
American Diplomat

PRIMARY SOURCE

"[The] USSR still [believes] in antagonistic 'capitalist encirclement' with which in the long run there can be no permanent peaceful coexistence. . . . At bottom of [the] Kremlin's neurotic view of world affairs is traditional and instinctive Russian sense of insecurity. . . . And they have learned to seek security only in patient but deadly struggle for total destruction of rival power, never in compacts and compromises with it.

. . . In summary, we have here a political force committed fanatically to the belief that . . . it is desirable and necessary that the internal harmony of our society be disrupted, our traditional way of life be destroyed, the international authority of our state be broken, if Soviet power is to be secure."

—Moscow Embassy Telegram #511, 1946

NO

Andrei Zhdanov
Advisor to Stalin

PRIMARY SOURCE

"The more the war recedes into the past, the more distinct becomes . . . the division of the political forces operating on the international arena into two major camps. . . . The principal driving force of the imperialist camp is the U.S.A. . . . The cardinal purpose of the imperialist camp is to strengthen imperialism, to hatch a new imperialist war, to combat socialism and democracy, and to support reactionary and antidemocratic profascist regimes. . . .

. . . As embodiment of a new and superior social system, the Soviet Union reflects in its foreign policy the aspirations of progressive mankind, which desires lasting peace and has nothing to gain from a new war hatched by capitalism."

—from *For a Lasting Peace for a People's Democracy*, no. 1, November 1947

DBQ Document-Based Questions

1. **Paraphrasing** What belief of the Soviets does Kennan say will prevent "permanent peaceful coexistence" with the United States?
2. **Identifying Central Issues** What does Zhdanov say are the goals of the "imperialist camp" led by the United States?

C Critical Thinking

Hypothesizing Ask: How can economic growth prevent a country from going to war? *(If a country is prosperous, has plenty of resources, and its people are gainfully employed, there is no reason for war.)* **OL**

✓ Reading Check

Answer: The Allies decided Poland's government, Europeans' right to choose their own governments, the division of Germany and Berlin into four zones, the addition of the Soviets in the war effort against Japan, and reparations from Germany.

Debates IN HISTORY

Answers:

1. antagonistic "capitalist encirclement"
2. to strengthen it in order to hatch an imperialist war that wants to defeat socialism and democracy

Hands-On Chapter Project Step 1

Role-Playing to Demonstrate McCarthyism in Action

Step 1: Researching the Army-McCarthy Hearings of 1954 Essential question: How did Senator Joe McCarthy conduct the Army-McCarthy hearings that were televised in 1954?

Directions Explain to students that they will be re-enacting or improvising the Army-McCarthy hearings that were so influential, and which turned the tide against McCarthyism. For background, they can consult sources found online or in the Library. Students can also research in books on McCarthy or McCarthyism to find direct quotations from the hearings or people who witnessed them.

Putting It Together Students should share their research and then discuss the essential elements they want to convey about McCarthyism in the performance they will do for the class. **OL** *(Chapter Project continued on page 771)*

R Reading Strategy

Determining Importance Truman was determined to demonstrate American resolve toward the Soviet Union. **Ask:** Why was President Truman's meeting with Molotov an important turning point in U.S.–Soviet diplomacy? *(Truman stood up to the Soviets. He demanded that Stalin hold free elections in Poland.)* **OL**

S Skill Practice

Interpreting a Map Have students look at the map. **Ask:** With which Communist countries did Austria share a border? *(Yugoslavia, Hungary, and Czechoslovakia)* **BL**

DBQ Document Based Questions

Answers:

1. a political and economic barrier between the Soviet sphere and Western Europe; The image provides a strong division between the world and the Soviets. Churchill wanted to illustrate that the Soviets would be a formidable enemy.
2. the Soviet attempts to establish communism in other countries across Europe

Additional Support

Teacher Tip

Collaborative Learning This activity requires students within each group to participate on some level. Have each group select a leader to help divide the work. A person from each group should be selected to lead the debate.

NATIONAL GEOGRAPHIC **The Iron Curtain in Europe, 1948**

Primary Source

"A shadow has fallen upon the scenes so lately light by the Allied victory. . . . From Stettin in the Baltic to Trieste in the Adriatic, an iron curtain has descended across the continent. Behind that line lie all the capitals of the ancient states of Central and Eastern Europe. Warsaw, Berlin, Prague, Vienna, Budapest, Belgrade, Bucharest and Sofia, all these famous cities and the populations around them lie in what I must call the Soviet sphere, and all are subject in one form or another, not only to Soviet influence, but to a very high and, in some cases, increasing measure of control from Moscow. . . .

The Communist parties, which were very small in all these Eastern States of Europe, have been raised to pre-eminence and power far beyond their numbers and are seeking everywhere to obtain totalitarian control. . . .

In front of the iron curtain which lies across Europe are other causes for anxiety . . . in a great number of countries, far from the Russian frontiers and throughout the world, Communist fifth columns are established and work in . . . absolute obedience to the directions they receive from the Communist center. . . . I do not believe that Soviet Russia desires war. What they desire is the fruits of war and the indefinite expansion of their power and doctrines."

—Winston Churchill, address to Westminster College, Fulton, Missouri, March 5, 1946

DBQ Document-Based Questions

1. **Finding the Main Idea** What was the "iron curtain," and why do you think Churchill described it in that way?
2. **Identifying Central Issues** What "other causes for anxiety" did Churchill say the Soviets were creating?

Ten days later, Truman did exactly that during a meeting with Soviet Foreign Minister Molotov. Truman immediately brought up the issue of Poland and demanded that Stalin hold free elections as he had promised at Yalta. Molotov took the unexpectedly strong message back to Stalin. The meeting marked an important shift in Soviet-American relations and set the stage for further confrontations.

The Potsdam Conference

In July 1945 with the war against Japan still raging, Truman finally met Stalin at **Potsdam,** near Berlin. Both men had come to Potsdam primarily to work out a deal on Germany.

Truman was now convinced that industry was critical to Germany's survival. Unless that nation's economy was allowed to revive, the rest of Europe would never recover, and the German people might turn to communism out of desperation.

Stalin and his advisers were equally convinced that they needed reparations from Germany. The war had devastated the Soviet economy. Soviet troops had begun stripping their zone in Germany of its machinery and industrial equipment for use back home, but Stalin wanted Germany to pay much more.

Activity: Collaborative Learning

Identifying Central Issues Ask students to imagine that they are delegates at the Potsdam Conference. Divide the class into two groups: one representing the Soviet Union, the other the United States. Have each group work together to write a paragraph defending their position on German reparations. Students may use the library or Internet to find primary sources to use in their presentations. Remind students that the Allies were no longer sympathetic toward Stalin. Stalin was worried about the destruction in the Soviet Union. Have a representative from each group engage in a debate. Ask the class to vote on the most convincing argument. **OL**

At the conference, Truman took a firm stand against heavy reparations. He insisted that Germany's industry had to be allowed to recover. Truman suggested that the Soviets take reparations from their zone, while the Allies allowed industry to revive in the other zones. Stalin opposed this idea since the Soviet zone was mostly agricultural. It could not provide all the reparations the Soviets wanted.

To get the Soviets to accept the agreement, Truman offered Stalin a small amount of German industrial equipment from the other zones, but required the Soviets to pay for part of it with food shipments from their zone. He also offered to accept the new German-Polish border the Soviets had established.

D

Stalin did not like Truman's proposal. At Potsdam, Truman learned that the atomic bomb had been successfully tested, and he hinted to Stalin that the United States had developed a new, powerful weapon. Stalin suspected that Truman was trying to bully him into a deal and that the Americans were trying to limit reparations to keep the Soviets weak.

Despite his suspicions, Stalin had to accept the terms. American and British troops controlled Germany's industrial heartland, and there was no way for the Soviets to get any reparations except by cooperating. Nevertheless, the Potsdam conference marked yet another increase in tensions between the Soviets and the Americans.

The Iron Curtain Descends

Although Truman had won the argument over reparations, he had less success on other issues at Potsdam. The Soviets refused to make any stronger commitments to uphold the Declaration of Liberated Europe. The presence of the Soviet army in Eastern Europe ensured that pro-Soviet Communist governments would eventually be established in Poland, Romania, Bulgaria, Hungary, and Czechoslovakia. "This war is not as in the past," Stalin commented. "Whoever occupies a territory also imposes his own social system. . . . It cannot be otherwise."

The Communist countries of Eastern Europe came to be called **satellite nations** because they were controlled by the Soviets, as satellites are tied by gravity to the planets they orbit. These nations had to remain Communist and friendly to the Soviet Union. They also had to follow policies that the Soviets approved.

After watching the Communist takeover in Eastern Europe, Winston Churchill coined a phrase to describe what had happened. In a 1946 speech delivered in Fulton, Missouri, he referred to an "iron curtain" falling across Eastern Europe. The press picked up the term and, for the next 43 years, when someone referred to the Iron Curtain, they meant the Communist nations of Eastern Europe and the Soviet Union. With the **Iron Curtain** separating the Communist nations of Eastern Europe from the West, the World War II era had come to an end. The Cold War was about to begin.

Reading Check **Explaining** How did the Potsdam Conference hurt Soviet-American relations?

Section 1 REVIEW

Vocabulary

1. **Explain** the significance of: Yalta, Cold War, Potsdam, satellite nations, Iron Curtain.

Main Ideas

2. **Identifying** At Yalta, what agreement did the "Big Three" come to about Germany's future after World War II?
3. **Summarizing** What concerns made the Soviets suspicious of the Western Allies?
4. **Explaining** How did the Potsdam Conference help bring about the Cold War?

Critical Thinking

5. **Big Ideas** How did different economic systems cause tensions between the United States and the Soviet Union?
6. **Organizing** Use a graphic organizer similar to the one below to list events that led to the Cold War.

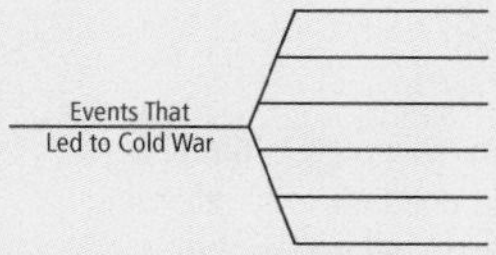

7. **Analyzing Visuals** Study the map on page 764. Why did the Soviet Union want to have control over the countries on its western border?

Writing About History

8. **Expository Writing** Suppose that you are an adviser to Truman. Write a report explaining your interpretation of Churchill's "iron curtain" speech.

History ONLINE
Study Central™ To review this section, go to glencoe.com and click on Study Central.

D Differentiated Instruction

Visual/Spatial Bring in and discuss some political cartoons illustrating the Potsdam Conference and the Cold War. Then have students design their own political cartoons illustrating the tension between the Allies and the Soviets. OL

Reading Check

Answer: It increased tension because Stalin suspected that Truman wanted to limit reparations.

Assess

History ONLINE

Study Central™ provides summaries, interactive games, and online graphic organizers to help students review content.

Close

Assessing Have students use their graphic organizer from page 760 and evaluate the effectiveness of the conferences. OL

Section 1 REVIEW

Answers

1. All definitions can be found in the section and the Glossary.
2. Germany was divided into four zones controlled by Great Britain, France, the Soviet Union, and the United States.
3. The Soviets were suspicious that the Western Allies wanted to increase economic independence in Europe and establish free governments. They were also unwilling to make the Germans pay large reparations.
4. The conference increased the tension between the Soviet Union and the United States. It was clear that Truman, with the atomic bomb in his pocket, was not willing to make concessions.
5. The United States wanted to promote strong economic growth throughout Europe. The Soviet Union wanted only to rebuild its own country.
6. 

7. to protect itself from invasion by Germany
8. Reports will vary but should include specific references to Churchill's speech.

Focus

Bellringer

Daily Focus Transparency 22-2

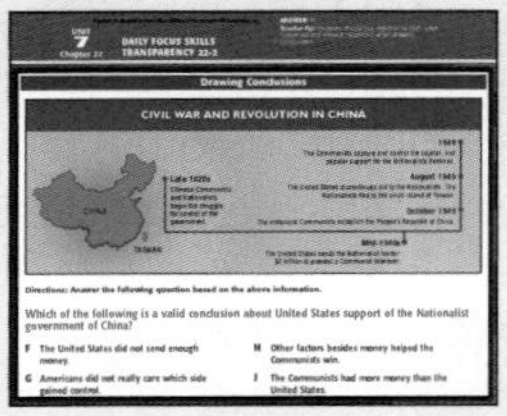

Guide to Reading

Answers:
Answers may include: 1945 Soviet-U.S. division of Korea;
June 1950 North Korea invades South Korea;
November 1950 China intervenes;
April 1951 MacArthur fired

Section Spotlight Video

To generate student interest and provide a springboard for class discussion, access the Chapter 22, Section 2 video at glencoe.com or on the video DVD.

Resource Manager

Section Audio   Spotlight Video

The Early Cold War Years

Guide to Reading

Big Ideas
Trade, War, and Migration As the Cold War began, the United States struggled to oppose Communist aggression in Europe and Asia through political, economic, and military measures.

Content Vocabulary
- containment *(p. 766)*
- limited war *(p. 773)*

Academic Vocabulary
- insecurity *(p. 766)*
- initially *(p. 769)*

People and Events to Identify
- George Kennan *(p. 766)*
- Long Telegram *(p. 766)*
- Marshall Plan *(p. 768)*
- NATO *(p. 769)*
- SEATO *(p. 773)*

Reading Strategy
Sequencing Complete a time line similar to the one below by recording the major events related to the Korean War.

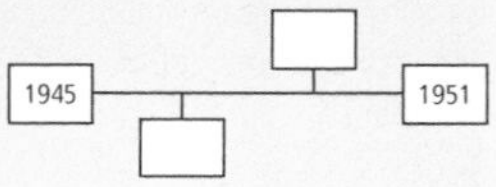

President Truman worked to contain communism by supporting Greece, Iran, and West Germany. When Communist North Korea invaded South Korea, Truman and the UN sent troops to aid South Korea.

Containing Communism

MAIN Idea The Truman Doctrine offered aid to any nation resisting communism; the Marshall Plan aided European countries in rebuilding.

HISTORY AND YOU Is there a conflict in the world today where you think the United States should intervene? Read on to learn how President Truman adopted policies designed to stop the spread of communism.

Despite growing tensions with the Soviet Union, many American officials continued to believe cooperation with the Soviets was possible. In late 1945 the foreign ministers of the former wartime Allies met first in London, then in Moscow, to discuss the future of Europe and Asia. Although both British and American officials pushed for free elections in Eastern Europe, the Soviets refused to budge. "Our relations with the Russians," the British foreign minister gloomily concluded, "are drifting into the same condition as that in which we had found ourselves with Hitler."

The Long Telegram

Increasingly exasperated by the Soviets' refusal to cooperate, officials at the State Department asked the American Embassy in Moscow to explain Soviet behavior. On February 22, 1946, diplomat **George Kennan** responded with what became known as the **Long Telegram,** a 5,540-word message explaining his views of the Soviets.

According to Kennan, the Soviets' view of the world came from a traditional "Russian sense of **insecurity**" and fear of the West, intensified by the communist ideas of Lenin and Stalin. Because communists believed that they were in a long-term historical struggle against capitalism, Kennan argued, it was impossible to reach any permanent settlement with them.

Kennan therefore proposed what became the basic American policy throughout the Cold War: "a long-term, patient but firm and vigilant **containment** of Russian expansive tendencies." Kennan explained that, in his opinion, the Soviet system had several major economic and political weaknesses. If the United States could keep the Soviets from expanding their power, it would be only a matter of time before the Soviet system would fall apart. Communism could be beaten without going to war. The Long Telegram circulated widely in

R Reading Strategies	C Critical Thinking	D Differentiated Instruction	W Writing Support	S Skill Practice
Teacher Edition • Identifying, p. 768 • Summarizing, p. 770 • Inferring, p. 771 **Additional Resources** • Guided Reading Act., URB p. 117 • Reading Skills Act., URB p. 89	**Teacher Edition** • Analyzing Prim. Sources, p. 767 • Drawing Con., pp. 768, 772 • Det. Cause/Effect, pp. 770, 773 **Additional Resources** • Quizzes/Tests, p. 316	**Teacher Edition** • Visual/Spatial p. 768 **Additional Resources** • English Learner Act., URB p. 93	**Teacher Edition** • Persuasive Writing, p. 769 • Personal Writing, p. 772	**Teacher Edition** • Using Geo. Skills, pp. 767, 771 **Additional Resources** • Reading Skills Act., URB p. 89 • Reinf. Skills Act., URB p. 99 • Read. Essen., p. 250

PRIMARY SOURCE
The Truman Doctrine

▲ *President Truman signs the Foreign Aid Assistance Act, providing aid to Greece and Turkey; the use of aid to support nations resisting Communist pressure became known as the Truman Doctrine.*

PRIMARY SOURCE

"The peoples of a number of countries of the world have recently had totalitarian regimes forced upon them against their will. The Government of the United States has made frequent protests against coercion and intimidation, in violation of the Yalta agreement in Poland, Romania, and Bulgaria. At the present moment in world history nearly every nation must choose between alternative ways of life. The choice is too often not a free one. . . . I believe that it must be the policy of the United States to support free peoples who are resisting attempted subjugation by armed minorities or by outside pressures. I believe that we must assist free peoples to work out their own destinies in their own way."

—Truman's address to Congress, March 12, 1947

C

DBQ Document-Based Questions

1. **Finding the Main Idea** What was the stated goal of the Truman Doctrine?
2. **Drawing Conclusions** Which nation received the most aid through the Marshall Plan? Why do you think this might be?

Marshall Plan Aid to Major Countries

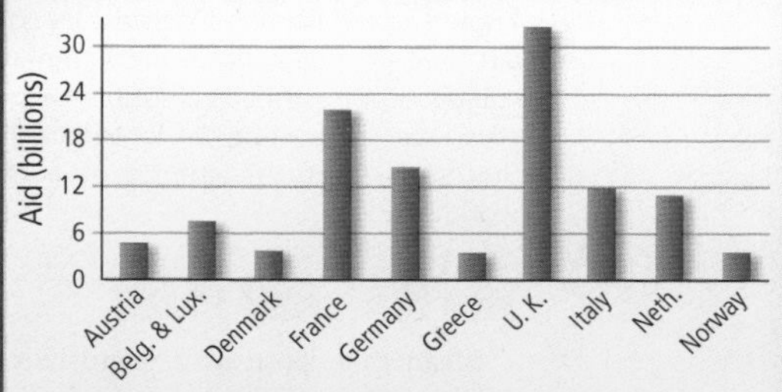

Source: *The Marshall Plan Fifty Years Later.*

Truman's administration. The administration based its policy of containment—keeping communism within its present territory through the use of diplomatic, economic, and military actions—on this document.

Crisis in Iran

While Truman's administration discussed Kennan's ideas, a series of crises erupted during the spring and summer of 1946. These crises seemed to prove that Kennan was right about the Soviets. The first crisis began in Iran in March 1946.

During World War II, the United States had put troops in southern Iran while Soviet troops occupied northern Iran to secure a supply line from the Persian Gulf. After the war, instead of withdrawing as promised, the Soviet troops remained in northern Iran. Stalin then began demanding access to Iran's oil supplies. To increase the pressure, Soviet troops helped local Communists in northern Iran establish a separate government.

To American officials, these actions signaled a Soviet push into the Middle East. The secretary of state sent Stalin a strong message demanding that Soviet forces withdraw. At the same time, the battleship USS *Missouri* sailed into the eastern Mediterranean. The pressure seemed to work. Soviet forces withdrew, having been promised a joint Soviet-Iranian oil company, although the Iranian parliament later rejected the plan.

The Truman Doctrine

Frustrated in Iran, Stalin turned northwest to Turkey. There, the straits of the Dardanelles were a vital route from Soviet Black Sea ports to the Mediterranean. For centuries, Russia had wanted to control this strategic route. In August 1946, Stalin demanded joint control of the Dardanelles with Turkey. S

For more of the text of Truman's Address to Congress, see page R54 in **Documents in American History.**

Teach

C Critical Thinking

Analyzing Primary Sources Ask students if the United States still practices the policy as set forth by Truman—that the U.S. "must assist free peoples." Have students use current examples to support their statements. **AL**

S Skill Practice

Using Geography Skills Provide students with a map of Eastern Europe. Ask them to identify the following: Turkey, the straits of Dardanelles, the Black Sea, and the Mediterranean Sea. **Ask:** Why did the Soviet Union want to gain influence over Turkey? *(To secure access to the Mediterranean.)* **BL**

DBQ Document Based Questions

Answers:
1. to support free peoples, fight Soviet aggression, and stop the spread of communism
2. U.K.; It had been bombed and was America's closest ally.

Additional Support

Activity: Economics Connection

Analyzing Information The Tripartite Treaty of Alliance of January 29, 1942, was an agreement between Russia, Britain, and Iran. Allied troops agreed to withdraw from Iran within six months after the end of World War II. British and American troops left Iran, but Stalin did not. Iranian Prime Minister Ahmad Qavam tried to persuade Stalin to remove his troops by agreeing to a Soviet oil concession and a peace agreement with the Azerbaijani Republic, a Soviet puppet republic set in the Soviet military zone in Northern Iran. When the *USS Missouri* arrived and the Soviets finally left Iran, Qavam then reclaimed his concessions. **Ask:** Why was Iran important to the Allies? Why did Stalin refuse to honor the treaty? Have students look at a current map identifying oil and gas production areas. They should then write a one-page report answering the above questions. **OL**

R Reading Strategy

Identifying Ask: How much money did Truman ask Congress to appropriate to fight communism? *($400 million)* Remind students of the value of the dollar in 1947. **Ask:** Why did the United States have to support the Greek government? *(The British did not have the resources to help Greece.)* **BL**

D Differentiated Instruction

Visual/Spatial Have students draw a map of the German zones in 1948. Instruct students to use a transparency to show what West Germany and West Berlin looked like after the United States, Britain, and France merged their zones. **Ask:** Why was this merger not welcomed by the Soviets? *(The Soviets saw this as an attempt to undermine their reparations plan.)* **OL**

Presidential adviser Dean Acheson saw this move as part of a Soviet plan to control the Middle East. He advised Truman to make a show of force. The president ordered the new aircraft carrier *Franklin D. Roosevelt* to join the *Missouri* in protecting Turkey and the eastern Mediterranean.

Meanwhile, Britain tried to help Greece. In August 1946 Greek Communists launched a guerrilla war against the Greek government. British troops helped fight the guerrillas, but in February 1947 Britain informed the United States that it could no longer afford to help Greece due to Britain's weakened postwar economy.

On March 12, 1947, Truman went before Congress to ask for $400 million to fight Communist aggression in Greece and Turkey. His speech outlined a policy that became known as the Truman Doctrine. Its goal was to aid "free peoples who are resisting attempted subjugation by armed minorities or by outside pressures." In the long run, it pledged the United States to fight the spread of communism worldwide.

The Marshall Plan

Meanwhile, postwar Western Europe faced grave problems. Economies were ruined, people were nearing starvation, and political chaos was at hand. In June 1947 Secretary of State George C. Marshall proposed the European Recovery Program, or **Marshall Plan,** which would give European nations American aid to rebuild their economies. Truman saw the Marshall Plan and the Truman Doctrine as "two halves of the same walnut," both essential for containment. Marshall offered help to all nations planning a recovery program:

PRIMARY SOURCE

"Our policy is directed not against any country or doctrine but against hunger, poverty, desperation and chaos. Its purpose should be the revival of a working economy in the world so as to permit the emergence of political and social conditions in which free institutions can exist."

—quoted in *Marshall: Hero for Our Times*

Although the Marshall Plan was offered to the Soviet Union and its satellite nations in Eastern Europe, those nations rejected the offer. Instead, the Soviets developed their own economic program. This action further separated Europe into competing regions. The Marshall Plan pumped billions of dollars worth of supplies, machinery, and food into Western Europe. Western Europe's recovery weakened the appeal of communism and opened new markets for trade.

In his 1949 Inaugural Address, President Truman also proposed assistance for underdeveloped countries outside the war zone. The Point Four Program aimed to make "scientific advances and industrial progress available for the improvement and growth of underdeveloped areas" regardless of region. The Department of State administered Point Four assistances from 1950 until its merger with other foreign aid programs in 1953.

The Berlin Airlift

President Truman and his advisers believed that Western Europe's prosperity depended on Germany's recovery. The Soviets, however, still wanted Germany to pay reparations to the Soviet Union. This dispute brought these nations to the brink of war.

By early 1948, U.S. officials had concluded that the Soviets were trying to undermine Germany's economy. In response, the United States, Great Britain, and France announced that they were merging their zones in Germany and allowing the Germans to have their own government. They also agreed to merge their zones in Berlin and to make West Berlin part of the new German republic.

The new nation was officially called the Federal Republic of Germany, but it became known as West Germany. The Soviet zone eventually became the German Democratic Republic, also known as East Germany. West Germany was not allowed to have a military, but in most respects, it was independent.

The decision to create West Germany convinced the Soviets that they would never get the reparations they wanted. In late June 1948, Soviet troops cut all road and rail traffic to West Berlin hoping to force the United States to either reconsider its decision or abandon West Berlin. President Truman sent bombers with atomic weapons to bases in Britain and the American commander in Germany warned: "If we mean to hold Europe against communism,

Differentiated Instruction

Leveled Activities

BL Reading Skills Activity, URB p. 89

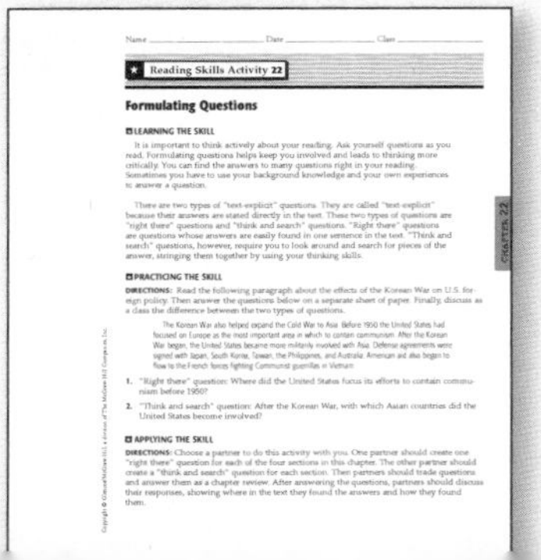

OL Content Vocabulary Activity, URB p. 95

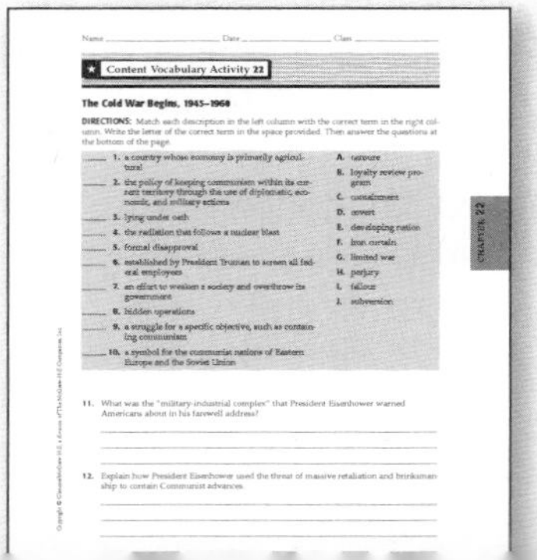

AL Primary Source Reading, URB p. 103

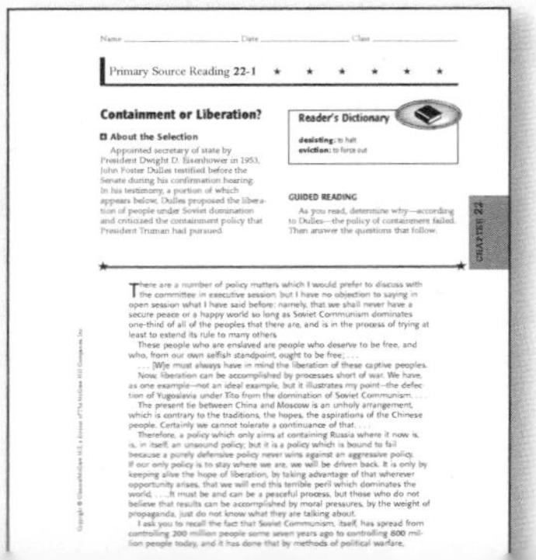

ELL English Learner Activity, URB, p. 93

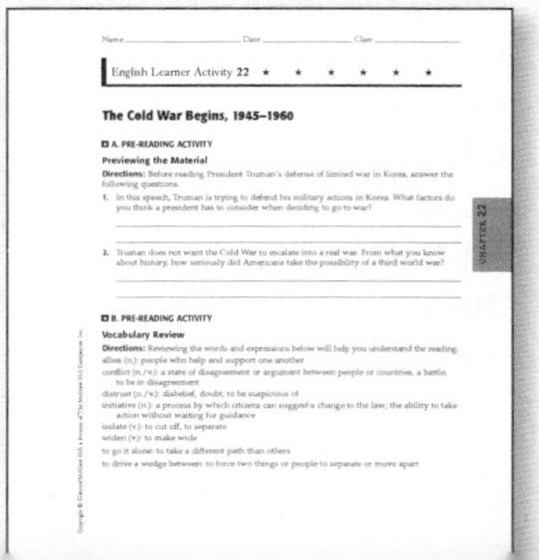

then we must not budge."The challenge was to keep West Berlin alive without provoking war with the Soviets. Instead of ordering troops to fight their way to Berlin, and thereby triggering war with the Soviet Union, Truman ordered the air force to fly supplies into Berlin instead.

The Berlin airlift began in June 1948 and continued through the spring of 1949, bringing in more than 2 million tons of supplies to the city. Stalin finally lifted the blockade on May 12, 1949. The airlift symbolized American determination to contain communism and not give in to Soviet demands.

NATO

The Berlin blockade convinced many Americans that the Soviets were bent on conquest. The public began to support a military alliance with Western Europe. By April 1949, an agreement had been reached to create the North Atlantic Treaty Organization (NATO)—a mutual defense alliance.

NATO initially included 12 countries: the United States, Canada, Britain, France, Italy, Belgium, Denmark, Portugal, the Netherlands, Norway, Luxembourg, and Iceland. NATO members agreed to come to the aid of any member who was attacked. For the first time in its history, the United States had committed itself to maintaining peace in Europe. Six years later, NATO allowed West Germany to rearm and join its organization. This decision alarmed Soviet leaders. They responded by organizing a military alliance in Eastern Europe known as the Warsaw Pact. **W**

Reading Check **Evaluating** What triggered the beginning of the Berlin airlift?

History ONLINE
Student Web Activity Visit glencoe.com and complete the activity on the Berlin Airlift.

PRIMARY SOURCE
The Berlin Airlift, 1948–1949

After the Soviet Union blockaded West Berlin, the United States delivered 4,000 tons of food, medicine, coal and other supplies that were needed every day to keep the city functioning. A cargo plane had to land with supplies every three and a half minutes. To keep the airlift running, crews stayed onboard and food was brought to them while the planes were unloaded and refueled. Meanwhile, 20,000 volunteers in Berlin built a third airport, enabling the flow of supplies to increase to 13,000 tons a day.

NATIONAL GEOGRAPHIC NATO Is Born, 1949

Analyzing VISUALS

1. **Interpreting** Which nations are the founding members of NATO?
2. **Identifying** Which NATO nations shared a border with one or more Warsaw Pact nations?

W Writing Support

Persuasive Writing Have students write an editorial supporting the creation of NATO. **OL**

Did You Know?

During the Berlin airlift, a plane flew into the city every three minutes. Without the supplies those planes carried, West Berliners would have had to back down.

Analyzing VISUALS

Answers:
1. United Kingdom, France, Italy, Belgium, Denmark, Portugal, the Netherlands, Norway, Luxembourg, and Iceland
2. Greece, Turkey, West Germany

Reading Check

Answer: Soviet blockade of West Berlin

Additional Support

Extending the Content

Point Four Program In his 1949 inaugural address, President Harry Truman announced (as the fourth point of his speech) "a bold new program for making the benefits of our scientific advances and industrial progress available for the improvement and growth of underdeveloped areas" around the globe. The program was intended to encourage development and economic growth in poorer countries and thereby diminish the appeal of socialist or communist doctrines. Officially titled the United States Technical Assistance Plan, the Point Four Program focused on providing technical assistance to developing nations.

R Reading Strategy

Summarizing Have students state why China suspended its civil war during World War II and what happened at the end of the war. *(Communist forces and the Nationalist government suspended fighting to make sure Japan would not try to invade. Once the war was over, they continued fighting since a resolution was never obtained.)* **OL**

C Critical Thinking

Determining Cause and Effect Ask: What happened in China when the United States discontinued financial aid? *(The Chinese Nationalists fled to Taiwan, and China became an established Communist country.)* What effect did this have on American policy and why? *(The new strategy was to help Japan recover quickly from the war, due to its strategic location. The Americans believed that by strengthening Japan, they could fend off communism in the rest of Asia.)* **OL**

The Korean War

MAIN Idea Attempts to keep South Korea free from communism led the United States to military intervention.

HISTORY AND YOU What happens to someone who disobeys a coach, employer, or teacher? Read on to learn what happened to General MacArthur when he criticized the president.

The Cold War eventually spread beyond Europe. Conflicts also emerged in Asia, where events in China and Korea brought about a new attitude toward Japan and sent American troops back into battle in Asia less than five years after World War II had ended.

The Chinese Revolution

In China, Communist forces led by Mao Zedong had been struggling against the Nationalist government led by Chiang Kai-shek since the late 1920s. During World War II, the two sides suspended their war to resist Japanese occupation. With the end of World War II, however, civil war broke out again. Although Mao made great gains, neither side R could win nor agree to a compromise.

To prevent a Communist revolution in Asia, the United States sent the Nationalist government $2 billion in aid beginning in the mid-1940s, but the Nationalists squandered this advantage through poor military planning and corruption. By 1949, the Communists had captured the Chinese capital of Beijing, while support for the Nationalists declined.

In August 1949 the U.S. State Department discontinued aid to the Chinese Nationalists. The defeated Nationalists then fled to the small island of Taiwan (Formosa). The victorious Communists established the People's Republic of China in October 1949.

China's fall to communism shocked Americans. To make matters worse, in September 1949 the Soviet Union announced C that it had successfully tested its first atomic weapon. Then, early in 1950, the People's Republic of China and the Soviet Union signed a treaty of friendship and alliance. Many Western leaders feared that China and the Soviet Union would support Communist revolutions in other nations.

The United States kept formal diplomatic relations with only the Nationalist Chinese in Taiwan. It used its veto power in the UN Security Council to keep representatives of the new Communist People's Republic of China out of the UN, allowing the Nationalists to retain their seat.

New Policies in Japan

C The Chinese revolution brought about a significant change in American policy toward Japan. At the end of World War II, General Douglas MacArthur had taken charge of occupied Japan. His mission was to introduce democracy and keep Japan from threatening war again. Once the United States lost China as its chief ally in Asia, it adopted policies to encourage the rapid recovery of Japan's industrial economy. Just as

INFOGRAPHIC

The Korean War, 1950–1953

▲ **June–September 1950**

North Korean troops invade South Korea, driving South Korean and UN forces south into a small perimeter around Pusan.

0 — 400 kilometers
0 — 400 miles
Miller projection

- North Korean-controlled territory
- South Korean-controlled territory
- North Korean advance
- UN counteroffensive
- Front line
- Chinese counteroffensive
- Armistice line

Additional Support

Activity: Collaborative Learning

Contrasting In 1949, Nationalists fled the Chinese mainland to the island of Taiwan. While mainland China became a Communist stronghold, Taiwan remained tied to the West. Have students work in groups and trace the development of China and Taiwan over the last 55 years. Groups should create a time line to document and illustrate main events and crises between China and Taiwan. Have groups present their time lines in class. **Ask:** Why does China want Taiwan? How far will China go to ensure Taiwan does not become independent? What do the Taiwanese people want? **OL**

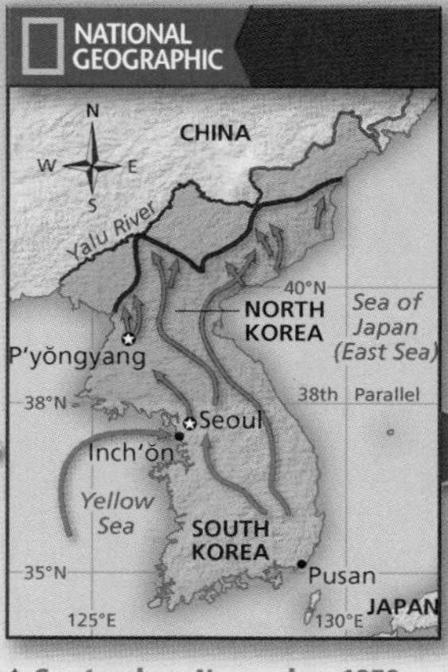

▲ **September–November 1950**
Led by General MacArthur, UN troops land behind North Korean lines at the port of Inchon. North Korean forces fall back rapidly, and the UN forces head north into North Korea.

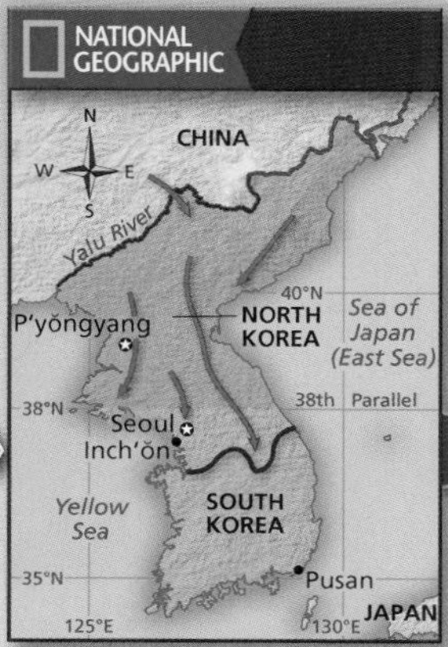

▲ **November 1950–January 1951**
As UN forces near the Chinese border, Chinese troops cross into North Korea driving the UN back. MacArthur wants to attack Chinese territory. He publicly argues with Truman and is fired.

▲ **January 1951–July 1953**
Led by U.S. General Matthew Ridgway, the UN forces push the Chinese and North Korean forces out of South Korea. The war bogs down into a stalemate along the 38th parallel.

S

◀ *Soldiers of the U.S. 2nd Infantry Division man a machine gun near the Chongchun River in Korea, December 15, 1950.*

Analyzing GEOGRAPHY

1. **Human-Environment Interaction** What occurred at the port of Inchon in 1950?
2. **Location** What geographical feature forms the border between China and North Korea?

the United States viewed West Germany as the key to defending all of Europe against communism, it saw Japan as the key to defending Asia.

The Korean War Begins

At the end of World War II, American and Soviet forces entered Korea to disarm the Japanese troops stationed there. The Allies divided Korea at the 38th parallel of latitude. Soviet troops controlled the north, while American troops controlled the south.

As the Cold War began, talks to reunify Korea broke down. A Communist Korean government was organized in the north, while an American-backed government controlled the south. Both governments claimed authority over Korea, and border clashes were common. The Soviet Union provided military aid to the North Koreans, who quickly built up an army. On June 25, 1950, North Korean troops invaded the south, rapidly driving back the poorly equipped South Korean forces.

Truman saw the Communist invasion of South Korea as a test of the containment policy and ordered United States naval and air power into action. He then called on the United Nations to act. Truman succeeded because the Soviet delegate was boycotting the UN Security Council over its China policy and was not present to veto the American proposal. With the pledge of UN troops, Truman ordered General MacArthur to send American troops from Japan to Korea. R

S Skill Practice

Using Geography Skills Have students look at the map of Korea. Ask them to identify the 38th parallel of latitude. **Ask:** Why did the Allies divide Korea at the 38th parallel? *(It looks like an even division.)* What is the importance of Korea's geographic location? *(It is close to China and the Soviet Union.)* **BL**

R Reading Strategy

Inferring Ask: Why do you think Truman called on the UN to assist the United States troops in Korea? *(Students might suggest that he did not want the world to think the United States was a "military bully." He wanted international approval and support.)* **OL**

Analyzing GEOGRAPHY

Answers:
1. U.N. forces under General MacArthur landed and cut off the North Korean army.
2. The Yalu River.

Hands-On Chapter Project Step 2

Role-Playing to Demonstrate McCarthyism in Action

Step 2: Creating the Roles and the Script Essential question: How much of a hearing can student cast members perform and who will write the script?

Directions From reading about the hearings or even seeing them if a historical video exists, students will create their script and cast different students in the lead and supporting roles. These roles should include Senator McCarthy, army lawyer Joseph Welch, other senators on the committee, and a witness.

Putting It Together Students should meet to finalize the product—a script outline (some improvisation might be allowed), and a definite beginning and an end that will make sense to viewers. **OL**

(Chapter Project continued on page 777)

W Writing Support

Personal Writing Have students write a journal entry expressing what they think about the MacArthur/Truman debate. **Ask:** **Should a country use all the military force at its disposal to guarantee a victory, or should a country fight a limited war, hoping to avoid a nuclear war?** OL

C Critical Thinking

Drawing Conclusions When the Chinese came to the aid of the North Koreans, MacArthur wanted to attack China but Truman disagreed. **Ask:** **Why was Truman against expanding the war to China?** *(Truman wanted to fight a limited war. The Chinese would be a formidable enemy. He didn't want to drop another atomic bomb.)* OL

Analyzing VISUALS

Answers:

1. the one on the right
2. make decisions reserved for the president

Additional Support

POLITICAL CARTOONS — PRIMARY SOURCE

Truman vs. MacArthur

▲ *President Truman, Secretary of State Dean Acheson, and "The Pentagon" are held over the flame of public opinion for firing General MacArthur. "John Q." refers to "John Q. Public," or the American people.*

▲ *Entitled "Not a General's Job," this cartoon suggests that MacArthur had overstepped his authority in Korea.*

Analyzing VISUALS

1. **Identifying Points of View** Which of the cartoons supports President Truman's decision to fire General MacArthur? Explain.
2. **Making Inferences** What does the cartoon on the right imply MacArthur was trying to do in Asia?

The American and South Korean troops were driven back into a small pocket of territory near the port of Pusan. Inside the "Pusan perimeter," as it came to be called, the troops stubbornly resisted the North Korean onslaught, buying time for MacArthur to organize reinforcements.

On September 15, 1950, MacArthur ordered a daring invasion behind enemy lines at the port of Inchon. The Inchon landing took the North Koreans by surprise. Within weeks they were in full retreat back across the 38th parallel. Truman then gave the order to pursue the North Koreans beyond the 38th parallel. MacArthur pushed the North Koreans north to the Yalu River, the border with China.

China Enters the War The Communist People's Republic of China saw the advancing UN troops as a threat and warned the forces to halt their advance. When those warnings were ignored, Chinese forces crossed the Yalu River in November. Hundreds of thousands of Chinese troops flooded across the border, driving the UN forces back across the 38th parallel.

As his troops fell back, an angry MacArthur demanded approval to expand the war against China. He asked for a blockade of Chinese ports, the use of Chiang Kai-shek's Nationalist forces, and the bombing of Chinese cities with atomic weapons.

Truman Fires MacArthur President Truman refused MacArthur's demands because he did not want to expand the war into China or to use the atomic bomb. MacArthur persisted. He publicly criticized the president, arguing that it was a mistake to keep the war limited. "There is no substitute for victory," MacArthur insisted, by which he meant that if the United States was going to go to war, it should use all of its power to win. Keeping a war limited was, in his view, a form of appeasement, and appeasement he argued, "begets new and bloodier war."

Determined to maintain control of policy and to show that the president commanded the military, an exasperated Truman fired MacArthur for insubordination in April 1951. Later, in private conversation, Truman explained:

Activity: Collaborative Learning

Identifying Central Issues A controversy between Harry S. Truman and General Douglas MacArthur began shortly after the outbreak of the Korean War. It reached a climax when the president relieved MacArthur of his command. Truman believed in limited war; MacArthur wanted total victory.

Have students review the Constitutional powers of the president. Then ask students to use the library or the Internet to locate and read the letter from Truman to MacArthur, dated April 11, 1951. Have students work in groups to discuss if President Truman made the correct choice. **Ask:** **Do you think President Truman exercised his presidential powers according to the Constitution? Should Truman have dealt differently with MacArthur?** After groups have reached their conclusions, lead a class discussion, writing major ideas on the board. OL

"I was sorry to have to reach a parting of the way with the big man in Asia, but he asked for it and I had to give it to him."

MacArthur, who remained popular despite being fired, returned home to parades and a hero's welcome. Many Americans criticized the president. Congress and other military leaders, however, supported Truman's decision and his Korean strategy. American policy in Asia remained committed to **limited war**—a war fought to achieve a limited objective, such as containing communism. Truman later explained why he favored limited war in Korea:

PRIMARY SOURCE

"The Kremlin [Soviet Union] is trying, and has been trying for a long time, to drive a wedge between us and the other nations. It wants to see us isolated. It wants to see us distrusted. It wants to see us feared and hated by our allies. Our allies agree with us in the course we are following. They do not believe we should take the initiative to widen the conflict in the Far East. If the United States were to widen the conflict, we might well have to go it alone."

—from "Address to the Civil Defense Conference," May 7, 1951

As Truman also noted, America's allies in Europe were much closer to the Soviet Union. If war broke out, Europe would suffer the most damage and might well be attacked with atomic bombs. This concern—that all-out war in Korea might lead to nuclear war—was the main reason why Truman favored limited war. This concern shaped American foreign policy throughout the Cold War.

Changes in Policy

By mid-1951, the UN forces had pushed the Chinese and North Korean forces back across the 38th parallel. The war then settled down into a series of relatively small battles over hills and other local objectives. In November 1951, peace negotiations began, but an armistice would not be signed until July 1953. More than 33,600 American soldiers died in action in the Korean War, and more than 2,800 died from accidents or disease.

The Korean War marked an important turning point in the Cold War. Until 1950, the United States had preferred to use political pressure and economic aid to contain communism. After the Korean War began, the United States embarked on a major military buildup.

The Korean War also helped expand the Cold War to Asia. Before 1950, the United States had focused on Europe as the most important area in which to contain communism. After the Korean War began, the United States became more militarily involved in Asia. In 1954 the United States signed defense agreements with Japan, South Korea, Taiwan, the Philippines, and Australia, forming the Southeast Asia Treaty Organization (**SEATO**). American aid also began flowing to French forces fighting Communists in Vietnam. C

Reading Check **Analyzing** How did President Truman view the Communist invasion of South Korea?

Section 2 REVIEW

Vocabulary

1. **Explain** the significance of: George Kennan, Long Telegram, containment, Marshall Plan, NATO, limited war, SEATO.

Main Ideas

2. **Explaining** How did the Truman Doctrine and the Marshall Plan address the spread of communism?
3. **Describing** What originally led to the formation of two Koreas?

Critical Thinking

4. **Big Ideas** How did the Long Telegram influence U.S. foreign policy?
5. **Categorizing** Use a graphic organizer similar to the one below to list early conflicts between the Soviet Union and the United States.

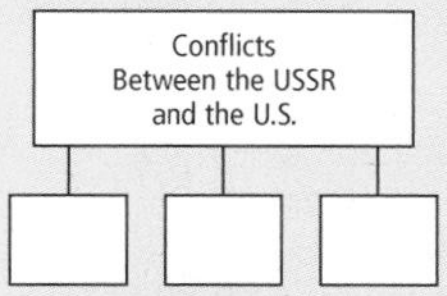

6. **Analyzing Visuals** Study the maps of the Korean War on pages 770–771. When did the United Nations control the most territory in Korea? When did both sides finally agree on an armistice line?

Writing About History

7. **Persuasive Writing** Write a letter to the editor of a newspaper explaining why you agree or disagree with President Truman's firing of General MacArthur.

History ONLINE

Study Central™ To review this section, go to glencoe.com and click on Study Central.

C Critical Thinking

Determining Cause and Effect Ask: How did the Korean War change U.S. policy in regard to communism? *(Prior to the Korean War, the U.S. preferred to use political and economic pressures. After Korea, the U.S. turned toward a militaristic approach by building up its army and its arsenals.)* **OL**

Reading Check

Answer: He saw it as a test of the U.S. containment policy.

Assess

History ONLINE

Study Central™ provides summaries, interactive games, and online graphic organizers to help students review content.

Close

Cause and Effect Have students work in groups to create two cause and effect graphic organizers—one for the Cold War and the other for the Korean War. **OL**

Section 2 REVIEW

Answers

1. All definitions can be found in the section and the Glossary.
2. The Truman Doctrine pledged U.S. military involvement to fight the spread of communism, and the Marshall Plan provided economic aid to strengthen resistance to communism.
3. At the end of World War II, the Soviet Union and the United States both entered Korea to disarm Japanese troops. The Soviets took control of Korea north of the 38th parallel, and the U.S. took control south of the 38th parallel. Talks to unite the country broke down with the Soviets establishing a Communist government in the north and the U.S. organizing a non-Communist government in the south.
4. In the Long Telegram, George Kennan recommended a policy of containment of the Soviet Union's expansion, which became a mainstay of U.S. foreign policy throughout the Cold War.
5. Students should include: Crisis in Iran, Berlin crisis, Korean War, Crisis with Turkey
6. November 1950; July 27, 1953
7. Letters will vary but should express a point of view based on facts.

Focus

Bellringer

Daily Focus Transparency 22-3

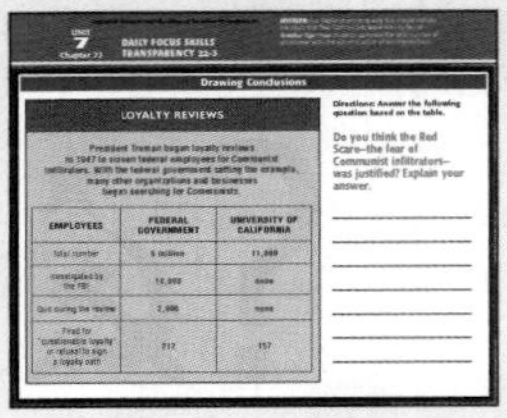

Guide to Reading

Answers: Students should complete the outline by including all headings in the section.

Section Spotlight Video

To generate student interest and provide a springboard for class discussion, access the Chapter 22, Section 3 video at glencoe.com or on the video DVD.

Section 3

Section Audio Spotlight Video

The Cold War and American Society

Guide to Reading

Big Ideas

Struggles for Rights In the early part of the Cold War, the fear of communism led to a hunt for spies and to intolerance and suspicion of people with radical ideas in the United States.

Content Vocabulary

- subversion *(p. 774)*
- loyalty review program *(p. 774)*
- perjury *(p. 776)*
- censure *(p. 778)*
- fallout *(p. 781)*

Academic Vocabulary

- manipulate *(p. 775)*
- convince *(p. 776)*

People and Events to Identify

- Red Scare *(p. 774)*
- Alger Hiss *(p. 776)*
- McCarran Act *(p. 778)*
- McCarthyism *(p. 778)*

Reading Strategy

Summarizing As you read, summarize the section content by using the major headings to create an outline similar to the one below.

The Cold War and American Society
I. A New Red Scare
  A. The Loyalty Review Program
  B.
  C.

Fearing subversive activity, the government tried to root out Communists in government, Hollywood, and labor unions, while Americans learned to live with the threat of nuclear attack.

A New Red Scare

MAIN Idea Public accusations and trials followed in the wake of fears of communism and spies.

HISTORY AND YOU Do you remember reading about the fears of communism during the early twentieth century? Read on to learn of a second major scare in the 1950s.

During the 1950s, thousands of ordinary people—from teachers to autoworkers to high government officials—shared a disturbing experience. Rumors and accusations of Communists in the United States and of Communist infiltration of the government tapped into fears that Communists were trying to take over the world.

The **Red Scare** began in September 1945, when a clerk named Igor Gouzenko walked out of the Soviet Embassy in Ottawa, Canada, and defected. Gouzenko carried documents revealing a massive effort by the Soviet Union to infiltrate organizations and government agencies in Canada and the United States, with the specific goal of obtaining information about the atomic bomb.

The Gouzenko case stunned Americans. It implied that spies had infiltrated the American government. Soon, however, the search for spies escalated into a general fear of Communist **subversion.** Subversion is the effort to weaken a society secretly and overthrow its government.

The Loyalty Review Program

In early 1947, just nine days after his powerful speech announcing the Truman Doctrine, the president established a **loyalty review program** to screen all federal employees. Rather than calm public suspicion, Truman's action seemed to confirm fears that Communists had infiltrated the government and helped to increase the fear of communism sweeping the nation.

Between 1947 and 1951, more than 6 million federal employees were screened for their loyalty—a term difficult to define. A person might become a suspect for reading certain books, belonging to various groups, traveling overseas, or even seeing certain foreign films. About 14,000 employees were subject to scrutiny by the Federal Bureau of Investigation (FBI). Some 2,000 employees quit their jobs

Resource Manager

R Reading Strategies	C Critical Thinking	D Differentiated Instruction	W Writing Support	S Skill Practice
Teacher Edition • Making Connections, pp. 775, 781 • Inferring, p. 775 **Additional Resources** • Guided Reading Act., URB p. 118 • Prim. Source Reading, URB p. 105	**Teacher Edition** • Recognizing Bias, p. 776 • Det. Cause/Effect, p. 777 • Interpreting, p. 778 **Additional Resources** • Supreme Court Case Studies, p. 69 • Link. Past and Present, URB p. 102 • Interpret. Political Cartoons, URB p. 109 • Quizzes/Tests, p. 317	**Teacher Edition** • Visual/Spatial, pp. 776, 780 • Kinesthetic, p. 777 **Additional Resources** • Differentiated Instruct. Act., URB p. 91	**Teacher Edition** • Descriptive Writing, p. 778	**Teacher Edition** • Visual Literacy p. 780 **Additional Resources** • Read. Essen., p. 253 • Historical Analysis Skills Act., URB p. 90

PRIMARY SOURCE

The Hunt for Spies, 1947–1954

▲ *Hiss v. Chambers*, 1948

In 1948, Whittaker Chambers, a *TIME* magazine editor and former Communist Party member, testified that U.S. diplomat Alger Hiss was a Communist. Hiss denied being a spy or a member of the Communist Party. Evidence provided by Chambers led to Hiss being convicted of perjury.

▲ **Loyalty and Dissent, Oppenheimer, 1953**

Although he had led the effort to develop the atomic bomb, Dr. Robert Oppenheimer's left-wing views and opposition to the hydrogen bomb led to the suspension of his security clearance and controversial public hearings.

▶ **The Rosenbergs Are Convicted, 1950**

In 1950 the hunt for spies who had given U.S. nuclear secrets to the Soviets led to the arrest of Julius and Ethel Rosenberg. Accused of running a Soviet spy network, the Rosenbergs became the first civilians executed for espionage in 1953. Their case was controversial and led to public protests.

Analyzing VISUALS

1. **Summarizing** What were the Rosenbergs accused of and what was the result?
2. **Explaining** Why was Robert Oppenheimer's security clearance suspended?

during the check, many under pressure. Another 212 were fired for "questionable loyalty," although no actual evidence against them was uncovered. R1

House Un-American Activities Committee (HUAC)

Although the FBI helped screen federal employees, FBI Director J. Edgar Hoover was not satisfied. In 1947 Hoover went before the House Un-American Activities Committee (HUAC). Formed in 1938 to investigate both Communist and Fascist activities in the United States, HUAC was a minor committee until Hoover expanded its importance.

Hoover urged HUAC to hold public hearings on Communist subversion. The committee, Hoover said, could reveal "the diabolic machinations of sinister figures engaged in un-American activities." Hoover's aim was to expose not just Communists but also "Communist sympathizers" and "fellow travelers." Under Hoover's leadership, the FBI sent agents to infiltrate groups suspected of subversion and wiretapped thousands of telephones.

Hollywood on Trial One of HUAC's first hearings in 1947 focused on the film industry as a powerful cultural force that Communists might **manipulate** to spread their ideas and influence. HUAC's interviews routinely began, "Are you now, or have you ever been, a member of the Communist Party?" Future American president Ronald Reagan was head of the Screen Actors Guild at the time and, when called before HUAC, he testified that there were Communists in Hollywood. R2

Teach

R1 Reading Strategy

Making Connections Have students work in small groups and come up with a definition for *loyalty*. Discuss as a class why it is difficult to define an abstraction in absolute terms. OL

R2 Reading Strategy

Inferring HUAC was concerned that Communists were using the American film industry to disseminate their ideas. **Ask:** Why did this tactic seem plausible? *(Students might say that films reached large audiences, so many Americans would be exposed to Communist ideas—and it would happen without their knowledge or consent.)* OL

Analyzing VISUALS

Answers:

1. They were accused of running a Soviet spy network. They were executed.
2. He opposed the hydrogen bomb and had left-wing views.

Additional Support

Activity: Collaborative Learning

Identifying Points of View Many members of Hollywood were brought before the HUAC; half provided names for the committee to investigate, the other half refused to name names. Nine screenwriters and one director went to jail. Nearly 300 writers, directors, and actors were "blacklisted," or unable to get jobs. One actor, Charlie Chaplin, left the United States. Others changed their names to get work. Have students work in groups to research HUAC versus Hollywood. They may use actual transcripts or articles, many of which can be found on the Internet. **Ask:** Is it un-American to produce a film that contains Communist propaganda? What films were identified as "Communistic"? Does the entertainment business have the power to manipulate public opinion? Was Hollywood a menace to society? Did HUAC violate citizens' right to free speech? Have students prepare a five minute presentation, offering their views on these questions. Ask students to use specific examples to support their findings. OL

D Differentiated Instruction

Visual/Spatial Have students write two newspaper headlines about the execution of the Rosenbergs. One headline should be from the point of view of someone who believes that the Rosenbergs were innocent of the charges, and the other should be from the point of view of someone who is convinced of their guilt. OL

C Critical Thinking

Recognizing Bias Ask: Do you think union members, schools or universities, churches, or businesses have the right to make members divulge information about their political views? Why or why not? *(Responses will vary. Most students will suggest that political views are private and protected under the Constitution.)* OL

Reading Check

Answer: to discover Communists who might have infiltrated the U.S. government or areas of American society

Additional Support

During the hearings, ten screenwriters, known as the "Hollywood Ten," used their Fifth Amendment right to protect themselves from self-incrimination and refused to testify. The incident led producers to blacklist, or agree not to hire, anyone who was believed to be a Communist or who refused to cooperate with the committee. In 1950 a pamphlet called *Red Channels* was published, listing 151 blacklisted actors, directors, broadcasters, and screenwriters. The blacklist created an atmosphere of distrust and fear.

Alger Hiss In 1948 Whittaker Chambers, a *TIME* magazine editor and former Communist Party member, testified to HUAC that several government officials were also former Communists or spies.

The most prominent official named by Chambers was **Alger Hiss,** a diplomat who had served in Roosevelt's administration, attended the Yalta conference, and taken part in organizing the United Nations. After Hiss sued him for libel, Chambers testified before a grand jury that, in 1937 and 1938, Hiss had given him secret documents from the State Department. Hiss denied being either a spy or a member of the Communist Party, and he also denied ever having known Chambers.

The committee was ready to drop the investigation until Representative Richard Nixon of California **convinced** his colleagues to continue the hearings to determine whether Hiss or Chambers had lied. Chambers produced copies of secret documents, along with microfilm that he had hidden in a hollow pumpkin on his farm. These "pumpkin papers," Chambers claimed, proved Hiss was lying. A jury agreed and convicted Hiss of **perjury,** or lying under oath.

The Rosenbergs Another sensational spy case centered on accusations that American Communists had sold the secrets of the atomic bomb to the Soviets. Many people did not believe that the Soviet Union could have produced an atomic bomb in 1949 without help. This belief intensified the hunt for spies. D

In 1950 the hunt led to a British scientist who admitted sending information to the Soviet Union. After hearing his testimony, the FBI arrested Julius and Ethel Rosenberg, a New York couple who were members of the Communist Party. The government charged them with heading a Soviet spy ring.

The Rosenbergs denied the charges but were condemned to death for espionage. Many people believed that they were not leaders or spies but victims caught up in the wave of anti-Communist frenzy. Appeals, public expressions of support, and pleas for clemency failed, however, and the couple was executed in June 1953.

Project Venona The American public hotly debated the guilt or innocence of individuals, like the Rosenbergs, who were accused of being spies. There was, however, solid evidence of Soviet espionage, although very few Americans knew it at the time. In 1946 American and British cryptographers, working for a project code-named "Venona," cracked the Soviet spy code of the time, enabling them to read approximately 3,000 messages between Moscow and the United States collected during the Cold War.

The messages collected using Project Venona confirmed extensive Soviet spying and an ongoing effort to steal nuclear secrets. The government did not reveal Project Venona's existence until 1995. The Venona documents provided strong evidence that the Rosenbergs were indeed guilty.

The Red Scare Spreads

Following the federal government's example, many state and local governments, universities, businesses, unions, churches, and private organizations began their own efforts to find Communists. The University of California required its 11,000 faculty members to take loyalty oaths and fired 157 who refused to do so. Many Catholic groups became strongly anti-Communist and urged their members to identify Communists within the Church. C

The Taft-Hartley Act of 1947 required union leaders to take oaths that they were not Communists, but many union leaders did not object. Instead, they launched their own efforts to purge Communists from their organizations. The president of the CIO called Communist sympathizers "skulking cowards" and "apostles of hate." The CIO eventually expelled 11 unions that refused to remove Communist leaders from their organization.

Reading Check **Explaining** What was the purpose of the loyalty review boards and HUAC?

Activity: Interdisciplinary Connection

Civics Many people, including Albert Einstein and Pope Pius XII urged clemency for the Rosenbergs. Files released after the fall of the Soviet Union seem to indicate that the Rosenbergs were guilty. However, information revealed in a 1996 interview with David Greenglass, Ethel Rosenberg's brother, puts Ethel's guilt in doubt. Have students research the details of the trial. **Ask:** Who were the Rosenbergs? How did they come under suspicion? Why was the trial so highly publicized? What were the official charges? Why were they sentenced to death? How many people protested their execution? What exactly did the Venona transcripts reveal about them? Have students write a two-page summary of their findings to present in class. Encourage students to include photos in their reports. OL

McCarthyism

MAIN Idea Senator Joseph R. McCarthy used the fear of communism to increase his own power and destroy the reputations of many people.

HISTORY AND YOU Have you ever known anyone who spread untrue stories about others? Read on to find out about the false accusations that Senator McCarthy spread in the early 1950s.

In 1949 the Red Scare intensified even further. In that year, the Soviet Union successfully tested an atomic bomb, and China fell to communism. To many Americans, these events seemed to prove that the United States was losing the Cold War. Deeply concerned, they wanted to know why their government was failing. As a result, many continued to believe that Communists had infiltrated the government and remained undetected.

In February 1950, soon after Alger Hiss's perjury conviction, a little-known Wisconsin senator gave a political speech to a Republican women's group in West Virginia. Halfway through his speech, Senator Joseph R. McCarthy made a surprising statement:

PRIMARY SOURCE

"While I cannot take the time to name all the men in the State Department who have been named as members of the Communist Party and members of a spy ring, I have here in my hand a list of 205 that were known to the Secretary of State as being members of the Communist Party and who nevertheless are still working and shaping the policy of the State Department."

—quoted in *The Fifties*

The Associated Press picked up the statement and sent it to newspapers nationwide. **C** While at an airport, reporters asked McCarthy to see his list of Communists. McCarthy replied that he would be happy to show it to them, but unfortunately, it was in his bag on the plane. In fact, the list never appeared. McCarthy, however, continued to make charges and draw attention.

McCarthy's use of sensationalist charges was not new. When he ran for the Senate in 1946, he accused his opponent, Robert M. La Follette, Jr., of being "communistically inclined." McCarthy did not provide any evidence to support his accusation, but it helped him win the election.

POLITICAL CARTOONS — PRIMARY SOURCE
McCarthyism

▲ *President Eisenhower and CIA Director Allen Dulles try not to make any noise in the hope that the "bull," Joe McCarthy, will go away without doing much damage.*

◀ *The wall of the U.S. State Department is smeared by McCarthy.*

D

Analyzing VISUALS

1. **Explaining** What does the cartoon on the left imply about President Eisenhower's leadership during the McCarthy era?
2. **Assessing** Which cartoon do you think is more critical of McCarthy? Why?

C Critical Thinking

Determining Cause and Effect McCarthy accused people of being Communists with no evidence. **Ask:** Why was McCarthy so successful in getting the press to believe his claims, even though he had no evidence? *(People were extremely fearful.)* **OL**

D Differentiated Instruction

Kinesthetic Illustrate how baseless yet powerful McCarthy was by designating some students as "Communists" for a day. Arbitrarily assign these students to sit in a different part of the class. Do not call on them or let others talk to them. They can only rejoin the group if they identify someone else as a Communist. The accused will join the isolated group. **OL**

Analyzing VISUALS

Answers:
1. he refused to condemn McCarthy
2. Answers will vary. Students should support their choice.

Hands-On Chapter Project Step 3

Role-Playing to Demonstrate McCarthyism in Action

Step 3: Staging the Hearing Essential Question: Does the role-play or mock hearing succeed in reflecting what happened and give a sense of why McCarthy ultimately failed? *(Performers' Perspective)*

Directions Students will perform the role-play before the entire class. Viewers can take notes and ask questions after the performance.

Putting It Together After the performance, the students who created and performed the mock-hearing should meet. They can then decide if they need to revise it in any way based on audience feedback. **OL**

(Chapter Project continued on page 785)

C Critical Thinking

Interpreting Truman vetoed the McCarran Bill stating, "The basic error of this bill is that it moves in the direction of suppressing opinion and belief...that would make a mockery of the Bill of Rights and of our claims to stand for freedom in the world." Ask students if they agree with Truman or Congress, which overrode his veto. **Ask:** Do you think a bill such as the McCarran Act could become law in present times? *(Responses will vary.)* OL

W Writing Support

Descriptive Writing

McCarthyism was often called the "Witch Hunt of the 1950s." Have students research and explain the metaphor in a one-page paper. *(Students should compare McCarthyism to the Puritan persecution of women in Salem.)* AL

Reading Check

Answer: it ruined many careers, colored political life, and influenced popular culture

Additional Support

After becoming a senator, McCarthy continued to proclaim that Communists were a danger both at home and abroad. To some audiences, he distributed a booklet called "The Party of Betrayal," which accused Democratic Party leaders of corruption and of protecting Communists. Secretary of State Dean Acheson was a frequent target. According to McCarthy, Acheson was incompetent and a tool of Stalin. He also wildly accused George C. Marshall, the former army chief of staff and secretary of state, of disloyalty as a member of "a conspiracy so immense as to dwarf any previous such ventures in the history of man."

McCarthy was not alone in making such charges. In the prevailing mood of anxiety about communism, many Americans were ready to believe them.

The McCarran Act

In 1950, with the Korean War underway and McCarthy and others arousing fears of Communist spies, Congress passed the Internal Security Act, usually called the **McCarran Act.** Declaring that "world Communism has as its sole purpose the establishment of a totalitarian dictatorship in America," Senator Pat McCarran of Nevada offered a way to fight "treachery, infiltration, sabotage, and terrorism." The act made it illegal to "combine, conspire, or agree with any other person to perform any act which would substantially contribute to . . . the establishment of a totalitarian government." C

The McCarran Act required all Communist Party and "Communist-front" organizations to publish their records and register with the United States attorney general. Communists could not have passports to travel abroad and, in cases of a national emergency, Communists and Communist sympathizers could be arrested and detained. Unwilling to punish people for their opinions, Truman vetoed the bill, but Congress easily overrode his veto in 1950. Later Supreme Court cases, however, limited the scope of the McCarran Act.

McCarthy's Tactics

After the Republicans won control of Congress in 1952, McCarthy became chairman of the Senate subcommittee on investigations. Using the power of his committee to force government officials to testify about alleged Communist influences, McCarthy turned the investigation into a witch hunt—a search for disloyalty based on flimsy evidence and irrational fears. His tactic of damaging reputations with vague and unfounded charges became known as **McCarthyism.**

W McCarthy's sensational accusations drew the attention of the press, which put him in the headlines and quoted him widely. When he questioned witnesses, McCarthy would badger them and then refuse to accept their answers. His tactics left a cloud of suspicion that McCarthy and others interpreted as guilt. Furthermore, people were afraid to challenge him for fear of becoming targets themselves.

McCarthy's Downfall

In 1954 McCarthy began to look for Soviet spies in the United States Army. During weeks of televised Army-McCarthy hearings, millions of Americans watched McCarthy question and bully officers, harassing them about trivial details and accusing them of misconduct. His popular support began to fade.

Finally, to strike back at the army's lawyer, Joseph Welch, McCarthy brought up the past of a young lawyer in Welch's firm who had been a member of a Communist-front organization while in law school. Welch, who was fully aware of the young man's past, now exploded at McCarthy for possibly ruining the young man's career: "Until this moment, I think I never really gauged your cruelty or your recklessness. . . . You have done enough. Have you no sense of decency, sir, at long last? Have you left no sense of decency?"

Spectators cheered. Welch had said aloud what many Americans had been thinking. As Senator Stuart Symington of Missouri commented, "The American people have had a look at you for six weeks. You are not fooling anyone." McCarthy had lost the power to arouse fear. Newspaper headlines repeated: "Have you no sense of decency?"

Later that year, the Senate passed a vote of **censure,** or formal disapproval, against McCarthy—one of the most serious criticisms it can level against a member. Although he remained in the Senate, McCarthy had lost all influence. He died in 1957.

Reading Check **Evaluating** What were the effects of McCarthyism?

Activity: Technology Connection

Identifying Points of View News writers, radio broadcasters, average Americans, and even well-known and respected politicians were afraid to speak out against McCarthy for fear they would be next to face his committee (HUAC). When the McCarthy hearings were televised, it drew national attention. The American people were able to witness the bullying techniques of McCarthy. When McCarthy began attacking the United States Army, he had gone too far. Those who had remained silent finally spoke up, including Edward R. Murrow, an experienced television broadcaster. On March 9, 1954, Murrow used his television program, *See It Now*, to express his views on McCarthyism. Have students use the Internet and library to discover what Murrow said and how the American public reacted. Have students work in groups to present a "live" or "prerecorded" TV talk show that reflects Murrow's stance, public reaction, and McCarthy's spin on the broadcast. AL

ANALYZING SUPREME COURT CASES

Are There Limits on Congressional Power?

★ *Watkins* v. *United States*, 1957

Background to the Case

In 1954 labor organizer John Watkins testified before the House Un-American Activities Committee. He agreed to discuss his own connections with the Communist Party and to identify people he knew who were still members, but he refused to give information about those who were no longer members. Watkins received a misdemeanor conviction for refusing to answer questions "pertinent to the question under inquiry." In 1957 he appealed his case to the Supreme Court.

How the Court Ruled

The Watkins case raised the question: Is it constitutional for a congressional committee to ask any question or investigate any topic, whether or not it is directly related to Congress's law-making function? In a 6-to-1 decision—two members did not participate—the Supreme Court held that the activities of HUAC during its investigations were, indeed, beyond the scope of the stated aims of the committee, as well as the authority of congressional powers.

▲ Senator Joseph McCarthy (above) symbolized the fears of the early 1950s, when communist spies were suspected to have infiltrated all aspects of American society. Together, McCarthy's committee in the Senate and the House Un-American Activities Committee used their power to subpoena people to investigate their loyalty. As a result many reputations were smeared and careers ruined.

PRIMARY SOURCE

The Court's Opinion

"The power of the Congress to conduct investigations is inherent in the legislative process. That power is broad. . . . But, broad as is this power of inquiry, it is not unlimited. There is no general authority to expose the private affairs of individuals without justification in terms of the functions of the Congress. . . . Nor is the Congress a law enforcement or trial agency. These are functions of the executive and judicial departments of government. No inquiry is an end in itself; it must be related to, and in furtherance of, a legitimate task of the Congress. Investigations conducted solely for the personal aggrandizement of the investigators or to "punish" those investigated are indefensible."

—Chief Justice Earl Warren, writing for the majority in *Watkins* v. *United States*

PRIMARY SOURCE

Dissenting View

"It may be that at times the House Committee on Un-American Activities has, as the Court says, "conceived of its task in the grand view of its name." And, perhaps, as the Court indicates, the rules of conduct placed upon the Committee by the House admit of individual abuse and unfairness. But that is none of our affair. So long as the object of a legislative inquiry is legitimate and the questions propounded are pertinent thereto, it is not for the courts to interfere with the committee system of inquiry. To hold otherwise would be an infringement on the power given the Congress to inform itself. . . ."

—Justice Tom Campbell Clark, author of the dissenting opinion in *Watkins* v. *United States*

DBQ Document-Based Questions

1. **Explaining** On what does Warren say a congressional inquiry must always be based?
2. **Discussing** Why does Clark disagree with the majority opinion?
3. **Making Inferences** What opinion do you think Warren had of HUAC?

SUPREME COURT CASES

More About the Case

Watkins, who was an active leader in the labor movement, was identified by witnesses as Communist. Watkins testified freely about his own activities, admitting to participating in some Communist activities and to making contributions. As a union official, he also worked closely with the Communist Party. However, Watkins denied that he was ever a "card carrying member" of the Communist Party, and he refused to answer questions about others who may have been members of the Communist Party, claiming that information was not relevant to the Committee's work.

DBQ Document Based Questions

1. must be based on the law-making, or legislative duties, of Congress
2. He argued that Congress was pursuing an inquiry on a "legitimate" topic, and the judicial branch should not interfere.
3. Warren appears to have been hostile to HUAC.

Differentiated Instruction

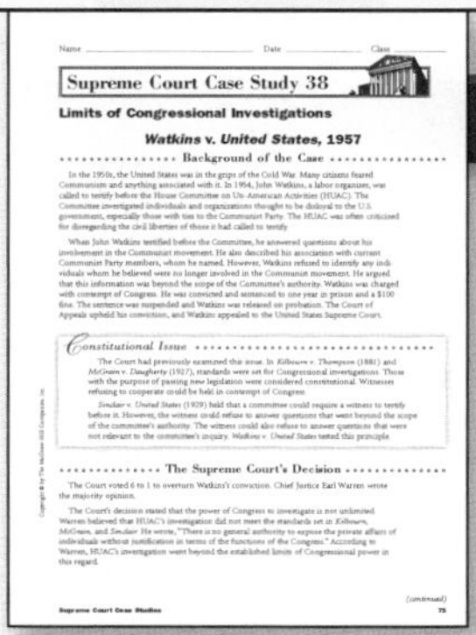

Supreme Court Case Study 38

Limits of Congressional Investigations

Watkins v. *United States*, 1957

Case Study 38: *Watkins* v. *United States*, p. 75

Analyzing a Supreme Court Decision

Objective: Learn how judicial review was applied to a refusal to answer questions of the HUAC.

Focus: Identify the central issue of the case: Congressional powers of investigation are not unlimited.

Teach: Discuss the Court's opinion.

Assess: Explain the importance of the case (First and Fifth Amendment rights).

Close: Write a paragraph summarizing the case.

Differentiated Instruction Strategies

BL Define *judicial review* using your own words.

AL Write a brief essay in which you argue against the Court's decision.

ELL Create a list of all of the unfamiliar words in the reading. Then work with a partner to define them.

D Differential Instruction

Visual/Spatial Have students create a chart that includes all the nations that have developed nuclear weapons since 1945. The chart should include the name of the country and the year it conducted its first nuclear test. **OL**

S Skill Practice

Visual Literacy Have students look at the school picture and the bomb shelter. **Ask:** How did people think they were going to survive a nuclear bomb? *(by covering their heads and eyes, hiding underground, eating canned food)* **Ask:** Have you seen any old fallout shelter signs in your community? If so, where are they located? *(Answers will vary.)* **BL**

Analyzing VISUALS

Answers:

1. to protect people from a nuclear bomb blast
2. If a nuclear bomb were dropped, most services would not be available. Each person would have to fend for himself.

Additional Support

Life During the Early Cold War

MAIN Idea Obsessed with fear of a nuclear attack, many Americans took steps to protect themselves.

HISTORY AND YOU Have you ever felt the need to protect yourself from something dangerous or scary? Read to learn more about how Americans tried to deal with their fears during the early 1950s.

The Red Scare and the spread of nuclear weapons had a profound impact on American life in the 1950s. Fear of communism and of nuclear war affected the thinking and choices of many ordinary Americans, as well as their leaders in government. Some Americans responded by preparing to survive a nuclear attack, while others became active in politics in an effort to shape government policy. Writers responded by describing the dangers of atomic war and the threat of communism—sometimes to convince people to take action and sometimes to protest policies they feared might lead to war.

Facing the Bomb

D Already upset by the first Soviet atomic test in 1949, Americans were shocked when the Soviets again successfully tested the much more powerful hydrogen bomb, or H-bomb, in 1953. The United States had tested its own H-bomb less than a year earlier.

Americans prepared for a surprise Soviet attack. Schools set aside special areas as bomb shelters. In bomb drills, students learned to

PRIMARY SOURCE
Living with the Bomb in the 1950s

The Cold War convinced many in American society that they needed to be prepared to survive a nuclear attack. While authorities made Civil Defense plans, individuals took it upon themselves to build bomb shelters and stockpile supplies.

▲ *The Civil Defense Agency set up bomb shelters in cities, and made plans to assist survivors after an attack. Today the Civil Defense Agency is known as FEMA—the Federal Emergency Management Agency.*

S ▶ *In the 1950s school children took part in "duck-and-cover" drills designed to give them a chance at surviving a nuclear blast if they were far enough from the epicenter.*

◀ *Some Americans invested in personal bomb shelters stocked with food to allow them to survive a bomb blast and the radiation that would follow.*

Analyzing VISUALS

1. **Explaining** What was the purpose of the "duck-and-cover "drills and bomb shelters?
2. **Making Inferences** Even if some preparations would not work, why might the government have wanted people to prepare for war?

Activity: Interdisciplinary Connection

Literature The literature and pop culture of the 1950s reflected themes that were often in conflict with one another. On one side, the view was annihilistic, filled with anti-Communism hysteria and the threat of nuclear war. Ray Bradbury's *The Martian Chronicles* features a doomsday view of the future. Science fiction movies such as *The Invasion of the Body Snatchers* were allegories for communist (alien) subversion. The other side portrayed an unrealistic view of family life in suburbia. Houses were filled with new appliances and perfect children. Television shows such as *Ozzie and Harriet* and *Leave It To Beaver* portrayed families who were not concerned about bomb shelters or communism.

Have students read some of Bradbury's stories, look at movie posters from the 1950s, and watch a few episodes of 1950s sitcoms to create a poster with a 1950s theme to be shared with the class. **OL** duck under their desks, turn away from the windows, and cover their heads with their hands. These "duck-and-cover" actions were supposed to protect them from a nuclear bomb blast.

Although "duck-and-cover" might have made people feel safe, it would not have protected them from deadly nuclear radiation. According to experts, for every person killed outright by a nuclear blast, four more would die later from **fallout,** the radiation left over after a blast. To protect themselves, some families built backyard fallout shelters and stocked them with canned food.

Popular Culture in the Cold War

Worries about nuclear war and Communist infiltration filled the public's imagination. Cold War themes soon appeared in films, plays, television, the titles of dance tunes, and popular fiction.

In 1953 Arthur Miller's thinly veiled criticism of the Communist witchhunts, *The Crucible,* appeared on Broadway. The play remains popular today as a cautionary tale about how hysteria can lead to false accusations. Matt Cvetic was an FBI undercover informant who secretly infiltrated the Communist Party in Pittsburgh, Pennsylvania. His story captivated magazine readers in the *Saturday Evening Post* in 1950 and came to movie screens the next year as *I Was a Communist for the FBI*. Another suspense film, *Walk East on Beacon* (1951), features the FBI's activities in an espionage case.

In 1953 television took up the theme with a series about an undercover FBI counterspy who was also a Communist Party official. Each week, *I Led Three Lives* kept television viewers on edge. Popular tunes such as "Atomic Boogie" and "Atom Bomb Baby" played on the radio.

In 1954 author Philip Wylie published *Tomorrow!* This novel describes the horrific effects of nuclear war on an unprepared American city. As an adviser on civil defense, Wylie had failed to convince the federal government to play a strong role in building bomb shelters. Frustrated, he wrote his novel to educate the public about the horrors of atomic war.

R One of the most famous and enduring works of this period is John Hersey's nonfiction book *Hiroshima*. Originally published as the entire contents of the August 1946 edition of *The New Yorker* magazine, the book provides the firsthand accounts of six survivors of the U.S. dropping of the atomic bomb on Hiroshima, Japan. Not only did it make some Americans question the use of the bomb, *Hiroshima* also underscored the real and personal horrors of a nuclear attack.

At the same time that these fears were haunting Americans, the country was enjoying postwar prosperity and optimism. That spirit, combined with McCarthyism, fears of Communist infiltration, and the threat of atomic attack, made the early 1950s a time of contrasts. As the 1952 election approached, Americans were looking for someone or something that would make them feel secure.

Reading Check **Describing** How did the Cold War affect life in the 1950s?

Section 3 REVIEW

Vocabulary

1. **Explain** the significance of: Red Scare, subversion, loyalty review program, Alger Hiss, perjury, McCarran Act, McCarthyism, censure, fallout.

Main Ideas

2. **Explaining** What was the result of President Truman's loyalty review program?
3. **Analyzing** Hearings to investigate Communist subversion in what organization led to McCarthy's downfall?
4. **Identifying** What event made Americans fearful of a nuclear attack by the Soviets?

Critical Thinking

5. **Big Ideas** How did the Red Scare and McCarthyism change American society and government?
6. **Organizing** Use a graphic organizer similar to the one below to list the causes and effects of the Red Scare of the 1950s.

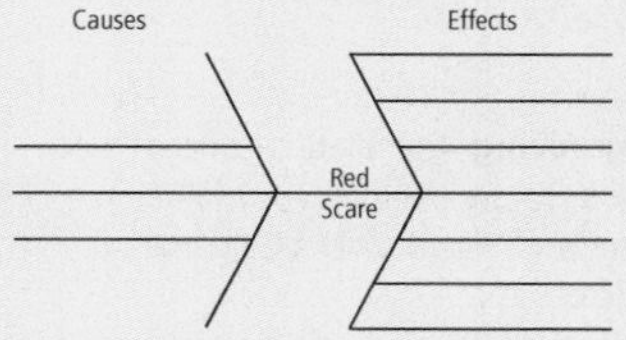

7. **Analyzing Visuals** Study the cartoons on page 777. Which cartoon do you think makes the stronger point? Explain.

Writing About History

8. **Persuasive Writing** Suppose that you are a newspaper editor during the Army-McCarthy hearings. Write an editorial giving reasons why people should support or condemn Senator McCarthy.

History ONLINE
Study Central™ To review this section, go to glencoe.com and click on Study Central.

R Reading Strategy

Making Connections Ask: Why would John Hersey's book *Hiroshima* have been so popular during the Cold War? *(It tied together the recent history of using an atomic bomb to people's fears that the U.S. would soon be victims of a nuclear attack.)* OL

Reading Check

Answer: Americans prepared for a surprise Soviet attack, worried about a nuclear war, and watched films and read books about Communist infiltrations.

Assess

History ONLINE

Study Central™ provides summaries, interactive games, and online graphic organizers to help students review content.

Close

Identifying Have students break into groups and discuss how American society reflected fears of the nuclear age. OL

Section 3 REVIEW

Answers

1. All definitions can be found in the section and the Glossary.
2. Six million federal employees were screened for their loyalty, 2,000 employees quit their jobs, and 212 were fired.
3. the U.S. Army
4. The Soviets successfully tested a hydrogen bomb in 1953.
5. While people were enjoying postwar prosperity and optimism, they feared communism and an atomic attack.
6. Causes: Alger Hiss Trial, Rosenbergs, Russia's successful test of an atomic bomb
Effects: Loyalty Review Program, HUAC, McCarran Act, McCarthyism, fallout shelters, blacklists, duck-and-cover, and so on
7. Responses will vary. Students should support their answers with sound reasoning.
8. Editorials will vary but should reflect a position supported with persuasive reasons.

Focus

Bellringer

Daily Focus Transparency 22-4

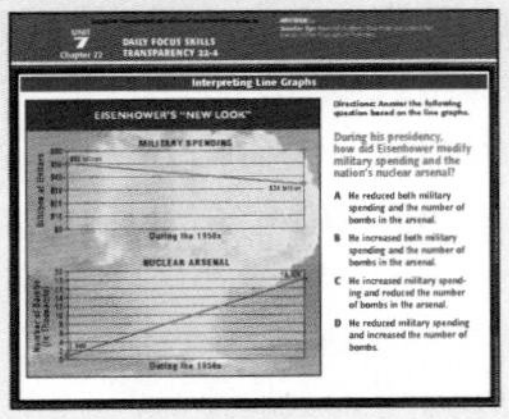

Guide to Reading

Answers:
brinkmanship, covert operations, massive retaliation

Section Spotlight Video

To generate student interest and provide a springboard for class discussion, access the Chapter 22, Section 4 video at glencoe.com or on the video DVD.

Section 4

Section Audio · Spotlight Video

Eisenhower's Cold War Policies

Guide to Reading

Big Ideas

Science and Technology Nuclear technology enabled Eisenhower to change U.S. military policy, while new missile technology marked the beginning of the space age.

Content Vocabulary

- massive retaliation *(p. 783)*
- brinkmanship *(p. 783)*
- covert *(p. 785)*
- developing nation *(p. 785)*
- military-industrial complex *(p. 787)*

Academic Vocabulary

- imply *(p. 786)*
- response *(p. 787)*

People and Events to Identify

- Central Intelligence Agency *(p. 785)*
- *Sputnik* *(p. 787)*

Reading Strategy

Organizing Complete a concept web similar to the one below by filling in aspects of Eisenhower's Cold War Policies.

President Eisenhower believed developing new technology to deliver nuclear weapons would help prevent war. He also directed the CIA to use covert operations in the struggle to contain communism.

Massive Retaliation

MAIN Idea Eisenhower fought the Cold War by increasing the U.S. nuclear arsenal and using the threat of nuclear war to end conflicts in Korea, Taiwan, and the Suez.

HISTORY AND YOU Do you know anyone who uses threats to get his or her way? Read further to learn about Eisenhower's use of nuclear threats to achieve foreign policy goals.

By the end of 1952, many Americans were ready for a change in leadership. The Cold War had much to do with that attitude. Many people believed that Truman's foreign policy was not working. The Soviet Union had tested an atomic bomb and consolidated its hold on Eastern Europe. China had fallen to communism, and American troops were fighting in Korea.

Tired of the criticism and uncertain he could win, Truman decided not to run again. The Democrats nominated Adlai Stevenson, governor of Illinois. The Republicans chose Dwight D. Eisenhower, the general who had organized the D-Day invasion. Stevenson had no chance against a national hero who had helped win World War II. Americans wanted someone they could trust to lead the nation in the Cold War. Eisenhower won in a landslide.

"More Bang for the Buck"

The Cold War shaped Eisenhower's thinking from the moment he took office. He was convinced that the key to victory in the Cold War was not simply military might but also a strong economy. The United States had to show the world that free enterprise could produce a better society than communism. At the same time, economic prosperity would prevent Communists from gaining support in the United States and protect society from subversion.

As a professional soldier, Eisenhower knew the costs associated with large-scale conventional war. Preparing for that kind of warfare, he believed, was too expensive. "We cannot defend the nation in a way which will exhaust our economy," the president declared. Instead of maintaining a large and expensive army, the nation "must be prepared to use atomic weapons in all forms." Nuclear weapons, he said, gave "more bang for the buck."

Resource Manager

R Reading Strategies	C Critical Thinking	D Differentiated Instruction	W Writing Support	S Skill Practice
Teacher Edition • Explaining, p. 787 **Additional Resources** • Guided Reading Act., URB p. 119 • Am. History in Graphic Novel, p. 57 • Prim. Source Reading, URB p. 103	**Teacher Edition** • Analyzing Info., p. 783 • Speculating, p. 784 • Drawing Con., p. 785 • Evaluating, p. 786 **Additional Resources** • Supreme Court Case Studies, p. 77 • Quizzes/Tests, p. 318 • Authentic Assess., p. 49	**Teacher Edition** • Visual/Spatial, p. 784 • Gifted and Talented, p. 786 **Additional Resources** • American Art and Music Act., URB p. 107 • Enrichment Act., URB p. 113 • Reteaching Act., URB p. 111	**Additional Resources** • Cont. Vocab. Act., URB p. 95 • Academic Vocab. Act., URB p. 97	**Teacher Edition** • Using Geo. Skills, p. 785 **Additional Resources** • Time Line Act., URB p. 101 • Read. Essen., p. 256

TECHNOLOGY & HISTORY

Cold War Technology President Eisenhower's emphasis on nuclear weapons required new technology to deliver them. Eisenhower wanted to make sure that the United States could wage nuclear war even if the Soviets destroyed American bases in Europe or Asia. This required technology that would allow the U.S. to strike the USSR without needing bases in Europe.

▲ **Long-Range Bombers**

In 1955 the U.S. Air Force unveiled the huge B-52 bomber (above), which could fly across continents to drop nuclear bombs. The B-52 is still in use today.

▶ **ICBMs**

Because bombers could be shot down, Eisenhower also approved the development of intercontinental ballistic missiles (ICBMs) that could reach anywhere in the world in less than 30 minutes. The Atlas missile (right) was the first American ICBM. It was also used to launch the first seven U.S. astronauts. It is still used today to launch satellites.

◀ **Missile Submarines**

Eisenhower also began a program to build submarines capable of launching nuclear missiles from underwater. The Polaris submarine (left) launched in 1960 and carried 16 nuclear missiles.

Analyzing VISUALS

1. **Determining Cause and Effect** How did Eisenhower's nuclear strategy lead to the development of new technologies?
2. **Defining** What is an ICBM and what is its purpose?

The Korean War had convinced Eisenhower that the United States could not contain communism by fighting a series of small wars. Such wars were unpopular and too expensive. Instead, wars had to be prevented from happening in the first place. The best way to do that seemed to be to threaten to use nuclear weapons. This policy came to be called **massive retaliation.** C

The new policy enabled Eisenhower to cut military spending from $50 billion to $34 billion. He did this by reducing the size of the army, which was expensive to maintain. At the same time, he increased the U.S. nuclear arsenal from about 1,000 bombs in 1953 to about 18,000 bombs in 1961.

Brinkmanship

President Eisenhower's willingness to threaten nuclear war to maintain peace worried some people. However, Secretary of State John Foster Dulles, the dominant figure in the nation's foreign policy in the 1950s, strongly defended this approach:

PRIMARY SOURCE

"You have to take chances for peace, just as you must take chances in war. Some say that we were brought to the verge of war. Of course we were brought to the verge of war. The ability to get to the verge without getting into the war is the necessary art. . . . If you try to run away from it, if you are scared to go to the brink, you are lost. We've had to look it square in the face. . . . We walked to the brink and we looked it in the face. We took strong action."

—quoted in *Rise to Globalism*

Critics called this **brinkmanship**—the willingness to go to the brink of war to force the other side to back down—and argued that it was too dangerous. During several crises, however, President Eisenhower felt compelled to threaten nuclear war.

Teach

C Critical Thinking

Analyzing Information Have students create a T-chart. One column should list the advantages of massive retaliation; the other column should list the disadvantages. Lead a discussion as to whether massive retaliation is a sound policy. **OL**

Analyzing VISUALS

Answers:

1. Nuclear weapons had to be delivered quickly and with little or no harm to Americans. Special planes required new technology—their range had to be longer with an ability to fly higher. Missiles that were launched from land and from submarines were also developed.
2. intercontinental ballistic missile; its purpose was to reach its target within 30 minutes—no pilot required.

Differentiated Instruction

Primary Source Reading 22-1
Containment or Liberation?
About the Selection
Reader's Dictionary
GUIDED READING

Primary Source Reading, URB p. 103

Writing a Narrative Essay

Objective: Examine a speech regarding the policy of containment.

Focus: Read the speech to determine the message.

Teach: List the reasons Dulles gives to support his argument.

Assess: Write an essay either supporting or contradicting Dulles' opinion.

Close: Ask students: In your opinion, why did containment fail?

Differentiated Instruction Strategies

BL List the examples Dulles gives. Why does he give these examples?

AL Find another primary source about containment.

ELL Outline the speech.

C Critical Thinking

Speculating Remind students that during the Korean War, Truman did not want to fight China; MacArthur wanted to use atomic weapons. Eisenhower "hinted" that he would use nuclear bombs, and the Chinese backed off. **Ask:** **Did Eisenhower do the right thing? Should Truman have used a similar threat?** Write student responses on the board and decide as a class which president took the best approach to end the war. **OL**

D Differentiated Instruction

Visual/Spatial Have students create a time line, listing actions the North Koreans have taken in the last ten years. **Ask:** **How should the U.S. and the world deal with North Korea?** *(Responses will vary.)* **OL**

Turning Point

Essays will vary but should include an opinion supported with information from the text.

Additional Support

History ONLINE **Student Skill Activity** To learn how to create a multimedia presentation visit glencoe.com and complete the skill activity.

The Korean War Ends

During his campaign for the presidency, Eisenhower had said, "I shall go to Korea," promising to end the costly and increasingly unpopular war. On December 4, 1952, he kept his promise. Bundled against the freezing Korean winter, the president-elect talked with frontline commanders and their troops.

C Eisenhower became convinced that the ongoing battle was costing too many lives and bringing too few victories. He was determined to bring the war to an end. The president then quietly let the Chinese know that the United States might continue the Korean War "under circumstances of our own choosing"—a hint at a nuclear attack.

D The threat to go to the brink of nuclear war seemed to work. In July 1953 negotiators signed an armistice. The battle line between the two sides in Korea, which was very near the prewar boundary, became the border between North Korea and South Korea. A "demilitarized zone" (DMZ) separated them. American troops are still based in Korea, helping to defend South Korea's border. There has never been a peace treaty to end the war.

The Taiwan Crisis

Shortly after the Korean War ended, a new crisis erupted in Asia. Although Communists had taken power in mainland China, the Nationalists still controlled Taiwan and several

Turning Point

Sputnik Launches a Space Race

As the United States began to develop ICBMs, Americans were stunned to discover that the Soviet Union already had them. On October 4, 1957, the Soviets demonstrated this technology by launching *Sputnik*, the first artificial satellite to orbit Earth.

Worried that the United States was falling behind, Congress created the National Aeronautics and Space Administration (NASA) to coordinate missile research and space exploration. It also passed the National Defense Education Act (NDEA), which provided funds for education in science, math, and foreign languages.

Sputnik marked the beginning of a new era—the use of satellites in space. Both nations in the Cold War began launching satellites to assist in communications and to spy on the other nation. Today, satellites are a vital part of modern communications and travel. They transmit television and cell phone signals, and the satellites of the Global Positioning System (GPS) help ships and airplanes to navigate. Hikers and drivers can also buy GPS receivers to help determine where they are.

ANALYZING HISTORY **Do you think missile and satellite technology helped prevent conflict during the Cold War or made the Cold War worse? Create a multimedia presentation on the Space Race and how it has changed American society.**

"All the News That's Fit to Print"

The New York Times. LATE CITY EDITION

SOVIET FIRES EARTH SATELLITE INTO SPACE; IT IS CIRCLING THE GLOBE AT 18,000 M. P. H.; SPHERE TRACKED IN 4 CROSSINGS OVER U. S.

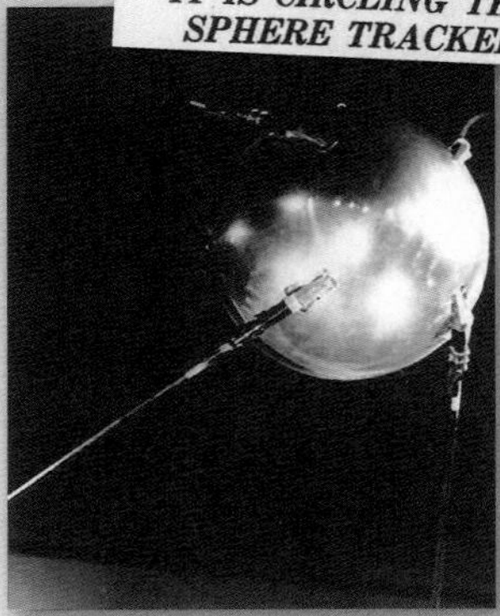

▲ Sputnik *(above) was the world's first artificial satellite. It made news around the world and launched the space race.*

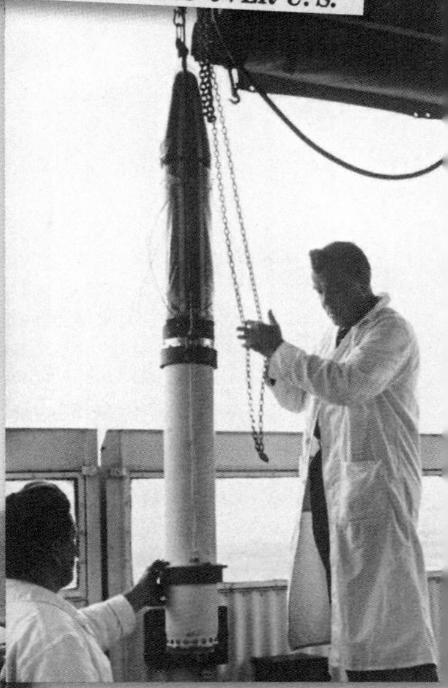

▲ *Scientists prepare the first U.S. satellite,* Explorer I, *for launch in 1958.*

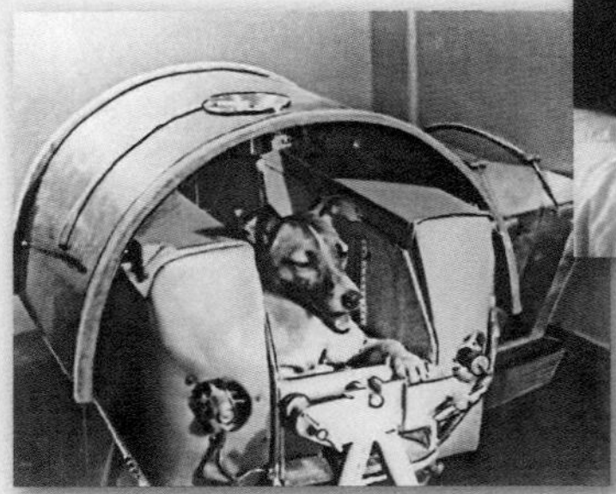

▲ Sputnik II, *launched only a month after* Sputnik, *carried the first living creature into orbit—an "astro" dog named Laika.*

Extending the Content

Space Race New technology led to planes that could fly across continents at very high altitudes and deliver nuclear bombs. Americans were sure they were ahead of the Russians in the arms race. But *Sputnik* shocked and terrified them.

Then, on November 3, 1957, the Soviets stunned the Americans again when they launched *Sputnik 2* with a live dog on board! America met this challenge head on. On January 31, 1958, *Explorer 1* lifted off from Cape Canaveral, Florida. The United States had just launched its first artificial satellite.

Less than a year after the launch of *Sputnik 1*, Congress approved the creation of the National Aeronautics and Space Administration (NASA). Its mission was to develop an unmanned moon probe, hoping to be the first to the moon. Its goal, however, was a human space exploration program.

small islands along China's coast. In the fall of 1954, China threatened to seize two of the islands. Eisenhower saw Taiwan as part of the "anti-Communist barrier" in Asia that needed to be protected at all costs.

When China began shelling the islands and announced that Taiwan would be liberated, Eisenhower asked Congress to authorize the use of force to defend Taiwan. He then warned the Chinese that any attack on Taiwan would be resisted by U.S. naval forces stationed nearby and hinted that they would use nuclear weapons to stop an invasion. Soon afterward, China backed down. C

The Suez Crisis

The following year, a serious crisis erupted in the Middle East. Eisenhower's goal in that region was to prevent Arab nations from aligning with the Soviet Union. To build support among Arabs, Secretary of State Dulles offered to help Egypt finance the construction of a dam on the Nile River.

The deal ran into trouble in Congress, however, because Egypt had bought weapons from Communist Czechoslovakia. Dulles was forced to withdraw the offer. A week later, Egyptian troops seized control of the Suez Canal from the Anglo-French company that had controlled it. The Egyptians intended to use the canal's profits to pay for the dam.

The British and French responded quickly to the Suez Crisis. In October 1956, British and French troops invaded Egypt. Eisenhower was furious with Britain and France. The situation became even more dangerous when the Soviet Union threatened rocket attacks on Britain and France and offered to send troops to help Egypt. Eisenhower immediately put U.S. nuclear forces on alert, noting, "If those fellows start something, we may have to hit them—and if necessary, with everything in the bucket." S

Under strong pressure from the United States, the British and French called off their invasion. The Soviet Union had won a major diplomatic victory, however, by supporting Egypt. Soon afterward, other Arab nations began accepting Soviet aid as well.

Reading Check **Identifying** What was brinkmanship?

Covert Operations

MAIN Idea Eisenhower directed the Central Intelligence Agency to use covert operations to limit the spread of communism and Soviet influence.

HISTORY AND YOU Do you enjoy reading spy novels? Read on to learn of the development and work of a spy agency in the United States.

President Eisenhower relied on brinkmanship on several occasions, but he knew it could not work in all situations. It could prevent war, but it could not, for example, prevent Communists from staging revolutions within countries. To prevent Communist uprisings in other countries, Eisenhower decided to use **covert,** or hidden, operations conducted by the **Central Intelligence Agency (CIA).**

Many of the CIA's operations took place in **developing nations**—nations with primarily agricultural economies. Many of these countries blamed European imperialism and American capitalism for their problems. Their leaders looked to the Soviet Union as a model of how to industrialize their countries. They often threatened to nationalize, or put under government control, foreign businesses operating in their countries.

One way to stop developing nations from moving into the Communist camp was to provide them with financial aid, as Eisenhower had tried to do in Egypt. In some cases, however, where the threat of communism seemed stronger, the CIA ran covert operations to overthrow anti-American leaders and replace them with pro-American leaders.

Iran and Guatemala

Two examples of covert operations that achieved U.S. objectives took place in Iran and Guatemala. By 1953, Iranian Prime Minister Mohammed Mossadegh had already nationalized the Anglo-Iranian Oil Company. He seemed ready to make an oil deal with the Soviet Union. The pro-American Shah of Iran tried to force Mossadegh out of office, but failed and fled into exile. The CIA quickly sent agents to organize street riots and arrange a coup that ousted Mossadegh and returned the shah to power.

C Critical Thinking

Drawing Conclusions First with Korea and then again with Taiwan, Eisenhower "hints" to China that the U.S. may use nuclear weapons. **Ask:** How many times do you think a threat like this will work? Is brinkmanship a good diplomatic tool? *(Answers will vary. Students may suggest that it will only work a few times.)* **OL**

S Skills Practice

Using Geography Skills Have students locate the Suez Canal on a map. **Ask:** What two bodies of water does the Suez Canal connect? *(the Mediterranean Sea and the Red Sea)* **BL**

Reading Check

Answer: Brinkmanship is the willingness to go to the brink of war to force the other side to back down.

Hands-On Chapter Project
Step 4

Role-Playing to Demonstrate McCarthyism in Action

Step 4: Critiquing the Performance

Essential Question: Does the role-play or mock hearing succeed in reflecting what happened and give a sense of why McCarthy ultimately failed? *(Viewers' Perspective)*

Directions Viewers of the performance should divide into groups or meet as whole to critique the performance. Using their notes, viewers should evaluate the performance by answering and discussing the following questions:

- What was the main message of the performance?
- How did the performance compare with the description of McCarthyism in the textbook?
- Why did McCarthy's early targets not challenge him when they stood accused?
- Why did support for McCarthy eventually fade?

Putting It Together After the discussion, have students divide into groups and each choose one of the questions cited above. Give groups a few minutes to agree on an answer. Then have each group recite their answers. **OL** *(Chapter Project continued on the Visual Summary page)*

C Critical Thinking

Evaluating Ask: Is secret aggression by the CIA, such as in Guatemala and Eastern Europe justifiable? Why or why not? What events in your lifetime have shaped your answer? *(Responses and examples will vary.)* **OL**

D Differentiated Instruction

Gifted and Talented Have interested students research the cultural, social, and historical factors that affected the Hungarians' reaction to Communist control. Have students present their findings in a brochure form, complete with photos and captions. **AL**

Analyzing VISUALS

Answers:
1. war
2. Because the U-2 flew so high, it might go undetected.

Additional Support

The following year, the CIA intervened in Guatemala. In 1951, with Communist support, Jacobo Arbenz Guzmán was elected president of Guatemala. His land-reform program took over large estates and plantations, including those of the American–owned United Fruit **C** Company. In May 1954, Communist Czechoslovakia delivered arms to Guatemala. The CIA responded by arming the Guatemalan opposition and training them at secret camps in Nicaragua and Honduras. Shortly after these CIA-trained forces invaded Guatemala, Arbenz Guzmán left office.

Trouble in Eastern Europe

Covert operations did not always work as Eisenhower hoped. Stalin died in 1953, and a power struggle began in the Soviet Union. By 1956, Nikita Khrushchev had emerged as the leader of the Soviet Union. That year, Khrushchev delivered a secret speech to Soviet officials. He attacked Stalin's policies and insisted that there were many ways to build a communist society. Although the speech was secret, the CIA obtained a copy of it. With Eisenhower's permission, the CIA arranged for it to be broadcast to Eastern Europe.

Many Eastern Europeans had long been frustrated with Communist rule. Hearing Khrushchev's speech further discredited communism. In June 1956 riots erupted in Eastern Europe. By late October, a full-scale uprising **D** had begun in Hungary. Although Khrushchev was willing to tolerate greater freedom in Eastern Europe, he had never meant to **imply** that the Soviets would tolerate an end to communism in the region. Soon after the uprising began, Soviet tanks rolled into Budapest, the capital of Hungary, and crushed the rebellion.

The Eisenhower Doctrine

The United States was not the only nation using covert means to support its foreign policy. President Gamal Abdel Nasser of Egypt had emerged from the Suez crisis as a hero to the Arab people, and by 1957 he had begun working

PRIMARY SOURCE

The U-2 Incident

In 1960, the Soviet Union shot down an American U-2 spy plane in Soviet air space. The incident led to a dramatic confrontation at the U.S-Soviet summit in Paris in 1960.

▲ *The U-2 (above left) was America's most sophisticated spy plane, able to fly higher than any other plane at the time. The pilot, Francis Gary Powers (above right), was captured but later released.*

◀ *Calling President Eisenhower "a thief caught red-handed," Soviet Premier Khrushchev warns the Paris summit that further spy flights will lead to war.*

Analyzing VISUALS

1. **Paraphrasing** What did Nikita Khrushchev say would be the result of further U.S. aerial spying?
2. **Making Inferences** Why was the U-2 used as a spy plane?

Activity: Collaborative Learning

Determining Cause and Effect In 1959 Premier Khrushchev visited several cities in the United States and met with President Eisenhower. The two leaders agreed to a summit in Paris the following year. The U-2 incident occurred just weeks before the summit. When Eisenhower thought the pilot was dead, he denied the allegations, but he admitted the truth when he learned pilot Francis Gary Powers was alive. Khrushchev left Paris before the meeting and withdrew an invitation to Eisenhower to visit the Soviet Union. The focus of the summit was disarmament. Have students use the Dwight D. Eisenhower Library on the Internet to create a poster of the U-2 incident and write a one-page report about what happened to Powers. **Ask:** Do you think Khrushchev overreacted or do you think he was justified in leaving the summit? **OL**

with Jordan and Syria to spread pan-Arabism—the idea that all Arab people should be united into one nation. Eisenhower and Dulles worried about Nasser's links to the Soviets and feared that he was laying the groundwork to take control of the Middle East. In late 1957 Eisenhower asked Congress to authorize the use of military force whenever the president thought it necessary to assist Middle East nations resisting Communist aggression. The policy came to be called the Eisenhower Doctrine. It essentially extended the Truman Doctrine and the policy of containment to the Middle East.

In February 1958 Eisenhower's concerns appeared to be confirmed when left-wing rebels, believed to be backed by Nasser and the Soviet Union, seized power in Iraq. Fearing that his government was next, the president of Lebanon asked the United States for help. Eisenhower immediately ordered 5,000 marines to Lebanon to protect its capital, Beirut. At the same time, British forces went into Jordan at the request of King Hussein to protect his government. Once the situation stabilized, the U.S. forces withdrew.

A Spy Plane Is Shot Down

After the Hungarian uprising, Khrushchev reasserted Soviet power and the superiority of communism. Although he had supported "peaceful coexistence" with capitalism, he began accusing the "capitalist countries" of starting a "feverish arms race." In 1957 after the launch of ***Sputnik,*** Khrushchev boasted, "We will bury capitalism. . . . Your grandchildren will live under communism."

Late the following year, Khrushchev demanded the withdrawal of Allied troops from West Berlin. Secretary of State Dulles rejected Khrushchev's demands. If the Soviets threatened Berlin, Dulles announced, NATO would respond, "if need be by military force." Brinkmanship worked again, and Khrushchev backed down.

At Eisenhower's invitation, Khrushchev visited the United States in late 1959. After the success of that visit, the two leaders agreed to hold a summit in Paris. A summit is a formal face-to-face meeting of leaders from different countries to discuss important issues.

Shortly before the summit was to begin in 1960, the Soviet Union shot down an American U-2 spy plane. At first, Eisenhower claimed that the aircraft was a weather plane that had strayed off course. Then Khrushchev dramatically produced the pilot. Eisenhower refused to apologize, saying the flights had protected American security. In **response,** Khrushchev broke up the summit.

In this climate of heightened tension, President Eisenhower prepared to leave office. In January 1961 he delivered a farewell address to the nation. In the address, he pointed out that a new relationship had developed between the military establishment and the defense industry. He warned Americans to be on guard against the influence of this **military-industrial complex** in a democracy. Although he had avoided war and kept communism contained, Eisenhower was also frustrated: "I confess I lay down my official responsibility in this field with a definite sense of disappointment. . . . I wish I could say that a lasting peace is in sight." R

Reading Check **Explaining** In what nations did the United States intervene with covert operations?

Section 4 REVIEW

Vocabulary

1. **Explain** the significance of: massive retaliation, brinkmanship, covert, Central Intelligence Agency, developing nation, *Sputnik,* military-industrial complex.

Main Ideas

2. **Summarizing** Why did Eisenhower want to depend on nuclear weapons instead of traditional military approaches to war?
3. **Defining** What was the goal of the Eisenhower Doctrine?

Critical Thinking

4. **Big Ideas** How did technology shape Eisenhower's military policy?
5. **Organizing** Use a graphic organizer similar to the one below to list Eisenhower's strategies for containing communism.

6. **Analyzing Visuals** Study the photograph of Khrushchev on page 786. How does this photograph illustrate the U.S. and Soviet relationship at this point in the Cold War?

Writing About History

7. **Persuasive Writing** Suppose that you are a member of Eisenhower's Cabinet. Defend or attack brinkmanship as a foreign policy tactic. Be sure to provide specific reasons for your opinions.

History ONLINE
Study Central™ To review this section, go to glencoe.com and click on Study Central.

R Reading Strategy

Explaining **Ask:** Why did Eisenhower warn the American people about the military-industrial power? *(He thought a military-industrial power would threaten democracy.)* OL

Reading Check

Answer:
Iran, Guatemala, and the countries of Eastern Europe

Assess

History ONLINE

Study Central™ provides summaries, interactive games, and online graphic organizers to help students review content.

Close

Evaluating Have groups debate the effectiveness of Eisenhower's foreign policy. OL

Section 4 REVIEW

Answers

1. All definitions can be found in the section and the Glossary.
2. He thought large-scale conventional wars were too expensive and would exhaust the economy. Nuclear weapons provided "more bang for the buck."
3. to extend military aid to the Middle East in order to contain communism
4. It allowed him to pursue the policy of brinkmanship since the nuclear arsenal was a real threat. It also allowed the U.S. to spy on other nations with satellites and spy planes.
5. 

strong economy
nuclear weapons for massive retaliation
brinkmanship
covert operations
6. Khrushchev looks strained and defensive, with his fists clenched, an image that reflects the strained relations between the U.S. and the Soviet Union.
7. Responses will vary but should express an opinion supporting or opposing brinkmanship.

Visual/Spatial Instruct students to use the information on the page and prepare two cause and effect graphic organizers—one for immediate causes of the Cold War and one for long term causes. **OL**

Evaluating Ask students to create a T-chart. In one column, have them identify positive effects of the Cold War *(rebuilding Europe, rebuilding Japan, NATO is created).* In the other column, have them list negative effects *(Germany is divided, China falls to communism, HUAC invades people's private lives, more weapons of mass destruction are built).* **Ask:** Which effects do you think are neutral? *(Responses will vary.)* **OL**

Chapter 22 Visual Summary

STUDY TO GO — You can study anywhere, anytime by downloading quizzes and flashcards to your PDA from glencoe.com.

Causes of the Cold War

Long-Range Causes

- Both the United States and the Soviet Union believe their economic and political systems are superior.
- Defeat of Germany creates a power vacuum in Europe and leaves U.S. and Soviet forces occupying parts of Europe.
- The U.S. wants to rebuild Europe's economy and support democratic governments to ensure peace and security.
- The USSR wants Germany weak and believes nations on the Soviet border should have Communist governments.

Immediate Causes

- At Yalta, Soviets promise to allow free elections in Eastern Europe but instead gradually impose Communist regimes.
- At Potsdam, Soviets want German reparations, but the U.S. supports rebuilding Germany's economy.
- Soviet troops help Communists in northern Iran, but U.S. pressure forces a withdrawal.
- George Kennan sends the Long Telegram to U.S. officials, explaining that the Soviets need to be contained.
- Soviets send aid to Communist rebels in Greece and demand Turkey share control of the Dardanelles with the USSR; Truman issues the Truman Doctrine and sends aid to Greece and Turkey.

▲ *From left to right: British Prime Minister Clement Attlee, U.S. President Harry Truman, and Soviet leader Joseph Stalin at the Potsdam Conference in 1945. The conference contributed to the onset of the Cold War because of disagreements over how to handle postwar Europe.*

Effects of the Cold War

Effects in Europe

- U.S. launches the Marshall Plan to rebuild Europe.
- Germany is divided into two separate nations.
- The USSR blockades Berlin; U.S. organizes the Berlin Airlift.
- The U.S. creates NATO; the USSR creates the Warsaw Pact.

Global Effects

- When China falls to communism, the U.S. responds by helping Japan build up its economy and military.
- When Communist North Korea invades South Korea, the U.S. organizes an international force to stop the invasion.

Effects on the United States

- Soviet spies are arrested.
- A new Red Scare leads to laws restricting the Communist Party in the U.S. and to investigations by the House Un-American Activities Committee and Senator Joseph McCarthy.
- Americans practice civil defense; some build bomb shelters.
- President Eisenhower orders the development of new rockets, bombers, and submarines that can carry nuclear weapons.
- Eisenhower uses the CIA to covertly contain communism.

▲ *The Soviet Union displays its nuclear capabilities in the form of these short-range missiles during celebrations commemorating the 40th anniversary of the Bolshevik Revolution in 1957. The nuclear arms race was a part of the Cold War for nearly 40 years.*

Hands-On Chapter Project
Step 5: Wrap Up

Role-Playing to Demonstrate McCarthyism in Action

Step 5: Wrap Up Essential Question: What was the impact of McCarthyism? How did it shape American history?

Directions Students should draw from each step of the chapter project to write a brief essay that answers the essential question (above). You may want to give students the option of recording their answer to the essential question and submitting it to you as an audio file.

Putting It Together Students will synthesize the information presented and the discussions following each step to summarize the big idea—how McCarthyism impacted the history of the United States. **OL**

Reviewing Vocabulary

Directions: Choose the word or words that best complete the sentence.

1. After World War II, the Soviet Union wanted to establish a buffer zone of ________ on its European border.
   A developing nations
   B capitalist nations
   C satellite nations
   D demilitarization

2. The policy of ________ became the main approach in U.S. foreign policy toward the Soviet Union during the Cold War.
   A democracy
   B limited war
   C free trade
   D containment

3. Once the Soviet Union tested an atomic bomb, Americans began to fear the effects of ________, assuming they initially survived a nuclear attack.
   A fallout
   B censure
   C subversion
   D duck-and-cover

4. In his farewell address, President Eisenhower warned the American people about the dangers of
   A the Central Intelligence Agency.
   B massive retaliation.
   C the military-industrial complex.
   D brinkmanship.

5. Though a professional soldier, President Eisenhower adopted ________ as the proper way to battle communism.
   A détente
   B implied response
   C inversion
   D massive retaliation

Reviewing Main Ideas

Directions: Choose the best answer for each of the following questions.

Section 1 *(pp. 760–765)*

6. Which of the following was a major outcome of the Yalta Conference?
   A the division of Germany
   B the terms of Germany's surrender
   C the establishment of satellite nations
   D the establishment of NATO

7. At Potsdam, the main conflict was over which of the following?
   A the United Nations
   B the invasion of Japan
   C German reparations
   D nuclear weapons

Section 2 *(pp. 766–773)*

8. George Kennan first suggested which foreign policy?
   A brinkmanship
   B containment
   C massive retaliation
   D the Marshall Plan

9. Which of the following events set off the Korean War?
   A The Japanese invaded South Korea.
   B Soviet-controlled North Korea invaded South Korea.
   C Chinese-controlled North Korea invaded South Korea.
   D The Soviet Union invaded North Korea.

TEST-TAKING TIP

When you first start a test, review it completely so that you can budget your time most efficiently. For example, if there are essay questions at the end, you will want to be sure you leave enough time to write complete answers.

Need Extra Help?

If You Missed Questions . . .	1	2	3	4	5	6	7	8	9
Go to Page . . .	765	766	780–781	787	783	760–761	764–765	766	771

GO ON

Answers and Analyses
Reviewing Vocabulary

1. C Developing nations are nations that are transforming economically, and are not relevant to the question. Capitalist nations are the opposite of what the USSR would want to set up. Demilitarization is an action, not an object, and does not make grammatical sense.

2. D The United States wanted to stop, or contain, the spread of communism. Democracy is not a foreign policy approach. Free trade does not make sense in the context of the Cold War.

3. A Fallout is the aftereffect of a nuclear attack. Censure is a political term. Subversion does not make sense in the context of the sentence. Duck and cover was an action that was to be taken during an attack, not after.

4. C Eisenhower issued the warning due to the new relationship that had developed between the military and the defense industry. He was afraid their influence would be too far reaching and warned Americans to be on guard.

5. D Eisenhower's theory of massive retaliation was that the threat of total nuclear destruction would prevent all war. Fighting small-scale wars would not bring an end to the Cold War.

Reviewing Main Ideas

6. A At the conference, Germany was divided into four parts, one each controlled by the U.S., Great Britain, France, and the Soviet Union. Berlin was also divided between the four nations. Satellite nations and NATO were not established until after the conference.

7. C Truman and Stalin met at Potsdam to discuss mainly what to do with Germany. Truman believed Germany needed industry to survive and needed money to fuel industry. Stalin wanted reparations from Germany. He was not concerned with the German economy, because the Soviet economy was so devastated.

8. B Kennan's proposal of containment of Communism became the basis for American Cold War foreign policy. Brinkmanship and massive retaliation were later policies instituted by Eisenhower's administration. The Marshall Plan was a plan to help rebuild Europe after WWII.

9. B It is important that students understand the Korean conflict was between North Korea and South Korea, which eliminates *A* and *D*. However, students may have trouble choosing between *B* and *C*. Students should remember that the Korean War involved the two main players in the Cold War: the U.S. and USSR.

10. B The Marshall Plan was aimed at rebuilding Europe after the war. An underlying motivation was to stop the spread of communism—strong European economies would help keep European nations from falling to communism.

11. A Remind students that HUAC stands for House Un-American Activities Committee. Un-American activities are anti-American. During the Red Scare that swept the nation in the years following WWII, Communists or those who were believed to be communist "sympathizers" were considered un-American—a threat to the nation.

12. C Although many local governments, businesses, unions, etc., asked employees to take loyalty oaths, such as the University of California, all government employees did not have to take an oath. The government did not order all Communist Party chapters to disband. The act did require these organizations to register with the government. The act was passed over Truman's veto.

13. B Students should relate attack to retaliation, which may help them remember the policy of massive retaliation. Containment was the policy under the Truman administration. Subversion is a rebellion or treason, and does not fit. Duck-and-cover was a plan to "survive" a nuclear attack.

14. D The Truman Doctrine offered aid to any nation resisting communism and was connected to the policy of containment. The Eisenhower Doctrine was issued in response to the Pan-Arabism movement, which some feared would lead to communism in the Middle East.

Chapter 22 Assessment

10. What was the underlying goal of the Marshall Plan?
- **A** to contain Soviet expansion in the Middle East and Asia
- **B** to rebuild European economies to prevent the spread of communism
- **C** to monitor the growth of the military-industrial complex in the United States
- **D** to Americanize Western European nations

Section 3 *(pp. 774–781)*

11. After World War II, the purpose of HUAC was to
- **A** hold public hearings on Communist subversion.
- **B** locate chapters of the Communist Party.
- **C** administer the loyalty review program.
- **D** create the McCarran Act.

12. The McCarran Act required
- **A** every government employee to take a loyalty oath.
- **B** all Communist Party chapters to disband.
- **C** all Communist organizations to register with the government.
- **D** the censure of members of Congress who would not support HUAC.

Section 4 *(pp. 782–787)*

13. Eisenhower's administration developed an approach to foreign policy based on the threat of nuclear attack, known as
- **A** containment.
- **B** massive retaliation.
- **C** subversion.
- **D** duck-and-cover.

14. The Eisenhower Doctrine extended the Truman Doctrine to which region?
- **A** Asia
- **B** Eastern Europe
- **C** South America
- **D** the Middle East

Critical Thinking

Directions: Choose the best answers to the following questions.

Base your answers to questions 15 and 16 on the map below and on your knowledge of Chapter 22.

Berlin After World War II, 1945

15. Why was Stalin initially able to control access to West Berlin?
- **A** West Berlin was in the Soviet Union.
- **B** West Berlin was ruled by Communists.
- **C** West Berlin was in the Soviet sector of Germany.
- **D** West Berlin had been invaded and occupied by the Red Army.

16. Why did Stalin order a blockade of West Berlin?
- **A** West Berlin was primarily agricultural and would help feed the Soviet army.
- **B** Stalin wanted to unite Berlin and organize free elections for Germany.
- **C** Stalin was afraid of the U.S. nuclear technology and wanted a larger buffer zone.
- **D** Stalin wanted the United States to abandon West Berlin.

Need Extra Help?

If You Missed Questions . . .	10	11	12	13	14	15	16
Go to Page . . .	768	775	778	782–783	786–787	768–769	768–769

GO ON

Critical Thinking

15. C Although the map is helpful, the incorrect answers are easily eliminated. The map is labeled East Germany, which eliminates *A*. West Berlin included the American, British, and French sectors, according to the map key, so it was not ruled by Communists and not occupied by the Soviet Army. Berlin was, however, in the Soviet sector.

16. D A blockade attempts to keep supplies and food out of a certain area. Keeping food out of West Berlin would not help feed the Soviet army. Stalin wanted to unite Berlin under his own control, and would not want free elections. He wanted the U.S. to leave. West Berlin would not create a significant buffer zone.

17. One historical lesson from the McCarthy era is the realization that

A loyalty oaths prevent spying.

B communism is attractive in prosperous times.

C Communist agents had infiltrated all levels of the U.S. government.

D public fear of traitors can lead to intolerance and discrimination.

Analyze the cartoon and answer the question that follows. Base your answer on the cartoon and on your knowledge of Chapter 22.

"So Russia Launched a Satellite, but Has It Made Cars With Fins Yet?"

18. In this cartoon, the cartoonist is expressing

A pride in America's technological know-how.

B anxiety that America is behind in the space race.

C a wish for larger, more elaborate cars.

D the need to share auto technology with Russia.

Document-Based Questions

Directions: Analyze the document and answer the short-answer questions that follow the document.

Margaret Chase Smith, a Republican senator from Maine, was a newcomer and the only woman in the Senate. Smith was upset by McCarthy's behavior and hoped that her colleagues would reprimand him. When they failed to do so, Smith made her "Declaration of Conscience" speech.

> *"As a United States Senator, I am not proud of the way in which the Senate has been made a publicity platform for irresponsible sensationalism. I am not proud of the reckless abandon in which unproved charges have been hurled from this side of the aisle. I am not proud of the obviously staged, undignified countercharges that have been attempted in retaliation from the other side of the aisle . . . I am not proud of the way we smear outsiders from the Floor of the Senate and hide behind a cloak of congressional immunity. . . .*
>
> *As an American, I am shocked at the way Republicans and Democrats alike are playing directly into the Communist design of 'confuse, divide, and conquer'. . . . I want to see our nation recapture the strength and unity it once had when we fought the enemy instead of ourselves."*
>
> —*from* Declaration of Conscience

19. In the speech, Smith expresses anger with whom? Why?

20. According to Smith, who is really dividing the nation?

Extended Response

21. Many factors contributed to the development of the Cold War, but could it have been avoided? Write a persuasive essay arguing that actions of the United States or the Soviet Union following World War II might have prevented the Cold War, or that it was inevitable.

STOP

History ONLINE
For additional test practice, use Self-Check Quizzes—Chapter 22 at glencoe.com.

Need Extra Help?

If You Missed Questions . . .	17	18	19	20	21
Go to Page . . .	777–778	R18	791	791	760–773

17. D The Red Scare during the McCarthy era led many people to discriminate and accept poor or legally suspect treatment of people considered to be Communists and subversives. The culture of fear during the era allowed this discrimination to take place.

18. B The car salesman in the cartoon is expressing pride in American know-how, but Uncle Sam looks concerned. Direct students to read the caption. The caption pokes fun at American technology; it says that Americans were making strides in frivolous things like fins on cars while the USSR had already launched a satellite into space.

Document-Based Questions

19. Smith expresses anger with the members of Senate, both Republican and Democrat, who took part in irresponsible charges and accusations against fellow Americans. She also expresses anger at the way they hide behind congressional immunity to do so.

20. Smith believes the Republicans and Democrats in Senate are dividing the nation, playing into the Soviet plan or "confuse, divide, and conquer."

Extended Response

21. Students must take a position either that the Cold War could have been prevented or could not have been prevented. Students should use evidence from the chapter, and possible topics for discussion include Yalta, the Marshall Plan, the Berlin Airlift, and the formation of NATO. Essays should adhere to the guidelines for writing a persuasive essay and should present a clear and well-reasoned argument.

History ONLINE
Have students visit the Web site at glencoe.com to review Chapter 22 and take the Self-Check Quiz.

Need Extra Help?
Have students refer to the pages listed if they miss any of the questions.

Chapter 23 Planning Guide

Key to Ability Levels	
BL Below Level	AL Above Level
OL On Level	ELL English Language Learners

Key to Teaching Resources	
Print Material	Transparency
CD-ROM or DVD	

Levels BL	OL	AL	ELL		Resources	Chapter Opener	Section 1	Section 2	Section 3	Chapter Assess
					FOCUS					
BL	OL	AL	ELL	Transparency	**Daily Focus Skills Transparencies**		23-1	23-2	23-3	
					TEACH					
BL	OL		ELL	Print Material	**Reading Essentials and Note-Taking Guide***		p. 259	p. 262	p. 265	
	OL			Print Material	**Historical Analysis Skills Activity, URB**		p. 124			
BL	OL		ELL	Print Material	**Guided Reading Activities, URB***		p. 150	p. 151	p. 152	
BL	OL	AL	ELL	Print Material	**Content Vocabulary Activity, URB***		p. 129			
BL	OL	AL	ELL	Print Material	**Academic Vocabulary Activity, URB**		p. 131			
	OL	AL		Print Material	**Critical Thinking Skills Activity, URB**				p. 134	
BL	OL		ELL	Print Material	**Reading Skills Activity, URB**			p. 123		
BL			ELL	Print Material	**English Learner Activity, URB**		p. 127			
	OL	AL		Print Material	**Reinforcing Skills Activity, URB**			p. 133		
BL	OL	AL	ELL	Print Material	**Differentiated Instruction Activity, URB**				p. 125	
BL	OL		ELL	Print Material	**Time Line Activity, URB**				p. 135	
	OL			Print Material	**Linking Past and Present Activity, URB**				p. 136	
BL	OL	AL	ELL	Print Material	**American Art and Music Activity, URB**			p. 141		
BL	OL	AL	ELL	Print Material	**Interpreting Political Cartoons Activity, URB**			p. 143		
	OL	AL		Print Material	**Economic Activity, URB**			p. 7		
		AL		Print Material	**Enrichment Activity, URB**			p. 147		
BL	OL	AL	ELL	Print Material	**American Biographies**			✓		
BL	OL	AL	ELL	Print Material	**Primary Source Reading, URB**			p. 139	p. 137	
BL	OL	AL	ELL	Print Material	**The Living Constitution***	✓	✓	✓	✓	✓
	OL	AL		CD-ROM or DVD	**American History Primary Source Documents Library**	✓	✓	✓	✓	✓
BL	OL	AL	ELL	Transparency	**Unit Map Overlay Transparencies**	✓	✓	✓	✓	✓
BL	OL	AL	ELL	Print Material	**Differentiated Instruction for the American History Classroom**	✓	✓	✓	✓	✓
BL	OL	AL	ELL	CD-ROM or DVD	**StudentWorks™ Plus**	✓	✓	✓	✓	✓

Note: Please refer to *Unit 7 Resource Book* for this chapter's URB materials.

* Also available in Spanish

TeacherWorks Plus
All-In-One Planner and Resource Center

- Interactive Lesson Planner
- Interactive Teacher Edition
- Fully editable blackline masters
- Section Spotlight Videos Launch
- Differentiated Lesson Plans
- Printable reports of daily assignments
- Standards Tracking System

Levels				Resources	Chapter Opener	Section 1	Section 2	Section 3	Chapter Assess
BL	OL	AL	ELL						
				TEACH *(continued)*					
BL	OL	AL	ELL	American Music Hits Through History CD	✓	✓	✓	✓	✓
BL	OL	AL	ELL	Unit Time Line Transparencies and Activities	✓	✓	✓	✓	✓
BL	OL	AL	ELL	Cause and Effect Transparencies, Strategies, and Activities	✓	✓	✓	✓	✓
BL	OL	AL	ELL	Why It Matters Transparencies, Strategies, and Activities	✓	✓	✓	✓	✓
BL	OL	AL	ELL	American Issues	✓	✓	✓	✓	✓
	OL	AL	ELL	American Art and Architecture Transparencies, Strategies, and Activities	✓	✓	✓	✓	✓
BL	OL	AL		High School American History Literature Library	✓	✓	✓	✓	✓
BL	OL	AL	ELL	*The American Vision* Video Program	✓	✓	✓	✓	✓
Teacher Resources				Strategies for Success	✓	✓	✓	✓	✓
Teacher Resources				Success with English Learners	✓	✓	✓	✓	✓
Teacher Resources				Reading Strategies and Activities for the Social Studies Classroom	✓	✓	✓	✓	✓
Teacher Resources				Presentation Plus! with MindJogger CheckPoint	✓	✓	✓	✓	✓
				ASSESS					
BL	OL	AL	ELL	Section Quizzes and Chapter Tests*		p. 327	p. 328	p. 329	p. 331
BL	OL	AL	ELL	Authentic Assessment With Rubrics					p. 51
BL	OL	AL	ELL	Standardized Test Practice Workbook					p. 52
BL	OL	AL	ELL	*ExamView® Assessment Suite*		23-1	23-2	23-3	Ch. 23
				CLOSE					
BL			ELL	Reteaching Activity, URB					p. 145
BL	OL		ELL	Reading and Study Skills Foldables™	p. 77				

✓ Chapter- or unit-based activities applicable to all sections in this chapter.

Using Study-to-Go

Teach With Technology

What is Study-to-Go?
Study-to-Go provides portable textbook-based content direct from the Glencoe Web site to your students whenever and wherever they want!

How can Study-to-Go help my students?
Study-to-Go content can be downloaded to a personal digital assistant (PDA) or a cell phone. Students can download Study Sets that include:

- Self Quiz—a series of multiple choice quizzes that provides instant answer feedback
- Key Terms—definitions for textbook vocabulary
- Flashcards—an assessment tool to help students study textbook key terms

Visit glencoe.com and enter a ***QuickPass***™ code to go to the Study-to-Go.

History ONLINE
Visit glencoe.com and enter ***QuickPass***™ code TAV9399c23T for Chapter 23 resources.

You can easily launch a wide range of digital products from your computer's desktop with the McGraw-Hill Social Studies widget.

	Student	Teacher	Parent
Media Library			
• Section Audio	●		●
• Spanish Audio Summaries	●		●
• Section Spotlight Videos	●	●	●
***The American Vision* Online Learning Center (Web Site)**			
• StudentWorks™ Plus Online	●	●	●
• Multilingual Glossary	●	●	●
• Study-to-Go	●	●	●
• Chapter Overviews	●	●	●
• Self-Check Quizzes	●	●	●
• Student Web Activities	●	●	●
• ePuzzles and Games	●	●	●
• Vocabulary eFlashcards	●	●	●
• In Motion Animations	●	●	●
• Study Central™	●	●	●
• Web Activity Lesson Plans		●	
• Vocabulary PuzzleMaker	●	●	●
• Historical Thinking Activities		●	
• Beyond the Textbook	●	●	●

Reading Support From Jamestown Education

- **Timed Readings Plus in Social Studies** helps students increase their reading rate and fluency while maintaining comprehension. The 400-word passages are similar to those found on state and national assessments.
- **Reading in the Content Area: Social Studies** concentrates on six essential reading skills that help students better comprehend what they read. The book includes 75 high-interest nonfiction passages written at increasing levels of difficulty.
- **Reading Social Studies** includes strategic reading instruction and vocabulary support in Social Studies content for both ELLs and native speakers of English.

www.jamestowneducation.com

Biography — A&E Home Video — The History Channel

The following videotape programs are available from Glencoe as supplements to this chapter:

- Dwight D. Eisenhower: Commander-in-Chief (ISBN 1-56-501807-9)
- The Class of the 20th Century; Vol. 3: 1952–1961 (ISBN 1-56-501049-3)

To order, call Glencoe at 1-800-334-7344. To find classroom resources to accompany many of these videos, check the following home pages:

A&E Television: www.aetv.com

The History Channel: www.historychannel.com

Reading List Generator CD-ROM — Glencoe BookLink 3

Use this database to search more than 30,000 titles to create a customized reading list for your students.

- Reading lists can be organized by students' reading level, author, genre, theme, or area of interest.
- The database provides Degrees of Reading Power™ (DRP) and Lexile™ readability scores for all selections.
- A brief summary of each selection is included.

Leveled reading suggestions for this chapter:

For students at a Grade 8 reading level:
- ***October Sky***, by Homer H. Hickam

For students at a Grade 9 reading level:
- ***Plain Speaking: An Oral Biography of Harry S. Truman***, by Merle Miller

For students at a Grade 10 reading level:
- ***Elvis Presley***, by Bobbie Ann Mason

For students at a Grade 11 reading level:
- ***Harry S. Truman***, by Caroline Evenson Lazo

For students at a Grade 12 reading level:
- ***Polio***, by Allison Stark Draper

National Geographic

Index to National Geographic Magazine:

The following articles relate to this chapter:

- "He Refused to Leave. (Harry Truman)," January 1981.
- "Alone Across the Arctic Crown," by Berge Ousland, November 1993.

National Geographic Society Products To order the following, call National Geographic at 1-800-368-2728:

- *ZipZapMap! USA Windows* (ZipZapMap! USA)

Access National Geographic's new, dynamic MapMachine Web site and other geography resources at:

www.nationalgeographic.com
www.nationalgeographic.com/maps

Introducing Chapter 23

Focus

MAKING CONNECTIONS

What Does It Mean to Be Prosperous?

Ask students to imagine that each of them just received $10,000 to spend, save, or invest as they choose. Have students brainstorm what they would do with this money and list their ideas on the board. Explain that many Americans had extra money to spend in the 1950s. Discuss with the students how Americans in the 1950s spent this extra money. **OL**

Teach

The Big Ideas

As students study the chapter, remind them to consider the section-based Big Ideas included in each section's Guide to Reading. The **Essential Questions** in the activities below tie in to the Big Ideas and help students think about and understand important chapter concepts. In addition, the Hands-on Chapter Projects with their culminating activities relate the content from each section to the Big Ideas. These activities build on each other as students progress through the chapter. Section activities culminate in the wrap-up activity on the Visual Summary page.

Chapter 23

Postwar America

1945–1960

SECTION 1 Truman and Eisenhower
SECTION 2 The Affluent Society
SECTION 3 The Other Side of American Life

Teens enjoy milkshakes while studying in a 1950's-style diner.

U.S. PRESIDENTS

Truman 1945–1953

U.S. EVENTS

1944
- GI Bill is enacted

1946
- Strikes erupt across country

1947
- Congress passes Taft-Hartley Act over Truman's veto

1951
- The *I Love Lucy* television show airs its first show

1944 — 1948 — 1952

WORLD EVENTS

1946
- Churchill gives "Iron Curtain" speech

1948
- South Africa introduces apartheid

1952
- Scientists led by Edward Teller develop hydrogen bomb

Section 1

Truman and Eisenhower

Essential Question: How did Truman and Eisenhower guide the nation after World War II? *(Both presidents worked to keep the nation strong as it returned to a peacetime economy.)* Tell students that in this section they will learn about how the differing policies of presidents Truman and Eisenhower kept the nation's economy strong after World War II. **OL**

Section 2

The Affluent Society

Essential Question: What were the characteristics of affluent Americans in the 1950s? *(Most people had more money to spend; many people moved to the suburbs; leisure time increased.)* Tell students that this section will focus on how many Americans enjoyed their newfound affluence. **OL**

Chapter Audio

MAKING CONNECTIONS

What Does It Mean to Be Prosperous?

After World War II, the United States experienced years of steady economic growth. Although not everyone benefited, the economic boom meant most Americans enjoyed more prosperity than earlier generations.

- ***How did Americans spend this new wealth?***
- ***How does prosperity change the way people live?***

FOLDABLES

Categorizing Information Make a Folded-Table Foldable on popular culture in the 1950s and present. List the following for both time periods: data on the types of mass media and size of the audiences for them, characteristics of youth culture, and groups represented in the mass media.

Popular Culture	1950s	Present
Mass Media Types		
Youth Culture		
Groups Represented in Media		

Eisenhower 1953–1961

1955
- Salk polio vaccine becomes widely available

1956
- Congress passes Federal Highway Act

1957
- Estimated 40 million television sets in use in the United States

1956

1960

1954
- Gamal Abdel Nasser takes power in Egypt

1956
- Suez Canal crisis

1957
- USSR launches *Sputnik I* and *Sputnik II* satellites

History ONLINE Visit glencoe.com and enter **QuickPass™ code TAV9846c23 for Chapter 23 resources.**

Introducing
Chapter 23

More About the Photo

Visual Literacy In the 1950s, diners became popular places for young people to gather. The affluence of the 1950s allowed more teenagers to acquire cars, which they drove to school and then, after school, to the local diner or malt shop for milkshakes or soft drinks. Most diners had jukeboxes that played rock-and-roll music.

FOLDABLES Study Organizer **Dinah Zike's Foldables**

Dinah Zike's Foldables are three-dimensional, interactive graphic organizers that help students practice basic writing skills, review vocabulary terms, and identify main ideas. Instructions for creating and using Foldables can be found in the Appendix at the end of this book and in the *Dinah Zike's Reading and Study Skills Foldables* booklet.

History ONLINE

Visit glencoe.com and enter ***QuickPass***™ code TAV9399c23T for Chapter 23 resources, including a Chapter Overview, Study Central™, Study-to-Go, Student Web Activity, Self-Check Quiz, and other materials.

Section 3

The Other Side of American Life

Essential Question: What groups of Americans did not enjoy the affluence of the 1950s? *(people living in inner cities, people living in Appalachia, minorities, and Native Americans)* Tell students that in Section 3 they will learn about Americans who did not share in the prosperity of the 1950s. **OL**

Focus

Bellringer

Daily Focus Transparency 23-1

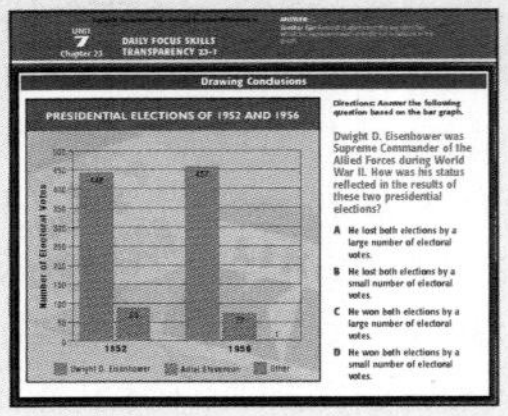

Guide to Reading

Answers:

Characteristics of a Postwar Economy:
increased consumer spending, higher prices, rising inflation, labor unrest

Section Spotlight Video

To generate student interest and provide a springboard for class discussion, access the Chapter 23, Section 1 video at glencoe.com or on the video DVD.

Section 1

Section Audio · Spotlight Video

Truman and Eisenhower

Guide to Reading

Big Ideas

Economics and Society Following World War II, the federal government supported programs that helped the American economy make the transition from wartime to peacetime production.

Content Vocabulary
- closed shop *(p. 794)*
- right-to-work laws *(p. 795)*
- union shop *(p. 795)*
- dynamic conservatism *(p. 798)*

Academic Vocabulary
- legislator *(p. 794)*
- abandon *(p. 796)*

People and Events to Identify
- GI Bill *(p. 794)*
- "Do-Nothing Congress" *(p. 796)*
- Fair Deal *(p. 797)*
- Federal Highway Act *(p. 799)*

Reading Strategy

Complete a graphic organizer similar to the one below by listing the characteristics of the U.S. postwar economy.

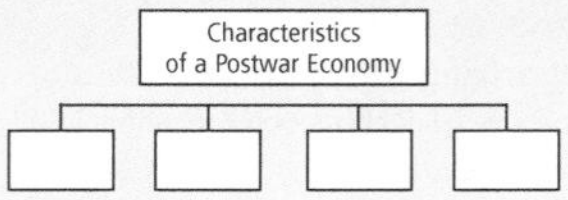

In the postwar era, Congress limited the power of unions and rejected most of President Truman's plan for a "Fair Deal." When Eisenhower became president, he cut back some government programs and launched the interstate highway system.

Return to a Peacetime Economy

MAIN Idea Despite inflation and strikes, the nation was able to shift to a peacetime economy without a recession.

HISTORY AND YOU Do you know you can get help paying for college if you serve in the military? Read to learn about the origins of the "GI Bill" and how it helped World War II veterans get a college education.

After the war many Americans feared the return to a peacetime economy. They worried that, after military production halted and millions of former soldiers glutted the labor market, unemployment and recession might sweep the country. Despite such worries, the economy continued to grow after the war as increased consumer spending helped ward off a recession. After 17 years of an economic depression and wartime shortages, Americans rushed out to buy the consumer goods they had long desired.

The Servicemen's Readjustment Act, popularly called the **GI Bill,** boosted the economy further. The act provided generous funds to veterans to help them establish businesses, buy homes, and attend college. The postwar economy did have problems, particularly in the first couple of years following the end of the war. A greater demand for goods led to higher prices, and this inflation soon triggered labor unrest. As the cost of living rose, workers in the automobile, steel, electrical, and mining industries went on strike for better pay.

Afraid that the nation's energy supply would be drastically reduced because of the striking miners, Truman ordered government seizure of the mines, while pressuring mine owners to grant the union most of its demands. The president also halted a strike that shut down the nation's railroads by threatening to draft the striking workers into the army.

Labor unrest and high prices prompted many Americans to call for a change. The Republicans seized on these sentiments during the 1946 congressional elections, winning control of both houses of Congress for the first time since 1930.

The new conservative Congress quickly set out to curb the power of organized labor. **Legislators** proposed a measure known as the Taft-Hartley Act, which outlawed the **closed shop,** or the practice of forcing business owners to hire only union members. Under this law,

Resource Manager

R Reading Strategies	C Critical Thinking	D Differentiated Instruction	W Writing Support	S Skill Practice
Teacher Edition • Organizing, p. 796 **Additional Resources** • Content Vocab. Act., URB p. 129 • Guided Reading Act., URB p. 150	**Teacher Edition** • Det. Cause/Effect, p. 795 **Additional Resources** • Historical Analysis Skills Act., URB p. 124 • Quizzes/Tests, p. 327	**Teacher Edition** • Interpersonal, p. 796 • Visual/Spatial, p. 798 **Additional Resources** • Eng. Learner Act., URB p. 127 • Academic Vocab. Act., URB p. 131	**Teacher Edition** • Personal Writing, p. 797 **Additional Resources** • Foldables, p. 77	**Teacher Edition** • Evaluating, p. 798 **Additional Resources** • Read. Essen., p. 259

PRIMARY SOURCE
The GI Bill of Rights

One reason the American economy rebounded so quickly after World War II ended was the Servicemen's Readjustment Act of 1944, popularly called the GI Bill of Rights. The act subsidized college tuition and provided zero down-payment, low-interest loans to veterans to help them buy homes and establish businesses.

Veterans flocked to colleges in large numbers after the war. Among them was William Oskay, Jr., (above) who attended Pennsylvania State University in 1946. By 1947, nearly half of all people attending college were veterans. At the University of Iowa (left), 60 percent of students were veterans in 1947. By 1956, when the GI program ended, 7.8 million veterans had used it to attend college. Another 2.4 million veterans used the program to obtain home loans.

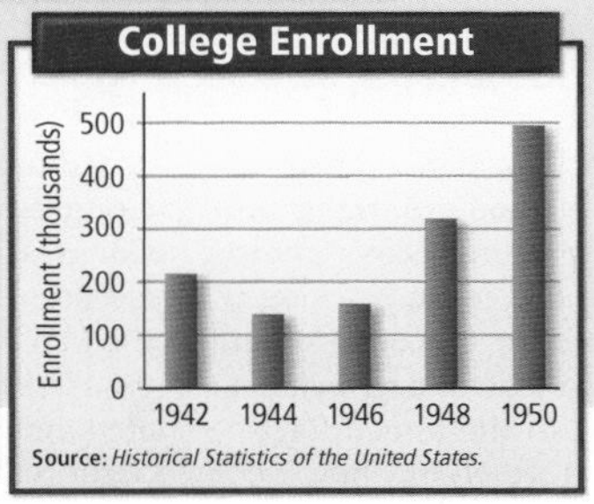

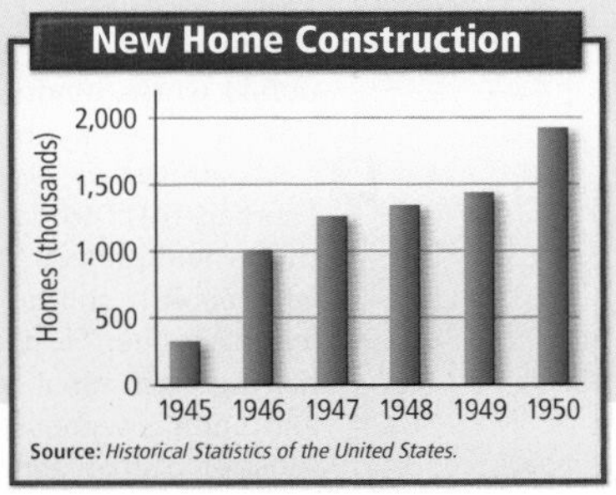

Analyzing VISUALS

1. **Calculating** Based on the graph, what was the increase in college enrollments between 1944 and 1950?
2. **Specifying** About how many new homes were constructed in 1950?

states could pass **right-to-work laws,** which outlawed **union shops** (shops in which new workers were required to join the union). The measure also prohibited featherbedding, the practice of limiting work output in order to create more jobs. Furthermore, the bill forbade unions from using their money to support political campaigns.

When the bill reached Truman, however, he vetoed it, arguing that it was a mistake:

PRIMARY SOURCE

"... [It would] reverse the basic direction of our national labor policy, inject the government into private economic affairs on an unprecedented scale, and conflict with important principles of our democratic society. Its provisions would cause more strikes, not fewer."

—quoted in *The Growth of the American Republic*

The president's concerns did little to sway Congress, which passed the Taft-Hartley Act in 1947 over Truman's veto. Its supporters claimed that the law held irresponsible unions in check, just as the Wagner Act of 1935 had restrained anti-union activities and employers. Labor leaders called the act a "slave labor" law and insisted that it erased many of the gains that unions had made since 1933.

Reading Check **Explaining** Why did Truman veto the Taft-Hartley Act?

History ONLINE
Student Web Activity Visit glencoe.com and complete the activity on the GI Bill.

Teach

C Critical Thinking

Determining Cause and Effect Tell students that in the late 1940s nearly half of college students were veterans. **Ask:** What accounted for the high percentage of veterans in college? *(The GI Bill subsidized tuition for veterans.)* **OL**

Analyzing VISUALS

Answers:
1. about 360,000
2. close to 2,000,000

Reading Check

Answer:
He felt that it brought the government into private economic affairs on an unprecedented scale and would cause more strikes without contributing to economic stability and progress.

Hands-On Chapter Project
Step 1

A New Peacetime America

Step 1: Facing the Future Students will focus on the amazing changes that took place in American government and culture following World War II, with their final product being a classroom display of items representing these changes.

Directions Have students review Section 1, noting the new government programs presented by presidents Truman and Eisenhower such as the system of interstate highways and the raising of the minimum wage. Have students meet in small groups to research and discuss these changes and how lasting the impact of each was.

Drawing Conclusions Have students regroup as a class and record what they have found in their research and discussions on the board. After comparing these government programs, then and now, have them draw some conclusions about the effectiveness of the government and the impact it has on their daily lives. **OL**

(Chapter Project continued on page 801)

R Reading Strategy

Organizing Have each student complete a three-column chart with the headings *Economic Measures, Social Measures,* and *Civil Rights Improvements* to list Truman's domestic agenda. *(Answers may include: Economic: expand Social Security benefits, raise minimum wage; Social: public housing, long-range environmental and public works planning, national health insurance; Civil Rights: civil rights bill, establish voting rights, bar workforce discrimination, integrate armed forces.)* **OL**

D Differentiated Instruction

Interpersonal Invite four students to represent the candidates in the 1948 presidential election campaign—Truman, Dewey, Thurman, and Wallace. Have the remaining students meet and greet the "candidates." Encourage the candidates to talk with their constituents and describe their qualifications and their proposed programs. **OL**

Additional Support

Truman's Program

MAIN Idea Truman pushed for a "Fair Deal" for Americans, despite the legislative conflicts he had with Congress.

HISTORY AND YOU Do you remember how close the last presidential election was? Read on to learn about Truman's surprise victory in 1948.

The Democratic Party's loss of control in Congress in the 1946 elections did not dampen President Truman's spirits or his plans. Shortly after taking office, Truman had proposed domestic measures seeking to continue the work of Franklin Roosevelt's New Deal. During his tenure in office, Truman worked to push this agenda through Congress.

Truman's Legislative Agenda

Truman's proposals included expansion of Social Security benefits; raising the minimum wage; a program to ensure full employment through aggressive use of federal spending and investment; public housing and slum clearance; and long-range environmental and public works planning. He also proposed a system of national health insurance.

R Truman also boldly asked Congress in February 1948 to pass a broad civil rights bill that would protect African Americans' right to vote, abolish poll taxes, and make lynching a federal crime. He issued an executive order barring discrimination in federal employment and ending segregation in the armed forces. Most of Truman's legislative efforts, however, met with little success, as a coalition of Republicans and conservative Southern Democrats defeated many of his proposals.

The Election of 1948

As the 1948 presidential election approached, most observers gave Truman little chance of winning. Some Americans still believed that he lacked the stature for the job, D and they viewed his administration as inept.

Divisions within the Democratic Party also seemed to spell disaster for Truman. At the Democratic Convention that summer, two factions **abandoned** the party altogether. Reacting angrily to Truman's support of civil rights, a group of Southern Democrats formed the States' Rights, or Dixiecrat, Party and nominated South Carolina Governor Strom Thurmond for president. At the same time, the party's more liberal members were frustrated by Truman's ineffective domestic policies and critical of his anti-Soviet foreign policy. They formed a new Progressive Party, with Henry A. Wallace as their presidential candidate.

The president's Republican opponent was New York Governor Thomas Dewey, a dignified and popular candidate who seemed unbeatable. After polling 50 political writers, *Newsweek* magazine declared three weeks before the election, "The landslide for Dewey will sweep the country."

Perhaps the only person who gave Truman any chance to win the election was Truman himself. "I know every one of those 50 fellows," he declared about the writers polled in *Newsweek*. "There isn't one of them has enough sense to pound sand in a rat hole." Truman poured his energy into the campaign, traveling more than 20,000 miles by train and making more than 350 speeches. Along the way, he attacked the majority Republican Congress as "do-nothing, good-for-nothing" for refusing to D enact his legislative agenda.

Truman's attacks on the "**Do-Nothing Congress**" did not mention that both he and Congress had passed the Truman Doctrine's aid program to Greece and Turkey, as well as the Marshall Plan. Congress had also enacted the National Security Act of 1947, which created the Department of Defense, the National Security Council, and the CIA; established the Joint Chiefs of Staff as a permanent organization; and made the Air Force an independent branch of the military. Congress also passed the Twenty-second Amendment, which limited a president to two terms in office. The 80th Congress did not "do nothing" as Truman charged, but its accomplishments were in areas that did not affect most Americans directly. As a result, Truman's charges began to stick.

With a great deal of support from laborers, African Americans, and farmers, Truman won a narrow but stunning victory over Dewey. Perhaps just as remarkable as the president's victory was the resurgence of the Democratic Party. On election day, Democrats regained control of both houses of Congress.

Activity: Collaborative Learning

Identifying Organize the class into groups of three or four and have students research the campaign slogans and strategies of the different candidates in the 1948 presidential election. Ask students to write a one-minute radio advertisement for the candidate of their choice. Ads should present the candidate's positions clearly and accurately. Students may incorporate music, dialogue, and sound effects in their radio spot. If possible, students can tape record their spots or simply present them "live" to the class. Encourage the class to discuss how effective the spots are. **Ask:** Did the radio advertisement present accurate information about the candidate? Did the spot influence your opinion of the candidate? How? **OL** **AL**

The Fair Deal

Truman's 1949 State of the Union address repeated the domestic agenda he had put forth previously. "Every segment of our population and every individual," he declared, "has a right to expect from . . . government a fair deal." Whether intentional or not, the president **W** had coined a name—the **Fair Deal**—to set his program apart from the New Deal. In February, he began to send his proposals to Congress.

The 81st Congress did not completely embrace Truman's Fair Deal. Legislators did raise the legal minimum wage to 75¢ an hour. They increased Social Security benefits by 75 percent and extended them to 10 million additional people. Congress also passed the National Housing Act of 1949, which provided for the construction of low-income housing, accompanied by long-term rent subsidies.

Congress refused, however, to pass national health insurance or to provide subsidies for **W** farmers or federal aid for schools. In addition, legislators, led by the same coalition of conservative Republicans and Dixiecrats, opposed Truman's efforts to enact civil rights legislation. His plans for federal aid to education were also not enacted.

Reading Check **Summarizing** What did Truman and the Congress accomplish in foreign relations?

PRIMARY SOURCE
The Election of 1948

▲ Harry Truman gleefully displays the erroneous *Chicago Daily Tribune* headline announcing his defeat by Thomas Dewey.

What Was the Fair Deal?

In 1949 Truman outlined in his State of the Union address an ambitious legislative program that became known as the Fair Deal. Some of its main features were:

- the expansion of Social Security benefits
- an increase in the minimum wage
- a program to ensure full employment
- a program of public housing and slum clearance
- a long-range plan for environmental and public works
- a system of national health insurance
- a broad program of civil rights legislation

Presidential Election of 1948

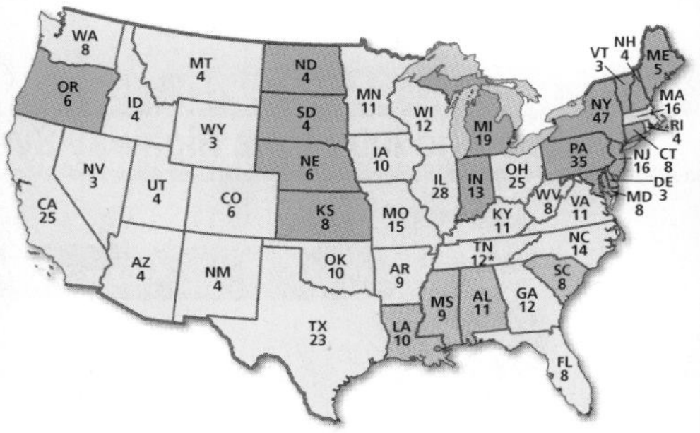

Presidential Candidate	Popular Votes	% of Popular Vote	Electoral Votes
Truman	24,105,695	49.51%	303
Dewey	21,969,170	45.13%	189
Thurmond	1,169,021	2.40%	39
Wallace	1,156,103	2.37%	

*Eleven electors voted for Truman, and one voted for Thurmond.

Analyzing VISUALS

1. **Interpreting** In what regions of the nation did Thomas Dewey receive the most votes?
2. **Calculating** What was the difference in percentage of the popular vote received by Truman and Dewey?

W Writing Support

Personal Writing Truman declared that every citizen has the right to expect a "fair deal" from the government. Ask students to write a few paragraphs expressing their personal feelings about what citizens should expect from government. **OL**

Analyzing VISUALS

Answers:
1. the Northeast and Midwest
2. 4.38%

Reading Check

Answer:
Truman and Congress passed the National Security Act, the Truman Doctrine's aid program to Greece and Turkey, as well as the Marshall Plan.

Additional Support

Activity: Economics Connection

Analyzing Tell students that Bill Clinton's presidential campaign of 1992 famously used the phrase, "It's the economy, stupid!" to underscore the importance of economic concerns for voters. Have students research the economic concerns of the various regions of the United States in 1948. Ask students to make a three-column chart listing the economic considerations of the country's different regions in one column, the presidential candidate's proposals in another column, and, finally, the candidate who got the most votes in each of the different regions. **Ask:** What correlations did you find between the economic concerns of a particular region and the policies of the candidate of its choice? **AL**

D Differentiated Instruction

Visual/Spatial Organize the class into groups of four. Have each group create two campaign posters for the election of 1952, one for Eisenhower and the other for Adlai Stevenson. Use the posters to discuss the key issues of the 1952 election. **OL**

S Skill Practice

Evaluating President Eisenhower used the phrase "middle of the road" to describe his political beliefs. Have students work in pairs to create a table listing Eisenhower's conservative policies in one column, and his liberal policies in the other.

Ask: Do you agree that Eisenhower's political beliefs could be described as "middle of the road?" Why or why not? *(Answers will vary.)* **OL**

Analyzing GEOGRAPHY

Answers:

1. in the Northeast, because of large population centers
2. It led to suburban sprawl and encouraged travel.

Additional Support

The Eisenhower Years

MAIN Idea President Eisenhower cut federal spending, supported business, funded the interstate highway system, and extended some New Deal programs.

HISTORY AND YOU Do you think it is important for a president to have served in the military? Read to learn how Americans chose a war hero as president in the 1950s.

In 1950 the United States went to war in Korea. The war consumed the nation's attention and resources and effectively ended Truman's Fair Deal. By 1952, with the war at a bloody stalemate and his approval rating dropping quickly, Truman declined to run again for the presidency.

D With no Democratic incumbent to face, Republicans pinned their hopes for regaining the White House in 1952 on a popular World War II hero: Dwight Eisenhower, former commander of the Allied Forces in Europe. The Democrats nominated Illinois Governor Adlai Stevenson.

The Republicans adopted the slogan: "It's time for a change!" The warm and friendly Eisenhower, known as "Ike," promised to end the war in Korea. "I like Ike" became the Republican rallying cry. Eisenhower won the election in a landslide, carrying the Electoral College, 442 votes to 89. The Republicans also gained an eight-seat majority in the House, while the Senate became evenly divided between Democrats and Republicans. **D**

Eisenhower Takes Office

President Eisenhower had two favorite phrases. "Middle of the road" described his political beliefs and "**dynamic conservatism**" meant balancing economic conservatism with activism in areas that would benefit the country. Eisenhower wasted little time in showing his conservative side. The new president's cabinet appointments included several business **S**

HISTORY AND GEOGRAPHY
Effects of the Interstate Highway System

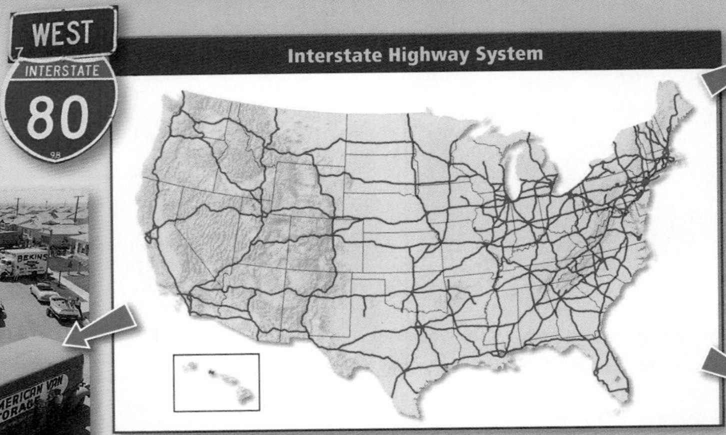

Commercial Trucking *Interstate highways made distribution of goods by transport truck fast and efficient. By the 1990s, trucks moved more than 6 billion tons of goods—mostly by interstate.*

Rise of Suburbs *Interstate highways contributed to the growth of suburbs and urban sprawl. Interstates let people commute long distances from home to work.*

Road Culture *Interstate travel encouraged the development of cheap hotel chains, roadside convenience stores, and fast food restaurants located near interstate exits.*

Analyzing GEOGRAPHY

1. **Location** Where were most of the interstate highways built? Why do you think that is?
2. **Movement** In what ways did the interstate highway system change daily life?

Extending the Content

Korea The Korean War sprang from a conflict between factions in Korea. Korean leftists wished to reform Korea's land ownership laws that kept a small group wealthy while many lived in poverty. The right opposed this. Following World War II, Korea was divided: Leftists controlled the North, and rightists controlled the South. Fighting soon broke out along the border, and in 1950 North Korean forces invaded the South. The United States, under the flag of the United Nations, joined the fight on behalf of the South. By the time a cease-fire was established in Korea, on July 27, 1953, the total death toll for both sides had reached 600,000 soldiers and as many as 2 million civilians. The border between North and South Korea was re-established in roughly the same place as before the war. In the early 2000s, it remained the most heavily fortified border in the world.

leaders. Under their guidance, Eisenhower ended government price and rent controls, which many conservatives viewed as unnecessary federal regulation of the economy. Eisenhower's administration believed business growth was vital to the nation. His secretary of defense, formerly the president of General Motors, declared to the Senate that "what is good for our country is good for General Motors, and vice versa."

Eisenhower's conservatism showed itself in other ways as well. In an attempt to cut federal spending, the president vetoed a school construction bill and agreed to slash government aid to public housing. Along with these cuts, he supported some modest tax cuts.

Eisenhower also targeted the federal government's continuing aid to businesses, or what he termed "creeping socialism." Shortly after taking office, the president abolished the Reconstruction Finance Corporation (RFC), which since 1932 had lent money to banks, railroads, and other large institutions in financial trouble. Another Depression-era agency, the Tennessee Valley Authority (TVA), also came under Eisenhower's scrutiny. During his presidency, appropriations for the TVA fell from $185 million to $12 million.

In some areas, President Eisenhower took an activist role. For example, he pushed for two large government projects. During the 1950s, as the number of Americans who owned cars increased, so too did the need for greater and more efficient travel routes. In 1956 Congress responded to this growing need by passing the **Federal Highway Act,** the largest public works program in American history. The act appropriated $25 billion for a 10-year effort to construct more than 40,000 miles (64,400 km) of interstate highways. Congress also authorized construction of the Great Lakes–St. Lawrence Seaway to connect the Great Lakes with the Atlantic Ocean through a series of locks on the St. Lawrence River. Three previous presidents had been unable to reach agreements with Canada to build this waterway to aid international shipping. Through Eisenhower's efforts, the two nations finally agreed on a plan to complete the project.

Extending Social Security

Although President Eisenhower cut federal spending and tried to limit the federal government's role in the economy, he agreed to extend the Social Security system to an additional 10 million people. He also extended unemployment compensation to an additional 4 million citizens and agreed to raise the minimum wage and continue to provide some government aid to farmers.

By the time Eisenhower ran for a second term in 1956, the nation had successfully shifted back to a peacetime economy. The battles between liberals and conservatives over whether to continue New Deal policies would continue. In the meantime, however, most Americans focused their energy on enjoying what had become a decade of tremendous prosperity.

Reading Check **Evaluating** What conservative and activist measures did Eisenhower take during his administration?

Section 1 REVIEW

Vocabulary

1. **Explain** the significance of: GI Bill, closed shop, right-to-work laws, union shop, "Do-Nothing Congress," Fair Deal, dynamic conservatism, Federal Highway Act.

Main Ideas

2. **Identifying** What difficulties could have hindered the return to a peacetime economy?
3. **Analyzing** Why did Congress oppose some of Truman's Fair Deal policies?
4. **Describing** How did Eisenhower describe his approach to politics?

Critical Thinking

5. **Big Ideas** How did President Eisenhower aid international shipping during his administration?
6. **Organizing** Use a graphic organizer like the one below to compare the agendas of the Truman and Eisenhower administrations.

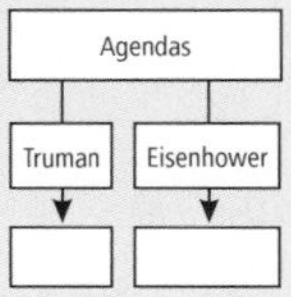

7. **Analyzing Visuals** Study the map on page 797. In which part of the country did Strom Thurmond receive the most votes? Why do you think this is?

Writing About History

8. **Persuasive Writing** Assume the role of a member of Congress during Truman's administration. Write a speech convincing Congress to pass or defeat Truman's Fair Deal measures.

History ONLINE
Study Central™ To review this section, go to glencoe.com and click on Study Central.

Reading Check

Answer:
He reduced government control over business, cut spending, passed the Federal Highway Act, extended the Social Security System, and increased the minimum wage.

Assess

History ONLINE

Study Central™ provides summaries, interactive games, and online graphic organizers to help students review content.

Close

Summarizing Ask: In what direction did the federal government take the country after World War II? *(The federal government supported programs such as the GI Bill, Social Security, public works projects, and civil rights.)* OL

Section 1 REVIEW

Answers

1. All definitions can be found in the section and the Glossary.
2. Military production had stopped, and millions of former soldiers glutted the labor market.
3. Republicans controlled Congress after 1946 and also formed a coalition with conservative Southern Democrats to defeat many of Truman's proposals.
4. Eisenhower described his approach to politics as "middle of the road" and "dynamic conservatism," meaning balancing economic conservatism with activism in those areas that would benefit the country.
5. He pushed for two major projects—the Federal Highway Act and the construction of the St. Lawrence Seaway. Both projects enabled goods to be moved more quickly and efficiently.
6. Truman: increase government involvement in business, expand federal spending, extend civil rights; Eisenhower: limit government involvement in business, curb federal spending
7. Thurmond received the most votes in the South. Thurmond was the candidate of the States' Rights, or Dixiecrat, Party made up of Southern Democrats who opposed federal action on civil rights.
8. Students' speeches will vary but should focus on several components of the Fair Deal.

Focus

Bellringer

Daily Focus Transparency 23-2

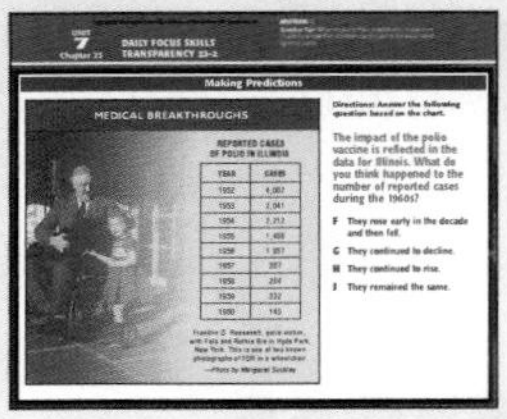

Guide to Reading

Answers:

1946: ENIAC computer developed
1950: Riesman's *The Lonely Crowd* published
1955: Salk polio vaccine widely available
1958: Galbraith's *The Affluent Society* published

Section Spotlight Video

To generate student interest and provide a springboard for class discussion, access the Chapter 23, Section 2 video at glencoe.com or on the video DVD.

Section 2

Section Audio   Spotlight Video

The Affluent Society

Guide to Reading

Big Ideas

Culture and Beliefs Postwar abundance and new technologies changed American society.

Content Vocabulary

- baby boom *(p. 801)*
- white-collar job *(p. 802)*
- blue-collar worker *(p. 802)*
- multinational corporation *(p. 802)*
- franchise *(p. 802)*
- rock 'n' roll *(p. 805)*
- generation gap *(p. 807)*

Academic Vocabulary

- phenomenon *(p. 800)*
- conform *(p. 802)*

People and Events to Identify

- Levittown *(p. 800)*
- Jonas Salk *(p. 803)*
- Elvis Presley *(p. 805)*
- Jack Kerouac *(p. 807)*

Reading Strategy

Sequencing Use a time line to record major events of science, technology, and popular culture during the 1950s.

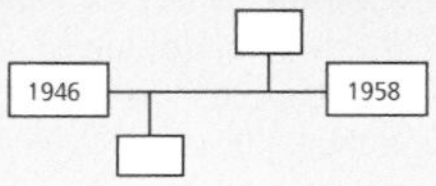

For many Americans, the 1950s was a time of affluence, with many new technological breakthroughs. In addition, new forms of entertainment created a generational divide between young people and adults.

American Abundance

MAIN Idea America entered a period of postwar abundance, with expanding suburbs, growing families, and more white-collar jobs.

HISTORY AND YOU Have you ever noticed that every restaurant in a pizza chain looks alike? Read on to learn about the rise of franchises.

The 1950s was a decade of incredible prosperity. Between 1940 and 1955, the average income of American families roughly tripled. Americans in all income brackets—poor, middle-class, and wealthy—experienced this rapid rise in income. In 1958 economist John Kenneth Galbraith published *The Affluent Society,* in which he claimed that the nation's postwar prosperity was a new **phenomenon.** In the past, Galbraith said, all societies had an "economy of scarcity," meaning that a lack of resources and overpopulation had limited economic productivity. Now, the United States had created what Galbraith called an "economy of abundance." New business techniques and improved technology enabled the nation to produce an abundance of goods and services, thereby dramatically raising the standard of living for Americans.

The economic boom of the 1950s provided most Americans with more disposable income than ever before and, as in the 1920s, they began to spend it on new consumer goods, including refrigerators, washing machines, televisions, and air conditioners. Advertising helped fuel the nation's spending spree. Advertising became the fastest-growing industry in the United States, as manufacturers employed new marketing techniques to sell their products. These techniques were carefully planned to whet the consumer's appetite. A second car became a symbol of status, a freezer became a promise of plenty, and mouthwash was portrayed as the key to immediate success.

The Growth of Suburbia

Advertisers targeted consumers who had money to spend. Many of these consumers lived in new mass-produced suburbs that grew up around cities in the 1950s. **Levittown,** New York, was one of the earliest of the mass-produced suburbs. The driving force behind this planned residential community was Bill Levitt, who mass-produced hundreds of simple and similar-looking homes in a potato field 10 miles east of New York City. Between 1947 and 1951, thousands of

Resource Manager

R Reading Strategies	C Critical Thinking	D Differentiated Instruction	W Writing Support	S Skill Practice
Teacher Edition • Questioning, p. 802 • Making Connections, p. 804 **Additional Resources** • Guided Reading Act., URB p. 151 • Prim. Source Reading, URB p. 139	**Teacher Edition** • Pred. Conseq., p. 802 • Det. Cause/Effect, p. 806 • Anal. Primary Sources, p. 806 **Additional Resources** • Inter. Political Cartoons, URB p. 143 • Quizzes/Tests, p. 328 • Enrichment Act., URB p. 147	**Teacher Edition** • Interpersonal, pp. 801, 805 **Additional Resources** • Econ. Act., URB p. 7 • Am. Art and Music Act., URB p. 141	**Teacher Edition** • Persuasive Writing, p. 805	**Teacher Edition** • Reading Graphs, p. 801 • Evaluating, p. 804 **Additional Resources** • Reading Skills Act., URB p. 123 • Reinf. Skills Act., URB p. 133 • Read. Essen., p. 262

PRIMARY SOURCE

A New America: Suburbs and Highways

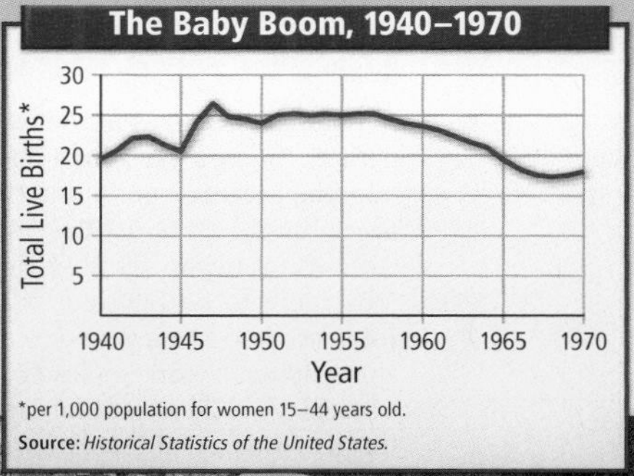

Thanks to the GI Bill, many people could afford the cheap mass-produced houses of suburban developments, such as Levittown, New York (above). Suburban living led to crowded highways (right) as commuters headed to work.

Analyzing VISUALS

1. **Interpreting** In what year was there the greatest increase in the number of live births? Why might this be?
2. **Drawing Conclusions** Why might the number of live births have started to decline by the late 1950s?

families rushed to buy the inexpensive homes. These new suburbs multiplied throughout the United States. Suburbs became increasingly popular during the 1950s, accounting for about 85 percent of new home construction. The number of suburban dwellers doubled, while the population of cities rose only 10 percent.

Reasons for the rapid growth of suburbia varied. Some people wanted to escape the crime and congestion of city neighborhoods. Others believed the suburbs would provide a better life for themselves and their children. For millions of Americans, the suburbs came to symbolize the American dream.

Affordability was a key reason that home buyers moved to the suburbs. With the GI Bill providing low-interest loans to veterans, buying a new house was more affordable than at any previous time in American history. The government's decision to give income tax deductions for home-mortgage interest payments and property taxes made owning a home even more attractive. Between 1940 and 1960, the number of Americans who owned their own homes rose from about 41 percent to about 61 percent.

The Baby Boom

The American birthrate exploded after World War II. From 1945 to 1961, a period known as the **baby boom,** more than 65 million children were born in the United States. At the height of the baby boom, a child was born every seven seconds.

Several factors contributed to the baby boom. First, young couples who had delayed marriage during World War II and the Korean War could now marry, buy homes, and begin their families. In addition, the government encouraged the growth of families by offering generous GI benefits for home purchases. Finally, on television and in magazines, popular culture celebrated pregnancy, parenthood, and large families.

Teach

S Skill Practice

Reading a Graph Ask: Between what years did the birth rate remain steady? *(1950–1958)* OL

D Differentiated Instruction

Interpersonal Organize students into groups of three or four. Have them work together to write a one-minute radio spot attracting home buyers to a new suburban development. *(Radio spots will vary but should note affordability, good schools, safety, and more space.)* Invite students to share their advertisements with the class and vote on which one is most convincing. OL

Analyzing VISUALS

Answers:
1. 1947; veterans were now able to start a family
2. Most returning GIs had completed their families.

Hands-On Chapter Project
Step 2

A New Peacetime America

Step 2: New Technologies Americans' buying power increased during this boom time following the war.

Directions Have students read Section 2 and remind them that many Americans had new-found wealth in the 1950s and 60s. What did they spend their money on? Have students note all of the new inventions created and discoveries made in postwar America and research others not mentioned in their text.

Putting It Together During their research have them collect photos or drawings of the new developments to be displayed on poster board in their final class presentation. OL

(Chapter Project continued in Section 3 on page 811)

C Critical Thinking

Predicting Consequences Sociologist David Riesman argued that the conformist urge of the 1950s changed people from being "inner-directed" (judging themselves on the basis of their own values) to being "other-directed" (concerned with winning the approval of others). **Ask:** What consequences might this produce for individuals and society? *(Answers will vary.)* **AL**

R Reading Strategy

Questioning Have students brainstorm a list of diseases that affect Americans today for which there are no vaccines, such as cancer, AIDS, diabetes, and so forth. **Ask:** What are reasons why vaccines for these diseases still do not exist? *(Students may note the expense of medical research, mutation of the diseases, and so on.)* **OL**

Reading Check

Answer:
Causes: new business methods and improved manufacturing technology; Effects: average family income tripled and the number of white-collar jobs increased

The Changing Workplace

Dramatic changes in the workplace accompanied the country's economic growth. The ongoing mechanization of farms and factories accelerated in the 1950s. As a result, more Americans began working in offices. These jobs came to be referred to as **white-collar jobs,** because employees typically wore a white shirt and tie to work, instead of the blue denim of factory workers and laborers. In 1956, for the first time, white-collar workers outnumbered **blue-collar workers.**

Many white-collar employees worked for large corporations. As these businesses competed with each other, some expanded overseas. These **multinational corporations** located themselves closer to important raw materials and benefited from a cheaper labor pool, which made them more competitive.

The 1950s also witnessed the rise of **franchises,** in which a person owns and runs one or several stores of a chain operation. Because many business leaders believed that consumers valued dependability and familiarity, the owners of chain operations often demanded that their franchises present a uniform look and style.

C Like franchise owners, many corporate leaders expected their employees to **conform** to company standards. In general, they did not want free-thinking individuals or people who might speak out or criticize the company. Some observers criticized this trend. In his 1950 book *The Lonely Crowd,* sociologist David Riesman argued that this conformity was changing people. Formerly, he claimed, people were "inner-directed," judging themselves on the basis of their own values and the esteem of their families. Now, however, people were becoming "other-directed"—concerned with winning the approval of the corporation or community.

In his 1956 book, *The Organization Man,* William H. Whyte, Jr., attacked the similarity many business organizations cultivated to keep any individual from dominating. "In group doctrine," Whyte wrote, "the strong personality is viewed with overwhelming suspicion," and the person with ideas is considered "a threat."

Reading Check **Interpreting** Describe two causes and effects of the economic boom of the 1950s.

Scientific Advances

MAIN Idea Computers began a business revolution, and doctors discovered new ways to fight disease.

HISTORY AND YOU Do you own a computer? Read on to learn about the earliest computers.

As the United States experienced many social changes during the postwar era, the nation also witnessed several important scientific advances. In electronics, manufacturing, and medicine, American scientists broke new ground during the 1950s.

Advances in Electronics

The electronics industry made rapid advances after World War II. In 1947 three American physicists—John Bardeen, Walter H. Brattain, and William Shockley—developed the transistor, a tiny electric generator that made it possible to miniaturize radios from large pieces of furniture to small portable items.

The age of computers also dawned in the postwar era. In 1946 scientists working under a U.S. Army contract developed one of the nation's earliest computers—known as ENIAC (Electronic Numerical Integrator and Computer)—to make military calculations. Several years later, a newer model called UNIVAC (Universal Automatic Computer) would process business data and launch the computer revolution. The jet airline age also progressed rapidly with an increased use of plastics and light metals, the development of the jet engine, the swept-back wing design—all of which improved fuel effeciency—and a longer flight range. These developments reduced consumer costs, making airline travel available to the masses.

Medical Miracles

R The medical breakthroughs of the 1950s included the development of new, powerful antibiotics and vaccines to fight infection and the introduction of new techniques to fight cancer and heart disease.

Prior to the 1950s, cancer had been thought to be untreatable. The development of radiation treatments and chemotherapy in the 1950s

Differentiated Instruction

Economics and History, URB p. 7

Money and the Affluent Society

Objective: Read about money, the money supply, and America's affluence during the 1950s.

Focus: How is money and the money supply important in American society?

Teach: Explain how the money supply is a measure of affluence.

Assess: List the functions of money.

Close: Using evidence from the textbook, show three images of the affluence of the American society in the 1950s.

Differentiated Instruction Strategies

- **BL** List the characteristics of money.
- **AL** Develop an economic system based on something other than money. Does it meet the characteristics of money?
- **ELL** Explain how the money of another country or your native country meets the characteristics of money listed in the reading.

People IN HISTORY

Dr. Jonas Salk
1914–1995

The man who developed the vaccine for one of the nation's most feared diseases almost did not go into medicine. Jonas Salk enrolled in college as a prelaw student but soon changed his mind. Salk switched his major to premed and went on to become a research scientist.

Every so often, Salk would make rounds in the overcrowded polio wards of a hospital near his lab, where nurses described their feelings of helpless rage. One nurse said, "I can remember how the staff used to kid Dr. Salk—kidding in earnest—telling him to hurry up and do something."

Salk became famous for the polio vaccine he developed in 1952. About becoming a celebrity, Salk observed that it was "a transitory thing and you wait till it blows over. Eventually people will start thinking, 'That poor guy,' and leave me alone. Then I'll be able to get back to my laboratory."

What character traits do you think made Dr. Salk a successful research scientist?

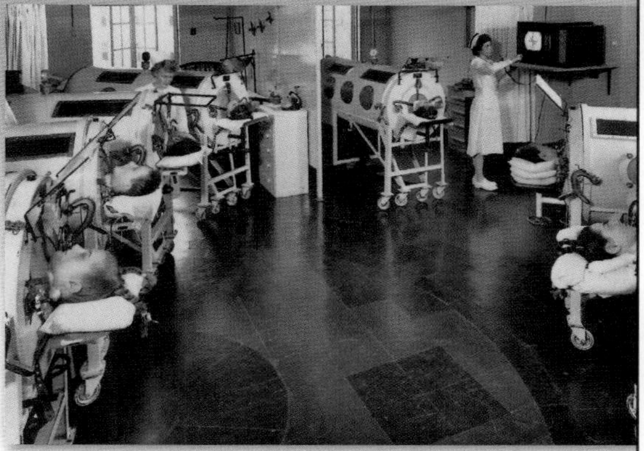

▲ *In the 1940s and 1950s, Americans fought the epidemic of polio cases that struck many children. Here, a device known as an iron lung helps polio patients to breathe.*

helped many cancer patients survive. Similarly, treatments for heart disease had eluded scientists for decades, and when someone suffered a heart attack, nothing could be done. In 1950, however, doctors developed cardiopulmonary resuscitation (CPR), a technique that has saved many lives. Doctors also began replacing worn-out heart valves with mechanical valves and implanted the first pacemakers in 1952.

A third disease that had frightened Americans for decades was tuberculosis, a lung disease also known as the white plague. The disease was both highly infectious and contagious, so patients lived in isolation in sanatoriums. In 1956 for the first time, tuberculosis fell from the list of the top ten fatal diseases. New antibiotics and a blood test for the disease finally put an end to fear of tuberculosis.

Polio, too, finally yielded to science. Polio epidemics had been occurring in the United States since 1916. The viral disease had struck Franklin Roosevelt as a young man and forced him to use a wheelchair and wear steel braces on his legs. In the 1940s and 1950s, widespread polio epidemics terrorized the nation. Every summer, polio broke out somewhere in the country. Many died; those who did not were often confined to iron lungs—large metal tanks with pumps that helped patients breathe. Even if they eventually recovered, they were often paralyzed for life.

Each summer, parents searched for ways to safeguard their families from the dreaded disease. Some sent their children to the country to avoid excessive contact with others. Public swimming pools and beaches were closed. Parks and playgrounds across the country stood deserted. Nevertheless, the disease continued to strike. In 1952 a record 58,000 new cases were reported.

Finally, research scientist **Jonas Salk** developed an injectable vaccine to prevent polio. Salk first tested the vaccine on himself, his wife, and his three sons, and then on 2 million schoolchildren. In 1955 the vaccine became available to the general public. American scientist Albert Sabin then developed an oral vaccine for polio. Safer and more convenient than Salk's injection vaccine, the Sabin vaccine became the most common method for preventing the disease. The threat of polio nearly disappeared.

✔ Reading Check **Examining** What medical and technological advances met specific needs in the late 1940s and 1950s?

People IN HISTORY

Answer:
Besides being very intelligent, Dr. Salk had to be patient, persistent, and concerned about others.

✔ Reading Check

Answer:
antibiotics, treatments for cancer and heart disease; drugs and a test for tuberculosis, a vaccine for polio

Additional Support

Activity: Technology Connection

Plastics: Use and Development Humans have been developing and perfecting plastics since the late 1800s. Alexander Parkes unveiled the first man-made version in 1862. He claimed that the material could do anything that the natural material, rubber, could do. However, the product proved too expensive. Since then plastics have been refined, and now they touch many aspects of our lives. Divide the class into two teams. One team will create a time line of the development of plastics. The other team will create a collage of how we use plastics today. **OL**

R Reading Strategy

Making Connections Ask: Why have different types of shows been popular in different periods of television history? *(Students may point out that television shows usually reflect the culture and specific concerns of their time.)* **BL**

S Skill Practice

Evaluating Have students watch a rerun of a program that was popular in the 1950s such as *I Love Lucy* or *The Many Loves of Dobie Gillis*. Tell them to make a list of the styles, slang expressions, attitudes, and behaviors that are different from those of today. Discuss the lists and then compile them into a 1950s culture dictionary. **OL**

Analyzing VISUALS

Answers:

1. They were a middle-class family in which the father worked and mom raised the children.
2. a middle-class audience

Additional Support

The New Mass Media

MAIN Idea The rise of television led to changes in the movie and radio industries.

HISTORY AND YOU How many hours of television do you watch weekly? Read to find out about the early days of television broadcasting.

Although regular television broadcasts had begun in the early 1940s, there were few stations, and sets were expensive. There were estimated to be no more than 8,000 sets in use in the entire United States in 1946. By the late 1950s, however, small black-and-white-screened televisions sat in living rooms across the country. Nearly 40 million televisions had been sold by 1957, and more than 80 percent of families had at least one television.

The Rise of Television

Early television programs fell into several main categories, including comedy, action and adventure, and variety entertainment. In 1953 Lucille Ball and her real-life husband, Desi Arnaz, starred in one of the most popular shows ever to air on American television, a situation comedy (sitcom) called *I Love Lucy*. The episode in which Lucy gave birth (which paralleled Lucille Ball's actual pregnancy) had an audience of 44 million viewers. Fewer people tuned in to watch the presidential inauguration the following day.

Comedy proved popular in other formats. Many early comedy shows, such as those starring Bob Hope and Jack Benny, were adapted from radio programs. Variety shows, such as Ed Sullivan's *Toast of the Town*, provided a mix of comedy, music, dance, acrobatics, and juggling. Quiz shows also drew large audiences after the 1955 debut of *The $64,000 Question*. In this show and its many imitators, two contestants tried to answer questions from separate, soundproof booths.

Television viewers also enjoyed action shows. Westerns such as *Hopalong Cassidy*, *The Lone Ranger*, and *Gunsmoke* grew quickly in popularity. Viewers also enjoyed police shows

PRIMARY SOURCE
Television in the 1950s

▲ *I Love Lucy, a comedy about housewife Lucy, husband Ricky, and friends Fred and Ethel was the most popular show of the 1950s.*

▲ *Howdy Doody was the first network kids' show ever broadcast in color.*

▲ *The Adventures of Ozzie and Harriet was a comedy featuring the life of Ozzie and Harriet Nelson and their sons in a middle-class American suburb. Their portrayal of family life was idealized—father worked, mother stayed at home raising the children, and there was always plenty of food and consumer goods available.*

Analyzing VISUALS

1. **Explaining** How did *The Adventures of Ozzie and Harriet* reflect an idealized American family?
2. **Making Generalizations** To what type of audience were most of these television programs designed to appeal?

Activity: Interdisciplinary Connection

Language Arts Have students work in small groups to write a short scene in which a character from a 1950s television show, such as *I Love Lucy*, or *Howdy Doody*, is magically transported to the present day. Students should begin by borrowing and viewing a tape of a 1950s program from the library. Next, have students select a character from the program they viewed to use in their original scenes. Students should create a scene in which the behaviors and attitudes of today are explained to their 1950s characters. Encourage students to allow their 1950s characters to express how they feel about life in the present versus life in the 1950s. Have groups present their scenes to the class. **Ask:** Which current attitudes and behaviors were most difficult for the 1950s characters to understand? Which 1950s attitudes and behaviors are most difficult to understand today? *(Answers will vary, but should reflect an understanding of section content.)* **AL**

such as *Dragnet*, a hugely successful show featuring Detective Joe Friday and his partner hunting down a new criminal each week. By the late 1950s, television news had also become an important vehicle for information, and televised athletic events had made professional and college sports a popular choice for entertainment.

Hollywood Responds

As the popularity of television grew, movies lost viewers. Weekly movie attendance dropped from 82 million in 1946 to 36 million by 1950. By 1960, when some 50 million Americans owned televisions, one-fifth of the nation's movie theaters had closed.

Throughout the 1950s, Hollywood struggled to recapture its audience. When contests, door prizes, and advertising failed to lure people back, Hollywood tried 3-D films that required **D** the audience to wear special glasses. Viewers soon tired of the glasses and the often ridiculous plots of 3-D movies.

Cinemascope—a process that showed movies on large, panoramic screens—finally gave Hollywood something television could not match. Wide-screen, full-color spectacles like *The Robe, The Ten Commandments,* and *Around the World in 80 Days* cost a great deal of money to produce. These blockbusters, however, made up for their cost by attracting huge audiences and netting large profits.

Radio Draws Them In

Television also forced the radio industry to change in order to keep its audience. Television made radio comedies, dramas, and soap operas obsolete. Radio stations responded by broadcasting recorded music, news, weather, sports, and talk shows.

Radio also had one audience that television could not reach—people traveling in their cars. In some ways, the automobile saved the radio industry. People commuting to and from work, running errands, or traveling on long road trips relied on radio for information and entertainment. As a result, radio stations survived and even flourished. The number of radio stations more than doubled between 1948 and 1957.

Reading Check **Identifying** How did the television industry affect the U.S. economy?

New Music and Poetry

MAIN Idea Young people developed their own popular culture based largely on rock 'n' roll music and literature of the beat movement.

HISTORY AND YOU How do the adults you know feel about your favorite music? Read on to learn of the conflicts over musical taste that began during the 1950s.

Many teens in every generation seek to separate themselves from their parents. One way of creating that separation is by embracing different music. In that respect, the 1950s were no different from earlier decades, but the results were different for two reasons.

For the first time, teens had large amounts of disposable income that could be spent on entertainment designed specifically for them. In addition, the new mass media meant that teens across the country could hear the same music broadcast or watch the same television shows. The result was the rise of an independent youth culture separate from adult culture. The new youth culture became an independent market for the entertainment and advertising industries.

Rock 'n' Roll

In 1951 at a record store in downtown Cleveland, Ohio, radio disc jockey Alan Freed noticed white teenagers buying African American rhythm-and-blues records and dancing to the music in the store. Freed convinced his station manager to play the music on the air. Just as the disc jockey had suspected, the listeners went crazy for it. Soon, white artists began making music that stemmed from these African American rhythms and sounds, and a new form of music, **rock 'n' roll,** was born. **W**

With a loud and heavy beat that made it ideal for dancing, along with lyrics about romance, cars, and other themes that appealed to young people, rock 'n' roll became wildly popular with the nation's teens. Before long, teenagers around the country were rushing out to buy recordings from such artists as Buddy Holly, Chuck Berry, and Bill Haley and the Comets. In 1956 teenagers found their first rock 'n' roll hero in **Elvis Presley,** who became known as the "King of Rock 'n' Roll."

D Differentiated Instruction

Interpersonal Have groups create murals that illustrate the theme "Hollywood in the 1950s." The murals should depict the challenges and changes that defined Hollywood during this era. **OL**

W Writing Support

Persuasive Writing Have students write a paragraph that persuades others about the excellence of a particular style of music, group, or singer. **OL**

Reading Check

Answer:
Television drew audiences away from the film and radio industries and forced these industries to change their approaches. Hollywood tried various film processes, and Cinemascope proved to be successful. Radio stations changed their programming from comedies, dramas, and variety shows to sports, news, weather reports, and recorded music.

Additional Support

Extending the Content

Television Television became popular in the 1940s. Viewers could tune in to such shows as *The Texaco Star Theater* starring comedian Milton Berle. Many children wouldn't miss *Howdy Doody*, a popular show aimed at youngsters. The television news came to Americans from two news programs lasting only 15 minutes. The 1948 news program *Camel News Caravan* was sponsored by a tobacco company that insisted its news anchor always have a burning cigarette visible when he presented the news. Over the years, Americans began spending more and more time watching television, and some worried that it was taking away from other activities such as reading or socializing. However, by 1960 nearly 90 percent of American families owned at least one TV set. Although the Columbia Broadcasting System presented the first commercial color telecast in 1951, color television remained too expensive during the 1950s for widespread use. Most people watched their shows in black and white.

C1 Critical Thinking

Determining Cause and Effect **Ask:** Why did Ed Sullivan change his mind about allowing Elvis Presley to perform on his television show? *(Elvis appeared on another show, and it received better ratings than the Ed Sullivan Show.)* **BL**

C2 Critical Thinking

Analyzing Primary Sources Have students use Internet or library sources to locate the lyrics to a popular rock'n'roll song of the 1950s. Ask students to write one paragraph summarizing some of the key images, ideas, or themes in the song. Then have them write a second paragraph describing how these lyrics represented the concerns of American teenagers of the period. **AL**

Analyzing VISUALS

Answers:

1. They found it shocking and suggestive.
2. Teenagers rebelled against their parents and embraced rock'n'roll.

Additional Support

For an excerpt from *On the Road*, see page R77 in the **American Literature Library.**

Elvis Presley was born in rural Mississippi and grew up poor in Memphis, Tennessee. While in high school, Presley learned to play guitar and sing by imitating the rhythm-and-blues music he heard on the radio. By 1956, the handsome young Elvis had a record deal with RCA Victor, a movie contract, and had made public appearances on several television shows. C1 At first, the popular television variety show host Ed Sullivan refused to invite Presley to appear, insisting that rock 'n' roll music was not fit for a family-oriented show. When a competing show featuring Presley upset Sullivan's high ratings, however, he relented. He ended up paying Presley $50,000 per performance for three appearances, more than triple the amount he had paid any other performer.

Presley owed his wild popularity as much to his moves as to his music. During his performances he would gyrate his hips and dance in ways that shocked many in the audience. Not surprisingly, parents—many of whom listened to Frank Sinatra and other more mellow, mainstream artists—condemned rock 'n' roll as loud, mindless, and dangerous. The city council of San Antonio, Texas, actually banned rock 'n' roll from the jukeboxes at public swimming pools.

The rock 'n' roll hits that teens bought in record numbers united them in a world their parents did not share. Thus, in the 1950s,

PRIMARY SOURCE
Rock 'n' Roll Sweeps the Nation

C2

African American singers such as Chuck Berry (left), Little Richard (below left), and Fats Domino (below right) became huge stars in the popular music industry of the 1950s.

Bill Haley and His Comets (above) was one of the first popular rock 'n' roll bands. Elvis Presley (left) became rock 'n' roll's first superstar, but many disapproved of his dance moves.

▲ *Little Richard*

▲ *Fats Domino*

Analyzing VISUALS

1. **Explaining** Why did adults disapprove of rock 'n' roll?
2. **Describing** How did this disapproval contribute to the generation gap?

Extending the Content

Hall of Fame The Rock and Roll Hall of Fame Museum opened in Cleveland, Ohio, on September 2, 1995. Artists and musical groups become eligible for induction into the Hall of Fame 25 years after the release of their first records. One of the earliest inductees was Chuck Berry. Named Charles Edward Berry by his parents, he was born in St. Louis on October 18, 1926. In the 1950s, Berry worked as a musician at night leading a popular blues trio. During the day he worked as a beautician. Berry also played fast, energetic music such as his famous song "Maybellene." It was this music that got him a recording contract. The Rock and Roll Hall of Fame Web site says of Berry, "While no individual can be said to have invented rock and roll, Chuck Berry comes the closest of any single figure to being the one who put all the essential pieces together."

rock 'n' roll helped to create what became known as the **generation gap,** or the cultural separation between children and their parents.

The Beat Movement

If rock 'n' roll helped to create a generation gap, a group of mostly white writers and artists who called themselves beats, or beatniks, highlighted a values gap in 1950s America. The term "beat" may have come from the feeling among group members of being "beaten down" by American culture, or from jazz musicians who would say, "I'm beat right down to my socks."

Beat poets, writers, and artists harshly criticized what they considered the sterility and conformity of American life, the meaninglessness of American politics, and the emptiness of popular culture. In 1956, 29-year-old beat poet Allen Ginsberg published a long poem titled "Howl," which blasted modern American life. Another beat member, **Jack Kerouac,** published *On the Road* in 1957. Although Kerouac's book about his freewheeling adventures with a car thief and con artist shocked some readers, the book went on to become a classic in modern American literature. Although the beat movement remained relatively small, it laid the foundations for the more widespread youth cultural rebellion of the 1960s.

African American Entertainers

African American entertainers struggled to find acceptance in a country that often treated them as second-class citizens. With a few notable exceptions, television tended to shut out African Americans. In 1956 NBC gave a popular African American singer named Nat King Cole his own 15-minute musical variety show. In 1958, after 64 episodes, NBC canceled the show after failing to secure a national sponsor for a show hosted by an African American.

African American rock 'n' roll singers faced fewer obstacles. The talented African Americans who recorded hit songs in the 1950s included Chuck Berry, Little Richard, Fats Domino, and Ray Charles. The late 1950s and early 1960s also saw the rise of several female African American groups, including the Crystals, the Shirelles, and the Ronettes. With their catchy, popular sound, these groups were the musical predecessors of the famous late 1960s groups Martha and the Vandellas and the Supremes.

Over time, the music of the early rock 'n' roll artists had a profound influence on popular music throughout the world. Little Richard and Chuck Berry, for example, provided inspiration for the Beatles, whose music swept Britain and the world in the 1960s. Elvis Presley's music transformed generations of rock 'n' roll bands that followed him and other pioneers of rock.

Despite the innovations in music and the economic boom of the 1950s, not all Americans were part of the affluent society. For many of the country's minorities and rural poor, the American dream remained well out of reach.

Reading Check **Summarizing** How did rock 'n' roll help create the generation gap?

Section 2 REVIEW

Vocabulary

1. **Explain** the significance of: Levittown, baby boom, white-collar job, blue-collar worker, multinational corporation, franchise, Jonas Salk, rock 'n' roll, Elvis Presley, generation gap, Jack Kerouac.

Main Ideas

2. **Organizing** Use a graphic organizer like the one below to list the causes and effects of the economic boom of the 1950s.

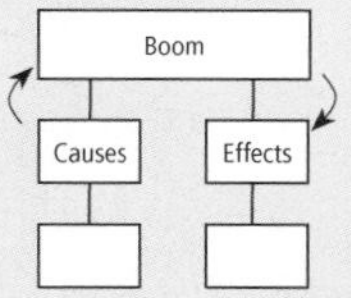

3. **Listing** What major technological breakthroughs occurred in the 1950s?
4. **Explaining** How did television affect other forms of mass media?
5. **Identifying** How did young people of the 1950s express their own culture?

Critical Thinking

6. **Big Ideas** What were the roots of rock 'n' roll, and how did it reach a mass audience?
7. **Analyzing Visuals** Study the photographs on page 804. These programs have been criticized for presenting a one-sided view of American life. Do you agree? Why or why not?

Writing About History

8. **Expository Writing** Assume the role of a media critic in the 1950s, and use the information in this section to write a critique of one television show, movie, music concert, or piece of literature.

History ONLINE
Study Central™ To review this section, go to glencoe.com and click on Study Central.

Reading Check

Answer:
It generated conflict between children and parents based on musical taste and mores of the time, and created a bond among members of the younger generation.

Assess

History ONLINE

Study Central™ provides summaries, interactive games, and online graphic organizers to help students review content.

Close

Summarizing Ask: How did American society change after World War II? *(America entered a period of postwar abundance with expanding suburbs, growing families, more white collar jobs, an increased expectation of social conformity, and technological advances.)* OL

Section 2 REVIEW

Answers

1. All definitions can be found in the section and the Glossary.
2. Causes: new business techniques, improved technology; Effects: consumerism, suburban growth
3. The transistor was developed, as was the first computer. In medicine, antibiotics and vaccines were created. Also television sets became available to the average American.
4. Television caused changes in radio and film industries. Hollywood tried new film processes, and radio started broadcasting more news, weather, and sports instead of radio dramas and comedies.
5. through rock 'n' roll music and artistic movements such as the Beat movement
6. Its roots were in African American rhythms and sounds. It reached the mass media when a radio DJ in Cleveland, Ohio, named Alan Freed noticed that teenagers were buying African American rhythm and blues records. Freed then received permission to play the music on the air.
7. Student responses will vary but should provide a detailed explanation of opinions.
8. Students' critiques will vary. Critiques should provide a reasoned opinion on a specific television show, movie, musical act, or piece of literature based on the information in this section.

Focus

Tell students that actor James Dean was a favorite with 1950s teenagers. He projected a rebellious image expressing anger, confusion, and hurt. **Ask:** What does the popularity of actor James Dean with teenagers tell you about 1950s youth? What impact do you think his early death had on American youth? *(Answers will vary, but students might say that 1950s teenagers identified with his rebellious image. His early death must have been quite painful for his fans.)* **OL**

Teach

C Critical Thinking

Identifying Central Issues

Have students review the quotes in the Verbatim section and discuss each item as it relates to the people and themes found in the textbook. **OL**

Additional Support

TIME NOTEBOOK

BETTMANN/CORBIS

JAMES DEAN *had a brief but spectacular career as a film star. His role in* Rebel Without a Cause *made him an icon for American youth in the mid-50s. In 1955 Dean was killed in a car crash. He was 24.*

"I guess I have as good an insight into this rising generation as any other young man my age. Therefore, when I do play a youth, I try to imitate life. *Rebel Without a Cause* deals with the problems of modern youth. . . . If you want the kids to come and see the picture, you've got to try to reach them on their own grounds. If a picture is psychologically motivated, if there is truth in the relationships in it, then I think that picture will do good."

—*from an interview for* Rebel Without a Cause

VERBATIM

"It will make a wonderful place for the children to play in, and it will be a good storehouse, too."

MRS. RUTH CALHOUN,
mother of three, on her backyard fallout shelter, 1951

"Riddle: What's college? That's where girls who are above cooking and sewing go to meet a man they can spend their lives cooking and sewing for."

ad for Gimbel's department store campus clothes, 1952

"Radioactive poisoning of the atmosphere and hence annihilation of any life on Earth has been brought within the range of technical possibilities." C

ALBERT EINSTEIN,
physicist, 1950

"If the television craze continues with the present level of programs, we are destined to have a nation of morons."

DANIEL MARSH,
President of Boston University, 1950

"Every time the Russians throw an American in jail, the House Un-American Activities Committee throws an American in jail to get even."

MORT SAHL,
comedian, 1950s

WINNERS & LOSERS

Poodle Cut

UNDERWOOD & UNDERWOOD/CORBIS

POODLE CUTS
Short, curly hairstyle gains wide popularity and acceptance

TV GUIDE
New weekly magazine achieves circulation of 6.5 million by 1959

PALMER PAINT COMPANY OF DETROIT
Sells 12 million paint-by-number kits ranging from simple landscapes and portraits to Leonardo da Vinci's The Last Supper

THE DUCKTAIL
Banned in several Massachusetts schools in 1957

COLLIER'S
The respected magazine loses circulation, publishes its final edition on January 4, 1957

LEONARDO DA VINCI'S *THE LAST SUPPER*
Now everyone can paint their own copy to hang in their homes

The Ducktail

SUPER STOCK

808 **Chapter 23** Postwar America

Extending the Content

Movie Magazines Americans had always been interested in the movies and the lives of movie stars. The new medium of television gave Americans a whole new medium with which to become fascinated. That medium was television and just as movie magazines had given fans an inside look at the movies, a new magazine did the same for television. That magazine was *TV Guide*. The first issue came out in 1953 and had Lucille Ball on its cover. The magazine let readers know what shows were on their televisions every day and night of the week. It also contained stories on the programs and stars of television. This proved to be exactly what television viewers wanted. Sales soared, and *TV Guide* became the best-selling weekly magazine in the United States.

1950S WORD PLAY

Translation, Please!

Match the word to its meaning.

D

Teen-Age Lingo

1. cool
2. hang loose
3. hairy
4. yo-yo

a. a dull person, an outsider
b. worthy of approval
c. formidable
d. don't worry

answers: 1. b; 2. d; 3. c; 4. a

American Scene, 1950–1960

(MILLIONS)

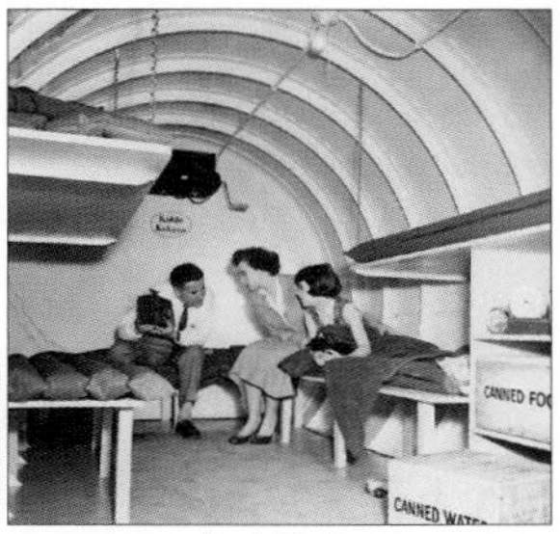

BETTMANN/CORBIS

Bomb Shelter

Be Prepared

"Know the Bomb's True Dangers. Know the Steps You Can Take to Escape Them!—You Can Survive."

Government pamphlet, 1950

DIGGING YOUR OWN BOMB SHELTER? Better go shopping. Below is a list of items included with the $3,000 Mark I Kidde Kokoon, designed to accommodate a family of five for a three-to five-day underground stay.

- air blower
- radiation detector
- protective apparel suit
- face respirator
- radiation charts (4)
- hand shovel (for digging out after the blast)
- gasoline driven generator
- gasoline (10 gallons)
- chemical toilet
- toilet chemicals (2 gallons)
- bunks (5)
- mattresses and blankets (5)
- air pump (blowing up mattresses)
- incandescent bulbs (2) 40 watts
- fuses (2) 5 amperes
- clock—non-electric
- first aid kit
- waterless hand cleaner
- sterno stove
- canned water (10 gallons)
- canned food (meat, powdered milk, cereal, sugar, etc.)
- paper products

NUMBERS 1957

3¢ Cost of first-class postage stamp

19¢ Cost of loaf of bread

25¢ Cost of issue of *Sports Illustrated*

35¢ Cost of movie ticket

50¢ Cost of gallon of milk (delivered)

$2.05 Average hourly wage

$2,845 Cost of new car

POPPERFOTO/ARCHIVE PHOTO

$5,234 Median income for a family of four

$19,500 Median price of a home

CRITICAL THINKING

1. *Predicting* If the number of American children continued to grow, how would that affect bicycle production and Scout membership? How could that growth affect the American economy?

2. *Hypothesizing* How have attitudes towards women changed since the 1952 department store ad for campus clothes? What do you think are some reasons for the change in attitude?

Teach

D Differentiated Instruction

Interpersonal Have students interview friends and relatives who lived during the 1950s to learn more about teenage lingo. Make a list of all the words and definitions that students bring in. BL

CRITICAL THINKING

Answers:

1. It could lead to greater demand for these things and spur the economy.
2. Women are seen as having lives beyond being wives and mothers; this is partly due to the women's movement.

Assess/Close

Visit the TIME Web site at www.time.com for up-to-date news, weekly magazine articles, editorials, online polls, and an archive of past magazine and Web articles.

Additional Support

Activity: Interdisciplinary Connection

Sociology In the 1950s, the response of citizens to societal dangers such as atomic war was more often an individual rather than a group effort. As early as the 1960s, with efforts such as the civil rights and anti-war movements, this began to change. Ask students to read newspapers and search the Internet for current examples of citizens' responses to public concerns such as global warming and war. Have students write a paragraph comparing and contrasting the response of Americans in the 1950s to the threat of atomic war with the responses of Americans to threats today. Have them write a second paragraph expressing their thoughts on the responsibility of citizens to address public concerns and the best ways to do so. OL

Focus

Bellringer

Daily Focus Transparency 23-3

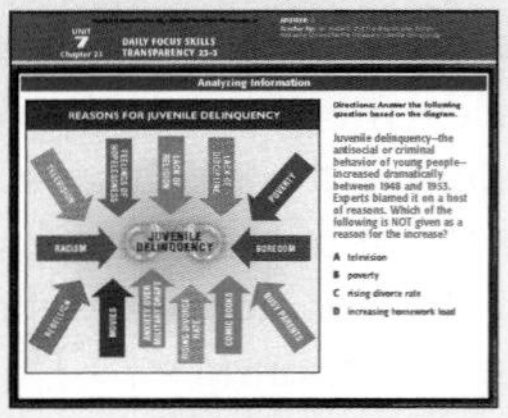

Guide to Reading

Answers:

The Other Side of American Life

I. Poverty Amidst Prosperity
- A. The Decline of the Inner City
- B. African Americans
- C. The Inner City's Ongoing Problems
- D. Hispanics
- E. Native Americans
- F. Appalachia

II. Juvenile Delinquency

Section Spotlight Video

To generate student interest and provide a springboard for class discussion, access the Chapter 23, Section 3 video at glencoe.com or on the video DVD.

Section 3 — Section Audio — Spotlight Video

The Other Side of American Life

Guide to Reading

Big Ideas

Economics and Society The postwar prosperity did not extend to all Americans. For some groups, poverty and discrimination continued during the apparent abundance of the 1950s.

Content Vocabulary
- poverty line *(p. 810)*
- urban renewal *(p. 811)*
- termination policy *(p. 813)*
- juvenile delinquency *(p. 815)*

Academic Vocabulary
- income *(p. 810)*
- entity *(p. 813)*

People and Events to Identify
- Lorraine Hansberry *(p. 812)*
- Bracero Program *(p. 812)*
- Appalachia *(p. 814)*

Reading Strategy

Taking Notes As you read about social problems in the United States in the 1950s, use the major headings of this section to create an outline similar to the one below.

The Other Side of American Life
I. Poverty Amidst Prosperity
A.
B.
C.
D.
E.
II.

During the 1950s, about 20 percent of the American population—particularly people of color and those living in the inner cities and Appalachia—did not share in the general prosperity. Experts also worried about the rise in juvenile delinquency.

Poverty Amidst Prosperity

MAIN Idea Despite the growing affluence of much of the nation, many groups still lived in poverty.

HISTORY AND YOU Are the pockets of poverty in America today the same as they were in the 1950s? Read on to learn about the people and regions most affected by poverty in the 1950s.

The 1950s saw a tremendous expansion of the middle class. At least one in five Americans, or about 30 million people, however, lived below the **poverty line.** This imaginary marker is a figure the government sets to reflect the minimum **income** required to support a family. Such poverty remained invisible to most Americans, who assumed that the country's general prosperity had provided everyone with a comfortable existence.

The writer Michael Harrington, however, made no such assumptions. During the 1950s, Harrington set out to chronicle poverty in the United States. In his book *The Other America,* published in 1962, he alerted those in the mainstream to what he saw in the run-down and hidden communities of the country:

PRIMARY SOURCE

"To be sure, the other America is not impoverished in the same sense as those poor nations where millions cling to hunger as a defense against starvation. . . . That does not change the fact that tens of millions of Americans are, at this very moment, maimed in body and spirit, existing at levels beneath those necessary for human decency. If these people are not starving, they are hungry, and sometimes fat with hunger, for that is what cheap foods do. They are without adequate housing and education and medical care."

—from *The Other America*

The poor included single mothers and the elderly; minorities such as Puerto Ricans and Mexican immigrants; rural Americans—both African American and white—and inner city residents, who remained stuck in crowded slums as wealthier citizens fled to the suburbs. Many Native Americans endured grinding poverty whether they stayed on reservations or migrated to cities.

Resource Manager

R Reading Strategies	C Critical Thinking	D Differentiated Instruction	W Writing Support	S Skill Practice
Teacher Edition • Content Vocab., p. 811 • Inferring, p. 813 **Additional Resources** • Guided Reading Act., URB p. 152 • Prim. Source Read., URB p. 137	**Teacher Edition** • Analyzing Info., p. 811 • Drawing Con., p. 813 **Additional Resources** • Critical Thinking Skills Act., URB p. 134 • Linking Past and Present, URB p. 136 • Quizzes/Tests, p. 329	**Teacher Edition** • Gifted/Talented, p. 812 • Kinesthetic, p. 814 **Additional Resources** • Differentiated Act., URB p. 125 • Reteaching Act., URB p. 145 • Enrich. Act., URB p. 147	**Teacher Edition** • Expository Writing, p. 812	**Additional Resources** • Authentic Assess., p. 51 • Read. Essen., p. 265 • Time Line Act., URB p. 135

PRIMARY SOURCE

The Other America

Amid the prosperity of the 1950s, many lived in terrible poverty. While suburbs boomed, the poor, many of whom were minorities, were relegated to inner-city slums. Native Americans suffered extreme poverty and the breakdown of their culture on reservations, while Mexican migrant workers in the Southwest barely made enough to feed, clothe, and shelter themselves and their children.

▲ *Children play in the littered streets of a Chicago slum in 1954.*

▲ *A poor Navajo family stands outside their home on an Arkansas reservation in 1948.*

▲ *The Cervantes family lived in a one-room shack at a ranch camp near Fresno, California, in 1950.*

Analyzing VISUALS

1. **Examining** Based on the photos, what aspect of life does it seem the hardest for the poor in America to obtain?
2. **Hypothesizing** What do you think might account for minorities having a lower average income than whites in the United States in the 1940s and 1950s?

The Decline of the Inner City

The poverty of the 1950s was most apparent in the nation's urban centers. As middle-class families moved to the suburbs, they left behind the poor and less-educated. Many city centers deteriorated because the taxes that the middle class paid moved out with them. Cities no longer had the tax dollars to provide adequate public transportation, housing, and other services.

When government tried to help inner-city residents, it often made matters worse. During the 1950s, for example, **urban renewal** programs tried to eliminate poverty by tearing down slums and erecting new high-rise buildings for poor residents. These crowded, high-rise projects, however, often created an atmosphere of violence. The government also unwittingly encouraged the residents of public housing to remain poor by evicting them as soon as they began earning a higher income.

In the end, urban renewal programs actually destroyed more housing space than they created. Too often, the wrecking balls destroyed poor people's homes to make way for roadways, parks, universities, tree-lined boulevards, or shopping centers.

Teach

C Critical Thinking

Analyzing Information Have students conduct additional research on one urban renewal project of the 1950s and the changes this project has undergone from the 1950s to today. They should determine the problems the project created, the steps government undertook to remedy the problems, and any new problems that developed. Have students present their findings in a written report. **OL**

R Reading Strategy

Content Vocabulary Ask: Why was the term *urban renewal* descriptive of the changes in inner cities? *(Old slums were being torn down and new housing was being built.)* **BL**

Analyzing VISUALS

Answers:
1. adequate housing
2. racism; less access to education and good jobs

Hands-On Chapter Project Step 3

A New Peacetime America

Step 3: Create a Brochure America was bursting with new gadgets after the war years.

Directions Organize students into groups. Have each group select one of the new inventions that appeared in this time period, whether a home device or one used in business or manufacturing. Their task is to create a brochure to sell that product to whomever their buying audience might be—homemakers, businessmen, choir children, for example. They should write and illustrate their brochures in whatever design they choose. Have the groups present their brochures to the rest of the class, explaining their selling approach and purpose.

Representing Information Give students time to prepare for their presentations. They may role play or use media other than their posters to present the information. Encourage students to state the topic clearly, describe it, and summarize the information. **OL**

(Chapter Project continued on the Visual Summary page)

W Writing Support

Expository Writing Have students use library or Internet resources to find Langston Hughes's poem "A Dream Deferred," from which Lorraine Hansberry's play *A Raisin In the Sun* drew its name. Instruct students to read the poem and write one-page responses. **Ask:** What key images do you remember from the poem? What does Hughes seem to be saying about dreams that remain unrealized? Why do you think that Lorraine Hansberry chose the phrase "a raisin in the sun" for the title of her play? Invite students to share their responses. OL

D Differentiated Instruction

Gifted and Talented Tell students that music has long been a way for people to express their emotions. Challenge interested students to take the impressions they have gained while reading the chapter to compose and perform a song expressing the plight of Mexican laborers in the 1950s. AL

Additional Support

African Americans

Many of the citizens left behind in the cities were African American. By 1960, more than 3 million African Americans had migrated from the South to Northern cities in search of greater economic opportunity and to escape violence and racial intimidation. For many of these migrants, however, the economic boom of the war years did not continue in the 1950s.

Long-standing patterns of racial discrimination in schools, housing, hiring, and salaries in the North kept many inner-city African Americans poor. The last hired and the first fired for good jobs, they often remained stuck in the worst-paying occupations. In 1958 African Americans' salaries, on average, were only 51 percent of what whites earned. Poverty and racial discrimination also deprived many African Americans of other benefits, such as decent medical care.

In 1959 the play *A Raisin in the Sun* opened on Broadway. Written by African American author **Lorraine Hansberry,** the play told the story of a working-class African American family struggling against poverty and racism. W The title referred to a Langston Hughes poem that wonders what happens to an unrealized dream:"Does it dry up like a raisin in the sun?" The play won the New York Drama Critics Circle Award for the best play of the year. Responding to a correspondent who had seen the play, Lorraine Hansberry wrote:"The ghettos are killing us; not only our dreams . . . but our very bodies. It is not an abstraction to us that the average [African American] has a life expectancy of five to ten years less than the average white." W

Hispanics

African Americans were not the only minority group that struggled with poverty. Much of the nation's Hispanic population faced the same problems. During the 1950s and early 1960s, the **Bracero Program** brought nearly 5 million Mexicans to the United States D to work on farms and ranches in the Southwest. Braceros were temporary contract workers. Many later returned home, but some 350,000 settled permanently in the United States.

These laborers, who worked on large farms throughout the country, lived with extreme poverty and hardship. They toiled long hours, for little pay, in conditions that were often

PAST & PRESENT

The Inner-City's Ongoing Problems

By the end of the 1950s, many major U.S. cities were in decline. "White flight" and lowered tax revenues, as well as racial discrimination and a lack of sympathy for the less fortunate, combined to create islands of decay and poverty in urban centers.

Although numerous programs were launched in the 1960s to try to improve living conditions and eliminate poverty, the problem has proven more difficult than first anticipated. Fifty years separate the two photos of inner-city slums to the right, yet, tragically, the quality of life has barely changed.

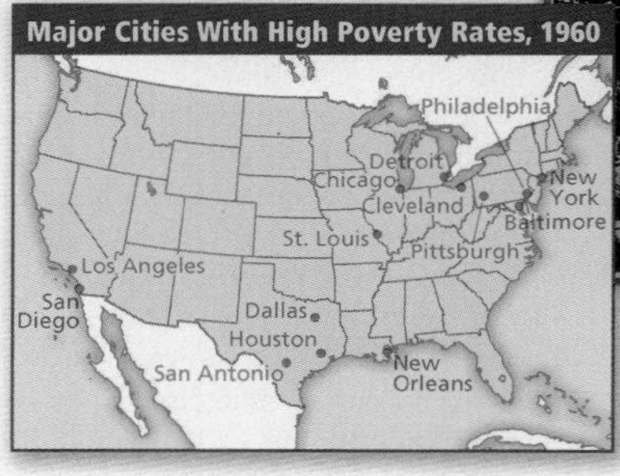

▲ *Even in the 1940s, urban decay was characteristic of many American cities, including Washington, D.C., where people lived in dire poverty within sight of the Capitol.*

Activity: Interdisciplinary Connection

Performing Arts Organize students into small groups and have them discuss what life was like in the 1950s for one of the groups mentioned in this section. Then have students produce a skit depicting one aspect of life for the group they selected. Encourage students to use appropriate music to set the tone for their skits. Make arrangements for students to perform for their classmates. OL unbearable. In *The Other America,* Michael Harrington noted:

PRIMARY SOURCE

"[Migrant laborers] work ten-eleven-twelve hour days in temperatures over one hundred degrees. Sometimes there is no drinking water. . . . Women and children work on ladders and with hazardous machinery. . . . Babies are brought to the field and are placed in 'cradles' of wood boxes."

—from *The Other America*

R Away from the fields, many Mexican families lived in small, crudely built shacks, while some did not even have a roof over their heads. "They sleep where they can, some in the open," Harrington noted about one group of migrant workers. "They eat when they can (and sometimes what they can)." The nation paid little attention to the plight of Mexican farm laborers until the 1960s, when the workers began to organize for greater rights.

Native Americans

Native Americans also faced challenges throughout the postwar era. By the middle of the 1900s, Native Americans—who made up less than one percent of the population—were the poorest ethnic group in the nation. Average annual family income for Native American families, for example, was $1,000 less than that of African American families.

After World War II, during which many Native American soldiers had served with distinction, the United States government launched a program to bring Native Americans into mainstream society—whether they wanted to assimilate or not.

Under the plan, which became known as the **termination policy,** the federal government withdrew all official recognition of the Native American groups as legal **entities** and made them subject to the same laws as white citizens. Native American groups were then C placed under the responsibility of state governments. At the same time, the government encouraged Native Americans to blend in with the larger society by helping them move off reservations to cities.

Although the idea of integrating Native Americans into mainstream society began with good intentions, some of its supporters had more selfish goals. Speculators and developers sometimes gained rich farmland at the expense of destitute Native American groups.

1990

▼ *By the early 1990s, conditions were not much improved as this North Baltimore neighborhood suggests.*

MAKING CONNECTIONS

1. **Comparing** How did conditions change, if at all, from 1940 to 1990?
2. **Identifying Central Issues** Which groups suffered most from issues of urban decline? Why?

Activity: Interdisciplinary Connection

Daily Life Have students work in groups to research Native American life in the 1950s. Within each group, pairs of students should investigate such aspects of daily life as housing, food, education, religious life, culture, work and leisure. Student pairs should present the results of their research to their groups. Together, each group should then make decisions about how to present the information they have gathered. Some groups might wish to present their findings in the form of a written report. Others might make an oral presentation. Still others might wish to create an interactive Web site with their findings. Have students present their final products to the class. **Ask:** Did the termination policy change the lives of Native Americans? In what ways? **OL**

R Reading Strategy

Inferring Ask: Why did Mexican migrant laborers put up with poor housing, dangerous working conditions, and long days? *(Jobs were scarce, and a job as a hard working migrant laborer was better than no job at all.)* **BL**

C Critical Thinking

Drawing Conclusions Ask: Why did the federal government promote the plan known as the termination policy? *(It wanted to assimilate Native Americans into mainstream society, with the hope that they would be better off in cities than on the reservations.)* **BL**

MAKING CONNECTIONS

Answers:
1. Conditions did not improve much.
2. minorities and the poor; the decreased tax base did not allow governments to provide needed services

Additional Support

D Differentiated Instruction

Kinesthetic Organize students into small groups and have them discuss what life was like in the 1950s for people living in Appalachia. Have students produce skits depicting one aspect of Appalachian life. Encourage them to use appropriate music to set the tone for their skits. Make arrangements for students to perform for their classmates. **OL**

Analyzing VISUALS

Answers:

1. Mississippi, Alabama, Tennessee, Kentucky, Virginia, West Virginia
2. high unemployment in mining communities

Reading Check

Answer:
African Americans, Hispanics, and Native Americans

For most Native Americans, termination was a disastrous policy that only deepened their poverty. In the mid-1950s, for example, the Welfare Council of Minneapolis described Native American living conditions in that city as miserable: "One Indian family of five or six, living in two rooms, will take in relatives and friends who come from the reservations seeking jobs until perhaps fifteen people will be crowded into the space."

During the 1950s, Native Americans in Minneapolis could expect to live only 37 years, compared to 46 years for all Minnesota Native Americans and 68 years for other Minneapolis residents. Similar patterns existed elsewhere. Benjamin Reifel, a Sioux, described the despair that the termination policy produced:

PRIMARY SOURCE

"The Indians believed that when the dark clouds of war passed from the skies overhead, their rising tide of expectations, though temporarily stalled, would again reappear. Instead they were threatened by termination. . . . Soaring expectations began to plunge."

—quoted in *The Earth Shall Weep*

Appalachia

Residents of rural **Appalachia** also failed to share in the prosperity of the 1950s. The scenic beauty of the mountainous region, which stretches from New York to Georgia, often hid desperate poverty. Coal mining had long been the backbone of the Appalachian economy. With mechanization of mining in the 1950s, unemployment soared. With no work to be had, some 1.5 million people abandoned Appalachia to seek a better life in the cities. "Whole counties," wrote one reporter, "are precariously held together by a flour-and-dried-milk paste of surplus foods. . . . The men who are no longer needed in the mines and the farmers who cannot compete . . . have themselves become surplus commodities in the mountains." **D**

Appalachia had fewer doctors per thousand people than the rest of the country. Studies revealed high rates of nutritional deficiency and infant mortality. In addition, schooling in the region was considered even worse than in inner-city slums.

Reading Check **Identifying** Which groups were left out of the economic boom of the 1950s?

PRIMARY SOURCE
Poverty in Appalachia

▲ *Eight family members lived in this three-room house lined with newspaper in Appalachia in the 1950s.*

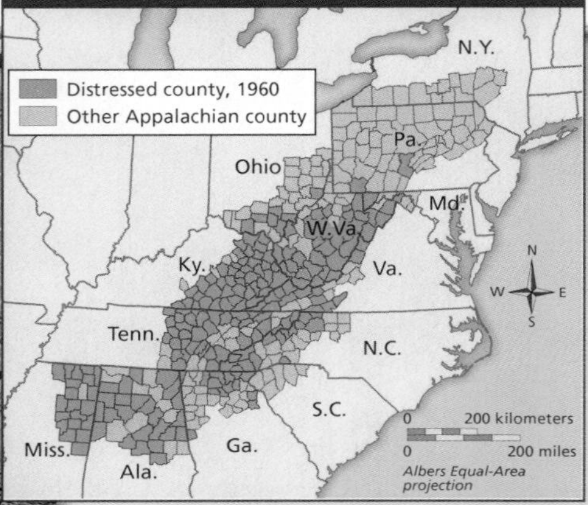

Analyzing VISUALS DBQ

1. **Identifying** Which states had the highest concentration of distressed counties in 1960?
2. **Explaining** What might have accounted for this high number?

Differentiated Instruction

Leveled Activities

BL Reteaching Activity, URB p. 145

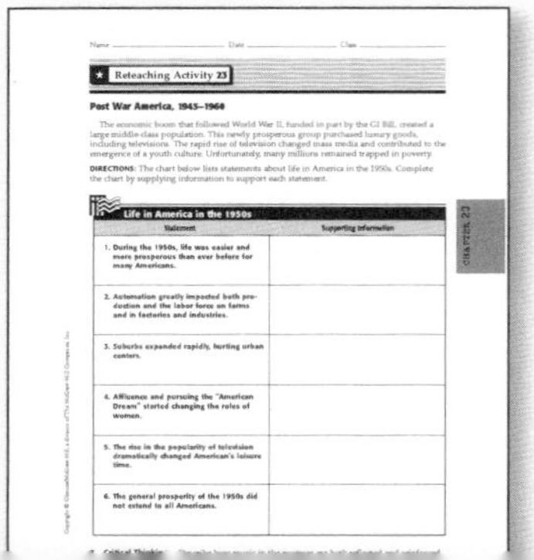

OL Academic Vocabulary Activity, URB p. 131

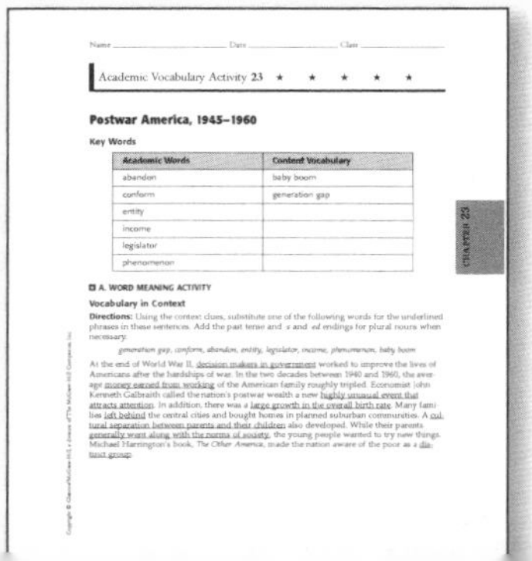

AL Primary Source Reading, URB p. 137

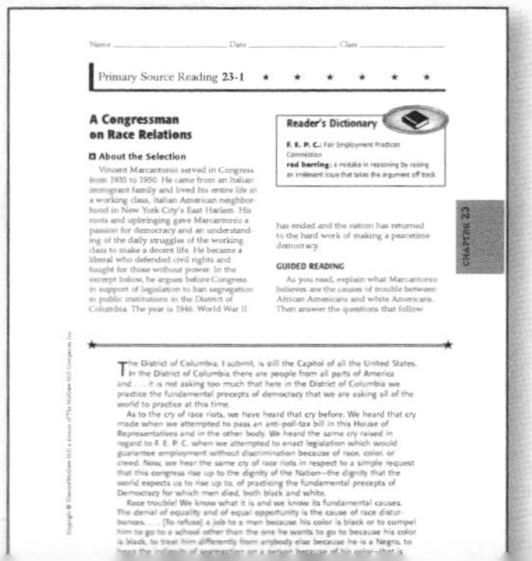

ELL Reinforcing Skills Activity, URB p. 133

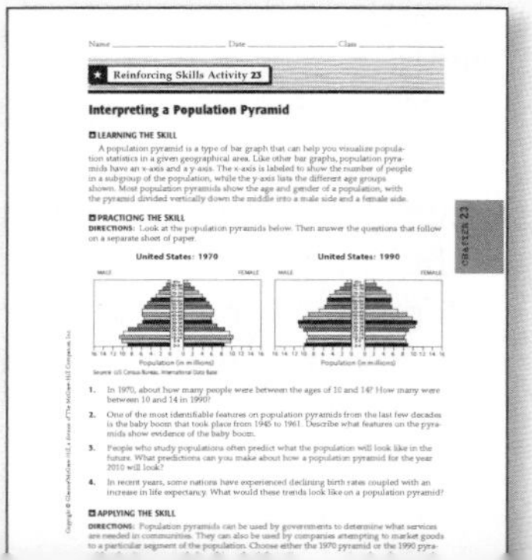

Juvenile Delinquency

MAIN Idea Juvenile crime rates rose during the 1950s; a crisis in education occurred when the baby boomers began school.

HISTORY AND YOU Has your school placed a greater emphasis on science and math classes recently? Read to learn about a push in science and math education during the 1950s.

During the 1950s, many middle-class, white Americans found it easy to ignore the poverty and racism that afflicted many of the nation's minorities, since they themselves were removed from it. Some social problems, however, became impossible to ignore.

One problem at this time was a rise in, or at least a rise in the reporting of, **juvenile delinquency**—antisocial or criminal behavior of young people. Between 1948 and 1953, the United States saw a 45 percent rise in juvenile crime rates. A popular 1954 book titled *1,000,000 Delinquents* correctly predicted that in the following year, about 1 million young people would be involved in some kind of criminal activity.

Americans disagreed on what had triggered the rise in delinquency. Experts blamed television, movies, comic books, racism, busy parents, a rising divorce rate, lack of religion, and anxiety over the military draft. Some cultural critics claimed that young people were rebelling against the conformity of their parents. Others blamed a lack of discipline. Doting parents, complained Bishop Fulton J. Sheen, had raised bored children who sought new thrills, such as "alcohol, marijuana, even murder." Still others pointed at social causes, blaming teen violence on poverty. The problem, however, cut across class and racial lines—the majority of car thieves, for example, had grown up in middle-class homes.

Most teens, of course, steered clear of gangs, drugs, and crime. Nonetheless, the public tended to stereotype young people as juvenile delinquents, especially those teens who favored unconventional clothing and long hair, or used street slang.

Concerned about their children, many parents focused on the nation's schools as a possible solution. When baby boomers began entering the school system in the 1950s, enrollments increased by 13 million. School districts struggled to pay for new buildings and hire more teachers.

Americans' education worries only intensified in 1957 after the Soviet Union launched the world's first space satellites, *Sputnik I* and *Sputnik II.* Many Americans felt that the nation had fallen behind its Cold War enemy and blamed what they felt was a lack of technical education in the nation's schools. *Life* magazine proclaimed a "Crisis in Education" and offered a grim warning: "What has long been an ignored national problem, *Sputnik* has made a recognized crisis." In the wake of the *Sputnik* launches, efforts began to improve math and science education. Profound fears about the country's young people, it seemed, dominated the end of a decade that had brought prosperity and progress for many Americans.

Reading Check **Evaluating** What were some suggested explanations of the increase in juvenile crime?

Section 3 REVIEW

Vocabulary

1. **Explain** the significance of: poverty line, urban renewal, Lorraine Hansberry, Bracero Program, termination policy, Appalachia, juvenile delinquency.

Main Ideas

2. **Evaluating** How did the federal government's termination policy affect Native Americans?
3. **Analyzing** What effects did the baby boomers have on schools?

Critical Thinking

4. **Big Ideas** Why did urban renewal fail to improve the lives of the poor in the inner cities?
5. **Organizing** Use a graphic organizer similar to the one below to list groups of Americans left out of the country's postwar economic boom.

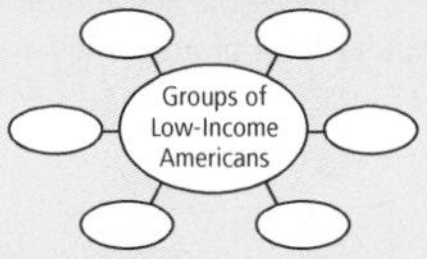

6. **Analyzing Visuals** Study the photographs on page 811. Why were minority groups hit so hard by poverty, compared to whites, in the 1950s?

Writing About History

7. **Expository Writing** Choose a current social problem that you observe among adolescents. Describe the problem and its causes, and then recommend a solution.

History ONLINE
Study Central™ To review this section, go to glencoe.com and click on Study Central.

Reading Check

Answer:
Answers may include: television, movies, comic books, racism, busy parents, a rising divorce rate, lack of religion, anxiety over the military draft, teenage rebellion, lack of discipline, doting parents, boredom, poverty.

Assess

History ONLINE

Study Central™ provides summaries, interactive games, and online graphic organizers to help students review content.

Close

Summarizing Ask: What was the major cause of deteriorating cities in the 1950s? *(The tax base of city governments dropped as middle-class residents moved to the suburbs.)* OL

Section 3 REVIEW

Answers

1. All definitions can be found in the section and the Glossary.
2. They lost much of their cultural uniqueness and valuable land, and they were often as poor in the cities as they would have been on the reservations.
3. As the wave of baby boomers entered the education system, school districts had to find the money to build new buildings and hire more teachers.
4. The high-rise projects that were built to replace older buildings were crowded and destroyed more housing space than they created. They also often created an atmosphere of violence.
5. single mothers, the elderly, minority immigrants, inner-city poor, people in Appalachia
6. Minority groups did not have access to the new higher-paying, white-collar jobs that whites did.
7. The social problems and solutions students cover will vary. Students should provide a current problem among juveniles and a relevant, reasoned solution to that problem.

Drawing Conclusions After World War II, the GI Bill provided generous funds to veterans. **Ask:** What effect did this government spending have on the economy? *(It boosted the economy by putting money in the hands of veterans to start businesses, buy homes and goods, and get an education.)* **OL**

Determining Cause and Effect During the 1950s Americans experienced a baby boom. **Ask:** What were the reasons for the baby boom of the 1950s? *(Young couples who had delayed marriage during the war were now starting families, generous GI benefits helped veterans afford homes in which to raise families, popular culture celebrated large families.)* **OL**

Personal Writing During the 1950s, television did not usually portray women as independent and strong. Minorities were largely absent from television. **Ask:** What impact do you think this may have had on women and minorities in the 1950s? **OL**

Chapter 23 Visual Summary

STUDY TO GO You can study anywhere, anytime by downloading quizzes and flashcards to your PDA from glencoe.com.

The Prosperity of the 1950s

Economy and Society

- The GI Bill provided funds and loans to millions of war veterans.
- Consumer spending increased rapidly.
- More Americans owned homes than ever before.

Population Patterns

- The U.S. population experienced a "baby boom."
- Millions of Americans moved out of cities to the suburbs.

Science, Technology, and Medicine

- Improvements in communication, transportation, and electronics allowed Americans to work more efficiently.
- Medical breakthroughs included the polio vaccine, antibiotics, and treatments for tuberculosis, cancer, and heart disease.

Popular Culture

- New forms of music, radio, cinema, and literature emerged.
- Television replaced movies and radio as the nation's new and most popular form of mass media.

▲ *The huge, stylized automobiles of the 1950s, such as this Cadillac convertible, symbolized the good life to many Americans of the time.*

▲ *While many prospered in the 1950s, many were excluded from achieving the American Dream.*

The Problems of the 1950s

Economy and Society

- Workers went on strike for higher wages.
- Congress would not pass Truman's civil rights legislation.
- Eisenhower cut back on New Deal programs.

Population Patterns

- Financially able people moved from crowded cities to new suburbs.
- Poverty increased in the inner city and the poor faced ongoing social problems.
- Crime increased among young people.

Science, Technology, and Medicine

- Poor people in inner cities and rural areas had limited access to modern health care.

Popular Culture

- Not everyone could afford to buy the new consumer goods available, such as televisions.
- African Americans and other minorities were, for the most part, not depicted on television.
- Many television programs promoted stereotypical gender roles.

Hands-On Chapter Project Step 4: Wrap Up

A New Peacetime America

Step 4: Wrap Up This activity will synthesize the information that students have collected about the society and culture of this time period.

Directions Divide the class into six teams. Each team should select one presenter to take on the role of an individual who lived during this time period. To avoid duplication among the teams, have each team announce which role their presenter will play. If there are duplicates, assign another role to one of the teams.

Analyzing Information Team members will collaboratively write a journal page from the perspective of the presenter. Each journal page should describe vividly the person's life at this time. Presenters will read the group's journal page to the class. The rest of the class may want to ask the presenters questions. To make the presentations more lively and memorable, presenters may wish to carry relevant signs, dress in costumes, or hold up photos. **OL**

Chapter 23 Assessment

Reviewing Vocabulary

Directions: Choose the word or words that best complete the sentence.

1. The Taft-Hartley Act outlawed the ________, opening some industries to nonunion workers.

A closed shop
B labor unions
C right-to-work laws
D open shop

2. During the 1950s, the number of ________ grew, as more Americans worked in offices.

A computers
B blue-collar jobs
C franchises
D white-collar jobs

3. After World War II, Native Americans suffered from the government policy of ________, which forced them into mainstream society.

A urban renewal
B termination
C migrant work
D reservation planning

4. ________ tried to eliminate poverty in cities by replacing slums with high-rise buildings for poor residents.

A Urban renewal
B Termination policy
C Franchising
D Dynamic conservatism

5. The poem "Howl," by Allen Ginsberg, is a work that came out of the ________ movement.

A rock 'n' roll
B generation gap
C beat
D jazz

Reviewing Main Ideas

Directions: Choose the best answer for each of the following questions.

Section 1 *(pp. 794–799)*

6. Which of the following were two characteristics of the U.S. economy after World War II?

A high unemployment and scarce goods
B abundant goods and low unemployment
C low unemployment and scarce goods
D abundant goods and high unemployment

7. Which of the following was achieved under Truman's Fair Deal?

A a large increase in Social Security benefits
B a broad program of civil rights reforms
C a decrease in funding for the TVA
D a federal highway bill

Section 2 *(pp. 800–807)*

8. One major cause of the growth of the suburbs was the

A rise in blue-collar jobs.
B Korean War.
C affordability of homes.
D television.

9. Jonas Salk developed the first vaccine for which illness?

A tuberculosis
B cancer
C heart disease
D polio

TEST-TAKING TIP

Before answering, read the entire question and all answer choices. Then choose the answer that makes the most sense.

Need Extra Help?

If You Missed Questions . . .	1	2	3	4	5	6	7	8	9
Go to Page . . .	794–795	802	813–814	811	807	794–795	797	800–801	802–803

GO ON

Answers and Analyses
Reviewing Vocabulary

1. A The closed shop was an industry that was closed to nonunion workers. The question states that the act opened some industries to "nonunion" workers. The opposite of the closed shop is the open shop—industries open to all workers.

2. D Computers did not come into popular use in offices until decades after the 1950s. Franchises are a type of business, and usually include retail establishments, not offices. Blue-collar workers work in factories and as laborers. White-collar workers are office workers.

3. B An easy way for students to remember this is to think that the government attempted to "terminate" the Native American way of life by assimilating them into American culture and refusing to recognize tribes as legal entities.

4. A The urban renewal program had unforeseen consequences. The crowded high-rise buildings created an atmosphere of violence. The policy of evicting residents with higher incomes also encouraged families to remain poor.

5. C Poetry is an art form associated more with the beat movement than with other movements listed. Rock 'n' roll and jazz were styles of musical innovation. The generation gap was a fact of life, not a movement.

Reviewing Main Ideas

6. B The answer choices in this question can confuse students who do not read carefully. Remind students that the economy after WWII was good. Therefore, they can eliminate any answer choices that include a negative. All three incorrect choices include at least one negative, and *A* includes two negatives.

7. A Like FDR's New Deal, the Fair Deal was aimed at improving domestic affairs. Have students who answer incorrectly review "What Was the Fair Deal?" on page 797. Listed first is an increase in Social Security benefits.

8. C This is a cause-and-effect question; students must choose the answer that is most likely responsible for growing suburbs. *A* may be tempting for students, because any rise in jobs might equal a rise in money for housing. However, this connection is too tenuous. It is not likely a war would cause suburbs to grow. Nor is it likely that television would cause suburbs to grow. Affordable homes caused more people to be able to buy homes, which caused suburbs to grow.

9. D Have students who have trouble reread "Medical Miracles" on page 802. Jonas Salk invented the first injected polio vaccine. The other choices discussed are not associated with any single scientist.

10. C This is another cause-and-effect question. The baby boom increased the population. An increase in population would not cause a decrease in housing demand, nor would it cause people to migrate en masse to one part of the nation. Although there is concern for the Social Security system today because of the increasing amount of boomers who are eligible, it is not yet bankrupt.

11. C This question may confuse students, who may be tempted to choose *D*. However, as students read in the chapter, radio stations actually increased after television, because TV forced radio stations to make changes to continue to draw audiences in. The car helped save the radio, because people used the radio for entertainment when driving.

12. B Urban renewal was an action or movement, not an object. Delinquency is criminal behavior or wrongdoing. Income tax does not make sense. An easy way for students to remember this definition is to think of an actual line marking the threshold for poverty.

13. A The Bracero Program began during World War II, when men were brought from Mexico to help harvest crops and work on ranches. They were not citizens of the U.S., they were here on work contracts, but many of their families came over to the U.S. with them and settled. You might tie this in with a current events discussion on Mexican immigration today.

Critical Thinking

14. B The GI Bill was instrumental in helping returning veterans gain access to education, housing, and services. Housing loans helped contribute to the growth of suburbs. Builders, such as William Levitt, developed a system of mass-produced housing that took advantage of the fact that the GI Bill made housing affordable to returning veterans.

15. D Study the graph with students. It shows an overall upward trend in the number of suburban dwellers between 1910 and 1980. In 1970, approximately 36 percent of the population lived in suburbs, according to the chart. In 1980, approximately 45 percent of the population lived in suburbs.

16. C There were approximately twice as many suburban residents in 1950.

Chapter 23 ASSESSMENT

10. How did the post–World War II baby boom affect American society between 1945 and 1960?

A It decreased the demand for housing.
B It bankrupted the Social Security system.
C It increased the need for educational resources.
D It encouraged people to migrate to the Sun Belt.

11. How did television affect the radio industry?

A One-fifth of the nation's movie theaters closed.
B Radio stations started to broadcast soap operas.
C The number of radio stations increased as the car created a larger audience.
D Radio stations declined in number as the audience turned to television.

Section 3 *(pp. 810–815)*

12. The imaginary government marker setting the minimum income required to support a family is called the

A urban renewal.
B poverty line.
C income tax.
D delinquency.

13. The purpose of the Bracero Program was to

A bring workers into the United States from Mexico.
B send workers from the United States to Mexico.
C find housing for new immigrants.
D deport illegal immigrants.

Critical Thinking

Directions: Choose the best answers to the following questions.

14. The GI Bill boosted the postwar economy by

A instituting a military draft.
B providing veterans with generous loans.
C requiring all veterans to go to college.
D providing veterans with white-collar jobs.

Base your answers to questions 15 and 16 on the graph below and on your knowledge of Chapter 23.

Suburban Dwellers, 1910–1980

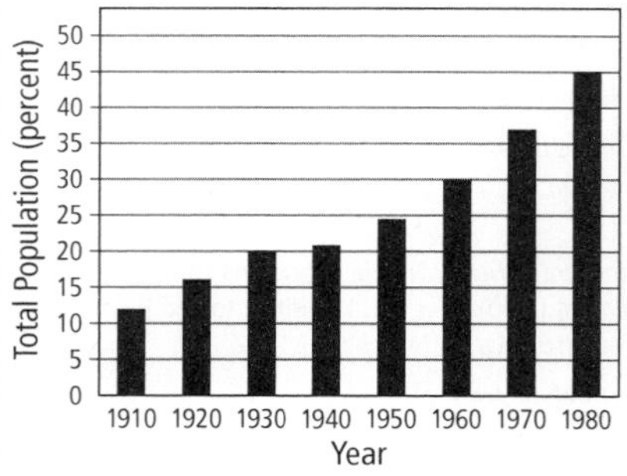

Source: *The First Measured Century.*

15. What trend in the percentage of suburban dwellers does this graph show?

A Fewer people were moving from the cities to the suburbs each year.
B More people lived in the suburbs in 1910 than 1950.
C More people lived in the cities in 1960 than 1950.
D More people lived in the suburbs in 1980 than 1970.

16. In what year was there approximately twice the percentage of suburban residents as there had been in 1910?

A 1930
B 1940
C 1950
D 1960

Need Extra Help?

If You Missed Questions . . .	10	11	12	13	14	15	16
Go to Page . . .	801	805	810	812–813	794–795	R16	R16

GO ON

17. Many Americans responded to the Soviet launching of *Sputnik* by demanding that schools

A focus more on math and science.

B offer more physical fitness training.

C require students to learn a foreign language.

D require the recitation of the Pledge of Allegiance.

Analyze the cartoon and answer the questions that follow. Base your answers on the cartoon and on your knowledge of Chapter 23.

"He never wastes a minute, J.P.—that's his lunch."

18. The main idea of this cartoon is that 1950s white-collar workers were

A lazy and useless.

B unstable and untrustworthy.

C extremely good at what they did.

D overly dedicated to their jobs.

Document-Based Questions

Directions: Analyze the document and answer the short-answer questions that follow the document.

George Gallup, one of the nation's first pollsters, spoke at the University of Iowa in 1953 about the importance of mass media in the United States. Below is an excerpt from his remarks:

> "One of the real threats to America's future place in the world is a citizenry which duly elects to be entertained and not informed. From the time the typical citizen arises and looks at his morning newspaper until he turns off his radio or television set before going to bed, he has unwittingly cast his vote a hundred times for entertainment or for education. Without his knowing it, he has helped to determine the very character of our three most important media of communication—the press, radio, and television."
>
> —quoted in *Legacy of Freedom, Vol. 2: United States History from Reconstruction to the Present*

19. According to Gallup, what is a threat to the future of the United States in the world?

20. How do American citizens "cast their votes" to determine what is read, seen, and heard in the mass media?

Extended Response

21. Harry Truman was a Democrat, and Dwight Eisenhower was a Republican. However, the two men did not always act along party lines and, in some cases, took similar approaches to governing. In an expository essay, compare and contrast the domestic agendas of these two presidents of the postwar era. Include an introduction and at least three paragraphs with supporting details that explain how Truman's and Eisenhower's ideas and approaches to domestic issues were different and similar.

STOP

History ONLINE
For additional test practice, use Self-Check Quizzes—Chapter 23 at glencoe.com.

Need Extra Help?

If You Missed Questions . . .	17	18	19	20	21
Go to Page . . .	815	R18	819	819	794–799

17. A They demanded schools focus more on math and science.

18. D Study the cartoon with students. The man at the desk is working and "eating" lunch. His lunch, though, is being given intravenously. The implication is that he doesn't want to let eating lunch get in the way of his work. This is overdedication. He is not lazy; he is working hard. It appears he never leaves his desk, even to eat lunch, so he is not unstable. He might be good at what he does, but *D* better fits the cartoon.

Document-Based Questions

19. According to Gallup, the threat was that Americans had chosen to be entertained rather than informed or educated. The focus on entertainment and lack of education might cause the U.S. to lag behind in intellectual accomplishments.

20. American citizens cast their votes by what they choose to watch, read, and listen to. If most people choose entertainment over education in the mass media, then the mass media will respond by providing more, or only, entertainment.

Extended Response

21. Students' essays will vary, but should make clear and logical comparisons, with supporting details from the chapter, between Truman's and Eisenhower's domestic agendas and policies. Discussions should include discussion of Truman's Fair Deal and Eisenhower's Dynamic Conservatism.

History ONLINE
Have students visit the Web site at glencoe.com to review Chapter 23 and take the Self-Check Quiz.

Need Extra Help?
Have students refer to the pages listed if they miss any of the questions.

Unit 8 Planning Guide

UNIT PACING CHART						
	Unit 8	Chapter 24	Chapter 25	Chapter 26	Chapter 27	Unit 8
Day 1	Unit Opener	Chapter 24 Opener, Section 1	Chapter 25 Opener, Section 1	Chapter 26 Opener, Section 1	Chapter 27 Opener, Section 1	Wrap-Up/Project, Unit Assessment
Day 2		Section 2	Section 2	Section 2	Section 2	
Day 3		Section 3	Section 3	Section 3	Section 3	
Day 4		Chapter Assessment	Chapter Assessment	Chapter Assessment	Chapter Assessment	

Teacher to Teacher

Erin Johnston
South Caldwell High School
Hudson, North Carolina

History Music Video Project Have students select a figure, event, or era from world and American history as well as a song. (I generally try to have them use one that is no more than 5 minutes to keep the file size down. You may want them to bring a copy of the lyrics to you so you can determine appropriateness.) If you are uncertain about the choice you should ask students to explain their "vision" to you. Tell them that they are telling a story through images, songs, and quotes to their audience. I have been surprised at how insightful my students have been in selecting their songs.

There are many programs that allow you to make videos, and many students already know how to use this technology and may help demonstrate it in class. The media programs are fairly simple "click and drag" programs that have directions on the screen. I generally have my students save 30–50 images for their projects. These programs allow you to include actual film footage and add quotes/passages as "eyewitness accounts."

These videos have become powerful teaching tools in helping my students understand historical periods such as the civil rights movement.

Author Note

Dear American History Teacher,

The 25 years covered in this unit represented an era of dramatic change in American history. The Cold War served as the backdrop to many of these events and should be reemphasized as you discuss the social and political upheavals of the 1960s and 1970s. The United States emerged from World War II as one of two superpowers, along with the Soviet Union. This fact may help students understand why the United States felt obligated to become immersed in so many foreign policy entanglements.

Indeed, the decades of the 1950s and 1960s witnessed some of the greatest social movements of the twentieth century—the civil rights movement, the student movement, the women's movement, the environmental movement, and the counterculture movement. These movements touched nearly every corner of American society. New leaders emerged on college campuses, in local communities, and on the national stage. American colleges and universities served as forums for many of the movements.

These were years of relative prosperity, rising expectations, and the desire to end poverty and suffering among all Americans, as illustrated in President Lyndon Johnson's Great Society. Historians continue to debate the significance of Johnson's presidency and his Great Society programs, but there is little doubt that many of these programs such as Medicaid, Medicare, Head Start, the Child Nutrition Act, and the Clean Water Act improved the quality of life for millions of Americans.

Students should also, however, get a sense of how deeply the nation divided over American foreign policy, especially U.S. involvement in the Vietnam War. The legacy of that war is still being debated by historians as well. Finally, the struggle for civil rights and racial equality were central to this era, and students are generally excited to learn about the roles of leaders such as Martin Luther King, Jr., Rosa Parks, Thurgood Marshall, and Malcolm X.

Albert S. Broussard

Senior Author

Introducing **Unit 8**

Focus

Why It Matters

Ask students to interview someone who came of age during the 1960s or 1970s. Ask them to focus interview questions on how that era has influenced the person's life and how it has affected national policy. Invite volunteers to share what they learned from the interviews. **OL**

Connecting to Past Learning

In previous units, students have learned about other presidential policies, such as the Square Deal and the New Deal. In this unit, they will learn of the New Frontier and the Great Society. They also learned about other wars. They will learn about the Vietnam War in this unit.

Unit Launch Activity

Write the Scene Have students skim the unit for a photograph that interests them. Then challenge them to write a paragraph describing the photograph or its setting and why they were drawn to it. **OL**

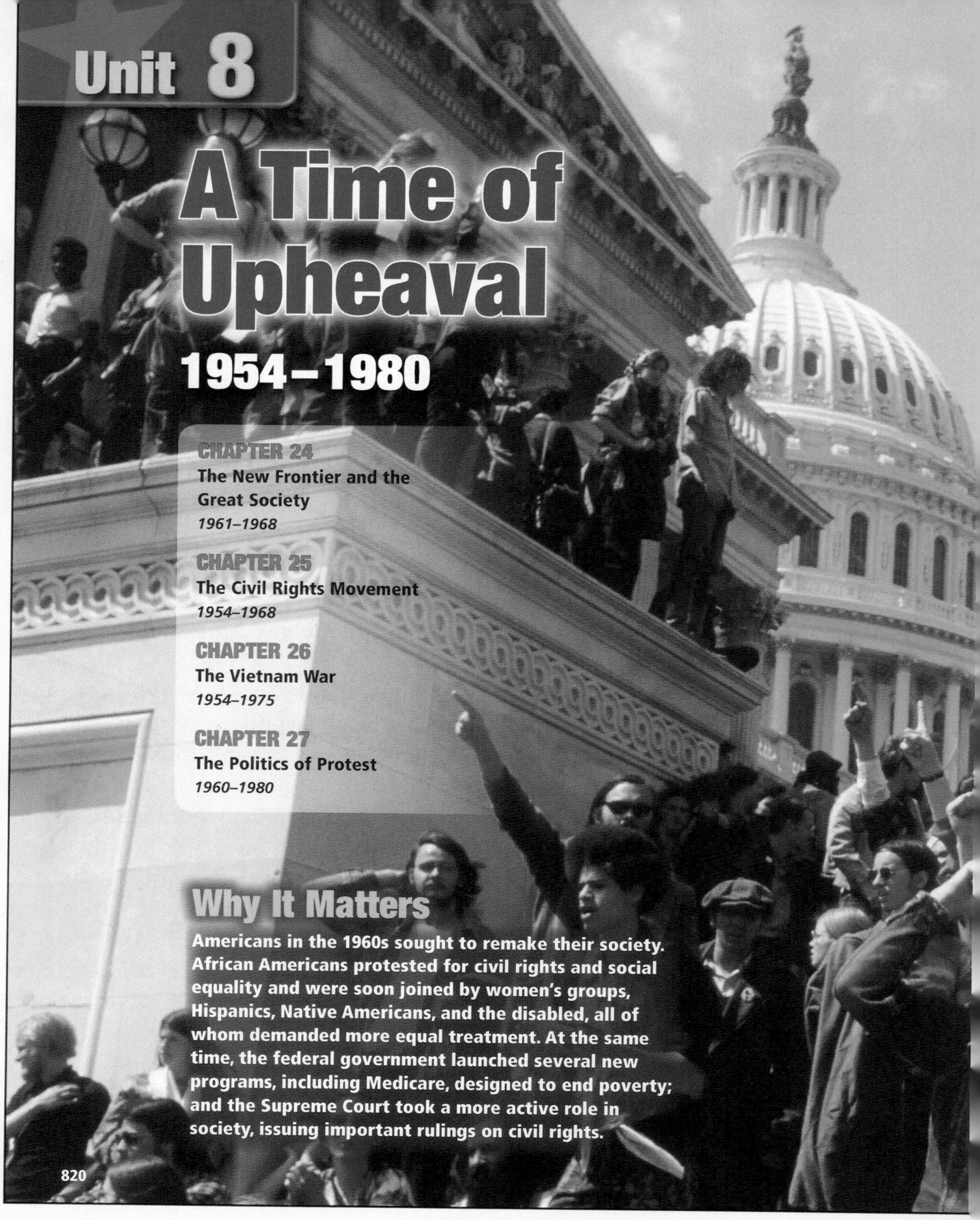

Unit 8

A Time of Upheaval

1954–1980

Why It Matters

Americans in the 1960s sought to remake their society. African Americans protested for civil rights and social equality and were soon joined by women's groups, Hispanics, Native Americans, and the disabled, all of whom demanded more equal treatment. At the same time, the federal government launched several new programs, including Medicare, designed to end poverty; and the Supreme Court took a more active role in society, issuing important rulings on civil rights.

820

Team Teaching Activity

Political Science Invite a political science teacher to the class to discuss the impact of visual media on presidential and congressional elections since the 1960 election. Ask him or her to show clips of effective and ineffective use of advertisements, debates, or interviews. Use the clips as background for a discussion on how candidates create positive images for constituents. **OL**

Demonstrators block the entrance to the House of Representatives as part of the "May Day" protest against the Vietnam War, 1971

821

Introducing **Unit 8**

Teach

Skill Practice

Using Geography Skills Ask students to use the world maps in their textbooks to locate Vietnam and its relation to France and to the United States. Have students suggest why its location was significant for the domino theory of the spread of communism. *(Vietnam is near Communist China. The spread of communism could logically extend to the Philippines, in which the United States had a military and economic interest.)* BL

Skill Practice

Reading a Time Line Draw students' attention to the time lines of each chapter. Ask them to preview those time lines to prepare for new information they will learn in this unit OL

More About the Photo

Visual Literacy Ask students to describe the people who are protesting. *(Most are young and informally dressed; the men wear their hair longer than what was then considered normal.)* Tell them that the early protests were conducted primarily by college students and often on college campuses. At Columbia University in 1968, about 500 students took control of five buildings on campus, including the president's office. Protests increased in other parts of the world as well, notably in Paris, London, and Prague. Protests became more widespread, including many different groups of people, not just college students who did not want to be drafted to fight a war they could not support. One of the most significant ones occurred at the Democratic National Convention in Chicago in 1968, when an estimated 10,000 demonstrators clashed outside the convention center with perhaps 20,000 police and National Guard troops.

NCLB No Child Left Behind

Teaching Tip The NCLB Act places an emphasis on computer literacy. Assist students doing online research in selecting only reputable sources. For example, Web sites ending in *.gov, .org,* or *.edu* are generally trustworthy. Encourage students to look for historical museum sites and presidential libraries as they do their research for this chapter.

Chapter 24 Planning Guide

Key to Ability Levels	
BL Below Level	AL Above Level
OL On Level	ELL English Language Learners

Key to Teaching Resources	
Print Material	Transparency
CD-ROM or DVD	

BL	OL	AL	ELL		Resources	Chapter Opener	Section 1	Section 2	Section 3	Chapter Assess
					FOCUS					
BL	OL	AL	ELL	Transparency	Daily Focus Transparencies		24-1	24-2	24-3	
					TEACH					
	OL	AL		Print Material	Geography and History Activity, URB	p. 3				
BL	OL	AL		Print Material	Economics and History Activity, URB					p. 7
BL	OL		ELL	Print Material	Reading Skills Activity, URB				p. 21	
	OL			Print Material	Historical Analysis Skills Activity, URB			p. 22		
BL	OL	AL	ELL	Print Material	Differentiated Instruction Activity, URB				p. 23	
BL	OL		ELL	Print Material	English Learner Activity, URB		p. 25			
BL	OL	AL	ELL	Print Material	Content Vocabulary Activity, URB*		p. 27			
BL	OL	AL	ELL	Print Material	Academic Vocabulary Activity, URB		p. 29			
	OL	AL		Print Material	Reinforcing Skills Activity, URB		p. 31			
	OL	AL		Print Material	Critical Thinking Skills Activity, URB				p. 32	
BL	OL		ELL	Print Material	Time Line Activity, URB			p. 33		
	OL			Print Material	Linking Past and Present Activity, URB		p. 34			
BL	OL	AL	ELL	Print Material	Primary Source Reading, URB			p. 35	p. 37	
BL	OL	AL	ELL	Print Material	American Art and Music Activity, URB	p. 39				
BL	OL	AL	ELL	Print Material	Interpreting Political Cartoons Activity, URB			p. 41		
		AL		Print Material	Enrichment Activity, URB			p. 45		
BL	OL		ELL	Print Material	Guided Reading Activity, URB*		p. 48	p. 49	p. 50	
BL	OL	AL	ELL	Print Material	Reading Essentials and Note-Taking Guide*		p. 268	p. 271	p. 274	
BL	OL	AL	ELL	Print Material	Differentiated Instruction for the American History Classroom	✓	✓	✓	✓	✓
BL	OL	AL	ELL	Transparency	Unit Map Overlay Transparencies	✓	✓	✓	✓	✓
BL	OL	AL	ELL	Print Material	Unit Time Line Transparencies, Strategies, and Activities	✓	✓	✓	✓	✓
BL	OL	AL	ELL	Print Material	Cause and Effect Transparencies, Strategies, and Activities	✓	✓	✓	✓	✓
BL	OL	AL	ELL	Print Material	Why It Matters Chapter Transparencies, Strategies, and Activities	✓	✓	✓	✓	✓

Note: Please refer to the *Unit 8 Resource Book* for this chapter's URB materials.

* Also available in Spanish

TeacherWorks Plus
All-In-One Planner and Resource Center

- Interactive Lesson Planner
- Interactive Teacher Edition
- Fully editable blackline masters
- Section Spotlight Videos Launch
- Differentiated Lesson Plans
- Printable reports of daily assignments
- Standards Tracking System

Levels				Resources	Chapter Opener	Section 1	Section 2	Section 3	Chapter Assess
BL	OL	AL	ELL						
				TEACH *(continued)*					
BL	OL	AL	ELL	The Living Constitution	✓	✓	✓	✓	✓
BL	OL	AL	ELL	American Issues	✓	✓	✓	✓	✓
	OL	AL	ELL	American Art and Architecture Transparencies, Strategies, and Activities	✓	✓	✓	✓	✓
BL	OL	AL		High School American History Literature Library	✓	✓	✓	✓	✓
	OL	AL		American History Primary Source Documents Library	✓	✓	✓	✓	✓
BL	OL	AL	ELL	American Music: Hits Through History CD	✓	✓	✓	✓	✓
BL	OL	AL	ELL	StudentWorks™ Plus	✓	✓	✓	✓	✓
BL	OL	AL	ELL	*The American Vision* Video Program	✓	✓	✓	✓	✓
Teacher Resources				Reading Strategies and Activities for the Social Studies Classroom	✓	✓	✓	✓	✓
Teacher Resources				Strategies for Success	✓	✓	✓	✓	✓
Teacher Resources				Presentation Plus! with MindJogger CheckPoint	✓	✓	✓	✓	✓
Teacher Resources				Success With English Learners	✓	✓	✓	✓	✓
				ASSESS					
BL	OL	AL	ELL	Section Quizzes and Chapter Tests*		p. 347	p. 348	p. 349	p. 351
BL	OL	AL	ELL	Authentic Assessment With Rubrics					p. 53
BL	OL	AL	ELL	Standardized Test Practice Workbook					p. 54
BL	OL	AL	ELL	*ExamView® Assessment Suite*		24-1	24-2	24-3	Ch. 24
				CLOSE					
BL			ELL	Reteaching Activity, URB					p. 43
BL	OL		ELL	Reading and Study Skills Foldables™	p. 78				

✓ Chapter- or unit-based activities applicable to all sections in this chapter.

Using a Widget

Teach With Technology

What is a widget?
The McGraw-Hill Social Studies widget is a program for any computer with Internet access that acts as a one-stop launching pad for both software- and online-based programs.

How can the widget help my students and me?
The widget is a convenient way for you and your students to access McGraw-Hill's technology tools, both software-based and online. Some of the features of the widget include:

- customizable links to frequently used Glencoe Web pages
- recognition of, and compatibility with, Glencoe DVD and CD-ROM programs
- QuickPass entry for fast access to chapter content and activities

Visit glencoe.com to download the free student and teacher versions of the McGraw-Hill Social Studies widget.

History ONLINE
Visit glencoe.com and enter ***QuickPass***™ code TAV9399c24T for Chapter 24 resources.

You can easily launch a wide range of digital products from your computer's desktop with the McGraw-Hill Social Studies widget.

	Student	Teacher	Parent
Media Library			
• Section Audio	●		●
• Spanish Audio Summaries	●		●
• Section Spotlight Videos	●	●	●
***The American Vision* Online Learning Center (Web Site)**			
• StudentWorks™ Plus Online	●	●	●
• Multilingual Glossary	●	●	●
• Study-to-Go	●	●	●
• Chapter Overviews	●	●	●
• Self-Check Quizzes	●	●	●
• Student Web Activities	●	●	●
• ePuzzles and Games	●	●	●
• Vocabulary eFlashcards	●	●	●
• In Motion Animations	●	●	●
• Study Central™	●	●	●
• Web Activity Lesson Plans		●	
• Vocabulary PuzzleMaker	●	●	●
• Historical Thinking Activities		●	
• Beyond the Textbook	●	●	●

Reading Support From Jamestown Education

- **Timed Readings Plus in Social Studies** helps students increase their reading rate and fluency while maintaining comprehension. The 400-word passages are similar to those found on state and national assessments.
- **Reading in the Content Area: Social Studies** concentrates on six essential reading skills that help students better comprehend what they read. The book includes 75 high-interest nonfiction passages written at increasing levels of difficulty.
- **Reading Social Studies** includes strategic reading instruction and vocabulary support in Social Studies content for both ELLs and native speakers of English.

www.jamestowneducation.com

Biography / A&E Home Video / The History Channel

The following videotape programs are available from Glencoe as supplements to this chapter:

- John F. Kennedy: A Personal Story (ISBN 0-76-700010-2)
- Lyndon Johnson: Triumph and Tragedy (ISBN 0-76-700109-5)

To order, call Glencoe at 1-800-334-7344. To find classroom resources to accompany many of these videos, check the following home pages:

A&E Television: www.aetv.com
The History Channel: www.historychannel.com

Reading List Generator CD-ROM — Glencoe BookLink 3

Use this database to search more than 30,000 titles to create a customized reading list for your students.

- Reading lists can be organized by students' reading level, author, genre, theme, or area of interest.
- The database provides Degrees of Reading Power™ (DRP) and Lexile™ readability scores for all selections.
- A brief summary of each selection is included.

Leveled reading suggestions for this chapter:

For students at a Grade 8 reading level:
- ***John Fitzgerald Kennedy: America's Youngest President,*** by Lucy Post Frisbee

For students at a Grade 9 reading level:
- ***John F. Kennedy,*** by Lucia Raatma

For students at a Grade 10 reading level:
- ***The First Moon Landing,*** by Sabina Crewe and Dale Anderson

For students at a Grade 11 reading level:
- ***John F. Kennedy,*** by Michael Burgan

For students at a Grade 12 reading level:
- ***Footprints on the Moon,*** by Alexandra Siy

National Geographic

Index to National Geographic Magazine:

The following articles relate to this chapter:

- "Selma to Montgomery: The Road to Equality," by Chuck Stone and Meria Joel Carstarphen, February 2000.
- "A Generation After Sputnik: Are the Soviets Ahead in Space?," by Thomas Y. Canby, October 1986.

National Geographic Society Products To order the following, call National Geographic at 1-800-368-2728:

- *ZipZapMap! USA Windows* (ZipZapMap! USA)

Access National Geographic's new, dynamic MapMachine Web site and other geography resources at:

www.nationalgeographic.com
www.nationalgeographic.com/maps

Introducing Chapter 24

Focus

MAKING CONNECTIONS

Can Government Fix Society?

Ask students to brainstorm ways in which society needs to be "fixed." Have them suggest ways in which these needs have or have not been met by local, state, or national governments. Remind students of the great changes that the New Deal brought about in terms of providing a social safety net for citizens. Have them identify areas that the New Deal did not address. *(Possible answers include: universal health care, women's issues, and minority issues.)* **OL**

Teach

The Big Ideas

As students study the chapter, remind them to consider the section-based Big Ideas included in each section's Guide to Reading. The **Essential Questions** in the activities below tie in to the Big Ideas and help students think about and understand important chapter concepts. In addition, the Hands-on Chapter Projects with their culminating activities relate the content from each section to the Big Ideas. These activities build on each other as students progress through the chapter. Section activities culminate in the wrap-up activity on the Visual Summary page.

Chapter 24

The New Frontier and the Great Society

1961–1968

SECTION 1 The New Frontier
SECTION 2 JFK and the Cold War
SECTION 3 The Great Society

Future President John F. Kennedy waves to a crowd while campaigning, January 1960.

U.S. PRESIDENTS

Kennedy 1961–1963

U.S. EVENTS

1961
- Bay of Pigs invasion
- Peace Corps is created

Oct. 1962
- Cuban missile crisis

Nov. 1963
- Kennedy is assassinated; Johnson becomes president

Johnson 1963–1969

1961 — 1963

WORLD EVENTS

1961
- Construction of Berlin Wall begins

1964
- South Africa's Nelson Mandela sentenced to life in prison

Section 1

The New Frontier

Essential Question: What social issues did the Kennedy administration address? *(affordable housing, minimum wage, women's equality, disability rights)* Tell students that in Section 1 they will learn about Kennedy's domestic agenda and struggles with an unsupportive Congress. **OL**

Section 2

JFK and the Cold War

Essential Question: What efforts to achieve peace did the Kennedy administration follow? *(diplomacy, foreign aid, Peace Corps, expansion of military, space exploration)* Inform students that in this section they will learn about Kennedy's creative efforts to prevent the further spread of communism and war. **OL**

Chapter Audio

MAKING CONNECTIONS

Can Government Fix Society?

President John F. Kennedy and President Lyndon B. Johnson supported programs intended to end poverty and racism at home and promote democracy abroad. The War on Poverty and the Great Society programs marked the greatest increase in the federal government's role in society since the New Deal. Kennedy's aid programs for developing nations also marked a dramatic shift in American foreign policy towards promoting economic development abroad.

- ***How do you think Presidents Kennedy and Johnson changed American society? What programs from the 1960s still exist today?***

FOLDABLES

Categorizing Information Make a Four-Door Book Foldable listing the various programs of Lyndon Johnson's Great Society. Sort the programs into these four categories: War on Poverty, Health and Welfare, Education, and Consumer and Environmental Protection. As you read the chapter, list programs inside your Foldable under the four major categories.

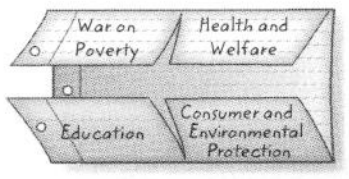

1965
- Congress establishes Medicare and Medicaid

1966
- Congress passes the Child Nutrition Act

1968
- Lyndon Johnson decides not to run for reelection

1965 — 1967 — 1968

1966
- Indira Gandhi becomes prime minister of India

1968
- Student riots paralyze France

History ONLINE Visit glencoe.com and enter ***QuickPass***™ code TAV9846c24 for Chapter 24 resources.

Introducing
Chapter 24

More About the Photo

Visual Literacy Kennedy received the Democratic Party's nomination on the first ballot in July 1960. He was the youngest person ever to be elected, a sharp contrast to then-President Dwight Eisenhower, who was, at 70, the oldest person up to that point to serve as president. Kennedy was a son of privilege. His father, Joseph Kennedy, one of the richest men in the United States, nourished and supported the political ambitions of his sons. In 1953 Kennedy had married Jacqueline Bouvier, an elegant and gracious woman whose presence on the campaign trail was an asset.

FOLDABLES Study Organizer Dinah Zike's Foldables

Dinah Zike's Foldables are three-dimensional, interactive graphic organizers that help students practice basic writing skills, review vocabulary terms, and identify main ideas. Instructions for creating and using Foldables can be found in the Appendix at the end of this book and in the *Dinah Zike's Reading and Study Skills Foldables* booklet.

Section 3

The Great Society

Essential Question: What groups of people did Lyndon Johnson's Great Society assist? *(the poor, minorities, the elderly and uninsured, those unable to get an education)* Tell students that in this section they will read about the massive reform efforts the Johnson administration supported. **OL**

History ONLINE

Visit glencoe.com and enter ***QuickPass***™ code TAV9399c24T for Chapter 24 resources, including a Chapter Overview, Study Central™, Study-to-Go, Student Web Activity, Self-Check Quiz, and other materials.

Focus

Bellringer

Daily Focus Transparency 24-1

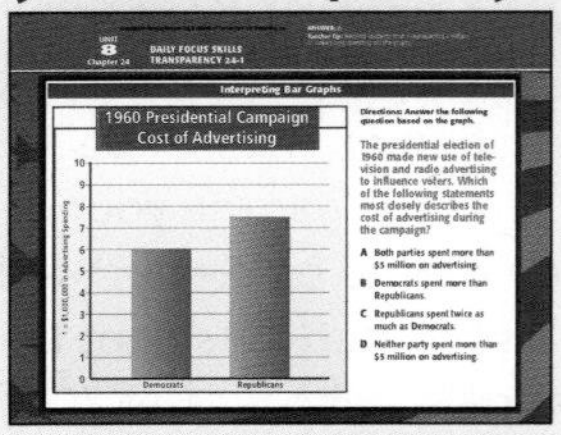

Guide to Reading

Successes	Setbacks
more funds in defense and space exploration	health insurance for senior citizens
some advance in women's rights	a Department of Urban Affairs
economic improvement	federal aid for education
assistance to the disabled	

Section Spotlight Video

To generate student interest and provide a springboard for class discussion, access the Chapter 24, Section 1 video at glencoe.com or on the video DVD.

Section 1

Section Audio   Spotlight Video

The New Frontier

Guide to Reading

Big Ideas

Government and Society Under the programs and policies of the Kennedy administration, women, persons with disabilities, and others gained a greater share of civil rights.

Content Vocabulary
- missile gap *(p. 824)*
- reapportionment *(p. 828)*
- due process *(p. 829)*

Academic Vocabulary
- commentator *(p. 824)*
- arbitrary *(p. 829)*

People and Events to Identify
- New Frontier *(p. 825)*
- Earl Warren *(p. 828)*

Reading Strategy

Categorizing As you read about the presidency of John F. Kennedy, complete a graphic organizer similar to the one below by listing the domestic successes and setbacks of his administration.

Successes	Setbacks

In the presidential election campaign of 1960, John F. Kennedy promised to move the nation into "the New Frontier." After narrowly winning the election, Kennedy succeeded in getting only part of his agenda enacted.

The Election of 1960

MAIN Idea In 1960 a youthful John F. Kennedy narrowly defeated Richard M. Nixon in the presidential election.

HISTORY AND YOU Have you ever watched a televised political debate? Did you pay attention to the candidates' looks and mannerisms? Read on to learn how television changed people's perception of candidates.

On September 26, 1960, at 9:30 P.M. Eastern Standard Time, an estimated 75 million people sat indoors, focused on their television sets, watching the first televised presidential debate. The debate marked a new era of television politics.

During the 1960 presidential race, both parties made substantial use of television. The Democrats spent more than $6 million on television and radio spots, while the Republicans spent more than $7.5 million. Not everyone was happy with this new style of campaigning. Television news **commentator** Eric Sevareid complained that the candidates had become "packaged products" and declared, "the Processed Politician has finally arrived."

The candidates in the first televised debate differed in many ways. The Democratic nominee, John F. Kennedy, was a Catholic from a wealthy and influential Massachusetts family. Richard M. Nixon, the Republican nominee and Eisenhower's vice-president, was a Quaker from California; he had grown up in a family that struggled financially. Kennedy seemed outgoing and relaxed, while Nixon struck many as formal and even stiff in manner.

The campaign centered on the economy and the Cold War. Although the candidates presented different styles, they differed little on these two issues. Both promised to boost the economy, and both portrayed themselves as "Cold Warriors," determined to stop the forces of communism. Kennedy expressed concern about a suspected "**missile gap,**" claiming the United States lagged behind the Soviets in weaponry. Nixon warned that the Democrats' fiscal policies would boost inflation, and that only he had the necessary foreign policy experience to guide the nation.

Kennedy's Catholic faith became an issue, as Al Smith's Catholicism had in 1928. The United States had never had a Catholic president, and many Protestants had concerns about Kennedy. Kennedy decided to confront this issue openly in a speech.

Resource Manager

R Reading Strategies	C Critical Thinking	D Differentiated Instruction	W Writing Support	S Skill Practice
Teacher Edition • Act. Prior Know., p. 825 • Inferring, p. 826 • Using Word Parts, p. 829 **Additional Resources** • Guid. Read. Act., URB p. 48 • Foldables, p. 78	**Additional Resources** • Geo. and History Act., URB p. 3 • Quizzes and Tests, p. 347 • Linking Past and Present, URB p. 34	**Teacher Edition** • Kinesthetic, p. 826 **Additional Resources** • Eng. Learner Act., URB p. 25 • Acad. Vocab. Act., URB p. 29 • Am. Art & Music Act., p. 39	**Teacher Edition** • Expository Writing, p. 828 **Additional Resources** • Content Vocab. Act., URB p. 27	**Additional Resources** • Reinforcing Skills Act., URB p. 31 • Read. Essen., p. 268

The Presidential Election of 1960

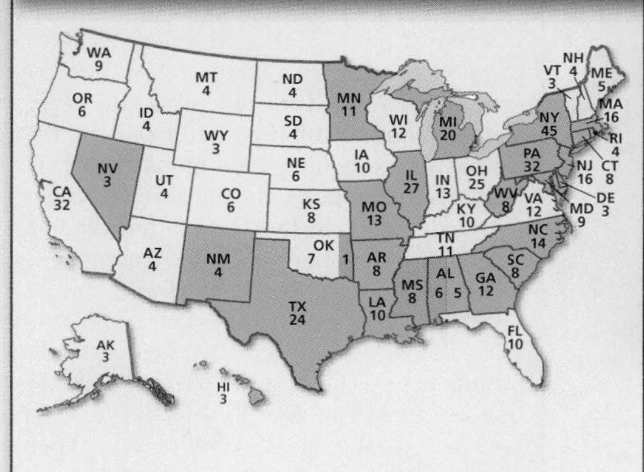

Presidential Candidate	Popular Votes	% of Popular Vote	Electoral Votes
Kennedy	34,227,096	49.72%	303
Nixon	34,107,646	49.55%	219
Byrd	501,643	0.73%	15

PRIMARY SOURCE

The Election of 1960

▲ *The Kennedy-Nixon debates marked the first televised presidential campaign. Senator Kennedy matched Vice President Nixon's well-known debating skills, grasped facts about the way government worked, and showed he cared about Americans.*

Analyzing VISUALS

1. **Assessing** What region of the nation went most solidly Republican?
2. **Identifying** Which states gave one or more electoral votes to Harry Byrd?

R "I believe in an America where the separation of the church and state is absolute," he said, "where no Catholic prelate would tell the president, should he be a Catholic, how to act."

The four televised debates influenced the election's outcome, one of the closest in American history. Kennedy won the popular vote by 119,000 out of 68 million votes cast, and the Electoral College by 303 votes to 219.

Despite his narrow victory, John F. Kennedy captured the imagination of the American public as few presidents had before him. During the campaign, many had been taken with Kennedy's youth and optimism, and his Inaugural Address reinforced this impression.

In the speech, the new president declared that "the torch has been passed to a new generation" and called on citizens to take a more active role in making the nation better. "My fellow Americans," he exclaimed, "ask not what your country can do for you—ask what you can do for your country."

✓Reading Check **Identifying** What were the two main issues of the 1960 presidential election?

Kennedy Takes Office

MAIN Idea Despite an uneasy relationship with Congress, President Kennedy managed to get parts of his domestic agenda passed.

HISTORY AND YOU Do you think there are enough women in top government positions today? Read on to learn how Kennedy's programs were designed to help women.

Upon entering office, President Kennedy set out to implement a legislative agenda that became known as the **New Frontier.** He hoped to increase aid to education, provide health insurance to the elderly, and create a Department of Urban Affairs. He would soon find that transforming lofty ideals into real legislation was no easy task on Capitol Hill.

Although the Democrats had majorities in both houses of Congress, Kennedy was unable to push through many of his programs. Kennedy had trailed Nixon in many Democratic districts and had not helped many Democrats get elected. Those who did win, therefore, did not feel they owed him anything.

Teach

R Reading Strategy

Activating Prior Knowledge

Direct students' attention to the quotation by Senator Kennedy. **Ask:** Who had been the first Roman Catholic candidate chosen by a major party to run for president and in what election year did he run for that office? *(Alfred Smith, 1928)*

Analyzing VISUALS

Answers:

1. the West
2. Mississippi, Alabama, Oklahoma

✓Reading Check

Answer:
The issues were the economy and the Cold War

Hands-On Chapter Project
Step 1

What Is a Great Society?

Step 1: How Court Decisions Affect Society Today In the first of four activities relating to what makes a great society, students will use information in the section to relate 1960s Supreme Court decisions to modern American life.

Directions Have students review the Court decisions made during the 1960s. Then ask them to research newspaper, library, or Internet sources to find a recent event or legal decision that relates to decisions made by the Supreme Court during the 1960s. Have them explain the connection between the recent event and the original Court decision.

Comparing and Contrasting In their presentations, students will discuss ways in which the current event is similar to or different from an event that led to a 1960s Supreme Court decision. **OL** *(Project continued on page 831)*

R Reading Strategy

Inferring Although born into wealth and privilege, Jacqueline Kennedy worked as a photographer and journalist before marrying John Kennedy. As a photographer (the "Inquiring Camera Girl") with the *Washington Times-Herald*, she earned a regular salary. Invite students to consider if her experiences and influence might have shaped Kennedy's push for women's rights. **BL**

D Differentiated Instruction

Kinesthetic Ask students to investigate local involvement in the Special Olympics program. Suggest that students help with a local event as part of their community service. **OL**

Reading Check

Answers:
The legislation was perceived as too expensive and too broad in scope.

Additional Support

Southern Democrats—who were a large part of the Democratic majority in Congress—viewed the New Frontier as too expensive and, together with Republicans, were able to defeat many of Kennedy's proposals. Senator Everett Dirksen, Republican minority leader from Illinois, claimed that Kennedy's efforts to increase the power of the federal government would push the nation down an ominous path.

Successes and Setbacks

Kennedy did achieve some victories, particularly in his efforts to improve the economy. Although the economy had soared through much of the 1950s, it had slowed by the end of the decade. In an effort to increase economic growth and create more jobs, Kennedy advocated deficit spending. The new president convinced Congress to invest more funds in defense and space exploration. Such spending did indeed create more jobs and stimulate economic growth.

In addition, Kennedy asked businesses to hold down prices and labor leaders to hold down pay increases. The labor unions in the steel industry agreed to reduce their demands for higher wages, but several steel companies raised prices sharply. In response, Kennedy threatened to have the Department of Defense buy cheaper foreign steel, and instructed the Justice Department to investigate whether the steel industry was fixing prices. The steel companies backed down and cut their prices, but the victory had strained the president's relations with the business community.

Kennedy also pushed for a cut in tax rates. When opponents argued that a tax cut would help only the wealthy, Kennedy asserted that lower taxes meant businesses would have more money to expand, which would create new jobs and benefit everybody. "A rising tide lifts all boats," Kennedy explained to illustrate how tax cuts would help all Americans.

Congress refused to pass the tax cut because of fears that it would cause inflation. Congress also blocked his plans for health insurance for senior citizens and federal aid to education. However, they did agree to Kennedy's request to raise the minimum wage and his proposal for an Area Redevelopment Act and a Housing Act. These acts helped to create jobs and build low-income housing in poor areas.

Expanding Women's Rights

The issue of women's rights also received attention during the Kennedy administration. In 1961 Kennedy created the Presidential Commission on the Status of Women. The commission called for federal action against gender discrimination and affirmed the right of women to equally paid employment. The commission proposed the Equal Pay Act, which **R** Kennedy signed in 1963. The commission also inspired the creation of similar groups on the state level to study the status of women.

Although he never appointed a woman to his cabinet, a number of women worked in prominent positions in the Kennedy administration, including Esther Peterson, assistant secretary of labor and director of the Women's Bureau of the Department of Labor.

A New View of the Disabled

In 1961 Kennedy convened the President's Panel on Mental Retardation. The panel's first report, containing 112 recommendations, called for funding of research into developmental disabilities and educational and vocational programs for people with developmental disabilities; a greater reliance on residential—as opposed to institutional—treatment centers; and grants to provide prenatal services to women in low-income groups to promote healthy pregnancies.

Responding to the report, Congress enacted the Mental Retardation Facilities and Community Mental Health Centers Construction Act of 1963. This legislation provided grants for construction of research centers; funds to train educational personnel to work with people with developmental disabilities; and grants to states for construction of mental health centers.

In 1962 Eunice Kennedy Shriver, the president's sister, began a day camp at her home for children with developmental disabilities. Camp **D** Shriver, as it was first known, offered people with disabilities a chance to be physically competitive. That effort later grew into the Special Olympics program. The first Special Olympics Games were held in Chicago in 1968.

Reading Check **Evaluating** Why did Kennedy have difficulty getting his agenda enacted?

Activity: Economics Connection

Tax Cuts Does a rising tide really lift all boats, as Kennedy suggested? Invite a teacher from the business or economics department to class to discuss the idea of lower taxes helping to create new jobs and thus benefiting everyone. Encourage interested students to track the federal stance on tax cuts for the past two decades and chart the results. Ask them to consider the effect of tax cuts on real wages and gross domestic product. **AL**

ANALYZING SUPREME COURT CASES

Does Each Vote Really Count?

★ ***Baker* v. *Carr*, 1962**
★ ***Reynolds* v. *Sims*, 1964**

Background of the Cases

Although many more Americans were living in urban areas, most states had not redrawn their political districts to reflect this shift. This gave rural voters more political influence than urban voters. In *Baker* v. *Carr*, the Supreme Court ruled on whether federal courts had jurisdiction in lawsuits seeking to force states to redraw their electoral districts. In *Reynolds* v. *Sims*, the court decided whether uneven electoral districts violated the equal protection clause of the 14th Amendment.

How the Court Ruled

In *Baker* v. *Carr*, the Supreme Court ruled that federal courts can hear lawsuits seeking to force state authorities to redraw electoral districts. In *Reynolds* v. *Sims*, the Court ruled that the inequality of representation in the Alabama legislature did violate the equal protection clause. These rulings forced states to reapportion their political districts according to the principle of "one person, one vote."

PRIMARY SOURCE

The Court's Opinion

"Legislators represent people, not trees or acres. Legislators are elected by voters, not farms or cities or economic interests. As long as ours is a representative form of government . . . the right to elect legislators in a free and unimpaired fashion is a bedrock of our political system. . . .

And, if a State should provide that the votes of citizens in one part of the State should be given two times, or five times, or 10 times the weight of votes of citizens in another part of the State, it could hardly be contended that the right to vote of those residing in the disfavored areas had not been effectively diluted.

—Justice William Brennan, Jr., writing for the court in *Reynolds* v. *Sims*

▲ The 1962 Supreme Court. Seated left to right, Associate Justices Tom Clark and Hugo Black, Chief Justice Earl Warren, Associate Justices William O. Douglas and John Harlan; standing, left to right, Associate Justices Byron White, William Brennan, Potter Stewart, and Arthur Goldberg. Justices Byron White and Arthur Goldberg were appointed by Kennedy.

PRIMARY SOURCE

Dissenting Views

"As of 1961, the Constitutions of all but 11 States . . . recognized bases of apportionment other than geographic spread of population. . . . The consequence of today's decision is that . . . state courts, are given blanket authority and the constitutional duty to supervise apportionment. . . . It is difficult to imagine a more intolerable and inappropriate interference by the judiciary with the independent legislatures of the States. . . . [The Court] says only that 'legislators represent people, not trees or acres,'. . . . But it is surely equally obvious . . . that legislators can represent their electors only by speaking for their interests—economic, social, political—many of which do reflect the place where the electors live. . . . These decisions also cut deeply into the fabric of our federalism."

—Justice John Marshall Harlan dissenting in *Reynolds* v. *Sims*

DBQ Document-Based Questions

1. **Summarizing** What is the main idea of the majority decision in *Reynolds* v. *Sims*?
2. **Explaining** Why does Justice Harlan disagree with the majority in *Reynolds* v. *Sims*?
3. **Making Inferences** How do you think reapportionment according to "one person, one vote" changed state politics?

SUPREME COURT CASES

Analyzing Supreme Court Cases

Does Each Vote Really Count?

Teach

More About the Case The notion of "one person, one vote" had already been articulated in the 1963 case *Gray* v. *Sanders* and extended to the legislative and congressional districts in *Wesberry* v. *Sanders* the following year. Over the next decade, the nation's political map was redrawn in response to the many lawsuits subsequently filed on behalf of urban residents.

DBQ Document Based Questions

Answers:

1. uneven electoral districts violated the equal protection clause.
2. He believes it is a state, not a federal, issue.
3. Students may suggest that urban dwellers gained more influence.

Differentiated Instruction

Leveled Activities

BL **Reinforcing Skills Activity, URB p. 31**

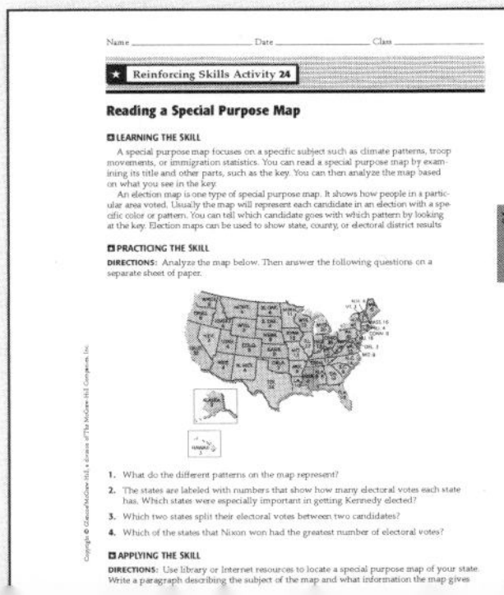

Reinforcing Skills Activity 24

Reading a Special Purpose Map

OL **Reading Skills Activity, URB p. 21**

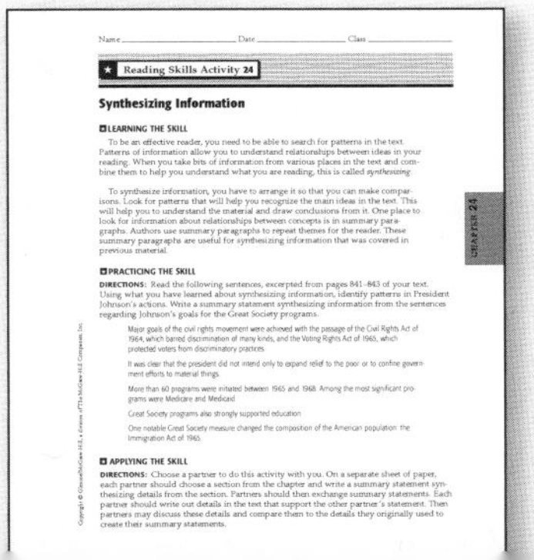

Reading Skills Activity 24

Synthesizing Information

AL **Linking Past and Present Activity, URB p. 34**

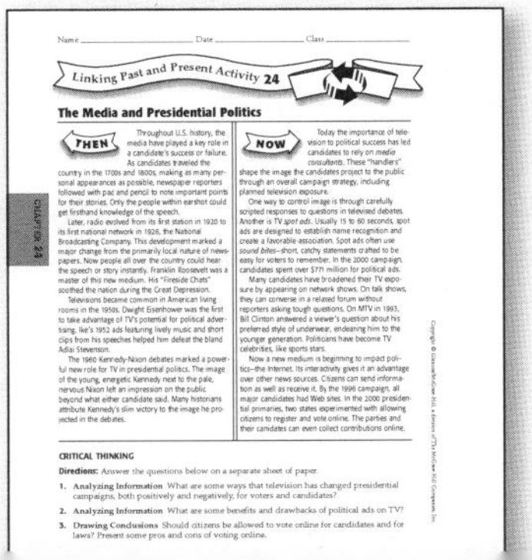

Linking Past and Present Activity 24

The Media and Presidential Politics

ELL **English Learner Activity, URB p. 25**

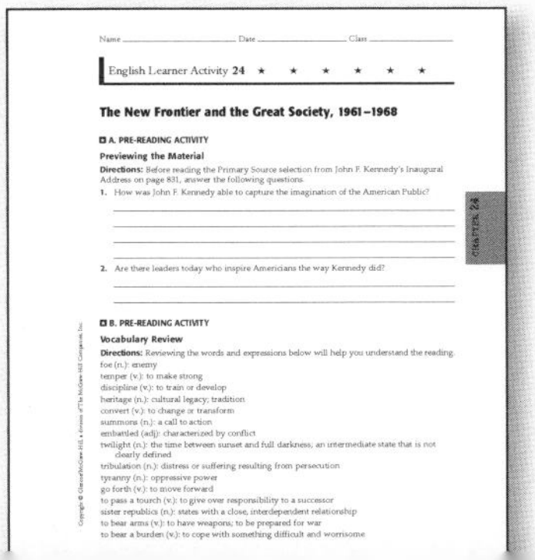

English Learner Activity 24

The New Frontier and the Great Society, 1961–1968

W Writing Support

Expository Writing Ask students to investigate the 2002 Texas redistricting case that went to the Supreme Court and the aftermath of the decision. Have them summarize their findings in a short essay agreeing or disagreeing with the Court's ruling. **AL**

Analyzing VISUALS

Answers:

1. *Brown* v. *Board of Education* made segregation of public schools unconstitutional, requiring they be desegregated. *Reynolds* v. *Sims* led to a major restructuring of legislative voting districts.
2. civil rights, due process, and freedom of speech and religion

Warren Court Reforms

MAIN Idea Under Chief Justice Earl Warren, the Supreme Court issued a number of decisions that altered the voting system, expanded due process, and reinterpreted aspects of the First Amendment.

HISTORY AND YOU Do you ever watch cop shows in which police officers read suspects their "Miranda rights"? Read on to learn about the origin of this process.

For further information on the Supreme Court cases referenced on this page, see pages R58–R61 in **Supreme Court Case Summaries.**

In 1953 President Eisenhower nominated **Earl Warren,** governor of California, to be Chief Justice of the United States. Under Warren's leadership, the Supreme Court issued several rulings that dramatically reshaped American politics and society.

"One Man, One Vote"

W Some of the Warren Court's more notable decisions concerned **reapportionment,** or the way in which states draw up political districts based on changes in population. By 1960, many more Americans resided in cities and suburbs than in rural areas. Yet many states had failed to change their electoral districts to reflect that population shift.

In Tennessee, for example, a rural county with only 2,340 voters had one representative in the state assembly, while an urban county with 133 times more voters had only seven. Thus, rural voters had far more political influence than urban voters. Some Tennessee voters took the matter to court and their case wound up in the Supreme Court. In *Baker* v. *Carr* (1962), the Court ruled that the federal courts had jurisdiction to hear lawsuits seeking to force states to redraw electoral districts.

The Supreme Court subsequently ruled, in *Reynolds* v. *Sims* (1964), that the current apportionment system in most states was unconstitutional. The Warren Court required states to reapportion electoral districts along the principle of "one man, one vote," so that all citizens' votes would have equal weight. The decision was a momentous one, for it shifted political

What Were the Major Decisions of the Warren Court?

Civil Rights	
Brown v. Board of Education (1954)	Declared segregation in public schools unconstitutional
Baker v. Carr (1962)	Established that federal courts can hear lawsuits seeking to force state authorities to redraw electoral districts
Reynolds v. Sims (1964)	Mandated that state legislative districts be approximately equal in population
Heart of Atlanta Motel v. United States (1964)	Upheld the Civil Rights Act of 1964 provision requiring desegregation of public accommodations
Loving v. Virginia (1967)	Forbade state bans on interracial marriage
Due Process	
Mapp v. Ohio (1961)	Ruled that unlawfully seized evidence cannot be used in a trial
Gideon v. Wainwright (1963)	Established suspects' right to a court-appointed attorney if suspects were unable to afford one
Escobedo v. Illinois (1964)	Affirmed right of the accused to an attorney during police questioning
Miranda v. Arizona (1966)	Required police to inform suspects of their rights during the arrest process
Freedom of Speech and Religion	
Engel v. Vitale (1962)	Banned state-mandated prayer in public schools
Abington School District v. Schempp (1963)	Banned state-mandated Bible reading in public schools
New York Times v. Sullivan (1964)	Restricted circumstances in which celebrities could sue the media

Analyzing VISUALS

1. **Interpreting** How did *Brown* v. *Board of Education* and *Reynolds* v. *Sims* affect the nation?
2. **Summarizing** What three major policy areas did the Warren Court's decisions affect?

Additional Support

Activity: Interdisciplinary Connection

Civics Tell students that Eleanor Roosevelt remained politically active following her husband's death. During the 1960 campaign, she appeared in a television commercial supporting John Kennedy for president. Her appearance signaled to women and traditional Democrats that Kennedy should be elected. Invite a civics teacher to class to discuss with students the pitfalls of such "celebrity" endorsements and their effect on recent elections. **OL**

power from rural and often conservative areas to urban areas, where more liberal voters resided. The Court's decision also boosted the political power of African Americans and Hispanics, who often lived in cities.

Extending Due Process

In a series of rulings, the Supreme Court began to use the Fourteenth Amendment to apply the Bill of Rights to the states. Originally, the Bill of Rights applied only to the federal government. Many states had their own bills of rights, but some federal rights did not exist at the state level. The Fourteenth Amendment states that "no state shall . . . deprive any person of life, liberty, or property without due process of law." **Due process** means that the law may not treat individuals unfairly, **arbitrarily,** or unreasonably, and that courts must follow proper procedures when trying cases. Due process is meant to ensure that all people are treated the same by the legal system. The Court ruled in several cases that due process meant applying the federal bill of rights to the states. R

In 1961 the Supreme Court ruled in *Mapp* v. *Ohio* that state courts could not consider evidence obtained in violation of the federal Constitution. In *Gideon* v. *Wainwright* (1963), the Court ruled that a defendant in a state court had the right to a lawyer, regardless of his or her ability to pay. The following year, in *Escobedo* v. *Illinois*, the justices ruled that suspects must be allowed access to a lawyer and must be informed of their right to remain silent before being questioned by the police. *Miranda* v. *Arizona* (1966) went even further, requiring that authorities immediately inform suspects that they have the right to remain silent; that anything they say can and will be used against them in court; that they have a right to a lawyer; and that, if they cannot afford a lawyer, the court will appoint one for them. Today these warnings are known as the Miranda rights.

Prayer and Privacy

The Supreme Court also handed down decisions that reaffirmed the separation of church and state. The Court applied the First Amendment to the states in *Engel* v. *Vitale* (1962). In this ruling, the Court decided that states could not compose official prayers and require those prayers to be recited in public schools. The following year, in *Abington School District* v. *Schempp*, it ruled against state-mandated Bible readings in public schools. Weighing in on another issue, the Court ruled in *Griswold* v. *Connecticut* (1965) that prohibiting the sale and use of birth-control devices violated citizens' constitutional right to privacy.

As with most rulings of the Warren Court, these decisions delighted some and deeply disturbed others. What most people did agree upon, however, was the Court's pivotal role in shaping national policy. The Warren Court, wrote *New York Times* columnist Anthony Lewis, "has brought about more social change than most Congresses and most Presidents."

Reading Check **Examining** What was the significance of the "One Man, One Vote" ruling?

Section 1 REVIEW

Vocabulary

1. **Explain** the significance of: missile gap, New Frontier, Earl Warren, reapportionment, due process.

Main Ideas

2. **Interpreting** In what ways was the 1960 presidential election a turning point in political campaign history?
3. **Summarizing** What progress was made for women's rights during Kennedy's administration?
4. **Describing** Name three decisions of the Warren Court and explain how each protected civil rights.

Critical Thinking

5. **Big Ideas** What were some successes and failures of Kennedy's New Frontier? How did the new programs change the lives of Americans?
6. **Organizing** Use a graphic organizer similar to the one below to list the economic policies of the Kennedy administration.

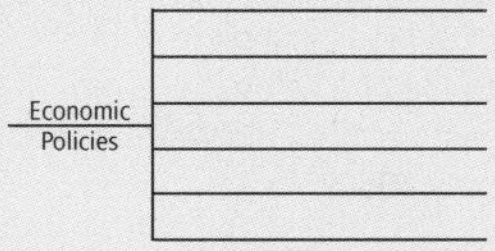

7. **Analyzing Visuals** Look at the election map on page 825. Which states split their electoral votes?

Writing About History

8. **Expository Writing** In his Inaugural Address, President Kennedy asked his fellow Americans to "ask what you can do for your country." Respond to this statement in an essay.

History ONLINE
Study Central™ To review this section, go to glencoe.com and click on Study Central.

829

R Reading Strategy

Using Word Parts Point out to students the academic vocabulary term *arbitrarily*. Ask them to identify the root word (*arbitrary*) and to note the change in spelling when a suffix is added. EL

Reading Check

Answer:
All citizens' votes would have equal weight regardless of where they lived.

Assess

History ONLINE

Study Central™ provides summaries, interactive games, and online graphic organizers to help students review content.

Close

Summarizing Ask: How was Kennedy's term truly a New Frontier? *(Students may suggest space exploration, court-mandated reforms, and new opportunities for women and people with developmental disabilities.)*

Section 1 REVIEW

Answers

1. All definitions can be found in the section and the Glossary.
2. Television played a more influential role.
3. Presidential Commission on the Status of Women, ending gender discrimination in federal civil service, and the Equal Pay Act
4. Answers should include any of the civil rights decisions listed on page 828 and include explanations of how each influenced civil rights.
5. successes: federal action against gender discrimination, assistance to people with disabilities, development in lower income areas, and raising the minimum wage; failures: no increase in federal aid for education or to senior citizens; changes: more money for cost of living, educational and work opportunities for people with disabilities, and better housing for lower-income families
6. answers may include: a cut in tax rates, an increase in funds for defense and space exploration, an increase in the minimum wage, housing and redevelopment
7. Oklahoma and Alabama
8. Students' essays will vary but should focus on the meaning of Kennedy's statement.

Focus

Bellringer

Daily Focus Transparency 24-2

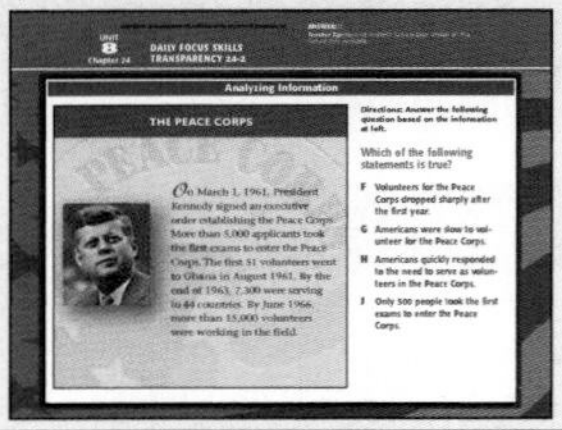

Guide to Reading

Answers may include:
January 1959: Castro's overthrow of Batista; April 17, 1961: Bay of Pigs; June 1961: Kennedy and Khrushchev meet in Vienna; October 1962: Cuban missile crisis; October 1962: Soviets agree to remove missiles from Cuba; November 1963: Kennedy assassinated

Section Spotlight Video

To generate student interest and provide a springboard for class discussion, access the Chapter 24, Section 2 video at glencoe.com or on the video DVD

Resource Manager

Section 2

Section Audio · Spotlight Video

JFK and the Cold War

Guide to Reading

Big Ideas

Economics and Society The Kennedy administration used foreign aid to improve relations with Latin American countries and lessen the appeal of left-wing movements.

Content Vocabulary
- flexible response *(p. 830)*
- space race *(p. 832)*

Academic Vocabulary
- conventional *(p. 830)*
- institute *(p. 833)*
- remove *(p. 835)*

People and Events to Identify
- Peace Corps *(p. 832)*
- Berlin Wall *(p. 834)*
- Warren Commission *(p. 835)*

Reading Strategy

Sequencing As you read about the crises of the Cold War, complete a time line similar to the one below to record the major events of the Cold War in the 1950s and early 1960s.

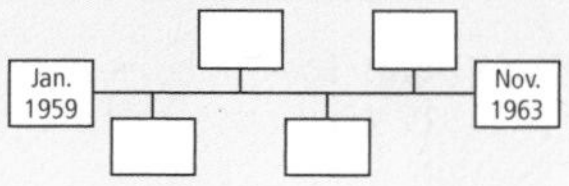

During the Kennedy Administration, ongoing tensions with the Soviet Union led to crises over Cuba and West Berlin. To contain communism and stay ahead of the Soviet Union in technology, President Kennedy created aid programs for developing nations and expanded the space program.

Containing Communism

MAIN Idea President Kennedy developed new programs to combat the spread of communism.

HISTORY AND YOU Would you consider joining the Peace Corps and serving in a foreign country? Read on to learn about Kennedy's diplomatic efforts in Latin America.

When John F. Kennedy entered the White House, he had to devote much of his time to foreign policy. The Cold War with the Soviet Union dominated all other concerns at the time, and Kennedy attempted to stop the spread of communism with a range of programs. These included a **conventional** weaponry program to give the nation's military more flexibility, a program to provide economic aid to Latin America, and the creation of the Peace Corps to help developing nations worldwide.

A More Flexible Response

Kennedy took office at a time of growing global instability. Nationalism was exploding throughout the developing world, and the Soviet Union actively supported "wars of national liberation."

Kennedy felt that Eisenhower had relied too heavily on nuclear weapons, which could be used only in extreme situations. To allow for a "**flexible response**" if nations needed help resisting Communist movements, the president pushed for a buildup of troops and conventional weapons. Kennedy also expanded the Special Forces, an elite army unit created in the 1950s to wage guerrilla warfare in limited conflicts, and allowed the soldiers to wear their distinctive "Green Beret" headgear.

Aid to Other Countries

Kennedy wanted to renew diplomatic focus on Latin America. Conditions in many Latin American societies were not good: Governments were often in the hands of the wealthy few and many

R Reading Strategies	C Critical Thinking	D Differentiated Instruction	W Writing Support	S Skill Practice
Teacher Edition • Act. Prior Know., p. 834 **Additional Resources** • Prim. Source Read., URB p. 35 • Guid. Read. Act., URB p. 49 • Enrichment Act., URB p. 45	**Teacher Edition** • Making Inferences, p. 833 **Additional Resources** • Quizzes and Tests, p. 348 • Interpret. Pol. Cartoons Act., URB p. 41	**Teacher Edition** • Advanced Learners, p. 832	**Teacher Edition** • Narrative Writing, p. 833	**Teacher Edition** • Visual Literacy, p. 831 • Using Geo. Skills, p. 834 **Additional Resources** • Hist. Analysis Skill, URB p. 22 • Read. Essen., p. 271 • Time Line Act., URB p. 33

PRIMARY SOURCE
John F. Kennedy's Inaugural Address

S

▲ *John F. Kennedy delivers his inaugural speech, January 20, 1961. He spoke of the obligation of his generation to defend liberty. To his right is incoming Vice President Lyndon Johnson.*

PRIMARY SOURCE

"Let the word go forth from this time and place, to friend and foe alike, that the torch has been passed to a new generation of Americans—born in this century, tempered by war, disciplined by a hard and bitter peace, proud of our ancient heritage—and unwilling to witness or permit the slow undoing of those human rights to which this Nation has always been committed. . . . Let every nation know, whether it wishes us well or ill, that we shall pay any price, bear any burden, meet any hardship, support any friend, oppose any foe, in order to assure the survival and the success of liberty. . . .

To those old allies whose cultural and spiritual origins we share, we pledge the loyalty of faithful friends. . . . To those peoples in the huts and villages across the globe struggling to break the bonds of mass misery, we pledge our best efforts to help them help themselves . . . To our sister republics south of our border, we offer a special pledge—to convert our good words into good deeds—in a new alliance for progress—to assist free men and free governments in casting off the chains of poverty. . . .

Now the trumpet summons us again—not as a call to bear arms, though arms we need; not as a call to battle, though embattled we are—but a call to bear the burden of a long twilight struggle, year in and year out, "rejoicing in hope, patient in tribulation"—a struggle against the common enemies of man: tyranny, poverty, disease, and war itself. . . .

And so, my fellow Americans: ask not what your country can do for you—ask what you can do for your country. My fellow citizens of the world: ask not what America will do for you, but what together we can do for the freedom of man."

—Inaugural Address delivered January 20, 1961

DBQ Document-Based Questions

1. **Expressing** What commitment does Kennedy make with respect to human rights?
2. **Classifying** To what three specific groups does Kennedy promise aid, and what aid is promised?
3. **Finding the Main Idea** What does Kennedy indicate are the common enemies of humankind?

of their citizens lived in extreme poverty. In some countries, these conditions spurred the growth of left-wing movements aimed at overthrowing their governments.

When the United States became involved in Latin America, it usually did so to help existing governments stay in power and to prevent Communist movements from flourishing. Poor Latin Americans resented this intrusion, just as they resented American corporations, whose presence was seen as a kind of imperialism.

The Alliance for Progress To improve relations between the United States and Latin America, Kennedy proposed an Alliance for Progress, a series of cooperative aid projects with Latin American governments. The alliance was designed to create a "free and prosperous Latin America" that would be more stable and less likely to support Communist-inspired revolutions.

Over a 10-year period, the United States pledged $20 billion to help Latin American countries establish better schools, housing, health care, and fairer land distribution. The results were mixed. In some countries—notably Chile, Colombia, Venezuela, and the Central American republics—the alliance did promote real reform. In others, local rulers used the money to keep themselves in power.

Teach

S Skill Practice

Visual Literacy

Ask students to look carefully at the photograph of Kennedy giving his Inaugural Address

Ask: How do Kennedy and Johnson differ from the other men in the photograph? *(They are not wearing hats.)* Tell students that this difference in style led to a decline in men wearing hats.

DBQ Document Based Questions

Answers:

1. He is not willing to see or allow the slow undoing of human rights.
2. to old allies: the loyalty of faithful friends; to peoples struggling to break free of misery: our best efforts to help them help themselves; to republics south of our border; to help cast off the chains of poverty
3. tyranny, poverty, disease, and war

Hands-On Chapter Project
Step 2

What Is a Great Society?

Step 2: Motivational Speeches Students will research memorable speeches made by leaders, writers, and citizens that relate to the building of a great society.

Directions Have students conduct newspaper, library, or Internet research to find speeches made by people throughout history. Speeches may be historical or current. Students may research speeches made by Americans or other citizens of the world.

Encourage students to find a speech that is aimed at the building of an improved or just society. Students should find speeches that are inspirational to them.

Analyzing Primary Sources Students will select the parts of the speech that are most relevant and inspirational to share with the rest of the class, either as oral presentations or in typed papers. OL

(Project continued on page 839)

D Differentiated Instruction

Advanced Learners Ask students to investigate the controversies surrounding violence against Peace Corps volunteers. Have them present their findings. **AL**

Did You Know?

By the mid-1960s, NASA (National Aeronautics and Space Administration) had about 400,000 people in space programs, with 35,000 focused on the Apollo mission of getting a man to the Moon. Between 1969 and 1972, twelve astronauts walked on the Moon, collected rock samples, set up experiments, and took photographs.

Reading Check

Answer:
the spread of communism, Latin American relations, reducing the threat of nuclear war, and winning the space race

Additional Support

The Peace Corps Another program aimed at helping less-developed nations fight poverty was the **Peace Corps,** an organization that sent Americans to provide humanitarian services in less-developed nations.

D After rigorous training, volunteers spent two years in countries that requested assistance. They laid out sewage systems in Bolivia and trained medical technicians in Chad. Others taught English or helped to build roads. Today, the Peace Corps is still active and remains one of Kennedy's most enduring legacies.

The Cold War in Space

In 1961 Yuri Gagarin (YHOO•ree gah•GAHR•ihn), a Soviet astronaut, became the first person to orbit Earth. Again, as in 1957 when they launched *Sputnik,* the first satellite, the Soviets had beaten the United States in the **space race.** President Kennedy worried about the impact of the flight on the Cold War. Soviet successes in space might convince the world that communism was better than capitalism.

Less than six weeks after the Soviet flight, the president went before Congress and declared: "I believe this nation should commit itself to achieving the goal, before this decade is out, of landing a man on the moon."

Kennedy's speech set in motion a massive effort to develop the necessary technology. In 1962 John Glenn became the first American to orbit Earth. Three years later, the United States sent three men into orbit in a capsule called *Apollo. Apollo* was launched using the Saturn V, the most powerful rocket ever built. The Saturn V was able to give both *Apollo* and the lunar module—which astronauts would use to land on the moon—enough velocity to reach the moon.

On July 16, 1969, a Saturn V lifted off in Florida, carrying three American astronauts: Neil Armstrong, Edwin "Buzz" Aldrin, and Michael Collins. On July 20 Armstrong and Aldrin boarded the lunar module, named *Eagle,* and headed down to the moon. Minutes later, Armstrong radioed NASA's flight center in Texas: "Houston . . . the *Eagle* has landed."

Armstrong became the first human being to walk on the moon. As he set foot on the lunar surface, he announced: "That's one small step for a man, one giant leap for mankind." The United States had won the space race and decisively demonstrated its technological superiority over the Soviet Union.

Reading Check **Examining** What global challenges did Kennedy face during his presidency?

TECHNOLOGY & HISTORY

Space Technology Cold War tensions between the United States and the Soviet Union fueled the space race. Both countries vied for superiority in aeronautical technology and dominance in space exploration.

▲ American astronaut John Glenn is loaded into his space capsule, named *Friendship 7*, on February 20, 1962, shortly before being launched into orbit.

▲ John Glenn in orbit around Earth

◀ NASA recruited seven astronauts for its first manned space program. Each astronaut would ride in a *Mercury* capsule atop an ICBM reconfigured to lift them into space. The first American astronaut to ride into space in the capsule was Alan Shepard. The first American to orbit Earth was John Glenn.

Activity: Collaborative Learning

Investigating Peace Corps Projects Organize the class into three groups, assigning each group one of the following regions: Africa, Asia, or Latin America. Have each group use library or Internet resources to research and prepare a visual report using charts and maps on the current work of the Peace Corps in their assigned region. Suggest that groups provide both an overview of the work and an in-depth look at one project of special interest. Have groups share their completed reports with the class. **OL**

Crises of the Cold War

MAIN Idea President Kennedy faced foreign policy crises in Cuba and Berlin.

HISTORY AND YOU Do you think the embargo against Cuba should be lifted? Read on to learn about the crises President Kennedy faced over Cuba.

President Kennedy's efforts to combat Communist influence in other countries led to some of the most intense crises of the Cold War. At times these crises left Americans and people in many other nations wondering whether the world would survive.

The Bay of Pigs

The first crisis occurred in Cuba, only 90 miles (145 km) from American shores. There, Fidel Castro had overthrown the corrupt Cuban dictator Fulgencio Batista in 1959. Almost immediately, Castro established ties with the Soviet Union, **instituted** drastic land reforms, and seized foreign-owned businesses, many of which were American. Cuba's alliance with the Soviets worried many Americans. The Communists were now too close for comfort, and Soviet premier Nikita Khrushchev was also expressing his intent to strengthen Cuba militarily.

Fearing that the Soviets would use Cuba as a base from which to spread revolution throughout the Western Hemisphere, President Eisenhower had authorized the CIA to secretly train and arm a group of Cuban exiles, known as *La Brigada,* to invade the island. The invasion was intended to set off a popular uprising against Castro.

When Kennedy became president, his advisers approved the plan. In office less than three months and trusting his experts, Kennedy agreed to the operation with some changes. On April 17, 1961, some 1,400 armed Cuban exiles landed at the Bay of Pigs on the south coast of Cuba. The invasion was a disaster. *La Brigada*'s boats ran aground on coral reefs; Kennedy canceled their air support to keep the United States' involvement a secret; and the expected popular uprising never happened. Within two days, Castro's forces killed or captured almost all the members of *La Brigada.* C W

The Bay of Pigs was a dark moment for the Kennedy administration. The action exposed an American plot to overthrow a neighbor's government, and the outcome made the United States look weak and disorganized.

◀ Apollo capsule carried three astronauts.

▲ To reach the Moon, NASA developed the giant Saturn V rocket, which lifted a three-person capsule, called *Apollo,* and a landing craft, called the Lunar Module, into space. Once *Apollo* and the Lunar Module entered orbit around the Moon, the Lunar Module carried two astronauts from the Apollo capsule down to the Moon's surface.

▲ Neil Armstrong was the first person to walk on the Moon.

▲ Buzz Aldrin descended to the Moon's surface, July 20, 1969, becoming the second man to walk on the Moon.

Analyzing VISUALS

1. **Calculating** What analysis can you make about the size of the space capsules and modules used in space?
2. **Describing** How does the Moon's surface appear in these photos?
3. **Identifying** What was the purpose of the Lunar Module?

C Critical Thinking

Making Inferences Draw students' attention to the second paragraph of the second column, which alludes to Kennedy's inexperience and his trust of his advisors. Ask students to infer what the text is suggesting in this sentence. *(Students may say that if Kennedy had had more experience or less trust in his experts, the invasion might not have failed.)* **OL**

W Writing Support

Narrative Writing Invite students to imagine an alternative ending to the Bay of Pigs invasion, in which the uprising succeeded as planned. Have them write this alternative ending, considering the effect it would have on U.S.–Latin American relations **AL**

Analyzing VISUALS

Answers:

1. lots of extra space for fuel
2. gray, barren
3. to carry crew members from the space capsule to the Moon's surface

Additional Support

Activity: Interdisciplinary Connection

Science Organize students into small groups and explain that they will investigate the practical outcomes of the U.S. space program. Ask students to use library or Internet resources to find out how the work of the space program has affected everyday life for all Americans. Suggest that each group select an area such as medicine, robotics, or safety devices on which to focus. Have groups present their findings to the class. **OL**

R Reading Strategy

Activating Prior Knowledge
Ask students to recall the division of Germany following World War II as well as the subsequent merging of Allied zones. **OL**

S Skill Practice

Using Geography Skills
Direct students' attention to the map of Cuba and the site of the Bay of Pigs invasion. **Ask:** Why do you think that site was chosen? *(Students may say it was far from Havana and that the CIA hoped the rebels could land unnoticed. Also, there was probably a good harbor there.)* **BL**

Analyzing GEOGRAPHY

Answers:
1. Havana
2. about 250 miles
3. a bay southeast of Havana

NATIONAL GEOGRAPHIC **The Cuban Missile Crisis, October 1962**

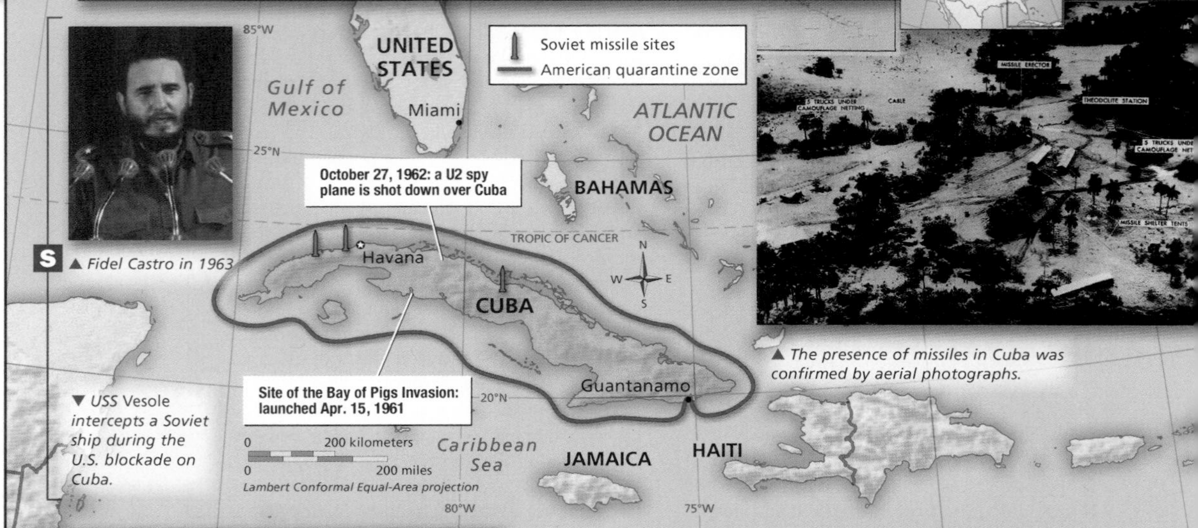

▲ Fidel Castro in 1963

▲ The presence of missiles in Cuba was confirmed by aerial photographs.

▼ USS Vesole intercepts a Soviet ship during the U.S. blockade on Cuba.

Analyzing GEOGRAPHY

1. **Location** Near what major Cuban city are the missiles placed?
2. **Regions** What is the distance from those missiles to Miami?
3. **Place** Where in Cuba did the Bay of Pigs invasion begin?

Maps in Motion See *StudentWorks™ Plus* or glencoe.com.

The Berlin Wall Goes Up

Kennedy faced another foreign policy challenge beginning in June 1961, when he met with Soviet Premier Nikita Khrushchev in Vienna, Austria. Khrushchev wanted to stop the flood of Germans pouring out of Communist East Germany into West Berlin. **R** He demanded that the Western powers recognize East Germany and that the United States, Great Britain, and France withdraw from Berlin, a city lying completely within East Germany. Kennedy refused and reaffirmed the West's commitment to West Berlin.

Khrushchev retaliated by building a wall through Berlin, blocking movement between the Soviet sector and the rest of the city. Guards posted along the wall shot at many of those attempting to escape from the East. For nearly 30 years afterward, the **Berlin Wall** stood as a visible symbol of Cold War divisions.

The Cuban Missile Crisis

By far the most terrifying crisis of the Kennedy era occurred the next year. During the summer of 1962, American intelligence agencies learned that Soviet technicians and equipment had arrived in Cuba and that military construction was in progress. On October 22, President Kennedy announced on television that American spy planes had taken aerial photographs showing that the Soviet Union had placed long-range missiles in Cuba. Enemy missiles stationed so close to the United States posed a dangerous threat.

Kennedy ordered a naval blockade to stop the delivery of more missiles, demanded the existing missile sites be dismantled, and warned that if attacked, the United States would respond fully against the Soviet Union. Still, work on the missile sites continued. Nuclear holocaust seemed imminent.

Differentiated Instruction

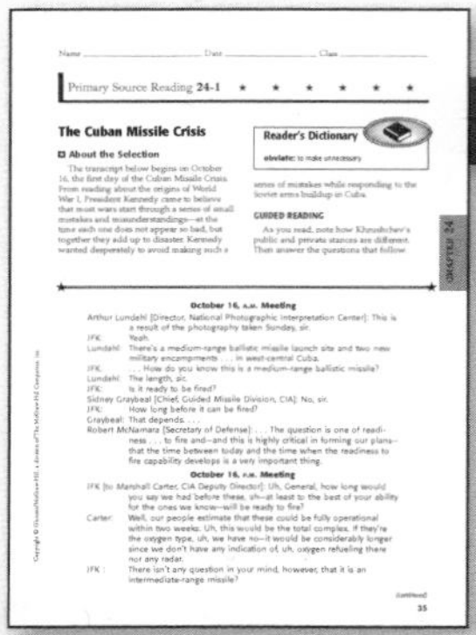
Primary Source Reading, URB p. 35

Reading Primary Sources: The Cuban Missile Crisis

Objective: Read primary sources to understand key events in history.
Focus: Identify the main issue of the transcript.
Teach: Explain the background of the Cuban missile crisis.
Assess: Discuss Kennedy's reaction to the discovery of missiles in Cuba.
Close: Summarize the transcript.

Differentiated Instruction Activities

- **BL** Create a time line sequencing the information Kennedy received.
- **AL** Find out more about the communications between Kennedy and Khrushchev. How are their negotiation strategies similar or different?
- **ELL** Create a list of unfamiliar words, and define the words using a dictionary.

Then, after a flurry of secret negotiations, the Soviet Union offered a deal. It would **remove** the missiles if the United States promised not to invade Cuba and to remove its missiles from Turkey near the Soviet border. The reality was that neither Kennedy nor Khrushchev wanted nuclear war. "Only lunatics . . . who themselves want to perish and before they die destroy the world, could do this," wrote the Soviet leader. On October 28, the leaders reached an agreement. Kennedy publicly agreed not to invade Cuba and privately agreed to remove the Turkish missiles; the Soviets agreed to remove their missiles from Cuba. The world could breathe again.

The Cuban missile crisis forced the United States and the Soviet Union to consider the consequences of nuclear war. In August 1963, the two countries concluded years of negotiation by agreeing to a treaty that banned testing nuclear weapons in the atmosphere.

In the long run, however, the missile crisis had ominous consequences. The humiliating retreat the United States forced on the Soviet leadership undermined the position of Nikita Khrushchev and contributed to his fall from power a year later. The crisis also exposed the Soviets' military inferiority and prompted a dramatic Soviet arms buildup over the next two decades. This buildup contributed to a comparable military increase in the United States in the early 1980s.

Death of a President

Soon after the Senate ratified the test ban treaty, John F. Kennedy's presidency ended shockingly and tragically. On November 22, 1963, Kennedy and his wife traveled to Texas. As the presidential motorcade rode slowly through the crowded streets of Dallas, gunfire rang out. Someone had shot the president twice—once in the throat and once in the head. Horrified government officials sped Kennedy to a nearby hospital, where he was pronounced dead moments later.

Lee Harvey Oswald, the man accused of killing Kennedy, appeared to be a confused and embittered Marxist who had spent time in the Soviet Union. He himself was shot to death while in police custody two days after the assassination. The bizarre situation led some to speculate that the second gunman, local nightclub owner Jack Ruby, killed Oswald to protect others involved in the crime. In 1964 a national commission headed by Chief Justice Warren concluded that Oswald was the lone assassin. The report of the **Warren Commission** left some questions unanswered, and theories about a conspiracy to kill the president have persisted, though none has gained wide acceptance.

In the wake of the assassination, the United States and much of the world went into mourning. Thousands traveled to Washington, D.C., and waited in a line several miles long outside the Capitol to walk silently past the president's flag-draped casket.

Kennedy was president for little more than 1,000 days. Yet he made a profound impression on most Americans. Kennedy's successor, Vice President Lyndon Baines Johnson, set out to promote many of the programs that Kennedy left unfinished.

Reading Check **Summarizing** How was the Cuban missile crisis resolved?

Section 2 REVIEW

Vocabulary

1. **Explain** the significance of: flexible response, Peace Corps, space race, Berlin Wall, Warren Commission.

Main Ideas

2. **Explaining** What were the goals of the Alliance for Progress?

3. **Discussing** How did Kennedy and Khrushchev reach an agreement to end the Cuban missile crisis? What were the details of this agreement?

Critical Thinking

4. **Big Ideas** What was the role of foreign aid in relations between the United States and Latin America?

5. **Organizing** Use a graphic organizer similar to the one below to list the programs that Kennedy used to reduce the threat of nuclear war and to try to stem communism.

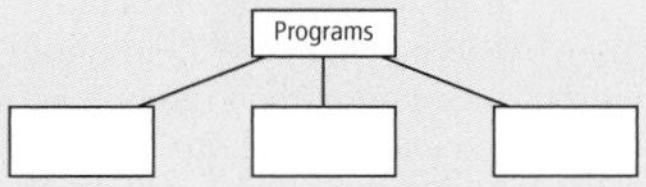

6. **Analyzing Visuals** Look at the photograph of John Glenn on page 832. What is the name of his craft, and why do you think the name might have been chosen?

Writing About History

7. **Descriptive Writing** Assume the role of an American citizen during the Cuban missile crisis. Write a journal entry describing the mood of the country during that time.

History ONLINE
Study Central™ To review this section, go to glencoe.com and click on Study Central.

Assess

History ONLINE

Study Central™ provides summaries, interactive games, and online graphic organizers to help students review content.

Close

Summarizing Ask: What difference do you think it might have made if Kennedy had been able to complete a term in office? *(Students may suggest that some of his goals would have been accomplished over time and that he would have found a way to work effectively with Congress and other world leaders.)*

Reading Check

Answer:
Through negotiations, the Soviet Union agreed to remove the missiles, and Kennedy agreed not to invade Cuba and to remove missiles from Turkey.

Section 2 REVIEW

Answers

1. All definitions can be found in the section and the Glossary.
2. The goals were to create cooperative aid projects that helped establish better schools, improve housing, distribute land more equitably, and improve health care in Latin America.
3. They communicated through secret negotiations. The Soviets would remove the missiles from Cuba, while Kennedy promised publicly not to invade Cuba and privately to remove missiles from Turkey.
4. to help governments stay in power and prevent communist revolutions
5. conventional weaponry program, aid to foreign governments, the Peace Corps
6. The craft is called the *Friendship 7*. It may signal a desire to indicate coming in peace.
7. Journal entries will vary but should focus on emotions.

Focus

Introducing TIME Notebook

Inform students that in this speech, given six months after Kennedy's assassination, LBJ set forth his domestic agenda. **Ask:** Why was this speech important to the new president and to the nation? *(Students may suggest that the speech gives hope after the sadness of Kennedy's death and calls on people to do their part toward making a new, richer life.)* Ask students to identify particular phrases they find inspiring. Then **Ask:** What political ideals have recent leaders held out to the nation? How do they compare with Johnson's ideas?

Teach

D Differentiated Instruction

Auditory/Musical Invite interested students to locate recordings of the great hits by the groups listed and to play them for the class. Ask students to compare and contrast the music and lyrics with current hit songs. BL

Additional Support

TIME NOTEBOOK

BETTMANN/CORBIS

On May 22, 1964, **PRESIDENT LYNDON JOHNSON** *delivered a speech in Ann Arbor, Michigan, outlining his domestic agenda that would become known as "The Great Society." Speechwriter and policy adviser Richard Goodwin watched the speech on videotape the next morning back in Washington. He recalls his reaction:*

Then, with the cheers, at first muted as if the audience were surprised at their own response, then mounting toward unrestrained, accepting delight, Johnson concluded: "There are those timid souls who say . . . we are condemned to a soulless wealth. I do not agree. We have the power to shape civilization. . . . But we need your will, your labor, your hearts. . . . So let us from this moment begin our work, so that in the future men will look back and say: It was then, after a long and weary way, that man turned the exploits of his genius to the full enrichment of his life."

Watching the film in the White House basement, almost involuntarily I added my applause to the tumultuous acclaim coming from the sound track. . . . I clapped for the President, and for our country.

WHAT IS A PIP, ANYWAY?

Match these rock 'n' roll headliners with their supporting acts.

D

1. Paul Revere and	**a.** the Union Gap
2. Martha and	**b.** the Supremes
3. Gary Puckett and	**c.** the Miracles
4. Gladys Knight and	**d.** the Vandellas
5. Smokey Robinson and	**e.** the Raiders
6. Diana Ross and	**f.** the Pips

answers: 1. e; 2. d; 3. a; 4. f; 5. c; 6. b

VERBATIM

"Is there any place we can catch them? What can we do? Are we working 24 hours a day? Can we go around the moon before them?"

PRESIDENT JOHN F. KENNEDY, *to Lyndon B. Johnson, after hearing that Soviet cosmonaut Yuri Gagarin had orbited the Earth, 1961*

"It was quite a day. I don't know what you can say about a day when you see four beautiful sunsets. . . . This is a little unusual, I think."

COLONEL JOHN GLENN, *in orbit, 1962*

"There are tens of millions of Americans who are beyond the welfare state. Taken as a whole there is a culture of poverty . . . bad health, poor housing, low levels of aspiration and high levels of mental distress. Twenty percent of a nation, some 32,000,000."

MICHAEL HARRINGTON, The Culture of Poverty, *1962*

"I have a dream."

MARTIN LUTHER KING JR., *1963*

"I don't see an American dream; . . . I see an American nightmare . . . . Three hundred and ten years we worked in this country without a dime in return."

MALCOLM X, *1964*

"The Great Society rests on abundance and liberty for all. It demands an end to poverty and racial injustice."

LYNDON B. JOHNSON, *1964*

"In 1962, the starving residents of an isolated Indian village received 1 plow and 1,700 pounds of seeds. They ate the seeds."

PEACE CORPS AD, *1965*

Extending the Content

Lyndon Johnson's Rhetorical Skills LBJ came from a political family; his maternal grandfather was a Texas secretary of state and his father was a member of the Texas legislature. Lyndon was handing out pamphlets and attending political rallies by the time he was six. At ten, he accompanied his father to sessions of the legislature to watch the activity from the gallery. Teaching Mexican-American children in real poverty the year he dropped out of college to earn money, he honed their English skills with recitations, debates, and spelling bees. In college, working as a janitor, he made speeches and told stories to walls and doormats as he worked. One Senate Committee assistant recalled that Johnson "said the only power he had was the power to persuade. That's like saying the only wind we have is a hurricane."

Space Race

Want to capture some of the glamour and excitement of space exploration? Create a new nickname for your city. You won't be the first.

CITY	NICKNAME
Danbury, CT	Space Age City
Muscle Shoals, AL	Space Age City
Houston, TX	Space City, USA
Galveston, TX	Space Port, USA
Cape Kennedy, FL	Spaceport, USA
Blacksburg, VA	Space Age Community
Huntsville, AL	~~Rocket City, USA~~ ~~Space City, USA~~ ~~Space Capital of the Nation~~ Space Capital of the World

John Glenn, first American to orbit Earth

RALPH MORSE/TIMEPIX

Milestones

PERFORMED IN ENGLISH, 1962. THE CATHOLIC MASS, following Pope John XXIII's Second Vatican Council. "Vatican II" allows the Latin mass to be translated into local languages around the world.

ENROLLED, 1962. JAMES MEREDITH, at the University of Mississippi, following a Supreme Court ruling that ordered his admission to the previously segregated school. Rioting and a showdown with state officials who wished to bar his enrollment preceded Meredith's entrance to classes.

BROKEN, 1965. 25-DAY FAST BY CÉSAR CHÁVEZ, labor organizer. His protest convinced others to join his nonviolent strike against the grape growers; shoppers boycotted table grapes in sympathy.

STRIPPED, 1967. MUHAMMAD ALI, of his heavyweight champion title, after refusing induction into the army following a rejection of his application for conscientious objector status. The boxer was arrested, given a five-year sentence, and fined $10,000.

PICKETED, 1968. THE MISS AMERICA PAGEANT in Atlantic City, by protesters who believe the contest's emphasis on women's physical beauty is degrading and minimizes the importance of women's intellect. **C**

AP

NUMBERS

7% Percentage of African American adults registered to vote in Mississippi in 1964 before passage of the Voting Rights Act of 1965

67% Percentage of African American adults in Mississippi registered to vote in 1969

70% Percentage of white adults registered to vote in 1964, nationwide

90% Percentage of white adults registered to vote nationwide in 1969

57 Number of days senators filibustered to hold up passage of the Civil Rights Bill in 1964

14½ Hours duration of all-night speech delivered by Senator Robert Byrd before a cloture vote stopped the filibuster

72% Percentage of elementary and high school teachers who approved of corporal punishment as a disciplinary measure in 1961

$80–90 Weekly pay for a clerk/typist in New York in 1965

CRITICAL THINKING

1. ***Determining Cause and Effect*** Who did the Voting Rights Act of 1965 help more—whites or African Americans? Explain your answer.

2. ***Speculating*** Why do you think President Kennedy was eager to best the Soviets in space?

C Critical Thinking

Identifying Central Issues

The Miss America Pageant and other beauty contests continue to generate controversy. Ask students to debate the value of such competitions today. **OL**

Assess/Close

Visit the Time Web site at www.time.com for up-to-date news, weekly magazine articles, editorials, online polls, and an archive of past magazine and Web articles.

Critical Thinking Answers:

1. Students may suggest that it helped African Americans, since a larger percentage of them were registered to vote, or that it helped whites, because they were the majority, and a 20 percent increase in voter registration would be significant.
2. Students' responses will vary but may conclude that the United States was not used to thinking of itself as less than first in anything.

Additional Support

Activity: Collaborative Learning

Predicting Consequences Ask a volunteer to read the information about Muhammad Ali to the class. **Ask:** What effect do you think Ali's refusal to serve in the army had on others who claimed conscientious objector status? How might it have affected those already serving in the army? *(Ask students to share their responses in a class discussion.)*

Focus

Bellringer

Daily Focus Transparency 24-3

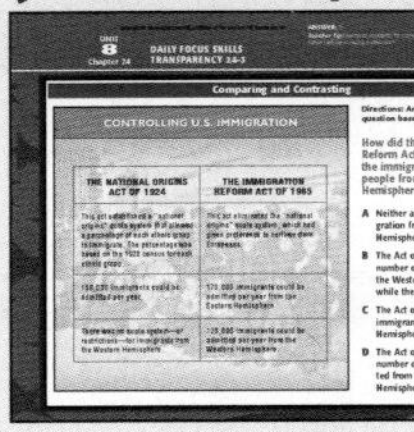

Guide to Reading

Answers:
programs include Higher Education Act, HUD, Job Corps, Medicaid, Medicare, and Project Head Start (see the chart on p. 842 for summary)

Section Spotlight Video

To generate student interest and provide a springboard for class discussion, access the Chapter 24, Section 3 video at glencoe.com or on the video DVD.

Section 3 — Section Audio — Spotlight Video

The Great Society

Guide to Reading

Big Ideas
Individual Action President Lyndon B. Johnson relied on his experience and persuasiveness to get civil rights and antipoverty bills enacted.

Content Vocabulary
- consensus *(p. 839)*

Academic Vocabulary
- confine *(p. 841)*
- subsidy *(p. 842)*

People and Events to Identify
- War on Poverty *(p. 839)*
- VISTA *(p. 840)*
- Barry Goldwater *(p. 840)*
- Great Society *(p. 841)*
- Medicare *(p. 841)*
- Medicaid *(p. 841)*
- Head Start *(p. 842)*
- Robert Weaver *(p. 842)*

Reading Strategy
Organizing As you read about Lyndon Johnson's presidency, complete a graphic organizer similar to the one below to list the social and economic programs started during his administration.

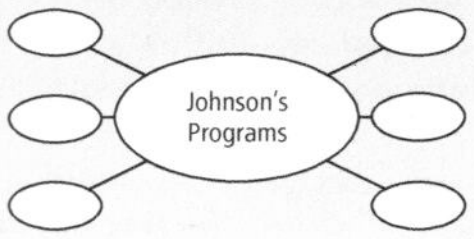

Lyndon B. Johnson had decades of experience in Congress and was skilled in getting legislation enacted. When he became president, he moved quickly to push for passage of a civil rights bill and antipoverty legislation.

Johnson Takes the Reins

MAIN Idea President Johnson's experience in Congress helped him push through a civil rights bill and new laws to fight poverty.

HISTORY AND YOU How do you think someone's early life affects his or her career choices? Read on to learn how Lyndon Johnson's early life prepared him for the presidency.

At 2:38 P.M. on November 22, 1963, just hours after President Kennedy had been pronounced dead, Lyndon B. Johnson stood in the cabin of *Air Force One*, the president's plane, with Kennedy's widow on one side of him and his wife, Claudia, known as "Lady Bird," on the other. Johnson raised his right hand, placed his left hand on a Bible, and took the oath of office.

Within days of the assassination, Johnson appeared before Congress and urged the nation to move forward and build on Kennedy's legacy: "The ideas and ideals which [Kennedy] so nobly represented must and will be translated into effective action," he declared. "John Kennedy's death commands what his life conveyed—that America must move forward."

The United States that President Lyndon B. Johnson inherited from John F. Kennedy appeared to be a booming, bustling place. Away from the nation's affluent suburbs, however, was another country, one inhabited by the poor, the ill-fed, the ill-housed, and the ill-educated. Writer Michael Harrington examined the nation's impoverished areas in his 1962 book, *The Other America*. Harrington claimed that, while the truly poor numbered almost 50 million, they remained largely hidden in city slums, in Appalachia, in the Deep South, and on Native American reservations. Soon after taking office, Lyndon Johnson decided to launch an antipoverty crusade.

Johnson's Leadership Style

Lyndon Baines Johnson was born and raised in the "hill country" of central Texas, near the banks of the Pedernales River. He remained a Texan in his heart, and his style posed a striking contrast with Kennedy's. He was a man of impressive stature who spoke directly, convincingly, and even roughly at times.

Resource Manager

R Reading Strategies	C Critical Thinking	D Differentiated Instruction	W Writing Support	S Skill Practice
Teacher Edition • Academic Vocab., p. 839 • Using Word Parts, p. 842 **Additional Resources** • Read. Skills Act., URB p. 21 • Guid. Read. Act., URB p. 50 • Prim. Source Reading, URB p. 37	**Teacher Edition** • Making Inferences, p. 840 • Analyzing Prim. Sources, p. 841 • Compare. & Contrast., p. 843 **Additional Resources** • Critical Thinking Skills Act., URB p. 32 • Quizzes and Tests, p. 349 • Auth. Assess, p. 53	**Teacher Edition** • Logical/Math., p. 841 • Naturalist, p. 842 **Additional Resources** • Differentiated Instruction, URB p. 23 • Reteach. Act., URB p. 43	**Teacher Edition** • Persuasive Writing, p. 840	**Teacher Edition** • Reading a Chart, p. 839 **Additional Resources** • Read. Essen., p. 274

PRIMARY SOURCE
The Other America

When President Johnson launched the War on Poverty in 1964, he wanted programs that would help all impoverished Americans, rural and urban.

▲ This unemployed miner and his family pose on the porch of their Kentucky home in 1964.

▲ *Low-income residents sweep the front stoops of their row houses in Baltimore, Maryland, in the early 1960s.*

Poverty Rate in America, 1960–2000

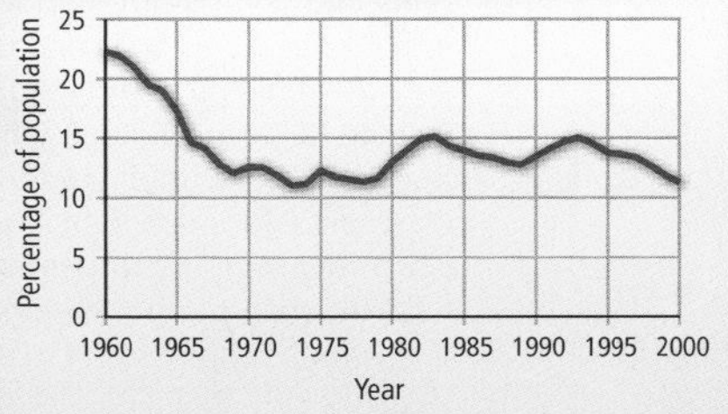

Source: U.S. Census Bureau.

Analyzing VISUALS DBQ

1. **Evaluating** Do you find anything hopeful in the photographs shown?
2. **Interpreting** Based on the data in the chart, how successful was Johnson's War on Poverty?

Johnson had honed his style in long years of public service. By the time he became president at age 55, he already had 26 years of congressional experience behind him. He had been a congressional staffer, a member of the House of Representatives, a senator, Senate majority leader, and vice president.

During his career Johnson earned a reputation as a man who got things done. He did favors, twisted arms, bargained, flattered, and threatened. With every technique he could think of, Johnson sought to find **consensus,** R or general agreement. His ability to build coalitions had made him one of the most effective and powerful leaders in the Senate's history.

A War on Poverty

Why was this powerful man so concerned about poor people? Although Johnson liked to exaggerate the poor conditions of his childhood for dramatic effect, he had in fact known hard times. He had also seen extreme poverty firsthand in a brief career as a teacher in a low-income area. Johnson believed deeply in social action. He felt that a wealthy, powerful government could and should try to improve the lives of its citizens. Kennedy himself had said of Johnson, "He really cares about this nation." Finally, there was Johnson's ambition. He wanted history to portray him as a great president. Attacking poverty was a good place to begin.

Kennedy had plans for an antipoverty program and a civil rights bill before his death. President Johnson knew that any program linked to the slain president would be very popular. In his State of the Union address in 1964, Johnson told his audience: "Unfortunately, many Americans live on the outskirts of hope, some because of their poverty and some because of their color and all too many because of both." He concluded by declaring an "unconditional **War on Poverty** in America."

Teach

S Skill Practice

Reading a Chart Direct students' attention to the chart on poverty rates. **Ask:** In what year did the poverty rate begin a climb of nearly 5 percentage points? *(1979)* Encourage students to keep that fact in mind as they continue their study of American history to interpret why the climb might have begun. BL

R Reading Strategy

Academic Vocabulary Remind students that the prefix *con-* means *with.* This knowledge can help them remember the meaning of *consensus.* BL

Analyzing VISUALS

Answers:
1. Students' responses will vary.
2. Between 1960 and 1970, the poverty rate dropped 10 percent, a steeper drop than in any subsequent decade. That would be considered a success.

Hands-On Chapter Project
Step 3

What Is a Great Society?

Step 3: Creating a Peace Corps or VISTA Work Plan Students will explore responsibilities of citizenship by taking on the role of a Peace Corps or VISTA volunteer.

Directions Discuss why the VISTA and Peace Corps programs are part of a "great society" in terms of a nation's responsibility to its citizens and to other nations. Have students research the types of projects that VISTA and the Peace Corps tackle. Then have each student choose an area of the United States or of another country in which to "volunteer." Ask each student to create a work plan that includes identification of a problem, a specific goal they hope to accomplish, equipment or resources needed, tasks required to achieve the goal, and a schedule for completing the tasks.

Identifying Problems and Solutions By breaking societal problems into achievable steps, students will learn how to find and implement solutions. OL

(Project continued on the Visual Summary page)

C Critical Thinking

Making Inferences Ask students to define the word *vista.* ("a distant view") **Ask:** Why do you think this word was chosen as the appropriate acronym for the program? *(Students may suggest that it was offering people a new view of their lives.)* OL

W Writing Support

Persuasive Writing Providing adequate day care services for the children of women who work outside the home has continued to be a major challenge. Have students take a position on whether this should be part of federal programs, as it was during World War II. Ask them to write a persuasive essay detailing their arguments. OL

Reading Check

Answer: The pockets of extreme poverty in a generally prosperous society; as a former member of Congress, Johnson understood how to play politics to gain consensus on important issues.

By the summer of 1964, Johnson had convinced Congress to pass the Economic Opportunity Act. This legislation attacked inadequate public services, illiteracy, and unemployment as three major causes of poverty. The act established 10 new programs within a new government agency, the Office of Economic Opportunity (OEO). Many of the new programs were directed at young Americans living in inner cities.

The Neighborhood Youth Corps provided work-study programs to help underprivileged young men and women earn a high school diploma or college degree. The Job Corps helped unemployed people ages 16–21 acquire job skills. One of the more dramatic programs introduced was **VISTA** (Volunteers in Service to America), which was essentially a domestic C Peace Corps. VISTA put young people with skills and community-minded ideals to work in poor neighborhoods and rural areas to help people overcome poverty. Additional programs included Upward Bound, which offered tutoring to high school students, and a W Work Experience Program, which provided day care and other support for those in poor households to enable them to work.

The Election of 1964

In April 1964 *Fortune* magazine observed, "Lyndon Johnson has achieved a breadth of public approval few observers would have believed possible when he took office." Johnson had little time to enjoy such praise, for he was soon to run for the office he had first gained through a tragic event.

The Republican candidate in the 1964 election was Senator **Barry Goldwater** of Arizona. Known for his strong conservatism, he set the tone for his campaign when he accepted his party's nomination, declaring, "Extremism in the defense of liberty is no vice! And let me remind you also that moderation in the pursuit of justice is no virtue!"

Few Americans were ready to embrace Goldwater's message, which seemed too aggressive for a nation nervous about nuclear war. On Election Day, Johnson won in a landslide, gaining more than 61 percent of the popular vote and winning all but six states in the Electoral College.

Reading Check **Examining** What inspired the War on Poverty? Why was Johnson able to convince Congress to pass it?

PAST & PRESENT

VISTA Continues the War on Poverty

Volunteers in Service to America (VISTA) began in 1965 as part of President Johnson's War on Poverty. Its focus was to help people help themselves, offering money and programs to low-income communities. Many young people during the idealistic 1960s who weren't able to serve abroad in the Peace Corps program chose instead to work with VISTA. Since the program began, more than 140,000 people have served.

In 1993 VISTA became part of the government agency AmeriCorps. Today, more than 1,200 projects across the nation attempt to make gains in bridging the technology gap, increase housing opportunities, improve health care services, and strengthen community organizations. Volunteers, who must be at least 18, usually work for a year in VISTA-sponsored projects through local, state, or federal agencies or nonprofit, public, or private organizations. In 2006 VISTA had nearly 6,000 volunteers.

1973

▲ *In 1973, Leroy Sneed was a VISTA member in his hometown of Mitchellville, South Carolina, where he was involved in home-repair and community organizing. Here he talks with a homeowner about rebuilding or repairing her home.*

Additional Support

Activity: Collaborative Learning

Investigate the Work of VISTA Have students work in small groups and use library and Internet sources to find out more about the current work of VISTA. Ask students to present their findings using visual aids, such as maps and charts, to portray the work and its locations. Have each group select one project or region of the country on which to focus their research. Discuss and compare groups' findings as a class. OL

The Great Society

MAIN Idea Great Society programs provided assistance to disadvantaged Americans.

HISTORY AND YOU What reforms do you think might help reduce poverty today? Read on to learn about the antipoverty programs initiated by President Johnson.

After his election, Johnson began working with Congress to create the "**Great Society**" he had promised during his campaign. In this same period, major goals of the civil rights movement were achieved through the Civil Rights Act of 1964, which barred discrimination of many kinds, and the Voting Rights Act of 1965, which protected voters from discriminatory practices.

Johnson's goals were consistent with the times for several reasons. The civil rights movement had brought the grievances of African Americans to the forefront, reminding many that equality of opportunity had yet to be realized. Economics also supported Johnson's goal. The economy was strong, and many believed it would remain so indefinitely. There was no reason to believe, therefore, that poverty could not be significantly reduced.

Johnson elaborated on the Great Society's goals during a speech at the University of Michigan in May of 1964. It was clear that the president did not intend only to expand relief to the poor or to **confine** government efforts to material things. The president wanted, he said, to build a better society "where leisure is a welcome chance to build and reflect, . . . where the city of man serves not only the needs of the body and the demands of commerce but the desire for beauty and the hunger for community." **C**

This ambitious vision encompassed more than 60 programs that were initiated between 1965 and 1968. Among the most significant programs were **Medicare** and **Medicaid.** Health care reform had been a major issue since the days of Harry Truman. By the 1960s, public support for better health care benefits had solidified. Medicare had especially strong support since it was directed at all senior citizens. In 1965 approximately half of all Americans over the age of 65 had no health insurance. **D**

◄ *Members of AmeriCorps clear debris from a home in Pass Christian, Mississippi, following Hurricane Katrina in 2005.*

MAKING CONNECTIONS

1. **Analyzing** How does volunteering help both the volunteer and the communities served?
2. **Problem Solving** What challenges in your town or city could AmeriCorps help address? What would you do to solve these challenges?

C Critical Thinking

Analyzing Primary Sources Invite a volunteer to read the quotation from Johnson's speech. **Ask:** Why would these words appeal to a college audience? *(Students may say that college students are idealistic.)* Discuss with students whether they feel Johnson's goals for leisure, beauty, and community have been met. **OL**

D Differentiated Instruction

Logical/Mathematical Ask students to find out the current statistics on the number of Americans without health insurance. Have them break down the figures by age groups and present their findings in chart or graph form. **OL**

MAKING CONNECTIONS

Answers:

1. Students may say that volunteering extends a person's compassion and may enhance useful life skills. The persons being helped are given tangible assistance.
2. Students' responses to both questions will vary.

Additional Support

Extending the Content

Since 1994, more than 400,000 men and women have served in AmeriCorps. Over 50,000 volunteers each year work with nonprofit organizations to provide assistance to other Americans.

Once a person has completed a year of full-time service, he or she receives an education grant of $4725. This can be used for college, graduate school, or to pay back student loans. Those who serve part-time receive a partial award.

R Reading Strategy

Using Word Parts Point out the academic vocabulary term in the second column. **Ask:** What does the prefix *sub-* mean? *(below, under)* Have students come up with other terms using the prefix. (Possible answers include *subatomic, submarine, substandard,* and so on.) **OL**

D Differentiated Instruction

Naturalist Invite interested students to find out how the Water Quality and Clean Air Acts have improved environmental conditions since 1965. Ask them to include information about local efforts on preserving clean water and air. Have them present their findings to the class. **OL**

Analyzing VISUALS

Answers:

1. They supported the development of standards and goals for water and air quality.
2. Students' responses will vary but should be supported.

Additional Support

INFOGRAPHIC

What Was the Great Society?

Health and Welfare

Medicare (1965) established a comprehensive health insurance program for all senior citizens; financed through the Social Security system.

Medicaid (1965) provided health and medical assistance to low-income families; funded through federal and state governments.

Child Nutrition Act (1966) established a school breakfast program and expanded the school lunch and milk programs to improve nutrition.

Education

Elementary and Secondary Education Act (1965) targeted aid to students and funded related activities such as adult education and education counseling.

Higher Education Act (1965) supported college tuition scholarships, student loans, and work-study programs for low- and middle-income students.

Project Head Start (1965) funded a preschool program for disadvantaged children.

The War on Poverty

Office of Economic Opportunity (1964) oversaw many programs to improve life in inner cities, including Job Corps, an education and job training program for at-risk youth.

Housing and Urban Development Act (1965) established new housing subsidy programs and made federal loans and public housing grants easier to obtain.

Demonstration Cities and Metropolitan Development Act (1966) revitalized urban areas through a variety of social and economic programs.

Consumer and Environmental Protection

Water Quality Act and Clean Air Acts (1965) supported development of standards and goals for water and air quality.

Highway Safety Act (1966) improved federal, state, and local coordination and created training standards for emergency medical technicians.

Fair Packaging and Labeling Act (1966) required all consumer products to have true and informative labels.

Analyzing VISUALS

1. **Interpreting** What was the purpose of the Water Quality and Clean Air Acts of 1965?
2. **Evaluating** Which of the Great Society programs do you think had the most effect on American life? Why do you think so?

Johnson convinced Congress to set up Medicare as a health insurance program funded through the Social Security system. Medicare's twin program, Medicaid, financed health care for welfare recipients who were living below the poverty line. Like the New Deal's Social Security program, both programs created what have been called "entitlements," that is, they entitle certain categories of Americans to benefits. Today, the cost of these programs has become a permanent part of the federal budget.

Great Society programs also strongly supported education. For Johnson, who had taught school as a young man, education was a personal passion. Vice President Hubert Humphrey once said that Johnson "was a nut on education. . . . [He] believed in it, just like some people believe in miracle cures."

The Elementary and Secondary Education Act of 1965 granted millions of dollars to public and private schools for textbooks, library materials, and special education programs. Efforts to improve education also extended to preschoolers through Project **Head Start.** Administered by the Office of Economic Opportunity, Head Start was directed at disadvantaged children who had "never looked at a picture book or scribbled with a crayon." Another program, Upward Bound, was designed to prepare low-income teenagers for college.

Improvements in health and education were only the beginning of the Great Society programs. Conditions in the cities—poor schools, crime, slum housing, poverty, and pollution—blighted the lives of those who dwelled there. Johnson urged Congress to act on several pieces of legislation addressing urban issues. One created a new cabinet agency, the Department of Housing and Urban Development, in 1965. Its first secretary, **Robert Weaver,** was the first African American to serve in the cabinet. A broad-based program informally called "Model Cities" authorized federal **subsidies** to many cities. The funds, matched by local and state contributions, supported programs to improve transportation, health care, housing, and policing. Since many

Extending the Content

Robert Weaver Although Weaver's great-grandfather had been enslaved, Weaver, born in 1907, graduated from Harvard with a doctorate in economics and served in several government positions nationally and at the state level. He also was a member of Franklin Roosevelt's "Black Cabinet." He served a year as the national chair for the National Association for the Advancement of Colored People. President Kennedy appointed him in 1960 to lead the federal Housing and Home Finance Agency before he became secretary of HUD in 1965. After leaving HUD at the end of 1968, Weaver served as president of Bernard Baruch College and taught at several institutions of higher learning. Weaver is credited with beginning the revitalization of urban centers in the United States, working to pass the Fair Housing Act, and increasing available affordable housing. In 2000 the Department of Housing and Urban Development named their building, which Weaver had opened and dedicated in 1968, in his honor.

urban areas lacked sufficient or affordable housing, legislation also authorized about $8 billion to build houses for low- and middle-income people.

One notable Great Society measure changed the composition of the American population: the Immigration Act of 1965. This act eliminated the national origins system established in the 1920s, which had given preference to northern European immigrants. The new measure opened wider the door of the United States to newcomers from all parts of Europe, as well as from Asia and Africa.

The Great Society's Legacy

The Great Society programs touched nearly every aspect of American life and improved thousands, perhaps millions, of lives. In the years since President Johnson left office, however, debate has continued over whether the Great Society was truly a success.

In many ways, the impact of the Great Society was limited. In his rush to accomplish as much as possible, Johnson did not calculate exactly how his programs might work. As a result, some of them did not work as well as hoped. Furthermore, the programs grew so quickly they were often unmanageable and difficult to evaluate. C

Cities, states, and groups eligible for aid began to expect immediate and life-changing benefits. These expectations left many feeling frustrated and angry. Other Americans opposed the massive growth of federal programs and criticized the Great Society for intruding too much into their lives.

A lack of funds also hindered the effectiveness of Great Society programs. When Johnson attempted to fund both his grand domestic agenda and the increasingly costly war in Vietnam, the Great Society eventually suffered. Some Great Society initiatives have survived to the present, however. These include Medicare and Medicaid, two cabinet agencies—the Department of Transportation and the Department of Housing and Urban Development (HUD)—and Project Head Start. Overall, the programs provided some important benefits to poorer communities and gave political and administrative experience to minority groups.

An important legacy of the Great Society was the questions it produced. How can the federal government help disadvantaged citizens? How much government help can a society provide without weakening the private sector? How much help can people receive without losing motivation to fight against hardships on their own?

Lyndon Johnson took office determined to change the United States in a way few other presidents had attempted. If he fell short, it was perhaps that the goals he set were so high. In evaluating the administration's efforts, the *New York Times* wrote, "The walls of the ghettos are not going to topple overnight, nor is it possible to wipe out the heritage of generations of social, economic, and educational deprivation by the stroke of a Presidential pen."

Reading Check **Summarizing** What were the Great Society programs, and what was their impact?

Section 3 REVIEW

Vocabulary

1. **Explain** the significance of: consensus, War on Poverty, VISTA, Barry Goldwater, Great Society, Medicare, Medicaid, Head Start, Robert Weaver.

Main Ideas

2. **Analyzing** How did Johnson's War on Poverty strive to ensure greater fairness in American society?
3. **Describing** Which Great Society programs supported education? How did these programs help?

Critical Thinking

4. **Big Ideas** How did President Johnson carry on the ideals of President Kennedy?
5. **Organizing** Use a graphic organizer similar to the one below to list five of the Great Society initiatives that have survived to the present.

Great Society Initiatives

6. **Analyzing Visuals** Look at the graph on page 839. When was poverty at its lowest in the U.S.?

Writing About History

7. **Descriptive Writing** Assume the role of a biographer. Write a chapter in a biography of Lyndon Johnson in which you compare and contrast his leadership style to that of John Kennedy.

History ONLINE
Study Central™ To review this section, go to glencoe.com and click on Study Central.

C Critical Thinking

Comparing and Contrasting Ask students to compare and contrast two major social programs in the twentieth century. They might design graphic organizers to analyze the New Frontier and New Deal, for example. OL

Reading Check

Answer: programs for health, housing, jobs, and education that changed the nation

Assess

History ONLINE

Study Central™ provides summaries, interactive games, and online graphic organizers to help students review content.

Close

Summarizing Ask: What programs from the Great Society do you feel had the most lasting significance? Why do you think so? *(Answers will vary.)*

Section 3 REVIEW

Answers

1. All definitions can be found in the section and the Glossary.
2. by offering the less fortunate education, training, and access to jobs
3. Elementary and Secondary Education Act: money to schools for textbooks, library materials, and special education programs; Project Head Start: improved education for preschoolers; Upward Bound: college preparation for low-income teenagers; Higher Education Act: college tuition scholarships, student loans and work-study for low- and middle-income students
4. Johnson pushed through Kennedy initiatives including major civil rights bills and anti-poverty programs.
5. answers may include: Medicare, Medicaid, Department of Transportation, Department of Housing and Urban Development, Project Head Start
6. 1973
7. Chapters should include specific information about the leadership styles of the two men.

Expository Writing Have students select one of the domestic programs listed and explain why it was important for the Great Society and its legacy for today. **OL**

Taking Notes Have students create graphic organizers to identify the major Supreme Court cases and their provisions. Remind them to use this as a study aid. **OL**

Chapter 24 Visual Summary

You can study anywhere, anytime by downloading quizzes and flashcards to your PDA from glencoe.com.

Domestic Programs of the 1960s

- A growing awareness of poverty, as well as concern for women's rights and the rights of various minority groups, leads to a series of new programs known as the War on Poverty and the Great Society.
- The President's Commission on the Status of Women is established and the Equal Pay Act of 1963 is passed.
- New programs aid the developmentally disabled.
- Office of Economic Opportunity is established to fight poverty, illiteracy, unemployment, and disease.
- Civil Rights Act of 1964 prohibits race discrimination and social segregation, and the Voting Rights Act protects universal suffrage.
- Medicare and Medicaid Acts are passed to provide federal medical aid to senior citizens and poor.
- Elementary and Secondary Education Act is passed to increase aid for public schools.

▲ *VISTA volunteers work to curb delinquency by counseling and helping troubled children and their families.*

▲ *The U.S. Navy ship, the* Vesole, *intercepts the missile-carrying Soviet ship* Potzunov *as it leaves Cuba during the Cuban Missile Crisis.*

Foreign Policy of the 1960s

- Kennedy pledges to end Eisenhower's reliance on nuclear weapons and to use new methods to prevent the spread of communism.
- Kennedy introduces the "flexible response" policy—building up both nuclear missiles and conventional forces.
- The United States pledges aid to struggling Latin American nations.
- Peace Corps sends volunteers to help in poor countries.
- The United States aids Cuban exiles trying to overthrow Castro, but their landing at the Bay of Pigs fails.
- Soviet missiles in Cuba lead to the Cuban missile crisis; the United States blockades Cuba and the Soviets remove the missiles.
- The U.S. and Soviet Union sign the Nuclear Test Ban Treaty.

Supreme Court Cases of the 1960s

- Led by Chief Justice Earl Warren, the Supreme Court makes a series of decisions that dramatically change American society and the federal government's relationship to citizens.
- In *Reynolds* v. *Sims* the Court requires states to adhere to the principle of one person, one vote.
- In four cases, *Mapp* v. *Ohio*, *Gideon* v. *Wainwright*, *Escobedo* v. *Illinois*, and *Miranda* v. *Arizona*, the Court extends due process, giving more protection to those accused of crimes.
- In *Abington School District* v. *Schemp*, the Court rules that states cannot require prayer and Bible readings in public schools.

▲ *Clarence Earl Gideon was denied counsel during a trial in Florida in 1961. His case eventually went to the Supreme Court.*

Hands-On Chapter Project Step 4

What Is a Great Society?

Step 4: Wrap Up Creating a Great Society Poster Students will discuss what qualities make up a society that can be considered "great" and create a poster illustrating those qualities.

Directions Hang a poster on the wall with the title "A Great Society." Ask the class what societies they have studied—such as ancient Greece—that they consider great. Then ask them to list the qualities that are important in a great society. Use their list as headings for columns on the poster.

Analyzing Information Students will analyze the domestic programs, foreign policies, and court decisions of the 1960s and list below the headings on the poster those items that illustrate each quality. **OL**

Chapter 24 ASSESSMENT

Reviewing Vocabulary

Directions: Choose the word or words that best completes the sentence.

1. Reapportionment, as ruled on by the Warren Court, is
- **A** the requirement of separate but equal facilities for schools.
- **B** the process courts must follow when trying cases to treat individuals fairly.
- **C** the way in which political districts are drawn based on population changes.
- **D** the separation of church and state for schools.

2. The policy called ________ helped nations resist Communism by building up conventional troops and weapons.
- **A** military-industrial complex
- **B** containment
- **C** mutual assured destruction
- **D** flexible response

3. ________ means that the law may not treat individuals unfairly or unreasonably and must treat all individuals equally.
- **A** Reapportionment
- **B** Consensus
- **C** Due process
- **D** Judicial review

4. Following World War II, the Cold War era featured competition between the United States and the Soviet Union in everything from diplomacy and the military to
- **A** architecture.
- **B** the space race.
- **C** television.
- **D** population growth.

5. President Johnson was successful at building coalitions and finding a ________, or general agreement.
- **A** discord
- **B** consensus
- **C** accord
- **D** variance

Reviewing Main Ideas

Directions: Choose the best answers to the following questions.

Section 1 *(pp. 824–829)*

6. During the presidential election of 1960, Kennedy focused his campaign message on
- **A** bridging the "missile gap" between the United States and the Soviet Union.
- **B** continuing the foreign policy of the current administration.
- **C** how the Democrats' fiscal policies would boost inflation and harm the economy.
- **D** how Catholicism would influence his decision-making as president.

7. Congress defeated which of the following proposals of Kennedy's New Frontier?
- **A** raising the minimum wage
- **B** investing funds in defense and space exploration
- **C** health care for senior citizens
- **D** providing funds to build low-income housing

8. The Warren Court decision requiring that a defendant in a state court had the right to a lawyer, regardless of his or her ability to pay, was
- **A** *Engel* v. *Vitale.*
- **B** *Griswold* v. *Connecticut.*
- **C** *Plessy* v. *Ferguson.*
- **D** *Gideon* v. *Wainwright.*

TEST-TAKING TIP

To answer vocabulary questions, first look at the terms listed as answers. See if you can mentally define each one. Then read the question to select the right answer.

Need Extra Help?

If You Missed Questions . . .	1	2	3	4	5	6	7	8
Go to Page . . .	828	830	829	832	839	824	826	829

GO ON

Answers and Analyses

Reviewing Vocabulary

1. C The clue to the correct answer is in the term *reapportionment.* If students spot the prefix *re-*, meaning "again," with the word *changes* in the answer, they can eliminate other distractors.

2. D Students should recall that the flexible response was deemed preferable to the expansion of nuclear weapons that Eisenhower had begun, which led to the military-industrial complex against which he warned. The question asks them to choose the answer that helps resist communism, not contain or destroy it.

3. C By linking the idea of something due to a benefit, students can eliminate the other distractors and select the correct answer.

4. B The Soviets took the early lead in the space race. Soviet astronaut Yury Gagarin was the first person to orbit Earth, and the *Sputnik* satellite was launched before the United States' own satellite.

5. B Students need only a basic knowledge of prefix meanings to see that *dis-* and *con-* are opposing ideas; therefore, one of them must be correct. The other choices can be eliminated. Knowing that *dis-* means "not" can help students select a synonym for *agreement*.

Reviewing Main ideas

6. A The three incorrect responses are each unlikely to be the work of a Democratic presidential candidate who was also the first Roman Catholic to run in more than three decades. Even without knowing what a missile gap was, students knowing Kennedy's political and religious background could eliminate wrong answers.

7. C Students should recall that Medicaid was a breakthrough program that Johnson succeeded in getting passed after Kennedy had failed. JFK succeeded in the other efforts listed as distractors.

8. D Students should be able to eliminate *Plessy* v. *Ferguson* by recalling the landmark case upholding separate but equal facilities for African Americans and whites. By careful attention to the chart of Supreme Court cases in the Warren years, they can select the correct answer.

9. C None of the other answers proposes an effective solution to reducing nuclear war, even if they may be attractive options for stopping the spread of communism. Students should be able to link creating the Peace Corps with not having war.

10. B Students should be able to eliminate the two options that pertain to Cuba. The Berlin blockade had already occurred, leaving only option B.

11. A The key to the correct answer is for students to link the terms *young people* and *youth,* ignoring the more generic-sounding programs. They may know that AmeriCorps is a current program.

12. D Given chapter content, *A* and *C* can be eliminated at once. To derive the correct answer, students then need only recall that Johnson was able to push through reforms that Kennedy could not.

13. B Students can ignore distractors with negative words such as *eliminating* and *opposing.* Foreign aid to Cuba would not make America a Great Society. The correct answer deals with an increase; students may also recall that the text mentions Johnson's passion for education.

Chapter 24 Assessment

Section 2 *(pp. 830–835)*

9. Kennedy attempted to reduce the threat of nuclear war and stop the spread of communism by

A withdrawing aid from Latin American countries.
B withdrawing troops from limited military conflicts.
C creating the Peace Corps.
D encouraging growth in the automotive industry to assure that capitalism was superior to communism.

10. How did Soviet Premier Nikita Khrushchev respond when Western powers refused to withdraw from West Berlin?

A He sent long-range missiles to Cuba.
B He had a wall built through Berlin to keep East Germans from escaping to West Berlin.
C He enlisted *La Brigada* to invade Cuba and remove Castro from power.
D He had food and supplies airlifted to Berlin to end a blockade by American forces.

Section 3 *(pp. 838–843)*

11. Which Johnson program provided work-study opportunities to help young people earn high school diplomas or attend college?

A the Neighborhood Youth Corps
B VISTA
C the Peace Corps
D AmeriCorps

12. Medicare and Medicaid were major accomplishments of

A Franklin Roosevelt's New Deal.
B John F. Kennedy's New Frontier.
C Richard Nixon's New Federalism.
D Lyndon Johnson's Great Society.

13. Which idea was part of Johnson's Great Society?

A eliminating government-funded health care for senior citizens
B providing federal aid for education
C opposing civil rights legislation
D increasing foreign aid to Cuba

Critical Thinking

Directions: Choose the best answers to the following questions.

14. How did the Immigration Reform Act of 1965 change the composition of the American population?

A It set strict limits on the number of immigrants admitted to the United States.
B It did not allow any immigrants to enter the United States from Eastern Europe.
C It continued the national origins system, which gave preference to northern European immigrants.
D It opened the United States to individuals from all over the world, including Asia and Africa.

Base your answer to question 15 on the map below and on your knowledge of Chapter 24.

Election of 1960

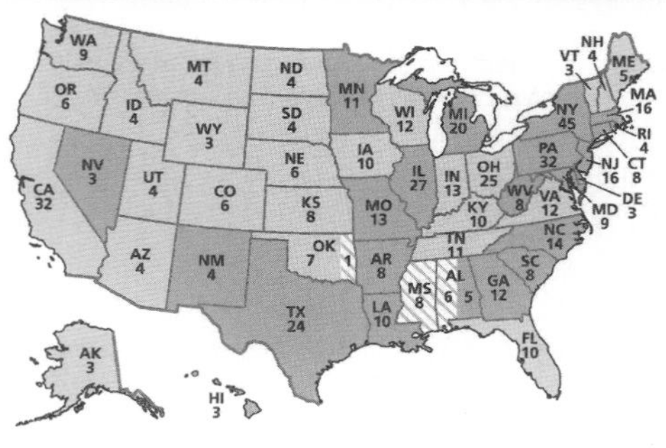

Presidential Candidate	Popular Votes	% of Popular Vote	Electoral Votes
Kennedy	34,227,096	49.72%	303
Nixon	34,107,646	49.55%	219
Byrd	501,643	0.73%	15

15. Which region of the country gave Kennedy the most electoral votes?

A Pacific Northwest
B Northeast
C Southwest
D Midwest

Need Extra Help?

If You Missed Questions . . .	9	10	11	12	13	14	15
Go to Page . . .	832	834	840	841–842	842	843	R15

GO ON

Critical Thinking

14. D The key term in the question is the title of the act itself. To reform would be to improve; only opening the country to people from more nations fits that description.

15. B By carefully looking at the map, students can see that simply combining votes from New York and Pennsylvania provided a majority.

16. President Lyndon B. Johnson's Great Society is similar to President Franklin D. Roosevelt's New Deal in that both programs
   - **A** sought ratification of the Equal Rights Amendment to guarantee equality for women.
   - **B** advocated passage of civil rights laws to help African Americans.
   - **C** approved efforts by states to reduce taxes for the middle class.
   - **D** supported federal funding of programs for the poor.

Analyze the cartoon and answer the question that follows. Base your answer on the cartoon and on your knowledge of Chapter 24.

HERBLOCK'S CARTOON

"Kindly Move Over A Little, Gentlemen"

17. According to the cartoon, what is Johnson trying to do?
   - **A** Johnson wants to give more money to the arms race and military establishments.
   - **B** Johnson is trying to give health, education, and welfare programs more money.
   - **C** Military establishments and arms costs are giving money to social programs.
   - **D** Social programs are receiving more money than the military.

Document-Based Questions

Directions: Analyze the document and answer the short-answer questions that follow the document.

Although the standard of living for most Americans rose dramatically throughout the 1960s, some Americans remained mired in poverty. Read the excerpt below in which John Rath discusses his personal experiences with coping with poverty in his sparely furnished room in Chicago:

> *"I come home to an empty room. I don't even have a dog. . . . No, this is not the kind of life I would choose. If a man had a little piece of land or something, a farm, or well . . . anyway, you've got to have something. You sit down in a place like this, you grit your teeth, you follow me? So many of them are doing that, they sit down, they don't know what to do, they go out. I see 'em in the middle of the night, they take a walk. Don't know what to do. Have no home environment, don't have a dog, don't have nothing . . . just a big zero."*
>
> —quoted in *Division Street: America*

18. What does Rath think might help him to have some purpose in his life?
19. What does he mean when he says: "You sit down in a place like this, you grit your teeth . . . "?

Extended Response

20. Discuss why President Johnson proposed the Great Society and how his initiatives were intended to bring about social change. Then evaluate the extent to which the Great Society succeeded in meeting its goals. Write a well-organized essay that includes an introduction, several paragraphs, and a conclusion. Establish a framework that goes beyond a simple restatement of facts and draws a conclusion about the effectiveness of Johnson's programs.

STOP

History ONLINE
For additional test practice, use Self-Check Quizzes—Chapter 24 at glencoe.com.

Need Extra Help?

If You Missed Questions . . .	16	17	18	19	20
Go to Page . . .	842	R18	847	R19	838–843

Extended Response

20. Students' essays will vary but should include an introduction, several paragraphs, and a conclusion. Essays should address Johnson's Great Society and evaluate its results.

16. D The question asks students to recall the provisions of the New Deal. By doing so, they will recall that none of the first three items were part of FDR's explicit agenda. *D* is the only common thread.

17. B Johnson is asking the arms race and the military to make way for health, education, and welfare. Johnson is trying to improve these programs by giving them milk (budgetary funds) to help them grow.

Document-Based Questions

18. Rath thinks that owning a piece of land or a farm would give him purpose.

19. He means that the situation is so unpleasant that a person grits his or her teeth to avoid screaming.

History ONLINE
Have students visit the Web site at glencoe.com to review Chapter 24 and take the Self-Check Quiz.

Need Extra Help?
Have students refer to the pages listed if they miss any of the questions.

Chapter 25 Planning Guide

Key to Ability Levels	
BL Below Level	AL Above Level
OL On Level	ELL English Language Learners

Key to Teaching Resources	
Print Material	Transparency
CD-ROM or DVD	

Levels				Resources	Chapter Opener	Section 1	Section 2	Section 3	Chapter Assess
BL	OL	AL	ELL						
FOCUS									
BL	OL	AL	ELL	**Daily Focus Skills Transparencies**		25-1	25-2	25-3	
TEACH									
	OL	AL		**History Simulations and Problem Solving, URB**		p. 9			
		AL		**American Literature Reading, URB**		p. 13			
BL	OL		ELL	**Reading Essentials and Note-Taking Guide***		p. 277	p. 280	p. 283	
	OL			**Historical Analysis Skills Activity, URB**		p. 54			
BL	OL		ELL	**Guided Reading Activities, URB***		p. 80	p. 81	p. 82	
BL	OL	AL	ELL	**Content Vocabulary Activity, URB***		p. 59			
BL	OL	AL	ELL	**Academic Vocabulary Activity, URB**		p. 61			
	OL	AL		**Critical Thinking Skills Activity, URB**				p. 64	
BL	OL		ELL	**Reading Skills Activity, URB**			p. 53		
BL			ELL	**English Learner Activity, URB**		p. 57			
	OL	AL		**Reinforcing Skills Activity, URB**		p. 63			
BL	OL	AL	ELL	**Differentiated Instruction Activity, URB**			p. 55		
BL	OL		ELL	**Time Line Activity, URB**				p. 65	
	OL			**Linking Past and Present Activity, URB**			p. 66		
BL	OL	AL	ELL	**American Art and Music Activity, URB**			p. 71		
BL	OL	AL	ELL	**Interpreting Political Cartoons Activity, URB**			p. 73		
		AL		**Enrichment Activity, URB**			p. 77		
BL	OL	AL	ELL	**American Biographies**		✓	✓		
BL	OL	AL	ELL	**Primary Source Reading, URB**			p. 67	p. 69	
BL	OL	AL	ELL	**Supreme Court Case Studies**		p. 73	p. 97		
BL	OL	AL	ELL	**The Living Constitution***	✓	✓	✓	✓	✓
	OL	AL		**American History Primary Source Documents Library**	✓	✓	✓	✓	✓
BL	OL	AL	ELL	**Unit Map Overlay Transparencies**	✓	✓	✓	✓	✓
BL	OL	AL	ELL	**Differentiated Instruction for the American History Classroom**	✓	✓	✓	✓	✓

Note: Please refer to the *Unit 8 Resource Book* for this chapter's URB materials.

* Also available in Spanish

TeacherWorks Plus
All-In-One Planner and Resource Center

- Interactive Lesson Planner
- Interactive Teacher Edition
- Fully editable blackline masters
- Section Spotlight Videos Launch
- Differentiated Lesson Plans
- Printable reports of daily assignments
- Standards Tracking System

BL	OL	AL	ELL		Resources	Chapter Opener	Section 1	Section 2	Section 3	Chapter Assess
					TEACH *(continued)*					
BL	OL	AL	ELL	CD	StudentWorks™ Plus	✓	✓	✓	✓	✓
BL	OL	AL	ELL	CD	American Music Hits Through History CD	✓	✓	✓	✓	✓
BL	OL	AL	ELL	Folder	Unit Time Line Transparencies and Activities	✓	✓	✓	✓	✓
BL	OL	AL	ELL	Folder	Cause and Effect Transparencies, Strategies, and Activities	✓	✓	✓	✓	✓
BL	OL	AL	ELL	Folder	Why It Matters Transparencies, Strategies, and Activities	✓	✓	✓	✓	✓
BL	OL	AL	ELL	Folder	American Issues	✓	✓	✓	✓	✓
	OL	AL	ELL	Folder	American Art and Architecture Transparencies, Strategies, and Activities	✓	✓	✓	✓	✓
BL	OL	AL		Folder	High School American History Literature Library	✓	✓	✓	✓	✓
BL	OL	AL	ELL	CD	*The American Vision* Video Program	✓	✓	✓	✓	✓
Teacher Resources				Folder	Strategies for Success	✓	✓	✓	✓	✓
				Folder	Success with English Learners	✓	✓	✓	✓	✓
				Folder	Reading Strategies and Activities for the Social Studies Classroom	✓	✓	✓	✓	✓
				CD	Presentation Plus! with MindJogger CheckPoint	✓	✓	✓	✓	✓
					ASSESS					
BL	OL	AL	ELL	Folder	Section Quizzes and Chapter Tests*		p. 359	p. 360	p. 361	p. 363
BL	OL	AL	ELL	Folder	Authentic Assessment With Rubrics					p. 55
BL	OL	AL	ELL	Folder	Standardized Test Practice Workbook					p. 57
BL	OL	AL	ELL	CD	*ExamView® Assessment Suite*		25-1	25-2	25-3	Ch. 25
					CLOSE					
BL			ELL	Folder	Reteaching Activity, URB					p. 75
BL	OL		ELL	Folder	Reading and Study Skills Foldables™	p. 79				

✓ Chapter- or unit-based activities applicable to all sections in this chapter.

Using Reproducible Lesson Plans

Teach With Technology

What are Reproducible Lesson Plans?

Reproducible Lesson Plans (RLPs) are detailed lesson plans that teachers may use to prepare their lessons throughout the year.

How can RLPs help me teach?

RLPs are organized by chapter and also by section, suggesting where the wide variety of technology and ancillary products can be used within the book. RLPs are organized two ways:

- Teaching activities and ancillaries are presented using the FOCUS, TEACH, ASSESS, CLOSE organization of the Teacher Wraparound Edition.
- Teaching activities and ancillaries are also grouped by skill level, which helps you identify the activities that are appropriate for the students in your classroom.

RLPs are available on TeacherWorks™ Plus.

History ONLINE
Visit glencoe.com and enter ***QuickPass***™ code TAV9399c25T for Chapter 25 resources.

You can easily launch a wide range of digital products from your computer's desktop with the McGraw-Hill Social Studies widget.

	Student	Teacher	Parent
Media Library			
• Section Audio	●		●
• Spanish Audio Summaries	●		●
• Section Spotlight Videos	●	●	●
The American Vision **Online Learning Center (Web Site)**			
• StudentWorks™ Plus Online	●	●	●
• Multilingual Glossary	●	●	●
• Study-to-Go	●	●	●
• Chapter Overviews	●	●	●
• Self-Check Quizzes	●	●	●
• Student Web Activities	●	●	●
• ePuzzles and Games	●	●	●
• Vocabulary eFlashcards	●	●	●
• In Motion Animations	●	●	●
• Study Central™	●	●	●
• Web Activity Lesson Plans		●	
• Vocabulary PuzzleMaker	●	●	●
• Historical Thinking Activities		●	
• Beyond the Textbook	●	●	●

Reading Support From Jamestown Education

- **Timed Readings Plus in Social Studies** helps students increase their reading rate and fluency while maintaining comprehension. The 400-word passages are similar to those found on state and national assessments.
- **Reading in the Content Area: Social Studies** concentrates on six essential reading skills that help students better comprehend what they read. The book includes 75 high-interest nonfiction passages written at increasing levels of difficulty.
- **Reading Social Studies** includes strategic reading instruction and vocabulary support in Social Studies content for both ELLs and native speakers of English.

www.jamestowneducation.com

Biography / A&E Home Video / The History Channel

The following videotape programs are available from Glencoe as supplements to this chapter:

- Martin Luther King, Jr.: The Man and the Dream (ISBN 0-76-701057-4)
- The Class of the 20th Century; Vol. 4 1961–1968 (ISBN 1-56-501050-7)

To order, call Glencoe at 1-800-334-7344. To find classroom resources to accompany many of these videos, check the following home pages:

A&E Television: www.aetv.com

The History Channel: www.historychannel.com

National Geographic

Index to National Geographic Magazine:

The following articles relate to this chapter:

- "On the Civil Rights Trail," by Charles E. Cobb, Jr., February 2005.
- "Selma to Montgomery: The Road to Equality," by Chuck Stone and Meria Joel Carstarphen, February 2000.

National Geographic Society Products To order the following, call National Geographic at 1-800-368-2728:

- *Civil Rights* (CD-ROM)

Access National Geographic's new, dynamic MapMachine Web site and other geography resources at:

www.nationalgeographic.com
www.nationalgeographic.com/maps

Reading List Generator CD-ROM — Glencoe BookLink 3

Use this database to search more than 30,000 titles to create a customized reading list for your students.

- Reading lists can be organized by students' reading level, author, genre, theme, or area of interest.
- The database provides Degrees of Reading Power™ (DRP) and Lexile™ readability scores for all selections.
- A brief summary of each selection is included.

Leveled reading suggestions for this chapter:

For students at a Grade 8 reading level:
- ***Neil Armstrong: Young Flyer,*** by Montrew Dunham

For students at a Grade 9 reading level:
- ***One Giant Leap: The Story of Neil Armstrong,*** by Don Brown

For students at a Grade 10 reading level:
- ***The Civil Rights Movement,*** by Stuart Kallen

For students at a Grade 11 reading level:
- ***The Civil Rights Movement,*** by Michael Anderson

For students at a Grade 12 reading level:
- ***Great African Americans in Civil Rights,*** by Pat Rediger

Introducing
Chapter 25

Focus

MAKING CONNECTIONS
What Causes Societies to Change?

Ask students to give suggestions as to why societies change. Students may list economic, political, and social reasons. Have students surmise why the civil rights movement gathered momentum after World War II. Students may recall the effects of the Holocaust on people's views of human rights as well as the fact that the contributions of African Americans in the armed forces during the conflict made American citizens sensitive to the need for social equality. Have students hypothesize whether nonviolent or violent strategies work best in bringing about positive social change. **OL**

Teach

The Big Ideas

As students study the chapter, remind them to consider the section-based Big Ideas included in each section's Guide to Reading. The **Essential Questions** and the activities below tie in to the Big Ideas and help students think about and understand important chapter concepts. In addition, the Hands-on-Chapter Projects with their culminating activities relate the content from each section to the Big Ideas. These activities build on each other as students progress through the chapter. Section activities culminate in the wrap-up activity on the Visual Summary page.

Chapter 25

The Civil Rights Movement

1954–1968

Martin Luther King, Jr., and his wife Coretta lead the civil rights march in Selma, Alabama, 1965.

U.S. PRESIDENTS
Eisenhower 1953–1961
Kennedy 1961–1963

U.S. EVENTS
- 1954 • *Brown* v. *Board of Education* ruling is issued
- 1955 • Montgomery bus boycott begins in Alabama
- 1957 • Eisenhower sends troops to Little Rock to ensure integration of a high school
- 1960 • Greensboro sit-in begins
- 1963 • The March on Washington, D.C., is held to support the Civil Rights bill

1953 — 1957 — 1961

WORLD EVENTS
- 1955 • West Germany is admitted to NATO
- 1957 • Russia launches *Sputnik* into orbit
- 1960 • France successfully tests nuclear weapons
- 1962 • Cuban missile crisis erupts

Section 1

The Movement Begins

Essential Question: How might people work to bring about social change in a democracy? *(People can contact public officials, bring their cases to the courts, vote in elections, and carry out peaceful demonstrations.)* Point out that in Section 1 students will learn about the steps taken by African Americans to desegregate public places. **OL**

Section 2

Challenging Segregation

Essential Question: What effect do you think young people can have on the political system? *(Young people can effect change by writing to political leaders, participating in meetings, and going door-to-door to appeal for support.)* Point out in Section 2 students will learn how African American students took part in efforts to end segregation and register voters throughout the South. **OL**

Chapter Audio

MAKING CONNECTIONS

What Causes Societies to Change?

The civil rights movement gained momentum rapidly after World War II. Decisions by the Supreme Court combined with massive protests by civil rights groups and new federal legislation to finally end racial segregation and disfranchisement in the United States more than 70 years after Southern states had put it in place.

- ***Why do you think the civil rights movement made gains in postwar America? What strategies were most effective in winning the battle for civil rights?***

Johnson 1963–1969

1964
- Civil Rights Act of 1964 passes

1965
- Voting Rights Act passes
- Malcolm X is assassinated

1968
- Civil Rights Act of 1968 is passed
- Martin Luther King, Jr., is assassinated

1965 — 1969

1965
- China's Cultural Revolution begins

1967
- Arab-Israeli War brings many Palestinians under Israeli rule

FOLDABLES™

Sequencing Civil Rights Events Create an Accordion Book Foldable to gather information on a time line about various events of the civil rights movement. As you read the chapter, complete the time line by filling in events for roughly 20 years, starting with Roosevelt's Executive Order 8802 of June 1941. The time line should include brief notes on each event.

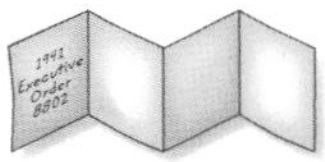

History ONLINE Visit glencoe.com and enter QuickPass™ code TAV9846c25 for Chapter 25 resources.

Introducing **Chapter 25**

More About the Photo

Visual Literacy Ask students: What type of activity is taking place in the photo? What people are participating? *(a protest march; African American leaders, such as Martin Luther King, Jr., and Coretta Scott King, as well as some white American citizens)* The main contribution of Martin Luther King, Jr.'s, Southern Christian Leadership Conference (SCLC) to the civil rights movement was a series of highly publicized protest campaigns in Southern cities during the early and mid-1960s. The protests were aimed at forcing white officials and business leaders to end segregation and to allow African Americans to vote.

FOLDABLES™ Study Organizer Dinah Zike's Foldables

Dinah Zike's Foldables are three-dimensional, interactive graphic organizers that help students practice basic writing skills, review vocabulary terms, and identify main ideas. Instructions for creating and using Foldables can be found in the Appendix at the end of this book and in the *Dinah Zike's Reading and Study Skills Foldables* booklet.

Section 3

New Civil Rights Issues

Essential Question: How do you think people might respond when their hopes for change are not realized? *(Some people might protest peacefully; others might take a violent course of action.)* Point out to students that in Section 3 they will learn how African Americans responded to the slow pace of change in American society. **OL**

History ONLINE

Visit glencoe.com and enter QuickPass™ code TAV9399c25T for Chapter 25 resources, including a Chapter Overview, Study Central™, Study-to-Go, Student Web Activity, Self-Check Quiz, and other materials.

Focus

Bellringer

Daily Focus Transparency 25-1

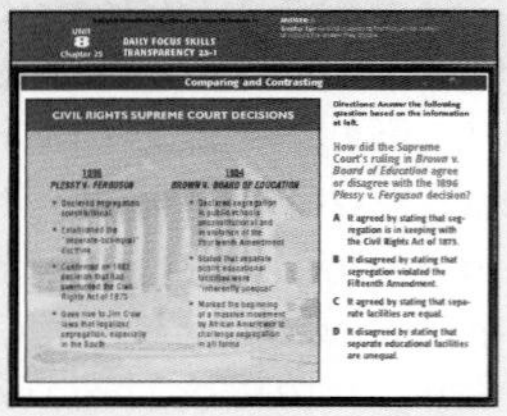

Guide to Reading

Answers:
segregation
lack of voting rights
African American experiences in World War II

Section Spotlight Video

To generate student interest and provide a springboard for class discussion, access the Chapter 25, Section 1 video at glencoe.com or on the video DVD.

Section 1

Section Audio   Spotlight Video

The Movement Begins

Guide to Reading

Big Ideas

Struggles for Rights In the 1950s, African Americans began a movement to win greater legal and social equality.

Content Vocabulary

- "separate but equal" *(p. 850)*
- de facto segregation *(p. 851)*
- sit-in *(p. 852)*

Academic Vocabulary

- facility *(p. 850)*

People and Events to Identify

- Rosa Parks *(p. 850)*
- National Association for the Advancement of Colored People (NAACP) *(p. 850)*
- Thurgood Marshall *(p. 852)*
- Linda Brown *(p. 852)*
- Martin Luther King, Jr. *(p. 854)*
- Southern Christian Leadership Conference (SCLC) *(p. 855)*

Reading Strategy

Organizing Complete a graphic organizer similar to the one below by listing the causes of the civil rights movement.

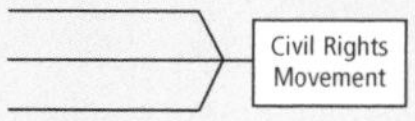

After World War II, African Americans and other civil rights supporters challenged segregation in the United States. Their efforts were vigorously opposed by Southern segregationists, but the federal government began to take a firmer stand for civil rights.

The Origins of the Movement

MAIN Idea African Americans won court victories, increased their voting power, and began using "sit-ins" to desegregate public places.

HISTORY AND YOU Are you registered to vote, or do you plan to register when you are 18? Read on to learn how African Americans increased their voting power and worked to desegregate public places.

Prior to the mid 1950s, African Americans struggling for equality had few successes. Jackie Robinson's integration of baseball in 1947 was a dramatic symbol of opportunity, but one baseball player could not transform normal citizens' daily mistreatment. On December 1, 1955, **Rosa Parks** left her job as a seamstress in Montgomery, Alabama, and boarded a bus to go home. In 1955 buses in Montgomery reserved seats in the front for whites and seats in the rear for African Americans. Seats in the middle were open to African Americans, but only if there were few whites on the bus.

Rosa Parks took a seat just behind the white section. Soon, all of the seats on the bus were filled. When the bus driver noticed a white man standing, he told Parks and three other African Americans in her row to get up and let the white man sit down. When Parks did not, the driver then called the Montgomery police.

News of the arrest soon reached E. D. Nixon, a former president of the local chapter of the **National Association for the Advancement of Colored People (NAACP).** Nixon told Parks, "With your permission we can break down segregation on the bus with your case." Parks replied, "If you think it will mean something to Montgomery and do some good, I'll be happy to go along with it."

Rosa Parks did not know that her decision would spark a new era in the civil rights movement. African Americans in Montgomery quickly organized a boycott of the bus system. After decades of segregation and inequality, many African Americans had decided the time had come to demand equal rights.

The struggle would not be easy. The Supreme Court had declared segregation to be constitutional in *Plessy* v. *Ferguson* in 1896. The ruling had established the **"separate but equal"** doctrine. Laws that segregated African Americans were permitted as long as equal **facilities** were provided for them.

Resource Manager

R Reading Strategies	C Critical Thinking	D Differentiated Instruction	W Writing Support	S Skill Practice
Teacher Edition • Summarizing, p. 852 • Inferring, p. 854 **Additional Resources** • Guid. Read. Act., URB p. 80 • Am. Literature Reading, URB p. 13	**Teacher Edition** • Analyzing Pri. Sources, pp. 854, 856 **Additional Resources** • Supreme Court Case Studies, p. 73 • Quizzes and Tests, p. 359 • Hist. Sim. and Prob. Solv., URB p. 9	**Teacher Edition** • English Learners, p. 852 • Visual/Spatial, p. 855 **Additional Resources** • Academic Vocab. Act., URB p. 61 • English Learner Act., URB p. 57	**Teacher Edition** • Personal Writing, p. 851 • Persuasive Writing, p. 855 • Expository Writing, p. 856 **Additional Resources** • Content Vocab. Act., URB p. 59	**Additional Resources** • Read. Essen., p. 277 • Hist. Skills Act., URB p. 54 • Reinforcing Skills Act., URB p. 63

People IN HISTORY

Thurgood Marshall
1908–1993

Over his lifetime, Thurgood Marshall made many contributions to the civil rights movement. Perhaps his most famous accomplishment was representing the NAACP in the *Brown* v. *Board of Education* case.

Marshall's speaking style was simple and direct. During the Brown case, Justice Frankfurter asked Marshall for a definition of *equal.* Marshall replied: "*Equal* means getting the same thing, at the same time and in the same place."

Born into a middle-class Baltimore family in 1908, Marshall earned a law degree from Howard University Law School. The school's dean, Charles Hamilton Houston, enlisted Marshall to work for the NAACP. Together, the two laid out the legal strategy for challenging discrimination in many areas of American life. In 1935 Marshall won his first case regarding segregation in state institutions. The decision forced the University of Maryland to integrate. Marshall went on to win 29 of the 32 cases he argued before the Supreme Court, and became known as "Mr. Civil Rights." In 1967 Marshall became the first African American to serve on the Supreme Court, where he continued to be a voice for civil rights. In his view, the Constitution was not perfect, because it had accepted slavery. "The true miracle of the Constitution," he once wrote, "was not the birth of the Constitution, but its life."

How did Thurgood Marshall contribute to the civil rights movement?

The NAACP's Legal Strategy in Action

Even before the famous *Brown* v. *Board of Education* case, Thurgood Marshall had won several cases for the NAACP that chipped away at segregation in the South.

Smith* v. *Allwright (1944): Political parties cannot deny voting rights in party primaries on the basis of race.

Shelley* v. *Kraemer (1948): States cannot enforce private agreements to discriminate on the basis of race in the sale of property.

Sweatt* v. *Painter (1950): Law schools segregated by race are inherently unequal.

After the *Plessy* decision, laws segregating African Americans and whites spread quickly. These laws, nicknamed "Jim Crow" laws, segregated buses, trains, schools, restaurants, pools, parks, and other public facilities. Usually the "Jim Crow" facilities provided for African Americans were of poorer quality than those provided for whites. Areas without laws requiring segregation often had **de facto segregation**—segregation by custom and tradition.

Court Challenges Begin

The civil rights movement had been building for a long time. Since 1909, the NAACP had supported court cases intended to overturn segregation. W Over the years, the NAACP achieved some victories. In 1935, for example, the Supreme Court ruled in *Norris* v. *Alabama* that Alabama's exclusion of African Americans from juries violated their right to equal protection under the law. In 1946 the Court ruled in *Morgan* v. *Virginia* that segregation on interstate buses was unconstitutional. In 1950 it ruled in *Sweatt* v. *Painter* that state law schools had to admit qualified African American applicants, even if parallel black law schools existed.

New Political Power

In addition to a string of court victories, African Americans enjoyed increased political power. Before World War I, most African Americans lived in the South, where they were largely excluded from voting. During the Great Migration, many moved to Northern cities, where they were allowed to vote. Increasingly, Northern politicians sought their votes and listened to their concerns.

During the 1930s, many African Americans benefited from FDR's New Deal programs and began supporting the Democratic Party. This gave the party new strength in the North. This wing of the party was now able to counter Southern Democrats, who often supported segregation.

Teach

People IN HISTORY

Answer:
He worked as a lawyer with the NAACP to win many important cases that ended segregation or made strides in other areas of civil rights, such as *Brown* v. *Board of Education*. Later, he became the first African American to sit on the Supreme Court.

W Writing Support

Personal Writing Have students write a paragraph they believe would convince other people of the importance of equal protection under the law. They may include personal experiences, an anecdote, or an example. OL

Hands-On Chapter Project
Step 1

A Freedom Drama

Step 1: We Shall Overcome Remind students that American history is filled with dramatic events. In Step 1 students will create the first of a theatrical presentation that chronicles the history of freedom for African Americans in the United States.

Directions Write the Big Idea on the board. Discuss the experiences of African Americans under Jim Crow laws. Have students give their views on how they would have felt in similar circumstances. Organize students into groups. Assign each group to research a different African American (a farmer, a teacher, a civil rights activist) during the days of Jim Crow. Each group should write a monologue about the experiences of their person. Encourage students to share sensory elements in their monologues. Have the characters let the class know what they saw, heard, smelled, and felt.

Summarizing Have group members read the monologues aloud. Have the class comment on the effectiveness of the monologues in helping them understand the experiences of African Americans under Jim Crow. OL

(Chapter Project continues on page 860)

D Differentiated Instruction

English Learners Explain to students that a sit-in occurs when protesters sit down in an office, restaurant, or other place of business and refuse to leave. Ask students if they are aware of any recent sit-ins, and have them consider the possible impact of such actions. ELL BL

R Reading Strategy

Summarizing Have students read the second paragraph under "Southern Resistance" and then summarize what they have just read. Remind them that only the main ideas should be included in a summary but that all the main ideas should be included. OL ELL

Reading Check

Answer:
The ruling marked a dramatic reversal of the precedent established in the *Plessy* v. *Ferguson* case.

Additional Support

The Push for Desegregation

During World War II, African American leaders began to use their political power to demand more rights. Their efforts helped end discrimination in wartime factories and increased opportunities for African Americans in the military.

D In Chicago in 1942, James Farmer and George Houser founded the Congress of Racial Equality (CORE). CORE began using **sit-ins,** a form of protest first used by union workers in the 1930s. In 1943 CORE attempted to desegregate restaurants that refused to serve African Americans. Using the sit-in strategy, members of CORE went to segregated restaurants. If they were denied service, they sat down and refused to leave. The sit-ins were intended to shame restaurant managers into integrating their restaurants. Using these protests, CORE successfully integrated many restaurants, theaters, and other public facilities in Northern cities including Chicago, Detroit, Denver, and Syracuse.

Brown v. *Board of Education*

To better understand the court ruling in *Brown* v. *Board of Education*, read an excerpt from the Court's ruling on page R55 in **Documents in American History.**

After World War II, the NAACP continued to challenge segregation in the courts. From 1939 to 1961, the NAACP's chief counsel and director of its Legal Defense and Education Fund was the brilliant African American attorney **Thurgood Marshall.** After the war, Marshall focused his efforts on ending segregation in public schools.

In 1954 the Supreme Court decided to combine several cases and issue a general ruling on segregation in schools. One of the cases involved a young African American girl named **Linda Brown,** who was denied admission to her neighborhood school in Topeka, Kansas, because of her race. She was told to attend an all-black school across town. With the help of the NAACP, her parents then sued the Topeka school board.

On May 17, 1954, the Supreme Court ruled unanimously in *Brown* v. *Board of Education of Topeka, Kansas,* that segregation in public schools was unconstitutional and violated the equal protection clause of the Fourteenth Amendment. Chief Justice Earl Warren summed up the Court's decision, declaring: "In the field of public education, the doctrine of separate but equal has no place. Separate educational facilities are inherently unequal."

Southern Resistance

The Brown decision marked a dramatic reversal of the precedent established in the *Plessy* v. *Ferguson* case in 1896. *Brown* v. *Board of Education* applied only to public schools, but the ruling threatened the entire system of segregation. Although it convinced many African Americans that the time had come to challenge segregation, it also angered many white Southerners, who became even more determined to defend segregation, regardless of what the Supreme Court ruled.

Although some school districts in border states integrated their schools, anger and opposition was a far more common reaction. In Washington, D.C., Senator Harry F. Byrd of Virginia called on Southerners to adopt "massive resistance" against the ruling. Across the South, hundreds of thousands of white Americans joined citizens' councils to pressure their local governments and school boards into defying the Supreme Court. Many states adopted pupil assignment laws. These laws established elaborate requirements other than race that schools could use to prevent African Americans from attending white schools. R

The Supreme Court inadvertently encouraged white resistance when it followed up its decision in *Brown* v. *Board of Education* a year later. The Court ordered school districts to proceed "with all deliberate speed" to end school segregation. The wording was vague enough that many districts were able to keep their schools segregated for many more years.

Massive resistance also appeared in the halls of Congress. In 1956 a group of 101 Southern members of Congress signed the "Southern Manifesto," which denounced the Supreme Court's ruling as "a clear abuse of judicial power" and pledged to use "all lawful means" to reverse the decision. Although the "Southern Manifesto" had no legal standing, the statement encouraged white Southerners to defy the Supreme Court. Not until 1969 did the Supreme Court order all school systems to desegregate "at once" and operate integrated schools "now and hereafter."

Reading Check **Examining** Why was the ruling in *Brown* v. *Board of Education* so important?

Activity: Interdisciplinary Connection

Daily Life In 1947 Jackie Robinson became the first African American to play major-league baseball. Other professional sports integrated at different times. Professional football, for example, had the first African American player (Charles W. Follis) in 1904, and African American prizefighters and jockeys had been successful before that. Have students research and share more about these and other milestones (such as Olympic triumphs). Have students hypothesize about why integration took place sooner in some sports than in others. OL

Analyzing Supreme Court Cases

Is Segregation Unconstitutional?

★ ***Brown* v. *Board of Education*, 1954**

Background to the Cases

One of the most important Supreme Court cases in American history began in 1952, when the Supreme Court agreed to hear the NAACP's case *Brown* v. *Board of Education of Topeka, Kansas,* along with three other cases. They all dealt with the question of whether the principle "separate but equal" established in *Plessy* v. *Ferguson* was constitutional with regard to public schools.

How the Court Ruled

In a unanimous decision in 1954, the Court ruled in favor of Linda Brown and the other plaintiffs. In doing so, it overruled *Plessy* v. *Ferguson* and rejected the idea that equivalent but separate schools for African American and white students were constitutional. The Court held that racial segregation in public schools violates the Fourteenth Amendment's equal protection clause because "Separate educational facilities are inherently unequal." The Court's rejection of "separate but equal" was a major victory for the civil rights movement and led to the overturning of laws requiring segregation in other public places.

▲ *The children involved in the* Brown v. Board of Education *case are shown in this 1953 photograph. They are, from front to back, Vicki Henderson, Donald Henderson, Linda Brown (of the case title), James Emanuel, Nancy Todd, and Katherine Carper. Together, their cases led to the Supreme Court decreeing that public schools could not be segregated on the basis of race.*

Primary Source

The Court's Opinion

"In these days, it is doubtful that any child may reasonably be expected to succeed in life if he is denied the opportunity of an education. Such an opportunity, where the state has undertaken to provide it, is a right which must be made available to all on equal terms. We come then to the question presented: Does segregation of children in public schools solely on the basis of race, even though the physical facilities and other 'tangible' factors may be equal, deprive the children of the minority group of equal educational opportunities? We believe that it does."

—Chief Justice Earl Warren writing for the Court in *Brown* v. *Board of Education of Topeka, Kansas*

Primary Source

Dissenting Views

"We regard the decisions of the Supreme Court in the school cases as a clear abuse of judicial power. . . . In the case of *Plessy* v. *Ferguson* in 1896 the Supreme Court expressly declared that under the 14th Amendment no person was denied any of his rights if the States provided separate but equal facilities. . . . This interpretation, restated time and again, became a part of the life of the people of many of the States and confirmed their habits, traditions, and way of life. It is founded on elemental humanity and commonsense, for parents should not be deprived by Government of the right to direct the lives and education of their own children."

—from the "Southern Manifesto"

DBQ Document-Based Questions

1. **Explaining** Why did the Supreme Court find in favor of Linda Brown?
2. **Drawing Conclusions** What is the main argument against the *Brown* decision in the excerpt from the "Southern Manifesto"?
3. **Making Inferences** Do you think that the authors of the "Southern Manifesto" were including African Americans in the last sentence of the excerpt? Why or why not?

Supreme Court Cases

Teach

When the Supreme Court delivered its opinion in the *Brown* v. *Board of Education* case, 17 Southern states and the District of Columbia required segregation of public schools. In a few states outside the South, including Kansas, individual school districts could decide whether to racially segregate public schools. In 1954 the few racially integrated schools in the South consisted of federally run schools on military bases and some private schools.

DBQ Document Based Questions

Answers:

1. Segregation deprived African American children of equal educational opportunities.
2. Government should not deprive parents of the right to direct the education of their children.
3. Answers will vary but should mention the long-standing practice of racial discrimination in the South.

Additional Support

Activity: Collaborative Learning

Separate but Equal Organize the class into two groups to research the "separate but equal" doctrine. One group should research the *Plessy* v. *Ferguson* case, which set the legal precedent for "separate but equal" schools. The other group should research the *Brown* v. *Board of Education of Topeka, Kansas* case, which overturned the "separate but equal" doctrine. Groups should then come together for a class discussion of their findings—or group spokespersons may be selected for class presentations. **OL**

R Reading Strategy

Inferring Ask: What does the text mean in saying that the Montgomery bus boycott "marked the start of a new era of the civil rights movement?" *(The struggle for civil rights now included organized protests as well as court cases.)* **OL** **ELL**

C Critical Thinking

Analyzing Primary Sources

Ask: How did King justify his movement's use of the "weapon of protest?" *(Peaceful protest for rights was a basic practice of American democracy.)* **OL**

Turning Point

Analyzing HISTORY

Answer:
It showed that even small acts of defiance could empower people to create change.

Additional Support

The Civil Rights Movement Begins

MAIN Idea The *Brown* v. *Board of Education* ruling ignited protest and encouraged African Americans to challenge other forms of segregation.

HISTORY AND YOU Do you think that one person has the power to change things for the better? Read on to learn how the courage and hard work of individuals helped reform society.

In the midst of the uproar over the *Brown* v. *Board of Education* case, Rosa Parks made her decision to challenge segregation of public transportation. Outraged by Parks's arrest, Jo Ann Robinson, head of a local organization called the Women's Political Council, called on African Americans to boycott Montgomery's buses on the day Rosa Parks appeared in court.

R The boycott marked the start of a new era of the civil rights movement among African Americans. Instead of limiting the fight for their rights to court cases, African Americans in large numbers began organizing protests, defying laws that required segregation, and demanding they be treated as equal to whites.

The Montgomery Bus Boycott

The Montgomery bus boycott was a dramatic success. On the afternoon of Rosa Parks's court appearance, several African American leaders formed the Montgomery Improvement Association to run the boycott and to negotiate with city leaders for an end to segregation. They elected a 26-year-old pastor named **Martin Luther King, Jr.,** to lead them.

On the evening of December 5, 1955, a meeting was held at Dexter Avenue Baptist Church, where Dr. King was the pastor. In the deep, resonant tones and powerful phrases that characterized his speaking style, King encouraged the people to continue their protest. "There comes a time, my friends," he said, "when people get tired of being thrown into the abyss of humiliation, where they experience the bleakness of nagging despair." He cautioned, however, that the protest had to be peaceful:

PRIMARY SOURCE

"Now let us say that we are not advocating violence. . . . The only weapon we have in our hands this evening is the weapon of protest. If we were incarcerated behind the iron curtains of a communistic nation—we couldn't do this. If we were trapped in the dungeon of a totalitarian regime—we couldn't do this. But the great glory of American democracy is the right to protest for right!" C

—quoted in *Parting the Waters: America in the King Years*

King had earned a Ph.D. in theology from Boston University. He believed that the only moral way to end segregation and racism was through nonviolent passive resistance. He told his followers, "We must use the weapon of love. We must realize that so many people are taught to hate us that they are not totally responsible for their hate." African Americans, he urged, must say to racists: "We will soon wear you down by our capacity to suffer, and in winning our freedom we will so appeal to your heart and conscience that we will win you in the process."

Turning Point

The Montgomery Bus Boycott

The act of one woman on a bus and the subsequent bus boycott in Montgomery, Alabama, brought civil rights out of the legal arena and turned it into a struggle in which ordinary Americans realized that they could make a difference. Rosa Parks's refusal to give up her seat on the bus to a white man showed that even small acts of defiance could empower people to create change.

The Montgomery bus boycott, which was begun to show support for Parks, became a huge success. It started a chain reaction—the beginning of a mass movement that would dramatically change American society over the next 20 years, and bring to prominence many influential African American leaders, including Martin Luther King, Jr.

ANALYZING HISTORY Drawing Conclusions How did the bus boycott create a mass movement for change?

Activity: Interdisciplinary Connection

Philosophy Martin Luther King, Jr., took many of his nonviolent ideas from Mohandas Gandhi, the leader of India's movement for independence from Britain. Ask students to research Gandhi's philosophy and his work. Have them compare the two men's philosophies. **Ask:** How are their ideas similar? How are they different? How successful was each man in reaching his goals? Have students present their findings orally for class discussion. **OL**

King drew upon the philosophy and techniques of Indian leader Mohandas Gandhi, who had used nonviolent resistance effectively to challenge British rule in India. Believing in people's ability to transform themselves, King was certain that public opinion would eventually force the government to end segregation.

Stirred by King's powerful words, African Americans in Montgomery continued their boycott for over a year. Instead of riding the bus, they organized car pools or walked to work. Meanwhile, Rosa Parks's legal challenge to bus segregation worked its way through the courts. In November 1956, the Supreme Court affirmed the decision of a special three-judge panel declaring Alabama's laws requiring segregation on buses unconstitutional.

African American Churches

W Martin Luther King, Jr., was not the only prominent minister in the bus boycott. Many of the other leaders were African American ministers. The boycott could not have succeeded without the support of the African American churches in the city. As the civil rights movement gained momentum, African American churches continued to play a critical role. They served as forums for many of the protests and planning meetings, and mobilized many of the volunteers for specific civil rights campaigns.

After the Montgomery bus boycott demonstrated that nonviolent protest could be successful, African American ministers led by King established the **Southern Christian Leadership Conference (SCLC)** in 1957. The SCLC set out to eliminate segregation from American society and to encourage African Americans to register to vote. Dr. King served as the SCLC's first president. Under his leadership, the organization challenged segregation at voting booths and in public transportation, housing, and accommodations.

History ONLINE
Student Web Activity Visit glencoe.com and complete the activity on Rosa Parks.

Reading Check **Summarizing** What role did African American churches play in the civil rights movement?

▲ *Rosa Parks rides a newly integrated bus after the successful boycott.*

D

▲ *African Americans walk to work during the third month of the Montgomery bus boycott (above). The Dexter Avenue Baptist Church in Montgomery, Alabama (right), was the Reverend Dr. Martin Luther King, Jr.'s, first church as a minister and headquarters for the organizers of the bus boycott.*

W Writing Support

Persuasive Writing Ask students to write an editorial explaining why African American churches should support the Montgomery bus boycott. **AL**

D Differentiated Instruction

Visual/Spatial Have students look at the four images on the page. **Ask:** What do the events, people, or places shown in these photos have in common? *(Each records an aspect of the civil rights movement—protest marches, Rosa Parks' challenge to bus segregation, an African American church—a center of civil rights activity, and civil rights leader Martin Luther King, Jr.)* **BL**

Reading Check

Answer:
African American churches served as forums for many of the protests and planning meetings, and mobilized many of the volunteers for civil rights campaigns.

Additional Support

Activity: U.S./World Connections

Making Connections Ask: What philosophy and techniques did Martin Luther King, Jr., draw from Indian leader Mohandas Gandhi? Have students gather information from the library and the Internet on the life and ideas of Indian independence leader Mohandas Gandhi. Tell them to create a chart comparing and contrasting the ideas of Gandhi and King. Then have student volunteers explain to the class what the connections are between the two leaders. Students may also research the links among King, Gandhi, Henry David Thoreau, and Jesus. **OL**

W Writing Support

Expository Writing Ask: Why did President Eisenhower refuse to endorse the *Brown* ruling but still enforced it? Ask students to conduct research to learn how Eisenhower came to this decision. Then have them write an essay explaining their answer. **OL**

C Critical Thinking

Analyzing Primary Sources
Ask: What can you infer from the photos about the response of many people in Little Rock to the integration of their public schools? *(Many white residents were opposed to integration and tried to intimidate students trying to register; state officials used state forces to oppose the federal government.)* **AL**

Analyzing VISUALS

Answers
1. They opposed integration.
2. to protect African American students and to prevent states from blocking integration efforts

Additional Support

Eisenhower Responds

MAIN Idea President Eisenhower sent the U.S. Army to enforce integration in Arkansas.

HISTORY AND YOU Do you believe that the president should uphold Supreme Court rulings? Read to learn how Eisenhower responded to events in Little Rock, Arkansas.

President Eisenhower sympathized with the civil rights movement and personally disagreed with segregation. Following the precedent set by President Truman, he ordered navy shipyards and veterans' hospitals to desegregate. At the same time, however, Eisenhower disagreed with those who wanted to end segregation through protests and court rulings. He believed segregation and racism would end gradually, as values changed. With the nation in the midst of the Cold War, he worried that challenging white Southerners might divide the nation at a time when the country needed to pull together. Publicly, he refused to endorse the *Brown v. Board of Education* decision. Privately, he remarked, "I don't believe you can change the hearts of men with laws or decisions."

Although he believed that the *Brown v. Board of Education* decision was wrong, Eisenhower knew he had to uphold the authority of the federal government. As a result, he became the first president since Reconstruction to send troops into the South to protect the rights of African Americans.

Crisis in Little Rock

In September 1957, the school board in Little Rock, Arkansas, won a court order requiring that nine African American students be admitted to Central High, a school with 2,000 white students. The governor of Arkansas, Orval Faubus, was known as a moderate on racial issues, but he was determined to win reelection and began to campaign as a defender of white supremacy. He ordered troops from the Arkansas National Guard to prevent the nine students from entering the school. The next day, as the National Guard troops sur-

PRIMARY SOURCE
Little Rock School Crisis, Arkansas, 1957

▲ In 1957 Elizabeth Eckford (left center) was one of nine courageous African American students determined to integrate Central High School in Little Rock.

▲ Arkansas governor Orval Faubus sought to block the school's integration. He is shown holding up a paper making his argument that the federal government was abusing its power in forcibly integrating Central High in Little Rock.

▶ Federal troops protect African American students at Central High.

Analyzing VISUALS

1. **Explaining** Why do you think the crowd is shouting at Elizabeth Eckford?
2. **Identifying Central Issues** Why did President Eisenhower send troops to Little Rock?

Activity: Collaborative Learning

Questioning Have students write journal entries about how it might have felt to be one of the first few African Americans to attend all-white schools. Ask them to focus on why a student would be willing to go through the stress of entering a school where he or she was, for the most part, unwanted. Encourage students to be creative but also to include some of the factual details from the text. Work with students to present the results as a whole-class presentation. **AL**

rounded the school, an angry white mob joined the troops to protest and to intimidate the students trying to register.

Faubus had used the armed forces of a state to oppose the federal government—the first such challenge to the Constitution since the Civil War. Eisenhower knew that he could not allow Faubus to defy the federal government. After a conference between Eisenhower and Faubus proved fruitless, the district court ordered the governor to remove the troops. Instead of ending the crisis, however, Faubus simply left the school to the mob. After the African American students entered the building, angry whites beat at least two African American reporters and broke many of the school's windows.

The violence finally convinced President Eisenhower that he had to act. Federal authority had to be upheld. He immediately ordered the Army to send troops to Little Rock. In addition, he federalized the Arkansas National Guard. By nightfall, 1,000 soldiers of the elite 101st Airborne Division had arrived. By 5:00 A.M., the troops had encircled the school, bayonets ready. A few hours later, the nine African American students arrived in an army station wagon and walked into the high school. Federal authority had been upheld, but the troops had to stay in Little Rock for the rest of the school year.

Officials in Little Rock, however, continued to resist integration. Before the start of the following school year, Governor Faubus ordered the three public high schools in Little Rock closed. Steps to integrate the schools in Little Rock resumed only in 1959.

New Civil Rights Legislation

In the same year that the Little Rock crisis began, Congress passed the first civil rights law since Reconstruction. The Civil Rights Act of 1957 was intended to protect the right of African Americans to vote. Eisenhower believed firmly in the right to vote, and he viewed it as his responsibility to protect voting rights. He also knew that if he sent a civil rights bill to Congress, conservative Southern Democrats would try to block the legislation. In 1956 he did send the bill to Congress, hoping not only to split the Democratic Party but also to convince more African Americans to vote Republican.

Several Southern senators did try to stop the Civil Rights Act of 1957, but the Senate majority leader, Democrat Lyndon Johnson, put together a compromise that enabled the act to pass. Although its final form was much weaker than originally intended, the act still brought the power of the federal government into the civil rights debate. It created a civil rights division within the Department of Justice and gave it the authority to seek court injunctions against anyone interfering with the right to vote. It also created the United States Commission on Civil Rights to investigate allegations of denial of voting rights. After the bill passed, the SCLC announced a campaign to register 2 million new African American voters.

Reading Check **Explaining** Why did Eisenhower intervene in the Little Rock controversy?

Section 1 REVIEW

Vocabulary

1. **Explain** the significance of: Rosa Parks, NAACP, "separate but equal," de facto segregation, sit-in, Thurgood Marshall, Linda Brown, Martin Luther King, Jr., Southern Christian Leadership Conference.

Main Ideas

2. **Explaining** What was CORE and what were some of its tactics?
3. **Identifying** What event set off the civil rights movement of the 1950s?
4. **Summarizing** Why did Eisenhower send the 101st Airborne Division to Little Rock, Arkansas?

Critical Thinking

5. **Big Ideas** Why did the role of the federal government in civil rights enforcement change?
6. **Organizing** Use a graphic organizer similar to the one below to list the efforts made to end segregation.

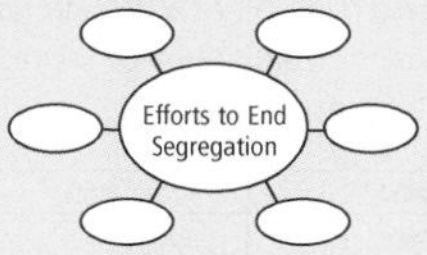

7. **Analyzing Visuals** Study the photograph of Elizabeth Eckford on page 856. Describe Eckford's demeanor compared to those around her. What might this indicate about her character?

Writing About History

8. **Expository Writing** Assume the role of an African American soldier returning from World War II. Write a letter to the editor of a newspaper describing your expectations of civil rights.

History ONLINE
Study Central™ To review this section, go to glencoe.com and click on Study Central.

Reading Check

Answer:
Although Eisenhower believed the *Brown* ruling was wrong, he knew he had to uphold the authority of the federal government when the Arkansas governor blocked student registration.

Assess

History ONLINE

Study Central™ provides summaries, interactive games, and online graphic organizers to help students review content.

Close

Predicting Consequences
Have students explain how the events discussed in this section advanced the cause of civil rights in the United States. OL

Section 1 REVIEW

Answers

1. All definitions can be found in the section and the Glossary.
2. CORE stood for Congress of Racial Equality and was begun in 1942 to fight segregation. CORE applied a union tactic called the sit-in to fight segregation in restaurants.
3. Rosa Parks's arrest and the consequent Montgomery bus boycott.
4. Eisenhower personally did not approve of forcing segregation through the courts or laws. Governor Faubus's use of the National Guard, however, was a challenge to the federal government, and Eisenhower felt that he had no choice but to intervene in Arkansas to uphold the *Brown* ruling.
5. Organizations, such as the NAACP, appealed segregation cases to the Supreme Court. When individual states challenged these decisions, the federal government intervened to enforce the Court's decisions.
6. Founding of CORE, sit-ins, NAACP court challenges, bus boycott, voter registration drives
7. Students' answers will vary, but should recognize her courage and dignity.
8. Student letters will vary but should include specific expectations supported by reasoned arguments and evidence.

Focus

Bellringer

Daily Focus Transparency 25-2

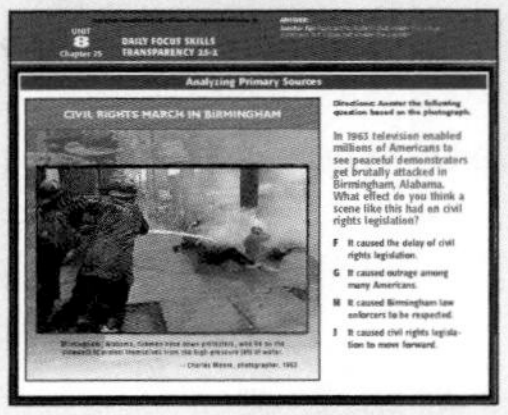

Guide to Reading

Answers:

Cause	Effect
Sit-in Movement	brought attention to the civil rights movement
Freedom Riders	Kennedy's decision to stop violence
King's release from jail	African American support for Kennedy
Selma march	African American voter registration

Section Spotlight Video

To generate student interest and provide a springboard for class discussion, access the Chapter 25, Section 2 video at glencoe.com or on the video DVD.

Section 2

Section Audio   Spotlight Video

Challenging Segregation

Guide to Reading

Big Ideas

Group Action African American citizens created organizations that directed protests to demand full civil rights.

Content Vocabulary

- filibuster *(p. 864)*
- cloture *(p. 864)*

Academic Vocabulary

- register *(p. 859)*

People and Events to Identify

- Student Nonviolent Coordinating Committee (SNCC) *(p. 859)*
- Freedom Riders *(p. 860)*
- James Meredith *(p. 862)*
- Civil Rights Act of 1964 *(p. 865)*
- Voting Rights Act of 1965 *(p. 867)*

Reading Strategy

Organizing Complete a graphic organizer about the challenges to segregation in the South.

Cause	Effect
Sit-In Movement	
Freedom Riders	

In the early 1960s, the struggle for civil rights intensified. African American citizens and white supporters created organizations that directed protests, targeted specific inequalities, and attracted the attention of the mass media and the government.

The Sit-in Movement

MAIN Idea African American students staged sit-ins and formed the Student Nonviolent Coordinating Committee (SNCC) to organize efforts for desegregation and voter registration throughout the South.

HISTORY AND YOU Would you risk your personal safety to participate in a sit-in? Read on to learn of the response of young people to the sit-in movement of the early 1960s.

In the fall of 1959, four young African Americans—Joseph McNeil, Ezell Blair, Jr., David Richmond, and Franklin McCain—enrolled at North Carolina Agricultural and Technical College, an African American college in Greensboro. The four freshmen spent evenings talking about the civil rights movement. In January 1960, McNeil suggested a sit-in at the whites-only lunch counter in the nearby Woolworth's department store.

"All of us were afraid," Richmond later recalled, "but we went and did it." On February 1, 1960, the four friends entered the Woolworth's. They purchased school supplies and then sat at the lunch counter and ordered coffee. When they were refused service, Blair asked, "I beg your pardon, but you just served us at [the checkout] counter. Why can't we be served at the counter here?" The students stayed at the counter until it closed, and then announced that they would sit at the counter every day until they were given the same service as white customers.

As they left the store, the four were excited. McNeil recalled, "I just felt I had powers within me, a superhuman strength that would come forward." McCain was also energized, saying, "I probably felt better that day than I've ever felt in my life."

News of the daring sit-in at the Woolworth's store spread quickly across Greensboro. The following day, 29 African American students arrived at Woolworth's determined to sit at the counter until served. By the end of the week, over 300 students were taking part.

Starting with just four students, a new mass movement for civil rights had begun. Within two months, sit-ins had spread to 54 cities in nine states. They were staged at segregated stores, restaurants, hotels, and movie theaters. By 1961, sit-ins had been held in more than 100 cities.

Resource Manager

R Reading Strategies	C Critical Thinking	D Differentiated Instruction	W Writing Support	S Skill Practice
Teacher Edition • Act. Prior Knowl., p. 862 • Outlining, p. 864 • Questioning, p. 864 • Read. Pri. Sources, p. 865 **Additional Resources** • Guid. Read. Act., URB p. 81 • Prim. Source Read., URB p. 67	**Teacher Edition** • Ident. Cent. Iss., p. 859 • Making Inf., p. 860 • Analyze Info., pp. 861, 862, 866 • Cause/Effect, p. 861 • Analyze Pri. Sources, p. 864 **Additional Resources** • Quizzes and Tests, p. 360 • Linking Past and Present Act., URB p. 66	**Teacher Edition** • English Learners, p. 866 **Additional Resources** • Differen. Instr. Act., URB p. 55 • Enrichment Act., URB p. 77 • Am. Art and Music Act., URB p. 71 • Interpret. Pol. Cartoons Act., URB p. 73	**Teacher Edition** • Expository Writing, p. 860 • Narrative Writing, p. 867 **Additional Resources** • Supreme Court Case Studies, p. 97	**Teacher Edition** • Visual Literacy, p. 863 **Additional Resources** • Read. Essen., p. 280 • Read. Skills Act., URB p. 53

PRIMARY SOURCE
The Sit-ins Begin in Greensboro

◀ Joseph McNeil, Franklin McCain, Billy Smith, and Clarence Henderson begin the second day of their sit-in at the whites-only Woolworth's counter in Greensboro, North Carolina, in 1960.

▲ *Nonviolent protests, such as this pray-in in Albany, Georgia, in 1962, spread across the nation as the civil rights movement gained momentum.*

Analyzing VISUALS DBQ

1. **Explaining** Why did the four African American students begin the sit-in at the Woolworth's counter?
2. **Drawing Conclusions** Why was nonviolence so effective as a form of protest?

The sit-in movement brought large numbers of idealistic and energized college students into the civil rights struggle. Many African American students had become discouraged by the slow pace of desegregation. Students like Jesse Jackson, a student leader at North Carolina Agricultural and Technical College, wanted to see things change more quickly. The sit-in offered them a way to take matters into their own hands.

C At first, the leaders of the NAACP and the SCLC were nervous about the sit-in campaign. They feared that students did not have the discipline to remain nonviolent if they were provoked enough. For the most part, the students proved them wrong. Those conducting sit-ins were heckled by bystanders, punched, kicked, beaten with clubs, and burned with cigarettes, hot coffee, and acid—but most did not fight back. Their heroic behavior grabbed the nation's attention.

As the sit-ins spread, student leaders in different states realized they needed to coordinate their efforts. The person who brought them together was Ella Baker, a former NAACP official and the executive director of the SCLC. In April 1960 Baker invited student leaders to attend a convention at Shaw University in Raleigh, North Carolina. There she urged students to create their own organization instead of joining the NAACP or the SCLC. Students, she said, had "the right to direct their own affairs and even make their own mistakes."

The students agreed with Baker and established the **Student Nonviolent Coordinating Committee (SNCC).** Among SNCC's early leaders were Marion Barry, who later served as mayor of Washington, D.C., and John Lewis, who later became a member of Congress. African American college students from all across the South made up the majority of SNCC's members, although many whites also joined. Between 1960 and 1965, SNCC played a key role in desegregating public facilities in dozens of Southern communities. SNCC also began sending volunteers into rural areas of the Deep South to **register** African Americans to vote.

Teach

C Critical Thinking

Identifying Central Issues

Ask: Why were African American leaders at first doubtful about student involvement in sit-ins? *(They feared that students did not have the discipline to remain nonviolent if they were provoked.)* What effect did student sit-ins have on public opinion? *(Their heroic behavior won the nation's respect.)* **OL**

Analyzing VISUALS

Answers:

1. They wanted to be served at the whites-only counter, so they refused to move until they were served to protest the segregated counter.
2. Answers will vary, but students should note that nonviolence gives protesters a way to make a strong point and gives them a moral "upper hand" if they are mistreated.

Differentiated Instruction

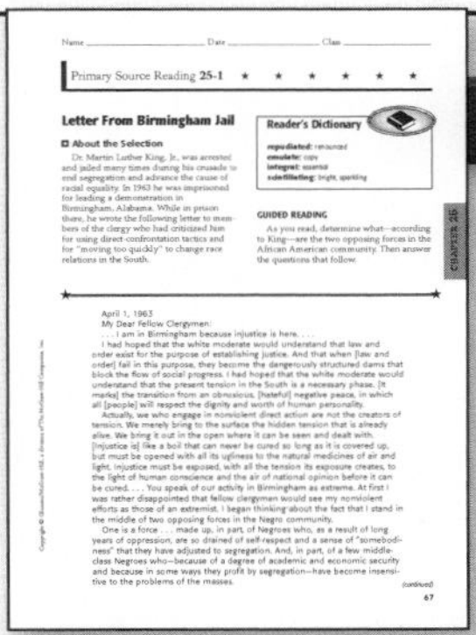

Primary Source Reading 25-1

Letter From Birmingham Jail

Primary Source Reading, URB pp. 67–68

Letter from a Birmingham Jail

Objective: Read to discover how Dr. Martin Luther King, Jr., explained his arrest.

Focus: Have students define *injustice.*

Teach: Associate King's letter with the active civil rights movement.

Assess: Have students identify the "forces" that King describes.

Close: Have students speculate about how the clergy reacted to King's letter.

Differentiated Instruction Strategies

BL Have students reference a map of Alabama and locate Birmingham.

AL Have students write a series of questions they would ask King as a news reporter.

ELL Have students select three terms from the letter. They should look up the terms and provide the definitions in their own words.

W Writing Support

Expository Writing Have students choose one of the activities carried on by SNCC and learn about how it began and what its purpose was. Then have them take the role of a leader, such as Robert Moses or Fannie Lou Hamer. Ask students to write a brief speech arguing in support of the cause the leader organized. **AL**

C Critical Thinking

Making Inferences Ask: What qualities would a person have needed to participate as a Freedom Rider? *(bravery, courage, dedication, sharp thinking, and clear speaking)* **OL**

Reading Check

Answer:
Sit-ins attracted the nation's attention and gave people, especially students, a way to become involved in the civil rights movement.

The idea for what came to be called the Voter Education Project began with Robert Moses, an SNCC volunteer from New York. Moses pointed out that the civil rights movement tended to focus on urban areas. He urged the SNCC to start helping rural African Americans, who often faced violence if they tried to register to vote. Despite the danger, many SNCC volunteers headed to the Deep South. Moses himself went to Mississippi. Several had their lives threatened; others were beaten, and in 1964, local officials brutally murdered three SNCC workers. **W**

One SNCC organizer, a sharecropper named Fannie Lou Hamer, had been evicted from her farm after registering to vote. She was arrested in Mississippi for urging other African Americans to register. Police severely beat her while she was in jail. She then helped organize the Mississippi Freedom Democratic Party and challenged the legality of Mississippi's segregated Democratic Party at the 1964 Democratic National Convention.

Reading Check **Explaining** What were the effects of the sit-in movement?

The Freedom Riders

MAIN Idea Teams of African Americans and whites rode buses into the South to protest the continued illegal segregation on interstate bus lines.

HISTORY AND YOU Is it acceptable to risk provoking violence in order to advance a cause you support? Read to learn about the violence that erupted against the Freedom Riders and against Martin Luther King, Jr.'s march in Birmingham.

Despite rulings outlawing segregation in interstate bus service, bus travel remained segregated in much of the South. In 1961 CORE leader James Farmer asked teams of African American and white volunteers, many of whom were college students, to travel into the South to draw attention to its refusal to integrate bus terminals. The teams became known as the **Freedom Riders.** **C**

In early May 1961, the first Freedom Riders boarded several southbound interstate buses. When the buses arrived in Anniston, Birmingham, and Montgomery, Alabama, angry white mobs attacked them. The mobs

The Civil Rights Movement, 1954–1965

May 1954 In *Brown* v. *Board of Education*, Supreme Court declares segregated schools unconstitutional

December 1955 Rosa Parks is arrested and Montgomery Bus Boycott begins

December 1956 Supreme Court declares separate-but-equal doctrine is no longer constitutional

January 1957 Martin Luther King, Jr., and other Southern ministers create SCLC

September 1957 Arkansas governor Faubus blocks desegregation of Little Rock High School, forcing Eisenhower to send troops to the school

February 1960 Students in Greensboro, North Carolina, stage a sit-in at a local lunch counter; as sit-ins spread, student leaders form SNCC in April

May 1961 James Farmer organizes the first Freedom Riders to desegregate interstate bus travel

1955 1957 1959 1961

Hands-On Chapter Project Step 2

A Freedom Drama

Step 2: Freedom News Students will continue their theatrical presentation by writing news stories about the Montgomery bus boycott.

Directions Write the Big Idea on the board. Discuss the events related to the Montgomery bus boycott, such as the arrest of Rosa Parks and Martin Luther King's leadership of the movement. Have groups write scripts for a TV news report about the bus boycott. Students should feel free to imply the feelings of the people represented in their news story while sticking to the known facts.

Putting it Together Have groups read their news scripts to the class. **OL** *(Chapter Project continued on page 874)*

slit the bus tires and threw rocks at the windows. In Anniston, someone threw a firebomb into one bus, but fortunately no one was killed.

In Birmingham the riders emerged from a bus to face a gang of young men armed with baseball bats, chains, and lead pipes. The gang beat the riders viciously. One witness later reported, "You couldn't see their faces through the blood." The head of the police in Birmingham, Public Safety Commissioner Theophilus Eugene "Bull" Connor, explained that there had been no police at the bus station because it was Mother's Day, and he had given many of his officers the day off. FBI evidence later showed that Connor had contacted the local Ku Klux Klan and told them to beat the Freedom Riders until "it looked like a bulldog got a hold of them." C1

The violence in Alabama made national news, shocking many Americans. The attack on the Freedom Riders came less than four months after President John F. Kennedy took office. The new president felt compelled to get the violence under control.

Kennedy and Civil Rights

While campaigning for the presidency in 1960, John F. Kennedy promised to actively support the civil rights movement if elected. His brother, Robert F. Kennedy, had used his influence to get Dr. King released from jail after a demonstration in Georgia. African Americans responded by voting overwhelmingly for Kennedy. Their votes helped him narrowly win several key states, including Illinois, which Kennedy carried by only 9,000 votes. C2

Once in office, however, Kennedy at first seemed as cautious as Eisenhower on civil rights, which disappointed many African Americans. Kennedy knew he needed the support of many Southern senators to get other programs through Congress and that any attempt to push through new civil rights legislation would anger them. Congressional Republicans repeatedly reminded the public of Kennedy's failure to follow through on his campaign promise to push for civil rights for African Americans.

May 1963 Martin Luther King, Jr., leads protests in Birmingham, Alabama; police assault the protestors and King is jailed

March 1965 King leads a march in Selma, Alabama, to build support for a new voting rights law; police brutally attack marchers

August 3, 1965 Congress passes the Voting Rights Act of 1965

1963 — 1965

September 1962 James Meredith tries to register at University of Mississippi; riots force Kennedy to send troops

August 1963 King delivers his "I Have a Dream" speech during the March on Washington in support of new civil rights act

July 1964 Johnson signs Civil Rights Act of 1964 into law

Analyzing TIME LINES

1. **Identifying** According to the time line, what was the first major event in the civil rights movement?
2. **Analyzing** How many years were there between the *Brown* decision and the passage of the Civil Rights Act of 1964?
3. **Stating** When were the Freedom Riders organized?

C1 Critical Thinking

Analyzing Information Have students look at the quotations on this page. **Ask:** What do these quotations reveal about the feelings and actions of the people opposed to the Freedom Riders? *(Opponents hated the Freedom Riders and the civil rights cause so much they were willing to use extreme force and violence.)* OL

C2 Critical Thinking

Determining Cause and Effect Ask: What effect did the civil rights struggle have on the outcome of the 1960 presidential election? *(African American voters responded to Kennedy's support for King by voting overwhelmingly for Kennedy in the election. Their votes helped Kennedy win several key states.)* OL

Analyzing TIME LINES

Answers:

1. the Supreme Court decision in *Brown* v. *Board of Education*
2. ten years
3. 1961

Differentiated Instruction

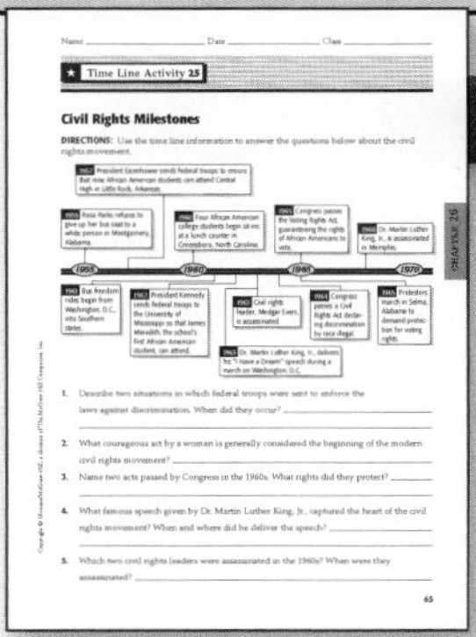

Time Line Activity 15

Civil Rights Milestones

Time Line Activity, URB p. 65

Civil Rights Milestones

Objective: To understand milestone events of the civil rights movement.

Focus: Have students identify and use information on the time line.

Teach: Discuss the causes and effects of various civil rights events.

Assess: Have students design time lines to include other civil rights events.

Close: Have students share their time lines.

Differentiated Instruction Activities

BL Discuss the meaning of civil rights and the key issues involved.

AL Research the strategies and activities of the civil rights movement. Which were the most effective? Why?

ELL Define *discrimination* and propose synonyms for the word.

C Critical Thinking

Analyzing Information

Ask: How did Kennedy's response to the civil rights movement change during the course of his presidency? *(Kennedy was reluctant at first to become actively involved in the civil rights struggle, but the pressure of events forced him to take a stand in supporting an end to segregation.)* **OL**

R Reading Strategy

Activating Prior Knowledge

In earlier text chapters, students have studied the discrimination and mistreatment of African Americans before the civil rights era. **Ask:** What did James Farmer mean when he said "If we cool off anymore, we'll be in a deep freeze." *(African Americans have been waiting far too long—over 350 years—for their right to equality, and their patience had finally ended).* **OL**

Kennedy did, however, name approximately 40 African Americans to high-level positions in the government. He also appointed Thurgood Marshall to a federal judgeship on the Second Circuit Appeals Court in New York—one level below the Supreme Court and the highest judicial position an African American had attained to that point. Kennedy created the Committee on Equal Employment Opportunity (CEEO) to stop the federal bureaucracy from discriminating against African Americans in hiring and promotions.

The Justice Department Takes Action Although President Kennedy was unwilling to challenge Southern Democrats in Congress, C he allowed the Justice Department, run by his brother Robert, to actively support the civil rights movement. Robert Kennedy tried to help African Americans register to vote by having the civil rights division of the Justice Department file lawsuits across the South.

When violence erupted against the Freedom Riders, the Kennedys came to their aid as well, although not at first. At the time the Freedom Riders took action, President Kennedy was preparing for a meeting with Nikita Khrushchev, the leader of the Soviet Union. Kennedy did not want violence in the South to disrupt the meeting by giving the impression that his country was weak and divided.

After the Freedom Riders were attacked in Montgomery, the Kennedys publicly urged them to stop the rides and give everybody a "cooling off" period. James Farmer replied that African Americans "have been cooling off now for 350 years. If we cool off anymore, we'll R be in a deep freeze." Instead, he announced that the Freedom Riders planned to head into Mississippi on their next trip.

To stop the violence, President Kennedy made a deal with Senator James Eastland of Mississippi, a strong supporter of segregation. If Eastland would use his influence in Mississippi to prevent violence, Kennedy would not object if the Mississippi police arrested the Freedom Riders. Eastland kept the deal. No violence occurred when the buses arrived in Jackson, Mississippi, but the riders were arrested.

The cost of bailing the Freedom Riders out of jail used up most of CORE's funds, which meant that the rides would have to end unless more money could be found. When Thurgood Marshall learned of the situation, he offered James Farmer the use of the NAACP Legal Defense Fund's huge bail bond account to keep the rides going.

When President Kennedy returned from meeting with Khrushchev and found that the Freedom Riders were still active, he changed his approach. He ordered the Interstate Commerce Commission (ICC) to tighten its regulations against segregated bus terminals. In the meantime, Robert Kennedy ordered the Justice Department to take legal action against Southern cities that maintained segregated bus terminals. The actions of the ICC and the Justice Department finally produced results. By late 1962, segregation in interstate bus travel had come to an end.

James Meredith As the Freedom Riders were trying to desegregate interstate bus lines, efforts continued to integrate Southern schools. On the day John F. Kennedy was inaugurated, an African American air force veteran named **James Meredith** applied for a transfer to the University of Mississippi. Up to that point, the university had avoided complying with the Supreme Court ruling ending segregated education.

In September 1962, Meredith tried to register at the university's admissions office, only to find Ross Barnett, the governor of Mississippi, blocking his path. Meredith had a court order directing the university to register him, but Governor Barnett stated emphatically, "Never! We will never surrender to the evil and illegal forces of tyranny."

Frustrated, President Kennedy dispatched 500 federal marshals to escort Meredith to the campus. Shortly after Meredith and the marshals arrived, an angry white mob attacked the campus, and a full-scale riot erupted. The mob hurled rocks, bottles, bricks, and acid at the marshals. Some people fired shotguns at them. The marshals responded with tear gas, but they were under orders not to fire.

The fighting continued all night. By morning, 160 marshals had been wounded. Reluctantly, Kennedy ordered the army to send several thousand troops to the campus. For the rest of the year, Meredith attended classes at the University of Mississippi under federal guard. He graduated in August.

Additional Support

Activity: Collaborative Learning

Using Graphic Organizers To examine groups affected by the civil rights movement, organize students into four teams. Supply each team with poster board and markers. Within each team, have some students specialize in NAACP, SNCC, SCLC, and CORE. Ask each team to create a concept web with the phrase *My Rights* in the center of the page, branching out to show the kinds of rights sought and noting a few details about each group discussed. Encourage teams to compare and discuss their webs. **OL**

PRIMARY SOURCE
Protests in Birmingham, 1963

▲ A protester in Birmingham, Alabama, is attacked by police dogs—a scene that outraged Americans across the nation.

Primary Source

"Since we so diligently urge people to obey the Supreme Court's decision of 1954 outlawing segregation in the public schools, at first glance it may seem rather paradoxical for us consciously to break laws. One may well ask: "How can you advocate breaking some laws and obeying others?" The answer lies in the fact that there are two types of laws: just and unjust. . . . [and] one has a moral responsibility to disobey unjust laws. I would agree with St. Augustine that 'an unjust law is no law at all.'

. . . . Any law that uplifts human personality is just. Any law that degrades human personality is unjust. All segregation statutes are unjust because segregation distorts the soul and damages the personality. It gives the segregator a false sense of superiority and the segregated a false sense of inferiority. . . . An unjust law is a code that a numerical or power majority group compels a minority group to obey but does not make binding on itself. This is difference made legal. By the same token, a just law is a code that a majority compels a minority to follow and that it is willing to follow itself. This is sameness made legal."

—from Martin Luther King, Jr., "Letter from Birmingham Jail, 1963"

S

DBQ Document-Based Questions

1. **Classifying** According to Dr. King, what are the two types of laws? What is the difference between them?
2. **Determining Cause and Effect** What does King say are the effects of segregation on the segregator? On the segregated?

Violence in Birmingham

The events in Mississippi frustrated Martin Luther King, Jr., and other civil rights leaders. Although they were pleased that Kennedy had intervened, they were disappointed that the president had not seized the moment to push for a new civil rights law.

Reflecting on the problem, Dr. King came to a difficult decision. It seemed to him that only when violence got out of hand would the federal government intervene. "We've got to have a crisis to bargain with," one of his advisers observed. King agreed. In the spring of 1963, he decided to launch demonstrations in Birmingham, Alabama, knowing they would provoke a violent response. He believed it was the only way to get President Kennedy to actively support civil rights.

The situation in Birmingham was volatile. Public Safety Commissioner Bull Connor, who had arranged for the attack on the Freedom Riders, was now running for mayor. Eight days after the protests began, King was arrested. While in jail, King began writing on scraps of paper that had been smuggled into his cell. The "Letter from Birmingham Jail" that he produced is one of the most eloquent defenses of nonviolent protest ever written.

In his letter, King explained that although the protesters were breaking the law, they were following a higher moral law based on divine justice. Injustice, he insisted, had to be exposed "to the light of human conscience and the air of national opinion before it can be cured."

After King was released, the protests, which had been dwindling, began to grow again. Bull Connor responded with force. He ordered the Birmingham police to use clubs, police dogs, and high-pressure fire hoses on the demonstrators. Millions of Americans watched the graphic violence on the nightly news on television. Outraged by the brutality and worried that the government was losing control, Kennedy ordered his aides to prepare a new civil rights bill.

✓ Reading Check **Evaluating** How did President Kennedy help the civil rights movement?

S Skill Practice

Visual Literacy Have students study the image on this page. Lead a discussion in which students pose questions raised by the image. *(Questions might include: What people are shown in the image? How are they interacting with each other? How do their actions reflect attitudes of both sides in the civil rights struggle in Birmingham?)* AL

DBQ Document Based Questions

Answers:

1. just and unjust; a law uplifting humanity is just; one that degrades human personality is unjust
2. Segregation gives the segregator a false sense of superiority, while it gives the segregated a false sense of inferiority.

✓ Reading Check

Answer:
Kennedy appointed African Americans to some federal positions, protected civil rights through involvement with the states, and prepared a civil rights bill.

Differentiated Instruction

Leveled Activities

BL Content Vocabulary Activity, URB p. 59

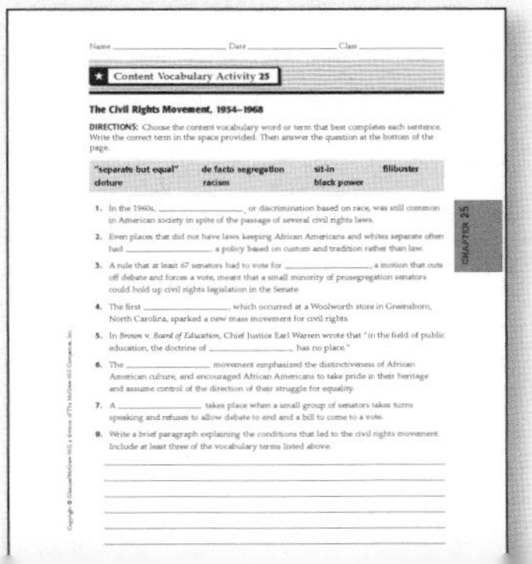

OL Linking Past and Present Activity, URB p. 66

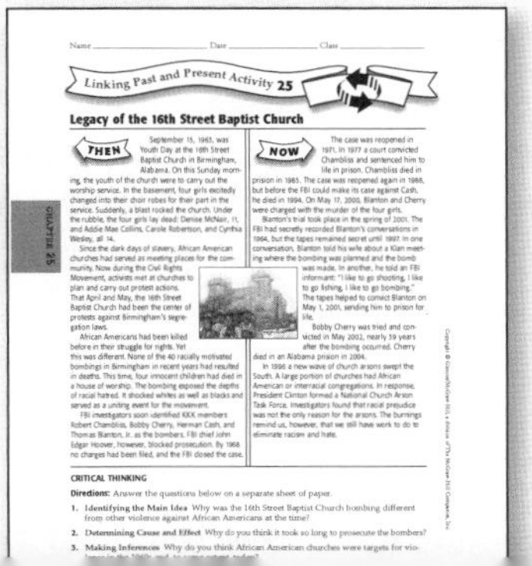

AL Primary Source Reading, URB p. 67

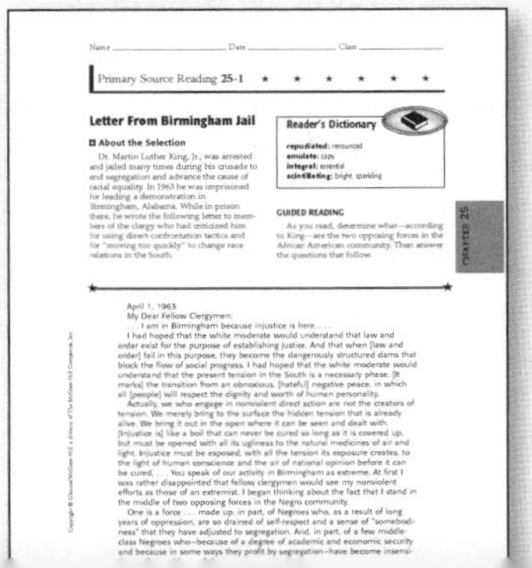

ELL English Learner Activity, URB p. 57

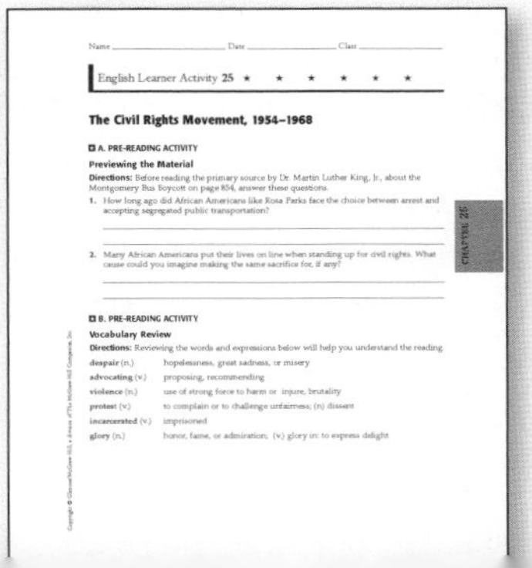

R1 Reading Strategy

Outlining Encourage students to outline the section on the Civil Rights Act of 1964. Suggest they group the information under two main headings: *The March on Washington* and *The Bill Becomes Law.* BL

C Critical Thinking

Analyzing Primary Sources Ask students why Kennedy refers to Lincoln's freeing of enslaved African Americans in his address. *(Kennedy states that the step begun by Lincoln in the past needs to be completed in the present by ensuring full freedom and equality to African Americans.)* OL

R2 Reading Strategy

Questioning Ask: Why did some U.S. senators stage a filibuster during the debate for civil rights legislation in 1964? *(By taking turns speaking and refusing to stop the debate, the senators wanted to keep the civil rights bill from coming to a vote.)* OL

Additional Support

The Civil Rights Act of 1964

MAIN Idea President Johnson used his political expertise to get the Civil Rights Act of 1964 passed.

HISTORY AND YOU Do you remember the constitutional amendments that granted African Americans civil rights after the Civil War? Read on to learn about new legal steps taken during the 1960s.

Determined to introduce a civil rights bill, Kennedy now waited for a dramatic moment to address the nation on the issue. Alabama's governor, George Wallace, gave the president his chance. At his inauguration as governor, Wallace had stated, "I draw a line in the dust . . . and I say, Segregation now! Segregation tomorrow! Segregation forever!" On June 11, 1963, Wallace stood in front of the University of Alabama's admissions office to block two African Americans from enrolling. He stayed until federal marshals ordered him to move.

The next day a white segregationist murdered Medgar Evers, a civil rights activist in Mississippi. President Kennedy seized the moment to announce his civil rights bill. That evening, he spoke to Americans about a "moral issue . . . as old as the scriptures and as clear as the American Constitution":

PRIMARY SOURCE

"The heart of the question is whether . . . we are going to treat our fellow Americans as we want to be treated. If an American, because his skin is dark, cannot eat lunch in a restaurant open to the public, if he cannot send his children to the best public school available, if he cannot vote for the public officials who represent him . . . then who among us would be content to have the color of his skin changed and stand in his place?

One hundred years of delay have passed since President Lincoln freed the slaves, yet their heirs, their grandsons, are not fully free. . . . And this Nation, for all its hopes and all its boasts, will not be fully free until all its citizens are free. . . . Now the time has come for this Nation to fulfill its promise."

—from Kennedy's White House address, June 11, 1963

The March on Washington

Dr. King realized that Kennedy would have a very difficult time pushing his civil rights bill through Congress. Therefore, he searched for a way to lobby Congress and to build more public support. When A. Philip Randolph suggested a march on Washington, King agreed.

On August 28, 1963, more than 200,000 demonstrators of all races flocked to the nation's capital. The audience heard speeches and sang hymns and songs as they gathered peacefully near the Lincoln Memorial. Dr. King then delivered a powerful speech outlining his dream of freedom and equality for all Americans.

King's speech and the peacefulness and dignity of the March on Washington built momentum for the civil rights bill. Opponents in Congress, however, continued to do what they could to slow the bill down, dragging out their committee investigations and using procedural rules to delay votes.

The Bill Becomes Law

Although the civil rights bill was likely to pass the House of Representatives, where a majority of Republicans and Northern Democrats supported the measure, it faced a much more difficult time in the Senate. There, a small group of determined Southern senators would try to block the bill indefinitely.

In the U.S. Senate, senators are allowed to speak for as long as they like when a bill is being debated. The Senate cannot vote on a bill until all senators have finished speaking. A **filibuster** occurs when a small group of senators take turns speaking and refuse to stop the debate and allow a bill to come to a vote. Today a filibuster can be stopped if at least 60 senators vote for **cloture,** a motion that cuts off debate and forces a vote. In the 1960s, however, 67 senators had to vote for cloture to stop a filibuster. This meant that a minority of senators opposed to civil rights could easily prevent the majority from enacting a new civil rights law.

Worried that the bill would never pass, many African Americans became even more disheartened. Then, President Kennedy was assassinated in Dallas, Texas, on November 22, 1963, and his vice president, Lyndon Johnson, became president. Johnson was from Texas and

Extending the Content

The March on Washington Because of racial violence in June 1963, President Kennedy urged Martin Luther King, Jr., not to hold the civil rights march in Washington, D.C., but King and his colleagues held firm. March organizer Bayard Rustin later said, "What made the march was that black people . . . came from every state, they came in jalopies, on trains, buses, anything they could get—some walked . . . And after [members of Congress] . . . saw that there was fantastic determination that there were all kinds of people there other than black people, they know there was a consensus in this country for a civil rights bill." Have students find the definition of *consensus* in the dictionary. Ask them, based on their reading of the text, if they agree or disagree with Rustin's view about public support for civil rights legislation. Have students hypothesize about the impact of the march on the final passage of the 1964 Civil Rights Act.

PRIMARY SOURCE

Martin Luther King, Jr.'s Address, Washington, 1963

PRIMARY SOURCE

"And so even though we face the difficulties of today and tomorrow, I still have a dream. It is a dream deeply rooted in the American dream.

I have a dream that one day this nation will rise up and live out the true meaning of its creed: 'We hold these truths to be self-evident, that all men are created equal.'

I have a dream that one day on the red hills of Georgia, the sons of former slaves and the sons of former slave owners will be able to sit down together at the table of brotherhood. . . .

I have a dream that my four little children will one day live in a nation where they will not be judged by the color of their skin but by the content of their character.

I have a dream today!

. . . And when this happens, when we allow freedom to ring, when we let it ring from every village and every hamlet, from every state and every city, we will be able to speed up that day when all of God's children, black men and white men, Jews and Gentiles, Protestants and Catholics, will be able to join hands and sing in the words of the old Negro spiritual:

Free at last! Free at last!

Thank God Almighty, we are free at last!"

—Martin Luther King, Jr., "Address in Washington," 1963

R

DBQ Document-Based Questions

1. **Identifying Central Issues** What was Martin Luther King, Jr.'s dream?
2. **Interpreting** What did King mean when he said that he hoped that one day the nation will "live out the true meaning of its creed"?

had been the leader of the Senate Democrats before becoming vice president. Although he had helped pass the Civil Rights Acts of 1957 and 1960, he had done so by weakening their provisions and by compromising with other Southern senators.

To the surprise of the civil rights movement, Johnson committed himself wholeheartedly to getting Kennedy's program, including the civil rights bill, through Congress. Johnson had served in Congress for many years and was adept at getting legislation enacted. He knew how to build public support, how to put pressure on Congress, and how to use the rules and procedures to get what he wanted.

In February 1964, President Johnson's leadership began to produce results. The civil rights bill passed the House of Representatives by a majority of 290 to 130. The debate then moved to the Senate. In June, after 87 days of filibuster, the Senate finally voted to end debate by a margin of 71 to 29—four votes over the two-thirds needed for cloture. The Senate then easily passed the bill. On July 2, 1964, President Johnson signed the **Civil Rights Act of 1964** into law.

The Civil Rights Act of 1964 was the most comprehensive civil rights law Congress had ever enacted. It gave the federal government broad power to prevent racial discrimination in a number of areas. The law made segregation illegal in most places of public accommodation, and it gave citizens of all races and nationalities equal access to public facilities. The law gave the U.S. attorney general more power to bring lawsuits to force school desegregation and required private employers to end discrimination in the workplace. It also established the Equal Employment Opportunity Commission (EEOC) as a permanent agency in the federal government. This commission monitors the ban on job discrimination by race, religion, gender, and national origin.

Reading Check **Examining** How did Dr. King lobby Congress to pass a new civil rights act?

To read more of Martin Luther King, Jr.'s "I Have a Dream" speech, see page R56 in **Documents in American History.**

R Reading Strategy

Reading Primary Sources

Ask: What is the tone of King's speech? *(King's speech is inspirational and upbeat.)* **Ask:** To what extent has King's dream been fulfilled today? In what ways has it yet to be fulfilled? *(Answers will vary, but students should point to gains and continuing challenges in relations between ethnic groups.)* OL

DBQ Document Based Questions

Answers:

1. complete legal and social equality for all races
2. He hopes one day the United States will actually practice the principles of the Declaration of Independence, the country's founding document.

Reading Check

Answer:

King organized and led the March on Washington.

Additional Support

Activity: Interdisciplinary Connection

Language Arts Locate a recording of King's "I Have a Dream" speech and play it for the class. Remind students to focus on the tone and cadence of King's voice. Then have students pause to make a few notes about the "sound" of the speech. Discuss with students any examples of phrasing and ideas in the speech that they found memorable. Ask them to comment about the inspiration they heard in those ideas—and in the sound of King's voice. BL ELL

C Critical Thinking

Analyzing Information Ask: Why did African Americans face hurdles in voting despite the passage of the Twenty-fourth Amendment? *(The amendment ended poll taxes in federal elections, not state elections; also, voter registration efforts met open resistance in the South.)* **OL**

D Differentiated Instruction

English Learners Have students explain the text when it says that Sheriff Clark's "posse terrorized African Americans." *(Sheriff Clark gave a group of citizens the authority to deal with the situation, in this case, to attack African Americans.)* **OL**

Analyzing VISUALS

Answers:

1. It made segregation illegal in virtually all areas of public life.
2. Counties with low voter registrations may have been keeping people from registering.

Additional Support

The Struggle for Voting Rights

MAIN Idea President Johnson called for a new voting rights law after hostile crowds severely beat civil rights demonstrators.

HISTORY AND YOU Do you remember the tactics Southern states adopted to keep African Americans from voting? Read on to learn about the Voting Rights Act of 1965.

Even after the Civil Rights Act of 1964 was passed, voting rights were far from secure. The act had focused on segregation and job discrimination, and it did little to address voting issues. The Twenty-fourth Amendment, ratified in 1964, helped somewhat by eliminating **C** poll taxes, or fees paid in order to vote, in federal (but not state) elections. African Americans still faced hurdles, however, when they tried to vote. As the SCLC and SNCC stepped up their voter registration efforts in the South, their members were often attacked and beaten, and several were murdered.

Across the South, bombs exploded in African American businesses and churches. Between June and October 1964, arson and bombs destroyed 24 African American churches in Mississippi alone. Convinced that a new law was needed to protect African American voting rights, Dr. King decided to stage another dramatic protest.

The Selma March

In January 1965, the SCLC and Dr. King selected Selma, Alabama, as the focal point for their campaign for voting rights. Although African Americans made up a majority of Selma's population, they comprised only 3 percent of registered voters. To prevent African Americans from registering to vote, Sheriff Jim Clark had deputized and armed dozens of white citizens. His posse terrorized African Americans and frequently attacked demonstrators with clubs and electric cattle prods. **D**

In December 1964, Dr. King received the Nobel Peace Prize in Oslo, Norway, for his work in the civil rights movement. A few weeks

PRIMARY SOURCE
Marching for Freedom, Selma, 1965

The Civil Rights Act of 1964
- Gave the federal government power to prevent racial discrimination and established the Equal Employment Opportunity Commission (EEOC).
- Made segregation illegal in most places of public accommodation.
- Gave the U.S. attorney general more power to bring lawsuits to force school desegregation.
- Required employers to end workplace discrimination.

The Voting Rights Act of 1965
- Authorized the U.S. attorney general to send federal examiners to register qualified voters.
- Suspended discriminatory devices, such as literacy tests, in counties where less than half of all adults had been allowed to vote.

Analyzing VISUALS

1. **Making Connections** How did the Civil Rights Act of 1964 work to end segregation?
2. **Drawing Conclusions** Why do you think counties where less than half of all adults were allowed to vote were a focus of the Voting Rights Acts of 1965?

Activity: Interdisciplinary Connection

Music Have students write a civil rights song based on the sit-in movement or the Freedom Riders. Suggest that students use library or Internet resources to find and review examples of civil rights songs, such as "We Shall Overcome." Organize students into three groups, and have each group write a song that expresses the meaning of the civil rights movement and its impact on American culture and society. Encourage students to experiment with rhyme, rhythm, and figurative language. Once groups have completed their song, ask them to perform the song for the class. **OL**

later, King announced, "We are not asking, we are demanding the ballot." King's demonstrations in Selma led to the arrest of approximately 2,000 African Americans, including schoolchildren, by Sheriff Clark. Clark's men attacked and beat many of the demonstrators, and Selma quickly became a major story in the national news.

To keep pressure on the president and Congress to act, Dr. King joined with SNCC activists and organized a "march for freedom" from Selma to the state capitol in Montgomery, a distance of about 50 miles (80 km). On Sunday, March 7, 1965, the march began. The SCLC's Hosea Williams and SNCC's John Lewis led 500 protesters toward U.S. Highway 80, the route that marchers had planned to follow to Montgomery.

As the protesters approached the Edmund Pettus Bridge, which led out of Selma, Sheriff Clark ordered them to disperse. While the marchers kneeled in prayer, more than 200 state troopers and deputized citizens rushed the demonstrators. Many were beaten in full view of television cameras. This brutal attack, known later as "Bloody Sunday," left 70 African Americans hospitalized and many more injured.

W The nation was stunned as it viewed the shocking footage of law enforcement officers beating peaceful demonstrators. Watching the events from the White House, President Johnson became furious. Eight days later, he appeared before a nationally televised joint session of the legislature to propose a new voting rights law.

The Voting Rights Act of 1965

On August 3, 1965, the House of Representatives passed the voting rights bill by a wide margin. The following day, the Senate also passed the bill. The **Voting Rights Act of 1965** authorized the U.S. attorney general to send federal examiners to register qualified voters, bypassing local officials who often refused to register African Americans. The law also suspended discriminatory devices, such as literacy tests, in counties where less than half of all adults had been registered to vote.

The results were dramatic. By the end of the year, almost 250,000 African Americans had registered as new voters. The number of African American elected officials in the South also increased. In 1965, only about 100 African Americans held elected office; by 1990 more than 5,000 did.

The passage of the Voting Rights Act of 1965 marked a turning point in the civil rights movement. The movement had now achieved its two major legislative goals. Segregation had been outlawed and new federal laws were in place to prevent discrimination and protect voting rights. After 1965, the movement began to shift its focus to the problem of achieving full social and economic equality for African Americans. As part of that effort, the movement turned its attention to the problems of African Americans trapped in poverty and living in ghettos in many of the nation's major cities.

✓ Reading Check **Summarizing** How did the Twenty-fourth Amendment affect African American voting rights?

Section 2 REVIEW

Vocabulary

1. **Explain** the significance of: SNCC, Freedom Riders, James Meredith, filibuster, cloture, Civil Rights Act of 1964, Voting Rights Act of 1965.

Main Ideas

2. **Describing** What was the purpose of the SNCC?
3. **Summarizing** How did the Freedom Riders help the civil rights movement?
4. **Explaining** Why did Dr. King lead the March on Washington in 1963?
5. **Analyzing** What was "Bloody Sunday"? How did President Johnson respond?

Critical Thinking

6. **Big Ideas** How did television help the civil rights movement?
7. **Sequencing** Use a time line similar to the one below to sequence the events in the civil rights movement.

Feb. 1960 | May 1961 | Sept. 1962 | Aug. 1963 | July 1964 | March 1965

8. **Analyzing Visuals** Study the photographs in this section. What elements of the photographs show the sacrifices African Americans made in the civil rights movement?

Writing About History

9. **Descriptive Writing** Assume the role of a journalist working for a college newspaper in 1960. Write an article for the newspaper describing the sit-in movement, including its participants, goals, and achievements.

History ONLINE

Study Central™ To review this section, go to glencoe.com and click on Study Central.

W Writing Support

Narrative Writing Have students take the role of a reporter covering the Selma march and write a story detailing the events that led President Johnson to propose a new voting rights law. OL

Assess

History ONLINE

Study Central™ provides summaries, interactive games, and online graphic organizers to help students review content.

✓ **Reading Check**

Answer: The amendment eliminated poll taxes in federal elections.

Close

Drawing Conclusions During the late 1950s and early 1960s, the federal government became actively involved in civil rights issues. **Ask:** How successful was the federal government in achieving equality for African Americans? *(Answers will vary.)* OL

Section 2 REVIEW

Answers

1. All definitions can be found in the section and the Glossary.
2. The purpose of SNCC, or the Student Nonviolent Coordinating Committee, was to organize students in the desegregation effort.
3. The Freedom Riders focused public attention on bus segregation; media coverage made President Kennedy aware that he needed to take action to stop the violence against the Freedom Riders.
4. King's leadership of the march was a way of lobbying Congress for the passage of a major civil rights bill.
5. "Bloody Sunday" was the brutal attack against African American protestors in Selma, Alabama. President Johnson was so angered that he immediately proposed a new voting rights law.
6. Television coverage focused national attention on the civil rights movement and brought sympathy to the protestors because of the way they were treated.
7. 1960: sit-ins in Greensboro; 1961: Freedom Riders; 1962: James Meredith enters University of Mississippi; 1963: March on Washington; 1964: Civil Rights Act; 1965: Selma March, Voting Rights Act
8. The photographs show the humiliations and dangers African Americans endured in their fight for equal rights.
9. Student articles will vary but must be historically accurate.

ANALYZING PRIMARY SOURCES

Focus

The Civil Rights Movement
Have students share their thoughts on the extent of segregation in the South. **Ask:** **What were the names and goals of some major civil rights organizations?** *(CORE traveled around the South in buses to test a Supreme Court decision that segregation was illegal in bus stations open to interstate travel. SNCC organized voter registration campaigns.)*

Teach

Have students point out details and describe the events shown in the photos. **Ask:** **What do the photographs on pages 868 and 869 reveal about the kinds of activities in which civil rights supporters participated?** *(teaching literacy, voter registration, and sit-ins)* Then have students brainstorm the reasons why they continued their involvement even though the threat of violence was always near. **OL**

Additional Support

ANALYZING PRIMARY SOURCES

The Civil Rights Movement

Although major figures of the civil rights movement such as Martin Luther King, Jr., are widely remembered today, the movement drew its strength from the dedication of grass-roots supporters. In rural and urban areas across the South, ordinary individuals advanced the movement through their participation in marches, boycotts, and voter registration drives. Those who dared to make a stand against discrimination risked being fired from their job, evicted from their home, and becoming the target of physical violence.

Study these primary sources and answer the questions that follow.

PRIMARY SOURCE 1

Public Testimony, 1964

In 1964, the "Mississippi Freedom Democratic Party" challenged the right of Mississippi's established (all white) Democratic Party representatives to seats at the party's national convention on the grounds that African Americans had been systematically denied the right to vote.

"[M]y husband came, and said the plantation owner was raising cain because I had tried to register [to vote] and before he quit talking the plantation owner came, and said, 'Fannie Lou, do you know—did Pap tell you what I said?' And I said, 'Yes sir.' He said, 'I mean that . . . If you don't go down and withdraw . . . well—you might have to go because we are not ready for that.' . . .

And I addressed him and told him and said, 'I didn't try to register for you. I tried to register for myself.'

I had to leave the same night.

On the 10th of September, 1962, 16 bullets was fired into the home of Mr. and Mrs. Robert Tucker for me. That same night two girls were shot in Ruleville, Mississippi. Also Mr. Joe McDonald's house was shot in.

And in June, the 9th, 1963, I had attended a voter registration workshop, was returning back to Mississippi. . . . I stepped off the bus . . . and somebody screamed . . . 'Get that one there,' and when I went to get in the car, when the man told me I was under arrest, he kicked me.

I was carried to the county jail. . . . [The patrolmen] left my cell and it wasn't too long before they came back. He said 'You are from Ruleville all right,' and he used a curse word, he said, 'We are going to beat you until you wish you was dead.'. . .

All of this on account we want to register, to become first-class citizens, and if the freedom Democratic Party is not seated now, I question America, is this America, the land of the free and the home of the brave where we have to sleep with our telephones off the hooks because our lives be threatened daily because we want to live as decent human beings in America?"

—Fannie Lou Hamer testifying before the Credentials Committee of the Democratic National Convention, August 22, 1964

PRIMARY SOURCE 2

Photograph, c. 1964

"Freedom Schools" taught literacy and African American history and encouraged voter registration.

PRIMARY SOURCE 3

Strategy Memo, April 1960

"The choice of the non-violent method, 'the sit-in,' symbolizes both judgment and promise. It is a judgment upon middle-class conventional half-way efforts to deal with radical social evil. It is specifically a judgment upon contemporary civil rights attempts. As one high school student from Chattanooga exclaimed, 'We started because we were tired of waiting for you to act. . . .'"

—James M. Lawson, Jr., "From a Lunch-Counter Stool," April 1960, Student Nonviolent Coordinating Committee Papers

Activity: Collaborative Learning

Comparing and Contrasting Have students prepare questions to interview someone who lived through the civil rights movement. Organize students into groups and help them prepare questions that encourage more than a yes/no answer, such as: *When were you first aware that civil rights was a movement and not just a need? What forms of protest most impressed you? How did your life change as a result of the civil rights movement? How do you think the civil rights movement should be remembered today?* Discuss how responses to the questions compare with information in the text. **OL**

PRIMARY SOURCE 4

Autobiography, 1968

"[At Tougaloo College] I had become very friendly with my social science professor, John Salter, who was in charge of NAACP activities on campus. All during the year, while the NAACP conducted a boycott of the downtown stores in Jackson, I had been one of Salter's most faithful canvassers and church speakers. During the last week of school, he told me that sit-in demonstrations were about to start in Jackson and that he wanted me to be the spokesman for a team that would sit-in at Woolworth's lunch counter. The two other demonstrators would be classmates of mine, Memphis and Pearlena. . . .

Seconds before 11:15 we were occupying three seats at the previously segregated Woolworth's lunch counter. In the beginning the waitresses seemed to ignore us, as if they really didn't know what was going on. Our waitress walked past us a couple of times before she noticed we had started to write our own orders down and realized we wanted service. She asked us what we wanted. We began to read to her from our order slips. She told us that we would be served at the back counter, which was for Negroes.

'We would like to be served here,' I said.

The waitress started to repeat what she had said, then stopped in the middle of the sentence. She turned the lights out behind the counter, and she and the other waitresses almost ran to the back of the store, deserting all their white customers. I guess they thought that violence would start immediately after the whites at the counter realized what was going on.

At noon, students from a nearby white high school started pouring in to Woolworth's. When they first saw us they were sort of surprised. . . . Then the white students started chanting all kinds of anti-Negro slogans. We were called a little bit of everything. . . .

Memphis suggested that we pray. We bowed our heads, and all hell broke loose. A man rushed forward, threw Memphis from his seat, and slapped my face. Then another man who worked in the store threw me against an adjoining counter. . . . The mob started smearing us with ketchup, mustard, sugar, pies, and everything on the counter. . . .

About ninety policemen were standing outside the store; they had been watching the whole thing through the windows, but had not come in to stop the mob or do anything. . . .

After the sit-in, all I could think of was how sick Mississippi whites were. They believed so much in the segregated Southern way of life, they would kill to preserve it. . . . Now I knew it was impossible for me to hate sickness. The whites had a disease, an incurable disease in its final stage. What were our chances against such a disease?"

—Anne Moody, *Coming of Age in Mississippi*

PRIMARY SOURCE 5

Photograph, 1963

▼ *Lunch counter sit-in May 28, 1963, in Jackson, Mississippi. Seated (from left to right) are John Salter, Joan Trumpauer, and Anne Moody.*

DBQ Document-Based Questions

1. **Identifying** In Source 1, what sorts of repercussions did Fannie Lou Hamer endure for daring to register to vote? How do you think such tactics affected the civil rights movement?
2. **Interpreting** Study the photograph in Source 2. Who seems to be teaching whom? Why do you think the civil rights movement attracted so many young people?
3. **Evaluating** Read the passage in Source 3 and study the photograph in Source 5. Why do you think nonviolent demonstrations were effective for the civil rights movement?
4. **Making Inferences** Read Source 4. Why do you think Anne Moody wanted to try to force integration of the lunch counter? Why would she risk physical harm to do so?

ANALYZING PRIMARY SOURCES

Assess/Close

Have students answer the Document-Based Questions. Then have them use the Internet and resource books to create a bulletin board display of events in which civil rights supporters participated. Have students agree on a bulletin board title.

DBQ Document Based Questions

Answers:

1. She suffered physical attacks and was jailed. They strengthened awareness of the justice of the cause and won support for civil rights.
2. The younger person is the teacher. The civil rights movement appealed to their idealism and desire for change.
3. They showed the courage and commitment of the participants, and they appealed to the moral conscience of the nation.
4. She wanted African Americans to be served the same way whites were and was tired of having to endure segregation. She believed in the rightness of her cause.

Extending the Content

Facing Violence Just as the Freedom Riders faced violence in Alabama, Melba Patillo Beals faced violence in school. She was another student brought into Central High School under guard in 1957. She recalls some of the challenges: "You'd be walking out to the volleyball court and someone would break a bottle and trip you on the bottle . . . first you're in pain, then you're angry, then you try to fight back . . . And then you mellow out and just realize that survival is day-to-day and you start to grasp the depth of the human spirit, you start to understand your own ability to cope no matter what. This is the greatest lesson I learned."

Focus

Bellringer

Daily Focus Transparency 25-3

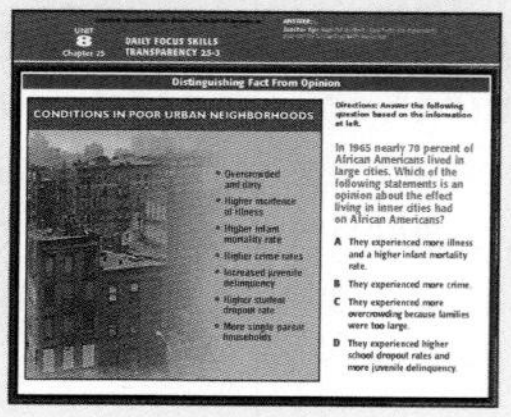

Guide to Reading

Answers:

Event	Result
Watts Riot	Kerner Commission report
Malcolm X breaks with Nation of Islam	Malcolm X assassinated
King's support of sanitation strikers	King assassinated

Section Spotlight Video

To generate student interest and provide a springboard for class discussion, access the Chapter 25, Section 3 video at glencoe.com or on the video DVD.

Section 3

Section Audio   Spotlight Video

New Civil Rights Issues

Guide to Reading

Big Ideas

Struggles for Rights In the late 1960s, the civil rights movement tried to address the persistent economic inequality of African Americans.

Content Vocabulary

- racism *(p. 870)*
- black power *(p. 872)*

Academic Vocabulary

- enforcement *(p. 874)*

People and Events to Identify

- Kerner Commission *(p. 871)*
- Chicago Movement *(p. 872)*
- Richard J. Daley *(p. 872)*
- Stokely Carmichael *(p. 872)*
- Malcolm X *(p. 873)*
- Black Panthers *(p. 874)*

Reading Strategy

Organizing Complete a graphic organizer like the one below by listing five major violent events in the civil rights movement and their results.

Event	Result

By the mid-1960s, much progress had been made in the arena of civil rights. However, leaders of the movement began to understand that merely winning political rights for African Americans would not completely solve their economic problems. The struggle would continue to try to end economic inequality.

Urban Problems

MAIN Idea African Americans became impatient with the slow pace of change; this frustration sometimes boiled over into riots.

HISTORY AND YOU Have you ever seen news coverage of a riot in the United States or overseas? What triggered the outburst? Read on to learn about the factors that fed into the riots of the 1960s.

Despite the passage of civil rights laws in the 1950s and 1960s, **racism**—prejudice or discrimination toward someone because of his or her race—was still common in American society. Changing the law could not change people's attitudes, nor did it help most African Americans trapped in poverty in the nation's big cities.

In 1965 nearly 70 percent of African Americans lived in large cities. Many had moved from the South to the big cities of the North during the Great Migration of the 1920s and 1940s. There, they often found the same prejudice and discrimination that had plagued them in the South.

Even if African Americans had been allowed to move into white neighborhoods, poverty trapped many of them in inner cities. Many African Americans found themselves channeled into low-paying jobs with little chance of advancement. Those who did better typically found employment as blue-collar workers in factories, but most did not advance beyond that. In 1965 only 15 percent of African Americans held professional, managerial, or clerical jobs, compared to 44 percent of whites. The average income of an African American family was only 55 percent of that of the average white family, and almost half of African Americans lived in poverty. Their unemployment rate was typically twice that of whites.

Poor neighborhoods in the nation's major cities were overcrowded and dirty, leading to higher rates of illness and infant mortality. At the same time, the crime rate increased in the 1960s, particularly in low-income neighborhoods. Juvenile delinquency rates rose, as did the rate of young people dropping out of school. Complicating matters even more was a rise in the number of single-parent households. All poor neighborhoods suffered from these problems, but because

Resource Manager

R Reading Strategies	C Critical Thinking	D Differentiated Instruction	W Writing Support	S Skill Practice
Teacher Edition • Understanding Vocabulary, p. 871 • Questioning, p. 872 • Determining Importance, p. 874 **Additional Resources** • Guid. Read. Act., URB p. 82 • Prim. Source Read., URB p. 69	**Teacher Edition** • Identifying Central Issues, p. 871 • Comparing & Contrasting, p. 873 **Additional Resources** • Crit. Think. Skills, URB p. 64 • Quizzes and Tests, p. 361	**Additional Resources** • Differen. Instr. Act., URB p. 55	**Additional Resources** • Content Vocabulary Act., URB p. 59 • Academic Vocabulary Act., URB p. 61	**Additional Resources** • Read Essen., p. 283 • Time Line Act., URB p. 65

POLITICAL CARTOONS — PRIMARY SOURCE

The Problem of Urban Poverty

◀ *Barry Goldwater tries to persuade President Johnson to stop creating programs to end urban poverty.*

▶ *Congress is compared to the Roman emperor Nero, who was said to have played music as Rome burned.*

Analyzing VISUALS — DBQ

1. **Making Inferences** In the cartoon on the left, what does the man suggest about urban problems?
2. **Drawing Conclusions** Based on the cartoon above, what should Congress have done to stop the rioting?

more African Americans lived in poverty, their communities were disproportionately affected.

Many African Americans living in urban poverty knew the civil rights movement had made enormous gains, but when they looked at their own circumstances, nothing seemed to be changing. The movement had raised their hopes, but their everyday problems continued. As a result, their anger and frustration began to rise—until it finally erupted.

The Watts Riot

Just five days after President Johnson signed the Voting Rights Act, a riot erupted in Watts, an African American neighborhood in Los Angeles. Allegations of police brutality had served as the catalyst for this uprising, which lasted for six days and required over 14,000 members of the National Guard and 1,500 law officers to restore order. Rioters burned and looted entire neighborhoods and destroyed about $45 million in property. They killed 34 people and injured about 900 others.

More rioting was yet to come. Riots broke out in dozens of American cities between 1965 and 1968. The worst riot took place in Detroit in 1967. Burning, looting, and skirmishes with police and National Guard members resulted in 43 deaths and over 1,000 wounded. C

Eventually the U.S. Army sent in tanks and soldiers armed with machine guns to get control of the situation. Nearly 4,000 fires destroyed 1,300 buildings, and the damage in property loss was estimated at $250 million.

The Kerner Commission

In 1967 President Johnson appointed the National Advisory Commission on Civil Disorders, headed by Governor Otto Kerner of Illinois, to study the causes of the urban riots and to make recommendations to prevent them from happening again. The **Kerner Commission,** as it became known, conducted a detailed study of the problem. The commission blamed racism for most of the problems in the inner city. "Our nation is moving toward two societies, one black, one white—separate and unequal," it concluded. R

Teach

C Critical Thinking

Identifying Central Issues After the Watts riot, other riots broke out in American cities during the late 1960s. **Ask:** Why do you think this series of riots took place? *(Answers will vary but should focus on economic grievances as well as on high hopes for change but slow results.)* OL

R Reading Strategy

Understanding Vocabulary Explain that a *commission* is a group authorized to carry out a particular task. BL

Analyzing VISUALS

Answers:

1. He is suggesting that if people ignore the problems, they will eventually "drown" and just go away.
2. The cartoonist is suggesting that Congress could have put out the "fire" in the inner cities with urban programs and antigun legislation.

Additional Support

Activity: Collaborative Learning

Conducting a Debate Organize students into two groups to conduct a class debate. One group will present arguments in support of African American nationalism, the other will present arguments in opposition to African American nationalism. Give students time to consider their arguments and conduct further research if necessary. Have each side present its views to the class. Make sure each side presents evidence to support its views. As the students discuss the pros and cons, encourage the class to reach a consensus. OL

W Writing Support

Expository Writing Have students take the role of a government official serving during the 1960s and write a brief speech either supporting or opposing the recommendations of the Kerner Commission. Remind students to have a clear thesis and supporting details. OL

R Reading Strategy

Questioning Ask students to write five questions, with answers, about the content of the subsection "Black Power." Have them write each question on a strip of paper, with the answer on the reverse side. Then put all the questions in a hat. Have one student act as quizmaster, drawing a slip and asking the question to the class. OL

Reading Check

Answer:
They hoped to work with local leaders to call attention to poverty and to support open housing.

W The commission recommended the creation of 2 million inner-city jobs, the construction of 6 million new units of public housing, and a renewed federal commitment to fight de facto segregation. President Johnson's War on Poverty, which addressed some of the concerns about inner-city jobs and housing, was already underway. Saddled with spending for the Vietnam War, however, Johnson never endorsed the recommendations of the commission.

The Shift to Economic Rights

By the mid-1960s, a number of African American leaders were becoming increasingly critical of Martin Luther King, Jr.'s nonviolent strategy. They felt it had failed to improve the economic position of African Americans. Dr. King came to agree with this criticism, and in 1965 he decided to address economic issues.

Dr. King decided to focus on the problems that African Americans faced in Chicago. King had never conducted a civil rights campaign in the North, but by tackling a large Northern city, he believed he could call greater attention to poverty and other racial problems that lay beneath the urban race riots.

To call attention to the deplorable housing conditions that many African American families faced, Dr. King and his wife Coretta moved into a slum apartment in an African American neighborhood in Chicago. Dr. King and the SCLC hoped to work with local leaders to improve the economic status of African Americans in poor neighborhoods.

The **Chicago Movement,** however, made little headway. When Dr. King led a march through the all-white suburb of Marquette Park to demonstrate the need for open housing, he was met by angry white mobs similar to those in Birmingham and Selma. Mayor **Richard J. Daley** ordered the Chicago police to protect the marchers, and he was determined to prevent violence. He met with Dr. King and proposed a new program to clean up the slums. Associations of realtors and bankers also agreed to promote open housing. In theory, mortgages and rental property would be available to everyone, regardless of race. In practice, little changed.

Reading Check **Describing** How did Dr. King and SCLC leaders hope to address economic concerns?

Black Power R

MAIN Idea Impatient with the slower gains of Martin Luther King, Jr.'s movement, many young African Americans called for "black power."

HISTORY AND YOU How did Dr. King work to avoid violence? Read on to find out how some African Americans broke with Dr. King's approach.

Dr. King's failure in Chicago seemed to show that nonviolent protests could do little to solve economic problems. After 1965, many African Americans, especially urban young people, began to turn away from King. Some leaders called for more aggressive forms of protest. Their strategies ranged from armed self-defense to promoting the idea that the government should set aside a number of states where African Americans could live separate from whites. As African Americans became more assertive, some organizations, including CORE and SNCC, voted to expel all whites from leadership positions in their organizations. They believed that African Americans alone should lead their struggle.

Many young African Americans called for **black power,** a term that had many meanings. A few interpreted black power to mean that physical self-defense and even violence were acceptable—a clear rejection of Dr. King's philosophy. To most, including **Stokely Carmichael,** the leader of SNCC in 1966, the term meant that African Americans should control the social, political, and economic direction of their struggle:

PRIMARY SOURCE

"This is the significance of black power as a slogan. For once, black people are going to use the words they want to use—not just the words whites want to hear. . . . The need for psychological equality is the reason why SNCC today believes that blacks must organize in the black community. Only black people can . . . create in the community an aroused and continuing black consciousness. . . ."

—from the *New York Review of Books*, September 1966

Black power stressed pride in the African American cultural group. It emphasized racial distinctiveness rather than assimilation—the process by which minority groups adapt to the dominant culture in a society. African Americans showed pride in their racial

Additional Support

Teacher Tip

Invite a local civil rights leader or organizer to explain their philosophy, work, and experiences to the class. Ask them to give their views on how the civil rights movement of the 1950s and 1960s changed American society.

Activity: Collaborative Learning

Comparing and Contrasting To review the civil rights movement, ask students to consider four types of protest: (1) student sit-ins, (2) SCLC marches, (3) Freedom Rides, and (4) speeches by Stokely Carmichael. **Ask:** **How was each form of protest different?** *(Student sit-ins: nonviolent protests to desegregate public facilities; SCLC marches: nonviolent protests to end segregation and promote voter registration; Freedom Rides: nonviolent protest to desegregate buses; Stokely Carmichael speeches: advocacy of self-defense, even violence, to bring equality)* Conclude by taking a class vote on which form of protest was the most effective. Have students share the reasons for their choices with the class. OL heritage by adopting new Afro hairstyles and African-style clothing. Many also took African names. In universities, students demanded that African and African American studies courses be made part of the standard school curriculum. Dr. King and some other leaders criticized black power as a philosophy of hopelessness and despair. The idea was very popular, however, in poor neighborhoods where many African Americans resided.

Malcolm X

By the early 1960s, a young man named **Malcolm X** had become a symbol of the black power movement. Born Malcolm Little in Omaha, Nebraska, he experienced a difficult childhood and adolescence. He drifted into a life of crime and, in 1946, was convicted of burglary and sent to prison for six years.

Prison transformed Malcolm. He began to educate himself and played an active role in the prison debate society. Eventually, he joined the Nation of Islam, commonly known as the Black Muslims, who were led by Elijah Muhammad. Despite their name, the Black Muslims do not hold the same beliefs as mainstream Muslims. The Nation of Islam preached black nationalism. Like Marcus Garvey in the 1920s, Black Muslims believed that African Americans should separate themselves from whites and form their own self-governing communities.

Shortly after joining the Nation of Islam, Malcolm Little changed his name to Malcolm X. The "X" symbolized the family name of his African ancestors who had been enslaved. He delcared that his true name had been stolen from him by slavery, and he would no longer use the name white society had given him.

The Black Muslims viewed themselves as their own nation and attempted to make themselves as self-sufficient as possible. They ran their own businesses and schools, and published their own newspaper, *Muhammad Speaks*. They encouraged their members to respect each other and to strengthen their families. Black Muslims did not advocate violence, but they did advocate self-defense. Malcolm X's criticisms of white society and the mainstream civil rights movement gained national attention for the Nation of Islam. **C**

C Critical Thinking

Comparing and Contrasting

Ask: How were the system of segregation and the later idea of African American separation similar? How were they different? *(Both stressed separation of the races, but segregation made African Americans subservient and unequal to whites. The idea of African American separation, on the other hand, was inspired by African Americans and would give them control of their lives apart from whites).*

DBQ Document Based Questions

Answers:

1. Malcolm X stated that African Americans can integrate with whites or separate from them.
2. Answers will vary. After reading the excerpt, most students will probably think that Malcolm X opposed integration because he viewed whites as oppressors.

PRIMARY SOURCE

Black Power in the 1960s

In the late 1960s, a new group of African American leaders, such as Malcolm X, had lost patience with the slow progress of civil rights and felt that African Americans needed to act more militantly and demand equality, not wait for it to be given.

PRIMARY SOURCE

"Since the black masses here in America are now in open revolt against the American system of segregation, will these same black masses turn toward integration or will they turn toward complete separation? Will these awakened black masses demand integration into the white society that enslaved them or will they demand complete separation from that cruel white society that has enslaved them? Will the exploited and oppressed black masses seek integration with their white exploiters and white oppressors or will these awakened black masses truly revolt and separate themselves completely from this wicked race that has enslaved us?"

—Malcolm X, from his speech "The Black Revolution," 1964

▲ *Medalists Tommie Smith and John Carlos give the black power salute at the 1968 Olympics. Above right, Stokely Carmichael speaks at a protest rally in Mississippi in 1966.*

DBQ Document-Based Questions

1. **Identifying** What are two options Malcolm X thinks African Americans have regarding their relationship with whites?
2. **Drawing Conclusions** Do you think Malcolm X supported integration? Why or why not?

Differentiated Instruction

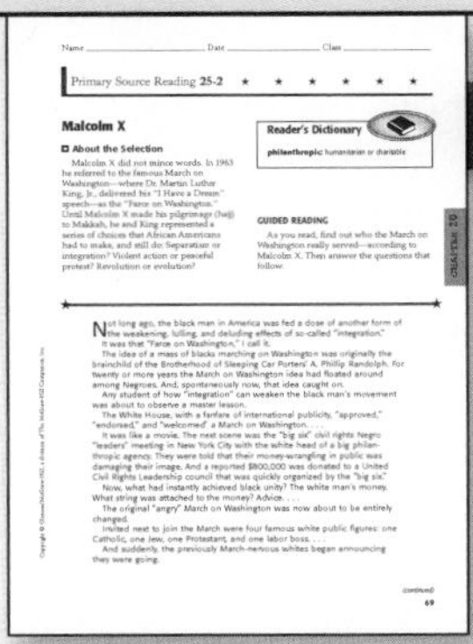

Primary Source Reading, URB p. 69

Malcolm X

Objective: To identify Malcolm X's influence on the civil rights movement.

Focus: Have students describe what they already know about Malcolm X.

Teach: Have students read the reading aloud, and then summarize Malcolm X's message.

Assess: Have students write a paragraph describing Malcolm X's greatest achievement.

Close: Play a recording or video of one of Malcolm X's speeches.

Differentiated Instruction Strategies

BL Have students draw a time line of Malcolm X's political activities.

AL Have students analyze Malcolm X's impact on civil rights and explain it on a poster.

ELL Have students try to paraphrase the reading aloud as a class.

R Reading Strategy

Determining Importance

Ask: Why was Malcolm X's trip to the Muslim holy city of Makkah an important event in the black power movement? *(After seeing Muslims of many races worshipping together, Malcolm X believed that an integrated society was possible, and he turned from the idea of racial separation.)* **BL**

Analyzing VISUALS

Answers:

1. city and county offices
2. Answers will vary, but students may note that education levels are connected to economic success.

Reading Check

Answer:
King believed in nonviolence and cooperation with supportive whites; the black power movement called for more aggressive forms of protests and believed that African Americans alone should lead their struggle.

INFOGRAPHIC

The Civil Rights Movement's Legacy

There have been many changes in the status of African Americans in the United States since the 1960s. Changes have taken place in politics, economics, and education.

Economic Status of African Americans

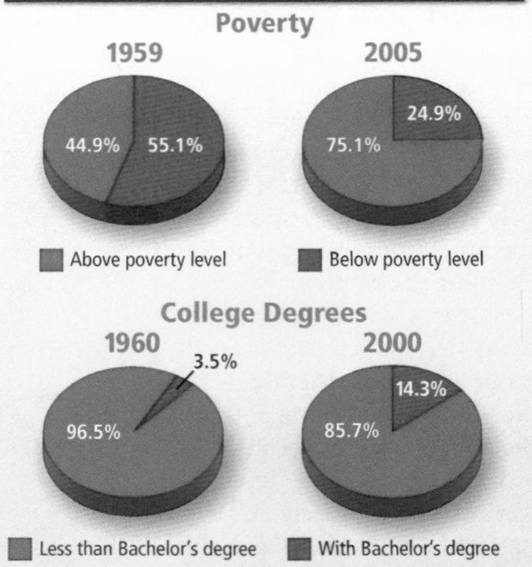

African-Americans in House of Representatives and Senate, 1961–2001

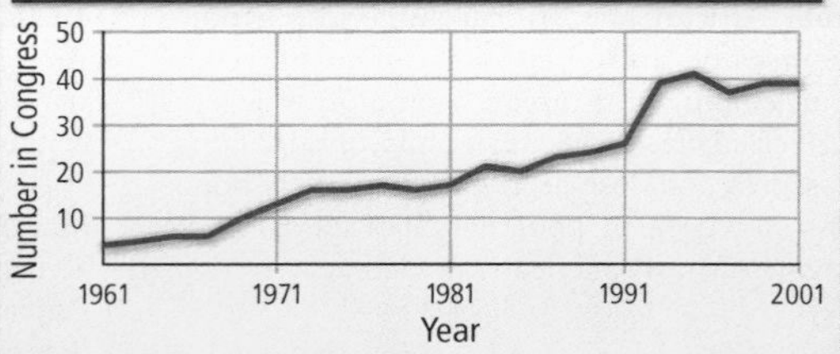

Source: *Statistical Abstract of the United States.*

African Americans Elected by Office

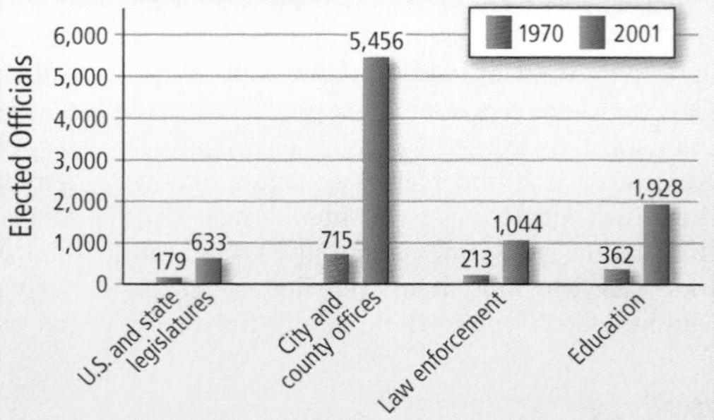

Source: *Statistical Abstract of the United States.*

Analyzing VISUALS

1. **Interpreting** In which elected offices did African Americans see the greatest increase in representation?
2. **Drawing Conclusions** Does the data presented suggest that the civil rights movement was a success? Why or why not?

R By 1964, Malcolm X had broken with the Black Muslims. Discouraged by scandals involving the Nation of Islam's leader, he went to the Muslim holy city of Makkah (also called Mecca) in Saudi Arabia. After seeing Muslims from many races worshipping together, he concluded that an integrated society was possible after all.

After Malcolm X broke with the Nation of Islam, he continued to criticize the organization. Because of this, organization members shot and killed him in February 1965. Although Malcolm X left the Nation of Islam before his death, his speeches and ideas from those years with the Black Muslims have influenced African Americans to take pride in their own culture and to believe in their ability to make their way in the world.

Malcolm X's ideas influenced a new generation of militant African American leaders who also preached black power, black nationalism, and economic self-sufficiency. In 1966 in Oakland, California, Huey Newton, Bobby Seale, and Eldridge Cleaver organized the **Black Panthers.**

The Black Panthers believed that a revolution was necessary in the United States, and they urged African Americans to arm themselves and prepare to force whites to grant them equal rights. Black Panther leaders called for an end to racial oppression and control of major institutions in the African American community, such as schools, law **enforcement,** housing, and hospitals. Eldridge Cleaver, who served as the minister of culture, articulated many of the organization's aims in his 1967 best-selling book, *Soul on Ice.*

Reading Check **Describing** What disagreements split Dr. Martin Luther King, Jr., and the black power movement?

Hands-On Chapter Project Step 3

A Freedom Drama

Step 3: Securing Voting Rights Students will continue work on their theatrical presentations of the civil right movement by writing a voting rights debate scene.

Directions Discuss African American struggles to gain voting rights and the opposition they faced. Once again, organize students into groups. Ask each group to research viewpoints on either side of the voting rights debate. Have groups use their research to write a debate scene representing viewpoints for and against a voting rights act. Encourage students to incorporate quotes from their research into their debate scenes. Students should also create posters as props for the scene. The posters should use actual slogans from the period.

Summarizing Have groups present their scenes. Ask students to compare past and present attitudes about the role of African Americans in politics.

(Chapter Project continued on Visual Summary page)

King Is Assassinated

MAIN Idea After Dr. King was assassinated in Memphis, Tennessee, Congress passed the Civil Rights Act of 1968.

HISTORY AND YOU Do you know someone who remembers Dr. King's assassination? Read about the events surrounding King's death.

By the late 1960s, the civil rights movement had fragmented into dozens of competing organizations with differing philosophies for reaching equality. At the same time, the emergence of black power and the call by some African Americans for violent action angered many white civil rights supporters. This made further legislation to help African Americans economically less likely.

In this atmosphere, Dr. King went to Memphis, Tennessee, to support a strike of African American sanitation workers in March 1968. At the time, the SCLC had been planning a national "Poor People's Campaign" to promote economic advancement for all impoverished Americans. The purpose of this campaign, the most ambitious one that Dr. King would ever lead, was to lobby the federal government to commit billions of dollars to end poverty and unemployment in the United States. People of all races and nationalities were to converge on the nation's capital, as they had in 1963 during the March on Washington, where they would camp out until both Congress and President Johnson agreed to pass the requested legislation to fund the proposal.

On April 4, 1968, as he stood on his hotel balcony in Memphis, Dr. King was assassinated by a sniper. Ironically, the previous night he had told a gathering at a local church, "I've been to the mountaintop. . . . I've looked over and I've seen the Promised Land. I may not get there with you, but I want you to know tonight that we as a people will get to the Promised Land."

Dr. King's death touched off both national mourning and riots in more than 100 cities, including Washington, D.C. The Reverend Ralph Abernathy, who had served as a trusted assistant to Dr. King for many years, led the Poor People's Campaign in King's absence. The demonstration, however, did not achieve any of the major objectives that either King or the SCLC had hoped it would.

In the wake of Dr. King's death, Congress did pass the Civil Rights Act of 1968. The act contained a fair-housing provision outlawing discrimination in housing sales and rentals and gave the Justice Department authority to bring suits against such discrimination.

Dr. King's death marked the end of an era in American history. Although the civil rights movement continued, it lacked the unity of purpose and vision that Dr. King had given it. Under his leadership, and with the help of tens of thousands of dedicated African Americans, many of whom were students, the civil rights movement transformed American society. Although many problems remain to be solved, the achievements of the civil rights movement in the 1950s and 1960s dramatically improved the lives of African Americans, creating opportunities that had not existed before.

Reading Check **Summarizing** What were the goals of the Poor People's Campaign?

Section 3 REVIEW

Vocabulary

1. **Explain** the significance of: racism, Kerner Commission, Chicago Movement, Richard J. Daley, black power, Stokely Carmichael, Malcolm X, Black Panthers.

Main Ideas

2. **Describing** What were the findings and the recommendations of the Kerner Commission?
3. **Assessing** How did Malcolm X's ideas about the relationship between African Americans and white Americans change by the time of his murder?
4. **Explaining** What was the general effect of Dr. King's assassination?

Critical Thinking

5. **Big Ideas** How was the Civil Rights Act of 1968 designed to improve the economic status of African Americans?
6. **Categorizing** Use a graphic organizer similar to the one below to list the main views of each leader.

Leader	Views
Dr. Martin Luther King, Jr.	
Malcolm X	
Eldridge Cleaver	

7. **Analyzing Visuals** Study the cartoons on page 871. Together, what do they imply about government response and responsibility for the problems of the inner cities?

Writing About History

8. **Expository Writing** Assume the role of a reporter in the late 1960s. Suppose that you have interviewed a follower of Dr. King and a member of the Black Panthers. Write a transcript of each interview.

History ONLINE
Study Central™ To review this section, go to glencoe.com and click on Study Central.

Assess

History ONLINE

Study Central™ provides summaries, interactive games, and online graphic organizers to help students review content.

Reading Check

Answer:
The goal of the campaign was to promote economic advancement for all impoverished Americans.

Close

Identifying Central Issues
Have students list the problems that African Americans faced in the late 1960s and suggest what they would have done to solve them. *(Answers will vary but students should focus on economic as well as social issues.)* **OL**

Section 3 REVIEW

Answers

1. All definitions can be found in the section and the Glossary.
2. The Commission found that racism was the root cause of the urban riots and that two separate but unequal societies—one white, the other black—were emerging. It called for funding to create jobs and public housing as well as ending de facto segregation.
3. Malcolm X came to believe that an integrated society was possible.
4. The civil rights movement lacked the unity and direction that King had given it.
5. By outlawing housing discrimination, the act made it easier for African Americans to buy and invest in homes.
6. King: nonviolent protest; Malcolm X: self-defense and separatism; Cleaver: revolution
7. Possible answer: They both imply that the government is not doing anything or not doing enough, and that it does not really care about the people who live in the inner city.
8. Students' transcripts should vary, but should use details from the section to create an accurate approximation of an interview with each subject.

Identifying Main Ideas Draw students' attention to the civil rights legislation summarized in the left-hand column. **Ask:** These laws were important results of the civil rights movement. What does this tell you about the nature of the nation's law? *(Answer: The law is not static but responds to changes and movements in society. It has moved gradually toward an ideal of equal and fair treatment for all citizens.)* **OL**

Visual Literacy **Ask:** Look at the three images on the page. What do the three events chronicled in these images have in common? *(Each image records a landmark in the civil rights movement—school desegregation, peaceful protest for voter registration and other rights, and a march for an end to segregation in housing. Each event was an attempt to bring an injustice to the attention of citizens and leaders so that the unjust situation would be changed.)* **OL**

Chapter 25 Visual Summary

STUDY TO GO You can study anywhere, anytime by downloading quizzes and flashcards to your PDA from glencoe.com.

Origins of the Civil Rights Movement

Long-Range Causes

- Widespread racial segregation in the American South
- Lack of voting rights for African Americans in the American South

Immediate Causes

- The arrival of large numbers of African Americans in the North after the Great Migration gives them increased political influence and greater voting power.
- African American contributions during World War II lead many African Americans to believe it is time to take action to demand change.
- NAACP strategy of using lawsuits to weaken segregation scores a major victory in 1954 with the *Brown* v. *Board of Education* ruling.
- African American churches serve as organizational bases, and pastors rally African Americans and organize protests.

▶ *Linda Brown was the main plaintiff in* Brown v. Board of Education.

▲ *Civil rights activists march to protest a pro-segregationist speech by Alabama governor George Wallace in 1964.*

Major Results of the Civil Rights Movement

- Civil Rights Act of 1957
- Civil Rights Act of 1964
- Voting Rights Act of 1965
- Civil Rights Act of 1968
- End of legal segregation in schools and public facilities
- Restoration of voting rights for African Americans
- Ban on discrimination based on race in the workplace
- Increased federal power to protect civil rights

Major Events of the Civil Rights Movement

- African American community in Montgomery, Alabama, led by Dr. Martin Luther King, Jr., organizes the Montgomery bus boycott.
- African American students are blocked from entering Little Rock High School. President Eisenhower sends in federal troops and asks Congress to pass the Civil Rights Act of 1957.
- Sit-ins begin in Greensboro, and soon young people are staging sit-ins across the South to integrate public facilities.
- Freedom Riders end segregation on interstate bus travel.
- Martin Luther King, Jr., leads a march in Birmingham, then a March on Washington to support the Civil Rights Act of 1964.
- Martin Luther King, Jr., leads a march in Selma to pressure Congress to pass the Voting Rights Act of 1965.

▲ *A civil rights march in Montgomery, Alabama, in 1965*

Hands-On Chapter Project

Step 4: Wrap Up

A Freedom Drama

Step 4: Wrap Up Students will finish the process they started in Step 1.

Directions As a class, review the news reports, debate scenes, and monologues that each group created. Decide if any scenes should be shortened or combined. Make any revisions needed to the writing, including corrections for spelling, mechanics, and word choice. Next, decide on the order in which the scenes will be presented. The teacher should assign roles to student actors. Have the class select a student to act as director to oversee staging the drama.

Putting It Together Finally, have the class present their drama to another class or to the school. Encourage the class and audience to discuss their thoughts and feelings about the civil rights movement and its impact on the growth of freedom and democracy in the United States. **OL**

Chapter 25 Assessment

Reviewing Vocabulary

Directions: Choose the word or words that best complete the sentence.

1. In *Brown* v. *Board of Education,* the Supreme Court overturned the precedent of ______ established in *Plessy* v. *Ferguson.*

A reading requirements
B de facto segregation
C "separate but equal"
D discrimination

2. During World War II, the Congress of Racial Equality used the ______ to desegregate public restaurants.

A cloture
B sit-in
C filibuster
D March on Washington

3. Some Southern senators used a ______ to try to prevent civil rights legislation from passing.

A filibuster
B cloture
C closed vote
D walk-out

4. Prejudice and discrimination against a person because of his or her race is called

A black power.
B cloture.
C segregation.
D racism.

5. The concept of ______ was supported by militant African American leaders.

A racism
B black power
C nonviolent resistance
D freedom marches

Reviewing Main Ideas

Directions: Choose the best answer to the following questions.

Section 1 *(pp. 850–857)*

6. Which event led to the bus boycott in Montgomery, Alabama?

A a riot in Montgomery
B the CORE sit-in
C the arrest of Rosa Parks
D a church bombing

7. In 1957 the Southern Christian Leadership Conference (SCLC) set out to

A march on Washington and pass a civil rights bill.
B encourage demonstrations and boycotts.
C increase church attendance and promote brotherhood.
D end segregation and encourage voter registration.

8. *Brown* v. *Board of Education* was a significant case because

A it declared it illegal to prevent African Americans from voting.
B it declared it illegal to segregate restaurants.
C it declared it illegal to segregate public schools.
D it declared it illegal to discriminate in the selling of a house.

9. Which of the following statements best describes President Eisenhower's thoughts on civil rights?

A The government should end segregation immediately.
B Integration should only occur in government agencies.
C Segregation and racism would end as generational attitudes changed.
D Only governmental power could change people's beliefs.

TEST-TAKING TIP

Look for clues in the question that help you to eliminate certain answer choices right away. For example, if a question asks for a difference between two political leaders, you know that you can eliminate answer choices that show what they have in common.

Need Extra Help?

If You Missed Questions . . .	1	2	3	4	5	6	7	8	9
Go to Page . . .	852	852	864–865	870–871	872–873	854	855	852	857

GO ON

Answers and Analyses
Reviewing Vocabulary

1. C Students may be confused because the answers all refer to legal or administrative matters. Reading requirements concern a decision by an educational institution and not by a court. De facto segregation and discrimination were addressed by courts, but they are not specific legal precedents. Thus, C is the answer.

2. B Cloture is a debate-ending motion used in the Senate; filibuster is a Senate method to kill unwanted bills by preventing a vote; the March on Washington did not take place until 1963.

3. A Students may be able to eliminate closed vote and walk-out, because these terms do not refer to standard congressional practices discussed in the chapter. Cloture can be associated with the word "close," to stop a debate and to move along legislation to final passage. Filibuster conveys a stalling tactic to disrupt the process of lawmaking.

4. D By using the term "race," the question itself provides a clue to the answer that students may recognize. Also, black power can be eliminated because "power" indicates a positive view of identity held by African Americans. Segregation is a result of prejudice and discrimination, not their cause.

5. B Students can eliminate nonviolent resistance and freedom marches because the question relates to a militant activity. Racism was directed at African Americans by whites. This leaves as the answer black power, a way that forcefully affirmed African American identity.

Reviewing Main Ideas

6. C Rosa Parks's refusal to give up her seat and sit in the back of the bus reserved for African Americans was an example of the nonviolent protest against discrimination carried out by the civil rights movement.

7. D The major goals of African American civil rights leaders in the late 1950s were an end to segregation and the advancement of voter registration. Later, in 1963, a march in Washington, D.C., took place to promote support for civil rights legislation.

8. C The *Brown* ruling was an important landmark toward the goal of ensuring that African American children would have the same educational opportunities as white children.

9. C Eisenhower did not favor immediate action by the federal government. Though he personally disliked racism, he felt lasting change would only come as attitudes and opinions changed over time.

10. A The Selma march was the focal point for the nonviolent Southern Christian Leadership Conference (SCLC) campaign for voting rights. To prevent African Americans from voting, white police and deputized citizens brutally attacked Selma marchers in view of television cameras.

11. D The Civil Rights Act of 1964 gave the U.S. attorney general more power to bring lawsuits to force school desegregation. It also made segregation illegal in most public facilities and required private employers to end job discrimination. The EEOC was established as a permanent agency to monitor the ban on job discrimination.

12. D In 1967 President Johnson set up the Kerner Commission to study the causes of the urban riots and make recommendations to prevent them from happening again. The Commission determined that racism was the root cause, dividing the country into two separate and unequal societies. The Commission recommended efforts to fight de facto segregation and to provide jobs and public housing.

13. B Black Muslims called on African Americans to separate from whites and form their own self-governing communities. They ran their own businesses and schools and had their own publications. Black Muslims did not advocate violence, but they did support self-defense. They also were highly critical of the mainstream civil rights movement and its support of integration.

Chapter 25 Assessment

Section 2 *(pp. 858–867)*

10. "Bloody Sunday" occurred in reaction to which event?

A the Selma march
B the passage of the Civil Rights Act of 1964
C the March on Washington
D the assassination of Dr. Martin Luther King, Jr.

11. How did the Civil Rights Act of 1964 help African Americans?

A The act authorized the U.S. attorney general to send federal employees to register voters.
B The act suspended literacy tests in counties where less than half of all adults had been allowed to vote.
C The act outlawed discrimination in housing sales and rentals.
D The act gave the federal government more power to force school desegregation.

Section 3 *(pp. 870–875)*

12. In response to the race riots in the mid-1960s, the federal government established which of the following?

A SNCC
B EEOC
C Chicago Movement
D Kerner Commission

13. What did the Nation of Islam, or the Black Muslims, advocate?

A African Americans should use nonviolent resistance to fight for civil rights.
B African Americans should separate from whites and form their own self-governing communities.
C African Americans should use violence to overthrow the government and establish their own nation.
D African Americans should sue the federal government to establish equality among the nation's citizens.

Critical Thinking

Directions: Choose the best answers to the following questions.

14. Which group worked to fight segregation and other inequalities primarily through the courts?

A NAACP
B SNCC
C SCLC
D CEEO

Base your answers to questions 15 and 16 on the map below and on your knowledge of Chapter 25.

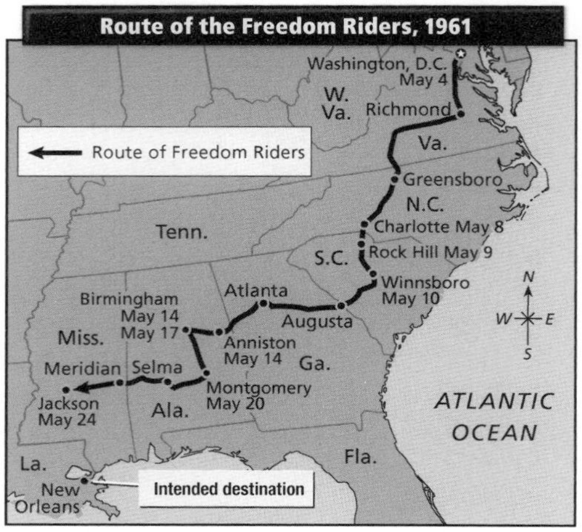

15. The route of the Freedom Riders focused on which region of the United States?

A the Midwest
B the South
C New England
D the West

16. The final destination of the Freedom Riders was

A Montgomery, Alabama.
B Washington, D.C.
C Selma, Alabama.
D Jackson, Mississippi.

Need Extra Help?

If You Missed Questions . . .	10	11	12	13	14	15	16
Go to Page . . .	866–867	864–865	871–872	873	850–851	R15	R15

GO ON

Critical Thinking

14. A The National Association for the Advancement of Colored People (NAACP) supported court cases intended to overturn segregation. It achieved a string of court victories that led to the landmark *Brown* v. *Board of Education* ruling in 1954 that segregation in public schools was unconstitutional.

15. B In 1961, teams of African American and white volunteers known as Freedom Riders rode buses into the South to protest the continued illegal segregation on interstate bus lines. Violence against the Freedom Riders forced President Kennedy to take more action on behalf of civil rights.

16. D The Freedom Ride ended in Jackson, Mississippi, where the Riders were met by an angry mob of segregationists and arrested by local police. Attorney General Robert Kennedy had agreed to the arrests in return for a guarantee of the Riders' safety.

17. Huey Newton, Eldridge Cleaver, and Bobby Seale founded which militant African American group?
   - **A** the Black Muslims
   - **B** the Black Panthers
   - **C** SNCC
   - **D** the Chicago Movement

Analyze the cartoon and answer the questions that follow. Base your answers on the cartoon and on your knowledge of Chapter 25.

18. In this cartoon, American cities are represented by
   - **A** riots.
   - **B** water.
   - **C** mines.
   - **D** ships.

19. Which of the following describes the main idea of this cartoon?
   - **A** American cities are being destroyed by racial issues.
   - **B** American cities are much like ships.
   - **C** American cities need to change direction.
   - **D** American cities should avoid racial issues.

Document-Based Questions

Directions: Analyze the document and answer the short-answer questions that follow the document.

On the evening of July 2, 1964, as he prepared to sign the historic Civil Rights Act of 1964, President Lyndon Johnson made a televised address to the American people. Below is an excerpt:

> "I want to take this occasion to talk to you about what . . . [the Civil Rights Act of 1964] means to every American. . . . We believe that all men are created equal. Yet many are denied equal treatment. . . . We believe that all men are entitled to the blessings of liberty. Yet millions are being deprived of those blessings—not because of their own failures, but because of the color of their skin. The reasons are deeply imbedded in history and tradition and the nature of man. We can understand—without rancor or hatred—how this all happened. But it cannot continue. Our Constitution, the foundation of our Republic, forbids it. The principles of our freedom forbid it. Morality forbids it. And the law I will sign tonight forbids it."
>
> —Lyndon Johnson

20. According to Johnson, what are the origins of racism?

21. What does Johnson say forbids the continuation of racism in the United States?

Extended Response

22. Select one of the African American leaders who advocated a more militant approach to the problems of racism in America than did Martin Luther King, Jr. Write an essay comparing and contrasting the ideas of that figure with King's ideas, providing your views on which approach was more effective and why. Your essay should include an introduction and at least three paragraphs with supporting details from the chapter.

STOP

History ONLINE
For additional test practice, use Self-Check Quizzes—Chapter 25 at glencoe.com.

Need Extra Help?

If You Missed Questions . . .	17	18	19	20	21	22
Go to Page . . .	873–874	R18	R18	879	879	870–875

Extend Response

22. Student essays will vary but should coherently compare and contrast the ideas of King with one of the militant African American leaders, and provide a reasoned opinion about the greater efficacy of one of the approaches.

17. B The Black Panthers, founded by Huey Newton, Eldridge Cleaver, and Bobby Seale, believed that a revolution by African Americans was necessary to force whites to grant equal rights. Black Panther leaders called for control of major institutions in the African American community, such as schools and housing.

18. D American cities, represented by ships, are threatened by riots, tension, and racial violence, all symbolized as a minefield.

19. A The cartoon states that, in the summer of 1966, cities in the United States were being destroyed by racial issues.

Document-Based Questions

20. The origins of racism are deeply embedded in history, tradition, and human nature.

21. According to President Johnson, the U.S. Constitution, the principles of freedom, morality, and the Civil Rights Act (1964) forbid racism in the United States.

History ONLINE
Have students visit the Web site at glencoe.com to review Chapter 25 and take the Self-Check Quiz.

Need Extra Help?
Have students refer to the pages listed if they miss any of the questions.

Chapter 26 Planning Guide

Key to Ability Levels	
BL Below Level	AL Above Level
OL On Level	ELL English Language Learners

Key to Teaching Resources	
Print Material	Transparency
CD-ROM or DVD	

Levels				Resources	Chapter Opener	Section 1	Section 2	Section 3	Chapter Assess
BL	OL	AL	ELL						
FOCUS									
BL	OL	AL	ELL	Daily Focus Transparencies		26-1	26-2	26-3	
TEACH									
BL	OL		ELL	Reading Skills Activity, URB			p. 85		
	OL			Historical Analysis Skills Activity, URB		p. 86			
BL	OL	AL	ELL	Differentiated Instruction Activity, URB		p. 87			
BL	OL		ELL	English Learner Activity, URB			p. 89		
BL	OL	AL	ELL	Content Vocabulary Activity, URB*		p. 91			
BL	OL	AL	ELL	Academic Vocabulary Activity, URB		p. 93			
	OL	AL		Reinforcing Skills Activity, URB				p. 95	
	OL	AL		Critical Thinking Skills Activity, URB		p. 96			
BL	OL		ELL	Time Line Activity, URB				p. 97	
	OL			Linking Past and Present Activity, URB				p. 98	
BL	OL	AL	ELL	Primary Source Reading, URB		p. 99		p. 101	
BL	OL	AL	ELL	American Art and Music Activity, URB			p. 103		
BL	OL	AL	ELL	Interpreting Political Cartoons Activity, URB		p. 105			
		AL		Enrichment Activity, URB				p. 109	
BL	OL		ELL	Guided Reading Activity, URB*		p. 112	p. 113	p. 114	
BL	OL	AL	ELL	Reading Essentials and Note-Taking Guide*		p. 286	p. 289	p. 292	
BL	OL	AL	ELL	Differentiated Instruction for the American History Classroom	✓	✓	✓	✓	
BL	OL	AL	ELL	Unit Map Overlay Transparencies	✓	✓	✓	✓	✓
BL	OL	AL	ELL	Unit Time Line Transparencies, Strategies, and Activities	✓	✓	✓	✓	✓
BL	OL	AL	ELL	Cause and Effect Transparencies, Strategies, and Activities	✓	✓	✓	✓	✓
BL	OL	AL	ELL	Why It Matters Chapter Transparencies, Strategies, and Activities	✓	✓	✓	✓	✓
BL	OL	AL	ELL	American Biographies			✓		

Note: Please refer to the *Unit 8 Resource Book* for this chapter's URB materials.

* Also available in Spanish

TeacherWorks Plus
All-In-One Planner and Resource Center

- Interactive Lesson Planner
- Interactive Teacher Edition
- Fully editable blackline masters
- Section Spotlight Videos Launch
- Differentiated Lesson Plans
- Printable reports of daily assignments
- Standards Tracking System

Levels				Resources	Chapter Opener	Section 1	Section 2	Section 3	Chapter Assess
BL	OL	AL	ELL						
				TEACH *(continued)*					
BL	OL	AL		Supreme Court Case Studies				p. 109	
BL	OL	AL	ELL	The Living Constitution	✓	✓	✓	✓	✓
BL	OL	AL	ELL	American Issues	✓	✓	✓	✓	✓
	OL	AL	ELL	American Art and Architecture Transparencies, Strategies, and Activities	✓	✓	✓	✓	✓
BL	OL	AL		High School American History Literature Library	✓	✓	✓	✓	✓
	OL	AL		American History Primary Source Documents Library	✓	✓	✓	✓	✓
BL	OL	AL	ELL	American Music: Hits Through History CD	✓	✓	✓	✓	✓
BL	OL	AL	ELL	StudentWorks™ Plus	✓	✓	✓	✓	✓
BL	OL	AL	ELL	*The American Vision* Video Program	✓	✓	✓	✓	✓
Teacher Resources				Reading Strategies and Activities for the Social Studies Classroom	✓	✓	✓	✓	✓
				Strategies for Success	✓	✓	✓	✓	✓
				Presentation Plus! with MindJogger CheckPoint	✓	✓	✓	✓	✓
				Success With English Learners					
				ASSESS					
BL	OL	AL	ELL	Section Quizzes and Chapter Tests*		p. 371	p. 372	p. 373	p. 375
BL	OL	AL	ELL	Authentic Assessment With Rubrics					p. 57
BL	OL	AL	ELL	Standardized Test Practice Workbook					p. 39
BL	OL	AL	ELL	*ExamView® Assessment Suite*		26-1	26-2	26-3	Ch. 26
				CLOSE					
BL			ELL	Reteaching Activity, URB					p. 107
BL	OL		ELL	Reading and Study Skills Foldables™	p. 80				
BL	OL	AL	ELL	*American History* in Graphic Novel					p. 65

✓ Chapter- or unit-based activities applicable to all sections in this chapter.

Using Chapter Overviews

Teach With Technology

What is a Chapter Overview?

A Chapter Overview provides an online section-by-section summary of the content of each chapter. It can help students review—or preview—chapter content to increase comprehension of main ideas.

How can a Chapter Overview help my students and me?

A Chapter Overview helps you and your students review the main points from each chapter section-by-section. It can help:

- students preview chapter content
- students focus on the main ideas
- students review chapter content
- students practice reading and comprehension skills
- you devise discussion points
- you summarize the chapter for your students

Visit glencoe.com and enter a ***QuickPass***™ code to go to Chapter Overview.

History ONLINE
Visit glencoe.com and enter ***QuickPass***™ code TAV9399c26T for Chapter 26 resources.

You can easily launch a wide range of digital products from your computer's desktop with the McGraw-Hill Social Studies widget.

TeacherWorks

	Student	Teacher	Parent
Media Library			
• Section Audio	●		●
• Spanish Audio Summaries	●		●
• Section Spotlight Videos	●	●	●
***The American Vision* Online Learning Center (Web Site)**			
• StudentWorks™ Plus Online	●	●	●
• Multilingual Glossary	●	●	●
• Study-to-Go	●	●	●
• Chapter Overviews	●	●	●
• Self-Check Quizzes	●	●	●
• Student Web Activities	●	●	●
• ePuzzles and Games	●	●	●
• Vocabulary eFlashcards	●	●	●
• In Motion Animations	●	●	●
• Study Central™	●	●	●
• Web Activity Lesson Plans		●	
• Vocabulary PuzzleMaker	●	●	●
• Historical Thinking Activities		●	
• Beyond the Textbook	●	●	●

Reading Support From Jamestown Education

- **Timed Readings Plus in Social Studies** helps students increase their reading rate and fluency while maintaining comprehension. The 400-word passages are similar to those found on state and national assessments.
- **Reading in the Content Area: Social Studies** concentrates on six essential reading skills that help students better comprehend what they read. The book includes 75 high-interest nonfiction passages written at increasing levels of difficulty.
- **Reading Social Studies** includes strategic reading instruction and vocabulary support in Social Studies content for both ELLs and native speakers of English.

www.jamestowneducation.com

Biography / A&E Home Video / The History Channel

The following videotape programs are available from Glencoe as supplements to this chapter:

- Vietnam: A Soldier's Diary (ISBN 0-76-700772-7)
- War Memorials - Great American Monuments (ISBN 1-56-501643-2)

To order, call Glencoe at 1-800-334-7344. To find classroom resources to accompany many of these videos, check the following home pages:

A&E Television: www.aetv.com
The History Channel: www.historychannel.com

Reading List Generator CD-ROM — Glencoe BookLink 3

Use this database to search more than 30,000 titles to create a customized reading list for your students.

- Reading lists can be organized by students' reading level, author, genre, theme, or area of interest.
- The database provides Degrees of Reading Power™ (DRP) and Lexile™ readability scores for all selections.
- A brief summary of each selection is included.

Leveled reading suggestions for this chapter:

For students at a Grade 8 reading level:
- ***Young Man in Vietnam,*** by Charles Coe

For students at a Grade 9 reading level:
- ***Dear America: Letters Home from Vietnam,*** by Bernard Edelman

For students at a Grade 10 reading level:
- ***Getting to Know the Two Vietnams,*** by Fred West

For students at a Grade 11 reading level:
- ***Voices from Vietnam,*** by Barry Denenberg

For students at a Grade 12 reading level:
- ***The Vietnam War,*** by Debbie Levy

National Geographic

Index to National Geographic Magazine:

The following articles relate to this chapter:

- "Hanoi: Shedding the Ghosts of War," by David Lamb, May 2004.
- "Saigon: Fourteen Years After," by Peter T. White, November 1989.

Access National Geographic's new, dynamic MapMachine Web site and other geography resources at:
www.nationalgeographic.com
www.nationalgeographic.com/maps

Introducing Chapter 26

Focus

MAKING CONNECTIONS

Should Citizens Support the Government During Wartime?

Invite a volunteer to read the paragraph and questions presented. Use the questions provided to begin a discussion about the Vietnam conflict. Have students write the two questions in their notebooks, adding to their answers as they read the chapter. **OL**

Teach

The Big Ideas

As students study the chapter, remind them to consider the section-based Big Ideas included in each section's Guide to Reading. The **Essential Questions** in the activities below tie in to the Big Ideas and help students think about and understand important chapter concepts. In addition, the Hands-on Chapter Projects with their culminating activities relate the content from each section to the Big Ideas. These activities build on each other as students progress through the chapter. Section activities culminate in the wrap-up activity on the Visual Summary page.

Chapter 26

The Vietnam War

1954–1975

American soldiers march up a hill in Vietnam in 1968, as fires behind them send smoke into the air.

U.S. PRESIDENTS

Eisenhower 1953–1961

Kennedy 1961–1963

Johnson 1963–1969

U.S. EVENTS

1955
- U.S. military aid and advisers are sent to South Vietnam

1964
- Congress passes Gulf of Tonkin Resolution

1965
- U.S. combat troops arrive in Vietnam

1955 — 1960 — 1965

WORLD EVENTS

1954
- France leaves Indochina; Geneva Accords divide Vietnam in two

1958
- U.S. troops land in Lebanon

1960
- U-2 spy plane is shot down

Section 1

Going to War in Vietnam

Essential Question: What created the conflict in Vietnam and how did America become involved? *(The desire for independence from France fueled rebellion. The United States became involved first by aiding the French and later by committing military advisers and troops to prevent the fall of Vietnam to communism.)* Tell students they will learn in this section how the United States began fighting in Vietnam. **OL**

Section 2

Vietnam Divides the Nation

Essential Question: How did Americans protest against the war in Vietnam? *(Teach-ins were held at universities; some men burned draft cards; people held protest marches.)* Inform students that in this section they will read about the protest movement, which helped to change the culture of the United States and its relationship to the federal government. **OL**

Chapter Audio

MAKING CONNECTIONS

Should Citizens Support the Government During Wartime?

During the Cold War, the United States sent troops to Vietnam to stop the spread of communism. Winning in Vietnam proved to be difficult and, as the war dragged on, many Americans began to protest. Eventually, the United States pulled out of Vietnam.

- ***Why do you think the United States sent troops to Vietnam?***
- ***Why do you think Vietnam divided Americans?***

1968
- Tet Offensive begins
- Anti-war protest in Chicago

Nixon 1969–1974

1970
- National Guard troops kill student protesters at Kent State

1973
- Last U.S. troops leave Vietnam

1970 — 1975

1970
- Nixon orders invasion of Cambodia

1975
- Saigon falls to North Vietnamese invasion

FOLDABLES™

Defining Vietnam Terminology

Make a Vocabulary Book Foldable to aid your review of the Vietnam War. Select terms for a 10-tab Vocabulary Book. Example terms include: *Ho Chi Minh, Containment,* and *Gulf of Tonkin Resolution.* Define the terms under the appropriate tab.

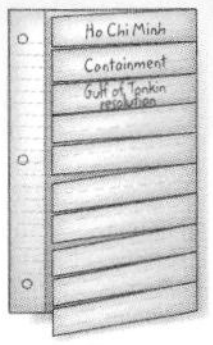

History ONLINE Visit glencoe.com and enter *QuickPass*™ code TAV9846c26 for Chapter 26 resources.

Introducing Chapter 26

More About the Photo

Visual Literacy In 1969, the year after this photo was taken, the number of American troops reached their peak of about 540,000. Many of the soldiers were a year or two out of high school. Both civilian and military photographers covered the war, enduring the same hardships and risks as soldiers with some losing their lives. Thousands of the photographs taken by military photographers are housed at the National Archives in Washington, D.C.

FOLDABLES™ Study Organizer **Dinah Zike's Foldables**

Dinah Zike's Foldables are three-dimensional, interactive graphic organizers that help students practice basic writing skills, review vocabulary terms, and identify main ideas. Instructions for creating and using Foldables can be found in the Appendix at the end of this book and in the *Dinah Zike's Reading and Study Skills Foldables* booklet.

History ONLINE

Visit glencoe.com and enter *QuickPass*™ code TAV9399c26T for Chapter 26 resources, including a Chapter Overview, Study Central™, Study-to-Go, Student Web Activity, Self-Check Quiz, and other materials.

Section 3

The War Winds Down

Essential Question: How did the war end and how did it affect Americans? *(Negotiations dragged on while the military implemented Vietnamization. Ultimately, American troops were withdrawn and South Vietnam fell to communism. Americans became cynical about the war and their government.)* Tell students that this section will describe the end of the war. **OL**

Focus

Bellringer
Daily Focus Transparency 26-1

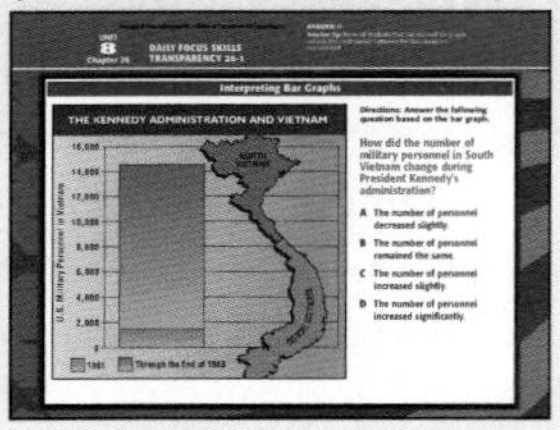

Guide to Reading

Answers: fall of China to communism, the outbreak of the Korean War

Section Spotlight Video

To generate student interest and provide a springboard for class discussion, access the Chapter 26, Section 1 video at glencoe.com or on the video DVD.

Section 1

Section Audio Spotlight Video

Going to War in Vietnam

Guide to Reading

Big Ideas

Trade, War, and Migration American involvement in the war in Vietnam was the result of its Cold War strategy.

Content Vocabulary
- domino theory *(p. 883)*
- guerrilla *(p. 883)*
- napalm *(p. 889)*
- Agent Orange *(p. 889)*

Academic Vocabulary
- strategic *(p. 885)*
- traditional *(p. 885)*

People and Events to Identify
- Ho Chi Minh *(p. 882)*
- Dien Bien Phu *(p. 884)*
- Geneva Accords *(p. 884)*
- Ngo Dinh Diem *(p. 884)*
- Vietcong *(p. 885)*
- Gulf of Tonkin Resolution *(p. 886)*
- Ho Chi Minh trail *(p. 889)*

Reading Strategy

Organizing Complete a graphic organizer similar to the one below by providing reasons why the United States aided France in Vietnam.

Reasons for U.S. Support of France → [ ] → [ ]

In the late 1940s and early 1950s, most Americans knew little about Indochina, France's colony in Southeast Asia. During the Cold War, however, American officials became concerned the region might fall to communism. Eventually, American troops were sent to fight in Vietnam.

American Involvement in Vietnam

MAIN Idea The Cold War policy of containment led the United States to become increasingly involved in events in Vietnam.

HISTORY AND YOU Have you met anyone who was born in Vietnam? Do you know why he or she left? Read to learn about Vietnam's complicated and tragic history.

In 1940, the Japanese invaded Vietnam. The occupation was only the latest example of foreigners ruling the Vietnamese people. The Chinese Empire had controlled the region for hundreds of years. Then, beginning in the late 1800s and lasting until World War II, France ruled Vietnam as well as neighboring Laos and Cambodia—a region known collectively as French Indochina.

The Growth of Vietnamese Nationalism

The Vietnamese did not want to be ruled by foreigners, and by the early 1900s, nationalism had become a powerful force in the country. The Vietnamese formed several political parties to push for independence or for reform of the French colonial government. One of the leaders of the nationalist movement for almost 30 years was Nguyen That Thanh—better known by his assumed name, **Ho Chi Minh.** At the age of 21, Ho Chi Minh traveled to Europe where he lived in London and then Paris. In 1919 he presented a petition for Vietnamese independence at the Versailles Peace Conference, but the peace treaty ignored the issue. Ho Chi Minh later visited the Soviet Union where he became an advocate of communism. In 1930 he returned to Southeast Asia, helped found the Indochinese Communist Party, and worked to overthrow French rule.

Ho Chi Minh's activities made him a wanted man. He fled Indochina and spent several years in exile in the Soviet Union and China. In 1941 he returned to Vietnam. By then, Japan had seized control of the country. Ho Chi Minh organized a nationalist group called the Vietminh. The group united both Communists and non-Communists in the struggle to expel the Japanese forces. Soon afterward, the United States began sending aid to the Vietminh.

Resource Manager

R Reading Strategies	C Critical Thinking	D Differentiated Instruction	W Writing Support	S Skill Practice
Teacher Edition • Act. Prior Know., p. 883 • Making Connections, p. 885 **Additional Resources** • Prim. Source Read, URB p. 99 • Guide Read Act., URB p. 112	**Teacher Edition** • Analyzing, p. 883 • Det. Cause and Effect, p. 885 • Making Generalizations, p. 886 • Contrasting, p. 888 **Additional Resources** • Crit. Think Skills, URB p. 96 • Quizzes and Tests, p. 371 • Interpret. Pol. Cartoons Act., URB p. 105	**Teacher Edition** • English Learners, p. 886 • Logical/Math., p. 888 • Naturalist, p. 889 **Additional Resources** • Diff. Instruction Act., URB p. 87 • Foldables, p. 80	**Additional Resources** • Content Vocab. Act., URB p. 91 • Academic Vocab. Act., URB p. 93	**Teacher Edition** • Using Geo. Skills, p. 884 **Additional Resources** • Read Essen., URB p. 286 • Hist. Analysis Skills Act., URB p. 86 • Time Line Act., URB p. 97

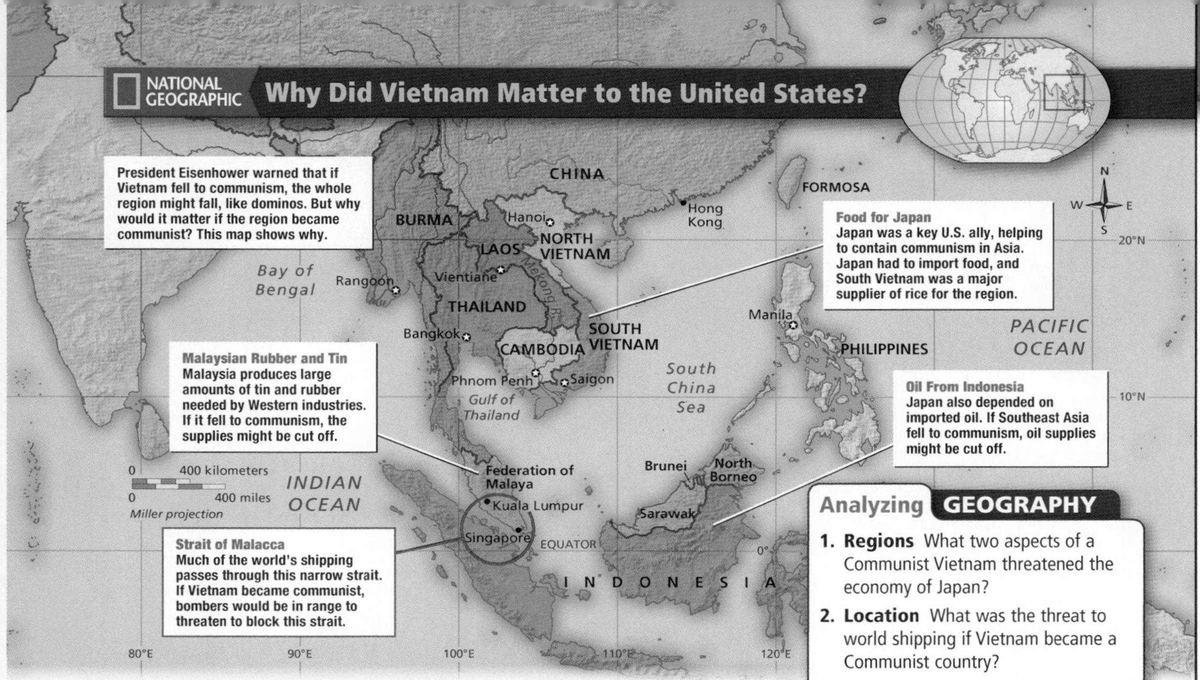

Analyzing GEOGRAPHY

1. **Regions** What two aspects of a Communist Vietnam threatened the economy of Japan?
2. **Location** What was the threat to world shipping if Vietnam became a Communist country?

America Aids the French

When Japan surrendered to the Allies in 1945, it gave up control of Indochina. Ho Chi Minh quickly declared Vietnam to be an independent nation. France, however, had no intention of allowing Vietnam to become independent. Seeking to regain their colonial empire in Southeast Asia, French troops returned to Vietnam in 1946 and drove the Vietminh forces into hiding in the countryside.

The Vietminh fought back against the French-dominated regime and slowly gained control of large areas of the countryside. As the fighting escalated, France appealed to the United States for help. The request put American officials in a difficult position. The United States opposed colonialism. It had pressured the Dutch to give up their empire in Indonesia and supported the British decision to give India independence in 1947. In Vietnam, however, the independence movement had become entangled with the Communist movement. American officials did not want France to control Vietnam, but they also did not want Vietnam to be communist.

Two events convinced President Truman to help France—the fall of China to communism and the outbreak of the Korean War. The latter, in particular, seemed to indicate that the Soviet Union had begun a major push to impose communism on East Asia. Shortly after the Korean War began, Truman authorized military aid to French forces in Vietnam. President Eisenhower continued Truman's policy and defended his decision with what became known as the **domino theory**—the idea that if Vietnam fell to communism, the rest of Southeast Asia would follow:

PRIMARY SOURCE

"You have a row of dominoes set up, you knock over the first one, and what will happen to the last one is the certainty that it will go over very quickly. . . . Asia, after all, has already lost some 450 million of its peoples to Communist dictatorship, and we simply can't afford greater losses." **C**

—President Eisenhower, quoted in *America in Vietnam*

Defeat at Dien Bien Phu

Despite aid from the United States, the French continued to struggle against the Vietminh, who consistently frustrated the French with hit-and-run and ambush tactics. **R** These are the tactics of **guerrillas,** irregular troops who blend into the civilian population and are difficult for regular armies to fight.

Teach

C Critical Thinking

Analyzing Invite a volunteer to read the quotation by Eisenhower. **Ask:** What is the "flaw" in this argument? *(It is based on a presupposition that nations act like game pieces. Students should question the validity of Eisenhower's reference to "the certainty that it will go over very quickly.")* **AL**

R Reading Strategy

Activating Prior Knowledge
Ask: What previous experience did Americans have with guerrilla warfare? *(They had fought Filipino guerillas.)* **OL**

Analyzing GEOGRAPHY

Answers:
1. Japan depended on Vietnam for food and a communist Vietnam could threaten its oil supply from Indonesia
2. Vietnam might control the Straits of Malacca.

Hands-On Chapter Project
Step 1

Create a Documentary of the Vietnam War

Step 1: Determining the Theme
Essential question: What were the milestones in the Vietnam War?

Directions Write the essential question on the board and explain to students that in this first step, different groups will create the basic storyline for a documentary of the Vietnam War. For example, a documentary could describe the battles of the war, the U.S. presidents conducting the war, army life, or life at home during the war.

Putting It Together Later, each group should make a presentation to persuade the others about the merits of their choice. (Students could think about the arguments and style a young filmmaker might use to persuade potential backers about backing his or her project.) **OL**
(Chapter Project continued on page 893)

S Skill Practice

Using Geography Skills Ask students to calculate the distance from Dien Bien Phu to Hanoi, the North Vietnamese capital, and to Saigon, which had been the French capital. *(about 200 miles to Hanoi and 800 miles to Saigon)* OL

Analyzing GEOGRAPHY

Answers:

1. For security reasons, it was better for communist China to have a communist neighbor.
2. Shipping by sea would have been difficult because of American ships guarding the South China Sea; shipping overland through hundreds of miles of jungle was time-consuming and dangerous.

Reading Check

Answer: He sought independence for Vietnam.

Additional Support

NATIONAL GEOGRAPHIC **Vietnam, 1959**

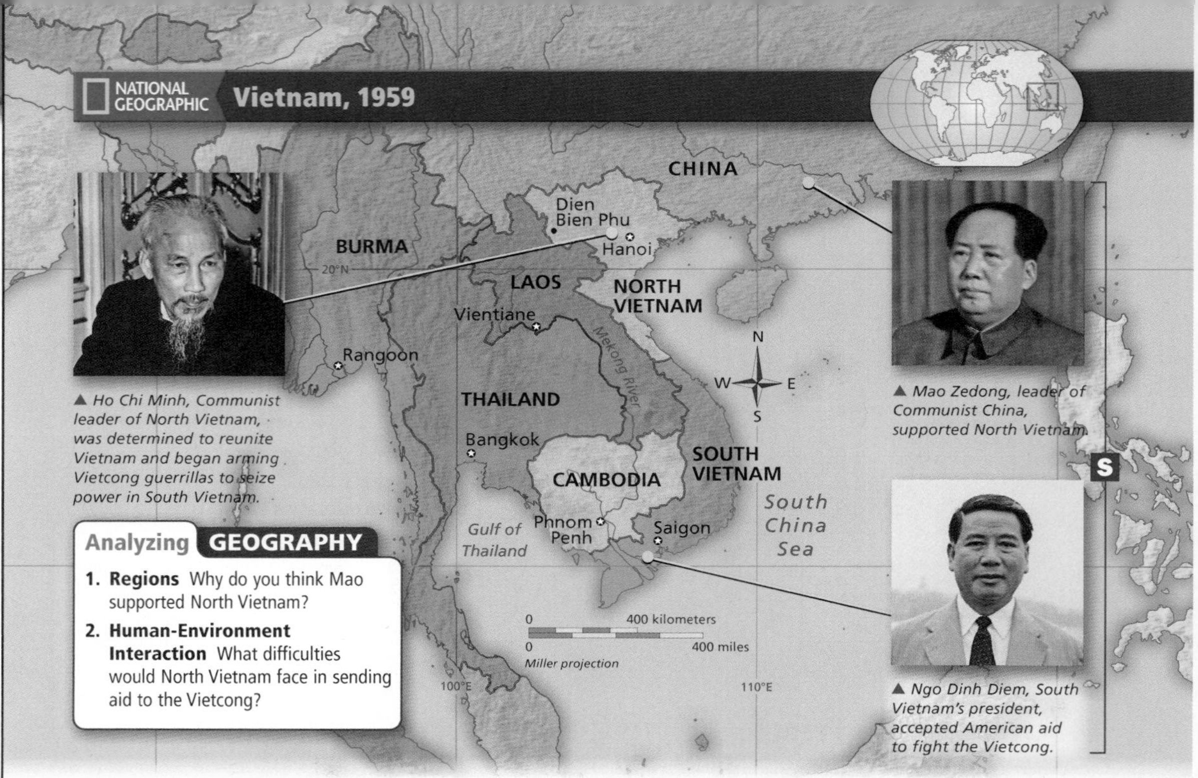

▲ *Ho Chi Minh, Communist leader of North Vietnam, was determined to reunite Vietnam and began arming Vietcong guerrillas to seize power in South Vietnam.*

▲ *Mao Zedong, leader of Communist China, supported North Vietnam.*

▲ *Ngo Dinh Diem, South Vietnam's president, accepted American aid to fight the Vietcong.*

Analyzing GEOGRAPHY

1. **Regions** Why do you think Mao supported North Vietnam?
2. **Human-Environment Interaction** What difficulties would North Vietnam face in sending aid to the Vietcong?

The mounting casualties and the inability of the French to defeat the Vietminh made the war very unpopular in France. Finally, in 1954 the struggle reached a turning point when the French commander ordered his forces to occupy the mountain town of **Dien Bien Phu.** Seizing the town would interfere with the Vietminh's supply lines and force them into open battle. Soon afterward, a huge Vietminh force surrounded Dien Bien Phu and began bombarding the town. On May 7, 1954, the French force at Dien Bien Phu fell to the Vietminh. The defeat convinced the French to make peace and withdraw from Indochina.

Geneva Accords

Negotiations to end the conflict were held in Geneva, Switzerland. The **Geneva Accords** divided Vietnam along the 17th parallel, with Ho Chi Minh and the Vietminh in control of North Vietnam and a pro-Western regime in control of the South. In 1956 elections were to be held to reunite the country under a single government. The Geneva Accords also recognized Cambodia's independence. Laos had gained independence in the previous year.

Shortly after the Geneva Accords partitioned Vietnam, the French troops left. The United States became the principal protector of the new government in the South, led by a nationalist leader named **Ngo Dinh Diem** (NOH DIHN deh•EHM). Like Ho Chi Minh, Diem had been educated abroad, but, unlike the North Vietnamese leader, Diem was pro-Western and fiercely anti-Communist. A Catholic, he welcomed the roughly one million North Vietnamese Catholics who migrated south to escape Ho Chi Minh's rule.

The elections mandated by the Geneva Accords never took place. In a special referendum, Diem became president of the new Republic of Vietnam in the South. He then refused to permit the 1956 elections, fearing Ho Chi Minh would win. Eisenhower approved Diem's actions and increased American aid to South Vietnam.

Reading Check **Summarizing** Why did Ho Chi Minh lead a resistance movement against France?

Extending the Content

Ngo Dinh Diem Diem's ancestors had converted to Catholicism. They were also a noble family with connections to the imperial family. Frustrated at the French unwillingness to implement legislative reforms he suggested, in 1933 Diem resigned his post as Minister of the Interior.

In 1945 Diem was captured by forces of Ho Chi Minh, who hoped he would join an independent government in the north. Diem refused, however, and lived outside the country for most of the following decade. He returned at the emperor's request to serve as prime minister in 1954; the following year, after a government-controlled referendum, Diem made himself president and staffed his regime with family members. Diem imprisoned and killed hundreds of Buddhists, whom he accused of aiding the Communists. This action in a land primarily Buddhist cost him the support not only of his own people but of the United States.

America Becomes Involved in Vietnam

MAIN Idea Political pressures in the United States led the nation to become deeply involved in the civil war in Vietnam.

HISTORY AND YOU Do you have a relative or family friend who fought in the Vietnam War? Read on to find out why the United States got involved in this complicated conflict.

After Ngo Dinh Diem refused to hold national elections and began to crack down on Communist groups in South Vietnam, Ho Chi Minh and the Communists began an armed struggle to reunify the nation. They organized a new guerrilla army of South Vietnamese Communists, which became known as the **Vietcong.** As fighting began between the Vietcong and South Vietnam's forces, President Eisenhower sent hundreds of military advisers to train South Vietnam's army.

Despite American assistance, the Vietcong continued to grow more powerful because many Vietnamese opposed Diem's government. The Vietcong's use of terror was also effective. By 1961, the Vietcong had assassinated thousands of government officials and established control over much of the countryside. In response Diem looked increasingly to the United States for help.

Kennedy Takes Over

On taking office in 1961, President Kennedy continued the nation's policy of support for South Vietnam. Like Presidents Truman and Eisenhower before him, Kennedy saw the Southeast Asian country as vitally important in the battle against communism.

C In political terms, Kennedy needed to appear tough on communism, since Republicans often accused Democrats of having lost China to communism during the Truman administration. From 1961 to late 1963, the number of American military personnel in South Vietnam jumped from about 2,000 to around 15,000.

American officials believed that the Vietcong continued to grow because Diem's government was unpopular and corrupt. They urged him to create a more democratic government and to introduce reforms to help Vietnam's peasants. Diem introduced some limited reforms, but they had little effect.

One program Diem introduced, at the urging of American advisers, made the situation worse. The South Vietnamese created special fortified villages known as **strategic** hamlets. These villages were protected by machine guns, bunkers, trenches, and barbed wire. C Vietnamese officials then moved villagers to the strategic hamlets. The program proved to be extremely unpopular. Many peasants resented being uprooted from their villages, where they had worked to build farms and where many of their ancestors lay buried.

The Overthrow of Diem

Diem made himself even more unpopular by discriminating against Buddhism, one of the country's most widely practiced religions. In the spring of 1963, Diem, a Catholic, banned the **traditional** religious flags for Buddha's birthday. When Buddhists took to the streets in protest, Diem's police killed 9 people and injured 14 others. In the demonstrations that R followed, a Buddhist monk poured gasoline over his robes and set himself on fire, the first of several Buddhists to do so. Images of their self-destruction horrified Americans as they watched the footage on television news reports. These extreme acts of protest were a disturbing sign of the opposition to the Diem regime.

In August 1963 American ambassador Henry Cabot Lodge arrived in Vietnam. He quickly learned that Diem's unpopularity had so alarmed several Vietnamese generals that they were plotting to overthrow him. When Lodge expressed American sympathy for their cause, the generals launched a military coup. They seized power on November 1, 1963, and executed Diem shortly afterward.

Diem's overthrow only made matters worse. Despite his unpopularity with some Vietnamese, Diem had been a respected nationalist and a capable administrator. After his death, South Vietnam's government grew increasingly weak and unstable. The United States became even more deeply involved in order to prop it up. Coincidentally, three weeks after Diem's death, President Kennedy was assassinated. The presidency, as well as the growing problem of Vietnam, now belonged to Kennedy's vice president, Lyndon Johnson.

C Critical Thinking

Determining Cause and Effect Invite students to create graphic organizers showing the cause-and-effect relationships in the segment "Kennedy Takes Over." *(Possible answers include: Cause: Kennedy does not want to appear soft on communism. Effect: number of military personnel in South Vietnam increases. Cause: American officials believe the corruption and unpopularity of Diem's government increased Vietcong growth. Effect: They were sympathetic to his overthrow. Cause: Diem created strategic hamlets. Effect: Program was unpopular among the people.)* OL

R Reading Strategy

Making Connections Remind students that in the early 2000s some nations, such as France, banned young female Muslims from wearing their traditional head scarves to schools. In the Netherlands, the government proposed banning female Muslims from wearing a burka, a garment that covers both the head and body. Lead a discussion about the rights of religious minorities and majorities. OL

Additional Support

Activity: Collaborative Learning

Model a Diplomatic Mission Divide the class into small groups. Ask students to imagine they are the diplomatic team given the task of planning what ought to be done in South Vietnam in 1961 to prevent the nation from collapsing. Have students present their ideas in panel discussion form or as a dialogue between American and South Vietnamese diplomats. OL

D Differentiated Instruction

English Learners Point out the expression "the battle . . . must be joined" in the quotation by President Johnson. Explain to students that in this case the term *joined* does not refer to a putting together of different parts. Rather, it means that the battle must begin. Remind students that every language has its own idioms that must simply be learned and not to be discouraged by the oddities of English. Encourage students to share an example of an idiom in their own language. **ELL**

C Critical Thinking

Making Generalizations Point out the reference to Johnson's sensitivity to accusations of being soft on communism and to Kennedy's equal sensitivity, discussed on page 885. Remind students that these sensitivities were related to earlier accusations against Truman and to the McCarthy era. Lead a discussion on the question of how much the decisions or mistakes of previous administrations influence current foreign or domestic policies. **OL**

Additional Support

Johnson and Vietnam

D Initially, President Johnson exercised caution and restraint regarding the conflict in Vietnam. "We seek no wider war," he repeatedly promised. At the same time, Johnson was determined to prevent South Vietnam from becoming communist. "The battle against communism," he declared shortly before becoming president, "must be joined . . . with strength and determination."

Politics also played a role in Johnson's Vietnam policy. Like Kennedy, Johnson remembered that many Republicans blamed the Truman administration for the fall of China to communism in 1949. Should the Democrats also "lose" Vietnam, Johnson feared, it might cause a "mean and destructive debate that would shatter my Presidency, kill my administration, and damage our democracy."

For the text of the Gulf of Tonkin Resolution see R57 in **Documents in American History.**

The Gulf of Tonkin Resolution On August 2, 1964, President Johnson announced that North Vietnamese torpedo boats had fired on two American destroyers in the Gulf of Tonkin. Two days later, the president reported that another similar attack had taken place. **C** Johnson was campaigning for the presidency and was very sensitive to accusations of being soft on communism. He insisted that North Vietnam's attacks were unprovoked and immediately ordered American aircraft to attack North Vietnamese ships and naval facilities. Johnson did not reveal that the American warships had been helping the South Vietnamese conduct electronic spying and commando raids against North Vietnam.

Johnson then asked Congress for the authority to defend American forces and American allies in Southeast Asia. Congress agreed to Johnson's request with little debate. Most members of Congress agreed with Republican representative Ross Adair of Indiana, who defiantly declared, "The American flag has been fired upon. We will not and cannot tolerate such things."

On August 7, 1964, the Senate and House passed the **Gulf of Tonkin Resolution,** authorizing the president to "take all necessary measures to repel any armed attack against the forces of the United States and to prevent further aggression." With only two dissenting votes, Congress had, in effect, handed its war powers over to the president.

The United States Sends in Troops Shortly after Congress passed the Gulf of Tonkin Resolution, the Vietcong began to attack bases where American advisers were stationed in South Vietnam. The attacks began in the fall of 1964 and continued to escalate. After a Vietcong attack on a base at Pleiku in February 1965 left eight Americans dead and more than 100 wounded, President Johnson decided to respond. Less than 14 hours after the attack, American aircraft bombed North Vietnam.

After the air strikes, one poll showed that Johnson's approval rating on his handling of Vietnam jumped from 41 percent to 60 percent. Further, nearly 80 percent of Americans agreed that without American assistance, Southeast Asia would fall to the Communists. An equivalent number believed that the United States should send combat troops to Vietnam

Debates IN HISTORY

Should America Fight in Vietnam?

As the war in Vietnam dragged on, Americans became increasingly divided about the nation's role in the conflict. In January 1966, George W. Ball, undersecretary of state to President Johnson, delivered an address to indicate "how we got [into Vietnam] and why we must stay." George Kennan, a former ambassador to the Soviet Union, testified before the Senate Foreign Relations Committee in that same year, arguing that American involvement in Vietnam was "something we would not choose deliberately if the choice were ours to make all over again today."

Activity: Interdisciplinary Connection

Civics Invite students to find out who voted against the Gulf of Tonkin Resolution and why they voted against it. Students may decide to extend their research to find out who were the other members of Congress who voted against going to war in previous and subsequent clashes. Ask them to see if there is a common thread among these dissenting voters. Suggest they present their findings as a skit or news interview with one of the dissenters. **OL**

to prevent that from happening. The president's actions also met with strong approval from his closest advisers, including Secretary of Defense Robert McNamara and National Security Adviser McGeorge Bundy.

Some officials disagreed, chief among them Undersecretary of State George Ball, who initially supported involvement in Vietnam but later turned against it. He warned that if the United States got too involved, it would be difficult to get out. "Once on the tiger's back," he warned, "we cannot be sure of picking the place to dismount."

Most of the advisers who surrounded Johnson, however, firmly believed the nation had a duty to halt communism in Vietnam, both to maintain stability in Southeast Asia and to ensure the United States's continuing power and prestige in the world. In a memo to the president, Bundy argued:

PRIMARY SOURCE

"The stakes in Vietnam are extremely high. The American investment is very large, and American responsibility is a fact of life which is palpable in the atmosphere of Asia, and even elsewhere. The international prestige of the U.S. and a substantial part of our influence are directly at risk in Vietnam."

—quoted in *The Best and the Brightest*

In March 1965, President Johnson expanded American involvement by beginning a sustained bombing campaign against North Vietnam code-named Operation Rolling Thunder. That same month, the president also ordered the first combat troops into Vietnam. American soldiers would now fight alongside South Vietnamese troops against the Vietcong.

Reading Check **Describing** How did politics play a role in President Johnson's Vietnam policy?

YES

George W. Ball
Undersecretary of State

PRIMARY SOURCE

"[T]he conflict in Viet-Nam is a product of the great shifts and changes triggered by the Second World War. . . . [T]he Soviet Union under Stalin exploited the confusion to push out the perimeter of its power and influence in an effort to extend the outer limits of Communist domination by force or the threat of force. . . .

The bloody encounters in [Vietnam] . . . are thus in a real sense battles and skirmishes in a continuing war to prevent one Communist power after another from violating internationally recognized boundary lines fixing the outer limits of Communist dominion. . . .

In the long run our hopes for the people of South Vietnam reflect our hopes for people everywhere. What we seek is a world living in peace and freedom."

—Speech delivered January 30, 1966

NO

George F. Kennan
Former Diplomat

PRIMARY SOURCE

"Vietnam is not a region of major military-industrial importance. . . . Even a situation in which South Vietnam was controlled exclusively by the Vietcong, . . . would not present in my opinion, dangers great enough to justify our direct military intervention.

And to attempt to crush North Vietnamese strength to a point where Hanoi could no longer give any support to Vietcong political activity in the South would . . . have the effect of bringing in Chinese forces at some point. . . .

Our motives are widely misinterpreted; and the spectacle of Americans inflicting grievous injury on the lives of a poor and helpless people . . . produces reactions among millions of people throughout the world profoundly detrimental to the image we would like them to hold of this country."

—Testimony before the Senate Foreign Relations Committee, February 10, 1966

DBQ Document-Based Questions

1. **Summarizing** Why does Ball believe that the United States is justified in fighting in Vietnam?
2. **Explaining** What are the three main points of Kennan's argument?
3. **Contrasting** What is the fundamental difference between the views of Ball and Kennan?
4. **Evaluating** With which position do you agree? Write a paragraph to explain your choice.

Debates IN HISTORY

Answers:
1. Ball argues that the United States wants to protect the Vietnamese from communism. He also sees Vietnam as part of the larger Cold War.
2. Vietnam is unimportant; if the U.S. tried to crush North Vietnam, the Chinese would enter the conflict; the war is giving the world a negative view of the U.S.
3. Ball: Vietnam is strategically important in the Cold War, it is the duty of the U.S. to help maintain its freedom; Kennan: Vietnam is not important and that the U.S. is losing good will around the world over it.
4. Students' paragraphs will vary.

Reading Check

Answer: Johnson thought his presidency would be ruined and democracy damaged if the Democrats lost Vietnam.

Additional Support

Extending the Content

The War in Vietnam One of the contentions of those who did not support the war was that it was a civil war in which the United States had no business intervening. Others thought the conflict was one nation, North Vietnam, conducting a war of aggression against another nation, South Vietnam. In a White Paper issued in February 1965, the State Department argued that Vietnam was a new type of war, a covert war of aggression intended to bring about a communist regime. It described the people of South Vietnam as having courageously resisted these efforts for years, which violated the Geneva Accords, the United Nations Charter, and other international agreements. Many felt that in coming to the aid of South Vietnam, without a desire for military bases or territory there, the United States was acting as a friend to the people of that nation.

D Differentiated Instruction

Logical/Mathematical Ask students to use the data on this page and on page 885 to graph the increase of American troops in Vietnam from 1961 to 1966. Tell them to use a bar graph or line graph to chart their findings. BL

C Critical Thinking

Contrasting Invite a volunteer to read the quotation by Linda Martin. **Ask:** In what earlier wars might American soldiers have felt they were more certain and safe? Why? *(Students may say that in previous wars the enemy was readily recognizable and that conventional warfare felt safer than guerrilla attacks.)* OL

Analyzing GEOGRAPHY

Answers:

1. Laos, Cambodia
2. South Vietnam had a long border with Cambodia and Laos that passed through jungle regions.

Additional Support

A Bloody Stalemate

MAIN Idea The failure of United States forces to defeat the Vietcong and the deaths of thousands of American soldiers led many Americans to question the nation's involvement in Vietnam.

HISTORY AND YOU Have you ever heard people compare a contemporary military conflict to the Vietnam War? Read on to find out why some people fear becoming involved in a similar conflict today.

By the end of 1965, more than 180,000 American combat troops were fighting in Vietnam. In 1966 that number doubled. Since the American military was extremely strong, it **D** marched into Vietnam with great confidence. "America seemed omnipotent then," wrote Philip Caputo, one of the first marines to arrive. "We saw ourselves as the champions of a 'cause that was destined to triumph.'"

Lacking the firepower of the Americans, the Vietcong used ambushes, booby traps, and other guerrilla tactics. Ronald J. Glasser, an American army doctor, described the devastating effects of one booby trap:

PRIMARY SOURCE

"Three quarters of the way through the tangle, a trooper brushed against a two-inch vine, and a grenade slung at chest high went off, shattering the right side of his head and body. . . . Nearby troopers took hold of the unconscious soldier and, half carrying, half dragging him, pulled him the rest of the way through the tangle."

—quoted in *Vietnam, A History*

The Vietcong also frustrated American troops by blending in with the general population and then quickly vanishing. "It was a sheer physical impossibility to keep the enemy from slipping away whenever he wished," explained one American general. Journalist Linda Martin noted, "It's a war where nothing is ever quite certain **C** and nowhere is ever quite safe."

NATIONAL GEOGRAPHIC **The Vietnam War, 1965–1973**

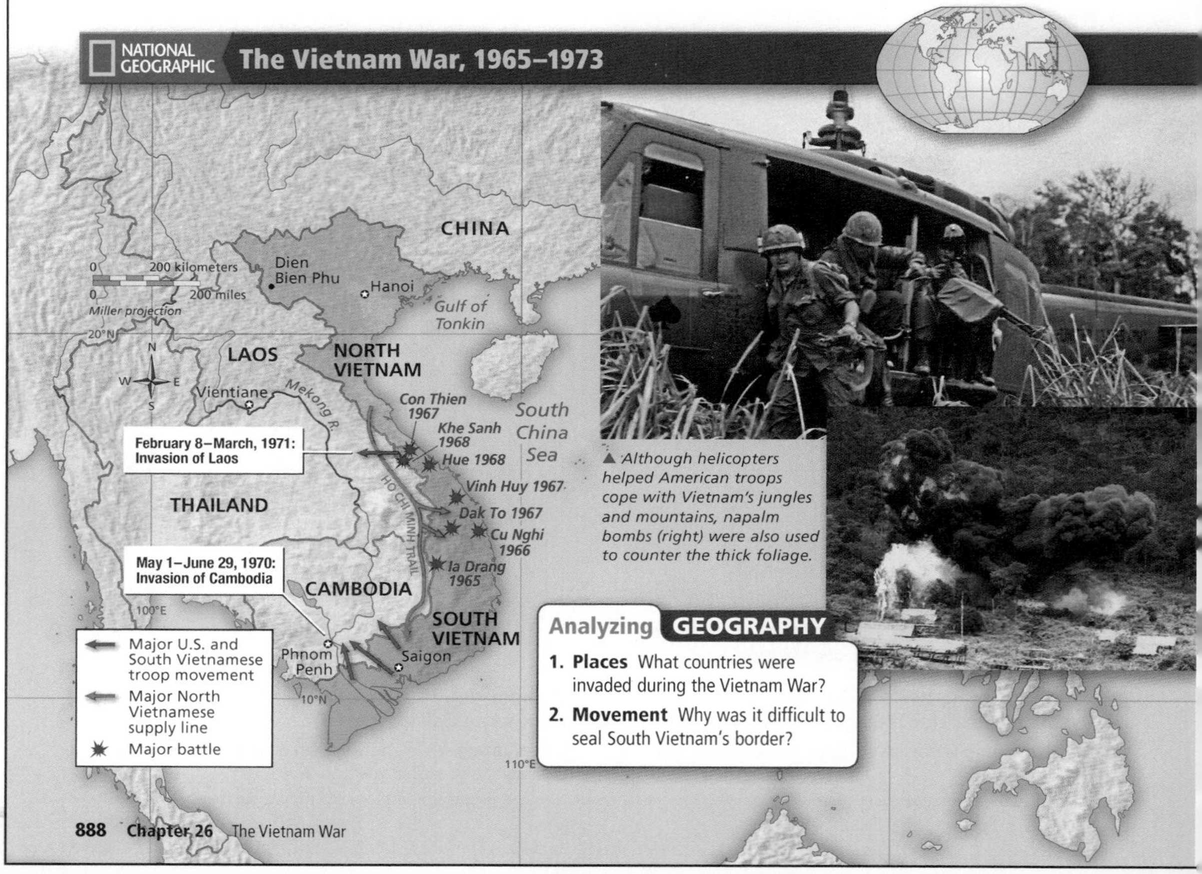

▲ Although helicopters helped American troops cope with Vietnam's jungles and mountains, napalm bombs (right) were also used to counter the thick foliage.

Analyzing GEOGRAPHY

1. **Places** What countries were invaded during the Vietnam War?
2. **Movement** Why was it difficult to seal South Vietnam's border?

888 Chapter 26 The Vietnam War

Extending the Content

Robert McNamara Robert McNamara's training was in business, with an interest in efficiency. He further developed that interest during World War II, serving in the Air Force's Statistical Control Office, and at the Ford Motor Company, where he became the first nonfamily member to rise to the presidency of the company. Tapped as Secretary of Defense by John Kennedy, McNamara wanted to streamline both the Defense Department's bureaucracy and its defense force. An architect of military strategy, he became disillusioned with the progress of the war and resigned in 1968, going on to become president of the World Bank. A 1996 memoir reveals the mistakes McNamara perceives were made in Vietnam.

"Search and Destroy"

To counter the Vietcong's tactics, American troops went on "search and destroy" missions. They tried to find enemy troops, bomb their positions, destroy their supply lines, and force them out into the open for combat.

D The Vietcong evaded American forces by hiding out in the thick jungle or escaping through tunnels dug in the earth. To take away the Vietcong's ability to hide, American forces literally destroyed the landscape. American planes dropped **napalm,** a jellied gasoline that explodes on contact. They also used **Agent Orange,** a chemical that strips leaves from trees and shrubs, turning farmland and forest into wasteland. For those South Vietnamese still living in the countryside, danger lay on all sides.

United States military leaders underestimated the Vietcong's strength. They also misjudged the enemy's stamina and the support they had among the South Vietnamese. American generals believed that continuously bombing and killing large numbers of Vietcong would destroy the enemy's morale and force them to give up. The guerrillas, however, had no intention of surrendering, and they were willing to accept huge losses to achieve their goals.

The Ho Chi Minh Trail

In the Vietcong's war effort, North Vietnamese support was a major factor. Although the Vietcong forces were made up of many South Vietnamese, North Vietnam provided arms, advisers, and leadership. As Vietcong casualties mounted, North Vietnam began sending North Vietnamese Army units to fight.

North Vietnam sent arms and supplies south by way of a network of jungle paths known as the **Ho Chi Minh trail.** The trail wound through the countries of Cambodia and Laos, bypassing the border between North and South Vietnam. Because the trail passed through countries not directly involved in the war, President Johnson refused to allow a full-scale attack on the trail to shut it down.

North Vietnam itself received military weapons and other support from the Soviet Union and China. One of the main reasons President Johnson refused to order a full-scale invasion of North Vietnam was his fear that such an attack would bring China into the war, as had happened in Korea. By placing limits on the war, however, Johnson made it very difficult to win. Instead of conquering enemy territory, American troops were forced to fight a war of attrition—a strategy of defeating the enemy forces by wearing them down. This strategy led troops to conduct grisly body counts after battles to determine how many enemy soldiers had been killed. The U.S. military began measuring "progress" in the war by the number of enemy dead.

Bombing from American planes killed as many as 220,000 Vietnamese between 1965 and 1967. By the end of 1966, more than 6,700 American soldiers had been killed. The notion of a quick and decisive victory grew increasingly remote. As a result, many citizens back home began to question the nation's involvement in the war.

Reading Check **Describing** What tactics did the United States adopt to fight the Vietcong?

Section 1 REVIEW

Vocabulary

1. **Explain** the significance of: Ho Chi Minh, domino theory, guerrilla, Dien Bien Phu, Geneva Accords, Ngo Dinh Diem, Vietcong, Gulf of Tonkin Resolution, napalm, Agent Orange, Ho Chi Minh trail.

Main Ideas

2. **Explaining** What convinced the French to pull out of Vietnam?
3. **Determining Cause and Effect** What was the result of the overthrow of Diem in Vietnam?
4. **Analyzing** Why did fighting in Vietnam turn into a stalemate by the mid-1960s?

Critical Thinking

5. **Big Ideas** How did American Cold War politics lead to the United States fighting a war in Vietnam?
6. **Sequencing** Use a graphic organizer similar to the one below to sequence events that led to U.S. involvement in Vietnam.

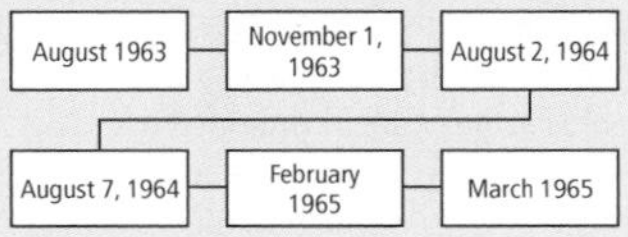

7. **Analyzing Visuals** Study the map on page 883. Why is China's location significant in relation to the Cold War struggles in Southeast Asia?

Writing About History

8. **Persuasive Writing** Suppose you are a member of Congress in August 1964. Write a statement supporting or opposing the Gulf of Tonkin Resolution.

History ONLINE
Study Central™ To review this section, go to glencoe.com and click on Study Central.

D Differentiated Instruction

Naturalist Invite interested students to find out more about the effects of napalm and Agent Orange on both Vietnam and American soldiers. Have them present their findings to the class using visual aids. **AL**

Assess

History ONLINE

Study Central™ provides summaries, interactive games, and online graphic organizers to help students review content.

Close

Summarizing Ask: How did America become involved in Vietnam? *(Presidents committed advisers and troops gradually, hoping to prevent the spread of communism.)* **OL**

Reading Check

Answer: search and destroy missions, bombing, the use of napalm and Agent Orange

Section 1 REVIEW

Answers

1. All definitions can be found in the section and the Glossary.
2. The French troops were unable to defeat the Vietminh guerrillas, and casualties made the war increasingly unpopular with the French people. When the French lost Dien Bien Phu to the Vietminh, they decided to make peace and withdraw from Indochina.
3. Diem's overthrow made the situation in South Vietnam more unstable. The U. S. then had to use more resources to keep the government in power.
4. The Vietcong showed no signs of surrendering, and Johnson refused to order a full-scale invasion for fear of involving China in the conflict.
5. As Democrats, both Kennedy and Johnson were concerned about being accused by Republicans of losing Vietnam to Communists. This made them express their clear belief in the Cold War domino theory, and to dedicate more and more forces to efforts against the Vietnamese Communists.
6. August 1963: Henry Cabot Lodge arrives in Vietnam; November 1, 1963: Diem is overthrown; August 2, 1964: Gulf of Tonkin incident; August 7, 1964: Gulf of Tonkin resolution; February 1965: attack on Pleiku base; March 1965: Johnson expands bombing campaign
7. China borders North Vietnam, Laos, and Burma, which all seemed vulnerable to Communist influence.
8. Students' statements should express a clear and reasoned point of view.

GEOGRAPHY & HISTORY

Focus

Explain that American pilots could see war supplies, military equipment, and weapons being moved on railroad trains in North Vietnam. For fear of escalating the war, however, Navy and Air Force strikes were rare in North Vietnam. Only after the shipments were divided into small loads moving south on the Ho Chi Minh Trail were bombers allowed to strike.

Teach

C Critical Thinking

Making Inferences Ask: What advantages did the North Vietnamese have in following the natural physical features of the trail? *(They didn't have to build bridges or roads; the tunnels and forest cover helped to hide them.)* **OL**

Additional Support

NATIONAL GEOGRAPHIC

GEOGRAPHY & HISTORY

The Ho Chi Minh Trail

North and South Vietnam were long narrow countries. As a result, the border between them was very narrow and easy to defend. In order to send supplies and troops to the south, the North Vietnamese had to find a way around the border. They achieved this by crossing (illegally) into Laos and Cambodia, two neutral nations to the west, then heading south bypassing South Vietnam's northern border. The mountains and rain forests of the region provided cover for people using the trails and roads that ran south. The Americans referred to the elaborate network of roads, trails, forest paths, bridges, tunnels, and shelters as the Ho Chi Minh Trail.

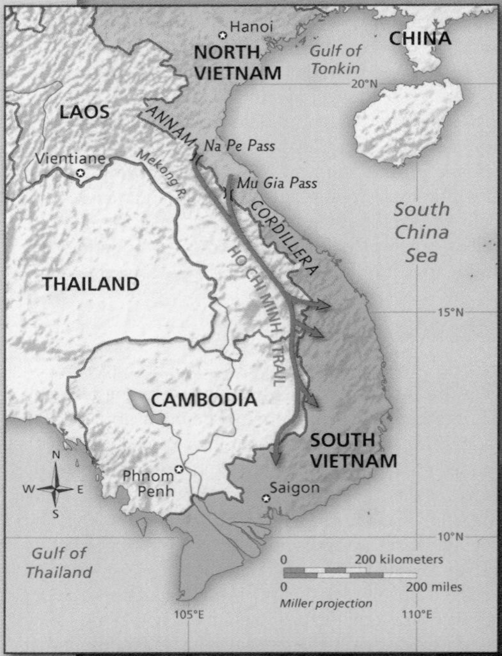

How Did Geography Influence the Ho Chi Minh Trail?

C The Ho Chi Minh Trail followed the topography—or natural physical features—of the region. When viewed from aircraft, the trail often disappeared and blended into the surrounding countryside, making it very difficult to attack. Furthermore, it provided access to multiple points along South Vietnam's long western border, which was much harder for American and South Vietnamese troops to defend. By 1967, an estimated 20,000 Vietnamese soldiers traveled the route each month. The American military tried to disrupt the flow of people and goods, but this proved very difficult to do. By the end of the war, the Ho Chi Minh Trail stretched some 12,000 miles (19,312 km) through the canopied rain forests.

Analyzing GEOGRAPHY

1. **Movement** What diplomatic and international problems were caused by the route of the Ho Chi Minh Trail?
2. **Human-Environment Interaction** What kinds of challenges did the geography of Southeast Asia pose for fighting a war?

Extending the Content

The Ho Chi Minh Trail The route that Americans dubbed the Ho Chi Minh Trail was an elaborate patchwork of jungle paths, bridges, and shelters which began in North Vietnam and extended through southern Laos and northeastern Cambodia into South Vietnam. Much of this "trail" existed long before the Vietnam War. Over centuries, the people who lived in this jungle region had carved out the paths as they hunted tigers, elephants, and other prey. In addition the paths had long been used by caravans of traders who traveled through Southeast Asia.

During the Vietnam War, this web of paths carried soldiers and military supplies from North Vietnam into South Vietnam. In following the trail as it snaked through the rain forests of Southeast Asia, travelers endured leeches, mosquitoes, and attacks by wild animals (in addition to the dangers posed by human enemies).

▲ In an effort to close the trail and ambush enemy troops using it, American troops set up "firebases" on hilltops overlooking part of the trail. Helicopters helped American troops overcome the region's difficult terrain. They could quickly move men and supplies over the rain forest.

▲ The Vietnamese moved goods along the trail in many ways. Most porters carried goods on their back; others strapped goods to bicycles. Trucks carried supplies and people on wider parts of the trail.

American aircraft tried to destroy troops and vehicles on the trail by dropping bombs, including napalm—a jellied gasoline that would catch fire and burn a wide area.

To deprive the enemy of cover, American aircraft sprayed areas near the trail with defoliants that killed all plant life, leaving a barren area. The most famous chemical used was Agent Orange.

GEOGRAPHY & HISTORY

C Critical Thinking

Predicting Consequences Ask students to predict what the effect of napalm and Agent Orange would be on the landscape and economy of Vietnam. *(Students may say that the land would be spoiled through the fires and chemicals used, and would probably not be able to be cultivated for some time.)* **OL**

Assess/Close

Analyzing GEOGRAPHY

Answers:

1. The Ho Chi Minh Trail went through countries that were supposed to be neutral.
2. Vietnam was a land of mountains and of dense rain forests, which were difficult to penetrate and to see into.

Additional Support

Activity: Economics Connection

Defending the Border The United States shares a border with Mexico to the south. Because this border stretches for 1,900 miles, it is difficult to prevent people and goods from coming illegally into the United States. This flow of people and goods has an enormous effect on the American economy, both in Mexico and in the United States. Have students use library or Internet resources to investigate both the cost of defending the border and the contributions made by people coming from Mexico to work in the United States. Hold a panel discussion focusing on the economic effects of this exchange. **OL**

Focus

Bellringer

Daily Focus Transparency 26-2

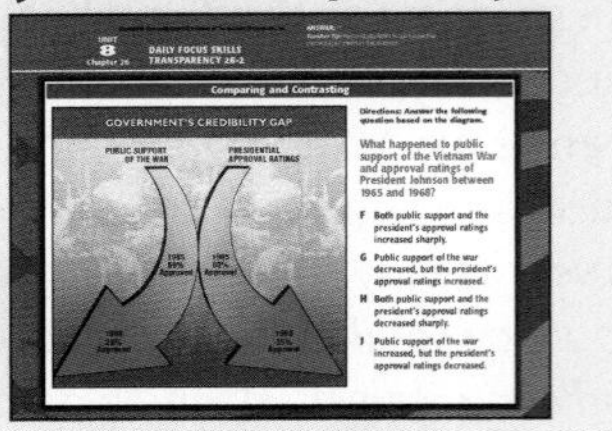

Guide to Reading

Answers: credibility gap, unfair draft system, immorality of defending a corrupt dictatorship in South Vietnam, belief that it was a civil war that was not the business of the United States

Section Spotlight Video

To generate student interest and provide a springboard for class discussion, access the Chapter 26, Section 2 video at glencoe.com or on the video DVD.

Section 2

Section Audio   Spotlight Video

Vietnam Divides the Nation

Guide to Reading

Big Ideas

Group Action Many Americans protested to end their country's involvement in the Vietnam War.

Content Vocabulary

- credibility gap *(p. 892)*
- teach-in *(p. 893)*
- dove *(p. 895)*
- hawk *(p. 895)*

Academic Vocabulary

- media *(p. 892)*
- disproportionate *(p. 893)*

People and Events to Identify

- William Westmoreland *(p. 892)*
- Tet Offensive *(p. 895)*

Reading Strategy

Organizing Complete a graphic organizer similar to the one below to list the reasons for opposition to the Vietnam War.

As casualties mounted in Vietnam, many Americans began to protest against the war. Discouraged by domestic conflict over the war, rising violence, and the apparent lack of progress in Vietnam, President Johnson announced he would not seek another term as president.

An Antiwar Movement Emerges

MAIN Idea The Vietnam War produced sharp divisions between Americans who supported the war and those who did not, and the resulting political turmoil led President Johnson to decide not to run again for president.

HISTORY AND YOU Do you know people who did not support the war in Iraq and those who did? Read on to find out how differences over the Vietnam War began to divide the country.

When American troops first entered the Vietnam War in the spring of 1965, many Americans supported the military effort. A Gallup poll published soon afterward showed that 66 percent of Americans approved of the policy in Vietnam. As the war dragged on, however, public support began to drop. Suspicion of the government's truthfulness about the war was a significant reason. Throughout the early years of the war, the American commander in South Vietnam, General **William Westmoreland,** reported that the enemy was on the brink of defeat. In 1967 he confidently declared that the "enemy's hopes are bankrupt" and added, "we have reached an important point where the end begins to come into view."

Contradicting such reports were less optimistic **media** accounts, especially on television. Vietnam was the first "television war," with footage of combat appearing nightly on the evening news. Day after day, millions of people saw images of wounded and dead Americans and began to doubt government reports. In the opinion of many people, a **credibility gap** had developed, meaning it was hard to believe what the Johnson administration said about the war.

Congress, which had given the president a nearly free hand in Vietnam, soon grew uncertain about the war. Beginning in February 1966 the Senate Foreign Relations Committee held "educational" hearings on Vietnam, calling in Secretary of State Dean Rusk and other policy makers to explain the administration's military strategy. The committee also listened to critics, such as American diplomat George Kennan. Although Kennan had helped to create the policy of containment, he argued that Vietnam was not strategically important to the United States.

Resource Manager

R Reading Strategies	C Critical Thinking	D Differentiated Instruction	W Writing Support	S Skill Practice
Teacher Edition • Using Word Parts, p. 893 • Read. Prim. Sources, p. 894 • Making Connections, p. 894 **Additional Resources** • Guide Read Act., URB p. 113	**Additional Resources** • Quizzes and Tests, p. 372	**Teacher Edition** • Verbal/Ling., p. 895 • Adv. Learners, p. 897 **Additional Resources** • Inter. Pol. Cartoons, URB pp. 105–106 • Eng. Learner Act., URB p. 89 • Am. Art and Music Act., URB p. 103	**Teacher Edition** • Expository Writing, p. 895	**Additional Resources** • Read Skills Act., URB p. 85 • Read. Essen., p. 289

POLITICAL CARTOONS PRIMARY SOURCE
Should America Stay in Vietnam?

▲ An axe labeled "Vietnam Issue" splits the nation in two.

◀ Ho Chi Minh sends a telegram praising antiwar protesters.

Analyzing VISUALS

1. **Finding the Main Idea** What is the main message of the cartoon on the left?
2. **Making Inferences** The cartoon on the right was drawn before the one on the left. Do you think that differences between the two indicate a change in attitude toward antiwar protests? Explain.

Teach-ins Begin

In March 1965, a group of faculty members and students at the University of Michigan joined together in a **teach-in.** They discussed the issues surrounding the war and reaffirmed their reasons for opposing it. In May 1965, 122 colleges held a "National Teach-In" by radio for more than 100,000 antiwar demonstrators.

People who opposed the war did so for different reasons. Some saw the conflict as a civil war in which the United States had no business interfering. Others viewed South Vietnam as a corrupt dictatorship and believed that defending it was immoral and unjust.

Anger at the Draft

Young protesters especially focused on what they saw as an unfair draft system. Until 1969, a college student was often able to defer military service until after graduation. By contrast, young people from working-class families were more likely to be drafted and sent to Vietnam because they were unable to afford college. Draftees in the military were most likely to be assigned to dangerous combat units. In 1969 draftees made up 62 percent of battle deaths.

The majority of soldiers who served in Vietnam, however, were volunteer enlistees. Holding out the military as an avenue to vocational training and upward social mobility, military recruiters encouraged youth in poor and working-class communities to enlist. Thus, a **disproportionate** number of working-class youths, many of them minorities, were among the volunteers who served in Vietnam. R

The Vietnam War coincided with the high tide of the civil rights movement, so the treatment of African American soldiers came under scrutiny. Between 1961 and 1966, African Americans constituted about 10 percent of military personnel while African Americans comprised about 13 percent of the total population of the United States. Because African Americans were more likely to be assigned to combat units, however, they accounted for almost 20 percent of combat-related deaths.

This unequal death rate angered African American leaders. In April 1967 Dr. Martin Luther King, Jr. publicly condemned the conflict:

Teach

R Reading Strategy

Using Word Parts Tell students that taking apart a long word, such as *disproportionate*, may help them reach the word's meaning. By removing the prefix and suffix, they can see the word *proportion*. Recalling that *dis-* means "not" will help them define the word. BL

Analyzing VISUALS

Answers:
1. the differing opinions on Vietnam issues threatens to split the nation
2. The cartoon on the right is openly critical of draft card burners, while the one on the left sees the war as dividing all Americans.

Hands-On Chapter Project Step 2

Create a Documentary of the Vietnam War

Step 2: Planning the Video Essential question: What were the key developments in the chosen story and what were the historical results?

Directions Students should use their textbook and other research to outline the basic issue and the chronology. A second team could concentrate on thinking visually. This team would have to collaborate closely with the first and research photos in magazines and newspapers or video clips of the period.

Putting It Together When the teams meet, they can decide on the "storyboards" for the video—sketches representing each shot in the 10 scenes (or whatever number seems appropriate) so that the topic is covered from beginning to end. OL

(Chapter Project continued on page 899)

R1 Reading Strategies

Reading Primary Sources Invite a volunteer to read Dr. King's words. **Ask:** According to Dr. King, who is really paying the cost of the war in Vietnam? *(the poor of both the United States and Vietnam)* **BL**

R2 Reading Strategies

Making Connections Military recruiters are occasionally visitors to high school campuses. Discuss with students their perceptions of whether this practice should be allowed and whether reinstating the draft would be a good idea. **OL**

PRIMARY SOURCE

R1 "I speak for the poor of America who are paying the double price of smashed hopes at home and death and corruption in Vietnam. . . . The great initiative in this war is ours. The initiative to stop it must be ours."

—quoted in *A Testament of Hope*

In response, military officials tried to lower the number of African American casualties. At war's end, African Americans made up about 12 percent of America's dead, roughly the same as their national population percentage.

R2 As the war escalated, an increased draft call put many college students at risk. An estimated 500,000 draftees refused to go. Some burned their draft cards, or did not show up for induction, or fled the country. Between 1965 and 1968, officials prosecuted over 3,300 Americans who refused to serve in a war they opposed. In 1969 the government introduced a lottery system in which only those with low lottery numbers were subject to the draft.

Anger against the war was not confined to college campuses. Demonstrators held large and small protests against the war in towns across the country. In April 1965 Students for a Democratic Society (SDS), a left-wing student organization, organized a march on Washington, D.C., that drew over 20,000 people. Two years later, in October 1967, a rally at the Lincoln Memorial drew tens of thousands of protesters as well. When a group of Iowa public school students protested the war by wearing black armbands to school, school district administrators suspended them to maintain "the disciplined atmosphere of the classroom." The Supreme Court decision for the case, *Tinker* v. *Des Moines Independent Community School District* (1969), supported the students' actions, saying that the armbands were a form of symbolic speech, and therefore protected by the First Amendment.

Anger over the draft also fueled discussions about the voting age. Many draftees argued that if they were old enough to fight, they were old enough to vote. In 1971 the Twenty-sixth Amendment to the Constitution was ratified, giving all citizens age 18 and older the right to vote in all state and federal elections.

PRIMARY SOURCE

A Divided Nation

▲ An antiwar protest in New York City in 1969

▲ The war split the nation. Above, construction workers march in New York City in support of the war effort.

◄ Antiwar demonstrators burn their draft cards in front of the Pentagon in 1972.

Additional Support

Activity: Collaborative Learning

Investigate Younger Voters Divide the class into small groups. Ask each group to conduct interviews with at least six people between the ages of 18 and 25, three who voted in the last presidential election and three who did not. Have students summarize the participants' answers to questions about why they did or did not vote. Have them also look at and evaluate the work of organizations such as Rock the Vote that attempt to make voting popular among younger people. Have them present their findings to the class as a panel discussion about the question "Have young people effectively used the right to vote?" **OL**

Hawks and Doves

In the face of growing opposition to the war, President Johnson remained determined to continue fighting. He assailed his critics in Congress as "selfish men who want to advance their own interests." He dismissed the college protesters as too naive to appreciate the importance of resisting communism.

The president was not alone in his views. In a poll taken in early 1968, 53 percent of the respondents favored stronger military action in Vietnam, compared to 24 percent who wanted an end to the war. Of those Americans who supported the policy in Vietnam, many openly criticized the protesters for a lack of patriotism.

By 1968 the nation seemed to be divided into two camps. Those who wanted the United States to withdraw from Vietnam were known as **doves.** Those who insisted that the country stay and fight came to be known as **hawks.** As the two groups debated, the war appeared to take a dramatic turn for the worse, and the nation endured a year of shock and crisis.

Reading Check **Explaining** What led to the ratification of the Twenty-sixth Amendment?

Opposition to the Vietnam War

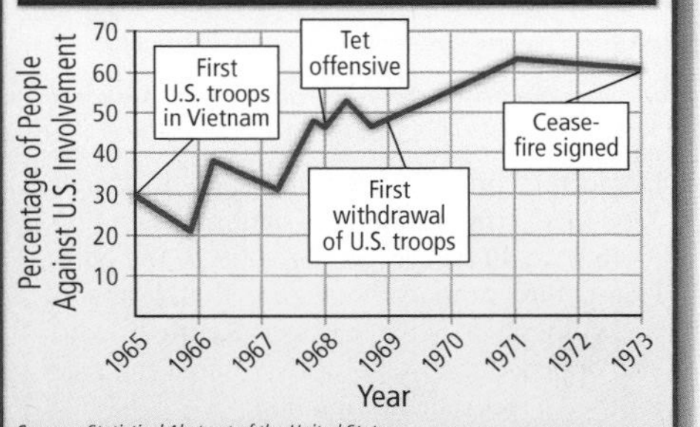

Source: *Statistical Abstract of the United States.*

Analyzing VISUALS

1. **Interpreting** During which two years was opposition to the war lowest? What event occurred around that time?
2. **Synthesizing** In what year did opposition to the war peak? How was this sentiment logically related to the withdrawal of American troops?

1968: The Pivotal Year

MAIN Idea The Tet Offensive increased doubt that the United States could win in Vietnam.

HISTORY AND YOU Have you ever participated in a public-opinion poll? Read how Johnson's plummeting approval rating made him decide not to run for re-election in 1968.

The most turbulent year of the chaotic 1960s was 1968. The year saw a shocking political announcement, two traumatic assassinations, and a political convention held amid strident anti-war demonstrations. First, however, the nation endured a surprise attack in Vietnam.

The Tet Offensive

On January 30, 1968, during Tet, the Vietnamese New Year, the Vietcong and North Vietnamese launched a massive surprise attack. In this **Tet Offensive,** guerrilla fighters attacked most American airbases in South Vietnam and most of the South's major cities. Vietcong even blasted their way into the American embassy in Saigon. D

Militarily, Tet was a disaster for the Vietcong. After about a month of fighting, the American and South Vietnamese soldiers repelled the enemy troops, inflicting heavy losses on them. President Johnson triumphantly noted that the enemy's effort had ended in "complete failure." Later, historians confirmed that Tet nearly destroyed the Vietcong.

The North Vietnamese, however, had scored a major political victory. The American people were shocked that an enemy supposedly on the verge of defeat could launch such a large-scale attack. When General Westmoreland requested 209,000 troops in addition to the 500,000 already in Vietnam, he seemed to be admitting the United States could not win.

To make matters worse, the media, which had tried to remain balanced in their war coverage, now openly criticized the effort. "The American people should be getting ready to accept, if they haven't already, the prospect that the whole Vietnam effort may be doomed," declared the *Wall Street Journal.* Television newscaster Walter Cronkite announced that it seemed "more certain than ever that the bloody experience in Vietnam is to end in a stalemate." W

D Differentiated Instruction

Verbal/Linguistic Invite students to hold a debate on the role of protest in a democratic society. Ask them to consider the question of whether the answer changes if that nation is at war. OL

W Writing Support

Expository Writing Ask students to write brief essays explaining the role of the media in telling unpleasant truths. Have them cite specific examples to support their views. OL

Reading Check

Answer: Protests concerning the draft led to discussion about the fact that draft-age citizens did not at that time have the right to vote.

Analyzing VISUALS

Answers:
1. 1965, 1966; first U.S. troops arrive
2. 1971; the government did not believe the war could be won.

Extending the Content

Walter Cronkite By the time of the Vietnam War, veteran journalist Walter Cronkite had plenty of experience with war. He had gone ashore with the troops on D-Day and covered the Nuremberg trials as a United Press reporter. In 1950 he joined CBS, becoming news anchor in 1962 and retiring from that position in 1981.

Initially Cronkite was a hawk, and he went to Vietnam after the Tet Offensive. After that trip, he addressed his audience with a changed attitude about the war. In his television broadcast, Cronkite said, "It seems now more certain than ever that the bloody experience of Vietnam is a stalemate." President Lyndon Johnson listened to Cronkite's verdict as did the rest of the nation. According to one of Johnson's aides, the president said, "If I've lost Cronkite, I've lost Middle America."

As media analysts have observed, Cronkite's influence was substantial for two reasons. First, most Americans believed that he was objective, trustworthy, and patriotic. Second, Cronkite worked during an era when the vast majority of Americans regularly tuned in to one of the three major networks.

Did You Know?

In 1972 during his second run for the presidency, this time as a Democratic Party candidate, Governor Wallace was the victim of an assassination attempt. Although he survived the attack, Wallace was paralyzed in both legs. He stopped his campaign for the presidency but continued to govern Alabama until 1979 and again was elected governor from 1983 until 1987.

Analyzing VISUALS

Answers:
1. the South
2. Students may say that voters who would have supported Wallace would be unlikely to vote for Humphrey, thus giving Nixon an even bigger victory.

PRIMARY SOURCE

1968: A Year of Turmoil

The election year 1968 was tumultuous. The country was divided over Vietnam. President Johnson chose not to run again. Protesters fought with police at the Democratic National Convention. Race riots erupted in several American cities and both Martin Luther King, Jr., and Robert Kennedy were killed.

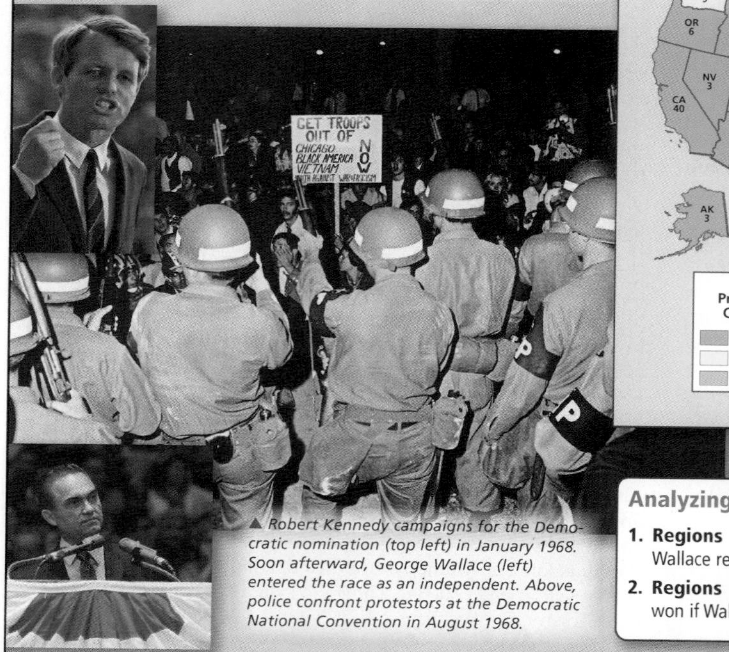

▲ *Robert Kennedy campaigns for the Democratic nomination (top left) in January 1968. Soon afterward, George Wallace (left) entered the race as an independent. Above, police confront protestors at the Democratic National Convention in August 1968.*

Presidential Candidate	Popular Votes	% of Popular Vote	Electoral Votes
Nixon	31,710,470	43.60%	301
Humphrey	30,898,055	42.48%	191
Wallace	9,906,473	13.62%	46

Analyzing VISUALS

1. **Regions** In what area of the country did George Wallace receive the most votes?
2. **Regions** Do you think Richard Nixon would have won if Wallace had not been in the race?

Public opinion no longer favored the president. In the weeks following the Tet Offensive, the president's approval rating plummeted to a dismal 35 percent, while support for his handling of the war fell even lower, to 26 percent. The administration's credibility gap now seemed too wide to repair.

Johnson Leaves the Race

With the war growing increasingly unpopular and Johnson's credibility all but gone, some Democrats began looking for an alternative candidate to nominate for president in 1968. In November 1967, even before the Tet disaster, a little-known liberal senator from Minnesota, Eugene McCarthy, became the first dove to declare he would challenge Johnson for the Democratic presidential nomination. In March 1968 McCarthy stunned the nation by winning more than 40 percent of the votes in the New Hampshire primary. Realizing that Johnson was vulnerable, Senator Robert Kennedy, who also opposed the war, quickly entered the race for the Democratic nomination.

With both the country and his own party deeply divided, Johnson addressed the public on television on March 31, 1968. He stunned viewers by announcing, "I have concluded that I should not permit the presidency to become involved in the partisan divisions that are developing in this political year. Accordingly, I shall not seek, and I will not accept, the nomination of my party for another term as your President."

Additional Support

Activity: Economics Connection

The Cost of War Lyndon Johnson challenged Congress to fund both "guns and butter" programs, but Congress refused, rendering some of Johnson's Great Society programs all but useless. Have students use the Internet to find out what modern wars cost per day and on what items the money is spent. Suggest that they do a comparative study of the costs of the wars in Vietnam and in Iraq. **OL**

A Season of Violence

Following Johnson's announcement, the nation endured even more shocking events. In April, James Earl Ray was arrested for killing Dr. Martin Luther King, Jr. Just two months later, another assassination rocked the country—that of Robert Kennedy. Kennedy, who appeared to be on his way to winning the Democratic nomination, was gunned down on June 5. The assassin was Sirhan Sirhan, an Arab nationalist angry over the candidate's pro-Israeli remarks a few nights before.

The violence that seemed to plague the country in 1968 culminated with a chaotic and well-publicized clash between antiwar protesters and police at the Democratic National Convention in Chicago. Thousands of protesters surrounded the convention center, demanding that the Democrats adopt an antiwar platform.

Despite the protests, the delegates chose Hubert Humphrey, President Johnson's vice president, as their presidential nominee. Meanwhile, in a park not far from the convention hall, the protesters and police began fighting. As officers tried to disperse demonstrators with tear gas and billy clubs, demonstrators taunted the authorities with the chant, "The whole world is watching!" A subsequent federal investigation of the incident described the event as a "police riot."

Nixon Wins the Presidency

The violence and chaos now associated with the Democratic Party benefited the 1968 Republican presidential candidate, Richard Nixon. Although defeated by John Kennedy in the 1960 election, Nixon had remained active in national politics. A third candidate, Governor George Wallace of Alabama, decided to run in 1968 as an independent. Wallace, an outspoken segregationist, sought to attract Americans who felt threatened by the civil rights movement and urban social unrest.

Public opinion polls gave Nixon a wide lead over Humphrey and Wallace. Nixon's campaign promise to unify the nation and restore law and order appealed to Americans who feared their country was spinning out of control. Nixon also declared that he had a plan for ending the war in Vietnam.

At first Humphrey's support of President Johnson's Vietnam policies hurt his campaign. After Humphrey broke with the president and called for a complete end to the bombing of North Vietnam, he began to move up in the polls. A week before the election, President Johnson helped Humphrey by announcing that the bombing had halted and that a cease-fire would follow.

D Johnson's announcement had come too late, however. In the end, Nixon's promises to end the war and restore order at home were enough to sway the American people. On Election Day, Nixon defeated Humphrey by more than 100 electoral votes, although he won the popular vote by a slim margin of 43 percent to 42 percent. Wallace partially accounted for the razor-thin margin by winning 46 electoral votes and more than 13 percent of the popular vote.

✓ Reading Check **Explaining** Why did President Johnson say he would not run for reelection in 1968?

Section 2 REVIEW

Vocabulary

1. **Explain** the significance of: William Westmoreland, credibility gap, teach-in, dove, hawk, Tet Offensive.

Main Ideas

2. **Explaining** Why did some people view the draft as unfair?
3. **Summarizing** What are three important events that made 1968 such a violent year in the United States?

Critical Thinking

4. **Big Ideas** Why did support of the war dwindle by the late 1960s?
5. **Organizing** Use a graphic organizer similar to the one below to list the effects of the Tet Offensive.

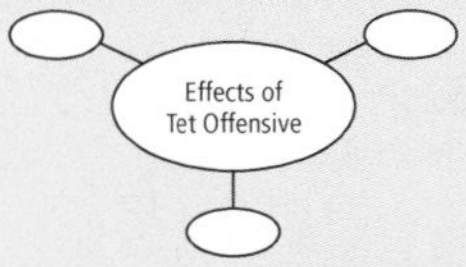

6. **Analyzing Visuals** Study the cartoon on the right on page 893. What is the message of the telegram beyond its literal meaning?

Writing About History

7. **Expository Writing** Suppose that you are living in 1968. Write a letter to the editor of a local newspaper in which you explain your reasons for either supporting or opposing the Vietnam War.

History ONLINE
Study Central™ To review this section, go to glencoe.com and click on Study Central.

897

D Differentiated Instruction

Advanced Learners Invite students to find out how third party candidates have fared in presidential elections since 1900. Ask them to present their findings to the class using visual aids such as graphs or charts. **AL**

Assess

History ONLINE

Study Central™ provides summaries, interactive games, and online graphic organizers to help students review content.

Close

Summarizing Ask: **What event eroded public confidence in America's role in Vietnam?** *(failure to win the war, especially after the Tet Offensive)* **OL**

✓ Reading Check

Answer: He did not want the presidency to become involved in partisan division.

Section 2 REVIEW

Answers

1. All definitions can be found in the section and the Glossary.
2. Poor men, including a high proportion of minorities, who were unable to afford college, were more likely to be drafted than those who could afford college and thus get deferments.
3. the assassination of Martin Luther King, Jr., the assassination of Robert Kennedy, and the riots at the Democratic National Convention
4. Media coverage of the mounting casualties fueled anger and distrust of government officials' reports on the progress of the war, and many were angry over the unfair draft system.
5. support for the war dropped, the media became critical of the war effort, the president's approval rating plummeted
6. Students may say that the message is that draft card burners were unpatriotic or Communist sympathizers.
7. Students' letters should express a clear and reasoned argument for supporting or opposing the war.

Focus

Bellringer

Daily Focus Transparency 26-3

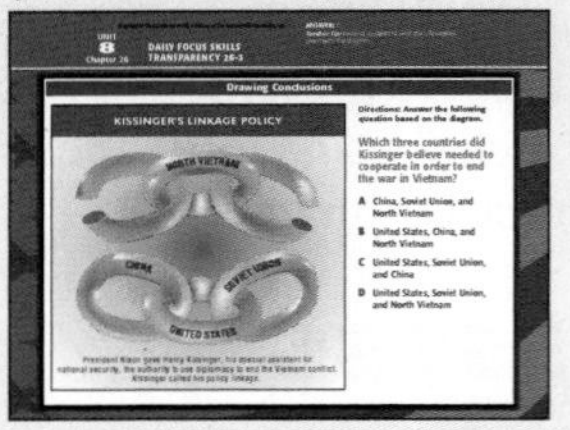

Guide to Reading

Answers may include: Kissinger appointment, linkage policy, Vietnamization, bombing campaign, Cambodian invasion

Section Spotlight Video

To generate student interest and provide a springboard for class discussion, access the Chapter 26, Section 3 video at glencoe.com or on the video DVD.

Resource Manager

Section 3

Section Audio   Spotlight Video

The War Winds Down

Guide to Reading

Big Ideas

Trade, War, and Migration
The Vietnam War changed the way Americans viewed the government and the military, and led them to question how the armed forces were deployed.

Content Vocabulary
- linkage *(p. 898)*
- Vietnamization *(p. 898)*

Academic Vocabulary
- generation *(p. 899)*
- unresolved *(p. 903)*

People and Events to Identify
- Henry Kissinger *(p. 898)*
- Pentagon Papers *(p. 900)*
- War Powers Act *(p. 903)*

Reading Strategy
Organizing Complete a graphic organizer similar to the one below by listing the steps that President Nixon took to end American involvement in Vietnam.

Steps Nixon Took

Shortly after taking office, President Nixon moved to end the nation's involvement in the Vietnam War. The final years of the conflict, however, yielded more bloodshed and turmoil, as well as a growing cynicism in the minds of Americans about the honesty and effectiveness of the United States government.

Nixon Moves to End the War

MAIN Idea While unrest and suspicion of the government grew, the United States finally withdrew its troops from Vietnam.

HISTORY AND YOU Have you ever protested against something you felt was wrong? Read on to find out how college students reacted to what they viewed as a widening of the Vietnam War.

As a first step to fulfilling his campaign promise to end the war, Nixon appointed Harvard professor **Henry Kissinger** as special assistant for national security affairs and gave him wide authority to use diplomacy to end the conflict. Kissinger embarked upon a policy he called **linkage,** which meant improving relations with the Soviet Union and China—suppliers of aid to North Vietnam—so that he could persuade them to cut back on their aid.

Kissinger also rekindled peace talks with the North Vietnamese. In August 1969 Kissinger entered into secret negotiations with North Vietnam's negotiator, Le Duc Tho. In their talks, which dragged on for four years, Kissinger and Le Duc Tho argued over a possible cease-fire, the return of American prisoners of war, and the ultimate fate of South Vietnam.

Meanwhile, Nixon reduced the number of American troops in Vietnam. Known as **Vietnamization,** this process involved the gradual withdrawal of U.S. troops while the South Vietnamese assumed more of the fighting. On June 8, 1969, Nixon announced the withdrawal of 25,000 soldiers, but he was determined to keep a strong American presence in Vietnam to ensure bargaining power during peace negotiations. In support of that goal, the president increased air strikes against North Vietnam and—without informing Congress or the public—began secretly bombing Vietcong sanctuaries in neighboring Cambodia.

Turmoil at Home Continues

Even though the United States had begun scaling back its involvement in Vietnam, the American home front remained divided and volatile, as Nixon's war policies stirred up new waves of protest.

R Reading Strategies	C Critical Thinking	D Differentiated Instruction	W Writing Support	S Skill Practice
Teacher Edition • Act. Prior Know., p. 899 • Making Inferences, p. 900 • Read. Prim. Sources, p. 903 **Additional Resources** • Guide Read Act., URB p. 114 • Am. History in Graphic Novel, p. 65 • Prim. Source Read., URB p. 101	**Teacher Edition** • Analyzing Prim. Sources, p. 899 **Additional Resources** • Linking Past and Present Act., URB p. 98 • Authentic Assess, p. 57 • Quizzes and Tests, p. 373 • Supreme Court Case Studies, p. 109	**Teacher Edition** • Visual/Spatial, p. 900 **Additional Resources** • Enrich. Act., URB p. 109	**Additional Resources** • Linking Past/Present, URB p. 98	**Additional Resources** • Read Essen., p. 292 • Reinforcing Skills, URB p. 95 • Time Line Act., URB p. 97

PRIMARY SOURCE
Protests and Peace Talks

▲ *To convince North Vietnam to settle for a negotiated peace, Nixon ordered troops into Cambodia to destroy North Vietnamese bases there. The invasion led to mass protests in the United States and to the tragic shooting of four students by National Guard troops at Kent State University (above).*

▲ *President Nixon (above) describes the invasion of Cambodia in 1970. Two years later, Secretary of State Henry Kissinger met for peace talks with North Vietnam's representative Le Duc Tho (right).*

U.S. Troops in Vietnam, 1964–1974

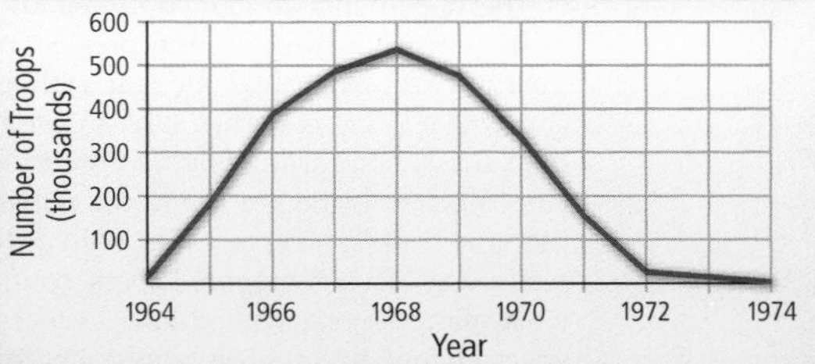

Source: *Statistical Abstract of the United States.*

Analyzing VISUALS

1. **Determining Cause and Effect** How did the invasion of Cambodia lead to the shootings at Kent State?
2. **Specifying** In what year did the troop level in Vietnam reach its peak?

Massacre at My Lai In late 1969 Americans learned that, in the spring of 1968, an American platoon under the command of Lieutenant William Calley had massacred unarmed South Vietnamese civilians in the hamlet of My Lai. Most of the victims were old men, women, and children. Calley eventually went to prison for his role in the killings.

Most American soldiers acted responsibly and honorably during the war. The actions of a small group, however, convinced many people that the war was brutal and senseless. Jan Barry, a founder of the Vietnam Veterans Against the War, viewed My Lai as a symbol of the dilemma his **generation** faced in the conflict:

C **PRIMARY SOURCE**

"To kill on military orders and be a criminal, or to refuse to kill and be a criminal is the moral agony of America's Vietnam war generation. It is what has forced upward of sixty thousand young Americans, draft resisters and deserters to Canada, and created one hundred thousand military deserters a year. . . ." C

—quoted in *Who Spoke Up?*

The Invasion of Cambodia Sparks Protest Americans heard more startling news when Nixon announced in April 1970 that American troops had invaded Cambodia. The R troops were ordered to destroy Vietcong military bases there.

Many viewed the Cambodian invasion as a widening of the war, and it set off many protests. At Kent State University on May 4, 1970, Ohio National Guard soldiers, armed with tear gas and rifles, fired on demonstrators without an order to do so. The soldiers killed four students. Ten days later, police killed two African American students during a demonstration at Jackson State College in Mississippi.

Teach

C Critical Thinking

Analyzing Primary Sources

Read the quotation aloud. **Ask:** What were the two results of the difficult choices young American men faced? *(about 60,000 went to Canada and another 100,000 deserted the military)* BL

R Reading Strategy

Activating Prior Knowledge

Ask students why Nixon's announcement of the invasion of Cambodia was so startling to many. *(The U.S. had invaded a neutral country without a declaration of war.)* OL

Analyzing VISUALS

Answers:

1. The protests at Kent State were among many that resulted from the invasion of Cambodia.
2. 1968

Hands-On Chapter Project Step 3

Create a Documentary of the Vietnam War

Step 3: Creating the Script or Voiceover Essential question: What is the core of the message and how shall it be conveyed with the images?

Directions Students may need to re-assess their storyboards and edit them as they go through them to write the script or "voiceover" for the video or as they create the visuals. The writing will need to be concise and focus on the essential point of what is happening in each scene. Students can divide up in teams to write the voiceover for two or more storyboards.

Putting It Together The teams can meet to review and edit their final script. OL

(Chapter Project continued on Visual Summary page)

R Reading Strategy

Making Inferences Have students read the first paragraph under the heading "The United States Pulls Out." **Ask:** What can you infer about the timing of Kissinger's announcement? *(it was timed to influence the outcome of the presidential election)* **OL**

D Differentiated Instruction

Visual/Spatial Invite students to make a timeline of the war, showing major events. **BL**

Reading Check

Answer: that the government had not been honest with them

In addition to sparking violence on campuses, the invasion of Cambodia cost Nixon significant congressional support. Numerous legislators expressed outrage over the president's failure to notify them of the action. In December 1970 an angry Congress repealed the Gulf of Tonkin Resolution, which had given the president nearly complete power in directing the war in Vietnam.

The Pentagon Papers Support for the war weakened further in 1971 when Daniel Ellsberg, a disillusioned former Defense Department worker, leaked what became known as the **Pentagon Papers** to the *New York Times.* The documents revealed that many government officials during the Johnson administration privately questioned the war while publicly defending it.

The documents contained details of decisions that were made by the presidents and their advisers to expand the war without the consent of Congress. They also showed how the various administrations had tried to convince Congress, the press, and the public that the situation in Vietnam was better than it really was. The Pentagon Papers confirmed what many Americans had long believed: the government had not been honest with them.

The United States Pulls Out

R By 1971, polls showed that nearly two-thirds of Americans wanted to end the Vietnam War as quickly as possible. In April 1972 President Nixon dropped his longtime insistence that North Vietnamese troops had to withdraw from South Vietnam before any peace treaty could be signed. In October, less than a month before the presidential election, Kissinger emerged from his secret talks with Le Duc Tho to announce that "peace is at hand."

A month later, Americans went to the polls to decide on a president. Senator George McGovern, the Democratic candidate, was an outspoken critic of the war. He did not appeal to many middle-class Americans, however, who were tired of antiwar protesters. Nixon was reelected in a landslide, winning 60.7 percent of the popular vote.

Just weeks after the presidential election, the peace negotiations broke down. South Vietnam's president, Nguyen Van Thieu, refused to agree to any plan that left North Vietnamese troops in the South. Henry Kissinger tried to win additional concessions from the Communists, but talks broke off on December 16, 1972.

The next day, to force North Vietnam to resume negotiations, the Nixon administration began the most destructive air raids of the entire war. In what became known as the "Christmas bombings," American B-52s dropped thousands of tons of bombs on North Vietnamese targets for 11 straight days, pausing only on Christmas Day.

In the wake of the bombing campaign, the United States and North Vietnam returned to the bargaining table. Thieu finally gave in to American pressure and allowed North Vietnamese troops to remain in the South. On January 27, 1973, the warring sides signed an agreement "ending the war and restoring the peace in Vietnam."

The United States promised to withdraw its troops, and both sides agreed to exchange prisoners of war. The parties did not resolve the issue of South Vietnam's future, however. After almost eight years of war—the longest war in American history—the nation ended its direct involvement in Vietnam.

South Vietnam Falls

D Two years after the United States pulled its troops out of Vietnam, the peace agreement collapsed. In March 1975 the North Vietnamese army launched a full-scale invasion of the South. Thieu desperately appealed to Washington, D.C., for help.

President Nixon had assured Thieu during the peace negotiations that the United States "[would] respond with full force should the settlement be violated by North Vietnam." Nixon, however, had resigned under pressure following Watergate, a scandal that broke as the war was winding down. The new president, Gerald Ford, asked for funds to aid the South Vietnamese, but Congress refused.

Without American assistance, the South Vietnamese Army was unable to stop the invasion. On April 30, the North Vietnamese captured Saigon, South Vietnam's capital, and united Vietnam under Communist rule. They then renamed the city Ho Chi Minh City.

Reading Check **Evaluating** What did the Pentagon Papers confirm for many Americans?

Differentiated Instruction

Leveled Activities

BL Historical Analysis Skills Activity, URB p. 86

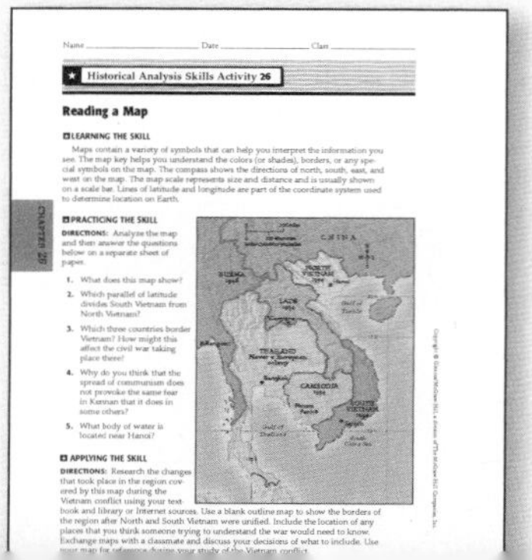

OL Reinforcing Skills Activity, URB p. 95

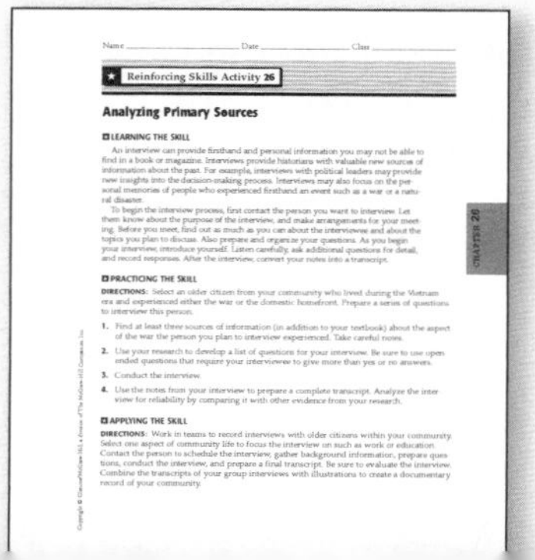

AL Critical Thinking Skills Activity, URB p. 96

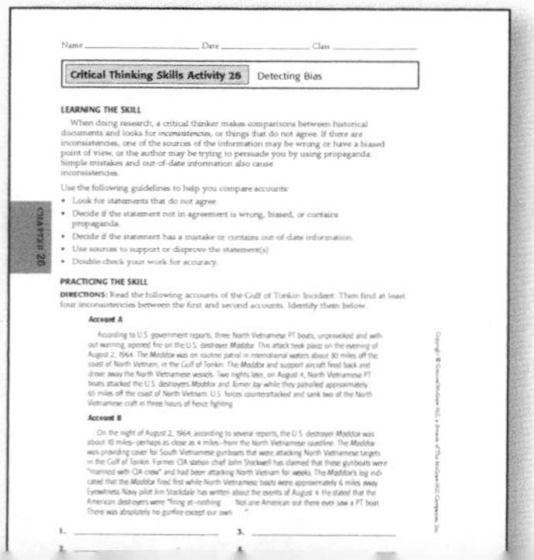

ELL Content Vocabulary Activity, URB p. 91

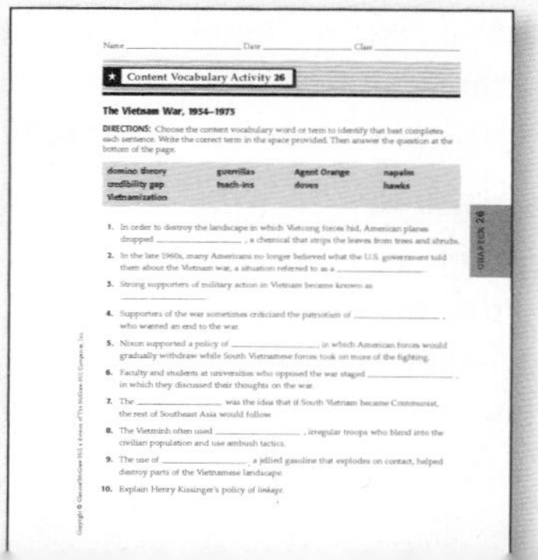

ANALYZING SUPREME COURT CASES

Can the Government Put Limits on the Press?

★ *New York Times* v. *United States*, 1971

Background to the Case

In 1971 Daniel Ellsberg leaked classified documents, known as the Pentagon Papers, to the *New York Times* and the *Washington Post*. When the newspapers attempted to publish these documents, the Nixon administration argued that publication would threaten national security. The case centered on the First Amendment guarantee of a free press.

How the Court Ruled

In a 6-to-3 per curiam opinion—*per curiam* meaning that the decision was issued by the whole Court and not specific justices—the Court found that the Nixon administration had failed to prove that publication of the Pentagon Papers would imperil the nation in any way. The *New York Times* and the *Washington Post* could publish the Pentagon Papers.

▲ Daniel Ellsberg (above, left) leaked the classified documents known as the Pentagon Papers.

PRIMARY SOURCE

Concurring View

"The Government's power to censor the press [via the First Amendment] was abolished so that the press would remain forever free to censure the Government. . . . And paramount among the responsibilities of a free press is the duty to prevent any part of the government from deceiving the people and sending them off to distant lands to die of foreign fevers and foreign shot and shell. In my view, far from deserving condemnation for their courageous reporting, the *New York Times*, the *Washington Post*, and other newspapers should be commended for serving the purpose that the Founding Fathers saw so clearly. In revealing the workings of government that led to the Vietnam War, the newspapers did precisely that which the Founders hoped and trusted they would do."

—Justice Hugo Black in *New York Times* v. *United States*

PRIMARY SOURCE

Dissenting View

The First Amendment, after all, is only one part of an entire Constitution. Article II of the great document vests in the Executive Branch primary power over the conduct of foreign affairs and places in that branch the responsibility for the Nation's safety. . . . What is needed here is a weighing, upon properly developed standards, of the broad right of the press to print and of the very narrow right of the Government to prevent. Such standards are not yet developed. The parties here are in disagreement as to what those standards should be. But even the newspapers concede that there are situations where restraint is in order and is constitutional."

—Justice Harry Blackmun, dissenting in *New York Times* v. *United States*

DBQ Document-Based Questions

1. **Explaining** Why did Justice Black agree with the Court's decision? What did he imply about the government's actions?
2. **Contrasting** Why did Justice Blackmun disagree with the Court's decision?
3. **Assessing** Do you think the government can ever justify media censorship, even based on national security concerns? Explain.

More About the Case

Daniel Ellsberg, a former bureaucrat working in national security, was unhappy with the course of the war. His leak of the Pentagon Papers did not at first trouble officials in the Nixon administration. Nixon, however, feared that if he did not have control over classified documents, he would later be embarrassed. For his role in the case, Ellsberg was indicted and tried for the leak.

DBQ Document Based Questions

Answers:

1. He feels that the First Amendment guarantees a free press to keep the government from oppressing the people. He implies that the government lied by sending troops off to die for dishonest reasons.
2. He felt the executive branch would know best about issues of national security and thus should be able to restrain the media if necessary.
3. Students' answers will vary.

Differentiated Instruction

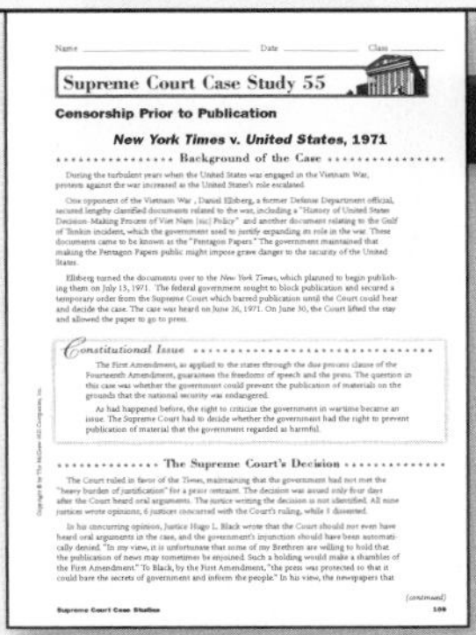
Supreme Court Case Study 55
Censorship Prior to Publication
New York Times v. United States, 1971
Background of the Case
Constitutional Issue
The Supreme Court's Decision

Case Study 55: *New York Times* v. *United States*, p. 109

Analyzing a Supreme Court Decision

Objective: Learn how the Supreme Court determined whether the government could prevent the publication of materials on the grounds that national security was endangered.

Focus: Identify the central issue of the case.

Teach: Discuss the Court's opinion.

Assess: Explain the importance of the case (interpretation of the First Amendment).

Close: Write a paragraph summarizing the case.

Differentiated Instruction Strategies

BL Explain the role the Vietnam War played in the case.

AL Paraphrase the Court's decision. Read your version to the class.

ELL Explain the First Amendment in your own words.

Analyzing VISUALS

Answers:

1. It required the president to consult with Congress before making troop commitments and to inform Congress of any troops committed abroad within 48 hours. Also, unless Congress approved the commitment, troops had to be withdrawn in 60 to 90 days.
2. Students' responses will vary but should be supported by reasons.

The Legacy of Vietnam

MAIN Idea The Vietnam War made a negative impact on the way in which Americans viewed international conflicts, as well as their own government.

HISTORY AND YOU Do you think that leaders at the highest levels of the federal government are trustworthy? Read on to find out how the Vietnam War and other events led Americans to lose some trust in their leaders.

History ONLINE Student Web Activity Visit glencoe.com and complete the activity on the Vietnam Veterans Memorial.

"The lessons of the past in Vietnam," President Ford declared in 1975, "have already been learned—learned by Presidents, learned by Congress, learned by the American people—and we should have our focus on the future." Vietnam had a deep and lasting impact on American society.

The War's Human Toll

The United States paid a heavy price for its involvement in Vietnam. The war had cost the nation over $170 billion in direct costs and much more in indirect economic expenses. It had also resulted in the deaths of approximately 58,000 young Americans and the injury of more than 300,000. In Vietnam, around one million North and South Vietnamese soldiers died in the conflict, as did countless civilians.

PRIMARY SOURCE
The Legacy of Vietnam

▲ The Vietnam Veterans Memorial is inscribed with the names of the 58,249 people killed or missing in Vietnam.

The War Powers Act

- Requires the president in all cases to consult with Congress before making any troop commitments
- Requires the president to inform Congress of any commitment of troops abroad within 48 hours
- Requires the president to withdraw troops in 60 to 90 days, unless Congress explicitly approves the troop commitment

▲ Along with returning troops, many freed prisoners of war, or POWs, such as Lt. Colonel Robert Stirm, were joyfully greeted by their families. Sadly, some did not come home and were labeled as MIAs, or "missing in action," and remain so to this day.

Analyzing VISUALS

1. **Explaining** How did the War Powers Act seek to curb the power of the president?
2. **Assessing** Do you think that the legacy of Vietnam has been a lasting one? Why or why not?

Additional Support

Extending the Content

The Vietnam Memorial The names of eight women nurses who died in Vietnam are inscribed on The Wall of the Vietnam Veterans Memorial. Many more women served; a former army nurse began working for a monument to highlight the contributions of women in the war. A sculpture of three women with a soldier, designed by Glenna Goodacre, was dedicated in 1993. No specific records on women in the military were kept during the war, but it is estimated that as many as 8,000 may have served in Vietnam.

The Vietnam Veterans Memorial was itself controversial. In the fall of 1980, the Vietnam Veterans Memorial Fund sponsored a national competition for the design, to be judged by a panel whose members would not know the creators of the more than 1400 designs submitted. When 21-year-old Maya Lin, still a student at Yale University, won the competition, many people were dismayed by Lin's youth, gender, and ethnicity, as well as by the design itself, a "black gash of shame," as some called it. The Wall was dedicated in 1982, becoming one of the nation's most-visited public monuments.

Even after they returned home from fighting as in other wars, soldiers found it hard to escape the war's psychological impact. Army Specialist Doug Johnson recalled the problems he faced:

PRIMARY SOURCE

"It took a while for me to recognize that I did suffer some psychological problems in trying to deal with my experience in Vietnam. The first recollection I have of the effect took place shortly after I arrived back in the **R** States. One evening . . . I went to see a movie on post. I don't recall the name of the movie or what it was about, but I remember there was a sad part, and that I started crying uncontrollably. It hadn't dawned on me before this episode that I had. . . succeeded in burying my emotions."

—quoted in *Touched by the Dragon*

One reason why it may have been harder for some Vietnam veterans to readjust to civilian life was that many considered the war a defeat. Many Americans wanted to forget the war. Thus, the sacrifices of many veterans often went unrecognized. There were relatively few welcome-home parades and celebrations after the war.

The war also remained **unresolved** for the American families whose relatives and friends were classified as prisoners of war (POWs) or missing in action (MIA). Despite many official investigations, these families were not convinced that the government had told the truth about POW/MIA policies.

The nation finally began to come to terms with the war almost a decade later. In 1982 the nation dedicated the Vietnam Veterans Memorial in Washington, D.C., a large black granite wall inscribed with the names of those killed and missing in action in the war. "It's a first step to remind America of what we did," veteran Larry Cox of Virginia said at the dedication of the monument.

The War's Impact on the Nation

The war also left its mark on the nation as a whole. In 1973 Congress passed the **War Powers Act** as a way to reestablish some limits on executive power. The act required the president to inform Congress of any commitment of troops abroad within 48 hours, and to withdraw them in 60 to 90 days, unless Congress explicitly approved the troop commitment. No president has recognized this limitation, and the courts have tended to avoid the issue as a strictly political question. Nonetheless, every president since the law's passage has asked Congress to authorize the use of military force before committing ground troops to combat. In general, the war shook the nation's confidence and led some to embrace isolationism, while others began to question the policy of containing communism and instead urged more negotiation with the Soviet Union.

On the domestic front, the Vietnam War increased Americans' cynicism about their government. Many felt the nation's leaders had misled them. Together with Watergate, Vietnam made Americans more wary of their leaders.

Reading Check **Describing** How did the Vietnam War affect Americans' attitudes toward international conflicts?

Section 3 REVIEW

Vocabulary

1. **Explain** the significance of: Henry Kissinger, linkage, Vietnamization, Pentagon Papers, War Powers Act.

Main Ideas

2. **Explaining** Why was the United States unable to help South Vietnam following the full-scale invasion by North Vietnam in 1975?
3. **Describing** How was the aftermath of the Vietnam War different for its veterans than postwar periods had been for veterans of earlier U.S. wars?

Critical Thinking

4. **Big Ideas** Why did Congress pass the War Powers Act? How did it reflect distrust of the executive branch of government?
5. **Organizing** Use a graphic organizer similar to the one below to list the effects of the Vietnam War on the nation.

Effects of Vietnam War

6. **Analyzing Visuals** Study the left photo on page 902. Why do you think it is important for society to have war memorials?

Writing About History

7. **Descriptive Writing** Suppose you are a college student in 1970. Write a journal entry expressing your feelings about the events at Kent State University and Jackson State College.

History ONLINE
Study Central™ To review this section, go to glencoe.com and click on Study Central.

R Reading Strategy

Reading Primary Sources Invite a volunteer to read aloud the quotation by Doug Johnson. **Ask:** What event triggered Johnson's realization that the war was affecting him emotionally? *(crying uncontrollably at a movie being shown on post)* **BL**

Assess

History ONLINE

Study Central™ provides summaries, interactive games, and online graphic organizers to help students review content.

Close

Summarizing Ask: What events led to America pulling out of Vietnam? *(protests over Cambodia, leaking of Pentagon Papers)* **OL**

Reading Check

Answer: They became more reluctant to intervene in other nations' affairs.

Section 3 REVIEW

Answers

1. All definitions can be found in the section and the Glossary.
2. Nixon, who had promised to help, had resigned due to Watergate, and Congress refused to give President Ford the funds.
3. Unlike the periods following other wars, many Americans just wanted to forget the Vietnam War. There was also no sense of having won the conflict, and so there were few welcome-home parades or other celebrations for the returning troops.
4. It wanted to limit executive power. There was a general sense that the presidents had misused the power granted to them in the Gulf of Tonkin Resolution, and it had been found through the Pentagon Papers and other sources that presidents had lied to the American public about the course of the war in Vietnam.
5. Answers may include the following: American cynicism toward government, war dead and casualties, cost, and War Powers Act.
6. Students' responses will vary but may suggest it is important to recall the human costs of war.
7. Students' journal entries should focus on feelings about the events and include descriptive language.

Expository Writing Ask students to select one cause or one effect and write a paragraph further explaining the event in its historical context. **OL**

Visual/Spatial Ask students why so many photographs capture people touching the names on the wall. *(Students may say that it is a concrete way to connect with the person whose name is written there.)* **BL**

Chapter 26 Visual Summary

STUDY TO GO You can study anywhere, anytime by downloading quizzes and flashcards to your PDA from glencoe.com.

Causes of the Vietnam War

- During World War II, the United States helps the people of Indochina fight the Japanese, who had invaded the region.
- After World War II, France refuses to give independence to the people of Indochina and sends troops to reestablish control.
- Led by Ho Chi Minh, the Vietminh fight the French. Ho Chi Minh wants Vietnam to be independent but also wants to build a Communist society in Vietnam.
- Concerned about the spread of communism, President Eisenhower sends aid to help the French retain control in Vietnam.
- After losing the battle of Dien Bien Phu, France pulls out of Vietnam. The Geneva Accords create North and South Vietnam.
- Ho Chi Minh becomes the leader of North Vietnam and makes it a Communist nation allied with the USSR and China. North Vietnam begins arming guerrillas to fight the South Vietnamese government.
- American leaders become worried that a "domino effect" might cause all of Southeast Asia to fall to communism if South Vietnam falls.
- President Kennedy sharply increases military aid to South Vietnam.
- President Johnson escalates U.S. involvement and gains war powers after the Gulf of Tonkin incident.

► *U.S. troops arrive in Vietnam in 1965 (above). Fighting communist guerrillas proved difficult in the dense jungle terrain (right).*

▲ *The Vietnam Veterans Memorial in Washington, D.C., is a stark reminder of the costs of the Vietnam War.*

Effects of the Vietnam War

- Americans applaud President Johnson's response to a Vietcong attack with aggressive air strikes.
- The United States commits over 380,000 ground troops to fighting in Vietnam by the end of 1966.
- American people question the government's honesty about the war, creating the so-called "credibility gap."
- The war casualties and the unfair draft system cause civil unrest.
- The wartime economy hurts domestic spending for programs such as the Great Society.
- President Nixon is elected largely on promises to end the war and unite a divided country.
- Congress passes the War Powers Act to limit the power of the president during wartime.

Hands-On Chapter Project Step 4

Create a Documentary of the Vietnam War

Step 4: Presenting the Documentaries Ask: What is the message of the documentary?

Directions Allow class time to view the completed documentaries. After each showing, engage the class by asking them to answer the following questions during a class discussion:

- What was the message of the documentary?
- How was the message conveyed? Was it clear?
- What information was "left out" of the documentary?
- What were the best parts of the documentary? Why?
- How could the documentary be improved?

Putting It Together The class should determine as a whole if the documentaries reflected information from the textbook, and if the information was portrayed accurately. **OL**

Chapter 26 Assessment

Reviewing Vocabulary

Directions: Choose the word or words that best complete the sentence.

1. Eisenhower cited the ________ as the reason why the United States had to support South Vietnam.
   - **A** credibility gap
   - **B** self-determination theory
   - **C** domino theory
   - **D** Communist way

2. A person who supported the war effort in Vietnam might be called a
   - **A** hawk.
   - **B** dove.
   - **C** guerrilla.
   - **D** linkage.

3. As the war in Vietnam escalated, a ________ developed as Americans began to find it hard to believe what the Johnson administration said about the conflict.
   - **A** linkage
   - **B** credibility gap
   - **C** domino theory
   - **D** teach-in

4. The Vietcong were Communist ________ located in South Vietnam.
   - **A** elected officials
   - **B** generals
   - **C** diplomats
   - **D** guerrillas

5. President Nixon's plan to withdraw U.S. troops and replace them with South Vietnamese troops was known as
   - **A** linkage.
   - **B** the Tet Offensive.
   - **C** the domino theory.
   - **D** Vietnamization.

Reviewing Main Ideas

Directions: Choose the best answer for each of the following questions.

Section 1 *(pp. 882–889)*

6. Who was the leader of the North Vietnamese?
   - **A** Mao Zedong
   - **B** Ho Chi Minh
   - **C** Dien Bien Phu
   - **D** Ngo Dinh Diem

7. One reason why President Johnson did not order a full-scale attack on North Vietnam was because
   - **A** he did not think that the United States could win.
   - **B** the military lacked the manpower to launch an assault.
   - **C** he did not want to bring China into the war.
   - **D** he did not want to lose the 1968 election.

8. Which of the following temporarily established North and South Vietnam and recognized Cambodia's independence?
   - **A** the Treaty of Paris
   - **B** Gulf of Tonkin Resolution
   - **C** the Truman Doctrine
   - **D** the Geneva Accords

Section 2 *(pp. 892–897)*

9. Many Americans objected to the draft because they believed it
   - **A** forced young men to flee to Canada.
   - **B** unfairly targeted the poor and minorities.
   - **C** did not include women.
   - **D** did not raise the necessary number of troops.

TEST-TAKING TIP

Do not spend too much time trying to figure out the right answer to a question. Move on, and then come back to that question when you have answered all the questions you do know. If you still do not know the answer, select the one that you think is the most logical.

Need Extra Help?

If You Missed Questions . . .	1	2	3	4	5	6	7	8	9
Go to Page . . .	883	895	892	885	898	882	886	884	893

GO ON

Answers and Analyses Reviewing Vocabulary

1. C Students may note that two answers are labeled theories, giving a clue that one of those two answers must be correct. By observing that self-determination does not describe the idea of supporting, they can select the domino theory.

2. A Option *D* is easily eliminated, because it is not a term that applies to a person. Because *dove* and *hawk* are contrasting terms, students can also eliminate *C*. Considering the different natures of doves and hawks, students can select the correct answer.

3. B Students with a firm grasp of vocabulary will quickly see that *believe* and *credible* are related words, thus eliminating all false choices.

4. D This question requires simple memorization and identification. There are no real clues in the possible answers themselves, since any of the options could describe Communists.

5. D Nixon announced the withdrawal of 25,000 soldiers in June 1969. He did not, however, wish to completely remove U.S. troops because he wanted to maintain negotiating power at the peace talks.

Reviewing Main ideas

6. B Students should be able to ignore the distraction of Mao Zedong, recalling that he is Chinese. They will have to resort to basic recall, knowing that Dien Bien Phu is a place and that Ngo Dinh Diem was the leader of South Vietnam.

7. C Knowing that Johnson decided not to run in 1968 will allow students to ignore answer *D*. Options *A* and *B* are also easy to discard as options, since the United States was used to winning wars and the military was at the ready.

8. D Students can eliminate *C* because it is a doctrine and does not sound like a peace treaty. They need to recall that the Gulf of Tonkin Resolution granted Johnson the power to wage the war. They might also connect the ideas of accord and peace to arrive at the correct answer.

9. B Students can eliminate *A*, which was an unintended effect of the draft. Not including women would not raise an objection, especially in the 1960s. Students should recall that many thousands of military personnel served in the war. They may also recall the objections of Dr. Martin Luther King, Jr., and so choose the correct answer.

10. D The question asks for a turning point against the war. Only *A* and *D* are directly related to the war. None of the other options, although they affected some Americans, influenced public opinion about the war to a great extent. While teach-ins were important in the antiwar movement, they did not turn the majority of public opinion against the war. The Tet Offensive was a major political victory for the North Vietnamese. It led many to believe the war could not be won and widened the credibility gap.

11. D Students should be able to omit Agent Orange, recalling that it was used to deforest Vietnam. Although this leaves three options, they should recall that the suffix *-tion* refers to a process, which aligns it to the idea of a gradual removal.

12. A After abandoning the stalemated war, Americans did not have greater belief in containment as effective nor confidence in their ultimate victory in the Cold War. Within two years the North Vietnamese conquered the South Vietnamese, so there was no need for paranoia about their intentions.

13. B The incorrect options all extend the president's power. Only *B* limits executive power, so it is most likely to be correct.

Critical Thinking

14. A The resolution gave President Johnson the authority to use force in Vietnam.

15. D If students look carefully at the map, they will see that *D* is the only possible answer.

Chapter 26 Assessment

10. Which of the following events was significant in turning American public opinion against the war in Vietnam?

A the National Teach-in
B the 1968 Democratic National Convention
C the assassination of President Kennedy
D the Tet Offensive

Section 3 *(pp. 898–903)*

11. The gradual removal of U.S. troops from Vietnam was known as

A Agent Orange.
B containment.
C linkage.
D Vietnamization.

12. Which of the following was part of the legacy of the Vietnam War?

A Americans' increased cynicism about their government
B Americans' belief that the policy of containment worked
C Americans' confidence that the United States would win the Cold War
D Americans' paranoia about the intentions of the North Vietnamese government

13. The purpose of the War Powers Act was to ensure that the president would

A have greater authority over the military.
B consult Congress before committing troops in extended conflicts.
C have the authority to sign treaties without Senate approval.
D have a freer hand in fighting the spread of communism.

Critical Thinking

Directions: Choose the best answers to the following questions.

14. Why is the Gulf of Tonkin Resolution important?

A It authorized the use of force in Vietnam.
B It ordered U.S. forces to withdraw from Vietnam.
C It divided Vietnam into two countries.
D It required the president to consult Congress before committing troops.

Base your answer to question 15 on the map below and on your knowledge of Chapter 26.

15. The Ho Chi Minh trail ran through which two nations?

A Laos and Japan
B Laos and Thailand
C Laos and China
D Laos and Cambodia

Need Extra Help?

If You Missed Questions . . .	10	11	12	13	14	15
Go to Page . . .	895–896	898	902–903	903	886	R15

GO ON

16. On which idea is the Twenty-sixth Amendment based?

A Women should be allowed to serve in the armed forces.

B The president, not Congress, should decide where and when troops will fight.

C A person who is old enough to fight is old enough to vote.

D A draft is an old-fashioned and unworkable system for selecting soldiers.

Analyze the cartoon and answer the questions that follow. Base your answers on the cartoon and on your knowledge of Chapter 26.

17. This cartoon depicts what aspect of the Vietnam War's effect on the United States?

A disagreements in Congress between hawks and doves

B disagreements among military leaders about war strategy

C disagreements between pro-war and antiwar groups among civilians

D disagreements on Nixon's plan to pull out of Vietnam

18. The cartoonist is expressing the opinion that

A the war was dividing the country.

B President Johnson should ask the country to remain patient during the war.

C Vietnam is a conflict with an easy solution.

D President Johnson is a great leader with a solution to the problems in Vietnam.

Document-Based Questions

Directions: Analyze the document and answer the short-answer questions that follow the document.

In the 1960s many young Americans enlisted or were drafted for military service. Some believed that they had a duty to serve their country. Many had no clear idea of what they were doing or why. In the following excerpt, a young man expresses his thoughts about going to war:

> *"I read a lot of pacifist literature to determine whether or not I was a conscientious objector. I finally concluded that I wasn't. . . .*
>
> *The one clear decision I made in 1968 about me and the war was that if I was going to get out of it, I was going to get out in a legal way. I was not going to defraud the system in order to beat the system. I wasn't going to leave the country, because the odds of coming back looked real slim. . . .*
>
> *With all my terror of going into the Army . . . there was something seductive about it, too. I was seduced by World War II and John Wayne movies. . . . I had been, as we all were, victimized by a romantic, truly uninformed view of war."*
>
> —*quoted in* Nam

19. What options did the young man have regarding the war?

20. Do you think World War II movies gave him a realistic view of what fighting in Vietnam would be like?

Extended Response

21. The conflict in Vietnam has been called the first "television war." Americans could watch scenes of death and destruction unfold in front of them from their living rooms. Write an expository essay about how television changed the way Americans view war in general and how it contributed to the unpopularity of the Vietnam War specifically. Your essay should include an introduction and at least three paragraphs that explore this issue.

STOP

History ONLINE

For additional test practice, use Self-Check Quizzes—Chapter 26 at glencoe.com.

Need Extra Help?

If You Missed Questions . . .	16	17	18	19	20	21
Go to Page . . .	894–895	R18	R18	907	907	892–900

16. C Students familiar with the type of content in constitutional amendments will readily eliminate the false possibilities, even if they cannot recall the subject of the Twenty-Sixth Amendment. Other students may remember that protest of the draft also raised questions about the voting age.

17. C The cartoon depicts pro-war and antiwar groups that divided the home front during the Vietnam War.

18. A The other options are clearly false. No one is pulling on Johnson, who appears to be feeling his way in the dark, thus indicating the lack of easy solutions.

Document-Based Questions

19. He could declare he was a conscientious objector, avoid service in a legal way, leave the country, or become part of the military.

20. No; the young man realized that the view of war he had from World War II and the movies was romanticized and not at all like what real war would be like.

Extended Response

21. Students' essays will vary but should clearly and logically express the changing effects of television on Americans' perceptions of the Vietnam war and war in general.

History ONLINE

Have students visit the Web site at glencoe.com to review Chapter 26 and take the Self-Check Quiz.

Need Extra Help?

Have students refer to the pages listed if they miss any of the questions.

Chapter 27 Planning Guide

Key to Ability Levels	
BL Below Level	AL Above Level
OL On Level	ELL English Language Learners

Key to Teaching Resources	
Print Material	Transparency
CD-ROM or DVD	

Levels BL	OL	AL	ELL		Resources	Chapter Opener	Section 1	Section 2	Section 3	Chapter Assess
					FOCUS					
BL	OL	AL	ELL	Transparency	Daily Focus Skills Transparencies		27-1	27-2	27-3	
					TEACH					
		AL		Print Material	American Literature Reading, URB			p. 17		
BL	OL		ELL	Print Material	Reading Essentials and Note-Taking Guide*		p. 295	p. 298	p. 301	
	OL			Print Material	Historical Analysis Skills Activity, URB				p. 118	
BL	OL		ELL	Print Material	Guided Reading Activities, URB*		p. 144	p. 145	p. 146	
BL	OL	AL	ELL	Print Material	Content Vocabulary Activity, URB*		p. 123			
BL	OL	AL	ELL	Print Material	Academic Vocabulary Activity, URB		p. 125			
	OL	AL		Print Material	Critical Thinking Skills Activity, URB		p. 128			
BL	OL		ELL	Print Material	Reading Skills Activity, URB		p. 117			
BL	OL		ELL	Print Material	English Learner Activity, URB				p. 121	
	OL	AL		Print Material	Reinforcing Skills Activity, URB			p. 127		
BL	OL	AL	ELL	Print Material	Differentiated Instruction Activity, URB			p. 119		
BL	OL		ELL	Print Material	Time Line Activity, URB		p. 129			
	OL			Print Material	Linking Past and Present Activity, URB			p. 130		
BL	OL	AL	ELL	Print Material	American Art and Music Activity, URB		p. 135			
BL	OL	AL	ELL	Print Material	Interpreting Political Cartoons Activity, URB			p. 137		
		AL		Print Material	Enrichment Activity, URB		p. 141			
BL	OL	AL	ELL	Print Material	American Biographies			✓	✓	
BL	OL	AL	ELL	Print Material	Primary Source Reading, URB		p. 131		p. 133	
BL	OL	AL		Print Material	Supreme Court Case Studies		p. 105	p. 115	p. 107	
BL	OL	AL	ELL	Print Material	The Living Constitution*	✓	✓	✓	✓	✓
	OL	AL		CD-ROM or DVD	American History Primary Source Documents Library	✓	✓	✓	✓	✓
BL	OL	AL	ELL	Transparency	Unit Map Overlay Transparencies	✓	✓	✓	✓	✓
BL	OL	AL	ELL	Print Material	Differentiated Instruction for the American History Classroom	✓	✓	✓	✓	✓
BL	OL	AL	ELL	CD-ROM or DVD	StudentWorks™ Plus	✓	✓	✓	✓	✓

Note: Please refer to the *Unit 8 Resource Book* for this chapter's URB materials.

* Also available in Spanish

TeacherWorks Plus
All-In-One Planner and Resource Center

- Interactive Lesson Planner
- Interactive Teacher Edition
- Fully editable blackline masters
- Section Spotlight Videos Launch
- Differentiated Lesson Plans
- Printable reports of daily assignments
- Standards Tracking System

Levels: BL	OL	AL	ELL	Resources	Chapter Opener	Section 1	Section 2	Section 3	Chapter Assess
				TEACH *(continued)*					
BL	OL	AL	ELL	American Music Hits Through History CD	✓	✓	✓	✓	✓
BL	OL	AL	ELL	Unit Time Line Transparencies and Activities	✓	✓	✓	✓	✓
BL	OL	AL	ELL	Cause and Effect Transparencies, Strategies, and Activities	✓	✓	✓	✓	✓
BL	OL	AL	ELL	Why It Matters Chapter Transparencies, Strategies, and Activities	✓	✓	✓	✓	✓
BL	OL	AL	ELL	American Issues	✓	✓	✓	✓	✓
	OL	AL	ELL	American Art and Architecture Transparencies, Strategies, and Activities	✓	✓	✓	✓	✓
BL	OL	AL		High School American History Literature Library	✓	✓	✓	✓	✓
BL	OL	AL	ELL	*The American Vision* Video Program	✓	✓	✓	✓	✓
BL	OL	AL	ELL	Reading Strategies and Activities for the Social Studies Classroom	✓	✓	✓	✓	✓
Teacher Resources				Strategies for Success	✓	✓	✓	✓	✓
				Success with English Learners	✓	✓	✓	✓	✓
				Presentation Plus! with MindJogger CheckPoint	✓	✓	✓	✓	✓
				ASSESS					
BL	OL	AL	ELL	Section Quizzes and Chapter Tests*		p. 383	p. 384	p. 385	p. 387
BL	OL	AL	ELL	Authentic Assessment With Rubrics					p. 59
BL	OL	AL	ELL	Standardized Test Practice Workbook					p. 61
BL	OL	AL	ELL	*ExamView® Assessment Suite*		27-1	27-2	27-3	Ch. 27
				CLOSE					
BL			ELL	Reteaching Activity, URB					p. 139
BL	OL		ELL	Reading and Study Skills Foldables™	p. 81				
BL	OL	AL	ELL	*American History* in Graphic Novel		p. 45			

✓ Chapter- or unit-based activities applicable to all sections in this chapter.

Using Glencoe's Vocabulary Tools

Teach With Technology

What Glencoe technology products improve students' vocabulary?

Vocabulary eFlashcards, ePuzzles and Games, and **Vocabulary PuzzleMaker** all build students' vocabulary and help students understand key words and concepts from the textbook.

How can these products help my students?

Vocabulary eFlashcards help students review and test their recall of content vocabulary, academic vocabulary, and people, places, and events for each chapter. **ePuzzles and Games** are an entertaining way for students to study the key facts, concepts, and vocabulary introduced in each chapter. The **Vocabulary PuzzleMaker** lets you quickly create word searches, crosswords, and jumbles that students can use to practice vocabulary from each chapter.

For **Vocabulary eFlashcards** and **ePuzzles and Games,** visit glencoe.com and enter a student QuickPass™ code to go directly to student resources for the chapter. For **Vocabulary PuzzleMaker,** enter a teacher code to go to teacher resources.

History ONLINE
Visit glencoe.com and enter QuickPass™ code TAV9399c27T for Chapter 27 resources.

You can easily launch a wide range of digital products from your computer's desktop with the McGraw-Hill Social Studies widget.

	Student	Teacher	Parent
Media Library			
• Section Audio	●		●
• Spanish Audio Summaries	●		●
• Section Spotlight Videos	●	●	●
***The American Vision* Online Learning Center (Web Site)**			
• StudentWorks™ Plus Online	●	●	●
• Multilingual Glossary	●	●	●
• Study-to-Go	●	●	●
• Chapter Overviews	●	●	●
• Self-Check Quizzes	●	●	●
• Student Web Activities	●	●	●
• ePuzzles and Games	●	●	●
• Vocabulary eFlashcards	●	●	●
• In Motion Animations	●	●	●
• Study Central™	●	●	●
• Web Activity Lesson Plans		●	
• Vocabulary PuzzleMaker	●	●	●
• Historical Thinking Activities		●	
• Beyond the Textbook	●	●	●

READING SUPPORT FROM JAMESTOWN EDUCATION

- **Timed Readings Plus in Social Studies** helps students increase their reading rate and fluency while maintaining comprehension. The 400-word passages are similar to those found on state and national assessments.
- **Reading in the Content Area: Social Studies** concentrates on six essential reading skills that help students better comprehend what they read. The book includes 75 high-interest nonfiction passages written at increasing levels of difficulty.
- **Reading Social Studies** includes strategic reading instruction and vocabulary support in Social Studies content for both ELLs and native speakers of English.

www.jamestowneducation.com

NATIONAL GEOGRAPHIC

Index to National Geographic Magazine:

The following articles relate to this chapter:

- "Latinos Rise Nationwide: America's New Majority Minority," by A.R. Williams, November 2003.
- "Philadelphia's African Americans: A Celebration of Life," by Roland L. Freeman, August 1990.

Access National Geographic's new, dynamic MapMachine Web site and other geography resources at:

www.nationalgeographic.com
www.nationalgeographic.com/maps

Biography A&E HOME VIDEO THE HISTORY CHANNEL

The following videotape programs are available from Glencoe as supplements to this chapter:

- Jimmy Carter (ISBN 1-56-501530-4)
- Drive for the American Dream (ISBN 1-56-501221-6)

To order, call Glencoe at 1-800-334-7344. To find classroom resources to accompany many of these videos, check the following home pages:

A&E Television: www.aetv.com
The History Channel: www.historychannel.com

Reading List Generator CD-ROM

GLENCOE BOOKLINK 3

Use this database to search more than 30,000 titles to create a customized reading list for your students.

- Reading lists can be organized by students' reading level, author, genre, theme, or area of interest.
- The database provides Degrees of Reading Power™ (DRP) and Lexile™ readability scores for all selections.
- A brief summary of each selection is included.

Leveled reading suggestions for this chapter:

For students at a Grade 8 reading level:
- ***Learning about Justice from the Life of Cesar Chavez***, by Jeanne Strazzabosco

For students at a Grade 9 reading level:
- ***Cesar Chavez: Labor Leader***, by Maria E. Cedeno

For students at a Grade 10 reading level:
- ***Warriors Don't Cry***, by Melba Pattillo Beals

For students at a Grade 11 reading level:
- ***The Beatles***, by Michael Burgan

For students at a Grade 12 reading level:
- ***Andy Warhol: Prince of Pop***, by Jan Greenburg & Sandra Jordan

Focus

MAKING CONNECTIONS

Can Protests Bring Change?

Ask students to give examples of why groups today use public protest to achieve change. Have students discuss whether protesters in the 1960s and 1970s might have achieved comparable change using other approaches. Then ask whether the protests of the 1960s and 1970s continue to influence the rights, workplaces, and economic opportunities of students, women, and Latinos today. Students should evaluate their answers after they have completed the chapter. **OL**

Teach

The Big Ideas

As students study the chapter, remind them to consider the section-based Big Ideas included in each section's Guide to Reading. The **Essential Questions** in the activities below tie in to the Big Ideas and help students think about and understand important chapter concepts. In addition, the Hands-on Chapter Projects with their culminating activities relate the content from each section to the Big Ideas. These activities build on each other as students progress through the chapter. Section activities culminate in the wrap-up activity on the Visual Summary page.

Chapter 27

The Politics of Protest

1960–1980

SECTION 1 Students and the Counterculture
SECTION 2 The Feminist Movement
SECTION 3 Latino Americans Organize

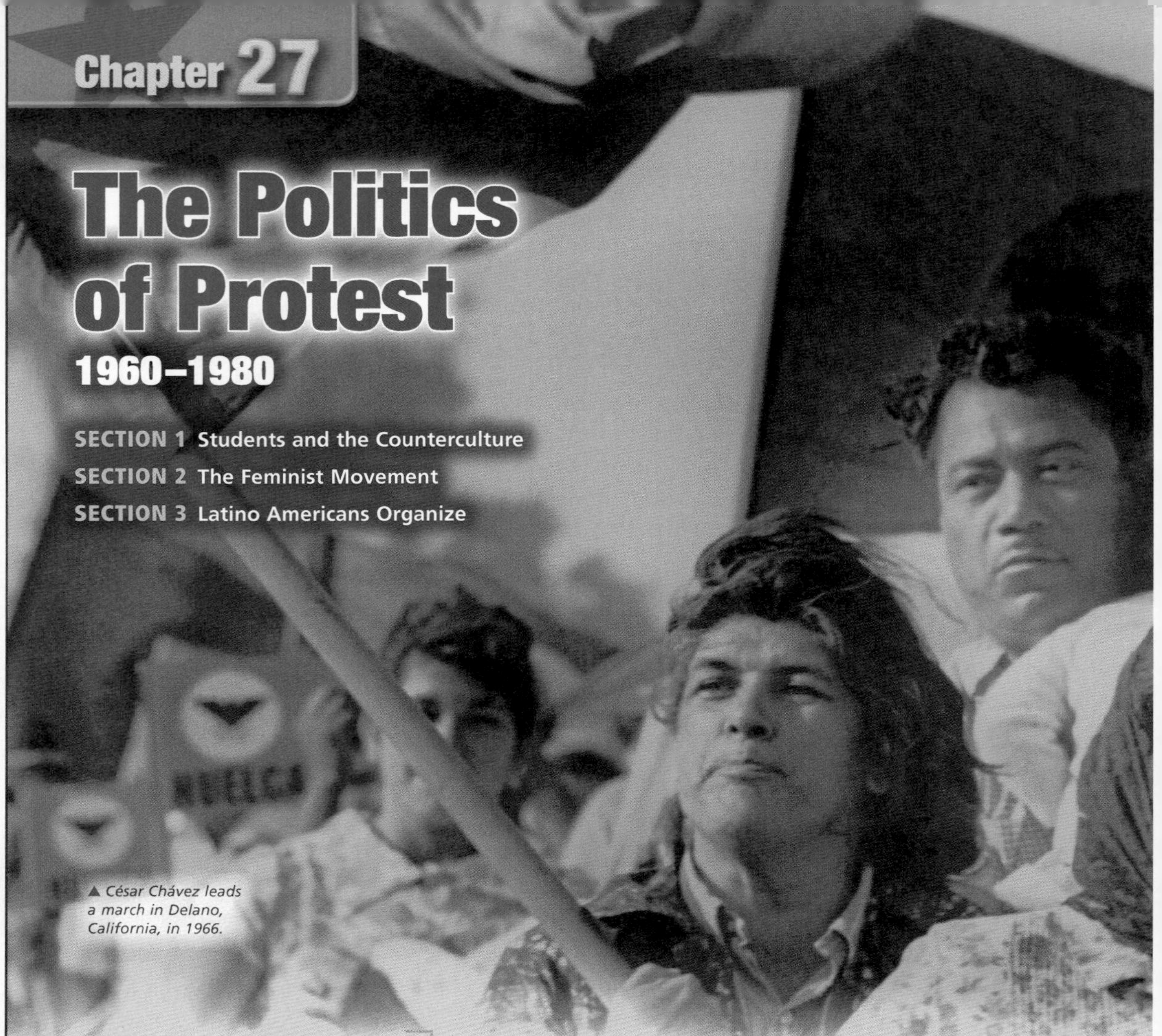

▲ *César Chávez leads a march in Delano, California, in 1966.*

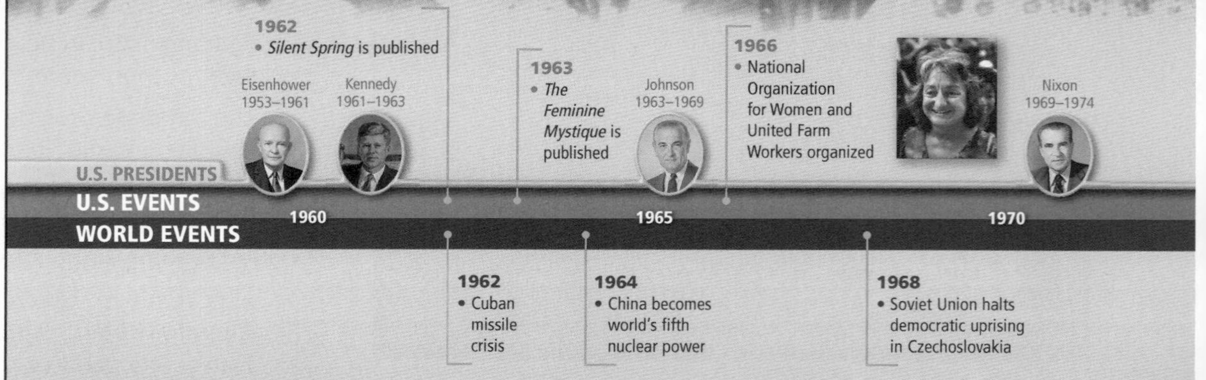

Section 1

Students and the Counterculture

Essential Question: How did students and the counterculture want to change society? *(They wanted a society that was free of war, poverty, pressure to conform, and materialism; was tolerant; and offered equal justice and opportunity for all.)* Point out that in Section 1 students will learn about the impact of protest and the counterculture on society. **OL**

Section 2

The Feminist Movement

Essential Question: What were the goals of the feminist movement that began in the 1960s? *(Women wanted equal pay for equal work, better educational and career opportunities, more career choices, and reproductive choice.)* Point out that in Section 2 students will learn about the impact of the renewed women's movement on society. **OL**

Chapter Audio

MAKING CONNECTIONS

Can Protests Bring Change?

The civil rights movement that began in the 1950s inspired other groups in American society to stage protests in the 1960s and 1970s. Students, women, and Latinos all formed organizations and began demanding changes in how American society treated them. Instead of trying to lobby legislatures or educate voters, all of these groups used mass protests and demonstrations to draw attention to their cause.

- ***Why do you think these groups decided to use public protests to achieve change?***
- ***How has society changed for students, women, and Latinos?***

1973
- *Roe* v. *Wade* decision on abortion
- Native Americans clash with FBI at Wounded Knee

Ford 1974–1977

Carter 1977–1981

1979
- Nuclear accident at Three Mile Island

1975

1980

1975
- Last European colonies in Africa gain independence from Portugal

1979
- Ayatollah Khomeini leads revolution against the Shah of Iran

FOLDABLES

Organizing Information Make a Four-Door Book Foldable about the Berkeley Free Speech Movement, Students for a Democratic Society (SDS), or the National Organization for Women. As you read, complete the Four-Door Book by answering the questions *who, what, when,* and *why.*

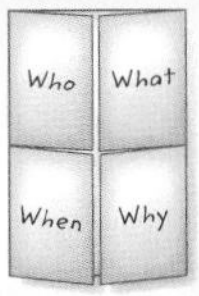

History ONLINE Visit glencoe.com and enter **QuickPass™** code TAV9846c27 for Chapter 27 resources.

Introducing Chapter 27

More About the Photo

Visual Literacy César Chávez was born in 1927 on a small farm near Yuma, Arizona. When his father lost his land during the Depression, Chávez began working as a migrant farm worker to help support the family. After serving in the navy during World War II, he returned to farm labor. Soon he became committed to improving the lives of farm workers. For his leadership, he received the Presidential Medal of Freedom.

FOLDABLES™ Study Organizer **Dinah Zike's Foldables**

Dinah Zike's Foldables are three-dimensional, interactive graphic organizers that help students practice basic writing skills, review vocabulary terms, and identify main ideas. Instructions for creating and using Foldables can be found in the Appendix at the end of this book and in the *Dinah Zike's Reading and Study Skills Foldables* booklet.

History ONLINE

Visit glencoe.com and enter **QuickPass™** code TAV9399c27T for Chapter 27 resources, including a Chapter Overview, Study Central™, Study-to-Go, Student Web Activity, Self-Check Quiz, and other materials.

Section 3

Latino Americans Organize

Essential Question: What were the goals of the Latinos who organized? *(They wanted an end to discrimination; improved working conditions, and greater pay, especially for farm workers; increased Latino voter participation and more Latino candidates elected.)* Point out that in Section 3 students will learn about the impact of Latino organizations and movements. **OL**

Focus

Bellringer

Daily Focus Transparency 27-1

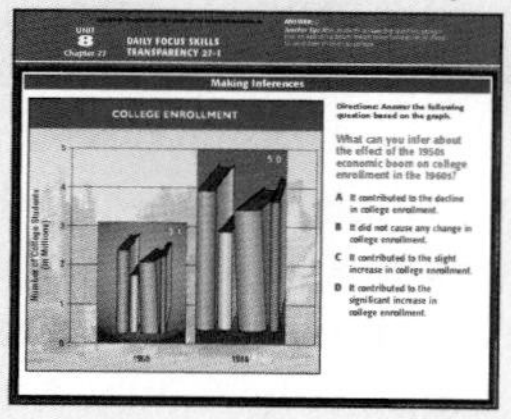

Guide to Reading

Answer to the Graphic:

I. The Rise of the Youth Movement
 A. SDS
 B. The Free Speech Movement
II. The Counterculture
 A. Hippie Culture
 B. The Impact of Counterculture
  1. Fashion
  2. Music

Section Spotlight Video

To generate student interest and provide a springboard for class discussion, access the Chapter 27, Section 1 video at glencoe.com or on the video DVD.

Section 1

Section Audio Spotlight Video

Students and the Counterculture

Guide to Reading

Big Ideas

Struggles for Rights During the 1960s, many of the country's young people raised their voices in protest against numerous aspects of American society.

Content Vocabulary

- counterculture *(p. 912)*
- hippies *(p. 912)*
- communes *(p. 913)*

Academic Vocabulary

- rationality *(p. 912)*
- conformity *(p. 913)*

People and Events to Identify

- Port Huron Statement *(p. 911)*
- Tom Hayden *(p. 911)*
- Free Speech Movement *(p. 911)*
- Haight-Ashbury district *(p. 913)*
- Woodstock *(p. 913)*
- Bob Dylan *(p. 913)*

Reading Strategy

Organizing Use the major headings of this section to create an outline similar to the one below.

Students and the Counterculture
I. The Rise of the Youth Movement
 A.
 B.
II.
 A.
 B.

The 1960s was one of the most tumultuous decades in American history. The decade also gave birth to a youth movement that challenged the American political and social system and conventional middle-class values.

The Rise of the Youth Movement

MAIN Idea The youth protest movement of the 1960s included Students for a Democratic Society and the Free Speech Movement.

HISTORY AND YOU Do you know of any groups that work to improve society? Read how the youth of the 1960s protested social injustice.

The roots of the 1960s youth movement stretched back to the 1950s. In the decade after World War II, the country had enjoyed a time of peace and prosperity. Prosperity did not extend to all, however, and some, especially the artists and writers of the beat movement, had openly criticized American society. They believed American society valued conformity over independence and financial gain over spiritual and social advancement.

At the same time, the turmoil of the civil rights movement had raised serious questions about racism in American society, and the nuclear arms race between the United States and the Soviet Union made many of the nation's youth uneasy about the future. For many young people, the events of the 1950s had called into question the wisdom of their parents and their political leaders.

The youth movement originated with the baby boomers, the huge generation born after World War II. By 1970, 58.4 percent of the American population was 34 years old or younger. (By comparison, those 34 or younger in 2000 represented an estimated 48.9 percent.) The early 1960s also saw a rapid increase in enrollment at colleges. The economic boom of the 1950s meant more families could afford to send their children to college. Between 1960 and 1966, enrollment in four-year colleges rose from 3.1 million to almost 5 million. College life gave young people a sense of freedom and independence. It also allowed them to meet and bond with others who shared their feelings about society and fears about the future. It was on college campuses across the nation that youth protest movements began and reached their peak.

Students for a Democratic Society

Some young people were concerned most about the injustices they saw in the country's political and social system. In their view, a small wealthy elite controlled politics, and wealth itself was unfairly

Resource Manager

R Reading Strategies	C Critical Thinking	D Differentiated Instruction	W Writing Support	S Skill Practice
Teacher Edition • Taking Notes, p. 916 • Academic Vocab., p. 917 **Additional Resources** • Pri. Source Read., URB p. 131 • Guid. Read. Act., URB p. 144 • Reading Skills Act., URB p. 117	**Teacher Edition** • Analyzing Pri. Sources, pp. 911, 915, 918 **Additional Resources** • Critical Thinking Skills Activity, URB p. 128 • Quizzes and Tests, p. 383 • Supreme Court Case Studies, p. 105	**Additional Resources** • Am. Art and Music Act., p. 135 • Am. History in Graphic Novel, p. 45 • Academic Vocab. Act., URB p. 123 • Enrichment Act., URB p. 141	**Teacher Edition** • Descriptive Writing, p. 912 • Persuasive Writing, p. 916 • Content Vocab. Act., URB p. 125	**Additional Resources** • Read. Essen., p. 295 • Time Line Act., URB p. 129

PRIMARY SOURCE

The Student Movement

▼ Members of SDS protest the Vietnam War

PRIMARY SOURCE

In 1962 Students for a Democratic Society issued the Port Huron Statement explaining SDS and the reasons for their actions:

"We are people of this generation, bred in at least modest comfort, housed now in universities, looking uncomfortably to the world we inherit. . . .

When we were kids the United States was the wealthiest and strongest country in the world . . . Freedom and equality for each individual, government of, by, and for the people—these American values we found good. . . .

As we grew, however, our comfort was penetrated by events too troubling to dismiss. First, the permeating and victimizing fact of human degradation, symbolized by the Southern struggle against racial bigotry, compelled most of us from silence to activism. Second, the enclosing fact of the Cold War, symbolized by the presence of the Bomb, brought awareness that we ourselves, and our friends, and millions of abstract 'others' . . . might die at any time.

. . . Our work is guided by the sense that we may be the last generation in the experiment with living. . . . The search for truly democratic alternatives to the present, and a commitment to social experimentation with them, is a worthy and fulfilling human enterprise, one which moves us and, we hope, others today.

—from the *Port Huron Statement*, 1962

C

DBQ Document-Based Questions

1. **Determining Cause and Effect** What two issues led to the activism of the members of SDS?
2. **Summarizing** What were the two goals of the group?

divided. These young people formed what came to be known as the New Left. (The "new" left differed from the "old" left of the 1930s, which had advocated socialism and communism.)

A prominent organization within the New Left was Students for a Democratic Society (SDS), founded in 1959. It defined its views in a 1962 declaration known as the **Port Huron Statement.** Written largely by **Tom Hayden,** editor of the University of Michigan's student newspaper, the declaration called for an end to apathy and urged citizens to stop accepting a country run by big corporations and big government.

SDS chapters focused on protesting the Vietnam War, but they also addressed other issues, including poverty, campus regulations, nuclear power, and racism. In 1968, for example, SDS leaders assisted in an eight-day occupation of several buildings at Columbia University to protest the administration's plan to build a new gym in an area that had served as a neighborhood park near Harlem.

The Free Speech Movement

Another movement that captured the nation's attention in the 1960s was the **Free Speech Movement,** led by Mario Savio and others at the University of California at Berkeley. The movement began when the university decided, in the fall of 1964, to restrict students' rights to distribute literature and to recruit volunteers for political causes on campus. The protesters, however, quickly targeted more general campus matters as well.

Like many college students, those at Berkeley were dissatisfied with practices at their university. Officials divided huge classes into sections taught by graduate students, while many professors claimed they were too busy with research to meet with students. Faceless administrators made rules that were not always easy to obey and imposed punishments for violations. Feeling isolated in this impersonal environment, many Berkeley students rallied to support the Free Speech Movement.

Teach

C Critical Thinking

Analyzing Primary Sources
Have students read the Primary Source on page 911. **Ask:** How did the American values the students had embraced as children help motivate their later protests? *(Racism and inequality were at odds with these values.)* BL

DBQ Document Based Questions

Answers:
1. Accept any two: racism, the Cold War, threat of nuclear attack
2. truly democratic alternatives to the present and social experimentation

Hands-On Chapter Project
Step 1

Presenting a Historical Drama

Step 1: Assigning Groups Small groups of students receive their assignments.

Directions Organize the class into groups and have each prepare a dramatic presentation on one of the situations below or another of their choice. Encourage all students to participate and have each group present their skit to the rest of the class.

- a brother and sister in college trying to explain the counterculture to their parents
- a group of women at the first meeting of the National Organization for Women, setting goals and planning action
- a group of Latino farm workers discussing the benefits and risks of a strike

Putting It Together Encourage students to begin a separate section of their notebooks to take notes on the chapter from the perspective of the Americans they will role-play. OL

(Chapter Project continued on page 915)

W Writing Support

Descriptive Writing Have students study the photo on page 912 and the outward signs that defined the student protest movement. Tell them to write a letter from the viewpoint of a student from a traditional mainstream town arriving at an urban college. The letter should describe the students, sights, sounds, and activities to a friend at home. **OL**

DBQ Document Based Questions

Answers:

1. members of Congress/the government and parents/the older generation
2. Sample answer: He is telling them to either be helpful and understanding or stay out of the way of the young generation.

Reading Check

Answer:
criticism of conformity and materialism; injustices in the political system and society; increased college enrollment

Additional Support

The struggle between Berkeley's students and administrators peaked on December 2, 1964, with a sit-in and powerful speech by Savio. Early the next morning, 600 police officers entered the campus and arrested more than 700 protesters.

The arrests set off an even larger protest movement. Within days, a campus-wide strike had stopped classes and many members of the faculty also voiced their support for the Free Speech Movement. In the face of this growing opposition, the administration gave in to the students' demands.

Soon afterward, the Supreme Court upheld students' rights to freedom of speech and assembly on campuses. In a unanimous vote, the Court upheld the section of the Civil Rights Act assuring these rights in places offering public accommodations, which, by definition, included college campuses. The Berkeley revolt was one of the first major student protests in the 1960s, and it became a model for others. The tactics the Berkeley protesters had used were soon being used in college demonstrations across the country.

Reading Check **Synthesizing** What were three reasons for the growth of the youth movement of the 1960s?

The Counterculture

MAIN Idea Counterculture youths tried to create an alternative to mainstream culture.

HISTORY AND YOU Do you know anyone today who rejects mainstream society? Read on to learn about the ideas of the 1960s counterculture.

While many young Americans in the 1960s sought to reform the system, others rejected it entirely and tried to create a new lifestyle based on flamboyant dress, rock music, drug use, and communal living. They created what became known as the **counterculture** and were commonly called "**hippies.**"

Hippie Culture

Originally, hippies rejected **rationality,** order, and traditional middle-class values. They wanted to build a utopia—a society that was freer, closer to nature, and full of love, empathy, tolerance, and cooperation. Much of this was a reaction to the 1950s stereotype of the white-collar "man in the gray flannel suit" who led a constricted and colorless life.

As the counterculture grew, many newcomers did not understand these ideas. For them, what mattered were the outward signs that

PRIMARY SOURCE

The Counterculture

▲ *Hippies at a festival in New Orleans, Louisiana in 1971*

W

Come senators, congressmen
Please heed the call
Don't stand in the doorway
Don't block up the hall
For he that gets hurt
Will be he who has stalled
There's a battle outside
And it is ragin'.
It'll soon shake your windows
And rattle your walls
For the times they are a-changin'.

Come mothers and fathers
Throughout the land
And don't criticize
What you can't understand
Your sons and your daughters
Are beyond your command
Your old road is
Rapidly agin'.
Please get out of the new one
If you can't lend your hand
For the times they are a-changin'.

—from *"The Times They Are A-Changin'"*

▲ *Bob Dylan performs at the Newport Folk Festival in 1965.*

DBQ Document-Based Questions

1. **Identifying** What two groups does Dylan address in these two stanzas?
2. **Finding the Main Idea** What is Dylan asking these groups to do?

Activity: Interdisciplinary Connection

Music Encourage students to use library and Internet resources to find lyrics for songs that expressed the sentiments of protesters or the counterculture of the 1960s. Have students select three different sets of lyrics and write a paragraph explaining how each one represents these sentiments. Find recordings of one or more of the songs to play for the class. Then discuss with students whether any of the song lyrics could apply to sentiments held by people today. **OL**

defined the movement—long hair, Native American headbands, cowboy boots, long dresses, shabby jeans, and the use of drugs.

Many hippies wanted to drop out of society by leaving home and living together in **communes**—group living arrangements in which members shared everything and worked together. Some hippies established rural communes, while others lived together in parks or crowded apartments in large cities. One of the most famous hippie destinations was San Francisco's **Haight-Ashbury district.** By the mid-1960s, thousands of hippies had flocked there.

The Impact of the Counterculture

After a few years, the counterculture movement began to decline. Some urban hippie communities became dangerous places where muggings and other criminal activity took place. The glamour of drug use waned as more and more young people became addicted or died from overdoses. In addition, many people in the movement had gotten older and moved on. Although the counterculture declined without achieving its utopian ideals, it did change some aspects of American culture.

Fashion Protesters and members of the counterculture often expressed themselves with their clothing. By wearing cheap surplus clothes recycled from earlier decades and repaired with patches, they showed that they were rejecting both consumerism and the social class structure. Ethnic clothing was popular for similar reasons. Beads and fringes imitated Native American costumes, while tie-dyed shirts borrowed techniques from India and Africa.

Perhaps the most potent symbol of the era was hair. Long hair, beards, and mustaches on young men symbolized defiance of both 1950s **conformity**—when buzz cuts were popular—and the military, which required all recruits to have short hair. School officials at the time debated the acceptable length of a student's hair. Over time, however, longer hair on men and more individual clothing for both genders became generally accepted. What was once the clothing of defiance became mainstream.

Music Counterculture musicians made use of folk music and the rhythms of rock 'n' roll and wrote heartfelt lyrics that expressed the hopes and fears of their generation. At festivals such as **Woodstock,** held in upstate New York in August 1969, and in Altamont, California, later that year, hundreds of thousands of people gathered to listen to the new music.

Major folk singers included **Bob Dylan,** who became an important voice of the movement, as did singers Joan Baez and Pete Seeger. Rock musicians popular with the counterculture included Jimi Hendrix, Janis Joplin, and The Who. These musicians used electrically amplified instruments that drastically changed the sound of rock, and their innovations continue to influence musicians today.

Reading Check **Evaluating** What lasting impact did the counterculture have on the nation?

Section 1 REVIEW

Vocabulary

1. **Explain** the significance of: Port Huron Statement, Tom Hayden, Free Speech Movement, counterculture, hippies, communes, Haight-Ashbury district, Woodstock, Bob Dylan.

Main Ideas

2. **Describing** With what issues did SDS concern itself?
3. **Summarizing** What were the core ideals of the members of the counterculture?

Critical Thinking

4. **Big Ideas** How did the U.S. Supreme Court validate the actions of the members of the Free Speech Movement?
5. **Organizing** Use a graphic organizer similar to the one below to list the causes of the youth movement.

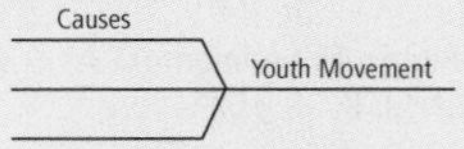

6. **Analyzing Visuals** Study the image on page 911. Why do you think that older adults were frightened or threatened by the student movement?

Writing About History

7. **Descriptive Writing** Suppose that you are a journalist in the 1960s. Write an article in which you visit a commune and describe the hippie culture of the day.

History ONLINE
Study Central™ To review this section, go to glencoe.com and click on Study Central.

Reading Check

Answer:
changes in fashion and music and the idea that alternatives to mainstream culture were possible

Assess

History ONLINE

Study Central™ provides summaries, interactive games, and online graphic organizers to help students review content.

Close

Summarizing Ask: What were the goals and accomplishments of the student movement and the counterculture? *(They wanted a society that was free of war, poverty, pressure to conform, and materialism; was tolerant; and offered equal justice and opportunity for all. Students won freedom of speech, assembly, and public protest in general. The counterculture liberalized fashion, influenced music and lessened pressure to conform.)*

Section 1 REVIEW

Answers

1. All definitions can be found in the section and the Glossary.
2. It focused on protesting the Vietnam War, but it also addressed other issues, including poverty, racism, freedom of speech and assembly, and nuclear power, unequal distribution of wealth.
3. They wanted a society that was freer, closer to nature, and full of love, empathy, tolerance, and cooperation.
4. It upheld the rights to freedom of speech and of assembly on campuses.
5. criticism of conformity and materialism, baby boom and increased college enrollments, social and political injustice
6. Possible answer: The students' culture was completely different from the culture of their parents. The young people appeared unkempt, they seemed disrespectful of the values of their parents, and they were vocal and angry.
7. Students' articles will vary. Articles should include descriptions of hippie commune life based on the section and students' prior knowledge.

Focus

Bellringer

Daily Focus Transparency 27-2

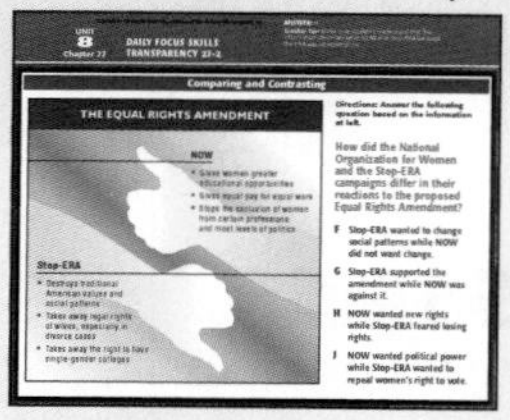

Guide to Reading

Answers: League of Women Voters: promoted laws to protect women and children; National Woman's Party: opposed protective legislation because it reinforced workplace discrimination

Section Spotlight Video

To generate student interest and provide a springboard for class discussion, access the Chapter 27, Section 2 video at glencoe.com or on the video DVD.

Section 2 — Section Audio — Spotlight Video

The Feminist Movement

Guide to Reading

Big Ideas

Struggles for Rights Women organized to claim their rights and responsibilities as citizens.

Content Vocabulary

- feminism *(p. 914)*

Academic Vocabulary

- gender *(p. 915)*
- compatible *(p. 919)*

People and Events to Identify

- Equal Pay Act *(p. 915)*
- Betty Friedan *(p. 915)*
- National Organization for Women (NOW) *(p. 916)*
- Gloria Steinem *(p. 916)*
- Equal Rights Amendment (ERA) *(p. 917)*
- Phyllis Schlafly *(p. 918)*
- Title IX *(p. 918)*

Reading Strategy

Categorizing Use a graphic organizer similar to the one below to list the main arguments for and against the Equal Rights Amendment (ERA).

For ERA	Against ERA

By the 1960s, many women had become increasingly dissatisfied with society's perception of women and their place in society. Some women began to join organizations aimed at improving their role in society. The Equal Rights Amendment stirred a national debate.

A Renewed Women's Movement

MAIN Idea Women in the 1960s and 1970s began creating organizations to change society through education and legislative action.

HISTORY AND YOU Have you ever read a book that spurred you to action or got you excited? Read on to learn about a book that helped define and reawaken the women's movement.

African Americans and college students were not the only groups seeking to change American society in the 1960s. By the middle of the decade, a new women's movement had emerged as many women became discontent with their status and treatment in American society. This movement became known as the feminist movement, or the women's liberation movement.

Feminism—the belief that men and women should be equal politically, economically, and socially—had been a weak and often embattled force since the adoption of the Nineteenth Amendment guaranteeing women's voting rights in 1920. Soon after the amendment was ratified, the women's movement split into two camps. For the next 40 years, it had very little political influence.

The onset of World War II provided women with greater opportunity, at least temporarily. With many men enlisted in the army, women became an integral part of the nation's workforce. After the war, however, many women returned to their traditional role of homemaker. Even though 8 million American women had gone to work during the war, the new postwar emphasis on having babies and establishing families discouraged women from seeking employment. Many Americans assumed that a good mother should stay home to raise her children.

Despite the popular emphasis on homemaking, however, the number of women who held jobs outside the home actually increased during the 1950s. Most women who went to work did so in order to help their families maintain their comfortable lifestyles. By 1960, nearly one-third of all married women were part of the paid workforce. Yet many people continued to believe that women, even college-educated women, could better serve society by remaining in the home to influence the next generation of men.

Resource Manager

R Reading Strategies	C Critical Thinking	D Differentiated Instruction	W Writing Support	S Skill Practice
Teacher Edition • Taking Notes, p. 916 • Academic Vocab., p. 917 **Additional Resources** • American Lit. Read., URB p. 17 • Guided Read., URB p. 145	**Teacher Edition** • Analyzing Prim. Sources, pp. 915, 918 **Additional Resources** • Linking Past and Present, URB p. 130 • Interp. Pol. Cartoons Act., URB p. 137 • Supreme Court Case Studies, p. 115 • Quizzes and Tests, p. 384	**Additional Resources** • Interp. Pol. Cartoons, URB p. 137 • Differentiated Instr. Act., URB p. 119	**Teacher Edition** • Persuasive Writing, p. 916	**Additional Resources** • Read. Essen., p. 298 • Reinforcing Skills Act., URB p. 127

PRIMARY SOURCE

What Caused the Women's Movement?

The women's movement was revitalized in the 1960s, partly because of the efforts of the President's Commission on the Status of Women, and partly because writers, such as Betty Friedan, convinced women the time had come to take action.

▲ *President Kennedy meets with Eleanor Roosevelt, Representative Edith Green (center) and Esther Peterson, director of the Women's Bureau at the Department of Labor (right) in early 1962 to discuss the findings of the President's Commission on the Status of Women.*

PRIMARY SOURCE

In 1963 Betty Friedan tried to describe the feelings that would lead to the rebirth of the women's movement:

▲ *Betty Friedan, 1972*

"The problem lay buried, unspoken, for many years in the minds of American women. . . . Each suburban housewife struggled with it alone. As she made the beds, shopped for groceries, matched slipcover material, ate peanut butter sandwiches with her children, chauffeured Cub Scouts and Brownies . . . she was afraid to ask even of herself the silent question—'Is this all?'

. . . In the fifteen years after World War II, this mystique of feminine fulfillment became the cherished and self-perpetuating core of contemporary American culture. Millions of women lived their lives in the image of those pretty pictures of the American suburban housewife . . . Words like 'emancipation' and 'career' sounded strange and embarrassing. . . .

But on an April morning in 1959, I heard a mother of four, having coffee with four other mothers in a suburban development . . . say in a tone of quiet desperation, 'the problem.' And the others knew, without words, that she was not talking about a problem with her husband, or her children, or her home. Suddenly they realized they all shared the same problem, the problem that has no name.

. . . Sometimes a woman would say 'I feel empty somehow . . . incomplete.' Or she would say, 'I feel as if I don't exist.'"

—from *The Feminine Mystique*

C

DBQ Document-Based Questions

1. **Making Inferences** What was the "feminine mystique"?
2. **Drawing Conclusions** What do you think "the problem" was?
3. **Hypothesizing** Why might President Kennedy have wanted Eleanor Roosevelt to head the commission studying the status of women?

Origins of the Movement

By the early 1960s, many women were increasingly resentful of a world where newspaper ads separated jobs by **gender,** banks denied them credit, and, worst of all, they often were paid less for the same work. Women found themselves shut out of higher-paying professions such as law, medicine, and finance. By the mid-1960s, about 47 percent of American women were in the workforce, but three-fourths of them worked in lower paying clerical, sales, or factory jobs, or as cleaning women and hospital attendants.

Workplace Rights One stimulus that invigorated the women's movement was the President's Commission on the Status of Women, established by President Kennedy and headed by Eleanor Roosevelt. The commission's report highlighted the problems faced by women in the workplace and helped create a network of feminist activists who lobbied Congress for women's legislation. In 1963, with the support of organized labor, they won passage of the **Equal Pay Act,** which in most cases outlawed paying men more than women for the same job.

The Feminine Mystique Although many working women were angry about inequality in the workplace, many other women who had stayed home were also discontent. **Betty Friedan** tried to describe the reasons for their discontent in her book *The Feminine Mystique,* published in 1963.

Teach

C Critical Thinking

Analyzing Primary Sources
Have students read the Primary Source quotation. **Ask:** Do you agree that the only way women in the 1960s could go was up? *(Answers will vary. Some students may point out that they could have lost rights gained earlier, such as the right to vote and own property. Others might point out that these women enjoyed more rights than some women around the world enjoy today.)* **OL**

DBQ Document Based Questions

Answers:

1. The "feminine mystique" was the postwar myth that all women should be completely fulfilled as wives and mothers and not seek professional interests outside the home.
2. "The problem" was that many women felt incomplete and unfulfilled as wives and mothers operating solely in the home.
3. The former First Lady had a history of support for civil rights and human rights.

Hands-On Chapter Project
Step 2

Presenting a Historical Drama

Step 2: Write and Plan the Drama Students begin to write their scripts, including lines and stage directions. They create any props they might need, such as posters, signs, buttons, or headbands.

Directions Remind students that their dramas should be based on the content of the section. Written scripts can be rough guides, with students free to improvise. Props should be appropriate to protests of the time and the situation they will enact.

Putting It Together Ask students to read each others' drafts and suggest changes for the second draft. **OL**

(Chapter Project continued on page 921)

R Reading Strategy

Taking Notes Have students use the heads of the section to create a study outline. As they complete each subhead, have them write notes about the important points. Then encourage them to discuss their outlines with a partner and make any modifications that would improve their notes. BL

W Writing Support

Persuasive Writing Have students write an editorial supporting or challenging the EEOC's decision that jobs and want ads could be gender-specific. Then have them write a letter to the editor arguing against the position taken in the editorial. OL

Reading Check

Answer:
the mass protests of ordinary women and the President's Commission on the Status of Women

Additional Support

Friedan had traveled around the country interviewing women who had graduated with her from Smith College in 1942. She found that while most of these women reported having everything they could want in life, they still felt unfulfilled.

Friedan's book became a best-seller. Many women began reaching out to one another, pouring out their anger and sadness in what came to be known as consciousness-raising sessions. While they talked informally about their unhappiness, they were also building the base for a nationwide mass movement.

R **The Civil Rights Act and Women** Congress gave the women's movement another boost by including them in the 1964 Civil Rights Act. Title VII of the act outlawed job discrimination not only on the basis of race, color, religion, and national origin, but also on the basis of gender. The law provided a strong legal basis for the changes the women's movement would later demand.

Given the era's attitudes about what kind of work was proper for women, simply having the law on the books was not enough. Even the agency charged with administering the civil rights act—the Equal Employment W Opportunity Commission (EEOC)—accepted the idea that jobs could be gender-specific. In 1965 the commission ruled that gender-segregated help-wanted ads were legal.

R The Time Is NOW

By June 1966, Betty Friedan returned to an idea that she and other women had been considering—the need for an organization to promote feminist goals. On the back of a napkin she scribbled that it was time "to take the actions needed to bring women into the mainstream of American society, now . . . in fully equal partnership with men." Friedan and others then set out to form the **National Organization for Women** (NOW).

In October 1966, a group of about 300 women and men held the founding conference of NOW. "The time has come," its founders declared, "to confront with concrete action the conditions which now prevent women from enjoying the equality of opportunity and freedom of choice which is their right as individual Americans and as human beings."

The new organization responded to frustrated housewives by demanding greater educational opportunities for women. The group also focused much of its energy on aiding women in the workplace. NOW leaders denounced the exclusion of women from certain professions and from most levels of politics. They lashed out against the practice of paying women less than men for equal work, a practice the Equal Pay Act had not eliminated.

When NOW set out to pass an Equal Rights Amendment to the Constitution, its membership rose to over 200,000. By July 1972, the movement had its own magazine, *Ms.*, which kept readers informed about women's issues. The editor of the magazine was **Gloria Steinem,** an author who became one of the movement's leading figures.

Reading Check **Identifying** What two forces helped bring the women's movement to life again?

Debates IN HISTORY

Should the Equal Rights Amendment Be Ratified?

In the 1970s ratification of the Equal Rights Amendment (ERA) was a hotly debated issue. Organizations such as NOW and other supporters of the amendment fought hard for its ratification. One of these was U.S. Representative Shirley Chisholm, who spoke out in support of the ERA in a speech to Congress in 1970. In 1971 conservative activist Phyllis Schlafly formed the group Stop-ERA to fight the legislation.

Extending the Content

Equal Rights Amendment In 1923 the National Woman's Party (NWP) introduced an Equal Rights Amendment to the U.S. Constitution. Some version of the ERA was introduced into every session of Congress between 1923 and 1972, when it was passed. It was sent to the states for ratification with a seven-year time limit, which was extended to 1982. The opposition that defeated the 1973 ERA was similar in many ways to opposition that derailed the earlier amendment. People concerned about women's welfare feared that legal equality threatened laws that protected women.

Successes and Failures

MAIN Idea The women's movement made gains for women in education and employment but has not achieved complete equality for women.

HISTORY AND YOU Have you ever seen men and women treated differently because of their gender? Read to learn how the women's movement tried to get equal treatment for women in the 1960s and 1970s.

During the late 1960s and early 1970s, the women's movement fought to amend the Constitution and enforce Title VII of the Civil Rights Act, lobbied to repeal laws against abortion, and worked for legislation against gender discrimination in employment, housing, and education. The movement had many successes, but also encountered strong opposition to some of the reforms it wanted.

The Equal Rights Amendment

The women's movement seemed to be off to a strong start when Congress passed the **Equal Rights Amendment** (ERA) in March 1972. The amendment specified that "Equality of rights under the law shall not be denied or abridged by the United States or by any State on account of sex." To become part of the Constitution, the amendment had to be ratified by 38 states. Many states did so—35 by 1979—but by then, significant opposition to the amendment had begun to build up. R

Opponents of the ERA argued that it would take away some traditional rights, such as the right to alimony in divorce cases or the right to have single-gender colleges. They also feared it would allow women to be drafted into the military and eliminate laws that provided special protection for women in the workforce.

YES

Shirley Chisholm
Member of the U.S. House of Representatives

PRIMARY SOURCE

"Discrimination against women . . . is so widespread that it seems to many persons normal, natural and right. . . .

It is time we act to assure full equality of opportunity . . . to women.

The argument that this amendment will not solve the problem of sex discrimination is not relevant. . . . Of course laws will not eliminate prejudice from the hearts of human beings. But that is no reason to allow prejudice to continue to be enshrined in our laws. . . . The Constitution they wrote was designed to protect the rights of white, male citizens. As there were no black Founding Fathers, there were no founding mothers—a great pity, on both counts. It is not too late to complete the work they left undone."

—speech before Congress, August 10, 1970

NO

Phyllis Schlafly
Author and Conservative Activist

PRIMARY SOURCE

"This Amendment will absolutely and positively make women subject to the draft. Why any woman would support such a ridiculous and un-American proposal as this is beyond comprehension. . . . Foxholes are bad enough for men, but they certainly are *not* the place for women—and we should reject any proposal which would put them there in the name of 'equal rights.'. . .

Another bad effect of the Equal Rights Amendment is that it will abolish a woman's right to child support and alimony . . .

Under present American laws, the man is *always* required to support his wife and each child he caused to be brought into the world. Why should women abandon these good laws . . . ?"

—from the *Phyllis Schlafly Report*, February 1972

DBQ Document-Based Questions

1. **Summarizing** Why does Chisholm believe that the ERA is necessary?
2. **Explaining** What does Schlafly say was the main flaw in the arguments of the ERA supporters?
3. **Evaluating** With which position do you agree? Write a paragraph to explain your choice.

R Reading Strategy

Academic Vocabulary Point out the term *abridged* in the second column. Help students use a dictionary and the context to define the word as "reduced." Ask them in what ways equality under the law might be abridged because of gender. Remind them that many words have different meanings or shades of meaning depending on their context. ELL

Debates IN HISTORY

Answers:

1. To assure equality of opportunity in a society where discrimination is so ingrained that many people consider it right.
2. That it will subject women to the military draft and abolish a woman's right to alimony and child support.
3. Students' paragraphs will vary. Paragraphs should be based on points from both women, as well as personal experience and observation.

Activity: Collaborative Learning

Role Playing Have students work in pairs. One partner in each pair should list what women in 1972 had to lose with the passage of the Equal Rights Amendment, while the other partner lists what women stood to gain. Tell students to draw on chapter content and their own knowledge. Students may also use library or Internet sources to conduct further research. After students have completed their lists, have them share the list with their partner. After partners have studied each other's lists, invite pairs to role-play for the class two state legislators discussing whether or not to vote for ratification. AL

C Critical Thinking

Analyzing Primary Sources
Have students study the graphs in the Primary Source feature. **Ask:** What might account for the continuing gap between women's and men's median incomes? *(Answers will vary. Some may say that women are still ending up in lower paid professions. Others may say women's roles as primary parents may exert downward pressure on a self-employed woman's income or the ability of a salaried woman to advance.)* **OL**

Analyzing VISUALS

Answers:
1. from 30% to 60% (a 100% increase between 1950 and 2000)
2. They made no real gains compared to men—the difference between women's and men's median income was still about the same in 2000 as it was in 1970.

One outspoken opponent was **Phyllis Schlafly,** who organized the Stop-ERA campaign. By the end of 1979, four states had voted to rescind their approval. Many people had become worried that the amendment would give federal courts too much power to interfere with state laws. Unable to achieve ratification by three-fourths of the states by the deadline set by Congress, the Equal Rights Amendment finally failed in 1982.

Equality in Education

One major achievement of the movement came in the area of education. Kathy Striebel's experience illustrated the discrimination female students often faced in the early 1970s. In 1971 Striebel, a high school junior in St. Paul, Minnesota, wanted to compete for her school's swim team, but the school did not allow girls to join. Kathy's mother, Charlotte, was a member of the local NOW chapter. Through it, she learned that St. Paul had recently banned gender discrimination in education. She filed a grievance with the city's human rights department, and officials required the school to allow Kathy to swim.

For further information on the case of *Roe* v. *Wade*, see page R60 in **Supreme Court Case Summaries.**

Shortly after joining the team, Kathy beat out one of the boys and earned a spot at a meet. As she stood on the block waiting to swim, the opposing coach declared that she was ineligible because the meet was outside St. Paul and thus beyond the jurisdiction of its laws. "They pulled that little girl right off the block," Charlotte Striebel recalled angrily.

Recognizing the problem, leaders of the women's movement lobbied Congress to ban gender discrimination in education. In 1972 Congress responded by passing a law known collectively as the Educational Amendments. One section, **Title IX,** prohibited federally funded schools from discriminating against women in nearly all aspects of its operations, from admissions to athletics.

Right to Privacy and *Roe* v. *Wade*

One aspect of the feminist movement was securing the right to make private decisions, including reproductive decisions. A constitutional right to marital privacy was introduced in 1965 when the Supreme Court outlawed state bans on contraceptives for married couples in *Griswold* v. *Connecticut.* The right to privacy was

PRIMARY SOURCE

The Changing Status of Women

Women's roles were changing in society. Although the ERA failed, more women entered the workforce and gender discrimination in schools was banned with the passage of Title IX.

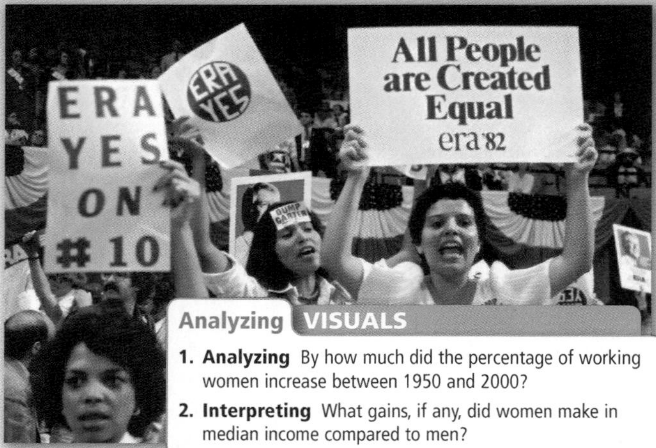

Analyzing VISUALS

1. **Analyzing** By how much did the percentage of working women increase between 1950 and 2000?
2. **Interpreting** What gains, if any, did women make in median income compared to men?

Women in the Workforce

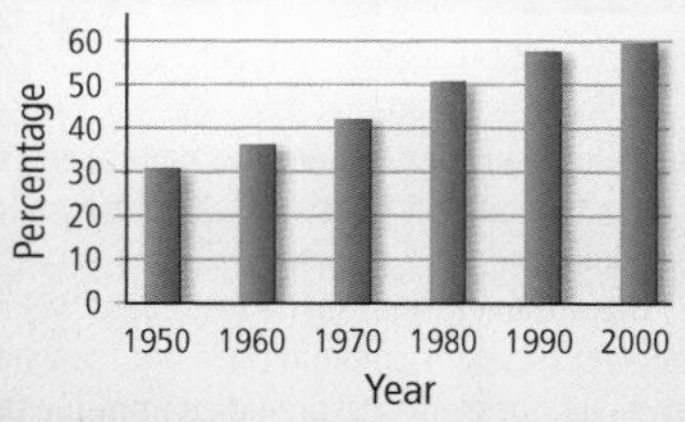

Source: *Historical Statistics of the United States: Earliest Times to the Present, Volume 2.*

Median Income, 1970–2000

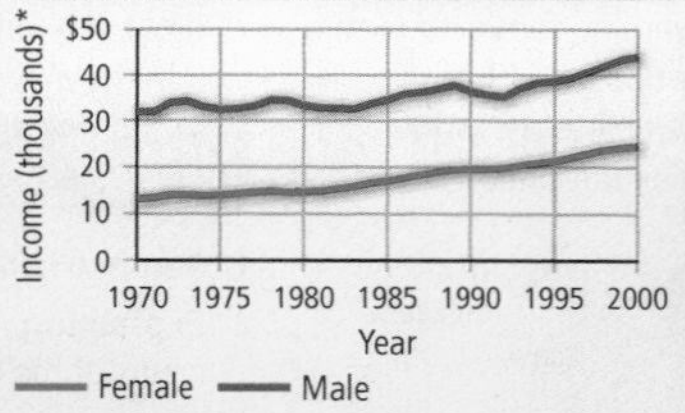

*Amount is in 2004 dollars.

Source: U.S. Census Bureau.

C

Additional Support

Activity: Technology Connection

Title IX Tell students that Title IX of the 1972 Educational Amendments is still a frequently debated topic. Share these statistics: Girls' participation in high school athletics has increased from fewer than 300,000 in the 1970s to almost 3 million; but girls still receive fewer opportunities to participate than boys do. Male college athletes receive $133 million more in athletic scholarship assistance. Coaches of women's teams receive about 35 percent less than coaches of men's teams. Have students discuss the participation of girls in their school's athletics program and other school activities. **Ask:** How might these activities have been different before the Educational Amendments? *(Answers will vary, but may mention the fact that most schools have women participating on athletic teams that may not have been funded before 1972.)* Ask students to choose a female student athlete and use the Internet to find information for a brief written report. Encourage them to download photographs to illustrate their reports. **OL**

expanded beyond married couples when activists began challenging laws against abortion. Until 1973, the right to regulate abortion was reserved to the states. This matched the original plan of the Constitution, which reserved all police power—the power to control people and property in the interest of safety, health, welfare, and morals—to the state. Early in the country's history, some abortions were permitted in the early stages of pregnancy, but by the mid-1800s, states had passed laws prohibiting abortion, except to save the life of the mother.

In the late 1960s, some states began adopting more liberal abortion laws. For example, several states allowed abortion if carrying a baby to term might endanger the woman's mental health or if she was a victim of rape or incest. The big change came with the 1973 Supreme Court decision in *Roe* v. *Wade,* which stated that state governments could not regulate abortion during the first three months of pregnancy, a time that was said to be within a woman's constitutional right to privacy. During the second three months of pregnancy, states could regulate abortions on the basis of the health of the mother. States could ban abortion in the final three months except in cases of a medical emergency. Those in favor of abortion rights cheered *Roe* v. *Wade* as a victory, but the issue was far from settled politically. The decision gave rise to the right-to-life movement, whose members consider abortion morally wrong and advocate its total ban.

After the *Roe* v. *Wade* ruling, the two sides began an impassioned battle that continues today. In the 1992 case *Planned Parenthood* v. *Casey,* the Supreme Court modified *Roe* v. *Wade*. The court decided that states could place some restrictions on all abortions, such as requiring doctors to explain the risks and require their patients to give "informed consent," or requiring underage girls to inform their parents before obtaining an abortion. The court struck down laws requiring women to notify their husbands before having an abortion, and abandoned the rule that states could ban abortion only in the final three months. Technology had now made it possible for the fetus to be viable outside the womb much earlier in a pregnancy. States could now restrict abortion based on the viability of the fetus.

The Impact of the Feminist Movement

The women's movement has profoundly changed society. Since the 1970s, many women have pursued college degrees and careers outside of the home, and two-career families are much more common than they were in the 1950s and 1960s. Many employers now offer options to help make work more **compatible** with family life, including flexible hours, on-site child care, and job sharing.

Even with those changes, a significant income gap between men and women still exists. A major reason for the gap is that many working women still hold lower-paying jobs such as bank tellers, administrative assistants, cashiers, schoolteachers, and nurses. It is in professional jobs that women have made the most dramatic gains since the 1970s. By 2000, women made up over 40 percent of the nation's graduates receiving medical or law degrees.

Reading Check **Summarizing** What successes and failures did the women's movement experience during the late 1960s and early 1970s?

Section 2 REVIEW

Vocabulary

1. **Explain** the significance of: feminism, Equal Pay Act, Betty Friedan, National Organization for Women (NOW), Gloria Steinem, Equal Rights Amendment (ERA), Phyllis Schlafly, Title IX.

Main Ideas

2. **Explaining** Why did more women work outside the home in the 1950s?
3. **Explaining** Why were some people against passage of the ERA?

Critical Thinking

4. **Big Ideas** What gains have been made in women's rights since the 1960s?
5. **Organizing** Use a graphic organizer similar to the one below to list the major achievements of the women's movement.

6. **Analyzing Visuals** Study the bar graph on page 918. What was the first year in which approximately half of all women were in the workforce?

Writing About History

7. **Persuasive Writing** Assume the role of a supporter or an opponent of the ERA. Write a letter to the editor of your local newspaper to persuade people to support your position.

History ONLINE
Study Central™ To review this section, go to glencoe.com and click on Study Central.

Reading Check

Answer:
Successes: the Educational Amendments/Title IX, abortion rights, and improved working conditions and educational opportunities; Failures: not passing the ERA, lingering income gap, most women still hold low-paying jobs

Assess

History ONLINE

Study Central™ provides summaries, interactive games, and online graphic organizers to help students review content.

Close

Summarizing Ask: What were the goals and accomplishments of the feminist movement that began in the 1960s? *(Women wanted, and achieved, better educational and career opportunities, more career choices, laws requiring equal pay for equal work, and reproductive choice.)*

Section 2 REVIEW

Answers

1. All definitions can be found in the section and the Glossary.
2. Women worked outside the home to help the family enjoy a more comfortable lifestyle.
3. They were afraid of losing traditional protections and rights, such as the exemption from military combat service, the right to alimony, and the right to have single-gender colleges.
4. More women have achieved equal pay for equal work, better educational opportunities, more career choices, and more political power.
5. Equal Pay Act, Title VII in the Civil Rights Act, Title IX, *Roe* v. *Wade*, more career possibilities
6. 1980
7. Students' letters will vary but should express a clear and logically reasoned viewpoint.

Focus

Bellringer

Daily Focus Transparency 27-3

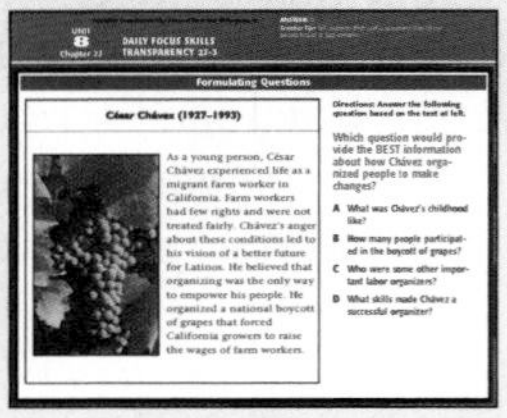

Guide to Reading

Answers may include: 1929: LULAC founded; 1947: *Mendez* v. *Westminster* ends school segregation in California; 1954: *Hernandez* v. *Texas* increases Latino rights in Texas; 1966: Chávez and Huerta form the United Farm Workers; 1967: José Angel Gutiérrez founds MAYO; 1968: Bilingual Education Act passes; 1969: Gutiérrez founds La Raza Unida

Section Spotlight Video

To generate student interest and provide a springboard for class discussion, access the Chapter 27, Section 3 video at glencoe.com or on the video DVD.

Section 3 — Section Audio — Spotlight Video

Latino Americans Organize

Guide to Reading

Big Ideas

Struggles for Rights Latinos organized to fight discrimination and to gain access to better education and jobs.

Content Vocabulary
- repatriation *(p. 922)*
- bilingualism *(p. 925)*

Academic Vocabulary
- likewise *(p. 920)*
- adequate *(p. 924)*

People and Events to Identify
- League of United Latin American Citizens *(p. 923)*
- American GI Forum *(p. 924)*
- César Chávez *(p. 925)*
- Dolores Huerta *(p. 925)*
- United Farm Workers *(p. 925)*
- *La Raza Unida* *(p. 925)*
- Bilingual Education Act *(p. 925)*

Reading Strategy

Organizing Complete a time line similar to the one below to record major events in the struggle of Latinos for equal civil and political rights.

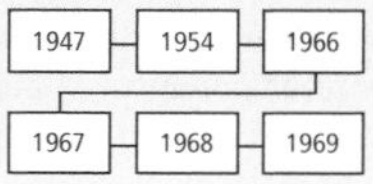

Most Mexican Americans and Mexican immigrants lived in the Southwest, where many faced discrimination in jobs and housing. By the mid-twentieth century, more immigrants arrived from various parts of Latin America. Latinos formed civil rights organizations to challenge discrimination.

Latinos Migrate North

MAIN Idea Mexicans, the largest Spanish-speaking immigrant group, faced discrimination and segregation in the West and Southwest.

HISTORY AND YOU Have you ever heard of immigrants getting their "green cards," which permit them to work in the United States? Read on to learn how the Bracero Program allowed some Mexicans to work on a temporary basis.

Americans of Mexican heritage have lived in what is now the United States since before the founding of the republic. Their numbers steadily increased in the 1800s, in part because the United States acquired territory where Mexicans already lived, and in part because Mexicans began migrating north to live in the United States. In the twentieth century, Mexican immigration rose dramatically.

In 1910 the Mexican Revolution began and the resulting turmoil prompted a wave of emigration from Mexico that lasted more than a decade. During the 1920s, half a million Mexicans immigrated to the United States through official channels, and an unknown number entered the country through other means. Precise population estimates are impossible to determine because many Mexicans frequently moved back and forth across the border.

Not surprisingly, persons of Mexican heritage remained concentrated in the areas that were once the northern provinces of Mexico. In 1930, 90 percent of ethnic Mexicans in the United States lived in Texas, California, Arizona, New Mexico, and Colorado. In Texas, the favorite destinations for Mexican immigrants, cities such as San Antonio and El Paso, had large populations of Mexican Americans and Mexican immigrants. As a result of heavy Mexican immigration, the ethnic Mexican population in Texas grew from 71,062 in 1900 to 683,681 in 1930. Southern California, **likewise,** had a large Spanish-speaking population.

Of course, not all Mexican Americans remained in the West and Southwest. In the 1910s and 1920s, along with Americans of other ethnic backgrounds, many Mexican Americans headed for the cities of the Midwest and Northeast, where they found jobs in factories.

Resource Manager

R Reading Strategies	C Critical Thinking	D Differentiated Instruction	W Writing Support	S Skill Practice
Teacher Edition • Read. Prim. Sources, p. 924 **Additional Resources** • Guid. Read. Act., URB p. 146 • Prim. Source Reading, URB p. 133	**Teacher Edition** • Analyzing Prim. Sources, pp. 922, 923 **Additional Resources** • Quizzes and Tests, p. 385 • Supreme Court Case Studies, p. 107	**Teacher Edition** • Logical/Math, p. 921 **Additional Resources** • English Learner Act., URB p. 121	**Additional Resources** • Academic Vocab. Act., URB p. 126	**Additional Resources** • Hist. Skills Analysis, URB p. 118 • Read. Essen., p. 301

PRIMARY SOURCE

Latinos Arrive in America, 1910–1950

In the twentieth century, Latinos, mainly Mexicans, began to enter the United States in large numbers settling mostly in the West and Southwest. Others, who came from Puerto Rico or Cuba, often settled in the barrios of the large cities in the East.

▲ *These refugees, guarded by U.S. troops at Fort Bliss, Texas, were some of the more than 500,000 who came to the United States to escape the turmoil of the Mexican Revolution.*

▲ *Family of Mexican migrant workers, who came to the United States as part of the Bracero program during World War II*

Growth of Latino Population in the U.S.

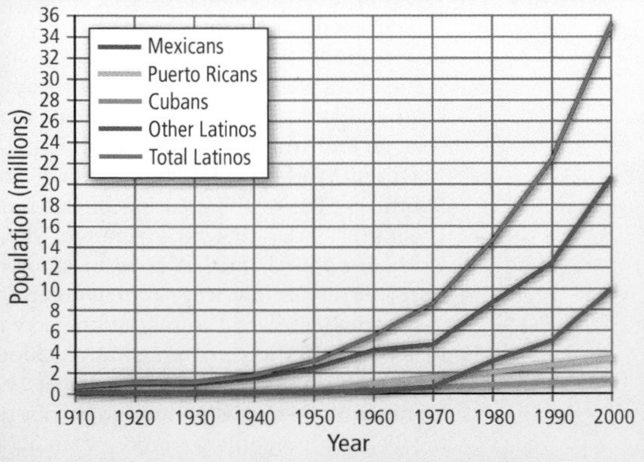

Source: *Historical Statistics of the United States: Earliest Times to the Present, Volume 1.*

Analyzing VISUALS

1. **Interpreting** The U.S. Latino population is made up of which main groups?
2. **Drawing Conclusions** Why have Latino Americans experienced a growing political influence in recent years?

Mexicans Face Discrimination

Across the Southwest, most Mexican Americans lived in barrios. Barrios were the product of a combination of the region's history and discrimination against Latinos. Los Angeles, for example, was founded as a Spanish town in 1781. When English-speaking settlers arrived a century later, they built around the older Spanish-speaking district.

Residential segregation, however, also had roots in ethnic discrimination. With heavy Mexican immigration in the early twentieth century, the ethnic Mexican population of Los Angeles grew from 5,000 in 1900 to around 190,000 in 1930. By that time, the Spanish-speaking population was segregated in the eastern part of the city, where most lived in small, dilapidated housing and suffered high rates of infant mortality and disease. **D**

In California and across the Southwest, discrimination in employment meant that most ethnic Mexicans could find work only in low-paying jobs. Many lived in rural areas where they worked as agricultural laborers. Ernesto Galarza was eight years old when his family immigrated to California and settled in Sacramento in 1913. In his autobiography, he recalled the importance of the barrio to new immigrants:

Teach

D Differentiated Instruction

Logical/Mathematical Have students read the figures in the first two lines of the second column. **Ask:** Of the Mexican Americans living in Los Angeles in 1930, what percentage had arrived since 1900? *(97.4)* **OL**

Analyzing VISUALS

Answers:

1. Mexican, Puerto Rican, and Cuban
2. growing numbers and political and labor organizations

Hands-On Chapter Project
Step 3

Presenting a Historical Drama

Step 3: Present the Drama Students rehearse and present their dramas. They watch the dramas of other groups.

Directions Remind students that scripts can be rough guides. They are free to improvise during the dramatization, as long as any ad-libbed lines are based on the content of the section. Have students rehearse until they are comfortable and ready to present. Students should be attentive during the presentations of other groups.

Putting It Together As students do their presentations ask the class to take notes as to the historical accuracy of the presentation. **OL**

(Chapter Project continued on Visual Summary page)

C Critical Thinking

Analyzing Primary Sources Direct students to the Primary Source quotation. **Ask:** How did the barrio both help Latino immigrants and hold them back economically? *(The barrio helped them meet basic needs and gave them a supportive community. It also resulted in de facto segregation, which leads to de facto segregation in schools and may have tended to keep Latino immigrants out of areas where better economic opportunities were available. Living in a Spanish-speaking area may have discouraged learning of English, which also restricted economic opportunities.)* OL

Reading Check

Answer: The program sometimes targeted people for "looking Mexican" and often did not distinguish between legal and illegal immigrants.

Additional Support

PRIMARY SOURCE

C "For the Mexicans the *barrio* was a colony of refugees. We came to know families from Chihuahua, Sonora, Jalisco, and Durango. . . . As poor refugees, their first concern was to find a place to sleep, then to eat and find work. In the *barrio* they were most likely to find all three, for not knowing English, they needed something that was even more urgent than a room, a meal, or a job, and that was information in a language they could understand."

—from *Barrio Boy*

During the Great Depression of the 1930s, approximately one-third of the Mexican population in the United States returned to Mexico. Some left voluntarily, believing it would be easier to get by in Mexico. Many Mexican Americans, however, faced increased hostility and discrimination as unemployment rates soared in the early 1930s.

Then, federal officials launched a series of deportations that not only included immigrants from Mexico but often their American-born children as well. This return to Mexico became known as the **repatriation.**

During World War II, labor shortages in the Southwest led to the creation of the Bracero Program. Under this arrangement, Mexican workers entered into short-term labor contracts, mostly as low-wage farm workers.

Meanwhile, illegal immigration increased. In 1954 Eisenhower's administration launched a program intended to deport illegal Latino immigrants. Police swept through barrios seeking illegal immigrants, and more than 3.7 million Mexicans were deported over the next three years. The raids were criticized in the United States and in Mexico for intimidating people for simply looking "Mexican." In addition, the program often failed to distinguish between individuals legally in the country (some of whom were U.S. citizens) and those who had entered illegally.

Other Latinos Arrive

Although Mexicans remained the largest group of Spanish-speaking newcomers in the 1950s, large numbers of Puerto Ricans arrived as well. American citizens since 1917, Puerto Ricans may move freely within American territory. After World War II, economic troubles in Puerto Rico prompted over a million Puerto Ricans to move to the mainland United States. American factory owners and employment agencies had also begun to recruit in Puerto Rico for workers, and the advent of relatively cheap air travel made immigration easier. The majority of Puerto Ricans settled in New York City. There, they suffered racial discrimination and alarmingly high levels of poverty.

The United States also became home to more than 350,000 Cuban immigrants in the decade after the Cuban Revolution of 1959. Many Cubans fleeing the Communist regime were professionals or business owners who settled in and around Miami, Florida. Most were welcomed in the United States because they were middle class or affluent and viewed as refugees fleeing Communist oppression. In 1960 about 3 million Latinos lived in the United States. By the late 1960s, more than 9 million Latinos lived in the United States.

Reading Check **Summarizing** What were some of the criticisms of Eisenhower's deportation program?

PRIMARY SOURCE

Latinos in the United States

By the late 1960s, approximately 9 million Latinos lived in the United States. Although many were citizens, they still faced segregation, discrimination, and other forms of racial prejudice. However, with their increasing population and through political protest and legal action they began to work to improve conditions.

▲ *Latino dancers in a traditional dance at a fiesta in Taos, New Mexico*

Extending the Content

Puerto Rican Immigrants During the 1940s, Puerto Rico began to industrialize. Many Puerto Ricans moved from rural to urban areas, causing a jump in the urban population. Between 1940 and 1970, the proportion of the Puerto Rican population living in rural areas dropped from 70 percent to 42 percent. With so many people moving from rural areas to cities, the number of workers grew faster than jobs. As a result, migration from Puerto Rico to the mainland United States was extensive from the early 1940s through the 1960s as Puerto Ricans left to find work. Unemployment in Puerto Rico rose again during the 1970s, when worldwide inflation and a recession in the U.S. economy stalled Puerto Rico's economic growth.

Latinos Organize

MAIN Idea Latino civil rights organizations, such as LULAC and the American GI Forum, fought against discrimination.

HISTORY AND YOU Recall what you learned about the decision in the Supreme Court case *Brown* v. *Board of Education.* Read on to find out how LULAC filed similar lawsuits challenging discrimination against Mexican Americans.

The Latino community in the West and Southwest included American citizens and immigrant noncitizens. Regardless of their citizenship status, however, people of Mexican heritage were often treated as outsiders by the English-speaking majority. Latinos formed several organizations to work for equal rights and fair treatment.

In 1929 a number of Mexican American organizations came together to create the **League of United Latin American Citizens** (LULAC). The purpose of this organization was to fight discrimination against persons of Latin American ancestry. The organization limited its membership to people of Latin American heritage who were American citizens. LULAC encouraged assimilation into American society and adopted English as its official language.

LULAC achieved many advances for Latinos. One of its early crusades ended segregation of public places in Texas where Mexican Americans (along with African Americans) had been barred from "whites only" sections. The organization also ended the practice of segregating Spanish-speaking children in "Mexican schools."

In *Mendez* v. *Westminster* (1947), a group of Mexican parents won a lawsuit that challenged school segregation in California. Two years later, LULAC filed a similarly successful suit in Texas. During the 1950s, the organization was a frequent and vocal critic of the excesses and abuses of deportation authorities. In 1954 the Supreme Court's ruling in *Hernandez* v. *Texas* extended more rights to Latino citizens. The case ended the exclusion of Mexican Americans from juries in Texas.

▼ *Many migrant workers lived in terrible conditions, such as this family who shared one small room.*

▲ *Every member of the family had to work to survive, such as these Mexican children picking cotton in Texas.*

Analyzing VISUALS

1. **Describing** What types of treatment did many Latinos experience in the United States?
2. **Differentiating** What challenges were presented by the living and working conditions for Latino families in the United States?

C Critical Thinking

Analyzing Primary Sources Direct students' attention to the photo of children working in the fields. Ask them how the need for children's labor can deprive future generations of equal opportunity to improve their status. *(Working in the fields can deprive children of the education they need to improve their status. It also isolates them from the larger culture, where they could learn to interact with Americans who enjoy economic opportunities the workers might pursue in the future.)* **BL**

Analyzing VISUALS

Answers:

1. They faced segregation, discrimination, and other forms of racial prejudice.
2. Overcrowded substandard housing; long workdays doing hard, manual labor in fields

Additional Support

Activity: Interdisciplinary Connection

Language Arts Refer students to "A Farm Worker's Story" on page 133 of the Unit Resource Book. Read students this excerpt by Roberto Acuna, in which he explains why he joined United Farm Workers: "I began to see how everything was so wrong. When growers can have an intricate watering system to irrigate their crops but they can't have running water inside the houses of workers. Veterinarians tend the needs of domestic animals but they can't have medical care for the workers. They can have land subsidies for the growers but they can't have adequate unemployment compensation for the workers. They treat him like a farm implement. In fact, they treat their implements better and their domestic animals better. They have heat and insulated barns for the animals but the workers live in beat-up shacks with no heat at all. Illness . . . is 120 percent higher than the average rate for industry. . . . back trouble, rheumatism and arthritis. . . . Tuberculosis is high. And now because of the pesticides, we have many respiratory diseases." **Ask:** What conditions do you think you—and all workers—have a right to expect at a job? *(Students should be able to defend their answers.)* **OL**

R Reading Strategy

Reading Primary Sources
Ask students why becoming citizens and voting are important for Latino Americans, as Chávez points out. *(A group with a large number of voters has political power and can demand changes in laws and legal protection.)* BL

DBQ Document Based Questions

Answers:
1. Mohandas Gandhi
2. It ended talk of violence and showed the power of nonviolent protest.

Reading Check

Answer:
They were treated as outsiders, kept in low-paying, menial jobs, and segregated in the community and in schools.

Additional Support

History ONLINE
Student Web Activity Visit glencoe.com and complete the activity on protest movements.

Another Latino organization, the **American GI Forum,** was founded to protect the rights of Mexican American veterans. After World War II, Latino veterans were excluded from veterans' organizations and denied medical services by the Veterans Administration.

The GI Forum's first effort to combat racial injustice involved a Mexican American soldier who was killed during World War II. A funeral home refused to hold his funeral because he was Mexican American. The GI Forum drew national attention to the incident and, with the help of Senator Lyndon Johnson, the soldier's remains were buried in Arlington National Cemetery. Initially concerned only with issues directly affecting Latino veterans, the organization later broadened its scope to challenge segregation and other forms of discrimination against all Latinos.

Reading Check **Analyzing** How did American society discriminate against Latinos?

Protests and Progress

MAIN Idea Many Latinos worked as poorly paid agricultural laborers; the United Farm Workers tried to improve their working conditions.

HISTORY AND YOU Do you think the United States should have a national language? Read how school districts set up bilingual education classes to teach immigrant students in their own language while they were still learning English.

As the 1960s began, Latino Americans continued to face prejudice and limited access to **adequate** education, employment, and housing. Encouraged by the achievements of the African American civil rights movement, Latinos launched a series of campaigns to improve their economic situation and end discrimination.

One major campaign was the effort to improve conditions for farmworkers. Most Mexican American farm laborers earned little pay, received few benefits, and had no job

PRIMARY SOURCE

César Chávez Promotes Nonviolence

▲ *Activist César Chávez was instrumental in improving conditions for Latino migrant workers.*

PRIMARY SOURCE

"Farmworkers had been trying to organize a union for more than one hundred years. In 1965 they began a bitter five-year strike against grape growers around Delano, California. Two and one-half years later, in the hungry winter of 1968 with no resolution in sight, they were tired and frustrated.

Among some of them, particularly some of the young men, there began the murmurs of violence. . . . But Cesar rejected that part of our culture 'that tells young men that you're not a man if you don't fight back.' The boycott had followed in the tradition of Cesar's hero, Mahatma Gandhi, whose practice of nonviolence he embraced. And now, like Gandhi, Cesar announced he would undertake a fast . . . .

After twenty-five days, Cesar was carried to a nearby park where the fast ended during a mass with thousands of farmworkers. He had lost thirty-five pounds, but there was no more talk of violence among the farmworkers. . . .

Cesar was too weak to speak, so his statement was read by others in both English and Spanish. 'It is my deepest belief that only by giving our lives do we find life,' they read. 'The truest act of courage . . . is to sacrifice ourselves for others in a totally nonviolent struggle for justice.'"

—Marc Grossman, UFW spokesman, quoted in *Stone Soup for the World*

R

DBQ Document-Based Questions

1. **Identifying** Whose ideas inspired César Chávez to begin his fast?
2. **Explaining** What effect did the fast have on the striking farmworkers?

Extending the Content

The Three-Hundred Mile March In 1965, when grape vineyard owners in Delano, California, cut the already pitiful pay of their workers, farmworker César Chávez called a strike at one of the farms. He knew that, when ripe, grapes do not last long. After attacks on strikers by the grape company, Chávez organized a march of more than three hundred miles from Delano to the state capitol in Sacramento. There, he would ask for the government's help.

The march began with Chávez and sixty-seven others. For about fifteen miles a day, they marched on blistered and bloody feet. Meanwhile, the unharvested grapes in Delano rotted on the vine.

As the marchers passed, farmworkers fed them and offered places to sleep. Some joined the march. Every day, more marchers followed Chávez. The marchers arrived in Sacramento on Easter Sunday, and a parade of ten thousand people marched through the streets to the capitol. There, they learned that the grape company had signed a contract with the National Farm Workers Association, promising a pay raise and better conditions.

security. In the early 1960s, **César Chávez** and **Dolores Huerta** organized two groups that fought for farmworkers. In 1965 the groups went on strike in California to demand union recognition, increased wages, and better benefits.

When employers resisted, Chávez enlisted college students, churches, and civil rights groups to organize a national boycott of table grapes, one of California's main agricultural products. An estimated 17 million citizens stopped buying grapes, and industry profits tumbled. In 1966, under the sponsorship of the American Federation of Labor and Congress of Industrial Organization (AFL-CIO), Chávez and Huerta merged their two organizations into one—the **United Farm Workers** (UFW). The new union kept the boycott going until 1970, when the grape growers finally agreed to raise wages and improve working conditions.

During the 1960s and 1970s, a growing number of Latino youths became involved in civil rights. In 1967 college students in San Antonio, Texas, led by José Angel Gutiérrez, founded the Mexican American Youth Organization (MAYO). MAYO organized walk-outs and demonstrations to protest discrimination. In 1968 about 1,000 Mexican American students and teachers in East Los Angeles walked out of their classrooms to protest racism. In Crystal City, Texas, protests organized by MAYO in 1969 led to the creation of bilingual education at the local high school.

MAYO's success and the spread of protests across the West and Southwest convinced Gutiérrez to found a new political party, ***La Raza Unida,*** or "the United People," in 1969. *La Raza* promoted Latino causes and supported Latino candidates in Texas, California, Colorado, Arizona, and New Mexico. The group mobilized Mexican American voters with calls for job-training programs and greater access to financial institutions. By the early 1970s, it had elected Latinos to local offices in several cities with large Latino populations.

La Raza was part of a larger civil rights movement among Mexican Americans (many of whom began calling themselves Chicanos). This "Brown Power" movement fought against discrimination and celebrated ethnic pride. On September 16, 1969 (Mexican Independence Day), students at the University of California at Berkeley staged a sit-in demanding a Chicano Studies program. Over the next decade, more than 50 universities created programs dedicated to the study of Latinos in the United States.

One issue many Latino leaders promoted in the late 1960s was **bilingualism**—the practice of teaching immigrant students in their own language while they also learned English. Congress supported their arguments, passing the **Bilingual Education Act** in 1968. This act directed school districts to set up classes for immigrants in their own language while they were learning English.

Later, bilingualism became politically controversial. Many Americans worried that bilingualism made it difficult for Latino immigrants to assimilate. Beginning in the 1980s, an English-only movement began, and by the 2000s, legislatures in 25 states had passed laws or amendments making English the official language of their state.

Reading Check **Explaining** How did Latino Americans increase their economic opportunities in the 1960s?

Section 3 REVIEW

Vocabulary

1. **Explain** the significance of: repatriation, League of United Latin American Citizens, American GI Forum, César Chávez, Dolores Huerta, United Farm Workers, *La Raza Unida*, bilingualism, Bilingual Education Act.

Main Ideas

2. **Identifying** What are the national origins of the three main groups of Latinos in the United States?
3. **Describing** Under what circumstances did the American GI Forum first take action?
4. **Explaining** Why did some Americans worry about the Bilingual Education Act?

Critical Thinking

5. **Big Ideas** How did the judicial system support Latino civil rights in the last century? Cite two relevant court cases and their decisions.
6. **Categorizing** Use a graphic organizer similar to the one below to identify Latino groups and their achievements.

Civil Rights Group	Achievement

7. **Analyzing Visuals** Study the graph on page 921. What was the total U.S. Latino population in 2000? Which group had the largest population?

Writing About History

8. **Expository Writing** Write a magazine article about the conditions that gave rise to the Latino civil rights movement in the postwar period.

History ONLINE
Study Central™ To review this section, go to glencoe.com and click on Study Central.

Reading Check

Answer:
By forming the UFW and *La Raza Unida* and staging boycotts, they increased their wages, won contracts, improved working conditions, and lobbied successfully to achieve the Bilingual Education Act.

Assess

History ONLINE

Study Central™ provides summaries, interactive games, and online graphic organizers to help students review content.

Close

Summarizing Ask: Why did Latino Americans organize? *(They wanted an end to discrimination; improved working conditions and better pay, especially for farmworkers; increased Latino voter participation; more Latino elected officials; and bilingual education in schools.)*

Answers

1. All definitions can be found in the section and the Glossary.
2. Mexico, Puerto Rico, Cuba
3. A Latino American soldier was killed during World War II, and a funeral home in Texas refused to hold his funeral.
4. They were concerned that it would make it harder for Latino Americans to assimilate.
5. *Mendez* v. *Westminster*: ended school segregation in California; *Hernandez* v. *Texas*: extended greater rights to Latino citizens, including the right to serve on a jury
6. Answers may include the following: LULAC: brought cases to court that ended many discriminatory practices; American GI Forum: fought for Latino veterans' rights and to end discrimination in general; UFW: fought for improved working conditions and pay for farmworkers; *La Raza Unida*: worked to increase Latino voter participation and got Latino candidates elected; MAYO: held protests against discrimination and got bilingual education added to a high school in Texas
7. about 35 million; Mexicans
8. Students' articles will vary, but should focus on the reasons for and results of the Latino civil rights movement.

Determining Cause and Effect Invite students to write at least one cause-and-effect statement for the student protest movement, the feminist movement, and the Latino movement. **Ask:** What was the overall effect of the protest movements that began or gained momentum during the 1960s? **OL**

Expository Writing Have students select one of the three groups mentioned in the Determining Cause and Effect activity above and write a one-page summary of their achievements during the 1960s and 1970s. **Ask:** Of the movements covered in this chapter, which do you think had the most lasting and important effect? **OL**

Chapter 27 Visual Summary

STUDY TO GO You can study anywhere, anytime by downloading quizzes and flashcards to your PDA from glencoe.com.

Causes of the New Protest Movements

- The earlier "beat" movement questioned American values.
- The successes of African Americans' fight for civil rights demonstrated to other groups that change was possible if people demanded change.
- Many in the baby boom generation became frustrated with society as they entered college and began to advocate for social reform.
- The Vietnam War and the draft led many students to join protests.
- Women began to question their position in postwar society. Betty Friedan's book *The Feminine Mystique* influenced many young women.
- The Kennedy administration began to pay attention to women's issues, passing the Equal Pay Act and creating the President's Commission on the Status of Women.
- The Latino American population increased through immigration; Latino newcomers, as well as citizens, faced discrimination.

◄ *Mario Savio speaks at a 1966 sit-in.*

► *Latinos began to fight for improved labor conditions through the work of the United Farm Workers who held rallies such as this one in 1979.*

▲ *Women's rights leaders, such as Bella Abzug (left, in hat) and Betty Friedan (right, in red coat) fought for greater equality for women.*

Effects of the New Protest Movements

- New student groups, including Students for a Democratic Society (SDS), were formed. Court cases affirmed student rights to free speech on campus.
- New women's groups, such as the National Organization of Women (NOW), emerged. They fought for equal economic rights in the workplace and in society, and they demanded equal opportunities in education.
- A campaign began for the Equal Rights Amendment, but the amendment was not ratified.
- The *Roe* v. *Wade* decision affirmed a constitutional right to abortion, with some limits.
- New Latino organizations emerged, such as the United Farm Workers (UFW) and *La Raza Unida*, fighting for increased economic opportunity and greater representation in political institutions.
- Latinos made substantial gains politically and economically, and many were elected to positions in Congress and state governments.

Hands-On Chapter Project
Step 4: Wrap Up

Presenting a Historical Drama

Step 4

Directions Ask groups to write a review of the dramas presented by the other two groups. Have groups share the reviews with each other.

Putting It Together After groups have read the reviews, ask them to make any corrections for accuracy and present the dramas to the class again. **OL**

Chapter 27 ASSESSMENT

Reviewing Vocabulary

Directions: Choose the word or words that best complete the sentence.

1. In the 1960s young people known as hippies began the ________ movement.
- **A** beat
- **B** counterculture
- **C** student
- **D** commune

2. One way that hippies separated themselves from typical society was by living in group arrangements with other hippies known as
- **A** communes.
- **B** countercultures.
- **C** barrios.
- **D** Woodstocks.

3. A newly energized belief in ________ led to the fight to pass the Equal Rights Amendment.
- **A** communism
- **B** environmentalism
- **C** fascism
- **D** feminism

4. In the 1930s U.S. officials began to return Mexican immigrants to Mexico in what became known as the
- **A** counterculture.
- **B** barrio.
- **C** repatriation.
- **D** *La Raza Unida.*

5. Latinos lobbied successfully for the addition of ________ in public education.
- **A** bilingualism
- **B** repatriation
- **C** feminism
- **D** legalism

Reviewing Main Ideas

Directions: Choose the best answer for each of the following questions.

Section 1 *(pp. 910–913)*

6. SDS was begun by Tom Hayden at which university?
- **A** Harvard University
- **B** University of California at Berkeley
- **C** Kent State University
- **D** University of Michigan

7. Which of the following was an outgrowth of hippie culture?
- **A** SDS
- **B** rock 'n' roll music
- **C** communes
- **D** buzz cuts

Section 2 *(pp. 914–919)*

8. The work of the President's Commission on the Status of Women led to
- **A** the Equal Employment Opportunity Commission.
- **B** the Equal Rights Amendment.
- **C** the Equal Pay Act.
- **D** the National Organization for Women.

9. Title IX of the Educational Amendments prohibited federally funded schools
- **A** from paying male teachers more than female teachers.
- **B** from discriminating against minorities.
- **C** from providing same-gender education.
- **D** from discriminating on the basis of gender.

TEST-TAKING TIP

Read each question carefully to understand exactly what it is asking. Then review all the answer choices before finally choosing the ***best*** answer to the question.

Need Extra Help?

If You Missed Questions . . .	1	2	3	4	5	6	7	8	9
Go to Page . . .	912	913	914–919	922	925	910–911	913	915	918

GO ON

Answers and Analyses
Reviewing Vocabulary

1. B Counter means "against" or "opposing." The beat movement was a precursor to the counterculture movement. Communes grew out of the counterculture movement. Student is too general.

2. A Counterculture was the term used to describe the hippie lifestyle. Barrios were Hispanic neighborhoods within larger English-speaking communities. Woodstock was the 1969 music and arts festival held in New York State.

3. D Feminism is the belief in the need for equal rights for women. Communism and fascism are forms of government. Environmentalism is work to help conserve the environment.

4. C Help students break down the word *repatriation.* "Re-" is a prefix that means "back" or "again." The suffix "-ation" means action or a process. In the middle, "patri" derives from the Latin word *patria* meaning native country. Repatriation = the process of returning someone to their country of origin.

5. A Latinos come from Latin America and usually are Spanish-speakers. Bilingual means two languages. Latinos sought bilingual education in English and Spanish. The lobbying efforts for bilingual education grew out of the Latino civil rights movement.

Reviewing Main Ideas

6. D Tom Hayden wrote the Port Huron Statement, which stated the goals of SDS. To help remember that SDS began at the University of Michigan, students should relate the Port Huron Statement to Lake Huron, one of the Great Lakes.

7. C Here, students can use the process of elimination. *A* is incorrect, SDS was founded in 1959, before hippie culture had really begun. Rock 'n' roll also predated the hippie culture. Long hair was a symbol of the hippie movement, not a conservative buzz cut. This leaves communes, which were places where hippies practiced communal living.

8. C When the same word appears in more than one answer choice, it is vital that students read each answer choice carefully, to avoid making a careless mistake. Headed by Eleanor Roosevelt, the Commission won the passage of the Equal Pay Act. The Equal Employment Opportunity Commission had to implement the Equal Pay Act. The Equal Rights Amendment was never passed. NOW was an independent group. It was not formed due to a presidential commission.

9. D Title IX today is mostly associated with sports programs. It is somewhat controversial, as the need to have a balance between men's and women's athletic programs sometimes leads to programs simply being cut.

10. C The purpose of the ERA was to ensure equal rights for women, not to gain advantages, like free schooling. The ERA did not concern abortion. *D* represents a possible opposite effect of the passage of the amendment. *C* correctly represents the fears of some—that full equality would mean no consideration for traditional rights of women.

11. B Remind students to consider the time period; 1959 was in the middle of the Cold War, when communists were the "enemy." This culture created an environment where refugees from communism were welcomed. This was a bit unique, as the 1950s and 1960s saw much discrimination against other Spanish-speaking immigrant groups.

12. C The NAACP experienced much success in the struggle for equality for African Americans through the court system, with cases such as *Brown* v. *Board of Education of Topeka, Kansas*. The LULAC took a similar path, with cases such as *Mendez* v. *Westminster*. An easy way for students to remember that these organizations had similar methods is to think that both are represented by acronyms (and both acronyms have five letters).

13. C Mexican American veterans of World War II were excluded from the veterans' benefits that other veterans were entitled to, including medical services.

Chapter 27 Assessment

10. Why did some people oppose the Equal Rights Amendment?

A It said that state governments could not regulate abortion during the first three months of pregnancy.
B It allowed women to go to college and vocational schools for free.
C People feared that it would take away traditional rights such as receiving alimony and exemption from the military draft.
D People feared that more women would choose to stay at home with their families rather than having a career.

Section 3 *(pp. 920–925)*

11. Cuban immigrants arriving after the Cuban Revolution in 1959 were welcomed by Americans because

A there was a shortage of cheap labor.
B they were considered refugees from communism.
C most of them were fluent in English.
D there was a need for more doctors and other professionals.

12. Using a tactic the NAACP had used to advance the rights of African Americans, LULAC fought discrimination against Latinos mainly through

A lobbying efforts.
B demonstrations and other protests.
C the court system.
D periodicals and other mass media.

13. Who was the American GI Forum founded to protect?

A African American veterans
B women veterans
C Mexican American veterans
D Veterans of Pacific Battles

Critical Thinking

Directions: Choose the best answers to the following questions.

14. The Supreme Court upheld the Free Speech protesters' rights to free speech and assembly under which law?

A the Civil Rights Act of 1964
B the Equal Rights Amendment
C the Educational Amendments
D the Twenty-sixth Amendment

Base your answers to questions 15 and 16 on the map below and on your knowledge of Chapter 27.

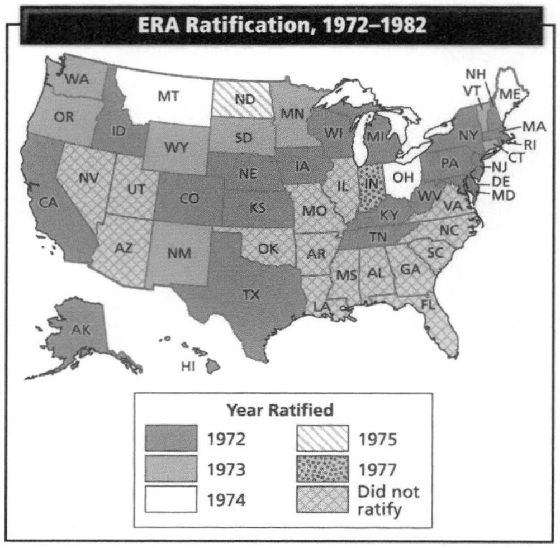

15. How many states had ratified the ERA by 1977?

A 20
B 25
C 30
D 35

16. In what region did most states fail to ratify the ERA?

A the South
B New England
C the West
D the Midwest

Need Extra Help?

If You Missed Questions . . .	10	11	12	13	14	15	16
Go to Page . . .	917–918	922–923	923	924	911–912	R15	R15

GO ON

Critical Thinking

14. A The Civil Rights Act supported the right of people to assemble in public places. The Supreme Court ruled that this applied to college campuses. The Equal Rights Amendment was never passed, so it cannot be correct. The term Educational Amendments is too broad, and would not apply, even though the protest took place on a college campus. The Twenty-sixth Amendment lowered the voting age to 18, and would not apply.

15. D Students may be confused and just look at the states that ratified the ERA in 1977. However, the question asks how many states had ratified it *by* 1977. So, students must count all of the states that match the shading for 1972, 1973, 1974, 1975, and 1977.

16. A The states that did not ratify the ERA are shaded with a crosshatch pattern. From the map, it is apparent that most of the states in the South did not ratify the amendment.

17. The United Farm Workers' boycott against California grape growers was effective because
   - **A** the grape growers gave in so quickly to the union's demands.
   - **B** no one thought that they could organize so well.
   - **C** grapes were a major agricultural product of California.
   - **D** the union had the support of the U.S. government.

Base your answers to questions 18 and 19 on the cartoon below and on your knowledge of Chapter 27.

18. What did the cartoonist imply with this cartoon?
   - **A** Hippies know a great deal of information.
   - **B** Parents do not listen to their children.
   - **C** Hippies were wrong to question the older generation when they still accepted money from them.
   - **D** The older generation thought hippies were lazy and unintelligent.

19. Based on this cartoon and what you learned in the chapter, which of the following best describes the hippies shown in the cartoon?
   - **A** They reject everything about their parents' lifestyle.
   - **B** They were most interested in reforming society.
   - **C** They only cared about music and communal living.
   - **D** They were more interested in the outward signs of a hippie lifestyle.

Document-Based Questions

Directions: Analyze the document and answer the short-answer questions that follow the document.

On December 2, 1964, Mario Savio, the leader of the Free Speech Movement, led a protest at the University of California at Berkeley. Before the protest, Savio made a speech in reaction to comments by Berkeley's president, Clark Kerr. Kerr had said that he would not speak out in favor of students' demands in opposition to the Board of Regents, in the same way that a manager would not speak out against a board of directors. Savio used Kerr's metaphor of the university as a corporation in the following excerpt from his speech:

> "[I]f this is a firm, and if the Board of Regents are the board of directors, and if President Kerr in fact is the manager, then I'll tell you something: the faculty are a bunch of employees, and we're the raw material! But we're a bunch of raw material[s] that don't mean to have any process upon us, don't mean to be made into any product. . . . We're human beings! . . . you've got to put your bodies upon the gears and upon the wheels, upon the levers, upon all the apparatus, and you've got to make it stop. And you've got to indicate to the people who run it, to the people who own it, that unless you're free, the machine will be prevented from working at all!"
>
> —from Mario Savio's speech to Free Speech Movement demonstrators

20. According to Savio, if the university is a company, then what are the students?
21. What is Savio asking his fellow students to do, both literally and figuratively?

Extended Response

22. Write an expository essay explaining why so many protest movements emerged in the United States during the 1960s and 1970s. Your essay should include an introduction and at least three paragraphs that explore this issue, including facts and examples from the chapter.

STOP

History ONLINE
For additional test practice, use Self-Check Quizzes—Chapter 27 at glencoe.com.

Need Extra Help?

If You Missed Questions . . .	17	18	19	20	21	22
Go to Page . . .	925	R18	929	929	R19	R12

Document-Based Questions

20. The students are the product or material produced by the company. Savio calls the students "raw material" as far as the university is concerned, but asserts that they are in fact, real people.

21. Literally: Savio is asking students to protest personally against the problems they see with the university and bring the workings of the university to a halt. Figuratively: Savio is asking them to put themselves "in the works" of the machine. This is a good place to review metaphors with students: the factory as a metaphor for the university.

Extended Response

22. Students' essays will vary, but should clearly and logically express their ideas about why this era was an active period of protest and change. Essays should include at least two examples of protest movements and supporting details from the chapter.

17. C Grapes were a major agricultural product in California, therefore, the UFW boycott had a major financial impact. This financial impact is what made the boycott successful, because it forced the growers to negotiate with the UFW. Had the boycott been of a less profitable product, it may not have had as much impact.

18. C Study the cartoon with students. One hippie is chastising/making fun of his father for being old-fashioned, while another in the background reminds the first hippie to "tell him he's late with our allowance." The message is that the hippies had no respect for the older generation, but had no problem being supported by them.

19. D These people wore hippie fashions and seemed to reject the ideas of their parents, but they were also interested in attending college. Therefore, you can correctly say that they were most interested in the outward appearance of the hippie lifestyle, rather than rejecting traditional values completely.

History ONLINE
Have students visit the Web site at glencoe.com to review Chapter 27 and take the Self-Check Quiz.

Need Extra Help?
Have students refer to the pages listed if they miss any of the questions.

Unit 9 Planning Guide

UNIT PACING CHART						
	Unit 9	Chapter 28	Chapter 29	Chapter 30	Chapter 31	Unit 9
Day 1	Unit Opener	Chapter 28 Opener, Section 1	Chapter 29 Opener, Section 1	Chapter 30 Opener, Section 1	Chapter 31 Opener, Section 1	Wrap-Up/Project, Unit Assessment
Day 2		Sections 2 & 3	Section 2	Section 2	Section 2	
Day 3		Section 4	Section 3	Section 3	Section 3	
Day 4		Section 5	Section 4	Section 4	Section 4	
Day 5		Chapter Assessment	Chapter Assessment	Chapter Assessment	Chapter Assessment	

Teacher to Teacher

Philip Prale
Oak Park and River Forest High School
Oak Park, IL

Into the New Century—The Keeper's Project The purpose of this project is to analyze developments of the 1900s and explain why they are worth keeping in this new twenty-first century.

Ask students to construct a list of five to ten items that are Twentieth Century Keepers. Variations include:

1. Draw keepers from specific categories—Political, Economic, Social, Cultural, Religious, or Environmental.
2. Add one item that you would want to eliminate in this new century.
3. For each item write a description of the item and how it fits into the category.
4. Write an introductory paragraph explaining the general connection, besides time, of the keepers. What is the theme or central idea?
5. Make a poster with images or produce a slide show presentation of the material.

Author Note

Dear American History Teacher:

As you begin to teach this unit, there are themes that recur throughout the chapters that you will want to point out to students.

The last unit in this textbook offers some unique opportunities for connecting students to the major themes of American history. The trends and events that this unit covers occurred during their lifetimes and may have directly affected them. This unit deals with sweeping changes, both nationally and globally, at the end of the twentieth century. It follows political and demographic shifts within the United States, as well as the collapse of the Soviet Union, the end of the Cold War, and the plunge into a war on terrorism.

Vast changes have taken place around us. When I began teaching, essentially the only available equipment was the mimeograph machine. When I went to work at the Capitol in the 1970s, reporters there were writing their stories on typewriters and sending them to their newspapers by telegraph. In short order, equipment that seemed so essential became museum pieces. Personal computers, electronic mail, and the Internet created a communications revolution, in the classroom as well as in the newsroom and the halls of Congress. Digital resources provided instant access to vast amounts of information on a previously unimaginable global scale.

In studying this unit, most students can readily relate to the development of personal computers and the rise of the Internet. They can recall a recent election that was in the news. Most students will have memories of the tragic events on September 11, 2001. Such personal links should enable them to better understand the impact of earlier forms of science and technology, of previous elections, and of other traumatic national events. You might consider teaching the material from the last chapter first to frame the past through students' present experiences.

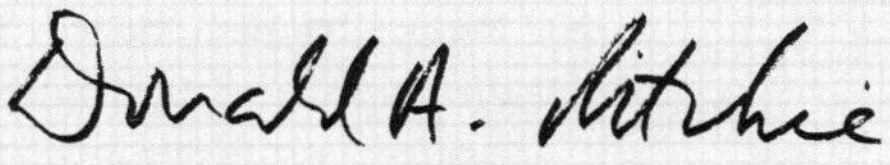

Senior Author

Introducing
Unit 9

Focus

Why It Matters

Ask students to think about the hot wars that have replaced the Cold War, the globalization of the economy, the issues of global warming, and the political climate today. Have them discuss whether they think Americans are more or less secure economically and politically than they were in 1960 and whether they have more or less personal freedom. **OL**

Connecting to Past Learning

Have students recall the Progressive Era in U.S. history, in which people began to be aware of the environmental damage that industry was causing. **Ask:** How did government help correct the environmental problems in the early twentieth century? *(The government passed new health and safety codes and created national parks.)* Tell students that in this unit they will learn about the changing society in the late twentieth century, the return to conservatism, and the changes caused by terrorism. **AL**

Unit Launch Activity

Making Connections Have students write one fact they know or opinion they hold about each of the following presidents: President Reagan, President George H.W. Bush, President Clinton, and President George W. Bush. Ask volunteers to share their statements, and have the class identify the statement as fact or opinion as they study the unit. **OL**

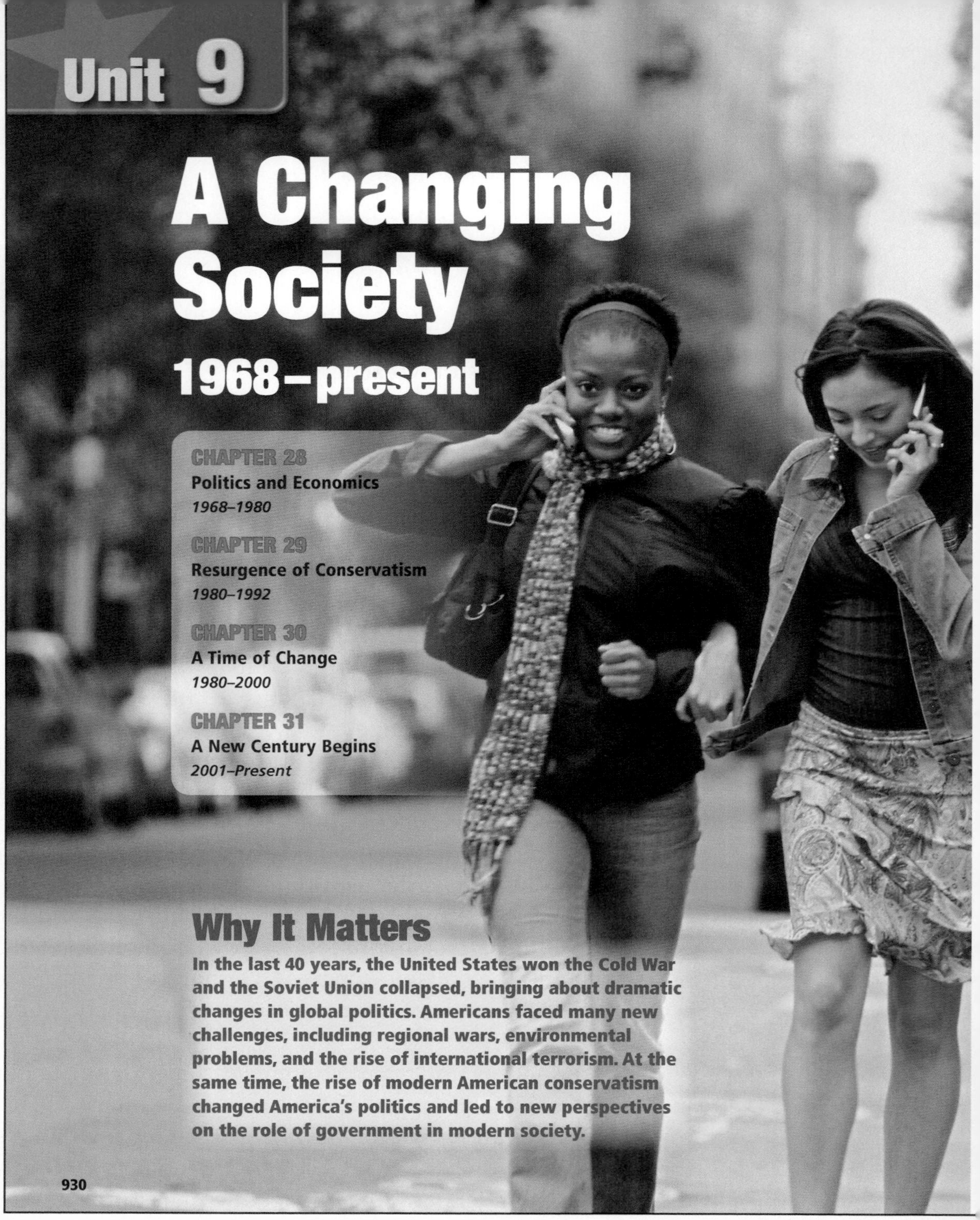

Unit 9

A Changing Society

1968–present

Why It Matters

In the last 40 years, the United States won the Cold War and the Soviet Union collapsed, bringing about dramatic changes in global politics. Americans faced many new challenges, including regional wars, environmental problems, and the rise of international terrorism. At the same time, the rise of modern American conservatism changed America's politics and led to new perspectives on the role of government in modern society.

Team Teaching Activity

Economics Invite an economics teacher to the class to discuss how trade agreements, globalization, and technology have affected the economy, employment opportunities, and consumer choices in the last part of the twentieth and the beginning of the twenty-first century. Ask the teacher to include a basic discussion of how microchip technology has affected the economy and society. Encourage students to ask questions to stimulate a class discussion. **OL**

By the early twenty-first century, American society was becoming increasingly diverse even as technology enabled people to become more interconnected.

931

Skill Practice

Predicting Consequences Ask students to consider what they associate with the terms *liberalism* and *conservatism*. As they respond, list their responses on the chalkboard. Clarify the terms briefly, and ask students to predict how a resurgence of conservatism would affect foreign policy, the economy, and daily life. Tell them to verify their predictions as they read. **OL**

Skill Practice

Describing Have students look at the photograph again and describe how the people in the photographs reflect the changing population of the United States. *(Answers may include that the population is more diverse now, that females make up more than 50% of the population, and that young people embrace new technologies.)* **OL**

NCLB No Child Left Behind

Teaching Tip The NCLB Act emphasizes reading. One strategy that helps students who are having difficulty understanding information is to have them use graphic organizers, such as flowcharts, to understand the sequence of events in the text. Have students work in groups of four. Each group member should maintain a flowchart showing major events and changes in one of these areas: foreign policy, domestic policy, economy, and society. After they have finished the unit, have them share their charts and discuss the political, economic, and social impacts of these events and changes.

More About the Photo

Visual Literacy Cell phones on the street are a common sight today, but on April 3, 1973, people stared as Martin Cooper walked down the street talking on a portable cellular phone. People knew about cellular phones in cars, but Cooper, general manager of Motorola's Communications Systems Division, was making the first public telephone call from a handheld portable cell phone. He called his rival at AT&T's Bell Labs. Cooper's cell phone looked like a brick and weighed 30 ounces. Ten years later, his company brought a 16-ounce cell phone to market at a price of $3,500. Today, mobile phones can weigh as little as a few ounces. The cell phone is just one of many advances in communications technology that have brought distant and diverse peoples closer.

Chapter 28 Planning Guide

Key to Ability Levels	
BL Below Level	AL Above Level
OL On Level	ELL English Language Learners

Key to Teaching Resources	
Print Material	Transparency
CD-ROM or DVD	

Levels				Resources		Chapter Opener	Section 1	Section 2	Section 3	Section 4	Section 5	Chapter Assess
BL	OL	AL	ELL									
FOCUS												
BL	OL	AL	ELL	Transparency	**Daily Focus Transparencies**		28-1	28-2	28-3	28-4	28-5	
TEACH												
	OL	AL		Print Material	**History Simulations and Problem Solving, URB**			p. 9				
	OL	AL		Print Material	**American Literature Reading, URB**					p. 13		
BL	OL		ELL	Print Material	**Reading Skills Activity, URB**		p. 21					
	OL			Print Material	**Historical Analysis Skills Activity, URB**			p. 22				
BL	OL	AL	ELL	Print Material	**Differentiated Instruction Activity, URB**		p. 23					
BL	OL		ELL	Print Material	**English Learner Activity, URB**		p. 25					
BL	OL	AL	ELL	Print Material	**Content Vocabulary Activity, URB***		p. 27					
BL	OL	AL	ELL	Print Material	**Academic Vocabulary Activity, URB**		p. 29					
	OL	AL		Print Material	**Reinforcing Skills Activity, URB**				p. 31			
	OL	AL		Print Material	**Critical Thinking Skills Activity, URB**			p. 32				
BL	OL		ELL	Print Material	**Time Line Activity, URB**			p. 33				
	OL			Print Material	**Linking Past and Present Activity, URB**					p. 34		
BL	OL	AL	ELL	Print Material	**Primary Source Reading, URB**			p. 35	p. 37			
BL	OL	AL	ELL	Print Material	**American Art and Music Activity, URB**						p. 39	
BL	OL	AL	ELL	Print Material	**Interpreting Political Cartoons Activity, URB**						p. 41	
		AL		Print Material	**Enrichment Activity, URB**					p. 45		
BL	OL		ELL	Print Material	**Guided Reading Activity, URB***		p. 48	p. 49	p. 50	p. 51		
BL	OL	AL	ELL	Print Material	**Reading Essentials and Note-Taking Guide***		p. 304	p. 307	p. 310	p. 313	p. 316	
BL	OL	AL	ELL	Print Material	**Differentiated Instruction for the American History Classroom**	✓	✓	✓	✓	✓	✓	✓
BL	OL	AL	ELL	Transparency	**Unit Map Overlay Transparencies**	✓	✓	✓	✓	✓	✓	✓
BL	OL	AL	ELL	Print Material	**Unit Time Line Transparencies, Strategies, and Activities**	✓	✓	✓	✓	✓	✓	✓
BL	OL	AL	ELL	Print Material	**Cause and Effect Transparencies, Strategies, and Activities**	✓	✓	✓	✓	✓	✓	✓
BL	OL	AL	ELL	Print Material	**Why It Matters Chapter Transparencies, Strategies, and Activities**	✓	✓	✓	✓	✓	✓	✓

Note: Please refer to the *Unit 9 Resource Book* for this chapter's URB materials.

* Also available in Spanish

TeacherWorks Plus
All-In-One Planner and Resource Center

- Interactive Lesson Planner
- Interactive Teacher Edition
- Fully editable blackline masters
- Section Spotlight Videos Launch
- Differentiated Lesson Plans
- Printable reports of daily assignments
- Standards Tracking System

Levels				Resources	Chapter Opener	Section 1	Section 2	Section 3	Section 4	Section 5	Chapter Assess
BL	OL	AL	ELL								
				TEACH *(continued)*							
BL	OL	AL	ELL	**American Biographies**						✓	
BL	OL	AL		**Supreme Court Case Studies**			p. 117		p. 121		
BL	OL	AL	ELL	**The Living Constitution**	✓	✓	✓	✓	✓	✓	✓
BL	OL	AL	ELL	**American Issues**	✓	✓	✓	✓	✓	✓	✓
	OL	AL	ELL	**American Art and Architecture Transparencies, Strategies, and Activities**	✓	✓	✓	✓	✓	✓	✓
BL	OL	AL		**High School American History Literature Library**	✓	✓	✓	✓	✓	✓	✓
	OL	AL		**American History Primary Source Documents Library**	✓	✓	✓	✓	✓	✓	✓
BL	OL	AL	ELL	**American Music: Hits Through History CD**	✓	✓	✓	✓	✓	✓	✓
BL	OL	AL	ELL	**StudentWorks™ Plus**	✓	✓	✓	✓	✓	✓	✓
BL	OL	AL	ELL	***The American Vision* Video Program**	✓	✓	✓	✓	✓	✓	✓
Teacher Resources				**Reading Strategies and Activities for the Social Studies Classroom**	✓	✓	✓	✓	✓	✓	✓
Teacher Resources				**Strategies for Success**	✓	✓	✓	✓	✓	✓	✓
Teacher Resources				**Presentation Plus! with MindJogger CheckPoint**	✓	✓	✓	✓	✓	✓	✓
Teacher Resources				**Success With English Learners**	✓	✓	✓	✓	✓	✓	✓
				ASSESS							
BL	OL	AL	ELL	**Section Quizzes and Chapter Tests***		p. 403	p. 404	p. 405	p. 406	p. 407	p. 409
BL	OL	AL	ELL	**Authentic Assessment With Rubrics**							p. 61
BL	OL	AL	ELL	**Standardized Test Practice Workbook**							p. 64
BL	OL	AL	ELL	***ExamView® Assessment Suite***		28-1	28-2	28-3	28-4	28-5	Ch. 28
				CLOSE							
BL			ELL	**Reteaching Activity, URB**							p. 43
BL	OL		ELL	**Reading and Study Skills Foldables™**	p. 82						
BL	OL	AL	ELL	***American History* in Graphic Novel**		p. 73					

✓ Chapter- or unit-based activities applicable to all sections in this chapter.

Using the Media Library

Teach With Technology

What is the Media Library?
The Media Library is an all-in-one online resource center that provides students with access to digital media associated with the textbook.

How can the Media Library help my students?
The Media Library contains Section Audio and Section Spotlight Videos. Section Audio can help struggling readers and English Language Learners better comprehend the textbook. Section Spotlight Videos engage visual learners and generate student interest. Students can download audio to their digital media player or listen from their computer screen.

Visit glencoe.com and enter a *QuickPass*™ code to go to the Media Library.

History ONLINE
Visit glencoe.com and enter *QuickPass*™ code TAV9399c28T for Chapter 28 resources.

You can easily launch a wide range of digital products from your computer's desktop with the McGraw-Hill Social Studies widget.

	Student	Teacher	Parent
Media Library			
• Section Audio	●		●
• Spanish Audio Summaries	●		●
• Section Spotlight Videos	●	●	●
***The American Vision* Online Learning Center (Web Site)**			
• StudentWorks™ Plus Online	●	●	●
• Multilingual Glossary	●	●	●
• Study-to-Go	●	●	●
• Chapter Overviews	●	●	●
• Self-Check Quizzes	●	●	●
• Student Web Activities	●	●	●
• ePuzzles and Games	●	●	●
• Vocabulary eFlashcards	●	●	●
• In Motion Animations	●	●	●
• Study Central™	●	●	●
• Web Activity Lesson Plans		●	
• Vocabulary PuzzleMaker	●	●	●
• Historical Thinking Activities		●	
• Beyond the Textbook	●	●	●

Reading Support From JAMESTOWN EDUCATION

- **Timed Readings Plus in Social Studies** helps students increase their reading rate and fluency while maintaining comprehension. The 400-word passages are similar to those found on state and national assessments.
- **Reading in the Content Area: Social Studies** concentrates on six essential reading skills that help students better comprehend what they read. The book includes 75 high-interest nonfiction passages written at increasing levels of difficulty.
- **Reading Social Studies** includes strategic reading instruction and vocabulary support in Social Studies content for both ELLs and native speakers of English.

www.jamestowneducation.com

Biography | A&E Home Video | The History Channel

The following videotape programs are available from Glencoe as supplements to this chapter:

- Richard Nixon: Man and President (ISBN 1-56-501742-0)
- The Secret Service (ISBN 1-56-501521-5)

To order, call Glencoe at 1-800-334-7344. To find classroom resources to accompany many of these videos, check the following home pages:

A&E Television: www.aetv.com
The History Channel: www.historychannel.com

NATIONAL GEOGRAPHIC

Index to National Geographic Magazine:

The following articles relate to this chapter:

- "Widespread as Rain and Deadly as Poison: Our Polluted Runoff," by John G. Mitchell, February 1996.
- "The Great Lakes' Troubled Waters," by Charles E. Cobb Jr., Bob Sacha, and Richard Olsenius, July 1987.

National Geographic Society Products To order the following, call National Geographic at 1-800-368-2728:

- *Civil Rights* (Transparencies)

Access National Geographic's new dynamic MapMachine Web site and other geography resources at:
www.nationalgeographic.com
www.nationalgeographic.com/maps

Reading List Generator CD-ROM

GLENCOE BOOKLINK 3

Use this database to search more than 30,000 titles to create a customized reading list for your students.

- Reading lists can be organized by students' reading level, author, genre, theme, or area of interest.
- The database provides Degrees of Reading Power™ (DRP) and Lexile™ readability scores for all selections.
- A brief summary of each selection is included.

Leveled reading suggestions for this chapter:

For students at a Grade 8 reading level:
- ***Andrew Young: Freedom Fighter,*** by Naurice Roberts

For students at a Grade 9 reading level:
- ***Habitat for Humanity***

For students at a Grade 10 reading level:
- ***Andrew Young: A Matter of Choice,*** by Jan Simpson

For students at a Grade 11 reading level:
- ***All the President's Men,*** by Carl Bernstein & Bob Woodward

For students at a Grade 12 reading level:
- ***White House Years,*** by Henry Kissinger

Introducing
Chapter 28

Focus

MAKING CONNECTIONS

What Stops Government Abuse of Power?

Ask students to give examples from the news of legal and ethical challenges facing individuals in government. Ask them how much people today trust government leaders. Then ask them how they think Watergate affected peoples' attitudes toward government. Students should evaluate their answers after they have completed the chapter. **OL**

Teach

The Big Ideas

As students study the chapter, remind them to consider the section-based Big Ideas included in each section's Guide to Reading. The **Essential Questions** in the activities below tie in to the Big Ideas and help students think about and understand important chapter concepts. In addition, the Hands-On Chapter Projects with their culminating activities relate the content from each section to the Big Ideas. These activities build on each other as students progress through the chapter.

Chapter 28

Politics and Economics

1968–1980

SECTION 1 The Nixon Administration

SECTION 2 The Watergate Scandal

SECTION 3 Ford and Carter

SECTION 4 New Approaches to Civil Rights

SECTION 5 Environmentalism

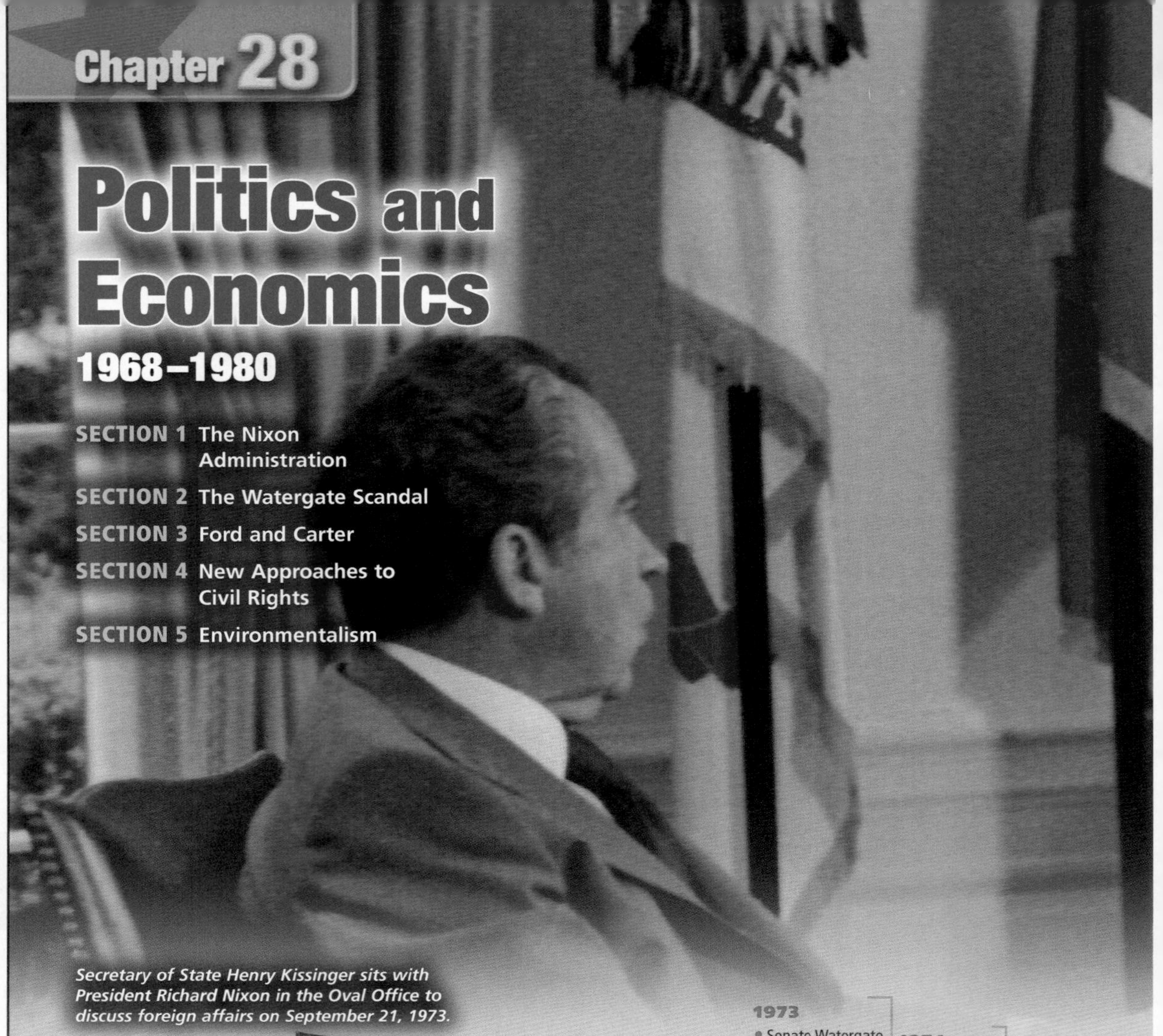

Secretary of State Henry Kissinger sits with President Richard Nixon in the Oval Office to discuss foreign affairs on September 21, 1973.

U.S. PRESIDENTS

Nixon 1969–1974

Ford 1974–1977

U.S. EVENTS

1970
- First Earth Day observed
- Environmental Protection Agency created

1972
- Nixon visits China and the Soviet Union
- Watergate burglars are arrested

1973
- Senate Watergate investigations begin
- AIM and government clash at Wounded Knee, South Dakota

1974
- Nixon resigns

1970 1972 1974

WORLD EVENTS

1971
- People's Republic of China admitted to UN

1973
- Britain, Ireland, and Denmark join Common Market

1974
- India becomes world's sixth nuclear power

Section 1

The Nixon Administration

Essential Question: How did Nixon's presidency change the country and its position in the world? *(He appointed conservative judges, eliminated some of Johnson's programs, and established détente with the Soviet Union and China.)* Tell students that in Section 1 they will learn about the Nixon presidency. **OL**

Section 2

The Watergate Scandal

Essential Question: What were the causes and effects of the Watergate scandal? *(Causes: Nixon's conviction that people were out to get him led to the break-in and cover up. Effects: Nixon's resignation, public distrust of government leaders, new anti-corruption laws.)* Point out that in Section 2 students will learn about the causes and impact of the Watergate scandal. **OL**

Section 3

Ford and Carter

Essential Question: How did Ford and Carter respond to energy and economic challenges? *(Ford cut spending and kept taxes low, while Carter vetoed spending bills, delayed tax cuts, urged the public to curb energy use, created a Department of Energy, and deregulated oil.)* Point out that in Section 3 students will study the Ford and Carter administrations. **OL**

Chapter Audio

MAKING CONNECTIONS

What Stops Government Abuse of Power?

The Watergate scandal forced Richard Nixon to become the first president to resign from office. The legacy of Watergate, together with the Vietnam War and the economic downturn of the late 1970s, caused many people to distrust the government and worry about the nation's future.

- ***How do you think Watergate affected people's attitudes toward government?***
- ***Do you think Nixon should have been punished for his role in the scandal?***

1975
- President Ford signs Helsinki Accords

Carter 1977–1981

1977
- Human rights manifesto is signed by 241 Czech activists and intellectuals

1976

1978

1979
- Sandinista guerrillas overthrow Nicaraguan dictator Somoza
- Margaret Thatcher becomes prime minister of Great Britain

1979
- Iranian revolutionaries seize U.S. embassy in Tehran

FOLDABLES

Analyzing Cause and Effect After you have read about the Watergate scandal, create a Shutter Fold Foldable to analyze critical information. Write a summary of Watergate events in the large middle section inside the Shutter Foldable. On the left-hand tab, list the causes of the Watergate scandal. On the right-hand tab, list the effects of Watergate on the political system.

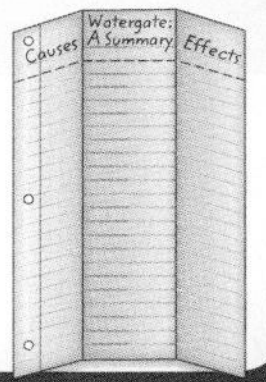

History ONLINE Visit glencoe.com and enter ***QuickPass***™ code TAV9846c28 for Chapter 28 resources.

More About the Photo

Visual Literacy Working together, Henry Kissinger and President Nixon reshaped U.S. foreign policy. They placed limits on U.S. commitments to allies. They also began to rely more heavily on negotiation and building relationships with traditional foes. In his inaugural address, Nixon announced, "After a period of confrontation we are entering an era of negotiation." Nixon relied on Kissinger both as an adviser and a negotiator. Together, Nixon and Kissinger worked to build bridges with the Soviet Union, the People's Republic of China, and Egypt.

FOLDABLES Study Organizer **Dinah Zike's Foldables**

Dinah Zike's Foldables are three-dimensional, interactive graphic organizers that help students practice basic writing skills, review vocabulary terms, and identify main ideas. Instructions for creating and using Foldables can be found in the Appendix at the end of this book and in the *Dinah Zike's Reading and Study Skills Foldables* booklet.

Section 4

New Approaches to Civil Rights

Essential Question: What were the goals of the African Americans, Native Americans, and Americans with disabilities when they organized? *(They wanted an end to discrimination. Native Americans also wanted sovereignty.)* Point out that in Section 4 students will learn about these movements. **OL**

Section 5

Environmentalism

Essential Question: What conditions did the environmental movement address? *(controls on pollution; cleanups; and protection of land, plant, wildlife, air, and water resources)* Tell students that in Section 5 they will learn about the origins of the modern enviornmental movement. **OL**

History ONLINE

Visit glencoe.com and enter ***QuickPass***™ code TAV9399c28T for Chapter 28 resources, including a Chapter Overview, Study Central™, Study-to-Go, Student Web Activity, Self-Check Quiz, and other materials.

Focus

Bellringer

Daily Focus Transparency 28-1

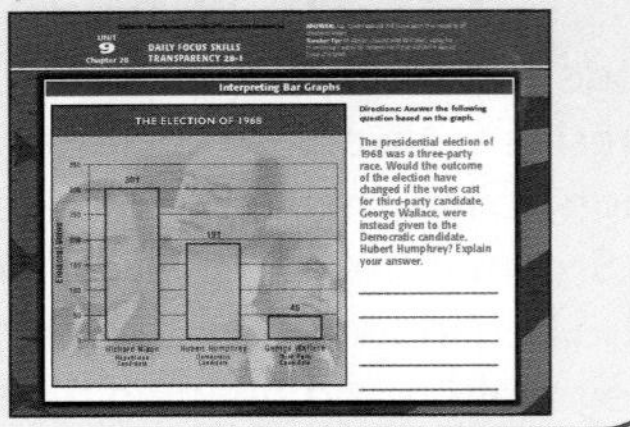

Guide to Reading

Answers:
Students should list Nixon's policies discussed in this section under the appropriate headings.

Section Spotlight Video

To generate student interest and provide a springboard for class discussion, access the Chapter 28, Section 1 video at glencoe.com or on the video DVD.

Section 1 — Section Audio — Spotlight Video

The Nixon Administration

Guide to Reading

Big Ideas

Individual Action One of President Nixon's most dramatic accomplishments was changing the United States's relationship with the People's Republic of China and the Soviet Union.

Content Vocabulary
- revenue sharing *(p. 936)*
- impound *(p. 936)*
- détente *(p. 938)*
- summit *(p. 939)*

Academic Vocabulary
- welfare *(p. 936)*
- liberal *(p. 936)*

People and Events to Identify
- Southern strategy *(p. 935)*
- New Federalism *(p. 936)*
- Henry Kissinger *(p. 937)*
- Vietnamization *(p. 937)*
- SALT I *(p. 939)*

Reading Strategy

Organizing Complete a graphic organizer similar to the one below by listing Nixon's domestic and foreign policies.

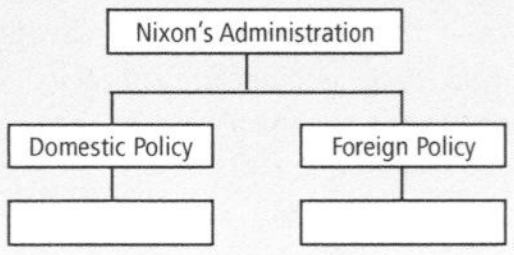

After he won the 1968 presidential election, Richard Nixon sought to restore law and order at home. His greatest accomplishments, however, were in foreign policy, where he worked to ease Cold War tensions with China and the Soviet Union.

Appealing to Middle America

MAIN Idea Nixon won the 1968 election by appealing to a "silent majority" of Americans.

HISTORY AND YOU Do you view your community as politically and socially liberal or conservative? Read on to find out about the strategies Nixon used to convince conservative Southerners to vote for him.

While they did not shout as loudly as the protesters, many Americans supported the government and longed for an end to the violence and turmoil that seemed to be plaguing the nation. The presidential candidate in 1968 who appealed to many of these frustrated citizens was Richard Nixon, a Republican. Nixon aimed many of his campaign messages at these Americans, whom he referred to as "Middle America" and the "silent majority." He promised them "peace with honor" in Vietnam, law and order, a more streamlined government, and a return to more traditional values at home.

Nixon's principal opponent in the 1968 presidential election was Democrat Hubert Humphrey, who had served as vice president under Lyndon Johnson. Nixon also had to wage his campaign against a strong third-party candidate, George Wallace, an experienced Southern politician and avowed supporter of segregation. In a 1964 bid for the Democratic presidential nomination, the former Alabama governor had attracted considerable support.

On Election Day, Wallace captured an impressive 13.5 percent of the popular vote, the best showing of a third-party candidate since 1924. Nixon managed a victory, however, receiving 43.4 percent of the popular vote to Humphrey's 42.7, and 301 electoral votes to Humphrey's 191.

The Southern Strategy

One of the keys to Nixon's victory was his surprisingly strong showing in the South. Even though the South had long been a Democratic stronghold, Nixon had refused to concede the region. To gain Southern support, Nixon had met with powerful South Carolina senator Strom Thurmond and won his backing by promising several things: to appoint only conservatives to the federal

Resource Manager

R Reading Strategies	C Critical Thinking	D Differentiated Instruction	W Writing Support	S Skill Practice
Teacher Edition • Taking Notes p. 936 • Reading Graphs p. 938 **Additional Resources** • Guid. Read. Act., URB p. 48	**Teacher Edition** • Analyzing Visuals pp. 935, 937 **Additional Resources** • Quizzes and Tests, p. 403	**Additional Resources** • Differentiated Instr. Act., URB p. 23 • English Learner Act., URB p. 25 • Foldables, p. 82 • Am. Hist. in Graphic Novel, p. 73	**Teacher Edition** • Expository Writing, p. 936 **Additional Resources** • Content Vocab. Act., URB p. 27 • Academic Vocab. Act., URB p. 29	**Additional Resources** • Read. Essen., p. 304 • Reading Skills Act., URB p. 21

POLITICAL CARTOONS PRIMARY SOURCE

The Election of 1968

▲ *Third-party presidential candidate George Wallace tailors an overcoat to cover the robe worn by one of his supporters.*

▲ *Republican Richard Nixon is fast on his feet as he spars with Democrat Hubert Humphrey. The man with the glasses represents John Q. Public, who is speaking to an elephant representing the Republican Party.*

C

Analyzing VISUALS DBQ

1. **Identifying** In the cartoon on the left, what is the cartoonist accusing Wallace of doing?
2. **Identifying Points of View** In the cartoon on the right, do you think the cartoonist approves of Nixon? Why or why not?

courts, to name a Southerner to the Supreme Court, to oppose court-ordered busing, and to choose a vice presidential candidate acceptable to the South. (Nixon ultimately chose Spiro Agnew, governor of the border state of Maryland.)

Nixon's efforts paid off on Election Day. Large numbers of white Southerners deserted the Democratic Party, granting Humphrey only one victory in that region—in Lyndon Johnson's home state of Texas. While Wallace claimed most of the states in the Deep South, Nixon captured Virginia, Tennessee, Kentucky, and North Carolina. Senator Strom Thurmond's support delivered his state of South Carolina for the Republicans as well.

Following his victory, Nixon set out to attract even more Southerners to the Republican Party, an effort that became known as the **Southern strategy.** Toward this end, he kept his agreement with Senator Thurmond and took steps to slow desegregation. During his tenure, Nixon worked to overturn several civil rights policies. He reversed a Johnson administration policy, for example, that had cut off federal funds for racially segregated schools.

A Law-and-Order President

During the campaign, Nixon had also promised to uphold law and order. His administration specifically targeted the nation's antiwar protesters. Attorney General John Mitchell declared that he stood ready to prosecute "hard-line militants" who crossed state lines to stir up riots. Mitchell's deputy, Richard Kleindienst, went even further with the boast, "We're going to enforce the law against draft evaders, against radical students, against deserters, against civil disorders, against organized crime, and against street crime."

Teach

C Critical Thinking

Analyzing Visuals Have students study the Political Cartoon on page 935, and think about what they have read about the election. **Ask:** Who is the other person in the ring with Nixon? *(Hubert Humphrey)* BL

Analyzing VISUALS DBQ

Answers:
1. Possible answer: He is accusing Wallace of trying to cover up the true nature of his constituency in order to be more attractive as a national presidential candidate.
2. Possible answer: No, the cartoonist does not really approve as he implies that Nixon does not have much of a punch—just fancy footwork.

Hands-On Chapter Project Step 1

Oral History of the 1970s

Step 1: Researching the Topic Divide the class into small groups. Ask groups to choose one of the following topics: the civil rights movement, the environmental movement, or the Watergate scandal.

Analyzing Visuals Have students use library and Internet sources to find photographs that show a dramatic moment relevant to their topic. (For example, Nixon flashing the "victory" sign after he resigned or photos of the first Earth Day.) Have students print out the photographs and save them for use later in the project. OL

(Chapter Project continued on page 942)

W Writing Support

Expository Writing Have students conduct research and write a report describing the ways in which the Burger Court disappointed conservatives. Remind students to include bibliographic references and footnotes in proper style. AL

R Reading Strategy

Taking Notes For better understanding of the New Federalism and Nixon's proposed Family Assistance Plan, have students use the heads of these sections to create a study outline. BL

Reading Check

Answer: The New Federalism was an attempt to lessen the power of the federal government by giving money back to the states and asking them to address their problems locally, while the Great Society was a program to alleviate social ills through federal aid. Under the New Federalism, Nixon also attempted to undermine some of the assistance programs of the Great Society.

Differentiated Instruction

President Nixon also went on the attack against the recent Supreme Court rulings that expanded the rights of accused criminals. Nixon openly criticized the Court and its chief justice, Earl Warren. The president promised to fill vacancies on the Supreme Court with judges who would support the rights of law enforcement over the rights of suspected criminals.

When Chief Justice Warren retired shortly after Nixon took office, the president replaced **W** him with Warren Burger, a respected conservative judge. He also placed three other conservative justices on the Court, including one from the South. The Burger Court did not reverse Warren Court rulings on the rights of criminal suspects. It did, however, refuse to expand those rights further. For example, in *Stone* v. *Powell* (1976), it agreed to limits on the rights of defendants to appeal state convictions to the federal judiciary. The Court also continued to uphold capital punishment as constitutional.

R The New Federalism

Nixon had campaigned promising to reduce the size of the federal government by dismantling several federal programs and giving more control to state and local governments. Nixon called this the **New Federalism.** He argued that such an approach would make government more effective.

"I reject the patronizing idea that government in Washington, D.C., is inevitably more wise and more efficient than government at the state or local level," Nixon declared. "The idea that a bureaucratic elite in Washington knows what's best for people . . . is really a contention that people cannot govern themselves." Under the New Federalism program, Congress passed a series of **revenue-sharing** bills that granted federal funds to state and local agencies to use.

Although revenue sharing was intended to give state and local agencies more power, over time it gave the federal government new power. As states came to depend on federal funds, the federal government could impose conditions on the states. Unless they met those conditions, their funds would be cut off.

As part of the New Federalism, Nixon sought to close down many of the programs of Johnson's Great Society. He vetoed funding for the Department of Housing and Urban Development, eliminated the Office of Economic Opportunity, and tried unsuccessfully to shut down the Job Corps.

While he worked to reduce the federal government's role, Nixon also sought to increase the power of the executive branch. The president did not have many strong relationships with members of Congress. The fact that the Republicans did not control either house also contributed to struggles with the legislative branch. Nixon often responded by trying to work around Congress. For instance, when Congress appropriated money for programs he opposed, Nixon **impounded,** or refused to release, the funds. By 1973, he had impounded an estimated $15 billion. The Supreme Court eventually declared the practice of impoundment unconstitutional.

The Family Assistance Plan

One federal program Nixon sought to reform was the nation's **welfare** system—Aid to Families with Dependent Children (AFDC). The program had many critics, Republican and Democratic alike. They argued that AFDC was structured so that it was actually better for poor people to apply for benefits than to take a low-paying job. A mother who had such a job, for example, would then have to pay for child care, sometimes leaving her with less income than she had on welfare.

In 1969 Nixon proposed replacing the AFDC with the Family Assistance Plan. The plan called for providing needy families a guaranteed yearly grant of $1,600, which could be supplemented by outside earnings. Many **liberals** applauded the plan as a significant step toward expanding federal responsibility for the poor. Nixon, however, presented the program in a conservative light, arguing it would encourage welfare recipients to become more responsible.

Although the program won approval in the House in 1970, it soon came under harsh attack. Welfare recipients complained that the federal grant was too low, while conservatives, who disapproved of guaranteed income, also criticized the plan. Such opposition led to the program's defeat in the Senate.

Reading Check **Evaluating** How did Nixon's New Federalism differ from Johnson's Great Society?

Leveled Activities

BL Reading Skills Activity 28
URB p. 21

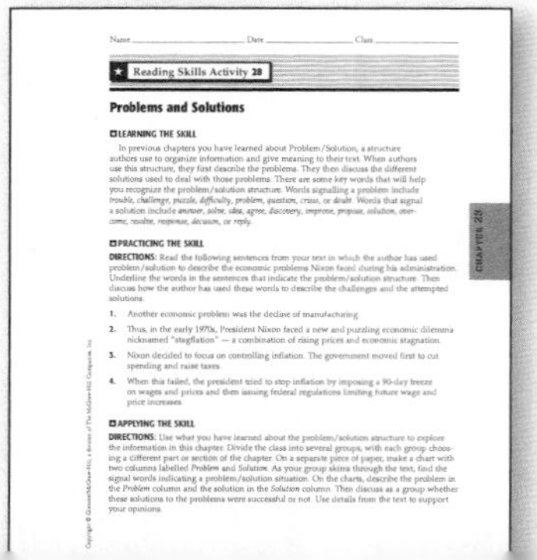
Reading Skills Activity 28

Problems and Solutions

OL Reteaching Activity 28
URB p. 43

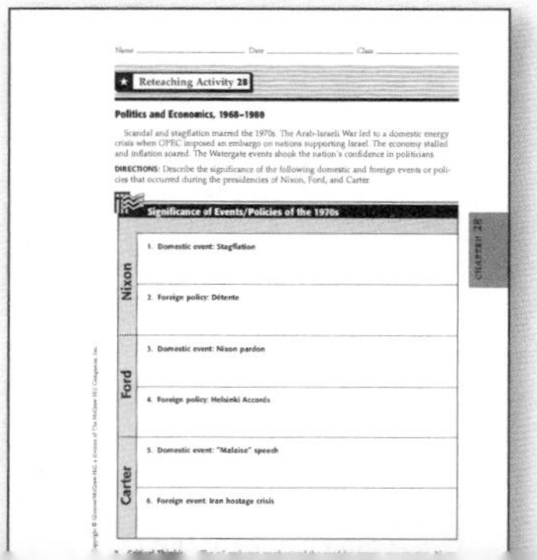
Reteaching Activity 28

Politics and Economics, 1968–1980

AL Reinforcing Skills Activity 28
URB p. 31

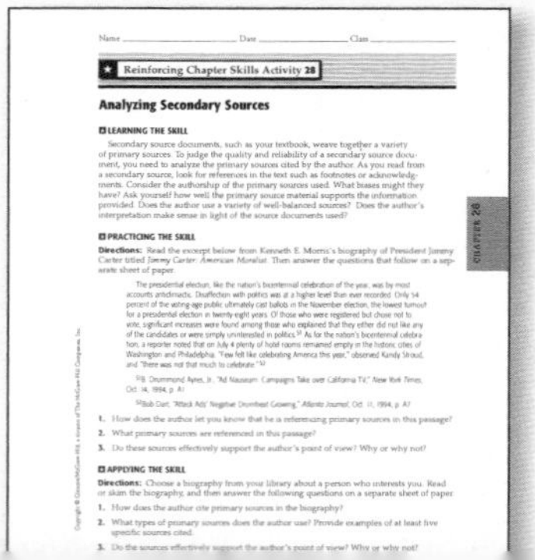
Reinforcing Chapter Skills Activity 28

Analyzing Secondary Sources

ELL English Learner Activity 28
URB p. 25

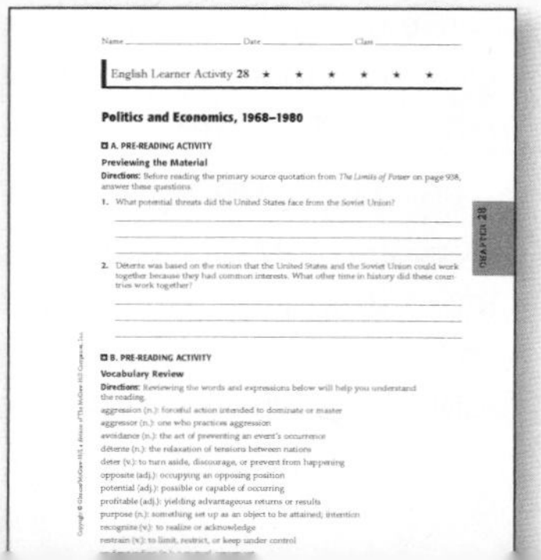
English Learner Activity 28

Politics and Economics, 1968–1980

Nixon's Foreign Policy

MAIN Idea With the support of national security adviser Henry Kissinger, Nixon forged better relationships with China and the Soviet Union.

HISTORY AND YOU How should a president balance his efforts between domestic and foreign affairs? Read on to learn about Nixon's strategies for dealing with communist countries.

Despite Nixon's domestic initiatives, a State Department official later recalled that the president had a "monumental disinterest in domestic policies." Nixon once expressed his hope that a "competent cabinet" of advisers could run the country. This would allow him to focus his energies on foreign affairs.

Nixon and Kissinger

In a move that would greatly influence his foreign policy, Nixon chose as his national security adviser **Henry Kissinger,** a former Harvard professor. Kissinger had served under Presidents Kennedy and Johnson as a foreign policy consultant. Although Secretary of State William Rogers outranked him, Kissinger soon took the lead in helping shape Nixon's foreign policy.

The Nixon Doctrine Nixon and Kissinger shared views on many issues. Both believed abandoning the war in Vietnam would damage the United States's position in the world. Thus, they worked toward a gradual withdrawal while simultaneously training the South Vietnamese to defend themselves.

This policy of **Vietnamization,** as it was called, was then extended globally in what came to be called the Nixon Doctrine. In July 1969, only six months after taking office, Nixon announced that the United States would now expect its allies to take care of their own defense. The United States would uphold all of the alliances it had signed, and would continue to provide military aid and training to allies, but it would no longer "conceive all the plans, design all the programs, execute all the decisions and undertake all the defense of the free nations of the world." America's allies would have to take responsibility for maintaining peace and stability in their own areas of the world.

People IN HISTORY

Henry Kissinger
1923–

Born in Germany, Henry Kissinger immigrated to the United States with his family in 1938 to escape Nazi persecution of Jews. During World War II, he served in U.S. military intelligence. After the war, Kissinger attended Harvard University and then joined the faculty there. He held various positions related to government, defense, and international affairs.

After acting as a consultant on national security under Presidents Kennedy and Johnson, Kissinger became President Nixon's national security adviser. In this capacity, he helped to establish the policy of détente with the Soviet Union and China. In 1973 he became secretary of state. Kissinger negotiated the cease-fire with North Vietnam, and along with Le Duc Tho, his co-negotiator, was awarded the Nobel Peace Prize in 1973.

In 1977 Kissinger was awarded the Presidential Medal of Freedom for his services to the nation. Today, he remains an unofficial adviser on international issues to leaders around the world.

How did Henry Kissinger influence foreign policy in the 1970s?

▲ *In 1971,* Time *magazine celebrated Kissinger as the driving force behind Nixon's trip to China.*

People IN HISTORY

Answer: As Nixon's Assistant for National Security Affairs he established the policy of détente with the Soviet Union and China. As secretary of state under Nixon, he negotiated the ceasefire with North Vietnam and developed the concept of "shuttle diplomacy" when he made numerous trips to the Middle East to broker a peace agreement in that region.

C Critical Thinking

Analyzing Visuals Call attention to the cartoon on the cover of *Time.* **Ask:** What does the cartoon suggest about Nixon's and Kissinger's roles in opening relations with mainland China? *(Nixon is relying on Kissinger's knowledge, skill, and activity to "steer" his foreign policy forward.)* **Ask:** What message does the cartoonist convey with the positions and relative sizes of Nixon and Kissinger? *(Nixon is receiving the recognition for negotiating with Peking. Kissinger remains in the background with less recognition, although he is the power behind Nixon's foreign policy achievements.)* **BL** **OL**

Additional Support

Activity: Collaborative Learning

Comparing Vietnamization with Foreign Policy in Iraq Tell students that the George W. Bush administration announced goals similar to Vietnamization during the Iraq war. Have interested students work in pairs to compare and contrast these policies. One partner should research Vietnamization and its results, while the other partner researches the goals stated by the Bush administration during 2006–2007. Allow time for partners to share their findings. Then have them work together to write a short essay comparing and contrasting these strategies and their results. **Ask:** How does Vietnamization compare to the goals and strategies of the Bush administration during the Iraq war? **OL**

R Reading Strategy

Reading Graphs Refer students to the graph in the Primary Source feature. Ask them about what year the Soviets and the United States had the same number of nuclear weapons. *(about 1978–1979)* OL

Analyzing VISUALS

Answers:

1. 1965
2. Answers will vary, but students should acknowledge that these two Communist nations had been the enemies of the United States during the Cold War, and still were.

Additional Support

PRIMARY SOURCE

Détente With the Soviet Union and China

▲ *President Nixon meets with Soviet premier Brezhnev to discuss limiting the number of nuclear weapons.*

R

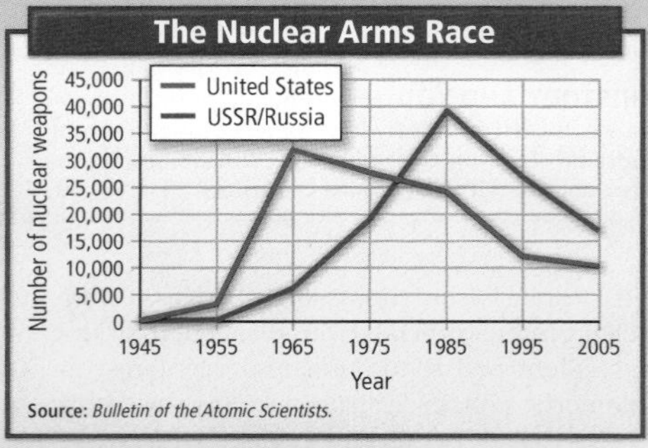

Source: *Bulletin of the Atomic Scientists.*

◀ *Mao Zedong, leader of China, greets Nixon in Beijing on February 21, 1972.*

Analyzing VISUALS

1. **Specifying** In what year did the number of nuclear weapons in the U.S. peak?
2. **Explaining** Why was establishing détente a significant accomplishment?

The New Policy of Détente The Soviet Union was not pleased when Nixon, a man with a history of outspoken anticommunist actions, became president. Nixon was still a staunch anticommunist, but he and Kissinger believed the United States needed to adjust to the growing role of China, Japan, and Western Europe. This emerging "multipolar" world demanded a different approach to American foreign policy.

Both Nixon and Kissinger wanted to continue to contain communism, but they believed that negotiation with Communists offered a better way for the United States to achieve its international goals. Nixon and Kissinger developed a new approach called **détente,** or relaxation of tensions, between the United States and its two major Communist rivals, the Soviet Union and China. In explaining détente to the American people, Nixon said that the United States had to build a better relationship with its main rivals in the interest of world peace:

PRIMARY SOURCE

"We must understand that détente is not a love fest. It is an understanding between nations that have opposite purposes, but which share common interests, including the avoidance of a nuclear war. Such an understanding can work—that is, restrain aggression and deter war—only as long as the potential aggressor is made to recognize that neither aggression nor war will be profitable."

—quoted in *The Limits of Power*

The successes of détente were diminished due to upheavals in smaller nations on the periphery of the Cold War. In Chile, President Salvador Allende was killed during a coup supported by the American CIA. Similarly, the Angolan Civil War, which began in 1975, featured covert aid from the United States. The conflicts in Chile and Angola were examples of proxy wars, conflicts during the Cold War that did not directly involve the United States and the Soviet Union but pursued Cold War aims of the two superpowers.

Activity: Interdisciplinary Connection

Art Have students work in groups to design a poster that might have been placed in China announcing president Richard M. Nixon's visit in 1972. Posters should include photos, newspaper clippings, and any other visuals that help communicate the Chinese reception of Richard Nixon. Encourage groups to conduct research using the Internet to find information about how the Chinese felt at the time of Nixon's visit. Post completed posters around the room and have each group give a brief summary of its poster. ELL OL

Nixon Visits China

Détente began with an effort to improve American-Chinese relations. Since 1949, when Communists took power in China, the United States had refused to recognize the Communists as the legitimate rulers. Instead, the American government recognized the exiled regime on the island of Taiwan as the Chinese government. Having long supported this policy, Nixon now set out to reverse it. He began by lifting trade and travel restrictions and withdrawing the Seventh Fleet from defending Taiwan.

After a series of highly secret negotiations between Kissinger and Chinese leaders, Nixon announced that he would visit China in February 1972. During the historic trip, the leaders of both nations agreed to establish "more normal" relations between their countries. In a statement that epitomized the notion of détente, Nixon told his Chinese hosts during a banquet toast, "Let us start a long march together, not in lockstep, but on different roads leading to the same goal, the goal of building a world structure of peace and justice."

In taking this trip, Nixon hoped not only to strengthen ties with the Chinese, but also to encourage the Soviets to more actively pursue diplomacy. Since the 1960s, a rift had developed between the Communist governments of the Soviet Union and China. Troops of the two nations occasionally clashed along their borders. Nixon believed détente with China would encourage Soviet premier Leonid Brezhnev to be more accommodating with the United States.

United States-Soviet Tensions Ease

Nixon's strategy toward the Soviets worked. Shortly after the public learned of American negotiations with China, the Soviets proposed an American-Soviet **summit,** or high-level diplomatic meeting, to be held in May 1972. On May 22, President Nixon flew to Moscow for a weeklong summit, becoming the first American president since World War II to visit the Soviet Union.

During the historic Moscow summit, the two superpowers signed the first Strategic Arms Limitation Treaty, or **SALT I,** a plan to limit nuclear arms the two nations had been working on for years. Nixon and Brezhnev also agreed to increase trade and the exchange of scientific information. Détente profoundly eased tensions between the Soviet Union and the United States.

By the end of Nixon's presidency, one Soviet official admitted that "the United States and the Soviet Union had their best relationship of the whole Cold War period." President Nixon indeed had made his mark on the world stage. As he basked in the glow of his 1972 foreign policy triumphs, however, trouble was brewing on the home front. A scandal was about to engulf his presidency and plunge the nation into one of its greatest constitutional crises.

Reading Check **Summarizing** What were the results of the 1972 American-Soviet summit?

Section 1 REVIEW

Vocabulary

1. **Explain** the significance of: Southern strategy, New Federalism, revenue sharing, impound, Henry Kissinger, Vietnamization, détente, summit, SALT I.

Main Ideas

2. **Describing** How did President Nixon attempt to increase the power of the presidency?
3. **Explaining** How did Nixon use his visit to China to improve relations with the Soviet Union?

Critical Thinking

4. **Big Ideas** What were the results of Nixon's policy of détente?
5. **Organizing** Use a graphic organizer similar to the one below to describe how President Nixon established détente in the listed countries.

China	
Soviet Union	

6. **Analyzing Visuals** Look at the *Time* cover on page 937. What does the image portray about Nixon's foreign policy?

Writing About History

7. **Expository Writing** Take on the role of a member of President Nixon's staff. Write a press release explaining either Nixon's domestic or foreign policies.

History ONLINE
Study Central™ To review this section, go to glencoe.com and click on Study Central.

Reading Check

Answer: signed SALT I, agreed to increase trade and exchange scientific information

Assess

History ONLINE

Study Central™ provides summaries, interactive games, and online graphic organizers to help students review content.

Close

Summarizing Ask: How would you characterize Nixon's domestic and foreign policies? *(Domestic: He increased presidential control, moved the courts and the country in a conservative direction, and eliminated some programs for the disadvantaged. Foreign policy: he found more peaceful ways of waging the Cold War, such as détente with the Soviet Union and improving relations with the People's Republic of China.)* **OL**

Section 1 REVIEW

Answers

1. All definitions can be found in the section and the Glossary.
2. Nixon often tried to work around Congress; for example, he impounded an estimated $15 billion that Congress had earmarked for various programs that the president did not support.
3. He thought that if the United States improved its relations with China, with whom the Soviets had had some friction, that the Soviets might want to improve U.S.-U.S.S.R. relations, and he was correct.
4. Détente led to more normal relations between the United States and China and eased tensions between the United States and Soviet Union.
5. China: lifted trade and travel restrictions, withdrew Seventh Fleet from Taiwan; Soviet Union: increased trade, signed SALT I, exchanged scientific information
6. Nixon is relying on Kissinger to "steer" his foreign policy.
7. Students' press releases will vary, but should include summaries of Nixon's domestic and foreign policies.

Focus

Bellringer

Daily Focus Transparency 28-2

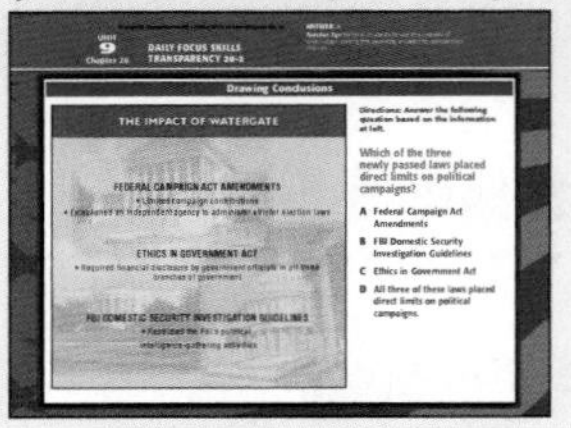

Guide to Reading

Answers:

I. The Roots of Watergate
  A. Mounting a Reelection Fight
  B. The Cover-Up Begins
II. The Cover-Up Unravels
  A. A Summer of Shocking Testimony
  B. The Case of the Tapes
  C. Nixon Resigns
  D. The Impact of Watergate

Section Spotlight Video

To generate student interest and provide a springboard for class discussion, access the Chapter 28, Section 2 video at glencoe.com or on the video DVD.

Section 2

Section Audio   Spotlight Video

The Watergate Scandal

Guide to Reading

Big Ideas

Government and Society The Watergate scandal intensified lingering distrust of government that had arisen during the Vietnam War.

Content Vocabulary
- executive privilege *(p. 944)*
- special prosecutor *(p. 944)*

Academic Vocabulary
- incident *(p. 940)*
- challenger *(p. 941)*

People and Events to Identify
- Sam J. Ervin *(p. 942)*
- John Dean *(p. 942)*
- Federal Campaign Act Amendments *(p. 945)*

Reading Strategy

Taking Notes Use the headings in this section to create an outline similar to the one below by recording information about the Watergate scandal.

The Watergate Scandal
I. The Roots of Watergate
  A.
  B.
II.
  A.
  B.

Despite a successful first term, Richard Nixon and his supporters worried about reelection. The tactics they resorted to led the president to become embroiled in a scandal known as Watergate, one of the United States's great constitutional crises.

The Roots of Watergate

MAIN Idea Tactics used by Nixon's supporters to try to ensure his reelection in 1972 led to the Watergate scandal.

HISTORY AND YOU What do you know about Richard Nixon and the Watergate scandal? Read on to learn how the president became involved in this major governmental crisis.

The Watergate scandal is perhaps the most famous scandal in modern American history. It certainly had momentous consequences, as it led to the only time in the nation's history when the president of the United States was forced to resign from office. As reporter Bob Woodward recounts in his book, *All the President's Men*, the scandal began on the morning of June 17, 1972.

Woodward was a young reporter for the *Washington Post* at that time. His editor had ruined his Saturday by asking him to cover a seemingly insignificant but bizarre **incident.** In the early hours of that morning, five men had broken into the Democratic National Committee (DNC) headquarters in the city's Watergate apartment-office complex. Woodward was ordered to attend the arraignment and see if there was a story worth reporting.

As Woodward sat near the back of the courtroom listening to the bail proceedings for the five defendants, the judge asked each man his occupation. One of the men, James McCord, answered that he was retired from government service.

"Where in government?" asked the judge. "CIA," McCord whispered. Woodward sprang to attention. Why was a former agent of the CIA involved in what seemed to be nothing more than a burglary? Over the next two years, Woodward and another reporter, Carl Bernstein, would investigate this question. In so doing, they uncovered a scandal that helped trigger a constitutional crisis and eventually forced President Nixon to resign.

Mounting a Reelection Fight

The Watergate scandal began when the Nixon administration tried to cover up its involvement in the break-in at the Democratic National Committee headquarters, along with other illegal

Resource Manager

R Reading Strategies	C Critical Thinking	D Differentiated Instruction	W Writing Support	S Skill Practice
Teacher Edition • Taking Notes p. 942 • Academic Vocabulary p. 943 **Additional Resources** • Prim. Source Read., URB p. 35 • Guid Read. Act., URB p. 49	**Teacher Edition** • Analyzing Primary Sources p. 941 **Additional Resources** • Hist. Sim. and Prob. Solve, URB p. 9 • Supreme Court Case Studies, p. 117 • Quizzes and Tests, p. 404	**Teacher Edition** • Visual/Spatial pp. 942, 944	**Additional Resources** • Content Vocabulary Act., URB p. 27 • Academic Vocabulary Act., URB p. 29	**Additional Resources** • Hist. Analysis Skills, URB p. 22 • Crit. Think. Skills Act., URB p. 32 • Time Line Act., URB p. 33 • Read. Essen., p. 307

PRIMARY SOURCE

The Watergate Scandal Erupts

In June 1972, five men were arrested attempting to place wiretaps on phones and stealing information from the Democratic National Headquarters at the Watergate Hotel. The subsequent investigation revealed a cover-up that reached to the White House.

▲ *The Watergate Complex gave its name to the resulting scandal. Security guard Frank Willis (right) reported to police evidence of the break-in.*

▲ *James McCord shows Congress the bugging device he installed. E. Howard Hunt (center) and G. Gordon Liddy (right) also testified.*

▶ *Counsel to the president John Dean testified that Nixon had been directly involved in the cover-up of the Watergate break-in.*

Analyzing VISUALS

1. **Speculating** If you had discovered the break-in, what might make you suspicious about the burglars?
2. **Explaining** Why was John Dean's testimony damaging to the president?

actions. Although the affair began with the Watergate burglary, many scholars believe the roots of the scandal lay in Nixon's character and the atmosphere that he and his advisers created in the White House.

Richard Nixon had fought hard to become president. He had battled back from numerous political defeats, including a loss to John F. Kennedy in the 1960 presidential election. Along the way, Nixon had grown defensive, secretive, and often resentful of his critics.

Furthermore, Nixon had become president when American society was in turmoil. There were race riots, and protests over the Vietnam War continued to consume the country. In Nixon's view, protesters and other "radicals" were trying to bring down his administration. Nixon was so consumed with his opponents that he compiled an "enemies list" filled with people—from politicians to members of the media—whom he considered a threat to his presidency.

When Nixon began his reelection campaign, his advisers were optimistic. Nixon had just finished triumphant trips to China and the Soviet Union. Former governor George Wallace, who had mounted a strong campaign in 1968, had dropped out of the race after an assassin's bullet paralyzed him, and the Democratic **challenger,** South Dakota Senator George McGovern, was viewed by many as too liberal.

Nixon's reelection was by no means certain, however. The unpopular Vietnam War still raged, and his staffers remembered how close the 1968 election had been. Determined to win at all costs, they began spying on opposition rallies and spreading rumors and false reports about their Democratic opponents.

Teach

C Critical Thinking

Analyzing Primary Sources Have students study the photos and captions on page 941. **Ask:** Whose testimony was most damaging to President Nixon? Why? *(Dean's testimony was most damaging, because he implicated Nixon directly in the cover-up.)* BL

Analyzing VISUALS

Answers:

1. Students' answers will vary. They may note that the burglars were caught wearing business suits and carrying bugging devices.
2. He was Nixon's lawyer and a White House insider, and he testified that Nixon tried to cover up evidence of the break-in.

Additional Support

Activity: Collaborative Learning

Think/Write–Pair–Share Use this strategy to engage your students in their subject matter through discussion. Tell students to Think silently about what they know of President Nixon and the Watergate scandal. Then ask them to Write three to five ideas down on a piece of paper. Students should then Pair with another student and Share their ideas. Conclude the activity with a class Share discussion. OL

D Differentiated Instruction

Visual/Spatial Have students work in groups to find photos in the library or online and create a photo essay about the Watergate scandal. Encourage students to use photographs and captions to tell how the Watergate scandal started, who was involved, when it happened, and how it concluded. OL ELL

R Reading Strategy

Taking Notes Have students use the heads of the section "The Cover-Up Unravels" to create a study outline. As they complete each subhead, have them write notes about the important points. Then encourage them to discuss their outlines with a partner and make any modifications that would improve their notes. BL

Reading Check

Answer: They intended to steal sensitive campaign information and place wiretaps.

As part of their efforts to help the president, Nixon's advisers ordered five men to break into the Democratic Party's headquarters at the Watergate complex and steal any sensitive campaign information. They were also to place wiretaps on the office telephones. While the burglars were at work, a security guard making his rounds spotted a piece of tape holding a door lock. The guard ripped off the tape, but when he passed the door later, he noticed that it had been replaced. He quickly called police, who arrived shortly and arrested the men.

The Cover-Up Begins

History ONLINE Student Web Activity Visit glencoe.com and complete the activity on the 1970s.

After the Watergate break-in, the media discovered that one burglar, James McCord, was not only an ex-CIA officer but also a member of the Committee for the Re-election of the President (CRP). Reports soon surfaced that the burglars had been paid from a secret CRP fund controlled by the White House.

At this point, the cover-up began. White House officials destroyed incriminating documents and gave false testimony to investigators. Meanwhile, President Nixon stepped in. The president may not have ordered the break-in, but he did order a cover-up. With Nixon's consent, administration officials asked the CIA to stop the FBI from investigating the source of the money paid to the burglars. The CIA told the FBI that the investigation threatened national security. To combat efforts to block the FBI investigation, the FBI's deputy director, W. Mark Felt, secretly leaked information about Watergate to the Washington Post.

Meanwhile, Nixon's press secretary dismissed the incident as a "third-rate burglary attempt," and the president told the American public, "The White House has had no involvement whatever in this particular incident." The strategy worked. Most Americans believed President Nixon, and despite efforts by the media, in particular the *Washington Post*, to keep the story alive, few people paid much attention during the 1972 presidential campaign. On Election Day, Nixon won reelection by one of the largest margins in history with nearly 61 percent of the popular vote, compared to 37.5 percent for George McGovern.

Reading Check **Examining** Why did members of the CRP break into the Democratic National Committee headquarters?

The Cover-Up Unravels

MAIN Idea The president's refusal to cooperate with Congress only focused attention on his possible involvement.

HISTORY AND YOU How far do you think that presidents should be able to go in the name of national security? Read on to learn how Nixon tried to invoke national security concerns to thwart an investigation of his involvement in Watergate.

In early 1973, the Watergate burglars went on trial. Under relentless prodding from federal judge John J. Sirica, McCord agreed to cooperate with the grand jury investigation. He also agreed to testify before the newly created Senate Select Committee on Presidential Campaign Activities. The chairman of the committee was Senator **Sam J. Ervin,** a Democrat from North Carolina.

McCord's testimony opened a floodgate of confessions, and a parade of White House and campaign officials exposed one illegality after another. Foremost among the officials was counsel to the president **John Dean,** a member of the inner circle of the White House who leveled allegations against Nixon himself.

A Summer of Shocking Testimony

In June 1973 John Dean testified before Senator Ervin's committee that former Attorney General John Mitchell had ordered the Watergate break-in and that Nixon had played an active role in attempting to cover up any White House involvement. As a shocked nation absorbed Dean's testimony, the Nixon administration strongly denied the charges.

Because Dean had no evidence to confirm his account, for the next month, the Senate committee attempted to determine who was telling the truth. Then, on July 16, the answer appeared unexpectedly. On that day, White House aide Alexander Butterfield testified that Nixon had ordered a taping system installed in the White House to record all conversations. The president had done so, Butterfield said, to help him write his memoirs after he left office. For members of the committee, however, the tapes would tell them exactly what the president knew and when he knew it, but only if the president could be forced to release them.

Hands-on Chapter Project: Step 2

Oral History of the 1970s

Step 2: Preparing for the Interview Tell students that each of them will be conducting an interview with someone who was a teenager or an adult in the 1970s.

Formulating Questions Have students in groups prepare a list of questions they want to ask interview subjects about their topic. Questions should center on the interviewee's recollections of the events related to the chosen topic. Each student will be conducting their own interview, but have students discuss amongst themselves who would be the most interesting interviewees. Whenever possible, encourage students to choose interviewees of different backgrounds and ages.

(Chapter Project continued on page 948)

Analyzing Supreme Court Cases

Is Executive Privilege Unlimited?

★ *United States* v. *Nixon*, 1974

Background to the Case

In 1974 Special Prosecutor Leon Jaworski issued a subpoena to gain access to tape recordings President Nixon had made of conversations in the Oval Office. Jaworski believed that the tapes would prove the active involvement of the president in the Watergate cover-up. Nixon filed a motion to prevent the subpoena, claiming executive privilege. The case went to district court, but that court withheld judgment pending the decision of the Supreme Court.

How the Court Ruled

In a unanimous 8-to-0 decision (Justice Rehnquist did not take part), the Supreme Court found that executive privilege did not protect Nixon's tape recordings, stating that while the president has a right to protect military secrets and other sensitive material and has a right to some confidentiality, the needs of a criminal trial must take precedence.

▲ The Senate committee overseeing the Watergate investigation, chaired by Senator Sam Ervin (fourth from left at the table), wanted access to Nixon's tape recordings.

PRIMARY SOURCE

The Court's Opinion

"In this case we must weigh the importance of the general privilege of confidentiality of Presidential communications in performance of the President's responsibilities against the inroads of such a privilege on the fair administration of criminal justice. The interest in preserving confidentiality is weighty indeed and entitled to great respect. However, we cannot conclude that advisers will be moved to temper the candor of their remarks by the infrequent occasions of disclosure because of the possibility that such conversations will be called for in the context of a criminal prosecution. On the other hand, the allowance of the privilege to withhold evidence that is demonstrably relevant in a criminal trial would cut deeply into the guarantee of due process of law and gravely impair the basic function of the courts. A President's acknowledged need for confidentiality in the communications of his office is general in nature, whereas the constitutional need for production of relevant evidence in a criminal proceeding is specific and central to the fair adjudication of a particular criminal case in the administration of justice. . . . The President's broad interest in confidentiality of communications will not be vitiated by disclosure of a limited number of conversations preliminarily shown to have some bearing on the pending criminal cases. We conclude that when the ground for asserting privilege as to subpoenaed materials sought for use in a criminal trial is based only on the generalized interest in confidentiality, it cannot prevail over the fundamental demands of due process of law in the fair administration of criminal justice. . . ."

—Chief Justice Warren Burger writing for the Court in *United States* v. *Nixon*

DBQ Document-Based Questions

1. **Finding the Main Idea** What is the main point of the decision in *United States* v. *Nixon*?
2. **Summarizing** What does Burger say that executive privilege in this case would violate?
3. **Expressing** Do you agree with the Supreme Court's decision in this case? Explain.

Supreme Court Cases

More About the Case

The Supreme Court's ruling in *United States* v. *Nixon* had two important results. It not only reaffirmed the power of the Court as the final authority in questions of constitutionality, but it also showed that no one, including the president of the United States, was above the law. **ELL**

DBQ Document Based Questions

Answers:

1. The ruling states that while executive privilege is important and necessary, it cannot be used to impede progress in a criminal proceeding.
2. He says that it would violate due process of law and hinder the activities of the courts.
3. Students' answers will vary; accept all reasoned arguments based on the information in the feature and in Section 2.

Differentiated Instruction

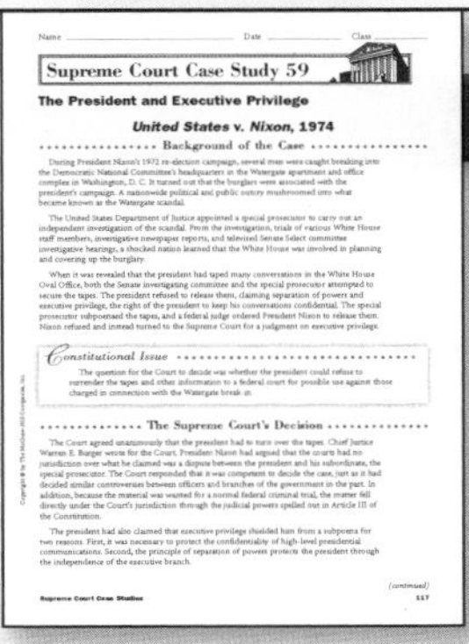

Supreme Court Case Study 59

The President and Executive Privilege

United States v. Nixon, 1974

Background of the Case

Case Study 59: *United States* v. *Nixon*, p. 117

Analyzing a Supreme Court Decision

Objective: Learn how the Supreme Court determined whether the president could refuse to surrender tapes and other information connected to the Watergate break-in.

Focus: Identify the central issue of the case.

Teach: Discuss the Court's opinion.

Assess: Explain the importance of the case (interpretation of executive privilege).

Close: Write a paragraph summarizing the case.

Differentiated Instruction Strategies

BL Explain the role President Nixon played in the case.

AL Paraphrase the Court's decision. Read your version to the class.

ELL Explain the concept of executive privilege in your own words.

D Differentiated Instruction

Visual/Spatial Have students study the Political Cartoons on page 944. **Ask:** Why was a "search dog" necessary during the Watergate investigation? BL

Analyzing VISUALS

Answers:
1. a tidal wave
2. Nixon is dressed like a detective, similar to Sherlock Holmes. It may be to signify that the president pretended to try to cooperate with the Watergate investigation, but really was guilty of involvement himself.

Additional Support

POLITICAL CARTOONS PRIMARY SOURCE

The Watergate Scandal

◀ *President Nixon clings to his desk as the Watergate scandal crashes like a tidal wave through the Oval Office.*

▲ *The Watergate investigation takes the form of a search dog who has tracked the evidence directly to the president.*

D

Analyzing VISUALS DBQ

1. **Specifying** What does the cartoon on the left use to symbolize the Watergate scandal?
2. **Explaining** What is the meaning of Nixon's appearance and the magnifying glass in the cartoon on the right?

The Case of the Tapes

At first, Nixon refused to hand over the tapes, pleading **executive privilege**—the principle that White House conversations should remain confidential to protect national security. **Special prosecutor** Archibald Cox, the government lawyer appointed by the president to handle the Watergate cases, took Nixon to court in October 1973 to force him to give up the recordings. Nixon ordered Attorney General Elliot Richardson to fire Cox, but Richardson refused and resigned. Nixon then ordered Richardson's deputy to fire Cox, but the deputy resigned as well. Nixon's solicitor general, Robert Bork, finally fired Cox, but the incident, nicknamed the "Saturday Night Massacre" in the press, badly damaged Nixon's reputation with the public.

The fall of 1973 proved to be a disastrous time for Nixon for other reasons, as well. His vice president, Spiro Agnew, was forced to resign in disgrace after investigators learned that he had taken bribes from state contractors while governor of Maryland and that he had continued to accept bribes while serving in Washington. Gerald Ford, the Republican leader of the House of Representatives, became the new vice president.

Nixon Resigns

In an effort to quiet the growing outrage over his actions, President Nixon appointed a new special prosecutor, Texas lawyer Leon Jaworski, who proved no less determined than Cox to obtain the president's tapes. In July the Supreme Court ruled that the president had to turn over the tapes, and Nixon complied.

Several days later, the House Judiciary Committee voted to impeach Nixon, or officially charge him with misconduct. The committee charged Nixon with obstructing justice in the Watergate cover-up; misusing federal agencies to violate the rights of citizens; and defying the authority of Congress by refusing to deliver tapes and other materials as requested. Before the House of Representatives

Activity: Interdisciplinary Connection

Civics Have students use library or Internet resources to conduct research on the order of succession for the president and the process for replacing a vice president who leaves office during his or her term. Have students use their findings to create a poster showing the steps prescribed by the Twenty-fifth Amendment to the Constitution. Remind students that they can review the Twenty-fifth Amendment on page 148 of their textbook. Ask students to share their posters with the class. Then discuss as a class why it is important to have an established procedure for replacing national leaders. OL could vote on whether Nixon should be impeached, investigators found indisputable evidence against the president. One of the tapes revealed that on June 23, 1972, just six days after the Watergate burglary, Nixon had ordered the CIA to stop the FBI's investigation. With this news, even the president's strongest supporters conceded that impeachment by the House and conviction in the Senate were inevitable. On August 9, 1974, Nixon resigned his office in disgrace. Gerald Ford took the oath of office and became the nation's 38th president.

The Impact of Watergate

Upon taking office, President Ford urged Americans to put the Watergate scandal behind them. "Our long national nightmare is over," he declared. On September 8, 1974, Ford announced that he would grant a "full, free, and absolute pardon" to Richard Nixon for any crimes he "committed or may have committed or taken part in" while president. "[This] is an American tragedy in which we all have played a part," he told the nation. "It could go on and on and on, or someone must write the end to it."

The Watergate crisis led to new laws intended to limit the power of the executive branch. The **Federal Campaign Act Amendments** limited campaign contributions and established an independent agency to administer stricter election laws. The Ethics in Government Act required financial disclosure by high government officials in all three branches of government. The FBI Domestic Security Investigation Guidelines Act restricted the Bureau's political intelligence-gathering activities. Congress also established a means for appointing an independent counsel to investigate and prosecute wrongdoing by high government officials.

Despite these efforts, Watergate left many Americans with a deep distrust of their public officials. On the other hand, some Americans saw the Watergate affair as proof that in the United States, no person is above the law. As Bob Woodward observed:

PRIMARY SOURCE

"Watergate was probably a good thing for the country; it was a good, sobering lesson. Accountability to the law applies to everyone. The problem with kings and prime ministers and presidents is that they think that they are above it . . . that they have some special rights, and privileges, and status. And a process that says: No. We have our laws and believe them, and they apply to everyone, is a very good thing."

—quoted in *Nixon: An Oral History of His Presidency*

After the ordeal of Watergate, most Americans attempted to put the affair behind them. In the years ahead, however, the nation encountered a host of new troubles, from a stubborn economic recession to a heart-wrenching hostage crisis overseas.

Reading Check **Evaluating** Why did Congress pass new laws after the Watergate scandal?

Section 2 REVIEW

Vocabulary

1. **Explain** the significance of: Sam J. Ervin, John Dean, executive privilege, special prosecutor, Federal Campaign Act Amendments.

Main Ideas

2. **Explaining** How did the Watergate cover-up involve the CIA and the FBI?
3. **Determining Cause and Effect** Why did President Nixon finally resign?

Critical Thinking

4. **Big Ideas** How did the Watergate scandal alter the balance of power between the executive and legislative branches of the federal government?
5. **Organizing** Use a graphic organizer similar to the one below to record the effects of the Watergate scandal.

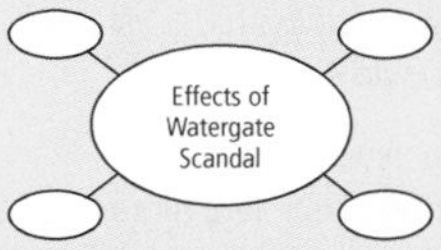

6. **Analyzing Visuals** Study the photographs on page 941. How did the Watergate hearings demonstrate the effectiveness of the system of checks and balances?

Writing About History

7. **Descriptive Writing** Take on the role of a television news analyst. Write a script in which you explain the Watergate scandal and analyze the factors that led to it.

History ONLINE
Study Central™ To review this section, go to glencoe.com and click on Study Central.

Reading Check

Answer: Congress wanted to put checks on the power of the presidency and the rest of the executive branch of the federal government.

Assess

History ONLINE

Study Central™ provides summaries, interactive games, and online graphic organizers to help students review content.

Close

Summarizing Ask: How did Nixon's nature and leadership style lead to his downfall? *(Causes: Nixon's distrustful, secretive nature, his need for control, and his conviction that people were out to get him led to the Watergate break-in. His belief that he was above the law led to the cover-up, eventually forcing his resignation.)* **OL**

Section 2 REVIEW

Answers

1. All definitions can be found in the section and the Glossary.
2. Nixon requested that the CIA tell the FBI to cease investigating the Watergate break-in on grounds of national security.
3. The House of Representatives was about to vote to impeach him and everyone felt that if impeached, he would be convicted by the Senate.
4. It led to laws intended to limit the power of the executive branch of the federal government.
5. Nixon's resignation, Federal Campaign Act Amendments, Ethics in Government Act, FBI Domestic Security Investigation Guidelines
6. The hearings demonstrated that the legislative branch could effectively check the power of the executive branch.
7. Students' scripts will vary; encourage students to include suggested visuals in their scripts.

Focus

Bellringer

Daily Focus Transparency 28-3

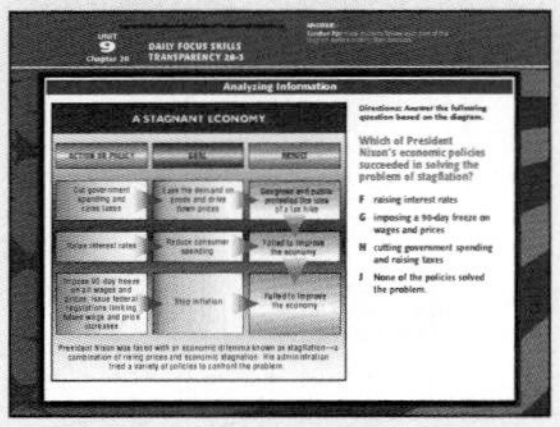

Guide to Reading

Causes

rising cost of raw materials and rising cost of oil → Economic Problems in the 1970s

increased international competition → Economic Problems in the 1970s

Section Spotlight Video

To generate student interest and provide a springboard for class discussion, access the Chapter 28, Section 3 video at glencoe.com or on the video DVD.

Resource Manager

R Reading Strategies	C Critical Thinking	D Differentiated Instruction	W Writing Support	S Skill Practice
Teacher Edition • Reading Primary Sources, p. 949 **Additional Resources** • Guid. Read. Act., URB p. 50 • Prim. Source Read., URB p. 37	**Teacher Edition** • Comparing and Contrasting, p. 948 • Analyzing Primary Sources p. 950 • Predicting Consequences, p. 951 **Additional Resources** • Quizzes and Tests, p. 405	**Additional Resources** • Differentiated Instruction Act., URB p. 23	**Teacher Edition** • Persuasive Writing, p. 948 **Additional Resources** • Academic Vocab. Act., URB p. 29	**Teacher Edition** • Reading a Graph, p. 947 **Additional Resources** • Reinforcing Skills Act., URB p. 31 • Read. Essen., p. 310

Section 3

Section Audio   Spotlight Video

Ford and Carter

Guide to Reading

Big Ideas

Economics and Society A weakening economy and growing energy crisis marred the terms of Presidents Ford and Carter.

Content Vocabulary

- inflation *(p. 946)*
- embargo *(p. 946)*
- stagflation *(p. 947)*

Academic Vocabulary

- theory *(p. 947)*
- deregulation *(p. 949)*

People and Events to Identify

- OPEC *(p. 946)*
- Helsinki Accords *(p. 948)*
- Department of Energy *(p. 949)*
- Camp David Accords *(p. 951)*

Reading Strategy

Organizing Complete a graphic organizer similar to the one below by listing the causes of economic problems in the 1970s.

Causes

[ ] → Economic Problems in the 1970s

[ ] → Economic Problems in the 1970s

By the time Richard Nixon resigned, the boom period Americans had experienced in the previous decades was coming to an end. Through the 1970s, Presidents Gerald R. Ford and Jimmy Carter attempted, with varying levels of success, to lead the United States through both domestic and foreign crises.

The Economic Crisis of the 1970s

MAIN Idea In the 1970s Americans had to face a slowing economy and an end to plentiful, cheap energy.

HISTORY AND YOU Have you ever heard anyone describe their experiences during the energy crisis of the 1970s? Read on to learn how politics and Americans' dependency on oil imports led to a serious crisis.

After World War II, American prosperity seemed normal. This prosperity relied on easy access to global raw materials and a strong manufacturing base at home. In the 1970s, however, prosperity gave way to a decade of hard times.

A Mighty Economic Machine Slows

Economic troubles began in the mid-1960s when President Johnson increased federal deficit spending, to fund both the Vietnam War and the Great Society programs, without raising taxes. This spending spurred **inflation** by pumping large amounts of money into the economy. One measure of inflation, the Consumer Price Index (CPI) calculates the average price of goods and services purchased by households. Comparing CPI on a yearly basis during the 1970s shows that the inflation rate rose more rapidly during this decade.

Another economic blow came when the price of oil began to rise. By 1970, the United States had become dependent on oil imports from the Middle East and Africa. This was not a problem as long as prices remained low, but in 1973, the **Organization of Petroleum Exporting Countries (OPEC)**—a cartel dominated by Arab countries—decided to use oil as a political weapon. In 1973 a war erupted between Israel and its Arab neighbors. OPEC announced an **embargo**, or trade ban, of petroleum to countries that supported Israel. OPEC also raised the price of crude oil by 70 percent, and then by another 130 percent a few months later.

Although the embargo ended within a few months, oil prices continued to rise. The price of a barrel of crude oil rose from $3 in 1973 to $30 in 1980. As oil and gasoline prices rose, Americans had less money for other goods, which contributed to a recession.

PRIMARY SOURCE

The Energy Crisis

OPEC's embargo caused long lines at gas stations and caused inflation to accelerate rapidly. The U.S. government responded by imposing price controls.

▲ *The oil embargo and price increases imposed by OPEC, whose members are shown above, severely decreased supply and increased prices in the United States.*

Price of Gasoline, 1970–1990

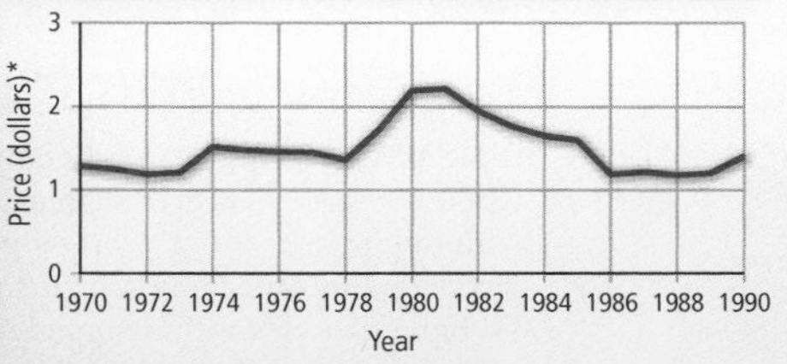

*Price of Leaded Regular Gasoline in Constant 2000 dollars.

Source: Energy Information Administration.

S

Analyzing VISUALS

1. **Drawing Conclusions** What problems did American consumers face because of the oil embargo?
2. **Specifying** In what year, between 1970 and 1990, did gasoline reach its highest price?

A Stagnant Economy

Another economic problem was the decline of manufacturing. By 1970, many American manufacturing plants were old and less efficient than the plants Japan and Germany had built after World War II. In 1971, for the first time since 1889, the United States imported more than it exported. Unable to compete, many factories closed, and millions of workers lost their jobs. Thus, in the early 1970s, President Nixon faced a new economic problem nicknamed **"stagflation"**—a combination of inflation and a stagnant economy with high unemployment.

Economists who emphasized the demand side of economic **theory,** including supporters of Keynesianism, did not think that inflation and recession could occur at the same time. They believed that demand drives prices and that inflation could only occur in a booming economy when demand for goods was high. As a result, they did not know what fiscal policy the government should pursue. Increased spending might help end the recession, but it would increase inflation. Raising taxes might slow inflation, but it would also keep the economy in recession.

Nixon decided to focus on controlling inflation. The government moved first to cut spending and raise taxes. The president hoped that higher taxes would prompt Americans to spend less, which would ease the demand on goods and drive down prices. Congress and much of the public, however, protested the idea of a tax hike. Nixon then tried to reduce consumer spending by getting the Federal Reserve Board to raise interest rates. When this failed, the president tried to stop inflation by imposing a 90-day freeze on wages and prices and then issuing federal regulations limiting future wage and price increases. This too met with little success.

✓Reading Check **Explaining** How did President Nixon attempt to stop stagflation?

Teach

S Skill Practice

Reading a Graph Ask students to find the years between 1970 and 1990 that gasoline prices were the lowest. *(1972–1973, 1986–1988)*

Analyzing VISUALS

Answers:
1. The embargo led to high gas prices and gas shortages.
2. 1981

✓**Reading Check**

Answers: The government cut spending and raised taxes, the Federal Reserve raised interest rates. The president imposed a 90-day freeze on wages and prices and issued regulations to limit future wage and price increases.

Additional Support

Activity: Interdisciplinary Connection

Economics Ask an economics teacher to present an explanation of cartels, including the fact that OPEC is the most long-lived cartel in history. Then have students use library or Internet sources to research other cartels, either past or present. Students should determine the purpose of cartels, what holds cartels together, and what types of problems bring an end to cartels. Have students report their findings in a three-page research report. Note that students' reports should use one of the cartels of the past or present as an example when discussing the purpose and problems of cartels. **AL**

Did You Know?

After his inauguration, Jimmy Carter and his family chose to walk up Pennsylvania Avenue from the Capitol to the White House instead of riding in the traditional limousine. The gesture symbolized Carter's desire to lead a simple life even while in the White House.

C Critical Thinking

Comparing and Contrasting Ask students to compare and contrast what Carter promised before the election and what he did in office. *(He promised new programs for energy and did address them, but his promises for tax reform, welfare reform, and health care reform were derailed by the need to manage the economic crisis he inherited.)* OL

W Writing Support

Persuasive Writing Have students write a campaign handout explaining why the public should vote for either Carter or Ford. OL

Ford and Carter Battle the Economic Crisis

MAIN Idea When Gerald Ford failed to solve the nation's problems, Americans turned to political outsider Jimmy Carter to lead the nation.

HISTORY AND YOU Do you think a president should be a Washington insider? Read how being an outsider affected Carter's ability to lead.

When Nixon resigned in 1974, inflation was still high, despite many efforts to reduce prices. Meanwhile, the unemployment rate was over 5 percent. It would now be up to the new president, Gerald Ford, to confront stagflation.

Ford Tries to "Whip" Inflation

By 1975, the American economy was in the worst recession since the Great Depression, with unemployment at nearly 9 percent. Ford responded by launching a plan called WIN—"Whip Inflation Now." He urged Americans to reduce their use of oil and gas, and take steps to conserve energy. The plan had little impact on the economic situation. The president then began cutting government spending and urged the Federal Reserve to raise interest rates to curb inflation. He also sought to balance the budget and keep taxes low. He vetoed more than 50 bills that the Democratic Congress passed during the first two years of his administration. These efforts failed to revive the economy.

Ford's Foreign Policy

In foreign policy, Ford continued Nixon's general strategy. Ford kept Kissinger on as secretary of state and continued to pursue détente with the Soviets and the Chinese. In August 1975, he met with leaders of NATO and the Warsaw Pact to sign the **Helsinki Accords.** Under the accords, the parties recognized the borders of Eastern Europe established at the end of World War II. The Soviets in return promised to uphold certain basic human rights, including the right to move across national borders. The subsequent Soviet failure to uphold these basic rights turned many Americans against détente.

Ford also met with problems in Southeast Asia. In May 1975, soon after Communists seized power in Cambodia, Cambodian forces captured the *Mayaguez,* an American cargo ship traveling near its shores. Calling the seizure an "act of piracy," Ford sent U.S. Marines to retrieve it. Cambodia secretly released the crew shortly before the marines arrived. Unaware the crew was safe, the marines attacked and recaptured the ship, but 41 servicemen died in the battle.

The Election of 1976

The presidential race pitted Gerald Ford against James Earl Carter, Jr., or Jimmy Carter, as he liked to be called. A former governor of Georgia, Carter had no political experience in Washington. Carter took advantage of his outsider status, promising to restore honesty to the federal government. He also promised new programs for energy development, tax reform, welfare reform, and national health care.

Ford characterized Carter as a liberal whose social programs would produce higher rates of inflation and require tax increases. For many voters, however, Carter's image as a moral and upstanding individual, untainted by Washington politics, made him an attractive candidate. In the end, Carter narrowly defeated Ford with 50.1 percent of the popular vote to Ford's 47.9 percent, while capturing 297 electoral votes to Ford's 240.

Carter's Economic Policies

Most of Carter's domestic policies were intended to fix the economy. At first he tried to end the recession and reduce unemployment by increasing government spending and cutting taxes. When inflation surged in 1978, he changed his mind. He delayed the tax cuts and vetoed the spending programs he had himself proposed. He tried to ease inflation by reducing the money supply and raising interest rates. In the end, none of his efforts succeeded.

Carter believed that the nation's most serious problem was its dependence on foreign oil. In one of his first national addresses, he asked Americans to support a "war" against rising energy consumption. "Our decision about energy will test the character of the American people and the ability of the president and Congress to govern this nation," Carter stated.

Hands-on Chapter Project: Step 3

Oral History of the 1970s

Step 3: Conducting the Interview Students should arrange the interview and be prepared to take notes. (Or, students may ask permission to record the interview.) In addition, students should show interviewees the photographs they selected and ask interviewees to comment on them.

Making Connections After the interview, students should meet back in their groups to discuss and compare what they have learned from the interviews.

(Chapter Project continued on page 953)

PRIMARY SOURCE

The Election of 1976

When President Ford failed to solve the nation's economic problems, voters decided to give Washington outsider Jimmy Carter a chance.

Inflation and Unemployment Rates

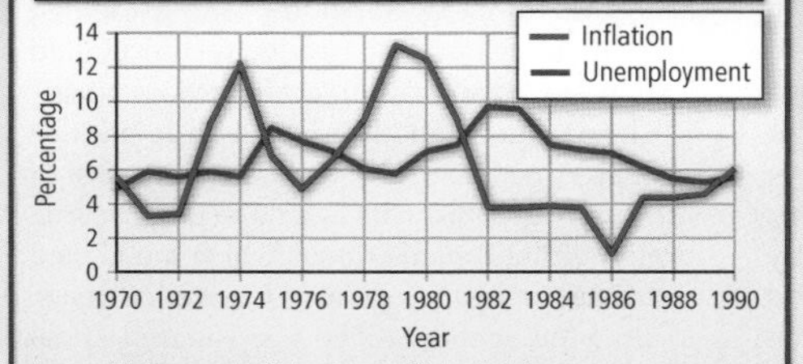

Source: U.S. Department of Labor; Bureau of Labor Statistics.

Presidential Election of 1976

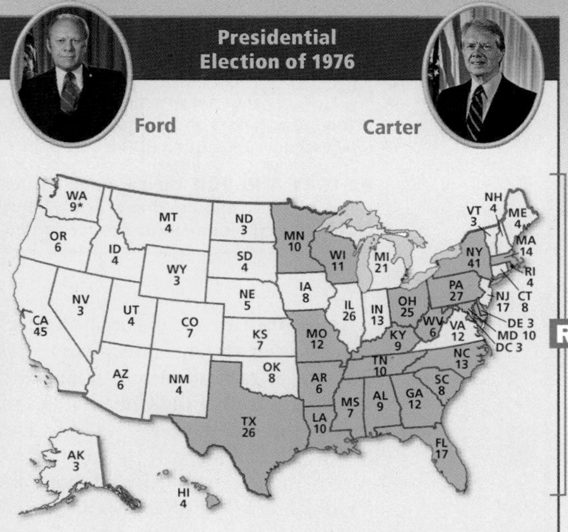

Presidential Candidate	Popular Votes	% of Popular Vote	Electoral Votes
Carter	40,825,839	50.15%	297
Ford	39,147,770	48.09%	240

* Eight electors in Washington voted for Ford and one voted for Reagan.

Analyzing VISUALS

1. **Analyzing** In what areas of the country did Carter receive the most votes? Why do you think this was so?
2. **Interpreting** What was the trend for both unemployment and inflation after 1976?

Carter proposed a national energy program to conserve oil and to promote the use of coal and renewable energy sources such as solar power. He also convinced Congress to create a **Department of Energy,** and asked Americans to reduce their energy consumption.

Meanwhile, many business leaders and economists urged the president and Congress to deregulate the oil industry. They believed that regulations, first imposed as part of President Nixon's price control plan, made it very difficult for oil companies to make a profit. They claimed they lacked the spare capital needed to invest in new domestic oil wells. This in turn kept the nation dependent on foreign oil.

Carter agreed to support **deregulation** but insisted on a "windfall profits tax" to prevent oil companies from overcharging consumers. Critics argued that the tax conflicted with the basic idea of deregulation, which was to free up capital for use in finding new sources of oil.

In the summer of 1979, instability in the Middle East produced a second major fuel shortage and deepened the nation's economic problems. Under increasing pressure to act, Carter made several proposals in a televised address. In the speech, Carter warned about a "crisis of confidence" that had struck "at the very heart and soul of our national will." The address became known as the "malaise" speech, although Carter had not specifically used that word. Many Americans felt that Carter was blaming the people for his failures.

President Carter's difficulties in solving the nation's economic problems lay partly in his inexperience and inability to work with Congress. Carter, proud of his outsider status, made little effort to reach out to Washington's legislative leaders. As a result, Congress blocked many of his energy proposals. The president also failed to set clear goals for the nation. Instead, he followed a cautious middle course that left people confused. By 1979, public opinion polls showed that Carter's popularity had dropped lower than President Nixon's during Watergate.

Reading Check **Summarizing** To what did President Carter devote much of his domestic agenda?

R Reading Strategy

Reading Primary Sources:
Ask: Which candidate carried more states during the election of 1976? *(Ford)* Ask why Carter won, despite carrying fewer states. *(Many of the states Ford carried had very few electoral votes.)* BL OL

Analyzing VISUALS

Answers:
1. Carter received the most votes in the East and in the South. This is probably because he is a Southerner, and in the North and East people tended to be more liberal as Carter was more liberal than Ford.
2. inflation increased sharply in the late 1970s, unemployment gradually declined

Reading Check

Answer: His main domestic focus was on the energy crisis.

Additional Support

Extending the Content

Life After the White House Carter continued his humanitarian policies after leaving office. He and his wife established a long-standing relationship with Habitat for Humanity, an organization promoting affordable housing in the United States and around the world. The organization builds thousands of houses for low-income families. Each house is built by volunteers, with the families themselves working alongside volunteers to build the homes. Many of the building supplies are donated or are purchased at cost.

C Critical Thinking

Analyzing Primary Sources Direct students' attention to the captions describing Carter's foreign policy actions. Remind students that Carter negotiated a peace agreement between longstanding enemies Egypt and Israel. Ask them why this major achievement may have weighed less heavily during the election of 1980 than such issues as boycotting the 1980 Summer Olympics or his inability to negotiate the release of the hostages. *(Americans were less directly affected by the peace agreement than by the other issues.)*

Analyzing VISUALS

Answers:

1. the Camp David Accords
2. The Middle East was a major source of oil. The U.S. wanted peace in the region but also U.S.-friendly governments. Good relations with countries in the Middle East would help solve the energy crisis.

Carter's Foreign Policy

MAIN Idea Carter attempted to reestablish the United States as a moral force for good on the international stage but had few successes.

HISTORY AND YOU Do you think a leader's personal morality should shape policy? Read how Carter applied his moral code to foreign policy.

In contrast to his uncertain leadership at home, Carter's foreign policy was more clearly defined. A man of strong religious beliefs, Carter argued that the United States must try to be "right and honest and truthful and decent" in dealing with other nations. Yet it was on the international front that Carter suffered one of his most devastating defeats.

Morality in Foreign Policy

President Carter set the tone for his foreign policy in his inaugural speech, when he said, "Our commitment to human rights must be absolute. . . . The powerful must not persecute the weak, and human dignity must be enhanced." Along with his foreign policy team—which included Andrew Young, the first African American ambassador to the United Nations—Carter strove to achieve these goals.

The president put his principles into practice in Latin America. To remove a major symbol of U.S. interventionism, he agreed to give Panama control of the Panama Canal, which the United States had built and operated for over 60 years. In 1978 the Senate ratified two Panama Canal treaties, which transferred control of the canal to Panama on December 31, 1999.

PRIMARY SOURCE

Jimmy Carter and the Middle East

During his administration, Jimmy Carter faced a number of challenges in the Middle East. His foreign policy there met with mixed success.

C

▲ **The Camp David Accords**

In 1978, Carter helped negotiate a peace treaty between Egypt and Israel. Above, Egyptian President Anwar Sadat, Carter, and Israeli Prime Minister Menachem Begin sign the accords.

▲ **The Soviet Invasion of Afghanistan**

The Soviet invasion of Afghanistan shattered détente. Carter responded by imposing a grain embargo, but it did not force the Soviets to pull back.

▼ **The Iranian Hostage Crisis**

The Ayatollah Khomeini (right) led a revolution in Iran in 1979. Fifty-two Americans were taken hostage. Carter's inability to negotiate their release hurt his reelection campaign.

Analyzing VISUALS

1. **Specifying** What was Carter's major success in foreign policy?
2. **Theorizing** Why was the Middle East a major focus of Carter's foreign policy?

Additional Support

Activity: Collaborative Learning

Organizing Information Have students work in groups of three, using a graphic organizer similar to the one below to indicate the domestic and foreign policy challenges Nixon, Ford, and Carter faced. Each group member should complete the chart for a different president. *(Answers will vary, but domestic challenges may include the Watergate scandal for Nixon, the pardoning of Nixon by Ford, and stagflation for Carter. Foreign challenges should include détente for Nixon, problems in Southeast Asia for Ford, and the Iranian hostage crisis for Carter.)* OL

Challenges	Nixon	Ford	Carter
Domestic			
Foreign			

Most dramatically, Carter singled out the Soviet Union as a violator of human rights. He strongly condemned, for example, the Soviet practice of imprisoning those who protested against the government. Relations between the two superpowers suffered a further setback when Soviet troops invaded the Central Asian nation of Afghanistan in December 1979. Carter responded by imposing an embargo on the sale of grain to the Soviet Union and boycotting the 1980 Summer Olympic Games in Moscow. Under the Carter administration, détente eroded further. C

Triumph and Failure in the Middle East

It was in the volatile Middle East that President Carter met both his greatest foreign policy triumph and his greatest failure. In 1978 Carter helped broker a historic peace treaty, known as the **Camp David Accords,** between Israel and Egypt—two nations that had been bitter enemies for decades. The treaty was formally signed in 1979. Most other Arab nations in the region opposed the treaty, but it marked a first step to achieving peace in the Middle East.

Just months after the Camp David Accords, Carter had to deal with a crisis in Iran. The United States had long supported Iran's monarch, the Shah, because Iran was a major oil supplier and a buffer against Soviet expansion in the Middle East. The Shah, however, had grown increasingly unpopular in Iran. He was a repressive ruler and had introduced Westernizing reforms to Iranian society. The Islamic clergy fiercely opposed the Shah's reforms. Opposition to the Shah grew, and in January 1979 protesters forced him to flee. An Islamic republic was then declared.

The new regime, led by religious leader Ayatollah Khomeini, distrusted the United States because of its support of the Shah. In November 1979, revolutionaries stormed the American embassy in Tehran and took 52 Americans hostage. The militants threatened to kill the hostages or try them as spies.

The Carter administration tried unsuccessfully to negotiate for the hostages' release. In April 1980, as pressure mounted, Carter approved a daring rescue attempt. To the nation's dismay, the rescue mission failed when several helicopters malfunctioned and one crashed in the desert. Eight servicemen died in the accident. Hamilton Jordan, President Carter's chief of staff, described the atmosphere in the White House the day after the crash. The president "looked exhausted and careworn. . . . The mood at the senior staff meeting was somber and awkward. I sensed that we were all uncomfortable, like when a loved one dies and friends don't know quite what to say."

The crisis continued into the fall of 1980. Every night, news programs reminded viewers how many days the hostages had been held. The president's inability to free them cost him support in the 1980 election. Negotiations continued right up to Carter's last day in office. On January 20, 1981, the day Carter left office, Iran released the Americans, ending their 444 days in captivity.

Reading Check **Summarizing** What was President Carter's main foreign policy theme?

Section 3 REVIEW

Vocabulary

1. **Explain** the significance of: inflation, OPEC, embargo, stagflation, Helsinki Accords, Department of Energy, Camp David Accords.

Main Ideas

2. **Describing** How did the OPEC embargo affect the U.S. economy?
3. **Specifying** What were two ingredients in Carter's failure to achieve success in his domestic policy?
4. **Identifying** What crisis in the Middle East occurred during the Carter administration?

Critical Thinking

5. **Big Ideas** How did Carter attempt to deal with the nation's energy crisis?
6. **Organizing** Complete a graphic organizer by listing the ways in which President Carter applied his human rights ideas to his foreign policy.

7. **Analyzing Visuals** Study the photograph of the hostages on page 950. What effect do you think images such as this one had on Americans who were living or traveling in other countries?

Writing About History

8. **Expository Writing** Write an essay identifying what you believe to be Carter's most important foreign policy achievement. Explain your choice.

History ONLINE
Study Central™ To review this section, go to glencoe.com and click on Study Central.

C Critical Thinking

Predicting Consequences
Ask: Who might be affected by the grain embargo other than Soviet leaders? *(Answers will vary, but may include U.S. farmers and Soviet consumers.)* OL

Reading Check

Answer: the need for the United States to be honest and decent in foreign relations

Assess

History ONLINE

Study Central™ provides summaries, interactive games, and online graphic organizers to help students review content.

Close

Summarizing Ask: What set Carter's domestic and foreign policy apart from Nixon's and Ford's? *(Domestically he focused on energy. In foreign policy, he made human rights a priority.)* OL

Section 3 REVIEW

Answers

1. All definitions can be found in the section and the Glossary.
2. The increase in oil prices caused by the embargo and later price increases accelerated inflation. As prices rose for oil-based products, Americans had less money for other goods, which helped cause a recession.
3. his inexperience and inability to work with Congress
4. the Iranian hostage crisis
5. He proposed a national energy program to conserve oil and promote the use of renewable energy sources, created the Department of Energy, and deregulated the oil industry.
6. Answers should reflect information in the text, particularly about the Soviet Union and Panama.
7. Answers will vary.
8. Students' essays will vary, but should include facts to support the position taken.

Focus

Bellringer

Daily Focus Transparency 28-4

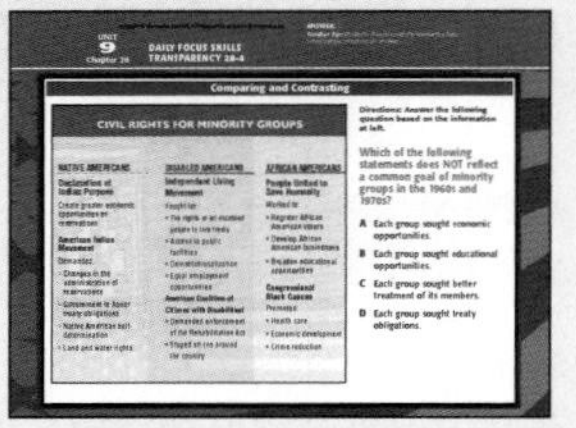

Guide to Reading

1969: AIM took over Alcatraz Island; 1971: PUSH organized voter registration, developed African American businesses, and broadened educational opportunities; CBC focused on African American concerns in Congress; 1973: AIM seized the town of Wounded Knee; 1977: Disability rights activists held a ten-city sit-in and occupied a federal building in San Francisco to force the federal government to enforce Section 504; 1994: Louis Farrakhan organized the Million Man March

Section Spotlight Video

To generate student interest and provide a springboard for class discussion, access the Chapter 28, Section 4 video at glencoe.com or on the video DVD.

Resource Manager

Section 4   Section Audio   Spotlight Video

New Approaches to Civil Rights

Guide to Reading

Big Ideas

Struggles for Rights African Americans, Native Americans, and people with disabilities organized to fight discrimination and gain access to better education and jobs.

Content Vocabulary
- busing *(p. 953)*
- affirmative action *(p. 953)*

Academic Vocabulary
- criteria *(p. 954)*
- appropriate *(p. 957)*

People and Events to Identify
- Allan Bakke *(p. 954)*
- Jesse Jackson *(p. 955)*
- Congressional Black Caucus *(p. 955)*
- Shirley Chisholm *(p. 955)*
- American Indian Movement (AIM) *(p. 955)*
- Section 504 *(p. 957)*

Reading Strategy

Sequencing Complete a time line similar to the one below by recording groups in the civil rights movement and their actions.

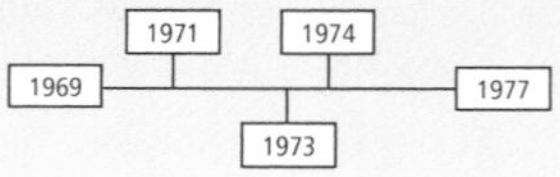

Throughout the 1960s and 1970s, reforms took place in many areas of society. In this period, minority groups, such as African Americans, Native Americans, and persons with disabilities, began to develop new ways to expand opportunities and assert their civil rights.

African Americans Seek Greater Opportunity

MAIN Idea During the 1960s and 1970s, African Americans built on the civil rights achievements of the 1950s to advance their social, political, and legal status.

HISTORY AND YOU Does your school district have a program of busing? Read on to learn how such programs originated as a way to integrate public schools.

By the end of the 1960s, many African American leaders felt a growing sense of frustration. Although most legal forms of racial discrimination had been dismantled, many African Americans saw little improvement in their daily lives. Increasingly, the problems facing most African Americans lay in their lack of access to good jobs and adequate schooling. As a result, leaders of the civil rights movement began to focus their energies on these problems.

Equal Access to Education

In the 1970s, African Americans began to push harder for improvements in public education and access to good schools. Although the Supreme Court had ordered an end to segregated public schools in the 1954 case *Brown* v. *Board of Education*, many schools remained segregated because children attended schools near where they lived. As a result many schools, especially in the North, remained segregated, not by law, but because whites and African Americans lived in different neighborhoods.

In many cases where de facto segregation existed, the white schools were superior, as Ruth Baston of the NAACP noted in 1965 after visiting Boston schools:

PRIMARY SOURCE

"When we would go to white schools, we'd see these lovely classrooms with a small number of children in each class. The teachers were permanent. We'd see wonderful materials. When we'd go to our schools, we'd see overcrowded classrooms, children sitting out in the corridors. And so then we decided that

R Reading Strategies	C Critical Thinking	D Differentiated Instruction	W Writing Support	S Skill Practice
Teacher Edition • Making Connections, p. 953 • Academic Vocabulary, p. 956 **Additional Resources** • Guid. Read. Act., URB p. 51	**Teacher Edition** • Comparing and Contrasting, p. 954 • Making Inferences, p. 955 **Additional Resources** • Linking Past and Present Act., URB p. 34 • Supreme Court Case Studies, p. 121 • Quizzes and Tests, p. 406	**Additional Resources** • Enrichment Act., URB p. 45	**Additional Resources** • Enrichment Act., URB p. 45	**Additional Resources** • Read. Essen., p. 313

PRIMARY SOURCE

Busing to End Segregation

To end segregation in public schools, state courts ordered the busing of children to schools outside of their neighborhoods. Reaction from parents to forced busing was often violent.

▲ *Anger over busing was particularly virulent in some neighborhoods in Boston, Massachusetts, where police often had to escort school buses along their routes.*

▲ *Supporters of busing took part in the National March on Boston in 1975. The NAACP sponsored the march to mark the anniversary of the* Brown v. Board of Education *decision, which outlawed segregation in schools.*

Analyzing VISUALS

1. **Explaining** Why were parents in Boston neighborhoods angry over busing?
2. **Making Inferences** Why are protesters holding signs that read "21 years is too long to wait" in the photograph on the right?

where there were a large number of white students, that's where the care went. That's where the books went. That's where the money went." **R**

—quoted in *Freedom Bound*

To solve this problem, state courts began ordering local governments to bus children to schools outside their neighborhoods to achieve greater racial balance. The practice led to protests and even riots in several white communities, including Boston. The Supreme Court, however, upheld the constitutionality of **busing** in the 1971 case *Swann* v. *Charlotte-Mecklenburg Board of Education.*

In response, many whites took their children out of public schools or moved to a district where busing had not been imposed. About 20,000 white students left Boston's public system for parochial and private schools. By late 1976, African Americans, Latinos, and other minorities made up the majority of Boston's public school students. This "white flight" also occurred in other cities. When Detroit tried to bus students from one school district to another in 1974, the Court held in *Milliken* v. *Bradley* that busing across district lines was unconstitutional unless districts had been deliberately drawn to create segregation.

For further information on the case of *Swann* v. *Charlotte-Mecklenburg Board of Education*, see page R61 in the *Supreme Court Case Summaries.*

Affirmative Action

In addition to supporting busing, civil rights leaders in the 1970s began advocating **affirmative action** as a new way to solve economic and educational discrimination. Enforced through executive orders and federal policies, affirmative action called for companies, schools, and institutions doing business with the federal government to recruit African Americans with the hope that this would lead to improved social and economic status. Officials later expanded affirmative action to include other minority groups and women.

Teach

R Reading Strategy

Making Connections Ask students how the Primary Source quote that ends on this page explains why courts might order busing. *(With de facto segregation, a greater share of resources went to the schools that served a predominantly white student body. Busing would prevent this injustice by mixing races at schools.)*

Analyzing VISUALS

Answers:

1. They did not want their children bused far from home where they might not be wanted and some probably did not want their children going to school with children of other races.
2. It refers to the 1954 Supreme Court decision *Brown* v. *Board of Education* that outlawed segregation in public schools and the fact that many schools were still segregated.

Hands-On Chapter Project
Step 4

Oral History of the 1970s

Step 4: Summarizing the Information Have students in groups collaboratively write an essay about their topic. Encourage students to draw upon information from Chapter 28 as well as their interviews.

Distinguishing Fact from Opinion In their essays, students should clearly delineate between the events that surrounded their topic and the reaction of people to those events at the time.

(Chapter Project continued on page 959)

C Critical Thinking

Comparing and Contrasting Ask students to compare and contrast the ways Jackson and Chisholm worked for civil rights. *(Answers may vary. Chisholm worked both within and outside the government, while Jackson worked mainly outside it.)* OL

People IN HISTORY

Answer: Jesse Jackson He worked with Dr. King, established PUSH and the Rainbow Coalition, ran for president and made African American issues important in the Democratic platform. **Answer: Shirley Chisholm** She worked on education and family issues and voted to increase daycare programs.

People IN HISTORY

Jesse Jackson
1941–

An ordained Baptist minister, Jesse Jackson first became involved in social causes as an aid to Martin Luther King, Jr. Jackson went on to form Operation PUSH, an organization based in Chicago, which was founded to promote economic opportunities for African Americans. In 1984 he founded the broader National Rainbow Coalition, which advocates for the rights of African Americans, women, and others. C

In the 1980s Jackson turned to politics. He ran for the Democratic presidential nomination in 1984 and 1988, placing third and then second to become the most successful African American presidential candidate to that point.

Jackson established the Wall Street Project in 1997 to increase opportunities for minorities in big business. Also in that year, President Clinton selected Jackson as a special envoy to Africa to promote democracy and human rights. In 2000 Jackson received the Presidential Medal of Freedom—the nation's highest civilian honor.

How has Jesse Jackson worked to improve the status of African Americans and promote civil rights for all Americans?

Shirley Chisholm
1924–2005

Shirley Chisholm once remarked, "Of my two 'handicaps,' being female put more obstacles in my path than being black." Her success in challenging both racism and sexism propelled the Brooklyn, New York, native into the national spotlight.

In 1968 Chisholm became the first African American woman to be elected to the United States Congress. There, Chisholm became an ardent defender of several causes, and helped to found the Congressional Black Caucus. She also worked on education and family issues and voted to increase day care programs.

In 1972 Chisholm ran for the Democratic nomination for president. Although she did not win the nomination, she did receive 28 delegates.

After the convention, Chisholm continued her crusade in Congress to help minorities and women for several more terms. She declined to run for re-election in 1982, citing the difficulties of campaigning for liberal issues in an increasingly conservative atmosphere.

On what issues did Shirley Chisholm focus?

For further information on the case of *University of California Regents v. Bakke*, see page R60 in the *Supreme Court Case Summaries*.

Supporters of the policy argued that because so few companies had hired from these groups in the past, they had not necessarily developed the required job skills. If businesses opened their doors wider to minorities, more of them could begin to acquire skills and build better lives.

In one example of affirmative action's impact, Atlanta witnessed a significant increase in minority job opportunities after Maynard Jackson became its first African American mayor in 1973. When Jackson took office, less than one percent of all city contracts went to African Americans, even though they made up about half of Atlanta's population. Jackson used the expansion of the city's airport to redress this imbalance. Through his efforts, small companies and minority firms took on 25 percent of all airport construction work, earning them some $125 million in contracts.

The *Bakke* Case

Affirmative action programs did not go unchallenged, however. Critics viewed them as a form of reverse racial discrimination. They claimed that qualified white male workers and students were kept from jobs, promotions, and places in schools because a certain number of such positions had been set aside for minorities or women.

Affirmative action was addressed by the Supreme Court in 1978. The case began in 1974, after officials at the medical school of the University of California at Davis turned down the admission of a white applicant named **Allan Bakke** for a second time. When Bakke learned that slots had been set aside for minorities, he sued the school. Bakke argued that by admitting minority applicants—some of whom had scored lower than Bakke on their exams—the school had discriminated against him based on his race.

In 1978, in *University of California Regents* v. *Bakke*, the Supreme Court, in a 5 to 4 ruling, declared that the university had violated Bakke's civil rights. It also ruled, however, that schools had an interest in maintaining a diverse student body. Thus, universities could consider race as one part of their admissions **criteria** as long as they did not use "fixed quotas," such as the slots the UC-Davis Medical School had reserved for minority students.

Additional Support

Activity: Collaborative Learning

Conducting a Debate Organize the class into two groups. Tell the groups that they are to prepare for a debate about affirmative action. Assign one group to concentrate on the pros of affirmative action; the other group should concentrate on the cons. Groups should conduct research using library or Internet sources to identify facts and theories to support their assigned point of view. Once both groups have completed their research, conduct an informal debate in which each side presents its case and rebuts the point of view of the other side. Encourage all students to participate. OL

New Political Leaders

New political leaders emerged in the African American community in the 1970s. **Jesse Jackson,** a former aid to Martin Luther King, Jr., was among this new generation of activists. In 1971 Jackson founded Operation PUSH (People United to Save Humanity), an organization dedicated to registering voters, developing African American businesses, and broadening educational opportunities. In 1984 and 1988, Jackson sought the Democratic presidential nomination. Although both attempts were unsuccessful, he won over millions of voters.

African Americans also became more influential in national politics for the first time since Reconstruction. In 1971 African American members of Congress organized the **Congressional Black Caucus** to more clearly represent their concerns. Another prominent leader of the era was **Shirley Chisholm** of New York. Chisholm was a founding member of the Congressional Black Caucus and the first African American woman to serve in Congress. In 1977 another former assistant to Martin Luther King, Jr., U.S. Representative Andrew Young, was selected by President Carter to become the first African American to serve as U.S. ambassador to the United Nations. He went on to become the mayor of Atlanta. By the early 1980s, African American mayors had been elected in Atlanta, Detroit, Chicago, Los Angeles, New Orleans, Philadelphia, and Washington, D.C.

Another leader who emerged in the 1980s was Louis Farrakhan, a prominent minister of the Nation of Islam. He organized the Million Man March, which attracted an enormous crowd in Washington, D.C., on October 16, 1995. Farrakhan had conceived of the march as a way to promote self-reliance and responsibility among African American men. In addition to Farrakhan, the event featured other prominent speakers, including Jesse Jackson and the poet Maya Angelou.

In 1990, voters in Virginia elected L. Douglas Wilder, who became the first African American to serve as governor of a state. In that same year, David Dinkins took office as the first African American mayor of New York City.

Reading Check **Examining** What were the goals of affirmative action policies?

Native Americans Raise Their Voices

MAIN Idea The most impoverished minority group in America, Native Americans, began organizing for civil rights.

HISTORY AND YOU What do you recall about the Black Power Movement in the 1960s? Read on to learn how some Native Americans formed the American Indian Movement.

In 1970 Native Americans were one of the nation's smallest minority groups, constituting less than one percent of the U.S. population, yet they faced enormous problems. The unemployment rate for Native Americans was ten times the national rate. Their average annual family income was $1,000 less than that of African Americans. Unemployment was very high on reservations, where nearly half of all Native Americans lived. Those living in cities often had little education or training. The bleakest statistic of all showed that the life expectancy for Native Americans was almost seven years below the national average.

A Protest Movement Emerges

In 1961 more than 400 members of 67 Native American groups gathered in Chicago to discuss ways to address their problems. They issued a manifesto, known as the Declaration of Indian Purpose, asking for federal programs to create greater economic opportunities on reservations.

Unlike some groups who wanted to be accepted by mainstream society, many Native Americans wanted more independence from it. They took a step toward this goal in 1968 when Congress passed the Indian Civil Rights Act. The legislation guaranteed reservation residents the protections of the Bill of Rights, but it also recognized local reservation law.

Native Americans who viewed the government's efforts as too modest formed more militant groups, which typically employed a more combative style. One such group, the **American Indian Movement (AIM),** staged a symbolic protest in 1969 by occupying the abandoned federal prison on Alcatraz Island in San Francisco Bay for 19 months, claiming ownership "by right of discovery." C

C Critical Thinking

Making Inferences What did AIM mean by "right of discovery"? *(They are making a statement about the Europeans who "discovered" Native American lands and claimed them.)* OL

Reading Check

Answer: to improve educational opportunities for African Americans and to actively recruit minorities and women for jobs

Additional Support

Activity: Interdisciplinary Connection

Art Have students design a postage stamp to commemorate progress in the pursuit of equal rights in the United States. The stamp should feature an event, person, or group that made a significant contribution to equal rights. Encourage students to choose a subject they feel is particularly worthy. In addition to a sketch of the stamp, ask students to prepare a short news release announcing the stamp and explaining its significance. Ask students to share their sketches and read their news releases to the class. OL

R Reading Strategy

Academic Vocabulary Point out the term *relinquish* in the first paragraph of the second column. Help students define the word as "part with or let go of." Ask them what they or others have relinquished. **ELL**

Reading Check

Answer: high unemployment, limited education and training, discrimination, and poor life expectancy

Analyzing VISUALS

Answers:

1. They struggled for equality in education, employment, and housing. They also worked for equal access to public facilities.
2. There is a ramp and lift on the bus and the sign shows that a spot is for people with disabilities only.

The most famous protest by AIM took place at Wounded Knee, South Dakota, where U.S. troops had killed hundreds of Sioux in 1890. In February 1973, AIM members seized the town of Wounded Knee for 70 days. They demanded that the government honor its past treaty obligations to Native Americans and insisted that radical changes be made in the administration of reservations. A brief clash between AIM members and the FBI resulted in two Native Americans dead and several wounded on both sides. Shortly thereafter, the siege came to an end.

Native American Gains

By the mid-1970s, the Native American movement had begun to achieve some of its goals. In 1975 Congress passed the Indian Self-Determination and Educational Assistance Act, which increased funds for Native American education and expanded local control over federal programs. More Native Americans also moved into policy-making positions at the Bureau of Indian Affairs, and the agency pushed for more Native American self-determination.

Native Americans also won several court cases involving land and water rights. The people of the Pueblo of Taos, New Mexico, regained property rights to Blue Lake, a place sacred to their religion. In 1980 a federal court settled a claim of the Passamaquoddy and the Penobscot peoples. The government paid them $81.5 million to relinquish their claim to land in Maine. Other court decisions gave Native American governments the authority to tax businesses on their reservations.

Since Native Americans first began to organize, many reservations have improved their economic conditions by actively developing businesses, such as electric plants, resorts, cattle ranches, and oil and gas wells. More recently, gambling casinos have become a successful enterprise. Because of rulings on sovereignty, Native Americans in some areas are allowed to operate gaming establishments under their own laws even though state laws prevent others from doing so.

Reading Check **Analyzing** What conditions led Native Americans to organize in the 1960s?

PRIMARY SOURCE

The Disability Rights Movement

In the 1970s, people with disabilities struggled for greater rights in education, employment, and housing. They met with success in the passage of legislation such as the Rehabilitation Act of 1973.

▲ *On April 5, 1977, the American Coalition of Citizens with Disabilities organized sit-ins demanding equal rights.*

▲ *Section 504 of the Rehabilitation Act and, later, the Americans with Disabilities Act specified that disabled people must have equal access to public facilities, such as transportation and parking.*

Analyzing VISUALS

1. **Listing** What rights did people with disabilities struggle for in the 1970s?
2. **Specifying** What two accommodations for people with disabilities are shown in the photograph on the right?

Additional Support

Activity: Interdisciplinary Connection

Language Arts After students have read the section, have them pose questions such as those below that could be used to interview someone who lived through the civil rights movement. Help students prepare open-ended questions. Then use the responses to evaluate the movement's impact on the American public. **OL**

- When were you first aware that "civil rights" was a broad movement?
- Which forms of protest most impressed you? In which, if any, did you participate?
- How did your life change as a result of the civil rights movement?
- How do you think the civil rights movement should be remembered today?

The Disability Rights Movement

MAIN Idea During the 1970s, people with disabilities fought for greater rights and access to education and jobs.

HISTORY AND YOU Do you or someone you know have a disability? Read on to learn about how people with disabilities achieved new legislation to help protect their civil rights.

The struggle for disability rights had its early expression in the independent living movement begun at the University of California at Berkeley in the early 1970s. The movement advocated for the right of people of all levels of abilities to choose to live freely in society. This was part of a new attitude that encouraged deinstitutionalization of people with disabilities.

People with disabilities also looked to the federal government to protect their civil rights. Access to public facilities and prohibitions on discrimination in employment led their demands. One victory was passage, in 1968, of the Architectural Barriers Act, which mandated that new buildings constructed with federal funds be accessible to disabled persons. The Rehabilitation Act of 1973 was even more significant. According to **Section 504,** "no otherwise qualified individual with a disability . . . shall . . . be excluded from participation in, be denied the benefits of, or be subjected to discrimination under any program or service or activity receiving Federal financial assistance . . ."

Unfortunately passage of the Rehabilitation Act meant little until procedures for enforcing its provisions were established. As of 1977, the Department of Health, Education, and Welfare (HEW) had issued no such regulations. Frustrated, the American Coalition of Citizens with Disabilities, headed by Frank Bowe, organized protests. On April 5, 1977, some 2,000 persons with disabilities in 10 cities began sit-ins at regional HEW offices. Although most protests lasted only a day or two, protesters in San Francisco maintained their sit-in for over three weeks—leaving only when HEW's director signed the regulations banning discrimination.

Changes also occurred in special education. In 1966 Congress created the Bureau for the Education of the Handicapped, which provided grants to develop programs for educating children with disabilities. In 1975 the Education for All Handicapped Children Act required that all students with disabilities receive a free, **appropriate** education. One trend was to mainstream, or bring into the regular classroom, students with disabilities.

In 1990 Congress enacted the Americans with Disabilities Act. This far-reaching legislation banned discrimination against persons with disabilities in employment, transportation, public education, and telecommunications.

Today, new technologies are important assets to people with disabilities. Innovations such as closed-captioned television broadcasts, devices for telephones, and screen readers allow people with disabilities to access information in new ways.

Reading Check **Explaining** Why did the American Coalition of Citizens with Disabilities stage sit-ins in 1977?

Section 4 REVIEW

Vocabulary

1. **Explain** the significance of: busing, affirmative action, Allan Bakke, Jesse Jackson, Congressional Black Caucus, Shirley Chisholm, American Indian Movement (AIM), Section 504.

Main Ideas

2. **Specifying** How did some critics characterize affirmative action?
3. **Identifying Central Issues** What was significant about AIM's claim to Alcatraz Island?
4. **Explaining** What was the significance of the independent living movement?

Critical Thinking

5. **Big Ideas** How did the Supreme Court support civil rights during the 1970s?
6. **Organizing** Use a graphic organizer to identify civil rights leaders and their causes.

Civil Rights Leaders	Causes

7. **Analyzing Visuals** Study the images on page 953 of busing in the 1970s. Why do you think reactions to busing were so strong and at times even violent?

Writing About History

8. **Expository Writing** Write a magazine article about conditions that provoked the Native American protest movement of the 1960s and 1970s. Be sure to discuss the movement's goals and activities.

History ONLINE
Study Central™ To review this section, go to glencoe.com and click on Study Central.

Reading Check

Answer: They were protesting the federal government's inaction over Section 504 of the Rehabilitation Act.

Assess

History ONLINE

Study Central™ provides summaries, interactive games, and online graphic organizers to help students review content.

Close

Summarizing Ask: What did African Americans, Native Americans, and Americans with disabilities gain by organizing? *(They all faced less discrimination and gained better employment, educational, and economic opportunities. Native Americans gained more sovereignty and some land and water rights. People with disabilities were supported in their desire to live independently and participate fully in the community.)* OL

Section 4 REVIEW

Answers

1. All definitions can be found in the section and the Glossary.
2. as reverse discrimination
3. They claimed ownership "by right of discovery," as Europeans had claimed their lands.
4. It was at the root of the disability rights movement.
5. *Swann v. Charlotte-Mecklenburg Board of Education:* constitutionality of busing; *University of California Regents v. Bakke:* constitutionality of affirmative action
6. Jackson: political power for African Americans; AIM: equal rights and improved conditions for Native Americans; American Coalition of Citizens with Disabilities/Frank Bowe: equal rights for people with disabilities
7. Possible answer: It was forcing integration, which people did not want. Also children were bused out of their own neighborhoods.
8. Students' articles will vary, but should focus on the reasons for the protest movement.

Focus

Bellringer

Daily Focus Transparency 28-5

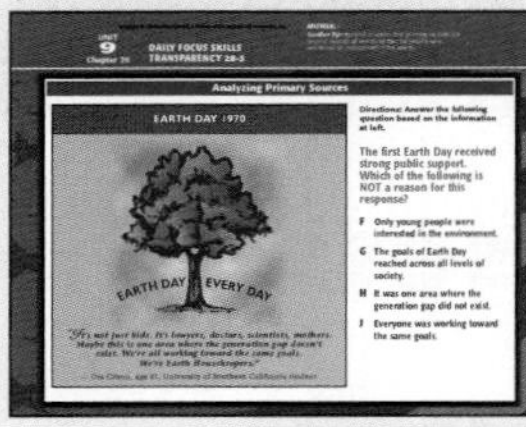

Guide to Reading

Answers: Clean Air Act, Clean Water Act, Earth Day celebration, Endangered Species Act, creation of the Environmental Protection Agency

Section Spotlight Video

To generate student interest and provide a springboard for class discussion, access the Chapter 28, Section 5 video at glencoe.com or on the video DVD.

Section 5

Section Audio Spotlight Video

Environmentalism

Guide to Reading

Big Ideas

Group Action Increased awareness of environmental issues inspired a grassroots campaign to protect nature.

Content Vocabulary

- smog *(p. 959)*
- fossil fuel *(p. 961)*

Academic Vocabulary

- intensify *(p. 961)*
- alternative *(p. 961)*

People and Events to Identify

- Rachel Carson *(p. 958)*
- Environmental Protection Agency *(p. 960)*
- Love Canal *(p. 960)*
- Three Mile Island *(p. 961)*

Reading Strategy

Organizing Complete a graphic organizer similar to the one below by including actions taken to combat the nation's environmental problems in the 1960s and 1970s.

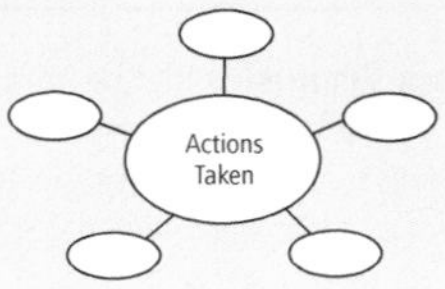

Americans became increasingly aware of the damage being done to the environment. Soon environmental issues became national concerns, and individuals, local groups, and the government acted to address the damage and protect natural resources.

The Origins of Environmentalism

MAIN Idea Concerns about the effects of a deadly pesticide, the visible signs of pollution in American cities, and an influential book inspired a movement to protect the environment.

HISTORY AND YOU Do you take action personally or with others to preserve and protect the environment? Read on to learn how one woman inspired the environmental movement.

In 1966 Carol Yannacone of Patchogue, a small community on Long Island, New York, learned that officials were using the powerful pesticide DDT as part of a mosquito control operation at a local lake. Alarmed that the pesticide might poison the lake and local streams, Yannacone and her husband Victor, an attorney, contacted several local scientists who confirmed their suspicions.

The Yannacones then successfully sued to halt the use of the pesticide. In so doing, they had discovered a new strategy for addressing environmental concerns. Shortly after the Yannacones' court victory, the scientists involved in the case established the Environmental Defense Fund and used its contributions for a series of legal actions across the country to halt DDT spraying. Their efforts led to a nationwide ban on the use of the pesticide in 1972.

The effort to ban DDT was only one part of a new environmental movement that took shape in the 1960s and 1970s. The person who helped trigger this new movement was not a political leader or prominent academic, but a soft-spoken marine biologist named **Rachel Carson.** Carson's 1962 book *Silent Spring* assailed the increasing use of pesticides, particularly DDT. She contended that while pesticides curbed insect populations, they also killed birds, fish, and other creatures that might ingest them. Carson warned Americans of a "silent spring," in which there would be no birds left to usher spring in with their songs. *Silent Spring* became a bestseller and one of the most controversial and influential books of the 1960s. The chemical industry was outraged and began an intense campaign to discredit Carson and her arguments.

Many Americans believed Carson's warnings, however, largely because of what they were seeing around them and reading in news reports. Rivers across the nation were no longer safe for

Resource Manager

R Reading Strategies	C Critical Thinking	D Differentiated Instruction	W Writing Support	S Skill Practice
Teacher Edition • Outlining, p. 960 **Additional Resources** • Guid. Read. Act., URB p. 52	**Teacher Edition** • Making Inferences, p. 960 **Additional Resources** • Quizzes and Tests, p. 407 • Interpret. Pol. Cartoons, URB p. 41	**Additional Resources** • Reteaching Act., URB p. 43 • Auth. Assess., p. 61	**Teacher Edition** • Expository Writing, p. 959 **Additional Resources** • American Art and Music, URB p. 39	**Additional Resources** • Read. Essen., p. 316

PRIMARY SOURCE

Origins of the Environmentalist Movement

▲ *Industrial pollution in cities like Newark, New Jersey (above) led to thick clouds of smog that caused breathing problems for some people. Tired of the dirty air, many Americans began to demand an end to pollution.*

▲ *Volunteers work to clean up an oil spill off the coast of California in 1969. News of the spill helped mobilize the new environmentalist movement.*

◀ *In 1969, the Cuyahoga River in Ohio caught fire. The incident gained national attention and contributed to the passage of the Clean Water Act in 1972.*

Analyzing VISUALS

1. **Summarizing** What events raised awareness of the need to protect the environment?
2. **Discussing** Why do you think the fire on the Cuyahoga River convinced many people of the need for action?

fishing or swimming. **Smog,** or fog made heavier and darker by smoke and chemical fumes, hung perpetually over many major cities. In the Northwest, timber companies were cutting down acres of forest. In 1969 a major oil spill off Santa Barbara, California, ruined miles of beach and killed scores of birds and aquatic animals. A dike project in Florida's Everglades indirectly killed millions of birds and animals. Pollution and garbage caused nearly all the fish to disappear from Lake Erie. By 1970, many citizens were convinced it was time to do something about protecting the environment.

W

A Grassroots Effort Begins

Many observers point to April 1970 as the unofficial beginning of the environmentalist movement. That month, the nation held its first Earth Day celebration, a day devoted to addressing environmental concerns. The national response was overwhelming. On 2,000 college campuses, in 10,000 secondary schools, and in hundreds of communities, millions of Americans participated in activities to show their environmental awareness.

After Earth Day, many citizens formed local environmental groups. Long-standing nonprofit organizations such as the Audubon Society, the Sierra Club, and the Wilderness Society grew rapidly in membership and political influence. These organizations worked to protect the environment and promote the conservation of natural resources. In 1970 activists started the Natural Resources Defense Council to coordinate a nationwide network of scientists, lawyers, and activists working on environmental issues.

Many communities and businesses responded to these organizations. Many city planners sought to reduce urban sprawl and expand green space. Architects and builders tried to make their structures more energy efficient, and the forestry industry began reforestation programs.

✓Reading Check **Identifying** What natural resources did environmental groups want to protect?

Teach

Analyzing VISUALS

Answers:

1. oil spills, terrible industrial pollution, fire on the Cuyahoga River
2. If something made of water can catch on fire, that indicates a serious level of pollution.

W Writing Support

Expository Writing Have interested students write a book review of *Silent Spring* by Rachel Carson or a more recent book about the environment. **AL**

✓Reading Check

Answer: plant, wildlife, air, and water resources

Hands-On Chapter Project Step 5

Oral History of the 1970s

Step 5: Presenting the Project Visually Students should try to integrate the information presented in this chapter, their research, and their notes based on the interviews.

Illustrating Have students create a poster presenting an overview of their topic using the photographs and excerpts from their interviews.

(Chapter Project continued on the Visual Summary page)

R Reading Strategy

Outlining To help students identify main ideas as they read the rest of the section, have them create an outline or draw a graphic organizer. **BL**

C Critical Thinking

Making Inferences Have students read the political cartoon on the left and its caption.

Ask: Why would industrial interests resist efforts to protect the environment? *(It can add to their cost of doing business, or in some cases, prevent their doing business. Manufacturers of toxic chemicals have much to lose if their chemicals are banned, and preventing or cleaning up pollution from doing business is expensive.)* **OL**

Analyzing VISUALS

Answers:

1. strip-mining interests
2. that Earth needs our help to recover from the damage it has already experienced, and to save it from further destruction

Additional Support

The Environmental Movement Blossoms

MAIN Idea Pressure from citizens and activist groups led Congress to pass major environmental legislation.

HISTORY AND YOU Can you think of a recent environmental disaster that has been in the news? Read on to learn about two of the worst environmental disasters in American history.

As the environmental movement gained support, the federal government took action. In 1970 President Nixon signed the National Environmental Policy Act, which created the **Environmental Protection Agency (EPA).** The EPA set and enforced pollution standards, promoted research, and directed antipollution activities with state and local governments.

The Clean Air Act also became law in 1970 after Congress overrode President Nixon's veto. This act established emissions standards for factories and automobiles. It also ordered all industries to comply with such standards within five years.

In following years, Congress passed two more pieces of significant environmental legislation. The Clean Water Act (1972) restricted the discharge of pollutants into the nation's lakes and rivers, and the Endangered Species Act (1973) established measures for saving threatened animal and plant species. These laws succeeded in reducing smog, and the pollution of many lakes, streams, and rivers declined dramatically.

Love Canal

Despite the flurry of federal environmental legislation, Americans continued to mobilize on the community level throughout the 1970s. One of the most powerful displays of community activism occurred in a housing development near Niagara Falls, New York, known as **Love Canal.**

POLITICAL CARTOONS PRIMARY SOURCE
A New Focus on the Environment

By the 1970s, the environmental movement was a strong force for change in the nation and around the world. In response, Congress passed a series of laws designed to protect the air, water, and wildlife.

◀ *President Ford and others are criticized for supporting industrial interests rather than protecting the environment.*

▶ *Events, such as the annual Earth Day celebrations, helped environmentalists increase public awareness of environmental problems.*

Analyzing VISUALS DBQ

1. **Identifying** Who does the large figure represent in the cartoon on the left?
2. **Summarizing** What is the main idea being expressed in the Earth Day poster?

Activity: Interdisciplinary Connection

Science Invite a scientist or science teacher to address your class about an environmental issue. Ask the speaker to address how science has helped to create some of the current environmental issues, how science helps prevent other environmental problems, and how science is helping to correct existing problems. For example, the speaker might address how science and technology helped to create many of the disposable products that we use today and how science is being used to help make those products more environmentally friendly. **OL**

During the 1970s, residents of Love Canal began to notice increasingly high incidences of health problems in their community, including nerve damage, blood diseases, cancer, miscarriages, and birth defects. The residents soon learned that their community sat atop a decades-old toxic waste dump. Over time, its hazardous contents had spread through the ground.

Led by a local woman, Lois Gibbs, the residents joined together and demanded that the government take steps to address these health threats. Hindered at first by local and state officials, the residents refused to back down, and by 1978 they had made their struggle known to the entire nation. That year, in the face of mounting public pressure and evidence of the dangers posed by the dump, the state permanently relocated more than 200 families.

In 1980, after hearing protests from the families who still lived near the landfill, President Carter declared Love Canal a federal disaster area and moved over 600 remaining families to new locations. In 1983 Love Canal residents sued the company that had created the dump site and settled the case for $20 million. The site was cleaned up by sealing the waste within an underground bunker and burning homes located above the dumping ground.

Concerns About Nuclear Energy

During the 1970s, a number of citizens also became concerned about the use of nuclear reactors to generate electricity. As nuclear power plants began to dot the nation's landscape, the debate over their use **intensified.** Supporters of nuclear energy hailed it as a cleaner and less expensive **alternative** to **fossil fuels,** such as coal, oil, and natural gas, which are in limited supply. Opponents warned of the risks nuclear energy posed, particularly the devastating consequences of an accidental radiation release into the air.

The debate gained national attention in a shocking fashion in 1979. In the early hours of March 28, one of the reactors at the **Three Mile Island** nuclear facility outside Harrisburg, Pennsylvania, overheated after its cooling system failed. Two days later, as plant officials scrambled to fix the problem, low levels of radiation escaped from the reactor.

Officials evacuated many nearby residents, while others fled on their own. Citizens and community groups expressed outrage at protest rallies. Officials closed down the reactor and sealed the leak. The Nuclear Regulatory Commission, the federal agency that regulates the nuclear power industry, eventually declared the plant safe. President Carter even visited the site in order to allay the public's concerns.

Although no one was hurt, the accident at Three Mile Island had a powerful impact politically. Many people now doubted the safety of nuclear energy. Such doubts have continued. Since Three Mile Island, some 60 nuclear power plants have been shut down or abandoned, and no new facilities have been built since 1973.

Reading Check **Summarizing** What is the environmental movement's main goal?

Section 5 REVIEW

Vocabulary

1. **Explain** the significance of: Rachel Carson, smog, Environmental Protection Agency, Love Canal, fossil fuel, Three Mile Island.

Main Ideas

2. **Summarizing** What were some of the dangers of DDT?
3. **Explaining** Why was Love Canal a dangerous place to live?

Critical Thinking

4. **Big Ideas** What were some groups that lobbied for legislation to protect the environment in the 1960s and 1970s?
5. **Categorizing** Use a graphic organizer similar to the one below to list the environmental laws passed in the 1970s, and explain their purposes.

Environmental Legislation	Purpose

6. **Analyzing Visuals** Study the cartoon on the left-hand side of page 960. What is the meaning of the piece of paper that reads "O.K. Gerald Ford" in the main figure's pocket?

Writing About History

7. **Descriptive Writing** Take on the role of an investigative reporter, and describe the environmental disaster at either Love Canal or Three Mile Island. Explain how community activism brought the issue to the nation's attention.

History ONLINE
Study Central™ To review this section, go to glencoe.com and click on Study Central.

Reading Check

Answer: protecting and preserving natural resources

Assess

History ONLINE

Study Central™ provides summaries, interactive games, and online graphic organizers to help students review content.

Close

Summarizing Ask: What did the environmental movement achieve during the 1970s? *(controls on pollution, cleanups; laws such as the Clean Air Act, Clean Water Act, and Endangered Species Act; creation of the Environmental Protection Agency; and establishment of Earth Day)* OL

Section 5 REVIEW

Answers

1. All definitions can be found in the section and the Glossary.
2. It killed many of the birds that ate it and the animals that then ate the birds, and it poisoned some lakes and streams.
3. It was built on a toxic waste dump and caused serious health problems to the people who lived there.
4. Natural Resource Defense Council, Sierra Club, Audubon Society, Wilderness Society
5. Clean Air Act: set emission standards for vehicles and factories; Clean Water Act: restricted discharge of pollutants into lakes and rivers; Endangered Species Act: established measures to save plant and animal species
6. The cartoonist is implying that President Ford basically gave the strip-mining interests permission to destroy the land and that he is "in their pocket."
7. Students' reports will vary, but should include details about the chosen disaster provided in the section.

Visual/Spatial Have students make a two-column problem/solution chart matching challenges of the 1970s with solutions attempted. Tell them to list at least two domestic challenges and two foreign policy challenges in the left column and the attempted solutions in the right column. *(Sample entries for domestic might include racial problems and environmental threats in the left column, with affirmative action and creation of the EPA in the right column. Sample entries for foreign policy might include Cold War tensions and conflicts between Israel and neighbors in the left column, with Nixon's détente and Carter's brokered peace treaty in the right.)* OL

Expository Writing Have students select a foreign policy or domestic challenge that faced all three presidents. Have them write an essay comparing and contrasting the three presidents' responses to the issue. OL

Chapter 28 Visual Summary

STUDY TO GO You can study anywhere, anytime by downloading quizzes and flashcards to your PDA from glencoe.com.

An Era of Challenges

Major Domestic Issues of the 1970s

- A nation is divided and angry over the Vietnam War.
- An energy crisis is triggered by OPEC's raising of oil prices.
- A stagnant economy exists with both inflation and high unemployment.
- Ongoing racial problems occur in major cities.
- Growing awareness of environmental problems including air and water pollution, toxic waste (at Love Canal and other sites), the overuse of pesticides, plus a crisis with the nuclear power plant at Three Mile Island.

Major Foreign Policy Issues of the 1970s

- Cold War tensions continue with the Soviet Union and China.
- The Soviet Union invades Afghanistan.
- War between Israel and its Arab neighbors breaks out in 1973, and ongoing violence occurs in the Middle East.
- A revolution in Iran leads to the taking of American hostages.

▲ *In the 1970s, state courts order the forced desegregation of public schools through busing, despite protests such as the one above in Memphis, Tennessee.*

▲ *Americans wait in long lines to purchase gasoline during the energy crisis of the 1970s.*

◀ *The first Earth Day in 1970 is often seen as the start of an organized environmentalist movement, which continues to have a major influence on politics and society today.*

New Policies and Activism

Responding to Domestic Issues

- Nixon attempts to win over Southern conservatives, but his administration's determination to win leads to the Watergate cover-up and Nixon's subsequent resignation.
- Ford's WIN campaign fails to overcome inflation.
- Carter urges Americans to conserve energy, creates the Department of Energy, and asks Congress to pass legislation deregulating the oil industry.
- Civil rights leaders propose affirmative action policies to reduce discrimination; the Supreme Court upholds some types of affirmative action in the *Bakke* case.
- Busing begins in northern cities to integrate schools.
- Environmentalist movement begins; Nixon creates the EPA.

Responding to Foreign Policy Issues

- Nixon and Kissinger introduce the policy of détente and begin talks with both the USSR and China.
- Carter mediates negotiations between Israel and Egypt leading to the first Arab-Israeli peace treaty.
- The United States imposes a grain embargo on the USSR for invading Afghanistan and boycotts the Moscow Olympics.
- The hostage crisis with Iran drags on for more than a year; an American rescue attempt fails, and the hostages are not released until Carter leaves office.

Hands-On Chapter Project
Step 6: Wrap Up

Oral History of the 1970s

Step 6: Wrap Up Students should present their final project to the class. They should explain what they learned in their research and interviews. Display final projects in the classroom.

Evaluating Ask students to evaluate their completed projects by answering the following questions in writing:

- Which part of the project was most demanding? Why?
- Which part of the project was the most interesting to me? Why?
- What did I learn from this project about American history? OL

Reviewing Vocabulary

Directions: Choose the word or words that best complete the sentence.

1. Richard Nixon used the ________ to attract more Southerners to the Republican Party.
   - **A** détente
   - **B** revenue sharing
   - **C** Southern strategy
   - **D** Dixiecrats

2. In *United States* v. *Nixon*, the Supreme Court found that President Nixon could not invoke _________ to prevent his tapes from being used as evidence in a criminal trial.
   - **A** revenue sharing
   - **B** habeas corpus
   - **C** détente
   - **D** executive privilege

3. During the 1970s, the U.S. economy was threatened by an oil ________ established by OPEC.
   - **A** embargo
   - **B** boycott
   - **C** importation
   - **D** duty

4. _________ was a new way to address the social and economic inequalities that kept African Americans as second-class citizens.
   - **A** Détente
   - **B** The Southern strategy
   - **C** Affirmative action
   - **D** Stagflation

5. In the 1960s and 1970s, environmentalists began to combat issues such as _________ and other types of air pollution.
   - **A** chemical runoff
   - **B** DDT
   - **C** smog
   - **D** toxic waste

Reviewing Main Ideas

Directions: Choose the best answer for each of the following questions.

Section 1 *(pp. 934–939)*

6. Nixon developed a new program to try to make government more efficient known as
   - **A** New Federalism.
   - **B** the Silent Majority.
   - **C** States' Rights.
   - **D** the Great Society.

Section 2 *(pp. 940–945)*

7. Members of the Committee for the Re-election of the President broke into Democratic Party headquarters at the Watergate to
   - **A** leave incriminating evidence of Democratic wrongdoing.
   - **B** install a tape-recording device so that Nixon could write his memoirs.
   - **C** find information to use in the case *United States* v. *Nixon*.
   - **D** steal sensitive information and install wiretaps.

8. In the wake of the Watergate scandal, Congress passed a series of laws to accomplish which of the following goals?
   - **A** to stop tape recordings in the White House
   - **B** to limit the power of the presidency
   - **C** to pardon Richard Nixon for his part in the cover-up
   - **D** to remove police power from the FBI

Section 3 *(pp. 946–951)*

9. In the early 1970s, OPEC began to use oil as a political weapon against countries that
   - **A** would not join their organization.
   - **B** supported Israel's right to exist.
   - **C** refused to pay the new per-barrel oil price.
   - **D** supported Arab countries' disapproval of Israel.

TEST-TAKING TIP

Always manage your time during a test so you can go back and review all your answers.

Need Extra Help?

If You Missed Questions . . .	1	2	3	4	5	6	7	8	9
Go to Page . . .	934–935	943	946	953	959	936	940–942	945	946

GO ON

Answers and Analyses Reviewing Vocabulary

1. C This is a good place to reinforce the importance of reading the question carefully. The question asks about Nixon's strategy to attract more *Southerners* to the Republican Party—the Southern strategy.

2. D Revenue sharing, or the sharing of profits, does not make sense. Habeas corpus deals with lawful imprisonment. Détente is an easing of tensions. Executive privilege is literally the right of the executive branch to refuse to disclose information it feels would be harmful to the administration.

3. A A boycott is a refusal to buy a certain product. OPEC produced oil, it did not buy it from the U.S., so it would not boycott U.S. oil. The U.S. economy would not be hurt by simple importation of oil. A duty is a tax or tariff, usually on foreign or incoming goods. OPEC caused economic problems when the OPEC embargo caused an oil shortage.

4. C Détente was a Cold War diplomatic strategy; the Southern strategy helped Nixon win support in the traditionally Democratic South; stagflation describes the economic stagnation and rising inflation of the 1970s.

5. C The key words in the question are "air pollution." Only smog is air pollution. The other answer choices refer to polluted land and water.

Reviewing Main Ideas

6. A Federalism refers to a system of government in which power is shared/divided between the federal government and state governments. New Federalism was Nixon's plan to reduce federal programs and pass them on to the states. The Great Society was LBJ's plan.

7. D During a break-in, something is usually taken. The break-in was not meant to plant evidence of any kind. It was an attempt to gain information. *B* does not make sense; Nixon would not need to secretly record the Democrats to write his own memoir. *U.S.* v. *Nixon* was a result of the break-in.

8. B This is a cause-and-effect question. Students must choose the answer that was an effect of the Watergate scandal. Part of the scandal was the liberties taken by the executive branch. New laws affected things like campaign contribution and election laws.

9. B *A* does not make sense; OPEC is an organization of oil-producing nations that used its control of oil supply to try to influence the foreign policies of other nations by withholding product or raising prices. *C* is incorrect because if a nation did not want to buy the oil in the first place, OPEC would have no recourse. *D* is the opposite of the correct answer.

10. D Carter did not send troops to Afghanistan. *B* and *C* would not be appropriate actions to take to show displeasure with another nation; they are more like acts to prepare for war. An embargo on grain shipments to the USSR, however, was an attempt to punish the USSR directly for its invasion of Afghanistan.

11. A The case clearly relates to education, so students should be able to immediately eliminate *D.* The fact that the case involved a board of education should tell students that the case dealt with high-school or lower. This eliminates affirmative action, which applied to higher education. Segregation was illegal by 1971, so a case in 1971 would not uphold it.

12. C Section 504 was a landmark because it banned all discrimination on the basis of disability in all federally–funded programs. The Rehabilitation Act was not meant specifically for veterans, nor was it an education bill. The Architectural Barriers Act mandated physical access to new buildings built with federal funds.

13. B Students should associate "beginning" with "first" Earth Day. *A* was a precursor to the first Earth Day. The Clean Air Act was passed after the first Earth Day, and the Love Canal was found to be poisoned after that.

Critical Thinking

14. B This is another cause-and-effect question. Students who are unsure of the answer should ask themselves what they think is the most likely effect listed in the answer choices. China is a communist nation. The most likely effect is that, if the U.S. improved its relations with China, it would be open to improving its relationship with the USSR, which it did. *B* is the only positive answer choice.

15. C Nixon carried most of the West and Midwest.

Chapter 28 Assessment

10. To protest the Soviet Union's invasion of Afghanistan, President Carter took which of the following actions?

A He sent U.S. Army troops to fight with the Afghans.
B He put NATO forces in Europe on high alert.
C He approved a buildup of U.S. nuclear weapons.
D He placed an embargo on grain shipments to the USSR.

Section 4 *(pp. 952–957)*

11. The 1971 case *Swann* v. *Charlotte-Mecklenburg Board of Education* upheld the constitutionality of

A busing.
B affirmative action.
C segregation.
D revenue sharing.

12. Section 504 of the Rehabilitation Act of 1973 was significant because it

A set aside money for helping injured veterans in their recovery.
B mandated physical access to federal buildings.
C banned discrimination against people with disabilities by any organization receiving federal funds.
D guaranteed all young people a free and appropriately designed education.

Section 5 *(pp. 958–961)*

13. The unofficial beginning of the environmentalist movement occurred

A when the Yannacones complained about the use of DDT.
B on the first Earth Day in 1970.
C when Congress passed the Clean Air Act.
D after Love Canal was found to be poisoned.

Critical Thinking

Directions: Choose the best answers to the following questions.

14. What effect did the United States's improved relations with China have on its relations with the Soviet Union?

A Tensions increased between the two nations.
B The two nations were able to establish détente.
C The Warsaw Pact began to break up.
D The Soviet Union began to boycott American goods.

Base your answer to question 15 on the map below and your knowledge of Chapter 28.

The Election of 1968

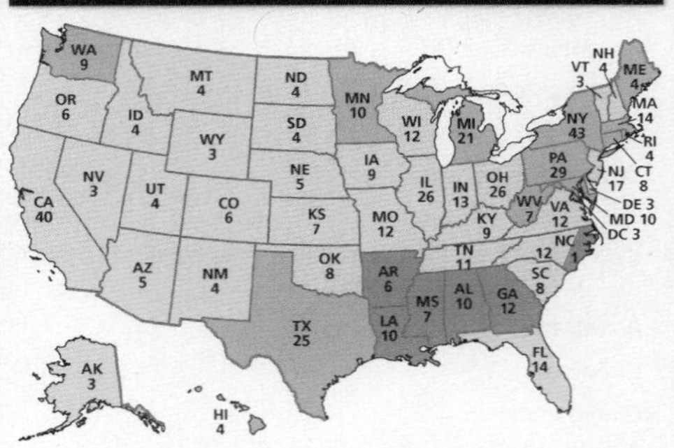

Presidential Candidate	Popular Votes	% of Popular Vote	Electoral Votes
Nixon	31,710,470	43.60%	301
Humphrey	30,898,055	42.48%	191
Wallace	9,906,473	13.62%	46

15. In the election of 1968, Nixon received the most support in the

A North and South.
B North and Midwest.
C Midwest and West.
D South and West.

Need Extra Help?						
If You Missed Questions . . .	10	11	12	13	14	15
Go to Page . . .	951	953	957	958	939	934

GO ON

16. In 1961, 67 Native American tribes issued the Declaration of Indian Purpose, which
   - A demanded federal programs to create greater opportunities on reservations.
   - B demanded that the Bill of Rights be recognized on reservations.
   - C established the militant group American Indian Movement (AIM).
   - D announced their decision to separate completely from the United States.

17. The result of the environmentalist legislation Congress passed in the 1970s was that
   - A many corporations went bankrupt.
   - B new renewable energy sources were developed.
   - C air and water pollution were greatly reduced.
   - D Rachel Carson published *Silent Spring.*

Analyze the cartoon and answer the question that follows. Base your answer on the cartoon and on your knowledge of Chapter 28.

Ranan Lurie, 1970

18. According to this cartoon, who ultimately suffered over the arms buildup between the United States and the Soviet Union?
   - A the military-industrial complex
   - B the generals of both nations
   - C the politicians of both nations
   - D the taxpayers of both nations

Document-Based Questions

Directions: Analyze the document and answer the short-answer questions that follow the document.

The following excerpt is from a magazine article that details the growing energy problems in the United States during the 1970s.

> *"Evidence of the full dimensions of the energy crisis in this country is becoming more clear every day. . . .*
> - *As a first step to cut gasoline use, President Nixon was reportedly ready to order closing of service stations nationwide from 9 P.M. Saturday to midnight Sunday. . . .*
> - *Immediate rationing of gasoline and fuel oil is being urged on the President by top oil-industry executives. . . .*
>
> *One major piece of legislation . . . directs the President to take measures necessary to reduce the nation's energy demands by 25 percent within four weeks.*
>
> *Speed limits would be cut nationally; lighting and heating of public and commercial buildings would be curtailed; home-owners would be given tax deductions to winterize their homes. . . .*
>
> *Other pending measures would impose year-round daylight saving time and would open naval oil reserves for intense exploration."*
>
> —from *U.S. News & World Report,* December 3, 1973

19. What proposals did the U.S. government make to deal with the energy crisis?
20. What lessons do you think the United States might have learned from this crisis?

Extended Response

21. Beginning in the mid 1970s, during what some historians have called a "reverse migration," African Americans moved back to Southern cities. For example, approximately 30,000 African Americans moved to Atlanta, Georgia, during this time. Based on what you have learned about new approaches to civil rights during this period, explain in a persuasive essay what encouraged this change in population movement.

STOP

History ONLINE
For additional test practice, use Self-Check Quizzes—Chapter 28 at glencoe.com.

Need Extra Help?

If You Missed Questions . . .	16	17	18	19	20	21
Go to Page . . .	955	960	939	965	R19	952–957

Document-Based Questions

19. Proposals included cutting speed limits, curtailing heat and lighting in public buildings, giving tax deductions to homeowners who winterized their homes, imposing year-round daylight savings time, and opening naval oil reserves for exploration. This is a good opener to discuss similarities and differences in energy conservation today.

20. Answers will vary, but students might note that after several years, Americans returned to driving large vehicles and other activities that did not conserve oil.

Extended Response

21. Essays will vary, but should express a clear point of view on the question and support their point of view with reasoned arguments and details from the chapter. Essays should demonstrate an understanding of the events of the Watergate scandal and the political changes it brought about.

16. A Students should remember that the Declaration of Indian Purpose was created by more than 400 members of 67 tribes and represented a moderate stance on Native American affairs. *B* is incorrect because the application of the Bill of Rights to reservations did not happen until 1968, seven years after the Declaration. AIM was a more militant group, and was not formed by the Declaration.

17. C *Silent Spring* was published in 1962; it could not have resulted from legislation in the 1970s. Remind students that the legislation passed in the 1970s included the Clean Air Act and the Clean Water Act, which led to a reduction of air and water pollution.

18. D At the bottom of each "pile" in the cartoon, is a Soviet taxpayer and a U.S. taxpayer, being crushed by the piles. They are clearly suffering.

History ONLINE
Have students visit the Web site at glencoe.com to review Chapter 28 and take the Self-Check Quiz.

Need Extra Help?
Have students refer to the pages listed if they miss any of the questions.

Chapter 29 Planning Guide

Key to Ability Levels	
BL Below Level	AL Above Level
OL On Level	ELL English Language Learners

Key to Teaching Resources	
Print Material	Transparency
CD-ROM or DVD	

Levels					Resources	Chapter Opener	Section 1	Section 2	Section 3	Section 4	Chapter Assess
BL	OL	AL	ELL								
FOCUS											
BL	OL	AL	ELL	Transparency	**Daily Focus Skills Transparencies**		29-1	29-2	29-3	29-4	
TEACH											
	OL	AL		Print Material	**Geography and History Activity, URB**				p. 3		
	OL	AL		Print Material	**American Literature Reading, URB**				p. 17		
BL	OL		ELL	Print Material	**Reading Essentials and Note-Taking Guide***		p. 319	p. 322	p. 325	p. 328	
	OL			Print Material	**Historical Analysis Skills Activity, URB**				p. 56		
BL	OL		ELL	Print Material	**Guided Reading Activities, URB***		p. 80	p. 81	p. 82	p. 83	
BL	OL	AL	ELL	Print Material	**Content Vocabulary Activity, URB***		p. 61				
BL	OL	AL	ELL	Print Material	**Academic Vocabulary Activity, URB**		p. 63				
	OL	AL		Print Material	**Critical Thinking Skills Activity, URB**					p. 66	
BL	OL		ELL	Print Material	**Reading Skills Activity, URB**					p. 55	
BL			ELL	Print Material	**English Learner Activity, URB**			p. 59			
	OL	AL		Print Material	**Reinforcing Skills Activity, URB**					p. 65	
BL	OL	AL	ELL	Print Material	**Differentiated Instruction Activity, URB**				p. 57		
BL	OL		ELL	Print Material	**Time Line Activity, URB**					p. 67	
	OL			Print Material	**Linking Past and Present Activity, URB**				p. 68		
BL	OL	AL	ELL	Print Material	**American Art and Music Activity, URB**						p. 73
BL	OL	AL	ELL	Print Material	**Interpreting Political Cartoons Activity, URB**			p. 75			
		AL		Print Material	**Enrichment Activity, URB**					p. 78	
BL	OL	AL	ELL	Print Material	**American Biographies**				✓		
BL	OL	AL	ELL	Print Material	**Primary Source Reading, URB**			p. 69	p. 71		
BL	OL	AL	ELL	Print Material	**Supreme Court Case Studies**		p. 127		p. 129		
BL	OL	AL	ELL	Print Material	**The Living Constitution***	✓	✓	✓	✓	✓	✓
	OL	AL		CD-ROM or DVD	**American History Primary Source Documents Library**	✓	✓	✓	✓	✓	✓
BL	OL	AL	ELL	Transparency	**Unit Map Overlay Transparencies**	✓	✓	✓	✓	✓	✓
BL	OL	AL	ELL	Print Material	**Differentiated Instruction for the American History Classroom**	✓	✓	✓	✓	✓	✓

Note: Please refer to the *Unit 9 Resource Book* for this chapter's URB materials.

* Also available in Spanish

TeacherWorks Plus
All-In-One Planner and Resource Center

- Interactive Lesson Planner
- Interactive Teacher Edition
- Fully editable blackline masters
- Section Spotlight Videos Launch
- Differentiated Lesson Plans
- Printable reports of daily assignments
- Standards Tracking System

Levels				Resources	Chapter Opener	Section 1	Section 2	Section 3	Section 4	Chapter Assess
BL	OL	AL	ELL							
				TEACH *(continued)*						
BL	OL	AL	ELL	StudentWorks™ Plus	✓	✓	✓	✓	✓	✓
BL	OL	AL	ELL	American Music Hits Through History CD	✓	✓	✓	✓	✓	✓
BL	OL	AL	ELL	Unit Time Line Transparencies and Activities	✓	✓	✓	✓	✓	✓
BL	OL	AL	ELL	Cause and Effect Transparencies, Strategies, and Activities	✓	✓	✓	✓	✓	✓
BL	OL	AL	ELL	Why It Matters Transparencies, Strategies, and Activities	✓	✓	✓	✓	✓	✓
BL	OL	AL	ELL	American Issues	✓	✓	✓	✓	✓	✓
	OL	AL	ELL	American Art and Architecture Transparencies, Strategies, and Activities	✓	✓	✓	✓	✓	✓
BL	OL	AL		High School American History Literature Library	✓	✓	✓	✓	✓	✓
BL	OL	AL	ELL	*The American Vision* Video Program	✓	✓	✓	✓	✓	✓
Teacher Resources				Strategies for Success	✓	✓	✓	✓	✓	✓
Teacher Resources				Success with English Learners	✓	✓	✓	✓	✓	✓
Teacher Resources				Reading Strategies and Activities for the Social Studies Classroom	✓	✓	✓	✓	✓	✓
Teacher Resources				Presentation Plus! with MindJogger CheckPoint	✓	✓	✓	✓	✓	✓
				ASSESS						
BL	OL	AL	ELL	Section Quizzes and Chapter Tests*		p. 417	p. 418	p. 419	p. 420	p. 421
BL	OL	AL	ELL	Authentic Assessment With Rubrics						p. 63
BL	OL	AL	ELL	Standardized Test Practice Workbook						p. 66
BL	OL	AL	ELL	*ExamView® Assessment Suite*		29-1	29-2	29-3	29-4	Ch. 29
				CLOSE						
BL			ELL	Reteaching Activity, URB						p. 77
BL	OL		ELL	Reading and Study Skills Foldables™	p. 83					
BL	OL	AL	ELL	*American History* in Graphic Novel				p. 87		

✓ Chapter- or unit-based activities applicable to all sections in this chapter.

Using PresentationPlus!

Teach With Technology

What is PresentationPlus! with MindJogger CheckPoint?

Glencoe's PresentationPlus! with MindJogger CheckPoint offers ready-made presentations and review activities for each chapter or section in the textbook.

How can PresentationPlus! help me?

PresentationPlus! allows you to create your presentations quickly and includes links to glencoe.com, In Motion Animations (maps, graphs, and charts), and a selection of transparencies that enhance the classroom discussion. Additionally, MindJogger CheckPoint offers entertaining ask-the-audience games that review content and generate student interest.

PresentationPlus! with MindJogger CheckPoint is one of Glencoe's technology resources available for teachers.

History ONLINE
Visit glencoe.com and enter ***QuickPass***™ code TAV9399c29T for Chapter 29 resources.

TeacherWorks
You can easily launch a wide range of digital products from your computer's desktop with the McGraw-Hill Social Studies widget.

	Student	Teacher	Parent
Media Library			
• Section Audio	●		●
• Spanish Audio Summaries	●		●
• Section Spotlight Videos	●	●	●
The American Vision **Online Learning Center (Web Site)**			
• StudentWorks™ Plus Online	●	●	●
• Multilingual Glossary	●	●	●
• Study-to-Go	●	●	●
• Chapter Overviews	●	●	●
• Self-Check Quizzes	●	●	●
• Student Web Activities	●	●	●
• ePuzzles and Games	●	●	●
• Vocabulary eFlashcards	●	●	●
• In Motion Animations	●	●	●
• Study Central™	●	●	●
• Web Activity Lesson Plans		●	
• Vocabulary PuzzleMaker	●	●	●
• Historical Thinking Activities		●	
• Beyond the Textbook	●	●	●

Reading Support From Jamestown Education

- **Timed Readings Plus in Social Studies** helps students increase their reading rate and fluency while maintaining comprehension. The 400-word passages are similar to those found on state and national assessments.
- **Reading in the Content Area: Social Studies** concentrates on six essential reading skills that help students better comprehend what they read. The book includes 75 high-interest nonfiction passages written at increasing levels of difficulty.
- **Reading Social Studies** includes strategic reading instruction and vocabulary support in Social Studies content for both ELLs and native speakers of English.

www.jamestowneducation.com

Biography / A&E Home Video / The History Channel

The following videotape programs are available from Glencoe as supplements to this chapter:

- Ronald Reagan: The Role of a Lifetime (ISBN 1-56-501808-7)
- The Class of the 20th Century; Vol. 6 1976–1990 (ISBN 1-56-501052-3)

To order, call Glencoe at 1-800-334-7344. To find classroom resources to accompany many of these videos, check the following home pages:

A&E Television: www.aetv.com
The History Channel: www.historychannel.com

Reading List Generator CD-ROM — Glencoe BookLink 3

Use this database to search more than 30,000 titles to create a customized reading list for your students.

- Reading lists can be organized by students' reading level, author, genre, theme, or area of interest.
- The database provides Degrees of Reading Power™ (DRP) and Lexile™ readability scores for all selections.
- A brief summary of each selection is included.

Leveled reading suggestions for this chapter:

For students at a Grade 8 reading level:
- ***The Cold War: An Uneasy Peace: 1945–1980,*** by Craig E. Blohm

For students at a Grade 9 reading level:
- ***The Persian Gulf War: The War Against Iraq,*** by Don Nardo

For students at a Grade 10 reading level:
- ***The Iran-Iraq War,*** by David Schaffer

For students at a Grade 11 reading level:
- ***Challenger,*** by Sandra Bricker

For students at a Grade 12 reading level:
- ***The Cold War Ends: 1980 to the Present,*** by Britta Bjornlund

National Geographic

Index to National Geographic Magazine:

The following articles relate to this chapter:

- "A Broken Empire," by Mike Edwards, March 1993.
- "Persian Gulf Pollution: Assessing the Damage One Year Later," by Sylvia Earle, February 1992.

National Geographic Society Products To order the following, call National Geographic at 1-800-368-2728:

- *ZipZapMap! USA* (ZipZapMap!)

Access National Geographic's new, dynamic MapMachine Web site and other geography resources at:

www.nationalgeographic.com
www.nationalgeographic.com/maps

Introducing
Chapter 29

Focus

MAKING CONNECTIONS

Are There Cycles in American Politics?

Have students read the Making Connections paragraph. Then ask students to think of any other time when voters elected a conservative president. Students may recall the election of 1920, in which voters elected Republican Warren G. Harding after the changes of the Progressive Era and World War I; students may also note that voters elected Republican Dwight D. Eisenhower in 1952 after the traumas of the Great Depression and World War II. In 1980 conservative ideas may have appealed to voters after the Vietnam War, Watergate, and the energy crisis of the early 1970s. **OL**

Teach

The Big Ideas

As students study the chapter, remind them to consider the section-based Big Ideas included in each section's Guide to Reading. The **Essential Questions** in the activities below tie in to the Big Ideas and help students think about and understand important chapter concepts. In addition, the Hands-on Chapter Projects with their culminating activities relate the content from each section to the Big Ideas. These activities build on each other as students progress through the chapter. Section activities culminate in the wrap-up activity on the Visual Summary page.

Chapter 29

Resurgence of Conservatism

1980–1992

SECTION 1 The New Conservatism
SECTION 2 The Reagan Years
SECTION 3 Life in the 1980s
SECTION 4 The End of the Cold War

President Ronald Reagan, his wife Nancy, Vice-President George H.W. Bush, and his wife Barbara at Reagan's Second Inauguration.

U.S. PRESIDENTS

Carter 1977–1981

Reagan 1981–1989

U.S. EVENTS

1979
- Jerry Falwell's "Moral Majority" movement begins

1981
- Launch of *Columbia*, first space shuttle
- American hostages released in Iran

1983
- Reagan announces the Star Wars program
- U.S. Marine barracks bombed in Lebanon

1979 — 1982 — 1985

WORLD EVENTS

1979
- Iranian revolution brings down Shah
- Soviets invade Afghanistan

1980
- War begins between Iran and Iraq

1985
- Mikhail Gorbachev becomes leader of Soviet Union

Section 1

The New Conservatism

Essential Question: What political changes following World War II supported the growth of political conservatism? *(The focus on defeating the Soviet Union renewed debate about the role and power of the federal government. Some saw the Cold War as a religious fight between good and evil, which increased the influence of conservatives in politics.)* Tell students that Section 1 will discuss the rise of the new conservative coalition in the early 1980s. **OL**

Section 2

The Reagan Years

Essential Question: Are American politics characterized by conflict or cooperation? *(Government is actually designed for both, but excessive conflict makes it run less effectively.)* Tell students that many citizens in the early 1980s were ready to combat a government they believed was increasingly controlling their lives. Section 2 tells how the Reagan presidency brought a different attitude and approach to government. **OL**

Chapter Audio

MAKING CONNECTIONS

Are There Cycles in American Politics?

After several decades where progressive and liberal ideas dominated American politics, conservatism began making a comeback in the 1970s, and in 1980 voters elected the conservative Ronald Reagan president. Reagan's commitment to less government regulation, a stronger military, and uncompromising anticommunism seemed to meet voters' concerns.

- ***Why do you think conservative ideas appealed to more Americans in the 1980s?***
- ***How do you think conservative ideas have changed society?***

1986
- Iran-Contra scandal enters the news

1987
- INF Treaty between U.S. and USSR

1988
- More than 35,000 cases of AIDS diagnosed for the year

G. Bush 1989–1993

1991
- Persian Gulf War occurs between Iraq and UN coalition

1988

1991

1989
- Tiananmen Square protest in China
- Communist governments in Eastern Europe collapse

1990
- Germany reunites as one nation

1991
- Soviet Union dissolves

FOLDABLES™

Analyzing Information Create a Folded Chart Foldable to organize information about the government under Ronald Reagan. List domestic and foreign policy for three eras: before the Reagan era, the Reagan administration, and the post-Reagan years.

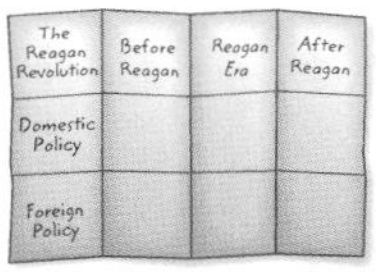

History ONLINE Visit glencoe.com and enter ***QuickPass***™ code TAV9846c29 for Chapter 29 resources.

Section 3

Life in the 1980s

Essential Question: What are the greatest social problems in the United States today? Have students list the problems they see as the most important today. *(drugs, AIDS, alcoholism, crime)* Tell students that Section 3 will examine how activists in the 1980s addressed the social issues of the decade. **OL**

Section 4

The End of the Cold War

Essential Question: What areas of problems do presidents face? *(foreign policy: diplomacy, treaties, trade policies, military; domestic policy: homeland security, education, health care, taxes, transportation)* Tell students that as they read Section 4, they will learn how the first President Bush's foreign policy was popular, while his domestic agenda was not. **OL**

Introducing **Chapter 29**

More About the Photo

Visual Literacy When the Watergate scandal forced Richard Nixon to resign from the presidency in 1974, most political observers assumed that it would take at least a generation for the Republican Party to restore its integrity in the eyes of American voters. Instead, the election of Ronald Reagan in 1980 reflected the continuing strength of conservatism. Reagan appealed to economic conservatives, social conservatives, and "tough on communism" conservatives.

FOLDABLES™ Study Organizer **Dinah Zike's Foldables**

Dinah Zike's Foldables are three-dimensional, interactive graphic organizers that help students practice basic writing skills, review vocabulary terms, and identify main ideas. Instructions for creating and using Foldables can be found in the Appendix at the end of this book and in the *Dinah Zike's Reading and Study Skills Foldables* booklet.

History ONLINE

Visit glencoe.com and enter ***QuickPass***™ code TAV9399c29T for Chapter 29 resources, including a Chapter Overview, Study Central™, Study-to-Go, Student Web Activity, Self-Check Quiz, and other materials.

Focus

Bellringer
Daily Focus Transparency 29-1

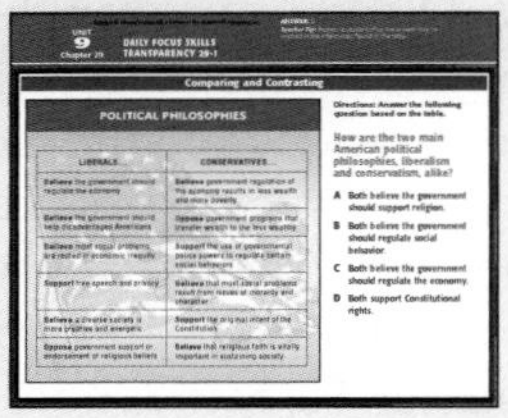

Guide to Reading
Answers:
Students should complete the outline by including all headings in the section.

I. Liberalism and Conservatism
   A. Liberalism
   B. Conservatism
II. Conservatism Revives
   A. The Role of the Cold War
   B. Conservatives Organize
   C. The Rise of the Sunbelt
   D. Sunbelt Conservatism
   E. Suburban Conservatism
   F. The Religious Right
   G. A New Coalition

Section Spotlight Video
To generate student interest and provide a springboard for class discussion, access the Chapter 29, Section 1 video at glencoe.com or on the video DVD.

Resource Manager

R Reading Strategies	C Critical Thinking	D Differentiated Instruction	W Writing Support	S Skill Practice
Teacher Edition • Summarizing, p. 969 **Additional Resources** • Guided Read. Act., URB p. 80	**Teacher Edition** • Making Generalizations, p. 971 **Additional Resources** • Quizzes/Tests, p. 417 • Supreme Court Case Studies, p. 127	**Teacher Edition** • Visual/Spatial, p. 972	**Teacher Edition** • Persuasive Writing, p. 972 • Narrative Writing, p. 971 **Additional Resources** • Cont. Vocab. Act., URB p. 61 • Academic Vocab. Act., URB p. 63	**Teacher Edition** • Analyzing Visuals, p. 969 • Reading a Map, p. 970 **Additional Resources** • Read. Essen., p. 319

Section 1
Section Audio   Spotlight Video

The New Conservatism

Guide to Reading

Big Ideas
Economics and Society High taxes as well as economic and moral concerns led the country toward a new conservatism.

Content Vocabulary
- liberal *(p. 968)*
- conservative *(p. 968)*
- "televangelist" *(p. 973)*

Academic Vocabulary
- indicate *(p. 973)*
- stability *(p. 973)*

People and Events to Identify
- William F. Buckley *(p. 971)*
- Sunbelt *(p. 971)*
- Billy Graham *(p. 973)*
- Jerry Falwell *(p. 973)*
- "Moral Majority" *(p. 973)*

Reading Strategy
Taking Notes Use the major headings of this section to outline information about the rise of the new conservatism in the United States.

The New Conservatism
I. Liberalism and Conservatism
   A.
   B.
II.
   A.

By the 1980s, new levels of discontent with government and society had left many Americans concerned about the direction of the nation. Some began to call for a return to more conservative approaches and values.

Liberalism and Conservatism

MAIN Idea Conservatives and liberals disagreed on the role of government.

HISTORY AND YOU Do you consider yourself liberal or conservative? Why? Read on to learn more about conservative and liberal ideas of government.

Midge Decter, a New Yorker and a writer for the conservative publication *Commentary*, was appalled at the violence that hit her city on a hot July night in 1977. On the night of July 13, the power failed in New York City. The blackout left millions of people in darkness, and looting and arson rocked the city. City officials and the media blamed the lawlessness on the anger and despair of youth in neglected areas. Decter disagreed:

PRIMARY SOURCE

"[T]hose young men went on their spree of looting because they had been given permission to do so . . . by all the papers and magazines, movies and documentaries—all the outlets for the purveying of enlightened liberal attitude and progressive liberal policy—which had for years and years been proclaiming that race and poverty were sufficient excuses for lawlessness. . . ."

—quoted in *Commentary*, September 1977

Midge Decter's article blaming liberalism for the New York riots illustrates one side of a debate in American politics that continues to the present day. On one side are people who call themselves **liberals;** on the other side are those who identify themselves as **conservatives.** Liberal ideas had dominated American politics in the 1960s, but conservative ideas regained significant support in the 1970s, and in 1980 Ronald Reagan, a strong conservative, was elected president.

Liberalism

In American politics today, people who call themselves liberals believe several basic ideas. In general, liberals believe that the government should regulate the economy to protect people from the

POLITICAL CARTOONS PRIMARY SOURCE

Liberalism vs. Conservatism

▲ *Conservatives believe the liberal concern with achieving social equality and alleviating poverty is often taken to excess. They also disapprove of the idea of using the power of government to redistribute wealth from one group to another, preferring that the free market determine the distribution of wealth.*

▲ *Liberals believe that the conservative concern with keeping taxes low comes at the expense of other social needs and that conservatives who want low taxes are uncaring when it comes to helping the less fortunate.*

Analyzing VISUALS

1. **Interpreting** In the cartoon on the left, what is the artist implying about Democratic policies?
2. **Identifying** In the cartoon on the right, what criticisms of tax breaks does the artist illustrate?

power of large corporations and wealthy elites. Liberals also believe that the government, particularly the federal government, should play an active role in helping disadvantaged Americans, partly through social programs and partly by putting more of society's tax burden on wealthier people.

Although liberals favor government intervention in the economy, they are suspicious of any attempt by the government to regulate social behavior. They are strong supporters of free speech and privacy, and are opposed to the government supporting or endorsing religious beliefs. They believe that a diverse society made up of different races, cultures, and ethnic groups will be more creative and energetic.

Liberals often support higher taxes on the wealthy, partly because they believe that those with greater assets should shoulder more of the costs of government and partly because it allows the government to redistribute wealth through government programs and thereby make society more equal.

Conservatism

Unlike liberals, conservatives distrust the power of government. They believe governmental power should be divided into different branches and split between the state and federal levels to limit its ability to intrude into people's lives.

Conservatives believe that when government regulates the economy, it makes the economy less efficient, resulting in less wealth and more poverty. They believe that free enterprise is the best economic system, and argue that if people and businesses are free to make their own economic choices, there will be more wealth and a higher standard of living for everyone.

For this reason, conservatives generally oppose high taxes and government programs that transfer wealth from the rich to those who are less wealthy. They believe that taxes and government programs discourage investment, take away people's incentive to work hard, and reduce the amount of freedom in society.

Teach

S Skill Practice

Analyzing Visuals Have students study the political cartoons on this page. **Ask:** Based on the cartoons, what are two major differences between the liberal and conservative philosophies? *(taxation and the redistribution of wealth)* **OL**

R Reading Strategy

Summarizing Have students write two paragraphs, one summarizing the key beliefs of liberals and one summarizing the key beliefs of conservatives. Encourage students to share their summaries with the class. **OL**

Analyzing VISUALS

Answers:

1. Democrats support the redistribution of wealth through high taxes.
2. Tax breaks negatively affect manufacturing, industry, and welfare.

Hands-On Chapter Project Step 1

Conducting an Opinion Poll

Step 1: Listing Priorities Tell students they will be conducting an opinion poll on President Ronald Reagan's performance as president.

Organizing Have students review the material presented in Section 1 to compile a list of the issues that were most important to Americans in the 1980s. **OL**

(Chapter Project continued on page 975)

S Skill Practice

Reading a Map Have students study the map. **Ask:** What Sunbelt states did not experience significant growth between 1950 and 1980? *(North Carolina, South Carolina, Tennessee, Alabama, Mississippi, and Arkansas)* BL

Analyzing GEOGRAPHY

Answers:

1. California, Texas, and Florida
2. Answers will vary, but students might note that people moved to states that already had a strong infrastructure and a health care system.

Reading Check

Answer:
Liberals often look to government to solve problems and seek government intervention in the economy to protect people from the power of big business; conservatives prefer small government and look to the free enterprise system to guide the economy.

The more the government regulates the economy, conservatives argue, the more it will have to regulate every aspect of people's behavior. Ultimately, conservatives fear, the government will so restrict people's economic freedom that Americans will no longer be able to improve their standard of living and get ahead in life.

Many conservatives believe that religious faith is vitally important in sustaining society. They believe most social problems result from issues of morality and character—issues, they argue, that are best addressed through commitment to a religious faith and through the private efforts of churches, individuals, and communities to help those in need. Despite this general belief, conservatives do support the use of the governmental police powers to regulate social behavior in some instances.

Reading Check **Contrasting** How do liberal and conservative opinions about government differ?

Conservatism Revives

MAIN Idea Geographical regions tend to support either liberal or conservative ideas.

HISTORY AND YOU Politically, how would you define yourself or the region in which you live? Read on to learn about the growing political power of voters in the Southwest.

During the New Deal era of the 1930s, conservative ideas lost much of their influence in national politics. Following World War II, however, conservatism began to revive.

The Role of the Cold War

Support for conservative ideas began to revive for two major reasons, both related to the Cold War. First, the struggle against communism revived the debate about the role of the government in the economy. Some Americans believed that liberal economic ideas

NATIONAL GEOGRAPHIC **The Rise of the Sunbelt, 1950–1980**

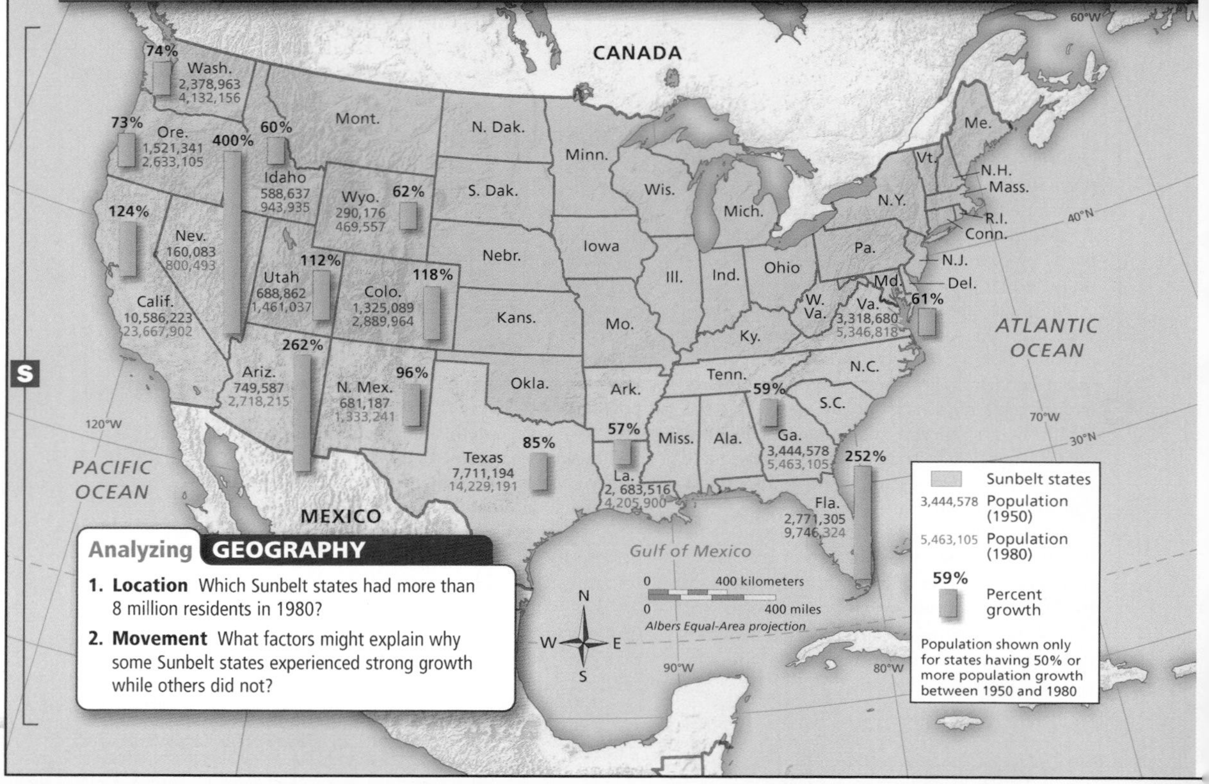

Analyzing GEOGRAPHY

1. **Location** Which Sunbelt states had more than 8 million residents in 1980?
2. **Movement** What factors might explain why some Sunbelt states experienced strong growth while others did not?

Additional Support

Activity: Interdisciplinary Connection

Mathematics Provide the population data for the United States and selected Sunbelt states, as shown below. Explain that although you can see that the population of these states increased between 1950 and 1980, the real significance appears when you express each state's population as a percentage of the country's total population. Have students calculate each state's population, in the selected years, as a percentage of the total U.S. population. OL

	1950	1960
U.S. Total	151,868,000	179,975,000
Arizona	750,000	1,302,000
California	10,586,000	15,717,000
Florida	2,771,000	4,952,000
Texas	7,712,000	9,580,000
	1970	**1980**
U.S. Total	203,302,000	226,546,000
Arizona	1,775,000	2,718,000
California	19,971,000	23,668,000
Florida	6,791,000	9,746,000
Texas	11,199,000	14,229,000

were slowly leading the United States toward communism and set out to stop this trend. They also thought the United States had failed to stop the spread of Soviet power because liberals did not fully understand the need for a strong anticommunist foreign policy.

At the same time, many Americans viewed the Cold War in religious terms. Communism rejects religion and emphasizes the material side of life. To Americans with a deep religious faith, the struggle against communism was a struggle between good and evil. Liberalism, which emphasizes economic welfare, gradually lost the support of many religious Americans, who increasingly turned to conservatism.

Conservatives Organize

In 1955 a young conservative named **William F. Buckley** founded a new magazine called *National Review.* Buckley's magazine helped to revive conservative ideas in the United States. Buckley debated in front of college students and appeared on radio and television shows, spreading conservative ideas to an even wider audience.

W Within the Republican Party, conservatives, particularly young conservatives, began to demand a greater role in party decision-making. In 1960 some 90 young conservative leaders met at Buckley's family estate and founded Young Americans for Freedom (YAF), an independent conservative group, to push for their ideas and to support conservative candidates.

By 1964 the new conservative movement had achieved enough influence within the Republican Party to enable the conservative Barry Goldwater to win the nomination for president. To the dismay of the conservatives, however, President Johnson easily defeated Goldwater and won the election in a landslide.

The Rise of the Sunbelt

One of the problems facing conservatives in the 1950s and early 1960s was that their votes were split between the Republicans and the Democrats. Two regions of the country, the South and the West, were more conservative than other areas. Southern conservatives, however, usually voted for the Democrats, while conservatives in the West voted Republican. This meant that the party that won the heavily populated Northeast would win the election. Since the Northeast strongly supported liberal ideas, both parties were pulled toward liberal policies.

This pattern began to change during World War II, when large numbers of Americans moved south and west to take jobs in the war factories. The movement to the South and West—together known as the **Sunbelt**—continued after the war. As the Sunbelt's economy expanded, Americans living in those regions began to view the federal government differently from people living in the Northeast.

Sunbelt Conservatism

Industry in the Northeast was in decline, leading to the region's nickname—the Rust Belt. This region had higher unemployment than any other, and its cities were congested and polluted. These problems prompted Americans in the Northeast to look to the government for programs and regulations that would help them solve their problems.

In contrast, many Americans in the Sunbelt opposed high taxes and federal regulations that might interfere with their region's growth. Many white Southerners were also angry with the Democrats for supporting civil rights, which they interpreted as an effort by the federal government to impose its policies on the South.

When Barry Goldwater argued in 1964 that the federal government was becoming too strong, many Southerners agreed. For the first time since Reconstruction, they began voting Republican in large numbers. Although Goldwater lost, he showed Republicans that the best way to attract Southern votes was to support conservative policies. C

Americans living in the West also responded to conservative criticism of the federal government. Westerners were proud of their frontier heritage and spirit of "rugged individualism." They resented federal environmental regulations that limited ranching, controlled water use, and restricted the development of the region's natural resources. Western anger over such policies inspired the "Sagebrush Rebellion" of the early 1970s—a widespread protest led by conservatives against federal laws that they felt were hindering the region's development.

W Writing Support

Narrative Writing Invite students to use library and Internet resources to write a one-page biography of William F. Buckley. Students should include a discussion of his early life and of his successes in organizing the conservative movement. Encourage students to share their biographies with the class. **OL**

C Critical Thinking

Making Generalizations Have interested students use library or Internet resources to find out more information about the growth of the Republican Party in the South during the 1960s and 1970s. **Ask:** Do you think racism played a role in the growth of the Republican Party during the 1960s and 1970s? Why or why not? *(Answers will vary, but students should base their answers on their research.)* **AL**

Additional Support

Activity: Interdisciplinary Connection

Civics Have students examine the income, property, and sales tax rate structure in their state. Then have them prepare a visual display of the rates to use during a brief oral presentation in which they either support the state's current tax policies or propose a plan to raise or lower taxes. **OL**

D Differentiated Instruction

Visual/Spatial Have students research the last presidential election to see whether the Sunbelt states followed recent trends by voting for the conservative candidate. Have them create a chart, or map showing their results. **OL**

W Writing Support

Persuasive Writing Have students use library or Internet resources to learn more about Howard Jarvis and other proponents of tax cuts. Have them use their findings to decide whether they favor tax cuts or not. Then have them write a letter to their governor persuading him or her to support their point of view. **OL**

Analyzing VISUALS

Answers:

1. They are white; answers will vary.
2. Students might note that those whose primary concern was the Cold War might leave after the Soviet Union collapsed in 1991.

Differentiated Instruction

PRIMARY SOURCE

The Conservative Coalition

The new conservative coalition that emerged in the 1970s was made up of people from the South and West, particularly middle class suburban voters, evangelical Christians, and people concerned about high taxes and resisting the Soviet Union in the Cold War.

▲ *Evangelical Christians including supporters of Jerry Falwell (photo left corner) were a major force behind the conservative resurgence.*

▲ *Voters in the suburbs (top) and rural west (above) increasingly voted conservative in the 1980s.*

Analyzing VISUALS

1. **Inferring** What do you notice about the ethnicity of most people in the conservative coalition? Why do you think other groups were not as well represented?
2. **Speculating** What groups in the coalition would be most likely to leave it in the future? Why?

D By 1980, the population of the Sunbelt had surpassed that of the Northeast. This gave the conservative regions of the country more electoral votes. With Southerners also shifting to the Republican Party, conservatives began to build a coalition that could elect a president.

Suburban Conservatism

As riots erupted and crime soared during the 1960s and 1970s, many Americans moved to suburbs to escape the chaos of the cities. Even there, however, they found the quiet middle-class lifestyle they desired to be in danger. The rapid inflation of the 1970s had caused the buying power of middle-class families to shrink while taxes remained high.

W Many Americans resented the taxes they had to pay for New Deal and Great Society programs when they themselves were losing ground economically. In 1978 Howard Jarvis, a conservative activist, launched the first successful tax revolt in California with Proposition 13, a referendum on the state ballot that greatly reduced property taxes.

W Soon afterward anti-tax movements appeared in other states, and tax cuts quickly became a national issue. For many Americans, the conservative idea that the government had become too big meant simply that taxes were too high. As conservatives began to call for tax cuts, the middle class flocked to their cause.

The Religious Right

While many Americans turned to conservatism for economic reasons, others were drawn to it because they feared that American society had lost touch with its traditional values. For many Americans of conservative religious faith, the events of the 1960s and 1970s were shocking. The Supreme Court decision in *Roe* v. *Wade,* which established that the right to have an abortion was protected by the Constitution, greatly concerned them. They were also critical of other Supreme Court decisions that limited

Leveled Activities

BL Guided Reading Activities, URB p. 82

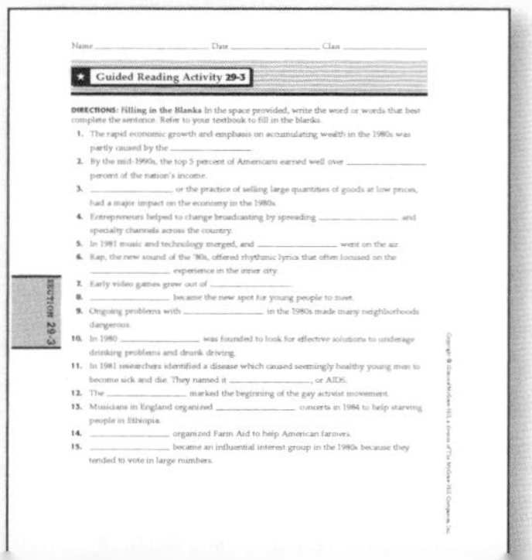

Guided Reading Activity 29-3

OL Content Vocabulary Activity, URB p. 61

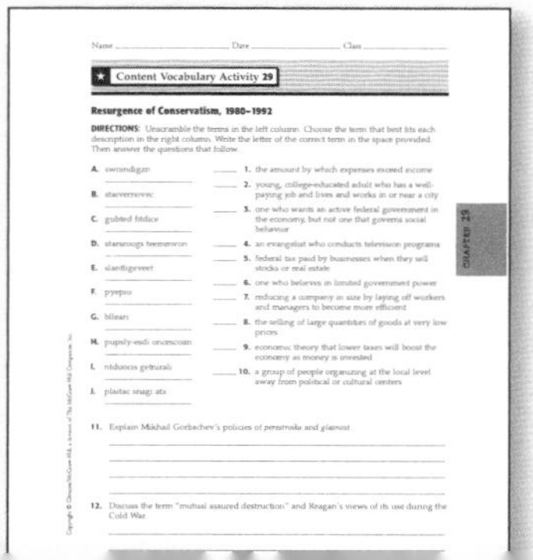

Content Vocabulary Activity 29

Resurgence of Conservatism, 1980–1992

AL Academic Vocabulary Activity, URB p. 63

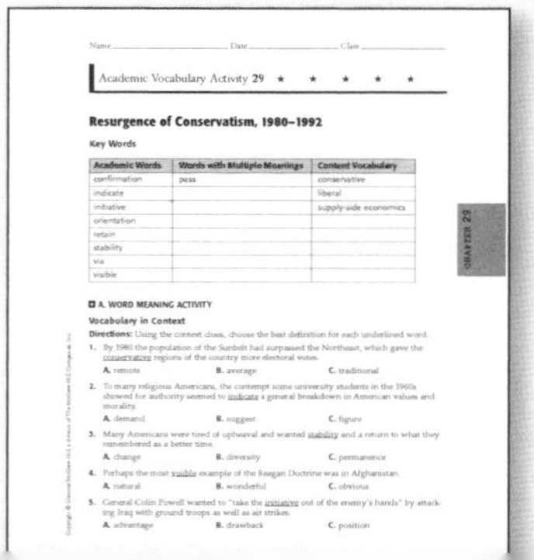

Academic Vocabulary Activity 29

Resurgence of Conservatism, 1980–1992

ELL English Learner Activity, URB p. 59

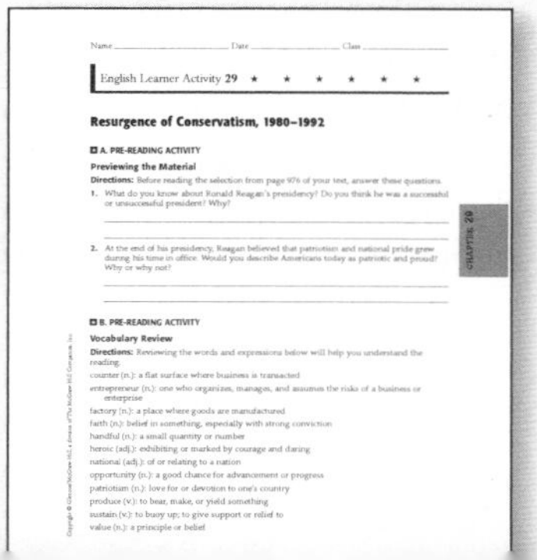

English Learner Activity 29

Resurgence of Conservatism, 1980–1992

prayer in public schools and expanded protections for people accused of crimes.

The feminist movement and the push for the Equal Rights Amendment (ERA) also upset some religious Americans because it seemed to represent an assault on the traditional family. Many religious conservatives were shocked by the behavior of some university students in the 1960s, whose contempt for authority seemed to **indicate** a general breakdown in American values and morality. These concerns helped expand the conservative cause into a mass movement.

Although religious conservatives included people of many faiths, the largest group was evangelical Protestants. Evangelicals believe that they are saved from their sins through conversion (which they refer to as being "born again") and a personal commitment to follow Jesus Christ, whose death and resurrection reconciles them to God.

After World War II, a religious revival began in the United States among Protestant evangelicals. Protestant ministers, such as **Billy Graham** and Oral Roberts, built national followings. By the late 1970s, about 70 million Americans described themselves as "born again." Protestant evangelicals owned their own newspapers, magazines, radio stations, and television networks.

Television in particular allowed evangelical ministers to reach a large nationwide audience. These **"televangelists,"** as they were soon called, included Marion "Pat" Robertson, who founded the Christian Broadcasting Network, and **Jerry Falwell,** who used his television show *The Old-Time Gospel Hour* to found a movement that he called the **"Moral Majority."** Using television and mail campaigns, the Moral Majority built up a network of ministers to register new voters who backed conservative candidates and issues. Falwell later claimed to have registered 2 million new voters by 1980.

A New Coalition

By the end of the 1970s, a new conservative coalition of voters had begun to come together. Although the members of this coalition were concerned with many different issues, they were held together by a common belief that American society had somehow lost its way.

The Watergate scandal, high taxes, and special interest politics had undermined many Americans' faith in their government. Rising unemployment, rapid inflation, and the energy crisis had shaken their confidence in the economy. Riots, crime, and drug abuse suggested that society itself was falling apart. The retreat from Vietnam, the hostage crisis in Iran, and the Soviet invasion of Afghanistan seemed to make the nation look weak and helpless internationally. Many Americans were tired of change and upheaval. They wanted **stability** and a return to what they remembered as a better time. For some, the new conservatism and its most prominent spokesperson, Ronald Reagan, offered hope to a nation in distress.

Reading Check **Summarizing** Why did many Americans begin to support the conservative movement?

Section 1 REVIEW

Vocabulary

1. **Explain** the significance of: liberal, conservative, William F. Buckley, Sunbelt, Billy Graham, "televangelist," Jerry Falwell, "Moral Majority."

Main Ideas

2. **Explaining** Why do liberals sometimes support higher taxes on the wealthy?
3. **Determining Cause and Effect** What was the cause of the Sagebrush Rebellion in the 1970s?

Critical Thinking

4. **Big Ideas** What kind of economy do conservatives want?
5. **Organizing** Use a graphic organizer similar to the one below to list conservative beliefs.

Conservative Beliefs

6. **Analyzing Visuals** Study the map of the Sunbelt on page 970. What impact would the migration patterns shown have on representation in the U.S. House of Representatives?

Writing About History

7. **Persuasive Writing** Many conservatives believe that "government that governs least, governs best." Write a paragraph supporting or opposing this statement.

History ONLINE
Study Central™ To review this section, go to glencoe.com and click on Study Central.

Assess

History ONLINE

Study Central™ provides summaries, interactive games, and online graphic organizers to help students review content.

Close

Summarizing Ask: Why did many Americans become more conservative in the 1960s and 1970s? *(They believed the federal government was too big and interfering in their lives; they wanted stability and longed for a return to what they remembered as better times.)* **OL**

Reading Check

Answer:
They wanted stability and a return to what they remembered as a better time.

Section 1 REVIEW

Answers

1. All definitions can be found in the section and the Glossary.
2. They believe the government should play an active role in helping disadvantaged Americans, partly by putting more of society's tax burden on wealthier people.
3. Westerners believed that government policies were hindering the region's development.
4. Conservatives want a free enterprise system.
5. free enterprise, emphasis on religious values, little government regulation of the economy
6. The number of representatives from the Sunbelt would increase.
7. Paragraphs will vary, but students should use information from the textbook and outside resources as needed.

Focus

Bellringer

Daily Focus Transparency 29-2

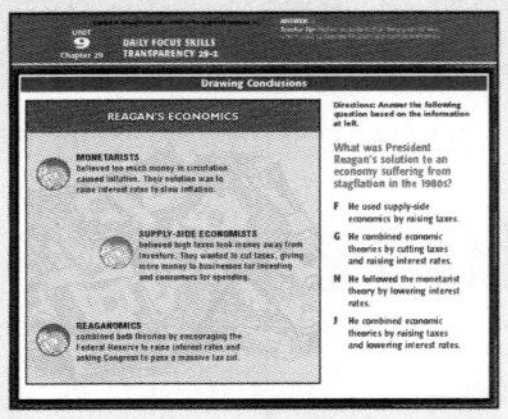

Guide to Reading

Answers may include:
High taxes take away money that could be invested; Cutting taxes will generate capital to make new and larger businesses and new jobs; Larger supply of consumer goods will cause more spending.

Section Spotlight Video

To generate student interest and provide a springboard for class discussion, access the Chapter 29, Section 2 video at glencoe.com or on the video DVD.

Section 2

Section Audio Spotlight Video

The Reagan Years

Guide to Reading

Big Ideas

Trade, War, and Migration During the Cold War, President Reagan reinforced the idea that the United States had to take strong action to resist the spread of Communist influence abroad.

Content Vocabulary
- supply-side economics *(p. 976)*
- budget deficit *(p. 977)*
- "mutual assured destruction" *(p. 981)*

Academic Vocabulary
- confirmation *(p. 978)*
- visible *(p. 979)*

People and Events to Identify
- Reaganomics *(p. 976)*
- Iran-Contra scandal *(p. 980)*
- Mikhail Gorbachev *(p. 981)*

Reading Strategy

Organizing Complete a graphic organizer similar to the one below by filling in the major points of the supply-side theory of economics.

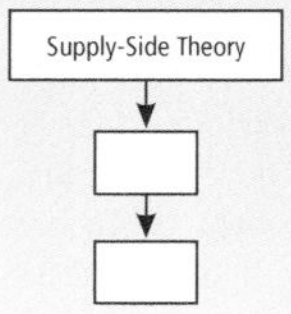

In 1980 Americans elected Ronald Reagan president. Reagan cut taxes, deregulated several industries, and appointed conservative justices. He began a massive military buildup that greatly increased the deficit and sent aid to insurgent groups fighting communism.

The Road to the White House

MAIN Idea President Reagan's experiences in Hollywood and as governor of California led to his successful campaign for the presidency.

HISTORY AND YOU How could a previous career as a movie star help someone get elected to public office? Read on to learn more about the way that President Reagan's background helped to make him an attractive presidential candidate.

In 1926, at age fifteen, Ronald Reagan earned $15 a week working as a lifeguard on the Rock River in Illinois. Being a lifeguard, Reagan later wrote, taught him quite a bit about human nature:

PRIMARY SOURCE

"Lifeguarding provides one of the best vantage points in the world to learn about people. During my career at the park, I saved seventy-seven people. I guarantee you they needed saving—no lifeguard gets wet without good reason. . . . Not many thanked me, much less gave me a reward, and being a little money-hungry, I'd done a little daydreaming about this. They felt insulted. . . . I got to recognize that people hate to be saved. . . ."

—from *Where's the Rest of Me?*

The belief that people do not want to be saved by someone else was one of the ideas that Ronald Reagan took with him to the White House. It reflected his philosophy of self-reliance and independence.

Becoming a Conservative

Reagan grew up in Dixon, Illinois, the son of an Irish American shoe salesman. After graduating from Eureka College in 1932, Reagan worked as a sports broadcaster at an Iowa radio station. In 1937 he took a Hollywood screen test and won a contract from a movie studio. During the next 25 years he made more than 50 movies. As a broadcaster and an actor, Reagan learned how to speak publicly and how to project a strong, attractive image—skills that proved invaluable when he entered politics.

In 1947 Reagan became president of the Screen Actors Guild—the actors' union. Soon afterward, he testified about communism in

Resource Manager

R Reading Strategies	C Critical Thinking	D Differentiated Instruction	W Writing Support	S Skill Practice
Teacher Edition • Act. Prior Know., p. 975 **Additional Resources** • Guided Read. Act., p. 81 • Prim. Source Read., URB p. 69	**Teacher Edition** • Analyzing Prim. Sources, p. 975 • Drawing Conclusions, p. 976 **Additional Resources** • Interp. Polit. Cartoon, URB p. 75 • Quizzes/Tests, p. 418	**Teacher Edition** • English Learners, p. 979 • Interpersonal, p. 980 **Additional Resources** • English Learner Act., URB p. 59	**Teacher Edition** • Descriptive Writing, pp. 976, 979 • Persuasive Writing, pp. 977, 978	**Teacher Edition** • Describing, p. 978 • Read. Prim. Sources, p. 979 **Additional Resources** • Read. Essen., p. 322

POLITICAL CARTOONS — PRIMARY SOURCE
The Election of 1980

▲ *When Ronald Reagan ran for the Republican presidential nomination, he was still best known to most Americans as an actor. Critics said that while he was scripted and polished, he lacked any real substance.*

▼ *By 1980, Carter was so unpopular that other Democrats did not want his help in their own campaigns. Reagan soundly defeated Carter in the Election of 1980.*

' I PLEDGE TO COME OUT CAMPAIGNING VIGOROUSLY FOR ALL DEMOCRATS!...'

Analyzing VISUALS

1. **Making Inferences** In the cartoon above, what does the artist infer about Reagan's campaign?
2. **Interpreting** What is the artist in the cartoon to the right saying about Carter's place in the Democratic Party?

R Hollywood before the House Un-American Activities Committee. Reagan had been a staunch Democrat and a supporter of the New Deal, but dealing with Communists in the union shifted him toward conservative ideas.

In 1954 Reagan became the host of the television show "General Electric Theater" and agreed to be a motivational speaker for General Electric. As he traveled the country speaking to people, he became increasingly conservative. Over and over again, he said later, he heard average Americans describe how high taxes and government regulations made it impossible for them to get ahead.

By 1964 Reagan had become such a popular national speaker that Barry Goldwater asked him to make a televised speech on behalf of Goldwater's campaign. The speech impressed several wealthy entrepreneurs in California. They convinced Reagan to run for governor of California in 1966 and helped finance his campaign. Reagan won the election and was reelected in 1970. Ten years later he won the Republican presidential nomination.

The Election of 1980

Reagan's campaign appealed to Americans who were frustrated with the economy and worried that the United States had become weak internationally. Reagan promised to cut taxes and increase defense spending. He won the support of social conservatives by calling for a constitutional amendment banning abortion. During one debate with President Carter, C Reagan asked voters, "Are you better off than you were four years ago?" On Election Day, the voters answered "No." Reagan won nearly 51 percent of the popular vote and 489 electoral votes, easily defeating Carter in the Electoral College. For the first time since 1954, Republicans also gained control of the Senate.

✓ Reading Check **Describing** What event jump-started Ronald Reagan's political career as a conservative leader?

Teach

C Critical Thinking

Analyzing Primary Sources Reagan once said that "people hate to be saved." **Ask:** How does this quote relate to the conservative political ideology? *(Conservatives believe that people should rely more on themselves to solve problems rather than expect the government to fix their problems for them.* **AL**

R Reading Strategy

Activating Prior Knowledge In 1947 Ronald Reagan testified before the House Un-American Activities Committee. **Ask:** What was the goal of HUAC? *(to uncover evidence of Communist infiltration in the U.S. government)* **OL**

Analyzing VISUALS

Answers:

1. Reagan's campaign is being run as if it were a movie.
2. Carter is not popular with other members of the Democratic Party.

Hands-On Chapter Project
Step 2

Conducting an Opinion Poll

Step 2: Preparing the Poll Keeping in mind the list of issues they compiled in Step 1, students should review the material presented in Section 2.

Evaluating Ask students to compose five statements that assess President Reagan's job performance on five significant issues of the 1980s. **OL**

(Chapter Project continued on page 983)

W Writing Support

Descriptive Writing Have students reread the passage about supply-side economics on this page. Then organize the class into three groups and ask each group to write a letter to President Reagan about the impact of his economic policies. One group should represent business, another group should represent workers in manufacturing industries, and the third group should represent people on fixed incomes. **AL**

C Critical Thinking

Drawing Conclusions Discuss in class the question posed by the Debates in History feature. Have students use library or Internet resources to find out more about Reagan's tax cuts and their effects on the nation's economy. **Ask:** Based on your research, what effects did the Reagan tax cuts have? *(Answers will vary. Some students might note that the economy grew steadily while others might mention problems such as the savings and loan crisis.)* **OL**

Additional Support

Domestic Policies

MAIN Idea Believing that government was part of the problem, President Reagan cut social service programs, sponsored tax cuts, and deregulated industry.

HISTORY AND YOU Do you think that cutting social programs is a good way to help the economy? Read on to learn more about Reagan's economic policies.

Ronald Reagan believed that the key to restoring the economy and overcoming problems in society was to get Americans to believe in themselves again. He expressed this idea in his Inaugural Address:

PRIMARY SOURCE

"We have every right to dream heroic dreams. . . . You can see heroes every day going in and out of factory gates. Others, a handful in number, produce enough food to feed all of us. . . . You meet heroes across a counter. . . . There are entrepreneurs with faith in themselves and faith in an idea who create new jobs, new wealth and opportunity. . . . Their patriotism is quiet but deep. Their values sustain our national life."

—from Reagan's First Inaugural Address

Reagan also told Americans that they should not expect government to help: "In this present crisis, government is not the solution to our problem. Government is the problem."

Reaganomics

History ONLINE Student Web Activity Visit glencoe.com and complete the activity on the 1980s.

Reagan's first priority was the economy, which was suffering from stagflation—a combination of high unemployment and high inflation. According to most economists, the way to fight unemployment was to increase government spending. Increasing spending, however, made inflation worse. Conservative economists offered two competing ideas for fixing the economy. One group, known as monetarists, argued that inflation was caused by too much money in circulation. They believed the best solution was to raise interest rates. Another group supported **supply-side economics.** They argued that the economy was weak because taxes were too high.

Supply-side economists believed that high taxes took too much money away from investors. If taxes were cut, businesses and investors could use their extra capital to make new investments. Businesses would expand and create new jobs, and the result would be a larger supply of goods for consumers, who would now have more money to spend because of the tax cuts.

Reagan combined monetarism and supply-side economics. He encouraged the Federal Reserve to keep interest rates high, and asked Congress to pass a massive tax cut. Critics called his approach **Reaganomics** or "trickle-down economics." They believed Reagan's policy would help corporations and wealthy Americans, but little wealth would "trickle down" to middle-class or poor Americans.

Reagan made deals with conservative Democrats in the House and moderate Republicans in the Senate. Eventually Congress passed a 25 percent tax cut.

Debates IN HISTORY

Are Tax Cuts Good for the Economy?

Ronald Reagan believed that government regulation of the economy was harmful and that taxes should be as low as possible to promote private spending and investment. During the 1984 presidential campaign, Reagan ran against Jimmy Carter's vice president, Walter Mondale. In these excerpts from the first debate between the two candidates, Reagan and Mondale discuss their fundamentally different approaches to government. Mondale advocated for tax increases and that is often cited as a main reason why he lost the election.

Extending the Content

Presidential Campaigns Political opponents unflatteringly compared Ronald Reagan to Calvin Coolidge, pointing out the similarity between Reaganomics and Coolidge's "trickle-down" economic policies. They also noted that Reagan, like Coolidge, seemed rather detached from the process of government. Far from being insulted, Reagan reveled in the comparison. He hung Coolidge's portrait in a prominent place in the White House and regularly quoted Coolidge's philosophy on business and government.

Cutting Programs Cutting tax rates meant that the government would receive less money, at least until the economy started to grow. This would increase the **budget deficit**—the amount by which expenditures exceed income. To keep the deficit under control, Reagan proposed cuts to social programs. Welfare benefits, including the food-stamp program and the school-lunch program, were cut back. Medicare payments, unemployment compensation, student loans, and housing subsidies were also reduced.

After a struggle, Congress passed most of these cuts. The fight convinced Reagan that he would never get Congress to cut spending enough to balance the budget. He decided that cutting taxes and building up the military were more important than balancing the budget. He accepted a rapidly rising deficit as the price of getting his other programs passed.

Deregulation Reagan believed that excessive government regulation was another cause of the economy's problems. His first act as president was to sign an executive order to end price controls on oil and gasoline. Critics said that ending controls would drive prices up, but in fact they fell. Falling energy prices freed up money for businesses and consumers to spend elsewhere, helping the economy to recover.

Other deregulation soon followed. The Federal Communications Commission stopped trying to regulate the cable television industry. The National Highway Traffic and Safety Administration reduced requirements for air bags and higher fuel efficiency for cars. Carter had already begun deregulating the airline industry, and Reagan encouraged the process, which led to price wars, cheaper fares, and the founding of new airlines.

YES

Ronald Reagan
President

PRIMARY SOURCE

"...[T]he plan that we have had and that we are following is a plan that is based on growth in the economy.... Our tax cut, we think, was very instrumental in bringing about this economic recovery.

...So, we believe that as we continue to reduce the level of government spending...and, at the same time, as the growth in the economy increases the revenues the government gets, without raising taxes, those two lines will meet.... The deficit is the result of excessive government spending.... I don't believe that Mr. Mondale has a plan for balancing the budget; he has a plan for raising taxes.... And for the 5 years previous to our taking office, taxes doubled in the United States, and the budgets increased $318 billion. So, there is no ratio between taxing and balancing a budget."

—from the first presidential debate, Oct. 7, 1984

NO

Walter Mondale
Presidential candidate

PRIMARY SOURCE

"...[E]ven with historically high levels of economic growth, we will suffer a $263 billion deficit.... Real interest rates—the real cost of interest—will remain very, very high, and many economists are predicting that we're moving into a period of very slow growth.... I proposed over a hundred billion dollars in cuts in federal spending over 4 years, but I am not going to cut it out of Social Security and Medicare and student assistance and things ... that people need.... The rate of defense spending increase can be slowed.... And there are other ways of squeezing this budget without constantly picking on our senior citizens and the most vulnerable in American life."

—from the first presidential debate, Oct. 7, 1984

DBQ Document-Based Questions

1. **Specifying** What does Reagan say his administration has done to improve economic growth?
2. **Explaining** How does Reagan propose to balance the federal budget?
3. **Summarizing** How does Mondale respond to Reagan's plan? What effects does he foresee from that course?
4. **Evaluating** Which approach do you feel will be the most effective? Why? Explain your answer.

W Writing Support

Persuasive Writing Have interested students use library or Internet resources to find out more information about the Reagan budget cuts of the early 1980s. Based on their research, have them decide whether they favor Reagan's proposals. Then have students write a letter to a member of Congress urging him or her to either support or oppose the president's proposals. Encourage volunteers to read their letters to the class. AL

Debates IN HISTORY

Answers:

1. cut taxes
2. the growth in the economy will increase revenues
3. Mondale says the nation will suffer a $263 billion deficit and that some economists are predicting that the nation is moving into a period of very slow growth.
4. Answers will vary, but students should support their answers with examples.

Activity: Collaborative Learning

Reaganomics Posters Organize students into five or six groups. Have students prepare posters that explain the assumptions and the results of Reaganomics. Remind the groups that each person should have a part in the project. Group members will need to plan the poster, divide the work fairly, and complete the project. Posters might include charts, graphs, or other visual aids. Some groups may want to explain their posters to the rest of the class. Display all the posters in the classroom. OL

W Writing Support

Persuasive Writing Ask students to carefully read the People in History feature about Sandra Day O'Connor. Have them write two-page essays either supporting or opposing O'Connor's nomination to the Supreme Court. Students may use library or Internet resources to find information supporting their arguments. OL

S Skill Practice

Describing Have students discuss the impact the Reagan administration had on the make-up of the Supreme Court. *(more conservative justices were appointed; the Court was less willing to continue the reforms of the Warren Court Era)* OL

People IN HISTORY

Answer:
because she is a woman

Reading Check

Answer:
Supply-side economics proposes low taxes as an incentive to generate more investment in business.

Additional Support

People IN HISTORY

Sandra Day O'Connor
1930–

When a Supreme Court vacancy opened up in 1981, President Reagan chose Sandra Day O'Connor, an Arizona appeals court judge. Unlike many Supreme Court justices, O'Connor had broad political experience. Appointed to a state senatorial vacancy in 1969, she successfully ran for the seat and became the state senate's first woman majority leader in 1972. O'Connor won election as a superior court judge in 1974 and was later appointed to the court of appeals.

O'Connor's nomination was opposed by the Moral Majority because she had supported the Equal Rights Amendment (ERA), and had refused to back an anti-abortion amendment, or criticize the decision in *Roe* v. *Wade*. Others, however, praised her legal judgment and conservative approach to the law. As a moderate conservative, she quickly became an important swing vote on the Court, between more liberal and more conservative justices.

Why do you think that O'Connor supported the Equal Rights Amendment?

▲ *(Above photo) From left, front row are Thurgood Marshall; William Brennan, Jr.; William Rehnquist; Byron White; and Harry Blackmun. Back row from left are Antonin Scalia; John Paul Stevens; Sandra Day O'Connor; and Anthony M. Kennedy. (Right photo) Robert Bork failed to be confirmed.*

Reagan's secretary of the interior, James Watt, increased the public land that companies could use for oil drilling, mining, and logging. Watt's actions angered environmentalists, as did the EPA's decision to ease regulations on pollution-control equipment and to reduce safety checks on chemicals and pesticides.

In 1983 the economy began to recover. By 1984, the United States had begun the biggest economic expansion in its history up to that time. The median income of families climbed steadily, rising 15 percent by 1989. Five million new businesses and 20 million new jobs were created. By 1988, unemployment had fallen to 5.5 percent, the lowest in 14 years.

Reagan Wins Reelection By 1984, the economic recovery had made Reagan very popular. Democrats nominated Jimmy Carter's vice president, Walter Mondale. He chose as his running mate Representative Geraldine Ferraro, the first woman nominated to run for vice president for a major party. Instead of arguing issues with his opponent, Reagan emphasized the good economy. In an overwhelming landslide, he won about 59 percent of the popular vote and all the electoral votes except those from Mondale's home state of Minnesota and the District of Columbia.

Shifting the Judicial Balance

Reagan did not apply his conservative ideas only to the economy. He also tried to bring a strict constructionist outlook to the federal judiciary. Reagan wanted judges who followed the original intent of the Constitution. He also changed the Supreme Court by nominating Sandra Day O'Connor, the first woman on the Supreme Court.

In 1986 Chief Justice Warren Burger retired. Reagan chose the most conservative associate justice, William Rehnquist, to succeed him. He then named Antonin Scalia, a conservative, to fill Rehnquist's vacancy. In 1987 his attempt to put Robert Bork on the Court led to a bitter fight in the Senate. Democrats saw Bork as too conservative and blocked his **confirmation.** Reagan then nominated Anthony Kennedy, a moderate, to become the new associate justice.

Reading Check **Explaining** What is supply-side economics?

Activity: Collaborative Learning

Voting Blocs During the 1970s, 1980s, and 1990s, about 55 percent of all qualified voters voted in presidential elections. More women voted than men, and there were more voters in the 55–75 age range than in any other age group. Organize the class into cooperative groups, and have them research why some groups of people vote more than others. How does being from a group that is likely to vote affect a person's clout with politicians? (For example, are politicians careful not to anger senior citizens because they vote in such large numbers?) Students will want to divide up the work and decide on a method of presentation. They may also want to create charts to show differences in voting patterns by region, age, education level, income, and so forth. OL

Reagan Oversees a Military Buildup

MAIN Idea President Reagan began a massive military buildup to weaken the Soviet economy and deter Soviet aggression.

HISTORY AND YOU Do you remember President Eisenhower's warning about the military as he left office? Read to learn how President Reagan sought to use military power to defeat the Soviets.

Reagan also adopted a new foreign policy that rejected both containment and détente. He called the Soviet Union "an evil empire." In his view, the United States should not negotiate with or try to contain evil. It should try to defeat it.

"Peace Through Strength"

In Reagan's opinion, the only option open to the United States in dealing with the Soviet Union was "peace through strength"—a phrase he used during his campaign. The military buildup Reagan launched was the largest peacetime buildup in American history. It cost about $1.5 trillion over five years.

D

Reagan believed that, if the Soviets tried to match the American buildup, it might put so much pressure on their economy that they would be forced to reform their system or it would collapse. In 1982 Reagan told students at Eureka College that Soviet defense spending would eventually cause the Communist system to fall apart:

PRIMARY SOURCE

S

"The Soviet empire is faltering because rigid centralized control has destroyed incentives for innovation, efficiency, and individual achievement. . . . But in the midst of social and economic problems, the Soviet dictatorship has forged the largest armed force in the world. It has done so by preempting the human needs of its people and in the end, this course will undermine the foundations of the Soviet system."

—from *A Time for Choosing*

The United States also tried to stop nations from supporting terrorism. After Libya backed a terrorist bombing in Berlin, the United States launched an air attack on Libya on April 14, 1986. The raids killed 37 and injured about 200.

Reagan's military buildup created new jobs in defense industries. Supply-side economists had predicted that, despite the spending, lower taxes combined with cuts in government programs would generate enough growth to increase tax revenues and balance the budget. Tax revenues did rise, but other programs were too popular for Reagan to cut significantly. As a result, the annual budget deficit went from $80 billion to over $200 billion.

The Reagan Doctrine

Reagan also believed that the United States should support guerrilla groups who were fighting to overthrow Communist or pro-Soviet governments. This policy became known as the Reagan Doctrine. This doctrine led to involvement in places as geographically diverse as Africa's Angola, Middle America's Nicaragua and Grenada, and the Middle East's Afghanistan and Lebanon.

D

Aid to the Afghan Rebels Perhaps the most **visible** example of the Reagan Doctrine was in Afghanistan. In late December 1979 the Soviet Union invaded Afghanistan to support a Soviet-backed government. The Soviets soon found themselves fighting Afghan guerrillas known as the mujahadeen.

President Carter sent about $30 million in military aid to the Afghan guerrillas, but Reagan sent $570 million more. The Soviets were soon trapped in a situation similar to the American experience in Vietnam. As casualties mounted, the war strained the Soviet economy, and in 1988 the Soviets decided to withdraw.

W

Nicaragua and Grenada Reagan was also concerned about Soviet influence in Nicaragua. Rebels known as the Sandinistas had overthrown a pro-American dictator in Nicaragua in 1979. The Sandinistas set up a socialist government and accepted Cuban and Soviet aid. They then began aiding rebels in nearby El Salvador. The Reagan administration responded by secretly arming an anti-Sandinista guerrilla force known as the contras, from the Spanish word for "counterrevolutionary." When Congress learned of this policy, it banned further aid to the contras.

D Differentiated Instruction

English Learners Ask students to read the text under the head "Reagan Oversees a Military Buildup" and then, working in pairs, summarize what they have just read. **ELL**

S Skill Practice

Reading Primary Sources Read aloud Reagan's quote on this page about the Soviet Union. **Ask:** What did Reagan mean when he said the Soviet Union had achieved its military might by "preempting the human needs of its people"? *(The Soviets had denied their citizens basic freedoms.)* **OL**

W Writing Support

Descriptive Writing Have interested students do library or Internet research to find out more about the Reagan administration's policies toward one of the following: the Afghan rebels, Nicaragua, or Grenada. Then have students write a one-page report describing America's policy concerning the nation or group they chose. **OL**

Activity: Interdisciplinary Connection

Geography Organize the class into groups of six to research the island country of Grenada, located in the southeastern Caribbean Sea. It is composed of 8 separate islands, with the island of Grenada being the largest and most populous. Have each group member use library or Internet sources to learn more about one of the following topics: geography, climate, vegetation, history, government, or economy. Then have the groups create a travel poster highlighting the features of the islands and encouraging tourists to visit. Students should illustrate their posters with magazine clippings, drawings, and maps. Have each group present its poster to the class. **OL**

D Differentiated Instruction

Interpersonal As students read "Arms Control," have them work in groups to trace the changes in relations between the Soviet Union and the United States on a time line. Groups should present their time lines to the class. ELL

Analyzing VISUALS

Answers:

1. One photograph depicts support of the Afghans against the Soviet Union and the other photograph shows President Reagan talking with Mikhail Gorbachev, the Soviet leader. The photographs indicate that the president was willing to use military power, as well as dialogue, when dealing with the Soviet Union.
2. to clearly state American policy and perhaps to embarrass the other nation; it might be effective because of international pressure

PRIMARY SOURCE
Reagan's Foreign Policy

President Reagan launched a massive weapons buildup, believing it would weaken the Soviet Union. He also provided aid to Afghan rebels fighting Soviet forces and engaged in a series of meetings with the Soviet leader that produced a nuclear arms treaty (at right).

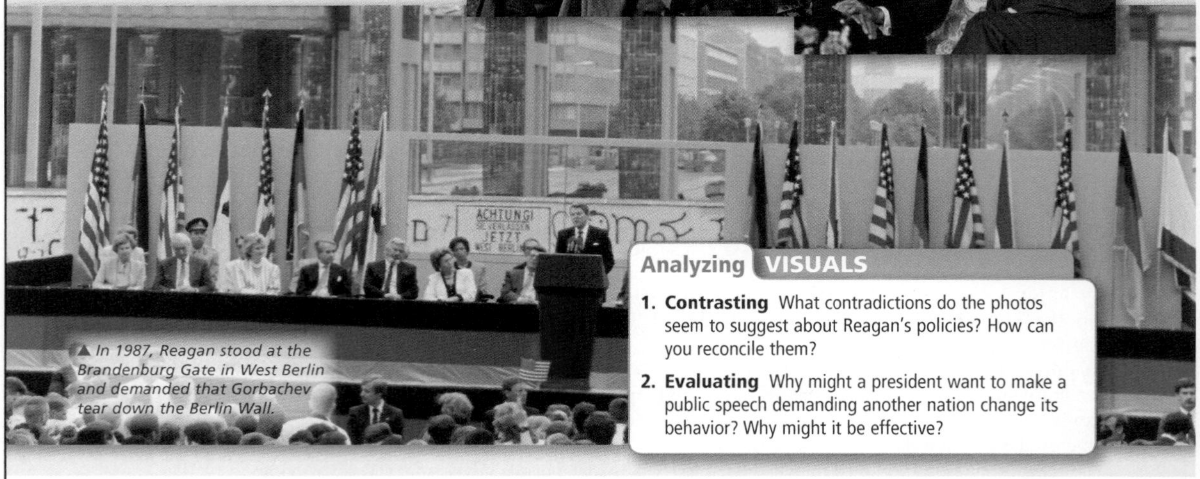

▲ In 1987, Reagan stood at the Brandenburg Gate in West Berlin and demanded that Gorbachev tear down the Berlin Wall.

Analyzing VISUALS

1. **Contrasting** What contradictions do the photos seem to suggest about Reagan's policies? How can you reconcile them?
2. **Evaluating** Why might a president want to make a public speech demanding another nation change its behavior? Why might it be effective?

Aiding the contras was not Reagan's only action in Latin America. In 1983 radical Marxists overthrew the left-wing government on the island of Grenada. In October, Reagan sent in American troops, who quickly defeated the Cuban and Grenadian soldiers. A new anti-Communist government was put in place.

The Iran-Contra Scandal Although Congress had prohibited aid to the Nicaraguan contras, individuals in Reagan's administration continued to illegally support the rebels. They secretly sold weapons to Iran, considered an enemy and sponsor of terrorism, in exchange for the release of American hostages being held in the Middle East. These hostages were taken by the Hezbollah terrorist group because the United States was supporting Israel's involvement in Lebanon's civil war. Profits from these sales were then sent to the contras.

News of the illegal operations broke in November 1986. One of the chief figures in the **Iran-Contra scandal** was Marine colonel Oliver North, an aide to the National Security Council (NSC). He and other senior NSC and CIA officials testified before Congress and admitted to covering up their actions.

President Reagan had approved the sale of arms to Iran, but the congressional investigation concluded that he had had no direct knowledge about the diversion of the money to the contras. The scandal tainted his second term in office.

Arms Control

As part of the military buildup, Reagan decided to place missiles in Western Europe to counter Soviet missiles in Eastern Europe. This decision triggered tens of thousands of protesters to push for a "nuclear freeze"—no more deployment of new nuclear missiles. D

Reagan offered to cancel the deployment of the new missiles if the Soviets removed their

Additional Support

Extending the Content

Divestment and Apartheid In 1984 an estimated $14 billion was invested in South Africa by multinational corporations; U.S. federal, state, and municipal governments; and American universities. Many college students wanted to support black South Africans' attempts to end apartheid—an official policy of discrimination against non-whites. Between 1977 and 1985, campus protests convinced 150 U.S. universities to divest—or remove—all or part of their investments from South Africa. In 1986 Congress banned new investments in South Africa. By 1991, more than 200 U.S. companies had divested, and 28 states, 24 counties, and 92 cities had imposed sanctions. The divestment movement and economic problems caused by apartheid policies themselves devastated the South African economy. Long imprisoned for his anti-apartheid activities, Nelson Mandela was freed in 1990. In 1994 he helped to craft a new constitution for South Africa that ended white minority rule.

missiles from Eastern Europe. He also proposed Strategic Arms Reduction Talks (START) to cut the number of missiles on both sides in half. The Soviets refused and walked out of the arms control talks.

"Star Wars" Despite his decision to deploy missiles in Europe, Reagan generally disagreed with the military strategy known as nuclear deterrence, sometimes called **"mutual assured destruction."** This strategy assumed that, as long as the United States and Soviet Union could destroy each other with nuclear weapons, they would be afraid to use them.

Reagan believed that mutual assured destruction was immoral because it depended on the threat to kill massive numbers of people. He also knew that if nuclear war did begin, there would be no way to defend the United States. In March 1983 Reagan proposed the Strategic Defense Initiative (SDI). This plan, nicknamed "Star Wars," called for the development of weapons that could intercept and destroy incoming missiles.

A New Soviet Leader In 1985 **Mikhail Gorbachev** became the leader of the Soviet Union and agreed to resume arms-control talks. Gorbachev believed that the Soviet Union had to reform its economic system or it would soon collapse. It could not afford a new arms race with the United States.

Reagan and Gorbachev met in a series of summits. The first of these was frustrating for both, as they disagreed on many issues. Gorbachev promised to cut back Soviet nuclear forces if Reagan would agree to give up SDI, but Reagan refused.

Reagan then challenged Gorbachev to make reforms. In West Berlin, Reagan stood at the Brandenburg Gate of the Berlin Wall, the symbol of divided Europe, and declared: "General Secretary Gorbachev, if you seek peace, if you seek prosperity for the Soviet Union and Eastern Europe . . . tear down this wall!"

Relations Improve By 1987, Reagan was convinced that Gorbachev did want to reform the Soviet Union and end the arms race. While some politicians distrusted the Soviets, most people welcomed the Cold War thaw and the reduction in the danger of nuclear war. In December 1987 the two leaders signed the Intermediate Range Nuclear Forces (INF) Treaty. It was the first treaty to call for the destruction of nuclear weapons.

No one realized it at the time, but the treaty marked the beginning of the end of the Cold War. With an arms control deal in place, Gorbachev felt confident that Soviet military spending could be reduced. He pushed ahead with economic and political reforms that eventually led to the collapse of communism in Eastern Europe and in the Soviet Union.

With the economy booming, the American military strong, and relations with the Soviet Union rapidly improving, Ronald Reagan's second term came to an end. As he prepared to leave office, Reagan assessed his presidency: "They called it the Reagan revolution. Well, I'll accept that, but for me it always seemed more like the great rediscovery, a rediscovery of our values and our common sense."

Reading Check **Identifying** What was the Reagan Doctrine?

Section 2 REVIEW

Vocabulary

1. **Explain** the significance of: supply-side economics, Reaganomics, budget deficit, Iran-Contra scandal, "mutual assured destruction," Mikhail Gorbachev.

Main Ideas

2. **Specifying** What political office did Ronald Reagan hold before he was elected president?
3. **Explaining** How did Reagan aim to change the Supreme Court?
4. **Summarizing** What was the goal of the U.S. military buildup under President Reagan?

Critical Thinking

5. **Big Ideas** What was President Reagan's approach to foreign policy?
6. **Organizing** Use a graphic organizer similar to the one below to list the ways in which the Reagan Doctrine was implemented.

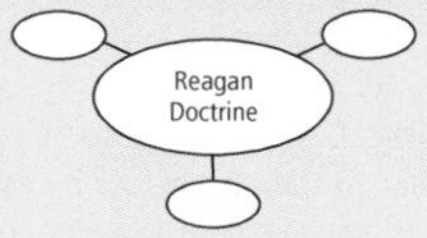

7. **Analyzing Visuals** Study the political cartoons on page 975. How do the cartoons portray Reagan and Carter?

Writing About History

8. **Expository Writing** Take on the role of a newspaper editor during the Reagan administration. Write an editorial in which you present your opinion of Reagan's plans for a military buildup.

History ONLINE
Study Central™ To review this section, go to glencoe.com and click on Study Central.

Reading Check

Answer:
The Reagan Doctrine was a policy of supporting guerrilla groups that were fighting to overthrow Communist or pro-Soviet governments.

Assess

History ONLINE

Study Central™ provides summaries, interactive games, and online graphic organizers to help students review content.

Close

Summarizing Ask: How did Ronald Reagan's presidency change the United States? *(taxes were reduced; some social programs were cut; military spending increased; most citizens were optimistic about the future; relations with the Soviet Union eventually improved)* **OL**

Section 2 REVIEW

Answers

1. All definitions can be found in the section and the Glossary.
2. Governor of California
3. Reagan planned to appoint conservative justices.
4. to bring about the fall of the Soviet Union
5. aggressive stance toward Communism everywhere; military buildup to weaken Soviets
6. answers may include: supported Afghan guerrillas and anti-Sandinista guerrillas in Nicaragua, sent American troops to Grenada
7. Reagan is leading a group of filmmakers; Carter is causing other Democrats to run away.
8. Students' editorials will vary.

Focus

Bellringer

Daily Focus Transparency 29-3

Guide to Reading

Answers may include:
AIDS, alcohol and drug abuse, crime, homelessness, gay and lesbian rights

Section Spotlight Video

To generate student interest and provide a springboard for class discussion, access the Chapter 29, Section 3 video at glencoe.com or on the video DVD.

Section 3

Section Audio   Spotlight Video

Life in the 1980s

Guide to Reading

Big Ideas
Science and Technology
Achievements in technology during the 1980s symbolized the optimism many associated with the Reagan era.

Content Vocabulary
- yuppie *(p. 982)*
- discount retailing *(p. 983)*

Academic Vocabulary
- via *(p. 984)*
- orientation *(p. 987)*

People and Events to Identify
- Mothers Against Drunk Driving (MADD) *(p. 986)*
- AIDS *(p. 987)*
- Stonewall Riot *(p. 987)*
- American Association of Retired Persons (AARP) *(p. 987)*

Reading Strategy
Organizing Complete a graphic organizer similar to the one below by listing the kinds of social issues that Americans faced in the 1980s.

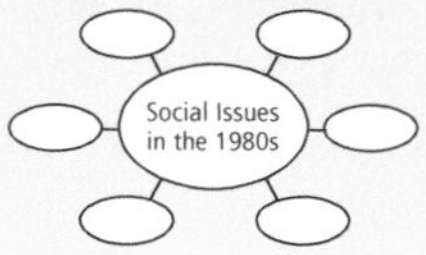

The 1980s was a period of increased wealth for many, as areas of the economy improved and new technologies came to market. However, cuts in social programs left many Americans in need, leading to a new sense of activism.

A Booming Economy

MAIN Idea Innovation in the retailing and broadcast industries changed American society and generated new businesses and jobs.

HISTORY AND YOU What technological devices are part of your everyday life? Read on to find out about the inventions of the 1980s.

By late 1983, the American economy had revived after the stagflation of the 1970s. Stock prices soared as many companies reported record profits. Stockbrokers, speculators, and real estate developers made multimillion-dollar deals, buying and selling hundreds of companies. Perhaps the most famous real estate developer of the era was Donald Trump, who opened Trump Tower in New York City in 1982. Many of the new moneymakers were young, ambitious, and hard-working. Journalists called them **yuppies,** from "young urban professionals."

The rapid economic growth and emphasis on accumulating wealth in the 1980s was partly caused by the baby boom. By the 1980s, many baby boomers had finished college, entered the job market, and begun building their careers. Young people entering the workforce often placed an emphasis on acquiring goods and getting ahead in their jobs. Because baby boomers were so numerous, their concerns tended to shape the culture.

The strong economic growth of the 1980s mostly benefited middle- and upper-class Americans. As a result, the emphasis on acquiring wealth had another effect on society. From 1967 to 1986, the amount of money earned by the top 5 percent of Americans fluctuated between 15.6 and 17.5 percent of the nation's total income. In the late 1980s, their share of the nation's income began to rise. By the mid-1990s, the top 5 percent of Americans earned well over 21 percent of the nation's income.

A Retail Revolution

In addition to the booming real-estate and stock markets, the economy of the 1980s witnessed a revolution in retail sales. Several entrepreneurs pioneered a new approach to retailing—or selling goods to

Resource Manager

R Reading Strategies	C Critical Thinking	D Differentiated Instruction	W Writing Support	S Skill Practice
Teacher Edition • Summarizing, p. 984 • Setting a Purpose, p. 986 **Additional Resources** • Prim. Source Read., URB p. 71 • Guided Read. Act., URB p. 82 • Am. Literature Reading, URB p. 17	**Teacher Edition** • Det. Cause/Effect, p. 984 **Additional Resources** • Historical Skills Act., URB p. 56 • Supreme Court Case Studies, p. 129 • Quizzes/Tests, p. 419 • Geography and History Act., URB p. 3	**Teacher Edition** • Special Ed., p. 983 **Additional Resources** • Differ. Instr. Act., URB p. 57	**Additional Resources** • American History in Graphic Novel, p. 87	**Teacher Edition** • Visual Literacy, p. 985 **Additional Resources** • Link. Past and Present Act., URB p. 68 • Read. Essen., p. 325

PRIMARY SOURCE

The Booming Economy of the 1980s

The American economy grew rapidly in the 1980s for several reasons—lower taxes spurred investment and spending while new methods of retailing lowered prices and new technology led to new businesses and the creation of many new jobs.

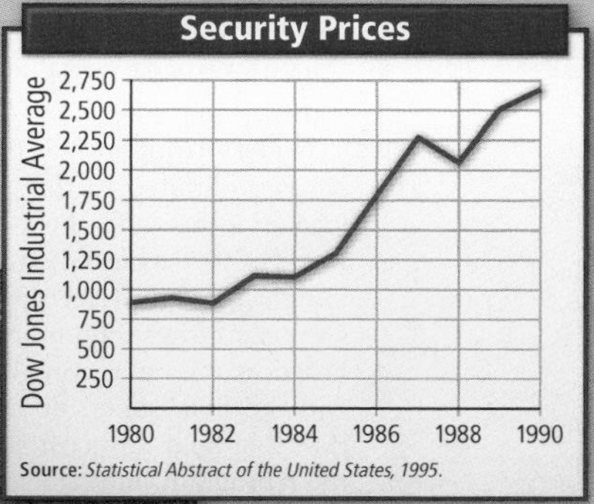

Source: *Statistical Abstract of the United States, 1995.*

Discount retail stores (above) and cable television (right) took off in the 1980s, helping to further fuel economic growth.

Analyzing VISUALS

1. **Identifying** In what year of the late 1980s did the Dow Jones sharply decline?
2. **Explaining** Examine the photos and then write a brief essay explaining how they demonstrate economic trends of the 1980s.

consumers—that greatly reduced prices for Americans.

D This new type of retailing, known as **discount retailing**, had actually begun to emerge in the 1960s—but it did not have a major impact on the economy until the 1980s. Discount retailers sell large quantities of goods at very low prices, trying to sell the goods quickly to turn over their entire inventory in a short period of time. By selling a lot of products at very low prices, they could make more money than traditional retailers who sold fewer products at higher prices. During the 1960s many new discount retail chains were founded, including K Mart, Woolco, Target, and Wal-Mart. Annual sales by discount stores grew from about $2 billion in the mid-1960s to almost $70 billion by 1985.

The most successful discount retailer was Sam Walton, the founder of Wal-Mart. Walton developed a system of distribution centers to rapidly re-supply his stores. He was one of the first retailers to use a computer database to track inventory and sales. By 1985, he was the richest person in the United States.

Others soon copied Walton's approach. By the late 1970s, discount retailers had begun to build huge "superstores" that enabled them to sell large quantities of goods very quickly at low prices. One such entrepreneur was Arthur Blank, who opened Home Depot—a chain of giant home-improvement stores—in 1978. In 1983 Richard Schulze, a former air force officer, used his technical training to found Best Buy, a huge discount retailer of consumer electronics. Dozens of other entrepreneurs started discount stores in other industries. Their innovations created millions of new jobs in the 1980s and helped fuel the era's rapid economic growth.

Teach

D Differentiated Instruction

Special Education As students read the section, they might encounter text or other information they do not understand, and they should adjust their reading strategies to clarify ideas. Model how this is done by reading part of the section aloud. As you read, ask yourself questions aloud, such as, "What do I think the main focus of the 1980s will turn out to be?" (predicting) and "What discount retail stores have I shopped in or are in my community?" (activating prior knowledge). Modeling how you check your comprehension helps students to think about strategies they can use as they read independently. BL

Analyzing VISUALS

Answers:

1. 1988
2. In their essays, students should note economic trends such as discount retailing and the rise of cable television.

Hands-On Chapter Project
Step 3

Conducting an Opinion Poll

Step 3: Conducting the Poll Each student should arrange to interview at least one person who was of voting age in the 1980s. The student should then read each of the statements composed during Step 2 and ask the respondent if he or she agrees or disagrees with the statement.

Classifying Respondents should be given five options, ranked by number: (1) strongly disagree; (2) disagree; (3) neutral; (4) agree; or (5) strongly agree. Encourage students to ask follow up questions if respondents express a strong opinion on an issue. OL

(Chapter Project continued on page 991)

C Critical Thinking

Determining Cause and Effect Discuss with students the changes in television in the 1980s. **Ask:** In what areas of broadcasting or on what new audiences did the new networks focus? *(CNN provided 24-hour news, BET focused on African Americans, MTV focused on youth.)* What do you think are some effects that the new television networks may have had on consumerism and culture in the United States? *(Students may note that new groups were represented more in popular culture with the new networks, but they were also exposed to advertising. CNN created a 24-hour news cycle, which may have led to a huge broadening in the definition of "news" as networks scrambled to fill air time.)* OL

R Reading Strategy

Summarizing Dr. Sally Ride became the first American woman to orbit Earth when she flew aboard the space shuttle *Challenger*. **Ask:** What are some innovations that occurred in the nation's space program in the 1980s? *(space shuttle, Hubble Space Telescope, experiments, women astronauts)* OL

Additional Support

A Revolution in Media

In the 1980s other entrepreneurs began transforming the news and entertainment industries. Until the late 1970s television viewers were limited to three national networks, local stations, and the public television network. In 1970 a businessman named Ted Turner bought a failing television station in Atlanta, Georgia. Turner then pioneered a new type of broadcasting by creating WTBS in 1975. WTBS was the first "superstation"—a television station that sold low-cost sports and entertainment programs **via** satellite to cable companies throughout the nation.

The Rise of Cable Television Turner's innovation changed broadcasting and helped spread cable television across the country. Dozens of networks soon appeared. Many of the new networks specialized in one type of broadcasting, such as sports (ESPN), movies (HBO), or news. In 1980 Turner himself founded the Cable News Network (CNN)—the first 24-hour, all-news network.

Other new networks focused on specific audiences, such as churchgoers, shoppers, or minorities. In 1980 entrepreneur Robert Johnson created Black Entertainment Television (BET). Johnson—who had been born into a poor, rural family in Mississippi and gone on to earn a master's degree from Princeton University—was convinced that television had tremendous power to promote African American businesses and culture. BET was the first, and is still the largest, African American-owned network on cable television.

In 1981 music and technology merged when Music Television (MTV) went on the air. MTV broadcast performances of songs and images, or music videos. MTV was an instant hit, though the videos it showed were often criticized for violence and sexual content. Many performers began to produce videos along with each of their new albums. Music videos boosted the careers of artists such as Madonna and Michael Jackson.

Rap music was the new sound of the 1980s. This musical style originated in local clubs in New York City's South Bronx. Emphasizing heavy bass and very rhythmic sounds, rap artists did not usually sing but rather spoke over the music and rhythmic beats. Rap's lyrics frequently focused on the African American expe-

PAST & PRESENT

New Space Technology

After the series of moon landings of the 1970s, NASA concentrated on the space shuttle. Although it looks like a huge airplane, the shuttle is rocketed into space, then glides back to Earth for another flight. Unlike earlier spacecraft, the shuttle is reusable. Astronauts John Young and Roger Crippen made the first space shuttle flight in April 1981.

Between April 1981 and December 2006, shuttle astronauts completed 114 missions. They have placed many satellites in orbit, including the Hubble Space Telescope, and conducted numerous experiments. Tragedy has struck twice during shuttle missions. In 1986, the space shuttle *Challenger* exploded shortly after liftoff. In 2003, the shuttle *Columbia* came apart while reentering the atmosphere. Seven astronauts died in each of these accidents.

As the shuttle nears the end of its service life, both NASA and several independent companies have begun work on vehicles capable of reaching orbit. Shuttle launches are very expensive and many entrepreneurs are seeking to develop low-cost alternatives to the shuttle that will enable business to move into space and develop new industries there.

▲ *On April 12, 1981, the shuttle* Columbia *lifted off on the first space shuttle flight.*

Activity: Interdisciplinary Connection

Science Have students review the history of the space program and research its future goals. Tell students that during times of economic struggle, some have questioned the ongoing usefulness of the space program and have proposed to reduce funding for it. Others see the potential future value to Americans and all humans of continued space exploration. Have students write a persuasive essay either supporting the continued expansion of the space program or call for reduced funding for it. **Ask:** What are the benefits of space exploration to the American public? What are the drawbacks? *(Students' answers will vary, but should be supported with logical reasons.)* AL rience in the inner city. While rap was initially popular among East Coast African Americans, it grew in popularity, becoming a multimillion-dollar industry that appealed to music lovers across the country.

Technology and Media In the 1980s technology also transformed how people accessed their entertainment. Until the 1980s, most people listened to music on large stereo systems in their homes or relied on radio-station programming when they were driving. In the 1980s, the Sony Walkman made music portable. The Sony Walkman played cassette tapes, but it marked the beginning of a new way for people to access music. In the 1990s, portable compact disc (CD) players replaced the Walkman, and in the early 2000s digital audio players, such as the iPod and MP3 players, advanced the technology even further.

Video technology also began to change. Until the 1980s most people had to watch television shows when they aired. By the end of the 1980s, many people had videocassette recorders (VCRs), enabling them to tape television shows or watch taped films whenever they wished. By the 2000s, VCRs were being replaced by digital video disk (DVD) recorders. The growing use of VCRs changed the movie industry, as people increasingly chose to rent taped movies to watch at home rather than go to the theater.

Even as technology changed the music and television industries, it also brought about a new form of entertainment that competed with music and movies—the video game. Early video games grew out of military computer technology. The first video arcade game was a game called *Pong*, released in 1972. Home video games developed quickly. In the early 1980s sales reached about $3 billion with the sale of games such as *Pac-Man* and *Space Invaders*. Video arcades became the new spot for young people to meet. By the mid-1980s, home video games were able to compete with arcade games in graphics and speed. Video games have continued to grow in popularity to the present day and three major companies—Sony, Nintendo, and Microsoft—have emerged as the major developers of video games and game devices.

Reading Check **Describing** What forms of entertainment gained popularity in the 1980s?

June 2004

In the early 2000s, many private companies were working on building spaceships. SpaceShipOne (below) was the first privately-built ship to carry a person to space. Another company is working on the Goddard (right)—a ship designed to take off and land vertically, without needing wings.

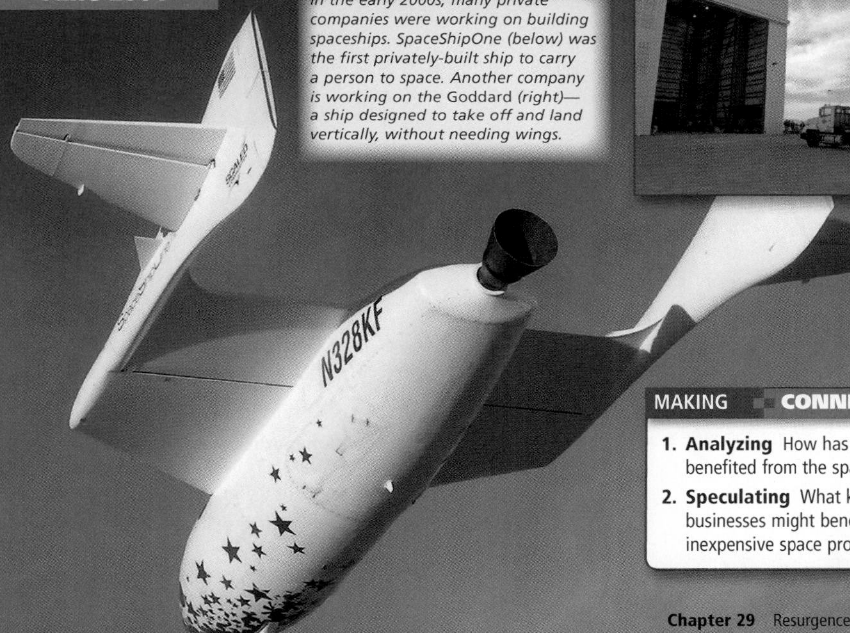

MAKING CONNECTIONS

1. **Analyzing** How has the United States benefited from the space program?
2. **Speculating** What kinds of private businesses might benefit from easy, inexpensive space programs?

S Skill Practice

Visual Literacy Have students study the examples of some of the latest spacecraft. **Ask:** **What features of *SpaceShipOne* and *Goddard* are similar to and different from the space shuttles?** *(All three vehicle types are aerodynamic and are meant to escape Earth's orbit. The newer craft seem to have simpler designs;* Goddard *does not have any type of wing.)* **OL**

MAKING CONNECTIONS

Answers:

1. Students should note that United States benefited from the space program in prestige and also through the many important scientific discoveries that were made and the materials, tools, and machines that were developed for space.
2. possible answer: satellite communications companies

Reading Check

Answer:
listening to music such as rap; watching taped movies, cable or satellite TV, and music videos; and playing video games

Differentiated Instruction

Leveled Activities

BL **Guided Reading Activity, URB p. 82**

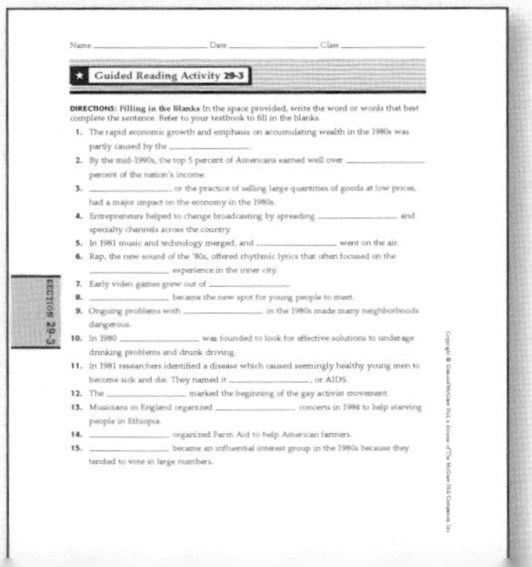

OL **Linking Past and Present Activity, URB p. 68**

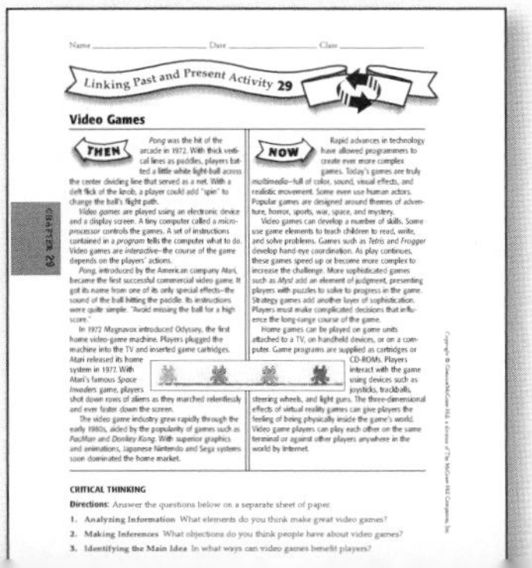

AL **Primary Source Reading, URB p. 71**

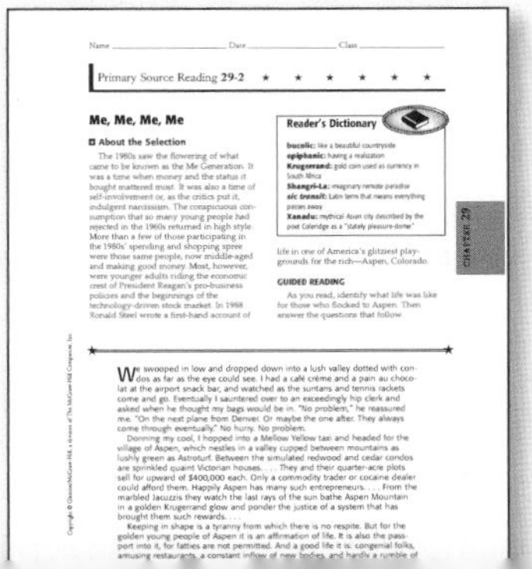

ELL **Differentiated Instruction Activity, URB, p. 57**

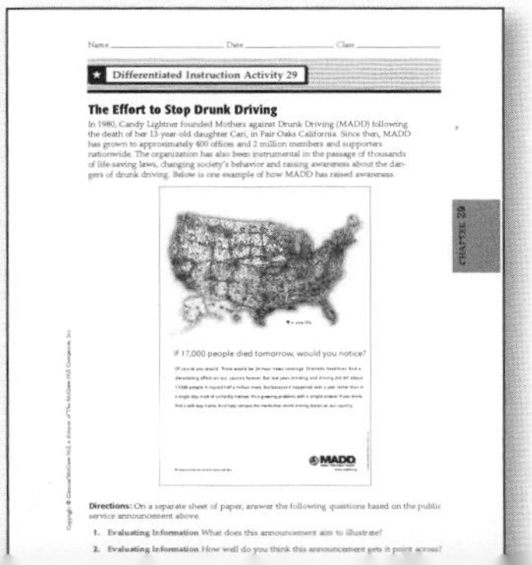

R Reading Strategy

Setting a Purpose Point out to students that they can use the Main Idea statements that follow each main heading in a section to help them preview and prepare to read. Instruct students to change the Main Idea statements into a question. For example, the statement on this page could be changed to "What social problems affected many people during the 1980s and what new groups formed to solve them?" Tell students that they should be able to answer the question as they read. **BL**

Analyzing VISUALS

Answers:

1. high interest rates and low food prices
2. low crop prices

Additional Support

New Social Activism

MAIN Idea Social problems affected many people during the 1980s, and new groups formed to try to solve them.

HISTORY AND YOU Does your school have organizations such as Students Against Drunk Driving? Read on to learn more about attempts to limit teen alcohol abuse.

The 1980s was a decade of wealth and prosperity. At the same time, many social problems continued to plague the nation, such as drugs, poverty, homelessness, and disease.

Social Problems

Ongoing problems with drug abuse in the 1980s made many neighborhoods dangerous. Drug users often committed crimes to get money for drugs. Drug use also spread from cities to small towns and rural areas.

Fighting Drugs in Schools In an effort to reduce teen drug use, some schools began searching student bags and lockers for concealed drugs. In 1984 one teen who had been arrested for selling drugs challenged the school's right to search her purse without a warrant. In 1985, the Supreme Court case *New Jersey* v. *T.L.O.* upheld the school's right to search without a warrant if it had probable cause. Although students did have a right to privacy, they did not have the same Fourth Amendment rights as adults. Similarly, the 1995 case of *Vernonia School District* v. *Acton* held that random drug tests do not violate students' Fourth Amendment rights.

Efforts to Stop Drunk Driving Abuse of alcohol was also a serious concern. In 1980 **Mothers Against Drunk Driving (MADD)** was founded to try to stop underage drinking and drunk driving in general. In 1984 Congress cut highway funds to any state that did not raise the legal drinking age to 21. Within four years, all states complied.

The AIDS Epidemic Begins In 1981 researchers identified a disease that caused healthy young people to become sick and die. They named it "acquired immune deficiency syndrome," or **AIDS.** AIDS weakens the

PRIMARY SOURCE

The Farm Debt Crisis of the 1980s

Although the high interest rates of the 1980s helped reduce inflation, when they were combined with the low food prices of the era, they created a debt crisis for American farmers who could not make their loan payments and were forced out of business. By the end of the 1980s, the total number of farms in the United States had sharply declined.

Farm Income and Debt

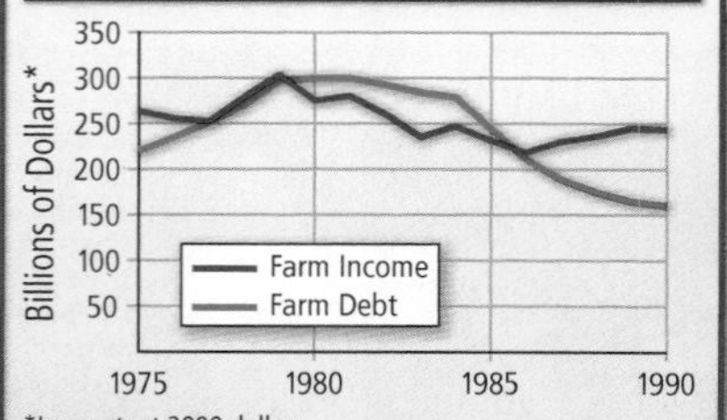

*In constant 2000 dollars

Source: U.S. Department of Agriculture.

◀ *As farmers faced a debt crisis, some began holding demonstrations, such as this one in Washington D.C. in 1984.*

Analyzing VISUALS

1. **Hypothesizing** What factors explain why farm debt increased between 1975 and 1980?
2. **Interpreting** What are the farmers at left complaining about?

Activity: Interdisciplinary Connection

Civics Invite someone who works in a mental health facility, free clinic, or other social agency to make a presentation to the class about ways in which students can help address an ongoing social problem, such as drug abuse, AIDS, or drunk driving. Be sure to brief the speaker beforehand on any guidelines your school may have about sensitive subjects. Allow time for students to ask questions of the guest speaker. Conclude with a discussion on civic participation. **Ask:** What are some ways in which you can make a difference in your community? **OL** **BL** **ELL**

immune system. HIV, the virus that causes AIDS, is spread through bodily fluids.

In the United States, AIDS was first noticed among homosexual men, but it soon spread among heterosexual men and women. Many people were infected by sexual partners. A few got the disease from blood transfusions. Other victims included drug users who shared needles. Between 1981 and 1988, the Centers for Disease Control and Prevention identified more than 100,000 cases in the United States.

New Activist Groups

AIDS increased the visibility of the country's gay and lesbian community, but some homosexuals had been engaged in efforts to defend their civil rights since the 1960s. On June 27, 1969, New York City police raided a nightclub called the Stonewall Inn. The police had often raided the nightclub because of the sexual **orientation** of its patrons. Frustration among the gay and lesbian onlookers led to a riot. The **Stonewall Riot** marked the beginning of the gay activist movement. Soon after, organizations such as the Gay Liberation Front began efforts to increase tolerance of homosexuality.

Rock 'n' Rollers Become Activists Many musicians and entertainers in the 1980s began using their celebrity to raise awareness about social issues. To help starving people in Ethiopia, Irish rocker Bob Geldof organized musicians in England to present "Band Aid" concerts in 1984. In the next year, the event grew into "Live Aid." People in some 100 countries watched benefit concerts televised from London, Philadelphia, and Sydney, Australia. The organization's theme song, "We Are the World," was a best-seller. In the same year, country singer Willie Nelson organized "Farm Aid" to help American farmers who were going through hard times. Musicians also publicized efforts to end the segregated apartheid social system in South Africa. In the late 1980s, the United States and other nations were attempting to end apartheid in South Africa by imposing economic sanctions against the country.

Senior Citizens Begin to Lobby Another group that became politically active in the 1980s was senior citizens. Decades of improvements in medicine had resulted in more Americans surviving to an older age. In addition, the birthrate had declined, so younger people represented a comparatively smaller proportion of the population. The fact that more Americans were receiving Social Security payments created budget pressures for the government.

Older Americans became very vocal in the political arena, opposing cuts in Social Security or Medicare. Because they tend to vote in large numbers, senior citizens are an influential interest group. Their major lobbying organization is the **American Association of Retired Persons (AARP),** founded in 1958.

✓Reading Check **Summarizing** On what issues did some entertainers focus in the 1980s?

Section 3 REVIEW

Vocabulary

1. **Explain** the significance of: yuppie, discount retailing, Mothers Against Drunk Driving (MADD), AIDS, Stonewall Riot, American Association of Retired Persons (AARP).

Main Ideas

2. **Summarizing** How did retailing change in the 1980s?
3. **Listing** What are three social problems that gained focus in the 1980s?

Critical Thinking

4. **Big Ideas** What new innovations occurred in the consumer electronics industry in the 1980s?
5. **Organizing** Use a graphic organizer similar to the one below to list the changes in entertainment in the 1980s.

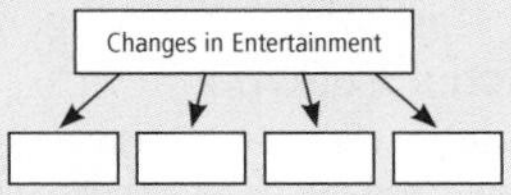

6. **Analyzing Visuals** Study the graph of the stock market rise on page 983. How is this graph indicative of what you have read about in this section?

Writing About History

7. **Persuasive Writing** Choose one of the social problems of the 1980s. Write a letter to members of your favorite band asking them to perform a concert to benefit your cause. Your letter should explain why the cause is important.

History ONLINE
Study Central™ To review this section, go to glencoe.com and click on Study Central.

✓Reading Check

Answer:
aid to starving people in Africa; aid to American farmers

Assess

History ONLINE

Study Central™ provides summaries, interactive games, and online graphic organizers to help students review content.

Close

Summarizing Ask: What was life like in the United States in the 1980s? *(The economy was booming, there was a revolution in the media, and there were advances in space technology. However, the decade was also marked by an increase in social problems, such as drug use and the AIDS epidemic, although many groups also began to fight to solve these problems.)* **OL**

Section 3 REVIEW

Answers

1. All definitions can be found in the section and the Glossary.
2. Some companies began to grow in the area of discount retailing.
3. drug abuse, alcohol abuse, AIDS
4. the Sony Walkman, VCRs, video games
5. Innovations include rap music; listening to music on tiny portable cassette players; watching movie and music videos and cable or satellite TV; and playing video games.
6. It indicates a booming economy.
7. Students' letters will vary but should use standard grammar, use correct letter format, and be persuasive.

GEOGRAPHY & HISTORY

Focus

Ask students to define basic terms such as urban, rural, and suburban. Explain the meaning of "exurbs." Have students identify the type of community in which they live.

Teach

R Reading Skill

Determining Importance

Ask: What are the possible advantages in several of the high growth areas that have made people and industry move there? *(Students might suggest climate, large labor pool, and infrastructure already in place.)* **BL**

C Critical Thinking

Analyze Information Have students work in teams to create surveys about local community development. Tell students to devise 10 questions that can be answered with a range of responses. *(One example could be: Do you favor increased mass transit options? Sample responses might be Strongly Favor, Favor, Neutral, Oppose, and Strongly Oppose.)* **OL**

Additional Support

NATIONAL GEOGRAPHIC

GEOGRAPHY & HISTORY

Urban America on the Move

R After World War II, cities grew into vast metropolitan areas—a development referred to as "urban sprawl." Inner cities, often inhabited by lower-income people, lost tax revenue, resulting in deteriorating infrastructure and shortages of affordable housing. As the map shows, many high-growth areas are in Southern Sunbelt states.

In response, some cities sought to improve urban neighborhoods and encourage reinvestment in the city core. These policies have had only limited effect, as suburbs and new "exurbs"—communities located in the country beyond the suburbs, continue to grow.

▲ *Urban sprawl, traffic congestion, long commutes, and air pollution are part of the price Atlanta paid for rapid growth.*

How Has Urban Geography Affected Politics?

C The rapid growth of the suburbs and exurbs plays an important role in American politics. Inner city communities tend to vote for Democrats, while voters in outer suburbs and exurbs tend to vote for Republicans. The reason for this pattern is unclear. In part, it reflects the preference of many minorities who live in the inner city to vote for Democrats. In addition, some political geographers believe that since city-dwellers rely more on government services, they tend to support liberal policies that favor government activism. People in the suburbs and exurbs want more independence and more often distrust government—a conservative perspective. They believe large city governments have done a poor job running schools and controlling crime.

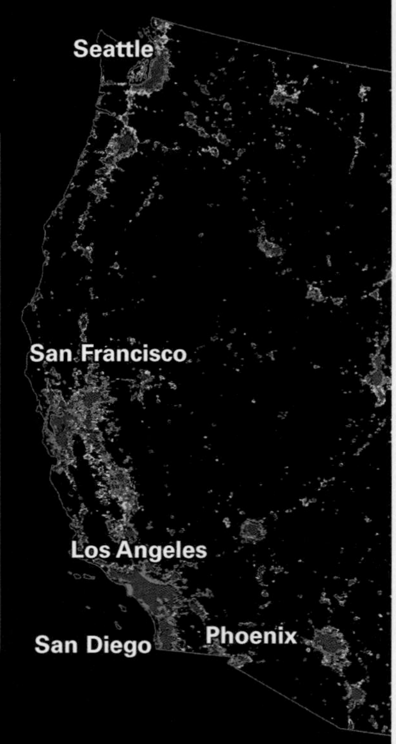

Analyzing GEOGRAPHY

1. **Movement** Which regions experienced the most growth after 1993?
2. **Human-Environment Interaction** How does the urban geography of American cities shape voting patterns and preferences?

Collaborative Learning

Create an Urban Plan Divide the class into small groups. Challenge each group to imagine that they are a firm of urban planners specializing in "smart growth" and "green building." Have them use the Internet or library resources to find out more about these concepts. Then have them outline a plan with rough sketches for the new community they have designed. Remind them to take climate into account; a development planned for the Sunbelt states will look different than one in northern states.

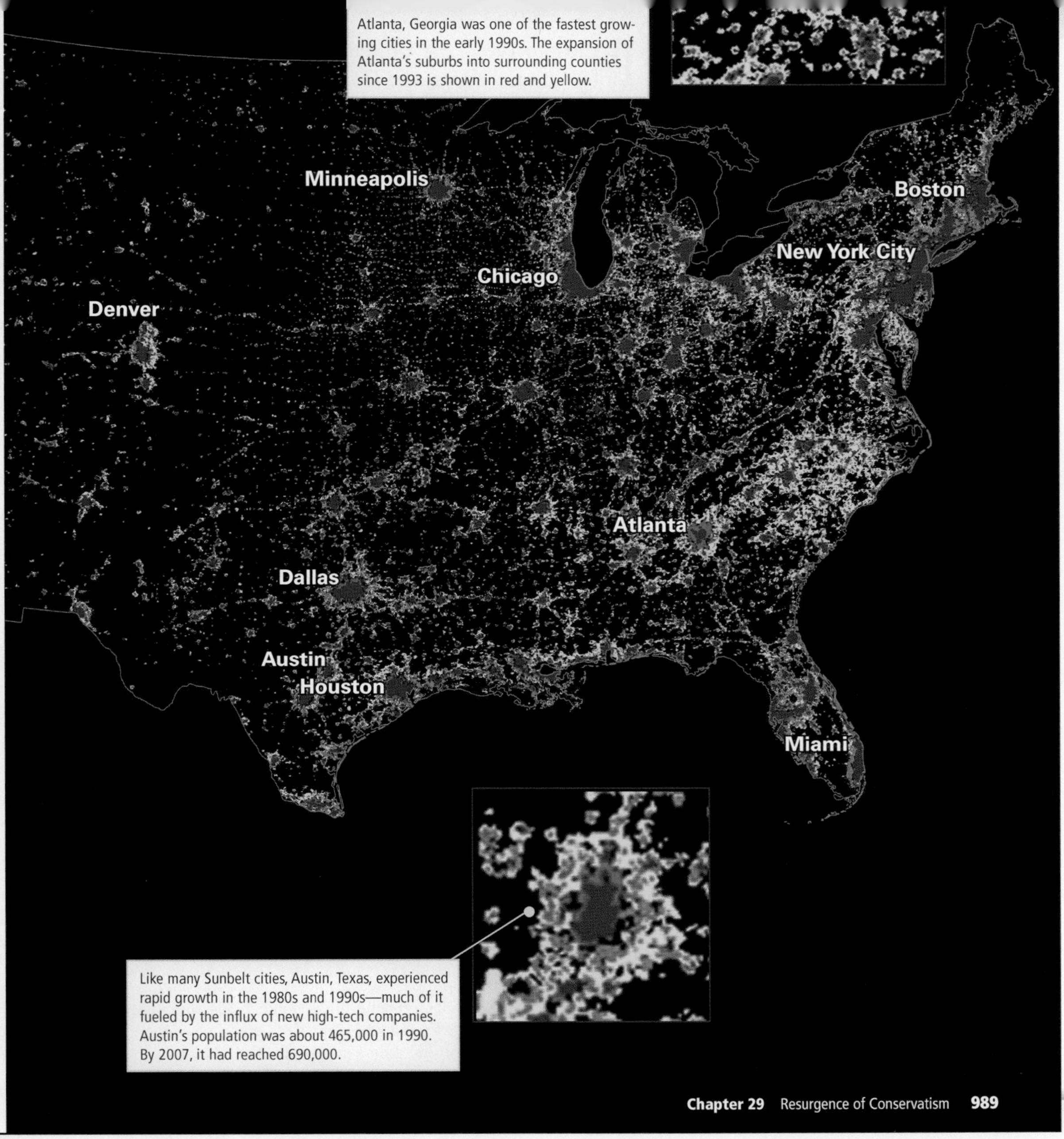

Assess/Close

Activity: Top Ten Cities Ask students to use an almanac or other reference source to find the top ten most populous cities in the United States. Have them locate those places on the map. Do they observe any changes or new patterns emerging?

Analyzing GEOGRAPHY

Answers:
1. the south and west
2. Urban voters tend to vote Democratic, while suburban and exurban voters tend to vote Republican. This may reflect the tendency of urban dwellers to rely on and be willing to support government services, while suburban and exurban dwellers tend to distrust government and prefer independence.

Technology Connection

Urban Planning in China Have students working in pairs use the Internet to find reputable sources on the problems of growing industrial cities in China. Ask students to read and summarize at least three articles suggesting ways that China can continue to modernize and still follow the Kyoto Protocols.

Focus

Bellringer

Daily Focus Transparency 29-4

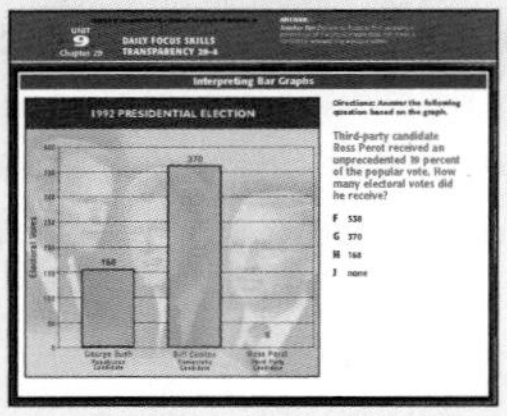

Guide to Reading

Answers:

Soviet Union: cooperated with reform leader Gorbachev; China: halted arms sales and reduced diplomatic contact; Panama: invaded and seized dictator and helped people hold elections and organize a new government; Middle East: imposed economic sanctions against Iraq and carried out Operation Desert Storm

Section Spotlight Video

To generate student interest and provide a springboard for class discussion, access the Chapter 29, Section 4 video at glencoe.com or on the video DVD.

Section 4

Section Audio Spotlight Video

The End of the Cold War

Guide to Reading

Big Ideas

Economics and Society The deficit and an economic slowdown hurt George H.W. Bush's attempt to win reelection in 1992.

Content Vocabulary

- perestroika *(p. 991)*
- glasnost *(p. 991)*
- downsizing *(p. 994)*
- capital gains tax *(p. 995)*
- grassroots movement *(p. 995)*

Academic Vocabulary

- initiative *(p. 993)*
- retain *(p. 995)*

People and Events to Identify

- Boris Yeltsin *(p. 992)*
- Tiananmen Square *(p. 993)*
- Saddam Hussein *(p. 993)*
- H. Ross Perot *(p. 995)*

Reading Strategy

Categorizing Complete a graphic organizer similar to the one below by describing U.S. foreign policy in each of the places listed.

Place	Foreign Policy
Soviet Union	
China	
Panama	
Middle East	

In the late 1980s, the United States faced a series of international crises. The Cold War came to an end in Europe, but events in the Middle East soon led the United States into its first major war since Vietnam.

The Soviet Union Collapses

MAIN Idea The Soviet Union's attempts at reforming its social and economic systems failed, leading to the collapse of the Communist eastern bloc.

HISTORY AND YOU What can you recall about the division of Europe after World War II? Read on to learn about the massive changes that took place in Eastern Europe at the end of the 1980s.

When Ronald Reagan left office, few Americans were thinking about foreign policy. Many generally wanted a continuation of Reagan's domestic policies—low taxes and less government action. When Republicans nominated George H. W. Bush for president in 1988, he reassured Americans he would continue Reagan's policies by making a promise: "Read my lips: No new taxes."

The Democrats hoped to regain the White House in 1988 by promising to help working-class Americans, minorities, and the poor. One candidate for the nomination, civil rights leader Jesse Jackson, tried to create a "rainbow coalition"—a broad group of minorities and the poor—by speaking about homelessness and unemployment. Jackson finished second in the primaries, the first African American to make a serious run for the nomination.

The Democrats nominated Massachusetts governor Michael Dukakis. The Bush campaign portrayed him as too liberal and "soft on crime." The Democrats questioned Bush's leadership abilities, but Bush had Reagan's endorsement and, with the economy still doing well, most Americans felt that Bush was the more able candidate. Bush easily defeated Dukakis in the general election, although Democrats kept control of Congress.

Voters had focused on domestic issues during the election campaign, but soon after taking office President Bush had to focus most of his time and energy on foreign policy as change swept through Eastern Europe and the Cold War came to an abrupt end.

Revolution in Eastern Europe

As president, Bush continued Reagan's policy of cooperation with Soviet leader Mikhail Gorbachev. By the late 1980s, the Soviet economy was suffering from years of inefficient central planning and huge expenditures on the arms race. To save the economy,

Resource Manager

R Reading Strategies	C Critical Thinking	D Differentiated Instruction	W Writing Support	S Skill Practice
Teacher Edition • Making Connections, p. 991 • Read. Prim. Sources, p. 992 • Act. Prior Know., p. 993 • Taking Notes, p. 994 **Additional Resources** • Read. Skill Act., URB p. 55 • Guided Read. Act., URB p. 83	**Additional Resources** • Critical Thinking Skills Act., URB p. 66 • Quizzes/Tests, p. 420 • Auth. Assess., p. 63 • Standard. Test Practice, p. 66	**Additional Resources** • Reinforcing Skill Act., p. 65 • Enrichment Act., URB p. 78	**Teacher Edition** • Narrative Writing, p. 991 **Additional Resources** • Enrichment Act., URB p. 78	**Additional Resources** • Reinforcing Skill Act., URB p. 65 • Time Line Act., URB p. 67 • Read. Essen., p. 328

Revolutions in Eastern Europe

◄ *The Berlin Wall fell on November 10, 1989.*

▲ *Boris Yeltsin rallies the crowd against the military coup on August 19, 1991.*

Analyzing GEOGRAPHY

1. **Regions** Which Eastern European countries abandoned communism first?
2. **Place** Why was the fall of communism in East Germany significant?

Gorbachev instituted **perestroika,** or "restructuring," and allowed some private enterprise and profit making.

The other principle of Gorbachev's plan was **glasnost,** or "openness." It allowed more freedom of religion and speech, enabling people to discuss politics openly. With Gorbachev's support, glasnost spread to Eastern Europe. In 1989 revolutions replaced Communist rulers with democratic governments in Bulgaria, Czechoslovakia, Hungary, Poland, and Romania. W The tide of revolution then swept over East Germany, and at midnight on November 9, 1989, guards at the Berlin Wall opened the gates. Within days, bulldozers leveled the hated symbol of Communist repression. Within a year, East and West Germany had reunited to form one nation—the Federal Republic of Germany. W

The Soviet Union Collapses

As Eastern Europe abandoned communism, Gorbachev faced mounting criticism from opponents at home. In August 1991 a group of Communist officials and army officers tried to stage a coup—an overthrow of the government. They arrested Gorbachev and sent troops into Moscow.

Teach

Analyzing GEOGRAPHY

Answers:
1. Poland, Hungary, Bulgaria, and Romania
2. It was particularly significant because it meant that Germany could be reunified.

R Reading Strategy

Making Connections To help students understand the impact of the Berlin Wall coming down, engage them in this pre-reading activity. Use a large map of your community and draw a line down the center of it. Ask students to look at the map closely and make a list of all the aspects of their lives that would be affected if they could not cross "the wall." OL

W Writing Support

Narrative Writing Have students conduct some research about the division and reunification of Germany. Tell them to write a letter that might have been written by a German teenager after the Berlin wall fell. OL

Hands-On Chapter Project Step 4

Conducting an Opinion Poll

Step 4: Analyzing the Findings Have students return to their groups and compare their poll results.

Identifying Points of View Ask students to calculate the average response to each of their statements and then write a brief paragraph for each in which they attempt to interpret their findings. OL

(Chapter Project continued on Visual Summary page)

R Reading Strategy

Reading Primary Sources
Ask students where U.S. forces launched attacks before they attacked the invading Iraqis in Kuwait. *(Iraq)* **BL**

Analyzing VISUALS

Answers:

1. Coalition forces most likely chose to launch their invasion from Saudi Arabia because Saudi Arabia, unlike Iran, was an ally, needed some protection anyway, and shared a border with Kuwait, unlike Syria and Turkey.
2. Saudi Arabia and Israel

Reading Check

Answer:
It was intended to save the Soviet economy by allowing some private enterprise and profit-making.

In Moscow, Russian president **Boris Yeltsin** defied the coup leaders from his offices in the Russian Parliament. About 50,000 people surrounded the Russian Parliament to protect it from troops. President Bush telephoned Yeltsin to express the support of the United States. Soon afterward, the coup collapsed, and Gorbachev returned to Moscow.

The defeat of the coup brought change swiftly. All 15 Soviet republics declared their independence from the Soviet Union. Yeltsin outlawed the Communist Party in Russia. In late December 1991 Gorbachev announced the end of the Soviet Union. Most of the former Soviet republics then joined in a federation called the Commonwealth of Independent States (CIS). Although CIS member states remained independent, they agreed to form a common economic zone in 1993.

Reading Check **Explaining** Why did Mikhail Gorbachev institute the policy of *perestroika*?

A "New World Order"

MAIN Idea Bush used his foreign policy expertise to deal with crises in China, Panama, and the Persian Gulf.

HISTORY AND YOU Do you remember learning about student protests in the 1960s? Read on to learn about a student protest in China.

After the Cold War, the world became increasingly unpredictable. President Bush noted that a "new world order" was emerging. This new world order introduced new military challenges around the globe. For example, U.S. troops led Operation Restore Hope, providing humanitarian assistance and famine relief to refugees in Somalia, which had collapsed when the Cold War motivations were removed. Several other crises requiring military action emerged in China, Panama, and the Middle East.

NATIONAL GEOGRAPHIC The Persian Gulf War, 1991

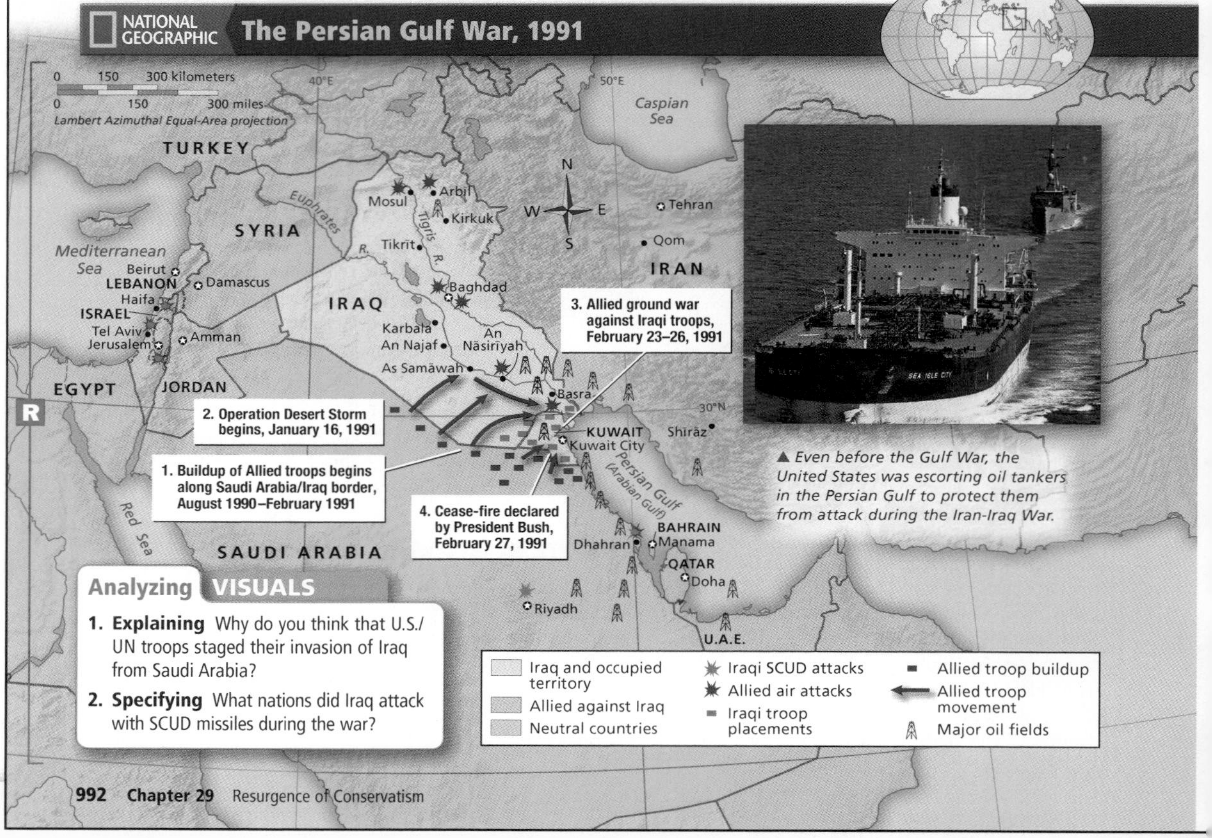

▲ Even before the Gulf War, the United States was escorting oil tankers in the Persian Gulf to protect them from attack during the Iran-Iraq War.

Analyzing VISUALS

1. **Explaining** Why do you think that U.S./UN troops staged their invasion of Iraq from Saudi Arabia?
2. **Specifying** What nations did Iraq attack with SCUD missiles during the war?

Additional Support

Extending the Content

Strait of Hormuz The Strait of Hormuz is a narrow shipping lane that connects the Persian Gulf, the Gulf of Oman, and the Arabian Sea. Most of the crude oil produced in the Middle East passes through the Strait of Hormuz. In 1997 about 14 million barrels of crude oil passed through the strait every day. Since the waterway is only about 40 miles (64 km) across at its widest point, it is possible that a country might block or hamper the passage of ships. During the 1980s, the United States began escorting oil tankers through the strait to protect them from Iranian attacks. If the passage were ever closed, oil would have to be shipped overland by pipeline—a much more expensive option.

Tiananmen Square

Despite the collapse of communism in Eastern Europe and the Soviet Union, China's Communist leaders were determined to stay in power. China's government had relaxed controls on the economy, but it continued to repress political speech and dissent. In May 1989, Chinese students and workers held demonstrations for democracy. The center of the protests was **Tiananmen Square** in Beijing, China's capital. In early June government tanks and soldiers crushed the protests. Many people were killed and hundreds of pro-democracy activists were arrested. Many were later sentenced to death.

R Shocked, the United States and several European countries halted arms sales and reduced their diplomatic contacts with China. The World Bank suspended loans. President Bush resisted harsher sanctions, believing that trade and diplomacy would eventually moderate China's behavior.

Panama

While President Bush struggled to deal with global events elsewhere, a crisis developed in Panama. In 1978 the United States had agreed to give Panama control over the Panama Canal by the year 2000. Because of the canal's importance, American officials wanted to make sure Panama's government was both stable and pro-American.

By 1989, Panama's dictator, General Manuel Noriega, had stopped cooperating with the United States. He also aided drug traffickers, cracked down on opponents, and harassed American military personnel defending the canal. In December 1989, Bush ordered American troops to invade Panama. The troops seized Noriega, who was sent to the United States to stand trial on drug charges. The troops then helped the Panamanians hold elections and organize a new government.

The Persian Gulf War

President Bush faced perhaps his most serious crisis in the Middle East. In August 1990 Iraq's dictator, **Saddam Hussein,** sent his army to invade oil-rich Kuwait. American officials feared that the invasion might be only the first step and that Iraq's ultimate goal was to capture Saudi Arabia and its vast oil reserves. American troops rushed to the Middle East and took up positions in Saudi Arabia in response.

President Bush persuaded other UN member countries to join a coalition to stop Iraq. Led by the United States, the United Nations imposed economic sanctions on Iraq and demanded that the Iraqis withdraw. The coalition included troops from the United States, Canada, Europe, and Middle Eastern nations. The UN set a deadline for the Iraqis' withdrawal, after which the coalition would use force to remove them. Congress also voted to authorize the use of force if Iraq did not withdraw.

On October 31, 1990, General Colin Powell, chairman of the Joint Chiefs of Staff, Secretary of Defense Dick Cheney, and other high-ranking officials met with President Bush. It was clear that Iraq would not obey the UN deadline. Powell presented the plan for attacking Iraq. Several advisers gasped at the numbers, which called for over 500,000 American troops. "Mr. President," Powell began, "I wish . . . that I could assure you that air power alone could do it but you can't take that chance. We've gotta take the **initiative** out of the enemy's hands if we're going to go to war." Cheney later recalled that Bush "never hesitated." He looked up from the plans and said simply, "Do it."

On January 16, 1991, the coalition forces launched Operation Desert Storm. Dozens of cruise missiles and thousands of laser-guided bombs fell on Iraq, destroying its air defenses, bridges, artillery, and other military targets. After about six weeks of bombardment, the coalition launched a massive ground attack. Waves of tanks and troop carriers smashed through Iraqi lines and encircled the Iraqi forces defending Kuwait.

The attack killed thousands of Iraqi soldiers, and hundreds of thousands more surrendered. Fewer than 300 coalition troops were killed. Just 100 hours after the ground war began, President Bush declared Kuwait to be liberated. Iraq accepted the coalition's cease-fire terms, and American troops returned home to cheering crowds.

Reading Check **Examining** Why did President Bush take action when Iraqi troops invaded Kuwait?

R Reading Strategy

Activating Prior Knowledge Before students read, ask them to recall how President Carter responded to human rights abuses around the world. Tell them they will read about how President George H. W. Bush responded to abuses in China. BL

Did You Know?

Iraqi leader Saddam Hussein liked to be called by his first name. When pronounced correctly, with the emphasis on the second syllable, *Saddam* means "leader" or "learned one." During the Persian Gulf War, President George H. W. Bush insisted on pronouncing the name with the emphasis on the first syllable. Pronounced this way, *Saddam* means "a boy who fixes or cleans shoes."

Reading Check

Answer:
American officials feared that Iraq's ultimate goal was to capture Saudi Arabia and its vast oil reserves.

Activity: Collaborative Learning

Comparing Invasions In the debate over whether to use force against Saddam Hussein, some who favored military action used the example of Hitler to justify their stance. Those who opposed action used the example of Vietnam. Have students work in pairs. One partner is to review the chapters about World War II; the other, the chapter about the Vietnam war. Ask them to share their information and decide whether each of these historical examples applied to the situation in Kuwait. Then ask students to consider the war that began with Iraq in 2003. **Ask:** **Which example best fits that war?** *(Students' answers will vary but should be supported with facts.)* OL

R Reading Strategy

Taking Notes Suggest that students take notes by creating cause-and-effect charts. They should identify the causes and effects of the recession and the causes of the election results in 1992. BL

Did You Know?

Many companies began using the term *downsizing* rather than *layoff* because *layoff* sounded too negative. After several years of downsizing, some companies started to use the term *rightsizing* to imply that cuts were being made to adjust the workforce to the correct size.

Analyzing VISUALS

Answers:

1. They are hurting mainstream parties. The cartoon of Perot is riding Bush, attached like a parasite.
2. The Northeast is a more liberal area, and more likely to vote Democratic.

Additional Support

Domestic Challenges

MAIN Idea To reduce the deficit, President Bush raised taxes, an unpopular decision that helped Bill Clinton win the election.

HISTORY AND YOU How are your school and community designed to provide access for people who use wheelchairs? Read on to find out more about the Americans with Disabilities Act of 1990.

President Bush spent much of his time dealing with foreign policy, but he could not ignore domestic issues. He inherited a growing deficit and a slowing economy. With the Persian Gulf crisis, the economy plunged into a recession and unemployment rose.

The Economy Slows

The recession that began in 1990 was partly caused by the end of the Cold War. As the Soviet threat faded, the United States began reducing its armed forces and canceling orders for military equipment. Thousands of soldiers and defense industry workers were laid off.

Other companies also began **downsizing**—laying off workers and managers to become more efficient. The nation's high level of debt made the recession worse. Americans had borrowed heavily during the 1980s and now faced paying off large debts. R

In addition, the huge deficit forced the government to borrow money to pay for its programs. This borrowing kept money from being

HISTORY AND GEOGRAPHY

The Election of 1992

The election of 1992 marked the first time since 1968 that no candidate won at least 50 percent of the popular vote and for much the same reason. A strong third party challenger, Ross Perot (below, center), took votes from both major candidates.

◄ The success of Perot's campaign surprised many Americans.

Presidential Candidate	Popular Votes	% of Popular Vote	Electoral Votes
Clinton	44,909,889	43.02%	370
Bush	39,104,545	37.46%	168
Perot	19,742,267	18.91%	0

Analyzing VISUALS

1. **Interpreting** What does the cartoon suggest about independent candidates?
2. **Speculating** What factors might explain Clinton's popularity in the Northeast?

Activity: Interdisciplinary Connection

Mathematics Have students use the figures in the map legend above to create a circle graph showing the proportion of total votes for each candidate in 1992. Point out that the percentages listed do not total 100 percent. Tell students to create a category labeled "other" for the remaining votes. Then have students create circle graphs showing the proportion of total votes each candidate received in the west (west of the Mississippi River) and the proportion of total votes each candidate received in the east (east of the Mississippi River). OL available to businesses. The government also had to pay interest on its debt, money that might otherwise have been used to fund programs or boost the economy.

As the economy slowed, hundreds of savings-and-loan institutions collapsed. After President Reagan had allowed them to be deregulated, many had made risky or even dishonest investments. When these investments failed, depositors collected on federal programs to insure deposits. The cost to the public may have reached $500 billion.

Gridlock in Government

Shortly after taking office, Bush tried to improve the economy. He called for a cut in the **capital gains tax**—the tax paid by businesses and investors when they sell stocks or real estate for a profit. Bush believed that the tax cut would encourage businesses to expand. Calling the idea a tax break for the rich, Democrats in Congress defeated it.

Aware that the growing federal deficit was hurting the economy, Bush broke his "no new taxes" campaign pledge. After meeting with congressional leaders, he agreed to a tax increase in exchange for cuts in spending. This decision turned many voters against Bush.

The 1992 Election

Although the recession had weakened his popularity, Bush won the Republican nomination. Bush promised to address voters' economic concerns and he blamed congressional Democrats for the gridlock that seemingly paralyzed the nation's government.

The Democrats nominated Arkansas governor William Jefferson Clinton, despite stories that questioned his character and the fact that he did not serve in Vietnam. Calling himself a "New Democrat" to separate himself from more liberal Democrats, Clinton promised to cut middle-class taxes, reduce government spending, and reform the nation's health care and welfare programs. His campaign repeatedly blamed Bush for the recession.

Some Americans were not happy with either Bush or Clinton. This enabled an independent candidate, billionaire Texas businessman **H. Ross Perot,** to make a strong challenge. Perot stressed the need to end deficit spending. His no-nonsense style appealed to many Americans. A **grassroots movement**—groups of people organizing at the local level—put Perot on the ballot in all 50 states.

Bill Clinton won the election with 43 percent of the popular vote and 370 electoral votes. The Democrats also **retained** control of Congress. Bush won 37 percent of the popular vote, while Perot received 19 percent—the best showing for a third-party candidate since 1912—but no electoral votes.

As the first president born after World War II, the 46-year-old Clinton was the first person from the baby boom generation to enter the White House. It was his task to revive the economy and guide the United States in a rapidly changing world.

Reading Check **Summarizing** Why did President Bush lose popularity as the 1992 election approached?

Section 4 REVIEW

Vocabulary

1. **Explain** the significance of: perestroika, glasnost, Boris Yeltsin, Tiananmen Square, Saddam Hussein, downsizing, capital gains tax, H. Ross Perot, grassroots movement.

Main Ideas

2. **Explaining** How did perestroika and glasnost create conditions that led to the fall of the Soviet Union?
3. **Describing** What actions did the United States take in Panama in 1989?
4. **Determining Cause and Effect** How did the huge deficits from the Reagan years lead to economic problems under George Bush?

Critical Thinking

5. **Big Ideas** How did the economy affect the 1992 election?
6. **Organizing** Use a graphic organizer similar to the one below to list the causes of the recession of the early 1990s.

Budget Problems	Economic Problems	Foreign Developments

7. **Analyzing Visuals** Examine the map on page 992. Which nations have significant oil resources?

Writing About History

8. **Descriptive Writing** Suppose that you are traveling in West Germany in 1989 when the Berlin Wall is being torn down. Write a letter to a friend at home to describe the event and how you think it will affect the United States.

History ONLINE
Study Central™ To review this section, go to glencoe.com and click on Study Central.

Assess

History ONLINE

Study Central™ provides summaries, interactive games, and online graphic organizers to help students review content.

Reading Check

Answer:
The economy was failing, and Bush broke his promise not to raise or introduce new taxes.

Close

Summarizing Ask: How did Clinton gain support in the 1992 election? *(He set himself apart from other Democrats by calling himself a "new Democrat." He also promised to cut taxes and spending.)* OL

Section 4 REVIEW

Answers

1. All definitions can be found in the section and the Glossary.
2. They created a more open economy and society; people were allowed to discuss politics and to protest, and this led to the overthrow of several Communist regimes in the eastern bloc and, eventually, to the fall of the Soviet Union.
3. U.S. troops invaded Panama, arrested its dictator, Manuel Noriega, and then helped the people hold elections and establish a democratic government.
4. The huge deficit forced the government to borrow money to pay for its programs. This borrowing kept money from being available to businesses. The government also had to pay interest, money that might otherwise have been used to fund programs or boost the economy.
5. The recession hurt Bush's efforts to win reelection.
6. Budget Problems: tax increase; Economic Problems: recession, high consumer debt, federal deficit; Foreign Developments: fall of the Soviet Union, Persian Gulf War
7. Saudi Arabia, Kuwait, Iraq, Iran, and Syria
8. Students' letters will vary but should be descriptive and use standard grammar and punctuation.

Activity: Collaborative Learning

Government Priorities As described in this chapter, conservatives and liberals believe in different types of spending, government control, and freedom from government. Have students work in groups. Ask them to discuss what spending, controls, and freedoms are most important. **Ask:** Is it more important for citizens to have personal freedoms or for business to have freedom from control? Should military spending be more or less important than programs that aid citizens personally? *Have students make a three-column chart headed "Spending," "Controls," and "Freedoms" and then rank their items in order of priority. Have a member from each group report the results, including disagreements among group members, to the class.* **OL**

Narrative Writing Have interested students create a narrative history of U.S. involvement in China, the Middle East, or Latin America during Reagan's and George H. W. Bush's presidencies. **AL**

Chapter 29 Visual Summary

STUDY TO GO You can study anywhere, anytime by downloading quizzes and flashcards to your PDA from glencoe.com.

Causes of the New Conservatism

- The Cold War promotes strong foreign policy and an emphasis on minimal government interference in economics.
- Cold War fears of communism encourage many religious Americans to turn to conservative ideas.
- Many Americans are disturbed by the protests, demonstrations, and violence of the 1960s.
- The population growth in the Sunbelt increases support for conservative politicians.
- The rise of an evangelical movement willing to use politics to change society and defend its values helps mobilize conservative voters.
- Frustration with rising taxes and government regulation, especially in the South and West, turns many voters to conservative ideas.
- Both Western conservatives and Southern conservatives come to see the Republican Party as the more conservative party.

▲ *Part of the new conservative movement drew support from Americans who were fed up with high taxes.*

▲ *The summit between President Reagan and Mikhail Gorbachev created an easing of tensions between the U.S. and Soviet Union.*

The Reagan Administration

- Ronald Reagan is elected president in 1980 and 1984.
- Reagan promotes supply-side economics and pushes large tax cuts through Congress.
- Many industries are deregulated, helping spur a boom in the oil, transportation, and communications industries.
- A political debate over cutting government programs rather than expanding them shapes the domestic politics of the era.
- Reagan's administration takes a strong anti-Communist stance in Latin America, the Caribbean, and the Middle East, providing aid to groups that resist communism.
- The nation begins a sustained military buildup to put pressure on the Soviet economy; in addition the United States begins work on anti-missile "Star Wars" technology.
- The failure to cut domestic programs, combined with increased military spending, drives the growing budget deficit to record levels.
- Energy prices fall, the economy grows rapidly, and stock market values soar.
- The farm debt crisis and deregulation of the banks leads to the collapse of many family farms, and many savings and loan institutions.
- Under great economic stress, the Soviet Union introduces perestroika and glasnost; communism falls across Eastern Europe in 1989, and then the Soviet Union collapses in 1991.

Hands-On Chapter Project
Step 5: Wrap Up

Conducting an Opinion Poll

Step 5: Wrap Up Have groups share their results with the rest of the class. Encourage students to discuss why President Reagan scored higher on some students' polls than others.

Putting It Together Have students evaluate the project by answering the following questions:

- What was the most difficult part of the project? Why?
- What was the best part of the project? Why?
- What was the most important thing I learned by completing this project?

Ask students to record their responses in their journal. **OL**

Chapter 29 ASSESSMENT

Reviewing Vocabulary

Directions: Choose the word or words that best complete the sentence.

1. Political views held by ______ include the belief that the government should regulate the economy to protect people from the power of large corporations.
- **A** economists
- **B** liberals
- **C** conservatives
- **D** televangelists

2. Reagan based his policies on ______, a philosophy that advocates tax cuts to improve the economy.
- **A** monetarist economics
- **B** supply-and-demand economics
- **C** microeconomics
- **D** supply-side economics

3. A new business model known as ______ had a major impact on the economy starting in the 1980s.
- **A** superstations
- **B** wholesale retailing
- **C** discount retailing
- **D** direct mail

4. One part of Mikhail Gorbachev's plan to improve conditions in the Soviet Union was to allow ______, or increased freedom in speech, religion, and political discussion.
- **A** glasnost
- **B** perestroika
- **C** contra
- **D** rights of assembly

5. To combat the recession of the late 1980s, and searching for greater efficiency, many corporations began laying off employees, a process called
- **A** downsizing.
- **B** mass firing.
- **C** horizontal integration.
- **D** vertical integration.

Reviewing Main Ideas

Directions: Choose the best answer for each of the following questions.

Section 1 *(pp. 968–973)*

6. One main difference between liberals and conservatives is that, generally,
- **A** conservatives believe in government regulation of the economy, while liberals do not.
- **B** liberals believe in government regulation of the economy, while conservatives do not.
- **C** conservatives believe that all power should be held by the national government, while liberals do not.
- **D** liberals believe that all power should be held by the states, while conservatives do not.

7. Which of the following two groups had added their support to conservatives by the 1980s?
- **A** African Americans and urbanites
- **B** Northerners and Easterners
- **C** Democrats and women
- **D** Sunbelters and suburbanites

Section 2 *(pp. 974–981)*

8. Critics of Reagan's economic policy referred to it as "trickle-down economics" because they
- **A** believed that the plan would work, allowing wealth to "trickle down" to the middle and lower classes.
- **B** ridiculed the idea that much wealth would "trickle down" to the middle and lower classes.
- **C** believed that the plan was messy and would cause a great deal of wasteful government spending.
- **D** agreed that the richest people would share their wealth with the neediest in society.

TEST-TAKING TIP

Read each answer choice and eliminate the ones that simply do not make sense for the given question.

Need Extra Help?

If You Missed Questions . . .	1	2	3	4	5	6	7	8
Go to Page . . .	968–970	976	983	990–991	994	968–970	971	976

GO ON

Answers and Analyses
Reviewing Vocabulary

1. B Review the general differences between liberals and conservatives with students, who will most likely have trouble choosing between *B* and *C*. Economists are people who study economics. They can be liberal or conservative. Televangelists are preachers on television.

2. D Reaganomics was based on supply-side economics. Basically, the theory says that lower taxes lead to more money being spent (including investments), thereby stimulating the economy and leading to economic growth. Basically, supply-side economics seeks to increase the *supply* of capital. Greater money supply = greater investment.

3. C Discount retailing offered goods at a discount. Discount retailers are prevalent today. Ask students to discuss how they think shopping was different in the years before discount retailing.

4. A *Glasnost* means "openness." A way for students to remember its meaning is to think of *glass*, which is clear, and relate it to openness. *Perestroika* dealt with restructuring the economy. To remember this, students should think of the "rest" in *Pe**rest**roika* to "restructuring."

5. A Downsizing was a popular way to combat rising business costs during this era and was the focus of much media coverage. Downsizing was replaced by outsourcing in the later 1990s.

Reviewing Main Ideas

6. B Review the sections on liberals and conservatives. Generally, conservatives support a more hands-off government with a laissez-faire approach to economics.

7. D Review "Sunbelt Conservatism" and "Suburban Conservatism" on pages 971–972 with students. The groups/areas listed in *A* and *B in general* tend to be liberals. *C* does not make sense because it includes "Democrats."

8. B Critics believed Reagan's policies would help the wealthy, but that it would not help, or trickle-down to, the middle and lower classes. The question asks about critics' opinions, so *A* and *D* are incorrect, because they are supportive of the plan, not critical.

9. C The key word in SDI is *defense*. Only *C* includes an action that is a directly defensive maneuver.

10. B VCRs revolutionized the way people watched TV and movies at home. The DVD and the PDA were not available in the 1980s. The digital watch was invented in the 1970s.

11. C Nancy Reagan's "Just Say No" campaign sums up a major focus of 1980s activism. As first lady for most of the decade, Nancy Reagan was able to keep the program in the forefront of public focus. She believed that eliminating drug abuse would lead to a reduction in crime.

12. B Boris Yeltsin was the president of Russia at the time of the coup. He was instrumental in dismantling it. The Berlin Wall had come down in 1989. *D* is irrelevant.

13. B The events in Tiananmen Square sparked protest in the U.S. and other nations, so students can reason that the actions of those nations expressed displeasure with China. Therefore, *A* can be eliminated. Making plans to express their concerns at a meeting would not be harsh enough. The U.S. did not send troops into China.

Critical Thinking

14. A The religious right is conservative in morals and values. Their concern for morals and values led them to join the conservative movement. Liberals generally favor increased social-welfare programs, not conservatives. The religious right was more concerned with the domestic agenda rather than with foreign relations. *D* would not make sense.

Chapter 29 Assessment

9. The Strategic Defense Initiative (SDI) was proposed to strengthen defense by

A preventing the expansion of Communist countries.
B re-emphasizing the use of infantry troops in future wars.
C developing weapons to intercept incoming missiles.
D severely reducing the number of American troops stationed worldwide.

Section 3 *(pp. 982–987)*

10. Which technology became available during the 1980s?

A the digital video recorder
B the video cassette recorder
C the personal digital assistant
D the digital watch

11. A major focus of U.S. social activism in the 1980s was

A gun control.
B illiteracy.
C drug abuse.
D poverty.

Section 4 *(pp. 990–995)*

12. The result of the failed Communist coup in Moscow in August 1991 was that

A Boris Yeltsin became president of the Soviet Union.
B the Soviet republics declared independence.
C the Berlin Wall was taken down by bulldozers.
D the United States sent troops into Saudi Arabia.

13. In response to events in Tiananmen Square in China, the United States and other nations

A sent weapons and money to the rebels.
B halted arms sales and reduced their diplomatic contacts with China.
C made plans for a summit meeting with China to express their concerns.
D sent in troops to help free the imprisoned protesters.

Critical Thinking

Directions: Choose the best answers to the following questions.

14. The religious right joined the conservative movement because they

A were concerned about American values and morality.
B wanted more liberal social welfare programs.
C felt that the U.S. had been too aggressive with the U.S.S.R.
D wanted government regulation of local churches.

15. The huge number of baby boomers affected the economy of the 1980s because they

A were driven to acquire material goods and social success.
B pushed for increased government spending for the poor.
C rejected worldly success as members of the Moral Majority.
D were beginning to draw Social Security benefits.

Base your answer to question 16 on the graph below and your knowledge of Chapter 29.

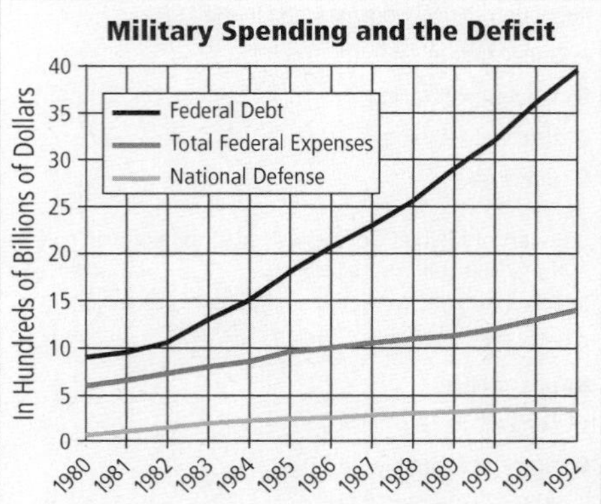

Sources: Departments of Commerce and Treasury; Office of Management and Budget.

16. How much money was spent on national defense in 1986?

A approximately 500 billion dollars
B more than 500 billion dollars
C approximately 250 billion dollars
D less than 250 million dollars

Need Extra Help?

If You Missed Questions . . .	9	10	11	12	13	14	15	16
Go to Page . . .	981	985	986–987	991–992	992–993	972–973	982	R16

GO ON

15. A Choices *C* and *D* can be immediately eliminated. Baby boomers spent money and sought out success, they did not reject it. Baby boomers are *now* affecting the economy because they are becoming eligible for Social Security, but were too young then for this to be a concern.

16. C The bottom line on the graph represents defense spending.

17. The beginning of the collapse of communism in Eastern Europe is most closely associated with the

A fall of the Berlin Wall.

B admission of Warsaw Pact nations to the North Atlantic Treaty Organization (NATO).

C intervention of the North Atlantic Treaty Organization (NATO) in Yugoslavia.

D formation of the European Union.

Analyze the cartoon and answer the question that follows. Base your answer on the cartoon and on your knowledge of Chapter 29.

18. What is the cartoonist saying about Gorbachev's policies?

A Marx, Lenin, and Stalin would approve of his policies of glasnost and perestroika.

B Marx, Lenin, and Stalin would disapprove of restructuring the Soviet economy and allowing some private enterprise.

C Marx, Lenin, and Stalin would approve of glasnost, or allowing more freedom of religion and speech.

D Marx, Lenin, and Stalin would disapprove of the expansion of communism to Eastern Europe.

Document-Based Questions

Directions: Analyze the document and answer the short-answer questions that follow the document.

President Ronald Reagan addressed the American people at the end of his presidency in 1988. The following is an excerpt from that address:

> The way I see it, there were two great triumphs, two things that I'm proudest of. One is the economic recovery, in which the people of America created—and filled—19 million new jobs. The other is the recovery of our morale. America is respected again. . . .
>
> Common sense told us that when you put a big tax on something, the people will produce less of it. So, we cut the people's tax rates, and the people produced more than ever before. The economy bloomed. . . . Common sense told us that to preserve the peace, we'd have to become strong again after years of weakness and confusion. So, we rebuilt our defenses, and this New Year we toasted the new peacefulness around the globe. . . .
>
> —from *Speaking My Mind*

19. What did Reagan believe were his greatest accomplishments?

20. How did Reagan feel his administration preserved peace?

Extended Response

21. In the late 1980s, the Cold War came to an end with the disintegration of the Warsaw Pact, the fall of the Berlin Wall, and the collapse of the Soviet Union. In an expository essay trace the events that led to the end of this global conflict and explain why you think the conflict ended when it did. In your essay, include an introduction, a conclusion, and at least three paragraphs with details from the chapter.

STOP

History ONLINE

For additional test practice, use Self-Check Quizzes—Chapter 29 at glencoe.com.

Need Extra Help?

If You Missed Questions . . .	17	18	19	20	21
Go to Page . . .	991	R18	999	R19	990–995

Extended Response

21. Essays must demonstrate a strong understanding of the events that led to the end of the Cold War. Events should be presented with an understanding of their chronological order, and opinions on why the Cold War ended when it did should be supported with well-reasoned arguments.

17. A This question does not ask what caused the collapse of communism in Eastern Europe; it asks what event is *associated* with it. The fall of the Berlin Wall was the culmination of a series of revolutions. Students should relate the *collapse* of communism with the *collapse* of the wall.

18. B In the cartoon, Marx, Lenin, and Stalin can be seen peering down with looks of disapproval. They did not believe in private enterprise, so *perestroika* would not please them. Stalin especially would not approve of greater freedoms of religion and speech.

Document-Based Questions

19. Reagan believed his greatest accomplishments were economic recovery and the recovery of American morale and international respect.

20. Reagan felt his administration preserved peace by becoming strong by rebuilding defenses.

History ONLINE

Have students visit the Web site at glencoe.com to review Chapter 29 and take the Self-Check Quiz.

Need Extra Help?

Have students refer to the pages listed if they miss any of the questions.

Chapter 30 Planning Guide

Key to Ability Levels	
BL Below Level	**AL** Above Level
OL On Level	**ELL** English Language Learners

Key to Teaching Resources	
Print Material	Transparency
CD-ROM or DVD	

Levels				Resources	Chapter Opener	Section 1	Section 2	Section 3	Section 4	Chapter Assess
BL	OL	AL	ELL							
				FOCUS						
BL	OL	AL	ELL	**Daily Focus Transparencies**		30-1	30-2	30-3	30-4	
				TEACH						
	OL	AL		**Geography and History Activity, URB**					p. 3	
BL	OL	AL		**Economics and History Activity, URB**		p. 7				
		AL		**American Literature Reading, URB**					p. 13	
BL	OL		ELL	**Reading Skills Activity, URB**					p. 87	
	OL			**Historical Analysis Skills Activity, URB**			p. 88			
BL	OL	AL	ELL	**Differentiated Instruction Activity, URB**		p. 89				
BL	OL		ELL	**English Learner Activity, URB**			p. 91			
BL	OL	AL	ELL	**Content Vocabulary Activity, URB***		p. 93				
BL	OL	AL	ELL	**Academic Vocabulary Activity, URB**				p. 95		
	OL	AL		**Reinforcing Skills Activity, URB**			p. 97			
	OL	AL		**Critical Thinking Skills Activity, URB**				p. 98		
BL	OL		ELL	**Time Line Activity, URB**		p. 99				
	OL			**Linking Past and Present Activity, URB**		p. 100				
BL	OL	AL	ELL	**Primary Source Reading, URB**		p. 101	p. 103			
BL	OL	AL	ELL	**American Art and Music Activity, URB**					p. 105	
BL	OL	AL	ELL	**Interpreting Political Cartoons Activity, URB**			p. 107			
		AL		**Enrichment Activity, URB**				p. 111		
BL	OL		ELL	**Guided Reading Activity, URB***		p. 114	p. 115	p. 116	p. 117	
BL	OL	AL	ELL	**Reading Essentials and Note-Taking Guide***		p. 331	p. 334	p. 337	p. 340	
BL	OL	AL	ELL	**Differentiated Instruction for the American History Classroom**	✓	✓	✓	✓	✓	✓
BL	OL	AL	ELL	**Unit Map Overlay Transparencies**	✓	✓	✓	✓	✓	✓
BL	OL	AL	ELL	**Unit Time Line Transparencies, Strategies, and Activities**	✓	✓	✓	✓	✓	✓
BL	OL	AL	ELL	**Cause and Effect Transparencies, Strategies, and Activities**	✓	✓	✓	✓	✓	✓
BL	OL	AL	ELL	**Why It Matters Chapter Transparencies, Strategies, and Activities**	✓	✓	✓	✓	✓	✓
BL	OL	AL	ELL	**American Biographies**		✓	✓	✓		

Note: Please refer to the *Unit 9 Resource Book* for this chapter's URB materials.

* Also available in Spanish

TeacherWorks Plus
All-In-One Planner and Resource Center

- Interactive Lesson Planner
- Interactive Teacher Edition
- Fully editable blackline masters
- Section Spotlight Videos Launch
- Differentiated Lesson Plans
- Printable reports of daily assignments
- Standards Tracking System

Levels BL	Levels OL	Levels AL	Levels ELL	Resources	Chapter Opener	Section 1	Section 2	Section 3	Section 4	Chapter Assess
				TEACH *(continued)*						
BL	OL	AL		Supreme Court Case Studies			p. 155	p. 157		
BL	OL	AL	ELL	The Living Constitution	✓	✓	✓	✓	✓	✓
BL	OL	AL	ELL	American Issues	✓	✓	✓	✓	✓	✓
	OL	AL	ELL	American Art and Architecture Transparencies, Strategies, and Activities	✓	✓	✓	✓	✓	✓
BL	OL	AL		High School American History Literature Library	✓	✓	✓	✓	✓	✓
	OL	AL		American History Primary Source Documents Library	✓	✓	✓	✓	✓	✓
BL	OL	AL	ELL	American Music: Hits Through History CD	✓	✓	✓	✓	✓	✓
BL	OL	AL	ELL	StudentWorks™ Plus	✓	✓	✓	✓	✓	✓
BL	OL	AL	ELL	*The American Vision* Video Program	✓	✓	✓	✓	✓	✓
Teacher Resources				Reading Strategies and Activities for the Social Studies Classroom	✓	✓	✓	✓	✓	✓
Teacher Resources				Strategies for Success	✓	✓	✓	✓	✓	✓
Teacher Resources				Presentation Plus! with MindJogger CheckPoint	✓	✓	✓	✓	✓	✓
Teacher Resources				Success With English Learners	✓	✓	✓	✓	✓	✓
				ASSESS						
BL	OL	AL	ELL	Section Quizzes and Chapter Tests*		p. 430	p. 431	p. 432	p. 433	p. 434
BL	OL	AL	ELL	Authentic Assessment With Rubrics						p. 65
BL	OL	AL	ELL	Standardized Test Practice Workbook						p. 69
BL	OL	AL	ELL	*ExamView® Assessment Suite*		30-1	30-2	30-3	30-4	Ch. 30
				CLOSE						
BL			ELL	Reteaching Activity, URB						p. 109
BL	OL		ELL	Reading and Study Skills Foldables™	p. 84					

✓ Chapter- or unit-based activities applicable to all sections in this chapter.

Using Student Web Activities

Teach With Technology

What is a Student Web Activity?

A Student Web Activity uses the Internet to enrich chapter content. It also helps students to enhance their online research skills.

How can a Student Web Activity help my students?

A Student Web Activity can teach students how to conduct research online and extends the content provided in the textbook. Features include:

- a research topic based on the chapter
- links to Web sites with more information on the topic
- short answer questions to assess comprehension
- a form to e-mail answers to you or to themselves

Visit glencoe.com and enter a *QuickPass*™ code to go to a Student Web Activity.

History ONLINE

Visit glencoe.com and enter *QuickPass*™ code TAV9399c30T for Chapter 30 resources.

You can easily launch a wide range of digital products from your computer's desktop with the McGraw-Hill Social Studies widget.

	Student	Teacher	Parent
Media Library			
• Section Audio	●		●
• Spanish Audio Summaries	●		●
• Section Spotlight Videos	●	●	●
***The American Vision* Online Learning Center (Web Site)**			
• StudentWorks™ Plus Online	●	●	●
• Multilingual Glossary	●	●	●
• Study-to-Go	●	●	●
• Chapter Overviews	●	●	●
• Self-Check Quizzes	●	●	●
• Student Web Activities	●	●	●
• ePuzzles and Games	●	●	●
• Vocabulary eFlashcards	●	●	●
• In Motion Animations	●	●	●
• Study Central™	●	●	●
• Web Activity Lesson Plans		●	
• Vocabulary PuzzleMaker	●	●	●
• Historical Thinking Activities		●	
• Beyond the Textbook	●	●	●

Reading Support From Jamestown Education

- **Timed Readings Plus in Social Studies** helps students increase their reading rate and fluency while maintaining comprehension. The 400-word passages are similar to those found on state and national assessments.
- **Reading in the Content Area: Social Studies** concentrates on six essential reading skills that help students better comprehend what they read. The book includes 75 high-interest nonfiction passages written at increasing levels of difficulty.
- **Reading Social Studies** includes strategic reading instruction and vocabulary support in Social Studies content for both ELLs and native speakers of English.

www.jamestowneducation.com

Biography / A&E Home Video / The History Channel

The following videotape programs are available from Glencoe as supplements to this chapter:

- Bill Clinton: In the Running (ISBN 1-56-501824-9)
- Yitzhak Rabin (ISBN 1-56-501714-5)

To order, call Glencoe at 1-800-334-7344. To find classroom resources to accompany many of these videos, check the following home pages:

A&E Television: www.aetv.com
The History Channel: www.historychannel.com

Reading List Generator CD-ROM — Glencoe BookLink 3

Use this database to search more than 30,000 titles to create a customized reading list for your students.

- Reading lists can be organized by students' reading level, author, genre, theme, or area of interest.
- The database provides Degrees of Reading Power (DRP) and Lexile™ readability scores for all selections.
- A brief summary of each selection is included.

Leveled reading suggestions for this chapter:

For students at a Grade 8 reading level:
- ***Bill Clinton: President of the 90s,*** by Robert Cwiklik

For students at a Grade 9 reading level:
- ***Bill Gates: Helping People Use Computers,*** by Charnan Simon

For students at a Grade 10 reading level:
- ***Bill Gates: Computer King,*** by Josepha Sherman

For students at a Grade 11 reading level:
- ***Internet: Electronic Global Village,*** by David Jefferis

For students at a Grade 12 reading level:
- ***Bill Clinton and His Presidency,*** by Elaine Landau

National Geographic

Index to National Geographic Magazine:

The following articles relate to this chapter:

- "Robot Revolution," by Curt Suplee, July 1997.
- "Unveiling the Universe," by Kathy Sawyer, October 1999.

National Geographic Society Products To order the following, call National Geographic at 1-800-368-2728:

- *ZipZapMap! USA (ZipZapMap!)*

Access National Geographic's new, dynamic MapMachine Web site and other geography resources at:
www.nationalgeographic.com
www.nationalgeographic.com/maps

Introducing
Chapter 30

Focus

MAKING CONNECTIONS
How Has Technology Changed Society?

Have students imagine their lives without cell phones, computers, or the Internet. Have them brainstorm how their lives would be different without these technologies. Discuss with students how Americans in the 1990s reacted to new technologies. **OL**

Teach

The Big Ideas

As students study the chapter, remind them to consider the section-based Big Ideas included in each section's Guide to Reading. The **Essential Questions** in the activities below tie in to the Big Ideas and help students think about and understand important chapter concepts. In addition, the Hands-on Chapter Projects with their culminating activities relate the content from each section to the Big Ideas. These activities build on each other as students progress through the chapter. Section activities culminate in the wrap-up activity on the Visual Summary page.

Chapter 30

A Time of Change

1980–2000

President Bill Clinton looks over the new White House Web site on July 8, 2000

U.S. PRESIDENTS
U.S. EVENTS
WORLD EVENTS

1980 · 1982 · 1984 · 1986 · 1988 · 1990 · 1992

1981
- IBM introduces their version of the PC or Personal Computer

1984
- Apple's Macintosh introduces the mouse and on-screen icons

1986
- Immigration Control and Reform Act passed

1991
- U.S. and other nations liberate Kuwait from Iraqi occupation

G. Bush 1989–1993

1980
- Lech Walesa organizes trade union Solidarity in Poland

1987
- Soviet Union and United States sign INF Treaty

1989
- The Berlin Wall falls

1990
- The World Wide Web is developed in Switzerland.

Section 1

The Technological Revolution

Essential Question: How did the technological revolution change American society? *(Computers became essential in the workplace and common in most homes. Communication became easier with the development of cell phones, e-mail, and instant messaging.)* Tell students that in this section they will learn about the technological revolution of the 1990s and its impact on American society. **OL**

Section 2

The Clinton Years

Essential Question: What were the successes and shortcomings of the Clinton administration? *(Successes: balancing the federal budget; Family Medical Leave Act; Americorps; welfare reform. Shortcomings: failure to get a comprehensive health care package; impeachment; no peace in the Middle East.)* Tell students that this section will focus on the Clinton presidency's successes and failures. **OL**

Chapter Audio

MAKING CONNECTIONS

How Has Technology Changed Society?

In the late twentieth century, the development of new technology, including personal computers, mobile phones, and the Internet, revolutionized the way people lived.

- ***What other eras in American history experienced rapid technological change?***
- ***Has the computer revolution changed society for the better? Why or why not?***

Clinton 1993–2001

1993
- Mosaic, the first popular Web browser, is released

1993
- Israeli-Palestinian peace accord signed

1994
- U.S., Mexico, and Canada found NAFTA

1995
- Cease-fire signed in Bosnian war

1997
- Britain returns Hong Kong to China

1998
- House of Representatives impeaches President Clinton

1999
- Senate acquits Clinton

G. W. Bush 2001–2009

1994 1996 1998 2000

FOLDABLES

Identifying Technological Changes
Research how computers have changed the way Americans live. Organize the information you learn in a Layered-Look Book Foldable by the following categories: business, communications, and entertainment. Describe how computers are applied in each field and how they have changed the way people live.

The Computer Revolution
Business
Communications
Entertainment

History ONLINE Visit glencoe.com and enter ***QuickPass***™ code TAV9846c30 for Chapter 30 resources.

More About the Photo

Visual Literacy In the 1990s, more and more American homes had desktop computers and Internet access—and this new technology could be found in the Oval Office of the White House. President Clinton had the White House fully wired in 1993.

FOLDABLES™ Study Organizer **Dinah Zike's Foldables**

Dinah Zike's Foldables are three-dimensional, interactive graphic organizers that help students practice basic writing skills, review vocabulary terms, and identify main ideas. Instructions for creating and using Foldables can be found in the Appendix at the end of this book and in the *Dinah Zike's Reading and Study Skills Foldables* booklet.

History ONLINE
Visit glencoe.com and enter ***QuickPass***™ code TAV9399c30T for Chapter 30 resources, including a Chapter Overview, Study Central™, Study-to-Go, Student Web Activity, Self-Check Quiz, and other materials.

Section 3

A New Wave of Immigration

Essential Question: How did new immigration laws change American society? *(Large numbers of non-European immigrants came to the United States, some legally, some illegally.)* Tell students that in Section 3 they will learn about how immigration laws have changed the ethnic makeup of the United States. **OL**

Section 4

An Interdependent World

Essential Question: Why did the world become more interdependent in the 1990s? *(Computers helped make the world's economies interconnected; the Internet helped link the world together culturally; more people realized that environmental issues are global in nature.)* Tell students that in Section 4 they will learn about how the world grew more interdependent in the 1990s. **OL**

Focus

Bellringer

Daily Focus Transparency 30-1

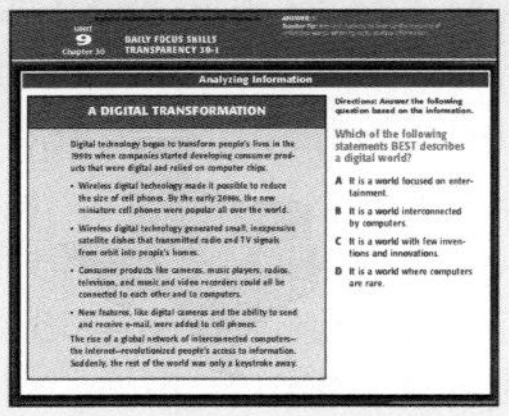

Guide to Reading

Answers:

	How it Revolutionized
Microprocessors	much faster and smaller computers
Apple II	practical, affordable home computers
Macintosh	simplified operating system with mouse-activated, on-screen icons
Windows	enabled PCs to use mouse-activated, on-screen graphic icons

Section Spotlight Video

To generate student interest and provide a springboard for class discussion, access the Chapter 30, Section 1 video at glencoe.com or on the video DVD.

Section 1 — Section Audio — Spotlight Video

The Technological Revolution

Guide to Reading

Big Ideas

Computers, Telecommunications, and the Internet The introduction of the first electronic digital computer in 1946 launched a technological revolution.

Content Vocabulary
- integrated circuit *(p. 1002)*
- microprocessor *(p. 1002)*
- telecommute *(p. 1003)*
- blogs *(p. 1005)*

Academic Vocabulary
- device *(p. 1002)*
- refinement *(p. 1003)*
- communications *(p. 1004)*

People and Events to Identify
- ENIAC *(p. 1002)*
- Silicon Valley *(p. 1002)*
- Steve Jobs *(p. 1002)*
- Bill Gates *(p. 1003)*

Reading Strategy

Categorizing As you read about the computer age, complete a chart similar to the one below to describe products that revolutionized the computer industry.

	How It Revolutionized Computer Industry
Microprocessors	
Apple II	
Macintosh	
Windows	

The computers we use today bear little resemblance to the first electronic computers that were built in the 1940s. Since the 1980s, computer technology has advanced dramatically, with the creation of home computers and then the expansion of the Internet.

The Computer Changes Society

MAIN Idea A computer revolution changed the workplace and the way people communicate.

HISTORY AND YOU What computer devices do you use regularly? Read on to learn about the earliest electronic computers.

The development of electronic computers began at the end of World War II. The world's first electronic digital computer, called **ENIAC** (Electronic Numerical Integrator and Computer), went into operation in February 1946. ENIAC weighed over 30 tons and was the size of a small house. In early 1959, Robert Noyce designed the first **integrated circuit**—a complete electronic circuit on a single chip of silicon—which made circuits much smaller and very easy to manufacture. Noyce's company was located south of San Francisco. As new companies sprang up nearby to make products using integrated circuits, the region became known as **Silicon Valley.**

In 1968 Noyce and colleague Gordon Moore formed Intel, for "Integrated Electronics," a company that revolutionized the computer industry by combining on a single chip several integrated circuits containing both memory and computing functions. Called **microprocessors,** these new chips made computers much faster and smaller.

Computers for Everyone

Using microprocessor technology, Stephen Wozniak and his 20-year-old friend **Steve Jobs** set out to build a small computer suitable for personal use. In 1976 they founded Apple Computer and completed the Apple I. The following year they introduced the Apple II, the first practical and affordable home computer.

Apple's success sparked intense competition in the computer industry. In 1981 International Business Machines (IBM) introduced its own compact machine, which it called the "Personal Computer" (PC). Apple responded in 1984 with the revolutionary Macintosh, a new model featuring a simplified operating system using on-screen graphic symbols called icons, which users could manipulate with a hand-operated **device** called a mouse.

Resource Manager

R Reading Strategies	C Critical Thinking	D Differentiated Instruction	W Writing Support	S Skill Practice
Teacher Edition • Making Connections, p. 1003 **Additional Resources** • Guided Reading Act., URB p. 114 • Prim. Source Reading, URB p. 101 • Quizzes/Tests, p. 429	**Teacher Edition** • Making Inferences, p. 1003 • Compare/ Contrast, p. 1004 **Additional Resources** • Economics and History, URB p. 7 • Linking Past/Present, URB p. 100	**Additional Resources** • Differentiated Instruction, URB p. 89	**Teacher Edition** • Persuasive Writing, p. 1005 **Additional Resources** • Content Vocab. Act., URB p. 93	**Teacher Edition** • Reading Graphs, p. 1004 **Additional Resources** • Time Line Act., URB p. 99 • Read. Essen., p. 331

TECHNOLOGY & HISTORY

Computers Beginning in the late 1970s and continuing to the present, changes in computer and telecommunications technology have transformed how people live and work.

▲ **Integrated Circuit**

The integrated circuit allowed literally millions of tiny circuits to be mass produced and for manufacturers to greatly reduce the size of computer-based products.

◀ **Mobile Phone**

Microprocessors and digital technology made small mobile phones (cell phones) possible. Improvements in light metals and plastics manufacturing made cell phones and other computerized devices portable. Combined with wireless access to the Internet, the cell phone allows people to stay in communication and to view videos, text messages, and photos no matter where they are.

Personal Computer ▶

The Apple Macintosh introduced in 1984 was the first mass-produced personal computer to use a mouse and on-screen icons to help users interact with the software. The new interface made computers far easier to use and encouraged Americans who were not technically trained to begin using computers. The first mouse (shown above) was invented by Douglas Englebart in 1964.

Analyzing VISUALS

1. **Explaining** What aspects of life do computer-based devices make easier?
2. **Inferring** Why do you think it was important for integrated circuits to be so small?

As Jobs and Wozniak were creating Apple, 19-year-old Harvard dropout **Bill Gates** co-founded Microsoft to design PC software, the instructions used to program computers to perform desired tasks. In 1980 IBM hired Microsoft to develop an operating system for its new PC. Gates paid a Seattle programmer $50,000 for the rights to his software, and with some **refinements,** it became MS-DOS (Microsoft Disk Operating System). In 1985 Microsoft introduced the "Windows" operating system, which enabled PCs to use mouse-activated, on-screen graphic icons.

Compact computers soon transformed the workplace, linking employees within an office or among office branches. They became essential tools in almost all businesses. By the late 1990s, workers used home computers and electronic mail (E-mail) to **"telecommute,"** or do their jobs from home via computer. C

New Telecommunications

A parallel revolution in telecommunications coincided with the development of personal computers. In the 1970s, the government started deregulating the telecommunications industry. Then, in 1996 Congress passed the Telecommunications Act, which allowed phone companies to compete with each other and to send television signals. It also allowed cable television companies to offer telephone service. This led to much greater competition, and many new technologies were developed. R

One major telecommunications technology that became very popular was the cell phone. Cell phones had been invented in the 1940s, and the first large-scale cellular networks were built in the 1980s, but the phones were large and the service was very expensive. All that began to change in the 1990s.

Teach

C Critical Thinking

Making Inferences Ask: What is the advantage of linking employees by computer? *(Answers will vary but may include that they can better work together and share ideas and information.)* BL

R Reading Strategy

Making Connections Ask: What phone and cable TV options are available locally? *(Answers will vary.)* OL

Analyzing VISUALS

Answers:

1. enhanced telecommunications with smaller and more powerful telephones and computers
2. to greatly reduce the size of computer-based products

Hands-On Chapter Project
Step 1

Art Show

Step 1: Researching the History of the Period Essential Question: What events occurred in American history from 1980 to 2000, and how can they be captured in images?

Directions Explain to students that they are going to create an art show of perhaps 10 images that they will hang in the classroom, a school hall or foyer, complete with a title, brief introduction near the beginning and the accompanying explanatory tags that will identify the images. In this step, two teams of students will: a) describe the events occurring in the United States between 1980 and 2000; and b) depict themes of the period. Each team will discuss how to depict the subject using images. (Students may choose to use graphic organizers, maps, charts, paintings, or drawings. Students may create their own images or find historical images online or in the library.)

Putting It Together After the two teams have determined four or five image selections, they should each either obtain the images (photocopies) or sketch them in a rough draft. OL

(Chapter Project continued on page 1012)

C Critical Thinking

Comparing and Contrasting
Ask: How are wireless digital cell phones different from older phones? *(They are smaller and portable.)* **BL**

S Skill Practice

Reading Graphs **Ask:** Based on the graph, which computer technology developed last? *(broadband Internet)* **ELL**

Reading Check

Answer:
They could be connected to each other and to computers.

Analyzing VISUALS

Answers:
1. E-mail or Instant Messaging
2. accelerating; Answers will vary but may include the idea that more households now have computers.

Additional Support

History ONLINE
Student Web Activity Visit glencoe.com and complete the activity on the technological revolution.

Wireless digital technology made it possible to miniaturize cell phones, and they quickly became very popular. By the early 2000s, they were in widespread use around the world. Wireless digital technology also made it possible to manufacture small inexpensive satellite dishes that could receive video and radio beamed from orbit into people's homes.

C Digital technology rapidly transformed many consumer products. Various companies developed music players, cameras, radios, televisions, and music and video recorders that used digital technology. Because they were digital and relied on computer chips, it became possible to connect them to each other and to computers. Modern cell phones, for example, often have digital cameras built in, and can send and receive E-mail and instant text messages. Computers can play the same videos that can be played on digital television. Further accelerating the interoperability and connections between the technologies was the rise of a global network of interconnected computers that came to be called the Internet.

Reading Check **Describing** How did digital technology change consumer products?

The Rise of the Internet

MAIN Idea A computer resource that linked government agencies developed into the Internet.

HISTORY AND YOU Have you ever used the Internet to do research for a class? Read on to learn about the origins of the Internet.

In 1969 the U.S. Defense Department's Advanced Research Project Agency created a system of networked computers known as ARPANET. The system linked computers at government agencies, defense contractors, and several universities, enabling them to communicate with one another.

In 1986 the National Science Foundation built NSFNet, a network connecting several super computer centers across the country. NSFNet was soon linked to ARPANET, and as the connections to other computer networks across the world grew, the system became known as the Internet. The Internet is not the World Wide Web or E-mail. Those are systems that use the Internet. The Internet is the physical network of computers connected together by phone lines, cable lines, and wireless **communications.**

PRIMARY SOURCE

The Rise of the Internet

As the Internet grew in size and people obtained access to faster computers and faster "broadband" connections, people began to use it for almost everything.

How People Use Computers

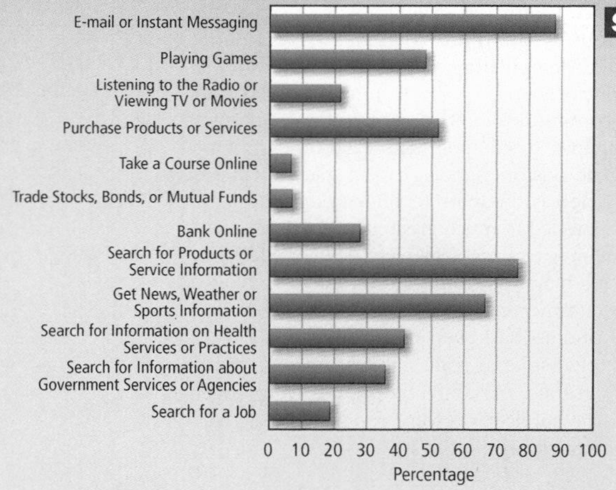

S

Computer and Internet Use, 1997–2003

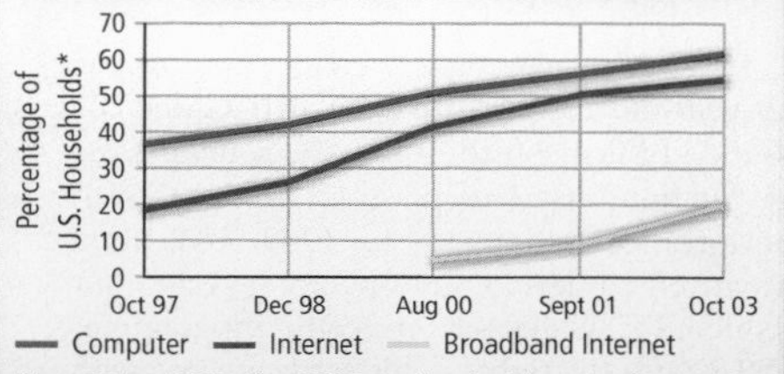

*Note: 2001 and 2003 reflect 2000 Census-based weights and earlier years use 1990 Census-based weights.

Source: Economics and Statistics Administration.

Analyzing VISUALS

1. **Classifying** Which category of activities is the Internet used for the most?
2. **Hypothesizing** Is the growth in the use of the internet slowing or accelerating? Why might this be so?

Activity: Technology Connection

Organizing an Internet Business Ask: How can a company use the Internet to conduct business? *(Answers may include advertising, taking orders, distributing information, communicating with customers, and so on.)* Show students the home page of a dot-com business, such as Amazon.com. Discuss the features of the Web site and the functions they serve. Have students work in groups of five or six to form a mock dot-com business. After groups have chosen a product line, ask them to design a mock-up of an Internet Web site for their business. Remind them to use their Internet sites to inform, persuade, and communicate with customers, as well as sell their products. Encourage creativity with the use of product illustrations and descriptions that will appeal to consumers. Ask groups to share their "Web sites" with the class. **OL**

As personal computers became cheaper and more widely available, more and more people began signing up with Internet Service Providers (ISPs) who could connect their computers to the Internet. By the late 1990s, the Internet had become wildly popular as businesses began experimenting with it to sell goods and services and to improve their productivity and communications. By 2007, more than 1 billion people were regularly using the Internet.

Birth of the World Wide Web

In 1990, researchers at CERN, a physics laboratory in Switzerland, developed a new way to present information on computers linked to the Internet. Known as the World Wide Web, this system used hypertext (what today are referred to as "links" on Web pages) and could be accessed with software known as a Web browser. The system allowed users to post information in the form of Web pages and click on links to jump from Web site to Web site.

Enthusiasm for the World Wide Web spawned a "dot-com" economy. A wide variety of dot-com companies made millions of dollars for stock investors without making any actual profits. Internet-related stocks helped fuel the prosperity of the 1990s, but fell dramatically in 2000 when many unprofitable online companies went out of business. Though the dot-com economy did not last, the computerization of the economy required the American labor force to acquire new skills. This retraining increased productivity as well as the nation's Gross Domestic Product (GDP), the total value of goods and services produced by the domestic economy. The GDP during the mid- to late-1990s rose over twenty percent. This increase was driven by the information technology industry, which includes computer and Internet router manufacturers.

A few companies have, however, become major success stories. Amazon.com, founded by Jeff Bezos, has become a highly successful online bookseller. The companies Google and Yahoo both created search engines that help people locate information on the Web. Many media companies have also found success on the Web in the same way that they did in print and on television —by charging fees for advertising.

The Internet Changes Society

For many people, the World Wide Web has become a way to build a sense of community. People with common interests visit Web sites about those interests to post comments and interact with each other.

Individuals and families share stories and photos about themselves on **blogs**—short for Web logs—Web sites that function as a kind of public diary or notebook. Web sites such as MySpace serve a similar function, while sites such as YouTube enable people to post video clips they want to share with others. Blogs have also led to a renaissance in essay writing and commentary as they enable people to publicly comment on news stories and other events. They have also helped mobilize people for political action. For many, accessing the Web has become a routine and important part of their daily life. **W**

✓ Reading Check **Analyzing** How have the Internet and World Wide Web changed society?

Section 1 REVIEW

Vocabulary

1. **Explain** the significance of: ENIAC, integrated circuit, Silicon Valley, microprocessor, Steve Jobs, Bill Gates, telecommute, blogs.

Main Ideas

2. **Describing** How have personal computers transformed the workplace?
3. **Contrasting** What is the difference between the World Wide Web and the Internet?

Critical Thinking

4. **Big Ideas** How have advances in telecommunications and the rise of the Internet affected the standard of living in the United States?
5. **Organizing** Complete a graphic organizer similar to the one below by listing developments that led to the technological revolution.

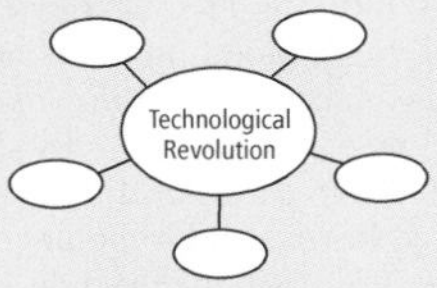

6. **Analyzing Visuals** Study the photograph of the Apple Computer on page 1003. How have computers changed since the 1980s?

Writing About History

7. **Descriptive Writing** Write two paragraphs describing the ways that you and your family use the Internet and how your way of life would be different without it.

History ONLINE
Study Central™ To review this section, go to glencoe.com and click on Study Central.

W Writing Support

Persuasive Writing
Ask: Should the Internet be censored? Have students write an essay arguing for or against censorship. **AL**

✓ Reading Check

Answer:
They built a sense of community, led to more commentary, and helped mobilize people for political action.

Assess

History ONLINE

Study Central™ provides summaries, interactive games, and online graphic organizers to help students review content.

Close

Summarizing Ask: How did computer technology change in the 1970s and 1980s? *(Microprocessors made them smaller and faster; simplified operating systems made them user-friendly.)* **OL**

Section 1 REVIEW

Answers

1. All definitions can be found in the section and the Glossary.
2. They have linked employees within an office or among office branches.
3. The Internet is a physical network of computers connected by phone lines, cable lines, and wireless communications. The World Wide Web is a system that allows Internet users to post information on Web pages and click on links to move from Web site to Web site.
4. People can better communicate; they can share information and interact with others who share common interests. They can publicly comment on news stories and other events and mobilize for political action.
5. Answers may include any of the following: electronic computer, integrated circuit, microprocessor, simplified operating system, cell phone, wireless digital technology, the Internet, the World Wide Web.
6. Answers will vary but may include the following: smaller, optional larger monitors, different varieties of the mouse device, laptop technology.
7. Paragraphs will vary but should describe students' personal Internet use and its affect on students' lives.

1005

TIME NOTEBOOK

Focus

Ask: What efforts have been made to address the issue of AIDS in the United States? *(Answers will vary but may include education, fund-raising, and government subsidized research.)* Explain that, in late 1990, Congress passed the Ryan White Comprehensive AIDS Resources Emergency Act (CARE), which annually provides about $1.5 billion to care for people living with AIDS/HIV.

Teach

R Reading Strategy

Activating Prior Knowledge
Ask: Why were Africans in need at this time? *(Answers will vary but may include that AIDS, civil unrest, and famine caused great suffering.)* AL

S Skill Practice

Reading a Time Line Ask: Which event on the time line has most impacted your life? Explain. *(Answers will vary but should relate to one of the advances listed on the time line.)* OL

Additional Support

TIME NOTEBOOK

KIM KOMENICH/GETTY IMAGES

In 1985, **RYAN WHITE** *became a symbol of the intolerance that is inflicted on some people suffering from HIV/AIDS.*

Ryan White was 13 years old when he learned that he had contracted HIV through blood products he was taking for hemophilia, a disease he had since birth. At the time, many people thought the AIDS virus could be passed by casual contact—by shaking hands, sneezing, or coughing. Even though AIDS can't be caught that way, people in Ryan's school in Kokomo, Indiana, were afraid to be near him. School officials banned him from classes, and Ryan had to fight in court to win the right to attend school.

In 1987, his family moved to another Indiana town, Cicero, where he was treated more kindly. Ryan died on April 8, 1990. At his funeral, a family friend, Rev. Ray Probasco, said: "It was Ryan who first humanized the disease called AIDS. He allowed us to see the boy who just wanted, more than anything else, to be like other children and to be able to go to school."

VERBATIM

"Just say no."
—NANCY REAGAN,
in 1983, launching her antidrug campaign

"Show me the money!"
—ACTOR CUBA GOODING, JR.'S CHARACTER,
in the 1996 movie Jerry Maguire

"Mr. Gorbachev, tear down this wall!"
—PRESIDENT RONALD REAGAN,
in 1987 addressing the head of the USSR while standing next to the Berlin Wall, which still divided East and West Berlin.

"Can we all get along?"
—RODNEY KING,
pleading in 1992 with the rioters in Los Angeles and other cities, after violence erupted following a jury's acquittal of the police officer who had beaten him.

R **"We are the world."**
—FORTY-FIVE POP STARS,
including Lionel Richie, Ray Charles, and Bruce Springsteen, known as USA for Africa. The group recorded the song "We Are the World" in 1985 to raise money for Africans in need.

"I do not like broccoli. And I haven't liked it since I was a little kid and my mother made me eat it. And I'm President of the United States and I'm not going to eat any more broccoli."
—PRESIDENT GEORGE H. W. BUSH,
1990

FIRSTS IN TECH

S *Important Dates in the Technology Revolution*

1981	1982	1983	1984	1985	1991	1995	1997
Columbia makes the first space shuttle flight	First use of emoticons in an e-mail: :-) and :-(	Music CDs go on sale in the United States The first American cell phone system goes into operation	Apple Macintosh computer is released	Nintendo Entertainment System comes to America	World Wide Web is created by Tim Berners-Lee of Great Britain	Release of first DVDs (digital video disks)	Dolly the sheep is the first animal made by cloning adult cells

NASA

Steve Jobs presents the first Macintosh computer

AP PHOTO/PAUL SAKUMA

NAJLAH FEANNY/CORBIS

Extending the Content

Sandra Day O'Connor Justice O'Connor traveled a long way to become the first female U.S. Supreme Court Justice. A top graduate in her Stanford law class, she experienced repeated rejection from law firms who refused to hire women. One firm did offer her employment—as a legal secretary. Determined, O'Connor accepted a position as a deputy county attorney in California. Later, after moving to Arizona, she served the state as assistant attorney general and state senator, becoming the first woman in any state to hold the office of majority leader in 1972. After her subsequent election to a state judgeship, she served five years before being appointed to the Arizona Court of Appeals. A short two years later, O'Connor replaced Justice Potter Stewart on the U.S. Supreme Court. On July 1, 2005, she announced her retirement. Justice Samuel Alito was sworn in on Feb. 1, 2006, marking the end of O'Connor's distinguished judicial career.

Time Capsule

In 1992, TIME *magazine ran a short story, "Things to Show How We Live Now," as a way to highlight what was important to the public at the time. Here are 15 items from the list. How do they compare with what you think is important?*

- REMOTE CONTROL
- GARTH BROOKS CD
- 8-MM CAMCORDER
- CASH-MACHINE CARD
- INFLATABLE GLOBE
- DISPOSABLE CAMERA
- DOLPHIN-SAFE TUNA
- BAGGY JEANS
- PALMTOP COMPUTER
- SPF 15 SUNSCREEN
- POCKET T-SHIRT
- BOTTLED WATER FROM THE ALPS
- IN-LINE SKATES
- AIR BAG
- BEEPER

JAMES KEYSER/GETTY IMAGES

Milestones

LOST, 1986. THE SPACE SHUTTLE *CHALLENGER* exploded 73 seconds after liftoff. Millions watched in horror as the 25th shuttle mission blew up, killing all seven crew members, including high school teacher Christa McAuliffe. **C**

RECONCILED, 1992. U.S. PRESIDENT GEORGE H.W. BUSH AND RUSSIAN PRESIDENT BORIS YELTSIN formally declared an end to the Cold War. **R**

RELEASED, 1981. FIFTY-TWO U.S. HOSTAGES IN IRAN were set free after 444 days in captivity. The crisis played a significant part in Jimmy Carter's failure to win a second presidential term.

AIRED, 1981. FORMER RADIO EXECUTIVES CREATED MTV (MUSIC TELEVISION). They knew that advertisers wanted to reach young people, who loved rock music. So they decided to run music videos on a cable channel.

ERUPTED, 1980. MOUNT ST. HELENS IN WASHINGTON STATE erupted after being dormant for 123 years. A stupendous explosion blew the entire top off the volcano.

NAMED, 1981. SANDRA DAY O'CONNOR became the first female justice on the U.S. Supreme Court after being appointed to the position by President Ronald Reagan.

WALLY MCNAMEE/CORBIS

Justice Sandra Day O'Connor

HONORED, 1995. BALTIMORE ORIOLES SHORTSTOP CAL RIPKEN, JR. became a national hero just by going to work every day for 13 years. On September 6, 1995, Ripken showed up at his 2,131st game in a row, breaking the 1939 record set by Lou Gehrig.

NUMBERS

168 **Number of people killed in the 1995 bombing of Oklahoma City's Federal Building by two Americans, Terry Nichols and Timothy McVeigh**

12 **Age of Valerie Ambrose, who won a NASA contest in 1997 by coming up with "Sojourner Truth" as the name for a robot explorer to Mars**

11,000,000 **Number of gallons of crude oil spilled into Prince William Sound by the tanker *Exxon Valdez* in 1989**

NATALIE FOBES/CORBIS

An oil-soaked whale after the Exxon Valdez *spill*

20,000,000 **Number of albums Michael Jackson's *Thriller* sold, making it the best-selling record of all time as of 1982**

Forever **Amount of time former player Pete Rose was banned from baseball after the discovery in 1989 that he was gambling on baseball games**

CRITICAL THINKING

1. ***Synthesizing*** Do you think people's attitudes have changed towards people with HIV/AIDS since 1985? Explain your answer.

2. ***Hypothesizing*** Why might celebrities be better able than the "average" citizen to focus public attention on serious global issues and problems?

C Critical Thinking

Speculating Ask: How might the Challenger's experience have affected attitudes toward the U.S. space program? *(Answers will vary but may speculate that people began to question the worth or necessity of the program.)* **OL**

R Reading Strategies

Activating Prior Knowledge
Ask: What was the Cold War? *(Answers may vary but should include the idea of a struggle for power between Communist bloc countries and Western powers.)* **OL**

Critical Thinking Answers:

1. Answers will vary. Some students may feel attitudes have changed because of the efforts of the government and private groups to educate Americans about HIV/AIDS. Others may feel that people with HIV or AIDS still suffer under a social stigma.
2. Answers will vary but could include the idea that people often emulate the views and actions of celebrities, giving famous people tremendous influence over public opinion and actions.

Activity: Technology Connection

Assessing Ask: What technology is most effective in the classroom? Why? *(Answers will vary but may include videos and DVDs, live TV broadcasts, computers, digital cameras, and CDs.)* Have students form groups. Ask each group to prepare a presentation for a classroom of new immigrants on an event or person from the decades of the 1980s or 1990s. Have students assess and select the forms of technology that will be most appropriate for the audience and the subject of their presentations. Encourage groups to appeal to various senses: sight, hearing, taste, touch, and/or smell. Ask groups to give their presentations to the class. Have audience members list and evaluate the effectiveness of the types of technology each presentation utilizes. **OL**

Focus

Bellringer

Daily Focus Transparency 30-2

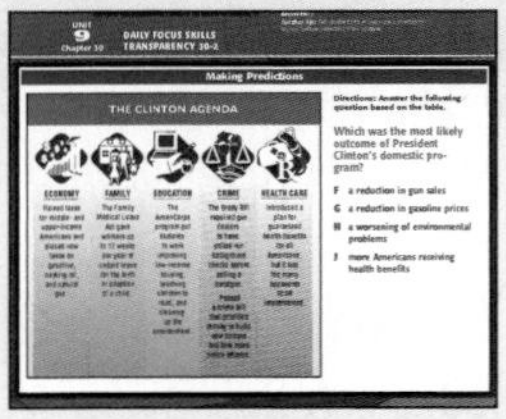

Guide to Reading

Answers:

I. Clinton's Agenda
- A. Raising Taxes, Cutting Spending
- B. Stumbling on Health Care
- C. Families and Education
- D. Crime and Gun Control

II. Republicans Gain Control of Congress
- A. The Contract With America
- B. The Budget Battle
- C. Clinton Wins Reelection

III. Clinton's Second Term
- A. Putting Children First
- B. Clinton Is Impeached

IV. Clinton Foreign Policy
- A. The Haitian Intervention
- B. Bosnia and Kosovo
- C. Peacemaking in the Middle East

Section Spotlight Video

To generate student interest and provide a springboard for class discussion, access the Chapter 30, Section 2 video at glencoe.com or on the video DVD.

Resource Manager

Section 2

Section Audio   Spotlight Video

The Clinton Years

Guide to Reading

Big Ideas

Government and Society President Clinton pushed through laws to help families and strengthen gun control, but he also raised taxes and failed to reform health care.

Content Vocabulary
- perjury *(p. 1013)*
- ethnic cleansing *(p. 1015)*

Academic Vocabulary
- modify *(p.1009)*
- unprecedented *(p.1009)*
- participant *(p. 1015)*

People and Events to Identify
- AmeriCorps *(p. 1010)*
- Contract with America *(p. 1011)*
- Kenneth Starr *(p. 1013)*
- Dayton Accords *(p. 1015)*

Reading Strategy

Taking Notes As you read about the administration of President Clinton, use the major headings of the section to create an outline similar to the one below.

The Clinton Years
I. Clinton's Agenda
A.
B.
C.
D.
II.

When William Jefferson Clinton was elected in 1992, he became the first Democrat to win the presidency in 12 years. After achieving only part of his agenda, he faced a new Republican Congress that had very different plans. His second term focused on foreign policy and scandal.

Clinton's Agenda

MAIN Idea President Clinton took office in 1993 with plans for improving health care, cutting the federal deficit, aiding families, and increasing gun control.

HISTORY AND YOU Do you know anyone who has worked for AmeriCorps? Read on to learn about the beginnings of this program.

Only 46 years old when he took office, Bill Clinton was the third-youngest person ever to serve as president and the first of the "baby boom" generation to reach the Oval Office. The new president put forth an ambitious domestic program focusing on five major areas: the economy, the family, education, crime, and health care.

Raising Taxes, Cutting Spending

As he had promised in his election campaign, Clinton focused first on the economy. The problem, in his view, was the federal deficit. Under Reagan and Bush, the deficit had nearly quadrupled, adding billions of dollars annually to the national debt. High deficits forced the government to borrow large sums of money, which helped to drive up interest rates. Clinton believed that the key to economic growth was to lower interest rates. Low interest rates would enable businesses to borrow more money to expand and create more jobs. Low rates would also make it easier for consumers to borrow money for mortgages, car loans, and other items, which in turn would promote economic growth.

One way to bring interest rates down was to reduce the federal deficit. In early 1993, Clinton sent Congress a deficit reduction plan. In trying to cut the deficit, however, Clinton faced a serious problem. About half of all government spending went to entitlement programs, such as Social Security, Medicare, and veterans' benefits. These programs are hard to cut because so many Americans depend on them. Faced with these constraints, Clinton decided to raise taxes, even though he had promised to cut them during his campaign. Clinton proposed raising tax rates for middle- and upper-income Americans and placed new taxes on gasoline, heating oil, and natural

R Reading Strategies	C Critical Thinking	D Differentiated Instruction	W Writing Support	S Skill Practice
Teacher Edition • Activ. Prior Knowledge, pp. 1010, 1011 • Identifying, p. 1012 • Sequencing Info., p. 1014 **Additional Resources** • Guided Reading Act., URB p. 115 • Prim. Source Read., URB p. 103	**Teacher Edition** • Speculating, p. 1009 • Drawing Con., p. 1011 • Defending, p. 1013 • Analyzing Primary Sources, p. 1014 • Making Inferences, p. 1015 **Additional Resources** • Inter. Political Cartoons, URB p. 107 • Quizzes/Test, p. 430	**Teacher Edition** • Visual/Spatial, p. 1012 • Logical/Math., p. 1013 **Additional Resources** • English Learner, URB p. 91	**Teacher Edition** • Personal Writing, p. 1010 **Additional Resources** • Supreme Court Case Studies, p. 155	**Teacher Edition** • Analyzing Visuals, p. 1009 **Additional Resources** • Reinf. Skills, URB p. 97 • Hist. Analysis Skills, URB p. 88 • Read. Essen., p. 334

POLITICAL CARTOONS PRIMARY SOURCE

The Debate Over Health Care

During his first term in office, President Clinton launched an ambitious program to reform the nation's health care system. The reforms faced much opposition and never materialized.

▲ The cartoonist shows President Clinton resolving to be very cautious throughout the rest of his administration.

▲ President Clinton explains the proposed Health Security card in a speech to Congress in October 1993.

▲ Hillary Clinton speaks about her health care plan in front of a counter showing one person losing health insurance every 1.17 seconds.

Analyzing VISUALS DBQ

1. **Inferring** How does the cartoonist compare Clinton's failed attempt to change health care to an accident?
2. **Analyzing** Why does Clinton resolve to be cautious in the future?

gas. The tax increases were very unpopular, and Republicans in Congress refused to support them. Clinton pressured Democrats, and after many amendments, a **modified** version of Clinton's plan narrowly passed.

Stumbling on Health Care

During his campaign, Clinton had promised to reform the health care system. Some 40 million Americans, or roughly 15 percent of the nation, did not have health insurance. The president created a task force and appointed his wife, Hillary Rodham Clinton, to head it—an **unprecedented** role for a first lady. The task force developed a plan to guarantee health benefits for all Americans, but it put much of the burden of paying for the benefits on employers. Small-business owners feared they could not afford it. The insurance industry and doctors' organizations also opposed the plan and mounted a nationwide advertising campaign on television and radio to build public opposition to the plan. C

Republicans argued that the plan was too complicated, costly, and relied too much on government control. Democrats were divided. Some supported alternative plans, but no plan had enough support to pass. Faced with public opposition, Clinton's plan died without a vote.

Teach

S Skill Practice

Analyzing Visuals Ask: Which frame explains Clinton's first reaction to the failure of his health care reform? *(the embarrassment)* BL

C Critical Thinking

Speculating Ask: Why might the insurance industry and doctors' organizations have opposed Clinton's national health care plan? *(Answers will vary but may include that doctors didn't want government regulating care and insurance companies didn't want to be told what to cover.)* OL

Analyzing VISUALS

Answers:
1. It shows him having to recover from it in stages.
2. Answers will vary but may include that it took him a long time to recover from his health care mistake.

Additional Support

Extending the Content

Health Insurance According to the Census Bureau, in 2004

- 45.8 million or 15.7 percent of the country's population had no health insurance.
- 11.2 percent of children under the age of 18 were uninsured.
- While 8.4 percent of Americans with incomes over $75,000 were uninsured, about 24.3 percent of those with incomes less than $25,000 lacked insurance.
- African-Americans (19.7 percent) and Hispanics (32.7 percent) were more likely to lack insurance than white, non-Hispanic Americans (11.3 percent).

According to a survey of the time,

- More than one-third of adults, both insured and uninsured, were having problems paying medical bills or accessing medical care.
- Low-income people with chronic health conditions had the most difficulty paying health expenses.
- While company profits rose by 16 percent in 2004, employment-based health insurance fell.

R Reading Strategies

Activating Prior Knowledge
Ask: To what international program is AmeriCorps similar? *(the Peace Corps)* How does it differ from the other program? *(AmeriCorps employs students, rather than adults, and operates domestically, rather than in foreign countries.)* **BL**

W Writing Support

Personal Writing Have students write one or two paragraphs to explain their views on gun control. **OL**

Reading Check

Answers:
Republicans felt it was too costly and heavy on government control; some Democrats supported other plans.

Families and Education

Clinton did manage to push several major pieces of legislation through Congress. During his campaign, he had stressed the need to help American families. His first success was the Family Medical Leave Act. This law gave workers up to 12 weeks per year of unpaid family leave for the birth or adoption of a child or for the illness of a family member.

R Clinton also persuaded Congress to create the **AmeriCorps** program. This program put students to work improving low-income housing, teaching children to read, and cleaning up the environment. AmeriCorps incorporated the VISTA program that John F. Kennedy had created. AmeriCorps volunteers earn a salary and are awarded a scholarship to continue their education. In September 1994, the first group of AmeriCorps volunteers—some 20,000 in number—began serving in more than 1,000 communities.

Crime and Gun Control

W Clinton had also promised to get tough on crime during his campaign, and he strongly endorsed new gun-control laws. Despite strong opposition from many Republicans and the National Rifle Association (NRA), the Democrats in Congress passed a gun-control law known as the Brady Bill. It was named after James Brady, President Reagan's press secretary who had been severely injured by a gunshot during the assassination attempt on the former president. His wife, Sarah Brady, became an advocate of gun control and lobbied Congress to pass the bill. The Brady Handgun Violence Prevention Act imposed a waiting period before people could buy handguns. It also required gun dealers to have police run a background check for a criminal record before selling someone a handgun.

The following year, Clinton introduced another crime bill. The bill provided extra funds for states to build new prisons, and put 100,000 more police officers on the streets. It banned 19 kinds of assault weapons and provided money for crime prevention programs, such as "midnight" basketball leagues that would get young people off the streets.

Reading Check **Explaining** Why did President Clinton's proposed health care plan fail?

Republicans Gain Control of Congress

MAIN Idea Republican victories in Congress led to conflicts between the executive and legislative branches of the federal government.

HISTORY AND YOU Have you ever refused to back down when you felt sure you were in the right? Read on to learn about a showdown between Congress and the president.

Despite his successes, Clinton was very unpopular by late 1994. He had raised taxes, instead of lowering them as he had promised, and he had failed to fix health care. Although the economy was improving, many companies were still downsizing. Several personal issues involving President Clinton further weakened

Debates IN HISTORY

Is a Balanced Budget Amendment a Good Idea?

One of the ideas that congressional Republicans put forth in the "Contract with America" was a balanced budget amendment to the Constitution. A balanced budget amendment would force Congress to pass a federal budget that balanced projected revenues and expenditures. Would such an amendment force Congress to be more responsible in how it spends the taxpayers' money, resulting in a more efficient, limited government? Or, would it dangerously limit Congress's ability to respond to economic and national security emergencies?

Additional Support

Teacher Tip

Collaborative Learning
Design collaborative projects that allow all members of a group to participate and share ideas. Encourage products that appeal to a variety of learning styles.

Activity: Collaborative Learning

Analyzing AmeriCorps Ask: Why might young people sign up for AmeriCorps? *(Answers will vary but could include the idea that it gives young people opportunities to serve the country, earn money for college, and see other parts of the country.)* Have students work in pairs to research AmeriCorps on the Internet at www.americorps.org/. Ask partners to focus on the following aspects: recruiting requirements, types of programs, and service areas. Have student pairs design a poster for one AmeriCorps program. Display the posters in the classroom. Discuss how the various programs contribute to American society and/or the environment. **OL**

public confidence in him. In response, many Americans decided to vote Republican in 1994.

The Contract With America

As the 1994 midterm elections neared, congressional Republicans, led by Newt Gingrich of Georgia, created the **Contract with America.** This program proposed 10 major changes, including lower taxes, welfare reform, tougher anticrime laws, term limits for members of Congress, and a balanced budget amendment. Republicans won a stunning victory—for the first time in 40 years, they had a majority in both houses of Congress.

In their first 100 days in office, House Republicans passed almost the entire Contract with America, but they soon ran into trouble. C The Senate defeated several proposals, while the president vetoed others.

The Budget Battle

In 1995 the Republicans clashed with the president over the new federal budget. Clinton vetoed several Republican budget proposals, claiming they cut into social programs too much. Gingrich believed that if Republicans stood firm, the president would back down R and approve the budget. Otherwise, the entire federal government would shut down for lack of funds. Clinton, however, refused to budge, and allowed the federal government to close.

By standing firm against Republican budget proposals and allowing the government to shut down, Clinton regained much of the support he had lost in 1994. The Republicans in Congress realized they needed to work with the president to pass legislation. Soon afterward, they reached an agreement with Clinton to balance the budget.

C Critical Thinking

Drawing Conclusions Ask: What conclusion can be drawn about the Senate from its defeat of several Contract with America proposals? *(Republicans did not vote along party lines.)* OL

R Reading Strategies

Activating Prior Knowledge Ask: What concept is illustrated by the presidential veto of proposed legislation? *(checks and balances)* AL

Debates IN HISTORY

YES

Strom Thurmond
U.S. Senator

PRIMARY SOURCE

"While Congress could achieve a balanced budget by statute, past efforts . . . have failed. It is simply too easy for Congress to change its mind. . . . The constitutional amendment is unyielding in its imposition of discipline on Congress to make the tough decisions necessary to balance the federal budget. Over the past half-century, Congress has demonstrated a total lack of fiscal discipline evidenced by an irrational and irresponsible pattern of spending. This reckless approach has seriously jeopardized the Federal government and threatens the very future of this Nation. As a result, I believe we must look to constitutional protection from a firmly entrenched fiscal policy which threatens the liberties and opportunities of our present and future citizens."

—Statement to the Judiciary Committee, February 16, 1994

NO

Bill Clinton
President

PRIMARY SOURCE

"The balanced budget amendment is, in the first place, bad economics. . . . [T]he Federal deficit depends not just on Congressional decisions, but also on the state of the economy. In particular, the deficit increases automatically whenever the economy weakens. If we try to break this automatic linkage by a Constitutional amendment, we will have to raise taxes and cut expenditures whenever the economy is weak. That not only risks turning minor downturns into serious recessions, but would make recovery from recession far more difficult. Let's be clear: This is not a matter of abstract economic theory. . . . A balanced budget amendment could threaten the livelihoods of millions of Americans. I cannot put them in such peril."

—Letter to Congressional leaders, November 5, 1993

DBQ Document-Based Questions

1. **Finding the Main Idea** Why does Senator Thurmond believe that a constitutional amendment, rather than simply a law, is necessary?
2. **Theorizing** How might Congress's "irresponsible pattern of spending" threaten the nation's future?
3. **Specifying** What specific reasons does President Clinton give to explain his opposition to the balanced budget amendment?
4. **Drawing Conclusions** Which argument do you find more convincing? Why?

Answers:

1. Congress has demonstrated a lack of fiscal discipline.
2. Answers may suggest that continued deficit spending could jeopardize the government's ability to make payments such as Social Security.
3. The economy is linked to the federal deficit, so in a weak economy taxes would increase and spending would decrease, possibly causing recession.
4. Answers should be supported with sound reasoning.

Extending the Content

The Balanced Budget Amendment Under the proposed Balanced Budget Amendment, congressional spending could not exceed revenues, or income. Exceptions could be made if three-fifths of each house approved specific instances of excess spending by a roll call vote. In addition, the national public debt could not be increased without that same three-fifths roll call vote. Finally, the president's annual budget would have had to be balanced when it was submitted to Congress. During years in which the country engaged in a declared war, the provisions of the amendment could be waived. Congress failed to pass this, and other, proposed balanced budget amendments.

D **Differentiated Instruction**

Visual/Spatial Ask students to make pie graphs to illustrate the popular and electoral voting results of the 1996 election. **ELL**

R **Reading Strategies**

Identifying Ask: What are four accomplishments of Clinton's domestic agenda during his second term? *(child tax credit, Adoption and Safe Families Act, ban on cigarette advertising aimed at children, Children's Health Insurance Program)* **BL**

Reading Check

Answers:
Health Insurance Portability Act, Welfare Reform Act

In the months before the 1996 election, the president and the Republicans worked together to pass new legislation. In August Congress passed the Health Insurance Portability Act. This act improved health coverage for people who changed jobs and reduced discrimination against people who had preexisting illnesses.

Later that month, Congress passed the Welfare Reform Act, which limited people to no more than two consecutive years on welfare and required them to work to receive welfare benefits. The law also increased child-care spending and gave tax breaks to companies that hired new employees who had been on welfare.

Clinton Wins Reelection

As the 1996 campaign began, Clinton took credit for the economy. The economic boom of the 1990s was the longest sustained period of growth in American history. Unemployment and inflation fell to their lowest levels in 40 years. The stock market soared, wages rose, crime rates fell, and the number of people on welfare declined. With the economy booming, Clinton's popularity climbed rapidly.

The Republican Party nominated Senator Bob Dole of Kansas, the Republican leader in the Senate, to run against Clinton. Dole chose as his running mate Jack Kemp, a former member of Congress from New York. Dole promised a 15 percent tax cut and attempted to portray Clinton as a tax-and-spend liberal.

H. Ross Perot also ran again as a candidate as he had in the 1992 election. This time he ran as the candidate of the Reform Party, which he had created. Once again Perot made the deficit the main campaign issue.

D President Clinton won reelection, winning a little more than 49 percent of the popular vote and 379 electoral votes. Dole received almost 41 percent and 159 electoral votes, and Perot won about 8.4 percent of the popular vote and no electoral votes. Despite Clinton's victory, Republicans retained control of Congress. Two years later, after the 1998 elections, Republicans kept control of Congress, although the Democrats gained 5 seats in the House of Representatives.

Reading Check **Identifying** What two reforms did Clinton and Congress agree to support?

Clinton's Second Term

MAIN Idea Clinton tried to focus the domestic agenda on the needs of children, but personal problems marred his second term.

HISTORY AND YOU Do you remember learning about the impeachment trial of Andrew Johnson? Read on to learn about the second president ever to be impeached.

During Clinton's second term, the economy continued its expansion. As people's incomes rose, so too did the amount of taxes they paid to all levels of government. At the same time, despite their differences, the president and Congress continued to shrink the deficit. In 1997, for the first time in 24 years, the president was able to submit a balanced budget to Congress. Beginning in 1998, the government began to run a surplus—that is, it collected more money than it spent.

Despite these achievements, Clinton's domestic agenda was less aggressive in his second term. Much of his time was spent on foreign policy and in struggling against a personal scandal.

Putting Children First

R During his second term, Clinton's domestic agenda shifted toward helping the nation's children. He began by asking Congress to pass a $500 per child tax credit. He also signed the Adoption and Safe Families Act and asked Congress to ban cigarette advertising aimed at children. In August 1997, Clinton signed the Children's Health Insurance Program—a plan to provide health insurance for children whose parents could not afford it.

Clinton also continued his efforts to help American students. "I come from a family where nobody had ever gone to college before," Clinton said. "When I became president, I was determined to do what I could to give every student that chance." To help students, he asked for a tax credit, a large increase in student grants, and an expansion of the Head Start program for disadvantaged preschoolers.

Clinton Is Impeached

The robust economy and his high standing in the polls allowed Clinton to regain the initiative in dealing with Congress. By 1998, how-

Hands-on Chapter Project: Step 2

Art Show

Step 2: Review and Critique Essential Question: Do the selections of the two groups merge well to form a cohesive presentation?

Directions Student teams will share their selected images and see how they fit together. The class as a whole will determine how the pieces work or do not work together to illustrate the topic at hand. Groups will critique the choices with the goal of presenting a cohesive art show.

Putting It Together Students should create a storyboard or blueprint for the presentation, determining how the selected pieces should be revised to present the whole picture of this period in American history. **OL**

(Chapter Project continued page 1018)

PRIMARY SOURCE

Impeaching a President

The Constitution gives Congress the power to remove the president from office "upon impeachment for and conviction of, treason, bribery, or other high crimes and misdemeanors." The House of Representatives has the sole power over impeachment—the formal accusation of wrongdoing in office. If the majority of the House votes to impeach the president, the Senate conducts a trial. A two-thirds vote of those present is needed for conviction. If the president is being impeached, the chief justice of the United States presides. **D**

▲ *House Judiciary Committee Chairman, Representative Henry Hyde, stands surrounded by boxes of evidence against President Clinton.*

▲ *Chief Justice Rehnquist is sworn in for the impeachment trial of President Clinton in the Senate.*

Analyzing VISUALS

1. **Hypothesizing** Why do you think the Founders required the House to impeach the president but the Senate to hold the trial?
2. **Theorizing** Why might impeachment only require a majority vote in the House, but conviction requires a two-thirds vote in the Senate?

ever, he had become entangled in a serious scandal that threatened to undermine his presidency.

The scandal began in Clinton's first term, when he was accused of arranging illegal loans for Whitewater Development—an Arkansas real estate company—while he was governor of that state. Attorney General Janet Reno decided that an independent counsel should investigate the president. A special three-judge panel appointed **Kenneth Starr,** a former federal judge, to this position. **C**

In early 1998, a new scandal emerged involving a personal relationship between the president and a White House intern. Some evidence suggested that the president had committed **perjury,** or had lied under oath, about the relationship. The three-judge panel directed Starr to investigate this scandal as well. In September 1998, after examining the evidence, Starr sent his report to the Judiciary Committee of the House of Representatives. Starr argued that Clinton had obstructed justice, abused his power as president, and committed perjury.

After the 1998 elections, the House began impeachment hearings. Clinton's supporters accused Starr of playing politics. Clinton's accusers argued that the president was accountable if his actions were illegal.

On December 19, 1998, the House of Representatives passed two articles of impeachment, one for perjury and one for obstruction of justice. The vote split almost evenly along party lines, and the case moved to the Senate for trial. On February 12, 1999, the senators cast their votes. The vote was 55 to 45 that Clinton was not guilty of perjury, and 50–50 on the charge of obstruction of justice. Although both votes were well short of the two-thirds needed to remove the president from office, Clinton's reputation had suffered.

✓Reading Check **Examining** What events led to the impeachment of President Clinton?

C Critical Thinking

Defending Ask: Should a president be investigated for acts committed before he took office? *(Answers will vary.)* **OL**

D Differentiated Instruction

Logical/Mathematical

Ask: What vote in the Senate would have removed Clinton from office? *(67 to 33).* **OL**

Analyzing VISUALS

Answers:

1. The House was closer to the people and more subject to voter passions; the Senate was calmer and more likely to judge fairly.
2. Conviction is more serious than charging someone with a crime, so a two-thirds vote is a safeguard against mistakes.

✓Reading Check

Answer:
Whitewater, Ken Starr's investigation, the House votes on articles of impeachment

Additional Support

Activity: Interdisciplinary Connection

Civics Ask: What expectations do you have of the president of the United States? Are they different from your expectations of a neighbor, classmate, or friend? Explain. *(Answers will vary but may include the idea that, because the president has a great deal of power, he or she must be especially honest and trustworthy.)* Have students work in pairs to read the presidential oath of office, which is available on the Internet at memory.loc.gov/ammem/pihtml/pioaths.html. Ask partners to list the duties of the president as listed in Article II, Sections 2–4 of the U.S. Constitution. Then ask students to rewrite the oath of office, incorporating additional pledges they feel the president should make to the people of the country as he or she takes office. Ask partners to share their oaths with the class. **OL**

R Reading Strategies

Sequencing Information

Ask: What chain of events led the U.S. to send troops to Haiti? *(Aristide is overthrown, U.N. embargo causes economic crisis, Haitian refugees flee to U.S., Clinton orders invasion, Carter convinces Haiti's rulers to step aside.)* BL

C Critical Thinking

Analyzing Primary Sources

Ask: How did many Haitians respond to the U.S. presence in their country? *(They seemed happy.)* ELL

Analyzing VISUALS

Answers:

1. Answers will vary. Possible problems: overextension of U.S. resources, foreign resentment.
2. Answers will vary but could include the idea that America's democratic system is threatened by the fall of other democracies.

Clinton Foreign Policy

MAIN Idea During Clinton's second term, the United States worked to end violence in Haiti, southeastern Europe and the Middle East.

HISTORY AND YOU Do you remember when and why NATO was created? Read on to find out how the United States and NATO worked to resolve a crisis in southeastern Europe.

Although Clinton's domestic policies became bogged down in struggles with Congress, he was able to engage in a series of major foreign policy initiatives. On several occasions, President Clinton used force to try to resolve regional conflicts.

The Haitian Intervention

R In 1991 military leaders in Haiti overthrew Jean-Bertrand Aristide, the country's first democratically elected president in many decades. Aristide sought refuge in the United States. Seeking to restore democracy, the Clinton administration convinced the United Nations to impose a trade embargo on Haiti. The embargo created a severe economic crisis in that country. Thousands of Haitian refugees fled to the United States in small boats, and many died at sea. Determined to end the crisis, Clinton ordered an invasion of Haiti. With the troops on the way, former president Jimmy Carter convinced Haiti's rulers to step aside. The American troops then landed to serve as peacekeepers.

Bosnia and Kosovo

The United States also was concerned about mounting tensions in southeastern Europe. During the Cold War, Yugoslavia had been a single federated nation made up of many different ethnic groups under a strong Communist government. In 1991, after the collapse of communism, Yugoslavia split apart.

In Bosnia, one of the former Yugoslav republics, a vicious three-way civil war erupted

PRIMARY SOURCE
Striving for Peace Around the World

With the Cold War over, the Clinton administration focused on bringing stability to the Middle East and southeastern Europe, where religious and ethnic strife had contributed to ongoing violence. In addition, Clinton sent peacekeepers into Haiti to help rebuild the nation's democracy.

▲ *Haitians gather outside the fence of the U.S. camp in Haiti to talk to American peacekeepers.*

C

▲ *Israeli Prime Minister Yitzhak Rabin and Palestinian leader Yasir Arafat shake hands after signing the 1993 Declaration of Principles.*

▼ *U.S. troops work with Bosnian Serbs in 1996 to set up boundaries between opposing forces.*

Analyzing VISUALS

1. **Predicting** Do you think the United States should intervene in conflicts in the world? What problems can result from such a policy?
2. **Explaining** Why would the United States think intervening in Haiti and Bosnia was important to its own security?

Differentiated Instruction

Leveled Activities

BL Reading Skills Activity, URB p. 87

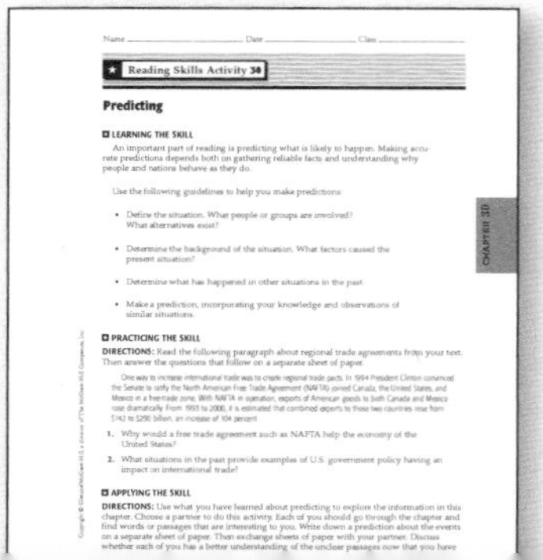

Reading Skills Activity 30

Predicting

OL Content Vocabulary Activity, URB p. 93

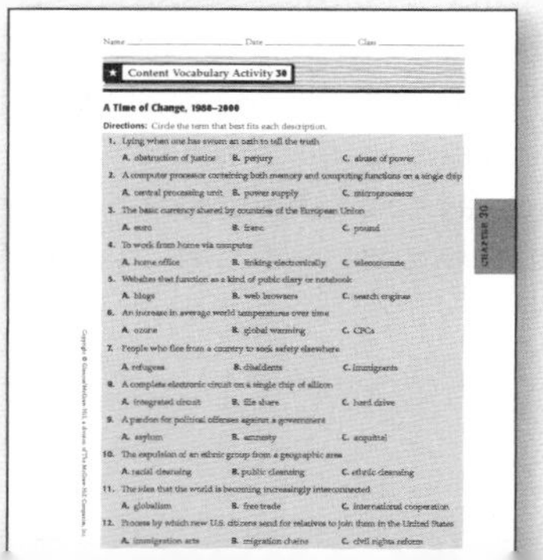

Content Vocabulary Activity 30

A Time of Change, 1980–2000

AL Historical Analysis Skills Activity, URB p. 88

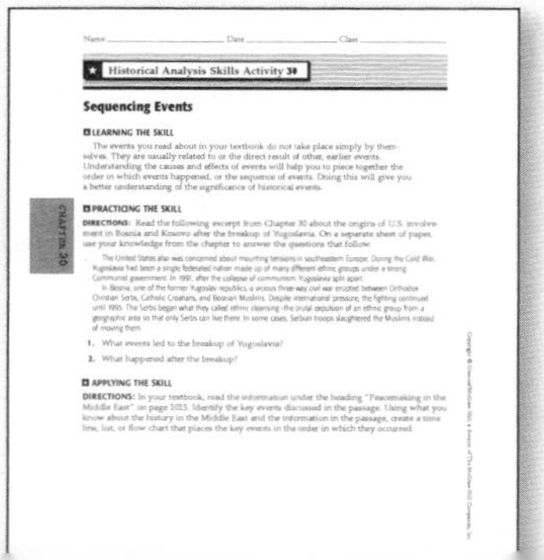

Historical Analysis Skills Activity 30

Sequencing Events

ELL Academic Vocabulary Activity, URB p. 95

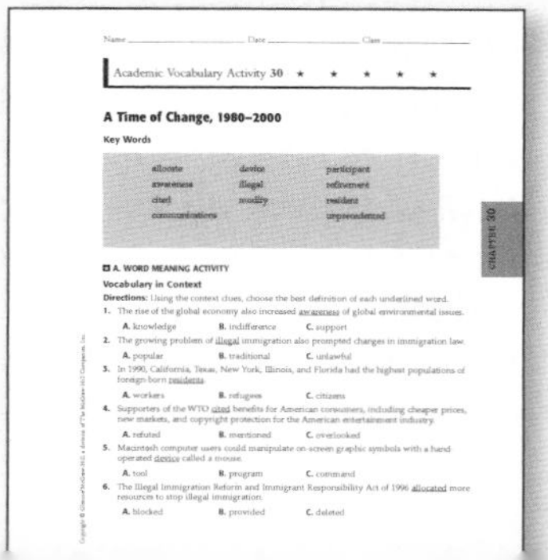

Academic Vocabulary Activity 30

A Time of Change, 1980–2000

between Orthodox Christian Serbs, Catholic Croatians, and Bosnian Muslims. Despite international pressure, the fighting continued until 1995. The Serbs began what they called **ethnic cleansing**—the brutal expulsion of an ethnic group from a geographic area so that only Serbs lived there. In some cases, Serbian troops slaughtered the Muslims instead of moving them.

The United States convinced its NATO allies that military action was necessary. NATO warplanes attacked the Serbs in Bosnia, forcing them to negotiate. The Clinton administration then arranged peace talks in Dayton, Ohio. The **participants** signed a peace plan known as the **Dayton Accords.** In 1996 some 60,000 NATO troops, including 20,000 Americans, entered Bosnia to enforce the plan. C

In 1998 another war erupted, this time in the Serbian province of Kosovo. Kosovo has two major ethnic groups—Serbs and Albanians. Many of the Albanians wanted Kosovo to separate from Serbia. To keep Kosovo in Serbia, Serbian leader Slobodan Milosevic ordered a crackdown. The Albanians then organized their own army to fight back. Worried by Serbian violence against Albanian civilians, President Clinton convinced European leaders that NATO should use force to stop the fighting. In March 1999, NATO began bombing Serbia. In response, Serbia pulled its troops out of Kosovo.

Peacemaking in the Middle East

Although Iraq had been defeated in the Persian Gulf War, Iraqi President Saddam Hussein remained determined to hang onto power. In 1996 Iraqi forces attacked the Kurds, an ethnic group whose homeland lies in northern Iraq. To stop the attacks, the United States fired cruise missiles at Iraqi military targets.

Relations between Israel and the Palestinians were even more volatile. In 1993 Israeli Prime Minister Yitzhak Rabin and Palestine Liberation Organization leader Yasir Arafat reached an agreement. The PLO recognized Israel's right to exist, and Israel recognized the PLO as the representative of the Palestinians. President Clinton then invited Arafat and Rabin to the White House, where they signed the Declaration of Principles—a plan for creating a Palestinian government. Opposition to the peace plan emerged. Radical Palestinians exploded bombs in Israel, killing 256. In 1995 a right-wing Israeli assassinated Prime Minister Rabin.

In 1994, with U.S. help, Jordan and Israel signed a peace treaty. In 1998 Israeli and Palestinian leaders met with President Clinton at the Wye River Plantation in Maryland. The agreement they reached, however, did not address the contested status of Jerusalem or the ultimate dimensions of a projected Israeli withdrawal from the West Bank and Gaza.

In July 2000, President Clinton invited Arafat and Israeli Prime Minister Ehud Barak to Camp David to discuss unresolved issues. Barak agreed to the creation of a Palestinian state in all of Gaza and about 95 percent of the West Bank, but Arafat rejected the deal. In October 2000, a Palestinian uprising began. The region was as far from peace as ever.

Reading Check **Identifying** In what three regions of the world did Clinton use force to support his foreign policy?

Section 2 REVIEW

Vocabulary

1. **Explain** the significance of: AmeriCorps, Contract with America, Kenneth Starr, perjury, ethnic cleansing, Dayton Accords.

Main Ideas

2. **Identifying** What were two reasons President Clinton's health care plan failed?
3. **Explaining** Why did the federal government shut down in 1995?
4. **Describing** How could Clinton be impeached but remain in office?
5. **Organizing** Complete a chart similar to the one below by explaining the foreign policy issues facing President Clinton in each of the areas listed.

Region	Issue
Latin America	
Southeastern Europe	
Middle East	

Critical Thinking

6. **Big Ideas** What did President Clinton do to help families during his presidency?
7. **Analyzing Visuals** Study the photograph on page 1013 of Clinton's impeachment trial. What elements in the photograph reflect the seriousness of the occasion?

Writing About History

8. **Persuasive Writing** Take on the role of a member of Congress. Write a letter in which you attempt to persuade other lawmakers to vote either for or against the impeachment of President Clinton. Provide reasons for your position.

History ONLINE
Study Central™ To review this section, go to glencoe.com and click on Study Central.

C Critical Thinking

Making Inferences Ask: Why did the United States not act on its own? *(Members of treaty organizations, such as NATO, pledge common defense. The Bosnian problem affected all NATO members, not just the United States.)* OL

Reading Check

Answers:
Bosnia, Kosovo, northern Iraq

Assess

History ONLINE

Study Central™ provides summaries, interactive games, and online graphic organizers to help students review content.

Close

Evaluating Ask: Was Clinton's presidency successful? *(Answers should be supported with information from the text.)* OL

Section 2 REVIEW

Answers

1. All definitions can be found in the section and the Glossary.
2. Republicans felt it was too costly and heavy on government control; some Democrats supported other plans.
3. In a clash over the budget, Clinton vetoed some Republican proposals, Republicans stood firm, and Clinton allowed the government to shut down for lack of funds rather than give in.
4. Unless convicted in the Senate, the president remains in office.
5.

Region	Issue
Latin America	military coup in Haiti
Southeastern Europe	civil wars in Bosnia and Kosovo
Middle East	Iraqi attacks on Kurds and volatile relations between Israel and Palestine

6. Answers should include some or all of the following: Family Medical Leave Act, AmeriCorps, child tax credit, Adoption and Safe Families Act, ban on cigarette advertising aimed at children, Children's Health Insurance Program, student tax credit, increased student grants, expanded Head Start
7. Answers will vary but could include the solemn expressions on the faces of people in the photo, the swearing in of the Chief Justice, and the large boxes of information to be presented.
8. Letters will vary.

Focus

Bellringer

Daily Focus Transparency 30-3

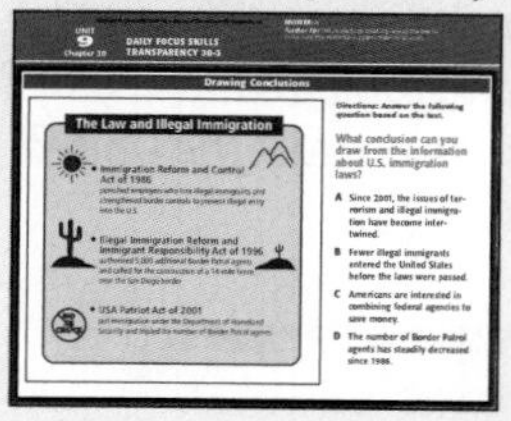

Guide to Reading

Answers:

abolished the national origins quota system; gave preference to skilled persons; established migration chains

Section Spotlight Video

To generate student interest and provide a springboard for class discussion, access the Chapter 30, Section 3 video at glencoe.com or on the video DVD.

Resource Manager

Section 3

Section Audio   Spotlight Video

A New Wave of Immigration

Guide to Reading

Big Ideas

Trade, War, and Migration A new immigration law allowed more people to immigrate to the United States.

Content Vocabulary

- migration chains *(p. 1016)*
- refugees *(p. 1017)*
- amnesty *(p. 1017)*

Academic Vocabulary

- illegal *(p. 1017)*
- allocate *(p. 1018)*
- resident *(p. 1018)*

People and Events to Identify

- Immigration Act of 1965 *(p. 1016)*
- Immigration Reform and Control Act of 1986 *(p. 1017)*
- Illegal Immigration Reform and Immigrant Responsibility Act of 1996 *(p. 1018)*

Reading Strategy

Determining Cause and Effect

Use a graphic organizer similar to the one below to list the effects of the Immigration Act of 1965.

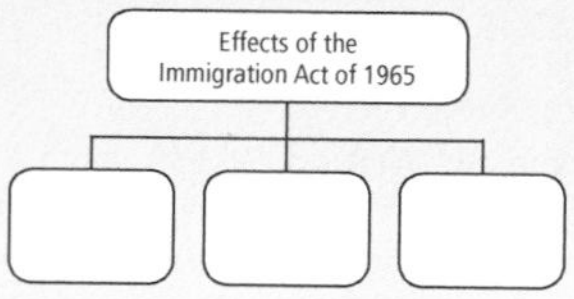

In the late twentieth century, the number of immigrants in the United States hit an all time high. Large numbers of non-European immigrants changed the ethnic composition of the United States. Immigration—legal and illegal—emerged as a difficult political issue.

Changes in Immigration Law

MAIN Idea The Immigration Act of 1965 eliminated preferences for certain European immigrants; illegal immigration became a problem.

HISTORY AND YOU Do you remember the controversial elements of the National Origins Act of 1924? Read on to learn how the repeal of the national origins system led to major changes in American society which few people had anticipated.

After the introduction of the national origins quota system in the 1920s, the sources and character of immigration to the United States changed dramatically. For the next few decades, the total number of immigrants arriving annually remained markedly lower. The quota system which gave preference to immigrants from northern and western European countries, although occasionally modified by Congress, remained largely intact until 1965.

In the midst of the flurry of civil rights and antipoverty legislation of the mid-1960s, the **Immigration Act of 1965** received scant attention when it was enacted. The law abolished the national origins quota system. It also gave preference to skilled persons and persons with close relatives who are U.S. citizens—policies which remain in place today. The preference given to the children, spouses, and parents of U.S. citizens meant that **migration chains** were established. As newcomers acquired U.S. citizenship, they too could send for relatives in their home country. Also, for the first time, the legislation introduced limits on immigration from the Western Hemisphere. The act further provided that immigrants could apply for U.S. citizenship after five years of legal residency.

At the time of its passage, few people expected that the new law would radically change the pattern or volume of immigration to the United States. Supporters of the law presented it as an extension of America's growing commitment to equal rights for non-European peoples. As U.S. Representative Philip Burton of California stated, "Just as we sought to eliminate discrimination in our land through the Civil Rights Act, today we seek by phasing out the national origins quota system to eliminate discrimination in immigration to this nation composed of the descendants of immigrants." Supporters of the new law also assumed that the new equal quotas

R Reading Strategies	C Critical Thinking	D Differentiated Instruction	W Writing Support	S Skill Practice
Teacher Edition • Activ. Prior Knowledge, p. 1019 **Additional Resources** • Guided Reading Act., URB p. 116 • Enrichment Act., URB p. 111	**Teacher Edition** • Compare/ Contrast, p. 1017 **Additional Resources** • Critical Thinking Skills Act., URB p. 98 • Supreme Court Case Studies, p. 157 • Quizzes/Tests, p. 431	**Teacher Edition** • Visual/Spatial, p. 1018 **Additional Resources** • Academic Vocab., URB p. 95	**Teacher Edition** • Persuasive Writing, p. 1017	**Teacher Edition** • Analyzing Graphs, p. 1018 **Additional Resources** • Read. Essen., p. 337

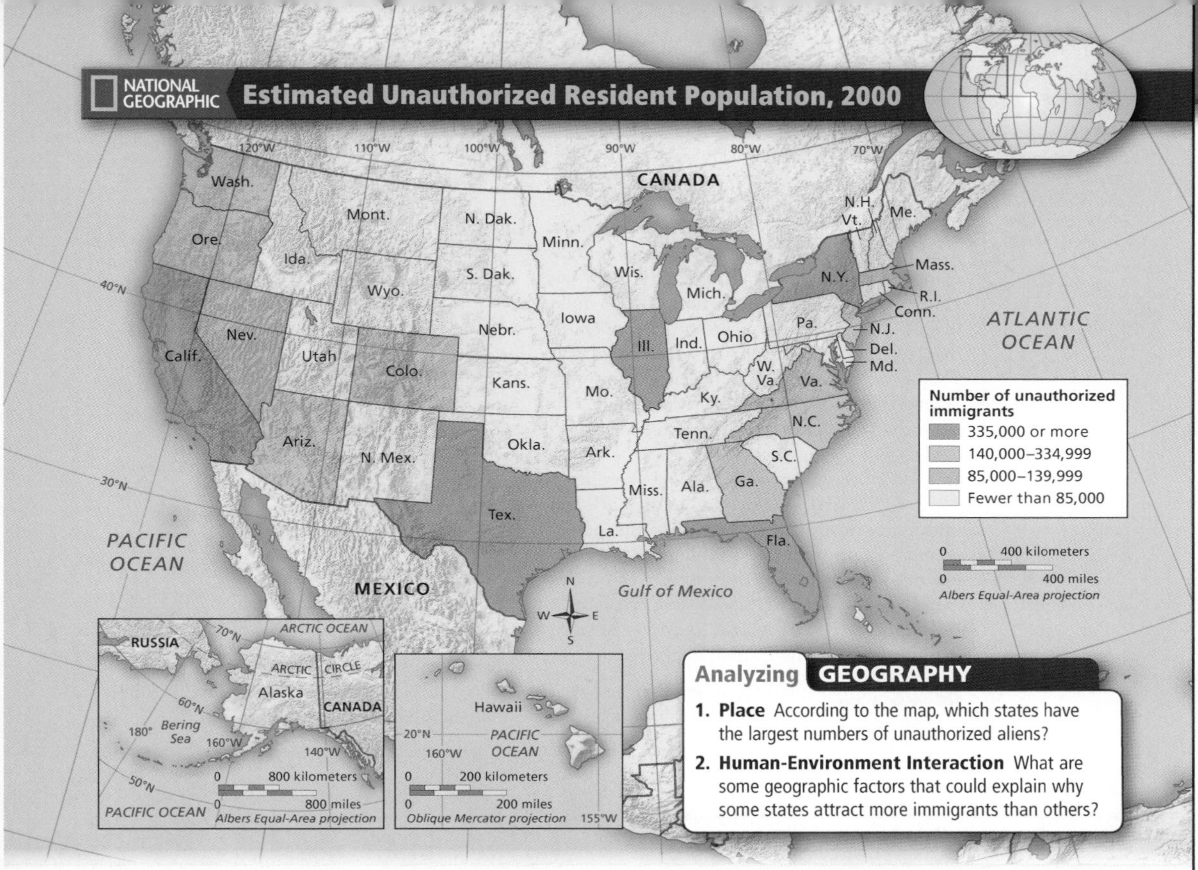

Analyzing GEOGRAPHY

1. **Place** According to the map, which states have the largest numbers of unauthorized aliens?
2. **Human-Environment Interaction** What are some geographic factors that could explain why some states attract more immigrants than others?

for non-European nations would generally go unfilled. In fact, immigration from non-European countries soared in subsequent decades.

In addition to those arriving through traditional immigration channels, some newcomers arrived in the United States as **refugees.** Beginning in 1948, refugees from countries ravaged by World War II were admitted, although they were counted as part of their nation's quota. The Cold War led to another class of refugees. According to the McCarran-Walter Act of 1952, anyone who was fleeing a Communist regime could be admitted as a refugee. Refugee policy was further broadened under the Refugee Act of 1980, which defined a refugee as someone leaving his or her country due to a "well founded fear of persecution on account of race, religion, nationality, membership in a particular group, or political opinion." C

The growing problem of **illegal** immigration also prompted changes in immigration law. During the Reagan administration, Congress passed the **Immigration Reform and Control Act of 1986.** This law established penalties for employers who knowingly hire unauthorized immigrants and strengthened border controls to prevent illegal entry into the United States. It also established a process to grant **amnesty** (in other words, a pardon) and legal papers to any undocumented alien who could prove that he or she had entered the country before January 1, 1982, and had resided in the United States since then. W

Despite these changes, illegal immigration persisted and the number of unauthorized immigrants continued to grow. By 1990, an estimated 3.5 million unauthorized immigrants resided in the United States. By the mid-1990s, Congress was debating new ways to combat illegal immigration.

Teach

C Critical Thinking

Comparing and Contrasting
Ask: How did the 1952 and 1980 refugee acts differ? *(The first defined a refugee as one who flees from a communist regime; the second broadened the definition to one who flees from fear of persecution for multiple reasons.)* **BL**

W Writing Support

Persuasive Writing Have students write an editorial supporting or criticizing the granting of amnesty. **AL**

Analyzing GEOGRAPHY

Answers:
1. Florida, Texas, California, Illinois, New York
2. Answers will vary but may state that coastal states offer easier access and warm climates attract farm workers.

Additional Support

Activity: Connecting with the United States

Analyzing Visas Tell students that there is no application fee for a visa to enter the United States legally. **Ask:** Why do so many immigrants enter illegally? *(Answers will vary but may include that many immigrants do not qualify for admission.)* Have students form five groups. Ask each group to research the requirements and processes for one of the types of visas available to immigrants who wish to settle permanently in the United States: family immigration, adoption of a foreign child, marriage to a foreign national, Diversity Visa Program, and employment visas. This information is available on the Internet at travel.state.gov/visa/immigrants/types/types_1326.html. Ask groups to create booklets that explain their visa to a prospective immigrant. Encourage students to illustrate their booklets and choose simple language to make information clear and understandable. Ask groups to exchange booklets until everyone has read the information about each visa type. **Ask:** What limitations do these visa types place on immigration? **OL**

D Differentiated Instruction

Visual/Spatial Have students diagram the provisions of the Illegal Immigration Reform and Immigrant Responsibility Act of 1996. BL

S Skill Practice

Analyzing Graphs Ask: What year saw the highest number of border deaths? *(2000)* ELL

Reading Check

Answers:
a well-founded fear of persecution because of race, religion, nationality, group membership, or political opinion

Analyzing VISUALS

Answers:
1. To identify with the revolutionaries of 1776.
2. Answers will vary but should be supported.

History ONLINE Student Skill Activity To learn how to create and modify spreadsheets, visit glencoe.com and complete the skill activity.

The law that resulted from these debates was the **Illegal Immigration Reform and Immigrant Responsibility Act of 1996,** which made several changes to U.S. immigration law. First, it required families sponsoring an immigrant to have an income above the poverty level. Second, it **allocated** more resources to stop illegal immigration, by authorizing an additional 5,000 Border Patrol agents and calling for the construction of a 14-mile fence along the border near San Diego. Third, the law toughened penalties for smuggling people or providing fraudulent documents. Finally, the law made it easier for immigration authorities to deport undocumented aliens. D

Another change in immigration law was spurred by the terrorist attacks of September 11, 2001. The USA Patriot Act of 2001 put immigration under the control of the newly created Department of Homeland Security. Furthermore, it tripled the number of Border Patrol agents, Customs Service inspectors, and Immigration and Naturalization Service inspectors along the Canadian border.

Reading Check Identifying For what reasons may a foreigner be admitted to the United States as a refugee?

Recent Immigration

MAIN Idea In the late twentieth century, immigrants from Latin America and Asia outnumbered European immigrants.

HISTORY AND YOU Do you remember the reasons that some Americans objected to immigration in the late 1800s? Read on to learn how the debate resurfaced in the 1980s and continues today.

Although immigrants headed for all parts of the United States, certain states experienced a larger influx than others. In 1990, California, Texas, New York, Illinois, and Florida had the highest populations of foreign-born **residents.** High numbers of immigrants also increased the ethnic diversity of these states, as their Latino and Asian populations grew. Among the immigrants who arrived in the 1990s, just over 10 percent came from Europe. More than half of new immigrants came from Latin America, while approximately another 25 percent came from Asia. By 2001, the top five countries of origin for legal immigrants to the United States were Mexico, India, China, the Philippines, and Vietnam.

PRIMARY SOURCE
Securing the Border

After the attacks of September 11, 2001, many Americans became increasingly concerned about border security. Many agreed on the need for increased border patrols. Others proposed building a continuous wall from Texas to California to prevent illegal immigration. Critics of such proposals, however, claimed such actions would not stop people who were determined to enter the country illegally, but rather force them to take more dangerous risks.

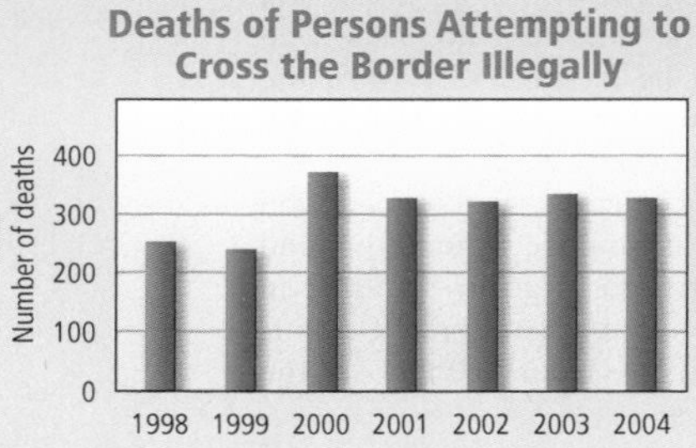

Source: United States Government Accountability Office.

▲ *On May 27, 2006, a volunteer organization called the Minutemen Civil Defense Corps built a fence along the Mexican border on private property.*

Analyzing VISUALS

1. **Making Connections** Why do you think the organization pictured above decided to call themselves the "minutemen"?
2. **Theorizing** Do you think building a fence along the border would lead to fewer deaths? Why or why not?

Hands-on Chapter Project: Step 3

Art Show

Step 3: Selecting the Images for the Art Exhibit Essential Question: How do the selected images reflect the period? What is most important about them?

Directions Student teams will continue to create their images. In this step, students will determine which members of their team will create the informational tags that will accompany the images in the art show. The informational tags should be typed sheets that include the following information:

- Image title
- Brief summary of how the image relates to the historical period
- Media (oil, watercolor, drawing, and so on)
- Date of completion
- Any other pertinent information

Putting It Together In one or two sittings, students should review the submissions and decide which will be hung in the exhibit. (School policy and space may determine if this ends up being an actual exhibit or a virtual exhibit.) OL

(Chapter Project continued on page 1024)

Refugees added to the growing immigrant population. In the 25 years following the Cuban Revolution of 1959, more than 800,000 Cubans arrived in the United States. So many of these immigrants settled in the Miami, Florida, area that only the city of Havana, Cuba, is home to more Cubans. In addition, the Vietnam War created refugees. Some 600,000 immigrants from Vietnam, Laos, and Cambodia arrived in the decade after 1974. R

In addition to the immigrants entering through legal channels, others arrived without official permission. The largest number of unauthorized immigrants came from Mexico, El Salvador, and Guatemala. The Reagan administration's amnesty program in 1986 had been designed to eliminate the problem of undocumented aliens, but over the next 20 years the number of unauthorized immigrants tripled. American public opinion divided over whether unauthorized immigrants should be able to obtain driver's licenses or send their children to public schools and receive other government services. Some believed that unauthorized immigrants should be deported. Others favored allowing them to apply for temporary work visas so the government could keep track of them, and permitting them to earn permanent residence if they learned English, paid back taxes, and had no criminal record.

In 2006, President George W. Bush made immigration reform a top priority, but members of Congress strongly disagreed over how to solve the problem. A bipartisan majority of the Senate favored legislation that blended tougher enforcement of immigration laws with some form of earned citizenship for the estimated 12 million undocumented aliens living and working in the country. The Senate bill included a provision that undocumented aliens who grew up in the United States and graduated from high school could apply for citizenship. Conservative Republicans who held the majority in the House objected that this would reward illegal behavior. The House rejected any form of amnesty and called for the United States to build a wall along its Mexican border—although the United States had already tripled the size of its border patrol without reducing illegal immigration. As Congress debated a bill that would subject unauthorized aliens to criminal prosecution, Latinos held rallies across the country, carrying signs that read: "We are not criminals."

Advocates of immigration reform promoted alternatives such as expanding quotas through a guest-worker program and establishing a means of legalization for those already in the country. Some undocumented aliens had lived in the United States for years, and had raised families here. Deporting them would mean separating husbands, wives, and children. Some undocumented aliens arrived as children and had lived in the United States most of their lives. Their own children, born in the United States, were native-born citizens even though their parents lacked legal status. Among those who became legal citizens, most wanted other family members to join them, so the reunification of families accounted for three-quarters of all legal immigration.

Reading Check **Explaining** Why did some members of Congress oppose amnesty for undocumented aliens? Why did others support it?

Section 3 REVIEW

Vocabulary

1. **Explain** the significance of: Immigration Act of 1965, migration chains, refugees, Immigration Reform and Control Act of 1986, amnesty, Illegal Immigration Reform and Immigrant Responsibility Act of 1996.

Main Ideas

2. **Summarizing** What problems arose that caused changes in the immigration laws?
3. **Describing** What alternatives to immigration reform did advocates for reform suggest?

Critical Thinking

4. **Big Ideas** What two acts were instrumental in helping refugees?
5. **Organizing** Use a graphic organizer similar to the one below to list the immigration laws and what they intended.

Immigration Law	Intent
Immigration Act of 1965	
Immigration Reform and Control Act of 1986	
Illegal Immigration Reform and Immigrant Responsibility Act of 1996	

6. **Analyzing Visuals** Study the map on page 1017. Research the number of unauthorized immigrants in the United States and create a spreadsheet that lists the states where these immigrants settled and the estimated numbers in 2000 and 2005.

Writing About History

7. **Persuasive Writing** After reading about the problem of illegal immigration, write a letter to your representative in Congress explaining what you feel he or she should do about the problem.

History ONLINE
Study Central™ To review this section, go to glencoe.com and click on Study Central.

1019

R Reading Strategies

Activating Prior Knowledge
Ask: How were the Cubans' and Southeast Asians' immigrations similar? *(Both fled communism.)* AL

Reading Check

Answers:
Some felt amnesty would reward illegal behavior. Supporters felt immigrants who had lived in the U.S. for years deserved to stay.

Assess

History ONLINE

Study Central™ provides summaries, interactive games, and online graphic organizers to help students review content.

Close

Problem-Solving Ask: How has the government tried to regulate immigration? *(by restricting immigrant eligibility, guarding borders, and deportation)* OL

Section 3 REVIEW

Answers

1. All definitions can be found in the section and the Glossary.
2. Immigration, both legal and illegal, soared. Terrorists entered the country.
3. expanding quotas through a guest-worker program, establishing a means of legalization for undocumented aliens already in the country
4. the McCarran-Walter Act of 1952 and the Refugee Act of 1980
5. **Immigration Act of 1965:** abolished the national origins quota system, gave preference to skilled persons and persons related to U.S. citizens, limited immigration from the Western hemisphere, let immigrants apply for citizenship after 5 years of legal residency; **Immigration Reform and Control Act**: penalized employers who knowingly hired unauthorized immigrants, strengthened border controls, established amnesty processes for certain immigrants; required sponsor families to have an income above poverty level; **Illegal Immigration Reform and Immigrant Responsibility Act**: allocated more resources to stop illegal immigration; toughened penalties for smuggling people or providing fraudulent documents
6. In addition to creating the spreadsheet, have students give a citation for their source.
7. Letters will vary but should offer a solution to the illegal immigration problem.

ANALYZING PRIMARY SOURCES

Focus

In general, people who immigrate illegally do so for two main reasons: family and jobs. They typically work for less than an American performing the same job. Many employers are happy to hire these low-cost, obedient workers.

Teach

R Reading Strategy

Summarizing Ask: How would you best summarize why the Vietnamese immigrant wants to return to Vietnam? *(Answers will vary but should describe the immigrant's lack of community connectedness in the United States.)* BL

D Differentiated Instruction

Verbal/Linguistic As a class, compose a poem or song to describe the feelings of these immigrants. OL

Additional Support

ANALYZING PRIMARY SOURCES

The New Immigrants

In the decades since the Immigration Act of 1965 was enacted, the number of immigrants in the United States has risen dramatically. By 2000, immigrants comprised more than 10 percent of the population. The largest groups of these new immigrants came from Latin America and Asia. Immigration has become a topic of political debate. Should the U.S. make it easier to immigrate legally? Should the U.S. decrease the number of persons allowed to immigrate? How should unauthorized immigrants be treated?

Study these primary sources and answer the questions that follow.

PRIMARY SOURCE 1

Oral Interview

"On our third attempt, my wife, children, and I escaped by boat from Vietnam and arrived in Hong Kong, where we remained for three months. Then my brother, who came to America in 1975, sponsored us, and we arrived in America in 1978. . . .

R Although in America we live with everything free, to move, to do business, we still have the need to return to Vietnam one day. This is our dream. In Vietnam, before the Communists came, we had a sentimental life, more [mentally] comfortable and cozy, more joyful. . . .

Here in America, we have all the material comforts, very good. But the joy and sentiment are not like we had in Vietnam. There, when we went out from the home, we laughed, we jumped. And we had many relatives and friends to come to see us at home. Here in America, I only know what goes on in my home; my neighbor knows only what goes on in his home. . . . In America, when we go to work, we go in our cars. When we return, we leave our cars and enter our homes [and do not meet neighbors]. We do not need to know what goes on in the houses of our neighbors. That's why we do not have the kind of being at ease that we knew in Vietnam."

—Vietnamese immigrant

PRIMARY SOURCE 3

Oral Interview

"The buzzword is diversity. It's on TV, politics, and this school [university], but then people like me are seen as foreigners and worse, illegals. The logic is if you look Mexican you are an immigrant, don't speak English and are illegal. I get tired of saying that's not me, oh well, except for the Mexican part. I don't look at an Anglo with an Italian name and say, 'Hey, do you speak Italian and when did you come to the United States?'"

—Diana, second-generation Mexican American

PRIMARY SOURCE 2

Photograph, c. 2006

▼ *Tijuana (on the left) lies just south of San Diego; a fence marks the Mexico-U.S. border.*

PRIMARY SOURCE 4

Photograph, 2006

D ▼ *Jorge Urbina of Nicaragua and his brother Carlos take the oath of citizenship during a naturalization ceremony for 250 immigrants.*

Activity: Collaborative Learning

Comparing and Contrasting Organize students into pairs and have them read Primary Source 1 above. **Ask:** How is America different from Vietnam? Have pairs respond to this question by creating a list of differences between Vietnamese life and American life according to the immigrant speaking in the excerpt. Then have student pairs share their lists with the class. Discuss with the class whether they agree with this view of America. Ask student pairs to use library or Internet sources to learn more about the lives of Vietnamese communities in the United States and in Vietnam and prepare a presentation of their findings. After students' presentations, discuss with the class how their findings influence their thoughts on the Vietnamese immigrant's view of America as described in Primary Source 1. OL

ANALYZING PRIMARY SOURCES

PRIMARY SOURCE 5

Photograph, 2006

▼ *Woman protests illegal immigration.*

PRIMARY SOURCE 7

Photograph, 2006

▼ *Marchers oppose passage of a bill that would make it a felony to be in the country illegally.*

PRIMARY SOURCE 6

Oral Interview

"Usually we catch young men, who are looking for work to support their families back in Mexico. But more and more we are seeing entire families. They start coming around 7:30 P.M. over the mesa near Cristo Rey Mountain. A steady stream of people all night. We use our night-vision 'infrared' equipment to spot a lot of illegals who would otherwise go unnoticed.

Sometimes border patrolmen ride horseback to patrol these hills. It's an interesting contrast—high-tech infrared machines directing cowboys on horseback. Other times we patrol in small trucks, which provide maneuverability. Before we began using night-vision equipment, aliens had an easier time coming through this area without getting caught. Now we can sit on top of a hill, spot undocumented aliens, then radio for patrol vehicles to come apprehend the groups or individuals after they enter into Texas or New Mexico.

This time of year, in late winter, the aliens try to find work on farms in the Upper Rio Grande Valley. This is the time when farm laborers start pulling weeds and preparing the ground for planting. Between New Year and June, on the northbound highways to Las Cruces, many of the aliens we apprehend are usually agricultural workers or people heading for cities further north, like Denver or Chicago.

Perhaps our greatest concern is the trafficking of drugs tied to the smuggling of illegal aliens. Smuggling of all sorts has become big business in the border regions. Some smugglers have set up networks that may start in Central America or Cuba. We catch illegal immigrants who come from as many as eighty-five countries around the world. Even people from Eastern Europe, who are smuggled in for large fees through South America and Mexico City."

—Michael Teague, U.S. Border Patrol

DBQ Document-Based Questions

1. **Contrasting** How does the speaker in Source 1 contrast his life in America with his life in Vietnam?
2. **Describing** Study the photograph in Source 2. Write a description of the Mexican side of the border and a description of the U.S. side of the border.
3. **Analyzing** Examine Sources 3 and 4. How do they reflect the ethnicities of the new immigrants?
4. **Speculating** Study the photograph in Source 5. What might be some reasons that the woman opposes illegal immigration?
5. **Making Connections** According to the speaker in Source 6, why do so many people risk crossing the border illegally? What other illegal traffic occurs at the border?

C Critical Thinking

Making Inferences Ask: Why might some Hispanic Americans oppose illegal immigration? *(Answers will vary but could include the following: fear of competition for jobs, resent public services provided to people who pay no taxes.)* **OL**

R Reading Strategies

Identifying Ask: What two activities draw the main focus of the Border Patrol? *(drug trafficking and smuggling of illegal aliens)* Why might these be more crucial than other activities? *(Answers will vary but could include that both endanger lives.)* **OL**

Assess/Close

Have students work in groups to list how aspects of local and state culture, such as language, foods, recreation, and religion, have been affected by immigrant groups.

Answers

DBQ Document Based Questions

Answers:

1. In Vietnam, he felt more of a sense of community. In the U.S., he does not know his neighbors.
2. Students' answers will vary.
3. The largest group of new immigrants comes from Mexico and other parts of Latin America.
4. Students' responses will vary, but should note that the woman's concerns are probably similar to those of other opponents of illegal immigration.
5. People take the risks because they are desperate to find work and make money to support their families. Drugs also get smuggled across the border.

Focus

Bellringer

Daily Focus Transparency 30-4

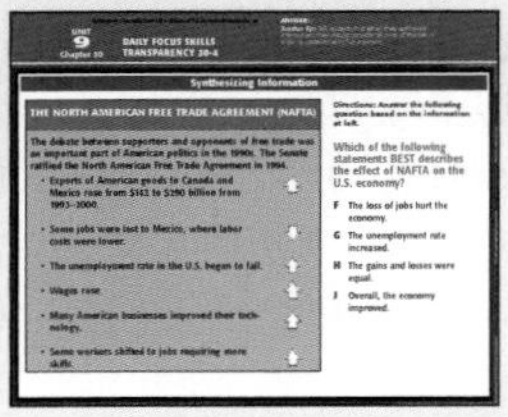

Guide to Reading

Answers:
interdependent economies, international trade, ozone depletion, global warming

Section Spotlight Video

To generate student interest and provide a springboard for class discussion, access the Chapter 30, Section 4 video at glencoe.com or on the video DVD.

Resource Manager

Section Audio   Spotlight Video

An Interdependent World

Guide to Reading

Big Ideas

Economics and Society As the twentieth century drew to a close, world trade and environmentalism became increasingly more important during a period of globalization.

Content Vocabulary
- globalism *(p. 1022)*
- euro *(p. 1023)*
- global warming *(p. 1025)*

Academic Vocabulary
- cited *(p. 1024)*
- awareness *(p. 1025)*

People and Events to Identify
- North American Free Trade Agreement (NAFTA) *(p. 1023)*
- European Union (EU) *(p. 1023)*
- Asia Pacific Economic Cooperation (APEC) *(p. 1024)*
- World Trade Organization (WTO) *(p. 1024)*
- Kyoto Protocol *(p. 1025)*

Reading Strategy

Organizing Complete a graphic organizer like the one below to chart the major political and economic problems facing the world at the turn of the century.

As the world economy became more interconnected in the 1990s, Americans debated whether the elimination of trade barriers was more beneficial or detrimental for the nation. Concerns about environmental damage led to an international conference in Kyoto, Japan.

The New Global Economy

MAIN Idea Regional trade agreements, such as the North American Free Trade Agreement (NAFTA), reflected the growing interdependence of the global economy.

HISTORY AND YOU Do you remember how tariffs were a hotly debated issue in earlier periods of American history? Read on to learn about NAFTA and the fierce political debate it sparked.

In the 1990s Americans began to realize that their relationship with the rest of the world was changing. The economies of individual countries were becoming much more interdependent, and events in one part of the world could dramatically affect the economy of another country thousands of miles away. Computer technology and the Internet played a big role in forging this new global economy. So too did the conviction of many of the world's political and business leaders that free trade and the global exchange of goods contributed to prosperity and economic growth.

At the same time, the Internet and digital satellite technology helped link the world together culturally. For example, people in the United States could read Australian newspapers on the Web, while Chinese students could download American popular music, and an African doctor could consult a British medical database. This idea that the world is becoming increasingly interconnected is sometimes referred to as **globalism,** and the process is called globalization.

Selling American-made goods abroad had long been important to American prosperity. From World War II to the present, Republican and Democratic administrations have worked to lower barriers to international trade. They reasoned that trade helps the American economy: American businesses make money selling goods abroad, and American consumers benefit by having the option to buy goods that are less expensive than those made in the United States. Importing low-cost goods would also keep inflation and interest rates low.

Opponents warned that embracing the global economy would cause manufacturing jobs to move from the United States to nations where wages were low and there were fewer environmental regulations. They suggested that having cheap imports available to buy

R Reading Strategies	C Critical Thinking	D Differentiated Instruction	W Writing Support	S Skill Practice
Teacher Edition • Activ. Prior Knowledge, p. 1023 **Additional Resources** • Guided Reading Act., URB p. 117	**Teacher Edition** • Drawing Conclusions, p. 1023 **Additional Resources** • Geography and History, URB p. 3 • Quizzes/Tests, p. 432	**Teacher Edition** • Visual/ Spatial, p. 1025 **Additional Resources** • American Lit., URB p. 13 • American Art/Music, p. 105	**Teacher Edition** • Personal Writing, p. 1024	**Teacher Edition** • Reading Graphs, p. 1024 **Additional Resources** • Authentic Assess., p. 65 • Read. Essen., p. 340

The Global Auto Industry

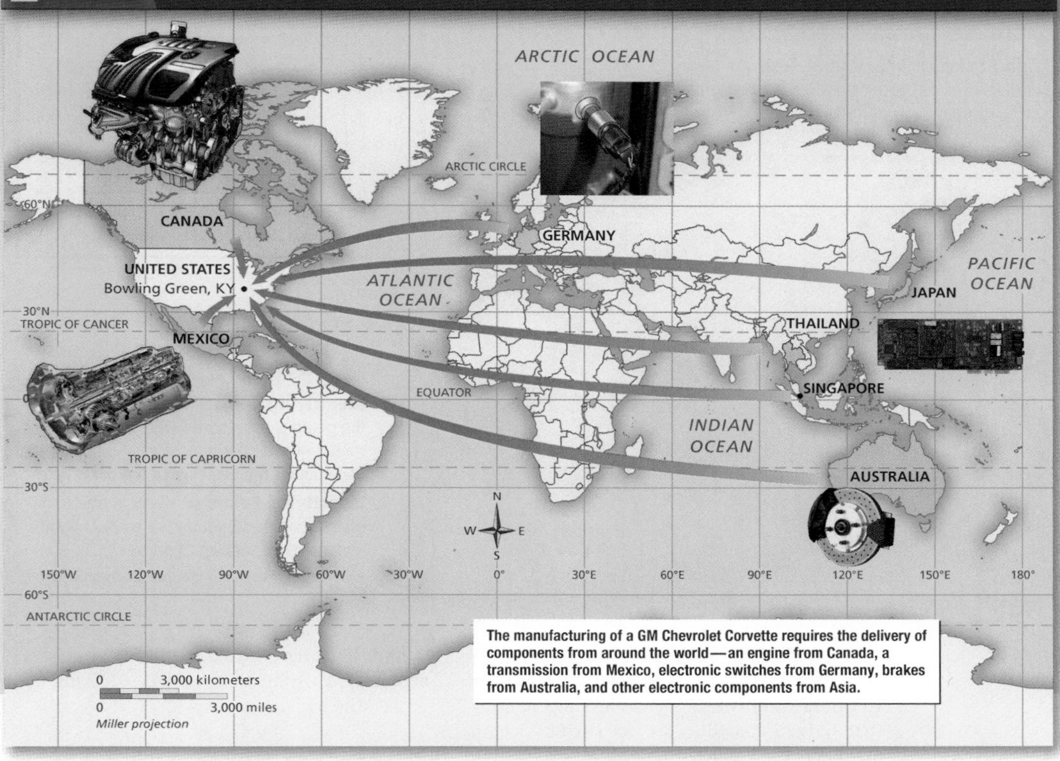

The manufacturing of a GM Chevrolet Corvette requires the delivery of components from around the world—an engine from Canada, a transmission from Mexico, electronic switches from Germany, brakes from Australia, and other electronic components from Asia.

would not help those Americans who no longer could find work because their industries had moved overseas. By the 1990s, the debate between supporters of free trade and those who wanted to limit trade had become an important part of American politics.

Regional Blocs

One way to increase international trade was to create regional trade pacts. In 1993 President Clinton convinced Congress to ratify the **North American Free Trade Agreement** (NAFTA). This agreement joined Canada, the United States, and Mexico in a free-trade zone. R With NAFTA in operation, exports of American goods to both Canada and Mexico rose dramatically. From 1993 to 2000, it is estimated that combined exports to those two countries rose from $142 to $290 billion, an increase of 104 percent.

Many Americans feared that NAFTA would cause industrial jobs to move to Mexico, where labor costs were lower. Some jobs were indeed lost, as foreign-owned factories, known as *maquiladoras*, opened in Mexico near the American border. At the same time, however, the unemployment rate in the United States began to fall and wages rose. Many American businesses upgraded their technology, and workers shifted to more skilled jobs or to the service industry.

Regional trade blocs also formed in Europe and Asia. In 1993, the **European Union** (EU) was created to promote economic and political cooperation among many European nations. The EU created a common bank and the **euro,** a common currency for member nations. C The organization also removed trade barriers between its members and set policies on imports from nations outside the community.

Teach

C Critical Thinking

Drawing Conclusions Ask: Why did the EU create a common bank and currency for member nations? *(to make it easier to trade within the member nations)* OL

R Reading Strategies

Activating Prior Knowledge Ask: What is the term for a trade barrier that taxes imported goods? *(tariff)* OL

Differentiated Instruction

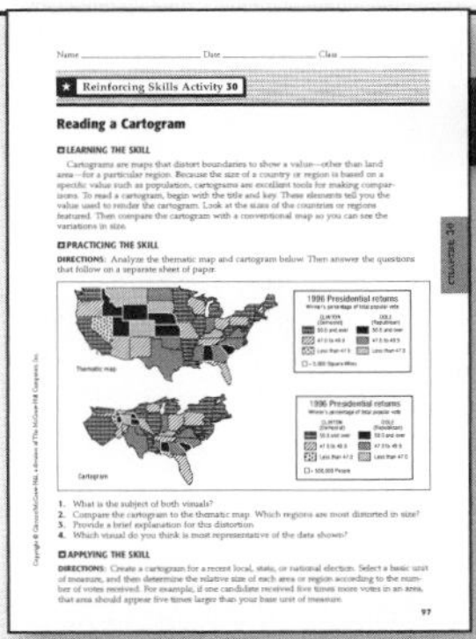

Reinforcing Skills Activity, URB p. 97

Reading a Cartogram

Objective: Read a cartogram.

Focus: Define a cartogram.

Teach: What is the purpose of a cartogram?

Assess: Explain why the size of the states are distorted in the cartogram.

Close: Use the cartogram to explain which states have the most popular votes.

Differentiated Instruction Strategies

- BL Explain the difference between a cartogram and a thematic map.
- AL Create a cartogram on a topic other than an election.
- ELL Explain the purpose of the title and key on a cartogram.

S Skill Practice

Reading Graphs **Ask:** What seems to be the correlation between trade and GDP? *(As trade increases, so does GDP.)* Between what years was there little expansion of trade and GDP? *(2000 and 2001)* **ELL**

W Writing Support

Personal Writing Have students write a personal response to the slogan *Buy American.* **AL**

Reading Check

Answer:
It created global economic interdependence.

Analyzing VISUALS

Answers:
1. Because increased trade increases GDP, countries are more prosperous. However, one country's economic woes can affect other countries.
2. Answers will vary but could include national autonomy and human rights.

PRIMARY SOURCE

Debating Free Trade

Globalization and the steady reduction of trade barriers between nations has led to many protests and political debates around the globe.

▲ *Demonstrators in Seattle protest a meeting of the WTO on November 30, 1999.*

S

Rise of Global Trade and Global GDP

Source: *Australia's Foreign and Trade Policy White Paper.*

Analyzing VISUALS

1. **Identifying Central Issues** How does the graph support those who want free trade? How do the protestors of globalization counter the evidence of the bar graph?
2. **Identifying Points of View** If free trade brings prosperity, what other values might opponents be seeking to protect?

Another trade bloc that came together in the early 1990s was the **Asia Pacific Economic Cooperation** (APEC). It includes most nations that have a coastline on the Pacific Ocean, including the United States, Canada, China, Japan, South Korea, Mexico, and Russia. APEC represented the fastest-growing region in the world and controlled 47 percent of global trade in 2001. APEC began as a forum to promote economic cooperation and lower trade barriers, but major political differences kept its members from acting together.

The World Trade Organization

In 1994 some 120 nations formed the **World Trade Organization** (WTO) to administer international trade agreements and help settle trade disputes. President Clinton convinced Congress to pass legislation enabling the United States to participate in the WTO. Supporters of the WTO **cited** benefits for American consumers, including cheaper imports, new markets, and copyright protection for the American entertainment industry. Opponents noted that the United States would be bound to accept the WTO's rulings in trade disputes even if they hurt the American economy. Despite their concerns, Congress passed the legislation.

Trade With China

China's huge population offered potential as a market for American goods, but many people had reservations about trading with China. These critics cited China's suppression of protests in Tiananmen Square in 1989, its record on human rights, and its threats to invade Taiwan. Despite these concerns, President Clinton argued that expanding trade with China would help bring it into the world community.

W After negotiating a new trade agreement, Clinton urged Congress to grant China permanent normal trade relation status. Unions opposed the deal, fearing that inexpensive Chinese goods would flood U.S. markets; conservatives objected to China's military ambitions; and environmentalists worried about pollution from Chinese factories. Over such objections, the bill passed in late 2000.

Reading Check **Analyzing** How did international trade change the world economy?

Hands-On Chapter Project Step 4

Art Show

Step 4: Hanging the Show **Essential Question:** How should the images best be presented to illustrate this time of change in American history?

Directions The final job is to hang the show, but this requires decisions about the best order in which to present the images for the audience. Students may choose to hang the images by chronological order, by date of the artwork, by the artists, or by a perceived theme in the images. Another task is to review the informational tags that will accompany the images. Will the tags give the audience enough information to clearly see the topic?

Putting It Together If there is space for the show to actually be hung; getting the materials to hang it is the last step. Students from other classes might view it and review it. **OL**

(Chapter Project continued on the Visual Summary page)

Global Environmentalism

MAIN Idea As scientists learned that certain chemicals could damage the Earth's ozone layer, they worked to ban their use; concern about global warming became a serious political issue.

HISTORY AND YOU Are there groups in your school or community that work to improve the environment? Read on to learn about efforts to reduce damage to the environment.

The rise of a global economy also increased **awareness** of environmental issues. Environmentalists began thinking of the environment as a global system. Increasingly, they began addressing issues that they believed were of global, not just local, concern.

Concern About Ozone

In the 1980s scientists discovered that chlorofluorocarbons (CFCs) had the ability to break down the ozone layer in the Earth's atmosphere. Ozone is a gas that protects life on Earth from the ultraviolet rays of the sun. At that time, CFCs were widely used in air conditioners and refrigerators. Environmental activists began to push for a ban on CFC production. In the late 1980s, public awareness of the issue increased dramatically when scientists documented a large ozone "hole" over Antarctica. In 1987 the United States and 22 other nations agreed to phase out the production of CFCs and other chemicals that might be weakening the ozone layer.

Global Warming

In the early 1990s, another global environmental issue developed when some scientists found evidence of **global warming**—an increase in average world temperatures over time. Such a rise in temperature could eventually lead to more droughts and other forms of extreme weather. A furious debate began over how to measure the Earth's temperature and what the results meant.

D

Many experts concluded that carbon dioxide emissions from factories and power plants caused global warming, but others disagreed. The issue became very controversial because the cost of controlling emissions would affect the global economy. Industries would have to pay the cost of further reducing emissions, and those costs would eventually be passed on to consumers. Developing nations trying to industrialize would be hurt the most, but economic growth in wealthier nations would be hurt, too.

Concern about global warming led to an international conference in Kyoto, Japan, in 1997. Thirty-eight nations and the EU signed the Kyoto Protocol promising to reduce emissions, but very few have actually complied with its requirements and reduced their emissions. President Clinton did not submit the Kyoto Protocol to the Senate for ratification because most senators were opposed to it. In 2001 President George W. Bush withdrew the United States from the **Kyoto Protocol,** citing flaws in the treaty.

Reading Check **Describing** Why did environmentalists think CFCs were dangerous?

Section 4 REVIEW

Vocabulary

1. **Explain** the significance of: globalism, North American Free Trade Agreement, European Union, euro, Asia Pacific Economic Cooperation, World Trade Organization, global warming, Kyoto Protocol.

Main Ideas

2. **Explaining** Why was China an important factor in world trade?
3. **Describing** What was the international response to concerns about global warming?

Critical Thinking

4. **Big Ideas** How did NAFTA affect exports of American goods?
5. **Organizing** Complete a graphic organizer by listing and describing the regional trade blocs that formed in the 1990s.

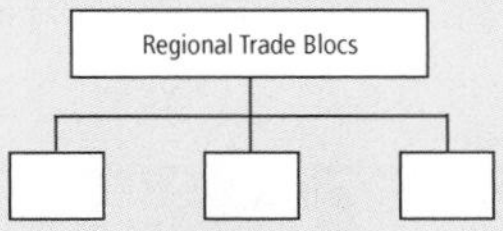

6. **Analyzing Visuals** Examine the image on page 1024. Why do some people or groups protest globalization?

Writing About History

7. **Expository Writing** Decide which issue of global concern is the most serious. In an essay, explain why you think it is the most serious problem, and provide some possible solutions.

History ONLINE
Study Central™ To review this section, go to glencoe.com and click on Study Central.

D Differentiated Instruction

Visual/Spatial Have students create posters or cartoons to illustrate the debate over global warming.

Reading Check

Answer:
Environmentalists grew concerned that CFCs may have caused a large ozone "hole" over Antarctica.

Assess

History ONLINE

Study Central™ provides summaries, interactive games, and online graphic organizers to help students review content.

Close

Identifying Ask: In what ways is today's world interdependent? *(economically, environmentally)* **OL**

Section 4 REVIEW

Answers

1. All definitions can be found in the section and the Glossary.
2. China's huge population offered great potential as a market for U.S. goods.
3. The EU and 38 nations signed the Kyoto Protocol promising to reduce emissions; few have complied, however.
4. With NAFTA in operation, American exports to Canada and Mexico rose dramatically, an estimated 104 percent.
5. NAFTA, EU, APEC
6. Answers will vary but could include that some fear that the U.S. will lose its economic autonomy, that the U.S. economy will be negatively affected by downturns in the economies of other countries, and that jobs will be lost as businesses seek cheaper labor and production costs overseas.
7. Essays will vary but should describe a global problem, provide rationale for the selection, and offer possible solutions.

Analyzing Visuals **Ask:** How did computers change job requirements for American workers? *(Workers had to demonstrate computer proficiency or be willing to learn.)* How might computers have affected work output? *(Answers will vary but could include the ideas that work could be produced and revised more quickly, that employees could share or consult on work, and that uniform appearance was possible.)* **ELL**

Drawing Conclusions **Ask:** How did increased taxes reduce the federal deficit? *(The increased tax revenues were used to pay off existing debt.)* **BL**

Chapter 30 VISUAL SUMMARY

STUDY TO GO You can study anywhere, anytime by downloading quizzes and flashcards to your PDA from glencoe.com.

A Changing Society

The Technological Revolution

- The invention of the integrated circuit and microprocessors enables small personal computers built by Apple and IBM.
- The telecommunications revolution leads to the development of small portable cell phones, and digital video and audio players.
- The rise of the Internet and World Wide Web provide new ways for people to retrieve information, build communities, and do business.

A New Wave of Immigrants

- New immigration laws in 1965 and 1986 contribute to a rise in Hispanic immigration and an increase in immigrants from Asia, Africa, and the Middle East.
- The American population becomes increasingly culturally diverse.

The Rise of a Global Economy

- Free trade, in combination with the technological revolution, creates a new global marketplace.
- Increasing awareness of the global economy also sparks a new global environmentalist movement.

▲ *Today, almost all businesses, such as this public relations firm, rely on computers to help employees perform their day-to-day duties.*

▲ *President Bill Clinton delivers his State of the Union address to a joint session of Congress on January 24, 1995.*

The Clinton Years

First-Term Achievements and Failures

- Raised taxes to help cut the deficit
- Proposal for a national health care program fails
- Signed the Family Medical Leave Act into law
- Persuaded Congress to create AmeriCorps
- Signed the Brady Handgun Bill into law
- Worked with Republicans to push the Health Insurance Portability Act and the Welfare Reform Act through Congress

Second-Term Achievements and Failures

- Submits a balanced budget to Congress
- Convinces Congress to pass a new tax credit for children and a children's health insurance program
- Impeached on charges of perjury and obstruction of justice but is acquitted by the Senate

Foreign Policy Achievements

- Dispatched troops to Haiti to restore democracy
- Dispatched troops to Bosnia and bombed Serbia to end the civil war and ethnic cleansing that followed the breakup of Yugoslavia
- Mediated negotiations between Israel and the PLO

Hands-On Chapter Project
Step 5: Wrap Up

Art Show

Step 5: Wrap Up After students have hung the presentation, they will acquire feedback and learn from the feedback.

Directions After the audience has had a chance to review the art show, ask them for their feedback. (You may want to put comment cards out for audience members.) As a class, review the comments, as well as discuss your own reactions to the show.

Ask the following questions to start the discussion:

- What was good about the show?
- Did the images illustrate the topics clearly? Why or why not?
- How could the show have been improved?
- What would you do differently if you did this project again?

Putting It Together As a final close to the project, have students write a brief summary of their reactions to the project, explaining how it illustrated the time period. **OL**

Chapter 30 Assessment

Reviewing Vocabulary

Directions: Choose the word or words that best complete the sentence.

1. The company Intel revolutionized computers by combining several integrated circuits on a single chip called a
   - **A** minicomputer.
   - **B** nanocomputer.
   - **C** microprocessor.
   - **D** microcomputer.

2. As the workplace became increasingly reliant on computers, some workers had the option to ________, or work from home via computer.
   - **A** blog
   - **B** allocate
   - **C** telecommute
   - **D** globalize

3. Clinton was impeached because he committed
   - **A** perjury.
   - **B** ethnic cleansing.
   - **C** overtaxation.
   - **D** robbery.

4. The Immigration Reform and Control Act of 1986 granted ________ to immigrants who entered the country before January 1, 1982.
   - **A** leniency
   - **B** citizenship
   - **C** a pardon
   - **D** amnesty

5. The process of the world becoming increasingly interconnected is called
   - **A** globalization.
   - **B** internationalism.
   - **C** Americanism.
   - **D** Nationalism.

Reviewing Main Ideas

Directions: Choose the best answer for each of the following questions.

Section 1 *(pp. 1002–1005)*

6. The government began to deregulate the telecommunications industry in the
   - **A** 1950s.
   - **B** 1960s.
   - **C** 1970s.
   - **D** 1980s.

7. In 1990, researchers at CERN developed a new way to present information known as
   - **A** the Internet.
   - **B** the computer.
   - **C** the Ethernet.
   - **D** the World Wide Web.

Section 2 *(pp. 1008–1015)*

8. Democrats passed a law during President Clinton's administration that tightened gun control called
   - **A** the Gun Law.
   - **B** the Anti-Gun Bill.
   - **C** the Brady Bill.
   - **D** the NRA Law.

9. The Contract with America was proposed by
   - **A** Hillary Clinton.
   - **B** President Clinton.
   - **C** Al Gore.
   - **D** Newt Gingrich.

TEST-TAKING TIP

Consider each answer choice individually and cross out choices you have eliminated. You will save time and stop yourself from choosing an answer you have mentally eliminated.

Need Extra Help?

If You Missed Questions . . .	1	2	3	4	5	6	7	8	9
Go to Page . . .	1002	1003	1013	1017	1022	1003	1005	1010	1011

GO ON

Answers and Analyses
Reviewing Vocabulary

1. C The question asks for the name of a computer chip. All of the answer choices except for *C* have prefixes attached to computer, as in minicomputer. A chip is not a computer.

2. C The ability to telecommute depended upon having a personal computer to access e-mails from work. This allowed them to communicate with people in the office while remaining at home.

3. A Ethnic cleansing is the attempt to kill off a certain group of people who share a certain ethnicity. Over-taxation is not a crime. Robbery would result in a criminal trial. Clinton was accused of lying under oath, perjury, about his relationship with an intern.

4. D Students may have trouble choosing between *C* and *D*, because amnesty is a type of pardon. However, amnesty is the more precise term.

5. A -ization is a suffix that means an action or a process. Globalization is the process of increasing global connections. Internationalism is a tempting choice, but its meaning is slightly different; it is more of an interest in other nations or describes cooperation between nations, but does not describe the process of increasing global connections.

Reviewing Main Ideas

6. C Review "New Communications" on page 1003 with students. It states that deregulation began in the 1970s.

7. D The Internet preceded the World Wide Web and began to be developed as early as 1969. The computer was also developed before the 1990s. The Ethernet uses cables to exchange messages between computers.

8. C Remind students that James Brady was shot and injured during the assassination attempt on Reagan. This should help them relate Brady to gun control.

9. D The Contract with America was proposed by congressional Republicans led by Newt Gingrich. Students should remember that the contract was a Republican movement. All answer choices besides *D* are Democrats.

10. B Admittance of refugees fleeing communist regimes was part of the McCarran-Walter Act of 1952. The national origin quota system was introduced in the 1920s. Allocation of more resources was part of the Illegal Immigration Reform and Immigrant Responsibility of 1996.

11. C As mentioned above, the act allocated more resources. *A* is incorrect because the law toughened penalties for smugglers.

12. A Both Republicans and Democrats would most likely support a policy that was beneficial to the U.S. A shows the most direct benefit to Americans. It was reasoned that international trade is beneficial because it provides overseas markets for American goods and provides choices for American consumers. *C* is an effect of lowered barriers that some use as an argument against international trade.

13. C It is important that students read the question carefully. All of the answer choices are reasons why people opposed trade with China. However, the question asks why *environmentalists* were concerned. Only *C* relates to the environment.

Critical Thinking

14. D Newspapers are not digital. They are not even electronic. Therefore, they are not an example of digital technology.

15. C Examine the graph with students. The percentage of Native Americans in 2005 was 1.0%. This is the lowest.

16. D Explain to students that it is important to read all aspects of graphs and tables, especially asterisked or footnoted information.

Chapter 30 Assessment

Section 3 *(pp. 1016–1019)*

10. The Immigration Reform and Control Act of 1986 established

- **A** admittance of any refugee fleeing a communist regime.
- **B** legal papers to any undocumented immigrant who could prove he or she entered the country before 1982.
- **C** the national origins quota system.
- **D** allocation of more resources to stop illegal immigration.

11. The Illegal Immigration Reform and Immigrant Responsibility Act of 1996

- **A** relaxed penalties for smuggling people or providing fraudulent documents.
- **B** established more schools for immigrant children.
- **C** allocated more resources to stop illegal immigration.
- **D** called for a wall to be built at the U.S. border.

Section 4 *(pp. 1022–1025)*

12. Since WWII, Republicans and Democrats have worked to lower barriers to international trade because

- **A** it helps the American economy.
- **B** it supports foreign policy.
- **C** it moves manufacturing jobs overseas.
- **D** it helps economically depressed countries.

13. Environmentalists were concerned about trade with China because

- **A** there was concern about the protests in Tiananmen Square.
- **B** they believed the goods should be manufactured in the United States.
- **C** there was concern about pollution from Chinese factories.
- **D** China had made threats to invade Taiwan.

Critical Thinking

Directions: Choose the best answers to the following questions.

14. Which of the following is not an example of digital technology?

- **A** cell phones that can receive e-mails
- **B** MP3 players
- **C** satellite radio
- **D** newspapers

Base your answers to questions 15 and 16 on the graph below and your knowledge of Chapter 30.

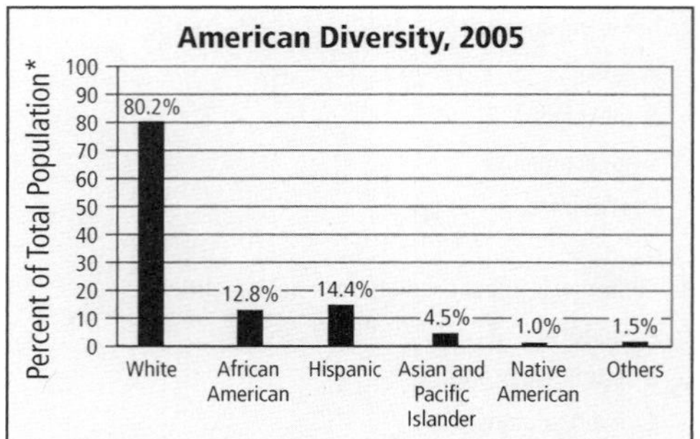

* Percentages add to more than 100 percent because Hispanics may be of any race.

Source: U.S. Census Bureau.

15. Which group was the smallest percentage of the population in 2005?

- **A** African American
- **B** White
- **C** Native American
- **D** Multiracial

16. Why do the percentages add up to more than 100 percent?

- **A** They did not record data carefully.
- **B** There can be more than 100 percent.
- **C** There is no way to determine exact numbers of the population.
- **D** Hispanics may be of any race.

Need Extra Help?

If You Missed Questions . . .	10	11	12	13	14	15	16
Go to Page . . .	1017	1017–1018	1022–1023	1024	1002–1005	R16	R16

GO ON

17. The North American Free Trade Agreement (NAFTA) joined Canada, Mexico and the United States in a free trade zone. Why was this beneficial?
   - **A** Exports to Canada and Mexico increased.
   - **B** Jobs were lost to Mexico.
   - **C** Unemployment in the United States rose.
   - **D** It provided free goods to Canada and Mexico.

Analyze the cartoon and answer the question that follows. Base your answer on the cartoon and on your knowledge of Chapter 30.

18. What is the main idea of this cartoon?
   - **A** Clinton needs to raise taxes to decrease the federal deficit.
   - **B** Clinton should lower taxes to provide relief to taxpapers.
   - **C** Clinton has increased the federal deficit to record levels.
   - **D** The taxpayers are taking advantage of the tax cuts.

19. The presence of increased levels of chlorofluorocarbons (CFCs) concerns scientists because
   - **A** they make the air hard to breathe.
   - **B** they cause global warming.
   - **C** they have the ability to break down ozone.
   - **D** they can enter the water supply.

Document-Based Questions

Directions: Analyze the document and answer the short-answer questions that follow the document.

Global warming became an important topic during the Clinton administration. It was debated across the country, with many different viewpoints.

> *"The world is getting warmer, and by the end of the 21st century could warm by another 6 degrees Celsius (10.8 degrees Fahrenheit). . . . And climate scientists at the heart of the research are now convinced that human action is to blame for some or most of this warming. . . .*
>
> *Everywhere climatologists look—at tree-ring patterns, fossil succession in rock strata, ocean-floor corings. . . they see evidence of dramatic shifts from cold to hot to cold again. . . . None of these ancient shifts can be blamed on humans. . . . There is still room for argument about the precise role of the sun or other natural cycles in the contribution to global warming. . . .*
>
> —from *World Press Review,* February 2001

20. Why are some scientists not convinced humans are to blame for global warming?

21. What evidence do these scientists cite?

Extended Response

22. After the 1992 election, what did President Clinton's domestic agenda include? Explain in detail the successes and failures of the Clinton administration. Your essay should include an introduction, several paragraphs, and a conclusion. Use relevant facts and details to support your conclusion.

STOP

History ONLINE
For additional test practice, use Self-Check Quizzes—Chapter 30 at glencoe.com.

Need Extra Help?

If You Missed Questions . . .	17	18	19	20	21	22
Go to Page . . .	1023	R18	1025	1025	1025	1008–1010

17. A The question asks about benefits, so *B* and *C* can be eliminated, because they describe negative effects. *D* does not make sense. The agreement is for free trade, not free goods. Free trade increased exports to Mexico and Canada because it became more economically feasible/beneficial to U.S. based manufacturers to export.

18. B The cartoon indicates that Clinton should lower taxes to provide relief to taxpayers, even if that means running a deficit.

19. C Students may be tempted to choose *B*, because the weakening of the ozone layer caused by CFCs has been linked to global warming. *B* is the best answer because it is the most specific and directly related to CFCs.

Document-Based Questions

20. Some scientists are not convinced that humans are to blame because there is evidence of dramatic shifts in temperature throughout history, so it can still be argued that there are natural causes or cycles of global temperature change.

21. The scientists cite evidence such as tree-ring patterns, fossil succession, and ocean floor corings that show evidence of past dramatic temperature shifts.

Extended Response

22. Students' essays will vary, but should contain a balance between successes and failures, using the text to provide well-reasoned support. Essays should contain a detailed description of Clinton's domestic agenda that is then clearly tied to either a success or failure.

History ONLINE
Have students visit the Web site at glencoe.com to review Chapter 30 and take the Self-Check Quiz.

Need Extra Help?
Have students refer to the pages listed if they miss any of the questions.

Chapter 31 Planning Guide

Key to Ability Levels	
BL Below Level	**AL** Above Level
OL On Level	**ELL** English Language Learners

Key to Teaching Resources	
Print Material	Transparency
CD-ROM or DVD	

Levels					Resources	Chapter Opener	Section 1	Section 2	Section 3	Section 4	Chapter Assess
BL	OL	AL	ELL								
FOCUS											
BL	OL	AL	ELL	Transparency	**Daily Focus Skills Transparencies**		31-1	31-2	31-3	31-4	
TEACH											
BL	OL		ELL	Print Material	**Reading Essentials and Note-Taking Guide***		p. 343	p. 346	p. 349	p. 352	
	OL			Print Material	**Historical Analysis Skills Activity, URB**		p. 122				
BL	OL		ELL	Print Material	**Guided Reading Activities, URB***		p. 148	p. 149	p. 150	p. 151	
BL	OL	AL	ELL	Print Material	**Content Vocabulary Activity, URB***		p. 127				
BL	OL	AL	ELL	Print Material	**Academic Vocabulary Activity, URB**		p. 129				
	OL	AL		Print Material	**Critical Thinking Skills Activity, URB**					p. 132	
BL	OL		ELL	Print Material	**Reading Skills Activity, URB**					p. 121	
BL			ELL	Print Material	**English Learner Activity, URB**			p. 125			
	OL	AL		Print Material	**Reinforcing Skills Activity, URB**					p. 131	
BL	OL	AL	ELL	Print Material	**Differentiated Instruction Activity, URB**			p. 123			
BL	OL		ELL	Print Material	**Time Line Activity, URB**		p. 133				
	OL			Print Material	**Linking Past and Present Activity, URB**					p. 134	
BL	OL	AL	ELL	Print Material	**American Art and Music Activity, URB**					p. 139	
BL	OL	AL	ELL	Print Material	**Interpreting Political Cartoons Activity, URB**		p. 141				
		AL		Print Material	**Enrichment Activity, URB**		p. 145				
BL	OL	AL	ELL	Print Material	**American Biographies**		✓			✓	
BL	OL	AL	ELL	Print Material	**Primary Source Reading, URB**			p. 135		p. 137	
BL	OL	AL	ELL	Print Material	**Supreme Court Case Studies**					p. 161	
BL	OL	AL	ELL	Print Material	**The Living Constitution***	✓	✓	✓	✓	✓	✓
	OL	AL		CD-ROM or DVD	**American History Primary Source Documents Library**	✓	✓	✓	✓	✓	✓
BL	OL	AL	ELL	Transparency	**Unit Map Overlay Transparencies**	✓	✓	✓	✓	✓	✓
BL	OL	AL	ELL	Print Material	**Differentiated Instruction for the American History Classroom**	✓	✓	✓	✓	✓	✓
BL	OL	AL	ELL	CD-ROM or DVD	**StudentWorks™ Plus DVD**	✓	✓	✓	✓	✓	✓

Note: Please refer to the *Unit 9 Resource Book* for this chapter's URB materials.

* Also available in Spanish

Planning Guide Chapter 31

TeacherWorks Plus
All-In-One Planner and Resource Center

- Interactive Lesson Planner
- Interactive Teacher Edition
- Fully editable blackline masters
- Section Spotlight Videos Launch
- Differentiated Lesson Plans
- Printable reports of daily assignments
- Standards Tracking System

Levels				Resources	Chapter Opener	Section 1	Section 2	Section 3	Section 4	Chapter Assess
BL	OL	AL	ELL							
				TEACH *(continued)*						
BL	OL	AL	ELL	American Music Hits Through History CD	✓	✓	✓	✓	✓	✓
BL	OL	AL	ELL	Unit Time Line Transparencies and Activities	✓	✓	✓	✓	✓	✓
BL	OL	AL	ELL	Cause and Effect Transparencies, Strategies, and Activities	✓	✓	✓	✓	✓	✓
BL	OL	AL	ELL	Why It Matters Transparencies, Strategies, and Activities	✓	✓	✓	✓	✓	✓
BL	OL	AL	ELL	American Issues	✓	✓	✓	✓	✓	✓
	OL	AL	ELL	American Art and Architecture Transparencies, Strategies, and Activities	✓	✓	✓	✓	✓	✓
BL	OL	AL		High School American History Literature Library	✓	✓	✓	✓	✓	✓
BL	OL	AL	ELL	*The American Vision* Video Program	✓	✓	✓	✓	✓	✓
Teacher Resources				Strategies for Success	✓	✓	✓	✓	✓	✓
Teacher Resources				Success with English Learners	✓	✓	✓	✓	✓	✓
Teacher Resources				Reading Strategies and Activities for the Social Studies Classroom	✓	✓	✓	✓	✓	✓
Teacher Resources				Presentation Plus! with MindJogger CheckPoint	✓	✓	✓	✓	✓	✓
				ASSESS						
BL	OL	AL	ELL	Section Quizzes and Chapter Tests*		p. 441	p. 442	p. 443	p. 444	p. 445
BL	OL	AL	ELL	Authentic Assessment With Rubrics						p. 67
BL	OL	AL	ELL	Standardized Test Practice Workbook						p. 71
BL	OL	AL	ELL	*ExamView® Assessment Suite*		31-1	31-2	31-3	31-4	Ch. 31
				CLOSE						
BL			ELL	Reteaching Activity, URB						p. 143
BL	OL		ELL	Reading and Study Skills Foldables™	p. 84					
BL	OL	AL	ELL	*American History* in Graphic Novel						p. 79

✓ Chapter- or unit-based activities applicable to all sections in this chapter.

Chapter 31 Integrating Technology

Using Study-to-Go: Teach With Technology

What is Study-to-Go?

Study-to-Go provides portable textbook-based content direct from the Glencoe Web site to your students whenever and wherever they want!

How can Study-to-Go help my students?

Study-to-Go content can be downloaded to a personal digital assistant (PDA) or a cell phone. Students can download Study Sets that include:

- Self Quiz—a series of multiple choice quizzes that provides instant answer feedback
- Key Terms—definitions for textbook vocabulary
- Flashcards—an assessment tool to help students study textbook key terms

Visit glencoe.com and enter a ***QuickPass***™ code to go to the Study-to-Go.

History ONLINE
Visit glencoe.com and enter ***QuickPass***™ code TAV9399c31T for Chapter 31 resources.

You can easily launch a wide range of digital products from your computer's desktop with the McGraw-Hill Social Studies widget.

TeacherWorks

	Student	Teacher	Parent
Media Library			
• Section Audio	●		●
• Spanish Audio Summaries	●		●
• Section Spotlight Videos	●	●	●
***The American Vision* Online Learning Center (Web Site)**			
• StudentWorks™ Plus Online	●	●	●
• Multilingual Glossary	●	●	●
• Study-to-Go	●	●	●
• Chapter Overviews	●	●	●
• Self-Check Quizzes	●	●	●
• Student Web Activities	●	●	●
• ePuzzles and Games	●	●	●
• Vocabulary eFlashcards	●	●	●
• In Motion Animations	●	●	●
• Study Central™	●	●	●
• Web Activity Lesson Plans		●	
• Vocabulary PuzzleMaker	●	●	●
• Historical Thinking Activities		●	
• Beyond the Textbook	●	●	●

Reading Support From Jamestown Education

- **Timed Readings Plus in Social Studies** helps students increase their reading rate and fluency while maintaining comprehension. The 400-word passages are similar to those found on state and national assessments.
- **Reading in the Content Area: Social Studies** concentrates on six essential reading skills that help students better comprehend what they read. The book includes 75 high-interest nonfiction passages written at increasing levels of difficulty.
- **Reading Social Studies** includes strategic reading instruction and vocabulary support in Social Studies content for both ELLs and native speakers of English.

www.jamestowneducation.com

Biography / A&E Home Video / The History Channel

The following videotape programs are available from Glencoe as supplements to this chapter:

- Colin Powell: A Soldier's Campaign (ISBN 1-56-501701-3)
- The White House—Great American Monuments (ISBN 1-56-501643-2)

To order, call Glencoe at 1-800-334-7344. To find classroom resources to accompany many of these videos, check the following home pages:

A&E Television: www.aetv.com

The History Channel: www.historychannel.com

Reading List Generator CD-ROM — Glencoe BookLink 3

Use this database to search more than 30,000 titles to create a customized reading list for your students.

- Reading lists can be organized by students' reading level, author, genre, theme, or area of interest.
- The database provides Degrees of Reading Power™ (DRP) and Lexile™ readability scores for all selections.
- A brief summary of each selection is included.

Leveled reading suggestions for this chapter:

For students at a Grade 8 reading level:
- ***September 11, 2001: Attack on New York City,*** by Wilborn Hampton

For students at a Grade 9 reading level:
- ***September 11, 2001: The Day that Changed America,*** by Jill C. Wheeler

For students at a Grade 10 reading level:
- ***President George W. Bush: Our Forty-Third President,*** by Beatrice Gormley

For students at a Grade 11 reading level:
- ***Thura's Diary: My Life in Wartime Iraq,*** by Thura Al-Windawi

For students at a Grade 12 reading level:
- ***Iraq and the Fall of Saddam Hussein,*** by Jason Richie

National Geographic

Index to National Geographic Magazine:

The following articles relate to this chapter:

- "Time to Hit the Panic Button? How We Decide What's Risky," by Joel Achenbach, September 2003.
- "Where Have You Gone New Orleans?," by Ernest J. Gaines, August 2006.

National Geographic Society Products To order the following, call National Geographic at 1-800-368-2728:

- *ZipZapMap! USA* (ZipZapMap!)

Access National Geographic's new, dynamic MapMachine Web site and other geography resources at:

www.nationalgeographic.com
www.nationalgeographic.com/maps

Introducing Chapter 31

Focus

MAKING CONNECTIONS

How Does the Passage of Time Affect the Way Events are Understood?

Have students reflect on a memorable past event or situation in their lives **Ask:** How was your life permanently changed by the event or situation? What lessons did you learn from the experience? Explain that a nation like the United States can also experience moments when its path in history dramatically alters and when unexpected decisions have to be made. Ask them to name episodes in American history that aroused Americans and suddenly changed the course of the nation's policies and actions. Most students will probably include the 9/11 terrorist attacks and their effect on the nation. Conclude by having students give their ideas about how the United States should respond to terrorism.

Teach

The Big Ideas

As students study the chapter, remind them to consider the section-based Big Ideas included in each section's Guide to Reading. The **Essential Questions** and the activities below tie in to the Big Ideas and help students think about and understand important chapter concepts. In addition, the Hands-on-Chapter Projects with their culminating activities relate the content from each section to the Big Ideas. These activities build on each other as students progress through the chapter. Section activities culminate in the wrap-up activity on the Visual Summary page. **BL** **OL**

Chapter 31

A New Century Begins

2001–Present

SECTION 1 America Enters A New Century
SECTION 2 The War on Terrorism Begins
SECTION 3 The Invasion of Iraq
SECTION 4 A Time of Challenges

On September 11, 2006, the Tribute in Light commemorated the fifth anniversary of the attack on the World Trade Center.

G. W. Bush 2001–2009

U.S. PRESIDENTS

U.S. EVENTS

- **November 2000** • A close vote in Florida causes a contested election
- **Sept. 11, 2001** • Terrorists attack World Trade Center and Pentagon
- **October 2001** • U.S. begins bombing Afghanistan • Patriot Act enacted
- **January 2002** • President Bush signs No Child Left Behind Act
- **March 2003** • U.S. invades Iraq

2001 · 2002 · 2003 · 2004

WORLD EVENTS

- **2001** • Terrorists attack the Indian Parliament
- **2002** • Suicide bombings in Israel
- **2004** • Tsunami in Indian Ocean devastates Indonesia and surrounding regions • Terrorists bomb trains in Spain

Section 1

America Enters a New Century

Essential Question: When an election's results are uncertain or disputed, how do you think the problem should be resolved? *(by compromise, vote counts, the courts, holding run-off elections)* Point out that in Section 1 students will learn about the close presidential election of 2000 and how its outcome was settled peacefully. **OL**

Section 2

The War on Terrorism Begins

Essential Question: What challenges might governments face in fighting terrorism? *(the need to enact tough measures against terrorism that at the same time are respectful of citizens' rights)* Point out in Section 2 students will learn about the terrorist attacks of September 11, 2001 and the response of the Bush Adminstration with the "War on Terror." **OL**

Chapter Audio

MAKING CONNECTIONS

How Does the Passage of Time Affect the Way Events Are Understood?

As the United States entered the twenty-first century, combating terrorism at home and abroad became a national priority. The attacks on the World Trade Center and the Pentagon resulted in wars in Afghanistan and Iraq. The wars as well as new security policies led to great controversy in American politics.

- ***What previous events in American history have forced the nation to dramatically change its policies and actions?***
- ***How should the United States respond to terrorism to prevent it from happening again?***

November 2004
- George W. Bush defeats John Kerry in the election

2005
- Terrorists bomb London subway system

August 2005
- Hurricane Katrina devastates Louisiana and Mississippi; levees fail and New Orleans floods

2006
- Israel invades Lebanon in response to Hezbollah attack
- Over 1 billion people worldwide use the Internet

January 2007
- Nancy Pelosi becomes first female Speaker of the House

2005 · 2006 · 2007

FOLDABLES

Organizing Information Compile facts about the terrorist attacks at the World Trade Center and Pentagon on September 11, 2001. Then, make a Four-Door Book Foldable that explains what, where, when, and why these events occurred.

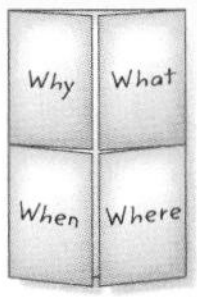

History ONLINE Visit glencoe.com and enter ***QuickPass***™ code TAV9846c31 for Chapter 31 resources.

Section 3

The Invasion of Iraq

Essential Question: How do you think the United States carries out its foreign policy? *(through diplomacy, trade, war, humanitarian aid, public relations)* Explain that in Section 3 students will learn about how the United States became militarily involved in Iraq and Afghanistan and the effects of U.S. actions on these two countries. **OL**

Section 4

A Time of Challenges

Essential Question: How might unexpected events affect a country's politics and government? *(Citizens' votes are based on how well or how badly the government responds to these emergencies.)* Explain that in Section 4 students will learn how scandal and natural disaster weakened Republican control of government and benefited Democrats in congressional elections. **OL**

More About the Photo

Visual Literacy Ask students: What city is shown in the photo? What type of event is taking place? *(New York City; a commemoration or memorial using light beams)* The "Tribute in Light" memorial lies near the site of the World Trade Center in lower Manhattan. The two beams of light, which represent the fallen twin towers of the Center, light up the evening sky to remember the people who lost their lives as a result of the terrorist attacks on September 11, 2001.

FOLDABLES™ Study Organizer **Dinah Zike's Foldables**

Dinah Zike's Foldables are three-dimensional, interactive graphic organizers that help students practice basic writing skills, review vocabulary terms, and identify main ideas. Instructions for creating and using Foldables can be found in the Appendix at the end of this book and in the *Dinah Zike's Reading and Study Skills Foldables* booklet.

History ONLINE

Visit glencoe.com and enter ***QuickPass***™ code TAV9399c31T for Chapter 31 resources, including a Chapter Overview, Study Central™, Study-to-Go, Student Web Activity, Self-Check Quiz, and other materials.

Focus

Bellringer

Daily Focus Transparency 31-1

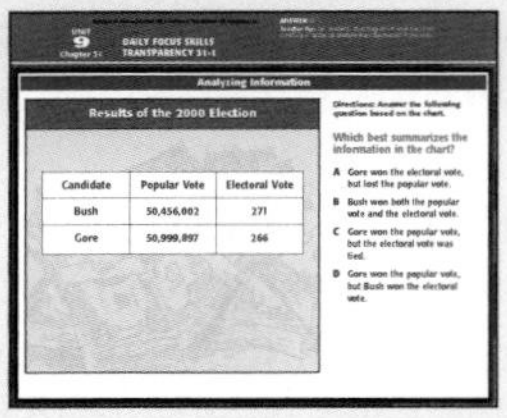

Guide to Reading

Answers:

Fla. recounts; Bush certified winner

Fla. Supreme Court decides for hand recount

U.S. Supreme Court rules in *Bush* v. *Gore* against hand recount

Bush's Victory

Section Spotlight Video

To generate student interest and provide a springboard for class discussion, access the Chapter 31, Section 1 video at glencoe.com or on the video DVD.

Section 1

Section Audio | Spotlight Video

America Enters a New Century

Guide to Reading

Big Ideas

Government and Society A very close presidential election saw a shift in power in the White House, as George W. Bush became the forty-third President of the United States.

Content Vocabulary

- chad *(p. 1033)*
- strategic defense *(p. 1035)*

Academic Vocabulary

- priority *(p. 1035)*
- controversial *(p. 1035)*

People and Events to Identify

- Al Gore *(p. 1032)*
- George W. Bush *(p. 1032)*
- Ralph Nader *(p. 1033)*

Reading Strategy

Organizing Complete a graphic organizer similar to the one below by charting the key postelection events culminating in George W. Bush's victory.

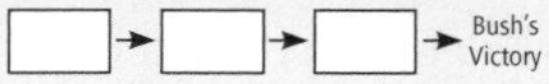

In the election of 2000, Democrat Al Gore faced Republican George W. Bush. After a dispute over the outcome in Florida, Bush became president. Bush then focused on cutting taxes and introducing health care and education reforms.

The Election of 2000

MAIN Idea In one of the closest presidential races in history, involving vote recounts and the Supreme Court, George W. Bush became president.

HISTORY AND YOU Do you think the Electoral College should be modified or eliminated? Read on to learn how the 2000 election ultimately came down to a decision about Florida's disputed electoral votes.

As he prepared to leave office, President Clinton's legacy was uncertain. He had balanced the budget and presided over a period of rapid economic growth. His presidency was marred, however, by the impeachment trial, which had divided the nation and widened the divide between liberals and conservatives. In the election of 2000, that division led to one of the closest elections in American history.

The Candidates Campaign

The Democrats nominated Vice President **Al Gore** for president in 2000. Gore, a former senator from Tennessee, was regarded as a moderate and his Southern roots were expected to help him win votes in the South. For his running mate, Gore chose Senator Joseph Lieberman from Connecticut, the first Jewish American ever to run for vice president on a major party ticket.

The Republican contest for the presidential nomination came down to two men: Governor **George W. Bush** of Texas, son of former president George H.W. Bush, and Senator John McCain of Arizona, a former navy pilot and prisoner of war in North Vietnam. Most Republican leaders endorsed Bush, who was especially popular with conservatives. He easily won the nomination, despite some early McCain victories in the primaries. Bush chose Richard "Dick" Cheney as his vice presidential running mate. Cheney had served as President George H.W. Bush's secretary of defense.

The election campaign revolved around the question of what to do with surplus tax revenues. Both Bush and Gore agreed that Social Security needed reform, but they disagreed on the details. Both promised to cut taxes, although Bush proposed a much larger tax cut than Gore. Both men also promised to improve public education and to support plans to help senior citizens pay for prescription drugs.

Resource Manager

R Reading Strategies	C Critical Thinking	D Differentiated Instruction	W Writing Support	S Skill Practice
Teacher Edition • Summarizing, p. 1034 **Additional Resources** • Guided Reading Act., URB p. 148	**Teacher Edition** • Making Inferences, p. 1035 **Additional Resources** • Hist. Analysis Skills, URB p. 122 • Interpret. Political Cartoons, URB p. 141 • Quizzes/Tests, p. 441	**Additional Resources** • Enrichment Act., URB p. 145 • Foldables, p. 84	**Additional Resources** • Content Vocabulary Act., URB p. 127 • Academic Vocabulary Act., URB p. 129	**Teacher Edition** • Interpret. Maps, p. 1033 **Additional Resources** • Time Line Act., p. 133 • Read. Essen., p. 343

HISTORY AND GEOGRAPHY

The Election of 2000

Presidential Candidate	Popular Votes	% of Popular Vote	Electoral Votes
Bush	50,456,002	47.88%	271
Gore	50,999,897	48.40%	266*
Nader	2,882,955	2.74%	0

*One Gore elector from Washington, D.C., abstained from casting an electoral vote.

▲ *The recount of the vote in Florida meant vote counters had to examine ballots individually to determine the intention of the voter.*

Analyzing VISUALS

1. **Making Generalizations** What characteristics do the states that voted for Bush share? What characteristics do the states that voted for Gore share?
2. **Assessing** Do you think the Florida ballot was easy to understand or confusing? Why?

Frustrated by what he viewed as the fundamental similarities between Bush and Gore, well-known consumer advocate **Ralph Nader** entered the race as the nominee of the Green Party. Nader was known for his strong environmentalist views and his criticism of the power of large corporations. Nader argued that both Bush and Gore depended on campaign funds from large companies and were unwilling to support policies that favored American workers and the environment.

A Close Vote

The 2000 election was one of the closest in American history. No candidate won a majority of the votes cast, but Gore received the most votes, winning 48.4 percent of the popular vote compared to 47.9 percent for Bush. (Nader won about 3 percent of the vote.) To win the presidency, however, candidates must win 270 electoral votes—not lead in the popular vote.

The election came down to the Florida vote—both men needed its 25 electoral votes to win. The results in Florida were so close that state law required a recount of the ballots using vote-counting machines. There were, however, thousands of ballots that had been thrown out because the counting machines could not read the voting cards. Gore then asked for a hand recount of ballots in several strongly Democratic counties. After the machine recount showed Bush still ahead, a battle began over the manual recounts.

Most Florida ballots required voters to punch a hole. The little piece of cardboard punched out of the ballot is called a **chad.** The problem for vote counters was how to count a ballot if the chad was still partially attached. On some, the chad was still in place, and the voter had left only a dimple on the surface. When looking at the ballots, vote counters had to determine what the voter intended—and different counties used different standards.

Teach

S Skill Practice

Interpreting Maps Point out to students that the 2000 election marked the first election since 1888 in which the candidate who won the popular vote did not win the electoral vote. **Ask:** Which states had more than 20 electoral votes? *[California (54), New York (33), Texas (32), Florida (25), Pennsylvania (23), Illinois (22), and Ohio (21)]* What candidate won the electoral votes in each of these states? *(Bush won Texas, Florida, and Ohio. Gore won California, New York, Pennsylvania, and Illinois.)* **OL**

Analyzing VISUALS

Answers:

1. Most Bush states were in the South and Interior West; most Gore states were in the Northeast, upper Midwest, and Pacific Coast.
2. Answers will vary but should focus on the readability and physical appearance of the ballot cards.

Hands-On Chapter Project
Step 1

Exploring the "Blogosphere"

Step 1: Making a Blog Chart Groups of students will use a blog search engine to search the Internet and identify a variety of blogs. They will chart the information.

Directions Tell groups of students to use a blog search engine to find blogs on different topics. Groups will then chart the information they have collected in three columns. The first column will give the name and Web address of the site. The second column will describe the topic of site information. Topics may cover a range of subjects—from politics to pop culture. The third column will cite what kind of blog it is (private, political, or commercial) and its creator's name.

Summarizing Have students share what they learned about how people use the Internet to communicate. Encourage the class to speculate about the goals of each of the blogs on their charts. **OL**

(Project continues on page 1039)

R Reading Strategy

Summarizing Have students read the first two paragraphs under "Bush v. Gore" and then summarize what they have just read. Remind them that only the main ideas should be included in a summary but that all the main ideas should be included. OL ELL

Analyzing VISUALS

Answers:

1. Answers will vary, but students should support their opinions.
2. The election of 2000 was an extremely close one. Every vote counts in such a close race.

Reading Check

Answer:
The Supreme Court ruled that the hand recounts violated the equal protection clause of the Constitution. Because different vote counters used different standards, the recount did not treat all voters equally.

POLITICAL CARTOONS PRIMARY SOURCE

The Election of 2000

▲ *The candidates are presented as two turkeys arguing over the results with closed captioning provided to translate what they are saying into what they really mean.*

▲ *The close presidential election of 2000 illustrated clearly how important it is for everyone to exercise the right to vote.*

Analyzing VISUALS DBQ

1. **Evaluating** Based on the cartoon on the left, do you think the cartoonist supported Bush or Gore?
2. **Analyzing** Why are the three characters in the cartoon above angry at the man on the right?

Under state law, Florida officials had to certify the results by a certain date. When it became clear that not all of the recounts could be finished in time, Gore went to court to challenge the deadline. The Florida Supreme Court agreed to set a new deadline. At Bush's request, the United States Supreme Court then intervened to decide whether the Florida Supreme Court had acted constitutionally.

While lawyers for Bush and Gore prepared their arguments for the Supreme Court, the hand recounts continued. Despite having more time, not all of the counties where Gore wanted recounts were able to meet the new deadline. On November 26, Florida officials certified Bush the winner by 537 votes.

For more on *Bush* v. *Gore* read the case summary on page R58 in **Supreme Court Case Summaries.**

Bush v. *Gore*

R Although Bush had been declared the winner in Florida, Gore's lawyers headed back to court arguing that thousands of ballots were still uncounted. The Florida Supreme Court ordered all Florida counties to begin a hand recount of ballots rejected by the counting machines. As counting began, the United States Supreme Court ordered the recount to stop until it had issued its ruling.

On December 12, in *Bush* v. *Gore,* the United States Supreme Court ruled 7–2 that the hand recounts in Florida violated the equal protection clause of the Constitution. The Court argued that because different vote counters used different standards, the recount did not treat all voters equally. R

Both federal law and the Constitution require the electoral votes for president to be cast on a certain day. If Florida missed that deadline, its electoral votes would not count. The Court ruled 5–4 that there was not enough time left to conduct a manual recount that would pass constitutional standards. This ruling left Bush the certified winner in Florida. The next day, Gore conceded the election.

Reading Check **Analyzing** Why did the U.S. Supreme Court stop the manual recounts in Florida?

Differentiated Instruction

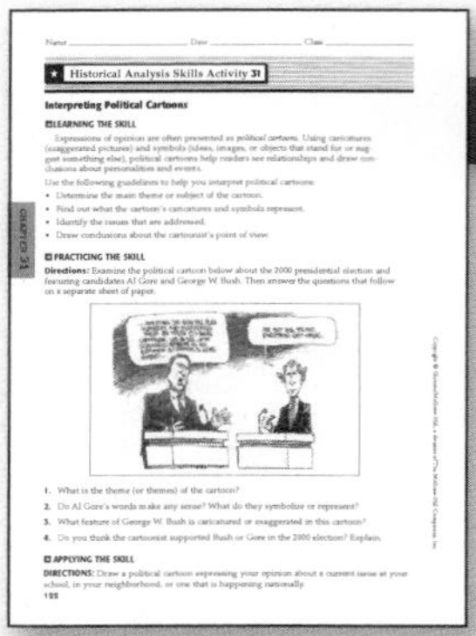

Historical Analysis Skills Activity, URB p. 122

Interpreting Political Cartoons

Objective: Understand how to interpret political cartoons.
Focus: Ask: What is the purpose of political cartoons?
Teach: List the steps to interpreting political cartoons.
Assess: Explain the main idea of this political cartoon.
Close: Find a political cartoon in a recent newsmagazine or newspaper. Bring it to class and interpret it.

Differentiated Instruction Strategies

- **BL** Create a political cartoon on a current national issue.
- **AL** Create a different political cartoon on the same topic.
- **ELL** Explain to a classmate how to interpret a political cartoon.

Bush Becomes President

MAIN Idea George W. Bush supported the enactment of a tax cut, the No Child Left Behind program, and a strategic defense system.

HISTORY AND YOU Have new education policies affected the testing process at your school? Read on to learn more about No Child Left Behind.

On January 20, 2001, George W. Bush became the forty-third president of the United States. In his Inaugural Address, Bush promised to improve the public schools, to cut taxes, to reform Social Security and Medicare, and to build up the nation's defenses.

After taking office, the president's first **priority** was to cut taxes to try to boost the economy. During the election campaign, the stock market dropped sharply, unemployment began to rise, and many new Internet-based companies went out of business. Despite opposition from some Democrats, Congress passed a large $1.35 trillion tax cut to be phased in over 10 years. In the summer of 2001, Americans began receiving tax rebate checks that put about $40 billion back into the economy in an effort to prevent a recession.

C Soon after Congress passed the tax cut plan, President Bush proposed two major reforms in education. He wanted public schools to give annual standardized tests, and he wanted to allow parents to use federal funds to pay for private schools if their public schools were doing a poor job. Although Congress refused to give federal funds to private schools, it did vote in favor of annual reading and math tests in public schools for grades 3–8. This law became known as the No Child Left Behind Act.

President Bush also focused on Medicare reform. By the summer of 2002, Congress had introduced a bill adding prescription drug benefits to Medicare. The bill was **controversial.** Some opponents feared it would cost too much, while others argued that it did not go far enough. The program finally became law in November 2003.

Congress also reacted to a rash of corporate scandals—the most famous taking place at a large energy trading company called Enron. Corporate leaders there cost investors and employees billions of dollars before the company went bankrupt. Congress passed a new law—the Public Company Accounting Reform and Investor Protection Act—also known as the Sarbanes-Oxley Act, after the members of Congress who introduced it. The law tightened accounting rules and toughened penalties for dishonest executives.

Shortly after taking office, President Bush also pushed for new military programs designed to meet the needs of the post–Cold War world. One program Bush strongly favored was **strategic defense**—the effort to develop missiles and other devices that could shoot down nuclear missiles. Bush argued that missile defense was needed because many hostile nations were developing long-range missiles.

As the debate about the nation's military programs continued in the summer of 2001, a horrific event changed everything. On September 11, 2001, terrorists crashed passenger jets into the World Trade Center and the Pentagon. A new war had begun.

Reading Check **Explaining** What was President George W. Bush's first priority when he took office?

Section 1 REVIEW

Vocabulary

1. **Explain** the significance of: Al Gore, George W. Bush, Ralph Nader, chad, strategic defense.

Main Ideas

2. **Paraphrasing** What did the U.S. Supreme Court decide in *Bush* v. *Gore?*
3. **Describing** What did the No Child Left Behind Act mandate?

Critical Thinking

4. **Big Ideas** What caused the vote-count controversy in Florida in the 2000 election?
5. **Organizing** Use a graphic organizer similar to the one below by listing President Bush's goals when he took office.

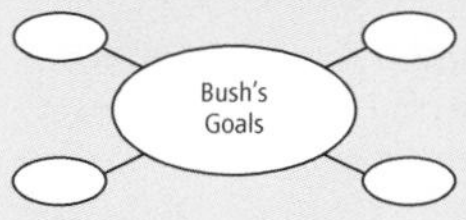

6. **Analyzing Visuals** Study the photos on page 1033. Explain how you would change the voting process following the controversy of the 2000 election.

Writing About History

7. **Persuasive Writing** Take on the role of a Supreme Court justice. Write a statement explaining how you voted in *Bush* v. *Gore* and why you took this position.

History ONLINE
Study Central™ To review this section, go to glencoe.com and click on Study Central.

1035

C Critical Thinking

Making Inferences Ask: What does the phrase "No Child Left Behind" reveal about Bush's reasons for education reform. *(Students may state that Bush wanted to improve learning and ensure that all students have equal access to good schools)* **OL**

Reading Check

Answer:
Bush's first priority was to cut taxes to try to boost the economy.

Assess

History ONLINE

Study Central™ provides summaries, interactive games, and online graphic organizers to help students review content.

Close

Drawing Conclusions
Ask: Why do you think the 2000 presidential election was so close? **OL**

Section 1 REVIEW

Answers

1. All definitions can be found in the section and the Glossary.
2. The Supreme Court decided that hand recounts in Florida were unconstitutional because different voting standards were used that did not treat all voters equally.
3. It mandated annual standardized tests in public schools.
4. Thousands of ballots had been thrown out because the counting machines could not read the voting cards. Then, in the hand recount, different counties used different standards to determine what the voter had intended.
5. Bush's goals were to improve public schools, to cut taxes, to reform Social Security and Medicare, and to build up the nation's defenses.
6. Answers will vary but should focus on simplifying the voting process and ensuring that all votes are counted.
7. Answers will vary but should be supported by reasoned arguments and evidence.

Focus

Bellringer

Daily Focus Transparency 31-2

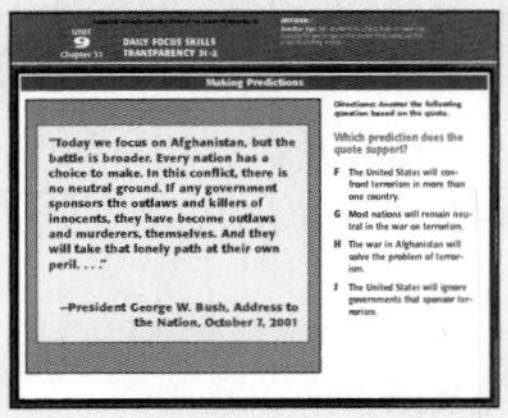

Guide to Reading

Answers:

Causes of Terrorism:
oil wealth and poverty
opposition to Western culture
U.S. support of ruling families
U.S. support of Israel

Section Spotlight Video

To generate student interest and provide a springboard for class discussion, access the Chapter 31, Section 2 video at glencoe.com or on the video DVD.

Resource Manager

Section 2

Section Audio Spotlight Video

The War on Terrorism Begins

Guide to Reading

Big Ideas

Government and Society Acts of terrorism against the United States prompted George W. Bush to declare "War on Terror."

Content Vocabulary

- terrorism *(p. 1038)*
- state-sponsored terrorism *(p. 1039)*
- anthrax *(p. 1041)*

Academic Vocabulary

- resolve *(p. 1037)*
- interpretation *(p. 1038)*
- obtain *(p. 1040)*

People and Events to Identify

- Osama bin Laden *(p. 1037)*
- al-Qaeda *(p. 1037)*

Reading Strategy

Organizing Complete a graphic organizer similar to the one below to show causes of terrorism.

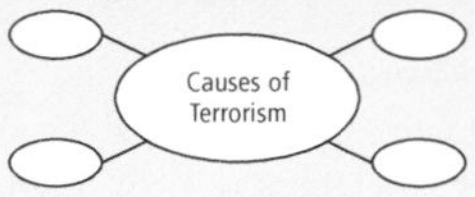

On September 11, 2001, terrorists attacked the United States killing over 3,000 people. The attacks united the nation as Americans worked to help the survivors. President George W. Bush and Congress launched a war on terrorism to prevent such attacks in the future.

September 11, 2001

MAIN Idea The terrorist attacks on the World Trade Center and the Pentagon shocked and alarmed Americans; almost immediately, combating terrorism became the nation's top priority.

HISTORY AND YOU Do you recall learning about the 1919 bombings that triggered government raids and roundups of foreigners? Read on to learn how the United States reacted to the more deadly attacks of 2001.

At 8:45 A.M. Eastern Daylight Time on September 11, 2001, a Boeing 767 passenger jet slammed into the North Tower of the World Trade Center in New York City. As people below gazed in horror, a second plane collided with the South Tower. Soon afterward, a third plane crashed into the Pentagon in Washington, D.C. At 9:50 A.M., the South Tower collapsed in a billowing cloud of dust and debris. The North Tower fell about 40 minutes later. The falling towers killed thousands of people, burying them beneath a vast mound of rubble.

The airplanes did not crash accidentally. Hijackers deliberately crashed them into the buildings. Hijackers also seized a fourth airplane, United Airlines Flight 93, probably hoping to crash it into the White House or the Capitol. Many passengers on Flight 93 had cell phones. After hearing about the World Trade Center, four passengers—Todd Beamer, Thomas Burnett, Jeremy Glick, and Mark Bingham—decided to do something. An operator listening over a cell phone heard Todd Beamer's voice: "Are you ready guys? Let's roll."

Soon afterward, Flight 93 crashed in a field in Pennsylvania. At that moment, Vice President Dick Cheney was in a bunker under the White House. After hearing Flight 93 had crashed, he turned to the others in the room, and said: "I think an act of heroism just took place on that plane."

A National Emergency

The attacks of 9/11, as the day came to be called, killed all 266 passengers and crewmembers on the four hijacked planes. Another 125 people died in the Pentagon. In New York City, nearly 3,000 people died. More Americans were killed in the attacks of September 11,

R Reading Strategies	C Critical Thinking	D Differentiated Instruction	W Writing Support	S Skill Practice
Teacher Edition • Academic Vocab., pp. 1037, 1038 **Additional Resources** • Content Vocab., URB p. 127 • Guided Reading Act., URB p. 149 • Prim. Source Read., URB p. 135	**Teacher Edition** • Determining Cause/Effect, p. 1038 • Evaluating, p. 1039 • Drawing Concl., p. 1039 **Additional Resources** • Quizzes/Tests, p. 442	**Teacher Edition** • Visual/Spatial, p. 1040 **Additional Resources** • English Learner Act., URB p. 125 • Differentiated Instruct. Act., URB p. 123	**Teacher Edition** • Narrative Writing, p. 1037	**Teacher Edition** • Analyz. a Map, p. 1038 **Additional Resources** • Read. Essen., p. 346

Turning Point

The Attacks of September 11, 2001

The terrorist attacks of September 11, 2001, altered the lives of millions of Americans and shifted the priorities of the federal government. At home the United States launched a new war against terrorists and their supporters. Globally, the United States took aggressive and preemptive steps to stop terrorism. At home, the balance between civil liberties and national security shifted, with passage of the USA Patriot Act, which gave broad new powers to the federal government.

MAKING CONNECTIONS How are the terrorist attacks and their aftermath still affecting American society and foreign policy?

Above, the South Tower of the World Trade Center bursts into flames after being struck by an airliner while the North Tower burns from an attack a few minutes earlier. At left, one side of the Pentagon was badly damaged. Part of the building later collapsed. At right, after the World Trade Center towers collapsed, the resulting debris coated the city with dust.

2001, than died at Pearl Harbor or on D-Day in World War II.

The attacks shocked Americans, but they responded rapidly to the crisis. Medical workers and firefighters from other cities raced to New York to help. Across the nation, Americans donated blood and collected food, blankets, and other supplies. Within weeks, Americans also donated over $1 billion. From around the world came sympathy. "We are all Americans!" wrote one French journalist.

Everywhere across the nation, Americans put up flags to show their unity and **resolve.** They held candlelight vigils and prayer services as they searched for ways to help. If the terrorists had hoped to divide Americans, they failed. As the Reverend Billy Graham noted at a memorial service, "A tragedy like this could have torn our country apart. But instead it has united us and we have become a family."

The American government also responded quickly to the crisis. All civilian airplanes were grounded. The armed forces were put on high alert. Across the nation, Americans in the National Guard left their civilian jobs and reported for duty. The Air National Guard began patrolling the skies over major cities, and Army National Guard troops were deployed to airports to strengthen security.

On September 14, President Bush declared a national emergency. Congress authorized the use of force to fight whoever had attacked the United States. Intelligence sources and the FBI quickly identified the attacks as the work of a man named **Osama bin Laden** and his organization, **al-Qaeda** (al KY•duh).

Teach

W Writing Support

Narrative Writing Have students research the response of American public to the 9/11 attacks. Then have them write a descriptive essay explaining how they think the terrorist attacks united Americans and brought a great sense of patriotism to the country. Have volunteers read their essays to the class. AL

R Reading Strategy

Academic Vocabulary Ask students to read the sentence that contains the word *resolve*. Have students list the synonyms and antonyms for the word.

Turning Point

Answer:
Answers will vary but might point out remembrances for those who lost their lives in the 9/11 attacks, the ongoing wars in Afghanistan and Iraq, the effect of the Iraq war on the 2006 congressional elections, and public debate over government intelligence-gathering and citizens' rights.

Additional Support

Activity: Collaborative Learning

Analyzing Information Have students find and bring to class an example of an article that uses both primary and secondary sources to tell the story of the September 11, 2001, terrorist attacks or of the massive relief effort that followed. Have students write a one-page summary of their article identifying the various points of view and explaining how the writer used a variety of source material to paint a picture of the events. As a class, discuss the importance of both types of sources in explaining historical events. OL

S Skill Practice

Analyzing a Map Have the students answer the following questions to help them learn more about current terrorist threats. **Ask:** On what continents have attacks occurred? *(North America, Europe, Africa, and Asia)* What place was attacked twice, and why? *(New York Trade Center; symbol of U.S. economic power)* Why might terrorist attacks have occurred in places other than the United States? *(Countries supporting U.S. policies or having Western residents or visitors)* **OL**

R Reading Strategy

Academic Vocabulary Ask students to read the sentence that contains the word *interpretation*. Then ask them to rewrite the sentence in their own words. **OL**

C Critical Thinking

Determining Cause and Effect Ask: What is the relationship between the oil industry and Middle East terrorism? *(The U.S. invested in the oil industry and supported the ruling families. Many Muslims resented this support, as well as the influence of Western ideas.)* **OL**

Additional Support

NATIONAL GEOGRAPHIC **Major Terrorist Attacks Involving Al-Qaeda, 1993–Present**

S

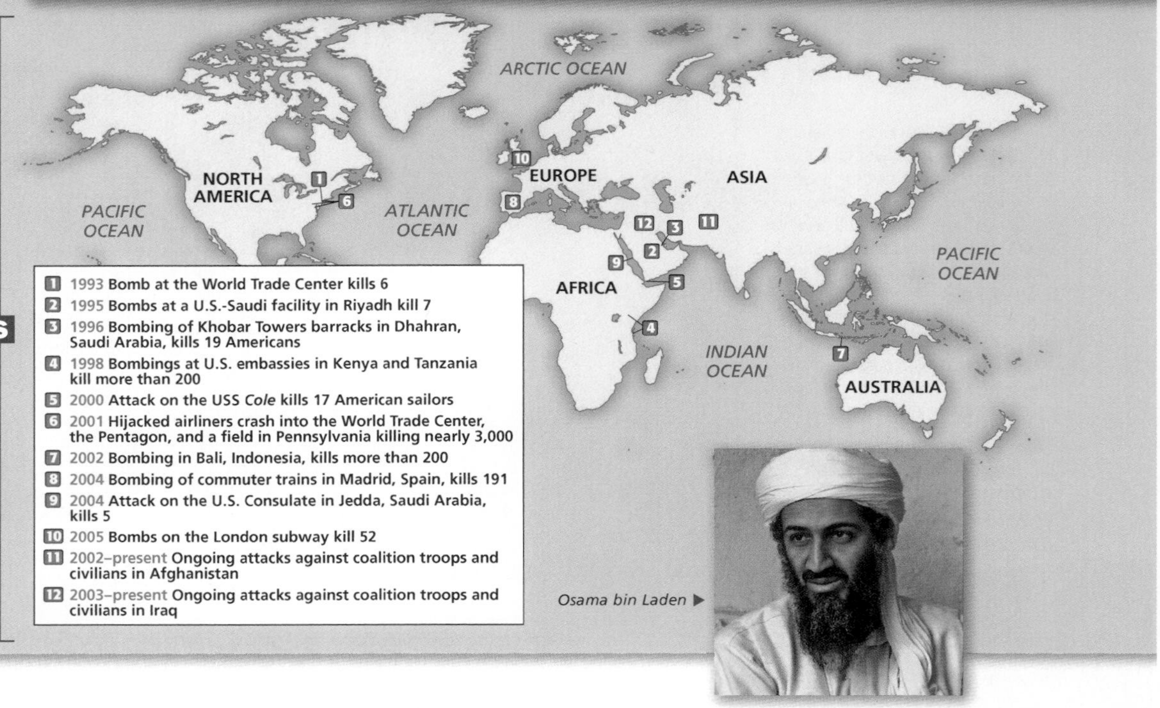

Osama bin Laden ▶

Middle East Terrorism and the United States

The attacks on the World Trade Center and the Pentagon were acts of terrorism. **Terrorism** is the use of violence by nongovernmental groups against civilians to achieve a political goal. Terrorist acts are intended to instill fear in people and to force governments into changing their policies.

Most terrorist attacks on Americans since World War II have been carried out by Middle Eastern groups. The reason Middle Eastern terrorists have targeted Americans can be traced back to events early in the twentieth century.

C As oil became important to the American economy in the 1920s, the United States invested heavily in the Middle East oil industry. This industry brought great wealth to the ruling families in some Middle Eastern kingdoms, but most people remained poor. Some became angry at the United States for supporting the wealthy kingdoms and families.

The rise of the oil industry also led to the spread of Western ideas in the region, and many Muslims feared that their traditional values were being weakened. Islamic movements that had been calling for a strict **interpretation** of the Quran—the Muslim holy book—and a return to traditional Muslim religious laws during the previous two centuries now gained more support. Their ideas gave birth to Muslim organizations that wanted to overthrow pro-Western governments in the Middle East and create a pure Islamic society. Muslims who support these organizations are referred to as fundamentalist militants. Some militants began using terrorism to achieve their goals. R C

American support of Israel angered many in the Middle East. In 1947, following the global outrage over the Jewish Holocaust, the UN proposed to divide the British Mandate of Palestine into an Arab state and a Jewish state. The Jews accepted and established Israel in 1948. Arab states responded by attacking Israel. The territory that the UN had proposed as an Arab state

Activity: Connecting with the United States

International Response to Terrorism Have students work in groups and use the library or Internet resources to research three of the terrorist attacks that occurred outside of the United States. Have the groups write and present oral reports describing the attacks and the response in the particular countries where the attacks took place. Students' reports should include photos, maps, or other visual aids. Then ask the class to compare these events to those of the attacks of 9/11 in the United States. Discuss how responses vary from country to country. **OL**

came under the control of Israel, Jordan, and Egypt. In the 1950s, Palestinians began staging guerrilla raids and terrorist attacks against Israel. Since the United States gave aid to Israel, it became the target of Muslim hostility. In the 1970s, several Middle East nations realized they could fight Israel and the United States by providing terrorists with money, weapons, and training. This is called **state-sponsored terrorism.** The governments of Libya, Syria, Iraq, and Iran have all sponsored terrorists.

The Rise of Al-Qaeda

In 1979 the Soviet Union invaded Afghanistan. In response, Muslims from across the world headed to Afghanistan to help fight the Soviets. Among them was a wealthy 22-year-old Saudi Arabian named Osama bin Laden. In 1988 he founded an organization called al-Qaeda or "the Base." Al-Qaeda recruited Muslims and channeled money and arms to the Afghan resistance.

Bin Laden believed that superpowers could be beaten. He also believed that Western ideas had contaminated Muslim society and was outraged by Saudi Arabia's decision to allow American troops to be based on Saudi soil after Iraq invaded Kuwait.

At first, bin Laden ran al-Qaeda from camps in Sudan, but in 1996, he moved back to Afghanistan after the Taliban, a militant Muslim fundamentalist group, took power there. Bin Laden dedicated himself to driving Westerners out of the Middle East. In 1998 he called on Muslims to kill Americans. His followers set off bombs at the American embassies in Kenya and Tanzania.

After these bombings, President Clinton ordered cruise missiles fired at terrorist camps in Afghanistan and Sudan, but bin Laden was not deterred. In 1999, al-Qaeda terrorists were arrested while trying to smuggle explosives into the United States in an attempt to bomb Seattle. In October 2000, al-Qaeda terrorists crashed a boat loaded with explosives into the *USS Cole*, an American warship, while it was docked in Yemen. Then, on September 11, 2001, al-Qaeda struck again, hijacking four American passenger planes and executing the most devastating terrorist attack in history.

Reading Check **Explaining** Why was Osama bin Laden able to create a terrorist organization?

A New War Begins

MAIN Idea The war on terrorism involved halting terrorists' access to funding and launching a war in Afghanistan.

HISTORY AND YOU Does your school have plans for coping with an emergency? Read on to learn about the national response to the terrorist attacks.

In an address to Congress on September 20, 2001, President Bush demanded the Taliban regime in Afghanistan turn over bin Laden and his supporters and shut down all terrorist camps. The president then made it clear that although the war on terrorism would start by targeting al-Qaeda, it would not stop there. "It will not end," the president announced, "until every terrorist group of global reach has been found, stopped, and defeated." While Secretary of State Colin Powell began building an international coalition to support the United States, Secretary of Defense Donald Rumsfeld began deploying troops, aircraft, and warships to the Middle East.

The president also announced that the United States would no longer tolerate states that aided terrorists: "From this day forward," the president proclaimed, "any nation that continues to harbor or support terrorism will be regarded by the United States as a hostile regime." The war would not end quickly, but it was a war the nation had to fight: C1

Primary Source

"Great harm has been done to us. We have suffered great loss. And in our grief and anger we have found our mission and our moment. . . . Our Nation—this generation—will lift a dark threat of violence from our people and our future."

—President George W. Bush, *Address to Joint Session of Congress*, September 20, 2001

In a letter to the *New York Times*, Secretary of Defense Rumsfeld warned Americans that "this will be a war like none other our nation has faced." The enemy, he explained, "is a global network of terrorist organizations and their state sponsors, committed to denying free people the opportunity to live as they choose." Fighting terrorism would not be easy. Military force would be used, but terrorism had to be fought by other means as well. C2

For a longer excerpt from this speech read, "President Bush's Address to Joint Session of Congress, September 20, 2001" on page R57 of **Documents in American History.**

C1 Critical Thinking

Evaluating Ask students to draw up a list for determining if the United States's war on terror is succeeding. Remind them to look at both short term and long-term success. Have them suggest changes to the nation's policies that may lead to better success. **OL**

C2 Critical Thinking

Drawing Conclusions Ask: What did Defense Secretary Rumsfeld mean when he said in 2001 that the war on terror would be "a war like none other our nation has faced"? *(Past wars involved fighting other countries that had standing armies, while the war on terror involves dealing with underground groups, in some cases sponsored by governments, who carry out attacks on civilians.)* **OL**

Reading Check

Answer:
He used his personal wealth to build a terrorist organization and relied on fighters trained during the Afghan resistance against the Soviet Union.

Hands-On Chapter Project Step 2

Exploring the "Blogosphere"

Step 2: Blog Quotes Students will make posters using quotes from blogs selected from the chart they compiled in Step 1.

Directions Write the Big Idea on the board. Have student groups select a quote from three of the blogs found on their charts. Ask students to make a poster for each quote. Each poster should include the quote in large enough type to be easily read. The posters should also include photographs from newspapers, magazines, and the Internet that illustrate the meaning of the quote.

Summarizing Have students present their posters to the class. Ask the class to match the posters to blogs on the chart compiled in Step 1. Have them discuss in what ways, if any, the blogs from which they have quoted strengthen or threaten democracy. **OL**

(Project continued on page 1044)

D Differentiated Instruction

Visual/Spatial Have students work in pairs to design a memorial to the victims and heroes of the September 11, 2001, terrorist attacks. Encourage students to use library and Internet resources to learn about the designs of other memorials. Have students note how symbolism is used in the design of many memorials. Have the pairs write a paragraph explaining the symbolism they chose for their memorial. **OL**

Analyzing VISUALS

Answers:

1. They felt a sense of personal loss because the attacks were carried out on innocent people living their everyday lives.
2. Answers will vary but might include more security checks at public places, especially at airports.

PRIMARY SOURCE

Responding to 9/11

After the attacks, Americans held vigils and prayer services to remember and honor those who had died. For months after the attacks, Americans closely followed the efforts of firefighters and rescue workers. Despite increased airport security, the attacks left some Americans wary of air travel.

At left, Alana Milawski, waves an American flag during a candlelight vigil in Las Vegas on September 12, 2001. Above, firefighters work in the rubble of the World Trade Center. The attacks led to an increase in airline security (right) resulting in long lines at airports while passengers waited to be screened.

Analyzing VISUALS

1. **Theorizing** Why do you think so many people participated in group vigils and memorials after the attacks?
2. **Evaluating** In what ways were Americans most immediately affected by the attacks of September 11, 2001?

Cutting Terrorist Funding One effective way to fight terrorist groups is to cut off their funding. On September 24, President Bush issued an executive order freezing the financial assets of several individuals and groups suspected of terrorism. As information about terrorist groups increased, more names and organizations were added to the list. President Bush asked other nations to help, and within weeks, some 80 nations had issued orders freezing the assets of the organizations and individuals on the American list.

Homeland Security and the Patriot Act

As part of the effort to protect the American people from further terrorist attacks, President Bush created a new federal agency—the Office of Homeland Security—to coordinate the dozens of federal agencies and departments working to prevent terrorism. He then appointed Pennsylvania governor Tom Ridge to serve as the agency's director.

History ONLINE Student Web Activity Visit glencoe.com and complete the activity on the war on terrorism.

The president also asked Congress to pass legislation to help law enforcement agencies track down terrorist suspects. Drafting the legislation took time. Congress had to balance Americans' Fourth Amendment protections against unreasonable search and seizure with the need to increase security. President Bush signed the antiterrorist bill—known as the USA Patriot Act—into law in October 2001. In cases involving terrorism, the law permitted secret searches to avoid tipping off suspects and allowed authorities to **obtain** a nationwide search warrant useable in any jurisdiction. The law also made it easier to wiretap suspects and allowed authorities to track Internet communications and seize voice mail.

In the months following the attack, the Office of Homeland Security struggled to coordinate all of the federal agencies fighting terrorism. In June 2002, President Bush asked Congress to combine all of the agencies responsible for the public's safety into a new

Additional Support

Activity: Connecting with the United States

Identifying Ask: **Do you know what agencies are included in the Department of Homeland Security?** Divide the class into groups, and have each group research the structure of the Department of Homeland Security and the agencies it now includes. Tell the groups to use their findings to create an organizational chart that shows the following directorates of the department: Border and Transportation Security, Emergency Preparedness and Response, Science and Technology, Information Analysis and Infrastructure Protection; describes the general responsibilities of each; and lists the agencies under the umbrella of each. Students' charts also should include agencies in the department that are not part of a directorate. Then ask each student to select an agency and find out how it contributes to the protection of the United States. Have students share what they discover in a class discussion. **AL**

department called the Department of Homeland Security. The plan called for the largest reorganization of the federal government since 1947, when Congress created the Department of Defense, the National Security Council, and the CIA.

The president's proposal led to an intense debate in Congress, and it did not pass until after the midterm elections in November 2002. The new Department of Homeland Security controls the Coast Guard, the Border Patrol, the Immigration and Naturalization Service, the Customs Service, the Federal Emergency Management Agency, and many other agencies. It also analyzes information collected by the FBI, the CIA, and other intelligence agencies.

Bioterrorism Strikes the United States As the nation struggled to cope with the attacks on the Pentagon and the World Trade Center, another terrorist attack began. On October 5, 2001, a newspaper editor in Florida died from an anthrax infection. **Anthrax** is a type of bacteria. Several nations, including the United States, Russia, and Iraq, have used anthrax to create biological weapons. Antibiotics can cure anthrax, but if left untreated, it can quickly become lethal.

Soon after its appearance in Florida, anthrax was found at the offices of news organizations in New York City. In Washington, D.C., a letter containing anthrax arrived at Senator Tom Daschle's office. It was now clear that terrorists were using the mail to spread anthrax. Traces of anthrax were found at several government buildings. Several postal workers who had handled letters containing anthrax contracted the disease, and two workers died. The FBI began investigating the attack, but no suspects were arrested.

The War in Afghanistan Begins

On October 7, 2001, the United States began bombing al-Qaeda's camps and the Taliban's military forces in Afghanistan. In an address to the nation, President Bush explained that Islam and the Afghan people were not the enemy, and that the United States would send food, medicine, and other supplies to Afghan refugees. The president also explained that the attack on the Taliban was only the beginning. The war on terrorism would continue until victory was achieved:

PRIMARY SOURCE

"Today we focus on Afghanistan, but the battle is broader. Every nation has a choice to make. In this conflict, there is no neutral ground. If any government sponsors the outlaws and killers of innocents, they have become outlaws and murderers, themselves. And they will take that lonely path at their own peril. . . . The battle is now joined on many fronts. We will not waver; we will not tire; we will not falter; and we will not fail. Peace and freedom will prevail. Thank you. May God continue to bless America."

—President George W. Bush, Address to the Nation, October 7, 2001

Reading Check **Outlining** What steps did the president take in response to the terrorist attacks?

Section 2 REVIEW

Vocabulary

1. **Explain** the significance of: Osama bin Laden, al-Qaeda, terrorism, state-sponsored terrorism, anthrax.

Main Ideas

2. **Describing** What factors have contributed to the rise of anti-American terrorism based in the Middle East?
3. **Listing** What major actions marked the beginning of the United States' war on terrorism?

Critical Thinking

4. **Big Ideas** Why do Islamic fundamentalists in the Middle East disagree with U.S. foreign policy?
5. **Categorizing** Use a graphic organizer similar to the one below to list the responses of individual Americans and the federal government to the attacks on September 11, 2001.

6. **Analyzing Visuals** Study the map of terrorist attacks on page 1038. How would you describe the scope of al-Qaeda's operation?

Writing About History

7. **Persuasive Writing** The Patriot Act gave law enforcement new ways to fight terrorism. Write a letter to a newspaper explaining why you are either for or against giving up some freedoms in exchange for increased security.

History ONLINE
Study Central™ To review this section, go to glencoe.com and click on Study Central.

Reading Check

Answer:
He froze financial assets of terrorist groups, created a new federal department to coordinate government efforts to prevent terrorism, signed legislation empowering government officials to hunt down terrorists, and sent the military to overthrow the pro-terrorist Taliban government in Afghanistan.

Assess

History ONLINE

Study Central™ provides summaries, interactive games, and online graphic organizers to help students review content.

Close

Summarizing Ask: How did the United States respond to the terrorist attacks of September 11, 2001? OL

Section 2 REVIEW

Answers

1. All definitions can be found in the section and the Glossary.
2. U.S. support of wealthy oil countries and ruling families, Western influences undermining traditional values and beliefs, U.S. troops stationed in Saudi Arabia and Kuwait, and American support for Israel
3. Freezing terrorist assets, more government anti-terrorist programs, increased security, and more U.S. forces in the Middle East
4. They resent the use of American power to spread Western political, cultural, and economic influences to the Middle East; they oppose U.S. support for the Jewish nation of Israel.
5. Individuals: medical workers and firefighters helped in New York, citizens donated blood, collected supplies, gave money to relief efforts, and commemorated the dead; Government: froze terrorist funds, reorganized bureaucracy and expanded efforts to hunt down terrorists, mandated security procedures, and used the military to remove pro-terrorist Taliban government in Afghanistan
6. Answers will vary but might mention the world-wide scope of terrorist operations from North America to Europe and Southeast Asia.
7. Answers will vary but should be supported by reasoned arguments and evidence.

Focus

Bellringer

Daily Focus Transparency 31-3

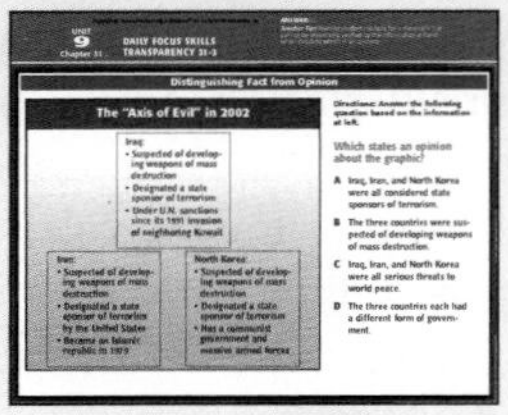

Guide to Reading

Answers:

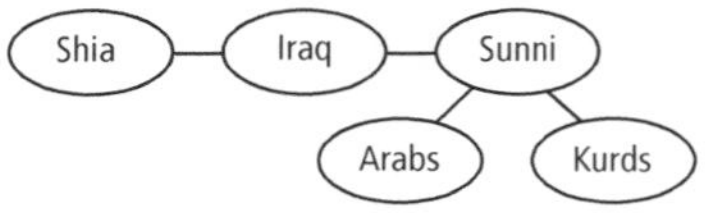

Section Spotlight Video

To generate student interest and provide a springboard for class discussion, access the Chapter 31, Section 3 video at glencoe.com or on the video DVD.

Section 3

Section Audio   Spotlight Video

The Invasion of Iraq

Guide to Reading

Big Ideas

Trade, War, and Migration In an effort to fight terrorism, the United States launched attacks in both Afghanistan and Iraq.

Content Vocabulary

- weapons of mass destruction (WMD) *(p. 1044)*

Academic Vocabulary

- inspector *(p. 1045)*
- significantly *(p. 1046)*
- eliminate *(p. 1047)*

People and Events to Identify

- Northern Alliance *(p. 1042)*
- Khalid Shaikh Mohammed *(p. 1043)*
- "axis of evil" *(p. 1044)*
- Saddam Hussein *(p. 1045)*

Reading Strategy

As you read this section on the Invasion of Iraq, complete a graphic organizer similar to the one below to show the different groups in Iraq.

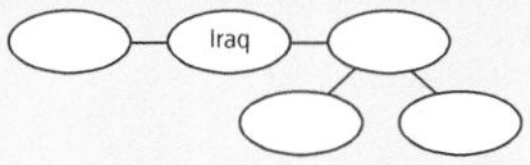

After the attacks of September 11, 2001, the United States invaded Afghanistan, the Central Asian nation that had sheltered many al-Qaeda members. In March 2003, the United States invaded Iraq and toppled the regime of Saddam Hussein.

The War on Terror Continues

MAIN Idea After forcing Taliban leaders in Afghanistan to flee, the United States and its allies sent more troops as peacekeepers and worked to create a stable and democratic government.

HISTORY AND YOU Can you think of a nation or region today where peacekeepers are stationed while a new government is established? Read on to learn about the role of peacekeepers in Afghanistan.

Less than a month after the September 11 attacks, the United States launched a war in Afghanistan with the goal of bringing down the Taliban regime that had sheltered Osama bin Laden and other members of al-Qaeda. Americans also hoped that bin Laden would be captured and brought back for trial in the United States.

While American warplanes bombed the Taliban's forces, the United States began sending military aid to the **Northern Alliance,** a coalition of Afghan groups that had been fighting the Taliban for several years. U.S. Special Forces also entered Afghanistan to advise the Northern Alliance and identify targets for American aircraft. The American bombing campaign quickly shattered the Taliban's defenses. The Northern Alliance then launched a massive attack. In December 2001, the Taliban government collapsed, and surviving Taliban fled to the mountains of Afghanistan.

Rebuilding Afghanistan

After the Taliban fled, the United States and its allies helped local Afghan leaders create a new government. Meanwhile, thousands of American and allied troops arrived to act as peacekeepers. In 2003 NATO took command of peacekeeping in Afghanistan.

Since 2002 Afghanistan has begun to slowly recover from decades of war. The economy has grown rapidly, although the people remain very poor. The United States and its allies have donated some $24 billion to help rebuild the country. In December 2004, Afghanistan held its first nationwide democratic election, and Hamid Karzai was elected president. One year later, the Afghan people elected a National Assembly. Despite these successes, Afghanistan continues to suffer from violence. Taliban insurgents have staged guerrilla

Resource Manager

R Reading Strategies	C Critical Thinking	D Differentiated Instruction	W Writing Support	S Skill Practice
Teacher Edition • Activate. Prior Knowl., p. 1044 **Additional Resources** • Guided Reading Act., URB p. 150	**Teacher Edition** • Identify Issues, p. 1043 • Analyz. Info., p. 1044 **Additional Resources** • Quizzes/Tests, p. 443	**Teacher Edition** • Special Education, p. 1046	**Teacher Edition** • Persuas. Writing, p. 1046	**Teacher Edition** • Reading a Time Line, p. 1045 **Additional Resources** • Read. Essen., p. 349

PRIMARY SOURCE

The War in Afghanistan

The United States invaded Afghanistan to overthrow the Taliban regime. Helping to establish a democratic government was the next step.

▲ American soldiers were sent to act as peacekeepers while the new Afghan government tried to establish order in the mountainous country.

▲ The new Afghan constitution granted equal rights to women, including the right to vote.

▶ Hamid Karzai was elected president in 2004.

Analyzing VISUALS

1. **Speculating** What part of their duties do you think these soldiers find most difficult?
2. **Predicting** How may voting rights for women affect the development of the new Afghan government?

attacks and suicide bombings. The Afghan government has little control over the mountainous regions of southern Afghanistan and fighting continues between NATO and Taliban forces in the south.

Bin Laden Goes Into Hiding

According to news reports, American intelligence agencies believe Osama bin Laden crossed into Pakistan to hide in the mountainous region of Waziristan where the local people were friendly to al-Qaeda and the Taliban. Between 2002 and 2006, bin Laden released a number of audiotapes and one videotape urging his followers to continue the fight.

C Pakistan has not officially allowed American troops to enter its territory to find bin Laden, although news reports suggest U.S. Special Forces may be operating in the area. Pakistan has itself launched several military operations in Waziristan in search of al-Qaeda and Taliban forces. Although many al-Qaeda operatives have been arrested in Pakistan, Osama bin Laden remains at large.

Tracking Down Al-Qaeda

Since 2001, the United States and its allies have continued their worldwide hunt for al-Qaeda members. Hundreds of people have been captured or killed, including several top leaders of al-Qaeda. In November 2002, the CIA used an unmanned remote-controlled flying drone to fire a missile at a car in Yemen killing everyone in the vehicle. The car had been carrying top al-Qaeda leaders who had planned the attack on the USS *Cole* in 1998.

In 2003, Pakistan and the United States captured **Khalid Shaikh Mohammed**—one of the highest ranking members of al-Qaeda, and the man suspected of planning the September 11 attacks. Between 2002 and 2006, the American government believes that at least 10 major attacks by al-Qaeda, including at least three attacks on the United States and two on Great Britain, have been prevented.

✓Reading Check **Describing** What strategy has the United States used to prevent the Taliban from regaining power?

Teach

C Critical Thinking

Identifying Central Issues

Ask: Would the finding of Osama bin Laden bring a significant end to terrorist activities by groups such as al-Qaeda? *(Answers will vary. Some students might state that finding bin Laden would be a severe blow; others might state that other terrorist leaders would arise)* **AL**

Analyzing VISUALS

Answers:

1. Answers will vary but might mention dealing with unexpected terrorist attacks as well as handling cultural differences between Afghan and American ways of life
2. Women will be able to have influence on government policies.

✓Reading Check

Answer:
The U.S. has helped set up a democratic government, has sent aid to rebuild the country, and contributes military support.

Additional Support

Activity: Interdisciplinary Connection

Geography Provide students with an outline map of Afghanistan. Have students create a series of maps showing the progress of Northern Alliance forces against the Taliban forces. Each map should show major cities and major physical features of Afghanistan. The maps should indicate the approximate areas controlled by opposing sides on each date chosen. Encourage students to create a minimum of five maps, using October 7, 2001 as the date of the first map. Have students display the completed maps in time line fashion. **AL**

R Reading Strategy

Activating Prior Knowledge Remind students that they studied the term *state-sponsored terrorism* in Section 1. Have them explain its relationship to the phrase *axis of evil*. *(Governments, such as those of the axis of evil, sponsor terrorism by supplying arms and funding to terrorist groups to fight wars instead of committing their own military forces.)* **OL**

C Critical Thinking

Analyzing Information Ask: In what way are weapons of mass destruction more dangerous today than during the Cold War? *(During the Cold War, the threat of counterattack kept the superpowers from using the weapons. Today, the weapons can be spread secretly by nations to terrorists who could use them without being known or located.)* **OL**

Iraq and Weapons of Mass Destruction

MAIN Idea Concern that Iraq might be producing WMDs that could be given to terrorists led to an ultimatum.

HISTORY AND YOU Do you think the UN is an effective mediator of world affairs? Read on to learn about UN actions before the Iraq War.

The terrorist attacks of September 11, 2001 showed that groups such as al-Qaeda were determined to kill as many Americans as possible. President Bush and his advisers were deeply concerned that terrorist groups might acquire **weapons of mass destruction** (WMD). Weapons of mass destruction can kill large numbers of people all at once. Nuclear, chemical, and biological weapons are all examples of weapons of mass destruction.

C During the Cold War, very few nations had weapons of mass destruction, and the United States relied upon a policy of deterrence to prevent their use. The United States announced that if any nation used weapons of mass destruction against the United States, the United States would counterattack with its own weapons of mass destruction. Deterrence worked during the Cold War, but the rise of state-sponsored terrorism created a new problem. If a nation secretly gave weapons of mass destruction to terrorists who then used them against the United States, the American military might not know where the weapons came from, or whom to attack in response. C

The "Axis of Evil"

In his State of the Union speech in 2002, President Bush warned that an **"axis of evil"** made up of Iraq, Iran, and North Korea posed a grave threat to the world. Each of these nations had been known to sponsor terrorism, and was suspected of developing weapons of mass destruction. The president warned that "The United States of America will not permit the world's most dangerous regimes to threaten us with the world's most destructive weapons." R

Of the three nations in the "axis of evil," the president and his advisers believed Iraq to be the most immediate danger. It had used chem-

THE Global War ON Terror, 2001–2007

Oct. 7, 2001 The United States launches attacks on Taliban positions in Afghanistan

March 20, 2003 American and coalition forces begin the invasion of Iraq

2001 2002 2003

Sept. 11, 2001 Terrorists highjack four planes and attack the World Trade Center and the Pentagon

Nov. 2002 UN Resolution warns Iraq to allow weapons inspectors to return

March 1, 2003 Khalid Shaikh Mohammed, suspected of planning the 9/11 attacks, is captured

Sept. 2003 Eleven countries form the Proliferation Security Initiative to intercept shipments of materials used to make weapons of mass destruction

Hands-On Chapter Project Step 3

Exploring the "Blogosphere"

Step 3: Blogging Students will work in groups to create their own blog.

Directions Write the Big Idea on the board. Remind students that they have the responsibility to practice free speech in a constructive manner. Any criticism they make should be useful and not abusive. Have student groups use the charts and posters they created in Steps 1 and 2 to brainstorm ideas for a blog topic. Remind students that the content of their blog must meet school standards. When students have selected a topic and a name for their blogs, have them collaborate on writing the first entries for their blogs.

Summarizing Have students read their blog entries to the class. Encourage the class to discuss how they chose their blog topics and how school standards influenced what they wrote. **OL**

(Project continued on page 1054)

ical weapons against the Kurds, an ethnic group in northern Iraq, and after the 1991 Gulf War, UN **inspectors** had also found evidence that Iraq had developed biological weapons and had been working on a nuclear bomb.

Between 1991 and 1998, Iraq appeared to be hiding its weapons of mass destruction from UN inspectors. In 1998 the Iraqi government ordered the inspectors to leave the country. In response, President Clinton ordered a massive bombing attack on Iraq to destroy its ability to make such weapons. Despite the attack, intelligence agencies continued to believe Iraq was hiding weapons of mass destruction.

An Ultimatum to Iraq

In 2002 President Bush decided the time had come to deal with Iraq. On September 12, he delivered a speech to the United Nations asking for a new resolution against Iraq. If Iraq's dictator, **Saddam Hussein,** wanted peace he would have to give up Iraq's weapons of mass destruction, readmit the UN weapons inspectors, stop supporting terrorism, and stop oppressing his people. Although he was asking the UN to pass a resolution, the president made it clear that the United States would act with or without UN support.

While the UN Security Council debated a new resolution, President Bush asked Congress to authorize the use of force against Iraq, which it did. With the midterm elections only weeks away, Democrats wanted to focus on the nation's high unemployment rate and the slow economy. Instead, President Bush successfully kept the focus on national security issues. In 2002 Republicans picked up seats in the House of Representatives and regained control of the Senate.

Soon after the American elections, the UN approved a new resolution setting a deadline for Iraq to readmit weapons inspectors. It also required Iraq to declare its weapons of mass destruction, to stop supporting terrorism, and to stop oppressing its people. It threatened "serious consequences" if Iraq did not comply.

Reading Check **Analyzing** Why did the United States think stopping the spread of weapons of mass destruction was linked to the war on terror?

Oct. 29, 2004 Osama bin Laden releases a video warning Americans that they will never have security if they continue their attacks

Oct., 2004 Iraq Survey Group issues its final report concluding Iraq did not have weapons of mass destruction at the time the war began

Jan. 31, 2005 Iraqis go to the polls in their first free election

Oct. 2005 American deaths in the war in Iraq surpass 2,000

June 2006 Al-Zarqawi, the leader of al-Qaeda in Iraq, is killed in a U.S. attack

Jan. 2007 President Bush announces he will send 20,000 more troops to Iraq to restore order in Baghdad

2004 | 2005 | 2006 | 2007

Analyzing TIME LINES

1. **Sequencing** Which happened first—the U.S. attack on Afghanistan or the invasion of Iraq?
2. **Specifying** When did Iraqis hold their first free election?

S Skill Practice

Reading a Time Line Ask: What was the major report released in October 2004? *(a report on Iraqi weapons of mass destruction)* Who released the report? *(the Iraq Survey Group)* What did the report conclude? *(Iraq did not have weapons of mass destruction at the time the Iraq War began.)* Why were the report's findings important? *(Bush had justified going to war on the basis of intelligence reports claiming that Iraq had weapons of mass destruction. The report cast doubt on this justification.)* **OL**

Analyzing TIME LINES

Answers:
1. Invasion of Afghanistan
2. January 31, 2005

Reading Check

Answer:
The U.S. feared the spread of weapons of mass destruction to terrorist groups.

Differentiated Instruction

Leveled Activities

BL Content Vocabulary Activity, URB, p. 127

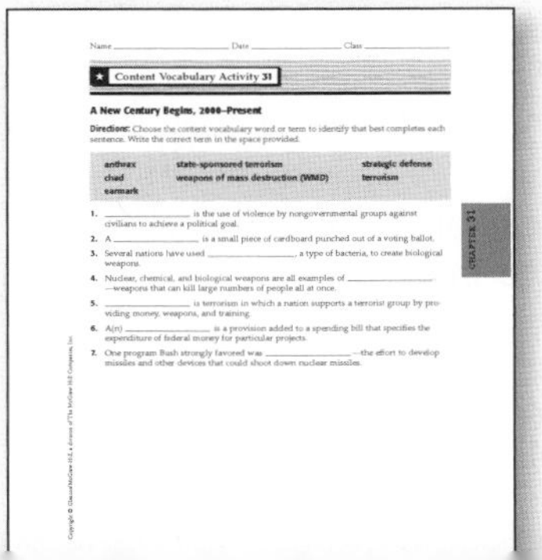

OL Reading Skills Activity, URB p. 121

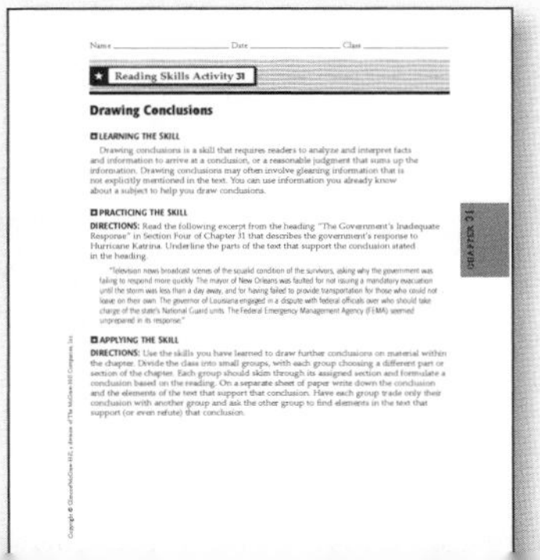

AL Linking Past and Present Activity, URB p. 134

ELL English Learner Activity, URB p. 125

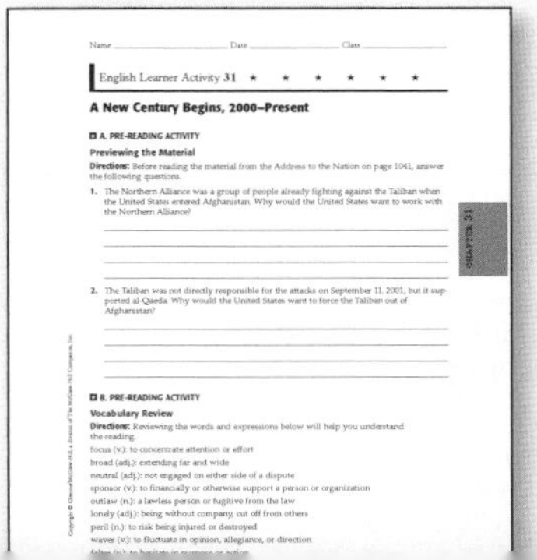

W Writing Support

Persuasive Writing Have students write a newspaper editorial supporting or opposing President Bush's decision to attack Iraq without UN Security Council support. Students should provide reasons for their positions. **AL**

D Differentiated Instruction

Special Education Help students identify the pointers that connect each picture with its caption. Explore what additional information the image teaches about the topic discussed in the caption. **OL**

Analyzing VISUALS

Answers:

1. Answers will vary but might include bringing peace, order, or security to Iraq.
2. Answers will vary but might mention the need for cooperation among Iraq's ethnic groups in order for democracy to work.

Confronting Iraq

MAIN Idea Coalition forces defeated the Iraqi military, but then factions in Iraq took up arms against coalition forces and each other.

HISTORY AND YOU In retrospect, do you believe the invasion of Iraq was justified? Read on to learn more about the different stages of the war.

In November 2002, Iraq agreed to readmit UN weapons inspectors. It then submitted a statement admitting it had weapons of mass destruction before the Gulf War, but denying it currently had weapons of mass destruction. Secretary of State Colin Powell declared that Iraq's declaration contained lies and was in "material breach" of the UN resolution.

W As the United States and a coalition of some 30 nations prepared for war with Iraq, others at the UN Security Council argued that the inspectors should be given more time to find evidence of Iraq's WMD programs. By March 2003, the inspectors still had found nothing, and the United States began pressing the UN to authorize the use of force against Iraq.

France and Russia, two Security Council members with veto power, refused to back such a resolution. As war became imminent, world opinion divided between those who supported the United States and those who opposed an attack on Iraq. Around the world antiwar protestors staged rallies and marches. Several nations that had supported the United States in its war on terror, and had sent troops to Afghanistan, including France, Germany, and Canada, refused to join the coalition against Iraq. Saudi Arabia and Turkey—both American allies—refused to allow the United States to attack Iraq from their territories. The only nation bordering Iraq that granted permission to use its territory was Kuwait. W

The Invasion Begins

On March 20, 2003, the U.S.-led coalition forces attacked Iraq. Over 150,000 American troops, some 45,000 British troops, as well as a few hundred special forces from Australia and Poland took part in the invasion.

Much of the Iraqi army dissolved as soldiers refused to risk their lives for Hussein. A few fierce battles took place, but the Iraqis were unable to slow the coalition advance **significantly.** On May 1, President Bush declared

PRIMARY SOURCE
The Invasion of Iraq

Overthrowing Saddam Hussein to ensure he could not give WMDs to terrorists was the primary objective of the invasion. Ousting his regime, however, proved easier than establishing a new government.

D

▲ U.S. and Iraqi soldiers face the difficult challenge of urban warfare in Iraq where the enemy can be very close, hiding behind walls or in buildings.

▲ After decades of sham elections, Iraqi voters get to make real choices when they vote during Iraq's 2005 elections.

Analyzing VISUALS

1. **Speculating** What do you suppose these soldiers hope to accomplish in fulfilling their duties?
2. **Predicting** Will regularly-scheduled elections lead to a more stable national government?

Differentiated Instruction

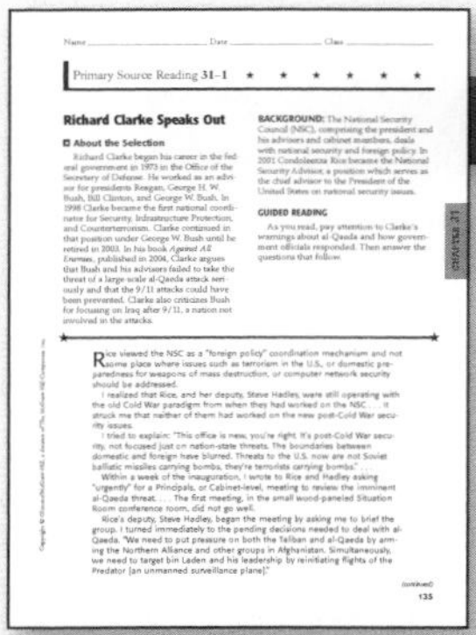

Primary Source Reading, URB p. 135

Richard Clarke Speaks Out

Objective: To review high-level discussions of foreign policy

Focus: Have students discuss the scene of this excerpt.

Teach: Outline the message of the excerpt.

Assess: Summarize Clarke's warnings.

Differentiated Instruction Strategies

BL Summarize Clarke's warning and the reaction to it.

AL Research to find other primary sources regarding the U.S. government's response to al-Qaeda. Summarize the content to share with the class.

ELL What is the NSC?

that the major combat was over. About 140 Americans and several thousand Iraqis had died. Saddam Hussein was captured in late 2003. After a prolonged trial, an Iraqi court found him guilty of ordering mass executions. He was executed in 2006.

Insurgents and Reconstruction

The quick victory did not end the fighting. Soon after the coalition took control of the country, small groups of Iraqis began staging bombings, sniper attacks, and sporadic battles against coalition forces. Some of the groups carrying out the attacks were former members of Saddam Hussein's military. Others were affiliated with al-Qaeda and other radical Muslim groups who believed the invasion offered a chance to build support in the Muslim world by organizing resistance to the Americans.

Some of the attacks were carried out by militias belonging to the different religious and ethnic groups in Iraq. The majority of Iraq's population is Shia Muslim, but there is a large Sunni Muslim minority as well. The Sunni are themselves divided between Sunni Arabs, who ruled the country under Saddam Hussein's leadership, and Sunni Kurds. The collapse of Hussein's dictatorship renewed old hostilities between these groups, forcing coalition troops to protect them from attacks from each other's militias.

Having gone to war in Iraq to overthrow a tyrant and **eliminate** the possibility of weapons of mass destruction being given to terrorists, the United States found itself trying to suppress an insurgency, prevent a civil war, and establish a new Iraqi government. The United States and its allies spent more than $30 billion to improve Iraq's electrical generating capacity, provide clean water, build schools, and improve health care, but insurgent attacks slowed these efforts. Despite the problems, Iraq's economy began to grow rapidly and a substantial improvement in living standards took place.

Between 2003 and 2006, insurgents killed over 3,000 American soldiers, many more than had died in the initial invasion. Many Americans had expected the war to be over quickly and as the fighting dragged on, support for the war began to decline. The failure to find any weapons of mass destruction also added to the growing controversy as to whether the war was a mistake.

American policy makers now faced a dilemma. If they pulled troops out too soon, Iraq might fall into civil war and provide a safe haven and breeding ground for terrorist groups. At the same time, the longer the United States stayed, the more its presence might stir resentment and support for terrorist groups. The best solution seemed to be to get a functioning and democratic Iraqi government up and running as fast as possible and then train its forces to take over the security of the country. As part of this plan, in January 2005, the Iraqi people went to the polls in huge numbers for the first free elections in their country's history. After much debate, voters then overwhelmingly approved a new constitution in October 2005.

Reading Check **Summarizing** Why did it prove so difficult to end the Iraq War quickly?

Section 3 REVIEW

Vocabulary

1. **Explain** the significance of: Northern Alliance, Khalid Shaikh Mohammed, weapons of mass destruction, "axis of evil," Saddam Hussein.

Main Ideas

2. **Explaining** Why did the United States send military aid to the Northern Alliance?
3. **Identifying** Why did Bush choose to focus military attention in Iraq?
4. **Summarizing** Why did fighting continue in Iraq after President Bush declared the major combat was over?

Critical Thinking

5. **Big Ideas** Why did the United States declare war on Afghanistan?
6. **Organizing** Use a graphic organizer to list the reasons why President Bush ordered the invasion of Iraq.

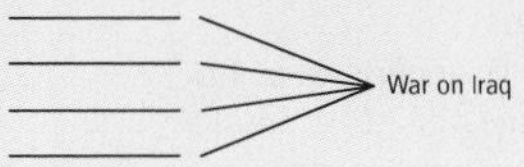

7. **Analyzing Visuals** Examine the photos on page 1046. How does the style of warfare in Iraq differ from the fighting in Afghanistan?

Writing About History

8. **Descriptive Writing** Suppose you are an Iraqi who has recently voted in your first election. Write a journal entry that explains how you feel following your vote.

History ONLINE
Study Central™ To review this section, go to glencoe.com and click on Study Central.

Reading Check

Answer:
Groups of Iraqis opposed to the U.S. invasion attacked American forces; conflicts broke out among Iraq's ethnic groups, adding to the turmoil.

Assess

History ONLINE

Study Central™ provides summaries, interactive games, and online graphic organizers to help students review content.

Close

Identifying Central Issues
Ask students to identify the challenges the United States faces in its occupation of Iraq. Ask students to suggest solutions to the challenges. OL

Section 3 REVIEW

Answers

1. All definitions can be found in the section and the Glossary.
2. The Northern Alliance had been fighting the Taliban for several years.
3. Bush believed that Iraq was a direct threat because of intelligence reports that Iraq was hiding weapons of mass destruction.
4. Insurgent groups supporting militant causes attacked American forces, and conflict broke out among militias of Iraq's ethnic/religious groups.
5. The Taliban government of Afghanistan had given shelter to the al-Qaeda terrorist movement.
6. He believed Iraq sponsored terrorism and had weapons of mass destruction; also, Iraq had refused to cooperate with the international community and had oppressed its own people.
7. The fighting in Afghanistan took place in mountainous areas; much of the fighting in Iraq occurred in urban areas.
8. Answers will vary but might refer to happiness at having the vote after years of being ruled by kings or dictators.

Focus

Bellringer

Daily Focus Transparency 31-4

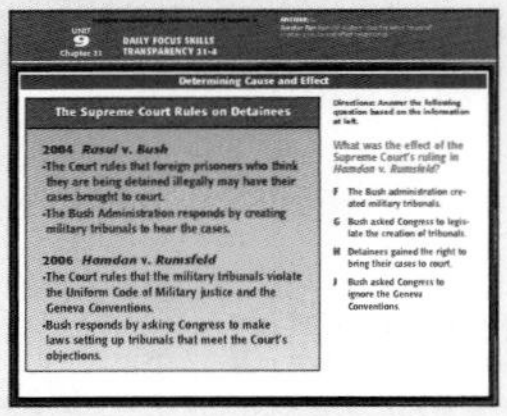

Guide to Reading

Answers:
Student outline notes should follow the major heading structure of the section

Section Spotlight Video

To generate student interest and provide a springboard for class discussion, access the Chapter 31, Section 4 video at glencoe.com or on the video DVD.

Reading Check

Answers:
the slow progress of the Iraq war, the Abu Ghraib prison scandal, and the failure to find weapons of mass destruction

Resource Manager

Section 4

Section Audio   Spotlight Video

A Time of Challenges

Guide to Reading

Big Ideas

Government and Society During President Bush's second term, the Republicans faced scandal and a national disaster that led to the Democrats gaining control of the White House and Congress in 2008.

Content Vocabulary

- "earmark" *(p. 1052)*

Academic Vocabulary

- procedure *(p. 1049)*
- monitor *(p. 1050)*

People and Events to Identify

- Abu Ghraib *(p. 1048)*
- Guantanamo Bay *(p. 1049)*
- National Security Agency (NSA) *(p. 1050)*
- John G. Roberts, Jr. *(p. 1052)*
- Samuel Alito, Jr. *(p. 1052)*
- Nancy Pelosi *(p. 1052)*

Reading Strategy

Taking Notes As you read about events from the 2004 election to the present day, use the major headings of the section to create an outline.

A Time of Challenges
I. The Election of 2004
II. Security vs. Liberty
A.
B.

After a close campaign, President Bush won a second term in 2004, but scandals and continued difficulties in Iraq helped Democrats win control of Congress in 2006. In 2008, as the economy began experiencing difficulties, voters elected Barack Obama to be president. Obama was the first African American president of the United States.

The Election of 2004

MAIN Idea After a campaign that centered on the war in Iraq and the war on terror, Bush was reelected.

HISTORY AND YOU Have you ever participated in an election at your school? Read on to learn about the election of 2004.

In early 2004, President Bush's approval ratings began to fall. The ongoing war in Iraq and the failure of inspectors to find any weapons of mass destruction weakened his support, as did the scandal at the Iraqi prison of **Abu Ghraib,** where some prisoners were abused by American soldiers. These events gave Democrats the opportunity to mount a serious challenge in the 2004 election.

President Bush and Vice President Cheney were renominated by the Republicans. The Democrats nominated Massachusetts Senator John Kerry for president and North Carolina Senator John Edwards for vice president. Bush promised to cut taxes while continuing the war on terrorism. He opposed abortion and called for a constitutional amendment to ban same-sex marriages. Senator Kerry promised to raise taxes on the wealthy to fund wider health care coverage, and to strengthen Social Security. He also took the opposite stand from Bush on most social issues. Bush's campaign portrayed Kerry as an untrustworthy "flipflopper." Kerry's campaign argued that Bush was too stubborn to change course when events required it.

Although September 11, 2001, had united the nation emotionally, the country remained as divided politically as it had been in 2000. Bush's support was strongest in the South and on the Great Plains, as well as in rural areas and the outer suburbs of major cities. Kerry's base was in the Northeast and on the West Coast, as well as in cities and inner suburbs. Both candidates focused on the upper Midwest where voters were narrowly divided. Nationwide, President Bush won a majority of the popular vote as well as 286 electoral votes. Despite the problems in Iraq, voters felt it safer to stay the course.

Reading Check **Analyzing** Why did President Bush's popularity decline in the year before the 2004 election?

R Reading Strategies	C Critical Thinking	D Differentiated Instruction	W Writing Support	S Skill Practice
Teacher Edition • Academic Vocab., p. 1051 • Prior Knowl., p. 1052 • Make Connect., p. 1052 **Additional Resources** • Guided Reading Act., URB p. 151 • Am. History in Graphic Novel, p. 79	**Teacher Edition** • Making Inferences, p. 1050 • Cause/Effect, pp. 1051, 1054 • Identify. Issues, p. 1053 **Additional Resources** • Prim. Source Reading, URB p. 137 • Supreme Court Case Studies, p. 161	**Teacher Edition** • Visual/Spatial, p. 1049 • Auditory/Musical, p. 1053 **Additional Resources** • Am. Art and Music Act., p. 139 • Reteaching Act., URB p. 143 • Authentic Asses., p. 67	**Additional Resources** • Linking Past/Present, URB p. 134	**Additional Resources** • Reading Skills Act., URB p. 121 • Read. Essen., p. 352 • Critical Thinking Skills Act., URB p. 132 • Quizzes/Tests, p. 444 • Reinforcing Skills Act., URB p. 131

PRIMARY SOURCE

Abu Ghraib and Guantanamo Bay

The revelation that some American troops had mistreated prisoners at the Abu Ghraib prison in Iraq shocked many people. Photographs of prisoners being abused and humiliated diminished the international image of the United States. Similarly, the lack of judicial proceedings and the secrecy surrounding the detainees at Guantanamo Bay prompted international criticism.

▲ Soldiers escort a detainee at Camp X-Ray at the military base at Guantanamo Bay, Cuba.

▲ A U.S. soldier points to prison cells where high risk detainees are held.

Analyzing VISUALS

1. **Interpreting** What might make a detainee "high risk"?
2. **Analyzing** In the photograph above, what elements show the level of security at the detention center?

Security vs. Liberty

MAIN Idea The Supreme Court rejected President Bush's interpretation of the rights and legal status of prisoners at Guantanamo Bay.

HISTORY AND YOU Do you believe all prisoners deserve a right to a trial? Read about the unusual status of prisoners at Guantanamo Bay.

The war on terror heightened the tension between America's national security and its civil liberties. In order to prevent another major terrorist attack, was the government justified in limiting the rights of citizens? Did captured terrorists have any rights at all?

Prisoners at Guantanamo

C As American forces captured members of al-Qaeda, a decision had to be made as to what to do with them. In 2004 President Bush decided to hold them at the American military base in **Guantanamo Bay,** Cuba, where they could be interrogated. This decision was very controversial. Some people argued that the prisoners should have the right to a lawyer, formal charges, and eventually a proper trial.

The Bush administration insisted that the prisoners were illegal enemy combatants, not suspects charged with a crime, and as such, they did not have the right to appeal their detentions to an American court. The administration also declared that the **procedures** regarding the treatment of prisoners, as specified in the Geneva Conventions, did not apply to terrorists since they were not part of any nation's armed forces. C

The Supreme Court disagreed with the administration. In 2004, in *Rasul* v. *Bush,* the Court ruled that foreign prisoners who claimed they were being unlawfully imprisoned had the right to have their cases heard in court. In response, the Bush administration created military tribunals to hear each detainee's case.

Teach

C Critical Thinking

Making Inferences Refer students to a map of North America and the Caribbean area that shows the location of Guantanamo Bay in Cuba in relation to the United States. **Ask:** **Why might United States officials have selected Guantanamo Bay as a place to hold people suspected of terrorism?** *(Students might point out Guantanamo's location outside of the country and beyond the reach of U.S. laws, allowing for secrecy and greater leeway in interrogating suspects.)* **AL**

Analyzing VISUALS

Answers:

1. association with terrorist groups; vocal or financial support for a terrorist cause
2. barbed wire, armed guards, prison cells

Additional Support

Activity: Collaborative Learning

Identifying Central Issues Remind students that Americans are strongly divided on many important issues. **Ask:** **What are some important national or local issues facing our nation?** *(the war in Iraq, illegal immigration, taxes, and so on)* Organize the class into small groups and assign each group a different issue. Ask groups to research their issues. The categories students should research include the nature of the issue, its impact on the public, and at least two different points of view about the issue. Have groups script and perform a mock debate that dramatizes the findings. **AL**

Teacher Tip

This activity requires students to do research, to write, and to perform. It allows students with different levels of academic skills and intelligences to work together. As you form groups, consider the needed skills and choose students accordingly.

C Critical Thinking

Determining Cause and Effect **Ask:** How did the U.S. Supreme Court ruling in *Hamdan* v. *Rumsfeld* affect the Bush administration policy on detainees? How did the administration react to the court ruling? *(The Supreme Court ruled that Bush's creation of military tribunals to hear cases violated U.S. military code and the Geneva Conventions regarding the treatment of prisoners. The Bush administration responded by allowing prisoners the right to see evidence and by agreeing to uphold the Geneva Conventions.)* **OL**

R Reading Strategy

Academic Vocabulary Have students read the sentence that contains the word *monitoring*. Then ask a student to define the word. **OL**

Reading Check

Answer:
The Bush administration held that the detainees were illegal enemy combatants, not suspects charged with a crime, and as such, they did not have a right to appeal their cases to an American court.

Additional Support

The Supreme Court struck this plan down in 2006 in *Hamdan* v. *Rumsfeld*, ruling that the military tribunals violated the Uniform Code of Military Justice and the Geneva Conventions.

President Bush then asked Congress to establish new tribunals that met the Court's objections. The president agreed that prisoners would have the right to see the evidence against them, and that evidence obtained by torture was inadmissible. The president also agreed to uphold the Geneva Conventions. Congress then passed the Military Commissions Act.

C The Military Commissions Act stated that non-citizens captured as enemy combatants had no right to file writs of habeas corpus. If a tribunal determined that they were being lawfully held, they could be held indefinitely without trial. In 2008, in *Boumediene* v. *Bush*, the Supreme Court ruled that the detainees had a right to habeas corpus and declared the section of the Military Commissions Act suspending that right to be unconstitutional.

Domestic Surveillance

As part of the war on terror, the **National Security Agency** (NSA) began wiretapping domestic telephone calls made to overseas locations when they believed one party in the call was a member of al-Qaeda or affiliated with R al-Qaeda. When the **monitoring** program became public in 2005, it created a controversy.

Civil rights groups argued that the program violated the Fourth Amendment. They pointed out that Congress had created the Foreign Intelligence Surveillance Court to issue warrants secretly in highly classified security cases. The president argued that the court was too slow and that he had the authority as commander in chief to expand wiretapping to help fight the war on terror. In 2006, a federal judge declared the wiretapping to be unconstitutional, but the following year an appeals court overturned the judge's decision. When Congress began drafting legislation to address the issue, the Bush administration suspended the program and announced that future wiretaps would require a warrant from the Foreign Intelligence Surveillance Court.

Reading Check **Explaining** Why did the Bush administration believe detainees at Guantanamo Bay had no right to take their case to a U.S. court?

PRIMARY SOURCE

Hurricane Katrina

Hurricane Katrina was one of the worst natural disasters in the history of the United States. The storm ravaged much of the Gulf Coast region. In New Orleans, the breach of the levees caused even more devastation.

▲ *An aerial photograph shows how the flooding in New Orleans ruined entire neighborhoods.*

A Stormy Second Term

MAIN Idea Bush appointed two new Supreme Court justices; his second term was marred by a hurricane, the ongoing war, and scandals.

HISTORY AND YOU Do you remember Hurricane Katrina? Read on to learn how the handling of the crisis hurt the Bush administration.

Having won a second term with a majority of the popular vote, President Bush concluded the American people had given him a mandate to continue his policies. He began his second term by announcing plans to overhaul the Social Security system and to create a prescription drug program for senior citizens.

Debating Social Security

To fix Social Security, President Bush proposed that workers be allowed to put 4 percent of their income in private accounts rather than in Social Security. This money could then be invested in stocks and bonds. The president

Activity: Collaborative Learning

Evaluating **Ask:** How do the government's efforts to protect the nation affect you? *(Answers will vary depending on students' personal experiences and where they live.)* Use the question to elicit ideas and anecdotes from students about ways that they have been affected by measures taken by the government to protect Americans from different kinds of attacks or disasters. Ask students what kinds of disasters have happened or might happen where they live and what they would expect the government to do to help before, during, and after a catastrophic event. Close the activity by discussing the impact of terrorist attacks and other disasters, and why such events matter to everyone in the country. **OL**

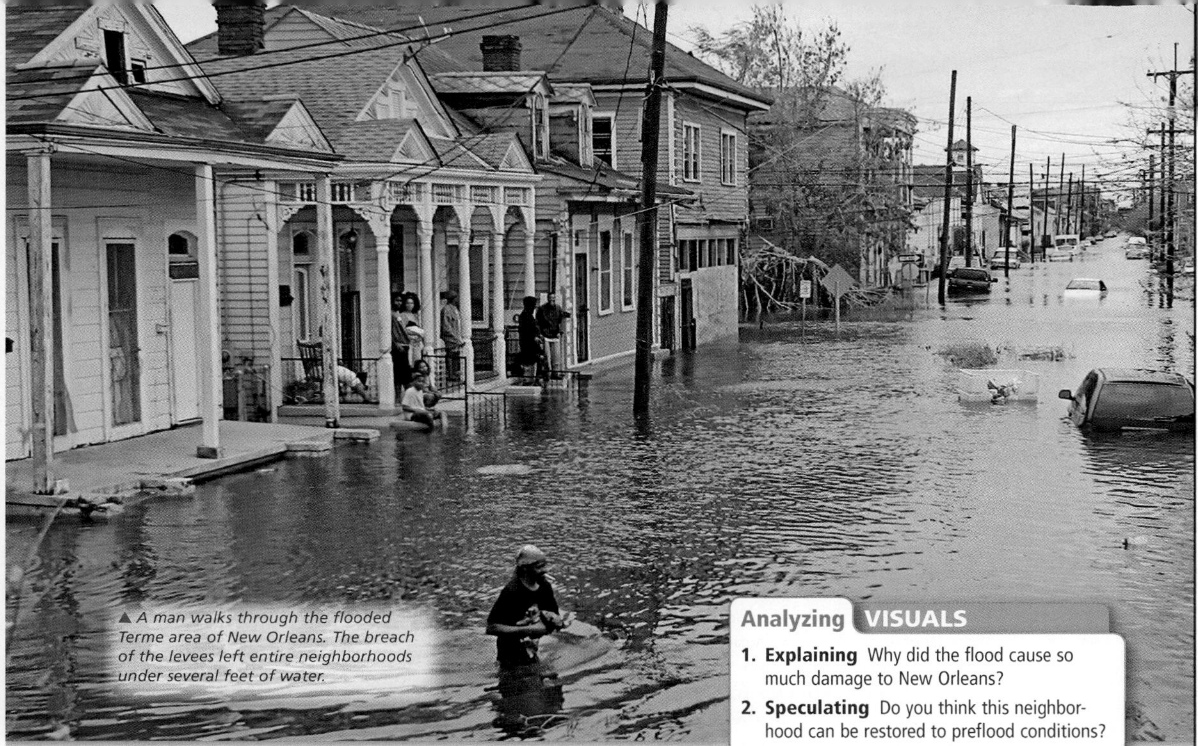

▲ A man walks through the flooded Terme area of New Orleans. The breach of the levees left entire neighborhoods under several feet of water.

Analyzing VISUALS

1. **Explaining** Why did the flood cause so much damage to New Orleans?
2. **Speculating** Do you think this neighborhood can be restored to preflood conditions?

believed that private accounts would grow rapidly and help cover the expected shortfall in Social Security accounts. Democrats argued that the danger to Social Security was overstated and that privatizing any part of Social Security was dangerous. With the American public unenthusiastic, the plan was never brought to a vote in Congress.

Although his plan to reform Social Security failed, President Bush did convince Congress to enact a new prescription drug program for seniors despite the concerns of many of his conservative supporters that the plan would cost too much money. Under the new program, provided by Medicare, people 65 and older can sign up for insurance that helps cover the cost of prescription drugs.

Hurricane Katrina

R On August 29, 2005, Hurricane Katrina smashed into the Gulf Coast of the United States, spreading devastation from Florida to Louisiana. The fierce winds, rain, high tides, and storm surges destroyed buildings, roads, and electrical lines, left thousands of people homeless, and cost at least 1,200 lives. After the hurricane had passed, rising waters breached levees protecting the low-lying city of New Orleans. As water flooded the city, R those who had stayed behind were forced to flee onto their roofs to await rescue. As the water rose 15 feet in some neighborhoods, many people drowned. Thousands more took shelter in the convention center and at the Superdome, a covered football stadium. There they waited for days without much food, clean water, or information from authorities.

Television news showed the condition of the survivors and asked why the government was not responding more quickly. The mayor of New Orleans was faulted for not issuing a mandatory evacuation until the storm was less than a day away, and for having failed to provide transportation for those who could not C leave on their own. The governor of Louisiana argued with federal officials over who was in charge of the state's National Guard units. The Federal Emergency Management Agency (FEMA) seemed unprepared in its response.

R Reading Strategy

Making Connections Ask students to think about images they have seen and reports they have read of the people of New Orleans and the Gulf Coast struggling to recover from the effects of Hurricane Katrina. **Ask:** If a disaster like Katrina hit this community, what factors would encourage people to stay and rebuild? *(Answers will vary. Encourage discussions.)* **OL**

C Critical Thinking

Identifying Central Issues Ask: Do you think that the federal government or local government should be more responsible for addressing a disaster like Hurricane Katrina? Why? *(Answers will vary; some students may claim that the responsibility should be shared equally.)* **OL**

Analyzing VISUALS

Answers:

1. Rising waters breached the levees that protected the low-lying city.
2. Answers will vary but might mention the need for federal funds to rebuild.

Additional Support

Activity: Interdisciplinary Connection

Science Ask: Are levees an effective method of flood control? *(Students may note that levees can help control flooding but also can be overwhelmed by floodwaters in certain circumstances.)* Have interested students research levee systems and present their findings in an oral presentation. Tell students to look for answers to these questions during their research: *What is a natural levee? Why do people build levees? Where are levees used in the United States? Where else in the world are levees used? How do levees help control flooding? Why are they ineffective?* Encourage students to create visuals or a model to illustrate how a levee works and how it can fail. **OL**

R Reading Strategy

Summarizing **Ask:** Why was the retirement of Justice Sandra Day O'Connor particularly significant? *(Students should remember that any opportunity for a president to name a Supreme Court justice is an opportunity to shape judicial interpretation, but Justice O'Connor's role as a swing voter in controversial cases made her retirement more important.)* OL

C Critical Thinking

Analyzing Primary Sources
Ask: What challenges do people living in Iraq face today? *(Answers will vary but may include summaries of the news headlines that describe the situation in the country.)* Have students search online news sources for first-hand reports that examine how the Sunnis, the Shias, and the Kurds are or are not cooperating with each other. Direct students to look for quotations about unsolved problems and feelings about Iraq's immediate future. Tell students to select two quotations to read aloud to the class and explain what each taught them about the current situation. AL

Additional Support

Only the Coast Guard seemed able to act, as its helicopters and boats began rescuing stranded citizens. Eventually troops and transportation arrived and moved the evacuees to other cities.

As New Orleans remained flooded, President Bush flew over the devastated areas a few days later. Photographs of the president viewing the scene from high above made him appear detached. With polls showing a sharp drop in confidence in his administration, President Bush fired the head of FEMA and then traveled to New Orleans to pledge federal funds for rebuilding the city.

New Supreme Court Judges

In 2005, President Bush filled two vacancies on the Supreme Court. In the spring of 2005, Justice Sandra Day O'Connor announced her retirement. Although appointed by President Reagan, Justice O'Connor had been a pivotal swing vote on the Court, sometimes siding with conservatives, sometimes with liberals. As her replacement, Bush nominated federal judge **John G. Roberts, Jr.,** a conservative who was well regarded in the Senate. Before the Senate could act, however, Chief Justice William Rehnquist died. Bush then named Roberts to replace him. Roberts easily won Senate confirmation as chief justice.

Again attempting to fill Justice O'Connor's vacancy, President Bush nominated his White House counselor Harriet Miers. Many conservative Republicans were unhappy with Miers because of her lack of experience as a judge. As Republican opposition mounted, President Bush withdrew Miers' name and nominated federal judge **Samuel Alito, Jr.,** a well-known conservative justice. The Senate voted 58 to 42 to confirm Alito.

The 2006 Midterm Elections

The first two years of President Bush's second term had not gone well. He had failed to reform Social Security, and the public was angry with his administration's response to Hurricane Katrina. His prescription drug plan and decision to nominate Harriet Miers to the Supreme Court had angered many conservatives. Many people were also angry at his plan to create a guest-worker program and a path to citizenship for immigrants who had entered the country illegally.

At the same time, Americans had grown frustrated with Congress. The Republican majority seemed awash in scandals. Two Republicans had resigned from Congress after being convicted of corruption, and House Majority Leader Tom DeLay had resigned after being indicted for violating campaign finance laws. Congress also seemed unable to control spending, partly because Republicans and Democrats had been adding an increasing number of **"earmarks"** to spending bills. An earmark requires federal money be spent on a specific project, such as building a bridge, or funding medical research, usually in the sponsor's own state or district.

Problems in Iraq Although government scandals and overspending angered many Americans, the most important reason voters were frustrated was the situation in Iraq. A year earlier, many Americans had taken heart when large numbers of Iraqis had turned out to vote in democratic elections, but their hope for peace in Iraq soon faded. Although the Sunni Kurds and Iraqi Shia generally supported the new Iraqi constitution, it had much less support among Sunni Arabs. Rather than bring peace, the elections were followed by a rise in sectarian violence. In February 2006, the bombing of the Shia Golden Mosque in Samarra set Sunni and Shia militias against each other.

Further complicating the situation was an insurgent group known as Al-Qaeda in Iraq (AQI) that controlled large areas of western Iraq and was determined to defeat American forces and impose a strict militant version of Islam. In addition, the government of Iran had begun covertly sending weapons to the Iraqi insurgents.

The ongoing suicide bombings, kidnappings, and attacks on American soldiers turned a majority of Americans against the war. Democrats demanded the president set a timetable for withdrawing U.S. troops, a policy that President Bush described as "cut and run."

The Democrats Gain Control of Congress Voters expressed their unhappiness with the president and the Republican Congress in 2006. The Democrats won a majority in both the House and the Senate for the first time since 1992. House Democrats then elected California Representative **Nancy Pelosi** to be the first female Speaker of the House of Representatives.

Activity: Collaborative Learning

Political Science Organize the class into four groups. Assign each group one of the following topics: Bush's goals for his second term, the public's reception to the president's goals, Congressional scandals during Bush's second term, and results of the 2006 midterm election. Have the groups research their topic. Then have each group prepare an oral report and a visual display that summarizes their research findings. OL

People IN HISTORY

Condoleezza Rice
1954–

Born in Birmingham, Alabama, the same year as the landmark *Brown* v. *Board of Education* decision, Condoleezza Rice rose to become the first African American female secretary of state.

Before becoming involved in politics, Rice had a distinguished career in academia. She started her college studies at age 15 and went on to earn advanced degrees in economics and international studies. Dr. Rice then became a professor at Stanford University. Due to her expertise in Eastern and Central Europe, Rice served as an adviser on foreign affairs to President Ronald Reagan and President George H.W. Bush. She later returned to her post at Stanford.

When George W. Bush decided to run for president, he asked Rice to be his foreign policy adviser. During his first term, she served as head of the National Security Council and supported the attacks on Afghanistan and the invasion of Iraq. She became secretary of state during Bush's second term.

How did Rice's academic studies prepare her for her future role in politics?

Nancy Pelosi
1940–

Originally from Baltimore, Maryland, Nancy Pelosi's interest in politics began at an early age. Her father was a supporter of Democrat Franklin D. Roosevelt's New Deal and held political office.

Pelosi has spent most of her adult life in the San Francisco area. There, she attracted attention as an effective fund-raiser for the Democratic Party. She became the chair of the California State Democratic Party in 1981 and served for two years.

In 1987 she was elected to Congress in a special election to fill a vacancy caused by the death of her predecessor. The following year she was reelected for a full term and has held that office ever since.

In 2002 Pelosi was elected minority whip and tried to forge greater unity among different factions of her party. In that post, she emerged as one of President Bush's toughest critics. When the Democrats regained control of the House of Representatives after the 2006 elections, she became Speaker, the first woman elected to that post.

Why would Pelosi's position give her a platform from which to criticize the president?

Despite promises to end the war and change how Congress operated, Speaker Pelosi and other Democrats opposed to the war were not able to get enough votes to cut funding for the war, or to force the president to set a deadline for pulling the troops out of Iraq. In addition, spending was not reduced and, after a brief moratorium, earmarks were again permitted.

Troops Surge to Iraq The day after the 2006 midterm elections, Secretary of Defense Donald Rumsfeld resigned. Rumsfeld admitted that the war in Iraq was not going well. "In my view it is time for a major adjustment," he wrote. "Clearly what U.S. forces are currently doing in Iraq is not working well enough or fast enough."

President Bush chose Robert Gates to replace Rumsfeld and put a new commander, General David Petraeus, in charge of operations in Iraq. The president then announced a plan to "surge" some 20,000 more troops to Iraq to restore order in Baghdad, where the violence was concentrated.

With the additional troops provided by the surge, General Petraeus began clearing and holding areas of Baghdad that had been plagued by crime and insurgent attacks. At the same time, his forces began reaching out to Sunni groups in western Iraq that had been opposed to the American presence.

By late 2006, Al-Qaeda in Iraq's campaign to impose a militant version of Islam in western Iraq through murder and intimidation had begun to backfire. The Sunni tribes of Anbar—the large western province of Iraq—began working with the American forces to fight the insurgents. Their organization, known as the Anbar Awakening, helped change the course of the war. Increasingly, Sunni militias stopped fighting the Americans and turned against Al-Qaeda in Iraq. In the meantime, Iraq's government continued to make reforms and became increasingly effective, as did the Iraqi army.

By the fall of 2008, violence in Iraq had been dramatically reduced. Coalition forces had handed over control of 12 of Iraq's 18 provinces to the Iraqi government and coalition casualties were lower than at any time since the war began in 2003. The United States began negotiating a new security pact with the Iraqi government to establish the terms and conditions for a continued American presence in the country.

✓Reading Check **Explaining** What events in the first two years of Bush's second term contributed to Republicans losing control of Congress?

People IN HISTORY

Answers: Rice earned advanced degrees in economics and international studies and was an expert in Eastern and Central Europe. As Speaker of the House, Pelosi has the power to shape legislation, especially regarding government finances and spending. As a talented student, Rice had many interests and was not sure about a future career. She was a skilled pianist and considered majoring in music before finally deciding on international studies. As Speaker of the House, Pelosi ranks second in the line of presidential succession, after the vice president. No woman has ever been as close in line to the U.S. presidency.

✓Reading Check

Answers:
dissatisfaction with the Republican administration's handling of the Iraq war and the Katrina emergency, congressional scandals involving Republicans, and conservative disenchantment with some of Bush's domestic agenda

Hands-On Chapter Project
Step 4

Exploring the "Blogosphere"

Step 4: Responding to Blogs Student groups respond to blog entries created in Step 3.

Directions Have student groups trade the blogs they created in Step 3. As a group, have students write a response to the blog entry. Remind students that readers contribute to blogs in many ways. They may rebut opinions stated in blogs. They sometimes add helpful information such as links. They may point out errors in information and make corrections. Sometimes they may simply express admiration for the blog. Have students weight their rights to free speech with their responsibility for civility as they respond to each other's blogs.

Summarizing Have groups share their blog responses with the class. Encourage the class to discuss what they learned about the Big Ideas of this chapter as they explored the "blogosphere." **OL**

(Chapter Project continued on the Visual Summary page)

D Differentiated Instruction

Visual/Spatial Ask students to draw political cartoons that reflect the candidates and major issues of the 2008 presidential election race. BL

Analyzing VISUALS

Answers:

1. Virginia and Indiana
2. three; California, New York, and Florida

Did You Know?

Barack Obama is not only the first African American president. He is also the first president to be born outside of the mainland United States. Obama was born in Hawaii.

Additional Support

HISTORY AND GEOGRAPHY

The Election of 2008

▲ *Barack Obama waves to the crowd in Chicago's Grant Park on election night. He is the nation's first African American president.*

Presidential Candidate	Popular Votes	% of Popular Vote	Electoral Votes
Obama	66,057,075	53%	364
McCain	57,839,810	46%	163
Nader	687,124	1%	0

Analyzing VISUALS

1. **Comparing** Compare Obama's election map to Clinton's 1992 victory and Carter's 1976 victory. What states did Obama win that neither Carter nor Clinton won?
2. **Analyzing** What is the fewest number of states that would have had to switch their votes to McCain for him to win the election?

D The Election of 2008

MAIN Idea A major financial crisis and public disapproval of President Bush enabled Barack Obama to win the 2008 election.

HISTORY AND YOU Do you remember Martin Luther King, Jr.'s, dream? Read on to learn about the first African American to become president.

In 2006, a financial crisis began when millions of Americans began to default on their mortgages. The crisis developed because banks had made too many subprime loans—risky loans that were not as likely to be repaid. In addition to the financial crisis, oil prices began to rise steeply. By the summer of 2008, a gallon of gasoline cost nearly twice what it had in 2006. As the 2008 election approached, the economy had replaced the war in Iraq as the most important issue for most Americans.

The Candidates Are Chosen

The election of 2008 was unusual in that neither party had an incumbent president or vice president running for the nomination.

Four Republicans emerged as frontrunners for their party's nomination: former New York mayor Rudy Giuliani, Governor Mike Huckabee of Arkansas, Senator John McCain of Arizona, and Governor Mitt Romney of Massachusetts. With many conservatives split between Romney and Huckabee, John McCain emerged the winner. Many Republican voters admired McCain's heroism during the Vietnam War and believed his reputation as a reformer would help the party win over voters who were angry at President Bush.

Knowing that many conservative Republicans distrusted him, John McCain selected Sarah Palin, the popular conservative governor of

Activity: Technology Connection

Evaluating Information The 2008 presidential election was notable in the greatest use of the Internet and candidate Web sites to raise campaign funds. **Ask:** **What factors helped contribute to more and more successful use of Web-based fund-raising?** *(the small successes made during the 2004 presidential election, the growing popularity of social networking sites such as Facebook).* Have students examine current political Web sites to see how these sites attempt to inform the voting population about critical issues and evaluate any methods or design elements that try to establish a direct connection between the administration and the population. Tell students to take notes on what they discover and report their evaluations to the class. OL

Alaska, to be his running mate. Palin was the first woman to be nominated by the Republican Party to run for vice president.

Three Democrats emerged as frontrunners for their party's nomination: Former First Lady and New York Senator Hillary Clinton; former Senator John Edwards, who had been John Kerry's running mate; and Senator Barack Obama from Illinois. Obama first gained national attention at the 2004 Democratic National Convention, where he delivered the convention's keynote address. His speech greatly impressed Democrats and made Obama a national figure in American politics.

Hillary Clinton was heavily favored to win the 2008 Democratic nomination, but Obama was able to build a large grassroots network of supporters and used the Internet to raise several hundred million dollars, far more than any previous candidate. Clinton tried to portray Obama as inexperienced, but Democrats decided that Obama was more likely to change the country's direction. After winning the nomination, Obama selected Senator Joe Biden of Delaware to be his running mate, probably because Biden's 35 years in the Senate would help offset charges that Obama was too inexperienced to be president.

With the approval ratings of the president and Congress at all-time lows, McCain and Obama both promised change. McCain stressed his experience and reputation for being a maverick—someone who is willing to go against his party and try new approaches to solving problems. Obama argued that McCain's policies were too similar to those of President Bush. Both candidates presented plans that would cut taxes, address the energy crisis, put people back to work, and reform health care.

Obama led in the polls in the summer of 2008, but McCain took the lead following the Republican convention in early September. Obama regained the lead, however, when President Bush announced that the economy was in serious danger because there was no longer enough credit available. In response, Bush and Congress passed a $700 billion dollar bailout for the nation's financial institutions. The crisis increased voter disapproval of the president and the Republican party.

Obama Wins

On election day, Obama won 53% of the popular vote and 364 electoral votes, the biggest victory for a Democratic candidate since 1964. Barack Obama became the first African American to win the presidency. Soon after the networks projected he would win, Obama spoke to his supporters at Grant Park in Chicago:

PRIMARY SOURCE

"... This is our moment. This is our time—to put our people back to work and open doors of opportunity for our kids; to restore prosperity and promote the cause of peace; to reclaim the American Dream and reaffirm that fundamental truth—that out of many, we are one; that while we breathe, we hope, and where we are met with cynicism, and doubt, and those who tell us that we can't, we will respond with that timeless creed that sums up the spirit of a people: Yes We Can."

—Barack Obama, Address at Grant Park, November 4, 2008

Reading Check **Analyzing** What events enabled Obama to win the presidency? Why was his election important in American history?

Section 4 REVIEW

Vocabulary

1. **Explain** the significance of: Abu Ghraib, Guantanamo Bay, National Security Agency, John G. Roberts, Jr., Samuel Alito, Jr., "earmarks," Nancy Pelosi.

Main Ideas

2. **Identifying** What issues did President Bush support in his reelection campaign? What did Kerry support?
3. **Explaining** What did the Supreme Court declare unlawful with the *Hamdan v. Rumsfeld* ruling?
4. **Describing** How did Bush propose to fix Social Security?

Critical Thinking

5. **Big Ideas** Why did Donald Rumsfeld resign as secretary of defense? Who did Bush choose to replace Rumsfeld?
6. **Organizing** Use a graphic organizer like the one below to list the reasons for Republican losses in the 2006 election.

Reasons for Republican Losses in 2006
I. The Election of 2004
II. Security vs. Liberty
A.
B.

7. **Analyzing Visuals** Examine the map on page 1054. How is Obama's victory different from Bush's victory shown on page 1033? Which states switched to the Democrats in 2008?

Writing About History

8. **Persuasive Writing** Write a journal entry describing current events that will be read by students 50 years in the future. Be clear and concise with your description of these events.

History ONLINE
Study Central™ To review this section, go to glencoe.com and click on Study Central.

1055

Reading Check

Answers:
The economic credit slowdown and bailout for the nation's financial institutions increased voter disapproval of the president and the Republican Party.

Assess

History ONLINE

Study Central™ provides summaries, interactive games, and online graphic organizers to help students review content.

Close

Evaluating Ask students what they think are the successes and failures of Bush's second term to date. **OL**

Section 4 REVIEW

Answers

1. All definitions can be found in the section and the Glossary.
2. Bush pledged to continue cutting taxes while building a strong national defense. Kerry favored raising taxes on the wealthy to fund wider health care coverage and strengthen social security.
3. the Bush administration's creation of military tribunals to hear detainees' cases
4. Bush proposed that workers be allowed to put some of their income in private accounts for investment use rather than in Social Security.
5. Rumsfeld acknowledged that the administration's Iraq strategy was not working and a change of course was needed.
6. Answers will vary but should include dissatisfaction with the war, anger at Republican scandals in Congress, and unpopular domestic policies.
7. Obama won states in the West, the Upper Midwest, and in the South that were Bush states in 2000. These states were Nevada, Colorado, Indiana, Ohio, North Carolina, Virginia, and Florida.
8. Student journals will vary but should use details from the section and reflect understanding of the key issues presented.

Identifying Main Idea Ask: Why do you think that 9/11 stunned the country? *(Many students will cite the unexpectedness of 9/11, the sheer scale of the destruction, and the knowledge that the United States was opposed and even hated by some people of the world.)* **OL**

Visual Literacy Ask: Look at the four images on the page. How do the images relate to the causes and effects of 9/11? *(The first two images show al-Qaeda leaders and the training of terrorists at special camps. The last two images show the public response to the loss of life in the 9/11 attacks and the involvement of American forces to eliminate terrorism and allow democracy to develop in Afghanistan and Iraq.)*

Chapter 31 Visual Summary

STUDY TO GO You can study anywhere, anytime by downloading quizzes and flashcards to your PDA from glencoe.com.

Causes of the Attacks of 9/11

- The rise of the oil industry in the Middle East makes many elites wealthy but leaves many people poor and resentful.
- The oil trade with Europe and the United States brings Western ideas and culture into the Middle East; many feel their traditional Muslim values are being undermined, and militant Muslim movements form.
- The founding of Israel in 1948 angers many Arabs, especially Palestinians. European and American support for Israel angers many in the Middle East.
- The Soviets invade Afghanistan in 1979; Muslims from across the Middle East, including Osama bin Laden, go to fight the Soviet troops.
- Osama bin Laden forms al-Qaeda to help drive the Soviets out of Afghanistan and all Westerners out of the Middle East.
- Iraq invades Kuwait leading to the deployment of American troops in Saudi Arabia, angering Muslim militants, including Osama bin Laden.
- The Soviet pullout from Afghanistan leads to a militant group, the Taliban, taking power and offering aid and shelter to bin Laden.
- Al-Qaeda, based in Afghanistan, stages a series of attacks on Americans, culminating in the attack on September 11, 2001.

The Taliban let al-Qaeda train at camps in Afghanistan (above). Osama bin Laden and his second in command, Ayman al-Zawahiri (right), often sent taped messages to Arab television networks.

American troops fight in rugged Afghan terrain (above) shortly after the 9/11 attacks. On the left, Americans attend a memorial service for the victims of the attacks.

Effects of the Attacks of 9/11

- Initially, the 9/11 attack unifies Americans and leads to an outpouring of support to the people of New York.
- President Bush declares a global war on terror to put an end to terrorist groups that threaten Americans.
- The United States launches attacks on the Taliban and helps local forces overthrow their regime. NATO troops then enter Afghanistan to serve as peacekeepers.
- Congress passes the Patriot Act giving the FBI additional powers to help prevent another attack in the United States.
- Congress creates the Department of Homeland Security.
- The Bush administration decides that preventing terrorist groups from getting weapons of mass destruction is a high priority.
- The United States, backed by a coalition of allies, invades Iraq to destroy its weapons of mass destruction.
- The invasion of Iraq is controversial; many traditional allies do not support it, and it divides the American people.
- An insurgency begins in Iraq that keeps American troops fighting for several years.

Hands-On Chapter Project
Step 5: Wrap Up

Exploring the "Blogosphere"

Step 5: Wrap Up Students will write an informational essay on blogs.

Directions Direct students to write an essay in which they use what they have learned in Steps 1 through 4 of this project. Student essays should answer the following questions:

- What are blogs?
- What purpose do blogs serve in today's society?
- Are blogs beneficial to American society? Why or why not?
- What other purposes might blogs be used for to benefit society?

Summarizing Students should write and turn in their essays individually, however, you may want to share interesting responses with the entire class. **OL**

Chapter 31 ASSESSMENT

Review Vocabulary

Directions: Choose the word or words that best complete the sentence.

1. ______ ran for the Green Party in the 2000 presidential election.
   A Al Gore
   B Ralph Nader
   C George W. Bush
   D Dick Cheney

2. Osama bin Laden heads the terrorist group known as
   A Al Jazeera.
   B guerrillas.
   C Hamas.
   D al-Qaeda.

3. The majority of Iraq's population is
   A Shia Muslim.
   B Sunni Muslim.
   C Sunni Arabs.
   D Sunni Kurds.

4. What military base held captured members of al-Qaeda in 2004?
   A Abu Ghraib
   B Guantanamo Bay
   C Pearl Harbor
   D Geneva

5. Projects that spend federal money but usually benefit a single congressional district are known as ______ .
   A gerrymanders
   B earmarks
   C isograms
   D the spoils system

Reviewing Main Ideas

Directions: Choose the best answer for each of the following questions.

Section 1 *(pp. 1032–1035)*

6. In the 2000 election, Al Gore won
   A the popular vote.
   B a majority of electoral votes.
   C the state of Florida.
   D a pivotal Supreme Court case.

7. After Bush took office, Congress passed which of the following educational reforms?
   A federal funding to parents to pay for private schools if their public school was performing poorly
   B annual standardized testing in reading and math for grades 3–8
   C prohibiting federally funded schools from discriminating against girls and young women
   D transporting children to schools outside their neighborhood to achieve a greater racial balance

Section 2 *(pp. 1036–1041)*

8. After the bombing of American embassies in Kenya and Tanzania, President Clinton
   A ordered the invasion of Iraq.
   B created the office of Homeland Security.
   C ordered the bombing of terrorist camps in Afghanistan.
   D signed the Patriot Act into law.

TEST-TAKING TIP

If a question involves a table, skim the table before reading the question. Then, read the question and interpret the information from the table.

Need Extra Help?

If You Missed Questions . . .	1	2	3	4	5	6	7	8
Go to Page . . .	1033	1037	1047	1049	1052	1033	1035	1039

GO ON

Answers and Analyses

Reviewing Vocabulary

1. B Ralph Nader has long been associated with environmentalism. Al Gore was the Democratic candidate. George W. Bush was the Republican candidate. Dick Cheney was the Republican vice-presidential candidate.

2. D Al Jazeera is a television network in the Middle East. Members of al-Qaeda can be considered to be guerrillas, but that is not the name of an organization. Hamas is not headed by bin Laden.

3. A The split between Shia and Sunni Muslims came about after the death of Muhammad. Shia Muslims believed the Muslim leader should be a direct descendant of Muhammad and a religious leader. Sunni Muslims believed the leader could be from Muhammad's tribe and should be a political leader. The majority of Muslims today are Sunni (who are the minority in Iraq).

4. B Abu Ghraib was a former prison, not a military base. Guantanamo Bay in Cuba is a U.S. military base where the captured members of al-Qaeda were held. Pearl Harbor is a naval base in the Pacific. Geneva is a city in Switzerland, not a military base.

5.B Congress had difficulty controlling federal spending because of the number of earmarks added to legislation by both political parties.

Reviewing Main Ideas

6. A This is a good opportunity to review the electoral system with students. Al Gore won the majority of the popular votes, but he did not win the majority of electoral votes. Make sure students understand that some states have more electoral votes than others.

7. B Standardized testing was part of the No Child Left Behind Act. Choice *A* was a reform that President Bush pushed for as part of the education act, but it was rejected by Congress. *C* and *D* are examples of past education reform.

8. C The bombing of terrorist camps was in response to the embassy bombings. President Bush ordered the invasion of Iraq in the wake of concern that Iraq had WMDs and Iraq's denial of having weapons. The Office of Homeland Security and the Patriot Act were created in response to the September 11 attacks.

Chapter 31 ASSESSMENT

9. B Anthrax was sent through the mail to a number of places, including a newspaper in Florida where one man died. The investigation and contamination shut down several major postal sorting facilities where contaminated mail was suspected or confirmed to have passed through.

10. C Iraq was believed to have WMDs and to be a danger to the U.S. Iraq was not the most vulnerable, nor was it responsible for the September 11 attacks and did not attack the U.S.

11. D Kuwait allowed the U.S. to launch offensives. The other nations were not supportive of the U.S. attacks. Kuwait had been invaded by Iraq in 1990, and the U.S. was instrumental in leading the coalition that expelled Iraq from Kuwait in Operation Desert Storm.

12. B Students who have trouble remembering this fact will be helped by the map question on this exam, which clearly shows that Bush's support was strongest in the South and the Great Plains.

13. D None of the other answer choices occurred. The severe financial crisis involving defaulted home mortgages, investment bank failures, and a downturn in consumer spending reflected negatively on the Bush administration.

Critical Thinking

14. A Discuss the cases in each of the answer choices with students. *A* is correct; the decision resulted in the creation of military tribunals to try the detainees. *C*, *Hamdan* v. *Rumsfeld*, struck down the military tribunal plan. *Bush* v. *Gore* dealt with disputed election results. *Gideon* v. *Wainwright* was decided in 1963. In it, the Court ruled that defendants have the right to a lawyer, and if they cannot afford one, the court should appoint one.

9. In the fall of 2001, bioterrorists attacked news organizations and political figures with
- **A** smallpox.
- **B** anthrax.
- **C** arsenic.
- **D** radioactive material.

Section 3 *(pp. 1042–1047)*

10. President Bush targeted Iraq, one of the three countries in the "axis of evil," before the other two countries because Iraq
- **A** was the most vulnerable.
- **B** was responsible for the September 11 attacks.
- **C** was believed to pose the most imminent danger to the United States.
- **D** attacked the United States first.

11. Which country was the only nation bordering Iraq to allow the United States to launch offensives from their territory?
- **A** Saudi Arabia
- **B** Turkey
- **C** Iran
- **D** Kuwait

Section 4 *(pp. 1048–1055)*

12. During the 2004 presidential election, George W. Bush's support was strongest in
- **A** the Northeast.
- **B** the South and the Great Plains.
- **C** the Midwest and Great Lakes.
- **D** all urban areas.

13. Which factor helped Barack Obama win the 2008 election?
- **A** President Bush's high popularity
- **B** the U.S. withdrawal from Iraq
- **C** Hillary Clinton's victory
- **D** a severe financial crisis

Critical Thinking

Directions: Choose the best answers to the following questions.

14. Which Supreme Court ruling stated that foreign prisoners who claim they were unlawfully imprisoned had the right to have their cases heard in court?
- **A** *Rasul* v. *Bush*
- **B** *Bush* v. *Gore*
- **C** *Hamdan* v. *Rumsfeld*
- **D** *Gideon* v. *Wainwright*

Base your answer to question 15 on the map below and on your knowledge of Chapter 31.

Election of 2000

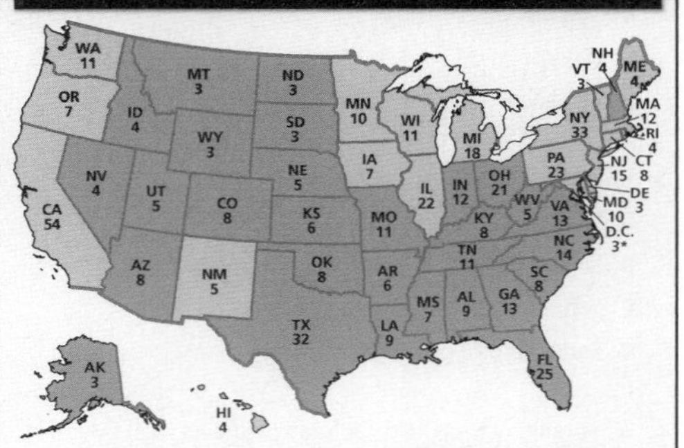

Presidential Candidate	Popular Votes	% of Popular Vote	Electoral Votes
Bush	50,456,002	47.88%	271
Gore	50,999,897	48.40%	266
Nader	2,882,955	2.74%	0

*One Gore elector from Washington, D.C., abstained from casting an electoral vote.

15. In the election of 2000, George W. Bush won
- **A** the popular vote.
- **B** fewer states than Al Gore.
- **C** a majority of electoral votes.
- **D** California and New York.

Need Extra Help?							
If You Missed Questions . . .	9	10	11	12	13	14	15
Go to Page . . .	1041	1044	1046	1049	1055	1049	1033

GO ON

15. C The states that George Bush won are shaded dark gray. Gore's states are light gray. It is clear that Bush won more states. However, the answer can be found in the key/chart that accompanies the map. Bush won 271 electoral votes, and Gore won 266. Therefore, George Bush won the election. Gore won the popular vote and California and New York.

Chapter 31 ASSESSMENT

16. Which the following is under the control of the Department of Homeland Security?
   - **A** Central Intelligence Agency (CIA)
   - **B** Defense Intelligence Agency (DIA)
   - **C** Federal Bureau of Investigation (FBI)
   - **D** Federal Emergency Management Agency (FEMA)

Analyze the cartoon and answer the question that follows. Base your answer on the cartoon and your knowledge of Chapter 31.

17. According to the cartoon, what is the artist saying about the 2004 presidential election?
   - **A** The world is excited about another four years with President Bush.
   - **B** The world is disappointed George Bush was reelected.
   - **C** The United States made a mistake reelecting Bush.
   - **D** Kerry was detached from Middle America therefore he lost the election.

18. Why did the United States think stopping the spread of weapons of mass destruction was linked to the war on terror?
   - **A** Saddam Hussein declared an allegiance with al-Qaeda.
   - **B** Bin Laden was believed to be hiding in the mountains of Iraq.
   - **C** Terrorists might buy or steal weapons of mass destruction and use them against the United States.
   - **D** Terrorist groups had already stolen weapons of mass destruction from Iraq.

Document-Based Questions

Directions: Analyze the document and answer the short-answer questions that follow the document.

In October 2001, President Bush signed the highly controversial Patriot Act.

> "If we were to take the position, reflected in provisions in the USA PATRIOT Act, that the government can invade our privacy and gather evidence that can be used against us based on no suspicion whatsoever that we've done anything wrong, but simply because the government wants to gather evidence as part of some generalized, 'anti-terrorism' or 'foreign intelligence' investigation, then we will have rendered that Fourth Amendment principle essentially meaningless."
>
> —Congressman Bob Barr (R-GA), "Problems with the USA PATRIOT Act"
>
> "Zero. That's the number of substantiated USA PATRIOT Act civil liberties violations. Extensive congressional oversight found no violations."
>
> —Congressman James Sensenbrenner (R-WI), "No rights have been violated"

19. According to Congressman Barr, which constitutional right does the Patriot Act violate and how?

20. What is Congressman Sensenbrenner's response to the accusation that the Patriot Act violates civil rights?

Extended Response

21. The decision to invade Iraq was controversial. Choose to either support a continued U.S. presence in Iraq or immediate troop withdrawal. Write a persuasive essay that includes an introduction and at least three paragraphs that support your position.

STOP

History ONLINE

For additional test practice, use Self-Check Quizzes—Chapter 31 at glencoe.com.

Need Extra Help?

If You Missed Questions . . .	16	17	18	19	20	21
Go to Page . . .	1041	R18	1044	1059	R19	1054

Document-Based Questions

19. Congressman Barr believes the Patriot Act violates the Fourth Amendment by invading privacy and gathering evidence with no warrant, proof or suspicion of a crime.

20. Congressman Sensenbrenner counters that the Patriot Act does not violate any civil rights and that the congressional committee that investigated it found no violations of civil rights.

Extended Response

21. This is currently a controversial topic. Accept any well-reasoned and reasonable answer. Students' essays should follow the proper format for a persuasive essay and include an acknowledgment and rebuttal of the opposing position.

16. D If students have trouble with this question, review "Homeland Security and Patriot Act" on page 1040. It makes sense that FEMA would be under Homeland Security because the agency would be responsible for helping with rescue and clean up for a domestic disaster.

17. B In the cartoon, the "world" is wearing a suit and watching TV. He is pointing at the TV and looks distraught. His speech bubble says "Oh No!!" On the TV, President Bush is seen holding up his arms making the "V for victory" sign. The world is clearly not happy with the reelection of George W. Bush.

18. C There was no evidence found of an allegiance between Hussein and al-Qaeda. Bin Laden was believed to be hiding in the mountains of Afghanistan. Iraq was not proved to have had WMDs, so *D* is incorrect.

History ONLINE

Have students visit the Web site at glencoe.com to review Chapter 31 and take the Self-Check Quiz.

Need Extra Help?

Have students refer to the pages listed if they miss any of the questions.

Appendix

Contents

Skills Handbook Table of Contents

Critical Thinking Skills

Social Studies Skills

Teach

Introduction

The following **Skills Handbook** offers opportunities to practice individual critical thinking and social studies skills. Students can benefit in multiple ways from completing the lessons. First, being equipped with these skills makes students' reading more meaningful and supports the content of the text. Second, the lessons give students practice in using skills they will need to complete standardized tests successfully since many of these skills are assessed on standardized tests.

You may use these lessons at any point in the text and in any order that you wish. You can also use these lessons as review for students who need extra practice with these skills.

Teach

S Skill Practice

Analyzing Tell students that being able to identify the main idea is a key reading skill whether they are reading fact or fiction. Have students think about a fictional story they have read recently or about a movie they have seen. Have students tell the rest of the class the title of the book or movie and give a two-minute statement that tells what the main idea of the movie or story was. **Ask:** Was the main idea presented at the beginning of the story or did it become apparent at the end of the story? OL

Identifying the Main Idea

Migrant mother and children in California, 1936

Why Learn This Skill?

S Finding the main idea in a reading passage will help you see the "big picture" by organizing information and determining the most important concepts to remember.

Learning the Skill

Follow these steps to learn how to make a valid generalization. Then answer the questions below.

"In this nation I see tens of millions of its citizens . . . who at this very moment are denied the greater part of what the very lowest standards of today call the necessities of life. I see millions of families trying to live on incomes so meager that the pall of family disaster hangs over them day by day. . . . see one-third of a nation ill-housed, ill-clad, ill-nourished.

It is not in despair that I paint you that picture. I paint it for you in hope—because the Nation, seeing and understanding the injustice in it, proposes to paint it out. We are determined to make every American citizen the subject of his country's interest and concern. . . . The test of our progress is not whether we add more to the abundance of those who have much; it is whether we provide enough for those who have too little."

—Franklin D. Roosevelt, Second Inaugural Address, January 20, 1937

1. Determine the setting of the passage.

2. Skim the material to identify its general subject. Look at headings and subheadings.

3. Notice any details that support a larger idea or issue.

4. Identify the central issue. Ask: What part of the selection conveys the main idea?

As you read the material, ask yourself: What is the purpose of this passage—why was it written?

Practicing the Skill

1. On what occasion was this speech given?
2. When was this speech given?
3. What was the condition of the people mentioned in this passage?
4. What did Roosevelt think should be done about the situation discussed?

Applying the Skill

Bring to class an article about American history from the Internet or another source. Identify the main idea and explain why it is important.

Practicing the Skill: Answers

1. This speech was given by Franklin D. Roosevelt as his Second Inaugural Address.
2. This speech was documented on January 20, 1937.
3. Many citizens are deprived of the basic necessities of human life. They are poor and hungry.
4. Roosevelt proposes that the government (the Nation) help these people.

Determining Cause and Effect

The effect of pesticides on wildlife

Why Learn This Skill?

Determining cause and effect involves considering *why* an event occurred. That helps you analyze how to encourage or prevent the same event in the future. A *cause* is an action or a situation that produces an event. What happens as a result of a cause is an *effect*.

Learning the Skill

To identify cause-and-effect relationships, follow these steps:

D **1.** Identify two or more events or developments.

2. Decide whether one event caused the other. Look for "clue words" such as *because, led to, brought about, so that, after that, produced, as a result of, since, in the wake of, as a result.*

C **3.** Identify the outcomes of events. Remember that some effects have more than one cause, and some causes lead to more than one effect. Also, an effect can become the cause of yet another effect.

Look for logical relationships between events, such as "She overslept, so she missed her bus."

"*. . . in 1957, there was a startling wildlife mortality in the wake of a mosquito-control campaign near Duxbury, Mass., followed by a pointless spraying of a DDT/fuel-oil mix over eastern Long Island for eradication of the gypsy moth. Next, an all-out war in the Southern states against the fire ant did such widespread harm to other creatures that its beneficiaries cried for mercy; and after that a great furor arose across the country over the spraying of cranberry plants with aminotriazole, which led to an Agriculture Department ban against all cranberry marketing just in time for Thanksgiving 1959. . . .*

Even before publication [of Rachel Carson's indictment of pesticides, Silent Spring,*] Carson was violently assailed by threats of lawsuits and derision. . . . A huge counterattack was organized and led by . . . the whole chemical industry.*"

—*Time,* March 29, 1999

Practicing the Skill

Categorize the items below as *cause, effect, both,* or *neither.*

1. Rachel Carson published *Silent Spring*, criticizing chemical pesticides.
2. Duxbury's wildlife mortality rate rose significantly in 1957.
3. The gypsy moth is a common insect on Long Island.
4. The Agriculture Department banned cranberry marketing.
5. Southern states used pesticides to eradicate the fire ant.
6. The chemical industry threatened Carson with lawsuits.

Applying the Skill

In a newspaper, read an article describing a current event. Determine at least one cause and one effect of that event, and complete a flowchart like the one below.

Cause → Event → Effect

Practicing the Skill: Answers

1. Both
2. Effect
3. Cause
4. Effect
5. Both
6. Effect

Teach

C Critical Thinking

Determining Cause and Effect The statement in item 3 under Learning the Skill states "... an effect can become the cause of yet another effect." This is a cause-and-effect chain. Have students consider such cause-and-effect chains and choose one to research and write about. Tell students that the chain can affect the environment, human population, animal population, or all of the above. Tell them to describe this chain in as much detail as they can. If possible, ask them to create a graphic to illustrate their cause-and-effect chain. AL

D Differentiated Instruction

Below Grade Level Ask: What might the effects of the spraying of DDT/fuel-oil mix be? *(The effects could be damage to the population's health, environment, and water systems.)* BL

Teach

C Critical Thinking

Making Generalizations
Have students research print or online sources to find out more about the roles of women in World War II. Then have them write three paragraphs that make generalizations about women on America's home front during World War II. Ask them to provide evidence from the article to support their generalizations. OL

Making Generalizations

Why Learn This Skill?

Generalizations are conclusions that are usually accurate, based on the facts at hand. Generalizations are useful in studying history because they help you see trends. If you say, "Most Mexican immigrants to the United States in the early twentieth century worked in agriculture," that's a generalization. To support it, you could mention that federal funding of irrigation projects in the Southwest in 1902 gave rise to large farms requiring thousands of workers. Not all Mexican immigrants at that time became farmworkers, but many did.

Women workers install fixtures and assemblies to a tail fuselage section of a B-17 bomber at Douglas Aircraft Company's, Long Beach, California, plant.

Learning the Skill

To learn how to make a valid generalization, follow these steps:

1. Identify the subject matter.
2. Collect factual information and examples relevant to the topic.
3. Identify similarities among these facts.

Use these similarities to form some general ideas about the subject.

C

"*The war years had a tremendous impact on women. . . . it was the first time I had a chance to get out of the kitchen and work in industry and make a few bucks. This was something I had never dreamed would happen. In Sapulpa [Oklahoma] all that women had to look forward to was keeping a house and raising families. The war years offered new possibilities. You came out to California, put on your pants and took your lunch pail to a man's job. In Oklahoma a woman's place was in the home, and men went to work and provided. This was the beginning of women's feeling that they could do something more.*"

—Sybil Lewis, quoted in *The Homefront: America During World War II*

Practicing the Skill

After reading the excerpt above, determine whether each generalization that follows is valid or invalid. Explain your answers.

1. During World War II, women did not want to work outside the home.
2. Women have careers only so that they can afford luxuries.
3. During the war, women had more choices in California than in Oklahoma.

Applying the Skill

Read three editorials in a newspaper and make a generalization about each.

Practicing the Skill: Answers

1. invalid; Students should note that the excerpt tells of a woman working outside the home for the first time.
2. invalid; There is no information in the excerpt that describes working to afford luxuries.
3. valid; The author compares women's roles in California and Oklahoma in this way.

Distinguishing Fact from Opinion

Why Learn This Skill?

R To make reasonable judgments about what others say or write, it is important to distinguish facts from opinions. Facts can be proved by evidence such as records, documents, or historical sources. Opinions are based on people's differing values and beliefs.

Richard M. Nixon

Learning the Skill

To learn how to separate facts from opinions, follow these steps:

1. Identify the facts. Ask: Which statements can be proved? Where would I find information to verify this statement? If the information is a statistic, it may sound impressive, but you won't know if it's accurate unless you check the source.

2. Identify opinions by looking for statements of feelings or beliefs. Opinions sometimes contain words like *should, would, could, best, greatest, all, every,* or *always.*

> *"In speaking of the consequences of a precipitate withdrawal [from Vietnam], I mentioned that our allies would lose confidence in America. Far more dangerous, we would lose confidence in ourselves. . . .*
>
> *In San Francisco a few weeks ago, I saw demonstrators carrying signs reading: "Lose in Vietnam, bring the boys home."*
>
> *Well, one of the strengths of our free society is that any American has a right to reach that conclusion and to advocate that point of view. But as President of the United States, I would be untrue to my oath of office if I allowed the policy of this Nation to be dictated by the minority who hold that point of view and who try to impose it on the Nation by mounting demonstrations in the street.*
>
> *. . . If a vocal minority, however fervent its cause, prevails over reason and the will of the majority, this Nation has no future as a free society."*
>
> —Richard M. Nixon speech, November 3, 1969

Practicing the Skill

D The excerpt above is from a televised speech given by President Richard M. Nixon in 1969, when a Gallup poll showed that 58 percent of Americans believed the Vietnam War was a mistake. Reread the excerpt and answer the questions that follow.

1. Which statements in the passage are factual?
2. Which statements are opinions? Explain.
3. What was the speaker's purpose?

Applying the Skill

Watch a television interview. Then list three facts and three opinions that you hear.

Teach

R Reading Strategy

Activating Prior Knowledge Have students review the various critical thinking skills they have encountered to determine which skills rely more on facts and which rely on opinion. **Ask:** Which skills utilize facts to form an opinion? *(drawing conclusions, making generalizations, predicting, making inferences)* **AL**

D Differentiated Instruction

Interpersonal Tell students that debates are forums in which facts and opinions are shaped into organized arguments for or against a specific question. Have students work in two groups to gather facts and form opinions about an issue at your school or from your community. Schedule a debate between the two sides. **OL**

Practicing the Skill: Answers

1. The factual statements include:
   Demonstrators were carrying signs in San Francisco.
   Americans have the right to advocate their point of view.
2. The opinions include:
   Our allies would lose confidence in America.
   We would lose confidence in ourselves.
   He would be untrue to his oath of office.
   If a vocal minority prevails, this Nation would not be a free society.
3. Nixon is defending his decision to not withdraw troops from Vietnam.

Teach

S Skill Practice

Applying **Ask:** What do you do when you can't find an answer to your question? *(ask another question)* Have students develop three questions about the critical thinking skill of formulating questions. Tell them to be sure that the questions are not the ones posed in Learning the Skill. The questions should be about asking questions, not about the chart in Practicing the Skill. After students have formed their questions, have them ask the questions for the rest of the class to try to answer. OL

Formulating Questions

Why Learn This Skill?

Asking questions helps you to understand and remember what you read. Learning increases when you ask yourself what is important about the topic and what you would like to know about the people, places, and events. S

Jackie Robinson

Learning the Skill

Follow these steps to formulate questions:

1. Think of questions you would like to have answered.
2. Ask *who, what, when, where, why,* and *how* about the main ideas, people, places, and events.
3. Reread the section to be sure all your questions have been answered.

> *"In 1947 life in America . . . was segregation. . . . But Jackie Robinson, God bless him, was bigger than all of that.*
>
> *. . . He had to be bigger than the Brooklyn teammates who got up a petition to keep him off the ball club, bigger than the pitchers who threw at him or the base runners who dug their spikes into his shin, bigger than the bench jockeys who hollered for him to . . . shine their shoes, bigger than the so-called fans who . . . wrote him death threats.*
>
> *. . . Somehow, though, Jackie had the strength to . . . sacrifice his pride for his people's. It was an incredible act of selflessness that brought the races closer together than ever before and shaped the dreams of an entire generation."*
>
> —Henry "Hank" Aaron, holder of major-league career home-run record, *Time*, June 14, 1999

Practicing the Skill

The excerpt above is about the first African American major-league baseball player. After reading it, use a chart like the one below and find the answers in the excerpt.

	Question	Answer
Who?		
What?		
Where?		
When?		
Why?		
How?		

Applying the Skill

Select any section of this textbook to read or reread. Make a question chart to help you ask and answer five or more questions about the section as you read.

Practicing the Skill: Answers

	Question	Answer
Who?	Who is the excerpt about?	Jackie Robinson
What?	What is the main idea of the excerpt?	Jackie overcoming racism
Where?	Where did these events take place?	Jackie played baseball in Brooklyn.
When?	When did the events take place?	1947
Why?	Why did Jackie choose to do this?	He chose to withstand the difficulties to uphold his race and dignity.
How?	How did Jackie overcome segregation?	He had the strength to withstand all those people who threatened and attempted to keep him from playing.

Analyzing Information

Why Learn This Skill?

The ability to analyze information is important in deciding what you think about a subject. For example, you need to analyze the benefits of social services versus the benefits of small government to decide where you stand on the issue of Social Security.

Gloria Steinem (right) with Adelaide Abankwah, a Ghanian asylum-seeker, in 1999

S

Learning the Skill

To analyze information, use the following steps:

1. Identify the topic being discussed.
2. Examine how the information is organized. What are the main points?
3. Summarize the information in your own words, and then make a statement of your own based on your understanding of the topic and on what you already know.

"Having spent most of my adult life in social justice movements—from living in post-Gandhian India to working in the civil rights, farm worker and peace movements here, and most of all, in the feminist movement—I've seen constant proof that revolutions are like houses: They can't be built from the top down. Leaders can issue blueprints, which we then adapt to our needs or quietly sabotage. They can prevent us from following our own plan, divide the work force against itself and otherwise slow or stop progress. But what they can't do is create organic and lasting change from the top. Attempts to do so, even in the most authoritarian of systems, eventually end in reversion to old ways, as we see in the countries where Communism and artificial national boundaries were once imposed by Moscow."

—Gloria Steinem, from *The Nation*, July 20–27, 1992

Practicing the Skill

After reading the excerpt above, answer the following questions:

1. What topic is being discussed?
2. What are the writer's main points?
3. Summarize the information in this excerpt, and then provide your analysis, based on this information and what you already know about the subject.

W

Applying the Skill

Select an issue that is currently in the news, such as Social Security, oil prices, global warming, or taxation. Read an article or watch a news segment about the issue. Analyze the information and make a brief statement of your own about the topic. Explain your thinking.

Practicing the Skill: Answers

1. social justice movements and how they arise
2. Revolutions cannot be started by governments, they need to be started by people.
3. Students' summaries should include the idea that governments cannot produce lasting change. It must be a grassroots movement. Students' analyses will vary.

Teach

S Skill Practice

Analyzing Tell students that the Learning the Skill section talks about social issues. Have students work in groups to research issues in various parts of the United States. As students identify an area to be researched, have them analyze the information they find on that area. Tell students to document their research and share it with the class. As students present their research, plot the information on a U.S. map. **Ask: Does your collective research show that this is a growing problem?** OL

W Writing Support

Persuasive Writing Have students write a one-page persuasive argument for or against the need to prevent global warming. OL

Teach

C Critical Thinking

Evaluating a Web Site Point out that virtually anyone can create and post a Web page. There are hosting sites that allow individuals to post Web pages at no charge. This means that when you search for Jimmy Carter, it is likely that your results will include authoritative sites with content developed by historians and a site that showcases a child's third-grade homework assignment. Ask students to search for Web sites about a topic or person in American history. Have students find a site that they consider authoritative. Have them print out the home page of the site and write a brief explanation of why they rate the site as authoritative. **OL**

Evaluating Information

Why Learn This Skill?

We live in an information age. Because the amount of information available can be overwhelming, it is sometimes difficult to tell which information is accurate and useful. To do this, you have to evaluate what you read and hear. **C**

Soaring gas prices in the early 2000s frustrated consumers.

Learning the Skill

To figure out how reliable information is, ask yourself the following questions as you read:

> *"The single biggest factor in . . . the increase in the inflation rate last year was from one cause: the skyrocketing prices of OPEC oil. We must take whatever actions are necessary to reduce our dependence on foreign oil—and at the same time reduce inflation."*
>
> —former president Jimmy Carter, January 23, 1980

> *"Oil prices are so high, becuz big oil companys are tryng to goug us. Greedy oil executives, are driven up prices to get richer."*
>
> —on an individual's Internet "blog"

> *"It's certainly clear that high oil prices aren't dulling demand for energy products. According to the Energy Dept.'s Energy Information Administration (EIA), U.S. demand for gasoline in June was 9.5 million barrels per day, a record."*
>
> —*BusinessWeek,* July 7, 2006

1. Is the author or speaker identified? Is he or she an authority on the subject?
2. Is there bias? Does the source unfairly present just one point of view, ignoring any arguments against it?
3. Is the information printed in a credible, reliable publication?
4. Is the information backed up by facts and other sources? Does it seem to be accurate?
5. Is it well written and well edited? Writing filled with errors in spelling, grammar, and punctuation is likely to be careless in other ways, too.

Also notice whether the information is up-to-date.

Practicing the Skill

After reading the statements above, rank them in order of most reliable to least reliable. Explain why you ranked them as you did.

Applying the Skill

Find an advertisement that contains text and bring it to class. In a brief oral presentation, tell the class whether the information in the advertisement is reliable or unreliable, and why.

Practicing the Skill: Answers

1. Students' rankings will vary. Students should be prepared to provide reasons for their rankings.

Making Inferences

Why Learn This Skill?

To *infer* means to evaluate information and arrive at a conclusion. When you make inferences, you "read between the lines," or use clues to figure something out that is not stated directly in the text.

Men read posters at an office of the National Association Opposed to Woman Suffrage.

Learning the Skill

Follow these steps to make inferences:

1. Read carefully for facts and ideas, and list them.
2. Summarize the information.
3. Consider what you may already know about the topic.
4. Use your knowledge and insight to develop logical conclusions.

"*Because the suffrage is not a question of right or of justice, but of policy and expediency. . . .*

. . . Because it means simply doubling the vote, and especially the undesirable and corrupt vote of our large cities.

. . . Because the great advance of women in the last century—moral, intellectual and economic—has been made without the vote; which goes to prove that it is not needed for their further advancement along the same lines.

. . . Because our present duties fill up the whole measure of our time and ability, and are such as none but us can perform. Our appreciation of their importance requires us to protest against all efforts to infringe upon our rights by imposing upon us those obligations which can not be . . . performed by us without the sacrifice of the highest interests of our families and our society."

—from Northern California Association Opposed to Woman Suffrage, 1912

Practicing the Skill

After reading the statement above, answer the following questions:

1. What points do the authors make?
2. Which points does your experience contradict?
3. What inferences might you draw about the women who wrote the document?

Applying the Skill

S Read an editorial printed in today's newspaper. What can you infer about the importance of the topic being addressed? Can you tell how the writer feels about the topic? Explain your answer.

Teach

S Skill Practice

Applying Bring in a copy of a front page of a daily newspaper to class. Put the front page up on the board and have students study it from their seats. Most students will not be able to read more than the headlines of the paper. Have students write a page of inferences they make based on what they can see. After students have had a chance to note their inferences, have them share them with the class. **Ask:** **What does this exercise tell you about inferences?** *(that much of what a person infers is dependent upon prior knowledge and facts at hand)*

Practicing the Skill: Answers

1. Students should include the following:
   Suffrage is not a right.
   Woman suffrage would just double the vote.
   Women have advanced without suffrage.
   Women are too busy to vote.
2. Student answers will vary, but many students will understand that voting is a right and that it enables progress to be made.
3. Students should infer that the authors did not want suffrage, instead seeing it as an unnecessary obligation.

Teach

S Skill Practice

Analyzing After students have read the lesson and engaged in practicing the skill, have them study the images on the page. Working with partners, have the students compare and contrast the two images. Possible comparisons include content, topic, style, and colors. As students begin to accumulate data that reflects similarities and differences, have them create a chart or graph that clearly shows their findings. **OL**

Comparing and Contrasting

Why Learn This Skill?

When you make comparisons, you determine similarities among ideas, objects, or events. When you contrast, you are noting differences between ideas, objects, or events. Comparing and contrasting are important skills because they help you choose among several possible alternatives.

Learning the Skill

To compare or contrast items, follow these steps:

1. Select the items to compare or contrast.
2. To compare, determine a common area or areas in which comparisons can be drawn, such as topic, style, or point of view. Look for similarities within these areas.
3. To contrast, look for differences that set the items apart from each other.

S

Practicing the Skill

After studying the paintings above, answer these questions:

1. How are the paintings similar?
2. How are they different?
3. What do the answers to questions 1 and 2 tell you about the two artists' attitudes toward their subject?

Applying the Skill

Survey 10 of your classmates about an issue in the news, and summarize their responses. Then write a paragraph or two comparing and contrasting their opinions.

Practicing the Skill: Answers

1. Students may mention that they are both paintings depicting people.
2. Students should note that the styles are different. Whereas one is realistic, the other is contemporary.
3. Answers will vary. Students should note that whereas the first artist shows a very noble and serious style, the other takes a more abstract approach.

Detecting Bias

Why Learn This Skill?

Most people have a point of view, or bias. This bias influences the way they interpret and write about events and issues.

A politician running for reelection, for example, may claim the economy is strong because 20,000 new jobs were created last month. His or her opponent may say the economy is weak because 40,000 people also lost jobs last month. Recognizing bias helps you judge the accuracy of what you hear or read.

Southerners seize abolitionist literature from a local post office in South Carolina in the 1840s.

Learning the Skill

To recognize bias, follow these steps:

1. Consider the author's identity, location, and motivation. Does the writer or a group he or she represents benefit from an outcome supported in the article?
2. Identify statements of fact, if any.
3. Identify any expressions of opinion or emotion. Look for words with positive or negative overtones for clues about the author's feelings on a topic.
4. Determine the author's point of view.
5. Notice how the author's point of view is reflected in the work.

"*The great conservative institution of slavery, so excellent in itself, and so necessary to civil liberty and the dignity of the white race, is one of the grand objects of our struggle. It should never be lost sight of, nor under any pressure should we ever take any step incompatible with the relation of master and slave. . . . Our theory is, that he is better off as a slave; and even if he were not, we could not safely have an emancipated class of them amongst us. Much less can we put arms in his hands. . . . Slavery afterwards would become impossible.*"

—Editorial from the Washington, Arkansas, *Telegraph*, January 13, 1865

Practicing the Skill

Read the passage above and then answer the following questions:

1. What is the purpose of this passage?
2. What statements of fact and/or opinion are presented?
3. What evidence of bias do you find?
4. How does the author attempt to convince the audience?

Applying the Skill

C Find an editorial in the newspaper that deals with a topic of interest to you. Apply the steps for recognizing bias to the editorial. Write a paragraph summarizing your findings.

Teach

C Critical Thinking

Detecting Bias Ask students to find letters to the editor on the editorial page of the newspaper they employ in Applying the Skill. Have students continue their exercise from Applying the Skill to these letters. Have students write a sentence or two summarizing the bias of the writer. **Ask:** Do any of the letters conflict with each other? Do any of the letters conflict with the opinions of the newspaper? *(Answers will vary.)* **AL**

Practicing the Skill: Answers

1. The purpose is to support the institution of slavery.
2. Many opinions are presented—that African Americans are better off as slaves, they cannot live free safely, that we cannot arm them.
3. Students should note that the author sees only one side of slavery.
4. The author uses arguments to justify slavery because, he or she says, it is a better state for African Americans.

Teach

S Skill Practice

Synthesizing Tell students to research the situation in Vietnam starting in the 1960s, apply the critical thinking skill of synthesizing information, and report on what their conclusions are. **Ask:** What are your sources? What did your sources add to your understanding of the situation? What are your conclusions based on your synthesis of information? *(Answers will vary.)* OL

W Writing Support

Personal Have students write a one-page statement that expresses their personal conclusion about the war in Vietnam based on the information they read. Tell them to be sure and support their conclusion with facts. OL

Synthesizing Information

Why Learn This Skill?

Synthesizing information involves combining information from two or more sources. Each source may shed new light on other information.

Antiwar rally, Miami Beach, Florida, 1972

Learning the Skill

Follow these steps to learn how to synthesize information:

1. Analyze each source separately to understand its meaning.

2. Determine what information and whose perspective each source adds to the subject.

Source A "*We should declare war on North Vietnam. . . . It's silly talking about how many years we will have to spend in the jungles of Vietnam when we could pave the whole country and put parking stripes on it and still be home for Christmas.*"

—future president Ronald Reagan, 1965

Source B "*Vietnam presumably taught us that the United States could not serve as the world's policeman; it should also have taught us the dangers of trying to be the world's midwife to democracy when the birth is scheduled to take place under conditions of guerrilla war.*"

—Jeane Kirkpatrick, future UN ambassador and foreign policy adviser to Ronald Reagan, 1979

Source C "*People say we could have won the [Vietnam] war—we know we could not. People say the anti-war movement harassed and betrayed the soldiers . . . the people who supported the war, the folks who favored intervention, the people who sent us crusading against communism—they betrayed us, their own sons and daughters. Anti-war veterans are the witnesses against them . . . we saw the system was not working, we knew the war had to stop.*"

—Ben Chitty, member Vietnam Veterans Against the War, April, 2000

3. Identify points of agreement and disagreement among the sources. Ask: Can Source B or C give me new ways of thinking about Source A?

4. Determine how the sources relate to each other.

Practicing the Skill

After reading the passages above, answer the questions that follow.

1. What is the main subject of each source?
2. Does Source B support or contradict Source A? Does Source C support or contradict source A? Explain.
3. Summarize what you learned from the three sources.
4. Which source do you consider the most reliable? Explain why.

Applying the Skill

Find two sources of information on any period of history that interests you. What are the main ideas in the sources? How does each source add to your understanding of the topic?

Practicing the Skill: Answers

1. the Vietnam War
2. Source B contradicts Source A. Whereas Source A states that the war in Vietnam will be quick and easy, Source B refers to the dangers of the war. Source C contradicts Source A. Source C states that the war was not easy; we could not have won it.
3. Answers will vary, but students should conclude that there are many opinions about the war in Vietnam.
4. Students should support their opinions. Be sure that students note the sources of each excerpt.

Drawing Conclusions

Why Learn This Skill?

D1 A conclusion is a logical understanding that you reach based on details or facts that you read or hear. When you draw conclusions, you use stated information to formulate ideas that are unstated.

Victorian-era house for sale

D2 Learning the Skill

Follow these steps to draw conclusions:

1. Read the text and labels carefully, looking for facts and ideas.
2. Summarize the information. List trends or important facts.
3. Apply related information that you may already have.
4. Use your knowledge and insight to develop some logical conclusions.

Homeownership in the U.S., 1890–2005

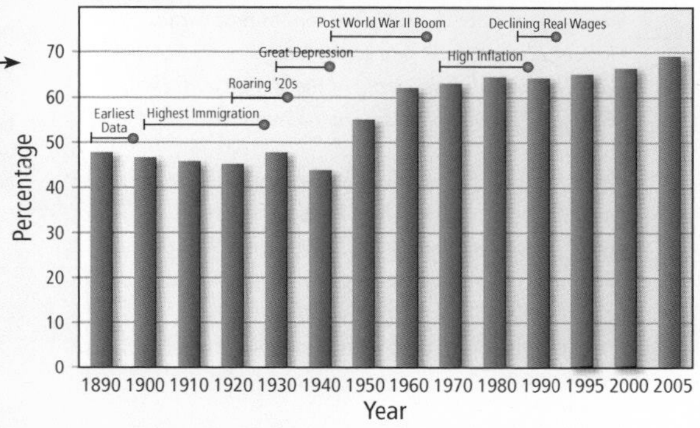

Source: U.S. Bureau of the Census; U.S. Department of Commerce

Practicing the Skill

The bar graph above shows the percentage of Americans who owned their own homes during various time periods. Study the graph and answer the following questions:

1. When was the home ownership rate the lowest? Why do you think this was so?
2. During what 20-year period did home ownership rates increase the most? Why do you think this happened?
3. What conclusions can you draw about trends in home ownership?

Applying the Skill

Read one of the People in History profiles in this book. Using the information in the profile, what conclusions can you draw about the life of the person described?

Teach

D1 Differentiated Instruction

Interpersonal Tell students that people draw conclusions all the time. Ask students to write down three facts (real or hypothetical) about themselves—such as "I've always had pets; I enjoy science; I want to work with animals"—and read them aloud to the class. See if classmates can draw the correct conclusions from the facts provided. OL

D2 Differentiated Instruction

Logical/Mathematical Ask students to research a measurable trend in the United States, then have them explain the topic in terms of numbers and percentages. **Ask:** How can numbers support the conclusion? OL

Practicing the Skill: Answers

1. 1940; few people owned homes during this era of the Great Depression.
2. Home ownership increased the most between 1940 and 1950 as Americans moved out of the Depression and to an age of prosperity in the post-war boom.
3. Home ownership increases in times of prosperity.

Teach

C Critical Thinking

Activating Prior Knowledge
Explain to students that predictions are not based on random guesses. Instead, they are based on extending knowledge of facts, events, reactions, patterns, and trends to new circumstances. Ask students to offer examples of how this skill is used in business, government, and personal situations. *(Students' answers will vary. For example, a business has to predict consumer behavior before a product is launched.)* BL

Predicting Consequences

Why Learn This Skill?

Predicting most future events is difficult, but the more information you have, the more accurate your predictions will be. Making good predictions will help you to make better decisions based on their likely outcomes. Using these skills can also help you to understand the outcomes of historical events. C

Lois Gibbs

Learning the Skill

To help you make predictions, follow these steps:

1. Gather information about the topic.

"In the mid-1950s, the Niagara Falls board of education built an elementary school adjacent to a site where Hooker Chemical and Plastics Corporation had dumped more than 22,000 tons of toxic waste. Housing also was built next to the landfill, called Love Canal. Chemicals leached out of the landfill and, by 1976, had shown up in yards and basements.

Residents were frequently sick and eventually were found to have extremely high rates of cancer, birth defects, miscarriages, and stillborns. In 1978 Lois Gibbs and other residents began a 3-year battle against Hooker and many levels of government, which claimed the health issues were not related to the chemicals.

By 1980, President Jimmy Carter declared Love Canal a federal emergency and more than 1,000 families were relocated and paid for their homes. The tragedy led to "Superfund" legislation that collects taxes from gas and chemical companies, to be used to clean up similar sites."

2. Use your experience and your knowledge of history and human behavior to predict what consequences could result.

3. Analyze each consequence by asking yourself: How likely is it that this will happen?

Practicing the Skill

1. Do you think the problem described in the passage is likely to reoccur elsewhere?
2. On what do you base your prediction?
3. What are the possible benefits and drawbacks of the "Superfund" legislation described in the passage?

Applying the Skill

Analyze three newspaper articles about an event affecting your community or the nation. Make an educated prediction about what will happen, and explain your reasoning. Then write a letter to the editor, summarizing your prediction. You may want to check back later to see if your prediction came true.

Practicing the Skill: Answers

1. Students should recognize that the problem could occur in other places if companies have dumped waste.
2. Students should base their prediction on the cause and effects given in the excerpts and knowledge that some companies produce toxic waste.
3. Students may note the benefits are penalties to companies for dumping waste, which may prevent this practice from occurring in the future. Drawbacks are that if companies can afford the penalties, they may continue the practice.

Reading a Special-Purpose Map

Why Learn This Skill?

Special-purpose maps show more than the location of places. They are useful because they show trends or movements of people or things in a concise, visual way.

Learning the Skill

To read a special-purpose map, follow these steps:

1. Read the title to see what topic is illustrated. If the time period being covered is part of the title, notice that.
2. Read the legend and any other text.
3. Notice the movement shown on the map, if any, including the direction of any arrows, where paths lead, or the concentration of several things in certain places.
4. Ask yourself: What have I learned from this map? What can I conclude from this information?

NATIONAL GEOGRAPHIC **Migration in the United States, 1940–1950**

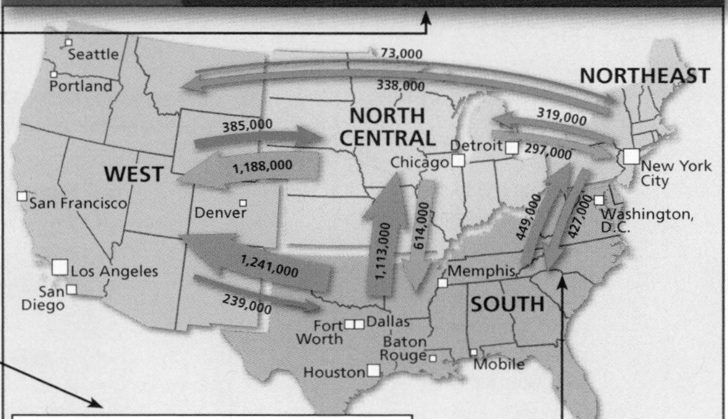

Urban Population Increase, 1940–1947

- 400,000 and over
- 200,000–399,999
- 100,000–199,999
- 50,000–99,999
- Population migration between regions

S

Practicing the Skill

Answer the following questions about the map above:

1. What period in history does the map cover?
2. Was the U.S. population fairly mobile or stationary during this time?
3. Name two cities that gained 400,000 or more residents.
4. From what part of the country did most immigrants to the West come?

Applying the Skill

Study the map in Section 3 of the "Settling the West" chapter. Then answer these questions.

1. Name three states through which Chief Joseph traveled in 1877.
2. What part of the country had the largest number of reservations at this time?
3. What does the map tell you about the compromises Native Americans made to the settlers?

Teach

S Skill Practice

Using a Map Looking at a map allows the user to see the big picture, including the physical relationship of the various areas depicted. To take advantage of seeing the big picture, it is important for students to understand the parts of the map. Have students describe what trend this map is showing. *(migration in the United States from 1940 to 1950)* **OL**

Practicing the Skill: Answers

1. 1940–1950
2. The U.S. population was mobile at this time.
3. Los Angeles and New York City
4. the South

Teach

S Skill Practice

Applying Have students research the ethnic makeup of their community based on the most recent census. Then, have them show that makeup in the form of a graph of their choosing. **OL**

W Writing Support

Expository After students have developed their graph that shows the ethnic makeup of their community, have them write a one-page expository paper that explains and interprets the graph, its results, and how the data was collected. **AL**

Interpreting Graphs

Bar graphs are often used to compare quantities. By presenting similar categories of information visually, often on a grid, they make it easy to see the relationships among the categories. **S**

Why Learn This Skill?

Being able to read bar graphs makes it easy to understand and analyze data quickly.

Learning the Skill

Follow these steps to learn how to understand and use bar graphs. Then answer the questions below.

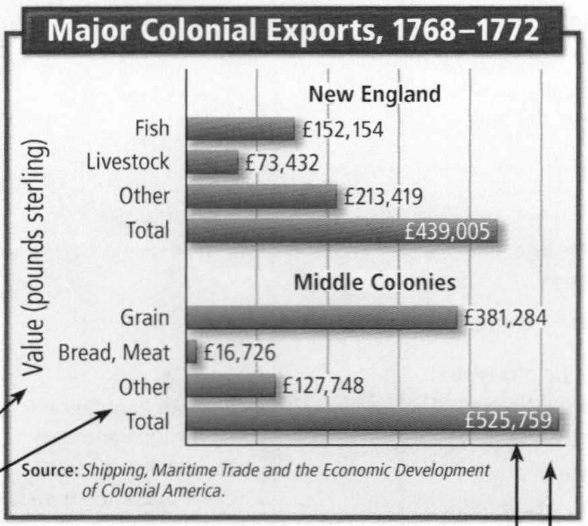

1. Read the title to see what topic is being illustrated. Notice whether the period of time covered or other information is included within or just below the title.
2. Read the labels to see what categories are being compared, and what measure is being used; for example, dollars, thousands of people, bushels of grain, etc.
3. Notice the numbers that correlate to the ends of the bars.
4. Compare the lengths of the bars and draw a conclusion about the relationships being shown.

Practicing the Skill

1. What is the topic of this bar graph?
2. In what currency does the graph measure the products?
3. Which type of exports were the least valuable?
4. If you were going into the export business in 1770, which product would you want to export? Why?

Applying the Skill

Ask five students what their favorite food is. Then create a bar graph showing which foods are the most popular. **W**

Practicing the Skill: Answers

1. major colonial exports from 1768 to 1772
2. British pounds
3. bread and meat
4. grain, because it has the highest value

Sequencing Events

Why Learn This Skill?

C Sequencing involves placing facts in the order in which they occurred. Sequencing helps you deal with large quantities of information in an understandable way. In studying history, sequencing can help you understand cause-and-effect relationships among events. This in turn helps analysts to predict outcomes of various events or policies.

John Wilkes Booth escaping Ford's Theatre after shooting President Lincoln

Learning the Skill

To sequence events, follow these steps:

1. Look for dates or clue words: *in 1920, later that year, first, then*, and so on.
2. Arrange facts in the order in which they occurred. Events are not always presented in sequential order. Ask: Would this logically have happened next?

Consider using an organizational tool such as a time line, which makes it easy to see the chronology as well as any cause-and-effect relationships between events.

> *"This evening [April 14] at about 9:30 P.M., at Ford's Theatre, the President, while sitting in the private box with Mrs. Lincoln . . . was shot by an assassin, who suddenly entered the box and approached behind the President.*
>
> *The assassin then leaped upon the stage brandishing a large dagger or knife, and made his escape in the rear of the theatre.*
>
> *. . . It is not probable that the President will live through the night.*
>
> *. . . Gen. Grant and wife were advertised to be at the theatre this evening, but he started to Burlington at six o'clock this evening.*
>
> *At a Cabinet meeting, at which Gen. Grant was present, the subject of the state of the country and the prospect of a speedy peace was discussed. The President was very cheerful and hopeful, and spoke very kindly of Gen. Lee and others of the confederacy."*
>
> —War Department statement of April 14, 1865, printed in *New York Times*, April 15

Practicing the Skill

Read the passage above and answer the questions that follow.

1. What dates or clue words in this passage help you determine the sequence of the events?
2. Complete a time line such as the one at right to show the sequence of events described in the selection.

Applying the Skill

Find a newspaper or magazine article about a recent event. Sequence the information presented in the article in a time line or chart.

Teach

C Critical Thinking

Sequencing This skill emphasizes the importance of chronological thinking to the study of history. By learning to put things in chronological order, students gain an appreciation for relationships among events. Have students choose several events that occurred in the 1900s. Ask them to write the events down, and then place them in the correct sequence on a time line. **OL**

Practicing the Skill: Answers

1. April 14, around 9:30 PM, then, this evening, six o'clock this evening
2. Students' time lines should show the following sequence of events:

   First Event: Cabinet meeting

   Second Event: General Grant and his wife started to Burlington

   Third Event: President shot

   Final Event: Assassin escaped; President not thought to live

Teach

C Critical Thinking

Interpreting Tell students that political cartoons have long been used as an effective means of expressing opinions about events, laws, and political figures. Bring several current political cartoons from local or national newspapers to class. Ask students to identify and interpret the caricatures and symbols used in the cartoons. Have students write a sentence summarizing the point being made by each of the political cartoonists. **OL**

Interpreting Political Cartoons

Why Learn This Skill?

Political cartoons are drawings that express an opinion about public figures, political issues, or economic or social conditions. They appear in newspapers, magazines, books, and on the Internet. They are **C** intended to convince readers of the artist's or the publication's opinion in an amusing way. Knowing how to interpret a political cartoon is useful because it helps you put issues and candidates in perspective.

Learning the Skill

To interpret a political cartoon, follow these steps:

1. Read the title, caption, conversation balloons, and other text to identify the subject of the cartoon.
2. Identify the characters, people, or symbols shown.
3. Ask yourself: What action is occurring? Who is taking the action?
4. Determine the cartoonist's purpose: is it to persuade, criticize, or just make people think? What idea is the cartoonist trying to get across?
5. Ask yourself whether the publication or the cartoonist has a bias that is being expressed in the cartoon.

Practicing the Skill

Study the cartoon. Then use the cartoon and your knowledge of history to answer the questions that follow.

1. What is the topic of the cartoon?
2. Who are the participants, and what are they doing?
3. What point do you think the cartoonist is trying to make? Is the cartoon relevant to any of today's political issues?

Applying the Skill

Bring a newspaper or magazine to class. With a partner, analyze the message and detect any bias in the cartoons you find.

Practicing the Skill: Answers

1. separation of powers between the three branches of government
2. Congress is requesting FBI help from the executive branch (President Truman)
3. Students should note that Congress is overstepping its boundaries by stepping on the executive branch's territory. The separation of powers is an issue that is relevant today.

Analyzing Primary Sources

Why Learn This Skill?

C To determine what happened in the past, historians do some detective work. They comb through bits of written and illustrated evidence from the past to reconstruct events. These bits of evidence are called "primary sources." They include letters, diaries, photographs, newspaper articles, ads, and legal documents.

A blind student using a device to take notes in Braille

Learning the Skill

Primary sources yield several important types of information. They often provide details of events or personal perspectives. But remember: any source reflects only one perspective. Before drawing any conclusions, you should examine as many perspectives as possible. To analyze primary sources, follow these steps:

"No person in the United States shall, on the ground of blindness or severely impaired vision, be denied admission in any course of study by a recipient of Federal financial assistance for any education program or activity; but nothing herein shall be construed to require any such institution to provide any special services to such person because of his blindness or visual impairment."

—United States Code, Title IX, Education Amendments of 1972

1. Identify the author, the publication, or the document.
2. Determine when and where the document was written or illustrated.
3. Read the document or study the illustration for its content. Try to answer the five "W" questions: Whom is it about? What is it about? When did it happen? Where did it happen? Why did it happen?

Practicing the Skill

The primary source above is a small part of a United States legal document. Read the source and then answer these questions:

1. When was the document written?
2. Who is affected by this document?
3. What is the purpose of this document?
4. Why do you think this document was written?

Applying the Skill

D Find a primary source from your past, such as a photo, a report card, an old newspaper clipping, or your first baseball card. Bring the source to class and explain what it shows about that time in your life.

Teach

C Critical Thinking

Analyzing Primary Sources Have students use a newspaper or other periodical to identify a current event or news story. After they have identified this news item, have them use an Internet search engine and type in the event. Tell students to choose five entries from the first results page and evaluate the entries for usefulness as primary sources. As the students evaluate their entries, have them keep notes and report to the class what their findings were. **OL**

D Differentiated Instruction

Intrapersonal To help students understand the factor of perspective when reading primary sources, ask students to recall an event in their lives. **Ask:** Would you be able to give a full account of that event to another person? Would someone else give a different account of the event? **BL**

Practicing the Skill: Answers

1. 1972
2. persons in the United States who are blind or have severely impaired vision
3. This document explains legislation enabling persons who are blind to attend universities without discrimination.
4. to halt discrimination

Teach

C Critical Thinking

Analyzing When researching a topic, recommend that students use several secondary sources in order to evaluate all aspects of the topic and to identify various writers' points of view. Assign students various passages from this book. Have students identify the portions of the information that are primary sources and which are secondary sources. Have volunteers share their findings with the class. **OL**

Analyzing Secondary Sources

Why Learn This Skill?

C This textbook, like many other history books, is a secondary source. It was written by using primary sources to explain the topics covered. The value of a secondary source depends on how well the author has used those primary sources. Learning to analyze secondary sources will help you figure out whether they are presenting topics completely and accurately.

Painting of Mark Twain by John White

Learning the Skill

Read the passage to the right, which discusses the controversy over the United States's occupation of the Philippines after the Spanish-American War. To analyze secondary sources, ask yourself these questions:

1. Are there references to primary sources in the text? Who are the sources?
2. What insights or biases might these people have?
3. Does the author use the sources effectively to support his or her points?
4. Does the author consider different kinds of sources? Do they represent varying viewpoints?

> *". . . [The anti-imperialists] denounced the extension of American rule by force in the Philippines, not because of what it might do to the Filipinos, but because of what they were convinced it was bound to do to American democratic ideals. They saw in the American seizure and retention of the Islands 'the infamy of the doctrine that a people may be governed without their consent.'. . .*
>
> *. . . The expansionists' reply . . . was the twin slogan: duty and destiny. . . . In the words of the archexpansionist Theodore Roosevelt: 'Peace cannot be had until the civilized nations have expanded in some shape over the barbarous nations.'*
>
> *. . . Mark Twain was one literary figure who was won over . . . 'I left these shores at Vancouver,' he wrote, 'a red-hot imperialist. I wanted the American eagle to go screaming into the Pacific. . . . Why not spread its wings over the Philippines, I asked myself? . . .' But . . . in 1900 he wrote to Joseph Twichell: 'Apparently we are not proposing to set the Filipinos free and give their islands to them. . . . If these things are so, the war out there has no interest for me.'"*
>
> —Harold A. Larrabee, in *Historical Viewpoints*

Practicing the Skill

1. What primary sources does the author use?
2. Does the author cite where the quotations he used first appeared?
3. How reliable do you think these sources are?
4. Which source do you agree with?

Applying the Skill

In a newspaper or online, read an in-depth article about a topic that interests you. Then list the primary sources the article uses and analyze how reliable you think they are.

Practicing the Skill: Answers

1. The author uses writings by Mark Twain and Theodore Roosevelt.
2. No, he does not cite the sources.
3. Students should find that the sources are reliable. They can be verified.
4. Answers should be supported.

Foldables

Dinah Zike's Foldables are three-dimensional, interactive graphic organizers used to help organize and retain information. Every chapter in your text uses a Foldable to help you identify and learn about the Big Ideas discussed in each section. The following pages provide complete folding instructions for the 14 different Foldables used throughout your Student Edition text.

Table of Contents

Basic Foldable Shapes

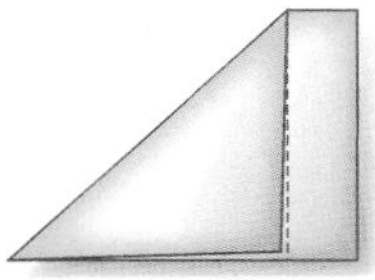
Taco Fold

Hamburger Fold

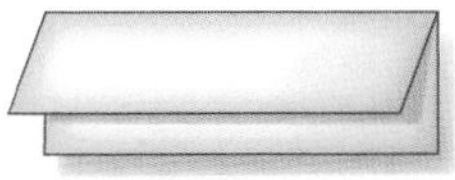
Hot Dog Fold

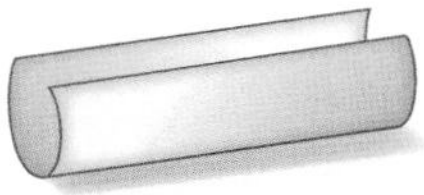
Burrito Fold

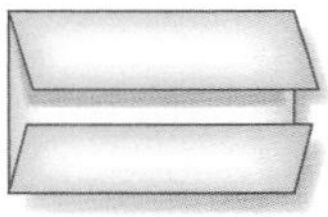
Shutter Fold

Valley Fold

Mountain Fold

Accordion Book

NOTE: *Steps 1 and 2 should be done only if paper is too large to begin with.*

1. Fold the selected paper into *hamburgers.*
2. Cut the paper in half along the fold lines.
3. Fold each section of paper into *hamburgers,* but fold one side one half inch shorter than the other side. This will form a tab that is one half inch long.
4. Fold this tab forward over the shorter side, and then fold it back away from the shorter piece of paper; in other words, fold it the opposite way.
5. To form an *accordion,* glue a straight edge of one section into the *valley* of another section.

NOTE: *Stand the sections on end to form an accordion to help students visualize how to glue them together. (See illustration.)*

Always place the extra tab at the back of the book so you can add more pages later.

Use this book for time lines, student projects that grow, sequencing events or data, and biographies.

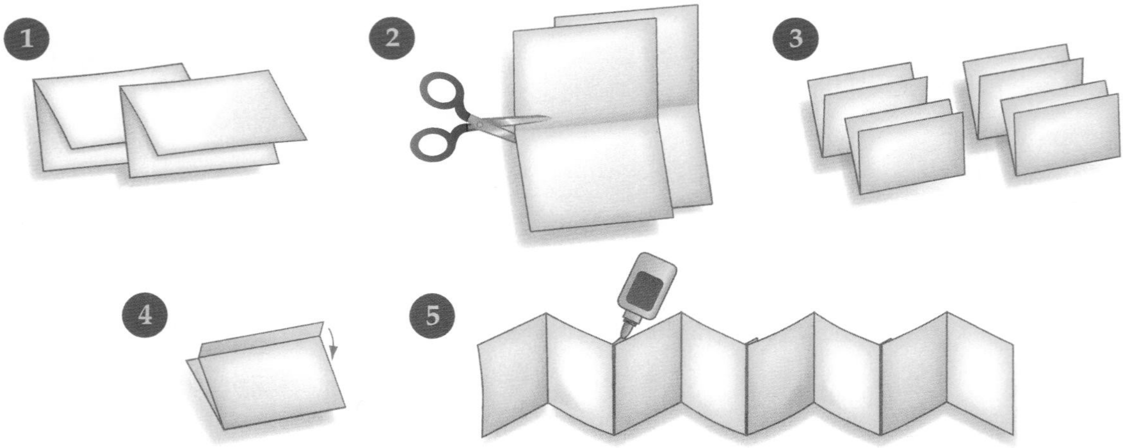

Concept-Map Book

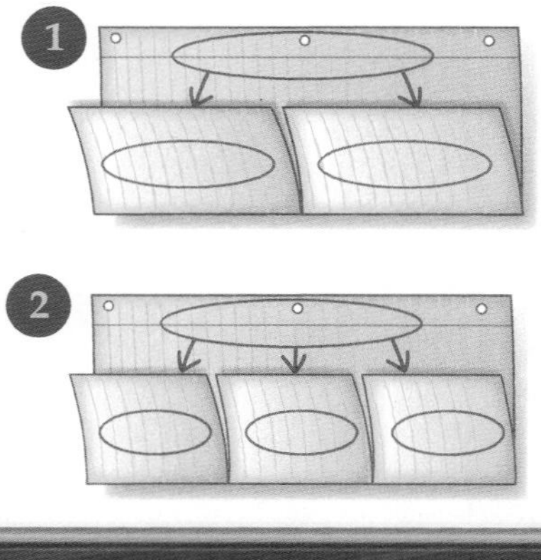

1. Fold a sheet of paper along the long or short axis, leaving a two-inch tab uncovered along the top.
2. Fold in half or in thirds.
3. Unfold and cut along the inside fold line(s) to create two or three flaps.

Folded Table or Chart

1. Fold the number of vertical columns needed to make the table or chart.
2. Fold the horizontal rows needed to make the table or chart.
3. Label the rows and columns.

Remember: Tables are organized along vertical and horizontal axes, while charts are organized along one axis, either horizontal or vertical.

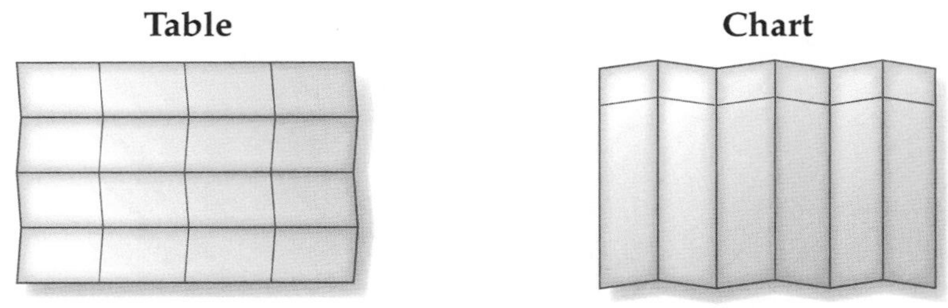

Four-Tab Book

1. Fold a sheet of paper (8½" × 11") in half like a *hot dog.*
2. Fold this long rectangle in half like a *hamburger.*
3. Fold both ends back to touch the *mountain top* or fold it like an *accordion.*
4. On the side with two *valleys* and one *mountain top,* make vertical cuts through one thickness of paper, forming four tabs.

Use this book for data occurring in fours.

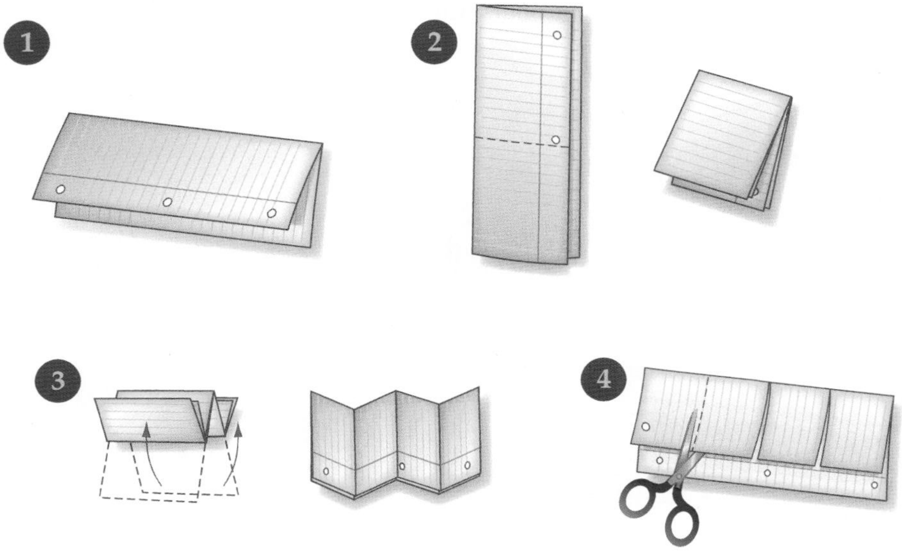

Foldables

Four-Door Book

1. Make a *shutter fold* using 11" × 17" or 12" × 18" paper.
2. Fold the *shutter fold* in half like a *hamburger.* Crease well.
3. Open the project and cut along the two inside *valley* folds.
4. These cuts will form four doors on the inside of the project.

Use this fold for data occurring in fours. When folded in half like a *hamburger,* a finished *four-door book* can be glued inside a large (11" × 17") *shutter fold* as part of a larger project.

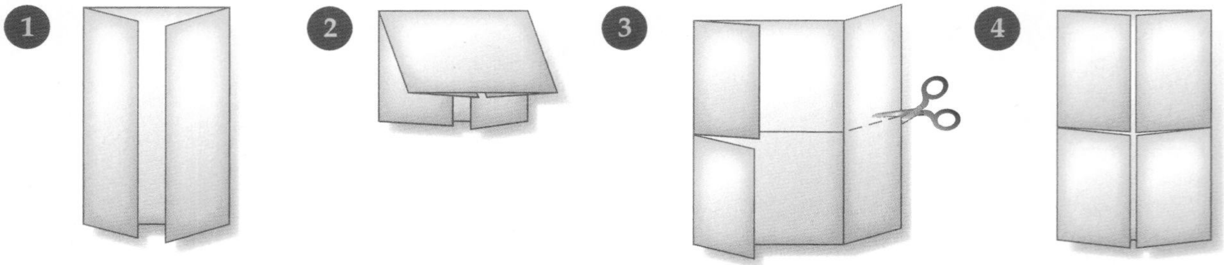

Half-Book

Fold a sheet of paper (8½" × 11") in half.

1. This book can be folded vertically like a *hot dog* or . . .
2. . . . it can be folded horizontally like a *hamburger.*

Use this book for descriptive, expository, persuasive, or narrative writing, as well as for graphs, diagrams, or charts.

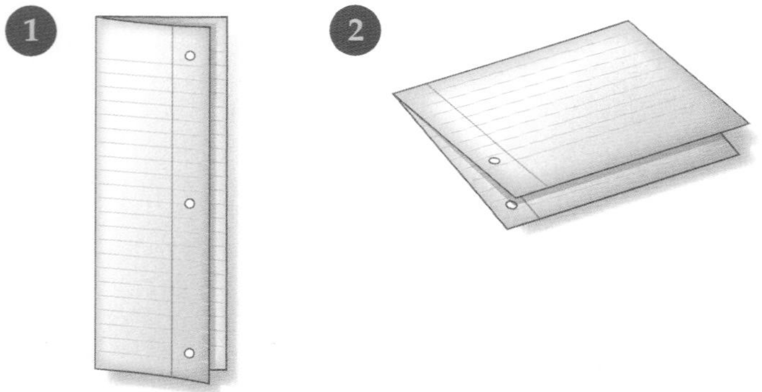

Layered-Look Book

1. Stack two sheets of paper (8½" × 11") so that the back sheet is one inch higher than the front sheet.
2. Bring the bottom of both sheets upward and align the edges so that all of the layers or tabs are the same distance apart.
3. When all tabs are an equal distance apart, fold the papers and crease well.
4. Open the papers and glue them together along the *valley,* or inner center fold, or staple them along the *mountain.*

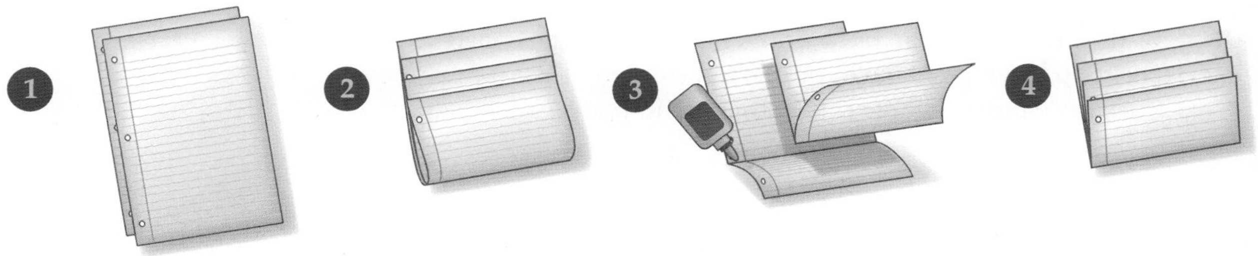

Pocket Book

1. Fold a sheet of paper (8½" × 11") in half like a *hamburger.*
2. Open the folded paper and fold one of the long sides up two inches to form a pocket. Refold along the *hamburger* fold so that the newly formed pockets are on the inside.
3. Glue the outer edges of the two-inch fold with a small amount of glue.
4. **Optional:** Glue a cover around the *pocket book.*

   Variation: Make a multi-paged booklet by gluing several pockets side-by-side. Glue a cover around the multi-paged *pocket book.*

Use 3" × 5" index cards inside the pockets. Store student-made books, such as two-tab books and folded books in the pockets.

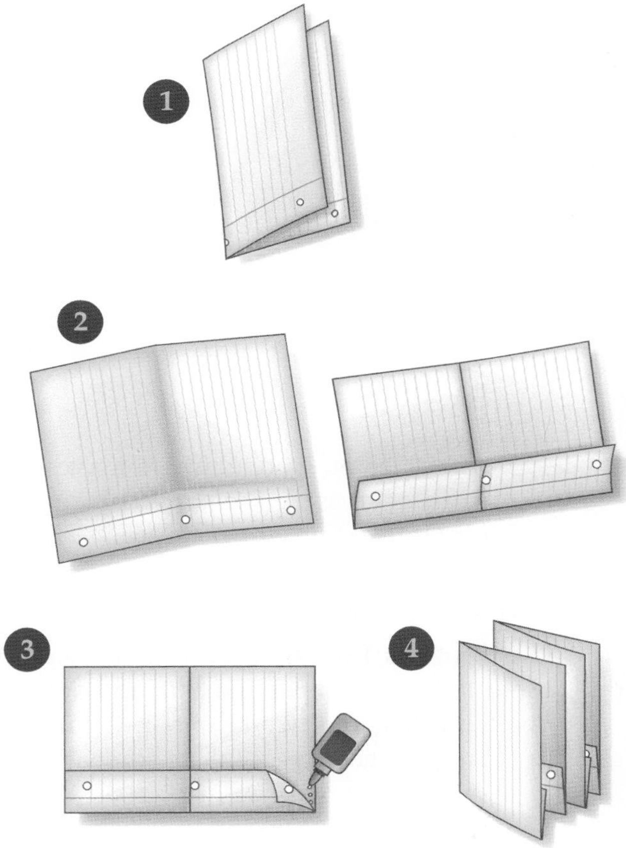

Sentence Strips

1. Take two sheets of paper (8½" × 11") and fold into *hamburgers*. Cut along the fold lines making four half sheets. *(Use as many half sheets as necessary for additional pages to your book.)*
2. Fold each sheet in half like a *hot dog*.
3. Place the folds side-by-side and staple them together on the left side.
4. One inch from the stapled edge, cut the front page of each folded section up to the *mountain top*. These cuts form flaps that can be raised and lowered.

To make a half-cover, use a sheet of construction paper one inch longer than the book. Glue the back of the last sheet to the construction paper strip leaving one inch, on the left side, to fold over and cover the original staples. Staple this half-cover in place.

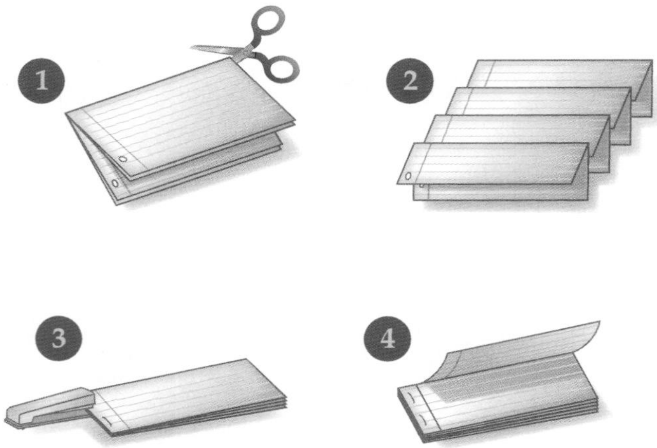

Shutter Fold

1. Begin as if you were going to make a *hamburger* but instead of creasing the paper, pinch it to show the midpoint.
2. Fold the outer edges of the paper to meet at the pinch, or mid-point, forming a *shutter fold*.

Use this book for data occurring in twos. Or, make this fold using 11" × 17" paper and smaller books—such as the half-book, journal, and two-tab book—that can be glued inside to create a large project full of student work.

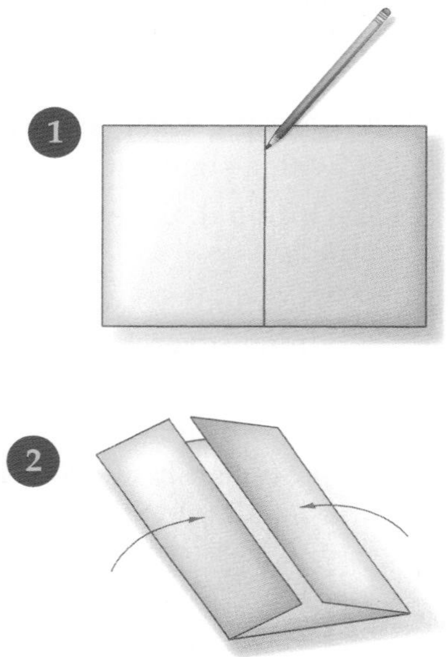

Three-Tab Book

1. Fold a sheet of paper like a *hot dog*.
2. With the paper horizontal, and the fold of the *hot dog* up, fold the right side toward the center, trying to cover one half of the paper.

   NOTE: *If you fold the right edge over first, the final graphic organizer will open and close like a book.*
3. Fold the left side over the right side to make a book with three folds.
4. Open the folded book. Place your hands between the two thicknesses of paper and cut up the two *valleys* on one side only. This will form three tabs.

Use this book for data occurring in threes, and for two-part Venn diagrams.

Variation A:

Draw overlapping circles on the three tabs to make a Venn diagram.

Variation B:

Cut each of the three tabs in half to make a six-tab book.

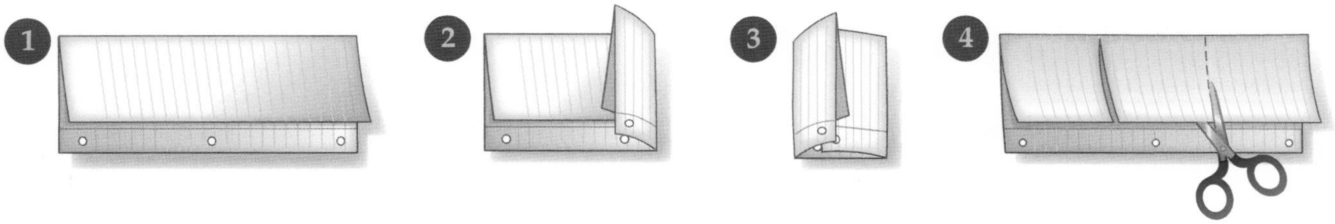

Trifold Book

1. Fold a sheet of paper (8½" × 11") into thirds.
2. Use this book as is, or cut into shapes. If the trifold is cut, leave plenty of fold on both sides of the designed shape, so the book will open and close in three sections.

Use this book to make charts with three columns or rows, large Venn diagrams, or reports on data occurring in threes.

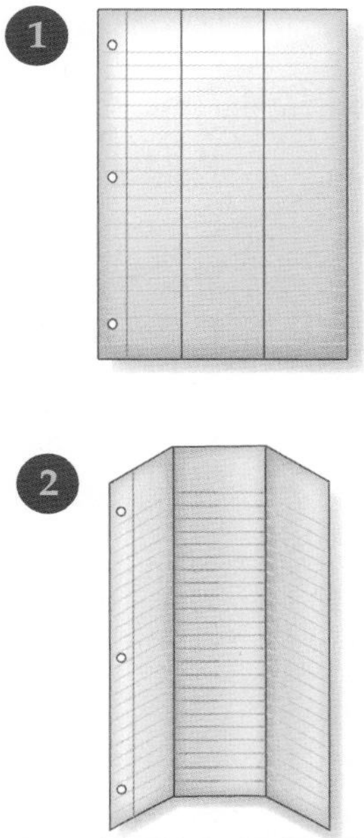

Two-Tab Book

1. Take a *folded book* and cut up the *valley* of the inside fold toward the *mountain top*. This cut forms two large tabs that can be used front and back for writing and illustrations.
2. The book can be expanded by making several of these folds and gluing them side-by-side.

Use this book with data occurring in twos. For example, use it for comparing and contrasting, determining cause and effect, finding similarities and differences, and more.

1
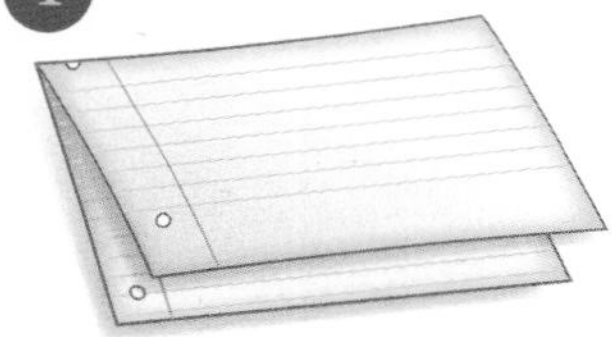

2

3

Vocabulary Book

1. Fold a sheet of notebook paper in half like a *hot dog*.
2. On one side, cut every third line. This results in ten tabs on wide-ruled notebook paper and twelve tabs on college-ruled.
3. Label the tabs.

1
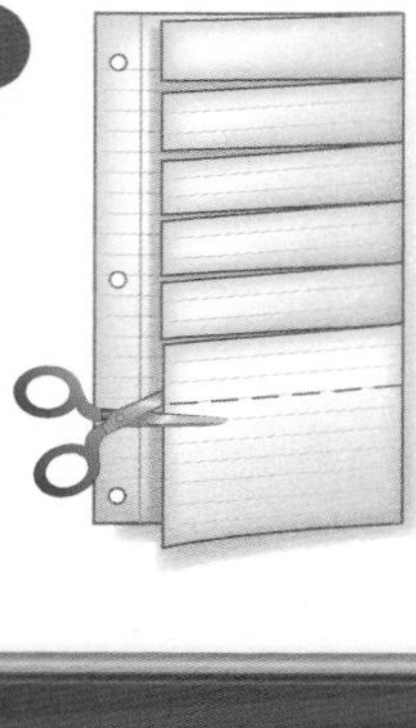

Presidents of the United States

In this resource you will find portraits of the individuals who served as presidents of the United States, along with their occupations, political party affiliations, and other interesting facts.

***The Republican Party during this period developed into today's Democratic Party. Today's Republican Party originated in 1854.*

1 George Washington

Presidential term: 1789–1797
Lived: 1732–1799
Born in: Virginia
Elected from: Virginia
Occupations: Soldier, Planter
Party: None
Vice President: John Adams

2 John Adams

Presidential term: 1797–1801
Lived: 1735–1826
Born in: Massachusetts
Elected from: Massachusetts
Occupations: Teacher, Lawyer
Party: Federalist
Vice President: Thomas Jefferson

3 Thomas Jefferson

Presidential term: 1801–1809
Lived: 1743–1826
Born in: Virginia
Elected from: Virginia
Occupations: Planter, Lawyer
Party: Republican**
Vice Presidents: Aaron Burr, George Clinton

4 James Madison

Presidential term: 1809–1817
Lived: 1751–1836
Born in: Virginia
Elected from: Virginia
Occupation: Planter
Party: Republican**
Vice Presidents: George Clinton, Elbridge Gerry

5 James Monroe

Presidential term: 1817–1825
Lived: 1758–1831
Born in: Virginia
Elected from: Virginia
Occupation: Lawyer
Party: Republican**
Vice President: Daniel D. Tompkins

6 John Quincy Adams

Presidential term: 1825–1829
Lived: 1767–1848
Born in: Massachusetts
Elected from: Massachusetts
Occupation: Lawyer
Party: Republican**
Vice President: John C. Calhoun

7 Andrew Jackson

Presidential term: 1829–1837
Lived: 1767–1845
Born in: South Carolina
Elected from: Tennessee
Occupations: Lawyer, Soldier
Party: Democratic
Vice Presidents: John C. Calhoun, Martin Van Buren

8 Martin Van Buren

Presidential term: 1837–1841
Lived: 1782–1862
Born in: New York
Elected from: New York
Occupation: Lawyer
Party: Democratic
Vice President: Richard M. Johnson

9 William H. Harrison

Presidential term: 1841
Lived: 1773–1841
Born in: Virginia
Elected from: Ohio
Occupations: Soldier, Planter
Party: Whig
Vice President: John Tyler

10 John Tyler

Presidential term: 1841–1845
Lived: 1790–1862
Born in: Virginia
Elected as V.P. from: Virginia
Succeeded Harrison
Occupation: Lawyer
Party: Whig
Vice President: None

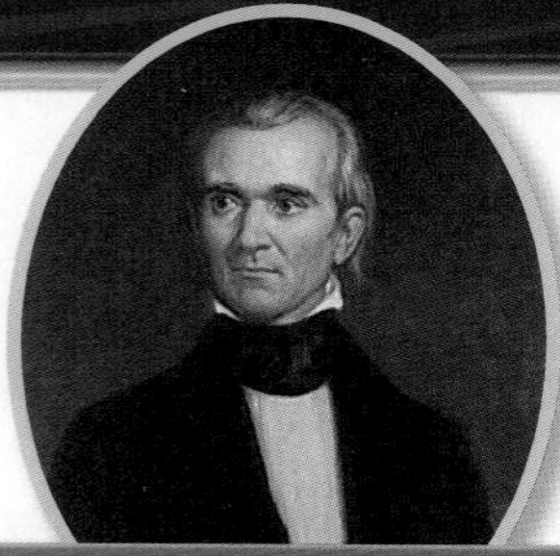

11 James K. Polk

Presidential term: 1845–1849
Lived: 1795–1849
Born in: North Carolina
Elected from: Tennessee
Occupation: Lawyer
Party: Democratic
Vice President: George M. Dallas

12 Zachary Taylor

Presidential term: 1849–1850
Lived: 1784–1850
Born in: Virginia
Elected from: Louisiana
Occupation: Soldier
Party: Whig
Vice President: Millard Fillmore

13 Millard Fillmore

Presidential term: 1850–1853
Lived: 1800–1874
Born in: New York
Elected as V.P. from: New York
Succeeded Taylor
Occupation: Lawyer
Party: Whig
Vice President: None

14 Franklin Pierce

Presidential term: 1853–1857
Lived: 1804–1869
Born in: New Hampshire
Elected from: New Hampshire
Occupation: Lawyer
Party: Democratic
Vice President: William R. King

15 James Buchanan

Presidential term: 1857–1861
Lived: 1791–1868
Born in: Pennsylvania
Elected from: Pennsylvania
Occupation: Lawyer
Party: Democratic
Vice President: John C. Breckinridge

16 Abraham Lincoln

Presidential term: 1861–1865
Lived: 1809–1865
Born in: Kentucky
Elected from: Illinois
Occupation: Lawyer
Party: Republican
Vice Presidents: Hannibal Hamlin, Andrew Johnson

17 Andrew Johnson

Presidential term: 1865–1869
Lived: 1808–1875
Born in: North Carolina
Elected as V.P. from: Tennessee
Succeeded Lincoln
Occupation: Tailor
Party: Democratic; National Unionist
Vice President: None

18 Ulysses S. Grant

Presidential term: 1869–1877
Lived: 1822–1885
Born in: Ohio
Elected from: Illinois
Occupations: Farmer, Soldier
Party: Republican
Vice Presidents: Schuyler Colfax, Henry Wilson

19 Rutherford B. Hayes

Presidential term: 1877–1881
Lived: 1822–1893
Born in: Ohio
Elected from: Ohio
Occupation: Lawyer
Party: Republican
Vice President: William A. Wheeler

20 James A. Garfield

Presidential term: 1881
Lived: 1831–1881
Born in: Ohio
Elected from: Ohio
Occupations: Laborer, Professor
Party: Republican
Vice President: Chester A. Arthur

21 Chester A. Arthur

Presidential term: 1881–1885
Lived: 1830–1886
Born in: Vermont
Elected as V.P. from: New York
Succeeded Garfield
Occupations: Teacher, Lawyer
Party: Republican
Vice President: None

22 Grover Cleveland

Presidential term: 1885–1889
Lived: 1837–1908
Born in: New Jersey
Elected from: New York
Occupation: Lawyer
Party: Democratic
Vice President: Thomas A. Hendricks

23 Benjamin Harrison

Presidential term: 1889–1893
Lived: 1833–1901
Born in: Ohio
Elected from: Indiana
Occupation: Lawyer
Party: Republican
Vice President: Levi P. Morton

24 Grover Cleveland

Presidential term: 1893–1897
Lived: 1837–1908
Born in: New Jersey
Elected from: New York
Occupation: Lawyer
Party: Democratic
Vice President: Adlai E. Stevenson

25 William McKinley

Presidential term: 1897–1901
Lived: 1843–1901
Born in: Ohio
Elected from: Ohio
Occupations: Teacher, Lawyer
Party: Republican
Vice Presidents: Garret Hobart, Theodore Roosevelt

26 Theodore Roosevelt

Presidential term: 1901–1909
Lived: 1858–1919
Born in: New York
Elected as V.P. from: New York
Succeeded McKinley
Occupations: Historian, Rancher
Party: Republican
Vice President: Charles W. Fairbanks

27 William H. Taft

Presidential term: 1909–1913
Lived: 1857–1930
Born in: Ohio
Elected from: Ohio
Occupations: Lawyer
Party: Republican
Vice President: James S. Sherman

28 Woodrow Wilson

Presidential term: 1913–1921
Lived: 1856–1924
Born in: Virginia
Elected from: New Jersey
Occupation: College Professor
Party: Democratic
Vice President: Thomas R. Marshall

29 Warren G. Harding

Presidential term: 1921–1923
Lived: 1865–1923
Born in: Ohio
Elected from: Ohio
Occupations: Newspaper Editor, Publisher
Party: Republican
Vice President: Calvin Coolidge

30 Calvin Coolidge

Presidential term: 1923–1929
Lived: 1872–1933
Born in: Vermont
Elected as V.P. from: Massachusetts, Succeeded Harding
Occupation: Lawyer
Party: Republican
Vice President: Charles G. Dawes

31 Herbert C. Hoover

Presidential term: 1929–1933
Lived: 1874–1964
Born in: Iowa
Elected from: California
Occupation: Engineer
Party: Republican
Vice President: Charles Curtis

32 Franklin D. Roosevelt

Presidential term: 1933–1945
Lived: 1882–1945
Born in: New York
Elected from: New York
Occupation: Lawyer
Party: Democratic
Vice Presidents: John N. Garner, Henry A. Wallace, Harry S. Truman

33 Harry S. Truman

Presidential term: 1945–1953
Lived: 1884–1972
Born in: Missouri
Elected as V.P. from: Missouri Succeeded Roosevelt
Occupations: Clerk, Farmer
Party: Democratic
Vice President: Alben W. Barkley

34 Dwight D. Eisenhower

Presidential term: 1953–1961
Lived: 1890–1969
Born in: Texas
Elected from: New York
Occupation: Soldier
Party: Republican
Vice President: Richard M. Nixon

35 John F. Kennedy

Presidential term: 1961–1963
Lived: 1917–1963
Born in: Massachusetts
Elected from: Massachusetts
Occupations: Author, Reporter
Party: Democratic
Vice President: Lyndon B. Johnson

36 Lyndon B. Johnson

Presidential term: 1963–1969
Lived: 1908–1973
Born in: Texas
Elected as V.P. from: Texas
Succeeded Kennedy
Occupation: Teacher
Party: Democratic
Vice President: Hubert H. Humphrey

37 Richard M. Nixon

Presidential term: 1969–1974
Lived: 1913–1994
Born in: California
Elected from: New York
Occupation: Lawyer
Party: Republican
Vice Presidents: Spiro T. Agnew, Gerald R. Ford

38 Gerald R. Ford

Presidential term: 1974–1977
Lived: 1913–2006
Born in: Nebraska
Appointed as V.P. upon Agnew's resignation; succeeded Nixon
Occupation: Lawyer
Party: Republican
Vice President: Nelson A. Rockefeller

39 James E. Carter, Jr.

Presidential term: 1977–1981
Lived: 1924–
Born in: Georgia
Elected from: Georgia
Occupations: Business, Farmer
Party: Democratic
Vice President: Walter F. Mondale

40 Ronald W. Reagan

Presidential term: 1981–1989
Lived: 1911–2004
Born in: Illinois
Elected from: California
Occupations: Actor, Lecturer
Party: Republican
Vice President: George H.W. Bush

41 George H.W. Bush

Presidential term: 1989–1993
Lived: 1924–
Born in: Massachusetts
Elected from: Texas
Occupation: Business
Party: Republican
Vice President: J. Danforth Quayle

42 William J. Clinton

Presidential term: 1993–2001
Lived: 1946–
Born in: Arkansas
Elected from: Arkansas
Occupation: Lawyer
Party: Democratic
Vice President: Albert Gore, Jr.

43 George W. Bush

Presidential term: 2001–2009
Lived: 1946–
Born in: Connecticut
Elected from: Texas
Occupation: Business
Party: Republican
Vice President: Richard B. Cheney

44 Barack Obama

Presidential term: 2009–
Lived: 1961–
Born in: Hawaii
Elected from: Illinois
Occupation: Lawyer
Party: Democratic
Vice President: Joseph R. Biden, Jr.

United States Facts

The states are listed in the order they were admitted to the Union.

Washington, D.C.
Population: 572,059
Land area: 61 sq. mi.

Population figures are based on U.S. Bureau of the Census for 2000. House of Representatives figures are from the Clerk of the House of Representatives. States are not drawn to scale.

U.S. Territories

Puerto Rico
Population: 3,808,610
Land area: 3,425 sq. mi.

Guam
Population: 155,000 (est.)
Land area: 209 sq. mi.

U.S. Virgin Islands
Population: 121,000 (est.)
Land area: 134 sq. mi.

American Samoa
Population: 65,000 (est.)
Land area: 77 sq. mi.

1 Delaware
Year Admitted: 1787
Population: 783,600
Land area: 1,955 sq. mi.
Representatives: 1

2 Pennsylvania
Year Admitted: 1787
Population: 12,281,054
Land area: 44,820 sq. mi.
Representatives: 19

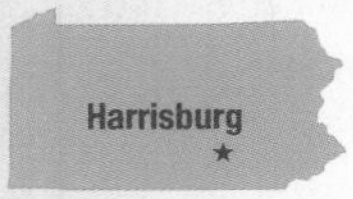

3 New Jersey
Year Admitted: 1787
Population: 8,414,350
Land area: 7,419 sq. mi.
Representatives: 13

4 Georgia
Year Admitted: 1788
Population: 8,186,453
Land area: 57,919 sq. mi.
Representatives: 13

5 Connecticut
Year Admitted: 1788
Population: 3,405,565
Land area: 4,845 sq. mi.
Representatives: 5

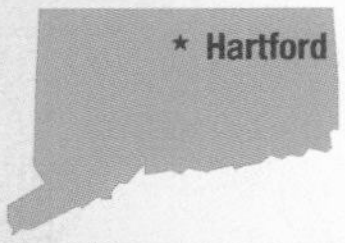

6 Massachusetts
Year Admitted: 1788
Population: 6,349,097
Land area: 7,838 sq. mi.
Representatives: 10

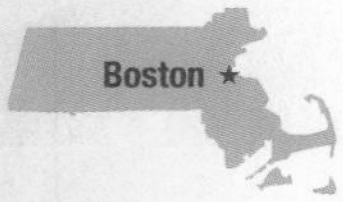

7 Maryland
Year Admitted: 1788
Population: 5,296,486
Land area: 9,775 sq. mi.
Representatives: 8

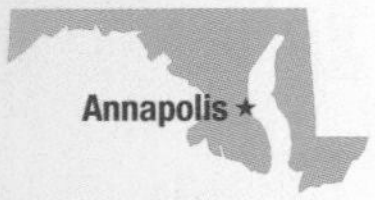

8 South Carolina
Year Admitted: 1788
Population: 4,012,012
Land area: 30,111 sq. mi.
Representatives: 6

9 New Hampshire
Year Admitted: 1788
Population: 1,235,786
Land area: 8,969 sq. mi.
Representatives: 2

10 Virginia
Year Admitted: 1788
Population: 7,078,515
Land area: 39,598 sq. mi.
Representatives: 11

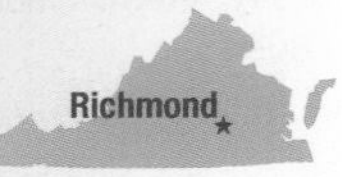

11 New York
Year Admitted: 1788
Population: 18,976,457
Land area: 47,224 sq. mi.
Representatives: 29

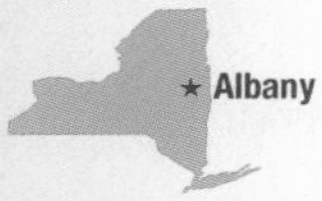

12 North Carolina
Year Admitted: 1789
Population: 8,049,313
Land area: 48,718 sq. mi.
Representatives: 13

13 Rhode Island
Year Admitted: 1790
Population: 1,048,319
Land area: 1,045 sq. mi.
Representatives: 2

14 Vermont
Year Admitted: 1791
Population: 608,827
Land area: 9,249 sq. mi.
Representatives: 1

15 Kentucky
Year Admitted: 1792
Population: 4,041,769
Land area: 39,732 sq. mi.
Representatives: 6

16 Tennessee
Year Admitted: 1796
Population: 5,689,283
Land area: 41,220 sq. mi.
Representatives: 9

17 Ohio
Year Admitted: 1803
Population: 11,353,140
Land area: 40,953 sq. mi.
Representatives: 18

18 Louisiana
Year Admitted: 1812
Population: 4,468,976
Land area: 43,566 sq. mi.
Representatives: 7

19 Indiana
Year Admitted: 1816
Population: 6,080,485
Land area: 35,870 sq. mi.
Representatives: 9

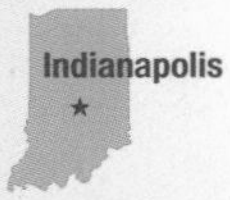

20 Mississippi
Year Admitted: 1817
Population: 2,844,658
Land area: 46,914 sq. mi.
Representatives: 4

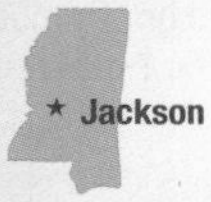

21 Illinois
Year Admitted: 1818
Population: 12,419,293
Land area: 55,593 sq. mi.
Representatives: 19

22 Alabama
Year Admitted: 1819
Population: 4,447,100
Land area: 50,750 sq. mi.
Representatives: 7

23 Maine
Year Admitted: 1820
Population: 1,274,923
Land area: 30,865 sq. mi.
Representatives: 2

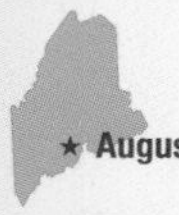

24 Missouri
Year Admitted: 1821
Population: 5,595,211
Land area: 68,898 sq. mi.
Representatives: 9

25 Arkansas
Year Admitted: 1836
Population: 2,673,400
Land area: 52,075 sq. mi.
Representatives: 4

26 Michigan
Year Admitted: 1837
Population: 9,938,444
Land area: 56,809 sq. mi.
Representatives: 15

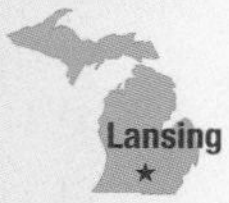

27 Florida
Year Admitted: 1845
Population: 15,982,378
Land area: 53,997 sq. mi.
Representatives: 25

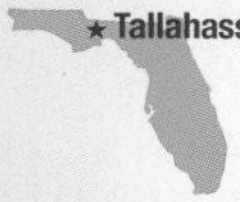

28 Texas
Year Admitted: 1845
Population: 20,851,820
Land area: 261,914 sq. mi.
Representatives: 32

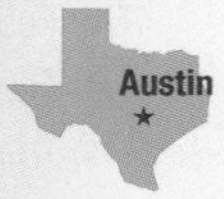

29 Iowa
Year Admitted: 1846
Population: 2,926,324
Land area: 55,875 sq. mi.
Representatives: 5

30 Wisconsin
Year Admitted: 1848
Population: 5,363,675
Land area: 54,314 sq. mi.
Representatives: 8

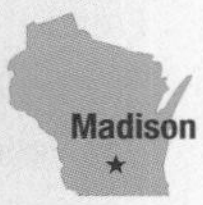

31 California
Year Admitted: 1850
Population: 33,871,648
Land area: 155,973 sq. mi.
Representatives: 53

32 Minnesota
Year Admitted: 1858
Population: 4,919,479
Land area: 79,617 sq. mi.
Representatives: 8

33 Oregon
Year Admitted: 1859
Population: 3,421,399
Land area: 96,003 sq. mi.
Representatives: 5

34 Kansas
Year Admitted: 1861
Population: 2,688,418
Land area: 81,823 sq. mi.
Representatives: 4

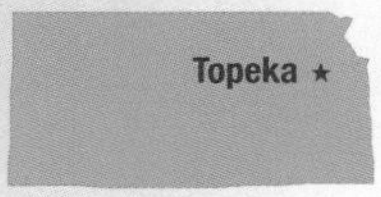

35 West Virginia
Year Admitted: 1863
Population: 1,808,344
Land area: 24,087 sq. mi.
Representatives: 3

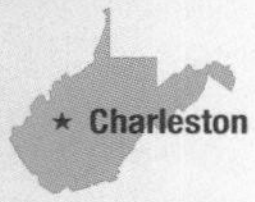

36 Nevada
Year Admitted: 1864
Population: 1,998,257
Land area: 109,806 sq. mi.
Representatives: 3

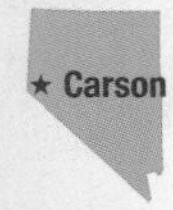

37 Nebraska
Year Admitted: 1867
Population: 1,711,263
Land area: 76,878 sq. mi.
Representatives: 3

38 Colorado
Year Admitted: 1876
Population: 4,301,261
Land area: 103,730 sq. mi.
Representatives: 7

39 North Dakota
Year Admitted: 1889
Population: 642,200
Land area: 68,994 sq. mi.
Representatives: 1

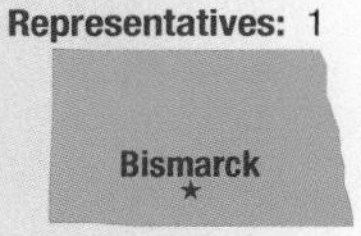

40 South Dakota
Year Admitted: 1889
Population: 754,844
Land area: 75,898 sq. mi.
Representatives: 1

41 Montana
Year Admitted: 1889
Population: 902,195
Land area: 145,556 sq. mi.
Representatives: 1

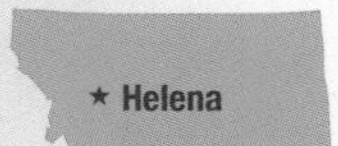

42 Washington
Year Admitted: 1889
Population: 5,894,121
Land area: 66,582 sq. mi.
Representatives: 9

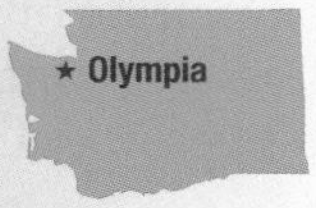

43 Idaho
Year Admitted: 1890
Population: 1,293,953
Land area: 82,751 sq. mi.
Representatives: 2

44 Wyoming
Year Admitted: 1890
Population: 493,782
Land area: 97,105 sq. mi.
Representatives: 1

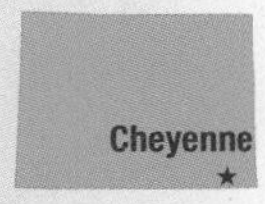

45 Utah
Year Admitted: 1896
Population: 2,233,169
Land area: 82,168 sq. mi.
Representatives: 3

46 Oklahoma
Year Admitted: 1907
Population: 3,450,654
Land area: 68,679 sq. mi.
Representatives: 5

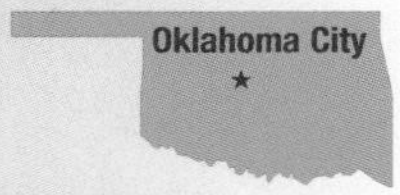

47 New Mexico
Year Admitted: 1912
Population: 1,819,046
Land area: 121,365 sq. mi.
Representatives: 3

48 Arizona
Year Admitted: 1912
Population: 5,130,632
Land area: 113,642 sq. mi.
Representatives: 8

49 Alaska
Year Admitted: 1959
Population: 626,932
Land area: 570,374 sq. mi.
Representatives: 1

50 Hawaii
Year Admitted: 1959
Population: 1,211,537
Land area: 6,432 sq. mi.
Representatives: 2

Documents of American History

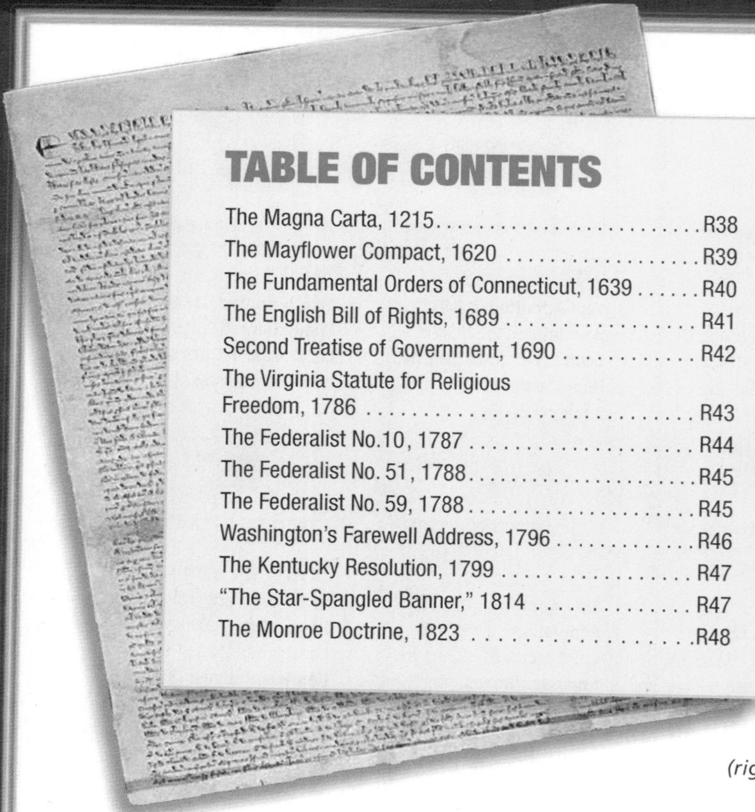

TABLE OF CONTENTS

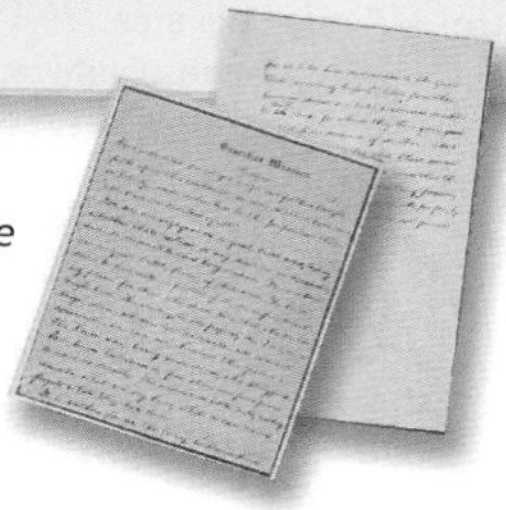

(right) Lincoln's drafts of the Gettysburg Address

Magna Carta

Why They Matter

Documents are often public statements by a president or an official body, such as a legislature, on an important issue. They have become documents because they define a particular issue so well that Americans continue to refer to them. Many documents here address fundamental American beliefs, such as the rights of the individual and the proper limits of government. Other documents, such as the Monroe Doctrine or the Truman Doctrine, address the nation's position and responsibilities in the world.

Documents matter because they are guides to American government and values. Sometimes people study them to learn how Americans came to believe in certain principles. Other times people read documents simply because these writings express certain principles passionately.

Signing the Mayflower Compact

Founding Documents of the American Republic

The first seven documents in this collection represent some of the founding documents of American democracy. Each contributed an essential building block for American political principles. Ultimately these principles were embodied in the Declaration of Independence, the Bill of Rights, and the Constitution.

DOCUMENT	WHY IT MATTERS
The Magna Carta In signing this charter in 1215, King John of England granted his subjects certain permanent liberties or rights, such as the right to a fair trial by a jury of their peers.	Over the centuries, English people believed that the Magna Carta gave them certain rights. They took this idea with them when they settled the American colonies. Some provisions of the Bill of Rights reflect ancient Magna Carta liberties.
The Mayflower Compact In 1620 the Pilgrims signed a compact while still aboard the *Mayflower.* This document laid out a plan for self-government the Pilgrims would use once they landed in America.	This document is the first plan for self-government put into effect in the English colonies. It reflected the idea that government should be based on a consensus of the entire community.
The Fundamental Orders of Connecticut Connecticut settlers agreed they would be governed according to a certain set of laws and through certain institutions. All citizens, not only those of a certain religion, could vote.	This document, the first written constitution drawn up in America, strengthened the colonists' beliefs about governing themselves.
The English Bill of Rights In 1689, after the Glorious Revolution, Parliament forced the king to accept this Bill of Rights guaranteeing basic civil rights.	This document clearly established that English subjects had certain rights and that the king could be removed from power for violating those rights.
Second Treatise of Government English philosopher John Locke wrote this document during the 1680s. One of his basic arguments was that government should be based on a contract between a ruler and those who are ruled. Rebellion is justified if a ruler violates the contract.	During the American Revolution, the colonists drew from Locke's theories of government and especially his ideas about the right to rebel.
The Virginia Statute for Religious Freedom This 1786 statute declared that the state of Virginia should not support Anglicanism or any other religious denomination.	The religious clauses of the Bill of Rights protecting the free exercise of religion and prohibiting an official religion were based on this statute.
The Federalist No. 10 In 1787 James Madison wrote this paper, one of a series arguing for stronger central government as reflected in the new Constitution.	The framework for American government today—a representative government with a strong federal government—was laid out in the Federalist Papers.

*Use the **American History Primary Source Document Library CD-ROM** to find additional primary sources about American heritage.*

The Magna Carta

The Magna Carta, signed by King John of England in 1215, marked a decisive step forward in the development of English constitutional government. Later it served as a model for the colonists, who carried the Magna Carta's guarantees of political rights to America.

John, by the grace of God, king of England, lord of Ireland, duke of Normandy and Aquitaine, and count of Anjou: to the archbishops, bishops, abbots, earls, barons, justiciaries, foresters, sheriffs, reeves, ministers, and all bailiffs and others his faithful subjects, greeting. . . .

1. We have, in the first place, granted to God, and by this our present charter, confirmed for us and our heirs forever that the English church shall be free. . . .

9. Neither we nor our bailiffs shall seize any land or rent for any debt so long as the debtor's chattels are sufficient to discharge the same. . . .

12. No scutage [tax] or aid shall be imposed in our kingdom unless by the common counsel thereof. . . .

14. For obtaining the common counsel of the kingdom concerning the assessment of aids. . . or of scutage, we will cause to be summoned, severally by our letters, the archbishops, bishops, abbots, earls, and great barons; we will also cause to be summoned generally, by our sheriffs and bailiffs, all those who hold lands directly of us, to meet on a fixed day . . . and at a fixed place. . . .

20. A free man shall be amerced [punished] for a small fault only according to the measure thereof, and for a great crime according to its magnitude. . . . None of these amercements shall be imposed except by the oath of honest men of the neighborhood.

21. Earls and barons shall be amerced only by their peers, and only in proportion to the measure of the offense. . . .

38. In the future no bailiff shall upon his own unsupported accusation put any man to trial without producing credible witnesses to the truth of the accusation.

39. No free man shall be taken, imprisoned, disseised [seized], outlawed, banished, or in any way destroyed, nor will we proceed against or prosecute him, except by the lawful judgment of his peers and by the law of the land.

40. To no one will we sell, to none will we deny or delay, right or justice. . . .

42. In the future it shall be lawful . . . for anyone to leave and return to our kingdom safely and securely by land and water, saving his fealty to us. Excepted are those who have been imprisoned or outlawed according to the law of the land. . . .

61. Whereas we, for the honor of God and the amendment of our realm, and in order the better to allay the discord arisen between us and our barons, have granted all these things aforesaid. . . .

63. Wherefore we will, and firmly charge . . . that all men in our kingdom shall have and hold all the aforesaid liberties, rights, and concessions . . . fully, and wholly to them and their heirs . . . in all things and places forever. . . . It is moreover sworn, as well on our part as on the part of the barons, that all these matters aforesaid will be kept in good faith and without deceit. Witness the above named and many others. Given by our hand in the meadow which is called Runnymede. . . .

The Mayflower Compact

On November 21, 1620, 41 colonists drafted the Mayflower Compact while still aboard the* Mayflower. *It was the first self-government plan ever put into effect in the English colonies. The compact was drawn up under these circumstances, as described by Governor William Bradford:

"This day, before we came to harbor, observing some not well affected to unity and concord, but gave some appearance of faction, it was thought good there should be an association and agreement that we should combine together in one body, and to submit to such government and governors as we should by common consent agree to make and choose, and set our hands to this that follows word for word."

In the Name of God, Amen. We, whose names are underwritten, the Loyal Subjects of our dread Sovereign Lord King James, by the Grace of God, of Great Britain, France, and Ireland, King, Defender of the Faith, etc.

Having undertaken for the Glory of God, and Advancement of the Christian Faith, and the honor of our King and Country, a Voyage to plant the first Colony in the northern Parts of Virginia, Do by these Presents, solemnly and mutually, in the Presence of God and one another, covenant and combine ourselves together into a civil Body Politick, for our better Ordering and Preservation, and Furtherance of the Ends aforesaid; And by Virtue hereof do enact, constitute, and frame, such just and equal Laws, Ordinances, Acts, Constitutions, and Offices, from time to time, as shall be thought most meet and convenient for the general Good of the Colony; unto which we promise all due Submission and Obedience. In Witness whereof we have hereunder subscribed our names at Cape Cod the eleventh of November, in the Reign of our Sovereign Lord King James of England, France, and Ireland, the eighteenth and of Scotland, the fifty-fourth. Anno Domini, 1620.

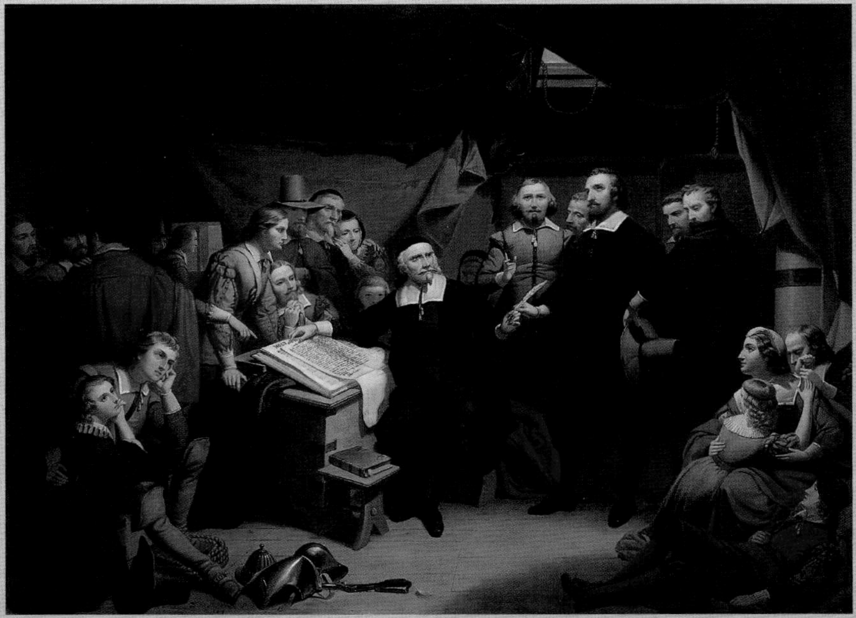

Signing of the Mayflower Compact

The Fundamental Orders of Connecticut

In January 1639, settlers in Connecticut, led by Thomas Hooker, drew up the Fundamental Orders of Connecticut—America's first written constitution. It is essentially a body of laws and a compact among the settlers.

Forasmuch as it has pleased the Almighty God by the wise disposition of His Divine Providence so to order and dispose of things that we, the inhabitants and residents of Windsor, Hartford, and Wethersfield are now cohabiting and dwelling in and upon the river of Conectecotte and the lands thereunto adjoining; and well knowing where a people are gathered together the Word of God requires that, to maintain the peace and union of such a people, there should be an orderly and decent government established according to God, . . . do therefore associate and conjoin ourselves to be as one public state or commonwealth. . . . As also in our civil affairs to be guided and governed according to such laws, rules, orders, and decrees as shall be made, ordered, and decreed, as follows:

1. It is ordered . . . that there shall be yearly two general assemblies or courts; . . . The first shall be called the Court of Election, wherein shall be yearly chosen . . . so many magistrates and other public officers as shall be found requisite. Whereof one to be chosen governor . . . and no other magistrate to be chosen for more than one year; provided always there be six chosen besides the governor . . . by all that are admitted freemen and have taken the oath of fidelity, and do cohabit within this jurisdiction. . . .

4. It is ordered . . . that no person be chosen governor above once in two years, and that the governor be always a member of some approved congregation, and formerly of the magistracy within this jurisdiction; and all the magistrates freemen of this Commonwealth. . . .

5. It is ordered . . . that to the aforesaid Court of Election the several towns shall send their deputies. . . . Also, the other General Court . . . shall be for making of laws, and any other public occasion which concerns the good of the Commonwealth. . . .

7. It is ordered . . . that . . . the constable or constables of each town shall forthwith give notice distinctly to the inhabitants of the same . . . that . . . they meet and assemble themselves together to elect and choose certain deputies to be at the General Court then following to [manage] the affairs of the Commonwealth; . . .

10. It is ordered . . . that every General Court . . . shall consist of the governor, or someone chosen to moderate the Court, and four other magistrates, at least, with the major part of the deputies of the several towns legally chosen. . . . In which said General Courts shall consist the supreme power of the Commonwealth, and they only shall have power to make laws or repeal them, to grant levies, to admit of freemen, dispose of lands undisposed of to several towns or person, and also shall have power to call either Court or magistrate or any other person whatsoever into question for any misdemeanor. . . .

Connecticut settlers on their way to Hartford

Documents

The English Bill of Rights

In 1689 William of Orange (pictured at right) and his wife Mary became joint rulers of England after accepting a list of conditions that later became known as the English Bill of Rights. This document assured the English people of certain basic civil rights and limited the power of the English monarchy.

An act declaring the rights and liberties of the subject and settling the succession of the crown. Whereas the lords spiritual and temporal and commons assembled at Westminster lawfully, fully and freely representing all the estates of the people of this realm did upon the thirteenth day of February in the year of our Seal of William and Mary Lord one thousand six hundred eighty-eight [-nine] present unto their majesties . . . William and Mary prince and princess of Orange . . . a certain declaration in writing made by the said lords and commons in the words following viz [namely]:

Whereas the late king James the second, by the assistance of divers evil counsellors, judges, and ministers employed by him did endeavor to subvert and extirpate the Protestant religion and the laws and liberties of this kingdom.

By assuming and exercising a power of dispensing with and suspending of laws and the execution of laws without consent of parliament. . . .

By levying money for and to the use of the crown by pretence of prerogative for other time and in other manner than the same was granted by parliament.

By raising and keeping a standing army within this kingdom in time of peace without consent of parliament and quartering soldiers contrary to law. . . .

By violating the freedom of election of members to serve in parliament. . . .

And excessive bail hath been required of persons committed in criminal cases to elude the benefit of the laws made for the liberty of the subjects.

And excessive fines have been imposed.

And illegal and cruel punishments inflicted. . . .

And thereupon the said lords spiritual and temporal and commons . . . do . . . declare that the pretended power of suspending of laws or the execution of laws by regal authority without consent of parliament is illegal. . . .

That levying money for or to the use of the crown . . . without grant of parliament for longer time or in other manner than the same is or shall be granted is illegal.

That it is the right of the subjects to petition the king and all commitments and prosecutions for such petitioning are illegal.

That the raising or keeping a standing army within the kingdom in time of peace unless it be with consent of parliament is against law. . . .

That election of members of parliament ought to be free. . . .

That excessive bail ought not to be required nor excessive fines imposed nor cruel and unusual punishments inflicted. . . .

The said lords . . . do resolve that William and Mary, prince and princess of Orange, be declared king and queen of England, France, and Ireland. . . .

Second Treatise of Government

English philosopher John Locke (above) wrote "Two Treatises of Government" in the early 1680s. Published in 1690, the "Second Treatise of Government" argues that government should be based on an agreement between the people and their ruler, and that if the ruler violates the agreement, a rebellion by the people may be justified.

Of the State of Nature

To understand Political Power right, and to derive it from its Original, we must consider what State all Men are naturally in, and that is, a State of perfect Freedom to order their Actions, and dispose of their Possessions, and Persons as they think fit, within the bounds of the Law of Nature, without asking leave, or depending upon the Will of any other Man. . . .

Of the Beginning of Political Societies

Men being, as has been said, by Nature, all free, equal and independent, no one can be put out of this Estate, and subjected to the Political Power of another, without his own Consent. The only way whereby any one divests himself of his Natural Liberty, and puts on the bonds of Civil Society is by agreeing with other Men to joyn and unite into a Community, for their comfortable, safe, and peaceable living one amongst another, in a secure Enjoyment of their properties, and a greater Security against any that are not of it. This any number of Men may do, because it injures not the Freedom of the rest; they are left as they were in the Liberty of the State of Nature. . . .

Whosoever therefore out of a state of Nature unite into a Community, must be understood to give up all the power, necessary to the ends for which they unite into Society, to the majority of the Community. . . .

Of the Dissolution of Government

Governments are dissolved from within . . . when the Legislative is altered. . . . First, that when such a single Person or Prince sets up his own Arbitrary Will in place of the Laws, which are the Will of the Society, declared by the Legislative, then the Legislative is changed. . . . Secondly, when the Prince hinders the legislative from . . . acting freely, pursuant to those ends, for which it was Constituted, the Legislative is altered. . . . Thirdly, When by the Arbitrary Power of the Prince, the Electors, or ways of Election are altered, without the Consent, and contrary to the common Interest of the People, there also the Legislative is altered. . . .

In these and the like Cases, when the Government is dissolved, the People are at liberty to provide for themselves, by erecting a new Legislative, differing from the other, by the change of Persons, or Form, or both as they shall find it most for their safety and good. For the Society can never, by the fault of another, lose the Native and Original Right it has to preserve itself. . . .

Documents

The Virginia Statute for Religious Freedom

This statute, excerpted below, was the basis for the religion clauses in the Bill of Rights. Thomas Jefferson drafted the statute, and James Madison guided it through the Virginia legislature in 1786. The issue it addresses arose when the new state considered whether citizens should continue to support the Anglican Church, as they had in colonial times, or whether they should support any or all other denominations.

Whereas Almighty God hath created the mind free; that all attempts to influence it by temporal punishments . . . tend only to beget habits of hypocrisy and meanness, and are a departure from the plan of the Holy author of our religion; . . . that the impious presumption of legislators and rulers, civil as well as ecclesiastical, who being themselves but fallible and uninspired men, have assumed dominion over the faith of others, setting up their own opinions and modes of thinking as the only true and infallible, and as such endeavouring to impose them on others, hath established and maintained false religions over the greatest part of the world, and through all time; . . . that to compel a man to furnish contributions of money for the propagation of opinions which he disbelieves, is sinful and tyrannical; . . . that our civil rights have no dependence on our religious opinions, any more than our opinions in physics or geometry; that therefore the proscribing any citizen as unworthy the public confidence by laying upon him an incapacity of being called to offices of trust . . . unless he profess or renounce this or that religious opinion, is depriving him injuriously of those privileges and advantages to which in common with his fellow-citizens he has a natural right; that it tends only to corrupt the principles of that religion it is meant to encourage, by bribing with a monopoly of worldly honours and emoluments, those who will externally profess and conform to it . . . :

Be it enacted by the General Assembly, That no man shall be compelled to frequent or support any religious worship, place, or ministry whatsoever, nor shall be enforced, restrained, molested, or burthened in his body or goods, nor shall otherwise suffer on account of his religious opinions or belief; but that all men shall be free to profess, and by argument to maintain, their opinion in matters of religion, and that the same shall in no wise diminish enlarge, or affect their civil capacities. . . .

Thomas Jefferson

Documents

The Federalist No. 10

James Madison (pictured at right) wrote several articles for a New York newspaper supporting ratification of the Constitution. In the excerpt below, he argues for the idea of a federal republic as a guard against factions, or overzealous parties, in governing the nation.

The latent causes of faction are thus sown in the nature of man; and we see them everywhere. . . . A zeal for different opinions concerning religion, concerning government, and many other points; . . . an attachment to different leaders ambitiously contending for preeminence and power . . . have, in turn, divided mankind into parties . . . disposed to vex and oppress each other than to cooperate for their common good. . . . But the most common and durable source of factions has been the various and unequal distribution of property. Those who hold and those who are without property have ever formed distinct interests in society. Those who are creditors, and those who are debtors, fall under a like discrimination. A landed interest, a manufacturing interest, a mercantile interest, a moneyed interest, with many lesser interests, grow up of necessity in civilized nations, and divide them into different classes, actuated by different sentiments and views. The regulation of these various and interfering interests forms the principal task of modern legislation and involves the spirit of party and faction in the necessary and ordinary operations of government. . . .

The inference to which we are brought is that the causes of faction cannot be removed and relief is only to be sought in the means of controlling its effects. . . .

By what means is this object attainable? Evidently by one of two only. Either the existence of the same passion or interest in a majority at the same time must be prevented, or the majority, having such coexistent passion or interest, must be rendered, by their number and local situation, unable to concert and carry into effect schemes of oppression. . . .

From this . . . it may be concluded that a pure democracy, by which I mean a society consisting of a small number of citizens, who assemble and administer the government in person, can admit of no cure for the mischiefs of faction. A common passion or interest will, in almost every case, be felt by a majority of the whole; a communication and concert results from the form of government itself; and there is nothing to check the inducements to sacrifice the weaker party or an obnoxious individual. Hence it is that such democracies have ever been spectacles of turbulence and contention. . . .

A republic, by which I mean a government in which the scheme of representation takes place, opens a different prospect and promises the cure for which we are seeking. . . .

The two great points of difference between a democracy and a republic are: first, the delegation of the government in the latter to a small number of citizens elected by the rest; secondly, the greater number of citizens and great sphere of country over which the latter may be extended.

Documents

The Federalist No. 51

The author of this Federalist paper is not known. It may have been either James Madison or Alexander Hamilton. The author argues that the Constitution's federal system and separation of powers will protect the rights of the people.

In order to lay a due foundation for that separate and distinct exercise of the different powers of government, which to a certain extent is admitted on all hands to be essential to the preservation of liberty, it is evident that . . . the great security against a gradual concentration of the several powers in the same department, consists in giving to those who administer each department the necessary constitutional means and personal motives to resist encroachments of the others. . . .

Ambition must be made to counteract ambition. . . . A dependence on the people is, no doubt, the primary control on the government; but experience has taught mankind the necessity of auxiliary precautions. . . . The constant aim is to divide and arrange the several offices in such a manner as that each may be a check on the other. . . . In the compound republic of America, the power surrendered by the people is first divided between two distinct governments, and then the portion allotted to each subdivided among distinct and separate departments. . . .

In a free government the security for civil rights must be the same as that for religious rights. It consists in the one case in the multiplicity of interests, and in the other in the multiplicity of sects. . . . In the extended republic of the United States, and among the great variety of interests, parties, and sects which it embraces, a coalition of a majority of the whole society could seldom take place on any other principles than those of justice and the general good. . . . It is no less certain than it is important . . . that the larger the society, provided it lie within a practical sphere, the more duly capable it will be of self-government.

The Federalist No. 59

In this Federalist paper, Alexander Hamilton explains why Congress, and not the states, should have the final say in how federal elections are conducted.

The natural order of the subject leads us to consider . . . that provision of the Constitution which authorizes the national legislature to regulate, in the last resort, the election of its own members. . . . Its propriety rests upon the evidence of this plain proposition, that every government ought to contain in itself the means of its own preservation. . . . Nothing can be more evident, than that an exclusive power of regulating elections for the national government, in the hands of the state legislatures, would leave the existence of the union entirely at their mercy. They could at any moment annihilate it, by neglecting to provide for the choice of persons to administer its affairs. . . .

It is certainly true that the state legislatures, by forbearing the appointment of senators, may destroy the national government. But it will not follow that, because they have a power to do this in one instance, they ought to have it in every other. . . . It is an evil; but it is an evil which could not have been avoided without excluding the states . . . from a place in the organization of the national government. If this had been done, it would doubtless have been interpreted into an entire dereliction of the federal principle; and would certainly have deprived the state governments of that absolute safeguard which they will enjoy under this provision. . . .

Washington's Farewell Address

Washington never orally delivered his Farewell Address. Instead, he arranged to have it printed in a Philadelphia newspaper on September 19, 1796. Designed in part to remove him from consideration for a third presidential term, the address also warned about dangers the new nation was facing, especially the dangers of political parties and sectionalism.

Washington preparing to leave office

Friends and Fellow Citizens:

The period for a new election of a citizen to administer the executive government of the United States being not far distant . . . I should now apprise you of the resolution I have formed to decline being considered. . . .

The unity of government which constitutes you one people is . . . a main pillar in the edifice of your real independence; the support of your tranquility at home, your peace abroad; of your safety; of your prosperity in every shape; of that very liberty which you so highly prize. But as it is easy to foresee that, from different causes and from different quarters, much pains will be taken, many artifices employed to weaken in your minds the conviction of this truth. . . .

The name of American, which belongs to you, in your national capacity, must always exalt the just pride of patriotism more than any appellation derived from local discriminations. . . .

In contemplating the causes which may disturb our Union, it occurs as matter of serious concern that any ground should have been furnished for characterizing parties by geographical discriminations: Northern and Southern; Atlantic and Western; whence designing men may endeavor to excite a belief that there is a real difference of local interests and views. . . .

Let me now take a more comprehensive view and warn you in the most solemn manner against the baneful effects of the spirit of party generally. . . .The alternate domination of one faction over another, sharpened by the spirit of revenge natural to party dissension . . . is itself a frightful despotism. . . .

Of all the dispositions and habits which lead to political prosperity, religion and morality are indispensable supports. . . . A volume could not trace all their connections with private and public felicity. Let it simply be asked where is the security for property, for reputation, for life, if the sense of religious obligation desert the oaths, which are the instruments of investigation in courts of justice? And let us with caution indulge the supposition, that morality can be maintained without religion. Whatever may be conceded to the influence of refined education on minds of peculiar structure—reason and experience both forbid us to expect that national morality can prevail in exclusion of religious principle.

The great rule of conduct for us, in regard to foreign nations, is in extending our commercial relations to have with them as little political connection as possible. . . .

In offering you, my countrymen, these counsels of an old and affectionate friend, I dare not hope that they will make the strong and lasting impression I could wish. . . . But if I may even flatter myself that they may be productive of some partial benefit. . . .

The Kentucky Resolution

The Alien and Sedition Acts of 1798 made it easier for the government to suppress criticism and to arrest political enemies. This Federalist legislation inspired fierce opposition among Republicans, who looked to the state governments to reverse the acts. Two states, Kentucky and Virginia, passed resolutions stating their right to, in effect, disregard federal legislation. The resolutions laid the groundwork for the states' rights often cited during the Civil War. Thomas Jefferson wrote the Kentucky Resolution, excerpted below, which was adopted in 1799.

RESOLVED, . . . that if those who administer the general government be permitted to transgress the limits fixed by that compact, by a total disregard to the special delegations of power therein contained, annihilation of the state governments, and the erection upon their ruins, of a general consolidated government, will be the inevitable consequence; that the principle and construction contended for by sundry of the state legislatures, that the general government is the exclusive judge of the extent of the powers delegated to it, stop nothing short of despotism; . . . that the several states who formed that instrument, being sovereign and independent, have the unquestionable right to judge of its infraction; and that a nullification, by those sovereignties, of all unauthorized acts done under colour of that instrument, is the rightful remedy; . . .

"The Star-Spangled Banner"

Francis Scott Key

During the British bombardment of Fort McHenry during the War of 1812, a young Baltimore lawyer named Francis Scott Key was inspired to write the words to "The Star-Spangled Banner." Although it became popular immediately, it was not until 1931 that Congress officially declared "The Star-Spangled Banner" as the national anthem of the United States.

O! say can you see, by the dawn's early light,
What so proudly we hail'd at the twilight's last gleaming,
Whose broad stripes and bright stars through the perilous fight,
O'er the ramparts we watch'd, were so gallantly streaming?
And the Rockets' red glare, the Bombs bursting in air,
Gave proof through the night that our Flag was still there;
O! say, does that star-spangled Banner yet wave,
O'er the Land of the free, and the home of the brave?

Fort McHenry flag

The Monroe Doctrine

When Spain's power in South America began to weaken, other European nations seemed ready to step in. The United States was developing trade and diplomatic relations with South America, and it wanted to curb European influence there. The following is a statement President Monroe made on the subject in his annual message to Congress on December 2, 1823.

The occasion has been judged proper for asserting, as a principle in which the rights and interests of the United States are involved, that the American continents, by the free and independent condition which they have assumed and maintain, are henceforth not to be considered as subjects for future colonization by any European powers. . . .

. . . We owe it, therefore, to candor and to the amicable relations existing between the United States and those [European] powers to declare that we should consider any attempt on their part to extend their system to any portion of this hemisphere as dangerous to our peace and safety. With the existing colonies or dependencies of any European power we have not interfered and shall not interfere. But with the Governments who have declared their independence and maintain it, and whose independence we have, on great consideration and on just principles, acknowledged, we could not view any interposition for the purpose of oppressing them, or controlling in any other manner their destiny, by any European power in any other light than as the manifestation of an unfriendly disposition toward the United States. . . .

Our policy in regard to Europe, which was adopted at an early stage of the wars which have so long agitated that quarter of the globe, nevertheless remains the same, which is, not to interfere in the internal concerns of any of its powers; to consider the government de facto as the legitimate government for us; to cultivate friendly relations with it, and to preserve those relations by a frank, firm, and manly policy, meeting in all instances the just claims of every power, submitting to injuries from none.

The Seneca Falls Declaration

One of the first documents to call for equal rights for women was the Declaration of Sentiments and Resolutions, issued in 1848 at the Seneca Falls Convention in Seneca Falls, New York. Led by Lucretia Mott and Elizabeth Cady Stanton, the delegates at the convention used the language of the Bill of Rights to call for women's rights.

We hold these truths to be self-evident: that all men and women are created equal; that they are endowed by their Creator with certain inalienable rights; that among these are life, liberty, and the pursuit of happiness; that to secure these rights governments are instituted, deriving their just powers from the consent of the governed. Whenever any form of government becomes destructive of these ends, it is the right of those who suffer from it to refuse allegiance to it, and to insist upon the institution of a new government. . . .

The history of mankind is a history of repeated injuries and usurpations on the part of man toward woman, having in direct object the establishment of an absolute tyranny over her.

Now, in view of this entire disfranchisement . . . we insist that they have immediate admission to all the rights and privileges which belong to them as citizens of the United States. . . .

Lucretia Mott

Documents

The Emancipation Proclamation

On January 1, 1863, President Abraham Lincoln issued the Emancipation Proclamation, which freed all enslaved persons in states under Confederate control. The Proclamation was a significant step toward the passage of the Thirteenth Amendment (1865), which ended slavery in the United States.

Whereas, on the 22nd day of September, in the year of our Lord 1862, a proclamation was issued by the President of the United States, containing, among other things, the following, to wit:

That on the 1st day of January, in the year of our Lord 1863, all persons held as slaves within any state or designated part of a state, the people whereof shall then be in rebellion against the United States, shall be then, thenceforward, and forever free; and the executive government of the United States, including the military and naval authority thereof, will recognize and maintain the freedom of such persons and will do no act or acts to repress such persons, or any of them, in any efforts they may make for their actual freedom.

That the executive will, on the 1st day January aforesaid, by proclamation, designate the states and parts of states, if any, in which the people thereof, respectively, shall then be in rebellion against the United States; and the fact that any state or the people thereof shall on that day be in good faith represented in the Congress of the United States by members chosen thereto at elections wherein a majority of the qualified voters of such states shall have participated shall, in the absence of strong countervailing testimony, be deemed conclusive evidence that such state and the people thereof are not then in rebellion against the United States.

Now, therefore, I, Abraham Lincoln, President of the United States, by virtue of the power in me vested as commander in chief of the Army and Navy of the United States, in time of actual armed rebellion against the authority and government of the United States, and as a fit and necessary war measure for suppressing said rebellion, do, on this 1st day of January, in the year of our Lord 1863, and in accordance with my purpose so to do, publicly proclaimed for the full period of 100 days from the day first above mentioned, order, and designate as the states and parts of states wherein the people thereof, respectively, are this day in rebellion against the United States. . . .

And, by virtue of the power and for the purpose aforesaid, I do order and declare that all persons held as slaves within said designated states and parts of states are, and henceforward shall be, free; and that the executive government of the United States, including the military and naval authorities thereof, will recognize and maintain the freedom of said persons. . . .

And upon this act, sincerely believed to be an act of justice, warranted by the Constitution upon military necessity, I invoke the considerate judgment of mankind and the gracious favor of Almighty God. . . .

Abraham Lincoln

The Gettysburg Address

National monument at Gettysburg

President Abraham Lincoln delivered the Gettysburg Address on November 19, 1863, during the dedication of the Gettysburg National Cemetery. The dedication was in honor of the more than 7,000 Union and Confederate soldiers who died in the Battle of Gettysburg earlier that year. Lincoln's brief speech is often recognized as one of the finest speeches in the English language. It is also one of the most moving speeches in the nation's history.

There are five known manuscript copies of the address, two of which are in the Library of Congress. Scholars debate about which, if any, of the existing manuscripts comes closest to Lincoln's actual words that day.

Four score and seven years ago our fathers brought forth on this continent a new nation, conceived in liberty and dedicated to the proposition that all men are created equal.

Now we are engaged in a great civil war, testing whether that nation or any nation so conceived and so dedicated can long endure. We are met on a great battlefield of that war. We have come to dedicate a portion of that field as a final resting-place for those who here gave their lives that that nation might live. It is altogether fitting and proper that we should do this.

But in a larger sense, we cannot dedicate, we cannot consecrate, we cannot hallow this ground. The brave men, living and dead, who struggled here have consecrated it far above our poor power to add or detract. The world will little note nor long remember what we say here, but it can never forget what they did here. It is for us the living, rather, to be dedicated here to the unfinished work which they who fought here have thus far so nobly advanced. It is rather for us to be here dedicated to the great task remaining before us—that from these honored dead we take increased devotion to that cause for which they gave the last full measure of devotion—that we here highly resolve that these dead shall not have died in vain, that this nation under God shall have a new birth of freedom, and that government of the people, by the people, for the people, shall not perish from the earth.

The Pledge of Allegiance

Students in a New York City school reciting the Pledge of Allegiance

In 1892 the nation celebrated the 400th anniversary of Columbus's landing in America. In connection with this celebration, Francis Bellamy, a magazine editor, wrote and published the Pledge of Allegiance. The words "under God" were added by Congress in 1954 at the urging of President Dwight D. Eisenhower.

I pledge allegiance to the Flag of the United States of America and to the Republic for which it stands, one Nation under God, indivisible, with liberty and justice for all.

President Harrison on Hawaiian Annexation

An early expression of American imperialism came in the annexation of Hawaii. With the support of the American government, a small number of American troops overthrew the Hawaiian monarchy in January 1893. The excerpt below is from President Benjamin Harrison's written message to Congress. He sent the message along with the treaty for annexation to Congress on February 15, 1893.

I do not deem it necessary to discuss at any length the conditions which have resulted in this decisive action. It has been the policy of the administration not only to respect but to encourage the continuance of an independent government in the Hawaiian Islands so long as it afforded suitable guarantees for the protection of life and property and maintained a stability and strength that gave adequate security against the domination of any other power. . . .

The overthrow of the monarchy was not in any way promoted by this government, but had its origin in what seems to have been a reactionary and revolutionary policy on the part of Queen Liliuokalani, which put in serious peril not only the large and preponderating interests of the United States . . . but all foreign interests. . . . It is quite evident that the monarchy had become effete and the queen's government is weak and inadequate as to be the prey of designing and unscrupulous persons. The restoration of Queen Liliuokalani . . . is undesirable . . . and unless actively supported by the United States would be accompanied by serious disaster and the disorganization of all business interests. The influence and interest of the United States in the islands must be increased and not diminished.

Only two courses are now open—one the establishment of a protectorate by the United States, and the other annexation, full and complete. I think the latter course, which has been adopted in the treaty, will be highly promotive of the best interest of the Hawaiian people and is the only one that will adequately secure the interests of the United States. These interests are not wholly selfish. It is essential that none of the other great powers shall secure these islands. Such a possession would not consist with our safety and with the peace of the world. This view of the situation is so apparent and conclusive that no protest has been heard from any government against proceedings looking to annexation.

The American's Creed

In the patriotic fervor of World War I, national leaders sponsored a contest in which writers submitted ideas for a national creed that would be a brief summary of American beliefs. Of the 3,000 entries, the judges selected that of William Tyler Page as the winner. In a 1918 ceremony in the House of Representatives, the Speaker of the House accepted the creed for the United States.

I believe in the United States of America as a Government of the people, by the people, for the people, whose just powers are derived from the consent of the governed; a democracy in a republic; a sovereign Nation of many sovereign States; a perfect union, one and inseparable; established upon those principles of freedom, equality, justice, and humanity for which American patriots sacrificed their lives and fortunes.

I therefore believe it is my duty to my Country to love it; to support its Constitution; to obey its laws; to respect its flag, and to defend it against all enemies.

The Fourteen Points

On January 8, 1918, President Woodrow Wilson went before Congress to offer a statement of war aims called the Fourteen Points. They reflected Wilson's belief that if the international community accepted certain basic principles of conduct and set up institutions to carry them out, there would be peace in the world.

We entered this war because violations of right had occurred. . . . What we demand in this war, therefore, is . . . that the world be made fit and safe to live in. . . .

The only possible programme, as we see it, is this:

I. Open covenants of peace, openly arrived at, after which there shall be no private international understandings of any kind but diplomacy shall proceed always frankly and in the public view.

II. Absolute freedom of navigation upon the seas, outside territorial waters, alike in peace and in war. . . .

III. The removal, so far as possible, of all economic barriers and the establishment of an equality of trade conditions among all the nations. . . .

IV. Adequate guarantees given and taken that national armaments will be reduced to the lowest point consistent with domestic safety.

V. A free, open-minded, and absolutely impartial adjustment of all colonial claims, based upon a strict observance of the principle that in determining all such questions of sovereignty the interests of the populations concerned must have equal weight with the equitable claims of the government whose title is to be determined.

VI. The evacuation of all Russian territory and . . . opportunity for the independent determination of her own political development and national polity. . . .

VII. Belgium . . . must be evacuated and restored. . . .

VIII. All French territory should be freed and the invaded portions restored, and the wrong done to France by Prussia in 1871 in the matter of Alsace-Lorraine should be righted. . . .

IX. A readjustment of the frontiers of Italy should be effected along clearly recognizable lines of nationality.

X. The peoples of Austria-Hungary . . . should be accorded the freest opportunity of autonomous development.

XI. Roumania, Serbia, and Montenegro should be evacuated; occupied territories restored . . . the relations of the several Balkan states to one another determined by friendly counsel along historically established lines of allegiance and nationality. . . .

XII. The Turkish portions of the present Ottoman Empire should be assured a secure sovereignty. . . .

XIII. An independent Polish state should be erected which should include the territories inhabited by indisputably Polish populations. . . .

XIV. A general association of nations must be formed under specific covenants for the purpose of affording mutual guarantees of political independence and territorial integrity. . . .

Discussion of the Fourteen Points at the Versailles peace conference

Documents

The Four Freedoms

President Franklin D. Roosevelt delivered this address on January 6, 1941, in his annual message to Congress. In it, Roosevelt called for a world founded on "four essential human freedoms": freedom of speech and expression, freedom of worship, freedom from want, and freedom from fear.

Just as our national policy in internal affairs has been based upon a decent respect for the rights and dignity of all our fellow men within our gates, so our national policy in foreign affairs has been based on a decent respect for the rights and dignity of all nations, large and small. And the justice of morality must and will win in the end.

Our national policy is this:

First, by an impressive expression of the public will and without regard to partisanship, we are committed to all-inclusive national defense.

Second, by an impressive expression of the public will and without regard to partisanship, we are committed to full support of all those resolute peoples, everywhere, who are resisting aggression and are thereby keeping war away from our Hemisphere. . . .

Third . . . we are committed to the proposition that principles of morality and considerations for our own security will never permit us to acquiesce in a peace dictated by aggressors. . . .

Let us say to the democracies, "We Americans are vitally concerned in your defense of freedom. We are putting forth our energies, our resources, and our organizing powers to give you the strength to regain and maintain a free world. We shall send you, in ever increasing numbers, ships, planes, tanks, guns. This is our purpose and our pledge." In fulfillment of this purpose we will not be intimidated by the threats of dictators that they will regard as a breach of international law and as an act of war our aid to the democracies which dare to resist their aggression. . . .

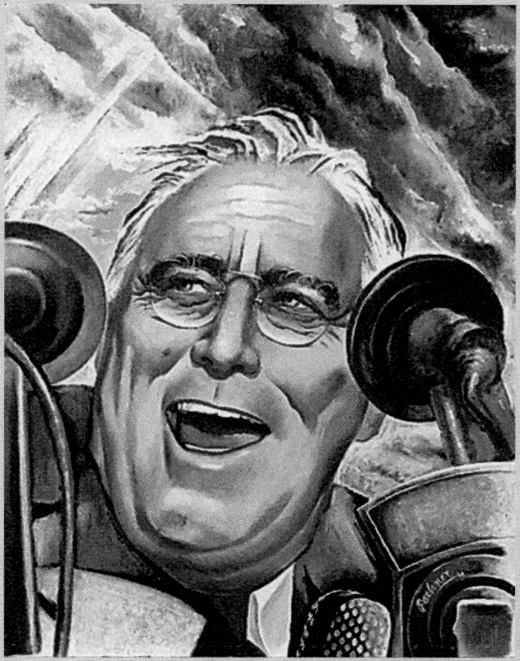

Caricature of President Roosevelt

In the future days, which we seek to make secure, we look forward to a world founded upon four essential human freedoms.

The first is freedom of speech and expression everywhere in the world.

The second is freedom of every person to worship God in his own way everywhere in the world.

The third is freedom from want, which, translated into world terms, means economic understandings which will secure to every nation a healthy peacetime life for its inhabitants everywhere in the world.

The fourth is freedom from fear—which, translated into world terms, means a world-wide reduction of armaments to such a point and in such a thorough fashion that no nation will be in a position to commit an act of physical aggression against any neighbor—anywhere in the world. . . .

The Truman Doctrine

President Harry S. Truman addressed a joint session of Congress on March 12, 1947, to request aid to fight Communist influence in Greece and Turkey. His message that communism had to be contained represents the central idea of American foreign policy during the Cold War.

The United States has received from the Greek Government an urgent appeal for financial and economic assistance. . . .

When forces of liberation entered Greece they found that the retreating Germans had destroyed virtually all the railways, roads, port facilities, communications, and merchant marine. More than a thousand villages had been burned. Eighty-five percent of the children were tubercular. Livestock, poultry, and draft animals had almost disappeared. Inflation had wiped out practically all savings. As a result of these tragic conditions, a militant minority, exploiting human want and misery, was able to create political chaos which, until now, has made economic recovery impossible.

Greece is today without funds to finance the importation of those goods which are essential to bare subsistence. Under these circumstances the people of Greece cannot make progress in solving their problems of reconstruction. Greece is in desperate need of financial and economic assistance to enable it to resume purchases of food, clothing, fuel and seeds. These are indispensable for the subsistence of its people and are obtainable only from abroad. Greece must have help to import the goods necessary to restore internal order and security, so essential for economic and political recovery. . . .

Meanwhile, the Greek Government is unable to cope with the situation. The Greek army is small and poorly equipped. It needs supplies and equipment if it is to restore the authority of the government throughout Greek territory. Greece must have assistance if it is to become a self-supporting and self-respecting democracy.

The United States must supply that assistance. We have already extended to Greece certain types of relief and economic aid but these are inadequate. There is no other country to which democratic Greece can turn. . . .

No government is perfect. One of the chief virtues of a democracy, however, is that its defects are always visible and under democratic processes can be pointed out and corrected.

The Government of Greece is not perfect. Nevertheless it represents eighty-five percent of the members of the Greek Parliament who were chosen in an election last year. . . .

Greece's neighbor, Turkey, also deserves our attention. The future of Turkey as an independent and economically sound state is clearly no less important to the freedom-loving peoples of the world than the future of Greece. The circumstances in which Turkey finds itself today are considerably different from those of Greece. Turkey has been spared the disasters that have beset Greece. And during the war, the United States and Great Britain furnished Turkey with material aid. Nevertheless, Turkey now needs our support.

. . . To ensure the peaceful development of nations, free from coercion, the United States has taken a leading part in establishing the United Nations. The United Nations is designed to make possible lasting freedom and independence for all its members. We shall not realize our objectives, however, unless we are willing to help free peoples to maintain their free institutions . . . against aggressive movements that seek to impose upon them totalitarian regimes. . . .

This is an investment in world freedom and world peace. . . . The seeds of totalitarian regimes are nurtured by misery and want. They spread and grow in the evil soil of poverty and strife. They reach their full growth when the hope of a people for a better life has died. We must keep that hope alive. . . . If we falter in our leadership, we may endanger the peace of the world—and we shall surely endanger the welfare of our own nation.

Brown v. Board of Education

On May 17, 1954, the Supreme Court ruled in* Brown *v.* Board of Education of Topeka, Kansas, *that racial segregation in public schools was unconstitutional. This decision provided the legal basis for court challenges to segregation in every aspect of American life.

These cases come to us from the States of Kansas, South Carolina, Virginia, and Delaware. They are premised on different facts and different local conditions, but a common legal question justifies their consideration together in this consolidated opinion.

In each of the cases, minors of the Negro race, through their legal representatives, seek the aid of the courts in obtaining admission to the public schools of their community on a nonsegregated basis. In each instance, they had been denied admission to schools attended by white children under laws requiring or permitting segregation according to race. This segregation was alleged to deprive the plaintiffs of the equal protection of the laws under the Fourteenth Amendment.

The plaintiffs contend that segregated public schools are not "equal" and cannot be made "equal," and that hence they are deprived of the equal protection of the laws. Because of the obvious importance of the question presented, the Court took jurisdiction. . . .

. . . Our decision . . . cannot turn on merely a comparison of these tangible factors in the Negro and white schools involved in each of the cases. We must look instead to the effect of segregation itself on public education.

In approaching this problem, we cannot turn the clock back to 1868 when the Amendment was adopted, or even to 1896 when *Plessy* v. *Ferguson* was written. We must consider public education in the light of its full development and its present place in American life throughout the nation. Only in this way can it be determined if segregation in public schools deprives these plaintiffs of the equal protection of the laws.

Today, education is perhaps the most important function of state and local governments. Compulsory school attendance laws and the great expenditures for education both demonstrate our recognition of the importance of education to our democratic society. . . . In these days, it is doubtful that any child may reasonably be expected to succeed in life if he is denied the opportunity of an education. Such an opportunity, where the state has undertaken to provide it, is a right which must be made available to all on equal terms.

Linda Brown

We come then to the question presented: Does segregation of children in public schools solely on the basis of race, even though the physical facilities and other "tangible" factors may be equal, deprive the children of the minority group of equal educational opportunities? We believe that it does.

. . . We conclude that, in the field of public education, the doctrine of "separate but equal" has no place. Separate educational facilities are inherently unequal. Therefore, we hold that the plaintiff and others similarly situated for whom the actions have been brought are, by reason of the segregation complained of, deprived of the equal protection of the laws guaranteed by the Fourteenth Amendment. . . .

"I Have a Dream"

On August 28, 1963, while Congress was debating broad civil rights legislation, Martin Luther King, Jr., led more than 200,000 people in a march on Washington, D.C. On the steps of the Lincoln Memorial, King gave a stirring speech in which he eloquently spoke of his dreams for African Americans and for the United States.

Martin Luther King, Jr., speaking at the march

Five score years ago, a great American, in whose symbolic shadow we stand, signed the Emancipation Proclamation. This momentous decree came as a great beacon light of hope to millions of Negro slaves who had been seared in the flames of withering injustice. It came as a joyous daybreak to end the long night of captivity.

But one hundred years later, we must face the tragic fact that the Negro is still not free. One hundred years later, the life of the Negro is still sadly crippled by the manacles of segregation and the chains of discrimination. . . .

There are those who are asking the devotees of civil rights, "When will you be satisfied?"

We can never be satisfied as long as the Negro is the victim of the unspeakable horrors of police brutality.

We can never be satisfied as long as our bodies, heavy with the fatigue of travel, cannot gain lodging in the motels of the highways and the hotels of the cities.

We cannot be satisfied as long as the Negro's basic mobility is from a smaller ghetto to a larger one. . . .

We cannot be satisfied as long as a Negro in Mississippi cannot vote and a Negro in New York believes he has nothing for which to vote.

No, no, we are not satisfied, and we will not be satisfied until "justice rolls down like waters and righteousness like a mighty stream." . . .

I say to you today, my friends, so even though we face the difficulties of today and tomorrow, I still have a dream. It is a dream deeply rooted in the American dream.

I have a dream that one day this nation will rise up and live out the true meaning of its creed: "We hold these truths to be self-evident; that all men are created equal."

I have a dream that one day on the red hills of Georgia the sons of former slaves and the sons of former slaveowners will be able to sit down together at the table of brotherhood.

I have a dream that one day even the state of Mississippi, a state sweltering with the heat of injustice and oppression, will be transformed into an oasis of freedom and justice.

I have a dream that my four little children will one day live in a nation where they will not be judged by the color of their skin but by the content of their character. . . .

And when this happens, when we allow freedom to ring, when we let it ring from every village and every hamlet, from every state and every city, we will be able to speed up that day when all of God's children, black men and white men, Jews and Gentiles, Protestants and Catholics, will be able to join hands and sing in the words of the old Negro spiritual, "Free at last! Free at last! Thank God Almighty, we are free at last!"

Gulf of Tonkin Resolution

On August 7, 1964, Congress passed the Gulf of Tonkin Resolution, which stood as the legal basis for the Vietnam War.

Resolved by the Senate and House of Representatives of the United States of America in Congress assembled,

That the Congress approves and supports the determination of the President, as Commander in Chief, to take all necessary measures to repel any armed attack against the forces of the United States and to prevent further aggression.

Section 2. The United States regards as vital to its national interest and to world peace the maintenance of international peace and security in southeast Asia. Consonant with the Constitution of the United States and the Charter of the United Nations and in accordance with its obligations under the Southeast Asia Collective Defense Treaty, the United States is, therefore, prepared, as the President determines, to take all necessary steps, including the use of armed force, to assist any member or protocol state of the Southeast Asia Collective Defense Treaty requesting assistance in defense of its freedom.

President Bush's Address to Joint Session of Congress, September 20, 2001

On September 11, 2001, terrorists crashed airplanes into the World Trade Center in New York City and the Pentagon in Washington, D.C. Thousands of people were killed. In his address, President George W. Bush announced a new kind of war against terrorism.

. . . On September the eleventh, enemies of freedom committed an act of war against our country. . . . Americans have known surprise attacks—but never before on thousands of civilians. All of this was brought upon us in a single day—and night fell on a different world, a world where freedom itself is under attack. . . .

The evidence we have gathered all points to a collection of loosely affiliated terrorist organizations known as al-Qaeda. . . . Our war on terror begins with al-Qaeda, but it does not end there. It will not end until every terrorist group of global reach has been found, stopped, and defeated.

Americans are asking: Why do they hate us? They hate what we see right here in this chamber—a democratically elected government. Their leaders are self-appointed. They hate our freedoms. . . . By sacrificing human life to serve their radical visions—by abandoning every value except the will to power—they follow in the path of fascism, and Nazism, and totalitarianism. And they will follow that path all the way, to where it ends: in history's unmarked grave of discarded lies.

. . . We will direct every resource at our command—every means of diplomacy, every tool of intelligence, every instrument of law enforcement, every financial influence, and every necessary weapon of war—to the disruption and defeat of the global terror network. . . .

I know there are struggles ahead, and dangers to face. But this country will define our times, not be defined by them. . . . Great harm has been done to us. We have suffered great loss. And in our grief and anger we have found our mission and our moment. . . . Our Nation—this generation—will lift a dark threat of violence from our people and our future. We will rally the world to this cause, by our efforts and by our courage. We will not tire, we will not falter, and we will not fail.

Supreme Court Case Summaries

The following case summaries explain the significance of major Supreme Court cases mentioned in the text.

Abington School District* v. *Schempp **(1963)** struck down a Pennsylvania statute requiring public schools in the state to begin each school day with Bible readings and a recitation of the Lord's Prayer. The Court held that the Constitution's establishment clause leaves religious beliefs and religious practices to each individual's choice and expressly commands that government not intrude into this decision-making process.

Abrams* v. *United States **(1919)** upheld a conviction under the Sedition Act and Espionage Act of 1917. The Court ruled that freedom of speech could be limited if there was a threat to the country.

Baker* v. *Carr **(1962)** established that federal courts can hear suits seeking to force state authorities to redraw electoral districts. In this case, the plaintiff wanted the population of each district to be roughly equal to the population in all other districts. The plaintiff claimed that the votes of voters in the least populous districts counted as much as the votes of voters in the most populous districts.

Brown* v. *Board of Education **(1954)** overruled *Plessy* v. *Ferguson* (1896) and abandoned the separate-but-equal doctrine in the context of public schools. In deciding this case, the Supreme Court rejected the idea that equivalent but separate schools for African Americans and white students would be constitutional. The Court stated that the Fourteenth Amendment's command that all persons be accorded the equal protection of the law (U.S. Const. amend. XIV, sec. 1) is not satisfied by ensuring that African American and white schools "have been equalized, or are being equalized, with respect to buildings, curricula, qualifications, and salaries, and other tangible factors."

The Court then held that racial segregation in public schools violates the equal protection clause because it is inherently unequal. In other words, the separation of schools by race marks the separate race as inferior. The ruling in this case has been extended beyond public education to virtually all public accommodations and activities.

Bush* v. *Gore **(2000)** found that a manual recount of disputed presidential ballots in Florida lacked a uniform standard of judging a voter's intent, thus violating the equal protection clause of the Constitution. The Court also ruled that there was not enough time to conduct a new manual recount that would meet constitutional standards. The case arose when Republican candidate George W. Bush asked the Court to stop a hand recount. This decision ensured that Bush would receive Florida's electoral votes and win the election.

Chisholm* v. *Georgia **(1793)** stripped the immunity of the states to lawsuits in federal court. The Supreme Court held that a citizen of one state could sue another state in federal court without that state consenting to the suit. The Court's decision created a furor and led to the adoption of the Eleventh Amendment, which protects states from federal court suits by citizens of other states.

Dred Scott* v. *Sandford **(1857)** was decided before the Fourteenth Amendment. The Fourteenth Amendment provides that anyone born or naturalized in the United States is a citizen of the nation and of his or her state. In this case, the Supreme Court held that a slave was property, not a citizen, and thus had no rights under the Constitution. The decision was a prime factor leading to the Civil War.

Engel* v. *Vitale **(1962)** held that the establishment clause (U.S. Const. amend. I, cl. 1) was violated by a public school district's practice of starting each school day with a prayer which began, "Almighty God, we acknowledge our dependence upon Thee." The Supreme Court ruled that religion is a personal matter and that government should not align itself with a particular religion in order to prevent religious persecution.

Escobedo v. Illinois (1964) held that Danny Escobedo's right to counsel, as provided by the Sixth Amendment, had been violated. Throughout police questioning, Escobedo asked repeatedly, but unsuccessfully, to see his attorney. The Supreme Court reversed Escobedo's murder conviction, holding that an attorney could have assisted Escobedo in invoking his Fifth Amendment right against self-incrimination. This case served as a forerunner to *Miranda* v. *Arizona*.

Gibbons v. Ogden (1824) made it clear that the authority of Congress to regulate interstate commerce (U.S. Const. art. I, sec. 8, cl. 3) includes the authority to regulate intrastate commercial activity that relates to interstate commerce. Before this case, it was thought that the Constitution would allow a state to close its borders to interstate commercial activity. This ruling says that a state can only regulate internal commercial activity, but Congress can regulate commercial activity that has both intrastate and interstate dimensions.

Gideon v. Wainwright (1963) ruled that poor defendants in criminal cases have the right to a state-paid attorney under the Sixth Amendment. The ruling in this case has been refined to apply only when the defendant, if convicted, can be sentenced to more than six months in jail.

Griswold v. Connecticut (1965) overturned the conviction of two Planned Parenthood employees charged with violating an 1879 state law banning the use of contraceptives. In deciding this case, the Court went beyond the actual words of the Constitution to protect a right—the right to privacy—which is not listed in the Constitution. The case also served as a forerunner to the *Roe* v. *Wade* decision that legalized abortion on the same basis.

Heart of Atlanta Motel, Inc. v. United States (1964) upheld the Civil Rights Act of 1964, which prohibits racial discrimination by those who provide goods, services, and facilities to the public. The Georgia motel in the case drew its business from other states but refused to rent rooms to African Americans. The Supreme Court explained that Congress had the authority to prohibit such discrimination under both the equal protection clause (U.S. Const. amend. XIV, sec. 1) and the commerce clause (art. I, sec. 8, cl. 3). With respect to the commerce clause, the Court explained that Congress had ample evidence to conclude that racial discrimination by hotels and motels impedes interstate commerce.

Korematsu v. United States (1944) allowed the federal government's authority to exclude Japanese Americans, many of whom were citizens, from designated military areas that included almost the entire West Coast. The government defended the orders as a necessary response to Japan's attack on Pearl Harbor. Yet, in upholding the orders, the Court established that government actions that discriminate on the basis of race would be subject to strict scrutiny.

Loving v. Virginia (1967) ruled that state laws that outlaw interracial marriages are unconstitutional under the Fourteenth Amendment. The Court explained that such laws violated the equal protection clause and deprived "citizens of liberty without due process of law." The Court went on to say, "Marriage is one of the basic civil rights of man, fundamental to our very existence and survival."

Mapp v. Ohio (1961) established that evidence seized in violation of the Fourth Amendment could not be used by the prosecution as evidence of a defendant's guilt at the federal, state, or local level.

Marbury v. Madison (1803) established one of the most important principles of American constitutional law. The Supreme Court held that the Court itself has the final say on what the Constitution means. It is also the Supreme Court that has the final say whether or not an act of government—legislative or executive at the federal, state, or local level—violates the Constitution.

Martin v. Hunter's Lessee (1816) affirmed that the Supreme Court has the authority to review state court decisions and is the nation's final court of appeal. The Supreme Court ruled that section 25 of the Judiciary Act of 1789 was constitutional. This section granted the Supreme Court appellate jurisdiction over state courts in certain situations, such as a state court denying the authority of federal law.

McCulloch v. Maryland (1819) established the basis for the expansive authority of Congress. The Supreme Court held that the necessary and proper clause (U.S. Const. art. I, sec. 8, cl. 18) allows Congress to do more than the Constitution specifically authorizes it to do. This case holds that Congress can enact almost any law that will help it achieve the ends established by Article I, Section 8 of the Constitution. For example, Congress has the power to regulate interstate commerce; the necessary and proper clause permits Congress to do so in ways not specified in the Constitution.

***Miranda* v. *Arizona* (1966)** held that a person in police custody may not be held unless reminded of his or her rights. These rights include: 1) the right to remain silent, 2) the right to an attorney (at government expense if the person is unable to pay), and 3) that anything the person says after acknowledging that he or she understands these rights can be used as evidence of guilt at a trial.

The Supreme Court explained that a person alone in police custody may not understand, even if told, that he or she can remain silent and thus might be misled into answering questions. The presence of an attorney is essential.

***Morgan* v. *Virginia* (1946)** challenged racial segregation in the South. Irene Morgan was convicted for refusing to give up her seat on an interstate bus bound from Virginia to Maryland. The Court ruled that the Virginia law posed an undue burden on interstate commerce and struck down the statute. However, segregation on southern buses continued on an informal basis.

***National Labor Relations Board* v. *Jones and Laughlin Steel Corp.* (1937)** upheld President Franklin Roosevelt's New Deal legislation, the National Labor Relations Act, which allowed workers to organize unions in businesses operating or affecting interstate commerce. Employers were prohibited from discriminating against their employees because of union membership. Prior to this case, the Supreme Court had ruled much New Deal legislation unconstitutional. This ruling came less than a week after Roosevelt's proposed court-packing plan. The president intended on "packing" the Supreme Court with additional justices in order to obtain a pro-New Deal majority on the Court.

***New York Times Co.* v. *Sullivan* (1964)** extended the protections afforded to the press by the free press clause (U.S. Const. amend. I). In this case, the Supreme Court held that a public official or public figure suing a publisher for libel (i.e., defamation) must prove that the publisher published a story that he or she knew was false or published the story in "reckless disregard of its truth or falsity," which means that the publisher did not take professionally adequate steps to determine the story's truth or falsity.

***Norris* v. *Alabama* (1935)** overturned the conviction of Clarence Norris, an African American sentenced to death for a crime in Alabama. The Supreme Court held that the grand jury and trial jury had systematically eliminated African American jurors. Thus, the Court reversed the conviction because it violated the equal protection clause of the Fourteenth Amendment.

***Northern Securities Company* v. *United States* (1904)** dealt with the application of congressional antitrust legislation. The party involved held three-fourths of the stock in two parallel railroad lines. By a narrow 5–4 decision, the Court upheld the application of the Sherman Antitrust Act. The Court ruled that the holding company clearly intended to eliminate competition between the two railroads, violating the constitutional right of Congress to regulate interstate commerce.

***Plessy* v. *Ferguson* (1896)** upheld the separate-but-equal doctrine used by Southern states to perpetuate segregation after the Civil War officially ended law-mandated segregation. The decision upheld a Louisiana law requiring passenger trains to have "equal but separated accommodations for the white and colored races." The Court held that the Fourteenth Amendment's equal protection clause required only equal public facilities for the two races, not equal access. This case was overruled by *Brown* v. *Board of Education* (1954).

***Regents of the University of California* v. *Bakke* (1978)** was the first Supreme Court decision to suggest that an affirmative action program could be justified on the basis of diversity. The Court explained that racial quotas were not permissible under the equal protection clause of the Fourteenth Amendment. However, the justices ruled that the diversity rationale was a legitimate interest that would allow a state medical school to consider an applicant's race in evaluating his or her application for admission. (Recent Supreme Court cases suggest that the diversity rationale is no longer enough to defend an affirmative action program.)

***Reynolds* v. *Sims* (1964)** extended the one-person, one-vote doctrine announced in *Wesberry* v. *Sanders* to state legislative elections. The Court held that the inequality of representation in the Alabama legislature violated the equal protection clause of the Fourteenth Amendment.

***Roe* v. *Wade* (1973)** held that women have the right under various provisions of the Constitution—most notably, the due process clause of the Fourteenth Amendment—to decide whether or not to terminate a pregnancy. The Court's ruling in this case was the most significant in a long line of decisions over a period of 50 years that recognized a constitutional right of privacy, even though the word *privacy* is not found in the Constitution.

Schechter Poultry Corporation* v. *United States **(1935)** overturned the conviction of the employers, who were charged with violating the wage and hour limitations of a law adopted under the authority of the National Industrial Recovery Act. The Court held that because the defendants did not sell poultry in interstate commerce, they were not subject to federal regulations on wages and hours.

Schenck* v. *United States **(1919)** upheld convictions under the Federal Espionage Act. The defendants were charged under the act with distributing leaflets aimed at inciting draft resistance during World War I; their defense was that antidraft speech was protected under the First Amendment.

The Supreme Court unanimously rejected the defense, explaining that whether or not speech is protected depends on the context in which it occurs. Because the defendants' antidraft rhetoric created a "clear and present danger" to the success of the war effort, it was not protected.

Stone* v. *Powell **(1976)** reversed a Court of Appeals decision that evidence was seized illegally and should therefore be excluded. The Court ruled that the defendant was provided a fair and legal opportunity to claim a Fourth Amendment violation before a trial jury. The trial jury found that the search was constitutional and the evidence should not be excluded. The Court stated, "Where the state has provided an opportunity for full and fair litigation of a Fourth Amendment claim, a state prisoner may not be granted federal habeas corpus relief."

Swann* v. *Charlotte-Mecklenburg Board of Education **(1971)** established a new plan to ensure that public schools were not segregated. Many school systems were slow to desegregate after *Brown* v. *Board of Education* and used various tactics to appear to be resolving the problem. This case ordered that busing students, reorganizing school boundaries, and racial ratios all be used as methods to obtain desegregated public school systems.

Sweatt* v. *Painter **(1950)** held that it was unconstitutional for African Americans to be denied admission to the University of Texas Law School based on race. An inferior law school established for African Americans did not give the state justification to deny admission to the main school. This act was a violation of the Fourteenth Amendment.

Wabash* v. *Illinois **(1886)** held that states have no authority to regulate railroad rates for interstate commerce. The Supreme Court held that the commerce clause (U.S. Const. art. I, sec. 8, cl. 3) allowed states to enforce "indirect" but not "direct" burdens on interstate commerce. State railroad rates were ruled "direct" burdens and therefore could not be enforced by states. The decision created a precedent by establishing rate regulation of interstate commerce as an exclusive federal power.

Wickard* v. *Filburn **(1942)** indicated how far the Supreme Court had come in complying with President Franklin Roosevelt's economic philosophies. The Court upheld specific parts of the Second Agricultural Adjustment Act. In its ruling, the Supreme Court held that marketing quotas could be applied to wheat that never left the farm. Using the commerce clause (U.S. Const. art. I, sec. 8, cl. 3) as the basis for its decision, the Court ruled that wheat that never left the farm still had an effect on interstate commerce. Farmers growing their own grain depressed the overall demand and market price of wheat. The decision further extended the power of the commerce clause.

Worcester* v. *Georgia **(1832)** overturned the conviction of Samuel A. Worcester, a missionary among the Cherokee. Worcester was imprisoned under a Georgia law forbidding whites to reside in Cherokee country without taking an oath of allegiance to the state and obtaining a permit. The Supreme Court voided the state law, ruling that the Cherokee were an independent nation based on a federal treaty and free from the jurisdiction of the state. Georgia ignored the decision, and President Jackson refused to enforce it, instead supporting the removal of the Cherokee to the Indian Territory.

American Literature Library

TABLE OF CONTENTS

What Is Literature?

Literature is art created with words. Some people use the term "literature" to include anything written—from newspaper articles and how-to books to pamphlets in a doctor's office. On the other hand, some insist that only creative writing can be literature. Still others suggest that some essays, or written opinions, and even speeches are of such high quality that they may be considered literature.

Just as there are many forms of the visual arts, there are many forms and styles of literature. Reading the literature of a certain period of history helps to bring the people and issues of the time to life.

A Good Story

Have you ever created a story to entertain a younger person? That's fiction: a story invented by the author. Writing that describes or explains real events or activities is referred to as "nonfiction."

The most popular type of fiction is the novel, a long story that usually has many people, or characters, and a complex plot, or action. Novels are written in prose, or everyday language, rather than poetry.

Some novels are inspired by actual events the author witnessed or people he or she has known. But a fiction writer is not attempting to report events or describe people accurately. By telling a good story, the author tries to lead the reader to discover universal truths. Other types of fiction include short stories and novellas, or short novels.

Time and Timelessness

Some writers set their stories in the present; some write historical novels; others write science fiction tales set in the future. All writers hope their work expresses truths that will be valid long after their lifetimes.

Throughout history, writers have addressed major themes such as good and evil, freedom, religion, power, corruption, love, death, and the relationship of humans to the natural world. Works of literature from a specific period of history often reflect their time in several ways:

- the language used
- the form of the work
- the general attitudes of the characters and the issues they face
- the morality expressed by the outcome

Approaching Poetry

Poetry is writing that is intended first and foremost to evoke emotion, not just convey information or tell a story. The first job of poetry is to create feeling—not to stimulate thought. For this reason it often has a rhythm like music, and it is often easier to understand if read aloud.

Eighteenth- and nineteenth-century poets—and some modern ones—wrote in one of many traditional forms. Each form requires a certain rhyme frequency and pattern of accented syllables, or meter. It also requires a specific number of lines of certain lengths.

Modern poetry does not always follow these conventions; words do not always rhyme, and sometimes the rhythm is to be found in how the words are arranged on the page, not how they sound. Despite these modern touches, the poet's goal remains constant—to evoke specific emotions that illuminate some aspect of life.

The Eras of Literature in American History

Writers reflect world events and issues in their work. Some write directly about those events and issues. Others express values or beliefs that were changed by historical events.

The Early National Period During the early years of the United States, authors often wrote about the challenges of settling a new land. They also focused on religion, morality, and the new form of government. Native Americans already had a rich tradition of oral literature.

After the War of 1812, writers such as James Fennimore Cooper and Washington Irving created a uniquely American style of writing with tales of adventures in the New World. Ralph Waldo Emerson and Henry David Thoreau wrote of the spiritual power of nature.

The Civil War Era During the Civil War and in every decade since, the tragedies of that conflict and the nature of race relations in American society have inspired some of America's best writers, from Mark Twain and Harriet Beecher Stowe in the nineteenth century to William Faulkner and Richard Wright in the twentieth century, and contemporary writers such as August Wilson and Toni Morrison.

Naturalism and Realism As industrialization attracted immigrants from around the globe, writers created art out of the attainment—and the failure—of their dreams. In *The Rise of Silas Lapham,* William Dean Howells told the rags-to-riches story of a Northern industrialist. Early in the twentieth century, "realist" writers, such as Theodore Dreiser, aided the work of Progressive reformers by exposing the underside of industry and the lives of laborers. Other major writers of the era included Mark Twain, Henry James, Stephen Crane, and Edith Wharton.

Modernism in the 1920s and 1930s World War I and its aftermath challenged traditional values, family life, and individual identity. Perhaps the best-known writer of this era is Ernest Hemingway, who along with other "lost generation" writers such as John dos Passos, Gertrude Stein, and F. Scott Fitzgerald described their sense of disillusionment with modern life.

The era also witnessed the appearance of several major African American writers and poets, including Langston Hughes and Claude McKay, in what became known as the Harlem Renaissance.

The tragedy of the Great Depression and the struggles of average Americans to survive provided inspiration for many writers. John Steinbeck's novel *The Grapes of Wrath* about Dust Bowl refugees is perhaps best known.

The second world war spawned a flood of war novels as writers reexamined human beings' relationship to evil, religion, and the meaning of life in the wake of the Jewish Holocaust, and what such an event said about human nature and its capacity for evil.

The 1950s and 1960s In the 1950s, beat writers, such as Jack Kerouac and Tom Robbins, shunned the conformity and materialism of affluent postwar America in favor of spontaneity and experimentation. But history had more shocks in store for American society including the social upheaval of the 1960s, the Vietnam War, and the transformation of a society from one based on reading to a mass-media consumer culture.

Postmodern Writers of Today The events of the late twentieth century led to "postmodern" writing. Postmodern writers are skeptical about any single version of reality in the Information Age. Their writing is full of irony and doubt about modern culture.

Creating a Nation

When white settlers arrived in America, the Native Americans living there already had a highly developed civilization dating back thousands of years. They also had their own form of literature—not written, but handed down from generation to generation orally. A theme common to many Native American stories is their relationship to nature. Many are also parables—stories that use symbols or animals to teach lessons. "Bald Eagle Sends Mud-turtle to the End of the World," written down by Jeremiah Curtin, is an example of a parable.

The second selection here is a portion of a famous speech given by Chief Red Jacket (Native American name Sagoyoweha). Red Jacket was an influential leader of the Seneca nation and the Iroquois confederation of tribes from the 1770s until the 1820s. He fought on the side of the British during the American Revolution, but in the War of 1812, he influenced his people to support the United States.

An ardent advocate of the Native American mode of life, he opposed the introduction of white customs, laws, schools, and especially conversion of Seneca to Christianity. In 1820 or 1821 he successfully petitioned Governor Clinton for the removal of missionaries and white teachers from Buffalo Creek reservation near Buffalo, New York. This speech was given at an 1805 meeting to discuss establishment of missions among six Iroquois nations. In it, Red Jacket argues forcefully for the religious freedom that many white settlers had left Europe to enjoy.

forefathers: ancestors

American Literature Library

"Bald Eagle Sends Mud-turtle to the End of the World"

Once upon a time, a bald-headed old man lived on the top of a mountain, and his wife and three children lived near a lake about half way to the summit of the same mountain.

Each day the old man went down to fish in the lake. On his way home he stopped and gave some of the fish to his wife, and thus they lived well and happily. After they had passed many years in this manner, the old man became curious to know how large the world is.

Being chief of his people he called a council, and said, "I want to know how large the world is. I wish some man would volunteer to find out."

One young man said, "I will go and find out."

"Very well," said the chief, "How long will you be gone?"

"I can't tell, for I don't know how far I shall have to travel."

"Go," said the chief, "and when you return you will tell us about your journey."

The young man started and after traveling two moons he came to a country where everything was white—the forests, the water, the grass. It hurt his feet to walk on the white ground, so he hurried back. When he reached home he notified the chief. The chief said, "I don't believe that he has been to the end of the world, but I will call a council and we will hear what he has to say."

When the people were assembled, the young man said: "I did not go very far, but I went as far as I was able." And he told all he knew of the White Country.

The chief said, "We must send another man." . . . Many men were sent, one after another, and each returned with a story a little different from that told by others, but still no one satisfied the chief. At last a man said, "I will start and I will go to the end of the world before I come back."

The chief looked at the man and saw that he was very homely, but very strong, and he said, "I think you will do as you promise. You may go." The chief called a council of the whole nation and each man agreed to make a journey by himself . . . The chief and his men went and were gone forty moons. When they came home a council was held and each told what he had seen. When the man came who had promised to go to the end of the world, he said, "I have been to the end of

Chief Red Jacket

the world, I have seen all kinds of people, all kinds of game, all kinds of forests and rivers. I have seen things which no one else has ever seen."

The chief was satisfied. He said, "I am chief of all the people, you will be next to me. You'll be second chief." This was the pay the man got for his journey. He took his position as second chief.

The old chief was Bald Eagle. The first man sent out was Deer. His feet were tender, he could not endure the ice and snow of the White Country. The homely man who went to the end of the world was Mud-turtle.

Chief Red Jacket's Speech

"BROTHER: Our seats were once large and yours were small. You have now become a great people, and we have scarcely a place left to spread our blankets. You have got our country, but you are not satisfied; you want to force your religion upon us. . . . You say that you are right and we are lost. How do we know this to be true? We understand that your religion is written in a book. If it was intended for us as well as you, why has not the Great Spirit given to us, and not only to us, but why did he not give to our **forefathers,** the knowledge of that book, with the means of understanding it rightly? We only know what you tell us about it. How shall we know when to believe, being so often deceived by the white people.

BROTHER: You say there is but one way to worship and serve the Great Spirit. If there is but one religion, why do you white people differ so much about it? Why not all agreed, as you can all read the book?

BROTHER: We do not understand these things. We are told that your religion was given to your forefathers, and has been handed down from father to son. We also have a religion, which was given to our forefathers, and has been handed down to us their children. We worship in that way. It teaches us to be thankful for all the favors we receive, to love each other, and to be united. We never quarrel about religion.

BROTHER: The Great Spirit has made us all, but He has made a great difference between his white and red children. He has given us different complexions and different customs. To you he has given the arts. To these He has not opened our eyes. . . . Since He has made so great a difference between us in other things, why may we not conclude that he has given us a different religion according to our understanding? The Great Spirit does right. He knows what is best for his children; we are satisfied. . . . We do not wish to destroy your religion, or take it from you. We only want to enjoy our own."

American Literature Library

The Young Republic

Sixty years after declaring independence, American culture was still heavily influenced by Europe. In 1836 Ralph Waldo Emerson's groundbreaking essay, "Nature", established a new way for Americans to look at the world. For the first time in history, there was a road-map showing how to escape from traditional cultures and build a new, American identity. A large part of that identity was the belief in individuality, expressed in another Emerson essay, "Self-Reliance," a portion of which follows.

Born in Boston in 1803, Emerson was descended from a long line of New England clergymen. He began his career as a Unitarian minister, but left the church because of doubts about orthodox doctrine. Still, he spent the rest of his life as a teacher of ethics, through his lectures and his writing.

Emerson wrote against the rising tide of American materialism and conformity in his time—themes that are as relevant today as they were a century ago. As he worded it, "Things are in the saddle/And ride mankind."

Emerson is considered the father of a philosophical, religious, and literary movement called transcendentalism. Along with Walt Whitman, Henry David Thoreau, Margaret Fuller, and other writers of the day, Emerson believed that the divine spirit was present in every man and in all of nature. In nature, man could ***intuitively*** *discover all universal laws at work. If God is good and just, then so is man. Evil exists only when man has an imperfect awareness of his essential goodness. This belief led some transcendentalists to social activism.*

intuitively: understanding immediately without the need of logic or rational thought

particulars: areas of life

asinine: marked by a failure to use intelligence or good judgment

loath: unwilling

hobgoblin: a mischievous goblin, or ugly sprite

gazetted: announced in a periodical

"Self-Reliance"

Ralph Waldo Emerson

What I must do is all that concerns me, not what the people think. This rule, equally arduous in actual and in intellectual life, may serve for the whole distinction between greatness and meanness. It is the harder, because you will always find those who think they know what is your duty better than you know it. It is easy in the world to live after the world's opinion; it is easy in solitude to live after our own; but the great man is he who in the midst of the crowd keeps with perfect sweetness the independence of solitude.

The objection to conforming to usages that have become dead to you is that it scatters your force. It loses your time and blurs the impression of your character. If you maintain a dead church, contribute to a dead Bible-society, vote with a great party either for the government or against it, spread your table like base housekeepers,—under all these screens I have difficulty to detect the precise man you are. And, of course, so much force is withdrawn from your proper life. But do your work, and I shall know you. Do your work, and you shall reinforce yourself. . . .

Well, most men have bound their eyes with one or another handkerchief, and attached themselves to some one of these communities of opinion. This conformity makes them not false in a few **particulars,** authors of a few lies, but false in all particulars. Their every truth is not quite true. . . . Meantime nature is not slow to equip us in the prison-uniform of the party to which we adhere. We come to wear one cut of face and figure, and acquire by degrees the gentlest **asinine** expression . . . the forced smile which we put on in company where we do not feel at ease in answer to conversation which does not interest us. The muscles, not spontaneously moved, but moved by a low usurping wilfulness, grow tight about the outline of the face with the most disagreeable sensation.

For nonconformity the world whips you with its displeasure. And therefore a man must know how to estimate a sour face. The by-standers look askance on him in the public street or in the friend's parlour. . . . but the sour faces of the multitude, like their sweet faces, have no deep cause, but are put on and off as the wind blows and a newspaper directs.

Ralph Waldo Emerson

. . . The other terror that scares us from self-trust is our consistency; a reverence for our past act or word, because the eyes of others have no other data for computing our orbit than our past acts, and we are **loath** to disappoint them. But why . . . drag about this corpse of your memory . . . ? Suppose you should contradict yourself; what then? It seems to be a rule of wisdom never to rely on your memory alone, scarcely even in acts of pure memory, but to bring the past for judgment into the thousand-eyed present, and live ever in a new day.

. . . A foolish consistency is the **hobgoblin** of little minds, adored by little statesmen and philosophers and divines. With consistency a great soul has simply nothing to do. He may as well concern himself with his shadow on the wall. Speak what you think now in hard words, and to-morrow speak what to-morrow thinks in hard words again, though it contradict every thing you said to-day.—'Ah, so you shall be sure to be misunderstood.'—Is it so bad, then, to be misunderstood? Pythagoras was misunderstood, and Socrates, and Jesus, and Luther, and Copernicus, and Galileo, and Newton, and every pure and wise spirit that ever took flesh. To be great is to be misunderstood.

. . . I hope in these days we have heard the last of conformity and consistency. Let the words be **gazetted** and ridiculous henceforward. . . . Man is timid and apologetic; he is no longer upright; he dares not say 'I think,' 'I am,' but quotes some saint or sage. He is ashamed before the blade of grass or the blowing rose. These roses under my window make no reference to former roses or to better ones; they are for what they are; they exist with God to-day. There is no time to them. There is simply the rose; it is perfect in every moment of its existence. . . . But man postpones or remembers; he does not live in the present, but with reverted eye laments the past, or, heedless of the riches that surround him, stands on tiptoe to foresee the future. He cannot be happy and strong until he too lives with nature in the present, above time.

The Crisis of the Union

Harriet Beecher Stowe witnessed the harsh realities of slavery while living in Cincinnati, Ohio, just across the Ohio River from the slave state of Kentucky. Because of these experiences, she became an active abolitionist.

Before the Civil War, many Northerners believed slavery was a constitutionally guaranteed right, and that opposition to it endangered the Union. Even those who agreed with Stowe considered it dangerous to oppose slavery openly and assisted slaveholders in recovering fugitives.

Stowe believed they were able to do this because they did not understand what they were defending. While in church one day in 1851, after she had moved to Brunswick, Maine, she was overcome with a vision of a slave being beaten to death. Sobbing, she ran home and began writing Uncle Tom's Cabin.

The book depicts the life of a long-suffering enslaved person, and the slaveholders and fellow enslaved people in his life. Its 1852 publication attracted threat letters to Stowe, forced closings of bookstores that sold it, and initiated proslavery novels by Southern writers. When Abraham Lincoln met Stowe, he reportedly said, "So this is the little lady who made this big [Civil] war."

In the first year after publication, Uncle Tom's Cabin *sold more than 300,000 copies in the United States. It became the best-selling novel of the nineteenth century, inspired songs and was presented as a play that is still performed today.*

wormwood: A European plant whose leaves yield a bitter oil used to make a liqueur.

dray horse: a horse that hauls heavy loads

Uncle Tom's Cabin

Harriet Beecher Stowe

In this excerpt the enslaved George is visiting his wife, Eliza. They were sold to different slaveholders, but have been allowed to visit each other when not working. George had been hired out to a factory, where he was treated well and had invented a work-saving machine. But when the slaveholder saw George's pride in his accomplishment, he moved George back to the plantation and gave him mindless physical work in order to restore his humility.

Harriet Beecher Stowe

From Chapter 3

"You are the handsomest woman I ever saw, and the best one I ever wish to see; but, oh, I wish I'd never seen you, nor you me!"

"O, George, how can you!"

"Yes, Eliza, it's all misery, misery, misery! My life is bitter as **wormwood;** the very life is burning out of me. I'm a poor, miserable, forlorn drudge; I shall only drag you down with me, that's all. What's the use of our trying to do anything, trying to know anything, trying to be anything? What's the use of living? I wish I was dead!"

"O, now, dear George, that is really wicked! I know how you feel about losing your place in the factory, and you have a hard master; but pray be patient, and perhaps something—"

"Patient!" said he, interrupting her; "haven't I been patient? Did I say a word when he came and took me away, for no earthly reason, from the place where everybody was kind to me? I'd paid him truly every cent of my earnings,—and they all say I worked well."

"Well, it *is* dreadful," said Eliza; "but, after all, he is your master, you know."

"My master! and who made him my master? That's what I think of—what right has he to me? I'm a man as much as he is. I'm a better man than he is. I know more about business than he does; I am a better manager than he is; I can read better than he can; I can write a better hand,—and I've learned it all myself, and no thanks to him,—I've learned it in spite of him;

and now what right has he to make a **dray-horse** of me?—to take me from things I can do, and do better than he can, and put me to work that any horse can do? He tries to do it; he says he'll bring me down and humble me, and he puts me to just the hardest, meanest and dirtiest work, on purpose!"

"O, George! George! you frighten me! Why, I never heard you talk so; I'm afraid you'll do something dreadful. I don't wonder at your feelings, at all; but oh, do be careful—do, do—for my sake—for Harry's! . . . O, George, we must have faith. Mistress says that when all things go wrong to us, we must believe that God is doing the very best."

"That's easy to say for people that are sitting on their sofas and riding in their carriages; but let 'em be where I am, I guess it would come some harder. I wish I could be good; but my heart burns, and can't be reconciled, anyhow. You couldn't in my place,—you can't now, if I tell you all I've got to say. You don't know the whole yet."

"What can be coming now?"

"Well, lately Mas'r has been saying that he was a fool to let me marry off the place; that . . . I shall take a wife and settle down on his place . . . or he would sell me down river."

"Why—but you were married to *me* by the minister, as much as if you'd been a white man!" said Eliza, simply.

"Don't you know a slave can't be married? There is no law in this country for that; I can't hold you for my wife, if he chooses to part us. That's why I wish I'd never seen you,—why I wish I'd never been born; it would have been better for us both,—it would have been better for this poor child if he had never been born. All this may happen to him yet!"

"O, but [my] master is so kind!"

"Yes, but who knows?—he may die—and then [our son] may be sold to nobody knows who. What pleasure is it that he is handsome, and smart, and bright? I tell you, Eliza, that a sword will pierce through your soul for every good and pleasant thing your child is or has; it will make him worth too much for you to keep."

The words smote heavily on Eliza's heart; the vision of the trader came before her eyes, and, as if some one had struck her a deadly blow, she turned pale and gasped for breath.

. . . "So, Eliza, my girl," said the husband, mournfully, "bear up, now; and good-by, for I'm going."

"Going, George! Going where?"

"To Canada," said he, straightening himself up; "and when I'm there, I'll buy you; that's all the hope that's left us. You have a kind master, that won't refuse to sell you. I'll buy you and the boy;—God helping me, I will!"

"O, dreadful! if you should be taken?"

"I won't be taken, Eliza; I'll *die* first! I'll be free, or I'll die!"

Eliza flees across the icy Ohio River

The Birth of Modern America

Carl Sandburg was the son of Swedish immigrants who settled in Galesburg, near Chicago. His father worked on the Chicago, Burlington and Quincy railroad at a time when advances in transportation, communications, and manufacturing technology were changing American commerce and life. By the end of the 1800s, the city had become an industrial hub for the lumber, grain, meatpacking, and mail-order businesses.

Sandburg's poem, "Chicago," captures the bustling activity of the city where many African Americans immigrated from the segregated South. It also exposes the evolving urban morality against which many Americans recoiled.

From the time he was a young boy, Sandburg had a variety of jobs—delivering mail, harvesting ice, laying bricks, thrashing wheat, and shining shoes. In 1897 he traveled as a hobo, seeing firsthand the sharp contrast between rich and poor. During his long career, he won two Pulitzer Prizes, one for poetry and another for a five-volume biography of Abraham Lincoln.

Following "Chicago" is a portion of an address by Samuel Clemens to the citizens of another city—his adopted home, San Francisco. It was written in 1866, as he prepared to revisit the town of his youth, Hannibal, Missouri. In this address, Clemens predicts the changes that he sees beginning to occur as San Francisco evolved from a "straggling town" to a modern ***mecca*** *for multicultural immigration.*

mecca: a center of activity sought as a goal by people with a common interest

heedlessly: without thinking

hither: here

American Literature Library

"Chicago"
Carl Sandburg

Hog Butcher for the World,
Tool Maker, Stacker of Wheat,
Player with Railroads and the Nation's Freight Handler;
Stormy, husky, brawling,
City of the Big Shoulders:

They tell me you are wicked and I believe them, for I
have seen your painted women under the gas lamps
luring the farm boys.
And they tell me you are crooked and I answer: Yes, it
is true I have seen the gunman kill and go free to
kill again.
And they tell me you are brutal and my reply is: On the
faces of women and children I have seen the marks
of wanton hunger.
And having answered so I turn once more to those who
sneer at this my city, and I give them back the sneer
and say to them:
Come and show me another city with lifted head singing
so proud to be alive and coarse and strong and cunning.
Flinging magnetic curses amid the toil of piling job on
job, here is a tall bold slugger set vivid against the
little soft cities;
Fierce as a dog with tongue lapping for action, cunning
as a savage pitted against the wilderness,
Bareheaded,
Shoveling,
Wrecking,
Planning,
Building, breaking, rebuilding,
Under the smoke, dust all over his mouth, laughing with
white teeth,
Under the terrible burden of destiny laughing as a young
man laughs,
Laughing even as an ignorant fighter laughs who has
never lost a battle,
Bragging and laughing that under his wrist is the pulse.
and under his ribs the heart of the people,
Laughing!
Laughing the stormy, husky, brawling laughter of
Youth, half-naked, sweating, proud to be Hog
Butcher, Tool Maker, Stacker of Wheat, Player with
Railroads and Freight Handler to the Nation.

Chicago grain elevator, 1900

"Farewell"
Samuel Clemens

"I am now about to bid farewell to San Francisco for a season, and to go back to that common home we all tenderly remember in our waking hours and fondly revisit in dreams of the night—a home which is familiar to my recollection, but will be an unknown land to my unaccustomed eyes. I shall share the fate of many another longing exile who wanders back to his early home to find gray hairs where he expected youth, graves where he looked for firesides, grief where he had pictured joy—everywhere change . . . where he had **heedlessly** dreamed that desolating Time had stood still! . . . And while I linger here upon the threshold of this, my new home . . . I accept the warning that mighty changes will have come over this home also when my returning feet shall walk these streets again.

I read the signs of the times, and I, that am no prophet, behold the things that are in store for you. Over slumbering California is stealing the dawn of a radiant future! The great China Mail Line is established, the Pacific Railroad is creeping across the continent, the commerce of the world is about to be revolutionized. California is Crown Princess of the new dispensation! She stands in the centre of the grand highway of the nations; she stands midway between the Old World and the New, and both shall pay her tribute. From the far East and from Europe, multitudes of stout hearts and willing hands are preparing to flock **hither;** to throng her hamlets and villages; to till her fruitful soil; to unveil the riches of her countless mines; to build up an empire on these distant shores that shall shame the bravest dreams of her visionaries. . . . Half the world stands ready to lay its contributions at her feet! Has any other State so brilliant a future? Has any other city a future like San Francisco?

"This straggling town shall be a vast metropolis; this sparsely populated land shall become a crowded hive of busy men; your waste places shall blossom like the rose, and your deserted hills and valleys shall yield bread and wine for unnumbered thousands; railroads shall be spread hither and thither and carry the invigorating blood of commerce to regions that are languishing now; mills and workshops, yea, and factories shall spring up everywhere, and mines that have neither name nor place to-day shall dazzle the world with their affluence. The time is drawing on apace when the clouds shall pass away from your firmament, and a splendid prosperity shall descend like a glory upon the whole land!

"I am bidding the old city and my old friends a kind, but not a sad farewell, for I know that when I see this home again, the changes that will have been wrought upon it . . . will be brighter, happier and prouder a hundred fold than it is this day."

San Francisco, 1890

American Literature Library

Imperialism and Progressivism

Theodore Dreiser and other writers, such as Frank Norris and Upton Sinclair, were Progressive Era "muckrakers." They exposed the scandals and corruption of urban American life at the turn of the twentieth century in a literary **genre** *(ZHAHN•ruh) known as American Realism. In this style, writers present everyday life as it actually is, rather than in a* **romanticized** *style, as many earlier writers had done. Norris and Sinclair were also considered naturalist writers, since they believed that humans had to overcome their environment, their ego, and their "brute instincts."*

Dreiser was born "on the wrong side of the tracks," and learned early that middle-class Americans looked on his impoverished family as outsiders. Because of that, his writing shows a compassionate understanding of life's outcasts and failures, and sympathy for those who desperately crave wealth, love, and power. His famous novel, An American Tragedy, *follows the descent of an ordinary young man who commits a ruthless murder, and the social and political pressures that assail him.*

The life of Madeleine, an impoverished young woman, is the theme of this selection, from the short story "Sanctuary." In it we glimpse some of the urban conditions that inspired the work of many progressive reformers of the day.

genre: a category of artistic composition characterized by form, style, or content

romanticized: presented in a fanciful, imaginative way rather than based on fact

"Sanctuary"
Theodore Dreiser

Theodore Dreiser

Primarily, there were the conditions under which [Madeleine] was brought to fifteen years of age: the crowded, scummy tenements; the narrow green-painted halls with their dim gas jets, making the entrance look more like that of a morgue than a dwelling place; the dirty halls and rooms with their green or blue or brown walls painted to save the cost of paper; the bare wooden floors, long since saturated with every type of grease and filth from oleomargarine and suet leaked from cheap fats or meats, to beer and whiskey and tobacco juice. . . .

And then the streets outside—any of the streets by which she had ever been surrounded—block upon block of other red, bare, commonplace tenements crowded to the doors with human life, the space before them sped over by noisy, gassy trucks and vehicles of all kinds. . . .

In this atmosphere were always longshoremen, wagon drivers, sweepers of floors, washers of dishes, waiters, janitors, workers in laundries, factories—mostly in indifferent or decadent or despairing conditions. And all of these people existed, in so far as she ever knew, upon that mysterious, evanescent and fluctuating something known as the weekly wage.

Always about her there had been drunkenness, fighting, complaining, sickness or death; the police coming in, and arresting one and another; the gas man, the rent man, the furniture man, hammering at doors for their due. . . .

It is not surprising that Madeleine came to her twelfth and thirteenth years without any real understanding of the great world about her and without any definite knowledge or skill. Her drunken mother was now more or less dependent upon her, her father having died of pneumonia and her brother and sister having disappeared to do for themselves. . . .

The child actually went hungry at times. . . . a neighbor perceiving her wretched state and suggesting that some extra helpers were wanted in a department store at Christmastime, she applied there, but so wretched were her clothes by now that she was not even considered. . . . she was able to get a place as a servant in a family.

Those who know anything of the life of a domestic know how thoroughly unsatisfactory it is—the leanness, the lack of hope. . . . she had only the kitchen for her chief chamber or a cubby-hole under the roof. . . .

And then, as was natural, love in the guise of youth, a rather sophisticated gallant somewhat above the world in which she was moving, appeared and paid his all but worthless court to her. . . .

A single trip to Wonderland, a single visit to one of its halls where music sounded to the splash of the waves and where he did his best to teach her to dance, a single meal in one of its gaudy, noisy restaurants . . . were given to hope, a new and seemingly realizable dream of happiness implanted in her young mind. The world was happier than she had thought, or could be made so; not all people fought and screamed at each other. There were such things as tenderness, soft words, sweet words.

But the way of so sophisticated a youth with a maid was brief and direct.

. . . Often in this hour she thought of the swift, icy waters of the river, glistening under a winter moon, and then again of the peace and quiet of the House of the Good Shepherd, its shielding remoteness from life, the only true home or sanctuary she had ever known. And so, brooding and repressing occasional sobs, she made her way toward it . . . thinking of the pathetically debasing love-life that was now over—the dream of love that never, never could be again, for her.

* * *

The stark red walls of the institution stood as before, only dim and gray and cold. . . . She had come a long way, drooping, brooding, half-freezing and crying. More than once on the way the hopelessness of her life and her dreams had given her pause, causing her to turn again with renewed determination toward the river—only the vivid and reassuring picture she had retained of this same grim and homely place, its restricted peace and quiet, the sympathy of Sister St. Agnes and Mother St. Bertha, had carried her on . . . the face of Mother St. Bertha, wrinkled and aweary, appeared at the square opening.

"What is it, my child?" she asked. . . .

"It is Madeleine. I was here four years ago. I was in the girls' ward. I worked in the sewing room."

She was so beaten by life . . . that even now and here she expected little more than an indifference which would send her away again. . . .

"Of course, my child," said the Mother, moving to the door and opening it. "You may come in. But what has happened, child?. . ."

"Mother," pleaded Madeleine wearily, "must I answer now? I am so unhappy! Can't I just have my old dress and my bed for tonight—that little bed under the lamp?"

"Why, yes, dear. . . . Now, my child," she said, "you may undress and bathe. . . . "

In a kind of dumbness of despair she . . . entered the warm, clean bath which had been provided. She stifled a sob as she did so, and others as she bathed. . . .

. . . Then she was led along other silent passages, once dreary enough but now healing in their sense of peace and rest, and so into the great room set with row upon row of simple white iron beds, covered with their snowy linen . . . beneath which so many like herself were sleeping.

. . . "Oh, Mother," she sobbed as the Sister bent over her, "don't ever make me go out in the world again, will you? You won't will you? I'm so tired! I'm so tired!"

"No, dear, no," soothed the Sister . . . "You need never go out in the world again unless you wish."

Family outside New York City tenement, 1890

American Literature Library

Boom and Bust

Writers sometimes create works of fiction inspired by or based on actual events in the news. The story of Nicola Sacco and Bartolomeo Vanzetti, Italian immigrants convicted of murder in 1921, was the inspiration for this selection by John Dos Passos, written in 1936. Large demonstrations were held in support of Sacco and Vanzetti, who claimed they were convicted for being immigrants and anarchists—not for committing a crime. They were executed in 1927, inspiring this passage, as well as the novel, Boston, *by Upton Sinclair.*

Dos Passos used his wartime experience as an ambulance driver in France as the background for several antiwar novels. In his ***trilogy,*** U.S.A, *he used an experimental form—fragments of songs, news headlines, monologues, and fragments from the lives of unrelated characters—to depict American* ***hypocrisy*** *and materialism between the two world wars. Dos Passos often combines separate words into one to shade its meaning and for the flow of a line. His* ***impressionistic*** *writing influenced several generations of American and European novelists.*

The lines in italics in the following passage from U.S.A. *are from actual letters written by Sacco and Vanzetti.*

trilogy: a work of fiction or nonfiction written in three separately published parts, or books

hypocrisy: acting in a way that contradicts what you say you believe in

impressionistic: using vivid details to create a sensory impression rather than objective reality

wardheeler: a worker for a political boss in a ward or local area

U.S.A., "Sacco and Vanzetti Must Die"

John Dos Passos

John Dos Passos

Shall be the human race.

Much I thought of you when I was lying in the death house—the singing, the kind tender voices of the children from the playground where there was all the life and the joy of liberty—just one step from the wall that contains the buried agony of three buried souls. It would remind me so often of you and of your sister and I wish I could see you every moment, but I feel better that you will not come to the death house so that you could not see the horrible picture of three living in agony waiting to be electrocuted.

The Camera Eye

they have clubbed us off the streets they are stronger they are rich they hire and fire the politicians the newspapereditors the old judges the small men with reputations the collegepresidents the **wardheelers** (listen businessmen collegepresidents judges America will not forget her betrayers) they hire the men with guns the uniforms the policecars the patrolwagons

all right you have won you will kill the brave men our friends tonight

there is nothing left to do we are beaten we the beaten crowd together in these old dingy schoolrooms on Salem Street shuffle up and down the gritty creaking stairs sit hunched with bowed heads on benches and hear the old words of the haters of oppression made new in sweat and agony tonight

our work is over the scribbled phrases the nights typing releases the smell of the printshop the sharp reek of newsprinted leaflets the rush for Western Union stringing words into wires the search for stinging words to make you feel who are your oppressors America

America our nation has been beaten by strangers who have turned our language inside out who have taken the clean words our fathers spoke and made them slimy and foul

their hired men sit on the judge's bench they sit back with their feet on the tables under the dome of the State House they are ignorant of our beliefs they have the dollars the guns the armed forces the powerplants

they have built the electricchair and hired the executioner to throw the switch

all right we are two nations

America our nation has been beaten by strangers who have bought the laws and fenced off the meadows and cut down the woods for pulp and turned our pleasant cities into slums and sweated the wealth out of our people and when they want to they hire the executioner to throw the switch

but do they know that the old words of the immigrants are being renewed in blood and agony tonight do they know that the old American speech of the haters of oppression is new tonight in the mouth of an old woman from Pittsburgh of a husky boilermaker from Frisco who hopped freights clear from the Coast to come here in the mouth of a Back Bay social-worker in the mouth of an Italian printer of a hobo from Arkansas the language of the beaten nation is not forgotten in our ears tonight

the men in the deathhouse made the old words new before they died

If it had not been for these things, I might have lived out my life talking at streetcorners to scorning men. I might have died unknown, unmarked, a failure. This is our career and our triumph. Never in our full life can we hope to do such work for tolerance, for justice, for man's understanding of man as now we do by an accident.

now their work is over the immigrants haters of oppression lie quiet in black suits in the little undertaking parlor in the North End the city is quiet the men of the conquering nation are not to be seen on the streets

they have won why are they scared to be seen on the streets? on the streets you see only the downcast faces of the beaten the streets belong to the beaten nation all the way to the cemetery where the bodies of the immigrants are to be burned we line the curbs in the drizzling rain we crowd the wet sidewalks elbow to elbow silent pale looking with scared eyes at the coffins

we stand defeated America

Nicola Sacco and Bartolomeo Vanzetti being arrested

American Literature Library

Global Struggles

Many Jews who survived concentration camps during World War II found it too painful to speak or write about their experiences until many years later. Elie Wiesel (vee•ZEHL) waited for 10 years to write the story of his experiences at Auschwitz, where his family was killed. The first passage is from his 1960 novel, Night. *Wiesel was a teenager when the Nazis invaded his town of Sighet in Transylvania in 1944. He became a U.S. citizen in 1963, and won the Nobel Peace Prize in 1986.*

World War II had shown the world an unprecedented scale of conflict. The science, technology, and industrialism—which were supposed to advance humanity—had been used instead for mass killing and devastation. It was not surprising that many postwar writers sought alternatives to traditional ways of thinking and writing.

The Beat Generation—a term coined by Jack Kerouac—was the first modern **subculture,** *or "alternative" culture. It was a group of writers during the late 1950s and early 1960s. Rejecting the intellectual, or mental, focus of traditional writing, the Beats sought spontaneity, emotion, and engagement in real, often gritty experience. Their writing has influenced artists, writers, rock musicians, and popular culture ever since.*

In 1947, Kerouac and a friend took a road trip around the country, which inspired his most famous novel, On the Road. *Published in 1957, it expresses both the quest for experience and the pessimism of the Beats as they struggled to find meaning in the shadow of the atomic bomb.*

subculture: a group that displays behavior different from that of society

Night
Elie Wiesel

Elie Wiesel

And then, one day all foreign Jews were expelled. . . .

Crammed into cattle cars by the Hungarian police, they cried silently. Standing on the station platform, we too were crying. The train disappeared over the horizon; all that was left was thick, dirty smoke.

Behind me, someone said, sighing, "What do you expect? That's war. . . ."

The deportees were quickly forgotten. A few days after they left, it was rumored that they were in Galicia, working, and even that they were content with their fate.

Days went by. Then weeks and months. Life was normal again. A calm, reassuring wind blew through our homes. The shopkeepers were doing good business, the students lived among their books, and the children played in the streets.

One day, as I was about to enter the synagogue, I saw Moishe the Beadle sitting on a bench near the entrance.

He told me what had happened to him and his companions. The train with the deportees had crossed the Hungarian border and, once in Polish territory, had been taken over by the Gestapo. The train had stopped. The Jews were ordered to get off and onto waiting trucks. The trucks headed toward a forest. There everybody was ordered to get out. They were forced to dig huge trenches. When they had finished their work, the men from the Gestapo began theirs. Without passion or haste, they shot their prisoners, who were forced to approach the trench one by one and offer their necks. Infants were tossed into the air and used as targets for the machine guns. This took place in the Galician forest, near Kolomay. How had he, Moishe the Beadle, been able to escape? By a miracle. He was wounded in the leg and left for dead.

On the Road
Jack Kerouac

Later in the afternoon we went out and played baseball with the kids in the sooty field by the Long Island railyard. We also played basketball so frantically the younger boys said, "Take it easy, you don't have to kill yourself." They bounced smoothly all around us and beat us with ease. Dean and I were sweating. At one point Dean fell flat on his face on the concrete court. We huffed and puffed to get the ball away from the boys; they turned and flipped it away. Others darted in and smoothly shot over our heads. We jumped at the basket like maniacs, and the younger boys just reached up and grabbed the ball from our sweating hands and dribbled away. We were like hotrock blackbelly tenorman *Mad* of American back-alley go-music trying to play basketball against Stan Getz and Cool Charlie. They thought we were crazy. Dean and I went back home playing catch from each sidewalk of the street. We tried extra-special catches, diving over bushes and barely missing posts. When a car came by I ran alongside and flipped the ball to Dean just barely behind the vanishing bumper. He darted and caught it and rolled in the grass, and flipped it back for me to catch on the other side of a parked bread truck. I just made it with my meat hand and threw it back so Dean had to whirl and back up and fall on his back across the hedges. Back in the house Dean took his wallet, harrumphed, and handed my aunt the fifteen dollars he owed her from the time we got a speeding ticket in Washington. She was completely surprised and pleased. We had a big supper. "Well, Dean," said my aunt, "I hope you'll be able to take care of your new baby that's coming and stay married this time."

"Yes, yass, yes."

"You can't go all over the country having babies like that. Those poor little things'll grow up helpless. You've got to offer them a chance to live." He looked at his feet and nodded. In the raw red dusk we said good-by, on a bridge over a superhighway.

"I hope you'll be in New York when I get back," I told him.

"All I hope, Dean, is someday we'll be able to live on the same street with our families and get to be a couple of oldtimers together."

"That's right, man—you know that I pray for it completely mindful of the troubles we both had and the troubles coming, as your aunt knows and reminds me. I didn't want the new baby, Inez insisted, and we had a fight. Did you know Marylou got married to a used-car dealer in Frisco and she's having a baby?"

"Yes. We're all getting in there now." Ripples in the upside-down lake of the void, is what I should have said. The bottom of the world is gold and the world is upside down. He took out a snapshot of Camille in Frisco with the new baby girl. The shadow of a man crossed the child on the sunny pavement, two long trouser legs in the sadness. "Who's that?"

"That's only Ed Dunkel. He came back to Galatea, they're gone to Denver now. They spent a day taking pictures."

Ed Dunkel, his compassion unnoticed like the compassion of saints. Dean took out other pictures. I realized these were all the snapshots which our children would look at someday with wonder, thinking their parents had lived smooth, well-ordered, stabilized-within-the-photo lives and got up in the morning to walk proudly on the sidewalks of life, never dreaming the raggedy madness and riot of our actual lives, our actual night, the hell of it, the senseless nightmare road. All of it inside endless and beginningless emptiness. Pitiful forms of ignorance. "Good-by, good-by." Dean walked off in the long red dusk. Locomotives smoked and reeled above him. His shadow followed him, it aped his walk and thoughts and very being. He turned and waved coyly, bashfully. He gave me the boomer's highball, he jumped up and down, he yelled something I didn't catch. He ran around in a circle. All the time he came closer to the concrete corner of the railroad overpass. He made one last signal. I waved back. Suddenly he bent to his life and walked quickly out of sight. I gaped into the bleakness of my own days. I had an awful long way to go too.

A Time of Upheaval

After two world wars many writers began to describe a sense of separateness from nature and a growing sense of personal alienation. The upheaval of societies and cultures brought about by the wars led to a feeling that morality was relative. In other words, what may be immoral in one situation could be considered moral in another situation. These themes, later called modernism by literary critics, showed up in many works of the time.

The early work of poet Adrienne Rich, who was born in 1929 and wrote in careful, more traditional forms, seemed not to be part of this evolving modernist tradition. By the 1960s, her work increasingly confronted themes such as women's role in society, racism, and the Vietnam War, and was written in free verse. In 1973, amid the feminist and civil rights movements, she wrote Diving Into the Wreck, Poems 1971–1972, *which won the National Book Award the next year. The title poem uses the* ***metaphor*** *of a deep-sea diver to express the goal of looking deeply within to find the truth about ourselves.*

Leroy V. Quintana is a New Mexico native of Mexican ancestry. His poetry draws on his experiences as a Chicano outsider in American society, subject to ethnic and socioeconomic discrimination. His poem here, "Natural History," reflects both his sensitivity to nature and the horrors of the Vietnam War, in which he served during 1967 and 1968.

metaphor: a figure of speech in which one word or image is used to mean something else

sundry: miscellaneous

crenellated: notched

American Literature Library

"Diving into the Wreck"

Adrienne Rich

First having read the book of myths,
and loaded the camera,
and checked the edge of the knife-blade,
I put on
the body-armor of black rubber
the absurd flippers
the grave and awkward mask.
I am having to do this
not like Cousteau with his
assiduous team
aboard the sun-flooded schooner
but here alone.

There is a ladder.
The ladder is always there
hanging innocently
close to the side of the schooner.
We know what it is for,
we who have used it.
Otherwise
it is a piece of maritime floss
some **sundry** equipment.

I go down.
Rung after rung and still
the oxygen immerses me
the blue light
the clear atoms
of our human air.
I go down.
My flippers cripple me,
I crawl like an insect down the ladder
and there is no one
to tell me when the ocean
will begin.

First the air is blue and then
it is bluer and then green and then
black I am blacking out and yet
my mask is powerful
it pumps my blood with power
the sea is another story
the sea is not a question of power

I have to learn alone
to turn my body without force
in the deep element.

And now: it is easy to forget
what I came for
among so many who have always
lived here
swaying their **crenellated** fans
between the reefs
and besides
you breathe differently down here.

I came to explore the wreck.
The words are purposes.
The words are maps.
I came to see the damage that was done
and the treasures that prevail.
I stroke the beam of my lamp
slowly along the flank
of something more permanent
than fish or weed

the thing I came for:
the wreck and not the story of the wreck
the thing itself and not the myth

the drowned face always staring
toward the sun
the evidence of damage
worn by salt and away into this threadbare
 beauty
the ribs of the disaster
curving their assertion
among the tentative haunters.

This is the place.
And I am here, the mermaid whose dark hair
streams black, the merman in his armored
 body.
We circle silently
about the wreck
we dive into the hold.
I am she: I am he

whose drowned face sleeps with open eyes
whose breasts still bear the stress
whose silver, copper, vermeil cargo lies
obscurely inside barrels
half-wedged and left to rot
we are the half-destroyed instruments
that once held to a course
the water-eaten log
the fouled compass

We are, I am, you are
by cowardice or courage
the one who find our way
back to this scene
carrying a knife, a camera
a book of myths
in which
our names do not appear.

"Natural History"

Leroy Quintana

To cross a river meant leeches.
A company of NVAs crashing toward you
would be a troop of baboons.
A green snake named Mr. Two Step,
for the number you'd last after bitten.
It was said the NVAs carried flashlights.
One night frightening scores of them
turned out to be a swarm of fireflies.
The whir of birds' wings
turned out to be artillery rounds.
Threw stones at a cobra once,
the sun going down.
Fire at it
and the VC would know our position.
A VC moving slowly in the elephant grass
happened to be a water buffalo.
One night they overran the compound.
Loaded down with grenades, AK-47s
from North Vietnam, mines strapped to their
 chests:
these were only the mosquitos.
The VC only a little more than a whisper's
 reach away,
we called in the Cobras. They came in hissing,
cannons twice as fast as the old gunships.
It was also said the VC kept chickens leashed
 to strings.
So easily frightened they were perfect warning.
One night, shivering uncontrollably with fear,
knowing I would have to kill whatever was
 out there,
walking slowly, scratching.

A Changing Society

Dr. Maya Angelou is a poet, historian, author, actress, playwright, civil-rights activist, producer, and director. Born in St. Louis, Missouri, she has lived in many places. She was a newspaper editor in Egypt and Ghana, and has taught at the University of Ghana and, since 1981, at Wake Forest University in Winston-Salem, North Carolina.

In the 1960s Dr. Martin Luther King, Jr., asked her to be the Northern coordinator for the Southern Christian Leadership Conference. Angelou gained fame in the United States when her ***autobiographical*** *novel,* I Know Why the Caged Bird Sings, *received critical and popular success when it was published in 1969.*

Like many modern writers, she focuses a harsh spotlight on characters' frailties, failures, and ***dilemmas*** *in today's complex world. Unlike some, however, she also challenges our strengths and human potential. Former president Bill Clinton commissioned her to read her poem "On the Pulse of the Morning" at his 1993 inauguration. Although Angelou wrote her poem in the last decade of the twentieth century, it shows a focus on personal responsibility and peaceful coexistence that have been her lifelong quests and are her hopes for this millennium.*

autobiographical: written about the person's own life

dilemma: problems caused by a person's situation or world conditions

"On the Pulse of the Morning"

Maya Angelou

Maya Angelou

. . . .

You, created only a little lower than
The angels, have crouched too long in
The bruising darkness
Have lain too long
Facedown in ignorance,
Your mouths spilling words
Armed for slaughter.

. . . .

Come, clad in peace,
And I will sing the songs
The Creator gave to me when I and the
Tree and the Rock were one.
Before cynicism was a bloody sear across your brow
And when you yet knew you still knew nothing.
The River sang and sings on.

. . . .

Here, on the pulse of this new day,
You may have the grace to look up and out
And into your sister's eyes,
And into your brother's face,
Your country,
And say simply
With hope—
Good morning.

"Human Family"

Maya Angelou

I note the obvious differences
in the human family.
Some of us are serious,
some thrive on comedy.

Some declare their lives are lived
as true profundity,
and others claim they really live
the real reality.

. . . .

We love and lose in China,
we weep on England's moors,
and laugh and moan in Guinea,
and thrive on Spanish shores.

We seek success in Finland,
Are born and die in Maine.
In minor ways we differ,
In major we're the same.

I note the obvious differences
between each sort and type,
but we are more alike, my friends,
than we are unalike.

We are more alike, my friends,
than we are unalike.

. . . .

"Equality"

Maya Angelou

You declare you see me dimly
through a glass which will not shine
though I stand before you boldly,
trim in rank and marking time.

You do own to hear me faintly
as a whisper out of range,
while my drums beat out the message
and the rhythms never change.

Equality, and I will be free.
Equality, and I will be free.

. . . .

We have lived a painful history,
we know the shameful past,
but I keep on marching forward,
and you keep on coming last.

Equality, and I will be free.
Equality, and I will be free.

Flag Etiquette

For Americans, the flag has always had a special meaning. It is a symbol of our nation's freedom and democracy.

Rules and Customs

Over the years, Americans have developed rules and customs concerning the use and display of the flag. One of the most important things every American should remember is to treat the flag with respect.

- The flag should be raised and lowered by hand and displayed only from sunrise to sunset. On special occasions, the flag may be displayed at night, but it should be illuminated.

- The flag may be displayed on all days, weather permitting, particularly on national and state holidays and on historic and special occasions.

- No flag may be flown above the American flag or to the right of it at the same height.

- The flag should never touch the ground or floor beneath it.

- The flag may be flown at half-staff by order of the president, usually to mourn the death of a public official.

- The flag may be flown upside down only to signal distress.

- When the flag becomes old and tattered, it should be destroyed by burning. According to an approved custom, the Union (stars on blue field) is first cut from the flag; then the two pieces, which no longer form a flag, are burned.

Continental Colors
1775-1777

First Stars and Stripes
1777-1795

Betsy Ross Flag
c. 1790

15-Star Flag
1795-1818

20-Star Flag
1818

Great Star Flag
1818

35-Star Flag
1863-1865

38-Star Flag
1877-1890

48-Star Flag
1912-1959

50-Star Flag
1960

Glossary/Glosario

- Content vocabulary terms in this glossary are words that relate to history content. They are **highlighted** yellow in your text.
- Words below that have an asterisk (*) are academic vocabulary terms. They help you understand your school subjects and are **boldfaced** in your text.

English	Español
A	
***abandon** to withdraw protection, support, or help (p. 796)	***abandonar** retirar la protección, el apoyo o la ayuda (p. 796)
abolition the immediate ending of slavery (p. 243)	**abolición** el final inmediato de la esclavitud (p. 243)
***academic** associated with higher learning at a scholarly institution (p. 536)	***académico** relacionado con los estudios superiores en una institución especializada (p. 536)
***access** freedom or ability to obtain or make use of (p. 505)	***acceso** libertad o capacidad de obtener o hacer uso de (p. 505)
***acquire** to get as one's own; to come into possession or control of (p. 16)	***adquirir** obtener como propio, tener la posesión o el control de algo (p. 16)
***adapt** to change in order to meet the demands of a certain environment or circumstance (p. 390)	***adaptar** cambiar para cumplir con las exigencias de cierto entorno o circunstancia (p. 390)
***adequate** sufficient for a specific requirement; completed to its minimum requirements (pp. 567, 924)	***adecuado** suficiente para un requisito específico, que se completa con los requisitos mínimos (pp. 567, 924)
***advocate** to propose a certain position or viewpoint (p. 527)	***abogar** proponer cierta posición o punto de vista (p. 527)
affirmative action an active effort to improve employment or educational opportunities for minorities (p. 953)	**acción afirmativa** un esfuerzo activo para mejorar las oportunidades educacionales y de empleo para las minorías (p. 953)
Agent Orange a chemical defoliant used to clear Vietnamese jungles during the Vietnam War (p. 889)	**Agente naranja** defoliante químico utilizado para limpiar las junglas vietnamitas durante la Guerra de Vietnam (p. 889)
agrarianism philosophy that agriculture and owning land is the backbone of the economy (p. 159)	**agrarismo** filosofía de que la agricultura y la propiedad de tierras son los elementos principales de la economía (p. 159)
agricultural revolution period when early Americans learned how to plant and raise crops (p. 4)	**revolución agrícola** período cuando los primeros americanos aprendieron plantar y cultivar la cosecha (p. 4)
alien a person living in a country who is not a citizen of that country (p. 166)	**extranjero** una persona que vive en un país del cual no es ciudadano (p. 166)
***allocate** to set apart for something specific (p. 1018)	***asignar** diferenciar para algo específico (p. 1018)
allotment a plot of land assigned to an individual or a family for cultivation (p. 403)	**parcela** un terreno asignado a un individuo o familia para su cultivación (p. 403)
***alternative** existing or functioning outside the established cultural, social, or economic system (p. 961)	***alternativo** que existe o funciona fuera del sistema cultural, social o económico establecido (p. 961)
***ambiguous** to lack a definitive purpose (p. 208)	***ambiguo** falta de un propósito definitivo (p. 208)
amendment a change to the Constitution (p. 109)	**enmienda** un cambio a la Constitución (p.109)
Americanization causing someone to acquire American traits and characteristics (p. 467)	**americanización** causar que una persona adquiera características y rasgos americanos (p. 467)

English	Español
amnesty the act of granting a pardon to a large group of people (pp. 356, 1017)	**amnistía** el acto de otorgar perdón a un número grande de personas (pp. 356, 1017)
amphtrac an amphibious tractor used to move troops from ships to shore (p. 742)	**amphtrac** un tractor anfibio utilizado para mover tropas desde barcos a la orilla del mar (p. 742)
anarchist a person who believes that there should be no government (p. 604)	**anarquista** una persona que cree que no debe haber ningún gobierno (p. 604)
annexation incorporating a territory within the domain of a country (p. 269)	**anexión** incorporar un territorio dentro del dominio de un país (p. 269)
***annual** occurring or happening every year (p. 202)	***anual** que ocurre o sucede cada año (p. 202)
annuity money paid by contract at regular intervals (p. 398)	**anualidad** dinero pagado por contrato en intervalos regulares (p. 398)
anthrax a bacteria used to create biological weapons (p. 1041)	**ántrax** bacteria utilizada para crear armas biológicas (p. 1041)
***apparent** appearing to be fact as far as can be understood (p. 651)	***aparente** que parece ser cierto dentro de lo que puede comprenderse (p. 651)
appeasement accepting demands in order to avoid conflict (p. 689)	**apaciguamiento** demandas aceptadas a fin de evitar conflictos (p. 689)
***appropriate** (adjective) especially suitable or compatible (p. 957)	***apropiado** (adjetivo) especialmente adecuado o compatible (p. 957)
***approximately** an estimation of a figure that is close to the actual figure (p. 403)	***aproximadamente** cálculo de un número cercano al número real (p. 403)
***arbitrary** existing or coming about seemingly at random or as an unfair or unreasonable act of will (pp. 829)	***arbitrario** que existe u ocurre aparentemente al azar o como un acto de voluntad injusto o irrazonable (p. 829)
arbitration settling a dispute by agreeing to accept the decision of an impartial outsider (pp. 432, 529)	**arbitraje** arreglar una disputa acordando aceptar la decisión de una persona imparcial (pp. 432, 529)
armistice a temporary agreement to end fighting (p. 569)	**armisticio** acuerdo temporal de paz para terminar con una lucha (p. 569)
***assemble** to bring together in a certain place for a particular purpose (p. 324)	***reunirse** congregarse en cierto lugar con un objetivo concreto (p. 324)
assembly line a production system with machines and workers arranged so that each person performs an assigned task again and again as the item passes before him or her (p. 596)	**línea de montaje** sistema de producción con máquinas y trabajadores arreglados para que cada persona haga su trabajo designado una y otra vez mientras el artículo pasa frente a ellos (p. 596)
assimilate to absorb a group into the culture of a larger population (p. 403)	**asimilar** incorporar a un grupo dentro de la cultura de una población más grande (p. 403)
***assume** to take for granted or as true (p. 696)	***suponer** dar algo por sentado o considerarlo verdadero (p. 696)
astrolabe a device used to determine direction, latitude, and local time (p. 16)	**astrolabio** instrumento usado para determinar la dirección, latitud y la hora de una localidad (p. 16)
attrition the act of wearing down by constant harassment or attack (p. 319)	**atrición** acto de desalentar por constantes ataques o acoso (p. 319)

English	Spanish
***authorities** those who have control over determining and enforcing what is right or wrong (p. 580)	***autoridades** aquéllas que poseen control sobre la determinación y el cumplimiento de lo que es correcto o incorrecto (p. 580)
autonomy the quality or state of being self-governing (p. 498)	**autonomía** la cualidad o el estado de autogobernarse (p. 498)
***awareness** the state of having or showing realization, perception, or knowledge (p. 1025)	***conciencia** estado de poseer o mostrar comprensión, percepción o conocimiento (p. 1025)

B

English	Spanish
baby boom a marked rise in birthrate, such as occurred in the United States following World War II (p. 801)	**auge de nacimientos** aumento marcado en la taza de natalidad, tal como ocurrió en Estados Unidos después de la Segunda Guerra Mundial (p. 801)
bailiff minor officer of the courts (p. 634)	**alguacil** oficial en rango menor de las Cortes (p. 634)
bank holiday closing of banks during the Great Depression to avoid bank runs (p. 652)	**feriado bancario** cierre de bancos durante la Gran Depresión para evitar las corridas bancarias (p. 652)
bank run persistent and heavy demands from a bank's depositors, creditors, or customers (p. 631)	**corrida bancaria** demandas constantes y numerosas por parte de los depo sitantes, acreedores o clientes de un banco (p. 631)
beats short for "beatniks"; a group of mostly white writers and artists who, in 1950s America, harshly criticized what they considered the sterility and conformity of American life, the meaninglessness of American politics, and the emptiness of popular culture (p. 807)	**beats** nombre corto para "beatniks", un grupo de escritores y artistas en su mayoría blancos quienes en la década de 1950 en Estados Unidos criticaban duramente lo que ellos consideraban la esterilidad y conformismo de la vida estadounidense, el sin sentido de la política estadounidense y el vacío de la cultura popular (p. 807)
***benefit** to be useful or profitable (p. 663)	***beneficiar** ser útil o rentable (p. 663)
benevolent society an association focusing on spreading the word of God and combating social problems (p. 237)	**sociedad de beneficencia** una asociación enfocada en llevar la palabra de Dios y combatir problemas sociales (p. 237)
bilingualism the practice of teaching immigrant students in their own language (p. 925)	**bilingualismo** la práctica de enseñar a estudiantes inmigrantes en su propio lenguaje (p. 925)
bill of rights a summary of fundamental rights and privileges guaranteed to a people against violation by the state (p. 113)	**declaración de derechos** resumen de los derechos y privilegios fundamentales que el estado garantiza al pueblo que no se violarán (p. 113)
binding arbitration process whereby a neutral party hears arguments from two opposing sides and makes a decision that both must accept (p. 666)	**arbitraje obligatorio** proceso por el cual un partido neutral escucha argumentos de dos partidos opositores y toma una decisión que ambos deben aceptar (p. 666)
black codes laws passed in the South just after the Civil War aimed at controlling freedmen and enabling plantation owners to exploit African American workers (p. 360)	**códigos negros** leyes aprobadas en el Sur al terminar la Guerra Civil para controlar a los libertos y permitir a los dueños de plantaciones la explotación de los trabajadores afroamericanos (p. 360)
black power the mobilization of the political and economic power of African Americans, especially to compel respect for their rights and to improve their condition (p. 872)	**poder negro** mobilización del poder económico y político de afroamericanos especialmente para imponer respeto por sus derechos y para mejorar su condiciones (p. 872)
blacklist a list of persons who are disapproved of or who are to be punished or boycotted (p. 429)	**lista negra** lista de personas rechazadas o a las que se castigará o boicoteará (p. 429)
blitzkrieg name given to sudden violent offensive attacks the Germans used during World War II; "lightning war" (p. 690)	**guerra relámpago** nombre dado a los ataques repentinos ofensivos violentos que los alemanes usaron durante la Segunda Guerra Mundial (p. 690)
blockade runner ship that runs through a blockade, usually to smuggle goods through a protected area (p. 322)	**forzador de bloqueo** un barco que navega a través de un bloqueo, usualmente para pasar contrabando a través de un área protegida (p. 322)

English	Español
blog online journal where an individual, group, or corporation presents a record of activities, thoughts, or beliefs (p. 1005)	**blog** publicación en línea donde un individuo, grupo o empresa presenta un registro de actividades, ideas o creencias (p. 1005)
blue-collar workers workers in the manual labor field, particularly those requiring protective clothing (p. 802)	**collar azul trabajadors** trabajadors de mano de obra, particularmente aquellos que requieren ropa protectora (p. 802)
blues style of music evolving from African American spirituals and noted for its melancholy sound (p. 618)	**blues** estilo de música que evolucionó de la música espiritual de los afroamericanos, distinguida por su sonido melancólico (p. 618)
bohemian a person (as an artist or a writer) leading an unconventional lifestyle (p. 610)	**bohemio** una persona (como artista o escritor) que lleva un estilo de vida poco convencional (p. 610)
bonanza farm a large, highly profitable wheat farm (p. 397)	**granja en bonanza** extensa granja de trigo que produce muchas ganancias (p. 397)
***bond** a note issued by the government that promises to pay off a loan with interest (pp. 156, 470)	***bono** una obligación emitida por el gobierno que promete pagar un préstamo con interés (pp. 156, 470)
bounty money given as a reward, as to encourage enlistment in the army (p. 321)	**recompensa** dinero dado para animar el alistamiento en el ejército (p. 321)
***briefly** for a short time (p. 740)	***brevemente** por poco tiempo (p. 740)
brinkmanship the willingness to go to the brink of war to force an opponent to back down (p. 783)	**política arriesgada** la buena voluntad para ir al borde de guerra para forzar a un oponente a que se retracte (p. 783)
broker state role of the government to work out conflicts among competing interest groups (p. 673)	**estado intermediario** el papel del gobierno para resolver conflictos entre grupos con intereses competitivos (p. 673)
budget deficit the amount by which expenses exceed income (p. 977)	**déficit del presupuesto** la cantidad por la cual los gastos exceden los ingresos (p. 977)
bull market a long period of rising stock prices (p. 629)	**bolsa al alza** largo período durante el cual los precios de acciones en la bolsa se incrementan (p. 629)
busing a policy of transporting children to schools outside their neighborhoods to achieve greater racial balance (p. 953)	**traslado** obligatorio la política de transportar estudiantes a escuelas fuera de sus vecindarios para alcanzar un balance racial (p. 953)

C

cabinet a group of advisers to the president (p. 154)	**gabinete** grupo de consejeros al presidente (p. 154)
capital gains tax a federal tax paid by businesses and investors when they sell stocks or real estate (p. 995)	**impuestos a las ganancias del capital** impuesto federal pagado por inversionistas y negocios cuando ellos venden acciones y bienes raíces (p. 995)
caravel sailing ship capable of long-distance exploration (p. 16)	**carabela** buque capaz de explorar largas distancias (p. 16)
carpetbagger name given to many Northerners who moved to the South after the Civil War and supported the Republicans (p. 366)	**carpetbagger** nombre dado a muchos norteños que se mudaron al Sur después de la Guerra Civil y apoyaron a los republicanos (p. 366)
caucus system a system in which members of a political party meet to choose their party's candidate for president or decide policy (p. 224)	**sistema de junta** electoral sistema en el cual los miembros de un partido político se reúnen para escoger el candidato a la presidencia de su partido o para decidir políticas (p. 224)
cede to give up by treaty (p. 275)	**ceder** darse por vencido por un tratado (p. 275)

censure to express a formal disapproval of an action (p. 778)

censura expresar la desaprobación formal sobre una acción (p. 778)

chad a small piece of cardboard produced by punching a data card (p. 1033)

agujereado pedazo pequeño de cartón producido taladrando una tarjeta de computadora (p. 1033)

***challenger** one who enters a competition (p. 941)

***contendiente** el que ingresa a una competencia (p. 941)

charter a constitution (p. 753)

carta de privilegio una constitución (p. 753)

checks and balances the system in which each branch of government has the ability to limit the power of the other branches to prevent any from becoming too powerful (p. 109)

control y balances sistema en el cual cada ramo de gobierno tiene la habilidad para limitar el poder a los otros ramos para que ninguno vuelva a ser demasiado poderoso (p. 109)

circumnavigate to sail around (p. 19)

circunnavegar navegar alrededor de (p. 19)

***circumstance** a factor in a problem that determines its solution (p. 377)

***circunstancia** factor en un problema que determina su solución (p. 377)

***cite** to point out as an example in an argument or debate (p. 1024)

***citar** señalar como ejemplo en un argumento o debate (p. 1024)

***civil** of or relating to citizens (p. 261)

***civil** de los ciudadanos o relativo a ellos (p. 261)

closed shop an agreement in which a company agrees to hire only union members (pp. 434, 794)

taller cerrado acuerdo en el que una compañía contrata solamente a miembros del sindicato (pp. 434, 794)

cloture a motion that ends debate and calls for an immediate vote, possible in the U.S. Senate by a vote of 60 senators (p. 864)

clausura una moción que termina con el debate y requiere un voto inmediato, posible en el Senado de EEUU por un voto de 60 senadores (p. 864)

***code** a signal or symbol used to represent something that is to be kept secret (p. 724)

***código** señal o símbolo utilizado para representar algo que se mantendrá en secreto (p. 724)

***collapse** a sudden loss of force, value, or effect (p. 628)

***colapso** pérdida repentina de fuerza, valor o efecto (p. 628)

***colleague** a person who works in the same, or a similar, profession (p. 636)

***colega** persona que trabaja en la misma profesión o en una similar (p. 636)

collective a farm, especially in communist countries, formed from many small holdings collected into a single unit for joint operation under governmental supervision (p. 683)

granja colectiva una granja, especialmente en los países comunistas, formada por muchas tierras pequeñas reunidas en una sola unidad para operar conjuntamente bajo la supervisión del gobierno (p. 683)

***commentator** one who explains, discusses, or reports in an expository manner, especially news on radio or television (p. 824)

***comentarista** aquél que explica, discute o informa de manera expositiva, especialmente noticias por radio o televisión (p. 824)

***commissioner** the officer in charge of a department or bureau of the public service (p. 368)

***comisionado** funcionario a cargo de un departamento o agencia de servicios públicos (p. 368)

***commitment** an agreement or pledge to do something in the future (p. 306)

***compromiso** acuerdo o promesa de hacer algo en el futuro (p. 306)

committee of correspondence committee organized in each colony to communicate with and unify the colonies (p. 64)

comité de correspondencia comité organizado en cada colonia para comunicar entre las colonias y unificarlas (p. 64)

commune a group living arrangement in which members share everything and work together (p. 913)

comuna un arreglo de vivienda en el cual los miembros de un grupo trabajan juntos y comparten todo (p. 913)

***communications** the various medias and processes by which information is exchanged between individuals (p. 1004)

***comunicaciones** los diferentes medios y procesos mediante los cuales se intercambia información entre individuos (p. 1004)

***community** people with common characteristics living in the same area (p. 641)

***comunidad** personas con características comunes que viven en la misma área (p. 641)

Glossary/Glosario

English	Español
***compatible** capable of existing in harmony (p. 919)	***compatible** capaz de existir en armonía (p. 919)
***compensate** to offset an error, defect or undesired effect (p. 242)	***compensar** resarcir un error, defecto o efecto no deseado (p. 242)
***comprehensive** covering a broad range of topics (p. 369)	***integral** que cubre una amplia gama de temas (p. 369)
***concentrate** to bring or direct one's powers, efforts, or attention toward a common objective (p. 690)	***concentrar** orientar los poderes, esfuerzos o atención hacia un objetivo común (p. 690)
concentration camp a camp where persons are detained or confined (p. 698)	**campo de concentración** un campamento donde personas están detenidas o encerradas (p. 698)
***conference** a meeting of two or more persons for discussing matters of common concern (p. 495)	***conferencia** reunión entre dos o más personas para discutir asuntos de interés mutuo (p. 495)
conference committee a special joint committee organized to help the House and Senate work on a compromise bill acceptable to both houses (p. 124)	**comité de conferencia** una comisión paritaria especial organizada para ayudar a la Cámara y al Senado a forjar un compromiso de ley aceptable para ambas cámaras (p. 124)
***confine** to enclose or restrain (p. 841)	***confinar** encerrar o contener (p. 841)
***confirmation** the process of supporting a statement by evidence (p. 978)	***confirmación** proceso de sustentar una afirmación con evidencia (p. 978)
***conform** to change in a way that fits a standard or authority (p. 802)	***adecuarse** cambiar para ajustarse a un estándar o autoridad (p. 802)
***conformity** agreement in form, manner, or character (p. 913)	***conformidad** acuerdo en forma, modo o carácter (p. 913)
conquistador Spanish for *conqueror;* the men who led the expeditions to conquer the Americas (p. 20)	**conquistador** los hombres que condujeron las expediciones para conquistar las Américas (p. 20)
conscription requiring people to enter military service (p. 316)	**reclutamiento** requerir que personas ingresen en el servicio militar (p. 316)
consensus general agreement (p. 839)	**consenso** acuerdo general (p. 839)
conservative a person who believes government power, particularly in the economy, should be limited in order to maximize individual freedom (p. 968)	**conservador** una persona que cree que el poder del gobierno, particularmente en la economía, debe estar limitado para llevar al máximo la libertad individual (p. 968)
***constitute** to be composed of, made up of, or formed from (p. 435)	***constituir** estar compuesto de, hecho de o formado por (p. 435)
constitutional being in accordance with or regulated by a constitution (p. 170)	**constitucional** de acuerdo con una constitución o reglamentado por ella (p. 170)
***consumer** a person who buys what is produced by an economy (p. 424)	***consumidor** persona que compra lo que produce una economía (p. 424)
containment the policy or process of preventing the expansion of a hostile power (p. 766)	**contención** la política o proceso de prevenir la expansión de un poder hostil (p. 766)
contra Spanish for counterrevolutionary, an anti-Sandinista guerrilla force in Nicaragua (p. 979)	**contra** contrarevolucionario, la fuerza guerilla anti-Sandinista en Nicaragua (p. 979)
contraband goods whose importation, exportation, or possession is illegal (p. 554)	**contrabando** artículos de los que la importación, exportación o posesión es ilegal (p. 554)
***contract** a binding legal document between two parties (p. 43)	***contrato** documento legal vinculante entre dos partes (p. 43)

***contradiction** a situation in which inherent factors, actions, or propositions are inconsistent or contrary to one another (p. 86)

***contradicción** situación en la que acciones, propuestas o factores inherentes son incoherentes o contrarios entre ellos (p. 86)

***controversy** a prolonged public dispute (p. 213)

***controversia** discusión pública prolongada (p. 213)

***convention** an assembly of persons who meet for a common purpose (p. 266)

***convención** asamblea de personas reunidas con un fin común (p. 266)

***conventional** nonnuclear (p. 830)

***convencional** no nuclear (p. 830)

***convert** to bring over from one belief, view, or party to another (p. 255)

***convertir** cambiar una creencia, punto de vista o partido por otro (p. 255)

***convince** to bring to belief, consent, or a course of action (p. 776)

***convencer** hacer creer, conseguir el consentimiento o lograr un curso de acción (p. 776)

convoy a group that travels with something, such as a ship, to protect it (p. 567)

convoy un grupo que viaja junto con algo, tal como un barco, para protegerlo (p. 567)

convoy system a system in which merchant ships travel with naval vessels for protection (p. 727)

sistema de convoy un sistema en el cual barcos mercantes viajan con buques navales para protección (p. 727)

cooperative a store where farmers buy products from each other; an enterprise owned and operated by those who use its services (p. 471)

cooperativa tienda donde los granjeros compraban productos el uno del otro; empresa poseída y operada por los que usan sus servicios (p. 471)

cooperative individualism President Hoover's policy of encouraging manufacturers and distributors to form their own organizations and volunteer information to the federal government in an effort to stimulate the economy (p. 593)

individualismo cooperativo política del Presidente Hoover para alentar a los manufactureros y distribuidores a formar sus propias organizaciones y pasar información voluntariamente al gobierno federal en un esfuerzo para estimular la economía (p. 593)

***coordinate** to harmonize or bring into common action, movement, or condition (p. 731)

***coordinar** armonizar o realizar acciones o movimientos comunes o bien obtener condiciones comunes (p. 731)

corporation an organization that is authorized by law to carry on an activity but treated as though it were a single person (p. 422)

sociedad anónima organización autorizada por ley a montar una actividad, tratada como si fuera una sola persona (p. 422)

***correspondence** communication by letters (p. 294)

***correspondencia** comunicación a través de cartas (p. 294)

"corrupt bargain" an illegitimate agreement between politicians (p. 215)

trato corrupto un acuerdo ilegítimo entre políticos (p. 215)

cost of living the cost of purchasing goods and services essential for survival (p. 576)

costo de vida el costo de comprar artículos y servicios esenciales para la supervivencia (p. 576)

cost-plus a government contract to pay a manufacturer the cost to produce an item plus a guaranteed percentage (p. 716)

costo más beneficio contrato del gobierno para pagar el costo de fabricación para producir un artículo más un porcentaje garantizado (p. 716)

cotton gin a machine that removed seeds from cotton fiber (p. 202)

despepitadora de algodón máquina que sacaba las semillas de las fibras de algodón (p. 202)

counterculture a culture with values and beliefs different than those of the mainstream (p. 912)

contracultura una cultura con valores y creencias diferentes de los de la cultura principal (p. 912)

court-packing the act of changing the political balance of power in a nation's judiciary system whereby a national leader, such as the American president, appoints judges who will rule in favor of his or her policies (p. 670)

recomposición de la corte acto de modificar el equilibrio político de poder en el sistema judicial de una nación mediante el cual un líder nacional, como el presidente estadounidense, nombra jueces que decidirán a favor de las políticas de éste (p. 670)

covert not openly shown or engaged in (p. 785)

secreto no hecho o mostrado abiertamente (p. 785)

Glossary/Glosario

English	Español
creationism the belief that God created the world and everything in it, usually in the way described in Genesis (p. 608)	**creacionismo** la creencia que Dios creó al mundo y todo lo que hay en él, usualmente como se describe en Génesis (p. 608)
credibility gap lack of trust or believability (p. 892)	**barrera de credibilidad** falta de confianza (p. 892)
***credit** an amount or sum of money placed at a person's disposal by a bank on condition that it will be repaid with interest (p. 600)	***crédito** monto o suma de dinero que un banco pone a disposición de una persona con la condición de que se devolverá con intereses (p. 600)
***creditor** one to whom a debt is owed (p. 156)	***acreedor** aquél con quien se tiene una deuda (p. 156)
***criteria** standards on which a judgment or action may be based (p. 954)	***criterios** normas sobre las que puede basarse una opinión o acción (p. 954)
crop lien obligation placed on a farmer to repay a debt with crops (p. 377)	**derecho de cultivo** obligación impuesta a un agricultor para cubrir la deuda por medio de cosecha (p. 377)
***crucial** something considered important or essential (p. 326)	***crucial** algo que se considera importante o fundamental (p. 326)
***currency** paper money used as a medium of exchange (p. 471)	***moneda** dinero en papel que se utiliza como medio de cambio (p. 471)
customs duty a tax on imports and exports (p. 57)	**derecho de aduana** impuesto sobre importaciones y exportaciones (p. 57)

D

English	Español
de facto segregation segregation by custom and tradition (p. 851)	**segregación de facto** segregación por costumbre y tradición (p. 851)
debt peonage condition of sharecroppers who could not pay off their debts and, therefore, could not leave the property they worked (p. 377)	**esclavitud deudora** condición de aparceros que no podían pagar sus deudas y por lo tanto no podían abandonar la propiedad que trabajaban (p. 377)
***decline** a change to a lower state or level (p. 5)	***disminución** modificación a un nivel o estado inferior (p. 5)
deficit spending government practice of spending borrowed money rather than raising taxes, usually in an attempt to boost the economy (p. 662)	**gastos déficits** práctica del gobierno de gastar dinero prestado en vez de aumentar impuestos, usualmente una tentativa para levantar la economía (p. 662)
deflation a decline in the volume of available money or credit that results in lower prices, and, therefore, increases the buying power of money (pp. 428, 470)	**deflación** un decremento de la cantidad de dinero o crédito disponible el cual resulta en precios reducidos y por lo tanto aumenta el poder adquisitivo de la moneda (pp. 428, 470)
***demonstration** an outward expression or display (p. 245)	***demostración** expresión o exposición exterior (p. 245)
***denial** refusal to satisfy a request or desire (p. 331)	***rechazo** negativa a satisfacer una petición o deseo (p. 331)
***deny** to declare untrue (p. 608)	***negar** declarar que algo no es cierto (p. 608)
deport to expel individuals from the country (p. 580)	**deportar** expulsar del país a individuos (p. 580)
***deregulation** the act or process of removing restrictions or regulations (p. 949)	***desregulación** acción o proceso de eliminar restricciones o reglamentaciones (p. 949)
***despite** in spite of (p. 748)	***a pesar de** pese a que (p. 748)
détente a policy that attempts to relax or ease tensions between nations (p. 938)	**détente** una política que intenta relajar o borrar la tensión entre naciones (p. 938)

developing nation a nation whose economy is primarily agricultural (p. 785)	**nación en desarrollo** nación en donde la economía es principalmente agrícola (p. 785)
***device** a piece of equipment or a mechanism designed to serve a special purpose or perform a special function (p. 1002)	***dispositivo** pieza de un equipo o mecanismo diseñado para servir un propósito especial o para realizar una función específica (p. 1002)
direct primary a vote held by all members of a political party to decide their candidate for public office (p. 522)	**elección primaria** voto tomado por todos los miembros de un partido político para elegir a su candidato para un puesto público (p. 522)
discount retailing selling large quantities of goods at very low prices and trying to sell the goods quickly to turn over their entire inventory in a short period of time (p. 983)	**ventas minoristas de descuento** vender grandes cantidades de productos a precios muy bajos e intentar realizar ventas rápidas de productos para la rotación del inventario en un corto período de tiempo (p. 983)
***discrimination** different treatment or preference on a basis other than individual merit (p. 478)	***discriminación** un trato o preferencia diferente en base a toda cosa diferente del mérito individual (p. 478)
disenfranchise to deprive of the right to vote (p. 719)	**privación** civil privar el derecho al voto (p. 719)
***disposable** referring to the money remaining to an individual after deduction of taxes (p. 598)	***disponible** hace referencia al dinero que le queda a un individuo después de la deducción de impuestos (p. 598)
***disproportionate** lacking regularity or symmetry in size, degree, or intensity (p. 893)	***desproporcionado** que carece de regularidad o simetría en tamaño, grado o intensidad (p. 893)
***distinct** separate, apart, or different from others (p. 35)	***distinto** separado, apartado o diferente de otros (p. 35)
***distribution** the act or process of being given out or disbursed to clients, customers, or members of a group (p. 422)	***distribución** acción o proceso de repartir o desembolsar entre clientes, consumidores o miembros de un grupo (p. 422)
***diverse** being different from one another (p. 610)	***diferente** ser distinto de otros (p. 610)
dollar diplomacy a policy of joining the business interests of a country with its diplomatic interests abroad (p. 509)	**diplomacia del dólar** política de juntar los intereses comerciales de un país con sus intereses diplomáticos en el extranjero (p. 509)
***dominance** being in a state or position of command or control over all others (p. 54)	***dominio** encontrarse en un estado o posición de mando o control sobre todos los demás (p. 54)
domino theory the belief that if one nation in Asia fell to the Communists, neighboring countries would follow (p. 883)	**teoría dominó** la creencia que si una nación en Asia se derrumbara ante los comunistas, sus (p. 883)
dove a person in favor of the United States withdrawing from the Vietnam War (p. 895)	**paloma** persona a favor de que Estados Unidos se retirara de la guerra en Vietnam (p. 895)
downsizing reducing a company in size by laying off workers and managers to become more efficient (p. 994)	**reducción de personal** reducción del tamaño de una compañía despidiendo gerentes y trabajadores para llegar a ser una empresa más eficiente (p. 994)
***draft** to select a person at random for mandatory military service (p. 560)	***conscripción** selección de una persona al azar para el servicio militar obligatorio (p. 560)
dry farming a way of farming dry land in which seeds are planted deep in the ground where there is some moisture (p. 396)	**cultivo seco** manera de cultivar tierra seca plantando las semillas en la profundidad de la tierra donde hay algo de humedad (p. 396)
due process a judicial requirement that laws may not treat individuals unfairly, arbitrarily, or unreasonably, and that courts must follow proper procedures and rules when trying cases (p. 829)	**proceso justo** requerimiento judicial de que las leyes no deben tratar individuos injusta, arbitraria, o irracionalmente y que las cortes deben de seguir procesos y reglamentos justos al jurar casos (p. 829)

English	Español
duty a tax on imports (p. 101)	**impuesto** un impuesto sobre importaciones (p. 101)
dynamic conservatism policy of balancing economic conservatism with some activism (p. 798)	**conservatismo dinámico** política de alcanzar un balance entre el conservatismo económico y algún activismo (p. 798)

E

English	Español
"earmark" specifications added by both Republicans and Democrats for the expenditure of federal money for particular projects (p. 1052)	**destino de fondos** especificaciones que tanto Republicanos como Demócratas añadieron para el gasto del dinero federal en proyectos particulares, por ejemplo, la construcción de un puente o la financiación de investigaciones médicas, generalmente, en sus propios estados y distritos (p. 1052)
economies of scale the reduction in the cost of a good brought about especially by increased production at a given facility (p. 422)	**economía a gran escala** reducción del costo de un producto a causa de la producción aumentada en una fábrica de producción (p. 422)
***eliminate** to remove or get rid of (p. 1047)	***eliminar** quitar o deshacerse de algo (p. 1047)
emancipation the act or process of freeing enslaved persons (pp. 89, 244)	**emancipación** el proceso de liberar a personas esclavizadas (pp. 89, 244)
embargo a government ban on trade with other countries (pp. 173, 946)	**embargo** prohibición gubernamental contra el comercio con otros países (pp. 173, 946)
***emphasis** a special importance given to an object or idea (p. 550)	***énfasis** importancia especial que se le da a un objeto o idea (p. 550)
empresario a person who arranged for the settlement of Texas in the 1800s (p. 264)	**empresario** persona que arreglaba el asentamiento de tierras en Texas durante los años 1800 (p. 264)
***enable** to make possible, practical, or easy (p. 178)	***permitir** hacer posible, práctico o fácil (p. 178)
encomienda system of rewarding conquistadors tracts of land, including the right to tax and exact labor from Native Americans (p. 22)	**encomienda** sistema de recompensar a los conquistadores con extensiones de tierra y el derecho de recaudar impuestos y exigir mano de obra a los indígenas americanos (p. 22)
***encounter** to come upon face-to-face as an enemy or adversary (p. 339)	***encontrarse** enfrentarse cara a cara como enemigos o adversarios (p. 339)
***enforce** to urge or carry out using force (pp. 67, 874)	***hacer cumplir** instar o llevar a cabo por medio de la fuerza (pp. 67, 874)
***ensure** to guarantee or make certain (p. 400)	***asegurar** garantizar o hacer certero (p. 400)
***entity** something having independent, separate, or self-contained existence (p. 813)	***entidad** algo que tiene una existencia independiente, separada y autónoma (p. 813)
entrepreneur one who organizes, manages, and assumes the risks of a business or enterprise (p. 415)	**empresario** persona que organiza, dirige y asume el riesgo de un negocio o empresa (p. 415)
enumerated powers powers listed in the Constitution as belonging to the federal government (p. 157)	**poderes enumerados** poderes nombrados en la Constitución que pertenecen solamente al gobierno federal (p. 157)
***environmental** having to do with the environment; the complex system of plants, animals, water, and soil (p. 532)	***medioambiental** relacionado con el medioambiente; el complejo sistema de plantas, animales, agua y suelo (p. 532)
envoy a person delegated to represent one country to another (p. 272)	**enviado especial** persona delegada para representar un país en otro (p. 272)

*__equip__ to furnish with provisions; to make ready for action (p. 78)

*__equipar__ proporcionar suministros, alistar para la acción (p. 78)

*__equipment__ the articles or physical resources prepared or furnished for a specific task (p. 762)

*__equipos__ artículos o recursos físicos preparados o proporcionados para una tarea específica (p. 762)

*__erode__ to wear away at something until it fades (p. 554)

*__erosionar__ desgastar algo hasta que desaparece (p. 554)

espionage spying, especially to gain government secrets (p. 558)

espionaje espiar, especialmente para obtener secretos gubernamentales (p. 558)

*__ethnic__ relating to large groups of people classed according to common racial, national, tribal, religious, linguistic, or cultural origin or background (p. 444)

*__étnico__ relativo a grandes grupos de personas clasificadas de acuerdo con características comunes de origen racial, de nacionalidad, tribal, religioso, lingüístico o cultural (p. 444)

ethnic cleansing the expulsion, imprisonment, or killing of ethnic minorities by a dominant majority group (p. 1015)

purificación étnica expulsión, encarcelamiento o asesinato de minorías étnicas por un grupo mayoritario dominante (p. 1015)

euro the basic currency shared by the countries of the European Union since 1999 (p. 1023)

eurodólar moneda básica compartida por los países de la Unión Europea desde 1999 (p. 1023)

*__eventually__ at an unspecified time or day; in the end (p. 8)

*__finalmente__ en un momento o día no especificado; al final (p. 8)

*__evident__ clearly visible or understood (p. 223)

*__evidente__ claro, sin la menor duda (p. 223)

*__evolution__ the scientific theory that humans and other forms of life have evolved over time (pp. 459, 608)

*__evolución__ teoría científica que los humanos y otras formas de vida se han evolucionado tras el tiempo (pp. 459, 608)

executive privilege principle stating that communications of the executive branch should remain confidential to protect national security (p. 944)

privilegio ejecutivo el principio de que las comunicaciones del ramo ejecutivo deben de permanecer confidenciales para proteger la seguridad nacional (p. 944)

*__expansion__ the act or process of increasing or enlarging the extent, number, volume, or scope (p. 491)

*__expansión__ acción o proceso de aumentar o ampliar la extensión, número, volumen o alcance (p. 491)

*__explicit__ fully revealed or expressed and leaving no question as to meaning (p. 98)

*__explícito__ completamente revelado o expresado y sin dudas en cuanto a significado (p. 98)

*__exposure__ the condition of being unprotected, especially from severe weather (p. 227)

*__exposición__ la condición de estar desprotegido, especialmente del mal tiempo (p. 227)

extermination camp a camp where men, women, and children were sent to be executed (p. 698)

campo de exterminación campo donde los hombres, las mujeres, y los niños eran enviados para ser ejecutados (p. 698)

*__extract__ to remove by force (p. 388)

*__extraer__ quitar algo por la fuerza (p. 388)

*__extraction__ the act or process of drawing or pulling something out (p. 196)

*__extracción__ acción o proceso de sacar o separar algo (p. 196)

F

*__facility__ something that is built, installed, or established to serve a particular purpose (p. 850)

*__instalación__ algo que se construye, instala o establece para servir un propósito especial (p. 850)

fallout radioactive particles dispersed by a nuclear explosion (p. 781)

caída radioactiva partículas radioactivas dispersadas por una explosión nuclear (p. 781)

fascism a political system headed by a dictator that calls for extreme nationalism and racism and no tolerance of opposition (p. 682)

fascismo un sistema político encabezado por un dictador que pide por nacionalismo y racismo extremo y poca tolerancia de la oposición (p. 682)

"favorite son" men who enjoyed the support of leaders from their own state and region (p. 214)

hijo favorito hombres que disfrutaban del apoyo do los líderes de su estado y región natales (p. 214)

federalism political system in which power is divided between the national and state governments (p. 108)

federalismo sistema político en el cual el poder está dividido entre los estados y el gobierno federal (p. 108)

Glossary/Glosario

English	Español
feminism the belief that men and women should be equal politically, economically, and socially (p. 914)	**feminismo** la creencia que los hombres y las mujeres deben ser iguales política, económica y socialmente (p. 914)
filibuster an attempt to kill a bill by having a group of senators take turns speaking continuously so that a vote cannot take place (p. 864)	**filibustero** un atentado para acabar con un proyecto de ley hablando continuamente a turnos un grupo de senadores para que no pueda haber un voto (p. 864)
***finalize** to put in finished form (p. 193)	***finalizar** llevar algo a su conclusión (p. 193)
***finance** to provide money for a project (p. 664)	***financiar** proporcionar dinero para un proyecto (p. 664)
***financier** one who deals with finance and investment on a large scale (p. 104)	***financiero** el que maneja finanzas e inversiones a gran escala (p. 104)
fireside chats radio broadcasts made by FDR to the American people to explain his initiatives (p. 653)	**pláticas hogareñas** emisiones de radio transmitidas por FDR al pueblo americano para explicar sus iniciativas (p. 653)
flexible response the buildup of conventional troops and weapons to allow a nation to fight a limited war without using nuclear weapons (p. 830)	**respuesta flexible** formación de tropas y armas convencionales para permitir que un país entre en una guerra limitada sin usar armas nucleares (p. 830)
forage to search or raid for food (p. 337)	**forrajear** buscar alimento (p. 337)
foreclose to take possession of a property from a mortgagor because of defaults on payments (p. 643)	**ejecutar** una hipoteca tomar posesión de una propiedad por falta de pagos hipotecarios (p. 643)
***formulate** to prepare or devise according to a systematized statement or formula (p. 300)	***formular** preparar o crear de acuerdo con una fórmula o declaración sistematizada (p. 300)
fossil fuel a fuel formed in the earth from decayed plant or animal remains (p. 961)	**combustible fósil** un combustible formado en la tierra de los restos descompuestos de plantas o animales (p. 961)
***framework** a set of guidelines to be followed (p. 112)	***marco** conjunto de pautas por seguir (p. 112)
franchise the right or license to market a company's goods or services in an area, such as a store of a chain operation (p. 802)	**franquicia** derecho o licencia para comercializar los productos o servicios de una empresa en un área, como una tienda de operación en cadena (p. 802)
free enterprise system market economy in which privately owned businesses have the freedom to operate for a profit with limited government intervention (p. 197)	**sistema de libre empresa** economía de mercado en la que las empresas privadas tienen la libertad de operar para obtener una ganancia con poca intervención del gobierno (p. 197)
***fundamental** being of central importance (p. 658)	***fundamental** de central importancia (p. 658)

G

***gender** term applied to the characteristics of a male or female (p. 915)	***género** término aplicado a las características de un ser masculino o femenino (p. 915)
general strike a strike involving all the workers in a particular geographic location (p. 577)	**huelga general** una huelga por todos los trabajadores de un lugar geográfico (p. 577)
***generation** a classification of people who share the same experience throughout their lives (p. 899)	***generación** clasificación de personas que comparten las mismas experiencias a lo largo de sus vidas (p. 899)
generation gap a cultural separation between parents and their children (p. 807)	**barrera generacional** una separación cultural entre padres e hijos (p. 807)
glasnost a Soviet policy permitting open discussion of political and social issues and freer dissemination of news and information (p. 991)	**glasnost** política soviética que permitía discusión abierta de temas políticos y sociales y diseminación más libre de noticias e información (p. 991)

globalism the idea that the world is becoming increasingly interconnected (p. 1022)

globalismo idea de que el mundo se encuentra cada vez más interconectado (p. 1022)

global warming an increase in average world temperatures over time (p. 1025)

calentamiento global aumento en la temperatura promedio mundial tras un período (p. 1025)

gold standard a monetary standard in which one ounce of gold equals a set number of dollars (p. 652)

patrón oro norma monetaria en la cual una onza de oro igualaba a un número fijo de dólares (p. 652)

gradualism theory that slavery should be ended gradually (p. 242)

gradualismo teoría de que la esclavitud debería terminarse gradualmente (p. 242)

graduated income tax tax based on the net income of an individual or business and which taxes different income levels at different rates (p. 473)

impuesto graduado de utilidades impuesto basado en los ingresos netos de un individuo o empresa en el cual la taza del impuesto se diferencia de acuerdo a diferentes niveles de salario (p. 473)

graft the acquisition of money in dishonest ways, as in bribing a politician (pp. 368, 455)

soborno adquisición de dinero de manera deshonesta tal como el sobornar a un político (pp. 368, 455)

grandfather clause a clause that allowed individuals who did not pass the literacy test to vote if their fathers or grandfathers had voted before Reconstruction began; an exception to a law based on preexisting circumstances (p. 478)

cláusula de abuelo cláusula que permitió votar a los que no aprobaron el examen de leer si sus padres o sus abuelos habían votado antes de que empezara la Reconstrucción; excepción a una ley basada en circunstancias preexistentes (p. 478)

***grant** to give or bestow upon, especially by a formal act (p. 26)

***conceder** otorgar o conferir, especialmente a través de un acto formal (p. 26)

grassroots movement a group of people organizing at the local or community level, away from political or cultural centers (p. 995)

movimiento local grupo de personas que se organiza a nivel local y popular lejos de centros políticos o culturales (p. 995)

greenback a piece of U.S. paper money first issued by the North during the Civil War (pp. 315, 470)

billete dorso verde billete de papel moneda de EEUU expedido por primera vez por el Norte durante la Guerra Civil (pp. 315, 470)

gross national product the total value of goods and services produced by a country during a year (p. 410)

producto nacional bruto valor total de bienes y servicios producidos por un país durante un año (p. 410)

***guarantee** a statement of assurance (p. 254)

***garantía** declaración de seguridad (p. 254)

guerrilla member of an armed band that carries out surprise attacks and sabotage rather than open warfare (pp. 511, 883)

guerrilla banda armada que usa ataques sorpresas o sabotaje en vez de la guerra organizada (pp. 511, 883)

guerrilla warfare a hit-and-run technique used in fighting a war; fighting by small bands of warriors using tactics such as sudden ambushes (p. 78)

guerra de guerrillas técnica de tirar y darse a la huida usada en combates de guerra; peleas por pequeñas bandas de guerreros usando tácticas tales como emboscadas repentinas (p. 78)

H

habeas corpus a legal order for an inquiry to determine whether a person has been lawfully imprisoned (p. 316)

hábeas corpus orden legal para una encuesta para determinar si una persona ha sido encarcelada legalmente (p. 316)

hacienda a huge ranch (p. 392)

hacienda un rancho extenso (p. 392)

hardtack a hard biscuit made of wheat flour (p. 331)

hardtack galleta dura hecha de harina de trigo (p. 331)

hawk someone who believed the United States should continue its military efforts in Vietnam (p. 895)

halcón persona que creía que Estados Unidos debía continuar sus esfuerzos militares en Vietnam (p. 895)

headright system in which settlers were granted land in exchange for settling in Virginia (p. 27)

derecho de terreno sistema en el cual los colonizadores recibían tierra a cambio de establecerse en Virginia (p. 27)

hedgerow row of shrubs or trees surrounding a field, often on a dirt wall (p. 746)

seto fila de arbustos o árboles cercando un campo a menudo sobre un muro de tierra (p. 746)

English	Español
hemispheric defense zone national policy during World War II that declared the Western Hemisphere to be neutral and that the United States would patrol this region against German submarines (p. 704)	**zona de defensa hemisférica** política nacional durante la Segunda Guerra Mundial que declaró que el Hemisferio Oeste fue neutral y que Estados Unidos patrullaría esta región en contra de submarinos alemanes (p. 704)
heretic a dissenter from established church beliefs (p. 29)	**hereje** disidente de creencias establecidas por la iglesia (p. 29)
hippies refers to young Americans, especially during the 1960s, who reject the conventions of established society (p. 912)	**hippies** se refiere a los jóvenes estadounidenses, especialmente durante la década de 1960, que rechazaban las convenciones de la sociedad establecida (p. 912)
hobo a homeless and usually penniless wanderer (p. 634)	**vagabundo** persona errante sin hogar y usualmente sin dinero (p. 634)
holding company a company whose primary business is owning a controlling share of stock in other companies (p. 426)	**compañía de valores** compañía de la cual el negocio principal es poseer el control de acciones en otras compañías (p. 426)
homestead method of acquiring a piece of U.S. public land by living on and cultivating it (p. 395)	**posesionar** método de adquirir una extensión de tierra pública de EEUU viviendo en ella y cultivándola (p. 395)
horizontal integration combining of many firms engaged in the same type of business into one corporation (p. 425)	**integración horizontal** asociación do firmas competitivas en una sociedad anónima (p. 425)
hydraulic mining method of mining by which water is sprayed at a very high pressure against a hill or mountain, washing away large quantities of dirt, gravel, and rock, and exposing the minerals beneath the surface (p. 389)	**minería hidráulica** método de minería mediante el que se pulveriza agua a alta presión contra una colina o montaña, lo que elimina grandes cantidades de suciedad, grava y rocas y expone los minerales que se encuentran debajo de la superficie (p. 389)

I

English	Español
***ideology** a system of thought that is held by an individual, group, or culture (p. 652)	***ideología** sistema de ideas que posee un individuo, grupo o cultura (p. 652)
***ignorance** the state of being uneducated, uninformed, or unaware (p. 215)	***ignorancia** el estado de ser inculto, ignorante o carecer de conocimiento (p. 215)
***illegal** not according to or authorized by law (p. 1017)	***ilegal** que no está de acuerdo con la ley o ésta no lo autoriza (p. 1017)
***immigrant** one who enters and becomes established in a country other than that of their original nationality (p. 442)	***inmigrante** aquél que ingresa y se establece en un país que no es su país de origen (p. 442)
***impact** to make a lasting impression upon an individual or group (p. 620)	***impactar** dejar una impresión duradera en un individuo o grupo (p. 620)
impeach to formally charge a public official with misconduct in office (p. 363)	**acusar** acusar formalmente a un oficial público de mala conducta en la oficina (p. 363)
imperialism the actions used by one nation to exercise political or economic control over a smaller or weaker nation (p. 490)	**imperialismo** acciones usadas por una nación para ejercer el control político o económico sobre naciones más pequeñas o débiles (p. 490)
***implement** to put into action; to assemble (p. 319)	***implementar** poner en acción (p. 319)
implied powers powers not specifically listed in the Constitution but claimed by the federal government (p. 157)	**poderes implícitos** poderes no nombrados específicamente en la Constitución pero reclamados por el gobierno federal (p. 157)
***imply** to express indirectly (p. 786)	***insinuar** expresar indirectamente (p. 786)
***impose** to establish authority by force (p. 307)	***imponer** establecer autoridad por la fuerza (p. 307)

English	Español
***imposition** something established or brought about as if by force (p. 238)	***imposición** algo que se establece o se ocasiona por medio de la fuerza (p. 238)
impound to take possession of (p. 936)	**confiscar** tomar posesión de (p. 936)
impressment a kind of legalized kidnapping in which people are forced into military service (p. 173)	**requisición** un tipo de secuestro legalizado en el cual personas son forzadas a servir en el servicio militar (p. 173)
***incentive** something that motivates a person into action (p. 450)	***incentivo** algo que motiva a que una persona realice una acción (p. 450)
***incident** occurrence of a happening or situation that is a separate unit of experience (p. 940)	***incidente** acontecimiento de un suceso o situación que es una unidad separada de experiencia (p. 940)
***income** a gain or recurrent benefit usually measured in money derived from capital or labor (p. 810)	***ingresos** ganancia o beneficio recurrente que generalmente se mide en dinero proveniente de capital o trabajo (p. 810)
income tax a tax based on the net income of a person or business (p. 538)	**impuesto de utilidades** impuesto basado en el ingreso neto de una persona o empresa (p. 538)
indentured servant an individual who contracts to work for a colonist for a specified number of years in exchange for transportation to the colonies, food, clothing, and shelter (p. 34)	**sirviente contratado** individuo contratado para trabajar para un colono durante cierto número de años a cambio de transportación a las colonias, alimento, ropa y refugio (p. 34)
***indicate** to point out, point to, or demonstrate the necessity of (p. 973)	***indicar** señalar, describir o demostrar la necesidad de algo (p. 973)
individualism the thought that no matter what a person's background is, the person can still become successful (p. 458)	**individualismo** el pensamiento de que sin importar el origen de una persona, ésta puede ser exitosa (p. 458)
industrial union an organization of common laborers and craft workers in a particular industry (p. 429)	**sindicato industrial** organización de trabajadores comunes y obreros calificados en una industria (p. 429)
inflation the loss of value of money (pp. 58, 470, 946)	**inflación** pérdida del valor del dinero (pp. 58, 470, 946)
***initially** of or relating to the beginning (p. 769)	***inicial** relacionado con el comienzo (p. 769)
***initiative** the right of citizens to place a measure or issue before the voters or the legislature for approval (pp. 523, 993)	***iniciativa** derecho de los ciudadanos de poner una propuesta o tema ante los votantes o la legislatura para su aprobación (pp. 523, 993)
injunction a court order whereby one is required to do or to refrain from doing a specified act (p. 433)	**medida cautelar** orden judicial que exige o prohíbe la realización de una acción específica (p. 433)
***innovation** a new idea or method (p. 396)	***innovación** nueva idea o método (p. 396)
***insecurity** the state of not being confident or sure (p. 766)	***inseguridad** estado de desconfianza o indecisión (p. 766)
***inspector** a person appointed to examine foreign facilities, usually in search of weapons (p. 1045)	***inspector** persona designada para examinar instalaciones extranjeras, por lo general, en búsqueda de armas (p. 1045)
installment buying an item on credit with a monthly plan to pay off the value of the good (p. 633)	**pago a plazos** compra de un artículo a crédito con un plan de pago mensual para pagar el valor del artículo (p. 633)
***institute** to initiate or establish something (p. 833)	***instituir** iniciar o establecer algo (p. 833)
***institution** an established organization or corporation (p. 236)	***institución** organización o empresa establecida (p. 236)
insubordination disobedience (p. 535)	**insubordinación** desobediencia (p. 535)
insurrection an act of rebellion against the established government (p. 301)	**insurrección** un acto de rebelión en contra del gobierno establecido (p. 301)
***integrate** to combine two previously separate things (p. 419)	***integrar** combinar dos cosas previamente separadas (p. 419)

English	Español
integrated circuit a complete electronic circuit on a silicon chip that is small and easy to produce (p. 1002)	**circuito integrado** un circuito electrónico completo en un chip de silicona pequeño y fácil de producir (p. 1002)
***intense** existing in an extreme degree (p. 740)	***intenso** que existe en un grado extremo (p. 740)
***intensify** to become more frequent and powerful (p. 961)	***intensificar** volverse más frecuente y poderoso (p. 961)
interchangeable parts uniform pieces that can be made in large quantities to replace other identical pieces (p. 198)	**partes intercambiables** piezas uniformes que pueden ser hechas en grandes cantidades para reemplazar otras piezas idénticas (p. 198)
internationalism a national policy of actively trading with foreign countries to foster peace and prosperity (p. 687)	**internacionalismo** política nacional de intercambio comercial activo con países extranjeros para promover la paz y la prosperidad (p. 687)
interposition theory that a state should be able to intervene between the federal government and the people to stop an illegal action (p. 167)	**interposición** teoría que un estado debiera poder intervenir entre el gobierno federal y la gente para detener una acción ilegal (p. 167)
***interpret** to explain the meaning of complex material (p. 190)	***interpretar** explicar el significado de materiales complejos (p. 190)
***interpretation** the act or process of explaining or telling the meaning of (p. 1038)	***interpretación** acción o proceso de explicar o decir el significado de algo (p. 1038)
***intervene** to get involved in the affairs of another (p. 498)	***intervenir** involucrarse en los asuntos de otros (p. 498)
***invest** to put money into a company in order to gain a future financial reward (p. 629)	***invertir** colocar dinero en una empresa con el fin de obtener una recompensa financiera en el futuro (p. 629)
***investigation** a systematic examination or official inquiry (p. 591)	***investigación** examen sistemático o indagación oficial (p. 591)
***investor** one who puts money into a company in order to gain a future financial reward (p. 420)	***inversor** aquél que coloca dinero en una empresa con el fin de obtener una recompensa financiera en el futuro (p. 420)
Iron Curtain the political and military barrier that isolated Soviet-controlled countries of Eastern Europe after World War II (p. 765)	**cortina de hierro** barrera política y militar que aisló a los países de Europa Oriental controlados por los soviéticos después de la Segunda Guerra Mundial (p. 765)
isolationism a national policy of avoiding involvement in world affairs (p. 594)	**aislacionismo** política nacional de evitar el involucramiento en asuntos mundiales (p. 594)

J

English	Español
jazz American style of music that developed from ragtime and blues and that uses syncopated rhythms and melodies (p. 617)	**jazz** estilo de música americana que se desarrolló de ragtime y blues y que usa melodías y ritmos sincopados (p. 617)
Jim Crow laws statutes or laws created to enforce segregation (p. 478)	**Leyes de Jim Crow** leyes creadas para reforzar la segregación (p. 478)
jingoism extreme nationalism marked by aggressive foreign policy (p. 499)	**patriotismo** extremo nacionalismo marcado por la agresiva política extranjera (p. 499)
joint-stock company form of business organization in which many investors pool funds to raise large amounts of money for large projects (p. 25)	**compañía por acciones** forma de organización de negocios en la cual muchos inversionistas compran acciones para juntar grandes cantidades de dinero para grandes proyectos (p. 25)
judicial review power of the Supreme Court to determine whether laws of Congress are constitutional and to strike down those that are not (p. 170)	**revisión judicial** derecho de la Suprema Corte para determinar si las leyes del Congreso son constitucionales y para derribar aquellas que no lo son (p. 170)

*justify to prove or to show to be just, right, or reasonable (p. 732)

*justificar probar o demostrar que algo es justo, correcto y razonable (p. 732)

juvenile delinquency antisocial or criminal behavior of young people (p. 815)

delincuencia juvenil comportamiento antisocial o criminal de los jóvenes (p. 815)

K

kamikaze during World War II, a Japanese suicide pilot whose mission was to crash into his target (p. 743)

kamikase durante la Segunda Guerra Mundial un piloto suicida japonés de quien la misión fue chocar en su objetivo (p. 743)

kiva circular ceremonial room built by the Anasazi (p. 7)

kiva cuarto circular ceremonial construido por los Anasazi (p. 7)

L

*labor an action that produces a good or service (p. 17)

*mano de obra acción que produce un producto o servicio (p. 17)

labor union an organization of workers formed for the purpose of advancing its members' interests (p. 199)

sindicato organización de trabajadores formada con el propósito de promover los intereses de sus miembros (p. 199)

laissez-faire policy that government should interfere as little as possible in the nation's economy (p. 414)

laissez-faire política que el gobierno debe interferir tan poco como sea posible en la economía del país (p. 414)

land grant a grant of land by the federal government especially for roads, railroads, or agricultural colleges (p. 420)

concesión de tierras una concesión de terrenos por el gobierno federal especialmente para carreteras, vías de ferrocarril y colegios agrícolas (p. 420)

*legislation a proposed law to be voted on by a governing body (p. 523)

*legislación ley propuesta para que un órgano directivo la vote (p. 523)

*legislator one who makes laws as a member of a political, legislative body (p. 794)

*legislador aquél que elabora leyes como miembro de un órgano político legislativo (p. 794)

letters of marque licenses issued by Congress to private ship owners authorizing them to attack British merchant ships (p. 82)

patente de corso cédula autorizada por el Congreso para propietarios de naves privadas autorizándoles a atacar barcos mercantes británicos (p. 82)

*liberal a person who generally believes the government should take an active role in the economy and in social programs but should not dictate social behavior (pp. 936, 968)

*liberal persona que generalmente cree que el gobierno debe desempeñar un papel active en la economía y programas sociales pero que el gobierno no debe dictar el comportamiento social (pp. 936, 968)

*liberate to set free (p. 760)

*liberar dejar en libertad (p. 760)

*license permission or freedom to act (p. 173)

*licencia permiso o libertad de acción (p. 173)

*likewise in a like manner; similarly (p. 920)

*asimismo de la misma manera, igualmente (p. 920)

limited war a war fought with limited commitment of resources to achieve a limited objective, such as containing communism (p. 773)

guerra limitada guerra peleada con compromisos limitados de recursos para alcanzar un objetivo limitado, tal como la contención del comunismo (p. 773)

linkage policy of improving relations with the Soviet Union and China in hopes of persuading them to cut back their aid to North Vietnam (p. 898)

enlace política de mejorar relaciones con la Unión Soviética y China con la esperanza de persuadirlas a que redujeran su ayuda a Vietnam del Norte (p. 898)

lockout a company tool to fight union demands by refusing to allow employees to enter its facilities to work (p. 430)

cierre patronal práctica de una empresa para rechazar las demandas sindicales negándose a permitir a los empleados a entrar al área de trabajo (p. 430)

long drive driving cattle long distances to a railroad depot for fast transport and great profit (p. 391)

manejo largo conducción de ganado por largas distancias a estaciones de ferrocarril para la transportación rápida y grandes ganancias (p. 391)

Loyalist American colonist who supported Britain and opposed the War for Independence (p. 68)

lealista colono americano que apoyó a la Gran Bretaña y se opuso a la guerra para la independencia (p. 68)

English	Español
loyalty review program a policy established by President Truman that authorized the screening of all federal employees to determine their loyalty to the American government (p. 774)	**programa de verificación de la lealtad** política que estableció el presidente Truman y que autorizaba la investigación de todos los empleados federales para determinar la lealtad de éstos al gobierno estadounidense (p. 774)
lynching an execution performed without lawful approval (p. 480)	**linchamiento** ejecución hecha sin aprobación legal (p. 480)

M

English	Español
mandate authorization to act given to a representative (p. 348)	**mandato** autorización dado a un representante (p. 348)
***manipulate** to operate or arrange manually to achieve a desired effect (p. 775)	***manipular** operar o disponer manualmente para alcanzar un efecto deseado (p. 775)
manumission the voluntary freeing of enslaved persons (p. 90)	**manumisión** liberación voluntaria de personas esclavizadas (p. 90)
margin buying a stock by paying only a fraction of the stock price and borrowing the rest (p. 629)	**margen** comprar acciones pagando solamente una fracción del precio y pidiendo prestado el resto (p. 629)
margin call demand by a broker that investors pay back loans made for stocks purchased on margin (p. 629)	**llamada de reserva** demanda de un accionista a que los inversionistas paguen los préstamos hechos para la compra de acciones al margen (p. 629)
martial law the law administered by military forces that is invoked by a government in an emergency (p. 307)	**derecho marcial** derecho administrado por fuerzas militares que es invocado por un gobierno en una emergencia (p. 307)
mass media a medium of communication (as in television and radio) intended to reach a wide audience (p. 613)	**medios informativos** medios de comunicación (como televisión y radio) con la intención de llegar a la audiencia extensa (p. 613)
mass production the production of large quantities of goods using machinery and often an assembly line (p. 596)	**fabricación en serie** producción de grandes cantidades de productos usando máquinas y a menudo una línea de montaje (p. 596)
massive retaliation a policy of threatening a massive response, including the use of nuclear weapons, against a Communist state trying to seize a peaceful state by force (p. 783)	**represalia masiva** una política que amenaza una respuesta masiva, incluyendo el uso de armas nucleares, contra un estado comunista que trata de captar un país pacífico por la fuerza (p. 783)
***media** a means of expression or communication, especially in reference to the agencies of mass communication—newspapers, radio, television, and the Internet (p. 892)	***medios de comunicación** medios de expresión o comunicación, especialmente en referencia a las agencias de comunicación masiva periódicos, radio, televisión e Internet (p. 892)
***mediate** an attempt to resolve conflict between hostile people or groups (p. 673)	***mediar** intento de resolver un conflicto entre personas o grupos hostiles (p. 673)
mercantilism the theory that a state's power depends on its wealth (p. 40)	**mercantilismo** teoría que el poder de una estado depende de su riqueza (p. 40)
mestizo a person of mixed blood or ancestry (p. 262)	**mestizo** persona de ascendencia o sangre mixta (p. 262)
microprocessor a computer processor containing memory and computing functions on a single chip (p. 1002)	**microprocesador** procesador de computadora que contiene memoria y funciones de computación en un solo chip (p. 1002)
***migrate** to move from one location to another (p. 558)	***migrar** mudarse de un lugar a otro (p. 558)
***migration** movement from one location to another (p. 24)	***migración** desplazamiento de un lugar a otro (p. 24)
migration chain the process by which immigrants who have acquired U.S. citizenship can send for relatives in their home country to join them (p. 1016)	**cadena migratoria** proceso mediante el cual los inmigrantes que obtuvieron la ciudadanía estadounidense pueden llamar a sus familiares en sus países de origen para que se les unan (p. 1016)

militarism a policy of aggressive military preparedness (p. 549)

militarismo política de preparación militar agresiva (p. 549)

military-industrial complex an informal relationship that some people believe exists between the military and the defense industry to promote greater military spending and influence government policy (p. 787)

compejo militar industrial relación informal que algunas personas creen que existe entre lo militar y la industria de defensa para promover mayores gastos militares y para influenciar la política gubernamental (p. 787)

minutemen companies of civilian soldiers who boasted they were ready to fight on a minute's notice (p. 68)

minutemen compañías de soldados civiles que se jactaban de que podrían estar listos para tomar armas en sólo un minuto (p. 68)

missile gap belief that the Soviet Union had more nuclear weapons than the United States (p. 824)

diferencia de proyectiles creencia que la Unión Soviética tenía más armas nucleares que Estados Unidos (p. 824)

Model T automobile built by the Ford Motor Company from 1908 until 1927 (p. 596)

Modelo T automóvil construido por la Ford Motor Company desde 1908 hasta 1927 (p. 596)

***modify** to make changes or alter (p. 1009)

***modificar** realizar cambios o alterar (p. 1009)

***monitor** to observe, oversee, or regulate (p. 1050)

***controlar** vigilar, supervisar o regular (p. 1050)

monopoly total control of a type of industry by one person or one company (p. 425)

monopolio control total de una industria por una persona o una compañía (p. 425)

most-favored nation a policy between countries ensuring fair trading practices (p. 163)

nación más favorecida política entre países asegurando prácticas de tratado de comercio justo (p. 163)

muckraker a journalist who uncovers abuses and corruption in a society (p. 521)

muckraker periodista que revela abusos y corrupción en una sociedad (p. 521)

mudslinging attempt to ruin an opponent's reputation with insults (p. 215)

mudslinging intentar arruinar la reputación de un adversario con insultos (p. 215)

multinational corporation large corporations with overseas investments (p. 802)

corporación multinacional grandes corporaciones de inversión extranjera (p. 802)

mutual assured destruction the strategy assuming that, as long as two countries can destroy each other with nuclear weapons, they will be afraid to use them (p. 981)

destrucción mutua asegurada estrategia que supone que mientras dos países puedan destruirse mutuamente con armas nucleares, tendrán miedo de utilizarlas (p. 981)

N

napalm a jellied gasoline used for bombs (pp. 749, 889)

napalm gasolina gelatinosa utilizada para bombas incendiarias (pp. 749, 889)

national self-determination the free choice by the people of a nation of their own future political status (p. 570)

autodeterminación nacional es la libre elección que hacen los habitantes de un país sobre su propia situación política futura (p. 570)

nationalism loyalty and devotion to a nation (pp. 181, 550)

nacionalismo lealtad y devoción a una nación (pp. 181, 550)

nativism hostility toward immigrants (pp. 232, 446, 604)

nativismo sentimientos de hostilidad hacia imigrantes (pp. 232, 446, 604)

***network** an interconnected system (p. 564)

***red** sistema interconectado (p. 564)

***neutral** not aligned with any political or ideological group (p. 162)

***neutral** no alineado con ningún grupo político ni ideológico (p. 162)

nomad a person who continually moves from place to place, usually in search of food (p. 398)

nómada persona que se mueve de un lugar a otro, generalmente en busca de alimentos o pastos (p. 398)

nonimportation agreement a pledge by merchants not to buy imported goods from a particular source (p. 59)

acuerdo de no importación compromiso por mercaderes de no comprar artículos importados de una fuente indicada (p. 59)

English	Español
***nuclear** used in or produced by a nuclear reaction (p. 751)	***nuclear** que se utiliza en una reacción nuclear o que ésta lo produce (p. 751)
nullification theory that states have the right to declare a federal law invalid (p. 167)	**anulación** teoría que los estados tienen el derecho de declarar inválida una ley federal (p. 167)
O	
***objective** strategic position to be attained or a purpose to be achieved by a military operation (p. 83)	***objetivo** posición estratégica por lograr o propósito por alcanzar mediante una operación militar (p. 83)
***obtain** to gain possession of (p. 1040)	***obtener** lograr posesión de algo (p. 1040)
***occupy** to take control or possession of a location (p. 101)	***ocupar** tomar control o posesión de un lugar (p. 101)
***ongoing** being actually in process; continuing (p. 621)	***continuo** que está en proceso, en curso (p. 621)
Open Door policy a policy that allowed each foreign nation in China to trade freely in the other nations' spheres of influence (p. 505)	**política de Puertas Abiertas** política que permitió a cada nación extranjera en China intercambiar libremente en las esferas de influencia de otras naciones (p. 505)
open range vast areas of grassland owned by the federal government (p. 390)	**terreno abierto** gran extensión de pastos propiedad del gobierno federal (p. 390)
open shop a workplace where workers are not required to join a union (p. 602)	**taller abierto** lugar de trabajo donde los trabajadores no son requeridos de ser miembros del sindicato (p. 602)
***orientation** position relative to a standard (p. 987)	***orientación** posición relativa a un estándar (p. 987)
***outcome** something that follows as a result or consequence (p. 375)	***resultado** algo que sigue como efecto o consecuencia (p. 375)
overlander someone who travels overland to the West (p. 256)	**viajero** persona que viaja al oeste por tierra (p. 256)
***overseas** situated, originating in, or relating to lands beyond the sea (p. 177)	***extranjero** situado en, originado en o relacionado con las tierras al otro lado del mar (p. 177)
P	
***participant** one who takes part or shares in something (p. 1015)	***participante** que forma parte de algo o que comparte algo (p. 1015)
party boss the person in control of a political machine (p. 455)	**jefe de partido** persona que lleva el control de la maquinaria política (p. 455)
penitentiary prison whose purpose is to reform prisoners (p. 238)	**penitenciaría** prisión cuyo propósito es de reformar prisioneros (p. 238)
***perception** the capacity, degree, and accuracy of one's consciousness, awareness, or comprehension (p. 291)	***percepción** capacidad, grado y precisión del conocimiento, conciencia o comprensión de una persona (p. 291)
perestroika a policy of economic and government restructuring instituted by Mikhail Gorbachev in the Soviet Union in the 1980s (p. 991)	**perestroika** política de reestructuración económica y gubernamental instituida por Mikhail Gorbachev en la Unión Soviética en los años 1980 (p. 991)
periphery the outer boundary of something (p. 725)	**periferia** frontera externa de algo (p. 725)
perjury lying when one has sworn under oath to tell the truth (pp. 776, 1013)	**perjurio** mentir cuando uno ha jurado decir la verdad (pp. 776, 1013)

*phenomenon an exceptional, unusual, or abnormal person, thing, or occurrence (p. 800)

*fenómeno persona, cosa o acontecimiento excepcional, inusual o anormal (p. 800)

philanthropy providing money to support humanitarian or social goals (p. 460)

filantropía proporcionar dinero para apoyar metas humanitarias o sociales (p. 460)

*philosopher person who seeks wisdom or enlightenment (p. 234)

*filósofo persona que busca la sabiduría o la iluminación (p. 234)

pietism movement in the 1700s that stressed an individual's piety and an emotional union with God (p. 47)

piedad movimiento en los años 1700 que enfatizó la piedad individual y la unión emocional con Dios (p. 47)

pillage to loot or plunder (p. 347)

saquear botín y robo (p. 347)

pocket veto indirectly vetoing a bill by letting a session of Congress expire without signing the bill (p. 358)

veto indirecto vetar indirectamente un proyecto de ley permitiendo que una sesión del Congreso expire sin firmar el proyecto (p. 358)

polio abbreviated form of poliomyelitis, an acute infectious disease affecting the skeletal muscles, often resulting in permanent disability and deformity (p. 650)

polio abreviatura de poliomielitis, una enfermedad infecciosa aguda que afecta los músculos esqueléticos y a menudo provoca discapacidad y deformidad permanente (p. 650)

political machine an organization linked to a political party that often controlled local government (p. 455)

maquinaria política organización aliada con un partido político que a menudo controlaba el gobierno local (p. 455)

poll tax a tax of a fixed amount per person that had to be paid before the person could vote (p. 478)

impuesto de capitación impuesto de cantidad fija por cada persona, el cual tenía que ser pagado antes de que una persona pudiera votar (p. 478)

pool a group sharing in some activity; for example, among railroad owners who made secret agreements and set rates among themselves (p. 424)

consorcio grupo compartiendo una actividad; por ejemplo, dueños de ferrocarril que tomaban acuerdos secretos y fijaban tipos entre ellos mismos (p. 424)

popular sovereignty government subject to the will of the people (pp. 108, 120); before the Civil War, the idea that people living in a territory had the right to decide by voting if slavery would be allowed there (p. 285)

soberanía popular teoría política de que el gobierno está sujeto a la voluntad del pueblo (pp. 108, 120); antes de la Guerra Civil, la idea de que la gente que vivía en un territorio tenía el derecho de decidir votando si ahí sería permitida la esclavitud (p. 285)

populism political movement founded in the 1890s representing mainly farmers, favoring free coinage of silver and government control of railroads and other large industries (p. 470)

populismo movimiento político fundado en los años 1890 representando principalmente a los granjeros que favoreció libre acuñación de plata y el control gubernamental de ferrocarriles y otras industrias grandes (p. 470)

poverty line a level of personal or family income below which one is classified as poor by the federal government (p. 810)

línea de pobreza nivel de ingreso individual o familiar bajo del cual uno es clasificado por el gobierno federal como pobre (p. 810)

*practice to do something repeatedly so it becomes the standard (p. 415)

*práctica es la realización de algo repetidamente hasta que se convierte en hábito (p. 415)

*precedent an earlier occurrence of something that may serve as a model for similar occurrences in the future (p. 363)

*precedente acontecimiento anterior a algo que puede servir como modelo para acontecimientos similares en el futuro (p. 363)

*predominant being most frequent or common (p. 232)

*predominante más frecuente o común (p. 232)

*prior happening before an event (p. 390)

*previo que sucede antes de un acontecimiento (p. 390)

prisoner of war a person captured in war (p. 333)

prisionero de guerra persona capturada durante una guerra (p. 333)

privateer privately owned ship licensed by the government to attack ships of other countries (p. 26)

buque corsario buque de propiedad privada autorizado por el gobierno para atacar a buques de otros países (p. 26)

*procedure a particular way of conducting or engaging in an activity (p. 1049)

*procedimiento método particular de llevar a cabo una actividad o participar en ella (p. 1049)

Glossary/Glosario

English	Español
*__prohibit__ to make illegal by an authority (p. 694)	*__prohibir__ cuando una autoridad dictamina que algo es ilegal (p. 694)
__prohibition__ laws banning the manufacture, transportation, and sale of alcoholic beverages (p. 527)	__prohibición__ leyes que prohibían la manufactura, transportación y venta de bebidas alcohólicas (p. 527)
*__promote__ to advance in station, rank, or honor (p. 341)	*__ascender__ progresar en puesto, rango u honor (p. 341)
__propaganda__ the spreading of ideas about an institution or individual for the purpose of influencing opinion (p. 552)	__propaganda__ diseminación de ideas sobre una institución o individuo con el propósito de influenciar la opinión (p. 552)
__proprietary colony__ a colony owned by an individual (p. 27)	__colonia propietaria__ colonia propiedad de un individuo (p. 27)
*__prospective__ to be likely to, or have intentions to, perform an act (p. 394)	*__potencial__ que hay probabilidades o se tienen intenciones de realizar una acción (p. 394)
__protective tariff__ tax on imports designed to protect American manufacturers (p. 189)	__arancel protectora__ impuesto en importaciones diseñado para proteger a los manufactureros americanos (p. 189)
__protectorate__ a country that is technically independent but is actually under the control of another country (p. 490)	__protectorado__ país que es técnicamente independiente pero que en realidad queda bajo el control de otro país (p. 490)
__public works__ projects such as highways, parks, and libraries built with public funds for public use (p. 640)	__obras públicas__ proyectos como carreteras, parques y bibliotecas construidos con fondos públicos para uso público (p. 640)
*__publish__ to make a document available to the general public (p. 461)	*__publicar__ hacer que un documento esté disponible para el público en general (p. 461)
__pueblo__ Spanish for *village;* term used by early Spanish explorers to denote large housing structures built by the Anasazi (p. 7)	__pueblo__ término usado por los primeros exploradores españoles para denotar grandes estructuras habitacionales construidas por los Anasazi (p. 7)
*__purchase__ to gain by paying money or its equivalent (p. 702)	*__comprar__ adquirir algo pagando dinero o su equivalente (p. 702)

R

English	Español
__racism__ prejudice or discrimination against someone because of his or her race (p. 870)	__racismo__ prejuicio o discriminación en contra de alguien por su raza (p. 870)
*__radical__ one whose political views, practices, or policies are considered extreme (p. 162)	*__radical__ aquél cuyas ideas, prácticas o normas políticas se consideran extremas (p. 162)
__rationalism__ philosophy that emphasizes the role of logic and reason in gaining knowledge (p. 45)	__racionalismo__ filosofía que enfatiza el papel de la lógica y la razón para obtener el conocimiento (p. 45)
*__rationality__ the quality or state of being agreeable to reason (p. 912)	*__racionalidad__ la cualidad o el estado de estar dispuesto a razonar (p. 912)
__reapportionment__ the method states use to draw up political districts based on changes in population (p. 828)	__nueva repartición__ método usado por los estados para formar distritos políticos basados en los cambios de población (p. 828)
__recall__ the right that enables voters to remove unsatisfactory elected officials from office (p. 523)	__elección de revocación__ derecho que permite a los votantes quitar del cargo a los oficiales elegidos que son inadecuados (p. 523)
__recession__ an economic slowdown (p. 102)	__recesión__ retraso económico (p. 102)
*__recovery__ an economic upturn, as after a depression (p. 670)	*__recuperación__ repunte económico, como sucede después de una depresión (p. 670)

referendum the practice of letting voters accept or reject measures proposed by the legislature (pp. 298, 523)

referéndum práctica de permitir a los votantes aceptar o rechazar medidas propuestas por la legislatura (pp. 298, 523)

***refinement** the act or process of improving or perfecting (p. 1003)

***refinamiento** acción o proceso de mejorar o perfeccionar (p. 1003)

refugee someone leaving his or her country due to a well-founded fear of persecution on account of race, religion, nationality, membership in a particular group, or political opinion (p. 1017)

refugiado persona que abandona su país debido a un miedo fundado de persecución a causa de su raza, religión, nacionalidad, pertenencia a un grupo en particular u opinión política (p. 1017)

***regime** a form of government (p. 688)

***régimen** una forma de gobierno (p. 688)

***register** to file personal information in order to become eligible for an official event (p. 859)

***inscribirse** presentar información personal con el fin de ser elegible para un evento oficial (p. 859)

***regulate** to govern or direct according to rule (p. 530)

***regular** gobernar o dirigir según las normas (p. 530)

***reinforcement** to strengthen by additional assistance, material, or support (p. 268)

***refuerzo** fortalecer mediante asistencia, materiales o apoyo adicional (p. 268)

***reliable** dependable; giving the same results on successive trials (p. 40)

***confiable** fiable, que da los mismos resultados en pruebas sucesivas (p. 40)

relief aid for the needy; welfare (p. 642)

asistencia pública ayuda para los necesitados; beneficencia (p. 642)

***relocate** to move to a new place (p. 398)

***trasladar** llevar a un nuevo lugar (p. 398)

***remove** to change the location or position (p. 835)

***quitar** cambiar la ubicación o posición (p. 835)

reparations payment by the losing country in a war to the winner for the damages caused by the war (p. 572)

indemnización pago hecho por el país perdedor de una guerra al país ganador por los daños causados por la guerra (p. 572)

repatriation being restored or returned to the country of origin, allegiance, or citizenship (p. 922)

repatriación acción de devolver o regresar a una persona a su país de origen, lealtad o ciudadanía (p. 922)

republic form of government in which power resides in a body of citizens entitled to vote (p. 86)

república forma de gobierno en el cual el poder reside en un cuerpo de ciudadanos con derecho al voto (p. 86)

***requirement** something essential to the existence or occurrence of something else (p. 362)

***requisito** algo fundamental para la existencia o acontecimiento del algo más (p. 362)

***resident** one who lives in a place for some length of time (p. 1018)

***residente** que vive en un lugar durante algún tiempo (p. 1018)

***resolution** a formal expression of opinion, will, or intent voted by an official body or assembly (p. 272)

***resolución** expresión formal de una opinión, deseo o intención votada por una asamblea u organismo oficial (p. 272)

***resolve** to come to an agreement (pp. 570, 1037)

***resolver** llegar a un acuerdo (pp. 570, 1037)

***resource** material used in the production process, such as money, people, land, wood, or steel (p. 410)

***recurso** material utilizado en el proceso de producción, como dinero, personas, tierra, madera o acero (p. 410)

***response** something said or done as a reaction (p. 787)

***respuesta** algo que se dice o hace en reacción a algo (p. 787)

***restraint** the act of limiting, restricting, or keeping under control (p. 430)

* **restricción** acción de limitar, impedir o mantener bajo control (p. 430)

***retain** to keep in possession (p. 995)

***retener** conservar la posesión (p. 995)

***revelation** an act of revealing to view or making known (p. 592)

***revelación** acción de divulgar para hacer ver o conocer (p. 592)

revenue sharing federal tax money that is distributed among the states (p. 936)

participación en los ingresos dinero de los impuestos federales que se distribuye entre los estados (p. 936)

English	Español
revenue tariff tax on imports for the purpose of raising money (p. 189)	**arancel de ingresos** impuesto en las importaciones con el propósito de recaudar dinero (p. 189)
***revise** to make changes to an original document (p. 702)	***revisar** realizar cambios a un documento original (p. 702)
revival large public meeting for preaching and prayer (p. 47)	**asamblea evangelista** reunión pública grande para predicar y rezar (p. 47)
***revolutionary** constituting or bringing about a major or fundamental change (p. 88)	***revolucionario** que constituye o provoca un cambio importante o esencial (p. 88)
right-to-work law a law making it illegal to require employees to join a union (p. 795)	**derecho a trabajar** ley que hace ilegal la demanda que los trabajadores se unan a un sindicato (p. 795)
rock 'n' roll popular music usually played on electronically amplified instruments and characterized by a persistent, heavily accented beat, much repetition of simple phrases, and often country, folk, and blues elements (p. 805)	**rock 'n' roll** música popular que generalmente se toca con instrumentos amplificados electrónicamente y se caracteriza por un ritmo persistente y pesadamente acentuado, muchas repeticiones de frases simples y a menudo elementos del Country, Folk y Blues (p. 805)
romanticism a literary, artistic, and philosophical movement in the 1700s emphasizing the imagination and the emotions, advocating feeling over reason, inner spirituality over external rules, the individual above society, and nature over environments created by humans (p. 234)	**romanticismo** movimiento literario, artístico, y filosófico del siglo XVIII que enfatizó la imaginación y las emociones, promoviendo el sentido en lugar de la razón, la espiritualidad interior en lugar de reglas externas, el individuo en lugar de la sociedad, y la naturaleza en lugar de medios ambientes credos por los humanos (p. 234)
***route** an established or selected course of travel or action (p. 15)	***ruta** curso de acción o viaje establecido o seleccionado (p. 15)

S

English	Español
safety net something that provides security against misfortune; specifically, government relief programs intended to protect against economic disaster (p. 673)	**red de seguridad** algo que proporciona seguridad en contra de desgracias, específicamente, programas de beneficencia gubernamentales para proteger en contra del desastre económico (p. 673)
satellite nations nations politically and economically dominated or controlled by another more powerful country (p. 765)	**países satélite** naciones política y económicamente dominadas o controladas por otro país más poderoso (p. 765)
scalawag name given to Southerners who supported Republican Reconstruction of the South (p. 366)	**scalawag** nombre dado a los sureños que apoyaron la Reconstrucción republicana del Sur (p. 366)
secede to leave or withdraw (p. 225)	**separarse** abandonar o retirar (p. 225)
secession withdrawal from the Union (p. 287)	**secesión** retiro de la Unión (p. 287)
secularize to transfer the use, possession, or control of something from church to civil authority (p. 261)	**secularizar** transferir el uso, la posesión o el control de algo de una iglesia a las autoridades civiles (p. 261)
***secure** free from risk of loss (p. 275)	***seguro** libre de riesgo de pérdida (p. 275)
sedition incitement to rebellion (p. 166)	**sedición** incitación a la rebelión (p. 166)
segregation the separation or isolation of a race, class, or group (p. 478)	**segregación** separación o aislamiento de una raza, clase o grupo (p. 478)
separate-but-equal doctrine established by the 1896 Supreme Court case *Plessy* v. *Ferguson* that permitted laws segregating African Americans as long as equal facilities were provided (p. 850)	**separados pero iguales** doctrina establecida por la Suprema Corte en el caso Plessy contra Ferguson en 1896 que las leyes que segregaron a los afroamericanos fueron permitidas si facilidades iguales fueron proporcionadas (p. 850)

separation of powers government principle in which power is divided among different branches (p. 108)

separación de poderes principio de gobierno en el cual el poder está dividido entre diferentes ramos (p. 108)

***series** a number of events that come one after another (p. 640)

***serie** acontecimientos que suceden uno después de otro (p. 640)

settlement house institution located in a poor neighborhood that provided numerous community services such as medical care, child care, libraries, and classes in English (p. 467)

casa de beneficencia institución establecida en una vecindad pobre que proveía numerosos servicios comunitarios tal como cuidado médico, cuidado de niños, bibliotecas, e instrucción en inglés (p. 467)

sharecropper farmer who works land for an owner who provides equipment and seed and receives a share of the crop (p. 377)

aparcero agricultor que labra la tierra para un dueño que proporciona equipo y semillas y recibe una porción de la cosecha (p. 377)

siege a military blockade of a city or fortified place to force it to surrender (p. 337)

sitio bloqueo militar de una ciudad o un recinto fortificado para forzarlo a rendirse (p. 337)

***significantly** to affect something enough to be of some importance (p. 1046)

***considerablemente** afectar algo lo suficiente como para que sea de importancia (p. 1046)

sin tax federal tax on alcohol and tobacco (p. 372)

impuesto pecadero impuesto federal sobre el alcohol y tabaco (p. 372)

sit-down strike method of boycotting work by sitting down at work and refusing to leave the establishment (p. 666)

huelga de brazos caídos método de boicotear el trabajo por medio de sentarse en el lugar de trabajo y de rehusar a abandonar el establecimiento (p. 666)

sit-in a form of protest involving occupying seats or sitting down on the floor of an establishment (p. 852)

plantón forma de protesta ocupando las sillas o sentándose en el piso de un establecimiento (p. 852)

skyscraper a very tall building (p. 450)

rascacielos edificio de gran altura (p. 450)

slave code a set of laws that formally regulated slavery and defined the relationship between enslaved Africans and free people (p. 44)

código de esclavos leyes aprobadas que regularon formalmente la esclavitud y definieron la relación entre los africanos esclavizados y la gente libre (p. 44)

smog fog made heavier and darker by smoke and chemical fumes (p. 959)

smog niebla hecha más pesada y oscura por el humo y vapores químicos (p. 959)

soap opera a serial drama on television or radio using melodramatic situations (p. 637)

novela drama en serie de radio o televisión utilizando situaciones melodramáticas (p. 637)

Social Darwinism based on Charles Darwin's theories of evolution and natural selection, states that humans have developed through competition and natural selection with only the strongest surviving (pp. 459, 528)

Darwinismo social se basa en las teorías de evolución y de selección natural de Charles Darwin y expresa que los humanos han evolucionado a través de la competencia y de la selección natural, donde sólo sobrevive el más fuerte (pp. 459, 528)

sodbuster a name given to Great Plains farmers (p. 396)

rompeterrón nombre dado a los granjeros de las Grandes Planicies (p. 396)

***source** the point at which something is provided (p. 606)

***fuente** punto en el que se proporciona algo (p. 606)

space race refers to the Cold War competition over dominance of space exploration capability (p. 832)

carrera espacial se refiere a la competencia durante la Guerra Fría sobre el dominio de la exploración espacial (p. 832)

speakeasy a place where alcoholic beverages are sold illegally (p. 609)

speakeasy lugar donde son vendidas clandestinamente bebidas alcohólicas (p. 609)

special prosecutor a lawyer from outside the government appointed by an attorney general or Congress to investigate a government official for misconduct while in office (p. 944)

fiscal especial un abogado externo al gobierno nombrado por un procurador general o congreso para investigar a un funcionario del gobierno por mala conducta durante sus funciones (p. 944)

***specific** restricted to a particular individual, situation, relation, or effect (p. 113)

***específico** limitado a un individuo, situación, relación o efecto particular (p. 113)

Glossary/Glosario

English	Español
speculation act of buying stocks at great risk with the anticipation that the price will rise (p. 629)	**especulación** acciones compradas con alto riesgo con la anticipación que los precios subirán (p. 629)
speculator person who risks money in hopes of a financial profit (p. 157)	**especulador** persona que arriesga dinero con la esperanza de obtener una ganancia financiera (p. 157)
sphere of influence section of a country where one foreign nation enjoys special rights and powers (p. 504)	**esfera de influencia** sección de un país donde una nación extranjera tiene derechos y poderes especiales (p. 504)
spoils system practice of handing out government jobs to supporters; replacing government employees with the winning candidate's supporters (p. 224)	**sistema de despojos** práctica de dar puestos gubernamentales a los partidarios; reemplazando a los empleados del gobierno con los partidarios del candidato victorioso (p. 224)
squatter someone who settles on public land under government regulation with the hopes of acquiring the title to the land (p. 254)	**colono usurpador** persona que se establece en tierras públicas bajo reglamento gubernamental con la esperanza de adquirir el título de propiedad (p. 254)
***stability** a state of peace; free from social unrest (p. 973)	***estabilidad** estado de paz, libre de inquietud social (p. 973)
stagflation persistent inflation combined with stagnant consumer demand and relatively high unemployment (p. 947)	**stagflación** inflación persistente combinado con la demanda estancada y una taza de desempleo alta (p. 947)
state-sponsored terrorism violent acts against civilians that are secretly supported by a government in order to attack other nations without going to war (p. 1039)	**terrorismo patrocinado por el estado** actos violentos en contra de civiles que son secretamente apoyados por un gobierno con el motivo de atacar a otras naciones sin entrar en la guerra (p. 1039)
steerage cramped quarters on a ship's lower decks for passengers paying the lowest fares (p. 443)	**tercera clase** cuarteles apretados de las cubiertas bajas de un barco para los pasajeros que pagan los pasajes más bajos (p. 443)
stock money or capital invested or available for investment or trading (p. 422)	**reserva** dinero o capital invertido o disponible para inversiones u operaciones comerciales (p. 422)
stock market a system for buying and selling stocks in corporations (p. 628)	**bolsa de valores** sistema para comprar y vender acciones de corporaciones (p. 628)
***strategic** necessary to or important in the initiation, conduct, or completion of a military plan (p. 885)	***estratégico** necesario o importante para iniciar, realizar o completar un plan militar (p. 885)
strategic defense a plan to develop missiles and other devices that can shoot down nuclear missiles before they hit the United States (p. 1035)	**defensa estratégica** plan para desarrollar proyectiles y otras armas que pueden derribar proyectiles nucleares antes de que estos golpeen en Estados Unidos (p. 1035)
strategic materials materials needed for fighting a war (p. 706)	**materiales estratégicos** materiales necesarios para una guerra (p. 706)
***strategy** a plan or method for achieving a goal (p. 472)	***estrategia** plan o método para alcanzar una meta (p. 472)
strike work stoppage by workers to force an employer to meet demands (p. 199)	**huelga** paro de trabajo por los trabajadores para forzar al empresario a satisfacer sus demandas (p. 199)
***structure** something that is composed or arranged into a unified whole, as a building or edifice (p. 346)	***estructura** algo compuesto o dispuesto como un todo unificado, como puede ser una construcción o edificio (p. 346)
***submit** to put forward for consideration or judgment (p. 73)	***presentar** presentar algo para consideración o fallo (p. 73)
***subordinate** one who is under the authority of a superior (p. 344)	***subordinado** aquél que está bajo la autoridad de un superior (p. 344)

***subsidy** money granted by the government to achieve a specific goal that is beneficial to society (p. 842)	***subsidio** dinero que otorga el gobierno para alcanzar una meta específica que beneficia a la sociedad (p. 842)
***substitute** to put or use in the place of another (p. 59)	***sustituto** colocar o utilizar en lugar de otro (p. 59)
subversion a systematic attempt to overthrow a government by using persons working secretly from within (p. 774)	**subversión** intento sistemático para derrocar un gobierno utilizando personas que trabajan secretamente desde adentro (p. 774)
***sufficient** enough, adequate (p. 316)	***suficiente** bastante, adecuado (p. 316)
suffrage the right to vote (pp. 223, 524)	**sufragio** derecho al voto (pp. 223, 524)
***sum** a specified amount of money (p. 631)	***suma** cantidad específica de dinero (p. 631)
summit a meeting of heads of government (p. 939)	**cumbre** junta de jefes de gobiernos (p. 939)
Sunbelt a new industrial region in southern California and the Deep South, developing during World War II (p. 730)	**Región Solada** nueva región industrial en el sur de California y el Bajo Sur que se desarrolló durante la Segunda Guerra Mundial (p. 730)
***supplement** an addition to something, meant to make it complete (p. 331)	***complemento** una adición a algo con la intención de completarlo (p. 331)
supply-side economics economic theory that lower taxes will boost the economy as businesses and individuals invest their money, thereby creating higher tax revenue (pp. 593, 976)	**economía de oferta teoría** económica de que los impuestos bajos levantarían la economía invirtiendo su dinero los negocios y los individuos, así creando un alto ingreso del impuesto (pp. 593, 976)
***survival** the continuation of life or existence (p. 286)	***supervivencia** continuación de la vida o existencia (p. 286)
***suspend** to temporarily stop an operation (p. 634)	***suspender** detener temporalmente una operación (p. 634)
***symbolize** to represent, express, or identify by a symbol (p. 618)	***simbolizar** representar, expresar o identificar por medio de un símbolo (p. 618)

T

***target** something or someone fired on or marked for attack (p. 726)	***objetivo** algo o alguien a quien se dispara o a quien se marca para atacar (p. 726)
task system a method of organizing enslaved labor wherein workers were given a specific set of jobs to accomplish every day, after which they were allowed to spend their time as they chose (p. 206)	**sistema de tareas** método de organización del trabajo esclavizado en el que se les asignaba a los trabajadores un conjunto de tareas para realizar cada día, y una vez finalizadas, eran libres de hacer lo que quisieran con su tiempo (p. 206)
teach-in an extended meeting or class held to discuss a social or political issue (p. 893)	**plantón educacional** junta o clase extendida para discutir un asunto político o social (p. 893)
***technique** a method of achieving a desired task (p. 637)	***técnica** método para lograr una tarea determinada (p. 637)
***technology** the result of an improvement on an old or existing idea (p. 6)	***tecnología** el resultado del avance de una idea antigua o ya existente (p. 6)
telecommute to work at home by means of an electronic linkup with a central office (p. 1003)	**viajar electrónicamente** trabajar en casa por medio de conexión electrónica con una oficina central (p. 1003)
televangelist an evangelist who conducts regularly televised religious programs (p. 973)	**televangelista** evangelista que transmite regularmente programas evangélicos por televisión (p. 973)
temperance moderation in or abstinence from alcohol (p. 238)	**templanza** moderación o abstinencia del uso del alcohol (p. 238)
tenant farmer farmer who works land owned by another and pays rent either in cash or crops (p. 377)	**granjero arrendatario** granjero que labra la tierra de un terrateniente y paga la renta ya sea con dinero efectivo o cosecha (p. 377)

English	Español
tenement multifamily apartments, usually dark, crowded, and barely meeting minimum living standards (p. 453)	**casa de vecindad** apartamentos para varias familias, normalmente obscuros, apretados que apenas cumplen con los estándares mínimos de viviendas (p. 453)
termination policy a government policy to bring Native Americans into mainstream society by withdrawing recognition of Native American groups as legal entities (p. 813)	**política de terminación** política gubernamental para traer a los Nativos Americanos dentro de la sociedad principal retirando el reconocimiento de los grupos Nativos Americanos como entidades legales (p. 813)
terrorism the use of violence by non-governmental groups against civilians to achieve a political goal by instilling fear and frightening governments into changing policies (p. 1038)	**terrorismo** el uso de violencia por grupos no del gobierno en contra de civiles para alcanzar una meta política impartiendo miedo y amenazando gobiernos para que cambien su política (p. 1038)
***theory** a hypothesis meant for argument or investigation (p. 947)	***teoría** hipótesis pensada para un argumento o investigación (p. 947)
time zone a geographical region in which the same standard time is kept (p. 419)	**huso horario** región geográfica en la cual la misma norma horaria es mantenida (p. 419)
town meeting a gathering of free men in a New England town to elect leaders, which developed into the local town government (p. 38)	**junta municipal** asamblea de hombres libres de un pueblo de Nueva Inglaterra para elegir líderes la cual desarrolló en gobierno local (p. 38)
trade union an organization of workers with the same trade or skill (p. 429)	**gremio** organización de trabajadores con el mismo oficio o destreza (p. 429)
***traditional** relating to cultural continuity in social attitudes, customs, and institutions (p. 885)	***tradicional** relativo a la continuidad cultural en las actitudes sociales, costumbres e instituciones (p. 885)
transcendentalism a philosophy stressing the relationship between human beings and nature, spiritual things over material things, and the importance of the individual conscience (p. 234)	**transcendentalismo** filosofía que acentúa la relación entre los seres humanos y la naturaleza, cosas espirituales sobre las materiales y la importancia de la conciencia del individuo (p. 234)
transcontinental railroad a railway system extending across the continent (p. 291)	**ferrocarril transcontinental** sistema de ferrocarril que se extiende a través del continente (p. 291)
***transport** to convey from one place to another (p. 693)	***transportar** llevar de un lugar a otro (p. 693)
***transportation** method of travel from one place to another (p. 194)	***transporte** método para viajar de un lugar a otro (p. 194)
triangular trade a three-way trade route for exchanging goods between the American colonies and two other trading partners (p. 38)	**comercio triangular** una ruta comercial de tres ramas para intercambiar productos entre las colonias americanas y otros dos asociados comerciales (p. 38)
tribute a payment by one ruler or nation to another in acknowledgment of submission or as the price of protection (p. 6)	**tributo** pago de un gobernante o país a otro en reconocimiento de la sumisión o como precio por la protección brindada (p. 6)
***trigger** to cause an action that causes a greater reaction (p. 455)	***desencadenar** provocar una acción que desencadena una reacción mayor (p. 455)
trust a combination of firms or corporations formed by a legal agreement, especially to reduce competition (p. 426)	**cártel** combinación de empresas o sociedades anónimas formada por acuerdo legal, especialmente para reducir la competición (p. 426)

U

*ultimately in the end, finally, or eventually (p. 263)

*última instancia al final, finalmente, o por último (p. 263)

*unconstitutional not in accordance with or authorized by the constitution of a state or society (p. 540)

inconstitucional que no está de acuerdo con la constitución de un estado o sociedad o no posee la autorización de ésta (p. 540)

unfair trade practices trading practices that derive a gain at the expense of the competition (p. 539)

prácticas comerciales injustas prácticas comerciales que ganan el beneficio perjudicando a la competencia (p. 539)

*unify to bring a group together with a similar goal or thought pattern (p. 613)

*unificar juntar a un grupo con un objetivo o patrones de pensamiento similares (p. 613)

union shop a business that requires employees to join a union (p. 795)

taller sindicalizado comercio que requiere que los trabajadores se unan al sindicato (p. 795)

*unresolved not cleared up, understandable, or dealt with successfully (p. 903)

*no resuelto no esclarecido, no comprensible o tratado con éxito (p. 903)

urban renewal government programs that attempt to eliminate poverty and revitalize urban areas (p. 811)

renovación urbana programas gubernamentales que intentan eliminar la pobreza y revitalizar las áreas urbanas (p. 811)

utopia community based on a vision of a perfect society sought by reformers (p. 234)

utopía comunidad basada en una visión de la sociedad perfecta buscada por los reformistas (p. 234)

V

vaquero men who herded cattle on haciendas (p. 262)

vaquero hombres que conducían el ganado en las haciendas (p. 262)

*vehicle a means of carrying or transporting something (p. 717)

*vehículo medio para llevar o transportar algo (p. 717)

vertical integration the combining of companies that supply equipment and services needed for a particular industry (p. 425)

integración vertical asociación de compañías que abastecen equipo y servicios necesarios a una industria particular (p. 425)

veto power of the chief executive to reject laws passed by the legislature (p. 109)

veto poder del jefe del ejecutivo de rechazar leyes aprobadas por la legislatura (p. 109)

*via to have come by way of or through (p. 984)

*vía haber llegado mediante o a través de (p. 984)

victory garden gardens planted by American citizens during war to raise vegetables for home use, leaving more for the troops (pp. 556, 735)

huerto de victoria huertos plantados por ciudadanos americanos durante la guerra para cultivar vegetales para usar en casa así dejando más para las tropas (pp. 556, 735)

victory suit a men's suit with no vest, no cuffs, a short jacket, and narrow lapels, worn during World War II in order to save fabric for the war effort (p. 732)

victory suit traje de hombre sin chaleco ni puños, con una chaqueta corta y solapas angostas que se vestía durante la Segunda Guerra Mundial para ahorrar tela para la guerra (p. 732)

Vietnamization the process of making South Vietnam assume more of the war effort by slowly withdrawing American troops from Vietnam (p. 898)

vietnamización el proceso de hacer que el Vietnam del Sur asumiera más de los esfuerzos de la guerra sacando poco a poco a las tropas americanas de Vietnam (p. 898)

vigilance committee group of ordinary citizens formed by local law enforcement officers whose goal is to find criminals and bring them to justice (p. 387)

comité de vigilancia grupo de ciudadanos comunes formado por funcionarios locales encargados del cumplimiento de la ley, que deben encontrar criminales y ponerlos a disposición de la justicia (p. 387)

*violation the disregard or breaking of the law (p. 688)

*violación ignorar o quebrantar la ley (p. 688)

*virtually almost entirely; nearly (p. 699)

*prácticamente casi por completo, por poco (p. 699)

*visible what can be seen (p. 979)

*visible lo que puede verse (p. 979)

English	Español
W	
war on poverty antipoverty program under President Lyndon Johnson (p. 839)	**guerra contra la pobreza** programa anti-pobreza bajo el Presidente Lyndon Johnson (p. 839)
weapons of mass destruction (WMD) weapons—including nuclear, chemical, and biological—that can kill large numbers of people all at once (p. 1044)	**armas de destrucción masiva (ADM)** armas, incluidas las nucleares, químicas y biológicas, que pueden matar una gran cantidad de personas a la vez (p. 1044)
***welfare** aid in the form of money or necessities for those in need, especially disadvantaged social groups (p. 936)	***asistencia social** ayuda en forma de dinero o necesidades para los necesitados; grupos sociales que se encuentran especialmente en desventaja (p. 936)
welfare capitalism system in which companies enable employees to buy stock, participate in profit sharing, and receive benefits such as medical care common in the 1920s (p. 602)	**capitalismo de beneficencia** sistema en el cual las compañías permiten a los trabajadores comprar acciones, compartir las ganancias, y recibir beneficios tal como atención médica, común en los años 1920 (p. 602)
white-collar jobs jobs in fields not requiring work clothes or protective clothing, such as sales (p. 802)	**collar blanco trabajos** trabajos que no requieren ropa de protección o de trabajo, asi como los vendedores (p. 802)
***widespread** having influence on or affecting a large group (p. 47); widely diffused or prevalent (p. 577)	***generalizar** influir sobre algo/alguien o afectar a un grupo numeroso (p. 577)
writ of assistance a search warrant enabling customs officers to enter any location to look for evidence of smuggling (p. 60)	**escrito de asistencia** documento legal que permitió a los oficiales aduanales entrar cualquier lugar en busca de evidencia de contrabando (p. 60)
Y	
yellow journalism type of sensational, biased, and often false reporting for the sake of attracting readers (p. 497)	**periodismo amarillista** tipo de reportaje sensacional, tendencioso, y a menudo falso con el propósito de atraer a los lectores (p. 497)
yeoman farmer owner of a small farm with four or fewer enslaved persons, and usually none (p. 205)	**terrateniente menor** dueño de una granja pequeña con cuatro o menos esclavos, normalmente ninguno (p. 205)
yuppie a young, college-educated adult who is employed in a well-paying profession and who lives and works in or near a large city (p. 982)	**yuppie** adulto joven educado en la universidad empleado en una profesión de buen salario y que vive y trabaja en o cerca de una ciudad grande (p. 982)
Z	
zoot suit men's clothing of extreme cut typically consisting of a thigh-length jacket with wide padded shoulders and peg pants with narrow cuffs (p. 732)	**zoot suit** vestimenta de hombre de corte extremo que consiste típicamente de una chaqueta a la altura de los muslos con hombreras anchas y pantalón pirata con bocamanga angosta (p. 732)

Index

Italicized page numbers refer to illustrations. The following abbreviations are used in the index: m = map; c = chart; p = photograph or picture; g = graph; crt = cartoon; ptg = painting; q = quote

A

Index

Index

C

E

I

J

Index

M

Index

O

P

Q

R

Index

Acknowledgments and Photo Credits

TEXT AND ART

20, 51 from *The Broken Spears* by Miguel Leon-Portilla. Copyright © 1962, 1990 by Miguel Leon-Portilla. Expanded and Updated Edition © 1992 by Miguel Leon-Portilla. Reprinted by permission of Beacon Press, Boston; **545** From *The Century* by Peter Jennings, copyright © 1998 by ABC Television Network Group, a division of Capitol Cities, Inc. Used by permission of Doubleday, a division of Random House, Inc.; **611** Reprinted with the permission of Scribner, an imprint of Simon & Schuster Adult Publishing Group, from *The Great Gatsby* by F. Scott Fitzgerald. Copyright 1925 by Charles Scribner's Sons. Copyright renewed 1953 by Frances Scott Fitzgerald Lanahan; Excerpt from Part I of "The Hollow Men" in *Collected Poems 1909-1962* by T.S. Eliot, copyright 1936 by Harcourt, Inc., and renewed 1964 by T.S. Eliot, reprinted by permission of the publisher; **617** Excerpt from *Dust Tracks on a Road* by Zora Neale Hurston. Copyright 1942 by Zora Neale Hurston, renewed © 1970 by John C. Hurston. Reprinted by permission of HarperCollins Publishers, "If we must die" by Claude McKay, courtesy of the Literary Representative for the Works of Claude McKay, Schomburg Center for Research in Black Culture, The New York Public Library, Astor, Lennox and Tilden Foundations, "I, Too" from *The Collected Poems of Langston Hughes* by Langston Hughes, edited by Arnold Rampersad with David Roessel, Associate Editor, copyright © 1994 by The Estate of Langston Hughes. Used by permission of Alfred A. Knopf, a division of Random House, Inc; **630** From *1929: the Year of the Great Crash* by William K. Klingman. Copyright © 1989 by William K. Klingman. Reprinted by permission of HarperCollins Publishers; **637** Excerpt from Dust to Eat: Drought and Depression in the 1930s by Michael L. Cooper. Copyright © 2004 by Michael L. Cooper. Reprinted by permission of Clarion Books, an imprint of Houghton Mifflin Company. All rights reserved; **660** "Gardiner C. Means" and "Raymond Moley" from *Hard Times* by Studs Terkel. Copyright © 1970, 1986 by Studs Terkel. Reprinted by permission of Donadio & Olson, Inc.; **677** Excerpt from *The Autobiography of Eleanor Roosevelt* by Eleanor Roosevelt. Copyright 1937, 1949, © 1958, 1961 by Anna Eleanor Roosevelt. Copyright © 1958 by Curtis Publishing Company. Reprinted by permission of HarperCollins Publishers; **695** from "Kristallnacht" by Frederic Morton. *The New York Times*, November 10, 1978. Copyright © 1978 The New York Times Company. Reprinted by permission; **701** "Luther D. Fletcher" from World War II: From the Battle Front to the Home Front, Arkansans Tell Their Stories, copyright © 1995 by Kay B. Hall. Reprinted by permission of the University of Arkansas Press; **847** "John Rath, 61" from *Division Street* by Studs Terkel. Copyright © 1967 by Studs Terkel. Reprinted by permission of Donadio & Olson, Inc.; **863 865** Reprinted by arrangement with The Heirs to the Estate of Martin Luther King Jr., c/o Writers house as agent for the proprietor New York, NY. Copyright 1963 Martin Luther King, Jr.; copyright renewed 1991 Coretta Scott King; **869** From *Coming of Age in Mississippi* by Anne Moody, copyright © 1968 by Anne Moody. Used by permission of Doubleday, a division of Random House, Inc.; **873** Copyright © 1971 by Merlin House, Inc./Seaver Books. Reprinted from *The End of White World Supremacy* by Malcolm X, edited by Imam Benjamin Karim. Published by Seaver Books, New York, New York; **912** from "The Times They Are A-Changin'" by Bob Dylan. Copyright © 1963; renewed 1991 Special Rider Music. All rights reserved. International copyright secured. Reprinted by permission; **915** From The Feminine Mystique by Betty Friedan. Copyright © 1983, 1974, 1973, 1963 by Betty Friedan. Used by permission of W.W. Norton & Company, Inc.; **1021** "The Tortilla Curtain," from *New Americans: An Oral History* by Al Santoli, copyright © 1988 by Al Santoli. Used by permission of Viking Penguin, a division of Penguin Group (USA) Inc.; **1029** from "A Grim Picture" by Tim Radford. *The Guardian*, November, 15, 2000. Copyright Guardian News & Media Ltd, 2000. Reprinted by permission; **R7** From "Why I'm Not Running for President" by Gloria Steinem, from the July 20, 1992 issue of *The Nation*. Reprinted by permission. For subscription information call 1-800-333-8536. Portions of each week's Nation magazine can be accessed at http://www.thenation.com; **R74** "The Camera Eye (50)" from *The Big Money*, copyright 1933, 1934, 1935, 1936 and © renewed 1963, 1964 by John Dos Passos. Reprinted by permission of Lucy Dos Passos Coggin; **R77** "Part Four – 1" from *On the Road* by Jack Kerouac, copyright © 1955, 1957 by Jack Kerouac; renewed © 1983 by Stella Kerouac, renewed © 1985 by Stella Kerouac and Jan Kerouac. Used by permission of Viking Penguin, a division of Penguin Group (USA) Inc.; **R80** From *On the Pulse of Morning* by Maya Angelou, copyright © 1993 by Maya Angelou. Used by permission of Random House, Inc.

Glencoe would like to acknowledge the artists and agencies that participated in illustrating this program: American Artists Reps Inc.; Deborah Wolfe Ltd/illustrationOnLine.com; GeoNova LLC.

PHOTO CREDITS

Abbreviation Key: BC: Bettmann/CORBIS; GI: Getty Images; LOC: Library of Congress

Cover (tl)Steve Schapiro, (tc)CORBIS, (tr)National Portrait Gallery, Smithsonian Institution/Art Resource, NY, (cl)New York Historical Society/Library of Congress, (c)Thomas E. Franklin/Bergen Record/GI, (cr)Carl Van Vechten/The Granger Collection, New York/Reprinted with permission of the Van Vechten Trust, (b)Collection of The Butler Institute of American Art, Youngstown, Ohio; **endsheet** (bl)photolibrary.com/Index Open, (bkgd)GI; **vi** (t)SuperStock, (b)Boltin Picture Library/Bridgeman Art Library; **vii** (t)S uperStock, (c)Bridgeman Art Library, (b)akg-images; **viii** (t)Painting by Don Troiani, www.historicalartprints.com, (c)Art Archive/Metropolitan Museum of Art New York/Laurie Platt Winfrey, (b)Minnesota Historical Society/CORBIS; **ix** (t)Lowell Georgia/CORBIS, (c)William Henry Jackson/Cardoza Fine Art Gallery, (b)CORBIS; **x** (t)Nagasaki Museum of History and Culture, (c)The Granger Collection, New York, (b)CORBIS; **xi** (t)Howard A. Thain/Collection of the New York Historical Society/Bridgeman Art Library, (c)Roger-Viollet/Topham/The Image Works, (b)BC; **xii** (t)Mary Evans Picture Library, (c)BC, (b)SuperStock; **xiii** (t)Wally McNamee/CORBIS, (c)Bob Adelman/Magnum Photos, (b)Larry Burrows/Time Life Pictures/GI; **xiv** (t)Eli Reed/Magnum Photos, (c)The White House/Handout/GI, (b)Brooks Kraft/CORBIS; **xxviii** (t)Owaki/Kulla/CORBIS, (b)Pierce Rafferty/Petrified Collection/GI; **xxix** (t)Dynamic Graphics Group/Creatas/Alamy Images, (b)Eric Foltz/iStockphoto; **A16** (t)ThinkStock/SuperStock, (cl)Janet Foster/Masterfile, (cr)Mark Tomalty/Masterfile, (bl)age fotostock/SuperStock, (br)Jurgen Freund/Nature Picture Library; **GH2** BananaStock/PictureQuest; **GH13** Copyright © 2008 by David W. Boles. All Rights Reserved; **GH16-1** Boltin Picture Library/Bridgeman Art Library; **2** (t)The Granger Collection, New York, (b)SuperStock; **2-3** BC; **3** (t)Stock Montage/GI, (b)Michael Nicholson/CORBIS; **5** (l)Alison Wright/The Image Works, (r)Neil Setchfield/GI; **6** (l)Art Archive/National Anthropological Museum Mexico/Dagli Orti, (r)Art Archive; **9** (tl)George Catlin/GI, (tr bl)The Granger Collection, New York, (br)Photograph courtesy of the Schwarz Gallery, Philadelphia; **12** (t) CORBIS, (c)PunchStock, (bl)C Squared Studios/GI, (br)Iconotec/Alamy Images; **13** (l to r, t to b)GI, (2)LOC, LC-USZ62-242, (3)Ingram Publishing/Alamy Images, (4)Brand X Pictures/PunchStock, (5)Artvillle/GI, (6)Alan and Sandy Carey/GI, (7)Dynamic Graphics Group/IT Stock Free/Alamy Images, (8) PunchStock, (9)PhotoAlto/GI, (10)CORBIS, (11)GI, (12)Image Source Pink/GI, (13)C Squared Studios/GI, (14)LOC, LC-USZ62-242, (15)Creativ Studio Heinemann/GI, (16)Alamy Images; **15** (l)National Maritime Museum, (c)CORBIS, (r)The British Museum/Topham-HIP/The Image Works; **17** Theodore de Bry/The Granger Collection, New York; **19** (l)The City of Plainfield, NJ, (r)The Granger Collection, New York; **21** (l)SuperStock, (r)Bibliotheque Nationale/Art Resource, NY; **22** Biblioteca Colombina, Sevilla; **25** (tl)Sheffield Galleries and Museums Trust, UK/Bridgeman Art Library, (tr)Adam Woolfitt/Robert Harding World Imagery/CORBIS, (b)National Maritime Museum, London; **26** (l)Stock Montage/GI, (r)Association for the Preservation of Virginia Antiquities; **28** Private Collection; **30** (l)Kean Collection/Getty Image, (r)Schlesinger Library, Radcliffe Institute, Harvard University/Bridgeman Art Library; **35** Hulton Archive/GI; **40** (l)Private Collection/Getty Image, (r)The Print Collector/Alamy Images; **44** The Granger Collection, New York; **45** (l)Ariadne Van Zandbergen/GI, (r)Bridgeman Art Library; **46** BC; **48** (t)Erich Lessing/Art Resource, NY, (c)Association for the Preservation of Virginia Antiquities, (b)Private Collection; **51** BC; **52** (l) MPI/GI, (r)Colonial Williamsburg; **52-53** SuperStock; **55** (t)LOC, LC-USZC4-5315, (b)LOC; **57** National Portrait Gallery, London; **58** The Granger Collection, New York; **59** Christopher J. Morris/CORBIS; **60** (tl)The

Granger Collection, New York, (tr)John Carter Brown Library, (b)BC; **62** The Granger Collection, New York; **63** LOC, LC-DIG-ppmsca-01657; **65 66 67** BC; **69** The Granger Collection, New York; **71** (l)National Portrait Gallery/SuperStock, (r)The Granger Collection, New York; **72** (tl)William Walcutt, Pulling Down the Statue of George III, 1857/Lafayette College Art Collection, Easton, Pennsylvania, (tr)BC, (b)The Granger Collection, New York; **79** North Wind Picture Archives; **81** (t)BC, (b)Yale University Art Gallery/Trumbull Collection; **83** Fraunces Tavern Museum, New York City; **84 87 89** The Granger Collection, New York; **90** (l)Courtesy of the Massachusetts Historical Society, (r)The Granger Collection, New York; **92** (t)Hulton Archive/GI, (c)SuperStock, (b)The Granger Collection, New York; **95** Picture History; **96** (t)Signing of the Constitution of the United States by Thomas Pritchard Rossiter. Gift of John Schermerhorn Jacobus, 1960. Collection of Fraunces Tavern® Museum, New York City, (b)Picture Research Consultants; **97** National Postal Museum, Smithsonian Institution; **102** (l)The Granger Collection, New York, (r)Geoffrey Clements/CORBIS; **105** The Granger Collection, New York; **107** (l)American School/Bridgeman Art Library/GI, (r)National Portrait Gallery, Smithsonian Institution/Art Resource, NY; **113** (l)LOC, LC-USZC4-4097, (r)Stock Montage/GI; **114** The Granger Collection, New York; **116** (t)LOC, LC-USZ62-59464, (c b)The Granger Collection, New York; **119** American Antiquarian Society; **121** Comstock/PunchStock; **125 127** Brooks Kraft/CORBIS; **130** John Aikins/CORBIS; **150-151** Winterthur Museum; **152** National Museum of American History/Smithsonian Institution; **152-153** SuperStock; **153** Mary Evans Picture Library; **156** MPI/GI; **157** (l)Art Archive/National Gallery of Art Washington/Laurie Platt Winfrey, (c)Huntington Library/SuperStock, (r)courtesy Winterthur Museum; **158** (l)Art Archive/National Gallery of Art Washington/LauriePlatt Winfrey, (r)Huntington Library/SuperStock; **163** LOC; **165** National Portrait Gallery, Smithsonian Institution/Art Resource, NY; **166** BC; **169** The Granger Collection, New York; **171** Stock Montage/GI; **172** The Granger Collection, New York; **177** (t)The Granger Collection, New York, (cl)LOC, LC-USZC4-782, (cr)Bridgeman Art Library, (b)BC; **180** Anne S.K. Brown, Brown Military Collection/Brown University Library; **182** (t)North Wind Picture Archives, (b)SuperStock **185** LOC, LC-USZC4-2711; **186 186-187** The Granger Collection, New York; **189** The Landis Valley Museum; **191 192** The Granger Collection, New York; **195** Hermann J. Meyer/akg-images; **196** (l)BC, (r)Underwood & Underwood/CORBIS; **197** (l)Eric Long/National Museum of American History, Smithsonian Institution, (c)Photographer Unknown/SSPL/The Image Works, (r)The Granger Collection, New York; **198** (l)American Textile History Museum, Lowell, MA, (r)The Granger Collection, New York; **200** SuperStock; **203** (l)Art Archive/Yale University New Haven/Laurie Platt Winfrey, (r)National Museum of American History, Smithsonian Institution; **204** CORBIS; **205** (tl)The Granger Collection, New York, (tr)Carl G. Von Iwonski/Yanaguana Society gift/Daughters of the Republic of Texas Library (SC96.009A), (b)BC; **206** Collection of The New York Historical Society (48169); **208** The Granger Collection, New York; **210** The New York Public Library; **211** (t)BC, (b)Missouri Historical Society, St. Louis; **214** The Granger Collection, New York; **216** (t)The Granger Collection, New York, (b)Christie's Images/SuperStock; **219** LOC, LC-USZ62-41838; **220** David R. Barker/Ohio Historical Society; **220-221** Bridgeman Art Library, BC; **223** (tl)Collection of the New York Historical Society/Bridgeman Art Library, (tr)Art Archive/Chateau de Blerancourt/Dagli Orti, (c)BC, (b)The Granger Collec-tion, New York; **224** The Granger Collection, New York; **225** (l)Monika Graff/The Image Works, (r)Gary I. Rothstein/Reuters/CORBIS; **227** Super-Stock; **228** (l)The Granger Collection, New York, (r)BC; **231** (t)The Granger Collection, New York, (c)Mark Sexton/The Bostonian Society, (b)Museum of the City of New York/CORBIS; **232** (l)Old Dartmouth Historical Society/New Bedford Whaling Museum, (r)Picture History; **233** The Granger Collection, New York; **234** BC; **237** CORBIS; **238** The Granger Collection, New York; **239** (l)The Granger Collection, New York, (r)Museum of the City of New York, Harry T. Peters Collection; **240** Art Archive/Culver Pictures/Napoleon Sarony; **243** (t)BC, (c)Massachusetts Historical Society, Boston/Bridgeman Art Library, (b)Schlesinger Library, Radcliffe Institute, Harvard University/Bridgeman Art Library; **244** (l)Collection of J. Paul Getty Museum, (r)The Granger Collection, New York; **245** BC; **246** CORBIS; **248**(t)Francis G. Mayer/CORBIS, (c b)The Granger Collection, New York; **251** The New York Historical Society; **252** Texas Department of Highways and Public Transportation; **252-253** akg-images; **255** Christie's Images/CORBIS; **256** Bridgeman Art Library; **262** Courtesy of The Bancroft Library/University of California, Berkeley, 1963.002:1350-FR; **266** Texas State Library and Archives Commission; **267** (tl)Center for American History/Barker Collection/University of Texas at Austin, (tr)Texas State Preservation Board, (b)Texas Department of Transportation; **268** (t)Eric Beggs/Texas State Library & Archive Commission, (b)Randy Faris/CORBIS; **271** (tl tc)The Granger Collection, New York, (tr)LOC, LC-USZ62-10802, (b)LOC, LC-USZ62-1277; **273** (l)White House Historical Association, (r)Library of Congress/GI; **274** LOC, LC-USZC4-9950; **276** (t)The Granger Collection, New York, (c)North Wind Picture Archives, (b)MPI/GI; **280-281** Painting by Don Troiani, www.historicalart-prints.com; **282** The Kansas State Historical Society, Topeka; **282-283** Art Archive/Metropolitan Museum of Art New York/Laurie Platt Winfrey; **283** Chicago Historical Society; **285** CORBIS; **286** (l)California State Library, Sacramento, (r)LOC, LC-DIG-cwpbh-01232; **286-287** (br)The Granger Collection, New York, (t)Bridgeman Art Library, (b)The Granger Collection, New York; **289** The Granger Collection, New York; **290** (l)Syracuse Newspapers/Dick Blume/The Image Works, (r)BC; **292** CORBIS; **295** (t)LOC, LC-USZ62-92049, (b)LOC, LC-USZ62-92031; **297** (l)LOC, LC-USZ62-79305, (r)The Supreme Court of the United States Office of the Curator, #1991.402.2; **299** Picture History; **300** LOC, LC-USZ62-2890; **303** Steve Laschever/Museum of American Political Life; **304** (l)BC, (c r)The Granger Collection, New York; **305** (l)Bridgeman Art Library, (c)Henry Horner Lincoln Collection, (r)Art Archive/Culver Pictures; **306** The Granger Collection, New York; **308** (tl)Picture History, (tr)BC, (c)Library of Congress/Bridgeman Art Library, (b)The Granger Collection, New York; **311** LOC, LC-USZC4-7997; **312** Museum of the Confederacy; **312-313** Minnesota Historical Society/CORBIS; **313** LOC, LC-DIG-cwpb-06233; **315** (l)Medford Historical Society Collection/CORBIS, (r)BC; **317** (l)LOC, LCUSZ62-42025, (r)LOC, LC-USZ62-132934; **318** (tl)Collection of David & Kevin Kyle/Picture Research Consultants, (tc)Military & Historical Image Bank/Don Troiani, (tr)Medford Historical Society Collection/CORBIS, (b)War Department/National Archives/Time Life Pictures/GI; **321** (l)LOC, LC-USZC4-708, (r)LOC, LC-USZC2-2124; **322** (t)LOC, LC-USZC4-1910, (b)CORBIS; **323** G.H. Suydam Collection, Mss. 1394, Louisiana and Lower Mississippi Valley Collections, LSU Libraries, Baton Rouge, La.; **325** (t)CORBIS, (b)LOC, LC-USZ62-66616; **326** (tl)LOC, LC-USZC4-1768, (tr b)BC; **329** (tl)CORBIS, (tr b) BC; **330** (l)BC, (r)CORBIS; **331** LOC, LC-USZC4-507; **332** (tl)LOC, LC-USZC4-4582, (tr)LOC, LC-DIG-cwpb-01195, (b)CORBIS; **334** LOC, LC-USZ62-100066; **335** LOC, LC-USZC4-1425; **337** (l)LOC, LC-USZC4-1754, (r)US Naval Academy Museum/Beverly R. Robinson Collection/US Naval Historical Center; **338** BC; **339** CORBIS; **340** (l)Hulton-Deutsch Collection/CORBIS, (r)LOC, LC-DIG-cwpb-04402; **345** CORBIS; **346** (t)LOC, LC-DIG-cwpb-02226, (b)BC; **348** (l)BC, (r)The Granger Collection, New York; **350** (tl)The Granger Collection, New York, (tr)Bridgeman Art Library, (cl)CORBIS, (cr)Kunstler Enterprises, Ltd., (bl)LOC, LC-USZC4-1519, (br)Picture History; **353** LOC, LC-USZ62-132749; **354-355** Art Archive/National Archives, Washington DC, (t)LOC, (b)Art Archive/Musee d'Orsay Paris/Dagli Orti; **357** (t)CORBIS, (cl)Art Archive/National Archives, Washington DC, (cr)LOC, LC-USZ62-128709, (b)LOC, LC-DIG-ppmsca-05704; **359** (l)CORBIS, (r)Cook Collection/Valentine Museum; **361** (tl)Flip Schulke/CORBIS, (tc)Flip Schulke/Black Star, (tr)AP Images, (b)BC; **367** (tl)The Granger Collection, New York, (tr b)The Granger Collection, New York; **368** (l)Mother Bethel African Methodist Episcopal Church/Scurlock Records, Archives Center, National Museum of American History, Smithsonian Institution, (r)The Granger Collection, New York; **369** Patrick Zachmann/Magnum Photos; **370** (l br)The Granger Collection, New York, (tr)Dallas Historical Society/Bridgeman Art Library; **373** (t)LOC, LC-USZC4-8345, (b)LOC; **374** (l)SuperStock, (r)Art Archive/Culver Pictures; **374-375** LOC, LC-USZC4-2623; **376** CORBIS; **378** (t)Picture History, (b)CORBIS; **381** LOC, LC-USZC4-5606; **382-383** William Henry Jackson/Cardoza Fine Art Gallery; **384** The Granger Collection, New York; **384-385** Lowell Georgia/CORBIS; **388** LOC, LC-USZ62-9889; **389** (t)Calvin Larsen/Photo Researchers, (b)Scott T. Smith/CORBIS; **391** BC; **392** (l)Art Archive/Bill Manns, (r)GI; **395** Minnesota Historical Society/CORBIS; **396** (l)State Historical Society of Wisconsin, (r)akg-images; **401** (l)GI, (r)CORBIS; **402** (l)CORBIS, (r)The Granger Collection, New York; **404** (t b)The Granger Collection, New York, (c)CORBIS; **408** National Railway Museum/Science & Society Museum; **408-409** LOC, LC-USZ62-77541; **412** (t)Mary Evans Picture Library, (bl)The Granger Collection, New York, (bcl)Time Life Pictures/GI, (bcr)BC, (br)Schenectady Museum; Hall of Electrical History Foundation/CORBIS; **413** (tl)BC, (tr)Mary Evans Picture Library, (b)George Eastman House **414** (l)LOC, LC-USZ62-99122, (r)LOC, LC-USZ62-99407; **417** (tl)Union Pacific Museum, (tr)Private Collection, Peter Newark American Pictures/Bridgeman Art Library, (bl)GI, (bc)Union Pacific Museum, (br)BC; **420** GI; **423** BC; **426** (l)SuperStock, (r)CORBIS; **429** (tbl)

CORBIS, (br)Hulton Archive/Getty Images; **434** CORBIS **436** (t)Union Pacific Museum, (c)CORBIS, (b)Hulton Archive/GI; **439** Stock Montage/ Hulton Archive/GI; **440-441** CORBIS; **441** (l)Shore Line Trolley Museum Library, Sprague Collection, (r)London Stereoscopic Company/ GI; **444** (l)Michael Maslan Historic Photographs/CORBIS, (c)The Granger Collection, New York, (r)Art Archive/Culver Pictures; **446** The Granger Collection, New York; **448** (t)Picture Research Consultants, (b)Brown Brothers; **449** OSU Cartoon Research Library **451** (l)CORBIS, (c)LOC, LC-USZ62-54088, (r)Museum of the City of New York/CORBIS; **452** Hulton-Deutsch Collection/CORBIS; **453** (l)CORBIS, (c)The Granger Collection, New York, (r)BC; **454** The Granger Collection, New York; **459** (l)LOC, LC-USZ62-15566, (r)Frank & Marie Wood/The Picture Bank; **460** Geofferey Clements/CORBIS; **461** Museum of Art, Rhode Island School of Design; Jesse Metcalf and Walter H. Kimball Funds; **463** (l)The Granger Collection, New York, (r)GI; **465** (l)CORBIS, (r)Duke University; **466** (l)The Granger Collection, New York, (r)AP Images; **471** The Everett Collection; **472** The Granger Collection, New York; **474** (l)GI, (c r)CORBIS; **477** The Granger Collection, New York; **479** Snark/Art Resource, NY; **480** Brown Brothers; **482** (t)Brown Brothers, (c)Picture Research Consultants, (b)Lewis W. Hine/George Eastman House/GI; **485** Picture Research Consultants; **486-487** Franklin D Roosevelt Library; **488-489** CORBIS; **491** (t)CORBIS, (b)The Mariners' Museum/CORBIS; **493** (l)Nagasaki Museum of History and Culture, (r)James G. Evans/Chicago History Museum (1932.21); **494** (l)Hawaii State Archives, (r)The Granger Collection, New York; **497** (tl)LOC, LC-USZ62-99767, (tr)The Granger Collection, New York, (b)Kurz & Allison/The Granger Collection, New York; **498** BC; **499** (l)Hult on Archive/GI, (r)LOC; **501** (l)LOC, LC-USZ62-62631, (r)GI; **502** (l)LOC, LC-USZC4-5392, (r)LOC, LC-USZ62-91465; **505** The Granger Collection, New York; **506** BC; **507** Koichi Kamoshida/GI; **510** The Granger Collection, New York; **513** Morton Beebe/CORBIS; **514** (t)BC, (c b)Time Life Pictures/GI; **517** CORBIS; **518** (t)Museum of the City of New York Print Archives, (b)Key Color/Index Stock Imagery; **518-519** Jessie Beals/ Schlesinger Library, Radcliffe Institute, Harvard University/Bridgeman Art Library; **521** (t)BC, (b)Hulton-Deutsch Collection/CORBIS; **522-523** LOC, LC-USZ62-56437; **524** (t)LOC, LC-USZ62-46713, (bl)LOC, LC-USZ62-106109, (br)LOC, LC-ISZ62-28195; **525** BC; **526** (l)Keystone/GI, (r)UNITE HERE Archives, Kheel Center, Cornell University; **529** LOC, LC-USZC4-434; **531** The Granger Collection, New York; **533** (l)BC, (r)The Granger Collection, New York; **534** CORBIS; **537** (t)CORBIS, (b)The Granger Collection, New York; **540** (t)Underwood & Underwood/CORBIS, (b)BC; **542** (t)BC, (c)LOC, LC-USZ62-83858, (b)CORBIS; **545** LOC, LC-USZC4-6425; **546** (t)The Mariners' Museum/CORBIS, (b)BC; **546-547** BC; **547** BC; **550** (l)CORBIS, (c r)BC; **551** BC; **553** (l)LOC, LC-DIG-ggbain-05650, (r)CORBIS; **554** (t b)BC, (c)CORBIS; **557** (l)BC, (c)Swim Ink 2, LLC/ CORBIS, (r)K.J. Historical/CORBIS; **559** BC; **560** (l)LOC, LC-USZ62-116442, (r)LOC, LC-USZC4-2426; **562** (t)LOC, LC-USZC4-1539, (b)LOC, LC-USZC4-9928; **563** LOC, LC-USZC4-9861; **566** (l)Australian War Memorial Negative Number, E00921, (r)Hulton-Deutsch Collection/ CORBIS; **567 569** BC; **572** (l)By Permission of the Marcus Family, (r)Library of Congress/© 1919, The Washington Post. Reprinted with permission; **577** Underwood & Underwood/CORBIS; **578** Brown Brothers; **579** Neville Elder/CORBIS; **580** (l cr)White House Historical Association, (cl)Underwood & Underwood/CORBIS, (r)CORBIS; **582** (t)BC, (c b)CORBIS; **585** Chicago Tribune; **586-587** Howard A. Thain/Collection of the New York Historical Society/Bridgeman Art Library; **588** CORBIS; **588-589** Roger-Viollet/Topham/The Image Works; **589** National Air and Space Museum/Smithsonian Institution; **591 592** The Granger Collection, New York; **597** (tl)Hirz/GI, (tr)FPG/Hulton Archive/GI, (cl)Hulton Archive/GI, (cr)Topham/The Image Works, (bl)FPG/GI, (br)The Granger Collection, New York; **598** (l to r)Hulton Archive/GI, (2)The Image Works, (3)SSPL/The Image Works, (4)Ohio Historical Society; **599** (tl)Mary Evans Picture Library, (tr)LOC, LC-USZ62-119950, (c)Huntington Library/ SuperStock, (b)Minnesota Historical Society; **600** The Granger Collection, New York; **601** (l)Frank & Marie-Therese Wood, (r)The Granger Collection, New York; **602** Hulton Archive/GI; **605** (l)BC, (r)LOC, LC-USZ62-52584; **606** Underwood & Underwood/CORBIS; **607** (l)Mary Evans Picture Library, (r)Columbus Dispatch/Ohio Historical Society; **608** (l)Library Of Congress/GI, (r)CORBIS; **611** Francis G. Mayer/CORBIS; **612** (tl)Culver Pictures/SuperStock, (tc)National Archives, (tr)Art Archive/Culver Pictures, (b)The Kobal Collection; **617** (tl)Carl Van Vechten/The Granger Collection, New York/Reprinted with permission of the Van Vechten Trust, (tr b)The Granger Collection, New York; **618** (l)Art Archive/Culver Pictures, (r b)Frank Driggs Collection/GI; **619** (l)Frank Driggs Collection/GI, (c)Sasha/ GI, (r)Underwood & Underwood/CORBIS; **622** (t)Mary Evans Picture Library, (c)Frank Driggs Collection/GI, (b)General Photographic Agency/ GI **625** Library of Congress/© 1925, The Washington Post. Reprinted with permission; **626-627** BC; **627** BC; **629** (l)The Granger Collection, New York, (r)LOC, LC-USZ62-24155; **630** Hulton-Deutsch Collection/ CORBIS; **631** (l)BC, (r)American Stock/GI; **635** (l)Chicago History Museum, (r)Hulton Archive/GI; **636** (l)BC, (r)Margaret Bourke-White/Time Life Pictures/GI; **639** Russell Lee/CORBIS; **641** (l)The Granger Collection, New York, (r)GI; **642** (tl)BC, (tr)AP Images, (b)Picture History; **644** (t)Mary Evans Picture Library, (c)BC, (b)Scherl/SVBilderdienst/The Image Works; **647** John T. McCutcheon/The Granger Collection, New York; **648** (t)CORBIS, (b)akg-images; **648-649** BC; **649** BC; **651** Underwood & Underwood/CORBIS; **653** BC; **654** (tl)Picture History, (tr)LOC, LC-USF34-032948-D, (b)MPI/GI; **655** (tl)B, (tr)Underwood & Underwood/ CORBIS, (b)BC; **657** (l)Tom Brakefield/GI, (r)CORBIS; **658** The Granger Collection, New York; **660** The Granger Collection, New York; **661** (l)LOC, LC-DIG-ppmsca-12896, (r)The Granger Collection, New York; **663** (l c)BC, (r)The Granger Collection, New York; **665** (l)The Granger Collection, New York, (r)CORBIS; **666 669** BC; **671** The Granger Collection, New York; **672** (tl)BC, (tr)courtesy FDIC, (b)courtesy FHA; **674** (t)Underwood & Underwood/CORBIS, (c)U.S. Forest Servic, (b)BC; **677 678-679** The Granger Collection, New York; **680** Keystone/GI; **680-681** Mary Evans Picture Library; **681** (t)United States Holocaust Memorial Museum, (b)LOC, LC-USZ62-89348; **685** (t)Art Archive/Reina Sofia Museum, Madrid, (b)BC; **686** BC; **689** CORBIS; **691** (l c)BC, (r)The Granger Collection, New York; **692** (tl)Art Archive, (tr b)BC; **695** Mary Evans Picture Library, (bkgd)Roger Foley; **696** (l)Yivo Institute for Jewish Research, (r)Yad Vashem Photo Archives, courtesy of USHMM; **696-697** Roger Foley; **697** (l)AFP/GI, (r) National Archives: Suitland, courtesy of USHMM; **698 700** USHMM; **701** (l)USHMM, (r)By Permission of Alexandre Oler, the son of the Artist. Nice, France; **703** (l)The Granger Collection, New York, (r)LOC, LC-USZ62-52601; **704** SuperStock; **706** (t)CORBIS, (b)MPI/GI; **708** The Granger Collection, New York; **711** Chicago History Museum; **712 712-713** BC; **713** CORBIS; **715** BC; **716** GI; **718** BC; **719** (l)US Army Photo, (r)BC; **720** (l)Peter Stackpole/Time Life Pictures/GI, (r)CORBIS; **723** CORBIS; **725** Art Archive/National Archives Washington, DC; **726** (t)CORBIS, (b)Art Archive; **729** (l)LOC, LC-DIG-fsac-1a34953, (c)GI, (r)CORBIS; **730-731** John Vachon/Anthony Potter Collection/GI; **733** GI; **734** (l)United Artists/The Kobal Collection, (c)Walt Disney Pictures/The Kobal Collection;**734** (r)CORBIS; **738** (t)BC, (bl)CORBIS, (br)GI; **739** (t)Art Archive, (b)ullstein bild/The Granger Collection, New York; **740-741 742** CORBIS; **748** Digital Stock/ CORBIS; **749** (tl b)CORBIS, (tr)Naval Historical Foundation; **751** (l)Art Archive/Culver Pictures, (r)GI;**752** CORBIS; **754** (l)LOC, LC-DIG-fsac-1a35223, (r)Digital Stock/CORBIS; **757** Dr. Seuss Collection/Mandeville Special Collections Library/University of California, San Diego; **758** (t)BC, (b)Picture Research Consultants; **758-759** BC; **759** Smithsonian Institution; **761** The Granger Collection, New York; **763** (l)BC, (r)Hulton-Deutsch Collection/CORBIS; **767** GI; **769** Time Life Pictures/ GI; **771** BC; **772** The Granger Collection, New York; **775** CORBIS; **777** (l) Weber and Beyer/CORBIS, (r)The Granger Collection, New York; **779** BC; **780** (t)LOC, LC-USZC4-4431, (c b)BC; **783** (l c)CORBIS, (r)U.S. Air Force Photo; **784** (tl)NSSDC/NASA, (tr)The Granger Collection, New York, (bl)BC, (br)Donald Uhbrock/Time Life Pictures/GI; **786** (tl)NASA Dryden Flight Research Center, (tr)Time Life Pictures/GI, (b)CORBIS; **788** (t)Picture Research Consultants, (b)BC; **791** Ross Lewis Milwaukee Public Library; **792** (t)FPG, (b)CORBIS; **792-793** SuperStock; **793** Natural Museum of American History/Smithsonian Institution; **795** (l)GI, (r)CORBIS; **797** CORBIS; **798** (tl)Masterfile, (tr)Time Life Pictures/GI, (bl)J R Eyerman/Time Life Pictures/GI, (br)Marvin Koner/CORBIS; **801** (l)Time Life Pictures/GI, (r)CORBIS; **803** BC; **804** (l)BC, (c)National Museum of American History/Smithsonian Institution, (r)The Kobal Collection; **806** (tl) Brown Brothers, (tr br)Michael Ochs Archives/CORBIS, (c)Photofest, (bl)BC; **811** (tl tr)Time Life Pictures/GI, (b)AP Images; **812** BC; **813** Thomas Hoepker/Magnum Photos; **814** National Archives; **816** (t)SuperStock, (b)Time Life Pictures/GI; **819** B. Wiseman/from Hey, Can't You Forget Business? by Charles Preston, ©1953, E.P. Dutton & Co., Inc.; **820-821** Wally McNamee/CORBIS; **822** (tl)Art Resource, (tc)GI, (tr b)AP Images; **822-823** Time Life Pictures/GI; **825 827** BC; **831** George Silk/Time Life Pictures/GI; **832** (l)GI, (c)CORBIS SYGMA, (r)CORBIS; **833** (l)CORBIS SYGMA, (c)BC, (cr r)CORBIS; **834** (tl)Rene Burri/Magnum Photos, (tr)AP Images, (b)Carl Mydans/Time Life Pictures/GI; **839** (l)John Dominis/Time Life Pictures/GI, (r)CORBIS; **840** Americorps VISTA Archives; **841** Corporation photo by Peter Shifter, Office of Public Affairs/ AmeriCorps; **844** (t)Ameri-Corps Archive, (c)Carl Mydans/Time Life

Pictures/GI, (b)Flip Schulke/Black Star; **847** A 1965 Herblock Cartoon, copyright by The Herb Block Foundation; **848** (l)Carl Iwaski/Time Life Pictures/GI, (r)Art Resource, NY; **848-849** Bob Adelman/Magnum Photos; **849** Collection of Janice L. and David J. Frent; **851** Time Life Pictures/GI; **853** Carl Iwasaki/Time Life Pictures/GI; **855** (t br)Don Craven/Time Life Pictures/GI, (bl) Flip Schulke/CORBIS; **856** CORBIS; **859** (l)CORBIS, (r)AP Images; **860** (t br)BC, (bl)Don Craven/Time Life Pictures/GI; **861** (tl)Charles Moore 1963/Black Star, (tr)Steve Schapiro, (b)BC; **863** Bill Hudson/AP Images; **865** Francis Miller/Time Life Pictures/GI; **866** Flip Schulke/CORBIS; **868** Eve Arnold/Magnum Photos; **869** The Everett Collection; **871** (l)Atlanta Constitution, 1964, Clifford H. "Baldy" Baldowski Editorial Cartoons. Courtesy of the Richard B. Russell Library for Political Research and Studies, The University of Georgia Libraries, (r)A 1967 Herblock Cartoon, copyright by The Herb Block Foundation; **873** (l)Robert Parent/Time Life Pictures/GI, (c)AP Images, (r)Flip Schulke/CORBIS; **876** (t)Carl Iwasaki/Time Life Pictures/GI, (c)Francis Miller/Time Life Pictures/GI, (b)Flip Schulke/CORBIS; **879** Jon Kennedy/Arkansas Democrat-Gazette; **880** (t)Art Resource, NY, (b)Naval Historical Foundation; **880-881** Larry Burrows/Time Life Pictures/GI; **884** (tl)BC, (tr)AFP/GI, (b)AP Images; **887** (l)POPPERFOTO/Alamy Images, (r)CORBIS; **888** (t)MPI/GI, (b)Larry Burrows/Time Life Pictures/GI; **891** (l)BC, (r)AP Images; **893** (l)Library of Congress/Tom Francis Darcy, Newsday/Reprinted with permission from LA Times Reprints, (r)Atlanta Constitution, Oct. 18, 1965, Clifford H. "Baldy" Baldowski Editorial Cartoons. Courtesy of the Richard B. Russell Library for Political Research and Studies, The University of Georgia Libraries; **894** (l) Bernard Gotfryd/GI, (c)Hulton Archive/GI, (r)Paul Fusco/Magnum Photos; **896** (tl)Bob Gomel/Time Life Pictures/GI, (tc)CORBIS, (tr c)BC, (b)Bernard Gotfryd/GI; **899** (l)John Filo, (c)David Kennerly/BC, (r)Dirck Halstead/Time Life Pictures/GI; **901** (l)BC, (c)The Granger Collection, New York, (r)Time Life Pictures/GI; **902** (l)Alex Wong/GI, (r)Sal Veder/AP Images; **904** (t)AP Images, (c)Art Archive/Dept Defence Washington, (b)Wally McNamee/CORBIS; **907** The Granger Collection, New York; **908** (l)Art Resource, NY, (r)Charles Gatewood/The Image Works; **908-909** Take Stock; **909** AP Images; **911** BC; **912** (l)Vince Streano/CORBIS, (r)Andrew DeLory/Hulton Archive/GI; **915** (l)BC, (r)Charles Gatewood/The Image Works; **917** AP Images; **918** BC; **921** CORBIS; **922** LOC, LC-USF33-012870-M5; **923** (l)CORBIS, (r)Jim Sugar/CORBIS; **924** Arthur Schatz/Time Life Pictures/GI; **926** (t c)BC, (b)Steve Northup/Time Life Pictures/GI; **929** Jack Knox Estate/OSU Cartoon Research Library; **930-931** Michael Goldman/Master-file; **932** (l)Hulton Archive/GI, (r)BC; **932-933** AP Images, Tom Ebenhoh/Black Star; **935** (l)A 1968 Herblock Cartoon, copyright by The Herb Block Foundation, (r)Atlanta Constitution, 1968 Oct. 17, Clifford H. "Baldy" Baldowski Editorial Cartoons. Courtesy of the Richard B. Russell Library for Political Research and Studies, The University of Georgia Libraries; **937** (l)BC, (r)Time Life Pictures/GI; **938** (t)Dirck Halstead/Liasion/GI, (b)AFP/GI; **941** (tl)Adam Woolfitt/CORBIS, (tcl)Dennis Brack/Black Star, (tc tcr b)BC, (tr)Robert Maass/CORBIS; **943** Mark Godfrey/The Image Works; **944** (l)A 1973 Herblock Cartoon, copyright by The Herb Block Foundation, (r)Atlanta Constitution, 1973, Clifford H. "Baldy" Baldowski Editorial Cartoons. Courtesy of the Richard B. Russell Library for Political Research and Studies, The University of Georgia Libraries; **947** (l)Jason Laure/Woodfin Camp/Time Life Pictures/GI, (c r)BC; **949** (l)Brown Brothers, (r)Karl Schumacher/Time Life Pictures/GI; **950** (tl)David Rubinger/CORBIS, (tr)M. Lipschitz/AP Images, (bl)MPI/GI, (br)Sergio Gaudenti/Kipa/CORBIS; **953** (l)AP Images, (r)Scherl/SV-Bilderndienst/The Image Works; **954** (l)PA/Topham/The Image Works, (r)Charles Gatewood/The Image Works; **956** (l)Wally McNamee/CORBIS, (c)Ed Kashi/CORBIS, (r)Brand X/SuperStock; **959** (l c)BC, (r)Charles E. Rotkin/CORBIS; **960** (l)A 1975 Herblock Cartoon, copyright by The Herb Block Foundation, (r)Hulton Archive/GI; **962** (t)Charles Gatewood/The Image Works, (c)BC, (b)Julian Wasser/Time Life Pictures/GI; **965** Ranan R. Lurie, Cartoonews International Syndicate, New York City; **966** (t)AP Images, (b)Peter Turnley/CORBIS; **966-967** Eli Reed/Magnum Photos; **967** Lana Harris/AP Images; **969** (l)Gary McCoy/Cagle Cartoons, (r)Chris Slane/Cagle Cartoons; **972** (t)Index Stock Imagery, (bl)Cynthia Johnson/Time Life Pictures/GI, (bc)Annie Griffiths Belt/CORBIS, (br)Joe Raedle/Newsmakers/GI; **975** (t)Atlanta Constitution, 1976 Apr. 6, Clifford H. "Baldy" Baldowski Editorial Cartoons. Courtesy of the Richard B. Russell Library for Political Research and Studies, The University of Georgia Libraries, (b)Atlanta Constitution, 1981 Oct. 18, Clifford H. "Baldy" Baldowski Editorial Cartoons. Courtesy of the Richard B. Russell Library for Political Research and Studies, The University of Georgia Libraries; **977** (l)Wally McNamee/CORBIS, (r)Roger Ressmeyer/CORBIS; **978** (tl)Wally McNamee/CORBIS, (tr)Bob Daughtery/AP Images, (b)BC; **980** (tl)Robert Nickelsberg/Time Life Pictures/GI, (tr)Dirck Halstead/Time Life Pictures/GI, (b) CORBIS; **983** (l)Eli Reichman/Time Life Pictures/GI, (r)Bob Krist/CORBIS; **984** NASA/AP Images; **985** (inset)Blue Origin, (bkgd)HANDOUT/epa/CORBIS; **986** BC; **988** AP Images; **991** (l)Stephen Ferry/Liasion/GI, (r)Diane-Lu Hovasse/AFP/GI; **992** Thomas Hartwell/Time Life Pictures/GI; **994** (tl)Owen Franken/CORBIS, (tr)Markowitz Jeffrey/CORBIS SYGMA, (c)Wally McNamee/CORBIS, (b)Mike Lane/Cagle Cartoons; **996** (t)Tony Korody/Time Life Pictures/GI, (c)BC, (b)Alain Nogues/CORBIS SYGMA; **999** LOC, LC-DIG-ppmsc-07960; **1000** (tl)Roger Ressmeyer/CORBIS, (tr)Spec. Robert Elliott/CORBIS, (b)David Brauchli/Reuters/CORBIS; **1000-1001** The White House/Handout/GI; **1003** (tl)Ed Young/CORBIS, (tr)Douglas Engelbart/Bootstrap Alliance, (bl)TWPhoto/CORBIS, (br)Roger Ressmeyer/CORBIS; **1009** (l)TOLES © 1997 The Washington Post. Reprinted with permission of UNIVERSAL PRESS SYNDICATE. All rights reserved, (tr)Wally McNamee/CORBIS, (br)Markowitz Jeffrey/CORBIS SYGMA; **1011** (l)Terry Ashe/Time Life Pictures/GI, (r)SuperStock; **1013** (l)Wally McNamee/CORBIS, (r)Joe Marquette/AP Images; **1014** (tl)Peter Turnley/CORBIS, (tr)Les Stone/CORBIS SYGMA, (b)Leif Skoogfors/CORBIS; **1018** David Kadlubowski/CORBIS; **1020** (l)Fred Greaves/Reuters/CORBIS, (r)Carlos Barria/Reuters/CORBIS; **1021** (t)Stanley Rogouski, (b)Michael Newman/Photo-Edit; **1023** (t)GI, (b)Transtock/Alamy Images; **1024** Hamilton Karie/CORBIS SYGMA; **1026** (t)Michael Newman/PhotoEdit, (b)Ron Edmonds/AP Images; **1029** TOLES © 1998 The Washington Post. Reprinted with permission of UNIVERSAL PRESS SYNDICATE. All rights reserved.; **1030** (l)Alan Diaz/AP Images, (c)Evan Vucci/AP Images, (r)Dimas Ardian/GI; **1030-1031** Michael Macor/San Francisco Chronicle/CORBIS; **1033** (tl tc)Ron Sachs/CNP/CORBIS, (tr)Colin Braley/Reuters/CORBIS, (b)Najlah Feanny/CORBIS; **1034** Daryl Cagle/Cagle Cartoons; **1037** (t) Reuters/Sean Adair/CORBIS, (bl)Ron Sachs/CNP/CORBIS, (br)Stan Honda/AFP/GI; **1038** AP Images; **1040** (t)Matthew McDermott/CORBIS, (bl)Reuters/CORBIS, (br)Steve Liss/CORBIS; **1043** (t)Alexandra Boulat/VII/AP Images, (bl)Scott Peterson/GI, (br)David Guttenfelder/AP Images; **1044** (t)Ali Haider/AP Images, (b)Reuters/Jeff Christensen/CORBIS; **1045** (tl)Al Jazeera via APTN/AP Images, (tr)Lynsey Addario/CORBIS, (b)Wathiq Khuzaie/GI; **1046** (l)Lauren Frayer/AP Images, (r)Khalid al-Mousily/Reuters/CORBIS; **1049** (l)Khampha Bouaphanh/Knight Ridder/Tribune/Pool/Reuters/CORBIS, (r)Brooks Kraft/CORBIS; **1050** Smiley N. Pool/Dallas Morning News/CORBIS; **1051** Rick Wilking/Reuters/CORBIS; **1053** (l)Wathiq Khuzaie/GI, (r)Nancy Kaserman/ZUMA/CORBIS; **1054** (tl)Bruno Vincent/GI, (tr)Evan Agostini/GI, (b)Chris McGrath/GI; **1056** (t)AFP/GI, (cl)Kamal Kishore/AP Images, (cr)Al Jazeera/AP Images, (b)Evan Agostini/ImageDirect/GI; **1059** Olie Johannson/Political Cartoons; **R2** LOC, LC-USF34-T01-009095-C; **R3** Art Shay/Time Life Pictures/GI; **R4** LOC, LC-DIG-fsac-1a35337; **R5** Wally McNamee/CORBIS; **R6** Photo File/MLBPhotos/GI; **R7** Stan Honda/AFP/GI; **R8** GI; **R9** CORBIS; **R10** (l)Comstock/CORBIS, (r)Art Archive/Reina Sofia Museum, Madrid; **R11** CORBIS; **R12 R13** BC; **R14** Harry Scull Jr./GI; **R17** The Granger Collection, New York; **R18** Clifford K. Berryman/National Archives; **R19** Scott Lituchy/Star Ledger/CORBIS; **R20** Smithsonian Institution/CORBIS; **R29 through R33** White House Historical Association; **R33** (bl)Official White House Photo by Eric Draper, (br)Brooks Kraft/CORBIS; **R36** (t)Illinois State Historical Library, (b)Private Collection; **R39** Private Collection; **R40** The Wadsworth Atheneum; **R41 R42** Bridgeman Art Library; **R43 R44** National Portrait Gallery, Smithsonian Institution/Art Resource, NY; **R46** Chicago Historical Society; **R47** (t)Maryland Historical Society, Baltimore, Maryland, (b)National Museum of American History/Armed Forces History Collections/Smithsonian Institution; **R48** Picture Research Consultants; **R49** LOC; **R50** (t)Andre Jenny/Focus Group/PictureQuest, (b)BC; **R52** National Portrait Gallery, Smithsonian Institution, Washington, D.C./Art Resource. N.Y.; **R53** Courtesy Franklin D. Roosevelt Library; **R55** Carl Iwaski/Time Life Pictures/GI; **R56** Francis Miller/Time Life Pictures/GI; **R58 R60** GI; **R61** Picture Research Consultants; **R65** Stock Montage/GI; **R67** (t)Stock Montage/GI, (b)Frans Lanting/CORBIS; **R68** BC; **R69** Collection of the New York Historical Society/Bridgeman Art Library; **R71** (t)Erling Larson/GI, (b)Henry Guttmann/GI; **R72** Keystone/GI; **R73** General Photographic Agency/GI; **R74** Ray Fisher/Time Life Pictures/GI; **R75** Hulton Archive/GI; **R76** Stephen Jaffe/AFP/GI; **R80** Mitchell Gerber/CORBIS; **Time Line Presidential Paintings** White House Historical Association.